May, 4–8, 2015
Istanbul, Turkey

Association for Computing Machinery

Advancing Computing as a Science & Profession

AAMAS'15

Proceedings of the 2015 International Conference on Autonomous Agents & Multiagent Systems

Sponsored by:

IFAAMAS, NSF, Artificial Intelligence, ACM SIGAI, ARGELA, Microsoft Research, FOCAS, SIG-MACC, and teknoparkistanbul

In cooperation with:

ACM

Association for
Computing Machinery

Advancing Computing as a Science & Profession

The Association for Computing Machinery
2 Penn Plaza, Suite 701
New York, New York 10121-0701

ISBN: 978-1-4503-3413-6 (Digital)

ISBN: 978-1-4503-3769-4 (Print)

Additional copies may be ordered prepaid from:

ACM Order Department
PO Box 30777
New York, NY 10087-0777, USA

Phone: 1-800-342-6626 (USA and Canada)
+1-212-626-0500 (Global)
Fax: +1-212-944-1318
E-mail: acmhelp@acm.org
Hours of Operation: 8:30 am – 4:30 pm ET

Printed in the USA

Introduction

The Autonomous Agents and MultiAgent Systems (AAMAS) conference series brings together researchers from around the world to share the latest advances in the field. It is the premier forum for research in the theory and practice of autonomous agents and multi-agent systems. AAMAS 2002, the first of the series, was held in Bologna, followed by Melbourne (2003), New York (2004), Utrecht (2005), Hakodate (2006), Honolulu (2007), Estoril (2008), Budapest (2009), Toronto (2010), Taipei (2011), Valencia (2012), Saint Paul (2013), and Paris (2014). This volume constitutes the proceedings of AAMAS 2015, the fourteenth conference in the series, held in Istanbul in May 2015.

In line with previous editions, AAMAS 2015 attracted submissions for a general track and four special tracks: Innovative Applications, Robotics, Virtual Agents and Humans, and the Blue Sky Ideas track. The special tracks were chaired by leaders in their corresponding fields: Amal El Fallah Seghrouchni and Milind Tambe chaired the Innovative Applications track, Alessandro Farinelli and Gal Kaminka the Robotics track, Catholijn Jonker and Rui Prada the Virtual Agents and Humans track, and Victor Lesser the Blue Sky Ideas track. The special track chairs were responsible for appointing the Programme Committee (PC) members and the Senior Programme Committee members (SPC) for their tracks, and they made acceptance/rejection decisions for their tracks in consultation with Programme Chairs based on input provided by the track PC and SPC. Members of the PC and SPC of the special tracks also reviewed papers on topics of their expertise submitted to the general track.

Full paper submissions (8 pages plus bibliographic references) and Blue Sky Ideas paper submissions (4 pages plus references) were solicited for AAMAS 2015. Some of the full paper submissions were accepted as extended abstracts (2 pages). The papers were selected by means of a thorough review and discussion process, which included an opportunity for authors to respond to reviewer comments. All SPC members followed and contributed to the technical discussions on the papers they were overseeing.

AAMAS 2015 attracted a large number of high-quality submissions; the result of the reviewing process is summarised by the following table:

Track	*Reviewed*	*Accepted as full papers*		*Accepted as extended abstracts*	
Main Track Papers	520	127	24%	122	23%
Innovative Applications	47	15	32%	6	13%
Robotics	45	12	27%	9	20%
Virtual Agents and Humans	40	10	25%	10	25%
Blue Sky Ideas	18	3	17%	N/A	

Overall, out of 670 submissions, 167 (25%) were accepted as full papers and 147 (22%) were accepted as extended abstracts.

The acceptance rates by a paper's primary high-level keyword from the conference topics of interest are:

Topics	*Reviewed*	*Accepted as full papers*		*Accepted as extended abstracts*	
Agent Societies and Societal Issues	47	10	21%	11	23%
Agent Theories and Models	59	14	24%	14	24%
Agent-based Simulation	66	6	9%	17	26%
Agents and Mainstream Computing	12	2	17%	3	25%
Communication and Argumentation	22	5	23%	3	14%
Cooperation	50	13	26%	7	14%
Economic Paradigms	138	46	33%	32	23%
Engineering Agent-Based Systems	19	4	21%	1	5%
Innovative Applications	54	13	24%	7	13%
Knowledge Representation and Reasoning	36	7	19%	8	22%
Learning and Adaptation	51	14	27%	14	27%
Robotics	53	15	28%	11	21%
Verification and Validation	14	5	36%	4	29%
Virtual Agents and Humans	49	13	24%	15	31%

Full papers were presented orally in 15-minute slots; all extended abstracts and, optionally, full papers were presented as posters during the conference.

Out of the 670 submissions, 395 (59%) had a student as the primary author, 108 of these (27%) were accepted as full papers, and a further 91 (23%) were accepted as extended abstracts.

The proceedings also contain 30 Demonstration papers, 29 Doctoral Consortium papers, as well as abstracts of the invited talks and details of some of the awards given. The overall conference programme also had 26 workshops and 8 tutorials, although that material is not included in the proceedings.

We would like to thank the authors in our and closely-related communities for submitting a large number of top-quality papers, the PC and SPC members, additional reviewers, and the track chairs for their dedication in reviewing the submissions and for engaging in the technical discussions held during the reviewing process. We are indebted to Dave Shield for assisting us with ConfMaster throughout the process. We also thank Neil Yorke-Smith for arranging the conference proceedings and all the members of the local organising committee for their industrious work without which the conference would not have been possible.

Rafael H. Bordini and Edith Elkind
AAMAS 2015 Programme Chairs

Gerhard Weiss and Pınar Yolum
AAMAS 2015 General Chairs

Table of Contents

AAMAS 2015 Organizing Committee xxvii

AAMAS 2015 Senior Programme Committee xxviii

AAMAS 2015 Programme Committee xxx

AAMAS 2015 Additional Reviewers xxxvi

AAMAS 2015 Sponsors and Supporters xxxviii

AAMAS 2015 Awards xxxix

Book 1

Invited Talks

- **On the Full Organism Challenge: Or, Can We Computerize an Elephant?** 1
  David Harel *(The Weizmann Institute of Science in Israel)*
- **Learning Submodular Functions with Applications to Multi-Agent Systems** 3
  Maria Florina Balcan *(Carnegie Mellon University)*
- **Greta, an Interactive Expressive Embodied Conversational Agent** 5
  Catherine Pelachaud *(CNRS-LTCI - TELECOM ParisTech)*

Session: B1 — Game Theory I

- **Hierarchical Abstraction, Distributed Equilibrium Computation, and Post-Processing, with Application to a Champion No-Limit Texas Hold'em Agent** 7
  Noam Brown, Sam Ganzfried, Tuomas Sandholm *(Carnegie Mellon University)*
- **Decision-theoretic Clustering of Strategies** 17
  Nolan Bard *(University of Alberta)*, Deon Nicholas *(University of Waterloo)*, Csaba Szepesvári, Michael Bowling *(University of Alberta)*
- **Online Monte Carlo Counterfactual Regret Minimization for Search in Imperfect Information Games** 27
  Viliam Lisý *(Czech Technical University in Prague)*, Marc Lanctot *(Maastricht University)*, Michael Bowling *(University of Alberta)*
- **Endgame Solving in Large Imperfect-Information Games** 37
  Sam Ganzfried, Tuomas Sandholm *(Carnegie Mellon University)*
- **Discretization of Continuous Action Spaces in Extensive-Form Games** 47
  Christian Kroer, Tuomas Sandholm *(Carnegie Mellon University)*
- **Welfare Effects of Market Making in Continuous Double Auctions** 57
  Elaine Wah, Michael P. Wellman *(University of Michigan)*

Session: B2 — Social Choice I

- **Large-Scale Election Campaigns: Combinatorial Shift Bribery** 67
  Robert Bredereck *(TU Berlin)*, Piotr Faliszewski *(AGH University)*, Rolf Niedermeier, Nimrod Talmon *(TU Berlin)*
- **Manipulation with Bounded Single-Peaked Width: A Parameterized Study** 77
  Yongjie Yang *(Universität des Saarlandes)*
- **Kernelization Complexity of Possible Winner and Coalitional Manipulation Problems in Voting** 87
  Palash Dey, Neeldhara Misra, Y. Narahari *(Indian Institute of Science)*

- **On the Parameterized Complexity of Minimax Approval Voting** 97
  Neeldhara Misra, Arshed Nabeel *(Indian Institute of Science)*,
  Harman Singh *(BITS Pilani-K.K. Birla Goa Campus)*
- **Computational Aspects of Multi-Winner Approval Voting** 107
  Haris Aziz, Serge Gaspers *(NICTA & UNSW)*, Joachim Gudmundsson *(NICTA & University of Sydney)*,
  Simon Mackenzie, Nicholas Mattei, Toby Walsh *(NICTA & UNSW)*
- **Complexity of the Winner Determination Problem in Judgment Aggregation: Kemeny, Slater, Tideman, Young** 117
  Ulle Endriss *(University of Amsterdam)*, Ronald de Haan *(Technische Universität Wien)*
- **Parameterized Complexity Results for Agenda Safety in Judgment Aggregation** 127
  Ulle Endriss *(University of Amsterdam)*, Ronald de Haan, Stefan Szeider *(Technische Universität Wien)*

Session: B3 — Learning I

- **Adaptive Budgeted Bandit Algorithms for Trust Development in a Supply-Chain** 137
  Sandip Sen, Anton Ridgway, Michael Ripley *(The University of Tulsa)*
- **Improving the Performance of Mobile Phone Crowdsourcing Applications** 145
  Erfan Davami, Gita Sukthankar *(University of Central Florida)*
- **Selecting Robust Strategies in RTS Games via Concurrent Plan Augmentation** 155
  Abdelrahman Elogeel *(University of Washington, Tacoma)*, Andrey Kolobov *(Microsoft Corporation)*,
  Matthew Alden, Ankur Teredesai *(University of Washington, Tacoma)*
- **CFQI: Fitted Q-Iteration with Complex Returns** 163
  Robert Wright, Xingye Qiao, Lei Yu *(Binghamton University)*,
  Steven Loscalzo *(Air Force Research Laboratory)*
- **Counterfactual Exploration for Improving Multiagent Learning** 171
  Mitchell Colby, Sepideh Kharaghani *(Oregon State University)*, Chris HolmesParker *(Parflux LLC)*,
  Kagan Tumer *(Oregon State University)*
- **Policy Transfer Using Reward Shaping** 181
  Tim Brys, Anna Harutyunyan *(Vrije Universiteit Brussel)*, Matthew E. Taylor *(Washington State University)*,
  Ann Nowé *(Vrije Universiteit Brussel)*

Session: B4 — Logic I

- **Verifying Multi-Agent Systems by Model Checking Three-Valued Abstractions** 189
  Alessio Lomuscio, Jakub Michaliszyn *(Imperial College London)*
- **Parameterised Verification of Autonomous Mobile-Agents in Static But Unknown Environments** 199
  Sasha Rubin *(Università degli Studi di Napoli "Federico II")*
- **Decentralized Bisimulation for Multiagent Systems** 209
  Lei Song, Yuan Feng *(University of Technology Sydney)*, Lijun Zhang *(Chinese Academy of Sciences)*
- **Budget-Constrained Knowledge in Multiagent Systems** 219
  Pavel Naumov *(McDaniel College)*, Jia Tao *(Bryn Mawr College)*
- **Module Checking of Strategic Ability** 227
  Wojciech Jamroga *(Polish Academy of Sciences)*,
  Aniello Murano *(Università degli Studi di Napoli "Federico II")*
- **On the Formal Verification of Diffusion Phenomena in Open Dynamic Agent Networks** 237
  Francesco Belardinelli *(Université d'Evry)*, Davide Grossi *(University of Liverpool)*

Session: B5 — Bio-inspired Approaches

- **Determining Placements of Influencing Agents in a Flock** 247
  Katie Genter, Shun Zhang, Peter Stone *(University of Texas at Austin)*
- **Particle Field Optimization: A New Paradigm for Swarm Intelligence** 257
  Nathan Bell, B. John Oommen *(Carleton University)*

- **Bio-Inspired Practicalities: Collective Behaviour Using Passive Neighbourhood Sensing** 267
  Mansoor Shaukat, Mandar Chitre *(National University of Singapore)*
- **Firefly-Inspired Synchronization in Swarms of Mobile Agents** 279
  Fernando Perez-Diaz *(The University of Sheffield)*, Ruediger Zillmer *(Unilever R&D)*,
  Roderich Groß *(The University of Sheffield)*
- **Swarm Robot Foraging with Wireless Sensor Motes** 287
  Katherine Russell, Michael Schader, Kevin Andrea, Sean Luke *(George Mason University)*
- **Cooperative Coevolution of Partially Heterogeneous Multiagent Systems** 297
  Jorge Gomes *(BioMachines Lab & Universidade de Lisboa)*, Pedro Mariano *(Universidade de Lisboa)*,
  Anders Lyhne Christensen *(BioMachines Lab & Universidade de Lisboa)*

Session: C1 — Game Theory II

- **The Power of Verification for Greedy Mechanism Design** 307
  Dimitris Fotakis *(National Technical University of Athens)*, Piotr Krysta *(University of Liverpool)*,
  Carmine Ventre *(Teesside University)*
- **Computational Bundling for Auctions** 317
  Christian Kroer, Tuomas Sandholm *(Carnegie Mellon University)*
- **Mechanism Design for Daily Deals** 327
  Binyi Chen *(University of California, Santa Barbara)*, Tao Qin, Tie-Yan Liu *(Microsoft Research)*
- **Selling Tomorrow's Bargains Today** 337
  Melika Abolhassani, Hossein Esfandiari, MohammadTaghi Hajiaghayi, Hamid Mahini,
  David Malec, Aravind Srinivasan *(University of Maryland)*
- **Social Decision with Minimal Efficiency Loss: An Automated Mechanism Design Approach** 347
  Mingyu Guo, Hong Shen *(University of Adelaide)*, Taiki Todo, Yuko Sakurai,
  Makoto Yokoo *(Kyushu University)*
- **Complexity of Mechanism Design with Signaling Costs** 357
  Andrew Kephart, Vincent Conitzer *(Duke University)*

Session: C2 — Cooperation

- **To Ask, Sense, or Share: Ad Hoc Information Gathering** 367
  Adam Eck, Leen-Kiat Soh *(University of Nebraska-Lincoln)*
- **A Mechanism for Smoothly Handling Human Interrupts in Team Oriented Plans** 377
  Alessandro Farinelli, Nicolo' Marchi, Masoume M. Raeissi *(University of Verona)*,
  Nathan Brooks, Paul Scerri *(Carnegie Mellon University)*
- **Bounty Hunters and Multiagent Task Allocation** 387
  Drew Wicke, David Freelan, Sean Luke *(George Mason University)*
- **How to Form a Task-Oriented Robust Team** 395
  Tenda Okimoto *(Kobe University)*, Nicolas Schwind *(Transdisciplinary Research Integration Center)*,
  Maxime Clement, Tony Ribeiro *(The Graduate University for Advanced Studies)*,
  Katsumi Inoue *(National Institute of Informatics)*, Pierre Marquis *(CRIL - CNRS Université d'Artois)*
- **Dynamic Theoretical Analysis of the Distributed Stochastic and Distributed Breakout Algorithms** 405
  Anton Ridgway, Roger Mailler *(University of Tulsa)*
- **Efficient Inter-Team Task Allocation in RoboCup Rescue** 413
  Marc Pujol-Gonzalez, Jesus Cerquides *(IIIA-CSIC)*, Alessandro Farinelli *(University of Verona)*,
  Pedro Meseguer, Juan A. Rodriguez-Aguilar *(IIIA-CSIC)*

Session: C3 — Agent Societies

- **A Semantic Framework for Socially Adaptive Agents: Towards Strong Norm Compliance** 423
  M. Birna van Riemsdijk *(Delft University of Technology)*, Louise Dennis, Michael Fisher *(University of Liverpool)*, Koen V. Hindriks *(Delft University of Technology)*
- **Synthesising Liberal Normative Systems** 433
  Javier Morales *(Universitat de Barcelona & Research Institute)*, Maite Lopez-Sanchez *(Universitat de Barcelona & Artificial Intelligence Research Institute (IIIA-CSIC))*, Juan A. Rodriguez-Aguilar *(Artificial Intelligence Research Institute (IIIA-CSIC))*, Michael Wooldridge *(University of Oxford)*, Wamberto Vasconcelos *(University of Aberdeen)*
- **Practical Run-Time Norm Enforcement with Bounded Lookahead** 443
  Natasha Alechina, Nils Bulling *(Delft University of Technology)*, Mehdi Dastani *(Universiteit Utrecht)*, Brian Logan *(University of Nottingham)*
- **Generalized Commitment Alignment** 453
  Amit K. Chopra *(Lancaster University)*, Munindar P. Singh *(North Carolina State University)*
- **Monitoring Hierarchical Agent-based Simulation Traces** 463
  Benjamin Herd, Simon Miles, Peter McBurney, Michael Luck *(King's College London)*
- **A Framework for Institutions Governing Institutions** 473
  Thomas C. King *(Delft University of Technology)*, Tingting Li *(Imperial College London)*, Marina De Vos *(University of Bath)*, Virginia Dignum, Catholijn M. Jonker *(Delft University of Technology)*, Julian Padget *(University of Bath)*, M. Birna van Riemsdijk *(Delft University of Technology)*

Session: C4 — Applications I

- **DIRECT: A Scalable Approach for Route Guidance in Selfish Orienteering Problems** 483
  Pradeep Varakantham, Hala Mostafa, Na Fu, Hoong Chuin Lau *(Singapore Management University)*
- **Coordinating Measurements for Air Pollution Monitoring in Participatory Sensing Settings** 493
  Alexandros Zenonos, Sebastian Stein, Nicholas R. Jennings *(University of Southampton)*
- **Factored MDPS for Optimal Prosumer Decision-Making** 503
  Angelos Angelidakis, Georgios Chalkiadakis *(Technical University of Crete)*
- **Data-Driven Agent-Based Modeling, with Application to Rooftop Solar Adoption** 513
  Haifeng Zhang, Yevgeniy Vorobeychik *(Vanderbilt University)*, Joshua Letchford, Kiran Lakkaraju *(Sandia National Laboratories)*
- **Optimizing Efficiency of Taxi Systems: Scaling-up and Handling Arbitrary Constraints** 523
  Jiarui Gan *(University of Chinese Academy of Sciences)*, Bo An, Chunyan Miao *(Nanyang Technological University)*
- **HAC-ER: A Disaster Response System Based on Human-Agent Collectives** 533
  Sarvapali D. Ramchurn, Trung Dong Huynh, Yuki Ikuno, Jack Flann, Feng Wu, Luc Moreau, Nicholas R. Jennings *(University of Southampton)*, Joel E. Fischer, Wenchao Jiang, Tom Rodden *(University of Nottingham)*, Edwin Simpson, Steven Reece, Stephen J. Roberts *(University of Oxford)*

Session: C5 -- Virtual Agents and Humans I

- **Adaptive Advice in Automobile Climate Control Systems** 543
  Ariel Rosenfeld *(Bar-Ilan University)*, Amos Azaria *(Carnegie Mellon University)*, Sarit Kraus *(Bar-Ilan University)*, Claudia V. Goldman, Omer Tsimhoni *(General Motors Advanced Technical Center)*
- **Are Aggressive Agents as Scary as Aggressive Humans?** 553
  Romy Blankendaal, Tibor Bosse *(VU University Amsterdam)*, Charlotte Gerritsen *(Netherlands Institute for the Study of Crime and Law Enforcement)*, Tessa de Jong, Jeroen de Man *(VU University Amsterdam)*

- **The Fallacy of Endogenous Discounting of Trust Recommendations** 563
  Tim Muller, Yang Liu, Jie Zhang *(Nanyang Technological University)*
- **Composing Social Interactions via Social Games** 573
  Daniel G. Shapiro, Karen Tanenbaum *(University of California at Santa Cruz)*,
  Josh McCoy *(American University)*, Larry LeBron, Craig Reynolds, Andrew Stern,
  Michael Mateas *(University of California at Santa Cruz)*, Bill Ferguson, David Diller ,
  Kerry Moffitt, Will Coon, Bruce Roberts *(Raytheon-BBN Technologies)*
- **Human Behavior Models for Virtual Agents in Repeated Decision Making under Uncertainty** 581
  Ming Yin *(Harvard University)*, Yu-An Sun *(PARC)*
- **DJ-MC: A Reinforcement-Learning Agent for Music Playlist Recommendation** 591
  Elad Liebman, Maytal Saar-Tsechansky, Peter Stone *(The University of Texas at Austin)*

Book 2

Session: G1 — Game Theory III

- **Approximately Strategy-proof Mechanisms for (Constrained) Facility Location** 605
  Xin Sui, Craig Boutilier *(University of Toronto)*
- **Facility Location Games with Dual Preference** 615
  Shaokun Zou, Minming Li *(City University of Hong Kong)*
- **The Power of Swap Deals in Distributed Resource Allocation** 625
  Anastasia Damamme, Aurélie Beynier *(Univ Paris 06)*,
  Yann Chevaleyre *(Université Paris 13)*, Nicolas Maudet *(Univ Paris 06)*
- **Strategic Free Information Disclosure for Search-Based Information Platforms** 635
  Shani Alkoby, David Sarne *(Bar-Ilan University)*,
  Sanmay Das *(Washington University in St. Louis)*
- **Information Disclosure as a Means to Security** 645
  Zinovi Rabinovich *(Mobileye Vision Technologies Ltd.)*, Albert Xin Jiang *(Trinity University)*,
  Manish Jain *(Armorway)*, Haifeng Xu *(University of Southern California)*
- **Electric Boolean Games: Redistribution Schemes for Resource-Bounded Agents** 655
  Paul Harrenstein *(University of Oxford)*, Paolo Turrini *(Imperial College London)*,
  Michael Wooldridge *(University of Oxford)*

Session: G2 — Social Choice II

- **A Study of Human Behavior in Online Voting** 665
  Maor Tal *(Ben-Gurion University)*, Reshef Meir *(Harvard University)*,
  Ya'akov (Kobi) Gal *(Ben-Gurion University)*
- **Aggregating Partial Rankings with Applications to Peer Grading in Massive Online Open Courses** 675
  Ioannis Caragiannis, George A. Krimpas, Alexandros A. Voudouris *(University of Patras & CTI Diophantus)*
- **Computing Manipulations of Ranking Systems** 685
  Ethan Gertler, Erika Mackin, Malik Magdon-Ismail, Lirong Xia, Yuan Yi *(Rensselaer Polytechnic Institute)*
- **Every Team Deserves a Second Chance: Identifying When Things Go Wrong** 695
  Vaishnavh Nagarajan *(Indian Institute of Technology Madras)*,
  Leandro Soriano Marcolino, Milind Tambe *(University of Southern California)*
- **Adapting the Social Network to Affect Elections** 705
  Sigal Sina *(Bar Ilan University)*, Noam Hazon *(Ariel University)*,
  Avinatan Hassidim, Sarit Kraus *(Bar Ilan University)*
- **Multiple Referenda and Multiwinner Elections Using Hamming Distances: Complexity and Manipulability** 715
  Georgios Amanatidis *(Athens University of Economics and Business)*,
  Nathanaël Barrot, Jérôme Lang *(Université Paris Dauphine)*, Evangelos Markakis *(Athens University of Economics and Business)*,
  Bernard Ries *(Université Paris Dauphine)*

Session: G3 — Learning II

- **Learning Inter-Task Transferability in the Absence of Target Task Samples** ... 725
  Jivko Sinapov, Sanmit Narvekar, Matteo Leonetti, Peter Stone *(The University of Texas at Austin)*
- **R-HybrID: Evolution of Agent Controllers with a Hybrisation of Indirect and Direct Encodings** ... 735
  Fernando Silva *(BioMachines & BioISI)*, Luís Correia *(BioISI)*, Anders Lyhne Christensen *(BioMachines)*
- **Learning by Observation Using Qualitative Spatial Relations** ... 745
  Jay Young, Nick Hawes *(The University of Birmingham)*
- **Learning in Multi-Agent Systems with Sparse Interactions by Knowledge Transfer and Game Abstraction** ... 753
  Yujing Hu, Yang Gao *(Nanjing University)*, Bo An *(Nanyang Technological University)*
- **Knowledge Revision for Reinforcement Learning with Abstract MDPs** ... 763
  Kyriakos Efthymiadis, Daniel Kudenko *(University of York)*
- **Monte Carlo Hierarchical Model Learning** ... 771
  Jacob Menashe, Peter Stone *(The University of Texas at Austin)*

Session: G4 — Applications II

- **Supporting Reasoning with Different Types of Evidence in Intelligence Analysis** ... 781
  Alice Toniolo, Timothy J. Norman, Anthony Etuk, Federico Cerutti *(University of Aberdeen)*, Robin Wentao Ouyang, Mani Srivastava *(University of California, Los Angeles)*, Nir Oren *(University of Aberdeen)*, Timothy Dropps, John A. Allen *(Honeywell, USA)*, Paul Sullivan *(Intelpoint Incorporated)*
- **Using Information Theory to Improve the Robustness of Trust Systems** ... 791
  Dongxia Wang, Tim Muller, Athirai A. Irissappane, Jie Zhang, Yang Liu *(Nanyang Technological University)*
- **Learning Behavior Patterns from Video: A Data-Driven Framework for Agent-based Crowd Modeling** ... 801
  Jinghui Zhong, Wentong Cai *(Nanyang Technological University)*, Linbo Luo *(Xidian University)*, Haiyan Yin *(Nanyang Technological University)*
- **Signaled Queueing** ... 811
  Laura Brink *(Yale University)*, Robert Shorten, Jia Yuan Yu *(IBM Ireland Research Lab)*
- **Modeling the Management of Water Resources Systems Using Multi-Objective DCOPs** ... 821
  Francesco Amigoni, Andrea Castelletti, Matteo Giuliani *(Politecnico di Milano)*
- **A Multi-Agent Platform for Automating the Collection of Patient-Provided Clinical Feedback** ... 831
  Zina M. Ibrahim *(King's College London)*, Lorena Fernández de la Cruz *(Karolinska Institutet)*, Argyris Stringaris, Robert Goodman, Michael Luck, Richard J.B. Dobson *(King's College London)*

Session: G5 — Robotics I

- **Real-time Opinion Aggregation Methods for Crowd Robotics** ... 841
  Elliot Salisbury, Sebastian Stein, Sarvapali Ramchurn *(University of Southampton)*
- **Teaching Robots Parametrized Executable Plans Through Spoken Interaction** ... 851
  Guglielmo Gemignani *(Sapienza University of Rome)*, Emanuele Bastianelli *(University of Rome Tor Vergata)*, Daniele Nardi *(Sapienza University of Rome)*
- **Frontier-Based RTDP: A New Approach to Solving the Robotic Adversarial Coverage Problem** ... 861
  Roi Yehoshua, Noa Agmon, Gal A. Kaminka *(Bar Ilan University)*
- **Pervasive 'Calm' Perception for Autonomous Robotic Agents** ... 871
  Thiemo Wiedemeyer, Ferenc Bálint-Benczédi, Michael Beetz *(Universität Bremen)*
- **Effective Approximations for Multi-Robot Coordination in Spatially Distributed Tasks** ... 881
  Daniel Claes *(University of Liverpool)*, Philipp Robbel *(Massachusetts Institute of Technology)*, Frans A. Oliehoek *(University of Amsterdam & University of Liverpool)*, Karl Tuyls *(University of Liverpool)*, Daniel Hennes *(European Space Agency)*, Wiebe van der Hoek *(University of Liverpool)*

- **Adversarial Modeling in the Robotic Coverage Problem** 891
  Roi Yehoshua, Noa Agmon *(Bar Ilan University)*

Session: H1 — Game Theory IV

- **Waste Makes Haste: Bounded Time Protocols for Envy-Free Cake Cutting with Free Disposal** 901
  Erel Segal-Halevi, Avinatan Hassidim, Yonatan Aumann *(Bar Ilan University)*
- **Fairness and False-Name Manipulations in Randomized Cake Cutting** 909
  Shunsuke Tsuruta, Masaaki Oka, Taiki Todo, Yuko Sakurai, Makoto Yokoo *(Kyushu University)*
- **Bitcoin Mining Pools: A Cooperative Game Theoretic Analysis** 919
  Yoad Lewenberg *(The Hebrew University of Jerusalem)*, Yoram Bachrach *(Microsoft Research, Cambridge)*, Yonatan Sompolinsky, Aviv Zohar, Jeffrey S. Rosenschein *(The Hebrew University of Jerusalem)*
- **On Sex, Evolution, and the Multiplicative Weights Update Algorithm** 929
  Reshef Meir, David Parkes *(Harvard University)*
- **On the Susceptibility of the Deferred Acceptance Algorithm** 939
  Haris Aziz *(NICTA & UNSW)*, Hans Georg Seedig, Jana Karina von Wedel *(TU München)*
- **Dynamic Influence Maximization Under Increasing Returns to Scale** 949
  Haifeng Zhang *(Vanderbilt University)*, Ariel D. Procaccia *(Carnegie Mellon University)*, Yevgeniy Vorobeychik *(Vanderbilt University)*

Session: H2 — Logic II

- **A Dialogue Game for Recommendation with Adaptive Preference Models** 959
  Christophe Labreuche *(Thales Research & Technology)*, Nicolas Maudet *(Univ Paris 06)*, Wassila Ouerdane *(LGI- CentraleSupélec)*, Simon Parons *(University of Liverpool)*
- **Reasoning with PCP-nets in a Multi-Agent Context** 969
  Cristina Cornelio, Umberto Grandi *(University of Padova)*, Judy Goldsmith *(University of Kentucky)*, Nicholas Mattei *(NICTA & University of New South Wales)*, Francesca Rossi *(University of Padova)*, K. Brent Venable *(Tulane University & IHMC)*
- **A Logic for Collective Choice** 979
  Guifei Jiang *(University of Western Sydney & University of Toulouse)*, Dongmo Zhang *(University of Western Sydney)*, Laurent Perrussel *(University of Toulouse 1)*, Heng Zhang *(University of Western Sydney)*
- **Propositional Opinion Diffusion** 989
  Umberto Grandi, Emiliano Lorini, Laurent Perrussel *(University of Toulouse)*
- **Belief Merging versus Judgment Aggregation** 999
  Patricia Everaere *(Université de Lille 1)*, Sébastien Konieczny, Pierre Marquis *(Université d'Artois)*
- **A Syntactic Proof of Arrow's Theorem in a Modal Logic of Social Choice Functions** 1009
  Giovanni Ciná, Ulle Endriss *(University of Amsterdam)*

Session: H3 — Engineering Agent-Based Systems

- **Global Protocols as First Class Entities for Self-Adaptive Agents** 1019
  Davide Ancona, Daniela Briola, Angelo Ferrando, Viviana Mascardi *(University of Genova)*
- **A Self-Organizing Virtual Environment for Agent-Based Simulations** 1031
  Mohammad Al-Zinati, Rym Wenkstern *(University of Texas at Dallas)*
- **An Approach to Quantify Workload in a System of Agents** 1041
  Richard Stocker, Neha Rungta *(NASA Ames Research Center)*, Eric Mercer *(Brigham Young University)*, Franco Raimondi *(Middlesex University)*, Jon Holbrook, Colleen Cardoza *(San Jose State University)*, Michael Goodrich *(Brigham Young University)*
- **Agent Oriented Modelling of Tactical Decision Making** 1051
  Rick Evertsz, John Thangarajah, Nitin Yadav *(RMIT University)*, Thanh Chi Ly *(DSTO)*

- **Metrics for Evaluating Modularity and Extensibility in HMAS Systems** 1061
  Massimo Cossentino, Carmelo Lodato, Salvatore Lopes,
  Patrizia Ribino *(National Research Council of Italy)*, Valeria Seidita *(University of Palermo)*
- **Early Detection of Design Faults Relative to Requirement Specifications in Agent-Based Models** 1071
  Yoosef Abushark, John Thangarajah *(RMIT University)*, Tim Miller *(University of Melbourne)*,
  James Harland *(RMIT University)*, Michael Winikoff *(University of Otago)*

Session: H4 — Applications III

- **Incentive Schemes for Participatory Sensing** 1081
  Goran Radanovic, Boi Faltings *(Ecole Polytechnique Federale de Lausanne)*
- **Truthful Interval Cover Mechanisms for Crowdsourcing Applications** 1091
  Pankaj Dayama *(IBM Research, India)*, Balakrishnan Narayanaswamy *(University of California, San Diego)*,
  Dinesh Garg *(IBM Research, India)*, Y. Narahari *(Indian Institute of Science)*
- **A Truthful Budget Feasible Multi-Armed Bandit Mechanism for Crowdsourcing Time Critical Tasks** 1101
  Arpita Biswas *(Xerox Research Centre)*, Shweta Jain *(Indian Institute of Science)*,
  Debmalya Mandal *(Harvard University)*, Y. Narahari *(Indian Institute of Science)*
- **TAC AdX'14: Autonomous Agents for Realtime Ad Exchange** 1111
  Bingyang Tao, Fan Wu, Guihai Chen *(Shanghai Jiao Tong University)*
- **Predicting Bundles of Spatial Locations From Learning Revealed Preference Data** 1121
  Truc Viet Le *(Singapore Management University)*, Siyuan Liu *(Carnegie Mellon University)*,
  Hoong Chuin Lau *(Singapore Management University)*, Ramayya Krishnan *(Carnegie Mellon University)*
- **A Multiagent Approach to Variable-Rate Electric Vehicle Charging Coordination** 1131
  Konstantina Valogianni, Wolfgang Ketter *(Erasmus University Rotterdam)*,
  John Collins *(University of Minnesota)*

Session: H5 — Planning I

- **Optimisation and Relaxation for Multiagent Planning in the Situation Calculus** 1141
  Toby O. Davies, Adrian R. Pearce, Peter J. Stuckey *(National ICT Australia & The University of Melbourne)*,
  Harald Søndergaard *(The University of Melbourne)*
- **Capability Models and Their Applications in Planning** 1151
  Yu Zhang, Sarath Sreedharan, Subbarao Kambhampati *(Arizona State University)*
- **Iterative Online Planning in Multiagent Settings with Limited Model Spaces and PAC Guarantees** 1161
  Yingke Chen, Prashant Doshi *(University of Georgia)*, Yifeng Zeng *(Teesside University)*
- **Managing Dynamic Multi-Agent Simple Temporal Network** 1171
  Guillaume Casanova, Cédric Pralet, Charles Lesire *(ONERA—The French Aerospace Lab)*
- **The Dependence of Effective Planning Horizon on Model Accuracy** 1181
  Nan Jiang, Alex Kulesza, Satinder Singh, Richard Lewis *(University of Michigan)*
- **Planning for Crowdsourcing Hierarchical Tasks** 1191
  Ece Kamar, Eric Horvitz *(Microsoft Research)*

Session: I1 — Blue Sky Ideas

- **Creating Socially Adaptive Electronic Partners: Interaction, Reasoning and Ethical Challenges** 1201
  M. Birna van Riemsdijk, Catholijn M. Jonker *(Delft University of Technology)*,
  Victor Lesser *(UMass, Amherst)*
- **Cybersecurity as an Application Domain for Multiagent Systems** 1207
  Munindar P. Singh *(North Carolina State University)*
- **Crowdsourcing Societal Tradeoffs** 1213
  Vince Conitzer, Markus Brill, Rupert Freeman *(Duke University)*

Session: I2 — Hedonic Games

- **Fractional Hedonic Games: Individual and Group Stability** ... 1219
  Florian Brandl, Felix Brandt, Martin Strobel *(TU München)*
- **Representing and Solving Hedonic Games with Ordinal Preferences and Thresholds** ... 1229
  Jérôme Lang *(Université Paris-Dauphine)*, Anja Rey, Jörg Rothe, Hilmar Schadrack, Lena Schend *(Heinrich-Heine-Universität Düsseldorf)*
- **On the Price of Stability of Fractional Hedonic Games** ... 1239
  Vittorio Bilò *(University of Salento)*, Angelo Fanelli *(CNRS)*, Michele Flammini, Gianpiero Monaco *(University of L'Aquila)*, Luca Moscardelli *(University of Chieti-Pescara)*

Session: I3 — Planning II

- **Incremental Policy Iteration with Guaranteed Escape from Local Optima in POMDP Planning** ... 1249
  Marek Grzes, Pascal Poupart *(University of Waterloo)*
- **Predictive State Representations with State Space Partitioning** ... 1259
  Yunlong Liu, Yun Tang *(Xiamen University)*, Yifeng Zeng *(Xiamen University & Teesside University)*
- **Effective Influence Abstractions for Organizational Design** ... 1267
  Jason Sleight, Edmund H. Durfee *(University of Michigan)*

Session: I4 — Applications IV

- **Near-Optimal Decentralized Power Supply Restoration in Smart Grids** ... 1275
  Pritee Agrawal, Akshat Kumar, Pradeep Varakantham *(Singapore Management University)*
- **Designing a Marketplace for the Trading and Distribution of Energy in the Smart Grid** ... 1285
  Jesus Cerquides *(IIIA-CSIC)*, Gauthier Picard *(Institut Henri Fayol, Mines Saint-Etienne)*, Juan A. Rodriguez-Aguilar *(CSIC)*
- **AdaHeat: A General Adaptive Intelligent Agent for Domestic Heating Control** ... 1295
  Athanasios Aris Panagopoulos, Muddasser Alam, Alex Rogers, Nicholas R. Jennings *(University of Southampton, UK)*

Session: I5 — Robotics II

- **Efficient Decision-Making in a Self-Organizing Robot Swarm: On the Speed versus Accuracy Trade-Off** ... 1305
  Gabriele Valentini *(Université Libre de Bruxelles)*, Heiko Hamann *(University of Paderborn)*, Marco Dorigo *(Université Libre de Bruxelles)*
- **Pipelined Consensus for Global State Estimation in Multi-Agent Systems** ... 1315
  Golnaz Habibi, Zachary Kingston *(Rice University)*, Zijian Wang, Mac Schwager *(Boston University)*, James McLurkin *(Rice University)*
- **Continuous Foraging and Information Gathering in a Multi-Agent Team** ... 1325
  Somchaya Liemhetcharat, Rui Yan, Keng Peng Tee *(Agency for Science, Technology and Research)*

Book 3

Session: L1 — Game Theory V

- **Robust Strategy Against Unknown Risk-Averse Attackers in Security Games** ... 1341
  Yundi Qian *(University of Southern California)*, William Haskell *(National University of Singapore)*, Milind Tambe *(University of Southern California)*
- **Keeping Pace with Criminals: Designing Patrol Allocation Against Adaptive Opportunistic Criminals** ... 1351
  Chao Zhang, Arunesh Sinha, Milind Tambe *(University of Southern California)*
- **It Pays to Pay in Bi-Matrix Games – A Rational Explanation for Bribery** ... 1361
  Anshul Gupta, Sven Schewe *(University of Liverpool)*

- **Two-Timescale Algorithms for Learning Nash Equilibria in General-Sum Stochastic Games** 1371
H. L. Prasad *(Streamoid Technologies, Inc.)*, Prashanth L.A., Shalabh Bhatnagar *(Indian Institute of Science)*
- **"A Game of Thrones": When Human Behavior Models Compete in Repeated Stackelberg Security Games** 1381
Debarun Kar, Fei Fang *(University of Southern California)*,
Francesco Maria Delle Fave *(Disney Research, Boston)*,
Nicole Sintov, Milind Tambe *(University of Southern California)*
- **Stackelberg Games for Vaccine Design** 1391
Swetasudha Panda, Yevgeniy Vorobeychik *(Vanderbilt University)*

Session: L2 — Social Choice III

- **General Tiebreaking Schemes for Computational Social Choice** 1401
Rupert Freeman, Markus Brill, Vincent Conitzer *(Duke University)*
- **Incentives for Participation and Abstention in Probabilistic Social Choice** 1411
Florian Brandl, Felix Brandt, Johannes Hofbauer *(TU München)*
- **Sample Complexity for Winner Prediction in Elections** 1421
Palash Dey, Arnab Bhattacharyya *(Indian Institute of Science)*
- **How Credible is the Prediction of a Party-Based Election?** 1431
Jiong Guo *(Shandong University)*, Yash Raj Shrestha *(ETH Zürich)*,
Yongjie Yang *(Universität des Saarlandes)*
- **Detecting Possible Manipulators in Elections** 1441
Palash Dey, Neeldhara Misra, Y. Narahari *(Indian Institute of Science)*
- **Manipulating the Probabilistic Serial Rule** 1451
Haris Aziz, Serge Gaspers, Simon Mackenzie, Nicholas Mattei *(NICTA & UNSW)*,
Nina Narodytska *(Carnegie Mellon University)*, Toby Walsh *(NICTA & UNSW)*

Session: L3 — Logic III

- **Efficient Reasoning with Consistent Proper Epistemic Knowledge Bases** 1461
Christian Muise, Tim Miller, Paolo Felli, Adrian R. Pearce, Liz Sonenberg *(University of Melbourne)*
- **Arbitrary Public Announcement Logic with Mental Programs** 1471
Tristan Charrier, François Schwarzentruber *(ENS Rennes)*
- **Neuro-Symbolic Agents: Boltzmann Machines and Probabilistic Abstract Argumentation with Sub-Arguments** 1481
Regis Riveret, Jeremy Pitt *(Imperial College London)*, Dimitrios Korkinof *(Cortexica Vision Systems)*,
Moez Draief *(Huawei Technologies Co., Ltd.)*
- **Agreeing to Agree: Reaching Unanimity via Preference Dynamics Based on Reliable Agents** 1491
Sujata Ghosh *(Indian Statistical Institute)*, Fernando R. Velázquez-Quesada *(Universidad de Sevilla)*
- **Analysis Problems for Graphical Dynamical Systems: A Unified Approach Through Graph Predicates** 1501
Daniel J. Rosenkrantz *(University at Albany — State University of New York)*,
Madhav V. Marathe *(Virginia Tech)*, Harry B. Hunt III, S. S. Ravi,
Richard E. Stearns *(University at Albany — State University of New York)*
- **Argumentation-based Ranking Logics** 1511
Leila Amgoud, Jonathan Ben-Naim *(IRIT – CNRS)*

Session: L4 — Virtual Agents and Humans II

- **Modeling Students Self-Studies Behaviors** 1521
Pedro Mota *(Instituto Superior Técnico & Carnegie Mellon University)*,
Francisco Melo, Luísa Coheur *(Universidade de Lisboa)*

- **Beyond Traits: Social Context Based Personality Model** 1529
  Jaroslaw Kochanowicz, Ah-Hwee Tan, Daniel Thalmann *(Nanyang Technological University)*
- **Incorporating Global and Local Knowledge in Intentional Narrative Planning** 1539
  Jonathan Teutenberg *(Independent)*, Julie Porteous *(Teesside University)*
- **Automated Extension of Narrative Planning Domains with Antonymic Operators** 1547
  Julie Porteous, Alan Lindsay, Jonathon Read, Mark Truran, Marc Cavazza *(Teesside University)*
- **Semi-feature Level Fusion for Bimodal Affect Regression Based on Facial and Bodily Expressions** 1557
  Yang Zhang, Li Zhang *(Northumbria University)*
- **An Effective Conversation Tactic for Creating Value over Repeated Negotiations** 1567
  Johnathan Mell, Gale Lucas, Jonathan Gratch *(Institute for Creative Technologies)*

Session: L5 — Robotics III

- **Adaptive Learning for Multi-Agent Navigation** 1577
  Julio Godoy, Ioannis Karamouzas, Stephen J. Guy, Maria Gini *(University of Minnesota)*
- **Detecting and Correcting Model Anomalies in Subspaces of Robot Planning Domains** 1587
  Juan Pablo Mendoza, Manuela Veloso, Reid Simmons *(Carnegie Mellon University)*
- **Solving Infrastructure Monitoring Problems with Multiple Heterogeneous Unmanned Aerial Vehicles** 1597
  Jakub Ondráček, Ondřej Vaněk, Michal Pěchouček *(Czech Technical University)*
- **Observation Modelling for Vision-Based Target Search by Unmanned Aerial Vehicles** 1607
  W. T. Luke Teacy *(University of Southampton)*, Simon J. Julier, Renzo De Nardi *(University College London)*, Alex Rogers, Nicholas R. Jennings *(University of Southampton)*
- **Sliding Autonomy for UAV Path-Planning: Adding New Dimensions to Autonomy Management** 1615
  Lanny Lin *(Vivint Inc.)*, Michael A. Goodrich *(Brigham Young University)*
- **Leading the Way: An Efficient Multi-Robot Guidance System** 1625
  Piyush Khandelwal *(University of Texas at Austin)*, Samuel Barrett *(Kiva Systems)*, Peter Stone *(University of Texas at Austin)*

Poster Session / Extended Abstracts (Part 1)

- **Multi-Objective Multiagent Credit Assignment in NSGA-II Using Difference Evaluations** 1635
  Logan Yliniemi *(Oregon State University)*, Drew Wilson *(Austin Peay State University)*, Kagan Tumer *(Oregon State University)*
- **Towards Agent-Based Simulation of Maritime Customs** 1637
  F. Jordan Srour *(Lebanese American University)*, Neil Yorke-Smith *(American University of Beirut)*
- **Ex post Efficiency of Random Assignments** 1639
  Haris Aziz, Simon Mackenzie *(NICTA & UNSW)*, Lirong Xia *(Rensselaer Polytechnic Institute)*, Chun Ye *(Columbia University)*
- **Multi-Scale Reward Shaping via an Off-Policy Ensemble** 1641
  Anna Harutyunyan, Tim Brys, Peter Vrancx, Ann Nowé *(Vrije Universiteit Brussel)*
- **Towards Consistency-Based Reliability Assessment** 1643
  Laurence Cholvy *(ONERA)*, Laurent Perrussel *(Université Toulouse 1 Capitole)*, William Raynaut *(ONERA, France)*, Jean-Marc Thévenin *(Université Toulouse 1 Capitole)*
- **Estimating the Progress of Maintenance Goals** 1645
  John Thangarajah, James Harland *(RMIT University)*, Neil Yorke-Smith *(American University of Beirut)*
- **Heuristic Collective Learning for Efficient and Robust Emergence of Social Norms** 1647
  Jianye Hao, Jun Sun *(Singapore University of Technology and Design)*, Dongping Huang, Yi Cai *(South China University of Technology)*, Chao Yu *(Dalian University of Technology)*
- **"I like this painting too": When an ECA Shares Appreciations to Engage Users** 1649
  Sabrina Campano, Chloé Clavel, Catherine Pelachaud *(Télécom-ParisTech)*

- **Towards Probabilistic Decision Making on Human Activities Modeled with Business Process Diagrams** 1651
  Hector G. Ceballos, Victor Flores-Solorio *(Tecnologico de Monterrey)*, Juan P. Garcia-Vazquez *(Universidad Autonoma de Baja California)*
- **Accounting for Circumstances in Reputation Assessment** 1653
  Simon Miles *(King's College London)*, Nathan Griffiths *(University of Warwick)*
- **A Game for Studying Maintenance Alerts' Effectiveness** 1655
  Avraham Shvartzon, Amos Azaria, Sarit Kraus *(Bar Ilan University)*, Claudia V. Goldman, Omer Tsimhoni *(General Motors Advanced Technical Center)*, Joachim Meyer *(Tel Aviv University)*
- **The Efficient Interaction of Costly Punishment and Commitment** 1657
  The Anh Han *(Teesside University)*, Tom Lenaerts *(Université Libre de Bruxelles & Vrije Universiteit Brussel)*
- **Approximating Difference Evaluations with Local Information** 1659
  Mitchell Colby, William Curran, Kagan Tumer *(Oregon State University)*
- **A Replicator Dynamics Analysis of Difference Evaluation Functions** 1661
  Mitchell K. Colby, Kagan Tumer *(Oregon State University)*
- **Defender Strategies in Domains Involving Frequent Adversary Interaction** 1663
  Fei Fang *(University of Southern California)*, Peter Stone *(The University of Texas at Austin)*, Milind Tambe *(University of Southern California)*
- **New Winning Strategies for the Iterated Prisoner's Dilemma** 1665
  Philippe Mathieu, Jean-Paul Delahaye *(Lille University)*
- **Filling Knowledge Gaps in Human-Robot Interaction Using Rewritten Knowledge of Common Verbs** 1667
  Dongcai Lu, Jianmin Ji, Xiaoping Chen, Jiangchuan Liu *(University of Science and Technology of China)*
- **Coping with Moral Emotions** 1669
  Cristina Battaglino, Rossana Damiano *(University of Torino)*
- **SMT-based Bounded Model Checking for Weighted Interpreted Systems and for Weighted Epistemic ECTL** 1671
  Agnieszka M. Zbrzezny, Bożena Woźna-Szcześniak, Andrzej Zbrzezny *(Jan Długosz University in Częstochowa)*
- **Bounded Rationality of Restricted Turing Machines** 1673
  Lijie Chen, Pingzhong Tang *(Tsinghua University)*
- **Synchronous Games in the Situation Calculus** 1675
  Giuseppe De Giacomo *(Università di Roma)*, Yves Lespérance *(York University)*, Adrian R. Pearce *(University of Melbourne)*
- **Private Revision in a Multi-Agent Setting** 1677
  Thomas Caridroit *(Université d'Artois & CNRS)*, Sébastien Konieczny *(CRIL & CNRS)*, Tiago de Lima, Pierre Marquis *(Université d'Artois & CNRS)*
- **Near Optimal Strategies for Targeted Marketing in Social Networks** 1679
  Ramakumar Pasumarthi *(American Express India)*, Ramasuri Narayanam *(IBM Research India)*, Balaraman Ravindran *(Indian Institute of Technology Madras)*
- **Towards Planning Uncertain Commitment Protocols** 1681
  Felipe Meneguzzi *(Pontifical Catholic University of Rio Grande do Sul)*, Pankaj R. Telang *(North Carolina State University)*, Neil Yorke-Smith *(American University of Beirut)*
- **Calibration of Multi-Agent Simulations through a Participatory Experiment** 1683
  Kévin Darty *(University Paris-Sud)*, Julien Saunier *(Normandie Université)*, Nicolas Sabouret *(University Paris-Sud)*
- **Trajectory Sampling Value Iteration: Improved Dyna Search for MDPs** 1685
  Yicheng Zhou, Quan Liu *(Soochow University)*, Qiming Fu *(Suzhou University of Science and Technology)*, Zongzhang Zhang *(Soochow University)*
- **Empirical Analysis of Reputation-aware Task Delegation by Humans from a Multi-Agent Game** 1687
  Han Yu, Han Lin, Su Fang Lim, Jun Lin, Zhiqi Shen, Chunyan Miao *(Nanyang Technological University)*

- **Quality and Budget Aware Task Allocation for Spatial Crowdsourcing** 1689
  Han Yu, Chunyan Miao, Zhiqi Shen *(Nanyang Technological University)*,
  Cyril Leung *(Nanyang Technological University & The University of British Columbia)*
- **Modelling of Personality in Agents: From Psychology to Logical Formalisation and Implementation** 1691
  Sebastian Ahrndt, Johannes Fähndrich, Marco Lützenberger, Sahin Albayrak *(Technische Universität Berlin)*
- **Validating Business Requirements Using MAS Analysis Models** 1693
  Nektarios Mitakides, Nikolaos Spanoudakis *(Technical University of Crete)*,
  Pavlos Delias *(Eastern Macedonia and Thrace Institute of Technology)*
- **Applying the Synergy Graph Model to Human Basketball** 1695
  Somchaya Liemhetcharat *(Institute for Infocomm Research)*, Yicheng Luo *(National Junior College)*
- **PrivHab: A Multiagent Secure Georouting Protocol for Podcast Distribution on Disconnected Areas** 1697
  Adrián Sánchez-Carmona, Sergi Robles, Carlos Borrego *(Universitat Autónoma de Barcelona (UAB))*
- **Survival of the Chartist: An Evolutionary Agent-Based Analysis of Stock Market Trading** 1699
  Daan Bloembergen *(University of Liverpool)*, Daniel Hennes *(European Space Agency, The Netherlands)*,
  Simon Parsons, Karl Tuyls *(University of Liverpool)*
- **A Dancing Virtual Agent to Evoke Human Emotions** 1701
  Deborah Richards, Jon Cedric Roxas, Ayse Bilgin, Nader Hanna *(Macquarie University)*
- **Influence-Optimistic Local Values for Multiagent Planning** 1703
  Frans A. Oliehoek *(University of Amsterdam & University of Liverpool)*,
  Matthijs T. J. Spaan *(Delft University of Technology)*,
  Stefan J. Witwicki *(Swiss Federal Institute of Technology (EPFL))*
- **Programming with Commitments and Goals in JaCaMo+** 1705
  Matteo Baldoni, Cristina Baroglio, Federico Capuzzimati, Roberto Micalizio *(Università di Torino)*
- **Voter Dissatisfaction in Committee Elections** 1707
  Dorothea Baumeister *(Heinrich-Heine Universität Duesseldorf)*,
  Sophie Dennisen *(Technische Universität Clausthal)*
- **Bidding in Non-Stationary Energy Markets** 1709
  Pablo Hernandez-Leal *(Instituto Nacional de Astrofísica, Óptica y Electrónica)*,
  Matthew E. Taylor *(Washington State University)*,
  Enrique Munoz de Cote, L. Enrique Sucar *(Instituto Nacional de Astrofísica, Óptica y Electrónica)*
- **Influencing the Learning Experience Through Affective Agent Feedback in a Real-World Treasure Hunt** 1711
  Mary Ellen Foster, Amol Deshmukh, Srinivasan Janarthanam, Mei Yii Lim,
  Helen Hastie, Ruth Aylett *(Heriot-Watt University)*
- **Verification of Multi-Agent Systems via SDD-Based Model Checking** 1713
  Alessio Lomuscio, Hugo Paquet *(Imperial College London)*
- **Multi-Agent Task Assignment for Mobile Crowdsourcing Under Trajectory Uncertainties** 1715
  Cen Chen, Shih-Fen Cheng, Archan Misra, Hoong Chuin Lau *(Singapore Management University)*
- **Evolution of Cooperation under Entrenchment Effects** 1717
  Jayati Deshmukh, Srinath Srinivasa *(International Institute of Information Technology)*
- **The Cost of Interference in Evolving Multiagent Systems** 1719
  The Anh Han *(Teesside University)*, Long Tran-Thanh, Nicholas R. Jennings *(University of Southampton)*
- **Playing Congestion Games with Bandit Feedbacks** 1721
  Po-An Chen *(National Chiao Tung University)*, Chi-Jen Lu *(Academia Sinica)*
- **A Hybrid Evolutionary and Multiagent Reinforcement Learning Approach to Accelerate the Computation of Traffic Assignment** 1723
  Ana L. C. Bazzan *(Univ. Federal do Rio Grande do Sul (UFRGS))*,
  Camelia Chira *(Technical University of Cluj-Napoca)*
- **How Hard is Bribery in Party Based Elections?** 1725
  Yongjie Yang *(Universität des Saarlandes)*, Yash Raj Shrestha *(ETH Zürich)*, Jiong Guo *(Shandong University)*

- **Reinforcement Learning for Nash Equilibrium Generation** 1727
  David Cittern, Abbas Edalat *(Imperial College London)*
- **How Hard is Control in Multi-Peaked Elections: A Parameterized Study** 1729
  Yongjie Yang *(Universität des Saarlandes)*, Jiong Guo *(Shandong University)*
- **Modeling Tipping Point Theory Using Normative Multi-Agent Systems** 1731
  Rahmatollah Beheshti, Gita Sukthankar *(University of Central Florida)*
- **Beyond Plurality: Truth-Bias in Binary Scoring Rules** 1733
  Svetlana Obraztsova *(Tel-Aviv University)*, Omer Lev *(Hebrew University of Jerusalem)*,
  Evangelos Markakis *(Athens University of Economics and Business)*,
  Zinovi Rabinovich *(Mobileye Vision Technologies Ltd.)*,
  Jeffrey S. Rosenschein *(Hebrew University of Jerusalem)*
- **An Efficient Knowledge Transfer Solution to a Novel SMDP Formalization of a Broker's Decision Problem** 1735
  Rodrigue T. Kuate, Maria Chli, Hai H. Wang *(Aston University)*
- **Controlling Elections by Replacing Candidates or Votes** 1737
  Andrea Loreggia *(University of Padova)*,
  Nina Narodytska *(University of Toronto and University of New South Wales)*,
  Francesca Rossi *(University of Padova and Harvard University)*,
  K. Brent Venable *(Tulane University and IHMC)*, Toby Walsh *(NICTA and UNSW)*
- **Social Contexts and Social Pragmatics** 1739
  Matteo Baldoni, Cristina Baroglio *(Università degli Studi di Torino)*, Amit K. Chopra *(Lancaster University)*,
  Munindar P. Singh *(North Carolina State University)*
- **Mechanism Design for Resource Allocation — With Applications to Centralized Multi-Commodity Routing** 1741
  Qipeng Liu, Yicheng Liu, Pingzhong Tang *(Tsinghua University)*
- **A Bayesian Approach to Norm Identification** 1743
  Stephen Cranefield, Tony Savarimuthu *(University of Otago)*,
  Felipe Meneguzzi *(Pontifical Catholic University of Rio Grande do Sul)*, Nir Oren *(University of Aberdeen)*
- **The RoboCup 2014 SPL Drop-In Player Competition: Encouraging Teamwork without Pre-Coordination** 1745
  Katie Genter *(University of Texas at Austin)*, Tim Laue *(University of Bremen)*,
  Peter Stone *(University of Texas at Austin)*
- **Emigration or Tax Evasion? Solutions for Portuguese to Escape from Its Economic Crisis** 1747
  Nuno Magessi, Luis Antunes *(Universidade de Lisboa)*
- **On Structure-Based Inconsistency Measures and Their Computations via Closed Set Packing** 1749
  Said Jabbour *(University Artois)*, Yue Ma *(LRI – University Paris-Saclay)*,
  Badran Raddaoui, Lakhdar Sais, Yakoub Salhi *(CRIL – University Artois)*
- **Crowdfunding Investment for Renewable Energy** 1751
  Ronghuo Zheng, Ying Xu *(Carnegie Mellon University)*, Nilanjan Chakraborty *(Stony Brook University)*,
  Katia Sycara *(Carnegie Mellon University)*
- **Profit Maximizing Prior-free Multi-Unit Procurement Auctions with Capacitated Sellers** 1753
  Arupratan Ray *(Indian Institute of Science)*, Debmalya Mandal *(Harvard University)*,
  Yadati Narahari *(Indian Institute of Science)*
- **Competitive Pricing for Cloud Computing in an Evolutionary Market** 1755
  Bolei Xu *(University of Nottingham)*, Tao Qin *(Microsoft Research Asia)*,
  Guoping Qiu *(University of Nottingham)*, Tie-Yan Liu *(Microsoft Research Asia)*
- **Towards Completely Decentralized Mustering for StarCraft** 1757
  Zachary Suffern, Craig Tovey *(Georgia Institute of Technology)*,
  Sven Koenig *(University of Southern California)*
- **An Agent-Based Simulation System for Dynamic Project Scheduling and Online Disruption Resolving** 1759
  Hui Xi, Chi Keong Goh, Partha Sarathi Dutta *(Rolls-Royce Singapore Pte Ltd.)*,
  Meng Sha, Jie Zhang *(Nanyang Technological University)*

- **Social Network Driven Traffic Decongestion Using Near Time Forecasting** 1761
  Deepika Pathania, Kamalakar Karlapalem *(IIIT Hyderabad)*
- **A Gillespie-based Computational Model for Integrating Event-driven and Multi-Agent Based Simulation** 1763
  Sara Montagna, Andrea Omicini *(Università di Bologna)*, Danilo Pianini *(Università di Bologna)*
- **New Mechanism for Reservation in Cloud Computing** 1765
  Changjun Wang *(Chinese Academy of Sciences)*,
  Weidong Ma, Tao Qin, Feidiao Yang, Tie-Yan Liu *(Microsoft Research, China)*,
  Xujin Chen, Xiaodong Hu *(Chinese Academy of Sciences)*
- **Competitive Influence in Social Networks: Convergence, Submodularity, and Competition Effects** 1767
  Aris Anagnostopoulos *(Sapienza University of Rome)*, Diodato Ferraioli *(University of Salerno)*,
  Stefano Leonardi *(Sapienza University of Rome)*
- **Now, Later, or Both: A Closed-Form Optimal Decision for a Risk-Averse Buyer** 1769
  Jasper Hoogland *(CWI Amsterdam)*, Mathijs De Weerdt *(TU Delft)*,
  Han La Poutré *(CWI Amsterdam & TU Delft)*
- **A Large-Scale Study of Agents Learning from Human Reward** 1771
  Guangliang Li *(University of Amsterdam)*, Hayley Hung *(Delft University of Technology)*,
  Shimon Whiteson *(University of Amsterdam)*
- **Game-Theoretic Algorithms for Optimal Network Security Hardening Using Attack Graphs** 1773
  Karel Durkota, Viliam Lisý *(Czech Technical University in Prague)*,
  Christofer Kiekintveld *(University of Texas at El Paso)*, Branislav Bošanský *(Aarhus University)*

Poster Session / Extended Abstracts (Part 2)

- **Social Insect-Inspired Multi-Robot Coverage** 1775
  Bastian Broecker, Ipek Caliskanelli, Karl Tuyls, Elizabeth Sklar *(University of Liverpool)*,
  Daniel Hennes *(European Space Agency)*
- **The Impact of Virtual Agent Personality on a Shared Mental Model with Humans during Collaboration** 1777
  Nader Hanna, Deborah Richards *(Macquarie University)*
- **Computing Pareto Optimal Agreements in Multi-issue Negotiation for Service Composition** 1779
  Claudia Di Napoli *(Istituto di Calcolo e Reti ad Alte Prestazioni C.N.R.)*,
  Dario Di Nocera, Silvia Rossi *(University of Naples "Federico II")*
- **A Model for Collaborative Runtime Verification** 1781
  Bas Testerink *(Utrecht University)*, Nils Bulling *(Delft University of Technology)*,
  Mehdi Dastani *(Utrecht University)*
- **An Overview of a Mapping from Processes to Agents** 1783
  Tobias Küster, Marco Lützenberger *(Technische Universität Berlin, DAI-Labor)*
- **Convention Emergence and Influence in Dynamic Topologies** 1785
  James Marchant, Nathan Griffiths, Matthew Leeke *(University of Warwick)*
- **A Multi-phase Approach for Improving Information Diffusion in Social Networks** 1787
  Swapnil Dhamal, Prabuchandran K. J., Yadati Narahari *(Indian Institute of Science)*
- **An Optimal Bidimensional Multi-Armed Bandit Auction for Multi-unit Procurement** 1789
  Satyanath Bhat, Shweta Jain *(Indian Institute of Science)*,
  Sujit Gujar *(École Polytechnique Fédérale de Lausanne)*, Yadati Narahari *(Indian Institute of Science)*
- **A Continuous Negotiation Based Model for Traffic Regulation at an Intersection** 1791
  Matthis Gaciarz, Samir Aknine *(Université Claude Bernard Lyon 1)*,
  Neïla Bhouri *(IFSTTAR/GRETTIA)*
- **Randomized Coordination Search for Scalable Multiagent Planning** 1793
  N. Kemal Ure, Jonathan P. How *(Massachusetts Institute of Technology)*,
  John Vian *(Boeing Research & Technology)*
- **Elements of Epistemic Crypto Logic** 1795
  Jan van Eijck *(CWI & ILLC)*, Malvin Gattinger *(ILLC)*

- **Using Kl Divergence for Credibility Assessment** 1797
  Thibaut Vallée, Grégory Bonnet *(Normadie University)*
- **A Heating Agent Using a Personalised Thermal Comfort Model to Save Energy** 1799
  Frederik Auffenberg, Sebastian Stein, Alex Rogers *(University of Southampton)*
- **A Multidimensional Environment Implementation for Enhancing Agent Interaction** 1801
  Stéphane Galland *(Université de Technologie de Belfort-Montbéliard)*,
  Flavien Balbo *(Ecole Nationale Supérieure des Mines de Saint-Etienne)*,
  Nicolas Gaud *(Université de Technologie de Belfort-Montbéliard)*, Sebastian Rodriguez *(UTN Tucuman)*,
  Gauthier Picard, Olivier Boissier *(Ecole Nationale Supérieure des Mines de Saint-Etienne)*
- **Computing Quantal Response Equilibrium for Sponsored Search Auctions** 1803
  Jiang Rong *(Chinese Academy of Sciences)*, Tao Qin *(Microsoft Research)*,
  Bo An *(Nanyang Technological University)*
- **When Opinion Request Meets Majority Search: Avoiding Fraud in On-Line Review Systems** 1805
  Roberto Centeno *(UNED)*, Ramón Hermoso *(University of Zaragoza)*
- **Strategies for Truth Discovery Under Resource Constraints** 1807
  Anthony Etuk, Timothy J. Norman, Nir Oren *(University of Aberdeen)*, Murat Şensoy *(Özyeğin University)*
- **Symbolic Model-checking for Resource-Bounded ATL** 1809
  Natasha Alechina, Brian Logan, Hoang Nga Nguyen *(University of Nottingham)*,
  Franco Raimondi *(Middlesex University)*, Leonardo Mostarda *(Universitá degli Studi di Camerino)*
- **Trusted Mediator Agents to Better Manage Complex and Competitive Supply Chains** 1811
  Moath Jarrah, Jie Zhang *(Nanyang Technological University)*
- **Strategy Effectiveness of Game-Theoretical Solution Concepts in Extensive-Form General-Sum Games** 1813
  Jiří čermák *(Czech Technical University in Prague)*, Branislav Bošanský *(Aarhus University)*,
  Nicola Gatti *(Politecnico di Milano)*
- **Some Performance Bounds of Strategies for Graph Exploration** 1815
  Alessandro Riva, Alberto Quattrini Li, Francesco Amigoni *(Politecnico di Milano)*
- **Laughing with a Virtual Agent** 1817
  Florian Pecune *(Telecom ParisTech)*, Maurizio Mancini *(Università di Genova)*,
  Beatrice Biancardi *(Telecom ParisTech)*, Giovanna Varni *(Università di Genova)*,
  Yu Ding, Catherine Pelachaud *(Telecom ParisTech)*, Gualtiero Volpe, Antonio Camurri *(Università di Genova)*
- **Norm Establishment Constrained by Limited Resources** 1819
  Samhar Mahmoud, Simon Miles, Adel Taweel, Brendan Delaney, Michael Luck *(King's College London)*
- **Verifying Normative System Specification Containing Collective Imperatives and Deadlines** 1821
  Luca Gasparini, Timothy J. Norman, Martin J. Kollingbaum, Liang Chen *(University of Aberdeen)*,
  John-Jules Ch. Meyer *(Utrecht University)*
- **Multi-Variable Agents Decomposition for DCOPs to Exploit Multi-Level Parallelism** 1823
  Ferdinando Fioretto, William Yeoh, Enrico Pontelli *(New Mexico State University)*
- **Computer Aided Tax Evasion Policy Analysis: Directed Search Using Autonomous Agents** 1825
  Jacob B. Rosen, Erik Hemberg *(Massachusetts Institute of Technology)*,
  Geoff Warner, Sanith Wijesinghe *(MITRE Corporation)*,
  Una-May O'Reilly *(Massachusetts Institute of Technology)*
- **Improving Value Function Approximation in Factored POMDPs by Exploiting Model Structure** 1827
  Tiago S. Veiga *(Universidade de Lisboa)*, Matthijs T. J. Spaan *(Delft University of Technology)*,
  Pedro U. Lima *(Universidade de Lisboa)*
- **Real-Time Bidding Based Vehicle Sharing** 1829
  Yinlam Chow *(Stanford University)*, Jia Yuan Yu *(IBM Research Ireland)*
- **Cascade Model with Contextual Externalities and Bounded User Memory for Sponsored Search Auctions** 1831
  Nicola Gatti, Marco Rocco *(Politecnico di Milano)*, Paolo Serafino, Carmine Ventre *(Teesside University)*

- **A Market for Reliability for Electricity Scheduling in Developing World Microgrids** 1833
Daniel Strawser, Brian C. Williams, Wardah Inam *(Massachusetts Institute of Technology)*
- **Large Neighborhood Search with Quality Guarantees for Distributed Constraint Optimization Problems** 1835
Ferdinando Fioretto, Federico Campeotto *(New Mexico State University)*, Agostino Dovier *(University of Udine)*, Enrico Pontelli, William Yeoh *(New Mexico State University)*
- **Multi-Robot Inverse Reinforcement Learning Under Occlusion with State Transition Estimation** 1837
Kenneth Bogert, Prashant Doshi *(University of Georgia)*
- **Improved Planning for Infinite-Horizon Interactive POMDPs Using Probabilistic Inference** 1839
Xia Qu, Prashant Doshi *(University of Georgia)*
- **Voting with Social Influence: Using Arguments to Uncover Ground Truth** 1841
Alan Tsang, John A. Doucette, Hadi Hosseini *(University of Waterloo)*
- **Cognitive Robots Learning Failure Contexts through Experimentation** 1843
Sertac Karapinar, Sanem Sariel *(Istanbul Technical University)*
- **Global Approximations for Principal Agent Theory** 1845
Federico Cerutti, Nir Oren, Christopher Burnett *(University of Aberdeen)*
- **The Evolutionary Perks of Being Irrational** 1847
Fernando P. Santos, Francisco C. Santos, Ana Paiva *(Universidade de Lisboa)*
- **A Computational Model of Trust Based on Message Content and Source** 1849
Célia da Costa Pereira, Andrea G. B. Tettamanzi *(University Nice Sophia Antipolis)*, Serena Villata *(Inria Sophia Antipolis)*
- **Probabilistic Copeland Tournaments** 1851
Sam Saarinen, Judy Goldsmith *(University of Kentucky)*, Craig Tovey *(Georgia Institute of Technology)*
- **Quantifier Learning: An Agent-based Coordination Model** 1853
Dariusz Kalociński, Nina Gierasimczuk, Marcin Mostowski *(University of Warsaw)*
- **Paving the Way for Large-Scale Combinatorial Auctions** 1855
Francisco Cruz-Mencia *(IIIA-CSIC & CAOS-UAB)*, Jesus Cerquides *(IIIA-CSIC)*, Antonio Espinosa, Juan Carlos Moure *(CAOS-UAB)*, Juan Antonio Rodriguez-Aguilar *(IIIA-CSIC)*
- **Towards Social Power Intelligent Agents** 1857
Gonçalo Pereira, Rui Prada, Pedro A. Santos *(Universidade Técnica de Lisboa)*
- **Exploring Social Power Intelligent Behavior** 1861
Gonçalo Duarte Garcia Pereira, Rui Prada, Pedro A. Santos *(Universidade Técnica de Lisboa)*
- **Considering Agent and Task Openness in Ad Hoc Team Formation** 1861
Bin Chen, Xi Chen, Anish Timsina, Leen-Kiat Soh *(University of Nebraska)*
- **Reducing Diffusion Time in Attitude Diffusion Models Through Agenda Setting** 1863
Kiran Lakkaraju *(Sandia National Laboratories)*
- **Incremental Knowledge Acquisition with Selective Active Learning** 1865
Batbold Myagmarjav *(Texas Tech University)*, Mohan Sridharan *(The University of Auckland)*
- **Towards Sketch Recognition by Mirroring** 1867
Mor Vered, Gal A. Kaminka *(Bar Ilan University)*
- **Exploiting Objects as Artifacts in Multi-Agent Based Social Simulations** 1869
Felicitas Mokom, Ziad Kobti *(University of Windsor)*
- **MAP: A Computational Model for Adaptive Persuasion** 1871
Yilin Kang, Ah-Hwee Tan *(Nanyang Technological University)*
- **Discovery, Evaluation, and Exploration of Human Supplied Options and Constraints** .. 1873
Jesse Rosalia, Guliz Tokadli, Charles L. Isbell Jr., Andrea Thomaz, Karen M. Feigh *(Georgia Institute of Technology)*
- **Nonparametric Bayesian Learning of Other Agents' Policies in Interactive POMDPs** 1875
Alessandro Panella, Piotr J. Gmytrasiewicz *(University of Illinois at Chicago)*
- **Selecting Robust Strategies Based on Abstracted Game Models** 1877
Oscar Veliz, Christopher Kiekintveld *(University of Texas at El Paso)*

- **On Task Recognition and Generalization in Long-Term Robot Teaching** 1879
  Guglielmo Gemignani *(Sapienza University of Rome)*, Steven D. Klee,
  Manuela Veloso *(Carnegie Mellon University)*, Daniele Nardi *(Sapienza University of Rome)*
- **Learning Payoffs in Large Symmetric Games** 1881
  Bryce Wiedenbeck, Michael P. Wellman *(University of Michigan)*
- **Managing Multi Robotic Agents to Avoid Congestion and Stampedes** 1883
  Garima Ahuja, Kamalakar Karlapalem *(IIIT Hyderabad)*
- **Parametric Mechanism Design via Quantifier Elimination** 1885
  Atsushi Iwasaki *(University of Electro-Communications)*,
  Etsushi Fujita, Taiki Todo *(Kyushu University)*,
  Hidenao Iwane, Hirokazu Anai *(Fujitsu Laboratories & National Institute of Informatics)*,
  Mingyu Guo *(University of Adelaide)*, Makoto Yokoo *(Kyushu University)*
- **Improving Fairness in Nonwasteful Matching with Hierarchical Regional Minimum Quotas** 1887
  Masahiro Goto, Ryoji Kurata, Naoto Hamada *(Kyushu University)*,
  Atsushi Iwasaki *(University of Electro-Communications)*, Makoto Yokoo *(Kyushu University)*
- **Behaviour Analysis of Mixed Game-Theoretic Learning Algorithms** 1889
  Michalis Smyrnakis, Hongyang Qu, Sandor M. Veres *(University of Sheffield)*
- **Generalized Plan Design for Autonomous Mobile Manipulation in Open Environments** 1891
  Jan Oliver Winkler, Michael Beetz *(University of Bremen)*
- **Spiteful Bidding in the Dollar Auction** 1893
  Marcin Waniek *(University of Warsaw)*,
  Agata Nieścieruk *(Polish-Japanese Academy of Information Technology)*,
  Tomasz Michalak *(University of Oxford & University of Warsaw)*,
  Talal Rahwan *(Masdar Institute of Science and Technology)*
- **Multiagent Fair Optimization with Lorenz Dominance** 1895
  Lucie Galand *(Université Paris-Dauphine)*, Thibaut Lust *(Univ Paris 06, CNRS)*
- **P-MARL: Prediction-Based Multi-Agent Reinforcement Learning for Non-Stationary Environments** 1897
  Andrei Marinescu, Ivana Dusparic, Adam Taylor, Vinny Cahill, Siobhán Clarke *(Trinity College Dublin)*
- **The "Favors Game": A Framework to Study the Emergence of Cooperation Through Social Importance** 1899
  Pedro Sequeira, Samuel Mascarenhas, Francisco S. Melo, Ana Paiva *(University of Lisbon)*
- **A Novel Abstraction Framework for Online Planning** 1901
  Ankit Anand, Aditya Grover, Mausam, Parag Singla *(Indian Institute of Technology)*

Demonstration Abstracts

- **Community Evacuation Planning for Bushfires Using Agent-Based Simulation** 1903
  Dhirendra Singh, Lin Padgham *(RMIT University)*
- **Agent-Based Adaptive Mobile Computing in Games: Demonstration** 1905
  Damian Burke, Axel Heßler, Sahin Albayrak *(TU Berlin)*
- **Enabling Intelligence Analysis through Agent-Support: The CISpaces Toolkit** 1907
  Alice Toniolo, Hengfei Li, Timothy J. Norman, Nir Oren *(University of Aberdeen)*,
  Robin Wentao Ouyang, Mani Srivastava *(University of California, Los Angeles)*,
  Timothy Dropps, John A. Allen *(Honeywell)*, Paul Sullivan *(INTELPOINT Incorporated)*
- **Every Team Deserves a Second Chance: An Interactive 9x9 Go Experience** 1909
  Leandro Soriano Marcolino *(University of Southern California)*,
  Vaishnavh Nagarajan *(Indian Institute of Technology Madras)*,
  Milind Tambe *(University of Southern California)*
- **Learning, Predicting and Planning Against Crime: Demonstration Based on Real Urban Crime Data** 1911
  Chao Zhang *(University of Southern California)*, Manish Jain, Ripple Goyal *(Armorway. Inc.)*,
  Arunesh Sinha, Milind Tambe *(University of Southern California)*

- **Shaping Mario with Human Advice** ... 1913
  Anna Harutyunyan, Tim Brys, Peter Vrancx, Ann Nowé *(Vrije Universiteit Brussel)*
- **Pnyx: A Powerful and User-Friendly Tool for Preference Aggregation** ... 1915
  Felix Brandt, Guillaume Chabin, Christian Geist *(TU München)*
- **SCANERGY: A Scalable and Modular System for Energy Trading Between Prosumers** ... 1917
  Mihail Mihaylov, Sergio Jurado, Narcís Avellana *(Sensing & Control Systems)*, Iván Razo-Zapata, Kristof Van Moffaert, Leticia Arco, Maite Bezunartea, Isel Grau, Adrian Cañadas, Ann Nowé *(Vrije Universiteit Brussel)*
- **Aerial Robotic Simulations for Evaluation of Multi-Agent Planning in GaTAC** ... 1919
  Kenneth Bogert, Sina Solaimanpour, Prashant Doshi *(University of Georgia)*
- **HAC-ER: A Disaster Response System Based on Human-Agent Collectives** ... 1921
  Sarvapali D. Ramchurn, Trung Dong Huynh, Yuki Ikuno, Jack Flann, Feng Wu, Luc Moreau, Nicholas R. Jennings, Joel E. Fischer, Wenchao Jiang, Tom Rodden *(University of Nottingham)*, Edwin Simpson, Steve Reece, Stephen J. Roberts *(University of Oxford)*
- **An Empathic Robotic Tutor in a Map Application** ... 1923
  Amol Deshmukh *(Heriot-Watt University)*, Aidan Jones *(University of Birmingham)*, Srinivasan Janarthanam, Helen Hastie *(Heriot-Watt University)*, Tiago Ribeiro *(GAIPS, INESC-ID & Instituto Superior Tecnico)*, Ruth Aylett *(Heriot-Watt University)*, Ana Paiva *(GAIPS, INESC-ID & Instituto Superior Tecnico)*, Ginevra Castellano *(Uppsala University & University of Birmingham)*, Mary Ellen Foster *(Heriot-Watt University)*, Lee J. Corrigan, Fotios Papadopoulos *(University of Birmingham)*, Eugenio Di Tullio, Pedro Sequeira *(GAIPS, INESC-ID & Instituto Superior Tecnico)*
- **How to Use OpenEASE: An Online Knowledge Processing System for Robots and Robotics Researchers** ... 1925
  Georg Bartels, Michael Beetz, Daniel Beßler, Moritz Tenorth, Jan Winkler *(Universität Bremen)*
- **Open Game Tournaments in STARLITE** ... 1927
  Jack Hopkins, Özgür Kafalı, Kostas Stathis *(Royal Holloway, University of London)*
- **Using Agent-Based Tactics Models to Control Virtual Actors in VBS3** ... 1929
  Rick Evertsz, John Thangarajah, Nik Ambukovski *(RMIT University)*
- **Extending NormLab to Spur Research on Norm Synthesis** ... 1931
  Javier Morales *(Universitat de Barcelona)*, Iosu Mendizabal *(IIIA-CSIC)*, David Sánchez-Pinsach *(Universitat de Barcelona)*, Juan A Rodríguez-Aguilar *(IIIA-CSIC)*, Maite López-Sánchez *(Universitat de Barcelona)*, Michael Wooldridge *(University of Oxford)*, Wamberto Vasconcelos *(University of Aberdeen)*
- **Multi-Agent Target Tracking Using Particle Filters Enhanced with Context Data** ... 1933
  Rik Claessens *(University of Liverpool & Thales Research and Technology Delft)*, Alta de Waal *(University of Pretoria)*, Pieter de Villiers *(University of Pretoria and Council for Scientific and Industrial Research)*, Ate Penders *(Thales Research & Technology, Delft & Delft University of Technology)*, Gregor Pavlin *(Thales Research & Technology Delft and University of Amsterdam)*, Karl Tuyls *(University of Liverpool and Delft University of Technology)*
- **A Tool for Defining Agent Protocols in HAPN** ... 1935
  Nitin Yadav, Lin Padgham *(RMIT University)*, Michael Winikoff *(University of Otaga)*
- **Multi-stage Smart Grid Optimisation with a Multiagent System** ... 1937
  Christopher-Eyk Hrabia, Francisco Denis Pozo Pardo, Tobias Küster, Sahin Albayrak *(Technische Universität Berlin)*
- **SE-Star: A Large-Scale Human Behavior Simulation for Planning, Decision-Making and Training** ... 1939
  Laurent Navarro, Fabien Flacher, Christophe Meyer *(Thales Services)*
- **A Knowledge-Based Approach to Robotic Perception Using Unstructured Information Management** ... 1941
  Ferenc Bálint-Benczédi, Thiemo Wiedemeyer, Moritz Tenorth, Daniel Beßler, Michael Beetz *(University of Bremen)*

- **PrivHab: A Multiagent Secure Georouting Protocol for Distributing Podcasts in Disconnected Areas** 1943
  Adrián Sánchez-Carmona, Sergi Robles, Carlos Borrego, Gerard Garcia-Vandellós *(Universitat Autónoma de Barcelona)*
- **PViz: Visualising P2P Multi-Agent Simulations** 1945
  Dimitris Giouroukis, Nikos Platis *(University of the Peloponnese)*, Christos Tryfonopoulos *(University of the Peloponnese & Max-Planck Institute for Informatics)*
- **An Affective Agent for Studying Composite Emotions** 1947
  Jun Lin, Han Yu, Chunyan Miao, Zhiqi Shen *(Nanyang Technological University)*
- **A Framework for Developing Multi-Agent Systems in Ambient Intelligence Scenarios** 1949
  Pablo Campillo-Sanchez, Jorge J. Gomez-Sanz *(Universidad Complutense de Madrid)*
- **Social Theatre: Showcasing Social Power Aware Agents** 1951
  Gonçalo Pereira, Rui Prada, Pedro A. Santos *(INESC-ID, Instituto Superior Técnico & Universidade Técnica de Lisboa)*
- **fNIRS-based BCI for Robot Control** 1953
  Kirill Tumanov, Rainer Goebel, Rico Möckel, Bettina Sorger, Gerhard Weiss *(Maastricht University)*
- **emigo: A Large-Scale Multi-Agent Platform for the Web** 1955
  Rym Wenkstern, Travis Steel, Dane Kuiper *(ZW Corp)*
- **Interfacing Agents with an Industrial Assembly System for "Plug and Produce"** 1957
  Nikolas Antzoulatos, Elkin Castro, Lavindra de Silva, Svetan Ratchev *(University of Nottingham)*
- **A Prototype for AUV Post-Mission Debrief Generation From Metadata** 1959
  Zhuoran Wang *(Toshiba Research Europe Ltd)*, Helen Hastie *(Heriot-Watt University)*

Doctoral Consortium Abstracts

- **To Handle, to Learn and to Manipulate the Attacker's (Uncertain) Payoffs in Security Games** 1961
  Yundi Qian *(University of Southern California)*
- **A Unifying Methodology for Confronting Uncertainties in Security Games: Advances and Algorithms** 1963
  Thanh H. Nguyen, Milind Tambe *(University of Southern California)*
- **Agent-based Coordination Mechanisms in Smart Electricity Markets** 1965
  Konstantina Valogianni *(Erasmus University Rotterdam)*
- **Three Fundamental Pillars of Multi-Agent Team Formation** 1967
  Leandro Soriano Marcolino, Milind Tambe *(University of Southern California)*
- **Robotic Adversarial Coverage** 1969
  Roi Yehoshua *(Bar Ilan University)*
- **Modeling, Learning and Defending against Opportunistic Criminals in Urban Areas** 1971
  Chao Zhang *(University of Southern California)*
- **Computational Complexity of Fundamental Problems in Social Choice Theory** 1973
  Palash Dey *(Indian Institute of Science)*
- **Representing and Reasoning about Game Strategies** 1975
  Guifei Jiang *(University of Western Sydney & University of Toulouse)*
- **Heterogeneous Facility Location without Money** 1977
  Paolo Serafino *(Teesside University)*
- **Dynamic Capacity Control and Balancing in the Medium Voltage Grid** 1979
  Frits de Nijs *(Delft University of Technology)*
- **A Reference Model for a Networked Organization** 1981
  Saad Alqithami *(Southern Illinois University)*

- **Intelligent Learning Agents for Music-Based Interaction and Analysis** 1983
  Elad Liebman *(University of Texas at Austin)*
- **Monte Carlo Hierarchical Model Learning** 1985
  Jacob Menashe, Peter Stone *(The University of Texas at Austin)*
- **Computational Models of Algorithmic Trading in Financial Markets** 1987
  Elaine Wah *(University of Michigan)*
- **Opponent Modeling Against Non-Stationary Strategies** 1989
  Pablo Hernandez-Leal, Enrique Munoz de Cote,
  L. Enrique Sucar *(Instituto Nacional de Astrofísica, Óptica y Electrónica)*
- **Emotional Interactions between Artificial Companion Agents and the Elderly** 1991
  Xinjia Yu, Charles Thomas Salmon *(Nanyang Technological University)*,
  Cyril Leung *(The University of British Columbia)*
- **Incremental Knowledge Acquisition with Selective Active Learning** 1993
  Batbold Myagmarjav *(Texas Tech University)*, Mohan Sridharan *(The University of Auckland)*
- **Machine Learning Methods for Multi Robot Navigation** 1995
  Julio Godoy *(University of Minnesota)*
- **Quantifying and Improving Robustness of Trust Systems** 1997
  Dongxia Wang *(Nanyang Technological University)*
- **Adaptation from Sparse Observations through Detection and Correction of Model Anomalies** 1999
  Juan Pablo Mendoza *(Carnegie Mellon University)*
- **Adaptation and Incentive Design in Large Scale Task Systems** 2001
  Avi Segal *(Ben-Gurion University)*
- **Stackelberg Games for Robust Vaccine Design** 2003
  Swetasudha Panda, Yevgeniy Vorobeychik *(Vanderbilt University)*
- **One-Sided Matching with Dynamic Preferences** 2005
  Hadi Hosseini *(University of Waterloo)*
- **Exploiting the Structure of Distributed Constraint Optimization Problems** 2007
  Ferdinando Fioretto *(New Mexico State University & University of Udine)*
- **Data-Driven Agent-Based Modeling of Innovation Diffusion** 2009
  Haifeng Zhang *(Vanderbilt University)*
- **Governing Government: A Framework for Multi-tier Institution Specification and Reasoning** 2011
  Thomas C. King *(Delft University of Technology)*
- **Verifying Conflicts Between Multiple Norms in Multi-Agent Systems** 2013
  Eduardo Augusto Silvestre *(Federal Fluminense University)*, Viviane Torres da Silva *(IBM Research)*
- **Toward Social-Emotional Virtual Humans** 2015
  Johnathan Mell *(University of Southern California)*
- **Engineering Online Evolution of Robot Behaviour** 2017
  Fernando Silva, Anders Lyhne Christensen *(BioMachines & BioISI)*, Luís Correia *(BioISI)*
- **Privacy Management in Agent-Based Social Networks** 2019
  Nadin Kökciyan *(Bogazici University)*
- **Selected Methods of Model Checking Using SAT and SMT-solvers** 2021
  Agnieszka M. Zbrzezny *(Jan Długosz University)*

Author Index 2023

AAMAS 2016 Call for Papers 2030

AAMAS 2015 Organizing Committee

General Chairs:	Gerhard Weiss *(Maastricht University, Netherlands)* Pınar Yolum *(Bogazici University, Turkey)*
Program Chairs:	Rafael H. Bordini *(PUCRS, Brazil)* Edith Elkind *(University of Oxford, UK)*
Innovative Applications Track Chairs:	Amal El Fallah Seghrouchni *(LIP6, France)* Milind Tambe *(University of Southern California, USA)*
Robotics Track Chairs:	Alessandro Farinelli *(University of Verona, Italy)* Gal Kaminka *(Bar Ilan University, Israel)*
Virtual Agents & Humans Track Chairs:	Catholijn Jonker *(Delft University of Technology, Netherlands)* Rui Prada *(Technical University of Lisbon, Portugal)*
Blue Sky Ideas Track Chair:	Victor Lesser *(University of Massachusetts, USA)*
Workshop Chairs:	Michal Pechoucek *(University of Prague, Czech Republic)* Longbing Cao *(University of Technology, Sydney, Australia)*
Tutorial Chairs:	Cristina Baroglio *(Università di Torino, Italy)* Thomas Ågotnes *(University of Bergen, Norway)*
Demonstration Chairs:	Paolo Torroni *(University of Bologna, Italy)* Karl Tuyls *(University of Liverpool, UK)*
Doctoral Student Mentoring Consortium Chairs:	M. Birna van Riemsdijk *(Delft University of Technology, Netherlands)* Ya'akov (Kobi) Gal *(Ben-Gurion University of the Negev, Israel)* Adrian Pearce *(University of Melbourne, Australia)*
Sponsorship Chairs:	Americas: Matthew E. Taylor *(Washington State University, USA)* Asia/Oceania: Toshiharu Sugawara *(Waseda University, Japan)* Europe: Vicent Botti *(Universidad Politécnica de Valencia, Spain)*
Student Scholarship Chairs:	Gita Sukthankar *(University of Central Florida, USA)* Sebastian Sardina *(RMIT University, Australia)*
Publicity Chair:	Amit Chopra *(Lancaster University, UK)*
Publications Chair:	Neil Yorke-Smith *(American University Beirut, Lebanon)*
Exhibition Chair:	Ulle Endriss *(University of Amsterdam, Netherlands)*
Finance Chair:	Murat Şensoy *(Ozyegin University, Turkey)*
Local Organization Chair:	Pınar Yolum *(Bogazici University, Turkey)*

AAMAS 2015 Senior Programme Committee

Main Track:

Thomas Agotnes *(University of Bergen, Norway)*
Natasha Alechina *(University of Nottingham, UK)*
Bo An *(Nanyang Technological University, Singapore)*
Matteo Baldoni *(University of Turin, Italy)*
Georgios Chalkiadakis *(Technical University of Crete, Greece)*
Bruce Edmonds *(Manchester Metropolitan University, UK)*
Piotr Faliszewski *(AGH University of Science and Technology, Poland)*
Enrico Gerding *(University of Southampton, UK)*
Andreas Herzig *(Paul Sabatier University, France)*
Katsutoshi Hirayama *(Kobe University, Japan)*
Christopher Kiekintveld *(University of Texas, USA)*
Sven Koenig *(University of Southern California, USA)*
Han La Poutre *(CWI, Netherlands)*
Jerome Lang *(CNRS, France)*
Kate Larson *(University of Waterloo, Canada)*
Yves Lesperance *(York University, Canada)*
Brian Logan *(University of Nottingham, UK)*
Alessio Lomuscio *(Imperial College London, UK)*
Viviana Mascardi *(University of Genova, Italy)*
Nicolas Maudet *(Paris Dauphine University, France)*
Felipe Meneguzzi *(PUCRS, Brazil)*
Emma Norling *(Manchester Metropolitan University, UK)*
Simon Parsons *(University of Liverpool, UK)*
Maria Polukarov *(University of Southampton, UK)*
Ariel Procaccia *(Carnegie Mellon University, USA)*
David Pynadath *(University of Southern California, USA)*
Alessandro Ricci *(University of Bologna, Italy)*
Avi Rosenfeld *(Jerusalem College of Technology, Israel)*
Francesca Rossi *(University of Padova, Italy)*
Michael Rovatsos *(University of Edinburgh, UK)*
Jordi Sabater-Mir *(IIIA-CSIC, Spain)*
Sebastian Sardina *(RMIT University, Australia)*
David Sarne *(Bar Ilan University, Israel)*
Sandip Sen *(University of Tulsa, USA)*
Gita Sukthankar *(University of Central Florida, USA)*
Matthew Taylor *(Washington State University, USA)*
Wamberto Vasconcelos *(University of Aberdeen, UK)*
Rineke Verbrugge *(University of Groningen, Netherlands)*
Shimon Whiteson *(University of Amsterdam, Netherlands)*
Cees Witteveen *(Delft University of Technology, Netherlands)*
Makoto Yokoo *(Kyushu University, Japan)*
Roie Zivan *(Ben Gurion University, Israel)*

Innovative Applications Track:

Yoram Bachrach *(Microsoft Research, USA)*
Lars Braubach *(University of Hamburg, Germany)*
Ruggerio Cavallo *(Yahoo Research, USA)*
James Harland *(RMIT University, Australia)*
Tom Holvoet *(University of Leuven, Belgium)*
Ece Kamar *(Microsoft Research, USA)*
Fernando Koch *(Samsung Research, Brazil)*
Michael Luck *(King's College London, UK)*
Janusz Marecki *(IBM Research, USA)*
Andrea Omicini *(Università di Bologna, Italy)*

Robotics Track:

Noa Agmon *(Bar Ilan University, Israel)*
Maria Gini *(University of Minnesota, USA)*
Alexander Kleiner *(Linköping University, Sweden)*
Daniele Nardi *(Sapienza University of Rome, Italy)*
Paul Scerri *(Carnegie Mellon University, USA)*
Elizabeth Sklar *(University of Liverpool, UK)*
Mohan Sridharan *(University of Auckland, New Zealand)*
Manuela Veloso *(Carnegie Mellon University, USA)*

Virtual Agents and Humans Track:
Elisabeth Andre *(Augsburg University, Germany)*
Ruth Aylett *(Heriot Watt University, UK)*
Timothy Bickmore *(Northeastern University, USA)*
Stefan Kopp *(Bielefeld University, Germany)*
Stacy Marsella *(University of Southern California, USA)*
Ana Paiva *(Technical University of Lisbon, Portugal)*
Catherine Pelachaud *(CNRS - LTCI Telecom-ParisTech, France)*
Mark Riedl *(Georgia Institute of Technology, USA)*
Hannes Vilhjalmsson *(Reykjavík University, Iceland)*

Blue Sky Ideas Track:
Ed Durfee *(University of Michigan, USA)*
Jeffrey S. Rosenschein *(Hebrew University of Jerusalem, Israel)*
Munindar Singh *(North Carolina State University, USA)*
Liz Sonenberg *(University of Melbourne, Australia)*

AAMAS 2015 Programme Committee

Main Track:

Sherief Abdallah *(British University in Dubai, UAE)*
Carole Adam *(University of Grenoble, France)*
Gul Agha *(University of Illinois at Urbana, USA)*
Adrian Agogino *(University of California at Santa Cruz and NASA Ames Research Center, USA)*
Stéphane Airiau *(Université Paris-Dauphine, France)*
Juan M. Alberola *(Universitat Politecnica de Valencia, Spain)*
Huib Aldewereld *(Delft University of Technology, Netherlands)*
Christopher Amato *(University of New Hampshire, USA)*
Frederic Amblard *(Universite Toulouse 1 Capitole, France)*
Leila Amgoud *(IRIT - CNRS, France)*
Ofra Amir *(Harvard University, USA)*
Alexander Artikis *(NCSR Demokritos, Greece)*
Katie Atkinson *(University of Liverpool, UK)*
Guillaume Aucher *(University of Rennes, France)*
Reyhan Aydogan *(Delft University of Technology, Netherlands)*
Amos Azaria *(Carnegie Mellon University, USA)*
Haris Aziz *(NICTA and University of New South Wales, Australia)*
Tim Baarslag *(University of Southampton, UK)*
Dirk Bade *(University of Hamburg, Germany)*
Costin Badica *(University of Craiova, Romania)*
Cristina Baroglio *(University of Torino, Italy)*
Dorothea Baumeister *(Heinrich-Heine-Universitaet Duesseldorf, Germany)*
Francesco Belardinelli *(Université d'Evry, France)*
Vaishak Belle *(University of Toronto, Canada and KU Leuven, Belgium)*
Jamal Bentahar *(Concordia University, Canada)*
Federico Bergenti *(University of Parma, Italy)*
Aurélie Beynier *(LIP6, University Pierre & Marie Curie, France)*
Elizabeth Black *(King's College London, UK)*
Guido Boella *(Universita di Torino, Italy)*
Frank S. de Boer *(Centrum Wiskunde en Informatica, Netherlands)*
Olivier Boissier *(Ecole des Mines de Saint-Etienne, France)*
Ladislau Bölöni *(University of Central Florida, USA)*
Elise Bonzon *(Université Paris Descartes, France)*
Juan Botia *(King's College London, UK)*
Vicent Botti *(Universitat Politècnica de València, Spain)*
Gauvain Bourgne *(Université Pierre et Marie Curie – Paris 6, France)*
Sylvain Bouveret *(Grenoble INP - Ensimag, France)*
Anarosa A. F. Brandão *(University of São Paulo, Brazil)*
Felix Brandt *(Technische Universität München, Germany)*
Frances Brazier *(Delft University of Technology, Netherlands)*
Robert Bredereck *(Technische Universität Berlin, Germany)*
Jean-Pierre Briot *(Laboratoire d'Informatique de Paris 6, France)*
Nils Bulling *(Delft University of Technology, Netherlands)*
Olivier Cailloux *(Université de Technologie de Compiègne, France)*
David Camacho *(Autonomous University of Madrid, Spain)*
Martin Caminada *(University of Aberdeen, UK)*
Ioannis Caragiannis *(University of Patras, Greece)*
C. Carrascosa *(Universitat Politècinca de València, Spain)*
Arthur Carvalho *(Erasmus University, Netherlands)*
Cristiano Castelfranchi *(ISTC-CNR, Italy)*
Sofia Ceppi *(Microsoft Research, UK)*
Michal Chalamish *(Ashkelon Academic College, Israel)*
Archie Chapman *(University of Sydney, Australia)*
Shih-Fen Cheng *(Singapore Management University, Singapore)*
Federico Chesani *(University of Bologna, Italy)*
Yann Chevaleyre *(University of Paris 13, France)*
Meenal Chhabra *(Square, USA)*
Amit Chopra *(Lancaster University, UK)*
Helder Coelho *(Universidade de Lisboa, Portugal)*
Rem Collier *(University College Dublin, Ireland)*
Marco Colombetti *(Politecnico di Milano, Italy)*
Flavio Correa da Silva *(University of Sao Paulo, Brazil)*

Vincent Corruble *(Université Pierre et Marie Curie – Paris 6, France)*
Stefania Costantini *(University of L'Aquila, Italy)*
Fabiano Dalpiaz *(Utrecht University, Netherlands)*
Hoa Dam *(University of Wollongong, Australia)*
Sanmay Das *(Washington Univ. in St Louis, USA)*
Mehdi Dastani *(Utrecht University, Netherlands)*
Patrick De Causmaecker *(KU Leuven, Belgium)*
Tiago de Lima *(Université d'Artois, France)*
Lavindra de Silva *(University of Nottingham, UK)*
Marina De Vos *(University of Bath, UK)*
Mathijs de Weerdt *(Delft University of Technology, Netherlands)*
Keith Decker *(University of Delaware, USA)*
Louise Dennis *(University of Liverpool, UK)*
Sam Devlin *(York Centre for Complex Systems Analysis, UK)*
Jilles Dibangoye *(INSA, France)*
Oguz Dikenelli *(Ege University, Turkey)*
Graçaliz Dimuro *(Universidade Federal do Rio Grande, Brazil)*
Prashant Doshi *(University of Georgia, USA)*
Sylvie Doutre *(Université Toulouse 1 Capitole - IRIT, France)*
Barbara Dunin-Keplicz *(University of Warsaw, Poland)*
Paul Dunne *(University of Liverpool, UK)*
Marcin Dziubinski *(Warsaw University, Poland)*
Artur d'Avila Garcez *(City University London, UK)*
Ulle Endriss *(University of Amsterdam, Netherlands)*
Gabor Erdelyi *(University of Siegen, Germany)*
Patricia Everaere *(LIFL, France)*
Moser Fagundes *(Instituto Federal Sul-Rio-Grandense, Brazil)*
Shaheen Fatima *(Loughborough University, UK)*
Guillaume Feuillade *(Université Paul Sabatier, France)*
Nicoletta Fornara *(Università della Svizzera Italiana, Switzerland)*
Lars-Åke Fredlund *(Universidad Politecnica de Madrid, Spain)*
Tim French *(University of Western Australia, Australia)*
Katsuhide Fujita *(Tokyo University of Agriculture & Technology, Japan)*
Martin Gairing *(University of Liverpool, UK)*
Maria Ganzha *(Polish Academy of Sciences, Poland)*
Serge Gaspers *(University of New South Wales and NICA, Australia)*
Les Gasser *(University of Illinois at Urbana-Champaign, USA)*
Nicola Gatti *(Politecnico di Milano, Italy)*
Benoit Gaudou *(Université Toulouse 1 Capitole, France)*
Kallirroi Georgila *(University of Southern California, USA)*
Aditya Ghose *(University of Wollongong, Australia)*
Paolo Giorgini *(University of Trento, Italy)*
Marie-Pierre Gleizes *(Université de Toulouse, France)*
Jorge Gomez-Sanz *(Universidad Complutense de Madrid, Spain)*
Guido Governatori *(NICTA, Australia)*
Umberto Grandi *(University of Toulouse, France)*
Gianluigi Greco *(Università della Calabria, Italy)*
Rachel Greenstadt *(Drexel University, USA)*
Francisco Grimaldo *(Universitat de València, Spain)*
Tal Grinshpoun *(Ariel University, Israel)*
Davide Grossi *(University of Liverpool, UK)*
Zahia Guessoum *(Universite de Paris 6, France)*
Laszlo Gulyas *(AITIA International, Inc., Hungary)*
Akin Gunay *(Nanyang Technological University, Singapore)*
Mingyu Guo *(University of Adelaide, Australia)*
Stephen J. Guy *(University of Minnesota, USA)*
Daisuke Hatano *(National Institute of Informatics, Japan)*
Noam Hazon *(Ariel University, Israel)*
Carlos Hernandez (UCSC, Chile)
Axel Heßler *(Technische Universität Berlin, Germany)*
Vincent Hilaire *(UTBM, France)*
Martin Hoefer *(Max-Planck Institut für Informatik, Germany)*
Jesse Hoey *(University of Waterloo, Canada)*
Chris Holmes-Parker *(Parflux LLC, USA)*
Mark Hoogendoorn *(VU University Amsterdam, Netherlands)*
Anthony Hunter *(University College London, UK)*
Takayuki Ito *(Nagoya Institute of Technology, Japan)*
Atsushi Iwasaki *(University of Electro-Commnunications, Japan)*
Michal Jakob *(Czech Technical University in Prague, Czech Republic)*

Nadeem Jamali *(University of Saskatchewan, Canada)*
Albert Xin Jiang *(Trinity University, USA)*
Ozgur Kafali *(Royal Holloway, University of London, UK)*
Michael Kaisers *(CWI, Netherlands)*
Chyon Hae Kim *(Iwate University, Japan)*
Akihiro Kishimoto *(IBM Research, Ireland)*
Tomas Klos *(Delft University of Technology, Netherlands)*
Franziska Klugl *(Orebro University, Sweden)*
Sebastien Konieczny *(CRIL-CNRS, France)*
Barteld Kooi *(University of Groningen, Netherlands)*
Martin Lackner *(TU Vienna)*
Kiran Lakkaraju *(Sandia National Labs, USA)*
Steffen Lamparter *(Siemens AG Corporate Research and Technologie, Germany)*
Jimmy Lee *(The Chinese University of Hong Kong, Hong Kong)*
Michael Lees *(University of Amsterdam, Netherlands)*
João Leite *(Universidade Nova de Lisboa, Portugal)*
Julien Lesca *(Paris Dauphine University, France)*
Raz Lin *(Bar-Ilan University, Israel)*
Dominique Longin *(IRIT-CNRS, France)*
Manuel Lopes *(INRIA, France)*
Maite Lopez-Sanchez *(University of Barcelona, Spain)*
Emiliano Lorini *(IRIT-CNRS, France)*
Ulf Lotzmann *(University of Koblenz-Landau, Germany)*
Marco Lützenberger *(Technische Universität Berlin, Germany)*
Roger Mailler *(University of Tulsa, USA)*
Elisa Marengo *(Free University of Bozen-Bolzano, Italy)*
Vangelis Markakis *(Athens University of Economics and Business, Greece)*
Philippe Mathieu *(Lille 1 University, France)*
Eric Matson *(Purdue University, USA)*
Toshihiro Matsui *(Nagoya Institute of Technology, Japan)*
Nicholas Mattei *(NICTA and University of New South Wales, Australia)*
Reshef Meir *(Harvard University, USA)*
Amnon Meisels *(Ben-Gurion University of the Negev, Israel)*
Pedro Meseguer *(IIIA CSIC, Spain)*
João Messias *(University of Amsterdam, Netherlands)*
John-Jules Meyer *(Utrecht University, Netherlands)*
Ruth Meyer *(Manchester Metropolitan University, UK)*
Roberto Micalizio *(Università di Torino, Italy)*
Tomasz Michalak *(University of Oxford, UK and University of Warsaw, Poland)*
Jakub Michaliszyn *(Imperial College London, UK)*
Tim Miller *(The University of Melbourne, Australia)*
Marco Montali *(Free University of Bozen-Bolzano, Italy)*
Pavlos Moraitis *(Paris Descartes University, France)*
Alvaro Moreira *(Federal University of Rio Grande do Sul, Brazil)*
Koichi Moriyama *(Osaka University, Japan)*
Hala Mostafa *(United Technologies Research Center, Singapore)*
Enrique Munoz de Cote *(INAOE, Mexico)*
Aniello Murano *(University of Napoli Federico II, Italy)*
Dave Murray-Rust *(University of Edinburgh, UK)*
Nina Narodytska *(NICTA and University of New South Wales, Australia)*
Hoang Nga Nguyen *(University of Nottingham, UK)*
Jinzhong Niu *(City University of New York, USA)*
Itsuki Noda *(Center for Service Research, Japan)*
Timothy Norman *(University of Aberdeen, UK)*
Peter Novak *(Delft University of Technology, Netherlands)*
Ann Nowe *(Vrije Universiteit Brussel, Belgium)*
Svetlana Obraztsova *(National Technical University of Athens, Greece)*
Steven Okamoto *(Ben Gurion University of the Negev, Israel)*
Tenda Okimoto *(Kobe University, Japan)*
Eugenio Oliveira *(Universidade do Porto, Portugal)*
Nardine Osman *(IIIA-CSIC, Spain)*
Sascha Ossowski *(University Rey Juan Carlos, Spain)*
Julian Padget *(University of Bath, UK)*
Ioannis Partalas *(Viseo Research Lab, France)*
Juan Pavón *(Universidad Complutense de Madrid, Spain)*
Terry Payne *(University of Liverpool, UK)*
Wojciech Penczek *(IPIPAN Warsaw, Poland)*
Patrice Perny *(LIP6 - UPMC, France)*
Laurent Perrusel *(IRIT, University of Toulouse, France)*
Steve Phelps *(University of Essex, UK)*

Gauthier Picard *(Ecole des Mines de Saint-Etienne, France)*
Olivier Pietquin *(University Lille 1, France)*
Gabriella Pigozzi *(Univ. Paris Dauphine, France)*
Vedran Podobnik *(University of Zagreb, Croatia)*
Alexander Pokahr *(University of Hamburg, Germany)*
Daniele Porello *(ISTC-CNR, Italy)*
Henry Prakken *(Utrecht University and University of Groningen, Netherlands)*
Doina Precup *(McGill University, Canada)*
Marc Pujol-Gonzalez *(IIIA-CSIC, Spain)*
Martin Purvis *(University of Otago, New Zealand)*
Tao Qin *(Microsoft Research Asia, China)*
Hongyang Qu *(University of Sheffield, UK)*
Zinovi Rabinovich *(Mobileye Vision Technologies Ltd., Israel)*
Franco Raimondi *(Middlesex University, UK)*
Anita Raja *(The Cooper Union, USA)*
Subramanian Ramamoorthy *(The University of Edinburgh, UK)*
Sarvapali Ramchurn *(University of Southampton, UK)*
Wolfgang Renz *(Hamburg University of Applied Sciences, Germany)*
Deborah Richards *(Macquarie University, Australia)*
Ariella Richardson *(Lev Academic Center, Israel)*
M. Birna van Riemsdijk *(Delft University of Technology, Netherlands)*
David Robertson *(University of Edinburgh, UK)*
Valentin Robu *(Heriot-Watt University, UK)*
Antônio Carlos Rocha Costa *(FURG, Brazil)*
Nico Roos *(Maastricht University, Netherlands)*
Rosaldo J. F. Rossetti *(Universidade do Porto, Portgual)*
Joerg Rothe *(Heinrich-Heine-Universitaet Duesseldorf, Germany)*
Antonino Rotolo *(University of Bologna, Italy)*
Joshua Sack *(University of Amsterdam, Netherlands)*
Fariba Sadri *(Imperial College London, UK)*
Yuko Sakurai *(Kyushu University, Japan)*
Ken Satoh *(National Institute of Informatics, Japan)*
Henning Schnoor *(Christian-Albrechts-Universität zu Kiel, Germany)*
René Schumann *(HES-SO, Switzerland)*
Francois Schwarzentruber *(École normale supérieure de Rennes, France)*
Nicolas Schwind *(National Institute of Informatics, Japan)*
Murat Sensoy *(Ozyegin University, Turkey)*
Emilio Serrano *(Universidad Politécnica de Madrid, Spain)*
Paulo Shakarian *(Arizona State University, USA)*
Guy Shani *(Ben Gurion University, IL)*
Marius Silaghi *(Florida Institute of Technology, USA)*
Gerardo Simari *(Universidad Nacional del Sur in Bahia Blanca and CONICET, Argentina)*
Dhirendra Singh *(RMIT University, Australia)*
Arunesh Sinha *(University of Southern California, USA)*
Marjan Sirjani *(Reykjavik University, Iceland)*
Oskar Skibski *(Kyushu University, Japan)*
Piotr Skowron *(University of Warsaw, Poland)*
Marija Slavkovijk *(University of Bergen, Norway)*
Troels Bjerre Sørensen *(IT-University of Copenhagen, Denmark)*
Nikolaos Spanoudakis *(Technical University of Crete, Greece)*
Sebastian Stein *(University of Southampton, UK)*
Leon Sterling *(Swinburne University of Technology, Australia)*
Roni Stern *(Ben Gurion University of the Negev, Israel)*
Jose Such *(Lancaster University, UK)*
Pavel Surynek *(Charles University in Prague, Czech Republic)*
Samarth Swarup *(Virginia Tech, USA)*
Katia Sycara *(Carnegie Mellon University, USA)*
Suzanne Tamang *(Stanford University, USA)*
Valentina Tamma *(University of Liverpool, UK)*
Yuqing Tang *(Carnegie Mellon University, USA)*
Luke Teacy *(University of Southampton, UK)*
Pankaj Telang *(North Carolina State University, USA)*
Michael Thielscher *(University of New South Wales, Australia)*
Matthias Thimm *(University of Koblenz-Landau, Germany)*
Ingo J. Timm *(University of Trier, Germany)*
Taiki Todo *(Kyushu University, Japan)*
Leendert van der Torre *(University of Luxembourg, Luxembourg)*
Viviane Torres da Silva *(IBM Research, Brazil)*
Paolo Torroni *(University of Bologna, Italy)*
Long Tran-Thanh *(University of Southampton, UK)*
Jan Treur *(VU University Amsterdam, Netherlands)*

Nicolas Troquard *(Université Paris-Est Créteil, France)*
Paolo Turrini *(Imperial College London, UK)*
Suguru Ueda *(National Institute of Informatics, Japan)*
Volkan Ustun *(University of Southern California, USA)*
Pradeep Varakantham *(Singapore Management University, Singapore)*
Carlos Varela *(Rensselaer Polytechnic Institute, USA)*
Matteo Venanzi *(University of Southampton, UK)*
Salvatore Venticinque *(Second University of Naples, Italy)*
Carmine Ventre *(Teesside University, UK)*
Laurent Vercouter *(INSA de Rouen, France)*
Harko Verhagen *(Stockholm University, Sweden)*
Srdjan Vesic *(CRIL – CNRS, France)*
Ioannis Vetsikas *(NCSR Demokritos, Greece)*
Serena Villata *(INRIA Sophia Antipolis, France)*
Meritxell Vinyals *(Commissariat à l'Énergie Atomique, France)*
Mirko Viroli *(University of Bologna, Italy)*
Giuseppe Vizzari *(Università degli Studi di Milano-Bicocca, Italy)*
Yevgeniy Vorobeychik *(Vanderbilt University, US)*
Toby Walsh *(NICTA, Australia)*
Yanjing Wang *(Peking University, China)*
Yi Wang *(Zhejiang University, China)*
Martijn Warnier *(Delft University of Technology, Netherlands)*
Mark Wilson *(University of Auckland, New Zealand)*
Stefan Witwicki *(Swiss Federal Institute of Technology, Switzerland)*
Wayne Wobcke *(University of New South Wales, Australia)*
Lirong Xia *(Rensselaer Polytechnic Institute, USA)*
William Yeoh *(New Mexico State University, USA)*
Neil Yorke-Smith *(American University of Beirut, Lebanon)*
Han Yu *(Nanyang Technological University, Singapore)*
Yifeng Zeng *(Teesside University, UK)*
Jie Zhang *(Nanyang Technological University, Singapore)*
Jie Zhang *(University of Oxford, UK)*
Dengji Zhao *(University of Southampton, UK)*
Yair Zick *(Carnegie Mellon University, USA)*
Aviv Zohar *(Hebrew University, Israel)*

Programme Committee members in the special tracks also reviewed for the main track

Innovative Applications Track:
Tina Balke *(University of Surrey, UK)*
Lucas Bordeaux *(Microsoft Research, UK)*
Lawrence Cavedon *(RMIT University, Australia)*
Ricardo Choren *(IME, Brazil)*
Alice Gao *(University of British Columbia, Canada)*
Maira Gatti *(IBM Research, Brazil)*
Nathan Griffiths *(University of Warwick, UK)*
Christian Guttmann *(IVBAR & Karolinska Institute, Sweden and University of New South Wales, Australia)*
Benjamin Hirsch *(EBTIC / Khalifa University, UAE)*
Ian Kash *(Microsoft Research, UK)*
Michael Kirley *(The University of Melbourne, Australia)*
Andrew Koster *(Samsung Research Institute Brazil, Brazil)*
Hoong Chuin Lau *(Singapore Management University, Singapore)*
Samhar Mahmoud *(King's College London, UK)*
Simon Miles *(King's College London, UK)*
Karen Myers *(SRI International, USA)*
Ingrid Nunes *(Federal University of Rio Grande do Sul, Brazil)*
Nir Oren *(University of Aberdeen, UK)*
Kostas Stathis *(Royal Holloway, University of London, UK)*
Simon Thompson *(BT Research and Technology, UK)*
Eduardo Valle *(State University of Campinas, Brazil)*
Jose Vidal *(University of South Carolina, USA)*
Rym Z. Wenkstern *(University of Texas at Dallas, USA)*
Rong Yang *(Palo Alto Research Center, USA)*
Jia Yuan Yu *(IBM Research Ireland, Ireland)*

AAMAS 2015 Additional Reviewers

Luca Aceto
Aamir Ahmad
Sebastian Ahrndt
Charilaos Akasiadis
Mohammad Al-Zinati
Ashkan Aleali
Khalid Alhamed
Georgios Amanatidis
Alba Amato
Luis Antunes
John Atkinson
Jorge Baier
João Balsa
Laura Barbulescu
Nathanael Barrot
Nicola Basilico
Atef Ben Youssef
Martin Berger
Nathalie Bertrand
Holger Billhardt
Kenneth Bogert
Michael Borish
Matthieu Boussard
Florian Brandl
Erik Brinkman
Matthew Brown
Jesús Capitán
Henrique Cardoso
Alan Carlin
José Carlos Castillo Montoya
Roi Ceren
Mithun Chakraborty
Muthukumaran Chandrasekaran
Tristan Charrier
Chris Child
Mathieu Chollet
Caroline Chopinaud
Natalia Criado
Ionut Damian
Maximilien de Bayser
Bart de Keijzer
Elena del Val
Argyrios Deligkas
Dario Della Monica
Sophie Dennisen
Duarte Dias
Jan Drchal
Malcolm Egan
Mohamed El Menshawy
Anestis Fachantidis
Caroline Faur
Paolo Felli
Aris Filos-Ratsikas
Avelino Forechi
Christopher Frantz
Nurit Gal-Oz
Lucie Galand
Chris Geib
Christian Geist
Hongxing Geng
Mira Gonen
Ilaria Gori
Ruocheng Guo
Patricia Gutierrez
Rafik Hadfi
Chen Hajaj
Shivashankar Halan
James Hales
Chung-Wei Hang
Jens Ulrik Hansen
Paul Harrenstein
Chris Hazard
Pablo Hernandez-Leal
Tasuku Hiraishi
Johannes Hofbauer
Ping Hou
Christopher-Eyk Hrabia
Hung-Hsuan Huang
Thomas Huraux
Shigeru Imai
Athirai A. Irissappane
Ali Jafari
Marzieh Jahanbazi
Wafa Johal
Vicente Julián
Antonis Kakas
Julian Kalinowski
Maryam Kamali
Giorgos Karafotias
Majid Karimi
Ehsan Khamespanah
Piyush Khandelwal
Chyon Hae Kim
Thomas King
Kohei Kishida
Michal Knapik
Max Knobbout
Andrey Kolobov
Zohar Komarowsky
George Krimpas
Philipp Kulms
Akshat Kumar
Oded Lachish
Aron Laszka
Allen Lavoie
Michel Lemaître
Omer Lev
Vadim Levit
Yoad Lewenberg
Marco Lippi
Omer Litov
Miao Liu
Marin Lujak
Benny Lutati
Simon Mackenzie
Faustine Maffre
Vadim Malvone
Efrat Manisterski
Janusz Marecki
Clodéric Mars
Maria Vanina Martinez
Szymon Matejczyk
Mohamed Mehdi
Artur Meski
Jason Metcalf
Ahmed Abdel Moamen
Morteza Mohagheghi
Anahita Mohseni-Kabir
Julia S. Mollee

Luis Moniz
Eduardo Morales
Tim Muller
Paresh Nakhe
Ramasuri Narayanam
Ilan Nehama
Daniel Neugebauer
Nhan-Tam Nguyen
Thanh Nguyen
Truc-Vien T. Nguyen
Naoyuki Nide
Agata Niescieruk
Antoine Nongaillard
Eric Nunes
Joel Oren
Gabriel Orsini
Domenico Pascarella
Stacy Patterson
Alexandre Pauchet
José Nuno Pereira
Giuseppe Perelli
Alan Perotti
Dominik Peters
Rens Philipsen
Sebastien Picault
Bilal Piot
Fabio Piva
Gleb Polevoy
Emmanouil Pountourakis
Denis Pozo
Tiago Primo
Yann Prudent
Alberto Quattrini Li
David Rajaratnam
Cristian Ramirez Atencia
Anja Rey
Lisa Rey
Alessandro Riva
Victor Rodriguez Fernandez
Abdallah Saffidine
Baldoino Santos Neto
Alessandro Sapienza
Julien Saunier
Hilmar Schadrack
Lena Schend
Ann-Kathrin Selker
Pedro Sequeira
Paolo Serafino
Paolo Sernani
Elham Shaabani
Nisarg Shah
Benjamin Shih
Jivko Sinapov
Liat Sless
Yonatan Sompolinsky
Lei Song
Ekhlas Sonu
Roni Stern
Peter Stone
Alina Strachocka
Filipo Studzinski Perotto
Andrzej Szalas
Paweł Szmeja
Maciej Szreter
Seyed Amin Tabatabaei
Mateusz Tarkowski
Bas Testerink
Jesse Thomason
Satoshi Tojo
Andrea Turrini
Paulo Urbano
Joana Urbano
Mahsa Varshosaz
Tiago Veiga
Angelina Vidali
Marlo Vieira dos Santos e Souza
Alexandros Voudouris
Elaine Wah
David Wajc
Yonghong Wang
Bryce Wiedenbeck
Mason Wright
Fan Xie
Yuan Xu
Haifeng Xu
Amulya Yadav
Chun Ye
Logan Yliniemi
Alexandros Zenonos
Haifeng Zhang
Shiqi Zhang
Peng Zhou
Inon Zuckerm

AAMAS 2015 Sponsors and Supporters

Emerald:

Gold

Silver

Bronze

In cooperation with

Awards

ACM SIGART Autonomous Agents Research Award

The ACM SIGART Autonomous Agents Research Award is an annual award for excellence in research in the area of autonomous agents. The award is intended to recognize researchers in autonomous agents whose current work is an important influence on the field. The award is an official ACM award, funded by an endowment created by ACM SIGART from the proceeds of previous Autonomous Agents conferences. Candidates for the award are nominated through an open nomination process. Previous winners of the SIGART Autonomous Research Award were Michael Wellman (2014), Jeffrey S. Rosenschein (2013), Moshe Tennenholtz (2012), Joe Halpern (2011), Jonathan Gratch and Stacy Marsella (2010), Manuela Veloso (2009), Yoav Shoham (2008), Sarit Kraus (2007), Michael Wooldridge (2006), Milind Tambe (2005), Makoto Yokoo (2004), Nick Jennings (2003), Katia Sycara (2002), and Tuomas Sandholm (2001).

The selection committee for the ACM/SIGAI Autonomous Agents Research Award is pleased to announce that Dr. Catherine Pelachaud, Director of Research at CNRS at Telecom ParisTech is the recipient of the 2015 award. Dr. Pelachaud is honored for her sustained and substantial contributions to the area of intelligent virtual agents. Her seminal work in this area helped launch the area of intelligent virtual agents, and her many subsequent publications have exerted a strong influence on virtual agent research at AAMAS and the Intelligent Virtual Agents conferences. Furthermore, her research on the role that bodily communication plays in face-to-face interaction has helped set the agenda of embodied agent research. In the process, it has firmly established a research area of modeling the body, its relation to the mind and its role in social interaction. Overall, this work has filled critical gaps in agents research often ignored by the larger community.

IFAAMAS Victor Lesser Distinguished Dissertation Award

This award was started for dissertations defended in 2006 and is named for Professor Victor Lesser, a long standing member of the AAMAS community who has graduated a large number of outstanding PhD students in the area. To be eligible for the 2014 award, a dissertation had to have been written as part of a PhD defended during the year 2014, and had to be nominated by the supervisor with three supporting references. Selection is based on originality, depth, impact and written quality, supported by quality publications. Previous winners of this award were Manish Jain (2013), Birgit Endrass (2012), Daniel Villatoro (2011), Bo An (2010), Andrew Gilpin (2009), Ariel Procaccia (2008), Radu Jurca (2007), and Vincent Conitzer (2006).

The 2014 IFAAMAS Victor Lesser Distinguished Dissertation Award recipient is Dr. Yair Zick, whose thesis titled "Arbitration, Fairness and Stability: Revenue Division in Collaborative Settings" was supervised by Dr. Edith Elkind. The committee also wanted to recognise two other nominees (unordered): Dr. Tim Baarslag, whose thesis titled "What to Bid and When to Stop" was supervised by Prof. Catholijn Jonker and Dr. Koen Hindriks; and Dr. Xi (Alice) Gao, whose thesis titled "Eliciting and Aggregating Truthful and Noisy Information" was supervised by Assoc. Prof. Yiling Chen.

IFAAMAS Influential Paper Award

The International Foundation for Autonomous Agents and Multi-Agent Systems set up an influential paper award in 2006 to recognize publications that have made seminal contributions to the field. Such papers represent the best and most influential work in the area of autonomous agents and multi-agent systems. These papers might, therefore, have proved a key result, led to the development of a new sub-field, demonstrated a significant new application or system, or simply presented a new way of thinking about a topic that has proved influential. The award is open to any paper that was published at least 10 years before the award is made. The paper can have been published in any journal, conference, or workshop. The award is sponsored by the Agent Theories, Architectures and Languages foundation.

This year's IFAAMAS Influential Paper Award winner is Prof. Michael Littman, in recognition of his distinguished contributions to the field as exemplified by the following influential paper:

> *Michael L. Littman.* **Markov games as a framework for multi-agent reinforcement learning**. Proceedings of the Eleventh International Conference on Machine Learning (ICML-94), New Brunswick, NJ, pp. 157-163, 1994.

Best Paper Nominations

The following papers (in alphabetical order by author) have been nominated for Best Paper:

The Dependence of Effective Planning Horizon on Model Accuracy (Page 1181)
Nan Jiang (University of Michigan)
Alex Kulesza (University of Michigan)
Satinder Singh (University of Michigan)
Richard Lewis (University of Michigan)

Efficient Decision-Making in a Self-Organizing Robot Swarm: On the Speed versus Accuracy Trade-Off (Page 1305)
Gabriele Valentini (Université Libre de Bruxelles)
Heiko Hamann (University of Paderborn)
Marco Dorigo (Université Libre de Bruxelles)

Dynamic Influence Maximization Under Increasing Returns to Scale (Page 949)
Haifeng Zhang (Vanderbilt University)
Ariel D. Procaccia (Carnegie Mellon University)
Yevgeniy Vorobeychik (Vanderbilt University)

Best Paper of the Innovative Applications Track

The following papers (in alphabetical order by author) have been nominated for Innovative Applications Track Best Paper:

Improving the Performance of Mobile Phone Crowdsourcing Applications (Page 145)
Erfan Davami (University of Central Florida)
Gita Sukthankar (University of Central Florida)

A Mechanism for Smoothly Handling Human Interrupts in Team Oriented Plans (Page 377)
Alessandro Farinelli (University of Verona)
Nicolò L Marchi (University of Verona)
Masoume M. Raeissi (University of Verona)
Nathan Brooks (Carnegie Mellon University)
Paul Scerri (Carnegie Mellon University)

HAC-ER: A Disaster Response System Based on Human-Agent Collectives (Page 533)
Sarvapali D. Ramchurn (University of Southampton)
Trung Dong Huynh (University of Southampton)
Yuki Ikuno (University of Southampton)
Jack Flann (University of Southampton)
Feng Wu (University of Southampton)
Luc Moreau (University of Southampton)
Nicholas R. Jennings (University of Southampton)
Joel E. Fischer (University of Nottingham)
Wenchao Jiang (University of Nottingham)
Tom Rodden (University of Nottingham)
Edwin Simpson (University of Oxford)
Steven Reece (University of Oxford)
Stephen J. Roberts (University of Oxford)

Pragnesh Jay Modi Best Student Paper

The following papers (in alphabetical order by author) have been nominated for Pragnesh Jay Modi Best Student Paper:

Factored MDPs for Optimal Prosumer Decision-Making (Page 503)
Angelos Angelidakis (Technical University of Crete)
Georgios Chalkiadakis (Technical University of Crete)

Particle Field Optimization: A New Paradigm for Swarm Intelligence (Page 257)
Nathan Bell (Carleton University)
B. John Oommen (Carleton University)

Welfare Effects of Market Making in Continuous Double Auctions (Page 57)
Elaine Wah (University of Michigan)
Michael P. Wellman (University of Michigan)

Best Programme Committee Member

The following Programme Committee members (in alphabetical order) have been nominated:

Sylvain Bouveret

Reshef Meir

Timothy Norman

On the Full Organism Challenge: Or, Can We Computerize an Elephant?

Prof. David Harel
Weizmann Institute of Science in Israel
dharel@weizmann.ac.il

Abstract

We show how techniques from computer science and software engineering can be applied beneficially to research in the life sciences. I will discuss the idea of comprehensive and realistic modeling of biological systems, where we try to understand and analyze an entire system in detail, utilizing in the modeling effort all that is known about it. I will address the motivation for such modeling and the philosophy underlying the techniques for carrying it out, as well as the crucial question of when such models are to be deemed valid, or complete. The examples will be from among the biological modeling efforts my group has been involved in: T cell development, lymph node behavior, organogenesis of the pancreas, rat whisking, cancer tumor formation, and various projects regarding the C. elegans nematode. The ultimate long-term "grand challenge" is to produce an interactive, dynamic, computerized model of an entire multi-cellular organism, such as the C. elegans, which is extremely complex despite its small size, but well-defined in terms of anatomy and genetics. The sweeping potential benefits of such a model will be discussed.

ACM Classification

J.3 LIFE AND MEDICAL SCIENCES: Biology and genetics

Keywords

Biological modeling; full organism challenge; *C. elegans*; Statecharts.

Short Bio

Prof. David Harel has been at the Weizmann Institute of Science in Israel since 1980. He was Department Head from 1989 to 1995, and was Dean of the Faculty of Mathematics and Computer Science between 1998 and 2004. He was also co-founder of I-Logix, Inc. He received his PhD from MIT in 1978, and has spent time at IBM Yorktown Heights, and sabbaticals at Carnegie-Mellon, Cornell, and the University of Edinburgh. In the past he worked mainly in theoretical computer science (logic, computability, automata, database theory), and he now works mainly on software and systems engineering and on modeling biological systems. He is the inventor of Statecharts and co-inventor of live sequence charts (LSCs) and behavioral programming. He co-designed Statemate, Rhapsody, the Play-Engine and PlayGo.

Among his books are "Algorithmics: The Spirit of Computing" and "Computers Ltd.: What They Really Can't Do", and his awards include the ACM Karlstrom Outstanding Educator Award (1992), the Israel Prize (2004), the ACM Software System Award (2007), the Emet Prize (2010), and five honorary degrees. He is a Fellow of ACM, IEEE and AAAS, a member of the Academia Europaea and the Israel Academy of Sciences, and a foreign member of the US National Academy of Engineering and the American Academy of Arts and Sciences.

Appears in: Proceedings of the 14th International Conference on Autonomous Agents and Multiagent Systems (AAMAS 2015), Bordini, Elkind, Weiss, Yolum (eds.), May, 4–8, 2015, Istanbul, Turkey.

Learning Submodular Functions with Applications to Multi-Agent Systems

Maria Florina Balcan
School of Computer Science
Carnegie Mellon University
ninamf@cs.cmu.edu

Abstract

Machine learning can provide powerful tools for the design and analysis of multi-agent systems, as well as a novel lens on important questions in the area. In this talk I will focus on the use of machine learning for understanding submodular functions, an important class of discrete functions that model laws of diminishing returns and enjoy many important applications in multi-agent settings. For example, submodular functions are commonly used to model valuation functions for bidders in auctions, the influence of various subsets of agents in social networks, and the benefits of performing different actions in a variety of situations. Traditionally it is assumed that these functions are known to the decision maker; however, for large scale systems, in the age of big data, it is often the case they must be learned from observations.

In this talk, I will discuss a recent line of work on studying the learnability of submodular functions, and highlight its applications to the analysis of multi-agent systems. I will discuss both general algorithms for learning such functions, as well as even better guarantees that can be achieved for important classes appearing in multi-agent scenarios that exhibit additional structure. These classes include: probabilistic coverage functions that can be used to model the influence function in classic models of information diffusion in networks; functions with bounded complexity used in modeling bidder valuation functions in auctions, including XOS and gross-substitutes; and classes of functions appearing in cooperative game theory for expressing the values of various types of coalitions.

I will additionally discuss a large scale application of our algorithms for learning the influence functions in social networks, that significantly outperforms existing approaches empirically in both synthetic and real world data.

ACM Classification: I.2.6 [Learning], J.4 [Social and Behavioral Sciences]: Economics, F.2 [Analysis of Algorithms and Problem Complexity]

Keywords: Diminishing returns; learning submodular functions; influence of agents in social networks; valuation functions in auctions; values of coalitions

Short Bio

Maria Florina Balcan is an Associate Professor in the School of Computer Science at Carnegie Mellon University. Her main research interests are machine learning, computational aspects in economics and game theory, and algorithms. Her honors include the CMU SCS Distinguished Dissertation Award, an NSF CAREER Award, a Microsoft Faculty Research Fellowship, a Sloan Research Fellowship, and several paper awards at COLT. She is currently a board member of the International Machine Learning Society and was recently Program Committee chair for COLT 2014.

Appears in: Proceedings of the 14th International Conference on Autonomous Agents and Multiagent Systems (AAMAS 2015), Bordini, Elkind, Weiss, Yolum (eds.), May, 4–8, 2015, Istanbul, Turkey.

Greta, an Interactive Expressive Embodied Conversational Agent

Catherine Pelachaud
Director of Research CNRS
LTCI, TELECOM ParisTech
catherine.pelachaud@telecom-paristech.fr

Abstract

Greta is an interactive Embodied Conversational Agent platform. It is endowed with socio-emotional and communicative behaviors. Through its behaviors, the agent can sustain a conversation as well as show various attitudes and levels of engagement.

Through the years, we have integrated all our research in the Greta platform. By applying different methodologies, based on corpus analysis, user-centered, or motion capture, we have enriched the agent's palette of multimodal behaviors. We have conducted various studies to simulate communicative behaviors, emotional behaviors, social attitudes and behavior expressivity. In particular we have proposed models to go beyond the prototypical expressions of emotions. Through its behaviors patterns, the agent can display complex emotions such as masking one expression of emotions by another ones, its relationship towards its interlocutors, specific social signals such as smile and laughter. In an interaction, the agent can be a speaker or a listener. It can exhibit backchannels, mimic on the fly its interlocutor's behaviors. To develop our models, we rely on theoretical models from social psychology literature and on data analysis.

After describing our platform, we will first review our rationale; then we will introduce our model of socio-emotional behaviors. Finally we will present experiments where we measure the impact of the agent's copying behaviors on the user's level of engagement.

ACM Classification

H.5.1 Information Systems Applications [Multimedia Information Systems]: Artificial, augmented, and virtual realities; I.2.11 Artificial Intelligence [Distributed Artificial Intelligence]: Intelligent Agents;

Keywords

Embodied Conversational Agent; Multimodal behaviors; Socio-emotional agent

Short Bio

Catherine Pelachaud is a Director of Research at CNRS in the laboratory LTCI, TELECOM ParisTech. She participated to the elaboration of the first embodied conversation agent system, GestureJack, with Justine Cassell, Norman Badler and Mark Steedman when being a post-doctorate at the University of Pennsylvania. She went to Università di Roma "La Sapienza" with a Marie-Curie CEE scholarship. Her research interest includes embodied conversational agent, nonverbal communication (face, gaze, and gesture), expressive behaviors and socio-emotional agents. With her research team, she has been developing an interactive virtual agent platform GRETA that can display socio-emotional and communicative behaviors. She has been involved and is still involved in several European projects related to believable embodied conversational agents, emotion and social behaviors. She is associate editors of several journals among which IEEE Transactions on Affective Computing, ACM Transactions on Interactive Intelligent Systems and Journal on Multimodal User Interfaces. She has co-edited several books on virtual agents and emotion-oriented systems. She participated to the organization of international conferences such as IVA, ACII and AAMAS, virtual agent track.

Appears in: Proceedings of the 14th International Conference on Autonomous Agents and Multiagent Systems (AAMAS 2015), Bordini, Elkind, Weiss, Yolum (eds.), May, 4–8, 2015, Istanbul, Turkey.

Hierarchical Abstraction, Distributed Equilibrium Computation, and Post-Processing, with Application to a Champion No-Limit Texas Hold'em Agent*

Noam Brown, Sam Ganzfried, and Tuomas Sandholm
Computer Science Department
Carnegie Mellon University
{noamb, sganzfri, sandholm}@cs.cmu.edu

ABSTRACT

The leading approach for solving large imperfect-information games is automated abstraction followed by running an equilibrium-finding algorithm. We introduce a distributed version of the most commonly used equilibrium-finding algorithm, counterfactual regret minimization (CFR), which enables CFR to scale to dramatically larger abstractions and numbers of cores. The new algorithm begets constraints on the abstraction so as to make the pieces running on different computers disjoint. We introduce an algorithm for generating such abstractions while capitalizing on state-of-the-art abstraction ideas such as imperfect recall and earth-mover's distance. Our techniques enabled an equilibrium computation of unprecedented size on a supercomputer with a high inter-blade memory latency. Prior approaches run slowly on this architecture. Our approach also leads to a significant improvement over using the prior best approach on a large shared-memory server with low memory latency. Finally, we introduce a family of post-processing techniques that outperform prior ones. We applied these techniques to generate an agent for two-player no-limit Texas Hold'em, called Tartanian7, that won the 2014 Annual Computer Poker Competition, beating each opponent with statistical significance.

Categories and Subject Descriptors

I.2.11 [**Distributed Artificial Intelligence**]: Multiagent Systems; J.4 [**Social and Behavioral Sciences**]: Economics

General Terms

Algorithms, Economics, Theory

Keywords

Game Theory, Multiagent Systems, Equilibrium Finding, Game Abstraction, Imperfect Information, Distributed AI

*This material is based on work supported by the National Science Foundation under grant IIS-1320620, as well as XSEDE computing resources provided by the Pittsburgh Supercomputing Center.

Appears in: *Proceedings of the 14th International Conference on Autonomous Agents and Multiagent Systems (AAMAS 2015), Bordini, Elkind, Weiss, Yolum (eds.), May 4–8, 2015, Istanbul, Turkey.*

1. INTRODUCTION

The leading approach for creating strong agents for large imperfect-information games—which is used by all of the strongest Texas Hold'em (TH) poker agents—is to first create a sufficiently small strategic approximation of the full game, called an *abstraction*, then to apply an *equilibrium-finding algorithm* [27, 14] to the abstraction, and finally to apply *post-processing* techniques [11, 23, 6, 4] to obtain a strategy in the original game from the approximate equilibrium of the abstraction. Initially abstractions were created manually [24, 2], while nowadays they are created by algorithms [8, 9, 10, 26, 18, 5]. The equilibrium-finding algorithm used by today's strongest TH agents is a Monte Carlo version of the counterfactual regret minimization algorithm (MCCFR) [21]. That algorithm involves repeatedly sampling chance outcomes and actions down the tree, and updating regret and average strategy values that are stored at each information set.

On a shared-memory architecture, MCCFR can be parallelized straightforwardly. True shared-memory architectures typically come with relatively little memory and relatively few cores, however, and it would be desirable for scalability to be able to run on architectures that have more memory (in order to be able to run on larger, more detailed abstractions) and more cores (for speed). However, on distributed architectures and supercomputers with high inter-blade[1] memory access latency, straightforward MCCFR parallelization approaches lead to impractically slow runtimes because when a core does an update at an information set (extensive-form games and information sets therein are formally defined in Appendix C) it needs to read and write memory with high latency. A second issue in MCCFR (even on a shared-memory architecture) is that different cores working on the same information set may need to lock memory, wait for each other, possibly over-write each others' parallel work, and work on out-of-sync inputs. Our approach solves the former problem and also helps mitigate the latter issue.

To obtain these benefits, our algorithm creates an information abstraction that allows us to assign different components of the game tree to different blades so the trajectory of each sample only accesses information sets located on the

[1]Such supercomputers consists of *blades*, which are themselves computers that are plugged into racks. A core can access memory on its blade faster than memory on other blades—seven times faster on the computer we used. On regular distributed systems, the difference between local and remote memory access is even greater.

same blade. At a high level, the first stage of our hierarchical approach is to cluster public information at some early point in the game (public flop cards in the case of Texas Hold'em poker—see Appendix A for the rules), giving a global basis for distributing the rest of the game into non-overlapping pieces; then our algorithm conducts clustering of private information. A key contribution is the specific way to cluster the public information. As we will detail in Section 2, two prior abstraction algorithms motivated by similar considerations have been developed for poker by others [26, 15], but ours differs in that it does not use hand-crafted poker features, is applicable to the large, and does not have the conceptual weaknesses from which they suffer.

We developed an equilibrium-finding algorithm that can be applied to this abstraction. It is a modified version of external-sampling MCCFR [21]. Applied to TH, it samples one pair of preflop (i.e., first betting round) hands per iteration. For the later betting rounds, each blade samples public cards from its public cluster and performs MCCFR within each cluster. Our algorithm weighs the samples to remove bias. Ours is similar to the algorithm of Jackson [15]. However, we implement MCCFR instead of chance-sampled CFR, and split only based on public information (chance actions) rather than players' actions. Another related prior approach used vanilla CFR (which converges significantly slower in practice) and split based only on players' actions (which does support nearly as much parallelization) [16].

The new abstraction and equilibrium-finding algorithms enabled an equilibrium computation of unprecedented size on a supercomputer with high inter-blade memory access latency. Experiments also show that this run outperforms the strongest prior approach executed on a large shared-memory server with low memory latency but fewer cores.

Finally, post-processing techniques have been shown to be useful to mitigate the issues from overfitting to one's abstraction and approximate equilibrium finding. We introduce a family of post-processing techniques that outperform prior ones. Our techniques combine 1) the observation that rounding action probabilities mitigates the above-mentioned issues [6], 2) the new observation that similar abstract actions should be bucketed before such rounding so that fine-grained action discretization (aka action abstraction) does not disadvantage those actions, and 3) the new observation that biasing toward actions that reduce variance is helpful in a strong agent and our experiments show that this increases expected value as well.

We applied all of the above-mentioned techniques to generate an agent for two-player no-limit TH (NLTH). It won the 2014 Annual Computer Poker Competition (ACPC), beating each opponent with statistical significance.

2. ABSTRACTION ALGORITHM

The first contribution of this paper is a new hierarchical abstraction algorithm. It is domain independent, although in many places of the description we present it in the context of poker for concreteness. In order to enable distributed equilibrium finding, it creates an information abstraction that assigns disjoint components of the game tree to different blades so that sampling in each blade will only access information sets that are located on that blade.

At a high level, the first stage of our hierarchical abstraction algorithm is to cluster public information at some early point in the game (public flop boards, i.e., combinations of public flop cards, in the case of TH), giving a global basis for distributing the rest of the game into non-overlapping pieces. Then, as a second stage our algorithm conducts clustering of information states (that can include both public and private information) in a way that honors the partition generated in the first stage.

As an example, suppose that in the first stage we cluster public flop boards into 60 buckets. Suppose bucket 4 contains only the boards AsKhQd and AsKhJd. Then we cluster all private hands for each betting round, starting with the flop, i.e., the second round (we assume the abstraction for the preflop round has already been computed—the strongest agents, including ours, use no abstraction preflop). We perform abstraction over full (five-card) flop hands separately for each of the 60 blades. For blade 4, only the hands for which the public board cards are AsKhQd or AsKhJd are considered (for example, 5s4s-AsKhQd and QcJc-AsKhJd). There are 2,352 such hands. If we allowed an abstraction at the current round with 50 private buckets per blade, we would then group these 2,352 hands into 50 buckets (using some abstraction algorithm; we discuss ours in detail later). We then perform a similar procedure for the third (aka turn) and fourth (aka river) rounds, ensuring that the hands for each blade are limited only to the hands that contain a public flop board that was assigned to that blade in the first stage of the algorithm.

A game has *perfect recall* if, informally, no player ever forgets information that he knew at an earlier point in the game. This is a useful concept for several reasons. First, certain equilibrium-finding algorithms can only be applied to games with perfect recall [19, 14]. Second, other equilibrium-finding algorithms, such as CFR [27] and its sampling variants, have no theoretical guarantees in games that have imperfect recall, though they can still be applied. (One notable exception is recent work giving a theoretical guarantee of the performance of CFR in one class of imperfect-recall games called well-formed games [20].) And third, Nash equilibria are not even guaranteed to exist in general in behavioral strategies in games with imperfect recall.

Despite these limitations, poker agents using abstractions with imperfect recall have consistently been shown to outperform agents that use perfect recall abstractions [26]. Intuitively, perfect-recall abstractions force agents to distinguish all information at a later round in the tree that they were able to distinguish at an earlier round, even if such a distinction is not very significant at the later round. For example, if an agent can distinguish between Kh3c and Kh4c in the preflop round (as is the case in the abstractions of the best agents), then a perfect-recall abstraction would force them to be able to distinguish between Kh3c on a KsJd9h flop, and Kh4c on the same flop, despite the fact that the 3c vs. 4c distinction is extremely unlikely to play a strategic role in the hand. On the other hand, with imperfect recall, agents are not forced to remember all of these distinctions simply because they knew them at a previous round, and are free to group any hands together in a given round without regard to what information was known about them in prior rounds of the abstraction. The most successful prior abstraction algorithms use imperfect recall [18, 5].

Unfortunately, running CFR on imperfect-recall abstractions on a machine with high inter-blade memory access latency can be problematic, since regrets and strategy values at different buckets along a sample may be located on different blades. We now describe in detail our new approach that enables us to produce strong abstractions for this setting. Our approach requires players to remember certain information throughout the hand (public flop bucket), but does not force players to distinguish between other pieces of information that they may have been able to distinguish between previously (if such distinctions are no longer relevant). Thus, our approach achieves the benefits of imperfect recall to a large extent (though not the flexibility of full imperfect recall) while achieving partitioning of the game into disjoint pieces for different blades to work on independently.

2.1 Main Abstraction Algorithm

Our main abstraction algorithm, Algorithm 1, which is domain independent, works as follows. Let $\hat{r}$ be the special round of the game where we perform the public clustering. For the initial $\hat{r} - 1$ rounds, we compute a (potentially imperfect-recall) abstraction using an arbitrary algorithm A_r for round r. For example, in poker the strongest agents use no abstraction in the preflop round (and even if they did use abstraction for it, it would not require public clustering and could be performed separately). Next, the public states at round $\hat{r}$ are clustered into C buckets. The algorithm for this public clustering is described in Section 2.2. Once this public abstraction has been computed, we compute abstractions for each round from $\hat{r}$ to R over all states of private information separately for each of the public buckets that have been previously computed. These abstractions can be computed using any arbitrary approach, A_r. For our poker agent, we used an abstraction algorithm that had previously been demonstrated to perform well as the A_r's [18].

Algorithm 1 Main abstraction algorithm

Inputs: number of rounds R; round where public information abstraction is desired $\hat{r}$; number of public buckets C; number of desired private buckets per public bucket at round r, B_r; abstraction algorithm used for round r, A_r

```
for r = 1 to r̂ − 1 do
    cluster information states at round r using A_r
cluster public information states at round r̂ into C buckets
(e.g., using Algorithm 2)
for r = r̂ to R do
    for c = 1 to C do
        cluster private information states at round r that
        have public information in public bucket c into B_r
        buckets using abstraction algorithm A_r
```

2.2 Algorithm for Computing Abstraction of Public Information

The algorithm used to compute the abstraction of public information at round $\hat{r}$ is shown as Algorithm 2. For TH, this corresponds to computing a bucketing of the public flop boards. To do this, we need a distance function $d_{i,j}$ between pairs of public states (or, equivalently, a similarity function $s_{i,j}$ that can be transformed into a distance function). We use this distance function to compute the public abstraction using the clustering algorithm described in Section 2.3.

Two prior approaches have been applied to abstract public flop boards. One uses poker-specific features that have been constructed manually [15]. The second, due to Waugh et al., uses k-means clustering with L_2 distance over transition tables that were constructed from a small perfect-recall *base abstraction* with 10 preflop buckets and 100 flop buckets [26]. The entry $T[f][i][j]$ in the table gives the probability of transitioning from preflop bucket i to flop bucket j in the abstraction when the public flop board is f. In addition to potentially prohibitive computational challenges of scaling that approach to large base abstractions (such as the one we will use, which has 169 preflop and 5,000 flop buckets), there are also conceptual issues, as the following example illustrates. Consider the similar public flop boards AhKs3d and AhKs2d. Suppose the base abstraction does not perform abstraction preflop and places 4c3s-AhKs3d and 4c2s-AhKs2d into the same flop bucket, (which we would expect, as they are very similar—both have bottom pair with a 4 "kicker"), say bucket 12, while it places 4c3s-AhKs2d and 4c2s-AhKs3d into bucket 13 (these hands are also very similar—the worst possible non-pair hand with a "gutshot" straight draw). Suppose 4c3s is in bucket 7 preflop and 4c2s is in bucket 8. Then the transition table for AhKs2d would have value 0 for the probability of transitioning from preflop bucket 7 into flop bucket 12, while it would have value 1 for transitioning from preflop bucket 8 into flop bucket 12 (and the reverse for AhKs3d). So the L_2 distance metric would maximally penalize the boards for this component, despite the fact that they should actually be considered very similar based on this component, since they map hands that are extremely similar to the same bucket. Our new approach accounts for this problem by building a distance function based on how often public boards result in a given flop bucket in the base abstraction for *any* private cards (not necessarily the same private cards, as the prior approach has done).

We have developed an efficient approach that was able to use the strong 169-5,000-5,000-5,000 imperfect-recall abstraction as its base. We refer to this abstraction as A. The algorithm is game independent, and pseudocode (that is not specific to poker) is presented in Algorithm 2. As in Waugh's approach described above, we first compute a transition table T that will be utilized later in the algorithm, though our table will contain different information than theirs. For concreteness, and to demonstrate the implementation used by our agent so that it can be replicated, we will describe how the table is constructed in the context of TH poker.

We first construct a helper table called PublicFlopHands. The entry PublicFlopHands[i][j] for $1 \leq i \leq 1,755$, $1 \leq j \leq 3$ gives the j'th public flop card corresponding to index i, using a recently developed indexing algorithm that accounts for all suit isomorphisms [25] (there are $\frac{52 \cdot 51 \cdot 50}{6} = 22,100$ total public flop hands, but only 1,755 after accounting for all isomorphisms). We specify one such canonical hand for each index. Next, using this table, we create the transition table T, where the entry $T[i][j]$ for $1 \leq i \leq 1,755$, $1 \leq j \leq 5,000$ gives the number of private card combinations for which a hand with public flop i transitions into bucket j of the abstraction A, which has $B = 5,000$ buckets. This is computed by iterating over all public flop indices, then looking up the canonical hand in PublicFlopHands, and iterating over the $\frac{49 \cdot 48}{2} = 1,176$ possible private card combinations given that public flop hand. We then construct the 5-card flop hand by combining the two private cards with the given public flop hand, look up the index of this hand (again using Waugh's indexing algorithm), and then look up what bucket A places that flop hand index into. Thus, the creation of the transition table involves iterating over $1,755 \cdot 1,176 = 2,063,880$ combinations, which can be done quickly.

In poker-independent terms, $T[i][j]$ stores how often public state i will lead to bucket j of the base abstraction, aggregated over all possible states of private information. In contrast, Waugh's table stores separate transition probabilities for each state of private information.

We would like our distance function to assign a small value between public states that are frequently grouped into the same bucket by A, since we already know A to be a very strong abstraction. We compute distances by iterating over the B (private) buckets in round $\hat{r}$ of A. We initialize a variable $s_{i,j}$ which corresponds to the similarity between i and j to be zero. For each bucket b, let c_i denote the number of private states with public state i that are mapped to b under A (and similarly for c_j). For example, suppose i corresponds to the public flop board of AsQd6h and $b = 7$. Then c_i would denote the number of private preflop card combinations (x,y), such that the flop hand xy-AsQd6h is placed in bucket 7 under A. We then increment $s_{i,j}$ by the minimum of c_i and c_j. For example, if $c_i = 4$ and $c_j = 12$, this would mean that i and j are *both* placed into the current bucket b four times. Then the distance $d_{i,j}$ is defined as $\frac{V-s_{i,j}}{V}$, which corresponds to the fraction of private states that are not mapped to the same bucket of A when paired with public information i and j.[2]

Algorithm 2 Algorithm for computing abstraction of public information

Inputs: number of public buckets C; number of public states M; number of private information sets per public state V; prior abstraction A with B buckets; transition table T for public states into buckets of A; clustering algorithm L

```
for i = 1 to M − 1 do
    for j = i + 1 to M do
        s_{i,j} ← 0
        for b = 1 to B do
            c_i ← T[i][b], c_j ← T[j][b], s_{i,j} += min(c_i, c_j)
        d_{i,j} ← (V − s_{i,j}) / V
Cluster the M public states into C clusters using L with
distance function d
```

For our application of Algorithm 2 to poker, the number of public buckets we used is $C = 60$, the total number of private states for each public state is $V = 1,176$, and $B = 5,000$ as described above. The full number of public flop boards after accounting for all suit isomorphisms is $M = 1,755$. Thus, to compute all of the distances we must iterate over $\frac{BN(N-1)}{2} =$ 7.7 billion triples. This can be performed quickly in practice, since for each item we only need to perform lookups in the precomputed transition table.

2.3 Public Abstraction Clustering Algorithm

Given the distance function we have computed, we next perform the clustering of the public states into C public clusters, using the procedure shown in Algorithm 3. The initial clusters c^0 are computed by applying k-means++ [1], using the pairwise point distance function $d_{i,j}$, which is taken as an input. The k-means++ initialization procedure only requires knowing distances between data points, not distances from a point to a non-data-point. Next, for each iteration t, we iterate over all points i. We initialize clusterDistances to be an array of size K of all zeroes, which will denote the distance between point i and each of the current clusters. We then iterate over all other points $j \neq i$, and increment clusterDistances$[c^{t-1}[j]]$ by $d_{i,j}$. Once we have iterated over all values of j, we let $c^t[i]$ denote the cluster with smallest distance from i. If no clusters changed from the clustering at the previous iteration, we are done. Otherwise, we continue this procedure until T iterations have been performed, at which point we output $c^T[i]$ as the final abstraction.

Algorithm 3 Clustering algorithm for public abstraction

Inputs: Number of public states to cluster M; desired number of clusters K; distances $d_{i,j}$ between each pair of points; number of iterations to run T

```
Compute initial clusters c^0 (e.g., using k-means++)
for t = 1 to T do
    for i = 1 to M do
        clusterDistances ← array of size K of zeroes
        for j = 1 to M, j ≠ i do
            clusterDistances[c^{t−1}[j]] += d_{i,j}
        c^t[i] ← cluster with smallest distance
    if no clusters were changed from previous iteration
then break
```

This algorithm only takes into account distances between pairs of data points, and not distances between points in the space that are not data points (such as means). Clustering algorithms that are designed for metric spaces, such as k-means, are not applicable to this setting.[3]

3. EQUILIBRIUM-FINDING ALGORITHM

To solve the abstract game, one needs an algorithm that converges to a Nash equilibrium. The most commonly used equilibrium-finding algorithm for large imperfect-information extensive-form games is counterfactual regret minimization (CFR) and its extensions. We review CFR and the formal notation of extensive-form games in the appendix.

There is a large benefit to not needing to sample all actions at every iteration of CFR, and the variants that selectively sample more promising actions more often are Monte Carlo CFR (MCCFR) and Pure CFR. The external sampling variant of MCCFR converges faster than Pure CFR in practice but requires twice as much memory [7]. We build our equilibrium-finding algorithm starting from MCCFR because it converges faster and we are no longer memory constrained since we can run on distributed architectures.

External-Sampling MCCFR (ES-MCCFR) does a separate iteration for each player. On a player's iteration, ES-MCCFR samples opponent action and chance nodes down the tree (while exploring all of the player's actions). Actions

[2]Note that d is not a distance metric. It is possible to have $d_{i,j} = 0$ for boards that are different, if the boards send the same number of preflop hands into each flop bucket in A. Thus, we view d as an arbitrary matrix of distances rather than viewing the space as a metric space. This will affect selection of the clustering algorithm, described in Section 2.3.

[3]We could have used the k-medoid algorithm (though it has a significant computational overhead over our approach, both in terms of running time and memory), or used the objective of minimizing the average distance of each point from the points in a cluster (rather than the sum). It would be interesting to explore the effect of using different choices for the clustering objective on abstraction quality. We chose the sum objective because it is computationally feasible and gives a clustering with clusters of more balanced sizes than the average objective.

are selected according to regret minimization. Regret is updated in the player's information sets, while average strategy is updated for encountered opponent information sets. This is problematic on a machine with high inter-blade memory access latency because the information sets traversed on a single iteration can be located on different blades. On the supercomputer we used, for example, accessing memory on the same blade takes 130 nanoseconds, while accessing memory on different blades takes about one microsecond.

As discussed in the previous section, our new abstraction addresses this issue by ensuring that after a certain point (for the flop through river rounds in the case of TH) all remaining information sets encountered in the current MCCFR iteration are stored on the same blade (i.e., the blade that the public flop was assigned to in the first stage of the abstraction algorithm.)

We developed a modification of MCCFR specifically for architectures with high inter-blade memory access latency. It designates one blade as the "head" blade, which stores the regrets and average strategies for the top part of the game tree (preflop round in TH). The algorithm begins by sampling private information and conducting MCCFR on the head blade. When an action sequence is reached that transitions outside the top of the game tree (to the flop in TH), the algorithm sends the current state to each of the C child blades. Each child blade then samples public information from its public bucket and continues the iteration of MCCFR. Once all the child blades complete their part of the iteration, their values are returned to the head blade. The head blade calculates a weighted average of these values, weighing them by the number of choices of public information (possible flops in TH) that they sampled from. This ensures that the expected value is unbiased. The head node then continues its iteration of MCCFR, repeating the process whenever the sample exits the top part (a flop sequence is encountered), until the iteration is complete. Pseudocode of the detailed algorithm appears in Algorithm 4.

In practice, rather than communicating with the child nodes every time sampling passes beyond the top part of the tree (i.e., a flop sequence is encountered in TH), we instead use a two-pass approach. On the first pass, we only record which continuation (flop) sequences were encountered. These sequences are then sent to the child blades, so they can calculate values for those sequences; the child blades work in parallel, but within each child blade the continuation sequences assigned to that blade are handled one after another. The head blade then does a second pass that is identical to the first, except that values returned from the child blades are used whenever a sample gets beyond the top part of the tree (i.e., the flop is reached in TH).

Our algorithm encounters the inter-blade latency whenever the head node sends data to the cluster blades, and again when receiving the responses. This only amounts to around 60 microseconds per MCCFR iteration. Each iteration takes about 15 milliseconds, so this latency overhead is negligible. In settings where this overhead is significant, one can easily make it negligible by having the child blades take more samples on each iteration, thereby increasing the ratio of time spent sampling to time spent on latency; however, this reduces the role of sampling, and moves the algorithm closer to vanilla CFR, which converges slower than MCCFR.

Since the head node can only proceed after receiving a response from all the cluster blades, some clusters may be idle

Algorithm 4 Our equilibrium-finding algorithm

```
for all histories h at the end of the first part of the tree
do // combinations of the players' preflop hands
    for all clusters C_n, n ≠ 0 do // public (flop) clusters
        |F_{n,h}| ← number of public samples in C_n given h
for all information sets I and actions a do
    regret r_I[a] ← 0
    cumulative strategy s_I[a] ← 0
loop  // Keep iterating
    for all p ∈ N, p ≠ c do // Players other than chance
        Iter(∅, p, C_0)

function ITER(History h, Player p, Cluster C)
    if h ∈ Z then // Terminal state
        return u(h)
    else if P(h) = c then // Chance node
        Draw action a ∈ A(h) according to f_c(·|h)
        if C = C_0 and (h, a) ∉ TopOfTree then
            u⃗ ← 0
            for all C_n ∈ Clusters do
                u⃗ ← u⃗ + |F_{n,h}| · Iter((h, a), p, C_n)
            u⃗ ← u⃗ / Σ_n |F_{n,h}| // Remove bias
        else
            u⃗ ← Iter((h, a), p, C)
    else if P(h) = p then
        for all a ∈ A(h) do // Traverse all actions
            Pr(a) ← max{r_I[a],0} / Σ_{a'} max{r_I[a'],0} // Regret matching
            if C = C_0 and (h, a) ∉ TopOfTree then
                u⃗'[a] ← 0
                for all C_n ∈ ChildClusters do
                    u⃗'[a] ← u⃗'[a] + |F_{n,h}| · Iter((h, a), p, C_n)
                u⃗'[a] ← u⃗'[a] / Σ_n |F_{n,h}| // Remove bias
            else
                u⃗'[a] ← Iter((h, a), p, C)
            u⃗ ← u⃗ + Pr(a) · u⃗'[a]
        for all a ∈ A(h) do
            r_I[a] ← r_I[a] + u'_p[a] − u_p // Update regret
    else// Sample an action
        σ⃗_I ← max{r⃗_I,0} / Σ_{a'} max{r_I[a'],0}
        s⃗_I ← s⃗_I + σ⃗_I // Update cumulative strategy
        Draw action a ∈ A(h) from σ⃗_I
        if C = C_0 and (h, a) ∉ TopOfTree then
            u⃗ ← 0
            for all C_n ∈ Clusters do
                u⃗ ← u⃗ + |F_{n,h}| · Iter((h, a), p, C_n)
            u⃗ ← u⃗ / Σ_n |F_{n,h}| // Remove bias
        else
            u⃗ ← Iter((h, a), p, C)
    return u⃗
```

for a significant amount of time if their MCCFR iterations complete faster than other blades'. This happens despite the fact that our abstraction algorithm evenly divides the game tree among the child blades: on some blades the current strategies computed by MCCFR are such that the path of play ends sooner (e.g., by folding in poker).

In more detail, the algorithm begins by sampling private information and conducting MCCFR on the head blade. When an action sequence is reached that transitions beyond the top part of the tree (i.e., transitions to the flop in Texas

Hold'em), the algorithm sends the current state to each of the K child blades $C_1, C_2, ..., C_K$. Each child blade C_k then samples public information from its public bucket (i.e., a flop from the valid flops F_k assigned to it), and continues the iteration of MCCFR. Once all the children blades complete their part of the iteration, their calculated values $\vec{u}_k$ are returned to the head blade. The head blade calculates a weighted average of these values, weighing them by the number of choices of public information (possible flops in Texas Hold'em) that they sampled from: $\vec{u} = \frac{\sum_{k=1}^{K} F_k \vec{u}_k}{\sum_{k=1}^{K} F_k}$. This ensures that the expected value is unbiased, that is, in expectation each flop is weighed equally. The head node then continues its iteration of MCCFR, repeating the process whenever the sample exits the top part (a flop sequence is encountered), until the iteration is complete.

Within each child blade—i.e., each child cluster—we actually have, and use, multiple cores (not shown in the pseudocode for simplicity). Whenever a child cluster is reached, each core is given the same inputs but uses a different random number seed to select which public sample (public flop in Texas Hold'em) from within the cluster to work on, and how to randomly sample actions thereunder according to MCCFR. Given the nature of the game, the cores will do redundant work with very low probability, and iterates in different parts of the cluster will be stale by at most one iteration. (Another choice would be to lock parts of the tree within the cluster to prevent cores from working on the same information sets, but that would introduce overhead, and does not seem warranted at least in Texas Hold'em.)

4. POST-PROCESSING TECHNIQUE

Post-processing is important in solving imperfect-information games. In games where the action spaces are very large, action abstraction is typically used to select only some actions (e.g., bet sizes in poker) to include in the abstraction. However, the opponent may use actions that are not part of the abstraction. This begets the need to map the opponent's actions back into the abstract game. Throughout our experiments we used the leading reverse mapping approach, the pseudo-Harmonic mapping [4], which has been adopted broadly among the top NLTH agents over the last two years.

Post-processing techniques have also been shown to be useful for mitigating the issue of overfitting the equilibrium to one's abstraction and the issue that approximate equilibrium finding may end up placing positive probability on poor actions.[4] Two approaches have been studied, *thresholding* and *purification* [6]. In thresholding, action probabilities below some threshold are set to zero and then the remaining probabilities are renormalized. Purification is the special case of thresholding where the action with the highest probability is played with probability 1 (ties are broken uniformly at random).

We observe that combining reverse mapping and thresholding leads to the issue that discretizing actions finely in some area of the action space disfavors those actions because the probability mass from the equilibrium finding gets diluted among them. To mitigate this problem, we propose to *bucket* abstract actions into similarity classes for the purposes of thresholding (but not after thresholding). For example, in no-limit poker any bet size is allowed up to the number of chips a player has left. In a given situation our betting abstraction may allow the agent to fold, call, bet 0.5 pot, 0.75 pot, pot, 1.5 pot, 2 pot, 5 pot, and all-in. If the action probabilities are (0.1, 0.25, 0.15, 0.15, 0.2, 0.15,0,0,0), then purification would select the call action, while the vast majority of the mass (0.65) is on betting actions. In this example, our approach—detailed below—would make a pot-sized bet (the highest-probability bet action).

Finally, we observe that biasing toward conservative actions that reduce variance (e.g., the fold action in poker) is helpful in a strong agent (variance increases the probability that the weaker opponent will win). Our experiments will show that preferring the conservative "fold" action in TH increases expected value as well. One reason may be that if an agent is uncertain about what should be done in a given situation (the equilibrium action probabilities are mixed), the agent will likely be uncertain also later down that path and it may be better to end the game here instead of continuing to play into a part of the game where the agent is weak.

Our new post-processing technique combines all the ideas listed above. It first separates the available actions into three categories: fold, call, and bet. If the probability of folding exceeds a threshold parameter, we fold with probability 1. Otherwise, we follow purification between the three options of fold, call, and the "meta-action" of bet. If bet is selected, then we follow purification within the specific bet actions.

Clearly, there are many variations of this technique—so it begets a family—depending on what threshold for definitely using the conservative action (fold) is used, how the actions are bucketed for thresholding, what thresholding value is used among the buckets, and what thresholding value is used within (each of possibly multiple) meta-actions.

5. EXPERIMENTS

We experimented on the version of two-player no-limit Texas Hold'em (NLTH) used in the ACPC, which has 10^{165} nodes [17] in its game tree.

We used our new abstraction algorithm to create an information abstraction with 169 preflop buckets, 60 public flop buckets, and 500 private buckets for the flop, turn, and river for each of the public flop buckets, that is, 30,000 total private buckets for each of the three postflop rounds. Our action abstraction had 6,104,546 nodes (including leaves). In total, our abstract game then had $5.49 \cdot 10^{15}$ nodes (including leaves), $6.6 \cdot 10^{10}$ information sets (not including leaves), and $1.8 \cdot 10^{11}$ *infoset actions* (a new measure of game size that is directly proportional to the amount of memory that CFR uses [17]). This is six times larger than the largest abstractions used by prior NLTH agents—and, to our knowledge, the largest imperfect-information game ever tackled by an equilibrium-finding algorithm. This scale was enabled by our new, distributed approach.

We ran our equilibrium-finding algorithm for 1,200 hours on a supercomputer (Blacklight) with a high inter-blade memory access latency using 961 cores (60 blades of 16 cores each, plus one core for the head blade), for a total of 1,153,200 core hours. Each blade had 128 GB RAM.

The results from the 2014 ACPC against all opponents are shown in Table 1. The units are milli big blinds per hand (mbb/h), and the ± indicates 95% confidence intervals. Our

[4]Each of the post-processing techniques discussed can increase the agent's exploitability; however, opponents may have a hard time exploiting the agent in complex imperfect-information games. In the ACPC, post-processing has been shown to be beneficial in practice [6].

O1	O2	O3	O4	O5	O6	O7	O8	O9	O10	O11	O12	O13
261 ± 47	121 ± 38	21 ± 16	33 ± 16	20 ± 16	125 ± 44	499 ± 68	141 ± 45	214 ± 57	516 ± 61	980 ± 34	1474 ± 180	1819 ± 111

Table 1: Win rate (in mbb/h) of our agent in the 2014 Computer Poker Competition against opposing agents.

agent beat each opponent with statistical significance, with an average win rate of 479 mbb/h.

We also compared our algorithm's performance to using the prior best approach on a low-latency shared-memory server with 64 cores and 512 GB RAM. This is at the upper end of shared-memory hardware commonly available today. The algorithm run on the server used external sampling MC-CFR on a 169-5,000-5,000-5,000-bucket imperfect-recall card abstraction (this size was selected because it is slightly under the capacity of 512 GB RAM). We computed that information abstraction using the state-of-the-art non-distributed abstraction algorithm [5]. We used the same action abstraction as for the distributed case. The abstract game then had $1.5 \cdot 10^{14}$ nodes (including leaves), $1.1 \cdot 10^{10}$ information sets (not including leaves), and $3.1 \cdot 10^{10}$ infoset actions.

We benchmarked both against the two strongest agents from the 2013 competition, Figure 1.[5] The new approach outperformed the old against both agents for all timestamps tested. So, it is able to effectively take advantage of the additional distributed cores and RAM.

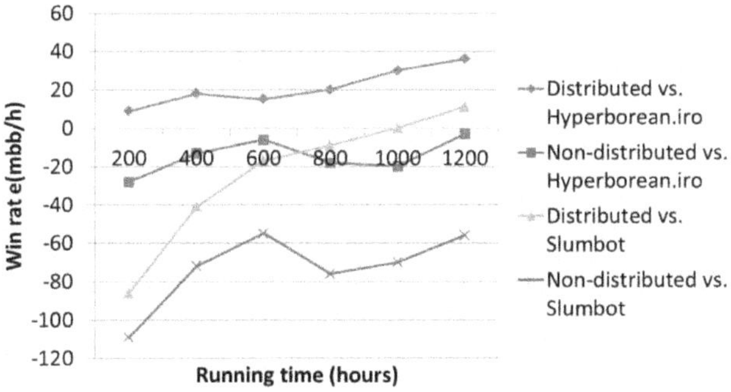

Figure 1: Win rates over time against the two strongest agents from the 2013 poker competition.

We also studied the effect of using our new post-processing techniques on the final strategies computed by our distributed equilibrium computation. We compared using no threshold, purification, a threshold of 0.15,[6] and using the new technique with a threshold of 0.2.[7] We tested against the same two strongest agents from the 2013 competition. Results are shown in Table 2. The new post-processor outperformed the prior ones both on average performance and on worst observed performance.

6. CONCLUSION

We introduced a distributed version of the most commonly used algorithm for large-scale equilibrium computation, counterfactual regret minimization (CFR), which enables CFR to scale to dramatically larger abstractions and numbers of cores. Specifically, we based our algorithm on external-sampling Monte Carlo CFR. The new algorithm begets constraints on the abstraction so as to make the pieces running on different computers disjoint. We introduced an algorithm for generating such abstractions while capitalizing on state-of-the-art abstraction ideas such as imperfect recall and the earth-mover's-distance similarity metric. Our techniques enabled an equilibrium computation of unprecedented size on a supercomputer with a high inter-blade memory latency. Prior approaches run slowly on this architecture. Our approach also leads to a significant improvement over using the prior best approach on a large shared-memory server with low memory latency. Finally, we introduced a family of post-processing techniques that outperform prior ones. We applied these techniques to generate an agent for two-player no-limit Texas Hold'em. It won the 2014 Annual Computer Poker Competition, beating each opponent with statistical significance.

The techniques are game independent. While we presented them for a setting that does not require abstraction before the public information arrives, and there is only one round of public information, they can be extended to settings with any sequence of interleaved public and private information delivery—while keeping the information sets on different blades disjoint. Also, while we presented techniques for two levels in the distribution tree (one blade to handle the top part and the rest split disjointly among the other blades), it is easy to see how the same idea can be directly extended to trees with more than two levels of blades.

[5]Both our distributed and parallel algorithms were evaluated in play with purification (except no post-processing of the first action), which had been shown to perform best among prior techniques. This is also one of the benchmarks we evaluate in the experiments presented in Table 2.

[6]This value was a prior benchmark [6]. Our exploratory data analysis concurred that it is a good choice.

[7]This was a good choice based on exploratory analysis, and it performed clearly better than 0.1 against both opponents.

	Hyperborean	Slumbot	Avg	Min
No Threshold	+30 ± 32	+10 ± 27	+20	+10
Purification	+55 ± 27	+19 ± 22	+37	+19
Thresholding-0.15	+35 ± 30	+19 ± 25	+27	+19
New-0.2	+39 ± 26	+103 ± 21	+71	+39

Table 2: Win rate (in mbb/h) of several post-processing techniques against strongest 2013 agents.

APPENDIX

A. RULES OF NO-LIMIT TEXAS HOLD'EM

Two players initially ante chips into a *pot*, which will go to the winner of the hand. Then, there is an initial round of betting (*preflop*). The player whose turn it is can:

- *Fold:* Give up on the hand, surrendering the pot.
- *Call:* Put in the minimum number of chips needed to match the amount put into the pot by the opponent.
- *Bet:* Put in chips beyond what is needed to call.

The initial round ends if a player has folded or if a bet has been called. If the round ends without a fold, then three public cards are revealed on the table (the *flop*) and a second round of betting occurs. This is followed by two additional betting rounds with one public card each (*turn* and *river*). If the final round is completed without a player folding, then both players reveal their private cards, and the player with the best hand wins the pot.

B. REGRET MATCHING

In regret-minimization algorithms, a strategy is determined through an iterative process. While there are a number of such algorithms (e.g., [13, 12]), this paper will focus on a typical one called *regret matching* (specifically, the polynomially weighted average forecaster with polynomial degree 2). We will now review how regret matching works, as well as the necessary tools to analyze it.

A normal-form (aka bimatrix) game is defined as follows. The game has a finite set N of players, and for each player $i \in N$ a set A_i of available actions. The game also has:

- For each player $i \in N$ a payoff function $u_i : A_i \times A_{-i} \to \Re$, where A_{-i} is the space of action vectors of the other agents except i. Define $\Delta_i = \max_{\langle a_i, a_{-i}\rangle} u_i(a_i, a_{-i}) - \min_{\langle a_i, a_{-i}\rangle} u_i(a_i, a_{-i})$ and define $\Delta = \max_i \Delta_i$.
- For each player i, a *strategy* σ_i is a probability distribution over his actions. The vector of strategies of players $N \setminus \{i\}$ is denoted by σ_{-i}. We define $u_i(\sigma_i, \sigma_{-i}) = \sum_{a, a_{-i}} p_{\sigma_i}(a) p_{\sigma_{-i}}(a_{-i}) u_i(a, a_{-i})$. We call the vector of strategies of all players a *strategy profile* and denote it by $\sigma = \langle \sigma_i, \sigma_{-i} \rangle$. Moreover, the *value* of σ to player i is defined as $v_i(\sigma) = u_i(\sigma_i, \sigma_{-i})$.

Let σ_i^t be the strategy used by player i on iteration t. The *instantaneous regret* of player i on iteration t for action a is

$$r_{t,i}(a) = u_i(a, \sigma_{-i}^t) - u_i(\sigma^t, \sigma_{-i}^t) \quad (1)$$

The *regret*, for player i on iteration T for action a is

$$R_{T,i}(a) = \frac{1}{T} \sum_{t=1}^{T} r_{t,i}(a) \quad (2)$$

Also, $R_{T,i} = \max_a \{R_{T,i}(a)\}$.

In the regret-matching algorithm, a player simply picks an action in proportion to his positive regret on that action, where positive regret is $R_{t,i}(a)_+ = \max\{R_{t,i}(a), 0\}$. Formally, at each iteration $t+1$, player i selects actions $a \in A_i$ according to probabilities

$$p_{t+1}(a) = \begin{cases} \frac{R_{t,i}(a)_+}{\sum_{a' \in A_i} R_{t,i}(a')_+}, & \text{if } \sum_{a' \in A_i} R_{t,i}(a')_+ > 0 \\ \frac{1}{|A|}, & \text{otherwise} \end{cases} \quad (3)$$

As shown in [3, p. 10], one can bound regret as

$$R_{T,i} \leq R_{T,i+} \leq \frac{\Delta_i \sqrt{|A_i|}}{\sqrt{T}} \quad (4)$$

Thus, as $T \to \infty$, $R_{T,i+} \to 0$.

C. EXTENSIVE-FORM GAMES

An extensive form game is defined as follows [22].

- A finite set N of players.
- A finite set H of sequences, the possible histories of actions, such that the empty sequence is in H and every prefix of a sequence in H is also in H. $Z \subseteq H$ are the terminal histories (those which are not a prefix of any other sequences). $A(h) = a : (h, a) \in H$ are the actions available after a nonterminal history $h \in H$.
- A function P that assigns to each nonterminal history (each member of $H \setminus Z$) a member of $N \cup c$. P is the player function. $P(h)$ is the player who takes an action after the history h. If $P(h) = c$ then chance determines the action taken after history h.
- A function f_c that associates with every history h for which $P(h) = c$ a probability measure $f_c(\cdot|h)$ on $A(h)$ ($f_c(a|h)$ is the probability that a occurs given h), where all pairs of measures are independent.
- For each player $i \in N$ a partition $\mathcal{I}_i$ of $\{h \in H : P(h) = i\}$ with the property that $A(h) = A(h')$ whenever h and h' are in the same member of the partition. For $I_i \in \mathcal{I}_i$ we denote by $A(I_i)$ the set $A(h)$ and by $P(I_i)$ the player $P(h)$ for any $h \in I_i$. We define $|A_i| = \max_{I_i} |A(I_i)|$ and $|A| = \max_i |A_i|$. $\mathcal{I}_i$ is the information partition of player i; a set $I_i \in \mathcal{I}_i$ is an information set of player i. We denote by $|\mathcal{I}_i|$ the number of information sets belonging to player i in the game and $|\mathcal{I}| = \max_i |\mathcal{I}_i|$.
- For each player $i \in N$ a payoff function u_i from Z to the reals. If $N = 1, 2$ and $u_1 = -u_2$, it is a zero-sum extensive game. Define $\Delta_i = \max_z u_i(z) - \min_z u_i(z)$ to be the range of payoffs to player i.

D. COUNTERFACTUAL REGRET MINIMIZATION (CFR)

Regret matching, described in Appendix B, is for normal-form games. However, it can be efficiently generalized to extensive-form games by using the counterfactual regret minimization (CFR) algorithm. CFR and its extensions are widely used in solving large imperfect-information games.

In CFR [27], $u_i(\sigma, h)$ is defined as the expected utility to player i given that history h has occurred, assuming all players then play according to σ. Next, *counterfactual utility* is defined as the expected utility given that information set I is reached and all players play according to σ except that player i plays to reach I. Formally, if $\pi^\sigma(h)$ is the probability of reaching history h according to σ, and $\pi^\sigma(h, h')$ is the probability of going from history h to history h', then

$$u_i(\sigma, I) = \frac{\sum_{h \in I, h' \in Z} \pi_{-i}^\sigma(h) \pi^\sigma(h, h') u_i(h')}{\pi_{-i}^\sigma(I)}$$

Further, for all $a \in A(I)$, $\sigma|_{I \to a}$ is defined to be a strategy profile identical to σ except that player i always chooses action a when in information set I. *Immediate counterfactual regret* for an action is defined as

$$R_{i,imm}^T(I, a) = \frac{1}{T} \sum_{t=1}^{T} \pi_{-i}^{\sigma^t}(I)(u_i(\sigma^t|_{I \to a}, I) - u_i(\sigma^t, I))$$

and for an information set as

$$R_{i,imm}^T(I) = \max_{a \in A(I)} R_{i,imm}^T(I, a)$$

In CFR, on iteration $T+1$ a player at an information set selects among actions $a \in A(I)$ by

$$p_{T+1}(a) = \begin{cases} \frac{R_i^{T,+}(I,a)}{\sum_{a \in A(I)} R_i^{T,+}(I,a)}, & \text{if } \sum_{a \in A(I)} R_i^{T,+}(I, a) > 0 \\ \frac{1}{|A(I)|}, & \text{otherwise} \end{cases}$$

Using CFR, one can bound regret in extensive-form games.

REFERENCES

[1] D. Arthur and S. Vassilvitskii. k-means++: The advantages of careful seeding. In *Proceedings of the Annual ACM-SIAM Symposium on Discrete Algorithms (SODA)*, 2007.

[2] D. Billings, N. Burch, A. Davidson, R. Holte, J. Schaeffer, T. Schauenberg, and D. Szafron. Approximating game-theoretic optimal strategies for full-scale poker. In *Proceedings of the 18th International Joint Conference on Artificial Intelligence (IJCAI)*, 2003.

[3] N. Cesa-Bianchi and G. Lugosi. *Prediction, learning, and games.* Cambridge University Press, 2006.

[4] S. Ganzfried and T. Sandholm. Action translation in extensive-form games with large action spaces: Axioms, paradoxes, and the pseudo-harmonic mapping. In *Proceedings of the International Joint Conference on Artificial Intelligence (IJCAI)*, 2013.

[5] S. Ganzfried and T. Sandholm. Potential-aware imperfect-recall abstraction with earth mover's distance in imperfect-information games. In *Proceedings of the AAAI Conference on Artificial Intelligence (AAAI)*, 2014.

[6] S. Ganzfried, T. Sandholm, and K. Waugh. Strategy purification and thresholding: Effective non-equilibrium approaches for playing large games. In *Proceedings of the International Conference on Autonomous Agents and Multi-Agent Systems (AAMAS)*, 2012.

[7] R. Gibson. *Regret Minimization in Games and the Development of Champion Multiplayer Computer Poker-Playing Agents.* PhD thesis, University of Alberta, 2014.

[8] A. Gilpin and T. Sandholm. A competitive Texas Hold'em poker player via automated abstraction and real-time equilibrium computation. In *Proceedings of the National Conference on Artificial Intelligence (AAAI)*, 2006.

[9] A. Gilpin and T. Sandholm. Better automated abstraction techniques for imperfect information games, with application to Texas Hold'em poker. In *Proceedings of the International Conference on Autonomous Agents and Multi-Agent Systems (AAMAS)*, 2007.

[10] A. Gilpin, T. Sandholm, and T. B. Sørensen. Potential-aware automated abstraction of sequential games, and holistic equilibrium analysis of Texas Hold'em poker. In *Proceedings of the AAAI Conference on Artificial Intelligence (AAAI)*, 2007.

[11] A. Gilpin, T. Sandholm, and T. B. Sørensen. A heads-up no-limit Texas Hold'em poker player: Discretized betting models and automatically generated equilibrium-finding programs. In *Proceedings of the International Conference on Autonomous Agents and Multi-Agent Systems (AAMAS)*, 2008.

[12] G. J. Gordon. No-regret algorithms for online convex programs. *Advances in Neural Information Processing Systems*, 19:489, 2007.

[13] A. Greenwald, Z. Li, and C. Marks. Bounds for regret-matching algorithms. In *ISAIM*, 2006.

[14] S. Hoda, A. Gilpin, J. Peña, and T. Sandholm. Smoothing techniques for computing Nash equilibria of sequential games. *Mathematics of Operations Research*, 35(2):494–512, 2010.

[15] E. Jackson. Slumbot NL: Solving large games with counterfactual regret minimization using sampling and distributed processing. In *AAAI Workshop on Computer Poker and Incomplete Information*, 2013.

[16] M. Johanson. Robust strategies and counter-strategies: Building a champion level computer poker player. Master's thesis, University of Alberta, 2007.

[17] M. Johanson. Measuring the size of large no-limit poker games. Technical report, University of Alberta, 2013.

[18] M. Johanson, N. Burch, R. Valenzano, and M. Bowling. Evaluating state-space abstractions in extensive-form games. In *Proceedings of the International Conference on Autonomous Agents and Multi-Agent Systems (AAMAS)*, 2013.

[19] D. Koller, N. Megiddo, and B. von Stengel. Fast algorithms for finding randomized strategies in game trees. In *Proceedings of the 26th ACM Symposium on Theory of Computing (STOC)*, pages 750–760, 1994.

[20] M. Lanctot, R. Gibson, N. Burch, M. Zinkevich, and M. Bowling. No-regret learning in extensive-form games with imperfect recall. In *Proceedings of the International Conference on Machine Learning (ICML)*, 2012.

[21] M. Lanctot, K. Waugh, M. Zinkevich, and M. Bowling. Monte Carlo sampling for regret minimization in extensive games. In *Proceedings of the Annual Conference on Neural Information Processing Systems (NIPS)*, 2009.

[22] M. J. Osborne and A. Rubinstein. *A Course in Game Theory.* MIT Press, 1994.

[23] D. Schnizlein, M. Bowling, and D. Szafron. Probabilistic state translation in extensive games with large action sets. In *Proceedings of the 21st International Joint Conference on Artificial Intelligence (IJCAI)*, 2009.

[24] J. Shi and M. Littman. Abstraction methods for game theoretic poker. In *CG '00: Revised Papers from the Second International Conference on Computers and Games*, London, UK, 2002. Springer-Verlag.

[25] K. Waugh. A fast and optimal hand isomorphism algorithm. In *AAAI Workshop on Computer Poker and Incomplete Information*, 2013.

[26] K. Waugh, M. Zinkevich, M. Johanson, M. Kan, D. Schnizlein, and M. Bowling. A practical use of imperfect recall. In *Proceedings of the Symposium on Abstraction, Reformulation and Approximation (SARA)*, 2009.

[27] M. Zinkevich, M. Bowling, M. Johanson, and C. Piccione. Regret minimization in games with incomplete information. In *Proceedings of the Annual Conference on Neural Information Processing Systems (NIPS)*, 2007.

Decision-theoretic Clustering of Strategies

Nolan Bard, †Deon Nicholas, Csaba Szepesvári, and Michael Bowling

University of Alberta
Edmonton, Alberta
{nolan,szepesva,bowling}@cs.ualberta.ca

†University of Waterloo
Waterloo, Ontario
dnichola@uwaterloo.ca

ABSTRACT

Clustering agents by their behaviour can be crucial for building effective agent models. Traditional clustering typically aims to group entities together based on a distance metric, where a desirable clustering is one where the entities in a cluster are spatially close together. Instead, one may desire to cluster based on actionability, or the capacity for the clusters to suggest how an agent should respond to maximize their utility with respect to the entities. Segmentation problems examine this decision-theoretic clustering task. Although finding optimal solutions to these problems is computationally hard, greedy-based approximation algorithms exist. However, in settings where the agent has a combinatorially large number of candidate responses whose utilities must be considered, these algorithms are often intractable. In this work, we show that in many cases the utility function can be factored to allow for an efficient greedy algorithm even when there are exponentially large response spaces. We evaluate our technique theoretically, proving approximation bounds, and empirically using extensive-form games by clustering opponent strategies in toy poker games. Our results demonstrate that these techniques yield dramatically improved clusterings compared to a traditional distance-based clustering approach in terms of both subjective quality and utility obtained by responding to the clusters.

Categories and Subject Descriptors

I.5.3 [**Pattern Recognition**]: Clustering—*Algorithms*; I.2.1 [**Artificial Intelligence**]: Applications and Expert Systems—*Games*

General Terms

Algorithms

Keywords

Clustering; decision-theory; extensive-form games; agent modelling; opponent modelling; maximum cover; poker

Appears in: *Proceedings of the 14th International Conference on Autonomous Agents and Multiagent Systems (AAMAS 2015), Bordini, Elkind, Weiss, Yolum (eds.), May 4–8, 2015, Istanbul, Turkey.*

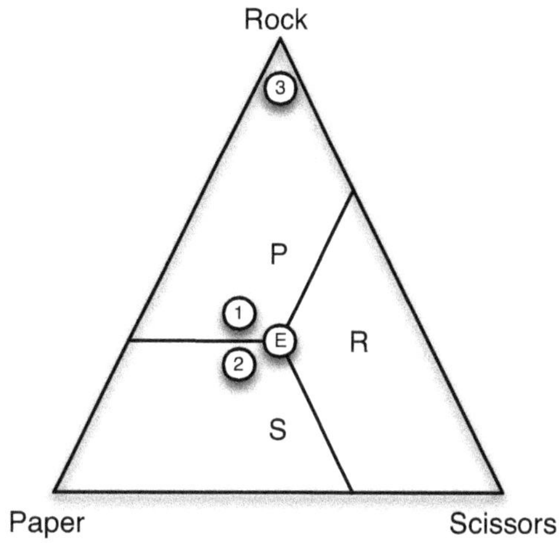

Figure 1: Rock-paper-scissors strategy simplex partitioned into best response regions. Despite their spatial proximity, 1 and 2 fall into distinct best response regions (P and S).

1. INTRODUCTION

In domains where maximizing an agent's utility is the primary goal, agents may need to model other agents or entities in their environment to improve their utility. Clustering techniques can be beneficial in these settings by allowing the agent to partition the set of entities into similar groups called clusters. In this setting, a clustering's *actionability* — its capacity to suggest responses with high utility to the agent — is the fundamental clustering objective. Contrast this with many traditional clustering problems, such as k-means and k-medians, where similarity is measured by some notion of *spatial* distance between the entities within the same cluster. For instance, the k-means objective is to minimize the within-cluster sum of squared Euclidean distances between each of the entities and their cluster's centroid. Despite an abundance of spatial clustering techniques, these techniques may fail to capture similarity in how the agent should respond to the entities.

To illustrate, we briefly examine the game of Rock-Paper-Scissors. In this game, a static agent's behaviour can be specified by their probability distribution over choosing rock, paper, and scissors. Figure 1 depicts a simplex representing the space of possible probability distributions over these three actions. The point E is the game's Nash equilibrium of 1/3 for each action. Consider the points labelled 1,2, and 3.

Although 1 and 2 are spatially close, an agent's **response** for how to act with respect to them should be different as their strategies do not share the same best response. In contrast, 1 and 3 share the same best response (always play paper) despite being spatially distant.

Although this type of decision-theoretic clustering may appear to be a niche problem at first glance, it is actually related to a range of optimization problems. Kleinberg and colleagues [5] introduced and formalized this style of clustering problem in the data mining community as *segmentation problems*. Their work showed that optimal solutions to this type of clustering induce optimal solutions to a form of maximum coverage optimization, and vice versa. Lu and Boutilier [10] highlighted several parallels between their budgeted social choice model and segmentation problems. Carlin and Zilberstein [3] also use a similar type of utility-based clustering to group observations in Dec-POMDPs, reducing the size of agent policies. Their algorithm, though, was presented with no approximation bounds.[1]

Due to the computational complexity of segmentation problems (and many other similar maximum coverage based problems) one typically forgoes exact solutions for efficient approximate solutions to these problems. In particular, Nemhauser and colleagues' [11] greedy algorithm for maximizing monotone submodular functions is often used to attack a segmentation problem's maximum coverage formulation. This approach iteratively constructs a solution by evaluating the marginal gain of each feasible response, adding the greedy-best response. Unfortunately, as Kleinberg *et al.* [6] noted, such greedy algorithms may not be efficient as even a single step can be an NP-complete problem.

In this paper, we examine segmentation problems where the response space is either exponential or infinite and the standard greedy approximation is computationally infeasible. We show that despite this, in certain cases where the utility function can be factored, an efficient response oracle can be constructed. We then use such a response oracle to operate directly on the partitioning formulation of a segmentation problem by greedily merging clusters together in an agglomerative (*i.e.*, "bottom up") clustering algorithm. Finally, we evaluate our technique both theoretically and empirically. Our theoretical results provide a guarantee on the worst-case performance of our greedy algorithm relative to the optimal clustering into k sets. This approximation bound is shown to be tight within a factor of 2. We empirically evaluate our technique using extensive-form games by clustering agent strategies in two toy games of poker: Kuhn poker and Leduc hold'em. Our results highlight the benefit of clustering strategies based on their actionability rather than their spatial similarity by contrasting our greedy method with a traditional k-means clustering approach.

2. BACKGROUND

We begin our exposition by introducing segmentation problems, followed by a brief description of our experimental domain of extensive-form games.

[1]The theoretical results from this paper can also be applied to their problem, giving an algorithm with approximation guarantees for the single-agent case. Whether the same principles can give an algorithm with approximation bounds for the multi-agent case is open.

2.1 Segmentation Problems

Segmentation problems [5] examine the challenge of determining how an agent should respond to maximize utility given information about different entities[2]. For example, a commercial enterprise with information about their customers could act homogeneously across the customers, but the enterprise may be able to increase its utility by tailoring their **response** (*e.g.*, marketing strategy, product line) to each customer's preferences. While such individual personalization is often impractical, a more limited form of personalization where the market of customers is segmented (*i.e.*, clustered) into k groups may still be beneficial.

One way to view segmentation problems is as clustering problems where the desired clustering depends on a utility function $u(e, r)$ that specifies the utility of **response** $r \in R$ with respect to an **entity** $e \in E$ being clustered. Unlike traditional clustering approaches, this approach directly optimizes for the actionability of the clustering.

More formally, let E and R be sets (E finite), and $u : E \times R \to \mathbb{R}$ be a **utility function**. For convenience, we let $\text{Part}(E)$ denote the **set of partitions of E**:

$$\text{Part}(E) = \left\{ P \in 2^{2^E} : \cup P = E; A, B \in P \Rightarrow A \cap B = \emptyset \right\}.$$

For $k \in \mathbb{N}$, we shall also use $\text{Part}_k(E)$ to denote the **set of k-element partitions of E**:

$$\text{Part}_k(E) = \{P \in \text{Part}(E) : |P| = k\}.$$

We abuse notation slightly to define several recurring terms for utility over subsets and partitions of E. For $P \in \text{Part}(E)$, $C \subset E$, $r \in R$, let

$$u(C, r) = \sum_{e \in C} u(e, r),$$
$$u(C) = \max_{r \in R} u(C, r), \text{and}$$
$$u(P) = \sum_{C \in P} u(C).$$

In words, $u(C, r)$ is the total utility of a "cluster" of entities $C \subset E$ when the response is r, $u(C)$ is the utility of C and $u(P)$ is the utility of partition P.

The partitioning form of a segmentation problem considers the problem of finding a partition of E that gives the highest utility amongst all k-element partitions:

$$P_k^* = \operatorname*{argmax}_{P \in \text{Part}_k(E)} u(P) = \operatorname*{argmax}_{P \in \text{Part}_k(E)} \sum_{C \in P} \max_{r \in R} \sum_{e \in C} u(e, r). \tag{1}$$

For clarity, note that this assumes clustering E is our ground truth objective: other potential entities are ignored. Finally, we let u_k^* denote the **utility of an optimal k-element partition**: $u_k^* = \max_{P \in \text{Part}_k(E)} u(P)$.

To provide more visual intuition of this problem, we can view the problem as an optimization on a matrix. Let U be an $|E| \times |R|$ matrix where the (i, j)-th entry $U_{i,j} = u(e_i, r_j)$. Then, given $k < |E|$, the goal of the optimization is to find a partition $P = \{C_1, \ldots, C_k\}$ of the rows of U that maximizes the sum of the utilities over the rows when all rows in the same cluster must share the same response column r_j. Figure 2 depicts an example of this matrix form.

[2]Kleinberg and colleagues referred to the entities and responses as customers and decisions, respectively.

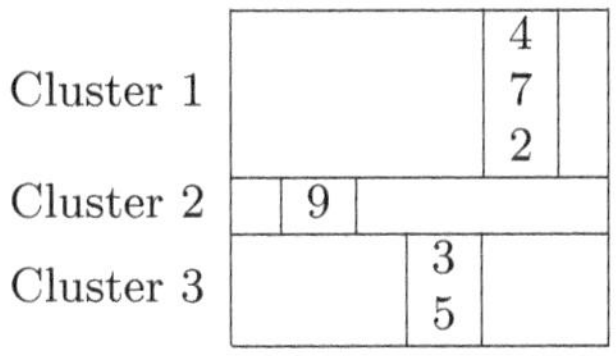

Figure 2: Matrix view of a segmentation problem with an objective value of 30.

Kleinberg and colleagues showed that this partitioning view of a segmentation problem is also equivalent to the following maximum coverage based optimization,

$$\underset{\substack{R' \subseteq R \\ |R'|=k}}{\operatorname{argmax}} \sum_{e \in E} \max_{r \in R'} u(e, r). \qquad (2)$$

In our matrix view of this problem, one can think of Equation 2 as choosing the set of k columns of the matrix U that maximally cover the rows of the matrix.

The utility of optimal solutions to these two views of a segmentation problem not only have equal value, u_k^*, but one can construct a solution to Equation 2 given a solution to Equation 1, and vice versa. Though straightforward, we show these constructions and their computational cost in the following two lemmas.

LEMMA 1. *Partitions induce covers.*
Given $P \in \text{Part}_k(E)$ where $v = u(P)$, one can construct $R' \subseteq R$ with $|R'| \leq k$ such that $\sum_{e \in E} \max_{r \in R'} u(e, r) \geq v$ in $O(|E||R|)$ evaluations of u.

PROOF. We prove this by constructing $R' \subseteq R$. Begin with $R' = \emptyset$. Then for each $C \in P$, add $r_C = \operatorname{argmax}_{r \in R} u(C, r)$ to R'. This adds at most k unique elements to R'. Finally, observe that R' has a maximum coverage value of at least v.

$$\begin{aligned} v = \sum_{C \in P} \max_{r \in R} \sum_{e \in C} u(e, r) &= \sum_{C \in P} \max_{r \in R'} \sum_{e \in C} u(e, r) \\ \leq \sum_{C \in P} \sum_{e \in C} \max_{r \in R'} u(e, r) &= \sum_{e \in E} \max_{r \in R'} u(e, r) \quad \square \end{aligned}$$

LEMMA 2. *Covers induce partitions.*
Given $R' = \{r_1, \ldots, r_k\}, R' \subseteq R$ such that $v = \sum_{e \in E} \max_{r \in R'} u(e, r)$, one can construct $P \in \text{Part}(E)$ where $|P| \leq k$ and $u(P) \geq v$ in $O(k|E|)$ evaluations of u.

PROOF. We prove this by constructing such a partition as follows. Initialize $P = \{C_1, \ldots, C_k\}$ where $C_i = \emptyset$. For each $e \in E$, add e to C_i where $i = \operatorname{argmax}_{j \in \{1, \ldots, k\}} u(e, r_j)$. Finally, remove C_i if it remained empty. P is clearly a partition of E of size at most k where $u(P) \geq v$ since for each $C_i \in P$, $u(C_i) \geq u(C_i, r_i)$. $\square$

The equivalence of these two problems means that techniques for solving the maximum coverage based problem in Equation 2 can also be used to solve the partitioning problem in Equation 1. Unfortunately, this type of weighted maximum coverage problem is known to be computationally hard. Cornuejols *et al.* [4] showed that when u is a nonnegative utility function, the weighted maximum coverage optimization in Equation 2 is NP-complete. Kleinberg *et al.* also showed on several constrained response spaces that for u a general linear function, the segmentation problems are still NP-complete [5], or more specifically MAXSNP-complete [6].

Due to these negative complexity results, approximate solutions to segmentation problems are typically sought in lieu of exact solutions. Nemhauser and colleagues [11] showed that when u is constrained to nonnegative values, the weighted maximum coverage problem is submodular and a $(1 - 1/e)$-approximation to the optimal solution can be computed using a greedy approximation algorithm. Their greedy algorithm iteratively constructs $R' \subseteq R$ by adding $r \in R \setminus R'$ that maximally increases the objective given the previously selected elements in R'. In many natural settings the response space R is either exponential or infinite and solving even a single step of such a greedy algorithm may be NP-complete. Kleinberg *et al.* [6] introduce several approximation algorithms for segmentation problems. In addition to some greedy approximations, which greedily add the response that maximizes the marginal gain like Nemhauser and colleagues' algorithm, they also introduce efficient approximation algorithms that avoid enumerating the response space by exploiting domain-specific assumptions about the utility function's structure.

In many domains, the utility function does not conform to the assumptions required by Kleinberg and colleagues' algorithms. In this work, we develop efficient approximation algorithms by assuming that the utility function's structure admits a specific type of efficient oracle. Before describing the details of our oracle, we introduce our experimental domain of extensive-form games: a broad class of problems that admit such oracles but do not satisfy the assumptions required by Kleinberg and colleagues' approaches.

2.2 Extensive-form Games

The experimental results in this paper will examine clustering strategies in extensive-form games. Extensive-form games provide a general model to represent sequential interactions between agents in an environment. Extensive-form games can be viewed as a tree consisting of nodes corresponding to states of the game where some player acts, and edges representing each of the actions available to a player. Leaves of the tree represent the end of the game and assign utilities to each of the players. In games with a stochastic element, a special chance player acts according to a known distribution. In games of imperfect information, some actions are not fully observed by some of the players. These players are then unable to distinguish which of several game states they are in. A set of these indistinguishable states is called an **information set**. A **strategy** for a player specifies a distribution for each information set over the available actions. One potential use for clustering strategies is to help produce a portfolio of "expert" responses that could be used to implicitly model agents in these games [2].

3. EXPLOITING STRUCTURED UTILITY

In settings where the response space is too large to enumerate efficiently, algorithms that avoid enumerating the candidate responses are necessary. We examine problems where structure in the utility function u allows the best response for a given set of entities to be efficiently computed despite a prohibitively large response space. Next, we formalize this response oracle, provide examples of problems where such an oracle exists, and show how one can incorporate a response oracle into an efficient greedy agglomerative clustering algorithm.

3.1 Response Oracles

In some settings the utility function u can be factored to enable the efficient computation of the response (*i.e.*, column of U) that maximally covers a given set of entities. Formally, given $C \subseteq E$ a **response oracle** $f : 2^E \to R$ is defined as

$$f(C) \equiv \operatorname*{argmax}_{r \in R} u(C, r).$$

By definition, this means $u(C, f(C))$, the utility obtained by the response oracle on C, is $u(C)$.

We provide some domains where such a response oracle can be computed efficiently, taking time logarithmic in the size of the response space, and then present a greedy algorithm that capitalizes on this oracle.

Example: Extensive-form Games.

Let the entities E consist of observed opponent strategies and let the response space R be the possible strategies that our agent could employ. Even if our agent only considers pure strategies (where a player acts deterministically at each of the game's information sets) the size of the response space is exponential in the number of the game's information sets. The response oracle $f(C)$ in this setting is a best response to the average of the sequence-form representations [7] of the strategies in C. Due to an extensive-form game's tree structure, this can be computed in time linear in the number of information sets.

Example: Budgeted Social Choice.

In the case of maximizing social welfare, Lu and Boutilier's [10] limited choice model of budgeted social choice is equivalent to the segmentation problem optimization in Equation 2 (with entities and responses instead called agents and alternatives, respectively). In their formulation, they assume that the responses can be enumerated and use Nemhauser and colleagues' greedy algorithm. Suppose the responses consist of products represented by feature vectors $r = (r_1, \ldots, r_n) \in R_1 \times \ldots \times R_n$ and that the utility function can be factored into $u(e, r) = \sum_{i=1}^{n} u_i(e, r_i)$ where $u_i : E \times R_i \to \mathbb{R}$. Then the response oracle $f(C)$ can compute each r_i of the optimal response as $\operatorname{argmax}_{r_i \in R_i} \sum_{e \in C} u_i(e, r_i)$. Instead of enumerating the $\prod_{i=1}^{n} |R_i|$ possible responses in R, the response oracle can be computed efficiently in time $O(|C| \sum_{i=1}^{n} |R_i|)$.

3.2 A Greedy Heuristic

Since both exact solutions and algorithms similar to Nemhauser and colleagues' greedy algorithm are infeasible on segmentation problems with a large response space, we propose an alternative greedy approximation algorithm. Like others, our approach acts greedily based on the marginal change in utility, but it does so when considering how to merge clusters in an agglomerative hierarchical clustering algorithm [13]. Our algorithm is efficient, requiring a polynomial number of oracle queries, provided an efficient response oracle.

In an agglomerative clustering algorithm, one starts with a partition of singletons and builds a solution in a "bottom up" manner by iteratively coarsening the partition. Unlike Nemhauser and colleagues' greedy algorithm, which acted greedily according to the *maximum marginal gain*, we greedily merge clusters that incur the *minimal marginal loss*. This is because the objective value of Equation 1 is vacuously maximized by the initial partition of singletons (when the size of the partition is unconstrained). One can view this as a greedy heuristic for the following optimization.

$$\min_{P \in \mathrm{Part}_k(E)} \left[\sum_{e \in E} \max_{r^* \in R} u(e, r^*) - u(P) \right] \quad (3)$$

Conceptually, this objective function represents the utility lost by responding to the entities in clusters rather than individually. Note that a partition that optimizes our original objective in Equation 1 also optimizes Equation 3, and vice versa.

Our algorithm starts with the trivial partition $P_0 = \{\{e\} : e \in E\}$ where every entity is in its own set. On each iteration we coarsen the partition by greedily merging together the two sets in the current partition that incur the minimal marginal loss in the objective value of Equation 3. This is repeated until we have a partition that satisfies the cardinality constraint k.

More formally, let Coarse(P) be all the 1-step coarsenings of partition $P = \{C_1, \ldots, C_k\}$:

$$\mathrm{Coarse}(P) = \{\mathrm{Merge}(P, C_i, C_j) : 1 \le i < j \le k\},$$

where

$$\mathrm{Merge}(P, C_i, C_j) = P \setminus \{C_i, C_j\} \cup \{C_i \cup C_j\}$$

is the partition that results from P by merging C_i and C_j. Then, the greedy algorithm can be written as in Algorithm 1. Note that the combination of sets $C_i, C_j \in P$ that produce the optimal coarsening are exactly those for which the marginal loss $u(C_i) + u(C_j) - u(C_i \cup C_j)$ is minimal.

Algorithm 1 Greedy response oracle clustering

Require: Set E of entities, a response oracle f, utility function u, k
  Initialization: $G = P_0 = \{\{e\} : e \in E\}$
  while $|G| > k$ **do**
    $G \leftarrow \operatorname{argmax}_{P \in \mathrm{Coarse}(G)} u(P)$
  end while
  return G

A naive implementation of this algorithm must compute the marginal loss for all combinations $C_i, C_j \in P$ on each of the $|E| - k$ iterations. This implementation would require $O(|E|^3)$ calls to the oracle. By noticing some structure in the computation, we can use memoization to improve this. After computing the marginal loss for all combinations $C_i, C_j \in P$ of candidate merges on the first iteration, the marginal losses for all candidates can be updated after each merge with at most $O(|E|)$ calls to the response oracle. If C_i and C_j are merged, we need only compute the marginal losses for all pairs of clusters that involve the new cluster $C_i \cup C_j$. This memoization implementation only needs a total of $O(|E|^2)$ calls to the oracle. Additionally, since we know that the marginal loss is always nonnegative, we can lazily update the marginal losses (only evaluating them while no zero loss candidate exists) to further reduce computation. Finally, each marginal loss computation is independent from the others and therefore amenable to parallelization.

Unlike clustering algorithms where the desired number of clusters k needs to be specified in advance (*e.g.*, Lloyd's algorithm for k-means), our greedy algorithm's iterative and deterministic nature means that it could be run a single time for $|E|$ iterations, reporting the partitions and objective value on each iteration. This enables users to directly evaluate the trade-off between the objective and the number of clusters.

In the remainder of the paper, we evaluate our greedy algorithm both theoretically, proving approximation bounds on the solution quality, and empirically by clustering agent strategies in toy poker games. We begin with our theoretical analysis.

4. THEORETICAL RESULTS

Our theoretical analysis examines the worst-case behaviour of our greedy clustering algorithm. Theorem 1 establishes a lower bound on the utility of a clustering produced by our greedy algorithm, relative to the optimal clustering into k sets. Theorem 2 then shows that this lower bound is tight (within a factor of 2) and cannot be improved substantially.

In this section we fix E and we denote its cardinality by m. Using the subsequent three lemmas, we prove the following result:

THEOREM 1. *Let u be a nonnegative valued utility function, $1 \le k \le m$. Then $u(G_k) \ge \max\left(\frac{1}{k}, \frac{k}{m}\right) u_k^* \ge \frac{1}{\sqrt{m}} u_k^*$, where G_k is a k-element partition of E returned by the greedy algorithm.*

Note that the second inequality follows trivially from $\max\left(\frac{1}{k}, \frac{k}{m}\right) \ge \min_{s>0} \max\left(\frac{1}{s}, \frac{s}{m}\right) = \frac{1}{\sqrt{m}}$. Hence, it remains to prove the first inequality. We prove this by showing that $u(G_k) \ge \frac{k}{m} u_k^*$ in Lemma 4, and that $u(G) \ge \frac{1}{k} u_k^*$ in Lemma 5. We begin by proving a lower bound on the utility for a single coarsening step of the greedy algorithm.

LEMMA 3. *Let u be a nonnegative valued utility function, $G \in \mathrm{Part}(E)$, $C = \mathrm{argmin}_{C \in G} u(C)$. Then, for any $C' \in G$, $C' \ne C$,*

$$\max_{P \in \mathrm{Coarse}(G)} u(P) \ge u(\mathrm{Merge}(G, C, C')) \ge \left(1 - \frac{1}{|G|}\right) u(G).$$

PROOF. The first inequality holds by the definition of Coarse. Hence, it remains to prove the second. For this, let $k = |G|$. By the choice of C and the definition of $u(G)$, $u(G) \ge k u(C)$, or $u(C) \le u(G)/k$. Pick any $C' \in G$, $C' \ne C$ and set $G' = \mathrm{Merge}(G, C, C')$. Let $r' = \mathrm{argmax}_{r \in R} u(C', r)$. Then,

$$\begin{aligned}
u(G') = \sum_{A \in G'} u(A) &= \overbrace{\sum_{A \in G} u(A)}^{u(G)} + u(C \cup C') - (u(C) + u(C')) \\
&\ge u(G) + u(C \cup C', r') - (u(C) + u(C')) \\
&= u(G) + u(C, r') + \cancel{u(C', r')} - u(C) - \cancel{u(C')} \\
&\ge u(G) - u(C) \qquad \text{(since } u \text{ is nonnegative)} \\
&\ge \left(1 - \frac{1}{k}\right) u(G). \qquad \text{(by the choice of } C\text{)}
\end{aligned}$$

□

LEMMA 4. *Assume that u is nonnegative valued. Fix $1 \le i \le m$ and let G_i denote the i-element partition returned by the greedy algorithm. Then, $u(G_i) \ge \frac{i}{m} u(G_m) \ge \frac{i}{m} u_i^*$.*

PROOF. By using Lemma 3 $(m - i)$-times, we get

$$u(G_i) \ge \left(\prod_{j=i}^{m-1} \frac{j}{j+1}\right) u(G_m),$$

which proves the first half of the lemma. For the second part just combine this with $u(G_m) = u_m^* \ge u_{m-1}^* \ge \cdots \ge u_i^*$. □

It remains to prove that the following lemma holds:

LEMMA 5. *Assume that u is nonnegative valued. Let $G \in \mathrm{Part}_k(E)$. Then, $u(G) \ge \frac{1}{k} u_k^*$.*

PROOF. Let $P_k^* = \mathrm{argmax}_{P \in \mathrm{Part}_k(E)} u(P)$, and $C = \mathrm{argmax}_{C' \in P_k^*} u(C')$. Then, $u_k^* = u(P_k^*) \le k u(C)$, hence it suffices to show that $u(G) \ge u(C)$. Let $r_C = \mathrm{argmax}_{r \in R} u(C, r)$. We have

$$\begin{aligned}
u(G) &= \sum_{C' \in G} u(C') \\
&\ge \sum_{C' \in G} u(C', r_C) = \sum_{e \in E} u(e, r_C) \\
&\ge u(C, r_C) \qquad \text{(since } u \text{ is nonnegative)} \\
&= u(C). \ \square
\end{aligned}$$

The next result establishes that the bound in Theorem 1 cannot be substantially improved:

THEOREM 2. *Let k be a positive integer. For each $\varepsilon > 0$, there exists a nonnegative utility function on a set of entities E of $m = k^2$ elements and on a set R of $k^2 + k$ responses such that if G_k is the k-element partition returned by the greedy algorithm when fed with k and u then $u(G_k) - \varepsilon \le \frac{2}{\sqrt{m}} u_k^*$.*

PROOF. We will construct a matrix of size $k^2 \times (k^2 + k)$ holding the values of the utility function. Let $E = \{1, \ldots, k^2\}$, I denote the $k \times k$ identity matrix, $\varepsilon > 0$ and define the $k \times k$ matrix Q_ε by

$$Q_\varepsilon = \begin{pmatrix} 2+\varepsilon & \varepsilon & \ldots & \varepsilon \\ \varepsilon & 2+\varepsilon & \ldots & \varepsilon \\ \vdots & \vdots & \ddots & \vdots \\ \varepsilon & \varepsilon & \ldots & 2+\varepsilon \end{pmatrix}.$$

Finally, as in Section 2.1, the $k^2 \times (k^2 + k)$ matrix representing the utility function u is given by

$$U = \begin{pmatrix} I & Q_\varepsilon & 0 & \ldots & 0 \\ I & 0 & Q_\varepsilon & \ldots & 0 \\ \vdots & \vdots & \vdots & \ddots & \vdots \\ I & 0 & 0 & \ldots & Q_\varepsilon \end{pmatrix}.$$

Let $C_1 = \{1, \ldots, k\}$, $C_2 = \{k+1, \ldots, 2k\}$, …, $C_k = \{k^2 - k + 1, \ldots, k^2\}$. Note that $\{C_1, \ldots, C_k\} \in \mathrm{Part}_k(E)$. We claim that the greedy algorithm returns the k-element partition $G_k = \{C_1, \ldots, C_k\}$.

To show this, let G_i denote the i-element partition computed by the greedy algorithm. We claim that for any $C \in G_i$, $C \subset C_p$ for some $1 \le p \le k$ (i.e., G_i is a refinement of G_k). This clearly suffices to prove that $G_k = \{C_1, \ldots, C_k\}$. Since $G_m = \{\{1\}, \ldots, \{k^2\}\}$, the claim holds for $i = m$.

Let us assume that it holds up to $k < i \le m$. Consider $C, C' \in G_i$. By the induction hypothesis, G_i is a refinement of G_k and therefore $C \subset C_p$ and $C' \subset C_q$ for some $1 \le p, q \le k$. Then, $u(C) = 2 + |C|\varepsilon$ and $u(C') = 2 + |C'|\varepsilon$. If C and C' were merged, the marginal loss due to merging is $\ell(C, C') = u(C) + u(C') - u(C \cup C')$. The greedy algorithm merges the two elements of G_i that minimize this loss. If $p = q$ then $u(C \cup C') = 2 + (|C| + |C'|)\varepsilon$ and $\ell(C, C') = 2$. If $p \ne q$ then $u(C \cup C') = 2 + \max(|C|, |C'|)\varepsilon$ and $\ell(C, C') = 2 + (|C| + |C'| - \max(|C|, |C'|))\varepsilon$. Since $\varepsilon > 0$, the loss due to merging two clusters within the same block is always smaller than that of when the two clusters belong to different blocks. Hence, the greedy algorithm will choose to merge clusters within the same block. This shows that the induction hypothesis also holds for $i - 1$, finishing the proof of the claim.

We also claim that as long as ε is small enough, the optimal k-element partition is $P_k^* = \{\{1, k+1, 2k+1, \ldots, k^2 - k+1\}, \{2, k+2, 2k+2, \ldots, k^2 - k+2\}, \ldots, \{2k, 3k, \ldots, k^2\}\}$. Let C_i^* be the ith cluster in P_k^*. Then, for any $C \subset E$, if $n_i = |C \cap C_i^*|$, $1 \le i \le k$, $n(C) = \max(n_1, \ldots, n_k)$, we have $n(C) \le k$ and $u(C) = \max(n_1, \ldots, n_k, 2 + n_1\varepsilon, \ldots, 2 + n_k\varepsilon) = \max(n(C), 2 + n(C)\varepsilon) \le \max(k, 2 + k\varepsilon) \le k$, as long as $\varepsilon \le 1 - \frac{2}{k}$. Hence, for such an ε, for any k-element partition, $P = \{A_1, \ldots, A_k\}$, $u(P) = \sum_{i=1}^k u(A_i) = \sum_{i=1}^k \max(n(A_i), 2 + n(A_i)\varepsilon) \le k^2 = u(P_k^*)$, showing that P_k^* is indeed an optimal partition.

Now, $u(G_k) = k(2 + k\varepsilon) = 2k + k^2\varepsilon$, while $u_k^* = u(P_k^*) = k^2$. Hence, $\frac{2}{\sqrt{m}} u_k^* = \frac{2}{k} k^2 = 2k \ge u(G_k) - k^2\varepsilon$, finishing the proof. □

While these theoretical results provide guarantees about our greedy algorithm's *worse-case* performance, it can perform much better in practice. In the next section, we empirically evaluate our greedy algorithm's practical performance by clustering agent strategies in two toy poker games.

5. EMPIRICAL RESULTS

We demonstrate the performance of our greedy heuristic algorithm by clustering agent strategies for extensive-form games. In particular, our experiments examine poker: a popular family of games that can be modelled as extensive-form games. We begin our empirical analysis with a brief introduction of poker and the two small poker games used in our experiments: Kuhn poker and Leduc hold'em. We then describe how we cast this problem as a segmentation problem, the design of our empirical evaluation, and finally present our results.

5.1 Poker

Poker is a family of stochastic imperfect information games where each agent's goal is to maximize their winnings against some opponents. While there are numerous poker variants, their rules share similar structure. A game begins with chance dealing cards from a deck to each player, and typically one or more players are forced to place bets. All bets contribute to the pot which is paid to the winner. The game proceeds through a number of betting rounds consisting of actions by the players. Players can fold (conceding the pot), call (matching the maximum previous bet), or raise (increasing the maximum bet). A betting round ends if every player except the last player to bet has called the outstanding bet or folded. If only one player remains, they win the pot and the game ends. Between betting rounds, players' hands change in some way due to chance events. One common way this happens is that chance deals some number of "community" cards which are visible and usable by all players. At the end of the final betting round, if more than one player remains, a showdown occurs. In a showdown, all remaining players reveal their cards, evaluate their hands based on their cards and any community cards, and the player with the strongest hand is awarded the pot (or it is split in the event of a tie). In limit poker variants, bets are of a fixed size and the maximum number of bets within a betting round is limited.

5.1.1 Kuhn Poker

Kuhn poker is a toy variant of poker that is small enough that a game theoretic analysis can be done by hand [8]. It is a two-player zero-sum poker game with a deck of three cards: jack, queen, and king. In Kuhn poker, both players must make an initial forced bet (ante) and are dealt a single private card. Betting occurs in a single betting round with betting limited to at most a single bet of a fixed size.

In Kuhn's analysis, he showed that strategies playing certain actions from certain information sets were dominated. For example, when holding the king (the strongest card) a player should never fold. If all such actions are eliminated, then strategies in the resulting undominated version of Kuhn poker can be parameterized with three parameters (α, β, γ) for player one, and two parameters (η, ξ) for player two. Our experiments examine this undominated Kuhn poker game.

5.1.2 Leduc Hold'em

Leduc hold'em [12] is another two-player zero-sum variant of poker which, though larger than Kuhn poker, is still small relative to common poker games played by humans. As in Kuhn poker, the game begins with both players forced to bet an ante and being dealt a single private card. The deck in Leduc hold'em consists of six cards with three ranks (jack, queen, and king) and two suits. Leduc has two betting rounds with betting limited to a maximum of two fixed-size bets per round. After the first betting round, chance deals a public community card. In a showdown, a pair of cards now beats any other hand.

5.2 Experimental Design

To evaluate our greedy decision-theoretic clustering algorithm, we contrast its performance with a k-means clustering algorithm in the domains of Kuhn and Leduc hold'em poker. We start by describing how clustering agents in an extensive-form game can be cast as a segmentation problem, and then detail our benchmark k-means algorithm before moving on to our empirical data.

In this setting, we seek a partition of a set E of static agent strategies that optimizes Equation 1. In our experiments, we generate the agents in E by sampling 200 strategies uniformly at random from the strategy space. Though not constructed explicitly, the utility matrix U can be viewed as having a column for each possible strategy and entries $u(e, r)$ corresponding to the expected utility of playing strategy r against static agent e. As mentioned previously, the response oracle $f(C)$ for a set of strategies C is the best response to the average of the sequence-form representations of the strategies in C.

Each of our experiments contrasts our greedy algorithm with the standard k-means clustering algorithm, *i.e.* Lloyd's algorithm [9], using the sequence-form representation [7]

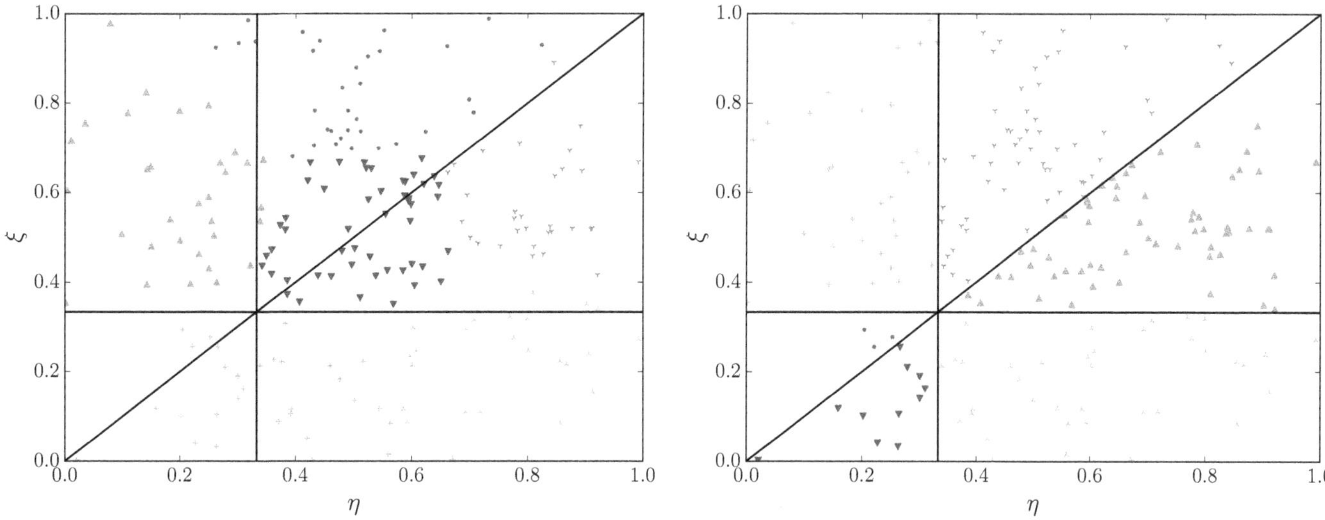

(a) k-means

(b) Greedy agglomerative clustering

Figure 3: Clusters of player two Kuhn poker agents found using k-means clustering over the sequence-form representations and our greedy heuristic algorithm ($k = 6$). Marker shape and colour indicate cluster membership.

of an agent's strategy as its feature vector. We initialize the cluster centroids using the k-means++ algorithm [1]. Note that while the locally optimal clustering found by Lloyd's algorithm may be arbitrarily bad in terms of the k-means objective, initializing with k-means++ provides an approximation guarantee on the solution quality. Despite this, the stochasticity of the k-means initialization impacts which local optimum is found. In our experiments, k-means is restarted 50 times and the clustering with the best k-means objective (*i.e.*, minimal within-cluster sum of squared Euclidean distances) is reported.

5.3 Results

We begin the analysis of our greedy clustering algorithm by examining both its qualitative and quantitative performance when clustering player two's strategies in undominated Kuhn poker.

5.3.1 Kuhn Poker

Figure 3 contrasts clusterings produced by k-means and our greedy algorithm to demonstrate the qualitative differences in these clustering approaches. These figures visualize each of the 200 agent strategies according to their two parameters, η and ξ. The marker shape and colour correspond to which cluster each strategy is assigned to. As with the rock-paper-scissors example, the boundary lines between each of the best response regions are plotted. This partitions the strategy space into six regions each with a distinct best response. The k-means and greedy algorithms were run with $k = 6$ clusters as this is sufficient to optimally partition the strategies. Figure 3a illustrates how k-means tends to produce relatively spherical clusters of similar size. Unsurprisingly, k-means' optimization of spatial distances results in clusters that fail to respect these boundaries. In contrast, our greedy algorithm (Figure 3b) is able to exactly partition the agents according to the best response regions.

Next, we examine the quantitative performance of these algorithms in terms of the utility lost due to responding to agents in clusters rather than as individuals (as in Equation 3). Figure 4a shows the loss incurred by k-means and our greedy algorithm as we vary the number of clusters for undominated Kuhn poker. In this domain we also compute the optimal clustering through enumerating all possible combinations of k of the six best responses and then inducing the corresponding partition as per Lemma 2. Results have been averaged over 50 trials each sampling a new set of 200 agents. The trend lines show the mean value for the loss and the surrounding shaded region indicates the 95% confidence interval (which is occasionally difficult to see as it is smaller than the line width). Values are in milli big blinds per game (*i.e.*, thousandths of the initial ante). While the greedy algorithm manages to achieve zero loss once allowed the six clusters required to guarantee the points can be properly partitioned, k-means is unable to reach zero loss even after being given twice as many clusters. This result also highlights how our greedy algorithm can obtain considerably more of the optimal clustering's utility than is guaranteed by our worst-case approximation bound.

5.3.2 Leduc Hold'em

Though Kuhn poker provides a convenient domain for visualizing strategies and best response regions, clustering agents in such small domains can be done through direct analysis of the game or brute force enumeration of a player's pure strategies. Leduc hold'em better demonstrates the value of a response oracle as the game is sufficiently large that such enumeration is infeasible. Figure 4b shows similar quantitative performance results for the domain of Leduc hold'em where strategies for player one are being clustered. Note that the results in Figure 4 exploit the fact that the greedy algorithm's performance can be computed for each k with little additional computation (though Figure 4b omits values over 64). It is clear in these results that our greedy clustering algorithm substantially outperforms k-means. In particular, the greedy algorithm achieves approximately the same performance with 7 clusters as k-means does with 64.

Finally, it is interesting to note the rate of improvement as we allow for more clusters. In particular, although the

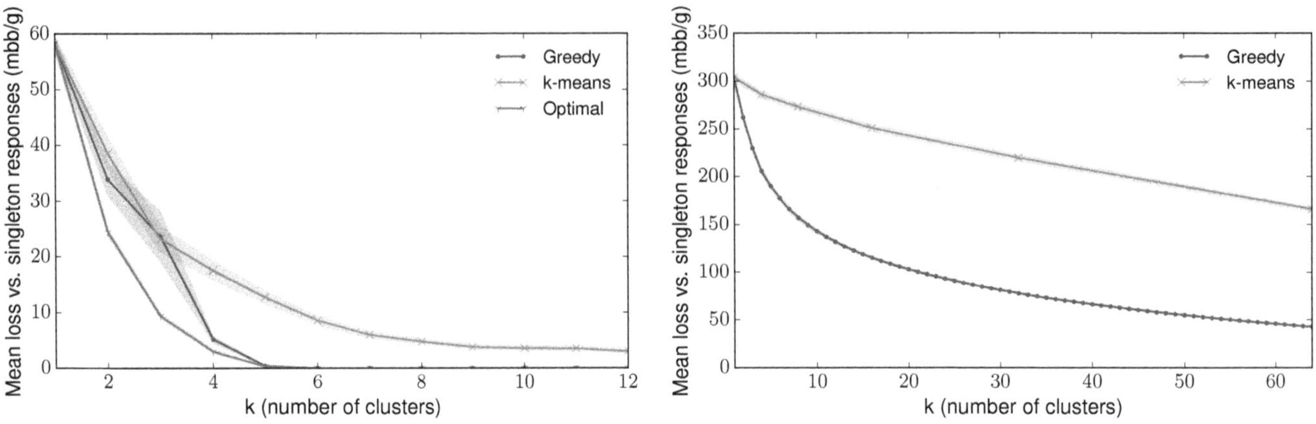

(a) Kuhn poker (b) Leduc hold'em

Figure 4: Performance of different clustering techniques in small poker domains

greedy algorithm initially improves rapidly as we increase the number of clusters, the rate of improvement quickly levels off and leaves a very long tail compared to Kuhn poker. This is likely due both to the increased complexity of the game and also the uniform random sampling of the strategy space. Unlike Kuhn poker where we would expect each best response region to contain multiple of the 200 sampled strategies, the more complex strategy space of Leduc hold'em likely means any given best response region is (at best) sparsely sampled. If the agents being clustered were covered by relatively few of a game's best response regions, then this long tail may not be present.

6. CONCLUSION

Agents seeking to maximize their utility may be able to improve their performance by exploiting models of other agents or entities in their environment. In these settings, clustering techniques can be beneficial for extracting similar groups of entities. Despite the ubiquity of spatial clustering techniques, spatial similarity may be insufficient for capturing similarity in how an agent should respond to these groups. Instead, practitioners with utilitarian clustering objectives may prefer to explicitly optimize the utility of an agent's responses to the clusters. Although work related to segmentation problems provide techniques to optimize for such actionable clusters, these techniques may be computationally infeasible for domains with large response spaces.

We introduced an efficient greedy algorithm for this type of decision-theoretic clustering that can exploit the structure of certain domains. We proved worst-case approximation bounds on the quality of solutions produced by our greedy algorithm. Finally, we showed how to apply this technique to extensive-form games, and empirically demonstrated the value of this approach by comparing it to k-means for clustering agent behaviours in two toy games of poker.

Acknowledgements

The authors would like to thank all of the members of the Computer Poker Research Group at the University of Alberta for helpful conversations pertaining to this research. This research was supported by NSERC and Alberta Innovates Technology Futures. Computing resources were provided by Calcul Québec, Westgrid, and Compute Canada.

REFERENCES

[1] D. Arthur and S. Vassilvitskii. K-means++: The advantages of careful seeding. In *Proceedings of the Eighteenth Annual ACM-SIAM Symposium on Discrete Algorithms*, SODA '07, pages 1027–1035, 2007.

[2] N. Bard, M. Johanson, N. Burch, and M. Bowling. Online implicit agent modelling. In *Proceedings of the Twelfth International Conference on Autonomous Agents and Multiagent Systems*, AAMAS '13, 2013.

[3] A. Carlin and S. Zilberstein. Value-based observation compression for DEC-POMDPs. In *Proceedings of the Seventh International Conference on Autonomous Agents and Multiagent Systems*, AAMAS '08, pages 501–508, 2008.

[4] G. Cornuejols, M. L. Fisher, and G. L. Nemhauser. Location of Bank Accounts to Optimize Float: An Analytic Study of Exact and Approximate Algorithms. *Management science*, 23(8):789–810, 1977.

[5] J. M. Kleinberg, C. H. Papadimitriou, and P. Raghavan. A microeconomic view of data mining. *Data Mining and Knowledge Discovery*, 2(4):311–324, 1998.

[6] J. M. Kleinberg, C. H. Papadimitriou, and P. Raghavan. Segmentation problems. *Journal of the ACM*, 51(2):263–280, 2004.

[7] D. Koller, N. Megiddo, and B. von Stengel. Fast algorithms for finding randomized strategies in game trees. In *Proceedings of the Twenty-Sixth Annual ACM Symposium on Theory of Computing*, STOC '94, pages 750–759, 1994.

[8] H. W. Kuhn. A simplified two-person poker. *Contributions to the Theory of Games*, 1:97–103, 1950.

[9] S. P. Lloyd. Least squares quantization in PCM. *IEEE Transactions on Information Theory*, 28(2):129–137, 1982.

[10] T. Lu and C. Boutilier. Budgeted social choice: From consensus to personalized decision making. In *Proceedings of the Twenty-Second International Joint Conference on Artificial Intelligence*, IJCAI '11, pages 280–286. AAAI Press, 2011.

[11] G. Nemhauser, L. Wolsey, and M. Fisher. An analysis

of approximations for maximizing submodular set functions — I. *Mathematical Programming*, 14(1):265–294, 1978.

[12] F. Southey, M. Bowling, B. Larson, C. Piccione, N. Burch, D. Billings, and C. Rayner. Bayes' bluff: Opponent modelling in poker. In *Proceedings of the 21st Annual Conference on Uncertainty in Artificial Intelligence*, UAI '05, pages 550–558, 2005.

[13] J. H. Ward. Hierarchical grouping to optimize an objective function. *Journal of the American Statistical Association*, 58(301):236–244, March 1963.

Online Monte Carlo Counterfactual Regret Minimization for Search in Imperfect Information Games

Viliam Lisý
Dept. Computer Science, FEE
Czech Technical University
in Prague, Czech Republic
lisy@agents.fel.cvut.cz

Marc Lanctot*
Dept. Knowledge Engineering
Maastricht University
The Netherlands
marc.lanctot@gmail.com

Michael Bowling
Dept. Computing Science
University of Alberta,
Edmonton, Canada
bowling@cs.ualberta.ca

ABSTRACT

Online search in games has been a core interest of artificial intelligence. Search in imperfect information games (*e.g.*, Poker, Bridge, Skat) is particularly challenging due to the complexities introduced by hidden information. In this paper, we present Online Outcome Sampling, an online search variant of Monte Carlo Counterfactual Regret Minimization, which preserves its convergence to Nash equilibrium. We show that OOS can overcome the problem of non-locality encountered by previous search algorithms and perform well against its worst-case opponents. We show that exploitability of the strategies played by OOS decreases as the amount of search time increases, and that preexisting Information Set Monte Carlo tree search (ISMCTS) can get more exploitable over time. In head-to-head play, OOS outperforms ISMCTS in games where non-locality plays a significant role, given a sufficient computation time per move.

Categories and Subject Descriptors

I.2.1 [**Artificial Intelligence**]: Applications and Expert Systems—*Games*

General Terms

Algorithms

Keywords

Imperfect information games; online search; Nash equilibrium; Monte Carlo tree search; regret minimization

1. INTRODUCTION

Algorithms for creating strong strategies in games have been a core interest of artificial intelligence research. Strong strategies are useful not only as research benchmarks and opponents in digital entertainment, but they are becoming increasingly important also in real world applications, such as critical infrastructure security [36]. Because these games are often played against unknown opponents, a good strategy should be sufficiently robust against any possible counterstrategy used by the adversary. In strictly competitive games, the strategy that is optimal with respect to this criterion is the Nash equilibrium. It is guaranteed to provide the maximal possible expected value against any strategy of the opponent. For example, an equilibrium defense strategy minimizes the maximal damage caused by any attack.

When preparation time is abundant and the exact problem definition is known in advance, an equilibrium strategy for a smaller abstract game can be pre-computed and then used during game play. This *offline approach* has been remarkably successful in Computer Poker [2, 12, 32, 31, 21]. However, the preparation time is often very limited. The model of the game may become known only shortly before acting is necessary, such as in general game-playing, search or pursuit in a previously unknown environment, and general-purpose robotics. In these circumstances, creating and solving an abstract representation of the problem may not be possible. In these cases, agents must *decide online*: make initial decisions quickly and then spend effort to improve their strategy while the interaction is taking place.

In this paper, we propose a search algorithm that can compute an approximate Nash equilibrium (NE) strategy in two-player zero-sum games *online*, in a previously unknown game, and with a very limited computation time and space. Online Outcome Sampling (OOS) is a simulation-based algorithm based on Monte Carlo Counterfactual Regret Minimization (MCCFR) [24]. OOS makes two novel modifications to MCCFR. First, OOS builds its search tree incrementally, like Monte Carlo tree search (MCTS) [7, 3, 22]. Second, when performing additional computation after some moves have been played in the match, the following samples are targeted primarily to the parts of the game tree, which are more relevant to the current situation in the game. We show that OOS is *consistent*, *i.e.* it is guaranteed to converge to an equilibrium strategy as search time increases. To the best of our knowledge, this is not the case for any existing online game playing algorithm, all of which suffer from the problem of *non-locality* in these games.

We compare convergence and head-to-head performance of OOS to Information Set MCTS [8, 37, 25] in three fundamentally different games. We develop a novel methodology for evaluating convergence of online algorithms that do not produce a complete strategy. The results show that OOS, unlike ISMCTS, consistently converges close to NE strat-

*This author has a new affiliation: Google DeepMind, London, United Kingdom.

Appears in: *Proceedings of the 14th International Conference on Autonomous Agents and Multiagent Systems (AAMAS 2015), Bordini, Elkind, Weiss, Yolum (eds.), May 4–8, 2015, Istanbul, Turkey.*

egy in all three games. In head-to-head performance, with sufficient time, OOS either ties or outperforms ISMCTS.

2. BACKGROUND AND RELATED WORK

Most imperfect information search algorithms are built upon perfect information search algorithms, such as minimax or Monte Carlo tree search (MCTS). One of the first popular applications of imperfect information search was Ginsberg's Bridge-playing program, GIB [15, 16]. In GIB, perfect information search is performed on a *determinized* instance of the game: one where all players can see usually hidden information. This approach has also performed well in other games like Scrabble [34], Hearts [35], and Skat [5].

Several problems have been identified with techniques based on determinization, such as Perfect Information Monte Carlo (PIMC) [28]. Two commonly reported problems are *strategy fusion* and *non-locality* [9]. Strategy fusion occurs when distinct actions are recommended in states that the player is not able to distinguish due to the imperfect information. Strategy fusion can be overcome by imposing the proper information constraints during search [9, 6, 30, 26, 8].

Non-locality occurs due to optimal payoffs not being recursively defined over subgames as in perfect information games. As a result, guarantees normally provided by search algorithms built on subgame decomposition no longer hold. Previous work has been done for accelerating offline equilibrium computation by solving subgames in end-game situations [13, 14, 11]. While these techniques tend to help in practice, non-locality can prevent them from producing equilibrium strategies; we discuss this further in Section 2.2.

The last problem is the need for randomized strategies in imperfect information games. In many games, any deterministic strategy predictable by the opponent can lead to arbitrarily large losses. To overcome this problem, MCTS algorithms sometimes randomize by sampling actions from its empirical frequency counts. Evidence suggests that the resulting strategies will not converge to the optimal solution even in very small imperfect information games like Biased Rock-Paper-Scissors and Kuhn poker [33, 30]. Our results show that, the empirical frequencies can *diverge away* from the equilibrium strategies. A little more promising are the MCTS approaches that use alternative selection functions, such as Exp3 or Regret Matching [25]. Variants of MCTS with these selection functions have been shown both formally and empirically [27, 23] to converge to Nash equilibrium in games with simultaneous moves, which are the simplest subclass of imperfect information games. However, we show that even these selection functions cannot help to overcome the problem of non-locality.

2.1 Extensive-Form Games

We focus on two-player zero-sum extensive form games and base our notation on [29]. These games model sequential decision making **players** denoted $i \in N = \{1, 2\}$. In turn, players choose **actions** leading to sequences called **histories** $h \in H$. A history $z \in Z$, where $Z \subseteq H$, is called a **terminal history** and represents a full game from start to end. At each terminal history z there is a payoff $u_i(z)$ to each player i. At each nonterminal history h, there is a single current player to act, determined by $P : H \backslash Z \to N \cup \{c\}$ where c is a special player called **chance** that plays with a fixed stochastic strategy. For example, chance is used to represent rolls of dice and card draws. The game starts in the empty

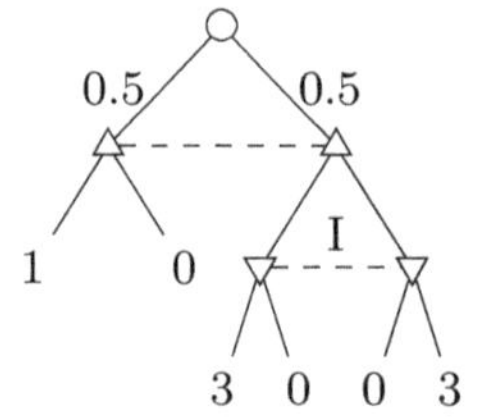

Figure 1: An extensive-form game demonstrating the problem of non-locality with maximizing △, minimizing ▽ and chance ○ players.

history $\emptyset$, and at each step, given the current history h, the current player chooses an action $a \in A(h)$ leading to successor history $h' = ha$; in this case we call h a **prefix** of h' and denote this relationship by $h \sqsubset h'$. Also, for all $h, h', h'' \in H$, if $h \sqsubset h'$ and $h' \sqsubset h''$ then $h \sqsubset h''$, and $h \sqsubset h$. Sets H and $A(h)$ are finite and histories have finite length.

Set $\mathcal{I}_i$ is an partition over $H_i = \{h \mid P(h) = i\}$ where each part is called an **information set**. Intuitively, an information set $I \in \mathcal{I}_i$ of player i represents a state of the game with respect to what player i knows. Formally, I is a set of histories that a player cannot tell apart (due to information hidden from that player). For all $h, h' \in I$, $A(h) = A(h')$ and $P(h) = P(h')$; hence, we extend the definition to $A(I)$, $P(I)$, and denote $I(h)$ the information set containing h.

A **behavioral strategy** for player i is a function mapping each information set $I \in \mathcal{I}_i$ to a probability distribution over the actions $A(I)$, denoted by $\sigma_i(I)$. For a profile σ, we denote the probability of reaching a terminal history z under σ as $\pi^\sigma(z) = \prod_{i \in N \cup c} \pi_i(z)$, where each $\pi_i(z) = \prod_{ha \sqsubset z, P(h)=i} \sigma_i(I(h), a)$ is a product of probabilities of the actions taken by player i along z. We use $\pi_i^\sigma(h, z)$ and $\pi^\sigma(h, z)$ for $h \sqsubset z$ to refer to the product of only the probabilities of actions along the sequence from the end of h to the end of z. Define Σ_i to be the set of behavioral strategies for player i. As is convention, $-i$ refers to player i's opponent.

An **ϵ-Nash equilibrium**, σ, is a set of σ_i for $i \in N$ such that the benefit of switching to some alternative σ_i' is limited by ϵ, i.e., $\forall i \in N : \max_{\sigma_i' \in \Sigma_i} u_i(\sigma_i', \sigma_{-i}) - u_i(\sigma) \leq \epsilon$. When $\epsilon = 0$, the profile is called a Nash equilibrium. When $|N| = 2$ and $u_1(z) + u_2(z) = k$ for all $z \in Z$, then the game is a zero-sum game. In these games, different equilibrium strategies result in the same expected payoff against any arbitrary opponent equilibrium strategy and at least the same payoff for any opponent strategy. The **exploitability** of a profile σ is the sum of strategies' distances from an equilibrium, $\epsilon_\sigma = \max_{\sigma_1' \in \Sigma_1} u_1(\sigma_1', \sigma_2) + \max_{\sigma_2' \in \Sigma_1} u_2(\sigma_1, \sigma_2')$.

In a **match** (online game), each player is allowed little or no preparation time before playing (preventing the offline computation of approximate equilibria solutions). The current **match history**, $\mathtt{m} \in H$, is initially the empty history $\emptyset$ representing the start of the match. Each turn, player $P(\mathtt{m})$ is given t time units to decide on a **match action** $\mathbf{a} \in A(\mathtt{m})$ and the match history then changes from $\mathtt{m}$ to $\mathtt{ma}$. There is a referee who knows $\mathtt{m}$, samples chance outcomes from $\sigma_c(\mathtt{m})$, and reveals $I(\mathtt{m})$ to player $P(\mathtt{m})$. The match terminates when $\mathtt{m} \in Z$, giving each player i a payoff of $u_i(\mathtt{m})$.

2.2 The Problem of Non-Locality

We demonstrate the problem of non-locality on the game in Figure 1. It starts with a decision of chance ○ which leads to two nodes that cannot be distinguished by the maximizing player △. On the left, the game ends after his actions. On the right, both his actions lead to information set I of the minimizing player ▽, whose utility is minus the depicted value. The optimal (Nash equilibrium) strategy in I depends on the value of the leftmost leaf, even though this outcome of the game cannot be reached once the game entered information set I. Because △ does not know at the time of his move if ▽ will play, he needs to randomize its decision so that ▽ cannot easily make the move that is more harmful for △. However, he would prefer to play left for the case that ▽ will not play. Player ▽ knows that △ has this dilemma and tries to exploit it as much as possible. Uniform strategy at I clearly motivates △ to play left, leading to expected utility $0.5 \cdot 1 + 0.5 \cdot 1.5 = 1.25$, instead of $0.5 \cdot 0 + 0.5 \cdot 1.5 = 0.75$. If ▽ plays right a little more often, △ is still motivated to play left and ▽ improves his payoff. This holds until ▽ plays (left,right) with probabilities $(\frac{1}{3}, \frac{2}{3})$, which results to expected reward of 1 for both actions of △. If △ plays $(\frac{1}{2}, \frac{1}{2})$, ▽ cannot lower the utility anymore and the pair of strategies is an equilibrium. If the leftmost leaf was 2 instead of 1, the optimal strategy in I would be $(\frac{1}{6}, \frac{5}{6})$.

Current approaches, after reaching the information set I, will repeatedly sample and search one of subtrees in I, aggregating the information collected to make a final recommendation. However, even if the information structure is kept intact, such as in ISMCTS [8], the problem still occurs. If subtrees of I are sampled equally often, a searching player will not have any preference between left and right and will recommend $(\frac{1}{2}, \frac{1}{2})$, which is suboptimal. Moreover, the uniform probability of being in each state of I corresponds to the distribution over the states given the optimal play, so the problem occurs even if subtrees are sampled from the correct belief distribution. Note that this is a simple example; in larger games, this problem could occur over much longer paths or many times in different parts of the game. The analysis in [28] suggests that the effect may be critical in games with low *disambiguation factor*, where private information is slowly (or never) revealed throughout a match.

To the best of our knowledge, OOS is the first online search algorithm that solves this problem. It does it by starting each sample from the root of the game. If the computed strategy tends to come closer to the uniform strategy in I, the updates in the maximizing player's information set will modify the strategy to choose left more often. The following samples will reach I more often at the left state and consequently modify the strategy in I in the right direction.

2.3 Offline Equilibrium Approximation

There are multiple algorithms for computing approximate equilibrium strategies offline [32]. We focus on a popular choice among Poker researchers due to its sampling variants.

Counterfactual Regret (CFR) is a notion of regret at the information set level for extensive-form games [38]. The CFR algorithm iteratively learns strategies in self-play, converging to an equilibrium. The **counterfactual value** of reaching information set I is the expected payoff given that player i played to reach I, the opponents played σ_{-i} and both players played σ after I was reached:

$$v_i(I, \sigma) = \sum_{(h,z) \in Z_I} \pi^{\sigma}_{-i}(h) \pi^{\sigma}(h, z) u_i(z), \qquad (1)$$

where $Z_I = \{(h, z) \mid z \in Z, h \in I, h \sqsubset z\}$. Suppose, at time t, player i plays with strategy σ_i^t. Define $\sigma^t_{I \to a}$ as identical to σ^t except at I action a is taken with probability 1. The counterfactual regret of not taking $a \in A(I)$ at time t is $r^t(I, a) = v_i(I, \sigma^t_{I \to a}) - v_i(I, \sigma^t)$. The algorithm maintains the cumulative regret $R^T(I, a) = \sum_{t=1}^{T} r^t(I, a)$, for every action at every information set. Then, the distribution at each information set for the next iteration $\sigma^{T+1}(I)$ is obtained using regret-matching [17]. The distribution is proportional to the positive portion of the individual actions' regret:

$$\sigma^{T+1}(I, a) = \begin{cases} R^{T,+}(I, a)/R^{T,+}_{sum}(I) & \text{if } R^{T,+}_{sum}(I) > 0 \\ 1/|A(I)| & \text{otherwise,} \end{cases}$$

where $x^+ = \max(0, x)$ for any term x, and $R^{T,+}_{sum}(I) = \sum_{a' \in A(I)} R^{T,+}(I, a')$. Furthermore, the algorithm maintains for each information set the average strategy profile

$$\bar{\sigma}^T(I, a) = \frac{\sum_{t=1}^{T} \pi_i^{\sigma^t}(I) \sigma^t(I, a)}{\sum_{t=1} \pi_i^{\sigma^t}(I)}, \qquad (2)$$

where $\pi_i^{\sigma^t}(I) = \sum_{h \in I} \pi_i^{\sigma^t}(h)$. The combination of the counterfactual regret minimizers in individual information sets also minimizes the overall average regret [38], and hence the average profile is a 2ϵ-equilibrium, with $\epsilon \to 0$ as $T \to \infty$.

Monte Carlo Counterfactual Regret Minimization (MCCFR) applies CFR to sampled portions of the games [24]. In the **outcome sampling** (OS) variant of the algorithm, a single terminal history $z \in Z$ is sampled in each iteration. The algorithm updates the regret in the information sets visited along z using the **sampled counterfactual value**,

$$\tilde{v}_i(I, \sigma) = \begin{cases} \frac{1}{q(z)} \pi^{\sigma}_{-i}(h) \pi^{\sigma}(h, z) u_i(z) & \text{if } (h, z) \in Z_I \\ 0 & \text{otherwise,} \end{cases}$$

where $q(z)$ is the probability of sampling z. If every $z \in Z$ has non-zero probability of being sampled, $\tilde{v}_i(I, \sigma)$ is an unbiased estimate of $v(I, \sigma)$ due to the importance sampling correction $(1/q(z))$. For this reason, applying CFR updates using these sampled counterfactual values on the sampled information sets values also eventually converges to the approximate equilibrium of the game with high probability.

3. ONLINE OUTCOME SAMPLING

When outcome sampling is used in the offline setting, data structures for all information sets are allocated before the first iteration. In each iteration, all sampled information sets get updated. We make two essential modifications to adapt outcome sampling to the online setting.

Incremental Game Tree Building. Before the match begins, only the very first (root) information set is added to memory. In each iteration, a single information set (at most) is added to memory. In particular, when an information set is reached that is not in memory, it is added to memory and then a default playout policy (*e.g.*, uniform random) takes over for the remainder of the simulation. Along the playout portion (tail) of the simulation, information sets are not added to memory nor updated. Along the tree portion (head), information sets are updated as normal. This way, only the relevant information sets are stored in the memory.

In-Match Search Targeting. Suppose several moves have been played since the start of the match leading to `m`. Plain outcome sampling would continue to sample from the root of the game (not the current match history `m`), rarely reaching the region of the game space that the match has headed toward. Hence, the second modification we propose

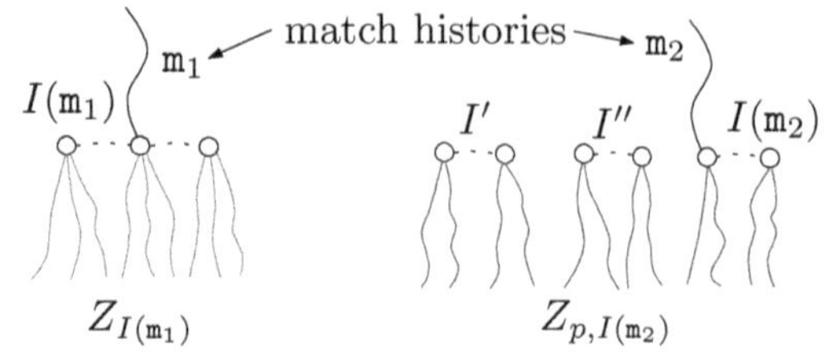

Figure 2: Example subgames targeted by IST (left) and PST (right). All histories $\{ h \mid h \in I' \cup I'' \cup I(\mathtt{m}_2) \}$ share a common public action sequence ($p(\mathtt{m}_2)$).

is directing the search towards the histories that are more likely to occur during the match currently played. Note that the complete history is typically unknown to the players, who know only their information sets. Unlike in ISMCTS, OOS always runs samples from the root of the game tree, even with non-empty match history. We now describe two specific targeting methods demonstrated in Figure 2.

3.1 Information Set Targeting (IST)

Suppose the match history is $\mathtt{m}$. IST samples histories reaching the current information set ($I(\mathtt{m})$), i.e., $(h, z) \in Z_{I(\mathtt{m})}$, with higher probability than other histories. The intuition is that these histories are particularly relevant since the searching player *knows* that one of these z will describe the match at its completion. However, focusing *only* on these histories may cause problems because of the non-locality and the convergence guarantees would be lost.

Consider again the game in Figure 1. If the minimizing player knows it is in the information set I and focuses all its search to this information set, she computes the suboptimal uniform strategy. Any fixed non-zero probability of sampling the left chance action eventually solves the problem. The regrets are multiplied by the reciprocal of the sampling probability; hence, they influence the strategy in the information set proportionally stronger if the samples are rare.

Note that previous methods, such as PIMC and ISMCTS, *never* update any information sets, which are not reachable from $I(\mathtt{m})$. In contrast, in IST *all* information sets in memory have positive probability of being reached and updated.

3.2 Public Subgame Targeting (PST)

IST may "reveal" information about the current information set available to only one of the players affecting the computed strategy (this vanishes in the limit due to consistency but could have a short-term effect). PST only uses information available to both players to target the search to prevent this effect. A **public action** is an action in the "public tree" defined in [20] and commonly used in offline CFR. Informally, an action is said to be public if it is observable by all players (e.g., bids in Liar's Dice and bets in Poker are public). Formally, an action a is public, iff $\forall i, \forall I \in \mathcal{I}_i, \forall h_1, h_2 \in I : a \in h_1 \Leftrightarrow a \in h_2$. For example, the extensive-form version of Rock, Paper, Scissors has two information sets $I_1 = \emptyset$ and $I_2 = \{r, p, s\}$; it has no public actions, because each history in I_2 contains a single unique action (the unobserved ones taken by the first player).

Given a history h, let $p(h)$ be the sequence of public actions along h in the same order that they were taken in h. Define the **public subgame** induced by I to be the one

OOS($h, \pi_i, \pi_{-i}, s_1, s_2, i$):
if $h \in Z$ **then**
return $(1, \delta s_1 + (1-\delta)s_2, u_i(z))$
else if $P(h) = c$ **then**
Sample an outcome a and let ρ_1, ρ_2 be its probability in targeted and untargeted setting
$(x, l, u) \leftarrow$ OOS$(ha, \pi_i, \rho_2\pi_{-i}, \rho_1 s_1, \rho_2 s_2, i)$
return $(\rho_2 x, l, u)$
$I \leftarrow$ getInfoset$(h, P(h))$
Let $(a, s_1', s_2') \leftarrow$ Sample(h, I, i, ϵ)
if I *is not in memory* **then**
Add I to memory
$\sigma(I) \leftarrow$ Unif$(A(I))$
$(x, l, u) \leftarrow$ Playout$(ha, \frac{\delta s_1 + (1-\delta)s_2}{|A(I)|})$
else
$\sigma(I) \leftarrow$ RegretMatching(r_I)
$\pi'_{P(h)} \leftarrow \sigma(I, a)\pi_{P(h)}$
$\pi'_{-P(h)} \leftarrow \pi_{-P(h)}$
$(x, l, u) \leftarrow$ OOS$(ha, \pi'_i, \pi'_{-i}, s'_1, s'_2, i)$
$c \leftarrow x$
$x \leftarrow x\sigma(I, a)$
for $a' \in A(I)$ **do**
if $P(h) = i$ **then**
$W \leftarrow u\pi_{-i} \,/\, l$
if $a' = a$ **then**
$r_I[a'] \leftarrow r_I[a'] + (c - x)W$
else
$r_I[a'] \leftarrow r_I[a'] - xW$
else
$s_I[a'] \leftarrow s_I[a'] + \frac{1}{\delta s_1 + (1-\delta)s_2}\pi_{-i}\sigma(I, a')$
return (x, l, u)

Algorithm 1: Online Outcome Sampling.

whose terminal history set is

$$Z_{p,I(h)} = \{(h', z) \mid z \in Z, h' \in H, p(h') = p(h), h' \sqsubset z\}.$$

With match history $\mathtt{m}$, PST samples $z \in Z_{p,I(\mathtt{m})}$ with higher probability than terminal histories outside this set.

In a game of poker, suppose the chance decides on the private cards of the players, the first player bets one chip and the second player calls. At this point, the public actions are: bet one chip and call. The public subgame $Z_{p,I(h)}$ contains every terminal history (including every combination of private chance outcomes for all players) whose first two public actions are: bet one chip and call.

3.3 Algorithm

The algorithm iteratively samples a single trajectory from the root $\emptyset$ to a terminal history. At each information set in memory, I, it maintains two tables: r_I stores cumulative regret for each action $a \in A(I)$, and s_I stores the cumulative average strategy probability of each action.

Depending on the targeting method (IST or PST), Z_{sub} is one of $Z_{I(\mathtt{m})}$ or $Z_{p,I(\mathtt{m})}$. The pseudo-code is presented as Algorithm 1. Each iteration is represented by two calls of OOS where the update player $i \in \{1, 2\}$ is alternated. Before each iteration, a *scenario* is decided: with probability δ the iteration targets the subgame and chooses $z \in Z_{sub}$ and with probability $(1 - \delta)$ the usual OS sampling determines

$z \in Z$. As a result, OOS with $\delta = 0$ becomes MCCFR with incremental tree building.

The first parameter of OOS is the current history. The next two are strategy's reach probabilities for the update player i and the opponent. The third and fourth parameters are initially the overall probabilities that the current sample is generated, one for each scenario: first the targeted and then the untargeted. With non-empty match history, these two parameters include an additional weighting factor w_T explained later. The last parameter is the update player. Initial calls have the form OOS$(\emptyset, 1, 1, 1/w_T, 1/w_T, i)$. For the return values, x is a suffix/tail reach probability for both players, l is the root-to-leaf sample probability, and u is the payoff of the trajectory in view of the update player.

The ϵ-on-policy sampling distribution used at each information set is defined as

$$\Phi(I,i) = \begin{cases} \epsilon \cdot \text{Unif}(A(I)) + (1-\epsilon)\sigma_i(I) & \text{if } P(I) = i \\ \sigma_i(I) & \text{otherwise,} \end{cases}$$

and denote $\Phi(I,i,a)$ the probability of sampling $a \in A(I)$.

The sampling at chance's choices on line 5 depends on the method and the scenario being used. For example, when using information set targeting, the outcome that is sampled must be consistent with match history.

A critical part of the algorithm is the action chosen and sample reach updates on line 9. If I is not in memory, then an action is sampled uniformly. Otherwise, in the targeted scenario, the current history h is always in the targeted part of the game and an action from $\{a \mid \exists z \in Z\ (ha,z) \in Z_{sub}\}$ is selected using the distribution $\Phi(I(h),i)$ normalized to one on this subset of actions. If we define $sum = \sum_{(ha,z)\in Z_{sub}} \Phi(I,i,a)$ then $s_1' = s_1\Phi(I,i,a)/sum$. In the untargeted scenario, any action $a \sim \Phi(I,i)$ can be sampled. If the action is not leaving the targeted part of the game (i.e., $(ha,z) \in Z_{sub}$) then $s_1' = s_1\Phi(I,i,a)/sum$ otherwise $s_1' = 0$. In all cases $s_2' = \Phi(I,i,a)s_2$.

These sample reach probabilities are combined into one at a terminal history on line 3, start of the playout on line 13, and when updating the average strategy on line 29.

The playout on line 13 samples to the end of the game with some playout policy at each step; we use uniform random, but in general one could use an informed policy based on domain knowledge as well. Unlike MCTS, the playout policy in OOS must compute l when reaching a terminal and update the tail probability x when returning as done on line 20. Lines 16 and 17 modify $P(h)$'s reach probability by multiplying it by $\sigma(I,a)$, keeping the other value the same. Lines 19 to 24 contain the usual outcome sampling updates. Note that regrets are updated at the update player histories, while average strategy tables at opponent histories.

Now we explain the role of the weighting factor w_T. Note that on lines 23 and 29, the regret and strategy updates are multiplied by the reciprocal of the probability of sampling the sample leaf and the current state. Consider the updates in the current information set of the game $I_{\mathtt{m}}$. In the initial samples of the algorithm with empty match history, this information set was on average sampled with a very low probability s_0. Let's say that out of 10^6 samples started from the root, 1000 samples reached this particular information set. In that case, $s_0 = 0.001$ and the regret updates caused by each of these samples were multiplied by $\frac{1}{s_0} = 1000$. Now the game has actually reached the history $\mathtt{m}$ and due to targeting, half of the next 10^6 samples reach $I(\mathtt{m})$. It means that $s_{\mathtt{m}} = 0.5$ and the regrets will be multiplied only by 2. As a results, the updates of the first (generally less precise) 1000 samples are all together weighted the same as the 5×10^5 later samples, which makes it almost impossible to compensate for the initial errors. In order to prevent this effect, we add the weighting factor w_T to compensate the change of targeting and make each of the samples have similar weight at $I(\mathtt{m})$. In our example, $w_T = \frac{s_{\mathtt{m}}}{s_0}$. More formally, when running the iterations from match history $\mathtt{m}$, we define the weighting factor as the probability of reaching $I(\mathtt{m})$ without any targeting divided by the probability of reaching $I(\mathtt{m})$ with the current targeting, assuming the players play according to the current mean strategy profile $\bar{\pi}$:

$$\frac{1}{w_T(\mathtt{m})} = (1-\delta) + \delta \frac{\sum_{(h,z)\in I(\mathtt{m})} \bar{\pi}(h)}{\sum_{z \in Z_{sub(\mathtt{m})}} \bar{\pi}(z)}. \quad (3)$$

OOS would quickly stop improving a strategy in information sets that are below an irrational move of the opponent ($\pi_{-i} = 0$). This cannot be avoided even if many samples are targeted to the information set. Therefore, we use a more explorative regret matching, $\sigma_\gamma^{T+1}(I,a) = \gamma/|A(I)| + (1-\gamma)\sigma^{T+1}(I,a)$, with $\gamma = 0.01$. This affects the worst-case regret bound at most by γ (due to the linearity of the expected utility), but allows for much better play.

3.3.1 Consistency

THEOREM 1. *Let $\bar{\sigma}_m^t(\delta,\mathtt{m})$ be a strategy produced by OOS with scheme IST or PST using $\delta < 1$ started from $\mathtt{m}$ run for t iterations, with exploration $\epsilon > 0$. For any $p \in (0,1], \varepsilon > 0$ there exists $t < \infty$ such that with probability $1-p$ the strategy $\bar{\sigma}_m^t(\delta,\mathtt{m})$ is a ε-equilibrium strategy.*

PROOF. (Sketch) Each terminal history has nonzero probability of being sampled, eventually every information set will be contained in memory. The algorithm then becomes MCCFR with a non-uniform sampling scheme. By [24, Theorem 5] OOS minimizes regret with high probability. The additional weighting of all updates of the algorithm by the same constant has no influence on the computed average strategy and the strategies computed by regret matching, because it uses only relative proportions of the regrets. □

4. EMPIRICAL EVALUATION

We now compare the exploitability and head-to-head performance of OOS and ISMCTS.

4.1 Information Set Monte Carlo Tree Search

We have implemented ISMCTS in the same framework with similar data representations as OOS. ISMCTS runs MCTS samples as in a perfect information game, but uses common statistics computed for the whole information set and not individual states in the selection phase. When initiated from a non-empty match history, it starts samples uniformly from the states in the current information set. We use two selection functions in our experiments. First, the commonly used UCT as suggested in [8]. We use two times the maximal game outcome as the exploration parameter C. In matches, we select the action with the highest number of iterations. For evaluating convergence, this would often have the maximum possible exploitability in the evaluated games.

Therefore, we use the distribution given by the empirical frequencies for this part of evaluation. Second, we use Regret Matching (RM) as the selection strategy, because it has been shown to empirically perform better in many games [25] and because it is based on the same principles that are behind CFR. For RM, we use exploration 0.2, the mean strategy for evaluating exploitability and samples from this strategy in head to head matches. In the following, we refer to ISMCTS with the corresponding selection function by only UCT/RM.

4.2 Evaluating Performance

In games like Poker and Liar's Dice, it is often critical to play in such a way that the opponent cannot easily infer the private information. This explains partly the success of CFR-based methods in the offline setting. In the online setting, since the tree is built incrementally, only partial strategies are produced. We are unaware of any methods for assessing the worst-case exploitability of strategies produced by an online search algorithm.

There is a brute-force approach that runs the search at each information set and computes exploitability of a strategy composed from strategies computed for these information sets. However, it requires $O(t|I|)$ seconds for a single run and multiple runs are required for statistically significant results. Instead, we propose an approximate multi-match **aggregate method**. It creates a global (accumulating) strategy data structure for each player. Then, it runs a fixed number of matches (500 in our experiments) of the search algorithm against a random opponent. In each information set reached in the match, the information computed (visit counts in ISMCTS, s_I in OOS) is added into the global strategy of the player who searched. Besides the information in the current information set, the information computed in all successor information sets is also added with a weight proportional to the number of visits of the information set. If an information set is never reached directly, this gives at least some estimate of how the strategy would behave there. If it is, the number of samples in the information set outweighs the less precise estimates from the cases where it is not. In the information sets not added to the global strategy, a fixed random action is selected. The result is the exploitability of the global strategy.

4.3 Domains

Imperfect Information Goofspiel In II-GS(N), each player is given a private hand of bid cards with values 0 to $N-1$. A different deck of N point cards is placed face up in a stack. On their turn, each player bids for the top point card by secretly choosing a single card in their hand. The highest bidder gets the point card and adds the point total to their score, discarding the points in the case of a tie. This is repeated N times and the player with the highest score wins. In II-Goofspiel, the players only discover who won or lost a bid, but not the bid cards played. Also, we assume the point-stack is strictly increasing: $0, 1, \dots N-1$. This way the game does not have non-trivial chance nodes, all actions are private and information sets have various sizes.

Liar's Dice LD(D_1,D_2), also known as Dudo, Perudo, and Bluff is a dice-bidding game. Each die has faces ⚀ to ⚄ and a star $\star$. Each player i rolls D_i of these dice without showing them to their opponent. Each round, players alternate by bidding on the outcome of all dice in play until one player "calls liar", *i.e.* claims that their opponent's latest bid does not hold. If the bid holds, the calling player loses; otherwise, she wins. A bid consists of a quantity of dice and a face value. A face of $\star$ is considered wild and counts as matching any other face. To bid, the player must increase either the quantity or face value of the current bid (or both). All actions in this game are public. The only hidden information is caused by chance at the beginning of the game. Therefore, the size of all information sets is identical.

Generic Poker GP(T, C, R, B) is a simplified poker game inspired by Leduc Hold'em. First, both players are required to put one chip in the pot. Next, chance deals a single private card to each player, and the betting round begins. A player can either *fold* (the opponent wins the pot), *check* (let the opponent make the next move), *bet* (add some amount of chips, as first in the round), *call* (add the amount of chips equal to the last bet of the opponent into the pot), or *raise* (match and increase the bet of the opponent). If no further raise is made by any of the players, the betting round ends, chance deals one public card on the table, and a second betting round with the same rules begins. After the second betting round ends, the outcome of the game is determined — a player wins if: (1) her private card matches the table card and the opponent's card does not match, or (2) none of the players' cards matches the table card and her private card is higher than the private card of the opponent. If no player wins, the game is a draw and the pot is split. The parameters of the game are the number of types of the cards (T), the number of cards of each type (C), the maximum length of sequence of raises in a betting round (R), and the number of different sizes of bets (i.e., amount of chips added to the pot) for *bet/raise* actions. This game is similar to Liar's Dice in having only public actions. However, it includes additional chance nodes later in the game, which reveal part of the information not available before. Moreover, it has integer results and not just win/draw/loss.

4.4 Results

We first focus on LD(1,1), II-GS(6), and GP(3,3,2,2). While these games are considered small by search algorithm standards, it is still possible to compute the exact worst case counterstrategies (i.e., best response) to measure exploitability. After analyzing the convergence, we proceed to performance in head-to-head matches also in larger variants of the games.

4.4.1 Convergence at the root

First we evaluate the speed of convergence of the proposed algorithm when run in the root of the games. The strategy in the information sets, which are not included in the tree yet, is assumed to be a fixed random action identical for all algorithms. The impact of the exploration parameters of the algorithms is not very strong here and we set it to 0.6 for OOS. The results are in Figures 3(a,d,h). OOS clearly converges the fastest in all games, eventually converging to the exact equilibrium. The exact convergence is not surprising, because the algorithm run from the root is MCCFR, only with incremental tree building.

In all three games, the empirical action frequencies in UCT first converge quite quickly towards less exploitable strategies, but they always start to become more exploitable at some point. This does not happen with RM, but its initial convergence is slower.

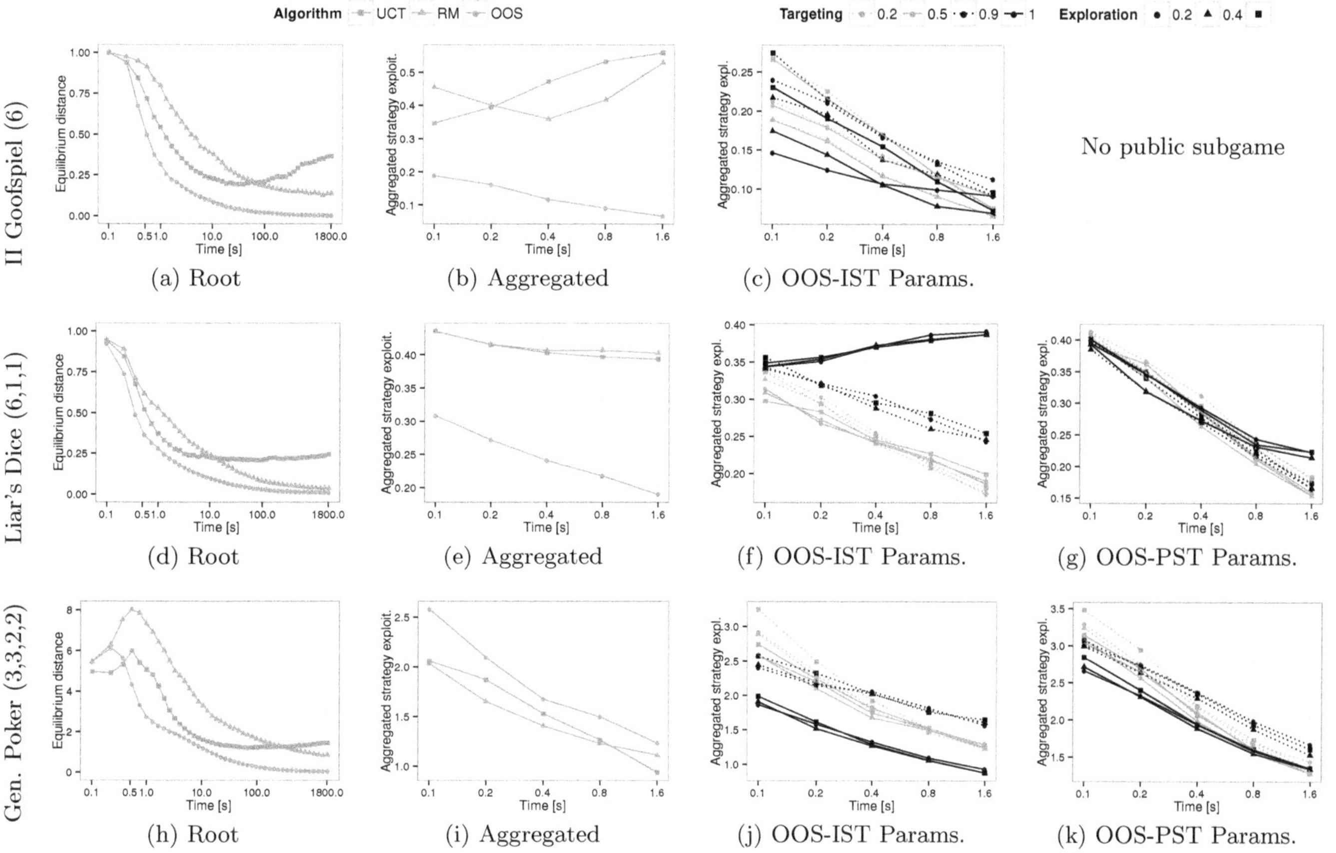

Figure 3: Exploitability ISMCTS with various selection functions and OOS with various parameter settings in the smaller game variants (rows).

4.4.2 Aggregated strategy exploitability

Figures 3(b,e,i) present the exploitability of the strategies computed by different algorithms estimated by the aggregate method. The OOS in this graphs is run with IST, $\gamma = 0.4$ for exploration and $\delta = 0.5$ for targeting. The x-axis denotes the amount of computation per move. In Goofspiel 3(b), both ISMCTS variants produce a more exploitable strategy with more computation time per move. For any of the evaluated time settings, OOS is substantially less exploitable. In Liar's Dice 3(e), ISMCTS does not seem to get worse with additional computation time, but it improves marginally with more than 0.4 seconds per move. OOS steadily approaches the equilibrium. In Poker 3(i), the exploitability is lower for ISMCTS variants than for OOS with the default settings. With the limited computation time, having more iterations to avoid bad moves seems to be more important than guessing and hiding the private information of the players.

The remaining plots in Figures 3 present how the exploitability of the strategies produced by OOS depends on the selected targeting scheme and parameters: the amount of targeting shown by color and the amount of exploration shown by point shapes. Figures 3(c,f,j) show the information set targeting and 3(g,k) show the public subgame targeting. Overall, OOS produces strategies closer to the equilibrium as the computation time per move increases. The only exception is IST with full targeting ($\delta = 1$) in Liar's Dice (Figure 3(f)). This confirms that sampling the histories that will certainly not occur in the game anymore is necessary to converge to the optimal strategy in LD. In the other two games, full targeting produces the least exploitable strategies with very short computation times. This indicates that sophisticated modeling of hidden information can be counterproductive with very short computation times. With more time per move, weaker targeting performs as well as the stronger targeting or even better in case of PST.

4.4.3 Head-to-head performance

After we confirmed that we achieved the goal of creating an online game playing algorithm that converges close to Nash equilibrium, we evaluate its game playing performance in head-to-head matches with ISMCTS. For each game, we focus on two sizes: the smaller variant, for which we analyzed the exploitability in the previous section and a substantially larger variant that is closer to the size of the domains where online search algorithms are typically applied. The largest domain is II-GS(13) with approximately 3.8×10^{19} terminal histories.

The results are summarized in Figure 4. For Goofspiel and Liar's Dice, we present the win-rate, where a tie is considered half win half loss. II-GS is perfectly balanced for both players. In LD, the first player has a slight disadvantage corresponding to approximately 1% in the win rate and we do not compensate for that. Poker is not balanced. If both players play the optimal strategy, the first player loses 0.11 chips on average. This value is practically the

0.1s	OOS	UCT	RM	RND
OOS	49.3(2.7)	50.0(1.3)	50.5(1.3)	83.1(1.5)
UCT	51.2(2.2)	62.9(2.6)	62.7(2.5)	84.0(2.1)
RM	52.3(1.4)	70.6(1.7)	73.1(2.1)	87.8(1.4)
RND	17.1(2.2)	15.7(2.2)	10.3(1.8)	49.7(3.0)

(a) II Goofspiel (6)

0.1s	OOS	UCT	RM	RND
OOS	48.5(2.0)	51.7(2.0)	56.8(2.8)	83.3(1.5)
UCT	45.7(2.0)	49.7(2.0)	52.9(2.8)	87.2(1.3)
RM	47.9(2.8)	49.0(2.8)	54.3(2.8)	84.8(2.0)
RND	16.9(1.5)	19.5(1.6)	18.1(2.2)	47.7(2.0)

(b) Liar's Dice (1,1)

0.1s	OOS	UCT	RM	RND
OOS	0.25(0.53)	-0.45(0.10)	-0.40(0.10)	1.85(0.16)
UCT	0.53(0.10)	0.21(0.15)	0.20(0.15)	1.35(0.36)
RM	0.39(0.13)	0.21(0.40)	-0.12(0.32)	1.75(0.44)
RND	-2.17(0.20)	-2.22(0.54)	-3.24(0.55)	1.07(0.61)

(c) Generic Poker (3,3,2,2)

1s	OOS	UCT	RM	RND
OOS	49.2(2.5)	28.3(3.9)	35.1(4.2)	83.0(3.2)
UCT	69.2(4.0)	70.0(2.8)	61.0(3.0)	90.6(1.8)
RM	67.5(4.0)	73.8(2.7)	67.5(2.9)	92.8(1.5)
RND	19.6(3.4)	6.2(1.5)	4.9(1.3)	49.0(3.0)

(d) II Goofspiel (13)

5s	OOS	UCT	RM	RND
OOS	49.9(3.7)	55.4(2.3)	53.3(3.7)	91.3(1.7)
UCT	49.8(2.2)	56.2(3.1)	49.8(3.1)	93.7(1.5)
RM	53.3(3.5)	51.7(4.0)	51.0(4.0)	88.7(2.0)
RND	7.3(1.6)	12.9(2.1)	12.7(2.1)	47.3(3.0)

(e) Liar's Dice (2,2)

1s	OOS	UCT	RM	RND
OOS	-0.54(0.47)	-1.79(0.27)	-2.19(0.32)	8.36(0.54)
UCT	-0.07(0.35)	0.22(0.10)	-0.76(0.18)	9.48(0.40)
RM	-0.12(0.38)	-0.28(0.17)	-0.97(0.22)	9.09(0.44)
RND	-3.25(0.43)	-3.91(0.27)	-4.12(0.31)	2.51(0.51)

(f) Generic Poker (4,6,4,4)

Figure 4: Head-to-head matches in small (a-c) and large (d-f) game variants. The top left corner indicates the computation time per move and the brackets show 95% confidence intervals. OOS run with IST for II-GS and PST for the other games, targeting $\delta = 0.9$ and exploration $\epsilon = 0.4$; UCT with $C = 2 \cdot \max$; RM with $\gamma = 0.2$.

same for both evaluated sizes of the game. For clarity, we present the difference between this game value and the mean reward obtained by the players in the matches. A value 0.1 in the tables means that the row player on average wins 0.1 more than the game value from the column player per match. Each entry in the tables presents the result of at least 500 mutual matches between two algorithms from the perspective of the one in the row header. The values in the brackets are the size of half of the 95% confidence intervals centered in the presented mean. If it is not specified otherwise, OOS was run with IST for II-Goofspiel and PST for the other games, targeting $\delta = 0.9$ and exploration $\epsilon = 0.4$.

Figure 4(a) presents the results for the smaller Goofspiel and 0.1 second of computation per move. Even though the game is balanced, the results of ISMCTS are strongly biased towards the first player. The second player has generally larger information sets and needs to better evaluate the hidden information to choose a good move. OOS does not have this problem in the smaller game. It is the only algorithm that managed to prevent ISMCTS from exploiting it. In both positions, the algorithm won approximately 50% of matches, which corresponds to the value of the game. On the other hand, the first line in the table shows that OOS did not exploit the weaker play of ISMCTS, even though it is possible. This is a common disadvantage of Nash equilibrium play. One simple way to overcome this would be to trade a bit of exploitability to gain some exploitation; computing a restricted Nash response using MCRNR [30] (a minor modification of MCCFR) allows the best possible trade-off for a given importance between exploitability and exploitation. In the large variant of Goofspiel (see Figure 4(d)) with one second per move, the situation is different. OOS does not manage to converge sufficiently close to the equilibrium and ISMCTS exploits it from both positions to a similar extent. Increasing the computation time to 5 seconds per move helps OOS to win 35% matches against UCT, but it would likely need a substantially longer time to reach the equilibrium.

The results on Liar's Dice are even more promising for OOS. In the smaller game with 0.1 second per move (Figure 4(b)), OOS statistically significantly wins over both variants of ISMCTS from at least one position. This is not the case for the larger game and 1 second per move, where OOS already wins only 45% and 40% of matches against UCT and RM from the first position and loses 69% and 66% from the second position. However, with 5 seconds and the exploration parameter set to $\epsilon = 0.8$ to balance the need for exploring a large number of actions in this game, OOS again wins over UCT and ties with RM (Figure 4(e)).

As indicated by the exploitability results, OOS performs the worst against ISMCTS in the Poker domain. In the smaller variant (Figure 4(c)), it is losing from both positions. The result of OOS from the first position against UCT improves to -0.22 with 5 seconds per move, but even more time would be required to tie. From the first (generally more difficult) position, the situation is similar also in the larger Poker (Figure 4(f)). It is not the case for the second position, where OOS is able to tie both ISMCTS variants. This could be because Poker games have very high variance.

5. CONCLUSION

We have introduced Online Outcome Sampling, the first online game playing algorithm for imperfect information games that is guaranteed to produce approximate equilibrium strategies as search time per move increases. In order to achieve this, we do not modify a perfect information search algorithm to avoid the main problems caused by imperfect information, as in previous work. We instead start from an offline equilibrium computation method and adapt it to make the most of the limited time it has by using the information about the current position in the match. Besides incremental tree building, we propose two methods for targeting relevant parts of the game based on the current match history. In empirical evaluation, we show that a player using ISMCTS can suffer almost arbitrarily large loss when the opponent knows the algorithm she uses. The expected worst-case loss of using OOS decreases close to its minimum with additional search time. Furthermore, even with these guarantees, we can achieve comparable game playing performance to ISMCTS in mutual matches.

In future work, we hope to investigate more and larger games and the effect of informed playout policies. We hope to compare practical performance against other baseline algorithms such as PIMC [28], MMCTS [1], IIMC [10], and Smooth UCT [18]. Finally, one interesting question is whether the subgame decomposition ideas of [4, 19] could be adapted to the online search setting.

6. ACKNOWLEDGMENTS

This work is partially funded by the Czech Science Foundation, grant P202/12/2054 and 15-23235S; and by the Netherlands Organisation for Scientific Research (NWO) in the framework of the project Go4Nature, grant 612.000.938.

REFERENCES

[1] D. Auger. Multiple tree for partially observable Monte-Carlo tree search. In *Applications of Evolutionary Computation (EvoApplications 2011), Part I*, volume 6624 of *LNCS*, pages 53–62, 2011.

[2] M. Bowling, N. Burch, M. Johanson, and O. Tammelin. Heads-up limit hold'em poker is solved. *Science*, 347(6218):145–149, 2015.

[3] C. Browne, E. Powley, D. Whitehouse, S. M. Lucas, P. I. Cowling, P. Rohlfshagen, S. Tavener, D. Perez, S. Samothrakis, and S. Colton. A survey of Monte Carlo tree search methods. *IEEE Transactions on Computational Intelligence and AI in Games*, 4(1):1–43, March 2012.

[4] N. Burch, M. Johanson, and M. Bowling. Solving imperfect information games using decomposition. In *28th AAAI Conference on Artificial Intelligence*, 2014.

[5] M. Buro, J. Long, T. Furtak, and N. Sturtevant. Improving state evaluation, inference, and search in trick-based card games. In *Proceedings of the AAAI Conference on Artificial Intelligence*, pages 1407–1413, 2009.

[6] P. Ciancarini and G. Favini. Monte Carlo tree search in Kriegspiel. *Artificial Intelligence*, 174(11):670–684, 2010.

[7] R. Coulom. Efficient selectivity and backup operators in monte-carlo tree search. In *Proceedings of the 5th international conference on Computers and games*, CG'06, pages 72–83. Springer-Verlag, 2007.

[8] P. I. Cowling, E. J. Powley, and D. Whitehouse. Information set Monte Carlo tree search. *IEEE Transactions on Computational Intelligence and AI in Games*, 4(2):120–143, December 2012.

[9] I. Frank, D. Basin, and H. Matsubara. Finding optimal strategies for imperfect information games. In *Proceedings of the Fifteenth National Conference on Artificial Intelligence*, pages 500–507, 1998.

[10] T. Furtak and M. Buro. Recursive Monte Carlo search for imperfect information games. In *IEEE Conference on Computational Intelligence in Games (CIG 2013)*, 2013.

[11] S. Ganzfried and T. Sandholm. Improving performance in imperfect-information games with large state and action spaces by solving endgames. In *AAAI Workshop on Computer Poker and Incomplete Information*, 2013.

[12] A. Gilpin. *Algorithms for Abstracting and Solving Imperfect Information Games.* PhD thesis, Carnegie Mellon University, 2009.

[13] A. Gilpin and T. Sandholm. A competitive Texas Hold'em poker player via automated abstraction and real-time equilibrium computation. In *Proceedings of the 21st AAAI Conference on Artificial Intelligence*, pages 1453–1454, 2006.

[14] A. Gilpin and T. Sandholm. Better automated abstraction techniques for imperfect information games, with application to Texas Hold'em poker. In *Proceedings of the International Joint Conference on Autonomous Agents and Multi-Agent Systems (AAMAS)*, 2007.

[15] M. Ginsberg. Partition search. In *Proceedings of the Thirteenth National Conference on Artitificial Intelligence (AAAI)*, pages 228–233, 1996.

[16] M. Ginsberg. GIB: Imperfect information in a computationally challenging game. *Journal of Artificial Intelligence Research*, 14:303–358, 2001.

[17] S. Hart and A. Mas-Colell. A simple adaptive procedure leading to correlated equilibrium. *Econometrica*, 68(5):1127–1150, 2000.

[18] J. Heinrich and D. Silver. Self-play Monte-Carlo tree search in computer poker. In *Proceedings of the AAAI Workshop on Computer Poker and Perfect Information*, 2014.

[19] E. Jackson. A time and space efficient algorithm for approximately solving large imperfect information games. In *Proceedings of the AAAI Workshop on Computer Poker and Perfect Information*, 2014.

[20] M. Johanson, N. Bard, M. Lanctot, R. Gibson, and M. Bowling. Efficient Nash equilibrium approximation through Monte Carlo counterfactual regret minimization. In *Proceedings of the Eleventh International Conference on Autonomous Agents and Multi-Agent Systems (AAMAS)*, 2012.

[21] M. Johanson, N. Burch, R. Valenzano, and M. Bowling. Evaluating state-space abstractions in extensive-form games. In *Proceedings of the 12th International Conference on Autonomous Agents and Multi-Agent Systems (AAMAS)*, 2013.

[22] L. Kocsis and C. Szepesvári. Bandit-based Monte Carlo planning. In *15th European Conference on Machine Learning*, volume 4212 of *LNCS*, pages 282–293, 2006.

[23] M. Lanctot, V. Lisý, and M. H. Winands. Monte Carlo tree search in simultaneous move games with applications to Goofspiel. In *Computer Games*, volume 408 of *Communications in Computer and Information Science*, pages 28–43. Springer, 2014.

[24] M. Lanctot, K. Waugh, M. Bowling, and M. Zinkevich. Sampling for regret minimization in extensive games. In *Advances in Neural Information Processing Systems (NIPS 2009)*, pages 1078–1086, 2009.

[25] V. Lisy. Alternative selection functions for information set Monte Carlo tree search. *Acta Polytechnica: Journal of Advanced Engineering*, 54(5):333–340, 2014.

[26] V. Lisy, B. Bosansky, and M. Pechoucek. Anytime algorithms for multi-agent visibility-based pursuit-evasion games. In *Proceedings of the 11th International Conference on Autonomous Agents and Multiagent Systems (AAMAS)*, pages 1301–1302, 2012.

[27] V. Lisy, V. Kovarik, M. Lanctot, and B. Bosansky. Convergence of Monte Carlo tree search in simultaneous move games. In *Advances in Neural Information Processing Systems 26*, pages 2112–2120, 2013.

[28] J. Long, N. R. Sturtevant, M. Buro, and T. Furtak. Understanding the success of perfect information Monte Carlo sampling in game tree search. In *Proceedings of the AAAI Conference on Artificial Intelligence*, pages 134–140, 2010.

[29] M. Osborne and A. Rubinstein. *A Course in Game Theory.* MIT Press, 1994.

[30] M. Ponsen, S. de Jong, and M. Lanctot. Computing approximate Nash equilibria and robust best-responses using sampling. *Journal of Artificial Intelligence Research*, 42:575–605, 2011.

[31] J. Rubin and I. Watson. Computer poker: A review. *Artificial Intelligence*, 175(5–6):958–987, 2011.

[32] T. Sandholm. The state of solving large incomplete-information games, and application to poker. *AI Magazine*, 31(4):13–32, 2010.

[33] M. Shafiei, N. R. Sturtevant, and J. Schaeffer. Comparing UCT versus CFR in simultaneous games. In *IJCAI Workshop on General Game-Playing (GIGA)*, pages 75–82, 2009.

[34] B. Sheppard. World-championship-caliber scrabble. *Artificial Intelligence*, 134:241–275, 2002.

[35] N. R. Sturtevant. An analysis of UCT in multi-player games. *ICGA Journal*, 31(4):195–208, 2008.

[36] M. Tambe. *Security and Game Theory: Algorithms, Deployed Systems, Lessons Learned.* Cambridge University Press, 2011.

[37] D. Whitehouse, P. Cowling, E. Powley, and J. Rollason. Integrating Monte Carlo tree search with knowledge-based methods to create engaging play in a commercial mobile game. In *9th Conference on Artificial Intelligence and Interactive Digital Entertainment (AIIDE)*, pages 100–106, 2013.

[38] M. Zinkevich, M. Johanson, M. Bowling, and C. Piccione. Regret minimization in games with incomplete information. In *Advances in Neural Information Processing Systems 20 (NIPS 2007)*, 2008.

Endgame Solving in Large Imperfect-Information Games*

Sam Ganzfried and Tuomas Sandholm
Computer Science Department
Carnegie Mellon University
{sganzfri, sandholm}@cs.cmu.edu

ABSTRACT

The leading approach for computing strong game-theoretic strategies in large imperfect-information games is to first solve an abstracted version of the game offline, then perform a table lookup during game play. We consider a modification to this approach where we solve the portion of the game that we have actually reached in real time to a greater degree of accuracy than in the initial computation. We call this approach endgame solving. Theoretically, we show that endgame solving can produce highly exploitable strategies in some games; however, we show that it can guarantee a low exploitability in certain games where the opponent is given sufficient exploitative power within the endgame. Furthermore, despite the lack of a general worst-case guarantee, we describe many benefits of endgame solving. We present an efficient algorithm for performing endgame solving in large imperfect-information games, and present a new variance-reduction technique for evaluating the performance of an agent that uses endgame solving. Experiments on no-limit Texas Hold'em show that our algorithm leads to significantly stronger performance against the strongest agents from the 2013 AAAI Annual Computer Poker Competition.

Categories and Subject Descriptors

I.2.11 [**Distributed Artificial Intelligence**]: Multiagent Systems; J.4 [**Social and Behavioral Sciences**]: Economics

General Terms

Algorithms, Economics, Theory

Keywords

Game Theory; Game Solving; Imperfect Information

1. INTRODUCTION

Sequential games of perfect information can be solved in linear time by a straightforward backward induction procedure in which solutions to endgames are propagated up the game tree.[1] However, this procedure does not work in general in imperfect-information games because different endgames can contain nodes that belong to the same information set and cannot be treated independently. More sophisticated algorithms are needed for this class of game. One algorithm for solving two-player zero-sum imperfect-information games is based on a linear program (LP) formulation [14], which scales to games with around 10^8 nodes in their game tree [7]. Many interesting games are significantly larger; for example, two-player limit Texas Hold'em has about 10^{17} nodes, and a popular variant of two-player no-limit Texas Hold'em has about 10^{165} nodes [12]. To address such large games, newer approximate equilibrium-finding algorithms have been developed that scale to games with around 10^{14} nodes, such as counterfactual regret minimization (CFR) [21] and an algorithm based on the excessive gap technique (EGT) [10]. These algorithms are iterative and guarantee convergence to equilibrium in the limit.

The leading approach for solving extremely large games such as Texas Hold'em (TH)[2] is to abstract the game down to a game with only around 10^{12} nodes, then to compute an approximate equilibrium in the abstract game using one of the algorithms described above [2, 7]. In order to perform such a dramatic reduction in size, significant abstraction is often needed. *Information* (aka *card*) *abstraction* involves reducing the number of nodes by bundling signals (e.g., forcing a player to play the same way with two different hands), and *action* (aka *betting*) *abstraction* involves reducing the number of actions by discretizing large action spaces into a small number of actions. All of the computation (both for constructing the abstraction and computing an approximate equilibrium in the abstraction) is done offline, and a table lookup is performed in real time to implement the strategy.

We consider a modification to this approach where we retain the abstract equilibrium strategies for the initial portion of the game tree (called the *trunk*), and discard the strategies for the final portion (called the *endgames*). Then, in real time, we solve the relevant endgame that we have reached to a greater degree of accuracy than the initial abstract strategy, where we use Bayes' rule to compute the distribution of players' private information leading into the endgames from the precomputed trunk strategies. This approach, which we call *endgame solving*, is depicted in Figure 1.

We present the first theoretical analysis of endgame solv-

*This material is based on work supported by the National Science Foundation under grants IIS-1320620, IIS-0964579, and CCF-1101668, as well as XSEDE computing resources provided by the Pittsburgh Supercomputing Center.

Appears in: *Proceedings of the 14th International Conference on Autonomous Agents and Multiagent Systems (AAMAS 2015), Bordini, Elkind, Weiss, Yolum (eds.), May 4–8, 2015, Istanbul, Turkey.*

[1]Prior work has shown that precomputing solutions to endgames offline can be effective in large perfect-information games [1, 18]. In contrast, we solve endgames online.
[2]See Appendix A for background on Texas Hold'em poker.

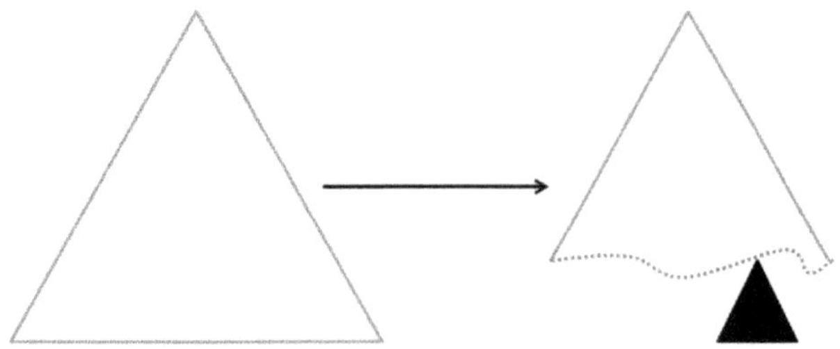

Figure 1: Endgame solving (re-)solves the relevant endgame that we have actually reached in real time to a greater degree of accuracy than in the offline computation.

ing in imperfect-information games, and show that it can actually produce highly exploitable strategies in some games. In fact, we show that it can fail even in a simple game with a unique equilibrium and a single endgame, even if our base strategy were an exact equilibrium (of the full game) and we were able to compute an exact equilibrium in the endgame. However, we show that endgame solving can guarantee a low *exploitability* (difference between game value and payoff against a nemesis) in some games when the opponent is given sufficient exploitative power within the endgame.

Endgame solving has been used by several prior agents for the limit variation of TH (where bets must be of a single fixed size). The agent GS1 precomputed strategies only for the first two rounds, using rough approximations for the payoffs at the leaves of that trunk based on the (unrealistic) assumption that there was no betting in future rounds [7]. Then in real time, the relevant endgame consisting of the final two rounds was solved using the LP algorithm. GS2 precomputed strategies for the first three rounds, using simulations to estimate the payoffs at the leaves; it then solved the endgames for the final two rounds in real time [8].

However endgame solving has not been implemented by any competitive agents for the significantly larger and more challenging domain of no-limit Texas Hold'em (NLTH) prior to our work. We present a new algorithm that is capable of scaling to extremely large games such as no-limit Texas Hold'em, and incorporates several algorithmic improvements over the prior approaches (the benefits described in this paragraph would be improvements over the prior approaches even for the limit variant). First, the prior approaches assume that the private hand distributions leading into the endgame are independent, while they are actually dependent and the full joint distribution should be computed. The naïve way of accomplishing this would require $O(n^2)$ strategy table lookups, where n is the number of private hands (1081 for the final round of poker), and computing these distributions would become the bottleneck of the algorithm and make the real-time computation intractable; however, we developed a technique for computing the joint distributions that requires just $O(n)$ strategy table lookups. Second, the prior approaches use a single perfect-recall card abstraction that has been precomputed offline (which assumes a uniform random distribution for the opponent's hand distributions). In contrast, we use an imperfect-recall card abstraction[3] that is computed in real time in a finer granularity than the initial offline abstraction and that is tailored specifically to the relevant distribution of the opponent's hands at the given hand history. Furthermore, the prior approaches did not compare performance between endgame solving and not using it (since the base strategies were not computed for the endgames), while we provide such a comparison.

Very recent work, which appeared subsequently to the first version of this work, has presented approaches for decomposing imperfect-information games into smaller games that can be solved independently offline, and provides some theoretical guarantees on full-game exploitability. One of these approaches has only been applied to the small domain of limit Leduc Hold'em, which has 936 information sets in its game tree, and is not practical for larger games such as NLTH due to its running time [3]. A second related (offline) approach includes counterfactual values for game states that could have been reached off the path to the endgames [11]. This approach has been demonstrated to be effective in limit Leduc Hold'em, and has also been implemented in NLTH, though no experimental results are given for that domain. For NLTH, it is implemented by first solving the game in a coarse abstraction, then fixing the strategies for the preflop (first) round, and re-solving for certain endgames starting at the flop (second round) after common preflop betting sequences have been played. All of this computation is done offline. In contrast, our approach enables us to solve endgames at the river (final round) in real time. It is infeasible to solve the river endgames using the prior approach for several reasons. First, there are far too many of them to be solved individually in advance (there is a different one for each sequence of public cards and betting actions). Second, by the time play gets down to the river, there are many possible alternative actions that a player could have taken to avoid reaching the given endgame, and counterfactual values for each of these would need to be computed and then included in the solution to the endgame solver; this would likely be infeasible to do in real time. Solving the river endgames, as opposed to the flop endgames which the prior approach does, is very important because CFR only occasionally samples from a specific river endgame during the course of the initial equilibrium computation, while it very frequently samples from the flop endgames that follow common preflop betting sequences. So, our approach is addressing a more pressing limitation.

Our approach has significant benefits over the standard approach for solving large imperfect-information games, including computation of exact (rather than approximate) equilibrium strategies (within a given abstraction), the ability to compute certain equilibrium refinements that cannot be computed in the full offline computation, finer-grained abstraction in the endgames, abstraction that takes into account realistic distributions of players' private information entering the endgame (as opposed to the typical assumption of uniform random distributions), and a solution to the "off-tree" problem that arises when the opponent has taken actions that are not allowed in the abstraction. We present an efficient algorithm for performing endgame solving in large imperfect-information games, and present a novel variance-reduction technique for evaluating the performance of an agent that uses endgame solving. Experiments on no-limit Texas Hold'em show that using our algorithm leads to a significantly stronger performance against the strongest 2013 poker competition agents.

[3]Imperfect-recall abstractions allow for greater flexibility in which hands can be grouped together, and significantly improve performance over perfect-recall abstractions [20, 13].

2. ENDGAME SOLVING

DEFINITION 1. *E is an* endgame *of game G if the following properties hold:*

1. *The set of E's nodes is a subset of the set of G's nodes.*
2. *If s' is a child of s in G and s is a node in E, then s' is also a node in E.*
3. *If s is in the same information set as s' in G and s is a node in E, then s' is also a node in E.*

For example, we can consider endgames in poker where several rounds of betting have taken place and several public cards have already been dealt. In these endgames, we can assume players have a joint distribution of private information from nodes prior to the endgame that are induced from the precomputed base approximate-equilibrium strategy using Bayes' rule. Given this distribution as input, we can then solve individual endgames in real time using more accurate abstractions.

Unfortunately, this approach has some fundamental theoretical shortcomings. It turns out that even if we computed an exact equilibrium in the trunk (which is an unrealistically optimistic assumption in large games) and in the endgame, the combined strategies for the trunk and endgame may fail to be an equilibrium in the full game. One obvious reason for this is that the game may contain many equilibria, and we might choose one for the trunk that does not match up correctly with the one for the endgame; or we may compute different equilibria in different endgames that do not balance appropriately. However, Proposition 1 shows that it is possible for this procedure to output a non-equilibrium strategy profile in the full game even if the full game has a unique equilibrium and a single endgame.

PROPOSITION 1. *There exist games—even with a unique equilibrium and a single endgame—for which endgame solving can produce a non-equilibrium strategy profile.*

PROOF. Consider a sequential version of Rock-Paper-Scissors where player 1 acts, then player 2 acts without observing player 1's action. This game has a single endgame—when it is player 2's turn to act—and a unique equilibrium—where each player plays each action with probability $\frac{1}{3}$. Now suppose we restrict player 1 to follow the equilibrium in the initial portion of the game. Any strategy for player 2 is an equilibrium in the endgame, because each one yields her expected payoff 0. In particular, suppose our equilibrium solver outputs the pure strategy Rock for her. This is clearly not an equilibrium of the full game. □

Rock-Paper-Scissors (RPS) is somewhat of an extreme example though, because player 1 does not actually make any moves in the endgame. At the other extreme, if the endgame were the entire game, then endgame solving would produce an exact equilibrium. As a slightly less extreme example, consider the game in Figure 2, where P1 selects an action a_i, and then a sequential imperfect-information game G_i is played. Suppose we are solving endgames after P1's initial action. Then we will solve the endgame G_i and produce strategies with zero exploitability in the full game. Endgame solving could be very useful in this game for several reasons. First, if the number of initial actions n for P1 were extremely large, it may be infeasible to solve and/or store solutions to all of the endgames in advance of game play. Endgame solving would only require solving the endgames that are actually reached during game play, and would be feasible even if n is extremely large as long as the number of game repetitions were relatively small. And second, the typical approach would actually not even involve solving each of the G_i separately in advance; it would be to solve the full game, which includes each of the G_i as well as P1's initial actions. It is very possible that equilibrium-finding algorithms would not scale to the full game and/or it would not fit in memory, while equilibria could be computed quickly and fit into memory for the individual endgames G_i.

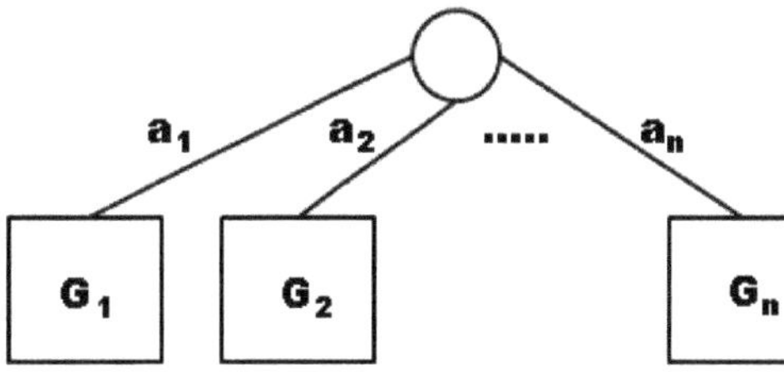

Figure 2: Player 1 selects his action a_i, then the players play imperfect-information game G_i.

One could imagine much more complex trunk games than the above example with imperfect information and multiple actions for both players where it is difficult to know for sure how "important" the trunk strategies are for the endgames. In such games, it may be possible for endgame solving to still guarantee a reasonably low exploitability in the full game. As Proposition 2 shows, in general, the more exploitative power the opponent has within the endgame, the lower the full-game exploitability of the strategies produced by (approximate) endgame solving are.

PROPOSITION 2. *If every strategy that has exploitability strictly more than ϵ in the full game has exploitability of strictly more than δ within the endgame, then the strategy output by a solver that computes a δ-equilibrium in the endgame induced by a trunk strategy t would constitute an ϵ-equilibrium of the full game when paired with t.*

PROOF. Suppose a strategy is a δ-equilibrium in the endgame induced by t, but not an ϵ-equilibrium in the full game when paired with t. Then by assumption, it has exploitability of strictly more than δ within the endgame, which leads to a contradiction. □

Intuitively, Proposition 2 says that endgame solving produces strategies with low exploitability in games where the endgame is a significant strategic portion of the full game, that is, in games where any endgame strategy with high full-game exploitability can be exploited by the opponent by modifying his strategy just within the endgame.

One could classify different games according to how they fall regarding the premise of Proposition 2, given a subdivision of the game into a trunk and endgames, and given fixed strategies for the trunk. If the premise is satisfied, then we can say that the game/subdivision satisfies the (ϵ, δ)-*endgame property*. An interesting property would be the smallest value $\epsilon^*(\delta)$ such that the game satisfies the (ϵ, δ)-endgame property for a given δ. For instance, the game in Figure 2 would have $\epsilon^*(\delta) = \delta$ for all $\delta \geq 0$, while RPS would only have $\epsilon^*(\delta) = 1$ for each $\delta \geq 0$. While Proposition 2 is admittedly somewhat trivial, such a classification could be useful in developing a better understanding of when endgame solving would be helpful in general.

3. BENEFITS OF ENDGAME SOLVING

Even though we showed in the previous section that endgame solving may lead to highly exploitable strategies in some games, it has many clear benefits in large imperfect-information games, which we now describe. These benefits and techniques are *enabled by* using endgame solving (rather than being techniques that help alongside endgame solving).

3.1 Exact Computation of Nash Equilibrium in Abstracted Endgames

The best algorithms for computing approximate equilibria in large games of imperfect information scale to about 10^{14} nodes. However, they are iterative and guarantee convergence only in the limit; in practice they only produce approximations of equilibrium strategies (within a given abstraction). Sometimes the approximation error is quite large. For example, a recent NLTH agent reported having an exploitability of 800 milli big blinds per hand (mbb/h) even within the abstract game [4] (an agent that folds every hand would only have an exploitability of 750 mbb/h). The best general-purpose LP algorithms find an exact equilibrium, though they only scale to games with around 10^8 nodes [7]. While the LP algorithms do not scale to reasonable abstractions of full TH, we can (and do) use them to exactly solve abstracted endgames that have up to around 10^8 nodes.

3.2 Ability to Compute Certain Equilibrium Refinements

The Nash equilibrium (NE) solution concept has some theoretical limitations, and several equilibrium refinements have been proposed which rule out NEs that are not rational in various senses. In general, these solution concepts guarantee that we behave sensibly against an opponent who does not follow his prescribed equilibrium strategy (i.e., he takes actions that should be taken with probability zero in equilibrium). Specialized algorithms have been developed for computing many of these concepts [15, 16, 17]. However, those algorithms do not scale to large games. In TH, computing a reasonable approximation of a single Nash equilibrium already takes months (using the leading algorithms, CFR or EGT), and there are no known algorithms for computing any of the common refinements that scale to games of that size. However, when solving endgames that are significantly smaller than the full game, it can be possible to compute certain refinements. An undominated Nash equilibrium (UNE) can be computed by solving two LPs instead of one and an ϵ-quasi-perfect-equilibrium by solving a single LP (though the second one is not technically a refinement and has documented numerical stability issues). We have implemented algorithms for computing both of these on large NLTH endgames, which demonstrates for the first time that they are feasible to compute in imperfect-information games of this magnitude. Preliminary experiments indicate that in NLTH endgames UNE is useful, though those results were not statistically significant, so we do not report on those experiments here.

3.3 Finer-Grained, History-Aware, and Strategy-Biased Abstraction

Another important benefit of endgame solving in large games is that we can compute better abstractions in the endgame that is actually played than if we are forced to abstract the entire game at once in advance. In addition to allowing us to compute finer-grained abstractions, endgame solving enables us to compute an abstraction specifically for the situation at hand. In other words, we can condition the abstraction on the path of play so far (both the players' actions and nature's actions). For example, in poker, we can condition the abstraction on the betting history (which offline game-solving approaches do not do) and on the board cards (which offline game-solving approaches cannot afford to do at an equally fine granularity).

The standard approach for performing information abstraction is to bucket information sets together for hands that perform similarly against a uniform distribution of the opponent's private information [7, 13].[4] However, the assumption that the opponent has a hand uniformly at random is extremely unrealistic in many situations; for example, if the opponent has called large bets throughout the hand, he is unlikely to hold a very weak hand. Ideally, a successful information abstraction algorithm would group hands together that perform similarly against the relevant distribution of hands the opponent actually has—not a naïve uniform random distribution. Fortunately, we can accomplish such *strategy-biased information abstraction* in endgames. Our algorithm is detailed in Section 4.

3.4 A Solution to the Off-Tree Problem

When we perform action abstraction, the opponent may take an action that falls outside of our action model for him. When this happens, an *action translation mapping* (aka *reverse mapping*) is necessary to interpret his action by mapping it to an action in our model [5, 19]. However, this mapping may ignore relevant game state information. In poker, action translation works by mapping a bet of the opponent to a 'nearby' bet size in our abstraction; however, it does not account for the size of the pot or remaining stacks. For example, suppose remaining stacks are 17,500, the pot is 5,000, and our abstraction allows for bets of size 5,000 and 17,500. Suppose the opponent bets 10,000, which we map to 5,000 (if we use a randomized mapping, we will do this with some probability). So we map his action to 5,000, and simply play as if he had bet 5,000. If we call his bet, we will think the pot has 15,000 and stacks are 12,500. However, in reality the pot has 25,000 and stacks are 7,500. These two situations are completely different and should be played very differently (for example, we should be more reluctant to bluff in the latter case because the opponent will be getting much better odds to call). This is known as the *off-tree problem.* Even if one is using a very sophisticated translation algorithm, one will run into the off-tree problem.

When performing endgame solving in real time, we can solve the off-tree problem completely. Regardless of the action translation used to interpret the opponent's actions prior to the endgame, we can take the stack and pot sizes (or any other relevant game state information) as inputs to the endgame solver. Our endgame solver in poker takes the current pot size, stack sizes, and prior distributions of the cards of both players as inputs. Therefore, even if we mapped the opponent's action to 5,000 in the above example, we correct the pot size to 25,000 (and the stack sizes accordingly) before solving the endgame.

[4]Recent work has also considered an approach where the opponent's preflop hands are first grouped into several buckets, then hands for the later rounds are grouped together if they perform similarly against each of the preflop buckets [13].

4. ENDGAME SOLVING ALGORITHM

In this section we present our algorithm for endgame solving in imperfect-information games with very large state and action spaces. Pseudocode is given in Algorithm 1. The core algorithm is domain independent, although we present the signals as card-playing hands for concreteness. An example poker hand illustrating each step of the algorithm is given in Appendix B.

Algorithm 1 Algorithm for endgame solving

Inputs: number of information buckets per agent k_i; abstraction parameter T; action abstractions B_i with b_i action sequences; clustering algorithms C_i; equilibrium-finding algorithm Q; number of private hands H; hand rankings $R[]$

```
Compute joint hand-strength distribution D[i][j]
E1, E2 ← array of dimension H of zeroes
for h1 = 1 to H do
    r1 ← R[h1], s1, s2 ← 0
    for h2 = 1 to H do
        r2 ← R[h2], s1 += D[h1][h2], s2 += D[h2][h1]
        if r2 < r1 then
            E1[h1] += D[h1][h2], E2[h1] += D[h2][h1]
        else if r1 == r2 then
            E1[h1] += D[h1][h2]/2, E2[h1] += D[h2][h1]/2
    E1[h1] = E1[h1]/s1, E2[h1] = E2[h1]/s2
k_i ← ⌊T/b_i⌋ for i = 1, 2
A_i ← information abstraction created by clustering elements of E_i into k_i buckets using C_i for i = 1, 2
Solve game with information abstractions A_i and action abstractions B_i using Q
```

The first step is to compute the joint input distribution of private information using Bayes' rule. The naïve approach for doing this would require iterating over all possible private hand combinations h_1, h_2 for the players, and for each pair looking up the probability that the base agent would have taken the given action sequence. This requires $O(n^2)$ lookups to the strategy table, where n is the number of possible hands ($n = 1081$ for the final round in poker). It turns out that this computation would become the bottleneck of the entire endgame-solving algorithm and would make real-time endgame solving computationally infeasible. For this reason, prior approaches for endgame solving have made the (significantly) simplifying assumption that the distributions are independent [7, 8]. However, we developed an algorithm that does this with just $O(n)$ table lookups. Pseudocode for our algorithm is given in Algorithm 2.

In short, the algorithm first computes the distributions separately for each player (as done by the independent approach), then multiplies the probabilities together for hands that do not share a common card (and setting the joint probability to zero otherwise). In order to make sure hands are indexed properly in the array, we must make use of two helper indexing functions, Algorithms 3 and 4. The former gives an algorithm for indexing the two-card private hands, and the latter gives an algorithm for indexing the 7-card river hand consisting of the two private cards and five public cards. Then, in Algorithm 2, we iterate over all sets of private hands (p_1, p_2), and create an array called IndexMap that maps the 7-card hand index to the corresponding 2-card hand index. In the course of this loop, we also look up the probability that each player would play according to the observed betting history in the precomputed trunk strategies, which we then normalize in accordance with Bayes' rule.

Algorithm 2 Algorithm for computing hand distributions

Inputs: Public board B; number of possible private hands H; betting history of current hand h; array of index conflicts IC[][]; base strategy s^*

```
D1, D2 ← array of dimension H of zeroes
for p1 = 0 to 50, p1 not already on B do
    for p2 = p1 + 1 to 51, p2 not already on B do
        I ← IndexFull(B, p1, p2)
        IndexMap[I] ← IndexHoles(p1, p2)
        P1 ← probability P1 would play according to h with p1, p2 in s*
        P2 ← probability P2 would play according to h with p1, p2 in s*
        D1[I] += P1, D2[I] += P2
Normalize D1 and D2 so all entries sum to 1
for i = 0 to H do
    for j = 0 to H do
        if !IC[IndexMap[i]][IndexMap[j]] then
            D[i][j] ← D1[i] · D2[j]
        else
            D[i][j] ← 0
Normalize D so all entries sum to 1 return D
```

Algorithm 3 Algorithm for computing private hand index

Inputs: Private hole cards h_1, h_2

```
if h2 < h1 then t ← h1, h1 ← h2, h2 ← t
return C(h2, 2) + C(h1, 1)
```

Algorithm 4 Algorithm for computing index of 7-card hands on a given board

Inputs: Private hole cards h_1, h_2, board B consisting of five public cards

```
if h2 < h1 then, t ← h1, h1 ← h2, h2 ← t
n1 ← 0, n2 ← 0
for i = 1 to 5 do
    for j = 1 to 2 do
        if B[i] < h_j then ++n_j
return C(h2 − n2, 2) + C(h1 − n1, 1)
```

In advance of applying Algorithm 2, we compute a table of the conflicts between each pair of private-hand indices, where we set IC$[i][j]$ to 1 if hand with indices i and j share a card in common, and 0 otherwise. Then, we set the joint probability $D[i][j]$ to equal the product of the two independent probabilities $D_1[i], D_2[j]$ if there is no constraint between the indices, and we set it to zero otherwise. Note that this algorithm actually runs in $O(n^2)$, where n is the number of private hands. However, the n^2 loop only involves the simple step of looking up an element in the IC array, which is performed extremely quickly. The time-consuming part of the computation is looking up the strategy probabilities P_1, P_2, which involves accessing several elements in the massive binary strategy file. Our algorithm performs this task only $O(n)$ times, while the naïve approach would do this $O(n^2)$ time, and make real-time endgame solving intractable. (Note that each private hand consists of the two cards p_1, p_2, so while the main loop in Algorithm 2 iterates over both p_1 and p_2, it is only iterating once over the H private hands and is $O(n)$).

Next we compute arrays E_1, E_2 that contain the *equities* for each state of private information against the opponent's distribution. For player 1, we do this by adding $D[h_1][h_2]$ to $E_1[h_1]$ for each hand h_2 such that the rank of it on the given board is lower than that of h_1, and adding $\frac{D[h_1][h_2]}{2}$ for each hand with equal rank.[5] We then normalize the entries of $E_1[h_1]$, and compute E_2 analogously. $E_1[h_1]$ is now the probability that player 2 has a hand worse than h_1, given the prior distribution D and the current history of betting and public cards.

In advance of gameplay, we have computed separate action abstractions for the endgame solver to use for each pot/stack size that could be encountered. This allows us to solve the "off-tree problem," since we are taking into account the actual pot size even the opponent took an action outside the action abstraction earlier in the hand. We have constructed these abstractions so that the larger pot sizes (which have shallower stacks) have more bet sizes available for each history, for several reasons; the first is that the tree is smaller in these situations due to the shallower stack sizes (once players are "all-in," no additional bets are allowed), and the second is that hands with larger pot sizes are more important, since more money is won and lost on them, and we would like to ensure that more bet sizes are accounted for on these hands. B_i denotes the action abstraction to use for the given pot size at hand, and b_i denotes the number of betting sequences of B_i, for $i = 1, 2$.

Next, we compute a card abstraction A_i by grouping E_i into k_i buckets, using some clustering algorithm C_i, for $i = 1, 2$. Here $k_i = \frac{T}{b_i}$, where T is a parameter of the algorithm (for our agent we used $T = 7500$). While much prior work on poker has used k-means as the standard clustering algorithm, the following example demonstrates why this would be problematic. Suppose there are many hands with an equity of 0.775, and also many hands with an equity of 0.772. Then k-means would likely create separate clusters for these two equity values, and possibly group hands with very different equities (e.g., 0.2 and 0.3) together if few hands have those equities. To address this concern we used percentile hand strength, which also happens to be easier to compute. To do this, we break up the interval [0,1] into k_i regions of equal length (each of size $\frac{1}{k_i}$). We then group hand h_i into bucket $\lfloor \frac{E_i[h_i]}{k_i} \rfloor$. (For our poker agent we actually use a slight modification of this approach where we create a special bucket just for the hands with $E_i[h_i] \geq \alpha$, to ensure that the strongest hands are grouped separately (we used $\alpha = 0.99$ for our agent). Then the remaining α mass is divided according to the previously described procedure.) Sometimes this algorithm results in significantly fewer than k_i buckets, since there may be zero hands with E_i within certain intervals. We take this into account, and reduce the number of buckets in the card abstraction accordingly before solving the endgame. Note that the card abstractions A_i may be very different for the two players (and have different numbers of buckets); this differs from all the standard approaches, which use the same abstraction for all players.

[5]The rank of a hand given a set of public cards is an integral-valued mapping such that stronger hands have a higher value; for example, a royal flush has the highest rank.

Algorithm 5 Algorithm for computing endgame information abstractions

Inputs: Equity arrays E_i; desired number of buckets per agent k_i; parameter for top bucket α; total number of possible private hands H

$J \leftarrow \frac{\alpha}{k_1 - 1}$
$A_1 \leftarrow$ array of zeroes of size H
$U_1 \leftarrow$ array of booleans initialized to false of size H
for $h = 1$ to H **do**
  if $E_1[h] \geq \alpha$ **then** $b \leftarrow k_1 - 1$
  else
    $b \leftarrow \lfloor \frac{E_1[h]}{J} \rfloor$
  if $U_1[b] ==$ FALSE **then** $U_1[h] \leftarrow$ TRUE
$M_1 \leftarrow$ array of zeroes of size k_1, $g \leftarrow 0$
for $i = 0$ to k_i **do**
  $M_1[i] \leftarrow g$
  if $U_1[i] ==$ TRUE **then** $g = g + 1$
for $h = 1$ to H **do**
  if $E_1[h] \geq \alpha$ **then** $A_1[h] \leftarrow M_1[k_1 - 1]$
  else
    $A_1[h] \leftarrow M_1\left[\lfloor \frac{E_1[h]}{J} \rfloor\right]$
Compute A_2 analogously

Finally, we compute an (exact) equilibrium in the abstracted endgame by applying an equilibrium-finding algorithm Q to the game with card abstractions A_i and betting abstractions B_i. While the card abstractions were computed independently (based on equities derived from the joint distribution), we use the joint distribution for determining the probabilities that players are dealt hands from their respective buckets when constructing the endgame. For our agent, we used Gurobi's parallel LP solver [9] as Q.

5. EXPERIMENTS ON NO-LIMIT TEXAS HOLD'EM

We tested our algorithm against the two strongest agents from the 2013 poker competition. The base agent was a version of the agent we submitted to the 2014 AAAI computer poker competition (that came in first place) from shortly before the competition. Ordinarily it would be very time consuming to differentiate the performance of the base strategies from the endgame solver with statistical significance, since the endgame solver plays relatively slowly (it averaged around 8 seconds per hand, which still kept us well within the competition time limit of 7 seconds per hand on average, since only around 25% of hands make it to the final betting round). A useful variance-reduction technique is to only consider hands where both agents make it to an endgame. In Appendix C we prove that this technique is unbiased. The results using this evaluation metric are given in Table 1, where the ± indicates 95% confidence intervals.

Hyperborean.iro	Slumbot
+87 ± 50	+29 ± 25

Table 1: Improvement by using endgame solving against the strongest agents from the 2013 poker competition over all hands where both agents made it to some endgame (i.e., to the river betting round). Units are milli big blinds per hand.

The base agent used a procedure called purification on all rounds (except for the first preflop action); this procedure selects the maximal probability action at each information set with probability 1 instead of randomizing according to the abstract equilibrium strategy (ties are broken uniformly at random) [6]. This parameter setting was shown to be the best in our thorough experiments in prior years, and we had used this as the standard setting when evaluating our base agent. The main motivation for purification is that it compensates for the failure of iterative equilibrium-finding algorithms to fully converge to equilibrium in the abstract game (a phenomenon that has been documented by prior agents, e.g., [4]). The endgame solving agent did not use any rounding for the river, as the endgame equilibria are exact (within the chosen abstraction), and the problem of the equilibrium-finding algorithm failing to converge is not present. Both agents used the pseudoHarmonic action translation mapping [5] for all rounds to interpret actions taken by the opponent that fall outside of the action abstraction.

The results are from 100 duplicate matches against Hyperborean and 155 duplicate matches against Slumbot. Since each match is 3,000 hands, this means we played 600,000 and 930,000 hands; out of these hands, both versions of our agent made it to the river round on 173,568 and 318,700 hands against the respective opponents. If we had used the standard duplicate approach for evaluating performance, we would not have been able to statistically differentiate the base agent from the endgame solver over this sample. However, we were able to obtain statistically significant results using our new evaluation approach.

6. CONCLUSION

We demonstrated that endgame solving can be successful in practice in large imperfect-information games despite the fact that the strategies it computes is not guaranteed to constitute an equilibrium in the full game (which we showed). We also showed that endgame solving guarantees a low exploitability in certain games, and presented a framework that can be used to evaluate its applicability more broadly. We described several benefits of endgame solving in large imperfect-information games, including exact computation of Nash equilibria in abstracted endgames, the ability to compute certain equilibrium refinements, the ability to compute finer-grained, history-aware, and strategy-biased abstractions in endgames, and a solution to the off-tree problem. We presented an efficient algorithm for performing endgame solving in very large imperfect-information games and showed that it led to a significantly stronger performance against the strongest no-limit Texas Hold'em agents from the 2013 computer poker competition, utilizing a new variance-reduction technique that we described.

This work opens many interesting avenues for future research. We showed that endgame solving can produce strategies with high exploitability in certain games, while it guarantees low exploitability in others. It would be interesting to study where different game classes fall on this spectrum. It is possible that for interesting classes of games—perhaps even classes that include variants of poker—endgame solving is guaranteed to produce strategies with low exploitability. We would also like to study various subdivisions of a game into a trunk and endgames, to experiment on additional game classes, to experiment with the refinements we described, and to develop improved variance-reduction techniques.

APPENDIX

A. NO-LIMIT TEXAS HOLD'EM POKER

No-limit Texas Hold'em is the most popular variant of poker among humans, and the two-player version is the game of most active research in the computer poker community currently. This game works as follows. Initially two players each have a *stack* of chips (worth \$20,000 in the computer poker competition). One player, called the *small blind*, initially puts \$50 worth of chips in the middle, while the other player, called the *big blind*, puts \$100 worth of chips in the middle. The chips in the middle are known as the *pot*, and will go to the winner of the hand.

Next, there is an initial round of betting. The player whose turn it is can choose from three available options:

- *Fold:* Give up on the hand, surrendering the pot to the opponent.
- *Call:* Put in the minimum number of chips needed to match the number of chips put into the pot by the opponent. For example, if the opponent has put in \$1000 and we have put in \$400, a call would require putting in \$600 more. A call of zero chips is also known as a *check*.
- *Bet:* Put in additional chips beyond what is needed to call. A bet can be of any size up to the number of chips a player has left in his stack. If the opponent has just bet, then our additional bet is also called a *raise*.

The initial round of betting ends if a player has folded, if there has been a bet and a call, or if both players have checked. If the round ends without a player folding, then three public cards are revealed face-up on the table (called the *flop*) and a second round of betting occurs. Then one more public card is dealt (called the *turn*) and a third round of betting, followed by a fifth public card (called the *river*) and a final round of betting. If a player ever folds, the other player wins all the chips in the pot. If the final betting round is completed without a player folding, then both players reveal their private cards, and the player with the best hand wins the pot (it is divided equally if there is a tie).

In the experiments, we will be solving endgames after the final public card is dealt but before the final round of betting. (Thus, the endgame contains no more chance events, and only publicly observable actions of both players remain.)

B. EXAMPLE

In this section we demonstrate the operation of our algorithm on an example hand of no-limit Texas Hold'em. Recall that blinds are \$50 and \$100 and that both players start with \$20,000. In the example hand, we are in the small blind with 8dTh. We raise to \$250, the opponent re-raises to \$750, and we call (there is now \$1500 in the pot). The flop is Jc6s2c. The opponent checks and we check. The turn is Kd. The opponent checks, we bet \$375, and he calls (there is now \$2250 in the pot). The river is Qc. Up until this point we have just played according to the precomputed base strategy; the endgame-solving algorithm begins now.

According to the pseudocode for Algorithm 1, the first step is to compute the joint prior hand distribution D from the base strategies, using Algorithm 2. This took 0.433 seconds. We then compute the equities E_i for each player, using Algorithm 1. This took 0.015 seconds.

The next step is to look at the betting abstraction that has been precomputed for this specific pot/stack size (pot size of \$2250 and stack sizes of \$18875). Note that for this particular hand all of the opponent's actions before the river fell inside of our betting abstraction; however, if they had not, and we were forced to use an action translation mapping to map his action to an action in our betting abstraction, we would be able to correct our misperception of the pot size at this point, by selecting the precomputed betting abstraction for the actual pot/stack size (as opposed to the size that assumed he played an action in our betting abstraction). This solves the "off-tree" problem, discussed in the paper.

The betting abstraction for a pot size of \$2250 has 196 betting sequences for each player. For this hand we used a betting abstraction parameter of $T = 10000$ (while for the experiments described in the paper, we used $T = 7500$). Therefore, we will use $k_i = \lfloor \frac{10000}{196} \rfloor = 51$ card buckets for each player for this hand.

Next, we compute card abstractions for both players We used used a top bucket parameter of $\alpha = 0.995$ (while for the experiments described in the paper, we used $\alpha = 0.99$). After applying our card abstraction algorithm for both players, the resulting abstractions had 38 and 35 buckets respectively for the two players (since not all of the 51 hand equity intervals contained hands). Computing these took 0.008 seconds.

Our actual hand (8dTh) had rank 296 (out of 1081) and actually had an equity of 0 vs. the opponent's hand distribution (we thought the opponent would never play the hand the way he did so far with a worse hand than 8dTh). This places us in bucket 0 (the worst bucket, out of 35). By contrast, if the opponent had our hand, he would have an equity of 0.336 against our hand distribution, and would be in bucket 8 (where his buckets range from 0–37).

We then construct the LP matrices for the resulting abstracted endgame, which took 0.15 seconds, and then compute an exact equilibrium by solving the LP using Gurobi's parallel LP solver (it took 1.051 seconds to construct the LP instance and 5.328 seconds to solve it). Overall, the endgame-solving algorithm took 6.985 seconds for this hand.

The opponent checked for his initial action on the river. The betting abstraction for this hand had nine available options for the first action for each player: check, 0.1 pot, $\frac{1}{3}$ pot, $\frac{2}{3}$ pot, pot, 1.5 pot, 2 pot, 3 pot, all-in. The strategy from our endgame solver said for us to check with probability 0.742, bet $\frac{2}{3}$ pot with probability 0.140, bet pot with probability 0.103, and bet 2 pot with probability 0.014.

C. VARIANCE-REDUCTION TECHNIQUE

When comparing the performance of one version of an agent A_1 to another version that is identical except that it plays differently on endgames A_2, one would like to take advantage of the fact that the agents play identically up until the endgames in order to evaluate the performance difference more efficiently. Ideally, we could play A_1 against a given opponent, and when the endgame is reached, evaluate how both A_1 and A_2 would do on that same endgame given the trunk history. However, such a technique is not possible on the poker competition test server. All that is allowed is to play A_1 and A_2 against an opponent for a full set of matches. The agents may reach endgames on different hands, or may reach different endgames even on the same hands (since both our agent and the opponent may be playing randomized strategies before the endgames).

One possible approach for reducing variance would be to only consider hands where both A_1 and A_2 arrive at the same endgame (the same betting history was played). It turns out that this approach is actually biased, so it cannot be applied to accurately measure performance. A second approach, that it turns out is unbiased, would be to only consider the hands where both agents arrive at *some* endgame (though not necessarily the same one). If we only consider these hands, then the difference in performance between the two agents is an unbiased estimator of their true performance difference. This would allow us to achieve statistical significance using a smaller sample of hands.

PROPOSITION 3. *Let A_1 and A_2 be two algorithms that differ in play only for endgames. Then the difference in performance looking at only the hands where both make it to the same endgame is not an unbiased estimator of the overall performance difference.*

PROOF. Suppose there were only two betting sequences and both make it to the river, where the first one (A) happens 99% of the time and the second one (B) happens 1% of the time. Then the probability that both hands hit the river with B on any particular hand is 0.01%, and the probability that both hands hit the river with A with any particular hand is 98.01%. So if you look at all hands where both hit the river with the same sequence, there would be only 1 (B) for every 9802 (A) sequences. □

PROPOSITION 4. *Let A_1 and A_2 be two algorithms that differ in play only for endgames. Then the difference in performance looking at only the hands where both make it to some (but not necessarily the same) endgame is an unbiased estimator of the overall performance difference.*

PROOF. For each history that leads into an endgame h_i, let p_i be the probability that h_i is played when we use the base strategy against the opponent O. Then the expectation of the difference in payoff between playing A_1 (base strategy) and A_2 (endgame solver) against O is

$$\begin{aligned} & \sum_i \left[p_i \left(U(A_1, O, h_i) - U(A_2, O, h_i)\right)\right] \\ = & \sum_i \left[p_i U(A_1, O, h_i)\right] - \sum_i \left[p_i U(A_2, O, h_i)\right] \end{aligned}$$

Suppose that we look at performance over all hands where both algorithms make it to some endgame. The probability that A_1 makes it to the endgame with history h_i and A_2 makes it to the endgame with history h_j is $p_i p_j$. Thus, the expectation of the payoff difference is

$$\begin{aligned} & \sum_i \sum_j \left[p_i p_j \left(U(A_1, O, h_i) - U(A_2, O, h_j)\right)\right] \\ = & \sum_i \sum_j \left[p_i p_j U(A_1, O, h_i)\right] - \sum_i \sum_j \left[p_i p_j U(A_2, O, h_j)\right] \\ = & \sum_i \left[p_i U(A_1, O, h_i) \sum_j p_j\right] - \sum_j \left[p_j U(A_2, O, h_j) \sum_i p_i\right] \\ = & \sum_i \left[p_i U(A_1, O, h_i)\right] - \sum_j \left[p_j U(A_2, O, h_j)\right] \\ = & \sum_i \left[p_i U(A_1, O, h_i)\right] - \sum_i \left[p_i U(A_2, O, h_i)\right] \end{aligned}$$

□

REFERENCES

[1] R. E. Bellman. On the application of dynamic programming to the determination of optimal play in chess and checkers. *National Academy of Sciences of the United States of America*, 53:244–247, 1965.

[2] D. Billings, N. Burch, A. Davidson, R. Holte, J. Schaeffer, T. Schauenberg, and D. Szafron. Approximating game-theoretic optimal strategies for full-scale poker. In *Proceedings of the 18th International Joint Conference on Artificial Intelligence (IJCAI)*, 2003.

[3] N. Burch, M. Johanson, and M. Bowling. Solving imperfect information games using decomposition. In *Proceedings of the AAAI Conference on Artificial Intelligence (AAAI)*, 2014.

[4] S. Ganzfried and T. Sandholm. Tartanian5: A heads-up no-limit Texas Hold'em poker-playing program. In *Computer Poker Symposium at the National Conference on Artificial Intelligence (AAAI)*, 2012.

[5] S. Ganzfried and T. Sandholm. Action translation in extensive-form games with large action spaces: Axioms, paradoxes, and the pseudo-harmonic mapping. In *Proceedings of the International Joint Conference on Artificial Intelligence (IJCAI)*, 2013.

[6] S. Ganzfried, T. Sandholm, and K. Waugh. Strategy purification and thresholding: Effective non-equilibrium approaches for playing large games. In *Proceedings of the International Conference on Autonomous Agents and Multi-Agent Systems (AAMAS)*, 2012.

[7] A. Gilpin and T. Sandholm. A competitive Texas Hold'em poker player via automated abstraction and real-time equilibrium computation. In *Proceedings of the National Conference on Artificial Intelligence (AAAI)*, 2006.

[8] A. Gilpin and T. Sandholm. Better automated abstraction techniques for imperfect information games, with application to Texas Hold'em poker. In *Proceedings of the International Conference on Autonomous Agents and Multi-Agent Systems (AAMAS)*, 2007.

[9] I. Gurobi Optimization. Gurobi optimizer reference manual, 2014.

[10] S. Hoda, A. Gilpin, J. Peña, and T. Sandholm. Smoothing techniques for computing Nash equilibria of sequential games. *Mathematics of Operations Research*, 35(2):494–512, 2010.

[11] E. Jackson. A time and space efficient algorithm for approximately solving large imperfect information games. In *AAAI Workshop on Computer Poker and Incomplete Information*, 2014.

[12] M. Johanson. Measuring the size of large no-limit poker games. Technical report, University of Alberta, 2013.

[13] M. Johanson, N. Burch, R. Valenzano, and M. Bowling. Evaluating state-space abstractions in extensive-form games. In *Proceedings of the International Conference on Autonomous Agents and Multi-Agent Systems (AAMAS)*, 2013.

[14] D. Koller, N. Megiddo, and B. von Stengel. Fast algorithms for finding randomized strategies in game trees. In *Proceedings of the 26th ACM Symposium on Theory of Computing (STOC)*, pages 750–760, 1994.

[15] P. B. Miltersen and T. B. Sørensen. Computing proper equilibria of zero-sum games. In *Computers and Games*, pages 200–211, 2006.

[16] P. B. Miltersen and T. B. Sørensen. Fast algorithms for finding proper strategies in game ttrees. In *Proceedings of the Annual ACM-SIAM Symposium on Discrete Algorithms (SODA)*, pages 874–883, 2008.

[17] P. B. Miltersen and T. B. Sørensen. Computing a quasi-perfect equilibrium of a two-player game. *Economic Theory*, 42(1):175–192, 2010.

[18] J. Schaeffer, Y. Björnsson, N. Burch, R. Lake, P. Lu, and S. Sutphen. Building the checkers 10-piece endgame databases. In *Advances in Computer Games 10*, 2003.

[19] D. Schnizlein, M. Bowling, and D. Szafron. Probabilistic state translation in extensive games with large action sets. In *Proceedings of the 21st International Joint Conference on Artificial Intelligence (IJCAI)*, 2009.

[20] K. Waugh, M. Zinkevich, M. Johanson, M. Kan, D. Schnizlein, and M. Bowling. A practical use of imperfect recall. In *Proceedings of the Symposium on Abstraction, Reformulation and Approximation (SARA)*, 2009.

[21] M. Zinkevich, M. Bowling, M. Johanson, and C. Piccione. Regret minimization in games with incomplete information. In *Proceedings of the Annual Conference on Neural Information Processing Systems (NIPS)*, 2007.

Discretization of Continuous Action Spaces in Extensive-Form Games

Christian Kroer
Computer Science Department
Carnegie Mellon University
5000 Forbes Ave
Pittsburgh, PA, USA
ckroer@cs.cmu.edu

Tuomas Sandholm
Computer Science Department
Carnegie Mellon University
5000 Forbes Ave
Pittsburgh, PA, USA
sandholm@cs.cmu.edu

ABSTRACT

Extensive-form games are a powerful tool for modeling a large range of multiagent scenarios. However, most solution algorithms require discrete, finite games. In contrast, many real-world domains require modeling with continuous action spaces. This is usually handled by heuristically discretizing the continuous action space without solution quality bounds. In this paper we address this issue. Leveraging recent results on abstraction solution quality, we develop the first framework for providing bounds on solution quality for discretization of continuous action spaces in extensive-form games. For games where the error is Lipschitz-continuous in the distance of a continuous point to its nearest discrete point, we show that a uniform discretization of the space is optimal. When the error is monotonically increasing in distance to nearest discrete point, we develop an integer program for finding the optimal discretization when the error is described by piecewise linear functions. This result can further be used to approximate optimal solutions to general monotonic error functions. Finally we discuss how our theory applies to several practical problems for which no solution quality bounds could be derived before.

Categories and Subject Descriptors

I.2.11 [**Distributed Artificial Intelligence**]: Multiagent systems; J.4.a [**Social and Behavioral Sciences**]: Economics

General Terms

Algorithms; Theory; Economics

Keywords

Extensive-form games; Nash equilibrium; equilibrium finding; discretization; continuous action spaces

1. INTRODUCTION

Game-theoretic equilibrium concepts play an increasingly important role in prescribing how agents should act in multiagent settings. The problem of computing Nash equilibria and related concepts has received significant attention in the literature (e.g., [28, 27, 12, 18]). Extensive-form games are an especially powerful class of games, that model many sequential real-world domains, such as sequential auctions, negotiation, security domains, cybersecurity, medical applications of game theory, and recreational games such as poker and billiards [1, 34, 29, 8, 9, 35].

The computational literature has largely focused on games where the action spaces are discrete at every node of the game. Indeed, most algorithms for solving extensive-form games require this (e.g. [39, 42, 25, 17, 32]). (One notable exception to this was introduced by Johanson et al. [20], where a technique was demonstrated for handling continuous action spaces for nature in a fairly restricted sense.) However, not all games encountered in practice are discrete. Sources of continuity include noise (e.g. Gaussian) being modeled by a nature node, bid sizes in auctions, betting sizes in poker games, type profiles in mechanism design, and power levels in jamming games.

In the past, such continuity has largely been handled by heuristic discretization, with no theoretical guarantees on solution quality. In contrast, we develop the first general bounds on solution quality for discretizations of continuous action spaces in a very broad class of games. Building on recent results on abstraction in extensive-form games [23], we show how to discretize continuous action spaces in a way that gives theoretical bounds on solution quality when using any Nash equilibrium computed in the discretized game to form a strategy in the full (continuous) game. This is highly nontrivial because abstraction in games is *pathological* unlike in single-agent settings such as MDPs: there are cases where the (best) equilibrium strategy computed from a fine-grained abstraction is worse (more exploitable) than the (worst) equilibrium computed from a coarser abstraction, when measured on the original unabstracted game [40]!

We then proceed to investigate the computation of discretizations that minimize an error bound. We first formulate the general problem, making only the assumption that the error bound function is *monotonic*, which intuitively requires that the error gets worse the farther a point gets from the discrete point to which it maps. Since our problem formulation consists of linear constraints, this immediately leads to the conclusion that convex error functions can typically be minimized in polynomial time. We then go on to consider error functions of the form derived in our theoretical solution-quality bounds. We show that when individual leaf and nature node error functions are linear, and nature always picks uniformly over continuous action intervals, the

Appears in: *Proceedings of the 14th International Conference on Autonomous Agents and Multiagent Systems (AAMAS 2015), Bordini, Elkind, Weiss, Yolum (eds.), May 4–8, 2015, Istanbul, Turkey.*

bound-minimizing solution is to uniformly discretize each continuous interval. We further show how to decompose the problem and we develop a general framework for optimizing the decomposed formulation for convex functions. We then develop a mixed-integer program (MIP) for computing optimal discretizations when only player action spaces are being discretized and the error functions are piecewise linear.

Our paper is similar in spirit to two recent strands of research in game solving. First is the bounded abstraction literature. Our bounds leverage recent results in game abstraction [23]. In addition to that work, solution-quality bounds have also been obtained for imperfect-recall games. Lanctot et al. [26] give solution-quality bounds for running the counterfactual regret minimization algorithm on an imperfect-recall abstraction of a perfect-recall game. Kroer and Sandholm [24] give solution-quality bounds on implementing Nash equilibria computed from imperfect-recall abstractions in the original perfect-recall game. Both sets of results allow only information abstraction, not action removal, and thus cannot discretize continuous actions. Gilpin and Sandholm [12] give lossless abstraction results and algorithms. These are for a specialized class of games called *games of ordered signals*, and apply only to finite-sized games. Similarly, Basilico and Gatti [2] give bounds for another finite specialized class of games called *Patrolling Security Games.* There have been several recent papers on evaluating the quality of an abstraction after the fact—typically for games with discrete action spaces [13, 19, 20, 21]. This is not feasible in most continuous games, and also our goal is to devise good abstractions up front rather than evaluating strategies computed using abstraction after the fact. Sandholm and Singh [36] give solution quality bounds for stochastic games. For the special case of our results where the game is a stochastic game, their results could also be applied, similarly to how we apply the results of Kroer and Sandholm [23]. However, the latter lead to stronger bounds.

Second is the literature on practical game abstraction, which has focused on poker. This literature is less related to our work, as our goal is to derive explicit general bounds, rather than experimentally constructing abstractions that work well for a particular game. The experimental game-specific approach could, of course, potentially yield discretizations with better bounds because specific games can have additional structure. Initially, game abstractions were created by hand, using domain dependent knowledge [38, 4]. More recently, automated abstraction has taken over [11, 12, 42]. This has typically been used for information abstraction, whereas action abstraction is still largely done by hand [14, 37]. Recently, automated action abstraction approaches have also started to emerge [15, 16, 6]. In addition to focusing on theoretical solution quality bounds, our work also does not distinguish between information and action abstraction, as we consider both discretization of nature (information) and player nodes.

2. EXTENSIVE-FORM GAMES

Extensive-form games provide a general framework for modeling scenarios where agents make decisions sequentially (or simultaneously), potentially with imperfect information about the state of the game. Here we give a short formal description. For a complete description see Osborne and Rubinstein [31]. An extensive-form game is a tuple $\Gamma = \langle N, A, S, Z, \mathcal{H}, \sigma_0, u, \mathcal{I} \rangle$. N is the set of players. A is the set of all actions in the game. S is a set of nodes corresponding to sequences of actions. They form a tree with root node $r \in S$. At each node s, it is the turn of some Player $P(s)$ who gets to choose an action from action set A_s. Each branch at s denotes a different choice in A_s. The set of all nodes where Player i is active is denoted by $S_i = \{s \in S : P(s) = i\}$. $Z \subset S$ is the set of leaf nodes, where $u_i(z)$ is the utility to Player i of node z. We assume, without loss of generality, that all utilities are non-negative. Z_s is the subset of leaf nodes reachable from node s. $\mathcal{H}_i \subseteq \mathcal{H}$ is the set of heights in the game tree where Player i acts. $\mathcal{H}_0$ is the set of heights where nature acts. σ_0 specifies the probability distribution for nature, with $\sigma_0(s, a)$ denoting the probability of nature choosing outcome a at node s.

$\mathcal{I}_i \subseteq \mathcal{I}$ is the set of information sets where Player i acts. $\mathcal{I}_i$ partitions S_i. For any two nodes s_1, s_2 in the same information set I, Player i cannot distinguish among them, and $A_{s_1} = A_{s_2}$.

Perfect recall means that no player forgets anything that that player observed. Formally, for every Player $i \in N$, information set $I \in \mathcal{I}_i$, and nodes $s_1, s_2 \in I$, the sequence of actions performed by Player i is the same for s_1 and s_2.

We denote by σ_i a *behavioral strategy* for Player i. For each information set I where it is the player's turn to move, it assigns a probability distribution over the actions A_I at the information set. $\sigma_i(I, a)$ is the probability of playing action a. A *strategy profile* $\sigma = (\sigma_0, \dots, \sigma_n)$ consists of a behavioral strategy for each player. We will often use $\sigma(I, a)$ to mean $\sigma_i(I, a)$, since the information set uniquely specifies which Player i is active. As described above, randomness external to the players is captured by the nature outcomes σ_0. Using this notation allows us to treat nature as a player when convenient. We let $\sigma_{I \to a}$ denote the strategy profile obtained from σ by having Player i deviate to taking action a at $I \in \mathcal{I}_i$. The probability of reaching node s is $\pi^\sigma(s) = \Pi_{\{\bar{s},\bar{a}\} \in X_s} \sigma(\bar{s}, \bar{a})$ where X_s is the set of pairs of nodes and actions on the path from the root to s. $\pi^\sigma(I) = \sum_{s \in I} \pi^\sigma(s)$ is the probability of reaching any node in I. For probabilities over nature, $\pi_0^\sigma = \pi_0^{\bar{\sigma}}$ for all $\sigma, \bar{\sigma}$, so we can ignore the strategy profile superscript and write π_0. Finally, for all behavioral strategies, the subscript $-i$ refers to the same definition, but without Player i. Given a strategy profile σ, we let $u_i(\sigma) = \sum_{z \in Z} \pi^\sigma(z) u_i(z)$ denote the expected utility of player i under σ. We let $u_i(\sigma_i, \sigma_{-i})$ denote the same quantity, allowing us to swap the strategy for player i.

We denote by t_a^s be the node transitioned to by performing action $a \in A_s$ at any node s.

2.1 Continuous action spaces

We will assume that we are dealing with a game Γ, where one or more nodes $s \in S$ have one or more continuous action intervals $A_{s,c} = [\alpha_{s,c}, \beta_{s,c}] \subseteq A_s$ for $c \in C_s$, where C_s is an index set of the continuous action spaces at s.

Let S_a be the set of nodes in the subtree reached by taking action $a \in A_{s,c}$ at node s. We assume there is a one-to-one mapping $\phi_{a,\hat{a}} = \phi_{\hat{a},a}$ between S_a and $S_{\hat{a}}$ for any two actions $a, \hat{a} \in A_{s,c}$, where nodes at a given height map onto nodes at the same height, and the condition of Definition 1 is satisfied. Intuitively, the condition requires that nodes that are mapped to each other are either (1) in the same information set, or (2) their information sets contain no nodes from outside the (infinitely large) set of subtrees reachable by taking

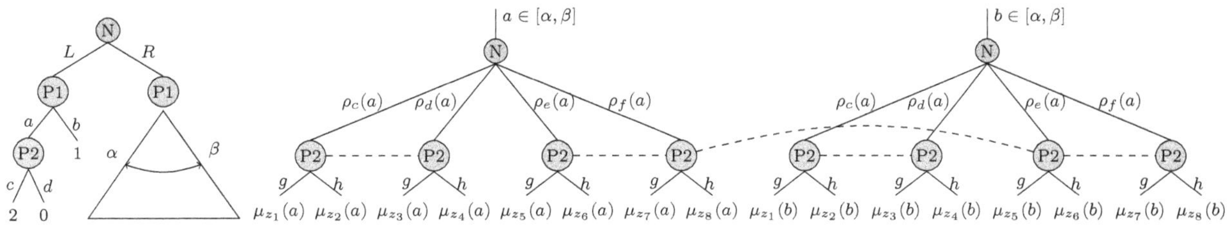

Figure 1: An example of a game tree with the triangle representing a subtree with a continuous action space at the node.

actions from $A_{s,c}$ at s, and for any other node in the same information set and same subtree, the nodes mapped to must similarly be in the same information set.

DEFINITION 1. *For any node $\hat{s} \in S_a$ in the subtree at $a \in A_{s,c}$, we require one of the two following conditions to hold for all a':*

1. $\phi_{a,a'}(\hat{s}) \in I_{\hat{s}}$
2. $I_{\hat{s}} \subset \bigcup_{\bar{a} \in [\alpha_{s,c}, \beta_{s,c}]} S_{\bar{a}}$, and for any other node $\bar{s} \in I_{\hat{s}}, \bar{s} \in S_a$: $\phi_{a,a'}(\bar{s}) \in I_{\phi_{a,a'}}(\hat{s})$

For each leaf node $z \in Z_{t^s_a}$ for some $a \in A_{s,c}$, we assume that the payoff to Player i can be described as $u_i(z) = \mu^i_z(a)$, where $\mu^i_z = \mu^i_{\phi_{a,\hat{a}}(z)}$ for all $\hat{a} \in A_{s,c}$. Intuitively, all leaf nodes that map to each other have their payoffs described by the same function, with the actual value depending on the choice of a. Similarly, the probability of each outcome at each nature node s' in the subtree rooted at t^s_a is described by a function $\rho_{s'}(a)$ where $\rho_{s'} = \rho_{\phi_{a,\hat{a}}}(s')$ for all $\hat{a} \in A_{s,c}$.

Since we require a bijection mapping $\phi_{a,\hat{a}}$ between the subtrees for any two actions $a, \hat{a} \in [\alpha_{s,c}, \beta_{s,c}]$ for each node s with continuous action interval c, the infinitely many subtrees can equivalently be thought of as infinitely many instantiations of a single game-tree prototype, where payoffs and nature outcome probabilities are parameterized by the choice of $a \in [\alpha_{s,c}, \beta_{s,c}]$, and the information set topology of the instantiations satisfy Definition 1.

An example game is shown in Figure 1. On the left is a game with three players: nature(N), Player 1 ($P1$), and Player 2 ($P2$). Nature first chooses between L and R (with some unspecified fixed probability distribution). If L is chosen, a discrete subgame is reached. If R is chosen, $P1$ has a continuous action space $[\alpha, \beta]$. In the middle and right are shown two specific subtrees under the continuous action space, for $P1$ choosing actions $a, b \in [\alpha, \beta]$, respectively. The information set that spans across the trees is an example of one that satisfies Condition 1 of Definition 1, while the one that does not span across the trees satisfies Condition 2.

So far we have described our notation in terms of discretizing a single continuous action space at some node. When there is more than one node with a continuous action space that is being discretized, we have to consider two groups of nodes with continuous action spaces.

The first group is the set of all nodes s that have one or more continuous action intervals, and s is the first node on the path from the root to s with a continuous action space. Let the set of all such nodes be $\mathcal{S}^1 \subseteq S$. These nodes are handled exactly as described above. If there are additional continuous action spaces in the subtree after taking some action $a \in A_{s,c}$ for some s, c, then the bijections between subtrees simply map uncountably many nodes.

The second group is the set of all nodes s' such that there is at least one node-action pair s, a on the path from the root to s', where s has a continuous action space $A_{s,c}$ such that $a \in A_{s,c}$. Let this set of nodes be called $\mathcal{S}^2 \subset S$. Let $\vec{a} \in \mathbb{R}^n$, where n is the number of continuous action spaces leading to s' and including the one at s', such that $a_i \in [\alpha_i, \beta_i]$ where $[\alpha_i, \beta_i]$ is the continuous action space for the i'th node with a continuous action space on the path to s'. We then require that the payoff and nature functions are functions of $\vec{a}$ rather than a single action choice. For fixed choices in the past, the functions then behave exactly as the functions for nodes in $\mathcal{S}^1$.

We fix some ordering of all continuous intervals, and define $\mathcal{A} = \times_{s \in \mathcal{S}^1 \cup \mathcal{S}^2, c \in C_s} A_{s,c}$ to be the Cartesian product over all continuous intervals. We will use j to denote indices into this ordering $\mathbb{I}$. We let $[\alpha_j, \beta_j]$ denote the endpoints of interval $j \in \mathbb{I}$. From now on we will use $\vec{a} \in \mathcal{A}$ to denote elements of this set. A *discretization* is a finite set of points $\mathcal{A}' \subset \mathcal{A}$. The size $|\mathcal{A}'| = m$ is the number of discrete points chosen for each interval. If fewer than m points are desired for some interval $A_{s,c}$ with index $j \in \mathbb{I}$, we can simply let $\vec{a}_j = \vec{a}'_j$ for distinct points $\vec{a}, \vec{a}' \in \mathcal{A}'$. For a node s, we will use $\vec{a}^s$ to refer to the subset of actions taken on the path to s such that the action is part of a continuous action interval. We will overload the notation of the payoff and nature error functions so that for a given f or h for a node s, they take elements $\vec{a} \in \mathcal{A}$ as input, with the implicit understanding that the value of the function depends only on $\vec{a}^s$. We will let $\pi_0(\vec{a})$ denote the product of probabilities over each index j into $\vec{a}$ such that nature acts at $\vec{a}_j$.

The game $\Gamma' = \langle N, A', S', Z', \mathcal{H}, \sigma_0, u, \mathcal{I}' \rangle$ is the discrete extensive-form game obtained by restricting players to selecting actions that are part of the discretization $\mathcal{A}'$.

2.2 Equilibrium notions

In this work, the kind of strategy profiles that we will focus on are ones that constitute an (approximate) *Nash equilibrium*. A Nash equilibrium is a strategy profile σ such that for each agent i and alternative strategy σ'_i: $u_i(\sigma_i, \sigma_{-i}) \geq u_i(\sigma'_i, \sigma_{-i})$. An *$\epsilon$-Nash equilibrium* is a strategy profile where each agent can gain at most ϵ by deviating, as long as the strategies of the other agents are kept fixed. Formally, for each agent i and alternative strategy σ'_i: $u_i(\sigma_i, \sigma_{-i}) + \epsilon \geq u_i(\sigma'_i, \sigma_{-i})$. In a Nash equilibrium, $\epsilon = 0$.

2.3 Discretization mapping and error terms

We will need to reason about the similarity of the full game Γ and the induced game Γ' for a given discretization $\mathcal{A}'$. To do this we will require a mapping of the continuous action space onto the discretization:

DEFINITION 2. *A discretization mapping is a surjective function $g : \mathcal{A} \to \mathcal{A}'$ that maps the continuous action space $\mathcal{A}$ onto the discretization $\mathcal{A}'$. We require that g is decomposable, so for all $\vec{a} \in \mathcal{A}$, $g(\vec{a})_j$ depends only on $\vec{a}_j$. $\mathcal{G}_{\mathcal{A}'}$ denotes the set of legal discretization maps for a given discretization $\mathcal{A}'$.*

The discretization mapping along with the bijections $\phi_{a,a'}$ for all $s \in S, c \in C_s, a, a' \in A_{s,c}$ immediately defines a mapping of the nodes S onto the nodes S'. Denote this node mapping function by $h : S \to S'$. For any node $s \in S \cap S'$, $h(s) = s$. For $s \in S, s \notin S'$, $h(s)$ is the node in S' reached by inductively applying the maps g and $\phi_{\vec{a}^s_j, g(\vec{a}^s)_j}$ at each continuous action space on the path to s.

Due to the constraints in Definition 1, g also leads to an information set mapping, as any two nodes $s_1, s_2 \in I$ for some I must map to the same information set: $h(s_1), h(s_2) \in I'$ for some I'. We let $f : \mathcal{I} \to \mathcal{I}'$ be this information set mapping.

For all three functions g, h, f we also define their inverses g^{-1}, h^{-1}, f^{-1}, that return all intervals $\bar{\mathcal{A}} \subseteq \mathcal{A}$, nodes $\bar{S} \subset S$, and information sets $\bar{\mathcal{I}} \subseteq \mathcal{I}$, respectively, that map onto given $\vec{a} \in \mathcal{A}', s' \in S'$, and $I' \in \mathcal{I}'$, respectively. We denote by $h_I^{-1}(s')$ the intersection $h^{-1}(s') \cap I$.

Given a discretization mapping g, it will be convenient to define aggregate utility error terms for nodes of the real game:

$$\epsilon^R_{s,i} = \begin{cases} \max_{a \in A_s} \epsilon^R_{t^s_a,i} & \text{if } s \text{ is a player node} \\ \int_{a \in A_s} \sigma_0(s,a) \epsilon^R_{t^s_a,i} & \text{if } s \text{ is a nature node} \\ |\mu^i_s(\vec{a}) - \mu^i_s(g(\vec{a}))| & \text{if } s \text{ is a leaf node} \end{cases}$$

Similarly, we define aggregate error terms for nature error. We define the nature distribution error of an information set I and node $s' \in f(I)$ to be

$$\epsilon^0_{I,s'} = \left| \frac{\int_{s \in h_I^{-1}(s')} \sigma_0(s)}{\sigma_0(I)} - \frac{\sigma'_0(s')}{\sigma'_0(f(I))} \right|$$

This is the difference between nature's probability of reaching s' and its probability of reaching any node in $h_I^{-1}(s')$, normalized by the probability of reaching the given information sets. The nature error for information set I is

$$\epsilon^0_I = \sum_{s' \in f(I)} \epsilon^0_{I,s'}$$

For a nature node s at height $k \in \mathcal{H}_0$ and $s' = h(s)$, we define the nature action $a' \in A_{s'}$ error and node error to respectively be

$$\epsilon^0_{s,s',a'} = \left| \sigma'_0(s',a') - \int_{a \in g^{-1}(a') \cap A_s} \sigma_0(s,a) \right|$$

$$\epsilon^0_s = \sum_{a' \in A_{s'}} \epsilon^0_{s,s',a'}$$

The nature error at height k is

$$\epsilon^0_k = \begin{cases} \int_{I \in \mathcal{I}_k} \pi(I) \epsilon^0_I & \text{if } k \notin \mathcal{H}_0 \\ \int_{s \in S_k} \pi(s) \epsilon^0_s & \text{if } k \in \mathcal{H}_0 \end{cases}$$

Finally, we let $\bar{W} = \max_{i \in N, z \in Z} u_i(z)$ be the maximum payoff at any leaf node.

2.4 Strategy mapping

Once a Nash equilibrium has been computed in the discretized game, we need to define a way of converting that strategy profile to a strategy profile for the full game. We perform this mapping in the following simple way. Since all subtrees under discretized intervals have the same shape (based on how we defined the discretization problem in Section 2.1) and thus same number of actions, we can simply implement the same strategy that we computed for a given discretized subtree at all subtrees that map to it. Specifically, let σ' be the strategy profile computed for the discretized game. Then for each real node $s \in S$, we set $\sigma(s,a) = \sigma'(h(s), a')$, where a' is the action at s' that leads to $h(t^s_a)$. For continuous intervals, we simply pick each discrete point a with the probability that it was chosen in the discrete game, and every other action with probability zero. This mapping yields a strategy profile that satisfies the following property, which we will use to derive bounds later:

PROPOSITION 1. *For a strategy profile σ' computed in a discretized game Γ', our method of strategy conversion leads to a strategy profile σ for the full game Γ so that for any information set pair I, I' such that I maps onto I', $\sigma_{-0}(I) > 0$, and $\sigma_i(I) > 0$,*

$$\left| \frac{\sigma(s')}{\sigma(I')} - \sum_{s \in g_I^{-1}(s')} \frac{\sigma(s)}{\sigma(I)} \right| \leq \epsilon^0_{I,s'}$$

PROOF. This follows immediately from how we defined the mapping. □

3. OVERVIEW OF OUR APPROACH

Given some game with continuous action spaces, the goal in this paper is to pick a finite set of points for each continuous action interval. This will induce a finite extensive-form game. A (potentially approximate) Nash equilibrium is then computed in the discrete game. The computed Nash equilibrium is then mapped to a strategy profile in the full (continuous) game. Figure 2 illustrates the approach.

Under reasonable assumptions, we will derive solution quality bounds for any Nash equilibrium computed in the abstraction when implemented in the full game. More specifically, we will show that such strategy profiles constitute ϵ-Nash equilibria in the full game, where the ϵ depends on the error terms we defined in the previous section. These results are anlogous to the solution-quality results for discrete games [23, 24].

4. DISCRETIZATION QUALITY BOUNDS

We start by showing an error bound on solution quality for any given discretization and discretization mapping, leveraging a recent result of Kroer and Sandholm [23].

THEOREM 2. *For any game Γ with continuous action spaces $\mathcal{A}$ that satisfy the constraint given in Definition 1, discretization $\mathcal{A}' \subset \mathcal{A}$, and discretization mapping $g : \mathcal{A} \to \mathcal{A}'$, any Nash equilibrium σ computed in Γ' constitutes an ϵ-Nash equilibrium when implemented in Γ, where*

$$\epsilon = \max_i \{2\epsilon^R_{s,i} + \sum_{k \in \mathcal{H}_i} \epsilon^0_k \bar{W}\} + 2 \sum_{k \in \mathcal{H}_0} \epsilon^0_k \bar{W}$$

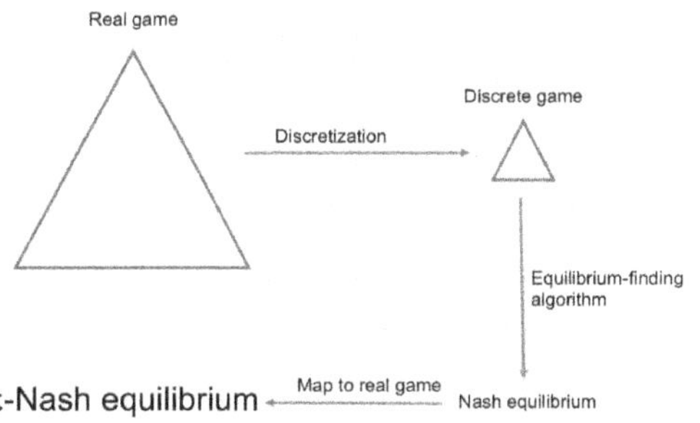

Figure 2: An overview of our discretization approach.

PROOF. We can view the game Γ' obtained by this discretization as an abstraction, where g defines a mapping of each real action a to some abstract action a'. Coupled with the bijection $\phi_{a,a'}$, this induces a node mapping h and information set mapping f, as argued in Section 2.3.

Theorem 4.2 of Kroer and Sandholm [23] gives error bound results for abstractions like this. To see that f indeed forms a surjective function that respects h, consider Conditions 1 and 2 of Definition 1, which ensure that any discretization induces an information set mapping. First consider when Condition 1 is satisfied. In this case the information set mapping is obviously respected, as the nodes that map to each other were already in the same information set.

Now consider any information set I such that a node $s \in I$ is mapped onto another node $\hat{s} \in \hat{I}, \hat{I} \neq I$. Condition 2 ensures that this only happens for information sets completely contained in the subtrees rooted at the continuous interval in question. We have to show that I is surjectively mapped onto $\hat{I}$. Condition 2 states that for any other node $\bar{s} \in I$, $\bar{s}$ must map to a node in the same information set as $\hat{s}$. Thus we just have to verify that every node $s^* \in \hat{I}$ has a node from I mapped onto it. This is immediately seen by applying Definition 1 to the bijection from the perspective if $\hat{I}$, as the bijection has to be the same when applying the definition in both directions.

Theorem 4.2 of Kroer and Sandholm [23] also requires that the strategy implemented in the full game is an *undivided lifted strategy*. We did not quite guarantee this property with our strategy mapping described in Section 2.4. However, this property is only used in the very last step of the proof of Theorem 4.2 in their paper, where they use it to apply Proposition 3.1 of their paper. Instead, we can apply our Proposition 1, which achieves the same effect.

The result as presented by Kroer and Sandholm [23] takes the maximum nature outcome error for each height. Their proof is easily modified to take the expected value, ϵ^0_k, instead, as we do in the theorem. (This approach was also taken by Kroer and Sandholm [24].) □

The bounds as given here are in their most general form. In particular, the two nature error terms $\sum_{k\in\mathcal{H}_i} \epsilon^0_k \overline{W}$ and $2\sum_{k\in\mathcal{H}_0} \epsilon^0_k \overline{W}$ are not given in terms of the functions ρ_s that describe the change in nature outcome probabilities. ϵ^0_k can easily be bounded for all k in $\mathcal{H}_i$ and $\mathcal{H}_0$ respectively:

$$\epsilon^0_k \leq \int_{I\in\mathcal{I}_k} \pi(I) \sum_{s'\in f(I)} \left| \int_{s\in h_I^{-1}(s')} \pi_0(\vec{a}^s) - \pi_0(\vec{a}^{s'}) \right| = \xi^0_k$$

$$\epsilon^0_k \leq \int_{s\in S_k} \pi(s) \sum_{a'\in A_{s'}} \left| \int_{a\in g_I^{-1}(a')} \sigma_0(s,a) - \sigma_0(s',a') \right| = \xi^0_k$$

This gives the following corollary:

COROLLARY 3. *For any game Γ with continuous action spaces $\mathcal{A}$ that satisfy the constraint given in Definition 1, discretization $\mathcal{A}' \subset \mathcal{A}$, and discretization mapping $g : \mathcal{A} \to \mathcal{A}'$, any Nash equilibrium σ computed in Γ' constitutes an ϵ-Nash equilibrium when implemented in Γ, where*

$$\epsilon = \max_i \{2\epsilon^R_{s,i} + \sum_{k\in\mathcal{H}_i} \xi^0_k \overline{W}\} + 2\sum_{k\in\mathcal{H}_0} \xi^0_k \overline{W}$$

The ξ^0_k terms do not diverge. While an infinite sum is taken in both cases, the terms are probability weighted, and $\int_{I\in\mathcal{I}_k} \pi(I) = 1, \int_{s\in S_k} \pi(s) = 1$. Since we are dealing with probability distributions, we can take the maximum over $\mathcal{I}_k$ or S_k. In practical settings, it may be desireable to take several maxima. First, in the current form of both Theorem 2 and Corollary 3, the bound depends on the strategy profile of the players, not just nature. To make the bound independent of player actions, one can take the maximum over player actions. Second, instead of computing the infinite sum of errors over $\mathcal{I}_k$ or S_k, it may be useful to take the probability-weighted sum of errors over discrete points, and then compute the maximum error over each discrete point.

5. DISCRETIZATION ALGORITHMS

In this section we consider general bounded discretization problems that are largely independent of the specific error bound to be minimized. This means that our algorithms will apply to the results from Section 4, and also to any (potentially stronger or more general) bounds obtained in the future, as long as they fall under the setting described in Section 5.1.

5.1 The optimization problem

We consider a more general class of problems than those described in Section 2.1. We consider a game Γ where one or more $s \in S$ has a continuous action space. We again let $\mathcal{A}$ be the set of all intervals to be discretized with index set $\mathbb{I}$ and let $\vec{a}^l_j$ refer to the k_j discrete points chosen for interval j. We assume the points in the discretization are ordered, so $\vec{a}^l_j < \vec{a}^{l+1}_j$ for all $j \in \mathbb{I}, l \in [k_j]$.

We start by formulating the optimization problem very generally. We assume that we have an error bounding function $\Psi : \mathcal{A}^k \times \mathcal{G}_{\mathcal{A}} \to \mathbb{R}$ that takes as input a discretization $\mathcal{A}'$ and discretization map g and returns a real-valued error bound $\Psi(\mathcal{A}', g)$. We make two innocuous assumptions about Ψ to represent the natural condition that the error increases the further an actual point is from the discrete point to which it maps.

First, each point maps to its nearest lower or upper discrete point. Formally, for all $j \in \mathbb{I}$, and any point a_l, $\vec{a}^l_j < a_l < \vec{a}^{l+1}_j$ not in the discretization, Ψ is minimized at $g(a_l) = \vec{a}^l_j$ or $g(a_l) = \vec{a}^{l+1}_j$.

Second, for all $j \in \mathbb{I}$, and any two points $a_l, \hat{a}_l$, $\vec{a}^l_j < a_l < \hat{a}_l < \vec{a}^{l+1}_j$ not in the discretization, if Ψ is minimized when $g(\hat{a}_l) = \vec{a}^l_j$ then Ψ is minimized when $g(a_l) = \vec{a}^l_j$, and if Ψ is minimized when $g(a_l) = \vec{a}^{l+1}_j$ then Ψ is minimized when $g(\hat{a}_l) = \vec{a}^{l+1}_j$.

We will say that an error function Ψ that satisfies our two assumptions is *monotonic*. Given a monotonic Ψ and a discretization $\mathcal{A}'$, the optimal mapping for each interval $j \in \mathbb{I}$ can be determined by finding the splitting point between each interval $\left[\vec{a}_j^l, \vec{a}_j^{l+1}\right]$ such that the left side of the splitting point is mapped onto $\vec{a}_j^l$ and right side is mapped onto $\vec{a}_j^{l+1}$.

For each interval $j \in \mathbb{I}$, we introduce real-valued variables $\vec{a}_j^l \in \mathcal{A}_j, l \in [k_j]$ and $g_{s,c}^{\tau}, \tau \in [k_j - 1]$, where k_j is the desired number of discrete points for interval $\mathcal{A}_j$. The variables $\vec{a}_j^l$ represent the discrete points, while g_j^{τ} represents the point between $\vec{a}_j^{\tau}$ and $\vec{a}_j^{\tau+1}$ that separates the interval, such that the points in the interval $\left[\vec{a}_j^{\tau}, g_j^{\tau}\right]$ map onto $\vec{a}_j^{\tau}$ and the points in the interval $\left[g_j^{\tau}, \vec{a}_j^{\tau+1}\right]$ map onto $\vec{a}_j^{\tau+1}$. Since any set of values for $\vec{a}_j^l, g_j^{\tau}$ over all $j \in \mathbb{I}, l \in [k_j], \tau \in [k_j - 1]$ completely specifies a discretization and discretization mapping, we let $\mathcal{A}_v', g_v$ denote the discretization and mapping obtained by a solution. The feasible set of this problem is

$$\mathcal{F} = \left\{ \mathcal{A}_v', g_v : \begin{array}{ll} \vec{a}_j^l \leq \vec{a}_j^{l+1} & \forall j \in \mathbb{I}, l \in [k_j - 1] \\ \vec{a}_j^{\tau} \leq g_j^{\tau} \leq \vec{a}_j^{\tau+1} & \forall j \in \mathbb{I}, \tau \in [k_j - 1] \\ \vec{a}_j^l \in \mathcal{A}_j & \forall j \in \mathbb{I}, l \in [k_j] \\ g_j^{\tau} \in \mathcal{A}_j & \forall j \in \mathbb{I}, \tau \in [k_j - 1] \end{array} \right\} \quad (1)$$

With this notation, we arrive at the most generic form of the optimal discretization problem for monotonic error functions:

$$\min \left\{ \Psi(\mathcal{A}_v', g_v) : (\mathcal{A}_v', g_v) \in \mathcal{F} \right\} \quad (2)$$

Setting $k = 1$, one can see that this is equivalent to minimizing *any* function, so this general form will not get us far. Fortunately, there is often further structure in practical games. In the rest of the algorithms section, we will consider various forms of structure that enable us to design efficient algorithms for finding good discretizations.

5.1.1 *Convex error function*

The constraints specified in (1) are all linear. Thus, if Ψ is convex, solving (2) becomes a convex minimization problem over linear constraints. These are solvable in polynomial time under mild assumptions [3][1]. Perhaps more importantly, large subsets of this class of error functions have practically efficient solution methods—e.g., an error function that is conic-quadratic or semi-definite representable (Ben-Tal and Nemirovski [3] give a thorough discussion of such representability [1]), smooth, or non-smooth with certain structure [30].

5.2 Decomposable error function

In Section 4, we considered error functions that are a mixture of maximums (player nodes) and probability-weighted sums (nature nodes) of the error functions at individual nodes. We now consider how to (recursively) represent such error functions using linear inequalities, for the purpose of computation.

Let $\xi_j : \mathcal{A}_j \times g_j \to \mathbb{R}$ be an error function that gives the error incurred at interval $j \in \mathbb{I}$ when choosing discretization $\mathcal{A}_j'$ and mapping g_j at $\mathcal{A}_j$. Recursively taking the maximum or weighted sum can be implemented by recursively applying the following linear inequalities, where variable e_δ represents the error at a given node or information set δ:

$$\mathcal{E} = \left\{ \begin{array}{l} e_s \geq \sum_{a \in A_s} \sigma_0(s,a) e_{t_a^s} \\ e_s \geq \max_{a \in A_s} e_{t_a^s} \\ e_s \geq \xi_j \end{array} \right\} \quad (3)$$

The same linear formulation can also be used to formulate the error bound in the case where $\xi_s : \mathcal{A} \times g$ are functions that give the error for each leaf and nature node. In a slight abuse of notation, we denote the set of error function solutions described in (3) by $\mathcal{E}$.

If each error function ξ_j depends only on the subset of $\mathcal{A}$ that consists of interval j and any descendant intervals, the discretization problem can be decomposed: find each interval $j \in \mathbb{I}$ that is the first continuous interval from the root to the interval. Each such interval, along with its subtrees and any intervals therein, can be minimized separately.

5.3 Minimizing our bound

We will now study the game class that satisfies Definition 1 and minimization of the bound given in Corollary 3. We will consider various types of error functions.

5.3.1 *Linear error functions*

In this section we consider games Γ where the utility and nature outcome distribution functions μ_z, ρ_s, at all $z \in Z, s \in S$ that are descendants of a continuous interval, are Lipschitz continuous with Lipschitz constant $L_{z/s}$. This encompasses two important practical classes of game: (1) all the functions μ and ρ are linear, and (2) the functions are non-linear but the bound being derived is based on knowing (only) that the functions are Lipschitz continuous.

If all continuous intervals at nature nodes have a uniform distribution, we get the following simple results: all intervals should be discretized into uniform interval sizes.

THEOREM 4. *For a game Γ with continuous action spaces $\mathcal{A}$, where each utility and nature outcome distribution function is Lipschitz continuous with constant $L_{z/s}$ for each leaf z or nature node s, and all continuous nature intervals are uniformly distributed, the bound-minimizing k_j-point discretization at each interval $\mathcal{A}_j'$ is:*

$$\vec{a}_j^l = \alpha_j + \left(l - \frac{1}{2}\right) \cdot \left(\frac{\beta_j - \alpha_j}{k_j}\right) \qquad \forall l \in [k_j]$$

$$g_j^{\tau} = \alpha_j + \tau \cdot \left(\frac{\beta_j - \alpha_j}{k_j}\right) \qquad \forall \tau \in [k_j - 1]$$

We will call this a uniform discretization.

PROOF. Consider such a discretization and mapping. We will show that any other discretization or mapping can not be better. For an interval $j \in \mathbb{I}$ at a player node, this is easily seen. The error of the interval is the maximum error over the interval. Since all functions are linear, this is simply the point $a \in \mathcal{A}_j$ with the largest distance to its discrete point. For a uniform discretization, this is either endpoint α_j, β_j or some inner point g_j^{τ}, which all have distance $\frac{\beta_j - \alpha_j}{2k_j}$. For any other discretization, some point must have distance strictly greater than this to its discrete point, thus worsening the bound.

[1] A heavily and continuously updated version of this book is at `http://www2.isye.gatech.edu/~nemirovs/`.

For an interval $j \in \mathbb{I}$ at some nature node s, we first observe that the error function is convex. The error at each leaf or nature node in the subtrees is linear (and thus convex). The error at each other node is the finite sum or maximum over descendant errors. The error over the interval is the integral over error at each subtree. Since taking finite sums, maxima, and integrals all preserve convexity (see Boyd and Vandenberghe [5] for a calculus of convex functions), we get that the error over the interval is convex. For convex functions, local minimizers are global minimizers. Thus, it is sufficient to show that the derivative is zero at the uniform discretization. Since the subtrees have the same structure, by the conditions given in Definition 1, and the fact that the error functions depends only on the distance, we get that the error between any two points $a_1, a_2 \in \mathcal{A}_j$ can be represented by some function $\Delta(|a_1 - a_2|)$. Using this representation, we consider the error of each interval $[\vec{a}_j^l, g_j^l]$:

$$\int_{\vec{a}_j^l}^{g_j^l} \frac{1}{\beta_j - \alpha_j} \Delta\left(\left|\vec{a}_j^l - t\right|\right) \mathrm{d}t$$

$$= \frac{1}{\beta_j - \alpha_j} \int_0^{g_j^l - \vec{a}_j^l} \Delta(t)\, \mathrm{d}t \tag{4}$$

Using exactly the same approach, we can also get the error of the interval $[g_j^l, \vec{a}_j^{l+1}]$:

$$\frac{1}{\beta_j - \alpha_j} \int_0^{\vec{a}_j^{l+1} - g_j^l} \Delta(t)\, \mathrm{d}t \tag{5}$$

We see that for any subgradient x of (4), $-x$ is a subgradient of (5). Using additivity of subdifferentials (see Rockafellar [33] chapter 23), we get that 0 is a subgradient of g_j^l. We can apply exactly the same approach to each $\vec{a}_j^l$ to see that 0 is a subgradient there as well. □

When the conditions of the above theorem do not hold, the decomposition results from Section 5.2 and the recursive linearization (3) still apply. In the following two subsections, we leverage this fact.

5.3.2 *Convex error functions*

As we pointed out above, taking the maximum, sum, and integral all preserve convexity. Thus, if the error

$$|\mu_z(a) - \mu_z(a')| \quad \text{or} \quad |\rho_s(a) - \rho(a')|$$

at each leaf or nature node can be represented by a convex function, the linear constraints in (3) can be used to represent the overall error as a convex function. As discussed in Section 5.1.1, this would, depending on the specific structure, allow the application of various efficient polynomial-time methods. We do not give specific algorithms here, but merely point out that optimal solutions can be found in polynomial time. In practice, the specific choice of which polynomial-time algorithm to apply should be informed by the exact structure of the error functions of the given game.

5.3.3 *Piecewise linear error functions*

We now consider piecewise linear utility error functions and piecewise linear nature probability error functions for discretizing continuous player action intervals. We do not consider discretizing nature actions here because even with linear functions and a uniform nature distribution, discretizing nature intervals would lead to quadratic error, as shown in the proof of Theorem 4. Even if the actual error functions are not piecewise linear, this can be used for arbitrarily accurate approximation.

Finding a bound-minimizing discretization, subject to a limit on the number of discretization points, is NP-hard. This is easily seen by considering the NP-hardness proof by Kroer and Sandholm [23], and representing their discrete game-abstraction problem using a step function.

However, it can be represented by a MIP, where the number of binary variables is equal to the number of pieces summed over all functions. This number can be significantly decreased if the interval pieces over the different functions μ, ρ under some interval $j \in \mathbb{I}$ align. We use the same variable formulation $\vec{a}_j^l, g_j^l$ as defined in (1), and the feasible set $\mathcal{F}$ remains the same. Consider an interval $j \in \mathbb{I}$ and the set of points where some function in the subtrees at j changes piece. This set of points divides the interval $[\alpha_j, \beta_j]$ into pieces. Let $\mathbb{P}_j$ be an index set into these pieces. The size of $\mathbb{P}_j$ is clearly bounded by the sum of pieces in functions in subtrees at j. We introduce a Boolean variable $b_j^{\gamma,l}, c_j^{\gamma,\tau}$ for each $\gamma \in \mathbb{P}_j$, $l \in [k_j]$, and $\tau \in [k_j - 1]$, representing whether $\vec{a}_j^l, g_j^\tau$ fall into the interval representing piece $\gamma \in \mathbb{P}_j$, respectively. When $b_j^{\gamma,l}(c_j^{\gamma,\tau}) = 1$, we restrict $\vec{a}_j^l(g_j^\tau)$ as follows:

$$\alpha_j^\gamma \cdot b_j^{\gamma,l} \le \vec{a}_j^l, \quad \vec{a}_j^l \le \beta_j^\gamma + (\beta_j - \beta_j^\gamma) \cdot b_j^{\gamma,l}$$

The sum $\sum_{\gamma \in \mathbb{P}_j} b_j^{\gamma,l} = 1$ ensures that only one interval is chosen. The constraints for $c_j^{\gamma,\tau}, g_j^\tau$ are completely analogous. For each leaf node z with piecewise payoff function μ_z^γ, and $l \in [k_j]$, we can then introduce price variables $p_z^l, p_z^l(\vec{a}_j^l), p_z^l(g_j^l) \in \mathbb{R}$, with the latter two for the interval $[\vec{a}_j^l, g_j^l]$, and constrain them linearly as follows:

$$\mathcal{P} = \left\{ \begin{array}{rll} p_z^l \ge & p_z^l(g_j^l) - p_z^l(\vec{a}_j^l) & \\ p_z^l(g_j^l) \ge & \mu_z^\gamma(g_j^l) - M \cdot c_j^{\gamma,\tau} & \forall \gamma \in \mathbb{P}_j \\ p_z^l(\vec{a}_j^l) \le & \mu_z^\gamma(\vec{a}_j^l) + M \cdot b_j^{\gamma,l} & \forall \gamma \in \mathbb{P}_j \end{array} \right\} \tag{6}$$

This is correct for sufficiently large $M \in \mathbb{R}$. We now have variables p_z^l representing each error function for the discrete points, and can apply the linear constraints from (3) to get a linear representation of the overall error. Thus we get the following MIP, where e_r is the objective value at the root according to (3):

$$\min\left\{e_r : e_r \in \mathcal{E}, (\mathcal{A}'_v, g_v) \in \mathcal{F} \cap \mathcal{P}, b_j^{\gamma,l}, c_j^{\gamma,\tau} \in \{0,1\}\right\} \tag{7}$$

6. APPLICATIONS

In this section, we discuss some applications of our results. We will focus on three recent problems that have included continuity in their problem formulation, or discretized away continuity: robust policy optimization under parameter uncertainty [8], security games [41, 22, 29], and sequential wifi-jamming under battery constraints [9].

Chen and Bowling [8] propose the use of zero-sum extensive-form game solving as a way of tractably computing optimally robust policies for Markov Decision Processes (MDPs) with parameter uncertainty. They design robustness criteria that can be implemented via nature first sampling parameter instances, and an opponent then choosing the worst of these. This sampling by nature was necessary in order to get games where the action space for the players is finite. Now, with our discretization-quality results, it is possible to use a broader class of robustness measures that allow continuous action spaces, while obtaining solution quality bounds.

Several papers have investigated continuous settings for security games. These have been for single-shot [22, 41] or repeated Bayesian Stackelberg games [29]. Since our framework is for the more general setting of extensive-form games, our solution-quality bounds apply to all these settings. Furthermore, they would also apply to more sophisticated models that include both sequential actions and imperfect information. Marecki et al. [29] mention as future work the setting where the follower also behaves strategically. Our results immediately yield solution quality bounds for discretizations for this setting.

Another area with continuity is wifi jamming. In recent work, sequential-interaction models were introduced for this domain [9]. These models employ discretized action spaces, where both the jammer and transmitter have a (small) finite set of possible power levels to transmit at. However, this is an abstraction of reality, where software-defined radios mean that action spaces can be continuous (at least up to the bit-precision of the hardware). Using the techniques developed in this paper, we can give solution quality bounds on the utility loss obtained from considering only a discrete number of possible power levels (possibly by padding the game tree with dummy actions to satisfy Definition 1). DeBruhl et al. [9] also mention that in a more realistic model, both transmitter and jammer would be modeled as observing only noisy signals of the actions taken by the other player. Since these observations would be of a continuum, the noise would likewise be continuous. The discretization quality bounds derived here would immediately apply to this setting.

7. DIFFERENCES TO ABSTRACTION PRACTICE IN POKER

We have already discussed how our framework can be used to give theoretical bounds on solution quality in practical scenarios. In particular, we showed that a uniform discretization is optimal for linear error functions (for discretizing nature this required a uniform distribution over the continuous action space). This stands somewhat in contrast to how practical abstractions are created for poker.

Consider no-limit Texas hold'em (NLHE). This game is the premier testbed for (discrete) extensive-form game solving algorithms [34]. Each year, the Annual Computer Poker Competition is held, where research groups submit highly-tuned poker-playing programs. The winning programs are based on computing Nash equilibrium approximations in abstractions of the full extensive-form game [34].

In NLHE, at each betting step, the acting player may bet any amount from the minimum bet to their entire stack of chips. To handle this action space, the top agents devise betting abstractions. These are completely analogous to the discretizations considered in this paper. The payoff functions under the subtrees are all linear in the specific actions chosen. At a cursory glance, one might say that Theorem 4 suggests that the optimal discretization would be uniform. However, the discretizations employed by the poker bots are more akin to a geometric progression. For example, Brown et al. [7] describe using a betting abstraction consisting of $0.5, 0.75, 1, 1.5, 2$ and 5 times the pot size, as well as the all-in action. At the start of betting, all-in is approximately 133 times the pot size. Both examples and experiments by Ganzfried and Sandholm [10] support the idea that the uniform mapping is not optimal.

A potential explanation for this is that the subtrees reached for different choices of bet size technically do not fall under the constraints of Definition 1. Consider a group of bets, say raising in the range of $[1, 2]$ (here we consider continuous bets in this small continuous range due to ease of exposition, one can construct similar examples with larger integer ranges) with a stack size of 2.5. The subtree where the player bets 2 exists as a subset of the subtree at every other betsize. These subsets all map to each other in a way that obeys Definition 1. However, if the player bets 1 instead, the opponent may reraise by 1, in which case the agent can call. This scenario does not exist when betting 2, as the player already bet her entire stack. For any two bet sizes $a_1 < a_2$, these discrepancies due to extra actions exist. To resolve this issue, one could pad the tree with extra actions such that Definition 1 is satisfied, but it is unclear how this would interact with the solution-quality bound, and could thus lead to nonoptimality of the uniform discretization.

8. CONCLUSIONS

We analyzed the problem of developing solution-quality bounds for discretization of extensive-form games with continuous action spaces. To our knowledge, we developed the first such bounds. We developed bounds for a very general class of continuous games: ones where there is a finite set of prototype trees, such that the instantiation of a given prototype has its nature probability outcomes and utilities parameterized by the choice on the continuous intervals. We developed bounds both where they depend on the specific Nash equilibrium (Theorem 2) and where they are independent of the Nash equilibrium chosen (Corollary 3).

We then considered the problem of computing bound-minimizing discretizations. First we developed very general bound-minimization formulations that allow a broad class of error-bounding functions. We discussed how such functions can be minimized in polynomial time when they are convex. We then considered the more specific problem of minimizing our bound developed for Corollary 3. For the case where all utility error and nature probability error functions are Lipschitz continuous (without additional structure), and nature chooses uniformly over each continuous interval, we showed that the bound-minimizing solution is to discretize uniformly. For the case where the error functions at individual nodes can be represented by convex functions, we showed how to generate a convex optimization formulation of the overall problem. We also developed a MIP for piecewise linear error functions, which can also be used for arbitrarily accurate approximation. We also showed how the problem can be decomposed into separately optimizable components.

Ganzfried and Sandholm [10] dicuss randomized mappings, where each real point has a probability distribution over which of its nearest discrete points it maps to. Their experiments strongly suggest that such randomization is desirable. Incorporating randomized mappings in our work could potentially lead to better discretizations, almost certainly in practice, and potentially also in theory. We leave this as future research.

Acknowledgements. This material is based on work supported by the National Science Foundation under grant IIS-1320620.

References

[1] C. Archibald and Y. Shoham. "Modeling Billiards Games". In: *International Conference on Autonomous Agents and Multi-Agent Systems (AAMAS)*. Budapest, Hungary, 2009.

[2] Nicola Basilico and Nicola Gatti. "Automated Abstractions for Patrolling Security Games". In: *Proceedings of the AAAI Conference on Artificial Intelligence (AAAI)*. 2011.

[3] Aharon Ben-Tal and Arkadi Nemirovski. *Lectures on modern convex optimization: analysis, algorithms, and engineering applications*. Vol. 2. Siam, 2001.

[4] Darse Billings, Neil Burch, Aaron Davidson, Robert Holte, Jonathan Schaeffer, Terence Schauenberg, and Duane Szafron. "Approximating Game-Theoretic Optimal Strategies for Full-scale Poker". In: *Proceedings of the 18th International Joint Conference on Artificial Intelligence (IJCAI)*. 2003.

[5] Stephen Boyd and Lieven Vandenberghe. *Convex Optimization*. Cambridge University Press, 2004.

[6] Noam Brown and Tuomas Sandholm. "Regret Transfer and Parameter Optimization". In: *Proceedings of the AAAI Conference on Artificial Intelligence (AAAI)*. 2014.

[7] Noam Brown, Sam Ganzfried, and Tuomas Sandholm. "Hierarchical Abstraction, Distributed Equilibrium Computation, and Post-Processing, with Application to a Champion No-Limit Texas Hold 'em Agent". In: *International Conference on Autonomous Agents and Multi-Agent Systems (AAMAS)*. 2015.

[8] Katherine Chen and Michael Bowling. "Tractable Objectives for Robust Policy Optimization". In: *Proceedings of the Annual Conference on Neural Information Processing Systems (NIPS)*. 2012.

[9] Bruce DeBruhl, Christian Kroer, Anupam Datta, Tuomas Sandholm, and Patrick Tague. "Power napping with loud neighbors: optimal energy-constrained jamming and anti-jamming". In: *Proceedings of the 2014 ACM conference on Security and privacy in wireless & mobile networks*. ACM. 2014, pp. 117–128.

[10] Sam Ganzfried and Tuomas Sandholm. "Action Translation in Extensive-Form Games with Large Action Spaces: Axioms, Paradoxes, and the Pseudo-Harmonic Mapping". In: *Proceedings of the International Joint Conference on Artificial Intelligence (IJCAI)*. 2013.

[11] Andrew Gilpin and Tuomas Sandholm. "A Competitive Texas Hold'em Poker Player via Automated Abstraction and Real-Time Equilibrium Computation". In: *Proceedings of the National Conference on Artificial Intelligence (AAAI)*. 2006, pp. 1007–1013.

[12] Andrew Gilpin and Tuomas Sandholm. "Lossless Abstraction of Imperfect Information Games". In: *Journal of the ACM* 54.5 (2007). Early version in EC-06.

[13] Andrew Gilpin and Tuomas Sandholm. "Expectation-Based versus Potential-Aware Automated Abstraction in Imperfect Information games: An Experimental Comparison Using Poker". In: *Proceedings of the AAAI Conference on Artificial Intelligence (AAAI)*. Short paper. 2008.

[14] Andrew Gilpin, Tuomas Sandholm, and Troels Bjerre Sørensen. "A Heads-Up No-Limit Texas Hold'em Poker Player: Discretized Betting Models and Automatically Generated Equilibrium-Finding Programs". In: *International Conference on Autonomous Agents and Multi-Agent Systems (AAMAS)*. 2008.

[15] John Hawkin, Robert Holte, and Duane Szafron. "Automated action abstraction of imperfect information extensive-form games". In: *Proceedings of the AAAI Conference on Artificial Intelligence (AAAI)*. 2011.

[16] John Hawkin, Robert Holte, and Duane Szafron. "Using sliding windows to generate action abstractions in extensive-form games". In: *Proceedings of the AAAI Conference on Artificial Intelligence (AAAI)*. 2012.

[17] Samid Hoda, Andrew Gilpin, Javier Peña, and Tuomas Sandholm. "Smoothing Techniques for Computing Nash Equilibria of Sequential Games". In: *Mathematics of Operations Research* 35.2 (2010). Conference version appeared in WINE-07, pp. 494–512.

[18] Albert Jiang and Kevin Leyton-Brown. "Polynomial-time computation of exact correlated equilibrium in compact games". In: *Proceedings of the ACM Conference on Electronic Commerce (EC)*. 2011.

[19] Michael Johanson, Kevin Waugh, Michael Bowling, and Martin Zinkevich. "Accelerating Best Response Calculation in Large Extensive Games". In: *Proceedings of the International Joint Conference on Artificial Intelligence (IJCAI)*. 2011.

[20] Michael Johanson, Nolan Bard, Neil Burch, and Michael Bowling. "Finding Optimal Abstract Strategies in Extensive-Form Games". In: *Proceedings of the AAAI Conference on Artificial Intelligence (AAAI)*. 2012.

[21] Michael Johanson, Neil Burch, Richard Valenzano, and Michael Bowling. "Evaluating State-Space Abstractions in Extensive-Form Games". In: *International Conference on Autonomous Agents and Multi-Agent Systems (AAMAS)*. 2013.

[22] Christopher Kiekintveld, Janusz Marecki, and Milind Tambe. "Approximation methods for infinite Bayesian Stackelberg games: modeling distributional payoff uncertainty". In: *10th International Conference on Autonomous Agents and Multiagent Systems AAMAS 2011*. 2011.

[23] Christian Kroer and Tuomas Sandholm. "Extensive-Form Game Abstraction With Bounds". In: *Proceedings of the ACM Conference on Economics and Computation (EC)*. 2014.

[24] Christian Kroer and Tuomas Sandholm. *Extensive-Form Game Imperfect-Recall Abstractions With Bounds.* arXiv. 2014.

[25] Marc Lanctot, Kevin Waugh, Martin Zinkevich, and Michael Bowling. "Monte Carlo Sampling for Regret Minimization in Extensive Games". In: *Proceedings of the Annual Conference on Neural Information Processing Systems (NIPS).* 2009, pp. 1078–1086.

[26] Marc Lanctot, Richard Gibson, Neil Burch, Martin Zinkevich, and Michael Bowling. "No-Regret Learning in Extensive-Form Games with Imperfect Recall". In: *International Conference on Machine Learning (ICML).* 2012.

[27] Richard Lipton, Evangelos Markakis, and Aranyak Mehta. "Playing Large Games Using Simple Strategies". In: *Proceedings of the ACM Conference on Electronic Commerce (ACM-EC).* 2003.

[28] Michael Littman and Peter Stone. "A polynomial-time Nash equilibrium algorithm for repeated games". In: *Proceedings of the ACM Conference on Electronic Commerce (ACM-EC).* 2003.

[29] Janusz Marecki, Gerald Tesauro, and Richard Segal. "Playing repeated Stackelberg games with unknown opponents". In: *International Conference on Autonomous Agents and Multiagent Systems, AAMAS 2012.* 2012.

[30] Yurii Nesterov. "Smooth Minimization of Non-Smooth Functions". In: *Mathematical Programming.* A 103 (2005), pp. 127–152.

[31] Martin J Osborne and Ariel Rubinstein. *A Course in Game Theory.* MIT Press, 1994.

[32] FranÃğois Pays. "An Interior Point Approach to Large Games of Incomplete Information". In: *AAAI Computer Poker Workshop.* 2014.

[33] R. Tyrell Rockafellar. *Convex Analysis.* Princeton University Press, 1970.

[34] Tuomas Sandholm. "The State of Solving Large Incomplete-Information Games, and Application to Poker". In: *AI Magazine* (2010). Special issue on Algorithmic Game Theory, pp. 13–32.

[35] Tuomas Sandholm. "Steering Evolution Strategically: Computational Game Theory and Opponent Exploitation for Treatment Planning, Drug Design, and Synthetic Biology". In: *AAAI Conference on Artificial Intelligence, Senior Member Track.* 2015.

[36] Tuomas Sandholm and Satinder Singh. "Lossy stochastic game abstraction with bounds". In: *Proceedings of the ACM Conference on Electronic Commerce (EC).* 2012.

[37] David Schnizlein, Michael Bowling, and Duane Szafron. "Probabilistic State Translation in Extensive Games with Large Action Sets". In: *Proceedings of the 21st International Joint Conference on Artificial Intelligence (IJCAI).* 2009.

[38] Jiefu Shi and Michael Littman. "Abstraction Methods for Game Theoretic Poker". In: *CG '00: Revised Papers from the Second International Conference on Computers and Games.* 2002.

[39] Bernhard von Stengel. "Efficient Computation of Behavior Strategies". In: *Games and Economic Behavior* 14.2 (1996), pp. 220–246.

[40] Kevin Waugh, David Schnizlein, Michael Bowling, and Duane Szafron. "Abstraction Pathologies in Extensive Games". In: *International Conference on Autonomous Agents and Multi-Agent Systems (AAMAS).* 2009.

[41] Zhengyu Yin and Milind Tambe. "A unified method for handling discrete and continuous uncertainty in Bayesian Stackelberg games". In: *International Conference on Autonomous Agents and Multiagent Systems, AAMAS 2012.* 2012.

[42] Martin Zinkevich, Michael Bowling, Michael Johanson, and Carmelo Piccione. "Regret Minimization in Games with Incomplete Information". In: *Proceedings of the Annual Conference on Neural Information Processing Systems (NIPS).* 2007.

Welfare Effects of Market Making in Continuous Double Auctions

Elaine Wah
ewah@umich.edu

Michael P. Wellman
wellman@umich.edu

Computer Science & Engineering
University of Michigan

ABSTRACT

We investigate the effects of market making on market performance, focusing on allocative efficiency as well as gains from trade accrued by background traders. We employ empirical simulation-based methods to evaluate heuristic strategies for market makers as well as background investors in a variety of complex trading environments. Our market model incorporates private and common valuation elements, with dynamic fundamental value and asymmetric information. In this context, we compare the surplus achieved by background traders in strategic equilibrium, with and without a market maker. Our findings indicate that the presence of the market maker strongly tends to increase not only total surplus across a variety of environments, but also background-trader surplus in thin markets with impatient investors, with urgency captured by a limited trading horizon. Comparison across environments reveals factors that influence the existence and magnitude of benefits provided by the market maker function.

Categories and Subject Descriptors

J.4 [**Social and Behavioral Sciences**]: Economics

Keywords

Market maker; agent-based simulation; allocative efficiency

1. INTRODUCTION

A *market maker* (MM) facilitates trade in a two-sided auction market by simultaneously maintaining offers to buy and sell. An ever-present MM supplies *liquidity* to the market. Liquidity refers to the availability of immediate trading opportunities at prices that reasonably reflect current market conditions. In compensation for liquidity provision, MMs profit from the *spread*, the difference between their buy and sell offers. MM activity is generally understood to stabilize prices and facilitate discovery of accurate prices in the market [43].

The exact role of market makers varies across market institutions. In a *pure dealer market*, multiple MMs competitively quote prices, and incoming market orders from investors trade at the best available MM price [31]. In a *pure limit-order market*, both investors and MMs submit orders with price limits, and whenever an incoming order matches an existing order, they trade at the incumbent order's limit price. This market mechanism is also called a *continuous double auction* (CDA), the name we use here. In a *specialist market*, there is a single MM designated to act as dealer, with an affirmative obligation to maintain fair and orderly markets [41]. With the transition to electronic markets, pure limit-order markets are becoming predominant [20, 23], thus this is the market mechanism we employ in our study.

Providing liquidity can generate profits from investors, but also runs the risk of *adverse selection*: when traders with newer or otherwise better information take advantage of the MM's standing offers. Much of the market making literature focuses on this tradeoff and its implications for MM strategies [24, 33]; other prior research has investigated the effects of MM on liquidity (e.g., as measured by price spreads) [18] and price discovery [34]. Although liquidity and price discovery are generally expected to be positive factors for market performance and therefore welfare, there has been a notable dearth of prior research modeling this directly. Of the existing work addressing welfare, the focus has been on the need for affirmative MM obligation due to adverse selection [4, 5], the cost structure of market participation in supplying liquidity [30], and trading mechanisms to incentivize market making [7].

In this study, we investigate the effects of MM on market performance, focusing on allocative efficiency as well as gains from trade accrued by background investors. In our model, a single security is traded via CDA mechanism in a market environment comprising a single market maker and multiple background traders. The fundamental value of the security evolves according to a mean-reverting stochastic process. An investor's value for units of the security is given by this fundamental plus an agent-specific private value that decreases with the number of units held. The background traders enter and reenter according to a stochastic arrival process, each time to offer to buy or sell a single unit of the security. The single MM has no private value, and thus aims to profit by maintaining buy and sell offers with a positive price spread.

To compare outcomes both with and without market making, we search for strategy configurations where traders best-respond to the environment and other-agent behavior. As analytic game-theoretic solution of this rich dynamic model appears intractable, we employ empirical simulation-based methods to derive equilibria over a restricted strategy space. For background traders, we consider parameterized strategies based on Zero Intelligence agents [25]. For the MM, we consider heuristic strategies loosely based on that defined by Chakraborty and Kearns [9]. From extensive simulation over thousands of strategy profiles, we estimate game models for various instances of the target scenario.

Analysis of the empirical games provides strong support for overall welfare benefits of market making and evidence for a general benefit for background investors in thin markets with limited trading horizons. We derive empirical equilibria with and without mar-

Appears in: *Proceedings of the 14th International Conference on Autonomous Agents and Multiagent Systems (AAMAS 2015), Bordini, Elkind, Weiss, Yolum (eds.), May 4–8, 2015, Istanbul, Turkey.*

ket making in a number of environments, finding that the mix of background-trader strategies in equilibrium varies depending on the presence and strategy choice of the MM. In all of our environments, market making is profitable in equilibrium, and in all but two equilibrium comparisons, the presence of MM increases overall welfare (background trader surplus combined with MM profit). In markets with impatient investors, we find typically that the background traders themselves are better off (in expectation), that is, welfare is improved net of MM profits. However, if the background traders have ample time horizons, then MM profits often exceed any improvement in overall efficiency, so the background investors are net worse off with the MM present.

In the next section we explain by way of example the potential role of market makers in alleviating allocative inefficiencies. We describe relevant work in Section 3. Section 4 discusses the market environment including background-trader strategies, and Section 5 describes our MM strategies. In Section 6 we present our empirical game-theoretic analysis, and we conclude in Section 7.

2. MOTIVATING EXAMPLE

We illustrate the problem of allocative inefficiency in CDAs, and the influence of market makers, with the following simple example. Suppose a market with four background traders: two buyers and two sellers. The buyers have values b_1 and b_2, and seller values are s_1 and s_2, with $b_1 > s_1 > b_2 > s_2$. Let us further assume for this illustration that the traders submit orders at their valuations.

Suppose that the orders arrive at the market in the order shown in Figure 1. Then buyer 1 trades with seller 1, and buyer 2 with seller 2, achieving a total surplus of $(b_1 - s_1) + (b_2 - s_2)$. The socially optimal allocation, in contrast, would have buyer 1 trading with seller 2, for a total surplus of $b_1 - s_2$. The difference between the optimal and achieved surplus is $\Delta = s_1 - b_2 > 0$. We can attribute this loss to the vagaries of the sequencing of limit orders, combined with the greedy matching implemented by the CDA mechanism. We choose to depict in the figure a sequence that leads to a suboptimal allocation; however, this is not the only one. In fact, only one-third of the possible orderings of these bids (8 out of 24) would result in the optimal allocation, with the remaining two-thirds under-performing by Δ.

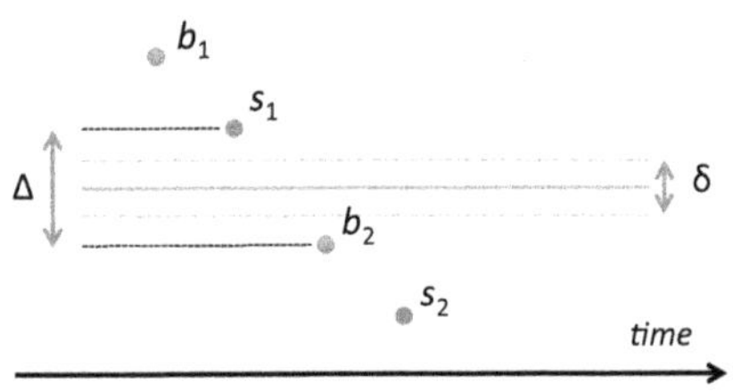

Figure 1: A sequence of CDA orders leading to a suboptimal allocation.

Now suppose there is a market maker who continually maintains buy and sell offers in the auction, with difference δ between them. As long as the MM's offer to buy is within the interval (s_2, s_1), and its offer to sell falls within (b_2, b_1), then for this sequence of order arrivals, buyer 1 and seller 2 will trade with the MM, and the allocation will be efficient. If the MM quotes lie within the narrower interval of *competitive equilibrium* prices[1] $[b_2, s_1]$, then the efficient allocation is achieved for *any* sequence. In such cases, the MM accrues a profit of δ, with the remaining surplus divided among background traders.

The MM promotes efficiency in this example by providing liquidity to the market. In the absence of MM, when buyer 1 arrives, it has nobody to trade with. Seller 1 fills the vacuum and makes a profitable trade with this buyer, but at a price quite removed from that which would match supply and demand aggregated over time. An MM with quotes approximating this long-run price, in contrast, allows arriving bidders to trade near prevailing prices. Equally important, it prevents bidders who should not trade based on their valuations from doing so.

Even assuming that the MM improves overall efficiency, does it make the background traders better off? In the specific scenario of Figure 1, the background traders benefit (in aggregate) if $\delta < \Delta$. If instead we consider the same set of four bids, but submitted in random order, then the background traders are clearly worse off in the third of instances where they would have achieved the efficient allocation without the MM's help. With random sequencing, the background traders benefit in expectation if and only if $\delta < \frac{2}{3}\Delta$.

More generally, we see that the question of whether MM presence is welfare-improving for background traders depends on specific details of the market setting. For background traders, the MM contribution may be sensitive to the distribution of valuations and bids, as well as their pattern of arrival over time. It also depends pivotally on the MM strategy—how well it tracks the prevailing market price and how large a spread the MM maintains between its buy and sell offers. In realistic environments, valuations include a combination of common and private elements and may evolve over time. Based on time and role, agents may have differential information about the common-value component. Thus for time-varying environments, we cannot assume the MM knows the underlying market equilibrium; it must instead act adaptively based on observations and statistical assumptions. Moreover, individual traders may reenter the market to revise bids or reverse transactions, or to trade multiple units of the good. If such reentry were costless, market making would not be necessary to achieve allocative efficiency, as the traders could exchange among themselves to quiescence. In other words, liquidity has economic value only if patience and market participation have costs or limits.

With such complications, it seems unlikely we will be able to establish general analytical conditions for the benefits of MM. We therefore adopt a simulation approach, employing empirical game-theoretic techniques to search for strategically stable background-trader and MM strategies. Our model includes all of the elements listed above, within an extensible framework that could incorporate (in future work) additional relevant features of financial markets.

3. RELATED WORK

Literature on market making lies predominantly within the field of *market microstructure*, which examines the process by which prices, information, and transactions are formed by detailed interactions of traders in a market mechanism [6, 36, 39]. Early work focused on dealer markets, in which a monopolistic MM (the dealer) controls trading by acting as the middleman. Garman [22] presents an explicit formulation of the market maker's optimization problem. O'Hara and Oldfield [40] and Amihud and Mendelson [3] concentrate on the impact of dealer inventory on spreads, while the seminal model of Glosten and Milgrom [24] frames spread as arising from adverse selection. Others focus on the consequences of informed trading on MM [33, 12, 17], as well as the role of market makers as liquidity providers [27, 44].

Much of the relevant theoretical literature, however, relies on simplifying assumptions of MM behavior and trader interactions

[1]A competitive equilibrium price balances supply and demand with price-taking bidders. Here the balance is with respect to cumulative orders over the time horizon.

[6]. Empirical studies have provided insight on the effects of market makers in real-world markets [38, 20, 42, 37, 29]. Historical data alone, however, cannot elucidate the strategic choices faced by market participants. Agent-based modeling (ABM) and simulation of financial markets has proven conducive to exploring these questions [35]; however, only a handful of ABM finance papers focus on market making [10, 14, 17].

Outside of microstructure, researchers have developed MM strategies for a variety of settings, including prediction markets [28, 11, 2], dealer-mediated markets [16, 32], CDAs [19], and environments where prices are generated exogenously [1]. In this last category, Chakraborty and Kearns [9] demonstrate the profitability of market making given a mean-reverting price series series. They propose a simple MM algorithm to submit a ladder of prices; the market makers we investigate can be viewed as variations on this strategy.

None of these studies, however, address questions about allocative efficiency in the market. To our knowledge, the literature on welfare effects of MM behavior is quite limited, and existing studies are largely concerned with how adverse selection affects allocative efficiency. For example, Bessembinder et al. [4] demonstrate that restricting spread widths improves allocative efficiency and encourages more traders to become informed. Their results suggest that MMs enhance efficiency primarily when information asymmetries are significant. Brusco and Jackson [7] illustrate the inefficiencies of competitive markets in a two-period model in which the market maker position is designated via an auction. They also design a system of trading rules to reach an efficient allocation by identifying and incentivizing MM agents. Huang and Wang [30] propose a model in which provision of liquidity is endogenous, finding that mandating participation tends to improve welfare, but that the welfare effects of lowering costs for liquidity provision per se are ambiguous. In a similar vein, Bessembinder et al. [5] present a model in which a firm can sell an asset to an investor in an IPO, with the option of paying a designated market maker (DMM) in exchange for liquidity provision in a secondary market. When the secondary market is illiquid due to asymmetric information and uncertainty regarding the asset's fundamental value, social welfare can be improved if the firm enters into a DMM contract.

4. MARKET ENVIRONMENT

To investigate the effect of market making on allocative efficiency, we construct a simple model of a single security traded in a continuous double auction market. Prices are fine-grained but discrete, taking values at integer multiples of the *tick size* p_{ts}. Time is likewise fine-grained and discrete, with finite horizon T. Agents arrive at designated times, and submit limit orders to the market. The CDA maintains price quotes reflecting the best outstanding orders. BID_t corresponds to the highest buy offer at time t, and ASK_t to the lowest offer to sell. Other bids in the order book are not visible to traders. The market environment is populated by multiple background traders, representing investors, and (optionally) one market maker. At any given time, the background investors are restricted to a single order to buy or sell one unit, whereas the MM may maintain orders to buy and sell any number of units at various prices.

4.1 Valuation Model

Each background trader has an individual valuation for the security comprised of private and common components. We denote by r_t the common *fundamental value* for the security at time t. The fundamental time series is generated by a mean-reverting stochastic process:

$$r_t = \max\left\{0,\ \kappa\bar{r} + (1-\kappa)\, r_{t-1} + u_t\right\}.$$

Parameter $\kappa \in [0,1]$ specifies the degree to which the fundamental reverts back to the mean $\bar{r}$, and parameter $u_t \sim \mathcal{N}\left(0, \sigma_s^2\right)$ is a random shock at time t.

The private component for agent i is a vector Θ_i representing differences in private benefits of trading given the trader's net position, similar to the model of Goettler et al. [26]. The vector is of size $2q_{\max}$, where $q_{\max} > 0$ is the maximum number of units the agent can be long or short at any time, with

$$\Theta_i = \left(\theta_i^{-q_{\max}+1}, \ldots, \theta_i^0, \theta_i^{+1}, \ldots, \theta_i^{q_{\max}}\right).$$

Element θ_i^q is the incremental private benefit obtained from selling one unit of the security given current position q, where positive (negative) q indicates a long (short) position. Similarly, θ_i^{q+1} is the marginal private gain from buying an additional unit given current net position q.

We generate Θ_i from a set of $2q_{\max}$ values drawn independently from a Gaussian distribution. Let $\hat{\theta} \sim \mathcal{N}\left(0, \sigma_{PV}^2\right)$ denote one of these drawn values. To ensure that the valuation reflects diminishing marginal utility, that is, $\theta^{q'} \geq \theta^q$ for all $q' \leq q$, we sort the $\hat{\theta}$ and set the θ_i^q to respective values in the sorted list.

Background trader i's valuation v for the security at time t is based on its current position q_t and the value of the global fundamental at time T, the end of the trading horizon:

$$v_i(t) = r_T + \begin{cases} \theta_i^{q_t+1} & \text{if buying 1 unit} \\ \theta_i^{q_t} & \text{if selling 1 unit.} \end{cases}$$

For a single-quantity limit order transacting at time t and price p, a trader obtains surplus:

$$\begin{cases} v_i(t) - p & \text{for buy transactions, or} \\ p - v_i(t) & \text{for sell transactions.} \end{cases}$$

Since the price and fundamental terms cancel out in exchange, the total surplus achieved when agent B buys from agent S is $\theta_B^{q(B)+1} - \theta_S^{q(S)}$, where $q(i)$ denotes the pre-trade position of agent i.

4.2 Background Trading Strategies

There is an extensive literature on autonomous bidding strategies for CDAs [21, 48, 15]. In this study, we consider trading strategies in the so-called *Zero Intelligence* (ZI) family [25].

The background traders arrive at the market according to a Poisson process with rate λ_a. On arrival, they are assigned to buy or sell (with equal probability), and accordingly submit an order to buy or sell a single unit. Traders subsequently reenter the market, with time between entries distributed exponentially at rate λ_r. Agents may trade any number of times, as long as their net positions do not exceed $q_{\max}$ (either long or short). At the end of the simulation period, background traders liquidate their accumulated inventory at r_T, the end-time fundamental. Background traders are notified of all transactions and current price quotes with zero delay, and may use this information in computing their bids.

A ZI trader assesses its valuation $v_i(t)$ at the time of market entry t, using an estimate $\hat{r}_t$ of the terminal fundamental r_T. The estimate is based on the current fundamental, r_t, adjusted to account for mean reversion:[2]

$$\hat{r}_t = \left(1 - (1-\kappa)^{T-t}\right)\bar{r} + (1-\kappa)^{T-t} r_t. \tag{1}$$

[2]We also implemented a version of this strategy that did not account for mean reversion, taking $\hat{r}_t = r_t$. This misestimating agent performed poorly with $\kappa > 0$, so we omit it from further discussion.

The ZI agent then submits a bid shaded from this estimate by a random offset—the degree of surplus it demands from the trade. The amount of shading is drawn uniformly from range $[R_{\min}, R_{\max}]$. Specifically, a ZI trader i arriving at time t with current position q submits a limit order for a single unit of the security at price

$$p_i \sim \begin{cases} \mathcal{U}\left[\hat{r}_t + \theta_i^{q+1} - R_{\max}, \hat{r}_t + \theta_i^{q+1} - R_{\min}\right] & \text{if buying} \\ \mathcal{U}\left[\hat{r}_t + \theta_i^{q} + R_{\min}, \hat{r}_t + \theta_i^{q} + R_{\max}\right] & \text{if selling.} \end{cases}$$

We also consider a threshold parameter $\eta \in [0, 1]$, whereby if the agent could achieve a fraction η of its requested surplus at the current price quote, it would simply take that quote rather than posting a limit order to the book. Setting $\eta = 1$ is equivalent to the strategy without employing the threshold.

In our model, background traders are permitted to reenter the market, thus we denote agents employing this strategy *ZI with Reentry* (ZIR). Upon each reentry, the ZIR trader withdraws its previous order (if not transacted yet) before executing the strategy described above.

5. MARKET MAKER STRATEGIES

Much of the prior work on MM strategies treats the market maker as a dealer [24, 16]. In our model, all trades execute through the CDA order book, therefore the MM submits limit orders just as background traders do. We consider a family of MM strategies that submit at time t a *ladder* of single-quantity buy and sell orders, comprised of K rungs spaced ξ ticks apart:

$$\begin{cases} [S_t, S_t + \xi, S_t + 2\xi, \ldots, S_t + K\xi] & \text{for sell orders} \\ [B_t - K\xi, \ldots, B_t - 2\xi, B_t - \xi, B_t] & \text{for buy orders} \end{cases}$$

with $S_t > B_t$ and $K, \xi > 0$. The MM arrives at time 0 and reenters the market according to a Poisson process with rate λ_{MM}. On reentry at time t, the MM observes the current fundamental r_t, which it may use in determining its ladder of buy and sell orders. It cancels any standing orders remaining from its previous ladder when submitting a new ladder.

Like the background traders, the MM liquidates its inventory at the end of the trading horizon. The liquidation price is the global fundamental value r_T. The MM's total profit is defined by the sum of trading cash flow plus liquidation proceeds.

To avoid crossing the current BID-ASK quote, the MM truncates its ladder. Specifically, if $BID_t > S_t$ (or similarly, $B_t > ASK_t$), the agent cuts the ladder off at the rung that is at or above (below) the current BID (ASK) price. The truncated ladder is:

$$\begin{cases} [S_t + (K - x)\xi, \ldots, S_t + K\xi] & \text{if } BID_t > S_t \\ [B_t - K\xi, \ldots, B_t - (K - x)\xi] & \text{if } B_t > ASK_t, \end{cases}$$

where $x > 0$ specifies the rung immediately above BID (for sell orders) or below ASK (for buy orders). That is, x satisfies the condition $S_t + (K - x - 1)\xi < BID_t < S_t + (K - x)\xi$ for sell orders in the ladder, and $B_t - (K - x)\xi < ASK_t < B_t - (K - x - 1)\xi$ for buy orders.

Within this family of of MM strategies, we define the *Fundamental Market Maker* (FUNDMM), which uses its observation of the current fundamental r_t to inform its ladder construction. FUNDMM computes an estimate $\hat{r}_t$ of the terminal fundamental r_T via (1), and centers its ladder around this estimate. It determines its spread ω either via the current quote (i.e., $\omega_t = ASK_t - BID_t$), or by a fixed value specified as a strategy parameter. The central ladder prices are:

$$S_t = \hat{r}_t + \frac{1}{2}\omega_t, \; B_t = \hat{r}_t - \frac{1}{2}\omega_t.$$

6. EMPIRICAL GAME-THEORETIC ANALYSIS

We have described a variety of strategies for the roles of background trader and MM, each with tunable parameters. Evaluating the effect of market making for all combinations of strategy choices would be infeasible; moreover, the various strategic contexts are not equally relevant. Generally speaking, we are most interested in the effect of market making when all agents are doing their best to generate profit. In other words, we wish to evaluate the impact of MM in equilibrium, that is, where both the background traders and MM are adopting the best strategies, given the environment and other agent strategy selections.

We qualify our equilibrium analysis in two ways. First, we consider only a restricted set of available strategy choices, defined by selected parameterized versions of the strategies introduced above. Second, we determine equilibria among these strategies through a simulation-based process, known as *empirical game-theoretic analysis* (EGTA) [47]. In EGTA, we use systematic simulation of strategy profiles in a specified environment to induce a game model of that environment. For the present study, we simulate an instance of the financial market described in Section 4, using an extension of the discrete-event market simulation system developed for our previous study of latency arbitrage [46]. We generate data for various combinations of the strategies introduced in Sections 4.2 and 5, each sampled over many runs (all environments in this study averaged at least 241 per profile, most over 5000) to account for stochastic effects (valuation schedules, trajectories of the market fundamental, agent arrival patterns). From this data we estimate game payoffs and derive equilibria with respect to the strategy space explored. We then take these equilibria as the basis for evaluating MM welfare effects.

6.1 Environment Settings

We evaluate the performance of background traders and the MM within thirty parametrically distinct environments. For each environment, we analyze two empirical games that differ in whether the MM is present. In all settings, there are $N \in \{25, 66\}$ background traders who arrive at a rate $\lambda_a = 0.075$. Each simulation run lasts T time steps. If present, the MM in each environment enters the market at the start of the simulation and reenters with rate $\lambda_{MM} = 0.005$, or approximately once every 200 time steps. The global fundamental has a mean value $\bar{r} = 10^5$ and mean-reversion parameter $\kappa = 0.05$. The minimum tick size p_{ts} is fixed at 1. If we interpret the tick size as a thousandth of a dollar ($0.001), then the mean fundamental is $100. The variance for the private value vector is $\sigma_{PV}^2 = 5 \times 10^6$. The maximum number of units the background trader can be long or short at any time is $q_{\max} = 10$.

The environments differ in number of background traders (N), background-trader reentry rate (λ_r), fundamental shock variance (σ_s^2), and time horizon (T). The configurations of parameter settings for $N \in \{25, 66\}$ background traders are as follows.

A $\lambda_r = 0.0005, \sigma_s^2 = 1 \times 10^6,$
$T \in \{1000, 2000, 4000, 12000, 60000\}$

B $\lambda_r = 0.005, \sigma_s^2 = 1 \times 10^6,$
$T \in \{1000, 2000, 4000, 12000, 120000\}$

C $\lambda_r = 0.005, \sigma_s^2 = 5 \times 10^5,$
$T \in \{1000, 2000, 4000, 12000, 120000\}$

We describe each environment by its configuration label, followed by time horizon (in thousands). For example, B12 is the environment labeled **B** above with $T = 12000$.

6.2 EGTA Process

We model our market as a *role-symmetric game*, in which players are partitioned into roles, each with a specified strategy set. The payoff for playing a strategy in a particular role depends on the number of other agents playing each strategy in this role and the others, but not on how the strategies are mapped to players within the roles. Our two roles are background trader (25 or 66 players) and market maker (one player).

Even exploiting symmetry, game size grows exponentially in players and strategies, so it is computationally infeasible to analyze games with this many traders. We therefore apply aggregation to approximate the many-player games as games with fewer players. The specific technique we employ, called *deviation-preserving reduction* (DPR) [49], defines reduced-game payoffs in terms of payoffs in the full game as follows. Consider an N-player symmetric game, reduced to a k-player game. The payoff for playing strategy s_1 in the reduced game, with other agents playing strategies $(s_2, \ldots, s_k)$, is given by the payoff of playing s_1 in the full N-player game when the other $N-1$ agents are evenly divided ($\frac{N-1}{k-1}$ each) among strategies $s_2, \ldots, s_k$.

We chose values for N in this study to facilitate DPR by ensuring that the required aggregations come out as integers: the approximation of an $(N, 1)$-size game (i.e., N background traders and 1 MM) by a $(k, 1)$-player reduced game works best when k divides N and $k-1$ divides $N-1$. Specifically, we use simulation data from the $(66, 1)$-agent environments to estimate reduced $(6, 1)$-player games, where six players represent the 66 background traders in the simulated environment. We similarly estimate $(5, 1)$-player games from the $(25, 1)$-agent cases.

We iteratively apply EGTA to guide our exploration of the strategy space. Exploration starts with the most promising profiles and spreads through their neighbors, that is, those profiles related by single-agent deviations. The goal in this process is to identify Nash equilibria, and we focus our search on role-symmetric (pure or mixed) Nash equilibria (RSNE). As the observed payoffs from our simulator for a given profile are incrementally added, we analyze each successive intermediate game model by computing (mixed) equilibria for each complete subgame, defined as a set of strategies for which we have simulated all profiles. These represent candidates for equilibria of the full game, which we can refute by finding a beneficial deviation outside the strategy set, or confirm by examining all deviations without refuting. We continue to refine the empirical game with additional simulations until at least one equilibrium is confirmed and all non-confirmed candidates are refuted. In this study, we successfully found at least one and at most six non-trivial RSNEs for each game evaluated, with support sizes (i.e., numbers of strategies played with positive probability) up to five for background traders and up to three for MMs.

We utilize the EGTAOnline infrastructure [8] for conducting and managing our experiments, and our simulations are run on the high-performance computing cluster at the Center for Advanced Computing at the University of Michigan. The process accumulates a dataset of profile simulation results, which we use to estimate payoff values for strategy profiles in the game.

For all the games we model, there exists a trivial pure RSNE in which all agents play a "NOOP" strategy that refrains from bidding. This exists because if none of the other agents (background traders or MM) submit limit orders, then there is nobody to trade with and there will be no transactions regardless of the strategy the subject agent employs. In our discussion below, we ignore this degenerate equilibrium, which obviously has payoff zero for all agents.

To provide a benchmark for efficiency, we calculate the social optimum based on the trader population and valuation distribution used in our environments (i.e., $N \in \{25, 66\}$ background traders with parameters $q_{\max} = 10$ and $\sigma^2_{PV} = 5 \times 10^6$). We determine the optimum for a particular draw of N valuation vectors by treating each as a demand curve and finding a uniform competitive equilibrium price. This is conveniently implemented in our simulation environment, where valuation vector Θ_i is represented by a background trader i, who submits $q_{\max}$ single-unit sell orders at prices $\bar{r} + \theta_i^s$, $s \in \{-q_{\max}+1, \ldots, 0\}$, and $q_{\max}$ single-unit buy orders at prices $\bar{r} + \theta_i^b$, $b \in \{+1, \ldots, q_{\max}\}$. A call market computes a uniform clearing price to match supply and demand, which defines the optimal allocation for the sample. From 20,000 samples, we find a mean social welfare of 44155 and 16306 for 66 and 25 background traders, respectively. Figure 2 presents histograms of trades per background trader in the social optima.

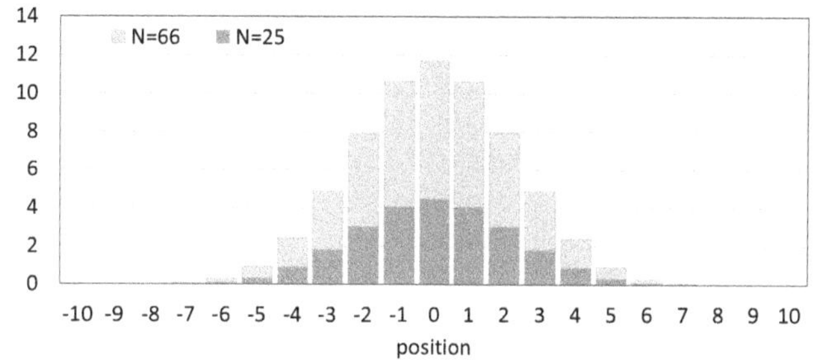

Figure 2: Distributions of the net position (equivalently, number of units traded) of N background traders in socially optimal allocations. The histograms (shown superimposed) are compiled from 20,000 samples.

6.3 Game without Market Making

The empirical games without MM cover 13 background-trader strategies: 12 versions of ZIR[3] (see Table 1), and the no-trade strategy NOOP. We identified at least 1–3 ZIR equilibria[4] for each of our thirty environments (see Tables 2 and 3). For each equilibrium, we calculated background-trader surplus by sampling 10,000 full-game profiles according to the equilibrium mixture, running one simulation per sampled profile and then recording the aggregate surplus.

6.4 Game with Market Making

Our games with MM include the 13 background-trader strategies from the no-MM treatment above, plus eight strategies for the MM role. The MMs employed in our game analysis are all parametric variants of FUNDMM (Section 5), with $K = 100$ rungs spaced ξ units apart. One variant sets its spread using the current price quote at reentry, whereas the others employ a constant spread $\omega \in \{64, 128, 256, 512, 1024, 2048\}$. Rung size ξ is 100, plus two variants with $\xi = 50$ for $\omega \in \{256, 512\}$. The equilibria found are presented in Tables 4 and 5. Background-trader surplus and MM profit are estimated for each equilibrium based on the sampling method described for the no-MM game above.

[3]Not every ZIR strategy appears in every environment; for instance, in the $N = 25$ case, agents playing strategies with $R_{\min} \geq 2500$ never trade, so we exclude such strategy variants from the analysis of those environments.

[4]We report only one equilibrium when multiple close equilibria (for which the mixture probabilities are nearly identical) exist. The full details of all equilibria in games both with and without MM are available in an online appendix (`http://hdl.handle.net/2027.42/110647`).

R_{min}	0	0	0	0	0	0	500	0	0	2500	5000	5000
R_{max}	125	125	250	500	1000	1000	1000	1500	2500	10000	10000	15000
η	0.8	1	1	1	0.8	1	0.4	0.6	1	1	1	1

Table 1: ZIR strategy combinations included in empirical game-theoretic analysis.

Env	surplus	R_{mid}	η
A1	12997	416	0.878
A1	11958	586	0.721
A2	16501	377	0.878
A4	22384	339	0.909
A12	34853	283	0.930
A12	36668	161	0.919
A12	34865	338	0.930
A60	43343	300	1
B1	27387	616	0.683
B2	35648	572	0.706
B4	39180	633	0.647
B12	42635	393	0.885
B120	41076	746	0.598
B120	41469	630	0.689
B120	41066	665	0.554
C1	29433	379	0.959
C2	37533	443	0.845
C4	40926	469	0.842
C12	43001	436	0.932
C120	43308	350	0.948

Table 2: Symmetric equilibria for games without market makers, $N = 66$, calculated from the 6-player DPR approximation. Each row of the table describes one equilibrium found and its average values for total surplus and two strategy parameters: R_{mid} (the midpoint of ZIR range $[R_{\text{min}}, R_{\text{max}}]$) and threshold η. Values presented are the average over strategies in the profile, weighted by mixture probabilities.

Env	surplus	R_{mid}	η
A1	4110	634	0.678
A2	5103	677	0.576
A4	8543	125	1
A4	8237	285	1
A12	13639	125	1
A60	15798	349	0.980
A60	15910	347	0.935
A60	15629	412	0.844
B1	9591	684	0.532
B2	12792	583	0.604
B4	13823	650	0.593
B12	15673	500	1
B12	15627	521	0.909
B12	15675	445	0.885
B120	15658	747	0.551
C1	9831	656	0.566
C1	10010	626	0.543
C2	12678	626	0.599
C2	13058	553	0.637
C4	13967	646	0.566
C12	14688	658	0.622
C12	15792	500	0.872
C120	16047	500	0.8
C120	15012	677	0.541

Table 3: Symmetric equilibria for games without market makers, $N = 25$, calculated from the 5-player DPR approximation. Data presented is as for Table 2.

6.5 Comparison of Market Performance

Our findings with regard to the central question in this paper are presented in Figure 3. For each environment, we compare equilibrium outcomes, with and without an MM, on two measures: social welfare and background-trader surplus. Since there are often multiple equilibria, the differences are presented as ranges, delimiting the most and least favorable comparisons.

In the scenarios with 66 background traders (Figure 3(a)), the change in overall welfare is generally positive, with only two environments (A60 and B120) providing small exceptions. The change in background-trader surplus, in contrast, varies widely across environments, with multiple examples of both positive and negative changes. The effect is strongly negative in the **A** environments with longer trading horizons, which may be explained by the significant information advantage of MMs over background traders due to their disparate reentry rates ($\lambda_{MM} = 0.005$ versus $\lambda_r = 0.0005$). For environments A60, B12, B120, C12, and C120, the total social welfare, regardless of whether MM is present, is very close to the socially efficient outcome of 44155. That is, the ZIR background traders in these environments extract nearly all the potential surplus in the market on their own. Intuitively, given sufficient time for reentry (as governed by horizon T and reentry rate λ_r), agents with private values on the right side of competitive prices will eventually trade, and any inefficient trades can effectively be reversed. When the background traders have sufficient time to reach efficient outcomes, the MM can provide little benefit to overall welfare, and its profits tend to come out of background-trader surplus.

The trading horizon T reflects whatever might limit an investor's patience (liquidity needs, portfolio hedging, cost of monitoring, etc.). By curbing agents' ability to find efficient trades, the time constraint limits their ability to extract all potential surplus solely by trading with each other. This problem is exacerbated in a thin market, where agents encounter fewer potential counterparties per unit time. Both factors increase the likelihood that agents trade inefficiently, as they lack sufficient time and opportunity to reverse poor transactions. In such scenarios, the MM can boost not only overall welfare but also background-trader surplus by facilitating trade among impatient investors arriving at different times. In our study, for markets populated by 25 background traders (Figure 3(b)), the market maker significantly improves both welfare and background-trader surplus for $T \in \{1000, 2000\}$. As for $N = 66$, the $N = 25$ background traders in environments with sufficiently long T get close to the social optimum without MM. The presence of the MM further improves overall social welfare in these environments up to the optimal value, enabling extraction of all surplus in the market at some loss to the background traders.

For both population sizes, background traders generally shade less when MM is present. In particular, for the $N = 25$ environments in which background-trader surplus improves with MM, the midpoint R_{mid} of the ZIR bid range is significantly lower in

Env	surplus	profit	R_{mid}	η	ω	ξ
A1	13379	1490	154	0.946	256	50
A2	17002	1558	151	0.935	256	50
A4	22520	2000	181	1	256	50
A12	34826	2745	182	1	256	50
A60	41049	2250	500	0.848	*var*	100
B1	29065	223	487	0.788	512	100
B2	36679	541	453	0.875	512	100
B2	37424	623	376	0.924	512	50
B4	40733	528	500	0.889	256	100
B12	42265	938	356	0.569	256	100
B12	42413	744	452	1	256	100
B120	40969	1837	673	0.607	256	100
B120	42282	1414	589	0.700	256	50
B120	42374	1272	621	0.682	311	61
B120	42648	994	621	0.682	312	61
B120	42769	1070	500	0.800	256	50
B120	42189	1268	556	0.735	128	100
C1	30049	794	311	0.962	512	100
C2	38551	1633	202	1	256	50
C4	39991	1403	500	0.903	256	79
C12	41488	2000	407	0.844	256	100
C120	41732	1702	455	0.909	256	54

Table 4: Role-symmetric equilibria for games with market makers, $N = 66$, calculated from the (6,1)-player DPR approximation. Each row of the table describes one equilibrium found and its average values for background-trader surplus, MM profit, and four strategy parameters: R_{mid} (the midpoint of ZIR range $[R_{\min}, R_{\max}]$), threshold η, MM spread ω, and rung size ξ. Values presented are the average over strategies in the profile, weighted by mixture probabilities. Spread *var* indicates context-varying spread based on current quotes, so an average is unavailable.

Env	surplus	profit	R_{mid}	η	ω	ξ
A1	4704	890	100	0.919	512	100
A2	6318	770	154	1	256	100
A4	8119	893	214	1	512	50
A12	12556	1861	109	1	256	50
A60	14335	2141	310	0.909	253	51
B1	11305	651	274	0.933	512	72
B2	13232	881	402	0.818	512	100
B4	14066	704	531	0.794	512	100
B12	15143	945	399	0.854	512	50
B12	15038	1277	504	0.833	256	100
B120	15234	1309	506	0.756	257	50
C1	10901	779	300	0.960	512	100
C1	11247	935	217	1	512	50
C2	13858	1054	247	1	512	50
C4	15319	911	223	1	256	88
C12	15030	1350	500	0.916	256	100
C120	15352	1313	511	0.904	256	50

Table 5: Role-symmetric equilibria for games with market makers, $N = 25$, calculated from the (5,1)-player DPR approximation. Data presented is as for Table 4.

equilibria with MM. This indicates that the MM facilitates optimal allocations; with MM present, background investors can demand less surplus per trade, yet still achieve greater payoff than without the market maker. We also find that MM spread ω tends to be larger for environments with shorter trading horizons, as we would expect when traders are more impatient.

Finally, we evaluate liquidity for the maximum-welfare RSNE (Figure 4), with and without MM, by sampling results from profiles at the RSNE proportions. We measure liquidity via the $BID\text{-}ASK$ spread (narrower spreads reflect greater liquidity) and background-trader execution time (interval between order submission and transaction). In general, both spreads and execution times drop with MM, which is indicative of the liquidity-provisioning capacity of the MM. In the thinner markets, spreads without MM are significantly wider than in the thicker markets, as would be expected. The presence of the MM serves to significantly narrow spreads nearly down to the levels present in the more populous environments. The fact that the liquidity proxy measures improve with MM in environments where background trader surplus does not, however, underscores that these measures are not adequate substitutes for direct evaluation of investor welfare.

7. CONCLUSIONS

In this study, we employed a simulation-based approach to compare several parameterized environments with and without a market maker. We modeled a single security traded in a CDA populated by multiple background traders, and we characterized the strategic play in the induced empirical game model. This enabled us to compare outcomes *in equilibrium*, that is, allowing the background traders and market makers to strategically react to each others' presence.

Our analysis demonstrates the generally beneficial effects of market making on efficiency, and shows that whether these benefits accrue to background investors depends on market characteristics. Specifically, we find a strong tendency of MMs to improve the welfare of impatient investors (those in environments with short time horizons), especially in thin markets, but no such benefit in environments comprising more patient investors.

Our study has several limitations, which must be taken into account in assessing our conclusions. First, our methods involve sampling, approximation, and limited search, all of which bear on the accuracy of equilibrium determinations. Sampling error is mitigated through the large number of simulation runs we gather over a breadth of environments and profiles, so not a fundamental concern for our conclusions here. The player reduction method we employ (DPR) has been shown to produce good approximate equilibrium estimates on other problems [49], and for our purposes approximate equilibria provide a sufficient basis for outcome comparison. However, DPR estimates are not guaranteed approximations, and it would be reassuring to confirm their quality in the context of our trading scenario. Even within the DPR game, we are unable to evaluate all profiles and cannot be sure that we have found all equilibria. Our search process attempts to evaluate all promising equilibrium candidates, but identifying these is not guaranteed.

A second area of limitation is the relatively narrow exploration of strategies. Further investigation may yield improved versions of ZIR or other strategies (for example adaptive variants [13, 45]) that could alter equilibrium findings. Similar improvements may be found on the MM side, for instance with strategies incorporating learning [1].

Finally, our exploration of environments is also far from exhaustive. Whereas covering all plausible environments is infeasible, a broader range of variation on number of players, valuation distributions, and fundamental dynamics could go a long way in illuminating and validating robust conditions for qualitative welfare effects of market making in continuous double auctions.

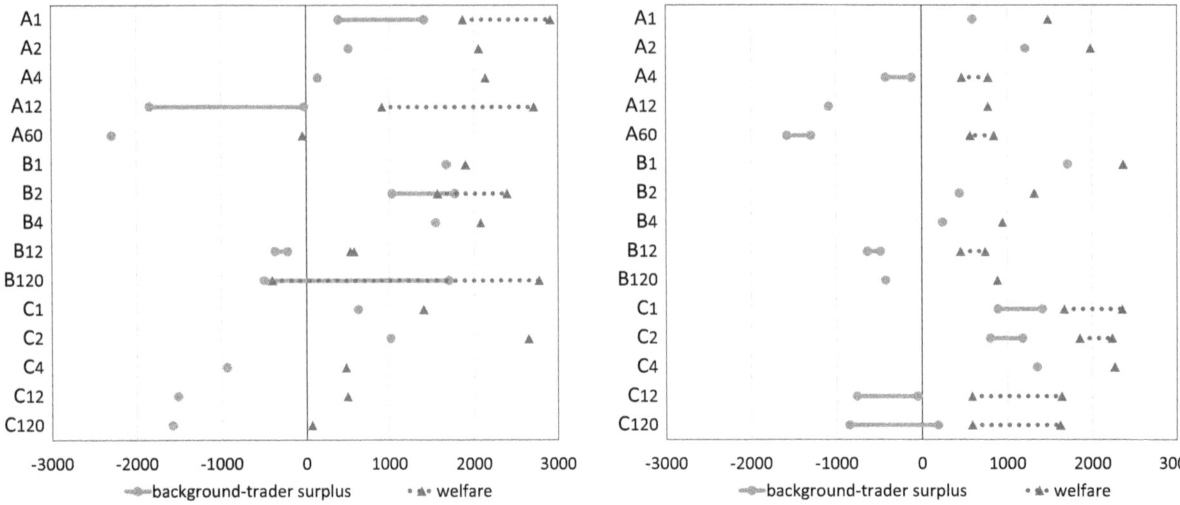

(a) $N = 66$ (b) $N = 25$

Figure 3: The effect of MM presence on background-trader surplus and social welfare in equilibrium, across all environments. Differences are presented as ranges, reflecting the multiplicity of equilibria found in some environments. The left point of each range is the minimum gain (in some cases a loss), that is, the lowest value observed with an equilibrium with MM minus the highest value observed in any equilibrium without MM. The right point is the maximum improvement observed: the difference between the highest value with MM and the lowest without MM.

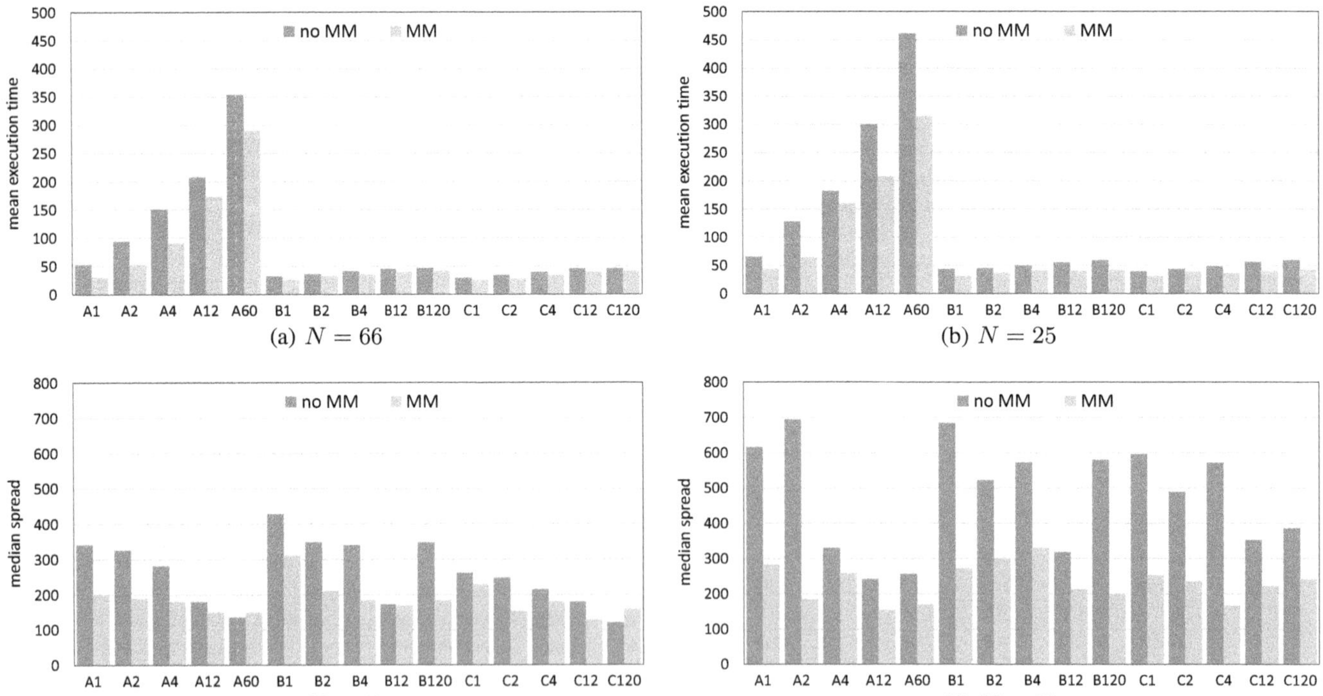

(a) $N = 66$ (b) $N = 25$

(c) $N = 66$ (d) $N = 25$

Figure 4: Comparison of background-trader execution time (Figures 4(a) and 4(b)) and median spread (Figures 4(c) and 4(d)) for the maximum-welfare RSNE in each environment, with and without MM. Mixed-strategy RSNE are approximated by profiles with trader population proportions corresponding to the strategy probabilities. Each bar is compiled from 10,000 samples.

Acknowledgments

Zhiyi Zhang's senior honors thesis served as a pilot study of MM strategies. Mason Wright improved our background-trader strategies. We are also grateful to Uday Rajan for helpful advice on this work, and to the anonymous reviewers for constructive feedback on our presentation. This work was supported in part by grant IIS-1421391 from the US National Science Foundation, and by the Microsoft Technology Policy Group.

References

[1] J. Abernethy and S. Kale. Adaptive market making via online learning. In *Advances in Neural Information Processing Systems*, pages 2058–2066, 2013.

[2] J. Abernethy, Y. Chen, and J. Wortman Vaughan. An optimization-based framework for automated market-making. In *12th ACM Conference on Electronic Commerce*, pages 297–306, 2011.

[3] Y. Amihud and H. Mendelson. Dealership market: Market-making with inventory. *Journal of Financial Economics*, 8(1):31–53, 1980.

[4] H. Bessembinder, J. Hao, and M. L. Lemmon. Why designate market makers? Affirmative obligations and market quality. Technical Report 989061, SSRN, 2011.

[5] H. Bessembinder, J. Hao, and K. Zheng. Market making contracts, firm value, and the IPO decision. Technical Report 2130875, SSRN, 2014.

[6] B. Biais, L. Glosten, and C. Spatt. Market microstructure: A survey of microfoundations, empirical results, and policy implications. *Journal of Financial Markets*, 8(2):217–264, 2005.

[7] S. Brusco and M. O. Jackson. The optimal design of a market. *Journal of Economic Theory*, 88(1):1–39, 1999.

[8] B.-A. Cassell and M. P. Wellman. EGTAOnline: An experiment manager for simulation-based game studies. In *Multi-Agent-Based Simulation XIII*, volume 7838 of *Lecture Notes in Artificial Intelligence*. Springer, 2013.

[9] T. Chakraborty and M. Kearns. Market making and mean reversion. In *11th ACM Conference on Electronic Commerce*, pages 307–314, 2011.

[10] N. T. Chan and C. Shelton. An electronic market-maker. Technical Report AI Memo 2001-005, Massachusetts Institute of Technology, 2001.

[11] Y. Chen and D. M. Pennock. A utility framework for bounded-loss market makers. In *23rd Conference on Uncertainty in Artificial Intelligence*, pages 49–56, 2007.

[12] B. Chowhdry and V. Nanda. Multimarket trading and market liquidity. *Review of Financial Studies*, 4(3):483–511, 1991.

[13] D. Cliff. ZIP60: Further explorations in the evolutionary design of online auction market mechanisms. *IEEE Transactions on Evolutionary Computation*, 13(1):3–18, 2009.

[14] V. Darley, A. Outkin, T. Plate, and F. Gao. Sixteenths or pennies? Observations from a simulation of the NASDAQ stock market. In *IEEE/IAFE/INFORMS Conference on Computational Intelligence for Financial Engineering*, pages 151–154, 2000.

[15] R. Das, J. E. Hanson, J. O. Kephart, and G. Tesauro. Agent-human interactions in the continuous double auction. In *17th International Joint Conference on Artificial Intelligence*, pages 1169–1176, 2001.

[16] S. Das. A learning market-maker in the Glosten–Milgrom model. *Quantitative Finance*, 5(2):169–180, 2005.

[17] S. Das. The effects of market-making on price dynamics. In *7th International Joint Conference on Autonomous Agents and Multiagent Systems*, volume 2, pages 887–894, 2008.

[18] S. Das and M. Magdon-Ismail. Adapting to a market shock: Optimal sequential market-making. In *Advances in Neural Information Processing Systems*, pages 361–368, 2008.

[19] Y. Feng, R. Yu, and P. Stone. Two stock-trading agents: Market making and technical analysis. In *Agent-Mediated Electronic Commerce V. Designing Mechanisms and Systems*, pages 18–36. Springer, 2004.

[20] S. Frey and J. Grammig. Liquidity supply and adverse selection in a pure limit order book market. *Empirical Economics*, 30(4):1007–1033, 2006.

[21] D. Friedman. The double auction market institution: A survey. In D. Friedman and J. Rust, editors, *The Double Auction Market: Institutions, Theories, and Evidence*, pages 3–25. Addison-Wesley, 1993.

[22] M. B. Garman. Market microstructure. *Journal of Financial Economics*, 3(3):257–275, 1976.

[23] L. R. Glosten. Is the electronic open limit order book inevitable? *Journal of Finance*, 49(4):1127–1161, 1994.

[24] L. R. Glosten and P. R. Milgrom. Bid, ask and transaction prices in a specialist market with heterogeneously informed traders. *Journal of Financial Economics*, 14(1):71–100, 1985.

[25] D. K. Gode and S. Sunder. Allocative efficiency of markets with zero-intelligence traders: Market as a partial substitute for individual rationality. *Journal of Political Economy*, 101 (1):119–137, 1993.

[26] R. L. Goettler, C. A. Parlour, and U. Rajan. Informed traders and limit order markets. *Journal of Financial Economics*, 93 (1):67–87, 2009.

[27] S. J. Grossman and M. H. Miller. Liquidity and market structure. *Journal of Finance*, 43(3):617–633, 1988.

[28] R. Hanson. Logarithmic market scoring rules for modular combinatorial information aggregation. *Journal of Prediction Markets*, 1(1):3–15, 2007.

[29] J. Hasbrouck and G. Sofianos. The trades of market makers: An empirical analysis of NYSE specialists. *Journal of Finance*, 48(5):1565–1593, 1993.

[30] J. Huang and J. Wang. Market liquidity, asset prices, and welfare. *Journal of Financial Economics*, 95(1):107–127, 2010.

[31] R. D. Huang and H. R. Stoll. Dealer versus auction markets: A paired comparison of execution costs on NASDAQ and the NYSE. *Journal of Financial Economics*, 41(3):313–357, 1996.

[32] J. Jumadinova and P. Dasgupta. A comparison of different automated market-maker strategies. In *12th Workshop on Agent-Mediated Electronic Commerce*, pages 141–154, 2010.

[33] A. S. Kyle. Continuous auctions and insider trading. *Econometrica*, 53(6):1315–1335, 1985.

[34] J. C. Leach and A. N. Madhavan. Intertemporal price discovery by market makers: Active versus passive learning. *Journal of Financial Intermediation*, 2(2):207–235, 1992.

[35] B. LeBaron. Agent-based computational finance. In L. Tesfatsion and K. L. Judd, editors, *Handbook of Agent-Based Computational Economics*, pages 1187–1233. Elsevier, 2006.

[36] A. Madhavan. Market microstructure: A survey. *Journal of Financial Markets*, 3(3):205–258, 2000.

[37] S. Manaster and S. C. Mann. Life in the pits: Competitive market making and inventory control. *Review of Financial Studies*, 9(3):953–975, 1996.

[38] A. J. Menkveld. High frequency trading and the new market makers. *Journal of Financial Markets*, 16(4):712–740, November 2013.

[39] M. O'Hara. *Market Microstructure Theory*, volume 108. Blackwell Cambridge, 1995.

[40] M. O'Hara and G. Oldfield. The microeconomics of market making. *Journal of Financial and Quantitative Analysis*, 21 (4):361–376, 1986.

[41] G. Saar. Specialist markets. In *Encyclopedia of Quantitative Finance*. Wiley Online Library, 2010.

[42] P. Sandås. Adverse selection and competitive market making: Empirical evidence from a limit order market. *Review of Financial Studies*, 14(3):705–734, 2001.

[43] R. A. Schwartz and L. Peng. Market makers. In *Encyclopedia of Finance*, pages 487–489. Springer, 2013.

[44] D. J. Seppi. Liquidity provision with limit orders and a strategic specialist. *Review of Financial Studies*, 10(1): 103–150, 1997.

[45] P. Vytelingum, D. Cliff, and N. R. Jennings. Strategic bidding in continuous double auctions. *Artificial Intelligence*, 172(14):1700–1729, 2008.

[46] E. Wah and M. P. Wellman. Latency arbitrage, market fragmentation, and efficiency: A two-market model. In *14th ACM Conference on Electronic Commerce*, pages 855–872, 2013.

[47] M. P. Wellman. Methods for empirical game-theoretic analysis (Extended abstract). In *21st National Conference on Artificial Intelligence*, pages 1552–1555, 2006.

[48] M. P. Wellman. *Trading Agents*. Morgan & Claypool, 2011.

[49] B. Wiedenbeck and M. P. Wellman. Scaling simulation-based game analysis through deviation-preserving reduction. In *11th International Conference on Autonomous Agents and Multiagent Systems*, pages 931–938, 2012.

Large-Scale Election Campaigns: Combinatorial Shift Bribery

Robert Bredereck[*]
TU Berlin, Berlin, Germany
robert.bredereck@tu-berlin.de

Piotr Faliszewski[†]
AGH University,
Krakow, Poland
faliszew@agh.edu.pl

Rolf Niedermeier
TU Berlin, Berlin, Germany
rolf.niedermeier@tu-berlin.de

Nimrod Talmon[‡]
TU Berlin, Berlin, Germany
nimrodtalmon77@gmail.com

ABSTRACT

We study the complexity of a combinatorial variant of the SHIFT BRIBERY problem in elections. In the standard SHIFT BRIBERY problem, we are given an election where each voter has a preference order over the candidate set and where an outside agent, the briber, can pay each voter to rank the briber's favorite candidate a given number of positions higher. The goal is to ensure the victory of the briber's preferred candidate. The combinatorial variant of the problem, introduced in this paper, models settings where it is possible to affect the position of the preferred candidate in multiple votes, either positively or negatively, with a single bribery action. This variant of the problem is particularly interesting in the context of large-scale campaign management problems (which, from the technical side, are modeled as bribery problems). We show that, in general, the combinatorial variant of the problem is highly intractable (NP-hard, hard in the parameterized sense, and hard to approximate), but we provide some (approximation) algorithms for natural restricted cases.

Categories and Subject Descriptors

I.2.11 [**Artificial Intelligence**]: Distributed Artificial Intelligence—*Multiagent systems*

Keywords

campaign management, preference aggregation, voting, computational complexity, parameterized complexity, fixed-parameter tractability, approximation algorithms

[*]Supported by the DFG, project PAWS (NI 369/10).

[†]Supported by the DFG, project PAWS (NI 369/10) and by AGH University grant 11.11.230.124 (statutory research).

[‡]Supported by the DFG, RTG MDS (GRK 1408).

Appears in: *Proceedings of the 14th International Conference on Autonomous Agents and Multiagent Systems (AAMAS 2015), Bordini, Elkind, Weiss, Yolum (eds.), May 4–8, 2015, Istanbul, Turkey.*

1. INTRODUCTION

We study the computational complexity of election campaign management, for the case where campaign actions (such as airing a TV advertisement, launching a web-based campaign, or organizing meetings with voters) may have large-scale effects which affect multiple voters. Further, we are interested in settings where these actions can have both positive effects (for example, some voters may choose to rank the promoted candidate higher because they find arguments presented in a given advertisement appealing) as well as negative ones (for example, because some other voters find the advertisement to be too aggressive). Thus, in our settings, the two major issues faced by a campaign manager are (a) choosing actions that positively affect as many voters as possible, and (b) balancing the negative effects of campaigning actions (for example, by concentrating these negative effects on voters who disregard the promoted candidate anyway).

Our research falls within the field of computational social choice, a subarea of multiagent systems. We use the standard election model, where we are given a set C of candidates and a collection V of voters, each represented by his or her preference order (that is, a ranking of the candidates from the most preferred one to the least desired one). That is, we assume that we know the preferences of all the voters. While having such perfect knowledge is impossible in practice, this assumption is a convenient simplification modeling the information we have from preelection polls.

We consider two voting rules, the Plurality rule (where we pick the candidate who is ranked first by most voters) and the Borda rule (where each candidate c gets from each voter v as many points as there are candidates that v prefers c to, and we pick the candidate with the most points). We chose these rules because the Plurality rule is the most widespread rule in practice and because the Borda rule is very well-studied in the context of campaign management.

Within computational social choice, the term *campaign management* (introduced by Elkind et al. [11, 12]) is an alternative name for the bribery family of problems (introduced by Faliszewski et al. [13]) that focuses on modeling actions available during election campaigns: as a result of money spent by a campaign manager, some of the voters change their votes. In this paper we focus on campaign management as modeled by the SHIFT BRIBERY problem [5, 11, 12]. In SHIFT BRIBERY we have a candidate p whom we want to win, for each voter v we have a price $\pi_v(i)$ for which this voter is willing to shift p forward by i positions in his or her preference order[1], and we ask for the lowest cost of ensuring that p is a winner (see "Related Work" below for references to other campaign management problems).

SHIFT BRIBERY has one major drawback as a model for campaign management: it is incapable of modeling large-scale effects of campaign actions. In particular, if one puts out a TV spot promoting a given candidate, then some voters will react positively and rank the candidate higher, some will be oblivious to it, and some will react negatively, by ranking the candidate lower. SHIFT BRIBERY cannot model such correlated effects. In this paper we introduce and study the COMBINATORIAL SHIFT BRIBERY problem, allowing campaign actions to have effects, positive or negative, on whole groups of voters.

We are interested in seeing how such a more realistic model of campaign management affects the complexity of the problem. Indeed, SHIFT BRIBERY is, computationally, a very well-behaved problem. For example, for the Plurality rule it is solvable in polynomial time and for the Borda rule it is NP-complete [12], but there is a polynomial-time 2-approximation algorithm [11, 12] and there are fixed-parameter tractable (FPT) algorithms, either exact or capable of finding solutions arbitrarily close to the optimal ones [5]. We ask to what extent do we retain these good computational properties when we allow large-scale effects. The results are surprising both positively and negatively:

1. COMBINATORIAL SHIFT BRIBERY becomes both NP-complete and W[1]-hard even for the Plurality rule, even for very restrictive choice of parameters, even if the correlated effects of particular campaign actions are limited to at most two voters. These hardness results also imply that good, general approximation algorithms do not exist, and are particularly strong when we allow negative effects of some campaign actions.

2. In spite of the above, it is still possible to derive relatively good (approximation) algorithms, both for the Plurality rule and for the Borda rule, provided that we restrict the effects of the campaign actions to be only positive and to either only involve few voters each, or to only involve groups of consecutive voters.

Due to space constraints several proof details are deferred to a full version of the paper.

Related Work. Our work builds on top of two main research ideas: first, on studying campaign managment/bribery problems, and second, on studying combinatorial variants of election problems.

The study of the computational complexity of bribery in elections was initiated by Faliszewski et al. [13], and continued by a number of researchers [14, 18, 21, 22]. Elkind et al. [11, 12] realized that the formalism of election bribery problems is useful from the point of view of planning election campaigns. In particular, they defined the SWAP BRIBERY problem and its restricted variant, SHIFT BRIBERY. In the former it is possible, at a given price, to swap any two adjacent candidates in a given vote. In the latter, we are only allowed to shift the preferred candidate forward. Various problems, modeling different flavors of campaign management, have been studied, including, for example, the possibility to alter the number of approved/ranked candidates [2, 15, 26]. Different (positive) applications of bribery problems have been revealed. For example, in the MARGIN OF VICTORY view of the problem, the goal of the briber is to prevent some candidate from winning; if it is possible to do so at low cost, then this suggests that the election could have been tampered with [6, 20, 27].

The most related works are those of Elkind et al. [11, 12], Bredereck et al. [5], and Dorn and Schlotter [9]. The former ones study SHIFT BRIBERY, which we generalize (with the work of Bredereck et al. [5] focusing on parameterized complexity), whereas the work of Dorn and Schlotter [9] pioneers the use of parameterized complexity analysis for bribery problems.

Our work is largely inspired by the work of Chen et al. [7], who introduced and studied a combinatorial variant of voter control (control is a very well-studied topic in computational social choice, initiated by Bartholdi et al. [1]). We stress that by combinatorial election problems, in this case, we do not mean the large line of work on modeling combinatorial candidate spaces (see, for example, the papers [3, 8, 22]), but use the same jargon from the mentioned literature with the term "Combinatorial" refering to the "combinations" of voters affected by each bribery action.

2. PRELIMINARIES

Elections. An election $E = (C, V)$ consists of a set $C = \{c_1, \dots, c_m\}$ of candidates and a collection $V = (v_1, \dots, v_n)$ of voters. Each voter is represented through his or her preference order, that is, a linear ranking of the candidates from the most preferred one to the least preferred one. For example, if $C = \{c_1, c_2, c_3\}$, then voter v_1 may have preference order $v_1 \colon c_1 \succ c_2 \succ c_3$ to indicate that he or she likes c_1 best, then c_2, and then c_3. We assume that an arbitrary (but fixed) canonical order over the set of candidates exists (for example, one could order the candidates lexicographically, by their names). If A is some subset of candidates, then writing $\overrightarrow{A}$ within a preference order means listing the candidates from A in this canonical order.

Voting Rules. A voting rule $\mathcal{R}$ is a function that, given an election $E = (C, V)$, outputs a set $\mathcal{R}(E) \subseteq C$ of (tied) election winners. We consider two election rules, the Plurality rule and the Borda rule. Each of these rules assigns points to candidates and outputs those with the highest score. Under the Plurality rule, each candidate receives one point for each voter ranking him or her first. Under the Borda rule, each candidate receives i points for each voter that preferring this candidate to exactly i other ones.

We use the nonunique-winner model. That is, all the candidates output by a given voting rule are viewed as equally successful winners (in practice, of course, one has to use some sort of a tie-breaking rule to resolve the situation, but disregarding ties simplifies the analysis; however, an interested reader should consult papers on the effects of tie-breaking on the complexity of election problems [24, 25]).

[1]Of course, this price does not necessarily reflect a direct money transfer to the voter, but rather the cost of convincing the voter to change his or her mind.

Parameterized Complexity. We assume that the familiarity with standard notions regarding algorithms and complexity theory, but briefly review notions regarding parameterized complexity theory [10, 16, 23].

In parameterized complexity theory, we measure the complexity of a given problem with respect to both the input size and a particular *parameter* of the problem. Typical parameters for election problems include the number of candidates, the number of voters, and the solution size (for example, the number of campaign actions one can perform). We say that a parameterized problem is *fixed-parameter tractable* (is in FPT) if there is an algorithm that, given an input instance I with parameter k, solves the problem in time $g(k)|I|^{O(1)}$, where g is some computable function and $|I|$ is the length of the encoding of I. There is also a hierarchy of hardness classes for parameterized problems, of which the two most important levels are formed by the classes W[1] and W[2]. The most convenient way of defining these classes is through an appropriate reduction notion and their complete problems. Specifically, we say that a parameterized problem A reduces to a parameterized problem B if there are two computable functions, g and g', with the following properties: given an instance I of A with parameter k, $g(I)$ outputs in FPT time an instance I' of B with parameter $k' \leq g'(k)$, such that I is a "yes"-instance of A if and only if I' is a "yes"-instance of B. In other words, g is a standard many-one reduction from A to B, which is allowed to run in FPT time, but such that the parameter parameter of the output instance must be upper-bounded by a function of the input instance's parameter.

The class W[1] is defined as the class of problems that parameterically reduce to the CLIQUE problem, and W[2] as the class of problems that parameterically reduce to the SET COVER problem, where both problems are parameterized by the solution size.

Definition 1. In the CLIQUE problem, we are given an undirected graph $G = (V(G), E(G))$ and an integer h. We ask for the existence of a set H of h vertices such that there is an edge between each pair of vertices from H.

Definition 2. In the SET COVER problem, we are given a universe set X, a family $\mathcal{S}$ of subsets of X, and an integer h. We ask for the existence of at most h sets from $\mathcal{S}$ whose union gives X.

A parameterized problem is contained in the class XP if there is an algorithm that, given an instance I for it with parameter k, solves it in time $|I|^{g(k)}$, where g is some computable function. It holds that FPT $\subseteq$ W[1] $\subseteq$ W[2] $\subseteq$ XP.

3. THE PROBLEM

In this section, we define our COMBINATORIAL SHIFT BRIBERY problem (CSB) in its full generality and describe why and how we simplify it for the remainder of our study.

The Definition. Let $\mathcal{R}$ be some voting rule. The definition of $\mathcal{R}$-CSB is somewhat involved therefore we first define some necessary components. We are given an election $E = (C, V)$ and a *preferred candidate* p. The goal is to ensure that p is an $\mathcal{R}$-winner of the election. To this end, we have a number of possible actions to choose from.

Let $m := |C|$ be the number of candidates in E and let $n := |V|$ be the number of voters. A *shift action* f is an n-dimensional vector of (possibly negative) integers, $f = (f^{(1)}, \ldots, f^{(n)})$. In $\mathcal{R}$-CSB we are given a family $F = (f_1, \ldots, f_\zeta)$ of shift actions. Each particular shift action models a possible campaigning action, such as airing a TV spot or organizing a meeting with the voters. The components of a given shift action measure the effect of the corresponding campaigning action on the particular voters. Further, each shift action f_j $(1 \leq j \leq \zeta)$ comes with a nonnegative integer cost $w(f_j)$ for applying this shift action. For a given subset $F' \subseteq F$ of available shift actions, we define the effect of F' on voter v_i $(1 \leq i \leq n)$ as $\mathcal{E}^{(i)}(F') = \sum_{f_j \in F'} f_j^{(i)}$.

Each voter v_i $(1 \leq i \leq n)$ has his or her individual *threshold function* $\pi_i : \mathbb{Z} \to \mathbb{Z}$ describing how shift actions affect this voter. We require that $\pi_i(0) = 0$ and that π_i is nondecreasing. Let F' be a collection of shift actions. After applying the shift actions from F', each voter v_i $(1 \leq i \leq n)$ shifts the preferred candidate p by $t > 0$ positions forward exactly if (a) $\mathcal{E}^{(i)}(F') > 0$, and (b) $\pi_i(t) \leq \mathcal{E}^{(i)}(F') < \pi_i(t+1)$. The shift is by $t > 0$ positions back if (a) $\mathcal{E}^{(i)}(F') < 0$, and (b) $\pi_i(-t) \geq \mathcal{E}^{(i)}(F') > \pi_i(-t-1)$.

Finally, we are given a nonnegative integer B, the *budget*. We ask for the existence of a collection $F' \subseteq F$ of available shift actions with total cost $\sum_{f_j \in F'} w(f_j)$ at most B and such that after applying them, p is an $\mathcal{R}$-winner of the given election. If this is the case, then we say that F' is *successful*.

Example 1. Consider an election with $C = \{a, b, c, p\}$, where p is the preferred candidate, and with three voters, $v_1 : c \succ b \succ p \succ a$, $v_2 : b \succ a \succ c \succ p$, and $v_3 : p \succ a \succ b \succ c$. We are using the Borda rule. Candidates a, b, c, and p have, respectively, 4, 6, 4, and 4 points. There are three available shift actions: $f_1 = (2, 4, 0)$, $f_2 = (6, 0, -3)$, and $f_3 = (0, 2, 0)$. The threshold functions are such that: (1) $\pi_1(-1) = -4$, $\pi_1(0) = 0$, $\pi_1(1) = 6$, $\pi_1(2) = 100$, (2) $\pi_2(0) = 0$, $\pi_2(1) = 2$, $\pi_2(2) = \pi_2(3) = 100$, and (3) $\pi_3(-3) = \pi_3(-2) - 100$, $\pi_3(-1) = -3$, $\pi_3(0) = 0$. Each shift action has the same cost, $w(f_1) = w(f_2) = w(f_3) = 1$.

It is easy to see that applying any single shift action does not ensure p's victory. However, applying shift actions $F' = \{f_2, f_3\}$ results in p being a winner. The total effect of these two shift actions is $(6, 2, -3)$. According to the threshold functions, this means that p is shifted forward by one position in v_1 and v_2, and is shifted backwards by one position in v_3. After these shifts, the modified election has the following votes: $v_1' : c \succ p \succ b \succ a$, $v_2' : b \succ a \succ p \succ c$, and $v_3' : a \succ p \succ b \succ c$. Therefore, candidate c has 3 points, while all other candidates have 5 points each; a, b, and p are tied winners. Therefore, F' is successful.

Formally, given a voting rule $\mathcal{R}$, we define the $\mathcal{R}$-CSB problem as follows:

> $\mathcal{R}$-COMBINATORIAL SHIFT BRIBERY ($\mathcal{R}$-CSB)
> **Input:** An election $E = (C, V)$, where $C = \{c_1, \ldots, c_m\}$ is the set of candidates and $V = (v_1, \ldots, v_n)$ is the collection of voters, a set $F = \{f_1, \ldots, f_\zeta\}$ of shift actions with costs $w(f_1), \ldots, w(f_\zeta)$, threshold functions $\pi_1, \ldots, \pi_n$, and a nonnegative integral budget B. One of the candidates is designated as the preferred candidate p.
> **Question:** Is there a subset $F' \subseteq F$ of shift actions with total cost at most B such that, after

we apply the shift actions from F', candidate p is an $\mathcal{R}$-winner of the resulting election?

While this definition is quite complicated, it captures some important features of campaigning. For example, the use of threshold functions allows us to model voters who are unwilling to change the position of the preferred candidate beyond a certain range, irrespective of the strength of the campaign. The fact that different shift actions have different costs models the fact that particular actions (for example, airing TV spots or organizing meetings) may come at different costs.

Relation to Standard Shift Bribery. It is now necessary to comment on the relation between our COMBINATORIAL SHIFT BRIBERY problem and its noncombinatorial variant, SHIFT BRIBERY [11, 12]. If we restrict our shift actions such that each shift action has a positive entry for exactly one voter, then—in effect—we obtain SHIFT BRIBERY for the case of *convex price functions* [5]. This is a very general variant of the SHIFT BRIBERY problem (but nonetheless not the most general one) for which, for example, all the known NP-hardness results hold. We decided not to complicate our definition further, to obtain a full generalization. As we will see below, doing so would obfuscate the problem without visible gain.

Hardness Result. The problem as defined above is so general that it allows for the following, sweeping, hardness result.[2]

THEOREM 1. *Both Plurality*-CSB *and Borda*-CSB *are (weakly)* NP*-hard even for five voters and two candidates.*

PROOF (CONSTRUCTION ONLY). We reduce from the following (weakly NP-hard) variant of the SUBSET SUM problem. We are given a set $A := \{a_1, \ldots, a_n\}$ of integers and we ask for the existence of a nonempty set A', $A' \subseteq A$, such that $\sum_{a_i \in A'} a_i = 0$.

Note that for elections with two candidates Plurality and Borda coincide. Given an instance $A = \{a_1, \ldots, a_n\}$ of our variant of SUBSET SUM, we construct an instance of Plurality-CSB with two candidates (indeed, since Borda and Plurality coincide for elections with two candidates, our hardness result transfers to Borda-CSB).

We take two candidates d and p, two voters, v_1 and v_2, preferring p, and three voters, v_3, v_4, and v_5, preferring d. For each element $a_i \in A$ we create one shift action f_i with effect a_i on v_1, effect $-a_i$ on v_2, effect 1 on v_3, and no effect on the other two voters. Each shift action has the same unit cost. The voter threshold functions are as follows. Candidate p is shifted to the last position for v_1 and v_2 if the effect on these voters is negative (that is, $\pi_1(-1) = \pi_2(-1) = -1$). Candidate p is shifted to the top position for the third voter if the effect is positive (that is, $\pi_3(1) = 1$). We set the cost of each shift action to be one and we set our budget to be n. □

Effectively, Theorem 1 shows that studying large-scale effects of campaign actions through the full-fledged $\mathcal{R}$-CSB problem leads to a hopelessly intractable problem as we obtain hardness even for elections with both a fixed number of candidates and a fixed number of voters.

[2]Note, however, that we prove weak NP-hardness. That is, our result may not hold if we assume that all occurring numbers are encoded in unary. On the contrary, all other hardness proofs in this paper give strong hardness results and are independent of such number encoding issues.

Restriction of CSB. Throughout the rest of the paper, we assume the individual threshold functions to be identity functions (that is, for each voter i and each integer t, it holds that $\pi_i(t) = t$) and we assume each shift action to have the same unit cost. Note that the instances built in the proof of Theorem 1 satisfy these restrictions and, so, considering harder instances is beyond point. Notably, however we will consider restricted types of shift actions as well (see Section 4).

Our restrictions on the costs and on the threshold functions require discussion. First, identity threshold functions mean that we model societies that are prone to propaganda. Second, assuming that every shift action has the same unit cost models settings where the costs of particular campaign actions are similar enough that small differences between them are irrelevant; the actual number of actions we choose to perform is a sufficiently good approximation of the real cost. This is true, for example, for the case of organizing meetings with voters, which often have comparable prices. It is also likely to be the case when shift actions model actions such as airing TV spots: each spot has a similar cost to produce/broadcast. The greatest disadvantage of assuming unit costs is that we no longer can model mixed campaigns that use actions of several different types (meetings with voters, TV spots, web campaigns, etc.).

Considered Parameters. We consider the influence of the following parameters on the computational complexity of our CSB problems: (1) the number n of voters, (2) the number m of candidates, (3) the budget B, (4) the maximum effect Γ of a single shift action (that is, $\Gamma := \max_{f \in F} \max_{1 \le i \le n} f^{(i)}$ where $f^{(i)}$ denotes the ith position of the vector f), and (5) the maximum number Λ of voters affected by a single shift action (that is, $\Lambda := \max_{f \in F} |\{i : f^{(i)} \neq 0\}|$).

4. RESULTS

It turns out that even with the above restrictions in place, COMBINATORIAL SHIFT BRIBERY is computationally hard in many settings. Thus, what we present here is our quest for understanding the border between tractability and intractability of CSB. To this end, we employ the following techniques and ideas: (1) we seek both regular complexity results (NP-hardness results) and parameterized complexity results (FPT algorithms, W[1] and W[2]-hardness results, XP algorithms) (2) we consider structural restrictions on the sets of shift actions available, and (3) we seek approximation algorithms and inapproximability results.

We consider the following families of shift actions:

Unrestricted Shift Actions. Here we put no restrictions on the allowed shift actions; this models the most general (and, naturally, the least tractable) setting.

Bounded-Effect Shift Actions. Here we consider a parameter Γ, and require that for each shift action $f = (f^{(1)}, \ldots, f^{(n)})$, it holds that for each j ($1 \le j \le n$), we have $|f^{(j)}| \le \Gamma$. This is still a very general setting, where we assume that each campaigning action has only a limited impact on each voter.

Unit-Effect Shift Actions. This is a class of bounded-effect shift actions for $\Gamma = 1$. For each given voter, applying a given shift action can either leave the preferred candidate p unaffected or it can shift p one position up or down.

Interval Shift Actions. This a subclass of unit-effect shift actions that never affect voters negatively, and where for each shift action there is an interval of voters that are affected positively (the interval is with respect to the order of the voters in the input collection V). This class of shift actions models campaigns associated with a time window where certain voters can be reached or campaigns that are local to given neighborhoods[3] (for example, that include putting up multiple posters, organizing meetings, etc.).

Unit-Effect on Two Voters Shift Actions. This is a subclass of unit-effect shift actions that affect two voters at most. We focus on shift actions that affect both voters positively, denoted as $(+1, +1)$-shift actions, and that affect one voter positively and one voter negatively, denoted as $(+1, -1)$-shift actions. The reason for studying these families is not because they model particularly natural types of election campaigns, but rather to establish the limits of tractability for our problem. For example, we consider $(+1, -1)$-shift actions to understand how intractable are shift actions that have negative effects; $(+1, -1)$-shift actions are the simplest shift actions of this type that may be useful in the campaign (one would never deliberately use $(-1, -1)$-shift actions).

Figure 1 presents graphically the difference between interval shift actions and unit-effect on two voters shift actions.

The remainder of this section has the following structure. First, in Section 4.1, we show relations of Plurality-CSB to the problem of combinatorial control by adding voters, establishing quite general hardness results (applied already to unit-effect shift actions). Then, in Section 4.2, we present a series of strong hardness results covering all our classes of shift actions for very restrictive sets of parameters (for example, many of our results apply already to the case of two candidates). Then, in Sections 4.3 and 4.4, we present some ways of dealing with our hardness results. Table 1 gives an overview of our main results.

4.1 Connection to Combinatorial Control

The study of combinatorial variants of problems modeling ways of affecting election results was initiated by Chen et al. [7], who considered combinatorial control by adding voters (COMB-CCAV) for the Plurality rule and the Condorcet rule. It turns out that for the Plurality rule we can reduce the problem of (COMBINATORIAL) CCAV to that of (COMBINATORIAL) SHIFT BRIBERY. For the non-combinatorial variants of these problems this does not give much since both are easily seen to be polynomial-time solvable. However, there are strong hardness results for Plurality-COMB-CCAV which we can transfer to the case of Plurality-CSB. Formally, Plurality-COMBINATORIAL-CCAV is defined as follows [7].

Definition 3. An instance of Plurality-COMB-CCAV consists of a set C of candidates with a preferred candidate $p \in C$, a collection V of registered voters, a collection W of unregistered voters, a bundling function $\kappa \colon W \to 2^W$ (for each $w \in W$, it holds that $w \in \kappa(w)$), and a nonnegative integer k. Each voter has a preference order over C. We ask for the existence of a collection $W' \subseteq W$ of at most k voters such that p is a winner of the modifed election $(C, V \cup \bigcup_{w' \in W'} \kappa(w'))$.

[3]In the neighborhood scenario, we take the simplified view that a society of the voters lives on a line. Of course, it would be more natural to take two-dimensional neighborhoods into account. We view this as an interesting direction for future research, but for the time being we consider as simple settings as possible. In the time window scenario, a natural ordering of the voters is the point of time when they cast their votes or can be affected by the campaign.

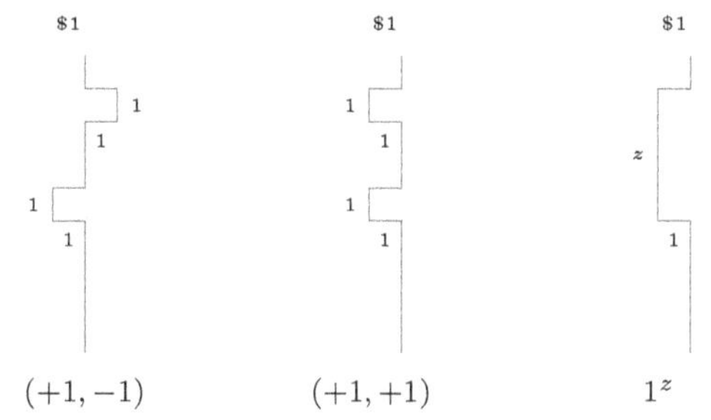

Figure 1: Restrictions on the shift actions. We visualize (from left to right) a shift action "$(+1, -1)$" with effect of $+1$ on one voter and effect of -1 on another voter, a shift action "$(+1, +1)$" with effect of $+1$ on two voters, and a shift action with effect of $+1$ on an interval of size z "1^z". The intended interpretation is that voters are listed vertically, from top to bottom.

Intuitively, for each unregistered voter $w \in W$, we have his or her bundle, $\kappa(w)$ (given explicitly in the input), such that when we add w to the election (for example, by somehow convincing him or her to vote), all the voters in his or her bundle also join the election (for example, people choose to vote under an influence of a friend).

THEOREM 2. *Plurality-*COMB-CCAV *is polynomial-time many-one reducible to Plurality-*CSB. *For an instance of Plurality-*COMB-CCAV *with m candidates, the reduction outputs an instance with $m + 1$ candidates.*

The idea of the proof is as follows. We create an election with both the registered and unregistered voters present. For the unregistered voters that rank p first, we put a new candidate d on top, such that shifting p forward has the effect of "adding" this voter. For the unregistered voters that rank some candidate other than p first, we shift p to the top, such that shifting p back (with a negative effect of a shift action) has the effect of "adding" this voter (we also need some additional voters to maintain the same score differences as in the original control instance). Using this reduction and the results of Chen et al. [7], we obtain the following.

COROLLARY 3. *Plurality-*CSB *is $W[2]$-hard with respect to parameter B even if $m = 3$, it is $W[1]$-hard with respect to parameter B even for shift actions with unit effect on up to 6 voters, and it is* NP*-hard even for shift actions with unit effects on up to 4 voters.*

4.2 Hardness Results

The results from the previous section show that we are bound to hit hard instances for COMBINATORIAL SHIFT BRIBERY even in very restricted settings. Now, we explore how restrictive these hard settings are.

We start by considering unit-effect shift actions. If the allowed effects are positive only, then we obtain NP-

Table 1: Overview of our results. We show exact algorithms and approximation algorithms for Plurality-CSB and Borda-CSB, for different restrictions on the shift actions (see Figure 1). Note that all of the variants are XP for parameter B. Recall that n denotes the number of voters and m denotes the number of candidates.

shift actions	rule	exact complexity	approximability
regular SHIFT BRIBERY (convex prices)	Plurality	polynomial-time solvable ([12])	—
	Borda	NP-complete but in FPT for B [5, 12]	2-approximable in poly. time [11, 12] FPT-approximation scheme for n [5]
unit effect	Both	W[2]-h for B even if $m = 2$ (Thm. 4) XP for n (Prop. 10)	inapproximable even in FPT-time for B and $m = 2$ (Thm. 5)
$(+1, -1)$	Plurality	FPT for n (Thm. 11)	—
	Borda	W[1]-hard for n (Thm. 8)	—
	Both	NP-h even if $m = 2$ (Thm. 6) W[1]-h for B and m combined (Thm. 7)	inapproximable even if $m = 2$ (Thm. 6)
$(+1, +1)$	Plurality	FPT for n (Thm 11)	—
	Both	W[1]-h for B and m combined (Thm. 7)	2-approximable in poly. time (Thm. 12)
1^z-intervals	Plurality	FPT for n (Thm. 11)	z-approximable in poly. time (Thm. 12)
	Borda	—	$2z$-approximable in poly. time (Thm. 12)
	Both	W[1]-h for B (Thm. 9)	2-approximable in m^z time (Thm. 14)

hardness/W[2]-hardness for parameterization by the budget B. If we allow also negative unit-effects, we even go beyond any hope for an approximation algorithm, even if the approximation algorithm was allowed to run in FPT time for parameter B. Quite strikingly, these results hold even if we only have two candidates.

THEOREM 4. *Plurality*-CSB *and Borda*-CSB *are both* NP*-hard and* W[2]*-hard for the parameter B, even for two candidates and even if each shift action has effects of either* $+1$ *or* 0 *on each voter.*

THEOREM 5. *Unless* W[2] = FPT, *both Plurality*-CSB *and Borda*-CSB *are inapproximable even in* FPT*-time for the parameter B, even for two candidates and even for unit-effect shift actions.*

PROOF. Let $(\mathcal{S}, X, h)$ be a SET COVER instance. We construct an instance of Plurality-CSB with two candidates. Since Borda and Plurality coincide for elections with two candidates, our hardness result transfers to Borda-CSB.

For each element $x_i \in X$, create $|\mathcal{S}|$ *element voters* $v_i^1, \ldots, v_i^{|\mathcal{S}|}$, each with preference order $d \succ p$, and for each set $S_j \in \mathcal{S}$ create a *set voter* v_j^0 with preference order $p \succ d$. Create $|\mathcal{S}| \cdot |X| + |\mathcal{S}| - 2h$ *dummy voters*, each with preference order $d \succ p$. The set F of shift actions contains, for each set S_j, a shift action f_j having an effect of 1 on each element voter corresponding to an element of the set and an effect of -1 on the set voter corresponding to the set. Finally, set $B := h$. This completes the construction.

Next, we show that there is a set cover of size h if and only if there is a successful set of shift actions of size h.

For the "only if" part, assume that there is a set cover $\mathcal{S}'$ of size at most h. Then, $F' = \{f_j \mid S_j \in \mathcal{S}'\}$ is a successful set of shift actions: since $\mathcal{S}'$ is a set cover, p will be the preferred candidate for all $|\mathcal{S}| \cdot |X|$ element voters and $|\mathcal{S}| - h$ set voters (corresponding to the sets not from the set cover) and d will be the preferred candidate for all $|\mathcal{S}| \cdot |X| + |\mathcal{S}| - 2h$ dummy voters and for h set voters (corresponding to the sets from the set cover). Hence, d and p tie as winners.

For the "if" part, assume that there is a successful set of shift actions $F' \subseteq F$ of size at most h. Then, p must be the preferred candidate for all element voters in the bribed election: if there is an element voter with $d \succ p$, then there are $|\mathcal{S}| - 1$ further element voters with $d \succ p$ (namely those being identical with respect to the effect of the shift actions). However, there will be in total at most $|\mathcal{S}|(|X| - 1)$ element voters and $|\mathcal{S}|$ set voters preferring p, but at least $|\mathcal{S}| \cdot |X| + |\mathcal{S}| - 2h$ dummy voters and $|\mathcal{S}|$ element voters preferring d. It follows that $\mathcal{S}' := \{S_j \mid f_j \in F'\}$ must be a set cover in order to make p win the election, and the size of the set $\mathcal{S}'$ is at most h due to the budget being h.

Finally, we show that Plurality-CSB is inapproximable even in FPT time when parameterized by the budget. Assume, towards a contradiction, that a set of shift actions $F' \subseteq F$ with $|F'| > B$ exists. Then, in the bribed election, at least $|\mathcal{S}| \cdot |X| + |\mathcal{S}| - 2h$ dummy voters and also $|F'| \geq h+1$ set voters prefer d, but at most $|\mathcal{S}| \cdot |X|$ element voters and at most $|\mathcal{S}| - (h + 1)$ set voters prefer p. Thus, d is the unique winner. Hence, *any* successful bribery action must be optimal and any FPT-algorithm for Plurality-CSB (parameterized by the budget) would solve the W[2]-hard problem SET COVER (parameterized by the solution size) in FPT time; a contradiction to FPT $\neq$ W[2]. □

In the above theorems we do not limit the number of voters affected by each shift action. Even if we consider only $(+1, -1)$-shift actions, then the problem remains NP-hard and hard to approximate even for two candidates.

THEOREM 6. *Unless* P = NP, *both Plurality*-CSB *and Borda*-CSB *neither can be solved exactly nor can be approximated in polynomial time even for two candidates and even if we only have $(+1, -1)$-shift actions.*

Note that, compared to Theorem 5, Theorem 6 does not yield W[2]-hardness for the parameter budget B; our proof uses a reduction from SET COVER in which the value of the budget is the size of the universe set X. If we insist on parameterized hardness for unit effects on two voters, then we have to accept larger sets of candidates. However, this increase is not too large: we show W[1]-hardness of CSB jointly parameterized by the budget and the number of candidates.

THEOREM 7. *Both Plurality-CSB and Borda-CSB are W[1]-hard for the combined parameter (m, B), even if we either only have $(+1, -1)$-shift actions or only have $(+1, +1)$-shift actions.*

PROOF. We give a parameterized reduction from the W[1]-hard CLIQUE problem, parameterized by the solution size, to Plurality-CSB, parameterized by (m, B), with $(+1, +1)$-shift actions (we omit the other cases due to space constraints).

Let (G, h) be an instance of CLIQUE with $V(G) = \{u_1, \ldots, u_{n'}\}$ and $E(G) = \{e_1, \ldots, e_{m'}\}$. We create an instance of Plurality-CSB as follows. The set of candidates is $\{p\} \cup D$, where $D = \{d_1, \ldots, d_{h-1}\}$. For each vertex $u_i \in V(G)$, we create a *vertex voter* v_i with preference order $\overrightarrow{D} \succ p$. Moreover, we create h *dummy voters* with preference order $\overrightarrow{D} \succ p$ each, and $n' - h$ *dummy voter* with preference order $p \succ \overrightarrow{D}$ each. For each edge $\{u_i, u_j\} \in E(G)$, we create a shift action $f_{\{u_i, u_j\}}$ with effect 1 on the vertex voters v_i and v_j and effect 0 on all other voters. Finally, we set the budget to $B := \binom{h}{2}$. This completes the construction.

We assume that d_1 is ranked first in the order $\overrightarrow{D}$. Observe that we have n' vertex voters and h dummy voters that rank d_1 first. We also have $n' - h$ dummy voters that rank p first. Hence, to make p win the election, one needs h additional voters to rank p first (and, in effect, not rank d_1 first).

It remains to show that (G, h) contains a clique of size at most h if and only if our constructed instance contains a successful set of shift actions F' of size at most h.

For the "only if" part, let $H \subseteq V(G)$ be a set of h vertices forming a clique and $E' \subseteq E(G)$ be the set of edges between vertices from H. Then, observe that $F' = \{f_{\{u_i, u_j\}} \mid \{u_i, u_j\} \in E'\}$ is a successful set of shift actions: for each vertex voter v_i with $u_i \in H$, candidate p is shifted $h - 1$ positions forward. This means that h vertex voters rank p first and p ties as a winner of the election.

For the "if" part, let F' be a successful set of shift actions. To make p a winner of the election, p must be shifted to the top position in at least h vertex voters (dummy voters cannot be affected). That is, in total p must be shifted $h \cdot (h - 1)$ positions forward. Since F' is of size at most $B = \binom{h}{2} = h \cdot (h - 1)/2$ and each shift action affects only two vertex voters, F' must be of size exactly $\binom{h}{2}$ affecting exactly h vertex voters. By construction, this implies that there are $\binom{h}{2}$ edges in G incident to exactly h different vertices which is only possible if these h vertices form a clique. □

It is quite natural to consider CSB also from a different perspective. Instead of asking what happens for a small number of candidates, we might ask about the complexity of CSB for a small number of voters (see, for example, the work of Brandt et al. [4] for some motivation as to why looking at elections with few voters is interesting). In this case we obtain hardness for Borda only; we will show later that Plurality-CSB is in FPT for this parameter.

THEOREM 8. *Borda-CSB is W[1]-hard with respect to the number n of voters, even for $(+1, -1)$-shift actions.*

Finally, we consider interval shift actions. In the above theorems we allowed shift actions to have non-zero effects on two voters each, but these two voters could have been chosen arbitrarily. Now we show a hardness result for the case where we can positively affect multiple voters, but these voters have to form a consecutive interval in the election.

THEOREM 9. *Both Plurality-CSB and Borda-CSB are NP-hard even if each shift action has effect 1 on a consecutive interval interval of z voters and effect 0 on all other voters.*

A brief summary of the results from this section is that $\mathcal{R}$-CSB is highly intractable. Theorems 4, 5, and 6 show that it is computationally hard (in terms of NP-hardness, W[2]-hardness, and inapproximability even by FPT algorithms) both for Plurality and Borda even for various very restricted forms of unit-effect shift actions, even for two candidates. This means that, in essence, the problem is hard for all natural voting rules, because for two candidates all natural voting rules boil down to the Plurality rule.

Further, Theorems 7 and 9 show that our problems are W[1]-hard even if we take the number of candidates and the budget as a joint parameter, even for extremely restricted shift actions. The problem remains hard (for the case of Borda) when parameterized by the number of voters (Theorem 8). On the contrary, for the case of Plurality, for this parameter we will show tractability.

4.3 Exact Algorithms

In spite of the pessimism looming from the previous section, we now show two exact FPT and XP algorithms for $\mathcal{R}$-CSB; in Section 4.4 we present some efficient approximation algorithms.

We show an XP algorithm for the case of bounded-effect shift actions (which include all unit-effect shift actions) for our problem, when parameterized by the number of voters.

PROPOSITION 10. *If the maximum effect is upper-bounded by a constant, then both Plurality-CSB and Borda-CSB are in XP for the parameter budget B.*

Proposition 10 holds even if each shift action comes at an individual cost and if each voter has an individual threshold function. By expressing our problem as an integer linear program (ILP) and by using a famous result of Lenstra [19], we can strengthen the XP-membership to FPT-membership, for the case of Plurality.

THEOREM 11. *For bounded-effect shift actions, Plurality-CSB is in FPT for the parameter number n of voters.*

PROOF. Given an instance I of Plurality-CSB with n voters, our algorithm proceeds as follows. First, we guess a subset of the voters for whom we will guarantee that p is ranked first (there are 2^n guesses to try). For each guessed set of voters, we test whether p would be a winner of the election if p was shifted to the top position by the guessed voters and was not ranked first by the remaining voters. For each set of guessed subset V' of voters for which this test is positive, we check whether it is possible to ensure (by applying shift actions whose cost does not exceed the budget) that the voters from V' rank p first. We do so as follows.

Let Γ be the value bounding, component-wise, the effect of each shift action. Observe that there are at most $(2\Gamma+1)^n$ types of different shift actions. For each shift action type z, we introduce a variable x_z denoting the number of times a shift action of type z is present in the solution. For each voter v_i, denote by $s_{v_i}(p)$ the position of p in the original preference order of v_i. For each voter $v_i \in V'$, we add the following constraint:

$$\sum_{\gamma\in[-\Gamma,\Gamma]} \left(\gamma \sum_{\{z:f_z \text{ has an effect of } \gamma \text{ on } v_i\}} x_z\right) \geq s_{v_i}(p).$$

This ensures that p is indeed shifted to the top position in v_i's preference list. We add another constraint: $\sum x_z \leq B$, ensuring that the solution respects the budget. Finally, for each shift action type z we add a constraint ensuring that we use at most as many shift actions of type z as there are available in the input. This finishes the description of the ILP. By a result of Lenstra [19], we can solve this ILP in FPT time, because we have at most $(2\Gamma + 1)^n$ integer variables.

Correctness follows from the fact that, for any "yes"-instance, there must be at least one good guess of V'; for this V', the ILP will compute a correct answer. □

Theorem 11 is the reason why Theorem 8 applies to Borda only.

4.4 Approximation Algorithms

We now explore the possibility of finding approximate solutions for COMBINATORIAL SHIFT BRIBERY. Theorems 5 and 6 show that we cannot hope for approximate results when shift actions have negative effects. Thus, in this section, we focus on unit-effect shift-actions with positive effects only. We can make good use of the approximation algorithms for the non-combinatorial variant of SHIFT BRIBERY.

THEOREM 12. *If each shift action has effects of either 0 or 1 on each voter, then Plurality-*CSB *can be Λ-approximated in polynomial-time and Borda-*CSB *can be 2Λ-approximated in polynomial time, where Λ denotes the maximum number of voters affected by a shift action.*

PROOF. We consider the case of Borda-CSB first. The idea is to translate the instance into a regular Borda-SHIFT BRIBERY instance with convex price functions and apply the known 2-approximation algorithm [11, 12] and "greedily reconstruct" the corresponding solution with combinatorial shift actions.

Let $\lambda(i)$ denote the number of shift actions affecting voter i. We copy the election from our Borda-CSB instance and set the price function for each voter i such that, for $j \leq \lambda(i)$, shifting p by j positions costs j and for $j > \lambda(i)$ shifting p by j positions costs B^j (note that the exponential function B^j ensures that the price functions are convex and that one cannot shift p by more than $\lambda(i)$ positions). Then, we apply the 2-approximation algorithm whose solution yields, for each voter i, the number $s(i)$ of positions p is shifted in the preference list of voter i. The cost of this solution is $\sum_{1\leq i\leq n} s(i)$. To obtain a solution F' for the Borda-CSB instance we greedily select shift actions until p was shifted at least $s(i)$ positions for each voter i. Observe that $|F'| \leq \sum_{1\leq i\leq n} s(i)$. Now, assume towards a contradiction that there is a successful set of shift actions F'' smaller than $|F'|/2\Lambda$. Then, in this solution p was shifted less than $|F'|/2$ positions in total, because each shift action affects at most Λ voters. However, then there would also be a solution for the regular SHIFT BRIBERY instance with costs smaller than $\sum_{1\leq i\leq n} s(i)/2$; a contradiction to the fact that we applied a 2-approximation.

The case of Plurality-CSB follows analogously, but we use an exact polynomial-time algorithm for Plurality-SHIFT BRIBERY instead of the 2-approximate one. □

We can achieve better approximation guarantees for Borda, when further restricting the allowed shift actions. The next result follows by finding (in polynomial-time) a b-matching [17] in a naturally constructed multigraph, followed by using a general framework for 2-approximation algorithms for SHIFT BRIBERY [11].

THEOREM 13. *Borda-*CSB *is 2-approximable in polynomial time for $(+1,+1)$-shift actions.*

The above result is mostly of theoretical value: it shows that indeed we can retain high-quality polynomial-time approximation algorithms when some combinatorial shift-action effects are allowed. However, from a practical point of view, it is more interesting to see what we can achieve for, say, interval shift actions. Using the ideas of Elkind and Faliszewski [11] and a natural generalization of the maximum interval cover algorithm of Gabow [17], we obtain a 2-approximation algorithm for CSB with interval shift actions. Unfortunately, the algorithm requires XP time, parameterized by the longest interval's length.

THEOREM 14. *Both Plurality-*CSB *and Borda-*CSB *can be 2-approximated in* XP*-time for interval shift actions, provided that we take z, the upper bound on the number of voters affected by each shift action, as the parameter.*

We see that it is still possible to achieve some approximation algorithms for our problems. However, the settings in which our algorithms are efficient are quite restrictive. This means that in practice one should seek good heuristics and use our algorithms only to guide the initial search.

5. CONCLUSIONS

We have defined and studied the computational complexity of a combinatorial variant of the SHIFT BRIBERY problem [5, 11, 12]. Our research was motivated by the desire to understand the computational difficulty imposed by correlated, large-scale effects of campaign actions. In this respect, our work was motivated by the combinatorial study of election control [7]. We have found that our problem, COMBINATORIAL SHIFT BRIBERY, is highly worst-case intractable in multiple ways. Nonetheless, we found some initial positive results. Our results suggest studying further restrictions of the problem: for example, parameterization by the number of available shift actions gives immediate FPT results, so maybe there are other natural parameterizations that lead to more positive results? It would be also interesting to consider domain restrictions regarding voters' preferences (single-crossing seems particularly natural in the context of interval shift actions).

REFERENCES

[1] J. J. Bartholdi, III, C. A. Tovey, and M. A. Trick. How hard is it to control an election. *Mathematical and Computer Modelling*, 16(8–9):27–40, 1992.

[2] D. Baumeister, P. Faliszewski, J. Lang, and J. Rothe. Campaigns for lazy voters: Truncated ballots. In *Proceedings of the 11th International Conference on Autonomous Agents and Multiagent Systems (AAMAS '12)*, pages 577–584. IFAAMAS, 2012.

[3] C. Boutilier, R. I. Brafman, C. Domshlak, H. H. Hoos, and D. Poole. CP-nets: A tool for representing and reasoning with conditional *ceteris paribus* preference statements. *Journal of Artificial Intelligence Research*, 21:135–191, 2004.

[4] F. Brandt, P. Harrenstein, K. Kardel, and H. Seedig. It only takes a few: On the hardness of voting with a constant number of agents. In *Proceedings of the 12th International Conference on Autonomous Agents and Multiagent Systems (AAMAS '13)*, pages 375–382. IFAAMAS, 2013.

[5] R. Bredereck, J. Chen, P. Faliszewski, A. Nichterlein, and R. Niedermeier. Prices matter for the parameterized complexity of shift bribery. In *Proceedings of the 28th AAAI Conference on Artificial Intelligence (AAAI '14)*, pages 1398–1404. AAAI Press, 2014.

[6] D. Cary. Estimating the margin of victory for instant-runoff voting. Presented at the 2011 Electronic Voting Technology Workshop/Workshop on Trustworthy Elections, 2011.

[7] J. Chen, P. Faliszewski, R. Niedermeier, and N. Talmon. Combinatorial voter control in elections. In *Proceedings of the 39th International Symposium on Mathematical Foundations of Computer Science (MFCS '14)*, volume 8635 of *LNCS*, pages 153–164. Springer, 2014.

[8] V. Conitzer, J. Lang, and L. Xia. How hard is it to control sequential elections via the agenda? In *Proceedings of the 21st International Joint Conference on Artificial Intelligence (IJCAI '10)*, pages 103–108. AAAI Press, 2009.

[9] B. Dorn and I. Schlotter. Multivariate complexity analysis of swap bribery. *Algorithmica*, 64(1):126–151, 2012.

[10] R. G. Downey and M. R. Fellows. *Fundamentals of Parameterized Complexity*. Springer, 2013.

[11] E. Elkind and P. Faliszewski. Approximation algorithms for campaign management. In *Proceedings of the 6th International Workshop On Internet And Network Economics (WINE '10)*, volume 6484 of *LNCS*, pages 473–482. Springer, 2010.

[12] E. Elkind, P. Faliszewski, and A. Slinko. Swap bribery. In *Proceedings of the 2nd International Symposium on Algorithmic Game Theory (SAGT '09)*, volume 5814 of *LNCS*, pages 299–310. Springer, 2009.

[13] P. Faliszewski, E. Hemaspaandra, and L. A. Hemaspaandra. How hard is bribery in elections? *Journal of Artificial Intelligence Research*, 35:485–532, 2009.

[14] P. Faliszewski, E. Hemaspaandra, L. A. Hemaspaandra, and J. Rothe. Llull and Copeland Voting Computationally Resist Bribery and Constructive Control. *Journal of Artificial Intelligence Research*, 35:275–341, 2009.

[15] P. Faliszewski, Y. Reisch, J. Rothe, and L. Schend. Complexity of manipulation, bribery, and campaign management in Bucklin and fallback voting. In *Proceedings of the 13th International Conference on Autonomous Agents and Multiagent Systems (AAMAS '14)*, pages 1357–1358. IFAAMAS, 2014.

[16] J. Flum and M. Grohe. *Parameterized Complexity Theory*. Springer, 2006.

[17] H. N. Gabow. An efficient reduction technique for degree-constrained subgraph and bidirected network flow problems. In *Proceedings of the 15th Annual ACM Symposium on Theory of Computing (STOC '83)*, pages 448–456. ACM, 1983.

[18] N. Hazon, R. Lin, and S. Kraus. How to change a group's collective decision? In *Proceedings of the 23rd International Joint Conference on Artificial Intelligence (IJCAI '13)*, pages 198–205. AAAI Press, 2013.

[19] H. W. Lenstra. Integer programming with a fixed number of variables. *Mathematics of Operations Research*, 8(4):538–548, 1983.

[20] T. Magrino, R. Rivest, E. Shen, and D. Wagner. Computing the margin of victory in IRV elections. Presented at the 2011 Electronic Voting Technology Workshop/Workshop on Trustworthy Elections, 2011.

[21] N. Mattei, J. Goldsmith, and A. Klapper. On the complexity of bribery and manipulation in tournaments with uncertain information. In *Proceedings of the 25th International Florida Artificial Intelligence Research Society Conference (FLAIRS '12)*, pages 549–554. AAAI Press, 2012.

[22] N. Mattei, M. Pini, F. Rossi, and K. Venable. Bribery in voting over combinatorial domains is easy. In *Proceedings of the 11th International Conference on Autonomous Agents and Multiagent Systems (AAMAS '12)*, pages 1407–1408. IFAAMAS, 2012.

[23] R. Niedermeier. *Invitation to Fixed-Parameter Algorithms*. Oxford University Press, 2006.

[24] S. Obraztsova and E. Elkind. On the complexity of voting manipulation under randomized tie-breaking. In *Proceedings of the 22nd International Joint Conference on Artificial Intelligence (IJCAI '11)*, pages 319–324. AAAI Press, 2011.

[25] S. Obraztsova, E. Elkind, and N. Hazon. Ties matter: Complexity of voting manipulation revisited. In *Proceedings of the 10th International Conference on Autonomous Agents and Multiagent Systems (AAMAS '11)*, pages 71–78, 2011.

[26] I. Schlotter, P. Faliszewski, and E. Elkind. Campaign management under approval-driven voting rules. In *Proceedings of the 25th AAAI Conference on Artificial Intelligence (AAAI '11)*, pages 726–731. AAAI Press, 2011.

[27] L. Xia. Computing the margin of victory for various voting rules. In *Proceedings of the 13th ACM Conference on Electronic Commerce (EC '12)*, pages 982–999. ACM Press, 2012.

Manipulation with Bounded Single-Peaked Width: A Parameterized Study

Yongjie Yang
Universität des Saarlandes
Campus E 1.7 (MMCI), D-66123 Saarbrücken, Germany
yyongjie@mmci.uni-saarland.de

ABSTRACT

We study the manipulation problem in elections with bounded single-peaked width from the parameterized complexity point of view. In particular, we focus on the Borda, Copeland$^\alpha$ and Maximin voting correspondences. For Borda, we prove that the unweighted manipulation problem with two manipulators is fixed-parameter tractable with respect to single-peaked width. For Maximin and Copeland$^\alpha$ for every $0 \leq \alpha \leq 1$, we prove that the unweighted manipulation problem is fixed-parameter tractable with respect to the combined parameter (k, t), where k denotes the single-peaked width and t denotes the number of manipulators. In addition, we study the weighted manipulation problem for Maximin and Copeland$^\alpha$ for every $0 \leq \alpha \leq 1$ in single-peaked elections and achieve several polynomial-time solvability results.

Categories and Subject Descriptors

F.2 [**Theory of Computation**]: Analysis of Algorithms and Problem Complexity; G.2.1 [**Combinatorics**]: Combinatorial algorithms; J.4 [**Computer Applications**]: Social Choice and Behavioral Sciences

General Terms

Algorithms

Keywords

single-peaked width; fixed-parameter tractable; parameterized complexity; Borda; Maximin; Copeland; weighted election

1. INTRODUCTION

Voting is a common method for preference aggregation and collective decision-making, and has applications in multi-agent systems [11], political elections, web spam reduction, pattern recognition, etc. For instance, in multiagent systems, it is often necessary for a group of agents to make a collective decision by means of voting in order to reach a joint goal. Unfortunately, by Arrow's impossibility theorem [1], there is no (rank-based) voting system which satisfies a certain set of desirable criteria (see [1] for the details) when more than two candidates are involved. One possible way to bypass Arrow's impossibility theorem is to restrict the domain of the preferences, for instance, the single-peaked domain introduced by Black [3]. Intuitively, in a single-peaked election, one can order the candidates from left to right such that every voter's preference increases first and then decreases after some point as the candidates are considered from left to right.

Recently, the complexity of various voting problems in single-peaked elections has been attracting attention of many researchers from both theoretical computer science and social choice communities [4, 13, 15]. It turned out that many voting problems being $\mathcal{NP}$-hard in general become polynomial-time solvable when restricted to single-peaked elections [4, 15]. However, most elections in practice are not purely single-peaked, which motivates researchers to study more general models of elections. We refer to [5, 8, 10, 12, 14] for some variants of the single-peaked model.

In this paper, we consider a newly introduced generalization of single-peaked elections, the so-called elections with bounded single-peaked width [7]. Other nearly single-peakedness concepts like κ-maverick, κ-global swaps, κ-candidate deletion, and multi-peaked elections have also been considered to cope with voting problems [5, 12, 14, 23, 25]. Cornaz et al. [7] first introduced single-peaked width into the context of complexity studies of voting problems. In particular, they considered a multi-winner determination problem and proved that this problem is fixed-parameter tractable ($\mathcal{FPT}$) with single-peaked width as parameter. Recall that a *parameterized problem* consists of instances of the form (I, κ), where I denotes the *main part* and κ is an integer *parameter*. A parameterized problem is $\mathcal{FPT}$ if it can be solved in $f(\kappa) \cdot |I|^{O(1)}$ time, where f is a computable function in the parameter κ. Later, Cornaz et al. [8] showed that the Kemeny winner determination is $\mathcal{FPT}$ with single-peaked width as parameter. Recently, Yang and Guo [24] studied control problems under Condorcet, Maximin and Copeland in elections with bounded single-peaked width. They showed that the destructive control problems (making someone not win the election by adding/deleting votes) are generally $\mathcal{FPT}$ with respect to single-peaked width, while the constructive control problems (making someone win the election by adding/deleting votes) are generally $\mathcal{NP}$-hard even when the single-peaked width is bounded by a small constant.

We mainly focus on the manipulation problem for Maximin, Copeland$^\alpha$ for every $0 \leq \alpha \leq 1$ and Borda. In the following, unless stated otherwise, manipulation refers to unweighted manipulation. In the *manipulation* problem, we are given a set of candidates including a distinguished candidate, a multiset of votes cast by the voters (nonmanipulators), and a set of manipulators who have not cast their votes yet. The question is whether the manipulators can cast their votes in a way so that the distinguished candidate becomes the winner. In the general case (the domain of the votes is not restricted), the manipulation problem for Maximin, Copeland$^\alpha$ for every $0 \leq \alpha \leq 1$ and Borda is polynomial-

Appears in: *Proceedings of the 14th International Conference on Autonomous Agents and Multiagent Systems (AAMAS 2015), Bordini, Elkind, Weiss, Yolum (eds.), May 4–8, 2015, Istanbul, Turkey.*

		number of manipulators t		
		$t=1$	$t=2$	$t \geq 3$
Borda	Gen	$\mathcal{P}$	$\mathcal{NP}$-hard	
	SPW		$\boldsymbol{\mathcal{FPT}}$	?
Maximin	Gen	$\mathcal{P}$	$\mathcal{NP}$-hard	
	SPWNM		$\boldsymbol{\mathcal{FPT}}$	
Copeland$^\alpha$ $\alpha \in [0, 0.5) \cup (0.5, 1]$	Gen	$\mathcal{P}$	$\mathcal{NP}$-hard	
	SPWNM		$\boldsymbol{\mathcal{FPT}}$	
Copeland$^{0.5}$	Gen	$\mathcal{P}$	?	
	SPWNM		$\boldsymbol{\mathcal{FPT}}$	

Table 1: A summary of the complexity of the unweighted manipulation problem. Let k denote the single-peaked width. Here, 'Gen' should be read as 'the general case', 'SPW' should be read as "with respect to k", and 'SPWNM' should be read as "with respect to the combined parameter (k, t)". Moreover, '$\mathcal{P}$' stands for polynomial-time solvable. Our results are shown in bold. The polynomial-time solvability results are from [20], and the $\mathcal{NP}$-hardness results are from [2, 9, 16, 17, 20]. All the results shown in this table apply to both the unique-winner model and the non-unique winner model. Entries with '?' means that the corresponding problems are open.

	number of candidates m				
	General			Single-Peaked	
	$m=2$	$m=3$	$m \geq 4$	$m=3$	$m \geq 4$
Borda	$\mathcal{P}$	$\mathcal{NP}$-h	$\mathcal{NP}$-h	$\mathcal{P}$	$\mathcal{NP}$-h
Maximin	$\mathcal{P}$	$\mathcal{P}$	$\mathcal{NP}$-h	$\mathcal{P}$	$\mathcal{P}$
Copeland^0	$\mathcal{P}$	$\mathcal{NP}$-h	$\mathcal{NP}$-h	$\boldsymbol{\mathcal{P}}$	$\boldsymbol{\mathcal{P}}$
Copeland^1	$\mathcal{P}$	$\mathcal{P}$	$\mathcal{P}$: $m=4$? : $m>4$	$\mathcal{P}$	$\mathcal{P}$
Copeland$^\alpha$ $0<\alpha<1$	$\mathcal{P}$	$\mathcal{NP}$-h: NON $\mathcal{P}$: UNI	$\mathcal{NP}$-h	$\boldsymbol{\mathcal{P}}$	$\boldsymbol{\mathcal{P}}$

Table 2: A summary of the complexity of the weighted manipulation problem. Here '$\mathcal{NP}$-h' stands for $\mathcal{NP}$-hard, and $\mathcal{P}$ stands for polynomial-time solvable. Moreover, 'NON' and 'UNI' in the entry in the last row means the nonunique-winner model and the unique-winner model, respectively. All the other results apply to both the unique-winner model and the nonunique-winner model. Our results are in bold. The polynomial-time solvability results for Maximin in single-peaked elections follow from several lemmas in [4]. Other results are from [4, 6, 15, 16, 18]. The entry with "?" means that the corresponding problem is open.

time solvable if there is only one manipulator [20]. However, if there are two manipulators all these problems, except the manipulation for Copeland$^{0.5}$, turned out to be $\mathcal{NP}$-hard [2, 9, 16, 17, 20]. To the best of our knowledge, the complexity of the Copeland$^{0.5}$ manipulation problem with two manipulators is still open. In the special case, Yang and Guo [22] proved that the Borda manipulation problem with two manipulators is polynomial-time solvable in single-peaked elections. In this paper, we explore the parameterized complexity of these problems. In particular, we prove that the manipulation problem with two manipulators for Borda is $\mathcal{FPT}$ with respect to single-peaked width. For Maximin and Copeland$^\alpha$ for every $0 \leq \alpha \leq 1$, we prove that the manipulation problem is $\mathcal{FPT}$, when parameterized by the combined parameter (k, t), where k denotes the single-peaked width and t the number of manipulators[1]. To this end, we derive several properties of elections with bounded single-peaked width. We believe that these properties are also helpful in solving further voting problems. Our results imply that the manipulation problem with any constant number of manipulators is polynomial-time solvable for Maximin and Copeland$^\alpha$ for every $0 \leq \alpha \leq 1$, in single-peaked elections, in contrast to the $\mathcal{NP}$-hardness of the problem in the general case. We remark in our analysis, the single-peaked width is based on all the votes; that is, the votes by the nonmanipulators union the votes by the manipulators. Moreover, all the above mentioned results apply to both the unique-winner model and the non-unique winner model (definition is in Section 2). Our results concerning the above problems are summarized in Table 1.

In addition, we study the weighted manipulation problem, where each voter (manipulator or nonmanipulator) has a non-negative integer weight, in single-peaked elections. Conitzer et al. [6] proved that the weighted manipulation problem with four or more candidates for Maximin is $\mathcal{NP}$-hard in general. Faliszewski et al. [16] studied the weighted manipulation for Copeland$^\alpha$. They proved that the problem with three candidates is $\mathcal{NP}$-hard for Copeland$^\alpha$ with $0 \leq \alpha < 1$, except for the unique-winner model for Copeland$^\alpha$ for every $0 < \alpha < 1$ which is polynomial-time solvable. Moreover, the weighted manipulation problem with three candidates is polynomial-time solvable for Copeland^1 [16]. We discuss the unique-winner model and the nonunique-winner model in detail latter. Unless stated otherwise, all the results mentioned throughout this paper apply to both the unique-winner and the nonunique-winner models. In this paper, we show that the weighted manipulation for both Maximin and Copeland$^\alpha$ for every $0 \leq \alpha \leq 1$ in single-peaked elections is polynomial-time solvable even when the number of candidates is not bounded by a constant. Table 2 summarizes the complexity of the above problems.

2. PRELIMINARIES

Elections: An *election* is a tuple $\mathcal{E} = (\mathcal{C}, \mathcal{V})$, where $\mathcal{C}$ is a set of candidates and $\mathcal{V}$ is a multiset of votes (for convenience, the terminologies "vote" and "voter" are used interchangeably throughout this paper), each of which is defined as a linear order $\succ$ over $\mathcal{C}$. For two candidates c and c' and a vote $\succ$, we say c is *ranked above* c' or $\succ$ prefers c to c' if $c \succ c'$. We use $N_{\mathcal{E}}(c, c')$ to denote the number of votes ranking c above c' in $\mathcal{E}$. We drop the index $\mathcal{E}$ if it is clear from the context. We say c *beats* c' if $N(c, c') > N(c', c)$, and c ties c' if $N(c, c') = N(c', c)$. For two subsets C and C' of candidates, $C \succ C'$ means that every candidate in C is ranked above every candidate in C' in the vote $\succ$. A *voting correspondence*[2] φ is

[1] An instance of a parameterized problem with combined parameter (κ_1, κ_2) can be considered as an instance of the same problem with the single parameter $\kappa = \kappa_1 + \kappa_2$.

[2] A related terminology is *voting rule* which is defined as a function mapping an election to a single candidate. A voting correspondence can be modified to a voting rule using a tie-breaking method.

a function that maps an election $\mathcal{E} = (\mathcal{C}, \mathcal{V})$ to a nonempty subset $\varphi(\mathcal{E})$ of $\mathcal{C}$. We call the elements in $\varphi(\mathcal{E})$ the *winners* of $\mathcal{E}$. If $\varphi(\mathcal{E})$ contains only one winner, we call it a *unique winner*; otherwise, we call them *co-winners*. For an election $\mathcal{E} = (\mathcal{C}, \mathcal{V})$ and a subset $C \subseteq \mathcal{C}$, we use $\mathcal{E}|_C$ to denote the election restricted to C. Precisely, the restricted election $\mathcal{E}|_C$ has C as the candidate set, and the votes of $\mathcal{E}|_C$ are obtained from $\mathcal{E}$ by replacing each vote $\succ$ of $\mathcal{E}$ by a new vote $\succ'$ such that for every two candidates $a, b \in C$, $a \succ' b$ whenever $a \succ b$.

Single-Peaked Width: An election $(\mathcal{C}, \mathcal{V})$ is *single-peaked* if there is an order $\mathcal{L}$ of $\mathcal{C}$, from left to right, such that for every vote $\succ$ and every three candidates $a, b, c \in \mathcal{C}$ with $a \mathcal{L} b \mathcal{L} c$ or $c \mathcal{L} b \mathcal{L} a$, $c \succ b$ implies $b \succ a$, where $a \mathcal{L} b$ means a lies on the left-side of b in $\mathcal{L}$. We call $\mathcal{L}$ a *harmonious order*. See Figure 1 for an example.

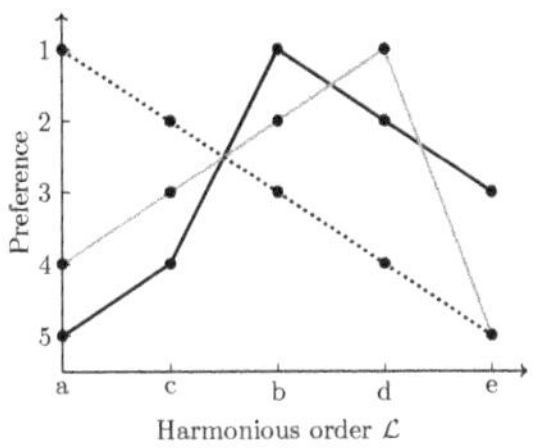

Figure 1: A single-peaked election with three votes (1) $b \succ_u d \succ_u e \succ_u c \succ_u a$; (2) $d \succ_v b \succ_v c \succ_v a \succ_v e$; and (3) $a \succ_w c \succ_w b \succ_w d \succ_w e$. The votes $\succ_u$, $\succ_v$ and $\succ_w$ are illustrated by the dark line, the gray line, and the dotted line, respectively.

A subset $C \subseteq \mathcal{C}$ is called an *interval* if all candidates in C are ranked contiguously in every vote. For example, for the election with candidates $\{a, b, c, d, e\}$ and votes $\{a \succ_1 b \succ_1 c \succ_1 d \succ_1 e,\ d \succ_2 c \succ_2 b \succ_2 e \succ_2 a,\ a \succ_3 e \succ_3 b \succ_3 d \succ_3 c\}$, $\{b, c, d\}$ is an interval. *Contracting* an interval C is the operation that first adds a new candidate c' to the election such that $C \cup \{c'\}$ forms a new interval and the preference between any two candidates of $\mathcal{C}$ in each vote preserves the same as before, and then deletes all candidates in C. For example, after contracting the interval $\{b, c, d\}$ in the above example, we get the new election with candidates a, c', e and votes $\{a \succ_1 c' \succ_1 e,\ c' \succ_2 e \succ_2 a,\ a \succ_3 e \succ_3 c'\}$, where c' is the newly introduced candidate.

Let $P = (C_1, C_2, ..., C_\omega)$ be an ordered partition of $\mathcal{C}$ with each C_i being an interval. We say P is a *single-peaked partition* if contracting all intervals in P results in a single-peaked election with respect to the harmonious order $(c_1, c_2, ..., c_\omega)$, where each c_i is the newly introduced candidate for the interval C_i. We say a vote *has its peak at C_i with respect to P* if the interval C_i is ranked above every other interval by the vote. The *width* of P is defined as $\max_{1 \le i \le \omega}\{|C_i|\}^3$. The *single-peaked width* of an election is the minimum width among all its single-peaked partitions. Cornaz et al. [8] proved that calculating the single-peaked width of an election and constructing an optimal single-peaked partition can be done in polynomial time.

Median Group: Let $P = (C_1, C_2, ..., C_\omega)$ be a single-peaked partition of the election $(\mathcal{C}, \mathcal{V})$, and let $(\succ_1, \succ_2, ..., \succ_n)$ be an order of $\mathcal{V}$ such that for every i, j with $1 \le i < j \le n$ the peak of $\succ_i$ does not lie on the right-side of the peak of $\succ_j$ in P. The set of all intervals lying between the peak C_l of $\succ_{\lceil n/2 \rceil}$ and the peak C_r of $\succ_{\lfloor n/2+1 \rfloor}$, together with C_l and C_r, denoted $\mathcal{G}[C_l, C_r]$, is called the *median group*. If there is only one interval in the median group, we call it a *median interval*. See Figure 2 for an example.

Voting Correspondences: We mainly study the following voting correspondences.

[3] Cornaz et al. [7] defined the width of the partition P as $\max_{1 \le i \le \omega}\{|C_i|\} - 1$, the size of the maximum group minors one. However, this does not affect the results of this paper.

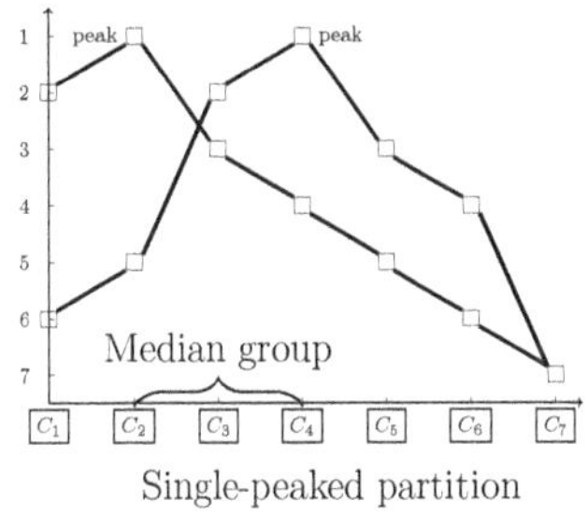

Figure 2: An illustration of median group. There are two votes, where the first vote has preference $C_2 \succ C_1 \succ C_3, ..., \succ C_7$ over the intervals, and the second vote has the preference $C_4 \succ C_3 \succ C_5 \succ C_6 \succ C_2 \succ C_1 \succ C_7$. The peak C_2 of the first vote is on the left side of the peak C_4 of the second vote.

Borda: In a Borda election, every voter gives 0 points to its last-ranked candidate, 1 point to its second-last ranked candidate and so on. A candidate with the highest score is a winner.

Copeland$^\alpha$ **($0 \le \alpha \le 1$):** For a candidate c, let $B(c)$ be the set of candidates who are beaten by c and $T(c)$ the set of candidates who tie with c. The Copeland$^\alpha$ score of c is then defined as $|B(c)| + \alpha \cdot |T(c)|$. A Copeland$^\alpha$ winner is a candidate with the highest score.

Maximin: For a candidate c, the Maximin score of c is defined as $\min_{c' \in \mathcal{C} \setminus \{c\}} N(c, c')$. A Maximin winner is a candidate with the highest Maximin score.

Problem Definitions. In the *unweighted manipulation problem* studied in this paper, we are given an election $\mathcal{E} = (\mathcal{C} \cup \{p\}, \mathcal{V})$ with single-peaked width k, an optimal single-peaked partition P and a set of voters who have not cast their votes yet. Here, p is the distinguished candidate. We call the set of voters who have not cast their votes the *manipulators*. The question is whether the manipulators can cast their votes according to the single-peaked partition P so that the distinguished candidate p becomes the winner under a specific voting correspondence, e.g., Maximin, Copeland$^\alpha$ and Borda. In the *weighted manipulation problem*, each voter (manipulator or nonmanipulator) has a nonnegative integer weight. Each vote defined as $\succ$ and with weight w is regarded as w individual votes each of which is defined as $\succ$. The assumption that the single-peaked partition is given in the input is based on the observation that in many real-world applications, the single-peaked partition is known in advance. This is actually one of the reasons why domain restricted elections can arise in practice. For example, in real-world single-peaked political elections, the voters are thought to agree upon that the candidates are ordered on a common known left-right dimension. See [3] for related discussion. Moreover, in this scenario, if the manipulators do not cast their votes according to the given single-peaked partition, they will be easily recognized as manipulators. See also [4, 14, 15, 19] for further study of manipulation problems where the domain of the manipulative votes is restricted.

Remark. All our results apply to both the unique-winner and the nonunique-winner models. In the unique-winner model, the objective is to make the distinguished candidate the unique winner, while in the nonunique-winner model the objective is to make the distinguished candidate a winner (that is, either a unique winner or a co-winner). For simplicity, all our proofs and algorithms are solely based on the unique-winner model.

3. MAXIMIN

In this section, we explore the parameterized complexity of the manipulation problem for Maximin. In particular, we prove that the manipulation problem for Maximin is $\mathcal{FPT}$, when parameterized by the combined parameter (k, t), where k is the single-peaked width and t is the number of manipulators. To this end, we introduce some properties of Maximin elections with bounded single-peaked width. These properties are also helpful in understanding the behavior of the Maximin correspondence. The first property is formally stated in Lemma 1. In an informal way, it states that for each candidate c, the closer another candidate c' lies to c according to the single-peaked partition, the less is the number of voters who prefer c to c'. For a positive integer n, let $[n]$ be the set $\{1, 2, ..., n\}$.

LEMMA 1. *Let $(C_1, C_2, ..., C_\omega)$ be the single-peaked partition and c be a candidate in a certain interval C_i. Then, $N(c, b_1) \leq N(c, b_2)$ for all $b_1 \in C_{x_1}$ and $b_2 \in C_{x_2}$ with $i < x_1 < x_2$, and $N(c, a_1) \leq N(c, a_2)$ for all $a_1 \in C_{z_1}$ and $a_2 \in C_{z_2}$ with $z_2 < z_1 < i$.*

PROOF. We first prove the first part of the claim. Let b_1 and b_2 be the two candidates as stated in the claim. For all $j \in [\omega]$, we denote the set of votes with peaks at C_j or on the right-side of C_j by $\mathcal{V}_j^r$, and denote the set of votes with peaks at C_j or on the left-side of C_j by $\mathcal{V}_j^l$. It is obvious that all votes in $\mathcal{V}_i^l$ prefer c to b_1 to b_2 and all votes in $\mathcal{V}_{x_1}^r$ prefer b_1 to c. Let $\mathcal{V}_{i,x_1}^{c \succ b_1}$ be the set of votes with peaks between C_i and C_{x_1} and prefer c to b_1. Thus, $N(c, b_1) = |\mathcal{V}_i^l| + |\mathcal{V}_{i,x_1}^{c \succ b_1}|$. Due to the definition of single-peaked partition, all votes in $\mathcal{V}_{i,x_1}^{c \succ b_1}$ prefer c to b_2. Therefore, $N(c, b_2) \geq |\mathcal{V}_i^l| + |\mathcal{V}_{i,x_1}^{c \succ b_1}| = N(c, b_1)$.
Due to symmetry, the second part is also correct. □

Recall that the Maximin score of a candidate c is equal to $N(c, c')$ where c' achieves the minimum value of $N(c, \cdot)$. Let c be a candidate from a certain interval C_i. Let $MIN(c)$ be the set of candidates that achieve the minimum value of $N(c, \cdot)$; hence, we have that $Maximin(c) = N(c, c')$ for every $c' \in MIN(c)$. According to Lemma 1, we have that $(C_{i-1} \cup C_i \cup C_{i+1}) \cap MIN(c) \neq \emptyset$. Therefore, to determine the Maximin score of c, it is sufficient to consider the election restricted to $C_{i-1} \cup C_i \cup C_{i+1}$ whose size is bounded by $3k$, where k is the single-peaked width. In the following, we introduce another property which helps to improve the upper bound.

LEMMA 2. *Let c be a candidate and C' be an interval with $c \notin C'$. Then, $N(c, a) = N(c, b)$ for every two candidates $a, b \in C'$.*

PROOF. Since C' is an interval, all votes rank the candidates in C' contiguously. Therefore, each vote either prefers c to all candidates in C' or prefers all candidates in C' to c, implying that for every two candidates $a, b \in C'$, $N(c, a) = N(c, b)$. □

According to Lemmas 1 and 2, the Maximin score of a candidate c is determined by all candidates in the interval including c, together with any two arbitrary candidates from the two neighbor intervals of the interval including c, one from each.

LEMMA 3. *Let $\mathcal{E} = (\mathcal{C}, \mathcal{V})$ be an election with single-peaked partition $P = (C_1, C_2, ..., C_\omega)$ and c be a candidate in an interval C_i. Then the Maximin score of c in $\mathcal{E}$, denoted by $Maximin_{\mathcal{E}}(c)$, is*

$$Maximin_{\mathcal{E}}(c) = Maximin_{\mathcal{E}|C_i \cup \{a,b\}}(c)$$

Here, a and b are any two arbitrary candidates in C_{i-1} and C_{i+1}, respectively (only b appears if $i = 1$ and only a appears if $i = \omega$).

It is clearly true that in the general case the optimal choice for the manipulators is to rank the distinguished candidate in the top. This is because of the monotonicity of Maximin. Recall that a voting correspondence τ is *monotonic* if in every τ election (that is, election where winners are selected according to τ), ranking a winner higher in some vote does not exclude the winner from the winning set [20]. However, when the election has a bounded single-peaked width, the correctness of the statement is not straightforward anymore, since improving one's position in a vote may destroy the single-peakedness. In the following, we provide a formal proof to support the above claim in elections with bounded single-peaked width.

LEMMA 4. *Every Yes-instance of the manipulation problem for Maximin in elections with bounded single-peaked width has a solution where all manipulators rank the interval C_p including the distinguished candidate p above every other interval. Moreover, p is ranked above every other candidate.*

PROOF. We prove this lemma by showing that if there is a solution which does not satisfy the lemma, we can construct another solution which satisfies the lemma. Observe first that it is always optimal to rank p above every other candidate in C_p, since there is no single-peaked restriction inside C_p. Therefore, it is sufficient to prove that ranking C_p in the top is the optimal choice for all the manipulators.

Assume that v is a manipulator who did not rank the interval C_p in the top. Let $(L_a, L_{a-1}, ..., L_1, C_p, R_1, ..., R_b)$ be the single-peaked partition. Let $\mathcal{C}_l = \{L_a, L_{a-1}, ..., L_1\}$ be the set of intervals on the left-side of C_p according to the single-peaked partition and $\mathcal{C}_r = \{R_1, ..., R_b\}$ be the set of intervals on the right-side of C_p. Without loss of generality, assume that $a, b \geq 1$, that is, $\mathcal{C}_l, \mathcal{C}_r \neq \emptyset$. Furthermore, assume that the manipulator v ranked some interval $L \in \mathcal{C}_l$ in the top. Due to the single-peakedness, the manipulator v has the following preference over the intervals in $C_p \cup \mathcal{C}_r$: $C_p \succ R_1 \succ R_2 \succ, ..., \succ R_b$. We consider two cases.

The first case is that for each $L \in \mathcal{C}_l$, $L \succ C_p$. In this case, we can create a new solution by recasting the vote of v with $\succ'$ defined as $C_p \succ' L_1, ..., \succ' L_a \succ' R_1 \succ', ..., \succ' R_b$. Here, the preference between every two candidates in the same interval preserves the same as before. That is, for every two candidates c and c' in the same interval, c is ranked above c' in the new vote whenever c is ranked above c' in the original vote.

The second case is that there is an $L \in \mathcal{C}_l$ with $L \prec C_p$. In this case, there must be a $z \in [a]$ such that $L_j \succ C_p$ for all $j \in [z-1]$ and $L_j \prec C_p$ for all $a \geq j \geq z$. Let $\widetilde{\mathcal{C}} = \mathcal{C}_r \cup \{L_z, L_{z+1}, ..., L_a\}$. We can get a new solution by recasting the vote $\succ$ of v as $\succ'$ with preference $C_p \succ' L_1 \succ', ..., \succ' L_{z-1} \succ' \widetilde{\mathcal{C}}$, where among $\widetilde{\mathcal{C}}$, we have $C \succ' C'$ if and only if $C \succ C'$ for every $C, C' \in \widetilde{\mathcal{C}}$. Moreover, the preference between every two candidates in the same interval preserves the same as before. See Figure 3 for an illustration.

Now we prove the correctness. Let $\mathcal{E} = (\mathcal{C} \cup \{p\}, \mathcal{V})$ be the original election and $\mathcal{E}' = (\mathcal{C} \cup \{p\}, \mathcal{V}')$ be the election obtained from $\mathcal{E}$ by replacing the vote $\succ \in \mathcal{V}$ by $\succ'$, as discussed above. We need to prove $Maximin_{\mathcal{E}'}(p) > Maximin_{\mathcal{E}'}(c)$ for every $c \in \mathcal{C}$, given that $Maximin_{\mathcal{E}}(p) > Maximin_{\mathcal{E}}(c)$. For a candidate c, let $MIN(c)$ be the set of candidates c' such that $Maximin_{\mathcal{E}}(c) = N_{\mathcal{E}}(c, c')$. Let $peak(c, right)$ be the number of votes with peaks not on the left side of the interval including c. We prove for the second case (the proof for the first case is analogous). Let

$$C' = \mathcal{C}_l \setminus \widetilde{\mathcal{C}} = \{L_1, ..., L_{z-1}\}.$$

Observe first that with recasting $\succ$, only the candidates in $C' \cup C_p$ have chance to increase their scores. Moreover, each candidate can increase his score by at most one. Therefore, it is sufficient

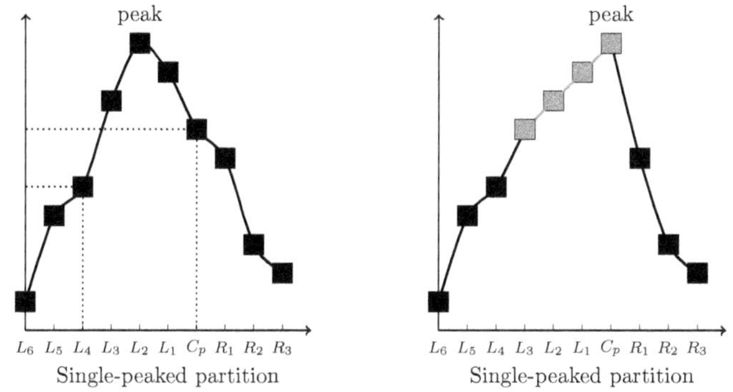

Figure 3: Case 2 in the proof of Lemma 4. The figure on the left side shows the original vote $\succ$ with $L_2 \succ L_1 \succ L_3 \succ C_p \succ R_1 \succ L_4 \succ L_5 \succ R_2 \succ R_3 \succ L_6$. The figure on the right side shows the new recast vote $\succ'$ with $C_p \succ' L_1 \succ' L_2 \succ' L_3 \succ' R_1 \succ' L_4 \succ' L_5 \succ' R_2 \succ' R_3 \succ' L_6$. Here we have $\widetilde{\mathcal{C}} = \{L_4, L_5, L_6, R_1, R_2, R_3\}$.

to prove that $Maximin_{\mathcal{E}'}(p) > Maximin_{\mathcal{E}'}(c)$ for every $c \in \mathcal{C}' \cup C_p$. This clearly holds for every candidate in C_p, since the new vote preserves the preference between every two candidates in C_p. We prove the correctness for every candidate in $\mathcal{C}'$ by contradiction. Suppose that $c \in L_i$ with $L_i \in \mathcal{C}'$ is a candidate with $Maximin_{\mathcal{E}}(p) > Maximin_{\mathcal{E}}(c)$ but $Maximin_{\mathcal{E}'}(p) \leq Maximin_{\mathcal{E}'}(c)$. Since recasting the vote $\succ$ does not decrease the score of p, we know that the score of c is increased by one after recasting the vote $\succ$. This happens only if $L_i \cap MIN(c) = \emptyset$ and $L_{i+1} \cap MIN(c) \neq \emptyset$. In this case, $Maximin_{\mathcal{E}}(c) = N_{\mathcal{E}}(c, c') = peak(c, right)$, where c' is any arbitrary candidate in L_{i+1} (the first equation is due to Lemma 2 and the second is due to the single-peakedness). Let c'' be any arbitrary candidate in L_1. Then, due to the definition of the Maximin correspondence, $Maximin_{\mathcal{E}}(p) \leq N_{\mathcal{E}}(p, c'') = peak(p, right) \leq peak(c, right) = Maximin_{\mathcal{E}}(c)$, contradicting with the fact that $Maximin_{\mathcal{E}}(p) > Maximin_{\mathcal{E}}(c)$ for every $c \in \mathcal{C}$. The lemma is proved. □

Now we are ready to show the main result of this section.

THEOREM 1. *The manipulation problem for Maximin is $\mathcal{FPT}$ with respect to the combined parameter (k, t), where k is the single-peaked width and t is the number of manipulators.*

PROOF. We prove the theorem by proposing an $\mathcal{FPT}$ algorithm. The algorithm ranks all the intervals first and then ranks the candidates in each interval.

Let $(C_1, C_2, ..., C_i, ..., C_\omega)$ be the single-peaked partition with width k, and C_i be the interval including the distinguished candidate p. Due to Lemma 4, all manipulators can safely rank C_i in the top. Let c be any arbitrary candidate. Without loss of generality, assume c is in the interval C_j. Then, for every candidate $c' \in C_{j-1} \cup C_{j+1}$, $N(c, c')$ is known. Precisely, $N(c, c') = |\mathcal{V}_j^l|$ if $c' \in C_{j+1}$, and $N(c, c') = |\mathcal{V}_j^r|$ otherwise. Here, $\mathcal{V}_j^l$ (resp. $\mathcal{V}_j^r$) is the set of votes with peaks at C_j or on the left-side (resp. right-side) of C_j. Due to Lemma 3 and the above analysis, the Maximin score of c is $\min\{|\mathcal{V}_j^l|, |\mathcal{V}_j^r|, \text{Maximin}_{\mathcal{E}|C_j}(c)\}$. Since $\text{Maximin}_{\mathcal{E}|C_j}(c)$ does not depend on how the manipulators rank the intervals, all manipulators can safely rank the intervals in any way which is consistent with the single-peaked partition. For example all the manipulators can rank the intervals as follows.

$$C_i \succ C_{i-1} \succ C_{i-2} \succ, ..., \succ C_1 \succ C_{i+1} \succ C_{i+2} \succ, ..., \succ C_\omega$$

It remains to rank the candidates in each interval. Let t be the number of manipulators. We begin with the interval C_i including p. We enumerate all the possible combinations of t linear orders over the candidates in C_i, each linear order is assumed to be the partial vote over C_i cast by a manipulator. Since $|C_i| \leq k$, there are at most $k!^t$ combinations. Moreover, each combination gives p a Maximin score by adding the partial votes corresponding to the t linear orders of the combination to the election. The algorithm chooses one combination which gives p the maximum Maximin score in the election restricted to C_i. Then, the manipulators rank the candidates in C_i according to the t linear orders of the chosen combination. Now the final Maximin score of p is known. It remains to rank the candidates in other intervals. We use a similar method. In particular, for each remaining interval C, we enumerate all possibilities of ranking the candidates in C until we find one which does not prevent p from being the winner. If for every possibility there is a candidate in C which has an equal or greater score than that of p, we immediately return "No"; otherwise, we proceed with the next interval. The algorithm runs in $O(\omega \cdot k!^t)$ time since ranking the candidates in each interval takes $k!^t$ time and we have ω intervals to consider. □

4. COPELAND

In this section, we study the manipulation problem for Copeland$^\alpha$ for every $0 \leq \alpha \leq 1$. In particular, we prove that the manipulation problem for Copeland$^\alpha$ for every $0 \leq \alpha \leq 1$ is $\mathcal{FPT}$, when parameterized by the combined parameter (k, t), where k is the single-peaked width and t is the number of manipulators. We start with some useful properties.

LEMMA 5. *Every Yes-instance of the manipulation problem for Copeland$^\alpha$ in elections with bounded single-peaked width has a solution where all manipulators rank the interval including the distinguished candidate in the top.*

The proof for the above lemma is similar to the one for Lemma 4. We omit the proof, due to space limitations.

The following lemma states that the Copeland$^\alpha$ scores of the candidates in different intervals strictly increase when the intervals are considered from either side to the median group.

LEMMA 6. *Let $\mathcal{G}[C_l, C_r]$ be the median group of an election with candidates set $\mathcal{C}$, with respect to the single-peaked partition $(C_1, C_2, ..., C_\omega)$. Let $a_1 \in C_{z_1}, a_2 \in C_{z_2}, b_1 \in C_{x_1}, b_2 \in C_{x_2}$ be any four arbitrary candidates with $z_2 < z_1 \leq l$ and $r \leq x_1 \leq x_2$. Then, the Copeland$^\alpha$ score of b_1 (resp. a_1) is strictly greater than that of b_2 (resp. a_2), for every $0 \leq \alpha \leq 1$.*

PROOF. Due to symmetry, we prove only for b_1 and b_2. Let $\mathcal{C}_1$ be the set of candidates included in intervals on the right-side of C_{x_1}. Clearly, $b_2 \in \mathcal{C}_1$. Since all votes with peaks at C_r or on the left-side of C_r, which amount to more than half of the votes, rank every candidate in C_{x_1} above every candidate in $\mathcal{C}_1$, we know that every candidate in C_{x_1} beats every candidate in $\mathcal{C}_1$. Thus, b_1 beats every candidate in $\mathcal{C}_1$, implying that the candidates in $\mathcal{C}_1$ contribute at least one more point (from b_2) to b_1 than to b_2. Now consider the candidates in $\mathcal{C}_2 = \mathcal{C} \setminus (\mathcal{C}_1 \cup C_{x_1})$. That is, the candidates included in intervals on the left-side of C_{x_1}. Due to the definitions of single-peaked election and single-peaked partition, for every candidate $c \in \mathcal{C}_2$, every vote which prefers b_2 to c also prefers b_1 to c. Thus, if b_2 beats (resp. ties) a candidate $c \in \mathcal{C}_2$, so does b_1 (resp.

b_1 beats c or ties c). Thus, the candidates in $\mathcal{C}_2$ contribute to b_1 at least the same points as to b_2. Since every candidate in C_{x_1} beats b_2, the lemma follows. □

Due to Lemma 6, we know that for every candidate c which is not in the median group, there exists at least one candidate who has a strictly greater Copeland$^\alpha$ score than that of c. This implies that the Copeland$^\alpha$ winners must be included in the median group.

LEMMA 7. *Every Copeland$^\alpha$ winner for all $0 \leq \alpha \leq 1$ is from the median group.*

Now we come to the main result of this section.

THEOREM 2. *The manipulation problem for Copeland$^\alpha$ for every $0 \leq \alpha \leq 1$ is $\mathcal{FPT}$ with respect to the combined parameter (k, t), where k denotes the single-peaked width and t the number of manipulators.*

PROOF. To prove the theorem, we derive an $\mathcal{FPT}$-algorithm. Let t be the number of manipulators and k be the single-peaked width of the given election. The algorithm first ranks the interval C including the distinguished candidate p in the top in all the manipulative votes. If p is not in the median group, we can immediately return "No", due to Lemma 7. Otherwise, we enumerate all possible combinations of t linear orders over the candidates in C. Since C has at most k candidates, there are at most $k!^t$ combinations. Moreover, each combination of t linear orders gives a Copeland$^\alpha$ score of p in the election restricted to C by asking the t manipulators to rank the candidates in C according to the t linear orders of the combinations. The algorithm chooses one combination which gives p the maximum Copeland$^\alpha$ score in the election restricted to C. Then, the manipulators rank the candidates in C according to the linear orders in the combination. Without loss of generality, assume that the single-peaked partition is $(C_1, C_2, ..., C_l, ..., C_r, C_{r+1}, ..., C_\omega)$, and the median group $\mathcal{G}[C_l, C_r]$ contains C_l, C_r and all intervals between C_l and C_r (C_l and C_r may be identical. In this case the algorithm becomes easier). Since all manipulators rank C in the top and C is in the median group, we have that either $p \in C_l$ or $p \in C_r$ (that is, $C = C_l$ or $C = C_r$). Without loss of generality, assume that $p \in C_l$. Due to Lemma 7, to make p the winner, we need only to make sure that every candidate included in $\mathcal{G}[C_l, C_r]$ has no equal or greater score than that of p. Hence, the optimal solution for all manipulators is to rank the intervals as follows.

$$C_l \succ C_{l-1} \succ, ..., C_1 \succ C_{l+1} \succ, ..., \succ C_\omega$$

In this case, every candidate in $\mathcal{G}[C_l, C_r] \setminus C_l$ gets the least points from the candidates in $\bigcup_{i=1}^{i=l-1} C_i$. It remains to rank the candidates in each interval. Due to Lemmas 6 and 7, for each interval which is not in $\mathcal{G}[C_l, C_r]$, no matter how the candidates in this interval are ranked, none of the candidates can have an equal or greater score than that of p. Hence, we rank them arbitrarily. For each interval in $\mathcal{G}[C_l, C_r] \setminus \{C\}$, we rank the candidates with the similar method as for Maximin. That is, for each interval $C' \in \mathcal{G}[C_l, C_r] \setminus \{C\}$, we enumerate all the combinations of t linear orders over the candidates in C' until we find one which does not prevent p from being the winner. On the other hand, if no such combinatorial exists, we return "No". The running time of the algorithm is $O(\omega \cdot k!^t)$. □

5. BORDA

In this section, we study the Borda manipulation with two manipulators in elections with bounded single-peaked width. Recall that this problem is $\mathcal{NP}$-hard in general [2, 9] but polynomial-time solvable in single-peaked elections [22].

THEOREM 3. *The manipulation problem with two manipulators for Borda is $\mathcal{FPT}$ when parameterized by single-peaked width.*

Our $\mathcal{FPT}$ algorithm is based on the polynomial-time algorithm for the same problem in single-peaked elections [22]. The algorithm ranks the intervals according to the single-peaked partition, beginning with the one including the distinguished candidate and ending with a one on either side. To rank each interval, the algorithm first assigns respective contiguous positions for the interval, then ranks the candidates in the interval in a brute-force way. The procedure of ranking the intervals mimics the algorithm for Borda manipulation in single-peaked elections in [22], and thus takes polynomial time. Since each interval contains at most k candidates (k is the single-peaked width of the given election), ranking candidates in each interval takes $O(k!^2)$ time (each manipulator has at most $k!$ choices and there are two manipulators). The whole running time of the algorithm will be $O(k!^2 \cdot poly(|\mathcal{E}|))$, where $|\mathcal{E}|$ is the size of the given election[4].

Main Idea. We illustrate the algorithm according to Figure 4. In the first step, the interval C_p including p is ranked in the top of the two manipulative votes, and p is ranked in the top within C_p. The final score of p is known now. Assume that p is the current winner. Then we check all possibilities (at most $(k-1)!^2$) of ranking the candidates in $C_p \setminus \{p\}$ until we find one case which does not prevent p from being the winner. After this, due to the single-peakedness, only R_1 or L_1 can be ranked in the next free positions. We check whether at least one of them can be ranked in the next free positions of the two manipulative votes simultaneously, without preventing p from being the winner. This can be done in $k!^2$ time by enumerating all possibilities. Suppose that R_1 can be ranked in this way as shown in Figure 4. Then, again due to the single-peakedness, only R_2 or L_1 can be ranked in the next free positions. We do the same thing for these two intervals as discussed above for R_1 and L_1. Differently, suppose that at this time none of R_2 and L_1 can be ranked simultaneously without preventing p from being the winner. Then, if the given instance is a Yes-instance, the only possible case is that each of R_2 and L_1 is ranked in the next free positions of different manipulative votes, as shown in Figure 4. Note that at this moment we do not know how the manipulators rank the candidates in R_2 and L_1. We will rank them as follows. In fact, our algorithm will always do the following once there is an interval which has been ranked by one manipulator but not by the other one. Let's take R_2 as an example. In this case, we are going to rank R_2 in the highest possible free contiguous positions of the second manipulative vote. To this end, for all free contiguous positions, from the highest to the lowest, we check whether R_2 can be ranked in these positions so that p is still the winner. Each case can be checked in $k!^2$ time as discussed above. If no such case exists, the instance must be a No-instance. Suppose that R_2 is ranked as shown in Figure 4 without preventing p from being the winner. Then due to the single-peakedness, the free positions between L_1 and R_2 can only be occupied by L_2, L_3 and so forth (the interval R_2 may need to be moved to lower contiguous positions if there are no enough positions for L_4. This does not change the solvability.). We do the same thing for each interval which has been ranked by exactly one manipulator until none of them exists. Then, either we find a solution or the next free positions of the two manipulative votes are "neat" (the set of intervals that have ranked in the first manipulative vote is

[4] By employing a similar dynamic programming technique as in [22], ranking candidates in each interval can be done in $O(8^k)$ time. Hence, the whole running time can be improved to $O(8^k \cdot poly(|\mathcal{E}|))$.

the same as that in the second manipulative vote). If it is the latter case, we go back to the step where we shall consider whether one interval can be ranked in the next free positions simultaneously as discussed in the beginning of the algorithm. A formal description of the algorithm is given in Algorithm 1.

Algorithm 1: The $\mathcal{FPT}$ algorithm for the unweighted Borda manipulation with two manipulators in elections with bounded single-peaked width.

---

1 Both manipulators rank p in their highest positions;
2 **if** $C_p \setminus \{p\} \rightarrow \{(\pi_1, 2, |C_p|), (\pi_2, 2, |C_p|)\}$ **then**
3   extend(S_1, C_p) and extend(S_2, C_p);
4 **else**
5   Return "NO";
6 **end**
7 **while** $\bigcup_{s \in S_1} s = \bigcup_{s \in S_2} s \neq \mathcal{C} \cup \{p\}$ **do**
8   $S := S_1$;
9   **if** $\exists B \in N(S)$ *with* $B \rightarrow \{(\pi_1, |S|+1, |S|+|B|), (\pi_2, |S|+1, |S|+|B|)\}$ **then**
10   extend(S_1, B) and extend(S_2, B);
11   **end**
12   **else if** $|N(S)| = 1$ **then**
13   Return "No";
14   **end**
15   **else**
16   Let $N(S) = \{B, B'\}$;
17   **if** $B \rightarrow (\pi_1, |S_1|+1, |S_1|+|B|)$ *and* $B' \rightarrow (\pi_2, |S_2|+1, |S_2|+|B'|)$ **then**
18   extend(S_1, B) and extend(S_2, B');
19   **else**
20   Return "No";
21   **end**
22   **end**
23   **while** $S_1 \neq S_2$ **do**
24   Let B be any interval in $N(S_1 \cap S_2)$;
25   Let $z = 1$ if $B \in S_2$ and $z = 2$ if $B \in S_1$;
26   **while** $B \not\rightarrow (\pi_z, |S_z|+1, |S_z|+|B|)$ **do**
27   **if** $N(S_z) \setminus B = \emptyset$ **then**
28   Return "No";
29   **end**
30   **else**
31         $B' := N(S_z) \setminus B$;
32   **if** $B' \rightarrow (\pi_z, |S_z|+1, |S_z|+|B'|)$ **then**
33   extend(S_z, B');
34   **else**
35   Return "NO";
36   **end**
37   **end**
38   **end**
39   extend(S_z, B);
40   **end**
41 **end**
42 Return "Yes";

We use functions $\pi : \mathcal{C} \cup \{p\} \mapsto [|\mathcal{C} \cup \{p\}|]$ that map candidates to positions to represent a vote. In particular, π_1 and π_2 will be the first and the second manipulative votes, respectively. A candidate c with $\pi(c) = 1$ has the highest position and thus gets the maximum $|\mathcal{C}|$ points. Initially, we set $\pi_i(c) = 0$ for every candidate c.

For an interval C and two integers k_l and k_r with $1 \leq k_l \leq k_r \leq |\mathcal{C}|$ and $|C| = k_r - k_l + 1$, we use $C \rightarrow (\pi, k_l, k_r)$ (resp. $C \not\rightarrow (\pi, k_l, k_r)$) to denote that the candidates in C can (resp. cannot) be safely ranked in the positions $\{k_l, k_l+1, ..., k_r\}$ of π. Here, "safely" means that it is possible to rank the candidates in these positions of π without preventing p from being the winner. Similarly, we use $C \rightarrow \{(\pi_1, k_l^1, k_r^1), (\pi_2, k_l^2, k_r^2)\}$ (resp. $C \not\rightarrow \{(\pi_1, k_l^1, k_r^1), (\pi_2, k_l^2, k_r^2)\}$) to denote that it is possible (resp. not possible) to rank the candidates in C in the positions $\{k_l^1, k_l^1+1, ..., k_r^1\}$ of π_1 and in the positions $\{k_l^2, k_l^2+1, ..., k_r^2\}$ of π_2 simultaneously, without preventing p from being the winner. Checking whether $C \rightarrow (\pi, k_l, k_r)$ can be done in $|C|!$ time by enumerating all the linear orders over C, and checking whether $C \rightarrow \{(\pi_1, k_l^1, k_r^1), (\pi_2, k_l^2, k_r^2)\}$ can be done in $|C|!^2$ by enumerating all the two linear orders over C.

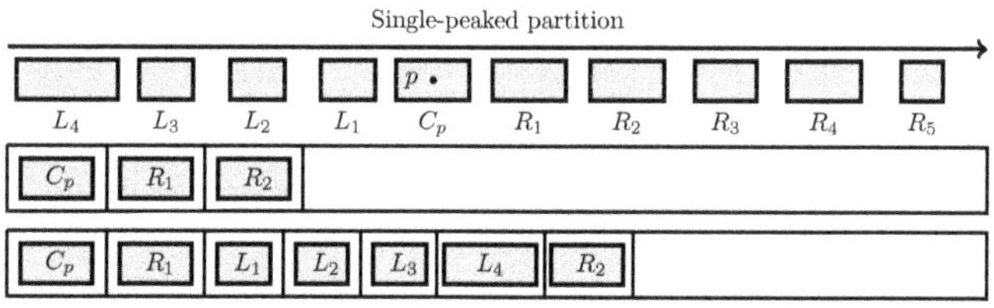

Figure 4: An illustration of the $\mathcal{FPT}$-algorithm for Borda. Inside C_p, the distinguished candidate is ranked in the top.

A *block* is a collection of intervals lying contiguously in the single-peaked partition. For example in Figure 4, $\{C_p, R_1, R_2\}$ is a block, but $\{C_p, R_2\}$ is not since there is an interval R_1 between C_p and R_2. For a block S, let $N(S)$ be the set of intervals lying directly on the left-side or on the right-side of S. For example in Figure 4, setting $S = \{C_p, R_1, R_2\}$, we have $N(S) = \{L_1, R_3\}$. Clearly, $|N(S)| \leq 2$ for every block S. In our algorithm, each manipulator maintains a block which initially is empty. Let S_i be the block maintained by the i-th manipulator, where $i = 1, 2$. For an interval $C \in N(S_i)$ and the block S_i, we use extend(S_i, C) to denote the operation $S_i := S_i \cup C$, where ':=' is the assignment operator that sets the left-hand operand equal to the right-hand expression value.

In Line 25, one of $B \in S_1$ or $B \in S_2$ must hold. We remark that the above algorithm can be adapted to handle the corresponding optimization problem, where instead of answering 'Yes' or 'No', the algorithm finds a solution for the given instance. For this purpose, extend(S_i, C) will denote both the operation $S_i := S_i \cup C$ and the following operation: ranks the candidates in C in the next contiguous positions of the i-th manipulative vote in a way that does not prevent p from being the winner. Due to space limitations, we omit further details.

6. WEIGHTED MANIPULATION

In this section, we study the weighted manipulation problem in single-peaked elections.

Faliszewski et al. [15] examined the weighted manipulation problem in single-peaked elections with three candidates for positional scoring correspondences, and proved that the problem is $\mathcal{NP}$-hard if and only if $a_1 - a_3 > 2(a_2 - a_3) > 0$, where (a_1, a_2, a_3) is the scoring vector with $a_1 \geq a_2 \geq a_3$. Recall that each positional scoring correspondence is defined by a non-negative integer scoring vector $(a_1, a_2, ..., a_m)$ with $a_1 \geq a_2 \geq, ..., \geq a_m$, where m is the number of candidates. Then every candidate c gets a_i points from each vote that ranks c in the i-th position. The winners are the candidates who have the maximum total score. Their result implies that the weighted Borda manipulation with three candidates is polynomial-time solvable in single-peaked elections. However, when the number of candidates increases to four, the weighted Borda manipulation problem becomes $\mathcal{NP}$-hard [15]. Brandt et al. [4] took the result in [15] a further step by deriving a dichotomy for the weighted manipulation problem for positional scoring correspondences with no restriction on the number of candidates.

In this section, we complement their results by exploring the weighted manipulation problem for Copeland$^\alpha$ and Maximin in single-peaked elections. A voting correspondence is *weakCondorcet-consistent* if the winners are exactly the weak Condorcet winners whenever there exists weak Condorcet winners [4]. First recall that both Maximin and Copeland^1 are weakCondorcet-consistent in single-peaked elections, and thus, the weighted manipulation problem for Maximin and Copeland^1 is polynomial-time solvable in single-peaked elections (we refer to [4] for the detailed arguments why the polynomial-time solvability holds). However, the Copeland$^\alpha$ voting for every $0 \leq \alpha < 1$ is not weakCondorcet-consistent even in single-peaked elections [4].

Our result of this section is summarized in the following theorem.

THEOREM 4. *The weighted manipulation problem for Copeland$^\alpha$ is polynomial-time solvable in single-peaked elections, for every* $0 \leq \alpha < 1$.

PROOF. We first give the proof for the unique-winner model with three candidates. To this end, we derive a polynomial-time algorithm. First observe that ranking the distinguished candidate p in the top is always the optimal choice. Hence, if p is not in the middle in the harmonious order, all the manipulators have only one way to cast their votes, and thus, the problem can be solved. Assume now that p is in the middle of the harmonious order. Without loss of generality, let a, b, p be the three candidates and (a, p, b) be the harmonious order. We consider the following cases to rank a and b. First observe that p beats at least one of a and b in the final election, no matter how the manipulators rank a and b. To check this, let x_a, x_p and x_b be the total weight of the votes (both manipulators and nonmanipulators) with their peaks at a, at p and at b, respectively. Since all manipulators have their peaks at p, we have that $x_p > 0$. Thus, one of $x_a + x_p > \frac{x_a+x_b+x_p}{2}$ and $x_b + x_p > \frac{x_a+x_b+x_p}{2}$ must hold, implying that p beats at least one of a and b. It remains to consider the following two cases. Note that since all the manipulators rank the distinguished candidate p in the top, the comparison between p and every a and b is known.

Case 1. p beats both a and b. In this case, p must be the unique winner no matter the comparison between a and b. Thus, we can immediately return 'Yes'.

Case 2. p beats exactly one of $\{a, b\}$. Without loss of generality, assume that p beats only a. Then, casting their votes as $p \succ a \succ b$ must be the optimal choice for the manipulators, since otherwise, b will beat a, implying p cannot be the unique winner.

The above algorithm directly applies to the nonunique-winner model. Due to space limitations, we only give the main idea of the algorithm for the weighted manipulation when the number of candidates is not bounded. Let $c_1, c_2, ..., c_i, p, c_{i+1}, ..., c_m$ be the harmonious order. The manipulators first rank the distinguished candidate in the top. Then, if $\{p\}$ is not in the median group (the median group in the weighted case is the median group in the unweighted case with each voter with weight w being considered as w individual unweighted voters), return "No". Otherwise, all the manipulators cast their votes as follows. If $\{p\}$ is on the left-side of the median group, then all the manipulators cast their votes as $p \succ c_i \succ ..., \succ c_1 \succ c_{i+1} \succ, ..., \succ c_m$. Otherwise, all the manipulators cast their votes as $p \succ c_{i+1} \succ ..., \succ c_m \succ c_i \succ, ..., \succ c_1$. The correctness of the algorithm is based on the weighted versions of Lemmas 5, 6 and 7. □

Note that the weighted manipulation with three candidates for Copeland$^\alpha$ for every $0 \leq \alpha < 1$ is $\mathcal{NP}$-hard in general, for the nonunique-winner model [6, 16]. Our polynomial-time algorithm in the above theorem does not apply to the general case since our algorithm relies heavily on the single-peaked restriction. For example, when the distinguished candidate is not in the middle of the harmonious order, all the manipulators have only one way to cast their votes. However, in the $\mathcal{NP}$-hardness reduction of the problem in the general case, the manipulators can cast their votes freely to balance the scores of a and b.

7. CONCLUDING REMARKS

We have studied the parameterized complexity of the unweighted manipulation problem under the Borda, Maximin and Copeland$^\alpha$ voting correspondences, and achieved several $\mathcal{FPT}$ results, with respect to the parameters "single-peaked width" and "number of manipulators". Moreover, we proposed several properties (Lemmas 1-7) of Maximin and Copeland$^\alpha$ elections with bounded single-peaked width. We believe that these properties are helpful in solving further voting problems. In addition, we proved that the weighted manipulation problem for Copeland$^\alpha$ for every $0 \leq \alpha < 1$ is polynomial-time solvable in single-peaked elections, regardless of the number of manipulators and the number of candidates. Tables 1 and 2 summarize our results.

The two $\mathcal{FPT}$-algorithms for Maximin and Copeland$^\alpha$ for every $0 \leq \alpha \leq 1$ run in $O(k!^t \cdot Poly)$ time, where k is the single-peaked width and t is the number of manipulators. The factorial $k!$ corresponds to the number of enumerations over a (candidate) set of size k. Several algorithms for generating all the permutations over a set of size k have been proved practical when k is a small number (see, e.g., http://theory.cs.uvic.ca/). It is plausible that our algorithms are implementable when both k and t are small (e.g., $k \leq 5$ and $t = 2, 3$). The number of candidates, however, can be very large. For lager k and t, more heuristic methods should be derived to speed up the algorithms.

We remark that our $\mathcal{FPT}$-algorithms for the unweighted manipulation problem for Maximin and Copeland$^\alpha$ can be extended to solve the weighted manipulation problem. Nevertheless, the extension for Copeland$^\alpha$ does not cover Theorem 4, since the polynomial-time solvability result stated in Theorem 4 holds regardless of the number of manipulators. The $\mathcal{FPT}$-algorithm for the unweighted manipulation for Borda, however, cannot be extended to the weighted manipulation since the polynomial-time algorithm in [22] does not apply to the weighted case.

We end with several open problems. First, it would be interesting to know whether the fixed-parameter tractability of the manipulation problem remains when parameterized by the single parameter "single-peaked width". Second, it would be interesting to explore the parameterized complexity of the manipulation problem for further voting correspondences with respect to the parameters "single-peaked width" and "number of manipulators", such as the second-order Copeland, STV and Ranked pair. In general, the unweighted manipulation problem under these voting correspondences is $\mathcal{NP}$-hard even when there is only two manipulators [21].

Acknowledgments

The author thanks the AAMAS-15 reviewers for their helpful comments. The author was supported by the DFG Cluster of Excellence (MMCI) and the China Scholarship Council (CSC).

REFERENCES

[1] K. J. Arrow. A difficulty in the concept of social welfare. *J. Polit. Econ.*, 58(4):328–346, 1950.

[2] N. Betzler, R. Niedermeier, and G. J. Woeginger. Unweighted coalitional manipulation under the Borda rule is NP-hard. In *IJCAI*, pages 55–60, 2011.

[3] D. Black. On the rationable of group decition-making. *J. Polit. Econ.*, 56:23–34, 1948.

[4] F. Brandt, M. Brill, E. Hemaspaandra, and L. A. Hemaspaandra. Bypassing combinatorial protections: Polynomial-time algorithms for single-peaked electorates. In *AAAI*, pages 715–722, 2010.

[5] R. Bredereck, J. Chen, and G. J. Woeginger. Are there any nicely structured preference profiles nearby? In *IJCAI*, pages 62–68, 2013.

[6] V. Conitzer, T. Sandholm, and J. Lang. When are elections with few candidates hard to manipulate? *J. ACM*, 54(3):1–33, 2007.

[7] D. Cornaz, L. Galand, and O. Spanjaard. Bounded single-peaked width and proportional representation. In *ECAI*, pages 270–275, 2012.

[8] D. Cornaz, L. Galand, and O. Spanjaard. Kemeny elections with bounded single-peaked or single-crossing width. In *IJCAI*, pages 76–82, 2013.

[9] J. Davies, G. Katsirelos, N. Narodytska, and T. Walsh. Complexity of and algorithms for Borda manipulation. In *AAAI*, pages 657–662, 2011.

[10] G. Demange. Single-peaked orders on a tree. *Math. Soc. Sci.*, 3(3):389–396, 1983.

[11] E. Ephrati and J. S. Rosenschein. A heuristic technique for multi-agent planning. *Ann. Math. Artif. Intell.*, 20(1-4):13–67, 1997.

[12] G. Erdélyi, M. Lackner, and A. Pfandler. Computational aspects of nearly single-peaked electorates. In *AAAI*, pages 283–289, 2013.

[13] B. Escoffier, J. Lang, and M. Öztürk. Single-peaked consistency and its complexity. In *ECAI*, pages 366–370, 2008.

[14] P. Faliszewski, E. Hemaspaandra, and L. A. Hemaspaandra. The complexity of manipulative attacks in nearly single-peaked electorates. *Artif. Intell.*, 207:69–99, 2014.

[15] P. Faliszewski, E. Hemaspaandra, L. A. Hemaspaandra, and J. Rothe. The shield that never was: Societies with single-peaked preferences are more open to manipulation and control. *Inf. Comput.*, 209(2):89–107, 2011.

[16] P. Faliszewski, E. Hemaspaandra, and H. Schnoor. Copeland voting: ties matter. In *AAMAS (2)*, pages 983–990, 2008.

[17] P. Faliszewski, E. Hemaspaandra, and H. Schnoor. Manipulation of copeland elections. In *AAMAS*, pages 367–374, 2010.

[18] P. Faliszewski, E. Hemaspaandra, and H. Schnoor. Weighted manipulation for four-candidate Llull is easy. In *ECAI*, pages 318–323, 2012.

[19] U. Grandi, A. Loreggia, F. Rossi, K. B. Venable, and T. Walsh. Restricted manipulation in iterative voting: Condorcet efficiency and Borda score. In *ADT*, pages 181–192, 2013.

[20] J. J. Bartholdi III, C. A. Tovey, and M. A. Trick. The computational difficulty of manipulating an election. *Soc. Choice. Welfare.*, 6(3):227–241, 1989.

[21] L. Xia, M. Zuckerman, A. D. Procaccia, V. Conitzer, and J. S. Rosenschein. Complexity of unweighted coalitional manipulation under some common voting rules. In *IJCAI*, pages 348–353, 2009.

[22] Y. Yang and J. Guo. Exact algorithms for weighted and unweighted Borda manipulation problems. In *AAMAS*, pages 1327–1328, 2013. http://arxiv.org/abs/1304.3145.

[23] Y. Yang and J. Guo. The control complexity of r-approval: from the single-peaked case to the general case. In *AAMAS*, pages 621–628, 2014.

[24] Y. Yang and J. Guo. Election controls with small single-peaked width. In *AAMAS*, pages 629–636, 2014.

[25] Y. Yang and J. Guo. Election control in multi-peaked elections: a parameterized study. In *AAMAS*, 2015. extended abstract.

Kernelization Complexity of Possible Winner and Coalitional Manipulation Problems in Voting

Palash Dey
Department of Computer Science and Automation
Indian Institute of Science, Bangalore, India.
palash@csa.iisc.ernet.in

Neeldhara Misra
Department of Computer Science and Automation
Indian Institute of Science, Bangalore, India.
mail@neeldhara.com

Y. Narahari
Department of Computer Science and Automation
Indian Institute of Science, Bangalore, India.
hari@csa.iisc.ernet.in

ABSTRACT

In the Possible Winner problem in computational social choice theory, we are given a set of partial preferences and the question is whether a distinguished candidate could be made winner by extending the partial preferences to linear preferences. Previous work has provided, for many common voting rules, fixed parameter tractable algorithms for the Possible Winner problem, with number of candidates as the parameter. However, the corresponding kernelization question is still open and in fact, has been mentioned as a key research challenge [10]. In this paper, we settle this open question for many common voting rules.

We show that the Possible Winner problem for maximin, Copeland, Bucklin, ranked pairs, and a class of scoring rules that include the Borda voting rule do not admit a polynomial kernel with the number of candidates as the parameter. We show however that the Coalitional Manipulation problem which is an important special case of the Possible Winner problem does admit a polynomial kernel for maximin, Copeland, ranked pairs, and a class of scoring rules that includes the Borda voting rule, when the number of manipulators is polynomial in the number of candidates. A significant conclusion of our work is that the Possible Winner problem is harder than the Coalitional Manipulation problem since the Coalitional Manipulation problem admits a polynomial kernel whereas the Possible Winner problem does not admit a polynomial kernel.

Categories and Subject Descriptors

F.2 [**Theory of Computation**]: Analysis of Algorithms and Problem Complexity;
I.2.11 [**Artificial Intelligence**]: Distributed Artificial Intelligence—*Multiagent Systems*

General Terms

Algorithms, Theory

Keywords

Computational social choice; possible winner; voting; kernelization; parameterized complexity

Appears in: *Proceedings of the 14th International Conference on Autonomous Agents and Multiagent Systems (AAMAS 2015), Bordini, Elkind, Weiss, Yolum (eds.), May, 4–8, 2015, Istanbul, Turkey.*

1. INTRODUCTION

In many real life situations including multiagent systems, agents often need to aggregate their preferences and agree upon a common decision (candidate). Voting is an immediate natural tool in these situations. Common and classical applications of voting rules in artificial intelligence include collaborative filtering [31], planning among multiple automated agents [19], etc.

Usually, in a voting setting, it is assumed that the votes are complete orders over the candidates. However, due to many reasons, for example, lack of knowledge of voters about some candidates, a voter may be indifferent between some pairs of candidates. Hence, it is both natural and important to consider scenarios where votes are partial orders over the candidates. When votes are only partial orders over the candidates, the winner cannot be determined with certainty since it depends on how these partial orders are extended to linear orders. This leads to a natural computational problem called the Possible Winner [25] problem: given a set of partial votes P and a distinguished candidate c, is there a way to extend the partial votes to linear ones to make c win? The Possible Winner problem has been studied extensively in the literature [2,5,6,8,14,22,26,27,32,33,35] following its definition in [25]. The Possible Winner problem is known to be in NPC for many common voting rules, for example, scoring rules, maximin, Copeland, Bucklin, and ranked pairs etc. [35]. Walsh [33] showed, for a constant number of candidates, that the Possible Winner problem can be solved in polynomial time for all the voting rules mentioned above. An important special case of the Possible Winner problem is the Coalitional Manipulation problem [1] where only two kinds of partial votes are allowed - complete preference and empty preference. The set of empty votes is called the manipulators' vote and is denoted by M. The Coalitional Manipulation problem is in NPC for maximin, Copeland, and ranked pairs voting rules even when $|M| \geq 2$ [20,21,36]. The Coalitional Manipulation problem is in P for the Bucklin voting rule [36]. We refer to [33,35,36] for detailed overviews.

1.1 Our Methodology

Preprocessing, as a strategy for coping with hard problems, is universally applied in practice. The main goal here is *instance compression* - the objective is to output a smaller instance while maintaining equivalence. In the classical setting, $\mathbb{NP}$-hard problems are unlikely to have efficient compression algorithms (since repeated application would lead to an efficient solution for the entire problem, which is unexpected). However, the breakthrough notion of *kernelization* in parameterized complexity provides a mathematical framework for analyzing the quality of preprocessing strategies. In parameterized complexity, each problem instance (x, k) comes with a parameter k. The parameterized problem is said to admit a *kernel* if there is a polynomial time algorithm (where the degree of polynomial is independent of k), called a *kernelization algorithm*, that reduces the input instance to an instance with size bounded by a function of k, while preserving the answer. This has turned out to be an important and widely applied notion in theory, and has also proven very successful in practice [28, 34]. Quantitatively, running a kernelization algorithm before solving it using an algorithm that runs in time $f(|x|)$ brings down the running time to $f(k)+p(|x|)$, where $|x|$ is the size of the input instance and the running time of the kernelization algorithm is $p(|x|)$.

A problem with parameter k is called *fixed parameter tractable* (FPT) if it is solvable in time $f(k) \cdot p(|x|)$, where f is an arbitrary function of k and p is a polynomial in the input size $|x|$. The existence of a fixed parameter tractable algorithm implies existence of a kernel for that problem. However, the size of the kernel need not be polynomial in the parameter. A polynomial kernel is said to exist if there is a kernelization algorithm that can output an equivalent problem instance of size polynomial in the parameter. We refer to [18, 30] for an excellent overview on fixed parameter algorithms and kernelization.

1.2 Contributions

Discovering kernelization algorithms is currently an active and interesting area of research in computational social choice theory [3–5,7,11,12,17,24]. Betzler et al. [8] showed that the Possible Winner problem has a kernelization algorithm when parameterized by the total number of candidates for scoring rules, maximin, Copeland, Bucklin, and ranked pairs voting rules. A natural and practical follow-up question is whether the problem admits a polynomial kernel when parameterized by the number of candidates. This question has been open ever since the work of Betzler et al. and in fact, has been mentioned as a key research challenge in parameterized algorithms for computational social choice theory [10]. Betzler et al. showed non-existence of polynomial kernel for the Possible Winner problem for the k-approval voting rule when parameterized by (t, k), where t is the number of partial votes [3]. The NPC reductions for the Possible Winner problem for scoring rules, maximin, Copeland, Bucklin, and ranked pairs voting rules given by Xia et al. [36] are from the Exact 3 Set-Cover problem. Their results do not throw any light on the existence of a polynomial kernel since Exact 3 Set-Cover has a trivial $O(m^3)$ kernel where m is the size of the universe. In our work in this paper, we show that there is no polynomial kernel for the Possible Winner problem for maximin, Copeland, Bucklin, ranked pairs, and a class of scoring rules that include the Borda voting rule, when parameterized by the total number of candidates unless CoNP $\subseteq$ NP/Poly. These hardness results are shown by a parameter-preserving many-to-one reduction from the Small Universe Set Cover problem for which there does not exist any polynomial kernel parameterized by universe size unless CoNP $\subseteq$ NP/Poly [16].

On the other hand, we show that the Coalitional Manipulation problem admits a polynomial kernel for maximin, Copeland, ranked pairs, and a class of scoring rules that includes the Borda voting rule when we have $O(poly(m))$ number of manipulators – specifically, we exhibit an $O(m^2|M|)$ kernel for maximin and Copeland, and an $O(m^4|M|)$ kernel for the ranked pairs voting rule, where m is the number of candidates and M is the set of manipulators. The Coalitional Manipulation problem for the Bucklin voting rule is in P [36] and thus the kernelization question does not arise.

A significant conclusion of our work is that, although the Possible Winner and Coalitional Manipulation problems are both NPC, the Possible Winner problem is harder than the Coalitional Manipulation problem since the Coalitional Manipulation problem admits a polynomial kernel whereas the Possible Winner problem does not admit a polynomial kernel.

The rest of the paper is organized as follows. We first establish the setup and general notions. Next, we discuss non-existence of polynomial kernels for the Possible Winner problem followed by existence of polynomial kernels for the Coalitional Manipulation problem.

2. PRELIMINARIES

Let $\mathcal{V} = \{v_1, \dots, v_n\}$ be the set of all *voters* and $\mathcal{C} = \{c_1, \dots, c_m\}$ the set of all *candidates*. From, here on, n is the number of voters and m is the number of candidates unless mentioned otherwise. Each voter v_i's *vote* is a *preference* $\succ_i$ over the candidates which is a linear order over $\mathcal{C}$. For example, for two candidates a and b, $a \succ_i b$ means that the voter v_i prefers a to b. We will use $a >_i b$ to denote the fact that $a \succ_i b, a \neq b$. We denote the set of all linear orders over $\mathcal{C}$ by $\mathcal{L}(\mathcal{C})$. The set of all preference profiles $(\succ_1, \dots, \succ_n)$ of the n voters is denoted by $\mathcal{L}(\mathcal{C})^n$. We use $x\%y$ to denote the modulus operation x mod y (for example, $5\%2$ is the same as 1). We denote the set $\{1, 2, \dots\}$ by $\mathbb{N}^+$ and the set $\{1, \cdots, k\}$ by $[k]$. Let $\uplus$ denote the disjoint union of sets. A map $r : \uplus_{n,|\mathcal{C}| \in \mathbb{N}^+} \mathcal{L}(\mathcal{C})^n \longrightarrow 2^{\mathcal{C}} \setminus \{\emptyset\}$ is called a *voting rule*. For a voting rule r and a preference profile $\succ$, we say a candidate x wins uniquely if $r(\succ) = \{x\}$. In this paper, unless mentioned otherwise, winning means winning uniquely. A more general setting is an *election* where the votes are only *partial orders* over candidates. A *partial order* is a relation that is *reflexive, antisymmetric*, and *transitive*. A partial vote can be extended to possibly more than one linear votes depending on how we fix the order for the unspecified pairs of candidates. For example, in an election with the set of candidates $\mathcal{C} = \{a, b, c\}$, a valid partial vote can be $a \succ b$. This partial vote can be extended to three linear votes namely, $a \succ b \succ c$, $a \succ c \succ b$, $c \succ a \succ b$. However, the voting rules always take as input a set of votes that are complete orders over the candidates. Some examples of common voting rules are as follows.

Positional scoring rules. Given an m-dimensional vector $\vec{\alpha} = (\alpha_1, \alpha_2, \dots, \alpha_m) \in \mathbb{R}^m$ with $\alpha_1 \geq \alpha_2 \geq \cdots \geq \alpha_m$, we can naturally define a voting rule - a candidate gets score α_i from a vote if it is placed at the ith position, and the score of a candidate is the sum of the scores it receives from all the votes. The winners are the candidates with maximum score. Scoring rules remain unchanged if we multiply every α_i by any constant $\lambda > 0$ and/or add any constant μ. Hence, we assume without loss of generality that for any score vector $\vec{\alpha}$, there exists a j such that $\alpha_j - \alpha_{j+1} = 1$ and $\alpha_k = 0$ for all $k > j$. We call such an $\vec{\alpha}$ a normalized score vector. A scoring rule is called a strict scoring rule if $\alpha_1 > \alpha_2 > \cdots > \alpha_m$. For $\alpha = (m-1, m-2, \dots, 1, 0)$, we get the *Borda* voting rule. With $\alpha_i = 1\ \forall i \leq k$ and 0 else, the voting rule we get is known as k-*approval*. *Plurality* is 1-*approval* and *veto* is $(m-1)$-*approval*.

Bucklin. A candidate x's Bucklin score is the minimum number l such that more than half of the voters rank x in their top l positions. The winners are the candidates with lowest Bucklin score.

Given an election E, we can construct a weighted graph G_E called *weighted majority graph* from E. The set of vertices in G_E is the set of candidates in E. For any two candidates x and y, the weight on the edge (x, y) is $D_E(x, y) = N_E(x, y) - N_E(y, x)$, where $N_E(x, y)(N_E(y, x))$ is the number of voters who prefer x to y (y to x). The following voting rules use weighted majority graph to select winner.

Maximin. The maximin score of a candidate x is $\min_{y \neq x} D(x, y)$. The winners are the candidates with maximum maximin score.

Copeland. The Copeland score of a candidate x is the number of candidates $y \neq x$ such that $D(x, y) > 0$. The winners are the candidates with maximum Copeland score.

Ranked pairs. We pick the pair $(c_i, c_j) \in \mathcal{C} \times \mathcal{C}$ such that $D(c_i, c_j)$ is maximum. We fix the ordering between c_i and c_j to be $c_i \succ c_j$ unless it contradicts previously fixed orders. We continue this process until all pairwise elections are considered. At this point, we have a complete order over the candidates. Now, the top candidate is chosen as the winner.

We use the parallel-universes tie breaking [13, 15] to define the winning candidate for the ranked pairs voting rule. In this setting, a candidate c is a winner if and only if there exists a way to break ties in all of the steps such that c is the winner. We say that a candidate is the unique winner of a ranked pairs election if the candidate is the sole winner in all possible tie breakings in all the steps.

We now briefly describe the framework in which we analyze the computational complexity of the POSSIBLE WINNER problem.

Parameterized Complexity.. A parameterized problem Π is a subset of $\Gamma^* \times \mathbb{N}$, where Γ is a finite alphabet. An instance of a parameterized problem is a tuple (x, k), where k is the parameter. A *kernelization* algorithm is a set of preprocessing rules that runs in polynomial time and reduces the instance size with a guarantee on the output instance size. This notion is formalized below.

Definition 1. **[Kernelization]** *[23, 30] A kernelization algorithm for a parameterized problem $\Pi \subseteq \Gamma^* \times \mathbb{N}$ is an algorithm that, given $(x, k) \in \Gamma^* \times \mathbb{N}$, outputs, in time polynomial in $|x| + k$, a pair $(x', k') \in \Gamma^* \times \mathbb{N}$ such that (a) $(x, k) \in \Pi$ if and only if $(x', k') \in \Pi$ and (b) $|x'|, k' \leq g(k)$, where g is some computable function. The output instance x' is called the kernel, and the function g is referred to as the size of the kernel. If $g(k) = k^{O(1)}$ then we say that Π admits a polynomial kernel.*

For many parameterized problems, it is well established that the existence of a polynomial kernel would imply the collapse of the polynomial hierarchy to the third level (or more precisely, CoNP $\subseteq$ NP/Poly). Therefore, it is considered unlikely that these problems would admit polynomial-sized kernels. For showing kernel lower bounds, we simply establish reductions from these problems.

Definition 2. **[Polynomial Parameter Transformation]** *[9] Let Γ_1 and Γ_2 be parameterized problems. We say that Γ_1 is polynomial time and parameter reducible to Γ_2, written $\Gamma_1 \leq_{Ptp} \Gamma_2$, if there exists a polynomial time computable function $f : \Sigma^* \times \mathbb{N} \to \Sigma^* \times \mathbb{N}$, and a polynomial $p : \mathbb{N} \to \mathbb{N}$, and for all $x \in \Sigma^*$ and $k \in \mathbb{N}$, if $f((x, k)) = (x', k')$, then $(x, k) \in \Gamma_1$ if and only if $(x', k') \in \Gamma_2$, and $k' \leq p(k)$. We call f a polynomial parameter transformation (or a PPT) from Γ_1 to Γ_2.*

This notion of a reduction is useful in showing kernel lower bounds because of the following theorem.

Theorem 1. *[9, Theorem 3] Let P and Q be parameterized problems whose derived classical problems are P^c, Q^c, respectively. Let P^c be NPC, and $Q^c \in \mathbb{NP}$. Suppose there exists a PPT from P to Q. Then, if Q has a polynomial kernel, then P also has a polynomial kernel.*

3. HARDNESS OF KERNELIZATION FOR POSSIBLE WINNER PROBLEM

In this section, we show non-existence of polynomial kernels for the POSSIBLE WINNER problem for maximin, Copeland, Bucklin, ranked Pairs, and a class of scoring rules that includes the Borda voting rule. We do this by demonstrating polynomial parameter transformations from the SMALL UNIVERSE SET COVER problem, which is the classic SET COVER problem, but now parameterized by the size of the universe and the budget.

SMALL UNIVERSE SET COVER	**Parameter:** $m + k$
Input: A set $\mathcal{U} = \{u_1, \ldots, u_m\}$ and a family $\mathcal{F} = \{S_1, \ldots, S_t\}$.	
Question: Is there a subfamily $\mathcal{H} \subseteq \mathcal{F}$ of size at most k such that every element of the universe belongs to at least one $H \in \mathcal{H}$?	

It is well-known [16] that RED-BLUE DOMINATING SET parameterized by k and the number of non-terminals does not admit a polynomial kernel unless CoNP $\subseteq$ NP/Poly. It follows, by the duality between dominating set and set cover, that SET COVER when parameterized by the solution size and the size of the universe (in other words, the SMALL UNIVERSE SET COVER problem defined above) does not admit a polynomial kernel unless CoNP $\subseteq$ NP/Poly.

We now consider the POSSIBLE WINNER problem parameterized by the number of candidates for maximin, Copeland, Bucklin, ranked pairs, and a class of scoring rules that includes the Borda rule, and establish that they do not admit a polynomial kernel unless CoNP $\subseteq$ NP/Poly, by polynomial parameter transformations from SMALL UNIVERSE SET COVER.

3.1 Scoring Rules

First, we prove hardness of kernelization for the POSSIBLE WINNER problem for a large class of scoring rules that includes the Borda rule. For that, we use the following lemma which has been used before [2].

Lemma 1. *Let $\mathcal{C} = \{c_1, \ldots, c_m\} \uplus D, (|D| > 0)$ be a set of candidates, and $\vec{\alpha}$ a normalized score vector of length $|\mathcal{C}|$. Then, for any given $\mathbf{X} = (X_1, \ldots, X_m) \in \mathbb{Z}^m$, there exists $\lambda \in \mathbb{R}$ and a voting profile such that the $\vec{\alpha}$-score of c_i is $\lambda + X_i$ for all $1 \leq i \leq m$, and the score of candidates $d \in D$ is less than λ. Moreover, the number of votes is $O(poly(|\mathcal{C}| \cdot \sum_{i=1}^{m} |X_i|))$.*

Theorem 2. *The* POSSIBLE WINNER *problem for any strict scoring rule, when parameterized by the number of candidates, does not admit a polynomial kernel unless* CoNP $\subseteq$ NP/Poly.

PROOF. Let $(\mathcal{U}, \mathcal{F}, k)$ be an instance of SMALL UNIVERSE SET COVER, where $\mathcal{U} = \{u_1, \ldots, u_m\}$ and $\mathcal{F} = \{S_1, \ldots, S_t\}$. We use T_i to denote $\mathcal{U} \setminus S_i$. We let $(\alpha_1, \alpha_2, \ldots, \alpha_t)$ denote the score vector of length t, and let δ_i denote the difference $(\alpha_i - \alpha_{i+1})$. Note that for a strict scoring rule, all the δ_i's will be strictly positive. We now construct an instance $(\mathcal{C}, V, c)$ of POSSIBLE WINNER as follows.

Candidates. $\mathcal{C} = \mathcal{U} \uplus \mathcal{V} \uplus \{w, c, d\}$, where $\mathcal{V} := \{v_1, \ldots, v_m\}$.

Partial Votes, P. The first part of the voting profile comprises t partial votes, and will be denoted by P_1. Let V_j denote the set $\{v_1, \ldots, v_j\}$. For each $1 \leq i \leq t$, we first consider a profile built on a total order η_i:

$$\eta_i := d \succ S_i \succ V_j \succ w \succ \cdots, \text{where } j = m - |S_i|.$$

Now, we obtain a partial order λ_i based on η_i as follows:

$$\lambda_i := \eta_i \setminus (\{w\} \times (\{d\} \uplus S_i \uplus V_j))$$

Let P_1' be the set of votes $\{\eta_i \mid 1 \leq i \leq t\}$. We will now add more votes, which we denote by P_2, such that $s(c) = s(u_i), s(d) - s(c) = (k-1)\delta_1, s(c) - s(w) = k(\delta_2 + \delta_3 + \cdots + \delta_{m+1}) + \delta_1, s(c) > s(v_i) + 1$, for all $1 \leq i \leq t$ where $s(\cdot)$ is the scores of the candidates from the combined voting profile $P_1' \uplus P_2$. From the proof of Lemma 1, we can see that such votes can always be constructed. In particular, also note that the voting profile P_2 consists of complete votes. Note that the number of candidates is $2m+3$, which is polynomial in the size of the universe, as desired. We now claim that the candidate c is a possible winner for the voting profile $P_1 \uplus P_2$ with respect to the strict scoring rule if, and only if, $(\mathcal{U}, \mathcal{F})$ is a YES-instance of Set Cover.

In the forward direction, suppose, without loss of generality, that $S_1, \ldots, S_k$ form a set cover. Then we propose the following extension for the partial votes $\lambda_1, \ldots, \lambda_k$:

$$w > d > S_i > V_j > \cdots,$$

and the following extension for the partial votes $\lambda_{k+1}, \ldots, \lambda_t$:

$$d > S_i > V_j > w > \cdots$$

For $1 \leq i \leq k$, the position of d in the extension of λ_i proposed above is δ_1 lower than its original position in η_i. Therefore, the final score of d is lower than the score of c. Similarly, the scores of all the u_i's decrease by at least $\min_{i=2}^{m}\{\delta_i\}$, which is strictly positive, since the S_i's together form a set cover, and the scoring rule is strict. Finally, the score of w increase by at most $k(\delta_2 + \delta_3 + \cdots + \delta_{m+1})$, since there are at most k votes where the position of w in the extension of λ_i improved from it's original position in η_i. Therefore, the score of c is greater than any other candidate, implying that c is a possible winner.

For the reverse direction, notice that there must be at least k extensions where d is in the second position, since the score of d is $(k-1)\delta_1$ more than the score of c. In these extensions, observe that w will be at the first position. On the other hand, placing w in the first position causes its score to increase by $(\delta_2 + \delta_3 + \cdots + \delta_{m+1})$, therefore, if w is in first position in ℓ extensions, its score increases by $\ell(\delta_2 + \delta_3 + \cdots + \delta_{m+1})$. Since the score difference between w and c is only $k(\delta_2+\delta_3+\cdots+\delta_{m+1})+1$, we can afford to have w in the first position in *at most* k votes. Therefore, apart from the extensions where d is in the second position, in all remaining extensions, w appears after V_j, and therefore the candidates from S_i continue to be in their original positions. We now claim that the sets corresponding to the k votes where d is on top form a set cover. Indeed, if not, suppose the element u_i is not covered. It is easily checked that the score of such a u_i remains unchanged in this extension, and therefore its score is equal to c, contradicting our assumption that we started with an extension for which c was a winner. □

The proof of Theorem 2 can be generalized to to a wider class of scoring rules as stated in the following corollary.

Corollary 1. *Let r be a positional scoring rule such that there exists a polynomial function $f : \mathbb{N} \to \mathbb{N}$, such that for every $m \in \mathbb{N}$, there exists an index l in the $f(m)$ length score vector $\vec{\alpha}$ satisfying following,*

$$\alpha_i - \alpha_{i+1} > 0, \forall l \leq i \leq l+m$$

Then, the Possible Winner *problem for r, when parameterized by the number of candidates, does not admit a polynomial kernel unless* CoNP $\subseteq$ NP/Poly.

3.2 Maximin Voting Rule

We will need the following lemma in subsequent proofs. The lemma has been used before [29,35].

Lemma 2. *For any function $f : \mathcal{C} \times \mathcal{C} \longrightarrow \mathbb{Z}$, such that*
1. *$\forall a, b \in \mathcal{C}, f(a,b) = -f(b,a)$.*
2. *either $\forall a, b \in \mathcal{C}, f(a,b)$ is even or $\forall a, b \in \mathcal{C}, f(a,b)$ is odd.*

there exists a n voters' profile such that for all $a, b \in \mathcal{C}$, a defeats b with a margin of $f(a,b)$. Moreover,

$$n = O\left(\sum_{\{a,b\}\in\mathcal{C}\times\mathcal{C}} |f(a,b)|\right)$$

We now describe the reduction for the Possible Winner parameterized by the number of candidates, for the maximin voting rule.

Theorem 3. *The* Possible Winner *problem for maximin voting rule, when parameterized by the number of candidates, does not admit a polynomial kernel unless* CoNP $\subseteq$ NP/Poly.

Proof. Let $(\mathcal{U}, \mathcal{F}, k)$ be an instance of Small Universe Set Cover, where $\mathcal{U} = \{u_1, \ldots, u_m\}$ and $\mathcal{F} = \{S_1, \ldots, S_t\}$. We use T_i to denote $\mathcal{U} \setminus S_i$. We now construct an instance $(\mathcal{C}, V, c)$ of the Possible Winner as follows.

Candidates. $C := \mathcal{U} \uplus W \uplus \{c, d, x\} \uplus L$. Where $W := \{w_1, w_2, \ldots, w_m, w_x\}, L := \{l_1, l_2, l_3\}$.

Partial Votes, P. The first part of the voting profile comprises t partial votes, and will be denoted by P. For each $1 \leq i \leq t$, we first consider a profile built on a total order η_i. We denote the order $w_1 \succ \cdots \succ w_m \succ w_x$ by $\vec{W}$. From this point onwards, whenever we place a set of candidates in some position of a partial order, we mean that the candidates in the set can be ordered arbitrarily. For example, the candidates in S_i can be ordered arbitrarily among themselves in the total order η_i below.

$$\eta_i := L \succ \vec{W} \succ x \succ S_i \succ d \succ c \succ T_i$$

Now, we obtain a partial order λ_i based on η_i as follows:

$$\lambda_i := \eta_i \setminus (W \times (\{c, d, x\} \uplus \mathcal{U}))$$

The profile P consists of $\{\lambda_i \mid 1 \leq i \leq t\}$.

Complete Votes, Q. We now describe the remaining votes in the profile, which are linear orders designed to achieve specific pairwise difference scores among the candidates. This profile, denoted by Q, is defined according to Lemma 2 to contain votes such that $D(c, w_1) = -2k, D(c, l_1) = -t, D(d, w_1) = -2k - 2, D(x, w_x) = -2k - 2, D(w_i, u_i) = -2t \ \forall\ 1 \leq i \leq m, D(a_i, l_1) = D(w_x, l_1) = -4t, D(l_1, l_2) = D(l_2, l_3) = D(l_3, l_1) = -4t, D(l, r) \leq 1$ for all other pairs $(l, r) \in C \times C$, are the pairwise score differences of $P \uplus Q$. We note that the for all $c, c' \in \mathcal{C}$, the difference $|D(c, c') - D_P(c, c')|$ is always even, as long as t is even and the number of sets in $\mathcal{F}$ that contain an element $u \in \mathcal{U}$ is always even. Note that the latter can always be ensured without loss of generality: indeed, if $u \in \mathcal{U}$ occurs in an odd number of sets, then we can always add the set $\{u\}$ if it is missing and remove it if it is present, flipping the parity in the process. In case $\{u\}$ is the only set containing the element u, then we remove the set from both $\mathcal{F}$ and $\mathcal{U}$ and decrease k by one. The number of sets t can be assumed to be even by adding a dummy element and a dummy pair of sets that contains the said element. Thus, the constructed instance of Possible Winner is $(\mathcal{C}, V, c)$, where $V := P \uplus Q$. We now turn to the proof of correctness.

In the forward direction, let $\mathcal{H} \subseteq \mathcal{F}$ be a set cover of size at most k. Without loss of generality, let $|\mathcal{H}| = k$ (since a smaller set cover can always be extended artificially) and let $\mathcal{H} = \{S_1, \ldots, S_k\}$ (by renaming).

$$\lambda_i^* := L \succ x \succ S_i \succ d \succ c \succ \vec{W} \succ T_i, \text{ if } i \leq k$$

$$\lambda_i^* := L \succ \vec{W} \succ x \succ S_i \succ d \succ c \succ T_i, \text{ if } i > k$$

Clearly λ_i^* extends λ_i for all $i \in 1 \leq i \leq k$. Let V^* denote the extended profile consisting of the votes $\{\lambda_i^* \mid 1 \leq i \leq k\} \uplus Q$.

We now claim that c is the unique winner with respect to maximin voting rule in V^*.

Since there are k votes in V^* where c is preferred over w_1 and $(t-k)$ votes where w_1 is preferred to c, we have:

$$\begin{aligned} D_{V^*}(c, w_1) &= D_V(c, w_1) + k - (t-k) \\ &= -2k + k - (t-k) = -t \end{aligned}$$

It is easy to check that maximin score of c is $-t$. Also, it is straightforward to verify that the maximin score of w_i is less than $-t$ for every $i \in [m]$, the maximin score of d and x is at most $-t-2$ and the maximin score of every other candidate is at most $-4t$. Therefore, c is the unique winner for the profile V^*.

We now turn to the reverse direction. Let P^* be an extension of P such that $V^* := P^* \uplus Q$ admits c as a unique winner. We first argue that P^* must admit a certain structure, which will lead us to an almost self-evident set cover for $\mathcal{U}$.

Let us denote by P_C^* the set of votes in P^* which are consistent with $c \succ w_1$, and let P_W^* be the set of votes in P^* which are consistent with $w_1 \succ c$. We first argue that P_C^* has at most k votes.

Claim 1. *Let P_C^* be as defined above. Then, $|P_C^*| \leq k$.*

PROOF. Suppose, for the sake of contradiction, that more than k extensions are consistent with $c \succ w_1$. Then we have:

$$\begin{aligned} D_{V^*}(c, w_1) &\geq D_V(c, w_1) + k + 1 - (t - k - 1) \\ &= -2k + 2k - t + 2 = -t + 2 \end{aligned}$$

Since $D_{V^*}(c, l_1) = -t$, the maximin score of c is $-t$. On the other hand, we also have that the maximin score of d is given by $D_{V^*}(d, w_1)$, which is now at least $(-t)$:

$$\begin{aligned} D_{V^*}(d, w_1) &\geq D_V(d, w_1) + k + 1 - (t - k - 1) \\ &= -2k - 2 + 2k - t + 2 = -t \end{aligned}$$

Therefore, c is no longer the unique winner in V^* with respect to the maximin voting rule, which is the desired contradiction. □

Next, we propose that a vote that is consistent with $w_1 \succ c$ must be consistent with $w_x \succ x$.

Claim 2. *Let P_W^* be as defined above. Then, any vote in P_W^* must respect $w_x \succ x$.*

PROOF. Suppose there are r votes in P_C^*, and suppose that in at least one vote in P_W^* where $x \succ w_x$. Notice that any vote in P_C^* is consistent with $x \succ w_x$. Now we have:

$$\begin{aligned} D_{V^*}(c, w_1) &= D_V(c, w_1) + r - (t - r) \\ &= -2k + 2r - t \\ &= -t - 2(k - r) \end{aligned}$$

And further:

$$\begin{aligned} D_{V^*}(x, w_x) &\geq D_V(x, w_x) + (r+1) - (t - r - 1) \\ &= -2k - 2 + 2r - t + 2 \\ &= -t - 2(k - r) \end{aligned}$$

It is easy to check that the maximin score of c in V^* is at most $-t - 2(k-r)$, witnessed by $D_{V^*}(c, w_1)$, and the maximin score of x is at least $-t-2(k-r)$, witnessed by $D_{V^*}(x, w_x)$. Therefore, c is no longer the unique winner in V^* with respect to the maximin voting rule, and we have a contradiction. □

We are now ready to describe a set cover of size at most k for $\mathcal{U}$ based on V^*. Define $J \subseteq [t]$ as being the set of all indices i for which the extension of λ_i in V^* belongs to P_C^*. Consider:

$$\mathcal{H} := \{S_i \mid i \in J\}.$$

The set $\mathcal{H}$ is our proposed set cover. Clearly, $|\mathcal{H}| \leq k$. It remains to be shown that $\mathcal{H}$ is a set cover.

Assume, for the sake of contradiction, that there is an element $u_i \in \mathcal{U}$ that is not covered by $\mathcal{H}$. This means that for all $i \in J$, $u_i \in T_i$, and in the corresponding extensions of λ_i in V^*, implying that $w_i \succ u_i$. Further, for all $i \notin J$, we have that the extension of λ_i in V^* is consistent with:

$$w_1 \succ \cdots \succ w_i \succ \cdots \succ w_x \succ x \succ S_i \succ c \succ T_i,$$

implying again that $w_i \succ u_i$ in these votes. Therefore, we have:

$$D_{V^*}(w_i, u_i) = D_V(w_i, u_i) + k + (t - k) = -2t + t = -t.$$

We know that the maximin score of c is less than or equal to $-t$, since $D_{V^*}(c, l_1) = -t$, and we now have that the maximin score of w_i is $-t$. This overrules c as the unique winner in V^*, contradicting our assumption to that effect. This completes the proof. □

3.3 Copeland Voting Rule

We now describe the reduction for POSSIBLE WINNER parameterized by the number of candidates, for the Copeland voting rule.

Theorem 4. *The* POSSIBLE WINNER *problem for the Copeland voting rule, when parameterized by the number of candidates, does not admit a polynomial kernel unless* CoNP $\subseteq$ NP/Poly.

PROOF. Let $(\mathcal{U}, \mathcal{F}, k)$ be an instance of SMALL UNIVERSE SET COVER, where $\mathcal{U} = \{u_1, \ldots, u_m\}$, and $\mathcal{F} = \{S_1, \ldots, S_t\}$. For the purpose of this proof, we assume (without loss of generality) that $m \geq 6$. We now construct an instance $(\mathcal{C}, V, c)$ of POSSIBLE WINNER as follows.

Candidates. $\mathcal{C} := \mathcal{U} \uplus \{z, c, d, w\}$.

Partial Votes, P. The first part of the voting profile comprises of m partial votes, and will be denoted by P. For each $1 \leq i \leq m$, we first consider a profile built on a total order:

$$\eta_i := \mathcal{U} \setminus S_i \succ z \succ c \succ d \succ S_i \succ w$$

Now, we obtain a partial order λ_i based on η_i as follows:

$$\lambda_i := \eta_i \setminus (\{z, c\} \times (S_i \uplus \{d, w\}))$$

The profile P consists of $\{\lambda_i \mid 1 \leq i \leq m\}$.

Complete Votes, Q. We now describe the remaining votes in the profile, which are linear orders designed to achieve specific pairwise difference scores among the candidates. This profile, denoted by Q, is defined according to lemma 2 to contain votes such that $D(c,d) = t - 2k + 1, D(z,w) = t - 2k - 1, D(c, u_i) = t - 1, D(c,z) = t+1, D(c,w) = -t-1 D(u_i, d) = D(z, u_i) = t+1$, for all $1 \leq i \leq m, D(z,d) = t+1, D(u_i, u_j) = t+1$, for all $j \in [i+1, i+\lfloor m/2 \rfloor]$, where addition is modulo m, are the pairwise score differences of $P \uplus Q$. We note that the for all $c, c' \in \mathcal{C}$, the difference $|D(c,c') - D_P(c,c')|$ is always even, as long t is odd and the number of sets in $\mathcal{F}$ that contain an element $a \in \mathcal{U}$ is always odd. Note that the latter can always be ensured without loss of generality: indeed, if $a \in \mathcal{U}$ occurs in an even number of sets, then we can always add the set $\{a\}$ if it is missing and remove it if it is present, flipping the parity in the process. The number of sets t can be assumed to be odd by adding a dummy element and a dummy set that contains the said element.

Thus the constructed instance of POSSIBLE WINNER is $(\mathcal{C}, V, c)$, where $V := P \uplus Q$. We now turn to the proof of correctness.

In the forward direction, let $\mathcal{H} \subseteq \mathcal{F}$ be a set cover of size at most k. Without loss of generality, let $|\mathcal{H}| = k$ (since a smaller set cover can always be extended artificially) and let $\mathcal{H} = \{S_1, \ldots, S_k\}$ (by renaming).

If $i \leq k$, let:

$$\lambda_i^* := \mathcal{U} \setminus S_i \succ z \succ c \succ d \succ S_i \succ w$$

If $i > k$, let:

$$\lambda_i^* := \mathcal{U} \setminus S_i \succ d \succ S_i \succ w \succ z \succ c$$

Clearly λ_i^* extends λ_i for all $i \in 1 \leq i \leq k$. Let V^* denote the extended profile consisting of the votes $\{\lambda_i^* \mid 1 \leq i \leq k\} \uplus Q$. We now claim that c is the unique winner with respect to the Copeland voting rule in V^*.

First, consider the candidate z. Between z and u_i, even if z loses to u_i in every λ_i^*, because $D(z, u_i) = t + 1$, z wins the pairwise election between z and u_i. The same argument holds between z and d. Therefore, the Copeland score of z, no matter how the partial votes were extended, is at least $(m + 1)$.

Further, note that all candidates (apart from c) have a Copeland score of less than $(m+1)$, because they are guaranteed to lose to at least three candidates (assuming $m \geq 6$). In particular, observe that u_i loses to at least $\lfloor m/2 \rfloor$ candidates, and d loses to all u_i (merely by its position in the extended votes), and w loses to all u_i (because of way the scores were designed). Therefore, the Copeland score of all candidates in $\mathcal{C} \setminus \{z, c\}$ is strictly less than the Copeland score of z, and therefore they cannot be possible winners.

Now we restrict our attention to the contest between z and c. First note that c beats every u_i: since the sets of $\mathcal{H}$ form a set cover, every u_i is present in some λ_i^* for $i \leq k$, in a position after c. Since the difference score between c and u_i was $(t - 1)$, even if c suffered defeat in every other extension, we have the pairwise score of c and u_i being at least $t - 1 - (t - 1) + 1 = 1$, which implies that c defeats every u_i in their pairwise election. Note that c also defeats d by getting ahead of d in k votes, making its final score $t - 2k + 1 + k - (t - k) = 1$. Finally, w defeats c, simply by the preset difference score. Hence, the Copeland score of c is $(m+2)$.

Now, all that remains to be done is to rule z out of the running. Note that z is defeated by w in their pairwise election: this is because z defeats w in k of the extended votes, and is defeated by w in the remaining. This implies that its final pairwise score with respect to w is at most $t - 2k - 1 + k - (t - k) = -1$. Also note that z loses to c because of its predefined difference score. Thus, the Copeland score of z in the extended vote is exactly $(m + 1)$, and thus c is the unique winner of the extended vote.

We now turn to the reverse direction. Let P^* be an extension of P such that $V^* := P^* \uplus Q$ admits c as an unique winner with respect to the Copeland voting rule. As with the argument for maximin voting rule, we first argue that P^* must admit a certain structure, which will lead us to an almost self-evident set cover for $\mathcal{U}$.

Let us denote by $P_{\mathcal{C}}^*$ the set of votes in P^* which are consistent with $c \succ d$, and let P_W^* be the set of votes in P^* which are consistent with $w \succ z$. Note that the votes in $P_{\mathcal{C}}^*$ necessarily have the form:

$$\lambda_i^* := \mathcal{U} \setminus S_i \succ z \succ c \succ d \succ S_i \succ w$$

and those in P_W^* have the form:

$$\lambda_i^* := \mathcal{U} \setminus S_i \succ d \succ S_i \succ w \succ z \succ c$$

It is easy to check that this structure is directly imposed by the relative orderings that are fixed by the partial orders.

Before we argue the details of the scores, let us recall that in any extension of P, z loses to c and z wins over d and all candidates in $\mathcal{U}$. Thus the Copeland score of z is at least $(m + 1)$. On the other hand, in any extension of P, c loses to w, and therefore the Copeland score of c is at most $(m + 2)$. (These facts follow from the analysis in the forward direction.)

Thus, we have the following situation. If z wins over w, then c cannot be the unique winner in the extended vote, because the score of z goes up to $(m + 2)$. Similarly, c cannot afford to lose to any of $\mathcal{U} \uplus \{d\}$, because that will cause its score to drop below $(m + 2)$, resulting in either a tie with z, or worse. These facts will successively lead us to the correctness of the reverse direction.

Now, let us return to the sets $P_{\mathcal{C}}^*$ and P_W^*. If $P_{\mathcal{C}}^*$ has more than k votes, then z wins over w: the final score of z is at least $t - 2k - 1 + (k + 1) - (t - k - 1) = 1$, and we have a contradiction. If $P_{\mathcal{C}}^*$ has fewer than k votes, then c loses to d, with a score of at most $t - 2k + 1 + (k - 1) - (t - k + 1) = -1$, and we have a contradiction.

Finally, suppose the sets corresponding to the votes of $P_{\mathcal{C}}^*$ do not cover $\mathcal{U}$. Consider an element u_i of $\mathcal{U}$ not covered by the union of these sets. Observe that c now loses the pairwise election between itself and u_i and is no longer in the running for being the unique winner in the extended vote. Therefore, the sets corresponding to the votes of $P_{\mathcal{C}}^*$ form a set cover of size exactly k, as desired. □

3.4 Bucklin Voting Rule

We now describe the reduction for Possible Winner parameterized by the number of candidates, for the Bucklin voting rule.

Theorem 5. *The* Possible Winner *problem for the Bucklin voting rule, when parameterized by the number of candidates, does not admit a polynomial kernel unless* CoNP $\subseteq$ NP/Poly.

Proof. Let $(\mathcal{U}, \mathcal{F}, k)$ be an instance of Small Universe Set Cover, where $\mathcal{U} = \{u_1, \ldots, u_m\}$, and $\mathcal{F} = \{S_1, \ldots, S_t\}$. Without loss of generality, we assume that $t > k + 1$, and that every set has at least two elements. We now construct an instance $(\mathcal{C}, V, c)$ of Possible Winner as follows.

Candidates. $\mathcal{C} := \mathcal{U} \uplus \{z, c, a\} \uplus W \uplus D_1 \uplus D_2 \uplus D_3$, where D_1, D_2, and D_3 are sets of *"dummy candidates"* such that $|D_1| = m$, $|D_2| = 2m$, and $|D_3| =$. $W := \{w_1, w_2, \ldots, w_{2m}\}$.

Partial Votes, P. The first part of the voting profile comprises of t partial votes, and will be denoted by P. For each $1 \leq i \leq t$, we first consider a profile built on a total order:

$$\eta_i := \mathcal{U} \setminus S_i \succ S_i \succ w_{i\%m} \succ w_{(i+1)\%m} \succ z \succ c \succ D_3 \succ \cdots$$

Now, we obtain a partial order λ_i based on η_i as follows:

$$\lambda_i := \eta_i \setminus ((\{w_{i\%m}, w_{(i+1)\%m}, z, c\} \uplus D_3) \times S_i)$$

The profile P consists of $\{\lambda_i \mid 1 \leq i \leq t\}$.

Complete Votes, Q.

$$\begin{aligned} t - k - 1 &: D_1 \succ z \succ c \succ \cdots \\ 1 &: D_1 \succ c \succ a \succ z \succ \cdots \\ k - 1 &: D_2 \succ \cdots \end{aligned}$$

We now show that $(\mathcal{U}, \mathcal{F}, k)$ is an Yes instance if and only if $(\mathcal{C}, V, c)$ is an Yes instance. Suppose, $\{S_j : j \in J\}$ forms a set cover. Then, consider the following extension of P :

$$(\mathcal{U} \setminus S_j) \succ w_{j\%m} \succ w_{(j+1)\%m} \succ z \succ c \succ D_3 \succ S_j \cdots, \text{ for } j \in J$$

$$(\mathcal{U} \setminus S_j) \succ S_j \succ w_{j\%m} \succ w_{(j+1)\%m} \succ z \succ c \succ D_3 \succ \cdots, \text{ for } j \notin J$$

We claim that in this extension, c is the unique winner with Bucklin score $(m+2)$. First, let us establish the score of c. The candidate c is within the top $(m+1)$ choices in $(t-k)$ of the complete votes. In all the sets that form the set cover, c is ranked within the first $(m + 2)$ votes in the proposed extension of the corresponding vote (recall that every set has at least two elements). Therefore, there are a total of t votes where c is ranked within the top $(m+2)$ preferences. Further, consider a candidate $v \in \mathcal{U}$. Such a candidate is not within the top $(m+2)$ choices of any of the complete votes. Let S_i be the set that covers the element v. Note that in the extension of the vote λ_i, v is not ranked among the top $(m+2)$ spots, since there are at least m candidates from D_3 getting in the way. Therefore, v has strictly fewer than t votes where it is ranked among the top $(m+2)$ spots, and thus has a higher Bucklin score than c.

Now, the candidate z is within the top $(m+2)$ ranks of at most $(t-k-1)$ voters among the complete votes. In the votes corresponding to the sets *not* in the set cover, z is placed beyond the first $(m+2)$ spots. Therefore, the number of votes where z is among the top $(m+2)$ candidates is at most $(t-1)$, which makes its Bucklin score strictly larger than $(m+2)$.

The candidates from W are within the top $(m+2)$ positions only in a constant number of votes. The candidates $D_1 \uplus \{a\}$ have $(t-k)$ votes (among the complete ones) in which they are ranked among the top $(m+2)$ preferences, but in all extensions, these candidates have ranks below $(m+2)$. Finally, the candidates in D_3 do not feature in the top $(m+2)$ positions of any of the complete votes, and similarly, the candidates in D_2 do not feature in the top $(m+2)$ positions of any of the extended votes. Therefore, the Bucklin scores of all these candidates is easily seen to be strictly larger than $(m+2)$, concluding the argument in the forward direction.

Now, consider the reverse direction. Suppose, $(\mathcal{C}, V, c)$ is an YES instance. For the same reasons described in the forward direction, observe that only the following candidates can win depending upon how the partial preferences get extended - either one of the candidates in $\mathcal{U}$, or one of z or c. Note that the Bucklin score of z in any extension is at most $(m+3)$. Therefore, the Bucklin score of c has to be $(m+2)$ or less. Among the complete votes Q, there are $(t-k)$ votes where the candidate c appears in the top $(m+2)$ positions. To get majority within top $(m+2)$ positions, c should be within top $(m+2)$ positions for at least k of the extended votes in P. Let us call these set of votes P'. Now notice that whenever c comes within top $(m+2)$ positions in a valid extension of P, the candidate z also comes within top $(m+2)$ positions in the same vote. However, the candidate z is already ranked among the top $(m+2)$ candidates in $(t-k-1)$ complete votes. Therefore, z can appear within top $(m+2)$ positions in *at most* k extensions (since c is the unique winner), implying that $|P'| = k$. Further, note that the Bucklin score of c cannot be strictly smaller than $(m+2)$ in any extension. Indeed, the candidate c features in only one of the complete votes within the top $(m+1)$ positions, and it would have to be within the top $(m+1)$ positions in at least $(t-1)$ extensions. However, as discussed earlier, this would give z exactly the same mileage, and therefore its score Bucklin score would be $(m-1)$ or even less; contradicting our assumption that c is the unique winner.

Now, we claim that the S_i's corresponding to the votes in P' form a set cover for $\mathcal{U}$. If not, then there is an element $x \in \mathcal{U}$ that is uncovered. Observe that x appears within top m positions in all the extensions of the votes in P', by assumption. Further, in all the remaining extensions, since z is not present among the top $(m+2)$ positions, we only have room for two candidates from W. The remaining positions must be filled by all the candidates corresponding to elements of $\mathcal{U}$. Therefore, x appears within the top $(m+2)$ positions of all the extended votes. Since these constitute half the total number of votes, we have that x ties with c in this situation, a contradiction. □

3.5 Ranked Pairs Voting Rule

We now describe the reduction for Possible Winner parameterized by the number of candidates, for the ranked pairs voting rule.

Theorem 6. *The* Possible Winner *problem for the ranked pairs voting rule, when parameterized by the number of candidates, does not admit a polynomial kernel unless* CoNP $\subseteq$ NP/Poly.

Proof. Let $(\mathcal{U}, \mathcal{F}, k)$ be an instance of Small Universe Set Cover, where $\mathcal{U} = \{u_1, \ldots, u_m\}$, and $\mathcal{F} = \{S_1, \ldots, S_t\}$. Without loss of generality, we assume that t is even. We now construct an instance $(\mathcal{C}, V, c)$ of Possible Winner as follows.

Candidates. $\mathcal{C} := \mathcal{U} \uplus \{a, b, c, w\}$.

Partial Votes, P. The first part of the voting profile comprises of t partial votes, and will be denoted by P. For each $1 \leq i \leq t$, we first consider a profile built on a total order:

$$\eta_i := \mathcal{U} \setminus S_i \succ S_i \succ b \succ a \succ c \succ \cdots$$

Now, we obtain a partial order λ_i based on η_i as follows:

$$\lambda_i := \eta_i \setminus (\{a, c\} \times (S_i \uplus \{b\}))$$

The profile P consists of $\{\lambda_i \mid 1 \leq i \leq t\}$.

Complete Votes, Q. We add complete votes such that along with the already determined pairs from the partial votes P, we have $D(v_i, c) = 2, \forall 1 \leq i \leq t, D(c, b) = 4t, D(c, w) = t + 2, D(b, a) = 2k + 4, D(w, a) = 4t, D(a, c) = t + 2, \forall 1 \leq i \leq m, D(w, v_i) = 4t$. We now show that $(\mathcal{U}, \mathcal{F}, k)$ is an Yes instance if and only if $(\mathcal{C}, V, c)$ is an Yes instance. Suppose, $\{S_j : j \in J\}$ forms a set cover. Then, consider the following extension of P :

$$\mathcal{U} \setminus S_j \succ a \succ c \succ S_j \succ b \succ \cdots, \forall j \in J$$

$$\mathcal{U} \setminus S_j \succ S_j \succ b \succ a \succ c \succ \cdots, \forall j \notin J$$

We claim that the candidate c is the unique winner in this extension. Note that the pairs $(w \succ a)$ and $(w \succ v_i)$ (for all $1 \leq i \leq t$) get locked first (since these differences are clearly the highest and unchanged). The pair (c, b) gets locked next, with a difference score of $(3t+2k)$. Now, since the votes in which $c \succ b$ are based on a set cover of size at most k, the the pairwise difference between b and a becomes at least $2k + 4 - k + (t-k) = t + 4$. Therefore, the next pair to get locked is $b \succ a$. Finally, for any element $v_i \in \mathcal{U}$, the difference $D(v_i, c)$ is at most $2 + (t-1) = t + 1$, since there is at least one vote where $c \succ v_i$ (given that we used a set cover in the extension). It is now easy to see that the next highest pairwise difference is between c and w, so the ordering $c \succ w$ gets locked, and at this point, by transitivity, c is superior to w, b, a and all v_i. It follows that c wins the election irrespective the sequence in which pairs are considered subsequently.

Now suppose, $(\mathcal{C}, V, c)$ is an Yes instance. Notice that, irrespective of the extension of the votes in P, $c \succ b, w \succ a, w \succ v_i, \forall 1 \leq i \leq t$, are locked first. Now, if $b \succ c$ in all the extended votes, then it is easy to check that $b \succ a$ gets locked next, with a difference score of $2k + 4 + t$; leaving us with $D(v_i, c) = t + 2 = D(c, w)$, where $v_i \succ c$ could be a potential lock-in. This implies the possibility of a v_i being a winner in some choice of tie-breaking, a contradiction to the assumption that c is the unique winner. Therefore, there are at least some votes in the extended profile where $c \succ b$. We now claim that there are at most k such votes. Indeed, if there are more, then $D(b, a) = 2k + 4 - (k+1) + (t-k-1) = t + 2$. Therefore, after the forced lock-ins above, we have $D(b, a) = D(c, w) = D(a, c) = t + 2$. Here, again, it is possible for $a \succ c$ to be locked in before the other choices, and we again have a contradiction.

Finally, we have that $c \succ b$ in at most k many extensions in P. Call the set of indices of these extensions J. We claim that $\{S_j :$

$j \in J\}$ forms a set cover. If not, then suppose an element v_i is not covered by $\{S_j : j \in J\}$. Then, the candidate v_i comes before c in all the extensions which makes $D(v_i, c)$ become $(t+2)$, which in turn ties with $D(c, w)$. This again contradicts the fact that c is the unique winner. Therefore, if there is an extension that makes c the unique winner, then we have the desired set cover. □

4. POLYNOMIAL KERNELS FOR COALITIONAL MANIPULATION

We now describe a kernelization algorithm for any scoring rule which has the following properties. For $m \in \mathbb{N}$, let $(\alpha_1, \dots, \alpha_m)$ and $(\alpha'_1, \dots, \alpha'_{m+1})$ be the normalized score vectors for a scoring rule for an election with m and $(m+1)$ candidates respectively. Then $\alpha_1 = O(poly(m))$ and $\alpha_i = \alpha'_i$ for all $1 \leq i \leq m$. For ease of exposition, we present the result for the Borda voting rule only.

Theorem 7. *The* Coalitional Manipulation *problem for the Borda voting rule admits a polynomial kernel when the number of manipulators is $O(poly(m))$.*

Proof. Let c be the candidate whom the manipulators aim to make winner. Let M be the set of manipulators and $\mathcal{C}$ candidate set. Let $s_{NM}(x)$ be the score of candidate x from the votes of the non-manipulators. Without loss of generality, we assume that, all the manipulators place c at top position in their votes. Hence, the final score of c is $= s_{NM}(c) + |M|(m-1)$, which we denote by $s(c)$. Now, if $s_{NM}(x) \geq s(c)$ for any $x \neq c$, then c cannot win and we output *no*. Hence, we assume that $s_{NM}(x) < s(c)$ for all $x \neq c$. Now let us define $s^*_{NM}(x)$ as follows.

$$s^*_{NM}(x) := \max\{s_{NM}(x), s_{NM}(c)\}$$

Also define $s^*_{NM}(c)$ as follows.

$$s^*_{NM}(c) := s_{NM}(c) - |M|$$

We define a Coalitional Manipulation instance with $(m+1)$ candidates as $(\mathcal{C}', NM, M, c)$, where $\mathcal{C}' = \mathcal{C} \uplus \{d\}$ is the candidate set, M is the set of manipulators, c is the distinguished candidate, and NM is the non-manipulators' vote is such that it generates score of $x \in \mathcal{C}$ to be $K + (s^*_{NM}(x) - s_{NM}(c))$, where $K \in \mathbb{N}$ is same for $x \in \mathcal{C}$, and the score of d is less than $K - m|M|$. The existence of such a voting profile NM of size $poly(m)$ is due to Lemma 1. Hence, once we show the equivalence of these two instances, we have a kernel whose size is polynomial in m. The equivalence of the two instances follows from the facts that (1) the new instance has $(m+1)$ candidates and c is always placed at the top position without loss of generality, c gets $|M|$ score more than the initial instance and this is compensated in $s^*_{NM}(c)$, (2) the relative score difference from the final score of c to the current score of every $x \in \mathcal{C} \setminus \{c\}$ is same in both the instances, and (3) in the new instance, we can assume without loss of generality that the candidate d will be placed in the second position in all the manipulators' votes. □

We now move on to the voting rules that are based on the weighted majority graph. The reduction rules modify the weighted majority graph maintaining the property that there exists a set of votes that can realize the modified weighted majority graph. In particular, the final weighted majority graph is realizable with a set of votes.

Theorem 8. *The* Coalitional Manipulation *problem for the maximin voting rule admits a polynomial kernel when the number of manipulators is $O(poly(m))$.*

Proof. Let c be the distinguished candidate of the manipulators. Let M be the set of manipulators. We can assume that $|M| \geq 2$ since for $|M| = 1$, the problem is in P [1]. Define s to be $\min_{x \in \mathcal{C}\setminus\{c\}} D_{(\mathcal{V}\setminus M)}(c, x)$. So, s is the maximin score of the candidate c from the votes except from M. Since, the maximin voting rule is monotone, we can assume that the voters in M put the candidate c at top position of their preferences. Hence, c's final maximin score will be $s + |M|$. This provides the following reduction rule.

Reduction rule 1. *If $s + |M| \geq 0$, then output* Yes.

In the following, we will assume $s + |M|$ is negative. Now we propose the following reduction rules on the weighted majority graph.

Reduction rule 2. *If $D_{(\mathcal{V}\setminus M)}(c_i, c_j) < 0$ and $D_{(\mathcal{V}\setminus M)}(c_i, c_j) > 2|M| + s$, then make $D_{(\mathcal{V}\setminus M)}(c_i, c_j)$ either $2|M| + s + 1$ or $2|M| + s + 2$ whichever keeps the parity of $D_{(\mathcal{V}\setminus M)}(c_i, c_j)$ unchanged.*

If $D_{(\mathcal{V}\setminus M)}(c_i, c_j) > 2|M| + s$,,then $D_{\mathcal{V}}(c_i, c_j) > |M| + s$ irrespective of the way the manipulators vote. Hence, whether or not the maximin score of c_i and c_j will exceed the maximin score of c does not gets affected by this reduction rule. Hence, reduction rule 2 is sound.

Reduction rule 3. *If $D_{(\mathcal{V}\setminus M)}(c_i, c_j) < s$, then make $D_{(\mathcal{V}\setminus M)}(c_i, c_j)$ either $s - 1$ or $s - 2$ whichever keeps the parity of $D_{(\mathcal{V}\setminus M)}(c_i, c_j)$ unchanged.*

The argument for the correctness of reduction rule 3 is similar to the argument for reduction rule 2. Here onward, we may assume that whenever $D_{(\mathcal{V}\setminus M)}(c_i, c_j) < 0$, $s - 2 \leq D_{(\mathcal{V}\setminus M)}(c_i, c_j) \leq 2|M| + s + 2$

Reduction rule 4. *If $s < -4|M|$ then subtract $s + 5|M|$ whenever $s - 2 \leq D_{(\mathcal{V}\setminus M)}(c_i, c_j) \leq 2|M| + s + 2$.*

The correctness of reduction rule 4 follows from the fact that it adds linear fixed offsets to all the edges of the weighted majority graph. Hence, if there a voting profile of the voters in M that makes the candidate c win in the original instance, the same voting profile will make c win the election in the reduced instance and vice versa. Now, we have an weighted majority graph with $O(|M|)$ weights for every edge. Also, all the weights have uniform parity and thus the result follows from lemma 2. □

The proof of the following theorem is analogous to the proof of Theorem 8. In the interest of space, we omit the proof.

Theorem 9. *The* Coalitional Manipulation *problem for the Copeland and ranked pairs voting rules admit a polynomial kernel when the number of manipulators is $O(poly(m))$.*

5. CONCLUSION AND FUTURE WORK

Here, we showed that the Possible Winner problem does not admit a polynomial kernel for many common voting rules under the complexity theoretic assumption that CoNP $\subseteq$ NP/Poly is not true. We also showed the existence of polynomial kernels for the Coalitional Manipulation problem for many common voting rules. This shows that the Possible Winner problem is a significantly harder problem than the Coalitional Manipulation problem, although both the problems are in NPC.

There are other interesting parameterizations of these problems for which fixed parameter tractable algorithms are known but the corresponding kernelization questions are still open. One such parameter is the total number of pairs s in all the votes for which an ordering has not been specified. With this parameter, a simple $O(2^s . \text{poly}(m, n))$ algorithm is known [8]. However, the corresponding kernelization question is still open.

REFERENCES

[1] J. Bartholdi, C. Tovey, and M. Trick. The computational difficulty of manipulating an election. *Social Choice and Welfare (SCW)*, 6(3):227–241, 1989.

[2] D. Baumeister, M. Roos, and J. Rothe. Computational complexity of two variants of the possible winner problem. In *The 10th International Conference on Autonomous Agents and Multiagent Systems (AAMAS)*, pages 853–860. International Foundation for Autonomous Agents and Multiagent Systems, 2011.

[3] N. Betzler. On problem kernels for possible winner determination under the k-approval protocol. In *Mathematical Foundations of Computer Science (MFCS)*, pages 114–125. Springer, 2010.

[4] N. Betzler, R. Bredereck, J. Chen, and R. Niedermeier. The multivariate algorithmic revolution and beyond. chapter Studies in Computational Aspects of Voting: Open Problems of Downey and Fellows, pages 318–363. Springer-Verlag, Berlin, Heidelberg, 2012.

[5] N. Betzler, R. Bredereck, and R. Niedermeier. Partial kernelization for rank aggregation: theory and experiments. In *International Symposium on Parameterized and Exact Computation (IPEC)*, pages 26–37. Springer, 2010.

[6] N. Betzler and B. Dorn. Towards a dichotomy of finding possible winners in elections based on scoring rules. In *Mathematical Foundations of Computer Science (MFCS)*, pages 124–136. Springer, 2009.

[7] N. Betzler, M. R. Fellows, J. Guo, R. Niedermeier, and F. A. Rosamond. Fixed-parameter algorithms for kemeny rankings. *Theoretical Computer Science (TCS)*, 410(45):4554–4570, 2009.

[8] N. Betzler, S. Hemmann, and R. Niedermeier. A Multivariate Complexity Analysis of Determining Possible Winners given Incomplete Votes. In *International Joint Conference on Artificial Intelligence (IJCAI)*, volume 9, pages 53–58, 2009.

[9] H. L. Bodlaender, S. Thomassé, and A. Yeo. Kernel Bounds for Disjoint Cycles and Disjoint Paths. In A. Fiat and P. Sanders, editors, *Proceedings of the 17th Annual European Symposium,on Algorithms (ESA 2009), Copenhagen, Denmark, September 7-9, 2009.*, volume 5757 of *Lecture Notes in Computer Science*, pages 635–646. Springer, 2009.

[10] R. Bredereck, J. Chen, P. Faliszewski, J. Guo, R. Niedermeier, and G. J. Woeginger. Parameterized algorithmics for computational social choice: Nine research challenges. In *Tsinghua Science and Technology*, volume 19, pages 358–373. IEEE, 2014.

[11] R. Bredereck, J. Chen, P. Faliszewski, A. Nichterlein, and R. Niedermeier. Prices matter for the parameterized complexity of shift bribery. 2014.

[12] R. Bredereck, J. Chen, S. Hartung, R. Niedermeier, O. Suchŷ, and S. Kratsch. A multivariate complexity analysis of lobbying in multiple referenda. In *International Conference on Artificial Intelligence (AAAI)*, 2012.

[13] M. Brill and F. A. Fischer. The price of neutrality for the ranked pairs method. In *International Conference on Artificial Intelligence (AAAI)*, 2012.

[14] Y. Chevaleyre, J. Lang, N. Maudet, and J. Monnot. Possible winners when new candidates are added: The case of scoring rules. In *International Conference on Artificial Intelligence (AAAI)*, 2010.

[15] V. Conitzer, M. Rognlie, and L. Xia. Preference functions that score rankings and maximum likelihood estimation. In *Proceedings of the 21st International Joint Conference on Artificial Intelligence (IJCAI)*, volume 9, pages 109–115, 2009.

[16] M. Dom, D. Lokshtanov, and S. Saurabh. Incompressibility through colors and IDs. In *Automata, Languages and Programming (ICALP), 36th International Colloquium, Part I*, volume 5555 of *LNCS*, pages 378–389, 2009.

[17] B. Dorn and I. Schlotter. Multivariate complexity analysis of swap bribery. *Algorithmica*, 64(1):126–151, 2012.

[18] R. G. Downey and M. R. Fellows. *Parameterized Complexity*, volume 3. springer Heidelberg, 1999.

[19] E. Ephrati and J. Rosenschein. The Clarke tax as a consensus mechanism among automated agents. In *Proceedings of the Ninth International Conference on Artificial Intelligence (AAAI)*, pages 173–178, 1991.

[20] P. Faliszewski, E. Hemaspaandra, and H. Schnoor. Copeland voting: Ties matter. In *Proceedings of the 7th International Conference on Autonomous Agents and Multiagent Systems (AAMAS)*, pages 983–990. International Foundation for Autonomous Agents and Multiagent Systems, 2008.

[21] P. Faliszewski, E. Hemaspaandra, and H. Schnoor. Manipulation of copeland elections. In *Proceedings of the 9th International Conference on Autonomous Agents and Multiagent Systems (AAMAS)*, pages 367–374. International Foundation for Autonomous Agents and Multiagent Systems, 2010.

[22] P. Faliszewski, Y. Reisch, J. Rothe, and L. Schend. Complexity of manipulation, bribery, and campaign management in bucklin and fallback voting. In *Proceedings of the 13th International Conference on Autonomous Agents and Multiagent Systems (AAMAS)*, pages 1357–1358. International Foundation for Autonomous Agents and Multiagent Systems, 2014.

[23] J. Flum and M. Grohe. *Parameterized Complexity Theory*, volume 3. Springer, 2006.

[24] V. Froese, R. Van Bevern, R. Niedermeier, and M. Sorge. A parameterized complexity analysis of combinatorial feature selection problems. In *Mathematical Foundations of Computer Science (MFCS)*, pages 445–456. Springer, 2013.

[25] K. Konczak and J. Lang. Voting procedures with incomplete preferences. In *Proceedings of the International Joint Conference on Artificial Intelligence-05 Multidisciplinary Workshop on Advances in Preference Handling*, volume 20, 2005.

[26] J. Lang, M. S. Pini, F. Rossi, D. Salvagnin, K. B. Venable, and T. Walsh. Winner determination in voting trees with incomplete preferences and weighted votes. *Autonomous Agents and Multiagent Systems*, 25(1):130–157, 2012.

[27] J. Lang, M. S. Pini, F. Rossi, K. B. Venable, and T. Walsh. Winner determination in sequential majority voting. In *Proceedings of the 20th International Joint Conference on Artificial Intelligence (IJCAI)*, volume 7, pages 1372–1377, 2007.

[28] D. Lokshtanov, N. Misra, and S. Saurabh. Kernelization–preprocessing with a guarantee. In *The Multivariate Algorithmic Revolution and Beyond*, pages 129–161. Springer, 2012.

[29] D. C. McGarvey. A theorem on the construction of voting paradoxes. *Econometrica: Journal of the Econometric Society*, pages 608–610, 1953.

[30] R. Niedermeier. Invitation to fixed-parameter algorithms. *Habilitationschrift, University of Tübingen*, 2002.

[31] D. M. Pennock, E. Horvitz, and C. L. Giles. Social choice theory and recommender systems: Analysis of the axiomatic foundations of collaborative filtering. In *Proceedings of the 17th International Conference on Artificial Intelligence (AAAI)*, 2000.

[32] M. S. Pini, F. Rossi, K. B. Venable, and T. Walsh. Incompleteness and incomparability in preference aggregation. In *Proceedings of the 20nd International Joint Conference on Artificial Intelligence (IJCAI)*, volume 7, pages 1464–1469, 2007.

[33] T. Walsh. Uncertainty in preference elicitation and aggregation. In *Proceedings of the International Conference on Artificial Intelligence (AAAI)*, volume 22, page 3, 2007.

[34] K. Weihe. Covering trains by stations or the power of data reduction. *Proceedings of Algorithms and Experiments, ALEX*, pages 1–8, 1998.

[35] L. Xia and V. Conitzer. Determining possible and necessary winners under common voting rules given partial orders. In *Proceedings of the International Conference on Artificial Intelligence (AAAI)*, volume 8, pages 196–201, 2008.

[36] L. Xia, M. Zuckerman, A. D. Procaccia, V. Conitzer, and J. S. Rosenschein. Complexity of unweighted coalitional manipulation under some common voting rules. In *Proceedings of the 21st International Joint Conference on Artificial Intelligence (IJCAI)*, volume 9, pages 348–352, 2009.

On the Parameterized Complexity of Minimax Approval Voting

Neeldhara Misra
Department of Computer Science and Automation
Indian Institute of Science, Bangalore, India.
mail@neeldhara.com

Arshed Nabeel
Department of Computer Science and Automation
Indian Institute of Science, Bangalore, India.
arshed.nabeel@gmail.com

Harman Singh
BITS Pilani-K.K. Birla Goa Campus.
harman28@gmail.com

ABSTRACT

In this work, we initiate a detailed study of the parameterized complexity of Minimax Approval Voting. We demonstrate that the problem is W[2]-hard when parameterized by the size of the committee to be chosen, but does admit a FPT algorithm when parameterized by the number of strings that is more efficient than the previous ILP-based approaches for the problem. We also consider several combinations of parameters and provide a detailed landscape of the parameterized and kernelization complexity of the problem. We also study the version of the problem where we permit outliers, that is, where the chosen committee is required to satisfy a large number of voters (instead of all of them). In this context, we strengthen an APX-hardness result in the literature, and also show a simple but strong W-hardness result.

Categories and Subject Descriptors

F.2 [**Theory of Computation**]: Analysis of Algorithms and Problem Complexity;
I.2.11 [**Artificial Intelligence**]: Distributed Artificial Intelligence—*Multiagent Systems*

General Terms

Algorithms, Theory

Keywords

Computational Social Choice; Fixed-Parameter Tractability; Kernelization; Approximation; Minimax Approval Voting

1. INTRODUCTION

Aggregating preferences of agents is a fundamental problem in artificial intelligence and social choice [10]. The typical setting is the following: agents (or voters) express their preferences over alternatives (or candidates), and subsequently, a voting rule selects a winner or a set of winners based on these preferences.

Appears in: *Proceedings of the 14th International Conference on Autonomous Agents and Multiagent Systems (AAMAS 2015), Bordini, Elkind, Weiss, Yolum (eds.), May 4–8, 2015, Istanbul, Turkey.*

A substantial fragment of research in computational social choice has been devoted to single-winner choice problems (sometimes admitting the possibility of ties, resulting in a collection of co-winners). However, there has been an emerging interest in the algorithmic aspects of multi-winner elections, where the goal is to elect a committee of size k, where k is fixed in advance. In other words, the goal is to determine a set of k "winners" based on an appropriate voting rule. Multi-winner problems have several important applications, such as the election of legislatures and committees using proportional representation. They are also heavily used in resource allocation problems, determining the top few movies, books, or products to be fed into recommendation systems, and so on. In a classroom setting (especially online, such as in a MOOC), using peer reviews to determine the best possible TA team of size, say, ten for a future edition of the course is also a scenario for multi-winner elections.

Approval Voting. This work is set in the framework of *approval voting systems*, where each voter may select and support at most some small number of candidates [6]. In such a system, each voter determines, for every single candidate, if he approves of him or not. A result is then obtained by applying a predefined election rule to the set of collected votes. We refer to such a collection of votes as an *approval ballot*. In contrast, *multi-winner voting rules*, also known as *choose-k rules*, use the standard election setup where every vote is a total order (or a full ranking) over the set of candidates, and the voting rule returns a collection of possible committees that are tied-for-winning [13]. Although there are connections between the two formats, as we will observe in a moment, our focus will be on the former setup.

Given an approval ballot $\mathcal{V} = \{v_1, \ldots, v_n\}$ that seeks to form a committee C of size k, there can be several measures for how well a particular committee performs with respect to the given ballot. Two such fundamental measures are:

- **Approval Voting.** Here, we seek to minimize the sum of the Hamming distances between C and v_i.
- **Minimax Approval Voting.** Here, we seek to minimize the maximum Hamming distance between C and any v_i.

Note that approval voting amounts to choosing the k "most popular" candidates. If every voter approved a subset of size k, then this would amount to a multi-winner extension of the k-approval rule. We note that there have been several other measures considered in this setting, for example

Satisfaction Approval, Proportional Approval, Reweighted approval, and so on. We refer the reader to [2] for some very recent work on these aspects of approval voting.

While approval voting has the advantage of being a rule where the winning committee is easy to compute, it can suffer from ignoring the preferences of many voters. For example, consider a ballot where a Y, which is some subset of k candidates, is approved by a subset X of voters. Note that if $|X|$ is even a little over half the total number of voters, then the committee Y will be a winning committee irrespective of the structure of the remaining votes. In such a situation, the minimax approach to approval voting tries to account for the opinion of every voter in its definition. On the other hand, note that the minimax approval voting rule can sometimes try too hard when satisfying every voter — it is possible that when, say, a large fraction of the ballot is accounted for, there exists a consensus with a small maximum distance threshold, while accounting for everyone pushes up the threshold by orders of magnitude. Therefore, a natural notion to incorporate into the problem to make it more robust in practice is that of *outliers*. We introduce and study this version of MINIMAX APPROVAL VOTING, which we believe has not been examined before, where we seek a committee of size k that has a Hamming distance of at most d from at least s votes. The original problem is the special case when $s = |\mathcal{V}|$.

Closest String. The MINIMAX APPROVAL VOTING problem is quite similar to the CLOSEST STRING problem, which is an intensely studied problem in the literature of string algorithms and bioinformatics. Most of our work builds on the work of [15] and [3] that explore the CLOSEST STRING problem from a parameterized perspective. In CLOSEST STRING, we are given a set of strings $\{s_1, \ldots, s_n\}$ and the goal is to find a string s that has a small Hamming distance from all the given strings. Note that MINIMAX APPROVAL VOTING is the CLOSEST STRING problem restricted to a binary alphabet, and accompanied with the additional constraint that the output string have exactly k ones. We note that our proposal for MINIMAX APPROVAL VOTING with outliers is inspired from the analogous question in the context of strings, namely CLOSEST TO MOST STRINGS, which is also a well-studied variant [5].

Our Framework. Our focus in this work is on the computational complexity of MINIMAX APPROVAL VOTING and several of its variations. We mostly use the paradigm of *parameterized complexity* [12, 19] but we also explore the hardness of approximation in suitable settings.

One of the fundamental types of parameterized algorithms is *kernelization*, where the main goal is *instance compression* - the objective is to output a smaller instance while maintaining equivalence. When outlining nine important future directions of research in computational social choice in a parameterized setting, one of the questions that emerged was the following [7]:

What is the kernelization complexity of fixed-parameter tractable voting problems with respect to the number m of alternatives, the number n of voters, or some parameter less than m or n? Can we derive polynomial (or even linear) problem kernels for some voting problems with the above parameters?

In this work we address several questions in the context of kernelization, hoping to demonstrate some progress on this theme. Another key challenge proposed in [7] is also regarding the use of ILP-based approaches:

Can the [...] ILP-based fixed-parameter tractability results be replaced by direct combinatorial (avoiding ILPs) fixed-parameter algorithms?

While the best known algorithm for CLOSEST STRING when parameterized by the number of strings was based on an ILP formulation, we give an argument here for its MAV analog that relies on the framework of Color Coding [1], which provides a completely different perspective, and we hope that our style of application will be of general interest.

Our Contributions and Related Work. We consider the MINIMAX APPROVAL VOTING problem and its variation where we allow for outliers, from a parameterized perspective. Despite its relationship with CLOSEST STRING, there are almost no "automatic" algorithmic or hardness implications. MINIMAX APPROVAL VOTING is already well-studied the perspective of approximation [9, 18], and is known to admit a PTAS [8]. We focus on the parameterized complexity of MINIMAX APPROVAL VOTING. Our results are summarized in Table 1, and include the following.

- MINIMAX APPROVAL VOTING, when parameterized by d and m is unlikely to admit a polynomial kernel, even though it is trivially FPT even when parameterized only by m (by trying all candidate committees in $\mathcal{O}(2^m)$ time).
- MINIMAX APPROVAL VOTING, when parameterized by d alone, is FPT and admits an algorithm with $\mathcal{O}^\star(d^d)$ running time. On the other hand, when parameterized by k alone, the problem is W[2]-hard. [1]
- MINIMAX APPROVAL VOTING, when parameterized by n, is FPT, however, it is unlikely to have a polynomial kernel even when parameterized by n and k. This is an adaptation of the proofs in [3]. Also, MINIMAX APPROVAL VOTING admits a randomized algorithm with running time $\mathcal{O}^\star(2^{kn}c^k)$.
- MINIMAX APPROVAL VOTING WITH OUTLIERS is W[1]-hard even when parameterized by s, d and n.
- MINIMAX APPROVAL VOTING WITH OUTLIERS, the version of the problem where we seek to minimize the number of outliers, is unlikely to admit a PTAS unless P = NP. An adaptation of our proof implies that CLOSEST TO MOST STRINGS is also unlikely to have a PTAS unless P = NP, strengthening a previous hardness result [5].

Summary of Results for MINIMAX APPROVAL VOTING		
Parameter	Kernel	FPT
d	No [Theorem 2]	Yes [Theorem 4]
d, m	No [Theorem 2]	Yes [Trivial]
k	N/A	No [Theorem 3]
n	No [Theorem 3]	Yes [ILP]
n, k	No [Theorem 3]	Yes [Theorem 6]

2. PRELIMINARIES

We work in the social choice setting where there are n *voters* and m *candidates*. We let $\mathcal{V} = \{v_1, \ldots, v_n\}$ denote

[1]We use the $\mathcal{O}^\star$ notation to suppress factors that are polynomial in the size of the instance.

the set of all voters and $\mathcal{C} = \{c_1, \ldots, c_m\}$ denote the set of all candidates. We use the notation $[n]$ to refer to the set $\{1, 2, \ldots, n\}$. A *bit vector* is a word over the binary alphabet $\{0, 1\}$. For a bit vector u, the character (or bit) at the ith position is denoted by $u[i]$. The *weight* of a bit vector u is defined to be the number of ones in the word u.

Let U be a finite set, and $\{u_1, \ldots, u_m\}$ be an arbitrary but fixed ordering of the elements of U. If S is a subset of U, we use $\overline{S}$ to denote the characteristic vector of S, which is a word of length $|U|$ over the binary alphabet $\{0, 1\}$, with a 1 in the ith position if and only if $u_i \in S$. Similarly, if s is a bit vector, we use $\mathcal{J}(s)$ to denote the corresponding set. We sometimes abuse language and refer interchangeably to a set and its characteristic vector. For bit vectors u and v of the same length, we use $d(u, v)$ to denote the Hamming distance between u and v, which is the number of positions i where $u[i] \neq v[i]$.

We now define the social choice problem that is central to this work.

Minimax Approval Voting
Input: A set of alternatives $\mathcal{C} := \{c_1, \ldots, c_m\}$, a collection of votes $\{v_1, \ldots, v_n\}$, where each vote v_i is an element of $\{0, 1\}^m$ (or equivalently a subset of $\mathcal{C}$), and positive integers d and k.
Question: Is there a subset of $\mathcal{X} \subseteq \mathcal{C}$ of size *exactly* k, such that the Hamming distance between $\overline{\mathcal{X}}$ and v_i is at most d for all $1 \leq i \leq n$?

The MINIMAX APPROVAL VOTING problem is closely related to the very well-studied CLOSEST STRING problem over the binary alphabet, which we describe below for completeness.

Closest String
Input: A set of n strings $s_1, \ldots, s_n$ over $\{0, 1\}$ of length m, and positive integers d and k.
Question: Is there a string s of length m such that the Hamming distance between s and s_i is at most d for all $1 \leq i \leq n$?

Note that the MINIMAX APPROVAL VOTING problem is exactly the CLOSEST STRING problem with the additional restraint that the output word has weight k. Note that despite the similarity, there is no trivial computational reduction between the two problems. Informally speaking, the additional constraint can either make the MINIMAX APPROVAL VOTING problem computationally easier or harder. However, we note that any algorithm that enumerates *all* closest strings to a given collection will also solve the MINIMAX APPROVAL VOTING problem.

For $\alpha \subseteq \{m, n, d, k\}$ use the notation $[\alpha]$–MINIMAX APPROVAL VOTING to refer to the MINIMAX APPROVAL VOTING problem when parameterized by the parameters in α. We also introduce the closely related problem of MINIMAX APPROVAL VOTING WITH OUTLIERS, which is inspired by the analogous and well-studied variant of the CLOSEST STRING problem, namely CLOSEST TO MOST STRINGS.

Minimax Approval Voting with Outliers
Input: A set of alternatives $\mathcal{C} := \{c_1, \ldots, c_m\}$, a collection of votes $\{v_1, \ldots, v_n\}$, where each vote v_i is an element of $\{0, 1\}^m$ (or equivalently a subset of $\mathcal{C}$), and positive integers s, d and k.
Question: Is there a subset of $\mathcal{X} \subseteq \mathcal{C}$ of size *exactly* k, and a subset $\mathcal{W} \subseteq \mathcal{V}$ of size *at least* s, such that the Hamming distance between $\overline{\mathcal{X}}$ and v_i is at most d for all $i \in \mathcal{W}$?

The analogous problem for binary strings is as follows.

Closest to Most Strings
Input: A set of n strings $s_1, \ldots, s_n$ over $\{0, 1\}$ of length m, and positive integers s, d and k.
Question: Is there a string w of length m for which at least s strings among $s_1, \ldots, s_n$ have Hamming distance at most d from w?

As before, for $\alpha \subseteq \{m, n, d, k, s\}$ we use the notation $[\alpha]$–MINIMAX APPROVAL VOTING WITH OUTLIERS to refer to the MINIMAX APPROVAL VOTING WITH OUTLIERS problem when parameterized by the parameters in α. For a special instance where every voter votes for a committee of a fixed size, we use t to denote the weight of each vote. Also, we use $s^\star$ to denote the *dual* parameter in the context of outliers, that is, when we are asking if there is a committee that is at a Hamming distance of at most d from *all but at most* $s^\star$ voters.

Parameterized Complexity. A parameterized problem Π is a subset of $\Gamma^* \times \mathbb{N}$, where Γ is a finite alphabet. An instance of a parameterized problem is a tuple (x, k), where k is the parameter. A *kernelization* algorithm is a set of preprocessing rules that runs in polynomial time and reduces the instance size with a guarantee on the output instance size. This notion is formalized below.

DEFINITION 1. **[Kernelization]** *[19, 14] A kernelization algorithm for a parameterized problem $\Pi \subseteq \Gamma^* \times \mathbb{N}$ is an algorithm that, given $(x, k) \in \Gamma^* \times \mathbb{N}$, outputs, in time polynomial in $|x| + k$, a pair $(x', k') \in \Gamma^* \times \mathbb{N}$ such that (a) $(x, k) \in \Pi$ if and only if $(x', k') \in \Pi$ and (b) $|x'|, k' \leq g(k)$, where g is some computable function. The output instance x' is called the kernel, and the function g is referred to as the size of the kernel. If $g(k) = k^{\mathcal{O}(1)}$ then we say that Π admits a polynomial kernel.*

For many parameterized problems, it is well established that the existence of a polynomial kernel would imply the collapse of the polynomial hierarchy to the third level (or more precisely, CoNP $\subseteq$ NP/Poly). Therefore, it is considered unlikely that these problems would admit polynomial-sized kernels. For showing kernel lower bounds, we simply establish reductions from these problems.

DEFINITION 2. **[Polynomial Parameter Transformation]** *[4] Let Γ_1 and Γ_2 be parameterized problems. We say that Γ_1 is polynomial time and parameter reducible to*

Γ_2, written $\Gamma_1 \leq_{Ptp} \Gamma_2$, if there exists a polynomial time computable function $f : \Sigma^* \times \mathbb{N} \to \Sigma^* \times \mathbb{N}$, and a polynomial $p : \mathbb{N} \to \mathbb{N}$, and for all $x \in \Sigma^*$ and $k \in \mathbb{N}$, if $f((x,k)) = (x', k')$, then $(x,k) \in \Gamma_1$ if and only if $(x', k') \in \Gamma_2$, and $k' \leq p(k)$. We call f a polynomial parameter transformation (or a PPT) from Γ_1 to Γ_2.

This notion of a reduction is useful in showing kernel lower bounds because of the following theorem.

THEOREM 1. *[4, Theorem 3] Let P and Q be parameterized problems whose derived classical problems are P^c, Q^c, respectively. Let P^c be NP-Complete, and $Q^c \in$NP. Suppose there exists a PPT from P to Q. Then, if Q has a polynomial kernel, then P also has a polynomial kernel.*

3. MINIMAX APPROVAL VOTING

In this section, we outline our results for MINIMAX APPROVAL VOTING. The problem was shown to be NP-hard in [17] using a reduction from the VERTEX COVER problem. This motivates the search for fixed-parameter tractable algorithms for MINIMAX APPROVAL VOTING.

Observe that MINIMAX APPROVAL VOTING is easily FPT by exhaustive search when parameterized by m. We now show that it is unlikely to admit a polynomial kernel even when parameterized by d and m. This follows from the proof of the hardness of CLOSEST STRING in [3], but adapted to ensure that the number of ones in the output string is fixed. We describe the details of the construction for completeness, but only sketch the proof of equivalence due to space constraints.

THEOREM 2. MINIMAX APPROVAL VOTING *does not admit a polynomial kernel when parameterized by d and m unless* CoNP $\subseteq$ NP/Poly.

PROOF. We prove the statement through a PPT reduction from CNF-SAT parameterized by the number of variables, adapting the ideas used in [3]. Given a CNF-SAT formula $F = C_1 \wedge C_2 \wedge \ldots \wedge C_q$ with variables $x_1, x_2, \ldots, x_p$, we obtain an instance of MINIMAX APPROVAL VOTING as follows. We begin by transforming F to F' with $2p$ variables, such that each clause has length p or 1, where p is the number of variables in F. To do this, we add p new variables $y_1, y_2, \ldots, y_p$. First, we add p new clauses to the formula. These new clauses have length 1 and are negations of the new variables. Next, for every clause C_i that has less than p variables, we replace it with C'_i where $C'_i = C_i \vee y_1 \vee y_2 \vee \ldots \vee y_{p-k}$ where $|C_i| = k$. So the transformed formula is given by:

$$F' = C'_1 \wedge C'_2 \wedge \ldots \wedge C'_q \wedge \neg y_1 \wedge \neg y_2 \wedge \ldots \wedge \neg y_p$$

To see that F is satisfiable if and only if F' is satisfiable, note that the satisfying assignment to F can be extended to a satisfying assignment of F' by setting all the y_i's to 0. Conversely, a satisfying assignment for F' must set all the y's to 0 to satisfy all the singleton clauses. The remaining clauses C'_i must each be satisfied by one of the original variables x_i, and so this assignment also satisfies the original clauses C_i. We will refer to each singleton clause $\neg y_i$ as C'_{q+i}.

We will now obtain an instance of MINIMAX APPROVAL VOTING from F'. The instance will have a total of $q+13p-8$ strings, each of length $6p-4$. The string set S consists of two types of strings. The first set S_1 will contain a string for each of the clauses in F', thus consisting of $q+p$ strings. The second set S_2 will contain 4 strings for each $i \in [3p-2]$, thus accounting for $12p-8$ strings. For each variable x_j (or y_j) and a clause C'_i we define a two bit string as follows.

$$X_{i,j}(\text{or } Y_{i,j}) = \begin{cases} 01 & \text{if } C_j \text{ contains } x_i \\ 10 & \text{if } C_j \text{ contains } \bar{x}_i \\ 00 & \text{otherwise} \end{cases}$$

- For every clause C'_i with $1 \leq i \leq q$, we add a string s_i to S_1, where $s_i = X_{i,1}X_{i,2}\ldots X_{i,p}Y_{i,1}Y_{i,2}\ldots Y_{i,p}\{10\}^{p-2}$.
- For every clause C'_{q+i} with $1 \leq i \leq p$, we add a string s_{q+i} to S_1, where $s_i = \{00\}^{p+i-1}10\{00\}^{2p-2-i}$.
- We add the following four strings to S_2 $\forall i \in [3p-2]$.

$$\begin{aligned} a_i &= \{00\}^{i-1}11\{00\}^{3p-2-i} \\ b_i &= \{00\}^{i-1}00\{00\}^{3p-2-i} \\ c_i &= \{11\}^{i-1}11\{11\}^{3p-2-i} \\ d_i &= \{11\}^{i-1}00\{11\}^{3p-2-i} \end{aligned}$$

Thus we get an instance of $(\mathcal{C}, \mathcal{V}, k, d)$MINIMAX APPROVAL VOTING by setting $\mathcal{V} = S_1 \uplus S_2$, the number of candidates (or the length of the strings) is $m = 6p-4$, the number of voters (or strings) is $n = q + 13p - 8$, and the maximum Hamming distance is $d = 3p-2$, where p and q are the number of variables and clauses respectively of the original CNF-SAT instance F.

The forward direction of the equivalence is established by translating an assignment to a string that is consistent with the construction described above. Towards the reverse direction, we make the following claim about the structure of a valid string in the reduced instance.

CLAIM 1. *If there exists a string s such that $d(s, v) \leq 3p - 2 \forall v \in S_2$, then $s[2i] \neq s[2i-1] \forall i \in [3p-2]$.*

PROOF. For any $i \in [3p-2]$ we look at the four strings corresponding to it in S_2. Then we look at two strings of length $6p-6$, which are $\{00\}^{i-1}\{00\}^{3p-2-i}$ and $\{11\}^{i-1}\{11\}^{3p-2-i}$. The first is subsequence of a_i and b_i, and the second is subsequence of c_i and d_i. These subsequences are also complements of each other, hence any string s has to be at a distance of $3p-3$ from at least one of them. If s has a distance at least $3p-3$ with the first, then it is at a distance at least $3n-3$ with a_i and b_i, else it is at a distance at least $3p-3$ with c_i and d_i. Now, (a_i, b_i) and (c_i, d_i) differ at only two positions, $2i-1$ and $2i$. In these two positions, one of the two strings has 00 while the other has 11, so if a string is to be at a distance of $3p-2$ from both of them, it must have 10 or 01 in these two positions. Otherwise it will differ at both positions with one of the strings, which in addition to the existing Hamming distance of $3p-3$ will result in a total distance of $3p-1$, which is a contradiction. So, if $d(s, v) \leq 3p - 2 \forall v \in S_2$, then $s[2i] \neq s[2i-1] \forall i \in [3p-2]$. Let us call such a string (i.e. a string that belongs to $\{01, 10\}^{6p-4}$) a 'well-formed' string. □

Thus, if the reduced instance admits a solution, then it clearly corresponds to a satisfying assignment. For arguing the reverse direction of the equivalence, it remains to be shown that this assignment is indeed satisfying. This is easily checked, and the details are deferred to a full version due to lack of space.

We note that MINIMAX APPROVAL VOTING is FPT when parameterized by the number of votes – the ILP approach used by [15] can be easily extended to accommodate the committee size constraint. However, we show that the problem is unlikely to admit a polynomial kernel even when parameterized by the number of votes and k.

THEOREM 3. MINIMAX APPROVAL VOTING, *parameterized by the number of votes n and k, does not admit a polynomial kernel unless* $\mathsf{CoNP} \subseteq \mathsf{NP/Poly}$.

PROOF. We show a *polynomial parametric transformation* from HITTING SET parameterized by the number of sets to MINIMAX APPROVAL VOTING. Since [11] shows kernelization hardness for HITTING SET, this rules out polynomial kernels for MINIMAX APPROVAL VOTING as well.

Consider a HITTING SET instance $(U, \mathcal{F}, k')$, where U is the universe of elements, $\mathcal{F}$ a family of subsets of U, $n' = |\mathcal{F}|$ and $m' = |U|$. Without loss of generality, assume that every set $S_i \in \mathcal{F}$ is of the same size l' – we will later show that this (seemingly) restricted version of the problem is equivalent to the original HITTING SET problem. We reduce this instance to a MINIMAX APPROVAL VOTING instance $(\mathcal{C}, \mathcal{V}, k, d)$, where the number of candidates $m = m'$, the number of voters $n = n'$, committee size $k = k'$ and the maximum permitted Hamming distance $d = k' + l' - 1$

Let $U = \{1 \ldots n\}$ and let $\mathcal{F} = \{S_1, \ldots S_m\}$ For each set $S_i \in \mathcal{F}$, let $v_i = \bar{S}_i$, the characteristic vector of S_i. Let $\mathcal{V} = \{v_1 \ldots v_n\}$ be our vote set.

CLAIM 2. *If $(U, \mathcal{F}, k')$ is a* YES*-instance for* HITTING SET, *then $(\mathcal{C}, \mathcal{V}, k, d)$ is a* YES*-instance for* MINIMAX APPROVAL VOTING.

PROOF. Let $S \subseteq U$ be a valid set of size at most k for $\mathcal{F}$, and let v be the indicator vector of S. Clearly, v has exactly k 1s. Also, each vote v_i has exactly l' 1s, at least one out of which overlaps with a 1 in v. Thus, $d(s, s_i) \leq k' + l' - 1 = d$ for every s_i. In other words, $(\mathcal{C}, \mathcal{V}, k, d)$ is a YES-instance for MINIMAX APPROVAL VOTING with v being a valid consensus. □

CLAIM 3. *If $(\mathcal{C}, \mathcal{V}, k, d)$ is a* YES*-instance for* MINIMAX APPROVAL VOTING *then $(U, \mathcal{F}, k')$ is a* YES*-instance for* HITTING SET.

PROOF. Let v be a consensus string for the MINIMAX APPROVAL VOTING instance $(\mathcal{C}, \mathcal{V}, k, d)$. We show that the corresponding set $S = \mathcal{J}(v)$, whose indicator vector is v, is a valid hitting set for the HITTING SET instance $(U, \mathcal{F}, k')$.

First of all, observe that $|S| = k = k'$, since v has exactly k 1s. Also, $d(v, v_i) \leq d = k' + l' - 1$ for every v_i, which means that some 1 in v overlaps with at least one 1 in each v_i. Rephrasing in HITTING SET terminology, S hits at least one element of every S_i, i.e. $(U, \mathcal{F}, k')$ is a YES-instance for HITTING SET, with S being a valid hitting set. □

To complete our proof, we also need to show that the general HITTING SET problem is equivalent to a restricted case where each set of $\mathcal{F}$ is of size exactly l. We call this version of the problem l-REGULAR HITTING SET, and show the following.

CLAIM 4. *Every instance of* HITTING SET *can be turned into an equivalent instance of* REGULAR HITTING SET.

PROOF. Let S_i be the largest set in $\mathcal{F}$, and let $l = |S_i|$. for every other set S_j with size l', add $l - l'$ dummy elements to S_j and to U. Let the modified instance be $(U', \mathcal{F}')$.

Clearly, a hitting set of size k for $(U, \mathcal{F})$ will indeed be a hitting set for $(U', \mathcal{F}')$. Conversely, consider a hitting set S' for $(U', \mathcal{F}')$. If S' does not contain any of the dummy elements, then S' is a hitting set for $(U, \mathcal{F})$ as well. On the other hand, any dummy element in S' will hit only one set from $\mathcal{F}'$, and hence can be replaced by any other element from that set. Thus, any solution for $(U', \mathcal{F}')$ can be transformed into an equivalent solution for $(U, \mathcal{F})$. □

We note that the reduction above also establishes the $W[2]$-hardness of the problem when parameterized by k alone.

We finally turn to two FPT algorithms. The first one is an algorithm when parameterized by d alone (extending the approach of [15]). The second algorithm considers the combined parameter n and k. The first algorithm uses a depth-bounded branching strategy, while the second one uses the method of color coding.

Algorithm 1: Recursive Procedure $\mathbf{MAVd}(v, \delta)$

```
input : Candidate string v and integer δ
        Global variables: Set of voters
  V = {v_1, v_2, ..., v_n}, integer d
output: A string v* with max_{i∈[n]} d(v*, v_i) ≤ d and
        d(v*, v) ≤ δ if it exists, and 'not found'
        otherwise.
if δ < 0 return NOT FOUND;
if d(v, v_i) > d + δ for some i ∈ [n] return NOT FOUND;
if d(v, v_i) ≤ d for all i ∈ [n] return v;
for some i ∈ [n] such that d(v, v_i) > d: do
    P_1 = {p | v[p] = 1, v_i[p] = 0};
    P_2 = {q | v[q] = 0, v_i[q] = 1};
    for all p ∈ P_1 do
        for all q ∈ P_2 do
            v' = v;
            v'[p] = 0;
            v'[q] = 1;
            v_ret = MAVd (v', δ − 2);
            If v_ret ≠ NOT FOUND then return v_ret;
return NOT FOUND;
```

We first discuss the FPT algorithm for the parameter d. The algorithm starts with some suitable string v having k 1's as the 'candidate string'. If there is some string v_i with $i \in [n]$ that differs from v at more than d positions, then we attempt to bring the candidate string 'closer' to v_i. We do this by removing some selected member of the committee that the voter corresponding to v_i did not vote for, and replacing him with another member that v_i did vote for, thus maintaining the strength of the committee at k. This means we change one of the k 1's in v to a zero, at a position p where $v_i[p] = 0$, and change one of the 0's in v to a one, at a position q where $v_i[q] = 1$. As in the approach used in [15], our algorithm stops either if the candidate string has moved too 'far away' from the initial string, or if it finds a solution. The size of the search tree for the recursion can be limited to $\mathcal{O}(d^d)$, as shown.

THEOREM 4. *Given a set of strings $\mathcal{V} = \{v_1, v_2, \dots, v_n\}$ and an integer d, Algorithm 1 determines in time $\mathcal{O}^\star(d^d)$ whether there is a string v such that $\max_{i\in[n]} d(v, v_i) \leq d$ and computes such a v if it exists.*

PROOF. **Running time.** The parameter δ is initialized to d and is decremented by 2 in each step of recursion. The recursion stops when $\delta < 0$. So the depth of the search tree is at most $d/2$. In a single step of recursion, the algorithm selects a string v_i such that $d(v, v_i) > d$. It creates a new subcase for each pair of positions from P_1 and P_2 where v_i differs from v. As $|P_1| + |P_2| = d + 1$, this results in a branching of at most $((d + 1)/2)^2$. Thus the tree size is bounded from above by $((d+1)/2)^{2\times \frac{d}{2}}$ or $\mathcal{O}(d^d)$. Every step of the recursion requires time that is polynomial in n and d, so the total running time is $\mathcal{O}^\star(d^d)$.

Correctness. We show that Algorithm 1 finds a string v such that $\max_{i\in[n]} d(v, v_i) \leq d$ if it exists. We explicitly show the correctness of only the first step of recursion; the correctness of the algorithm follows by inductive application of the same argument. For the initial candidate string, consider an arbitrary string from $\mathcal{V}$. Without loss of generality, we select v_1. Note that v_1 must contain at least $k - d$ 1's, otherwise it cannot be at a distance of less than $d + 1$ from any string that contains k 1's. If v_1 contains more than k 1's, we use the first k of these to create a candidate string v that adopts the first k 1's of v_1 and places 0 at all other positions. If v_1 contains less than k 1's, then we adopt the first $k - d$ 1's into v and add d more 1's to v at arbitrary locations. This gives us our initial candidate string.

In the situation that v satisfies $\max_{i\in[n]} d(v, v_i) \leq d$ for all $i \in [n]$, we immediately find the solution, i.e. v. If not, then there must exist some v_i such that $d(v, v_i) > d$. For the branching, we consider the positions where v and v_i differ, i.e. $P_1 = \{p \mid v[p] = 1, v_i[p] = 0\}$ and $P_2 = \{q \mid v[q] = 0, v_i[q] = 1\}$. The algorithm successively creates subcases for every pair of positions $p \in P_1$ and $q \in P_2$, and creates a new candidate by altering v to v' so that $v'[p] = 0$ and $v'[q] = 1$. Such a move is correct if the size of the committee, i.e. the number of 1's in v' remains k and the move brings the candidate string 'closer' to v^*, the solution string. It is clear that the number of 1's in the candidate string is always constant at k. We must show that at least one of the subcases is a correct move. We know that v^* differs from v_i in at most d locations. So, for all pairs p and q where $p + q = d + 1$, at least one pair must try a pair of positions that bring the candidate string closer to v^*.

Lemma 5 shows that it is correct to omit those branches where the candidate string v satisfies $d(v, v_i) > d + \delta$ for some $i \in [n]$.

CLAIM 5. *If there are two strings $v_i, v_j \in \mathcal{V}$ such that $d(v_i, v_j) > 2d$, then there is no string v such that $\max_{i\in[n]} d(v, v_i) \leq d$.*

PROOF. Hamming distance follows triangle inequality. So if given that $d(v_i, v_j) > 2d$, then $d(v_i, v) + d(v, v_j) > 2d$ for every v. Thus either $d(v_i, v) > d$ or $d(v, v_j) > d$ (or both). □

This completes the proof for Theorem 4. We now turn to a randomized algorithm parameterized by n and k. This based on the classic Color Coding approach introduced in [1].

THEOREM 5. MINIMAX APPROVAL VOTING *admits a randomized* FPT *algorithm, parameterized by the number of voters n and the committee size k.*

PROOF. Let $(\mathcal{C}, \mathcal{V} := \{v_1, \dots, v_n\}, k, d)$ be an instance of MINIMAX APPROVAL VOTING. We call a subset $\mathcal{X} \subseteq \mathcal{C}$ a *consensus committee* if $\mathcal{X}$ is a valid MINIMAX APPROVAL VOTING solution; in other words, the weight of $\mathcal{X}$ is k and further,$d(\overline{\mathcal{X}}, v) \leq d$ for all $v \in \mathcal{V}$.

We call a mapping $\phi : \mathcal{C} \to [k]$ a *k-coloring* of the candidate set $\mathcal{C}$. Note that a coloring partitions $\mathcal{C}$ into k color classes, $\mathcal{C}_1 \dots \mathcal{C}_k$. A coloring ϕ is a *good coloring* if there exists a consensus committee $\mathcal{X}$ which picks exactly one candidate of each color. Further, we call a consensus committee $\mathcal{X}$ to be *nice* to a vote v_i with respect to a color j if $\mathcal{X}$ contains some element of $\mathcal{J}(v_i) \cap \mathcal{C}_j$. We define $\omega(\mathcal{X}, v_i)$ to be the following k-length characteristic vector:

$$\omega(\mathcal{X}, v_i)[j] = \begin{cases} 1 & \text{if } \mathcal{X} \text{ is nice to } v_i \text{ on color } j, \\ 0 & \text{otherwise,} \end{cases}$$

and we refer to this as the *niceness vector* of v_i with respect to $\mathcal{X}$.

The algorithm. Assume that we have a good coloring ϕ. For every vote v_i, we guess a niceness vector ω_i. Given such a guess, our task now is to determine if there exists a consensus committee $\mathcal{Y}$ that respects all of these vectors, that is, if $\omega_i[j] = 1$, then $\mathcal{Y}$ picks some candidate in $\mathcal{J}(v_i) \cap \mathcal{C}_j$. This, however, is easily checked as follows. For every color j, let $\mathcal{V}_j$ be the set of votes v_i for which $\omega_i[j] = 1$. Note that $\mathcal{Y}$ must pick *one* candidate from $\mathcal{C}_j$ that intersects the sets $\mathcal{J}(v_i) \cap \mathcal{C}_j$ for every $i \in \mathcal{V}_j$. If the family:

$$\{\mathcal{J}(v_i) \cap \mathcal{C}_j \mid i \in \mathcal{V}_j\}$$

is an intersecting family, then we pick any element in the common intersection; otherwise it is clear that we must reject this guess as there is no $\mathcal{Y}$ that can intersect all sets while only picking one element from $\mathcal{C}_j$.

By repeating this procedure for all possible guesses for collections of nice vectors, we ensure that we will find a valid consensus committee whenever there exists one.

Correctness of the algorithm. Assume that there exists a consensus committee $\mathcal{X}$ of size k. We try sufficiently many different random colorings to ensure that we find a coloring that assigns each member of $\mathcal{X}$ a unique color.

Now, consider a good coloring ϕ and a consensus set $\mathcal{X}$. For a vote v_i, let $N_i = \{\phi(c_i) \mid c_i \in \mathcal{X} \cap \mathcal{J}(v_i)\}$, i.e. N_i is the set of all colors that $\mathcal{X}$ is nice on for the vote v_i. Our algorithm explores all possible choices of N_i – in particular, the algorithm cannot miss C_i induced by a valid consensus committee. Given the right collection of niceness vectors, our algorithm finds a consensus committee that respects all of them if one exists, so while the output of the algorithm may differ from $\mathcal{X}$, it is an equally valid choice of a consensus committee.

Running time. We start by guessing a random coloring ϕ for $\mathcal{C}$. By standard arguments, we will find a good coloring with high probability if we try $\mathcal{O}(e^k)$ different colorings.

Further, we need to guess what colors are nice for each votes. To get the nice colors right for one vote, this may take up to 2^k guesses in the worst case. Over all the votes, this adds an $(2^k)^n = 2^{kn}$ factor to the running time.

Determining whether a valid consensus exists for a given guess can be done in $\mathcal{O}(mnk)$ time. Thus, the overall running time of the algorithm is $\mathcal{O}(e^k \cdot 2^{kn} \cdot mnk) = c^{kn} \cdot m^{\mathcal{O}(1)}$ for a suitable choice of c. □

THEOREM 6. MINIMAX APPROVAL VOTING *is in* FPT, *parameterized by the number of voters* n *and the committee size* k.

4. MAV WITH OUTLIERS

In this section, we show the hardness of approximation of the MINIMAX APPROVAL VOTING WITH OUTLIERS problem, and also establish that it is W[2]-hard when parameterized by s, d and k. In [5], the authors show a randomized reduction from MAX-2-SAT to CLOSEST TO MOST STRINGS, and used the result in [16] to show that for some $\epsilon > 0$ there is no polynomial time $(1+\epsilon)$-approximation algorithm for CLOSEST TO MOST STRINGS unless P=NP. In this section, we adapt their reduction, using a tweak to fix the number of ones in the output, and a slightly different set of "fixing strings", replacing the randomized engine with a deterministic one. We now describe the details of our approach.

THEOREM 7. *For some* $\epsilon > 0$, *if there is a polynomial time* $(1+\epsilon)$*-approximation algorithm for* MINIMAX APPROVAL VOTING WITH OUTLIERS, *then* P=NP.

PROOF. We give a deterministic reduction from MAX-2-SAT to MINIMAX APPROVAL VOTING WITH OUTLIERS with a fixed k number of 1's in the output. As input, we take an instance of MAX-2-SAT comprised of q clauses $C_1, C_2, \ldots, C_q$ and p variables $x_1, x_2, \ldots, x_p$, where each clause is a disjunction of two literals appearing as either x_i or $\bar{x}_i$ for some $i \in [p]$, and r which is the number of clauses to be satisfied. The output of the reduction will be an instance of MINIMAX APPROVAL VOTING WITH OUTLIERS with a string set S consisting of $q + 2p(q-r+1)$ strings of length $2p$. Let $l = q - r + 1$. Here the $2pl$ strings are 'fixing' strings intended to force a structure in the solutions, while the first q strings represent an encoding of each clause as follows. For every clause C_j containing the variables from $x_1, x_2, \ldots, x_p$, the corresponding string $s_j = s_j(1)s_j(2)\ldots s_j(2p)$, where:

$$s_j(2i-1)s_j(2i) = \begin{cases} 01 & \text{if } C_j \text{ contains } x_i \\ 10 & \text{if } C_j \text{ contains } \bar{x}_i \\ 00 & \text{otherwise} \end{cases}$$

The fixing strings shall be of the form $\{00, 11\}^p$, or 'double strings'. There are l identical copies of a single 'block' of fixing strings. A block B_t is defined as follows. For every $i \in [p]$, we add two strings to the block.

$$a_i^t = \{00\}^{i-1}11\{00\}^{p-i}$$
$$b_i^t = \{11\}^{i-1}00\{11\}^{p-i}$$
$$B_t = \bigcup_{i\in[p]} \{a_i^t, b_i^t\}$$

Thus every block B_t consists of $2p$ strings of length $2p$. All $l = q - r + 1$ copies of the block together with the string encoding of each clause comprise the strings for our instance of MINIMAX APPROVAL VOTING WITH OUTLIERS, i.e. $S = B_1 \cup B_2 \cup \ldots B_l \cup \{s_1, s_2, \ldots, s_q\}$. So $\mid S \mid = n = q + 2p(q - r + 1)$ and the length of each string is $m = 2p$. The distance parameter is set $d = p$ and the number of strings that need to satisfy the constraint is $s = r + 2pl$ (i.e. the maximum number of outliers is $q - r$). The number of 1's in the output string is $k = p$.

For the forward direction, assume there exists an assignment ϕ to the variables $x_1, x_2, \ldots, x_p$ that satisfies r clauses. We encode this assignment in a string $\bar{\phi}$ of length $2p$ as follows. $\bar{\phi} = \bar{\phi}(1)\bar{\phi}(2)\ldots\bar{\phi}(2p)$, where:

$$\bar{\phi}(2i-1)\bar{\phi}(2i) = \begin{cases} 01 & \text{if } x_i \text{ is set to True} \\ 10 & \text{if } x_i \text{ is set to False} \end{cases}$$

Thus the assignment string $\bar{\phi}$ belongs to $\{01, 10\}^p$, i.e. it is 'well-formed' and has p 1's. The Hamming distance $d(\bar{\phi}, w)$ for any string w where w is a double string is exactly p, so $d(\bar{\phi}, w) \leq p$ for every $w \in B_1 \cup \ldots \cup B_l$. So the fixing strings are not outliers. Now, for every clause C_j where $j \in [q]$, the string s_j contains exactly $2p-4$ 0's for the $p-2$ variables that do not appear in C_j. This produces a Hamming distance of $p-2$ from the well-formed $\bar{\phi}$. Of the two variables that do appear in C_j, at least one must be set to true (or false if it appears negatively) in the assignment ϕ if C_j is satisfied by ϕ. The string locations for this variable must match exactly with its encoding in $\bar{\phi}$. So the Hamming distance caused by the variable that do appear in C_j cannot exceed 2. So for a clause C_j that is satisfied by ϕ, the distance $d(\bar{\phi}, s_j) \leq (p-2) + 2 = p$. Thus the satisfied clauses do not produce outliers. Since ϕ satisfies at least r clauses, there can be at most $q - r$ outliers, which satisfies the conditions of MINIMAX APPROVAL VOTING WITH OUTLIERS.

For the backward direction, let ψ be a string that satisfies $d(\psi, w) \leq n$ for $w \in S$ with a maximum of $q-r$ outliers and has exactly p 1's. We first show that ψ must necessarily be a well-formed string.

CLAIM 6. ψ *belongs to* $\{01, 10\}^p$.

PROOF. Assume to the contrary that $\exists i$ such that $\psi(2i-1)\psi(2i) = 00$ or 11.

- If $\psi(2i-1)\psi(2i) = 00$, consider the string $a_i^t = \{00\}^{i-1}11\{00\}^{p-i}$. At the locations $2i-1$ and $2i$, the Hamming distance is exactly 2. In the remaining locations of ψ there are exactly p 1's, which cause a further Hamming distance of p. The total distance $d(\psi, a_i^t) = p + 2$. Thus a_i^t is an outlier. However, S contains $l = q - r + 1$ copies of a_i^t in the blocks $B_1, B_2, \ldots, B_l$. This is a contradiction, as there can be at most $q - r$ outliers.
- If $\psi(2i-1)\psi(2i) = 11$, consider the string $b_i^t = \{11\}^{i-1}00\{11\}^{p-i}$. Again, there is a Hamming distance of 2 at the locations $2i-1$ and $2i$. The remaining length of ψ contains exactly $p-2$ 1's and $2p - 2 - (p-2) = p$ 0's, which cause a further Hamming distance of p. Thus the total distance is $p+2$ and b_i^t is an outlier. However, there are $l = q - r + 1$ copies of b_i^t in S. This is a contradiction.

So ψ must be a well-formed string, and none of the fixing strings are the outliers. □

There can be a maximum of $q - r$ outliers in the q remaining strings, so there must be at least r strings satisfying $d(\psi, p) \leq p$. For these r clause-encoding strings, a Hamming distance of exactly $p-2$ is caused by the $2p-4$ locations corresponding to variables not appearing in the clause. In the locations corresponding to the variables that do appear, the string contains 01 or 10. Note that ψ is well-formed, so the Hamming distance caused by these locations can be either 2 or 0 for each variable. If both variables cause a distance of 2, then total distance will be $p+2$ and the string will not satisfy $d(\psi, p) \leq p$. So at least one variable location produces a distance of 0, i.e. it matches with ψ. So if ψ is used as an assignment vector, setting x_i =True if $\psi(2i-1)\psi(2i) = 01$ and x_i =False if $\psi(2i-1)\psi(2i) = 10$, then as such clauses will be satisfied. As there are at least r such clauses, the assignment corresponding to ψ satisfies the conditions for MAX-2-SAT.

This completes the polynomial time reduction from MAX-2-SAT to MINIMAX APPROVAL VOTING WITH OUTLIERS. If there exists an $\epsilon > 0$ such that there is a polynomial time $(1+\epsilon)$-approximation algorithm for MINIMAX APPROVAL VOTING WITH OUTLIERS, then this would also give an approximation for MAX-2-SAT. However, it has been shown in [16] that it is NP-hard to compute a a 22/21-approximately optimal solution for MAX-2-SAT. So for some suitable $\epsilon > 0$, MINIMAX APPROVAL VOTING WITH OUTLIERS cannot have a $(1+\epsilon)$-approximation algorithm unless P=NP.

THEOREM 8. *For some $\epsilon > 0$, if there is a polynomial time $(1+\epsilon)$-approximation algorithm for* CLOSEST TO MOST STRINGS, *then* P=NP.

PROOF. In this reduction from MAX-2-SAT to CLOSEST TO MOST STRINGS we use a similar construct as in Theorem 7, but must ensure that the reasoning is valid even for the case where the output string of the reduced instance does not have exactly $k = p$ 1's. To accommodate this possibility, we include two new fixing strings in every block B_t of double strings. These new strings are simply:

$$c_t = \{00\}^p \; d_t = \{11\}^p$$

Thus every block B_t now contains $2p+2$ strings of length $2p$ and the total number of strings in S is $q + (2p+2)l$. The remaining parameters retain their values, so maximum outliers is $q - r$ and the required Hamming distance from each string is $d = p$.

For the forward direction of the reduction, note that both c_t and d_t for each value of $t \in [l]$ are double strings. So the encoded assignment string $\bar{\phi}$, which is a well-formed string, will have a Hamming distance of exactly p from all copies of the new fixing strings. The remainder of the argument is identical to that of the forward direction for Theorem 7.

For the backward direction, let ψ be the output string of the CLOSEST TO MOST STRINGS instance. Note that we cannot yet use Claim 6 to show that ψ is well-formed as that proof used that fact that the string contained exactly p 1's.

CLAIM 7. *ψ contains exactly p 1's.*

PROOF. Assume to the contrary that ψ contains either $> p$ or $< p$ 1's. Then:

- If ψ contains $> p$ 1's, then c_t is an outlier. However, in this case, every one of the $l = q - r + 1$ copies of c_t in S is an outlier. Because ψ cannot produce more than $q - r$ outliers, this is a contradiction.
- If ψ contain $< p$ 1's, then d_t is an outlier. in this case, every one of the $l = q - r + 1$ copies of d_t in S is an outlier. But the maximum number of outliers is $q - r$, so this is a contradiction.

Thus, ψ must contain exactly p 1's. □

The rest of the argument follows identically from that of Theorem 7. Thus there exists some $\epsilon > 0$ such that CLOSEST TO MOST STRINGS does not have a $(1+\epsilon)$-approximation algorithm, unless P=NP.

Note that both of the previous reductions have involved using string duplicates in the string set S. It is also possible to reduce an instance of MAX-2-SAT to an equivalent instance of CLOSEST TO MOST STRINGS which does not use duplicates, thus proving a stronger result. Due to space constraints, we state the following theorem without proof.

THEOREM 9. *For some $\epsilon > 0$, if there is a polynomial time $(1+\epsilon)$-approximation algorithm for* CLOSEST TO MOST STRINGS (WITHOUT DUPLICATES), *then* P=NP.

THEOREM 10. MINIMAX APPROVAL VOTING WITH OUTLIERS *is* W[1]-hard, *even when parameterized by s, d and k.*

PROOF. We show a reduction from the k-CLIQUE problem, parameterized by k.

Starting from a graph $G = (V, E)$. We construct an election instance $\mathcal{E} = (\mathcal{C}, \mathcal{V}, s, k, d)$, such that $\mathcal{E}$ has a k-consensus if and only if G has a clique of size k. We set s, the number of voters to satisfy, as $s = \binom{k}{2}$ and $d = k - 2$.

- For each vertex v in the graph, add a candidate c_v.
- Each vote is a bit string of length $|V|$, where each bit corresponds to a vertex. For each edge (u_1, u_2) in the graph, add a vote v_e which sets $v[u_1] = v[u_2] = 1$ and $s[i] = 0$ everywhere else.

Suppose that G has a clique C of size k, and let x be the characteristic vector of the vertices in C. Note that the weight of x is k. A clique of size k contains $\binom{k}{2}$ edges. Further, for every edge e contained in C, both endpoints of e are contained in C – thus, $d(x, v_e) = k - 2$. Therefore, x is a valid consensus vote for $\mathcal{E}$ and $\mathcal{E}$ is a YES-instance.

Conversely, assume that $\mathcal{E}$ is a YES-instance and let x be a valid consensus committee for $\mathcal{E}$. We show that $C = \mathcal{J}(x)$ will induce a clique on the graph G.

Indeed, $\mathcal{V}$ contains $\binom{k}{2}$ votes, with Hamming distance d to x. These votes correspond to edges in G – there are $\binom{k}{2}$ edges within C, hence C forms a clique of size k.

CLIQUE parameterized by the clique size k is a well-known W[1]-hard problem [12]. The above reduction bounds all the three parameters, s, d, k in terms of the clique size k in the original instance – it follows that MINIMAX APPROVAL VOTING WITH OUTLIERS is W[1]-hard even when parameterized by s, d and k together. □

5. ACKNOWLEDGMENTS

The first author is supported by the INSPIRE Faculty Scheme, DST India (project DSTO-1209). This work was carried out when the third author visited the Indian Institute of Science. His visit was sponsored by the INSPIRE fellowship of the first author.

REFERENCES

[1] Noga Alon, Raphael Yuster, and Uri Zwick. Color-coding. *Journal of the ACM (JACM)*, 42(4):844–856, 1995.

[2] Haris Aziz, Serge Gaspers, Joachim Gudmundsson, Simon Mackenzie, Nicholas Mattei, and Toby Walsh. Computational aspects of multi-winner approval voting. In *Proc. of the International Conference On Autonomous Agents & Multiagent Systems* (AAMAS), 2015 *To Appear.*

[3] Manu Basavaraju, Fahad Panolan, Ashutosh Rai, M.S. Ramanujan, and Saket Saurabh. On the kernelization complexity of string problems. In *Computing and Combinatorics*, volume 8591 of *Lecture Notes in Computer Science*, pages 141–153, 2014.

[4] Hans L. Bodlaender, Stéphan Thomassé, and Anders Yeo. Kernel Bounds for Disjoint Cycles and Disjoint Paths. In *Proceedings of the 17th Annual European Symposium,on Algorithms* (ESA), volume 5757 of *Lecture Notes in Computer Science*, pages 635–646, Springer 2009.

[5] Christina Boucher, Gad M. Landau, Avivit Levy, David Pritchard, and Oren Weimann. On approximating string selection problems with outliers. In Theor. Comput. Sci, pages 107–114, 2013.

[6] Steven J. Brams and Peter C. Fishburn. Going from theory to practice: the mixed success of approval voting. *Social Choice and Welfare*, 25(2-3):457–474, Springer 2005.

[7] Robert Bredereck, Jiehua Chen, Piotr Faliszewski, Jiong Guo, Rolf Niedermeier, and Gerhard J. Woeginger. Parameterized algorithmics for computational social choice: Nine research challenges. In *Tsinghua Science and Technology*, volume 19, pages 358–373. IEEE, 2014.

[8] Jaroslaw Byrka and Krzysztof Sornat. PTAS for minimax approval voting. In *Proc. of Web and Internet Economics - 10th International Conference* (WINE), volume 8877 of *Lecture Notes in Computer Science*, pages 203–217. Springer, 2014.

[9] Ioannis Caragiannis, Dimitris Kalaitzis, and Evangelos Markakis. Approximation algorithms and mechanism design for minimax approval voting. In *AAAI*. AAAI Press, 2010.

[10] Vincent Conitzer. Making decisions based on the preferences of multiple agents. *Commun. ACM*, 53(3):84–94, 2010.

[11] Michael Dom, Daniel Lokshtanov, and Saket Saurabh. Incompressibility through colors and ids. In *Automata, Languages and Programming* (ICALP), pages 378–389. Springer, 2009.

[12] Rodney G Downey and Michael R Fellows. *Fundamentals of Parameterized complexity*. Springer, 2013.

[13] Edith Elkind, Piotr Faliszewski, Piotr Skowron, and Arkadii Slinko. Properties of multiwinner voting rules. In *Proc. of the International Conference On Autonomous Agents & Multiagent Systems* (AAMAS), pages 53–60, IFAAMAS/ACM, 2014.

[14] Jörg Flum and Martin Grohe. *Parameterized Complexity Theory*, volume 3. Springer, 2006.

[15] Jens Gramm, Rolf Niedermeier, Peter Rossmanith, et al. Fixed-parameter algorithms for closest string and related problems. *Algorithmica*, 37(1):25–42, 2003.

[16] Johan Håstad. Some optimal inapproximability results. *Journal of the ACM (JACM)*, 48(4):798–859, July 2001.

[17] Rob LeGrand. Analysis of the minimax procedure. Technical report, Technical Report WUCSE-2004-67, Department of Computer Science and Engineering, Washington University, St. Louis, Missouri, 2004.

[18] Rob LeGrand, Evangelos Markakis, and Aranyak Mehta. Some results on approximating the minimax solution in approval voting. In *Proc. of the International Conference On Autonomous Agents & Multiagent Systems* (AAMAS), page 198. IFAAMAS, 2007.

[19] Rolf Niedermeier. Invitation to fixed-parameter algorithms. *Habilitationschrift, University of Tübingen*, 2002.

Computational Aspects of Multi-Winner Approval Voting

Haris Aziz Serge Gaspers
NICTA and UNSW
Sydney, Australia
{haris.aziz, serge.gaspers}@nicta.com.au

Joachim Gudmundsson
NICTA and University of Sydney
Sydney, Australia
joachim.gudmundsson@sydney.edu.au

Simon Mackenzie Nicholas Mattei Toby Walsh
NICTA and UNSW
Sydney, Australia
{simon.mackenzie, nicholas.mattei, toby.walsh}@nicta.com.au

ABSTRACT

We study computational aspects of three prominent voting rules that use approval ballots to select multiple winners. These rules are *proportional approval voting*, *reweighted approval voting*, and *satisfaction approval voting*. Each rule is designed with the intention to compute a representative winning set. We show that computing the winner for proportional approval voting is NP-hard, closing an open problem (Kilgour, 2010). As none of the rules we examine are strategyproof, we study various strategic aspects of the rules. In particular, we examine the computational complexity of computing a best response for both a single agent and a group of agents. In many settings, we show that it is NP-hard for an agent or agents to compute how best to vote given a fixed set of approval ballots of the other agents.

Categories and Subject Descriptors

F.2 [**Theory of Computation**]: Analysis of Algorithms and Problem Complexity; I.2.11 [**Distributed Artificial Intelligence**]: Multiagent Systems; J.4 [**Computer Applications**]: Social and Behavioral Sciences - Economics

General Terms

Economics, Theory and Algorithms

Keywords

Multi-winner voting; approval voting; computational social choice.

1. INTRODUCTION

The aggregation of possibly conflicting preferences is a central problem in artificial intelligence [9]. Agents express preferences over candidates and a voting rule selects a winner or winners based on these preferences. We focus here on rules that select k winners where k is fixed in advance. This covers a variety of important settings including parliamentary elections [25]; selecting committees [33, 26]; the hiring of faculty members [13]; understanding heredity and signals in DNA [20]; and movie recommendation systems [32, 14].

Appears in: *Proceedings of the 14th International Conference on Autonomous Agents and Multiagent Systems (AAMAS 2015), Bordini, Elkind, Weiss, Yolum (eds.), May 4–8, 2015, Istanbul, Turkey.*

Generally, in approval-based voting rules, an agent approves of (votes for) a subset of the candidates. The most straightforward way to aggregate these votes is to have every approval for a candidate contribute one point to that candidate; yielding the rule known as Approval Voting (AV). The same principle of selecting the candidate with the highest number of approvals can be extended to select multiple candidates the highest number of approvals. Unlike plurality voting, where agents only vote for their most preferred candidate, approval ballots permit agents to identify multiple candidates that they wish to win. Approval voting has many desirable properties in the single winner case [17, 6], including its 'simplicity, propensity to select Condorcet winners (when they exist), its robustness to manipulation and its monotonicity' [25]. However for the case of multiple winners, the merits of AV are 'less clear' [25]. In particular, for the multi-winner case, AV does not address more egalitarian concerns such as proportional representation.

Various methods for counting approvals have been introduced in the literature, each attempting to address the fairness and representation concerns when using AV for multiple winners (a *winning set* of candidates) [22]. In this paper we investigate three popular ways to count approvals that are designed with the intention of selecting a more representative set of winners than AV. First, under *Proportional Approval Voting (PAV)*, each agent's contribution to the committee's total score depends on how many candidates from the agent's approval set have been selected. A second way to promote fairness is to proceed across a set of rounds. In each round, the candidate with the most approvals wins. However, in each subsequent round we decrease the weight of agents who have already had a candidate selected in earlier rounds; this method is implemented in *Reweighted Approval Voting (RAV)*. Finally, *Satisfaction Approval Voting (SAV)* modulates the weight of approvals with a satisfaction score for each agent, based on the ratio of approved candidates appearing in the winning set to the agent's total number of approved candidates.

The three approaches we consider for generalizing approval voting to the case of multiple winners each have their own benefits and drawbacks. It is therefore necessary to understand the computational and axiomatic properties of these voting rules for the variety of domains for which they are typically deployed. In terms of computational properties, it is beneficial to have a voting rule which admits a polynomial algorithm to determine the winners. Otherwise, we cannot hope to use the rule in settings with large numbers of candidates or voters [21]. Another key problem studied in computational social choice is the complexity of computing a beneficial misreport (i.e., manipulation) [3, 15, 16]. If computing a beneficial misreport is computationally hard for a given rule, the rule is said to be resistant to manipulation. If it is computationally hard to compute a misreport, agents may decide to be truthful, since they cannot always easily manipulate. Connections also exist between manipulation and other important questions in social choice such as deciding when to terminate preference elicitation and determining possible winners [24, 37].

From the axiomatic perspective, studying the positive or negative properties of these multi-winner rules can help us make informed, objective decisions about which rule is better suited for the particular situation to which we are applying a multi-winner rule [14]. Though AV is the most widely known among these rules, RAV has been used, for example, in elections in Sweden. Rules other than AV may have better axiomatic properties in the multi-winner setting and thus, motivate our study. For example, each of PAV, RAV, and SAV have a more egalitarian objective than AV [2]. Brams, a proponent of AV when selecting a single winner, has argued that SAV is more suitable for equitable representation when multiple winners are to be selected [5].

We undertake a detailed study of the computational aspects of PAV, RAV, and SAV. We first consider the computational complexity of computing the winner. Although PAV was introduced over a decade ago, the computational complexity of determining the winners is an open question, having only been referred to as "computationally demanding" before [22]. We close this outstanding open problem, showing that winner determination for PAV is NP-hard. We then consider strategic voting for these rules. We show that, even with dichotomous preferences, PAV, RAV and SAV are not strategyproof. That is, it may be beneficial for agents to misreport their true preferences. We therefore consider computational aspects of manipulation. We prove that finding the best response given the preferences of other agents is NP-hard under a number of conditions for PAV, RAV, and SAV. In particular, we examine the complexity of checking whether an agent or a set of agents can make a given candidate or a set of candidates win. These results offer support for RAV over PAV or SAV as it is the only one of these three rules for which winner determination is computationally easy but manipulation is hard.

We stress here that our results are not restricted to AV, PAV, RAV and SAV. Our NP-hardness result for any rule implies NP-hardness for a more general class of rules that includes that rule. In certain cases, our precise reduction can be adapted to prove similar results for other variants of the rule. For example, our reduction to show that winner determination for PAV is NP-hard can be adapted to prove NP-hardness for winner determination for any variant of PAV in which the coefficient weight for the second approved candidate is less than the coefficient weight for the first approved candidate.

2. RELATED WORK

Surprisingly, there has only been limited consideration of computational aspects of selecting multiple-winners. Exceptions include work by Meir et al. [29] who consider single non-transferable voting, approval voting, k-approval, cumulative voting and the proportional schemes of Monroe, and of Chamberlin and Courant. Most relevant to our study is that for approval voting, Meir et al. prove that manipulation with general utilities and control by adding/deleting candidates are both polynomial to compute, but control by adding/deleting agents is NP-hard. Another work that considers computational aspects of selecting multiple-winners is Obraztsova et al. [32], but their study is limited to k-approval and scoring rules. Finally, the control and bribery problems for AV and two other approval voting variants are well catalogued by Baumeister et al. [4].

The Handbook of Approval Voting discusses various approval-based multi-winner rules including PAV, RAV and SAV. Another prominent multi-winner rule in the Handbook is *minimax approval voting* [7]. Each agent's approval ballot and the winning set can be seen as a binary vector. Minimax approval voting selects the set of k candidates that minimizes the maximum Hamming distance from the submitted ballots. Although minimax approval voting is a natural and elegant rule, LeGrand et al. [26] showed that computing the winning set is NP-hard. Strategic issues and approximation questions for minimax approval voting are covered by Caragiannis et al. [8] and Gramm et al. [20].

The area of multi-winner approval voting is closely related to the study of proportional representation when selecting a committee [34, 35]. Understanding approval voting schemes which select multiple winners, as the rules we consider do, is an important area in social choice with applications in a variety of settings from committee selection to multi-product recommendation [14].

3. FORMAL BACKGROUND

We consider the social choice setting (N, C) where $N = \{1, \dots, n\}$ is the set of agents and $C = \{c_1, \dots, c_m\}$ is the set of candidates. Each agent expresses an approval ballot $A_i \subset C$ that represents the subset of candidates that he approves of, yielding a set of approval ballots $A = \{A_1, \dots, A_n\}$. We will consider approval-based multi-winner rules that take as input (C, A, k) and return the subset $W \subseteq C$ of size k that is the winning set. We will assume a lexicographic tie-breaking rule over the candidate set.

Approval Voting (AV).

AV finds a set $W \subseteq C$ of size k that maximizes the total score $App(W) = \sum_{i \in N} |W \cap A_i|$. That is, the set of AV winners are those candidates that are approved by the largest number of agents. AV has been adopted by several academic and professional societies such as the American Mathematical Society (AMS), the Institute of Electrical and Electronics Engineers (IEEE), and the International Joint Conference on Artificial Intelligence (IJCAI).

Proportional Approval Voting (PAV).

In PAV, an agent's satisfaction score is $1 + 1/2 + 1/3 + \dots + 1/j$ where j is the number of his or her approved candidates that are selected in W. Formally, PAV finds a set $W \subseteq C$ of size k that maximizes the total score $PAV(W) = \sum_{i \in N} r(|W \cap A_i|)$ where $r(p) = \sum_{j=1}^{p} \frac{1}{j}$. PAV was proposed by the mathematician Forest Simmons in 2001 [22].

We observe that PAV is only one way to apply scores in a decreasing manner. Kilgour and Marshall [23] introduce the notion of Generalized Approval Voting (GAV) where the harmonic weights $1+1/2+1/3+\cdots+1/j$ are replaced by an arbitrary vector of weights $w(1), w(2), w(3), \ldots, w(m)$. We will focus on PAV in our results but show how they directly extend to the case of GAV. Moreover, we are interested in the harmonic weights as these are the *only* set of weights for GAV which satisfy a strong egalitarian axiomatic property called extended justified representation [2].

Reweighted Approval Voting (*RAV*).

RAV converts *AV* into a multi-round rule, selecting a candidate in each round and then reweighing the approvals for the subsequent rounds. In each of the k rounds, we select an unselected candidate to add to the winning set W with the highest "weight" of approvals. In each round we reweight each agents approvals, assigning the weight $\frac{1}{1+|W \cap A_i|}$ to each agent $i \in N$. *RAV* was invented by the Danish polymath Thorvald Thiele in the early 1900's. *RAV* has also been referred to as "*sequential proportional AV*" [5].

Satisfaction Approval Voting (*SAV*).

An agent's satisfaction is the fraction of his or her approved candidates that are selected. *SAV* maximizes the sum of such scores. Formally, *SAV* finds a set $W \subseteq C$ of size k that maximizes $Sat(W) = \sum_{i \in N} \frac{|W \cap A_i|}{|A_i|}$. The rule was proposed by Brams and Kilgour [5] with the aim of representing more diverse interests than *AV*.

Kilgour and Marshall [23] discuss several variants of SAV. We focus on SAV as it was the first rule in this family to be introduced and many open problems about strategic aspects of SAV remain open. As there is no consensus as to the best rule, our study will help understand the relative merits of different rules.

Tie-breaking is an important issue to consider when investigating the complexity of manipulation and winner determination problems as it can have a significant impact on the complexity of reasoning tasks [31, 30, 1]. We make the assumption that ties are broken lexicographically (both for individual elements and sets) with $a \succ b \succ c$, e.g., $\{a, b\}$ is preferred to $\{a, c\}$. We also note that many of our proofs are independent of the tie-breaking rule, in which case the hardness results transfer to any arbitrary tie-breaking rule.

EXAMPLE 1. *Consider a setting with 7 agents, a candidate set* $C = \{a, b, c, d\}$, $k = 2$, *and the following ballots:* $A_1 = A_2 = A_3 = \{a, b\}$; $A_4 = A_5 = \{c\}$; $A_6 = A_7 = \{d\}$.

Approval Voting (AV): *The approval scores of the candidates are* $App(\{a\}) = 3$, $App(\{b\}) = 3$, $App(\{c\}) = 2$, *and* $App(\{d\}) = 2$. *Hence, the set* $\{a, b\}$ *is selected.*

Proportional Approval Voting (PAV): *PAV scores are not additive and we can sum the satisfaction for each agent for each potential set of winners to determine the winner. For example,* $PAV(\{a, b\}) = 3 \cdot 1.5 = 4.5$. *Computing* $PAV(W)$ *for all* W *leaves us with a tie between the sets* $\{a, c\}, \{a, d\}, \{b, c\}, \{b, d\}$, *which is broken in favor of* $\{a, c\}$.

Reweighted Approval Voting (RAV): *In the first round,* a *is selected. This causes the weight of* A_1, A_2, *and* A_3 *to drop to* 0.5 *for the second round. Consequently,* c *is selected next, which gives the winning set* $\{a, c\}$.

Satisfaction Approval Voting (SAV): *As SAV scores are additive we can greedily add the agent which provides the most satisfaction, in order, to compute the result. Observe that the satisfaction obtained by adding* c *or* d *to the winning set is* 2, *the maximum of any candidate. Thus, the SAV rule selects* $\{c, d\}$.

4. WINNER DETERMINATION

We first examine one of the most basic computational questions, computing the winners of a voting rule. This problem should be computationally easy if we want to use a voting rule in practice [21].

Name: $\mathcal{R}$–WINNER DETERMINATION ($\mathcal{R}$–WD).
Input: A a set of approval ballots A over the set C of candidates and a winning set size $k \in \{1, \ldots, |C|\}$.
Output: Compute the winning set of size k under $\mathcal{R}$.

A related problem is the decision problem which tests whether a given set is the winning set.

Name: $\mathcal{R}$–TEST WINNING SET ($\mathcal{R}$–TESTWS).
Input: A a set of approval ballots A over the set C of candidates, a winning set size $k \in \{1, \ldots, |C|\}$, and a set $W \subseteq C$ with $|W| = k$.
Question: Is W the winning set under $\mathcal{R}$?

Since we consider resolute multi-winner rules, $\mathcal{R}$–WD is at least as hard as $\mathcal{R}$–TESTWS. Note that if there is a polynomial-time algorithm for $\mathcal{R}$–WD, then $\mathcal{R}$–TESTWS is in P as well: compute the unique winning set and check whether W coincides with the winning set. This means that if $\mathcal{R}$–TESTWS is coNP-complete, then there exists no polynomial-time algorithm for $\mathcal{R}$–WD unless $P = NP$.

We observe that *AV*–WD, *RAV*–WD, *SAV*–WD are all polynomial-time computable. We give a formal argument for *SAV*–WD as it is not formally stated in the literature whether the winning set can be computed in polynomial time.

THEOREM 1. *SAV–WD can be solved in linear time.*

PROOF. For $|W| = k$, $Sat(W) = \sum_{i \in N} \frac{|W \cap A_i|}{|A_i|} = \sum_{c \in W} \sum_{i \in N, c \in A_i} \frac{1}{|A_i|}$ where we say that $\sum_{i \in N, c \in A_i} \frac{1}{|A_i|}$ is the *Sat score of an individual candidate*. Hence computing a winning set of size k is equivalent to selecting k candidates with the highest Sat scores. □

Although *RAV*–WD is polynomial-time computable, it has been termed "computationally difficult" to analyze in [22]. We provide support for this claim by showing that computing a best response for *RAV* is NP-hard (Theorem 5). We close the computational complexity of *PAV*–TESTWS in this section.[1]

[1] Thm. 9 and 11 in Skowron et al. [36] independently show a similar result to Thm. 2 and Cor. 2. The framework of Skowron et al. [36] uses *order weighted averages* combined with voting [19] to select subsets of objects that have highest utility to the agents. Their results show that finding the set of winners is NP-hard for any weight vector that is non-increasing and non-constant. Our reduction *additionally* shows that it is computationally hard to even *verify* that a given set is a winning set, holds even when agents approve of only two objects, and shows Cor. 3.

Theorem 2. *PAV–TestWS is coNP-complete, even if each agent approves of 2 candidates.*

Proof. Consider the complement problem. A polynomial time checkable witness is simply a set of candidates of size k that has greater *PAV* score than W. For NP-hardness, we give a polynomial-time reduction from the NP-hard Independent Set problem [18], which is defined as follows. Given (G', t), where G' is a graph and t an integer, determine whether G' has an independent set of size t. An independent set is a subset of vertices S such that no edge of G' has both endpoints in S. For an instance (G', t) of Independent Set, we build a *PAV* instance such that G' has an independent set of size t if and only if the winning set for the *PAV* is not W.

Consider a graph G'. Obtain a new graph $G = (V, E)$ from G by adding a set I of t vertices to G', making them adjacent to all vertices in G', and adding exactly one edge between two arbitrary vertices of I. Note that a set of vertices $S \subseteq V$ of size at least t is independent in G if and only if it is independent in G'. Define the following *PAV* instance, $pav(G) = (N, C, A, k)$: We have a set of agents N and a set of candidates C. For each vertex $v \in V$, we create $deg(G) - deg(v)$ 'dummy' candidates in C, where $deg(G)$ is the maximum degree of G, $deg(G) > 1$, and $deg(v)$ the degree of vertex v. For each $v \in V$, we also create another candidate in C, labeled C_v. We create an agent in N for each edge $e \in E$. For each vertex we also create $deg(G) - deg(v)$ agents. Each of the "edge" agents we create approves of the two candidates corresponding to the two vertex candidates connected by the edge. Each vertex agent associated with vertex v approves of C_v and one of the dummy candidates associated with v, such that each dummy candidate has exactly one agent approving him. We also set $k = t$ and $W = \{C_v : v \in I\}$. The tie-breaking rule prefers the set W to any other set of k candidates. Observe that the satisfaction score for W is $deg(G) \cdot t - 1/2$, and a winning set distinct from W has satisfaction score at least $deg(G) \cdot t$.

We will show that $pav(G)$ has a winning set of size $k = t$ scoring a total approval of at least $s = deg(G) \cdot t$ if and only if G has an independent set of size t.

First, note that adding a candidate to a winning set increases its total score by at most $deg(G)$, since at most $deg(G)$ agents see their satisfaction score rise by at most one. Also, if adding a candidate c to a winning set increases the total score of the winning set by exactly $deg(G)$, then c corresponds to a vertex in G, since each dummy vertex is approved by only one agent, and the vertex corresponding to c is not adjacent to a vertex corresponding to any other candidate in the winning set. Thus, the candidates in a winning set of size $k = t$ scoring a total approval of s correspond to an independent set of size t in G and vice-versa. □

Corollary 1. *PAV–WD is NP-hard, even if each agent approves of 2 candidates.*

The proof of Theorem 2 does not rely on the particular score assigned to candidates assigned subsequently to the first one, as long as the second candidate contributes strictly less satisfaction score than the first. Thus, *PAV*–TestWS remains hard as long as the satisfaction score satisfies this strictly decreasing condition. Thus, we can state the following corollary.

Corollary 2. *GAV–TestWS is coNP-complete for any set of weights where $w(1) > w(2)$, even if each agent approves of 2 candidates.*

Since the reduction for Theorem 2 is a parameterized reduction from the W[1]-hard [12] Independent Set problem with parameter t to the complement of *PAV*–TestWS with parameter k, we have that *PAV*–TestWS is coW[1]-hard with parameter k. Therefore it is unlikely that the problem can be solved in time $f(k) \cdot m^{O(1)}$ for any function f. Thus, a factor m^k in the running time seems unavoidable.

Corollary 3. *PAV–TestWS is coW[1]-hard for parameter k, even if each agent approves of 2 candidates.*

5. STRATEGIC VOTING

As in the single winner case, agents may benefit from misreporting their true preferences when selecting multiple winners. Formally, we will assume that each agent $i \in N$ is equipped with a utility function $u_i : C \to \mathbb{R}^+$ and an agent i's utility for a winning set W is $\sum_{c \in W} u_i(c)$. We will mostly assume that agents have *Boolean* utilities: $u_i(c) \in \{0, 1\}$ for all $c \in C$. For agents with Boolean utilities, we say that a multi-winner approval-based voting rule is *strategyproof* if and only if there is no agent who will receive strictly greater utility by either approving candidates for whom he has utility 0 or not approving candidates for whom he has utility 1.

We begin by showing some results that are likely folklore but provide a useful starting point for our main results

Theorem 3. *PAV, RAV and SAV are not strategyproof with Boolean utilities.*

Proof. We treat each case separately. Ties are always broken lexicographically and $k = 2$. We show that we can construct instances where agent 1 has an opportunity to misreport his preference and get a more preferred set selected with respect to his true preferences.

For *PAV*, if we have $C = \{a, b, c\}$ and the votes:

$$A_1 = \{a, c\}, A_2 = A_3 = A_4 = \{a, b\}, A_5 = \{c\}, A_6 = \{a\}.$$

Then $\{a, b\}$ is the winning set due to tie-breaking (over the set $\{a, c\}$). However, if agent 1 only approves c, then we get $\{a, c\}$ as the winning set.

For *RAV*, consider the following votes:

$$A_1 = \{a, b\}, A_2 = A_3 = A_4 = \{a\}, A_5 = \{c\}, A_6 = \{b, c\}.$$

The outcome is $\{a, c\}$ for all reported preferences of agent 1 except if $A_1 = \{b\}$, in which case the outcome is $\{a, b\}$.

For *SAV*, if we have $C = \{a, b, c, d\}$ and the votes:

$$A_1 = \{a, b\}, A_2 = A_3 = \{a, c, d\}, A_4 = \{a\}.$$

Thus, $\{a, c\}$ and $\{a, d\}$ are the sets with highest SAV scores. Agent 1 is indifferent between them. If agent 1 only approves b, then we get $\{a, b\}$ as the winning set without tie-breaking. □

With *PAV*, *RAV* and *SAV*, it can therefore be beneficial for agents to vote strategically. Next, we consider the computational complexity of computing such strategic votes. Throughout the paper, we will denote by j the number of additional ballots submitted to achieve strategic goals such as getting a candidate, subset of candidates, or the exact set of candidates selected.

Name: $\mathcal{R}$–WINNER MANIPULATION ($\mathcal{R}$–WM)
Input: A set of approval ballots A over the set C of candidates, a winning size k, a number of agents j still to vote, and a preferred candidate c^*.
Question: Are there j additional approval ballots so that c^* is in the winning set W of size k (i.e., $c^* \in W, |W| = k$) under $\mathcal{R}$?

Name: $\mathcal{R}$–WINNING SET MANIPULATION ($\mathcal{R}$–WSM).
Input: A set of approval ballots A over the set C of candidates, a winning set size k, a number of agents j still to vote, and a set of preferred candidates $C^* \subseteq C$.
Question: Are there j additional approval ballots such that C^* is *exactly* the winning set of size k (i.e., $W = C^*, |W| = k$) under $\mathcal{R}$?

Note that our definitions for $\mathcal{R}$–WM and $\mathcal{R}$–WSM are for the basic computational problems. These problem definitions do not rely on our use of a particular utility model for the agents or lifting this model to sets of candidates. We also introduce the manipulation problem based on agent utilities.

Name: $\mathcal{R}$–UTILITY MANIPULATION ($\mathcal{R}$–UM).
Input: A set of approval ballots A over the set C of candidates, a winning set size k, a manipulating agent i with utility function $u : C \to \mathbb{R}^+$, a number of votes j still to be cast, and a target utility $t \in \mathbb{R}^+$
Question: Can the manipulator i submit j additional approval ballots so that he gets utility $u_i(W) \geq t$ from the winning set W of size k under rule R?

The problem of utility manipulation has been considered previously by Meir et al. [29]. We note that the problem of utility manipulation is at least as hard as $\mathcal{R}$–WM or $\mathcal{R}$–WSM. Hence, if $\mathcal{R}$–WM or $\mathcal{R}$–WSM is NP-hard for a single agent ($j = 1$), then the more general problem of maximizing the utility of an agent ($\mathcal{R}$–UM) is also NP-hard even for Boolean utilities. The reductions for WM and WSM to utility maximization involve giving desired candidates utility one and the rest utility zero. For AV, the utility maximizing best response of a single agent can be computed in polynomial time for both Boolean and general utilities [29, 28]. Note that AV is strategyproof for Boolean utilities and therefore an agent being able to compute a utility maximising vote is not a negative result. These single agent results for AV can be extended in a straightforward way to settings with multiple agents ($j \geq 1$).

Since j is encoded in binary in $\mathcal{R}$–WM, $\mathcal{R}$–WSM, and $\mathcal{R}$–UM, it is not entirely obvious that the problems are in NP as the the number of ballots of the manipulator could be exponential in the input size. However, notice that for $\mathcal{R} \in \{PAV, RAV, SAV\}$, $\mathcal{R}$–WM and $\mathcal{R}$–WSM instances are Yes-instances if $j > (n+1)(m+1)$, and likewise a utility-maximizing manipulation can be constructed for $\mathcal{R}$–UM if $j > (n+1)(m+1)$. Therefore, we may assume that $j \leq (n+1)(m+1)$, and as a result the problems are in NP since the manipulator ballots are polynomial-size certificates.

A summary of our results about strategic voting and winner determination can be found in Table 1. In the rest of this section we will investigate each of the rules in turn, examining the relationships between the complexity of computing various strategic behaviors for each.

5.1 Proportional Approval Voting (PAV)

Since PAV–TESTWS is coNP-complete, deciding if a coalition of agents who have yet to vote can ensure a given candidate or set of candidates wins is coNP-hard. Hence we can state the following corollary.

COROLLARY 4. *PAV–WM and PAV–WSM are coNP-hard.*

However the hardness of manipulation here comes from the hardness of winner determination even if the agents vote sincerely. This seems rather unsatisfying and motivates us to investigate the situation where a "real" manipulation is necessary, that is, whether a single manipulator can find a vote that will maximise his utility. The proof of Theorem 2 can be modified to show that a manipulator can compute a vote which maximises his utility if and only if he can decide the existence of an independent set of size t in G. We define an even more constrained problem:

Name: $\mathcal{R}$-BINARY CHOICE MANIPULATION ($\mathcal{R}$–BCM)
Input: A set of approval ballots A over the set C of candidates, a winning set size k, a set of preferred candidates $C^* \subseteq C$, and 2 ballots v_1 and v_2 such that the manipulator is guaranteed at least one of the two will ensure all his preferred candidates get selected.
Question: Will the manipulator choosing v_1 ensure all his preferred candidates get selected?

THEOREM 4. *PAV-BCM is NP-hard.*

PROOF. To show NP-hardness we leverage the construction from the proof of Theorem 2. Given an instance (G', t) of INDEPENDENT SET we create an instance of PAV–BCM, (C, A, k, C^*, v_1, v_2) where $k = t+5$ is the size of the committee. We first modify the provided graph G' by augmenting it in several ways. The resulting graph G will then be converted into a PAV instance through a modified version of the reduction described in Theorem 2. In the resulting instance, the manipulator will be able to decide on the vote which maximises his utility if and only if he can decide the existence of an independent set of size t in G'.

First, we obtain G from G' by adding three connected components: a simple 2-clique, and two bipartite graphs $K_{2,2}$. Let us label the vertices in the 2-clique q_1 and q_2. Let us label the vertices of the first $K_{2,2}$ graph $b_{1,1}$, $b_{1,2}$, $b_{2,1}$, $b_{2,2}$ and those of the second $d_{1,1}$, $d_{1,2}$, $d_{2,1}$ and $d_{2,2}$. The labeling is such that $b_{1,1}$ and $b_{1,2}$ are not connected by an edge, and neither are $d_{1,1}$ and $d_{1,2}$. Note that G' has an independent set of size t if and only if G has an independent set of size $t+5$. Now, we obtain a PAV instance $pav(G)$ from G as in Theorem 2. Then, we multiply the number of agents by 20, to ensure that the manipulator is not capable of having a meaningful impact on the candidates chosen in the graph G (by meaningful we mean that he cannot force two adjacent candidates to be chosen, which would invalidate the construction in Theorem 2). Note that multiplying the number of agents does not change the winning set.

In the resulting PAV instance, we delete 10 of the agents that correspond to the edges in the 2-clique and exactly 4 agents corresponding to the edges between q_2 and its dummy candidates. We now add 2 agents approving both q_2 and $d_{2,1}$ and 2 agents approving q_2 and $b_{1,2}$. We add 2 agents approving q_1 and one of its dummy candidates.

It only remains to specify the preferred candidates and the two approval ballots between which the manipulator needs to decide: $C^* = \{b_{1,1}, d_{1,1}\}$, $v_1 = \{d_{1,1}, d_{1,2}\}$ and $v_2 = \{b_{1,1}, b_{1,2}\}$.

If there is no independent set of size $t+5$ in G then q_1 and q_2 will be selected since adjacency is penalized less on these components. Else, if there is an independent set of size $t+5$ in G then only q_1 will be a part of the winning set, since q_1 gives slightly higher score than q_2 and other candidates.

Without the manipulator's vote, either q_2 is selected as part of the winning set – along with $b_{2,1}$, $b_{2,2}$, $d_{1,1}$ and $d_{1,2}$, or q_2 is not selected and $b_{1,1}$, $b_{1,2}$, $d_{2,1}$ and $d_{2,2}$ are selected. In either case the manipulator only gets one of his approved candidates.

It is possible for the manipulator to ensure the selection of both his approved candidates by either casting the approval vote $v_1 = \{d_{1,1}, d_{1,2}\}$ (if G' has an independent set of size t) or $v_2 = \{b_{1,1}, b_{1,2}\}$ (if G' has no independent set of size t). Therefore, the *PAV*–BCM is a YES-instance if and only if the INDEPENDENT SET instance is a YES-instance. □

5.2 Reweighted Approval Voting (RAV)

Though *RAV*–WD is polynomial-time computable, "computationally difficult" to analyze. This is because the decision for a single agent of whom to vote for in order to maximize his utility is not straightforward, as we show in the following observations.

OBSERVATION 1. *Under RAV an agent i who wants to include a single candidate c^* in the winning set may have incentive to approve other candidates.*

Suppose we are selecting a winning set of size $k = 2$ and $C = \{a, b, c, d\}$:

$$A_2 = \{b, d\}, A_3 = \{c, d\}, A_4 = \{a, b, c, d\}$$
$$A_5 = A_6 = \{b, c, d\}, A_7 = \{a, b\}, A_8 = \{c\}, A_9 = \{a\}.$$

If agent 1 is only interested in getting a to the winning set, then he may need to approve candidates other than a. If agent 1 casts the ballot $A_1 = \{a\}$ then in round 1, b is selected, in round 2, c is selected. However, if the agent casts the ballot $\{a, d\}$ then in round 1, d is selected, and in round 2, a is selected.

OBSERVATION 2. *Under RAV an agent i who wants to make C^* the winning set may need to approve a strict subset of C^*.*

Suppose we are selecting a winning set of size $k = 3$ with $C = \{a, b, c, d\}$, using lexicographic tie-breaking:

$$A_2 = \{b, d\}, A_3 = \{c, d\}, A_4 = A_5 = A_6 = \{b, c, d\}$$
$$A_7 = \{b\}, A_8 = \{c\}, A_9 = A_{10} = \{a\}.$$

If agent 1 has favored set $C^* = \{a, b, d\}$ and he approves all of them, then in round 1, b is selected, in round 2, c is selected, and in round 3, a is selected. However, if the agent casts the ballot $\{a, d\}$ then in round 1, d is selected, in round 2, a is selected, and in round 3, b is selected, exactly the favored set.

With these observations we are able to show *RAV*–WM is NP-complete.

THEOREM 5. *RAV–WM is NP-complete even for a single manipulator ($j = 1$).*

PROOF. To show that *RAV* is NP-complete to manipulate we reduce from the 3SAT decision problem [18]. Given an instance of 3SAT with w variables $\Phi = \{\phi_1, \ldots, \phi_w\}$, t clauses $\Psi = \{\psi_1, \ldots, \psi_t\}$, inducing $2w$ literals $\{l_1, \ldots, l_{2w}\}$, we construct an instance of *RAV*, (C, A, k) where a manipulator's preferred candidate c^* is in the winning set if and only if there is an assignment to the variables in Φ such that all clauses are satisfied.

For each variable ϕ_i introduce 2 candidates in C, corresponding to the positive and negative literal of that variable, and $2n - i$ agents approving the 2 candidates; note that $n \gg w + t$. For each clause ψ_j introduce two additional new candidates, corresponding to the clause being satisfied or unsatisfied, along with $2n - w - j$ new agents approving both new candidates. Additionally for each clause ψ_j, we add an agent in N approving each of the candidates that correspond to the positive and negative literals in ψ_j; this ensures that both the positive and negative literal have the same weight of approval in the set of agents. We also need to add 2 agents approving the candidate corresponding to the negation of the clause to maintain the weighting. Finally, add an extra 2 candidates to C, a and b. We add 2 agents approving the candidate corresponding to a clause being unsatisfied, and 2 agents approving the the candidate corresponding to each clause being satisfied and approving b.

Add t agents approving a. The size of the winning set k is equal to $|\Phi| + |\Psi| + 1$. Intuitively, the manipulator must approve of a setting of all the variables in the original 3SAT instance that satisfies all the clauses, plus the preferred candidate. We can now see that the manipulating agent is only capable of ensuring candidate a is selected by computing a solution to the initial 3SAT instance. □

The above proof also shows it is NP-complete to determine if C^* can be made a subset of the winning set, i.e. $C^* \subset W$. From the construction above, and setting $t = 1$, $u(c^*) = 1$, $u(c) = 0$ for all $c \in C \setminus \{c^*\}$, we can state the following corollary.

COROLLARY 5. *RAV–UM is NP-complete.*

Finally, the proof can also be modified to show the following:

THEOREM 6. *RAV–WSM is NP-complete even for a single manipulator ($j = 1$).*

The important observation is that for RAV, the order in which the candidates are included in the committee matters. Therefore we can modify the reduction so that all literals end up in the committee, but the manipulator will impact which ones are selected first. We can then ensure that the committee will consist of exactly all literal agents, the satisfied clause agents, and the preferred candidate if and only if the manipulator ensures that the literals corresponding to a satisfying assignment were chosen first.

5.3 Satisfaction Approval Voting (SAV)

We start this section with the following straightforward observation, namely to select a given candidate c^*, the manipulators need only approve c^*.

OBSERVATION 3. *SAV–WM is polynomial-time solvable.*

It follows that we can also construct the set of candidates that can possibly win in polynomial time.

It is more difficult to decide if a given k-set of candidates can possibly win. With certain voting rules, this problem simplifies if there exists an optimal strategy of j manipulating agents where they all approve the same set of candidates. This is not the case with *SAV*. Suppose $k = 3$ and $C = \{a, b, c, d, e, f, g\}$, one agent approves both a and b, and three agents approve d, e, f and g. If there are two more agents who want a, b and c to be selected, then one agent needs to approve c and the other both a and b, or one agent needs to approve a and b, and the other a and c. This makes it difficult to decide how a coalition of agents must vote. In fact, it is intractable in general to decide if a given set of candidates can be made winners.

THEOREM 7. *SAV–WSM is NP-complete.*

PROOF. The proof is by reduction from the permutation sum problem, inspired by the NP-hardness proof for Borda manipulation with two agents [11]. In the permutation sum problem, we are given integers $X_1 \leq \cdots \leq X_n$ with $\sum_i X_i = n(n+1)$ and the question is if there exist two permutations σ and π of 1 to n such that $\sigma(i) + \pi(i) = X_i$. We construct an instance such there is a strategic vote for $2n$ manipulating agents which ensures a given result if and only if there exists a solution to an instance of the permutation sum problem. In this instance, we want all the candidates alphabetically before e to win.

Our proof exploits the fact that for large m, an approval vote for $m+x$ candidates, all of whom win, results in a satisfaction score of $\frac{1}{m} - \frac{x}{m^2} + O(\frac{1}{m^3})$ for each of these candidates. For large m, terms in $O(\frac{1}{m^3})$ will only ensure we do not need to tie-break in favour of our preferred candidates. We will therefore ignore such terms. Note that the exact choice of m is not very critical other than to ensure such higher order terms are unimportant. For example, we could set $m = n^2$.

We construct an instance with the following candidates: b_y for $1 \leq y \leq n$, $c_{x,y}$ and $d_{x,y}$ for $1 \leq x \leq n$ and $1 \leq y \leq m + x - 1$, the danger candidate e, and some dummy candidates $f_{x,y,z}$, $g_{x,y,z}$ and $h_{y,z}$ for $1 \leq x \leq n$, $1 \leq y \leq m + x - 1$ and $1 \leq z \leq m^2 - 1$. We want all the candidates alphabetically before the danger candidate e to be selected. That is, $k = 2mn + n^2$ and we want b_y, $c_{x,y}$ and $d_{x,y}$ to be the winners.

We construct the votes in our instance as follows: there is one approval ballot for e, giving e a satisfaction score of 1. Hence, each candidate in the winning set will need to have a satisfaction score greater than or equal to 1. Next, for $x = 1$ to n and $y = 1$ to $m+x-1$, we have $m^2 - m + i$ votes, each of m^2 approvals for $c_{x,y}$ and $m^2 - 1$ dummy candidates $f_{x,y,z}$ where $z = 1$ to $m^2 - 1$. Similarly, for $x = 1$ to n and $y = 1$ to $m + x - 1$, we have $m^2 - m + x$ votes, each of m^2 approvals for $d_{x,y}$ and $m^2 - 1$ dummy candidates $g_{x,y,z}$ where $z = 1$ to $m^2 - 1$. Finally, for $y = 1$ to n, for each partial sum X_y, we have $m^2 - 2m + X_y$ votes, each of m^2 approvals for b_y and $m^2 - 1$ dummy candidates $h_{y,z}$ where $z = 1$ to $m^2 - 1$.

We now ask if we can cast $j = 2n$ additional votes so that the preferred candidates win. The candidates $c_{x,y}$ and $d_{x,y}$ each have a satisfaction score before the final agents vote of $1 - \frac{1}{m} + \frac{x}{m^2}$ ignoring higher order terms. For $c_{x,y}$ and $d_{x,y}$ to win, by a pigeonhole argument, they must each receive an approval vote from the $2n$ agents still to vote with between $m + x - 1$ and $m + x$ approvals. Similarly, the candidate b_y will have a satisfaction score before the agents vote of $1 - \frac{2}{m} + \frac{X_y}{m^2}$ ignoring higher order terms. Again, by a pigeonhole argument, each b_y must receive two approval ballots from the agents containing $m + \sigma(y)$ and $m + \pi(y)$ approvals respectively where $\sigma(y) + \pi(y) = X_y$. This also forces the approval ballots for $c_{x,y}$ and $d_{x,y}$ to win to contain exactly $m + x$ approvals. The winning ballots are thus of the form $\{c_{x,1}, \ldots, c_{x,m+y-1}, b_{\sigma(y)}\}$ and $\{d_{x,1}, \ldots, d_{x,m+y-1}, b_{\pi(y)}\}$. Note, we can swap $c_{x,l}$ and $d_{x,l'}$ between two such ballots without changing the result as long as the number of approvals in each ballot remains fixed. Hence, there is a manipulation if and only if there are two permutations with the appropriate sums. □

The proof requires neither the number of manipulating agents nor the size of the winning set to be constant. Thus, we turn to the special cases of a single agent and a pair of agents. Winning set manipulation is polynomial-time solvable with either one or two agents left to vote. This result holds even if the size of the winning set is not bounded (e.g. $k = m/2$).

On the other hand, *SAV–WSM* is polynomial-time solvable for $j = 1$ or 2. The main idea for the case for one manipulator is to identify the lexicographically minimum candidate $c \in W \setminus C^*$ with the highest satisfaction score when the manipulator does not vote. In order to ensure that C^* is the winning set (if possible), the manipulator approves all those candidates in C^* that either have smaller satisfaction score than c or the same score but lesser tie-breaking priority than c.

THEOREM 8. *If $j = 2$, then SAV–WSM can be solved in polynomial time.*

PROOF. Consider the satisfaction scores of the candidates in the winning set before agents 1 and 2 vote. Let s be the highest score of any candidate in $C^* \setminus W$. Let c be the lexicographically smallest candidate from $C^* \setminus W$ with score s.

Note that A_1 and A_2 will only include candidates in C^* since a vote on a candidate in $C \setminus C^*$ will never be beneficial. We show a simple algorithm such that if C^* can be made a winning set with two approval ballots of size at most j_1 and j_2 then the algorithm will produce two such ballots. Note that the manipulator ballots will add $1/j_1$ to the scores of the candidates approved by A_1 and $1/j_2$ to the scores of the candidates approved by A_2.

For every two integers j_1 and j_2, $k \geq j_1 \geq j_2 \geq 1$, the algorithm performs the following steps.

If there is a candidate $c' \in C^*$ such that c' has score less than $s - 1/j_2 - 1/j_1$ or c' has score equal to $s - 1/j_2 - 1/j_1$ and c is lexicographically smaller than c, then $C^* \neq W$ for any A_1 and A_2 with $|A_1| = j_1$ and $|A_2| = j_2$.

Otherwise, let C^*_- be the set of all candidates $c' \in C^*$ such that c' has score less than $s - 1/j_2$ or c' has score equal to $s - 1/j_2$ and c is lexicographically smaller than c'. The candidates in C^*_- must be in both A_1 and A_2 otherwise they will not reach a score of at least s. The candidates in C^* with score less than $s - 1/j_1$ (or equal to $s - 1/j_1$ if they are lexicographically larger than c) must be in A_2 and, finally, the remaining candidates in C^* with score smaller than s (or equal to s if they are lexicographically larger than c) must be in either A_1 or A_2. In the final step, one can distribute these candidates among A_1 and A_2 by guaranteeing, if possible, that $|A_1| \leq j_1$ and $|A_2| \leq j_2$.

	$\mathcal{R}$–WD	$\mathcal{R}$–TestWS	$\mathcal{R}$–WM	$\mathcal{R}$–WSM	$\mathcal{R}$–UM
AV	in P	in P	in P	in P	in P
PAV	**NP-hard** (Cor. 1)	**coNP-c** (Thm. 2)	**coNP-c** ($j = 1$) (Cor. 4)	**coNP-c** ($j = 1$) (Cor. 4)	**coNP-c** (Cor. 4)
RAV	in P	in P	**NP-c** ($j = 1$) (Thm. 5)	**NP-c** ($j = 1$) (Thm. 6)	**NP-c** ($j = 1$) (Cor. 5)
SAV	**in P** (Thm. 1)	**in P** (Thm. 1)	**in P** (Obs. 3)	**NP-c** (Thm. 7) **in P** ($j \in \{1, 2\}$) (Thm. 8)	**NP-c** (Thm. 10)

Table 1: Summary of computational results for approval-based multi-winner rules for **W**inner **D**etermination, **Test W**inning **S**et, **W**inner **M**anipulation, **W**inning **S**et **M**anipulation, and **U**tility **M**anipulation. Value j denotes the number of additional strategic ballots. Results in **bold** are from this paper; other results are from Kilgour [22] and Meir et al. [29].

If the size of A_1 is at most j_1 and the size of A_2 is at most j_2 then C^* is a winning set, otherwise there are no ballots with at most j_1 and j_2 approved candidates such that C^* is a winning set. □

In contrast to the complexity of *SAV*–WM, ensuring that a candidate c^* is *not* in the winning set of size k under rule *SAV* is intractable.

THEOREM 9. *The following problem is NP-complete: are there j additional approval ballots so that candidate c^* is* not *in the winning set of size k under rule SAV.*

Hence, in the case of multi-winner voting rules, destructive manipulation can be computationally harder than constructive manipulation. This contrasts to the single winner case where destructive manipulation is often easier than constructive manipulation [10]. It also follows from Theorem 9, simply by adding Boolean utilities to the winning set, that it is intractable for an agent (who can cast multiple ballots) to manipulate *SAV* to ensure at least a given utility.

THEOREM 10. *SAV–UM is NP-complete.*

6. CONCLUSIONS

We have studied some basic computational questions regarding three prominent rules for multi-winner approval voting: *PAV*, *RAV* and *SAV*. These three rules are designed with the intention of selecting a more representative set of winners than the more popular *AV* method. Our results are summarized in Table 1. We closed the computational complexity of computing the winner for *PAV* and studied the computational complexity of computing a best response for *PAV*, *RAV* and *SAV*. In many settings, we proved that it is NP-hard for an agent or agents to compute how best to vote given the other approval ballots.

Our most important conclusion is that among the three approval-based rules considered, *RAV* is the only rule for which winner determination is polynomial-time solvable but winner manipulation is NP-hard. From this computational perspective, *RAV* is more attractive than *AV*, *PAV*, and *SAV*. To complement this complexity study, it would be interesting to undertake further axiomatic and empirical analyses of prominent approval-based rules as well as considering other variants of the rules [23]. Such analyses would provide further insight into the relative merits of the voting methods. In addition, as several of our results are worst case, it would be interesting to undertake an empirical study that looks at the actual computational hardness in practice using, for instance, data from PrefLib.org [27].

Acknowledgments

NICTA is funded by the Australian Government through the Department of Communications and the Australian Research Council through the ICT Centre of Excellence Program. Serge Gaspers is the recipient of an Australian Research Council Discovery Early Career Researcher Award (project number DE120101761). Joachim Gudmundsson is funded by the Australian Research Council (project number FT100100755).

REFERENCES

[1] H. Aziz, S. Gaspers, N. Mattei, N. Narodytska, and T. Walsh. Ties matter: Complexity of manipulation when tie-breaking with a random vote. In *Proc. of the 27th AAAI Conference*, pages 74–80, 2013.

[2] H. Aziz, M. Brill, V. Conitzer, E. Elkind, R. Freeman, and T. Walsh. Justified representation in approval-based committee voting. In *Proc. of the 29th AAAI Conference*, 2015.

[3] J. Bartholdi, C. Tovey, and M. Trick. The computational difficulty of manipulating an election. *Social Choice and Welfare*, 6(3):227–241, 1989.

[4] D. Baumeister, G. Erdélyi, E. Hemaspaandra, L. A. Hemaspaandra, and J. Rothe. Computational aspects of approval voting. In *Handbook on Approval Voting*, chapter 10, pages 199–251. Springer, 2010.

[5] S. J. Brams and D. M. Kilgour. Satisfaction approval voting. In *Voting Power and Procedures*, Studies in Choice and Welfare, pages 323–346. Springer, 2014.

[6] S. J. Brams, D. M. Kilgour, and M. R. Sanver. Mathematics and democracy: Designing better voting and fair-division procedures. In *How to elect a representative committee using approval balloting*, pages 83–96. Springer, 2006.

[7] S. J. Brams, D. M. Kilgour, and M. R. Sanver. A minimax procedure for electing committees. *Public Choice*, 132:401–420, 2007.

[8] I. Caragiannis, D. Kalaitzis, and E. Markakis. Approximation algorithms and mechanism design for minimax approval voting. In *Proc. of the 24th AAAI Conference*, pages 737–742, 2010.

[9] V. Conitzer. Making decisions based on the preferences of multiple agents. *CACM*, 53(3):84–94, 2010.

[10] V. Conitzer, T. Sandholm, and J. Lang. When are elections with few candidates hard to manipulate? *JACM*, 54(3):14, 2007.

[11] J. Davies, G. Katsirelos, N. Narodytska, and T. Walsh. Complexity of and algorithms for Borda manipulation. In *Proc. of the 25th AAAI Conference*, pages 657–662, 2011.

[12] R. G. Downey and M. R. Fellows. *Fundamentals of Parameterized Complexity*. Texts in Computer Science. Springer, 2013.

[13] E. Elkind, J. Lang, and A. Saffidine. Choosing collectively optimal sets of alternatives based on the condorcet criterion. In *Proc. of the 22nd IJCAI*, pages 186–191, 2011.

[14] E. Elkind, P., Faliszewski, P. Skowron, and A. Slinko. Properties of multiwinner voting rules. In *Proc. of the 13th AAMAS Conference*, pages 53–60, 2014.

[15] P. Faliszewski and A. D. Procaccia. AI's war on manipulation: Are we winning? *AI Magazine*, 31(4):53–64, 2010.

[16] P. Faliszewski, E. Hemaspaandra, and L. A. Hemaspaandra. Using complexity to protect elections. *JACM*, 53(11):74–82, 2010.

[17] P. C. Fishburn. Axioms for approval voting: Direct proof. *Journal of Economic Theory*, 19(1):180–185, 1978.

[18] M. R. Garey and D. S. Johnson. *Computers and Intractability, A Guide to the Theory of NP-Completeness*. W.H. Freeman and Company, 1979.

[19] J. Goldsmith, J. Lang, N. Mattei, and P. Perny. Voting with rank dependent scoring rules. In *Proc. of the 28th AAAI Conference*, pages 698–704, 2014.

[20] J. Gramm, R. Niedermeier, and P. Rossmanith. Fixed-parameter algorithms for closest string and related problems. *Algorithmica*, 37(1):25–42, 2003.

[21] E. Hemaspaandra, L. Hemaspaandra, and J. Rothe. Exact analysis of Dodgson elections: Lewis Carroll's 1876 voting system is complete for parallel access to NP. *JACM*, 44(6):806–825, 1997.

[22] D. M. Kilgour. Approval balloting for multi-winner elections. In *Handbook on Approval Voting*, chapter 6. Springer, 2010.

[23] D. M. Kilgour and E. Marshall. Approval balloting for fixed-size committees. In *Electoral Systems*, Studies in Choice and Welfare, chapter 12, pages 305–326. Springer, 2012.

[24] K. Konczak and J. Lang. Voting procedures with incomplete preferences. In *Proc. of the 3rd MPREF Workshop*, 2005.

[25] J.-F. Laslier and M. R. Sanver, editors. *Handbook on Approval Voting*. Studies in Choice and Welfare. Springer, 2010.

[26] R. LeGrand, E. Markakis, and A. Mehta. Some results on approximating the minimax solution in approval voting. In *Proc. of the 6th AAMAS Conference*, pages 1193–1195, 2007.

[27] N. Mattei and T. Walsh. Preflib: A library for preferences, http://www.preflib.org. In *Proc. of the 3rd ADT Conference*, pages 259–270, 2013.

[28] R. Meir, A. D. Procaccia, and J. S. Rosenschein. A broader picture of the complexity of strategic behavior in multi-winner elections. In *Proc. of the 7th AAMAS Conference*, pages 991–998, 2008.

[29] R. Meir, A. D. Procaccia, J. S. Rosenschein, and A. Zohar. Complexity of strategic behavior in multi-winner elections. *JAIR*, 33:149–178, 2008.

[30] S. Obraztsova and E. Elkind. On the complexity of voting manipulation under randomized tie-breaking. In *Proc. of the 22nd IJCAI*, pages 319–324, 2011.

[31] S. Obraztsova, E. Elkind, and N. Hazon. Ties matter: Complexity of voting manipulation revisited. In *Proc. of the 10th AAMAS Conference*, pages 71–78, 2011.

[32] S. Obraztsova, Y. Zick, and E. Elkind. On manipulation in multi-winner elections based on scoring rules. In *Proc. of the 12th AAMAS Conference*, pages 359–366, 2013.

[33] T. C. Ratliff. Selecting committees. *Public Choice*, 126 (3/4):343–355, 2006.

[34] P. Skowron, P. Faliszewski, and A. Slinko. Fully proportional representation as resource allocation: Approximability results. In *Proc. of the 23rd IJCAI*, pages 353–359, 2013.

[35] P. Skowron, P. Faliszewski, and A. Slinko. Achieving fully proportional representation is easy in practice. In *Proc. of the 12th AAMAS Conference*, pages 399–406, 2013.

[36] P. Skowron, P. Faliszewski, and J. Lang. Finding a collective set of items: From proportional multi-representation to group recommendation. In *Proc. of the 4th COMSOC Workshop*, 2014.

[37] T. Walsh. Uncertainty in preference elicitation and aggregation. In *Proc. of the 22nd AAAI Conference*, pages 3–8, 2007.

Complexity of the Winner Determination Problem in Judgment Aggregation: Kemeny, Slater, Tideman, Young

Ulle Endriss
ILLC, University of Amsterdam
ulle.endriss@uva.nl

Ronald de Haan
Technische Universität Wien
dehaan@kr.tuwien.ac.at

ABSTRACT

Judgment aggregation is a collective decision making framework where the opinions of a group of agents is combined into a collective opinion. This can be done using many different judgment aggregation procedures. We study the computational complexity of computing the group opinion for several of the most prominent judgment aggregation procedures. In particular, we show that the complexity of this winner determination problem for analogues of the Kemeny rule, the Slater rule and the Young rule lies at the Θ_2^p-level of the Polynomial Hierarchy (PH). Moreover, we show that the problem has a complexity at the Δ_2^p-level of the PH for the analogue of Tideman's procedure with a fixed tie-breaking rule, and at the Σ_2^p-level of the PH for the analogue of Tideman's procedure without a fixed tie-breaking rule.

Categories and Subject Descriptors

F.2 [**Analysis of Algorithms and Problem Complexity**]: General

General Terms

Theory

Keywords

Judgment Aggregation; Winner Determination; Complexity Theory; Bounded Query Complexity

1. INTRODUCTION

Collective decision making is central in the area of multiagent systems [6]. Judgment aggregation is a collective decision making framework that can be used for many applications [12, 17, 23]. In judgment aggregation, the goal is to combine the opinions of a group of individuals (or agents) on a set of propositions into a collective opinion reflecting the views of the group as a whole. As such, judgment aggregation generalizes the setting of preference aggregation, where the opinions are restricted to preferences over a given domain of alternatives [9]. There are many ways (or procedures) to combine the individual opinions, and choosing between such procedures involves deciding between various desirable properties that such procedures can have. Some of the most salient desiderata for these procedures are that they are consistent (that is, the resulting group opinion is a tenable position) and complete (that is, for each proposition, the resulting group opinion takes a clear position).

Another important property of judgment aggregation procedures concerns their computational complexity, i.e., the amount of time it takes to compute the group opinion. In this paper, expanding on previous work [13, 21], we study the computational complexity of the winner determination problem for several of the most prominent judgment aggregation procedures that are complete and consistent. In particular, we study the judgment aggregation analogues of the Kemeny rule, the Slater rule and the Young rule, as well as two variants of Tideman's Ranked-Pairs rule (whose judgment aggregation analogue we call the Ranked-Agenda rule), all familiar from voting theory and preference aggregation [5].

Concretely, we study two different computational problems for the various procedures, one decision problem and one search problem. We consider the problem of deciding whether there exists an outcome that is deemed acceptable by the judgment aggregation procedure and that satisfies a number of additional requirements. In addition, we consider the computational task of producing one such acceptable outcome, if it exists. We argue that this latter formalization of the problem more adequately models the relevant computational properties of the various procedures. We show that the complexity (of both the decision and the search problem) for the Kemeny, Slater and Young rules lies at the Θ_2^p-level of the Polynomial Hierarchy (PH). Interestingly, these rules have exactly the same complexity in the setting of preference aggregation. In addition, we show that the complexity of Tideman's Ranked-Agenda procedure lies at the Δ_2^p-level of the PH, in case of a fixed tie-breaking rule, and lies at the Σ_2^p-level of the PH in case ties can be broken in arbitrary ways. It is interesting that both variants of the Ranked-Agenda rule are of higher computational complexity than the other three rules we consider in the setting of judgment aggregation, whereas in the case of preference aggregation both variants are of lower complexity than these rules. An overview of the complexity results that we obtain in this paper can be found in Table 1.

Understanding the complexity of the winner determination problem is a first step to making these important, but generally highly intractable, procedures amenable to practical use in multiagent systems and related fields requiring the consistent aggregation of information coming from several

Appears in: *Proceedings of the 14th International Conference on Autonomous Agents and Multiagent Systems (AAMAS 2015), Bordini, Elkind, Weiss, Yolum (eds.), May 4–8, 2015, Istanbul, Turkey.*

autonomous agents, or more generally, independent sources of information. Determining the exact location of these problems in the PH is very useful for determining what algorithmic approaches are best-suited to solve the problems in practice. For problems at the Θ_2^p-level and at the Δ_2^p-level, for instance, the method of iterative SAT solving could be used, which is generally more efficient than solving methods for problems at the Σ_2^p-level.

Related Work.

The computational complexity of the winner determination problem has been studied before, by Endriss et al. [13] for several procedures including the Kemeny rule, and by Lang and Slavkovik [21] for several procedures, including the Slater rule, the Kemeny rule and the variant of the Ranked-Agenda procedure without a fixed tie-breaking rule. However, those previous works consider different formalizations of the computational task of winner determination. First, they study only decision problems (and no search problems) [13, 21]. Second, the problems studied by Lang and Slavkovik involve checking whether all outcomes satisfy a certain property, rather than some outcome [21]. The computational complexity of various other computational tasks in judgment aggregation has also been studied, including problems related to manipulation, bribery and control [1, 3, 4, 8, 13].

Structure of the Paper.

We begin, in Section 2, with reviewing notions from logic, judgment aggregation and complexity theory. Then, in Section 3, we formally define the computational problems that we use to capture the task of winner determination, and we analyze their computational complexity for the various judgment aggregation procedures. Finally, in Section 4, we conclude, and suggest directions for further research.

2. PRELIMINARIES

In this section we review relevant material on logic, judgment aggregation and complexity theory.

2.1 Propositional Logic

A *literal* is a propositional variable x or a negated variable $\neg x$. For literals $l \in \{x, \neg x\}$, we let $\text{Var}(l) = x$ denote the variable occurring in l. A *clause* is a finite set of literals, not containing a complementary pair $x, \neg x$, and is interpreted as the disjunction of these literals. We let $\bot$ denote the empty clause. A formula in *conjunctive normal form (CNF)* is a finite set of clauses, interpreted as the conjunction of these clauses. We define the *size* $||\varphi||$ of a CNF formula φ to be $\sum_{c \in \varphi} |c|$; the number of clauses of φ is denoted by $|\varphi|$. For a CNF formula φ, the set $\text{Var}(\varphi)$ denotes the set of all variables x such that some clause of φ contains x or $\neg x$. We use the standard notion of *(truth) assignments* $\alpha : \text{Var}(\varphi) \to \{0, 1\}$ for Boolean formulas and *truth* of a formula under such an assignment. We let SAT denote the problem of deciding whether a given propositional formula is satisfiable. For every propositional formula φ, we let $\sim\varphi$ denote the *complement* of φ, i.e., $\sim\varphi = \neg\varphi$ if φ is not of the form $\neg\psi$, and $\sim\varphi = \psi$ if φ is of the form $\neg\psi$.

2.2 Judgment Aggregation

An *agenda* is a finite nonempty set Φ of propositional formulas that does not contain any doubly-negated formulas and that is closed under complementation. Moreover, if $\Phi = \{\varphi_1, \dots, \varphi_m, \neg\varphi_1, \dots, \neg\varphi_m\}$ is an agenda, then we let $[\Phi] = \{\varphi_1, \dots, \varphi_m\}$ denote the *preagenda* associated with the agenda Φ. A *judgment set* J for an agenda Φ is a subset $J \subseteq \Phi$. We call a judgment set J *complete* if either $\varphi \in J$ or $\sim\varphi \in J$, for all $\varphi \in \Phi$; we call it *complement-free* if for all $\varphi \in \Phi$ it is not the case that both φ and $\sim\varphi$ are in J; and we call it *consistent* if there exists a truth assignment that makes all formulas in J true.

In addition, we associate with each agenda Φ an integrity constraint Γ, that can be used to explicitly represent logical dependencies between agenda issues. Integrity constraints for agendas have been considered in previous literature [10, 21], and the notion bears resemblance to the framework of binary aggregation with integrity constraints [15, 16]. Such an integrity constraint Γ consists of a single propositional formula. In the remainder of the paper, if no integrity constraint is specified, we implicitly assume that $\Gamma = \top$. We say that a judgment set J is *Γ-consistent* if there exists a truth assignment that simultaneously makes all formulas in J and Γ true. Let $\mathcal{J}(\Phi, \Gamma)$ denote the set of all complete and Γ-consistent subsets of Φ.

Let $\mathcal{N}$ be a finite set of *individuals* (or *agents*). A *judgment aggregation procedure (or rule)* for the agenda Φ and the set $\mathcal{N}$ of individuals is a function F that takes as input a profile $\boldsymbol{J} \in \mathcal{J}(\Phi, \Gamma)^n$, consisting of a sequence $(J_1, \dots, J_n)$ of $n = |\mathcal{N}|$ complete and Γ-consistent judgment sets, and that produces a non-empty set of non-empty judgment sets, i.e., it produces an element in $\mathcal{P}(\mathcal{P}(\Phi)\backslash\{\emptyset\})\backslash\{\emptyset\}$. We call a judgment aggregation procedure F *resolute* if for any profile $\boldsymbol{J}$ it returns a singleton, i.e., $|F(\boldsymbol{J})| = 1$; otherwise, we call F *irresolute*. An example of a resolute judgment aggregation procedure is the *strict majority rule* F^{maj}, where $\varphi \in F^{\text{maj}}(\boldsymbol{J})$ if and only if φ occurs in the strict majority of judgment sets in $\boldsymbol{J}$, for all $\varphi \in \Phi$. We call F *complete*, *complement-free* and *(Γ-)consistent*, if J is complete, complement-free and (Γ-)consistent, respectively, for every $\boldsymbol{J} \in \mathcal{J}(\Phi, \Gamma)^n$ and every $J \in F(\boldsymbol{J})$.

As an example, consider the following profile for a judgment aggregation problem with preagenda $[\Phi] = \{p, q, p \vee q\}$, integrity constraint $\Gamma = \neg(p \wedge q)$, and three individuals:

	p	q	$p \vee q$
individual 1	no	yes	yes
individual 2	yes	no	yes
individual 3	no	no	no
majority	no	no	yes

Thus, respecting majorities leads to an inconsistent outcome for this profile. This is an instance of the well-known *discursive dilemma* [22]. In this paper, we will consider several judgment aggregation procedures that resolve this dilemma by always picking from the set of all consistent judgment sets. There currently is no consistent naming convention for these aggregation procedures in the literature. Here, to identify the procedures that we consider, we use names from well-known voting rules that most closely resemble them [5]. The procedures that we consider have been studied as judgment aggregation procedures before. We consider procedures that resemble the Kemeny rule [24, 25], the Slater rule [24], the Young rule [20], and the Ranked-Agenda rule [20, 26].

The former three aggregation procedures are based on a notion of score. For F $\in$ {Kemeny, Slater, Young}, we define Score_F as follows. Here J denotes a single consistent and complete judgment set, $\boldsymbol{J} \in \mathcal{J}(\Phi, \Gamma)^n$ denotes

F	WinDet(F)	FWinDet(F)	location in the PH
Kemeny	P^{NP}[log]-complete	$\mathrm{FP}^{\mathrm{NP}}$[log,wit]-complete	Θ_2^{p}-level
Slater	P^{NP}[log]-complete	$\mathrm{FP}^{\mathrm{NP}}$[log,wit]-complete	Θ_2^{p}-level
Young	P^{NP}[log]-complete	$\mathrm{FP}^{\mathrm{NP}}$[log,wit]-complete	Θ_2^{p}-level
Tideman (fixed tie-breaking)	P^{NP}-complete	$\mathrm{FP}^{\mathrm{NP}}$-complete	Δ_2^{p}-level
Tideman	Σ_2^{p}-complete	$\mathrm{F}\Sigma_2^{\mathrm{p}}$-complete	Σ_2^{p}-level

Table 1: Overview of complexity results.

a profile, and $d(J,J')$ denotes the Hamming distance between two consistent and complete judgment sets J, J'. We let $\mathrm{Score}_{\mathrm{Kemeny}}(J,\boldsymbol{J}) = \sum_{1 \leq i \leq n} d(J,J_i)$. Moreover, we let $\mathrm{Score}_{\mathrm{Slater}}(J,\boldsymbol{J}) = d(J,F^{\mathrm{maj}}(\boldsymbol{J}))$, where $F^{\mathrm{maj}}(\boldsymbol{J})$ denotes the (possibly inconsistent) majority outcome of a profile $\boldsymbol{J}$. Finally, we let $\mathrm{Score}_{\mathrm{Young}}(J,\boldsymbol{J}) = \min\{\, k :$ there exists a subprofile $\boldsymbol{J}'$ of $\boldsymbol{J}$ containing $n-k$ judgment sets such that $J = F^{\mathrm{maj}}(\boldsymbol{J}')\,\}$. Using these scores, we can define the aggregation procedures $\mathrm{Winner}_{\mathrm{F},\Phi,\Gamma}$, for $\mathrm{F} \in \{$Kemeny, Slater, Young$\}$, as follows. We say that a Γ-consistent and complete judgment set J^* is in $\mathrm{Winner}_{\mathrm{F},\Phi,\Gamma}(\boldsymbol{J})$ if and only if there is no Γ-consistent and complete judgment set J such that $\mathrm{Score}_{\mathrm{F}}(J,\boldsymbol{J}) < \mathrm{Score}_{\mathrm{F}}(J^*,\boldsymbol{J})$.

Intuitively, the *Kemeny* rule selects those complete and consistent judgment sets that minimize the cumulative Hamming distance to the judgment sets in the profile. The *Slater* rule selects those complete and consistent judgment sets that minimize the Hamming distance to the majority outcome. The *Young* rule selects those complete and consistent judgment sets that are the majority outcome of a subprofile of maximal size with a consistent majority outcome.

Next, we consider the *Ranked-Agenda* aggregation procedure. Given a profile $\boldsymbol{J} = (J_1,\dots,J_n) \in \mathcal{J}(\Phi,\Gamma)^n$ and a formula $\varphi \in \Phi$, we let the *majority strength* $\mathrm{ms}(\boldsymbol{J},\varphi)$ be the number of i's such that $\varphi \in J_i$, i.e., $\mathrm{ms}(\boldsymbol{J},\varphi) = |\{\, 1 \leq i \leq n : \varphi \in J_i \,\}|$. We define the partial order $\leq_{\boldsymbol{J}} \subseteq \Phi \times \Phi$ as follows. Let $\varphi, \varphi' \in \Phi$ be formulas. If $\mathrm{ms}(\boldsymbol{J},\varphi) < \mathrm{ms}(\boldsymbol{J},\varphi')$, we let $\varphi \leq_{\boldsymbol{J}} \varphi'$; and if $\mathrm{ms}(\boldsymbol{J},\varphi) = \mathrm{ms}(\boldsymbol{J},\varphi')$, we let $\varphi \not\leq_{\boldsymbol{J}} \varphi'$. We say that a total order $<_{\boldsymbol{J}}$ is a *Ranked-Agenda order (for $\boldsymbol{J}$)* if it extends $\leq_{\boldsymbol{J}}$. Given a Ranked-Agenda order $<_{\boldsymbol{J}}$, we define the judgment set $\mathrm{RA}(<_{\boldsymbol{J}},\Phi,\Gamma)$ as follows. Let $\Phi = \{\varphi_1,\dots,\varphi_m\}$ and assume that $\varphi_1 >_{\boldsymbol{J}} \cdots >_{\boldsymbol{J}} \varphi_{2m}$. We let $J_0 = \emptyset$. For each $1 \leq i \leq 2m$, we let $J_i = J_{i-1} \cup \{\varphi_i\}$ if $J_{i-1} \cup \{\varphi_i\}$ is Γ-consistent; otherwise, we let $J_i = J_{i-1}$. By definition, each J_i is Γ-consistent. (Note that we could equivalently let $J_i = J_{i-1} \cup \{\neg\varphi_i\}$ if $J_{i-1} \cup \{\varphi_i\}$ is not Γ-consistent.) We then let $\mathrm{RA}(<_{\boldsymbol{J}},\Phi,\Gamma) = J_{2m}$. Given any total order $<^A \subseteq \Phi \times \Phi$, and a partial order $\leq_{\boldsymbol{J}}$, we define the Ranked-Agenda order $<_{\boldsymbol{J}}^A$ to be the unique total order such that: (1) $\varphi <_{\boldsymbol{J}}^A \varphi'$ whenever $\varphi \leq_{\boldsymbol{J}} \varphi'$ and $\varphi' \not\leq_{\boldsymbol{J}} \varphi$; and (2) $\varphi <_{\boldsymbol{J}}^A \varphi'$ if and only if $\varphi <^A \varphi'$, whenever $\varphi =_{\boldsymbol{J}} \varphi'$. We now say that a Γ-consistent and complete judgment set $J^* \in \mathcal{J}(\Phi,\Gamma)$ is a *Ranked-Agenda winner*, denoted $J^* \in \mathrm{Winner}_{\mathrm{RA},\Phi,\Gamma}(\boldsymbol{J})$ if there is some Ranked-Agenda order $<_{\boldsymbol{J}}$ for $\boldsymbol{J}$ such that $J^* = \mathrm{RA}(<_{\boldsymbol{J}},\Phi,\Gamma)$. We say that a tie-breaking rule A is defined by a total order $<^A \subseteq \Phi \times \Phi$ for each agenda Φ. Moreover, we say that a Γ-consistent and complete judgment set $J^* \in \mathcal{J}(\Phi,\Gamma)$ is a *Ranked-Agenda winner for the fixed tie-breaking rule A*, denoted $J^* \in \mathrm{Winner}_{\mathrm{RA}_A,\Phi,\Gamma}(\boldsymbol{J})$ if $J^* = \mathrm{RA}(<_{\boldsymbol{J}}^A,\Phi,\Gamma)$. In voting, it is pairs (of alternatives) rather than propositions that are being ranked, which is why the corresponding voting rule is called the Ranked-Pairs rule.

2.3 Complexity Theory

Readers familiar with seach problems and bounded query complexity may skip this section.

Search Problems.

In this paper, we will assume knowledge of to the well-known complexity classes P and NP, consisting of decision problems. In addition, we will consider search problems. Let Σ be an alphabet. A *search problem* is a binary relation R over strings in Σ^*. For any input string $x \in \Sigma^*$, we let $R(x) = \{\, y \in \Sigma^* : (x,y) \in R \,\}$ denote the set of *solutions* for x. We say that a Turing machine T *solves* R if on input $x \in \Sigma^*$ the following holds: if there exists at least one y such that $(x,y) \in R$, then T accepts x and outputs some y such that $(x,y) \in R$; otherwise, T rejects x. With any search problem R we associate a decision problem S_R, defined by $S_R = \{\, x \in \Sigma^* :$ there exists some $y \in \Sigma^*$ such that $(x,y) \in R \,\}$. We will use the following notion of reductions for search problems. A *polynomial-time Levin reduction* from one search problem R_1 to another search problem R_2 is a pair of polynomial-time computable functions (g_1,g_2) such that (1) the function g_1 is a many-one reduction from S_{R_1} to S_{R_2}, i.e., for every $x \in \Sigma^*$ it holds that $x \in S_{R_1}$ if and only if $g_1(x) \in S_{R_2}$; and (2) for every string $x \in S_{R_1}$ and every solution $y \in R_2(g_1(x))$ it holds that $(x, g_2(x,y)) \in R_1$. For more details, we refer to textbooks on the topic [14].

Complexity Classes.

The complexity class FP consists of those search problems that can be computed by a polynomial-time deterministic Turing machine, and the class FNP consists of those search problems that can be computed by a polynomial-time nondeterministic Turing machine.

Moreover, we will use complexity classes that are based on Turing machines that have access to an oracle. Let C be a complexity class with decision problems. A Turing machine T with access to a *yes-no C oracle* is a Turing machine with a dedicated *oracle tape* and dedicated states q_{oracle}, q_{yes} and q_{no}. Whenever T is in the state q_{oracle}, it does not proceed according to the transition relation, but instead it transitions into the state q_{yes} if the oracle tape contains a string x that is a yes-instance for the problem C, i.e., if $x \in C$, and it transitions into the state q_{no} if $x \notin C$. Let C be a complexity class with search problems. Similarly, a Turing machine with access to a *witness C oracle* has a dedicated oracle tape and dedicated states q_{oracle}, q_{yes} and q_{no}. Also, whenever T is in the state q_{oracle} it transitions into the state q_{yes} if the oracle tape contains a string x such that there exists some y such that $C(x,y)$, and in addition the contents of the oracle tape are replaced by (the encoding of) such an y; it transitions into the state q_{no} if there exists no y such that $C(x,y)$. Such transitions are called *oracle queries*.

We point out that the notion of algorithms that have access to witness FNP oracles accurately models algorithms that can call a SAT solver (modulo the running time of the SAT solver), as SAT solvers also return a satisfying assignment if it exists.

In this paper, we will consider the following complexity classes that are based on oracle machines. The class $P^{NP}[\log]$ consists of all decision problems that can be decided by a deterministic polynomial-time Turing machine that has access to a yes-no NP oracle, and on any input of length n queries the oracle at most $O(\log n)$ many times. This class coincides with the class $P^{NP}_{||}$, and is also known as Θ^p_2.

The class $FP^{NP}[\log,wit]$ consists of all search problems that can be solved by a deterministic polynomial-time Turing machine that has access to a witness FNP oracle, and on any input of length n queries the oracle at most $O(\log n)$ many times. In a sense, it is the search variant of $P^{NP}[\log]$.

The class $F\Sigma^p_2$ consists of all search problems that can be computed by a nondeterministic polynomial-time Turing machine that has access to a witness FNP oracle. In a sense, it is the search variant of Σ^p_2.

We say that a decision problem P is complete for a complexity class C containing decision problems if any problem $Q \in C$ is polynomial-time (many-one) reducible to P. Similarly, we say that a search problem R is complete for a complexity class C containing search problems if for any problem $R' \in C$ there exists a polynomial-time Levin reduction from R' to R.

Complete Problems.

Next, we consider a number of search and decision problems that are complete for the various complexity classes that we consider in this paper. The decision problem SAT is NP-complete. This problem consists of deciding whether a given propositional formula φ has a satisfying assignment. The corresponding search problem, FSAT, consisting of all pairs (φ, α), where α is a satisfying assignment for φ, is FNP-complete. Next, consider the following problems.

> X-MAX-MODEL
> *Input:* a formula φ and a subset $X \subseteq \text{Var}(\varphi)$ of variables of φ.
> *Output:* a model M of φ that sets a maximum number of variables in X to true, if such a model exists.

> X-MAX-MODEL-PARITY
> *Instance:* a formula φ, a subset $X \subseteq \text{Var}(\varphi)$ of variables of φ, and a variable $x_0 \in X$.
> *Question:* is there a model M of φ such that X-MAX-MODEL(φ, M) and M sets x_0 to true?

The search problem X-MAX-MODEL is complete for $FP^{NP}[\log,wit]$ [7]. Moreover, the decision problem X-MAX-MODEL-PARITY is complete for $P^{NP}[\log]$. This follows from the fact that all predicates in $FP^{NP}[\log,wit]$ are computable in $P^{NP}[\log]$ [18, Corollary 6.3.5].

> FLEX-MAX-MODEL
> *Input:* a formula φ with $\text{Var}(\varphi) = \{x_1, \dots, x_n\}$.
> *Output:* a lexicographically maximal model M of φ, if such a model exists. (Here, the variables are ordered $x_1 < \dots < x_n$.)

> LEX-MAX-MODEL
> *Instance:* a formula φ and a variable $x_0 \in \text{Var}(\varphi)$.
> *Question:* is there a model M of φ such that FLEX-MAX-MODEL(φ, M) and M sets x_0 to true?

The search problem FLEX-MAX-MODEL is complete for FP^{NP}, and the decision problem LEX-MAX-MODEL is complete for P^{NP} [19].

> $FQSAT_2$
> *Input:* a quantified Boolean formula $\varphi = \exists X. \forall Y. \psi$, where ψ is quantifier-free.
> *Output:* an assignment α to the variables in X, such that $\forall Y. \psi[\alpha]$ is true, if it exists.

The decision problem $QSAT_2$ associated to $FQSAT_2$ is well-known to be Σ^p_2-complete. The search problem $FQSAT_2$ is complete for $F\Sigma^p_2$. This can be shown straightforwardly by modifying the proof of Σ^p_2-completeness for $QSAT_2$ [27, 28], which can also be found in many textbooks (e.g., [2]).

3. COMPLEXITY RESULTS

For the various judgment aggregation procedures F, we will consider the following decision problem.

> WINDET(F)
> *Instance:* an agenda Φ with an integrity constraint Γ, a profile $\boldsymbol{J} \in \mathcal{J}(\Phi, \Gamma)^n$ and a number of subsets $L_0, \dots, L_u \subseteq \Phi$ of the agenda, with $u \geq 0$.
> *Question:* is there a judgment set $J^* \in \text{Winner}_{F,\Phi,\Gamma}(\boldsymbol{J})$ such that $L_0 \subseteq J^*$ and $L_i \not\subseteq J^*$ for each $1 \leq i \leq u$?

In addition, we will consider the following search problem.

> FWINDET(F)
> *Input:* an agenda Φ with an integrity constraint Γ, a profile $\boldsymbol{J} \in \mathcal{J}(\Phi, \Gamma)^n$ and a number of subsets $L_0, \dots, L_u \subseteq \Phi$ of the agenda, with $u \geq 0$.
> *Output:* a judgment set $J^* \in \text{Winner}_{F,\Phi,\Gamma}(\boldsymbol{J})$ such that $L_0 \subseteq J^*$ and $L_i \not\subseteq J^*$ for each $1 \leq i \leq u$, if it exists.

In these problems, the set L_0 allows us to specify judgments that the outcome must contain. Moreover, using the sets $L_1, \dots, L_u$, we can specify a list of forbidden (combinations of) judgments that the outcome may not contain. This allows us, for instance, to enumerate several outcomes by using previously found outcomes as the sets $L_1, \dots, L_u$.

We make several observations about this formalization of the computational task of winner determination for the judgment aggregation procedures. In previous work [13, 21], only decision problems have been studied. We argue that the search problem formulation is a more accurate formalization of the computational task related to the winner determination problem in judgment aggregation. In general, for any judgment aggregation procedure, given a multiagent setting and individual opinions of the agents, one would like to compute a group opinion, which could then be used for various purposes. Given access to an algorithm that performs the computational task captured by the decision problem, one needs a linear number of calls to produce the description of an outcome. However, it turns out that (under some common complexity-theoretic assumptions) any such (deterministic) algorithm invokes an NP oracle only a small (sublinear) number of times in the worst case. This was known for the case of the Kemeny rule [13], and we show that it is also the case for the Slater and Young rules. Therefore, it could be that an algorithm that produces an outcome by simply calling an algorithm for the decision problem a linear number of times exceeds the minimum number of calls to the

NP oracle that are needed. In fact, we show that producing an outcome can be done in deterministic polynomial time with only a logarithmic number of calls to an oracle that produces witnesses for NP problems. Formalizing the task as a search problem in the first place circumvents this issue.

Secondly, these computational problems involve the question whether there exists an outcome that satisfies certain properties, rather than the question whether all outcomes satisfy certain properties (as studied by Lang and Slavkovik [21]). We think the former question is the more natural of these two, as computing outcomes for judgment aggregation procedures is arguably the most central computational task in judgment aggregation.

The third observation concerns the condition that the subsets $L_1, \dots, L_u$, given as part of the input to the problems, are not subsets of the judgment set $J^* \in \text{Winner}_{F,\Phi,\Gamma}(\boldsymbol{J})$. As can be seen in the proofs in the remainder of this section, this condition does not have an effect on the complexity analysis of the problem. However, it does allow us to use this formalization of the problem to devise an algorithm to enumerate outcomes of judgment aggregation procedures. In order to enumerate outcomes, one could use an algorithm that solves FWINDET(F) repeatedly, and rule out previously found outcomes by providing them as the subsets L_i (with $i > 0$).

We obtain the following complexity results for these two computational problems (summarized in Table 1).

THEOREM 1. *For each* F $\in$ {Kemeny, Slater, Young}*:*

a) WINDET(F) *is* P^{NP}[log]*-complete; and*

b) FWINDET(F) *is* FP^{NP}[log,wit]*-complete.*

THEOREM 2. *For any tie-breaking rule A, it holds that* WINDET(RA_A) *is in* P^{NP} *and* FWINDET(RA_A) *is in* FP^{NP}. *Moreover, there is some tie-breaking rule A such that* WINDET(RA_A) *is* P^{NP}*-complete and* FWINDET(RA_A) *is* FP^{NP}*-complete.*

THEOREM 3. WINDET(RA) *is* Σ_2^{p}*-complete and* FWINDET(RA) *is* $\text{F}\Sigma_2^{\text{p}}$*-complete.*

We would like to point out that the complexity result for WINDET(KEMENY) has been shown before [13]. We give an alternative proof of hardness for this problem. We prove hardness by giving a reduction directly from a canonical complete problem for P^{NP}[log], which allows us to extend this hardness result to the case of the search problem FWINDET(KEMENY), which would not have been at all straightforward with the known P^{NP}[log]-hardness proof for WINDET(KEMENY) from the literature.

We begin by proving Theorem 1 in Sections 3.1–3.3 (Propositions 5–9 and Corollaries 6–10). Then, we prove Theorems 2 and 3 in Section 3.4 (Propositions 11–12 and Corollaries 13–14, and Propositions 15–16 and Corollary 17, respectively).

3.1 Membership for Kemeny, Slater, Young

We will show FP^{NP}[log,wit]-membership of the problem FWINDET(F), for each F $\in$ {Kemeny, Slater, Young} by giving a polynomial-time algorithm that uses an FNP witness oracle at most $O(\log n)$ many times. Since P^{NP}[log] coincides with P^{NP}[log,wit], this algorithm can then easily be adapted to show P^{NP}[log]-membership of WINDET(F). The approach that we use to show these membership results is similar to the approach taken in the known P^{NP}[log]-membership proof of WINDET(KEMENY) [13].

For each F $\in$ {Kemeny, Slater, Young}, we will consider the following auxiliary problem.

> FSETSCORE(F)
> *Input:* an agenda Φ with an integrity constraint Γ, a profile $\boldsymbol{J} \in \mathcal{J}(\Phi, \Gamma)$, a number of subsets $L_0, \dots, L_u \subseteq \Phi$, with $u \geq 0$, and a positive integer m (in unary).
> *Output:* a consistent and complete judgment set J such that $L_0 \subseteq J$, $L_i \not\subseteq J$ for each $1 \leq i \leq u$, and $\text{Score}_F(J, \boldsymbol{J}) \leq m$, if it exists.

LEMMA 4. *For each* F $\in$ {Kemeny, Slater, Young}, *it holds that* FSETSCORE(F) $\in$ FNP.

PROOF (SKETCH). We describe a guess-and-check algorithm for FSETSCORE(F). The algorithm gets as input an agenda Φ with an integrity constraint Γ, a profile $\boldsymbol{J} \in \mathcal{J}(\Phi, \Gamma)$, a number of subsets $L_0, \dots, L_u \subseteq \Phi$ of the agenda, with $u \geq 0$, and a positive integer m in unary. The algorithm guesses a complete judgment set J, and an interpretation M that witnesses that J is Γ-consistent. Additionally, if F = Young, the algorithm guesses $\ell \leq m$ many judgment sets $J_{i_1}, \dots, J_{i_\ell}$ in $\boldsymbol{J}$ to remove from $\boldsymbol{J}$. Then, the algorithm verifies (1) whether M satisfies both J and Γ, (2) whether $\text{Score}_F(J, \boldsymbol{J}) \leq m$, (3) whether $L_0 \subseteq J$, and (4) whether $L_i \not\subseteq J$ for each $1 \leq i \leq u$. If F = Young, the verification of (2) uses the guessed judgment sets $J_{i_1}, \dots, J_{i_\ell}$. It is straightforward to verify that these checks can be done in polynomial time. If J satisfies conditions (1)–(4), the algorithm accepts and outputs J; otherwise, the algorithm rejects. ☐

PROPOSITION 5. *For each* F $\in$ {Kemeny, Slater, Young}, FWINDET(F) $\in$ FP^{NP}[log,wit].

PROOF (SKETCH). We describe a polynomial-time algorithm that computes FWINDET(F) by using an FSETSCORE(F) oracle. The algorithm firstly computes the minimal number m^* such that there is some Γ-consistent and complete judgment set J such that $\text{Score}_F(J, \boldsymbol{J}) \leq m^*$. For each F $\in$ {Kemeny, Slater, Young}, we know that m^* is polynomially bounded by the size of (the encoding of) $\boldsymbol{J}$. Therefore, we can employ a binary search strategy to compute m^* by asking $O(\log |\boldsymbol{J}|)$ many oracle queries of the form $(\Phi, \Gamma, \boldsymbol{J}, \emptyset, m)$. Then, the algorithm returns the answer to the oracle query $(\Phi, \Gamma, \boldsymbol{J}, L_0, \dots, L_u, m^*)$. ☐

COROLLARY 6. *For each* F $\in$ {Kemeny, Slater, Young}, WINDET(F) $\in$ P^{NP}[log].

3.2 Hardness for Kemeny and Slater

PROPOSITION 7. *The problems* FWINDET(KEMENY) *and* FWINDET(SLATER) *are* FP^{NP}[log,wit]*-hard, even with the restriction that* $\Gamma = \top$, *and* $u = 0$.

PROOF (SKETCH). We give a polynomial-time Levin reduction from X-MAX-MODEL. The same reduction works for both FWINDET(KEMENY) and FWINDET(SLATER). Let (φ, X) be an input to X-MAX-MODEL with $X = \{x_1, \dots, x_v\} \subseteq \text{Var}(\varphi)$. We construct an agenda Φ, an integrity constraint $\Gamma = \top$, an integer $u = 0$, a subset $L_0 \subseteq \Phi$, and a profile $\boldsymbol{J} \in \mathcal{J}(\Phi, \Gamma)^n$ as follows. We pick some w

such that $w > v^2$, e.g., $w = 2v^2$. For each $1 \leq i \leq v$ and $1 \leq j \leq w$, we introduce a fresh variable $z_{j,i}$. Moreover, we introduce a fresh variabe y. Then, we construct a propositional formula φ' that is true if and only if one of the following conditions holds: either (i) for some $1 \leq i \leq v$, x_i is set to false, y is set to false, and all $z_{j,i}$ for $1 \leq j \leq w$ are set to true, or (ii) all $z_{j,i}$ are set to false, y is set to true, and the assignment to the variables x_i satisfies φ. It is straightforward to construct in polynomial time some formula φ' that satisfies this property. Then we introduce w many syntactic copies φ'_j of φ'. We now define the agenda Φ by letting $[\Phi] = \{y\} \cup \{x_1, \dots, x_v\} \cup \{\, z_{j,i} : 1 \leq j \leq w, 1 \leq i \leq n \,\} \cup \{\varphi'_1, \dots, \varphi'_w\}$. Next, we construct the profile $\boldsymbol{J} = (J_1, \dots, J_v)$ as shown in Figure 1. Moreover, we let $L_0 = \{y\}$.

$\boldsymbol{J}$	J_1	J_2	$\dots$	J_{v-1}	J_v	$m(\boldsymbol{J})$
y	0	0	0	$\dots$	0	0
x_1	0	1	1	$\dots$	1	1
x_2	1	0	1	$\dots$	1	1
$\vdots$	$\vdots$		$\ddots$		$\vdots$	$\vdots$
x_{v-1}	1	$\dots$	1	0	1	1
x_v	1	$\dots$	1	1	0	1
$z_{1,1}$	1	0	0	$\dots$	0	0
$z_{1,2}$	0	1	0	$\dots$	0	0
$\vdots$	$\vdots$		$\ddots$		$\vdots$	$\vdots$
$z_{1,v-1}$	0	$\dots$	0	1	0	0
$z_{1,v}$	0	$\dots$	0	0	1	0
$\vdots$			$\vdots$			$\vdots$
$z_{w,1}$	1	0	0	$\dots$	0	0
$z_{w,2}$	0	1	0	$\dots$	0	0
$\vdots$	$\vdots$		$\ddots$		$\vdots$	$\vdots$
$z_{w,v-1}$	0	$\dots$	0	1	0	0
$z_{w,v}$	0	$\dots$	0	0	1	0
φ'_1	1	1	$\dots$		1	1
φ'_2	1	1	$\dots$		1	1
$\vdots$	$\vdots$		$\ddots$		$\vdots$	$\vdots$
φ'_{w-1}	1	$\dots$		1	1	1
φ'_w	1	$\dots$		1	1	1

Figure 1: construction of the profile in the proof of Proposition 7.

What remains is to specify a polynomial-time computable function g that takes some $J^* \in \text{Winner}_{\text{F},\Phi,\Gamma}(\boldsymbol{J})$ with $L_0 \subseteq J^*$, if it exists, and that produces a model M such that X-MAX-MODEL(φ, X, M). Let $J^* \in \text{Winner}_{\text{F},\Phi,\Gamma}(\boldsymbol{J})$ such that $L_0 \in J^*$. Then the function g outputs $J^* \cap \{x_1, \dots, x_v\}$.

The intuition behind this reduction is the following. The agenda and the profile are constructed in such a way that it is 'cheaper' to agree with the overall profile (respectively, with the majority outcome) on the formulas φ'_i and the formulas $z_{j,i}$, if possible. If φ is satisfiable, the cheapest way to agree with the overall profile (respectively, with the majority outcome) on the above formulas (in a consistent judgment set) is to set the variables x_i to a maximal assignment α to the variables in X that is extendable to a satisfying assignment to φ, and to set y to true. If φ is unsatisfiable, all consistent judgment sets that disagree with the majority outcome on a minimal number of formulas (e.g., setting $z_{j,i}$ to true for some $1 \leq i \leq v$ and all $1 \leq j \leq w$) do not contain y (and thus are not a superset of L_0). $\square$

COROLLARY 8. *The problems* WINDET(KEMENY) *and* WINDET(SLATER) *are* $\text{P}^{\text{NP}}[\log]$*-hard, even with the restriction that* $\Gamma = \top$*, and* $u = 0$.

PROOF (SKETCH). The reduction in the proof of Proposition 7 can be adapted to a many-one reduction from WINDET(KEMENY) (respectively, from WINDET(SLATER)) to X-MAX-MODEL-PARITY, by letting $L_0 = \{y, x_0\}$, where x_0 is given in the original input for the problem X-MAX-MODEL-PARITY. $\square$

3.3 Hardness for Young

PROPOSITION 9. FWINDET(YOUNG) *is* $\text{FP}^{\text{NP}}[\text{log,wit}]$*-hard, even with the restriction that* $\Gamma = \top$*, and* $u = 0$.

PROOF (SKETCH). We give a polynomial-time Levin reduction from X-MAX-MODEL. Let φ be an input to X-MAX-MODEL with $\text{Var}(\varphi) = \{x_1, \dots, x_v\}$. We may assume that any satisfying assignment (if there exists any) sets at least one variable in X to true, and that setting all variables in X to true does not satisfy φ. We construct an agenda Φ, an integrity constraint $\Gamma = \top$, an integer $u = 0$, a subset $L_0 \subseteq \Phi$, and a profile $\boldsymbol{J} \in \mathcal{J}(\Phi, \Gamma)^n$ as follows. We let $w = 2v + 1$. Then, we construct a propositional formula φ' that is satisfiable if and only if one of the following conditions holds: either (i) for some $1 \leq j \leq w$, y_j is set to true, or (ii) all y_j are set to false and the assignment to the variables x_i reduces φ to a satisfiable formula. It is straightforward to construct in polynomial time some formula φ' that satisfies this property. We now define the agenda Φ by letting $[\Phi] = \{x_1, \dots, x_v\} \cup \{\, y_j : 1 \leq j \leq w \,\} \cup \{\varphi'\}$. Next, we construct the profile $\boldsymbol{J} = (J_1, \dots, J_w)$ as shown in Figure 2. Moreover, we let $L_0 = \{\neg y_1, \dots, \neg y_w\}$.

What remains is to specify a polynomial-time computable function g that takes some $J^* \in \text{Winner}_{\text{Young},\Phi,\Gamma}(\boldsymbol{J})$ with $L_0 \subseteq J^*$, if it exists, and that produces a model M such that X-MAX-MODEL(φ, M). Let $J^* \in \text{Winner}_{\text{Young},\Phi,\Gamma}(\boldsymbol{J})$. Then the function g outputs $J^* \cap \{x_1, \dots, x_v\}$.

The intuition behind this reduction is the following. Since the profile is unanimous on φ', any winner must include φ'. Satisfying φ' can be done by either setting some y_i to true, or by satisfying the original formula φ. In the case that φ is satisfiable, a maximal assignment α to the variables in X that is extendable to a satisfying assignment for φ corresponds to the minimum number of judgment sets that need to be removed from the profile to get a consistent majority outcome (namely, remove exactly those J_i for which α sets x_i to false, and remove an equal number of judgment sets J_j for $v + 1 \leq j \leq w$). In the case that φ is unsatisfiable, the only subprofiles that have a consistent majority outcome are subprofiles consisting of a single judgment set J, for which all holds that $L_0 \not\subseteq J$. $\square$

COROLLARY 10. WINDET(YOUNG) *is* $\text{P}^{\text{NP}}[\log]$*-hard, even with the restriction that* $\Gamma = \top$*, and* $u = 0$.

PROOF (SKETCH). The reduction in the proof of Proposition 9 can be adapted to a many-one reduction from WINDET(YOUNG) to X-MAX-MODEL-PARITY, by letting $L_0 = \{x_0, x_1\}$, where x_0 is given in the original input for the problem X-MAX-MODEL-PARITY. $\square$

$\boldsymbol{J}$	J_1	J_2	J_3	$\ldots$	J_v	J_{v+1}	J_{v+2}	$\ldots$	J_w
φ'	1	1	1	$\ldots$	1	1	1	$\ldots$	1
x_1	1	0	0	$\ldots$	0	1	1	$\ldots$	1
x_2	0	1	0	$\ldots$	0	1	1	$\ldots$	1
$\vdots$	$\vdots$		$\ddots$		$\vdots$	$\vdots$	$\vdots$	$\ddots$	$\vdots$
x_{v-1}	0	$\ldots$	0	1	0	1	1	$\ldots$	1
x_v	0	$\ldots$	0	0	1	1	1	$\ldots$	1
y_1	1	0	$\ldots$				$\ldots$	0	0
y_2	0	1	$\ldots$				$\ldots$	0	0
$\vdots$	$\vdots$				$\ddots$				$\vdots$
y_{w-1}	0	0	$\ldots$				$\ldots$	1	0
y_w	0	0	$\ldots$				$\ldots$	0	1

Figure 2: construction of the profile in the proof of Proposition 9.

3.4 Completeness for Tideman

PROPOSITION 11. *Let $<^A$ be some tie-breaking rule. Then* FWINDET(RA_A) *is in* FP^{NP}.

PROOF (SKETCH). We describe a deterministic polynomial-time algorithm with access to a (yes-no) SAT oracle that solves FWINDET(RA_A). The algorithm takes as input an agenda Φ, an integrity constraint Γ, a profile $\boldsymbol{J} \in \mathcal{J}(\Phi,\Gamma)^n$, and a number of subsets $L_0,\dots,L_u$ of the agenda with $u \geq 0$. In polynomial time, the algorithm computes $\leq_{\boldsymbol{J}}$, and computes the Ranked-Agenda order $<^A_{\boldsymbol{J}}$, using the tie-breaking rule $<^A$. Let $\Phi = \{\varphi_1,\dots,\varphi_{2m}\}$, where $\varphi_1 >^A_{\boldsymbol{J}} \cdots >^A_{\boldsymbol{J}} \varphi_{2m}$. We compute $\text{RA}(<^A_{\boldsymbol{J}},\Phi,\Gamma) = J_{2m}$ by iteratively computing J_i, for all $0 \leq i \leq 2m$. Let $J_0 = \emptyset$. Given J_i, we compute J_{i+1} as follows, by querying the SAT oracle. We query the SAT solver whether $\psi_{i+1} = \bigwedge_{\varphi \in J_i} \varphi \wedge \varphi_{i+1}$ is Γ-consistent. If ψ_{i+1} is Γ-consistent, we let $J_{i+1} = J_i \cup \{\varphi_{i+1}\}$; otherwise, we let $J_{i+1} = J_i$. Clearly, this requires $2m = |\Phi|$ calls to the SAT oracle. Then, let $J^* = J_{2m} = \text{RA}(<^A_{\boldsymbol{J}},\Phi,\Gamma)$. Finally, the algorithm verifies whether $L_0 \subseteq J^*$ and $L_i \not\subseteq J^*$ for all $1 \leq i \leq u$. If these checks do not succeed, the algorithm rejects the input; otherwise, it returns J^*. □

PROPOSITION 12. FWINDET(RA_A) *is* FP^{NP}*-hard for some (fixed) tie-breaking rule A, even with the restriction that $\Gamma = \top$, and $u = 0$.*

PROOF (SKETCH). We give a polynomial-time Levin reduction from FLEX-MAX-MODEL. Let φ be an input for FLEX-MAX-MODEL, with $\text{Var}(\varphi) = \{x_1,\dots,x_v\}$. We construct an agenda Φ, an integrity constraint $\Gamma = \top$, an integer $u = 0$, a linear order $<^A \subseteq \Phi \times \Phi$, a profile $\boldsymbol{J} \in \mathcal{J}(\Phi,\Gamma)^n$, and a subset $L_0 \subseteq \Phi$, as follows. We pick some even w such that $w > v$, e.g., $w = 2v$. We introduce auxiliary variables $y_1,\dots,y_w$. Then, we construct a propositional formula φ' that is true if and only if one of the following conditions holds: either (i) for some $1 \leq j \leq w$, y_j is set to true, or (ii) the assignment to the variables x_i satisfies φ. We define the agenda Φ by letting $[\Phi] = \{\varphi'\} \cup \{y_1,\dots,y_w\} \cup \{x_1,\dots,x_v\}$. Then, we define the total order $<^A$ by letting $\varphi' >^A \neg y_1 >^A \cdots >^A \neg y_w >^A x_1 >^A \neg x_1 >^A \cdots >^A x_v >^A \neg x_v >^A y_1 >^A \cdots >^A y_w >^A \neg\varphi'$. Next, we construct the profile $\boldsymbol{J} = (J_1,\dots,J_w)$ as shown in Figure 3. Note that the Ranked-Agenda order $<^A_{\boldsymbol{J}}$ coindices with the order $<^A$. Finally, we let $L_0 = \{\neg y_w\}$.

$\boldsymbol{J}$	J_1	J_2	J_3	J_4	$\ldots$	J_{w-1}	J_w
φ'	1	1	1	1	$\ldots$	1	1
x_1	1	0	1	0	$\ldots$	1	0
x_2	1	0	1	0	$\ldots$	1	0
$\vdots$	$\vdots$	$\vdots$	$\vdots$	$\vdots$	$\ddots$	$\vdots$	$\vdots$
x_{v-1}	1	0	1	0	$\ldots$	1	0
x_v	1	0	1	0	$\ldots$	1	0
y_1	1	0	0	$\ldots$			0
y_2	0	1	0	$\ldots$			0
$\vdots$	$\vdots$			$\ddots$			$\vdots$
y_{w-1}	0	$\ldots$			0	1	0
y_w	0	$\ldots$			0	0	1

Figure 3: construction of the profile in the proof of Proposition 12.

What remains is to specify a polynomial-time computable function g that takes some $J^* \in \text{Winner}_{\text{RA}_A,\Phi,\Gamma}(\boldsymbol{J})$ with $L_0 \subseteq J^*$, and that produces a model M such that FLEX-MAX-MODEL(φ, M). The function g outputs $J^* \cap \{x_1,\dots,x_v\}$.

Note that for each instance φ of FLEX-MAX-MODEL, this reduction produces a different agenda Φ. Therefore, there is a single tie-breaking rule A that produces the correct order $<^A$ for each agenda Φ that is generated by this reduction (and moreover, this order $<^A$ clearly is computable in polynomial time, given φ).

The intuition behind this reduction is the following. If φ is satisfiable, the Ranked-Agenda winner (for the tie-breaking rule A) will contain φ' and $\neg y_1,\dots,\neg y_w$, because these are consistent (and are the first formulas in the order $>^A_{\boldsymbol{J}}$, and if φ is unsatisfiable, the winner will not contain $\neg y_w$, because φ' and $\neg y_1,\dots,\neg y_{w-1}$ are not consistent with $\neg y_w$. Moreover, if φ is satisfiable, the Ranked-Agenda order $>^A_{\boldsymbol{J}}$ forces the winner to contain the lexicographically maximal model of φ. □

COROLLARY 13. *Let $<^A$ be some tie-breaking rule. Then* WINDET(RA_A) *is in* P^{NP}.

COROLLARY 14. WINDET(RA_A) *is* P^{NP}*-hard for some (fixed) tie-breaking rule A, even with the restriction that $\Gamma = \top$, and $u = 0$.*

PROOF (SKETCH). The reduction in the proof of Proposition 12 can be adapted to a many-one reduction from

WINDET(RA_A) to LEX-MAX-MODEL, by letting $L_0 = \{\neg y_w, x_0\}$, where x_0 is given in the original input for the problem LEX-MAX-MODEL. □

Because the winner determination problem is hard for the Δ_2^p-level of the PH for some tie-breaking rule, we know that one cannot obtain lower complexity results without exploiting the structure of tie-breaking rules. In other words, any lower complexity results cannot hold for all tie-breaking rules, and their proofs will have to take into account some specific properties of any tie-breaking rules for which the results hold.

PROPOSITION 15. FWINDET(RA) *is in* $F\Sigma_2^p$.

PROOF (SKETCH). We describe a nondeterministic polynomial-time algorithm with access to a (yes-no) SAT oracle that solves FWINDET(RA). The algorithm takes as input an agenda Φ, an integrity constraint Γ, a profile $\boldsymbol{J} \in \mathcal{J}(\Phi,\Gamma)^n$, and a number of subsets $L_0, \dots, L_u \subseteq \Phi$ of the agenda. It is straightforward to compute $\leq_{\boldsymbol{J}}$ in polynomial time. Then, the algorithm guesses some total order $<_{\boldsymbol{J}}^A \subseteq \Phi \times \Phi$. It is straightforward to verify in polynomial time that $<_{\boldsymbol{J}}^A$ extends the partial order $\leq_{\boldsymbol{J}}$. (If $<_{\boldsymbol{J}}^A$ does not extend $\leq_{\boldsymbol{J}}$, the algorithm rejects.) Then, the algorithm proceeds similarly to the algorithm described in the proof of Proposition 11 to compute $J^* = \text{RA}(<_{\boldsymbol{J}}^A, \Phi, \Gamma)$. Also, the algorithm verifies whether $L_0 \subseteq J^*$ and $L_i \not\subseteq J^*$ for all $1 \leq i \leq u$. If these checks do not succeed, the algorithm rejects; otherwise, it returns J^*. □

PROPOSITION 16. FWINDET(RA) *is* $F\Sigma_2^p$*-hard, even with the restriction that* $\Gamma = \top$, *and* $u = 0$.

PROOF (SKETCH). We give a polynomial-time Levin reduction from FQSAT$_2$. Let $\varphi = \exists X.\forall Y.\psi$ be an instance of FQSAT$_2$, where $X = \{x_1, \dots, x_v\}$. We may assume without loss of generality that ψ is not a tautology. We construct an agenda Φ, an integrity constraint $\Gamma = \top$, an integer $u = 0$, a profile $\boldsymbol{J} \in \mathcal{J}(\Phi,\Gamma)^n$, and a subset $L_0 \subseteq \Phi$ of the agenda, as follows. We pick some w such that $w > v$, e.g., $w = 2v$. We introduce auxiliary variables $y_1, \dots, y_w$. Also, we introduce auxiliary variables z_l for each $l \in \{x_i, \neg x_i : 1 \leq i \leq v\}$. Then we construct a propositional formula χ that is true if and only if one of the following two conditions holds: either (i) some y_i is true, or (ii) for each $l \in \{x_i, \neg x_i : 1 \leq i \leq v\}$ it holds that l is true if and only if z_l is true. Moreover, we construct a propositional formula ψ' that is true if and only if both of the following two conditions holds: both (i) no y_i with $1 \leq i \leq 3$ is true, and (ii) either (ii.a) some y_i is true, or (ii.b) the formula $\neg\psi$ is satisfiable. It is straightforward to construct these formulas χ and ψ' in polynomial time. We now define the agenda Φ by letting $[\Phi] = \{\chi, \psi'\} \cup \{z_{x_i}, z_{\neg x_i} : 1 \leq i \leq v\} \cup \{y_1, \dots, y_w\}$. Next, we construct the profile $\boldsymbol{J} = (J_1, \dots, J_w)$ as shown in Figure 4. Note that $m(\boldsymbol{J}, \chi) = w$; $m(\boldsymbol{J}, \psi') = w - 3$; for each $1 \leq i \leq v$, $m(\boldsymbol{J}, z_{x_i}) = m(\boldsymbol{J}, z_{\neg x_i}) = w - 2$; for each $1 \leq j \leq w$, $m(\boldsymbol{J}, \neg y_j) = w - 1$. Therefore $\{\chi\} \leq_{\boldsymbol{J}} \{\neg y_j : 1 \leq j \leq w\} \leq_{\boldsymbol{J}} \{z_{x_i}, z_{\neg x_i} : 1 \leq i \leq v\} \leq_{\boldsymbol{J}} \{\psi'\}$. Moreover, we let $L_0 = \{\neg\psi'\}$.

What remains is to specify a polynomial-time computable function g that takes some $J^* \in \text{Winner}_{\text{RA},\Phi,\Gamma}(\boldsymbol{J})$ with $L_0 \subseteq J^*$, and that produces a model M such that FQSAT$_2(\varphi, M)$. Let $J^* \in \text{Winner}_{\text{RA},\Phi,\Gamma}(\boldsymbol{J})$. The function g outputs $\{x_i : 1 \leq i \leq v, z_{x_i} \in J^*\}$.

$\boldsymbol{J}$	J_1	J_2	J_3	J_4	...	J_w
χ	1	1	1	1	...	1
ψ'	0	0	0	1	...	1
z_{x_1}	0	0	1	...		1
$z_{\neg x_1}$	0	0	1	...		1
⋮	⋮	⋮	⋮			⋮
z_{x_v}	0	0	1	...		1
$z_{\neg x_v}$	0	0	1	...		1
y_1	1	0	0	...		0
y_2	0	1	0	...		0
⋮	⋮		⋱			⋮
				⋱		
y_{w-1}	0	...		0	1	0
y_w	0	...		0	0	1

Figure 4: construction of the profile in the proof of Proposition 16.

The intuition behind this reduction is the following. The profile is constructed in such a way that every Ranked-Agenda winner contains χ. If there is an assignment α to the variables $\{x_1, \dots, x_v\}$ such that $\forall Y.\psi[\alpha]$ is true, then there exists a winner containing all literals $\neg y_j$, the variables z_l for those literals l that are satisfied by α, and the formula $\neg\psi'$, because any set containing χ, the literals $\neg y_j$, and those variables z_l would be inconsistent with ψ', since such a set implies ψ (and thus forces $\neg\psi$ to be unsatisfiable). Moreover, any winner containing $\neg\psi'$ is of such a form, and thus corresponds to an assignment α with the property that $\forall Y.\psi[\alpha]$ is true. □

COROLLARY 17. WINDET(RA) *is* Σ_2^p*-complete. Hardness holds even with the restriction that* $\Gamma = \top$, *and* $u = 0$.

4. CONCLUSION

We studied the computational complexity of the winner determination problem for (the judgment aggregation analogues of) the Kemeny rule, the Slater rule and the Young rule, as well as two variants of the Ranked-Agenda rule. These computational tasks we formalized in the form of a search problem and a decision problem. We showed that the complexity for the Kemeny, Slater and Young rules lies at the Θ_2^p-level of the PH, and we showed that the complexity of the Ranked-Agenda rule, lies at the Δ_2^p-level of the PH, in case of a fixed tie-breaking rule, and lies at the Σ_2^p-level of the PH in case ties can be broken in arbitrary ways.

Future research should include investigating the computational complexity of the winner determination problem for other complete and consistent judgment aggregation procedures. One example of such a procedure is one based on the distance measure introduced by Duddy and Piggins [11]. Another direction for further research is to investigate the contribution of various aspects of the problem to its computational complexity, by analyzing the problems using the framework of parameterized complexity theory.

Acknowledgments

Ronald de Haan is supported by the European Research Council (ERC), project 239962, and the Austrian Science Fund (FWF), project P26200.

REFERENCES

[1] N. Alon, D. Falik, R. Meir, and M. Tennenholtz. Bundling attacks in judgment aggregation. In *Proceedings of the Twenty-Seventh AAAI Conference on Artificial Intelligence (AAAI 2013)*. AAAI Press, 2013.

[2] S. Arora and B. Barak. *Computational Complexity - A Modern Approach*. Cambridge University Press, 2009.

[3] D. Baumeister, G. Erdélyi, O. J. Erdélyi, and J. Rothe. Computational aspects of manipulation and control in judgment aggregation. In P. Perny, M. Pirlot, and A. Tsoukiàs, editors, *Proceedings of the Third International Conference on Algorithmic Decision Theory (ADT 2013), Brussels, Belgium, November 13–15, 2013*, volume 8176 of *Lecture Notes in Computer Science*, pages 71–85. Springer Verlag, 2013.

[4] D. Baumeister, G. Erdélyi, and J. Rothe. How hard is it to bribe the judges? A study of the complexity of bribery in judgment aggregation. In *Proceedings of the Second International Conference on Algorithmic Decision Theory (ADT 2011), Piscataway, NJ, USA, October 26–28, 2011*, volume 6992 of *Lecture Notes in Computer Science*, pages 1–15. Springer Verlag, 2011.

[5] S. J. Brams and P. C. Fishburn. Voting procedures. In K. J. Arrow, A. K. Sen, and K. Suzumura, editors, *Handbook of Social Choice and Welfare*, volume 1, chapter 4, pages 173–236. Elsevier Science Publishers, North-Holland, 2002.

[6] F. Brandt, V. Conitzer, and U. Endriss. Computational social choice. In G. Weiss, editor, *Multiagent Systems*, pages 213–283. MIT Press, 2013.

[7] Z.-Z. Chen and S. Toda. The complexity of selecting maximal solutions. *Information and Computation*, 119:231–239, June 1995.

[8] V. Conitzer, J. Lang, and L. Xia. How hard is it to control sequential elections via the agenda? In C. Boutilier, editor, *IJCAI 2009, Proceedings of the 21st International Joint Conference on Artificial Intelligence, Pasadena, California, USA, July 11-17, 2009*, pages 103–108, 2009.

[9] F. Dietrich and C. List. Arrow's Theorem in judgment aggregation. *Social Choice and Welfare*, 29(1):19–33, 2007.

[10] F. Dietrich and C. List. Judgment aggregation under constraints. In T. Boylan and R. Gekker, editors, *Economics, Rational Choice and Normative Philosophy*, Routledge Frontiers of Political Economy. Taylor & Francis, 2008.

[11] C. Duddy and A. Piggins. A measure of distance between judgment sets. *Social Choice and Welfare*, 39(4):855–867, 2012.

[12] U. Endriss. Judgment aggregation. In F. Brandt, V. Conitzer, U. Endriss, J. Lang, and A. D. Procaccia, editors, *Handbook of Computational Social Choice*. Cambridge University Press, 2015. Forthcoming.

[13] U. Endriss, U. Grandi, and D. Porello. Complexity of judgment aggregation. *J. Artif. Intell. Res.*, 45:481–514, 2012.

[14] O. Goldreich. *P, NP, and NP-Completeness: The Basics of Complexity Theory*. Cambridge University Press, 2010.

[15] U. Grandi. *Binary Aggregation with Integrity Constraints*. PhD thesis, University of Amsterdam, 2012.

[16] U. Grandi and U. Endriss. Lifting integrity constraints in binary aggregation. *Artificial Intelligence*, 199–200:45–66, 2013.

[17] D. Grossi and G. Pigozzi. *Judgment Aggregation: A Primer*. Synthesis Lectures on Artificial Intelligence and Machine Learning. Morgan & Claypool, 2014.

[18] J. Krajicek. *Bounded arithmetic, propositional logic and complexity theory*. Cambridge University Press, 1995.

[19] M. W. Krentel. Generalizations of OptP to the Polynomial Hierarchy. *Theoretical Computer Science*, 97(2):183–198, 1992.

[20] J. Lang, G. Pigozzi, M. Slavkovik, and L. van der Torre. Judgment aggregation rules based on minimization. In *Proceedings of the 13th Conference on Theoretical Aspects of Rationality and Knowledge (TARK-2011)*, 2011.

[21] J. Lang and M. Slavkovik. How hard is it to compute majority-preserving judgment aggregation rules? In *21st European Conference on Artificial Intelligence (ECAI 2014)*. IOS Press, 2014.

[22] C. List and P. Pettit. Aggregating sets of judgments: An impossibility result. *Economics and Philosophy*, 18(1):89–110, 2002.

[23] C. List and C. Puppe. Judgment aggregation: A survey. In P. Anand, P. Pattanaik, and C. Puppe, editors, *Handbook of Rational and Social Choice*. Oxford University Press, 2009.

[24] M. K. Miller and D. Osherson. Methods for distance-based judgment aggregation. *Social Choice and Welfare*, 32(4):575–601, 2009.

[25] G. Pigozzi. Belief merging and the discursive dilemma: An argument-based account of paradoxes of judgment aggregation. *Synthese*, 152(2):285–298, 2006.

[26] D. Porello and U. Endriss. Ontology merging as social choice. In *Proceedings of the 12th International Workshop on Computational Logic in Multiagent Systems (CLIMA-2011)*, volume 6814 of *Lecture Notes in Artificial Intelligence*, pages 157–170. Springer Verlag, July 2011.

[27] L. J. Stockmeyer. The polynomial-time hierarchy. *Theoretical Computer Science*, 3(1):1–22, 1976.

[28] C. Wrathall. Complete sets and the polynomial-time hierarchy. *Theoretical Computer Science*, 3(1):23–33, 1976.

Parameterized Complexity Results for Agenda Safety in Judgment Aggregation

Ulle Endriss
ILLC, University of Amsterdam
ulle.endriss@uva.nl

Ronald de Haan
Technische Universität Wien
dehaan@kr.tuwien.ac.at

Stefan Szeider
Technische Universität Wien
stefan@szeider.net

ABSTRACT

Many problems arising in computational social choice are of high computational complexity, and some are located at higher levels of the Polynomial Hierarchy. We argue that a parameterized complexity analysis provides valuable insight into the factors contributing to the complexity of these problems, and can lead to practically useful algorithms. As a case study, we consider the problem of agenda safety for the majority rule in judgment aggregation, consider several natural parameters for this problem, and determine the parameterized complexity for each of these. Our analysis is aimed at obtaining fixed-parameter tractable (fpt) algorithms that use a small number of calls to a SAT solver. We identify several positive results, including several results where the problem can be fpt-reduced to a single SAT instance. In addition, we identify several negative results. We hope that this work may help initiate a structured parameterized complexity investigation of problems arising in the field of computational social choice that are located at higher levels of the Polynomial Hierarchy.

Categories and Subject Descriptors

F.2 [**Analysis of Algorithms and Problem Complexity**]: General

General Terms

Theory

Keywords

Judgment Aggregation; Agenda Safety; Complexity Theory; Parameterized Complexity; Treewidth

1. INTRODUCTION

The field of computational social choice studies the interface of social choice theory and computer science. In particular, it is concerned with investigating properties of computational tasks related to procedures for collective decision making. Some of these computational tasks have a computational complexity that is 'beyond NP', and are thus considered to be highly intractable (cf. [2, 11, 29, 30]). We argue that the complexity analysis of problems arising in computational social choice that are 'beyond NP' benefits from a parameterized complexity approach [18, 19, 22, 37]. Recent advances in parameterized complexity theory [28] enable an investigation of the restrictions that allow an encoding of problems 'beyond NP' into the Boolean satisfiability problem (SAT). With the success that modern SAT solving algorithms have had in many practical settings over the last two decades [34, 39], this might lead to practically useful algorithms for problems that are traditionally considered to be highly intractable.

As a case study to underpin our argument, we consider the computational complexity of the problem of *agenda safety*, which is a computational problem that arises in the domain of judgment aggregation. Judgment aggregation studies the properties of procedures that combine the individual judgments on a set of related propositions (the *agenda*) of the members of a group into a collective judgment reflecting the views of the group as a whole [33]. Such procedures might, in general, yield inconsistent combined judgments. An example of a procedure whose outcome can be inconsistent is the *majority rule*, where for each issue the collective judgment agrees with the majority of the individual judgments on this issue. Because of such possible inconsistencies, it is useful to determine for a given agenda and some aggregation procedure whether there exists no combination of individual judgments such that the outcome of the procedure is inconsistent (we say that the agenda is *safe* if this is the case). This is relevant, for instance, in the setting of multiagent systems where agents need to coordinate their beliefs, intentions and actions repeatedly [42]. In this scenario, we might have to check whether the logical structure of the issues to be decided upon collectively is such that the majority decision can be guaranteed to be consistent for any combination of consistent choices made by the individual agents. The problem of agenda safety for the majority rule is complete for the second level of the Polynomial Hierarchy (PH) [20], and is thus 'beyond NP.'

Instances of hard computational problems that occur in practice often exhibit some kind of structure. A classical complexity analysis is insensitive to any such structure. A parameterized complexity analysis, on the other hand, can take into account different forms of structure in the problem instances, by means of problem parameters. The idea underlying parameterized complexity theory is that such parameters are expected to be small in problem instances occurring in practice. By restricting the high complexity of a problem to the parameter only, these structured instances

Appears in: *Proceedings of the 14th International Conference on Autonomous Agents and Multiagent Systems (AAMAS 2015), Bordini, Elkind, Weiss, Yolum (eds.), May 4–8, 2015, Istanbul, Turkey.*

of hard computational problems can often be solved reasonably efficiently. There has been a lot of research in the field of parameterized complexity over the last two decades [10]. Most of this research is aimed at problems that are in NP. Recently, tools have been developed to analyze the parameterized complexity of problems that are located higher in the PH [26, 27, 28]. The paradigm of parameterized complexity has been used to examine many problems in computational social choice [3, 4, 5, 17].

Contributions.

Concretely, we investigate what kind of structure helps to decrease the computational complexity of the problem of agenda safety for the majority rule. We do this by studying several natural parameterizations of the problem. The main concept of tractability that we have in mind is based on algorithms that run efficiently for small parameter values, and that use only a small number of SAT calls (depending on the parameter value only), preferably only a single call. Such parameterized algorithms are an improvement over polynomial-time algorithms, because the problem cannot be solved by a polynomial-time algorithm that can make calls to a SAT solver (unless the PH collapses). This notion of tractability is motivated by the enormous practical success of modern SAT solvers [8, 24, 34, 39]. For precise definitions, we refer to Section 2.

Several parameterizations that we consider correspond to simple syntactic restrictions on the agenda (i.e., bounds on the size of formulas, bounds on variable occurrence, and bounds on the number of formulas). Another several parameterizations that we consider capture structure in the agenda in terms of the 'tree-likeness' of various graphs associated to the agenda. Yet another parameterization corresponds to a bound on the size of counterexamples (to the logical characterization of agenda safety). These parameterizations have been applied successfully in other domains [6, 7, 25]. An overview of complexity results for these parameterizations can be found in Table 1.

We identify several positive cases, where structure present in the problem input allows us to solve the problem using a small number of SAT calls, in several cases even using a single call. These positive results could lead to algorithms that perform well in practice. Additionally, our parameterized complexity analysis allows us to pinpoint exactly what aspects of the problem play what role in the high computational complexity of the problem, and it helps to determine what algorithmic approach is well suited to solve the problem in practical settings. We hope that this work can help initiate a structured parameterized complexity investigation of problems arising in the field of computational social choice that are located at higher levels of the PH.

2. PRELIMINARIES

In this section, we formally define the problem of agenda safety and we provide a logical characterization of the problem for a particular aggregation procedure. Moreover, we review notions from complexity theory.

Propositional Logic and Agenda Safety.

A *literal* is a propositional variable x or a negated variable $\neg x$. A *clause* is a finite set of literals, not containing a complementary pair x, $\neg x$, and is interpreted as the disjunction of these literals. A formula in *conjunctive normal form (CNF)* is a finite set of clauses, interpreted as the conjunction of these clauses. We define the *size* $||\varphi||$ of a CNF formula φ to be $\sum_{c \in \varphi} |c|$; the number of clauses of φ is denoted by $|\varphi|$. For a CNF formula φ, the set $\text{Var}(\varphi)$ denotes the set of all variables x such that some clause of φ contains x or $\neg x$. We say that a clause is a *Horn clause* if it contains at most one positive literal; a CNF formula is a *Horn formula* if it contains only Horn clauses. We let the *degree* of a CNF formula φ be the maximum number of times that any variable $x \in \text{Var}(\varphi)$ occurs in φ. We use the standard notion of *(truth) assignments* $\alpha : \text{Var}(\varphi) \to \{0,1\}$ for Boolean formulas and *truth* of a formula under such an assignment. We let SAT denote the problem of deciding whether a given propositional formula is satisfiable, and we let UNSAT denote its co-problem, i.e., deciding whether a given formula is unsatisfiable. We say that a propositional formula is *doubly-negated* if it is of the form $\neg\neg\psi$. For every propositional formula φ, we let $\sim\varphi$ denote the *complement* of φ, i.e., $\sim\varphi = \neg\varphi$ if φ is not of the form $\neg\psi$, and $\sim\varphi = \psi$ if φ is of the form $\neg\psi$.

An *agenda* is a finite nonempty set Φ of formulas that does not contain any doubly-negated formulas and that is closed under complementation. Moreover, if $\Phi = \{\varphi_1, \dots, \varphi_n, \neg\varphi_1, \dots, \neg\varphi_n\}$ is an agenda, then we let $[\Phi] = \{\varphi_1, \dots, \varphi_n\}$ denote the *pre-agenda* associated to the agenda Φ. A *judgment set* J for an agenda Φ is a subset $J \subseteq \Phi$. We call a judgment set J *complete* if $\varphi \in J$ or $\sim\varphi \in J$ for all $\varphi \in \Phi$; we call it *complement-free* if for all $\varphi \in \Phi$ it is not the case that both φ and $\sim\varphi$ are in J; and we call it *consistent* if there exists an assignment that makes all formulas in J true. Let $\mathcal{J}(\Phi)$ denote the set of all complete and consistent subsets of Φ. Let $\mathcal{N}$ be a set of agents, with $|\mathcal{N}| = n$. We call a sequence $\boldsymbol{J} \in \mathcal{J}(\Phi)^n$ of complete and consistent subsets a *profile*. A (resolute) *judgment aggregation procedure* for the agenda Φ and the set of individuals $\mathcal{N}$ is a function $F : \mathcal{J}(\Phi)^n \to 2^\Phi$. An example is the *majority rule* F^{maj}, where $\varphi \in F^{\text{maj}}(\boldsymbol{J})$ if and only if φ occurs in the majority of judgment sets in $\boldsymbol{J}$, for all $\varphi \in \Phi$. We call F *complete*, *complement-free* and *consistent*, if $F(\boldsymbol{J})$ is complete, complement-free and consistent, respectively, for every $\boldsymbol{J} \in \mathcal{J}(\Phi)^n$. An agenda Φ is *safe* with respect to a class of aggregation procedures $\mathcal{F}$, if every procedure in $\mathcal{F}$ is consistent when applied to profiles of judgment sets over Φ. We say that an agenda Φ satisfies the *median property (MP)* if every inconsistent subset of Φ has itself an inconsistent subset of size at most 2. An agenda Φ is safe for the majority rule if and only if Φ satisfies the MP [20, 36]. There exist similar properties that characterize agenda safety for other aggregation procedures [20].

As an example, we consider the *discursive dilemma*, which concerns an agenda that is not safe for the majority rule. Consider the agenda $\Phi_{\text{dd}} = \{p, \neg p, q, \neg q, (p \to q), \neg(p \to q)\}$. Moreover, consider the profile $\boldsymbol{J} = (J_1, J_2, J_3)$, where $J_1 = \{p, q, (p \to q)\}$, $J_2 = \{p, \neg q, \neg(p \to q)\}$, and $J_3 = \{\neg p, \neg q, (p \to q)\}$. Each of these judgment sets are consistent. However, $F^{\text{maj}}(\boldsymbol{J}) = \{p, \neg q, (p \to q)\}$ is inconsistent. In other words, Φ_{dd} is not safe for the majority rule. Also, Φ_{dd} does not satisfy the MP, as it contains the subset $F^{\text{maj}}(\boldsymbol{J}) \subseteq \Phi$ that is inconsistent, but that itself contains no inconsistent subset of size 2. Intuitively, for each agenda that does not satisfy the MP, a similar discursive dilemma can be constructed, where the majority rule is forced to in-

Parameter	Complexity
maximum formula size (ℓ)	para-Π_2^P-complete, even when restricted to 2CNF $\cap$ HORN (Proposition 3)
maximum variable degree (d)	para-Π_2^P-complete, even when restricted to 2CNF $\cap$ HORN (Proposition 3)
agenda size	solvable in fpt-time with $f(k)$ many SAT calls, with $f(k) = 2^{O(k)}$ (Theorem 1) and $f(k) = \Omega(\log k)$ (Theorem 2)
counterexample size	$\forall^k\exists^*$-hard (Theorem 3)
formula primal treewidth	fixed-parameter tractable (Proposition 6)
clausal primal and incidence treewidth	para-co-NP-complete (Propositions 7 and 8)
formula incidence treewidth	para-Π_2^P-complete (Proposition 9)

Table 1: Complexity results for different parameterizations of agenda safety.

clude an inconsistent subset (of size larger than 2), whereas the individual profiles remain consistent.

In this paper, we consider several parameterizations of the following decision problem MAJ-AS, which is khown to be Π_2^P-complete [20]. The problem MAJ-AS consists of, given an agenda Φ, deciding whether Φ is safe for the majority rule. For our results, we will use the fact that deciding safety of an agenda Φ for the majority rule is equivalent to checking whether Φ satisfies the median property. In fact, the technical details behind our results involve only this alternative characterization.

The Boolean and Polynomial Hierarchies.

There are many natural decision problems that are apparently not contained in the classical complexity classes P or NP. The *Boolean Hierarchy* (BH) [12, 13, 31] consists of a hierarchy of complexity classes BH_i for all $i \geq 1$. Each class BH_i can be characterized as the class of problems that can be reduced in polynomial time to the problem BH_i-SAT, which is defined inductively as follows. The problem BH_1-SAT consists of all sequences (φ), where φ is a satisfiable propositional formula. For even $i \geq 2$, the problem BH_i-SAT consists of all sequences $(\varphi_1, \dots, \varphi_i)$ of propositional formulas such that both $(\varphi_1, \dots, \varphi_{i-1}) \in \text{BH}_{(i-1)}$-SAT and φ_i is unsatisfiable. For odd $i \geq 2$, the problem BH_i-SAT consists of all sequences $(\varphi_1, \dots, \varphi_i)$ of propositional formulas such that $(\varphi_1, \dots, \varphi_{i-1}) \in \text{BH}_{(i-1)}$-SAT or φ_i is satisfiable. The class BH_2 is also denoted by DP, and the problem BH_2-SAT is also denoted by SAT-UNSAT.

The *Polynomial Hierarchy* (PH) [35, 38, 43, 45] consists of a hierarchy of complexity classes, including the classes Σ_i^P, for all $i \geq 0$. The class Σ_2^P already contains the entire BH. We give a characterization of these classes based on the satisfiability problem of various classes of quantified Boolean formulas. A *(prenex) quantified Boolean formula* is a formula of the form $Q_1X_1Q_2X_2 \dots Q_mX_m\psi$, where each Q_i is either $\forall$ or $\exists$, the X_i are disjoint sets of propositional variables, and ψ is a Boolean formula over the variables in $\bigcup_{i=1}^m X_i$. The quantifier-free part of such formulas is called the *matrix* of the formula. Truth of such formulas is defined in the usual way. We let $\psi[\alpha]$ denote the formula obtained from ψ by instantiation variables by their truth values given by a (partial) truth assignment α. For each $i \geq 1$ we define the decision problem QSAT_i, where the problem is to decide whether a given quantified Boolean formula $\varphi = \exists X_1 \forall X_2 \exists X_3 \dots Q_i X_i \psi$ is true, where Q_i is a universal quantifier if i is even and an existential quantifier if i is odd. For each nonnegative integer $i \geq 0$, the complexity class Σ_i^P is the class of problems that can be reduced to QSAT_i in polynomial time [43, 45]. The Σ_i^P-hardness of QSAT_i holds already when the matrix of the input formula is restricted to 3CNF for odd i, and restricted to 3DNF for even i. Note that $\Sigma_0^P = \text{P}$, and that $\Sigma_1^P = \text{NP}$. For each $i \geq 1$, the class Π_i^P is defined as co-Σ_i^P.

Parameterized Complexity.

We introduce some core notions from parameterized complexity theory that we will use in this paper. For an in-depth treatment we refer to other sources [18, 19, 22, 28, 37]. A *parameterized problem* L is a subset of $\Sigma^* \times \mathbb{N}$ for some finite alphabet Σ. For an instance $(I, k) \in \Sigma^* \times \mathbb{N}$, we call I the *main part* and k the *parameter*. The following generalization of polynomial time computability is commonly regarded as the tractability notion of parameterized complexity theory. A parameterized problem L is *fixed-parameter tractable* if there exists a computable function f and a constant c such that there exists an algorithm that decides whether $(I, k) \in L$ in time $O(f(k)||I||^c)$, where $||I||$ denotes the size of I. Such an algorithm is called an *fpt-algorithm*, and this amount of time is called *fpt-time*. FPT is the class of all fixed-parameter tractable parameterized decision problems. If the parameter is constant, then fpt-algorithms run in polynomial time where the order of the polynomial is independent of the parameter. This provides a good scalability in the parameter in contrast to running times of the form $||I||^k$, which are also polynomial for fixed k, but are already impractical for, say, $k > 3$. By XP we denote the class of all problems L for which it can be decided whether $(I, k) \in L$ in time $O(||I||^{f(k)})$, for some fixed computable function f.

Let $L \subseteq \Sigma^* \times \mathbb{N}$ and $L' \subseteq (\Sigma')^* \times \mathbb{N}$ be two parameterized problems. An *fpt-reduction* from L to L' is a mapping $R : \Sigma^* \times \mathbb{N} \to (\Sigma')^* \times \mathbb{N}$ from instances of L to instances of L' such that there exist some computable function $g : \mathbb{N} \to \mathbb{N}$ such that for all $(I, k) \in \Sigma^* \times \mathbb{N}$: (i) (I, k) is a yes-instance of L if and only if $(I', k') = R(I, k)$ is a yes-instance of L', (ii) $k' \leq g(k)$, and (iii) R is computable in fpt-time.

Let C be a classical complexity class, e.g., NP. The parameterized complexity class para-C is then defined as the class of all parameterized problems $L \subseteq \Sigma^* \times \mathbb{N}$, for some finite alphabet Σ, for which there exists an alphabet Π, a computable function $f : \mathbb{N} \to \Pi^*$, and a problem $P \subseteq \Sigma^* \times \Pi^*$ such that $P \in C$ and for all instances $(x, k) \in \Sigma^* \times \mathbb{N}$ of L we have that $(x, k) \in L$ if and only if $(x, f(k)) \in P$. Intuitively, the class para-C consists of all problems that are in C after a precomputation that only involves the parameter [21].

In particular, the class para-NP contains those parameterized problems that can be fpt-reduced to a single instance of SAT. Another class containing problems that can be considered fpt-reducible to SAT is the class para-DP, based on the classical complexity class DP $= \{ L_1 \cap L_2 : L_1 \in$ NP$, L_2 \in$ co-NP$\}$. An instance of a parameterized problem in para-DP can be solved in fpt-time by firstly reducing it to an instance of the problem SAT-UNSAT $= \{ (\varphi_1, \varphi_2) : \varphi_1 \in$ SAT$, \varphi_2 \in$ UNSAT$\}$, and then solving this resulting instance by invoking a SAT oracle twice.

In addition to many-one fpt-reductions to SAT, we are also interested in Turing fpt-reductions. A *Turing fpt-reduction from a problem P to SAT* is an fpt-algorithm that has access to a SAT oracle and that decides P. We are mainly interested in fpt-algorithms that only use a small number of queries to the SAT oracle (*SAT calls*). We let $\text{FPT}^{\text{NP}[f(k)]}$ denote the class of all parameterized problems P for which there exists an fpt-algorithm that decides if $(x, k) \in P$ by using at most $f(k)$ many SAT calls, for some computable function f.

The notion of para-Σ_2^P-hardness can be employed to provide evidence against the existence of fpt-reductions to SAT. However, for many interesting parameterized problems for which we want to investigate the (non-)existence of fpt-reductions to SAT, hardness for para-Σ_2^P cannot be used. The class para-Σ_2^P contains problems that cannot be reduced to SAT in polynomial time if the parameter value is a constant (unless the Polynomial Hierarchy collapses at the first level), i.e., problems in para-Σ_2^P do not allow an xp-reduction to SAT. Since many problems we are interested in do allow such xp-reductions to SAT, it is unlikely that these problems can be shown to be hard for the complexity class para-Σ_2^P.

Recent work in parameterized complexity theory has resulted in complexity classes that can be used to provide evidence for the non-existence of fpt-reductions to SAT also for problems that do allow an xp-reduction to SAT [26, 28]. The parameterized complexity class $\forall^k\exists^*$ consists of all parameterized problems that can be fpt-reduced to the following variant of quantified Boolean satisfiability that is based on truth assignments of restricted (Hamming) weight (the Hamming weight of an assignment is the number of variables that it assigns to 1). The problem $\forall^k\exists^*$-WSAT consists of deciding, for a given quantified Boolean formula $\varphi = \forall X.\exists Y.\psi$ and a given integer k, whether for all truth assignments α to X of weight k there exists a truth assignment β to Y such that the assignment $\alpha \cup \beta$ satisfies ψ. The parameter is k.

For any problem in $\forall^k\exists^*$ there exists an xp-reduction to SAT. However, there is evidence that problems that are hard for $\forall^k\exists^*$ do not allow an fpt-reduction to SAT [26, 28]. Many natural parameterized problems from various domains are complete for the class $\forall^k\exists^*$, and for none of them an fpt-reduction to SAT has been found [26]. If there exists an fpt-reduction to SAT for any $\forall^k\exists^*$-complete problem then this is the case for all $\forall^k\exists^*$-complete problems. For an overview of parameterized complexity classes that are relevant to the results in this paper, we refer to Figure 1 (for a definition of the classes W[1], co-W[1] and Δ_2^P, referred to in this figure, we refer to other sources [18, 19, 22]). For a more detailed discussion on this topic, we refer to previous work in parameterized complexity [26, 28].

Treewidth.

Let $G = (V, E)$ be a graph. A tree decomposition of G is

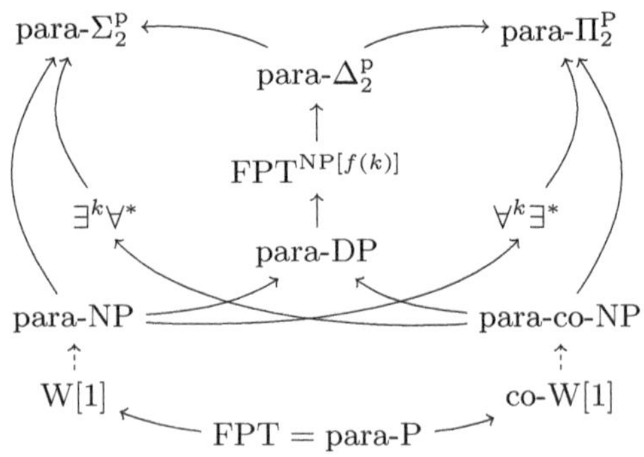

Figure 1: Parameterized complexity classes relevant to the results in this paper. Arrows indicate inclusion relations.

a pair $(\mathcal{T}, (B_t)_{t\in T})$ where $\mathcal{T} = (T, F)$ is a rooted tree and $(B_t)_{t\in T}$ is a family of subsets of V such that (1) for every $v \in V$, the set $B^{-1}(v) = \{ t \in T : v \in B_t \}$ is nonempty and connected in $\mathcal{T}$; and (2) for every edge $\{v, w\} \in E$, there is a $t \in T$ such that $v, w \in B_t$. The *width* of the decomposition is the number $\max\{ |B_t| : t \in T \} - 1$. The *treewidth* of G is the minimum of the widths of all tree decompositions of G. Let G be a graph and k a positive integer. There is an algorithm that computes a tree decomposition of G of width k, if it exists, and fails otherwise; this algorithm runs in linear time for fixed k [9].

Treewidth is often used as a parameter to represent the amount of structure present in CNF formulas. There are several ways of associating treewidth to a CNF formula. Two of the most common ways are the primal and incidence treewidth. Let φ be a CNF formula. The *primal graph* of φ has as vertices the variables occurring in φ, and two variables are connected by an edge if there exists a clause in which they both occur. The *incidence graph* of φ is a bipartite graph whose vertices consist of (1) the variables occurring in φ and (2) the clauses of φ. A variable x is connected by an edge to a clause c if x occurs in c. The *primal treewidth* of φ is the treewidth of its primal graph, and the *incidence treewidth* of φ is the treewidth of its incidence graph.

3. COMPLEXITY RESULTS

We start with showing that we can restrict our attention to agendas containing only formulas in CNF. We show how to transform any agenda Φ to an agenda Φ' of size polynomial in the size of Φ, containing only formulas in CNF (and their negations), that is safe if and only if Φ is safe. For this, we will need the following proposition, that can be shown by using the well-known Tseitin transformation [44] (we omit its straightforward proof).

PROPOSITION 1. *Let Φ be an agenda with $[\Phi] = \{\varphi_1, \dots, \varphi_n\}$. We can construct in polynomial time an agenda Φ' with $[\Phi'] = \{\varphi'_1, \dots, \varphi'_n\}$ such that each φ'_i is in CNF and any subset $\Psi = \{\varphi_{i_1}, \dots, \varphi_{i_{m_1}}, \neg\varphi_{j_1}, \dots, \neg\varphi_{j_{m_2}}\}$ of Φ is consistent if and only if $\Psi' = \{\varphi'_{i_1}, \dots, \varphi'_{i_m}, \neg\varphi'_{j_1}, \dots, \neg\varphi'_{j_{m_2}}\}$ is consistent.*

PROOF (SKETCH). Let Φ be an agenda with $[\Phi] = \{\varphi_1, \dots, \varphi_n\}$. By using the well-known Tseitin transformation [44], we can transform each φ_i in linear time to a CNF formula φ'_i such that $\text{Var}(\varphi'_i) \supseteq \text{Var}(\varphi_i)$ and for each truth assignment $\alpha : \text{Var}(\varphi_i) \to \{0,1\}$ we have that α satisfies φ_i if and only if there exists an assignment $\beta : (\text{Var}(\varphi'_i) \backslash \text{Var}(\varphi_i)) \to \{0,1\}$ such that the assignment $\alpha \cup \beta$ satisfies φ'_i. Because we can introduce fresh variables for constructing each φ'_i, we can assume without loss of generality that for each $1 \leq i < i' \leq n$ it is the case that $(\text{Var}(\varphi'_i)\backslash\text{Var}(\varphi_i)) \cap (\text{Var}(\varphi'_{i'})\backslash\text{Var}(\varphi_{i'})) = \emptyset$. Let $\Psi = \{\varphi_{i_1}, \ldots, \varphi_{i_{m_1}}, \neg\varphi_{j_1}, \ldots, \neg\varphi_{j_{m_2}}\}$ be an arbitrary subset of Φ. We claim that Ψ is consistent if and only if $\Psi' = \{\varphi'_{i_1}, \ldots, \varphi'_{i_{m_1}}, \neg\varphi'_{j_1}, \ldots, \neg\varphi'_{j_{m_2}}\}$ is consistent. □

Intuitively, the above results show that, using additional auxiliary variables, each agenda can be rewritten into another agenda that contains only formulas in CNF (or their negation) that are equivalent (with respect to satisfiability) to the formulas in the original agenda.

3.1 Simple Syntactic Restrictions

We consider the following parameterizations of the agenda safety problem that correspond to syntactic restrictions on the agenda Φ. We parameterize on the size of formulas $\varphi \in \Phi$, on the maximum number of times any variable occurs in Φ (i.e., the degree of Φ), and on the number of formulas occurring in Φ. Concretely, we consider the parameterized problems MAJ-AS(formula-size), where the parameter is $\ell = \max\{\, ||\varphi|| : \varphi \in \Phi \}$; MAJ-AS(degree), where the parameter is the degree d of Φ; MAJ-AS(degree + formula size), where the parameter is $\ell + d$; and MAJ-AS(ag.-size), where the parameter is $|\Phi|$. Here we define the *degree* of an agenda Φ to be the maximum number of times that any variable $x \in \text{Var}(\Phi)$ occurs in $[\Phi]$, i.e., $\max_{x\in\text{Var}(\Phi)}(\sum_{\varphi\in[\Phi]} \text{occ}(x,\varphi))$, where $\text{occ}(x,\varphi)$ denotes the number of times that x occurs in φ.

The assumption that the size of formulas in an agenda is small corresponds to the expectation that the separate statements that the individuals are judging are in a sense atomic, and therefore of bounded size. The assumption that the degree of an agenda is small corresponds to the expectation that each proposition that occurs in the statements to be judged occurs only a small number of times. The assumption that the number of formulas in the agenda is small is based on the fact that the individuals need to form an opinion on all formulas in the agenda.

Agendas with Small Formulas and Small Degree.

We start by showing that parameterizing on (the sum of) the maximum formula size and the degree of the agenda Φ does not decrease the complexity of deciding whether the agenda is safe, even when (the pre-agenda associated to) Φ contains only formulas in 2CNF $\cap$ HORN. Intuitively, these restrictions on the form and size of the formulas in the agenda do not rule out the complex interactions between the formulas in the agenda that involve many formulas simultaneously, and that give rise to the Π_2^{P}-hardness of the problem.

PROPOSITION 2. MAJ-AS(formula-size) *is para-*Π_2^{P}*-complete.*

PROOF (SKETCH). Membership in para-Π_2^{P} follows from the Π_2^{P}-membership of MAJ-AS. We show para-Π_2^{P}-hardness by giving a polynomial-time reduction from $\forall\exists$-SAT(3CNF) to the problem $\{\, x : (x,c) \in \text{MAJ-AS(formula-size)} \,\}$, where c is bounded by the size of formulas of the form $\neg((\neg x_1 \vee \neg x_2 \vee \neg x_3) \wedge \neg z)$. This reduction is a modified variant of a reduction given by Endriss et al. [20, Lemma 11]. Let $\varphi = \forall X.\exists Y.\psi$ be an instance of $\forall\exists$-SAT, where $\psi = c_1 \wedge \cdots \wedge c_m$ is in 3CNF, and where $X = \{x_1, \ldots, x_m\}$. We may assume without loss of generality that none of the c_i is a unit clause. We construct the agenda $\Phi = \{x_1, \neg x_1, \ldots, x_n, \neg x_n, (c_1 \wedge \neg z_1), \neg(c_1 \wedge \neg z_1), \ldots, (c_m \wedge \neg z_m), \neg(c_m \wedge \neg z_m)\}$, where $Z = \{z_1, \ldots, z_m\}$ is a set of fresh variables. We claim that Φ satisfies the median property if and only if φ is true. □

Next, using the following technical lemma (whose straightforward proof is omitted), and the reduction given in the proof of Proposition 2, we get para-Π_2^{P}-completeness of MAJ-AS(degree + formula size). The hardness result holds even when we restrict the formulas to be in HORN $\cap$ 2CNF.

LEMMA 1. *The problem* $\forall\exists$-SAT(3CNF) *is* Π_2^{P}*-hard even when restricted to instances* $\varphi = \forall X.\exists Y.\psi$ *where each* $x \in X$ *occurs at most* 2 *times in* ψ *and each* $y \in Y$ *occurs at most* 3 *times in* ψ.

PROPOSITION 3. MAJ-AS(degree + formula size) *is para-*Π_2^{P}*-hard even when restricted to agendas* Φ *such that all formulas* $\varphi \in [\Phi]$ *are in* HORN $\cap$ 2CNF.

PROOF. We consider the reduction used to show Proposition 2. The agenda Φ that we constructed contains only formulas of the form x_i or their negation, and formulas of the form $(c_i \wedge \neg z_i)$, where c_i is a clause, or their negation. Clearly, the formulas x_i and $\neg x_i$ are (equivalent to formulas) in HORN $\cap$ 2CNF. It suffices to show that each formula $\varphi \in \Phi$ with $\varphi = (c_i \wedge \neg z_i)$ is equivalent to a formula $\varphi' \in$ HORN $\cap$ 2CNF. Let $c_i = (l_1^i \vee l_2^i \vee l_3^i)$. Observe that $(c_i \wedge \neg z_i) = ((l_1^i \vee l_2^i \vee l_3^i) \wedge \neg z_i) \equiv (l_1^i \vee \neg z_i) \wedge (l_2^i \vee \neg z_i) \wedge (l_3^i \vee \neg z_i)$. Thus, we can construct Φ in such a way that $[\Phi]$ contains only formulas in HORN $\cap$ 2CNF. □

Agendas with Few Formulas.

Next, we parameterize the agenda safety problem on the number of formulas occurring in the agenda. We will show that instances (x,k) of the problem MAJ-AS(ag.-size) can be solved by an fpt-algorithm that uses $f(k)$ many SAT calls. Intuitively, the fpt-algorithm that we construct will exploit the fact that the agenda only contains few formulas, by considering all possible inconsistent subsets of the agenda, and using a SAT solver to verify that these all have an inconsistent subset of size at most 2. In particular, we will prove the following result.

THEOREM 1. *There exists an algorithm that decides* MAJ-AS(ag.-size) *in fpt-time using at most* $2^{O(k)}$ *SAT calls, where* k *is the parameter value.*

Moreover, we give evidence that this is the best one can do, i.e., there exists no fpt-algorithm that uses a significantly smaller number of SAT calls, assuming some widely believed complexity-theoretic assumptions (Theorem 2). In order to perform our lower-bound analysis, we will consider the parameterized complexity class $\text{FPT}^{\text{NP}[f(k)]}$. We will show that MAJ-AS(ag.-size) is complete for this class.

We begin with considering the following auxiliary problem BH(level)-SAT, and showing that it is $\text{FPT}^{\text{NP}[f(k)]}$-complete. Given a positive integer k and a sequence $\overline{\varphi} = (\varphi_1, \ldots, \varphi_k)$ of propositional formulas, the problem is to decide whether $\overline{\varphi} \in \text{BH}_k\text{-SAT}$. The parameter is k.

Lemma 2. BH(level)-Sat *is* $\mathrm{FPT}^{\mathrm{NP}[f(k)]}$*-complete.*

Proof (sketch). We first show membership. Let (x, k) be an instance of BH(level)-Sat, where $x = (\varphi_1, \dots, \varphi_{k'})$. Then, for each $1 \leq i \leq k$, it decides whether φ_i is satisfiable by a single SAT call. Since (x, k) corresponds to a Boolean combination of statements concerning the satisfiability of the formulas φ_i, the algorithm can then decide in fpt-time whether $(x, k) \in$ BH(level)-Sat.

We can prove hardness by showing the following. Let P be a parameterized problem and let A be an algorithm that decides P in fpt-time using at most $g(k)$ many SAT calls, where k is the parameter value and g is some computable function. Then there are at most $2^{g(k)}$ possible sequences of answers to these calls, that lead the algorithm to accept the input. We can encode the check whether a particular such sequence corresponds to the correct answers to the SAT calls, as a single instance of SAT-UNSAT. Then, the disjunction of all these instances can be encoded as a single instance (x', k') of BH(level)-Sat, where $k' \leq 2^{g(k)+1}$ [12]. We omit a full detailed proof of this claim. □

We now use this completeness result to show the upper bound on the number of SAT calls needed to solve Maj-AS(ag.-size).

Proof of Theorem 1. As a first step, we provide an fpt-algorithm that takes an instance Φ of Maj-AS(ag.-size) with $|\Phi| = k$ and produces $f(k)$ many instances $x_1, \dots, x_{f(k)}$ of co-SAT-UNSAT such that $\Phi \in$ Maj-AS(ag.-size) if and only if $\{x_1, \dots, x_{f(k)}\} \subseteq$ co-SAT-UNSAT. Let Φ be an agenda with $[\Phi] = \{\varphi_1, \dots, \varphi_k\}$. Let C denote the set of all complement-free subagendas $\Phi' \subseteq \Phi$ that are of size at least 3. Clearly, $|C| = 2^{O(k)}$. We know that Φ satisfies the MP if and only if for all $\Phi' \in C$ holds that either (1) Φ' is satisfiable, or (2) there exists some $\Phi'' \subseteq \Phi'$ of size 2 that is unsatisfiable.

Firstly, for each $\Phi' = \{\psi_1, \dots, \psi_\ell\} \in C$, we construct an instance $I(\Phi') = (\psi_1, \psi_2)$ of co-SAT-UNSAT such that $(\psi_1, \psi_2) \in$ co-SAT-UNSAT if and only if either (1) Φ' is satisfiable or (2) there exists some $\Phi'' \subseteq \Phi'$ of size 2 that is unsatisfiable. For any $1 \leq i < j \leq \ell$ and any propositional formula φ, we let $\varphi^{(i,j)}$ denote a copy of φ where each variable $x \in \mathrm{Var}(\varphi)$ is replaced with a copy $x^{(i,j)}$ indexed by the pair (i, j). We define $\psi_1 = \bigwedge_{\varphi \in \Phi'} \varphi$, and $\psi_2 = \bigwedge_{1 \leq i < j \leq \ell} (\psi_i^{(i,j)} \wedge \psi_j^{(i,j)})$. It is straightforward to verify that $I(\Phi')$ satisfies the required properties.

We now straightforwardly get that $\Phi \in$ Maj-AS(ag.-size) if and only if $\{ I(\Phi') : \Phi' \in C \} \subseteq$ co-SAT-UNSAT. Also, we know that $|C| = f(k) = 2^{O(k)}$ for a suitable computable function f. We know that the conjunction of $f(k)$ many instances of co-SAT-UNSAT can be reduced in polynomial time to an instance of co-$\mathrm{BH}_{2f(k)}$-Sat [12]. By Lemma 2, this implies that Maj-AS(ag.-size) is in $\mathrm{FPT}^{\mathrm{NP}[f(k)]}$. Moreover, the algorithm that witnesses this decides Maj-AS(ag.-size) in time $O(n \cdot 2^k)$ by making $O(2^k)$ many queries to a SAT solver consisting of formulas of size $O(n \cdot k^2)$, where n is the input size and k is the parameter value. □

Next, we will pursue the lower bound. We start with identifying an easier hardness result, which we will then extend to a hardness result for the class $\mathrm{FPT}^{\mathrm{NP}[f(k)]}$.

Lemma 3. Maj-AS(ag.-size) *is* para-co-DP*-hard.*

Proof (sketch). We prove hardness for para-co-DP by giving a polynomial-time reduction from SAT-UNSAT to co-Maj-AS, such that the resulting instance is an agenda of constant size. Let (φ_1, φ_2) be an instance of SAT-UNSAT. We construct the agenda Φ with $[\Phi] = \{\psi_1, \psi_2, \psi_3\}$ by letting $\psi_1 = r_1 \wedge p_1 \wedge \varphi_1$, $\psi_2 = r_2 \wedge p_2$, and $\psi_3 = r_3 \wedge ((p_1 \wedge p_2) \rightarrow \varphi_2)$, where $\{r_1, r_2, r_3, p_1, p_2\}$ are distinct fresh variables not occurring in φ_1 nor in φ_2. We claim that Φ does not satisfy the MP if and only if $(\varphi_1, \varphi_2) \in$ SAT-UNSAT. □

Proposition 4. Maj-AS(ag.-size) *is* $\mathrm{FPT}^{\mathrm{NP}[f(k)]}$*-hard.*

Proof. We give an fpt-reduction from BH(level)-Sat to co-Maj-AS(ag.-size). For the sake of simplicity, we assume that $k \geq 2$ is even. Let the sequence $(\varphi_1, \dots, \varphi_k)$ specify an instance of BH(level)-Sat. We know that we can construct in polynomial time a sequence of formulas $(\varphi_1, \psi_1, \dots, \varphi_\ell, \psi_\ell)$, where $\ell = k/2$, such that $(\varphi_1, \dots, \varphi_k) \in \mathrm{BH}_k$-Sat if and only if for some $1 \leq i \leq \ell$ it holds that $(\chi_i, \psi_i) \in \mathrm{BH}_2$-Sat = SAT-UNSAT [12].

Now, for each $1 \leq i \leq \ell$, we can use the reduction in the proof of Lemma 3 to construct in polynomial time an agenda Φ_i of constant size such that Φ_i does not satisfy the median property if and only if $(\chi_i, \psi_i) \in$ SAT-UNSAT. Moreover, we can ensure that the agendas Φ_i are variable-disjoint. We now construct the agenda $\Phi = \bigcup_{1 \leq i \leq \ell} \Phi_i$. We claim that Φ does not satisfy the median property if and only if $(\chi_i, \psi_i) \in$ SAT-UNSAT for some $1 \leq i \leq \ell$. We know this latter condition holds if and only if our original instance $(\varphi_1, \dots, \varphi_k) \in \mathrm{BH}_k$-Sat. Moreover, since $|\Phi| = O(k)$, we obtain a correct fpt-reduction. □

We will now use the $\mathrm{FPT}^{\mathrm{NP}[f(k)]}$-hardness of Maj-AS-(ag.-size), to obtain lower bounds on the number of SAT calls needed to solve Maj-AS(ag.-size).

Proposition 5. *Let P be any* $\mathrm{FPT}^{\mathrm{NP}[f(k)]}$*-hard problem. Then P is not solvable by an fpt-algorithm that uses only $O(1)$ many SAT calls, unless the PH collapses.*

Proof. Assume that P is solvable by an fpt-algorithm that uses only c many SAT calls, where c is a constant. We will show that the PH collapses. Since P is $\mathrm{FPT}^{\mathrm{NP}[f(k)]}$-hard, we know that there exists an fpt-reduction R_1 from BH(level)-Sat to P. Then, by (the proof of) Lemma 2, there exists an fpt-reduction R_2 from P to BH(level)-Sat, that reduces any instance (x', k') of P to an instance (x'', k'') of BH(level)-Sat, where $k'' \leq 2^{c+1}$. Then, the composition R of R_1 and R_2 is an fpt-reduction from BH(level)-Sat to itself such that any instance (x, k) of BH(level)-Sat is reduced to an equivalent instance (x'', k'') of BH(level)-Sat, where $k'' \leq 2^{c+1}$. We can straightforwardly modify this reduction to always produce an instance $(x'', 2^{c+1})$ of BH(level)-Sat, by adding trivial instances of SAT to the sequence x''.

We now show that the Boolean Hierarchy collapses to the m-th level, where $m = 2^{c+1}$. Let y be an instance of BH_{m+1}-Sat. We can then see the reduction R as a polynomial-time reduction from BH_{m+1}-Sat to BH_m-Sat: the fpt-reduction R runs in time $f(k) \cdot n^{O(1)}$, and since $k = m+1$ is a constant, the factor $f(k)$ is constant. From this we can conclude that $\mathrm{BH}_m = \mathrm{BH}_{m+1}$. Thus, the BH collapses, and consequently the PH collapses [13, 31]. □

The above lower bound holds for any $\mathrm{FPT}^{\mathrm{NP}[f(k)]}$-hard problem. We can improve this bound for the particular case of Maj-AS(ag.-size).

THEOREM 2. *Deciding whether* $(x, k) \in$ MAJ-AS(ag.-size) *is not solvable by an fpt-algorithm that uses* $o(\log k)$ *many SAT calls, unless the PH collapses.*

PROOF (SKETCH). The proof is analogous to the proof of Proposition 5. Since we know in addition that there exists an fpt-reduction from MAJ-AS(ag.-size) to BH(level)-SAT that increases the parameter value (only) exponentially, the argument from the proof of Proposition 5 gives us the lower bound on the number of SAT calls. □

3.2 Bounded Treewidth

Another type of structure that the agenda Φ can exhibit is the way in which the formulas $\varphi \in \Phi$ interact with each other. As an extreme example, consider the case of an agenda Φ with $[\Phi] = \{\varphi_1, \dots, \varphi_m\}$, and where all formulas φ_i are variable-disjoint. Clearly, any minimal inconsistent subset of this agenda has size 1, and thus this agenda is safe for the majority rule. In less extreme cases, the formulas of the agenda are allowed to interact (i.e., to have variables in common), but their interaction is structured in a particular way. The type of structured interaction that we consider in this section is the 'tree-likeness' of various graphs representing the interaction between formulas of the agenda, captured by the treewidth of these graphs. Treewidth is commonly used in the parameterized complexity analysis of hard problems in various fields, such as graph theory, Boolean satisfiability, constraint satisfaction, and Knowledge Representation and Reasoning. Recently, it has also been used to obtain fpt-reductions to SAT [27]. Intuitively, one could think of agendas of bounded treewidth as agendas where the propositional variables are divided into a number of (thematic) groups, where the interaction between such groups is tree-like. As an example, one could consider an agenda occurring in a court case, where propositions are grouped according to various claims made by the plaintiff, and where these claims support each other in a tree-shaped structure.

Let Φ be an agenda with $[\Phi] = \{\varphi_1, \dots, \varphi_m\}$, where each φ_i is a CNF formula. We define the following graphs that are intended to capture the interaction between formulas in Φ. The *formula primal graph* $\mathcal{G}^{fp}(\Phi)$ of Φ has as vertices the variables $\text{Var}(\Phi)$ occurring in the agenda, and two variables are connected by an edge if there exists a formula φ_i in which they both occur. The *formula incidence graph* $\mathcal{G}^{fi}(\Phi)$ of Φ is a bipartite graph whose vertices consist of (1) the variables $\text{Var}(\Phi)$ occurring in the agenda and (2) the formulas $\varphi_i \in \Phi$. A variable $x \in \text{Var}(\Phi)$ is connected by an edge with a formula $\varphi_i \in \Phi$ if x occurs in φ_i, i.e., $x \in \text{Var}(\varphi_i)$. The *clausal primal graph* $\mathcal{G}^{fp}(\Phi)$ of Φ has as vertices the variables $\text{Var}(\Phi)$ occurring in the agenda, and two variables are connected by an edge if there exists a formula φ_i and a clause $c \in \varphi_i$ in which they both occur. The *clausal incidence graph* $\mathcal{G}^{fi}(\Phi)$ of Φ is a bipartite graph whose vertices consist of (1) the variables $\text{Var}(\Phi)$ occurring in the agenda and (2) the clauses c occurring in formulas $\varphi_i \in \Phi$. A variable $x \in \text{Var}(\Phi)$ is connected by an edge with a clause c of the formula $\varphi_i \in \Phi$ if x occurs in c, i.e., $x \in \text{Var}(c)$.

Now, we consider the following parameterizations of the problem MAJ-AS. The problem MAJ-AS(f-tw) has as parameter the treewidth of the formula primal graph (the *formula primal treewidth*). The problem MAJ-AS(f-tw*) has as parameter the treewidth of the formula incidence graph (the *formula incidence treewidth*). Similarly, the parameterized problems MAJ-AS(c-tw) and MAJ-AS(c-tw*) have as parameters the treewidth of the clausal primal graph and the clausal incidence graph, respectively.

We show that the presence of tree-like structure in three of these four graphs leads to a reduction in the complexity of the problem MAJ-AS. Concretely, we show that in one case, the problem is fixed-parameter tractable, and in two other cases there exists an fpt-reduction to UNSAT.

PROPOSITION 6. MAJ-AS(f-tw) *is fixed-parameter tractable.*

PROOF (SKETCH). We give a high-level description how to prove this by using Courcelle's Theorem. One can encode the agenda Φ into a relational structure, representing by binary relations which formulas contain which clauses and which variables appear (positively or negatively) in which clauses. Moreover, one can do this in such a way that the treewidth of the Gaifman graph of this structure is at most a constant more than the treewidth of the formula primal graph of the agenda. Then, using these relation symbols, one can express the median property with a fixed monadic second-order logic sentence. The fixed-parameter tractability result then follows by Courcelle's Theorem. □

PROPOSITION 7. MAJ-AS(c-tw) *is* para-co-NP*-complete.*

PROOF. To show membership, it suffices to describe a nondeterministic fpt-algorithm that decides whether an instance is a no-instance of MAJ-AS(c-tw) [21]. The algorithm first guesses a subset $\Phi' \subseteq \Phi$ of the agenda of size > 2. Next, the algorithm verifies whether the formula $\psi = \bigwedge_{\varphi \in \Phi'} \varphi$ is unsatisfiable. Since the primal treewidth of ψ is bounded, this can be done in fpt-time [23, 15]. Next, the algorithm verifies whether for each $\varphi' \in \Phi'$ the formula $\psi' = \bigwedge_{\varphi \in \Phi \setminus \{\varphi'\}} \varphi$ is satisfiable. These are $|\Phi'| \leq |\Phi|$ many checks. Since each formula ψ' has bounded primal treewidth, each of these checks can be done in fpt-time. The algorithm accepts if and only if none of these checks fails, and thus it accepts if and only if there exists a minimal unsatisfiable subagenda of size > 2. Therefore, it checks whether a given instance is a no-instance of MAJ-AS in nondeterministic fpt-time. Hardness can be shown with an fpt-reduction from the parameterized variant of UNSAT where the parameter value is a constant. We omit a proof of hardness. □

PROPOSITION 8. MAJ-AS(c-tw*) *is* para-co-NP*-complete.*

PROOF (SKETCH). To show membership, it suffices to describe a nondeterministic fpt-algorithm that decides whether an instance is a no-instance of MAJ-AS(c-tw) [21]. The algorithm works exactly along the same lines as the algorithm given in the proof of membership for Proposition 7. Since satisfiability of CNF formulas of bounded incidence treewidth is also solvable in fpt-time [40], this algorithm also runs in (nondeterministic) fpt-time. Hardness can be shown similarly to the hardness proof of Proposition 7. We omit a proof of hardness. □

Finally, we show that bounding the formula incidence treewidth does not improve the complexity of the problem MAJ-AS.

PROPOSITION 9. MAJ-AS(f-tw*) *is* para-Π_2^P*-complete.*

PROOF. We observe that the Π_2^P-hardness proof of MAJ-AS given by Endriss, Grandi and Porello [20, Lemmas 22 and 24] shows that the problem MAJ-AS is already Π_2^P-hard for agendas with formula incidence treewidth 1. This implies that MAJ-AS(f-tw*) is para-Π_2^P-hard. □

3.3 Small Counterexamples

Another commonly identified "hidden" structure in problem instances is a restriction on the size of counterexamples. Many computational problems ask for the non-existence of a particular counterexample, and many of such problems show a decrease in complexity if attention can be restricted to counterexamples of a particular bounded size only.

One prominent example of a decrease in complexity induced by a restriction on the size of counterexamples is the method of Bounded Model Checking [6, 7]. In a nutshell, model checking is the problem of verifying whether a model of a system meets a given specification. This problem finds applications in a myriad of domains. A commonly used formalization is the problem of deciding whether a given transition systems satisfies a specification given in the form of a linear-time temporal logic (LTL) formula. This variant of the problem is PSPACE-complete (cf. [1, 14]). The problem is equivalent to deciding whether there exists no path (potentially of exponential length) in the transition system that serves as a counterexample to the specification. If the size of such counterexamples to consider is bounded (by an upper bound given in the input), the complexity of the problem decreases to NP [6, 7]. This result has been successfully applied in practice, by implementing algorithms that iteratively search for counterexamples of increasing size (cf. [6]). In the worst-case, there can be a counterexample of exponential size, but in many instances occurring in practice, small counterexamples can be found efficiently this way.

A natural question to investigate is whether we could apply a similar approach to deciding whether an agenda is safe for the majority rule. In order to do so, we would like to get an improvement in the computational complexity for the case where the size of counterexamples is bounded. Therefore, we consider the following parameterized variant MAJ-AS(c.e.-size) of the problem MAJ-AS. The problem consists of deciding, given an agenda Φ, and an integer k, whether every inconsistent subset Φ' of Φ of size k has itself an inconsistent subset of size at most 2? The parameter is k.

Assuming that counterexamples to the MP are small in practice corresponds to the supposition that whenever several statements together imply another statement, this latter statement is already implied by a small number of the former statements. In other words, the interaction between statements is, in a sense, local.

This problem is also related to agenda safety for supermajority rules. A supermajority rule accepts any proposition in the agenda if and only if a certain supermajority of the individuals, specified by a threshold $q \in (\frac{1}{2}, 1]$, accepts the proposition. Such rules always produce consistent outcomes if the threshold is greater than $\frac{k-1}{k}$, where k is the size of the largest minimally inconsistent subagenda (cf. [16, 32]).

Unfortunately, it turns out that this parameterization does not lead to a significant (practically exploitable) improvement in the computational complexity. In order to prove this, we will need the following technical lemma (we omit its straightforward proof).

LEMMA 4. *Let* (φ, k) *be an instance of* $\forall^k\exists^*$-WSAT. *In polynomial time, we can construct an equivalent instance* (φ', k) *of* $\forall^k\exists^*$-WSAT *such that: (1) for every assignment* $\alpha : X \rightarrow \{0,1\}$ *of weight* $m > k$*, the formula* $\exists Y.\psi[\alpha]$ *is false; and (2) for every assignment* $\alpha : X \rightarrow \{0,1\}$ *of weigth* $m < k$*, the formula* $\exists Y.\psi[\alpha]$ *is true.*

THEOREM 3. MAJ-AS(c.e.-size) *is* $\forall^k\exists^*$*-complete.*

PROOF (SKETCH). In order to show $\forall^k\exists^*$-hardness, we provide an fpt-reduction from $\forall^k\exists^*$-WSAT to MAJ-AS(c.e.-size). Let (φ, k) be an instance of $\forall^k\exists^*$-WSAT, where $\varphi = \forall X.\exists Y.\psi$ is a quantified Boolean formula, $X = \{x_1, \dots, x_n\}$, and k is a positive integer. We may assume without loss of generality that φ satisfies properties (1) and (2) described in Lemma 4. We define the agenda $\Phi = \{x_1, \neg x_1, \dots, x_n, \neg x_n, (\psi \wedge z), \neg(\psi \wedge z)\}$, where z is a fresh variable. We claim that for all assignments $\alpha : X \rightarrow \{0,1\}$ of weight k it is the case that $\exists Y.\psi[\alpha]$ is true if and only if every inconsistent subset Φ' of Φ of size $k+1$ has itself an inconsistent subset of size 2. □

Intuitively, restricting attention to counterexamples of size k, still leaves a search space of $O(n^k)$ many possible counterexamples (where n is the input size). Moreover, since there is no restriction on the agenda, searching this space for a counterexample (or verifying that no such counterexample exists) is computationally hard.

4. CONCLUSION

Our main aim, in this paper, was to argue that the complexity analysis of problems in computational social choice that are 'beyond NP' benefits from a parameterized complexity perspective, aiming at obtaining fpt-reductions to SAT in addition to fixed-parameter tractability results. As a concrete case study to kick-off this line of investigation, we provided a parameterized complexity analysis of the problem of agenda safety for the majority rule in judgment aggregation. We identified several positive cases, in addition to several negative cases. In several positive cases, the safety of the agenda can be decided by reducing the problem to a single SAT instance. In another positive case, we can decide whether the agenda is safe for the majority rule in fpt-time using a small number of SAT calls. Moreover, for this case, we identified lower bounds on the number of SAT calls needed to solve the problem in fpt-time.

We hope that the initial results obtained in this paper prove to be the beginning of a structured parameterized complexity investigation of problems in the field of computational social choice that are located at higher levels of the PH. One concrete direction for further research would be to explicitly develop fpt-reductions to SAT for the cases where this is possible, and to optimize them for practical use. In addition, it would be interesting to study the parameterized complexity of the problem of agenda safety for other judgment aggregation procedures.

Acknowledgments

Ronald de Haan and Stefan Szeider are supported by the European Research Council (ERC), project 239962 (COMPLEX REASON), and the Austrian Science Fund (FWF), project P26200 (Parameterized Compilation).

REFERENCES

[1] C. Baier and J.-P. Katoen. *Principles of Model Checking*. The MIT Press, 2008.

[2] D. Baumeister, F. Brandt, F. A. Fischer, J. Hoffmann, and J. Rothe. The complexity of computing minimal unidirectional covering sets. *Theory Comput. Syst.*, 53(3):467–502, 2013.

[3] D. Baumeister, G. Erdélyi, and J. Rothe. How hard is it to bribe the judges? A study of the complexity of bribery in judgment aggregation. In *Proceedings of the Second International Conference on Algorithmic Decision Theory (ADT 2011), Piscataway, NJ, USA, October 26–28, 2011*, volume 6992 of *Lecture Notes in Computer Science*, pages 1–15. Springer Verlag, 2011.

[4] N. Betzler, R. Bredereck, J. Chen, and R. Niedermeier. Studies in computational aspects of voting – a parameterized complexity perspective. In H. L. Bodlaender, R. Downey, F. V. Fomin, and D. Marx, editors, *The Multivariate Algorithmic Revolution and Beyond - Essays Dedicated to Michael R. Fellows on the Occasion of His 60th Birthday*, volume 7370 of *Lecture Notes in Computer Science*, pages 318–363. Springer Verlag, 2012.

[5] N. Betzler, J. Guo, and R. Niedermeier. Parameterized computational complexity of Dodgson and Young elections. *Information and Computation*, 208(2):165–177, 2010.

[6] A. Biere. Bounded model checking. In A. Biere, M. Heule, H. van Maaren, and T. Walsh, editors, *Handbook of Satisfiability*, volume 185 of *Frontiers in Artificial Intelligence and Applications*, pages 457–481. IOS Press, 2009.

[7] A. Biere, A. Cimatti, E. M. Clarke, and Y. Zhu. Symbolic model checking without BDDs. In R. Cleaveland, editor, *Proceedings of the 5th International Conference on Tools and Algorithms for the Construction and Analysis of Systems (TACAS), 1999*, volume 1579 of *Lecture Notes in Computer Science*, pages 193–207. Springer Verlag, 1999.

[8] A. Biere, M. Heule, H. van Maaren, and T. Walsh, editors. *Handbook of Satisfiability*, volume 185 of *Frontiers in Artificial Intelligence and Applications*. IOS Press, 2009.

[9] H. L. Bodlaender. A linear-time algorithm for finding tree-decompositions of small treewidth. *SIAM J. Comput.*, 25(6):1305–1317, 1996.

[10] H. L. Bodlaender, R. Downey, F. V. Fomin, and D. Marx, editors. *The Multivariate Algorithmic Revolution and Beyond – Essays Dedicated to Michael R. Fellows on the Occasion of His 60th Birthday*, volume 7370 of *Lecture Notes in Computer Science*. Springer Verlag, 2012.

[11] S. Bouveret and J. Lang. Efficiency and envy-freeness in fair division of indivisible goods: Logical representation and complexity. *J. Artif. Intell. Res.*, 32:525–564, 2008.

[12] J. Cai, T. Gundermann, J. Hartmanis, L. A. Hemachandra, V. Sewelson, K. W. Wagner, and G. Wechsung. The Boolean hierarchy I: Structural properties. *SIAM J. Comput.*, 17(6):1232–1252, 1988.

[13] R. Chang and J. Kadin. The Boolean hierarchy and the polynomial hierarchy: a closer connection. *SIAM J. Comput.*, 25:169–178, 1993.

[14] E. M. Clarke, D. Kroening, J. Ouaknine, and O. Strichman. Completeness and complexity of bounded model checking. In B. Steffen and G. Levi, editors, *Verification, Model Checking, and Abstract Interpretation, 5th International Conference (VMCAI 2004)*, volume 2937 of *Lecture Notes in Computer Science*, pages 85–96. Springer Verlag, 2004.

[15] R. Dechter and J. Pearl. Tree clustering for constraint networks. *Artificial Intelligence*, 38(3):353–366, 1989.

[16] F. Dietrich and C. List. Judgment aggregation by quota rules: Majority voting generalized. *J. of Theoretical Politics*, 19(4):391–424, 2007.

[17] B. Dorn and I. Schlotter. Multivariate complexity analysis of swap bribery. *Algorithmica*, 64(1):126–151, 2012.

[18] R. G. Downey and M. R. Fellows. *Parameterized Complexity*. Monographs in Computer Science. Springer Verlag, New York, 1999.

[19] R. G. Downey and M. R. Fellows. *Fundamentals of Parameterized Complexity*. Texts in Computer Science. Springer Verlag, 2013.

[20] U. Endriss, U. Grandi, and D. Porello. Complexity of judgment aggregation. *J. Artif. Intell. Res.*, 45:481–514, 2012.

[21] J. Flum and M. Grohe. Describing parameterized complexity classes. *Information and Computation*, 187(2):291–319, 2003.

[22] J. Flum and M. Grohe. *Parameterized Complexity Theory*, volume XIV of *Texts in Theoretical Computer Science*. Springer Verlag, Berlin, 2006.

[23] E. C. Freuder. A sufficient condition for backtrack-bounded search. *J. of the ACM*, 29(1):24–32, 1982.

[24] C. P. Gomes, H. Kautz, A. Sabharwal, and B. Selman. Satisfiability solvers. In *Handbook of Knowledge Representation*, volume 3 of *Foundations of Artificial Intelligence*, pages 89–134. Elsevier, 2008.

[25] G. Gottlob, R. Pichler, and F. Wei. Bounded treewidth as a key to tractability of knowledge representation and reasoning. *Artificial Intelligence*, 174(1):105–132, 2010.

[26] R. de Haan and S. Szeider. Compendium of parameterized problems at higher levels of the Polynomial Hierarchy. Technical Report TR14–143, *Electronic Colloquium on Computational Complexity* (ECCC), 2014.

[27] R. de Haan and S. Szeider. Fixed-parameter tractable reductions to SAT. In U. Egly and C. Sinz, editors, *Proceedings of the 17th International Symposium on the Theory and Applications of Satisfiability Testing (SAT 2014) Vienna, Austria, July 14–17, 2014*, volume 8561 of *Lecture Notes in Computer Science*, pages 85–102. Springer Verlag, 2014.

[28] R. de Haan and S. Szeider. The parameterized complexity of reasoning problems beyond NP. In C. Baral, G. De Giacomo, and T. Eiter, editors, *Proceedings of the Fourteenth International Conference on the Principles of Knowledge Representation and Reasoning (KR 2014), Vienna, Austria, July 20-24, 2014*. AAAI Press, 2014.

[29] E. Hemaspaandra, L. A. Hemaspaandra, and J. Rothe. Exact analysis of Dodgson elections: Lewis Carroll's 1876 voting system is complete for parallel access to NP. *J. of the ACM*, 44(6):806–825, 1997.

[30] E. Hemaspaandra, H. Spakowski, and J. Vogel. The complexity of Kemeny elections. *Theoretical Computer Science*, 349(3):382–391, 2005.

[31] J. Kadin. The polynomial time hierarchy collapses if the Boolean hierarchy collapses. *SIAM J. Comput.*, 17(6):1263–1282, Dec. 1988.

[32] C. List. The theory of judgment aggregation: an introductory review. *Synthese*, 187(1):179–207, 2012.

[33] C. List and C. Puppe. Judgment aggregation: A survey. In *Handbook of Rational and Social Choice*. Oxford University Press, 2009.

[34] S. Malik and L. Zhang. Boolean satisfiability from theoretical hardness to practical success. *Communications of the ACM*, 52(8):76–82, 2009.

[35] A. R. Meyer and L. J. Stockmeyer. The equivalence problem for regular expressions with squaring requires exponential space. In *SWAT*, pages 125–129. IEEE Computer Soc., 1972.

[36] K. Nehring and C. Puppe. The structure of strategy-proof social choice - part I: General characterization and possibility results on median spaces. *J. of Economic Theory*, 135(1):269–305, 2007.

[37] R. Niedermeier. *Invitation to Fixed-Parameter Algorithms*. Oxford Lecture Series in Mathematics and its Applications. Oxford University Press, 2006.

[38] C. H. Papadimitriou. *Computational Complexity*. Addison-Wesley, 1994.

[39] K. A. Sakallah and J. Marques-Silva. Anatomy and empirical evaluation of modern SAT solvers. *Bulletin of the European Association for Theoretical Computer Science*, 103:96–121, 2011.

[40] M. Samer and S. Szeider. Algorithms for propositional model counting. *J. Discrete Algorithms*, 8(1):50–64, 2010.

[41] J. Siekmann and G. Wrightson, editors. *Automation of reasoning. Classical Papers on Computer Science 1967–1970*, volume 2. Springer Verlag, 1983.

[42] M. Slavkovik. *Judgment Aggregation for Multiagent Systems*. PhD thesis, University of Luxembourg, 2012.

[43] L. J. Stockmeyer. The polynomial-time hierarchy. *Theoretical Computer Science*, 3(1):1–22, 1976.

[44] G. S. Tseitin. Complexity of a derivation in the propositional calculus. *Zap. Nauchn. Sem. Leningrad Otd. Mat. Inst. Akad. Nauk SSSR*, 8:23–41, 1968. English translation reprinted in [41].

[45] C. Wrathall. Complete sets and the polynomial-time hierarchy. *Theoretical Computer Science*, 3(1):23–33, 1976.

Adaptive Budgeted Bandit Algorithms for Trust Development in a Supply-Chain

Sandip Sen
Tandy School of Computer Science
The University of Tulsa
sandip@utulsa.edu

Anton Ridgway
Tandy School of Computer Science
The University of Tulsa
anton-ridgway@utulsa.edu

Michael Ripley
Tandy School of Computer Science
The University of Tulsa
michael-ripley@utulsa.edu

ABSTRACT

Recently, an AAMAS Challenges & Visions paper identified several key components of a comprehensive trust management has been understudied by the research community [13]. We believe that we can build on recent advances in closely related research in other sub-fields of AI and multiagent systems to address some of these issues. For example, the budgeted multi-armed bandit problem involves pulling multiple arms with stochastic rewards with the goal of maximizing the total reward generated from those arms, while keeping the cost of pulling the arms beneath a given budget. We argue that multi-armed bandit algorithms can be adapted to address research issues in trust engagement and evaluation components of a comprehensive trust management approach. To support this proposition, we consider a supply-chain application, where a tree of dependent supplier agents can be considered as an arm of the online bandit problem with budget constraints. Each of the nodes in the supply chain must then solve their local bandit problem in parallel to determine which of its sub-suppliers is most trustworthy. We use new arm-selection strategies, and demonstrate how they can be gainfully applied to the trust-based decision-making in the supply chain to reduce time to production and hence improve utility by timely delivery of products.

Categories and Subject Descriptors

I.2.11 [**Artificial Intelligence**]: Distributed Artificial Intelligence—*Multiagent systems*

General Terms

Performance, Reliability, Algorithms

Keywords

exploration-exploitation; trust management; contracting

1. INTRODUCTION

Research on trust in multiagent systems has given us a variety of conceptual frameworks to view trust and effective algorithms for evaluating the trustworthiness of other agents given the history of mutual interactions [7, 9, 11, 16, 17]. However, it has been posited that to fully harness the effectiveness of trust based decision making, it is critical to develop a more comprehensive approach to trust management that addresses not only trust evaluation but also provides strategic reasoning procedures that determine who to interact with, in what context, and how to best utilize the resultant knowledge about the trustworthiness of others [13]. The goal then is to develop proactive trust mechanisms that explore possible fruitful partnerships, create situations where interactions will provide discriminatory evidence of the trustworthiness of potential partners, and use a well-thought-out plan of how to best utilize the trusted partners given expectations of future goals, plans and resource requirements.

In this paper, we consider the problem of proactive engagement of potential long-term partners to determine who can be trusted for providing consistent service on which an agent's goal is critically dependent. Whereas most of the research on trust in multiagent systems focuses on after-the-event, offline evaluation of interaction histories to determine trustworthiness of partners, real-world scenarios demand forward-looking, online schemes that has to choose to engage interaction partners where the process of engagement incurs a cost. This "exploration cost" must be balanced against possible gain or "exploitation benefit" in the long run from the knowledge of who the more trustworthy partners are. Research in machine learning, and in particular, reinforcement learning has long confronted similar exploration versus exploitation dilemmas [12]. However, most of these research has ignored the time and cost of exploration, and focused primarily on proving convergence to optimal policies for solving the underlying Markov Decision processes in the limit, i.e., without time or budget constraints. In particular, the multi-armed bandit (MAB) problem has been proposed as a theoretical framework for evaluating the utility of interacting with multiple entities with stochastically varying performance [2, 1].

Though this approach would appear to be a natural mapping of the problem of evaluation of trust in new partners, on closer inspection a key missing aspect underlines the fundamental difference between the two. The basic MAB model does not consider any cost for pulling an arm, whereas interacting with a partner to gather further information to evaluate their trustworthiness involves risks, time and resource commitment, as well as other costs. More recently, however, researchers have considered augmentations of the basic MAB problem, that consider the cost of pulling arms in combination with a budget limit for exploration [8, 14, 15], i.e., a resource constraint that necessitates strategic engagement with potential partners to quickly identify partnerships which are likely to deliver maximal long-term benefits. We believe that solution approaches for the Fixed-Cost Multi-Armed Bandit Problem with Budget Constraints (MAB-BF) can be adapted to address the issue of strategic engagement and evaluation of potential partner's

Appears in: *Proceedings of the 14th International Conference on Autonomous Agents and Multiagent Systems (AAMAS 2015), Bordini, Elkind, Weiss, Yolum (eds.), May 4–8, 2015, Istanbul, Turkey.*

trustworthiness under a number of settings and trust metrics such as reliability, fairness, quality of performance, timeliness, etc. The MAB-BF has already been utilized for a wide range of reinforcement learning applications, including bidding in ad exchanges, bid optimization in search, and service provider selection in cloud computing [3, 5, 4, 6, 10].

Various metrics for determining the trustworthiness of a partner has been proposed. In this paper, we consider performance, in terms of reliability, as the objective criteria for trustworthiness. This choice is motivated by the following observation [13]: *Trust in another agent reduces the uncertainty over that agent's independent actions which positively correlates with the truster's utility.* We consider existing and recently developed approaches to addressing the MAB problem with cost and budget constraints to proactively engage and evaluate potential partners to gauge their reliability and hence long-term trustworthiness. To evaluate the efficacy of these approaches, we introduce a Supply Chain domain where a manufacturer has to procure raw materials from contractors of initially unknown reliability. Contractors in turn have to depend on sub-contractors to produce their deliverables. The goal of each agent in the supply chain is to reduce their time to delivery of their product for which they have to strategically engage their sub-contractors to discriminate sub-contractors of differing reliability.

We introduce three new algorithms for addressing the MAB-BF problem. First, we formally present the MAB-BF problem (Section 2); then, we introduce recent algorithms proposed for this variant of the MAB problem, together with our own proposed algorithms, highlighting their interrelationships and differences (Section 3). We then introduce the supply chain domain used for evaluating the effectiveness of the proposed algorithms in determining the trustworthiness of the sub-contractors under varying budget constraints and performance variability (Section 4). In Section 5 we describe the simulation framework used for experiments, and in Section 6 present a series of experimental results from a variety of scenarios , varying the branching factor of the arms in each tree, the payoff distributions of the arms, and the budget available to sample from the arms. In conclusion, in Section 7 we summarize the key findings from the comparative experimental evaluation and present thoughts for future research.

2. FIXED-COST MULTI-ARMED BANDIT WITH BUDGET CONSTRAINT

We now formally introduce the version of MAB-BF problem where the goal of the agent is to maximize the reward obtained by pulling a set of $\mathcal{A} = \{1, \ldots, K\}$ arms, the ith arm has a fixed cost c_i per pull, and arm rewards are drawn from an unknown distribution with a mean value of μ_i. The agent has at its disposal a total budget of B. Let $C = \langle c_1, \ldots, c_K \rangle$ and $\mu = \langle \mu_1, \ldots, \mu_K \rangle$ refer to the vector of pulling costs and mean rewards for the K arms. We refer to the above problem as the Fixed-Cost Multi-Armed Bandit with Budget Constraint (MAB-BF), defined by the tuple $P = (\mathcal{A}, B, C, \mu)$. The goal of an agent facing such a problem is to choose a sequence of arms that optimizes the expected reward without exceeding the total budget for arm pulls. Because the number of arm pulls in a given sequence is limited by the costs of the particular arms chosen, we generally consider the utility ratio $\frac{\mu_i}{c_i}$ rather than μ_i alone to determine the priority of a given arm i. It should be noted that while one could improve overall performance somewhat by incorporating the standard deviation of reward received, or any other statistical measures, together with the utility ratio to produce a more general utility index, the result would only be a general optimization, applicable to any of the algorithms we consider; for simplicity's sake, we choose to focus on the utility ratio only, and leave the determination of a best-case utility index for another setting. Finally, note that the μ values are not available to the agent.

The number of arm pulls that an agent can make is dependent on the multiset of arms it decides to pull. We now introduce some notations to refer to sequences of arm pulls:

- $S = \langle a_1, \ldots, a_t \rangle$ refers to the sequence of arms pulled by the agent in the first t attempts. We will use $|S|$ to refer to the number of arm pulls in the sequence S and $S(i), \forall i \in \{1, \ldots, |S|\}$ to refer to the ith arm pulled in that sequence. Also we denote the subsequence of pulls in S from $t = t_1, \ldots, t_2$ as S_{t_1,t_2}. We will use $a \in S$ to test for the existence of an arm a in the sequence S or to range over the set of arms in the sequence.
- n_a^S represents the number of times arm $a \in \mathcal{A}$ was pulled in sequence S.
- A_t is the set of arms which can still be pulled after the sequence of arm pulls $S_{1,t}$ with the remaining budget $B_t = B - \sum_{i=1}^{t} c_{S(i)}$, i.e., $A_t = \{a | a \in \mathcal{A} \wedge c_a \leq B_t\}$.
- A sequence S is *valid* if it does not violate the budget constraint, i.e., $\sum_{a \in S} c_a \leq B$.
- $\mathcal{S} = \{S | S \text{ is valid}\}$ is the set of all valid sequences. For the rest of the paper we will use the term 'sequence' for valid sequences.
- $G_S = \sum_i^{|S|} r_{a_i,i}$ is the total reward obtained from a valid sequence S, where $r_{a_i,i}$ is the reward returned from arm $a_i \in \mathcal{A}$ pulled at time i. As the rewards generated are non-deterministic, we are more interested the sum of the *mean* rewards in the sequence; that is, the *Expected Total Reward of sequence S*, $E[G_S] = \sum_i^{|S|} \mu_{a_i}$. Correspondingly, we are interested in the optimal sequence S^* if the reward distributions for the arms were known,

$$S^* = \arg\max_{S \in \mathcal{S}} E[G_S] \quad (1)$$

and the associated payoff $E[G_{S^*}]$. Note that since the mean rewards for the arms are not known *a priori*, we will only know G_S.
- Given a sequence of arm pulls, S, an estimate of the mean reward for each of the sampled arms, μ_S, can be formed. Then $\mu_S = \langle \mu_1^S, \ldots, \mu_K^S \rangle$ where $\mu_i^S, \forall i \in \mathcal{A}$, is the average reward obtained from the n_i^S pulls of arm i in the sequence S:

$$\mu_i^S = \frac{1}{n_i^S} \sum_{j=1}^{|S|} I(S(j) = i) r_{i,j} \quad (2)$$

where $I(\cdot)$ is the Indicator function.
- The expected regret, $\mathcal{R}(S)$ of the sequence S is then calculated as the difference: $\mathcal{R}(S) = E[G_{S^*}] - E[G_S]$. The desirability of a sequence of arm pulls can be measured by its expected regret and the problem of optimizing expected reward can be mapped into the problem of minimizing expected regret.

3. MAB-BF ALGORITHMS

In this section we introduce the different algorithms we experiment with. We first introduce some existing algorithms and then discuss our proposed approaches.

3.1 Existing Algorithms

We now describe some existing algorithms for the MAB problem; the first two (ϵ-first, Greedy) have an initial exploration phase for estimating the mean rewards of the K arms, and in the subsequent exploitation phase pull the arms in a greedy manner, and the last (fKDE) one stochastically integrates exploration and exploitation while narrowing its focus:

Budget-Limited ϵ-first: This algorithm, henceforth referred to as ϵ-first, uniformly selects from the set of arms, performing unordered sweeps of each before beginning again, until its exploration budget, ϵB, is exhausted (not enough budget remains to pull even the minimum cost arm[1]). Let $S^{explore}_{\epsilon-\text{first}}(P)$[2] be the sequence of arm pulls for the exploration phase for an ϵ-first approach with MAB-BF problem P. At the end of the exploration phase, an estimate of the mean rewards, $\mu_{S^{explore}_{\epsilon-\text{first}}}$ is calculated and subsequently used in the exploitation phase. Next, the arms are sorted by the ratio of their estimated mean to pulling cost (their reward-cost ratio). The best such arm, $I^{max} = \arg\max_{i \in \mathcal{A}} \frac{\mu_i^{S^{explore}_{\epsilon-\text{first}}}}{c_i}$, which we refer to as the *active arm*, is pulled until not enough of the exploitation budget, $(1-\epsilon)B$, is left for one more pull of that arm. This process is repeated with the rest of the arms until the budget is completely exhausted (not enough remains to pull even the lowest cost arm). We refer to the sequence of arms pulled in this exploration phase as $S^{exploit}_{\epsilon-\text{first}}(P)$ and the combined exploration-exploitation sequence as $S_{\epsilon-\text{first}} = S^{explore}_{\epsilon-\text{first}}(P) + S^{exploit}_{\epsilon-\text{first}}(P)$. This algorithm is presented in Algorithm 1.

One key difference between the original formulation of this algorithm[14] and our implementation of it is that our version continues to update the estimates of the arms during the exploitation phase, so that the active arm in that phase can change if its utility ratio drops below that of another arm, even if its cost is still affordable. We refer to our version of algorithms that behave this way as *online-exploitation* variants, in contrast to the original *offline-exploitation* variants. Experiments have shown that the online variants significantly outperform the offline variants in most scenarios and hence in this paper we present results with the online variants only, unless otherwise noted.

Greedy Algorithm: The Greedy algorithm is a special case of the ϵ-first algorithm where the exploration budget only allows each arm to be pulled once before the exploitation phase begins. This algorithm is remarkable because to our knowledge it has not been used before for the MAB-BF problem, but its online-exploration variant nevertheless performs exceptionally well on average. Note that since we require all arms to be pulled at least once, when $\epsilon \leq \frac{\sum_{i=1}^{K} c_i}{B}$, ϵ-first algorithms are reduced to the Greedy algorithm.

Fractional Knapsack-based Decreasing ϵ-greedy (fKDE): The fractional KDE algorithm [14] is a decreasing exploration over time approach which first pulls the arms uniformly γ times and thereafter pulls the arm with the highest estimated reward-cost ratio with increasing probability. The probability of uniform random exploration after t arm pulls is set to $\varepsilon_t = \min(1, \frac{\gamma}{t})$. Otherwise, the arm with the highest estimated reward-cost ratio, based on the sequence of arms pulled, is chosen.

Input : $P = (\mathcal{A}, B, C, \mu)$: MAB-BF problem;
ϵ, exploration fraction of budget
Output: S, a sequence of arm pulls;
μ', a vector of estimated mean rewards from the K arms;
G, total reward from all arm pulls;

Exploration phase:
$t \leftarrow 1$; $S \leftarrow \varnothing$; $G \leftarrow 0$; ExplorationRounds $\leftarrow \left\lfloor \frac{\epsilon B}{\sum_{i=1}^{K} c_i} \right\rfloor$;
for $i = 1 \rightarrow K$ **do**
    $\mu'_i \leftarrow 0$
for $n = 1 \rightarrow$ *ExplorationRounds* **do**
    for $i = 1 \rightarrow K$ **do**
        pull arm i to obtain $r_{i,t}$; $G \leftarrow G + r_{i,t}$;
        $S \leftarrow S + i$; // Add i to sequence S
        $\mu'_i \leftarrow \mu'_i + r_{i,t}$;
        $t \leftarrow t + 1$;
for $i = 1 \rightarrow K$ **do**
    $\mu'_i = \frac{\mu'_i}{n_i^S}$
; // form reward mean estimates
Exploitation phase:
RemainingBudget = $B -$ ExplorationRounds $* \sum_{i=1}^{K} c_i$;
$A' = \mathcal{A}$; // Initialize available arms
while *RemainingBudget* $\geq \min_{i \in \mathcal{A}'} c_i$ **do**
    $I^{max} = \arg\max_{i \in A} \frac{\mu_i}{c_i}$; // pick best arm
    if *RemainingBudget* $\geq c_{I^{max}}$ **then** // if budget allows to pull arm
        pull arm I^{max} to get reward $r_{I^{max},t}$;
        $G \leftarrow G + r_{I^{max},t}$;
        $\mu'_{I^{max}} \leftarrow \frac{\mu'_{I^{max}} * n^S_{I^{max}} + r_{I^{max},t}}{n^S_{I^{max}} + 1}$; // update mean reward estimate of arm
        $S \leftarrow S + I^{max}$;
        RemainingBudget $\leftarrow$ RemainingBudget$- c_{I^{max}}$;
        $t \leftarrow t + 1$;
    else
        $A' \leftarrow A' \setminus \{I^{max}\}$; // eliminate arm
return (S, μ', G);

Algorithm 1: The ϵ-first algorithm.

3.2 New Algorithms

Now, we present algorithms that we have developed for the MAB-BF problem. We believe these algorithms explore more intelligently compared to their predecessors; the choice of arms to be pulled during exploration is driven by either the number of arms $|\mathcal{A}|$, or the distribution of the arm rewards in μ and the costs in C; past algorithms only made use of uniform or minimal exploration phases, and fixed the exploration budget without consideration of the bandit at hand. Also note that all the algorithms that we introduce are *online* algorithms, i.e., an eliminated arm may be reconsidered if the reward-cost ratio of a sufficient number of previously preferred arms drops below the corresponding ratio of this arm upon further sampling.

l-split (lS): This is a generalized Greedy approach. Instead of eliminating all but one arm after the first pass, the `lS` algorithm successively eliminates $(1 - \frac{1}{l})$ of the arms after each pass: if $A_{lS}(p)$ is the number of surviving arms after p splitting passes of the algorithm, then $A_{lS}(p+1) = \lceil \frac{1}{l} A_{lS}(p) \rceil$. After $\lceil \log_l K \rceil$ passes, `lS` narrows down the choice to one, and thereafter performs greedy exploitation. The algorithm

[1] We only consider scenarios where the exploration budget allows us to pull every arm the same number of times in the exploration phase.

[2] We will omit the problem argument P in cases where the context is clear.

is presented in detail in Algorithm 2. The simplest of this family of algorithms is the 2-split (2S) or halving algorithm, which successively eliminates approximately half of the underperforming arms after each pass.

Progressive exploration ϵ-first (PEEF): The `PEEF` algorithm was developed upon a careful evaluation of the ϵ-first algorithm. Whereas the latter expends its exploration budget uniformly over the set of K arms, we conjectured that in a number of scenarios, particularly those with a large number of arms, there might be some low return arms that can be quickly discarded. More importantly, we believe that the exploration budget can be better utilized to tease out differences between similar, high reward-cost ratio arms by visiting them with increasing frequency. Hence, rather than uniform exploration, we propose a progressive exploration scheme where we perform a $l-$split operation, as in the `lS` algorithm after each pass. The difference with that algorithm is that in `PEEF` the splitting value l is calculated such that the number of remaining arm choices is reduced to 1 approximately at the end of the exploration phase. Given an exploration budget of ϵB then we want l to be such that the following condition holds:

$$\sum_{j=1}^{\log_l K} \frac{K}{j} c_{avg} = \epsilon B, \tag{3}$$

where $c_{avg} = \frac{1}{K} \sum_{i=1}^{K} c_i$, is the average cost of pulling an arm[3]. Solving this equation for l we obtain $l = \frac{\epsilon B - 1}{\epsilon B - K}$. For obvious reasons, we will perform a pairwise comparison of the ϵ-first algorithm and the corresponding `PEEF` algorithm for different scenarios in the experimental section.

Survival of the Above Average (SOAAv): This algorithm also successively narrows down the set of active arms by eliminating underperforming arms. But rather than eliminating a fixed number of arms after each pass, it eliminates arms whose estimated reward-cost ratio is below $(1+x)$ times the average of such ratios of the arms in the last pass.
Setting $x = 0$ means only above average individuals survive from one pass of the arms to the next. Note again that this is an online-exploration approach where a previously eliminated arm can come back into the active set if estimates of other active arms drop. This algorithm is presented in more detail in Algorithm 3.

Of the above algorithms, both `1S` and `PEEF` are rank-based algorithms, where arms are eliminated based on their ranking by reward-ratio cost ratios, whereas only the `SOAAv` algorithm is a *value-based* approach, where arms with estimated reward-cost ratios below a certain factor of the average of the currently active set are eliminated.

Input : $P = (\mathcal{A}, B, C, \mu)$: MAB-BF problem;
l, elimination factor
Output: S, a sequence of arm pulls;
μ', a vector of the arms' sample mean rewards;
G, total reward from all arm pulls;

$t \leftarrow 1$; $S \leftarrow \varnothing$; $G \leftarrow 0$; RemainingBudget $\leftarrow B$; NumPasses $\leftarrow 0$
for $i = 1 \rightarrow K$ **do**
    $\mu'_i \leftarrow 0$
$A' = \mathcal{A}$; `// Initialize available arms`
while $A' \neq \varnothing$ **do**
    foreach $a \in A'$ **do**
        if *RemainingBudget*$\geq c_{a_i}$ **then** `// if budget allows to pull arm`
            pull arm a to obtain reward $r_{a,t}$;
            $G \leftarrow G + r_{a,t}$;
            $\mu'_a \leftarrow \frac{\mu'_a * n_a^S + r_{a,t}}{n_a^S + 1}$; `// update mean reward estimate of arm`
            $S \leftarrow S + a$;
            RemainingBudget $\leftarrow$ RemainingBudget$-c_a$;
            $t \leftarrow t + 1$;
    $NumPasses \leftarrow NumPasses + 1$;
    $A' = \varnothing$;
    NumToPull $\leftarrow \lceil \frac{K}{l^{NumPasses}} \rceil$;
    while *NumToPull* > 0 *and* $A - A' \neq \varnothing$ **do**
        $A' \leftarrow A' \cup \{\arg\max_{i \in A} \frac{\mu_i}{c_i} \mid c_{a_i} \leq RemainingBudget, A_i \notin S'\}$;
        NumToPull $\leftarrow$ NumToPull - 1;
return (S, μ', G);

Algorithm 2: The $l-$`Split` algorithm.

4. SUPPLY-CHAIN MODEL

We now introduce the supply-chain model where contractors have to engage strategically with sub-contractors of initially-unknown reliability (trustworthiness). Each interaction has a cost and the contractor's goal is to distinguish the trustworthiness of all of its sub-contractors given a fixed budget to pay for the interactions. This domain allows us to examine how the algorithms developed for the budget-constrained MAB problem perform in complex, large-scale systems, while simultaneously examining the algorithms' efficiency in dealing with trust-based decision making. The trust that the agent places in each of its sub-contractors in the chain is based on its past observations while engagement decisions have to be predicated on remaining uncertainties about discriminating between potential partners.

In our supply-chain model, there is a root agent, which has access to a fixed set of contractor agents, represented as the set of arms $\mathcal{A}_{0,0} = \langle a_{1,0}, \ldots, a_{1,k} \rangle$, where k is the branching factor. Each of the other agents $a_{l,i}$, in turn, has access to its own set of sub-contractors $\mathcal{A}_{l,i} = \langle a_{l+1,0}, \ldots, a_{l+1,k} \rangle$, where l is the current level in the tree. This gives rise to a supply-chain tree, with the original agent $a_{0,0}$ at the root. Each agent besides the root agent possesses a fixed contracting cost $c_{l,i}$. The utility that each agent returns to its contracting agent is the inverse of the time that it takes to complete the task. This time is determined by the time returned by the agent's own sub-contractors, added to a value drawn from a Gaussian distribution internal to the agent, with mean $\mu_{l,i}$ and standard deviation $\sigma_{l,i}$; leaf agents' times are determined by their own distributions only. For our implementation of this model, we chose to hold the branching factor fixed for all the levels of each branch. Additionally, to maintain a reasonable level of variation in our experiments, we chose to give each agent in $\mathcal{A}_1$ identical sub-trees.

Especially important is that, because each algorithm must perform its own bandit problem on its sub-contractors simultaneously, and because no agent has the opportunity to sample arms when it is not pulled, most agents will not be able to complete their explo-

[3]Note that this calculation of l is necessarily approximate, both for the use of c_{avg} as the cost per unit pull during the exploration phase and in the use of $\log_l K$ as the number of passes during the exploration phase.

```
Input : P = (A, B, C, μ): MAB-BF problem;
        x, elimination factor
Output: S, a sequence of arm pulls;
        μ', a vector of the arms' sample mean rewards;
        G, total reward from all arm pulls;

t ← 1; S ← ∅; G ← 0; RemainingBudget ← B;
for i = 1 → K do
    μ'_i ← 0
A' = A ; // Initialize available arms
while RemainingBudget ≥ min_{i∈A'} c_i do
    numPullsInPass=0; passAverageRatio=0;
    foreach a ∈ A' do
        if RemainingBudget ≥ c_a then        // if budget allows to pull arm
            pull arm a to obtain reward r_{a,t};
            G ← G + r_{a,t};
            μ'_a ← (μ'_a * n^S_a + r_{a,t}) / (n^S_a + 1) ; // update mean reward estimate of arm
            S ← S + a;
            RemainingBudget ← RemainingBudget − c_a;
            t ← t + 1;
            passAverageRatio ← passAverageRatio + r_{a,t} / c_a ;
            numPullsInPass ← numPullsInPass+1;
        else
            A' ← A' \ {a} ; // eliminate arm
    if numPullsInPass > 0 then
        passAverageRatio ← passAverageRatio / numPullsInPass ;
        A' = ∅
        foreach a ∈ A do
            if c_a < RemainingBudget &
               μ'_a ≥ (1 + x)passAverageRatio then
                A' ← A' ∪ {a};
return (S, μ', G);
```

Algorithm 3: The `SOAAv` algorithm.

ration before the root agent has completed its budget. To remedy this, we set the budget of agent i on level l to be $B_{l,i,t} = kc_{l,i}$, if it is selected at time t. Thus, if an agent's budget is distributed evenly among all its sub-contractor agents, the budget of each sub-contractor will be equal to that of the original contractor, giving each agent the chance to explore its options and reach exploitation in time for its contractor to benefit. Though we chose for simplicity to fix the budget multiplier at a fairly neutral level (the parent's branching factor), this value could be altered per-agent or over time to introduce additional variability in the model. Additionally, because each agent in the tree is exploring simultaneously, we expected less aggressive bandit algorithms to have a slight advantage in this setting, since they will allow the sub-contractors more time to finish exploring before they begin exploitation.

It is also of note that, because of this set-up, no agent except for the root knows what its total budget will be until it has already spent it. Thus, for algorithms that fix their exploration budget in advance, we provided an estimated exploration budget of the same size as its contracting agent– since when budget is expended uniformly, each agent receives the same budget as its contracting agent, this seemed to be a reasonable measure that would allow these algorithms to be executed throughout the tree.

5. SIMULATION FRAMEWORK

In our simulation framework, we implemented fixed supply-chain trees where the ith agent in level l, agent $a_{l,i}$, was provided with a Gaussian reward distribution defined by $\{\mu_{l,i},\sigma_{l,i}\}$ and a fixed engagement or contracting cost of $c_{l,i}$. The algorithms' performance in each scenario was averaged over one thousand trials. As results in experiments where arm costs were selected randomly close to 1 were qualitatively similar to those where all arm costs were 1, we use the results from the latter scenario for uniformity in the results presented here. This fixed cost constraint could easily be lifted, and does not substantially affect our results.

To evaluate the algorithms under consideration for the supply-chain problem, and to help discover which situations each could function best in, we made use of the following test scenarios. There are two sets of experiments that use different allotment of MAB-BF algorithms to the different nodes in the supply-chain:

Root-Variation Trees: In the root-variation case, the root agent employs the algorithm under consideration, while each other contractor in the tree employs the same "basic" algorithm (we chose `lS`) in every case; because the sub-tree of contractors would perform the same for each algorithm tested, we use this case for comparing all MAB-BF algorithms.

Homogeneous Trees: In the homogeneous case, we employ the same algorithm at each level of the tree. We expected that this arrangement would help to amplify each algorithm's relative strengths and weaknesses. Because some algorithms require the total budget to be known initially, but no agent except for the root knows this in advance, estimated exploration budgets are needed for these to be allowed in the homogeneous configuration. So experiments with Homogeneous trees are run only for algorithms that does not require the knowledge of the total budget.

In addition, we use different function distributions to generate the performances of the contractors in the supply-chain. For each of the root-variation and homogeneous cases, therefore, we also experimented with several node performance distributions.

Curve Distributions: The simplest function type that we used is the linear *curve-based* distribution. That is, the values in the μ_l vector were chosen so that successive $\mu_{l,i}$ values followed some linear, superlinear (concave down), or sublinear (concave up) curve, with the average time for the first arm being $\mu_{l,1} = \frac{\mu_{l,max}}{k}$ and that of the last arm being $\mu_{l,k} = \mu_l^{max}$, where μ_l^{max} is the maximum mean time for any arm on level l of the tree. The standard deviation of processing time was held the same for all agents. Thus, in the linear set, arms' means were evenly distanced. In contrast, there were more (less) arms with high reward in the superlinear (sublinear) curve distributions compared to arms with low rewards. These configurations allowed us to examine the algorithms' performance in conditions where either more (superlinear) or less (sublinear) exploration would be beneficial.

Terraced Agents: We also considered "terraced" agent organizations, where for agents in the lth level, $a_{l,i}$, a single agent with a best μ was placed together with some percentage of "good" performers (around 80% μ values compared to the best), and the rest were "poor" performers (around 20%); the payoff variance was chosen to be large enough such that the best arm was difficult to identify. Contractors with such variable performance allowed us to better examine and evaluate how intelligently algorithms expended their exploration budget; the poor contractors were chosen to penalize algorithms that explore less intelligently, while the presence of the "good" contractors required focused sampling to discern which was the best– a single sweep or any myopic choice was unlikely to be sufficient.

6. EXPERIMENTAL RESULTS

In this section, we discuss the algorithms' performance for our trust-based supply-chain scenario. To evaluate the algorithms, we focused on the reward that they generated as the initial budget varied, and as the standard deviation of completion time of each contractor (fixed at the same value for every agent) varied. The parameters values chosen for these scenario were varied to determine when each algorithm would perform at its best, and in which situations it is less effective.

In general, our experimentation showed that at low budgets, the more aggressive algorithms, that performed the least exploration, tended to perform the best. The Greedy and `PEEF` algorithms converged with sufficiently small budget (they were not allowed to explore any less than the Greedy, since then some of the arms would go unexplored); `lS` and `SOAAv` were a little worse, while high-exploration ϵ-first and KDE were significantly worse (see Figure 1). As it turns out, the natural advantage that the model provides to less aggressive algorithms is not enough to overcome the advantage that more decisive algorithms accrue in a budget-limited environment.

As the budget increased, the `lS` and `SOAAv` algorithms quickly outperformed the other algorithms in nearly every case. Perhaps surprisingly, the low-exploration ϵ-first method also proved very strong (nearly on-par with `PEEF`), while KDE, despite its superior, asymptotically-optimal regret bounds [14], performed relatively worse for small budgets. By examining individual contractor-selection sequences, we determined that this was because, in many cases, the amount of exploration performed by KDE was not justified by the savings accrued in being able to locate the best contractor. By contrast, the ϵ-first method was still often able to determine the best contractor eventually, by reordering its contractor ranking after some number of mistakes during exploitation. With a sufficiently high budget, KDE was able to overtake the low-exploration ϵ-first method (see Figure 1), since the reward it missed from increased exploration was eventually surpassed by the savings it incurred over the Greedy algorithm's method, which accrued some regret over time on average, from the trials where it could not correctly identify the best contractor.

We also saw that while the `PEEF` algorithm performed well with small budget (it becomes identical to Greedy when budget is sufficiently small, since the algorithm must select each contractor at least once). Its average time to completion, like Greedy, drops off relative to the others once it begins spending more time exploring– that is, the other algorithms are able to explore more intelligently. As was expected, the `PEEF` method follows the general pattern of the equivalent ϵ-first algorithm, while their intelligent choice of contractors allows it to remain more competitive. The fact that the ϵ-first algorithms fall behind KDE in our experiments supports our understanding that these algorithms have asymptotically worse regret bounds than KDE.

Moreover, the juxtaposition of `lS` and `PEEF` emphasize the importance of how the algorithms are parameterized. The two algorithms are structurally identical, but because `PEEF`'s exploration budget is dependent on the size of the budget, while `lS`'s is dependent on the number of arms, `lS` is better able to cope with a variety of different datasets without altering its parameters, when the given budget is of a moderate to large size. For the same reason, `SOAAv`'s parameter is sufficiently general that the algorithm remains effectively adaptive without fine tuning.

6.1 Curve-Based Distributions for Base-Variation and Homogeneous Trees

When testing with the curve-based distributions, we consider cases where the $\sigma_{l,i}$ values were set at 20, and $\mu_{l,i}$ values were chosen 10 units apart. The branching factor was $k = 10$. All contracting costs were set to 1 unit, and contracting budgets ranged from 50 (five times the cost to pull all arms available to the root) to 500 (fifty times). Results from these experiments are plotted in Figures 1 and 2; here, time values are considered relative to the mean time values of all the algorithms to highlight differences between their performances. We can see that as budget increases, the differences between the KDE and ϵ-first algorithms become much smaller, while the other algorithms tend to spread out. The overall trends in the algorithms' rankings at low and high budgets matched those discussed earlier: the `lS` algorithm performed the best at large budgets, with `SOAAv` generally very close behind. While both `PEEF` and low-exploration ϵ-first were preferable to these for very small budgets, they became worse as budget became larger.

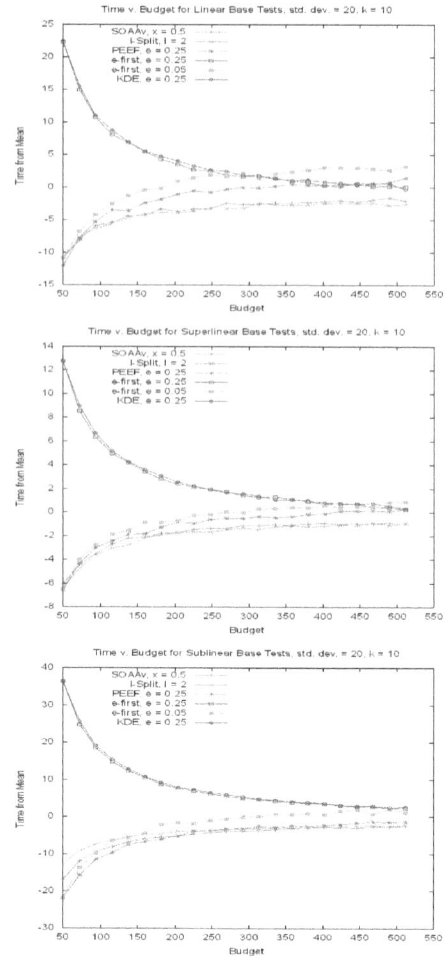

Figure 1: Time v. Budget for Curve-based Base-variation Trees - Linear (left), Superlinear (center), and Sublinear (right)

Also of note is the fact that KDE and ϵ-first are much less competitive to begin with, but begin to increase fast enough to overtake the other algorithms when budget becomes sufficiently large, as it does for ϵ-first and `PEEF` in the range of our experiments. This suggests that they could perform very well in very long-term cases. For the budget-limited scenario, however, this is of limited value.

In considering the sublinear and superlinear utility distribution trials, we found that the Greedy and `PEEF` algorithms tend to do relatively better in the sublinear case, and worse in the superlinear and linear cases. This makes sense, since these are more aggres-

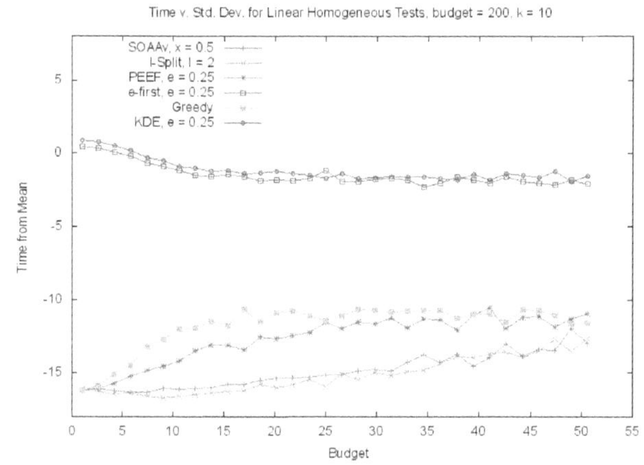

Figure 2: Time v. Standard Dev for Linear, Homogeneous Trees

sive algorithms, and are better able to take advantage of the more obvious best contractor location possible in the sublinear case. The other algorithms were fairly stably in their relative utility.

For the case of homogeneous trees we found that the algorithms' results were much closer together, and that the low-exploration ϵ-first and PEEF algorithms perform much closer to the adaptive algorithms as budget increased. This indicates that more aggressive algorithms tended to perform better when the other contractors in their sub-trees finished exploration at the same time that they did.

Finally, we also considered the completion time of each algorithm as standard deviation of task completion time of the bottom level contractors in the tree varied, as seen in Figure 4. Here, we considered the linear utility distribution case only, and found that, intriguingly, the same pattern applied. This observation reinforced the conjecture that the relative performance of the algorithms was directly related to the extent of their exploration. Increasing the contractor's standard deviation, and effectively bringing the agents' time distributions closer together, had the same effect as increasing the amount of interaction required to discriminate effectively between the contractors – the algorithms that acted more aggressively, `PEEF` and ϵ-first (ϵ = 0.1), became worse over time than the more deliberate algorithms KDE and ϵ-first (ϵ = 0.25), while the adaptive `SOAAv` and `lS` algorithms performed the best overall.

6.2 Terraced Distributions for Base-variation Trees

We also experimented with terraced arm configurations (see Figure 5), which provided key insights into the relative merits of these algorithms. We constructed a case where we used 1 best contractor (μ_i = 10), 4 good contractors (μ_i = 15), and 5 poor contractors (μ_i = 25), with σ_i = 20 for all but the best and σ_i = 0 for the best. We observed that the high-exploration ϵ-first algorithm and KDE was able to perform significantly better than any of the others at high budgets. The others performed somewhat worse, but retained the same ranking as before. What this case corroborated was the hypothesis that in cases where the best contractor has close competitors, more extensive exploration periods are more beneficial in the long-term (i.e., high budget) trials, even in the presence of the risk of contracting poor contractors that penalize continued sampling.

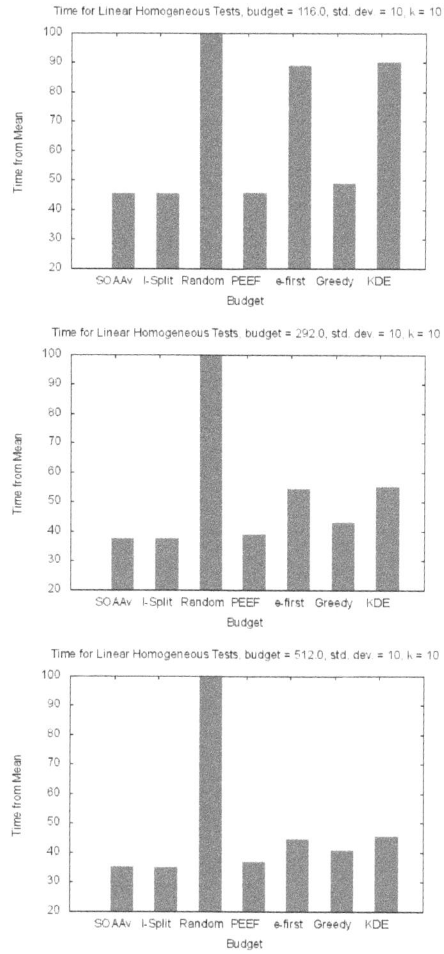

Figure 3: Time from Mean for Linear, Homogeneous Trees - at Low (left), Moderate (center), and High Budgets (right)

7. CONCLUSION AND DISCUSSIONS

In this paper we have evaluated the use of existing and recently-developed algorithms for solving the Fixed-Cost Multi-Armed Bandit Problem with Budget Constraint (MAB-BF) for addressing the core comprehensive trust management issues of engagement and evaluation of long-term reliability, and hence trustworthiness, of potential partners. We used a supply-chain domain where contractor agents have to depend on sub-contractors of initially unknown reliability to be able to fulfill their own production targets with the goal of minimizing time-to-completion of their orders. Algorithms that engage in strategic engagement, being cognizant of both current reliability estimates and remaining budgets for engagement before making final partner selections, have been used to develop trust estimates in potential long-term business partners.

Our experimental evaluation of the proposed algorithms show that our proposed algorithms are successful in discriminating between partners of variable reliability in the face of domain uncertainty, in the form of stochastic performance variation over multiple levels of the supply-chain, by effectively managing exploration budget and partial reliability estimates. Experiments over a wide range of problem scenarios show that the `lS` and `PEEF` methods' improvement on the weaknesses of the ϵ-first algorithm allowed them to be highly competitive in tightly-constrained cases where other algorithms with better theoretical bounds cannot excel. At the same time, the `SOAAv` algorithm was able to perform very well in general, consistently outperforming Greedy along with the others in the majority of our test cases. Surprisingly, the simple Greedy

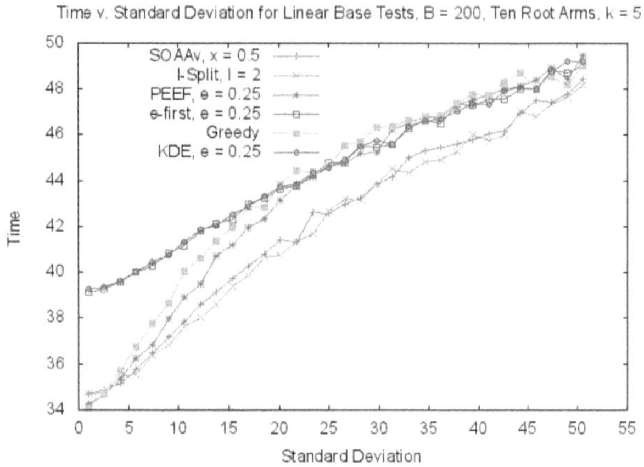

Figure 4: Time v. Standard Deviation for the Linear Case

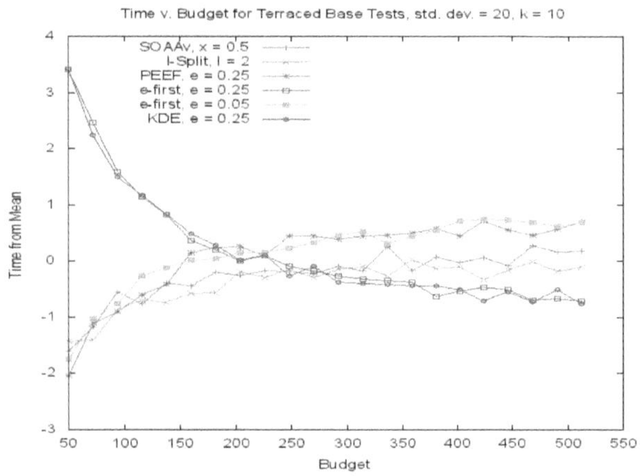

Figure 5: Time v. Budget for the Terraced Case

algorithm, not used in the literature earlier for the MAB-BF problem, held its own, underscoring the usefulness of maximizing the exploitation phase in most scenarios.

We plan to expand on this initial promising results of using MAB-BF algorithms for engagement and trust evaluation in a supply-chain domain by studying cases for variable, rather than uniform, topological configurations for each contractor below the first level in the supply-chains. It could be fruitful to study the effects of using algorithms in entire sub-trees, or entire levels of the tree.

We would like to develop variants of the proposed algorithms for the variable cost MAB problems which would be useful when contracting costs vary between contractors. We also plan to study an integrated approach that address, together with engagement and evaluation, other aspects of comprehensive trust management, e.g., the strategic use of known trustworthiness of contractors future contractor selection given expectations of upcoming task load distributions. Finally, we would like to characterize the applicability of the MAB-BF model and algorithms for trust management in diverse real-life problems.

Acknowledgments

Anton Ridgway and Michael Ripley were funded in part by the Tulsa Undergraduate Research Challenge (TURC) program at The University of Tulsa.

REFERENCES

[1] P. Auer, N. Cesa-Bianchi, and P. Fischer. Finitetime analysis of the multiarmed bandit problem. *Machine Learning*, 47(2):235–256, 2002.

[2] R. Agrawal, M. Hedge, and D. Teneketzis. Asymptotically efficient adaptive allocation rules for the multiarmed bandit problem with switching cost. *Automatic Control, IEEE Transactions on*, 33(10):899–906, 1988.

[3] D. Ardagna, B. Panicucci, and M. Passacantando. A game theoretic formulation of the service provisioning problem in cloud systems. In *Proceedings of the 20th international conference on World wide web*, pages 177–186. ACM, 2011.

[4] C. Borgs, J. Chayes, N. Immorlica, K. Jain, O. Etesami, and M. Mahdian. Dynamics of bid optimization in online advertisement auctions. In *Proceedings of the 16th international conference on World Wide Web*, pages 531–540. ACM, 2007.

[5] O. Ben-Yehuda, M. Ben-Yehuda, A. Schuster, and D. Tsafrir. Deconstructing amazon ec2 spot instance pricing. In *Cloud Computing Technology and Science (Cloud-Com), 2011 IEEE Third International Conference on*, pages 304–311. IEEE, 2011.

[6] T. Chakraborty, E. Even-Dar, S. Guha, Y. Mansour, and S. Muthukrishnan. Selective call out and real time bidding. In *Internet and Network Economics*, pages 145–157, 2010.

[7] C. Castelfranchi and R. Falcone. Principles of trust for MAS: Cognitive autonomy, social importance, and quantification. In *ICMAS-98* pages 72–79, Los Alamitos, CA, 1998. IEEE Computer Society.

[8] W. Ding, T. Qin, X.Zhang, and T. Liu. Multi-armed bandit with budget constraint and variable costs. In *AAAI-13*. AAAI Press, 2013.

[9] D. Gambetta. *Trust.* Basil Blackwell, Oxford, 1990.

[10] S. Guha and K. Munagala. Approximation algorithms for budgeted learning problems. In *Proceedings of the thirty-ninth annual ACM symposium on Theory of computing*, pages 104–113. ACM, 2007.

[11] T. D. Huynh, N. R. Jennings, and N. R. Shadbolt. An integrated trust and reputation model for open multi-agent systems. *Journal of Autonomous Agents and Multi-Agent Systems*, 13(2):119–154, 2006.

[12] R. S. Sutton and A. G. Barto. *Reinforcement Learning: An Introduction.* MIT Press, Cambridge, MA, 1998.

[13] S. Sen. A comprehensive approach to trust management. In *AAMAS'13*, pages 797–800, 2013.

[14] L. Tran-Thanh, A. Chapman, J. Munoz De Cote Flores Luna, A. Rogers, and N. Jennings. Epsilon-first policies for budget-limited multi-armed bandits. In *AAAI-10*, pages 1211–1216, 2010.

[15] L. Tran-Thanh, A. Chapman, A. Rogers, and N. Jennings. Knapsack based optimal policies for budget-limited multi-armed bandits. In *AAAI-12*, pages 1134–1140, 2012.

[16] P. Yolum and M. P. Singh. Engineering self-organizing referral networks for trustworthy service selection. *IEEE Transactions on System, Man, and Cybernetics*, 35(3):396–407, 2005.

[17] J. Zhang, R. Cohen, and K. Larson. Combining Trust Modeling and Mechanism Design for promoting Honesty in E-Marketplaces. *Computational Intelligence* 28(4): 549-578 (2012).

Improving the Performance of Mobile Phone Crowdsourcing Applications

Erfan Davami
Department of EECS
University of Central Florida
Orlando, FL, USA
erfand@knights.ucf.edu

Gita Sukthankar
Department of EECS
University of Central Florida
Orlando, FL, USA
gitars@eecs.ucf.edu

ABSTRACT

Mobile phone crowdsourcing is a powerful tool for many types of distributed sensing problems. However, a central issue with this type of system is that it relies on user contributed data, which may be sparse or erroneous. This paper describes our experiences developing a mobile phone crowdsourcing app, Kpark, for monitoring parking availability on a university campus. Our system combines multiple trust-based data fusion techniques to improve the quality of user submitted parking reports and is currently being used by over 1500 students.

Categories and Subject Descriptors

H.4 [**Information Systems Applications**]: Miscellaneous

General Terms

Experimentation

Keywords

mobile phone crowdsourcing; trust-based fusion

1. INTRODUCTION

Upon arriving on campus, there is a joke that one is never issued a parking permit but is granted a "hunting license" to search for elusive parking spaces. Although there has been extensive new construction, parking space availability often does not keep pace with student demand during peak periods of campus activity. Fortunately, the problem (having too many people on campus simultaneously) contains within it the germ of a solution—leverage the students and their mobile devices to form a large scale participatory sensing network. This network can be used to create a global parking lot occupancy map of the campus which can be made available to the users to further encourage them to contribute data. Data fusion and user modeling can then be used to reduce the error of the occupancy map, beyond the raw data. This approach doesn't require any additional instrumentation and hence scales well for the growing number of parking garages and can supplement the current parking counter system.

Appears in: *Proceedings of the 14th International Conference on Autonomous Agents and Multiagent Systems (AAMAS 2015), Bordini, Elkind, Weiss, Yolum (eds.), May 4–8, 2015, Istanbul, Turkey.*

This paper describes our experiences developing the mobile phone application for a participatory sensing network on the University of Central Florida campus. The Kpark app (Figure 1) is freely available for the IOS and Android platforms at `http://www.kparkapp.com/` and is currently being used by over 1500 users. Our back-end system maintains a worker quality model to account for every user's "trustworthiness" in correctly reporting the occupancy status of parking lots.[1] This paper describes several different methods for inferring the user's reliability. A key innovation of Kpark is that it combines multiple trust prediction approaches with a real-time data fusion method in order to create the final map. The real-time component of the system attempts to maintain data freshness by discounting older reports. We evaluated different variants of the occupancy prediction system vs. independently collected university parking data and determined that the best performing approach is to combine the output of multiple algorithms using an AdaBoost ensemble, which results in a substantial performance improvement over the baseline majority voting system.

The outline of the paper is as follows. The next section provides an overview of both commercial and academic mobile crowdsourcing systems. Section 3 describes the Kpark implementation and provides a brief summary of the user trust prediction techniques. Then we describe our methods for combining multiple prediction techniques and performing real-time updates. Section 5 presents our results: first we evaluate the performance of our system using data from an agent-based transportation simulation before presenting results from the large-scale campus deployment.

2. RELATED WORK

Mobile crowdsourcing systems have established themselves as a viable commercial technology for urban sensing; apps such as Waze (traffic prediction), GasBuddy (cheap fuel prices), and Yelp (restaurant ratings) have become a staple component of many people's smart phones. The problem of creating a worker pool for these types of applications was analyzed by Reddy et al. [15] in the context of documenting sustainability practices through geo-tagged photos. A recruitment framework can be used to identify a suitable group of participants, based on their transportation and participation habits, to accomplish specific data collection requirements outlined by the campaign organizers.

[1]Note that the current version of our trust model uses a single dimension to model user reliability and does not attempt to detect actively malicious behavior.

Figure 1: An app installed on each users' mobile device communicates with a webservice which manages the campus database (left). Potential parking spaces are displayed on an interactive map shown in the left middle panel. Red denotes parking sections that are full or close to full; green sections have a higher probability of vacancy. The right middle panel shows a more detailed view of the parking lot, divided into sections containing approximately 15 parking spots. Users have the option of reporting on the occupancy level for a specific parking section using the menu shown on the right.

Poor data is a potential problem for crowdsourcing applications that rely on low-cost labeling, but one that can often be addressed by soliciting redundant labels for the same task from different users. The most popular aggregation strategy is to use majority voting to fuse the labels or variations on majority vote such as absolute majority in which a majority opinion is only achieved when 50% of the labelers agree. However, our task is less easily framed as a consensus task, since we rely on opportunistic labels provided by workers who are either entering or leaving the parking garages, rather than tasking workers as has been done in crowdsourcing applications for disaster relief [23].

Understanding the demographics of the user population, particularly the user trust distribution, is important for designing a good crowdsourcing system. In a homogeneous population, the assumption is that all users have the same probability of producing the correct label, whereas in a heterogeneous population, users have different probabilities of producing the same label. In this paper, we assume a heterogeneous population and demonstrate the performance of our system under several realistic distributions of user trust. For more complicated tasks, such as disaster relief, where a single measure of user quality is insufficiently expressive, and having the users provide more information is valuable for the matching process [22].

One question which frequently arises is whether it is better to rely on the best labeler or to aggregate labels. Sheng et al. [18] model the effect of labeler skill variance on crowdsourcing performance in a simple three labeler case. Bachrach et al. [2] evaluate the IQ of the aggregate crowd by crowdsourcing IQ test questions. In homogeneous crowds with similar IQs, the crowd outperformed the individual both when using simple majority vote aggregation, as well as their machine learning method that infers user IQ values during the aggregation process. However, in a heterogeneous population, a large crowd is more likely to have one member with a very high IQ, capable of producing highly accurate answers. In this paper, we compare the strategy of relying on the most trusted user vs. other aggregation methods, such as weighted averaging using the user trust level to weight the vote. We also evaluate the performance of an iterative averaging method, robust averaging, used by Chou et al. [4] to successfully to track and compute the average of wireless sensor network measurements while accounting for sensor noise and error.

Bayesian models have been successfully used for aggregating labels, inferring worker reliability, as well as hiring and routing workers [11, 19, 20]. A Bayesian technique for user trust prediction was demonstrated to outperform other approaches in a simulated study of mobile phone crowdsourcing [5]. One commonly used approach is to model the labels as observable events in a probabilistic graphical model and to jointly estimate the correct label in combination with the user trust. In our mobile phone crowdsourcing problem, labels are provided opportunistically by community members who are parking their cars or walking by the lots. Our proposed framework assumes that user trust levels can change over time, as the user gains familiarity with the use of the app. There is a high rate of user turnover as new users adopt the app and former participants become inactive. We use a simple Bayesian model in which user trust estimates are only updated when they provide labels to avoid the computational costs of inferring large joint models.

A number of mobile phone apps such as Parkopedia [14], ParkJam [12], and SFPark [17] have emerged to assist users find parking and garages to manage parking pricing. Recently, a startup company, Anagog, has come to market with a parking analytics application that leverages mobile phone GPS data and uses limited crowdsourcing. In our application, relying exclusively on voluntary reporting makes the trust prediction problem harder, but does a better job of preserving the users' spatial privacy.

3. METHOD

Our mobile phone crowdsourcing system, Kpark, includes the following components: 1) trust prediction algorithms for inferring user reliability 2) a set of occupancy prediction algorithms for creating the parking availability map, 3) real-time processes for discounting/discarding stale data.

Each user report (tag) consists of a location (parking lot, level, and section number) and the perceived occupancy level of that section, ranging from 3 (fully occupied) to 1 (less than half empty).

$$Tag = \begin{cases} 1 & \text{if } Occupancy_{section} \in (0\%, 50\%) \\ 2 & \text{if } Occupancy_{section} \in (50\%, 95\%) \\ 3 & \text{if } Occupancy_{section} \in (95\%, 100\%) \end{cases} \quad (1)$$

The aim of our system is to fuse these user reports to produce the most accurate current global parking lot occupancy map. Code and data for our system can be found at `http://ial.eecs.ucf.edu/kpark.php`.

3.1 Trust Prediction

For privacy-preserving reasons, we opted not to use a strategy where we verify the user's location with GPS data. Instead the user's trustworthiness is inferred during a calibration period, when we compare the deviation of an individual user's reports against the average parking lot occupancy based on aggregated data indexed by the day and time. This data serves as a reasonable approximation to doing an actual majority vote across many user reports. If multiple reports from the same user deviate from the aggregated parking services data, it is likely to be the result of user error. We evaluated five standard trust prediction strategies drawn from the sensor network and machine learning communities: 1) beta reputation 2) Gompertz function 3) robust averaging 4) maximum likelihood estimation (MLE) and 5) a Bayesian model.

3.1.1 Beta Reputation Method

In the beta reputation system, user tag events are modeled as emanating from a binary process in which the new user's tag has a chance of agreeing or disagreeing with the previous data. Josang et al. [10] note that a beta distribution can be used to specify posteriori distributions of binary events and implemented a reputation system for e-commerce users. The beta function is parameterized by two values (α, β), and the expectation value of a beta distribution is given by $E(p) = \frac{\alpha}{\alpha+\beta}$. In their work, beta functions are used to model user reputation and to predict the future frequency of the binary events (customer satisfaction or dissatisfaction). In this paper we introduce two separate beta reputation systems for trust and occupancy prediction. The first system performs occupancy prediction by having the users rate the occupancy levels of parking sections. The second reputation system performs user trust prediction by having the parking section 'virtually' rate the users in order to update their trustworthiness based on previously submitted tags. Here we describe the trust prediction part of the system.

In this model, we tabulate a satisfactory rating (R_i) and unsatisfactory rating (S_i) score for every user i. New tags arriving from that user can alter these two scores based on the tag the user provides and also based on the aggregate tag for that section. The aggregate tag can be obtained from the consensus (robust averaging) strategy.

For any user i submitting the tag of x_i for a section in a given hour we define $v_i = |x_i - z|$ where z is the aggregate tag for that parking section for that hour. The value v_i can be interpreted as how accurately user i has tagged the parking section, thus the satisfactory and unsatisfactory rating (r and s respectively) of that section towards user i can be represented as: $r = \text{tag}_{\max} - v$ and $s = v + \text{tag}_{\min}$. It is also possible to have recent observations more heavily influence the reputation rating than older ones by including a forgetting factor, λ. The forgetting factor is a real number from 0 to 1 which indicates how much influence previous records should have on the quality of the user. With the forgetting factor, new values for the users' satisfactory and unsatisfactory ratings are updated according to the following procedure: $R_i \leftarrow \lambda R_i + r$ and $S_i \leftarrow \lambda S_i + s$. If the forgetting factor is 0, the previous satisfactory/unsatisfactory performance of the user will not influence the new trust values, whereas if the value is 1 all of the old data will be retained. Finally user trust is calculated as follows:

$$T_i = \frac{R_i}{R_i + S_i} \quad (2)$$

3.1.2 Gompertz Method

Huang et al. [9] proposed a method for updating the predicted trust value of hardware devices by using a Gompertz function to model increases and decreases in trust. This model has been shown to achieve good results in a synchronous and a data rich domain, but faces challenges in our sparse problem space. In the original paper, the assumption is that every device submits a report to the server every second, however for our parking occupancy prediction problem, very few people submit tags every hour for a particular parking section. In order to overcome the data sparsity obstacle, here we implemented a modified version of the Gompertz model. Given a group of users U reporting a set of tags X for a given section during one hour, the set of cooperative ratings P is initialized as $P_{i,0} = 1/n$ for every user i where n is the number of users providing tags. At each iteration l, the robust average value r for the user tags is updated according to the new p values:

$$r_l = \sum_{i=1}^{n} p_{i,l} x_i \quad (3)$$

Then the cooperative ratings of the users are updated with the new values of r:

$$p_{i,l} = \frac{\frac{1}{\frac{(x_i - r_l)^2}{\sum_{j=1}^{n}(x_j - r_l)^2} + \epsilon}}{\sum_{k=1}^{n} \frac{1}{\frac{(x_k - r_l)^2}{\sum_{j=1}^{n}(x_j - r_l)^2} + \epsilon}} + \epsilon \quad (4)$$

We iterate between Equations 3 and 4 until the following convergence is achieved: $|P_l - P_{l-1}| < 0.0001$.

The set of unnormalized cooperative ratings P ($P = \{p_i | i = 1, ..., n\}$) ranges from ϵ to infinity and is a representation of user reliability in comparison to other users who submitted reports for that section in that hour. These ratings are then normalized to the range [-1,1] (denoted by $\bar{p}_i$). However, when calculating the trustworthiness of a user, their history of cooperativeness also comes into effect. A person who has been trustworthy for a relatively long period of time should not entirely forfeit their high reputation rating after submitting a tag that does not follow the consensus vote. Conversely, we should not have complete trust towards a user with low reputation simply because they match the consensus value once. Given a particular user i with m previous ratings across all time frames and parking sections, the overall cooperative rating p_i' for user i takes into account their previous levels of cooperativeness and is calculated as:

$$p_i' = \sum_{j=1}^{m} \lambda_j^{m-j} \bar{p}_{j,i} \quad (5)$$

where

$$\lambda_j = \begin{cases} \lambda_{\text{standard}} & \text{if } \bar{p}_{j,i} > 0 \\ \lambda_{\text{penalty}} & \text{otherwise} \end{cases} \quad (6)$$

In this model, older cooperative ratings have less effect on the overall cooperativeness. The older a cooperative rating is, the less effect it has on determining the overall cooperativeness of a user. Including different λ terms that change depending on whether the user has been more cooperative ($\lambda_{\text{standard}}$) or is ranked in the bottom half of the user pool (λ_{penalty}) makes the process of gaining and losing trust asymmetric. Trust is gained slowly, but lost rapidly after uncooperative behavior. Finally the reputation (trust) of each user is calculated using a Gompertz function:

$$T_i = G(p_i') = ae^{be^{cp_i'}} \quad (7)$$

where a,b,c are model parameters.

3.1.3 Robust Averaging Method

Intuitively the cooperative ratings that emerge from the robust averaging process can be used to rate users' trustworthiness. Here we propose a simplified trust prediction method that uses the normalized cooperative ratings. Given the normalized cooperative ratings set of user i ($\bar{P}_i$) calculated by Equation 5, the trustworthiness of such user can be calculated as follows:

$$T_i = \frac{\sum_{j=1}^{m} \lambda_j^{m-j} \bar{p}_{j,i}}{\sum_{j=1}^{m} \lambda_j^{m-j}} \quad (8)$$

where m is the total number of cooperative ratings assigned to the user since the very beginning of the user's signup and λ_j is given by Equation 6.

3.1.4 Maximum Likelihood and Bayesian Estimation

Using maximum likelihood estimation, it is possible to estimate the trust of a particular user based on the likelihood of observing the training data set. With three reporting options, the possible gap, Δ, between the user report and the aggregated data falls in the set $\Delta = \{-2, -1, 0, 1, 2\}$. According to our trust model, given an unknown user trust t, the occurrence probability of each of these differences can be expressed as follows:

$$p(\Delta = k|\sigma(t)) = \frac{\int_{k-0.5}^{k+0.5} \frac{e^{-\frac{x^2}{2\sigma(t)^2}}}{\sigma(t)\sqrt{2\pi}} dx}{\int_{k_{\min}-0.5}^{k_{\max}+0.5} \frac{e^{-\frac{x^2}{2\sigma(t)^2}}}{\sigma(t)\sqrt{2\pi}} dx} \quad (9)$$

where $\sigma(t) = \frac{1}{t} - \alpha$. The expected tag difference of a user having a known trust value t for our trust model is simply:

$$\delta(t) = \sqrt{\frac{\sum_{i=1}^{N} p(\Delta = k, \sigma(t))\Delta_i}{\sum_{i=1}^{N} p(\Delta = k, \sigma(t))}} \quad (10)$$

in which N is the number of possible values for Δ and α=0.8. For a batch of user reports, the δ of all tags coming from a particular user, $\hat{\delta}$, can be calculated as: $\hat{\delta} = \sqrt{\frac{\sum_{i=1}^{N}(U_i - R_i)^2}{N}}$. Hence for a known value of $\hat{\delta}$ we can calculate a maximum likelihood estimate of the user's trust by performing a grid search over possible trust values to identify the t that satisfies $\arg\min_{t\in[0,1]} |\delta(t) - \hat{\delta}|$. We can use a similar approach to compute a Bayesian estimate of the user's trust.

3.2 Occupancy Calculation

Predicting user trust provides insight about which users are reporting the most accurate parking tags. Such information is vital for more accurate parking occupancy calculations, since giving more emphasis to data provided by trustworthy users has a potentially significant impact on the occupancy prediction accuracy. However it is only half the battle since the aim of our app is to provide accurate parking lot occupancy information. The final occupancy of parking lot sections can be predicted by fusing the user data, according to one of the following methods:

Weighted Average Trust The occupancy level for a section is the average of the report values weighted by the predicted trust of the user. Here everyone is allowed to vote on the occupancy level of a section; the more trustworthy a user is, the greater their influence in determining the final occupancy result.

Max Trust In this method, the occupancy level of a section is based solely on the report of the user with the maximum predicted user trust who has reported on that section. The other user reports do not contribute to the occupancy prediction.

3.3 Data Freshness

Failing to rapidly adapt to new parking status reports can cause errors during the transition from busy rush hour into the off peak traffic hours. We believe that discounting old data can lead to more accurate transportation prediction results in dynamic environments. Applying a discount factor on old information increases the influence of more recent reports, thus enabling the system to adapt to dynamic conditions. This adaptation is especially important when the number of reports is relatively low (e.g., on evenings and weekends). One solution to this problem is to periodically reset the parking section occupancy status to the most vacant tag until a new report is submitted for that parking section. In our initial experiments, this simple approach outperformed relying on the raw occupancy prediction calculation.

4. PROPOSED IMPROVEMENTS

Here we describe our two proposed improvements to the standard user modeling and data fusion systems. The first innovation is to combine the output of multiple trust and occupancy prediction algorithms; this is very similar in spirit to the use of algorithm portfolios for fast combinatorial search [13] or classifier ensembles [6, 8]. The second innovation is a more refined real-time updating system that accounts for the time of submission of individual reports, rather than periodically resetting the vacancy levels of the whole section. In the results section, we evaluate the benefits of these modifications.

4.1 Combining Prediction Models

The algorithm selection problem was first introduced by Rice et al. [16], along with a method to map algorithm-problem pairs to their performances. For some types of problems, a single algorithm will not necessarily perform optimally across the entire problem space [1, 21]. Machine learning can be applied to learn a good mapping from the problem space to the algorithm space using extracted features from the problem space [13]. A training phase is used to learn the performance of each algorithm, and the model obtained from this phase is then used to predict the performance of the algorithms on new problems.

During our initial simulation experiments, we noticed that different trust prediction methods seem to perform well under various conditions. Hence, leveraging the entire portfolio of algorithms may be a robust strategy for trust prediction. To do this we use adaptive boosting (AdaBoost), a machine learning algorithm presented by Freund et al. [8], that combines several weak-classifiers on order to form a strong classifier. In every training iteration of AdaBoost, a new weak-learner is added to the ensemble of learners in round *k+1* to focus on classifying data-points misclassified by weak-learning round *k*. The final strong-learner (classifier) is a weighted vote of all the learners in the ensemble, such that learners with the least error have the most influence in the final classification outcome. To extend this classification technique to a multi-class problem, we employ the method described in [7].

The core features given to our intelligent decision maker are:

- **Hour**: The hour of the day when the prediction is being performed
- **Weekday**: The day of the week in which the prediction is being performed
- **Fusion Method**: The trust-based fusion method being employed (max trust or weighted averaging)
- **Section Identifier**: The identifier of the parking lot section where occupancy prediction is being performed.

We created two versions of the system. In the classification version, the features are used to decide which trust-based prediction method to use. We train the AdaBoost classifier with 7 days worth of adaptation data (7 days after the trust prediction algorithm training is finished). The classifier maps the data to six possible classes: the majority vote class (labeled as 0) and the five other trust prediction algorithms described in Section 3.1. If the portfolio chooses the majority vote method to predict parking occupancy (i.e., label '0' is chosen by the classifier), the beta reputation model is then used for updating the trustworthiness of users.

In the regression version, the outcome of both the trust-based tag fusion and the majority vote are concatenated with the core features and this data is then mapped to the occupancy level (1–3). In the regression configuration the beta reputation model is always used for updating the estimates of user trustworthiness. Figure 2 illustrates the two configurations.

4.2 Real-time Data Fusion

The data flow of user reports varies substantially based on the time of day and day of the week. In some cases (the early evening), the low data flow occurs because there are few students on campus; however in other cases, there are dips in the data flow because the lots are already completely full and few people are entering/exiting the parking garages. The simple data freshness adaptation cannot distinguish between these two states. Our proposed real-time method asynchronously fuses reports and uses not only the trust of users who submitted the tags, but also how long ago they were submitted; it includes a tunable decay constant (σ) that ensures a continuous data freshness through time.

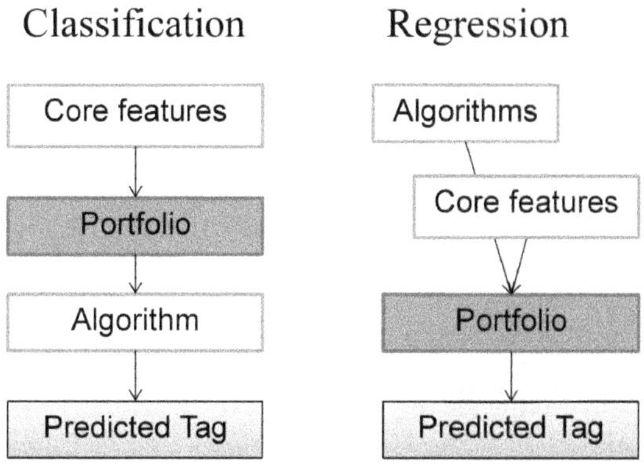

Figure 2: Two possible algorithm selection configurations. In the classification configuration (left), the selector is responsible for choosing one of the algorithms in the portfolio based on a set of core features (e.g., hour of the day, day of the week). That algorithm is then used to predict the occupancy of the parking selection and to update the user trust levels. In the regression configuration (right), the core features, along with the results of all algorithms, are sent to the selector, and the selector is ultimately responsible for predicting the section occupancy. The trustworthiness of the users is always updated with the top-performing beta reputation system.

Our proposed real-time fusion algorithm works as follows. Given the set U of tag updates $u_1, u_2, ..., u_N$ submitted for a parking section within a timeframe of 4 hours, the predicted occupancy of that section is calculated as $O = I + \sum_{i=1}^{N} \frac{\nu_i(u_i - I)}{\Delta t \sigma}$, where Δt is the time difference in minutes between the current time and the time the ith update was made, σ is a decay constant representing garage turnover, and I is the minimum occupancy level ($I = 1$). The validity of the report is calculated by $\nu_i = \tau_i \prod_{j=1}^{i-1}(1 - \tau_{i-j})$ where τ_i is the trustworthiness of the user who made the update i, and every user report within a time frame of 4 hours is considered in reverse order. The intuition is that earlier reports from more trustworthy users challenge the validity of the current report more than reports from less trustworthy users.

All user trustworthiness values are initialized to 50% (0.5). After a report, the trustworthiness is then updated by $\tau_i = \frac{\tanh(s_i/\varphi)+1}{2}$ where s_i is the data-quality score of user i and φ is the score coefficient constant which affects the magnitude of trust change. The data-quality score s_i itself depends on whether the users agreed on the tag. If the reported tag is the predicted value, the user's data-quality score will increase $\frac{\gamma}{\Delta t} \times \lambda_{\text{promote}}$ and if the user is a dissenter his/her score will decrease by $\frac{\gamma}{\Delta t} \times \lambda_{\text{punish}} \times (u_i - O)$, where γ is the certainty coefficient constant. Note that λ_{punish} is usually greater than λ_{promote} which causes participants to lose trust

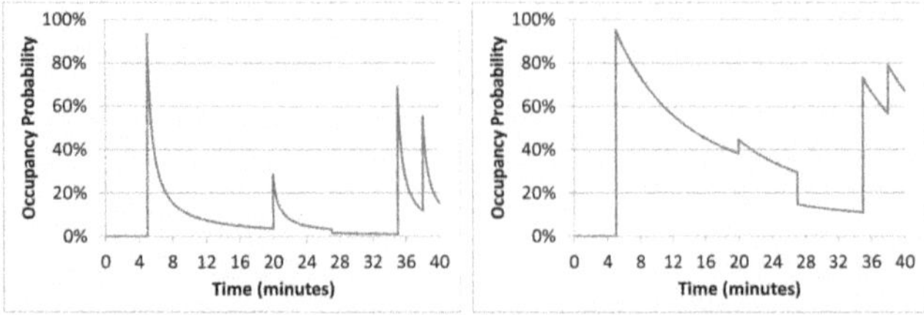

(a) (b)

Figure 3: The predicted occupancy levels of a parking section generated using the real-time data fusion algorithm over a timeframe of 40 minutes with constant values of $\lambda_{\text{promote}} = 1$, $\lambda_{\text{punish}} = 2$, $\gamma = 0.257$, and $\sigma = 1.7$ (a) vs. $\sigma = 0.1$ (b). Modifying the tunable decay parameter σ affects the length of time that a user report affects the parking lot occupancy prediction.

quicker than they obtain it [10]. Note that in cases where there is no recent report, there is little modification to the user's trustworthiness.

All of the constants were tuned to maximize the performance. The constant λ_{promote} is always set to be equal to 1. The tuning of the other four constants was done using Monte Carlo optimization; the final values of λ_{punish}, γ (certainty coefficient), φ (score coefficient) and σ (decay) were 3.7646, 7.1655, 0.7852 and 0.0017 respectively.

To better illustrate this process, we provide a simple example of a 40 minute timeframe where 5 reports are made by 4 users. Figure 3a illustrates the predicted occupancy of the parking section over time. The first report was made by user 1 5 minutes after the start (tag=3), and user 2 reported tag=2 at time 20. Finally users 3, 4, and again 3 reported tag values of 1, 3, and 3 at times 27, 35 and 38 respectively. Our initial estimate of the users' trustworthiness is 95%, 55%, 50% and 70%. The real-time data fusion process with constant values of $\lambda_{\text{promote}} = 1$, $\lambda_{\text{punish}} = 2$, $\gamma = 0.257$ and $\sigma = 1.7$ was used to update the occupancy probability of the parking section and also update the user trustworthiness. At the conclusion of 40 minutes the trustworthiness of users 1 to 4 has been updated to 94.21%, 53.72%, 48.07% and 67.79%. User 3's trust level fluctuates slightly between successive reports, moving from an initial 50% to 50.64% and finally to 48.07%.

Figure 3b illustrates the performance of the occupancy prediction with a decay of $\sigma = 0.1$. In this scenario, once all users submit their tag reports their trustworthiness levels are updated to values 91.29%, 57.43%, 47.52% and 61.09%. As shown in Figure 3 the real-time data fusion method can help ensure that the user receives a reasonable estimate of parking lot occupancy even in cases when no reports have been submitted to the system for some time.

5. RESULTS

We evaluated the performance of our system in several different ways. The first section focuses on evaluating the user modeling component. Since it was difficult to get ground truth data on user trustworthiness, this aspect of the evaluation uses data from a freely available agent-based urban transportation simulation [3]. We initialized the simulation with data collected from surveying 1008 community members about their daily habits. Several months of transportation patterns were simulated using the agent-based model and then validated against aggregate lot usage data collected by the campus parking services office on a monthly basis. The second section of the evaluation presents our occupancy prediction results on this simulated data, as compared to the baseline majority vote algorithm. The final section presents our results on the deployed system with almost 1600 users. The occupancy prediction of the real system was verified against independently collected data from university parking services. The real-time data fusion algorithm was only implemented and evaluated on the deployed system.

Table 1: Parameters for trust prediction models

Method	Parameters
MLE	$\alpha = 0.8$
Bayesian Update	$\alpha = 0.8$
Beta Reputation	$\lambda_{\text{user}} = 0.9$, $\lambda_{\text{section}} = 0.2$
Gompertz Method	$a = 1$, $b = -2.5$, $c = -0.85$
	$\lambda_{\text{standard}} = 0.7$, $\lambda_{\text{penalty}} = 0.8$
Robust Averaging	$\lambda_{\text{standard}} = 0.7$, $\lambda_{\text{penalty}} = 0.8$
Real-time Data Fusion	$\lambda_{\text{punish}} = 3.7646$, $\gamma = 7.1655$, $\varphi = 0.7852$, $\sigma = 0.0017$

The performance of the trust and occupancy algorithms under different user enrollment conditions was measured by varying the following population generation parameters within the urban simulation:

1. *User adoption:* This value represents the percentage of campus users who choose to install the application on their mobile phone.
2. *Tagging rate:* This variable represents the probability that an individual user will submit a tag while passing through a parking lot. Highly active users are more likely to use their app to submit reports.
3. *Population trust:* Our agent-based model simulates a population of users with varying user trust distributions. In the standard enrollment condition, we assume that user trust ratings, which are inversely proportional to the variance of their reports, are uniformly distributed. In addition to this scenario, we present results from scenarios in which the majority of users are very untrustworthy and generate data with a high variance. Also, we examined a bimodal population in which the users fall primarily at the extreme ends of the user trust scale.

5.1 Trust Prediction

The performance of the user trust model is reported as the complement of the average prediction errors. This is calculated by the L1-norm of the predicted and actual trust across all users:

$$\text{performance} = 1 - \frac{1}{N}\sum_{i=1}^{N} \|P(i) - A(i)\| \qquad (11)$$

where N is the number of users who made parking occupancy reports, P is the Predicted Trust set, and A is the Actual Trust set. Table 1 provides the parameters used by all the trust prediction methods.

Figure 4 compares the trust prediction results for all the methods in a scenario with standard values for user adoption, user activity, and population trust as well as scenarios with low user adoption, low tagging rate, and untrustworthy

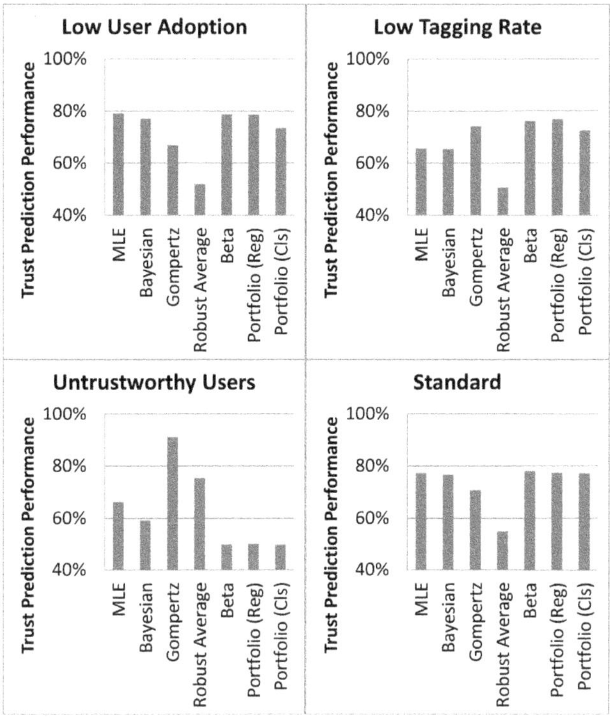

Figure 4: Trust prediction results as forecasted by the agent-based model with different potential user populations. The beta reputation system performs well, except in the case of untrustworthy user population. The portfolio approaches closely mirror the performance of the beta system.

users. An analysis of the individual trust prediction algorithms reveals that the beta reputation system is narrowly the best performer. However, the Gompertz model is excellent when most of the users are contributing unreliable data. The performance of the portfolio methods closely shadows the beta reputation system; this is unsurprising since by default the portfolio variants perform the trust prediction update using the beta reputation system. Disappointingly, it does not manage to leverage the better performing methods in the untrustworthy user case. Note that the aim of the portfolio was to improve occupancy prediction; our hope was that the trust prediction would improve as a byproduct, but that doesn't seem to be the case.

To show how the trust prediction is affected by the number of tags per user, we calculated the Spearman rank correlation coefficient of the actual and predicted user trust. The beta reputation system narrowly outperforms MLE and Bayesian models at correctly ranking the workers by the quality of their reports. The correlation between predicted and actual trust continues to improve over the number of reports and reaches a maximum of 0.54 (Figure 5).

5.2 Occupancy Prediction

In this section, we compare the performance of the data fusion approaches at predicting the parking lot occupancy over one semester (90 days of simulated data from the agent-based model). Occupancy prediction methods were scored according to their confusion matrices to create a model that more harshly penalizes mistakenly directing users toward full lots. To do this, we define a penalty matrix M. Each

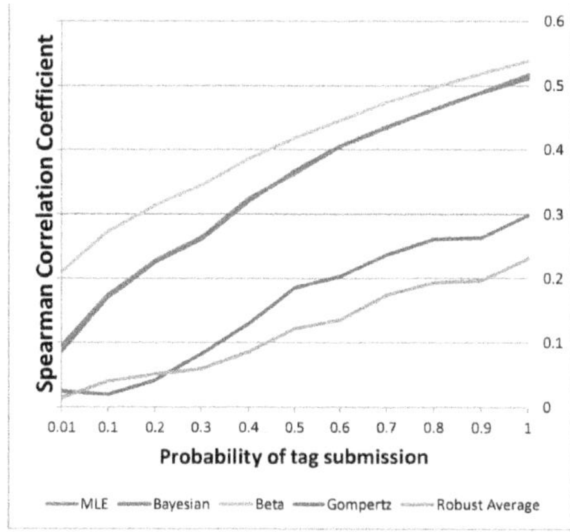

Figure 5: Spearman rank correlation of predicted user trust with actual user trust vs. user reports

element $m_{i,j}$ of M represents the penalty that the prediction method receives for falsely predicting outcome i as outcome j. All occupancy results were compared to a majority vote baseline (without any user trust modeling) and results were reported as improvements over that baseline.

$$\text{performance} = \frac{1}{N}\left(\sum_{i=1}^{N} M_{r_i,mv_i} - \sum_{i=1}^{N} M_{r_i,pr_i}\right) \tag{12}$$

where N is the number of hours during the test phase, M is the penalty matrix, r, pr_i and mv_i are the real tag, predicted tag and the majority vote tag of the section at hour i respectively.

Figure 6 shows the results of this evaluation on different testing scenarios (standard, low user adoption, and low tagging rate). The max trust data fusion variant was consistently the top performer so we only report the effect of different trust prediction methods and user populations on the final occupancy prediction. The two portfolio variants (regression and classification) outperformed the other methods; most of the time the beta reputation system is the best performing single algorithm. Interestingly the Gompertz model performs very poorly at the occupancy prediction problem, even though it does well on the trust prediction task, assuming an unreliable user population. It is conclusively outperformed by the portfolio (classification variant). In a population composed exclusively of high quality workers, all methods are comparable to the majority vote baseline.

5.3 Real Data

To perform our user study, we made the parking availability prediction app freely available for the IOS and Android platforms and announced the existence of the app through a mass campus email to all the students. At this time, participants are able to use the app in an unlimited fashion without providing any parking reports. There was enthusiastic response, and articles about the app appeared in several campus publications. Table 2 presents the overall statistics of the smartphone app usage since the release date.

To evaluate the occupancy prediction of our deployed app, we compare the app's predictions to hourly campus parking lot usage statistics independently collected from parking services. Figure 7 shows the results of this evaluation.

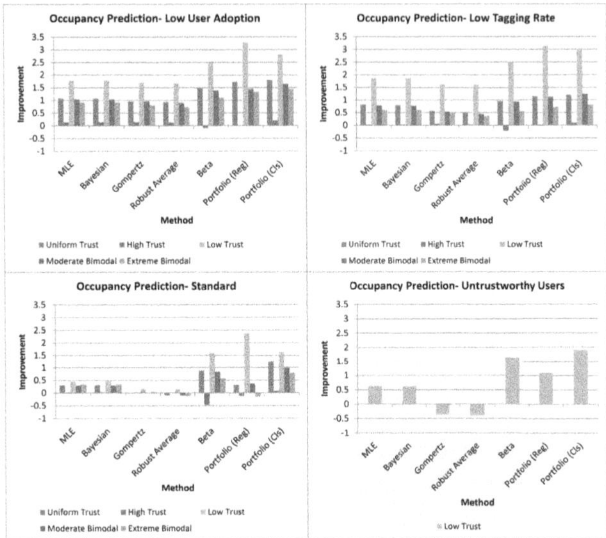

Figure 6: Occupancy prediction results as forecasted by agent-based model with different potential user populations. The portfolio approaches, which leverage information from multiple algorithms, show definite improvements over the other methods.

Table 2: Mobile phone app usage statistics

Participants	1586
Tag Reports	2842
Sections	351
Active Users (at least 1 tag)	129
Active User Ratio	0.0813
Avg Tags / Active User / Weekday	0.9948
Days since Release	31
Avg Tags / Section / Hour	0.0186

The results of the deployed app closely match the results from our simulated model, with the portfolio (regression variant) again exhibiting the best performance. The improvement relative to the majority vote baseline was even higher than predicted by the simulation. The real-time data fusion method performed respectively well and narrowly outperformed the beta-reputation system.

5.4 Discussion

The following list summarizes the pros and cons of the different methods:

- **Beta Reputation Model:** Fast to compute, performs acceptably well, and requires no training. Is outperformed by the other methods at occupancy prediction but performs equivalently well at trust prediction.
- **Real-time Data Fusion:** Improves on the beta reputation system. Requires parameter tuning to perform well. Is potentially more robust to low data flow rates since it propagates user reports from earlier time periods.
- **Portfolio:** Produces the best occupancy prediction results for all population groups in both simulation and the real data. Requires extensive training and may potentially perform poorly in cases when the simple data freshness technique too aggressively resets the section occupancy levels. The regression variant is generally the better performer.

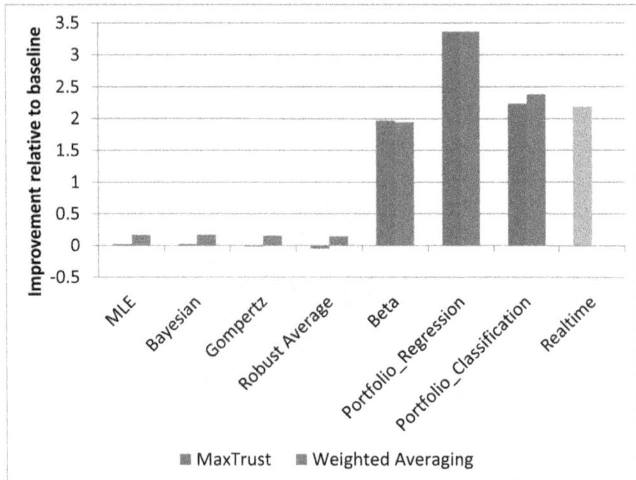

Figure 7: Occupancy prediction results for deployed application on real data. All our proposed techniques improve on the performance of the beta reputation system, with the portfolio (regression) approach being the top performer.

The current version of the system uses the real-time occupancy prediction but in the future we plan to adopt the portfolio approach (regression variant).

6. CONCLUSION AND FUTURE WORK

This paper reports on the development of Kpark, a freely available mobile phone application for crowdsourcing parking availability. Our smart phone app allows users to report on the occupancy level of the parking lots using a menu system; it relies solely on user reports and does not use the GPS sensors. To evaluate the performance of different back end data fusion choices pre-deployment, we constructed an agent-based transportation simulation to model users' parking and app usage habits.

This paper proposes two specific improvements to the user modeling and data fusion process: 1) use of an algorithm selection portfolio and 2) a novel real-time data fusion process. Results on both simulated and real data show that our techniques improve on the best previous performer (the beta reputation system). All of our proposed methods perform substantially better than the baseline majority voting system with no user modeling. Moreover we believe that these techniques are generally applicable to other types of participatory sensing applications.

Our app has nearly 1600 users, but we are still looking to both increase our user population and to increase the average reporting frequency. In the future, we plan to add additional functionality to the app, such as car finding, to incentivize the reporting process.

7. ACKNOWLEDGMENTS

This research was supported by NSF award IIS-0845159.

REFERENCES

[1] D. W. Aha. Generalizing from case studies: A case study. In *Proceedings of the International Conference on Machine Learning*, pages 1–10, 1992.

[2] Y. Bachrach, T. Graepel, G. Kasneci, M. Kosinski, and J. Van Gael. Crowd IQ: Aggregating opinions to boost performance. In *Proceedings of the International Conference on Autonomous Agents and Multiagent Systems*, pages 535–542, 2012.

[3] R. Beheshti and G. Sukthankar. Extracting agent-based models of human transportation patterns. In *Proceedings of the ASE/IEEE International Conference on Social Informatics, Washington, DC*, pages 157–164, 2012.

[4] C. T. Chou, A. Ignjatovic, and W. Hu. Efficient computation of robust average in wireless sensor networks using compressive sensing. *IEEE Transactions on Parallel and Distributed Systems*, 24(8), 2009.

[5] E. Davami and G. Sukthankar. Evaluating trust-based fusion models for participatory sensing applications (extended abstract). In *Proceedings of the International Conference on Autonomous Agents and Multi-agent Systems*, pages 1377–1378, Paris, France, May 2014.

[6] B. Efron and R. J. Tibshirani. *An introduction to the bootstrap*, volume 57. CRC press, 1994.

[7] H. Fleyeh and E. Davami. Multiclass AdaBoost based on an ensemble of binary AdaBoosts. *American Journal of Intelligent Systems*, 3(2):57–70, 2013.

[8] Y. Freund, R. Schapire, and N. Abe. A short introduction to boosting. *Journal of the Japanese Society For Artificial Intelligence*, 14(771-780):1612, 1999.

[9] K. L. Huang, S. S. Kanhere, and W. Hu. Are you contributing trustworthy data?: The case for a reputation system in participatory sensing. In *Proceedings of the ACM International Conference on Modeling, Analysis, and Simulation of Wireless and Mobile Systems*, pages 14–22, 2010.

[10] A. Josang and R. Ismail. The beta reputation system. In *In Proceedings of the Bled Electronic Commerce Conference*, 2002.

[11] E. Kamar, S. Hacker, and E. Horvitz. Combining human and machine intelligence in large-scale crowdsourcing. In *Proceedings of the International Conference on Autonomous Agents and Multiagent Systems*, pages 467–474, 2012.

[12] J. Kopecky. ParkJam. `https://play.google.com/store/apps/details?id=uk.ac.open.kmi.parking`, 2013.

[13] L. Kotthoff. Algorithm selection for combinatorial search problems: A survey. *arXiv preprint arXiv:1210.7959*, 2012.

[14] Parkopedia Ltd. Parkopedia Parking. `https://play.google.com/store/apps/details?id=com.parkopedia`, 2013.

[15] S. Reddy, D. Estrin, and M. Srivastava. Recruitment framework for participatory sensing data collections. In *Proceedings of the International Conference on Pervasive Computing*, 2010.

[16] J. R. Rice. The algorithm selection problem. Technical Report 75-152, Purdue University, 1975.

[17] SFMTA SFpark. SFpark. `https://play.google.com/store/apps/details?id=gov.sfmta.sfpark`, 2013.

[18] V. Sheng, F. Provost, and P. Ipeirotis. Get another label? Improving data quality and data mining using multiple, noisy labelers. In *Proceedings of the ACM SIGKDD Conference on Knowledge Discovery and Data Mining*, 2008.

[19] P. Welinder, S. Branson, P. Perona, and S. J. Belongie. The multidimensional wisdom of crowds. In *Advances in Neural Information Processing Systems*, pages 2424–2432, 2010.

[20] J. Whitehill, T.-f. Wu, J. Bergsma, J. R. Movellan, and P. L. Ruvolo. Whose vote should count more: Optimal integration of labels from labelers of unknown expertise. In *Advances in Neural Information Processing Systems*, pages 2035–2043, 2009.

[21] D. H. Wolpert and W. G. Macready. No free lunch theorems for optimization. *IEEE Transactions on Evolutionary Computation*, 1(1):67–82, 1997.

[22] D. Yang, D. Zhang, K. Frank, P. Robertson, E. Jennings, M. Roddy, and M. Lichtenstern. Providing real-time assistance in disaster relief by leveraging crowdsourcing power. *Personal and Ubiquitous Computing*, pages 1–10, 2014.

[23] Z. Yu, D. Zhang, D. Yang, and G. Chen. Selecting the best solvers: Toward community based crowdsourcing for disaster management. In *IEEE Asia-Pacific Services Computing Conference (APSCC)*, pages 271–277, 2012.

Selecting Robust Strategies in RTS Games via Concurrent Plan Augmentation

Abdelrahman Elogeel[♣] Andrey Kolobov[◇] Matthew Alden[♣] Ankur Teredesai[♣]

[♣]Institute of Technology
University of Washington, Tacoma
{elogeel,mealden,ankurt}@uw.edu

[◇]Microsoft Research
Redmond, WA, USA
akolobov@microsoft.com

ABSTRACT

The multifaceted complexity of real-time strategy (RTS) games forces AI systems to break down policy computation into smaller subproblems – strategic planning, tactical planning, reactive control, and others. To further simplify planning at the strategic and tactical levels, state-of-the-art automatic techniques for this task, such as case-based planning, produce deterministic plans for what is inherently an uncertain environment, and fall back on replanning when the game situation disagrees with the constructed plan. A major weakness of this approach is its lack of robustness: repairing a failed plan is often impossible or infeasible due to real-time computational constraints, causing a game loss. This paper presents a technique that selects a robust RTS game strategy by using ideas from contingency planning and by exploiting action concurrency of these games. Specifically, starting with a strategy and a linear tactical plan that realizes it, our algorithm identifies the plan's failure modes using available game traces and adds concurrent branches to it so that these failure modes are mitigated. In this manner, our approach may train an army reserve *concurrently with* an attack on the enemy, as defense against a possible counterattack. After augmenting each strategy from an available library (e.g., learned from human demonstration) our approach picks one with the most robust augmented tactical plan. An extensive evaluation on the popular RTS games of StarCraft and Wargus, which shares its engine with several other games, shows that concurrent augmentation significantly improves win rate and lets the agent prevail in scenarios where baseline strategy selection consistently leads to a loss.

1. INTRODUCTION

Ten years after real-time strategy (RTS) games were proposed as a challenge for AI [2], computational state of the art in them is still well short of the human performance level [13]. Among the aspects that make RTS games so difficult for computers to play well are the complexity and partial observability of the worlds they depict, their adversarial nature, and the necessity to plan in real time with durative actions and a high degree of concurrency. In an attempt to make RTS game policy computation more tractable, researchers have broken this problem into subproblems varying by planning timescale (strategy, tactics, reactive control) and by their function (opponent modeling, economy/resource management, infrastructure construction, and others). Some of them, e.g., planning at micro-timescales and terrain analysis, have been tackled with relative success using reinforcement and machine learning techniques [13], which affected at least one application area that shares characteristics with RTS games, combat environments simulation [11]. Nonetheless, AI agents in modern commercial RTS games are still far from intelligent. A major reason for this is that, despite progress in other areas, strategic and high-level tactical planning in RTS games have remained largely open problems; in this paper, we focus on them.

Selecting game strategy and high-level tactics are tightly intertwined tasks. On one hand, we would like to choose a strategy, i.e., a sequence of subgoals to achieve to win the game, for which a tactical plan that attains these subgoals is easy to find. On the other hand, tactical plans with a good chance of winning may be available only for specific subgoal sequences, thereby implicitly constraining strategy selection. Case-based planning [6] and the On-line Case-Based Planning (OLCBP) architecture derived from it [12] are among the few automatic approaches that have attempted to solve these planning problems jointly in RTS games.[1] Taking a set of subgoal specifications and gameplay logs (e.g., generated by humans) as inputs, OLCBP builds a hierarchical task network (HTN) [15] from them. It uses this HTN to produce a deterministic strategic and tactical plan at the start of a game. It follows this plan until the game state deviates from the plan's expectations, in which case OLCBP replans. While a significant step towards automating strategy selection, OLCBP doesn't explicitly attempt to maximize the chance of winning the game. Moreover, its reliance on replanning causes a game loss when the existing plan fails and no new one can be found [9].

The technique we present in this paper, which we call *concurrent plan augmentation (CPA)*, mitigates the drawbacks of OLCBP by aiming to select the strategy with a set of tactical plans that will empirically least likely require replanning when executed. We implement CPA in an architecture called *ROLCBP (Robust OLCBP)*. Like OLCBP, ROLCBP identifies promising strategies and tactical realizations for them from game logs *without using a conventional planner*. Importantly, the number of such distinct strategies in RTS games is usually small, allowing ROLCBP to analyze each such strategy with its tactical plans and try to address the plan's weaknesses. For each strategy, ROLCBP first identifies the likely steps at which its tactical plan will fail. Then ROLCBP searches for plans that can be executed *concurrently with* parts of the strategy's main tactical plan and can decrease its empirical chance of failure. For example, if the original plan calls for immediately attacking the enemy and the attack often fails in simulation, ROLCBP might propose to train an army reserve simultaneously with the attack so that the player's base does not get overrun by the opponent's counterattack if the player's attack peters out. Augmenting the tactical plans for each strategy and assessing their failure probability identifies

[1] See Related Work for a discussion of a hard-coded approaches.

Appears in: *Proceedings of the 14th International Conference on Autonomous Agents and Multiagent Systems (AAMAS 2015), Bordini, Elkind, Weiss, Yolum (eds.), May, 4–8, 2015, Istanbul, Turkey.*

the most empirically robust strategy, while storing the augmented plans reduces the need to replan in critical situations. The ability to produce robust tactical behavior automatically in the presence of action concurrency and without reliance on conventional deterministic or probabilistic planners is what makes ROLCBP functionally novel.

We conduct an extensive empirical evaluation of ROLCBP on the popular games of *StarCraft* and *Wargus* (an open-source clone of *Warcraft II* that shares its game engine with several other real-time strategies). It demonstrates CPA's broad applicability and shows that, thanks to CPA, ROLCBP not only has a significantly higher win rate against built-in AI than OLCBP, but can also win on maps where OLCBP always loses. Moreover, whenever CPA does not affect the strategy choice, it still improves the win rate by making tactical plans for the selected strategy much less failure-prone. Last but not least, the experiments reveal that ROLCBP easily wins against opponents very dissimilar from those encountered during training.

To sum up, our paper makes the following contributions:

- We present concurrent plan augmentation (CPA), a technique that helps pick robust strategic and tactical plans.
- We implement CPA in an OLCBP-based architecture called ROLCBP and extensively test it on complex commercial RTS games. The results indicate that CPA provides quantitative as well as qualitative win rate gains by improving decision-making at both strategic and tactical levels.

2. BACKGROUND

Real-time strategy games. RTS games are a genre that typically involves managing resources, building infrastructure, training an army, and ultimately defeating other players by destroying their units and infrastructure. *StarCraft*, an RTS developed by Blizzard Entertainment™, and *Wargus*, an open-source clone of *Warcraft II*, are popular games that we use as experimental testbeds in this paper. In *StarCraft*, every player controls one of three warrior races: Zerg, Protoss, or Terran. In *Wargus*, there are two of them: humans and orcs. In both games, warriors of each race differ in their combat characteristics and in the resources required to produce them. Accordingly, good choices of strategy and tactics vary among races, and also depend on the world configuration, called a *map*, where the game is played.

Strategic planning in RTS games. The objective of RTS game AI is to come up with a *policy* — a mechanism for deciding which actions to initiate at any point in time, given the agent's current belief about the state of the world and actions (both of the agent and of the opponents) that are already being executed. RTS games have several distinctive attributes that put them beyond the capabilities of most standard game tree search and reinforcement learning techniques: the size, complexity, and non-determinism of the game environment, durative and concurrent action execution, partial observability, and others. In fact, even simply finding action outcome trajectories that lead to victory under simplifying assumptions is difficult for modern planners due to actions having durations and being concurrent. For this reason, finding a policy in RTS games is broken down into several layers of abstraction, which effectively decomposes the problem into smaller, more manageable planning tasks. Strategic planning is the highest level in this abstraction hierarchy. It chooses a set of subgoals that need to be achieved to win the game, and the order in which they need to be achieved. While some of the lower levels of the abstraction hierarchy, e.g., unit control, can be tackled with automatic techniques, good strategic behavior in real-time games is very difficult to come by with existing planning technology and, as a result, is either scripted in game AI or relies on adapting plans gleaned from human gameplay. On-Line case-based planning is an example of the latter approach.

On-line case-based planning. OLCBP [12] is a planning architecture derived from hierarchical task networks (HTN) [15] and case-based reasoning. Its inputs, along with a game description, are a set of subgoal specifications and gameplay logs (e.g., generated by humans). OLCBP operates in a cycle with two main phases, behavior acquisition and online expansion-execution (Figure 1). During behavior acquisition, it heuristically matches up parts of the logged game traces with the subgoals, thereby identifying both the strategies used in the game and the tactical plans for achieving the subgoals. After some additional processing, OLCBP stores the extracted plans, called *cases*, in its *case base*.

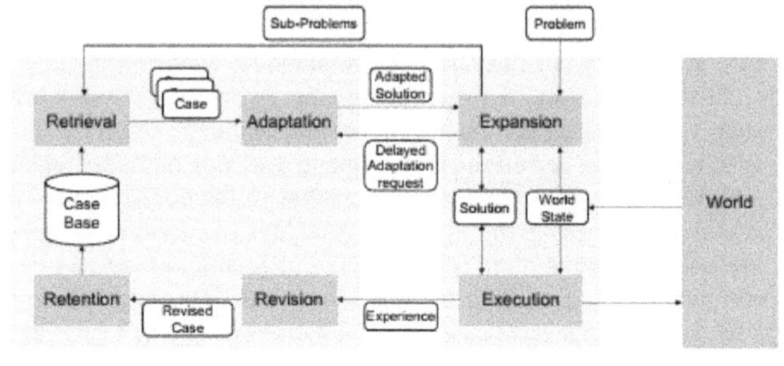

Figure 1: OLCBP cycle. Image taken from [12]

OLCBP assumes its opponents to be relatively static and views strategy and tactics selection as a classical planning problem with a possibility of replanning. OLCBP's expansion-execution step is responsible for dividing this planning problem into subproblems using an HTN constructed from the provided subgoals with the help of the game logs. The chosen strategy is passed to the retrieval submodule, which selects and adapts tactical plans for it from the case base. OLCBP executes these plans until the game situation deviates from the predicted one. In this case, it looks for a different tactical plan, strategy or both, given the player's current situation. Reliance on replanning is OLCBP's significant weakness. Replanning takes time, but even a small delay in acting may mean losing the game. In addition, OLCBP's case base my not contain a back-up plan for unforeseen circumstances, also leading to a game loss.

Contingency planning. In contingency planning [14], an agent situated in a partially observable non-deterministic environment needs to devise a policy for reaching the goal from any state in which the agent may end up. Unlike in (partially observable) Markov Decision Processes (MDPs), the agent does not know the probabilities of its actions' outcomes, only the sets of possible outcomes themselves. In this paper we show that, despite having been considered for non-adversarial settings so far, contingency planning can be potent in RTS game AI as well.

3. CONCURRENT PLAN AUGMENTATION

To address the drawbacks of existing strategy selection approaches such as OLCBP, we propose a technique called *concurrent plan augmentation* (CPA). CPA's high-level idea is to start with a tactical plan for each available strategy, analyze the ways in which the game situation can deviate from it, and come up with *contingent* plan branches that prevent the deviations from becoming catastrophic, to be executed *in parallel* with the main plan. Repeating these steps iteratively builds a partial *policy* for every strategy. This policy's ability to avoid failure is taken as a measure of the corresponding strategy's robustness; based on it, a strategy selection framework, e.g., OLCBP, can choose a strategy for playing the game. At first glance, CPA is reminiscent of contingency planning, but has several important differences:

- Most contingency planning algorithms assume that catastrophic failures cannot happen, i.e., that it is possible to reach the goal (win the game) starting from any state. Even the few exceptions such as [10] assume that failures can be fully avoided from any state. In contrast, failures impossible to avoid with certainty are common in RTS games, e.g., due to opponents' actions. For this reason, contingency planners can usually rely on replanning, whereas CPA attempts to preempt catastrophic events.
- Contingency planning mostly considers settings with no action concurrency, where actions must be executed one after another. CPA relies on concurrency for its operation.
- Unlike in contingency planning, which has no widely accepted measure of policy quality, characteristics of RTS games suggest gauging policy quality with its ability to avoid failures. CPA uses one such measure, a policy's failure probability. Although in a game this measure is only heuristic, since it depends on the training opponent's play, our experiments show that it works well in practice. In games with no draws, as is the case for most RTS games, failure probability minimization can be alternatively viewed as maximizing the win rate.

As described, CPA leaves many details unspecified. How to find contingent plan branches? When should a contingent branch's execution begin? Should the policy tree be computed eagerly before the start of the game or lazily as the game progresses? Their answers depend on the RTS game and strategy selection framework to which CPA is applied. This paper combines CPA with the OLCBP framework to produce the *Robust OLCBP* algorithm, which we describe next.

4. ROBUST OLCBP

The operation of CPA with OLCBP in an architecture we call Robust OLCBP (ROLCBP) is broken down into an offline stage (Algorithm 1) and an online stage (Algorithm 2). The offline stage is devoted to training, while the online stage exploits the learned knowledge for strategy and tactics selection. Throughout our explanations, we will be referring to ROLCBP's pseudocode, denoting line l of Algorithm a as "line l : a". In the following section, we illustrate the pseudocode's operation with an example from *StarCraft*.

Offline stage. At this stage, ROLCBP relies on the OLCBP's machinery to learn a set of strategies $\mathcal{S}$ and a case base of tactical plans $\mathcal{P}$ based on a human-specified set of subgoal descriptions $\mathcal{G}$, action descriptions $\mathcal{A}$, and a set of gameplay logs (line 10:1). The details of this step [12] are beyond the scope of our paper but, importantly for the rest of ROLCBP, each plan in the resulting case base $\mathcal{P}$ achieves a subgoal from $\mathcal{G}$ assuming some other subset of $\mathcal{G}$'s goals has already been achieved. Generally, $\mathcal{P}$ contains several plans that achieve a given subgoal.

After tactical plan extraction, ROLCBP gathers statistics for policy augmentation. Using a simulator for the RTS game to which

1 **Input:** M — a game map, $\mathcal{G} = \{g_i\}_{i=1}^{n}$ — a set of game subgoals, $\mathcal{A} = \{a_i\}_{i=1}^{m}$ — a set of game actions,
2 $\mathcal{L}$ — a set of gameplay logs,
3 *AugDegree* — augmentation degree
4
5 **Output:** *StarCraft* strategy & high-level tactical plan
6
7 *// Learn* $\mathcal{S} = \{S_i = (g_{j_1}, \ldots, g_{j_{n_i}})\}$ *— a set of strategies*
8 *// (subgoal sequences) &* $\mathcal{P} = \{P_i^g = (a_{j_1}, \ldots, a_{j_{m_i}})\}$ —
9 *// a set of high-level tactical plans, each for some subgoal g*
10 $\mathcal{S}, \mathcal{P} \leftarrow$ OLCBP-Learn($\mathcal{G}, \mathcal{A}, \mathcal{L}$)
11
12 **foreach** $P_i^g \in \mathcal{P}$, $a_j \in P_i^g$ **do**
13 $p_{\text{fail}}(a_j, P_i^g) \leftarrow$ *ProbOfCausingFailure*(a_j, P_i^g)

Algorithm 1: ROLCBP: **the offline stage**

it is applied, ROLCBP reproduces the initial conditions of each plan $P \in \mathcal{P}$ (i.e., generates a game state in which all subgoals that P assumes to be achieved have indeed been achieved). Then, with the help of game logs, it simulates the execution of P by an OLCBP-based bot against different opponents, recording the number of times each action in P was executed and failed.

For the purposes of CPA, we define an action a's failure probability $p_{\text{fail}}(a, P^g)$ as the fraction of times its execution caused a *deviation* from the corresponding tactical plan P^g and forced OLCBP to resort to replanning (lines 12:1-13:1). In reality, OLCBP's replanning is sometimes successful at attaining P^g's goal g. Therefore, $p_{\text{fail}}(a, P^g)$ is generally a pessimistic measure of a's quality in P^g. Nonetheless, the overestimation of a's probability of causing an unrecoverable failure actually helps CPA produce more robust policies.

Online stage. At runtime, ROLCBP follows the MainGameLoop method (lines 3:2-10:2). It begins by selecting a game strategy with the most *robust* tactical plan (line 4:2) as explained below, using the SelectStrategy&Tactics procedure. In addition to returning the tactical plan for the chosen strategy, SelectStrategy&Tactics augments it with concurrent contingent branches. In effect, this method constructs a tactical *policy tree*, although this tree may be only partial. ROLCBP plays according to the chosen tactical plan, launching its contingent branches prescribed by the policy tree, until OLCBP's mechanisms detect a deviation from it (line 6:2).

SelectStrategy&Tactics (lines 12:2 - 25:2) operates by iterating over all strategies S in library $\mathcal{S}$, letting OLCBP concoct a tactical plan P_S for each strategy, augmenting this tactical plan with contingent branches using CPA, and evaluating the *failure probability* of the policy tree based on this tactical plan. The failure probability of a strategy's augmented tactical plan serves as a proxy of the strategy's robustness; SelectStrategy&Tactics chooses the strategy with with lowest such probability.

The CPA logic at the heart of SelectStrategy&Tactics is captured in eponymous method (lines 27:2-41:2). CPA analyzes a tactical plan P_S by breaking it down into constituent plans P^g from case base $\mathcal{P}$. Recall that at the offline stage, ROLCBP estimated failure probabilities for each action in each such plan (lines 12:1-13:1). With the help of these estimates, CPA identifies actions with nonzero failure probabilities in P_S (line 29:2). For each of these actions a, CPA models the hypothetical situation immediately after a's failure by determining the "latest" subgoal g_j of strategy S that will remain achieved in that situation (line 31:2). In order to be considered a valid contingency branch for a's failure, a plan P_S^+ needs to

1 // *See Algorithm 1 for the description of* M, $\mathcal{G}$, $\mathcal{S}$, $\mathcal{P}$, *and AugDegree*
2
3 MainGameLoop(M, $\mathcal{G}$, $\mathcal{S}$, $\mathcal{P}$, *AugDegree*) **begin**
4     $S, P_S \leftarrow$ SelectStrategy&Tactics(M, $\mathcal{G}$, $\mathcal{S}$, $\mathcal{P}$, *AugDegree*)
5   **while** *game has not ended* **do**
6         $a_{\text{fail}}, P^g \leftarrow$ *PlayUntilActionFailure*(P_S)
7         $P_S \leftarrow$ *ContingentBranch*$[a_{\text{fail}}, P^g, P_S]$
8   **if** *AugDegree == 1* **then** CPA(M, S, P_S, $\mathcal{P}$)
9   **else if** *AugDegree == 0* **then** OLCBP(M, S, g, $\mathcal{P}$)
10   **else** *AugDegree* $\leftarrow$ *AugDegree* $- 1$
11
12 SelectStrategy&Tactics(M, $\mathcal{G}$, $\mathcal{S}$, $\mathcal{P}$, *AugDegree*) **begin**
13   **foreach** $S = (g_j, \ldots, g_k) \in \mathcal{S}$ **do**
14   // *Compose a tactical plan for strategy S*
15   // *by concatenating several plans from* $\mathcal{P}$
16         $P_S = (P^{g_j}_{i_j}, \ldots, P^{g_k}_{i_k}) \leftarrow$ OLCBP(M, S, $\emptyset$, $\mathcal{P}$)
17   *LeafBranches* $\leftarrow \{P_S\}$
18   **foreach** *d from 1 to AugDegree* **do**
19   *NewBranches* $\leftarrow \emptyset$
20   **foreach** *plan* $P \in$ *LeafBranches* **do**
21   *NewBranches* $\leftarrow$ *NewBranches* $\cup$
22                     $\cup$ CPA(M, S, P, $\mathcal{P}$)
23   *LeafBranches* $\leftarrow$ *NewBranches*
24         $p_{\text{fail}}(P_S) \leftarrow$ EvalFailProb(P_S)
25   **return** S, P_S *s.t.* $p_{fail}(P_S)$ *is the lowest*
26
27 CPA(M, S, P_S, $\mathcal{P}$) **begin**
28   *LeafBranches* $\leftarrow \emptyset$
29   **foreach** $a \in P^g \in P_S$ *s.t.* $p_{fail}(a, P^g) > 0$ **do**
30         $(g_1, \ldots, g_j) \leftarrow$ achieved prefix of S if a fails
31   during P^g's execution
32   // *Compose a plan for S's remaining subgoals*
33         $P^+_S \leftarrow$ *OLCBP*(M, S, $(g_1, \ldots g_j)$, $\mathcal{P}$)
34   // *Schedule* P^+_S *to start executing concurrently*
35   // *with* P_S *ASAP after* g_j *is achieved but*
36   // *before a starts executing, if possible*
37   **if** ScheduleConcurrentExec(P_S, P^+_S, g_j) **then**
38   *ContingentBranch*$[a, P^g, P_S] \leftarrow P^+_S$
39   *LeafBranches* $\leftarrow \{P^+_S\}$
40   **else** *ContingentBranch*$[a, P^g, P_S] \leftarrow \emptyset$
41   **return** *LeafBranches*
42
43 EvalFailProb(P_S) **begin**
44   **if** P_S *is* $\emptyset$ **then return** 1
45     $p_{\text{fail}}(P_S) \leftarrow 0$
46   **foreach** $a_i \in P_S$, *i ranging from* $|P_S|$ *to* 1 **do**
47         $p_{\text{fail}}(P_S) \leftarrow p_{\text{fail}}(a_i, P_S)\cdot$
48             $\cdot$EvalFailProb(*ContingentBranch*$[a_i, P^g, P_S]$)$+$
49             $+(1 - p_{\text{fail}}(a_i, P_S)) \cdot p_{\text{fail}}(P_S)$
50   **return** $p_{fail}(P_S)$

Algorithm 2: ROLCBP: **the online stage**

achieve all subgoals of S after g_j. CPA delegates it to OLCBP to find such a plan (line 33:2).

When/if P^+_S is found, it needs to be scheduled for execution. Intuitively, we would like to start P^+_S in parallel with P_S as early as possible after g_j is achieved. (By P^+_S's construction, we cannot start it before achieving all of S's subgoals up to g_j.) We would also like to schedule it before a, because otherwise in case of a's failure, while OLCBP is looking for another plan, for some time the player's units will not know what to do (and hence will be extremely vulnerable). Whether P^+_S's execution can start in this time window depends on game resource constraints. For example, it may be impossible to train several kinds of units concurrently without enough minerals. Scheduling P^+_S is again delegated to OLCBP (line 37:2). If it turns out to be possible, P^+_S is designated as P_S's contingency for a's failure (line 38:2). Otherwise, a's failure remains unaccounted for (line 40:2). Ultimately, CPA's inability to add contingency branches to a tactical plan may point to the plan's, and hence the strategy's, inherent weaknesses.

A single CPA invocation provides back-ups for the failure of a given tactical plan, but not for failures of the back-ups themselves. The latter would require applying CPA recursively to the contingent branches. SelectStrategy&Tactics provides the option of doing that via the *augmentation degree* (*AugDegree*) parameter. The first-degree augmentation applies CPA to a strategy's main tactical plan only, the second-degree one — to that plan and its contingent branches, and so on (lines 17:2-23:2). Intuitively, higher-degree augmentations reveal complete contingency structure and provide a more thorough assessment of a strategy's robustness. Independently of augmentation degree, evaluation of a strategy's failure probability can be done in a single pass. This is due to the fact that an augmented tactical plan is always a tree. Computing its failure probability is a matter of recursively propagating information from the tree's leaves to its root (lines 43:2 -50:2).

If augmentation degree is at least 1, deviating from the main tactical plan of the chosen strategy in ROLCBP's MainGameLoop likely does *not* cause replanning, as it would in OLCBP. This is because a contingent branch for this failure has already been launched, if this was possible given the game resource constraints. This branch becomes the main execution plan (line 7:2). However, this plan may be vulnerable: recall that, depending on augmentation degree, SelectStrategy&Tactics may not have scheduled any contingencies for it. Therefore, once ROLCBP switches to this plan, if necessary it augments it with contingent branches (line 8:2), to avoid hasty replanning in case of another failure.

Practical considerations. In its computations, ROLCBP iterates over all strategies in its library $\mathcal{S}$, and for each of them builds a policy tree whose size is influenced by the augmentation degree parameter. Thus, the size of $\mathcal{S}$ and augmentation degree are two major factors affecting ROLCBP's performance. Fortunately, the following observations imply that sensible values of these quantities are small in practice:

- *RTS games typically have few viable strategies, and OLCBP's learning from human demonstration naturally identifies them.* Indeed, although in theory there are many possible goal orderings for any scenario, human players tend to use only those belonging to a small set of successful ones. Since ROLCBP's strategy library $\mathcal{S}$ is populated by strategies extracted from human gameplay logs, it ends up containing only a few entries. This makes it possible to analyze each one of them in a short time at the beginning of the game.

- *High-degree augmentation does not pay off.* While n high-degree augmentation gives a better estimate of a strategy's robustness, and hence enables better-informed strategy choice, its computational cost grows exponentially in augmentation degree. ROLCBP can afford some deliberation time at the beginning of the game, but excessively long delay before committing to a strategy heightens the risk of the opponent's attack against the player's unprepared infrastructure. Moreover, most of the contingent branches in a highly augmented policy tree will end up not getting followed, wasting computational effort invested into them. Last but not least, high-degree contingencies are increasingly difficult to schedule because of the multiple resource conflict resolutions OLCBP needs to perform. In all our tests, *first-degree* augmentation, which applies CPA only to the main tactical plan of a policy, has provided the best balance of computational cost and strategy evaluation quality. Therefore, we set *AugDegree = 1* in all our experiments.

5. EXAMPLE

Suppose that after offline training (Algorithm 1), ROLCBP playing the game of *StarCraft* starts by analyzing a strategy whose subgoal ordering is depicted as a sequence of dark-gray rectangles on the *left* side of Figure 2. Suppose further that OLCBP, which ROLCBP uses to find a tactic for this strategy, composes a plan given by the white rectangles inside the dark-gray rectangles. Namely, the plan is *[GatherPrimaryResource, BuildBarracks, TrainMarine, AttackUnit]*, where several *TrainMarine* and several *AttackUnit* actions are executed in parallel. As Figure 2 shows, this tactical plan consists of primitive plans for achieving each subgoal given the previously achieved ones. For the simplicity of the example, each such subplan of the main tactical plan has only one step.

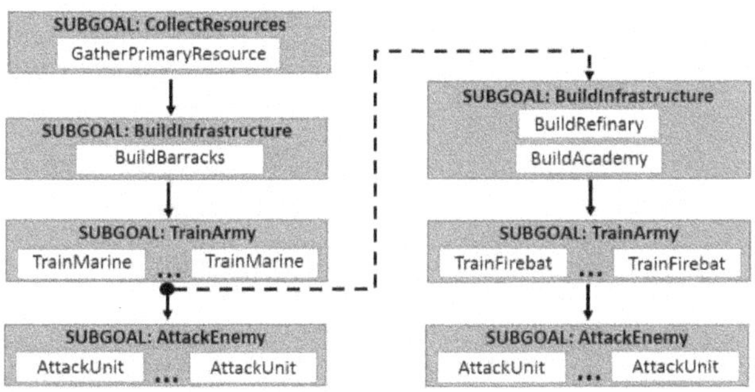

Figure 2: A tactical plan (left) with a contingent branch (right).

The analysis of this plan involves computing the failure probabilities of the steps that compose it. Imagine that during the offline stage (Algorithm 1), ROLCBP established that the first three subgoals, up to and including *TrainArmy*, are always achieved successfully, e.g., because at the start of the game the opponent has too little time to reach the player's base and disrupt the plan. However, ROLCBP may have discovered that the last subgoal of the plan, *AttackEnemy* is difficult to reach: the marine units, though quick to train, are fairly weak, and their attack often fails. When it does, the *TrainArmy* subgoal also gets "unachieved", because the army is destroyed in the attack.

Having performed this analysis, ROLCBP decides to inject a concurrent contingent plan before going for the *AttackEnemy* subgoal. This contingent branch needs to achieve all subgoals that remain unachieved if the main plan fails, i.e., *TrainArmy* and *AttackEnemy*. One such plan is shown on the right side of Figure 2. It trains an army of units more powerful than marines, which requires it to build additional infrastructure. This infrastructure takes a lot of resources, which are unavailable while the main army of marines is being trained, so it schedules this branch for execution right after the marines are trained and ready to attack. If the marines fail, a more potent army of firebats will be available to guard the base and attack the enemy soon afterwards.

After augmenting the main tactical plan, ROLCBP evaluates its failure probability. If more strategies are available, ROLCBP analyzes them too and picks the least likely to fail.

6. EVALUATION

We evaluated CPA by implementing it as part of ROLCBP in software bots for *StarCraft* and *Wargus* (an open-source clone of *Warcraft II*). Most of our experiments focus on *StarCraft*, since it is the more complicated of the two and has a better-developed publicly available experimentation infrastructure that greatly speeds up running tests on it. At the same time, *Wargus* shares its game engine *Stratagus*, the mechanism responsible for its planning capabilities, with a range of other RTS games such as *Aleona's Tales*, so our successful experiments on *Wargus* imply CPA's effectiveness on all these games as well and attest to the universality of our approach. Our experiments address the following questions: (1) How does concurrent policy augmentation affect the bot's performance if used purely at the tactical level when a strategy is fixed, by increasing the tactical plan's robustness? (2) How does CPA affect the bot's performance if used in both at the tactical and strategic levels in ROLCBP, by guiding the strategy selection process? (3) How successfully does CPA deal with opponents who are significantly different from those it plays during the offline training stage (Algorithm 1)? Note that demonstrating the overall superiority of our bot over state-of-the-art bots for *StarCraft* or *Wargus* is *not* an objective of our experiments. Building such a system would require extensive research into components other than strategy and tactics selection modules, which is beyond the scope of this work. Instead, our evaluation uses simple algorithms in bot modules such as those responsible for low-level control, and concentrates on the influence of CPA on strategic and high-level tactical performance.

Experimental setup. We gauge the performance of ROLCBP and the baselines (built-in AI, OLCBP, or both, depending on the experiments) by running many games against an opponent and measuring the *win rate* — the percentage of won games. Win rate subsumes all other gameplay characteristics of potential interest, such as speed or memory usage: if the player's AI is unacceptably slow or memory usage too high, this is reflected in a low win rate. We identify statistically significant performance differences in win rate with two-tailed z-test for equality of proportions at the 95% confidence level.

For *StarCraft*, we experiment on three maps frequently used in *StarCraft* tournaments: Blood Path, Binary Burghs, and Bottleneck. Each *StarCraft* map is characterized by the size of its grid, which is loosely correlated with the map's difficulty; Blood Path has size 64x64, Binary Burghs – 96x96, and Bottleneck – 128x128 cells. For *Wargus*, we use maps of similar sizes: Harrow (62x62), Hills of Glory (96x96), and Dust Storm (128x128). In all figures, map size increases along the x-axis. As mentioned previously, a *StarCraft* player can control one of three races and in *Wargus* — one of two, each with its own characteristics. Our bot always plays the *Terran* race in *StarCraft* and *orcs* in *Wargus*. For offline acquisition of strategies and tactical plans, our bot uses human gameplay logs. For *StarCraft*, they are available at http://www.teamliquid.net/replay/.

Our implementations of ROLCBP and OLCBP are in C++. The two differ only in strategy selection, and share all other components

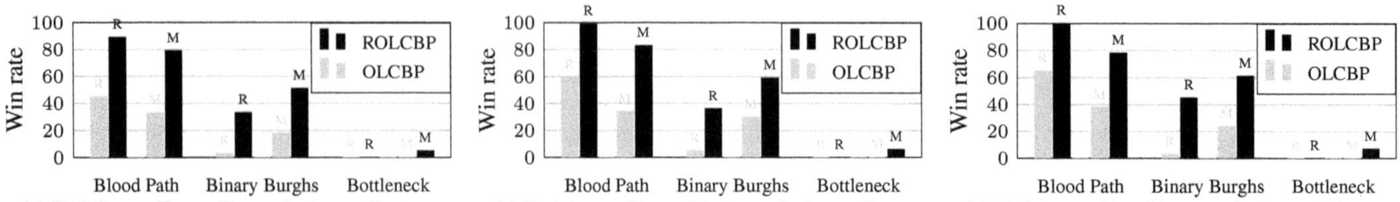

(a) Training vs Terran/Zerg, playing vs Protoss (b) Training vs Terran/Protoss, playing vs Zerg (c) Training vs Zerg/Protoss, playing vs Terran

Figure 3: Effect of CPA on the tactical performance of the rush attack **(R)** and mid-game attack **(M)** strategies in *StarCraft. The advantage of ROLCBP is statistically significant in all experiments except for rush attack on the Bottleneck map.*

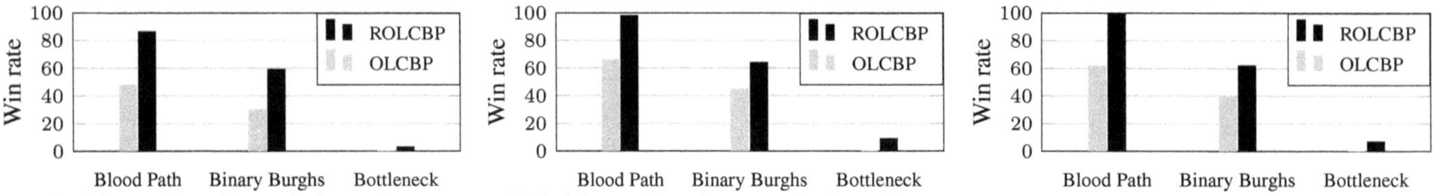

(a) Training vs Terran/Zerg, playing vs Protoss (b) Training vs Terran/Protoss, playing vs Zerg (c) Training vs Zerg/Protoss, playing vs Terran

Figure 4: Effect of CPA on overall performance in *StarCraft. The advantage of ROLCBP is statistically significant in all experiments.*

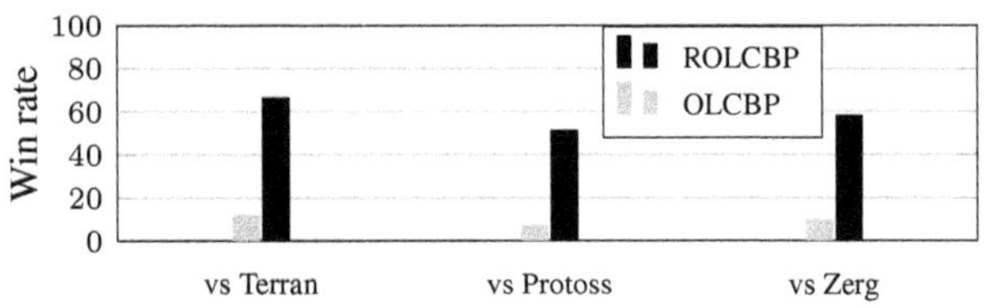

Figure 5: Effect of CPA on overall performance in *StarCraft* on the Bottleneck map with the Fabian strategy. In each case, ROLCBP trains on two races and plays versus the remaining one. *The advantage of ROLCBP is statistically significant in all experiments.*

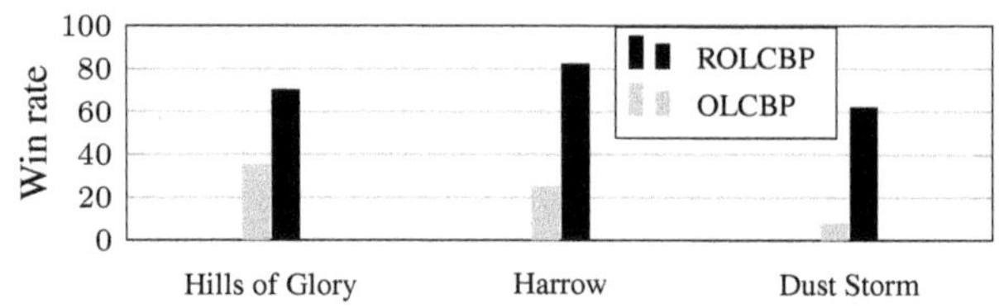

Figure 6: Effect of CPA on overall performance in *Wargus. The advantage of ROLCBP is statistically significant in all experiments.*

(modules for extracting strategies and tactical plans from game logs, low-level control, etc.) The augmentation degree parameter in ROLCBP was set to 1 (see the discussion at the end of the Robust OLCBP section). The experiments were run on an Intel Core i7 2.4GHz CPU with 12GB RAM under Windows 8.1.

Effects of Tactical-Level Augmentation. In this experiment, conducted on *StarCraft*, we measure how the win rate of individual strategies changes when first-degree CPA is applied to their main tactical plans. The results are shown in Figure 3. We focus on two strategies in this experiment. *StarCraft* has three different races, and we measure each strategy's win rate against each of the three races separately (Figures 3a, b, and c). Our bot always plays the Terran race.

To measure a strategy's win rate against a given race (e.g., Zerg) on a given map, we first run the offline training stage of ROLCBP and OLCBP on logs of games played against *the two other* races (e.g., Protoss and Terran) controlled by *StarCraft*'s built-in AI. Then we evaluate the strategy's performance against the target opponent race controlled by the built-in AI by comparing the win rates of OLCBP and ROLCBP when this strategy is the only one available in their strategy library. OLCBP and ROLCBP each ran every strategy 100 times against each race on each map.

The two strategies we use in this experiment are known among human *StarCraft* players as *rush attack* and *mid-game attack*. We chose these strategies because our bot judged them to be the most powerful ones it managed to extract from the game logs: in every game in the strategy selection experiments, whose results are presented later, our bot invariably choose one of these two strategies as the best one.

Figure 3, which summarizes the results on this experiment, reveals several patterns:

- *For most combinations of strategies, maps, and train-test splits in the experiment, ROLCBP's win rate is significantly higher than OLCBP's, i.e., CPA significantly improves strategies' robustness.* This happens because OLCBP resorts to replanning when a strategy's execution goes awry. Replanning is expensive, and if it does not yield a quick solution in a critical situation, the bot loses the game. CPA reduces the need for replanning in critical situations.

- *If a strategy is inherently unsuitable to a given map, applying CPA to it does not help.* For example, all tactical plans for the rush attack strategy on the Bottleneck map have fatal flaws that prevent them from winning even after CPA.

- *CPA can improve a strategy's tactical plan qualitatively, enabling it to win games that its non-augmented version would always lose.* For example, without CPA mid-game attack on the Bottleneck map always fails, while with CPA it is able to win a percentage (albeit small) of games.

Effects of CPA on Strategy Selection. Figures 4 and 6 show the main experimental results of this paper, which testify to the benefit of CPA for overall strategy selection in *StarCraft* and *Wargus*, respectively. For *StarCraft*, the experimental setup is the same as for the tactical-level augmentation experiments from the previous subsection, but now we allow ROLCBP and OLCBP to consider *all* strategies they extract from the game logs, instead of being restricted to any specific one. Thus, the quality of strategies' augmented tactical plans determines the strategy choice for the game. While ROLCBP makes this choice by minimizing strategies' empirical failure probability, OLCBP, our baseline, selects strategies heuristically based on the characteristics of the map and the races the players have picked, breaking ties randomly. In particular, for all *StarCraft* maps in our experiments both the rush and the mid-

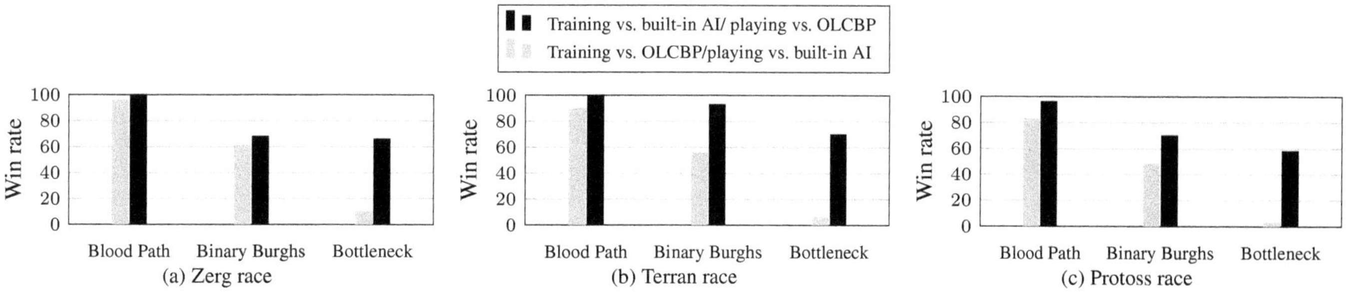

Figure 7: Training against OLCBP and playing against static AI and vice versa.

game attack strategies turn out to match OLCBP's criteria, so it decides randomly between them.

As the graphs in Figure 4 demonstrate, CPA gives ROLCBP a statistically significant advantage in strategy selection. At the same time, similar to the tactical-level experiments, they show that if no strategy learned from the logs is very suitable for a map, then ROLCBP cannot fundamentally change AI's performance — this is the case in the *Bottleneck* scenario. Fortunately, the fix for this issue is as simple as giving ROLCBP a more diverse set of logs. To ascertain this, we re-ran Figure 4's experiments after adding logs with plays of a third strategy, known among *StarCraft* players as Fabian, in addition to rush and mid-game attack discussed earlier. This strategy is not a good option on Blood Bath and Binary Burghs, and ROLCBP indeed does not choose it there, so the results on these two maps remain as in Figure 4. The performance on Bottleneck, however, shown in Figure 5, improves by a lot across each of the three train-test splits and allows ROLCBP to beat built-in AI most of the time. The role of plan augmentation in the decision to choose the Fabian strategy for this map is vital. If failure probabilities of the main tactical plans for mid-game attack, rush attack, and Fabian are evaluated (lines 43-50 of Algorithm 2) against training opponents *before* plan augmentation, rush attack's failure probability appears the lowest, implying that it is a better strategy. (Figure 3 does not reflect this, because it shows win rates of strategies against *testing* opponents.) However, this map's dynamics make deviations from rush attack's tactical plan hard to recover from. Performing CPA and re-evaluating the augmented plans' failure probabilities reveals this and leads to the correct decision to play the Fabian strategy.

For *Wargus*, due to the limitations of the testing framework, we measure ROLCBP's and OLCBP's win rates against the built-in AI playing the orc race only. ROLCBP and OLCBP, which also controlled orcs, each played 20 games on each map. Results on *Wargus* (Figure 6) confirm our findings from *StarCraft*: CPA implemented in ROLCBP drastically improves strategy selection compared to OLCBP. On all *Wargus* maps we have tested, ROLCBP wins over half of the games against built-in AI, whereas OLCBP does not on any single map. Last but not least, since many other RTS games share the *Stratagus* game engine with *Wargus*, we can expect ROLCBP to enjoy similar advantage on them as well.

CPA's performance against unfamiliar opponents. Besides its ability to improve gameplay at strategic and tactical levels, the experiments above hint at CPA's robustness to previously unencountered opponents. As evidence of this, note that in the aforementioned setups ROLCBP's win rate was evaluated on opponent races against which it did not play during training. Nonetheless, both in training and in testing ROLCBP's opponents were controlled by the same (built-in) AI, which prompts a question: does ROLCBP perform as well when the enemy AIs in training and testing are different?

In our final set of experiments on *StarCraft*, we answer this question positively. We consider two opponent AIs: *StartCraft*'s built-in AI and OLCBP. For each *StarCraft* race, we train ROLCBP on game logs against that race controlled by the built-in AI, and measure its win rate against that race played by OLCBP. We also experiment with the case when built-in AI's and OLCBP's roles are switched. As before, we let ROLCBP play 100 games for each race, map, and train-test AI combination.

Figure 7 presents ROLCBP's win rates in this experiment. With the exception of training against OLCBP and playing against built-in AI on the Bottleneck map, OLCBP consistently and convincingly outperforms its opponents. Nonetheless, ROLCBP's win rate noticeably depends on the specific combination of train and test opponent AIs; playing OLCBP after training on the built-in AI usually gives better results than vice versa. This is not surprising. OLCBP's inferior win rates against the built-in AI in Figure 4c suggest that the OLCBP bot is weaker. ROLCBP's win rate suffers when it trains against this weaker AI and then faces the stronger built-in one. The converse also holds: note that the training provided by the built-in AI is so powerful that ROLCBP outmatches OLCBP on Bottleneck (Figure 7) despite the fact that, as already mentioned, all of the strategies in its library are fundamentally unsuitable for this map.

7. RELATED WORK

Automatic strategy and high-level tactics selection methods have featured in several AI systems for playing RTS games; many, if not most, are derived from case-based planning. Darmok [12], I-Strategizer [4], and EISBot [17] use this technique with various additions. An agent developed for the DEFCON game employs a related technique, case-based reasoning, combining it with simulated annealing and decision trees [1]. This makes case-based planning and its variants de-facto state of the art in *automatic* strategy selection for RTS games.

Hierarchical Task Networks have also been used for strategy selection. Besides OLCBP, which is partly based on HTNs, they have been used for this purpose in first-person shooters [7] and role-playing games [8].

Hard-coded techniques for strategy and tactics selection are still strongly competitive with automatic ones, especially in complex games such as *StarCraft* [13]. Finite state machines have been particularly effective for specifying fixed patterns for strategic decision-making and other aspects of RTS games [5].

Besides strategy and tactics selection, RTS game AI's behavior depends on many other components, which are discussed in a recent survey on this topic [13].

Several approaches related to CPA have been proposed in the area of sequential decision-making under uncertainty. Possibly the closest is *incremental contingency planning*, devised for planning Mars rover missions [3]. At a high level, it operates similarly to CPA, but considers non-adversarial environments, doesn't face the strategy selection problem, has different mechanisms and utility for deciding where to add contingent branches, and, crucially, assumes the availability of a planner to construct them.

In probabilistic planning modeled by MDPs, a related approach is *incremental plan aggregation* [16]. RFF, the planner that implements it, finds a linear plan to the goal, determines states where an agent may end up if action outcomes deviate from this plan, adds linear plans to the goal from these states, and iteratively repeats the process. Like ROLCBP, between iterations RFF estimates the "failure probability" of exiting the partially constructed policy tree. Unlike ROLCBP, RFF assumes no action concurrency, which makes choosing branching points much easier, and generates contingent plans on-demand with a dedicated planner, whereas ROLCBP does not need such a planner, relying on plans from its case base. Lastly, ROLCBP's failure probability estimates are only a heuristic for adding contingency branches, because it works in an adversarial, possibly non-stationary environment.

8. CONCLUSION

This paper presented concurrent policy augmentation (CPA), a technique for addressing shortcomings of existing methods for automatic strategy and tactics selection in real-time strategy games. These existing methods, such as OLCBP, treat strategy selection as a hierarchical deterministic planning problem with a possibility of replanning. Replanning in critical situations often fails, leading to a game loss. In contrast, CPA analyzes tactical plans for available strategies to identify their potential failure points. It attempts to mitigate the consequences of these failures by adding contingent plan branches to be executed concurrently with the main plan. We implemented CPA in an OLCBP-based architecture ROLCBP that selects strategies by evaluating the failure probabilities of their augmented tactical plans. Our experiments on popular and complex RTS games *StarCraft* and *Wargus* show that CPA gives ROLCBP significant advantages in win rate compared to OLCBP by improving both tactical and strategic decision-making. It also lets ROLCBP outperform opponents with different behavior than those ROLCBP encounters during training. In the future, we plan to improve our ROLCBP implementation and turn it into a bot competitive with entries in the *StarCraft AI* competition. We have discovered that despite superior strategic performance, our bot's low-level unit control often causes it to lose skirmishes (and hence entire games) that state-of-the-art bots would easily win. Low-level control issues account for most of the games ROLCBP lost in this paper's experiments. Thus, despite being out of this paper's scope, low-level control is a clear area of improvement. We believe that the usefulness of CPA extends beyond case-based planning techniques. The hypothetical advent of planners capable of efficiently generating winning trajectories for RTS games would remove CPA's dependence on plans stored in the case base and would greatly increase CPA's potential.

REFERENCES

[1] R. Baumgarten, S. Colton, and M. Morris. Combining AI methods for learning bots in a real-time strategy game. *Int. J. Computer Games Technology*, 2009, 2009.

[2] M. Buro. Call for AI research in RTS games. In *In Proceedings of the AAAI Workshop on AI in Games*, pages 139–141. AAAI Press, 2004.

[3] R. Dearden, N. Meuleau, S. Ramakrishnan., D. E. Smith, and R. Wasington. Incremental Contingency Planning. In *ICAPS'03*, 2003.

[4] I. Fathy, M. Aref, O. Enayet, and A. Al-Ogail. Intelligent online case-based planning agent model for real-time strategy games. In *ISDA*, pages 445–450, 2010.

[5] D. Fu and R. Houlette. The ultimate guide to FSMs in games. *AI Game Programming Wisdom 2*, 2003.

[6] K. Hammond and R. Head. Case-based planning: A framework for planning from experience. *Cognitive Science*, 14:385–443, 1990.

[7] H. Hoang, S. Lee-urban, and H. MuÃśoz-avila. Hierarchical plan representations for encoding strategic game ai. In *In Proc. Artificial Intelligence and Interactive Digital Entertainment Conference (AIIDE-05*. AAAI Press, 2005.

[8] J.-P. Kelly, A. Botea, and S. Koenig. Offline planning with hierarchical task networks in video games. In *AIIDE'08*, 2008.

[9] I. Little and S. Thiébaux. Probabilistic planning vs replanning. In *Workshop on International Planning Competition: Past, Present and Future (ICAPS)*, 2007.

[10] C. Muise, V. Belle, and S. McIlraith. Computing contingent plans via fully observable non-deterministic planning. 2014.

[11] J. Muñoz, G. Gutiérrez, and A. Sanchis. A human-like TORCS controller for the Simulated Car Racing Championship. In *Proceedings 2010 IEEE Conference on Computational Intelligence and Games*, pages 473–480, August 2010.

[12] S. Ontañón, K. Mishra, N. Sugandh, and A. Ram. On-line case-based planning. *Computational Intelligence*, 26(1):84–119, 2010.

[13] S. Ontañón, G. Synnaeve, A. Uriarte, F. Richoux, D. Churchill, and M. Preuss. A survey of real-time strategy game AI research and competition in starcraft. *IEEE Trans. Comput. Intellig. and AI in Games*, 5(4):293–311, 2013.

[14] L. Pryor and G. Collins. Planning for contingencies: A decision-based approach. *Journal of Artificial Intelligence Research*, 4:287–339, 1996.

[15] E. D. Sacerdoti. The nonlinear nature of plans. In *Proceedings of the 4th International Joint Conference on Artificial Intelligence - Volume 1*, IJCAI'75, pages 206–214, San Francisco, CA, USA, 1975. Morgan Kaufmann Publishers Inc.

[16] F. Teichteil-Königsbuch, U. Kuter, and G. Infantes. Incremental plan aggregation for generating policies in MDPs. In *AAMAS'10*, pages 1231–1238, 2010.

[17] B. G. Weber, M. Mateas, and A. Jhala. Building human-level ai for real-time strategy games. In *AAAI Fall Symposium: Advances in Cognitive Systems*, volume FS-11-01 of *AAAI Technical Report*. AAAI, 2011.

CFQI: Fitted Q-Iteration with Complex Returns

Robert Wright*, Xingye Qiao, Lei Yu†
Binghamton University
Binghamton, NY 13902, USA
{rwright3,xqiao,lyu}@binghamton.edu

Steven Loscalzo
AFRL Information Directorate
26 Electronic Pkwy
Rome, NY 13441, USA
Steven.Loscalzo@us.af.mil

ABSTRACT

Fitted Q-Iteration (FQI) is a popular approximate value iteration (AVI) approach that makes effective use of off-policy data. FQI uses a 1-step return value update which does not exploit the sequential nature of trajectory data. Complex returns (weighted averages of the n-step returns) use trajectory data more effectively, but have not been used in an AVI context because of off-policy bias. In this paper we propose a new generalization of FQI called Complex Fitted Q-Iteration (CFQI) which allows for complex returns. Theoretical properties are proved that show CFQI does not break existing convergence properties. Two methods for integrating complex returns are presented. The first method uses a simple truncating procedure for reducing off-policy bias. Our second method applies a novel bounding operation that utilizes the off-policy bias. We provide an empirical evaluation of the proposed methods on several reinforcement learning benchmarks. The results demonstrate that our methods significantly improve over FQI in terms of value estimation accuracy, policy performance, and convergence speed.

Categories and Subject Descriptors

I.2.6 [**Artificial Intelligence**]: Learning

General Terms

Algorithms

Keywords

Reinforcement Learning; Approximate Value Iteration; Off-Policy; Fitted Q-Iteration; Complex Returns

1. INTRODUCTION

Fitted Q-Iteration (FQI) is a widely used approximate value iteration (AVI) framework for solving reinforcement learning (RL) problems [4]. Since its introduction FQI has been used and extended by numerous works [1, 8, 13, 17]. FQI's most compelling feature is its ability to learn effectively from varied sources of off-policy sample data. Off-policy data are generated from behavior policies that differ from the target policy, the policy being learned. Whereas, with on-policy data the behavior policy and target policy are the same. In a multi-agent context, this ability is analogous to learning from the aggregate experiences of heterogeneous agents solving a given problem. Most other RL methods make restrictive assumptions on sample data rendering such collections of data useless. In many realistic learning situations, where simulation is impractical and obtaining samples is difficult and costly, it is critically important to be able to use all available data. FQI is a means to use all available data to learn an approximation of the optimal policy.

Although FQI can use off-policy sample data effectively, it does not exploit this data to the fullest extent. The key operation of FQI, and its derivatives, is its Q-value update function which makes use of the greedy 1-step return [19]. This 1-step update treats each sample as an independent event and relies completely on bootstrapped value estimates. These bootstrapped estimates can have significant error due to the use of function approximation and irregularly distributed sample sets. Samples, however, are not typically gathered as single-step experiences and they are not independent of each other. Instead they are gathered as multi-step experiences known as trajectories and share sequential relationships that can be used to reduce this error.

Trajectory data has been used to great effect in on-policy and policy iteration RL contexts through the use of *complex returns*[5, 7, 9, 19]. Complex returns are weighted averages of the n-step returns, value estimates made by looking further down a trajectory. Through careful design, the aggregated value estimates produced by complex returns have low variance and are generally more accurate than 1-step return estimates. Despite this advantage and the general availability of trajectory data, complex returns have not been considered in an AVI context to the best of the author's knowledge. There are two primary reasons. First, off-policy trajectories introduce bias into estimates. Second, the target policy is unknown, making it impossible to apply importance sampling to mitigate off-policy biases [15].

To meet these challenges we propose Complex Fitted Q-Iteration (CFQI), a generalization of the FQI framework which allows for any general return based estimate, enabling the seamless integration of complex returns and AVI. We introduce and analyze two distinct methods for utilizing complex returns within the CFQI framework. The first method

*Dr. Wright is currently affiliated with AFRL. Email Robert.Wright.25@us.af.mil

†Dr. Yu is the last author who directed Wright's Ph.D. research including this work.

Appears in: *Proceedings of the 14th International Conference on Autonomous Agents and Multiagent Systems (AAMAS 2015), Bordini, Elkind, Weiss, Yolum (eds.), May 4–8, 2015, Istanbul, Turkey.*

is similar to the idea of $Q(\lambda)$ [19] and uses truncated portions of trajectories, that are consistent with the approximation of Q^*, to calculate complex return estimates without introducing off-policy bias. The second method is a more nuanced approach that makes use of the inherent negative bias of complex returns, due to the value iteration context, as a lower bound for value estimates. We provide statistical evidence and analysis that shows how an estimator with predictable, but unknown, bias can provide a bound on value estimates to produce a more accurate estimator. Additionally, we include convergence proofs showing that CFQI is guaranteed to converge under the same assumptions as FQI. Finally, we provide an empirical evaluation of our methods on several RL benchmarks that show how CFQI improves the accuracy of the learned Q^* approximation, the quality of the learned policy, and convergence behavior.

2. BACKGROUND

Our focus in this work is finding solutions to Markov Decision Processes (MDP) [16]. An MDP, M, is defined as a 5-tuple, $M = (S, A, P, \mathcal{R}, \gamma)$, where S is a fully observable finite set of states, A is a finite set of possible actions, P is the state transition model such that $P(s'|s,a) \in [0,1]$ describes the probability of transitioning to state s' after taking action a in state s, $\mathcal{R}^a_{s,s'}$ is the expected value of the immediate reward r after taking a in s, resulting in s', and $\gamma \in (0,1)$ is the discount factor on future rewards.

Solutions to MDPs are policies, which are functions on the state space that determine which action to take, $\pi : S \mapsto A$. The quality of a policy is determined by the expected value that can be obtained by following it from any given state. In RL we are concerned with Q-values which, given π, are defined as: $Q_\pi(s,a) = \mathbb{E}_\pi[\sum_{i=0}^{\infty} \gamma^i r_{i+1} | s_0 = s, a_0 = a]$, where r_{i+1} is the immediate reward given at time $i+1$.

Our goal is to derive an optimal policy, π^*, that maximizes this value for all $s \in S$. For this purpose we can estimate the optimal Q-function, Q^*, which is defined as the solution to the optimal Bellman equation: $Q^*(s,a) = \sum_{s' \in S} P(s'|s,a)[\mathcal{R}^a_{s,s'} + \gamma \max_{a' \in A} Q^*(s',a')]$. From this equation π^* can be extracted as: $\pi^*(s) = \arg\max_{a \in A} Q^*(s,a)$.

If P and $\mathcal{R}$ are known, Q^* can be solved for efficiently using dynamic programming. However, in RL scenarios P and $\mathcal{R}$ are unknown and Q^* must be learned from samples. Samples are single-step observations of transitions from the domain. They are represented by tuples, $(s_t, a_t, s_{t+1}, r_{t+1})$, consisting of a state s_t, an action a_t, the state s_{t+1} transitioned to by taking a_t in s_t, and r_{t+1}, the immediate reward for that transition. There are many different RL approaches for solving for Q^*. Here we focus on Fitted Q-Iteration.

2.1 Fitted Q-Iteration

Fitted Q-Iteration (FQI) [4] is a batch-mode, off-line, off-policy approach for solving RL problems. It is an approximate value iteration [12] framework that solves directly for Q^* through a sequence of standard supervised learning regression problems. As a batch-mode algorithm it makes efficient use of samples. It has also been proven that, under restrictive assumptions of the regression model, FQI is guaranteed to converge towards Q^* [14].

FQI starts with an arbitrarily initialized approximation of Q^*, $\hat{Q}_0$. This approximation of Q^* is then refined through an iterative process. In this process the estimated Q-values of each sample are calculated using the current $\hat{Q}$ approximation. These values are then used as target values for a regression algorithm that "fits" them with their corresponding sample state and action features producing the next approximation, $\hat{Q}_m$. The process is repeated for M iterations or until some other stopping criteria.

A crucial component of this process is how the sample value estimates are calculated. The accuracy of these estimates dictates the final accuracy of $\hat{Q}_M$ and in turn the quality of the derived policy. For this purpose FQI uses the greedy 1-step return estimate, $R_t^{(1)}$:

$$\hat{Q}_m(s_t, a_t) \leftarrow R_t^{(1)} = r_{t+1} + \gamma \max_{a \in A} \hat{Q}_{m-1}(s_{t+1}, a) \ , \quad (1)$$

which combines the single-step observed immediate reward with a greedy choice among all *bootstrapped* estimates of future returns provided by $\hat{Q}_{m-1}$. $R_t^{(1)}$ is a reasonable choice for a value estimator as it is unbiased with regard to the sampling policies. However, it is not the only choice and it is very sensitive to error caused by biases and variances in an imperfect function approximation model and irregular sample distributions. In the following we show how complex returns are more robust and can be used to provide more accurate estimates in an AVI context.

2.2 Complex Returns

Sample data are most commonly collected in sequences known as trajectories. A trajectory, T, is a sequentially ordered collection of observations where, $T = [(s_0, a_0, s_1, r_1), (s_1, a_1, s_2, r_2), \ldots]$. Trajectories provide an alternative to using just the $R_t^{(1)}$ return. Given trajectory data, the 1-step return estimate in Eq(1) can be generalized to produce the n-step returns:

$$R_t^{(n)} = \sum_{i=1}^{n-1} \gamma^{i-1} r_{t+i} + \gamma^n \max_{a \in A} \hat{Q}_{m-1}(s_{t+n}, a) \ . \quad (2)$$

It should be noted that this definition of the n-step returns differs from the standard on-policy definition of the n-step returns because of its use of the *max* operation. In principle each of the n-step returns can be used as approximations of $Q^*(s_t, a_t)$. Individually each estimator has its own distinct bias and variance. However, when combined, through averaging they can produce an estimator with lower variance than any one individual return [3]. It is this idea that motivated the development of *complex* returns [19, Chapter 7].

A complex return is a weighted average, with the weights summing to 1, of the n-step returns. The n-returns are weighted differently because of their assumed relative variance behaviors. The general assumption behind existing complex return methods is that the variance of the n-step returns increases as n increases. From the on-policy literature there are two competing complex return approaches. The classic complex return is the λ-return which serves as the basis for the TD(λ) family of algorithms [19]. More recently, the γ-return was introduced based upon different variance assumptions of the n-step returns [9]. The γ-return is defined as:

$$R_t^{\gamma} = \sum_{n=1}^{|T|} \frac{(\sum_{i=1}^{n} \gamma^{2(i-1)})^{-1}}{\sum_{m=1}^{|T|} (\sum_{i=1}^{m} \gamma^{2(i-1)})^{-1}} R_t^{(n)} \ . \quad (3)$$

The difficulty in applying complex returns to FQI is that

in an AVI context the trajectories can be sampled off-policy and the target policy is also unknown. Off-policy trajectories introduce undesirable bias into the n-step return estimates that cannot be reduced through averaging. If the target policy were known, as in policy iteration, importance sampling can be used to reduce off-policy bias [15]. However, the target policy is unknown in our AVI context. In the following section we will introduce two methods that utilize complex returns effectively in an AVI context.

3. COMPLEX FITTED Q-ITERATION

Here we introduce Complex Fitted Q-Iteration (CFQI) our generalization of the popular FQI framework that enables the use of complex return based value estimates. Algorithm 1 provides the details of the approach.

Algorithm 1 CFQI($\mathcal{T}, M, R^C$)

Input: $\mathcal{T}$: set of trajectories,
M: number of iterations, R^c: complex return function
1: $\hat{Q}_0 \leftarrow 0$
2: **for** $m = 1$ to M **do**
3: Let X and Y be empty sets.
4: **for** $k = 1$ to $|\mathcal{T}|$ **do**
5: **for** $t = 1$ to $|T_k|$ **do**
6: $X \leftarrow Append(X, (s_t^{T_k}, a_t^{T_k}))$
7: $Y \leftarrow Append(Y, R^C(t, T_k, \hat{Q}_{m-1}))$
8: **end for**
9: **end for**
10: $\hat{Q}_m \leftarrow Regression(X, Y)$
11: **end for**
12: **Return** $\hat{Q}_M$

The primary distinction between FQI and CFQI lies in the two update rules (line 7). FQI is limited to the $R^{(1)}$ return estimate, while CFQI makes use of any chosen complex return R^C to provide value estimates. A second difference between FQI and CFQI is that CFQI processes over trajectories, not unordered samples as in FQI. CFQI has the same computational complexity as FQI, since the derivations of the n-returns and complex returns can be performed efficiently by processing trajectories in reverse order. One of our contributions is to show that using complex returns as value estimates does not break the theoretical convergence guarantees of the original approach.

THEOREM 1. *CFQI converges w.p.1 if a normalized complex return, computed from fixed length trajectories, is used to derive value targets to be used in a kernel regression model, as defined by Eq(7) and Eq(8).*

The proof for Theorem 1 and equations Eq(7) and Eq(8) are provided in the Appendix. Still, although CFQI can be guaranteed to converge, the bias of off-policy n-step returns will introduce bias into the final result possibly eliminating any potential benefit from variance reduction. In the following subsections we propose two methods which aim to either mitigate or utilize this bias.

3.1 Method 1: Truncated Complex Returns

One way to handle the off-policy bias of the complex returns is to attempt to avoid it by truncating the trajectories where they appear to go off-policy. This idea is borrowed from the $Q(\lambda)$ [21] approach. However, this is the first work to the author's knowledge that has considered it for AVI. In this approach the current $\hat{Q}$ provides an approximation of the optimal policy that can be used to infer when a trajectory takes an off-policy sub-optimal action. During the process of calculating the complex return estimates, samples in a trajectory after the first off-policy action are not considered. Assuming $\hat{Q}$ is a close approximation of Q^* this approach should not introduce off-policy bias and can take advantage of portions of trajectories that follow the optimal policy to reduce variance and overall error. We refer to this method as CFQI-C.

However, the assumption that $\hat{Q}$ is an accurate approximation of Q^* is a poor one, especially early in the iterative process. Additionally, because the learned policy will likely change during the iterative process, the lengths of the trajectories used to calculate the complex returns will change dynamically from one iteration to the next. Changing lengths of the trajectories violates one of the assumptions made by Theorem 1 and convergence may no longer be guaranteed. This issue is examined further in the empirical study.

3.2 Method 2: Complex Returns as Bounds

Our second approach uses the off-policy n-step return bias rather than attempting to eliminate it. It exploits the predictability of this bias enabling the effective use of complex returns as a bound on the value of the $R^{(1)}$ return. In an AVI context, such as CFQI, this is possible due to the fact that the target policy is an optimal policy. Because the target policy is optimal, it is a safe assumption that any off-policy bias present in the n-step returns is negative in value. A complex return derived from the biased n-step returns will also be biased negatively, but should have relatively low variance. This insight directly leads to the derivation of a bounded complex return, R^B:

$$R^B = \max(R^{(1)}, R^C). \tag{4}$$

where R^C is some chosen complex return function. When integrated with CFQI, we refer to this method as CFQI-B.

To help motivate this approach we first consider a simple scenario. Let us assume $R^{(1)}$ is an unbiased estimator with non-zero variance and R^C is a constant that is known to be less than the target value being estimated. In this case it is always better to use $\max(R^{(1)}, R^C)$ in place of $R^{(1)}$ to estimate the value. When $R^{(1)}$ is less than R^C it must be farther away from the true value than R^C, in which case the greater observation R^C should be used. Realistically, however, R^C is not a constant and we must further examine the conditions under which R^C can provide an effective bound.

We now investigate when R^B improves $R^{(1)}$ using some distributional assumptions. The occurrence and degree of improvement depends on the underlying distribution of $R^{(1)}$ and R^C. Here we assume both estimators follow normal distributions. Further, let us also assume that $\text{bias}(R^{(1)}) = 0$ and $STD(R^{(1)}) = 1$. The bias and STD of R^C are chosen from the range $[-1.5, 1] \times (0, 2]$. For each pair of the bias and STD, we estimate the mean squared error of the estimators $R^{(1)}$ and R^B by Monte Carlo integration. Figure 1 provides a rendering of this model. The red solid curve is the boundary where R^B and $R^{(1)}$ are equally good. The area below the red curve is where R^B improves upon $R^{(1)}$.

The black contours in Figure 1 show the log ratio of MSE,

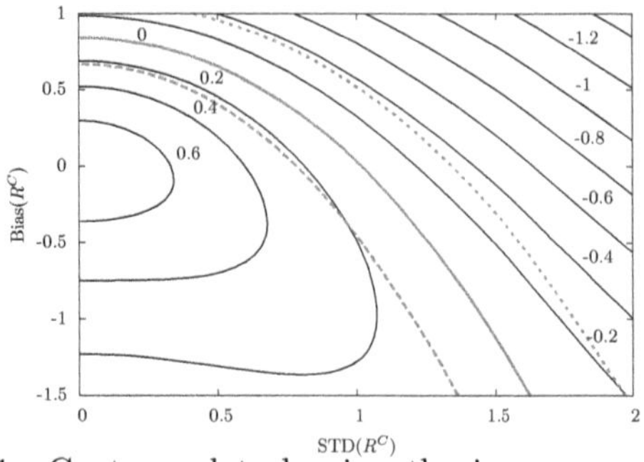

Figure 1: Contour plot showing the improvement of R^B over $R^{(1)}$. Red curves: boundaries between improvement and no improvement for cases of bias$(R^{(1)}) = 0$ (solid), 0.5 (dashed), and -0.5 (dotted).

$\log(MSE(R^{(1)})/MSE(\max(R^{(1)}, R^C)))$. The greater this value is, the more improvement $\max(R^{(1)}, R^C)$ has. Clearly the greatest improvement occurs at the unrealistic case where R^C is unbiased and has 0 variance. In general a combination of small bias and small variance is sufficient to guarantee an improvement. The more negative the bias is, the greater variance is allowed. However, if the bias is overly negative, then the improvement becomes negligible. Additionally, even if the bias of R^C is positive there is still a chance for the R^B to be a better estimator if $\text{Var}(R^C) < \text{Var}(R^{(1)})$.

We also show the boundaries under the cases where $R^{(1)}$ is biased. The dashed curve and the dotted curve correspond to bias 0.5 and -0.5 respectively. Compared to the solid curve, we have the impression that it is more likely for a maximum estimator such as $\max(R^{(1)}, R^C)$ to improve $R^{(1)}$, when $R^{(1)}$ is itself negatively biased; and vice versa. However, there is a potential risk of the bounding estimator R^C falls into the domain of loss (i.e., the northeast of the red curve). Such risk increases as bias$(R^{(1)})$ becomes more positive. Fortunately, $|\text{bias}(R^{(1)})|$ is generally under control in an AVI context. Ideally one would choose a model that fits well and thus does not have much bias without over-fitting.

We can now identify some characteristics about R^C that ensure an effective R^B:

1. The bias of R^C must be less than a positive value τ that satisfies $MSE(\max(R^{(1)}, \tau)) = MSE(R^{(1)})$. $\tau \approx 0.8399$ in the example given in Figure 1.
2. The variance of R^C should be small. It can be greater than that of $R^{(1)}$ as long as R^C has negative bias.
3. The bias of R^C should not be overly negative.

The first two criteria ensure a safe bound from below such that R^B is no worse than $R^{(1)}$. The third criterion is necessary to ensure there is a fair chance for $R^{(1)} < R^C$, enabling an effective bound.

The preceding analysis provides the motivation for our bounding approach. Given our AVI context the bias of off-policy n-step returns generally decreases as n increases. Hence, $\text{bias}(R^{(n)}) < \text{bias}(R^{(n-1)}) < \cdots < \text{bias}(R^{(1)})$. This bias behavior means if one was to use an n-step return or a complex return as the bounding estimator, it is very likely to satisfy the first criterion. Our choice in R^C will ultimately determine if the second and third criterion are satisfied.

In this paper we choose the γ-return as R^C for a proof of concept. Optimal design and selection of the bounding estimator is potentially an interesting future research direction. Given its proven variance reduction property [9], the γ-return is likely to have small variance, satisfying criterion 2. Since the γ-return includes non-negligible weights for all n-step returns its expected value is very likely to be negative, satisfying criterion 1. It is possible for this bias to become too negative, failing criterion 3. This can be remedied by restricting the length of the trajectory γ-return considers as was shown in [9].

Theorem 2 (proof in Appendix) below assures that CFQI with the bounding method also converges under the same conditions as FQI. This theorem can be further generalized to state that if CFQI converges with any two complex return estimates independently, then using one to bound the value of the other is also guaranteed to converge.

THEOREM 2. *CFQI converges w.p.1 if the $R^{(1)}$ return is bounded by a normalized complex return on fixed length trajectories to produce value estimates used in a kernel regression model, as defined by Eq(7) and Eq(8).*

4. RELATED WORK

Trajectory Fitted Q-Iteration (TFQI) [22] is a recently introduced FQI based algorithm that also makes use of the n-step returns. Instead of using a complex return, TFQI uses the n-step return that has the highest observed value as the sample Q-value estimate.

$$R^{Max} = \max(R^{(1)}, R^{(2)}, \ldots, R^{(|T|)}) \qquad (5)$$

Although there was no explicit mentioning of the bounding idea, it essentially uses the R^{Max} return as the bound for the $R^{(1)}$ return. The authors of this method reported significantly improved performance compared to that of FQI on two RL benchmark problems. However, our analysis in the previous subsections suggests that if any of the $R^{(n)}$ returns exhibits positive bias and/or high variance the R^{Max} return will likely overestimate values. In addition, the TFQI work did not provide any statistical explanation of why and when the R^{Max} return works or fails, and the experimental evaluation was conducted in deterministic environments.

There exists many approaches that enable the use of complex returns to improve value estimation in certain off-policy contexts through the use of importance sampling[5, 20]. These methods are similarly motivated but are limited to the policy iteration RL contexts where the target policy is known.

5. EMPIRICAL STUDY

In this section we provide an empirical evaluation of our approaches on several non-deterministic RL benchmarks. The methods are compared based upon accuracy of the learned value function, quality of the derived policy, and convergence behavior. We report comparative results for four methods, with the return used by each method listed in the following.

Method	Value Estimator
FQI	$R^{(1)}$
TFQI	R^{Max}
CFQI-C$_\gamma$	Truncated R^γ
CFQI-B$_\gamma(l)$	$R^B = max(R^{(1)}, R^{(\gamma)})$

For the CFQI-B$_\gamma(l)$ method, l denotes the limit on how many steps down the trajectory to use when computing the R^γ return. If l is not listed, it uses the full trajectory.

In all our experiments we use ridge linear regression with Fourier Basis functions [10]. AVI is known to exhibit divergence behavior when paired with this type of function approximation model [2]. We are able to circumvent this issue by bounding the values returned by the models with V_{max}. V_{max} is the maximum possible value for any state-action pair and can be calculated a priori as:

$$V_{max} = \frac{R_{max}}{(1-\gamma)} \tag{6}$$

where R_{max} is the maximum single step reward in the domain. This change was sufficient to ensure convergence for most methods we tested. In our experiments this form of function approximation provided results superior to the kernel averaging based methods that AVI is guaranteed to converge with. If the approximated values were not bounded by V_{max} we did observe divergence behavior from all methods. In our experimentation we examined a comprehensive set of parameters varying the complexity of the model, regularization, number of iterations, and trajectory counts. The results we report are consistent with the general trends we observed. Statistical significance is determined by performing a paired t-test. We report a result as significant in the following analysis if ($p < 0.005$).

5.1 Value Function Approximation Accuracy

In this series of experiments we examine how accurately the methods can derive Q^* using identical trajectory data sets. For this purpose we use a non-deterministic 51-state Markov chain similar to the one presented in [11]. This environment is chosen because Q^* can be calculated exactly using dynamic programming. The goal is to traverse the chain, starting from some random state, to one of the terminal states in as few steps as possible. There are three terminal states: 0, 25, and 50. From any non-terminal state the agent can take an action to move to one of the two neighboring states with a cost of -1. We set the discount factor, γ, to 0.9 and there is a 20% probability that an action taken will result in no transition. The function approximation model uses a 10th order Fourier basis with no regularization.

In order to evaluate the methods under varying levels of off-policy bias we generated multiple repositories of 10000 trajectories based on behavior policies that follow the optimal policy with probability 0.9 to 0.5 (equivalent to a random policy) at each step. For each run 1000 trajectories are randomly selected from a chosen repository to form a training data set. The reported results are the average of 200 runs. We evaluate each method based on the average MSE of the $\hat{Q}$ functions, comparing to the true Q^* function, after 50 iterations of learning (sufficient to ensure convergence).

For completeness, we also consider LSTD-Q [11], an alternative batch-mode algorithm. LSTD-Q's performance was nearly identical to FQI's, so we do not include that result. This finding is expected given that both LSTD-Q and FQI use $R^{(1)}$ and optimize the same objective function.

The results reported in Figure 2 show the CFQI based methods are stable and outperform FQI at most levels of off-policy bias. The only exception is with data from a 90% optimal policy, where CFQI performs comparably to FQI. TFQI on the other hand shows unstable results. It performs poorly when there is less off-policy bias, demonstrating that the R^{Max} return can be prone to overestimate. However, it is significantly better than all other methods on near random trajectory data. Comparing CFQI-C and CFQI-B, we see that the bounding approach can perform significantly better than its truncated complex return counterpart.

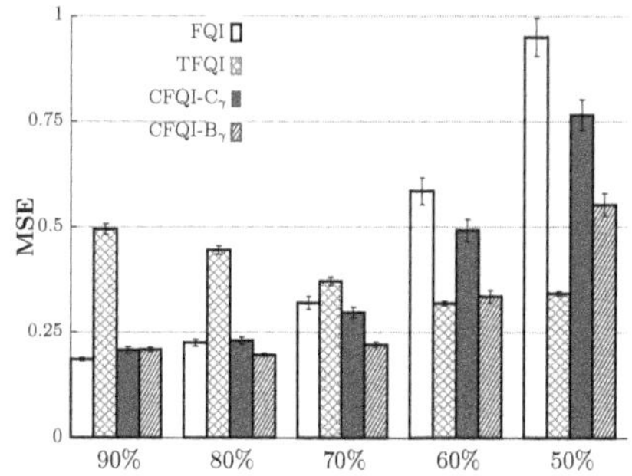

Figure 2: Average MSE of the $\hat{Q}$ functions for the various methods. The behavior policy is varied from 90% to 50% of the optimal policy. Error bars show standard deviation.

5.2 Policy Performance

In this set of experiments we examine the impact of improved value estimation on the policy quality on two RL benchmarks: the Acrobot (Acro) swing-up and the Cart Pole Balancing (CPB) [19]. These two particular problems were chosen because they represent different classes of domain: goal oriented and failure avoidance respectively. In the Acro domain the objective is to derive a policy that enables an under-actuated robot to swing-up in as few steps as possible, limited to 1000. A cost of -1 is given for every non-terminal transition. Whereas, in the CPB domain the goal is to avoid the failure conditions, for up to 10,000 steps, of dropping the pole or exceeding the bounds of the track. Here a positive reward of $+1$ is given for every non-terminal transition. We set the discount factor $\gamma = 0.9999$ for Acro and $\gamma = 0.99$ for CPB. Like the Markov chain these domains were made non-deterministic by incorporating a 20% probability that an action results in no action taken. Fourier basis of orders 2 and trained with small regularization penalties are used to represent $\hat{Q}$ in both domains.

Policy performance is measured by the mean aggregate reward obtained by running a given policy over 50 trials, necessary due to the non-determinism. Experiments are run on data sets comprised of increasing numbers of trajectories to examine the relative sample efficiency of the methods. NEAT [18] is used to generate diverse trajectory sets, comprised of over 5000 trajectories, for both domains as was done in the TFQI work [22]. This form of data violates LSTD-Q's assumptions on sampling distribution, so we do not include it in these experiments. The reported results are an average of 200 runs for each setting after 300 iterations of learning. Error bars are not included in the results, but statistically significant results are reported.

Figure 3 shows the policy performance results in the Acro domain. TFQI performs the best, significantly outperforming all other methods except at 100 trajectories. This observation suggests that there is significant negative bias stemming from either the trajectories, model, or both, making R^{Max} a safe estimator. The results for CFQI-C$_\gamma$ are purposely missing from Figure 3. CFQI-C$_\gamma$ has difficulty con-

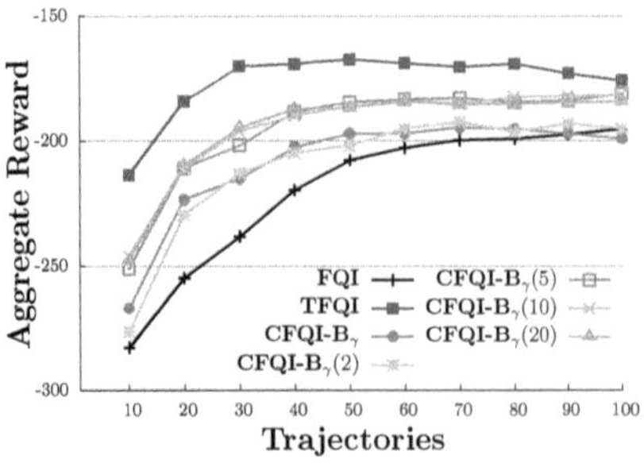

Figure 3: Policy performance after 300 iterations in the Acrobot domain using trajectory sets of increasing size.

verging on all data sets in this domain, confirming our suspicion from Section 3.1. The resulting policies all averaged an aggregate reward value of -700 or less.

CFQI-B$_\gamma$ performs well, but only significantly outperforms FQI in the 20 through 50 trajectory range. This demonstrates how the full γ-return can fail our third criterion by incorporating too much off-policy bias. In Section 3.2 we proposed a solution that limits the length of complex return. Figure 3 also shows results for CFQI-B$_\gamma(l)$ for various l settings. Setting $l = 2$ performs comparably to the default full length setting, CFQI-B$_\gamma$, which are representatives of the two extremes of the parameter's range. It is worth noting at $l = 1$ CFQI-B$_\gamma(l)$ reduces to FQI. From $l = 5$ to 20, CFQI-B$_\gamma(l)$ demonstrates significantly better performance than FQI at all trajectory counts. In terms of sample efficiency the improvement is dramatic. With just 30 trajectories CFQI-B$_\gamma$(10) achieves the same level of performance as FQI with 100 trajectories. These results show CFQI-B$_\gamma(l)$ provides effective bounds that enable significantly better policies to be learned on less data.

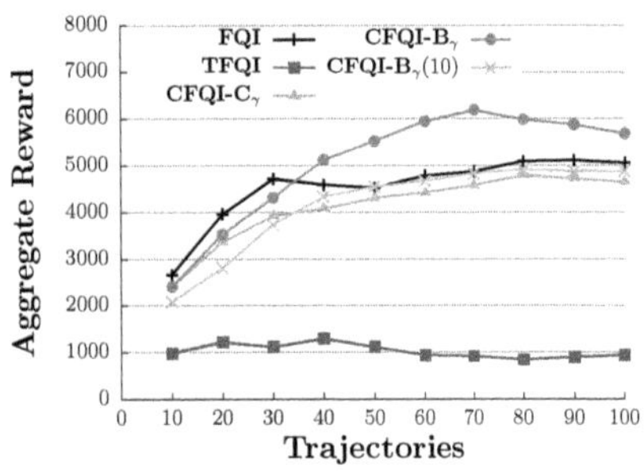

Figure 4: Policy performance after 300 iterations in the Cart Pole domain using trajectory sets of increasing size.

In Figure 4 we present the results from experiments on the CPB domain. In sharp contrast to the Acro results, TFQI performs the worst in this domain. It fails to find a competent policy at all trajectory counts, confirming that it can be an overly aggressive bound and an unstable approach. All other methods perform comparably with FQI with the exception of CFQI-B$_\gamma$. At higher trajectory counts CFQI-B$_\gamma$ learns a significantly better policy than all other methods. This observation can be explained by the γ-return's long-tail weighting and the specifics of the CPB domain. In the CPB domain all rewards are positive with the exception of transitions to failure states. As a result, it is hard to accumulate negative bias needed for the bounding estimator along a short trajectory segment.

5.3 Convergence Behavior

Convergence behavior is an important consideration because it determines how long before a consistent policy can be extracted or if the approach will succeed at all. Here we examine that behavior based on policy convergence and convergence of the approximated Q functions, $\hat{Q}$.

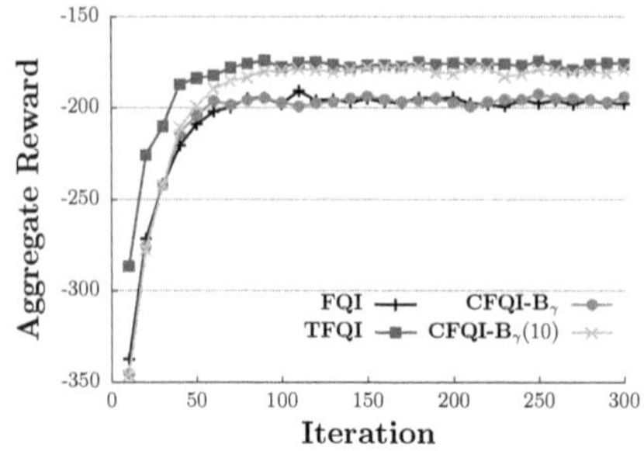

Figure 5: Mean policy performance at every 10 iterations in the Acrobot domain using 100 trajectories.

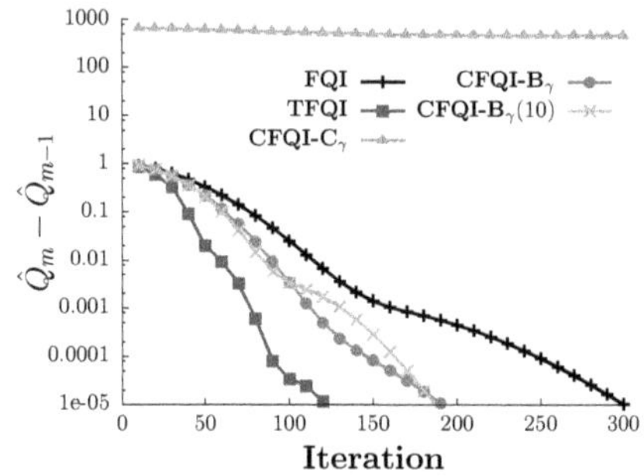

Figure 6: Mean per-iteration $\hat{Q}$ difference at every 10 iterations in Acrobot using 100 trajectories.

The results for the Acrobot domain are shown in Figures 5 and 6. Figure 5 shows the policy performance evaluated at every 10th iteration and Figure 6 shows the per-iteration difference in $\hat{Q}$ models. From Figure 5 it appears that the policy for the methods shown all converge around the 100th iteration. The explanation for this is that CFQI-C(γ) fails to converge as shown in Figure 6. The lack of convergence is caused by the non-fixed length of truncated trajectories. This finding suggests that the CFQI-C approach is not reliable. TFQI converges the fastest of all approaches followed by the CFQI-B methods, which all converge significantly faster than FQI.

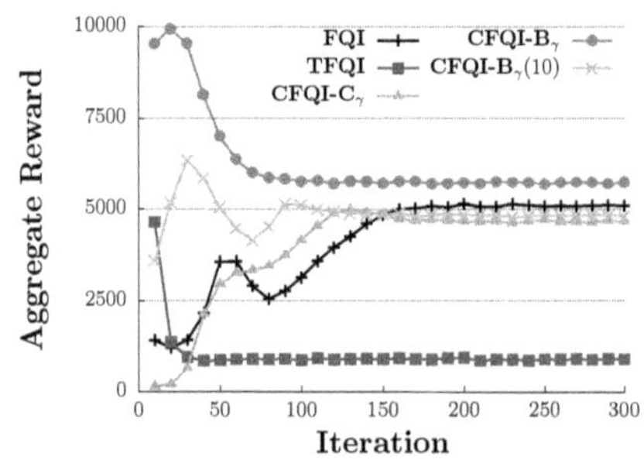

Figure 7: Mean policy performance at every 10 iterations in the Cart Pole Balancing domain using 100 trajectories.

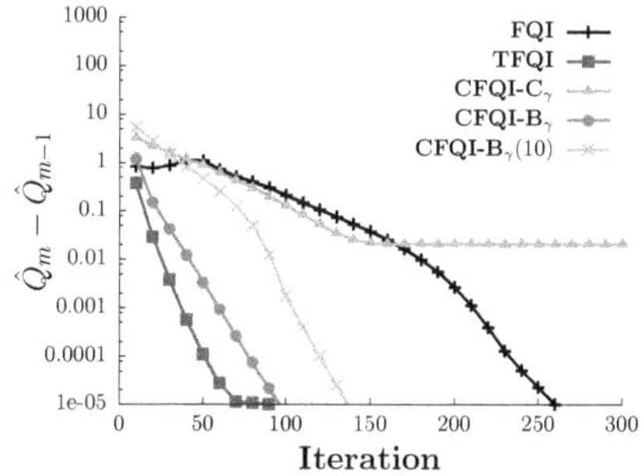

Figure 8: Mean per-iteration $\hat{Q}$ difference at every 10 iterations in the Cart Pole domain using 100 trajectories.

Figures 7 and 8 show the similar results for the CPB domain. FQI, CFQI-C$_\gamma$, and CFQI-B$_\gamma$(10) all converge to policies with similar performance after 100 iterations. It is somewhat odd that the CFQI-B$_\gamma$ runs produce near optimal policies early in the iterative process before converging to a lesser performing policy. This result demonstrates how there can be a disconnect between deriving an accurate value function and actual policy performance. TFQI also converges quickly, but to a poor policy. Figure 8, again, shows that CFQI-C$_\gamma$ fails to converge, even though it does manage to derive a stable policy. Truncating the trajectories dynamically causes oscillations in the policy and value estimates that prevent convergence. CFQI-B$_\gamma$ meanwhile, converges towards the best performing policy significantly quicker than FQI.

6. CONCLUSIONS AND FUTURE WORK

In this paper we have explored, for the first time, the idea of utilizing complex returns for AVI. A new AVI framework, CFQI, and two new approaches based on this framework, CFQI-C and CFQI-B, have been proposed. We have shown through statistical evidence how the sub-optimal off-policy bias, unique to the AVI context, can be exploited by using the complex returns as bounds on value estimates. We have provided proof that CFQI converges with fixed length complex returns and when bounding is used. Finally, we have provided an empirical evaluation that clearly demonstrates our bounding approach improves the accuracy of value estimates for AVI, resulting in significantly better policies, faster convergence, and improved sample efficiency.

Specialized bounding complex returns are a potential future direction for this research. In this paper we examined the γ-return as bound. It was not designed with this purpose and there are likely more effective bounding complex returns to be discovered. In addition, our empirical results show different methods perform best depending on the learning scenario. An adaptive method that mixes various approaches based upon the data and domain could lead to even better overall performance.

Acknowledgements

This work is supported in part by grants from NSF (# 0855204) and the AFRL's Visiting Faculty Research Program. Qiao's contribution was partially supported by a Collaboration Grant from the Simons Foundation (# 246649).

REFERENCES

[1] A. Antos, C. Szepesvári, and R. Munos. Fitted q-iteration in continuous action-space mdps. In J. Platt, D. Koller, Y. Singer, and S. Roweis, editors, *Advances in Neural Information Processing Systems 20*, pages 9–16. 2007.

[2] J. A. Boyan and A. W. Moore. Generalization in reinforcement learning: Safely approximating the value function. In *Advances in Neural Information Processing Systems 7*, pages 369–376, 1995.

[3] T. G. Dietterich. Ensemble methods in machine learning. In *Multiple classifier systems*, pages 1–15. Springer, 2000.

[4] D. Ernst, P. Geurts, L. Wehenkel, and L. Littman. Tree-based batch mode reinforcement learning. *J. Mach. Learning Research*, 6:503–556, 2005.

[5] M. Geist and B. Scherrer. Off-policy learning with eligibility traces: A survey. *J. Mach. Learn. Res.*, 15(1):289–333, Jan. 2014.

[6] G. J. Gordon. Approximate solutions to markov decision processes. *Robotics Institute*, page 228, 1999.

[7] H. Hachiya, T. Akiyama, M. Sugiayma, and J. Peters. Adaptive importance sampling for value function approximation in off-policy reinforcement learning. *Neural Networks*, 22(10):1399–1410, 2009.

[8] S. Kalyanakrishnan and P. Stone. Batch reinforcement learning in a complex domain. In *Proceedings of the 6th international joint conference on Autonomous agents and multiagent systems*, page 94. ACM, 2007.

[9] G. Konidaris, S. Niekum, and P. S. Thomas. Td$_\gamma$: Re-evaluating complex backups in temporal difference learning. In *Advances in Neural Information Processing Systems*, pages 2402–2410, 2011.

[10] G. Konidaris, S. Osentoski, and P. Thomas. Value function approximation in reinforcement learning using the Fourier basis. In *Proceedings of the Twenty-Fifth Conference on Artificial Intelligence*, pages 380–385, August 2011.

[11] M. G. Lagoudakis and R. Parr. Least-squares policy iteration. *J. Mach. Learn. Res.*, 4:2003, 2003.

[12] R. Munos. Error bounds for approximate value iteration. In *Proceedings of the 20th national conference on Artificial intelligence - Volume 2*, AAAI'05, pages 1006–1011. AAAI Press, 2005.

[13] A. Nouri and M. L. Littman. Multi-resolution exploration in continuous spaces. In *Advances in Neural Information Processing Systems*, pages 1209–1216, 2008.

[14] D. Ormoneit and Ś. Sen. Kernel-based reinforcement learning. *Machine learning*, 49(2-3):161–178, 2002.

[15] D. Precup, R. S. Sutton, and S. Dasgupta. Off-policy temporal-difference learning with function approximation. In *ICML*, pages 417–424, 2001.

[16] M. L. Puterman. *Markov decision processes: discrete stochastic dynamic programming*, volume 414. Wiley-Interscience, 2009.

[17] M. Riedmiller. Neural fitted Q iteration–first experiences with a data efficient neural reinforcement learning method. In *Machine Learning: ECML 2005*, pages 317–328. Springer, 2005.

[18] K. O. Stanley and R. Miikkulainen. Evolving neural

networks through augmenting topologies. *Evolutionary Computation*, 10(2):99–127, 2002.

[19] R. S. Sutton and A. G. Barto. *Introduction to reinforcement learning*. MIT Press, 1998.

[20] C. Thiery, B. Scherrer, et al. Least-squares λ policy iteration: Bias-variance trade-off in control problems. In *Int. Conference on Machine Learning*, 2010.

[21] C. J. C. H. Watkins. *Learning from Delayed Rewards*. PhD thesis, King's College, Cambridge, UK, 1989.

[22] R. Wright, S. Loscalzo, P. Dexter, and L. Yu. Exploiting multi-step sample trajectories for approximate value iteration. In *Machine Learning and Knowledge Discovery in Databases*, volume 8188, pages 113–128. Springer Berlin Heidelberg, 2013.

APPENDIX

A. PROOFS FOR THEOREMS 1 AND 2

In previous works AVI, using $R^{(1)}$ as the value estimator, has been shown to converge as long as the regression model is an averager such as a normalized kernel method [6, 14, 4]. Specifically, the supervised learning method learns a model, $\hat{Q}(s,a)$, defined by:

$$\hat{Q}(s,a) = \sum_{T_\ell \in \mathcal{T}} \sum_{t=1}^{|T_\ell|} k\left((s_t^{T_\ell}, a_t^{T_\ell}), (s,a)\right) R_{\ell,t}^c \tag{7}$$

where $R_{\ell,t}^c$ is the estimated value for sample t from T_ℓ. $R_{\ell,t}^c$ can be $R^{(1)}$, as in the standard AVI, or, as we will show, any normalized complex return. Additionally the kernel, $k : (S \times A)^2 \mapsto \mathbb{R}$, must satisfy the following condition:

$$\sum_{T_\ell \in \mathcal{T}} \sum_{t=1}^{|T_\ell|} \left| k\left((s_t^{T_\ell}, a_t^{T_\ell}), (s,a)\right) \right| = 1, \forall (s,a) \tag{8}$$

A.1 Proof for Theorem 1

PROOF. Following the proof from [4], the sequence of M Q-functions can be rewritten as, $\hat{Q}_m = \hat{H}\hat{Q}_{m-1}$ where $\hat{H}$ is an operator mapping any function in a Banach space $\mathcal{H}$ of functions over $S \times A$ to $\mathcal{H}$ itself. $\hat{H}$ is defined as:

$$(\hat{H}K)(s,a) = \sum_{T_\ell \in \mathcal{T}} \sum_{t=1}^{|T_\ell|} k\left((s_t^{T_\ell}, a_t^{T_\ell}), (s,a)\right) * \sum_{n=1}^{|T_\ell - t|} w(n) \left[\sum_{i=1}^{n-1} \gamma^{i-1} r_{t+i} + \gamma^n \max_{a' \in A} K(s_{t+n}, a') \right]$$

where $w(n)$ is the set of weights on the individual n-returns defined by the complex return. Next we show that $\hat{H}$ is a contraction in $\mathcal{H}$. Specifically we show $\|\hat{H}K - \hat{H}\bar{K}\|_\infty < \|K - \bar{K}\|_\infty$ for any K and $\bar{K} \in \mathcal{H}$

$$\begin{aligned}
&\|\hat{H}K - \hat{H}\bar{K}\|_\infty \\
&= \max_{(s,a)\in S\times A} \left| \sum_{T_\ell \in \mathcal{T}} \sum_{t=1}^{|T_\ell|} k((s_t^{T_\ell}, a_t^{T_\ell}), (s,a)) \sum_{n=1}^{|T_\ell - t|} w(n)\gamma^n \left[\max_{a' \in A} K(s_{t+n}, a') - \max_{a' \in A} \bar{K}(s_{t+n}, a') \right] \right| \\
&\leq \max_{(s,a)\in S\times A} \sum_{T_\ell \in \mathcal{T}} \sum_{t=1}^{|T_\ell|} k((s_t^{T_\ell}, a_t^{T_\ell}), (s,a)) * \sum_{n=1}^{|T_\ell - t|} w(n)\gamma^n \left| \max_{a' \in A} K(s_{t+n}, a') - \max_{a' \in A} \bar{K}(s_{t+n}, a') \right| \\
&< \gamma \max_{(s,a)\in S\times A} \sum_{T_\ell \in \mathcal{T}} \sum_{t=1}^{|T_\ell|} k((s_t^{T_\ell}, a_t^{T_\ell}), (s,a)) * \sum_{n=1}^{|T_\ell - t|} w(n) \max_{a' \in A} \left| K(s_{t+n}, a') - \bar{K}(s_{t+n}, a') \right| \\
&\leq \gamma \max_{(s,a)\in S\times A} \sum_{T_\ell \in \mathcal{T}} \sum_{t=1}^{|T_\ell|} k((s_t^{T_\ell}, a_t^{T_\ell}), (s,a)) * \max_{t' \geq t, (s_{t'}, a') \in S_{T_l} \times A} \left| K(s_{t'}, a') - \bar{K}(s_{t'}, a') \right| \\
&\leq \gamma \max_{(s,a)\in S\times A} \left| K(s,a) - \bar{K}(s,a) \right| \\
&= \gamma \|K - \bar{K}\|_\infty \\
&< \|K - \bar{K}\|_\infty
\end{aligned}$$

By fixed-point theorem, we have completed the proof. □

A.2 Proof for Theorem 2

PROOF. Following proof of Theorem 1, $\hat{H}$ is defined as:

$$(\hat{H}K)(s,a) = \sum_{T_\ell \in \mathcal{T}} \sum_{t=1}^{|T_\ell|} k\left((s_t^{T_\ell}, a_t^{T_\ell}), (s,a)\right) \max\left\{ r_{t+1} + \max_{a' \in A} K(s_{t+1}, a'), \sum_{n=1}^{|T_\ell - t|} w(n) \left[\sum_{i=1}^{n-1} \gamma^{i-1} r_{t+i} + \gamma^n \max_{a' \in A} K(s_{t+n}, a') \right] \right\}$$

We now show $\hat{H}$ is a contraction in $\mathcal{H}$.

$$\begin{aligned}
&\|\hat{H}K - \hat{H}\bar{K}\|_\infty \\
&= \max_{(s,a)\in S\times A} \left| \sum_{T_\ell \in \mathcal{T}} \sum_{t=1}^{|T_\ell|} k\left((s_t^{T_\ell}, a_t^{T_\ell}), (s,a)\right) \left(\max\left\{ r_{t+1} + \gamma \max_{a' \in A} K(s_{t+1}, a'), \sum_{n=1}^{|T_\ell - t|} w(n) \left[\sum_{i=1}^{n-1} \gamma^{i-1} r_{t+i} + \gamma^n \max_{a' \in A} K(s_{t+n}, a') \right] \right\} - \max\left\{ r_{t+1} + \gamma \max_{a' \in A} \bar{K}(s_{t+1}, a'), \sum_{n=1}^{|T_\ell - t|} w(n) \left[\sum_{i=1}^{n-1} \gamma^{i-1} r_{t+i} + \gamma^n \max_{a' \in A} \bar{K}(s_{t+n}, a') \right] \right\} \right) \right| \\
&\leq \max_{(s,a)\in S\times A} \left| \sum_{T_\ell \in \mathcal{T}} \sum_{t=1}^{|T_\ell|} k\left((s_t^{T_\ell}, a_t^{T_\ell}), (s,a)\right) \max\left\{ \gamma \max_{a' \in A} K(s_{t+1}, a') - \gamma \max_{a' \in A} \bar{K}(s_{t+1}, a'), \sum_{n=1}^{|T_\ell - t|} w(n) * \left[\gamma^n \max_{a' \in A} K(s_{t+n}, a') - \gamma^n \max_{a' \in A} \bar{K}(s_{t+n}, a') \right] \right\} \right|
\end{aligned}$$

At this point all that remains is to show that both choices in the second *max*{} function are less than $\|K - \bar{K}\|_\infty$ independently. The first choice was proven in [4]. Finally, the second choice is proven by Theorem 1. □

Counterfactual Exploration for Improving Multiagent Learning

Mitchell Colby
Oregon State University
Corvallis, OR, USA
colbym@engr.orst.edu

Sepideh Kharaghani
Oregon State University
Corvallis, OR, USA
kharaghs@onid.orst.edu

Chris HolmesParker
Parfulx LLC
chris@parflux.com

Kagan Tumer
Oregon State University
Corvallis, OR, USA
kagan.tumer@oregonstate.edu

ABSTRACT

In any single agent system, exploration is a critical component of learning. It ensures that all possible actions receive *some* degree of attention, allowing an agent to converge to good policies. The same concept has been adopted by multiagent learning systems. However, there is a fundamentally different dynamic in multiagent learning: each agent operates in a non-stationary environment, as a direct result of the evolving policies of other agents in the system. As such, exploratory actions taken by agents bias the policies of other agents, forcing them to perform optimally in the presence of agent exploration. CLEAN rewards address this issue by privatizing exploration (agents take their best action, but internally compute rewards for counterfactual actions). However, CLEAN rewards require each agent to know the mathematical form of the system evaluation function, which is typically unavailable to agents. In this paper, we present an algorithm to approximate CLEAN rewards, eliminating exploratory action noise without the need for expert system knowledge. Results in both coordination and congestion domains demonstrate the approximated CLEAN rewards obtain up to 95% of the performance of directly computed CLEAN rewards, without the need for expert domain knowledge while utilizing 99% less system information.

Categories and Subject Descriptors

I.2.11 [**Artificial Intelligence**]: Distributed Artificial Intelligence —*Multiagent systems*

Keywords

Multiagent learning; CLEAN Rewards

1. INTRODUCTION

As agents in a multiagent system learn policies, they frequently explore by taking random actions in order to determine if these actions improve system performance. Such exploration is critical to finding optimal agent policies. However, learning agents cannot typically differentiate between environmental dynamics and noise caused by the exploratory actions of other agents. This leads to agents learning policies which account for other agents taking random actions, rather than policies which perform well when all agents are following their target, or greedy, policies. Often, system performance can decrease once agents stop exploration, as learned policies depend on the random exploration of other agents [10]. CLEAN rewards address this problem by privatizing agent exploration, removing exploratory action noise from the feedback signals of learning agents.

CLEAN rewards effectively remove exploratory action noise, resulting in superior system performance as compared to more common reward shaping techniques such as difference rewards. When implementing CLEAN rewards, each agent in the system follows their target policy by greedily selecting actions with no exploration. Then, each agent privately computed the system reward if they had taken an exploratory action while all other agents in the system followed their target policies. In this manner, exploratory action noise caused by other agents is removed from an agent's feedback signal, because the exploration for each agent is privatized. This allows for agents to effectively determine if actions are good or not, without the noise caused by other agents in the system taking exploratory actions. Further, agents learn policies which do not depend on other agents in the system exploring, resulting in superior system performance when the learned policies are actually implemented.

Computing CLEAN rewards requires the mathematical form of the system evaluation function which the agents are optimizing, as well as information about the global joint state and joint action of all agents. This information is rarely known to agents in a multiagent system. Thus, although CLEAN rewards address the problem of exploratory action noise, they introduce a new problem of requiring the mathematical form of the system objective function. In order to obtain the benefits of CLEAN rewards while in a realistic setting, a technique to compute CLEAN rewards without the mathematical form of the system evaluation function or global state and action knowledge is needed.

In this paper, we present a generic method for approximating CLEAN rewards using only local state and action knowledge as well as a broadcast value of the system evaluation function (rather than the mathematical form of the

Appears in: *Proceedings of the 14th International Conference on Autonomous Agents and Multiagent Systems (AAMAS 2015), Bordini, Elkind, Weiss, Yolum (eds.), May 4–8, 2015, Istanbul, Turkey.*

function itself). We demonstrate how this approximation algorithm is implemented in a congestion and a coordination domain, both of which have extremely high coupling between agents, resulting in high sensitivity to exploratory action noise. Finally, we provide results demonstrating that approximate CLEAN rewards results in better system performance than difference evaluations, and attain up to 95% of the performance of directly computing CLEAN rewards while using 99% less system state and action information.

The specific contributions of this paper are to:

- present a novel algorithm for approximating CLEAN rewards using information easily available to each agent.
- demonstrate empirically that these approximate CLEAN rewards result in performance which is frequently comparable to, and in some cases outperforms, performance attained using directly computed CLEAN rewards.
- demonstrate empirically that these approximate CLEAN rewards provide better performance than rewards which use much more information to compute.
- demonstrate empirically the scalability of these rewards, in large multiagent systems containing up to 5000 agents.

The rest of the paper is organized as follows. Section 2 provides background material and related work. Section 3 details the proposed algorithm to approximate CLEAN rewards. Section 4 details the experimental domains used in this work. Section 5 provides the experimental results. Finally, Section 6 discusses the results and concludes the paper.

2. BACKGROUND

The following sections describe exploratory action noise, CLEAN rewards, difference rewards, and various techniques for approximating evaluation functions.

2.1 Exploratory Action Noise

In practice, agents learn by continuously taking actions in an effort to learn the underlying rewards associated with each action [17]. In order to allow for the expected values of different actions to be learned, exploration strategies are implemented. Agents must balance taking the best known action (exploitation) with taking actions which the agent doesn't know the value of (exploration). The way these two concepts are balanced is known as the exploration-exploitation dilemma [20]. A key problem associated with exploration is that in multiagent systems, this exploration may actually cause noise which leads to agents learning policies which are biased to expect some portion of agents taking random actions.

We present an example to demonstrate the effects of exploratory action noise. Agents learn in the Gaussian Squeeze Domain (Section 4) for 1000 episodes. During learning, agents select actions using ϵ-greedy selection, where $\epsilon = 0.1$. In this case, agents select their best known actions with probability 0.9, and take random exploratory actions with probability 0.1. After 1000 episodes, the agents policies are fixed. We then test performance for varying levels of exploration, by replacing some agents' policies with random exploratory actions. System performance as a function of the exploration level in the system is shown in Figure 1.

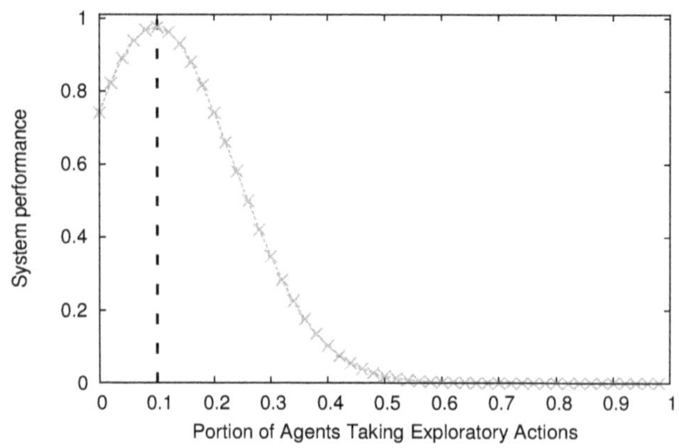

Figure 1: Demonstration of exploratory action noise: agents learned for 1000 episodes with ϵ-greedy action selection where $\epsilon = 0.1$. After learning, the policies are fixed, and we test performance of the learned policies under different amounts of exploration (some agents' policies are replaced with random exploratory policies). Agents perform better in the presence of exploration than they do with no exploration. The highest system performance is when the exploration rate is near ϵ, because agents have learned policies which are biased to include this level of random exploration by other agents in the system.

One of the fundamental difficulties in multiagent systems is the learning process where an agent may not only need to learn how to act in its environment, but may also need to account for the actions of the other learning agents [18]. As seen in Figure 1, exploratory action noise (when agents take random actions with probability 0.1) causes agents to learn policies which perform best when 10% of the agents in the system are taking random actions. This result is not intuitive, but occurs because agents have learned to depend on the exploratory actions of other agents in the system [9]. In particular, this phenomenon is caused by the fact that while learning in a system with agents taking exploratory actions, learning agents are unable to differentiate what parts of their feedback signal are caused by true environmental dynamics, and what parts are caused by exploratory action noise caused by other agents. CLEAN rewards were developed to remove exploratory action noise by privatizing agent exploration.

2.2 CLEAN Rewards

CLEAN rewards are defined as in [10]:

$$C_i = G(z_T - z_{T,i} + c_i) - G(z_T - z_{T,i} + c_i') \qquad (1)$$

where C_i is the CLEAN reward given to agent i, $G(z)$ is the system evaluation function, z_T is the target state which occurs if all agents act greedily, $z_{T,i}$ is the actual action of agent i, and c_i and c_i' are counterfactual actions of agent i (i.e. alternative actions the agent may have taken instead of following its target policy). CLEAN rewards replace the contribution of the agent's target action with two different counterfactual actions. The agent then is provided with a reward for the action c_i, rather than $z_{T,i}$.

CLEAN rewards remove exploratory action noise of other agents in the system, as all agents are actually following their target policies. Exploration is done offline, by computing the reward an agent would have received for exploring. CLEAN rewards have provided excellent empirical results in a variety of domains, including the Gaussian squeeze domain and defect combination problem [9, 10].

In order to compute them, CLEAN rewards require an accurate model of the underlying system objective $G(z)$, as all exploration is done privately by each agent. In practice, agents never have such information. Thus, although CLEAN rewards can improve learning by removing exploratory action noise, the requirement for an accurate model of $G(z)$ renders them unusable in most real world problems. In this paper, we demonstrate that CLEAN rewards may be approximated such that the performance gains from removing exploratory action noise are retained.

2.3 Difference Rewards

The agent specific Difference Reward $D_i(z)$ is defined as [2]:

$$D_i(z) = G(z) - G(z_{-i} + c_i) \tag{2}$$

where $G(z)$ is the global reward, and $G(z_{-i} + c_i)$ is the global reward when agent i is removed from the system and replaced with some counterfactual agent c_i. Intuitively, the difference reward gives agent i's specific impact on the overall system performance. Note that:

$$\frac{\partial D_i(z)}{\partial a(i)} = \frac{\partial G(z)}{\partial a_i} \tag{3}$$

where $a(i)$ is agent i. Thus, an agent acting to increase the value of the difference reward will also increase the global reward. This property is termed *alignment* [2]. Further, because the second term in the difference reward removes all portions of the system reward not related to agent i, noise in the learning signal caused by the actions of other agents is significantly reduced. This property is termed *sensitivity*. By being aligned with the global reward and sensitive to an individual agent's actions, difference rewards provide extremely effective feedback to each agent, allowing them to learn better policies than when using global rewards. Difference rewards have provided excellent empirical results in a variety of domains, including sensor coordination and mobile robot coordination [2, 19].

2.4 Approximation of Evaluation Functions

In cases where the system evaluation function is unknown, it may be approximated in order to provide better feedback to learning agents [3, 4]. In the case of reinforcement learning, reward functions are modeled; in the case of evolutionary algorithms, fitness functions are modeled. In either case, approximation of system evaluation functions allows for agent-specific evaluation functions to be easily shaped based on the overall system evaluation function. The following sections describe different approaches for approximating system evaluation functions, as well as previous work involving approximating difference evaluations.

Function approximation is commonly seen in reinforcement learning applications, where the value function or system state is approximated due to limited state information [8, 11, 14]. Value functions are often approximated when only partial state information is available, often using neural networks, maps, or some other type of function approximator [1, 5, 16]. The conclusion that only partial state information is necessary to accurately model value functions suggests these types of approaches can be successfully extended to multiagent learning problems, where only partial state information is available to each agent.

Fitness functions have also been approximated for use in evolutionary algorithms [6, 13]. This fitness approximation is typically used because the number of fitness function evaluations dominates the optimization cost in evolutionary algorithms, and fitness approximation typically decreases time to convergence [12, 15]. However, these approaches can easily be extended to cases in which the mathematical form of the fitness function is unknown, as in cases where the difference evaluation must be approximated. All of the methods described above are single agent cases, but there has also been research investigating approximating system evaluation functions in multiagent learning settings.

As seen above, there is a wide range of research involving approximation in reinforcement learning and evolutionary algorithms. However, to date, there has been no research involving approximating CLEAN rewards. This paper presents the first approximation of CLEAN rewards, demonstrating how they may be implemented in systems when agents do not have global knowledge about the system state or the system evaluation function.

3. CLEAN APPROXIMATION ALGORITHM

In this section, we introduce a general algorithm for approximating CLEAN rewards, and then demonstrate how this algorithm is implemented in a stateless discrete action domain. For the purpose of this analysis, we assume a cooperative multiagent system aims to coordinate in order to optimize some system level objective function $G(z)$, and that the true value of $G(z_T)$ is broadcast to each agent after a target joint action z_T is selected based on each agent's greedy policy. Recall that the CLEAN reward is defined as:

$$C_i = G(z_T - z_{T,i} + c_i) - G(z_T - z_{T,i} + c_i') \tag{4}$$

As we assume that the value of $G(z_T)$ is broadcast to each agent, approximating the CLEAN reward requires approximating $G(z)$ based on an agent's local information. Given the particular domain, a suitable function approximator is chosen. For a stateless domain with discrete actions, this approximator may simply be a tabular function approximator. For a stateful domain with continuous actions, this approximator may be a neural network. Note that these are not the only possible options for these function approximators, but are potential choices which match the domains they will be used in.

The CLEAN approximation algorithm is presented in Algorithm 1. At each time step, each agent takes a greedy action, and $G(z_T)$ is computed and broadcast to each agent, where z_T is the system state when each agent follows its target policy (greedily selects actions). Each agent i maintains a private approximation for $G(z)$, denoted as $\hat{G}_i(z_i)$. This is not a full approximation of the system evaluation function; rather, it is an approximation of $G(z)$ as a function of only one agent's state and action. The states and actions of other agents in the system are embedded into the function approximation. Note that the only information available to the agent includes the agent's state, action choice, and the

Initialize N agents
foreach *Agent* **do**
  Initialize private function approximator $\hat{G}_i(z_i)$
end
foreach *Learning Step* **do**
  foreach *Agent* **do**
    collect local state information s_i
    greedily select action a_i using agent's policy
    $z_{T,i} = \{s_i, a_i\}$
    $z_T = \{z_{T,1}, z_{T,2}, ..., z_{T,n}\}$
  end
  Calculate $G(z_T)$ based on joint action
  Broadcast $G(z_T)$ to each agent
  foreach *Agent* **do**
    Update $\hat{G}_i(z_i)$ using s_i, a_i, and $G(z_T)$
    $\hat{C}_i = \hat{G}(c_i) - \hat{G}(c_i')$
    Update policy/value table based on $\hat{C}_i$
  end
end

Algorithm 1: Approximation of CLEAN rewards. The functional form of $\hat{G}$ depends on the specific domain. For example, a stateless discrete action domain may use a tabular function approximator, while a continuous state and action domain may use a neural network.

broadcast value of $G(z_T)$. Each agent's approximation of $G(z)$ is therefore a mapping from that agent's state and action to the value of the system objective function. It is of note that this approximation is initially very noisy, because the state and action information used to approximate $G(z)$ is limited only to one agent's state and action. However, as learning progresses, the policies of each agent begin to converge; as the policies of other agents converge, approximating $G(z)$ using only one agent's state and action becomes less noisy, because the variance in the joint action for a particular system-level state is reduced. Given an agent's approximation $\hat{G}_i(z_i)$, the CLEAN reward can be estimated as:

$$\hat{C}_i(z_i) = \hat{G}_i(c_i) - \hat{C}_i(c_i') \qquad (5)$$

where $\hat{C}_i(z_i)$ is agent i's approximation of the CLEAN reward. In order to evaluate $\hat{C}_i(c_i)$, a default action c_i' is chosen for each agent at the beginning of each episode for evaluation, and a random action c_i is chosen to be evaluated at each time step. In other words, the approximation of the CLEAN reward determines *the difference between the system objective function for a random action c_i and a default action c_i', assuming all other agents in the system are following their target policies.*

The implementation of this approximation approach in a stateless discrete action domain is detailed in the following sections. We demonstrate how a multiagent reinforcement learning algorithm with an approximation of CLEAN rewards may be implemented in the stateless discrete action domain. The general algorithm presented in Algorithm 1 can be implemented in any domain where a broadcast value of $G(z)$ is available, whether the states or actions are continuous or discrete. For simplicity in demonstrating the CLEAN approximation algorithm, we choose to demonstrate this approximation approach in a stateless discrete action setting.

3.1 Stateless Discrete Action Domains

Initialize N agents
foreach *Agent* **do**
  Initialize private value table $V_i(a)$
  Initialize private function approximator $\hat{G}_i(a_i)$
end
foreach *Learning Step* **do**
  foreach *Agent* **do**
    greedily select action a_i using agent's policy
  end
  Calculate $G(a)$ based on joint action
  Broadcast $G(a)$ to each agent
  foreach *Agent* **do**
    $\hat{G}_i(a_i) \leftarrow \alpha_1 \cdot \hat{G}_i(a_i) + (1-\alpha_1) \cdot G(a)$
    $\hat{C}_i = \hat{G}_i(c_i) - \hat{G}_i(c_i')$
    $V_i(c_i) \leftarrow \alpha_2 \cdot V_i(c_i) + (1-\alpha_2) \cdot \hat{C}_i$
  end
end

Algorithm 2: Stateless Discrete-Action Multiagent Reinforcement Learning using $D_i(s, a)$ Approximation

We now demonstrate how Algorithm 1 may be implemented for a multiagent reinforcement learning algorithm in a stateless discrete action domain. The implementation of Algorithm 1 in a multiagent reinforcement learning problem with a stateless discrete action domain is given in Algorithm 2. Note that such problems may also be solved with coevolutionary algorithms. In a stateless discrete action domain, each agent maintains a value vector $V_i(a)$ containing the expected value of each possible action. Each agent also maintains an approximation of $G(a)$, which is simply a vector containing the estimated value of the system evaluation function corresponding to each action the agent may take. At each learning step, each agent i selects an action a_i. The system evaluation function $G(a)$ is then calculated based on the joint action $a = \{a_1, a_2, ..., a_n\}$, and this value is broadcast to each agent in the system. Each agent then updates its approximation $\hat{G}_i(a_i)$ according to:

$$\hat{G}_i(a_i) \leftarrow (1-\alpha_1) \cdot \hat{G}_i(a_i) + \alpha_1 \cdot G(a) \qquad (6)$$

Once each agent has updated its approximation of $G(a)$, the CLEAN for each agent is estimated as:

$$\hat{C}_i = \hat{G}_i(c_i) - \hat{C}_i(c_i') \qquad (7)$$

where c_i' is a randomly chosen action for evaluation, and c_i' is some default action. The value table is then updated using the estimate of the CLEAN reward:

$$Q_i(c_i) \leftarrow (1-\alpha_2) \cdot Q_i(c_i) + \alpha_2 \cdot \hat{C}_i \qquad (8)$$

4. EXPERIMENTAL DOMAINS

In the following sections, we detail the two experimental domains used in this work: the Defect Combination Problem (DCP) and the Gaussian Squeeze Domain (GSD). These domains were chosen for two reasons. First, the DCP is a coordination domain, while the GSD is a congestion domain. The inclusion of both of these types of domains illustrates how approximate CLEAN rewards perform in varying types of problems. Second, both of these domains are extremely sensitive to exploratory action noise; even in very large systems (e.g. 1000 agents), a single agent changing its policy can dramatically affect the overall system performance. As both of these domains are sensitive to exploratory action noise, they provide insight on how CLEAN rewards can improve system performance by privatizing agent exploration.

4.1 Defect Combination Problem

The Defect Combination Problem (DCP) assumes that there exists a set of imperfect sensors X which have constant measurement errors due to manufacturing defects or imperfections [7, 19]. Each sensor $x_i \in X$ has an attenuation a_i in its measurement. Thus, if sensor x_i is measuring some value A, its measurement is $A + a_i$. The individual sensor attenuation values are drawn from a Gaussian distribution with a mean of zero and some variance σ. Solving the DCP involves choosing a subset of the sensors such that the aggregate attenuation of the combined readings is minimized, which is equivalent to minimizing:

$$G(z) = \frac{\left|\sum_{i=1}^{N} n_i a_i\right|}{\sum_{i=1}^{N} n_i} \tag{9}$$

where N is the number of sensors in the system, $n_i \in \{0, 1\}$ is an indicator function based on whether the sensor is "on" or "off," and $G(z)$ is based on the aggregated attenuation of the combined sensor readings. The DCP is a large distributed agent coordination problem where each agent (device) needs to determine whether or not to be part of the aggregate device (determine whether to turn "on" or "off").

4.2 Gaussian Squeeze Domain

The Gaussian Squeeze Domain (GSD) is a problem involving agents which must coordinate their actions in order to optimize for a "capacity" in a Gaussian objective function [10]. The objective function to be maximized is:

$$G = xe^{\frac{-(x-\mu)^2}{\sigma^2}} \tag{10}$$

where $x = \sum_i x_i$ is the cumulative sum of the actions of agents (where x_i is the contribution of agent i), μ is the mean of the system objective's Gaussian (the target x the agents must coordinate to achieve), and σ is the standard deviation of the system objective's Gaussian. The goal of the agents is to choose their individual actions x_i such that the sum of their individual actions optimizes Equation 10. Each agent has n actions, ranging in value from zero to $(n-1)$. The Gaussian squeeze domain is a congestion domain, where each agent determines their allocation of resources, with the goal being that a set number of resources (defined by μ) is not over- or under-utilized. Adjusting the standard deviation σ affects the coordination complexity of the problem. For low values of σ, coordination complexity is high as the gradient around the optimal point is large. For high values of σ, coordination complexity is lower as the gradient around the optimal point is more gradual.

5. EMPIRICAL RESULTS

The following sections provide the results detailing the performance of the CLEAN approximation algorithm in both a coordination domain (Defect Combination Problem) and a congestion domain (Gaussian Squeeze Domain).

5.1 Defect Combination Problem

Approximate CLEAN rewards are tested in the DCP and compared to global rewards, difference rewards, and directly computed CLEAN rewards. For each experiment analyzed, 400 independent runs are conducted and we report the average performance over all runs. The first experiment involves analyzing the performance of 1000 agents, when the exploration rate ϵ is 0.01, the standard deviation for the sensor noise distribution σ is 1, the learning rate α_1 is 0.005, and the update rate for the agents' function approximators α_2 is 0.001. The results for this experiment are shown in Figure 2, where lower values (corresponding to lower sensor error) are preferable.

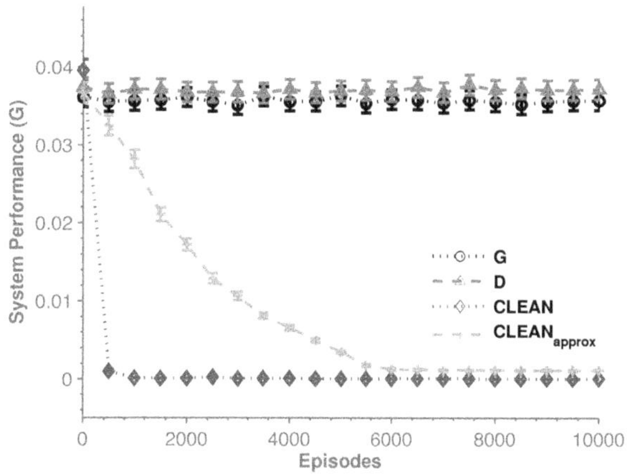

Figure 2: DCP results with 1000 agents, where $\epsilon = 0.01$, $\sigma = 1$, $\alpha_1 = 0.005$, and $\alpha_2 = 0.001$. Approximated CLEAN rewards outperform difference rewards and global rewards, and achieve 98% of the improvement over difference evaluations that the analytically computed CLEAN rewards attain.

As seen in Figure 2, approximate CLEAN rewards outperform global and difference rewards, and attain 98% of the performance of directly computed CLEAN rewards. It is of note that this 2% performance drop is accompanied by a 99.9% drop in system information used to compute the reward, as CLEAN rewards utilize the entire system joint action, while approximate CLEAN rewards only utilize an individual agent's action. This experiment demonstrates not only the ability of CLEAN rewards to effectively filter out exploration noise to improve performance, but that the benefits of CLEAN rewards can be attained with a small fraction of the overall information available within the system.

For the next experiment, the learning rate α_1 is changed to 0.01 rather than 0.005. This results in agents placing a higher emphasis on recently received rewards. The results for this experiment are shown in Figure 3.

As seen in Figure 3, approximate CLEAN rewards outperform not only global and difference rewards, but they actually outperform directly computed CLEAN rewards. This counter-intuitive result requires closer analysis. As agent exploration is privatized with CLEAN rewards, multiple agents may simultaneously change their policies while assuming that all other agents in the system will retain their current policies. For example, consider a system with one hundred agents. Suppose that during their private exploration,

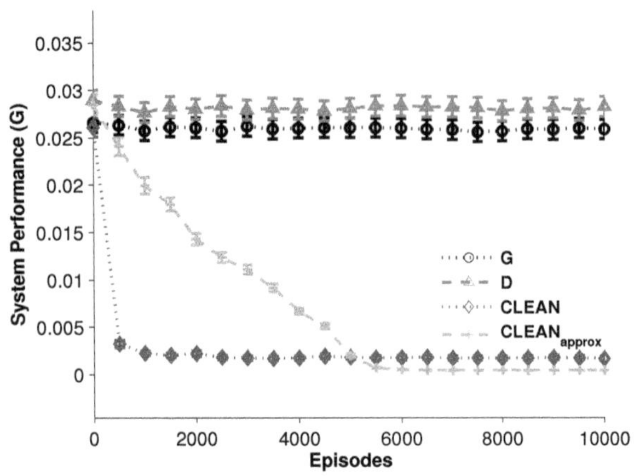

Figure 3: DCP results with 1000 agents, where $\epsilon = 0.01$, $\sigma = 1$, $\alpha_1 = 0.01$, and $\alpha_2 = 0.001$. Approximated CLEAN rewards outperform difference rewards and global rewards, as well as directly computed CLEAN rewards.

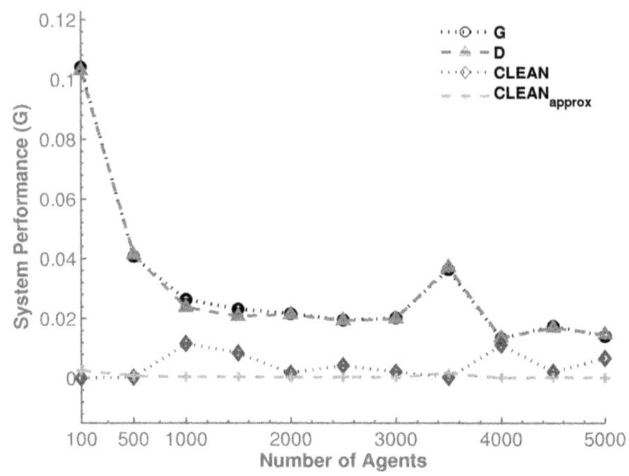

Figure 4: DCP results: Scaling. Regardless of system size, approximate CLEAN rewards outperform global and difference rewards, and outperform directly computed CLEAN rewards in some cases.

twenty of these agents determine that they should change their policies based on information derived from CLEAN rewards. When using CLEAN rewards, each agent in the system determines if an action they did not take would result in higher system performance, *assuming that every other agent in the system retains their current policy.* When all twenty of these agents change their actions simultaneously, the result may ultimately be a drop in system performance, as the assumption that other agents in the system remains static does not hold. Agents which approximate CLEAN rewards each have different local approximations of the system evaluation function, all of which focus on that particular agent's impact on the system evaluation function. This results in the number of agents altering their policies in any given time step to be lower than when directly computing CLEAN rewards. Intuitively, approximated CLEAN rewards slow down the process of agent's altering their policies, resulting in a less dynamic learning environment. This allows for individual agents to change their policies asynchronously, resulting in a lower frequency of decreased system performance as a result of widespread changes in the target policies of each agent. This counter-intuitive result only holds for cases where the approximation of the system evaluation function is sufficiently accurate, such that the benefit of breaking the symmetry of CLEAN actions overcomes the inaccuracies caused by the approximation.

The final experiment in the DCP involves analyzing the scalability of the system. For system sizes varying from 100 to 5000 agents, agents learn for 10000 episodes, using either difference, global, CLEAN, or approximate CLEAN rewards. Figure 4 shows converged system performance as a function of the number of agents in the system.

As seen in Figure 4, regardless of system size, approximate CLEAN rewards outperform both global and difference rewards. For some system sizes, approximate CLEAN rewards perform similarly to directly computed system rewards. For other system sizes (1000-1500 agents and 4000-5000 agents), approximate CLEAN rewards actually outperform directly computed CLEAN rewards. This result demonstrates that approximating CLEAN rewards provides the performance advantages of CLEAN rewards, without the restrictive requirement for global system information. In particular, global knowledge about the joint action becomes increasingly difficult to collect as the number of agents in the system grows. By approximating CLEAN rewards without requiring the global joint action, we have provided a technique to implement CLEAN rewards in large multiagent systems.

5.2 Gaussian Squeeze Domain

Approximate CLEAN rewards are tested in the GSD, and are compared to global rewards, difference rewards, and directly computed CLEAN rewards. All results are the average performance over 50 statistical runs. For all experiments, the standard deviation of the objective function σ is 400, the mean of the objective function μ is 200, the learning rate α_1 is 0.1, the update rate for agents' function approximators is 0.1, and the exploration rate ϵ is 0.1. The first experiment involves training 1000 agents, where each agent can select from 15 available actions. The results of this experiment are shown in Figure 5, where higher values are preferable.

As seen in Figure 5, approximate CLEAN rewards significantly outperform both global and difference rewards, and result in 94% of the performance of directly computed CLEAN rewards. In this case, the approximation of CLEAN rewards results in a 6% decrease in system performance while using 99.9% less information about the global joint action to compute. Further, approximate CLEAN rewards converge to their final policy faster than directly computed CLEAN rewards, due to the fact that the learning environment is less dynamic while approximating CLEAN rewards (see Section 5.1. The next experiment involves 1000 agents with 10 actions to choose from, with all other experimental parameters being held constant. These results are shown in Figure 6.

As seen in Figure 6, approximate CLEAN rewards significantly outperform global rewards, but only attain 75% of the performance of directly computed CLEAN rewards,

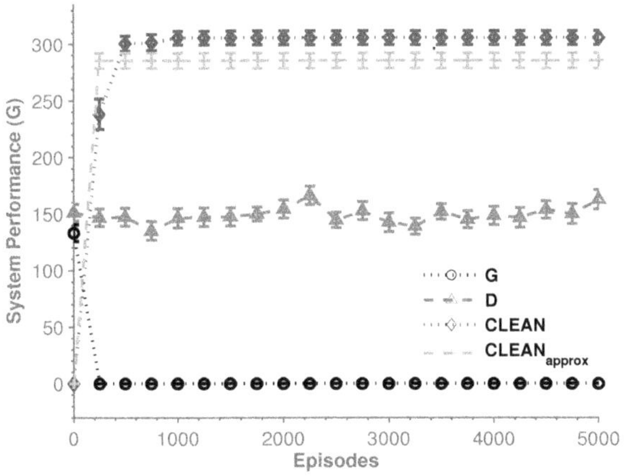

Figure 5: GSD results with 1000 agents, where agents can select from 15 available actions, the standard deviation of the objective function σ is 400, the mean of the objective function μ is 200, the learning rate α_1 is 0.1, the update rate for agents' function approximators is 0.1, and the exploration rate ϵ is 0.1. Approximate CLEAN rewards significantly outperform both global and difference rewards, and provide 94% of the performance of directly computed CLEAN rewards.

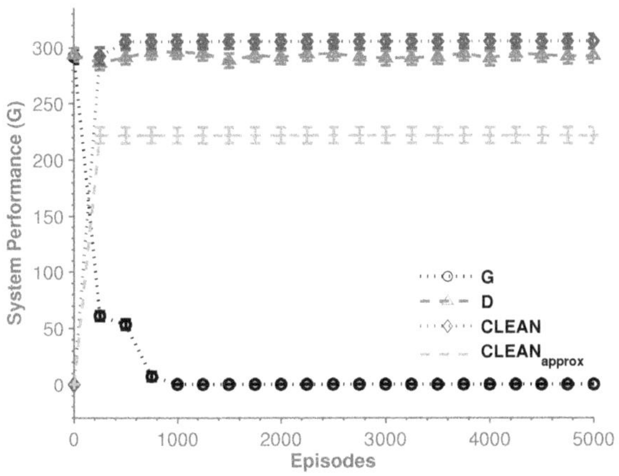

Figure 6: GSD results with 1000 agents, where agents can select from 10 available actions, the standard deviation of the objective function σ is 400, the mean of the objective function μ is 200, the learning rate α_1 is 0.1, the update rate for agents' function approximators is 0.1, and the exploration rate ϵ is 0.1. Approximate CLEAN rewards significantly outperform global rewards, but only achieve 75% of the performance of directly computed CLEAN rewards, and 78% of the performance of difference rewards.

and 78% of the performance of difference rewards. It is important to note that both CLEAN rewards and difference rewards require the global joint action of the system to compute, while approximated CLEAN rewards only depend on a single agent's action. As the size of this system is large (2000 agents), each agent would have difficulty learning the global joint action of the system. Thus, although approximate CLEAN rewards do not provide the performance of directly computed CLEAN rewards or difference rewards, they do not rely on information that is difficult or impossible for a single agent to obtain.

We now analyze the differences in results between Figures 5 and 6. The only difference in experimental setups is the number of actions which each agent may take, which determines how drastically exploratory action noise can affect system performance. In the case of the GSD, increasing from 10 to 15 actions per agents dramatically increases the effects of exploratory action noise. As seen in Figures 5 and 6, when exploratory action noise is not expected to have a large impact on the system (agents only pick from 10 actions), then difference rewards outperform approximate CLEAN rewards. When exploratory action noise does have a large impact on the system, then approximate CLEAN rewards outperform difference rewards. This result illustrates the tradeoff between exploratory action noise and the noise caused by the approximation of the system evaluation function in approximate CLEAN rewards. To further investigate this tradeoff, we analyzed converged system performance for each reward structure as a function of the number of actions each agent in the GSD could take for a 1000 agent system. These results are shown in Figure 7.

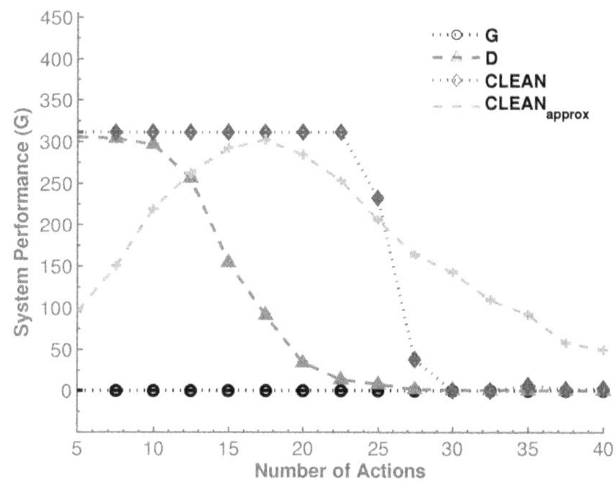

Figure 7: GSD results: scaling the number of actions.

As seen in Figure 7, as the level of potential exploratory action noise rises with the number of actions in the system, approximate CLEAN rewards overtake difference rewards and provide better performance. As the system complexity is increased further to 25 actions for each agent, approximate CLEAN rewards overtake CLEAN rewards. This is due to the less dynamic learning environment created by approximate CLEAN rewards; with CLEAN rewards, too many agents change their target policies on the assumption that the other agents in the system are remaining static. Approximate CLEAN rewards overcome this difficulty because the nature of their approximations results in a more asynchronous process of agents modifying their policies. To demonstrate the scalability of approximate CLEAN rewards, we conduct the final experiment in the GSD with 2000 agents and 15 actions. These results are shown in Figure 8.

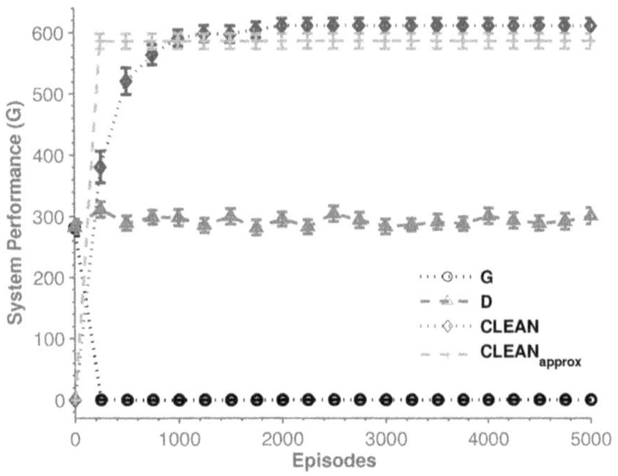

Figure 8: GSD results with 2000 agents, where agents can select from 15 available actions, the standard deviation of the objective function σ is 400, the mean of the objective function μ is 200, the learning rate α_1 is 0.1, the update rate for agents' function approximators is 0.1, and the exploration rate ϵ is 0.1. Approximate CLEAN rewards significantly outperform both global and difference rewards, and provide 96% of the performance of directly computed CLEAN rewards.

As seen in Figure 8, approximate CLEAN rewards now significantly outperform difference rewards, and result in 96% of the performance of directly computed CLEAN rewards. This result in addition to the results from Figure 6 demonstrate a tradeoff in approximating CLEAN rewards. While approximating CLEAN rewards, exploratory action noise is removed, but noise due to the approximation of the system evaluation function is added. In the case of 10 actions, a single agent has a smaller ability to drastically impact system performance, meaning that exploratory action noise has a smaller effect on system performance than in the case of 15 actions. As approximate CLEAN rewards result in superior system performance compared to difference rewards in the 15 action system, but perform worse in the 10 action system, we see that in the case where agents can only select 10 actions, exploratory action noise is less detrimental to system performance than noise caused by the approximation of the system evaluation function. However, in the 15 action case, exploratory action noise is more detrimental to system performance than noise caused by the approximation. This demonstrates that approximate CLEAN rewards should be used in cases where exploratory action noise can significantly impact system performance; these cases are characterized by the ability of a single agent to drastically impact the value of the system evaluation function.

6. DISCUSSION AND CONCLUSION

Agents in multiagent learning systems must often take exploratory actions in order to discover the mapping between actions and the expected value associated with those actions. However, agents are often unable to determine what portions of their feedback signal are caused by environmental dynamics, and what portions are caused by exploratory action noise from other agents. As a result, agents are biased to learn policies which depend on other agents taking exploratory actions, rather than policies which perform optimally when all agents are following their target policies.

CLEAN rewards address the problem of exploratory action noise by privatizing exploration, removing all noise from agent feedback signals caused by the exploratory actions of other agents. In systems where agent exploration can have a large impact on system performance, it is difficult for agents to evaluate the effectiveness of their selected actions. By privatizing exploration, CLEAN rewards allow agents to determine the value associated with the actions they select without being biased by noise caused by agent exploration. This results in policies which can outperform traditional reward signals such as difference rewards or global rewards.

However, CLEAN rewards require global state information, as well as the mathematical form of the system evaluation function in order to compute them. This information is typically unavailable to agents; thus, even though CLEAN rewards solve the problem of exploratory action noise, they introduce a problem of reward computability.

In this work, we demonstrate how CLEAN rewards may be approximated by learning agents using only local state and action information, as well as a broadcast value of the system evaluation function. This approximation approach does not require any global state or action knowledge, nor does it require expert knowledge about the system evaluation function. By approximating the global evaluation function in order to evaluate CLEAN rewards, the benefits of removing exploratory action noise are retained, while the restrictions of requiring expert system knowledge is removed.

Our results demonstrate that CLEAN rewards can be successfully approximated, and that these approximations typically outperform both global and difference rewards in both a congestion domain and coordination domain, with large systems containing up to 5000 agents. These results demonstrate that approximated CLEAN rewards can attain similar levels of performance as directly computed CLEAN rewards, and in some cases may attain even better performance. Results also demonstrate that approximate CLEAN rewards do not always result in superior system performance compared to difference rewards. In particular, in cases where exploratory action noise is relatively small compared to noise in the approximation of the system evaluation function, then approximate CLEAN rewards actually result in worse performance than difference rewards. This demonstrates that approximate CLEAN rewards should only be used in systems where exploratory action noise has a strong detrimental effect on system performance. In particular, approximate CLEAN rewards are most beneficial in systems where a single agent can dramatically impact system performance.

Future work on this research has multiple avenues. First, we will investigate the tradeoff between exploratory action noise and noise caused by the approximation, to determine if we can characterize systems to predict when approximate CLEAN rewards will be beneficial. Second, we will investigate CLEAN approximations when both terms (rather than one) are approximated, which could potentially improve sensitivity, but decrease alignment.

Acknowledgements

This work was partially supported by NETL DE-FE0011403.

REFERENCES

[1] J. Abounadi, D. Bertsekas, and V. Borkar. Stochastic Approximation for Non-Expansive Maps: Application to Q-Learning Algorithms. Technical report, SIAM Journal on Control and Optimization, 1998.

[2] A. K. Agogino and K. Tumer. Analyzing and visualizing multiagent rewards in dynamic and stochastic environments. *Journal of Autonomous Agents and Multi-Agent Systems*, 17(2):320–338, 2008.

[3] K. Anderson and Y. Hsu. Genetic crossover strategy using an approximation concept. In *In IEEE Congress on Evolutionary Computation*, pages 527–533.

[4] J. Branke, C. Schmidt, and H. Schmeck. Efficient Fitness Estimation in Noisy Environment. In *Proceedings of Genetic and Evolutionary Computation*, pages 243–250.

[5] D. Brillinger. Learning a Potential Function From a Trajectory. *Signal Processing Letters, IEEE*, 14(11):867–870, 2007.

[6] D. Buche, N. Schraudolph, and P. Koumoutsakos. Accelerating Evolutionary Algorithms Using Fitness Function Models. In *Proc. Workshops Genetic and Evolutionary Computation Conference*, 2003.

[7] D. Challet and N. Johnson. Optimal combinations of imperfect objects. *Physical Review Letters*, 89(2):028701, 2002.

[8] C. Gaskett, L. Fletcher, and A. Zelinsky. Reinforcement Learning for Visual Servoing of a Mobile Robot. In *In Proceedings of the Australian Conference on Robotics and Automation (ACRA 2000)*, 2000.

[9] C. HolmesParker. Clean learning to improve coordination and scalability in multiagent systems. 2013.

[10] C. HolmesParker, M. Taylor, A. Agogino, and K. Tumer. Clean rewards to improve coordination by removing exploratory action noise. 2014.

[11] Y. Isukapalli. An Analytically Tractable Approximation for the Gaussian Q-Function. In *IEEE Communications Letters*, volume 12, pages 669 – 671.

[12] Y. Jin. A Comprehensive Survey of Fitness Approximation in Evolutionary Computation. *Soft Comput.*, 9(1):3–12, Jan. 2005.

[13] J. Martikainen and S. Ovaska. Fitness Function Approximation by Neural Networks in the Optimization of MGP-FIR Filters. In *Adaptive and Learning Systems, 2006 IEEE Mountain Workshop on*, pages 7–12, 2006.

[14] H. Murao and S. Kitamura. Incremental State Acquisition for Q-Learning by Adaptive Gaussian Soft-Max Neural Network. In *Proceedings of the 1998 IEEE ISIC/CIRA/ISAS Joint Conference*, 1999.

[15] V. Oduguwa and R. Roy. Multiobjective Optimization of Rolling Rod Product Design Using Metamodeling Approach. pages 1164–1171, 2002.

[16] P. Pandey and D. Pandey. Reduct based q-learning: an introduction. In *Proceedings of the 2011 International Conference on Communication*, ICCCS '11, pages 285–288, New York, NY, USA, 2011. ACM.

[17] D. Ray, A. Mandal, S. Mazumder, and S. Mukhopadhay. Application of single-agent q-learning for light exploration. 2010.

[18] R. Sutton and A. Barto. *Reinforcement Learning, an Introduction.* MIT Press, 1998.

[19] K. Tumer. Designing agent utilities for coordinated, scalable and robust multiagent systems. In P. Scerri, R. Mailler, and R. Vincent, editors, *Challenges in the Coordination of Large Scale Multiagent Systems*, pages 173–188. Springer, 2005.

[20] K. Zhang and W. Pan. The two facets of the exploration-exploitation dilemma. 2006.

Policy Transfer using Reward Shaping

Tim Brys
Vrije Universiteit Brussel
timbrys@vub.ac.be

Anna Harutyunyan
Vrije Universiteit Brussel
aharutyu@vub.ac.be

Matthew E. Taylor
Washington State University
taylorm@eecs.wsu.edu

Ann Nowé
Vrije Universiteit Brussel
anowe@vub.ac.be

ABSTRACT

Transfer learning has proven to be a wildly successful approach for speeding up reinforcement learning. Techniques often use low-level information obtained in the source task to achieve successful transfer in the target task. Yet, a most general transfer approach can only assume access to the output of the learning algorithm in the source task, i.e. the learned policy, enabling transfer irrespective of the learning algorithm used in the source task. We advance the state-of-the-art by using a reward shaping approach to policy transfer. One of the advantages in following such an approach, is that it firmly grounds policy transfer in an actively developing body of theoretical research on reward shaping. Experiments in Mountain Car, Cart Pole and Mario demonstrate the practical usefulness of the approach.

Categories and Subject Descriptors

I.2.6 [**Learning**]: Miscellaneous

General Terms

Algorithms, Performance

Keywords

Reinforcement Learning; Transfer Learning;
Reward Shaping

1. INTRODUCTION

Reinforcement learning is a paradigm that allows an agent to learn how to control a system in order to achieve specific goals. The agent is guided by reward/punishment received for the behaviour it exhibits, adjusting its behaviour in order to maximize the cumulative reward. In complex tasks, or tasks with sparse rewards, learning can be excruciatingly slow (as many learning algorithms take the *tabula rasa* approach), and the agent cannot do better than behaving randomly until feedback is received.

A lot of research in this domain is therefore dedicated to speeding up the learning process, relying on the incorporation of various pieces of external knowledge. Particularly the use of knowledge transfer [20], i.e. transferring knowledge learned in a previous (source) task, has received a lot of attention in recent years, thanks to the publication of a few seminal papers that propose simple and intuitive techniques, achieving impressive improvements in learning [7, 11, 19]. Yet, many of these techniques involve the use of low level information obtained in the source task, which may not be transferrable to or incompatible with the agent learning in the new task, as the algorithms used in source and target task may differ in many ways. In the most basic case, one can only assume access to the learned behaviour, or policy, in the source task, which is the output of any reinforcement learning algorithm (and other techniques, such as learning from demonstration). This has lead to *policy transfer*, i.e. the use of an old policy to speed up learning in a new task, without any reference to a low level algorithm-specific representation of that policy [6, 22].

In this paper, we investigate the use of reward shaping to achieve policy transfer. Reward shaping is another popular approach used to speed up reinforcement learning. Shaping means modifying the basic reward signal with some extra reward to bias the agent's exploration. Potential-based reward shaping is a form that is firmly grounded in theory [3, 13] and has had many empirical successes [2, 4, 5]. While many heuristics can be easily formulated as potential functions (e.g. height in Mountain Car), it is a lot harder to define behaviour-based heuristics in that form without losing information (e.g. go left when the pole is leaning left in Cart Pole). However, recent research in shaping has lead to the development of a technique that allows any reward function to be transformed into a potential-based shaping function, therefore allowing any non-potential-based shaping function to benefit from the theoretical guarantees of potential-based shaping [8]. We exploit these results to achieve policy transfer through shaping, providing a theoretical basis for this approach to transfer. The connection between reward shaping and transfer learning is not an unnatural one, as these techniques are not only similar in purpose, but often are so on a technical level too, as e.g. static potential-based reward shaping is shown to be equivalent, given the same experiences, to Q-value initialization [24], which is exactly what many transfer learning techniques do [19, 21].

In the following sections, we provide the reader first with preliminaries on reinforcement learning, reward shaping and transfer learning, followed by an exposition of the proposed approach to policy transfer. In the experimental section, we show how this approach compares to state-of-the-art in policy transfer on three benchmark problems.

Appears in: *Proceedings of the 14th International Conference on Autonomous Agents and Multiagent Systems (AAMAS 2015), Bordini, Elkind, Weiss, Yolum (eds.), May, 4–8, 2015, Istanbul, Turkey.*

2. PRELIMINARIES

In this section we describe the body of research that is relevant to the work presented in this paper.

2.1 Reinforcement Learning

Reinforcement learning (RL) [17] is a paradigm that allows an agent to optimize its behaviour while operating in a given environment. It is rewarded or punished for the behaviour it exhibits, and its aim is to maximize the accumulated reward over time, which by definition amounts to solving the task. More formally, the environment is defined as a Markov Decision Process (MDP) $\langle S, A, T, \gamma, R \rangle$. $S = \{s_1, s_2, \ldots\}$ is the set of states the environment can be in, and $A = \{a_1, a_2, \ldots\}$ is the set of actions the learning agent can execute. Executing action a when the environment is in state s makes it transition to state s' with probability $T(s'|s, a)$, yielding $R(s, a, s')$ as reward for that transition. Finally, γ, the discounting factor, defines how important future rewards are. The goal is to learn a policy π that probabilistically maps states to actions in such a way that the expected discounted cumulative reward, the return, is maximized.

Reinforcement learning algorithms either directly search the policy space to find a policy that maximizes the return, or estimate the expected returns and derive a policy from those. The learning algorithms used in this paper are of the second type, and more specifically temporal-difference (TD) learning algorithms. These estimate state (V) or state-action (Q) value functions, that represent the return expected while following some behaviour policy. Algorithms such as Q-learning incrementally update these estimates based on the rewards observed while the agent is interacting with the environment:

$$Q(s, a) \leftarrow Q(s, a) + \alpha\delta$$

with α the learning rate, and δ the temporal-difference error:

$$\delta = R(s, a, s') + \gamma \max_{a'} Q(s', a') - Q(s, a)$$

Given certain conditions, such as the agent's exploration and learning rate going to zero, Q-learning is guaranteed to converge to the optimal values Q^*, from which the optimal policy π^* can easily be derived:

$$\pi^*(s) = \arg\max_{a} Q^*(s, a)$$

The basic form of this type of algorithm operates on a table that stores the values for every (s, a) pair. In continuous and/or very large state-spaces, the tabular approach is impractical or even impossible, and function approximation techniques are required. With linear function approximation techniques, such as the popular tile-coding [1], states are represented using a feature vector ϕ_s, and the Q-function is approximated using a set of weights θ:

$$Q(s, a) = \theta_a^T \phi(s)$$

The weight vector is updated using an update-rule similar to the one used in the tabular case:

$$\theta \leftarrow \theta + \alpha\delta$$

2.2 Reward Shaping

Reward shaping provides the agent with an extra reward signal F that is added to the environment's reward R, making the agent learn on the composite signal $R_F = R + F$. The shaping reward F usually encodes some kind of heuristic knowledge, and is intended to complement the typically sparser signal R. Since the agent's goal is defined by the reward function (solving the task optimally means finding a policy that achieves the maximum accumulated reward in expectation), changing the reward signal may actually change the task. Ng et al. [13] proved that the only sound way to shape without changing the task is through potential-based shaping. That is, define a potential function Φ over the state space, and define F as the difference between the potential of states s' and s, given observed transition (s, a, s'):

$$F(s, a, s') = \gamma\Phi(s') - \Phi(s)$$

This formulation preserves the total order over policies, and therefore the optimality of policies.

This result was extended to shaping over state-action pairs (s, a) by Wiewiora et al. [25]:

$$F(s, a, s', a') = \gamma\Phi(s', a') - \Phi(s, a)$$

This allows for the incorporation of more specific information, pertaining to both states and actions. Devlin et al. [3] extended Ng's potential-based reward shaping to dynamic potential-based shaping, allowing the shaping function to change over time:

$$F(s, t, s', t') = \gamma\Phi(s', t') - \Phi(s, t)$$

Finally, Harutyunyan et al. [8] combine these two extensions into dynamic shaping over state-action pairs:

$$F(s, a, t, s', a', t') = \gamma\Phi(s', a', t') - \Phi(s, a, t)$$

All of these extensions preserve the total order over policies and therefore do not change the task, given Ng's original assumptions.

Harutyunyan et al. developed this last extension to set the stage for their paper's main result: they show how any reward function $R^\dagger$ can be transformed into a potential-based shaping function, by learning a secondary Q-function $\Phi^\dagger$ in parallel on the negation of $R^\dagger$, and using that to perform dynamic shaping on the main reward R. The secondary value function $\Phi^\dagger$ must be learned on-policy, with a technique such as SARSA [15]:

$$\Phi^\dagger(s, a) \leftarrow \Phi^\dagger(s, a) + \beta\delta^{\Phi^\dagger}$$

where

$$\delta^{\Phi^\dagger} = -R^\dagger + \gamma\Phi^\dagger(s', a') - \Phi^\dagger(s, a)$$

When $\Phi^\dagger$ converges, $F(s, a, s', a') = R^\dagger(s, a)$ in expectation. In other words, when the secondary value function has converged, the main value function will be supplied with a potential-based reward shaping that is equivalent to the reward function $R^\dagger$. Of course, even before convergence, $\Phi^\dagger$ will reflect some useful information pertaining to $R^\dagger$, like the main Q-function will reflect useful information towards good policies before convergence to the optimal policy.

2.3 Transfer Learning

Transfer learning allows a learning agent to re-use knowledge obtained in a previous task, aiming to learn faster in the current task. Various approaches for transfer have been proposed, varying in the learning algorithms they work with, the type and representation of information that is transferred, allowed task differences, etc. [20].

Typically, transfer algorithms will be provided an inter-task mapping, to translate between the state and action spaces of the source and target task, in order to leverage the information transferred. Such mappings χ_S and χ_A, for state and action spaces respectively, take a state or action from the target task and map it onto a state or action in the source task:

$$\chi_S(s_{\text{target}}) = s_{\text{source}}$$

and

$$\chi_A(a_{\text{target}}) = a_{\text{source}}$$

Conversely, ρ represents a mapping from source task to target task:

$$\rho_S(s_{\text{source}}) = s_{\text{target}}$$

and

$$\rho_A(a_{\text{source}}) = a_{\text{target}}$$

Note that $\chi_S(\rho_S(s_{\text{source}})) = s_{\text{source}}$ need not always be true (and similarly for χ_A and ρ_A), as both χ and ρ need not be injective.

In this paper, we focus on policy transfer, the most general case with respect to the knowledge transferred, assuming the only available knowledge from the source task is the output of the learning algorithm, i.e. the policy. The target algorithms we consider are any value-based algorithms that can benefit from reward shaping.

Fernandez and Veloso [6] propose Probabilistic Policy Reuse (PPR) to transfer a policy to a TD learner. Whereas a typical reinforcement learning agent will probabilistically choose to either exploit the knowledge it has learned, or explore a random action (the exploration-exploitation trade-off), PPR adds a third option, which is the exploitation of a previous policy. With probability ψ, an action is selected according to the old policy; with probability $1-\psi$, a standard action selection mechanism, such as ϵ-greedy is used. ψ is decayed over time to allow the learner to emphasize new knowledge more as it learns more in the new task.[1] This adds a bias to the exploration of the agent, intended to guide it towards good policies in the new task. To use the old policy in the new task, the target task's state needs to be mapped to the source task's state, an action needs to be selected according to the source task's policy, and that action needs to be mapped to the target task:

$$\pi_{\text{PPR}}(s_{\text{target}}) = \rho_A(\pi_{\text{source}}(\chi_S(s_{\text{target}}))$$

There are other policy transfer algorithms besides PPR, but none, to the best of our knowledge, that transfer a full policy to TD-learners. Most such techniques will consider learning options in the source task and transfer those to the new task [10, 14]. Other popular transfer learning techniques transfer low-level information, such as Q or V values [21].

[1]In the original PPR algorithm, ψ is reset at the beginning of every episode and decays during the episode, so that the agent relies more on the old policy in the beginning of an episode and less at the end. This makes little sense in the domains considered here, as one would rather want ψ to decay over episodes, so that the agent relies more on the old policy in early episodes and less in later episodes. PPR was also interpreted this way in [23].

3. POLICY TRANSFER USING REWARD SHAPING

Given these preliminaries, we go on to describe our approach to policy transfer. To achieve policy transfer using reward shaping (PTS), we use the reward shaping technique developed by Harutyunyan et al. [8], which turns an arbitrary reward function into a potential-based shaping function, see Preliminaries. As the authors note, the approach is especially well-suited for the incorporation of behaviour-based knowledge, which is much harder to directly describe as a potential function without losing some information. Since a policy *is* behaviour-based knowledge, we build on this technique to realize policy transfer.

In order to use the technique, we need to define a reward function R^π in the new task that captures the policy π transferred from the source task. The idea is to reward the learning agent for taking action a in state s, proportionally to the probability of the mapped state-action pair $(\chi_S(s), \chi_A(a))$ in the transferred policy:

$$R^\pi(s, a, s') = \pi(\chi_S(s), \chi_A(a)) \quad (1)$$

Even though the formulation works for stochastic as well as deterministic policies, in this paper, we only focus on the latter. Therefore, R^π will always be either 0 or 1.

The negation of this reward function is then learned in a secondary value function Φ^π, whose values are used to shape the main reward R:

$$\begin{aligned} R_F(s, a, s', a') &= R(s, a, s') + F^\pi(s, a, t, s', a', t') \\ F^\pi(s, a, t, s', a', t') &= \gamma\Phi^\pi(s', a', t') - \Phi^\pi(s, a, t) \end{aligned}$$

Since this shaping is learned in parallel to the main learning, it is advisable to use a higher learning rate for the secondary value function, so that this information becomes available faster [8].

Note that a simpler approach to policy transfer using shaping could be taken, using a static potential function:

$$\Phi(s, a) = \pi(\chi_S(s), \chi_A(, a)) \quad (2)$$

The problem here, as argued in [8], is that when using this approach, a transition between two state-action pairs (s, a) with both high potential yields a very small shaping reward (as $F(s, a, s', a') = \gamma\Phi(s', a') - \Phi(s, a)$), while with the more elaborate technique, the actual shaping reward F would be high, which is desirable. We have evaluated the simpler approach empirically, and it proved to be inferior to the technique explained in this section. We omit these results from the experimental section for clarity of exposition.

In approaching policy transfer from a reward shaping perspective, we are able to ground this approach in the theory that has developed around potential-based reward shaping, leveraging the associated convergence guarantees for sound policy transfer.

4. EXPERIMENTS

To demonstrate the practical use of policy transfer using reward shaping as outlined in this paper, we evaluate the technique on two common reinforcement learning benchmarks, and a more complex domain: Mountain Car, Cart Pole and Mario. We compare with PPR, and evaluate the strengths and weaknesses of both techniques. Experiments in every domain are averaged over 100 trials, and the source task learning is rerun for every transfer trial. Whenever we say methods perform differently or similarly, this is supported by the Student's t-test ($p = 0.05$).

4.1 Mountain Car 3D

In the standard Mountain Car task [16], the agent is in control of a car and needs to drive this car up a hill. Yet, the car is underpowered, and therefore cannot drive up the hill in one go. The agent needs to learn to build up momentum driving the car up and down two opposite hills, until enough potential energy has built up to drive to the top of the hill where the goal is located. The state space is described by the position of the car and its velocity $(x, \dot{x})$, while the actions available to the agent involve applying either negative, positive, or no force to the car ($A = \{Left, Right, Neutral\}$). The agent receives a per-step reward of -1, encouraging it to find the goal as quickly as possible. The 3D version of the task [18] (or 4D as some would have it) is very similar, except that the terrain is three dimensional, and the car can apply force along two axes, although only one at a time ($A = \{East, West, North, South, Neutral\}$). The state space consists of the car's position and velocity in two dimensions $(x, \dot{x}, y, \dot{y})$.

To learn this task, we use Q(λ)-learning and SARSA(λ) with tile-coding in the 2D and 3D tasks respectively (each chosen because it yields the best performing base-line agent in its respective task). In the 2D task, parameters are $\alpha = \frac{0.1}{14}$, $\gamma = 1$, $\epsilon = 0.1$, $\lambda = 0.95$, with 14 10×10 tilings. In the 3D task, parameters are $\alpha = \frac{0.2}{14}$, $\gamma = 1$, $\epsilon = 0.05$, $\lambda = 0.95$, with 14 $10 \times 10 \times 10 \times 10$ tilings. Weights are initialized pessimistically to $-\frac{250}{14}$, which yields better performance in both base learner and agents using transfer.

In PPR, to take an action from the 2D Mountain Car policy, first the 3D state must be mapped to the 2D state, an action must be selected according to the transferred policy, and then that 2D action must be mapped onto a 3D action. Both of these mappings are ambiguous:

$$\chi_S((x, \dot{x}, y, \dot{y})) = \begin{cases} (x, \dot{x}) & \text{probability } 0.5 \\ (y, \dot{y}) & \text{probability } 0.5 \end{cases}$$

$$\rho_A(\text{Left}) = \begin{cases} \text{West} & \text{probability } 0.5 \\ \text{South} & \text{probability } 0.5 \end{cases}$$

$$\rho_A(\text{Right}) = \begin{cases} \text{East} & \text{probability } 0.5 \\ \text{North} & \text{probability } 0.5 \end{cases}$$

$$\rho_A(\text{Neutral}) = \text{Neutral}$$

This ambiguity prevents one to use the old policy to its full potential with PPR. ψ, the parameter controlling how frequently the old policy is used, is initially set to 1, and we tuned ψ to decay by 0.99 after every episode.

Unlike PPR, PTS can use the old policy completely, as the values obtained from both possible state mappings can be combined, and actions are mapped from 3D to 2D, which is an unambiguous mapping, as opposed to the mapping from 2D to 3D:

$$\chi_A(\text{West}) = \text{Left}$$

$$\chi_A(\text{South}) = \text{Left}$$

$$\chi_A(\text{East}) = \text{Right}$$

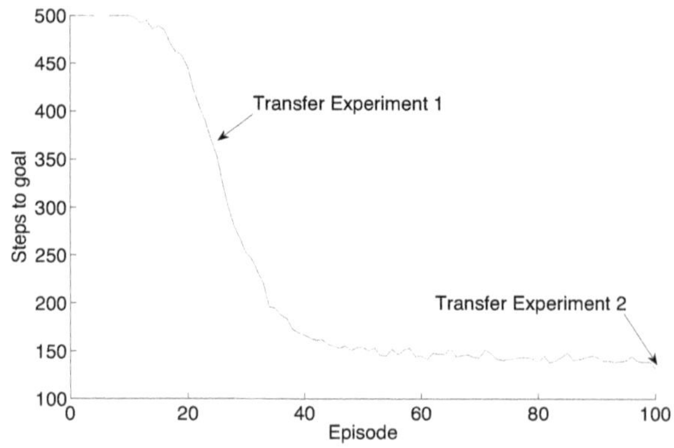

Figure 1: Basic Q(λ)-learner learning Mountain Car 2D. Convergence happens after about 50 **episodes.**

$$\chi_A(\text{North}) = \text{Right}$$

$$\chi_A(\text{Neutral}) = \text{Neutral}$$

The secondary reward function used for shaping is then:

$$R^{\pi}(s, a, s') = \frac{\pi(\chi_{S,1}(s), \chi_A(a)) + \pi(\chi_{S,2}(s), \chi_A(a))}{2}$$

with $\chi_{S,1}$ and $\chi_{S,2}$ indicating the two possible state mappings. The learning rate for the secondary value function, used for shaping, is $\beta = \frac{0.5}{14}$.

Figure 1 shows the basic Q-learner learning the 2D Mountain Car task. We perform two transfer experiments, either transferring after 25 or 100 episodes of learning in the 2D Mountain Car task. This allows us to investigate how these techniques perform when transferring either a suboptimal or near-optimal policy.

Figure 2 shows how both techniques perform when using a transferred policy that is suboptimal. Whereas PPR performs worse compared to the base learner, PTS results in faster learning, despite the transferred policy being far from optimal. When the transferred policy is near-optimal in the source task (Figure 3), PPR manages a big jumpstart in performance, as it immediately starts using the transferred policy. With the shaping approach on the other hand, a number of experiences are required before the transferred knowledge becomes apparrent in the learning process. Despite the jumpstart, PPR cannot maintain this level of performance and quickly degrades before improving again (we discuss this phenomenon at the end of the paper), while PTS again achieves a statistically significant improvement in learning.

Since PTS and PPR are complementary on a technical level (the former modifies the reward signal, the latter affects action selection), we can investigate how they perform combined. During initial episodes, PTS+PPR performs the same as PPR, as with high initial ψ, action selection is fully controlled by PPR. As ψ decays, PTS+PPR's performance does not drop as much as with PPR alone.

4.2 Cart Pole

Cart Pole [12] is a task in which the agent controls a cart with a pole on top. The goal is to keep the pole balanced for as long as possible. The agent can move the cart either left or right within a given interval in a single dimension. The

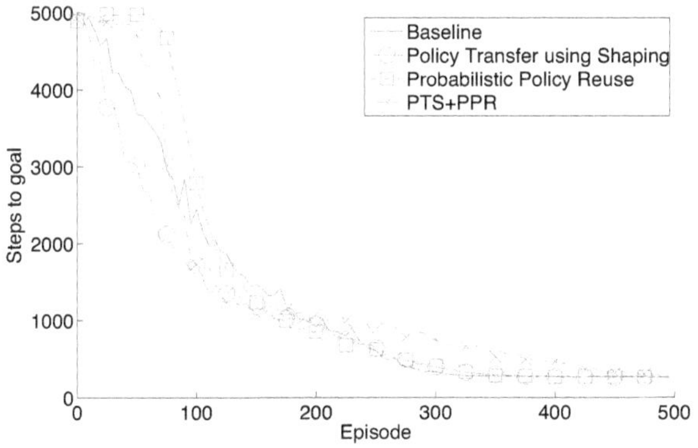

Figure 2: Policy transfer to Mountain Car 3D after having learned for 25 episodes in Mountain Car 2D, i.e. before convergence to the optimal policy. Nonetheless, PTS manages to improve performance over the base learner, while PPR cannot.

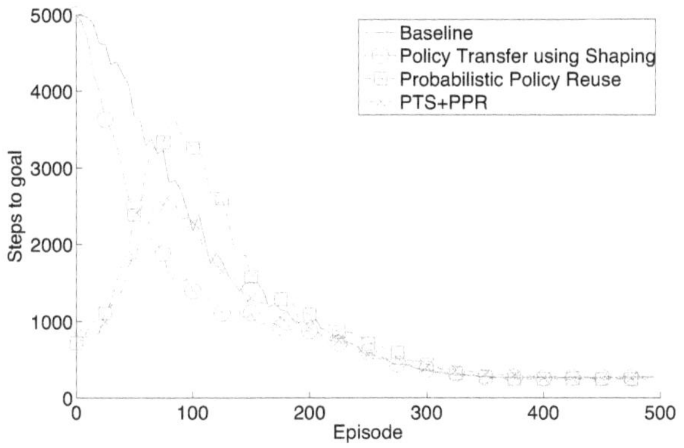

Figure 3: Policy transfer to Mountain Car 3D after having learned for 100 episodes in Mountain Car 2D, i.e. after convergence to a (near-) optimal policy. While PPR benefits from a jumpstart in performance, its performance deteriorates before improving again. PTS on the other hand exhibits more consistent learning, although it does not benefit from a jumpstart in performance.

state space consists of the position of the cart, its velocity, the angle of the pole and its angular velocity $(x, \dot{x}, \theta, \dot{\theta})$. We consider two versions of the task. The source task is the standard Cart Pole task, while we coin the target task the Heavy Cart Pole task, as we increase the weight of the pole from 0.1 to 1.0, making the task much harder. Since these two tasks only differ in transition function, no state or action mappings are required for transfer.

To learn the task, we use $Q(\lambda)$-learning with tile-coding. In the source task, we shape the learning with a static reward shaping function encouraging the angle of the pole to be 0, i.e. up ($\Phi(s) = 100(\pi - \bar{\theta})$), for faster learning; we add π to make the potential function positive, i.e. optimistic. Parameters are $\alpha = \frac{0.05}{32}$, $\gamma = 1$, $\epsilon = 0.05$, $\lambda = 0.95$, with 32 $10 \times 10 \times 10 \times 10$ tilings for both tasks. Weights are initialized optimistically to 0, except with PPR. For PPR, we need to initialize the weights pessimistically to $-\frac{1}{32}$ to avoid a

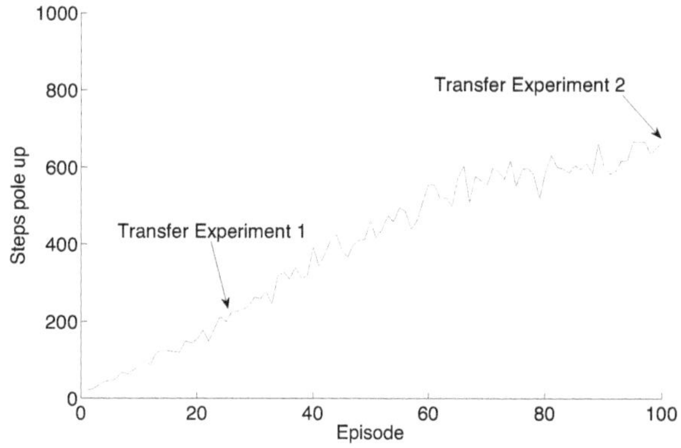

Figure 4: Basic $Q(\lambda)$-learner learning standard Cart Pole. It does not converge to the optimal policy within 100 episodes.

performance drop similar to the one seen in Mountain Car (we address this issue at the end of the paper). In PPR, ψ is initially set to 1, and decayed by 0.99 after every episode. In PTS, the secondary reward function is as described in Equation 1, and its value function is learned using the same parameters as the base learner, except with learning rate $\beta = \frac{0.5}{32}$.

We again perform two transfer experiments, one after learning for 25 episodes in the source task, and one after learning 100 episodes in the source task. In neither case will the agent have converged on the optimal policy, but the policy is much better after 100 episodes than after 25 episodes, as shown by the base-learner performance in the standard Cart Pole task, plotted in Figure 4.

Figure 5 shows the results for transfer after 25 learning episodes in the standard Cart Pole task. PPR again manages a good jumpstart in learning because it immediately starts using the transferred policy directly, while PTS needs learning experiences before the transferred knowledge affects the performance. Yet, PTS benefits much more from the transfer, despite the transferred policy's lack of quality, resulting in much better learning than PPR. The results for PPR are much better after 100 learning episodes in the source task (Figure 6), resulting in a jumpstart, and good learning from there on. PTS matches the performance of PPR and their combination only after some 600 episodes. Across the two experiments, PTS+PPR offers the best alternative.

4.3 Mario

The Mario benchmark problem [9] is a public reimplementation of the original Super Mario Bros® game. It involves an agent (Mario) that navigates a 2D level, collecting points for finishing the level, finding coins, getting hurt (negative points), etc. The goal is to collect as many points as possible. An episode is ended when time runs out, Mario dies, or when he finishes the level. The state space in Mario is fairly complex, as Mario observes the locations and types of enemies on the screen, he observes all information pertaining to himself, e.g. what mode he is in (small, big, fire), and furthermore he is surrounded by a gridlike receptive field in which each cell indicates what type of object is in it (a brick, a coin, a mushroom, an enemy, etc.). Mario can take 12 distinct 'super' actions, each being a combination of one action

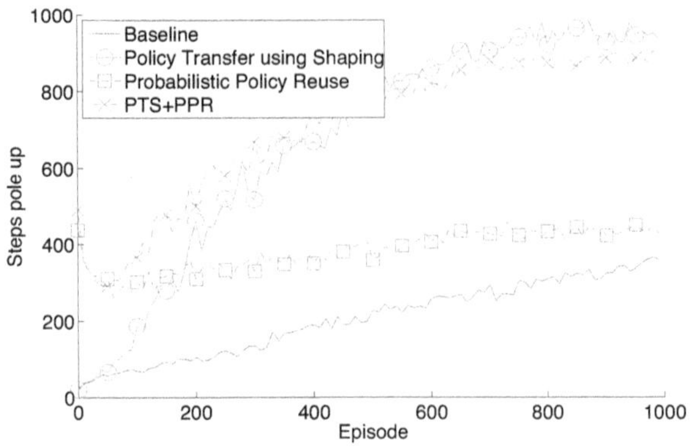

Figure 5: Policy transfer to Heavy Cart Pole, after having learned for 25 episodes in standard Cart Pole. Despite the low quality of the transferred policy, both PPR and PTS manage to leverage the transferred knowledge, although PTS is much more robust to the (lack of) quality of the transferred knowledge.

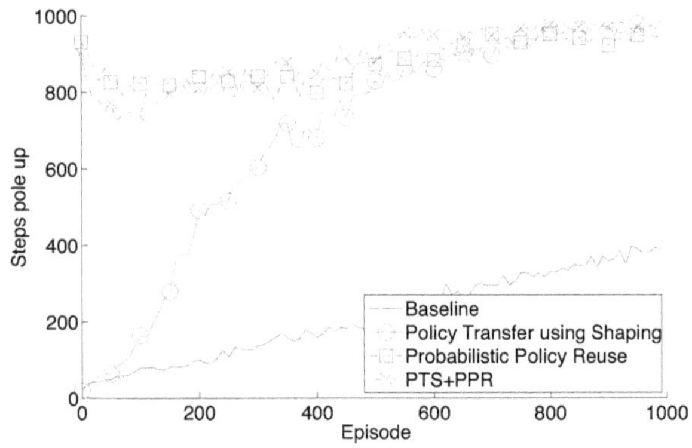

Figure 6: Policy transfer to Heavy Cart Pole, after having learned for 100 episodes in standard Cart Pole. PPR outperforms PTS in this case, as it manages to maintain the performance achieved after its jumpstart, while it takes PTS much longer to get to that level of performance.

from these three sets: {left, right, no direction}, {jump, do not jump} and {run, do not run}.

One part of the Mario game that can have a significant impact on performance is the presence of enemies. They are the source of most of the negative points Mario collects, by hurting, or worse, killing him. The latter ends the episode, preventing Mario from collecting more points. Therefore, a simple approach to transfer is to let Mario first figure out how to navigate and collect points in a level without enemies, and then transferring this information to a learning process in a level with enemies.

In these experiments, we use tabular $Q(\lambda)$-learning. The state-space in both source and target task consists of four boolean variables (indicating whether Mario is able to jump, on the ground, which direction he is facing, and whether he is able to shoot fireballs). In the target task, there are two additional variables indicating the relative position (x and

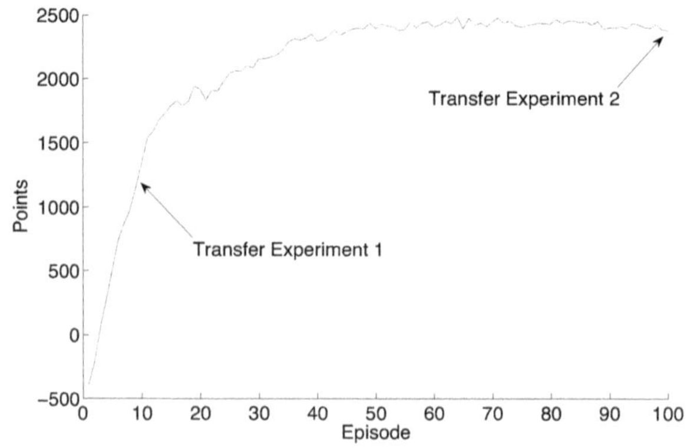

Figure 7: Basic $Q(\lambda)$-learner learning standard Mario without enemies. It converges after about 50 episodes.

y) of the closest enemy within a 21×21 grid surrounding Mario, making for a total of $2^4 \times (21^2 + 1) = 7072$ states (one extra for when there are no enemies in sight). Since we omit a lot of relevant state information, the agent operates in a non-Markovian state-space. Learning parameters are $\alpha = 0.01$, $\gamma = 0.9$, $\epsilon = 0.05$, and $\lambda = 0.5$. In PPR, ψ is initially set to 1, and decayed by 0.95 after every episode. In PTS, the secondary reward function is as described in Equation 1, and is learned using the same parameters as the base learner, except for its learning rate being $\beta = 0.05$.

The state-mapping from target to source task involves selecting only the four boolean variables, discarding the two state variables pertaining to enemies.

$$\chi_S(s_{target}) = s_{target,\{1..4\}}$$

The action spaces in source and target task are the same. Therefore no mapping is required.

Figure 7 shows the performance of the base learner in the Mario task without enemies (level generated with seed 0 and difficulty 0). We transfer to the same level, but with enemies, either after 10 or 100 learning episodes in the source task.

Results for transfer after learning only 10 episodes in the enemy-free level are depicted in Figure 8. PPR, PTS, and PTS+PPR all speed up learning, performing similarly, i.e. without statistically significant differences. Figure 9 shows the results for transferring the policy learned after 100 episodes. Transferring the better policy, PPR achieves a much better jumpstart, but PTS actually manages to converge to significantly better policies, which is possible due to the non-Markovian nature of the state-space.

5. DISCUSSION

Both Policy Transfer using Reward Shaping and Probabilistic Policy Reuse try to bias the agent's exploration in the target task using the transferred policy to achieve faster learning, but they do it in very dissimilar ways. PPR uses the transferred policy directly in the target task, while PTS rather uses the transferred policy to shape the state-action values being learned, which in turn biases exploration. The main advantage of PPR, is that using the transferred policy directly from the start can result in big jumpstarts in initial

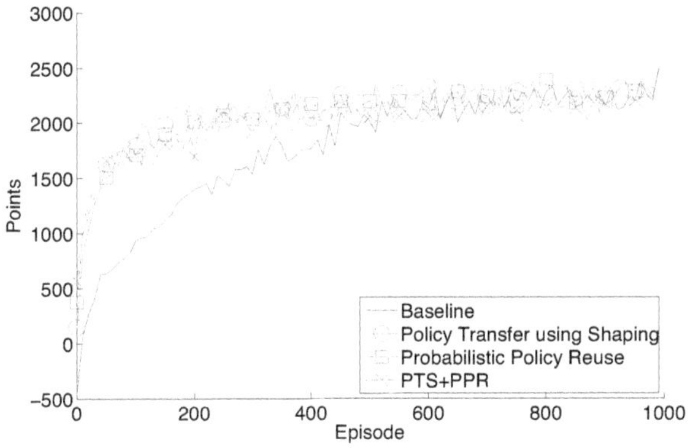

Figure 8: Policy transfer in Mario, after having learned for 10 episodes in the same level without enemies. PPR, PTS and their combination all improve performance, showing no statistically significant differences.

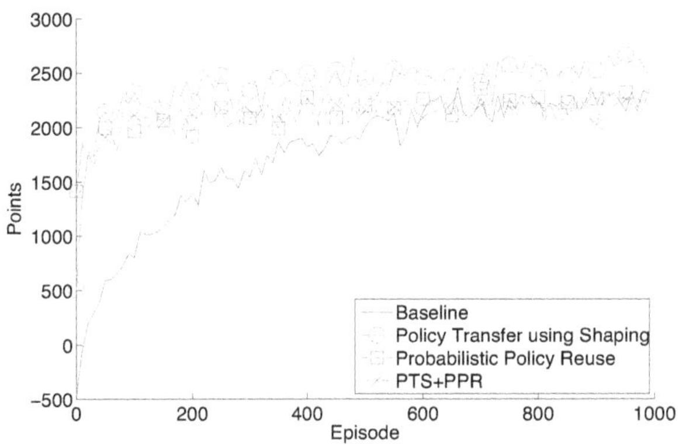

Figure 9: Policy transfer in Mario, after having learned for 100 episodes in the same level without enemies. PPR achieves a much greater jumpstart than PTS, but PTS quickly achieves the same level of performance, and actually converges to better policies than the base learner, PPR, or their combination.

performance. PTS on the other hand can only see the effect of the old policy after a state transition has been observed, and not before as PPR can.[2]

On the other hand, the shaping approach can easily exploit ambiguous state and action mappings, by combining the values obtained for each, while PPR is limited to taking a single action.[3] With respect to the quality of the transferred policy, PTS appeared to be more robust in our experiments, outperforming the base learner in every case, despite the suboptimality of transferred policies. PPR suffered more from the lack of quality in the transferred policy. A likely reason for this is that PPR always uses either only information from the old or the new task, while PTS always uses a combination of both, as its decisions will always be based on both the new environment's reward and the transferred policy's shaping.

Furthermore, PTS is firmly grounded in potential-based reward shaping theory, providing convergence guarantees for PTS, previously proven in that literature, without requiring special measures. PPR on the other hand needs to decrease the use of the transferred policy to preserve convergence guarantees.

Lastly, we need to address the drop in performance observed in Mountain Car for PPR (and in Cart Pole when not initializing pessimistically, results not included). For PPR to be effective, it needs to be able to affect the Q-values in such a way that its trajectories become positively reinforced. With Mountain Car, there is a step-reward of -1, which actually results in PPR's trajectories being negatively reinforced, except close to the goal, at least initially. In Cart Pole, initializing optimistically with 0, and receiving step rewards of 0, results in the old policy being unable to affect the Q-values in any way (positive or negative), and thus when the learner progressively relies less on the transferred policy, it will have learned little from those experiences. On the other hand, initializing the Q-values in Cart Pole to -1, will lead to every visited state-action pair's Q-value being positively reinforced due to the step-reward of 0, allowing PPR to carve a path in the Q-values.

Since PTS and PPR are compatible on a technical level, with PTS operating on the reward signal and PPR on the action selection mechanism, we have evaluated their combination too. PTS appears to be useful to improve the performance of PPR, as in our experiments PTS+PPR always outperformed or matched PPR performance. On the other hand, it is not true that PTS+PPR always outperforms PTS alone. As ψ is typically initialized to 1 (both in this paper and other works [6, 7, 23]), initial performance is completely determined by PPR. As ψ decays, PTS manages to affect learning more, but can not always overcome the initial bias set by PPR (as exemplified by the results in Mario, a non-Markovian environment), as opposed to when using PTS alone. Therefore, PTS appears to be a way to improve PPR, but not the reverse.

6. CONCLUSIONS AND FUTURE WORK

We presented a novel approach to policy transfer, encoding the transferred policy as a dynamic potential-based reward shaping function, benefiting from all the theory behind reward shaping. An experimental comparison between Policy Transfer using Reward Shaping (PTS) and Probabilistic Policy Reuse (PPR) has shown the weaknesses and strengths of both in several domains. Because PPR uses the transferred policy directly during action selection, it can achieve a big jumpstart in performance, but can not always maintain this level of performance as its effect on the value function being learned depends on factors such as the environment's step-reward and the value function's initialization. PTS needs more learning experiences before the effect of the transferred policy becomes apparent, but the technique appears much more robust against lack of quality of the transferred policy, and does not suffer from issues similar to PPR's. The combination of the two techniques is a way to improve PPR performance, while PTS alone may be a better option in some cases.

[2]We have experimented with initializing the Q-function with the static potential function (Eq. 2), aiming to achieve a similar jumpstart in PTS. This improved initial performance, but not dramatically so.

[3]One could approach this problem in an ensemble fashion, combining the different mappings through some voting mechanism, but that is beyond the scope of this article.

In a follow-up study, we are interested in looking at multi-task transfer. Recent developments in reward shaping have shown how learning with different shapings in parallel, and combining their estimates using ensemble techniques can speed up learning a lot [2]. In a transfer context, we can transfer multiple policies using PTS, learn estimates in parallel, and achieve multi-task transfer using an ensemble technique.

Furthermore, we want to look at transfer between agents using different learning algorithms (including humans), where policy transfer makes the most sense.

Acknowledgement

Tim Brys is funded by a Ph.D grant of the Research Foundation Flanders (FWO). Anna Harutyunyan is supported by the IWT-SBO project MIRAD (grant nr. 120057). This work was supported in part by NSF IIS-1149917.

7. REFERENCES

[1] J. S. Albus. *Brains, behavior, and robotics*. Byte books Peterborough, NH, 1981.

[2] T. Brys, A. Nowé, D. Kudenko, and M. E. Taylor. Combining multiple correlated reward and shaping signals by measuring confidence. In *Twenty-Eighth AAAI Conference on Artificial Intelligence*, pages 1687–1693, 2014.

[3] S. Devlin and D. Kudenko. Dynamic potential-based reward shaping. In *Proceedings of the 11th International Conference on Autonomous Agents and Multiagent Systems-Volume 1*, pages 433–440. International Foundation for Autonomous Agents and Multiagent Systems, 2012.

[4] S. Devlin, D. Kudenko, and M. Grześ. An empirical study of potential-based reward shaping and advice in complex, multi-agent systems. *Advances in Complex Systems*, 14(02):251–278, 2011.

[5] K. Efthymiadis and D. Kudenko. Using plan-based reward shaping to learn strategies in Starcraft: Broodwar. In *Computational Intelligence in Games (CIG), 2013 IEEE Conference on*, pages 1–8. IEEE, 2013.

[6] F. Fernández, J. García, and M. Veloso. Probabilistic policy reuse for inter-task transfer learning. *Robotics and Autonomous Systems*, 58(7):866–871, 2010.

[7] F. Fernández and M. Veloso. Probabilistic policy reuse in a reinforcement learning agent. In *Proceedings of the fifth international joint conference on Autonomous agents and multiagent systems*, pages 720–727. ACM, 2006.

[8] A. Harutyunyan, S. Devlin, P. Vrancx, and A. Nowé. Expressing arbitrary reward functions as potential-based advice. In *Proceedings of the Twenty-Ninth AAAI Conference on Artificial Intelligence*, 2015.

[9] S. Karakovskiy and J. Togelius. The Mario AI benchmark and competitions. *Computational Intelligence and AI in Games, IEEE Transactions on*, 4(1):55–67, 2012.

[10] G. Konidaris and A. G. Barto. Building portable options: Skill transfer in reinforcement learning. In *IJCAI*, volume 7, pages 895–900, 2007.

[11] A. Lazaric, M. Restelli, and A. Bonarini. Transfer of samples in batch reinforcement learning. In *Proceedings of the 25th international conference on Machine learning*, pages 544–551. ACM, 2008.

[12] D. Michie and R. Chambers. Boxes: An experiment in adaptive control. *Machine intelligence*, 2(2):137–152, 1968.

[13] A. Y. Ng, D. Harada, and S. Russell. Policy invariance under reward transformations: Theory and application to reward shaping. In *Proceedings of the Sixteenth International Conference on Machine Learning*, volume 99, pages 278–287, 1999.

[14] B. Ravindran and A. G. Barto. Relativized options: Choosing the right transformation. In *ICML*, pages 608–615, 2003.

[15] G. A. Rummery and M. Niranjan. *On-line Q-learning using connectionist systems*. University of Cambridge, Department of Engineering, 1994.

[16] S. P. Singh and R. S. Sutton. Reinforcement learning with replacing eligibility traces. *Machine learning*, 22(1-3):123–158, 1996.

[17] R. Sutton and A. Barto. *Reinforcement learning: An introduction*, volume 1. Cambridge Univ Press, 1998.

[18] M. E. Taylor, G. Kuhlmann, and P. Stone. Autonomous transfer for reinforcement learning. In *Proceedings of the 7th international joint conference on Autonomous agents and multiagent systems-Volume 1*, pages 283–290. International Foundation for Autonomous Agents and Multiagent Systems, 2008.

[19] M. E. Taylor and P. Stone. Behavior transfer for value-function-based reinforcement learning. In *Proceedings of the fourth international joint conference on Autonomous agents and multiagent systems*, pages 53–59. ACM, 2005.

[20] M. E. Taylor and P. Stone. Transfer learning for reinforcement learning domains: A survey. *The Journal of Machine Learning Research*, 10:1633–1685, 2009.

[21] M. E. Taylor, P. Stone, and Y. Liu. Transfer learning via inter-task mappings for temporal difference learning. *Journal of Machine Learning Research*, 8(1):2125–2167, 2007.

[22] M. E. Taylor, S. Whiteson, and P. Stone. Transfer via inter-task mappings in policy search reinforcement learning. In *Proceedings of the 6th international joint conference on Autonomous agents and multiagent systems*, pages 156–163. ACM, 2007.

[23] L. Torrey and M. E. Taylor. Help an agent out: Student/teacher learning in sequential decision tasks. In *Proceedings of the Adaptive and Learning Agents workshop (at AAMAS-12)*, 2012.

[24] E. Wiewiora. Potential-based shaping and Q-value initialization are equivalent. *J. Artif. Intell. Res. (JAIR)*, 19:205–208, 2003.

[25] E. Wiewiora, G. Cottrell, and C. Elkan. Principled methods for advising reinforcement learning agents. In *ICML*, pages 792–799, 2003.

Verifying Multi-Agent Systems by Model Checking Three-valued Abstractions

Alessio Lomuscio
Imperial College London
a.lomuscio@imperial.ac.uk

Jakub Michaliszyn
Imperial College London
j.michaliszyn@imperial.ac.uk

ABSTRACT

We develop the theoretical foundations of a predicate abstraction methodology for the verification of multi-agent systems. We put forward a specification language based on epistemic logic and a weak variant of the logic ATL interpreted on a three-valued semantics. We show that the model checking problem for multi-agent systems in this setting is tractable by giving a provably correct procedure which admits a PTIME bound. We give a constructive technique for generating abstract approximations of concrete multi-agent systems models and show that the truth values are preserved between abstract and concrete models. We evaluate the effectiveness of the methodology on a variant of the bit-transmission problem.

Categories and Subject Descriptors

D.2.4 [**Software/Program Verification**]: Model checking

General Terms

Verification

Keywords

Epistemic logic; ATL; model-checking; abstraction

1. INTRODUCTION

With an increasing number of applications of societal importance adopting a multi-agent systems (MAS) approach, there is an increasing need to verify formally that a MAS design is correct before deployment. Over the past ten years a number of approaches have been put forward to verify MAS by means of model checking [13]. These include explicit approaches [22, 4], symbolic techniques [20, 44] and translations into SAT [29, 48]. Most methods that have been introduced support agent-based specifications giving prominence to the mental states of the agents, notably their knowledge [19]. Symbolic approaches are normally considered to be the most powerful in terms of performance as they can comfortably verify systems generating 10^{15} states and beyond [20, 29, 36]. While these are large models, complex MAS inevitably produce state-spaces that are considerably larger when not infinite. To overcome this difficulty abstraction techniques have been put forward [18, 15, 14] with some success.

A considerable limitation of these approaches, however, is that they address the verification of *models* of the system and cannot be extended to the validation of actual *MAS programs*. This hinders the automatic applicability of the methods as any MAS needs first to be modelled before verification can take place. Techniques targeting the verification of MAS code directly have been developed [47, 8, 5, 6]. However, their actual applicability has proven to be very limited as scalability issues have severely affected their effectiveness beyond small scenarios. They have also typically supported only temporal specifications; any agent informational attitude (e.g., beliefs, knowledge, etc.) has so far been treated as a mere predicate and therefore nested statements cannot be expressed.

Verifying code correctness is undecidable in general. One of the leading techniques used in formal verification is predicate abstraction [21]. Predicate abstraction involves automatically generating Boolean predicates in key sections of the code, typically by means of SMT calls [32], which can be used to produce abstract models that under-approximate and over-approximate the concrete models of the actual executions. To reason about specifications on over- and under-approximations temporal specifications are interpreted on three or four truth values. Abstract models can be refined (abstract states can be expanded into finer approximations) if the truth value of a specification is not assessed to true or false by the approximation considered.

In this paper we intend to lay the theoretical foundations to develop a predicate abstraction technique for MAS specified by the strategic-epistemic logic ATLK. This includes epistemic specifications including common knowledge [19] and strategy constructs to represent what coalitions of agents may bring about in the system [2]. As we target the effective verification of MAS, efficiency is a key desideratum in our set-up. For this reason we operate in a setting where ATL operators are interpreted on non-uniform models [37]. This enables us to obtain a PTIME verification procedure albeit at a cost of a non-standard interpretation of the ATL operators. In scenarios where the reading of these operators is not suitable, we can simply use them to encode plain temporal-epistemic specifications by means of the logic CTLK, the combination of branching time logic CTL with epistemic logic [40], which is strictly subsumed by ATLK.

Scheme of the paper. In Section 2 we present and discuss the syntax and semantics for the novel three-valued

Appears in: *Proceedings of the 14th International Conference on Autonomous Agents and Multiagent Systems (AAMAS 2015), Bordini, Elkind, Weiss, Yolum (eds.), May, 4–8, 2015, Istanbul, Turkey.*

epistemic logic we develop and present an example. In Section 3 we define and give a procedure for the model checking problem in the three-valued setting we investigate. In Section 4 we introduce abstract models to approximate the concrete models and study preservation results in the semantics and between models. In Section 5 we introduce a constructive methodology for producing an initial abstraction and refine the model in case the verification is non-conclusive; we give an example to illustrate the technique in Section 6. We conclude in Section 7 where we also discuss related work.

2. THE THREE-VALUED LOGIC ATLK

In this section we put forward our rationale for the choice of the specification language for MAS that we adopt in this paper. Following these considerations we introduce a novel three-valued logic for knowledge and exemplify its use.

2.1 Desiderata for the Specification Language

Differently from reactive systems whose specifications typically involve temporal properties only, MAS are specified in terms of their informational states, notably the knowledge of the agents in the system [19]. The logics most commonly used [38, 40, 43] combine epistemic modalities with temporal operators. The assumptions on the underlying temporal model range from discrete [38] to continuous [35], from linear [38] to branching [43], from state interpretations to intervals [33]. Irrespective of the different expressive power of the various temporal logics used, the rationale in a MAS setting for including a temporal dimension beside epistemic operators is clear: temporal logic provides a way for reasoning about a changing world and, in combination with epistemic concepts, it can be used to specify the evolution of the agents' knowledge.

The past 10 years have also witnessed a growing attention to the need of specifying strategic properties arising from the interaction within a MAS. The logic ATL [2], originally put forward to reason about the outcome of games, has been widely adopted in the MAS domain and extended to reason about what agents can enforce in an exchange [23, 27, 11]. Since ATL strictly subsumes the branching time temporal logic CTL, it has gradually replaced it in several model checking approaches to the verification of MAS [2, 23, 45, 30, 10]. Recent techniques have featured specification languages even stronger than ATL, including Strategy Logic [39, 25, 24, 12]. The computational complexity of the model checking problem against ATL varies greatly; it ranges from linear complexity in the size of the model to full undecidability, depending on the assumptions made on the observability of the global state and the agents' memory.

While studies on the expressivity and complexity of powerful specification languages make an important contribution to the area and guide us the in the tradeoff between expressivity and efficiency, in this line of research we intend to address the need for the *practical* verification of MAS. Towards this end, we need to base our choice of a specification language not only on expressivity but also, crucially, on considerations of optimal efficiency. Indeed, due to the difficulty of the state explosion problem [13], experimental results show that even a linear complexity upper-bound against the model causes severe difficulties even for state-of-the-art BDD-based model checkers for MAS.

From a computational complexity standpoint, the easiest set up for ATL is complete information, where we to assume that the strategies of the agents depend on the whole state and not on their own private state only. In MAS this is an unrealistic assumption as the agents have access to their local state only. Unfortunately, incomplete information is problematic; for example the model checking problem for incomplete information and perfect recall, i.e., considering local states as local histories, is undecidable [17]. A notable set-up studied in the literature consists in considering incomplete information with local memoryless *uniform strategies* [28, 27]. Here it is assumed that the agents have access to their own local states only, but their non-deterministic strategies are selected consistently along a path. While this seems an appealing framework, its model checking problem is Δ_P^2 complete against an explicit description of the model [26]. Other sophisticated proposals have been made, including richer operators for memory and forgetting [9], but none of these have a PTIME bound.

Given the reasons above we here choose to adopt a framework where the agents have incomplete information and do not admit perfect recall, the strategies are local and not uniform. This set up has already been adopted previously in a two valued setting and referred to as "non-uniform" strategies [45] . As we clarify below, the reading of the modalities in this context is different from the usual one in ATL and does not capture the concept of "strict enforcement" typical of stronger versions of ATL. Our choice to adopt this setting is due to the fact that it enjoys good expressivity while its model checking problem is linear in size of both the model and formula. We regard it as the most expressive combination between epistemic and strategy operators which still has a PTIME model checking problem. If the reading of the ATL modalities is not suitable to a particular scenario, we can use CTL which is strictly subsumed by the fragment we consider; indeed our technique can more simply be reformulated for the weaker logic CTLK.

Our intention is to lay the foundation for a predicate abstraction methodologies where abstractions and their refinements are computed during verification. To do this we adopt a three-valued semantics where formulas may be true, false, or undefined at a given state.

2.2 Syntax and Semantics

We put forward a three-valued version of the logic ATLK, ATLK^{3v} for short, combining ATL modalities with epistemic modalities in a three-valued setting. The agents are assumed to have incomplete information and their strategies are based on their local states. We do not assume perfect recall; these systems are often called "memoryless". While as described in Section 7 our set-up is different, we follow [34] for some of the basic definitions.

Let $Ag = \{1, \ldots, m\}$ be a set of agents and $\mathcal{V}$ be a set of propositional variables. We use the letter Γ to denote subsets of agents, e.g., $\Gamma \subseteq Ag$; by $\overline{\Gamma}$ we denote the complementation of Γ, i.e., $Ag \setminus \Gamma$. We use $\overline{\mathcal{V}}$ to denote the set of all the literals containing propositional variables from $\mathcal{V}$, i.e., $\overline{\mathcal{V}} = \{q, \neg q \mid q \in \mathcal{V}\}$. We begin by introducing the models we will be using in the rest of the paper.

DEFINITION 1 (INTERPRETED SYSTEMS). *An* interpreted system *is a tuple* $IS = (\{L_i, Act_i, P_i, t_i\}_{i \in Ag}, I, \Pi)$ *such that for each agent i:*

- L_i *is a set of possible* local states*;*

- Act_i *is a set of possible* local actions*;*
- $P_i : L_i \to 2^{Act_i} \setminus \{\emptyset\}$ *is a* local protocol*;*
- $t_i \subseteq L_i \times ACT \times 2^{L_i}$ *is a* local transition relation *with* $ACT = Act_1 \times \cdots \times Act_m$*;*
- $I \subseteq L_1 \times \cdots \times L_m$ *is a set of* global initial states*;*
- $\Pi : L_1 \times \cdots \times L_m \to 2^{\overline{\mathcal{V}}}$ *is a* labelling function *such that for any variable* q *and a state* $s = (l_1, \ldots, l_m)$ *we either have* $q \notin \Pi(s)$ *or* $\neg q \notin \Pi(s)$.

Observe that our definition of interpreted systems extends the standard one [19] by admitting that a propositional variable nor its negation may hold at a state. This will form the basis for giving a three-valued interpretation on interpreted systems.

For a tuple $t = (t_1, \ldots, t_m)$, by $t.i$ we denote its i-th element t_i, with $i \leq m$. We will use this notation to identify individual local states and local actions.

For convenience we define models which are defined on the set of global states reachable from I via T.

Definition 2 (Models). *Given an interpreted system* $IS = (\{L_i, Act_i, P_i, t_i\}_{i\in Ag}, I, \Pi)$*, its* associated model *is a tuple* $M_{IS} = (S,\ T,\ \{\sim_i\}_{i\in Ag},\ I,\ \Pi)$ *such that:*

- $S \subseteq L_1 \times \cdots \times L_m$ *is the set of global states reachable via* T *from the set of initial global states* $I \subseteq S$,
- $T \subseteq S \times ACT \times S$ *is a global transition relation such that* $T((l_1, \ldots, l_m), a, (l'_1, \ldots, l'_m))$ *iff for all* $i \in Ag$ *we have* $t_i(l_i, a, l'_i)$ *and* $a.i \in P_i(l_i)$,
- $\sim_i \subseteq S^2$ *is such that* $s \sim_i s'$ *iff* $s.i = s'.i$*, for all* $i \in Ag$.

We omit IS in the subscript if it is clear from the context, i.e., we write M for M_{IS}. The intended meaning of $s \sim_i s'$ is that the global states s, s' are epistemically indistinguishable for the agent i [19]. We extend the notion to groups by defining, for each group Γ, the relation $\sim_\Gamma = (\bigcup_{i\in\Gamma} \sim_i)^+$, where $^+$ denotes the transitive closure operator. For convenience, we write $a \equiv_\Gamma a'$ iff for all $i \in \Gamma$ we have $a.i = a'.i$.

We only consider models such that for all global states $s \in S$ and joint actions $a \in ACT$ such that $a.i \in P_i(s.i)$ for all $i \in Ag$, there exists an $s' \in S$ such that $T(s, a, s')$.

We now introduce the common syntax for the logics ATLK and ATLK^{3v}.

Definition 3 (ATLK specifications). *The set of formulas for the logics ATLK and ATLK* ^{3v} *is defined from* $\mathcal{V}$ *by the following BNF expression:*
$\varphi ::= q \mid \neg\varphi \mid \varphi \wedge \varphi \mid \langle\langle\Gamma\rangle\rangle X\varphi \mid \langle\langle\Gamma\rangle\rangle(\varphi U \varphi) \mid \langle\langle\Gamma\rangle\rangle G\varphi \mid K_i\varphi \mid C_{\Gamma'}\varphi$
where $i \in Ag$, $\Gamma, \Gamma' \subseteq Ag$, $\Gamma' \neq \emptyset$ *and* $q \in \mathcal{V}$.

We use the standard abbreviations to define $\langle\langle\Gamma\rangle\rangle F\varphi, E_\Gamma\varphi$ and the Boolean connectives.

The formulas $K_i\varphi, C_{\Gamma'}\varphi$ are read as "the agent i knows that φ" and "in the group Γ' it is commonly known that φ", respectively. Their reading is standard [19]. The formula $\langle\langle\Gamma\rangle\rangle G\varphi$ stands for "the agents in Γ *may be able* to ensure that φ holds forever"; the meaning of the "until" modality U is analogous. This reading is the one given in [45] for ATL on non-uniform models and differs from some of the literature on ATL which assumes a definition of strategies on global histories. While our notion of the ATL modalities does not generally represent enforcement, this is retained for the next state operator "X" which can be read as "the agents in Γ can ensure that φ holds at the next state irrespective of the actions of the agents in $Ag \setminus \Gamma$". For computational complexity considerations as well as our previously discussed need to ground strategies on local states, our requirements are considerably weaker as we explain below.

Assume an interpreted system $IS = (\{L_i, Act_i, P_i, t_i\}_{i\in Ag}, I, \Pi)$. A (*local memoryless*) *strategy* for an agent $i \in \Gamma$, or simply a strategy, is a function $f_i : s.i \to 2^{Act_i} \setminus \{\emptyset\}$ such that for each local state $s.i \in L_i$ we have $f_i(s) \subseteq P_i(s.i)$. Notice that we do not assume perfect recall, i.e., all the strategies depend on the current local state only.

Given a path $p = s_0 s_1 \ldots$, by p^i we denote s_i, the i-th element of p. Assume a set of agents Γ and an indexed set of strategies $F_\Gamma = \{f_i \mid i \in \Gamma\}$. We say that a set of (infinite) paths X is F_Γ*-compatible* if it is a minimal non-empty set of paths such that for each path $p \in X$ and each position $j \geq 0$ there is a joint action a such that $T(p^j, a, p^{j+1})$, for all $i \in \Gamma$, $a.i \in f_i(s_j.i)$, and for all joint actions $a' \equiv_\Gamma a$ and all states s' such that $T(p^j, a', s')$, there exists a path $p' \in X$ starting with $p^0 \ldots p^j s'$. Let $out(s, F_\Gamma)$ be the family of all F_Γ-compatible sets of paths starting with s.

We do not assume uniformity [45, 41] in the definition of paths. In other words we do not require that the action choice of any agent $i \in \Gamma$ in a path is always the same, as long as it conforms to the strategy function f_i, hence to agent i's protocol P_i.

Two-valued semantics.

Having fixed the above we can now provide the definition for two-valued satisfaction.

Definition 4 (Two-valued Satisfaction). *Assume an interpreted system* $IS = (\{L_i, Act_i, P_i, t_i\}_{i\in Ag}, I, \Pi)$*, its associated model* $M = (S,\ T,\ \{\sim_i\}_{i\in Ag},\ I,\ \Pi)$ *and a global state* $s \in S$*. We inductively define the two-valued satisfaction relation* $\models^2$ *as follows.*

$M, s \models^2 q$	*iff* $q \in \Pi(s)$
$M, s \models^2 \neg\varphi$	*iff* $M, s \not\models^2 \varphi$
$M, s \models^2 \varphi_1 \wedge \varphi_2$	*iff* $M, s \models^2 \varphi_1$ *and* $M, s \models^2 \varphi_2$
$M, s \models^2 \langle\langle\Gamma\rangle\rangle X\varphi$	*iff for some strategy* F_Γ*, some* $X \in out(s, F_\Gamma)$ *and all* $p \in X$ *we have* $M, p^1 \models^2 \varphi$
$M, s \models^2 \langle\langle\Gamma\rangle\rangle \varphi_1 U \varphi_2$	*iff for some strategy* F_Γ*, some* $X \in out(s, F_\Gamma)$ *and all* $p \in X$*, there is a* $k \geq 0$ *s.t. we have* $M, p^k \models^2 \varphi_2$ *and for all* $0 \leq j < k$, $M, p^j \models^2 \varphi_1$
$M, s \models^2 \langle\langle\Gamma\rangle\rangle G\varphi$	*iff for some strategy* F_Γ*, some* $X \in out(s, F_\Gamma)$ *and all* $p \in X$, $i \geq 0$ *we have* $M, p^i \models^2 \varphi$
$M, s \models^2 K_i\varphi$	*iff for all* $s' \sim_i s$ *we have* $M, s' \models^2 \varphi$
$M, s \models^2 C_\Gamma\varphi$	*iff for all* $s' \sim_\Gamma s$ *we have* $M, s' \models^2 \varphi$

An interpreted system IS satisfies a property φ, written as $IS \models^2 \varphi$, iff for all the initial states s we have $M, s \models^2 \varphi$.

Three-valued semantics.

We now introduce the logic ATLK^{3v}. In ATLK^{3v}, a formula at a given state of an interpreted system can be true (tt), false (ff) or undefined (uu).

Assume an interpreted system $IS = (\{L_i, Act_i, P_i, t_i\}_{i \in Ag}, I, \Pi)$, its associated model $M = (S, T, \{\sim_i\}_{i \in Ag}, I, \Pi)$ and a global state $s \in S$. The inductive definition of the three-valued satisfaction $\models^3$ is given below.

We assume the Kleene semantics for the standard boolean connectivities.

$$M, s \models^3 q = \begin{cases} \text{tt iff } q \in \Pi(s), \\ \text{ff iff } \neg q \in \Pi(s), \\ \text{uu otherwise} \end{cases}$$

$$M, s \models^3 \neg\varphi = \begin{cases} \text{tt iff } M, s \models^3 \varphi = \text{ff} \\ \text{ff iff } M, s \models^3 \varphi = \text{tt} \\ \text{uu otherwise} \end{cases}$$

$$M, s \models^3 \varphi_1 \wedge \varphi_2 = \begin{cases} \text{tt iff } M, s \models^3 \varphi_i = \text{tt for all } i \in \{1,2\} \\ \text{ff iff } M, s \models^3 \varphi_i = \text{ff for any } i \in \{1,2\} \\ \text{uu otherwise} \end{cases}$$

For the ATL modalities, we adjust the semantics of [34].

$$M, s \models^3 \langle\langle\Gamma\rangle\rangle X\varphi = \begin{cases} \text{tt iff for some strategy } F_\Gamma, \text{ some } X \in out(s, F_\Gamma) \text{ and all } p \in X, \text{ we have } M, p^1 \models^3 \varphi = \text{tt} \\ \text{ff iff for some strategy } F_{\overline{\Gamma}}, \text{ all } X \in out(s, F_{\overline{\Gamma}}) \text{ and all } p \in X \text{ we have } M, p^1 \models^3 \varphi = \text{ff} \\ \text{uu otherwise} \end{cases}$$

$$M, s \models^3 \langle\langle\Gamma\rangle\rangle \varphi_1 U \varphi_2 = \begin{cases} \text{tt iff for some strategy } F_\Gamma, \text{ some } X \in out(s, F_\Gamma) \text{ and all } p \in X \text{ there is } k \geq 0 \text{ s.t. } M, p^k \models^3 \varphi_2 = \text{tt and for all } j < k, M, p^j \models^3 \varphi_1 = \text{tt} \\ \text{ff iff for some strategy } F_{\overline{\Gamma}}, \text{ all } X \in out(s, F_{\overline{\Gamma}}) \text{ and all } p \in X, k \geq 0 \text{ we have } M, p^k \models^3 \varphi_2 = \text{ff or there is } j < k \text{ s.t. } M, p^j \models^3 \varphi_1 = \text{ff} \\ \text{uu otherwise} \end{cases}$$

$$M, s \models^3 \langle\langle\Gamma\rangle\rangle G\varphi = \begin{cases} \text{tt iff for some strategy } F_\Gamma, \text{ some } X \in out(s, F_\Gamma) \text{ and all } p \in X, i \geq 0 \text{ we have } M, p^i \models^3 \varphi = \text{tt} \\ \text{ff iff for some strategy } F_{\overline{\Gamma}}, \text{ all } X \in out(s, F_{\overline{\Gamma}}) \text{ and all } p \in X \text{ there is } i \geq 0 \text{ s.t. } M, p^i \models^3 \varphi = \text{ff} \\ \text{uu otherwise} \end{cases}$$

Notice that in the cases above the requirements for tt are very similar to the conditions in the two-valued semantics. An ATL formula is ff if the complement of the agents in the modality may be able to ensure the formula is ff.

For the knowledge modalities, we propose the following.

$$M, s \models^3 K_i\varphi = \begin{cases} \text{tt iff } M, s' \models^3 \varphi = \text{tt for all } s' \sim_i s \\ \text{ff iff } M, s \models^3 \varphi = \text{ff} \\ \text{uu otherwise} \end{cases}$$

$$M, s \models^3 C_\Gamma\varphi = \begin{cases} \text{tt iff } M, s' \models^3 \varphi = \text{tt for all } s' \sim_\Gamma s \\ \text{ff iff } M, s \models^3 \varphi = \text{ff} \\ \text{uu otherwise} \end{cases}$$

As above, note that the condition for tt is similar to the one for the two-valued case. However, an epistemic formula is ff if the nested formula's valuation at the present state is ff. A weaker alternative, compatible with the two-valued semantics, is to assign $M, s \models^3 K_i\varphi = \text{ff}$ iff there is a state $s' \sim_i s$ such that $M, s' \models^3 \varphi = \text{ff}$. Such definition, however, would not enable us to ensure the transfer of the value ff from the abstract to concrete model (Theorem 11 below), an essential part of our abstraction technique.

We assign $IS \models^3 \varphi = \text{tt}$ iff for all $s \in I$ we have $M, s \models^3 \varphi = \text{tt}$, $IS \models^3 \varphi = \text{ff}$ iff there is $s \in I$ such that $M, s \models^3 \varphi = \text{ff}$, and $IS \models^3 \varphi = \text{uu}$ otherwise.

We now exemplify the above definitions.

EXAMPLE 1. *Let $Ag = \{1, 2\}$. Consider the interpreted system $IS = (\{L_i, Act_i, P_i, t_i\}_{i \in Ag}, I, \Pi)$ such that*

- $L_1 = \{l_=, l_{\neq}\}$, $L_2 = \{\epsilon\}$,
- $P_1(l_=) = P_1(l_{\neq}) = P_2(\epsilon) = Act_1 = Act_2 = \{a_1, a_2\}$,
- $t_1 = \{(l, (a_i, a_j), l_=) \mid l \in L_1 \wedge i = j\} \cup \{(l, (a_i, a_j), l_{\neq}) \mid l \in L_1 \wedge i \neq j\}$, $t_2 = \{(\epsilon, (a_i, a_j), \epsilon) \mid i, j \in \{1, 2\}\}$,
- $I = \{(l_=, \epsilon)\}$, $\Pi((l_=, \epsilon)) = \{q\}$ *and* $\Pi((l_{\neq}, \epsilon)) = \{\neg q\}$.

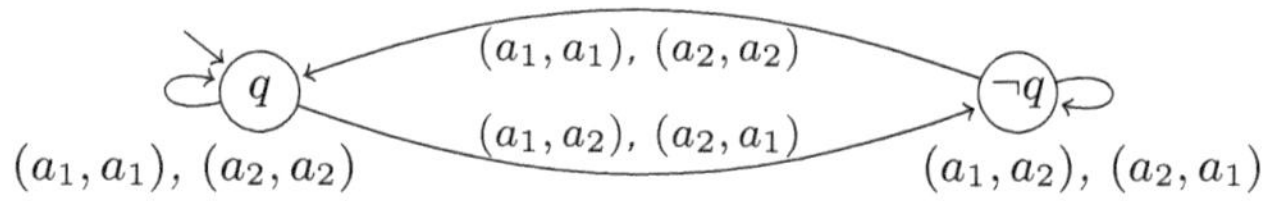

Consider the formula $\langle\langle 1\rangle\rangle Xq$ and the initial state $(l_=, \epsilon)$ indicated in the figure by the incoming arrow. It can be checked that agent 1 cannot enforce q in the next state as agent 2 can use a different action from that of agent 1. Therefore we have $IS \not\models^2 \langle\langle 1\rangle\rangle Xq$ and not $IS \models^3 \langle\langle 1\rangle\rangle Xq =$ tt. Similarly, regardless on the choice of the agent 2, if the agent 1 selects the same action at the initial state, then the next state is $(l_=, \epsilon)$. So it is not the case that $IS \models^3 \langle\langle 1\rangle\rangle Xq =$ ff, and therefore $IS \models^3 \langle\langle 1\rangle\rangle Xq =$ uu.

We have $IS \not\models^2 \langle\langle 1\rangle\rangle Xq$; so it is not the case that agent 1 may ensure q at the next state. We also have $IS \models^3 \langle\langle 1\rangle\rangle Xq =$ ff; so it is not the case that agent 2 has a strategy to avoid q.

Consider the formula K_2q at the initial state. Since both states of the model are indistinguishable for agent 2, we have $IS \not\models^2 K_2q$ and not $IS \models^3 K_2q =$ tt. However, since the initial state $(l_=, \epsilon)$ satisfies q, it is not the case that $IS \models^3 K_2q =$ ff; therefore we have $IS \models^3 K_2q =$ uu.

Note that in the setting we consider the strategies in both two-valued semantics and three-valued semantics can be replaced by agents' protocols.

3. CHECKING MAS AGAINST ATLK^{3V}

We give a definition of the model checking problem against ATLK^{3v} specifications and present a polynomial time algorithm to solve it. We phrase this as a decision procedure.

DEFINITION 5 (MODEL CHECKING PROBLEM). *Given an interpreted system IS, an ATLK specification φ and $b \in \{\text{tt}, \text{ff}, \text{uu}\}$, the* three-valued model checking problem *involves establishing whether $IS \models^3 \varphi = b$.*

We put forward Algorithm 1 to compute the truth value of a formula φ given a state s in an interpreted system IS. Propositional variables are labelled immediately with true

Algorithm 1 The model checking procedure for verifying an IS against ATLK^{3v} specifications.

procedure VERIFY(IS, φ)
  $(S_{tt}, S_{ff}) \leftarrow$ LABEL(IS, φ)
  if $\forall s \in I.s \in S_{tt}$ **then return** tt
  if $\exists s \in I.s \in S_{ff}$ **then return** ff
  return uu
procedure LABEL(IS, φ)
  if $\varphi = q$ **then**
    $S_{tt} \leftarrow \{s \mid q \in \Pi(s)\}$, $S_{ff} \leftarrow \{s \mid \neg q \in \Pi(s)\}$
  else if $\varphi = \varphi_1 \wedge \varphi_2$ **then**
    $(S^1_{tt}, S^1_{ff}) \leftarrow$ LABEL(IS, φ_1)
    $(S^2_{tt}, S^2_{ff}) \leftarrow$ LABEL(IS, φ_2)
    $S_{tt} \leftarrow S^1_{tt} \cap S^2_{tt}$, $S_{ff} \leftarrow S^1_{ff} \cup S^2_{ff}$
  else if $\varphi = \langle\langle\Gamma\rangle\rangle X\varphi'$ **then**
    $(S'_{tt}, S'_{ff}) \leftarrow$ LABEL(IS, φ')
    $S_{tt} \leftarrow$ PREIMAGE(IS, Γ, S'_{tt})
    $S_{ff} \leftarrow$ PREIMAGE($IS, \overline{\Gamma}, S'_{ff}$)
  else if $\varphi = \langle\langle\Gamma\rangle\rangle(\varphi_1 U \varphi_2)$ **then**
    $(S^1_{tt}, S^1_{ff}) \leftarrow$ LABEL(IS, φ_1)
    $(S_{tt}, S_{ff}) \leftarrow$ LABEL(IS, φ_2)
    repeat
      $S'_{tt} \leftarrow S_{tt}$
      $S_{tt} \leftarrow$ PREIMAGE(IS, Γ, S_{tt}) $\cap S^1_{tt}$
      $S_{tt} \leftarrow S_{tt} \cup S'_{tt}$
    until $S_{tt} = S'_{tt}$
    repeat
      $S'_{ff} \leftarrow S_{ff}$
      $S_{ff} \leftarrow$ PREIMAGE(IS, Γ, S_{ff}) $\cup S^1_{ff}$
      $S_{ff} \leftarrow S_{ff} \cap S'_{ff}$
    until $S_{ff} = S'_{ff}$
  else if $\varphi = \langle\langle\Gamma\rangle\rangle G\varphi'$ **then**
    $(S_{tt}, S_{ff}) \leftarrow$ LABEL(IS, φ')
    repeat
      $S'_{tt} \leftarrow S_{tt}$
      $S_{tt} \leftarrow$ PREIMAGE(IS, Γ, S_{tt}) $\cap S_{tt}$
    until $S_{tt} = S'_{tt}$
    repeat
      $S'_{ff} \leftarrow S_{ff}$
      $S_{ff} \leftarrow$ PREIMAGE(IS, Γ, S_{ff}) $\cup S'_{ff}$
    until $S_{ff} = S'_{ff}$
  else if $\varphi = K_i\varphi'$ **then**
    $(S'_{tt}, S_{ff}) \leftarrow$ LABEL(IS, φ')
    $S_{tt} \leftarrow S \setminus \{s \mid \exists s'.s' \sim_i s \wedge s' \notin S'_{tt}\}$
  else if $\varphi = C_\Gamma\varphi'$ **then**
    $(S'_{tt}, S_{ff}) \leftarrow$ LABEL(IS, φ')
    $S_{tt} \leftarrow S \setminus \{s \mid \exists s'.s' \sim_\Gamma s \wedge s' \notin S'_{tt}\}$
  return (S_{tt}, S_{ff})

and false. From those and by means of pre-image computations states are labelled with true and false for the relevant ATL and epistemic modalities, whenever possible.

For brevity, Algorithm 1 assumes that we have the relation $\sim_\Gamma$ to compute C_Γ; this can be obtained by means of fixpoint computation. The procedure PREIMAGE(IS, Γ, S') used in Algorithm 1 returns a set S_X of states from which Γ can *enforce* S' in one step. Formally, $s \in S_X$ iff there is a joint action $a \in ACT$ and a state s' such that $T(s, a, s')$ and for all $a' \equiv_\Gamma a$ and for all s'' if $T(s, a', s'')$, then $s'' \in S'$.

The algorithm can be shown to be correct.

THEOREM 6. *Consider an interpreted system IS, a state s, an ATLK specification φ and $(S_{tt}, S_{ff}) =$ VERIFY(IS, φ). We have that $IS, s \models^3 \varphi =$ tt iff $s \in S_{tt}$ and $IS, s \models^3 \varphi =$ ff iff $s \in S_{ff}$.*

PROOF. The proof is by induction on φ. The basic case and the Boolean cases are immediate. We prove the case for $\varphi = \langle\langle\Gamma\rangle\rangle X\varphi$; the others can be shown similarly.

Assume $\varphi = \langle\langle\Gamma\rangle\rangle X\varphi$ and let $(S_{tt}, S_{ff}) =$ VERIFY(IS, φ). For each state $s \in S_{tt}$ there is $a \in ACT$ and a state $s' \in S$ s.t. $T(s, a, s')$ and for all $a' \equiv_\Gamma a$ and all s'' s. t. $T(s, a', s'')$, we have $IS, s'' \models^3 \varphi =$ tt by the inductive hypothesis. Consider any strategy $F_\Gamma = \{f_i \mid i \in \Gamma\}$ such that $a.i \in f_i(s)$ for all $i \in \Gamma$. There is a set $X \in out(s, F_\Gamma)$ s.t. $p \in X$ and all each path of X starts with ss'' for some s'' satisfying φ. Therefore $IS, s \models^3 \varphi =$ tt.

If $IS, s \models^3 \varphi =$ tt, then there is a strategy F_Γ and a F_Γ-compatible set $X \in out(s, F_\Gamma)$ such that for all $p \in X$ we have $IS, p^1 \models^3 \varphi =$ tt. As X is F_Γ-compatible, there is a joint action a such that $T(p, a, p^1)$ for some path $p \in X$, and for all joint actions $a' \equiv_\Gamma a$ and states s'' such that $T(s, a', s'')$ we have $IS, s'' \models^3 \varphi =$ tt. Therefore, by the inductive hypothesis, we have $s \in S_{tt}$. □

From the above it follows, correctly, that $IS, s \models^3 \varphi =$ uu if neither $s \in S_{tt}$ nor $s \in S_{ff}$. Note that all operations in Algorithm 1 are either basic set operations or existential preimage computations. It is known that these can be efficiently implemented on BDD-based symbolic model checking [13].

Algorithm 1 can also be used to provide an upper bound for the verification problem.

THEOREM 7. *Three-valued model checking interpreted systems with imperfect information and memoryless local strategies against ATLK specifications is decidable in* PTIME.

PROOF SKETCH. For each subformula φ' of φ, the function LABEL(IS, φ') is run only once in the algorithm. Each of the fixed-point computations in the algorithm terminates after at most $|S|$ steps. The function PREIMAGE(IS, Γ, S') can be computed in polynomial time simply by checking all the states. Therefore, the computing time is polynomial. □

The results in this section give a provably correct polynomial time algorithm for the verification of ATLK^{3v} formulas. Not only is the algorithm attractive from a computational point of view, but it is amenable to symbolic implementation for efficient verification. In the next section we take this one step further and define methodologies to reduce the explicit model to more compact models.

4. ABSTRACTIONS

While the procedure put forward in the previous section is linear in the size of the model, verifying MAS still suffers from the state-space explosion, i.e., the fact that the models grow exponentially in the number of variables and agents in the system. To deal with this we use an abstraction methodology to reduce the size of the models considered. As we show below, this reduction generates an abstract model which depends on the specific characteristics of the interpreted system considered and the specification being checked.

First we recall the definitions below from [34]. A function f is *decomposable* if for any $x_1, \ldots, x_m$ we have that $f((x_1, \ldots, x_m)) = (f.1(x_1), \ldots, f.m(x_m))$, for some functions $f.i$, $i = 1, \ldots, m$.

DEFINITION 8 (STATE ABSTRACTION). *Consider an interpreted system $IS = (\{L_i, Act_i, P_i, t_i\}_{i \in Ag}, I, \Pi)$. A state* abstraction function *is a surjective and decomposable function $\sigma : S \to S^\sigma$, such that for each agent i and any two local states $l, l' \in L_i$, if $\sigma.i(l) = \sigma.i(l')$, then $P_i(l) = P_i(l')$, for some set S^σ of* abstract global states.

Given a state abstraction function σ, the state abstraction *of IS w.r.t. σ is the interpreted system $IS^\sigma = (\{L_i^\sigma, Act_i^\sigma, P_i^\sigma, t_i^\sigma\}_{i \in Ag}, I^\sigma, \Pi^\sigma)$ such that $\Pi^\sigma(s^\sigma) = \bigcap_{s \in \sigma^{-1}(\{s^\sigma\})} \Pi(s)$, $I^\sigma = \sigma(I)$ and, for each agent i,*

- $L_i^\sigma = \sigma.i(L_i)$,
- $Act_i^\sigma = Act_i$,
- $P_i^\sigma(l^\sigma) = \bigcup_{l \in \sigma.i^{-1}(\{l^\sigma\})} P_i(l)$,
- $t_i^\sigma(l^\sigma, a, l'^\sigma)$ *iff for some l, l' such that $\sigma.i(l) = l^\sigma$ and $\sigma.i(l') = l'^\sigma$ we have $t_i(l, a, l')$.*

EXAMPLE 2. *Consider an interpreted system with states s_1 labelled by $\{q, r\}$ and s_2 labelled by $\{\neg q, r\}$ such that $\sigma(s_1) = \sigma(s_2) = s^\sigma$. Then, $r \in \Pi^\sigma(s^\sigma)$ as both s_1 and s_2 are labelled by r, but neither $q \in \Pi^\sigma(s^\sigma)$ not $\neg q \in \Pi^\sigma(s^\sigma)$. Therefore, $IS^\sigma, s^\sigma \models^3 r = \mathrm{tt}$ and $IS^\sigma, s^\sigma \models^3 q = \mathrm{uu}$.*

The application of a state abstraction function results in the reduction of the number of states in an interpreted system, thereby generating an abstract one. One important requirement of the state abstraction function is that it can only merge states with the same protocol. In many applications this may be a significant limitation. To alleviate the impact of this, we provide a further abstraction function, called action abstraction. The goal of the action abstraction function is to reduce the number of actions and therefore the number of possible protocols in the system.

DEFINITION 9 (ACTION ABSTRACTION). *Consider an interpreted system $IS = (\{L_i, Act_i, P_i, t_i\}_{i \in Ag}, I, \Pi)$. An* action abstraction function *is a surjective and decomposable function $\alpha : ACT \to ACT^\alpha$, for some set ACT^α of* abstract joint actions.

Given an action abstraction function α, the action abstraction *of IS w.r.t. α is an interpreted system $IS^\alpha = (\{L_i^\alpha, Act_i^\alpha, P_i^\alpha, t_i^\alpha\}_{i \in Ag}, I^\alpha, \Pi^\alpha)$ such that $I^\alpha = I$, $\Pi^\alpha = \Pi$, and, for each agent i, all $l, l' \in L_i$ and all $a^\alpha \in ACT^\alpha$, we have $L_i^\alpha = L_i$, $Act_i^\alpha = \alpha.i(Act_i)$, $P_i^\alpha(l) = \alpha.i(P_i(l))$ and $t_i^\alpha(l, a^\alpha, l')$ iff there is $a \in ACT$ s.t. $\alpha.i(a) = a^\alpha$ and $t_i(l, a, l')$.*

In other words the application of an action abstraction function results in the reduction of the number of actions in an interpreted system, thereby generating an abstract one. A *full abstraction* is obtained by combining the action abstraction with the state abstraction.

DEFINITION 10 (ABSTRACTIONS). *Consider an interpreted system $IS = (\{L_i, Act_i, P_i, t_i\}_{i \in Ag}, I, \Pi)$. An* abstraction function *is a pair $\delta = (\alpha, \sigma)$, where α is an action abstraction function of IS and σ is an state abstraction function of IS^α.*

Given an abstraction function $\delta = (\alpha, \sigma)$, the abstraction *of IS w.r.t. δ is the interpreted system IS^δ, i.e., the state abstraction of IS^α w.r.t. σ.*

We can show that the truth values tt and ff are preserved from abstract model to concrete model if the abstract model is obtained from the concrete model by using the abstraction function above.

THEOREM 11. *Let $\delta = (\alpha, \sigma)$ be an abstraction function for an interpreted system IS . Then, for any state $s \in S$*

1. *If $M_{IS}^\delta, \sigma(s) \models^3 \varphi = \mathrm{tt}$, then $M_{IS}, s \models^3 \varphi = \mathrm{tt}$.*
2. *If $M_{IS}^\delta, \sigma(s) \models^3 \varphi = \mathrm{ff}$, then $M_{IS}, s \models^3 \varphi = \mathrm{ff}$.*

PROOF SKETCH. The proof is by induction on φ. We only present the key cases here; the others can be shown similarly.

Case of $\varphi = q$. If $M_{IS}^\delta, \sigma(s) \models^3 q = \mathrm{tt}$, then $q \in \Pi^\delta(s)$. By definition $q \in \bigcap_{s' \in \sigma^{-1}(\sigma(s))} \Pi^\alpha(\sigma(s'))$, and so $q \in \Pi^\alpha(s)$. Since $\Pi^\alpha = \Pi$, $q \in \Pi(s)$, we conclude that $M_{IS}, s \models^3 q = \mathrm{tt}$.

If $M_{IS}^\delta, \sigma(s) \models^3 q = \mathrm{ff}$, then $\neg q \in \Pi^\delta(s)$. By similar considerations we can conclude that $\neg q \in \bigcap_{s' \in \sigma^{-1}(s)} \Pi^\alpha(s')$, so $\neg q \in \Pi^\alpha(s) = \Pi(s)$ and $M_{IS}, s \models^3 q = \mathrm{ff}$.

Case of $\varphi = \neg\varphi'$. If $M_{IS}^\delta, \sigma(s) \models^3 \neg\varphi' = \mathrm{tt}$, then $M_{IS}^\delta, \sigma(s) \models^3 \varphi' = \mathrm{ff}$. By the inductive assumption $M_{IS}, s \models^3 \varphi' = \mathrm{ff}$, and therefore $M_{IS}, s \models^3 \neg\varphi' = \mathrm{tt}$. Similarly, if $M_{IS}^\delta, \sigma(s) \models^3 \neg\varphi' = \mathrm{ff}$, then $M_{IS}, s \models^3 \neg\varphi' = \mathrm{ff}$.

Case of $\varphi = \langle\langle\Gamma\rangle\rangle\varphi_1 U \varphi_2$. Assume that $M_{IS}^\delta, \sigma(s) \models^3 \langle\langle\Gamma\rangle\rangle \varphi_1 U \varphi_2 = \mathrm{tt}$ and let $F_\Gamma^\delta = \{f_i^\delta \mid i \in \Gamma\}$ be a strategy such that for some $X \in out(\sigma(s), F_\Gamma^\delta)$ and for all $p^\delta \in X$, there is $k \geq 0$ s.t. $M_{IS}^\delta, p^k \models^3 \varphi_2 = \mathrm{tt}$ and for all $0 \leq j < k$ we have $M_{IS}^\delta, p^j \models^3 \varphi_1 = \mathrm{tt}$.

Let $F_\Gamma = \{f_i \mid i \in \Gamma\}$ where $f_i(l) = \alpha^{-1}(\sigma.i^{-1}(f_i^\delta(\sigma.i(l))))$ (notice that α^{-1} and $\sigma.i^{-1}$ are the counter-images). One can show using the inductive hypothesis that there exists $X \in out(s, F_\Gamma)$ such that for all $p \in X$ there is $k \geq 0$ s.t. $M_{IS}, p^k \models^3 \varphi_2 = \mathrm{tt}$ and for all $0 \leq j < k$, $M_{IS}, p^j \models^3 \varphi_1 = \mathrm{tt}$. It follows that $M_{IS}, s \models^3 \langle\langle\Gamma\rangle\rangle\varphi_1 U \varphi_2 = \mathrm{tt}$.

Case of $\varphi = K_i\varphi'$. Assume that $M_{IS}^\delta, \sigma(s) \models^3 K_i\varphi' = \mathrm{tt}$. Observe that if $s_1 \sim_i s_2$, then $\sigma(s_1) \sim_i \sigma(s_2)$. Since for all $s^\gamma \sim_i \sigma(s)$ we have that $M_{IS}^\delta, s^\gamma \models^3 \varphi' = \mathrm{tt}$, then clearly for all $s' \sim_i s$ we have $M_{IS}, s' \models^3 \varphi' = \mathrm{tt}$, and therefore $M_{IS}, s \models^3 K_i\varphi' = \mathrm{tt}$.

If $M_{IS}^\delta, \sigma(s) \models^3 K_i\varphi' = \mathrm{ff}$, then $M_{IS}^\delta, \sigma(s) \models^3 \varphi' = \mathrm{ff}$, so $M_{IS}, s \models^3 \varphi' = \mathrm{ff}$ and thus $M_{IS}, s \models^3 K_i\varphi' = \mathrm{ff}$. □

In this section we have shown that constructions previously put forward in [34] for reasoning about ATL specifications with local strategies can be adapted to our present setting where epistemic modalities are also present and strategies are interpreted uniformly on the model.

5. MODEL CHECKING MAS VIA ABSTRACTION REFINEMENT

While in the previous section we presented the underlying principles of three-valued abstraction on interpreted systems, here we give a constructive methodology for generating and refining the abstract models from the concrete model. Our proposed algorithm for checking whether an interpreted system IS satisfies a specification φ is given by Algorithm 2.

The procedure VERIFY-ABS first constructs an initial abstraction and performs a finite number of refinement steps until one of two conditions holds: either no further refinement can be performed (the refinement function returns the identity) and the specification φ is undefined on the abstract model, or φ is calculated to be either ff or tt. Observe that

Algorithm 2 The verification procedure.

procedure VERIFY-ABS(IS, φ)
  $\delta \leftarrow \delta^I_{IS}(\varphi)$, $result \leftarrow$ uu
  while $\delta \neq (id, id)$ and $result =$ uu **do**
    $result \leftarrow$VERIFY(IS^δ, φ)
    $\delta \leftarrow$REFINE(IS, δ, φ)
  return $result$

the procedure VERIFY-ABS uses VERIFY which operates on the three valued semantics.

THEOREM 12 (CORRECTNESS). *Let IS be an interpreted system and φ be an ATLK specification. If* VERIFY-ABS(IS, φ) $=$ tt, *then $IS \models \varphi$; if* VERIFY-ABS(IS, φ) $=$ ff, *then $IS \not\models \varphi$.*

PROOF SKETCH. Observe from the constructions given below that all refinements are abstractions as per Definition 10; REFINE can only be invoked a finite number of times (see below). The results therefore follow by Theorem 11 and Theorem 6 by observing that if $M_{IS}, s \models^3 \varphi =$ tt, then $M_{IS}, s \models^2 \varphi$ and If $M_{IS}, s \models^3 \varphi =$ ff, then $M_{IS}, s \not\models^2 \varphi$. These two facts can be checked by induction on φ. □

We now constructively define the initial abstraction $\delta^I_{IS}(\varphi)$ and the procedure REFINE used above.

Assume an interpreted system $IS = (\{L_i, Act_i, P_i, t_i\}_{i \in Ag}, I, \Pi)$. Let α^Γ_{IS} be the action abstraction function α for IS that unifies actions of all the agents not in Γ, e.g., for every agent $i \in \Gamma$ we define $\alpha^\Gamma_{IS}.i(a_i) = a_i$, and for every $i \notin \Gamma$ we let $\alpha^\Gamma_{IS}.i(a_i) = \epsilon$. Consider an action abstraction function α and a set of literals V. Let $\sigma^{\alpha,V}_{IS}$ denote the state abstraction function σ for IS^α that unifies all the possible states that agree on the labelling by variables in V, i.e., for each agent $i \in Ag$, $\sigma^{\alpha,V}_{IS}.i(l) = \sigma^{\alpha,V}_{IS}.i(l')$ iff $P^\alpha_i(l) = P^\alpha_i(l')$ and $\Pi(l) \cap V = \Pi(l') \cap V$, where $\Pi(l) = \bigcap_{s \in S, s.i = l} \Pi(s)$. Finally, define $A(\varphi)$ as the set of agents in φ and $\mathcal{V}(\varphi)$ as the set of propositional variables in φ.

DEFINITION 13 (INITIAL ABSTRACTION). *Let IS be an interpreted system, φ be an ATLK specification. The* initial abstraction function *for IS is the pair $\delta^I_{IS}(\varphi) = (\alpha^I_{IS}, \gamma^I_{IS})$, where $\alpha^I_{IS} = \alpha^{A(\varphi)}_{IS}$ and $\gamma^I_{IS} = \sigma^{\alpha^I_{IS}, \mathcal{V}(\varphi)}_{IS}$. The* initial abstraction *of IS is the abstraction of IS w.r.t. $\delta^I_{IS}(\varphi)$.*

So the initial abstraction function groups together all the actions of the agents not referred to in the specification φ; all states with the same labelling and the same protocol are then further collapsed. Clearly any initial abstraction is an abstraction as in Definition 10; so Theorem 11 applies.

We conclude by presenting Algorithm 3 giving the refinement procedure REFINE which takes as input an interpreted system IS, an abstraction function δ, a specification φ and returns an abstraction function δ'. Intuitively if $IS^{\delta^I_{IS}(\varphi)} \models^3 \varphi =$ uu, then δ' refines δ by separating the states for which the value of some subformula is uu.

In the procedure the set $Sub(\varphi)$ stands for the set of all the subformulas of φ (including φ itself) and $\preceq$ is any linear order on $Sub(\varphi)$ such that if ψ is a subformula of ψ', then $\psi \preceq \psi'$. Let the set $\text{uu}^{IS}(\delta, \varphi)$ be the set of subformulas of φ that in at some abstract state of IS^δ corresponding to at least two concrete states have the unknown value.

As shown, REFINE computes the set $\Phi^{IS}((\alpha, \sigma), \varphi)$. If this is not empty, the smallest element ψ is considered and all

Algorithm 3 The refinement procedure.

procedure REFINE(IS, $\delta = (\alpha, \sigma)$, φ)
  if $\Phi^{IS}((\alpha, \sigma), \varphi) \neq \emptyset$ **then**
    $\alpha' \leftarrow \alpha$
    $\Phi_{uu} = min_{\preceq}(\text{uu}^{IS}((\alpha, \sigma), \varphi))$
    $(S_{\text{tt}}, S_{\text{ff}}) =$ LABEL(IS^σ, Φ_{uu})
    $S_{\text{uu}} \leftarrow \{s \in S \mid \sigma(s) \notin S_{\text{tt}} \cup S_{\text{ff}}\}$
    for $i \in Ag, l_i \in L_i$ **do**
      if $\exists s \in S_{\text{uu}}\ s.i = l_i$ **then**
        if $\exists s, s' \in S_{\text{uu}}.\exists i \in Ag.\sigma.i(s.i) = \sigma.i(s'.i)$ $\wedge\ \Pi(s.i) = \Pi(s'.i)$ **then**
          $\sigma'.i(l_i) \leftarrow (\sigma.i(l_i), \Pi(l_i))$
        else $\sigma'.i(l_i) \leftarrow l_i$
      else $\sigma'.i(l_i) \leftarrow \sigma.i(l_i)$
  else if $\alpha \neq id$ **then**
    $\alpha' \leftarrow id$, $\sigma' \leftarrow \sigma^{\alpha', \overline{\mathcal{V}(\varphi)}}_{IS}$
  else $\alpha' \leftarrow id$, $\sigma' \leftarrow id$
  return (α', σ')

the abstract states s^δ in which the value of ψ is uu are split. When this operation can no longer be performed the action abstraction function is refined. Since all sets considered are finite, the procedure terminates.

6. THE BIT TRANSMISSION PROTOCOL

In this section we consider a variation of the bit transmission protocol and show how the technique put forward so far can be used to verify it. We assume the system to be composed of three agents: a sender **S**, whose goal is to send 32 bits to a recipient **R**, who receives the bits and once all of these have been copied sends an acknowledgement to the sender; and the communication channel **CC** that controls whether messages are dropped. We refer to its original formulation and analysis for more details [19, 42].

We model the protocol as an interpreted system IS as follows. We take the communication channel agent as modelled by a single state ($L_{\mathbf{CC}} = \{\epsilon\}$) and four allowed actions, $Act_{\mathbf{CC}} = P_{\mathbf{CC}}(\epsilon) = \{-, \leftarrow, \rightarrow, \leftrightarrow\}$ intuitively corresponding to the direction in which communication is performed. The local transition function is defined as standard $t_{\mathbf{SS}}(\epsilon, \text{a}, \epsilon)$ for all the joint actions a.

The sender **S** is modelled through 2^{32} *regular* local states, one for each possible message to be sent, and two *special* states: $\perp$ denoting an internal problem and ✓ representing a state when the message was delivered. The actions of **S** are of the form $\text{b}^\text{v}_\text{i}$, where $i \in \{0, \ldots, 31\}$ and $v \in \{0, 1\}$. An action $\text{b}^\text{v}_\text{i}$ corresponds to sending the information that "the value of i-th bit is v". Formally, we consider the local states $L_{\mathbf{S}} = \{0, 1\}^{32} \cup \{\perp, \checkmark\}$, the local actions $Act_{\mathbf{S}} = \{\text{b}^\text{v}_\text{i} \mid i \in \{0, \ldots, 31\} \wedge v \in \{0, 1\}\}$, a fully non-deterministic protocol $P_{\mathbf{S}}(s) = Act_{\mathbf{S}}$ for all states S of the model, and a local transition function $t_{\mathbf{S}}(s, (\text{a}_{\mathbf{S}}, \text{a}_{\mathbf{CC}}, \text{a}_{\mathbf{R}}), s')$ iff

- $s = s'$ and $s \in \{\perp, \checkmark\}$, or
- $\text{a}_{\mathbf{CC}} \in \{\rightarrow, \leftrightarrow\}$, $\text{a}_{\mathbf{R}} = \text{ack}$, $s' = \checkmark$, or
- $s = b_0 b_1 \ldots b_{31}$, $\text{a}_{\mathbf{S}} = b^v_i$, $v = b_i$, $s' = s$, and either $\text{a}_{\mathbf{CC}} \notin \{\rightarrow, \leftrightarrow\}$ or $\text{a}_{\mathbf{R}} \neq \text{ack}$, or
- $s = b_0 b_1 \ldots b_{31}$, $\text{a}_{\mathbf{S}} = b^v_i$, $v \neq b_i$, $s' = \perp$.

The receiver **R** is modelled by considering 3^{32} states, $L_{\mathbf{R}} = \{0,1,?\}^{32}$, and two actions, $Act_{\mathbf{R}} = \{\epsilon, \text{ack}\}$. The protocol function is such that $P_{\mathbf{R}}(s) = \{\text{ack}\}$ if $s \in \{0,1\}^{32}$ and $P_{\mathbf{R}}(s) = \{\epsilon\}$ otherwise. The transitions are given by $t_{\mathbf{R}}(b_0 b_1 \dots b_{31}, (\mathrm{b}_i^v, \mathrm{a}_{\mathbf{CC}}, \mathrm{a}_{\mathbf{R}}), b'_0 b'_1 \dots b'_{31})$ iff

- $\mathrm{a}_{\mathbf{CC}} \in \{\rightarrow, \leftrightarrow\}$, $b'_i = v$ and for all $j \neq i$, $b'_j = b_j$, or
- $\mathrm{a}_{\mathbf{CC}} \notin \{\rightarrow, \leftrightarrow\}$ and for all j, $b'_j = b_j$.

The set of global initial states is given by $I = \{0,1\}^{32} \times \{\epsilon\} \times \{?^{32}\}$, representing the fact that **S** starts with any message to be sent and **R** has not copied any bit yet.

We use the propositional variable $\mathcal{ACK}$ to label the states where the state of **R** is ✓, *fail* to mark the states where the state of **R** is $\bot$, $\mathcal{S}_i^v$ to denote the states of the form $(b_0 b_1 \dots b_{31}, \epsilon, l_{\mathbf{R}})$, where $b_i = v$, and $\mathcal{R}_i^v$ to indicate the states of the form $(l_{\mathbf{S}}, \epsilon, b_0 b_1 \dots b_{31})$ where $b_i = v$.

By considering the global transition function from the initial state, we can compute the set of reachable global states S for the model M associated to the interpreted system IS here described. The size of S can be estimated as $4^{32} \approx 10^{19}$. This is beyond what any modern symbolic model checker would normally be able to compute.

We can use the logic ATLK defined earlier to state specifications of the protocol. For instance we may be interested to check whether **S** and **CC** may be able to ensure that eventually **R** knows the value v of the i-th bit, for some $i \in \{0, \dots, 31\}$ and $v \in \{0,1\}$:

$$\Phi_1 = (\mathcal{S}_i^v \rightarrow \langle\!\langle\{\mathbf{S}, \mathbf{CC}\}\rangle\!\rangle F K_{\mathbf{R}} \mathcal{R}_i^v)$$

Intuitively we would expect Φ_1 to be satisfied. Naturally, **S** is not on his own able to ensure the delivery of the messages. Indeed, we would expect the specification

$$\Phi_2 = \langle\!\langle\{\mathbf{CC}\}\rangle\!\rangle G \neg \mathcal{ACK}$$

to be satisfied as without any fairness assumption **CC** could simply block all messages.

Lastly, we may want to check whether **S** and **CC** may be able to guarantee that the whole message is delivered:

$$\Phi_3 = \langle\!\langle\{\mathbf{S}, \mathbf{CC}\}\rangle\!\rangle F \mathcal{ACK}$$

We illustrate the use of the abstraction technique above on the interpreted system IS and the specifications Φ_1, Φ_2, Φ_3.

The initial action abstraction for Φ_1 collapses all the actions of **R**. The state abstraction generates an interpreted system with four states only: $S^1 = \{(s_1^{\mathbf{S}}, \epsilon, s_1^{\mathbf{R}}), (s_1^{\mathbf{S}}, \epsilon, s_2^{\mathbf{R}}), (s_2^{\mathbf{S}}, \epsilon, s_1^{\mathbf{R}}), (s_2^{\mathbf{S}}, \epsilon, s_2^{\mathbf{R}})\}$. The initial states I are $(s_1^{\mathbf{S}}, \epsilon, s_1^{\mathbf{R}})$ and $(s_2^{\mathbf{S}}, \epsilon, s_1^{\mathbf{R}})$. It is easy to check that $\textsc{verify}(IS^1, \Phi_1)$ returns tt on this small system. By Theorem 6 we can deduce that $M \models \Phi_1$.

The initial abstraction for Φ_2 results in an interpreted system IS^2 with two global states only $S^2 = \{s, s'\}$ such that s satisfies $\mathcal{ACK}$ and s' satisfies $\neg\mathcal{ACK}$. The state s' is the only initial state; the transitions in the system are: $t(s', \mathrm{a}, s')$ for all the possible joint actions a, and $t(s', (\mathrm{a_S}, \mathrm{a_{CC}}, \mathrm{a_R}), s)$ for all the actions such that $\mathrm{a_{CC}} \in \{-, \Rightarrow\}$. Clearly, we have that $\textsc{verify}(IS^2, \Phi_2) = $ tt which, as above, enables us to conclude that $M \models \Phi_2$.

Verifying Φ_3 leads us to the same initial abstraction $IS^3 = IS^2$. The procedure $\textsc{Label}(IS, \Phi_3)$ returns $(\{s\}, \emptyset)$; so $\textsc{verify}(IS^3, \Phi_3) = $ uu. $\textsc{Verify-Abs}$ therefore calls for the refinement of IS^3 by means of the $\textsc{Refine}$ procedure that splits the abstract states into the concrete states, resulting in an interpreted system IS^4. The procedure determines that the smallest subformula whose value cannot be determined is Φ_3 itself and that its value is unknown at s'. Therefore, the procedure splits the abstract state s' into concrete states leading to the interpreted system IS^4. It can be checked that $\textsc{Verify}(IS^4, \Phi_3) = $ tt. As before, it therefore follows that $M \models \Phi_3$. Even after the refinement takes place on the resulting IS^4 all the states satisfying v are abstracted into one abstract state only; so IS^4 has $2^{32} - 1$ fewer states than the concrete model. It can be shown that no smaller abstraction would allow determining the truth value of Φ_3.

In summary, the abstraction refinement here put forward enabled us to determine the value of ATLK specifications on models that would be too large to verify by means of any state-of-the-art model checker.

7. CONCLUSIONS AND RELATED WORK

In this paper we have developed the theoretical underpinnings for a predicate abstraction methodology for verifying MAS against epistemic specifications. We put forward a temporal-epistemic specification language which includes some features expressing a weak form of strategic reasoning; we gave a three-valued semantics so that this can be used in an abstraction setting and showed that, differently from other approaches, its model checking problem has PTIME complexity. The initial abstraction and the refinement steps are given constructively and can be computed automatically; the scenario we discussed demonstrates potential significant gains of the technique.

Abstractions preserving epistemic properties of MAS have previously been introduced [14, 3, 31, 18]. However, all of these rely on ad-hoc constructions in which human intervention is required to generate the abstract model. Additionally, none of them is intended for three-valued model approximations as we do here. Much closer to our approach is instead [34] which markedly differs from the present investigation by addressing ATL specifications only. In contrast, we here show that these can be extended to the epistemic case. In addition to its increased expressivity, the present setup also offers a very attractive PTIME complexity for the model checking problem, whereas this is Δ_2^P in the case of [34]. This is essential for our future work in which we plan to investigate the verification of MAS when these are given by compact representations such as reactive modules [1] and ISPL [36]. In this case our technique is expected to have a PSPACE bound, whereas we would expect the technique from [34] to become doubly-exponential making any concrete application problematic.

Further ahead we intend to apply these ideas to limited classes of agent programs. Verification methods for MAS programs have of course been discussed prominently in the literature [16, 47, 5, 46, 7]. Even if these results have proven useful, the performance of these is limited due to the state-space explosion. One of the most promising techniques to overcome this is predicate abstraction. We see the development of MAS-oriented underpinnings as a necessary step before predicate abstraction methodologies for MAS can be implemented.

ACKNOWLEDGEMENTS

This research was funded by the EPSRC under grant EP/I00520X.

8. REFERENCES

[1] R. Alur, T. Henzinger, F. Mang, S. Qadeer, S. Rajamani, and S. Tasiran. MOCHA: Modularity in model checking. In *Proceedings of the 10th International Conference on Computer Aided Verification (CAV'98)*, volume 1427 of *LNCS*, pages 521–525. Springer-Verlag, 1998.

[2] R. Alur, T. A. Henzinger, and O. Kupferman. Alternating-time temporal logic. *Journal of the ACM*, 49(5):672–713, 2002.

[3] O. A. Bataineh and R. V. D. Meyden. Abstraction for epistemic model checking of dining cryptographers-based protocols. In *Proceedings of the 13th Conference on Theoretical Aspects of Rationality and Knowledge (TARK11)*, pages 247–256. ACM, 2011.

[4] F. Belardinelli, A. V. Jones, and A. Lomuscio. Model checking temporal-epistemic logic using alternating tree automata. *Fundamenta Informaticae*, 112(1):19–37, 2011.

[5] R. H. Bordini, L. A. Dennis, B. Farwer, and M. Fisher. Automated verification of multi-agent programs. In *23rd IEEE/ACM International Conference on Automated Software Engineering (ASE 2008)*, pages 69–78. IEEE, 2008.

[6] R. H. Bordini, M. Fisher, C. Pardavila, W. Visser, and M. Wooldridge. Model checking multi-agent programs with CASP. In *Proceedings of the 15th International Conference on Computer Aided Verification (CAV03)*, volume 2725 of *LNCS*, pages 110–113. Springer-Verlag, 2003.

[7] R. H. Bordini, M. Fisher, W. Visser, and M. Wooldridge. Verifying multi-agent programs by model checking. *Autonomous Agents and Multi-Agent Systems*, 12(2):239–256, 2006.

[8] R. H. Bordini, R. H. Hubner, and M. Wooldridge. *Programming Multi-Agent Systems in AgentSpeak using Jason.* John Wiley, 2007.

[9] T. Brihaye, A. D. Costa, F. Laroussinie, and N. Markey. ATL with strategy contexts and bounded memory. In *Logical Foundations of Computer Science*, pages 92–106. Springer, 2009.

[10] N. Bulling, J. Dix, and W. Jamroga. Model checking logics of strategic ability: Complexity. In *Specification and Verification of Multi-agent Systems*, pages 125–159. Springer, 2010.

[11] N. Bulling, J. Dix, and C. C. nevar. Modelling coalitions: ATL + argumentation. In *Proceedings of the 7th International Joint Conference on Autonomous Agents and Multiagent Systems (AAMAS08)*, pages 681–688. IFAAMAS, 2008.

[12] P. Čermák, A. Lomuscio, F. Mogavero, and A. Murano. MCMAS-SLK: A model checker for the verification of strategy logic specifications. In *Computer Aided Verification*, volume 8559 of *Lecture Notes in Computer Science*, pages 525–532. Springer, 2014.

[13] E. M. Clarke, O. Grumberg, and D. A. Peled. *Model Checking.* The MIT Press, Cambridge, Massachusetts, 1999.

[14] M. Cohen, M. Dam, A. Lomuscio, and H. Qu. A symmetry reduction technique for model checking temporal-epistemic logic. In *Proceedings of the 21st International Joint Conference on Artificial Intelligence (IJCAI09)*, pages 721–726, Pasadena, USA, 2009.

[15] M. Cohen, M. Dam, A. Lomuscio, and F. Russo. Abstraction in model checking multi-agent systems. In *Proceedings of the 8th International Conference on Autonomous Agents and Multiagent Systems (AAMAS09)*, pages 945–952. IFAAMAS Press, 2009.

[16] L. Dennis, M. Fisher, M. Webster, and R. H. Bordini. Model checking agent programming languages. *Automated Software Engineering*, 19(1):5–63, 2012.

[17] C. Dima and F. Tiplea. Model-checking ATL under imperfect information and perfect recall semantics is undecidable. *CoRR*, abs/1102.4225, 2011.

[18] C. Enea and C. Dima. Abstractions of multi-agent systems. In *Proceedings of 5th International Central and Eastern European Conference on Multi-Agent Systems (CEEMAS07)*, volume 4696 of *Lecture Notes in Computer Science*, pages 11–21. Springer, 2007.

[19] R. Fagin, J. Y. Halpern, Y. Moses, and M. Y. Vardi. *Reasoning about Knowledge.* MIT Press, Cambridge, 1995.

[20] P. Gammie and R. van der Meyden. MCK: Model checking the logic of knowledge. In *Proceedings of 16th International Conference on Computer Aided Verification (CAV04)*, volume 3114 of *LNCS*, pages 479–483. Springer-Verlag, 2004.

[21] S. Graf and H. Saïdi. Construction of abstract state graphs with pvs. In *Proceedings of the 9th International Conference on Computer Aided Verification (CAV97)*, volume 1254 of *Lecture Notes in Computer Science*, pages 72–83. Springer, 1997.

[22] W. Hoek and M. Wooldridge. Model checking knowledge and time. In *SPIN 2002 – Proceedings of the Ninth International SPIN Workshop on Model Checking of Software*, 2002.

[23] W. Hoek and M. Wooldridge. Cooperation, knowledge, and time: Alternating-time temporal epistemic logic and its applications. *Studia Logica*, 75(1):125–157, 2003.

[24] X. Huang and R. van der Meyden. Symbolic model checking epistemic strategy logic. In *AAAI*, pages 1426–1432, 2014.

[25] X. Huang and R. van der Meyden. A temporal logic of strategic knowledge. In *Proceedings of the 14th International Conference on Principles of Knowledge Representation and Reasoning (KR14)*. AAAI Press, 2014.

[26] W. Jamroga and J. Dix. Model checking abilities under incomplete information is indeed δ_p^2-complete. *EUMAS*, pages 14–15, 2006.

[27] W. Jamroga and W. van der Hoek. Agents that know how to play. *Fundamenta Informaticae*, 62:1–35, 2004.

[28] G. Jonker. Feasible strategies in alternating-time temporal epistemic logic. Master's thesis, University of Utrech, The Netherlands, 2003.

[29] M. Kacprzak, W. Nabialek, A. Niewiadomski, W. Penczek, A. Pólrola, M. Szreter, B. Woźna, and A. Zbrzezny. Verics 2007 - a model checker for knowledge and real-time. *Fundamenta Informaticae*, 85(1):313–328, 2008.

[30] M. Kacprzak and W. Penczek. Fully symbolic unbounded model checking for alternating-time temporal logic. *Autonomous Agents and Multi-Agent Systems*, 11(1):69–89, 2005.

[31] M. Koleini, E. Ritter, and M. Ryan. Model checking agent knowledge in dynamic access control policies. In *Tools and Algorithms for the Construction and Analysis of Systems*, volume 7795 of *Lecture Notes in Computer Science*, pages 448–462. Springer, 2013.

[32] S. Lahiri, R. Nieuwenhuis, and A. Oliveras. Smt techniques for fast predicate abstraction. In *Computer Aided Verification*, pages 424–437. Springer, 2006.

[33] A. Lomuscio and J. Michaliszyn. An epistemic Halpern-Shoham logic. In *Proceedings of the 23rd International Joint Conference on Artificial Intelligence (IJCAI13)*, pages 1010–1016. AAAI Press, 2013.

[34] A. Lomuscio and J. Michaliszyn. An abstraction technique for the verification of multi-agent systems against ATL specifications. In *Proceedings of the 14th International Conference on Principles of Knowledge Representation and Reasoning (KR14)*, pages 428–437. AAAI Press, 2014.

[35] A. Lomuscio, W. Penczek, and B. Woźna. Bounded model checking knowledge and real time. *Artificial Intelligence*, 171(16-17):1011–1038, 2007.

[36] A. Lomuscio, H. Qu, and F. Raimondi. MCMAS: A model checker for the verification of multi-agent systems. In *Proceedings of the 21th International Conference on Computer Aided Verification (CAV09)*, volume 5643 of *Lecture Notes in Computer Science*, pages 682–688. Springer, 2009.

[37] A. Lomuscio and F. Raimondi. Model checking knowledge, strategies, and games in multi-agent systems. In *Proceedings of the 5th International Joint Conference on Autonomous agents and Multi-Agent Systems (AAMAS06)*, pages 161–168. ACM Press, 2006.

[38] R. Meyden. Knowledge based programs: On the complexity of perfect recall in finite environments. In *Proceedings of the Sixth Conference on Theoretical Aspects of Rationality and Knowledge*, pages 31–50. Morgan Kaufmann Publishers, 1996.

[39] F. Mogavero, A. Murano, and M. Vardi. Reasoning About Strategies. In *IARCS Annual Conference on Foundations of Software Technology and Theoretical Computer Science (FSTTCS10)*, volume 8 of *Leibniz International Proceedings in Informatics (LIPIcs)*, pages 133–144. Schloss Dagstuhl, 2010.

[40] W. Penczek and A. Lomuscio. Verifying epistemic properties of multi-agent systems via bounded model checking. *Fundamenta Informaticae*, 55(2):167–185, 2003.

[41] J. Pilecki, M. Bednarczyk, and W. Jamroga. Synthesis and verification of uniform strategies for multi-agent systems. In *Computational Logic in Multi-Agent Systems*, volume 8624 of *Lecture Notes in Computer Science*, pages 166–182. Springer, 2014.

[42] F. Raimondi and A. Lomuscio. Automatic verification of deontic interpreted systems by model checking via OBDDs. In *Proceedings of the Sixteenth European Conference on Artificial Intelligence (ECAI04)*, pages 53–57. IOS PRESS, 2004.

[43] F. Raimondi and A. Lomuscio. Verification of multiagent systems via ordered binary decision diagrams: an algorithm and its implementation. In *Proceedings of the 3rd International Joint Conference on Autonomous Agents and Multiagent Systems (AAMAS'04)*, pages 630–637. ACM, 2004.

[44] F. Raimondi and A. Lomuscio. Automatic verification of multi-agent systems by model checking via OBDDs. *Journal of Applied Logic*, 5(2):235–251, 2005.

[45] F. Raimondi and A. Lomuscio. Model checking knowledge, strategies, and games in multi-agent systems. Technical Report RN/05/01, Department of Computer Science, UCL, London, UK, 2005.

[46] D. T. Trang, Y. Yao, N. Alechina, and B. Logan. Verifying heterogeneous multi-agent programs. In *Proceedings of the 13th International Conference on Autonomous Agents and Multiagent Systems (AAMAS 2014)*, pages 149–156, 2014.

[47] M. Wooldridge, M. Fisher, M. Huget, and S. Parsons. Model checking multiagent systems with MABLE. In *Proceedings of the First International Conference on Autonomous Agents and Multiagent Systems (AAMAS02)*, pages 952–959, Bologna, Italy, 2002.

[48] B. Woźna, A. Zbrzezny, and W. Penczek. Checking reachability properties for Timed Automata via SAT. *Fundamenta Informaticae*, 55(2):223–241, 2003.

Parameterised Verification of Autonomous Mobile-Agents in Static but Unknown Environments

Sasha Rubin*
Università degli Studi di Napoli "Federico II"
Naples, Italy
sasha.rubin@gmail.com

ABSTRACT

Automata walking on graphs are a mathematical formalisation of autonomous mobile agents with limited memory operating in discrete environments. This paper establishes a framework in which to model and automatically verify that autonomous mobile agents correctly perform their tasks. The framework consists of a logical language tailored for expressing agent tasks, and an algorithm solving the *parameterised* verification problem, where the graphs are treated as the parameter. We reduce the parameterised verification problem to classic questions in automata theory and monadic second order logic, i.e., universality and validity problems.

We illustrate the framework by instantiating it to a popular model of robot from the distributed computing literature.

This work clarifies the border between classes of mobile-agent systems that have decidable parameterised verification problem, and those that do not.

Categories and Subject Descriptors

D.2.4 [**Software/Program Verification**]: Formal Methods; F.1.1 [**Computation by Abstract Devices**]: Models of Computation—*Automata*; C.2.2 [**Computer Communication Networks**]: Network Protocols—*Protocol Verification*; C.2.4 [**Computer Communication Networks**]: Distributed Systems; I.2.11 [**Artificial Intelligence**]: Distributed Artificial Intelligence—*Multiagent systems*

Keywords

Model Checking; Logic; Automata Theory; Distributed Networks; Autonomous Mobile Agents; Robots; Parameterised Verification

1. INTRODUCTION

Autonomous mobile agents are designed to achieve some task in an environment, e.g., exploration, or rendezvous. They are in an *unknown* environment if they do not have global information about the environment, e.g., mobile software exploring hostile computer networks, or physical robots that rendezvous in an environment not reachable by humans. This paper studies a mathematical formalisation of autonomous mobile agents in discrete environments, i.e., robots on finite graphs.

The distributed computing community has recently proposed and studied a number of models of robot systems [5, 33, 28, 18, 21, 16, 27]. Theorems from this literature are *parameterised* i.e., they may involve graph-parameters (e.g., the maximum degree, the number of vertices, the diameter), memory parameters (e.g., the number of internal states of the robot protocol), and the number of robots may be a parameter.

However, until recently [31, 4, 35, 32] there has been little emphasis on formal analysis of correctness of robots in a parameterised setting. In this paper we apply formal methods to the parameterised verification problem in which it is the *environment that is parameterised.* This is how we model that robots operate in unknown environments. Formally, we address the following decision problem.

Parameterised Verification Problem: Given robots $\overline{R}$, decide if they solve the task T on all graphs $G \in \mathcal{G}$.

In contrast, the classic (non-parameterised) verification problem states:

Verification Problem: Given robots $\overline{R}$ and a graph $G \in \mathcal{G}$, decide if robots $\overline{R}$ solve the task T on G.

The non-parameterised verification problem is often handled using model-checking [14]. The parameterised verification problem corresponds to a family of model-checking problems (one for each $G \in \mathcal{G}$), or equivalently, a single infinite-state model-checking problem. A variety of techniques have been applied to such systems, fully discussed in Section 7 (Related Work), however none seem suited to the problem in which the environment is parameterised. Fortunately, the theory of automata and logic has produced a rich understanding of the expressive power of certain logics, e.g., monadic second-order logic MSOL, over certain classes of graphs, e.g., context-free sets of graphs [44, 45, 29, 17]. Our framework reduces the parameterised verification problem to classic questions in automata theory and MSOL, i.e., universality and validity problems. The key observations are that: i) robots are graph-walking automata, and can be defined in MSOL, and ii) robot tasks correspond to properties of runs of automata which are often definable in MSOL.

Modeling Choices.

There are a number of different modeling choices for mo-

*Marie Curie fellow of the Istituto Nazionale di Alta Matematica.

Appears in: *Proceedings of the 14th International Conference on Autonomous Agents and Multiagent Systems (AAMAS 2015), Bordini, Elkind, Weiss, Yolum (eds.), May 4–8, 2015, Istanbul, Turkey.*

bile agents [38]. We list them, and emphasise (using underlining) the choices made in this paper: (i) is the environment continuous (e.g., the plane) or discrete (e.g. a finite graph whose edges are labeled by directions or port numbers)? (ii) do agents act synchronously or asynchronously? (iii) are agents probabilistic or non-deterministic? (iv) is there one agent or are there multiple agents, and are the number of agents known or unknown? (v) is the environment static, or can agents affect their environment (e.g., by marking the nodes of a graph)? Moreover, (vi) how much information about the environment is known, a priori, to the agents? We assume agents do not have global knowledge of the environment, and in particular the size is not known and nodes in the environment do not have unique identifiers. And finally, (vii) how do agents communicate and sense their environment? We assume agents can *sense their positions in the graph* as well as those of the other agents (in the case of multiple agents), i.e., robots acquire information about the current state of the environment solely by vision (we use logical formulas, which we call tests, to define these sensing abilities).

Aim and Contributions.

The main aim of this work it to provide a clearer understanding of the border between classes of autonomous mobile-agent systems that have decidable parameterised verification problem, and those that do not.

In particular, we provide a quite general formalisation of robot systems (using the modeling choices above) in which all components (i.e., environments, robots, and tasks) are modeled separately. We formalise reasoning about robot systems as the parameterised verification problem (PVP) where the environment is treated as a parameter. We show how to reduce the PVP to problems about automata and logic, i.e., universality and validity problems. We then prove that the PVP is decidable for suitable restrictions of the components, notably the case of a single robot on context-free sets of graphs. We illustrate the power of the framework by instantiating it to a model of robot systems from the distributed computing literature. This instantiation falls into our decidable restrictions.

2. BACKGROUND: AUTOMATA THEORY

In order to make this paper self-contained, this section contains the necessary background. In particular, we will use basic notions from mathematical logic and automata theory to formalise the robot systems (a full logical background can be found in [22], and a smaller discussion of monadic second-order logic MSOL over graphs can be found in [17, Section 1.3.1]), and easy-to-state theorems (e.g., Kleene's Theorem about the equivalence of regular expressions and automata, and Courcelle's Theorem on satisfiability of MSOL over context-free sets of graphs [17]) to give an algorithm for solving the parameterised verification problem.

Write B^ω for the set of infinite sequences over alphabet B, and write B^* for the set of finite sequences. The empty sequence is denoted ϵ. Write $[n]$ for the set $\{1, 2, \cdots, n\}$.

Graphs.

A Σ-*graph*, or *graph*, G, is a tuple (V, E, Σ, λ) where V is a finite set of *vertices*, $E \subseteq V \times V$ is a relation called the *edge relation*, Σ is a finite set of *edge labels*, and $\lambda : E \to \Sigma$ is the *edge labeling function*. The *out-degree* of a vertex v, written $\mathsf{deg}(v)$, is the cardinality of the set $\{(v, w) \in E : w \in V\}$ of *outgoing edges* of v.

Sometimes the edge labels give a sense of direction:

EXAMPLE 1. *An* L-labeled grid *is a graph with* $V = [n] \times [m]$, $\Sigma = L \times \{N, S, E, W\}$, *and labels* $\lambda((x, y), (x + 1, y)) \in L \times \{E\}$, *etc., where* L *is a finite set and* $n, m \in \mathbb{N}$. *An* L-labeled line *is an* L*-labeled grid with* $V = [n] \times [1]$. *If* $|L| = 1$ *then we call the grid (or line)* unlabeled.

EXAMPLE 2. *A* Δ-ary tree *(for* $\Delta \in \mathbb{N}$*) is a* Σ*-graph* (V, E, Σ, λ) *where* (V, E) *is a tree,* $\Sigma = [\Delta] \cup \{up\}$, *and* λ *labels the edge leading to the node in direction* i *(if it exists) by* i, *and the edge leading to the parent of a node (other than the root) is labelled by* up. *We may rename the labels for convenience, e.g., for binary trees (*$\Delta = 2$*) we let* $\Sigma = \{lc, rc, up\}$ *where* lc *replaces* 1 *and* rc *replaces* 2.

First-order and Monadic Second-order Logic.

Formulas will be interpreted in Σ-graphs G (an exception are formulas in Section 4.3). Define the set of monadic second-order formulas $\mathsf{MSOL}(\Sigma)$ as follows. Formulas of $\mathsf{MSOL}(\Sigma)$ are built using *first-order variables* $x, y, \cdots$ that vary over vertices, and *set variables* $X, Y, \cdots$ that vary over sets of vertices. The *atomic formulas* (when interpreted over Σ-graphs) are: $x = y$ (denoting that vertex x is the same as vertex y), $x \in X$ (denoting that vertex x is in the set of vertices X), and $edg_\sigma(x, y)$ (denoting that there is an edge from x to y labeled $\sigma \in \Sigma$). The formulas of $\mathsf{MSOL}(\Sigma)$ are built from the atomic formulas using the Boolean connectives (i.e., $\neg, \vee, \wedge, \to$) and variable quantification (i.e., $\forall, \exists$ over both types of variables). The fragment of $\mathsf{MSOL}(\Sigma)$ which does not mention set variables is called *first-order logic*, denoted $\mathsf{FOL}(\Sigma)$. Write $\mathsf{MSOL}_k(\Sigma)$ for formulas with k-many free variables.

Here are some examples of formulas and their meanings:

MF1. The formula $\forall x(x \in X \to x \in Y)$ means that $X \subseteq Y$. Similarly, there are formulas for the set operations $\cup, \cap, =$, and relative complement $X \setminus Y$.

MF2. The formula $edg(x, y) := \bigvee_{\sigma \in \Sigma} edg_\sigma(x, y)$ means that there is an edge from x to y (here Σ is assumed to be finite).

MF3. The formula $\exists x \exists y(x \neq y \wedge edg(z, x) \wedge edg(z, y))$ means that $\mathsf{deg}(z) \geq 2$.

MF4. If $\phi(x, y)$ is an $\mathsf{MSOL}(\Sigma)$ formula then define $\phi^*(x, y)$ by $\forall Z[(closed_\phi(Z) \wedge x \in Z) \to y \in Z]$. Here $closed_\phi(Z)$ is defined as $\forall a \forall b[(a \in Z \wedge \phi(a, b)) \to b \in Z]$. Note that ϕ^* is an $\mathsf{MSOL}(\Sigma)$-formula.

Note that $\phi^*(x, y)$ holds in a graph G if and only if there exists a finite sequence of vertices $v_1 v_2 \cdots v_m \in V^*$ (here $m \geq 1$) such that $x = v_1, y = v_m$ and $\phi(v_i, v_{i+1})$ holds in G for all $i < m$. This shows that that if a binary relation is MSOL-definable, then so is its transitive-closure.

Similarly, define $\phi^\omega(x, y) := \phi^*(x, y) \wedge \exists z(\phi(y, z) \wedge \phi^*(z, y))$. Note $\phi^\omega(x, y)$ holds in a graph G if and only if there is an infinite sequence of vertices $v_1 v_2 \cdots \in V^\omega$ with $x = v_1$, $v_i = y$ for infinitely many $i \in \mathbb{N}$, and $\phi(v_i, v_{i+1})$ holds in G for all $i \in \mathbb{N}$. This uses the fact that V is finite.

MF5. The k-*ary transitive-closure operator* is the function that maps a $2k$-ary relation $\rho(\overline{x}, \overline{y})$ to the $2k$-ary relation $\rho^*(\overline{x}, \overline{y})$ such that, in every graph G: $\rho^*(\overline{x}, \overline{y})$ holds if and only if there exists a sequence $\overline{v}_1, \overline{v}_2, \cdots, \overline{v}_m$ such that $\overline{x} = \overline{v}_1$, $\overline{y} = \overline{v}_m$, and $\rho(\overline{v}_i, \overline{v}_{i+1})$ holds for every $i < m$. For $k > 1$, it is not the case that if a k-ary relation ϕ is MSOL-definable, then so is its k-ary transitive-closure, because, intuitively, this would require having k-ary relation variables Z.[1]

For a formula $\phi(x_1, \cdots, x_k)$, a graph G, and $v_1, \cdots, v_k \in V$, write $G \models \phi(v_1, \cdots, v_k)$ to mean that ϕ holds in G with variable x_i substituted by vertex v_i (for $i \leq k$).

The Validity Problem and Courcelle's Theorem.

A *sentence* is a formula with no free variables. Let Φ be a set of sentences, and let $\mathcal{G}$ be a set of graphs. The Φ-*validity problem of* $\mathcal{G}$ is to decide, given $\phi \in \Phi$, whether or not for all graphs $G \in \mathcal{G}$, it holds that $G \models \phi$. Unfortunately for us, the FOL(Σ)-validity problem for $\mathcal{G}$ = the set of all Σ-graphs is undecidable [22]. On the other hand, many interesting cases have decidable validity. One version of Courcelle's Theorem states that the MSOL-validity problem is decidable for every context-free set of graphs $\mathcal{G}$ [17].[2] Context-free sets of graphs are the analogue of context-free sets of strings, and are generated by graph grammars or equations using certain graph operations. Examples include, for a fixed alphabet, the set of labeled lines, the set of rings, the set of trees, the set of series-parallel graphs, the set of cliques, but not the set of all grids.

Automata and Regular Expressions.

Ordinary *regular-expressions* over a finite alphabet B are built from the sets $\emptyset$, $\{\epsilon\}$, and $\{b\}$ for $b \in B$, and the operations union $+$, concatenation $\cdot$, and Kleene-star *. Kleene's Theorem states that the languages recognised by regular expressions over alphabet B are exactly those recognised by finite automata over alphabet B.

An ω-*regular expression* over the finite alphabet B is inductively defined to be of the form: exp^ω, $exp \cdot r$, or $r + r'$, where exp is an ordinary regular-expression over B, and r, r' are ω-regular expressions over B. An ω-regular language is one defined by an ω-regular expression. A variation of Kleene's Theorem says that the languages recognised by ω-regular expressions over alphabet B are exactly the languages recognised by Büchi automata over alphabet B (which are like non-deterministic finite automata except that they take infinite words as input, and accept if some accepting state occurs infinitely often).

3. THE MODEL OF ROBOT SYSTEMS

We provide a framework for modeling multi-robot systems parameterised by their environment.

[1]To prove this formally, note that 2-ary transitive closure on finite words (i.e., binary-labeled lines) can define the non-regular language $\{0^n 1^n : n \in \mathbb{N}\}$; now use the fact that, over finite words, MSOL can only define the regular languages, part of a result known as the Büchi-Elgot-Trakhtenbrot Theorem, see [45].

[2]Actually, a strong form of the theorem states that there is an algorithm that given a description of a context-free set of graphs $\mathcal{G}$ and an MSOL-formula ϕ decides if every graph in $\mathcal{G}$ satisfies ϕ.

3.1 The model of robot systems

In this section we define robot systems, i.e., robot protocols, environments, and tasks.

Environments are modeled as Σ-graphs,[3] and robots are modeled as regular languages of instructions, as in [7]. An instruction either tells the robot to move along an edge, or it allows the robot to test the positions of the robots (e.g., a robot can learn which other robots are at the same vertex as it is, or if there is a robot north of it). Tests are formalised as logical formulas. As discussed in Section 5, our model is general enough to be able to express a popular model of robot systems found in the distributed computing literature [27, 21, 16, 33, 28, 18].

We first define robot systems consisting of a single robot, and then define multi-robot systems.

Robot Instruction Set.

A robot follows instructions from the *instruction set*

$$\text{INS}_{\Sigma,1} := \{\uparrow_\sigma : \sigma \in \Sigma\} \cup \mathsf{MSOL}_1(\Sigma).$$

Instructions are of two kinds, *moves* and *tests*:[4] $\uparrow_\sigma$ tells the robot to move from its current vertex along the edge labeled σ; and $\mathsf{MSOL}_1(\Sigma)$ consists of formulas $\tau(x)$ that allow the robot to test that $\tau(x)$ holds in G, where x is the current vertex of the robot in G. Typical tests include: is the degree of the current vertex at least d? is there an edge out of the current vertex labeled σ? Here is a more complex test: is there a path from the current vertex that only uses edges labeled σ to a vertex of degree d?

For a sequence $ins \in (\text{INS}_{\Sigma,1})^*$, write $[[ins]]_G \subseteq V^2$ for the set of pairs of vertices (u, v) such that, in G, one can reach v from u by following the instructions ins. Formally,

1. $(u, v) \in [[\epsilon]]_G$ iff $u = v$,
2. $(u, v) \in [[\uparrow_\sigma]]_G$ iff $\lambda(u, v) = \sigma$,
3. $(u, v) \in [[\tau(x)]]_G$ iff $u = v$ and $G \models \tau(u)$, and
4. $(u, v) \in [[d \cdot e]]_G$ for $d \in (\text{INS}_{\Sigma,1})^*$ and $e \in \text{INS}_{\Sigma,1}$ iff there exists $z \in V$ such that $(u, z) \in [[d]]_G$ and $(z, v) \in [[e]]_G$.

Robot Protocols.

Fix a set of edge-labels Σ. A 1-*robot*, or *robot*, R, is a pair (Q, δ) where Q is a finite set of *states*, and $\delta \subset Q \times \text{INS}_{\Sigma,1} \times Q$ is a finite *transition* relation.

We sometimes designate certain states of the robot to be *initial*, denoted $I \subseteq Q$ and certain states to be *repeating*, denoted $A \subseteq Q$. A state $p \in Q$ is called *halting* if the robot has the transition (p, true, p), i.e., state p is a sink. Thus we model a halting robot as one that stays in the same state forever. The set of halting states is denoted $H \subseteq Q$.

EXAMPLE 3. *The robot in Figure 1 does a (perpetual) depth-first search of trees in which every node has zero or two children.*[5] *Tests are written $leaf, lc, rc, root$ (whose meanings are "is the current node a leaf?", "left-child?", "right-child?", "the root?"), and move instructions are written $\uparrow_{up}$,*

[3]The fact that Σ-graphs are finite corresponds to our modeling assumption that environments are *discrete*.

[4]Looking at the instruction set we see that robots cannot alter the graph, i.e., the environment is *static*.

[5]To make the diagram readable, an edge may be labeled by multiple successive actions separated by semicolons.

$\uparrow_{lc}$, *and* $\uparrow_{rc}$ *(whose meanings are "move up to the parent", "to the left-child", "to the right-child").*

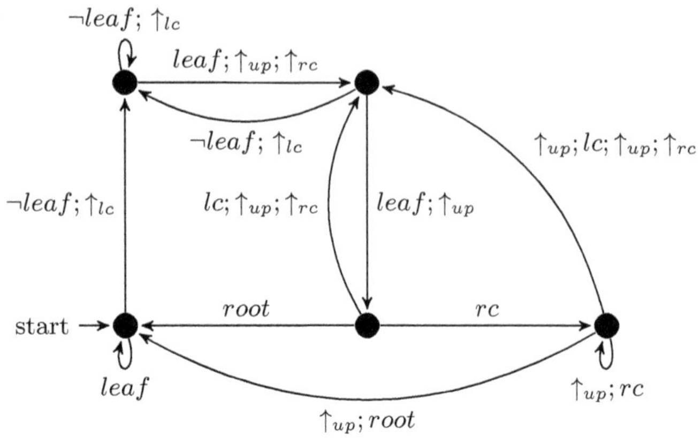

Figure 1: Robot that does a DFS on binary trees.

Configurations and Runs.

A robot walks about a Σ-graph G. Let $R = (Q, \delta)$ be a robot with instruction set $\text{INS}_{\Sigma,1}$. A *configuration* c of R on G is a pair $\langle v, q \rangle \in V \times Q$. Say that the configuration $\langle v, q \rangle$ has *position* v. A configuration is *initial* (resp. *halting, repeating*) if q is. The following definition expresses that one configuration results from another after the robot executes a single instruction: for configurations $c = \langle v, p \rangle$ and $d = \langle w, q \rangle$, say that d *results from* c iff there is a transition (p, ins, q) of δ such that $(v, w) \in [[ins]]_G$. A *run* α of R on G starting with an initial configuration c is an infinite sequence $c_1c_2c_3\cdots$ of configurations such that $c_1 = c$ and for all i, c_{i+1} results from c_i.

The *set of positions of a run* $\alpha = (v_1, q_1)(v_2, q_2)\cdots$ is the set of positions $\{v_1, v_2, \cdots\}$ of its configurations. The *sequence of positions of a run* α is the sequence of positions $v_1v_2\cdots$ of its configurations.

Multi-Robot Systems.

We extend the previous definitions to k-many of robots.

A *k-robot ensemble* is a sequence $\langle R_1, \cdots, R_k \rangle$ where, writing $R_i = (Q_i, \delta_i)$, each Q_i is a finite set of *states*, and each $\delta_i \subset Q_i \times \text{INS}_{\Sigma,k} \times Q_i$ is a finite *transition* relation, where the *instruction set* is $\text{INS}_{\Sigma,k} := \{\uparrow_\sigma : \sigma \in \Sigma\} \cup \mathsf{MSOL}_k(\Sigma)$. For a sequence $ins \in ((\text{INS}_{\Sigma,k})^k)^*$ define[6] $[[ins]]_G \subseteq V^{2k}$ such that $(\overline{u}, \overline{v}) \in [[ins]]_G$ if and only if, in G, one can reach $\overline{v}$ from $\overline{u}$ by following the instructions in ins.

Formally,

1. If $ins = \epsilon$, then $(\overline{u}, \overline{v}) \in [[ins]]_G$ if and only if $\overline{u} = \overline{v}$;
2. If $ins = (d_1, \cdots, d_k) \in \text{INS}_{\Sigma,k}$ then $(\overline{u}, \overline{v}) \in [[ins]]_G$ if, for each $i \leq k$:
   (a) if $d_i = \uparrow_\sigma$ then $\lambda(u_i, v_i) = \sigma$,
   (b) if $d_i = \tau(x_1, \cdots, x_k)$ then $u_i = v_i$ and $G \models \tau(u_1, \cdots, u_k)$.
3. If $ins = d \cdot e$ then $(\overline{u}, \overline{v}) \in [[ins]]_G$ if and only if there exists $\overline{z} \in V$ such that $(\overline{u}, \overline{z}) \in [[d]]_G$ and $(\overline{z}, \overline{v}) \in [[e]]_G$.

Fix a Σ-graph G. A *configuration* c of $\langle R_1, \cdots, R_k \rangle$ on graph G is a pair $\langle \overline{v}, \overline{q} \rangle \in V^k \times \prod_{i \leq k} Q_i$. A configuration is *initial* if q_i is the initial state of robot R_i (for all $i \leq k$). The following definition expresses that one configuration results from another after the robots simultaneously execute their own next instruction (which may be to move along an edge labeled σ, or to test the current position of all the robots):[7] configuration $\langle \overline{w}, \overline{q} \rangle$ *results from* $\langle \overline{v}, \overline{p} \rangle$ iff there are transitions $(p_i, ins_i, q_i) \in \delta_i$ (for $i \leq k$) such that $(\overline{v}, \overline{w}) \in [[(ins_1, \cdots, ins_k)]]_G$. *Runs* and their *sets of positions and sequences* are defined as before.

Robot Tasks.

Robots should achieve some task in their environment: a *k-robot task*, or simply a *task*, T, is a function that maps a graph G to a set of sequences of positions of G, i.e., $\mathrm{T}(G) \subseteq (V^k)^\omega$. A robot-ensemble $\overline{R}$ *achieves* T on G if for every run α of $\overline{R}$ on G it holds that $\alpha' \in \mathrm{T}(G)$, where α' is the sequence of positions of the run α.

We give some examples of foundational robot tasks [34]:

RT1. A robot *explores and halts* if, no matter where it starts, it a) eventually halts, and b) visits every vertex of the graph at least once.

RT2. A robot *perpetually explores* if, no matter where it starts, it visits every vertex of G infinitely often.

RT3. A robot *explores and returns* if, no matter where it starts, it a) eventually stops where it started, and b) visits every vertex of the graph at least once.

RT4. An ensemble of robots *collaboratively explores* a graph if, no matter where they start, every node is eventually visited by at least one robot.

RT5. A k-robot ensemble *gathers* if, no matter where each robot starts, there is a vertex z, such that eventually every robot is in z.

4. REASONING ABOUT ROBOT SYSTEMS

We formalise the parameterised verification problem for robot protocols, and then describe our solution to it (Theorem 2) which shows how to reduce parameterised verification in the case of a single robot to the logical validity problem of certain logics.

4.1 The Parameterised Verification Problem

The parameterised verification problem depends on a set of graphs $\mathcal{G}$, a set of robot ensembles $\mathcal{R}$, and a robot task T. Note that $\mathcal{G}$ is typically infinite.

DEFINITION 1. *The* ***parameterised verification problem*** $\mathsf{PVP}_{\mathrm{T}}(\mathcal{G}, \mathcal{R})$ *states: given a robot ensemble $\overline{R}$ from $\mathcal{R}$, decide whether or not $\overline{R}$ achieves the task* T *on every graph $G \in \mathcal{G}$.*

Unfortunately, this problem is easily undecidable for the types of systems we have:

[6]To improve readability, the notation $[[\ ]]_G$ does not mention k.

[7]This is where we model the assumption that robots act *synchronously*.

THEOREM 1. *There exists a task* T *and computable sets* $\mathcal{G}$ *and* $\mathcal{R}$ *such that* $\mathsf{PVP}_{\mathrm{T}}(\mathcal{G},\mathcal{R})$ *is undecidable.*

In particular, we can choose $k=1$, T *to be the task "never halt",* $\mathcal{G}$ *to be the set of unlabeled-grids, and* $\mathcal{R}$ *to be all robots; or we can choose* $k=2$, T *to be the task "no robot ever halts",* $\mathcal{G}$ *to be the set of unlabeled-lines, and* $\mathcal{R}$ *to be all robots.*

PROOF SKETCH. Since the proof technique is a standard, we merely sketch it. We reduce the non-halting problem for (Turing-powerful) two-counter machines to $\mathsf{PVP}_{\mathrm{T}}(\mathcal{G},\mathcal{R})$, i.e., given machine M build robot(s) $\overline{R}$ such that M accepts no input if and only if $\overline{R}$ achieves task T on all graphs in $\mathcal{G}$.

Case $k=1$: As observed by [8] for their "2-dimensional automata", one robot on a grid can simulate a two-counter machine: counter values $(n,m)\in\mathbb{N}^2$ are encoded by the robot being at position (n,m) of the grid. The only tests that are needed are to check whether or not the robot is on the boundary (this is to simulate the counter machine's "test for zero", as well as to alert about a counter overflow).

Case $k=2$: The idea is that two distinguishable robots on a line can simulate one robot on a square grid; the position of the ith robot on the line gives the ith co-ordinate of the single robot on the grid. The robots only need to be able to test if they are at the end points of the line. Alternatively, one can directly code computations of Turing machines, as was done by [40] to show that universality of 2-head one-way finite-state automata is undecidable. □

In light of this negative result, our main task is to understand in what way we can restrict the systems to get decidability.

4.2 Reducing Parameterised Verification to Validity

We first describe, at a high level, the approach we use to solve (restricted cases of) the parameterised verification problem $\mathsf{PVP}_{\mathrm{T}}(\mathcal{G},\mathcal{R})$. Suppose we can build, for every k-ensemble $\overline{R}$ of robots, a formula $\phi_{\overline{R},\mathrm{T}}$ such that for all graphs G the following are equivalent:

- $G\models\phi_{\overline{R},\mathrm{T}}$
- $\overline{R}$ achieves task T on G.

Then, for every $\mathcal{R}$ and $\mathcal{G}$, we would have reduced the parameterised verification problem $\mathsf{PVP}_{\mathrm{T}}(\mathcal{G},\mathcal{R})$ to the $\Phi_{\overline{R},\mathrm{T}}$-validity problem for $\mathcal{G}$ where $\Phi_{\overline{R},\mathrm{T}}$ is the set of formulas $\{\phi_{\overline{R},\mathrm{T}}:\overline{R}\in\mathcal{R}\}$.[8]

We now detail this approach in the case of a single robot, i.e., $k=1$.

LEMMA 1. *Let* $R=(Q,\delta)$ *be a robot over instruction set* $\mathrm{INS}_{\Sigma,1}$, *and let* $p,q\in Q$.

We can build $\mathsf{MSOL}(\Sigma)$ *formulas* $\psi_{R,p,q}(X,x,y)$ *so that for every graph* G: $G\models\psi_{R,p,q}(X,x,y)$ *if and only if there exists a run of* R *on* G *starting from configuration* $\langle x,p\rangle$ *that has a prefix that reaches the configuration* $\langle y,q\rangle$ *and the set of positions on the prefix is exactly* X.

We can build $\mathsf{MSOL}(\Sigma)$ *formulas* $\psi^{\infty}_{R,p,q}(X,x,y)$ *so that for every graph* G: $G\models\psi^{\infty}_{R,p,q}(X,x,y)$ *if and only if there is a run of* R *on* G *starting from configuration* $\langle x,p\rangle$ *that reaches the configuration* $\langle y,q\rangle$ *infinitely often and the set of positions on the run is exactly* X.

[8]Note that in our approach $\phi_{\overline{R},T}$ does not depend on $\mathcal{R}$ or on $\mathcal{G}$.

PROOF. A robot $R=(Q,\delta)$ is a finite automaton (without initial or final states) over a finite alphabet *Alph* of instructions, i.e., $Alph\subset\{\uparrow_\sigma\colon\sigma\in\Sigma\}\cup\mathsf{MSOL}_1(\Sigma)$. By Kleene's theorem — which states that every finite-state automaton can be translated into a regular expression — we can build a regular expression *exp* (that depends on R,p,q) over alphabet *Alph* for the language of the automaton R with initial state p and final state q.

By induction on the structure of regular expressions over alphabet *Alph* we build MSOL formulas:

- $\varphi_\emptyset:=\mathsf{false}$
- $\varphi_\epsilon(X,x,y):=x=y\wedge x\in X$
- $\varphi_{\uparrow_\sigma}(X,x,y):=edg_\sigma(x,y)\wedge x,y\in X$
- $\varphi_\tau(X,x,y):=x=y\wedge\tau(x)\wedge x\in X$
- $\varphi_{r+s}:=\varphi_r\vee\varphi_s$
- $\varphi_{r\cdot s}(X,x,y):=\exists z\,[\varphi_r(X,x,z)\wedge\varphi_s(X,z,y)]$
- $\varphi_{r^*}(X,x,y):=\forall Z[(cl_{\phi_r}(X,Z)\wedge x\in Z)\to y\in Z]$ where

$$cl_\phi(X,Z):=\forall a,b\,[(a\in Z\wedge\varphi(X,a,b))\to b\in Z]\,.$$

An easy induction shows that $G\models\varphi_r(X,x,y)$ if and only if there is a sequence of instructions $ins\in Alph^*$ accepted by the regular expression r and a path from x to y that follows instructions ins, and that only visits vertices in X (but not necessarily all of X). Finally, define the MSOL formula $\psi_{R,p,q}(X,x,y)$ to state that $\phi_{exp}(X,x,y)$ holds and X is minimal: $\phi_{exp}(X,x,y)\wedge\neg\exists Y(\phi_{exp}(Y,x,y)\wedge Y\subset X)$.

Similarly, by a variation of Kleene's Theorem, we can build an ω-regular expression *exp* over alphabet *Alph* for the language consisting of all infinite sequences that label infinite paths in R that start in p and see q infinitely often. Then, inductively build φ_{exp}, as before, with the following additional rule:

$$\varphi_{r^\omega}(X,x,y):=\exists z\,[\varphi_{r^*}(X,x,y)\wedge\varphi_r(X,y,z)\wedge\varphi_{r^*}(X,z,y)]$$

As before, define the MSOL formula $\psi^{\infty}_{R,p,q}(X,x,y)$ to state that X is minimal such that $\varphi_{exp}(X,x,y)$ holds. □

The idea of the proof of Lemma 1 follows [7] who built a formula expressing that there is a run starting in configuration $\langle x,p\rangle$ that reaches configuration $\langle y,q\rangle$. Our Lemma extends this in two ways, i.e., recording the visited states X, and expressing that a configuration occurs infinitely often.

NOTE 1. *The case of multiple robots* ($k>1$) *is more subtle. For instance, the analogue of Lemma 1 does not hold. Indeed, for* $k=2$, *let* $R_1=R_2$ *be robots that have one state* p *and that non-deterministically move in every direction. Then the statement "there is a run of the robots from configuration* $\langle x_1,x_2,p,p\rangle$ *to configuration* $\langle y_1,y_2,p,p\rangle$*" is equivalent to the statement that the* k*-ary transitive closure of the edge relation in graph* G *contains the tuple* $\langle x_1,x_2,y_1,y_2\rangle$. *However, the* k*-ary transitive closure is not expressible in* MSOL *(as was pointed out in Example MF5 in Section 2).*

4.3 Robot Task Logic — RTL

We now define a logic, called RTL, for expressing robot tasks in the case of one robot ($k = 1$).

Syntax. Formulas of RTL are built, as in the definition of MSOL from Section 2, from the following atomic formulas: $x = y$, $Reach(X, x, y), Halt(X, x, y), Infty(X, x, y)$, and $Rept(X, x, y)$.

Semantics. Formulas of RTL are interpreted with respect to graphs and robots. Thus, given a graph G and a robot R with state set Q, initial-state set I, repeating-state set A, and halting-state set H, define the satisfaction relation $\models_{\mathsf{RTL}}$:

$$\langle G, R\rangle \models_{\mathsf{RTL}} Reach(X, x, y) \quad \text{iff } G \models \bigwedge_{p\in I} \bigvee_{q\in Q} \psi_{R,p,q}(X, x, y)$$

$$\langle G, R\rangle \models_{\mathsf{RTL}} Halt(X, x, y) \quad \text{iff } G \models \bigwedge_{p\in I} \bigvee_{q\in H} \psi_{R,p,q}(X, x, y)$$

$$\langle G, R\rangle \models_{\mathsf{RTL}} Infty(X, x, y) \quad \text{iff } G \models \bigwedge_{p\in I} \bigvee_{q\in Q} \psi^{\infty}_{R,p,q}(X, x, y)$$

$$\langle G, R\rangle \models_{\mathsf{RTL}} Rept(X, x, y) \quad \text{iff } G \models \bigwedge_{p\in I} \bigvee_{q\in A} \psi^{\infty}_{R,p,q}(X, x, y)$$

The formulas $\psi_{R,p,q}$ and $\psi^{\infty}_{R,p,q}$ are from Lemma 1. Extend the satisfaction relation to all formulas of RTL in the natural way.

Examples. Here are some example RTL formulas and their meanings.

1. The atomic formula $Reach(X, x, y)$ expresses that the robot, starting in position x, reaches position y, and the set of visited vertices is X. The RTL formula $\forall x \exists y Reach(V, x, y)$ expresses that the robot explores the graph, no matter where it starts.

2. The RTL formula $\forall x \exists y Halt(V, x, y)$ expresses "explore and stop".

3. The RTL formula $\forall x Halt(V, x, x)$ expresses "explore and return".

4. The atomic formula $Infty(X, x, y)$ expresses that the robot, starting in position x, visits position y infinitely often, and the set of vertices the robot visits along this run is exactly X. Thus $\forall x Infty(V, x, x)$ is an RTL formula expressing that the robot "perpetually explores" the graph.

A task T is *captured* by an RTL formula ϑ if $\langle G, R\rangle \models_{\mathsf{RTL}} \vartheta$ is equivalent to the statement that every run of R on G is in $\mathrm{T}(G)$. The example formulas show that the first three tasks from Section 3.1 are captured by RTL formulas.

Here is the main theorem that solves the parameterised verification problem in the case of a single robot ($k = 1$). It reduces the PVP to MSOL-validity of the set of environments.

THEOREM 2. *Fix an edge-label set Σ. Let $\mathcal{R}$ be the set of all robots over $\mathrm{INS}_{\Sigma,1}$, let T be a task that is captured by an RTL formula, and let $\mathcal{G}$ be a set of Σ-graphs with decidable* MSOL*-validity problem. Then $\mathsf{PVP}_{\mathrm{T}}(\mathcal{G}, \mathcal{R})$ is decidable.*

PROOF. Say RTL formula ϑ captures T. Given $R \in \mathcal{R}$, build the formula $\phi_{R,\mathrm{T}}$ by replacing every atomic formula in ϑ by its definition with respect to R, e.g., $Reach(X, x, y)$ is replaced by $\bigwedge_{p\in I} \bigvee_{q\in Q} \psi_{R,p,q}(X, x, y)$. A routine induction on the structure of the formula ϑ gives: $\langle G, R\rangle \models_{\mathsf{RTL}} \vartheta$ if and only if $G \models \phi_{R,\mathrm{T}}$. But by Lemma 1 $\phi_{R,\mathrm{T}}$ is a formula in $\mathsf{MSOL}(\Sigma)$. Thus we can apply the fact that the MSOL-validity problem for $\mathcal{G}$ is decidable to decide whether or not $G \models \phi_{R,\mathrm{T}}$ for all $G \in \mathcal{G}$. □

COROLLARY 1. *If $\mathcal{R}$ and T are as in Theorem 2 and $\mathcal{G}$ is a context-free set of graphs, then $\mathsf{PVP}_{\mathrm{T}}(\mathcal{G}, \mathcal{R})$ is decidable.*

NOTE 2. *The case of multiple robots ($k > 1$) is harder to analyse. Indeed, Theorem 1 states that PVP is undecidable already for $k = 2$ on lines (which is a very basic context-free set of graphs) and simple reachability tasks. It is a challenging problem to find natural and useful restrictions on robots which allow the analogue of Corollary 1 (or Lemma 1) to hold in the case of multiple robots.*

5. ILLUSTRATION: DISTRIBUTED COMPUTING

We now instantiate our framework to a popular model of autonomous mobile-agent from the distributed computing literature, i.e., [27, 21, 16, 33, 28, 18]. To distinguish their agents from ours, we call theirs *DC-robots*. Here is their model: environments are modeled as undirected graphs, and each vertex is annotated with a local port numbering i.e., for every vertex v the set of labels of the edges of v are in bijection with $\{1, 2, \cdots, \mathsf{deg}(v)\}$. A DC-robot finding itself at vertex v can decide to exit via local port-number d and update its local state based on a) its current state, b) the identification of the robots at the same vertex v, c) the degree of v, and d) the local-port number of v of the edge it used when arriving at v. Thus graphs are assumed to have bounded degree Δ. Typical tasks from this literature are "perpetual exploration", "exploration with return", and "gathering". The main twist is that the robots should perform their task on a graph no matter the local port numbering.

Such robot systems are easily expressible in our framework. The edge-label set Σ is defined to be $[\Delta]$, the edge-relation E is assumed to be symmetric, and $\lambda(v, w) = i$ codes that i is v's port number for the undirected edge $\{v, w\}$. Note that $\lambda(v, w)$ need not equal $\lambda(w, v)$. The interesting aspect is how to simulate d) above. Our robot must store in its state both the state of the DC-robot, as well as the local-port number with which it entered the current vertex. It does this as follows: when our robot is at vertex v, and the DC-robot says to take exit i, our robot first determines the w such that $\lambda(v, w) = i$, and then it determines the $j \in \Delta$ such that $\lambda(w, v) = j$. It can do this with test-instructions in $\mathsf{FOL}(\Sigma)$.

Rotor-Robot We now give a simple but important example that can be analysed in our framework. The *rotor robot* operates as follows: when it enters a vertex v by port i it leaves by port $i+1$ modulo $\mathsf{deg}(v)$. This robot is known by various other names: Abelian mobile robot, rotor walk, ant walk, Eulerian walker, and Propp machine. It is important because it is a viable alternative to probabilistic robots that perform random walks [11]. It has the property that it explores all trees — a result that seems to be folklore, and that could be proved, for fixed degree Δ, using Theorem 2.

Label-Guided Tasks. The graphs in this paper are edge-labeled, but our results hold allowing vertex-labels. Moreover, our framework can incorporate questions of the form: given a robot and a task, decide if for every graph $G \in \mathcal{G}$ there exists a labeling of G such that the robot achieves the task on the graph with the help of the labeling. For instance, although there is no DC-robot that perpetually explores all graphs, there is a DC-robot and an algorithm that colours vertices by three colours, such that the robot can perpetually explore every such coloured graph [16]. Since the set of all graphs does not have decidable-validity, we might only hope to verify variations of this fact for restricted classes of graphs, e.g., fix a context-free set of graphs $\mathcal{G}$; then one can decide, given a DC-robot, whether or not for every $G \in \mathcal{G}$ the robot achieves the task "there is a colouring of G using three colours that the robot can use to perpetually explore G". The reason this fits into Theorem 2 is that this task is captured by an RTL formula — indeed, the property that $X_1, X_2, X_3 \subseteq V$ colour a graph is easily expressed in MSOL (just say that $\wedge_{i \neq j} X_i \cap X_j = \emptyset$ and $X_1 \cup X_2 \cup X_3 = V$).

6. COMPLEXITY CONSIDERATIONS

As discussed in Section 4.2, the framework reduces the parameterised verification problem $\mathsf{PVP}_{\mathrm{T}}(\mathcal{G}, \mathcal{R})$ to the $\Phi_{\overline{\mathcal{R}},\mathrm{T}}$-validity problem for $\mathcal{G}$ where $\Phi_{\overline{\mathcal{R}},\mathrm{T}}$ is the set of formulas $\{\phi_{\overline{R},\mathrm{T}} : \overline{R} \in \mathcal{R}\}$. Unfortunately, the complexity of the decision procedure for $\mathsf{PVP}_{\mathrm{T}}(\mathcal{G}, \mathcal{R})$ in Corollary 1 may be non-elementary, i.e., not bounded by any tower of exponentials in the size of the input robot R. Indeed: although the size of the computed formula $\phi_{R,\mathrm{T}}$ is exponential in the size of the robot R and linear in the size of the RTL formula capturing T, but the complexity of the MSOL-validity problem for $\mathcal{G}$ is non-elementary even taking $\mathcal{G}$ to be the set of binary-labeled lines [42].

Consequently, we illustrate that improved decision procedures can be found for interesting tasks and sets of graphs.

A robot is *deterministic* if for all $p \in Q$, either a) there exists $q, q' \in Q$ and $\tau \in \mathsf{MSOL}(\Sigma)$ and the only transitions out of p are (p, τ, q) and $(p, \neg\tau, q')$, or b) there exists $\sigma \in \Sigma, q, q' \in Q$ and the only transitions out of p are $(p, \uparrow_\sigma, q)$ and $(p, \neg\exists z(edg_\sigma(x, z)), q')$. In other words, a) says that if test τ holds goto state q else goto state q', and b) says that if there is an edge in the graph labeled σ then traverse it (in case of many such edges, pick one nondeterministically) and go to state q, otherwise goto state q'. A Σ-graph is *deterministic* if $\lambda(v, w) = \lambda(v, w')$ implies $w = w'$. For instance, Δ-ary trees are deterministic. Note that deterministic robots have at most one run on deterministic graphs.

THEOREM 3. *Fix $\Delta \in \mathbb{N}$. Let $\mathcal{G}$ be the Δ-ary trees, let $\mathcal{R}$ be all deterministic robots, and let* T *be the "explore and halt" task. Then* $\mathsf{PVP}_{\mathrm{T}}(\mathcal{G}, \mathcal{R})$ *is* EXPTIME-COMPLETE.

PROOF SKETCH. The idea is to inter-reduce the parameterised verification problem with the universality problem for deterministic tree-walking automata (DTWA). A DTWA is a deterministic machine that can recognise sets of trees: the automaton starts at the root, at any given time the automaton sits on a node of the input tree, can test if the current node is a leaf, the root, or the ith child (for $i \leq \Delta$), and based on these tests the machine updates its internal state and executes one of the commands: "accept the tree", "reject the tree", "go to the parent" or "go the ith child". The universality of DTWA is EXPTIME-COMPLETE. Indeed, from a DTWA A build a DTWA B that simulates A and rejects whenever A runs forever (this causes a quadratic blowup in the number of states [36]); then complement B by swapping accept and reject states to get a DTWA C; then convert C into an ordinary frontier-to-root tree automaton D using a subset construction that calculates loops of C [9, Fact 1] (this causes an exponential blowup); then test D for emptiness (which can be done in P).

Here is the reduction that gives the upper bound: given a deterministic robot R build a DTWA A_R that operates on trees t with marked nodes s and v, written (t, s, v), as follows: first it does a DFS from the root, and when it reaches s it begins the simulation of R; after the simulation begins, A_R remembers if v is visited; if R enters a halt state and v was visited then A_R accepts (t, s, v), and if R enters a halt state and v was not visited then A_R rejects input (t, s, v). Thus: R "explores and halts" iff for all (t, s, v) the run of R on t starting at s visits v and later enters a halt state iff A_R accepts all inputs of the form (t, s, v). The size of A_R is linear in the size of R.

Here is the reduction that gives the lower bound: given a DTWA A, build a robot R_A which first explores the input tree t (doing, say, a DFS), then simulates A from the root, and halts iff A accepts (thus R_A runs forever if A rejects). Since R_A always explores its input, A accepts t iff R_A explores and halts on t. The size of R_A is linear in the size of A. □

NOTE 3. *For every $\Delta \geq 2$, there is no robot that "explores and halts" on all local port-numbered Δ-ary trees [21]. The proof above is easily adapted to yield an algorithm that, given a robot R and $\Delta \geq 2$, returns a local-port numbered tree on which the robot does not succeed to "explore and halt".*

7. COMPARISON WITH RELATED WORK

Robot systems are considered distributed if they involve autonomous agents with no central control. In light of this, we first describe the relationship of our work to formal verification of distributed systems generally, and then to formal verification of robot protocols in particular.

Formal verification of distributed systems.

Typical parameters that arise in the study of distributed systems are the number of agents, the number of assumed faulty agents, etc. Since parameterised problems of distributed systems are, in general, undecidable [3, 43], the formal methods community developed sound but incomplete methods that require human intervention, e.g., counter- and predicate-abstractions, inductive invariants, regular model checking and acceleration techniques. See for instance [39, references on pages 2-3].

On the other hand, by simplifying the systems one can get decidable PVP. These use techniques from games, automata theory and logic, notably finite-model properties/cutoffs, reduction to Petri nets, and the theory of well-structured transition systems [24, 26, 23, 15, 31, 19, 1, 2].

Of all these models, token-passing systems (i.e., the models in [24, 15, 1, 2]) are the closest to robots — both tokens and robots move along the vertices of graphs. However, we now argue that the model in these cited papers is incomparable with our model. First, the translation of their token-passing systems into robot systems would require that robots can read and write to variables at the vertices (this is to model the fact that processes have states). However, we assumed environments are static (because otherwise the PVP is quickly undecidable). Conversely, translating robot-systems into the cited token-passing systems requires that the robot-systems satisfy the following unrealistic assumptions (that are used in their decidability proofs): when a robot decides to move, an adversary decides which edge it takes, as well as to which of its internal states to transition (i.e., even the robot's memory may be scrambled). Not even the simplest robots from the distributed computing literature (e.g., the rotor robot, or the DFS robot) satisfy this double restriction.

Formal verification of robot systems.

The formal methods community has only recently [30, 20, 12, 6, 4, 35] begun explicitly verifying and synthesising robot protocols (rather than distributed systems in general). However, half of these papers only treat small values of the parameters. For instance, one such paper concludes [6, page 11]:

> *While our method is parameterised by both k [the number of robots] and n [the size of the graph], it does not permit to verify whether a [robot] protocol is valid for every k and n satisfying a particular predicate.*

The papers that do treat parameterised robot protocols do not give sound and complete decision procedures for their systems, as we do. Indeed, [4] uses a proof assistant to provide certificates (formal proofs) of impossibility results about robot networks; [35] uses the theory of games on graphs to synthesise a robot protocol for gathering k robots on a ring of size n (for small values of k, n), and relies on a hand-proven induction to prove that the synthesised robot protocol works for all values of the parameters k, n; and [32] presents a sound technique that may identify cutoffs using a counter-abstraction in order to draw conclusions about certain swarm algorithms, independently of the number of swarming agents.

The quotation above continues:

> *Adapting recent advances in parameterised model checking [citation elided] would be a nice way to obtain such results.*

Both the methodology (reducing parameterised verification of robot systems to validity problems in logic) and the results of this paper (algorithms for automatic parameterised verification of robot systems consisting of a single robot in an unknown environment) are novel and have succeeded where other methods and "recent advances" (discussed in the previous subsection) have not.

Comparison with graph-walking automata.

Graph-walking automata. There is no canonical definition of automaton on graphs. Our model of a single robot is equivalent to graph-walking automata with MSOL-tests [7]. The proof idea of Lemma 1 (which compiles robots into formulas over graphs) is borrowed from [7, 25]. Other classical notions of automata on graphs (e.g., [8]) are often too expressive and lead to undecidable parameterised verification problems (see the proof of Theorem 1).

Multi-head automata. If agents are modeled as finite-state machines, then multi-agent systems are instances of multi-head automata, and the parameterised verification problem for reachability tasks is equivalent to the universality problem of such automata. A technical difference between our robot-ensembles and multi-head automata is that the k-many heads of a multi-head automaton are operated from a central control. In the language of robots this would mean that the robots can communicate their current local states to each other. Such communication is disallowed as it quickly results in undecidability. However, the proof of Theorem 1 shows that, similarly, even simple vision-based communication leads to undecidability.

Tree-walking automata (TWA) are a natural generalisation to trees of two-way automata on words. Tree-walking automata with a single head, and their corresponding regular expressions, have been studied for their own sake [9], in formal verification, e.g., [46, 10, 37], and as tree pattern-matching tools [13, 41]. TWA are used in Theorem 3 to reason about a single robot walking on unknown trees.

8. FUTURE CHALLENGES

This paper takes a step in the following general research agenda: find natural robot systems that have decidable or tractable PVP.

Regarding decidability, much work remains to be done. An important problem is to extend the methodology or results of this paper to multiple robots. Notes 1 and 2 discuss the challenges facing such an investigation.

Similarly, in light of the fact that PVP is quickly undecidable in a dynamic environment (e.g., this is the case for simple reachability tasks of a single robot that can read and write to every vertex on a line, cf. [43, 24]), what restrictions on the robot or the dynamic environment will result in decidable PVP?

On the other hand, we believe it is feasible to extend our framework to quantitative tasks, such as minimising the number of steps to complete a task.

Regarding complexity, we have seen that our general algorithm for solving the PVP (in Theorem 2) has high computational complexity, and we have seen (in Theorem 3) that a certain problem on trees is EXPTIME-COMPLETE. For which systems (tasks, classes of graphs, and classes of robots) is the PVP solvable in P, NP, or PSPACE?

We believe that tackling these questions will open avenues both in automata theory and in the verification of mobile multi-agent systems in unknown environments.

Acknowledgements

I thank the reviewers for their careful reading and provocative questions which helped improve the content and presentation of this paper.

REFERENCES

[1] B. Aminof, S. Jacobs, A. Khalimov, and S. Rubin. Parameterized model checking of token-passing systems. In *VMCAI*, pages 262–281, 2014.

[2] B. Aminof, T. Kotek, F. Spegni, S. Rubin, and H. Veith. Parameterized model checking of rendezvous systems. In *CONCUR*, pages 109–124, 2014.

[3] K. Apt and D. Kozen. Limits for automatic verification of finite-state concurrent systems. *Inf. Process. Lett.*, 15:307–309, 1986.

[4] C. Auger, Z. Bouzid, P. Courtieu, S. Tixeuil, and X. Urbain. Certified impossibility results for byzantine-tolerant mobile robots. In *SSS*, pages 178–190, 2013.
[5] M. A. Bender, A. Fernandez, D. Ron, A. Sahai, and S. Vadhan. The power of a pebble: Exploring and mapping directed graphs. *Information and Computation*, 176(1):1–21, 2002.
[6] B. Berard, L. Millet, M. Potop-Butucaru, Y. Thierry-Mieg, and S. Tixeuil. Formal verification of mobile robot protocols. Report <hal-00834061>, 2013.
[7] R. Bloem and J. Engelfriet. Monadic second order logic and node relations on graphs and trees. In *Structures in Logic and Computer Science*, pages 144–161, 1997.
[8] M. Blum and C. Hewitt. Automata on a 2-dimensional tape. *SWAT (FOCS)*, pages 155–160, 1967.
[9] M. Bojańczyk. Language and automata theory and applications. *Lecture Notes in Computer Science Volume 5196*, pages 1–2, 2008.
[10] P. A. Bonatti, C. Lutz, A. Murano, and M. Y. Vardi. The complexity of enriched μ-calculi. *Logical Methods in Computer Science*, 4(3:11):1–27, 2008.
[11] B. Bond and L. Levine. Abelian networks: foundations and examples. *CoRR*, abs/1309.3445, 2013.
[12] F. Bonnet, X. Defago, F. Petit, M. Potop-Butucaru, and S. Tixeuil. Brief announcement: Discovering and assessing fine-grained metrics in robot networks protocols. In *SSS*, pages 282–284. 2012.
[13] A. Brüggemann-Klein and D. Wood. Caterpillars: A context specification technique. *Markup Languages*, 2:81–106, 2000.
[14] E. Clarke, O. Grumberg, and D. Peled. *Model Checking*. MIT Press, 1999.
[15] E. Clarke, M. Talupur, T. Touili, and H. Veith. Verification by network decomposition. In *CONCUR 2004*, volume 3170, pages 276–291, 2004.
[16] R. Cohen, P. Fraigniaud, D. Ilcinkas, A. Korman, and D. Peleg. Label-guided graph exploration by a finite automaton. In *ICALP*, pages 335–346. 2005.
[17] B. Courcelle and J. Engelfriet. Book: Graph structure and monadic second-order logic. a language-theoretic approach. *Bull. EATCS*, 108:179, 2012.
[18] S. Das. Mobile agents in distributed computing: Network exploration. *Bull. EATCS*, 109:54–69, 2013.
[19] G. Delzanno. Parameterized verification and model checking for distributed broadcast protocols. In *ICGT*, pages 1–16, 2014.
[20] S. Devismes, A. Lamani, F. Petit, P. Raymond, and S. Tixeuil. Optimal grid exploration by asynchronous oblivious robots. *CoRR*, abs/1105.2461, 2011.
[21] K. Diks, P. Fraigniaud, E. Kranakis, and A. Pelc. Tree exploration with little memory. *Journal of Algorithms*, 51(1):38–63, 2004.
[22] H. Ebbinghaus and J. Flum. *Finite model theory.* Perspectives in Mathematical Logic. Springer, 1995.
[23] E. Emerson and V. Kahlon. Model checking guarded protocols. In *LICS*, pages 361–370, 2003.
[24] E. Emerson and K. Namjoshi. On reasoning about rings. *Int. J. Found. Comput. Sci.*, 14(4):527–550, 2003.
[25] J. Engelfriet and H. J. Hoogeboom. Nested pebbles and transitive closure. In *STACS*, pages 477–488, 2006.
[26] J. Esparza, A. Finkel, and R. Mayr. On the verification of broadcast protocols. In *LICS*, pages 352–359, 1999.
[27] P. Fraigniaud, D. Ilcinkas, G. Peer, A. Pelc, and D. Peleg. Graph exploration by a finite automaton. *Theoretical Computer Science*, 345:331 – 344, 2005.
[28] L. Gasieniec and T. Radzik. Memory efficient anonymous graph exploration. In H. Broersma, T. Erlebach, T. Friedetzky, and D. Paulusma, editors, *Graph-Theoretic Concepts in Computer Science*, volume 5344 of *LNCS*, pages 14–29. 2008.
[29] E. Grädel, W. Thomas, and T. Wilke, editors. *Automata, Logics, and Infinite Games: A Guide to Current Research*, volume 2500 of *LNCS*. Springer, 2002.
[30] X. Huang, P. Maupin, and R. Van Der Meyden. Model checking knowledge in pursuit evasion games. In *IJCAI*, pages 240–245, 2011.
[31] P. Kouvaros and A. Lomuscio. Automatic verification of parameterised multi-agent systems. In *AAMAS*, pages 861–868, 2013.
[32] P. Kouvaros and A. Lomuscio. A counter abstraction technique for the verification of robot swarms. To appear in *AAAI*, 2015.
[33] E. Kranakis, D. Krizanc, and S. Rajsbaum. Mobile agent rendezvous: A survey. *SIROCCO*, pages 1–9, 2006.
[34] E. Kranakis, D. Krizanc, and S. Rajsbaum. Computing with mobile agents in distributed networks. In S. Rajasekaran and J. Reif, editors, *Handbook of Parallel Computing: Models, Algorithms, and Applications*, pages 8–1 to 8–20. Chapman Hall/CRC Computer and Inf. Sci. Series, 2007.
[35] L. Millet, M. Potop-Butucaru, N. Sznajder, and S. Tixeuil. On the synthesis of mobile robots algorithms: The case of ring gathering. In *SSS*, pages 237–251, 2014.
[36] A. Muscholl, M. Samuelides, and L. Segoufin. Complementing deterministic tree-walking automata. *Inf. Process. Lett.*, 99(1):33–39, 2006.
[37] J. Obdržálek. Fast mu-calculus model checking when tree-width is bounded. In *CAV*, pages 80–92, 2003.
[38] A. Pelc. Disc 2011 invited lecture: Deterministic rendezvous in networks: Survey of models and results. In *DISC*, pages 1–15, 2011.
[39] A. Pnueli, J. Xu, and L. Zuck. Liveness with $(0,1,\infty)$-counter abstraction. In *CAV*, pages 93–111, 2002.
[40] A. Rosenberg. On multi-head finite automata. *IBM Journal of Research and Development*, 10(5):388–394, Sep 1966.
[41] T. Schwentick. Foundations of xml based on logic and automata: A snapshot. In *FoIKS*, pages 23–33, 2012.
[42] L. J. Stockmeyer. *The complexity of decision problems in automata theory and logic.* PhD thesis, MIT, 1974.
[43] I. Suzuki. Proving properties of a ring of finite-state machines. *Inf. Process. Lett.*, 28(4):213–214, July 1988.
[44] W. Thomas. Automata on infinite objects. In *Handbook of Theoretical Computer Science, Volume B: Formal Models and Semantics*, pages 133–192, 1990.

[45] W. Thomas. Languages, automata, and logic. In *Handbook of Formal Languages*, pages 389–455, 1996.

[46] M. Y. Vardi. Reasoning about the past with two-way automata. In *ICALP*, pages 628–641, 1998.

Decentralized Bisimulation for Multiagent Systems

Lei Song
Quantum Computation & Intelligent Systems
University of Technology, Sydney
lei.song@uts.edu.au

Yuan Feng
Quantum Computation & Intelligent Systems
University of Technology, Sydney
yuan.feng@uts.edu.au

Lijun Zhang
State Key Laboratory of Computer Science
Institute of Software, Chinese Academy of Sciences
zhanglj@ios.ac.cn

ABSTRACT

The notion of bisimulation has been introduced as a powerful way to abstract from details of systems in the formal verification community. When applying to multiagent systems, classical bisimulations will allow one agent to make decisions based on full histories of others. Thus, as a general concept, classical bisimulations are unrealistically powerful for such systems. In this paper, we define a coarser notion of bisimulation under which an agent can only make realistic decisions based on information available to it. Our bisimulation still implies trace distribution equivalence of the systems, and moreover, it allows a compositional abstraction framework of reasoning about the systems.

Categories and Subject Descriptors

F.1.2 [**Models of Computation**]Parallelism and concurrency, Probabilistic computation

General Terms

Theory, Verification

Keywords

Bisimulation; multiagent systems; decentralized

1. INTRODUCTION

Compositional theories have become a foundation for modeling and analyzing stochastic systems. In particular, the notion of compositional minimization [8, 5, 6] approaches has been introduced as a powerful way to abstract from details of systems in the formal verification community [23, 15].

Probabilistic automata (PA), also known as Markov Decision Processes in the planning community, were proposed by Segala in [29] as a compositional behavioral model, see Fig. 1 for some examples. Later, probabilistic automata were used to describe probabilistic multiagent systems [11].

Bisimulation is an important technique to cope with the infamous state-explosion problem in model checking [4]. Essentially, it tells whether two given systems exhibit the same behavior or should be distinguished. Intuitively, two systems are bisimilar if and only if each observable action of one of them can be simulated by the other by performing the same action, and furthermore, the resultant systems are again bisimilar. Ideally, a suitable notion of bisimulation for probabilistic multiagent systems should satisfy the following two natural requirements:

1. It should have an *appropriate distinguishing power.* If two agents output a sequence of observable actions with different probabilities, i.e., they are not trace distribution equivalent, then one can easily distinguish them by only observation (i.e., without interaction with the system). Therefore, a bisimulation should preserve trace distribution equivalence. On the other hand, for the sake of state space reduction, the bisimulation should be as coarse as possible, as coarser bisimulation means fewer states in the quotient system, which in turn means less effort in later verification and analysis.

2. It should be *compositional*, i.e., it is preserved by natural operators for constructing systems. As a multiagent system is typically built from more than one component agents, compositionality of bisimulation means that once we show two agents are bisimilar, no observer can distinguish them in any context. This is crucial in performing minimization compositionally. Note that trace distribution equivalence is not compositional.

Many variants of bisimulations have been proposed as powerful ways for equating behaviorally equivalent states [29, 16, 19]. However, as illustrated by the following example, which is inspired by [29, 17], these bisimulations are not suitable for probabilistic multiagent systems, thus motivating our definition of a coarser notion of distribution-based bisimulation and compositionality under realistic schedulers.

Example 1. *Consider a game with two players: Alice and Bob. Alice tosses a fair coin, while Bob tries to guess the result of the coin throw. If Bob guesses correctly, he wins; otherwise Alice wins. Suppose Alice can choose from two strategies to play the game: 1) She first informs Bob that the game starts and then tosses the coin, or 2) She first tosses the coin, keeps the result secret, and then asks Bob to guess. Formally, these two strategies are described in Fig. 1 (a) and (b), respectively, as probabilistic automata, where i denotes the announcement that the game begins, while h and t denote the coin tossing results "head" and "tail", respectively.*

Obviously, as the only difference between Alice's two strategies is whether or not the coin tossing is made before she announces the start of the game, which is unobservable

Appears in: *Proceedings of the 14th International Conference on Autonomous Agents and Multiagent Systems (AAMAS 2015), Bordini, Elkind, Weiss, Yolum (eds.), May, 4–8, 2015, Istanbul, Turkey.*

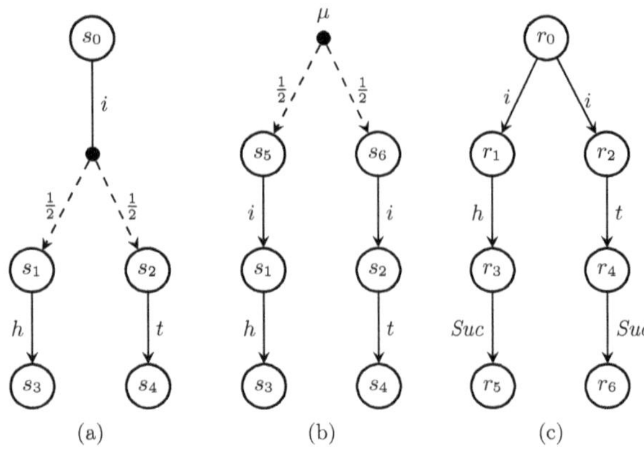

Figure 1: s_0 and μ represent two different strategies of Alice in playing the coin tossing game and r_0 denotes the guesser Bob.

for Bob, these strategies should work equally well for Alice. However, we can show that $s_0 \not\sim \mu$ for any state-based bisimulation $\sim$ defined as in, say [29]. To see this, note that state-based bisimulation is defined over states and then lifted to distributions. Thus, if $s_0 \sim \mu$, then we must have both $s_0 \sim s_5$ and $s_0 \sim s_6$, which is impossible.

The above argument motivates our first design decision to define bisimulation directly on distributions. In our notion of bisimulation, the distribution μ is regarded as a whole when compared with s_0. Thus we have both the transitions $s_0 \xrightarrow{i} \nu$ and $\mu \xrightarrow{i} \nu$ where $\nu = \{s_1 : \frac{1}{2}, s_2 : \frac{1}{2}\}$, making them bisimilar as expected.

To illustrate our second design decision, let us model the behaviors of Bob as in Fig. 1 (c): once he gets to know that Alice starts the game (by synchronizing with Alice through action i), he guesses Alice's coin tossing result by non-deterministically choosing the action h or t. Now consider a play of the game which is obtained by the parallel composition of Alice and Bob. We use a *CSP*-style parallel composition, where synchronization of corresponding actions of Alice and Bob in the set $A = \{i, h, t\}$ is enforced. If Bob wins (i.e., he successfully synchronizes with Alice through either h or t), he performs the action *Suc* to announce his success.

In view of our criterion (2) of an ideal bisimulation, we would like the two systems $s_0 \parallel_A r_0$ and $\mu \parallel_A r_0$ to be bisimilar. However, if a traditional way of defining compositionality is adopted, they are not bisimilar, even with the weaken notions of distribution-based bisimulation defined in this paper or [16, 19]. To see this, we depict the two systems $s_0 \parallel_A r_0$ and $\mu \parallel_A r_0$ in Fig. 2. For $s_0 \parallel_A r_0$, the probability of observing action *Suc* is exactly 0.5, no matter how a scheduler resolves the non-deterministic choice (which corresponds to how Bob guesses the outcome of the coin). In contrast, for system $\mu \parallel_A r_0$, an (unrestricted, as in the definition of classical bisimulations) scheduler can choose the lower i action from state $s_5 \parallel_A r_0$ while the upper i from state $s_6 \parallel_A r_0$. Obviously, this scheduler induces an execution for which action *Suc* is observed with probability 1.

To further explain why the traditional compositionality is a too strong requirement for multiagent systems, let us have a closer look at the scheduler that distinguishes $s_0 \parallel_A r_0$ and $\mu \parallel_A r_0$. The scheduler chooses different i actions for Bob in states $s_5 \parallel_A r_0$ and $s_6 \parallel_A r_0$. In other words, from Bob's view, the resolution of his non-deterministic choice of which transition to perform in state r_0 is based on the state Alice has reached by performing her internal probabilistic choice, namely either state s_5 or s_6. As in the context of multiagent systems, each agent runs autonomously and is partially observable to other agents as well as the environment, this is not a realistic scheduler. Specifically, Bob would need to see the internal state of Alice (actually the result of the coin throw) to make his decision. However, no communication between Alice and Bob has happened at this point in time, by which this information could have been conveyed. Thus, when agents only share the information they gain through explicit communication via observable actions [22], this behavior is prohibited. Note that it was also argued in [22] that in case all agents in a multiagent system share information with each other, the system can be transformed into an equivalent system with only one agent.

In this paper, we tackle this problem by restricting realistic schedulers to those which are decentralized [17], meaning that the scheduler can be decomposed into sub-schedulers of component agents, and with partial information [10], meaning that each sub-scheduler of component agents can only make decisions based on its local information obtained so far. The compositionality is then defined based on realistic schedulers instead of general schedulers considered in previous bisimulations. Both partial information and decentralized schedulers have been coined as principal means to exclude undesired or unrealistically powerful schedulers. We provide a co-inductive definition for distribution-based bisimulation which echoes these considerations on the automaton level, thereby resulting in a very coarse, yet reasonable, notion of equality for multiagent systems.

Summarizing, our contribution in this paper is a novel notion of bisimulation tailored for distributed systems, including multiagent systems, which

1. preserves observable behaviors, i.e., trace distribution equivalence, under partial information schedulers;
2. is compositional with respect to parallel operator under decentralized schedulers;
3. is proved to be the coarsest bisimulation relation satisfying the above two conditions.

Due to these results several things can be deduced directly, for instance (bounded and unbounded) reachability properties are preserved with respect to parallel composition by our bisimulation relations.

Organization of the Paper.

Section 2 recalls some notations used in the paper. In Section 3, a notion of distribution-based bisimulation is proposed and discussed, and its properties under realistic schedulers established in Section 4. Section 5 concludes the paper.

2. PRELIMINARIES

Let S be a finite set of states ranged over by $r, s, \ldots$. A *distribution* is a function $\mu : S \to [0, 1]$ satisfying $\mu(S) = \sum_{s \in S} \mu(s) \leq 1$. If $\mu(S) = 1$, it is called a *full distribution*, otherwise it is a *sub-distribution*. Let $Dist(S)$ denote the set of distributions over S, ranged over by $\mu, \nu, \gamma, \ldots$. Define $Supp(\mu) = \{s \mid \mu(s) > 0\}$ as the support set of μ. If $\mu(s) = 1$, then μ is called a *Dirac* distribution, written as δ_s. Let $|\mu| = \mu(S)$ denote the size of the distribution μ. Given

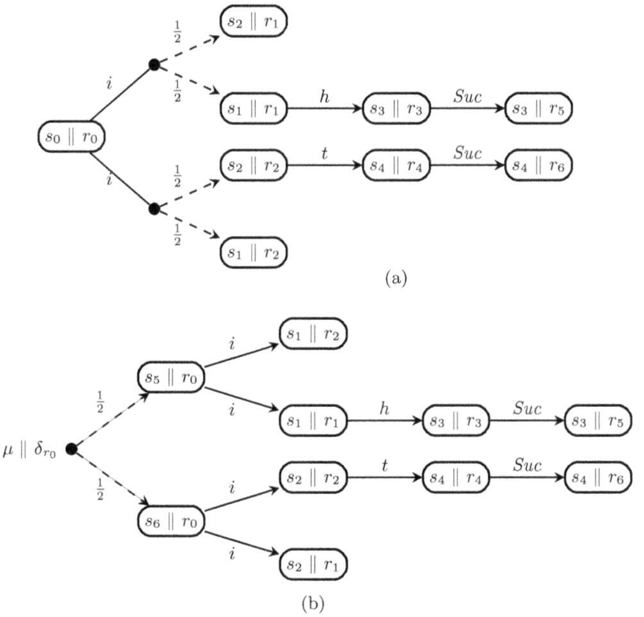

Figure 2: Executions of $s_0 \parallel_A r_0$ and $\mu \parallel_A \delta_{r_0}$ where A is omitted.

a real number $x \geq 0$, $x \cdot \mu$ is the distribution such that $(x \cdot \mu)(s) = x \cdot \mu(s)$ for each $s \in Supp(\mu)$ if $x \cdot |\mu| \leq 1$, while $\mu = \mu_1 + \mu_2$ whenever $\mu(s) = \mu_1(s) + \mu_2(s)$ for each $s \in S$ and $|\mu| \leq 1$. We often write $\{s : \mu(s) \mid s \in Supp(\mu)\}$ alternatively for a distribution μ. For instance, $\{s_1 : 0.4, s_2 : 0.6\}$ denotes a distribution μ such that $\mu(s_1) = 0.4$ and $\mu(s_2) = 0.6$.

2.1 Probabilistic Automata

We consider multiagent systems with probabilistic behaviors. In this paper, each agent as well as the environment is modeled as a probabilistic automaton [29].

Definition 1. *A* PA $\mathcal{P}$ *is a tuple* $(S, Act, \rightarrow, \bar{\mu})$ *where* $\bar{\mu} \in Dist(S)$ *is the initial distribution,* S *is a finite but non-empty set of states,* Act *is a set of actions, and* $\rightarrow \subseteq S \times Act \times Dist(S)$ *is a finite set of probabilistic transitions.*

Let $\alpha, \beta, \gamma, \ldots$ range over the actions in Act. We write $s \xrightarrow{\alpha} \mu$ if $(s, \alpha, \mu) \in \rightarrow$. Let $EA(s) = \{\alpha \in Act \mid \exists \mu . s \xrightarrow{\alpha} \mu\}$, i.e., $EA(s)$ is the set of actions enabled at state s. A *path* is a finite or infinite alternative sequence $\pi = s_0, \alpha_0, s_1, \alpha_1, s_2 \ldots$ of states and actions, such that for each $i \geq 0$ there exists a distribution μ with $s_i \xrightarrow{\alpha_i} \mu$ and $\mu(s_{i+1}) > 0$. We introduce some notations as follows:

- $|\pi|$, the length of π, i.e., the number of states on π, provided π is finite,
- $\pi\downarrow$, the last state of π, provided π is finite,
- $\pi[i] = s_i$ with $i \geq 0$, the $(i+1)$-th state on π if it exists,
- $\pi[0..i] = s_0, \alpha_0, s_1, \alpha_1, \ldots, s_i$, the prefix of π ending at state $\pi[i]$,

Let $Paths^\omega(\mathcal{P}) \subseteq S \times (Act \times S)^\omega$ and $Paths^*(\mathcal{P}) \subseteq S \times (Act \times S)^*$ denote the sets containing all infinite and finite paths of $\mathcal{P}$ respectively. Let $Paths(\mathcal{P}) = Paths^\omega(\mathcal{P}) \cup Paths^*(\mathcal{P})$. In case $\mathcal{P}$ is clear from the context, we simply omit it. We also let $Paths(s)$ be the set containing all paths starting from $s \in S$, similarly for $Paths^*(s)$ and $Paths^\omega(s)$.

Due to non-deterministic choices in PAs, a probability measure cannot be defined directly. As usual, we shall introduce the definition of *schedulers* to resolve the non-determinism. Intuitively, a scheduler will decide which transition to choose at each step, based on the history execution. Formally,

Definition 2. *A scheduler is a function* $\xi : Paths^* \mapsto Dist(Act \times Dist(S))$ *such that* $\xi(\pi)(\alpha, \mu) > 0$ *implies* $\pi\downarrow \xrightarrow{\alpha} \mu$. *A scheduler* ξ *is* deterministic *if it returns only Dirac distributions, that is,* $\xi(\pi)(\alpha, \mu) = 1$ *for some* α *and* μ.

In the sequel we will write $\xi(\pi) = \alpha$ to denote the fact that ξ only chooses transitions with the same label at each step, i.e., for all π, $\sum_{\mu \in Dist(S)} \xi(\pi)(\alpha, \mu) = 1$ for some α.

The *cone* of a finite path π, denoted C_π, is the set of infinite paths having π as their prefix, i.e., $C_\pi = \{\pi' \in Paths^\omega \mid \pi \leq \pi'\}$, where $\pi \leq \pi'$ iff π is a prefix of π'. Fixing a starting state s and a scheduler ξ, the measure $Pr_{\xi,s}$ of a cone C_π, where $\pi = s_0, \alpha_0, s_1, \alpha_1, \ldots, s_k$, is defined inductively as: $Pr_{\xi,s}(C_\pi) = 0$ if $s \neq s_0$, $Pr_{\xi,s}(C_\pi) = 1$ if $s = s_0$ and $k = 0$, and otherwise, $Pr_{\xi,s}(C_\pi) = Pr_{\xi,s}(C_{\pi[0..k-1]}) \times$

$$\left(\sum_{(s_{k-1}, \alpha_{k-1}, \mu) \in \rightarrow} \xi(\pi[0..k-1])(\alpha_{k-1}, \mu) \cdot \mu(s_k) \right).$$

Let $\mathcal{B}$ be the smallest algebra that contains all the cones and is closed under complement and countable unions. By standard measure theory [18, 26], this algebra is a σ-*algebra* and all its elements are measurable sets of paths. Moreover, $Pr_{\xi,s}$ can be extended to a unique measure on $\mathcal{B}$.

In this paper, a multiagent system is defined as a set of PAs running in parallel. For this, we recall the parallel operator for PAs [29].

Definition 3. *Let* $\mathcal{P}_i = (S_i, Act, \rightarrow_i, \bar{\mu}_i)$, $i = 1, 2$, *be two* PAs *and* $A \subseteq Act$, *then* $\mathcal{P}_1 \parallel_A \mathcal{P}_2 = (S, Act, \rightarrow, \bar{\mu})$ *such that*

1. $S = \{s_1 \parallel_A s_2 \mid (s_1, s_2) \in S_1 \times S_2\}$,
2. $s_1 \parallel_A s_2 \xrightarrow{\alpha} \mu_1 \parallel_A \mu_2$ *iff either* $\alpha \in A$ *and* $s_i \xrightarrow{\alpha}_i \mu_i$ *for each* $i \in \{1, 2\}$, *or* $\alpha \notin A$ *while* $s_i \xrightarrow{\alpha}_i \mu_i$ *and* $\mu_{3-i} = \delta_{s_{3-i}}$ *for some* $i \in \{1, 2\}$,
3. $\bar{\mu} = \bar{\mu}_1 \parallel_A \bar{\mu}_2$,

where $\mu_1 \parallel_A \mu_2$ *is a distribution over* S *such that* $(\mu_1 \parallel_A \mu_2)(s_1 \parallel_A s_2) = \mu_1(s_1) \cdot \mu_2(s_2)$.

Similar idea has been adopted in [11] to define the parallel composition of multiple probabilistic agents represented as *Markov Chains* (MCs) and the resulting composite system is described by a *Markov Decision Process* (MDP). Our definition of parallel operator generalizes the one in [11] in the sense that PAs subsume MDPs, hence also MCs. Note Definition 3 can be generalized to cases with more than two PAs in parallel, i.e.,

$$\parallel_A \{\mathcal{P}_i\}_{0 \leq i \leq n} \equiv (\parallel_A \{\mathcal{P}_i\}_{1 \leq i \leq n}) \parallel_A \mathcal{P}_0.$$

Below gives a simple example showing how the parallel operator works.

Example 2. *Let* s_0 *and* t_0 *be two states as in Fig. 3. Let* $A = \{\alpha\}$. *Intuitively,* $s_0 \parallel_A t_0$ *is a state obtained by running states* s_0 *and* t_0 *in parallel while imposing synchronization on the action* α. *By Definition 3,* $s_0 \parallel_A t_0$ *will have two transitions:* $s_0 \parallel_A t_0 \xrightarrow{\alpha} \nu_1 \equiv \mu_1 \parallel_A \mu_3$ *and* $s_0 \parallel_A t_0 \xrightarrow{\beta} \nu_2 \equiv$

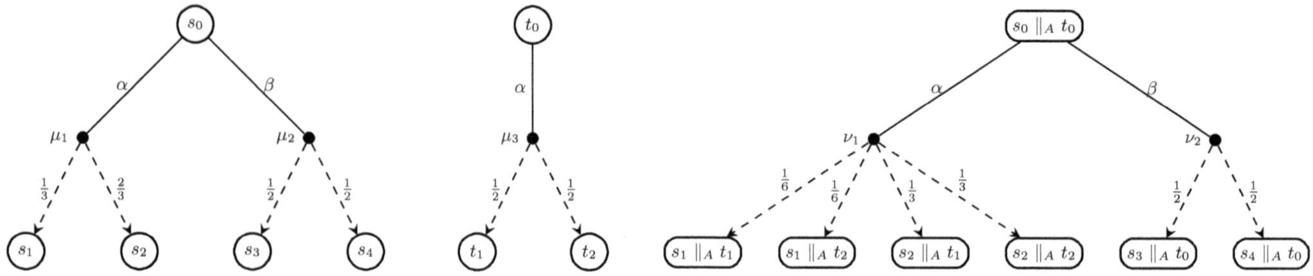

Figure 3: The parallel composition of s_0 and t_0 synchronizing on $A = \{\alpha\}$.

$\mu_2 \parallel_A \delta_{t_0}$*, where the transition with label* α *corresponds to the synchronization of* s_0 *and* t_0 *on* α*, while the transition labelled by* β *is the transition executed by* s_0 *spontaneously, as* t_0 *remains after the transition.*

Definition 4. *A probabilistic multiagent system (*PMA*)* $\mathcal{M}$ *is a set of* PA*s, called* local agents *and one of which may represent the environment, composed in parallel as* $\parallel_A \{\mathcal{P}_i\}_{0\leq i\leq n}$*. States of* $\mathcal{M}$ *are referred as* global states*, while states of local agents are called* local states.

Local agents execute actions not in A independently without synchronizing with others, while for actions in A, they need to synchronize with each other, which can be seen as a way to exchange information among all agents. It is easy to see from Definition 3 that each PMA is also a PA.

Note that we can also define a PMA hierarchically to model the case where some communication is only made between a subset of local agents. For example, in the PMA $(\mathcal{P}_1 \parallel_A \mathcal{P}_2) \parallel_B \mathcal{P}_3$, $\mathcal{P}_1$ and $\mathcal{P}_2$ may exchange information through actions in $A\backslash B$, while $\mathcal{P}_1$ or $\mathcal{P}_2$ may communicate with $\mathcal{P}_3$ through $B\backslash A$. Furthermore, information exchanged through $A \cap B$ becomes common knowledge shared among all the three agents.

3. BISIMULATIONS FOR PMAS

In this section, we first recall the definition of distribution-based bisimulation on probabilistic automata in [14, 12], which we have argued that may distinguish too many states in certain scenarios. We then propose a novel definition of distribution-based bisimulation for probabilistic multiagent systems.

Let $\mu \xrightarrow{\alpha} \mu'$ iff there exists a transition $s \xrightarrow{\alpha} \mu_s$ for each $s \in Supp(\mu)$ such that $\mu' = \sum_{s\in Supp(\mu)} \mu(s) \cdot \mu_s$. Given a transition relation $\rightsquigarrow \subseteq S \times Act \times Dist(S)$, we let $s \overset{\alpha}{\rightsquigarrow}_c \mu$ iff there exists a finite number of real numbers $w_i > 0$ and transitions $s \overset{\alpha}{\rightsquigarrow} \mu_i$ such that $\sum_i w_i = 1$, and $\sum_i w_i \cdot \mu_i = \mu$. We call $\rightsquigarrow_c$ *combined transitions* (of $\rightsquigarrow$).

Definition 5. *The distribution-based bisimulation defined in [14, 12] is a symmetric relation* $\mathcal{R} \subseteq Dist(S) \times Dist(S)$ *such that* $\mu \mathrel{\mathcal{R}} \nu$ *implies:*

1. *whenever* $\mu \xrightarrow{\alpha}_c \mu'$*, there exists a* $\nu \xrightarrow{\alpha}_c \nu'$ *such that* $\mu' \mathrel{\mathcal{R}} \nu'$*;*
2. *whenever* $\mu \equiv \sum_{0\leq i\leq n} p_i \cdot \mu_i$ *there exists a decomposition* $\nu \equiv \sum_{0\leq i\leq n} p_i \cdot \nu_i$ *such that* $\mu_i \mathrel{\mathcal{R}} \nu_i$ *for each* i*, where* $\sum_{0\leq i\leq n} p_i = 1$ *with* $p_i > 0$ *for each* i*.*

We say that μ *and* ν *are bisimilar, written as* $\mu \sim \nu$*, iff there exists such a bisimulation relation* $\mathcal{R}$ *with* $\mu \mathrel{\mathcal{R}} \nu$*. Moreover* $s \sim r$ *iff* $\delta_s \sim \delta_r$*.*

Clause 1 is standard. Clause 2 says that no matter how we split μ, there always exists a splitting of ν to simulate the splitting of μ. Clause 2 in Definition 5 is, in fact, the cause why this relation is unrealistically strong for scenarios as those discussed in Example 1. The reason is that in order to establish a bisimulation, *every* splitting of μ into distributions must be matched by ν. This also includes splittings into Dirac distributions. Intuitively, this means that still the individual behavior of each single state in $Supp(\mu)$ must be matched. In our scenarios, however, we want to focus on the behavior of distributions over states and not their individual supporting states. We will correct this in our definition of distribution-based bisimulation later.

Definition 6. *A distribution* μ *is* transition consistent*, written as* $\overrightarrow{\mu}$*, if for any* $s_1, s_2 \in Supp(\mu)$*,* $EA(s_1) = EA(s_2)$*.*

Intuitively, a distribution is transition consistent if and only if all states in its support have the same set of enabled actions. When a distribution is transition consistent, then $\mu \xrightarrow{\alpha}$ whenever there is a state $s \in Supp(\mu)$ with $s \xrightarrow{\alpha}$. This also means that when a distribution is *not* transition consistent, there must be a transition that a certain state in the support can perform but the distribution cannot. We then say that this state is *blocked* from taking this transition.

We are now ready to define our notion of distribution-based bisimulation in this paper, which serves as the basis for the decentralized bisimulation we are going to introduce in Section 4. To simplify notation, we simply call our bisimulation *distribution-based bisimulation*, which should not be confused with Definition 5.

Definition 7. *A symmetric relation* $\mathcal{R} \subseteq Dist(S) \times Dist(S)$ *is a* distribution-based bisimulation *iff* $\mu \mathrel{\mathcal{R}} \nu$ *implies:*

1. *whenever* $\mu \xrightarrow{\alpha}_c \mu'$*, there exists a* $\nu \xrightarrow{\alpha}_c \nu'$ *such that* $\mu' \mathrel{\mathcal{R}} \nu'$*;*
2. *if not* $\overrightarrow{\mu}$*, then there exists* $\mu \equiv \sum_{0\leq i\leq n} p_i \cdot \mu_i$ *and* $\nu \equiv \sum_{0\leq i\leq n} p_i \cdot \nu_i$ *such that* $\overrightarrow{\mu_i}$ *and* $\mu_i \mathrel{\mathcal{R}} \nu_i$ *for each* $0 \leq i \leq n$ *where* $\sum_{0\leq i\leq n} p_i = 1$ *with* $p_i > 0$ *for each* i*.*

We say that μ *and* ν *are distribution-based bisimilar, written as* $\mu \sim^d \nu$*, iff there exists a distribution-based bisimulation* $\mathcal{R}$ *such that* $\mu \mathrel{\mathcal{R}} \nu$*. Moreover* $s \sim^d r$ *iff* $\delta_s \sim^d \delta_r$*.*

The main difference between $\sim$ and $\sim^d$ is that in Definition 5 we require for *any* split $\mu \equiv \sum_{0\leq i\leq n} p_i \cdot \mu_i$ of μ, there exists $\nu \equiv \sum_{0\leq i\leq n} p_i \cdot \nu_i$ with $\mu_i \mathrel{\mathcal{R}} \nu_i$ for each i, while in Definition 7, we require to split μ *only if* it is not transition consistent. We further require that in the splitting, each distribution μ_i is transition consistent. We do not require this for ν_i. It can be shown, however, that $\overrightarrow{\mu_i}$ and $\mu_i \mathrel{\mathcal{R}} \nu_i$ implies $\overrightarrow{\nu_i}$. These conditions ensure that no states in the support of μ are blocked from executing certain transitions. Clearly, if μ is already transition consistent, we do not need to split μ further, since no transition of states in $Supp(\mu)$ is blocked, thus the distribution transitions in clause 1 suffice to capture every behavior.

Remark 1. *Essentially, in Definition 7 we keep all states with the same set of enabled actions together. This is similar to the idea in [10], where all states with the same enabled actions are non-distinguishable from the outside. Once a distribution becomes transition consistent, we will not try to split it anymore – but rather match the lifted transitions according to the first clause.*

The notion of consistent distributions defined in Definition 6 actually induces an equivalence relation $R = \{(s,t) \in S \times S \mid EA(s) = EA(t)\}$ over the state space, which is in turn used in Definition 7 to guide the splitting of a distribution. Therefore, our distribution-based bisimulation can be seen as defined upon R. The main purpose of R is to characterize indistinguishable states in a multiagent system, which is also referred to as an epistemic accessibility relation *in [32] or an* information function *in [27]. The relation R is the coarsest one for schedulers to be well defined in such systems, since otherwise an action scheduled at one state may not be enabled at all at another equivalent state. This is not acceptable, particularly in the setting of planning [27] and model checking with incomplete information [20], schedulers transferring [7] and so on. However, nothing hampers the usage of finer relations than R. By doing so, all results in this paper are preserved, as long as we change the definition of partial information scheduler accordingly, which we will introduce soon. Furthermore, like in [32, 27], we can also define different levels of accessibility (or distinguishability) for different agents such that two global states $\|_A \{s_i\}_{0\le i\le n}$ and $\|_A \{t_i\}_{0\le i\le n}$ are not distinguishable to the i-th agent iff s_i and t_i are not distinguishable. To simplify the presentation, we assume the same accessibility relation R to all agents in the sequel.*

Example 3. *Back to Example 1, we are going to show that in Fig. 1, $\delta_{s_0} \sim^d \mu$. Let $\mathcal{R} = \{(\delta_{s_0}, \mu), (\mu, \delta_{s_0})\} \cup \mathrm{ID}$ where* ID *is the identity relation. It is easy to show that $\mathcal{R}$ is a distribution-based bisimulation. The key point is that both δ_{s_0} and $\{s_5 : 0.5, s_6 : 0.5\}$ are transition consistent, thus we do not need to split them any further. Conversely, we can show that $\mathcal{R}$ is not a bisimulation in the settings of [14, 12]. According to clause* 1 *of Definition 5, we require that for any split of $\{s_5 : 0.5, s_6 : 0.5\}$, there must exist a matching split of δ_{s_0}, which cannot be established. For instance the split $\{s_5 : 0.5, s_6 : 0.5\} = 0.5 \cdot \delta_{s_5} + 0.5 \cdot \delta_{s_6}$ cannot be matched by any split of δ_{s_0}.* □

The following example shows that the transition consistency condition of Definition 7 is necessary to avoid equating states which should be distinguished.

Example 4. *Suppose there are two states s_0 and r_0 such that $s_0 \xrightarrow{\alpha} s_1$ and $r_0 \xrightarrow{\alpha} \{r_1 : 0.5, r_2 : 0.5\}$ where all of s_1, r_1, and r_2 have a transition to themselves with label α. In addition, $r_1 \xrightarrow{\beta} r_1$ where $\alpha \neq \beta$.*

If clause 2 in Definition 7 was dropped, then we would have $s_0 \sim^d r_0$. To see this, let $\mathcal{R}$ be the symmetric closure of $\{(\delta_{s_0}, \delta_{r_0}), (\delta_{s_1}, \{r_1 : 0.5, r_2 : 0.5\})\}$. Note that the distribution $\{r_1 : 0.5, r_2 : 0.5\}$ can only perform an α transition and then return to itself (the β transition of r_1 would be blocked as it is disabled in r_2). Thus $\mathcal{R}$ is a distribution-based bisimulation, and $s_0 \sim^d r_0$. However, s_0 and r_0 should be distinguished, because r_0 can reach state r_1 which is able to perform a β transition, while s_0 cannot.

According to our Definition 7, however, as the distribution $\{r_1 : 0.5, r_2 : 0.5\}$ is not transition consistent, we should split it further to a convex combination of δ_{r_1} and δ_{r_2}. Then $s_0 \not\sim^d r_0$ can be easily seen from the fact that δ_{r_1} cannot be matched by any distribution from s_1.

The following theorem shows that both $\sim$ and $\sim^d$ are equivalence relations. Moreover $\sim^d$ is strictly coarser than $\sim$, which is straightforward from Definitions 5 and 7.

Theorem 1. *1. $\sim$ and $\sim^d$ are equivalence relations; 2. $\sim \subsetneq \sim^d$.*

4. OBSERVABLE BEHAVIOR AND COMPOSITION

We consider important properties of distribution-based bisimulation in this section, namely preservation of trace distributions equivalence, and compositionality. While these properties do *not* hold if considering all schedulers, we establish them for the subclass of partial information decentralized schedulers. Partial information schedulers $\mathcal{S}_P$ have been coined by De Alfaro [10], and decentralized schedulers $\mathcal{S}_D$ stem from D'Argenio and Giro [17]. Both have been proposed to rule out unrealistic scheduling decisions such as the ones discussed in Fig. 2. We echo these arguments to back our claim that distribution-based bisimulation is a valuable relation in the context of realistic scheduling, especially in multiagent systems. To get started, we review some desirable properties we are going to discuss.

We first introduce the notion of trace distribution equivalence [28] adapted to our setting. Let $\varsigma \in Act^*$ denote a finite trace of a PA $\mathcal{P}$ consisting of an ordered sequence of actions. Moreover, the cylinder C_ς induced by ς is defined by: $C_\varsigma = \cup\{C_\pi \mid \pi \in Paths^* \wedge trace(\pi) = \varsigma\}$ where $trace(\pi) = \epsilon$ denotes an empty trace if $|\pi| \le 1$, and $trace(\pi) = trace(\pi') \circ \alpha$, where $\pi = \pi' \circ (\alpha, s')$. The measurability of C_ς is straightforward from its definition since it is a countable union of cylinders. Below we define a family of equivalences, parametrized by certain classes of schedulers.

Definition 8. *Let μ_1 and μ_2 be two distributions of a* PA, *and $\mathcal{S}$ a set of schedulers. Then, $\mu_1 \equiv_{\mathcal{S}} \mu_2$ iff for each scheduler $\xi_1 \in \mathcal{S}$ there exists a scheduler $\xi_2 \in \mathcal{S}$, such that*

$$\sum_{s\in Supp(\mu_1)} \mu_1(s) \cdot Pr_s^{\xi_1}(C_\varsigma) = \sum_{s\in Supp(\mu_2)} \mu_2(s) \cdot Pr_s^{\xi_2}(C_\varsigma)$$

for each finite trace ς and vice versa. If $\mathcal{S}$ is the set of all schedulers, we simply write $\equiv$. We write $s_1 \equiv_{\mathcal{S}} s_2$ iff $\delta_{s_1} \equiv_{\mathcal{S}} \delta_{s_2}$.

Below follow examples (and counterexamples) of trace distribution equivalent states:

Example 5. *Let s_0 and μ be as in Fig. 1, then we have $\delta_{s_0} \equiv \mu$, since the only trace distribution of δ_{s_0} and μ is $\{ih : \frac{1}{2}, it : \frac{1}{2}\}$. In contrast, δ_{s_0} and ν in Fig. 4 are not trace distribution equivalent, since there are two possible trace distributions for δ_{s_0} : $\{\beta : 1\}$ and $\{\alpha : 1\}$, but for ν there are four trace distributions: $\{\alpha : 1\}$, $\{\beta : 1\}$, $\{\alpha : \frac{1}{3}, \beta : \frac{2}{3}\}$, and $\{\beta : \frac{1}{3}, \alpha : \frac{2}{3}\}$. The last two distributions are induced*

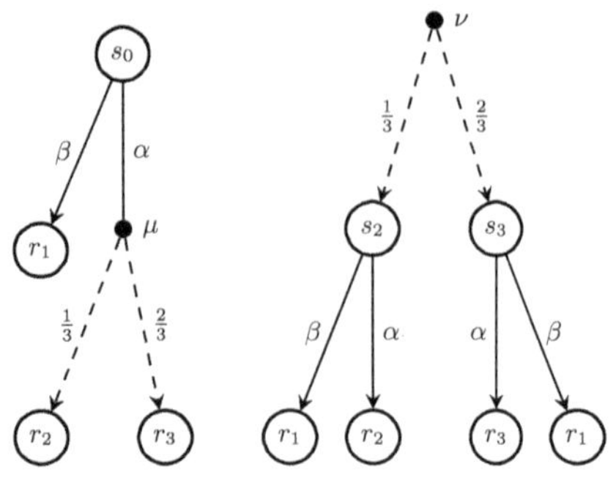

Figure 4: $\delta_{s_0} \sim^d \nu$.

by schedulers of ν *which choose transitions with different labels at states* s_2 *and* s_3*, which cannot be simulated by any scheduler of* s_0[1].

4.1 Realistic Schedulers

We now refine the very liberal Definition 2 where the set of all schedulers was introduced. As discussed, this class is too powerful for multiagent systems, since it includes unrealistic schedules such as the one which distinguishes the two automata in Fig. 2.

In the following we define two prominent sub-classes of schedulers, where only limited information is employed for scheduling. Recall $EA(s)$ denotes the set of actions enabled at s, which can be seen as the interface of s observable by other agents. We generalize the function EA to paths as follows: $EA(\pi) = EA(s)$ if $\pi = s$, and $EA(\pi) = EA(\pi')\alpha EA(s)$, where $\pi = \pi' \circ (\alpha, s)$. Other agents can only observe actions performed by s and its ancestors as well as their interfaces. We are now ready to define the *partial information schedulers* [10] as follows:

Definition 9. *A scheduler* ξ *is a partial information scheduler of* s *if for any* $\pi_1, \pi_2 \in Paths^*(s)$, $EA(\pi_1) = EA(\pi_2)$ *implies* $\xi(\pi_1) = \alpha$ *and* $\xi(\pi_2) = \alpha$ *for some* α*. We say* ξ *is a partial information scheduler of a* PMA *iff it is a partial information scheduler for all states in the* PMA.

We denote the set of all partial information schedulers by $\mathcal{S}_P$. Intuitively a partial information scheduler can only distinguish states via different enabled actions. It therefore excludes the possibility to schedule differently only because of different state identities. This fits well to a behavior-oriented rather than state-oriented view, as it is typical for multiagent systems. Consequently, for two different paths π_1 and π_2 with $EA(\pi_1) = EA(\pi_2)$, namely π_1 and π_2 are not distinguishable, a partial information scheduler chooses transitions labelled with the same action for both π_1 and π_2.

In order to exclude unrealistic schedulers when composing agents in parallel, another important sub-class of schedulers called *decentralized schedulers* has been introduced [17]. The idea is to assume that an agent running in parallel to other agents needs to make its local scheduling decisions in isolation, and thus can use only information about other agents that has been communicated to them beforehand. For instance the guesser Bob in Fig. 1 cannot base his local scheduling decision on the tossing outcome at the moment when his guess is to be scheduled. This fits perfectly in the setting of multiagent systems, as in such systems, each agent performs actions spontaneously and only interacts with other agents and the environment when necessary.

To formalize this locality idea, we first need to define the projection of a path to the path of its component agents. Let $s = \|_A \{s_i \mid 0 \le i \le n\}$ be a global state which is composed of $n+1$ local states with $n \ge 1$ in parallel such that all the local states synchronize on actions in A. Let π be a path starting from s, then the i-projection of π, denoted by $[\pi]_i$, is defined as follows: $[\pi]_i = [s]_i$ if $\pi = s$; otherwise if $\pi = \pi' \circ (\alpha, s')$,

$$[\pi]_i = \begin{cases} [\pi']_i \circ (\alpha, [s']_i) & \alpha \in A \vee (\alpha \notin A \wedge [\pi'\downarrow]_i \xrightarrow{\alpha} [s']_i) \\ [\pi']_i & \alpha \notin A \wedge (\exists j \neq i. [\pi'\downarrow]_j \xrightarrow{\alpha} [s']_j) \end{cases}$$

where $[s]_i = s_i$ with $0 \le i \le n$. Intuitively, given a path π of a state s, the i-projection of π is the path that only keeps track of the execution of the i-th agent of s during its execution. Also note any scheduler ξ of s can be decomposed into $n+2$ functions: a global scheduler $\xi_g : Paths^* \times \{0, \ldots, n\} \mapsto \{0, 1\}$ and $n+1$ local schedulers $\{\xi_i\}_{0 \le i \le n}$ such that for any π with $\pi\downarrow = \|_A \{s_i \mid 0 \le i \le n\}$, $\xi(\pi)(\alpha, \|_A \{\mu_i\}_{0 \le i \le n}) =$

$$\Pi_{0 \le i \le n}[\xi_g(\pi, i) \cdot \xi_i(\pi)(\alpha, \mu_i) + (1 - \xi_g(\pi, i)) \cdot Eq(\delta_{s_i}, \mu_i)],$$

where $Eq(\delta_{s_i}, \mu_i)$ returns 1 if $\delta_{s_i} = \mu_i$ and 0 otherwise. Intuitively, the global scheduler ξ_g chooses the agents which will participate in the next transition, while ξ_i guides the execution of s_i in case the i-th agent is chosen by ξ_g. In case the i-th agent is not chosen by the global scheduler, it will remain without changing its state. Below defines the decentralized schedulers:

Definition 10. *A scheduler* ξ *is* decentralized *for* $s = \|_A \{s_i \mid 0 \le i \le n\}$ *iff its corresponding global scheduler* ξ_g *and local schedulers* $\{\xi_i\}_{0 \le i \le n}$ *satisfy: for any* $\pi, \pi' \in Paths^*$ *and* $0 \le i \le n$, $[\pi]_i = [\pi']_i$ *implies* $\xi_g(\pi, i) = \xi_g(\pi', i)$ *and* $\xi_i(\pi) = \xi_i(\pi')$*. A decentralized scheduler for a* PMA *is a scheduler decentralized for all states in* PMA.

We denote the set of all decentralized schedulers by $\mathcal{S}_D$. In case $n = 1$, decentralized schedulers degenerate to ordinary schedulers defined in Definition 2. According to Definition 10, a scheduler ξ is decentralized, if ξ cannot distinguish different paths starting from s, provided the projections of these paths to each agent coincide. Note that the scheduler inducing the unrealistic execution in Fig. 2 is not decentralized, since the decision of r_0 depends on the execution history of μ, i.e., at state s_5, r_0 will choose the left transition, and it will choose the right transition while at state s_6. By restricting to the set of decentralized schedulers, we can avoid the unrealistic execution of $\mu \|_A \delta_{r_0}$ depicted in Fig. 2.

4.2 Properties of $\sim^d$

In this section we show properties of distribution-based bisimulation under realistic schedulers. We first introduce some notations: A transition from s to ν with label α is induced by a scheduler ξ, written as $s \xrightarrow{\alpha}_\xi \mu$, iff $\mu \equiv \sum_{\mu' \in Dist(S)} \xi(s)(\alpha, \mu') \cdot \mu'$. Accordingly, we write $\mu \xrightarrow{\alpha}_\xi \nu$ to denote that μ can evolve into ν by performing a transition with label α under the guidance of ξ, where $s \xrightarrow{\alpha}_\xi \nu_s$ for each $s \in Supp(\mu)$ and $\nu \equiv \sum_{s \in Supp(\mu)} \mu(s) \cdot \nu_s$. Intuitively, given a distribution μ, for each $s \in Supp(\mu)$ we use s as the history information for ξ to guide the execution — the so called *memoryless* schedulers which suffices to define bisimulations,

[1]For simplicity, we only consider deterministic schedulers here. A similar example can be constructed for general schedulers.

since it is the only priori information we have known so far. Based on the notations introduced above, we can modify Definition 7 with schedulers being considered explicitly.

Let $\mathcal{S}$ be a set of schedulers. We denote $\mu \xrightarrow{\alpha}_{\mathcal{S}} \mu'$ if $\mu \xrightarrow{\alpha}_{\xi} \mu'$ for some $\xi \in \mathcal{S}$.

Definition 11. *A symmetric relation $\mathcal{R} \subseteq Dist(S) \times Dist(S)$ is a distribution-based bisimulation with respect to a given set of schedulers $\mathcal{S}$ iff $\mu \mathrel{\mathcal{R}} \nu$ implies:*

1. *whenever $\mu \xrightarrow{\alpha}_{\mathcal{S}} \mu'$, there exists $\nu \xrightarrow{\alpha}_{\mathcal{S}} \nu'$ such that $\mu' \mathrel{\mathcal{R}} \nu'$;*
2. *if not $\overrightarrow{\mu}$, then there exists $\mu \equiv \sum_{0\leq i\leq n} p_i \cdot \mu_i$ and $\nu \equiv \sum_{0\leq i\leq n} p_i \cdot \nu_i$ such that $\overrightarrow{\mu_i}$ and $\mu_i \mathrel{\mathcal{R}} \nu_i$ for each $0 \leq i \leq n$ where $\sum_{0\leq i\leq n} p_i = 1$ with $p_i > 0$ for each i.*

We write $\mu \sim^d_{\mathcal{S}} \nu$, iff there exists a distribution-based bisimulation $\mathcal{R}$ with respect to $\mathcal{S}$ such that $\mu \mathrel{\mathcal{R}} \nu$. Moreover $s \sim^d_{\mathcal{S}} r$ iff $\delta_s \sim^d_{\mathcal{S}} \delta_r$.

Definition 11 is almost the same as Definition 7 except that we require every transition to be induced by a scheduler in $\mathcal{S}$. When $\mathcal{S}$ is taken to be the set of all possible schedulers, these two definitions are equivalent. Furthermore, as we shall prove later, partial information schedulers are already enough to make them equivalent.

As mentioned before, distribution-based bisimulation has a flavor similar to partial information schedulers in the sense that, due to the transition consistency requirement, there is no difference between states in the support of a distribution if the same set of actions is enabled. Indeed, distribution-based bisimulation and partial information schedulers are closely related. The following theorem states that partial information schedulers are enough to discriminate distribution-based bisimulation with respect to arbitrary schedulers, and that if restricting to partial information schedulers, distribution-based bisimulation implies trace distribution equivalence.

Theorem 2. *For any distributions μ_1 and μ_2, $\mu_1 \sim^d \mu_2 \iff \mu_1 \sim^d_{\mathcal{S}_P} \mu_2$; $\mu_1 \sim^d_{\mathcal{S}_P} \mu_2 \implies \mu_1 \equiv_{\mathcal{S}_P} \mu_2$.*

Theorem 2 does not hold if we consider general schedulers:

Example 6. *Let s_0 and ν be as in Fig. 4. In Example 5 we have shown that $\delta_{s_0} \not\equiv \nu$. It is also not hard to check that $\delta_{s_0} \sim^d \nu$. Therefore, if general schedulers were considered, $\sim^d$ does not always imply $\equiv$.*

However, we can show $\delta_{s_0} \equiv_{\mathcal{S}_P} \nu$. To see this, note that the trace distributions $\{\alpha : \frac{1}{3}, \beta : \frac{2}{3}\}$ and $\{\beta : \frac{1}{3}, \alpha : \frac{2}{3}\}$, which witness $\delta_{s_0} \not\equiv \nu$, can only be produced by a scheduler which chooses different transitions at states s_2 and s_3. As s_2 and s_3 have the same enabled actions, this scheduler is not a partial information one, thus should be excluded when the relation $\equiv_{\mathcal{S}_P}$ is considered.

For parallel composition, we need to restrict to decentralized schedulers to establish compositionality, as indicated by the following theorem:

Theorem 3. *For any distributions μ_1 and μ_2,*

$$\mu_1 \sim^d_{\mathcal{S}_D} \mu_2 \implies \mu_1 \parallel_A \mu_3 \sim^d_{\mathcal{S}_D} \mu_2 \parallel_A \mu_3$$

for any μ_3 and A.

Below is an example showing why Theorem 3 does not hold if general schedulers are considered.

Example 7. *Let s_0, μ, and r_0 be as in Fig. 1. We have shown in Example 3 that $\delta_{s_0} \sim^d \mu$. However, if general schedulers are considered, $\delta_{s_0} \parallel_A \delta_{r_0} \not\sim^d \mu \parallel_A \delta_{r_0}$, as the unrealistic execution of $\mu \parallel_A \delta_{r_0}$ depicted in Fig. 2 cannot be simulated by $\mu \parallel_A \delta_{r_0}$, no matter how the transitions of $\delta_{s_0} \parallel_A \delta_{r_0}$ are scheduled.*

In contrast, when restricting to decentralized schedulers, we can show that both $s_0 \parallel_A r_0$ and $\mu \parallel_A \delta_{r_0}$ can reach states $s_3 \parallel_A r_5$ and $s_4 \parallel_A r_6$ with probability 0.5 at most, since the scheduler of $\mu \parallel_A \delta_{r_0}$, which induces the unrealistic execution in Fig. 2 is not decentralized.

When restricting to the set of schedulers in $\mathcal{S} = \mathcal{S}_P \cap \mathcal{S}_D$, $\sim^d_{\mathcal{S}}$ will be called *decentralized bisimulation*. As we have demonstrated, decentralized bisimulation is compositional and implies trace distribution equivalence. Actually, we can show that decentralized bisimulation is the coarsest congruence preserving trace distribution equivalence, which in turn can be seen as the symmetric version of trace distribution precongruence defined in [24].

Theorem 4. *Let $\mathcal{S} = \mathcal{S}_P \cap \mathcal{S}_D$, then $\mu_1 \sim^d_{\mathcal{S}} \mu_2$ iff $\mu_1 \equiv^c_{\mathcal{S}} \mu_2$ for any μ_1 and μ_2, where $\mu_1 \equiv^c_{\mathcal{S}} \mu_2$ iff $\mu_1 \equiv_{\mathcal{S}} \mu_2$ and $\mu_1 \parallel_A \mu_3 \equiv_{\mathcal{S}} \mu_2 \parallel_A \mu_3$ for any μ_3 and A.*

4.3 Decision Algorithm

In this subsection we show that the problem of computing distribution-based bisimulation relations is decidable. For this, we first prove the linearity of $\sim^d$.

Lemma 1. *$\sim^d$ is (convex) linear, i.e., $\mu_1 \sim^d \nu_1$ and $\mu_2 \sim^d \nu_2$ imply that for any $p \in [0, 1]$,*

$$(p \cdot \mu_1 + (1-p) \cdot \mu_2) \sim^d (p \cdot \nu_1 + (1-p) \cdot \nu_2).$$

For systems with finite state space, we impose a fixed order for states in $S = (s_1, \ldots, s_n)$ with $n = |S|$ and identify a distribution μ with a vector $(\mu(s_1), \ldots, \mu(s_n))$. The algorithm presented in [19] can be applied for our bisimulation with some changes. The idea of the algorithm is to construct an $n \times m$ *bisimulation matrix* E such that $\mu \sim^d \nu$ iff $(\mu - \nu)E = 0$, where $0 < m \leq n$. Intuitively, E contains all linear constraints which should be satisfied for each variable $\mu(s_i) - \nu(s_i)$ with $1 \leq i \leq n$ for μ and ν being bisimilar. The following lemma shows that such bisimulation matrix always exists for $\sim^d$.

Lemma 2 ([19]). *For every linear bisimulation relation $R \subseteq Dist(S) \times Dist(S)$, there exists a bisimulation matrix E such that $\mu \mathrel{R} \nu$ iff $(\mu - \nu)E = 0$.*

We only sketch the algorithm here, interested readers can refer to [19] for details. Let $\mathcal{P}$ be a PA. For simplicity, we assume that $\mathcal{P}$ is deterministic, namely, for each state s in $\mathcal{P}$ and $\alpha \in Act$, whenever $s \xrightarrow{\alpha} \mu_1$ and $s \xrightarrow{\alpha} \mu_2$, it holds $\mu_1 = \mu_2$. In other words, all transitions of each state are labelled differently. For each $A \subseteq Act$ and $\alpha \in A$, let P^α_A be the matrix such that for all $s, t \in S$,

$$\mathsf{P}^\alpha_A(s,t) = \begin{cases} \mu(t) & EA(s) = A \text{ and } s \xrightarrow{\alpha} \mu \\ 0 & \textit{otherwise.} \end{cases}$$

Note for deterministic PAs, P^α_A is uniquely determined for any $A \subseteq Act$ and $\alpha \in A$.

To construct a bisimulation matrix E for $\mathcal{P}$, the algorithm starts with a matrix with only one column $\mathbf{1}$, i.e., every entry is 1. Then for each $A \subseteq Act$ and $\alpha \in A$, compute $E_A^\alpha = \mathcal{P}_A^\alpha E$ and let E be the new matrix by adding columns in E_A^α, but removing columns linearly dependent on the others. This process continues until E is stable, i.e., no independent column can be added. The algorithm terminates, since there are at most n independent columns for n variables. For deterministic PAs, the algorithm will terminate in polynomial time [30, 13].

For PAs which are not deterministic, $\mathcal{P}_A^\alpha$ may not be unique for some $A \subseteq Act$ and $\alpha \in A$, since a state may have more than one α-transitions and will induce uncountable many choices due to combined transitions. Fortunately, it was shown in [19] that it suffices to restrict to finitely many transitions to compute E. However, this will cause an exponential blow-up in the worst case and it is still an open problem whether polynomial algorithms exist for general PAs.

4.4 Related Work and Discussion

In this subsection we review some related work. In the classical setting of multiagent systems without probabilistic behavior, the notion of bisimulation has been introduced and studied intensively. For instance, [1] showed the relation between bisimulation and Alternating-time Temporal Logic [3] (ATL) under different semantics. Similar work has been done for epistemic logic [33]. In [2], bisimulation was adopted as an abstraction technique when performing epistemic model checking on dining cryptographers-based protocols. Apart from being an abstraction technique, bisimulation metrics (relaxed versions of bisimulations allowing some probability perturbation) have been used to transfer policies between Markov decision processes [25, 7]. The problem of planning [27] and model checking with incomplete information [21, 20] have also been investigated.

As state-based bisimulations are too distinguishable in certain scenarios, distribution-based bisimulation relations have attracted much attention recently [13, 14, 16, 19]. The equivalence in [13] was defined upon *reactive probabilistic automata*, i.e., PAs where each action has exactly one corresponding transition at all states. To the best of our knowledge, distribution-based bisimulation was first defined upon general PAs in [14] to cascade internal executions. It was shown that their definition of bisimulation is the coarsest one which is compositional and preserves trace distribution equivalence for general schedulers. However, their bisimulation still distinguishes the automata in Fig. 1 (a) and (b).

Later, two other variants of distribution-based bisimulation were defined in [16, 19], which equate the automata in Fig. 1 (a) and (b). However, they do not preserve observable behaviors, namely, trace distribution equivalence, even under the realistic classes of schedulers we will consider in the sequel. To see this, we show why bisimulations defined in [19] do not always imply trace distribution equivalence. Similar arguments can be applied to bisimulations in [16].

Before giving the formal definition, we first recall some notations. Let $S_A = \{s \in S \mid EA(s) \cap A \neq \emptyset\}$ be the set of states such that at least one of their transitions is labelled by an action in A. Let $\mu(A) = \mu(S_A)$ and $\mu \overset{A}{\hookrightarrow} \mu'$ iff $\mu(A) > 0$ and $\mu' = \frac{1}{\mu(A)} \sum_{s \in Supp(\mu) \cap S_A} \mu(s) \cdot \mu_s$, where for each $s \in Supp(\mu) \cap S_A$, $s \xrightarrow{\alpha} \mu_s$ for some $\alpha \in A$. Note, in $\mu \overset{A}{\hookrightarrow} \mu'$, states in $Supp(\mu)$ may perform transitions with different labels as long as they are in A. Below we recall their definition of bisimulations [19, Def. 2], which will be referred as HKK-bisimulation in the sequel.

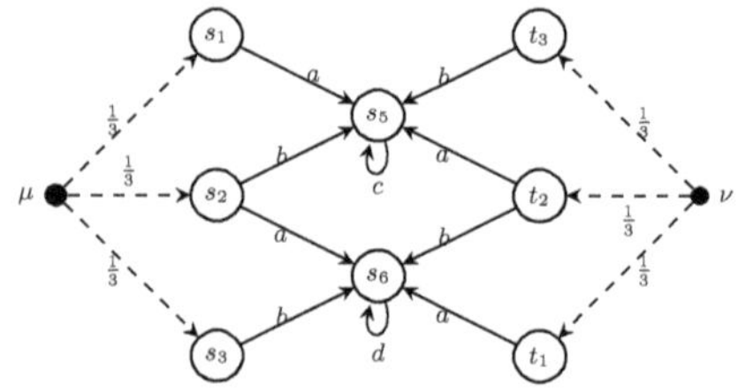

Figure 5: $\mu \sim_{\text{HKK}} \nu$ but $\mu \not\equiv_{SP} \nu$.

Definition 12. *A symmetric relation $\mathcal{R} \subseteq Dist(S) \times Dist(S)$ is an* HKK*-bisimulation iff $\mu \,\mathcal{R}\, \nu$ implies:*

1. *$\mu(A) = \nu(A)$ for each $A \subseteq Act$,*
2. *whenever $\mu \overset{A}{\hookrightarrow} \mu'$, there exists a transition $\nu \overset{A}{\hookrightarrow} \nu'$ such that $\mu' \,\mathcal{R}\, \nu'$.*

We write $\mu \sim_{\text{HKK}} \nu$, iff there exists an HKK*-bisimulation $\mathcal{R}$ such that $\mu \,\mathcal{R}\, \nu$. Moreover $s \sim_{\text{HKK}} r$ iff $\delta_s \sim_{\text{HKK}} \delta_r$.*

Now we are ready to show that $\sim_{\text{HKK}}$ is not strictly coarser than $\equiv_{SP}$. Let μ and ν be two distributions as in Fig. 5. Let $R = \{(\mu,\nu),(\nu,\mu)\} \cup ID$. By Definition 12, it is easy to see that R is an HKK-bisimulation. Therefore $\mu \sim_{\text{HKK}} \nu$. However, $\mu \not\equiv_{SP} \nu$. For instance, from μ we can obtain a trace distribution $\{\frac{1}{3} : ac, \frac{1}{3} : bc, \frac{1}{3} : bd\}$, which cannot be simulated by any scheduler of ν. Since all states in μ have different enabled actions, the scheduler induced the trace distribution is a partial information scheduler.

5. CONCLUSION AND FUTURE WORK

In this paper, we have presented a novel and very coarse bisimulation called distribution-based bisimulation for probabilistic multiagent systems, which has interesting properties under two well-known subclasses of schedulers: it implies trace distribution equivalence under partial information schedulers, while it is compositional under decentralized schedulers. Working in the intersection of both scheduler classes ensures a restricted form of compositionality for a reasonably coarse bisimulation, where the restriction excludes undesired or unrealistically powerful schedulers.

As shown in [31], model checking ATL [3] against multiagent systems is EXPTIME-complete, when the systems are represented by certain reactive languages, say "Simple Reactive Modules Language" (SRML). Therefore, abstraction and state space minimization are particularly important for these systems. For future work we will explore algorithms to compute our bisimulation in a symbolic and compositional manner. Another direction of future research is to investigate the relation between distribution-based bisimulation and some popular logics in multiagent setting, for instance probabilistic ATL [9]. The complexity of deciding distribution-based bisimulations will also be interesting.

6. ACKNOWLEDGMENTS

The authors are supported by Australian Research Council under Grant DP130102764, the National Natural Science Foundation of China (Grant Nos. 61428208, 61472473 and 61361136002), AMSS-UTS Joint Research Laboratory for Quantum Computation, Chinese Academy of Sciences, and the CAS/SAFEA International Partnership Program for Creative Research Team.

7. REFERENCES

[1] T. Ågotnes, V. Goranko, and W. Jamroga. Alternating-time temporal logics with irrevocable strategies. In *TARK*, pages 15–24, 2007.

[2] O. I. Al-Bataineh and R. van der Meyden. Abstraction for epistemic model checking of dining cryptographers-based protocols. In *TARK*, pages 247–256. ACM, 2011.

[3] R. Alur, T. A. Henzinger, and O. Kupferman. Alternating-time temporal logic. *J. ACM*, 49(5):672–713, 2002.

[4] C. Baier and J.-P. Katoen. *Principles of Model Checking*. MIT Press, 2008.

[5] E. Böde, M. Herbstritt, H. Hermanns, S. Johr, T. Peikenkamp, R. Pulungan, J. Rakow, R. Wimmer, and B. Becker. Compositional dependability evaluation for statemate. *IEEE Trans. Software Eng.*, 35(2):274–292, 2009.

[6] H. Boudali, P. Crouzen, and M. Stoelinga. A rigorous, compositional, and extensible framework for dynamic fault tree analysis. *IEEE Trans. Dependable Sec. Comput.*, 7(2):128–143, 2010.

[7] P. S. Castro and D. Precup. Using bisimulation for policy transfer in MDPs. In *AAAI*. AAAI Press, 2010.

[8] G. Chehaibar, H. Garavel, L. Mounier, N. Tawbi, and F. Zulian. Specification and Verification of the PowerScale^{TM} bus arbitration protocol: An industrial experiment with lotos. In *FORTE*, pages 435–450, 1996.

[9] T. Chen and J. Lu. Probabilistic alternating-time temporal logic and model checking algorithm. In *FSKD*, pages 35–39. IEEE, 2007.

[10] L. De Alfaro. The verification of probabilistic systems under memoryless partial-information policies is hard. Technical report, DTIC Document, 1999.

[11] C. A. D. M. Delgado and M. R. F. Benevides. Verification of epistemic properties in probabilistic multi-agent systems. In *MATES*, volume 5774 of *Lecture Notes in Computer Science*, pages 16–28. Springer, 2009.

[12] Y. Deng and M. Hennessy. On the semantics of markov automata. *Information and Computation*, 222:139–168, 2013.

[13] L. Doyen, T. A. Henzinger, and J. Raskin. Equivalence of labeled markov chains. *Int. J. Found. Comput. Sci.*, 19(3):549–563, 2008.

[14] C. Eisentraut, H. Hermanns, and L. Zhang. On probabilistic automata in continuous time. In *LICS*, pages 342–351, 2010.

[15] L. Feng, T. Han, M. Kwiatkowska, and D. Parker. Learning-based compositional verification for synchronous probabilistic systems. In *ATVA*, volume 6996 of *Lecture Notes in Computer Science*, pages 511–521. Springer, 2011.

[16] Y. Feng and L. Zhang. When equivalence and bisimulation join forces in probabilistic automata. In *FM*, volume 8442 of *Lecture Notes in Computer Science*, pages 247–262. Springer, 2014.

[17] S. Giro and P. R. D'Argenio. Quantitative model checking revisited: neither decidable nor approximable. In *FORMATS*, volume 4763 of *Lecture Notes in Computer Science*, pages 179–194. Springer, 2007.

[18] P. R. Halmos. *Measure theory*, volume 1950. Springer, 1974.

[19] H. Hermanns, J. Krcál, and J. Kretínský. Probabilistic bisimulation: Naturally on distributions. In *CONCUR 2014*, volume 8704 of *Lecture Notes in Computer Science*. Springer, 2014.

[20] X. Huang and C. Luo. A logic of probabilistic knowledge and strategy. In *AAMAS*, pages 845–852. IFAAMAS, 2013.

[21] X. Huang, K. Su, and C. Zhang. Probabilistic alternating-time temporal logic of incomplete information and synchronous perfect recall. In *AAAI*. AAAI Press, 2012.

[22] P. Kazmierczak, T. Ågotnes, and W. Jamroga. Multi-agency is coordination and (limited) communication. In *PRIMA*, volume 8861 of *Lecture Notes in Computer Science*, pages 91–106. Springer, 2014.

[23] M. Kwiatkowska, G. Norman, D. Parker, and H. Qu. Assume-guarantee verification for probabilistic systems. In *TACAS*, volume 6015 of *Lecture Notes in Computer Science*, pages 23–37. Springer, 2010.

[24] N. Lynch, R. Segala, and F. Vaandrager. Observing branching structure through probabilistic contexts. *SIAM J. Comput.*, 37(4):977–1013, Sept. 2007.

[25] C. Phillips. Knowledge transfer in Markov decision processes. Technical report, Technical report, McGill University, 2006.

[26] W. Rudin. *Real and complex analysis*. Tata McGraw-Hill Education, 2006.

[27] H. Schnoor. Strategic planning for probabilistic games with incomplete information. In *AAMAS*, pages 1057–1064. IFAAMAS, 2010.

[28] R. Segala. A compositional trace-based semantics for probabilistic automata. In *CONCUR*, volume 962 of *Lecture Notes in Computer Science*, pages 234–248. Springer, 1995.

[29] R. Segala. *Modeling and Verification of Randomized Distributed Realtime Systems*. PhD thesis, MIT, 1995.

[30] W.-G. Tzeng. A polynomial-time algorithm for the equivalence of probabilistic automata. *SIAM J. Comput.*, 21(2):216–227, 1992.

[31] W. van der Hoek, A. Lomuscio, and M. Wooldridge. On the complexity of practical ATL model checking. In *AAMAS*, pages 201–208. ACM, 2006.

[32] W. van der Hoek and M. Wooldridge. Tractable multiagent planning for epistemic goals. In *AAMAS*, pages 1167–1174. ACM, 2002.

[33] H. P. van Ditmarsch, D. F. Duque, and W. van der Hoek. On the definability of simulability and bisimilarity by finite epistemic models. In *CLIMA*, pages 74–87. Springer, 2011.

Budget-Constrained Knowledge in Multiagent Systems

Pavel Naumov
Mathematics and Computer Science
McDaniel College
Westminster, MD 20853
pavel@pavelnaumov.com

Jia Tao†
Department of Computer Science
Bryn Mawr College
Bryn Mawr, PA 19010
jtao@cs.brynmawr.edu

ABSTRACT

The paper introduces a modal logical system for reasoning about knowledge in which information available to agents might be constrained by the available budget. Although the system lacks an equivalent of the standard Negative Introspection axiom from epistemic logic S5, it is proven to be sound and complete with respect to an S5-like Kripke semantics.

Categories and Subject Descriptors

I.2.11 [**Distributed Artificial Intelligence**]: Multiagent systems; F.4.1 [**Mathematical Logic**]: Modal Logic

Keywords

modal logic; epistemology; axiomatization; completeness

General Terms

Theory, Economics

1. INTRODUCTION

There are many examples where large amount of data might be potentially accessible to an agent, but the agent is constrained by the available budget.

For instance, a recent ruling of the European Union Court of Justice [12] and the proposed EU regulation on "right to be forgotten"/"right to erasure" emphasize that this right is not absolute. The related European Commission memo [3] explicitly states that "... the right to be forgotten cannot amount to a right to re-write or erase history. Neither must the right to be forgotten take precedence over freedom of expression or freedom of the media. The right to be forgotten includes an explicit provision that ensures it does not encroach on the freedom of expression and information."

To balance individual privacy with freedom of media, these regulations, for example, require online search engines to remove links to certain newspaper articles from its search results, but they do not require libraries to remove the newspapers from their archives. As a result, the regulations enforce individual privacy not by completely eliminating access to certain information, but, instead, by making such access prohibitively time consuming or prohibitively expensive.

In this paper we study epistemic properties of budget-constrained knowledge. Consider a more specific example of such a situation based on Figure 1 that lists current criminal background check fees in several states in the US [11, 15, 14, 13, 2, 10, 16].

State	Fee (USD)
California	32
Florida	24
Hawaii	30
Iowa	15
Maryland	18
Pennsylvania	10
Virginia	15

Figure 1: Background Check Fees.

Let a hypothetical person John have criminal records in Florida and Maryland, but not in any other state. Any agent a who has at least 18 dollars has a chance to learn that John has criminal records in one of the states. We formally denote this as

$$\Box_a^{18}(\text{"John has criminal records in one of the states."}).$$

At the same time, if agent a has at least 42 dollars, then she could learn that John has at least two different criminal records:

$$\Box_a^{42}(\text{"John has at least two criminal records."}).$$

Furthermore, if agent a pays Florida and Maryland fees for background check, then this agent not only knows that John has at least two criminal records, but also learns that she can find out about this by paying only 42 dollars:

$$\Box_a^{42}\Box_a^{42}(\text{"John has at least two criminal records."}).$$

Note that no agent is able to discover that John has two criminal records with only 41 dollars:

$$\neg\Box_a^{41}(\text{"John has at least two criminal records."}).$$

The above statement is an example of a privacy claim about John's criminal records, that the "right to be forgotten" legislation is designed to provide.

Of course, if John's criminal records are different or if the states decide to change background check fees, then some

† The author gratefully acknowledges the support of Bryn Mawr College.

Appears in: *Proceedings of the 14th International Conference on Autonomous Agents and Multiagent Systems (AAMAS 2015), Bordini, Elkind, Weiss, Yolum (eds.), May, 4–8, 2015, Istanbul, Turkey.*

of the above statements might no longer be true. In this paper we study properties of budget-constrained knowledge that are universally true. An example of such properties is the monotonicity principle: $\Box^5_a\varphi \to \Box^7_a\varphi$. That is, more money buys you at least as much information as less money does. A more interesting example of such universal principle is the budget-constrained version of the standard modal Distributivity axiom:

$$\Box^c_a(\varphi \to \psi) \to (\Box^d_a\varphi \to \Box^{c+d}_a\psi). \tag{1}$$

In other words, if agent a can learn $\varphi \to \psi$ by spending at most c and she can learn φ by spending at most d, then she can learn ψ by spending at most $c + d$. The budget-constrained versions of Truth axiom and Positive Introspection axiom from epistemic logic [4, 7] are also true:

$$\Box^c_a\varphi \to \varphi,$$

$$\Box^c_a\varphi \to \Box^c_a\Box^c_a\varphi. \tag{2}$$

Negative Introspection. It is interesting to point out that budget-constrained version of Negative Introspection axiom from epistemic logic

$$\neg\Box^c_a\varphi \to \Box^c_a\neg\Box^c_a\varphi. \tag{3}$$

is not generally true. Indeed, suppose that another hypothetical person, say Frank, has no criminal records in any of the above states. Let statement φ be "Frank does have criminal records in one of the above states". Note that $\neg\Box^{100}_a\varphi$ is true because even for \$100 agent a can not find out something which simply is not true. At the same time, $\Box^{100}_a\neg\Box^{100}_a\varphi$ is false because the only way to learn $\neg\Box^{100}_a\varphi$ is to obtain criminal records from all states, which can not be done on \$100 budget. Thus, statement (3), for $c = 100$, is false.

The example above appears to rely on the fact that $c > 0$. One might wonder if the Negative Introspection axiom is true for zero-cost knowledge:

$$\neg\Box^0_a\varphi \to \Box^0_a\neg\Box^0_a\varphi. \tag{4}$$

The answer to this question is not trivial. Whether property (4) is universally true depends on exact details of the formal semantics definition. To illustrate the issue at hand, consider famous Hilbert Grand Hotel that has infinitely many rooms. Let us first assume that it costs one dollar to check if any particular room is occupied or not and that currently several rooms in this hotel are vacant. In this case any agent a, if she is lucky enough, spends one dollar and happens to check the room that is vacant. Then she learns that the hotel has vacancies:

$$\Box^1_a(\text{"The Grand Hotel has vacancies."}).$$

Now consider the case when the hotel is actually full and it costs nothing to check if any particular room is occupied. Note that in this situation statement

$$\neg\Box^0_a(\text{"The Grand Hotel has vacancies."}) \tag{5}$$

is true, because agent a can not learn something which is false. However, the only feasible way for any agent to learn that statement (5) is true is to open all doors and to see that the Grant Hotel has no vacancies. Let us consider the question whether statement

$$\Box^0_a\neg\Box^0_a(\text{"The Grand Hotel has vacancies."}) \tag{6}$$

is true. In other words, should we allow the agent to check infinitely many rooms and to make certain conclusion only after getting all the results? In this paper we assume that any agent can take only finitely many actions before making a logical conclusion. Thus, from our point of view, statement (6) is false. Hence, implication

$$\neg\Box^0_a(\text{"The Grand Hotel has vacancies."}) \to$$
$$\Box^0_a\neg\Box^0_a(\text{"The Grand Hotel has vacancies."})$$

is false, which shows that Negative Introspection principle is not always true even for zero-cost knowledge. We will further analyze this example after we give formal semantics of our logical system.

Multiagent Case. The logical system proposed in this paper supports reasoning about budget-constrained knowledge in multiagent systems. For example, the state of Virginia has lower background check fee if the request is for the purpose of volunteering for a non-profit organization. The current fee in this case is only eight dollars instead of fifteen [16]. Suppose that John is simultaneously applying for an internship with a for-profit organization (agent a) and for volunteering for a non-profit organization (agent b). Thus,

$$\neg\Box^{10}_a(\text{"John has no criminal records in Virginia"})$$

and

$$\Box^{10}_b(\text{"John has no criminal records in Virginia"}).$$

If agent a pays 15 dollars, then she learns that John has no criminal records in Virginia. Once she knows that this statement is true, she would also know that agent b may learn the same information for just eight dollars:

$$\Box^{15}_a\Box^8_b(\text{"John has no criminal records in Virginia"}).$$

Related Work. The idea to add numerical labels to epistemic modality goes back to Van der Hoek and Meyer's work [18] on graded modalities in epistemic logic. The numerical labels in their system, however, count the number of exceptions in which the statement is false, not the budget required to learn that statement is true. As a result, their axiomatic system is very different from the one proposed here.

The most popular logical system for reasoning about resource constraints is linear logic [6]. It treats propositional variables as resources without introducing any additional labeled modalities. Different from our system, linear logic reasons only about resources and does not deal with epistemology.

Our logical system is related to Artëmov's logic of justification [1]. Although logic of justification does not consider the cost of justification, the Distributivity axiom (1) could be viewed as a budget-constrained version of Application axiom from justification logic. Similarly, budget constrained version of Positive Introspection axiom (2) is related to Proof Checker axiom in justification logic: the costs of checking the proof, at least in our setting, is the same as the cost of the proof itself. Whereas justification logic deals with justifications syntactically, our logical system deals with them semantically. The superscript of the modal operator refers only to the cost of a justification. Thus, our logical system could be viewed, to some degree, as a more abstract version of justification logic. Note, however, that the formal semantics for budget-constrained knowledge that we propose in this paper is very different from Fitting's [5] semantics for justification logic. While Fitting's semantics extends S4 models with admissible evidence function, our S5-like semantics treats each justification as an equivalence relation.

Our system is also related to Moss and Parikh's work on topological semantics for epistemic logic [8], in which they developed a logical system that takes into account "effort" needed to acquire new knowledge. Unlike ours, their system treats efforts topologically without assigning them numerical costs.

Finally, in terms of a modality indexed with a real number subscript, this work is related to the author's article [9] on logic of confidence. In spite of this syntactic similarity, logic of confidence contains Negative Introspection axiom. Moreover, Distributivity axioms in these two systems are different.

Paper Structure. Section 2 introduces the syntax and the semantics of our logical system for budget-constrained knowledge. Formally equipped, we further analyze the Grand Hotel example and prove that statement (5) does not imply statement (6). The logical system is presented in Section 3 and a couple of example properties of budget-constrained knowledge followed from the logical system is shown in Section 4. In Section 5 and Section 6, the soundness and the completeness of the logical system are established. Finally, Section 7 discusses potential extensions to our work when our assumption of finitely many actions is relaxed to at most countably many actions, when one considers distributed knowledge with constrained budget, and when the budget becomes a function that relates time and money.

2. SYNTAX AND SEMANTICS

In this section we introduce formal syntax and semantics of our logical system. We assume that $\mathcal{A}$ is an arbitrary (possibly infinite) set of agents and $\mathcal{P}$ is a set of atomic propositions.

DEFINITION 1. *Let Φ be the minimal set of formulas such that*

1. $\mathcal{P} \subseteq \Phi$,
2. *if* $\varphi \in \Phi$, *then* $\neg\varphi \in \Phi$,
3. *if* $\varphi, \psi \in \Phi$, *then* $\varphi \to \psi \in \Phi$,
4. *if* $\varphi \in \Phi$, *then* $\Box_a^c \varphi \in \Phi$ *where* $a \in \mathcal{A}$ *and* $c \in [0, +\infty)$.

In the introduction we have seen that the cost of knowledge comes from costs associated with obtaining justifications for this knowledge. In some situations one might find it more natural to talk about costs of "efforts" [8], costs of "actions", or costs of "evidences". In our formal semantics we assume an existence of a set of justifications J_a for each agent $a \in A$. For technical convenience we assume that sets $\{J_a\}_{a\in\mathcal{A}}$ are disjoint for different agents a. The cost of justifications is captured by a cost function $\|j\|$ that maps each $j \in J_a$ into a non-negative real value. This function is not agent-dependent because any justification j uniquely determines the agent. Note that the same knowledge has different costs to different agents in the background check fees example. To account for this, in our model we assume that different agents have different sets of justifications. The difference in knowledge costs to different agents comes from the fact that they use agent-specific justifications for the same knowledge.

In our semantics, any justification $j \in J_a$ has an associated indistinguishability relation $\sim_j$. Informally, $u \sim_j w$ means that agent a can not distinguish epistemic worlds u and w with justification j. As mentioned in the introduction, this approach to capturing justifications, natural from epistemic logic point of view, is very different from Fitting's [5] models for justification logic.

Finally, the definition of formal semantics given below also includes function π that specifies, for each atomic proposition, the set of epistemic worlds in which the proposition is satisfied.

DEFINITION 2. *A budget-constrained epistemic model is a tuple* $(W, \{J_a\}_{a\in\mathcal{A}}, \{\{\sim_j\}_{j\in J_a}\}_{a\in\mathcal{A}}, \|\cdot\|, \pi)$, *where*

1. *W is a set (of "epistemic worlds"),*
2. *$\{J_a\}_{a\in\mathcal{A}}$ is family of disjoint sets of "justifications",*
3. *$\sim_j$ is an "indistinguishability" relation on W associated with justification $j \in J_a$ of an agent $a \in \mathcal{A}$,*
4. *$\|\cdot\|$ is the cost function that maps each justification $j \in \bigcup_{a\in\mathcal{A}} J_a$ into its price $\|j\| \in [0, +\infty)$,*
5. *π is a function that maps each $p \in \mathcal{P}$ into a subset of W.*

For any $J \subseteq J_a$, we write $u \sim_J w$ if $u \sim_j w$ for each $j \in J$. Informally, $u \sim_J w$ means that agent a can not distinguish epistemic worlds u and w while possessing all of the justifications in set J.

LEMMA 1. *For any $J \subseteq J_a$, relation $\sim_J$ is an equivalence relation on the set of epistemic worlds W.* ⊠

LEMMA 2. *If $J \subseteq J' \subseteq J_a$, then equivalence relation $\sim_{J'}$ is at least as strong as equivalence relation $\sim_J$.* ⊠

Recall from the introduction that, informally, $w \Vdash \Box_a^c \varphi$ means that in epistemic world w agent a has a *possibility* to learn φ with budget c. Below we capture this informal definition by saying that $\Box_a^c \varphi$ is satisfied in epistemic world w if there is a set of justifications J with a total cost of no more than c such that φ is satisfied in all epistemic worlds that are J-indistinguishable from w.

DEFINITION 3. *Satisfiability relation $\Vdash$ between epistemic worlds in W and all formulas in Φ is defined as follows:*

1. *$w \Vdash p$ if $w \in \pi(p)$, where $p \in \mathcal{P}$,*
2. *$w \Vdash \neg\varphi$ if $w \nVdash \varphi$,*
3. *$w \Vdash \varphi \to \psi$ if $w \nVdash \varphi$ or $w \Vdash \psi$,*
4. *$w \Vdash \Box_a^c \varphi$ if there is a finite set $J \subseteq J_a$ such that*
   (a) $\sum_{j\in J} \|j\| \le c$,
   (b) *for any $u \in W$, if $u \sim_J w$, then $u \Vdash \varphi$.*

Grand Hotel Example. We illustrate Definitions 2 and 3 using the Hilbert's Grand Hotel example from the introduction. The set of agents in this example consists of a single agent a. An epistemic world w is a possible hotel occupation state which can be represented as a Boolean function on hotel room numbers. That is, $w : \mathbb{N} \mapsto \{occupied, available\}$.

In this example, a justification could be thought of as an action of opening a single door in the hotel to check if the room is occupied. Thus, the set of all justifications can be identified with the set of room numbers $\mathbb{N}$. Such a justification j can not distinguish epistemic worlds $u : \mathbb{N} \mapsto \{occupied, available\}$ and $w : \mathbb{N} \mapsto \{occupied, available\}$ if $u(j) = w(j)$. In other words, $u \sim_j w$ if and only if $u(j) = w(j)$.

Suppose that the cost of opening any door is zero: $\|j\| = 0$ for each $j \in \mathbb{N}$ and that in epistemic world w_0 the hotel is full: $w_0(j) = occupied$ for each $j \in \mathbb{N}$.

Finally, let valuation $\pi(p_0)$ for some atomic proposition p_0 be defined to be the set of all epistemic worlds in which at least one room is vacant:

$$\pi(p_0) = \{w \in W \mid \exists n \in \mathbb{N}\ (w(n) = available)\}.$$

Informally, proposition p_0 is statement "The Grand Hotel has vacancies". For the sake of clarity, in what follows, we write "The Grand Hotel has vacancies" instead of atomic proposition p_0. The truth of statements (5) and (6) is formally shown below.

PROPOSITION 1.

$$w_0 \Vdash \neg\Box^0_a(\textit{“The Grand Hotel has vacancies.”}).$$

PROOF. Assume the opposite. Thus, there must exist a finite set $J \subseteq \mathbb{N}$ such that $\sum_{j\in J} \|j\| = 0$ and

$$u \Vdash \text{“The Grand Hotel has vacancies.”}$$

for each epistemic world u where $u \sim_J w_0$. By Lemma 1, $w_0 \sim_J w_0$. Thus, $w_0 \Vdash$ "The Grand Hotel has vacancies.", which contradicts the choice of world w_0. ⊠

PROPOSITION 2.

$$w_0 \nVdash \Box^0_a\neg\Box^0_a(\textit{“The Grand Hotel has vacancies.”}).$$

PROOF. Assume the opposite. Thus, there must exist a *finite* set $J \subseteq \mathbb{N}$ such that $\sum_{j\in J} \|j\| = 0$ and

$$u \Vdash \neg\Box^0_a(\text{“The Grand Hotel has vacancies.”})$$

for each epistemic world u where $u \sim_J w_0$. Since set J is finite, there must exist $n \in \mathbb{N} \setminus J$. Consider epistemic world u_0 such that

$$u_0(j) = \begin{cases} available, & \text{if } j = n, \\ occupied, & \text{otherwise.} \end{cases}$$

Note that $u_0 \sim_J w_0$ because $n \notin J$. Hence,

$$u_0 \Vdash \neg\Box^0_a(\text{“The Grand Hotel has vacancies.”}). \quad (7)$$

Consider set $J' = \{n\}$. Note that $\sum_{j\in J'} \|j\| = \|n\| = 0$. Thus, by Definition 3, statement (7) implies that there exists epistemic world v_0 such that $v_0 \sim_{J'} u_0$ and

$$v_0 \nVdash \text{“The Grand Hotel has vacancies.”}. \quad (8)$$

Finally, note that $v_0 \sim_{J'} u_0$ implies that $v_0(n) = u_0(n) = available$, which is a contradiction to statement (8). ⊠

3. AXIOMS

Our logical system, in addition to all propositional tautologies in language Φ, contains the following axioms:

1. Truth: $\Box^c_a\varphi \to \varphi$,
2. Positive Introspection: $\Box^c_a\varphi \to \Box^c_a\Box^c_a\varphi$,
3. Distributivity: $\Box^c_a(\varphi \to \psi) \to (\Box^d_a\varphi \to \Box^{c+d}_a\psi)$.

We write $\vdash \varphi$ if formula φ is provable from the propositional tautologies and the above axioms using Modus Ponens and Necessitation inference rules:

$$\frac{\varphi,\quad \varphi \to \psi}{\psi} \qquad\qquad \frac{\varphi}{\Box^c_a\varphi}.$$

We write $X \vdash \varphi$ if formula φ is provable from propositional tautologies, the above axioms, and the additional set of axioms X using only Modus Ponens inference rule.

4. EXAMPLES

The soundness of our logical system will be established in the next section. In this section we show how this system can be used to prove two additional properties of budget-constrained knowledge. We later use these results in the proof of completeness.

The first property is monotonicity of budget-constrained knowledge. Informally, it says that anything that can be learned on a smaller budget also can be learned with a larger budget.

LEMMA 3. *$\vdash \Box^c_a\varphi \to \Box^d_a\varphi$, where $c \le d$.*

PROOF. Note that $\varphi \to \varphi$ is a propositional tautology. Thus, $\vdash \Box^{d-c}_a(\varphi \to \varphi)$ by Necessitation rule. Note also that

$$\vdash \Box^{d-c}(\varphi \to \varphi) \to (\Box^c\varphi \to \Box^d\varphi)$$

is an instance of Distributivity axiom. Thus, from the two statements above, by Modus Ponens, $\vdash \Box^c_a\varphi \to \Box^d_a\varphi$. ⊠

The property expressed by the lemma below is something that, at first glance, might look as a more general version of Distributivity axiom. However, as we show below, it is provable from Positive Introspection axiom and the regular version of Distributivity axiom.

LEMMA 4. *$\vdash \Box^c_a(\Box^d_a\varphi \to \psi) \to (\Box^d_a\varphi \to \Box^{c+d}_a\psi)$.*

PROOF. By Distributivity axiom,

$$\vdash \Box^c_a(\Box^d_a\varphi \to \psi) \to (\Box^d_a\Box^d_a\varphi \to \Box^{c+d}_a\psi).$$

By Modus Ponens rule applied twice,

$$\Box^c_a(\Box^d_a\varphi \to \psi), \Box^d_a\Box^d_a\varphi \vdash \Box^{c+d}_a\psi.$$

By Positive Introspection axiom,

$$\Box^c_a(\Box^d_a\varphi \to \psi), \Box^d_a\varphi \vdash \Box^{c+d}_a\psi.$$

By Deduction theorem for propositional logic,

$$\vdash \Box^c_a(\Box^d_a\varphi \to \psi) \to (\Box^d_a\varphi \to \Box^{c+d}_a\psi).$$

⊠

5. SOUNDNESS

In this section we establish the soundness of our logical system with respect to the semantics given in Definition 3. The soundness of propositional tautologies and of Modus Ponens inference rule is straightforward. Below we prove the soundness of each of the remaining axioms and of Necessitation inference rule as a separate lemma. We assume that w is an arbitrary epistemic world of a budget-constrained epistemic model $(W, \{J_a\}_{a\in\mathcal{A}}, \{\{\sim_j\}_{j\in J_a}\}_{a\in\mathcal{A}}, \|\cdot\|, \pi)$.

LEMMA 5. *If $w \Vdash \Box_a^c\varphi$, then $w \Vdash \varphi$.*

PROOF. Suppose that $w \Vdash \Box_a^c\varphi$. Thus, there is a set $J \subseteq J_a$ such that $\sum_{j\in J}\|j\| \le c$ and $u \Vdash \varphi$ for each u such that $u \sim_J w$. Note that $w \sim_J w$ by Lemma 1. Therefore, $w \Vdash \varphi$. ⊠

LEMMA 6. *If $w \Vdash \Box_a^c\varphi$, then $w \Vdash \Box_a^c\Box_a^c\varphi$.*

PROOF. By assumption $w \Vdash \Box_a^c\varphi$, there must exist a set $J \subseteq J_a$ such that $\sum_{j\in J}\|j\| \le c$ and $u \Vdash \varphi$ for each $u \in W$ such that $u \sim_J w$. To prove $w \Vdash \Box_a^c\Box_a^c\varphi$, it is sufficient to show that $u \Vdash \Box_a^c\varphi$ for each $u \in W$ such that $u \sim_J w$. To show the latter, it is enough to justify that $v \Vdash \varphi$ for each $v \in W$ such that $v \sim_J u$. Indeed, consider any $v \in W$ such that $v \sim_J u$. By the assumption $u \sim_J w$ and Lemma 1, we have $v \sim_J w$. This, by the choice of the set J, implies that $v \Vdash \varphi$. ⊠

LEMMA 7. *If $w \Vdash \Box_a^c(\varphi \to \psi)$ and $w \Vdash \Box_a^d\varphi$, then $w \Vdash \Box_a^{c+d}\psi$.*

PROOF. Suppose that $w \Vdash \Box_a^c(\varphi \to \psi)$ and $w \Vdash \Box_a^d\varphi$. By the first assumption, there exists a set $J_1 \subseteq J_a$ such that $\sum_{j\in J_1}\|j\| \le c$ and $u \sim_{J_1} w$ implies $u \Vdash \varphi \to \psi$ for each $u \in W$. By the second assumption, there exists a set $J_2 \subseteq J_a$ such that $\sum_{j\in J_2}\|j\| \le d$ and $u \sim_{J_2} w$ implies $u \Vdash \varphi$ for each $u \in W$. Let $J = J_1 \cup J_2$. Then

$$\sum_{j\in J}\|j\| \le \sum_{j\in J_1}\|j\| + \sum_{j\in J_2}\|j\| \le c + d$$

and equivalence relation $\sim_J$, by Lemma 2, is at least as strong as both of the equivalence relations $\sim_{J_1}$ and $\sim_{J_2}$. Hence, $u \Vdash \varphi \to \psi$ and $u \Vdash \varphi$ for each $u \in W$ such that $u \sim_J w$. Thus, by Definition 3, $u \Vdash \psi$ for each $u \in W$ such that $u \sim_J w$. Therefore, again by Definition 3, $w \Vdash \Box_a^{c+d}\psi$. ⊠

LEMMA 8. *For any formula $\varphi \in \Phi$, if $w' \Vdash \varphi$ for each epistemic world $w' \in W'$ of each budget-constrained epistemic model $(W', \{J'_a\}_{a\in\mathcal{A}}, \{\{\sim'_j\}_{j\in J_a}\}_{a\in\mathcal{A}}, \|\cdot\|', \pi')$, then $w \Vdash \Box_a^c\varphi$.*

PROOF. Assume that $w \nVdash \Box_a^c\varphi$. Let $J = \varnothing \subseteq J_a$. Note that $\sum_{j\in J}\|j\| = 0 \le c$. Thus, by assumption $w \nVdash \Box_a^c\varphi$, there must exist $w' \in W$ such that $w' \sim_J w$ and $w' \nVdash \varphi$. The latter contradicts the assumption of the lemma. ⊠

6. COMPLETENESS

In this section we prove the completeness of our logical system with respect to the formal semantics given in Definition 3. This proof significantly deviates from the standard completeness proof techniques for modal logic systems due to the challenge that we describe below.

S5-like Semantics for S4-like Logic. If one ignores budget superscript on modalities in the language of our logical system, then the system is reduced to the multiagent S4 modal logic. The standard Kripke semantics for S4 is using Kripke frames with reflexive and transitive accessibility relations. However, the budget-constrained epistemic semantics in Definition 2, just like the standard S5 epistemic logic Kripke semantics, assumes that the indistinguishibility relation is not only reflexive and transitive, but also symmetric.

One might think that it would be possible to easily adopt the standard canonical Kripke model construction to our logical system. Unfortunately, in the absence of Negative Introspection axiom, this construction would yield nonsymmetric accessibility relations as it does in the case of S4 models.

The main challenge in the proof of the completeness of our logical system is to construct a Kripke-like model with symmetric accessibility relations in the absence of Negative Introspection axiom.

To overcome this challenge, we add extra information to each epistemic world. In the standard canonical model construction, an epistemic world is simply a maximal consistent set of formulas. In our construction, an epistemic world is a pair (X, β), where X is a maximal consistent set of formulas and β is a function of the type specified in Definition 4. Function β can be thought of as an array of "flags" that are used to fine-tune indistinguishability relations between epistemic worlds. The details of this "fine-tuning" are given in Definition 6.

We are now ready to define "canonical" budget-constrained epistemic model $(W, \{J_a\}_{a\in\mathcal{A}}, \{\{\sim_j\}_{j\in J_a}\}_{a\in\mathcal{A}}, \|\cdot\|, \pi)$.

DEFINITION 4. *The set of epistemic worlds W consists of all pairs (X, β), where X is a maximal consistent subset of Φ and β is a function that maps each tuple (c, φ), where $c \in [0, +\infty)$ and $\varphi \in \Phi$, into an integer value $\beta(c, \varphi) \in \mathbb{Z}$.*

DEFINITION 5. *For each agent $a \in \mathcal{A}$, the set of justifications J_a consists of all tuples of the form (a, b, c, φ), where $b \in \mathbb{Z}$, $c \in [0, +\infty)$, and $\varphi \in \Phi$.*

Informally, tuple (a, b, c, φ) justifies to agent a at cost c that statement φ is true. The component b of the tuple is a part of "fine-tuning" mechanism whose purpose is clarified in the next definition.

DEFINITION 6. *For any $(X_1, \beta_1) \in W$, any $(X_2, \beta_2) \in W$ and any $(a, b, c, \varphi) \in J_a$, let $(X_1, \beta_1) \sim_{(a,b,c,\varphi)} (X_2, \beta_2)$ if the following two conditions are either both true or both false:*

1. *$\Box_a^c\varphi \in X_1$ and $\beta_1(c, \varphi) = b$,*
2. *$\Box_a^c\varphi \in X_2$ and $\beta_2(c, \varphi) = b$.*

LEMMA 9. *For any $(a, b, c, \varphi) \in J_a$, relation $\sim_{(a,b,c,\varphi)}$ is an equivalence relation on set W.*

PROOF. The statement of the lemma follows from Definition 6 because biconditional is an equivalence relation on propositional formulas. ⊠

DEFINITION 7. *Let $\|(a, b, c, \varphi)\| = c$.*

In the standard construction of a canonical Kripke model, an atomic proposition is satisfied in an epistemic world if the maximal consistent set representing this world contains this proposition. We adopt the same approach in our construction without taking function β into consideration.

DEFINITION 8. *For any atomic proposition $p \in \mathcal{P}$, let $\pi(p)$ be the set $\{(X,\beta) \in W \mid p \in X\}$.*

The next two lemmas are at the core of the proof of the completeness theorem. They both have analogy in the standard completeness proofs for modal logics such as S4 and S5. In the case of these logics, we normally need to show that if a maximal consistent set representing world w contains formula $\Box\psi$, then ψ belongs to the maximal consistent set representing any world accessible from world w. In our case, such a property is stated as follows.

LEMMA 10. *If $(X,\beta) \in W$ and $\Box_a^c\psi \in X$, then $\psi \in Y$ for each $(Y,\gamma) \in W$ such that $(Y,\gamma) \sim_{(a,\beta(c,\psi),c,\psi)} (X,\beta)$.*

PROOF. Consider any $(Y,\gamma) \in W$ such that

$$(Y,\gamma) \sim_{(a,\beta(c,\psi),c,\psi)} (X,\beta).$$

Then, by Definition 6, $\Box_a^c\psi \in Y$. Hence, $Y \vdash \psi$ by Truth axiom. Therefore, $\psi \in Y$ due to maximality of set Y. ⊠

As mentioned earlier, tuple (a,b,c,ψ) justifies to agent a at cost c that statement ψ is true, where component b serves as a part of the "fine-tuning" mechanism. The above lemma clarifies the details of this mechanism. Namely, in epistemic world (X,β), such a justification is tuple $(a,\beta(c,\psi),c,\psi)$.

In a proof of completeness for classical modal logics such as S4 and S5, one shows that if formula $\Box\psi$ does not belong to the maximal consistent set of formulas representing world w, then there is a world u, accessible from world w, such that the maximal consistent set of formulas representing u does not contain formula ψ. Below is the corresponding statement in our proof of completeness.

LEMMA 11. *For any $(X,\beta) \in W$, any $\Box_a^d\psi \notin X$, and any finite $J \subseteq J_a$ such that $\sum_{j\in J}\|j\| \le d$, there is $(Y,\gamma) \in W$ such that $(Y,\gamma) \sim_J (X,\beta)$ and $\psi \notin Y$.*

PROOF. Define

$$\gamma(c,\varphi) = \begin{cases} \beta(c,\varphi), & \text{if } (a,\beta(c,\varphi),c,\varphi) \in J \text{ and } \Box_a^c\varphi \in X,\\ \omega, & \text{otherwise,}\end{cases}$$

where ω is an arbitrary integer such that $(a,\omega,c,\varphi) \notin J$. Such ω exists due to the finiteness of J. We next show that set

$$Y_0 \;=\; \{\neg\psi\} \cup \{\Box_a^c\varphi \mid \Box_a^c\varphi \in X, (a,\beta(c,\varphi),c,\varphi) \in J\}$$

is consistent. Assuming the opposite, there are formulas $\Box_a^{c_1}\varphi_1,\dots,\Box_a^{c_n}\varphi_n \in X$ such that $(a,\beta(c_i,\varphi_i),c_i,\varphi_i) \in J$ for each $i \le n$ and $\Box_a^{c_1}\varphi_1,\dots,\Box_a^{c_n}\varphi_n \vdash \psi$. Then, by Deduction theorem for propositional logic,

$$\vdash \Box_a^{c_1}\varphi_1 \to (\Box_a^{c_2}\varphi_2 \to \dots (\Box_a^{c_n}\varphi_n \to \psi)\dots).$$

By Necessitation rule,

$$\vdash \Box_a^{0}(\Box_a^{c_1}\varphi_1 \to (\Box_a^{c_2}\varphi_2 \to \dots (\Box_a^{c_n}\varphi_n \to \psi)\dots)).$$

By Lemma 4,

$$\vdash \Box_a^{c_1}\varphi_1 \to \Box_a^{c_1}(\Box_a^{c_2}\varphi_2 \to \dots (\Box_a^{c_n}\varphi_n \to \psi)\dots).$$

Note that $\Box_a^{c_1}\varphi_1 \in X$ by the choice of set Y_0. Thus, by Modus Ponens rule,

$$X \vdash \Box_a^{c_1}(\Box_a^{c_2}\varphi_2 \to \dots (\Box_a^{c_n}\varphi_n \to \psi)\dots).$$

Again by Lemma 4 and Modus Ponens inference rule,

$$X \vdash \Box_a^{c_2}\varphi_2 \to \Box_a^{c_1+c_2}(\Box_a^{c_3}\varphi_3 \to \dots (\Box_a^{c_n}\varphi_n \to \psi)\dots).$$

Note that $\Box_a^{c_2}\varphi_2 \in X$ again by the choice of set Y_0. Thus, by Modus Ponens rule,

$$X \vdash \Box_a^{c_1+c_2}(\Box_a^{c_3}\varphi_3 \to \dots (\Box_a^{c_n}\varphi_n \to \psi)\dots).$$

By repeating the last two steps $(n-2)$ times,

$$X \vdash \Box_a^{c_1+c_2+\dots+c_n}\psi.$$

Thus, $X \vdash \Box_a^d\psi$ by Lemma 3 and due to

$$\sum_i c_i = \sum_i \|(a,\beta(c_i,\varphi_i),c_i,\varphi_i)\| \le \sum_{j\in J}\|j\| \le d,$$

which is a contradiction to the assumption $\neg\Box_a^d\psi \in X$ and the consistency of the set X. Therefore, set Y_0 is consistent. Let Y be any maximal consistent extension of the set Y_0.

Note that $\neg\psi \in Y_0 \subseteq Y$ by the choice of Y_0 and Y. Thus, $\psi \notin Y$ due to consistency of the set Y. We are only left to show that $(X,\beta) \sim_J (Y,\gamma)$, which, by Definition 6, follows from the following claim:

CLAIM 1. *For each $(a,b,c,\varphi) \in J$, the following two conditions are either both true or both false:*

1. *$\Box_a^c\varphi \in X$ and $\beta(c,\varphi) = b$,*
2. *$\Box_a^c\varphi \in Y$ and $\gamma(c,\varphi) = b$.*

PROOF. 1) ⇒ 2) : Suppose that $\Box_a^c\varphi \in X$ and $\beta(c,\varphi) = b$. Thus, $\Box_a^c\varphi \in Y_0$ by the choice of Y_0. Hence, $\Box_a^c\varphi \in Y$ because Y is an extension of Y_0. Note also that $\Box_a^c\varphi \in X$ and $\beta(c,\varphi) = b$ implies, by the choice of γ, that $\gamma(c,\varphi) = \beta(c,\varphi)$. Therefore, $\gamma(c,\varphi) = \beta(c,\varphi) = b$.

2) ⇒ 1) : First, assume that $\Box_a^c\varphi \notin X$. Then, $\gamma(c,\varphi) = \omega$ where $(a,\omega,c,\varphi) \notin J$. Recall that $(a,b,c,\varphi) \in J$. Thus, $\omega \ne b$. Therefore, $\gamma(c,\varphi) \ne b$.

Next, suppose that $\Box_a^c\varphi \in X$ and $\beta(c,\varphi) \ne b$. There are two cases to consider. If $(a,\beta(c,\varphi),c,\varphi) \in J$, then $\gamma(c,\varphi) = \beta(c,\varphi)$, by the definition of function γ. Therefore, $\gamma(c,\varphi) = \beta(c,\varphi) \ne b$. Otherwise, suppose that $(a,\beta(c,\varphi),c,\varphi) \notin J$. Then, $\gamma(c,\varphi) = \omega$ where $(a,\omega,c,\varphi) \notin J$. Recall that $(a,b,c,\varphi) \in J$. Thus, $\omega \ne b$. Therefore, $\gamma(c,\varphi) \ne b$. ⊠

This concludes the proof of the lemma. ⊠

Next, we use Lemma 10 and Lemma 11 to show that a formula is satisfied in an epistemic world if and only if it belongs to the maximal consistent set of this world.

LEMMA 12. *$(X,\beta) \Vdash \varphi$ if and only if $\varphi \in X$, for each $\varphi \in \Phi$ and each $(X,\beta) \in W$.*

PROOF. We prove the lemma by induction on the structural complexity of formula φ. If φ is an atomic proposition, then the required follows from Definition 8. Cases of φ having form $\psi_1 \to \psi_2$ and $\neg\psi$ follow from Definition 3 and the maximality and consistency of set X in the standard way. Now suppose that φ has the form $\Box_a^c\psi$, for some $a \in \mathcal{A}$, $c \in [0,+\infty)$, and $\psi \in \Phi$.

(⇒) : Assume that $\Box_a^c\psi \notin X$. Consider any finite set $J \subseteq J_a$ such that $\sum_{j\in J}\|j\| \le c$. It is sufficient to show that there is $(Y,\gamma) \in W$ such that $(Y,\gamma) \sim_J (X,\beta)$ and $(Y,\gamma) \nVdash \psi$. Indeed, by Lemma 11, there is $(Y,\gamma) \in W$ such that $(Y,\gamma) \sim_J (X,\beta)$ and $\psi \notin Y$. Therefore, by the induction hypothesis, $(Y,\gamma) \nVdash \psi$.

(⇐) : If $\Box_a^c\psi \in X$, then by Definition 3, it is sufficient to show that $(Y,\gamma) \Vdash \psi$ for each $(Y,\gamma) \in W$ such that

$(X,\beta) \sim_{(a,\beta(c,\psi),c,\psi)} (Y,\gamma)$. Indeed, by Lemma 10, $\psi \in Y$ for each $(Y,\gamma) \in W$ such that $(Y,\gamma) \sim_{(a,\beta(c,\psi),c,\psi)} (X,\beta)$. Hence, by the induction hypothesis, $(Y,\gamma) \Vdash \psi$ for each $(Y,\gamma) \in W$ such that $(Y,\gamma) \sim_{(a,\beta(c,\psi),c,\psi)} (X,\beta)$. ⊠

We are now ready to state and prove the completeness theorem for our logical system.

THEOREM 1. *If $w \Vdash \varphi$ for each $w \in W$ of each budget-constrained model $(W, \{J_a\}_{a\in\mathcal{A}}, \{\{\sim_j\}_{j\in J_a}\}_{a\in\mathcal{A}}, \|\cdot\|, \pi)$, then $\vdash \varphi$.*

PROOF. Suppose that $\nvdash \varphi$. Let X be any maximal consistent subset of Φ containing formula $\neg\varphi$. Consider function β such that $\beta(c,\psi) = 0$ for each $c \in [0,+\infty)$ and each $\psi \in \Phi$. Note that $\neg\varphi \in X$ implies that $\varphi \notin X$ due to consistency of the set X. Therefore, $(X,\beta) \nVdash \varphi$, by Lemma 12. ⊠

7. CONCLUSION AND DISCUSSION

In this paper we introduced a formal logical system for reasoning about budget constrained knowledge. We provided a formal semantics for this system in terms of justifications with costs and proved the soundness and the completeness of our logical system with respect to this semantics. There are several issues related to this work that we want to discuss in the conclusion.

Infinite Sets of Justifications. In Definition 3, we have assumed that subset J is finite. Note that this assumption could be potentially weakened to subset J being *at most countable*. If the set J is countable, then the sum of costs in Definition 3 becomes an infinite series. Since all terms in this series are non-negative, if such series converges, then it converges absolutely and, thus, the value of the sum does not depend on the order of the terms [17, p. 78]. This means that semantics given by Definition 3 is well-defined for at most countable sets J. However, the proof of the completeness in given in Section 6 of this paper is no longer valid. Indeed, existence of integer ω in proof of Lemma 11 relies on the assumption of finiteness of set J. Furthermore, our logical system, although still sound, is no longer complete with respect to the semantics of at most countable sets of justifications, because Negative Introspection principle becomes true for zero-cost knowledge: $\neg\Box_a^0\varphi \to \Box_a^0\neg\Box_a^0\varphi$. We prove the soundness of this principle in such a setting in the following lemma:

LEMMA 13. *If $w \Vdash \neg\Box_a^0\varphi$, then $w \Vdash \Box_a^0\neg\Box_a^0\varphi$.*

PROOF. Consider set $J = \{j \in J_a \mid \|j\| = 0\}$. Thus, $\sum_{j\in J}\|j\| = 0$. By Definition 3, it is sufficient to show that for any $u \in W$ if $w \sim_J u$, then $u \Vdash \neg\Box_a^0\varphi$. We will prove this by contradiction. Consider any $u \in W$ such that $w \sim_J u$ and suppose that $u \Vdash \Box_a^0\varphi$. Thus, there is $J' \subseteq J_a$ such that $\sum_{j\in J'}\|j\| = 0$ and for each $v \in W$, if $u \sim_{J'} v$, then $v \Vdash \varphi$. Note that $\sum_{j\in J'}\|j\| = 0$ implies that $J' \subseteq J$.

Note that $\sum_{j\in J'}\|j\| = 0$ by the choice of J'. Thus, by Definition 3, the assumption $w \Vdash \neg\Box_a^0\varphi$ implies that there is $v_0 \in W$ such that $w \sim_{J'} v_0$ and $v_0 \Vdash \neg\varphi$. Recall that $w \sim_J u$ and that $J' \subseteq J$. Hence, $w \sim_{J'} u$. Thus, by Lemma 1, $u \sim_{J'} v_0$ and $v_0 \Vdash \neg\varphi$, which is a contradiction to our result from the previous paragraph. ⊠

However, under this modified semantics the negative introspection principle remains false for non-zero costs knowledge. To construct a specific example when this principle is false, consider again Hilbert's Grand Hotel example from the introduction, yet assuming that it costs one Turkish lira to open any door in the hotel: $\|j\| = 1$ for each $j \in \mathbb{N}$. In this case, if w_0 is, as before, the epistemic world in which the hotel has no vacancies, then

$$w_0 \nVdash \neg\Box_a^c(\text{“The Grand Hotel has vacancies.”}) \to \Box_a^c\neg\Box_a^c(\text{“The Grand Hotel has vacancies.”})$$

for each $c > 0$. The proof is very similar to the proofs of Proposition 1 and Proposition 2. In the proof of the second proposition, set J is still finite because $\sum_{j\in J}\|j\| \le c$ and, by our assumption, the cost of each justification is one lira.

Budget-Constrained Distributed Knowledge. In this paper each modality is labeled by only one agent. One can consider modality $\Box_A^c\varphi$, where A is a group of agents, meaning that, at cost no more than c, the group of agent A can obtain the distributed knowledge [4] of statement φ. Different from the single-agent knowledge case, the exact properties of budget-constrained distributed knowledge depend on the specific type of the constraints. Namely, for financial constraints we have:

$$\Box_a^{c_1}(\varphi \to \psi) \to (\Box_b^{c_2}\varphi \to \Box_{a,b}^{c_1+c_2}\psi),$$

because it is natural to assume that if agent a needs c_1 Turkish liras to learn $\varphi \to \psi$ and agent b needs c_2 liras to discover φ, then they together “distributively” know ψ after spending at most $c_1 + c_2$ liras.

However, for time constraints we have

$$\Box_a^{c_1}(\varphi \to \psi) \to (\Box_b^{c_2}\varphi \to \Box_{a,b}^{\max\{c_1,c_2\}}\psi),$$

assuming that the two agents can work simultaneously.

Production Possibility Frontiers. So far, we have been assuming that we either deal with a financial constraint or a time constraint. In many cases goods are priced based on delivery time. That is, a good could be obtained slow but cheap or faster but at a higher cost. Such a constraint could be described by a function that show how fast the good can be obtained within the given budget. In economics,

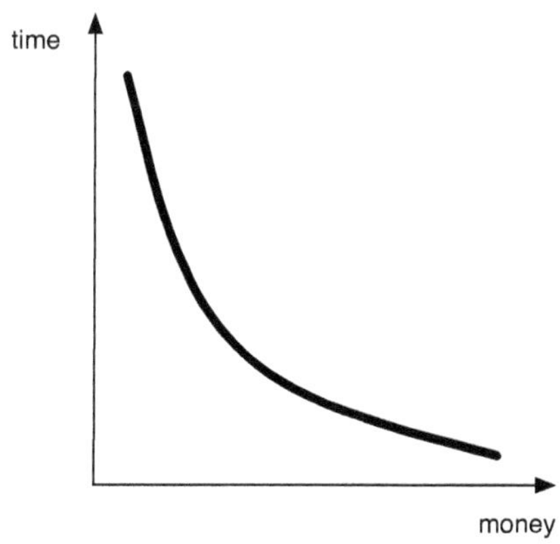

Figure 2: Production Possibility Frontier.

graphs of such functions (see Figure 2) are called production possibility frontiers. For any production possibility frontier f, by $\Box_a^f\varphi$ we mean the statement that for any given cost c, agent a can learn φ in time $f(c)$.

Suppose now that $\Box_a^f(\varphi \to \psi)$ and $\Box_a^g \varphi$, where f and g are two production possibility frontiers. To find function h such that $\Box_a^h \psi$, let us first fix any argument c of this function and decide what is the minimal time that agent a needs to learn both $\varphi \to \psi$ and φ. The agent can spend some part of this budget, say x, to learn $\varphi \to \psi$ in time $f(x)$ and the rest of the budget to learn ψ in time $g(c-x)$. Thus, $h(c) = \min_{0 \le x \le c}\{f(x) + g(c-x)\}$. In other words,

$$\Box_a^f(\varphi \to \psi) \to (\Box_a^g \varphi \to \Box_a^{f*g}\psi),$$

where

$$(f * g)(x) = \min_{0 \le x \le c} \{f(x) + g(c-x)\}.$$

Complete axiomatization of knowledge constrained by production possibility frontiers remains an open problem.

8. REFERENCES

[1] Sergei Artemov. The logic of justification. *The Review of Symbolic Logic*, 1(04):477–513, 2008.

[2] Hawaii Criminal Justice Data Center. HCJDC-073 request for criminal history record check, 2012.

[3] European Commission. Memo/14/186 12/03/2014, 2014.

[4] Ronald Fagin, Joseph Y. Halpern, Yoram Moses, and Moshe Y. Vardi. *Reasoning about knowledge*. MIT Press, Cambridge, MA, 1995.

[5] Melvin Fitting. The logic of proofs, semantically. *Annals of Pure and Applied Logic*, 132(1):1–25, 2005.

[6] Jean-Yves Girard. Linear logic. *Theoretical computer science*, 50:1–102, 1987.

[7] John-Jules Ch. Meyer and Wiebe Van Der Hoek. *Epistemic Logic for AI and Computer Science*. Cambridge University Press, 2004.

[8] Lawrence S Moss and Rohit Parikh. Topological reasoning and the logic of knowledge: preliminary report. In *Proceedings of the 4th conference on Theoretical aspects of reasoning about knowledge*, pages 95–105. Morgan Kaufmann Publishers Inc., 1992.

[9] Pavel Naumov and Jia Tao. Logic of confidence. *Synthese*, 2015. (to appear).

[10] Iowa Division of Criminal Investigation. Dci-76 (08/25/10) Criminal History Record Check Billing Form, 2010.

[11] California Department of Justice. Applicant fingerprint processing fees, 2012.

[12] The Court of Justice of the European Union. Judgment of the Court (Grand Chamber) of 13 May 2014. Google Spain SL and Google Inc. v Agencia Española de Protección de Datos (AEPD) and Mario Costeja González., 2014. Case: C-131/12.

[13] Florida Department of Law Enforcement. Criminal history information request, 2014.

[14] Maryland Department of Public Safety & Correctional Services. Background checks, 2014. www.dpscs.state.md.us/publicservs/bgchecks.shtml.

[15] Pennsylvania State Police. SP 4-164 (2-2013) Request for criminal record check, 2012.

[16] Virginia State Police. Sp-167: Criminal History Record Name Search Request, 2012.

[17] Walter Rudin. Principles of mathematical analysis (international series in pure & applied mathematics). 1976.

[18] W Van der Hoek and J-J Ch Meyer. Graded modalities in epistemic logic. *Logique et Analyse*, 34(133-134):251–270, 1991.

Module Checking of Strategic Ability

Wojciech Jamroga
Institute of Computer Science
Polish Academy of Sciences
w.jamroga@ipipan.waw.pl

Aniello Murano
Dipartimento di Ingegneria Elettrica e
Tecnologie dell'Informazione
Università degli Studi di Napoli Federico II, Italy
aniello.murano@unina.it

ABSTRACT

Module checking is a decision problem proposed in late 1990s to formalize verification of open systems, i.e., systems that must adapt their behavior to the input they receive from the environment. It was recently shown that module checking offers a distinctly different perspective from the better-known problem of *model* checking. So far, specifications in temporal logic CTL have been used for module checking. In this paper, we extend module checking to handle specifications in alternating-time temporal logic (ATL). We define the semantics of ATL module checking, and show that its expressivity strictly extends that of CTL module checking, as well as that of ATL itself. At the same time, we show that ATL module checking enjoys the same computational complexity as CTL module checking. We also investigate a variant of ATL module checking where the environment acts under uncertainty. Finally, we revisit the semantics of ability in the module checking problem, and propose a variant where strategies of agents in the module depend only on what the agents are able to observe.

Categories and Subject Descriptors

I.2.11 [**Artificial Intelligence**]: Distributed Artificial Intelligence—*Multiagent Systems*; I.2.4 [**Artificial Intelligence**]: Knowledge Representation Formalisms and Methods—*Modal logic*

General Terms

Theory, Verification

Keywords

Module checking, model checking, verification, alternating-time logic, strategic behavior

1. INTRODUCTION

Model checking is a well-established formal method to automatically check for global correctness of systems [10, 33]. In order to verify whether a system is correct with respect to a desired property, we describe its structure with a mathematical model, specify the property with a logical formula, and check formally if the model satisfies the formula. Model checking was first proposed for analysis of *closed systems* whose behavior is completely determined by their internal states and transitions. In this setting, models are often given as state transition graphs that usually include some degree of internal nondeterminism. An unwinding of the graph results in an infinite tree, formally called *computation tree*, that collects all possible evolutions of the system. Model checking of a closed system amounts to checking whether the tree satisfies the logical specification. Properties for model checking are usually specified in temporal logics CTL, LTL, CTL* [14], or strategic logics ATL, ATL* [2, 3].

In *module checking* [22, 25], the system is modeled as a *module* that interacts with its environment, and correctness means that a desired property must hold with respect to all possible interactions. The module can be seen as a transition system with states partitioned into ones controlled by the system and by the environment. Notice that the environment represents an external additional source of nondeterminism, because at each state controlled by the environment the computation can continue with any subset of its possible successor states. In other words, while in model checking we have only one computation tree to check, in module checking we have an infinite number of trees to handle, one for each possible behavior of the environment. Properties for module checking are usually given in CTL or CTL*.

It was believed for a long time that module checking of CTL/CTL* is a special (and rather simplistic) case of model checking ATL/ATL*. Because of that, active research on module checking subsided shortly after its conception. The belief has been recently refuted in [20]. There, it was proved that module checking includes two features inherently absent in the semantics of ATL, namely irrevocability and nondeterminism of strategies. This made module checking an interesting formalism for verification of open systems again.

In this paper, we extend module checking to handle specifications in the more expressive logic ATL. We define the semantics of ATL module checking, and show that its expressivity strictly extends that of CTL module checking, as well as that of ATL itself. At the same time, we show that ATL module checking enjoys the same computational complexity as CTL module checking. We also investigate a variant of ATL module checking where the environment acts under uncertainty, and show – again – that the computational price to pay is not high. Finally, we discuss the semantics of ability in the module checking problem. It turns out that the irrevocability of environment's strategies may yield counterintuitive interpretation of what agents can enforce. To deal

Appears in: *Proceedings of the 14th International Conference on Autonomous Agents and Multiagent Systems (AAMAS 2015), Bordini, Elkind, Weiss, Yolum (eds.), May 4–8, 2015, Istanbul, Turkey.*

with it, we propose a variant where strategies of agents in the module cannot depend on the whole strategy of the environment, but only on what the agents have so far observed.

Related work. Module checking was introduced in [22, 25], and later extended in several directions. In [23], the basic CTL/CTL* module checking problem was extended to the setting where the environment has imperfect information about the state of the system. In [8], it was extended to infinite-state open systems by considering pushdown modules. The pushdown module checking problem was first investigated for perfect information, and later, in [5, 7], for imperfect information; the latter variant was proved undecidable in [5]. [15, 4] extended module checking to μ-calculus specifications, and in [32] the module checking problem was investigated for bounded pushdown modules (or *hierarchical modules*). From a more practical point of view, [28, 29] built a semi-automated tool for module checking in the existential fragment of CTL, both in the perfect and imperfect information setting. Moreover, an approach to CTL module checking based on tableau was exploited in [6]. Finally, an extension of module checking was used to reason about three-valued abstractions in [17, 11, 18, 16].

It must be noted that literature on module checking became rather sparse after 2002, especially when compared to the body of work on model checking. This must be partially attributed to the popular belief that CTL module checking is nothing but a special case of ATL model checking. The belief has been refuted only recently [20], which will hopefully spark renewed interest in verification of open systems by module checking.

2. PRELIMINARIES

2.1 Models and Modules

In this paper, we consider several frameworks for modeling and verification of temporal properties. *Modules* in *module checking* [22] were proposed to represent open systems – that is, systems that interact with an environment whose behavior cannot be determined in advance. In their simplest form, modules are unlabeled transition systems with the set of states partitioned into those "owned" by the system, and the ones where the next transition is controlled by the environment. Models of *alternating-time temporal logic* [3], called *concurrent game structures*, are multi-player transition systems with transitions labeled by tuples of actions, one from each agent.

Definition 1 (Module). *A* module *is a tuple* $M = \langle AP, St_s, St_e, q_0, \rightarrow, PV\rangle$, *where* AP *is a finite set of (atomic) propositions,* $St = St_s \cup St_e$ *is a nonempty finite set of states partitioned into a set* St_s *of* system states *and a set* St_e *of* environment states, $\rightarrow \subseteq St \times St$ *is a (global) transition relation,* $q_0 \in St$ *is an initial state, and* $PV : St \rightarrow 2^{AP}$ *maps each state* q *to the set of atomic propositions true in* q.

Definition 2 (CGS). *A* concurrent game structure *is a tuple* $M = \langle AP, \mathbb{A}\mathrm{gt}, St, Act, d, o, PV\rangle$ *including nonempty finite set of propositions* AP, *agents* $\mathbb{A}\mathrm{gt} = \{1, \dots, k\}$, *states* St, *(atomic) actions* Act, *and a propositional valuation* $PV : St \rightarrow 2^{AP}$. *The function* $d : \mathbb{A}\mathrm{gt} \times St \rightarrow 2^{Act}$ *defines nonempty sets of actions available to agents at each state, and the (deterministic) transition function* o *assigns the outcome state* $q' = o(q, \alpha_1, \dots, \alpha_k)$ *to each state* q *and tuple of actions* $\alpha_i \in d(i, q)$ *that can be executed by* $\mathbb{A}\mathrm{gt}$ *in* q.

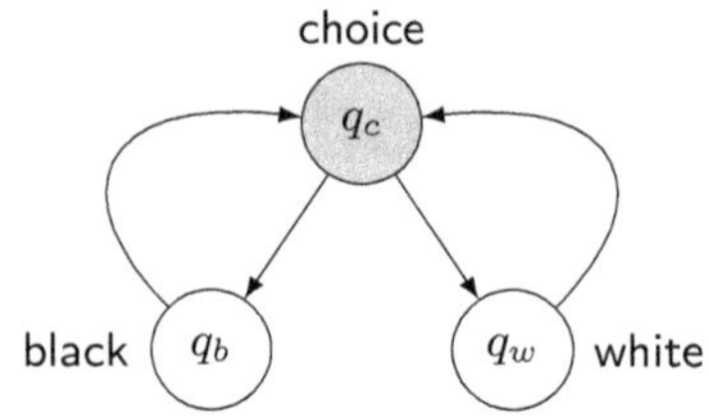

Figure 1: Coffee machine M_{caf}. Environment states are marked grey; system states are marked white.

A pointed CGS *is a pair* (M, q_0) *of a concurrent game structure and an initial state in it.*

Nondeterministic choices of agents in a CGS can be represented by sets of actions. In this sense, agent a can select at state q any nonempty set $\boldsymbol{\alpha} \subseteq d(a, q)$, and the set of successors of $\boldsymbol{\alpha}$ is simply the union of successor sets for each action in α. Then, modules can be seen as a subclass of concurrent game structures – more precisely, 2-player turn-based[1] pointed CGS's with agents $\mathbb{A}\mathrm{gt} = \{sys, env\}$.

Example 1. *Consider a coffee machine that allows customers to choose between ordering* black *or* white *coffee. After the selection, the machine delivers the product and waits for further selections, cf. Figure 1. The environment represents all possible infinite lines of customers, each with their own plans and preferences. We formally define the coffee machine as a module* $M_{caf} = \langle AP, St_s, St_e, q_0, \rightarrow, PV\rangle$ *such that* $AP = \{\mathsf{choice}, \mathsf{black}, \mathsf{white}\}$, $St_s = \{q_b, q_w\}$, $St_e = \{q_c\}$, $q_0 = q_c$, $\rightarrow = \{(q_c, q_b), (q_c, q_w), (q_b, q_c), (q_w, q_c)\}$, *and* $PV(black) = \{q_b\}$, $PV(white) = \{q_w\}$, $PV(choice) = \{q_c\}$. *We leave rewriting* M_{caf} *as a CGS to the reader.*

2.2 CTL Module Checking

CTL* is a branching–time temporal logic [12], where path quantifiers, E ("for some path") and A ("for all paths"), can be followed by an arbitrary linear-time formula, allowing boolean combinations and nesting over temporal operators X ("next"), U ("strong until"), F ("eventually"), and G ("always"). There are two types of formulas in CTL*: *state formulas* φ, whose satisfaction is related to a specific state (or node of a labeled tree), and *path formulas* γ, whose satisfaction is related to a specific path. Formally:

$$\varphi ::= \mathsf{p} \mid \neg\varphi \mid \varphi \wedge \varphi \mid \mathsf{E}\gamma,$$
$$\gamma ::= \varphi \mid \neg\gamma \mid \gamma \wedge \gamma \mid \mathrm{X}\gamma \mid \gamma\,\mathrm{U}\,\gamma.$$

where p is an atomic proposition. The other operators can be defined as: $\mathsf{A}\gamma \equiv \neg\mathsf{E}\neg\gamma$, $\mathrm{F}\gamma \equiv true\,\mathrm{U}\,\gamma$, and $\mathrm{G}\gamma \equiv \neg\mathrm{F}\neg\gamma$.

CTL [10] is a restricted subset of CTL*, obtained replacing the syntax of path formulas γ as follows: $\gamma := \mathrm{X}\varphi \mid \varphi\,\mathrm{U}\,\varphi \mid \varphi\,\mathrm{W}\,\varphi$ ("weak until"), i.e., every path quantifier must be immediately followed by a temporal operator.

We define the semantics of CTL* (and its fragment CTL) with respect to a St-labeled tree $\langle T, V\rangle$ with propositional valuation PV.[2] Let $x \in T$ and $\lambda \subseteq T$ be a path from x.

[1]A CGS is turn-based iff every state in it is controlled by (at most) one agent. That is, for every $q \in St$, there is an agent $a \in \mathbb{A}\mathrm{gt}$ such that $|d(a', q)| = 1$ for all $a' \neq a$.

[2]For the formal definition of labeled trees, cf. e.g. [22, 20].

By $\lambda[i]$ we denote the i-st element of λ and by $\lambda[1..\infty]$ the suffix of λ starting at $\lambda[1]$. For a state (resp., path) formula φ (resp. γ), the satisfaction relation $\langle T,V\rangle, PV, x \models_{\text{CTL}} \varphi$ (resp., $\langle T,V\rangle, PV, \lambda \models_{\text{CTL}} \gamma$) is defined as follows:

- $\langle T,V\rangle, PV, x \models_{\text{CTL}} \mathsf{p}$ *iff* $\mathsf{p} \in PV(x)$;
- $\langle T,V\rangle, PV, x \models_{\text{CTL}} \mathsf{E}\gamma$ *iff* there exists a path λ from x such that $\langle T,V\rangle, PV, \lambda \models_{\text{CTL}} \gamma$;
- $\langle T,V\rangle, PV, \lambda \models_{\text{CTL}} \varphi$ *iff* $\langle T,V\rangle, PV, \lambda[0] \models_{\text{CTL}} \varphi$;
- $\langle T,V\rangle, PV, \lambda \models_{\text{CTL}} \mathrm{X}\gamma$ *iff* $\langle T,V\rangle, PV, \lambda[1..\infty] \models_{\text{CTL}} \gamma$;
- $\langle T,V\rangle, PV, \lambda \models_{\text{CTL}} \gamma_1 \,\mathrm{U}\, \gamma_2$ *iff* there is $y \in \lambda$ such that $\langle T,V\rangle, PV, \lambda^y \models_{\text{CTL}} \gamma_2$ and $\langle T,V\rangle, PV, \lambda^z \models_{\text{CTL}} \gamma_1$ for all $z \in \lambda$ such that $z \prec y$.

The clauses for negation and conjunction are standard. Moreover, $\langle T,V\rangle, PV, \lambda \models_{\text{CTL}} \gamma_1 \,\mathrm{W}\, \gamma_2$ iff either $\langle T,V\rangle, PV, \lambda \models_{\text{CTL}} \gamma_1 \,\mathrm{U}\, \gamma_2$ or $\langle T,V\rangle, PV, \lambda \models_{\text{CTL}} \mathrm{G}\gamma_1$. Given a formula φ, we say that $\langle T,V\rangle$ satisfies φ if $\langle T,V\rangle, PV, \varepsilon \models_{\text{CTL}} \varphi$.

For a module $M = \langle AP, St_s, St_e, \rightarrow, q_0, PV\rangle$, the set of all (maximal) computations of M starting from the initial state q_0 is described by a St-labeled tree $\langle T_M, V_M\rangle$, called *computation tree*, which is obtained by unwinding M from the initial state in the usual way. The problem of deciding, for a given branching-time formula φ over AP, whether $\langle T_M, PV \circ V_M\rangle$ [3] satisfies φ, denoted $M \models_{\text{CTL}} \varphi$, is the usual *model-checking problem* [10, 33]. On the other hand, for an open system, $\langle T_M, V_M\rangle$ corresponds to a very specific environment, i.e. the maximal environment that never restricts the set of its next states. When we examine specification φ w.r.t. a module M, the formula φ should hold not only in $\langle T_M, V_M\rangle$, but in all the trees obtained by pruning some environment transitions from $\langle T_M, V_M\rangle$. The set of these trees is denoted by $exec(M)$ and is formally defined as follows. For each state $q \in St$, let $succ(q)$ be the ordered tuple of q' node successors of q, i.e., $q \rightarrow q'$. A tree $\langle T,V\rangle$ is in $exec(M)$ iff $T \subseteq T_M$, V is the restriction of V_M to the tree T, and for all $x \in T$ the following holds:

- if $V_M(x) = w \in St_s$ and $succ(q) = \langle q_1, \ldots, q_n\rangle$, then $children(T,x) = \{x \cdot 1, \ldots, x \cdot n\}$ (note that for $1 \le i \le n$, $V(x \cdot i) = V_M(x \cdot i) = q_i$);
- if $V_M(x) = w \in St_e$ and $succ(q) = \langle q_1, \ldots, q_n\rangle$, then there is a sub-tuple $\langle q_{i_1}, \ldots, q_{i_p}\rangle$ of $succ(q)$ such that $children(T,x) = \{x \cdot i_1, \ldots, x \cdot i_p\}$ (note that for $1 \le j \le p$, $V(x \cdot i_j) = V_M(x \cdot i_j) = q_{i_j}$).

Intuitively, when the module M is in a system state q_s, then all states in $succ(q_s)$ are possible successors. When M is in an environment state q_e, then the possible next states (that are in $succ(q_e)$) depend on the current environment. Since the behavior of the environment is nondeterministic, we have to consider all the nonempty sub-tuples of $succ(q_e)$.

For a module M and a CTL(*) formula φ, we say that M reactively satisfies φ, denoted by $M \models^r_{\text{CTL}} \varphi$, if all the trees in $exec(M)$ satisfy φ. The problem of deciding whether M reactively satisfies φ is called *module checking* [25]. Note that $M \models^r_{\text{CTL}} \varphi$ implies $M \models_{\text{CTL}} \varphi$ (since $\langle T_M, V_M\rangle \in exec(M)$), but the converse in general does not hold. Also, note that $M \not\models^r_{\text{CTL}} \varphi$ is *not* equivalent to $M \models^r_{\text{CTL}} \neg\varphi$.

[3] $PV \circ V_M$ denotes the composition of the functions PV and V_M that allows to re-label each state-labeled node u in $\langle T_M, V_M\rangle$ with $PV(V_M(u))$.

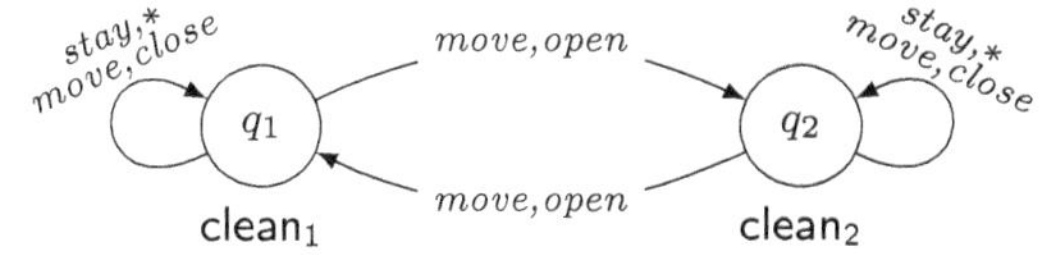

Figure 2: Vacuum cleaner vs. gate controller: M_{clean}

EXAMPLE 2. *Consider the coffee machine from Example 1. Clearly, $M_{caf} \models_{CTL}$ EFblack as it is (in principle) possible to deliver black coffee. On the other hand, $M_{caf} \not\models^r_{CTL}$ EFblack. Think of a line of customers who never order black coffee. It corresponds to an execution tree of M_{caf} with no node labeled with* black*, and such a tree does not satisfy* EFblack.

2.3 Alternating Time Logic ATL/ATL*

Alternating-time temporal logic [3] generalizes CTL* by replacing path quantifiers E, A with *strategic modalities* $\langle\langle A\rangle\rangle$. Informally, $\langle\langle A\rangle\rangle\gamma$ expresses that the group of agents A has a collective strategy to enforce temporal property γ. The language ATL* is given by the grammar below:

$$\varphi ::= \mathsf{p} \mid \neg\varphi \mid \varphi \wedge \varphi \mid \langle\langle A\rangle\rangle\gamma,$$
$$\gamma ::= \varphi \mid \neg\gamma \mid \gamma \wedge \gamma \mid \mathrm{X}\gamma \mid \gamma \,\mathrm{U}\, \gamma.$$

where $A \subseteq \mathbb{A}\mathrm{gt}$ is any subset of agents, and p is a proposition. "Sometime" and "always" are obtained like in CTL*. Also, we can use $[\![A]\!]\gamma \equiv \neg\langle\langle A\rangle\rangle\neg\gamma$ to express that no strategy of A can prevent property γ. Similarly to CTL, ATL is the syntactic variant in which every occurrence of a strategic modality is immediately followed by a temporal operator.

Given a CGS, we define the strategies and their outcomes as follows. A *perfect recall strategy* for agent a is a function $s_a : St^+ \rightarrow Act$ such that $s_a(q_0 q_1 \ldots q_n) \in d(a, q_n)$. A *memoryless strategy* for a is a function $s_a : St \rightarrow Act$ such that $s_a(q) \in d(a,q)$. A *collective strategy* for a group of agents $A = \{a_1, \ldots, a_r\}$ is simply a tuple of individual strategies $s_A = \langle s_{a_1}, \ldots, s_{a_r}\rangle$. The "outcome" function $out(q, s_A)$ returns the set of all paths that can occur when agents A execute strategy s_A from state q on. The semantics $\models_{\text{ATL}}$ of alternating-time logic is obtained from that of CTL* by replacing the clause for $\mathsf{E}\gamma$ as follows:

$M, q \models_{\text{ATL}} \langle\langle A\rangle\rangle\gamma$ iff there is a perfect recall strategy s_A for A such that for every $\lambda \in out(q, s_A)$ we have $M, \lambda \models_{\text{ATL}} \gamma$.

The problem of deciding whether a pointed CGS (M, q_0) satisfies the ATL formula φ is called *ATL model checking.*

EXAMPLE 3. *A vacuum cleaner robot can move between (and clean) two cubicles, while a controller can open/close the gate between the cubicles. A simple CGS modeling the scenario is depicted in Figure 2. The wildcard (*) stands for any action of the respective agent. We assume q_1 to be the initial state.*

Clearly, $M_{clean} \models_{ATL} \langle\langle robot, ctrl\rangle\rangle$F$\mathsf{clean}_1$ and $M_{clean} \models_{ATL} \langle\langle robot, ctrl\rangle\rangle$F$\mathsf{clean}_2$: if the robot and the controller cooperate, they can get any room cleaned. On the other hand, the robot cannot clean the other cubicle on its own, e.g., $M_{clean} \not\models_{ATL} \mathsf{clean}_1 \rightarrow \langle\langle robot\rangle\rangle$F$\mathsf{clean}_2$. Actually, the controller has a sure strategy to prevent that (by never opening

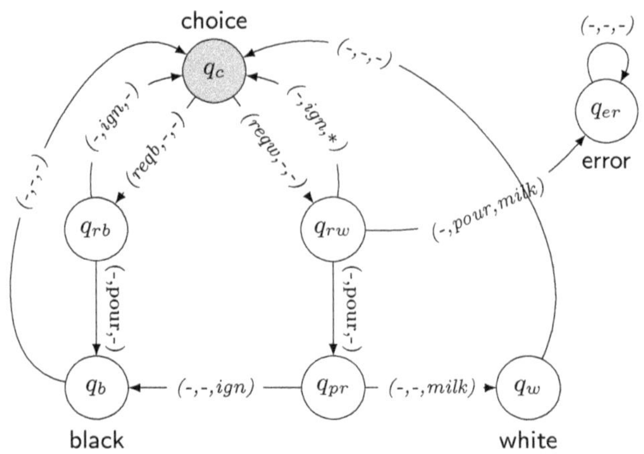

Figure 3: Multi-agent coffee machine M_{caf2}

the gate): $M_{clean} \models_{ATL} \mathsf{clean}_1 \to \langle\langle ctrl\rangle\rangle \mathrm{G}\neg\mathsf{clean}_2$. *The robot can also prevent cleaning the other room, by never deciding to move:* $M_{clean} \models_{ATL} \mathsf{clean}_1 \to \langle\langle robot\rangle\rangle \mathrm{G}\neg\mathsf{clean}_2$.

Embedding CTL* in ATL*. The path quantifiers of CTL* can be expressed in the standard semantics of ATL* as follows [3]: $\mathsf{A}\gamma \equiv \langle\langle\emptyset\rangle\rangle\gamma$ and $\mathsf{E}\gamma \equiv \langle\langle \mathbb{A}\mathrm{gt}\rangle\rangle\gamma$. We point out that the above translation of E does *not* work for several extensions of ATL*, e.g., with imperfect information, nondeterministic strategies, and irrevocable strategies. On the other hand, the translation of A into $\langle\langle\emptyset\rangle\rangle$ does work for all the semantic variants of ATL* considered in this paper. Thanks to that, we can define a translation $atl(\varphi)$ from CTL* to ATL* as follows. First, we convert φ so that it only includes universal path quantifiers, and then replace every occurrence of A with $\langle\langle\emptyset\rangle\rangle$. For example, $atl(\mathsf{EG}(\mathsf{p}_1 \wedge \mathsf{AF}\mathsf{p}_2)) = \neg\langle\langle\emptyset\rangle\rangle \mathrm{F}(\neg\mathsf{p}_1 \vee \neg\langle\langle\emptyset\rangle\rangle \mathrm{F}\mathsf{p}_2)$. Note that if φ is a CTL formula then $atl(\varphi)$ is a formula of ATL. By a slight abuse of notation, we will use path quantifiers A, E in ATL formulae whenever it is convenient.

3. ATL MODULE CHECKING

We are now ready to propose how module checking for ATL specifications can be defined.

3.1 Multi-Agent Modules

Definition 3 (Multi-agent module). *A* multi-agent module *is a pointed concurrent game structure that contains a special agent called "the environment" ($env \in \mathbb{A}\mathrm{gt}$). We call a module* k-agent *if it consists of k agents plus the environment (i.e., the underlying CGS contains $k+1$ agents).*

The module is alternating *iff its states are partitioned into those owned by the environment (i.e., $|d(a,q)| = 1$ for all $a \neq env$) and those where the environment is passive (i.e., $|d(env,q)| = 1$). That is, it alternates between the agents' and the environment's moves. Moreover, the module is* turn-based *iff the underlying CGS is turn-based.*

We remark in passing that the original modules [22] were turn-based (and hence also alternating). On the other hand, the version of module checking for imperfect information [23] assumed that the system and the environment can act simultaneously.

Example 4. *A multi-agent refinement of the coffee machine is presented in Figure 3. The module includes two agents: the brewer (br) and the milk provider (milky). The brewer's function is to pour coffee into the cup (action pour), and the milk provider can add milk on top (action milk). Moreover, each of them can be faulty and ignore the request from the environment (ign). Note that if br and milky try to pour coffee and milk at the same time, the machine gets jammed and needs repair. Finally, the environment has actions reqb, reqw available in state q_c, meaning that it requests black (resp. white) coffee. Since the module is alternating, we have kept the convention of marking system states as white, and environment states as grey.*

3.2 Multi-Agent Module Checking

We define the ATL module checking problem analogously to CTL module checking. Given a multi-agent module M and an ATL* formula φ, we say that M reactively satisfies φ, denoted $M \models^r_{\mathrm{ATL}} \varphi$, if all the trees in $exec(M)$ satisfy φ. Similarly to CTL, $M \models^r_{\mathrm{ATL}} \varphi$ implies $M \models_{\mathrm{ATL}} \varphi$ (since $\langle T_M, V_M\rangle \in exec(M)$ and $\langle T_M, V_M\rangle$ is strategically bisimilar to M [1]), but the converse in general does not hold. Again, note that $M \not\models^r_{\mathrm{ATL}} \varphi$ is *not* equivalent to $M \models^r_{\mathrm{ATL}} \neg\varphi$.

Example 5. *What questions can be answered with ATL module checking? Consider the multi-agent coffee machine M_{caf2} from Example 4. Clearly, $M_{caf2} \not\models^r_{ATL} \langle\langle br, milky\rangle\rangle \mathrm{F}\mathsf{white}$ because the environment can keep requesting black coffee. On the other hand, $M_{caf2} \models^r_{ATL} \langle\langle br, milky\rangle\rangle \mathrm{F}\mathsf{black}$: the agents can provide the user with black coffee whatever she requests. They can also deprive the user of coffee completely – in fact, the brewer alone can do it by consistently ignoring her requests: $M_{caf2} \models^r_{ATL} \langle\langle br\rangle\rangle \mathrm{G}(\neg\mathsf{black} \wedge \neg\mathsf{white})$.*

All the above formulae can be also be used for model checking, and they would actually generate the same answers. So, what's the benefit of module checking? In module checking, we can condition the property to be achieved on the behavior of the environment. *For instance, users who never order white coffee can be served by the brewer alone: $M_{caf2} \models^r_{ATL} \mathsf{AG}\neg\mathsf{reqw} \to \langle\langle br\rangle\rangle \mathrm{F}\mathsf{black}$. Note that the same formula in model checking does not express any interesting property. In fact, it trivially holds since $M_{caf2} \not\models_{ATL} \mathsf{AG}\neg\mathsf{reqw}$. Likewise, we have $M_{caf2} \models_{ATL} \mathsf{AG}\neg\mathsf{reqb} \to \langle\langle br\rangle\rangle \mathrm{F}\mathsf{white}$, whereas module checking gives a different and more intuitive answer: $M_{caf2} \not\models^r_{ATL} \mathsf{AG}\neg\mathsf{reqb} \to \langle\langle br\rangle\rangle \mathrm{F}\mathsf{white}$. That is, the brewer cannot handle requests for white coffee on his own, even if the user never orders anything else.*

More realistic examples can include a group of software agents serving customers on behalf of an online shop (each agent dealing with different merchandise), or a sensor network reacting to the stream of traffic data. We leave formal treatment of the examples to the reader's imagination.

4. EXPRESSIVE POWER OF ATL MODULE CHECKING

In this section, we show that ATL module checking strictly enhances the expressivity of both CTL module checking and ATL model checking.

4.1 ATL vs. CTL Module Checking

First, we prove that function $atl(\varphi)$ presented in Section 2.3 provides a sufficient syntactic translation to embed CTL module checking.

THEOREM 1. *For every module M and CTL* formula φ, we have $M \models^r_{CTL} \varphi$ iff $M \models^r_{ATL} atl(\varphi)$.*

PROOF. $M \models^r_{\mathrm{CTL}} \varphi$ iff for every $T \in exec(M)$ it holds that $T \models_{\mathrm{CTL}} \varphi$. Thus, equivalently, $\forall T \in exec(M) . T \models_{\mathrm{ATL}} atl(\varphi)$. But this is equivalent to $M \models^r_{\mathrm{ATL}} atl(\varphi)$. □

Note that, for a CTL formula φ, we have that $atl(\varphi)$ is a formula of ATL. Thus, Theorem 1 provides also an embedding of module checking for "CTL without star." The next theorem shows that there is no embedding the other way.

THEOREM 2. *There exists a pair of multi-agent modules M_1, M_2 that reactively satisfy the same formulae of CTL* (and hence also CTL), but are reactively distinguished by a formula of ATL (and hence also ATL*).*

PROOF. Take $M_1 = M_{caf2}$ and M_2 identical to M_1 except that state q_{rb} is controlled by *milky*.

Now, observe that *env* has the same "pruning strategies" in M_1, M_2, and that they yield bisimilar subtrees. More formally, for every $T_1 \in exec(M_1)$ there is bisimilar $T_2 \in exec(M_2)$, and vice versa. Thus, $M_1 \models^r_{\mathrm{CTL}} \varphi$ iff $\forall T \in exec(M_1) . T \models_{\mathrm{CTL}} \varphi$ iff $\forall T \in exec(M_2) . T \models_{\mathrm{CTL}} \varphi$ iff $M_2 \models^r_{\mathrm{CTL}} \varphi$.

Furthermore, take $\varphi \equiv \langle\langle milky \rangle\rangle \mathrm{G}(\neg \mathsf{black} \wedge \neg \mathsf{white})$. It is easy to see that $M_1 \not\models^r_{\mathrm{ATL}} \varphi$ but $M_2 \models^r_{\mathrm{ATL}} \varphi$. □

4.2 ATL Module vs. Model Checking

As we show below, ATL module checking subsumes ATL model checking modulo renaming. Moreover, there are properties captured by $\models^r_{\mathrm{ATL}}$ that cannot be discerned by $\models_{\mathrm{ATL}}$.

THEOREM 3. *For every module M and ATL* formula φ such that M and φ do not contain agent env, we have that $M \models^r_{ATL} \varphi$ iff $M \models_{ATL} \varphi$.*

PROOF. The equivalence is actually less straightforward than it seems, since $\models_{\mathrm{ATL}}$ evaluates nested cooperation modalities in new tree unfoldings starting from the current state of the model, whereas $\models^r_{\mathrm{ATL}}$ evaluates nested cooperation modalities in the original tree unfolding. Thus, $\models^r_{\mathrm{ATL}}$ comes close to the "no forgetting" semantics of ATL studied in [9]. Still, for perfect information, a pointed model is strategically bisimilar with its tree unfolding, and hence satisfies the same formulae of ATL* [1].

Formally, if $M \models^r_{\mathrm{ATL}} \varphi$ then $\langle T_M, V_M \rangle \models_{\mathrm{ATL}} \varphi$, and hence $M \models_{\mathrm{ATL}} \varphi$ (by the result from [1]). Conversely, if $M \models_{\mathrm{ATL}} \varphi$ then by the same result $\langle T_M, V_M \rangle \models_{\mathrm{ATL}} \varphi$, and hence also $M \models^r_{\mathrm{ATL}} \varphi$ as $exec(M) = \{\langle T_M, V_M \rangle\}$ when $env \notin M$. □

THEOREM 4. *There exists a pair of modules that satisfy the same formulae of ATL* (and hence also ATL), but are reactively distinguished by a formula of ATL (and hence also ATL*).*

PROOF. We know from [20] that there exists a pair of single-agent modules M_1, M_2 that satisfy the same formulae of ATL* but are reactively distinguished by an CTL formula. By Theorem 1, they are also reactively distinguished by an ATL formula. □

5. ALGORITHMS AND COMPLEXITY

Our algorithmic solution to the problem of ATL module checking exploits the automata-theoretic approach. More precisely, we make use of *parity tree automata* on infinite tress. We refer to [34] for an introduction. The approach we use combines and extends that ones used to solve the *CTL* module checking* and the *ATL* model checking* problems.

5.1 Trees for Strategies

Recall that $M \not\models^r_{\mathrm{ATL}} \langle\langle A \rangle\rangle \gamma$ iff there exists $\langle T_M, V_M \rangle \in exec(M)$ not satisfying $\langle\langle A \rangle\rangle \gamma$. Moreover, for memoryfull strategies, $M \models_{\mathrm{ATL}} \langle\langle A \rangle\rangle \gamma$ iff $\exists s_A \forall s_{\bar{A}} out(M, (s_A, s_{\bar{A}})) \models \gamma$, where $\bar{A}$ stands for the remaining agents not in A. Thus $\langle T_M, V_M \rangle \not\models_{\mathrm{ATL}} \langle\langle A \rangle\rangle \gamma$ means that for each possible strategy s_A for A there exists a strategy $s_{\bar{A}}$ for agents not in A such that γ does not hold on the resulting path(s).

Consider the tree $\langle T'_M, V_M \rangle$ that is obtained from $\langle T_M, V_M \rangle$ by pairing each possible perfect recall strategy for agents not in A with only one perfect recall strategy for agents in A. In other words, the tree is obtained from $\langle T_M, V_M \rangle$ by pruning at each node, for all strategies $s_{\bar{A}}$, all but one subtree among those induced by $s_{\bar{A}}$.

Then, $\langle\langle A \rangle\rangle \gamma$ does not hold according to the $\models^r_{\mathrm{ATL}}$ semantics iff there exists such a tree that satisfies the CTL* formula $\mathsf{A}\neg\gamma$. We denote the set of such trees by $exec(M, A)$, and call it the *A-executions* of M. This set is formally described below. The essence of our algorithm is to build an automaton that accepts all such trees. Then the emptiness of the automaton ensures that the multi-agent module satisfies the formula.

Let M be a multi-agent module and $A \subseteq \mathbb{A}\mathrm{gt}$ a set of agents. First observe that the tree unwinding $\langle T_M, V_M \rangle$ of M is done in such a way that looking at each node, by following backwards the path up to the root, it is possible to recover the sequence of states in St^* that leads to that node. This is important in ATL* as the strategies are memoryfull. Consequently, w.l.o.g. we can assume that each node in T_M belongs to St^*, as we do in the rest of this section. The set $exec(M, A)$ is defined below by refining the first bullet in the definition of $exec(M)$ as follows:

- if $V_M(x) = w \in St_s$ and $x = \lambda \cdot q' \in St^*$ then $children(T, x)$ contains all strings of the form $\lambda \cdot q' \cdot q''$ where q'' is such that there is a move vector $\langle \alpha_1, \ldots, \alpha_k \rangle$ such that (1) $\alpha_b = s_b(\lambda \cdot q') = d(b, q')$ for all agents $b \in \bar{A}$, (2) $o(q', \alpha_1, \ldots, \alpha_k) = q''$, and (3) $V(x \cdot q'') = q''$.

5.2 Automata-Based Procedure for ATL Module Checking

We will now sketch a module checking procedure that adapts the automata-theoretic approaches used in [25] and [3]. Given a module M and a CTL* formula, the former returns a Rabin tree automaton A_M accepting all trees in $exec(M)$ that do not satisfy the formula. The latter, given a CGS G and an ATL* formula $\langle\langle A \rangle\rangle \gamma$, returns a Rabin tree automaton A_G accepting all trees compatible with every strategy of agents in A.

Consider now a multi-agent module M'. We construct a Rabin tree automaton $A_{M'}$ that combines the ideas behind the constructions of A_M and A_G, and accepts all trees in $exec(M', A)$. That is, it accepts all trees compatible with the strategies in $\bar{A}$ and respecting all possible behaviors (i.e., prunings) from the environment. More precisely, $A_{M'}$ reproduces the transition relation of A_M over the environment states St_e and that of A_G over system states St_s. Note that, similarly to A_M and A_G, the automaton $A_{M'}$ turns out to have a doubly exponential number of states and an exponential number of pairs in the size of the formula. Now, it suffices to apply the classical algorithm that checks emptiness of the automaton [13], i.e., checks whether $L(A_{M'}) = \emptyset$.

THEOREM 5. *The algorithm returns "yes" iff $M \models^r_{ATL} \varphi$.*

PROOF. Follows from the construction. □

5.3 Complexity of Module Checking: ATL*

We start with the general result, and then consider the so called *program complexity*.

THEOREM 6. *The module-checking problem for ATL* is* 2EXPTIME*-complete.*

PROOF. For the lower bound, recall that both CTL* module checking and ATL* model checking are 2EXPTIME-hard. Since ATL* module checking embeds both problems through polynomial-time reductions, the hardness result immediately follows.

For the upper bound, consider the automata-theoretic procedure presented in Section 5.2. Recall that the automaton being constructed ($A_{M'}$) has a doubly exponential number of states and an exponential number of pairs in the size of the formula. Moreover, the algorithm for checking emptiness of the automaton is exponential in the number of pairs but polynomial in the number of states [13]. Thus, the overall algorithm runs in time which is doubly exponential in the size of the input formula. □

Similarly to model checking, the input to module checking typically consists of a large model (specifying the agents and their interaction with the environment) and a short formula (referring to a simple temporal pattern, e.g., reaching a state where some atomic formula p holds). Thus, the fact that the complexity is high wrt to the length of the formula is not significant in itself. It is much more important to see how the complexity scales in relation to the size of the model. To this end, *program complexity* is often used, where one assumes the length of the formula to be bounded by a constant, and hence not a parameter of the complexity function.

THEOREM 7. *For ATL* formulas of bounded size, the module checking problem is* P*-complete.*

PROOF. In case of an ATL* formula with bounded size, first note that, as both A_M and A_G are polynomial in the size of the model, it is also the case for the Rabin automaton $A_{M'}$. Then the polynomial-time upper bound follows from further observing that the number of pairs in all these automata is independent from the size of the model (i.e., it is a constant value in this case). For the lower bound we recall that both CTL* module checking and ATL* model checking are P-hard in case of bounded-size formulas. □

5.4 Complexity of Module Checking: ATL

We now look at the more restricted syntactic variant ATL.

THEOREM 8. *Module checking ATL is* EXPTIME*-complete.*

PROOF SKETCH. We use a similar approach to the one in Section 5.2. The construction yields a Buchi tree automaton (rather than a Rabin tree automaton) exponential in the size of the formula, whose emptiness is solvable in polynomial-time [35, 24]. For the lower bound, we recall that module checking of CTL is EXPTIME-hard. □

THEOREM 9. *Module checking ATL for formulae of bounded size is* P*-complete.*

PROOF. Straightforward, from Theorem 7 and the fact that CTL module checking and ATL model checking are P-hard in case of bounded-size formulas. □

Summary of complexity results. Summing up, we do not lose anything in terms of complexity by "upgrading" CTL* module checking to specifications written in ATL*. Both the general complexity results and the program complexities are exactly the same. Since ATL* module checking is more expressive than CTL* module checking, it seems we pay no (significant) price for the expressivity enhancement.

For "vanilla" ATL, module checking is EXPTIME-complete, which is the same as CTL module checking, but distinctly harder than for ATL model checking. Still, the complexity increase is only wrt the length of the formula; the program complexities in all the three cases are the same.

6. IMPERFECT INFORMATION

So far, we have only considered multi-agent modules in which the environment has complete information about the state of the system. In many practical scenarios this is not the case. Usually, the agents have some private knowledge that the environment cannot access. As an example, think of the coffee machine from Example 4. A realistic model of the machine should include some internal variables that the environment (i.e., the customer) is not supposed to know during the interaction, such as the amount of milk in the container or the amount of coins available for giving change. States that differ only in such hidden information are indistinguishable to the environment. While interaction with an "omniscient" environment corresponds to an arbitrary pruning of transitions in the module, in case of imperfect information the pruning must coincide whenever two computations look the same to the environment.

6.1 Imperfect Information Module Checking

To handle such scenarios, we extend the definition of multi-agent modules as follows.

DEFINITION 4 (MULTI-AGENT MODULE WITH IMP. INF.). A multi-agent module with imperfect information *is a multi-agent module further equipped with an indistinguishability relation* $\sim \subseteq St \times St$*. We assume* $\sim$ *to be an equivalence.*

We write $[St]$ for the set of equivalence classes of St under $\sim$. Clearly, in case of perfect information, $\sim$ is the equality relation, and $[St] = St$. Since the environment should know its own choices, we require that for every $q, q' \in St$ such that $q \sim q'$ we have that $d_{env}(q) = d_{env}(q')$. We also assume that if $q \sim q'$ then the set of atomic propositions holding in q and q' must coincide.

The ATL module checking problem is defined as in the perfect information case, with the following difference: $exec(M)$ consists only of trees that are consistent with the partial information available to the environment. Formally, two nodes v and v' in $\langle T_M, V_M \rangle$ are indistinguishable ($v \cong v'$) iff (1) the length of v, v' in $\langle T_M, V_M \rangle$ is the same, and (2) for each i, we have $v[i] \sim v'[i]$. Then, whenever $v \cong v'$ then each tree in $exec(M)$ must prune either both subtrees rooted at v, v', or none of them.

6.2 Automata and Complexity

As noted in [23], checking for consistency in pruned trees is the main source of difficulty in dealing with module checking with imperfect information. In consequence, the procedure we have used in Section 5 to solve ATL(*) module checking for perfect information is no longer valid. Instead, we will use an extension of the approach proposed in [23], which makes use of alternating tree automata. These are automata able to send several copies of themselves in the same direction of a tree [24]. We use this extra feature to send the same copy of the automaton to states that look the same to the environment. This will ensure the consistency of pruning. The idea leads to the following result.

THEOREM 10. *The module-checking problem is* 2EXPTIME-*complete for ATL* and* EXPTIME-*complete for ATL. For formulae of bounded size the problem is* EXPTIME-*complete in both cases.*

PROOF SKETCH. For the lower bounds, recall that module checking under imperfect information is 2EXPTIME-hard for CTL* and EXPTIME-hard for CTL. Also, for a fixed size formula, the problem is EXPTIME-hard in both cases [23].

For the upper bounds, we build alternating tree automata that adapt the constructions presented in the proofs of Theorems 6 and 8 regarding the transition relations involving environment states. More precisely, given a multi-agent module with imperfect information M having a set of states St and indistinguishability relation $\sim$, we use as directions the elements of [St] in a similar way to [23]. The constructed automaton requires, in case of ATL, a Büchi acceptance condition and its size is polynomial in both the formula and the system. In case of ATL*, a Rabin condition is required and the size of the automaton becomes exponential in size of the formula, while remaining polynomial in the size of the system. As checking the emptiness for Büchi and Rabin alternating tree automata is solvable in EXPTIME [24], the upper bounds follow, also in case of bounded-size formulae. □

7. REACTIVE VS. PROACTIVE SEMANTICS OF ATL MODULE CHECKING

The "r" in $\models^r_{\text{ATL}}$ stands for "reactive", and indeed $M \models^r_{\text{ATL}} \varphi$ is often read as "Module M reactively satisfies φ." It emphasizes that the system can react – and adapt – to the behavior of the environment in order to get formula φ satisfied. This poses no problem when φ is a CTL formula, i.e., φ requires a certain temporal pattern to be objectively possible (through the path quantifier E) or unavoidable (via A). However, things become trickier when φ refers to *strategic abilities* of agents. Recall that $M \models^r_{\text{ATL}} \langle\!\langle A \rangle\!\rangle\gamma$ expresses that the agents in A can adapt to every strategy of the environment so that they bring about γ. Among other things, it means that A can choose their strategy differently depending on the *future moves of the environment.* To make this observation more formal, we rephrase the semantics of ATL module checking from Section 3 in a similar way to the well known game semantics of first order logic [27, 19].

7.1 Module Checking as a Game

To make things simpler, we will only use ATL* formulae in negation normal form (NNF). That is, we add the disjunction and dual strategic modalities as primitives, and allow explicit negation only on the level of atomic propositions. It is easy to transform any formula of ATL to an equivalent formula in NNF by applying de Morgan laws and "flipping" modalities whenever necessary.

DEFINITION 5 (SEMANTIC GAME FOR $\models^r_{\text{ATL}}$). *We define the* semantic game $\Gamma(\varphi, M)$ *for formula φ in multi-agent module M as a turn-based extensive form game with two players $\mathbf{v}$ (the verifier) and $\mathbf{r}$ (the refuter). $\Gamma(\varphi, M)$ consists of the root, controlled by $\mathbf{r}$, with one move for each labeled tree $\langle T, V\rangle \in exec(M)$, leading to $\Gamma_0(\varphi, \langle T, V\rangle)$ constructed recursively as follows:.*

1. *If $\varphi \equiv p$ then $\Gamma_0(\varphi, \langle T, V\rangle)$ consists of a single node where $\mathbf{v}$ wins iff p holds in the initial state of $\langle T, V\rangle$;*
2. *If $\varphi \equiv \neg p$ then $\Gamma_0(\varphi, \langle T, V\rangle)$ consists of a single node where $\mathbf{v}$ wins iff p does not hold in the initial state of $\langle T, V\rangle$;*
3. *If $\varphi \equiv \varphi_1 \wedge \varphi_2$ then $\Gamma_0(\varphi, \langle T, V\rangle)$ consists of the root, controlled by $\mathbf{r}$, with two available moves: one leading to $\Gamma_0(\varphi_1, \langle T, V\rangle)$ and the other to $\Gamma_0(\varphi_2, \langle T, V\rangle)$;*
4. *$\varphi \equiv \varphi_1 \vee \varphi_2$: analogously to (3), but the root is controlled by $\mathbf{v}$;*
5. *If $\varphi \equiv \langle\!\langle A \rangle\!\rangle\gamma$ then $\Gamma_0(\varphi, \langle T, V\rangle)$ consists of the root, controlled by $\mathbf{v}$, with one move per strategy s_A of A. The move leads to a node of $\mathbf{r}$ with one move per path $\lambda \in out(\langle T, V\rangle, s_A)$, leading to $\Gamma_0(\gamma, \langle T, V\rangle, \lambda)$;*
6. *$\varphi \equiv [\![A]\!]\gamma$: analogously to (5), but the root is controlled by $\mathbf{r}$, and its successors by $\mathbf{v}$;*
7. *$\gamma \equiv \gamma \wedge \gamma$ and $\gamma \equiv \gamma \vee \gamma$: analogously to (3), (4);*
8. *If $\gamma \equiv \mathrm{X}\gamma_1$ then $\Gamma_0(\gamma, \langle T, V\rangle, \lambda) = \Gamma_0(\gamma_1, \langle T, V\rangle^{\lambda[1]}, \lambda[1..\infty])$, where $\langle T, V\rangle^x$ is the subtree of $\langle T, V\rangle$ starting from node x;*
9. *If $\gamma \equiv \gamma_1 \mathrm{U} \gamma_2$ then $\Gamma_0(\gamma, \langle T, V\rangle, \lambda)$ consists of the root, controlled by $\mathbf{v}$, with one move per $i = 0, 1, \ldots$. The move leads to a node of $\mathbf{r}$ with one move per $j = 0, \ldots, i-1$, leading to $\Gamma_0(\gamma_1, \langle T, V\rangle^{\lambda[j]}, \lambda[j..\infty])$, plus an additional move leading to $\Gamma_0(\gamma_2, \langle T, V\rangle^{\lambda[i]}, \lambda[i..\infty])$;*
10. *If $\gamma \equiv \gamma_1 \mathrm{W} \gamma_2$ then $\Gamma_0(\gamma, \langle T, V\rangle, \lambda)$ consists of the root, controlled by $\mathbf{v}$, with one move per $i = 0, 1, \ldots, \infty$. The move leads to a node of $\mathbf{r}$ with one move per $j = 0, \ldots, i-1$, leading to $\Gamma_0(\gamma_1, \langle T, V\rangle^{\lambda[j]}, \lambda[j..\infty])$, plus an additional move leading to $\Gamma_0(\gamma_2, \langle T, V\rangle^{\lambda[i]}, \lambda[i..\infty])$ in case $i < \infty$;*

The idea of the semantic game (sometimes also called *dialogical game*) is very simple. One player ($\mathbf{v}$) tries to prove that the formula holds, while the other ($\mathbf{r}$) tries to prevent. The verifier controls all the existentially quantified parts of the formula, and the refuter controls all the universal quantifiers. Moreover, when deciding on a subformula, the respective players can use their knowledge of the choices made for the outer operators. Now, the formula holds if the verify can prove it true no matter what the refuter does to prevent that.

DEFINITION 6 (GAME SEMANTICS FOR $\models^r_{\text{ATL}}$). *As usual for extensive form games, a strategy of player $\pi \in \{\mathbf{v}, \mathbf{r}\}$ in $\Gamma(M, \varphi)$ is a function that maps the nodes controlled by π to the available choices. To distinguish the strategies of agents in M from the strategies in $\Gamma(M, \varphi)$, we will call the latter* semantic strategies. *Note that semantic strategies are by definition deterministic. A verifier's strategy is* winning *if every full path in $\Gamma(M, \varphi)$ consistent with the strategy ends in a winning state.*

We say that $M \approx^r_{ATL} \varphi$ iff the verifier has a winning semantic strategy in $\Gamma(M, \varphi)$.

The semantics is correct in the following sense (the proof is straightforward, and we omit it due to lack of space):

PROPOSITION 11. *$M \approx^r_{ATL} \varphi$ iff $M \models^r_{ATL} \varphi$.*

7.2 Proactive Semantics of Module Checking

The game semantics of $\models^r_{\mathrm{ATL}}$ brings forward what we observed at the beginning of this section: that the strategy s_A of agents A in formula $\langle\langle A\rangle\rangle\gamma$ can be adapted to the *whole* strategy of the environment. That is because the success of s_A is evaluated not in the original model M, but in the tree corresponding to one of the environment's strategies. In many scenarios, this does not seem right. In particular, it corresponds to what some authors call *non-behavioral strategies* [31, 30]. Game semantics allows us to deal with the problem in a straightforward way, by defining a clustering of nodes in the semantic game that differ *only in the future behavior of the environment*, and changing the type of the verifier's strategies accordingly.

DEFINITION 7 (PROACTIVE SEMANTIC GAME). *Given M and φ, we construct the new semantic game $\Gamma^{pa}(M,\varphi)$ as an extensive game of imperfect information. $\Gamma^{pa}(M,\varphi)$ has the same players, nodes, and transitions as $\Gamma(M,\varphi)$. The only difference is that it adds an indistinguishability relation for the **v** player. Let $tree(\vartheta)$ denote the execution tree associated with the game node ϑ. Note that $tree(\vartheta)$ is always a subtree of some tree in $exec(M)$. Also, let $form(\vartheta)$ be the subformula of φ associated with ϑ, and $formpos(\vartheta)$ be its position within φ.*

*Now, two nodes ϑ_1, ϑ_2 controlled by **v** are indistinguishable iff: (i) $form(\vartheta_1) = form(\vartheta_2) = \langle\langle A\rangle\rangle\gamma$, (ii) $formpos(\vartheta_1) = formpos(\vartheta_2)$, and (iii) $root(tree(\vartheta_1)) = root(tree(\vartheta_2))$.*

Note that the root of *tree*(ϑ) is labeled by the sequence of states that have been visited between the initial state and the execution point behind ϑ. Thus, two **v**'s nodes in $\Gamma^{pa}(M,\varphi)$ are indistinguishable if the verifier is about to propose a strategy for some agents A, the nodes correspond to the same subformula of φ (meaning *exactly* the same subforumla, including its position within φ), and they consider the same history of execution in the module. The indistinguishability relation is an equivalence, and its abstraction classes are called *information sets*. In games with imperfect information, a strategy of player π is a function that maps π's information sets to π's choices.

DEFINITION 8 (PROACTIVE SEMANTICS). *We say that M* proactively satisfies *φ ($M \models^{pa}_{ATL} \varphi$) iff the verifier has a winning semantic strategy in $\Gamma^{pa}(M,\varphi)$.*

That is, we require the verifier to be able to win the semantic game without knowing the future choices of the environment in advance. The following is straightforward by the fact that we only constrain the choice of strategies for positive strategic modalities.

THEOREM 12. *If $M \models^{pa}_{ATL} \varphi$ then $M \models^r_{ATL} \varphi$*

More interestingly, the converse does not hold.

THEOREM 13. *$\models^{pa}_{ATL}$ is not equivalent to $\models^r_{ATL}$ even for turn-based single-agent modules.*

PROOF. Take module M_1 from Figure 4 and formula $\varphi \equiv \mathsf{EXAXp} \to \langle\langle a\rangle\rangle \mathrm{F}\mathsf{p}$. Now, $M_1 \models^r_{\mathrm{ATL}} \varphi$ but $M_1 \not\models^{pa}_{\mathrm{ATL}} \varphi$. □

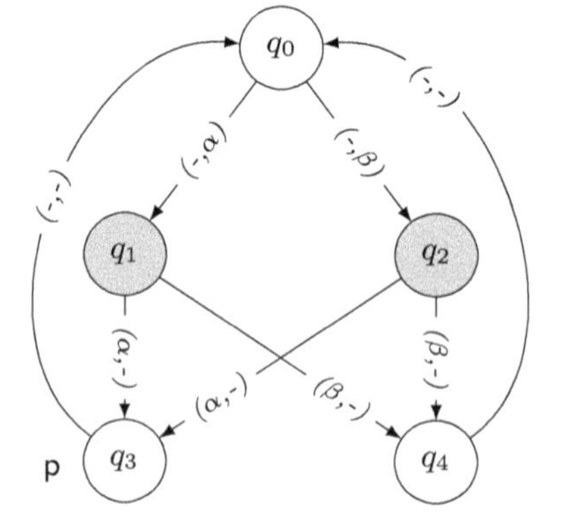

Figure 4: Single-agent module M_1

We observe that our proactive semantics of module checking comes close to the behavioral semantics of Strategy Logic in [31]. Note, however, that our definition is based on semantic strategies in a dialogical game, whereas the approach of [31] was based on Skolem dependence functions.

8. CONCLUSIONS

We have presented an extension of the module checking problem to specifications written in the strategic logic ATL*. As usual for computational problems, the key features are expressivity and complexity. We show that our proposal fares well in this respect. On one hand, the computational complexity of ATL/ATL* module checking is no worse than that of CTL/CTL* module checking, and its program complexity is the same as that of ATL/ATL* model checking. On the other hand, ATL/ATL* module checking has strictly more expressive power than both CTL/CTL* module checking and ATL/ATL* model checking. The results are encouraging, and can hopefully lead to a revival of research on practical verification procedures based on module checking.

In the rest of the paper, we consider two semantic variations of ATL module checking: one where we can model information internal to the module, and hence unaccessible to the environment, and another one where strategies of the agents in the module cannot be based on the *plans* of the environment. The former variation brings further encouraging complexity results. For the latter, we show that it brings a distinctly different interpretation of agents' ability when interacting with the outside world. We also conjecture that it should not increase the computational costs of module checking, but no concrete results have been obtained yet.

Interesting paths for future research include a formal characterization of the correspondence to model checking in the spirit of [20], and automata-based procedures as well as complexity and expressivity results for the proactive semantics of module checking. We are also going to look at the relation of module checking to model checking of temporal logics with propositional quantification [21, 26].

Acknowledgements. Aniello Murano acknowledges the support of the FP7 EU project 600958-SHERPA. Wojciech Jamroga acknowledges the support of the FP7 EU project ReVINK (PIEF-GA-2012-626398).

REFERENCES

[1] T. Ågotnes, V. Goranko, and W. Jamroga. Alternating-time temporal logics with irrevocable strategies. In D. Samet, editor, *Proceedings of TARK XI*, pages 15–24, 2007.

[2] R. Alur, T. A. Henzinger, and O. Kupferman. Alternating-time Temporal Logic. In *Proceedings of the 38th Annual Symposium on Foundations of Computer Science (FOCS)*, pages 100–109. IEEE Computer Society Press, 1997.

[3] R. Alur, T. A. Henzinger, and O. Kupferman. Alternating-time Temporal Logic. *Journal of the ACM*, 49:672–713, 2002.

[4] B. Aminof, A. Legay, A. Murano, O. Serre, and M. Y. Vardi. Pushdown module checking with imperfect information. *Inf. Comput.*, 223(1):1–17, 2013.

[5] B. Aminof, A. Murano, and M. Vardi. Pushdown module checking with imperfect information. In *Proceedings of CONCUR*, LNCS 4703, pages 461–476. Springer-Verlag, 2007.

[6] S. Basu, P. S. Roop, and R. Sinha. Local module checking for ctl specifications. *Electronic Notes in Theoretical Computer Science*, 176(2):125–141, 2007.

[7] L. Bozzelli. New results on pushdown module checking with imperfect information. In *Proceedings of GandALF*, volume 54 of *EPTCS*, pages 162–177, 2011.

[8] L. Bozzelli, A. Murano, and A. Peron. Pushdown module checking. *Formal Methods in System Design*, 36(1):65–95, 2010.

[9] N. Bulling, W. Jamroga, and M. Popovici. Agents with truly perfect recall: Expressivity and validities. In *Proceedings of ECAI*, pages 177–182, 2014.

[10] E. Clarke and E. Emerson. Design and synthesis of synchronization skeletons using branching time temporal logic. In *Proceedings of Logics of Programs Workshop*, volume 131 of *Lecture Notes in Computer Science*, pages 52–71, 1981.

[11] L. de Alfaro, P. Godefroid, and R. Jagadeesan. Three-valued abstractions of games: Uncertainty, but with precision. In *Proceedings of LICS*, pages 170–179. IEEE Computer Society, 2004.

[12] E. Emerson and J. Halpern. "sometimes" and "not never" revisited: On branching versus linear time temporal logic. *Journal of the ACM*, 33(1):151–178, 1986.

[13] E. Emerson and C. Jutla. Tree automata, mu-calculus and determinacy. In *Foundations of Computer Science, 1991. Proceedings., 32nd Annual Symposium on*, pages 368–377. IEEE, 1991.

[14] E. A. Emerson. Temporal and modal logic. In J. van Leeuwen, editor, *Handbook of Theoretical Computer Science*, volume B, pages 995–1072. Elsevier Science Publishers, 1990.

[15] A. Ferrante, A. Murano, and M. Parente. Enriched μ-calculi module checking. *Logical Methods in Computer Science*, 4(3:1):1–21, 2008.

[16] M. Gesell and K. Schneider. Modular verification of synchronous programs. In *Proceedings of ACSD*, pages 70–79. IEEE, 2013.

[17] P. Godefroid. Reasoning about abstract open systems with generalized module checking. In *Proceedings of EMSOFT*, volume 2855 of *LNCS*, pages 223–240. Springer, 2003.

[18] P. Godefroid and M. Huth. Model checking vs. generalized model checking: Semantic minimizations for temporal logics. In *Proceedings of LICS*, pages 158–167. IEEE Computer Society, 2005.

[19] J. Hintikka. Game-theoretical semantics: insights and prospects. *Notre Dame Journal of Formal Logic*, 23(2):219–241, 1982.

[20] W. Jamroga and A. Murano. On module checking and strategies. In *Proceedings of the 13th International Conference on Autonomous Agents and Multiagent Systems AAMAS 2014*, pages 701–708, 2014.

[21] O. Kupferman. Augmenting branching temporal logics with existential quantification over atomic propositions. *Journal of Logic and Computation*, 9(2):135–147, 1999.

[22] O. Kupferman and M. Vardi. Module checking. In *Procedings of CAV*, volume 1102 of *LNCS*, pages 75–86. Springer, 1996.

[23] O. Kupferman and M. Vardi. Module checking revisited. In *Proceedings of CAV*, volume 1254 of *LNCS*, pages 36–47. Springer, 1997.

[24] O. Kupferman, M. Vardi, and P. Wolper. An automata-theoretic approach to branching-time model checking. *Journal of the ACM*, 47(2):312–360, 2000.

[25] O. Kupferman, M. Vardi, and P. Wolper. Module checking. *Information and Computation*, 164(2):322–344, 2001.

[26] A. D. C. Lopes, F. Laroussinie, and N. Markey. Quantified CTL: expressiveness and model checking. In *Proceedings of CONCUR*, pages 177–192, 2012.

[27] K. Lorenz and P. Lorenzen. *Dialogische Logik*. Darmstadt, 1978.

[28] F. Martinelli. Module checking through partial model checking. Technical report, CNR Roma - TR-06, 2002.

[29] F. Martinelli and I. Matteucci. An approach for the specification, verification and synthesis of secure systems. *Electronic Notes in Theoretical Computer Science*, 168:29–43, 2007.

[30] F. Mogavero, A. Murano, G. Perelli, , and M. Vardi. What makes ATL* decidable? a decidable fragment of strategy logic. In *Proceedings of CONCUR*, pages 193–208, 2012.

[31] F. Mogavero, A. Murano, G. Perelli, and M. Vardi. Reasoning about strategies: On the model-checking problem. *ACM Transactions on Computational Logic*, 15(4):1–42, 2014.

[32] A. Murano, M. Napoli, and M. Parente. Program complexity in hierarchical module checking. In *Proceedings of LPAR*, volume 5330 of *Lecture Notes in Computer Science*, pages 318–332. Springer, 2008.

[33] J. Queille and J. Sifakis. Specification and verification of concurrent programs in Cesar. In *Symposium on Programming*, volume 137 of *LNCS*, pages 337–351. Springer, 1981.

[34] W. Thomas. Automata on infinite objects. *Handbook of Theoretical Computer Science*, 2, 1990.

[35] M. Vardi and P. Wolper. Automata-theoretic techniques for modal logics of programs. *Journal of Computer and System Sciences*, 32(2):183–221, 1986.

On the Formal Verification of Diffusion Phenomena in Open Dynamic Agent Networks

Francesco Belardinelli
Université d'Evry
France
belardinelli@ibisc.fr

Davide Grossi
University of Liverpool
United Kingdom
d.grossi@liverpool.ac.uk

ABSTRACT

The paper is a contribution at the interface of social network theory and multi-agent systems. As realistic models of multi-agent systems, we assume agent networks to be open, that is, agents may join or leave the network at run-time, and dynamic, that is, the network structure may change as a result of agents actions. We provide a formal model of open dynamic agent networks (ODAN) in terms of interpreted systems, and define the problem of model checking properties of diffusion phenomena, such as the spread of information or diseases, expressed in a first-order version of computation-tree logic. We establish the decidability of the model checking problem by showing that, under specific conditions, the verification of infinite-state ODAN can be reduced to model checking finite bisimulations.

Categories and Subject Descriptors

F.4.1 [**Mathematical Logic**]: Temporal Logic

General Terms

Theory,Verification

Keywords

Agent Networks; Diffusion Phenomena; First-order Temporal Logic

1. INTRODUCTION

Social network theory and analysis (SNA) is a thriving area of research (see [14, 11] for comprehensive introductions to the field) and its interaction with the field of multi-agent systems (MAS) has witnessed a steady growth over the last decade. On the one hand the MAS paradigm has established itself as a recognized tool within SNA, in particular for simulation purposes (e.g., [15]). On the other hand, concepts and methods from SNA are reaching the theory of MAS as a growing number of papers (e.g, [18, 19, 21], just to mention a few in the last edition of AAMAS) and events (e.g., the *Social Networks and Multi-Agent Systems Symposium* series) on the application of SNA to MAS testify.

Appears in: *Proceedings of the 14th International Conference on Autonomous Agents and Multiagent Systems (AAMAS 2015), Bordini, Elkind, Weiss, Yolum (eds.), May, 4–8, 2015, Istanbul, Turkey.*

The present paper contributes further to the application of SNA concepts to MAS, bringing them closer to standard MAS concerns such as openness, and deploying established methods in MAS research such as formal verification. We focus specifically on (non-probabilistic) diffusion phenomena, that is, how information, ideas, behaviors spread in networks of agents similarly to epidemics. We model a MAS as a network, that is, a set of agents – the nodes – which are linked via edges constraining their possible interactions. As typical in SNA, such links are abstractions of concrete relationships such as proximity, or the availability of communication channels, or trust relationships, and the like. However, although building on established concepts from SNA, the paper focuses on the type of networks that are of specific relevance for MAS, namely networks that are *open*, as agents can enter and leave the MAS at run-time; and *dynamic*, as the network links can change as the direct result of agents' actions.[1]

Aim of the paper and methodology. The paper investigates the applicability in principle of formal verification techniques to the analysis of diffusion phenomena in agent networks which may evolve over time as the result of agents' actions. More concretely, the paper establishes the decidability of the model-checking problem for properties of open and dynamic networks specified in a first-order temporal logic (FO-CTL). This result is obtained by modelling networks as a special type of infinite-state data-aware systems [7, 9]. This allows us to capitalize on recent results on the formal verification of artifact-centric systems [2, 3], and to extend them to MAS where agents can join or leave at run-time.

Related Work. From the technical point of view the paper builds on two strands of research: the *application of logic to SNA*, and the *verification of data-aware systems*. The application of logic-based methods to SNA is a very recent area of research. Researchers have focused in particular on the formalization of information dynamics phenomena, mainly using dynamic epistemic logic (DEL, [22]), over networks, e.g., [5, 6]. In particular, we are aware of only one study attempting the application of formal verification techniques to SNA, and in particular to the study of epidemics [20], which however does not focus on open and dynamic networks.

The verification of data-aware systems, i.e., systems where data play a crucial role in directing the system's execution, is in itself a subject of growing interest. In [10, 9] the verification of data-driven web services and business processes

[1] It may be worth noting that dynamic networks are themselves an open research area in SNA with no established models (cf. [14, Ch. 7])

is tackled by assuming syntactic restrictions on the specification language, and [13] investigated the verification of dynamic relational databases. With a different focus, networks have been used also in concurrency theory as an abstraction for modeling and verifying communicating processes (e.g., [16, 8]). More directly related to our contribution, [2, 3] put forward abstraction techniques for the verification of artifact-centric systems. While we make use of ideas and notions appearing therein, the motivation and setting for our paper are markedly different. First, the inspiration comes from SNA and the formal analysis of agents' behaviours in networked contexts. Second, the agent networks here introduced are open and dynamic, in particular agents can join or leave the network at run time. None of these features is considered in [2, 3].

Outline of the paper. The paper is structured as follows. In Section 2 we introduce a multi-agent, data-aware model for open dynamic agent networks (ODAN), and a first-order temporal specification language. Then, we state the model checking problem for this setting. Section 3 is devoted to show that the proposed framework is rich enough to express established network models such as the SIR (susceptible-infected-recovered) model for epidemics. The main technical results are presented in Section 4 and 5, where we prove that under specific conditions the model checking problem for ODAN is decidable. We conclude in Section 6. Proofs are omitted in the interest of space.

2. OPEN DYNAMIC AGENT NETWORKS

In this section we introduce open dynamic agent networks (ODAN) as multi-agent systems whose main feature is that agents can join or depart at run time. Then, we present a first-order version of the branching-time logic CTL, and state the model checking problem for this setting. We first present the basic terminology on databases that will be used throughout the paper; we refer to [1, 3] for further details.

DEFINITION 1 (DATABASE SCHEMA AND INSTANCE). *A* database schema *is a finite set* $\mathcal{D} = \{P_1/q_1, \ldots, P_n/q_n\}$ *of* predicate symbols P *with arity* $q \in \mathbb{N}$.

Given a (possibly infinite) interpretation domain X*, a* $\mathcal{D}$-instance *over* X *is a mapping* D *associating each predicate symbol* P *to a* finite *q-ary relation on* X*, i.e.,* $D(P) \subseteq X^q$.

Given a database schema $\mathcal{D}$, $\mathcal{D}(X)$ is the set of all $\mathcal{D}$-instances on domain X; while the *active domain* $adom(D)$ of a $\mathcal{D}$-instance D is the *finite* set of all individuals occurring in some predicate interpretation $D(P)$, i.e., $adom(D) = \bigcup_{P \in \mathcal{D}} \{u_1, \ldots, u_q \in X \mid \langle u_1, \ldots, u_q \rangle \in D(P)\}$. Further, the *primed version* of a database schema $\mathcal{D}$ as above is the schema $\mathcal{D}' = \{P'_1/q_1, \ldots, P'_n/q_n\}$. Then, the *disjoint union* $D \oplus D'$ of $\mathcal{D}$-instances D and D' is the $(\mathcal{D} \cup \mathcal{D}')$-instance such that *(i)* $D \oplus D'(P) = D(P)$, and *(ii)* $D \oplus D'(P') = D'(P)$. Intuitively, primed versions and disjoint unions will be used to describe the temporal evolution of a database schema from the previous state D to the next state D'.

2.1 Agents in ODAN

In this paper we focus on agents manipulating data organized in relational structures, according to some database schema. Specifically, hereafter we assume a finite number of *agent types* $T_0, \ldots, T_k$. Each agent type T is associated with *(i)* a *local database schema* $\mathcal{D}_T$, containing a reserved unary predicate symbol $N \in \mathcal{D}_T$ to represent the network structure, and *(ii)* a finite set Act_T of *parametric actions* $\alpha(\vec{x})$ with parameters $\vec{x}$. Hence, agents of the same type share the database schema and available actions. For every agent type T, let $Ag_T, Ag'_T, \ldots$ be possibly infinite sets of agent names. In the following we assume that the interpretation domain X for database schemas contains a set Ag_T of names for agents of type T, that is, $X = Ag \cup U$ for $Ag = \bigcup_{type\ T} Ag_T$ and some other set U of elements. Also, the interpretation $D(N)$ of predicate $N \in \mathcal{D}_T$ is a subset of Ag, i.e., intuitively $D(N)$ stores the agents related to a specific agent. To account for the temporal evolution of ODAN, we introduce protocols for agent types. First of all, we consider a notion of isomorphism between database instances.

DEFINITION 2 (INSTANCE ISOMORPHISM). *Two instances* $D \in \mathcal{D}(X)$ *and* $D' \in \mathcal{D}(X')$ *are* isomorphic*, or* $D \simeq D'$*, iff for some bijection* $\iota : adom(D) \mapsto adom(D')$*,*

(i) *ι preserves the type of agents, i.e., for every type T, ι is a bijection from $adom(D) \cap Ag_T$ into $adom(D') \cap Ag'_T$;*

(ii) *for every $P \in \mathcal{D}$, $\vec{u} \in X^q$, $\vec{u} \in D(P)$ iff $\iota(\vec{u}) \in D'(P)$.*

Then, we say that ι *is a* witness *for* $D \simeq D'$ *and write* $D \overset{\iota}{\simeq} D'$ *to state this explicitly.*

Once we have a notion of isomorphism between states, we can introduce the *local protocol* Pr_T for a type T as follows.

DEFINITION 3 (PROTOCOL). *Given an interpretation domain* X*,* Pr_T *is a function from* $\mathcal{D}_T(X)$ *to* $2^{Act_T(X)}$*, where* $Act_T(X)$ *is the set of* ground actions $\alpha(\vec{u})$*, for* $\alpha(\vec{x}) \in Act_T$ *and* $\vec{u} \in X^{|\vec{x}|}$.

Thus, the protocol Pr_T returns a ground action in $Act_T(X)$ for every $\mathcal{D}_T$-instance of type T. Hereafter we assume the following constraint on protocol functions: *for every instance* $D \in \mathcal{D}_T(X)$ *and* $D' \in \mathcal{D}_T(X')$*, if* $D \overset{\iota}{\simeq} D'$ *then* $\alpha(\vec{u}) \in Pr_T(D)$ *iff* $\alpha(\iota(\vec{u})) \in Pr_T(D')$. This constraint ensures that isomorphic states allow the same actions whenever "isomorphic" values are substituted to parameters. As an example, sending an email is allowed in all states where a valid receiver, subject and email body are provided, independently from the actual data content of these fields.

We finally introduce the notion of *agent*.

DEFINITION 4 (AGENT). *Given an agent name* $a \in Ag_T$ *of type* T*, an* agent *is a tuple* $a = \langle \mathcal{D}_T, Act_T, Pr_T \rangle$ *where* $\mathcal{D}_T$*,* Act_T*, and* Pr_T *are defined as above.*

Notice that above we assumed only a finite number of agent types. However, for each type we can have an infinite number of agents in priciple. This modelling choice is motivated by the use case scenario in Section 3. Also, in domains of interest typically it is possible to specify the relevant agent types at design time. However, it is much more difficult, viz. impossible, to know exactly how many agents of each type will appear during the system's execution. Accounting for incoming and outgoing agents is a major challenge we tackle in the proposed framework.

In what follows we often identify an agent with her name and write $a = \langle \mathcal{D}_a, Act_a, Pr_a \rangle$, omitting the type, whenever this is clear by the context. By Def. 4 at each moment agent a is in some local state $l \in \mathcal{D}_a(U \cup Ag)$ that represents the information she has about the system as well as fellow agents.

In this respect we follow the *interpreted systems* approach to MAS [17, 12, 23], but a fundamental difference is that here we require that the agent's information is structured as a relational database. Also, agent a is assumed to perform the actions in Act_a according to protocol function Pr_a. Finally, the database schema $\mathcal{D}_a$ contains the unary predicate symbol N to store the agents which a is related to.

Since we are interested in the interactions amongst agents and with the external environment, we define their synchronous composition, beginning with the notions of global state and network.

DEFINITION 5 (GLOBAL STATE). *Given a* finite *subset $A \subseteq Ag$ of agents $a_i = \langle \mathcal{D}_i, Act_i, Pr_i \rangle$ on domain $X = U \cup Ag$, for $i \leq n$, a* global state *is a tuple $s = \langle l_0, \ldots, l_n \rangle$ of instances $l_i \in \mathcal{D}_i(X)$ such that $\bigcup_{i \leq n} adom(l_i) \cap Ag \subseteq A$.*

By Def. 5 a global state accounts only for a finite set of agents, who are meant to be the *active* agents at a specific time in the system's execution. This assumption is consistent with the literature on MAS [17, 12, 23], where global states are tuples of fixed length. Also, by definition a global state s accounts at least for all agents appearing in its active domain $adom(s) = \bigcup_{i \leq n} adom(l_i)$. That is, if some agent a is mentioned in the local state of some other agent $b \in A$ (notably in the network relation N), and thus $a \in adom(s)$, then a also belongs to A. In what follows we implicitly identify global states containing the same local states for the same agents, only in a different order. This can be done w.l.o.g. by assuming a fixed enumeration of agents. Further, let ag be a function that for each global state $s = \langle l_0, \ldots, l_n \rangle$ returns the set $ag(s) = \{a_0, \ldots, a_n\}$ of agents such that $l_i \in \mathcal{D}_{a_i}(X)$ for $i \leq n$. By the constraint above on global states we have that for every state s, $adom(s) \cap Ag \subseteq ag(s)$. We write $\mathcal{S}$ to denote the set $\bigcup_{n \in \mathbb{N}}(\prod_{i \leq n} \mathcal{D}_{a_i}(X))$ of all global states. Notice that $\mathcal{S}$ is infinite whenever Ag is.

We already remarked that the unary predicate symbol N is used to encode the network structure of the global state. More precisely, given a state s we define the network induced by N as follows.

DEFINITION 6 (AGENT NETWORK). *The* agent network *induced by state s is the directed graph $\mathcal{N}_s = \langle ag(s), E \rangle$ where (i) $ag(s) \subseteq Ag$ is the set of vertices, and (ii) E is the binary relation on $ag(s)$ such that $E(a, b)$ iff $b \in l_a(N)$.*

The agent networks in Def. 6 are digraphs in general. However, by assuming suitable conditions on global states, namely that $b \in l_a(N)$ iff $a \in l_b(N)$, we can also model undirected graphs. The latter might be more appropriate when modelling particular agent networks, as in Section 3.

Finally, we introduce open dynamic agent networks.

DEFINITION 7 (ODAN). *Given a (possibly infinite) interpretation domain $X = Ag \cup U$ containing a (possibly infinite) set $Ag = \{a_0, a_1, \ldots\}$ of agents $a_i = \langle \mathcal{D}_i, Act_i, Pr_i \rangle$, an* open dynamic agent network *is a tuple $\mathcal{P} = \langle Ag, U, I, \tau \rangle$ where*

- *I is the set of* initial states *s_0 for some finite $ag(s_0) \subseteq Ag$;*
- *$\tau : \mathcal{S} \times Act(X) \mapsto 2^{\mathcal{S}}$ is the* global transition function, *where Act is the set of joint (parametric) actions, and $\tau(\langle l_0, \ldots, l_n \rangle, \langle \alpha_0(\vec{u}_0), \ldots, \alpha_n(\vec{u}_n) \rangle)$ is defined iff $\alpha_i(\vec{u}_i) \in Pr_i(l_i)$ for every $i \leq n$.*

An ODAN evolves from an initial state $s_0 \in I$ as specified by the global transition function τ, which returns a set $\tau(s, \alpha(\vec{u})) \in 2^{\mathcal{S}}$ of successor states for each current state s and joint ground action $\alpha(\vec{u})$ by all agents in s. Since the interpretation domain X is infinite in general, ODAN are infinite-state systems normally. In this respect, ODAN can be thought of as a natural extension of interpreted systems to a first-order setting. Moreover, ODAN are *open* and *dynamic* as global states may be tuples of different length, comprising a variable number of agents. The transition function is defined only for joint actions providing an individual action for each agent in the current global state, but the resulting state may include fewer or more agents. This is in marked contrast with most of the current literature on MAS [17, 12, 23], which assumes that the set of agents is finite and fully specified at design time.

Hereafter we introduce a further constraint on joint actions in ODAN. To present it we need to extend the notion of isomorphism to global states.

DEFINITION 8 (STATE ISOMORPHISM). *The global states $s \in \mathcal{S}$ and $s' \in \mathcal{S}'$ are* isomorphic, *or $s \simeq s'$, iff for some bijection $\iota : adom(s) \cup ag(s) \mapsto adom(s') \cup ag(s')$, (i) ι preserves the type of agents; and (ii) for every $a_j \in ag(s)$, $l_j \stackrel{\iota}{\simeq} l'_j$.*

Any function ι as above is a *witness* for $s \simeq s'$, also indicated as $s \stackrel{\iota}{\simeq} s'$. Obviously, $\simeq$ is an equivalence relation. Further, given an injective function $f : X \mapsto X'$ such that its restriction $f_{|Ag}$ is a type-preserving injection from Ag to Ag', $f(s)$ denotes the instance in $\mathcal{D}(X')$ obtained from s by renaming each $u \in adom(s) \cup ag(s)$ as $f(u)$. In particular, $f(s) \simeq s$. As a consequence of Def. 8, isomorphic states are tuples of the same length. Hereafter we consider the following constraint on the transition functions in ODAN: *for every state $s \in \mathcal{S}$ and $s' \in \mathcal{S}'$, if $s \stackrel{\iota}{\simeq} s'$ then $t \in \tau(s, \alpha(\vec{u}))$ iff $\iota(t) \in \tau(s', \alpha(\iota(\vec{u})))$.* Similarly to the condition on protocols, this constraint requires that actions performed with "isomorphic" values in isomorphic states, also return isomorphic states. In other words, "isomorphic" actions are invariant w.r.t. the relational structure of states. For instance, sending emails returns isomorphic states modulo the emails' actual data content.

It is important to stress that state isomorphism is an extremely natural condition. It amounts to the preservation of the interpretation of predicates in each local state up to renaming of corresponding agents and elements of the domain. In other words, it ensures that the behavior of the system does not depend on how agents or elements are named.

We now introduce some notation that will be used in the paper. We denote a joint (ground) action in $\prod_{i \leq n} Act_i(X)$, for $n \in \mathbb{N}$, as $\alpha(\vec{u})$, for $\alpha = \langle \alpha_0(\vec{x}_0), \ldots, \alpha_n(\vec{x}_n) \rangle$ and $\vec{u} = \langle \vec{u}_0, \ldots, \vec{u}_n \rangle$, and define the *transition relation* $s \rightarrow s'$ on global states iff $s \xrightarrow{\alpha(\vec{u})} s'$ for some joint action $\alpha(\vec{u})$, i.e., $s' \in \tau(s, \alpha(\vec{u}))$. When no risk of confusion arises, we will use the same symbols to denote parameters and ground values for actions. An *s-run* r is an infinite sequence $s^0 \rightarrow s^1 \rightarrow \cdots$, with $s^0 = s$. For $n \in \mathbb{N}$, we set $r(n) = s^n$. A state s' is *reachable* from s iff $s' = r(i)$ for some s-run r and $i \geq 0$. In what follows we assume that the transition relation $\rightarrow$ is serial. This can be ensured w.l.o.g. by assuming that each agent has a skip action enabled at each local state. Further, we define $\mathcal{R}$ as the set of states reachable from any initial state $s_0 \in I$, i.e., $\mathcal{R} = \{s \in \mathcal{S} \mid s \text{ is reachable from } s_0, \text{ for some } s_0 \in I\}$. Since the domain X may be infinite, the set $\mathcal{R}$ of reachable states is also infinite in principle. Indeed, in the general case our ODAN are infinite-state systems. Finally, for technical reasons we will refer to the *global* database schema $\mathcal{D}_s = \mathcal{D}_0 \cup \cdots \cup \mathcal{D}_n$ of a state $s = \langle l_0, \ldots, l_n \rangle$. Hence, every state s is associated with the $\mathcal{D}_s$-instance $D_s \in \mathcal{D}_s(X)$ such that $D_s(P) = \bigcup_{i \leq n} l_i(P)$, for $P \in \mathcal{D}_s$, that is, we assume that each agent has a truthful, yet limited, view of the global database $\mathcal{D}_s$. In particular, $adom(D_s)$ is equal to $adom(s)$. Notice that for every $s \in \mathcal{S}$, there is a unique instance D_s, while the converse is not true in general. Also, the disjoint union $s \oplus s'$ is defined as $\langle l_0 \oplus l'_0, \ldots, l_n \oplus l'_n \rangle$.

2.2 The Specification Language FO-CTL

We now introduce a formal language to specify properties of interest of open dynamic agent networks. The presence of data in ODAN calls for the use of first-order logic, whereas temporal operators are needed to account for the system's evolution. Hereafter we consider a set *Var* of *individual variables* and the database schema $\mathcal{D} = \bigcup_{type\ T} \mathcal{D}_T$.

Definition 9 (FO-CTL). *The FO-CTL formulas over the database schema $\mathcal{D}$ are defined in BNF as follows:*

$$\varphi \ ::= \ P(\vec{x}) \mid x = y \mid \neg\varphi \mid \varphi \rightarrow \varphi \mid \forall x \varphi \mid AX\varphi \mid A\varphi U \varphi \mid E\varphi U \varphi$$

where $x, y \in Var$, $P \in \mathcal{D}$, and $\vec{x}$ is a q-tuple of variables.

The language FO-CTL is a first-order extension of the propositional temporal logic CTL. The temporal formulas $AX\varphi$ and $A\varphi U\varphi'$ (resp. $E\varphi U\varphi'$) are read as "for all runs, next φ" and "for every (resp. some) run, φ until φ'". Free and bound variables are defined as standard, as well as formulas $EX\varphi$, $AF\varphi$, $AG\varphi$, $EF\varphi$, and $EG\varphi$. We write $\phi(\vec{x})$ to denote that the free variables of ϕ are among $\vec{x} = x_1, \ldots, x_n$. Notice that we use the same symbols to refer to individual variables and action parameters, the context will disambiguate. The present language can be enriched with constants for individuals. Since such an enhanced framework does not require significant new formal results, while making the notation more cumbersome, we consider only variables as individual terms. In the following we consider also first-order non-modal logic, as defined by the following syntax:

$$\varphi \ ::= \ P(\vec{x}) \mid x = y \mid \neg\varphi \mid \varphi \rightarrow \varphi \mid \forall x \varphi$$

To define the satisfaction of an FO-CTL formula on an ODAN, we introduce the notion of an *assignment* $\sigma : Var \mapsto X$. We denote by σ^x_u the assignment such that *(i)* $\sigma^x_u(x) = u$; and *(ii)* $\sigma^x_u(x') = \sigma(x')$ for every x' different from x.

Definition 10 (Semantics of FO-CTL). *We define whether an ODAN $\mathcal{P}$ satisfies a formula φ in a state s according to assignment σ, or $(\mathcal{P}, s, \sigma) \models \varphi$, as follows:*

$(\mathcal{P}, s, \sigma) \models P(\vec{x})$ iff $\langle \sigma(x_1), \ldots, \sigma(x_q) \rangle \in D_s(P)$
$(\mathcal{P}, s, \sigma) \models x = y$ iff $\sigma(x) = \sigma(y)$
$(\mathcal{P}, s, \sigma) \models N(x, y)$ iff $\sigma(y) \in l_{\sigma(x)}(N)$
$(\mathcal{P}, s, \sigma) \models \neg\varphi$ iff $(\mathcal{P}, s, \sigma) \not\models \varphi$
$(\mathcal{P}, s, \sigma) \models \varphi \rightarrow \varphi'$ iff $(\mathcal{P}, s, \sigma) \not\models \varphi$ or $(\mathcal{P}, s, \sigma) \models \varphi'$
$(\mathcal{P}, s, \sigma) \models \forall x \varphi$ iff for all $u \in adom(s)$, $(\mathcal{P}, s, \sigma^x_u) \models \varphi$
$(\mathcal{P}, s, \sigma) \models AX\varphi$ iff for all r, if $r(0) = s$ then $(\mathcal{P}, r(1), \sigma) \models \varphi$
$(\mathcal{P}, s, \sigma) \models A\varphi\mathcal{U}\varphi'$ iff for all r, if $r(0) = s$ then for some $k \geq 0$, $(\mathcal{P}, r(k), \sigma) \models \varphi'$, and for all j, $0 \leq j < k$ implies $(\mathcal{P}, r(j), \sigma) \models \varphi$
$(\mathcal{P}, s, \sigma) \models E\varphi\mathcal{U}\varphi'$ iff for some r, $r(0) = s$ and for some $k \geq 0$, $(\mathcal{P}, r(k), \sigma) \models \varphi'$, and for all j, $0 \leq j < k$ implies $(\mathcal{P}, r(j), \sigma) \models \varphi$

A formula φ is *true* at s, or $(\mathcal{P}, s) \models \varphi$, if $(\mathcal{P}, s, \sigma) \models \varphi$ for all assignments σ; φ is *true* in $\mathcal{P}$, or $\mathcal{P} \models \varphi$, if $(\mathcal{P}, s_0) \models \varphi$ for all $s_0 \in I$. Notice that in Def. 10 we adopt an *active domain* semantics, where quantifiers range over the active domain $adom(s)$ of a state s. This is a standard assumption in database theory that has been lifted to data-aware systems [3, 13]. Also, observe the particular clause for formulas of the form $N(x, y)$, according to the intution that $N(x, y)$ describes an edge from $\sigma(x)$ to $\sigma(y)$.

Finally, we state the model checking problem for ODAN with respect to the specification language FO-CTL.

Definition 11 (Model Checking Problem). *Given an ODAN $\mathcal{P}$ and an FO-CTL formula φ, determine whether for every initial state $s_0 \in I$, $(\mathcal{P}, s_0, \sigma_0) \models \varphi$ for some assignment σ_0.*

In the statement of the model checking problem we suppose that the transition function τ is given as some sort of computable function. Also, we assume finitary descriptions for the set I of initial states and the domain of interpretation. As it will be apparent in Section 3, these requirements are normally fulfilled in cases of interest. Also, for most of relevant applications the specification φ is an FO-CTL sentence, with no free variables. Hence, the model checking problem reduces to determine whether $\mathcal{P} \models \varphi$, as the satisfaction of FO-CTL sentences does not depend on bound variables.

Model checking general data-aware systems is known to be undecidable [10]. In [2, 3] the same problem is proved to be decidable for *bounded* and *uniform* systems. However, the set of agents is assumed to be fixed at design time. In the next section we illustrate and motivate the formal machinery introduced so far by means of a diffusion phenomenon.

3. THE SIR MODEL

In this section we show how an influential network diffusion model can be handled in our framework. The model at issue is the SIR (susceptible-infected-recovered) model for epidemics, i.e., the diffusion of a diseases in a population (see [11, Ch. 21] or [14, Ch. 7] for textbook introductions). In the SIR model a population of individuals is liable to go through three different stages during an epidemic. First, each agent is *susceptible* to be infected; she may actually get *infected* at a certain point; and finally she will eventually *recover*.[2] The SIR model typically assumes a finite population and a static network structure. In the following we show how the SIR model can be captured and generalized to an open and dynamic system within the framework of ODAN and how interesting properties of SIR can be expressed in FO-CTL. In Section 5 we will briefly discuss how the techniques developed in this paper can be deployed to verify the SIR model against FO-CTL specifications. We start with the standard case in which the topology of the network is assumed to be fixed and it does not change over time.

3.1 Static SIR Model

In the static SIR model the network topology is assumed to be fixed. This case is handy to introduce basic notation and terminology. More formally, we consider a unique

[2]Many variants of such model are of course possible, and many are indeed studied. For instance, the SIS model assumes a cycle from susceptibility to infection and back, without any recovered state.

type of agents with names in Ag. Also, the interpretation domain X is equal to Ag, i.e., for the time being we are only interested in facts concerning our agents. An *agent* in the static SIR model is a tuple $a = \langle \mathcal{D}_a, Act_a, Pr_a \rangle$ such that

- $\mathcal{D}_a = \{Sus/1, Inf/1, Rec/1, N/1\}$, where the intuitive meaning of *Sus* (resp. *Inf*, *Rec*) is that an agent is susceptible (resp. infected, recovered), while N is the network predicate expressing the proximity/contact relation between agents;
- $Act_a = \{\mathsf{skip}\}$, i.e., agents can only perform a skip;
- the protocol Pr_a is such that $Pr_a(l) = Act_a(X)$ for all $l \in \mathcal{D}_a(X)$, i.e., the skip action is enabled in any state.

Given the set Ag of agents as defined above, the *static SIR ODAN* is defined as the tuple $\mathcal{P} = \langle Ag, I, \tau \rangle$ such that

- I is the set of states where no agent is in the recovered state, and it is assumed that at least one agent is infected to rule out trivial models. Also, $Sus(b)$ (resp. $Inf(b)$, $Rec(b)$) belongs to l_a only if $b = a$, or $b \in l_a(N)$ and $Sus(b)$ (resp. $Inf(b)$, $Rec(b)$) belongs to l_b. Basically, we assume that each agent is exactly in one of the three possible states, and she knows only her local state and at most those of the agents she is directly related to.
- $s' \in \tau(s, \mathsf{skip})$ iff
  1. $Sus(a) \in l_a$, for some $b \in l_a(N)$, $Inf(b) \in l_b$, and either $Sus(a) \in l'_a$ or $Inf(a) \in l'_a$; or
  2. $Inf(a) \in l_a$ and either $Inf(a) \in l'_a$ or $Rec(a) \in l'_a$; or
  3. $Rec(a) \in l_a$ and $Rec(a) \in l'_a$;
  4. the consistency between an agent's information about the agents she is related to and said agents' local states is preserved.

Intuitively, by definition of the static SIR ODAN $\mathcal{P}$, in each moment a necessary but not sufficient condition for getting infected is that at least one related agent is such. Also, each infected agent non-deterministically recovers and remains so everafter. We observe that $\mathcal{P}$ is an infinite-state system as the set Ag of agents is infinite, thus allowing infinitely many initial states in I, according to the network topology. Nonetheless, notice that each $s_0 \in I$ defines a finite agent network. This observation is key for the developments in Section 5.

Further, we remark that the definitions of protocol Pr_a and transition function τ satisfy the constraints on both outlined in Section 2. Specifically, it is trivially true that in isomorphic local states the protocol Pr_a prescribes isomorphic actions (as it always prescribes skip); while τ returns isomorphic states provided isomorphic states and actions.

The formalisation of the SIR model here provided is extremely simple. More elaborate rules for infection spreading could be considered, especially if probabilities of infection are taken into account, which we abstract from here. Nonetheless, even this basic setting raises verificational issues. Indeed, the static SIR ODAN is an infinite-state system in general, and thus not amenable by standard model checking techniques for finite-state systems.

3.2 Dynamic SIR Model

To account for the agents' actions, in the dynamic SIR model agents are allowed to change the structure of the network given their current information on the other agents. Specifically, we suppose that agents disconnect from other agents in the network whenever the latter get infected. This can be seen for instance as a standard quarantine procedure during epidemics. Also in the present case we consider a unique type of agent. Then, an *agent* in the dynamic SIR model is introduced as a tuple $a = \langle \mathcal{D}_a, Act_a, Pr_a \rangle$ such that $\mathcal{D}_a$ is defined as in the static model and

- $Act_a = \{\mathsf{skip}, con(ag), disc(ag)\}$, where the intuitive meaning of $con(ag)$ (resp. $disc(ag)$) is that agent a connects with (resp. disconnects from) agent ag;
- the protocol Pr_a is such that $disc(b) \in Pr_a(l_a)$ whenever $b \in l_a(N)$ and $Inf(b) \in l_a$. Moreover, $\{\mathsf{skip}, con(b)\} \subseteq Pr_a(l)$ for all $l_a \in \mathcal{D}_a(X)$.

Notice that an agent can disconnect from another agent whenever she knows that the latter is infected. However, she can always connect to any other agent.

Given a set Ag of agents as defined above, the *dynamic SIR ODAN* is a tuple $\mathcal{P} = \langle Ag, I, \tau \rangle$ where I is defined as in the static SIR ODAN, and

- $s' \in \tau(s, \alpha)$ iff
  1. conditions (1)-(4) in the definition of τ for the static SIR ODAN hold;
  2. $\alpha_a = con(b)$, $l'_a(N) = l_a(N) \cup \{b\}$, and $l'_a = l_a \cup \{P(b) \mid P \in \mathcal{D}_b, P(b) \in l'_b\}$;
  3. $\alpha_a = dis(b)$, $l'_a(N) = l_a(N) \setminus \{b\}$, and $l'_a = l_a \setminus \{P(b) \mid P \in \mathcal{D}_b, P(b) \in l_b\}$.

We remark that when agent a connects to agent b, the health status of the latter become part of the local state of the former, as assumed to be the case already in the definition of the static model. Moreover, b may be a new agent, not appearing in $adom(s)$ nor $ag(s)$. If this is the case, the health status of b is initialised to *susceptible* for definiteness. Since agents can "be born" and "die" at run time, the lengths of tuples s and s' in the definition of τ will be different in general. This formal feature, which reflects the open and dynamic nature of ODAN, is in marked contrast with the standard literature on interpreted systems [17, 12, 23].

In the formalisation provided each agent disconnects or connects to a single agent at a time. We can generalize the model by allowing multiple connections/disconnections. Moreover, we may suppose that an agent not only sees the health status of directly reachable partners, but possibly of agents within a distance of k steps, for some $k \in \mathbb{N}$. These extra features, that can have an impact on the properties of the agent network, can be seamlessly modelled on ODAN.

3.3 Dynamic SIR Model with Health Workers

The third version of the SIR model is intended to account for the contribution of different *types* of agents to the diffusion process. For the case in hand, besides the standard agents of the static and dynamic SIR models, we introduce a new type of agent to mimick health workers. Containement policies are key to prevent the spreading of diseases. However, it is extremely challenging to assess the impact of such policies in real-life scenarios. In this endeavour formal verification techniques are surely of help (cf. [20]).

A *health agent* is defined as a tuple $h = \langle \mathcal{D}_h, Act_h, Pr_h \rangle$ where $\mathcal{D}_h$ and Act_h are the same as for standard agents; while the protocol Pr_h is such that

- $disc(b) \notin Pr_h(l_h)$ whenever $Inf(b) \in l_h$, but $disc(b) \in Pr_h(l_h)$ whenever $Inf(h) \in l_h$ and $b \in l_h(N)$.

Thus, differently from standard agents, health agents are not allowed to disconnect from infected agents. Nonetheless, they disconnect once they also become infected. As a result, health workers behave differently from standard agents as long as they are not infected. This modelling choice reflects the idea that health agent are also susceptible to infection.

Given sets Ag of agents and Ag_h of health agents, the *dynamic SIR ODAN with recovery threshold* $k \in \mathbb{N}$ is defined as a tuple $\mathcal{P} = \langle Ag \cup Ag_h, I, \tau \rangle$ such that the set I of initial states and the transition function τ are defined as for the dynamic model, but for the following clause:

- $s' \in \tau(s, \alpha)$ iff $Inf(a) \in l_a$, $Rec(a) \in l'_a$, and $|l_a(N) \cap Ag_h| > k$.

The ODAN $\mathcal{P}$ formalises, even though naively, the contribution provided by health workers to patient recovery. That is, we suppose that when an infected agent is in contact with more than k health workers, for some threshold $k \in \mathbb{N}$, then she is guaranteed to recover. Notice that, by definition of the procol Pr_h, these health workers are not infected and indeed capable of doing their job. By tweaking the threshold k we can simulate stricter or milder policies. Also, ODAN are expressive enough to accommodate communication amongst health agents in order to treat infected patients.

To summarize, the framework of ODAN is rich enough to model various assumptions on the network agents, including available actions, behaviour, and internal state. For systems such as the above SIR ODAN we will show in Section 5 that it is possible to develop verification techniques, even if we are dealing with infinite-state systems.

3.4 Specifications

We now consider specifications in FO-CTL that express interesting properties of the SIR models illustrated above. Firstly, a property that it is natural to consider is whether each agent goes through the susceptible-infected-recovered cycle. This can be easily expressed as an FO-CTL formula:

$$AG\ \forall x A(Sus(x) U A(Inf(x) U Rec(x))) \quad (1)$$

The same property can be recast by using the *weak until* operator defined as $A\phi W \phi' \equiv \neg E(\neg \phi' U(\neg \phi \wedge \neg \phi'))$:

$$AG\ \forall x A(Sus(x) W A(Inf(x) W Rec(x))) \quad (2)$$

We anticipate that, while (1) does not hold for some executions of the SIR model, its *weak until* version (2) is indeed satisfied.

Secondly, we might want to verify topological properties of the agent network, such as whether every agent either remains susceptible or will eventually become infected if she is continuously in contact with someone infected. This can be expressed in FO-CTL as follows:

$$AG\ \forall x(AG Sus(x) \vee E(\exists y(Inf(y) \wedge N(x,y)) U Inf(x))) \quad (3)$$

Another property of interest is whether each agent eventually disconnects from an infected neighbour:

$$AG\ \forall x, y(Inf(y) \wedge N(x,y) \rightarrow AF \neg N(x,y)) \quad (4)$$

Finally, we might want to assess the impact of health agents in the third version of the SIR model, for instance by evaluating whether an infected agent will always eventually recover if she is in contact with at least k health agents:

$$AG\ \forall x(\exists^{>k} y(Inf(x) \wedge Ag_h(y) \wedge N(x,y)) \rightarrow AF Rec(x)) \quad (5)$$

In (5) the bounded quantifier $\exists^{>k}$ can be defined by using equality $=$, while Ag_h is introduced as a new predicate in the language, true only of health agents.

Our aim in the present paper is to develop techniques to model check FO-CTL specifications as these on open dynamic agent networks. We remarked above that the SIR ODAN here provided are infinite-state systems in general, so their verification cannot be straightforwardly tackled by using techniques developed for finite-state systems. In the next section we prove novel results that make ODAN verification feasible.

4. BISIMULATION

In Section 2 we stated that model checking ODAN against FO-CTL specifications is undecidable in general. Clearly, for the verification of open dynamic agent networks it is crucial to isolate syntactic and semantical fragments with a decidable model checking problem. Hereafter we identify a rather natural subclass of ODAN that we call *bounded*. Bounded ODAN admit finite bisimilar abstractions, so that the verification of FO-CTL properties can be conducted on the latter, rather than on the original infinite-state system. We will discuss this in some detail in Section 5. To introduce finite abstractions we first present bisimulations and show that bisimilar ODAN satisfy the same FO-CTL formulas. The results presented in this section build on [2, 3]. However, the setting here is fundamentally different, as we consider networks where agents can join and leave at run time.

In the rest of the section we let $\mathcal{P} = \langle Ag, U, I, \tau \rangle$ and $\mathcal{P}' = \langle Ag', U', I', \tau' \rangle$ be two ODAN and assume that $s = \langle l_0, \ldots, l_n \rangle \in \mathcal{R}$ and $s' = \langle l'_0, \ldots, l'_n \rangle \in \mathcal{R}'$. First of all, according to Def. 8 isomorphic states have the same relational structure. However, they do not necessarily satisfy the same first-order formulas, as satisfaction depends also on the values assigned to free variables. To account for this, we introduce the following notion.

DEFINITION 12 (EQUIVALENT ASSIGNMENTS). *Given states $s \in \mathcal{R}$ and $s' \in \mathcal{R}'$, and a set $V \subseteq Var$ of variables, assignments $\sigma : Var \mapsto X$ and $\sigma' : Var \mapsto X'$ are* equivalent for V w.r.t. s and s' *iff for some bijection $\gamma : adom(s) \cup ag(s) \cup \sigma(V) \mapsto adom(s') \cup ag(s') \cup \sigma'(V)$,* (i) *the restriction $\gamma|_{adom(s) \cup ag(s)}$ is a witness for $s \simeq s'$; and* (ii) $\sigma'|_V = \gamma \circ \sigma|_V$.

Intuitively, equivalent assignments preserve agent types, the (in)equalities of the variables in V, as well as the active elements in s, s' up to renaming. Moreover, two assignments are *equivalent for an FO-CTL formula* φ (omitting states s and s' whenever clear by the context) if these are equivalent for its free variables $fr(\varphi)$.

We now state the following standard result on the preservation of first-order (non-modal) formulas.

LEMMA 1. *Given isomorphic states $s \in \mathcal{R}$ and $s' \in \mathcal{R}'$, an FO formula φ, and assignments σ and σ' equivalent for φ, we have that $(D_s, \sigma) \models \varphi$ iff $(D_{s'}, \sigma') \models \varphi$.*

As a result, isomorphic states cannot be distinguished by FO formulas (whenever equivalent assignments are considered). We make use of this observation to define bisimulations on ODAN. In particular, plain bisimulations are known to be satisfaction preserving in a modal propositional setting [4]. Hereafter we explore under which conditions this applies to ODAN as well.

DEFINITION 13 (SIMULATION). *A relation R on $\mathcal{R} \times \mathcal{R}'$ is a* simulation *if $\langle s, s' \rangle \in R$ implies* (i) *$s \simeq s'$; and* (ii) *for every $t \in \mathcal{R}$, if $s \rightarrow t$ then for some $t' \in \mathcal{R}'$, $s' \rightarrow t'$, $s \oplus t \simeq s' \oplus t'$, and $\langle t, t' \rangle \in R$;*

A state $s' \in \mathcal{R}'$ *simulates* $s \in \mathcal{R}$ iff $\langle s, s' \rangle \in R$ for some simulation R. Notice that similar states are isomorphic by condition 13.*(i)* above. Simulations can naturally be extended to bisimulations as follows.

Definition 14 (Bisimulation). *A relation B on $\mathcal{R} \times \mathcal{R}'$ is a* bisimulation *iff both B and $B^{-1} = \{\langle s', s\rangle \mid \langle s, s'\rangle \in B\}$ are simulations.*

Two states $s \in \mathcal{R}$ and $s' \in \mathcal{R}'$ are *bisimilar*, or $s \approx s'$, iff $\langle s, s'\rangle \in B$ for some bisimulation B. It can be shown that $\approx$ is the largest bisimulation, and an equivalence relation, on $\mathcal{R} \cup \mathcal{R}'$. Finally, $\mathcal{P}$ and $\mathcal{P}'$ are *bisimilar*, or $\mathcal{P} \approx \mathcal{P}'$, iff for every $s_0 \in I$, $s_0 \approx s_0'$ for some $s_0' \in I'$, and for every $s_0' \in I'$, $s_0 \approx s_0'$ for some $s_0 \in I$.

We remark that for general data-aware systems, bisimilarity is not sufficient to preserve FO-CTL formulas (please refer to [3] for a proof). This is in marked constrast with the modal propositional case. However, we show that ODAN, being *uniform*, admit bisimulations that preserve FO-CTL.

Lemma 2 (Uniformity). *Every ODAN $\mathcal{P}$ is* uniform, *that is, for every $s, t, s' \in \mathcal{R}$, $t' \in \mathcal{S}$, if $s \to t$ and $s \oplus t \simeq s' \oplus t'$, then $s' \to t'$.*

Intuitively, uniformity expresses that if t can be reached by executing the ground action $\alpha(\vec{u})$ in s, and we uniformly replace the element v with v' in s, $\vec{u}$ and t, obtaining s', $\vec{u}'$ and t' respectively, then t' can be reached by executing $\alpha(\vec{u}')$ in s'. This feature is a consequence of the invariance of the protocol and transition functions w.r.t. the actual data content of states and actions, as formalised in the requirements on ODAN in Section 2.

Now we state some lemmas, which are needed to prove the main preservation result Theorem 6. A further distinctive feature of ODAN is that isomorphic states are bisimilar.

Lemma 3. *For every ODAN $\mathcal{P}$, for every $s, s' \in \mathcal{R}$, $s \simeq s'$ implies $s \approx s'$.*

By Lemma 3 the submodels generated by isomorphic states are bisimilar.

The next two results guarantee that, under appropriate constraints, bisimulations preserve assignments equivalence.

Lemma 4. *Consider bisimilar ODAN $\mathcal{P}$ and $\mathcal{P}'$, bisimilar states $s \in \mathcal{R}$ and $s' \in \mathcal{R}'$, an FO-CTL formula φ, and assignments σ and σ' equivalent for φ w.r.t. s and s'.*

For every $t \in \mathcal{R}$, if (i) *$s \to t$,* (ii) *$|X'| \geq |adom(s) \cup ag(s) \cup adom(t) \cup ag(t) \cup \sigma(fr(\varphi))|$, and* (iii) *for every agent type T, $|Ag_T'| \geq |ag_T(s) \cup ag_T(t) \cup \sigma(fr(\varphi))|$, then for some $t' \in \mathcal{R}'$,* (i) *$s' \to t'$,* (ii) *$t \approx t'$, and* (iii) *σ and σ' are equivalent for φ w.r.t. t and t'.*

The proof of Lemma 4 makes essential use of Lemma 3 and uniformity. Thus, every time the cardinality constraints in Lemma 4 are satisfied, it is possible to extend equivalent assignments between pairs of bisimilar global states to their successors.

The next result relies on and generalises Lemma 4 to runs.

Lemma 5. *Consider bisimilar ODAN $\mathcal{P}$ and $\mathcal{P}'$, bisimilar states $s \in \mathcal{R}$ and $s' \in \mathcal{R}'$, an FO-CTL formula φ, and assignments σ and σ' equivalent for φ w.r.t. s and s'.*

For every s-run r in $\mathcal{P}$, if for all $i \geq 0$, (i) *$|X'| \geq |adom(r(i)) \cup ag(r(i)) \cup adom(r(i+1)) \cup ag(r(i+1)) \cup \sigma(fr(\varphi))|$, and* (ii) *$|Ag_T'| \geq |ag_T(r(i)) \cup ag_T(r(i+1)) \cup \sigma(fr(\varphi))|$ for every agent type T, then for some s'-run r' in $\mathcal{P}'$, for all $i \geq 0$,* (i) *$r(i) \approx r'(i)$;* (ii) *σ and σ' are equivalent for φ w.r.t. $r(i)$ and $r'(i)$; and* (iii) *if $r(i) \to r(i+1)$ then $r'(i) \to r'(i+1)$.*

By Lemma 5, if we have a sufficient number of elements in X' and of agents in each Ag_T', we can simulate the execution of an s-run by constructing a corresponding s'-run.

We finally prove that FO-CTL formulas cannot distinguish between bisimilar ODAN ($var(\varphi)$ is the set of variables in φ).

Theorem 6. *Consider bisimilar ODAN $\mathcal{P}$ and $\mathcal{P}'$, bisimilar states $s \in \mathcal{R}$ and $s' \in \mathcal{R}'$, an FO-CTL formula φ, and assignments σ and σ' equivalent for φ w.r.t. s and s'. If*

1. *for every s-run r, for every $k \geq 0$,* (i) *$|X'| \geq |adom(r(k)) \cup ag(r(k)) \cup adom(r(k+1)) \cup ag(r(k+1)) \cup \sigma(fr(\varphi))| + |var(\varphi) \setminus fr(\varphi)|$, and* (ii) *$|Ag_T'| \geq |ag_T(r(k)) \cup ag_T(r(k+1)) \cup \sigma(fr(\varphi))| + |var(\varphi) \setminus fr(\varphi)|$ for every type T;*
2. *for every s'-run r', for every $k \geq 0$,* (i) *$|X| \geq |adom(r'(k)) \cup ag(r'(k)) \cup adom(r'(k+1)) ag(r'(k+1)) \cup \sigma'(fr(\varphi))| + |var(\varphi) \setminus fr(\varphi)|$, and* (ii) *$|Ag_T| \geq |ag_T(r'(k)) \cup ag_T(r'(k+1)) \cup \sigma'(fr(\varphi))| + |var(\varphi) \setminus fr(\varphi)|$ for every type T;*

then $(\mathcal{P}, s, \sigma) \models \varphi$ iff $(\mathcal{P}', s', \sigma') \models \varphi$.

As a consequence of Theorem 6, bisimilar states satisfy the same FO-CTL formulas for equivalent assignments, whenever cardinality constraints (1) and (2) are satisfied. The proof of this result makes essential use of Lemma 5.

We now apply Theorem 6 to the model checking problem for ODAN. First of all, we introduce bounded ODAN.

Definition 15 (Bounded ODAN). *An ODAN $\mathcal{P}$ is b-*bounded, *for $b \in \mathbb{N}$, iff for all $s \in \mathcal{R}$, $|adom(s) \cup ag(s)| \leq b$.*

An ODAN $\mathcal{P}$ is *bounded* iff it is b-bounded for some $b \in \mathbb{N}$. Notice that bounded ODAN are still infinite-state systems in general. Hereafter let $\sup_{s \in \mathcal{R}}\{|adom(s) \cup ag(s)|\}$ be equal to ∞ whenever the ODAN $\mathcal{P}$ is unbounded. Similarly for $\sup_{s \in \mathcal{R}}\{|ag_T(s)|\}$.

Corollary 7. *Consider bisimilar ODAN $\mathcal{P}$ and $\mathcal{P}'$, and an FO-CTL formula φ. If*

1. *$|X'| \geq 2\sup_{s \in \mathcal{R}}\{|adom(s) \cup ag(s)|\} + |var(\varphi)|$ and $|Ag_T'| \geq 2\sup_{s \in \mathcal{R}}\{|ag_T(s)|\} + |var(\varphi)|$*
2. *$|X| \geq 2\sup_{s' \in \mathcal{R}'}\{|adom(s') \cup ag(s')|\} + |var(\varphi)|$ and $|Ag_T| \geq 2\sup_{s' \in \mathcal{R}'}\{|ag_T(s')|\} + |var(\varphi)|$*

then $\mathcal{P} \models \varphi$ iff $\mathcal{P}' \models \varphi$.

Corollary 7 shows that ODAN can in principle be verified by model checking a bisimilar system. Most importantly, this applies to any infinite ODAN $\mathcal{P}$ as well. Hence, by this result we can model check the corresponding, possibly finite $\mathcal{P}'$, as long as X' is sufficiently large for $\mathcal{P}'$ to bisimulate $\mathcal{P}$.

In the next section we show that finite abstractions can indeed be constructed for bounded ODAN, thus allowing for the verification of systems such as those of Section 3.

5. FINITE ABSTRACTION

In this section we state sufficient conditions to reduce the model checking problem for an infinite ODAN to the verification of a finite system. The main result is Theorem 8, which guarantees that boundedness is sufficient to obtain finite bisimilar abstractions that preserve FO-CTL formulas.

5.1 Reduction to finite-system verification

In Section 4 we specified that an ODAN is b-bounded if no active domain in its reachable state space contains more than

b distinct elements. Moreover, no more than b agents can be active at the same time. Observe that bounded ODAN may still contain infinitely many states, all bounded by some b. So, bounded ODAN are infinite-state systems in general, with a non-trivial model checking problem.

In order to verify ODAN we introduce abstractions in a modular manner by first defining abstract agents.

DEFINITION 16 (ABSTRACT AGENT). *Let $a = \langle \mathcal{D}, Act, Pr \rangle \in Ag_T$ be an agent of type T defined on a countable interpretation domain $X = U \cup Ag$. Given a countable set $X' = U' \cup Ag'$ of elements, the* abstract agent *$a' \in Ag'_T$ is a tuple $\langle \mathcal{D}', Act', Pr' \rangle$ on X' such that* (i) *$\mathcal{D}' = \mathcal{D}$;* (ii) *$Act' = Act$; and* (iii) *$Pr'$ is the smallest function defined as*

- *if $\alpha(\vec{u}) \in Pr(l)$, $l' \in \mathcal{D}'(X')$ and $l' \simeq l$ for some witness ι, then $\alpha(\iota(\vec{u})) \in Pr'(l')$.*

Given a set Ag_T of agents, let Ag'_T be the set of the corresponding abstract agents.

We remark that a', as defined in Def. 16, is indeed an agent of type T according to Def. 4. In particular, the protocol Pr' is well-defined provided Pr is, and it satisfies the assumption on protocols by definition. We now present abstractions.

DEFINITION 17 (ABSTRACTION). *Let $\mathcal{P} = \langle Ag, U, I, \tau \rangle$ be an ODAN, and Ag' the set of abstract agents given as in Def. 16. The ODAN $\mathcal{P}' = \langle Ag', U', I', \tau' \rangle$ is an* abstraction *of $\mathcal{P}$ iff* (i) *$I' = \{s'_0 \in \mathcal{D}'(X') \mid s'_0 \simeq s_0$ for some $s_0 \in I\}$, and* (ii) *τ' is the smallest function defined as follows*

- *if $s \xrightarrow{\alpha(\vec{u})} t$ in $\mathcal{P}$, $s', t' \in \mathcal{D}'(X')$, and $s \oplus t \simeq s' \oplus t'$ for some witness ι, then $s' \xrightarrow{\alpha(\iota(\vec{u}))} t'$.*

Notice that $\mathcal{P}'$ is indeed an ODAN as it satisfies the relevant conditions on protocols and transitions in Def. 7. Also, by varying X' we can obtain abstractions of different cardinalities. In particular, we are interested in finite ones.

The following result guarantees that for every bounded ODAN there exists a bisimilar abstraction, provided that the latter is built over a sufficiently large interpretation domain. In the following we assume that, for a bound $b \in \mathbb{N}$, N_b is the maximum numbers of parameters contained in any parametric joint actions, i.e., $N = b \cdot \max_{\{\alpha(\vec{x}) \in Act_T, type\ T\}}\{|\vec{x}|\}$.

THEOREM 8. *Consider a bounded ODAN $\mathcal{P}$ over an infinite interpretation domain X, an FO-CTL formula φ, and an interpretation domain X'. If* (i) *$|X'| \geq 2b + \max\{|var(\varphi)|, N_b\}$, and* (ii) *for every type T, $|Ag'_T| \geq 2b + \max\{|var(\varphi)|, N_b\}$, then there exists a bisimilar abstraction $\mathcal{P}'$ of $\mathcal{P}$ over X' such that $\mathcal{P} \models \varphi$ iff $\mathcal{P}' \models \varphi$*

We remark that each Ag'_T and X' in Theorem 8 might as well be finite. So, by using a sufficient number of abstract agents and values, we can in principle reduce the model checking problem for infinite-state ODAN to the verification of a finite abstraction. Specifically, we obtain the following corollary to Theorem 8.

COROLLARY 9. *Given a bounded ODAN $\mathcal{P}$ over an infinite interpretation domain X, and an FO-CTL formula φ, there exists an abstract ODAN $\mathcal{P}'$ over a finite interpretation domain X' such that φ holds in $\mathcal{P}$ iff $\mathcal{P}'$ satisfies φ.*

As a consequence of Corollary 9, we can verify an infinite-state, bounded ODAN, by model checking its finite, bisimilar abstraction.

For the time being we do not discuss efficient model checking procedure for finite ODAN, as it is beyond the scope of the paper. We only remark that the state space of ODAN is usually exponential in the number of agents and data. Thus, a major challenge for these systems is to develop efficient model checking algorithms. We leave this topic for future research and remind here that the main motivation and contribution of this paper is to show that under specific conditions (namely, boundedness) we can reduce the model checking problem for an infinite-state ODAN to the verification of its finite abstraction.

5.2 Model Checking SIR Models

In this section we outline how the properties listed in Section 3.4 can be verified on the SIR models provided in Section 3. We start by remarking the following.

Firstly, when studying the evolution of a diffusion phenomenon, such as epidemics, we can safely assume that the population will not exceed a certain bound at any given time, possibly determined by the resources of the environment. Hence, even though individual agents can join or leave the ODAN according to the cycle of births and deaths, their number is supposed to never exceed a given bound $b \in \mathbb{N}$.

Secondly, the computational capabilities of any real-life system are limited at each time-point. Specifically, system memories are capable of storing only a finite amount of data at each moment, even though these data can constantly change at run time.

Given the above, we can safely assume that the number of agents in any single state of the SIR ODAN in Section 3 is bounded by a value $b \in \mathbb{N}$. We can enforce this by modifying the definition of the SIR ODAN, by requiring that the initial states contain at most b agents, i.e., for every $s_0 \in I$, $|ag(s_0)| \leq b$. Further, we modify the definition of the transition function τ by specifying that recovered agents are discarded from the network and that existing agents can connect to new agents as long as the bound b is not met. Indeed, recovered agents no longer play an active role in the evolution of the SIR model, so they can be safely discarded.

Therefore, according to Theorem 8, to model check specification (1) in Section 3.4 on the dynamic SIR ODAN it is sufficient to consider a domain Ag' of agents of cardinality $|Ag'| = 2b + \max\{|var(\varphi)|, N_b\} = 3b$. The agents in Ag' generate a dynamic SIR ODAN $\mathcal{P}'$ that is bisimilar to the original concrete system $\mathcal{P}$ defined on some infinite set Ag of agents of the same type. In particular, $\mathcal{P}'$ is finite, so we can effectively verify specification (1) on $\mathcal{P}'$ and then transfer the result to $\mathcal{P}$.

6. CONCLUSIONS

In this paper we introduced a data-aware model for open dynamic agent networks (ODAN) and investigated the verification of first-order temporal specifications on such structures. The main technical result consists in proving that, under the boundedness assumption, the model checking problem for ODAN against FO-CTL is decidable. We also showed that the framework of ODAN is expressive enough to capture non-probabilistic diffusion phenomena such as epidemics in open and dynamic variants of the SIR model.

Future work should focus on exploring the complexity of the model-checking problem for ODAN possibly restricting the first-order expressivity of the underlying logic to a suitable modal fragment.

7. REFERENCES

[1] S. Abiteboul, R. Hull, and V. Vianu. *Foundations of Databases.* Addison-Wesley, 1995.

[2] F. Belardinelli, A. Lomuscio, and F. Patrizi. An Abstraction Technique for the Verification of Artifact-Centric Systems. In *Proc. of the 13th International Conference on Principles of Knowledge Representation and Reasoning (KR'12)*, pages 319 – 328, 2012.

[3] F. Belardinelli, F. Patrizi, and A. Lomuscio. Verification of agent-based artifact systems. *Journal of Artificial Intelligence Research*, 51:333–77, 2014.

[4] P. Blackburn, M. de Rijke, and Y. Venema. *Modal Logic*, volume 53 of *Cambridge Tracts in Theoretical Computer Science.* Cambridge University Press, 2001.

[5] Z. Christoff and J. U. Hansen. A two-tiered formalization of social influence. In *Proceedings of LORI'13*, number 8196 in LNCS, pages 68–81. Springer, 2013.

[6] Z. Christoff and J. U. Hansen. A logic for diffusion in social networks. *Journal of Applied Logic*, 13(1):48–77, 2015.

[7] D. Cohn and R. Hull. Business Artifacts: A Data-Centric Approach to Modeling Business Operations and Processes. *IEEE Data Eng. Bull.*, 32(3):3–9, 2009.

[8] M. Dam. Model checking mobile processes. *Information and Computation*, 129:35–51, 1996.

[9] A. Deutsch, R. Hull, F. Patrizi, and V. Vianu. Automatic Verification of Data-Centric Business Processes. In *Proc. of ICDT*, 2009.

[10] Alin Deutsch, Liying Sui, and Victor Vianu. Specification and Verification of Data-Driven Web Applications. *J. Comput. Syst. Sci.*, 73(3):442–474, 2007.

[11] D. Easley and J. Kleinberg. *Networks, Crowds, and Markets.* Cambridge University Press, 2010.

[12] R. Fagin, J.Y. Halpern, Y. Moses, and M.Y. Vardi. *Reasoning About Knowledge.* The MIT Press, 1995.

[13] B. Bagheri Hariri, D. Calvanese, G. De Giacomo, A. Deutsch, and M. Montali. Verification of relational data-centric dynamic systems with external services. In R. Hull and W. Fan, editors, *PODS*, pages 163–174. ACM, 2013.

[14] M. O. Jackson. *Social and Economic Networks.* Princeton University Press, 2008.

[15] S. Khan, R. Makkena, F. McGeary, K. Decker, W. Gillis, and C. Schmidt. A multi-agent system for the quantitative simulation of biological networks. In *Proceedings of the second international joint conference on Autonomous agents and multiagent systems (AAMAS'03)*, pages 385–392. ACM, 2003.

[16] R. Milner. The polyadic π-calculus: A tutorial. Technical Report ECS-LFCS-91-180, Laboratory for the Foundations of Computer Science, Department of Computer Science, University of Edinburgh, 1991.

[17] R. Parikh and R. Ramanujam. Distributed processes and the logic of knowledge. In *Logic of Programs*, pages 256–268, 1985.

[18] M. Rovatsos. Multiagent systems for social computation. In A. Lomuscio, P. Scerri, A. Bazzan, and M. Huhns, editors, *Proceedings of the 13th International Conference on Autonomous Agents and Multiagent Systems (AAMAS14).* IFAAMAS, 2014.

[19] A. Salehi-Abari and C. Boutilier. Empathetic social choice on social networks. In A. Lomuscio, P. Scerri, A. Bazzan, and M. Huhns, editors, *Proceedings of the 13th International Conference on Autonomous Agents and Multiagent Systems (AAMAS14).* IFAAMAS, 2014.

[20] G. Santhanam, Y. Suvorov, S. Basu, and V. Honavar. Verifying intervention policies to counter infection propagation over networks: A model checking approach. In *Proceedings of the 25th AAAI Conference on Artificial Intelligence.* AAAI Press, 2011.

[21] L. Sless, N. Hazon, M. Wooldridge, and S. Kraus. Forming coalitions and facilitating relationships for completing tasks in social networks. In A. Lomuscio, P. Scerri, A. Bazzan, and M. Huhns, editors, *Proceedings of the 13th International Conference on Autonomous Agents and Multiagent Systems (AAMAS14).* IFAAMAS, 2014.

[22] H. van Ditmarsch, B. Kooi, and W. van der Hoek. *Dynamic Epistemic Logic*, volume 337 of *Synthese Library Series.* Springer, 2007.

[23] M. Wooldridge. Computationally Grounded Theories of Agency. In *Proc. of ICMAS*, pages 13–22. IEEE Press, 2000.

Determining Placements of Influencing Agents in a Flock

Katie Genter, Shun Zhang and Peter Stone
Department of Computer Science, University of Texas at Austin
Austin, TX 78712 USA
{katie,menie482,pstone}@cs.utexas.edu

ABSTRACT

Flocking is a fascinating collective behavior exhibited by many different animals including birds and fish. As understood by biologists, the overall flocking behavior emerges from relatively simple local control rules by which each individual adjusts its own trajectory based on those of its closest neighbors. We consider the possibility of adding a small set of influencing agents, that are under our control, into a flock. Specifically, in this paper we consider where in the flock to place the influencing agents that we add to the flock. Following ad hoc teamwork methodology, we assume that we are given knowledge of, but no direct control over, the rest of the flock. We use the influencing agents to alter the flock's trajectory, for instance to avoid an obstacle. We define several methodologies for placing the influencing agents into the flock, and compare them via detailed experimental results.

Categories and Subject Descriptors

I.2.11 [**Distributed Artificial Intelligence**]: Multiagent systems

General Terms

Algorithms, Experimentation

Keywords

Ad Hoc Teamwork; Agent Placement; Flocking

1. INTRODUCTION

Flocking is an emergent swarm behavior found in various species in nature. Each animal in a flock follows a simple local behavior rule, but this simple behavior by individual agents often results in group behavior that appears well organized and stable. Flocking is often studied under the assumption that all of the agents are identical or represent a small set of well-defined behavior types. Indeed, various disciplines such as physics [12], graphics [9], biology [2], and distributed control theory [6, 7, 11] have studied flocking in order to characterize its emergent behavior. In our work, we instead consider how to lead a flock to adopt particular behaviors by adding a small amount of controllable agents to the flock.

As a motivating example, imagine that a flock of migrating birds is flying directly towards a dangerous area, such as an airport or wind farm. Our goal is to encourage the birds to avoid the dangerous area without significantly disturbing them. Since there is no way to directly control the flight path of the birds, we must instead alter the environment so as to encourage the flock to alter their flight path as desired. In this work, we choose to alter the environment by adding *influencing agents* to the flock. These influencing agents — which could be in the form of robotic birds[1], robotic bees [10], or ultralight aircraft[2] — follow our algorithms but are perceived by the rest of the flock to be one of their own.

Following a well-recognized flocking model [9], we assume that each bird in the flock dynamically adjusts its heading based on that of its immediate neighbors. Previous work has considered how *randomly* placed influencing agents should behave so as to influence the flock to face a particular direction or maneuver along a path so as to avoid an obstacle [4, 5]. In our work, we examine where the influencing agents should be placed in the flock. Specifically, our current research question is: *where should influencing agents be located within a flock to maximize their influence on the flock?*

The remainder of this paper is organized as follows. Section 2 situates our research in the literature and Section 3 introduces our problem and necessary terminology. Section 4 reviews past work on how the influencing agents decide how to behave. Section 5 introduces our graph-based method for deciding where to place the influencing agents and Section 6 introduces our approach for control of the influencing agents. We discuss our experiments in Section 7 and then Section 8 concludes.

2. RELATED WORK

Reynolds introduced the flocking model that we use in this work [9]. Reynolds focused on creating a flocking model that looked and behaved realistically. His model consisted of three simple steering behaviors that determine how each agent behaves based on the agents around it. Vicsek *et al.* considered only one aspect of Reynolds' model in physics work that studied the self-emergent nature of flocking [12]. However, neither of these lines of research considered how to influence the flock to adopt a particular behavior by introducing agents into the flock.

Appears in: *Proceedings of the 14th International Conference on Autonomous Agents and Multiagent Systems (AAMAS 2015), Bordini, Elkind, Weiss, Yolum (eds.), May, 4–8, 2015, Istanbul, Turkey.*

[1] www.mybionicbird.com
[2] www.operationmigration.org

Jadbabaie *et al.* considered the impact of adding a controllable agent to a flock [7]. They also used just one aspect of Reynolds' model and showed that a flock with a controllable agent will always converge to the controllable agent's heading. Su *et al.* also presented work that used a controllable agent to make the flock converge [11]. Celikkanat and Sahin used informed agents to lead the flock by their preference for a particular direction [1]. Our work is different from these lines of research in that they all influence the flock to converge to a target heading eventually, while we influence the flock to converge quickly.

Couzin *et al.* considered how animals in groups make informed, unanimous decisions [2]. They showed that only a very small proportion of informed agents is required for such decisions, and that the larger the group, the smaller the proportion of informed individuals required. Ferrante *et al.* used communication to coordinate a flock to move towards a common goal [3]. These two lines of research are different from ours because they do not consider how to control agents by considering and accounting for how the other agents will react. Instead, in these lines of research, each agent behaves in a fixed manner that is pre-decided or solely based on its type.

Han *et al.* assume that an influencing agent can be placed at any position at any time step [6]. Because of this assumption, the authors place the influencing agent at the position of the 'worst' flocking agent, which is the one that deviates from the desired orientation the most. In our work, we consider the assumption that the influencing agents can be placed as we want in the first time step. However, we do not allow teleporting and hence we can not continually place an influencing agent at the 'worst' flocking agent.

To the best of our knowledge, the work presented in this paper is the first that considers how to place controllable agents that aim to influence the flock towards a particular behavior into a flock.

3. PROBLEM DEFINITION

To fully define our problem, we must specify (1) a model of the flock, (2) the possible options for placing influencing agents initially, (3) the actions available to the influencing agents, and (4) the performance objective. This section does so, and also describes the concrete simulation environment that we use in our experiments. Our proposed methodologies for addressing the defined problem are presented in Sections 5 and 6.

3.1 Flocking Model

To model the flock, we use a simplified version of Reynolds' Boid algorithm for flocking [9] that is similar to the model utilized in our previous work [4]. Specifically, we only use the flock centering aspect of Reynolds' model, and do not use the collision avoidance and velocity matching aspects of his model.

The flock is comprised of two types of agents. Specifically, the n agents that comprise the flock consist of k *influencing* agents and m *flocking* agents, where $k + m = n$. The influencing agents $\{a_0, \ldots, a_{k-1}\}$ are agents whose behavior we can control, while the flocking agents $\{a_k, \ldots, a_{N-1}\}$ are agents that we cannot directly control.

Each agent in the flock has a velocity, a position in the environment, and an orientation. Each agent a_i moves with velocity v_i. At each time step t, each agent a_i has a position $p_i(t) = (x_i(t), y_i(t))$ in the environment and an orientation $\theta_i(t)$. Each agent's position $p_i(t)$ at time t is updated after its orientation is updated, such that $x_i(t) = x_i(t-1) + v_i \cos(\theta_i(t))$ and $y_i(t) = y_i(t-1) - v_i \sin(\theta_i(t))$. Hence, the current state of agent a_i at time t can be represented by its $(x_i(t),\ y_i(t), \theta_i(t))$ pose.

Agents in a flock update their orientations based on the orientations of the other agents in their *neighborhood*. Let $N_i(t)$ be the set of $n_i(t) \leq n$ agents (not including agent a_i) at time t which are located within a *visibility radius* r of agent a_i. This visibility radius defines each agent's *neighborhood*. The global orientation of agent a_i at time step $t+1$, $\theta_i(t+1)$, is set to be the average orientation of all agents in $N_i(t)$ (not including itself) at time t. Formally,

$$\theta_i(t+1) = \theta_i(t) + \frac{1}{n_i(t)} \sum_{a_j \in N_i(t)} \text{calcDiff}(\theta_j(t), \theta_i(t)) \quad (1)$$

We use Equation 1 instead of taking the average orientation of all agents because of the special cases handled by Algorithm 1. For example, the mathematical average of 350° and 10° is 180°, but by Algorithm 1 it is 0°. Throughout this paper, we restrict $\theta_i(t)$ to be within $[0, 2\pi)$.

Algorithm 1 calcDiff($\theta_i(t), \theta_j(t)$)

```
if ((θi(t) − θj(t) ≥ −π) ∧ (θi(t) − θj(t) ≤ π)) then
    return θi(t) − θj(t)
else if θi(t) − θj(t) < −π then
    return 2π + (θi(t) − θj(t))
else
    return (θi(t) − θj(t)) − 2π
```

3.2 Inf uencing Agent Initial Placement

The influencing agents join the flock in order to influence the flock to behave in a particular way. Our previous work only considered random placement of the influencing agents [5]. However, in this work we consider cases in which $\{p_0(0), \ldots, p_{k-1}(0)\}$ is under our control (Section 7.2) and cases in which it is not (Section 7.3).

In the cases where $\{p_0(0), \ldots, p_{k-1}(0)\}$ is under our control we may place the agents $\{a_0, \ldots, a_{k-1}\}$ wherever we wish. In the cases where it is not, we assume the agents $\{a_0, \ldots, a_{k-1}\}$ begin in designated starting spots and must then actively move to locate themselves within the flock, perhaps as the flock passes by their designated starting spots.

3.3 Inf uencing Agent Control

Influencing agents $\{a_0, \ldots, a_{k-1}\}$ are agents whose behavior we can control. Specifically, we control what type of behavior these agents display at each given time step: (1) control to *adjust position* or (2) control to *influence neighbors*. Our previous work only focused on control to influence neighbors [5]. In this work, Section 6 presents reasoning about control to adjust position and introduces a method to arbitrate between control to adjust position and control to influence neighbors.

3.4 Performance Representation

We define the *Agent Control and Placement Problem* as follows: Given a target orientation θ^* and a team of n agents $\{a_0, \ldots, a_{n-1}\}$, where the m flocking agents $\{a_k, \ldots a_{n-1}\}$ have positions $\gamma_m(t) = \{p_k(t), \ldots p_{n-1}(t)\}$ at time t and calculate their orientation based on Equation 1, determine placement $\pi(0)$ of influencing agents $\{a_0, \ldots a_{k-1}\}$ at time 0 and control $\Phi = \phi(0), \ldots, \phi(t)$ at times $t >= 0$ such that loss $l(\pi(0), \Phi)$ is minimized.

A k-agent placement specifies the positions that each influencing agent $\{a_0, \ldots a_{k-1}\}$ will take at time 0. The k-agent placement is denoted by $\pi_k(0) = \{p_0(0), \ldots, p_{k-1}(0)\}$ where $\{p_0(0), \ldots, p_{k-1}(0)\}$ is the set of positions for influencing agents $\{a_0, \ldots a_{k-1}\}$ at time 0.

We denote t^* as the earliest time step at which flocking agents $\{a_k, \ldots, a_{N-1}\}$ are oriented such that, for all $t \geq t^*$, $\{\theta_k(t), \ldots, \theta_{N-1}(t)\}$ are all within ϵ of θ^*. However, in some cases this will never occur because some of the m flocking agents may become permanently separated from the flock — we say these agents are *lost*. An agent a_i is considered lost if there exists a subset of flocking agents with cardinality $m' < m$ and orientations within ϵ of θ^* for more than 200 time steps and $|\theta_i(t^*) - \theta^*| > \epsilon$, where t^* is the time step at which the subset converged to θ^*. Let $\gamma_{m'}(t)$ denote the set of positions of the non-lost flocking agents at time t. Additionally, let $\alpha = \frac{\sum_{j \in \gamma_{m'}(t)} \|j - \overline{\gamma_{m'}(t)}\|}{m'}$. In other words, let α represent the average distance of the non-lost flocking agents at time t from the center of the flock.

The *loss* $l(\pi(0), \Phi)$ of a k-agent placement $\pi_k(0)$ and control Φ is a weighted function of four terms:

- w_1 is a weight that emphasizes the importance of minimizing the number of lost agents (minimize $\overline{m - m'}$)
- w_2 is a weight that emphasizes the importance of minimizing the number of simulation experiments in which any agent is lost (minimize simulation experiments in which $m - m' > 0$)
- w_3 is a weight that emphasizes the importance of minimizing the number of time steps needed for convergence (minimize $\overline{t^*}$)
- w_4 is a weight that emphasizes the importance of the flock being compactly spaced at time t^* (minimize $\overline{\alpha}$)

$$l(\pi(0), \Phi) = w_1\overline{m - m'} + w_2\overline{p(m - m' > 0)} + w_3\overline{t^*} + w_4\overline{\alpha} \tag{2}$$

An optimal placement $\pi^*(0), \Phi^*$ is one with minimal loss $l(\pi^*(0), \Phi)$.

In this work, we set $w_1 > w_2 > w_3 > w_4$. With these preferences for w_1, w_2, w_3, and w_4 we select influencing agent placements that generally lose the least number of agents on average but that also attempt to minimize the chances of losing any agents.

3.5 Simulation Environment

We situate our research within the MASON simulator [8]. This simulator encodes all the flock dynamics as described in this section and we augment it to compute the performance metric discussed Section 3.4. Pictures of the Flockers domain are shown in Figure 1. Each agent points and moves in the direction of its current velocity vector. We describe our experimental setup in detail in Section 7.1.

4. CONTROL OF INFLUENCING AGENTS

Birds in a flock dynamically update their headings based on the headings of their neighbors. In Section 3 we presented the models that we assume birds use when determining which nearby birds are in their neighborhood and when updating their headings. Our previous work has focused on how randomly placed influencing agents should behave so as to influence the flock towards a particular behavior [4, 5]. We shortly review this work below.

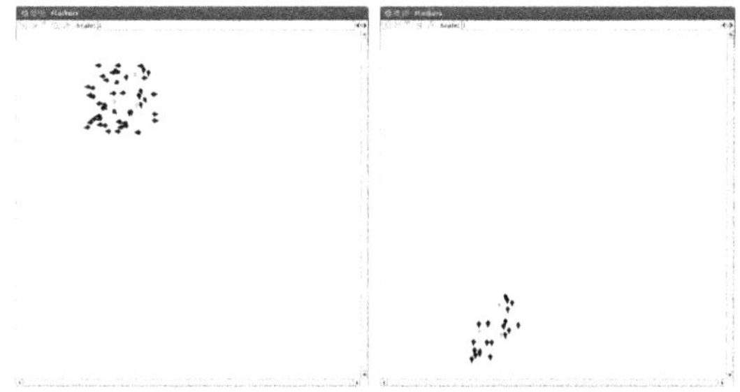

(a) (b)

Figure 1: Images of (a) the start of a trial and (b) the end of a trial. The gray agents are influencing agents while the black agents are other members of the flock.

Our first paper in this area considered how influencing agents should behave from a theoretical perspective [4]. This work presented a formal definition of the flocking model that served as a base for the model we use in the work presented in this paper. We presented multiple general flocking theorems that apply across all flocking scenarios before considering theorems specific to cases in which all agents are stationary ($v_i = 0 \ \forall \ i$) and cases in which only the influencing agents are non-stationary ($v_i = 0 \ \forall \ i \geq k$). In the case where all of the agents are stationary, we presented and then empirically evaluated an algorithm for determining the necessary orientations for influencing agents at each time step as well as the number of steps needed for the flocking agents to orient towards θ^*. In the case of non-stationary influencing agents attempting to influence stationary flocking agents, we empirically evaluated two heuristics for how the influencing agents should behave when they are not currently within the neighborhood of any flocking agents.

In more recent work we considered how to influence a large, non-stationary flock to (1) quickly *orient* towards a target orientation and (2) *maneuver* through turns quickly but with minimal agents becoming lost as a result of these turns [5]. We introduced a 1-step lookahead algorithm for determining the individual behavior of each influencing agent $a_i \in \{a_0, \ldots, a_{k-1}\}$. This 1-step lookahead algorithm considered all of the influences on the neighbors $N_i(t)$ of the influencing agent a_i and allowed the influencing agent to determine the best orientation to adopt (where best is defined as the behavior that exerts the most influence on the next step). We used this algorithm to determine the behavior of each influencing agent in empirical experiments, and showed that the 1-step lookahead algorithm did better in terms of the number of steps required for the flock to converge to θ^* than the baseline algorithm in both cases.

In the work presented in this paper, we used the 1-step lookahead algorithm from our previous work [5] as the behavior of the influencing agents once they are in their chosen positions within the flock. In order to maintain consistency with this previous work, in our experiments we set two control and task parameters in the same manner as we did previously. First, we only consider *numAngles* discrete angle choices for each influencing agent when performing 1-step lookahead, where *numAngles*=50. Thus the unit circle is equally divided into 50 segments beginning at 0 radians and each of these orientations is considered as a possible orientation for each influencing agent during 1-step lookahead. Second, we conclude that the flock has converged to θ^* when every agent (that is not an influencing agent or *lost*) is facing within 0.1 radians of θ^*.

5. DETERMINING INITIAL POSITIONS OF INFLUENCING AGENTS

The main contribution of this paper is a consideration of where to place the influencing agents $\{a_0, \ldots, a_{k-1}\}$ into the flock, assuming that once there, they will follow the 1-step lookahead behavior described above. We consider two different cases when determining how to place $a_i \in \{a_0, \ldots, a_{k-1}\}$ into the flock. In the **Drop** case, we are able to drop each influencing agent a_i into the flock at whatever location $p_i(0)$ we desire at time $t = 0$. In the **Dispatch** case, each influencing agent begins at one or more stations outside the flock at time $t = 0$ and is directed to travel to a particular location in the flock. Note that in the **Dispatch** case, each influencing agent will take time to reach its assigned location and may influence flocking agents along the way.

In the following subsections we discuss our approaches for placing influencing agents into the flock. Videos of these approaches are available on our web page.[3]

5.1 Random Approach

Our previous research randomly placed k influencing agents within the dimensions of the flock [5]. Hence, we use random placement as the base case for evaluating our placement approaches. Random placements are calculated for k influencing agents in constant time.

5.2 Grid Approach

Grid placement is another base case in which we place k influencing agents at predefined, well-spaced, gridded positions throughout flock. The placement of the influencing agents is dependent on the space covered by the flocking agents, and not on the positions of flocking agents. Hence, the placements of k influencing agents are determined in constant time. Grids are available that can fit at most x influencing agents, where we use the smallest grid in which $k \leq x$. Grids are available in which $x \in \{1, 2, 4, 9, 16, 25, 36, \ldots\}$. For each grid size, agents are spread out among the possible positions as much as possible. Examples of the grid approach for various values of k can be seen in Figure 2.

(a) $k = 2$ (b) $k = 4$ (c) $k = 6$

Figure 2: Images of influencing agent placement using the **grid approach** with (a) $k = 2$ (b) $k = 4$ and (c) $k = 6$. $n = 50$ in all three cases. The gray agents are influencing agents while the black agents are other members of the flock.

[3]http://www.cs.utexas.edu/~larg/index.php/Placement_Into_a_Flock

5.3 Border Approach

Our border approach works by placing k influencing agents as evenly as possible around the space covered by the flocking agents. As in the grid approach, the placement of the influencing agents is not dependent on the positions of flocking agents. Hence, the placements of k influencing agents are determined in constant time. We place influencing agents on the left side of the flock, right side of the flock, bottom of the flock, and top of the flock in order until all k influencing agents are placed. At most $\frac{k}{4}$ influencing agents are positioned on any particular side of the flock. If more than one influencing agent is placed on a particular side of the flock, the influencing agents spread out as much as possible on that side of the flock. Examples of the border approach for various values of k can be seen in Figure 3.

(a) $k = 2$ (b) $k = 4$ (c) $k = 6$

Figure 3: Images of influencing agent placement using the **border approach** with (a) $k = 2$ (b) $k = 4$ and (c) $k = 6$. $n = 50$ in all three cases. The gray agents are influencing agents while the black agents are other members of the flock.

5.4 Graph Approach

Our graph approach considers many possible k-sized sets of positions in which the k influencing agents could be placed, and then evaluates how well each of these sets connects the m flocking agents with the k influencing agents.

5.4.1 Creating the Graph

All $\{a_k, \ldots, a_{N-1}\}$ flocking agents are added to an initially empty graph G as nodes. Then, for each agent $a_i \in \{a_k, \ldots, a_{N-1}\}$, an undirected edge is added to G between a_i and each of its neighbors $a_b \in n_i(t)$ if such an edge does not already exist.

5.4.2 Calculating Sets of Inf uencing Agent Positions

Next we consider the positions at which we will consider adding influencing agents. For $a_i, a_j \in \{a_k, \ldots, a_{N-1}\}$, we consider adding an influencing agent at the mid-point $(\frac{x_i(t)+x_j(t)}{2}, \frac{y_i(t)+y_j(t)}{2})$ between $p_i(t)$ and $p_j(t)$ *only* if $p_i(t)$ and $p_j(t)$ are within $2r$ of each other. We consider this midpoint because placing an influencing agent here will allow the agent to influence both a_i and a_j. We also consider adding an influencing agent at $(x_i(t) + 0.1, y_i(t) + 0.1)$ for $a_i \in \{a_k, \ldots, a_{N-1}\}$ where $0.1 < r$. We consider this point, which is extremely close to a_i, since placing an influencing agent as this point will allow the agent to at least influence a_i. In cases where no or few flocking agents are within $2r$ of each other, placing influencing agents close to a flocking agent guaranteed that at least one flocking agent would be influenced by each influencing agent.

Once we have all of the positions at which we might add an influencing agents, we form all possible k-sized sets of these positions.

5.4.3 Evaluating Sets of Influencing Agent Positions

Finally, we take all possible k-sized sets and consider individually each set S of k influencing agent positions. In order to do this, we do the following for each S. Note that agents are 'directly' connected if they are neighbors and 'indirectly' connected if they have a neighbor, a neighbor of a neighbor, or a most distant agent in common.

- Add each influencing agent $a_i \in S$ to G
- For each agent $a_i \in S$, an edge is added to G between a_i and each of its neighbors $a_b \in n_i(t)$
- Run the Floyd Warshall shortest paths algorithm on G to obtain the following:
  - **numNoConn**: the number of flocking agents not connected to an influencing agent (directly or indirectly)
  - **numConn**: the number of connections between flocking agents and influencing agents (directly or indirectly)
  - **numDirectConn**: the number of direct connections between flocking agents and influencing agents
  - **numNoDirectConn**: the number of flocking agents not directly connected to an influencing agent
- Remove each influencing agent $a_i \in S$ from G

Once all possible k-sized sets T have been individually considered, we select a set based on the information we obtained. Specifically, we compare in order (lexicographically) criteria at four levels: (1) minimal **numNoConn**, (2) maximal **numConn**, (3) maximal **numDirectConn**, and (4) minimal **numNoDirectConn**. If only one set matches the criterion at a level, then we select it. Otherwise, all of the sets that matched the criterion at that level are considered at the next level. If multiple sets remain after the final level, we choose one of the remaining sets randomly.

In practice, we find that a set is usually selected using the first criterion. We have witnessed a few cases in which the fourth criterion has been used, but we have never witnessed a case in which the final criterion of selecting a remaining set randomly has been utilized.

The entire process of selecting placements for k influencing agents, given current placements of m flocking agents, has an algorithmic complexity of $O(n^3\binom{m^2+m}{k})$.

As can be seen in Figure 4, our graph approach places influencing agents in the areas in which their influence will be most impactful in decreasing loss of flocking agents.

(a) $k = 2$, $n = 10$ (b) $k = 4$, $n = 10$ (c) $k = 2$, $n = 20$

Figure 4: Images of influencing agent placement using the **graph approach** with (a) $k = 2$, $n = 10$ (b) $k = 4$, $n = 10$ and (c) $k = 2$, $n = 20$. The gray agents are influencing agents while the black agents are other members of the flock.

6. DETERMINING CONTROL OF INFLUENCING AGENTS

In the **Drop** case, the k influencing agents are at their desired positions at $t = 0$, so they can start influencing flocking agents directly via 1-step lookahead. In the **Dispatch** case, however, the influencing agents are initially positioned outside of the flock. They will only influence a limited number of flocking agents if they begin 1-step lookahead immediately. Hence, they must *reposition* themselves to their desired positions before they attempt to influence.

In the **Dispatch** case the influencing agents must approach and enter the flock in order to reach their desired positions and eventually influence more flocking agents. If they travel at the same speed as the flocking agents, they usually will not be able to catch up to the flocking agents. Instead, as the orientations of the flocking agents are affected by the influencing agents' directions, the flocking agents are likely to be driven away from the flock in the direction the influencing agents are traveling. Since the desired positions of the influencing agents are determined based on the current positions of the flocking agents, the influencing agents may never reach their desired positions if they travel at the same speed as the flocking agents. Hence, in the **Dispatch** case we assume the influencing agents are able to travel faster than the flocking agents. They do so when moving to their chosen position; when using 1-step lookahead to influence the flocking agents, they revert to the same speed as the flocking agents.

Influencing agents must always decide whether to attempt to move to their desired location *or* attempt to influence flocking agents in the **Dispatch** case. Once an influencing agent a_i reaches its desired position $p_i(t)$, it always enters the phase of influencing flocking agents via 1-step lookahead. However, behaving according to 1-step lookahead may cause a_i to leave its desired position (it could even leave the flock). As such, a_i should return to the repositioning phase if it strays too far from its desired position. However, if a_i switches between repositioning to its desired position and influencing flocking agents too frequently, it will oscillate between these two behaviors and not efficiently influence the flocking agents. To prevent excessive oscillation, we employ a hysteresis method to control the switch between these two phases. Specifically, when an influencing agent reaches a distance of h_1 away from its desired position, it returns to within h_2 of its desired position, where $h_1 > h_2$. In this way, the influencing agent will not reposition itself when it only deviates slightly from its desired position.

We examine the various types of desired positions described in Section 5 — random approach, grid approach, border approach, and graph approach. We use such placements as initial positions in the **Drop** case, and as desired positions in the **Dispatch** case. We report the empirical results in Section 7. However, we only report results for the graph approach in the **Drop** case. This is because as the desired positions need to be recalculated at each time step as the flocking agents update their positions, the graph approach was too computationally expensive to be evaluated in the **Dispatch** case. Moreover, the desired positions indicated by the graph approach are optimum points at one time step. They may change dramatically when the flock moves whereas the positions chosen by the border approach and grid approach change smoothly.

7. EXPERIMENTS

In this section we describe our experiments testing the various approaches for placing influencing agents into a flock in both the **Drop** case and the **Dispatch** case. We compare our novel approaches against baseline methods in both cases.

There are plenty of different metrics that can be used to access how 'good' a particular approach is — steps for the flock to converge, the number of trials in which any flocking agents were lost, the average number of flocking agents lost, and the average distance of the flocking agents from the center of flock at convergence are just some possible metrics. As discussed in Section 3.4, in this work we primarily focus on minimizing the average number of flocking agents lost. Our secondary focus is minimizing the number of trials in which any flocking agents are lost. Hence, for our experiments we set $w_1 = 0.45$, $w_2 = 0.4$, $w_3 = 0.1$, and $w_4 = 0.05$. However, our approach will be applicable as long as w_1 and w_2 are substantially greater than w_3 and w_4 — it is not sensitive to the exact values of these variables.

7.1 Experimental Setup

We utilize the MASON simulator [8] for our experiments in this paper. We introduced the MASON simulator in Section 3.5, but in this section we present the details of our experimental environment that are vital for completely understanding and replicating our experimental setup. We generally only discuss an experimental variable or control if we changed it from the default setting for the simulator.

The experimental settings for variables are given in Table 1 for both the **Drop** case and the **Dispatch** case.

Variable	**Drop Case**	**Dispatch Case**
toroidal domain	no	no
domain height	300	300
domain width	300	300
units moved by each flocking agent per time step ($v_k = \ldots = v_{N-1}$)	0.2	0.2
units moved by each influencing agent per time step ($v_0 = \ldots = v_{k-1}$)	0.2	0.2-1
number of agents in flock (n)	10-50	50
number of influencing agents (k)	1-5	5
neighborhood for each agent (radius)	*10*	*10*

Table 1: Experimental settings for variables in the **Drop** and **Dispatch** cases. Italicized values are default settings for the simulator.

Most of our experimental variables in Table 1, such as toroidal domain, domain height, domain width, and the units each agent moves per time step, are not set to the default settings for the MASON simulator. We chose to remove the toroidal nature of the domain in order to make the domain more realistic. Hence, if an agent moves off of one edge of our domain, it will not reappear. This is particularly important for *lost* agents remaining *lost*. We also increased the domain height and width, and decreased the units each agent moves per time step, in order to give agents a chance to converge with the flock before leaving the visible area. However, we have no reason to believe the exact values we chose for the experiments are of particular importance.

Flocking agents are randomly placed initially within a square in the top left of the domain, where this square occupies 4% of the domain. Agents are initially assigned random headings that are within 90 degrees of θ^*. If no influencing agents are added to the flock, some agents will likely be lost from the flock, the flock may separate into multiple smaller flocks, and the flock(s) will almost certainly not travel in the desired direction.

In all of our experiments, we run 100 trials for each experimental setting and we use the same set of 100 random seeds for each set of experiments. The random seeds are used to determine the exact placement and orientation of all of the flocking agents at the start of a simulation experiment. In all of the graphs in the following sections, the error bars depict the sample standard deviation.

7.2 Drop Experimental Results

In the **Drop** case, we are able to drop each influencing agent a_i into the flock at whatever location $p_i(0)$ we desire.

The left-hand side of Figure 5 shows graphs that depict the average number of flocking agents lost when $n = 10$, $n = 20$ and $n = 50$. We report results for $n = 50$ in order to allow comparison with results in Sections 7.2.1 and 7.3. However, results for flocks of $n = 10$ and $n = 20$ highlight the strength of the graph approach in the **Drop** case.

Note that the graph approach loses fewer flocking agents in comparison to the other approaches when the flock size is small ($n = 10$ and $n = 20$) because in these cases agents are more sparse in the environment and hence tend to have fewer neighbors. This is important because agents with fewer neighbors are less likely to be inadvertently influenced by distant influencing agents. Additionally, the graph approach also performs better than the other approaches when n is small and the percentage of influencing agents in the flock is high. This is because the graph approach focuses on minimizing the number of unconnected flocking agents, so as a higher percentage of the flock is composed of influencing agents, the number of unconnected — and hence uninfluenced — flocking agents will decrease quicker under the graph approach than under other the approaches. Finally, note that in Figure 5(a) no flocking agents are lost by the graph approach when 50% of the flock is composed of influencing agents. This is intuitively because the influencing agents will be placed such that each flocking agent is influenced by at least one influencing agent.

The right-hand side of Figure 5 shows how many trials out of 100 resulted in any flocking agents becoming lost. All of the methods begin to have more trials in which no flocking agents are lost as k increases. However, it is notable how stark the difference is between the number of trials in which no flocking agents are lost when using the graph approach versus any other approach. This supports our assertion that the graph approach places influencing agents in initial positions that minimize the number of disconnected — and hence uninfluenced — flocking agents.

7.2.1 Drop + Reposition Experimental Results

In the **Drop** case, the influencing agents are initially dropped at their desired positions. However, in this section we consider an extension to the **Drop** case which we call the **Drop + Reposition** case. In this case, we initially drop the influencing agents at their desired positions but also allow them to reposition as needed in order to stay near their desired positions. In order to reposition, the influencing agents employ the hysteresis method described in Section 6. To be consistent with Section 7.3, we set $h_1 = 5$ units and $h_2 = 3$ units for the border approach placements and $h_1 = 10$ units and $h_2 = 3$ for the grid approach placements.

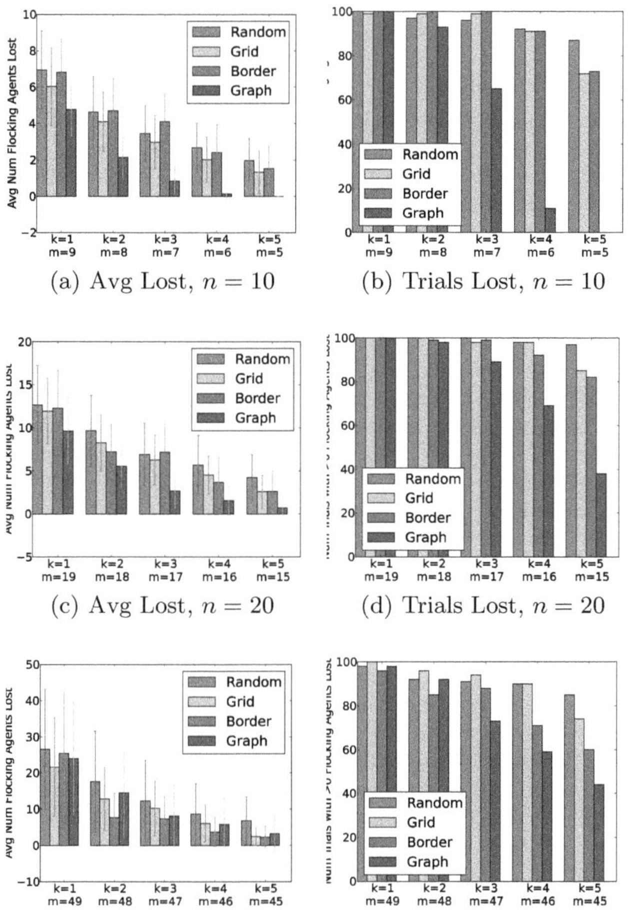

(a) Avg Lost, $n = 10$ (b) Trials Lost, $n = 10$

(c) Avg Lost, $n = 20$ (d) Trials Lost, $n = 20$

(e) Avg Lost, $n = 50$ (f) Trials Lost, $n = 50$

Figure 5: The average number of flocking agents lost (Avg Lost) when (a) $n = 10$ (c) $n = 20$ and (e) $n = 50$ and the number of trials in which any flocking agent was lost (Trials Lost) when (b) $n = 10$ (d) $n = 20$ and (f) $n = 50$. These results are obtained over 100 simulation experiments in the **Drop** case.

We present results using both the border approach and the grid approach for influencing agent placement in Figure 6(a). The influencing agents are initialized at their desired positions, and will return to these positions if they stray too far while attempting to influence the flock. Note that the difference in performance between different influencing agent speeds is small for both types of placement. This is because the influencing agents do not reposition very often, and since the speeds are only different while repositioning, the greater speeds do not have much affect on the results.

We can compare the results at speed **0.2** to the results for the border approach and the grid approach in Figure 5(e). These results look very similar, so we can conclude that, at least for these experimental settings, that the **Drop + Reposition** case does not provide any significant benefit over the **Drop** case. This is likely because there is not a significant need in this experimental setting for the influencing agents to reposition as they do not stray far from their desired positions. In the grid approach, the flock often converges before the influencing agents deviate from their desired positions by h_1 units. Hence, repositioning is rarely triggered. In the border approach, however, the influencing

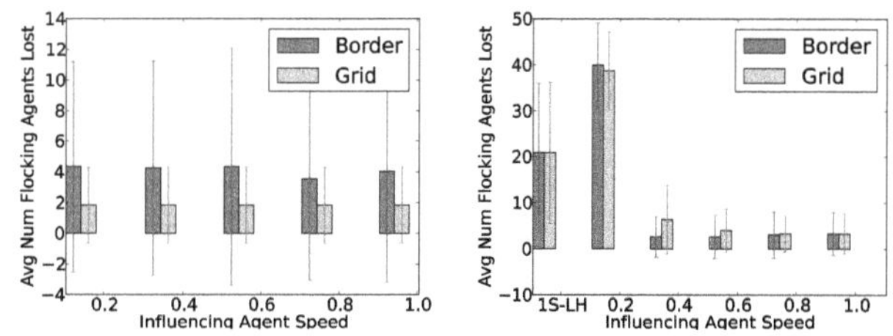

(a) **Drop + Reposition** case (b) **Dispatch** case

Figure 6: The average number of lost agents when $m = 45$ and $k = 5$. In (b), the influencing agents are initialized at two opposite corners.

agents sometimes travel away from their border positions, so repositioning is activated more frequently.

7.3 Dispatch Experimental Results

In the **Dispatch** case we initialize all of the influencing agents at one corner of the flock. The influencing agents first travel to their desired positions and then they focus on influencing the surrounding flocking agents in the **Dispatch** case. We use the hysteresis method described in Section 6 to control the switching of the influencing agents between repositioning to their desired position and attempting to influence nearby flocking agents. Based on a small amount of informal experimentation, we set $h_1 = 5$ units and $h_2 = 3$ units for the border approach and $h_1 = 10$ units and $h_2 = 3$ for the grid approach. In the border approach, the influencing agents are on the border and are more likely to leave the flock, so h_1 is smaller. In the grid approach, we are more tolerant on the distance that the influencing agents are away from their desired positions. In fact, a smaller h_1 in this case makes the influencing agents unnecessarily reposition inside the flock, which worsens performance. We do not use hysteresis for the random approach as there is no need to stay close to randomly chosen positions.

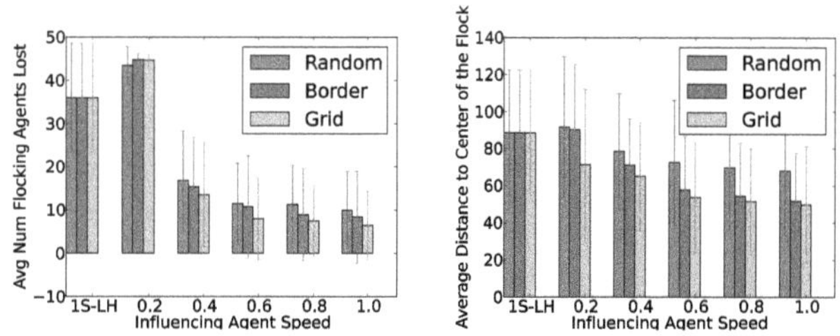

(a) Avg Lost, $n = 50$ (b) Avg Dist to Center

Figure 7: The average number of lost agents (Avg Lost) and the average distance to the center of the flock (Avg Dist to Center) when $m = 45$ and $k = 5$ in the **Dispatch** case.

In Figure 7 we show results in which the influencing agents are dispatched to three different types of positions: (1) random, (2) border and (3) grid. These positions are set as described in Section 5.

With regard to the x-axis labels of Figure 7, recall that in Section 6 we noted that in the **Dispatch** case, the influencing agents must move faster than the flocking agents when repositioning or otherwise the influencing agents may never reach their positions. In this graph we consider the effect of different influencing agent speeds on the number of lost flocking agents. **1S-LH** represents performance when, instead of repositioning, the influencing agents attempt to influence the flocking agents via performing 1-step lookahead from their initial positions. The flocking agents move 0.2 units per step, so **0.2** represents performance when the influencing agents move at the same speed as the flocking agents. Likewise, **0.4**, **0.6**, **0.8** and **1.0** represent the cases in which the influencing agents move two, three, four and five times as fast as the flocking agents, respectively.

A few trends stand out in the graphs of Figure 7; we discuss each of these trends in the following paragraphs.

We first consider Figure 7(a). These graphs show the average number of lost flocking agents in a flock where $m = 45$ and $k = 5$. As would be expected, **1S-LH** performs the same in each case since the influencing agents do not attempt to reposition. When $v_0 = \ldots = v_{n-1} = 0.2$, on average more flocking agents are lost than in **1S-LH** where the influencing agents do not attempt to reposition. This is because as the influencing agents enter the flock while traveling at the same velocity as the flocking agents, they push the flocking agents away and hence lose the entire flock in most cases. Across all of the positioning methods, faster speeds of the influencing agents results in fewer flocking agents becoming lost since the quicker speeds reduce the influence of the influencing agents on the flock while they are repositioning. However, the grid placement approach clearly loses fewer flocking agents across all of the cases in which the influencing agents are able to move quicker than the flocking agents.

Next we consider Figure 7(b). These graphs show the average distance of the flocking agents from the center of the flock at the point at which the flock converges. Faster influencing agents are able to reach their desired positions and begin influencing the flock towards θ^* much faster, which makes the flock more compact at convergence time.

When we consider both of the graphs from Figure 7 together, we conclude that the grid placement approach is best for this experimental setting in the **Dispatch** case. The grid approach loses fewer flocking agents than the border approach because the influencing agents in the border approach must travel longer distances across the flock in order to reach their desired positions. They must travel farther because some of the border positions are inherently located farther from the influencing agents' starting spot since they are located on the borders of the flock. This long distance traveling across the flock leads to lost flocking agents because it tends to push the flock to travel in the direction the influencing agents are traveling. This forces the influencing agents to work to reverse this effect once they are at their desired positions.

7.3.1 *Multiple Initialization Points*

We assume in the beginning of this section that the influencing agents are initialized at one point outside of the flock, which is, concretely, at one corner. Naturally, they can be initialized at multiple points instead of just one. In Figure 6(b), we examine the case in which the influencing agents are initialized at two opposite corners of the flock. In both the grid approach case and the border approach case, we initialize each influencing agent at the corner that is closest to its desired position. Initializing influencing agents in multiple corners generally has better performance than just initializing all agents at one corner. This is because the influencing agents do not have to travel as far to reach their desired positions. We leave a more thorough examination of multiple initialization points for future work.

7.4 Discussion

One impact of this work is to take a step towards the practical realization of influencing a flock by extending our previous positive results that showed that flocks could indeed be controlled if influencing agents are placed randomly in the flock [5]. In particular, the work presented in this paper contributes by determining that performance (1) can improve if we are able to control the initial positions of the influencing agents as in the **Drop** case and (2) is still generally positive even if influencing agents must be initialized outside the flock as in the **Dispatch** case.

The time that the influencing agents consume to travel to their desired destinations dominates in the **Dispatch** case. The border approach and grid approach have similar performance in the **Drop** case, as shown in Section 7.2. Their performance differs in the **Dispatch** case where the influencing agents take longer to reach their desired positions in the border approach. Our experiment in which influencing agents were dispatched from two initialization points shows that when less time is consumed traveling to desired positions, the border approach loses slightly fewer flocking agents on average than the grid approach when the influencing agents travel at faster speeds than the flocking agents.

Of course, we cannot completely compare the **Drop** case to the **Dispatch** case without being able to run the graph approach in the **Dispatch** case as well. The solid performance of the graph approach in the **Drop** case hints that it may perform well in the **Dispatch** case. We leave the task of implementing a more efficient or approximate graph approach for future work.

8. CONCLUSION

In this paper we consider where to place influencing agents that we add to a flock comprised of agents which we have no direct control over, but that we wish to influence towards a particular behavior. We present multiple methodologies as well as experimental results for placing influencing agents into a flock in two cases: (1) where we initially place the agents anywhere and (2) where the agents must travel to their desired positions after being initially placed outside the flock. Experimental results demonstrate that in (1), our graph approach performs better than other approaches in terms of the number of trials in which flocking agents are lost and the average number of flocking agents lost. In (2), the grid approach performs best in terms of the average number of lost flocking agents and flock compactness.

Positioning of influencing agents in a flock is a fertile research area with plenty of opportunities for future work. In our future work we plan to design a more efficient graph-based placement approach for use in the **Dispatch** case. Additionally, we intend to further consider the effect of utilizing multiple stations from which the influencing agents could emerge in the **Dispatch** case.

9. ACKNOWLEDGEMENTS

This work has taken place in the Learning Agents Research Group (LARG) at UT Austin. LARG research is supported in part by NSF (CNS-1330072, CNS-1305287), ONR (21C184-01), and AFOSR (FA8750-14-1-0070, FA9550-14-1-0087).

REFERENCES

[1] H. Celikkanat and E. Sahin. Steering self-organized robot flocks through externally guided individuals. *Neural Computing and Applications*, 19(6):849–865, September 2010.

[2] I. D. Couzin, J. Krause, N. R. Franks, and S. A. Levin. Effective leadership and decision-making in animal groups on the move. *Nature*, 433(7025):513–516, February 2005.

[3] E. Ferrante, A. E. Turgut, N. Mathews, M. Birattari, and M. Dorigo. Flocking in stationary and non-stationary environments: A novel communication strategy for heading alignment. In *Proceedings of the 11th International Conference on Parallel Problem Solving from Nature: Part II*, PPSN'10, pages 331–340. Springer-Verlag, 2010.

[4] K. Genter, N. Agmon, and P. Stone. Ad hoc teamwork for leading a flock. In *AAMAS'13*, May 2013.

[5] K. Genter and P. Stone. Influencing a flock via ad hoc teamwork. In *Ninth International Conference on Swarm Intelligence (ANTS'14)*, September 2014.

[6] J. Han, M. Li, and L. Guo. Soft control on collective behavior of a group of autonomous agents by a shill agent. *Systems Science and Complexity*, 19:54–62, 2006.

[7] A. Jadbabaie, J. Lin, and A. Morse. Coordination of groups of mobile autonomous agents using nearest neighbor rules. *IEEE Transactions on Automatic Control*, 48(6):988 – 1001, Jun 2003.

[8] S. Luke, C. Cioffi-Revilla, L. Panait, K. Sullivan, and G. Balan. Mason: A multi-agent simulation environment. *Simulation: Transactions of the Society for Modeling and Simulation International*, 81(7):517–527, 2005.

[9] C. W. Reynolds. Flocks, herds and schools: A distributed behavioral model. *SIGGRAPH*, 21:25–34, August 1987.

[10] J. Shang, S. Combes, B. Finio, and R. Wood. Artificial insect wings of diverse morphology for flapping-wing micro air vehicles. *Bioinspiration & Biomimetics*, 4(3), 2009.

[11] H. Su, X. Wang, and Z. Lin. Flocking of multi-agents with a virtual leader. *IEEE Transactions on Automatic Control*, 54(2):293–307, Feb 2009.

[12] T. Vicsek, A. Czirok, E. Ben-Jacob, I. Cohen, and O. Sochet. Novel type of phase transition in a system of self-driven particles. *PHYS REV LETT.*, 75:1226, 1995.

Particle Field Optimization: A New Paradigm for Swarm Intelligence

Nathan Bell
Carleton University
Ottawa, Ontario
Canada
nathanbell.42@gmail.com

B. John Oommen*
Carleton University
Ottawa, Ontario
Canada
oommen@scs.carleton.ca

ABSTRACT

Particle Swarm Optimization (PSO) has been a popular meta-heuristic for black-box optimization for almost two decades. In essence, within this paradigm, the system is fully defined by a swarm of "particles" each characterized by a set of features such as its position, velocity and acceleration. The consequent optimized global best solution is obtained by comparing the personal best solutions of the entire swarm. Many variations and extensions of PSO have been developed since its creation in 1995, and the algorithm remains a popular topic of research. In this work we submit a new, abstracted, perspective of the PSO system, where we attempt to move away from the swarm of individual particles, but rather characterize each particle by a field or distribution. The strategy that updates the various fields is akin to Thompson's sampling. By invoking such an abstraction, we present the novel Particle *Field* Optimization (PFO) algorithm which harnesses this new perspective to achieve a model and behavior completely distinct from the family of traditional PSO systems.

Categories:
G.1.6 [Optimization]: Global optimization;
I.2.11 [Distributed AI]: Multiagent systems
Keywords: *Particle Swarm Optimization/Intelligence.*

1. INTRODUCTION

The efficient use of resources is a fundamental problem which permeates every aspect of our lives. Nearly every decision we make can be interpreted, in some way, to involve the concept of minimizing the "cost", or maximizing the "returns" of our actions. In fact, this concept can be considered to be a core challenge of life of any kind, as resources and energy are inherently limited, and must be used efficiently in order to ensure long-term survival and prosperity. Any form of "intelligence", then, *must* have the ability to deal with problems of this type.

The field of function optimization presents a formalized framework for modelling and solving certain problems of this type. Given an "objective" function, which takes a number of parameters as its input, the goal is to find the combination of parameter values which returns the "best" value. This framework is abstract enough that a wide variety of different problems can be viewed as "function optimization" problems.

The objective function of an optimization problem can be any function which maps any number of parameters to a single final resultant value. Because of this non-specific definition, there are an extremely wide variety of distinct properties that these functions can have. This variety of properties presents a significant challenge when approaching function optimization. Many properties, such as discontinuities, multi-modal complexity, and elaborate constraints on the input values, render "standard" optimization methods impossible or infeasible, and so currently, new methods must be created and tailored to functions with specific properties.

"Black-box" optimization is a category of optimization problems dealing with functions about which no information is available. The fact that these functions are totally *unknown* presents a unique challenge for optimization. Without any knowledge of the function, algebraic manipulations (such as computing derivatives) are impossible. Thus, traditional analytical methods of discovering the optimum, no longer apply. In fact, it is unknown whether or not a single global optimum exists at all, and it is impossible to verify whether any solution found is globally optimal. The task of optimization, then, must be approached from a different perspective. Finding the optimal value becomes a search process within an unknown, and often infinite, solution space.

There exist a wide variety of strategies for approaching this search problem, each making use of its own distinct principles and perspectives. One such strategy is Particle Swarm Optimization (PSO). Created in 1995 as the result of experiments modelling a "collision-less" bird-flocking swarm behavior, the PSO algorithm has remained a popular subject of research and development. The PSO algorithm, briefly surveyed in Section 2.2, consists of a population of extremely basic individuals or particles which "fly" through the solution space. Through communication, these basic individuals find "good" solutions to the black-box optimization problem.

Many variations of the basic PSO algorithm have been proposed, seeking to improve the algorithm and introduce new behaviour to the algorithm. Among these variants is the Bare Bones Particle Swarm (BBPS), which applies an abstraction to the behavior of the particles within the swarm. In this paper, we show that inherent in the BBPS algorithm, there exists a previously-unexplored opportunity for an additional level of abstraction. Indeed, we show that each particle can be abstracted by a field or distribution,

*The second author is also an *Adjunct Professor* with the University of Agder in Grimstad, Norway.

Appears in: *Proceedings of the 14th International Conference on Autonomous Agents and Multiagent Systems (AAMAS 2015), Bordini, Elkind, Weiss, Yolum (eds.), May 4–8, 2015, Istanbul, Turkey.*

and where the form/parameters of the distribution are updated by using a scheme akin to Thompson's sampling, leading to a completely new and unique perspective on particle swarm systems. Taking advantage of this new perspective, we propose a novel search algorithm known as Particle *Field* Optimization (PFO), which, to the best of our knowledge, is both unique and pioneering.

The rest of the paper is organized as follows. Section 2 contains a fairly comprehensive overview of the field including that of black-box optimization, meta-heuristics and the PSO. The paper then continues to the submission of the new PFO paradigm in Section 3. Section 4 details the experimental results obtained by testing our scheme and comparing it with a benchmark algorithm on a *set* of internationally-recognized benchmark functions. Section 5 concludes the paper and presents possible avenues for future work.

2. SURVEY OF THE FIELD

2.1 Black-box Optimization: Meta-Heuristics

When dealing with black-box optimization, the only way of gaining information about the objective function is to generate and evaluate potential solutions. By observing the results of these function evaluations, some limited information can be deduced about the function, which can then be used to guide the search process. The most straightforward approach to this would be a basic, deterministic hill-climbing algorithm. A hill climbing algorithm simply generates a number of "adjacent" solutions to the current best-found solution, and updates that best-found solution if an adjacent solution is better. The process then loops until no better adjacent solution is discovered. This approach will quickly guarantee convergence to some *locally* optimal solution, but is not well suited to the problem of black-box optimization, in general. The majority of real-life applications involve functions with very complex, multi-modal solution spaces, and since nothing is known about the function being optimized, it must be assumed that these complexities are present. On such functions, a hill-climbing algorithm will perform poorly compared to other methods, exploiting the local information but becoming stuck in local optima.

In order to perform well on unknown functions, it is essential for the scheme to avoid stagnating or converging to a suboptimal point. If we consider the hill-climbing algorithm, the opposite extreme would be an algorithm which simply generates, and evaluates, totally random solutions within the solution space. Clearly, this strategy would not become stuck in local optima as the hill-climbing strategy would. However, simply generating random solutions is no better than one which sequentially generates and tests every possible solution, and so this strategy is not feasible either, due to potentially-infinite size of the solution space.

We thus argue that neither the extreme *exploitation* phase of a hill-climber, nor the extreme *exploration* phase of generating totally random solutions, are suitable for the problem of black-box optimization. To effectively and efficiently search the unknown space of a black-box function, an algorithm must strike a happy medium between these extremes. *Exploitation* is necessary to find the locally optimal solution in some area, and *exploration* is necessary to escape local optima and locate more areas for exploitation. This strategy of balancing exploitation with random exploration describes a category of algorithms known as "Meta-Heuristics".

The term "meta-heuristic" is a combination of the modifier "meta" ("beyond"), and the word "heuristic" ("proceeding to a solution by trial-and-error or by rules that are only loosely defined"). In general, a meta-heuristic algorithm is one which combines randomization with a higher-level guiding process to perform a search of some kind. This "higher guiding process" is what differentiates a meta-heuristic method from a *simple* heuristic method. The heuristic process within a meta-heuristic is modified by this guiding process, thus elevating the behavior to be *beyond* a simple heuristic.

Of particular interest to us in this work, are those algorithms that model so-called "swarming" behavior. In nature, there exist many examples of social creatures that cooperatively act together and display a behavior which, as a whole, is beyond the individual capabilities of the creatures themselves. This phenomenon is known as "Swarm Intelligence" (SI), and provides a very interesting perspective for problem solving. In an SI system, a population of rudimentary or primitive "individuals" work and interact with one another in order to solve a higher-level problem beyond the capabilities of any single individual.

2.2 Particle Swarm Optimization

The core PSO algorithm consists of a population of particles, which act according to individual behavior and influence each other via communication. A PSO particle i consists of a position $\vec{X_i}$ within the solution space, a velocity $\vec{V_i}$, and a personal best found point $\vec{P_i}$. The algorithm begins with an initialization stage, which is followed by an iterative simulation stage.

During initialization, the population of particles is created and their positions and velocities, are assigned random values. Following this, the simulation stage begins, and it runs indefinitely unless a termination criterion is met or the algorithm is manually stopped. At each step of the simulation, particles update their velocities, move accordingly, and evaluate their new location. Their corresponding personal best solution is also updated, if necessary. A particle i updates its velocity $\vec{V_i}$, and position $\vec{X_i}$, according to the equation:

$$\vec{V_i} = \omega\vec{V_i} + \vec{U}[0,\phi_p] \otimes (\vec{P_i} - \vec{X_i}) + \vec{U}[0,\phi_g] \otimes (\vec{P_g} - \vec{X_i})$$
$$\vec{X_i} = \vec{X_i} + \vec{V_i}.$$

Once a termination criterion is met, or the simulation is manually stopped, the position of the global best particle $\vec{P_g}$, which represents the best solution found by the algorithm, is returned as the output.

2.3 Variations/Extensions of the PSO

Due to the simple and flexible nature of the PSO algorithm, countless variations and extensions have been proposed since it's initial creation, and it remains an active topic of research today. The research and development of the PSO algorithm is also quite varied, with many distinct strategies and approaches being explored. Some of these strategies seek to improve existing components of the PSO algorithm [4], [8] [11], or to introduce adaptive behaviors to various levels of sophistication over the core algorithm to improve useability [15], [17], [19]. Other strategies include hybridizing the PSO algorithm with other population-based ideas such as genetic algorithms [1], [5], [10] [16].

Although the high level behavior of the PSO algorithm is very complex and difficult to analyze, analyses of simplified versions have been reported [2], [8], [13], [14]. This has shown that the PSO algorithm displays a number of biases, including a bias towards the center of the initialization area [12], and a bias favoring movement parallel to the axes [18].

2.4 Bare Bones Particle Swarm

The Bare Bones Particle Swarm (BBPS) algorithm [6] is a PSO variant which seeks to emulate the high-level behavior of the basic PSO algorithm, while simultaneously using a much simpler particle-update strategy. Observations of the basic PSO system suggested that very similar behavioral patterns could be achieved without the complicated velocity and acceleration components. Further, observations of a *single* particle using the standard velocity strategy, with the system in a state of swarm stagnation (i.e. when the personal and global best points remain constant), produced a histogram which displayed a distinct bell-curved shape. This phenomenon led to the conjecture that rather than dealing with the particle velocities and accelerations, each particle could be updated by merely sampling a random distribution constructed to approximate the observed histogram.

The BBPS algorithm entirely eliminates the velocity component of the particle and merely determines the particle's next position by sampling a Gaussian random distribution. This Gaussian distribution is constructed and sampled individually for each dimension. The mean of this distribution is set to be the midpoint between the global best found point and the particle's own best found point, and the variance is set as the absolute distance between the global and personal best points for each dimension. Given a particle i with position $\vec{X_i}$, whose personal best point is $\vec{P_i}$ and for which the global best point is $\vec{P_g}$, the particle's next position is determined according to:

$$\vec{P_m} = \frac{\vec{P_i} + \vec{P_g}}{2}, \qquad \vec{X_i} = \vec{\mathcal{N}}(\vec{P_m}, \vec{\sigma^2}),$$

where $\vec{\mathcal{N}}$ represents a function which creates a Gaussian random vector dimension-by-dimension, centred on $\vec{P_m}$. $\vec{\sigma}$ is a vector of standard deviations for each dimension, set to be proportional to the absolute values of the difference between the $\vec{P_i}$ and $\vec{P_g}$ points for each dimension.

This update strategy is marginally more abstract than the basic PSO velocity strategy, since the particles no longer "fly" through the space, but the general behavior of the swarm remains the same. At a higher level, the algorithm still involves a population of particles which move through the solution space, and which are influenced by the memories of their best found positions and the communication of the global best found position.

3. THE PARTICLE FIELD OPTIMIZATION (PFO) ALGORITHM

3.1 The Need for Further Abstraction

The BBPS model discards the velocity component of the basic PSO model and introduces a more abstract method for updating the positions of the particles. However, if we take a closer look at the consequences of this change, it is possible to take the abstraction to a level that is even higher, whence one discovers a completely new perspective and new avenues for development.

To motivate this abstraction, we first consider the issue of what constitutes a single particle in these two models. In the basic PSO model, an individual particle consists of: A current position, a current velocity and a personal best found position. Each of these components is required in order to determine the subsequent position of the particle for the next iteration. The particle's position in the next iteration depends upon its current position and the particle's velocity. The updated velocity, in turn, depends on the particle's current velocity, the particle's personal best found position and the population's global best found position. Each component of the particle contributes to the update function and must be maintained for use in the next iteration.

In the BBPS model, the velocity term is removed and an individual particle consists of only a current position and a personal best found position. However, unlike the basic PSO model, updating the particle does *not* require both of these components. Specifically, the position of the particle in the next iteration is independent of the position of the particle in the current iteration. When updating a particle, the next position is generated by *sampling* a Gaussian random distribution, which, in turn, is constructed using the particle's personal best, and the communicated global best points. After creation, the position is used for only *one* purpose, i.e., the updating of the particle's personal best found point. The global best point is, thereafter, updated using the population's personal best found points, and so does not rely *directly* on the particle's current position either.

As a result, it is possible to remove the particle's position component from the model entirely. Rather than storing and maintaining the particle's current position, we can modify the update operations to work directly with the particle's personal best point while maintaining equivalent behavior. A new point is generated by sampling the constructed random distribution. If the new point has a better value than the particle's personal best found point, the best found point is set equal to the new point. The only difference is that this newly generated point is temporary, rather than being maintained for the next iteration. The algorithm's behavior with this abstracted model is unchanged, but the metaphors and concepts of the original PSO may require re-examination.

After removing the particle's current position component, an individual particle now consists of only a personal best found position. The particle no longer exists as an explicit point in space. Conceptually, the particle's personal best point is a memory that the particle maintains of the best point it has evaluated so far, and the global best position which can be thought of as being the *collective* memory of the population. These two "memories" define the random distribution used to update the particle. Though the particle no longer exists as an explicit point in space, we can, instead, think of the particle's "position" in that space as being defined by the random *distribution* itself. This is because this distribution represents the probability field of possible positions for the particle. From this perspective, the particle exists as a random *field* defined by its own memory and the collective memory of the population.

With the new concept of what the population individuals are, the high-level perspectives of the algorithm change drastically. The metaphor of a swarm of particles "flying" through space no longer aptly describes the high-level concept of the algorithm. Rather, the algorithm now consists of a population of "particle fields" which move throughout the space in a different way. Because the "positions" of these "particle fields" are defined as random distributions, "evaluating" a "particle field's" current "position" is non-deterministic, and so these "particle fields" do not necessarily have to "move" to explore new points. These "particle fields" remain "stationary" in the space until either the individual's personal best point changes, or the population's global best point changes. This population of "particle fields" can, itself, be perceived as a random field of particles defined as a mixture distribution made up of each individual distribution. This population level distribution can be thought of as an abstract representation of a particle swarm, representing a probability distribution of all possible particle locations for the next iteration. This perspective of the high-level concept is significantly different than the BBPS algorithm, although their behaviors are analogous. However, with this new perspective, it is possible to explore new directions in improving or changing the behavior of the algorithm.

3.2 How the PFO Abstraction is Affected

With this new perspective of the BBPS algorithm, we can begin taking steps toward a new algorithm using this abstracted philosophy. In this abstracted BBPS model, each individual in the population would generate and evaluate a single new point per iteration so as to maintain the concept of an individual representing a single particle. However, it is not necessary to maintain this metaphor in our new model, and so we can approach the generation and evaluation of candidate solutions from a distinct perspective.

Rather than have each individual directly representing a candidate solution in and of itself as in traditional PSO algorithms, we use the population in a more indirect way to explore the solution space. Collectively, the population represents a complex, finite mixture distribution made up of an underlying set of simple multivariate Gaussian distributions, which are defined by the particle field individuals. Traditionally, each individual would generate, and evaluate exactly one new solution. However, this population distribution can be used to guide the search in a different way.

Candidate solutions are instead generated by sampling this population-level distribution. Although the population-level distribution is complex, the sampling process is simple. The population-level distribution is a finite mixture distribution with known component distributions. Therefore, sampling this complex population-level distribution is a simple matter of sampling one of the underlying component distributions, selected at random. In the context of the population, this means randomly selecting a particle field individual and then sampling the multivariate Gaussian distribution defining that particle field's "position".

Once the candidate solution points have been generated and evaluated, each particle field individual in the population is updated. Each individual is updated using the candidate solutions generated from that individual's own distribution. If a candidate solution is better than the individual's own personal best point, the personal best point is set equal to that solution. In this way, the population defines a random distribution which guides the search and generation of candidate solutions, which are then used to update the population and redefine the search area for the next iteration.

This concept of the population guiding the search leads us to the next step toward a new, distinct algorithm. Because the complex distribution created by the population is a finite mixture distribution, it is a simple matter to apply a weighting scheme to the distribution. By weighting the contribution of each particle field to the population distribution, it is possible to incorporate additional information into the search process, independent of the underlying PSO processes.

Finally, since the population of the particle field individuals no longer directly represents candidate solutions, it is no longer necessary that the number of candidate solutions generated and evaluated at each iteration equals the size of the population. Because of this, it is possible to further modify the behavior by using different relative population and candidate solution point pool sizes. Due to the nature of the population distribution, changing the number of particle field individuals in the population effects the "resolution" of this distribution.

3.3 Implementing the PFO Abstraction

With these changes taken into account, we have now moved away from the traditional PSO paradigm and arrived at a new, distinct algorithm, which will be hereafter referred to as Particle *Field* Optimization (PFO). This algorithm consists of a population of "particle field" individuals and a "point pool" of candidate solution points. The population of particle field individuals uses PSO principles to guide the search of the solution space, which is carried out by generating and evaluating, the pool of candidate solution points. Analogous to traditional PSO algorithms, the PFO algorithm consists of an initialization phase and a simulation phase which loops until some termination criteria is met, at which point the best solution found by the algorithm is returned as output. As its parameters, the algorithm takes an initialization range, a population size and a pool size. The population size parameter specifies the number of particle field individuals which form the population used to guide the search. The pool size parameter specifies the number of candidate solutions to be generated and evaluated, at each step of the simulation. A weighting function may be specified, which weights the contribution of each individual to the population-wide distribution.

The initialization phase initializes the population of particle field individuals. A particle field individual stores only a personal best found position, and so the initialization of these individuals is simple. Each individual is assigned an initial personal best point by sampling a uniform random distribution defined by the initialization range.

The simulation phase loops until a termination criteria is met, typically the maximum number of iterations. Each iteration consists of two phases. In the first phase, candidate solutions are generated. These candidate solutions are generated by sampling the mixture distribution defined by the population of particle field individuals. For each point in the point pool we do the following: A particle field individual is selected at random from the population, according to some weighting scheme. Then, the point is generated by sampling the random distribution defined by the selected individual. This random distribution is constructed using the individual's personal best, and the global (or neighborhood) best points in the same way as the BBPS method does. Given a particle field with personal best point $\vec{P_i}$ and for which the global (or neighborhood) best point is $\vec{P_g}$, the position of the candidate solution point, $\vec{c}$, is determined according to:

$$\vec{P_m} = \frac{\vec{P_i} + \vec{P_g}}{2}, \qquad \vec{\sigma^2} = |\vec{P_i} - \vec{P_g}|, \qquad \vec{c} = \vec{\mathcal{N}}(\vec{P_m}, \vec{\sigma^2}).$$

Once the candidate solution has been generated, the objective function is evaluated, using this generated point as its input, in order to assign it a value. After each candidate solution in the point pool has been generated, the second phase begins. In this phase, the population of particle field individuals is updated. Each individual updates its own best found point using the set of candidate solutions generated from its own distribution. Each individual selects the best point from the set of associated candidate solutions. If the best associated candidate solution is better than the individual's personal best found point, the individual sets its personal best found point to be equal to that candidate solution point. The pool of candidate solutions is then "emptied", and the simulation continues to the next iteration.

Once the termination criteria have been met, the global best found point is returned as output of the algorithm. The formal algorithm follows in Algorithm 1.

Algorithm 1 Particle Field Optimization Algorithm

Input:
Function $f()$ to be optimized
Initialization range *lbound, ubound*
Particle field population size n_{pop}
Candidate solution point pool size n_{pool}
Weighting function $w()$
Output:
Point $\vec{P_g}$ representing best found solution
Method:

```
create particle field population P with size n_pop
create candidate solution point pool C with size n_pool
for each particle field i ∈ P do
    P_i ⇐ U[lbound, ubound]
    if f(P_i) < f(P_g) then
        P_g ⇐ P_i
    end if
end for

while termination criteria not met do
    for each candidate solution point c ∈ C do
        select particle field i ∈ P with probability w(i) / Σ_{p∈P} w(p)
        c ⇐ N((P_i + P_g)/2, |P_i − P_g|)
        S_i ⇐ S_i ∪ {c}
    end for
    for each particle field i ∈ P do
        choose point c_min from S_i which minimizes f(c_min)
        if f(c_min) < f(P_i) then
            P_i ⇐ c_min
            if f(P_i) < f(P_g) then
                P_g ⇐ P_i
            end if
        end if
        S_i ⇐ ∅
    end for
end while
return P_g
```

4. THE PFO: EXPERIMENTAL RESULTS

4.1 The Experimental Test Bed

In order to accurately measure the performance of a black-box optimization algorithm, empirical testing must be carried out on a variety of test functions. The test suite selected to evaluate the PFO algorithm consists of a variety of different test functions commonly used for evaluating PSO related algorithms. This suite includes the Rosenbrock, Shaffer F6, Sphere, Rastrigin and Griewank functions. The full suite, including the choice of the dimensionality for each function, is presented in Table 1.

Table 1: The set of the test functions used in the test suite.

Function	Dim	Formula
Rosenbrock	2	$(1-x_1)^2 + 100(x_2 - x_1^2)^2$
Schaffer F6	2	$0.5 + \frac{sin^2(\sqrt{x_1^2+x_2^2})-0.5}{[1+0.001*(x_1^2+x_2^2)]^2}$
Sphere	10	$\sum_{i=1}^{d} x_i^2$
Rastrigin	10	$10d + \sum_{i=1}^{d}\left[x_i^2 - 10cos(2\pi x_i)\right]$
	20	
Griewank	2	$1 + \frac{1}{4000}\sum_{i=1}^{d} x_i^2 - \prod_{i=1}^{d}\cos\left(\frac{x_i}{\sqrt{i}}\right)$
	20	

4.2 Overview of Testing Strategy

The PFO algorithm can be configured using three primary parameters which modify the algorithm's behavior. These primary parameters are the "pool size" parameter, the "population size" parameter and the weighting scheme used by the algorithm. It is important to recall that the number of function evaluations performed by the PFO algorithm is dictated by the pool size parameter, rather than the population size parameter. For this reason, a single value was chosen for the pool size parameter for each function in order to ensure a consistent number of function evaluations. Testing was carried out on the PFO algorithm in order to investigate the range of behaviors possessed by the algorithm, and the effects of each parameter on that behavior. Consequently, a number of different values were chosen for each parameter, and tests were performed for each combination. A detailed justification of the parameter values and weighting schemes chosen for testing can be found in [3], and is omitted here in the interest of brevity.

The PFO algorithm was created by introducing a number of changes to the BBPS algorithm. As a result, the BBPS algorithm provides the best baseline point of comparison for assessing the effects of these changes. In addition to this, the BBPS algorithm takes only one parameter, which is the population size parameter. For each test, this parameter was set equal to the corresponding PFO pool size in order to ensure that the number of function evaluations remained consistent between the algorithms. Because of this, the BBPS algorithm required no parameter tuning itself, and so provides a very straightforward and dependable baseline of comparison.

4.3 Experimental Results

We now present the results of the testing carried out on the PFO algorithm. Due to the large number of tests required to adequately investigate the PFO algorithms, we summarize each set of tests rather briefly and include plot-

Table 2: A brief overview of the results for each test function.

Function	Dim	BBPS	Best PFO	Worst PFO
Sphere	2	$5.5282E^{-66}$	$1.3299E^{-89}$	$4.2189E^{-40}$
Rosenbrock	2	0.0170	$8.1423E^{-5}$	0.4980
Schaffer F6	2	0.0100	$7.6178E^{-3}$	0.0328
Rastrigin	10	4.4663	2.7609	6.5798
	20	17.5572	11.0465	21.3381
Griewank	2	0.0129	$5.6518E^{-3}$	0.2599
	20	0.0242	0.0206	0.0282

ted results for only a portion of the tests. Admittedly, due to space limitations, the results presented here are not comprehensive – a more detailed exegesis of the results of an exhaustive set of functions, dimensions, tests and parameter settings can be found in [3]. A brief overview of the best and worst results on each test function is presented in Table 2, and depicted graphically in the respective graphs.

4.3.1 Sphere Function

PFO configurations with a particle field population size smaller than the pool size performed best on the Sphere function, outperforming the baseline (i.e., the BBPS) considerably. When the population size was equal to the pool size, performance was similar to the BBPS, and when the population size was larger than the pool size, the performance was considerably degraded. In all cases, there was a relatively small amount of variance in performance between the tested schemes.

4.3.2 Rosenbrock Function

For the Rosenbrock function, PFO configurations using a population size of half the pool size performed poorly when compared to the baseline BBPS. Despite the Rosenbrock function being unimodal, these configurations quickly became stagnant and got stuck in a sub-optimal area within the first 50 iterations. Variations in the performance among the weighting schemes with this population size was also considerable, but with no particular outliers. Configurations with a population size equal to the pool size performed, on average, considerably better than the BBPS. The variation in performance among the weighting schemes with this population size was significant, with the Average weighting scheme performing dramatically worse than the others. All the PFO configurations with a population size of twice the pool size performed dramatically better than the baseline.

4.3.3 Schaffer F6 Function

In the case of the Schaffer F6 function, PFO configurations using a population size smaller than the pool size performed poorly compared to the baseline BBPS. The variation in performance among weighting schemes in this group was fairly significant, with two performing much worse than the others. These were the Personal Best and Relative Average weighting schemes. With a population size equal to the pool size and to twice the pool size, the PFO showed, on average, a small improvements over the baseline – which was a result unique to the Schaffer F6 function.

Figure 1: A selection of performance results for the Rosenbrock-2 function

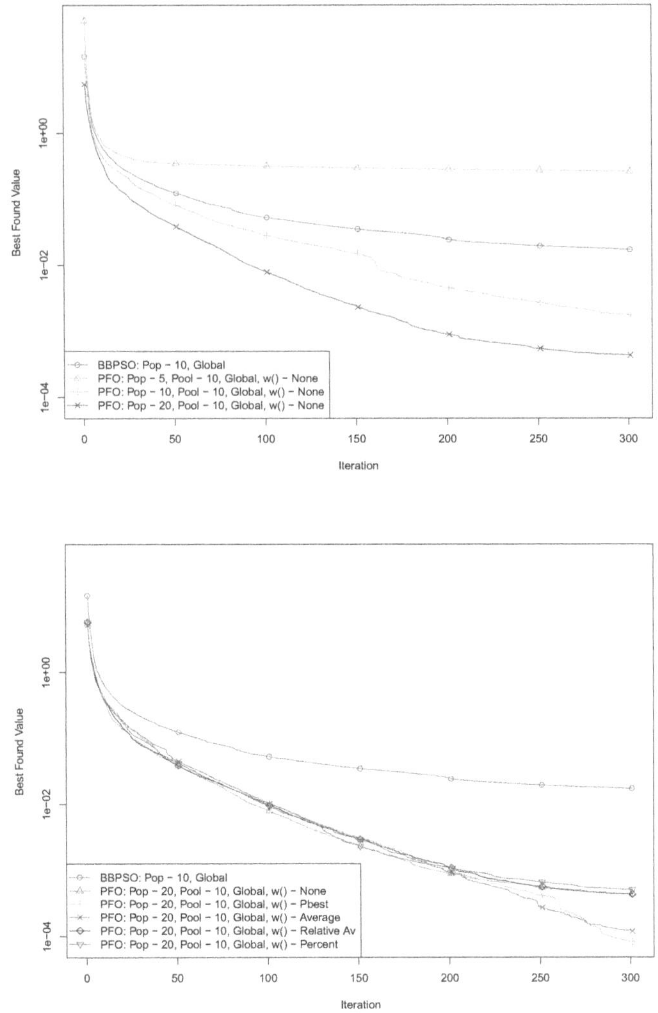

4.3.4 Rastrigin Function

Between the 10 and 20-dimensional versions of the Rastrigin function, the impact of the relative values of the particle field population size and pool size parameters were consistent. When using a population size less than the pool size, performance was poor compared to the BBPS. With a population size equal to the pool size the performance was, on average, similar to the baseline BBPS and with a population size greater than the pool size, performance was significantly improved over the baseline BBPS. The impact of the weighting scheme on performance was relatively insignificant.

4.3.5 Griewank Function

Results on the Griewank function varied between the function's 2 and 20 dimension versions. On the 2-dimensional Griewank function, PFO configurations using population sizes smaller than the pool size performed much worse than the baseline BBPS. PFO configurations with larger population sizes performed much better than the BBPS.

On the 20-dimensional Griewank function, the configurations with different relative population sizes performed about the same as one another. However, the smaller relative population size performed slightly *better* than the population size equal to the pool size, which, in turn, performed slightly better than the larger relative population size. This would suggest that as the dimensionality of the Griewank function increases, the larger population size becomes less beneficial, and more detrimental. Considering this along with the results of the Sphere function, this observation is in line with the idea that the Griewank function becomes "easier" as the number of dimensions is increased.

4.4 Discussions

From analyzing the results presented, it is possible to identify some patterns and gain insight into the behavior of the PFO algorithm, as well as the effects of the algorithm's parameters. From a cursory glance, the test results show a great amount of variation among the different configurations of the PFO algorithm on each test function, with many configurations performing significantly better than the baseline BBPS, and some performing significantly worse. This high variance among results shows that the different parameter values chosen had a significant impact on the PFO's behavior and performance.

We can summarize the overall results as below:

1. Among these results, a clear pattern emerges, suggesting a significant correlation between the particle field population size and the behavior of the PFO algorithm. On all the test functions, with the exception of the Griewank 20 function, the final results are divided by the particle field population size into distinct clusters. With the pool size parameter set as a single value for each function, the difference in the PFO configurations within these clusters is only the weighting scheme used. This suggests that the particle field population sizes chosen for each test "dominated" the choice of the weighting scheme, as there was no overlap between these groups.

2. In addition to this distinct grouping, a correlation between the relative order of these groups and the particle field population size can be observed. With the exception of the Sphere function, a larger particle field population size was correlated with a better best value found. On the Sphere function, the opposite is observed, where a smaller population size is correlated with a better best value found. In addition to this exception we observe the previously-mentioned exceptions of the Griewank 20 function, on which the particle field population size did not show such a distinct clustering on the final results. These exceptions can be explained when considering the plotted test results showing the average best value found at each iteration. Rather than make a correlation between the particle field population size and the final result, it is more accurate to correlate the particle field population size with the "exploratory" behavior of the algorithm. This correlation is in line with results on *all* test functions, including the Sphere and Griewank functions.

3. In the case of the Sphere function, a higher "exploratory" behavior would show poor performance compared to a more "exploitative" behavior, due to the simplicity of the function. This is in line with the plotted results, as configurations with smaller particle field population

Figure 2: A selection of performance results for the Rastrigin-10 function.

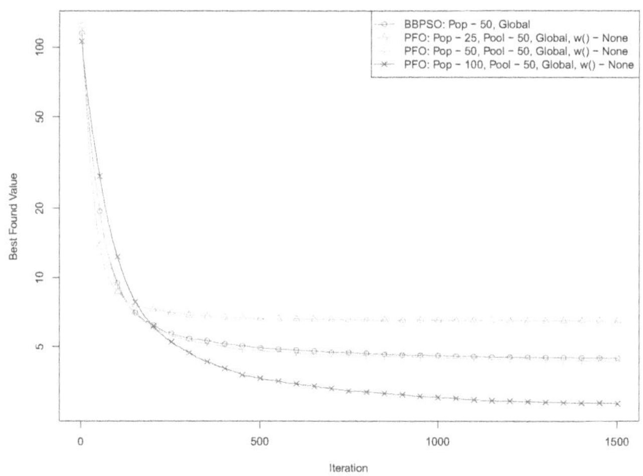

Figure 3: A selection of performance results for the Griewank-2 function.

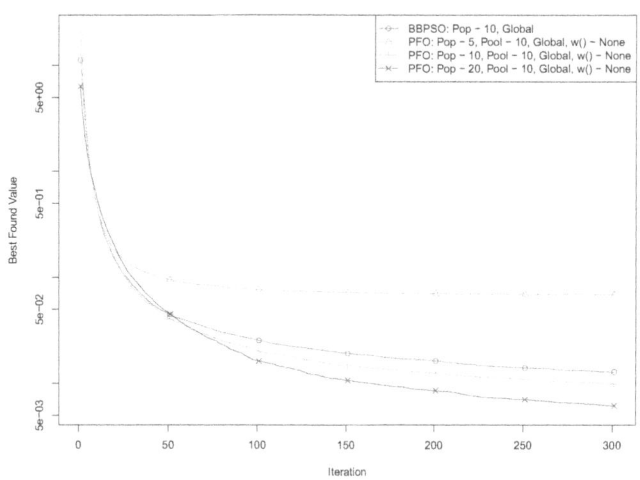

Figure 4: A selection of performance results for the Griewank-20 function.

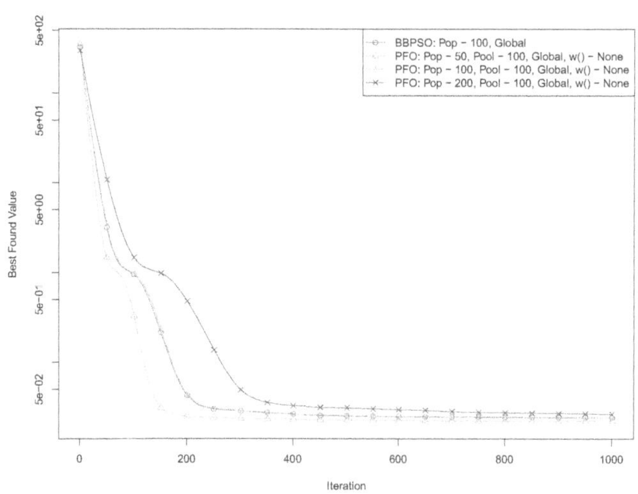

sizes were observed to converge much faster than configurations with larger population sizes.

4. The results on the Griewank function also suggest this correlation, though not as clearly. The plotted results show this correlation in the early iterations, although the final values are not distinctly separated by the particle field population sizes. In this connection, we mention that it has been shown that the Griewank function becomes "easier" as the number of dimensions are increased, and if we take this into account, these results, which are otherwise unexplainable on the Griewank functions, can be explained. Results on the Griewank 2 function support the correlation between the particle field population size and the "exploratory" behavior, with larger population sizes yielding dramatically better final results.

5. When comparing these observations with the results of tests on the Griewank 20 function, a possible pattern emerges which explains the observed exception. The results on the Griewank 20 function are not distinctly separated by particle field population sizes. However, the observed relation between the average final value for each group is, in fact, the opposite of the observed relation on the Griewank 2 function. In this case, the PFO configurations with a smaller population size performed, on average, slightly better than those with a larger population size. With the knowledge that the Griewank function becomes "easier" as the number of dimensions are increased [9], and recalling the results of tests on the Sphere function, a possible explanation for the results can be made. As the number of dimensions increases, the Griewank function becomes "easier", and so as the number of dimensions increases, "exploitative" behavior becomes more valuable than "exploratory" behavior, explaining the PFO's behavior that its "exploitative" nature of small populations begins to yield better results than its "exploratory" nature for large populations.

6. The weighting scheme was expected to have a large impact on the PFO algorithm's behavior. The test results, however, show that the weighting scheme chosen had a relatively small impact when compared with the particle field population size parameter. By grouping PFO configurations according to the particle field population sizes, the effects of the weighting schemes can be compared within these groups.

7. In addition to the tested weighting schemes, PFO configurations with no weighting scheme were tested [3] to provide a baseline point of comparison. The effectiveness of the weighting schemes varied greatly across the test functions and population size groups. On some functions there was a significant variation in performance between the weighting functions, and on some the variation was very small. Also, the relative performance of the weighting schemes within their groupings was inconsistent over the different test functions, with no significant patterns suggesting any clear correlation between the weighting schemes and specific behaviors. This is addressed in more detail in Section 5.2 which deals with the potential for more research in this area.

5. CONCLUSIONS AND FUTURE WORK

Particle swarm algorithms have been a popular topic of research and development since the inception of the original Particle Swarm Optimization (PSO) algorithm in 1995. Many different strategies have been explored to change, or improve, the PSO algorithm, with distinct motivations and results. The initial stages of our research into these various strategies led us to study the Bare Bones Particle Swarm (BBPS) algorithm, which simplified and abstracted the PSO algorithm. Upon discovering the potential for a further level of abstraction, we have been able to determine an even higher level of abstraction on which the particles were replaced by "fields", and to investigate the implications of the new perspective. As far as we know, such an abstraction is both novel and pioneering in the area of swarm-like algorithms, and in the field of AI, in general.

This work was written with two primary objectives in mind. The first objective was to present an abstracted perspective of the behavior of the BBPS algorithm. With this abstracted perspective came many new opportunities for the development of the algorithm. The second objective was to present the newly created PFO algorithm, which was designed by exploring some of the new opportunities presented by this abstracted perspective of the BBPS algorithm.

In this paper, we have thoroughly achieved and explored both of these objectives. The abstracted perspective of the behavior of the BBPS algorithm presents many new opportunities for development which are not evident with the traditional particle swarm perspective. With this perspective as a foundation, we have explored a number of these new opportunities, applying a number of changes and additions to the BBPS algorithm, resulting in the distinct Particle Field Optimization (PFO) algorithm. The PFO algorithm itself is a novel contribution, proving to be effective in the optimization of a variety of different functions of high and low dimensionalities and differing complexities. The PFO algorithm also presents a rich framework for further development and research of the new and abstracted perspective.

5.1 Application of PSO Concepts to the PFO

The PFO algorithm has an overall behavior which is distinct from traditional particle swarm algorithms, but the core particle swarm framework is still present within the population of particle field individuals. It is thus possible to incorporate many PSO-based facets, into the PFO paradigm. The PFO can also be applied in all the problem domains where PSO schemes are applicable.

5.2 Improvement of Weighting Schemes

The weighting scheme parameter of the PFO algorithm was originally intended as a way to introduce a dramatic change in the search behavior without interfering directly with the underlying particle swarm principles at work. However, the impact of the different weighting schemes tested was much less significant than we had hoped. The advantages gleaned were also very problem specific. Because of this, the improvement of the weighting scheme portion of the PFO algorithm presents a clear opportunity for further research and development. The observed effects of the weighting schemes were surprising, and so it is not yet clear *why* these different weighting schemes did not show the expected impact. Further investigation into the weighting schemes themselves, then, is required to understand this.

REFERENCES

[1] P. J. Angeline. Using selection to improve particle swarm optimization. *IEEE International Conference on Computational Intelligence*, 1998.

[2] M. Clerc and J. Kennedy. The particle swarm - explosion, stability, and convergence in a multidimensional complex space. *IEEE Transactions on Evolutionary Computation*, Vol. 6 pp. 58–73, 2002.

[3] N. Bell. *Swarm Optimization Using Agents Modeled as Distributions.* MCS Thesis, Carelton University, 2014.

[4] R. Eberhart and Y. Shi. Comparing inertia weights and constriction factors in particle swarm optimization. *Congress on Evolutionary Computation*, Vol. 1 pp. 84–88, 2000.

[5] N. Higashi and H. Iba. Particle swarm optimization with gaussian mutation. *IEEE Swarm Intelligence Symposium*, pp. 72–79, 2003.

[6] J. Kennedy. Bare bones particle swarms. *IEEE Swarm Intelligence Symposium*, pp. 80–87, 2003.

[7] J. Kennedy and R. Eberhart. Particle swarm optimization. *IEEE International Conference on Neural Networks*, Vol. 4 pp. 1942–1948, 1995.

[8] J. Kennedy and R. Mendes. Population structure and particle swarm performance. *Congress on Evolutionary Computation*, Vol. 2 pp. 1671–1676, 2002.

[9] M. Locatelli. A note on the griewank test function. *Journal of Global Optimization*, Vol. 25 pp. 169–174, 2003.

[10] M. Lovbjerg, T. K. Rasmussen, and T. Krink. Hybrid particle swarm optimiser with breeding and subpopulations. *Genetic and Evolutionary Computation Conference*, pp. 469–476, 2001.

[11] R. Mendes, J. Kennedy, and J. Neves. The fully informed particle swarm: Simpler, maybe better. *IEEE Transactions on Evolutionary Computation*, Vol. 8 pp. 204–210, 2004.

[12] C. K. Monson and K. D. Seppi. Exposing origin-seeking bias in pso. *Conference on Genetic and Evolutionary Computation*, GECCO '05, pp. 241–248, 2005.

[13] E. Ozcan and C. K. Mohan. Analysis of a simple particle swarm optimization system. *Intelligent engineering systems through artificial neural networks*, Vol. 8 pp. 253–258, 1998.

[14] E. Ozcan and C. K. Mohan. Particle swarm optimization: Surfing the waves. *Congress on Evolutionary Computation*, Vol. 3 pp. 1939–1944, 1999.

[15] A. Ratnaweera, S. Halgamuge, and H. C. Watson. Self-organizing hierarchical particle swarm optimizer with time-varying acceleration coefficients. *IEEE Transactions on Evolutionary Computation*, Vol. 8 pp. 240–255, 2004.

[16] M. Settles and T. Soule. Breeding swarms: a ga/pso hybrid. *Conference on Genetic and Evolutionary Computation*, GECCO '05, pp. 161–168, 2005.

[17] Y. Shi and R. Eberhart. Empirical study of particle swarm optimization. *Congress on Evolutionary Computation*, Vol. 3 pp. 1945–1950, 1999.

[18] W. M. Spears, D. T. Green, and D. F. Spears. Biases in particle swarm optimization. *Int. J. Swarm. Intell. Res.*, Vol. 1 pp. 34–57, April 2010.

[19] Z. H. Zhan, J. Zhang, and H. S. H. Chung. Adaptive particle swarm optimization. *IEEE Transactions on Systems, Man, and Cybernetics, Part B: Cybernetics*, Vol. 39 pp. 1362–1381, 2009. *IEEE Swarm Intelligence Symposium*, pp. 80–87, 2003.

Bio-inspired Practicalities: Collective Behaviour using Passive Neighbourhood Sensing

Mansoor Shaukat [*]
National University of Singapore
119222 Singapore
mansoor@arl.nus.edu.sg

Mandar Chitre [†]
National University of Singapore
119222 Singapore
mandar@arl.nus.edu.sg

ABSTRACT

Implementing collective behaviour in cooperative multi-agent systems requires several practical constraints to be addressed. In some environments, communication bandwidth is a critical constraint which may compromise the intended cooperative behaviour. This paper introduces a bio-inspired model which invokes collective behaviour in a multi-agent system using passive sensing without any explicit inter-agent communication. An agent looks for the majority of its neighbours either in its left or its right half space using two sensors. For a source localization problem, we compare performance of the proposed model using passive sensing against the well known school-of-fish collective behaviour models using ideal explicit inter-agent communication. For different cue strengths and neighbourhood radii, our results show that the proposed strategy boosts higher levels of group cohesion to make up for the information loss and in certain conditions performs better than the other collective behaviour models.

Categories and Subject Descriptors

I.2.9 [**Robotics**]: Autonomous Vehicles; I.2.11 [**Distributed Artificial Intelligence**]: Multiagent systems

Keywords

Biologically-inspired approaches and methods, Collective intelligence, Distributed problem solving, Emergent behavior

1. INTRODUCTION

With time, multi-agent systems have become a focal point in various fields of applied engineering research [54, 47, 52, 60] where researchers have formulated multi-agent strategies to solve different engineering problems [16, 46, 70]. A large contribution to the literature on physical multi-agent systems is biologically inspired [23, 41, 29, 26] from the collective behaviour in nature [64, 28]. In the domain of source localization, there are significant number of bio-inspired approaches and methods in the literature [20, 23, 40, 59]. Such implementations, either require explicit inter-agent communication, i.e., a deliberate act of invoking a signal transmission [45, 65] or use passive sensing of the environment or neighbours [51, 63].

In a nutshell, any cooperative source localization task requires some kind of information transfer which depends on the modality of a communication infrastructure, i.e., explicit or implicit [4]. Performance of explicit communication based strategies suffer substantially in the environments with severely limited communication bandwidth and delays, e.g., undersea environments [19, 17]. In such environments, having an implicit communication based strategy allows the multi-agent system to operate cooperatively potentially without a complete breakdown. However, implicit communication based strategies that appear in the literature are inspired from ants' pheromone sensing where an agent looks for other agents' passage trails in the environment [4, 51, 63]. In many practical scenarios, whether on land or underwater, explicitly depositing or implicitly leaving a pheromone-like trail may not be desirable or even possible.

We present a control strategy that invokes collective behaviour in multi-agent systems using only two passive sensors per agent. Fish schools or shoals are optimally evolved systems by the process of natural selection and find food [55] or acoustic [49, 56] sources benefitting from their collective behaviour. An ideal but a challenging approach is to translate this optimally evolved biological model into a practical control strategy for autonomous multi-agent systems. We discuss the practicalities of such a translation in Section 2 and present the passive sensing model in Section 3. In the proposed strategy, an agent uses the two sensors to look for where the *majority* of its neighbours are positioned, either in its left or right half space. Though similar notions pertaining to the dual sensors [11] or the neighbour majority [12] exist in the literature, the proposed strategy is novel in the way it integrates the two ideas to offer a practical collective behaviour based distributed control approach. We present the simulation setup in Section 4 and compare the performance of the proposed model against the biological models aided by explicit communication in Section 5. We finally conclude in Section 6 summarizing the important findings of this paper and sharing some thoughts pertaining to the future work.

---

[*]Mansoor Shaukat is a PhD scholar with the NUS Graduate School for Integrative Sciences & Engineering and works at the Acoustics Research Laboratory at National University of Singapore.

[†]Mandar Chitre is an Assistant Professor with the Electrical & Computer Engineering department and heads the Acoustics Research Laboratory at National University of Singapore.

Appears in: *Proceedings of the 14th International Conference on Autonomous Agents and Multiagent Systems (AAMAS 2015), Bordini, Elkind, Weiss, Yolum (eds.), May 4–8, 2015, Istanbul, Turkey.*

2. BIO-INSPIRED PRACTICALITIES

2.1 Biological Collective Behaviour Models

In a school of fish, the collective behaviour is believed to emerge from an individual's interaction with its neighbours [42, 32]. Many years of research [18, 2, 34] has classified three major rules that result in the collective behaviours, i.e., the long-range attraction, the short-range repulsion and the neighbour alignment. An individual fish is attracted towards its neighbour unless it gets too close, in which case repulsion takes over attraction – a phenomenon jointly known as the long-range attraction and short-range repulsion. Current literature on animal collective behaviour shows a lack of consensus on whether these animal interactions are based on metric/zonal interactions [58, 18, 31, 34] or topological interactions [7, 24, 10]. By metric interaction, one assumes the interaction of the focal animal with its neighbours within a fixed radius. There are three distinct zones defined within the fixed radius of interaction as shown in Fig. 1. For a distance, $r \in \mathbb{R}^+$ (m), away from the fish, there exists a repulsion zone such that $0 < r \leq r_\text{r}$, an orientation zone such that $r_\text{r} < r \leq r_\text{o}$ and an attraction zone such that $r_\text{o} < r \leq r_\text{a}$. By topological interaction, one assumes that the focal animal interacts with a fixed number of nearest neighbours but these models are more restricted in explaining the collective behaviour in some flocks of birds and their generic application is rather debatable [9, 42].

For metric/zonal interaction, there are numerous models having some very subtle differences between them but many of them fit the experimental data quite well. A very simple model [18, 9] is based on the unit vector information of the neighbour positions. For example, in case the focal fish, i, with position, $\mathbf{x}_i(t)$, at time, t, detects any neighbour(s), j, inside its repulsion zone, i.e., the inter-agent distance, $r_{ij}(t) = |\mathbf{x}_j(t) - \mathbf{x}_i(t)| \leq r_\text{r}$, it assumes heading according to the following direction vector

$$\mathbf{d}_{\text{r}_i}(t + \tau_\text{r}) = -\sum_{j \neq i}^{n_\text{r}(t)} \frac{\mathbf{x}_j(t) - \mathbf{x}_i(t)}{r_{ij}(t)} \tag{1}$$

where τ_r is the sampling time and $n_\text{r}(t)$ are the number of neighbours in the repulsion zone. Similarly for any neighbour(s), j, in the attraction zone such that $r_\text{o} < r_{ij}(t) \leq r_\text{a}$, the focal fish, i, would assume heading as

$$\mathbf{d}_{\text{a}_i}(t + \tau) = \sum_{j \neq i}^{n_\text{a}(t)} \frac{\mathbf{x}_j(t) - \mathbf{x}_i(t)}{r_{ij}(t)} \tag{2}$$

where τ is the sampling time and n_a are the total number of neighbours in the attraction zone. The repulsion zone holds the highest priority and in case a neighbour is found therein, other behaviours are suspended.

There are other collective behaviour models which build more directly on the significance of the centroid of the school's mass [5, 25, 30, 53]. Some of these models assume a somewhat unrealistic notion that a focal fish has the knowledge of the global centroid and tries to bias itself towards that center. Nevertheless, there are models that only assume knowledge of the centroid of neighbour positions within a fixed radius [56, 58, 50]. In fact, we can write a very simple centroid model by slightly modifying (1) and (2) such as

$$\mathbf{d}_{\text{r}_i}(t + \tau_\text{r}) = -\sum_{j \neq i}^{n_\text{r}(t)} (\mathbf{x}_j(t) - \mathbf{x}_i(t)) \tag{3}$$

and

$$\mathbf{d}_{\text{a}_i}(t + \tau) = \sum_{j \neq i}^{n_\text{a}(t)} (\mathbf{x}_j(t) - \mathbf{x}_i(t)) \tag{4}$$

respectively. By limiting the r_a in the centroid model, we can mimic knowledge of the local centroid and by increasing it to a very large number, we can mimic knowledge of the global centroid.

The orientation models serve the purpose of mimicking the *polarization* of a school, i.e., the mean of the angle deviation of each fish to the mean swimming direction of the school [34]. The long-range attraction and short-range repulsion model without the orientation model accounts well for the *expanse* of a school, i.e., the mean distance of all the fish from the school's centroid, but not so much for the polarization [42]. It is also known that the phenomenon of neighbour alignment in the orientation zone is dependent on the radial neighbour density. For example, a low density would result in a disordered orientation and only for a certain threshold of density, order emerges and increases thereafter as a function of group size [69, 21]. Such a transition from disorder to order (alignment) is seen in a group of locusts [13] where for small populations, there is no significant alignment among individuals. Similar transitions are observed in a school of fish [8]. These observations hint towards the possibility of alignment being an emergent property that is a consequence of long-range attraction and short-range repulsion phenomenon in a high density group. Also, from the perspective of a source localization problem, there is a high chance that alignment may result as an implicit consequence of following a certain cue. For example, a recent study has shown that alignment emerges from the long-range attraction and short-range repulsion phenomenon when agent speeds are varied as a function of instantaneous cue intensities [38]. Since this paper focuses on a team with small number of agents (1 – 20) and a source localization problem, we discount the orientation model in favour of keeping focus only on the role of the long-range attraction and the short-range repulsion behaviours.

To discount the orientation zone we set $r_\text{o} = r_\text{r}$ which applies to (2) and (4). For comparison of the biological models with the passive sensing model, we refer to the unit vector model as the UV model and the centroid model as the C model in the following text. Hence, UV model generates direction vectors for an autonomous agent based on (1) and (2) and C model generates direction vectors based on (3) and (4).

2.2 Practicalities of the Long-range Attraction

Long-range attraction is the key behaviour that contributes towards the cohesion and compactness of a group. It is interesting to investigate the advantages of having an attraction behaviour in multi-agent systems for some real-world problem. It has been shown that the long-range attraction behaviour without aid of any other collective behaviours (repulsion or orientation) can contribute towards increasing the efficiency of a source localization problem [59]. However, the implementation cost of behaviours given by (2) and (4) is in

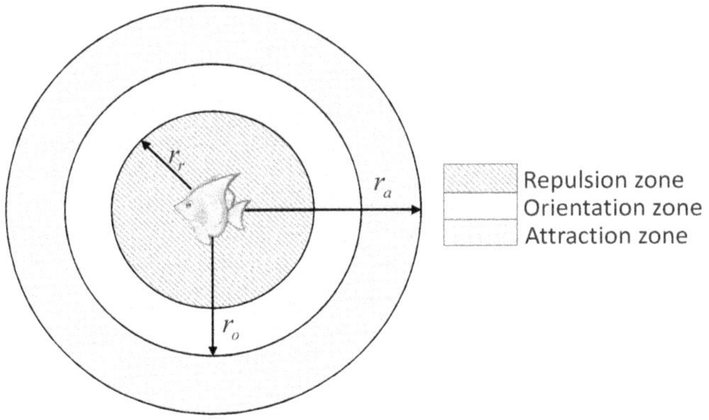

Figure 1: Zonal model of fish interaction.

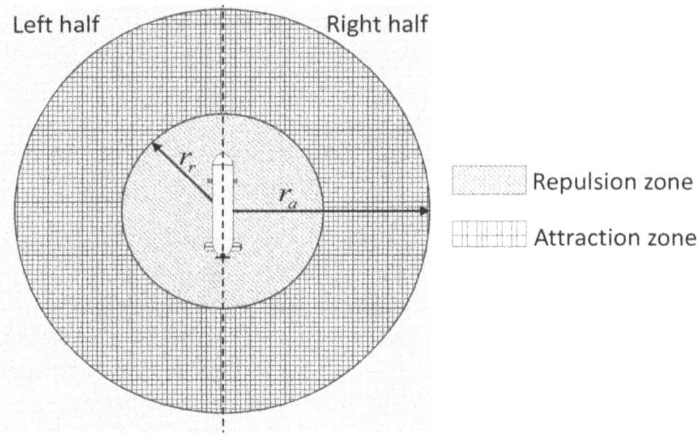

Figure 2: Passive sensing zonal model for detecting majority of neighbours either in left or right half space.

terms of an agent acquiring its own reliable position estimate and to establish communication with other agents to exchange the position information. Acquiring a reliable position estimate and/or communication with acceptable delays and bandwidth in certain environments is a hard and an expensive problem to solve [39, 62].

Having small interaction neighbourhoods may alleviate the communication issues to some extent [6, 36]. However from the perspective of a source localization problem, having a small neighbourhood may consequentially require a very large team of agents [55]. For example, a small team with agents having small neighbourhood radii will be potentially sampling a strong spatially-correlated cue which will have detrimental effects on its collective decision making [37]. Fish are known to have small neighbourhoods but some schools of fish undertaking distant migration are composed of several million individuals connected through small neighbourhoods over several kilometers [48, 43]. It is highly unlikely in the present times to build a massive swarm of autonomous agents with sufficient mission endurance to solve a real-world problem. Given a small number of agents (3 – 20), we show in Section 5 that C and UV models require a large neighbourhood (in hundreds of meters) for localizing an acoustic source 1000 m away.

2.3 Practicalities of the Short-range Repulsion

Repulsion allows more volume to a school allowing it to span more space. Also, increasing r_r results in decreasing cohesion in a school [34]. There is also a difference of opinion on the effect of repulsion on the overall schooling, e.g., some studies report that removing the repulsion zone causes school disintegration [2, 3], whereas some report that removal of the repulsion zone has insignificant effect on schooling [33, 34, 35]. Nevertheless, it is interesting to investigate the effect of the short-range repulsion on a school-of-fish or a team of autonomous agents in a source localization problem.

Short-range repulsion suffers from the same issues as discussed in the preceding section for the long-range attraction. Models defined in (1) and (3) also require the focal agent to acquire the position information of all the neighbouring agents. However, the short-range repulsion allows sophisticated multi-agent systems such as land robots, Unmanned Aerial Vehicles (UAVs) or AUVs to avoid collisions with their peers during a cooperative mission. From the perspective of an agent safety, collision avoidance control is indispensable in most physical multi-agent setups.

3. THE PASSIVE SENSING (PS) MODEL

As discussed in the preceding section, C and UV models require explicit communication of inter-agent position information. Our focus is an alternate collective behaviour model that builds on the biological counterparts but only requires passive sensing to achieve similar characteristics and performance. We assume that each agent is equipped with two passive sensors, one on its right side and one on its left side. This effectively partitions the two-dimensional sensing world of an agent as shown in Fig. 2 into right and left half plane. The passive sensing model requires an agent to have the following information

1. Where is the majority of neighbours in my attraction zone? Either to my right or to my left?

2. Are there any neighbours inside the repulsion zone? If so, what is the *estimated* distance to the closest one and which half is it located in?

Based on this information an agent exercises short-range repulsion and long-range attraction behaviours.

3.1 Collective behaviours of the PS Model

Short-range repulsion operates at the highest priority level. In case an agent detects a neighbour within its repulsion zone, it starts an evasive action and ignores any other behaviours such as going towards the goal or towards the neighbours etc. The evasion rules for an agent are:

1. If there are any number of neighbours inside the repulsion zone, estimate the distance to the nearest neighbour.

2. Determine the half (right or left) in which the nearest neighbour is located.

3. Initiate a turn in the opposite half (left or right) with a turning rate dependent on the estimated nearest neighbour distance.

The turning rate as a function of the distance between the focal agent, i, and the nearest neighbour, j, within the repulsion zone is given as

$$\dot{\theta}_{r_i}(t+\tau_r) = \begin{cases} \dot{\theta}_{\max}\left(\frac{r_r-\hat{r}_{i,j}(t)}{r_r-r_{\min}}\right) & \text{if } r_{\min} < \hat{r}_{i,j}(t) \leq r_r \\ \dot{\theta}_{\max} & \text{if } \hat{r}_{i,j}(t) \leq r_{\min} \end{cases} \quad (5)$$

where τ_r is the sampling time of the repulsion behaviour, $\hat{r}_{i,j}(t)$ is the estimated distance between the focal agent and the nearest neighbour through the sensor data (more on this in Section 3.2) and $r_{\min}$ is the minimum distance between the focal agent and the nearest neighbour where the focal agent starts turning with the maximum possible rate. Also, $r_{\min}$ needs to be greater than $2s\tau_r + l$ for an agent to detect all the potential collisions where s and l are the agent speed and length respectively. Then the focal agent, i, assumes heading according to the following direction vector

$$\mathbf{d}_{r_i}(t+\tau_r) = \mathbf{\Delta d}_{r_i}(t+\tau_r) + \mathbf{d}_i(t) \quad (6)$$

where $\mathbf{\Delta d}_{r_i}(t+\tau_r) = 1\angle\tau_r \cdot \dot{\theta}_{r_i}(t+\tau_r)$ and $\mathbf{d}_i(t)$ being the instantaneous unit directional vector of agent i.

For the long-range attraction behaviour, at every τ seconds, an agent calculates its desired heading towards the majority of its neighbours by detecting the majority either in its left or right half as

$$\mathbf{d}_{a_i}(t+\tau) = \begin{cases} R_\phi^+ \mathbf{d}_{w_i}(t) & \text{if more neighbours on left} \\ R_\phi^- \mathbf{d}_{w_i}(t) & \text{if more neighbours on right} \\ \mathbf{d}_{w_i}(t) & \text{otherwise} \end{cases} \quad (7)$$

where R_ϕ^+, R_ϕ^- are the counter clockwise and the clockwise rotation matrices for an angle of $\phi = 90°$ and $\mathbf{d}_{w_i}(t)$ is the previous weighted direction (see Section 4 for details on computation of the weighted direction).

3.2 Practicalities of the PS model

Here we provide some examples of using the dual sensor topology from the perspective of practical implementation. A very simple scenario is using two microphones or hydrophones per agent where the focal agent can *listen* for the presence of its neighbours. In most of the situations the drive or propulsion systems of land robots, UAVs or AUVs make a significant amount of noise which can be sensed easily by the focal agent within some local neighbourhood. Using the time-of-arrival analysis on the sensors' data can help the focal agent detect where the majority of neighbours is located. In fact in harsh environments, such as undersea environments, where communication bandwidth is severely limited, low frequency sound signals like the thruster noise can travel several hundreds of meters [22, 67, 15]. The thruster noise of a typical AUV or a ROV is in the range of 120 dB to 160 dB re 1 μPa at 1 m [27, 14]. AUVs can also be mounted with locator beacons which emit an acoustic pulse at a fixed rate in time. For example, a 20 kHz pinger with a source level of 180 dB re 1 μPa at 1 m can be heard over several kilometers undersea. In environments where light can travel, e.g., clear waters, the two sensors can simply be light detectors. For example, in the case of CoCoRo project, the researchers use small AUVs which can emit light [65]. Comparing the mean value of light intensity sensed by each sensor over some time window can give a good estimate of where the majority of the neighbours are. Cameras can also be an option as two passive sensors in many environments where robots can detect the neighbour majority using simple image processing techniques.

Where an estimate of the neighbour majority completely defines the long-range attraction behaviour, the short-range repulsion behaviour requires the estimated distance from the nearest neighbour in (5). In the PS model, the neighbour itself is a source. Given an agent has some prior knowledge of the source intensity and its propagation model, it can obtain a good estimate of the distance in close proximity to a source. This is especially true for sources which follow the inverse square law, i.e., the intensity is inversely proportional to the distance squared. Since the repulsion radius is generally small, the assumption pertaining to the knowledge of the estimated nearest neighbour distance is practically valid.

4. SIMULATION SETUP

Let us first define the source localization problem considered in this paper. We assume an acoustic point-source located at the origin of the search plane. Arrival time is defined as the time taken by a specific agent to enter a circular success zone around the source and not diverge from the success zone following its initial entry. The radius of the success zone, r_s is set to 50 m. For sensing the intensity of the source, we use a sound propagation model with spherical spreading suitable for deep underwater environments [66]. For the source, we assume a sound pressure level of 180 dB re 1 μPa at 1 m away in the bandwidth of interest. For the ambient noise, we assume noise levels of either 84 dB re 1 μPa or 118 dB re 1 μPa for comparative performance analysis of the collective behaviours in different Signal to Noise Ratio (SNR) conditions. Both the noise levels at 84 dB re 1 μPa and 118 dB re 1 μPa correspond to the deep sea noise and the shallow water noise respectively in a real-world scenario [22]. The source level correspond to the sound levels of many commercially available underwater locator beacons. We initialize a team of N AUVs, each with a random pose within a square region having an area of 20×20 m^2 and its center located 1000 m away from the acoustic source.

To bias an agent towards the source, we choose an individual behaviour that has the ability of helping an agent localize a source without the aid of collective behaviours [59]. According to the source bias model, an agent updates its direction as follows

$$\mathbf{d}_{s_i}(t+\tau) = \begin{cases} \mathbf{d}_{w_i}(t) & \text{if } I(t+\tau) \geq I(t) \\ R_\theta^+ \mathbf{d}_{w_i}(t) & \text{if } I(t+\tau) < I(t) \end{cases} \quad (8)$$

where I is the acoustic intensity and θ is the correction angle an agent adds to its previous weighted heading in case it is not going in the direction of increasing acoustic intensity. The corresponding weighted direction of an agent, i, based on (7) and (8) is computed every τ seconds as

$$\mathbf{d}_{w_i}(t) = b_s \cdot \mathbf{d}_{s_i}(t) + (1-b_s)\mathbf{d}_{a_i}(t) \quad (9)$$

where $b_s \in [0.5, 1]$ is the source biasing coefficient where any values of $b_s < 0.5$ fail in the source localization for any of the collective behaviour models. Note that higher values of b_s mean less team cohesion and vice versa. Now, we can write the desired direction of an agent, i, at time, t, as

$$\mathbf{d}_{d_i}(t) = \begin{cases} \mathbf{d}_{r_i}(t) & \text{if } n_r(t) \neq 0 \text{ and } r_r \neq 0 \\ \mathbf{d}_{w_i}(t) & \text{otherwise} \end{cases} \quad (10)$$

Table 1: Symbols, their description and values explored during simulation.

Sym.	Description	Value(s)
N	Total number of team members	$\{1, 3, 5, 10, 15, 20\}$
r_s	Radius of the success zone	50 m
r_a	Neighbourhood radius / Radius of the attraction zone	{150,300,600} (m)
r_r	Radius of the repulsion zone	$\{0, 7.6\}$ (m)
r_{min}	Minimum radius of the repulsion zone	3.8 m
l	Length of an agent	0.8 m
s	Speed of an agent	$1.5\,\mathrm{m\,s^{-1}}$
$\dot{\theta}_{max}$	Maximum turning rate of an agent	$35\,^{\circ}\,\mathrm{s}^{-1}$
τ_r	Sampling time of the short-range repulsion models	1 s
τ	Sampling time of the long-range attraction models and the source bias model	$[1, 1000]$ (s)
b_s	Source biasing coefficient	$[0.5, 1.0]$
θ	Correction angle	$[0, 180°]$

Also, note that (10) accounts for all the collective behaviour models, i.e., the short-range repulsion and the long-range attraction behaviours of UV, C and PS models.

A Genetic Algorithm [44] is used to optimize the parameters, b_s, θ and τ. The fitness function is the mean arrival time of 1024 simulation runs. Inspired by [1], the number of simulation runs is calculated from the Vargha-Delaney's A-measurement test [68] which ensures similar inter-simulation fitness distributions. We investigate the performance impact of varying the radius of the attraction zone (neighbourhood radius), r_a and SNR for different team size, N. A table for all the values of the parameters explored is given in Table 1. The agent length, speed and the maximum turning radius are taken from field experiments on a miniature submarine as shown in Fig. 3. We assume a constant speed operation in the simulations with speed, s, of each agent set to $1.5\,\mathrm{m\,s^{-1}}$.

Figure 3: A miniature submarine called Swarmbot during field experiments at Pandan Reservoir, Singapore.

5. RESULTS & DISCUSSION

The focus is to compare the PS model with limited neighbour information against the UV and C models with complete neighbour information under different operating conditions.

5.1 Without the Short-range Repulsion

First we investigate the effect of having only the long-range attraction in the UV, C and PS models, i.e., we set $r_r = 0$ for different team sizes as shown in Fig. 4. Figure 4(a) shows the mean arrival times of different team sizes. Each mean arrival time is representative of 49×10^3 simulation runs. It is interesting to note that for smaller teams, PS registers better performance in Fig. 4(a), using significantly more cohesion (lower b_s) than the other models in Fig. 4(b). However as the team size increases, the difference narrows down with all the three models displaying similar performance at $N = 15$. For all the simulated values of N, there is neither any significant difference between the performance of the UV and C models nor in their optimal control parameter values as can be seen in Fig. 4(b), Fig. 4(c) and Fig. 4(d). As for the correction angle, θ, all the three models use nearly the same values till $N = 5$ but for $N = 10$ and beyond, PS in Fig. 4(c) switches abruptly to a new correction angle strategy. This also corresponds in Fig. 4(b) to the cohesion levels switching abruptly to a higher value.

5.2 The Advantage Threshold

The dotted magenta line in Fig. 4(a) and Fig. 5(a) signifies the *advantage threshold* where the collective behaviours are inactive. The advantage threshold is important in the biological systems where researchers are interested in knowing if an individual enjoys any advantage living in a group rather than being alone and if there is an optimal group size [61, 57]. When the arrival times in a team ($N > 1$) remain below the advantage threshold, it signifies an individual benefitting from a group. It can be seen that all the collective behaviour models show significant improvement for small teams except at $N = 3$ in the case of the C and UV models.

5.3 With the Short-range Repulsion

We set $r_r = 2r_{min}$ in the UV, C and PS models to investigate the effect of the short-range repulsion on source localization arrival times. Figure 5(a) shows the arrival times for the neighbourhood radii of 300 m and 600 m. It is interesting to note the slight degradation in mean arrival times if we compare Fig. 4(a) and Fig. 5(a). The only exception is at $N = 3$ where the C and UV models have shown significant improvement. To show nearly the same performance as in the case of Fig. 4(a), the attraction radius needs to be twice as much when the short-range repulsion is also active. Also note that the PS model loses its slight advantage over the C and UV models once the neighbourhood radius is increased to 600 m. Fig. 5(b) emphasizes this fact where for the case of an increased neighbourhood radius, the C and UV models have utilized more cohesion than the PS model.

Also, in Fig. 5(a), increasing the team size up to a certain limit adds more benefit for an individual, however beyond that limit, the arrival times start degrading. In other words there seems to be an optimal team size for an individual in this case. The PS model suffers the most from this phenomenon where for $r_a = 600$ m, it is performing nearly at par with the C and UV models with $r_a = 300$ m at $N = 20$. The degradation in performance may have a link with the

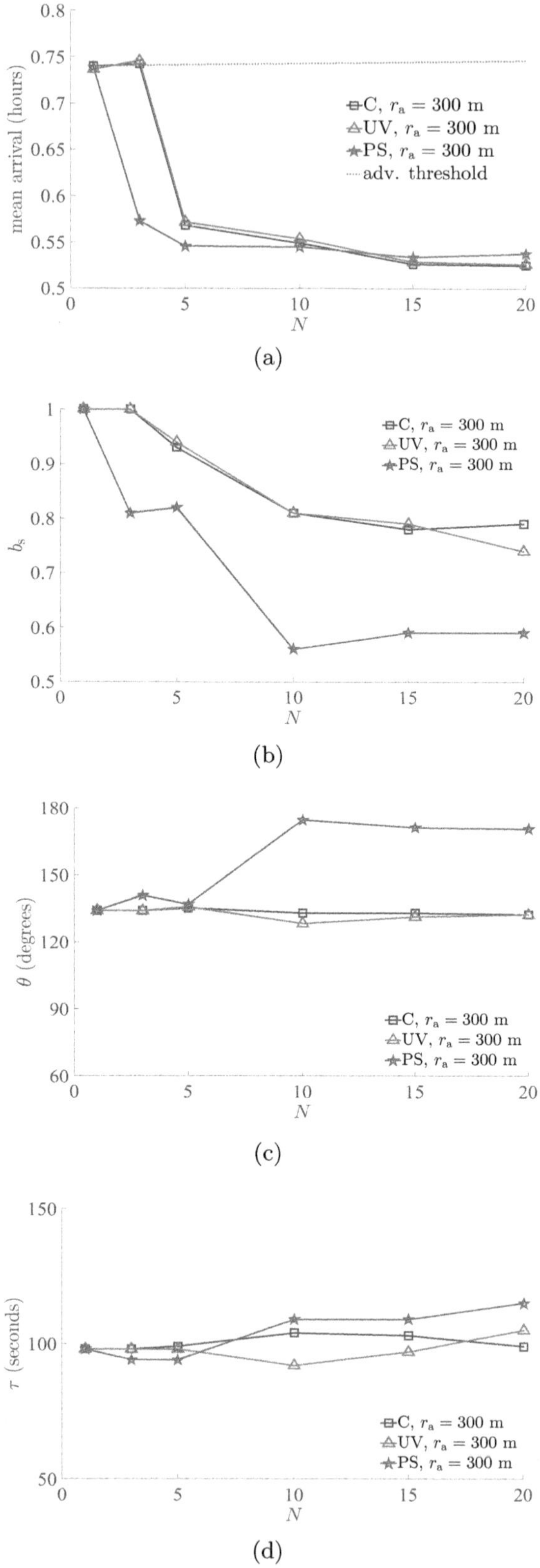

Figure 4: Comparative performance and optimal parameters of the Centroid (C) model, Unit Vector (UV) model and Passive Sensing (PS) model as a function of number of agents without short-range repulsion: (a) Mean arrival time (b) Source biasing coefficient. (c) Correction angle. (d) Sampling time.

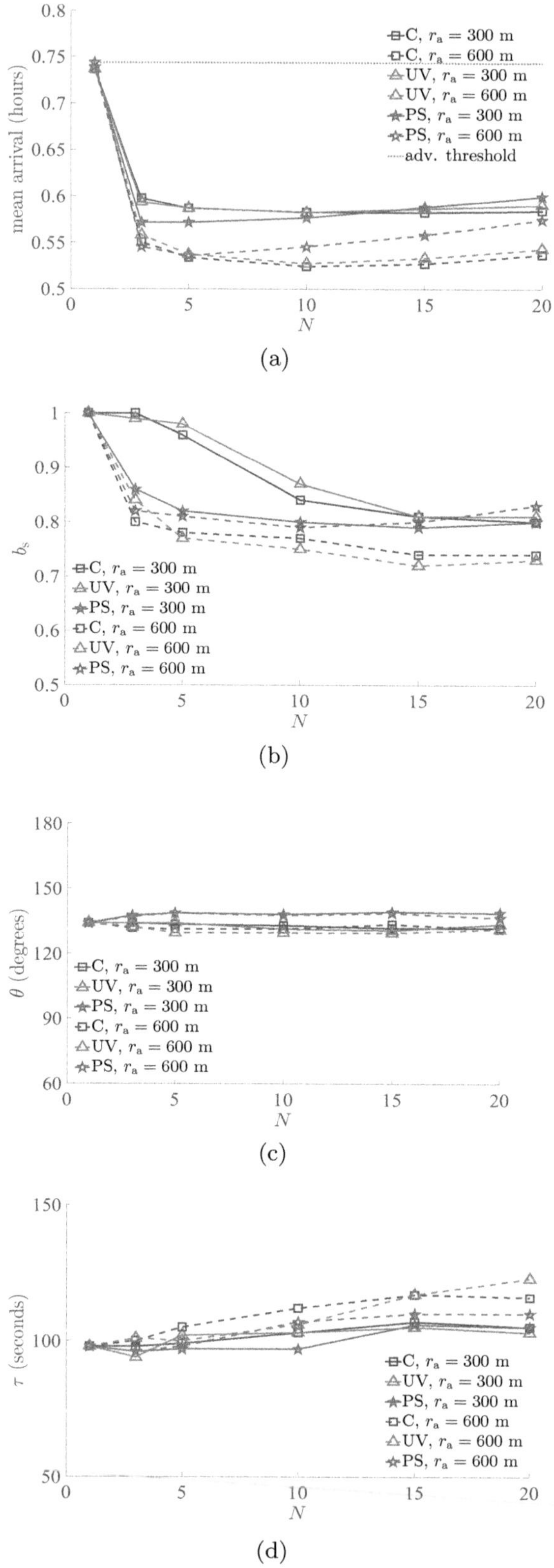

Figure 5: Comparative performance and optimal parameters of the Centroid (C) model, Unit Vector (UV) model and Passive Sensing (PS) model as a function of number of agents withshort-range repulsion: (a) Mean arrival time (b) Source biasing coefficient. (c) Correction angle. (d) Sampling time.

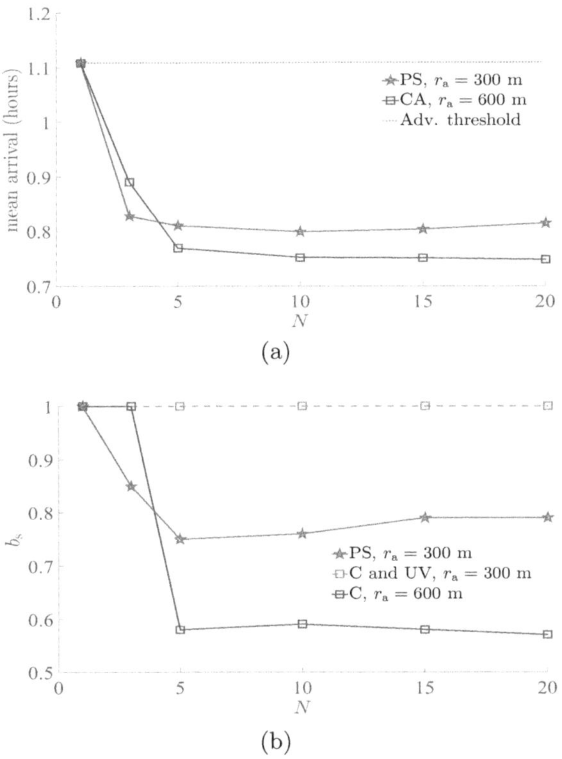

Figure 6: Performance of the Passive Sensing (PS) model in a reduced SNR scenario: a) Comparative performance against the advantage threshold and Centroid (C) model with double the neighbourhood radius. (b) Comparison of cohesion levels for PS, Centroid (C) and Unit Vector (UV) models.

increasing cohesion levels and number of agents. We can see the general trend in Fig. 5(b) where teams increase their cohesion levels as their size increases. However, this also increases the average number of times an individual has to avoid collisions during a mission. Since PS suffers from the incomplete neighbourhood information and consequentially responds only to the nearest neighbour, the behaviour may make the team confused with growing cohesion and team size [35]. The effect may be seen in Fig. 5(b) where PS starts retreating back to lower cohesion levels to perform optimally with larger team sizes.

The correction angle remains effectively constant for each of the collective behaviours in Fig. 5(c) throughout the range of the team size and also for both the neighbourhood radii.

Sampling times in Fig. 5(d) behave similarly for all the collective behaviours for the neighbourhood radius of 300 m. However, for the case of neighbourhood radius set to 600 m, UV displays a pattern of a slow increase in the sampling time as a function of team size. In general, a large sampling time in the range of 100 s to 110 s ensures enough agent traversal in the search space to collect an uncorrelated sample and contribute towards an implicit averaging process that would be beneficial as a whole.

5.4 Lower Intensity Cues

We assume a degraded SNR by increasing the ambient noise levels to 118 dB re 1 μPa. The comparative performance of the PS model for the degraded SNR is shown in Fig. 6(a) against the advantage threshold. It is interesting to note that for a neighbourhood radius of 300 m, both the C and UV models lose the ability of providing an agent with the benefit of team cohesion as shown in Fig. 6(b) where both operate with $b_s = 1$. However if we increase the neighbourhood radius to 600 m we can see that C model performs significantly better in Fig. 6(a) using higher cohesion levels as shown in Fig. 6(b).

The PS model keeps its trends in Fig. 6(a) and Fig. 6(b) as were described in Section 5.1 for Fig. 5(a) and Fig. 5(b). There seems to be an optimal group size between $N = 5$ and $N = 10$ in Fig. 6(a) where onwards, the PS model starts reducing its cohesion levels in Fig. 6(b).

5.5 Agent Trajectories

Agent trajectories from a simulated source localization mission for a team of 10 agents without the short-range repulsion behaviour are shown for the C, UV and PS models in Fig. 7(a), Fig. 7(b), Fig. 7(c) respectively. The red dots show the trajectory for a specific agent in a team, arrival of which marked the mission as a success. Since, the PS model boosts significantly higher cohesion levels in Fig. 4(b) for $N = 10$ as compared to the C and UV models, the agent trajectories for the PS model in Fig. 7(c) compliment that finding when compared to the trajectories of the C and UV models. As a whole, the team seems more cohesive and focussed towards the source for the PS model. For the short-range repulsion active, the three trajectories for C, UV and PS models are given in Fig. 7(d), Fig. 7(e), Fig. 7(f) respectively which are similar for nearly the same cohesion levels in Fig. 5(b). In summary, the trajectory response of the PS model is not significantly different than C and UV models and conserves the same pattern despite the loss of information.

6. CONCLUSION

We presented a bio-inspired model which invokes collective behaviour in a multi-agent system using passive sensing without any explicit inter-agent communication. The passive sensing model assumes two sensors per agent, one on its right side and one on its left side. Both the sensors help an agent detect the majority of its neighbours either in its left or right half space. For a source localization problem, we analyzed the comparative performance of the passive sensing model with the well-known school-of-fish collective behaviour models (C and UV) aided by ideal explicit communication. It was shown that the proposed approach performs better than or at par with C and UV models for teams with small number of agents (3 – 20) in certain conditions. Especially, in conditions involving constrained neighbourhood radii and higher background noise levels, C and UV models failed to extend any benefit to an individual agent whereas the passive sensing model extended significant benefit. Moreover, the proposed strategy was shown to make up for the information loss by boosting higher cohesion levels in a team than the other models. However, it was also shown that for larger teams, the passive sensing approach reduces the cohesion levels to avoid agent confusion due to the short-range repulsion behaviour.

In general, the proposed approach shares similar trends with the other collective behaviour approaches, e.g., in the effect of the long-range attraction and the short-range repulsion on performance, optimal parameter values and agent

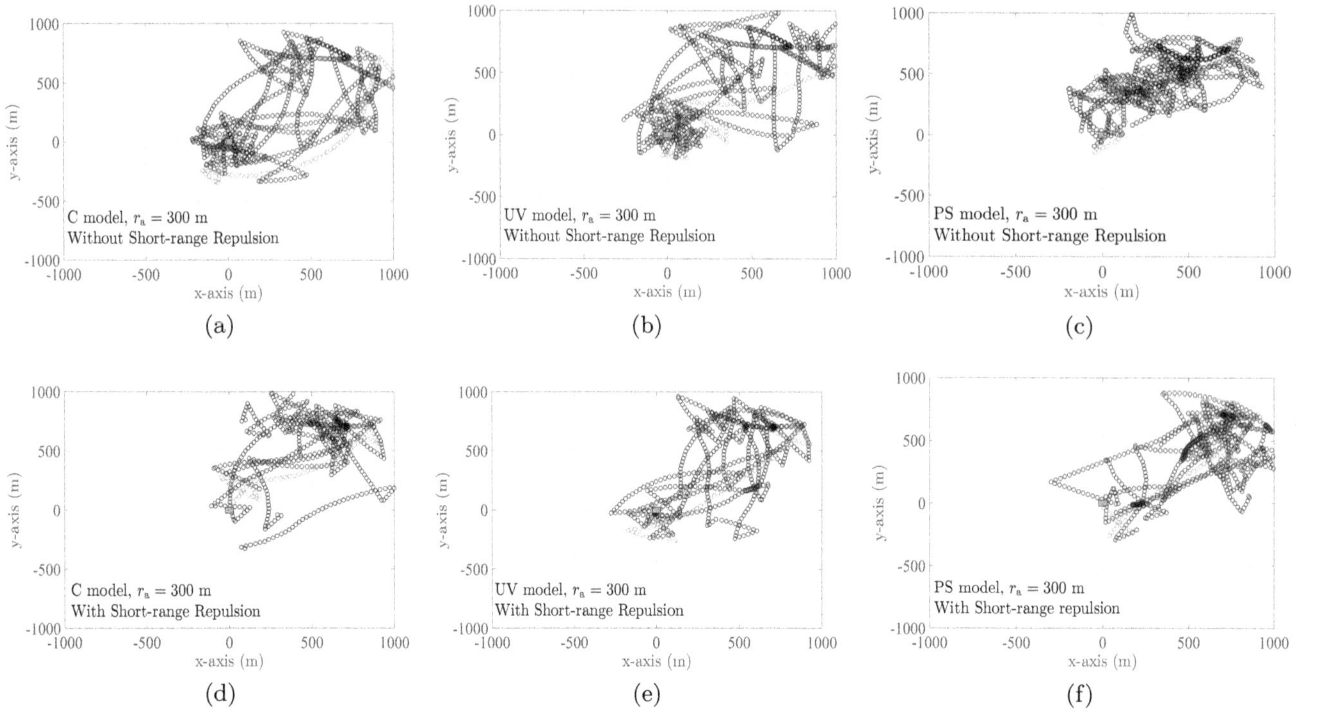

Figure 7: Trajectories of the collective behaviours without short-range repulsion: (a) C model. (b) UV model. (c) PS model. Trajectories with short-range repulsion: (d) C model. (e) UV model. (f) PS model.

trajectories. There is a need to investigate the short-range repulsion behaviour more in terms of the source localization problems. For all the collective behaviour models, the short-range repulsion shows some performance degradation. It may have to do with an agent facing competition near the source due to the earlier arrivals of other agents. Given the indispensable nature of collision avoidance control in many practical multi-agent systems, the short-range repulsion needs to be optimized such that it can accommodate larger team sizes.

We can also make some general conclusions from the results shown in this paper. It was shown that a small team requires a large enough neighbourhood radius to have sufficient uncorrelated cue samples. Collective implicit averaging works well with the uncorrelated cue samples but has a detrimental effect on the collective decision making of a team otherwise [37]. The cue sampling times also showed to have a complimentary effect. The sampling times were optimized by an evolutionary algorithm and the optimal values suggest that an agent needs to traverse more in space to gather uncorrelated samples of a cue. This warrants a more profound investigation of the relationship between the parameters like the neighbourhood radius, sampling time, team size and the spatial correlation of a cue.

7. ACKNOWLEDGMENTS

The authors would like to thank Prasad Anjangi from the Acoustics Research Lab for providing helpful suggestions in improving the layout of the manuscript. Also, the authors are thankful to the four anonymous reviewers for their detailed reviews, full of helpful critiques and insights which resulted in an improved manuscript and helped us in broadening our vision for the future research.

REFERENCES

[1] K. Alden, M. Read, J. Timmis, P. S. Andrews, H. Veiga-Fernandes, and M. Coles. Spartan: A comprehensive tool for understanding uncertainty in simulations of biological systems. *PLoS computational biology*, 9(2):e1002916, 2013.

[2] I. Aoki. A simulation study on the schoolng mechanism in fish. *Bull. Japan. Soc. Sci. Fish.*, 48, 1982.

[3] I. Aoki. Internal dynamics of fish schools in relation to inter-fish distance. *Bulletin of the Japanese Society of Scientific Fisheries*, 1984.

[4] T. Balch and R. Arkin. Communication in reactive multiagent robotic systems. *Autonomous Robots*, 1(1):27–52, 1994.

[5] J. G. Balchen. Mathematical modelling of fish behaviour. principles and applications. *Proc. IFAC 6th World Congr., Boston/Cambridge*, 1975.

[6] J. W. Bales and C. Chrissostomidis. High-bandwidth, low-power, short-range optical communication underwater. In *International Symposium on Unmanned Untethered Submersible Technology*, pages 406–415. University of New Hampshire Marine Systems, 1995.

[7] M. Ballerini, N. Cabibbo, R. Candelier, A. Cavagna, E. Cisbani, I. Giardina, V. Lecomte, A. Orlandi, G. Parisi, A. Procaccini, et al. Interaction ruling

animal collective behavior depends on topological rather than metric distance: Evidence from a field study. *Proceedings of the National Academy of Sciences*, 105(4):1232–1237, 2008.

[8] C. Becco, N. Vandewalle, J. Delcourt, and P. Poncin. Experimental evidences of a structural and dynamical transition in fish school. *Physica A: Statistical Mechanics and its Applications*, 367:487–493, 2006.

[9] A. Berdahl, C. J. Torney, C. C. Ioannou, J. J. Faria, and I. D. Couzin. Emergent sensing of complex environments by mobile animal groups. *Science*, 339(6119):574–576, 2013.

[10] N. W. Bode, D. W. Franks, and A. J. Wood. Limited interactions in flocks: relating model simulations to empirical data. *Journal of The Royal Society Interface*, 8(55):301–304, 2011.

[11] V. Braitenberg. Taxis, kinesis and decussation. *Progress in brain research*, 17:210–222, 1965.

[12] R. A. Brooks, P. Maes, M. J. Mataric, and G. More. Lunar base construction robots. In *Intelligent Robots and Systems' 90.'Towards a New Frontier of Applications', Proceedings. IROS'90. IEEE International Workshop on*, pages 389–392. IEEE, 1990.

[13] J. Buhl, D. Sumpter, I. Couzin, J. Hale, E. Despland, E. Miller, and S. Simpson. From disorder to order in marching locusts. *Science*, 312(5778):1402–1406, 2006.

[14] M. Cai, I. M. Sou, C. Layman, B. Bingham, and J. Allen. Characterization of the acoustic signature of a small remotely operated vehicle for detection. In *OCEANS 2010*, pages 1–7. IEEE, 2010.

[15] M. Calderon. Probability density analysis of ocean ambient and ship noise. Technical report, DTIC Document, 1964.

[16] Y. Cao, W. Yu, W. Ren, and G. Chen. An overview of recent progress in the study of distributed multi-agent coordination. *Industrial Informatics, IEEE Transactions on*, 9(1):427–438, 2013.

[17] M. Chitre, S. Shahabudeen, and M. Stojanovic. Underwater acoustic communications and networking: Recent advances and future challenges. *Oceanic Engineering, IEEE Journal of*, pages 103 –116, spring 2008.

[18] I. D. Couzin, J. Krause, R. James, G. D. Ruxton, and N. R. Franks. Collective memory and spatial sorting in animal groups. *Journal of theoretical biology*, 218(1):1–11, 2002.

[19] J.-H. Cui, J. Kong, M. Gerla, and S. Zhou. The challenges of building mobile underwater wireless networks for aquatic applications. *Network, IEEE*, 20(3):12 – 18, may-june 2006.

[20] X. Cui, C. T. Hardin, R. K. Ragade, and A. S. Elmaghraby. A swarm approach for emission sources localization. In *Tools with Artificial Intelligence, 2004. ICTAI 2004. 16th IEEE International Conference on*, pages 424–430. IEEE, 2004.

[21] A. Czirók, M. Vicsek, and T. Vicsek. Collective motion of organisms in three dimensions. *Physica A: Statistical Mechanics and its Applications*, 264(1):299–304, 1999.

[22] P. H. Dahl, J. H. Miller, D. H. Cato, and R. K. Andrew. Underwater ambient noise. *Acoustics Today*, 3(1):23–33, 2007.

[23] G. Ferri, E. Caselli, V. Mattoli, A. Mondini, B. Mazzolai, and P. Dario. Spiral: A novel biologically-inspired algorithm for gas/odor source localization in an indoor environment with no strong airflow. *Robotics and Autonomous Systems*, 57(4):393–402, 2009.

[24] A. Flack, Z. Ákos, M. Nagy, T. Vicsek, and D. Biro. Robustness of flight leadership relations in pigeons. *Animal Behaviour*, 86(4):723–732, 2013.

[25] S. Focardi and S. Toso. Foraging and social behaviour of ungulates: proposals for a mathematical model. In *Cognitive processes and spatial orientation in animal and man*, pages 295–304. Springer, 1987.

[26] T. Fong, I. Nourbakhsh, and K. Dautenhahn. A survey of socially interactive robots. *Robotics and autonomous systems*, 42(3):143–166, 2003.

[27] G. Griffiths, P. Enoch, and N. W. Millard. On the radiated noise of the autosub autonomous underwater vehicle. *ICES Journal of Marine Science: Journal du Conseil*, 58(6):1195–1200, 2001.

[28] D. Grünbaum, S. Viscido, and J. Parrish. Extracting interactive control algorithms from group dynamics of schooling fish. *Cooperative Control*, pages 447–450, 2005.

[29] A. Halász, M. Hsieh, S. Berman, and V. Kumar. Dynamic redistribution of a swarm of robots among multiple sites. In *Intelligent Robots and Systems, 2007. IROS 2007. IEEE/RSJ International Conference on*, pages 2320–2325. IEEE, 2007.

[30] W. D. Hamilton. Geometry for the selfish herd. *Journal of theoretical Biology*, 31(2):295–311, 1971.

[31] C. K. Hemelrijk and H. Hildenbrandt. Self-organized shape and frontal density of fish schools. *Ethology*, 114(3):245–254, 2008.

[32] C. K. Hemelrijk and H. Hildenbrandt. Schools of fish and flocks of birds: their shape and internal structure by self-organization. *Interface Focus*, page rsfs20120025, 2012.

[33] A. Huth and C. Wissel. The movement of fish schools: a simulation model. In *Biological Motion*, pages 577–595. Springer, 1990.

[34] A. Huth and C. Wissel. The simulation of the movement of fish schools. *Journal of theoretical biology*, 156(3):365–385, 1992.

[35] A. Huth and C. Wissel. The simulation of fish schools in comparison with experimental data. *Ecological modelling*, 75:135–146, 1994.

[36] J. Joe and S. Toh. Digital underwater communication using electric current method. In *OCEANS 2007-Europe*, pages 1–4. IEEE, 2007.

[37] A. B. Kao and I. D. Couzin. Decision accuracy in complex environments is often maximized by small group sizes. *Proceedings of the Royal Society B: Biological Sciences*, 281(1784):20133305, 2014.

[38] Y. Katz, K. Tunstrøm, C. Ioannou, C. Huepe, and I. Couzin. Inferring the structure and dynamics of interactions in schooling fish. *Proceedings of the*

National Academy of Sciences, 108(46):18720–18725, 2011.

[39] J. C. Kinsey, R. M. Eustice, and L. L. Whitcomb. A survey of underwater vehicle navigation: Recent advances and new challenges. In *IFAC Conference of Manoeuvering and Control of Marine Craft*, 2006.

[40] K. Krishnanand and D. Ghose. A glowworm swarm optimization based multi-robot system for signal source localization. In *Design and control of intelligent robotic systems*, pages 49–68. Springer, 2009.

[41] P. Leitão, J. Barbosa, and D. Trentesaux. Bio-inspired multi-agent systems for reconfigurable manufacturing systems. *Engineering Applications of Artificial Intelligence*, 25(5):934–944, 2012.

[42] R. Lukeman, Y. Li, and L. Edelstein-Keshet. Inferring individual rules from collective behavior. *Proceedings of the National Academy of Sciences*, 107(28):12576–12580, 2010.

[43] N. C. Makris, P. Ratilal, D. T. Symonds, S. Jagannathan, S. Lee, and R. W. Nero. Fish population and behavior revealed by instantaneous continental shelf-scale imaging. *Science*, 311(5761):660–663, 2006.

[44] K.-F. Man, K. S. TANG, and S. Kwong. *Genetic Algorithms: Concepts and Designs, Avec disquette*, volume 1. Springer, 1999.

[45] A. Marjovi, J. Nunes, P. Sousa, R. Faria, and L. Marques. An olfactory-based robot swarm navigation method. In *Robotics and Automation (ICRA), 2010 IEEE International Conference on*, pages 4958–4963. IEEE, 2010.

[46] T. Matsuda, T. Maki, T. Sakamaki, and T. Ura. Performance analysis on a navigation method of multiple auvs for wide area survey. *Marine Technology Society Journal*, 46(2):45–55, 2012.

[47] S. D. McArthur, E. M. Davidson, V. M. Catterson, A. L. Dimeas, N. D. Hatziargyriou, F. Ponci, and T. Funabashi. Multi-agent systems for power engineering applications – part i: Concepts, approaches, and technical challenges. *Power Systems, IEEE Transactions on*, 22(4):1743–1752, 2007.

[48] O. A. Misund. Dynamics of moving masses: variability in packing density, shape, and size among herring, sprat, and saithe schools. *ICES Journal of Marine Science: Journal du Conseil*, 50(2):145–160, 1993.

[49] J. C. Montgomery, A. Jeffs, S. D. Simpson, M. Meekan, and C. Tindle. Sound as an orientation cue for the pelagic larvae of reef fishes and decapod crustaceans. *Advances in marine biology*, 51:143–196, 2006.

[50] A. Okubo. Dynamical aspects of animal grouping: swarms, schools, flocks, and herds. *Advances in biophysics*, 22:1–94, 1986.

[51] L. Panait and S. Luke. A pheromone-based utility model for collaborative foraging. In *Proceedings of the Third International Joint Conference on Autonomous Agents and Multiagent Systems-Volume 1*, pages 36–43. IEEE Computer Society, 2004.

[52] D. C. Parker, S. M. Manson, M. A. Janssen, M. J. Hoffmann, and P. Deadman. Multi-agent systems for the simulation of land-use and land-cover change: a review. *Annals of the association of American Geographers*, 93(2):314–337, 2003.

[53] J. K. Parrish. Re-examining the selfish herd: are central fish safer? *Animal Behaviour*, 38(6):1048–1053, 1989.

[54] H. V. D. Parunak. "go to the ant": Engineering principles from natural multi-agent systems. *Annals of Operations Research*, 75:69–101, 1997.

[55] T. Pitcher, A. Magurran, and I. Winfield. Fish in larger shoals find food faster. *Behavioral Ecology and Sociobiology*, 10(2):149–151, 1982.

[56] J. Potter and M. Chitre. Do fish fry use emergent behaviour in schools to find coral reefs by sound. In *AGU Ocean Sciences Meeting, Honolulu, Hawaii*, 2006.

[57] H. R. Pulliam and T. Caraco. Living in groups: is there an optimal group size. *Behavioural ecology: an evolutionary approach*, 2:122–147, 1984.

[58] C. W. Reynolds. Flocks, herds and schools: A distributed behavioral model. *ACM SIGGRAPH Computer Graphics*, 21(4):25–34, 1987.

[59] M. Shaukat, M. Chitre, and S. H. Ong. A bio-inspired distributed approach for searching underwater acoustic source using a team of auvs. In *OCEANS 2013, Bergen*, 2013.

[60] W. Shen and D. H. Norrie. Agent-based systems for intelligent manufacturing: a state-of-the-art survey. *Knowledge and information systems*, 1(2):129–156, 1999.

[61] R. Sibly. Optimal group size is unstable. *Animal Behaviour*, 31(3):947–948, 1983.

[62] M. Stojanovic and J. Preisig. Underwater acoustic communication channels: Propagation models and statistical characterization. *Communications Magazine, IEEE*, 47(1):84 –89, january 2009.

[63] K. Sugawara, T. Kazama, and T. Watanabe. Foraging behavior of interacting robots with virtual pheromone. In *Intelligent Robots and Systems, 2004.(IROS 2004). Proceedings. 2004 IEEE/RSJ International Conference on*, volume 3, pages 3074–3079. IEEE, 2004.

[64] D. Sumpter. *Collective animal behavior*. Princeton University Press, 2010.

[65] D. Sutantyo, P. Levi, C. Moslinger, and M. Read. Collective-adaptive lévy flight for underwater multi-robot exploration. In *Mechatronics and Automation (ICMA), 2013 IEEE International Conference on*, pages 456–462. IEEE, 2013.

[66] R. J. Urick. Sound propagation in the sea. Technical report, DTIC Document, 1979.

[67] R. J. Urick. Ambient noise in the sea. Technical report, DTIC Document, 1984.

[68] A. Vargha and H. D. Delaney. A critique and improvement of the cl common language effect size statistics of mcgraw and wong. *Journal of Educational and Behavioral Statistics*, 25(2):101–132, 2000.

[69] T. Vicsek, A. Czirók, E. Ben-Jacob, I. Cohen, and O. Shochet. Novel type of phase transition in a system of self-driven particles. *Physical review letters*, 75(6):1226, 1995.

[70] Z. Wang and D. Gu. Cooperative target tracking control of multiple robots. *Industrial Electronics, IEEE Transactions on*, 59(8):3232–3240, 2012.

Firefly-Inspired Synchronization in Swarms of Mobile Agents

Fernando Perez-Diaz
Natural Robotics Lab
Sheffield Robotics &
Department of Computer Science
The University of Sheffield, UK
fernando.perez.diaz@sheffield.ac.uk

Ruediger Zillmer
Unilever R&D, Port Sunlight, UK
Ruediger.Zillmer@unilever.com

Roderich Groß
Natural Robotics Lab
Sheffield Robotics &
Department of Automatic Control and Systems Engineering
The University of Sheffield, UK
r.gross@sheffield.ac.uk

ABSTRACT

Recently, there has been growing interest in the synchronization of mobile pulse-coupled oscillators. We build on the work by Prignano et al. (Phys. Rev. Lett. 110, 114101) and show that agents that interact exclusively with others in their cone of vision can exhibit different synchronization regimes. Depending on their speed, synchronization emerges as a slow process through spreading of the local coherence, as a fast process where global synchronization dominates, or it is inhibited for a range of intermediate speeds. In addition, we show that, not only the speed of the agents, but also their angle and range of interaction can tune the appearance of this intermediate regime.

Categories and Subject Descriptors

I.2.11 [**Computing Methodologies**]: Distributed Artificial Intelligence—*Multiagent systems*

Keywords

Mobile Agents, Agent-Based Simulation, Emergent Behavior, Complex Systems, Swarm Robotics, Artificial Social Systems

1. INTRODUCTION

Rhythmic synchronous flashing by large groups of males of some firefly species, in particular, tropical fireflies in Southeast Asia, has been reported for hundreds of years. This phenomenon awoke the interest of biologist from the beginning of the 20th century, and a vast number of research articles appeared during that time, describing and modeling this behavior [4]. Each species of firefly may achieve this flash synchronization in a different manner, but the basic mechanism is as follows: each insect in the colony has an internal biological clock that indicates the timing of the flashes; by observing the firings of other individuals, either the timing or frequency of its own flashes gets slightly shifted in an attempt to match this external stimuli [15]. In such a way, spontaneous order appears without a leader, in a process of self-organization.

The synchronization of populations of pulse-coupled oscillators is not unique to fireflies. It is observed in numerous natural systems, such as pacemaker cells in the heart, pacemaker neurons in the brain (for instance, those producing the circadian rhythm), the unison chirping of crickets, or even the synchronization of women menstrual cycles [25, 13].

The ubiquity of synchronization in communities of locally interacting constituents gave rise to intensive research in mathematics, and complex networks and non-linear dynamics in physics [1], aiming for an understanding and a description of these multiple systems led by the seminal work of Winfree [24]. Most of this research focuses on static networks of oscillators. Recently, however, there has been increasing interest in the study of synchronization in networks of mobile oscillators [19, 7, 20]. These studies aim to understand what role topological changes, due to the mobility of the oscillators, play on the synchronization of theses systems.

In [20] and [19], Prignano et al. investigate a system similar to that of fireflies. Each oscillator moves in the plane and influences only the neighbors that lie within a certain range of interaction [20] (**case A**); or only its nearest neighbor [19] (**case B**). In *case A*, a monotonically descending relationship between the time it takes for the system to synchronize and the speed of the oscillators can be observed. This is what one would expect, given that at high speeds all the oscillators interact with each other frequently, whereas at low speeds the neighborhood of any particular individual does not often change, leading to a rapid local synchrony but taking a long time to achieve coherence at a global scale. Surprisingly, in *case B*, a non-monotonic dependence is found. While the slow and fast regimes remain the same, an intermediate regime appears where neither of these mechanisms work and synchronization is inhibited.

The self-organizing behavior of pulse-couple oscillators is akin to that of swarm intelligent systems, where a number of relatively simple and limited individuals can achieve a complex collective behavior through local interactions without any centralized control [3, 17, 2]. Therefore, it is natural to extend the aforementioned work to a swarms of robots. As a matter of fact, Christensen et al. [6] developed a swarm level fault detection behavior based on firefly synchroniza-

Appears in: *Proceedings of the 14th International Conference on Autonomous Agents and Multiagent Systems (AAMAS 2015), Bordini, Elkind, Weiss, Yolum (eds.), May 4–8, 2015, Istanbul, Turkey.*

tion, and implemented it on the *swarm-bot* robotic platform. In their work, similarly to *case A*, the agents interacted with others within a certain range. However, the effect of the speed of the robots and their radius of interaction was not investigated.

In this work we study a different kind of interaction, where the agents are influenced only by others in their cone of vision. This is a potentially more realistic scenario for robotics than *case B* given that, without knowledge of the position of every member of the population, a particular agent cannot know whether it is the nearest neighbor to another agent. We show that by tuning the angle and range of vision, both the monotonic and the non-monotonic behaviors of *case A* and *case B*, respectively, can be obtained.

Other recent works that researched pulse-coupled synchronization in swarms of robots include [5], which studied a synchronization based approach to task allocation; and [21, 22, 23], which utilize evolutionary approaches to obtain robot controllers that would lead to swarm synchronization. Some of these approaches involve the use a line of sight interaction, similar to the cone of vision. However, all of them deal with movement synchronization in the environment. Therefore, the impact of the speed of the agents was not examined.

This paper is organized as follows. Section 2 introduces the methods used, including the oscillator and neighborhood models as well as the synchronization metric. Section 3 presents the experiments performed in a particle simulator and compares the results with those of [19, 20]. Section 4 shows the effects of embodiment and physical constraints in a robot simulator. Section 5 concludes the paper.

2. METHODS

We consider a population of N agents moving with constant speed V in a bounded square 2-D environment of side length L. Each agent possesses an associated internal oscillator. When an agent reaches the scene boundary it will randomly reorient its motion to a direction uniformly selected from the range $\left[-\frac{\pi}{2}, \frac{\pi}{2}\right]$ with respect to the wall's normal. This is in contrast to the results of [20, 19], where periodical boundary conditions were considered (topologically equivalent to a torus). A bounded scenario was preferred here for realism and practical feasibility.

Two sets of simulations were realized. Firstly, we analyze an abstract model, where each oscillator behaves as a point-like particle. Secondly, we study the effects of physical constraints and embodiment on a robot simulator. The robot chosen for these simulations was the *e-puck* [14].

2.1 Oscillator Model

The model of the internal oscillator of each agent, i, is a simple integrate and fire oscillator,

$$\frac{d\phi_i}{dt} = \frac{1}{\tau}, \tag{1}$$

where its phase, $\phi_i \in [0, 1]$, grows linearly in time with period τ, until a threshold, $\phi_{thres} = 1$, is reached and a firing event occurs. Upon firing, the oscillator resets its phase to 0, and the phase of the neighbors, ϕ_n, is updated multiplicatively by a factor ϵ [20, 19, 6], as follows (see Fig. 1 left):

$$\phi_i\left(t^-\right) = 1 \Rightarrow \begin{cases} \phi_i\left(t^+\right) = 0 \\ \phi_n\left(t^+\right) = (1+\epsilon)\,\phi_n\left(t^-\right). \end{cases} \tag{2}$$

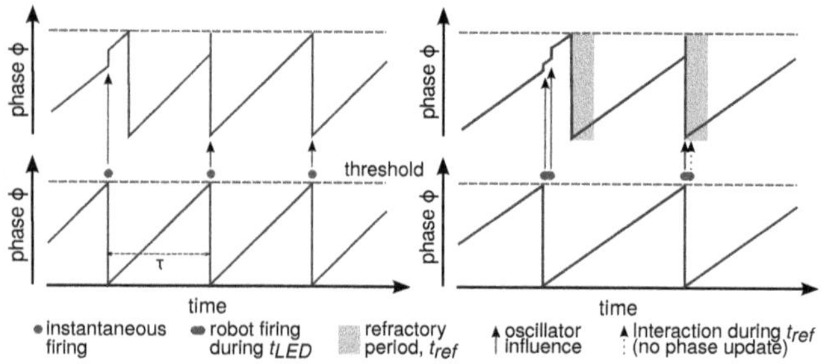

Figure 1: Dynamics of two oscillators, where the bottom one influences the top one. Left: Oscillator model and interaction as described in Sec. 2.1. Right: Oscillator as implemented in the robot simulations. During the refractory period (only shown for the upper oscillator) the oscillator is not influenced by any interaction. Outside the refractory period multiple consecutive interactions are allowed, as it will benefit synchronization.

Table 1: Dimensions of the Cone of Vision

Parameter	Value
R	$[0.05L, \infty]$
θ	$[10°, 360°]$

2.2 Neighborhood Model

An agent, A, is considered neighbor of another, B, if and only if B lies inside the **cone of vision** of A, that is, the circular sector centered in A, with radius R and angle θ, and oriented in the direction of motion of A (see Fig. 2 top-left). If A is a neighbor of B, then B will influence A when applying Eq. 2.

The bottom-left panel in Fig. 2 shows the *interaction range* used in *case A* [20]. In that case, agents that lie within a certain distance, R, from another are considered its neighbors. By contrast, regardless of the shape of the interaction region, our *cone* assigns the neighborhood in the opposite direction. That is, if B can be seen by A, then A is B's neighbor. This choice was made to emulate a natural scenario, where the flashing of a firefly would only be recognized by those insects that are currently seeing it. Note, however, that for $\theta = 360°$ this interaction becomes equivalent to *case A*.

In contrast to the *nearest neighbor interaction* (*case B*) described in [19] where each oscillator has precisely 1 neighbor, in our model any given agent could have from 0 to potentially $N-1$ neighbors (see Fig. 2 right for examples of different interactions). In this aspect, this is similar to the *interaction range* scenario of *case A*.

The dimensions of the cone of vision that were studied are shown in Table 1. Note that any R greater than $\sqrt{2}L$, the length of the diagonal, is equivalent to an infinite range.

2.3 Particle Simulation

The particle simulation was performed in an event-driven manner. The positions, phases and orientations of the oscillators were updated either when a wall was reached by a particle or when an oscillator reached the firing threshold. In this way we simulated pure continuous time and equation (1) is integrated exactly.

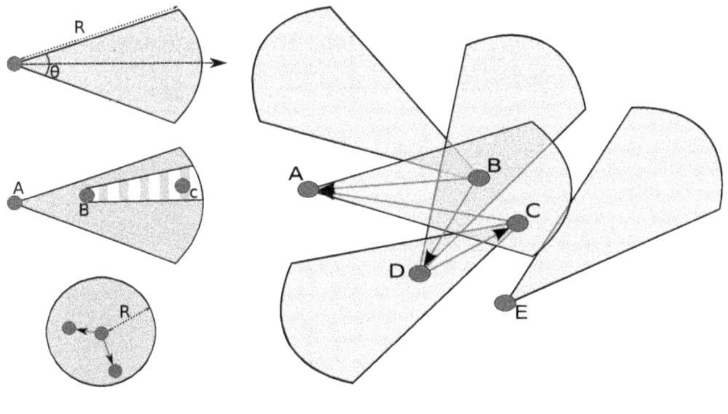

Figure 2: Top-left: Cone of interaction. Center-left: Occlusion in the robot simulation; C cannot be seen from A. Bottom-left: Interaction range used in [20]. The red arrows indicates the direction of the interaction. Right: Example of different interactions. A is neighbor of B and C; B has two neighbors, A and D; A and E have no neighbors and E is not a neighbor of any other agent.

Given that some agents may fire upon receiving a phase update from a firing neighbor and, it turn, could elicit further firings, in the particle simulation this interaction occurs instantaneously in frozen time. This also implies that, if two firings are received at the exact same time, a single phase update will take place.

2.4 Robot Simulation

2.4.1 Robot and Simulator

The robot simulation was performed using the open-source Enki simulation toolkit [12]. Enki provides a faster than real time simulation of the physics and dynamics of colonies of robots, and it contains a built-in model of the e-puck (see Fig. 3). This robot weighs 152 g and its body is modeled as a differential-wheeled cylinder of diameter 7.4 cm. The distance between the wheels is 5.1 cm. Their speed can be set independently within the range $[-12.8, 12.8]$ cm/s. The length of the control cycle was set to $\Delta t = 0.1$ s and the physics was updated 100 times per second.

The choice of simulator is supported by the work of Gauci et al. [8, 9] where swarm controllers synthesized using Enki were successfully validated with up to 40 physical e-pucks.

The e-puck is equipped with eight short-range infra-red proximity sensors and a proximity camera located at its front. The camera has a resolution of 640 (horizontal) by 480 (vertical) RGB pixels, with a corresponding 56° horizontal viewing angle. The full image cannot be processed or stored in the dsPIC of the robot. Nevertheless, a subsampled image can be acquired at 4 frames per second [14].

The proximity sensors are used to implement a simple wall avoidance algorithm. When the distance to a wall is smaller than a certain value, the robot reorients itself as described at the beginning of Section 2. In order to keep the robot simulation as close as possible to the particle simulation, no explicit robot-robot collision avoidance mechanism was employed. We carried out preliminary tests with ENKI and the physical e-pucks, and found that the circular shape of the robot allows two agents to come in contact and slide past each other.

2.4.2 Oscillator

The phase of the robot's oscillator is updated according to the discrete version of (1),

$$\phi_i(t_n) = \frac{\Delta t}{\tau}\phi_i(t_{n-1}), \tag{3}$$

where t_n represents the nth control step. Once the phase reaches the threshold and is reset to 0, the red LED ring on the contour of the robot is switched on and kept lit for a certain interval.

2.4.3 Cone and Interaction

The agents take snapshots using their camera, which is pointed in the direction of motion. In Enki, the camera can be set to capture images of objects within a certain distance range and angle of view, which directly implements the neighborhood model. If a certain robot is firing, and thus having its LEDs on, it will be detected by the camera of its neighbors and lead to an update of their phases according to (2). However, in contrast to the particle simulation, in this case a direct line of sight between the two agents is also required. Therefore, the effects of occlusion by other robots is taken into account (see center-left panel in Fig. 2).

In the particle simulation the interaction between oscillators occurs instantaneously. In a real robot scenario that would be impossible. For a robot to observe a flash it must record and process the snapshot of its camera [6]. This process inevitably gives rise to delays. For this reason, the LEDs are kept on for a certain time, t_{LED}. Because of the necessary latency of the flashing signal and the delays in processing it, an oscillator could get displaced from synchrony if it detects more than one firing. To compensate for this effect, a refractory period, t_{ref} was added immediately after each agent has fired. During this interval the oscillator is not influenced by any interaction [11, 18] (see Fig. 1 right). We have found experimentally that keeping the LEDs on for four control cycles, $t_{LED} = 4\Delta t$, while staying in the refractory period for eight cycles, $t_{ref} = 8\Delta t$ allowed the robots to achieve and sustain synchronization.

Even though the actual camera of the e-puck is directional and has a limited field of view (approx. 56°), we assumed that it can detect images of up to 360 degrees for the sake of completeness. In practice this could be implemented by rotating the robots on the spot to observe the full environment. To account for this the LEDs should be kept on for longer and the refractory period increased accordingly.

2.5 Synchronization Metric

In order to measure the level of synchrony of the system, a certain oscillator, ϕ_1, is selected as reference, and upon its kth firing, at time T_k, we calculate the order parameter [20, 19], defined as follows,

$$\eta(T_k) = \frac{1}{N}\sum_{i=1}^{N}\cos(2\pi\phi_i(T_k)). \tag{4}$$

As it is calculated at the moment of firing of the reference oscillator, this function measures the average phase difference between the other oscillators and the reference. It increases monotonically with the degree of synchronization, from $\eta(T_k) = 0$ for a totally uniform phase distribution, to $\eta(T_k) = 1$ for complete synchronization.

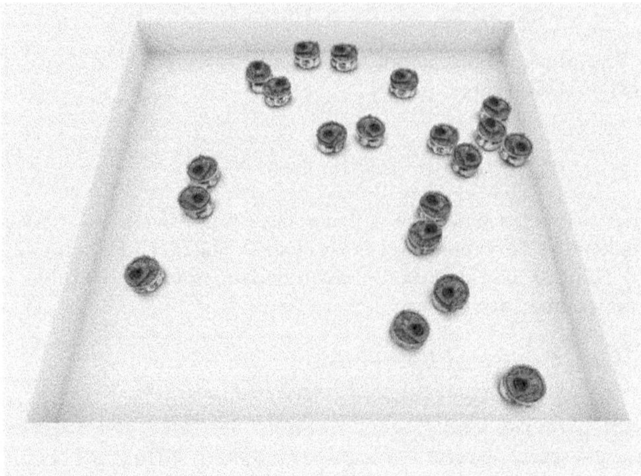

Figure 3: The robot environment in ENKI showing 20 e-pucks in a 100 cm square arena. The robots with the red LED ring turned on are firing.

Table 2: Parameters of the Particle Simulation

Parameter	Value
N	20
L	200 cm
τ	1 s
ϵ	0.1
V	$[10^{-2}, 10^{2}]$ cm/s
η_{sync}	$1 - 10^{-6}$
T_{cens}	10^{7}

The simulation is stopped once the order parameter arrives to a certain threshold, $\eta_{sync} \simeq 1$; in this case we consider the system to be synchronized. Moreover, we count the number of cycles, k, of the reference oscillator elapsed until synchronization. From this point, we will refer to this value as T_{sync}. This **synchronization time** is a good measure of how long it takes for a system to achieve coherence independently of the oscillation period.

For practical reasons, we halted any simulation where T exceeded a certain censoring threshold, T_{cens}, before synchronization is achieved. This censoring is taken into account when calculating the mean of T_{sync} over several repetitions (see Appendix A for further details).

3. PARTICLE SIMULATION RESULTS

We performed the particle simulations with the parameters shown in Table 2. We studied the effect of varying the cone dimensions for 30 different speeds, V. We explored a set of 18 angles of view, θ, and 14 radii, R, from the ranges in Table 1. For each combination of V, θ, R the simulations were repeated 100 times, where the initial phases, positions and orientations of the oscillators were randomly chosen.

Figure 4 shows the average synchronization time, T_{sync}, as a function of the speed of the oscillators, for several angles, θ, and radii, R, of the cone of interaction. We obtained both the monotonic dependence of *case A* and the non-monotonic relationship of *case B*. For large angles and large cone radii $Tsync$ is a strictly decreasing function of V. However, as the size of the cone decreases (either θ or R decrease), the monotonicity is broken, and an intermediate region appears where the synchronization is totally impeded. This intermediate regime varies from a small bump in the curve, to a drastic inhibition of synchronization, for relatively narrow and short interaction cones. Furthermore, we observe that, when present, the onset of the intermediate regime varies as a function of R. For comparison, the behavior for a nearest neighbor interaction (*case B*), for the same setup is depicted with a dashed-line. The resemblance to our case becomes apparent in the second plot in Fig. 4 ($R = 0.25L$), where the intermediate regime coincides for the same range of speeds.

For further insight, Figure 5 displays the dependence of T_{sync} as a function of the ranges of interaction for several angles of vision. Here we perceive three clearly distinct sectors corresponding to the three dynamical regimes. Narrow angles exhibit a low degree of synchronization and the three areas are visibly separated. As the cone widens, the intermediate regime gradually disappears and gets relegated to the small radii region of the graph. Concurrently, a monotonic gradient of $Tsync$ as a function of V appears and gradually spreads over all values of R. In the limit when $\theta \to 360°$, which is equivalent to *case A*, the synchronization time decreases monotonically with V and R as in [20].

The experiments corresponding to $R = 0.25$ were repeated for four additional environment sizes (L = 50, 100, 300 and 400 cm). In agreement with the results of [19], the location of the intermediate regime varies proportionally with the environment size. This relationship is not trivial, given that for a change of L not only the relative speed, V, changes but also the density of oscillators. Figure 7 shows the shift in speeds of T_{sync} from $L = 200$ cm to $L = 100$ cm.

Table 3: Parameters of the Robot Simulation

Parameter	Value
N	20
L	200 cm
τ	8 s
ϵ	0.1
V	$[10^{-2}, 12.8]$ cm/s
η_{sync}	0.95
T_{cens}	10^{4}
Δt	0.1 s
t_{LED}	0.4 s
t_{ref}	0.8 s

4. ROBOT SIMULATION RESULTS

We performed the robot simulations with the parameters shown in Table 3. For the initial experiments we used a scenario of the same size as in the particle simulation ($L =$ 200 cm). Nevertheless, the maximum speed of the e-pucks is 12.8 cm/s, which is significantly lower than the maximum investigated speed in the particle simulations (100 cm/s). We set $\tau = 8$ s in order to keep the number of cycles it takes for an agent to cover L approximately equal in both simulations.

Conditioned by the fact that embodied simulations are several orders of magnitude more costly to perform than particle simulations, we set lower synchronization and censoring thresholds compared to the particle simulation. By applying Eq. 4 to a system with 20 agents, $\eta_{sync} = 0.95$ implies that the firing time of any individual is not shifted further than 0.01τ from all other firings, which is equivalent

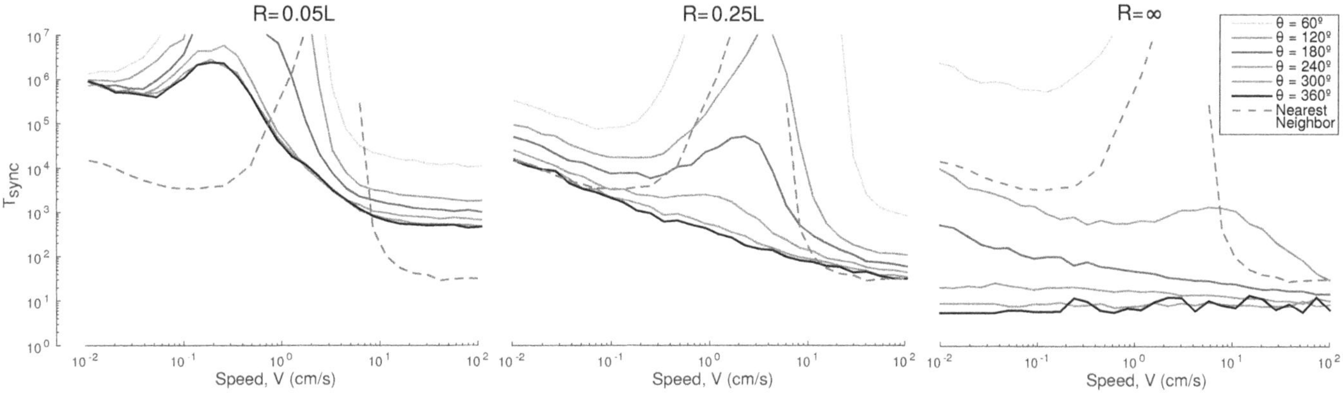

Figure 4: Log-log plot of T_{sync} as a function of the speed of the oscillators for the particle simulation. The results for three ranges of interaction, R, are shown. Different color lines represent different angles of interaction. The dashed line represents the nearest neighbor interaction of *case B* for the parameters of Table 2.

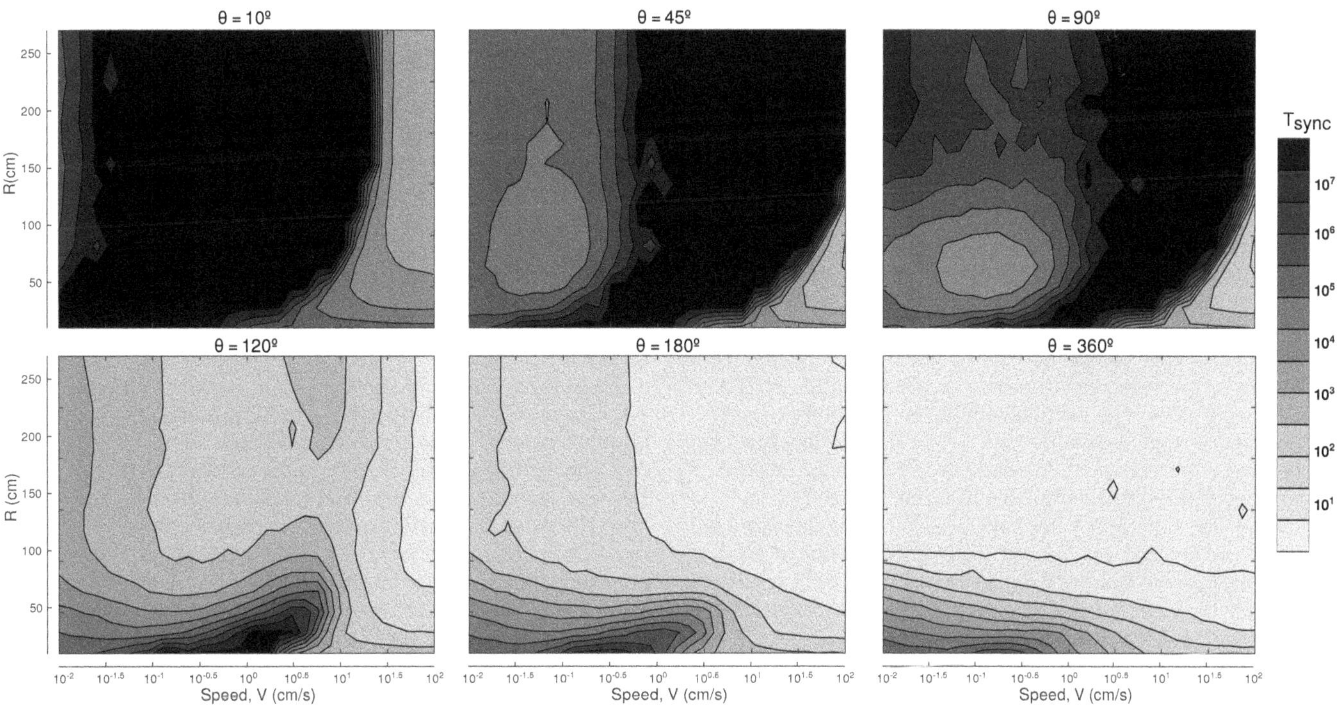

Figure 5: Contour plot showing the change in T_{sync} as a function of the speed of the oscillators, V, and their ranges of interaction, R, for the particle simulation. The results for six different angles of vision are shown. $\theta = 360$ is equivalent to *caseA*.

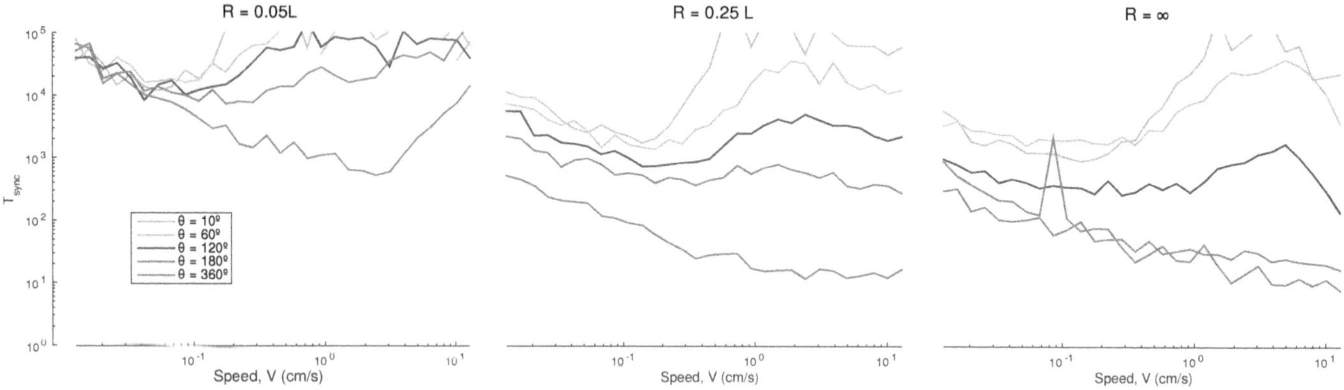

Figure 6: Log-log plot of T_{sync} as a function of the speed of the oscillators for the robot simulation. The results for three ranges of interaction, R, are shown. Different color lines represent different angles of interaction.

to the threshold suggested in [6]. $T_{cens} = 10^4$ with $\tau = 8$ s corresponds to 22 hours, much longer than what an e-puck can run continuously.

The effect of varying the cone dimensions was studied for 30 different speeds. We selected five different angles of interaction, θ, and six interaction radii, R, from the ranges in Table 1. For every combination of V, θ and R we performed 25 trials, where the initial phases, positions and orientations of the robots were randomly chosen. Additionally, we ensured that the random initial positions of the e-pucks were physically possible, i.e. no two individuals can occupy simultaneously the same space.

The results of these experiments are shown in Figure 6. Despite the changes in implementation with respect to the particle simulation, the same essential behavior is found (cf. Fig. 4). The non-monotonic relationship of T_{sync} with respect to V is observed. For cones of vision of increasing dimensions, a single monotonic regime dominates. However, in the case of embodied robot simulations, we observe a stronger prevalence of the intermediate regime than in the particle simulation. For instance, for $R = \infty$ and $\theta = 60°$ we still observe an inhibition of the synchronization in the robot simulation, whereas in the particle simulation this is almost completely smoothed out.

The simulations corresponding to $R = 0.25L$ were repeated for two smaller environment sizes ($L = 100$ and 150 cm). In contrast to the particle simulation, we observe that the inhibitory regime disappears for $L = 100$ cm for some of the studied angles (Fig. 8), instead of the shift in speeds previously obtained. We ascribe this difference to the effect of occlusion. For large environments, i.e. low robot densities, the effect of the physical size of the agents can be neglected. However, for an environment densely populated with robots, occlusion will occur more frequently. This will, inevitably, influence the rate at which agents change neighbors.

5. CONCLUSIONS

This paper has presented a new case study on the emergence and tuning of synchronization in mobile pusle-coupled oscillators and it has shown a possible implementation on a swarm of robots.

Prigano et al. [19] hypothesized that the occurrence of the intermediate regime in *case B* (that is, the case where only the agent that is nearest to a firing agent is influenced) might be related to the rate of change of neighbors. Our results support this hypothesis, given that a smaller cone of interaction (both in angle and range) implies a higher frequency of neighborhood change. Moreover, for very wide angles, our results approach those of *case A* [20] (that is, the case where all agents within a certain distance from a firing agent are influenced). The dimensions of the cone of vision allow to connect both cases, thus yielding a natural extension of the aforementioned work. We have shown that global synchrony can be tuned both with the speed of the agents and the characteristics of their interaction. Further analysis is needed to understand the underlying mechanism that governs the dynamical regimes of the system.

The work of [19] suggested a possible discontinuity in the intermediate regime of *case B*, where the synchronization is completely inhibited (i.e. $T_{sync} = \infty$). In our case, the synchronization time is computationally incalculable for small cones of vision. Nevertheless, we observe a gradual change of the behaviour for the intermediate range of speeds, from a slight impediment to a large inhibition of the synchronization. This could indicate that such a discontinuity might not exist in the present case until the size of the cone becomes infinitely small. However, this hypothesis remains unproven. In practice, the intermediate regime acts as a true boundary to synchronization.

In addition, an implementation on a swarm of e-pucks is simulated. For a sufficiently large environment, this yielded similar results to the particle simulation despite the physical constraints of the system, such as occlusion, collisions between agents and a non-instantaneous interaction. However, for a small environment, where the robots would be closer to each other, the effects of embodiment (i.e. occlusion, collision) become apparent. The intermediate regime is no longer present for some configurations. In the future, we intend to validate the results of this paper using a swarm of physical e-puck robots.

The cone of vision was chosen due to its applicability in a robotics scenario. We demonstrated that the synchronization of the system can be inhibited under certain conditions. This becomes relevant when applying algorithms that rely on synchronization to robots that interact with each other using an interaction akin to the cone of vision. An example would be to apply the fault-detection method proposed by [6] on robots with a directional camera, whereas it was originally implemented on robots with an omnidirectional camera. Our findings suggest that depending on the dimensions of their field of view, the speed of the agents would affect the performance of this algorithm.

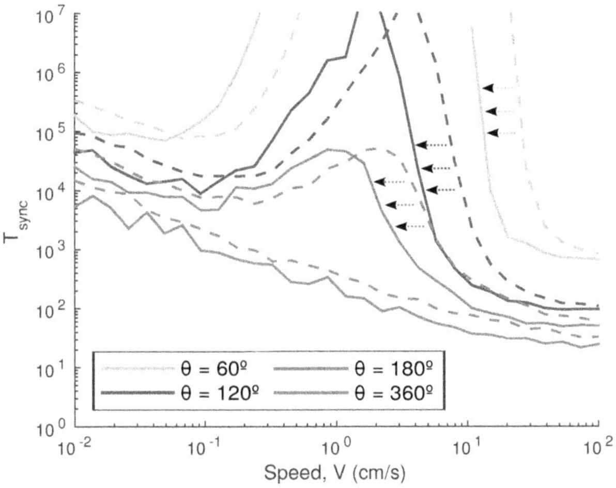

Figure 7: Effects of decreasing the environment size for $R = 0.25L$ in the particle simulation. The dashed lines represent the log-log plot of T_{sync} as a function of V for $L = 200\,\text{cm}$ whereas the solid lines depict the corresponding curves for $L = 100\,\text{cm}$.

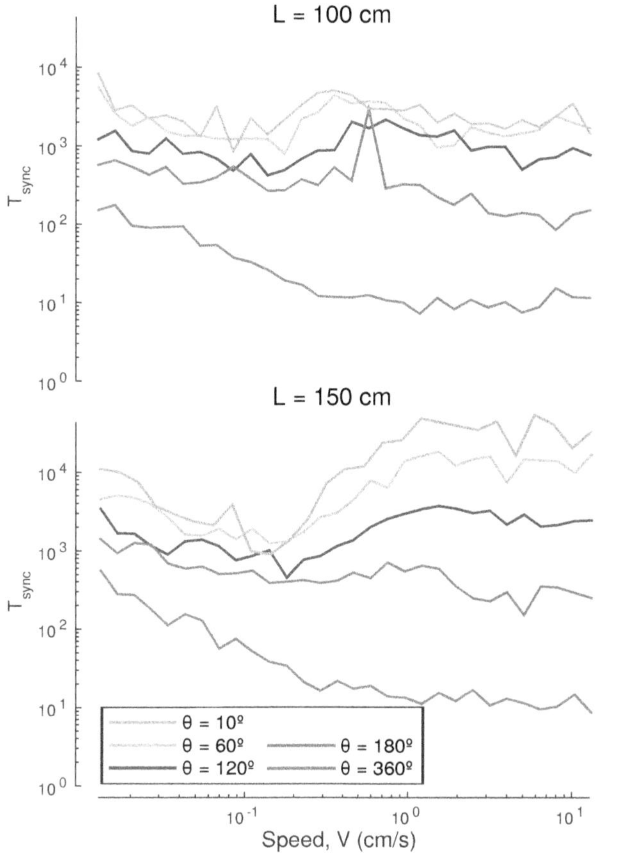

Figure 8: Effects of decreasing the environment size for $R = 0.25L$ in the robot simulation. The solid lines represent the log-log plot of T_{sync} as a function of V for $L = 100\,\text{cm}$ (top) and $L = 150\,\text{cm}$ (bottom).

REFERENCES

[1] A. Arenas, A. Díaz-Guilera, J. Kurths, Y. Moreno, and C. Zhou. Synchronization in complex networks. *Physics Reports*, 469(3):93–153, 2008.

[2] G. Beni. From swarm intelligence to swarm robotics. *Swarm Robotics. Lecture Notes in Computer Science*, 3342:1-9, 2005

[3] E. Bonabeau, M. Dorigo, and G. Theraulaz. *Swarm intelligence: From natural to artificial systems.* Oxford University Press, 1999.

[4] J. Buck. Synchronous rhythmic flashing of fireflies. II. *Quarterly Review of Biology*, Vol. 63, No. 3 265–289, 1988.

[5] M. Castillo-Cagigal, A. Brutschy, A. Gutiérrez, and M. Birattari. Temporal task allocation in periodic environments. *Lecture Notes in Computer Science*, 8667:182–193, 2014.

[6] A. L. Christensen, R. O'Grady, and M. Dorigo. From fireflies to fault-tolerant swarms of robots. *IEEE Transactions on Evolutionary Computation*, 13(4):754–766, 2009.

[7] N. Fujiwara, J. Kurths, and A. Díaz-Guilera. Synchronization in networks of mobile oscillators. *Physical Review E*, 83(2):025101, 2011.

[8] M. Gauci, J. Chen, W. Li, T. J. Dodd, and R. Groß. Clustering objects with robots that do not compute. *Proceedings of the 2014 International Conference on Autonomous Agents and Multi-Agent Systems.* International Foundation for Autonomous Agents and Multiagent Systems pages 421–428, 2014.

[9] M. Gauci, J. Chen, W. Li, T. J. Dodd, and R. Groß. Self-organized aggregation without computation. *The International Journal of Robotics Research*, 33(8):1145-1161, 2014

[10] E. L. Kaplan and P. Meier. Nonparametric estimation from incomplete observations. *Journal of the American Statistical Association*, 53(282):457–481, 1958.

[11] Y. Kuramoto. Collective synchronization of pulse-coupled oscillators and excitable units. *Physica D: Nonlinear Phenomena*, 50(1):15–30, 1991.

[12] S. Magnenat, M. Waibel, and A. Beyeler. Enki: The fast 2D robot simulator, 2007.

[13] R. E. Mirollo and S. H. Strogatz. Synchronization of pulse-coupled biological oscillators. *SIAM Journal on Applied Mathematics*, 50(6):1645–1662, 1990.

[14] F. Mondada, M. Bonani, X. Raemy, J. Pugh, C. Cianci, A. Klaptocz, S. Magnenat, J.-C. Zufferey, D. Floreano, and A. Martinoli. The e-puck, a robot designed for education in engineering. In *Proceedings of the 9th Conference on Autonomous Robot Systems and Competitions*, volume 1, pages 59–65. IPCB: Instituto Politécnico de Castelo Branco, 2009.

[15] J. D. Murray. *Mathematical Biology I: An Introduction, vol. 17 of Interdisciplinary Applied Mathematics.* Springer, New York, USA, 2002.

[16] M. Natrella. NIST/SEMATECH e-handbook of statistical methods. 2010.

[17] S. Nouyan, R. Groß, M. Bonani, F. Mondada, and M. Dorigo. Teamwork in self-organized robot colonies. *IEEE Transactions on Evolutionary Computation*, 13(4):695–711, 2009.

[18] K. Nymoen, A. Chandra, and J. Torresen. The challenge of decentralised synchronisation in interactive music systems. In *Self-Adaptation and Self-Organizing Systems Workshops (SASOW), 2013 IEEE 7th International Conference on*, pages 95–100. IEEE, 2013.

[19] L. Prignano, O. Sagarra, and A. Díaz-Guilera. Tuning synchronization of integrate-and-fire oscillators through mobility. *Physical Review Letters*, 110(11):114101, 2013.

[20] L. Prignano, O. Sagarra, P. M. Gleiser, and A. Diaz-Guilera. Synchronization of moving integrate and fire oscillators. *International Journal of Bifurcation and Chaos*, 22(07), 2012.

[21] V. Sperati, V. Trianni, and S. Nolfi. Self-organised path formation in a swarm of robots. *Swarm Intelligence*, 5(2):97–119, 2011.

[22] V. Trianni and S. Nolfi. Self-organizing sync in a robotic swarm: A dynamical system view. *IEEE Transactions on Evolutionary Computation*, 13(4):722–741, 2009.

[23] V. Trianni and S. Nolfi. Engineering the evolution of self-organizing behaviors in swarm robotics: A case study. *Artificial Life*, 17(3):183–202, 2011.

[24] A. T. Winfree. Biological rhythms and the behavior of populations of coupled oscillators. *Journal of Theoretical Biology*, 16(1):15–42, 1967.

[25] A. T. Winfree. *The geometry of biological time*, Interdisciplinary Applied Mathematics, vol. 12, Springer-Verlag New York, 2001.

APPENDIX

A. CENSORED DATA

As described in Sec. 2.5, any simulation exceeding T_{cens} is terminated. As a consequence, we will have a record of the repetitions where $T_{sync} < T_{cens}$ but no value of T_{sync} for the censored results. Despite the incompleteness of the data, we can estimate the cumulative distribution function, CDF, of the synchronization times by using the Kaplan-Meier, K-M, estimator [10]. Assume that out of M trials, there are K where $T_{sync} < T_{cens}$, the procedure for calculating K-M estimator is as follows [16]:

1. Sort T^i_{sync} in increasing order, from $i = 1$ to $i = K$.
2. Associate a number n_i for each T^i_{sync}. n_i is the number of trials that take longer than T^i_{sync} to synchronize.
3. Calculate $R(T^1_{sync}) = (n_1 - 1)/n_1$.
4. Calculate $R(T^i_{sync}) = R(T^{i-1}_{sync})(n_i - 1)/n_i$.
5. The CDF is estimated as $F(T^i_{sync}) = 1 - R(T^i_{sync})$

In this way, the censored values are counted up to the latest recorded synchronization time, T^K_{sync}. Note that the CDF is calculated without making any assumption about the form of the probability distribution function, PDF, of the data.

By examining our results we concluded that the data best fits a Weibull distribution for all the performed simulations. By adjusting the K-M estimator to the CDF of a Weibull distribution,

$$F(T_{sync}) = 1 - e^{-\left(\frac{T_{sync}}{\alpha}\right)^\gamma},$$

we obtain its two parameters, α and γ. Lastly, we can calculate the mean of T_{sync} as

$$\alpha\Gamma\left(1 + \frac{1}{\gamma}\right),$$

and its variance as

$$\alpha^2\Gamma\left(1 + \frac{2}{\gamma}\right) - \left[\alpha\Gamma\left(1 + \frac{1}{\gamma}\right)\right]^2,$$

where Γ is the Gamma function.

The accuracy of this method decreases as the number of censored values increases. Therefore, we required a minimum of 10% of the measures to be exactly obtained in order to calculate their average. If this condition is not met then we consider the mean value as undetermined.

Swarm Robot Foraging with Wireless Sensor Motes

Katherine Russell
Dept. Computer Science
George Mason University
Fairfax, Virginia USA
krussellc@gmu.edu

Michael Schader
Dept. Computer Science
George Mason University
Fairfax, Virginia USA
mschader@gmu.edu

Kevin Andrea
Dept. Computer Science
George Mason University
Fairfax, Virginia USA
kandrea@gmu.edu

Sean Luke
Dept. Computer Science
George Mason University
Fairfax, Virginia, USA
sean@cs.gmu.edu

ABSTRACT

We investigate the use of wireless sensor motes as mobile deployable waypoints for swarm robot navigation in a foraging scenario. Each robot can deploy, retrieve, and optimize the location of the sensor motes. After deployment, the robots treat the sensor motes as nodes in a sparse graph, and store and retrieve multiple pheromones and flags locally in each of them. Pheromone information stored in the sensor motes allows the robots to build up gradients to different targets of interest, and to determine which sensor motes are good candidates to optimize location, or to harvest for reuse elsewhere. Unlike many earlier pheromone-based foraging techniques, our method must deal with the physical reality of deploying and manipulating sensor motes, including a limited mote supply both onboard and in total, robustly dealing with occlusion and interference from other robots, and handling noise and robot or mote failure. We demonstrate the effectiveness of the technique both on differential drive robots of our own design, and in simulation, to examine its ability to robustly deal with various failure modes and changes in environment.

Categories and Subject Descriptors

I.2.11 [**Distributed Artificial Intelligence**]: Multiagent Systems

General Terms

Algorithms, Experimentation, Performance

Keywords

Beacons; Pheromone Robotics; Sensor Motes

1. INTRODUCTION

A major hurdle to realistic swarm robotics is performing scalable and reliable communication in difficult environments. A common solution has been to apply *indirect communication*, where the local environment itself is modified by the robots so as to leave information for future robots visiting the area. Examples include leaving trails of breadcrumbs, depositing pheromones, and erecting signs or directional markers. Indirect communication is attractive for several reasons. First, it scales to any arbitrary size area and number of agents. Second, it is potentially long-lasting. Third, information received through indirect communication is often highly relevant to a robot's current situation, since it was embedded locally in that environment. Fourth, it is robust in scenarios where global communication modes (such as a global wireless network) are infeasible.

Inspired by ants and termites, and following the lead of the artificial life literature, some swarm robotics research has examined simulating the embedding of *pheromones* directly in the environment, via drawing on surfaces with inks, scents, and phosphorescent dyes. We think these approaches have limited practical utility, partly because pheromones cannot store much information, and partly because they may mar the environments in which the robots operate.

A common alternative is to scatter some form of *breadcrumbs* or deployable *waypoints* in the environment. Robotic breadcrumbs may be small barcodes, QR codes, or RFID tags, for example. Because such objects often are read-only, much of the existing literature has augmented this kind of indirect communication with some other line-of-sight or global communication mode, or has treated such breadcrumbs as trivial environmental markers.

In this paper we study the use of wireless *sensor motes* as sophisticated read/write breadcrumbs in a food foraging scenario for a swarm of physical robots. A sensor mote is a tiny, low powered, wireless computer outfitted with an array of sensors and designed to run for months or years on batteries. Sensor motes are useful as breadcrumbs particularly because they are small, long-lived, easy to carry and deploy, and can store and retransmit significant amounts of data. Though many sensor motes can form ad-hoc networks among themselves, in this study they will only communicate with nearby robots as they pass by. Robots will not communicate with each other except indirectly through information stored in the motes.

Our experiments use small differential drive robots each outfitted with a sensor mote (for communications), and capable of picking up, moving, and releasing a single sensor mote in the environment. Robots may acquire sensor motes at a *nest* (a home base) or serendipitously in the environment, then deploy these motes as bread-crumbs. They can later optimize the location of these motes by physically adjusting their location, and can reacquire them if they are no longer needed. Robots may store and read various information in the sensor motes, including the values of different kinds of pheromones, flags, and atomic locks. The objective is for the robots to use the breadcrumbs to discover a *food source*, then optimize the breadcrumbs to shorten the trail between the nest and the food so as to maximize the amount of food being brought back to the nest.

The algorithm we will develop here is inspired by the approach we took in [9] and, as in that paper, we will likewise refer to our sensor motes as *beacons*. However the algorithm described in [9], while intended as a step in the direction of physical robots, cannot actually be deployed to real robots for a large number of reasons which we discuss later. Thus we have devised a major revision which is capable of deployment to real robots, and which deals

Appears in: *Proceedings of the 14th International Conference on Autonomous Agents and Multiagent Systems (AAMAS 2015), Bordini, Elkind, Weiss, Yolum (eds.), May 4–8, 2015, Istanbul, Turkey.*

robustly with sensor failure, occlusion, race conditions, noise, and other issues encountered in dealing with physical swarm robots in imprecise environments.

We will describe the algorithm in replicable detail, then discuss our robot platform. After this we will show an experiment with the physical robots, and validate a robot simulation with an identical experiment. The simulator affords us both faster runtime and environments with many more (virtual) robots. We will then perform experiments in simulation involving varying levels of occlusion, beacon reliability, and catastrophic beacon failure.

2. PREVIOUS WORK

Both pheromones and breadcrumbs are examples of *local indirect communication* among swarm agents, where such agents leave information in the environment for later agents to exploit. Early work in this area largely came from the artificial life community [2, 4, 12, 15, 19]. In this literature, simulated agents performed foraging on a virtual grid, using a single pheromone, and agents typically deposited and read pheromones on grid squares. Some work has extended this to multiple pheromone models [3, 25], and pheromones with rich semantics (such as different evaporation rates [16]).

Later work has come from the swarm robotics community. Some of this work directly draws pheromones on the ground using odiferous pens [20], ink [21], or phosphorescent paint [11]; or generally emitting odors [10] or other detectable chemicals [18]. Other work has approximated indirect communication using a breadcrumbs or beacons of some sort, but usually this is augmented with some other communication mode. For example, some work has used a global wireless network to simulate local indirect communication [22, 23, 24, 26]. Other work has used line-of-sight or short-range communication [13, 14, 17], or presumed fixed global communications devices embedded in the environment [1]. Robots have also communicated "pheromone"-like data by forming chains among themselves rather than fixing information in the environment directly (such as in [7, 8]). Finally, robots have themselves acted as mobile beacons for other classes of robots [5].

We are interested in a system which performs indirect communication by deploying and otherwise manipulating beacons which are capable of storing and transmitting rich information to local robots. We first proposed this approach in [9], where simulated swarm agents deployed, removed, and updated mobile beacons in the environment. These beacons would store local pheromone information deposited in them by the agents, and which acted as nodes in a sparse graph embedded in the environment. The agents used these beacons, and their pheromone information, to build up different gradients for other agents to follow. This model was meant as a first-step towards deployment to real physical robots, but the algorithm made a large number of simplifying assumptions which would prevent this, including:

- The agents shared a global, immediately available pool of beacons. An agent could immediately teleport a beacon from this pool to itself, or transport a beacon from the environment to the pool.
- The agents were point objects and could not collide with nor obstruct one another. Any number of agents could arrive at a given beacon at the same time.
- An agent could always see all beacons in its local environment: beacons were never occluded, nor difficult to identify.
- The beacons were reliably read from, written to, deployed, retrieved, and moved.
- The agents were not in parallel, and so could not encounter race conditions when working with the same beacon.
- The algorithm was generally not robust to noise.
- The algorithm was not sufficiently conservative when moving or retrieving beacons, and would often strand agents alone or on "islands" of beacons, with no way for them to find their way back home.

3. ALGORITHM DESCRIPTION

In this paper we describe a major revision of the technique described in [9] and demonstrate its deployment for the first time to actual physical robots. The "beacons" in our revised algorithm are mobile wireless sensor motes which communicate with nearby robots. One of the challenges in implementing this algorithm and deploying it to real physical robots is that there are a great number of corner cases and other critical implementation details necessary to describe for purposes of replicability. We beg the reader's indulgence as we discuss the algorithm in some detail here.

In the foraging scenario, robots emerge from a *nest* and search for a *food* source, then iteratively bring pellets of food back from the source to the nest. The sensor mote beacons deployed by the robots form a sparse embedded graph in the environment. For simplicity's sake, we also associate the nest and the food with unique, immobile beacons, though this is not a required feature of the environment. Robots have the ability to both add and remove beacons from the environment, as well as optimize beacon positions.

Each beacon stores several pieces of information. First, a beacon stores three real-valued *pheromones* which establish gradients in the environment to be followed by the robot: a pheromone associated with a gradient to the *nest*, one to a *food* source, and an additional *wandering* pheromone value meant to encourage exploration. As robots visit beacons, a negative wander pheromone builds up and encourages them to look elsewhere. A robot's behaviors are essentially finite-state automata, where depending on the mode of the robot, it will follow a certain pheromone gradient. Specifically, a robot may be either FORAGING for food (following the *food* gradient) or FERRYING food back to the nest (following the *nest* gradient). At all times, the robot updates the local gradients of all three pheromones based on new information.

Second, a beacon stores certain integer *indicators*: the first is the *id* of the robot, if any, that is presently "in control of" the beacon (this functions as an atomic lock when a robot wishes to move or control the beacon). The second is a *status* which can be set to one of two values: *deployed*, indicating that the beacon is in use in the environment, and *inactive*, meaning that it is not in use. New beacons, offered to robots at the nest or perhaps placed in the environment by the experimenter, are initially set to *inactive*. The status of a beacon may also be read as *faulty* if it is not operating properly. The third is a *last used* timestamp which allows the beacon to return a status of *disused* when it hasn't been updated in some period of time. This period is configurable: we set it to 3× the rough time it takes for a robot to travel from one beacon to another.

We note that that neither unique robot ids nor a global clock is required for the method proposed. Robot ids are merely a simple method of creating unique locks for small swarms, but other low conflict lock ids could be generated for larger swarms. Additionally, the *last used* timestamp mentioned above is based on the beacon's internal clock and could be (and likely often is) completely out of sync with the clocks of the robots and other beacons.

Beacon pheromones gradually decay by being iteratively multiplied by some value γ. The exact value is not important, but in our simulation experiments, we cut down by $\gamma = 0.99$ every timestep.

Robots iterate the following loop. First, they identify the beacons they can find in their immediate neighborhood (by looking about). If they are not presently associated with a beacon, they attempt to acquire one if it is available and appropriate. Then, if they are associated with a current beacon c they will read and write to it, and possibly move it. They also keep track of p, the beacon they were previously associated with, and with the next beacon n which with they intend to associate.

Below is that top-level loop. Note that initially $R_{ferrying}$ is set to some positive constant REWARD: a robot starts at the nest, believing it has just successfully ferried food back to the nest, has received a reward accordingly, and is now FORAGING. Probabilities, such as $P_{Acquire}$, will be discussed in more detail later.

TopLevel()

```
global variables
    mode ← FORAGING                      ▷ The robot's current state
    R_ferrying ← REWARD                  ▷ Reward just received while ferrying
    R_foraging ← 0                       ▷ Reward just received while foraging
    c ← □                                ▷ Current beacon, where □ means "null"
    p ← □                                ▷ Previous beacon
    n ← □                                ▷ Next beacon
    countdown ← 0                        ▷ Timer used to explore for a while
    deployFailed ← false                 ▷ Did beacon deployment fail last time?

loop
    {neighbors, inactiveBeacons} ← SurveySurroundings()
                                         ▷ Try to acquire a beacon if we don't have one
    if CanAcquireBeacon(inactiveBeacons) and Rand(P_Acquire)
        TryToAcquireBeacon(inactiveBeacons)
        {neighbors, inactiveBeacons} ←SurveySurroundings()
                                         ▷ Update the current beacon as needed
    if c ≠ □
        deployFailed ← false             ▷ Allow us to start deploying again
        UpdateCurrentBeacon(neighbors)   ▷ See Section 3.1
    DecideMode()
    DecideAndGo(neighbors)               ▷ See Section 3.2
```

The UpdateCurrentBeacon(...) and DecideAndGo(...) sub-algorithms will be described in later sections. For now, we describe the other functions here.

Rand(prob) Return true with probability *prob*, else false.

SurveySurroundings( ) Returns two (possibly empty) sets: one of nearby *deployed* beacons which are part of the network, and one of nearby *inactive* beacons. The robot's current beacon c is never included in either set. In our physical robots, these sets are built by rotating to visually observe nearby beacons, then querying the observed beacons for their status. Other methods of observing the local environment could easily replace this for robots with different capabilities.

CanAcquireBeacon(inactiveBeacons) Returns true if the robot could hold an additional beacon (in our scenario, this means that the robot is holding no beacons at present, as our robots can only carry one beacon at a time) and either *inactiveBeacons* is nonempty, or the current beacon c is the nest.

TryToAcquireBeacon(inactiveBeacons) If *inactiveBeacons* is nonempty, the robot chooses one at random and attempts to get a lock on it. If this is successful, it goes to the beacon, acquires it, and sets $c \leftarrow \square$, as the robot could now be at an unknown location. If *inactiveBeacons* is empty, the robot assumes it is at the nest, and so attempts to get a beacon from the nest's dispenser, acquire a lock on it, and set $c \leftarrow$ *nest*.

DecideMode( ) Sets the current mode to FERRYING if the following scenario is true: (1) the current mode is FORAGING, (2) the robot is not carrying any beacons, and (3) there is no trail to the food from the current beacon (the FORAGING pheromone at c is 0). This mode change is done when the robot has reached an edge in the beacon graph and decides it must expand the graph, but has no beacon to contribute to this goal. Since beacons are generally available at the nest, the robot changes its mode to head to the nest.

3.1 Updating the Current Beacon

The *UpdateCurrentBeacon(...)* sub-algorithm takes information from the survey step and uses it to decide on what to change about the current beacon c. The algorithm is as follows:

UpdateCurrentBeacon(*neighbors*)

```
UpdatePheromones(neighbors)
n ← NextBeacon(neighbors, mode)
if CanMoveBeacon(neighbors) and Rand(P_Optimize)
    MoveBeacon()
if CanRemoveBeacon(neighbors) and Rand(P_remove)
    RemoveBeacon()
UpdateLastUsed()
```

The process of updating the current beacon c involves updating its pheromone values, then optionally optimizing or deleting c. Updating the pheromone values follows essentially the same procedure as in [9]. We then determine $n \in$ *neighbors*, the next beacon to follow for the current *mode*. n is also used later in the calculations to determine whether c can be optimized or deleted.

UpdatePheromones(neighbors) As in [9], each pheromone value $U_p(c)(\forall p)$ at the current beacon c is updated using Equation 1, where c is the current beacon, $R_p(\forall p)$ is the reward for the given pheromone, and γ is a value between 0 and 1.

$$U_{foraging}(c) \leftarrow \max(U_{foraging}(c),\ R_{foraging} + \gamma \max_{i \in neighbors} U_{foraging}(i))$$
$$U_{ferrying}(c) \leftarrow \max(U_{ferrying}(c),\ R_{ferrying} + \gamma \max_{i \in neighbors} U_{ferrying}(i))$$
$$U_{wandering}(c) \leftarrow U_{wandering}(c) - 1 \qquad (1)$$

This is a form of value iteration which builds up the foraging and ferrying pheromone gradients in the environment. We want beacons with very small pheromone values to be considered disused. Thus if either $U_{foraging}(c)$ or $U_{ferrying}(c) < \varepsilon$, then it is simply set to 0 to indicate that the beacon is disused. In our experiments, we set $\varepsilon = 0.000000001$.

NextBeacon(neighbors, mode) Finds the beacon $n \in$ *neighbors*, if any, with the highest pheromone value for the given *mode*. If there is no such beacon, or if the associated pheromone for n is less than or equal to the same pheromone in c, returns $\square$, else returns n.

CanMoveBeacon(neighbors) Returns true if (1) the robot can carry more beacons, (2) there exists a path to optimize, that is: $c, p, n \neq \square$, the pheromones for the current mode in c, p, and n are in strictly increasing or decreasing order, and $n, p \in$ *neighbors*, (3) the robot is allowed to move the beacon (no other robot has locked c, p, or n) (4) the swarm is not presently expanding the network (c has both zero or both non-zero pheromone values for FORAGING and FERRYING) (5) the robot would not be breaking any other path between the *neighbors*. This last step can be defined as follows: there does not exist a strictly increasing or decreasing ordering $y \to c \to z$, where $y, z \in$ *neighbors*, for the FERRYING or FORAGING pheromones, other than $p \to c \to n$, which would be disrupted by the movement of c (so either there is no path $y \to c \to z$, or robots can travel directly between beacons y and z).

MoveBeacon( ) The robot attempts to acquire a lock on c, p, and n. If it cannot get a lock it releases all locks it has acquired and gives up moving the beacon. Otherwise it picks up c and attempts to move it directly between p and n. This fails if an obstacle is encountered in placing the beacon. There are two options for failure recovery: (1) attempt to put the beacon back, or (2) deposit the beacon at the robot's current location. We used option 2.

CanRemoveBeacon(neighbors) Performs a series of checks to determine if the current beacon c can be safely removed from the network. These are heuristics to determine if the beacon is either at an edge of the graph which not presently being expanded by the swarm, is redundant, or is on an island formed by erroneous past removals or optimizations. An *island* is a disconnected subgraph of beacons for which there is no path to the nest.

This function returns true if all of the following are true: (1) No one is using another beacon on this path (there is no lock on c, and p and n have no locks or are $\square$) (2) Neither the FERRYING nor FORAGING pheromone values at c are zero, or they both are (3) A heavily used but occluded path is not likely to be broken (any of the following are true: c is *disused*, there is more than one beacon in *neighbors*, or both pheromones FERRYING and FORAGING are zero) (4) p and n are within range of each other, if they exist: that is, removing c would not break the path from p to n (5) Any of the following is true: (a) Both FERRYING and FORAGING pheromones are zero. In other words, the robot believes it is on an island with no gradient to either food or the nest. Or: (b) *neighbors* is empty and the status of c is *disused*. This indicates that the beacon is likely an unimportant part of the network. Or: (c) there is a redundant beacon which can take the place of c. That is, there exists a beacon $b \in$ *neighbors* with higher pheromone values than c in both FERRYING and FORAGING, which is in range of all other beacons in *neighbors*.

RemoveBeacon( ) The robot sets the *deployed* status of c to false, resets all pheromones on c, and attempts to acquire c if the robot can carry more beacons. If it cannot acquire c, it will leave it on the field to be (potentially) acquired by robots at a later time.

UpdateLastUsed( ) Asks c to update its *last used* timestamp (so it will not report that it is *disused* for a while).

3.2 Deciding What To Do Next

Finally, the DecideAndGo(*neighbors*) sub-algorithm decides where to go next, attempts to travel there, and potentially deploys a beacon if appropriate. To begin, the robot tries to go to the food or nest if it exists, otherwise it considers *exploration*. Exploration is designed to add some amount of randomness to the algorithm, by making the robot do a random walk through the graph for some EXPLORECOUNTDOWN steps. This is done with probability $P_{Explore}$. Next, the robot will try *following* the current pheromone trail — the primary robot behavior — with probability P_{Follow}. If the robot can not follow the trail, it will try to *deploy* a beacon, if it can, with P_{Deploy} probability (or with 100% probability if it has no neighbors). If deployment is not an option, it may *wander* about, following the WANDERING pheromone, which is higher for beacons not frequently visited. As a last resort, the robot will *panic*.

DecideAndGo(*neighbors*)

```
if mode=FORAGING and food is within range
    GoTo(food)                    ▷ This will also update R_ferrying
else if mode=FERRYING and nest is within range
    GoTo(nest)                    ▷ This will also update R_foraging
else
    if countdown = 0 and Rand(p_Explore)
        countdown ← EXPLORECOUNTDOWN
    if countdown > 0 and neighbors is nonempty
        GoTo(random neighbor ∈ neighbors)
        countdown ← countdown−1
    else if n ≠ □ and Rand(p_Follow)
        GoTo(n)
    else if CanDeploy(neighbors) and either Rand(p_Deploy)
                                        or neighbors is empty
        Deploy(neighbors)
    else if neighbors is nonempty
        n ← NextWanderBeacon(neighbors)
        GoTo(n)
    else
        Panic( )
```

GoTo(beacon) Tries to move to the given *beacon*. If successful, c is set to *beacon* and n is set to $\square$. If *beacon* is the food source, the robot picks up a food pellet, sets $R_{foraging}$ to REWARD, and sets *mode* to FERRYING. If the beacon is the nest, the robot deposits any food it is carrying, sets $R_{ferrying}$ to REWARD, sets *mode* to FORAGING, and, if the robot arrived with food and with a beacon, returns the beacon to the nest if Rand(P_{return}) is true. Beacons are returned so that there are occasionally robots traversing the field who can pick up *inactive* beacons abandoned by other robots.

GoTo(*beacon*) can fail in some cases. It is possible to temporarily lose sight of the target beacon as the robot approaches it. To correct for this, if a robot loses sight of a beacon without sensing an obstacle (such as a robot or another beacon), it will wait for a few seconds to see if the beacon becomes visible again before declaring failure. However, if an obstacle is detected when sight is lost, the robot will attempt to go around the object and continue towards the target.

If GoTo(*beacon*) fails, c and n are both set to $\square$.

CanDeploy(neighbors) Returns true if all of the following are true: (1) *deployFailed* is false or the list of *neighbors* is empty, (2) the robot is carrying a beacon, (3) there is a reasonable place to deploy. On our robots, a reasonable place to deploy was determined by the fact that either the list of *neighbors* contains fewer than four neighbors or a pair of consecutive *neighbors* can be found in a rotational sweep of whose angle is greater than 90 degrees. Other methods would work as well and might be preferable with more capable robots or when a different density of beacons was desirable.

Deploy(neighbors) Attempts to place a beacon in the optimal direction (our robots chose the largest angle among those found as described in CanDeploy( )) at a distance slightly smaller than the range at which a robot can see a beacon from another beacon.

Deployment can fail if there is an obstacle (such as a robot) in the way of deploying at a given location. Deployment will also fail if doing so would deploy the beacon very close to previously-undetected beacons (because they were out of range at the time that

Figure 1: Physical Robot Setup. (Left) Differential-drive robot with sensor mote (at top), holding a beacon (a soda can wrapped in a unique bar code). The soda can is associated with a unique sensor mote. (Center) Larger food/nest beacon (to allow more robots to congregate) at left, also associated with a unique sensor mote, with regular beacon shown at right. (Right) Robots at work ferrying food to the nest in an environment of deployed beacons.

CanDeploy( ) was called). To detect this second situation, our robots walked some distance in the deploy direction and verified that there are no additional beacons near that location now visible which had not been previously.

If deployment fails, c is set to □ as it is now at an unknown location, and *deployFailed* is set to true. *deployFailed* prevents a second deployment without first returning to a beacon in the network. Without this, it is possible that a robot could make repeated attempts to deploy in bad locations (such as along a wall), and eventually form a single-beacon island. *deployFailed* will be reset next time that c is set in the main loop.

If deployment is successful, c is set to the deployed beacon, the lock is released for that beacon, and the *inactive* status on the beacon is set to false.

NextWanderBeacon(neighbors) Finds the beacon $n \in$ *neighbors*, if any, with the highest pheromone value WANDERING. If there is no such beacon, returns □.

Panic( ) p is set to □ and a spiral (or some other) search pattern is initiated. While the search pattern is running, the robot constantly searches for deployed beacons which are not c. The search pattern stops when such a beacon is found. c is then set to □.

4. EXPERIMENTS

Physical Robot Platform. Our test platform for the algorithm is shown in Figure 1, and consisted of multiple small robots, mobile beacons, and larger food and nest beacons.

The robots were small differential drive robots of our own design, capable of grasping a single beacon (in the form of a soda can) and moving it from place to place. These robots had an Arduino Uno microcontroller coupled with a Raspberry Pi Linux computer, and were outfitted with a camera, 802.11 wireless communication (not needed here), USB interfaces, five Sharp IR infrared distance sensors, two simple bump sensors, two encoded wheels, an embedded gripper capable of collecting small cans, a flat push surface, and an I2C-driven display. The robots acted entirely autonomously.

The robots were also outfitted with a Tmote Sky wireless sensor mote attached to the Raspberry Pi. The sensor motes used a version of Contiki OS, an operating system designed for wireless low-power and lossy networks (LLNs) [6]. The sensor motes communicated over 802.15.4, channel 26, via UDP multicast. Flooding was not used, but a double send was used to decrease the chance of missed messages.

A beacon was a soda can wrapped in a unique barcode which could be read by the robot's camera. Each such beacon was associated with a unique sensor mote. The food and nest were larger "beacons", also wrapped in a unique barcode each, and associated with unique sensor motes. These objects were larger to make it easier for more robots to congregate near them.

When a robot approached a beacon, the robot's onboard sensor mote could exchange messages with the beacon's sensor mote. Though our environment was small enough that most sensor motes could see one another, we required that robots would not communicate with one another, nor with distant beacons, nor would beacons communicate with one another.

Simulator. There were several physical limitations on both our robots and our environment. First, the battery life prevented us from running large numbers of robots for a prolonged period of time. Second, we were physically limited in the size of the field. Third, the speed of the physical experiments was too slow to gather more than a few runs per treatment. Fourth, it was not possible to smoothly "ramp down" the sensor motes to introduce noise and reliability issues. For these reasons we also developed a simulator testbed which tried to replicate the physical environment, robots, beacons, and many of the issues involved in their operation (such as occlusion, sensor mote failure, etc.).

We will begin with a physical robot experiment and a simulator validation, then discuss simulated experimental results under various conditions. We will discuss details special to the simulator later with its experiments.

Experimental Details. The robot system had the following user-defined parameters, expressed as probabilities. These will be specified in the experimental sections:

P_{Follow}	How often the robot tried to follow the gradient.
$P_{Explore}$	How often the robot would begin exploring.
$P_{Acquire}$	How often the robot tried to acquire a beacon.
P_{Return}	How often a robot would return a beacon upon arrival to the nest with food.
P_{Deploy}	How often the robot tried to deploy a beacon.
$P_{Optimize}$	How often the robot tried to optimize a beacon.
P_{Remove}	How often the robot tried to remove a beacon.

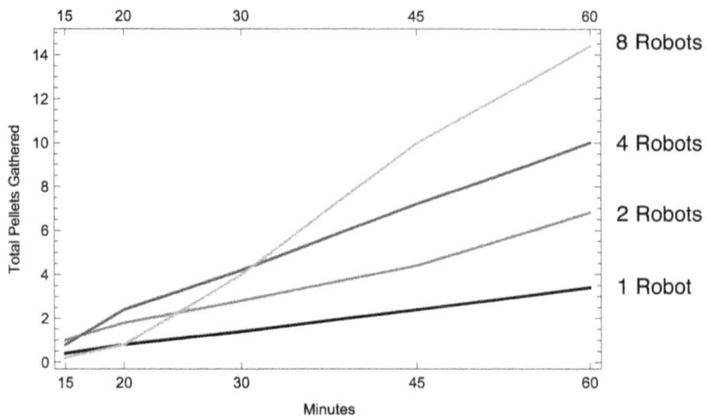

Figure 2: Performance of varying numbers of physical robots in environment with pre-deployed beacons. Measurement is sum total food pellets gathered so far.

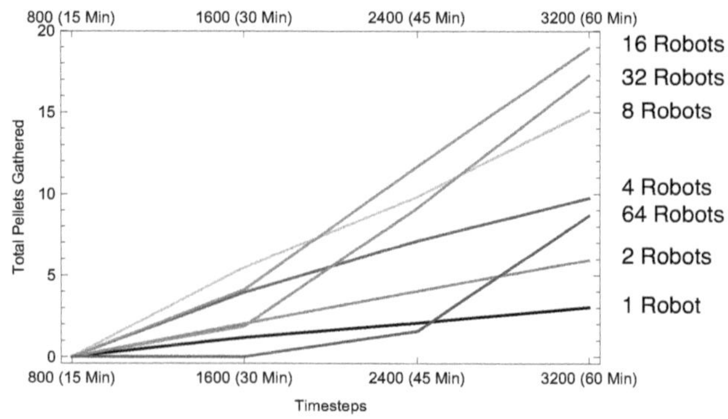

Figure 3: Validation of simulated model, with field size identical to physical robots in Figure 2. Note that 800 simulation timesteps roughly equals 15 minutes of physical robot time. Measurement is sum total food pellets gathered so far.

Additionally, the robots had the constant EXPLORECOUNTDOWN, which defined how many beacon-hops a robot would travel before it stopped exploring.

All experimental runs were done 100 times each, except for the physical robot tests. Experiments were verified for statistical significance using an ANOVA at $p = 0.05$ with a Tukey post-hoc test.

5. PHYSICAL ROBOT EXPERIMENT AND VALIDATION

Our first experiment exhibited the basic features of the algorithm and tested performance. We pre-deployed a grid of 28 beacons in the environment, including the nest and food. The grid of beacons included a reasonable trail from food to nest, but did not establish a pheromone gradient for the rest of the field. Since a path was already established, the robots were given parameters conducive to foraging: $P_{Follow} \leftarrow 0.95$, $P_{Explore} \leftarrow 0.05$. All other probabilities were set to 0. EXPLORECOUNTDOWN was set to 1, so that random walks were performed for only one step.

We varied the number of robots to observe performance. 5 runs each were performed for teams of 1, 2, 4, and 8 robots. Each run lasted one hour, and the amount of food gathered so far was recorded at 15, 20, 30, 45, and 60 minutes. Robots were released one at a time (half-way through the survey step of the previous robot) to avoid traffic jams near the nest and to prevent robots from panicking due to complete occlusion at the start.

Results. Figure 2 shows the performance results for various numbers of physical robots in our testbed. These results were verified with an ANOVA at the 60 minute mark: all differences are statistically significant.

While it might be expected that increasing the number of robots would have a beneficial effect on the amount of food gathered, this was in not certain at the outset. Occlusion was a serious issue in finding and using the optimal path, and traffic jams were common when multiple robots were on the field. However, robots would take advantage of their explore and wander behaviors to visit nearby beacons, establishing new paths or merely get out of the way of other robots. As a result the speedup was sublinear but substantial.

Of additional interest was the visibly slower start to the 8 robot experiments. This was due to early traffic jams among them. Once the robots had spread out, the collection rate sped up.

5.1 Simulation Validation

We next sought to validate the simulator against the physical robot results. Our simulator had several additional parameters meant to help approximate certain physical realities of interest:

$P_{Occlude}$ When two robots are near one another, one robot may occlude certain beacons normally visible to the other robot. Many variables determine the occlusion. To keep things simple, we defined an occlusion parameter ($P_{Occlude}$) which described the probability that a robot next to a beacon would occlude that beacon from another robot. Occluded beacons were removed from the *neighbors* list.

$P_{Unreliable}$ This described the (usually low) probability that a robot could not properly communicate with a sensor mote. A malfunctioning beacon was removed from the *neighbors* list. Additionally, if Rand($P_{Unreliable}$) was true, then UpdatePheromones(...) would immediately fail.

P_{GiveUp} When a robot bumps into another robot, it tries to maneuver around it and reestablish visual contact with its target beacon. This can be difficult if the area is crowded. In simulation this was handled with a probability P_{GiveUp} of giving up going to a target beacon after bumping into and going around a robot.

The time to do twelve iterations of the loop (roughly equivalent to crossing the field and returning) was measured in the simulator to be approximately 800 "steps" and on the physical robots to be about 15 minutes. Other configurable parameters include: the field size (65×100 units in the validation experiment), the nest location (50,95), the food location (7,7), the robot radius (2), the beacon range (15), the minimum distance from a beacon needed to interact with it (2), the robot forward speed (0.2 units per timestep), the robot rotation speed (1 radian per timestep), and the maximum number of beacons a robot could hold (1). The settings for these correspond with a translation of the real field into simulated space.

Using this simulator, we established the same setup as the physical robot experiment, with 28 predeployed beacons (including the food and nest) and a predefined path. Robots were introduced to the field one at a time. and parameters were set to either the same as the real robot experiments or, for the simulator specific parameters, they were set to mimic the physical attributes of the robots. Specifically, we set $P_{Occlude} \leftarrow 0.25$ based on the number of robots that could physically surround a beacon, and $P_{GiveUp} \leftarrow 0.5$ based

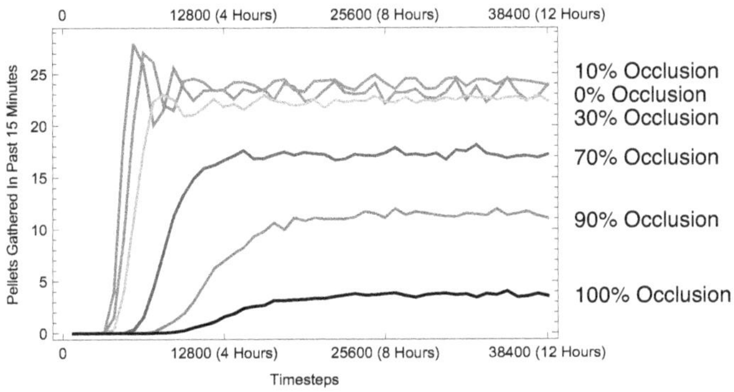

Figure 4: Occlusion results, with no beacon removal or optimization. Measurement is food pellets gathered in the past 15 minutes.

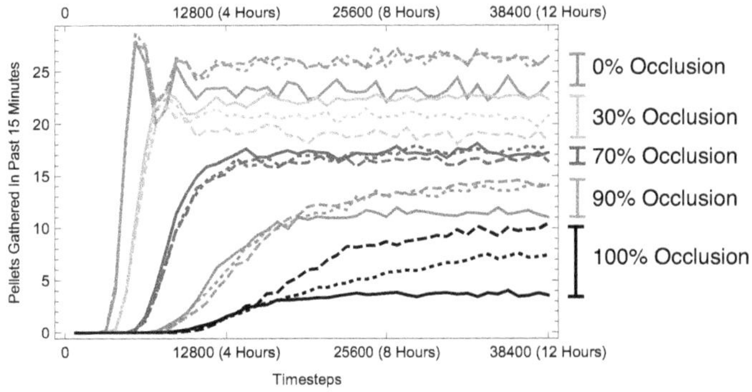

Figure 5: Full occlusion results. 10% Occlusion removed for clarity (they are similar to 30% Occlusion). Solid lines —— indicate no beacon removal or optimization (same as in Figure 4). Dotted lines - - - - indicate 25% probability of beacon removal or optimization. Dashed lines – – – indicate 50% probability of beacon removal or optimization. Measurement is food pellets gathered in the past 15 minutes. Compare to Table 1.

% Occlusion	% Removal and Optimization		
0%	0%	25%	50%
10%	50%	25%	0%
30%	50%	25%	0%
70%	50%	0%	25%
90%	0%	25%	50%
100%	0%	25%	50%

Table 1: Occlusion Results by Removal and Optimization Probability. The various removal and optimization behavior probability settings are sorted by performance, with higher performance further to the right. Overbars group together settings with no statistically significant differences among them. Compare to Figure 5.

on observation of the robots during the physical robot experiments. By default we also left $P_{Unreliable} \leftarrow 0$.

The number of robots in the field was varied in the same way as the physical robot experiments, except that 100 runs were performed for 1, 2, 4, 8, 16, 32, and 64 robots. Each run was a simulation of 1 hour (3200 steps) with the amount of food recorded at 15, 30, 45, and 60 minutes.

Results. Figure 3 shows the performance results for 1, 2, 4, 8, 16, 32, and 64 robots in the simulation environment. These results were verified with an ANOVA at the 3200 timestep (60 minute) mark. All differences are statistically significant.

The speedup was nearly the same as for the (1–8) physical robots, and continued until 16 robots. At this point crowding began to take its toll, causing performance to drop with 32 robots, then significantly drop with 64 (these also had increasingly slow start-up times). With 128 robots (not shown), the swarm was paralyzed. This was expected due to the relative size of the robots to the field.

6. SIMULATION EXPERIMENTS

We then used the simulation to examine the robustness of the method under different physical challenges. To test with more robots, we increased the size of the field (to 100×100, with the nest at $10, 10$ and the food at $90, 90$), reduced the size of the robots (to 0.5), and slightly increased the beacon range (to 20). We also extended the experiment length to 12 hours (38400 timesteps). We no longer used pre-deployed beacons: in all experiments, robots were responsible for deploying beacons and were permitted only a fixed number of beacons to use in the field (160 total beacons). These changes allowed us to use 100 robots in our simulation experiments.

For the parameters, we started with defaults similar to the physical robot experiments, and adjusted them to more efficiently explore the environment, forage, and ferry. They were: $P_{Follow} \leftarrow 0.9$, $P_{Explore} \leftarrow 0.05$, $P_{Acquire} \leftarrow 0.75$, $P_{Return} \leftarrow 0.5$, $P_{Deploy} \leftarrow 0.25$, $P_{Optimize} \leftarrow 0$, $P_{Remove} \leftarrow 0$, $P_{GiveUp} \leftarrow 0.05$, $P_{Occlude} \leftarrow 0.01$, $P_{Unreliable} \leftarrow 0$.

6.1 Beacon Occlusion

Resource blocking and occlusion is a common problem for swarm robots, especially when robots must share resources (such as the beacons). We expected our algorithm to behave robustly with regard to this issue. The default simulation parameters were used, except $P_{Occlude}$, which was given the values 0.0, 0.1, 0.3, 0.7, 0.9, and 1.0.

Results. Figure 4 shows the performance of the system over the simulated twelve hour period, measured by number of food pellets returned to the nest in the past fifteen minutes. An ANOVA of the sample at hour 12 indicates that the 0%, 10%, and 30% occlusion amounts are not statistically significantly different: but all other amounts are. It should be noted that 100% occlusion means that a robot using a beacon will always occlude it.

As can be seen, small amounts of occlusion are not particularly detrimental: but the effect quickly grows with more occlusion.

Effect of Beacon Removal and Optimization. As noted in [9], beacon removal and optimization would be expected to significantly improve performance as robots straighten out the path to the food. However occlusion can have a serious detrimental impact on both removal and optimization, as these behaviors are heavily reliant on being able to accurately see p and n as well as make changes based on the *neighbors* list. We wondered what impact varying levels of occlusion would have on them.

To this end, we re-ran the same occlusion experiment two more times, once with $P_{Optimize}$ and P_{Remove} both set to 0.25, then again with both of them set to 0.5.

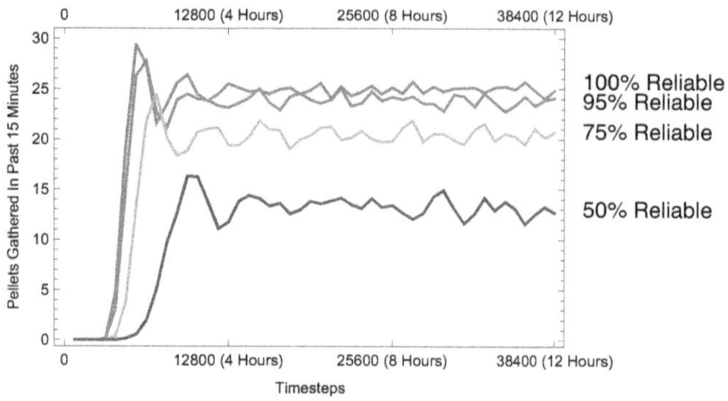

Figure 6: Beacon reliability results. Measurement is food pellets gathered in the past 15 minutes.

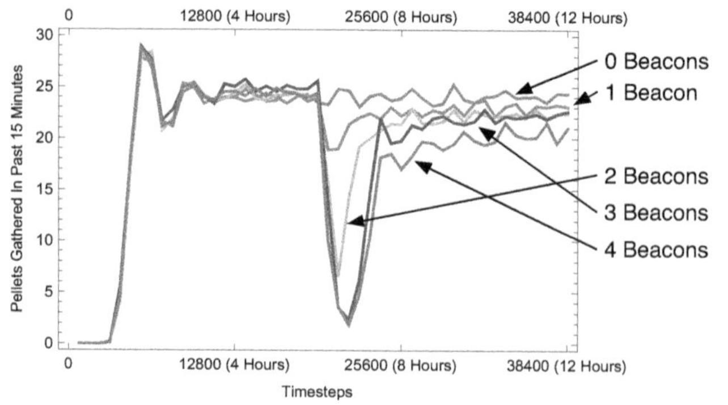

Figure 7: Beacon removal recovery results, for varying width strips removed (measured in number of beacon ranges across). Measurement is food pellets gathered in the past 15 minutes.

Figure 5 expands on Figure 4, including results when the robots use beacon removal or optimization with a 25% or 50% probability. For clarity the 10% occlusion results are not shown, as they are the same pattern as the 30% results. Table 1 summarizes the statistical significance results, verified with an ANOVA at hour 12.

With 0% occlusion, turning on removal and optimization at either level significantly increased its performance over the basic experiment. This result was expected.

As occlusion increased (10% and 30%), increasing removal and optimization *worsened* performance. This seemed natural as higher levels of occlusion would quickly hamper the ability to do removal or optimization: the robots were essentially wasting their time.

What wasn't expected was that at high levels of occlusion (90% and 100%), increasing removal and optimization once again significantly *improved* performance. A closer examination of the results revealed that this was an effect of the maximum number of beacons (160) allotted to the robots. With high levels of occlusion, the robots would deploy large numbers of beacons very densely near the nest, and only sparsely near the food source. When the robots ran out of beacons, optimization and removal enabled them to redistribute the beacons to provide new food routes; without optimization or removal, the robots were often stuck on a difficult-to-see single path.

6.2 Beacon Reliability

A large deployment of beacons might involve hundreds or thousands of sensor motes. This would require small, inexpensive disposable units likely to have reliability issues, especially if deployed over a period of years. We wanted to test the robustness of our approach over different amounts of beacon reliability. To this end the same default parameters were used, but we varied $P_{Unreliable}$. Optimize and deletion were not permitted for this experiment.

Figure 6 shows the results when the robots are operating under varying levels of beacon reliability. The differences between 100% and 95% reliability are not statistically significant, but all other differences are. The percentage of reliability almost perfectly linearly correlates with performance.

Since unreliability acts very much like a occlusion, but with additional consequences that can harm pheromone updates (keeping a beacon out-of-date compared to its neighbors) we expected that reliability would be an issue. However, small amounts of unreliability (for example, 5%) were handled robustly by the system.

6.3 Recovery from Beacon Removal

Finally, we wished to consider what would happen if beacons were removed wholesale from the environment, breaking existing paths to the food. Quite unlike the algorithm in [9], our method was meant to robustly handle this situation.

Our test scenario was as follows: The default parameters were used, such that removal and optimization were disabled. We then allowed the robots to deploy beacons and establish a path from the nest to the food. We then eliminated a roughly vertical strip of beacons centered in the field and pushed the robots in this area to the border of the strip (depending on which side they were closest to). This strip was some n number of beacon ranges wide: we chose values from 1 to 4 (20, 40, 60, and 80 units wide). This final value removed nearly all the beacons on the field between the nest and the food (the field being only 100 units wide). As a control, we included the scenario where no beacons were removed ($n = 0$).

Results. As shown in Figure 7, the robots were clearly capable of recovering from catastrophic beacon failure. Recovery was not total, but it was close. As expected, the rate and degree of recovery was largely related to the number of beacons removed.

7. CONCLUSION AND FUTURE WORK

We have demonstrated a multi-pheromone foraging algorithm deployed to real robots, and which uses stores pheromone information in mobile wireless sensor motes. We showed the technique running on real swarm robots and in simulation, and demonstrated how the algorithm deals robustly with noise, occlusion, and catastrophic beacon failure.

We have barely tapped into the potential of wireless sensor motes for with swarm robotics. Wireless sensor motes can hold much richer information than a few pheromones and flags and they have *sensors* on them which can assist robots. We intend to explore how this might benefit collaboration among the robots to do more complex behaviors other than collective foraging. Sensor motes can also easily *communicate with one another*, something ignored in our paper. This is no longer an indirect communication mode, but sensor motes are designed to do this communication efficiently and at extremely low power. We intend to further explore how this combination: robot-deployable and re-deployable beacons, plus both local and ad-hoc wireless communication, might enable much less trivial robot behaviors.

8. ACKNOWLEDGMENTS

The work presented in this paper is supported by NSF NRI grant 1317813.

REFERENCES

[1] E.J. Barth. A dynamic programming approach to robotic swarm navigation using relay markers. In *Proceedings of the 2003 American Control Conference*, volume 6, pages 5264–5269, June 2003.

[2] E. Bonabeau. Marginally stable swarms are flexible and efficient. *Phys. I France*, pages 309–320, 1996.

[3] Colin Chibaya and Shaun Bangay. A probabilistic movement model for shortest path formation in virtual ant-like agents. In *Proceedings of the Annual Research Conference of the South African Institute of Computer Scientists and Information Technologists on IT Research in Developing Countries*, pages 9–18. ACM, 2007.

[4] J. L. Deneubourg, S. Aron, S. Goss, and J. M. Pasteels. The self-organizing exploratory pattern of the argentine ant. *Insect Behavior*, 3:159–168, 1990.

[5] Frederick Ducatelle, Gianni A. Di Caro, Alexander Förster, and Luca Gambardella. Mobile stigmergic markers for navigation in a heterogeneous robotic swarm. In *Swarm Intelligence (ANTS)*, pages 456–463. Springer, 2010.

[6] Adam Dunkels, Björn Grönvall, and Thiemo Voigt. Contiki: A lightweight and flexible operating system for tiny networked sensors. In *IEEE International Conference on Local Computer Networks*, pages 455–462, 2004.

[7] S. Goss and J. L. Deneubourg. Harvesting by a group of robots. In *First European Conference on Artificial Life*, pages 195–204. MIT Press, 1992.

[8] Nicholas Hoff, Robert Wood, and Radhika Nagpal. Effect of sensor and actuator quality on robot swarm algorithm performance. In *IEEE/RSJ International Conference on Intelligent Robots and Systems (IROS)*. 2011.

[9] Brian Hrolenok, Sean Luke, Keith Sullivan, and Christopher Vo. Collaborative foraging using beacons. In *Proceedings of the Ninth International Conference on Autonomous Agents and Multiagent Systems (AAMAS 2010)*, pages 1197–1204, 2010.

[10] Gideon Kowadlo and R. Andrew Russell. Robot odor localization: A taxonomy and survey. *Int. J. Rob. Res.*, 27(8):869–894, August 2008.

[11] Ralf Mayet, Jonathan Rober, Thomas Schmickl, and Karl Crailsheim. Antbots: A feasible visual emulation of pheromone trails for swarm robots. In *International Conference on Swarm Intelligence*, 2010.

[12] M. Nakamura and K. Kurumatani. Formation mechanism of pheromone pattern and control of foraging behavior in an ant colony model. In C. G. Langton and K. Shimohara, editors, *Proceedings of the Fifth International Workshop on the Synthesis and Simulation of Living Systems*, pages 67–76. MIT Press, 1997.

[13] K.J. O'Hara and T.R. Balch. Distributed path planning for robots in dynamic environments using a pervasive embedded network. In *Proceedings of the Third International Joint Conference on Autonomous Agents and Multiagent Systems*, pages 1538–1539, 2004.

[14] K.J. O'Hara, V. Bigio, S. Whitt, D. Walker, and T. Balch. Evaluation of a large scale pervasive embedded network for robot path planning. In *Proceedings IEEE International Conference on Robotics and Automation*, pages 2072–2077, May 2006.

[15] Liviu Panait and Sean Luke. A pheromone-based utility model for collaborative foraging. In *Proceedings of the Third International Joint Conference on Autonomous Angents and Multi Agent Systems (AAMAS)*, pages 36–43, 2004.

[16] H. Van Dyke Parunak, Sven A. Brueckner, and John Sauter. *Digital Pheromones for Coordination of Unmanned Vehicles*, pages 246–263. Springer, 2005.

[17] D. Payton, M. Daily, R. Estkowski, M. Howard, and C. Lee. Pheromone Robotics. *Autonomous Robots*, 11(3):319–324, 2001.

[18] Anies Hannawati Purnamadjaja and R. Andrew Russell. Bi-directional pheromone communication between robots. *Robotica*, 28(1):69–79, March 2010.

[19] M. Resnick. *Turtles, Termites, and Traffic Jams: Explorations in Massively Parallel Microworlds*. MIT Press, 1994.

[20] Andrew Russell. Ant trails: an example for robots to follow? In *IEEE International Conference on Robotics and Automation*, 1999.

[21] J. Svennebring and S. Koenig. Building terrain-covering ant robots: A feasibility study. *Autonomous Robots*, 16(3):313–332, 2004.

[22] R. T. Vaughan, K. Støy, G. S. Sukhatme, and M. J. Matarić. Blazing a trail: insect-inspired resource transportation by a robot team. In *Proceedings of the International Symposium on Distributed Autonomous Robot Systems*, 2000.

[23] R. T. Vaughan, K. Støy, G. S. Sukhatme, and M. J. Matarić. Whistling in the dark: Cooperative trail following in uncertain localization space. In C. Sierra, M. Gini, and J. S. Rosenschein, editors, *Proceedings of the Fourth International Conference on Autonomous Agents*, pages 187–194. ACM, 2000.

[24] R. T. Vaughan, K. Støy, G. S. Sukhatme, and M. J. Matarić. LOST: Localization-space trails for robot teams. *IEEE Transactions on Robotics and Automation*, 18:796–812, 2002.

[25] M. Wodrich and G. Bilchev. Cooperative distributed search: The ants' way. *Control and Cybernetics*, 26, 1997.

[26] Vittorio Ziparo, A. Kleiner, B. Nebel, and Daniele Nardi. RFID-based exploration for large robot teams. In *IEEE International Conference on Robotics and Automation*, 2007.

Cooperative Coevolution of Partially Heterogeneous Multiagent Systems

Jorge Gomes
BioMachines Lab &
Instituto de Telecomunicações
& Faculdade de Ciências,
Universidade de Lisboa, BioISI
Lisboa, Portugal
jgomes@di.fc.ul.pt

Pedro Mariano
Faculdade de Ciências,
Universidade de Lisboa, BioISI
Lisboa, Portugal
plmariano@fc.ul.pt

Anders Lyhne Christensen
BioMachines Lab &
Instituto de Telecomunicações
& Instituto Universitário de
Lisboa (ISCTE-IUL)
Lisboa, Portugal
anders.christensen@iscte.pt

ABSTRACT

Cooperative coevolution algorithms (CCEAs) facilitate the evolution of heterogeneous, cooperating multiagent systems. Such algorithms are, however, subject to inherent scalability issues, since the number of required evaluations increases with the number of agents. A possible solution is to use partially heterogeneous (*hybrid*) teams: behaviourally heterogeneous teams composed of homogeneous sub-teams. By having different agents share controllers, the number of coevolving populations in the system is reduced. We propose *Hyb-CCEA*, an extension of cooperative coevolution to partially heterogeneous multiagent systems. In *Hyb-CCEA*, both the agent controllers and the team composition are under evolutionary control. During the evolutionary process, we rely on measures of behaviour similarity for the formation of homogeneous sub-teams (*merging*), and propose a stochastic mechanism to increase heterogeneity (*splitting*). We evaluate *Hyb-CCEA* in multiple variants of a simulated herding task, and compare it with a fully heterogeneous CCEA. Our results show that *Hyb-CCEA* can achieve solutions of similar quality using significantly fewer evaluations, and in most setups, *Hyb-CCEA* even achieves significantly higher fitness scores than the CCEA. Overall, we show that merging and splitting populations are viable mechanisms for the cooperative coevolution of hybrid teams.

Categories and Subject Descriptors

I.2.11 [**Artificial Intelligence**]: Distributed Artificial Intelligence

Keywords

Cooperative coevolution; emergent team composition; heterogeneity; scalability; partially heterogeneous teams.

1. INTRODUCTION

Cooperative coevolution algorithms (CCEAs) evolve solutions that consist of interacting, coadapted components [22]. CCEAs are commonly used for the evolution of multiagent behaviours [23]: the natural decomposition of the problem into sub-components makes the domain a good fit for cooperative coevolution, as each agent can represent a component of the solution. CCEAs are thus capable of evolving a heterogeneous set of agent behaviours, where each agent can have a specialised behaviour [23, 29]. CCEAs are, however, associated with inherent scalability issues [21, 28], since each agent behaviour typically evolves in a separate population. The computational complexity therefore increases at least linearly with the number of agents. Moreover, credit assignment issues might also arise in large multiagent systems: it can be hard to assess the contribution of each individual agent to the performance of the team as a whole [1].

In multiagent systems with large numbers of agents, successful solutions may contain agents with similar behaviours [16]. Nonetheless, if each population is isolated, as it is typically the case in CCEAs, similar agent behaviours might have to be learned multiple times in different populations. One way to increase the scalability of multiagent learning is through the reduction of the heterogeneity in the system [21]. Partially heterogeneous multiagent systems, also known as *hybrids*, are composed of multiple homogeneous sub-teams — sub-teams in which all agents have identical controllers. By allowing partial heterogeneity, the number of agent controllers that need to be evolved is reduced, improving the scalability of the learning process [14]. Most previous studies on the evolution of partially heterogeneous teams are focused on *team learning*, where one single genome encodes the behaviour and/or the composition of the whole team [2, 11, 13]. The cooperative coevolution of hybrid multiagent systems is still unexplored.

We propose an extension to the traditional cooperative coevolution architecture, *Hyb-CCEA*, that facilitates the emergence of partially heterogeneous teams. In *Hyb-CCEA*, both the team composition and the agent controllers are under evolutionary control. By forming homogeneous sub-teams inside the larger heterogeneous team, agent controllers can be shared by multiple agents in the team. This approach has potential to significantly improve scalability, as the number of populations can be much lower than the number of agents in the team, which translates in fewer individuals to evaluate. In *Hyb-CCEA*, populations can be *merged* if they are converging to the same region of the agent behaviour space, thereby avoiding the evolution of similar behaviours in separate populations. When two populations merge, a new and larger homogeneous sub-team is created, composed

Appears in: *Proceedings of the 14th International Conference on Autonomous Agents and Multiagent Systems (AAMAS 2015), Bordini, Elkind, Weiss, Yolum (eds.), May 4–8, 2015, Istanbul, Turkey.*

of the agents that were assigned to each former population. We also propose a stochastic *splitting* mechanism to complement the merging mechanism. The number of populations in the system is therefore dynamic, while the number of agents remains fixed. Multiple team compositions and levels of heterogeneity are thus explored throughout evolution.

We study the proposed approach in a simulated herding task, where each agent is controlled by a neural network. We explore multiple variations of the herding task, that involve different numbers of agents, require different degrees of specialisation, and that either benefit from the existence of sub-teams or not. We evaluate the performance improvements of *Hyb-CCEA* over a fully-heterogeneous CCEA. We additionally study the evolutionary dynamics of *Hyb-CCEA*, evaluating the dynamic of populations throughout evolution, the impact of the merge and split procedures, and the choice of the algorithm's main parameters.

2. RELATED WORK

2.1 Heterogeneous Multiagent Systems

Heterogeneous multiagent systems are characterised by the morphological and/or behavioural diversity of their agents. In morphologically heterogeneous systems, agents have varied actuation and sensing capabilities, and through collaboration, the system takes advantage of the collective set of capabilities [7]. In behaviourally heterogeneous systems, agents share the same morphology and capabilities, but have different controllers. In such systems, specialisation and division of labour are often paramount [23, 29, 4].

Heterogeneity in a multiagent system may significantly increase its capabilities, at the price of added complexity [25]. Heterogeneity complicates the multiagent learning process, as the search space becomes significantly larger [21]. In a heterogeneous system, behavioural control must integrate the abilities of different agents to work in synergy towards achieving a common goal. To solve the behavioural control problem, it is necessary to pursue a holistic approach, in which interactions between different agents are taken into account from the very beginning [7, 21]. Artificial evolution has proven to be a powerful tool for the synthesis of controllers for multiagent systems, both in homogeneous systems [3, 26] and in heterogeneous systems [23, 29].

To evolve controllers for heterogeneous systems, two main approaches can be considered [21]: *team learning* and *concurrent learning*. In *team learning*, all controllers for the whole team are encoded in a single genome [2, 27]. In *concurrent learning*, multiple learning processes for different parts of the team run in parallel, with the objective of improving the team as a whole. The most prominent *concurrent learning* algorithm is cooperative coevolution [22], where the controllers for the different agents are coevolved in separate populations that interact during the evaluation process. In this study, we focus on cooperative coevolution algorithms, which will be presented in the following section.

2.2 Cooperative Coevolution

Cooperative coevolution has a number of advantages over the non-coevolutionary approaches for the design of heterogeneous multiagent systems, such as: (i) the capability of working on a problem decomposition, comprised by more manageable sub-problems [12, 22], and (ii) the emergence of agent roles and specialisations [23, 29]. Some of the previous applications of CCEAs in the domain of embodied multiagent systems include the cooperative predator-prey task [29, 9, 18], multi-rover task [19], collective construction [16], herding [23], and keepaway soccer [9].

In a typical application of a CCEA, each agent is evolved in a separate population [23]. At every generation of the evolutionary algorithm, each population is evaluated in turn. To evaluate an individual from one population, teams are formed with representatives from the other populations. The teams are then evaluated by a fitness function in the problem domain, and the individual being evaluated receives the fitness score obtained by the team as a whole. The fitness differential is thus strictly a function of the individual's contribution to the problem-solving effort within the context of the other team members.

Cooperative coevolution has to deal with the intricate dynamics that stem from having multiple coevolving populations [28]. Some of the main challenges include premature convergence to *mediocre stable states* [20, 9], and the generally poor scalability of the algorithms [21]. The classic CCEA architecture is associated with inherent scalability issues with respect to the number of agents in the team. If each agent evolves in a separate population, the number of populations increases linearly with the number of agents, which opens the search space and increases computational complexity. Moreover, in large teams, the impact of a single agent in the behaviour of the team can be almost imperceptible, which can cause the fitness gradients to vanish [1].

The scalability issue is also related with the problem of *reinvention* [21]. CCEAs commonly separate agents into different populations, creating a strict separation between agents. In many multiagent tasks, however, there can be a high degree of overlap between the policies of each agent [16]. The evolutionary process can potentially waste many resources learning the same behaviour in multiple populations. In previous works, the problem of reinvention has been addressed by pre-programming the shared skillset in the robots [23], or by implementing a shaping phase to evolve the basic skillset for all robots [17]. An alternative approach was adopted in CONE-2 [16], where evolution starts with only one agent, and more agents, based on existing ones, can be added throughout evolution. CONE-2 thereby adapts the number of agents to the task at hand and mitigates the problem of reinvention.

2.3 Partially Heterogeneous MAS

One way of improving the scalability of multiagent learning is through the reduction of heterogeneity in the system [21]. By reducing heterogeneity, the number of agent controllers that need to be learned decreases, thus improving scalability [14]. With partial heterogeneity, the problem of reinvention can also be addressed: if different agents perform the same task, they can belong to the same homogeneous sub-team, thus avoiding the evolution of similar solutions in different populations.

Evolution of partially heterogeneous multiagent systems is a relatively unexplored field of research [27]. Previous works on the evolution of hybrid teams have been mostly restricted to team learning. Luke [14] evolved hybrid teams for the RoboCup challenge, with the team composition manually specified beforehand. Each genome was a forest of GP trees that encoded the behaviour of the multiple sub-teams. Hara [11] proposed a GP-based grouping technique, *Auto-*

matically Defined Groups (ADG), that automatically discovers the optimal number of groups and their compositions. Also based on genetic programming, Bongard [2] proposed the *Legion System*, where the genome encodes the composition of the team and one sub-tree for each behaviour class. In the context of team learning, Lichocki et al. [13] studied crossover operators for the evolution of hybrid teams, focusing on the exchange of agents between teams. A different neuroevolution approach was taken in [5]: the agent controllers were encoded in a single genome, and an indirect encoding technique, *HyperNEAT*, was used to exploit similarities in agents' policies. HyperNEAT allowed for sharing of policies between agents, while still exhibiting variations.

While encoding the whole team in one genome can facilitate the evolution of team compositions, such approaches lack the advantages provided by coevolutionary algorithms: the decomposition of the large search space into more tractable sub-problems. To cope with large heterogeneous multirobot systems, Nitschke [19] proposed CONE, a cooperative coevolution method that allows regulated breeding between different populations, each corresponding to a different agent. Crossover between different populations is allowed if the individuals of those populations share the same specialisation. The possible specialisations are specified manually by the experimenter. It was shown that CONE can improve the performance of coevolution when the tasks require a high degree of specialisation. The evolved teams are, however, still fully heterogeneous, as complete controllers are not shared by different agents.

In this paper, we propose a cooperative coevolution method that is capable of evolving partially heterogeneous teams. Both the team composition and the agent controllers are under evolutionary control. Our method draws inspiration from CONE [19], in the sense that it relies on agent specialisations to regulate interactions between different populations. In contrast to CONE, however, our method uses these specialisations to build homogeneous sub-teams, rather than only relying on them for the exchange of genetic material. Our approach is described in the following section.

3. HYB-CCEA: COOPERATIVE COEVOLUTION OF HYBRID TEAMS

We propose *Hyb-CCEA*, an extension of a CCEA to evolve agent controllers for physically homogeneous, behaviourally heterogeneous multiagent systems. In traditional applications of CCEAs in multiagent systems, there is a one-to-one mapping between agents and populations. Our approach departs from this concept: we allow population individuals to encode a controller that can be used by multiple agents, thus effectively forming homogeneous sub-teams inside heterogeneous teams. In *Hyb-CCEA*, each population is assigned to a subset of the agents in the team. The number of population individuals is constant across all populations, and two different populations cannot be assigned to the same agent.

During evaluation, all individuals of a given population are assigned to the same set of agents (see Figure 1). Each population thus become responsible for the evolution of a homogeneous sub-team, not just one specific agent. The rest of the coevolutionary evaluation operates the same way as a traditional CCEA [22]: individuals are joined with representative individuals from the other populations for evaluation, and the individual being evaluated receives the fitness

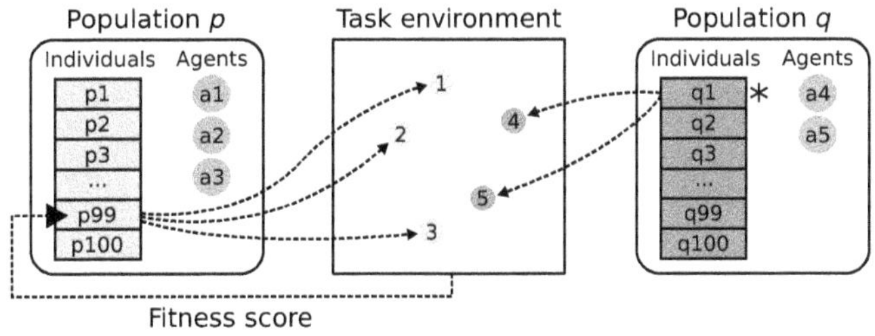

Figure 1: Illustration of the evaluation phase. In this example, the individual *p99* of population *p* is being evaluated. The representative individual of *q* is *q1*. The population individuals (controllers) are assigned to the respective agents, and the fitness of the whole team is assigned to individual *p99*.

Algorithm 1 *Hyb-CCEA* algorithm.

1: Let P be a set of populations, and A the set of all agents.
2: $P \leftarrow$ *createPopulations*()
3: **for** each generation **do**
4:     **for** $p \in P$ **do**
5:         **for** each individual $i \in p$ **do**
6:             $t \leftarrow$ Form a team with i and the representative r_q from each other population $q \neq p$.
7:             $fit_i \leftarrow evaluate(t)$, assigning each individual to the respective set of agents.
8:     $P \leftarrow attemptSplit(P)$
9:     $P \leftarrow attemptMerge(P)$
10:     **for** $p \in P$ **do**
11:         $r_p \leftarrow$ individual $i \in p$ with maximum *fit* score.
12:         Breed p, based on the fitness scores *fit* of the individuals.

score that the team as a whole obtained. The outline of the algorithm is shown in Algorithm 1. Throughout this study, only one collaboration is formed to evaluate each individual. Evaluations could, however, rely on more collaborations, for example using randomly chosen collaborators [20].

The distinctive aspect of *Hyb-CCEA* is that it does not assume that the optimal number of sub-teams and their composition are known beforehand: we extend the CCEA so that the number of composition of the sub-teams is also under evolutionary control. Different levels of heterogeneity can thus be explored throughout the evolutionary process. To this end, we propose: (i) a procedure for merging two populations (step 9), which creates a new population assigned to the agents of the two former populations, thus decreasing the heterogeneity of the system; and (ii) a procedure for splitting a population (step 8), which creates two populations assigned to different sets of agents, thus increasing heterogeneity. Both the split and merge procedures were implemented with the objective of minimising any immediate negative impact in the behaviour and performance of the teams. The evolutionary process can therefore follow the fitness gradients without major disruptions caused by sudden changes in team compositions. The following sections detail the initialisation, merge, and split procedures.

3.1 Initialisation Procedure

We consider two alternatives for the creation of the initial populations, which are studied and compared in Section 5.3.

Homogeneous start: There is only one population initially. All the agents of the multiagent system are assigned to this population.

Heterogeneous start: There is one population assigned to each agent of the multiagent system.

Another alternative would be to initialise the algorithm with a partially heterogeneous configuration, based on the experimenter's domain knowledge for instance. This alternative is fully compatible with the proposed algorithm, but we do not address it in this paper due to space restrictions.

3.2 Merge Procedure

Previous works have shown that cross-breeding between agents that share similar specialisations [19], or belong to the same sub-team [15], can be beneficial for the emergence of specialisations. We go beyond this concept by allowing behaviourally similar agents to become genetically homogeneous. If two separate populations are evolving similar agent behaviours, they can be merged into one population, see Figure 2. To identify behaviour similarities between agents, we rely on an *agent behaviour characterisation* [10] provided by the experimenter. This characterisation is a real-valued vector $\beta(a)$, composed of features that describe the state of the agent a during task execution, and/or the relation of the agent with the environment and other agents [10]. Characterisations are obtained during the evaluation phase: besides obtaining the fitness score of the individual, the behaviour of the respective agent(s) is also recorded.

The concept behind the *merge procedure*, described in Algorithm 2, is to first obtain a set of agent behaviours that is representative of each population, then measure the distance between these sets of behaviours, and finally merge populations with a high degree of behavioural similarity.

The behavioural set B of a population p is obtained (steps 2 and 5) by aggregating the agent behaviours recorded during the evaluation of p, considering the agents to which that population is currently assigned (A_p):

$$agentBehaviours(p) = \{\beta(i_a) : i \in p' \wedge a \in A_p\} \ . \quad (1)$$

Since the objective is to assess the behaviour space region to which a population is converging, we only consider the high-fitness portion of the population (p').[1]

The distance between two populations, including the distance between a population and itself, is then given by the mean pairwise distance between the respective sets of agent behaviours, $\mathcal{A}$ and $\mathcal{B}$:

$$pairwiseDistance(\mathcal{A}, \mathcal{B}) = \frac{1}{|\mathcal{A}||\mathcal{B}|} \sum_{x \in \mathcal{A}} \sum_{y \in \mathcal{B}} d(x, y) \ , \quad (2)$$

where d is the Euclidean distance between the behaviour characterisation vectors.

The distance between each two populations is then normalised (step 8), by dividing it by the respective intra-population distances (steps 3 and 6). The normalised distance measure $\delta_{p,q}$ represents the separation of two populations p and q in agent behaviour space. If two populations are converging to similar behaviours, their distance will be close to 1. The most similar populations are merged if the distance between them is inferior to the *merge threshold* T_D (step 10). Only populations older than a *stability threshold* T_G are allowed to merge. This threshold enforces a stability period that provides the population time to adapt to the current set of assigned agents. The new population replaces the two parent populations, and is comprised by the respective high-fitness individuals (steps 11–14). The number of individuals that are drawn from each population is proportional to the number of agents assigned to that population.

[1]In the experiments presented in this paper, we considered the high-fitness portion as the top 20% of each population, which is the same as the *survival threshold* of the NEAT algorithm we use. Preliminary experiments showed this parameter is robust to moderate variation.

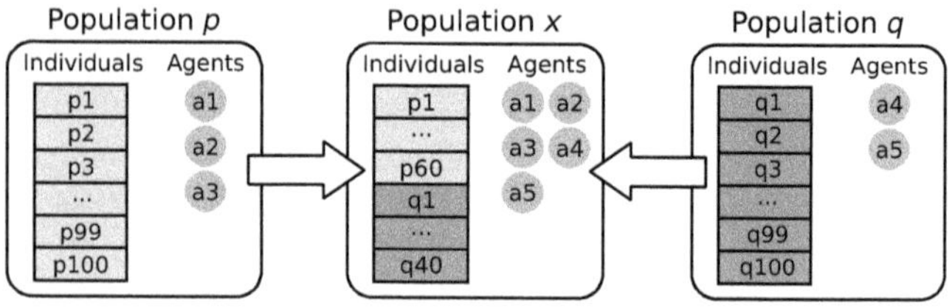

Figure 2: Merge procedure: the new population x replaces the two parents, p and q. The population x is formed by a subset of their individuals, and is assigned to all the parents' agents.

Algorithm 2 Merge procedure.

1: **for** each population $p \in P \wedge age(p) \geq T_G$ **do**
2: $B_p \leftarrow agentBehaviours(p)$
3: $\Delta_p \leftarrow pairwiseDistance(B_p, B_p)$
4: **for** each $q \in P \wedge q \neq p \wedge age(q) \geq T_G$ **do**
5: $B_q \leftarrow agentBehaviours(q)$
6: $\Delta_q \leftarrow pairwiseDistance(B_q, B_q)$
7: $\Delta_{p,q} \leftarrow pairwiseDistance(B_p, B_q)$
8: $\delta_{p,q} \leftarrow \frac{2\Delta_{p,q}}{\Delta_p + \Delta_q}$
9: Select p and q with the minimum $\delta_{p,q}$.
10: **if** $\delta_{p,q} \leq T_D$ **then**
11: Create a pop. x, assigned to the agents $A_p \cup A_q$.
12: Add to x the highest-fit individuals of p and q, in the proportions $\frac{|A_p|}{|A_q \cup A_q|}$ and $\frac{|A_q|}{|A_p \cup A_q|}$, respectively.
13: Remove p and q from P.
14: Add x to P.

3.3 Split Procedure

The *split procedure* increases the heterogeneity of the system by breaking up a homogeneous sub-team: two clones of a population are created, and each one is assigned to a different set of agents, see Figure 3. Since all agents assigned to a given population share the same controllers, they will most likely display very similar behaviours. Therefore, contrary to the merging process, we cannot rely on agent behaviour characterisations to regulate splits. We resort to a stochastic approach to splitting, described in Algorithm 3.

In the splitting process, each population is assigned a splitting pressure S_p (step 2). The splitting pressure increases linearly with the age of the population (number of generations since it was created) and the fraction of agents it is assigned to. The fraction of agents has a limited influence on the splitting pressure, in order to guarantee a healthy frequency of splits in multiagent systems of any size. The population with the highest pressure is split if S_p is above the stability threshold T_G (steps 3–4). The individuals of

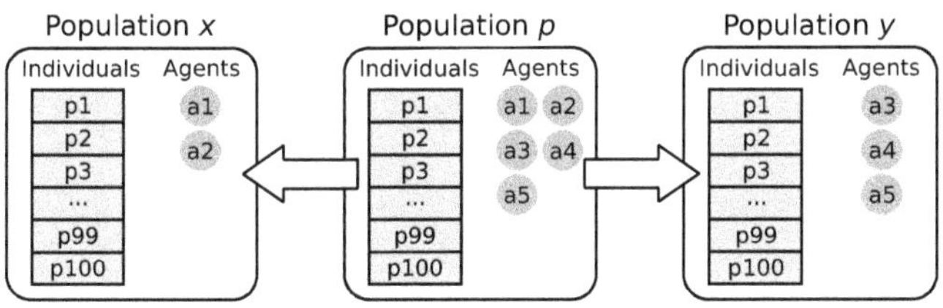

Figure 3: Split procedure: two new populations, x and y, replace the parent p. The populations x and y are copies of p, but each one is assigned to a disjoint set of agents.

Algorithm 3 Split procedure.

1: **for** each population $p \in P \wedge |A_p| \geq 2$ **do**

2: $S_p \leftarrow \frac{age(p)}{2}\left(1 + \frac{|A_p| - 2}{|A| - 2}\right), |A| > 2$

3: Select the population p with the maximum S_p.

4: **if** $S_p \geq T_G$ **then**

5: Randomly split the set of agents A_p into A_x and A_y such that: $A_x \cup A_y = A_p \wedge A_x \cap A_y = \varnothing$.

6: Create two copies of p, x and y, assigned to the set of agents A_x and A_y.

7: Remove p from P.

8: Add x and y to P.

---

the two resulting populations are exact copies of the individuals of the parent population (step 6). The set of agents of the parent population is randomly split into two (step 5), and each of the child populations is assigned to one of those subsets (step 6).

Stochastic splits are feasible because splits can be reverted later by the *merge procedure*. As both the merge and split procedures use the stability threshold T_G, new populations cannot be removed for at least T_G generations. This stability period provides the new populations time to converge to different regions of the agent behaviour space. If two recently split populations did not converge to different behaviours after the stability period, the distance between them will be relatively small, and they can therefore be merged again.

4. EXPERIMENTAL SETUP

Our experiments are based on a simulated version of the herding task [23]. In this task, a group of physically homogeneous shepherds must corral one or more sheep. To make the task more challenging, one or more foxes are present, which try to capture the sheep, and must be kept away by the shepherds. Only the controllers for the shepherds are evolved, and the other agents have a preprogrammed behaviour. The herding task requires behavioural heterogeneity in the team of shepherds [23], since there are different tasks that must be performed simultaneously: corral the sheep and keep away the foxes. We use multiple variants of the task in our experiments. The number of agent specialisations required to solve the task is varied by using different numbers of sheep and foxes. Additionally, we introduce two fox types: a *weak fox*, which can be kept away by just one shepherd, and an *evasive fox*, which requires more than one shepherd to be stopped. By introducing these variations to the herding task, we can study the algorithms in setups that require different sub-teams inside the larger team.

Table 1: Task setups.

Setup	Sheph.	Sheep	Foxes	Fox type	Eval. budget
W5	5	1	2	Weak	150K
E5	5	1	1	Evasive	150K
W7	7	2	2	Weak	300K
E7	7	1	2	Evasive	300K
W10	10	2	3	Weak	400K
E10	10	1	3	Evasive	400K

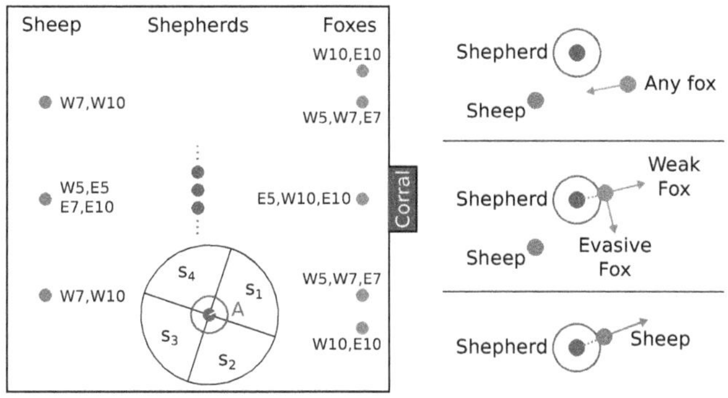

Figure 4: Left: Initial conditions for each setup. The labels on the sheep and foxes indicate the initial positions that are used in each setup. The shepherd on the bottom illustrates the sensor setup. Right: Illustration of the pre-programmed behaviour of the sheep and the different types of foxes.

The task variants are listed in Table 1, and the initial conditions are depicted in Figure 4 (left). The agents' initial positions for each variant are fixed. The task environment is a bounded square arena of size 150x150 units, with no obstacles. Each shepherd has the following sensors, which correspond to the inputs of the neural network: (i) four sensors that return the distance of the nearest shepherd (s_1–s_4), with a range of 25 units; and (ii) $2(f + s + 1)$ sensors that return the distance and relative orientation for each of the f foxes, each of the s sheep, and the centre of the corral. The two neural outputs control respectively the shepherd's linear speed (maximum of 1 unit/step) and turning speed (maximum of 22.5°/step).

When a shepherd approaches a sheep (distance less than 5 units), the sheep moves 1 unit in the opposite direction of that shepherd (see Figure 4, right). The sheep are otherwise passive. The behaviour of the foxes is preprogrammed: each fox tries to intercept the closest sheep by estimating its future position and by moving 1 unit in that direction. If a shepherd gets close to a fox (distance less than 5 units), the fox moves away from the shepherd. If the foxes are of the *weak* type, the fox moves in the opposite direction. If the foxes are of the *evasive* type, the fox moves in a perpendicular direction, choosing the side where the closest sheep is present. Figure 4 (right) illustrates the fox behaviours. A trial ends when all sheep enter the corral, all sheep are captured by a fox, or when 500 time steps have elapsed.

The fitness function F rewards the shepherds for getting the sheep closer to the corral, and in case a sheep is successfully corralled, for the amount of time it took to corral it. To bootstrap the evolutionary process, the fitness function also rewards the shepherds for getting close to the sheep at any point in the simulation trial.

$$F = \sum_{s \in S} \left[\frac{1 - m_s}{|S|} + \begin{cases} 2 - \tau_s / T & \text{if } s \text{ is corralled} \\ 1 - d_{f,s}/d_{i,s} & \text{otherwise} \end{cases} \right], \quad (3)$$

where S is the set of sheeps, m_s is the minimum distance of any shepherd to s (normalised to $[0, 1]$), τ_s is the number of time steps it took to corral s, T is the maximum trial length, $d_{f,s}$ is the final distance of s to the corral, and $d_{i,s}$ is the initial distance.

The agent behaviour characterisation $\beta(a)$ is a vector that describes the relation of shepherd a with the environment: (i) distance of a to every sheep, averaged over the simulation trial; (ii) mean distance of a to the corral, and (iii) mean distance of a to every fox. The length of the characterisation varies from 3 to 6, depending on the number of sheep and foxes. All features are normalised to the range [0,1].

The agent controllers are neural networks evolved by NEAT [24], a state-of-the-art neuroevolution algorithm that evolves both the weights and topology of the networks, and has been extensively used in evolutionary robotics. We use the NEAT4J[2] implementation and most of the default parameter values: each population has a fixed size of 100 individuals, the mutation probability is 25%, crossover probability is 20%, the probability of adding a connection is 5%, the probability of adding a neuron is 3%, and the target number of species is 5. The same evolutionary parameters were used in the experiments with *Hyb-CCEA* and *CCEA*. The task is implemented in MASON[3], and the evolutionary algorithms are implemented over the ECJ framework[4].

Although the two evolutionary algorithms are generational, we rely on the number of evaluations (i.e., number of evolved individuals) for a fair comparison, since *Hyb-CCEA* has a dynamic number of population individuals. The two algorithms were therefore given a fixed budget of evaluations for each task setup (see Table 1). Every evolutionary treatment is repeated in 30 independent evolutionary runs.

5. RESULTS

5.1 Comparison with Fully Heterogeneous Teams

To evaluate the potential improvements brought by *Hyb-CCEA*, we compare its performance with the underlying cooperative coevolution algorithm (*CCEA*), in which the teams are fully heterogeneous. The *CCEA* is implemented as described in Algorithm 1, but each agent is assigned to a separate population, and there are no split and merge procedures. *Hyb-CCEA* used the same parameter values in all tasks: $T_G = 20$ and $T_D = 1.25$ (these parameters are studied in Section 5.4). Figure 5 shows the highest fitness scores achieved after a given number of evaluations, averaged over 30 evolutionary runs for each method and task. The highest fitness scores achieved by *Hyb-CCEA* were significantly superior to those achieved by *CCEA* in all task setups (Mann-Whitney test, $p < 0.05$), except *W5* ($p = 0.14$). The results show that *Hyb-CCEA* not only achieves higher fitness scores in the end, it also displays a steeper initial increase in fitness scores across all tasks.

[2]http://neat4j.sourceforge.net

[3]http://cs.gmu.edu/~eclab/projects/mason

[4]http://cs.gmu.edu/~eclab/projects/ecj

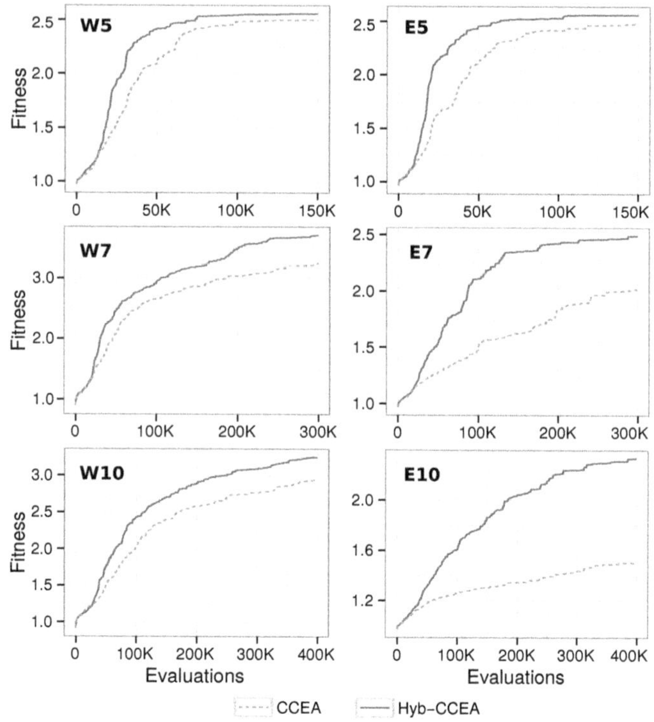

Figure 5: Mean of the highest fitness scores achieved after a given amount of evaluations.

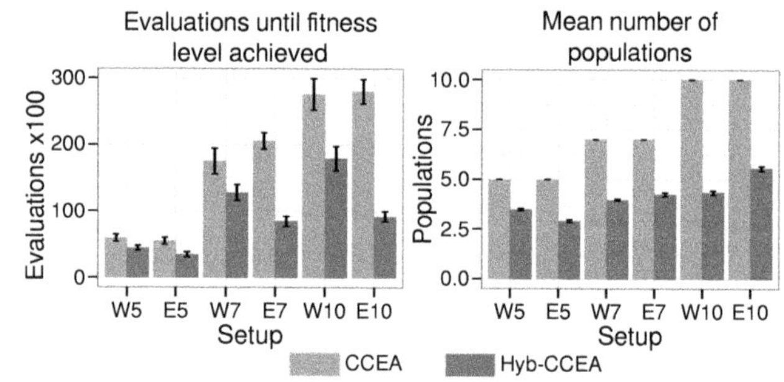

Figure 6: Left: Number of evaluations necessary to reach the following fitness levels – *W5* and *E5*: 2.5; *W7*: 3.0; *E7*: 1.75; *W10*: 2.75; *E10*: 1.5. Right: mean number of populations throughout evolution.

An analysis of how many evaluations were required on average to reach solutions with certain fitness levels is provided in Figure 6 (left). The fitness levels were chosen to be as high as possible while still being achieved by at least half the evolutionary runs of both *CCEA* and *Hyb-CCEA*. In all task setups, *Hyb-CCEA* requires significantly fewer evaluations to reach the same fitness levels (Mann-Whitney test, $p < 0.05$). Figure 6 (right) shows that in all task setups, *Hyb-CCEA* was able to form homogeneous sub-teams, since it used on average significantly fewer populations than the number of agents in the team. By reducing the number of populations, *Hyb-CCEA* could therefore achieve solutions with similar fitness scores with fewer evaluations, when compared with a fully heterogeneous *CCEA*.

The differences in both the number of evaluations and highest fitness scores are more pronounced in the setups with *evasive* foxes. In these setups, the shepherd team can benefit from the existence of sub-teams, since multiple shepherds are required to deal with each fox. This suggests that *Hyb-CCEA* is especially effective in domains where sub-teams should be formed. Nonetheless, in setups that do not require sub-teams (*weak* foxes), *Hyb-CCEA* still managed to achieve good solutions faster, without any sacrifice in terms of solution quality. These results highlight that *Hyb-CCEA* not only reduces the redundancy in the evolutionary process and improves scalability, it also takes advantage of the existence of homogeneous sub-teams to evolve higher quality solutions. In the following sections, we study the mechanisms contributing to the performance of *Hyb-CCEA*.

5.2 Evolutionary Dynamics Analysis

In this section, we analyse the evolutionary dynamics of *Hyb-CCEA* induced by the merge and split procedures. Figure 7 shows the mean number of populations throughout evolution in each task. In the early stages of evolution, there is a steep decrease in the number of populations, which suggests a low level of heterogeneity. This initial decrease is explained by the lack of agent specialisations in the early generations: since the agents display similar behaviours initially, the respective populations are merged. As evolution progresses, populations begin to converge to specific regions of the behaviour space: specialisations emerge. The number of populations therefore tends to increase. It is noteworthy that for setups with the same number of agents, evolution can converge to different number of populations (see *W5* and *E5*, and *W10* and *E10*), which confirms that *Hyb-CCEA* can adapt the level of heterogeneity to the task at hand.

The merging and splitting of populations should not lead to significant disruptions in the evolutionary process. This implies that the fitness of the highest scoring solutions in the system should not decrease substantially after a merge or a split. Table 2 lists the immediate impact of the merge and split procedures. In all setups, the immediate change in fitness after a split occurs is not significantly different from the change when no split or merge occurs (Mann-Whitney test, $p > 0.25$). This suggests that splits have no immediate impact in the performance of the teams, which is desirable, and explained by the fact that both new populations are initialised with the individuals of the parent population.

After a merge occurs, fitness scores tend to decrease slightly ($p < 0.001$ in all setups). In the merge procedure, only populations with *similar* agent behaviours are

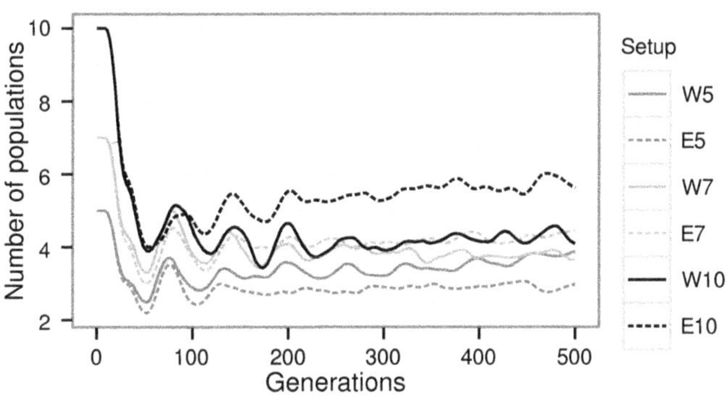

Figure 7: Mean number of populations at each generation. Results are only shown up to the 500th generation, the values remain relatively stable after.

Table 2: Mean variation of the highest fitness score after a merge/split, and mean number of merges/splits in each run. The *Stable* column shows the variation when no merge/split occurs.

Setup	Merges		Splits		Stable
	Num.	Var.	Num.	Var.	Var.
W5	13.26	-1.96%	12.20	+1.50%	+1.02%
E5	16.97	-3.01%	14.93	+0.60%	+0.55%
W7	25.57	-2.00%	22.43	+1.20%	+0.74%
E7	23.27	-2.67%	20.60	+1.00%	+0.76%
W10	41.50	-1.80%	35.03	+0.71%	+0.87%
E10	34.06	-0.76%	29.66	+0.27%	+0.51%

merged. There might, however, exist subtle differences in the behaviour of different agents that are beneficial for the behaviour of the team. If those agents become genetically homogeneous, these subtle differences disappear, potentially decreasing the performance of the teams. This impact, however, is relatively small on average (around 2% of the fitness score), and the results suggest that it does not compromise the effectiveness of *Hyb-CCEA*.

5.3 Initialisation Procedure

As discussed in Section 3.1, we consider two possible initialisations procedures: (i) each agent is assigned to a separate population (*heterogeneous start*); and (ii) all agents are assigned to the same population (*homogeneous start*).

Table 3 shows the highest fitness scores achieved with each approach. We could only find a significant difference in the *W7* setup (Mann-Whitney test, $p = 0.003$). In all other task setups, no differences were found ($p > 0.1$). We analysed the number of populations throughout evolution to discover the reason for the similarities in performance, see Table 4. As expected, there is a large difference in the number of populations in the initial generations (0–99th). As evolution progresses, however, the difference becomes smaller. After the 250th generation, there are no significant differences in the mean number of populations in the two approaches ($p > 0.1$). This result further reinforces that *Hyb-CCEA* can

Table 3: Highest fitness scores achieved with *Hyb-CCEA*, with a heterogeneous (*Het*) and homogeneous (*Hom*) initialisation.

	W5	E5	W7	E7	W10	E10
Het	2.56	2.56	3.71	2.49	3.25	2.33
Hom	2.56	2.57	3.40	2.48	3.07	2.38

Table 4: Mean number of populations at different stages of evolution.

Setup	Gen. 0–99		Gen. 100–249		Gen. 250–	
	Het	Hom	Het	Hom	Het	Hom
W5	3.47	2.22	3.23	3.14	3.61	3.38
E5	3.28	2.00	2.77	2.62	2.90	2.76
W7	4.75	2.33	3.85	3.46	3.87	3.55
E7	4.49	2.34	4.01	3.99	4.30	4.34
W10	5.90	2.44	4.07	3.63	4.18	3.73
E10	5.89	2.41	5.06	4.38	5.66	5.39

adapt the level of heterogeneity in the team to the task at hand, and is not significantly biased by the initial conditions.

5.4 Parameter Sensitivity

In this section, we study the sensitivity of *Hyb-CCEA* to the merge threshold T_D and the stability threshold T_G. The merge threshold dictates the maximum distance allowed between two mergeable populations. The distance between a population and itself is always 1 (see Section 3.2). A value $T_D = 1$ therefore means that two populations should cover exactly the same region of the behaviour space in order to be merged. The higher the threshold, the *easier* it is to merge two populations. The stability threshold T_G dictates the minimum age of a population: how many generations must pass before the population can be removed through a merge or a split. The stability threshold therefore controls the frequency of merges and splits in the evolutionary process. We evaluated the impact of these two parameters in two task setups, *W7* and *E7*, see Figure 8 for results. We evaluated T_D (left) with a fixed value of $T_G = 10$, and we evaluated T_G (right) with a value of $T_D = 1.25$.

The merge threshold T_D has a different impact on the performance of *Hyb-CCEA* in the two setups: in *W7*, there are no significant differences in the range $[1, 1.5]$ and there is a monotonic decrease in $[1.5, 2]$; in *E7*, there is a monotonic increase in the range $[1, 1.5]$, and no significant differences in $[1.5, 2]$. This is explained by the different nature of the two task variants: in *E7*, the existence of sub-teams is beneficial, while in *W7* there is no need of sub-teams, and more specialisations are required. Increasing the merge threshold facilitates the formation of sub-teams, but can hinder the evolution of subtly different specialisations. Considering the two setups, the optimal value of T_D is between $[1.25, 1.5]$.

The stability threshold only has a significant impact in the *E7* setup (Kruskal-Wallis test, $p = 0.50$ in *W7*, and $p = 0.004$ in *E7*). In the *E7* setup, higher values of T_G are preferred, although there are no significant differences in the range $[20, 60]$. Our results are insufficient to draw definite conclusions regarding the stability threshold. Although *Hyb-CCEA* is not overly sensitive to this parameter in our experiments, we are assessing the impact of T_G in different tasks in ongoing work.

Unlike the merge and split thresholds, the agent behaviour characterisation (see Section 3.2) is task-specific. The characterisation should have sufficient behaviour features to distinguish agents with evidently different behaviours. A very detailed characterisation should not be harmful to the algorithm, as the distance between populations is given by a relative measure. In ongoing work, we are empirically evaluating the impact of the behaviour characterisation in *Hyb-CCEA*, and experimenting with task-independent characterisations [6, 8].

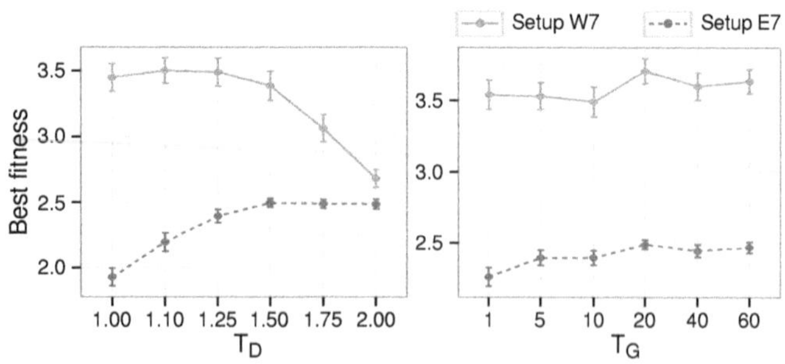

Figure 8: Highest fitness scores achieved at the end of the evolutionary runs, with different values for the merge threshold T_D and stability threshold T_G. Each point is the average of 30 evolutionary runs.

6. CONCLUSION

We proposed *Hyb-CCEA*, a novel method for the cooperative coevolution of partially heterogeneous (*hybrid*) teams. In *Hyb-CCEA*, each population can be assigned to an homogeneous sub-team, which departs from traditional CCEA applications where each agent evolves in a separate population. Both agent controllers and the team composition are under evolutionary control. The level of heterogeneity in the system is therefore dynamic: (i) heterogeneity can be decreased by *merging* two populations into a new one, forming an homogeneous sub-team with the respective agents, and (ii) heterogeneity can be increased by *splitting* one population into two new ones, where each is assigned to a different set of agents. We proposed a merge procedure that merges two populations if they are converging to similar regions of the agent behaviour space, and a stochastic split procedure based on populations' age.

We compared *Hyb-CCEA* with a fully heterogeneous CCEA in a simulated herding task. We used multiple task setups, varying the number of agents from 5 to 10, and varying the number and type of specialisations required. Our results were generally consistent across all tasks: *Hyb-CCEA* could reach good solutions for all tasks in significantly fewer evaluations, and it could also achieve significantly higher fitness scores in the end. We showed that *Hyb-CCEA* can adapt the level of heterogeneity in the system to the task at hand, and that it is especially effective in task variants that require the formation of sub-teams.

We studied the main parameters of *Hyb-CCEA*: the initialisation procedure, the merge threshold, which dictates the distance threshold for merging, and the stability threshold, which controls the minimum age of populations. Our experiments showed that *Hyb-CCEA* is not overly sensitive to variations in the parameter values. Additionally, the same parameter values were used across all the considered task setups, yielding promising results.

Our experiments revealed that the performance gains of *Hyb-CCEA* become higher as the number of agents increases. In ongoing work, we are evaluating the proposed approach in additional tasks, requiring a higher number of agents. Although the merge and split procedures proposed in this paper worked relatively well and did not disrupt the evolutionary process, we are currently studying alternative implementations of these procedures.

To the best of our knowledge, *Hyb-CCEA* is the first cooperative coevolution algorithm that allows for the emergence of partially heterogeneous teams. *Hyb-CCEA* improves the scalability of cooperative coevolution without sacrificing solution quality. Our study opens new interesting avenues of research, since it brings together the emergence of team compositions and the advantages of cooperative coevolution.

Acknowledgements This research is supported by Fundação para a Ciência e Tecnologia (FCT), with grant SFRH/BD/89095/2012 and projects UID/EEA/50008/2013, UID/Multi/04046/2013, and EXPL/EEI-AUT/0329/2013.

REFERENCES

[1] A. Agogino and K. Tumer. Efficient evaluation functions for evolving coordination. *Evolutionary Computation*, 16(2):257–288, 2008.

[2] J. C. Bongard. The legion system: A novel approach to evolving heterogeneity for collective problem solving. In *Genetic Programming*, volume 1802 of *LNCS*, pages 16–28. Springer, 2000.

[3] M. Brambilla, E. Ferrante, M. Birattari, and M. Dorigo. Swarm robotics: a review from the swarm engineering perspective. *Swarm Intelligence*, 7(1):1–41, 2013.

[4] A. Campbell and A. S. Wu. Multi-agent role allocation: issues, approaches, and multiple perspectives. *Autonomous Agents & Multi-Agent Systems*, 22(2):317–355, 2011.

[5] D. B. D'Ambrosio and K. O. Stanley. Generative encoding for multiagent learning. In *Genetic and Evolutionary Computation Conference (GECCO)*, pages 819–826. ACM Press, 2008.

[6] S. Doncieux and J.-B. Mouret. Behavioral diversity measures for evolutionary robotics. In *Congress on Evolutionary Computation (CEC)*, pages 1–8. IEEE Press, 2010.

[7] M. Dorigo, D. Floreano, L. Gambardella, F. Mondada, et al. Swarmanoid: A novel concept for the study of heterogeneous robotic swarms. *IEEE Robotics & Automation Magazine*, 20(4):60–71, 2013.

[8] J. Gomes and A. L. Christensen. Generic behaviour similarity measures for evolutionary swarm robotics. In *Genetic and Evolutionary Computation Conference (GECCO)*, pages 199–206. ACM Press, 2013.

[9] J. Gomes, P. Mariano, and A. L. Christensen. Avoiding convergence in cooperative coevolution with novelty search. In *International Conference on Autonomous Agents & Multiagent Systems (AAMAS)*, pages 1149–1156. IFAAMAS, 2014.

[10] J. Gomes, P. Mariano, and A. L. Christensen. Systematic derivation of behaviour characterisations in evolutionary robotics. In *International Conference on the Synthesis and Simulation of Living Systems (ALife)*, pages 212–219. MIT Press, 2014.

[11] A. Hara. Emergence of cooperative behavior using adg; automatically defined groups. In *Genetic and Evolutionary Computation Conference (GECCO)*, pages 1039–1046. Morgan Kaufmann, 1999.

[12] T. Jansen and R. P. Wiegand. Exploring the explorative advantage of the cooperative coevolutionary (1+1) EA. In *Genetic and Evolutionary Computation Conference (GECCO)*, volume 2723 of *LNCS*, pages 310–321. Springer, 2003.

[13] P. Lichocki, S. Wischmann, L. Keller, and D. Floreano. Evolving team compositions by agent swapping. *IEEE Transactions on Evolutionary Computation*, 17(2):282–298, 2013.

[14] S. Luke. Genetic programming produced competitive soccer softbot teams for RoboCup97. In *Genetic Programming*, pages 214–222. Morgan Kaufmann, 1998.

[15] S. Luke and L. Spector. Evolving teamwork and coordination with genetic programming. In *Genetic Programming*, pages 150–156. MIT Press, 1996.

[16] G. Nitschke. Behavioral heterogeneity, cooperation, and collective construction. In *Congress on Evolutionary Computation (CEC)*, pages 1–8. IEEE Press, 2012.

[17] G. S. Nitschke. *Neuro-evolution for emergent specialization in collective behavior systems*. PhD thesis, Vrije Universiteit Amsterdam, 2008.

[18] G. S. Nitschke, A. E. Eiben, and M. C. Schut. Evolving team behaviors with specialization. *Genetic Programming and Evolvable Machines*, 13(4):493–536, 2012.

[19] G. S. Nitschke, M. C. Schut, and A. E. Eiben. Collective neuro-evolution for evolving specialized sensor resolutions in a multi-rover task. *Evolutionary Intelligence*, 3(1):13–29, 2009.

[20] L. Panait. Theoretical convergence guarantees for cooperative coevolutionary algorithms. *Evolutionary Computation*, 18(4):581–615, 2010.

[21] L. Panait and S. Luke. Cooperative multi-agent learning: The state of the art. *Autonomous Agents & Multi-Agent Systems*, 11(3):387–434, 2005.

[22] M. A. Potter and K. A. D. Jong. Cooperative coevolution: An architecture for evolving coadapted subcomponents. *Evolutionary Computation*, 8(1):1–29, 2000.

[23] M. A. Potter, L. A. Meeden, and A. C. Schultz. Heterogeneity in the coevolved behaviors of mobile robots: The emergence of specialists. In *International Joint Conference on Artificial Intelligence (IJCAI)*, pages 1337–1343. Morgan Kaufmann, 2001.

[24] K. Stanley and R. Miikkulainen. Evolving neural networks through augmenting topologies. *Evolutionary Computation*, 10(2):99–127, 2002.

[25] P. Stone and M. Veloso. Multiagent systems: A survey from a machine learning perspective. *Autonomous Robots*, 8(3):345–383, 2000.

[26] V. Trianni, S. Nolfi, and M. Dorigo. Evolution, self-organization and swarm robotics. In *Swarm Intelligence*, Natural Computing Series, pages 163–191. Springer, 2008.

[27] M. Waibel, L. Keller, and D. Floreano. Genetic team composition and level of selection in the evolution of cooperation. *IEEE Transactions on Evolutionary Computation*, 13(3):648–660, 2009.

[28] R. P. Wiegand. *An Analysis of Cooperative Coevolutionary Algorithms*. PhD thesis, George Mason University, 2003.

[29] C. H. Yong and R. Miikkulainen. Coevolution of role-based cooperation in multiagent systems. *IEEE Transactions on Autonomous Mental Development*, 1(3):170–186, 2009.

The Power of Verification for Greedy Mechanism Design*

Dimitris Fotakis
National Technical Univ. of Athens, Greece
fotakis@cs.ntua.gr

Piotr Krysta
University of Liverpool, UK
pkrysta@liverpool.ac.uk

Carmine Ventre
Teesside University, UK
c.ventre@tees.ac.uk

ABSTRACT

Greedy algorithms are known to provide near optimal approximation guarantees for Combinatorial Auctions (CAs) with multidimensional bidders, ignoring incentive compatibility. Borodin and Lucier [5] however proved that truthful greedy-like mechanisms for CAs with multi-minded bidders do not achieve good approximation guarantees. In this work, we seek a deeper understanding of greedy mechanism design and investigate under which general assumptions, we can have efficient and truthful greedy mechanisms for CAs. Towards this goal, we use the framework of priority algorithms and weak and strong verification, where the bidders are not allowed to overbid on their winning set or on any subsets of this set, respectively. We provide a complete characterization of the power of weak verification showing that it is sufficient and necessary for any greedy fixed priority algorithm to become truthful with the use of money or not, depending on the ordering of the bids. Moreover, we show that strong verification is sufficient and necessary for the greedy algorithm of [20], which is 2-approximate for submodular CAs, to become truthful with money in finite bidding domains. Our proof is based on an interesting structural analysis of the strongly connected components of the declaration graph.

Categories and Subject Descriptors

F.2.0 [**Analysis of Algorithms and Problem Complexity**]: General; J.4 [**Social and Behavioral Sciences**]: Economics

General Terms

Algorithms, Theory, Economics

Keywords

Algorithmic Mechanism Design; Mechanisms with Verification; Combinatorial Auctions

*This work is partially supported by EPSRC through grants EP/K01000X/1 and EP/M018113/1 and by Greek NSRF grant Algorithmic Game Theory/THALES.

Appears in: *Proceedings of the 14th International Conference on Autonomous Agents and Multiagent Systems (AAMAS 2015), Bordini, Elkind, Weiss, Yolum (eds.), May, 4–8, 2015, Istanbul, Turkey.*

1. INTRODUCTION

Algorithmic mechanism design (AMD) is the study of optimization problems where part of the input data is private data of selfish agents. The goals of the protocol, called a *truthful mechanism*, are to incentivize the agents to truthfully report their private data to the mechanism and to optimize the objective function of the problem under consideration. AMD problems have numerous applications in areas like, e.g., e-commerce, online auctioning, shopping systems.

Combinatorial Auctions (CAs) with the objective to maximize the social welfare is a paradigmatic AMD problem. In a CA, we have a set U of m goods and a set of n bidders. Each bidder i has a *private* valuation function v_i mapping subsets of goods to nonnegative numbers. Valuations are monotone, i.e., for $S \supseteq T$, $v_i(S) \geq v_i(T)$, and normalized, i.e., $v_i(\emptyset) = 0$. The goal is to find a partition $S_1, \ldots, S_n$ of U such that the *social welfare* $\sum_{i=1}^n v_i(S_i)$ is maximized. Even the simplest versions of CAs are known to be **NP**-hard and even hard to approximate in polynomial time. For vast literature on the design of approximate polynomial-time mechanisms for various versions of CAs, see, e.g., [25].

We study CAs with bidders' valuation functions represented by *value oracles*, i.e., each bidder i submits such an oracle that given any subset of goods $S \subseteq \mathsf{U}$ outputs the value $v_i(S)$. This is the weakest possible assumption used in literature to tackle the issue of exponentially (in n and m) large valuations [4]. We aim at the design of truthful mechanisms that only use a polynomial number of calls to such value oracles and return solutions with best possible approximation guarantees with respect to social welfare. For CAs with single-minded bidders[1] a simple greedy truthful mechanism achieves the best possible $\sqrt{m}$-approximation [21].

Despite achieving an optimal approximation ratio for CAs with single-minded bidders, greedy truthful mechanisms perform much worse for more general valuation functions. Borodin and Lucier [5] studied limitations of a general class of greedy algorithms, *priority algorithms*, for truthful CAs with non single-minded bidders. They proved that any such truthful priority algorithm (i.e., mechanism using a priority algorithm to compute its outcome) has an approximation ratio $\Omega(m)$. The results of [5] imply that any truthful priority algorithm does not achieve a good approximation ratio.

A widely studied class of CAs with non single-minded, thus multidimensional, bidders assumes submodular valuation functions, modeling economies of scale. A well known

[1]Bidder i is single-minded if there exists a fixed subset $S_i \subseteq \mathsf{U}$ and a number $w_i \geq 0$ such that $v_i(S) = w_i$ for any S such that $\mathsf{U} \supseteq S \supseteq S_i$, and $v_i(S) = 0$ otherwise.

greedy approximation algorithm for submodular CAs gives an approximation guarantee of 2 [20]. This algorithm simply processes the goods in any fixed order and awards them to the bidder who has maximum marginal value for each good. However, there do not exist payments that make this algorithm truthful [20]. Moreover, Borodin and Lucier [5] considered the whole class of such greedy mechanisms (defined by a fixed order of the goods used) for submodular CAs and proved that no mechanism in this class is truthful!

Motivated by the dichotomy between a powerful algorithmic technique and its poor compatibility with bidders' incentives, we investigate here in which general circumstances of multi-dimensional CAs, we can have truthful greedy mechanisms. Inspired by [18], we focus on relaxations of truthfulness wherein some form of overbidding can be detected and prevented. This line of research, generally dubbed mechanisms with *verification*, is motivated by a number of real-life applications and has been considered by economists in the context of CAs (see, e.g., [7]). We want to understand what kind of relaxed notion of incentive-compatibility, i.e., verification, we can adopt to happily marry greedy algorithms with good approximation guarantees and truthfulness. A relaxation of truthfulness is necessary in general for efficient CAs with multidimensional bidders for otherwise no approximation better than m can be achieved [9].

Our Contribution. Priority algorithms comprise a widely accepted general model of greedy-like algorithms [6]. In the context of CAs and for our purposes, we consider *greedy priority algorithms* that sequentially process *elementary bids*, namely triples consisting of the identity i of a bidder, a subset S of goods, and bidder i's value $v_i(S)$ for S. Extending and generalizing previous results in [18, 14], we first prove that *weak verification*, namely verification that does not allow the bidders to overbid on their winning sets, is both sufficient and necessary for any greedy fixed priority algorithm to be truthful without money, if the elementary bids are processed in nonincreasing order of their values, or with money, if the order of the elementary bids is determined by, possibly bidder dependent, increasing functions of their values. We highlight that these results are not specific to only CAs but actually apply to any AMD problem Π and greedy fixed priority algorithm for Π that uses triples as elementary bids (S being an output component pertinent to Π), see Section 3. Observe that such general characterization-type results in AMD are scarce in literature.

To deal with the additional power of adaptive priority algorithms (cf. [5]), we introduce the concept of *strong verification*, where the bidders are not allowed to overbid on *any* subset of their winning set. We first characterize all mechanisms that are truthful without money and with strong verification. We observe that such mechanisms exhibit highly non-monotone behavior, thus suggesting that designing such mechanisms with good approximation guarantee is difficult. Thus, we study strong verification with money.

As our main technical result, we show that the 2-approximate (adaptive priority) greedy algorithm of [20] is truthful with money in finite bidding domains if and only if strong verification is used. We prove the existence of payments that make this algorithm truthful by using the well known cycle-monotonicity technique [27, 30], which basically requires to study the cycles of the so-called *declaration graph*. We unveil a surprising structural property of the declaration graph associated to this algorithm. It is well known that if the valuation domain is finite, a mechanism is truthful with money if and only if the corresponding declaration graph does not contain any negative cycles (see, e.g., [27, 30]). Here, carefully exploiting the greedy selection rule and strong verification, we prove that all cycles of the declaration graph consist of cliques of nodes linked by 0-weight edges. Thus, contracting the nodes of all such cliques, we obtain an acyclic declaration graph. Then, we can define payments for any given declaration (node of this graph) by computing essentially the shortest paths from this node to all the sinks. We also show that strong verification is necessary for making the greedy algorithm truthful with money, even if it is allowed to execute all possible orders of goods.

We finally turn our attention to the computational complexity of computing the payments, guaranteed to exist by our proof. The only general approach known to date to prove that computing payments is not harder than essentially executing the mechanism (once), is the technique of Babaioff et al. [3, 2]. We show, however, that this approach does not lead to the required payments in our case, indicating that the payment computation has to carefully take into account the structure of the declaration graph. The problem of computing payments can equivalently be formulated as computing a feasible solution to an appropriate linear program (of exponential size) defined on the declaration graph. It is easy to observe that shortest paths are only one of the feasible solutions to this linear program (the minimal), but any feasible solution can be used as a payment function. In fact, we are not interested in an entire feasible solution, but just on its component that corresponds to (and reveals the payment for) some given node of the declaration graph. We further prove that if the domain is represented succinctly, the problem of computing the payment corresponding to a shortest path solution to this linear program is **NP**-hard. The proof shows that computing such payments requires (and reveals) crucial information about a succinctly represented declaration graph of exponential size. This is true even for CAs with $n = 2$ submodular bidders and $m = 2$ goods.

We complement this result by showing that indeed, we can always efficiently find (non-shortest path) payments in our declaration graph in the restricted case with $m = 2$ goods and any number of bidders, by carefully exploiting the structure of the declaration graph in this case. We in fact prove that the associated outcome graph, i.e., the declaration graphs with its nodes leading to the same outcomes contracted to a single node, does not have any negative weight cycle. We are able to actually close the picture completely, by proving that there are instances with $n = 2$ and $m = 3$ for which the outcome graph has a negative weight cycle, meaning that for such instances the payment-per-outcome approach fails for payment computation.

Due to lack of space, some of the proofs are deferred to the full version of the paper.

Significance of Results and Related Work. Our work is among the very first studies which dig deeper into the mostly unexplored structure of the declaration graphs associated to interesting mechanisms. We are aware of only very few such similar studies, e.g., [19, 18].

To put our results in a broader mechanism design context, it is in place to compare them with the celebrated VCG mechanism [29, 8, 16]. Although, we do not know if payments for our greedy mechanism for submodular CAs can be computed in time independent of the size of the domain our results have significant implications. If one wants to use an auction mechanism in practice, the mechanism to choose would arguably be greedy, for its simplicity over the VCG, which requires an optimal solution to a computationally difficult problem (VCG does not need verification though). The crucial point is that the CAs setting relevant to applications is in fact the setting in which we *are able* to compute our payments efficiently. Think about submodular CAs where each bidder can declare valuation functions from a set of size polynomial in n and m. In this case, the allocation graph associated to the greedy mechanism has polynomial size and thus payments are computable in time polynomial time in n and m, i.e, in the combinatorial size of the allocation problem. For instance, valuations are numbers from $\{0, 1, 2, \ldots, M\}$, where M is a constant and, moreover, each bidder submits explicit bids on subsets of only fixed constant size subset of goods. Interestingly, for another such practically relevant setting of CAs with constant-size submodular valuations, Dobzinski and Vondrák [13] prove that the social welfare maximization problem is not only **NP**-hard but also **NP**-hard to approximate within any factor better than 1.225. Thus, we cannot run VCG in this setting in polynomial time. But since the declaration graph of the greedy algorithm is of size polynomial in n and m, we can compute the payments in polynomial time, see Theorem 8.

CAs with submodular bidders were widely studied both from algorithmic and AMD perspective, see, e.g., [22, 17, 31, 20, 11, 10, 12, 13]. CAs with submodular bidders given by value oracles as an optimization problem (without strategic consideration) is **NP**-hard to solve optimally and **NP**-hard to approximate with factors better than $e/(e-1)$ [17]; such factors cannot be obtained with using only polynomially many value oracles [22]. On the other hand, there are the following polynomial time algorithms: a deterministic greedy 2-approximation [20] and a randomized $e/(e-1)$-approximation algorithm [31]. Now, considering truthful mechanisms for this problem with payments, very strong non-constant lower bounds on the approximation ratios are known. Dobzinski [10] proved that every universally truthful randomized mechanism for CAs with submodular valuations with an approximation ratio of $m^{1/2-\varepsilon}$, for some $\varepsilon > 0$, must use exponentially many value oracles. There is a deterministic polynomial time truthful mechanism with an approximation ratio of $\sqrt{m}$, see [11], which is best possible by this hardness result. Moreover, Dobzinski and Vondrák [12] show that no deterministic polynomial time truthful mechanism provides an $m^{1/2-\varepsilon}$-approximation for a constant $\varepsilon > 0$ to this problem, even with succinctly represented submodular valuations, unless **NP** = **RP**. Similar strong non-constant lower bound holds even for randomized polynomial time truthful in expectation mechanisms for CAs with succinctly represented submodular valuations [12].[2] In light of such strong hardness results, our 2-approximate truthful mechanism assumes particular relevance (also considering its applicability to practical auction domains).

The concept of a posteriori verification (i.e., verification that depends on the output computed) in AMD dates back to the seminal work of Nisan and Ronen [24]; subsequently, it has been extensively studied in machine scheduling settings (see, [26] and references therein) and introduced to CAs in [18]. The feasibility of trading verification with money in mechanism design for CAs has been studied in [14].

[2] A valuation function is called succinctly represented if it can be encoded in a bit string of length polynomial in the problem size.

2. MODEL AND PRELIMINARIES

CAs and Verification Paradigms. For definition of CAs and basic notation, we refer to Section 1. Assuming that the values $v_i(S)$ are private knowledge of the bidders accessed by value oracles, we seek to design an *allocation algorithm* A and a payment function P. The auction (also called mechanism) (A, P) for a given input of bids from the bidders, outputs an assignment and charges the bidder i a payment P_i. Allocations and payments should be defined so that no bidder has an incentive to misreport her preferences and in order to maximize the social welfare. More formally, we let b_i be a valuation function of agent i, i.e., $b_i : 2^{\mathsf{U}} \to \mathbb{R}^+$. We call b_i a *declaration* of bidder i. We let v_i be the *true type* of agent i and D_i denote the set of all the possible declarations of agent i; we call D_i the *declaration domain* of bidder i. Let $\mathbf{b}_{-i}$ be the declarations of all the agents but i. For any $\mathbf{b}_{-i}$ and declaration $b_i \in D_i$, we let $A_i(b_i, \mathbf{b}_{-i})$ be the set in 2^{U} that A on input $\mathbf{b} = (b_i, \mathbf{b}_{-i})$ allocates to bidder i. We say that (A, P) is a truthful mechanism (or simply that A is a truthful algorithm) if for any i, $b_i \in D_i$ and $\mathbf{b}_{-i}$:

$$v_i(A_i(v_i, \mathbf{b}_{-i})) - P_i(v_i, \mathbf{b}_{-i}) \geq v_i(A_i(\mathbf{b})) - P_i(\mathbf{b}). \quad (1)$$

In the *(weak) verification model* [18, 14] each bidder can only declare lower valuations for the set she is awarded. More formally, bidder i whose type is v_i can declare a type b_i if and only if whenever $A_i(b_i, \mathbf{b}_{-i}) \neq \emptyset$:

$$b_i(A_i(b_i, \mathbf{b}_{-i})) \leq v_i(A_i(b_i, \mathbf{b}_{-i})). \quad (2)$$

The stronger variant of verification we consider here allows each bidder to underbid on the set awarded and its subsets (other declarations are unrestricted). Formally, in the *strong verification model*, bidder i can declare a type b_i if and only if whenever $A_i(b_i, \mathbf{b}_{-i}) \neq \emptyset$:

$$b_i(T) \leq v_i(T) \; \forall T \subseteq A_i(b_i, \mathbf{b}_{-i}). \quad (3)$$

When (2) or (3) is not satisfied, the bidder is caught lying by the relevant verification step and the mechanism punishes her so to make this behavior very undesirable (i.e., for simplicity we can assume that in such a case the bidder will have to pay a fine of infinite value). This way (1) is satisfied directly when the verification does catch lies – i.e., when (2) ((3), respectively) does not hold for the weak (strong, respectively) verification – as in such a case a lying bidder would have an infinitely bad utility because of the punishment/fine. Thus in this model, truthfulness with weak (strong, respectively) verification of a mechanism is fully captured by (1) holding only for any i, $\mathbf{b}_{-i}$ and $b_i \in D_i$ such that (2) ((3), respectively) is fulfilled. All the concepts can be adapted to the setting without money when $P_i(\mathbf{b}) = 0$ for any i and $\mathbf{b}$.

In CAs with submodular bidders, we have that D_i is comprised of submodular valuations, i.e., for all i, $b_i \in D_i$ and $S, T \subseteq \mathsf{U}$, $b_i(S) + b_i(T) \geq b_i(S \cup T) - b_i(S \cap T)$.

A Graph Theoretic Approach to Truthfulness. The technique we use to study truthful mechanisms with verification is the so-called cycle monotonicity. Consider an algorithm A. We set up a weighted graph for each bidder i depending on A, i's domain D_i, verification paradigm, and the declarations $\mathbf{b}_{-i}$. Non-existence of negative-weight cycles (respectively, edges) in this graph guarantees the truthfulness with money (respectively, without money) of A.

More formally, fix algorithm A, bidder i and declarations $\mathbf{b}_{-i}$. Let V denote the verification paradigm at hand; if a type a can declare to be of type b obeying V, we say that $a \rightarrow_V b$ (e.g., $a \rightarrow_V b$ if and only if (2) is true whenever V is weak verification). The *declaration graph* associated to algorithm A has a vertex for each possible declaration in the domain D_i. For the verification V, we add an arc between a and b in D_i whenever $a \rightarrow_V b$. For example, in the case of strong verification, from (3), edge (a, b) belongs to the graph if and only if $a(T) \geq b(T)$ for all $T \subseteq A_i(b, \mathbf{b}_{-i})$.[3] The weight of the edge (a, b) is defined as $a(A_i(a, \mathbf{b}_{-i})) - a(A_i(b, \mathbf{b}_{-i}))$ and thus encodes the loss that a bidder whose type is a incurs into by declaring b. The following known result relates the edges/cycles of the declaration graph to the existence of payments leading to truthful auctions.

PROPOSITION 1. *If each D_i is finite and each declaration graph associated to algorithm A does not have negative-weight cycles with verification V then there exists a payment function P s.t. (A, P) is a truthful mechanism with verification V. Similarly, if each (possibly infinite) graph does not have a negative-weight edge with verification V, then A is a truthful mechanism without money and with verification V.*

The proposition above is adapted from [27, 30] to the verification setting V as in [28]. Note that Proposition 1 requires the technical hypothesis of finite domains for mechanisms with money: this is because the payments P are defined as lengths of certain shortest paths on the declaration graph; shortest paths are well-defined only on finite graphs. This seems to be a limitation of the cycle-monotonicity technique for the design of mechanisms with verification in general [28].

A variant of the cycle-monotonicity technique described above, defines payments as a function of the outcome and the declarations of the others, using the following tool.

DEFINITION 1 ([28]). *For an algorithm A, verification paradigm V, every i and $\mathbf{b}_{-i} \in D_{-i}$, the* outcome graph *has a node for each possible outcome output of A. For every pair of outcomes, X, Y, $X \neq Y$, add an edge (X, Y) if there exist $a, b \in D_i$ such that $A(a, \mathbf{b}_{-i}) = X$, $A(b, \mathbf{b}_{-i}) = Y$ and $a \rightarrow_V b$. The weight of edge (X, Y) (if any) is $\inf_{a \in \mathcal{R}_X^Y} \{a(X) - a(Y)\}$, where $\mathcal{R}_X^Y = \{a \in \mathcal{R}_X | \exists b \in \mathcal{R}_Y \text{ s.t. } a \rightarrow_V b\}$ with $\mathcal{R}_Z = \{a \in D_i | A(a, \mathbf{b}_{-i}) = Z\}$ for any outcome Z.*

A theorem similar in spirit to Proposition 1 holds and then the absence of negative-weight cycles in the outcome graph is a condition which is necessary and sufficient for the existence of payments-per-outcome implementing algorithm A.

Greedy Priority Algorithms. We briefly introduce priority algorithms, following [6]. The input of a *priority algorithm* is a finite subset I of the class $\mathcal{I}$ of all permissible input atomic items. We consider (elementary) bids as input atomic items. Namely $\mathcal{I}$ consists of all possible triples $(i, S, b_i(S))$, where i is the bidder, S is an output component (e.g., subset of U for CAs) of the problem at hand, and $b_i(S)$ is i's valuation for S. For simplicity, we denote such an elementary bid as $b_i(S)$, or $b(S)$, if i is clear from the context.

[3]Formally, for strong verification, an edge (a, b) belongs to the graph if $a(T) \geq b(T)$, $\forall T \subseteq A_i(b, \mathbf{b}_{-i})$, only whenever $A_i(b, \mathbf{b}_{-i}) \neq \emptyset$ as this set (and its subsets) would be needed to verify. However, because of the monotonicity and normalization of valuations, $a(A_i(b, \mathbf{b}_{-i})) \geq b(A_i(b, \mathbf{b}_{-i}))$ holds also whenever $A_i(b, \mathbf{b}_{-i}) = \emptyset$, since $a(\emptyset) = b(\emptyset) = 0$.

The output of a priority algorithm consists of an irrevocable decision for each elementary bid processed. A (possibly adaptive) priority algorithm A receives as input a finite set of elementary bids I and proceeds in rounds, processing a single bid in each round. While there are unprocessed bids in I, A selects a total order $\mathcal{T}$ on $\mathcal{I}$ without looking at the set of unprocessed bids. It is important that $\mathcal{T}$ can be any total order on $\mathcal{I}$, and that for adaptive priority algorithms, the order may be different in each round. If the order is fixed before starting processing the bids, then the algorithm is called fixed priority. In each round, A receives the first (according to $\mathcal{T}$) unprocessed bid $x \in I$ and irrevocably accepts or rejects it. Then, x (and all bids preceding x in $\mathcal{T}$) are removed from I, and A proceeds to the next round. *Greedy priority algorithms* accept the current bid $b_i(S)$ if grating S to bidder i is feasible for the problem at hand (e.g., S is disjoint to the previously allocated subsets of U).

3. WEAK VERIFICATION AND GREEDY FIXED PRIORITY ALGORITHMS

We want to understand what kind of verification we can use with greedy fixed priority algorithms to implement them truthfully (with or without money). It turns out that the concept of weak verification (2) is sufficient and necessary for that. The role of money in truthfulness is strictly linked with the ordering of the bids used by the algorithm. Below, we call $A_i(\mathbf{b})$ the winning component of bidder i. Our first result concerns truthfulness without money.

THEOREM 1. *A greedy fixed priority algorithm processing the bids in non-increasing order of their value (and with a fixed bid-independent tie-breaking rule) is truthful with verification and without money if and only if the verification prevents overbidding on the (non-empty) winning component.*

PROOF. Fix i and $\mathbf{b}_{-i}$ and consider the declaration graph associated to the greedy priority algorithm A with a verification paradigm V. By Proposition 1, A is truthful without money if and only if the graph has no negative-weight edges. We prove that if V is weak verification (2), then there is no negative-weight edge, and conversely, if V is not weak verification (2), then there exist instances with a negative edge.

For the first claim, let (a, b) be an edge of the graph. By hypothesis, this edge exists iff $a(Y) \geq b(Y)$, $Y = A_i(b, \mathbf{b}_{-i})$. The edge weights $a(A_i(a, \mathbf{b}_{-i})) - a(Y)$. Consider the case in which the edge is negative, i.e., $a(A_i(a, \mathbf{b}_{-i})) < a(Y)$ (thus yielding $Y \neq A_i(a, \mathbf{b}_{-i})$). In such a case, due to the ordering of the bids, $a(Y)$ is considered by A before $a(A_i(a, \mathbf{b}_{-i}))$. But since A is greedy and since Y was not allocated to i, there must exist bids $b_j(Z)$, for $j \neq i$, and some other output components Z, conflicting with Y, such that $b_j(Z) \geq a(Y)$. Let $b_j^*(Z)$ be the highest of these bids. But then $b(Y) \geq b_j^*(Z) \geq a(Y)$, with at least one of the inequalities being strict (by the fixed tie-breaking rule). Thus, a contradiction.

For the second claim, since V is not (2), some bidder i is allowed to overbid on some winning component Y. We can, therefore, build an instance in which bidder i by declaring a does not win Y, with $a(A_i(a, \mathbf{b}_{-i})) < a(Y)$, while, she wins Y by declaring b. The construction amounts to define $\mathbf{b}_{-i}$ in a way similar to the above (i.e., bid $b_j^*(Z)$ in between $b(Y)$ and $a(Y)$). But then (a, b) would have negative weight. □

Let $f_i : \mathbb{R}^+ \rightarrow \mathbb{R}^+$ be a strictly increasing function and assume that the greedy fixed priority algorithm uses function f_i to rank the bids $b_i(S)$ of bidder i for component S. This generalization can add negative-weight edges (cf. [18, Example 2]) but no negative-weight cycle, as shown next.

THEOREM 2. *A greedy fixed priority algorithm that orders elementary bids using strictly monotone functions f_i of their value (and breaks ties in a fixed manner independent from the bids) is truthful with verification and with money if and only if the verification prevents bidder i from overbidding on the (non-empty) winning component.*

PROOF. For the "if" direction, fix i and $\mathbf{b}_{-i}$ and consider the declaration graph associated to the greedy priority algorithm A. (Accordingly, $\mathbf{b}_{-i}$ is dropped from the notation herein to increase readability.) We show that the cycles of this graph have non-negative weights. Consider a generic cycle $C := a^0 \to a^1 \to \ldots \to a^k \to a^{k+1} = a^0$.

Let us first consider the case in which for some $a = a^j$ in C, $A_i(a) = \emptyset$, meaning that the winning component of bidder i declaring a is empty. The claim is that for $b = a^{j+1}$, $A_i(b) = \emptyset$, thus implying that all the cycle has weight 0. Assume by sake of contradiction that $A_i(b) \neq \emptyset$ and note that since $A_i(a) = \emptyset$ then, for all non-empty output components X, there must exist bidder $j_X \neq i$ such that $Y_X = A_{j_X}(b_{j_X})$ conflicts with X and $f_{j_X}(b_{j_X}(Y_X)) \geq f_i(a(X))$. But then since $A_i(b) \neq \emptyset$ and as the edge (a, b) belongs to the graph, we have by the definition of verification, that $a(A_i(b)) \geq b(A_i(b))$ and then $f_i(b(A_i(b))) \leq f_i(a(A_i(b)))$. However, since $Z = A_i(b)$ is the winning component of i when declaring b it must be that $f_i(b(Z)) \geq f_{j_Z}(b_{j_Z}(A_{j_Z}(b_{j_Z}))) \geq f_i(a(Z))$. Therefore, $f_i(b(A_i(b))) = f_i(a(A_i(b)))$ which in turns yields, by the bid-independent fixed tie-breaking rule, that $A_i(a) = A_i(b) \neq \emptyset$, a contradiction.

Let us now focus on the case in which $A_i(a^j) \neq \emptyset$ for all $j \in \{0, \ldots, k\}$. By definition of the priority algorithm, for $0 \leq j \leq k$, $f_i(a^j(A_i(a^j))) \geq f_i(a^j(A_i(a^{j+1})))$; while the existence of edge (a^j, a^{j+1}) yields $a^j(A_i(a^{j+1})) \geq a^{j+1}(A_i(a^{j+1}))$ and then $f_i(a^j(A_i(a^{j+1}))) \geq f_i(a^{j+1}(A_i(a^{j+1})))$. Unfolding the two inequalities above for the cycle, we get

$$f_i(a^j(A_i(a^{j+1}))) = f_i(a^{j+1}(A_i(a^{j+1}))),$$

which implies that $a^j(A_i(a^{j+1})) = a^{j+1}(A_i(a^{j+1}))$. Then the weight of the cycle C is $\sum_{j=1}^{k} a^j(A_i(a^j)) - a^j(A_i(a^{j+1})) = 0$. This concludes this part of the proof by Proposition 1.

For the "only if" part, let us assume by contradiction that a fixed priority algorithm from the statement is truthful, yet it allows some bidder i to overbid on some non-empty winning component X. Consider the instance where X is the most preferred component of i and assume that X is the only component maximizing i's utility. Define $\mathbf{b}_{-i}$ in such a way that X is not allocated to i when she is truthtelling. Since A is greedy, there exist bidders $j \neq i$, such that $f_j(b_j(Y)) > f_i(a_i(X))$, $Y = A_j(b_j)$ and Y conflicting with X. Let j be such a bidder with the highest $f_j(b_j(Y))$. We are going to show a 3-cycle of negative weight thus showing that there are no payments for the algorithm (cf. Proposition 1).

Consider the bid b defined as a_i except that $b(X) > a_i(X)$ in such a way that $f_i(b(X)) > f_j(b_j(Y))$ and X is allocated to i. Since the verification allows this lie, then the declaration graph has the edge (a_i, b) of weight $\delta = a_i(A_i(a_i, \mathbf{b}_{-i})) - a_i(X) < 0$. Consider now b' defined as b with the exception that $a_i(A_i(a_i, \mathbf{b}_{-i})) \geq b'(A_i(a_i)) = b(X) - \epsilon$, with $\epsilon < -\delta$. (Since $f_i(b(X)) > f_i(a_i(A_i(a_i, \mathbf{b}_{-i})))$ and f_i is increasing such an ϵ exists.) Observe that $f_i(b'(X)) > f_i(b'(A_i(a_i, \mathbf{b}_{-i})))$ and then $A_i(b') = X$. Therefore, edges (b, b') and (b', a_i) belong to the graph, since there is no overbidding on winning component; (b, b') weighs 0, while (b', a_i) weighs ϵ. The cycle $a_i \to b \to b'$ has then negative weight. □

REMARK 1. *Theorems 1 and 2 hold for any AMD problem Π and greedy priority algorithm for Π that can be cast in our framework (i.e., input items are elementary bids). Recall that a greedy priority algorithm treats each input item as if it was the last one in the sequence and then optimizes the objective function of the algorithm on each item [6].*

For adaptive priority algorithm things can be more complex at least in the multidimensional case. Since bidders control more than one bid, they could lie on one of their bids to change the ordering of the adaptive priority algorithm and get an advantage. Therefore, it is not enough in general to prevent lies on the winning component, but a more stringent notion ought to be used. Next, we show that this is indeed the case for an adaptive priority algorithm for CAs with submodular bidders given in [20]. The concept of verification used to implement this algorithm turns out to be the strong verification introduced above.

4. STRONG VERIFICATION

Truthfulness without money. We begin by characterizing the algorithms that are truthful without money in the setting of strong verification. Interestingly, the characterizing property is algorithmic only.

DEFINITION 2. *An algorithm A is* strongly monotone *if the following holds for any i, any $\mathbf{b}_{-i}$, any $a \in D_i$: if $A_i(a, \mathbf{b}_{-i}) = S$ then for all $b \in D_i$ such that $b(T) \geq a(T)$ $\forall T \subseteq S$ it holds $b(A_i(b, \mathbf{b}_{-i})) \geq b(S)$.*

THEOREM 3. *An algorithm A is truthful without money and with strong verification for bidders given by value oracles if and only if A is strongly monotone.*

This characterization relates to those in [14] for moneyless mechanisms with weak verification. However, while in the latter case mechanisms are monotone, e.g., as in [23, 21] (i.e., to higher valuations there must correspond "better" sets), in our case the resulting mechanisms can be highly non-monotone. For example, it can be that for a known double-minded bidder[4] with valuation (v_1, v_2), the set $S_1 \supseteq S_2$ is won but for $b_i = (v_1 + \epsilon, v_2 - \epsilon)$ is not, i.e., there is a discontinuity in bids winning S_1. This makes the class of these mechanisms hard to design and then the hope to find one with good approximation guarantee appears slim. Therefore, we add money to our mechanisms in order to make the task of obtaining constant approximations tractable.

Strong verification with money. We focus on the greedy algorithm introduced in [20] (cf. Algorithm 1). We assume that the selection of the bidder with maximum marginal valuation in line 3 uses a fixed bid-independent tie-breaking rule. Algorithm 1 is a greedy adaptive priority algorithm. In particular, given the allocation $S_1, \ldots, S_n$ of goods considered so far and the current good, it orders first the elementary bids $v_j(S_j \cup \{e\})$ in nonincreasing order of their

[4]This terminology indicates a bidder only interested in two subsets of the universe; the two sets (denoted above as S_1 and S_2) are known to the mechanism and the bidders declare their two valuations rather than a value oracle.

Algorithm 1: Greedy algorithm

1 Set $S_1, \dots, S_n = \emptyset$
2 For each good $e \in \mathsf{U}$ do
3 Let j be the bidder with highest $v_j(S_j \cup \{e\}) - v_j(S_j)$
4 $S_j = S_j \cup \{e\}$
5 Return $S = (S_1, S_2, \dots, S_n)$

marginal valuations $v_j(S_j \cup \{e\}) - v_j(S_j)$ and next all other bids in an arbitrary order (note that [5, Section 4] uses a slightly different way of describing Algorithm 1 as a priority algorithm using goods as input atomic items).

THEOREM 4. *There exists a payment function that paired with Algorithm 1 gives rise to a truthful mechanism with strong verification for CAs with submodular bidders given by value oracles bidding from finite domains.*

PROOF. By Proposition 1, Algorithm 1 (denoted as A in the rest of the proof) is part of a truthful mechanism as long as no declaration graph associated to it has negative weight cycles. We will prove that this is indeed the case.

Fix i and $\mathbf{b}_{-i}$ and consider the declaration graph associated to A. Consider a generic cycle $C := a^0 \to a^1 \to \dots \to a^k \to a^{k+1} = a^0$ of this graph. By existence of edges, for all $j = 0, \dots, k$, we have:

$$a^j(T) \geq a^{j+1}(T) \; \forall T \subseteq A_i(a^{j+1}, \mathbf{b}_{-i}). \quad (4)$$

This yields that for all $j = 0, \dots, k$

$$a^j(U) = a^{j+1}(U) \; \forall U \subseteq \cap_{l=1}^{k} A_i(a^l, \mathbf{b}_{-i}). \quad (5)$$

Now let r be the first good of U in the order considered by the algorithm in line 2 that is in $\cup_{l=1}^{k} A_i(a^l, \mathbf{b}_{-i})$ but not in $\cap_{l=1}^{k} A_i(a^l, \mathbf{b}_{-i})$; let A_r be the set assigned to bidder i up to the point in which r is to considered. Without loss of generality, let $r \in A_i(a^1, \mathbf{b}_{-i})$. Since $r \in A_i(a^1, \mathbf{b}_{-i})$, then in $(a^1, \mathbf{b}_{-i})$ bidder i has the maximum marginal valuation for r. But then by (4) and (5), we have $a^0(A_r \cup \{r\}) \geq a^1(A_r \cup \{r\})$ and $a^0(A_r) = a^1(A_r)$, respectively. This yields $a^0(A_r \cup \{r\}) - a^0(A_r) \geq a^1(A_r \cup \{r\}) - a^1(A_r)$, which, in turn, implies that bidder i has maximum marginal for r also in bid vector $(a^0, \mathbf{b}_{-i})$. We then have that $r \in A_i(a^0, \mathbf{b}_{-i})$ as well. By reiterating the argument, we have that $r \in A_i(a^l, \mathbf{b}_{-i})$ for $l = 0, \dots, k$ and then $A_i(a^j, \mathbf{b}_{-i}) = A_i(a^{j+1}, \mathbf{b}_{-i}) \; \forall j = 0, \dots, k$. All edges in C have thus weight 0. □

The theorem above guarantees the existence of payments that enforce truthfulness when the bidding domains are finite. We are left with the question of how to efficiently compute payments. The first immediate observation is that whenever the size of the graph is polynomial in the number of players and goods, then we can simply compute shortest paths as from Rochet's theorem.

COROLLARY 1. *There exists a 2-approximate truthful mechanism with strong verification for CAs with submodular bidders given by value oracles bidding from finite domains. The allocation is computable in time polynomial in $n+m$. If bidders' domains are of polynomial size in $m+n$, then payments can also be computed efficiently.*

To remove the assumption of Corollary 1 on the domains, one would need to depart from shortest paths and find a different way to define payments (e.g., via a closed formula) allowing efficient computation. A common approach is to understand the structure of the graph. The graph is very well structured. Indeed, by the proof of Theorem 4 any cycle is a clique of nodes corresponding to declarations to which the algorithm assigns the same set S, $a(T) = b(T)$ for all $T \subseteq S$ and declarations a and b in the clique. Since all its edges have weight 0, the clique can be contracted and the same payment assigned to all these declarations. We are left with a directed acyclic graph, holding out the hope to compute payments efficiently.

Necessity of Strong Verification for the Truthfulness of Algorithm 1. We show that strong (no-overbidding) verification is necessary for the payments of Theorem 4 to exist. Namely, we give a domain for bidder 2 and a declaration for bidder 1 such that no matter what order Algorithm 1 uses in line 2, the declaration graph of bidder 2 has a negative-weight cycle, unless strong verification is used. We have $\mathsf{U} = \{\alpha, \beta\}$ and two submodular bidders $N = \{1, 2\}$. A valuation function v is represented as a triple (x, y, z), where $v(\{\alpha\}) = x$, $v(\{\beta\}) = y$, and $v(\{\alpha, \beta\}) = z$. Let $v_1 = (9.4, 6, 11)$ and $D_2 = \{b_2, b_2', b_2'', b_2'''\}$ where $b_2 = (11, 10, 18)$, $b_2' = (9, 10, 19)$, $b_2'' = (11, 7, 16.4)$ and $b_2''' = (11, 5.5, 16.5)$. Note that if Algorithm 1 considers first good α and then β, bidder 2 with declaration b_2 is allocated $\{\alpha, \beta\}$ and with declaration b_2' is allocated $\{\beta\}$. If the order of goods is reversed then we observe that $A_2(v_1, b_2'') = \{\alpha, \beta\}$ and $A_2(v_1, b_2''') = \{\alpha\}$. If no strong verification is used, e.g., weak verification would be adopted, then edges (b_2, b_2'), (b_2', b_2), for order α, β, and (b_2'', b_2''') and (b_2''', b_2''), for order β, α, are present in the declaration graph of bidder 2. Moreover, $b_2(\{\alpha, \beta\}) - b_2(\{\beta\}) = 18 - 10 = 8$ and $b_2'(\{\beta\}) - b_2'(\{\alpha, \beta\}) = 10 - 19 = -9$, and then $b_2 \to b_2' \to b_2$ is a negative cycle, if the order considered is α, β. Similarly, in the case in which the order is β, α, we have $b_2''(\{\alpha, \beta\}) - b_2''(\{\alpha\}) = 16.4 - 11 = 5.4$ and $b_2'''(\{\alpha\}) - b_2'''(\{\alpha, \beta\}) = 11 - 16.5 = -5.5$, and then $b_2'' \to b_2''' \to b_2''$ is a negative cycle. Note that strong verification would eliminate edges (b_2', b_2) and (b_2''', b_2'') in the respective cases. Therefore, Algorithm 1 does not admit truthful payments for any order in which the goods are processed, unless strong verification is used.

5. COMPUTING PAYMENTS

The complexity of payment computation is usually no harder than complexity of the corresponding algorithm for the combinatorial problem at hand. This is because explicit formulas for payments are either known (e.g., VCG, single-dimensional domains) or derived from the cycle-monotonicity analysis [19, 18]. However, when this fails, no other source of hardness for payment computation is sought [19, Section 4] [28]. We initiate here a study of the complexity of payment computation by decoupling the latter from the computational complexity of the combinatorial algorithm, using Algorithm 1 as a case study.

We begin by observing, via a connection with the implicit payment computation of [2, 3], that shortest-path payments cannot seem to overlook the structure of the declaration graph. Informed by this, and in order to prove hardness of payment computation, we enrich the classical mechanism design model by including bidding domains as input to the mechanisms. We will adapt standard black box approach and assume that in addition to bidders' declarations, the bidders' domains are either given explicitly as part of the input encoded in binary or they are represented succinctly and the mechanism can access them by queries. Running time of a mechanism is measured as a function of $m+n$ and the size of domains' description or the number of queries, where each query takes constant time.

Impossibility of Implicit Payment Computation. We present an example indicating that we need to carefully take the structure of the declaration graph into account when we compute the payments for Algorithm 1. As noted above, by Theorem 4, if we fix the declarations of all other bidders to $\mathbf{b}_{-i}$, the declaration graph of bidder i reduces to a directed acyclic graph. Among the nodes of the DAG, we are particularly interested in the node, that we call 0, containing all the declarations mapped by the algorithm to $\emptyset$.

We observe that 0 is a sink of the DAG. Fix i, $\mathbf{b}_{-i}$ and let $a \in D_i$ be a declaration mapped by Algorithm 1 (denoted as A below) to $\emptyset$. Assume that a could lie, according to (3), and say b such that $A_i(b, \mathbf{b}_{-i}) = S \neq \emptyset$, and let r be the first good of S according to the order considered by the algorithm in line 2. By the greedy rule in line 3 (and the fixed tie-breaking rule within), we have that $b(\{r\}) \geq \text{marg}_{-i}(r) \geq a(\{r\})$, with at least one of the inequalities being strict, where $\text{marg}_{-i}(r)$ denotes the maximum marginal on r of bidders other than i at this point. The above inequality chain shows that b is a lie which contradicts (3).

Proposition 1 for acyclic graphs can be proved by setting the payment of bidder i in the declarations profile $(b_i, \mathbf{b}_{-i})$ to the length of the shortest path from b_i to 0, denoted as $SP(b_i, 0)$. Indeed, fixed i and $\mathbf{b}_{-i}$, for an edge (a, b) of the declaration graph for bidder i, $SP(a, 0) \leq SP(b, 0) + a(A_i(a, \mathbf{b}_{-i})) - a(A_i(b, \mathbf{b}_{-i}))$ which simply rewrites (1). We note that this payment can be negative, i.e., we pay the bidders so that they do not underbid on their allocated set. Moreover, as noted in [18], scaling down all the payments so that they become non-negative (while remaining truthful) may require that the utility of some bidders becomes negative, i.e., violate voluntary participation.

One could try to compute (the length of the shortest path from b_i to 0 and) the payment of bidder i in $(b_i, \mathbf{b}_{-i})$ by considering the path from b_i to 0 consisting of all declarations obtained by uniformly scaling down all the coordinates b_i. Such a path would go down through all declarations λb_i, for all $\lambda \in [0, 1]$. Then, similarly to [1, 2, 3], one can set the payment of bidder i as follows:

$$P_i(b_i, \mathbf{b}_{-i}) = b_i(A_i(b_i, \mathbf{b}_{-i}) - \int_0^1 b_i(A_i(\lambda b_i, \mathbf{b}_{-i}))d\lambda. \quad (6)$$

It would be particularly interesting if the payments for Algorithm 1 can be computed in this way because [1, 2, 3] prove that random sampling w.r.t. λ yields an unbiased estimator of the integral in (6). Therefore, using the techniques of [1, 2, 3], we could estimate the payments in randomized polynomial time, thus turning Algorithm 1 into a truthful-in-expectation mechanism with strong verification. Our next example shows that (6) may not result in the right (shortest path length and) payments, thus indicating that this technique does not work with our declaration graph.

Our example uses 2 goods $\mathsf{U} = \{\alpha, \beta\}$ and 2 submodular bidders $N = \{1, 2\}$, and a valuation function v is a triple (x, y, z), where $v(\{\alpha\}) = x$, $v(\{\beta\}) = y$, and $v(\{\alpha, \beta\}) = z$. We let $v_1 = (11 - \varepsilon, 12, 12)$, for a small $\varepsilon > 0$, $b_2 = (23, 12, 23)$ and $b'_2 = (11, 12, 12)$. Algorithm 1 considers first α and next β. Then, $A_2(b_2, v_1) = A_2(b'_2, v_1) = \{\alpha\}$, while $A_2(\frac{10}{11}b'_2, v_1) = \{\beta\}$. Also, $A_2(\lambda b_2, v_1) = \{\alpha\}$ for all $\lambda \in (\frac{11-\varepsilon}{23}, 1]$, $A_2(\lambda b_2, v_1) = \{\beta\}$ for all $\lambda \in (\frac{1+\varepsilon}{12}, \frac{11-\varepsilon}{23}]$, and $A_2(\lambda b_2, v_1) = \emptyset$ for all $\lambda \in [0, \frac{1+\varepsilon}{12}]$. Thus, (6) yields that bidder 2 should give a positive payment of about $12.8 - 0.145\varepsilon + 0.052\varepsilon^2$ to the mechanism, while since the weight of edge (b_2, b'_2) is 0 and the weight of edge $(b'_2, \frac{10}{11}b'_2)$ is -1, we should pay bidder 2 at least 1 for declaration (b_2, v_1).

A Computational Criticism to Cycle-Monotonicity. We now show that if domains are represented succinctly, payment computation requires (and can reveal) crucial information about the declaration graph, and thus, it is **NP**-hard. Specifically, we show that, unless $\mathbf{P} = \mathbf{NP}$, we cannot efficiently compute minimum payments, i.e., payments defined as shortest paths on the declaration graph.

THEOREM 5. *The problem of computing the shortest-path payments for Algorithm 1 with strong verification is* **NP***-hard, even for $n = 2$ bidders and $m = 2$ goods, where bidders' domains are accessed by queries.*

PROOF. Suppose we are given an instance with two goods $\mathsf{U} = \{\alpha, \beta\}$ and two bidders $N = \{1, 2\}$ each with submodular valuation on the bundles of U. A valuation function v_i of bidder i is represented as above by a triple (x, y, z), where $v_i(\{\alpha\}) = x, v_i(\{\beta\}) = y, v_i(\{\alpha, \beta\}) = z$, and, because of monotonicity, we have that $x \leq z, y \leq z$, and, because of submodularity, we have that $y \geq z - x$.

We will define an instance of CA (and a particular domain) given an instance of the satisfiability problem which is specified by a CNF input Boolean formula ϕ with k Boolean variables. Let the domain of bidder 2 contain just one declaration $D_2 = \{(x, y, z)\}$ for some fixed positive numbers $x, y, z > 0$ such that $x < z, y < z$, and $y = z - x$. Let $S = \{s_j : j = 1, 2, \ldots, 2^k\}$ be the set of all possible $0 - 1$ truth assignments to the k Boolean variables of formula ϕ. The domain of bidder 1 is: $D_1 = \{(x + \varepsilon, y + \varepsilon, x + y + \varepsilon/2)\} \cup \{(x - \varepsilon/j, y + \varepsilon/2, x + y + \varepsilon/2 - \varepsilon/j) : s_j \text{ satisfies } \phi, j = 1, \ldots, 2^k\} \cup \{(x - \varepsilon/j, y + 2\varepsilon, x + y + 2\varepsilon - \varepsilon/j) : s_j \text{ does not satisfy } \phi, j = 1, \ldots, 2^k\}$, where $\varepsilon > 0$ is a small fixed constant, $\varepsilon \ll \min\{x, y\}$.

Since the declaration of bidder 2 is fixed to (x, y, z), the declaration graph for bidder 1 has D_1 as the set of its nodes, and before defining its arcs we will make some observations about the greedy algorithm, denoted as A, when α is considered first and β second. When we run A with bidder 1 declaring $(x + \varepsilon, y + \varepsilon, x + y + \varepsilon/2) \in D_1$, then the outcome for bidder 1 is $\{\alpha\}$ and $\{\beta\}$ for bidder 2. For any declaration of bidder 1 from $D_1 \setminus \{(x + \varepsilon, y + \varepsilon, x + y + \varepsilon/2)\}$ the A's outcome for bidder 1 is $\{\beta\}$ and $\{\alpha\}$ for bidder 2.

Given any node $b_1 \in D_1 \setminus \{(x + \varepsilon, y + \varepsilon, x + y + \varepsilon/2)\}$ and $b'_1 = (x + \varepsilon, y + \varepsilon, x + y + \varepsilon/2) \in D_1$, the declaration graph does not have the arc (b_1, b'_1). This follows from the fact that $b_1(\{\alpha\}) < x$ and $b'_1(\{\alpha\}) > x$, therefore if arc (b_1, b'_1) were present this would contradict the no-overbidding verification assumption. Similarly, there is no arc present from b'_1 to any node $b_1 \in \{(x - \varepsilon/j, y + 2\varepsilon, x + y + 2\varepsilon - \varepsilon/j) : s_j \text{ does not satisfy } \phi, j = 1, \ldots, 2^k\}$, as its presence would contradict the no-overbidding assumption for $\{\beta\}$: $b'_1(\{\beta\}) = y + \varepsilon < y + 2\varepsilon = b_1(\{\beta\})$.

Thus, node b'_1 is connected to the rest of the declaration graph by arc (b'_1, b_1), for some $b_1 \in \{(x - \varepsilon/j, y + \varepsilon/2, x + y + \varepsilon/2 - \varepsilon/j) : s_j \text{ satisfies } \phi, j = 1, \ldots, 2^k\}$. And, deciding if node b'_1 is connected to the rest of the declaration graph (and thus, whether Algorithm 1 requires a non-zero payment for b'_1) is equivalent to deciding if formula ϕ is satisfiable.

Therefore, the problem of computing the payment for node b'_1 is **NP**-hard provided that we can represent the declaration graph succinctly in time polynomial in k and the size of ϕ. Such a representation has been shown by small circuits by Galperin and Wigderson [15, Definition 2.2 and Lemma 2.2]. This representation essentially reduces to answering in polynomial time (in the size of ϕ) a question if given $b_1 \in D_1 \setminus \{(x+\varepsilon,\ y+\varepsilon,\ x+y+\varepsilon/2)\}$, does there exists arc (b'_1, b_1), which is just checking if the appropriate given 0/1 truth assignment s_j (defining node b_1) satisfies formula ϕ or not. Thus, our reduction represents the domain D_1 by presenting an encoding of formula ϕ to the mechanism and mechanism asks queries of type "does b_1 satisfy ϕ?". □

We complement this result by showing that for $m = 2$, it is indeed possible to compute efficiently different payments that are not defined as shortest paths on the declaration graph. Let α, β denote the two items and assume that Algorithm 1 considers α before β.

DEFINITION 3. *Let P_i^ω be the payment function defined as $P_i^\omega(b, \mathbf{b}_{-i}) = 0$ if $A_i(b, \mathbf{b}_{-i}) \in \{\{\alpha,\beta\},\{\beta\},\emptyset\}$; $P_i^\omega(b, \mathbf{b}_{-i}) = b_2(\beta)$ otherwise, $b_2(\beta)$ being the maximum of what the other bidders declare for $\{\beta\}$.*

THEOREM 6. *The payment P_i^ω leads to a truthful CA with strong verification when coupled with Algorithm 1 (even for infinite declaration domains).*

An important observation is that we use the outcome graph (i.e., same payment for all the nodes mapped by the algorithm to the same outcome) and therefore by Theorem 6, the outcome graph for $m = 2$ has no negative-weight cycles. There are many intuitive reasons for which the idea behind P_i^ω would not extend to three items α, β, γ considered in this order by the algorithm (e.g., marginals do not align neatly for all possible outcomes; hard to handle "jumps" from $\{\alpha\}$ to $\{\alpha,\beta,\gamma\}$). We give a formal argument for these intuitions. This approach of payment-per-outcome fails because the outcome graph might have negative weight cycles.

THEOREM 7. *There exists an instance of CAs with submodular bidder with $n = 2$ and $m = 3$, for which the outcome graph associated to Algorithm 1 has a negative weight cycle.*

PROOF. Let A denote Algorithm 1 with item order α, β, γ. Define the bid b_2 of bidder 2 to be $b_2(X) = |X|$ for each $X \subseteq \{\alpha, \beta, \gamma\}$. Consider the domain of bidder 1 to be $D_1 = \{a, b, c, d\}$ where for $\epsilon > 0$:

	a	b	c	d
$\{\alpha\}$	$1+\epsilon$	$1+\epsilon$	$1+\epsilon$	$1+\epsilon/3$
$\{\beta\}$	2	2	$1+\epsilon$	$1+\epsilon$
$\{\gamma\}$	2	2	$1+5/3\epsilon$	$1+5/3\epsilon$
$\{\alpha,\beta\}$	$2+2\epsilon$	2	$2+2/3\epsilon$	$2+2/3\epsilon$
$\{\alpha,\gamma\}$	$3+\epsilon$	$3+\epsilon$	$2+2\epsilon$	$2+2\epsilon$
$\{\beta,\gamma\}$	$3+\epsilon$	$3+\epsilon$	2	2
$\{\alpha,\beta,\gamma\}$	$3+\epsilon$	$3+\epsilon$	$2+2\epsilon$	$2+2\epsilon$

By inspection, the four bids are submodular and $A_1(a, b_2) = \{\alpha,\beta\}$, $A_1(b, b_2) = \{\alpha,\gamma\}$, $A_1(c, b_2) = \{\alpha,\gamma\}$ and $A_1(d, b_2) = \{\alpha,\beta\}$. It is also not hard to check that the edges (a, b) and (c, d) belong to the declaration graph. Their weight is $-1+\epsilon$ and $4/3\epsilon$, respectively. Therefore the outcome graph has the negative-weight cycle $\{\alpha,\beta\} \to \{\alpha,\gamma\} \to \{\alpha,\beta\}$. □

Comparison with the VCG mechanism. We now prove that there are settings of our model relevant to practical applications where we have a provable advantage over VCG.

THEOREM 8. *There is a setting of CAs with submodular bidders, for which the problem of computing payments for Algorithm 1 is solvable in polynomial time, but the problem of finding a social welfare maximizing allocation is* **NP**-*hard to approximate within a factor $2e/(2e-1)-\varepsilon$ for any $\varepsilon > 0$.*

PROOF. We will describe instances of CAs with submodular bidders for which Dobzinski and Vondrák [13] prove that the social welfare maximization problem is **NP**-hard to approximate within any constant factor better than $2e/(2e-1) \approx 1.225$. Fix any small $\varepsilon > 0$ and we are given a universe U of $|\mathsf{U}| = m$ goods and a set of n bidders. Dobzinski and Vondrák are the following instances of the Max n-Cover problem (see [13], page 9). Let $\mathcal{S} \subset 2^{\mathsf{U}}$ be a family of sets partitioned into subfamilies $\mathcal{S}_1, \ldots, \mathcal{S}_n$, such that: every set in $\mathcal{S}$ has the same size s; $|\mathcal{S}_1| = |\mathcal{S}_2| = \cdots = |\mathcal{S}_n| = g$; for every two sets $S, T \in \mathcal{S}$, $|S \cap T| \le \varepsilon \cdot s$. Note that s and g are absolute fixed constant integers.

The submodular valuation function v_i of any bidder $i \in \{1, \ldots, n\}$ is defined as function f in Definition 3.3 (page 5 in [13]), where we use the constant size family $\mathcal{S}_i \subset 2^{\mathsf{U}}$ in place of family $\mathcal{F}$ and $a = \frac{1}{2s}$, $b = \varepsilon \cdot s$. Observe that, given $\varepsilon > 0$ and the parameters m, n, s, g of this construction and the family $\mathcal{S}_i$, function v_i for bidder i is uniquely and succinctly defined. Suppose now that the declaration of any bidder $j \in \{1, \ldots, n\} \setminus \{i\}$ is fixed to his declared valuation v_j as defined above for his family $\mathcal{S}_j$. Then the set D_i of all possible declared valuations v_i of bidder i of the type defined above has size of at most the number of possible subfamilies $\mathcal{S}_i$. Subfamily $\mathcal{S}_i$ has g subsets of U each of size s, thus $|D_i| \le \left(\binom{m}{s}\right)^g$, which is polynomial in m because s and g are fixed constants. Thus, the declaration graph of Algorithm 1 has polynomial size and payments are polynomial time computable. □

6. CONCLUSIONS

We considered the question of how truthful greedy mechanisms are, by characterizing the kind of bidders' misbehavior that needs to be verified. In the context of CAs, we showed that *any* greedy fixed priority algorithm is truthful as long as bidders cannot overbid on the subset of goods they win (if any). We then proved that greedy adaptive priority algorithms require stronger assumptions, by proving that the 2-approximation algorithm for CAs with submodular bidders in [20] has to also verify overbidding on the subsets of the awarded set of goods.

The main question left open by our work concerns the computational complexity of computing the payments for the algorithm in [20]. Our results provide a first, meaningful case study for the problem of assessing the computational efficiency of the cycle-monotonicity technique. We conjecture that computing these payments is actually a hard problem. However, this appears hard to prove, given that the question is not about optimization but rather search (that is, the existence of a feasible solution is guaranteed and the question is about computing any feasible solution versus the shortest path solution); more specifically, tools adopted to prove the hardness of computing Nash equilibria seem to be required.

7. REFERENCES

[1] A. Archer, C. H. Papadimitriou, K. Talwar, and É. Tardos. An approximate truthful mechanism for combinatorial auctions with single parameter agents. In *Proc. of SODA*, pp. 205-214, 2003.

[2] M. Babaioff, R.D. Kleinberg, and A. Slivkins. Truthful mechanisms with implicit payment computation. In *Proc. of EC*, pp. 43-52, 2010.

[3] M. Babaioff, R.D. Kleinberg, and A. Slivkins. Multi-parameter mechanisms with implicit payment computation. In *Proc. of EC*, pp. 35-52, 2013.

[4] L. Blumrosen and N. Nisan. On the computational power of demand queries. *SIAM Journal on Computing*, 39(4):1372-1391, 2009.

[5] A. Borodin and B. Lucier. On the limitations of greedy mechanism design for truthful combinatorial auctions. In *Proc. of ICALP*, pp. 90-101, 2010.

[6] A. Borodin, M.N. Nielsen, and C. Rackoff. (Incremental) priority algorithms. *Algorithmica*, 37(4):295-326, 2003.

[7] G. Celik. Mechanism design with weaker incentive compatibility constraints. *Games and Economic Behavior*, 56(1):37-44, 2006.

[8] E.H. Clarke. Multipart Pricing of Public Goods. *Public Choice*, pp. 17-33, 1971.

[9] A. Daniely, M. Schapira, and S. Gal. Inapproximability of truthful mechanisms via generalizations of the VC dimension. In *Proc. of STOC*, 2015.

[10] S. Dobzinski. An impossibility result for truthful combinatorial auctions with submodular valuations. In *Proc. of STOC*, pp. 139-148, 2011.

[11] S. Dobzinski, N. Nisan, and M. Schapira. Approximation algorithms for combinatorial auctions with complement-free bidders. In *Proc. of STOC*, pp. 610-618, 2005.

[12] S. Dobzinski and J. Vondrák. The computational complexity of truthfulness in combinatorial auctions. In *Proc. of EC*, pp. 405-422, 2012.

[13] S. Dobzinski and J. Vondrák. Communication complexity of combinatorial auctions with submodular valuations. In *Proc. of SODA*, pp. 1205-1215, 2013.

[14] D. Fotakis, P. Krysta, and C. Ventre. Combinatorial auctions without money. In *Proc. of AAMAS*, pp. 1029-1036, 2014.

[15] H. Galperin and A. Wigderson. Succinct representations of graphs. *Information and Control*, 56(3):183-198, 1983.

[16] T. Groves. Incentive in Teams. *Econometrica*, 41:617-631, 1973.

[17] S. Khot, R.J. Lipton, E. Markakis, and A. Mehta. Inapproximability results for combinatorial auctions with submodular utility functions. In *Proc. of WINE*, pp. 92-101, 2005.

[18] P. Krysta and C. Ventre. Combinatorial auctions with verification are tractable. *Theoretical Computer Science*, 571:21-35, 2015.

[19] R. Lavi and C. Swamy. Truthful mechanism design for multidimensional scheduling via cycle monotonicity. *Games and Economic Behavior*, 67(1):99-124, 2009.

[20] B. Lehmann, D. J. Lehmann, and N. Nisan. Combinatorial auctions with decreasing marginal utilities. *Games and Economic Behavior*, 55(2):270-296, 2006.

[21] D. J. Lehmann, L. O'Callaghan, and Y. Shoham. Truth revelation in approximately efficient combinatorial auctions. *Journal of the ACM*, 49(5):577-602, 2002.

[22] V.S. Mirrokni, M. Schapira, and J. Vondrák. Tight information-theoretic lower bounds for welfare maximization in combinatorial auctions. In *Proc. of EC*, pp. 70-77, 2008.

[23] A. Mu'Alem and N. Nisan. Truthful approximation mechanisms for restricted combinatorial auctions. In *Proc. of AAAI*, pp. 379-384, 2002.

[24] N. Nisan and A. Ronen. Algorithmic Mechanism Design. *Games and Economic Behavior*, 35:166-196, 2001.

[25] N. Nisan, T. Roughgarden, E. Tardos, and V. Vazirani, editors. *Algorithmic Game Theory*. Cambridge University Press, 2007.

[26] P. Penna and C. Ventre. Optimal collusion-resistant mechanisms with verification. *Games and Economic Behavior*, 86:491-509, 2014.

[27] J. Rochet. A Condition for Rationalizability in a Quasi-Linear Context. *Journal of Mathematical Economics*, 16:191-200, 1987.

[28] C. Ventre. Truthful optimization using mechanisms with verification. *Theoretical Computer Science*, 518:64-79, 2014.

[29] W. Vickrey. Counterspeculation, Auctions and Competitive Sealed Tenders. *Journal of Finance*, pp. 8-37, 1961.

[30] R.V. Vohra. *Mechanism Design: A Linear Programming Approach*. Cambridge University Press, 2011.

[31] J. Vondrák. Optimal approximation for the submodular welfare problem in the value oracle model. In *Proc. of STOC*, pp. 67-74, 2008.

Computational Bundling for Auctions

Christian Kroer
Computer Science Department
Carnegie Mellon University
5000 Forbes Ave
Pittsburgh, PA, USA
ckroer@cs.cmu.edu

Tuomas Sandholm
Computer Science Department
Carnegie Mellon University
5000 Forbes Ave
Pittsburgh, PA, USA
sandholm@cs.cmu.edu

ABSTRACT

Revenue maximization in combinatorial auctions (and other multidimensional selling settings) is one of the most important and elusive problems in mechanism design. The optimal design is unknown, and is known to include features that are not acceptable in many applications, such as favoring some bidders over others and randomization. In this paper, we instead study a common revenue-enhancement approach—bundling—in the context of the most commonly studied combinatorial auction mechanism, the Vickrey-Clarke-Groves (VCG) mechanism. A second challenge in mechanism design for combinatorial auctions is that the prior distribution on each bidder's valuation can be doubly exponential. Such priors do not exist in most applications. Rather, in many applications (such as premium display advertising markets), there is essentially a point prior, which may not be accurate. We adopt the point prior model, and prove robustness to inaccuracy in the prior. Then, we present a branch-and-bound framework for finding the optimal bundling. We introduce several techniques for branching, upper bounding, lower bounding, and lazy bounding. Experiments on CATS distributions validate the approach and show that our techniques dramatically improve scalability over a leading general-purpose MIP solver.

Categories and Subject Descriptors

I.2.11 [**Distributed Artificial Intelligence**]: Multiagent systems; J.4.a [**Social and Behavioral Sciences**]: Economics

General Terms

Algorithms; Theory; Economics

Keywords

Bundling; search; integer programming; combinatorial auctions; VCG; revenue maximization

1. INTRODUCTION

Revenue maximization in combinatorial auctions (and other multidimensional selling settings) is one of the most important and most elusive problems in mechanism design. The optimal auction for a single item is known [32] and has been generalized to multiple units of one item [30], but the problem remains open even with just two items.[1] The fact that the general optimal combinatorial auction mechanism is unknown is not a coincidence: even a special case of the problem of designing the highest-revenue deterministic multi-item auction is NP-complete, even in the private values setting [15]. This suggests that, unlike for single-item settings, a concise characterization of optimal combinatorial auctions cannot exist. This is one of the key motivations for *automated mechanism design* where an algorithm is used to design the mechanism for the setting (prior probability distribution) at hand (e.g., [13, 14, 15, 37, 27, 28, 10]).

Even with automated design, and putting aside the computational complexity of the design problem, it is not clear that optimal combinatorial auctions are viable in practice, for the following reasons: (**a**) The revenue-optimal mechanism includes features that are not acceptable in many applications, such as favoring some bidders over others, and randomization. (**b**) The optimal mechanism is difficult to understand. This, itself, can be a deterrent to its adoption. (**c**) Even in the private values setting, the prior distribution on each bidder's valuation can have support the size of which is doubly exponential. Specifically, if there are m items and a bidder can have any of k values for each bundle, the support of the prior has k^{2^m-1} points because that is the size of the bidder's type space. Such prior distributions have not been (and cannot be) constructed in most applications. In this paper, we study a practical automated mechanism design setting where we avert these problems.

We avert the first two problems by only considering one common, practical way of increasing revenue, *bundling* items [33, 11, 24, 18, 6, 25, 9, 22, 45]. Our mechanisms will be fair in the sense that they are symmetric across bidders, and deterministic, unlike the optimal auction. Specifically, we will develop algorithms for optimal bundling in the context of the most commonly studied combinatorial auction mechanism, the *Vickrey-Clarke-Groves mechanism (VCG)* [43, 12, 19].[2] In the VCG—even with bundling—each bidder's dominant strategy is to bid truthfully.

We avert the third problem by not assuming that we have access to such a prior. In many (arguably most) applications there is essentially just a point prior, which may not be accurate. In other words, the seller has expectations about how much bidders would be willing to pay for various bundles, but the seller does not have a sophisticated probabilistic model about any bidder's valuations (which are not independent across bundles). This is the case, for example, in TV advertising sales and in premium, guaranteed display advertising sales. (In both of those markets, the sales occur manually, and the inventory is implicitly bundled in ad hoc ways today, with typically 2-4 targeting attributes.

[1]Relatively simple special cases have been solved, yielding interesting insights (e.g., [3, 5]).

[2]While the VCG itself has taken some time to get adopted in applications, it has been successfully adopted, for example, by Facebook for its advertising auctions.

Appears in: *Proceedings of the 14th International Conference on Autonomous Agents and Multiagent Systems (AAMAS 2015), Bordini, Elkind, Weiss, Yolum (eds.), May 4–8, 2015, Istanbul, Turkey.*

Another, very practically oriented, potential application of our work is to help an auction designer choose bundles through exploratory search. If no distribution is available, the auction designer could generate sets of reasonable bids in an iterative fashion, compute optimal bundlings, and choose a final bundling based on the intuitions gained from this.

Therefore, we adopt the point prior model. However, we also acknowledge the fact that in practice the point prior might not be accurate; we prove robustness of our approach to inaccuracy in the prior. One might also ask why we do not simply make take-it-or-leave-it offers to take the entire surplus for the seller given that we have a point prior. The reason we do not use that mechanism is that it is highly nonrobust to error in the prior: even slight overpricing on a bundle will cause the revenue from that bundle to drop to zero.

We develop a custom branch-and-bound framework for finding the optimal bundling. We show that algorithms in that framework scale significantly better than a leading general-purpose integer program solver, CPLEX. We design and compare several techniques for upper bounding, lower bounding, branching, and lazy child node evaluation. Experiments on the leading combinatorial auction test suite, CATS [26], validate the approach.

Our approach to bundling is computational. The goal is not to build insight from manual analysis that can then loosely be applied to practice—although the computational approach can help develop insight as well and fuel future theory. Rather, the goal is to develop a computational methodology that can be used in practice. It is therefore key that we make the computational techniques scalable.

1.1 Related work

Most prior work on bundling has been in the context of posted prices, for example, catalog pricing. Bundle pricing in economics has often focused on analyzing two-item settings [41, 1, 16, 20, 31, 40]. (One exception is that Armstrong [2] examines m-item settings, but places severe restrictions on buyers' utility functions. Another exception is that Manelli et al. [29] provide results for when bundled catalog sales are optimal, mainly in the two- and three-item settings.) There has been some computational work on bundle pricing, for example, mixed integer programming for optimizing bundle prices [21] and data-driven pricing of car configurations [35].

Benisch et al. [7] present a framework for automatically suggesting high-profit bundle discounts based on historical purchase data. There has also been work on pricing bundles of information goods, where it is usually assumed that valuations are based only on the size of the bundle and there are no marginal costs [25, 9, 6]. The operations research literature has also addressed the information goods setting. For example, Hitt et al. [22] and Wu et al. [45] consider a bundle pricing mechanism for information goods that allows customers to choose up to m' items from a larger pool of m items.

Walsh et al. [44] study inventory bundling in premium display advertisement campaign selling, with the goal of making the winner determination problem smaller and easier. Others have recently studied that problem as well [42, 23]. That objective is different than revenue maximization.

There has been some work on bundling in auctions. Several papers considered the problem of bundling all items versus separate sales [33, 11]. Armstrong [3] shows that in two-item auctions with two valuations per bidder, the revenue-maximizing auction is efficient. Avery et al. [5] show that this does not hold in general two-item settings, and that randomization can increase revenue.

Prior work on *automated mechanism design* has produced deterministic and randomized mechanisms for revenue-maximizing combinatorial auctions [14, 15, 27, 28]. Since our paper focuses on the VCG mechanism, our bundling is deterministic. There has been work on generalizing the VCG to higher-revenue dominant-strategy auction mechanisms. Likhodedov et al. [27, 28] study a generalization of VCG called *virtual valuations combinatorial auctions (VVCAs)* and a generalization of them, *affine maximizer combinatorial auctions*, which are auctions where the VCG is run on affine transformations of the bids. Those mechanism design algorithms scaled to a handful of items. For the restricted setting of additive valuations, Jehiel et al. [24] analyze a subclass of VVCAs called λ-*auctions*, which are nevertheless rich enough to allow the bundling to depend on the bids. Our approach of bundling first and then simply running VCG is easier for buyers and sellers to understand. Also, none of the prior papers present bundling algorithms. Core-selecting combinatorial auctions are another form of combinatorial auctions that has recently become popular in spectrum auctions [17]. They can generate higher revenue than the VCG. However, equilibria are not known (except in the known-valuations setting), so game-theoretic simulation of revenue properties is not possible. Core-selecting combinatorial auctions can also suffer from revenue deficiencies that bundling can alleviate.

To our knowledge, there has been no prior work on our setting.

2. PROBLEM FORMULATION

We assume that we have a set of bidders $N = \{1, \ldots, n\}$, a set of items $M = \{1, \ldots, m\}$, and a set of bids B. (The bids represent the, possibly inaccurate, point prior, and are given before actual bids are received.) B_i is the set of all bids for bidder i, and B_{-i} the set of all bids that do not belong to i. A bid is a tuple $\langle S_j, v_j \rangle$, where $S_j \subseteq M$ is the set of items that the bid wants and $v_j \geq 0$ is a valuation. For ease of exposition, we sometimes use $[k]$ to refer to the set $\{1, \ldots, k\}$ for $k \in \mathbb{N}$.

We denote an allocation of items to bidders by α, and α_i is the set of items allocated to bidder i in the allocation. We overload $v_i(\alpha)$ to be bidder i's valuation for α_i.

We work in the standard combinatorial auction setting with the XOR bidding language [36] so each bidder can have at most one of her bids win. Every item can be assigned to at most one bidder. There are *no externalities*: the valuation for each bidder i depends only on the items that i receives. There is *free disposal*: the value of a subset of items $M' \subseteq M$ for bidder i is less than (or equal to) the value of M. A bundle $b \subseteq M$ is a set of items from M. A *bundling* ϕ is a set of bundles that partitions M. We denote the set of all possible bundlings by Φ.

We say that two bids i, j *intersect* if their item sets overlap: $S_i \cap S_j \neq \emptyset$. Bundling can introduce additional overlap between bids, and for this reason we need a more general notion of overlap. Two bids i, j *bundling-intersect* in a given bundling ϕ if they intersect or there exists at least one item in each of the two bids so that those two items have been included in the same bundle. Formally, two bids i, j bundling-intersect in bundling ϕ if they intersect or $\exists a_i \in S_i, a_j \in S_j, b \in \phi$ such that $a_i \in b, a_j \in b$. We denote the set of bundling-intersecting items of the two sets by $S_i \sqcap S_j$.

We will be running the VCG to auction the bundles simultaneously. In the vanilla VCG without bundling, the allocation of items to bidders is computed so that it maximizes social welfare (henceforth referred to as welfare): $\alpha^* = \arg\max_\alpha \sum_{i=1}^n v_i(\alpha)$. The payment from each bidder i is $p_i = W^{*,-i}_{M,B} - W^{*,-i}_{M_{-i},B}$, where $W^{*,-i}_{M,B}$ is the optimal welfare where i receives no items, and we let $W^{*,-i}_{M_{-i},B} = \sum_{j \neq i} v_j(\alpha^*)$ be the welfare of the other agents in α^*. We denote by $W_B(\alpha)$ the welfare of an allocation α for bids B.

In our setting, we have to take the bundling into account in the VCG. For a given bundling $\phi \in \Phi$, the VCG allocation α^* is computed as before, but with the added constraint that no two items that are in the same bundle can be allocated to different bidders (i.e., for any two winning bids i and j, $S_i \sqcap S_j = \emptyset$). We denote the welfare of such an allocation by $W^*_{\phi,B} = \max_{\alpha \in A_\phi} \sum_{i \in N} v_i(\alpha)$, and the welfare of the welfare-maximizing allocation over the bundling, where bidder i is excluded, as $W^{*,-i}_{\phi,B} = \max_{\alpha \in A_\phi} \sum_{j \neq i} v_j(\alpha)$. Similarly, running VCG on bundling ϕ yields payments

$$p_i = W^{*,-i}_{\phi,B} - W^{*,-i}_{\phi_{-i},B}$$

from each bidder i. Here, ϕ_{-i} is the set of bundles from ϕ that are not allocated to bidder i. The goal in optimal bundling is to find a bundling ϕ^* such that the revenue $r_{\phi^*} = \sum_{i=1}^n p_i$ is maximized.

3. BASIC PROPERTIES OF THE SETTING

In this section we study some important basic properties of the proposed approach.

Number of bundlings The number of bundlings grows extremely rapidly with the number of items. The number of ways to bundle (exhaustively partition) m items is called the Bell number, $\mathcal{B}_m$. The Bell numbers can be defined recursively: $\mathcal{B}_m = \sum_{k=0}^{m-1} \binom{m-1}{k} \mathcal{B}_k$. Sandholm et al. [38] proved that $\mathcal{B}_m \in \omega(m^{\frac{m}{2}})$. Berend et al. [8] proved that $\mathcal{B}_m < (\frac{0.792m}{\ln(m+1)})^m$.

NP-hardness We first prove hardness of our problem (revenue-maximizing bundling in the VCG setting with a point prior).

THEOREM 1. *Finding the optimal bundling is NP-hard.*

PROOF. The proof is by reduction from bin packing. The bin packing problem is the following: Given a set of n objects of sizes $x_1, ..., x_n$, and positive integers k and V, is it possible to fit the n objects into k bins of size V?

For each bin $i = 1, ..., k$, we generate $n + 1$ items: a_i^{bin} and $G_i = \{g_1^i, ..., g_n^i\}$, and two bidders with bids $b_i^{bin}, b_{i'}^{bin}$ respectively, where $S_i^{bin} = \{a_i^{bin}\} \cup G_i, S_{i'}^{bin} = \{a_i^{bin}\}$, and valuations $v_i^{bin} = V + M, v_{i'}^{bin} = M$, for some $M > V, M > \sum_{j=1}^n x_j$. The set $G_i = \{g_1^i, ..., g_n^i\}$ is there to allow up to n other bids to intersect with b_i^{bin}, without having the bids themself intersecting. For each of the objects $j = 1, ..., n$, we generate an item a_j^{obj} and a bidder with bid b_j^{obj} with $S_j^{obj} = \{a_j^{obj}\}$, and valuation $v_j^{obj} = x_j$. Bundling an object item a_j^{obj} with some bin item g_i^l represents putting object j in bin i. The only pairs of bids that overlap before bundling are $b_i^{bin}, b_{i'}^{bin}$.

We claim that there is a solution to the bin packing problem iff there is some bundling with revenue $r = kM + \sum_{j=1}^n x_j$ for the above bundling problem. Now, assume that we have some solution with revenue $r \geq kM + \sum_{j=1}^n x_j$. Clearly, it cannot be the case that any two items such that $S_i^{bin} \cap S_j^{bin} \neq \emptyset$ for some bids b_i^{bin}, b_j^{bin} are bundled together, as this would cause revenue $r \leq (k-1)M + \sum_{j=1}^n x_j < kM$, since only $k-1$ bids with valuation above or equal to M can now win, and the remaining bids can have aggregate valuation at most $\sum_{j=1}^n x_j < M$. Hence, we are guaranteed kM revenue from the bids $\{b_i^{bin}, b_{i'}^{bin} : i = 1, ..., k\}$, and we know that they will not be bundled together. Now, each of the bids b_j^{obj} must be contributing x_j to revenue (either by paying that amount or causing one other bidder to pay that much more), since they are the only bids left that can be made bundling-intersecting with any other bid through bundling, and they have no competition if unbundled. We also know that any two bids b_i^{obj}, b_j^{obj} cannot be made bundling-intersecting. If they were, the revenue obtained from the two would be at most $\max(v_i^{obj}, v_j^{obj})$ (since they can be made bundling-intersecting with at most one winning bid, and alternatively if one of the two bids wins, its payment cannot exceed its valuation). It follows that the bids b_j^{obj} must bundling-intersect with the bids b_i^{bin}, which are already contributing kM revenue. Let B_i^{obj} be the set of bids b_j^{obj} that bundling-intersect with b_i^{bin}. We must have $M + \sum_{j \in B_i^{obj}} x_j \leq M + V$, since otherwise $r < kM + \sum_{j=1}^n x_j$, as some x_j is then not contributing its full valuation. Now, we can take the solution and turn it into a solution to the bin packing problem. Since we know that all b_j^{obj} bundling-intersect with one b_i^{bin} each, we take each such j and assign that object to bin i. Since $\sum_{j \in B_i^{obj}} x_j \leq V$ for all i, we know that this is a valid packing.

Conversely, if there is a solution to the bin packing problem, there is a bundling such that all bids b_j^{obj} bundling-intersect with one b_i^{bin} each, and $M + \sum_{j \in B_i^{obj}} v_j^{obj} = M + \sum_{j \in B_i^{obj}} x_j \leq V + M$ for all i. Hence we can get revenue at least $kM + \sum_{j=1}^n x_j$. □

In the instances generated by the reduction in the proof of Theorem 1, the winner determination problem is easy. This shows that the bundling problem is hard in itself. The NP-completeness of winner determination does, however, imply that the general optimal bundling problem is not contained in NP. Given a bundling with proposed revenue k, verification that it achieves revenue k requires computing the (exact, due to revenue nonmonotonicity) social-welfare maximizing outcomes, in order to compute payments.

Ghosh et al. [18] similarly show NP-hardness for the problem of computing the optimal bundling in their model, which assumes additive valuations. Their NP-hardness result relies on this, as their reduction uses the fact that bundle valuations can be expressed compactly in this setting. For the XOR language, representing the same valuations would take an exponential number of constraints, and thus hardness of our setting does not follow from theirs.

Revenue is nonmonotonic in bidders It is known that the VCG is not revenue monotonic in bidders [4], that is, adding bidders can decrease revenue. Rastegari et al. [34] characterize a broader class of mechanisms for which revenue monotonicity cannot be achieved. Our setting falls outside of this class of mechanism. Nevertheless, we can show revenue nonmonotonicity in our setting. Consider the valuations in Figure 1 Left. The optimal bundling is to sell the items separately, in which case bidders 3 and 4 receive items Y and X respectively, with payments 3 and 5, yielding total revenue of 8. If we remove bidder 4, the optimal bundling is still to sell the items separately, where bidder 1 wins both items, with a payment of 9, which is also the revenue. Thus removing bidder 4 can increase revenue.

	X	Y	XY
Bidder 1	0	0	10
Bidder 2	4	0	4
Bidder 3	0	5	5
Bidder 4	7	0	7

	X	Y	XY
Bidder 1	10	0	10
Bidder 2	5	0	5
Bidder 3	0	2	2
Bidder 4	0	1	1
Bidder 5	0	20	20

Figure 1: Left: Bidder valuations for a game with 4 bidders and 2 items. Right: Bidder valuations for a game with 5 bidders and 2 items. In both tables, the XY column denotes bidder valuations for the bundle.

Coarseness of the optimal bundling is nonmonotonic in bidders The optimal bundling can become coarser with the addition of a bidder. An example is given in Figure 1 Right. The optimal bundling without Bidder 5 is to sell X and Y separately, whereas with 5 it is optimal to bundle.

Low worst-case revenue It is well known that the VCG can be arbitrarily far from optimal in terms of revenue. Consider two bidders, and items X and Y, where bidder 1 bids v_a for X and bidder 2 bids v_b for Y, and there are no other bids. In this case the VCG revenue is 0. For settings such as this, optimal bundling can have arbitrarily high revenue lift over VCG since we can bundle X and Y, and earn $\min(v_a, v_b)$.

Even with optimal bundling in the VCG, we can have arbitrarily high loss compared to what is possible. This is because the seller would give away $|v_1 - v_2|$ of the surplus (and this part can be arbitrarily large) while with reserve prices of v_1, v_2 on the items, respectively, would allow the seller to capture the entire surplus.

Robustness of the proposed approach Another practical revenue-enhancement technique is reserve pricing. Since a point prior is typically imprecise in practice, using reserve pricing can lead to high revenue loss. Consider again the example in th previous paragraph, but where the point prior is that each bidder i has valuation $v_i = v$ and the bidder's true distribution p is $p(v_i = v) = \epsilon, p(v_i = v - \delta) = 1 - \epsilon$. In this case, if the reserve price is set between $v - \delta$ and v, the expected loss in revenue is $2(1-\epsilon)v$. In contrast to this, optimal bundling in the VCG would only have an expected loss of $2\epsilon v + (1-2\epsilon)(v-\delta) < v$. As shown in the example above, optimal bundling is more robust to inaccuracy in the point-prior than reserve-pricing. This is important, as the availability of precise point-priors is unlikely in real-world applications. In this section we make this notion of robustness more precise, as we show the following result. In contrast, bundling for the VCG is robust to error in the (point) prior:

THEOREM 2. *The revenue from the VCG with optimal bundling (which may change based on bidder valuations) is Lipschitz continuous in the valuations of the bidders with Lipschitz constant $n-1$. This bound is tight.*

To prove this, we first prove the following lemma.

LEMMA 3. *The revenue from the VCG with any fixed bundling is Lipschitz continuous in the valuations of the bidders with Lipschitz constant $n-1$.*

PROOF. The revenue obtained from VCG on a bundling ϕ can be written as

$$r_\phi = -(n-1) \cdot W^*_{\phi,B} + \sum_{i=1}^{n} W^{*,-i}_{\phi,B} \quad (1)$$

where $W^*_{\phi,B}$ is the welfare of the welfare-maximizing allocation for the bids B, and $W^{*,-i}_{\phi,B}$ denotes the same when bidder i's bids are excluded. Thus, it suffices to show that all the terms in Equation 1 are Lipschitz continuous in bidder valuations.

Assume that some bidder i changes his valuation for some bid j, and let B' be the new set of bids, where v'_j is the new valuation for bid j. We now show that the change in welfare $\Delta W = |W^*_{\phi,B} - W^*_{\phi,B'}|$ is bounded by $\Delta v_j = |v_j - v'_i|$. For any allocation α such that j is winning, we get that the change in welfare is Δv_j, whereas for any allocation α' such that j is not winning, the welfare remains the same. Hence, the previously winning allocation α can increase or decrease by at most Δv_j. Since $W_B(\alpha) \geq W_B(\alpha')$ for all α', the new winning allocation α^* satisfies $W_{B'}(\alpha^*) \leq W_B(\alpha) + \Delta v_j$. For the lower bound, we have $W_{B'}(\alpha) \geq W_B(\alpha) - \Delta v_j$, and hence α^* must satisfy $W_{B'}(\alpha^*) \geq W_B(\alpha) - \Delta v_j$.

Since all terms are welfare maximizations over different sets of bidders, this proves that r_ϕ is Lipshitz continuous in bidder valuations, with a Lipschitz constant of $n-1$ (because the $n-1$ term and n terms in the summation change in opposite directions, and the summation over n terms only has $n-1$ terms that can change, as $W^{*,-i}_{\phi,B}$ does not depend on v_j). □

With this lemma, we are now ready to prove Theorem 2.

PROOF. There are two possible cases. In the first case, the optimal bundling does not change, and in the second case it changes. The proof of the first case is immediate from Lemma 3. For the second case, let ϕ_1 and ϕ_2 be the old and new optimal bundlings, respectively. By Lemma 3 we can bound the revenue of a bundling under the new valuation using the old valuation:

$$r_B(\phi) - (n-1) \cdot \Delta v_i \leq r_{B'}(\phi) \leq r_B(\phi) + (n-1) \cdot \Delta v_i$$

By optimality,

$$r_{B'}(\phi_2) \geq r_{B'}(\phi_1) \geq r_B(\phi_1) - (n-1) \cdot \Delta v_i$$

From the fact that ϕ_1 is optimal for the original bids (B) we know that $r_B(\phi_2) \leq r_B(\phi_1)$ and hence

$$r_B(\phi_2) + (n-1) \cdot \Delta v_i \leq r_B(\phi_1) + (n-1) \cdot \Delta v_i$$

By Lemma 3, the left hand side of this inequality is an upper bound for $r_{B'}(\phi_2)$. Thus we get

$$r_B(\phi_1) - (n-1) \cdot \Delta v_i \leq r_{B'}(\phi_2) \leq r_B(\phi_1) + (n-1) \cdot \Delta B_i$$

So, the new optimal revenue is bounded both above and below as shown above, and is (by the formulas above) Lipschitz continuous with Lipschitz constant $n-1$.

Finally, we show that the bound is tight. Consider the case with 2 items X,Y and 3 bidders $\{b_1, b_2, b_3\}$, where b_1 has valuation 1 for X, b_2 has valuation 1 for Y and b_3 has valuation $\frac{1}{2}$ for X and for Y. The optimal bundling yields revenue 1, but if b_3 increases his valuation for both items to 1, the revenue increases to 2, and the increase in revenue is $1 = \frac{1}{2} \cdot (n-1)$. □

This shows that our approach is robust to inaccuracy in the prior in the following sense: If the point-prior turns out to be inaccurate, the change in revenue is at worst linear in the sum of inaccuracies in the prior. It is further worth pointing out that for m items, at most $3 \cdot m^2$ bids can affect the payments. Thus, the number of bids potentially being exponential in the number of items does not cause huge revenue shifts, even if there is inaccuracy for all bids.

4. MIXED INTEGER PROGRAM (MIP)

One approach to finding the revenue-maximizing bundling is to formulate the problem as a mixed integer program (MIP), and then use a general-purpose MIP solver—such as CPLEX—to solve the formulation. In this section we develop such a formulation.

Figure 2 shows the formulation. The basic idea behind this MIP is that we have m potential bundles, and the boolean variables $\delta_{a,b}$ denote whether item a is assigned to bundle b. Based on these assignments, the VCG payments are computed. To break symmetries, we only allow each item $a = 1, ..., m$ to be assigned to bundles $\{1, ..., a\}$. Furthermore, items with index $a > b$ can only be assigned to the bundle with index b if the item with index b is also assigned to the bundle. Each bid j has boolean variables I_j and I^{-i}_j that denote whether the bid wins in the optimal allocation and optimal allocation excluding bidder i, respectively. Each bidder has boolean variables $\Pi_j(b)$ and $\Pi^{-i}_j(b)$ that denote whether the bidder is allocated bundle b in the respective allocations, and boolean variables $\pi_j(a,b)$ and $\pi^{-i}_j(a,b)$ that denote whether the bidder is allocated item a through bundle b in the respective allocations. Finally, each real-valued variable p_i denotes the payment that bidder i must make. The objective function, (2), is the sum over the payment variables of the bidders. Constraint 3 sets the payment for bidder i equal to the externality she imposes on the other bidders, i.e., her VCG payment. Constraints 4-5 ensure that a bid j can only be winning if that bidder is assigned all the items in S_j for each allocation. Constraints 6-7 ensure that each bundle is assigned to only one bidder in each allocation. Constraints 8-11 ensure that a bidder can only receive item a through bundle b in each allocation if the bidder wins the bundle, and $\delta_{a,b} = 1$, i.e., the item is in the bundle. Constraints 12-13 ensure that each bidder wins only one item in each allocation. Constraints 14-15 ensure that each item is assigned to only one bundle and they break symmetries. Finally, Constraint 16 ensures that the welfare-maximizing allocation is chosen for each bundling ϕ by ensuring that if all the $\delta_{a,b}$ that are necessary to achieve ϕ are active, then the winning bids are active.

$$\max \sum_{i=1}^{n} p_i \tag{2}$$

$$p_i \leq \sum_{j \in B_{-i}} v_j \cdot I_j^{-i} - \sum_{j \in B_{-i}} v_j \cdot I_j \quad \forall i \in N \tag{3}$$

$$I_j \leq \sum_{b=1}^{m} \pi_i(a,b) \quad \forall i \in N, j \in B_i, a \in S_j \tag{4}$$

$$I_j^{-i} \leq \sum_{b=1}^{m} \pi_k^{-i}(a,b) \quad \forall i,k \in N, j \in B_k, a \in S_j \tag{5}$$

$$\sum_{i=1}^{n} \Pi_i(b) \leq 1 \quad \forall b \in [m] \tag{6}$$

$$\sum_{k=1}^{n} \Pi_k^{-i}(b) \leq 1 \quad \forall i \in N, b \in [m] \tag{7}$$

$$\pi_i(a,b) \leq \Pi_i(b) \quad \forall i \in N, a \in [m], b \in [m] \tag{8}$$

$$\pi_k^{-i}(a,b) \leq \Pi_k^{-i}(b) \quad \forall i,k \in N, a \in [m], b \in [m] \tag{9}$$

$$\pi_i(a,b) \leq \delta_{a,b} \quad \forall i \in N, a \in [m], b \in [m] \tag{10}$$

$$\pi_k^{-i}(a,b) \leq \delta_{a,b} \quad \forall i,k \in N, a \in [m], b \in [m] \tag{11}$$

$$\sum_{j \in B_i} I_j \leq 1 \quad \forall i \in N \tag{12}$$

$$\sum_{j \in B_k} I_j^{-i} \leq 1 \quad \forall i,k \in N \tag{13}$$

$$\sum_{b=1}^{a} \delta_{a,b} = 1 \quad \forall a = 1,...,m \tag{14}$$

$$\delta_{a,b} \leq \delta_{b,b} \quad \forall b = 1,...,m, a = b,...,m \tag{15}$$

$$\sum_{(a,b) \in \alpha_\phi^*} \delta_{a,b} - I_j \leq |\alpha_\phi^*| - 1 \quad \forall \phi \in \Phi, j \in B_{win(M')} \tag{16}$$

$$I_j, I_j^{-i}, \pi_j(a,b), \pi_j^{-i}(a,b) \in \{0,1\} \tag{17}$$

$$\Pi_j(a,b), \Pi_j^{-i}(a,b), \delta_{a,b} \in \{0,1\}, p_i \geq 0 \tag{18}$$

Figure 2: Mixed integer program for finding the optimal bundling.

The MIP model suffers from several limitations. First, the MIP has $\Omega(n|B|m^2)$ boolean variables, which rapidly becomes unmanageable. Second, and more importantly, Constraint 16 is required for every possible bundling, of which there are an extremely large number, as mentioned in Section 3; additionally, but less significantly, to generate each of these constraints, the welfare-maximizing allocation must be found, which is NP-hard in itself. This could potentially be alleviated by using constraint generation techniques but even this is unlikely to yield acceptable scalability, as each added constraint only cuts off solutions at that specific bundling, and nowhere else. In addition, this would require resolving the already large MIP every time a constraint is added.

5. CUSTOM BRANCH-AND-BOUND

We will now move on to discussing our custom branch-and-bound approaches. Later we show that these scale significantly better than general purpose MIP solving.

5.1 Branching scheme

To find the optimal bundling we introduce a custom branch-and-bound algorithm, FIND-BUNDLING. It is a tree search algorithm that branches on items. At each node in the search tree, the algorithm branches on an item, with each branch adding the item to a different bundle. One of the branches corresponds to adding it to the empty bundle. The algorithm explores nodes in best-first order. The revenue obtained from the best solution found so far is a global variable f^*; initially $f^* = 0$. The pseudocode is given in Algorithm 1.

ALGORITHM 1: FIND-BUNDLING

```
   Input: Set of items M, Set of bids B
   Output: Optimal revenue LB, Optimal bundling
1  LB ← 0
2  insert ({{BRANCHINGITEM(M, B)}}, ∞) in OPEN
   // Open is a priority queue of search tree fringe nodes,
   // sorted in descending order of the second argument
3  while OPEN not empty do
4      (CURRENT, VAL) ← next in OPEN
5      if UB(CURRENT,M, B)>LB then
6          i ← BRANCHINGITEM(CURRENT,M, B)
7          for b in CURRENT do
8              CHILD ← CURRENT with i added to b
9              f* = MAX(LB(CHILD,M, B),f*)
10             insert (CHILD, UB(CHILD,M, B)) in OPEN
11         CHILD ← CURRENT with {i} appended to the list of
           bundles
12         insert (CHILD, UB(CHILD,M, B)) in OPEN
```

FIND-BUNDLING starts out with a bundling consisting of a single item, chosen by the function BRANCHINGITEM(M,B) (Step 2). At each node, the next item i to branch on is chosen (Step 6), and in Step 7-10 FIND-BUNDLING creates a branch for each of the existing bundles, with i added to that bundle. For the last branch in Step 11-12, a new bundle is added with i as the lone item in that bundle. The branching factor at a given node is therefore the number of bundles already created plus one. For each node, the upper bound is used for deciding where in the ordered OPEN list the node is inserted.

5.2 Lower bounding

In Step 9 FIND-BUNDLING computes a lower bound at the node. If a high lower bound is found, we can update f^*, and thereby achieve better pruning.

We use the following technique for lower bounding. For any node v in the search tree, we simulate a VCG auction on the bundles decided on the search path from the root to v along with all the yet-undecided (i.e., yet unbundled) items. Our lower bound is then the sum of the VCG payments.

PROPOSITION 4. *The sum of the VCG payments from selling unbranched items separately is a valid lower bound.*

PROOF. One option for FIND-BUNDLING is to take the branch where every item is added in its own separate bundle for all yet-undecided items. This path yields exactly the auction that is used in the lower bound definition. □

In the rest of the paper, whenever we refer to the revenue of a node, we mean the value defined in this section.

To compute the lower bound, we make $n + 1$ calls (one overall and one with each bidder removed in turn) to a subroutine that does (optimal) combinatorial auction winner determination. We call that routine DETERMINE-WINNERS. We use the standard MIP formulation [36]. For the branch where the item is added alone in a bundle, we can reuse the bound from the parent node, as this is exactly the same MIP.

Typically in tree search/integer programming, if one does not use a lower-bounding technique for the yet-undecided variables, one simply (implicitly) uses a lower bound equal to the value from the variables that have been decided on the path from the root to the current node. For example, in winner determination for combinatorial auctions, one uses the sum of the values of the bids that have been accepted on that path (e.g., [36, 39]). Interestingly, in the bundling setting one needs to be more careful. For example, using just the bids that are only interested in items that have already been bundled on the path would not give a valid lower bound. The reason is that this could discard a bidder that causes revenue non-monotonicity (as shown in Figure 1.)

5.3 Upper bounding

In Steps 5 and 10, FIND-BUNDLING calls a function to upper bound the revenue obtainable in the subtree rooted at the node. In this paper we propose, and investigate the performance of, several such techniques. These techniques are discussed in each of the following subsubsections, respectively. If the technique indeed gives an upper bound (as opposed to sometimes giving a value that is below the actual revenue obtainable in the subtree rooted at the node), that is, the upper-bounding heuristic is *admissible*, FIND-BUNDLING will always give the optimal solution. We will also study their *monotonicity*, that is, whether the upper bound is non-increasing down each search path.[3]

WELFARE The first, and simplest, upper-bounding technique is to use the highest achievable welfare, constrained to honoring the bundling from the path so far. Specifically, the technique generates a set of "items" M' consisting of the *bundles* created so far in the search, and the remaining items unbundled, and then calls DETERMINE-WINNERS on the "item" set. We call this heuristic WELFARE.

PROPOSITION 5. WELFARE *is admissible and monotonic.*

PROOF. We prove monotonicity first. In the computation of WELFARE, all yet-undecided items at the search node are unbundled. So, WELFARE corresponds to the welfare of the finest bundling achievable in that subtree. Naturally, the optimal welfare is nondecreasing as we make strictly finer bundlings. It follows that WELFARE is monotonic.

We prove admissibility next. The welfare at a node upper bounds the revenue at the node. For any descendant d of the current node, we have that WELFARE at d upper bounds the revenue at d. From monotonicity we have that WELFARE at the current node is no less than WELFARE at d. Thus WELFARE at the current node is an upper bound. □

VCG$^+$ Our second upper-bounding technique is like computing VCG payments for the bundling at the node but with the negative term chosen so as to maximize payments (under the condition that no bidder pays more than her valuation). We call this VCG$^+$.

Let us now formalize this idea. The sum of payments like the VCG payments for the bundling at the node, but with the negative term chosen so as to maximize the payments, is

$$\max_{\alpha \in A_\phi} \sum_{i \in N} \sum_{j \neq i} [v_j(\alpha^*_{-i}) - v_j(\alpha)]$$

Here, $\alpha^*_{-i} \in A_\phi$ is the optimal allocation without bidder i, for the bundling, ϕ, at the node. A_ϕ is the set of allocations consistent with bundling ϕ. Also, $\alpha \in A_\phi$ is any allocation that satisfies the bundling at the node. We further tighten this upper bound by making sure that no bidder is charged more than her valuation. This gives us the formula for our upper-bounding technique VCG$^+$:

$$\max_{\alpha \in A_\phi} \sum_{i \in N} \min \left\{ \sum_{j \neq i} [v_j(\alpha^*_{-i}) - v_j(\alpha)],\ v_i(\alpha) \right\} \quad (19)$$

In the special case where α is the welfare-maximizing allocation at the current node, this equals the revenue of running VCG at the node.

$$\max \sum_{i=1}^{n} p_i \quad (20)$$

$$p_i \leq \sum_{j \in B_i} v_j \cdot I_j \qquad \forall i \in N \quad (21)$$

$$p_i \leq \sum_{j \in B_{-i}} v_j \cdot I_j^{-i} - \sum_{j \in B_{-i}} v_j \cdot I_j \quad \forall i \in N \quad (22)$$

$$\sum_{j \in B_{\sqcap b}} I_j \leq 1 \qquad \forall b \in \phi_p \quad (23)$$

$$\sum_{j \in B_{\sqcap b}} I_j^{-i} \leq 1 \qquad \forall i \in N, b \in \phi_p \quad (24)$$

$$\sum_{j \in B_i} I_j \leq 1 \qquad \forall i \in N \quad (25)$$

$$\sum_{j \in B_k} I_j^{-i} \leq 1 \qquad \forall i, k \in N \quad (26)$$

Figure 3: Mixed integer program for VCG$^+$. Here, $B_{\sqcap b} = \{j \in B | S_j \sqcap b \neq \emptyset\}$ is the set of all bids that are interested in some bundle b.

The MIP in Figure 3 implements this idea. Constraints 21 and 22 ensure that each bidder pays her VCG$^+$payment. Constraints 23 and 24 ensure that only one bidder can win each bundle in ϕ_p, the bundling at the node. Constraints 25 and 26 ensure that each bidder wins only one of his bids.

We now prove that VCG$^+$ gives an upper bound to the revenue found at any node in the subtree rooted at the current node.

PROPOSITION 6. VCG$^+$ *is admissible and monotonic.*

PROOF. Consider an arbitrary current node p. We prove admissibility first. VCG$^+$ selects the best set of winning bids from all legal allocations of winning bids for the bundling ϕ_p. For any descendant d, we get a bundling ϕ_d such that if two items $a, b \in M$ are bundled together in ϕ_p then they are also bundled together in ϕ_d. This means that any valid set of winning bids at d is also a valid set of winning bids at p. In particular, the welfare-maximizing allocation at d is a valid set of winning bids at p; call this allocation α_d. Since α_d is a valid allocation for VCG$^+$at p, we just need to show that the payment that VCG$^+$can obtain at p by selecting this allocation is no smaller than $r_d = \sum_{i=1}^{n} [W^{*,-i}_{\phi_d,B} - W^{*,-i}_{\phi_{d,-i},B}]$, the VCG revenue of ϕ_d. This is true because the negative term is the same (since the allocations are the same), and for the positive term $W^{*,-i}_{\phi_d,B}$, we have $W^{*,-i}_{\phi_d} \leq W^{*,-i}_{\phi_p}$ since optimal welfare is nonincreasing with more bundling.

Monotonicity follows from the fact that the VCG$^+$ MIP for any descendant of d of p is the VCG$^+$ MIP for p with additional constraints added. Adding constraints cannot increase the value. □

VCG$^+_{LB}$ We introduce a technique that tightens the bound of VCG$^+$ based on the observation that any constraint that does not cut off any of the welfare-maximizing allocations at any node in the subtree will preserve the upper bound. With this in mind, we add the constraint $\sum_{j \in B} v_j \cdot I_j \geq W_{LB}$ to the MIP of Figure 3, where W_{LB} is a lower bound on the welfare found at any node in the subtree.

[3]Unlike in typical tree (or graph) search in artificial intelligence, here monotonicity does not imply admissibility because there is no notion of the cost of the path from the root to the node.

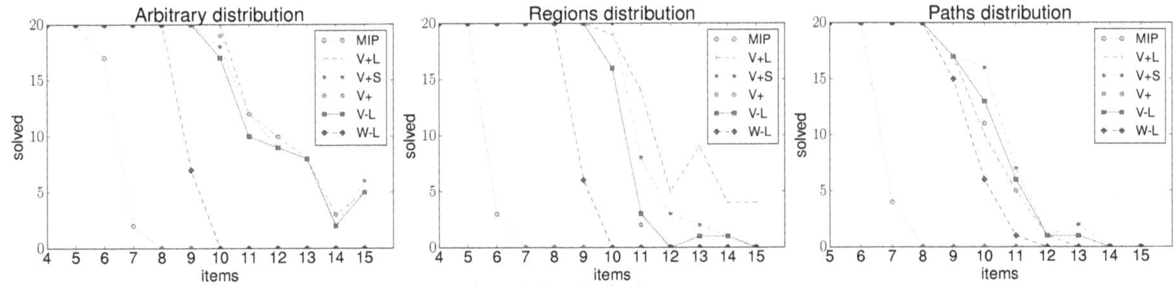

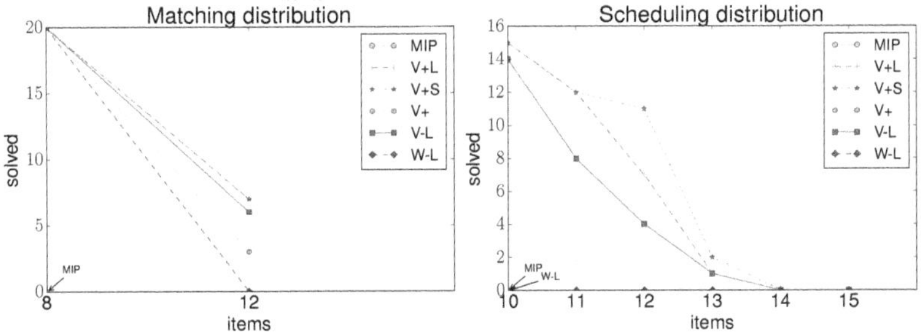

Distribution	MIP	V+L	V+S	V+	V-L	W-L
Arbitrary	59	178	175	177	171	107
Regions	43	175	154	140	141	106
Paths	44	113	123	115	118	102
Matching	0	27	27	23	26	20
Scheduling	0	35	40	27	27	0
Total	146	528	519	482	483	335

Figure 4: Plots showing the number of instances solved for varying numbers of items with the MIP, and various heuristic configurations for our branch-and-bound approach. The table shows the total number of instances solved for each algorithm and distribution pair.

At each search node, we use two different ways of computing a value for W_{LB}, and we use the larger of the two. The first is the maximum valuation of any single bid, which is obviously a lower bound since we can always let any single bid be the only winner. The second is obtained by running DETERMINE-WINNERS on the bids that do not use any of the yet-undecided items. This is clearly a lower bound on the welfare of any node in that subtree because the allocation that it finds remains feasible for all nodes the subtree.

PROPOSITION 7. VCG^+_{LB} *is admissible and monotonic.*

PROOF. Admissibility follows immediately from the admissibility of VCG^+ and the fact that both ways of computing W_{LB} indeed yield lower bounds as argued in Section 5.3.

Monotonicity follows from monotonicity of VCG^+ and the fact that both ways of computing W_{LB} yield W_{LB} values that are nondecreasing down each search path (because the set of bids to choose from grows or stays the same). □

5.4 Variable ordering

In Step 6, the function BRANCHINGITEM(node) chooses the item to branch on at the node. Any choice will yield a correct algorithm, but some choices lead to smaller trees than others and thus shorter run times. The motivation for our variable-selection heuristic is that we want to pick an item that most likely needs to be bundled so that we get a fairly balanced search tree (where the promising branches are the many branches where this item is bundled). In contrast, branching on an item that likely should not be bundled would render the one "unbundling" branch the most promising and would thus yield lopsided deep trees.

We introduce two branching heuristics, PRICE-GAP-SIZE and PRICE-GAP-LOG. They both work by first computing the highest and second-highest "normalized bid price" for each item. Then, the item that has the greatest difference between the highest and second-highest normalized bid price is chosen for branching. The idea is that such items are promising for bundling because there is not enough competition on them. PRICE-GAP-SIZE In PRICE-GAP-SIZE, we use the following formula for normalized bid price: $\frac{v_j}{|S_j|}$. In PRICE-GAP-LOG, we use the following formula for normalized bid price: $\frac{v_j}{log(|S_j|)}$.

Using the number of items in the bid, $|S_j|$, for normalization gives a more precise estimate of the valuation of each item, but using the logarithm of $|S_j|$ favors bids with a greater number of items, which can lead to more important decisions being made early. Logarithmic normalization has been experimentally shown to perform well in the winner determination problem [39] so we included that in our experiments as well.

6. EXPERIMENTS

We conducted experiments with all our different algorithmic approaches using the Combinatorial Auction Test Suite (CATS) [26], which is the leading combinatorial auction benchmark suite. We generated a test suite from all the CATS distributions (excluding the old, unrealistic "legacy" distributions): arbitrary, matching, paths, regions, and scheduling. For each distribution we generated instances with 4-15 items, and bids equal to 0.2, 0.5, 1, 2, 5, and 10 times the number of items, with 20 instances generated for each of these settings. For space reasons we include only the most interesting results here. All experiments were conducted on a cluster, with each experiment run on a core on AMD Opteron quad-core 2.0GHz processors and 10GB of RAM available. The operating system was Rocks Version 6.1. The MIP models were solved using CPLEX 12.5. We used a time limit of 15 minutes for each run.

In this paper we present the most interesting results from our experiments. For the interested reader, a full description and results for all our experiments can be found in a companion tech report that will be made available upon publication.

In addition to the techniques described above, we evaluated a node-ordering technique we call LAZY-BOUND, where the nodes' upper bounds are computed as the nodes are taken from the open list. This had a negligible positive impact on performance, and is discussed in the companion tech report. All algorithms presented here use the technique. We also designed and evaluated an upper-bounding technique we call EXTERNALITY-FLOW. Its performance was worse than that of VCG^+ and VCG^+_{LB}, its discussion is also relegated to the companion tech report.

Figure 4 shows five plots giving the number of instances solved by our various algorithmic configurations. A plot is given for each of the five CATS distribtutions. For each plot, the performance of the MIP and five heuristic configurations for FIND-BUNDLING are shown. The FIND-BUNDLING configurations are as follows: VCG^+_{LB} and PRICE-GAP-LOG(V+L), VCG^+_{LB} and PRICE-GAP-SIZE (V+S), VCG^+_{LB} with no variable ordering heuristic (V+), VCG^+ and PRICE-GAP-LOG (V-L), and WELFARE and PRICE-GAP-LOG (W-L). Finally, the table in Figure 4 shows the total number of instances solved for each distribution and algorithm pair.

The presented results are for using instances where we generate approximately ten times as many bids as there are items. The results are representative of algorithm performance for smaller numbers of bids, but these were hardest and thus best showed the performance difference. In the following sections we discuss the results in light of the various heuristics we developed.

MIP vs. our custom algorithm For the basic MIP approach, our experiments show that it is unable to scale beyond 7 items for all of the distributions (Figure 4). In contrast to this, our best algorithms (V+L and V+S) solve instances with up to 15 items. We also see that the total number of instances solved (table in Figure 4) by V+L and V+S is far greater than for the MIP approach.

Upper bounding heuristics We conducted experiments with each of the three upper-bounding techniques (WELFARE, VCG^+, and VCG^+_{LB}). All three use PRICE-GAP-LOG for variable ordering.

On the arbitrary and regions distributions, we see that VCG^+_{LB} is able to solve at least 3 out of 20 instances for all item sizes, and more than 10 for item sizes 11 and lower. On these distributions, VCG^+ performs almost as well, with only 7 fewer instances solved overall on the arbitrary distribution and 34 fewer on the regions distribution. WELFARE performs significantly worse on these two distributions, solving approximately 70 instances less on each. For the matching distribution, all algorithms have somewhat similar performance, but the relative order of the upper-bounding heuristics is the same. VCG^+_{LB} solves 27 out of 40 instances, whereas the MIP solves none. For the paths and scheduling distributions, all the upper-bounding techniques perform significantly worse. VCG^+_{LB} and VCG^+ only scale to 13 items, but still significantly outperform WELFARE, which scales to 11 items. Interestingly, the total number of instances solved is slightly higher for V-L than for V+L. Overall, VCG^+_{LB} and VCG^+ clearly outperform WELFARE by a significant margin. VCG^+_{LB} also outperforms VCG^+ on 4 out of 5 distributions, 2 by a significant margin.

Variable-ordering heuristics We experimented with all three settings for the variable ordering heuristic while using VCG^+_{LB} for upper bounding: PRICE-GAP-LOG (V+L) , PRICE-GAP-SIZE (V+S), and no heuristic (V+). The performance on the arbitrary and matching distributions is almost the same for all three heuristics, with PRICE-GAP-LOG solving three more instances than PRICE-GAP-SIZE. For the regions distribution, we see a more significant performance difference. PRICE-GAP-LOG solves 175 instances, where PRICE-GAP-SIZE solves 154 instances, and using no heuristic solves 140. Finally, for the paths and scheduling distributions, PRICE-GAP-SIZE performs somewhat better than PRICE-GAP-LOG. On paths, it solves 123 instances while PRICE-GAP-LOG solves 113. On scheduling, it solves 40 while PRICE-GAP-LOG solves 35. Overall, PRICE-GAP-LOG solved 9 instances more than PRICE-GAP-SIZE, both clearly outperforming not using a variable-ordering heuristic. However, even PRICE-GAP-LOG is outperformed by not using a variable-ordering heuristic on one distribution (although marginally).

6.1 Revenue increase and surplus extraction

Finally, we conducted experiments that empirically examine how well our approach both bridges the gap to the optimal revenue, and how much it improves over the VCG revenue. For low bids-to-items multipliers, the revenue increase was very often infinitely higher. This is because VCG often received no revenue in these settings, whereas VCG with optimal bundling usually achieves at leaft half the social welfare in revenue. These results are not shown here as they are trivially stated.

#items	arbitrary	regions	paths	matching	scheduling
4	5.9 / 89	4.6 / 91	- / -	- / -	- / -
5	1.6 / 90	7.6 / 87	0.6 / 89	- / -	- / -
6	4.4 / 90	0 / 82	1.7 / 86	- / -	- / -
7	6.3 / 87	0.1 / 84	7.6 / 85	- / -	- / -
8	9 / 88	1.6 / 84	2.2 / 87	3.4 / 84	- / -
9	2.6 / 92	4.7 / 91	3.9 / 88	- / -	- / -
10	2.2 / 91	4.1 / 92	1.2 / 89	- / -	5.4 / 88
11	3.8 / 92	- / -	3 / 91 11	- / -	5.1 / 88
12	8.6 / 92	- / -	- / -	8.4 / 89	3 / 86

Figure 5: The first column for each distribution shows the percentage increase in revenue from bundling compared to regular VCG with no bundling. The second shows the percentage of social welflare extracted as revenue.

Table 5 shows the results from running optimal bundling in the VCG, VCG (with no bundling), and welfare computation on each of the five CATS distributions, when the number of bids is 5 times the number of items. The percentages given are average increases over 10-20 instances for each parameter setting. Entries with - / - denote that not enough instances were generated or solved.

For the bids-to-items ratio 5 (Figure 5), the revenue increase over VCG tends to lie in the 2-20% range. About 90% of the social welfare is obtained in revenue for these settings.

In real-life applications, the revenue increase is likely to be even higher, as CATS tends to generate bids that span all items, with valuation for such bids being close to the optimal welfare, and thus causing artificially high compeition across all items. Similarly, CATS only generates undominated bids, that is, bids whose value is higher than what could be obtained in welfare from the items in the bid using other bids that only want those items. This means that CATS generates artificially strong competition, and thus revenue, for the given number of bids and items.

7. CONCLUSION AND FUTURE WORK

We studied bundling, a common revenue-enhancement approach, in the context of the most commonly studied combinatorial auction mechanism, VCG, adopting a point prior model. We proved robustness to inaccuracy in the prior, and showed that computing the optimal bundling is NP-hard even with a point prior. Then, we presented a custom branch-and-bound framework for finding the optimal bundling. In that framework, we introduced several techniques for branching, upper bounding, lower bounding, and lazy bounding. Experiments on CATS distributions validated the approach and showed that our techniques dramatically improve scalability over a leading MIP solver.

There are many interesting directions for future research. Affine maximizer auctions, virtual valuations combinatorial auctions, and λ-auctions all support unlimited, bidder-specific reserve prices. In contrast, we studied bundling alone as a revenue-enhancement tool. There are many interesting questions about the relative power of different forms of bundling, different forms of reserve pricing, and combinations thereof— both in the auction and catalog sales contexts. Second, we plan to extend our algorithms to settings with structure. For example, in many advertising markets, the inventory segments are defined by vectors of attributes, and that can, in some settings, provide additional structure.

Acknowledgements. This material is based on work supported by the National Science Foundation under grants CCF-1101668, IIS-0964579, and IIS-1320620.

References

[1] William James Adams and Janet L. Yellen. "Commodity Bundling and the Burden of Monopoly". In: *Quarterly Journal of Economics* 90.3 (1976), pp. 475–498.

[2] Mark Armstrong. "Multiproduct Nonlinear Pricing". In: *Econometrica* 64.1 (1996), pp. 51–75.

[3] Mark Armstrong. "Optimal Multi-Object Auctions". In: *Review of Economic Studies* 67 (2000), pp. 455–481.

[4] Lawrence M. Ausubel and Paul Milgrom. "The Lovely but Lonely Vickrey Auction". In: *Combinatorial Auctions*. Ed. by Peter Cramton, Yoav Shoham, and Richard Steinberg. MIT Press, 2006. Chap. 1.

[5] Christopher Avery and Terrence Hendershott. "Bundling and Optimal Auctions of Multiple Products". In: *Review of Economic Studies* 67 (2000), pp. 483–497.

[6] Yannis Bakos and Erik Brynjolfsson. "Bundling Information Goods: Pricing, Profits, and Efficiency". In: *Management Science* 45.12 (1999), pp. 1613–1630.

[7] Michael Benisch and Tuomas Sandholm. "A Framework for Automated Bundling and Pricing Using Purchase Data". In: *Proceedings of the Conference on Auctions, Market Mechanisms and Their Applications (AMMA)*. 2011.

[8] D Berend and T Tassa. "Improved Bounds on Bell Numbers and on Moments of Sums of Random Variables". In: *Probability and Mathematical Statistics* 30.2 (2010), pp. 185–205.

[9] Chirstopher H. Brooks and Edmund H. Durfee. "Toward Automated Pricing and Bundling of Information Goods". In: *AAAI Workshop on Knowledge-based Electronic Markets*. 2000, pp. 8–13.

[10] Yang Cai, Constantinos Daskalakis, and Matt Weinberg. "Optimal Multi-Dimensional Mechanism Design: Reducing Revenue to Welfare Maximization". In: *Proceedings of the Annual Symposium on Foundations of Computer Science (FOCS)*. 2012.

[11] I Chakraborty. "Bundling decisions for selling multiple objects". In: *Economic Theory* 13 (1999), pp. 723–733.

[12] Ed H. Clarke. "Multipart pricing of public goods". In: *Public Choice* 11 (1971), pp. 17–33.

[13] Vincent Conitzer and Tuomas Sandholm. "Complexity of Mechanism Design". In: *Proceedings of the 18th Annual Conference on Uncertainty in Artificial Intelligence (UAI)*. Edmonton, Canada, 2002, pp. 103–110.

[14] Vincent Conitzer and Tuomas Sandholm. "Applications of Automated Mechanism Design". In: *UAI-03 workshop on Bayesian Modeling Applications*. Acapulco, Mexico, 2003.

[15] Vincent Conitzer and Tuomas Sandholm. "Self-interested Automated Mechanism Design and Implications for Optimal Combinatorial Auctions". In: *Proceedings of the ACM Conference on Electronic Commerce (ACM-EC)*. New York, NY, 2004, pp. 132–141.

[16] Robert E. Dansby and Cecilia Conrad. "Commodity Bundling". In: *The American Economic Review* 74.2 (1984), pp. 377–381.

[17] Robert Day and Paul Milgrom. "Core-selecting package auctions". In: *International Journal of Game Theory* 36.3 (2008), pp. 393–407.

[18] Arpita Ghosh, Hamid Nazerzadeh, and Mukund Sundararajan. "Computing optimal bundles for sponsored search". In: *International Workshop On Internet And Network Economics (WINE)*. 2007, pp. 576–583.

[19] Theodore Groves. "Incentives in Teams". In: *Econometrica* 41 (1973), pp. 617–631.

[20] Joseph P. Guiltinan. "The Price Bundling of Services: A Normative Framework". In: *Journal of Marketing* 51.2 (1987), pp. 74–85.

[21] Ward Hanson and R. Kipp Martin. "Optimal bundle pricing". In: *Manage. Sci.* 36.2 (1990), pp. 155–174.

[22] Lorin M. Hitt and Pei-yu Chen. "Bundling with Customer Self-Selection: A Simple Approach to Bundling Low-Marginal-Cost Goods". In: *Management Science* 51.10 (2005), pp. 1481–1493.

[23] Ali Hojjat, John Turner, Suleyman Cetintas, and Jian Yang. "Delivering Guaranteed Display Ads under Reach and Frequency Requirements". In: *Proceedings of the AAAI Conference on Artificial Intelligence (AAAI)*. 2014.

[24] Philippe Jehiel, Moritz Meyer-Ter-Vehn, and Benny Moldovanu. "Mixed bundling auctions". In: *Journal of Economic Theory* 127.1 (2007), pp. 494–512.

[25] Jeffrey O. Kephart, Christopher H. Brooks, Rajarshi Das, Jeffrey K. MacKie-Mason, Robert Gazzale, and Edmund H. Durfee. "Pricing information bundles in a dynamic environment". In: *Proceedings of the ACM Conference on Electronic Commerce (ACM-EC)*. Tampa, Florida, USA: ACM Press, 2001, pp. 180–190.

[26] Kevin Leyton-Brown, Mark Pearson, and Yoav Shoham. "Towards a Universal Test Suite for Combinatorial Auction Algorithms". In: *Proceedings of the ACM Conference on Electronic Commerce (ACM-EC)*. Minneapolis, MN, 2000, pp. 66–76.

[27] Anton Likhodedov and Tuomas Sandholm. "Methods for Boosting Revenue in Combinatorial Auctions". In: *Proceedings of the National Conference on Artificial Intelligence (AAAI)*. San Jose, CA, 2004, pp. 232–237.

[28] Anton Likhodedov and Tuomas Sandholm. "Approximating Revenue-Maximizing Combinatorial Auctions". In: *Proceedings of the National Conference on Artificial Intelligence (AAAI)*. Pittsburgh, PA, 2005.

[29] Alejandro M Manelli and Daniel R Vincent. "Bundling as an optimal selling mechanism for a multiple-good monopolist". In: *Journal of Economic Theory* 127.1 (2006), pp. 1–35.

[30] Eric Maskin and John Riley. "Optimal Multi-Unit Auctions". In: *The Economics of Missing Markets, Information, and Games*. Ed. by Frank Hahn. Clarendon Press, Oxford, 1989. Chap. 14, pp. 312–335.

[31] R. Preston McAfee, John McMillan, and Michael D. Whinston. "Multiproduct Monopoly, Commodity Bundling, and Correlation of Values". In: *Quarterly Journal of Economics* 104.2 (1989), pp. 371–383.

[32] Roger Myerson. "Optimal auction design". In: *Mathematics of Operation Research* 6 (1981), pp. 58–73.

[33] Thomas Palfrey. "Bundling Decisions by a Multiproduct Monopolist with Incomplete Information". In: *Econometrica* 51 (1983), pp. 463–484.

[34] Baharak Rastegari, Anne Condon, and Kevin Leyton-Brown. "Revenue monotonicity in deterministic, dominant-strategy combinatorial auctions". In: *Artif. Intell.* 175.2 (2011), pp. 441–456.

[35] Paat Rusmevichientong, Benjamin Van Roy, and Peter W. Glynn. "A Nonparametric Approach to Multiproduct Pricing". In: *Oper. Res.* 54.1 (2006), pp. 82–98. ISSN: 0030-364X.

[36] Tuomas Sandholm. "Algorithm for Optimal Winner Determination in Combinatorial Auctions". In: *Artificial Intelligence* 135 (Jan. 2002), pp. 1–54.

[37] Tuomas Sandholm. "Automated Mechanism Design: A New Application Area for Search Algorithms". In: *International Conference on Principles and Practice of Constraint Programming (CP)*. Cork, Ireland, 2003, pp. 19–36.

[38] Tuomas Sandholm, Kate Larson, Martin Andersson, Onn Shehory, and Fernando Tohmé. "Coalition Structure Generation with Worst Case Guarantees". In: *Artificial Intelligence* 111.1–2 (1999), pp. 209–238.

[39] Tuomas Sandholm, Subhash Suri, Andrew Gilpin, and David Levine. "CABOB: A Fast Optimal Algorithm for Winner Determination in Combinatorial Auctions". In: *Management Science* 51.3 (2005), pp. 374–390.

[40] Richard Schmalensee. "Gaussian Demand and Commodity Bundling". In: *The Journal of Business* 57.1 (1984), S211–S230.

[41] George J. Stigler. "United States v. Loew's Inc.: A Note on Block-Booking". In: *The Supreme Court Review* 1963 (1963), pp. 152–157.

[42] John Turner. "The Planning of Guaranteed Targeted Display Advertising". In: *Operations Research* 60 (1 2012), pp. 18–33.

[43] William Vickrey. "Counterspeculation, Auctions, and Competitive Sealed Tenders". In: *Journal of Finance* 16 (1961), pp. 8–37.

[44] William Walsh, Craig Boutilier, Tuomas Sandholm, Robert Shields, George Nemhauser, and David Parkes. "Automated Channel Abstraction for Advertising Auctions". In: *Proceedings of the National Conference on Artificial Intelligence (AAAI)*. 2010.

[45] Shin-yi Wu, Lorin M. Hitt, Pei-yu Chen, and G. Anandalingam. "Customized Bundle Pricing for Information Goods: A Nonlinear Mixed-Integer Programming Approach". In: *Management Science* 54.3 (2008), pp. 608–622.

Mechanism Design for Daily Deals

Binyi Chen[1], Tao Qin[2], Tie-Yan Liu[2]
[1]University of California, Santa Barbara [2]Microsoft Research
[1]binyichen@cs.ucsb.edu [2]{taoqin, tyliu}@microsoft.com

ABSTRACT

Daily deals are very popular in today's e-commerce. In this work, we study the problem of mechanism design for a daily deal website to maximize its revenue and obtain the following results. (1) For the Bayesian setting, we first design a revenue-optimal incentive-compatible (IC) mechanism with pseudo-polynomial time complexity. Considering the high computational complexity of the mechanism, we then develop a greedy mechanism that is much more computationally efficient yet maintains a constant competitive ratio regarding the Bayesian optimal revenue in expectation. (2) For the prior-independent setting, we first propose a randomized IC mechanism with a pseudo-polynomial time complexity that can achieve a constant competitive ratio. Then, by leveraging the greedy mechanism designed for the Bayesian setting, we come up with a new mechanism that can achieve a good tradeoff between computational efficiency and competitive ratio. After that, we discuss the robustness issue regarding the two mechanisms (i.e., they both use the trick of random partition and may perform badly for the worst-case partition) and propose an effective way to guarantee a constant competitive ratio even for the worst-case partition.

Categories and Subject Descriptors

J.4 [**Computer Applications**]: Social and Behavioral Sciences–Economics

General Terms

Economics, Theory

Keywords

Mechanism Design, Daily Deals

1. INTRODUCTION

Daily deal services (e.g., Groupon) have become very popular nowadays. In daily deal services, a merchant demands and pays for a chunk of user impressions. [1] The demand of a merchant can be specified by a pair (l, u), where l and u denote the minimum and maximum numbers of user impressions that she would like to buy. The daily deal website can collect revenue from the merchant if the number of user impressions allocated to him/her (denoted as x) satisfies $l \leq x$: if $x < l$, the merchant will pay nothing because the deal is not tipped on; if $x > u$, the merchant will not pay extra money for the user impressions beyond u.

Daily deal services have been studied from many different perspectives, such as merchants' reputation [7] and profitability [11, 12], and customers' behaviors [6, 27, 21, 26]. Different from those work, we focus on the problem of revenue maximization by means of designing auction mechanisms.

1.1 Daily Deal Auctions

We define the Daily Deal Auctions (DDAs) as follows. Let N be the supply from the daily deal website, i.e., there are N web users visiting the website during a specific time period. Denote K as the maximum number of slots where the website can show deals to each web user. We follow the convention in previous work [13, 1, 19] and assume the qualities of the slots to be different from each other (e.g., a deal shown at the top slot is more likely to attract users' attention). Specifically, we use λ_k to denote the quality of slot k and assume that the slots are numbered in the descending order of their qualities: $1 \geq \lambda_1 > \lambda_2 > \cdots > \lambda_K \geq 0$.

If a deal is shown to x users at slot k, we say that the deal has obtained $x\lambda_k$ effective impressions. We define $N_k = N\lambda_k$ as the number of effective impressions of slot k in the entire time period (another way to understand N_k is to regard it as the expected number of users who have paid attention to the k-th slot). For simplicity and without much loss of accuracy, we assume N_k to be an integer. It is clear that $N_1 > N_2 > \cdots > N_K$.

Let M be the number of candidate deals participating in the auction. Each deal i is characterized by a tuple (l_i, u_i, v_i), where l_i and u_i denote the minimum and maximum number of effective impressions demanded by the deal, and v_i denotes the per-effective-impression value. We focus on the single-parameter setting, in which a merchant may strategically misreport her value v_i through a bid b_i.

[1]In daily deal services, merchants usually target at conversions/purchases, which can be easily transformed to impressions. For example, 10000 impressions is equivalent to 100 conversions if the conversion rate of the deal is 0.01. We choose to use the term *impression* throughout the paper because it is what the daily deal website can allocate in practice.

Appears in: *Proceedings of the 14th International Conference on Autonomous Agents and Multiagent Systems (AAMAS 2015), Bordini, Elkind, Weiss, Yolum (eds.), May 4–8, 2015, Istanbul, Turkey.*

Upon receiving the bids $\{b_i\}_{i\in[M]}$ from all the merchants, the website determines how to allocate the slots and how to charge merchants by using a mechanism. Let x_i be the number of effective impressions allocated to bidder i and p_i be the payment of bidder i. Then the utility of bidder i is

$$U_i = 1\{l_i \le x_i\}(\min\{x_i, u_i\}v_i - p_i),$$

where $1\{\}$ is the indicator function, and the revenue of the auctioneer is $\sum_{i\in[m]} p_i$. Note that the utility of any bidder should be non-negative for *individual rationality*.

A feasible allocation for DDAs must satisfy two conditions: (1) no more than one deal can be assigned to a slot for any user; (2) no deal can be assigned to more than one slot for any user. These feasibility conditions can be mathematically expressed by the following majorization constraints [19]:

$$\sum\nolimits_{j=1}^{i} x_{[j]} \le \sum\nolimits_{j=1}^{i} N_j, \forall i \in [M],$$

where $x_{[j]}$ denotes the j-th largest element in $\{x_i\}_{i\in[M]}$, and $N_i = 0, \forall K < i \le M$.

The goal of our work is to design computationally efficient mechanisms for DDAs, which are incentive compatible to the bidders and can (approximately) maximize the revenue of the auctioneer.

1.2 Our Results

Our main results can be summarized as follows.

We start with the *Bayesian setting*. (1) We first propose an incentive compatible (IC) mechanism $\mathcal{M}_1$ with a pseudo-polynomial time complexity, which can achieve the optimal expected revenue. This mechanism leverages the dynamic program proposed in [19] for the allocation, and uses a novel algorithm to calculate the payment. (2) Considering the high complexity of $\mathcal{M}_1$, we further propose a greedy mechanism $\mathcal{M}_2$ that is highly computationally efficient (e.g., $O(M^3)$) and can achieve a competitive ratio of 1/4.

We then consider the *prior-independent setting*. (1) Based on $\mathcal{M}_1$, we design a randomized IC mechanism $\mathcal{M}_3$ with a pseudo-polynomial time complexity and a competitive ratio of $\frac{\beta-1}{\beta}$, where $\beta > 1$ is a fixed constant. (2) To reduce the computational complexity of $\mathcal{M}_3$, we develop a greedy mechanism $\mathcal{M}_4$ with complexity is $O(M^3)$ and a competitive ratio of $\frac{\beta-1}{4\beta}$. (3) Considering that the above two mechanisms rely on random partition of the bidders and only have performance guarantee in the expected case, we then discuss how to improve their robustness, i.e., how to guarantee their performances even for the worst-case partition. As a showcase, we develop a mechanism $\mathcal{M}_5$ that can achieve a competitive ratio of $\frac{3}{7}$ and a robust ratio (see Definition 10) of $\frac{1}{4}$.

2. RELATED WORK

Daily deal services have been studied from many different perspectives. [7] studies how daily deal sites affecting the reputation of a business using evidences from Yelp reviews. [6] investigates hypotheses such as whether daily deal subscribers are more critical than their peers. [11] tries to answer the the question whether group-buying deals would be profitable for businesses. [12] finds that offering vouchers is more profitable for merchants which are patient or relatively unknown, and for merchants with low marginal costs. There are several papers [27, 21, 26] studying consumer purchase/repurchase behaviors towards daily deals. It is easy to see that the focuses of existing pieces of work are very different from ours. We stand on the position of a daily deal site and focus on the problem of revenue maximization by means of designing auction mechanisms.

A closely related work is [8], in which the authors also design auction mechanisms for daily deals. The difference is that they target at the maximization of a combination of the revenue of the auctioneer (website), welfare of the bidders (merchants), and the utility of the consumers, while we focus on the revenue of the website. Besides, they ignore the dynamic demand of merchants (i.e., from l_i to u_i) and do not consider the impression allocation problem.

The impression allocation problem in our work is related to the classical knapsack problem [9], which can be viewed as our special case by setting $l_i = u_i$ and $K = 1$. While some recent work on stochastic knapsack problem [10] consider items with stochastic volumes, the allocation of an item is binary (i.e., pack it or not). Our work is different in the sense that the allocation of a deal is not binary (zero or lower bounded by l_i and upper bounded by u_i). Our work is also highly related to [19] and [20], except that they ignore the incentive issues and assume that bidders truthfully report their valuations.

From the perspective of auction design, DDAs are related to knapsack auctions as studied in [2]. In fact, our problem will degenerate to the problem under their investigations by (1) setting $l_i = u_i, K = 1$ and (2) assuming bidders' private value are deterministic and fixed. Recently, [25] studies knapsack auctions in the Bayesian setting and obtain several approximation results, yet it is still a special case of our setting ($l_i = u_i$ and $K = 1$). DDAs are also related to multi-unit auctions [22, 16]. The difference is that the allocation in DDAs have a lower (l_i) and an upper (u_i) constraint.

[5] and [4] are the early pieces of work that consider payment computation in truthful mechanisms. Both of them and our work face the hinder that the computation involves the integral of a step function with possibly exponential breakpoints. Our method is different from them and we solve this issue in the specific setting of daily deal auctions.

The concept of competitive ratio comes from [18], which evaluates the performance of a mechanism by comparing its expected revenue against the Bayesian optimal expected revenue. The concept of "prior-independent setting" also comes from [18]. Our designed mechanisms for the prior-independent setting are inspired by [14], [15] and [3] in which bidders are partitioned into several sub markets to estimate the value distribution. Again, different from these pieces of work on digital goods, we consider bidders with dynamic demands (ranging from l_i to u_i).

3. PRELIMINARIES

3.1 Settings and Notations

We mainly investigate on two settings for DDAs, and use *competitive ratio* to measure the expected revenue that an auction mechanism can achieve.

In the *Bayesian setting*, it is assumed that the valuation v_i of bidder i is independently sampled from a distribution F_i, which is known to both the auctioneer and all the bidders. In this setting, the competitive ratio of a mechanism $\mathcal{M}$ is defined as $\frac{Rev(\mathcal{M})}{OPT}$, where OPT denotes the optimal expected revenue of an incentive compatible mechanism and $Rev(\mathcal{M})$ is the expected revenue of $\mathcal{M}$. Note that both expectations are taken over the joint distribution $F_1 \times F_2 \times \cdots \times F_M$.

In the *prior-independent setting*, it is assumed that the valuations of all the bidders are independently sampled from the same distribution F, but this distribution is unknown to the auctioneer. In this setting, the competitive ratio of a mechanism $\mathcal{M}$ is defined as $\inf_F \frac{Rev(\mathcal{M},F)}{OPT(F)}$, where $OPT(F)$ denotes the optimal expected revenue of an incentive compatible mechanism and $Rev(\mathcal{M}, F)$ is the expected revenue of $\mathcal{M}$. Both expectations are taken with respect to the distribution F.

In addition, throughout the paper, we use v_{-i} to denote the valuation profile of all the other bidders except i, use $x_i(v_i) = \mathbf{E}_{v_{-i}}[x_i(v_i, v_{-i})]$ to denote the expected number of effective impressions allocated to bidder i when her valuation is v_i, use $p_i(v_i)$ to denote the expected payment, and use $u_i(v_i) = v_i x_i - p_i$ to denote the expected utility. Since all the mechanisms designed in this paper are Bayesian incentive compatible, we will interchangeably use the valuation profile v and bid profile b, and so for v_i and b_i.

3.2 Myerson's Lemma

As mentioned in the introduction, we are concerned with the *single-parameter* auctions, in which each bidder's private information can be expressed by a one-dimensional value v_i. We can exploit the classical *Myerson Lemma* to design incentive compatible mechanisms for single-parameter auctions:

LEMMA 1. *The sufficient conditions for a mechanism to be Bayesian incentive compatible are as follows.*

1. *Allocation monotonicity: for all i and $v_i > v_i', x_i(v_i) \geq x_i(v_i')$.*
2. *Payment identity: for all i and v_i, $p_i(v_i) = v_i x_i(v_i) - \int_0^{v_i} x_i(v)dv$.*

Furthermore, we can leverage the following lemma to design incentive-compatible revenue-optimal mechanisms.

LEMMA 2. *[24] In a Bayesian incentive compatible mechanism with allocation rule $\mathbf{x}(\cdot)$, the expected payment of agent i satisfies $\mathbf{E}_{\mathbf{v}}[p_i(v)] = \mathbf{E}_{\mathbf{v}}[\phi_i(v_i)x_i(v)]$, where we denote the virtual value $\phi_i(v_i) = v_i - \frac{1-F_i(v_i)}{f_i(v_i)}$, and f_i and F_i are the probability density function and cumulative distribution function separately for bidder i's valuation.*

Following the common practice [24, 23] in mechanism design, we assume that the valuation distributions (all F_i's in the Bayesian setting and F in the prior-independent setting) are regular (i.e., the virtual value $\phi_i(v_i)$ is monotone with respect to v_i).

4. BAYESIAN SETTING

In this section, we design mechanisms for DDAs in the Bayesian setting. The goal is to (approximately) maximize the revenue through incentive compatible mechanisms.

4.1 Bayesian Optimal Mechanism

We design a mechanism $\mathcal{M}_1$ that leverages the dynamic program proposed for the Chunked Allocation Problem in [19] , together with a tie-breaking trick, to find the virtual surplus maximizing allocation, and charges bidders according to Eqn. (2). The details of the allocation and payment rules are discussed in Section 4.1.1 and 4.1.2 respectively. For ease of reference, we denote the dynamic program proposed in [19] as DP-CAP.

As will be shown in Section 4.1.3, $\mathcal{M}_1$ is Bayesian incentive compatible. In addition, because the allocation rule maximizes the virtual surplus, this mechanism is revenue optimal according to Lemma 2.

Algorithm 1 A Bayesian Optimal Mechanism ($\mathcal{M}_1$)

Input: $\{N_k\}_{k\in[K]}, \{b_i, l_i, u_i, F_i\}_{i\in[M]}$
Output: x_i, the number of effective impressions allocated to bidder i, and p_i, the payment of bidder i.

```
Compute bidders' virtual values, and remove bidders with negative virtual values.
Find an allocation that maximizes virtual surplus using DP-CAP plus the tie-breaking trick described in Section 4.1.1. Let x_i be the number of effective impressions allocated to bidder i.
for each bidder i ∈ [M] do
  if x_i = 0 then
    p_i ← 0.
  else
    For all a ∈ {0, l_i, l_i + 1, ··· , x_i}, compute Φ_{-i}(a), the maximum virtual surplus generated from all other bidders except i under the condition that i is allocated with exactly a effective impressions.
    Construct a convex hull by intersecting x_i − l_i + 2 half planes: f_a(y) = ay + Φ_{-i}(a) ≥ 0, ∀a ∈ {0, l_i, l_i + 1, ··· , x_i}. Each corner point of the convex hull can be represented by a pair, the first element of which indicates the virtual value of bidder i, and the second element of which is the number of effective impressions allocated to bidder i. We can get a set of pairs: (0, 0), (t_1, k_1), ..., (t_q, k_q), (φ_i(b_i), x_i), where 0 < t_1 < t_2 < ··· < t_q < φ_i(b_i).
    p_i ← x_i · z_q − Σ_{j=1}^{q} k_j · (z_j − z_{j−1}), where z_j = φ_i^{−1}(t_j).
  end if
end for
return {x_i, p_i}_{i∈[M]}
```

4.1.1 The Allocation Rule

While the allocation rule of $\mathcal{M}_1$ looks quite simple since it leverages an existing algorithm to find an optimal allocation, we would like to point out an unobvious pitfall here. Please note that the direct application of DP-CAP cannot guarantee the monotonicity of the allocation rule, when the optimal allocations are not unique. For example, suppose $\phi_i(b_i) = \phi_i(b_i')$ for $b_i' < b_i$. Since there may be multiple allocations that achieve the optimal virtual surplus, it is possible that for bidder i, the allocation that she obtains when bidding b_i is less than the allocation when bidding b_i'.

To address this issue, we need to break the ties so as to ensure the unique output of DP-CAP, and therefore ensure the monotonicity of the allocation rule of $\mathcal{M}_1$. Here we take the simple case of $K = 1$ (i.e., there is only one slot) as an example for illustration. For the case of multiple slots ($K > 1$), the same tie-breaking trick also applies.

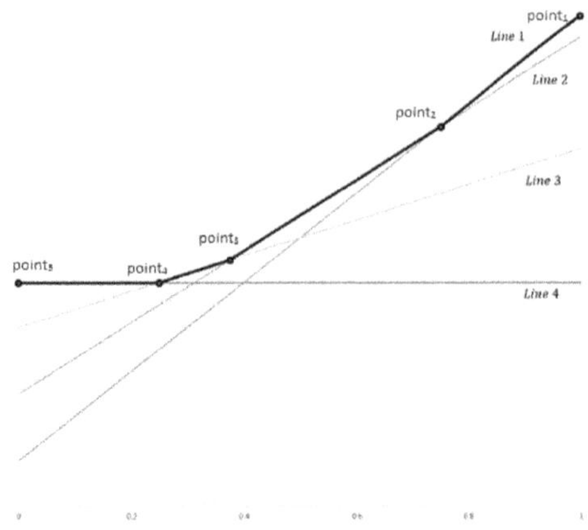

Figure 1: Computation of the Payment Rule

In this simple case, the transition equation of DP-CAP is

$$VS(i,n) = \max_{x_i}(VS(i-1,n-x_i)+x_i\phi_i) \quad x_i \in [l_i,u_i]\cup\{0\}, \tag{1}$$

where $VS(i,n)$ represents the maximum virtual surplus from n effective impressions and bidders $\{1,2,...,i\}$.

The key of ensuring the unique output of DP-CAP is as follows. When multiple x_i's make $VS(i-1,n-x_i)+x_i\phi_i$ maximal, we simply choose the minimum one among them. The optimal allocation is the one associated with $\max(VS(M,n))$ for $n \in [N]$. If there are multiple n's that achieve the maximum, we choose the minimum n.

4.1.2 The Payment Rule

According to Lemma 1, the payment rule for a Bayesian incentive compatible auction is:

$$p_i(v_i) = v_i x_i(v_i) - \int_0^{v_i} x_i(v)dv. \tag{2}$$

At first glance, given the above result, it seems trivial to design the payment rule for our problem. For example, when x_i takes binary values (e.g., win or lose), similar to the classical VCG payment [17], we can simply exploit the approach proposed in [18] to calculate the payment: let $p'_i = OPT(v_{-i}) - OPT_{-i}(v)$, where $OPT(v_{-i})$ is the optimal virtual surplus when i has been removed and $OPT_{-i}(v)$ is the original optimal virtual surplus minus i's virtual surplus, and charge i with the price $p_i = \phi_i^{-1}(p'_i)$.

However, we note that in daily deal auctions, x_i does not necessarily take binary values. In fact, it can take any value from$\{0, l_i, l_i+1, ..., \min(u_i, \text{allocated } N_j)\}$. In this case, the design of the payment rule becomes harder, and we need to explore the structural properties of the allocation rule. Since the allocation rule is monotone, fixing the bids of all the other bidders, x_i is a piecewise constant function of b_i. For simplicity, we call those bids corresponding to the change of x_i as breakpoints. To compute $p_i(v_i)$ in Eqn. (2), we need to know all the breakpoints of bidder i. As shown in Steps 7-9 of $\mathcal{M}_1$, we can find all the breakpoints by calling DP-CAP for at most $x_i(v_i)-l_i+2$ times, and thus the total complexity of payment computation is Poly(N,M,K). The remaining part of this subsection explains how Steps 7-9 work.

Consider the payment of bidder i when she is allocated with $x_i > 0$ effective impressions. Let $\Phi_{-i}(a)$ denotes the part of the maximum virtual surplus generated from all the other bidders under the condition that a fixed number of effective impressions (denoted as a) are allocated to bidder i. $\Phi_{-i}(a)$ can be easily calculated by calling DP-CAP and setting all its states with $x_i \neq a$ to negative infinity. Then for each allocation $a \in \{0, l_i, l_i+1, ..., x_i(v_i)\}$, the maximum virtual surplus (conditioned on that i gets a effective impressions) can be expressed as $a \cdot \phi_i + \Phi_{-i}(a)$, which is a linear function of ϕ_i with slope a and bias $\Phi_{-i}(a)$. After calling DP-CAP for $x_i(v_i)-l_i+2$ times, we get $x_i(v_i)-l_i+2$ lines with slopes $\{0, l_i, l_i+1, ..., x_i(v_i)\}$ and biases $\{\Phi_{-i}(0) \geq \Phi_{-i}(l_i) \geq \Phi_{-i}(l_i+1) \geq ..., \geq \Phi_{-i}(x_i(v_i))\}$.

As shown in Figure 4.1.2, the horizontal axis is the virtual value of bidder i and the vertical axis is the corresponding virtual surplus. First we set Cur to be the line with the largest slope (in Figure 4.1.2 it is line 1) and set (cx, cy) to be the point $(\phi_i(v_i), \Phi_{-i}(x_i) + x_i \cdot \phi_i(v_i))$. In each step, we can calculate the intersection points between the line Cur and other lines in $O(N)$ time, and choose the upmost point on the left side of the point (cx, cy). We use a pair to denote this upmost point: the first element of the pair is the virtual value of bidder i at the point and the second one is the number of effective impressions allocated to i. We then update (cx, cy) to be this point and update Cur to be the corresponding intersecting line. We terminate the process when $cx \leq 0$. Since each line can become Cur in at most one step, the procedure will terminate in $O(N)$ steps. Finally, we find those points (and their associated pairs) that build the convex hull of the lines (in Figure 4.1.2, they are $point_1, ..., point_5$). Assume those pairs are $(0,0), (t_1,k_1), ..., (t_q,k_q), (\phi_i(v_i), x_i(v_i))$, where $0 < t_1 < t_2 < \cdots < t_q < \phi_i(v_i)$. We set $t_0 = 0$. For all $j \in \{0, ..., q\}$, we set $z_j = \phi_i^{-1}(t_j)$, and compute the payment of bidder i as below:

$$p_i(v_i) = x_i(v_i) \cdot z_q - \sum_{j=1}^{q} k_j \cdot (z_j - z_{j-1}).$$

4.1.3 Incentive Compatibility

THEOREM 3. *$\mathcal{M}_1$ is Bayesian incentive compatible.*

PROOF. Lemma 1 has given the sufficient conditions for a mechanism to be Bayesian incentive compatible. It is easy to see that the payment rule of $\mathcal{M}_1$ satisfies the second condition. Therefore we only need to prove that $\mathcal{M}_1$ satisfies the first condition: its allocation rule is monotone.

Let $x^*(b)$ denote the unique optimal allocation vector outputted by the dynamic program for the bid profile b, and $x_i^*(b)$ denote the number of effective impressions allocated to bidder i. Without loss of generality, we assume $x_i^*(b) > 0$. Let $\Phi(x, b)$ denote the virtual surplus when the bid profile is b and allocation is x.

Now we prove the monotonicity of $x^*()$ by contradiction. If $x^*()$ is not monotone, there exist some $i, b_{-i}, b_i < b'_i$ such that $x_i^*(b) > x_i^*(b')$, where $b = (b_i, b_{-i})$ and $b' = (b'_i, b_{-i})$.

If $\phi_i(b_i) = \phi_i(b'_i)$ the allocation of i will not change, thus we can assume $\phi_i(b_i) < \phi_i(b'_i)$. Since $x_i^*(b) > 0$ is the optimal allocation for b and $x^*(b')$ is the optimal allocation for b', we have $\Phi(x^*(b), b) \geq \Phi(x^*(b'), b)$ and $\Phi(x^*(b'), b') \geq \Phi(x^*(b), b')$. Then we get

$$\Phi(x^*(b), b) - \Phi(x^*(b), b') \geq \Phi(x^*(b'), b) - \Phi(x^*(b'), b').$$
$$\Rightarrow x_i^*(b)(\phi_i(b_i) - \phi_i(b'_i)) \geq x_i^*(b')(\phi_i(b_i) - \phi_i(b'_i))$$
$$\Rightarrow x_i^*(b) \leq x_i^*(b')$$

Thus we arrive at a contradiction. □

4.2 A Greedy Mechanism

Although $\mathcal{M}_1$ is revenue optimal, it suffers from the huge computational complexity. Because it relies on DP-CAP to find the virtual surplus maximizing allocation, its running time is quadratic to N. This is not practically feasible because a typical publisher for daily deal auctions may have millions (even hundreds of millions) of user impressions every day. In this subsection, we propose a simple greedy mechanism $\mathcal{M}_2$ (see Algorithm 2), which is much more computationally efficient and has a revenue guarantee.

Algorithm 2 A $\frac{1}{4}$-Approximation Mechanism ($\mathcal{M}_2$)

Calculate bidders' virtual value. Remove those bidders with negative virtual values. Let $S = \{1, ..., t\}$ denote the remaining t bidders.

Sort bidders according to their virtual bidding values, w.l.o.g $\phi_1(b_1) \geq \phi_2(b_2) \geq ... \geq \phi_t(b_t)$.

Partition S into $\tilde{K}$ parts: $\{1, ..., t_1\}, \{t_1 + 1, ..., t_2\}, ..., \{t_{\tilde{K}-1} + 1, ..., t_{\tilde{K}}\}, \{t_{\tilde{K}} + 1, ..., t\}$ ($\tilde{K} < K$ if and only if $t_{\tilde{K}} = t$) as follows:

$$N_1 + u_{t_1} \geq u_1 + u_2 + ... + u_{t_1} > N_1$$
$$N_2 + u_{t_2} \geq u_{t_1+1} + u_{t_1+2} + ... + u_{t_2} > N_2$$
$$... \geq ... + ... + ... + ... > ...$$
$$N_{\tilde{K}} + u_{t_{\tilde{K}}} \geq u_{t_{\tilde{K}-1}+1} + u_{t_{\tilde{K}-1}+2} + ... + u_{t_{\tilde{K}}} > N_{\tilde{K}}$$

for each slot $i \leq \tilde{K}$ **do**

  With probability 1/2, each bidder $j \in \{t_{i-1}+1, ..., t_i - 1\}$ gets u_j effective impressions on slot i with payment computed according to Case 1 in Section 4.2.1 (here we set $t_0 = 0$).

  With probability 1/2, bidder t_i gets $\min(N_i, u_{t_i})$ effective impressions on slot i, with payment computed according to Cases 2 and 3 in Section 4.2.1.

end for

return $\{x_i, p_i\}_{i \in [M]}$.

4.2.1 *Payment Computation*

While the allocation rule is simple and clearly described in Algorithm 2, the payment rule is much more complicated. To compute the payments of all the winning bidders, we need to consider the following three cases.

Case 1: For bidder $j \in \{t_{i-1} + 1, ..., t_i - 1\}$, if j's expected allocation is non-zero, we calculate a set of critical bids $\{b_j(0), b_j(s), b_j(s+1), \cdots, b_j(\tilde{K})\}$ for him/her, where $s = \arg\min_k (N_k < u_j)$, $b_j(0)$ is the minimum bid for bidder j to win $\frac{u_j}{2}$ effective impressions in expectation when others' bids are fixed, and $b_j(k)$ is the minimum bid for him/her to win $\frac{N_k}{2}$ effective impressions in expectation when others' bids are fixed. It is easy to verify that $b_j(0) > b_j(s) > b_j(s+1) > \cdots > b_j(\tilde{K})$. $b_j(k)$ can be calculated by enumerating the bid from $\{\phi_j^{-1}(\phi_m(b_m))\}_{m=1}^t$ and finding the new slot that bidder j is allocated to. The complexity of calculating the set $b_j()$ for j is $O(M^2)$. Then the payment for bidder j is

$$p_j = b_j(0) \cdot u_j - (b_j(0) - b_j(s)) \cdot N_s - \sum_{l=s+1}^{\tilde{K}} (b_j(l-1) - b_j(l)) \cdot N_l.$$

Case 2: For bidder t_i, if t_i's expected allocation is non-zero and $\min(N_i, u_{t_i}) = u_{t_i}$, the payment can be computed in the same way as in the first case.

Case 3: For bidder t_i, if t_i's expected allocation is non-zero and $\min(N_i, u_{t_i}) = N_i$, we can compute the set of critical bids in the same way as in the first case, and then compute the payment as below.

$$p_{t_i} = b_{t_i}(i) \cdot N_i - \sum_{l=i+1}^{\tilde{K}} (b_{t_i}(l-1) - b_{t_i}(l)) \cdot N_l.$$

Since at most M bidders can win effective impressions and the complexity of payment computation for each bidder is $O(M^2)$, the complexity of $\mathcal{M}_2$ is $O(M^3)$, independent of the number of user impressions . In this regard, $\mathcal{M}_2$ is much more computationally efficient than $\mathcal{M}_1$, because the number of merchant (e.g., a typical daily deal website usually have hundreds of candidate deals at the same time.) is much smaller than that of the user impressions.

4.2.2 *Theoretical Analysis*

It is not difficult to verify that the allocation rule of $\mathcal{M}_2$ is monotone and the payment rule satisfies the condition in Lemma 1. As a consequence, $\mathcal{M}_2$ is Bayesian incentive compatible. Here we mainly investigate the competitive ratio of $\mathcal{M}_2$. We first prove two lemmas and then give the main theorem regarding the competitive ratio.

LEMMA 4. *Denote $OPT(\mathbf{N}, b)$ as the optimal virtual surplus for a bid profile b under the supply vector $\mathbf{N}$. For $\mathcal{M}_2$ we have*

$$\sum_{k=1}^{\tilde{K}} [\sum_{j=t_{k-1}+1}^{t_k - 1} \phi_j(b_j) \cdot u_j + \phi_{t_k}(b_{t_k}) \cdot N_k] \geq OPT(\mathbf{N}, b).$$

PROOF. Recall that the bidders are numbered according to the non-increasing order of their virtual values.

Let $\hat{x}$ be an allocation vector defined as below,

$$\hat{x} = (u_1, u_2, ..., u_{t_1 - 1}, N_1, u_{t_1+1}, ..., u_{t_2-1}, N_2, u_{t_2+1}, ..., u_{t_{\tilde{K}}-1}, N_{\tilde{K}}, 0, 0, ..., 0).$$

Note that $\hat{x}$ over allocates the effective impressions and therefore is not feasible. It will be used to upper bound the virtual surplus of the optimal allocation vector.

We use $\hat{x}_i$ to denote the i-th dimension of $\hat{x}$, i.e., the number of effective impressions allocated to bidder i in allocation vector $\hat{x}$.

Let x^* be the allocation profile given by the Bayesian optimal auction (i.e., mechanism $\mathcal{M}_1$). Let ϕ be the virtual value vector: $\phi = (\phi_1(b_1), ..., \phi_t(b_t))$. The left side of the inequality in the lemma therefore can be written as $\langle \phi, \hat{x} \rangle$, and the right side can be written as $\langle \phi, x^* \rangle$.[2] In addition, we use $\vec{1}$ to denote the t-dimensional identity vector.

First, we prove $\langle \vec{1}, \hat{x} \rangle \geq \langle \vec{1}, x^* \rangle$ by considering two possible cases with respect to $\tilde{K}$.

Case 1: $\tilde{K} < K$. In this case, we have $t_{\tilde{K}} = t$ and $\hat{x} = (u_1, u_2, ..., u_{t_1-1}, N_1, u_{t_1+1}, ..., u_{t_2-1}, N_2, u_{t_2+1}, ..., u_{t_{\tilde{K}}-1}, N_{\tilde{K}})$. It is clear $\forall i, u_i \geq x_i^*$. According to the majorization constraints, we have

$$\sum_{j=1}^{\tilde{K}} x_{t_j}^* \leq \sum_{j=1}^{\tilde{K}} x_{[j]}^* \leq \sum_{j=1}^{\tilde{K}} N_j.$$

Therefore we obtain $\langle \vec{1}, \hat{x} \rangle \geq \langle \vec{1}, x^* \rangle$.

Case 2: $\tilde{K} = K$. In this case, we have $\langle \vec{1}, \hat{x} \rangle \geq \sum_{j=1}^{K} N_K \geq \langle \vec{1}, x^* \rangle$.

---

[2]Here we use $\langle , \rangle$ to denote the inner product of two vectors.

Second, we prove $\langle \phi, \hat{x} \rangle \geq \langle \phi, x^* \rangle$. For ease of reference, we define $r_0 = \langle \phi, \hat{x} \rangle$. The basic idea of the proof is to construct another allocation vector x, which leads to a virtual surplus smaller than r_0 but larger than $\langle \phi, x^* \rangle$. We initialize $x = \hat{x}$, and then modify its elements one by one in the following steps.

(1) Considering $\min(N_1, u_1) \geq x_1^*$, in the first step, we decrease x_1 from $\hat{x}_1$ to x_1^* and increase x_2 from $\hat{x}_2$ to $\hat{x}_2 + \hat{x}_1 - x_1^*$. Define $r_1 = \phi \cdot x$. Then we have $r_1 \leq r_0$ because $\phi_1(b_1) \geq \phi_2(b_2)$. Now we show that after the update, $x_2 \geq x_2^*$:

- If $\hat{x}_2 = u_2$, we have $x_2 \geq \hat{x}_2 \geq x_2^*$.
- Otherwise, $\hat{x}_2 = N_p$. Considering the majorization constraints and $u_i \geq x_i^*$, we get

$$x_2 = N_p + \hat{x}_1 - x_1^* = \sum_{j=1}^{p} N_j + [\hat{x}_1 \neq N_1]u_1 - x_1^*$$
$$\geq x_1^* + x_2^* - x_1^* = x_2^*.$$

(2) In the i-th step ($i < t_{\tilde{K}}$), we have $x_i \geq x_i^*$. We increase x_{i+1} to $\hat{x}_{i+1} + x_i - x_i^*$ and decrease x_i to x_i^*. We define $r_i = \langle \phi, x \rangle$ and have $r_i \leq r_{i-1}$. Note that the allocation vector x has been updated and therefore r_i' s are different from each other. Similarly, we can verify that $x_{i+1} \geq x_{i+1}^*$.

By going through the above steps, we modify all the elements in x and obtain a sequence of r_i. Finally, we have the lemma proved as follows.

$$\langle \phi, \hat{x} \rangle = r_0 \geq r_{t_{\tilde{K}}-1}$$
$$= \sum_{j=1}^{t_{\tilde{K}}-1} \phi_j(b_j) \cdot x_j^* + \phi_{t_{\tilde{K}}}(b_{t_{\tilde{K}}}) \cdot (\langle \vec{1}, \hat{x} \rangle - \langle \vec{1}, x^* \rangle + \sum_{j=t_{\tilde{K}}}^{t} x_j^*)$$
$$\geq \sum_{j=1}^{t_{\tilde{K}}-1} \phi_j(b_j) \cdot x_j^* + \phi_{t_{\tilde{K}}}(b_{t_{\tilde{K}}}) \cdot (\sum_{j=t_{\tilde{K}}}^{t} x_j^*)$$
$$\geq \sum_{j=1}^{t} \phi_j(b_j) \cdot x_j^* = \langle \phi, x^* \rangle$$

Note that the second inequality holds because $\langle \vec{1}, \hat{x} \rangle \geq \langle \vec{1}, x^* \rangle$, and the third inequality holds because bidders are numbered in the descending order of their virtual values. ☐

LEMMA 5. *For $\mathcal{M}_2$, we have*

$$\sum_{k=1}^{\tilde{K}} [\sum_{j=t_{k-1}+1}^{t_k-1} \phi_j(b_j) \cdot u_j + \phi_{t_k}(b_{t_k}) \cdot \min(u_{t_k}, N_k)]$$
$$\geq \frac{1}{2} \{\sum_{k=1}^{\tilde{K}} [\sum_{j=t_{k-1}+1}^{t_k-1} \phi_j(b_j) \cdot u_j + \phi_{t_k}(b_{t_k}) \cdot N_k]\}.$$

PROOF. For ease of references, we define the following notations for each $k \leq \tilde{K}$,

$$\alpha_k = \phi_{t_k}(b_{t_k}) \cdot \min(u_{t_k}, N_k)$$
$$\beta_k = \sum_{j=t_{k-1}+1}^{t_k-1} \phi_j(b_j) \cdot u_j$$
$$\eta_k = \phi_{t_k}(b_{t_k}) \cdot N_k$$

Since $\sum_{j=t_{k-1}+1}^{t_k-1} u_j + \min(u_{t_k}, N_k) \geq N_k$ and for all $j \in \{t_{k-1}+1, ..., t_k\}$, $\phi_j(b_j) \geq \phi_{t_k}(b_{t_k})$, we have $\alpha_k + \beta_k \geq \eta_k$. It is clear $\alpha_k + \beta_k \geq \alpha_k$ due to the non-negativity of β_k.

Thus we have $(\alpha_k + \beta_k) \geq \frac{1}{2}(\alpha_k + \eta_k)$. By summing over k, we have the lemma proved. ☐

THEOREM 6. *When the value of bidder i follows a known regular distribution F_i, and $\forall i, l_i \leq N_K$, $\mathcal{M}_2$ achieves a competitive ration of at least $\frac{1}{4}$.*

PROOF. The expected allocation profile of $\mathcal{M}_2$ is

$$\hat{x}' = (\frac{u_1}{2}, ..., \frac{\min(u_{t_1}, N_1)}{2}, ..., \frac{\min(u_{t_{\tilde{K}}}, N_{\tilde{K}})}{2}, 0, ..., 0).$$

According to Lemma 4 and 5, we have that the virtual surplus $\langle \phi, \hat{x}' \rangle \geq \frac{1}{4} OPT(\mathbf{N}, b)$. Then the theorem is proven by taking expectation over the valuation/bid profile. ☐

REMARK 7. *The assumption, $l_i \leq N_K, \forall i$, means that the minimum demand of a merchant can be satisfied by displaying her deal to all the web users at the K-th slot. This assumption is reasonable since common merchants will not set the minimum demands too high so as not be rejected by the publisher.*

5. PRIOR-INDEPENDENT SETTING

In this section, we focus on the prior-independent setting, in which the valuations of all the bidders are i.i.d. drawn from an unknown distribution F. We assume that the number of bidders is sufficiently large so that the empirical distribution F' estimated from their bids (given that they make truthful bidding) can approximate the real distribution F very well.

5.1 Two Mechanisms

Based on $\mathcal{M}_1$, we can easily obtain a new mechanism $\mathcal{M}_3$ with a competitive ratio of $\frac{\beta-1}{\beta}$ (here $\beta > 1$ is an input parameter) for the prior-independent setting.

The new mechanism $\mathcal{M}_3$ consists of three steps. (1) Partition bids b at random into two sets: for each bid, with probability $\frac{1}{\beta}$ put it in set b' and otherwise b''. (2) Calculate the empirical distribution F' using the bid set b'. (3) Run $\mathcal{M}_1$ with all the effective impressions, distribution F' and bid set b''.

The estimation of the empirical distribution F' in $\mathcal{M}_3$ is independent of b'', the bids of the bidders included in the auction. Therefore, given $\mathcal{M}_1$ is Bayesian incentive compatible, $\mathcal{M}_3$ is also Bayesian incentive compatible. Furthermore, it is not difficult to prove Theorem 8 about the competitive ratio of the mechanism. We omit the proof here because of space limitations.

THEOREM 8. *If the valuations of the bidders are independently drawn from a regular distribution F and $\frac{M}{\beta}$ is statistically large enough, $\mathcal{M}_3$ achieves the competitive ratio of $\frac{\beta-1}{\beta}$.*

Similar to the case in the Bayesian setting, although $\mathcal{M}_3$ has a good competitive ratio, it suffers from the computational inefficiency in practice. Here we design a simple greedy mechanism $\mathcal{M}_4$ which can achieve a much lower computational complexity, by leveraging $\mathcal{M}_2$ as a building block.

$\mathcal{M}_4$ is very similar to $\mathcal{M}_3$. It also consists of three steps. The only difference between $\mathcal{M}_3$ and $\mathcal{M}_4$ is that we run $\mathcal{M}_2$ instead of $\mathcal{M}_1$ in the third step of $\mathcal{M}_4$.

It is easy to verify that $\mathcal{M}_4$ is also Bayesian incentive compatible, and to obtain the following theorem about the competitive ratio of $\mathcal{M}_4$. The detailed proof is omitted due to its simplicity.

THEOREM 9. *If the valuations of the bidders are independently drawn from a regular distribution F, $\frac{M}{\beta}$ is statistically large enough, and $\forall i, l_i \leq N_K$, $\mathcal{M}_4$ achieves a competitive ratio $\frac{\beta-1}{4\beta}$.*

5.2 Robust Approximation Mechanisms

In this subsection, we discuss a seemingly unobvious but practically important issue regarding mechanisms $\mathcal{M}_3$ and $\mathcal{M}_4$. That is, both mechanisms rely on random partition of the bidders, and thus might not be very robust in the following sense: although their competitive ratios are guaranteed in expectation, the revenue of the worst-case instantiation of the mechanism can be arbitrarily low as compared with the optimal revenue. For example, suppose $\beta = 2$, $K = 1$, $N_1 = 1000000$, $M = 200$, and every bidder's value is 1 with probability 1. Let us consider a specific partition b' and b'': $l_i = 10000, u_i = 20000$ for the 100 bidders in b' and $l_i = u_i = 1$ for the 100 bidders in b''. For such a partition, the revenue achieved by $\mathcal{M}_3$ is 100 while the Bayesian optimal revenue is 1000000, which corresponds to a very low competitive ratio.

To be formal, we introduce a concept called *robust ratio* to evaluate the worst-case performance of a mechanism, as defined below.

DEFINITION 10. *Let $OPT(F)$ denotes the optimal expected revenue of an incentive compatible mechanism under distribution F. Let σ be a random instance of the mechanism $\mathcal{A}$, and $Rev_\sigma(\mathcal{M}, F)$ be the expected revenue*[3] *of the random instance σ of $\mathcal{M}$ under distribution F. Then the robust ratio of a mechanism $\mathcal{M}$ is defined as $\inf_{\sigma,F} \frac{Rev_\sigma(\mathcal{M},F)}{OPT(F)}$.*

Note that the robust ratio ranges in $[0, 1]$, and the robust ratio of a mechanism is no larger than its competitive ratio.

To make mechanisms $\mathcal{M}_3$ and $\mathcal{M}_4$ robust (i.e., with a bounded robust ratio), we propose a technique called *supply partition*, i.e., partitioning the impressions. Due to space restrictions, we just take the modification to $\mathcal{M}_3$ as an example and present a new mechanism $\mathcal{M}_5$ as below.

Algorithm 3 A Robust Approximation Mechanism ($\mathcal{M}_5$)

```
Partition bids b at random into two sub sets: for each
    bid, with probability 1/2 put it in b' and otherwise b''.
Calculate an empirical distribution F' using the bid set
    b' and an empirical distribution F'' using the bid set b''.
for each slot i do
    If i is odd, offering the first N/2 impressions to set b'
    and the second N/2 impressions to set b''.
    If i is even, offering the first N/2 impressions to set
    b'' and the second N/2 impressions to set b'.
end for
Construct a new supply vector N' =
    ((N_1+N_2)/2, (N_3+N_4)/2, ..., (N_{⌈K/2⌉*2-1}+N_{⌈K/2⌉*2})/2, 0, ..., 0).
Run M_1 with the new supply vector N', distribution
    F'' and bid set b'. Run M_1 with the new supply vector
    N', distribution F' and bid set b''.
```

Note in $\mathcal{M}_5$, though the number of impressions allocated to bidders in slot i is $N/2$, the actual effective impressions is $N_i/2$ because of different conversion rate for each slot. It is easy to see that $\mathcal{M}_5$ is Bayesian incentive compatible. The following theorem shows that it has guarantee on both competitive ratio and robust ratio.

[3]Note that for "expected revenue", the expectation is taken over the randomness of bidders' valuations but not over the random instances of the mechanism.

THEOREM 11. *If bidders' valuations are independently drawn from a regular distribution F, the number of bidders is statistically large enough, and $l_i \le \frac{N_1+N_2}{2}, \forall i$, $\mathcal{M}_5$ achieves a competitive ratio of $\frac{3}{7}$ and a robust ratio of $\frac{1}{4}$.*

PROOF. To ease the proof, we give some notations first. Given the value profile v and the majorization constraint vector $\mathbf{N} = (N_1, N_2, ..., N_K)$, we denote $(x_1^*, ..., x_M^*)$ as the optimal allocation vector and $OPT(\mathbf{N}, b) = \sum_{i\in[M]} \phi_i \cdot x_i^*$ as the optimal virtual surplus[4] generated from the bidder set b when the constraint vector $\mathbf{N}$ is imposed and when F is known.

First, we prove the robust ratio of the mechanism.

For any partition (A, B) of the M bidders, we denote $OPT_A(\mathbf{N}, b) = \sum_{i\in A} \phi_i \cdot x_i^*$ and $OPT_B(\mathbf{N}, b) = \sum_{i\in B} \phi_i \cdot x_i^*$.

Let $OPT(\mathbf{N}', C)$ be the optimal virtual surplus generated from the bidder set C and the majorization constraint vector N', where C can be either A or B. As long as we can construct a feasible allocation under N' and C , whose virtual surplus is a constant approximation to $OPT_C(\mathbf{N}, b)$, we can say that $OPT(\mathbf{N}', C)$ is also a constant approximation to $OPT_C(\mathbf{N}, b)$.

We re-number the bidders in C according to the descending order of their allocated numbers of impressions: $x_1^* \ge x_2^* \ge ... \ge x_{|C|}^*$, where $|C|$ is the number of bidders in C. We focus on bidder 1 and consider the following two cases.

Case 1: If $\phi_1 x_1^* \ge \frac{N_1}{2\cdot N_1+N_2} \cdot OPT_C(\mathbf{N}, b)$, we allocate $\min(x_1^*, \frac{N_1+N_2}{2})$ effective impressions to bidder 1 under the constraint $\mathbf{N}'$, and the virtual surplus of this allocation is:

$$\phi_1 \cdot \min(x_1^*, \frac{N_1+N_2}{2}) = \frac{\min(x_1^*, \frac{N_1+N_2}{2})}{x_1^*} \cdot \phi_1 \cdot x_1^*$$
$$\ge \frac{N_1+N_2}{2N_1} \cdot \frac{N_1}{2\cdot N_1 + N_2} \cdot OPT_C(\mathbf{N}, b)$$
$$= \frac{1}{2} \cdot \frac{N_1+N_2}{2\cdot N_1+N_2} \cdot OPT_C(\mathbf{N}, b)$$

Case 2: If $\phi_1 x_1^* < \frac{N_1}{2\cdot N_1+N_2} \cdot OPT_C(\mathbf{N}, b)$, under $\mathbf{N}'$, for each pair of bidders $(2i, 2i+1)$, $i \in \{1, ..., \lfloor |C|/2 \rfloor\}$, if $\phi_{2i} \cdot x_{2i}^* \ge \phi_{2i+1} \cdot x_{2i+1}^*$, we allocate x_{2i}^* effective impressions to bidder $2i$; otherwise, we allocate x_{2i+1}^* effective impressions to bidder $2i+1$. Since $\{x_i^*\}$ are sorted and satisfy the majorization constraint vector $\mathbf{N}$, it is easy to see that for all $i \in \{1, ..., \lfloor K/2 \rfloor\}$,

$$\sum_{j=1}^{i} max(x_{2j}^*, x_{2j+1}^*) = \sum_{j=1}^{i} x_{2j}^* \le \sum_{j=1}^{i} \frac{N_{2j-1}+N_{2j}}{2},$$

$$\sum_{j=1}^{\lfloor |C|/2 \rfloor} max(x_{2j}^*, x_{2j+1}^*) \le \sum_{j=1}^{\lfloor |C|/2 \rfloor} x_{2j}^* \le \sum_{j=1}^{\lceil K/2 \rceil} \frac{N_{2j-1}+N_{2j}}{2}.$$

Therefore the allocation is feasible under $\mathbf{N}'$. Furthermore, we can lower bound the virtual surplus VS of this allocation:

$$VS \ge \frac{1}{2}\sum_{j=2}^{|C|} \phi_j x_j^* \ge \frac{1}{2} \cdot \frac{N_1+N_2}{2\cdot N_1+N_2} \cdot OPT_C(\mathbf{N}, b).$$

By jointly considering the two cases, for any partition (A, B) of the bidders, we can bound the total virtual surplus

[4]We can run the Bayesian optimal auction (i.e. $\mathcal{M}_1$) to get the optimal allocation vector and the optimal virtual surplus.

of $\mathcal{M}_5$ as follows,

$$Rev_{(A,B)}(\mathcal{M}_5) \geq OPT(\mathbf{N}', A) + OPT(\mathbf{N}', B)$$
$$\geq \frac{1}{2} \cdot \frac{N_1 + N_2}{2 \cdot N_1 + N_2} \cdot (OPT_A(\mathbf{N}, b) + OPT_B(\mathbf{N}, b))$$
$$= \frac{1}{2} \cdot \frac{N_1 + N_2}{2 \cdot N_1 + N_2} \cdot OPT(\mathbf{N}, b) \geq \frac{1}{4} \cdot OPT(\mathbf{N}, b).$$

By taking expectation of the leftmost side and the rightmost side of the above inequality over the distribution of bidders' valuations, we complete the proof of the robust ratio.

Second, we prove the competitive ratio of the mechanism. For this purpose, we re-number the bidders as $x_1^* \geq x_2^* \geq \ldots \geq x_M^*$. Denote $\alpha = \frac{\phi_1 x_1^*}{OPT(\mathbf{N},b)}$. Recall that $OPT(\mathbf{N}', A) + OPT(\mathbf{N}', B)$, the virtual surplus generated by the mechanism, is the optimal virtual surplus under partition (A, B) and the majorization constraint $\mathbf{N}'$. Given $\mathbf{N}'$ and (A, B), the virtual surplus of any feasible allocation lower bounds the virtual surplus of the mechanism. The basic idea of our proof is that we construct two feasible allocations, both of which can lower bound the virtual surplus of the mechanism, and show that the maximum of the two lower bounds is a constant approximation of $OPT(\mathbf{N}, b)$.

Allocation 1: No matter bidder 1 is partitioned to set A or B, we allocate $\min(x_1^*, \frac{N_1+N_2}{2})$ effective impressions to him/her. We then pair every adjacent two remaining bidders: $(2i, 2i+1)$, $i \in \{1, \ldots, \lfloor M/2 \rfloor\}$ and make allocation for each pair depending on which set the two bidders are partitioned into:

(1) With probability 1/4, bidder 1 and $2i$ are partitioned in the same set and bidder $2i+1$ is in the other set. For this case, we allocate x_{2i+1}^* effective impressions to bidder $2i+1$.

(2) With probability 1/4, bidder 1 and $2i+1$ are in the same set and bidder $2i$ is in the other set. For this case, we allocate x_{2i}^* effective impressions to bidder $2i$.

(3) With probability 1/4, bidder $2i$ and $2i+1$ are in the same set and bidder 1 is in the other set. For this case, if $\phi_{2i} \cdot x_{2i}^* > \phi_{2i+1} \cdot x_{2i+1}^*$, we allocate x_{2i}^* effective impressions to bidder $2i$; otherwise, we allocate x_{2i+1}^* effective impressions to bidder $2i+1$.

(4) With probability 1/4, bidder 1, $2i$ and $2i+1$ are partitioned into the same set. For this case, we do not allocate any impression to bidders $2i$ and $2i+1$.

In expectation, the virtual surplus (denoted as $VS(2i, 2i+1)$) generated from the pair $(2i, 2i+1)$ can be lower bounded as below.

$$VS(2i, 2i+1) \geq \frac{1}{4} \cdot \{\phi_{2i} \cdot x_{2i}^* + \phi_{2i+1} \cdot x_{2i+1}^*$$
$$+ \frac{1}{2}(\phi_{2i} \cdot x_{2i}^* + \phi_{2i+1} \cdot x_{2i+1}^*)\} = \frac{3}{8} \cdot (\phi_{2i} \cdot x_{2i}^* + \phi_{2i+1} \cdot x_{2i+1}^*)$$

For the set in which bidder 1 is partitioned to, since we only allocate impressions to bidder 1 and $l_1 \leq \frac{N_1+N_2}{2}$, the allocation is definitely feasible. In the other set, since for all i:

$$\sum\nolimits_{j=1}^{i} x_{2j}^* \leq \frac{1}{2} \sum\nolimits_{j=1}^{2i} x_j^* \leq \frac{1}{2} \sum\nolimits_{j=1}^{2i} N_j,$$
$$\sum\nolimits_{j=1}^{\lfloor M/2 \rfloor} x_{2j}^* \leq \frac{1}{2} \sum\nolimits_{j=1}^{M} x_j^* \leq \frac{1}{2} \sum\nolimits_{j=1}^{K} N_j,$$

the allocation is also feasible with respect to N'. The virtual surplus VS_1 of this allocation can be lower bounded as:

$$VS_1 = [\min(x_1^*, \frac{N_1 + N_2}{2})\phi_1 + \sum_{i=1}^{\lfloor M/2 \rfloor} VS(2i, 2i+1)$$
$$\geq [\frac{\min(x_1^*, \frac{N_1+N_2}{2})}{x_1^*}\alpha + \frac{3}{8}(1-\alpha)] \cdot \Phi^*$$
$$\geq [\frac{N_1 + N_2}{2N_1}\alpha + \frac{3}{8}(1-\alpha)] \cdot OPT(\mathbf{N}, b).$$

Allocation 2: We ignore bidder 1 and consider each pair of bidders $(2i, 2i+1)$, $i \in \{1, \ldots, \lfloor M/2 \rfloor\}$.

(1) With probability 1/2, two bidders in the same pair are located in the same set. If $\phi_{2i} \cdot x_{2i}^* \geq \phi_{2i+1} \cdot x_{2i+1}^*$, we allocate x_{2i}^* effective impressions to bidder $2i$; otherwise, we allocate x_{2i+1}^* effective impressions to bidder $2i+1$.

(2) With probability 1/2, two bidders in the same pair are in different sets. We allocate x_{2i}^* effective impressions to bidder $2i$ and x_{2i+1}^* effective impressions to bidder $2i+1$.

The above allocation still satisfies the majorization constraint $\mathbf{N}'$. The virtual surplus VS_2 of this allocation can be lower bounded as below.

$$VS_2 \geq \frac{1}{2} \cdot (1-\alpha) \cdot OPT(\mathbf{N}, b) + \frac{1}{2} \cdot \frac{1}{2} \cdot (1-\alpha) \cdot OPT(\mathbf{N}, b)$$
$$= \frac{3}{4} \cdot (1-\alpha) \cdot OPT(\mathbf{N}, b)$$

Denote $h(\alpha) = \max\{\frac{N_1+N_2}{2N_1}\alpha + \frac{3}{8}(1-\alpha), \frac{3}{4} \cdot (1-\alpha)\}$. It is easy to see that $\frac{3}{4} \cdot (1-\alpha)$ is a decreasing function of α. Since $\frac{N_1+N_2}{2N_1} > \frac{3}{8}$, $\frac{N_1+N_2}{2N_1}\alpha + \frac{3}{8}(1-\alpha)$ is an increasing function of α. Therefore $h(\alpha)$ achieves its minimal value when the two terms are equal, i.e., $\frac{N_1+N_2}{2N_1}\alpha + \frac{3}{8}(1-\alpha) = \frac{3}{4} \cdot (1-\alpha)$. Thus, we get

$$h(\alpha) \geq \frac{3(N_1 + N_2)}{4(N_1 + N_2) + 3N_1} = \frac{3}{7}.$$

That is, for any given bid/valuation profile b, the revenue of the mechanism averaged over the random partitions is lower bounded by $\frac{3}{7}OPT(\mathbf{N}, b)$. By further taking expectation over the value profile, we complete the proof of the competitive ratio. □

6. FUTURE WORK

As for future work, we plan to investigate the following aspects. First, we may prove the upper bound of competitive ratio for any polynomial mechanism in our model, thus to show our mechanisms are nearly the best that can do, or we may build other elegant mechanisms with better competitive ratio. Second, our approach for approximation mechanism may have significance on its own, we may find other interesting applications for our general analysis scheme. Third, we have assumed that the number of bidders is statistically large enough to get an accurate estimation of the distribution of bidders' valuations for the prior-independent setting. We will quantify how the number of bidders affect the revenue of the designed mechanisms. Finally, we have only considered offline auctions in this work, where the effective impressions in a future time period is known when the auction is executed. A more practical setting is online auctions.

REFERENCES

[1] G. Aggarwal, A. Goel, and R. Motwani. Truthful auctions for pricing search keywords. In *Proceedings of the 7th ACM conference on Electronic commerce*, pages 1–7. ACM, 2006.

[2] G. Aggarwal and J. D. Hartline. Knapsack auctions. In *Proceedings of the seventeenth annual ACM-SIAM symposium on Discrete algorithm*, pages 1083–1092. ACM, 2006.

[3] N. Alon, F. Fischer, A. D. Procaccia, and M. Tennenholtz. Sum of us: Truthful self-selection. In *TARK*.

[4] A. Archer, C. Papadimitriou, K. Talwar, and É. Tardos. An approximate truthful mechanism for combinatorial auctions with single parameter agents. *Internet Mathematics*, 1(2):129–150, 2004.

[5] A. Archer and É. Tardos. Truthful mechanisms for one-parameter agents. In *Foundations of Computer Science, 2001. Proceedings. 42nd IEEE Symposium on*, pages 482–491. IEEE, 2001.

[6] J. Byers, M. Mitzenmacher, and G. Zervas. Daily deals: Prediction, social diffusion, and reputational ramifications. In *Proceedings of the fifth ACM international conference on Web search and data mining*, pages 543–552. ACM, 2012.

[7] J. Byers, M. Mitzenmacher, and G. Zervas. The groupon effect on yelp ratings: a root cause analysis. In *Proceedings of the 13th ACM Conference on Electronic Commerce*, pages 248–265. ACM, 2012.

[8] Y. Cai, M. Mahdian, A. Mehta, and B. Waggoner. Designing markets for daily deals. In *Web and Internet Economics*, pages 82–95. Springer, 2013.

[9] G. B. Dantzig. Discrete-variable extremum problems. *Operations Research*, 5(2):266–288, 1957.

[10] B. C. Dean, M. X. Goemans, and J. Vondrdk. Approximating the stochastic knapsack problem: The benefit of adaptivity. In *Foundations of Computer Science, 2004. Proceedings. 45th Annual IEEE Symposium on*, pages 208–217. IEEE, 2004.

[11] U. Dholakia. What makes groupon promotions profitable for businesses? *Available at SSRN 1790414*, 2011.

[12] B. Edelman, S. Jaffe, and S. Kominers. To groupon or not to groupon: The profitability of deep discounts. *Harvard Business School NOM Unit Working Paper*, (11-063), 2011.

[13] B. Edelman, M. Ostrovsky, and M. Schwarz. Internet advertising and the generalized second price auction: Selling billions of dollars worth of keywords. Technical report, National Bureau of Economic Research, 2005.

[14] A. V. Goldberg, J. D. Hartline, A. R. Karlin, M. Saks, and A. Wright. Competitive auctions. *Games and Economic Behavior*, 55(2):242–269, 2006.

[15] A. V. Goldberg, J. D. Hartline, and A. Wright. Competitive auctions and digital goods. In *Proceedings of the twelfth annual ACM-SIAM symposium on Discrete algorithms*, pages 735–744. Society for Industrial and Applied Mathematics, 2001.

[16] R. Gonen and D. Lehmann. Optimal solutions for multi-unit combinatorial auctions: Branch and bound heuristics. In *Proceedings of the 2nd ACM conference on Electronic commerce*, pages 13–20. ACM, 2000.

[17] T. Groves. Incentives in teams. *Econometrica: Journal of the Econometric Society*, pages 617–631, 1973.

[18] J. D. Hartline. Approximation in economic design. *Lecture Notes*, 2012.

[19] W. Kong, J. Li, T.-Y. Liu, and T. Qin. Optimal allocation for chunked-reward advertising. In *Web and Internet Economics*, pages 291–304. Springer, 2013.

[20] W. Kong, J. Li, T. Qin, and T.-Y. Liu. Revenue optimization for group-buying websites. *arXiv preprint arXiv:1305.5946*, 2013.

[21] Y. Lvovskaya, S. Tan, and C. Zhong. *Online Discount Coupon Promotions & Repurchasing Behaviors: The Groupon Case*. PhD thesis, Mälardalen University, 2012.

[22] E. Maskin, J. Riley, and F. Hahn. Optimal multi-unit auctions. *The economics of missing markets, information, and games*, 1989.

[23] P. R. Milgrom and R. J. Weber. A theory of auctions and competitive bidding. *Econometrica: Journal of the Econometric Society*, pages 1089–1122, 1982.

[24] R. B. Myerson. Optimal auction design. *Mathematics of operations research*, 6(1):58–73, 1981.

[25] T. Roughgarden. Cs364a: Algorithmic game theory lecture# 4: Algorithmic mechanism design. 2013.

[26] M. Song, E. Park, B. Yoo, and S. Jeon. Is the daily deal social shopping?: An empirical analysis of purchase and redemption time of daily-deal coupons. *Working paper*, 2012.

[27] D. Zhao, W. Chen, and Q. Ye. Consumer purchase behavior under price promotion: Evidence from groupon daily deals. In *SIGBPS Workshop on Business Processes and Services (BPS'12)*, page 141, 2012.

Selling Tomorrow's Bargains Today

Melika Abolhassani
University of Maryland
College Park, MD, USA
melika@cs.umd.edu

Hossein Esfandiari
University of Maryland
College Park, MD, USA
hossein@cs.umd.edu

MohammadTaghi Hajiaghayi
University of Maryland
College Park, MD, USA
hajiagha@cs.umd.edu

Hamid Mahini
University of Maryland
College Park, MD, USA
hmahini@cs.umd.edu

David Malec
University of Maryland
College Park, MD, USA
dmalec@umiacs.umd.edu

Aravind Srinivasan
University of Maryland
College Park, MD, USA
srin@cs.umd.edu

ABSTRACT

Consider a good (such as a hotel room) which, if not sold on time, is worth nothing to the seller. For a customer who is considering a choice of such goods, their prices may change dramatically by the time the customer needs to use the good; thus a customer who is aware of this fact might choose to gamble, delaying buying until the last moment in the hopes of better prices. While this gamble can yield large savings, it also carries much risk. However, a coordinator can offer customers a compromise between these extremes and benefits in aggregate. Here we explore how a coordinator might profit from forecasts of such future price fluctuations. Our results can be used in a general setting where customers buy products or services in advance and where market prices may significantly change in the future.

We model this as a two-stage optimization problem, where the coordinator first agrees to serve some buyers, and then later executes all agreements once the final values have been revealed. Agreements with buyers consist of a set of acceptable options and a price where the details of agreements are proposed by the buyer. We investigate both the profit maximization and loss minimization problems in this setting. For the profit maximization problem, we show that the profit objective function is a non-negative submodular function, and thus we can approximate its optimal solution within an approximation factor of 0.5 in polynomial time. For the loss minimization problem, we first leverage a sampling technique to formulate our problem as an integer program. We show that there is no polynomial algorithm to solve this problem optimally, unless $P = NP$. In addition, we show that the corresponding integer program has a high integrality gap and it cannot lead us to an approximation algorithm via a linear-programming relaxation. Nevertheless, we propose a bicriteria-style approximation that gives a constant-factor approximation to the minimal loss by allowing a fraction of our options to overlap. Importantly, however, we show that our algorithm provides a strong, uniform bound on the amount the overlap per options. We propose our algorithm by rounding the optimal solution of the relaxed linear program via a novel dependent-rounding method.

Appears in: *Proceedings of the 14th International Conference on Autonomous Agents and Multiagent Systems (AAMAS 2015), Bordini, Elkind, Weiss, Yolum (eds.), May 4–8, 2015, Istanbul, Turkey.*

Categories and Subject Descriptors

F.2.2 [**Theory of Computation**]: Analysis of Algorithms and Problem Complexity—*Nonnumerical Algorithms and Problems*

General Terms

Algorithms

Keywords

two-stage optimization; matching; efficient algorithm

1. INTRODUCTION

Let us start with an example of a basic source of uncertainty in E-commerce. Google offers high-quality free services for retaining Internet users and makes over 96% of its revenue from advertisers by selling users' attention to them. For this purpose, Google provides its AdWords system, an online auction-based advertising system, that lets advertisers bid on keywords for showing their ads in Google's search results. Advertisers can participate in Google's on-line AdWords auction and bid on their keywords. However, the cost-per-click (CPC) amount that an advertiser should pay when users click on its ads depends heavily on the online demand and competitors' bids, and thus a (near-)optimal bidding strategy is not clear to advertisers at bidding time. This unknown behavior of prices may force advertisers to take too much risk at bidding time. Many risk-averse advertisers prefer to avoid such risk, and attempt to sign a contract which guarantees an appropriate number of clicks for a fixed price.

This phenomenon arises more generally due to uncertainty such as uncertain future demand, uncertainty in future costs, and uncertain competitors' behavior. While we started with an application in the online advertising industry, we continue with another example of this phenomenon in the hotel-reservation industry.[1] Consider a family that decides, on Monday, that they would like to go on vacation the following weekend. Perhaps they do some research, and find a convenient location that seems both pleasant and affordable. All that is left for them to do is actually reserve their accommodations. But this involves an interesting dilemma: should they book a room now, or wait until late in the week? Booking now assures them a place to stay that is affordable. On the other hand, many hotels offer last-minute deals, which could save the potential vacationers money if they decide to wait. Unfortunately, the latter

[1]A company in the hotel reservation market has based their business strategy around this phenomenon [13].

carries not only the chance for large savings, but the risk that prices will go up, perhaps even to the point where the vacation becomes impossible.

In this work, we study how a company might profit by offering customers a compromise between these options. While dealing with online prices typically carries too much risk and requires significant effort to appeal to individual customers, a coordinator has the advantage of spreading these risks across many contracts. By expending the effort to collect pricing data and form estimates of future prices, a company could reasonably hope to monetize this advantage by offering customers a reliable contract with an affordable price, while executing the contract when prices are as favorable as possible – while not every contract may be profitable, good price estimates should provide a profit in aggregate.

In fact, this opportunity arises more generally – the key relevant aspects of our examples are uncertain future prices. Thus, one could hope to exploit this sort of future arbitrage when selling stock options, airline tickets, rental cars, event tickets, or any product/service that typically faces price fluctuations. Our goal in this work is to answer this question: given estimates of future prices, what is the best way for an enterprising coordinator to offer contract to buyers?

Two-stage optimization.

We have a coordinator who can provide options from a set H, and who will have a chance to offer these options to a set of potential buyers B. This process, however, takes places in stages: in the first stage, the coordinator negotiates agreements; in the second stage, the prices will be realized, and the coordinator must serve options in the realized *scenario* to fulfill all of the previously made agreements. Each agreement with a buyer $b \in B$ specifies a *pack* $P \subseteq H$ of options that are acceptable to the buyer, and a *value* v_b the buyer must pay. The coordinator may satisfy the agreement by getting any option in the pack to the buyer, and it does not matter which one. The two-stage nature of our problem arises because the coordinator must make binding decisions about what agreements to make *before* the prices are revealed.

First stage: agreements.

The first stage of our optimization problem models the formation of agreements. In our model, all of the buyers arrive at once, and each proposes a pack of options and a price. The value v_b associated with each buyer is the price they propose, and the coordinator may accept a subset of offers[2]. Note that agreements are only formed when an offer is made and the coordinator accepts; therefore, we refer to the set S of buyers the coordinator chooses to form agreements with as the *served set*.

Second stage: execution.

In the second stage, the coordinator must match each buyer $b \in S$ to an option in their associated pack. At this point, the prices are revealed, and the coordinator's problem becomes one of maximum-weight matching. We call the collection of revealed prices a *scenario*, and denote it by I; we denote the full set of possible scenarios by $\mathcal{I}$. We denote the price of option h in scenario I by c_h^I. The I seen in the second stage is drawn according to a probability distribution, and the coordinator has the ability to sample from this distribution.

Objectives.

The coordinator's objective is to maximize *profit*. We denote the profit from a served set S as

$$P(S) = \sum_{b \in S} v_b + \mathrm{E}[\sum_{h \notin \mathcal{M}^I(S)} c_h^I],$$

where $\mathcal{M}^I(S)$ is the cheapest set of options that buyers in S can be matched to in scenario I, and the expectation is over which I occurs. The first term is the profit that is extracted from agreements in S, e.g., set of contracts in the Google advertising example. The second term is the profit that is made by selling the remaining options in the future, e.g., selling through online Google AdWords system.

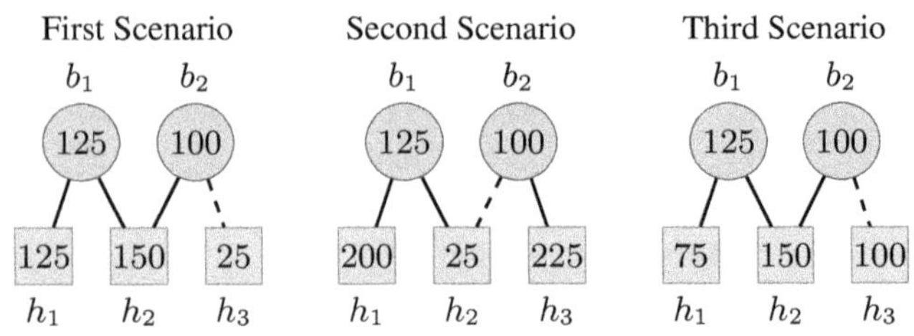

Figure 1: Each graph corresponds to one scenario. The upper vertices show the buyers and the price they are willing to pay. The lower vertices show the options and their realized values in each scenario. The edges indicate the buyers' interest in options. In this example, the best decision is to choose b_2, for which our best matches are shown with dashes.

EXAMPLE 1.1. *In this example, there are two buyers b_1 and b_2, three options h_1, h_2, and h_3, and three possible future scenarios. Each scenario can be represented by a vector of 3 elements indicating the realized values of the three options. Assume the future scenarios are $I_1 = \{125, 250, 25\}$, $I_2 = \{200, 25, 225\}$, and $I_3 = \{75, 150, 100\}$, and they happen with probabilities 0.4, 0.3, and 0.3, respectively. The first buyer is willing to pay a price equal to 125 dollars for being served, while the second buyer will pay 100 dollars. Figure 1 illustrates this example.*

In this case, if we only serve b_1, the best matches to this buyer in future scenarios I_1, I_2, and I_3 are h_1, h_2, and h_1 dollars, respectively. Therefore, our expected profit from choosing only b_1 to serve would be $125 + (0.4(150 + 25) + 0.3(200 + 225) + 0.3(150 + 100)) = 397.5$ dollars. On the other hand, if we only choose b_2, our expected profit would be $100 + (0.4(125 + 150) + 0.3(200 + 225) + 0.3(75 + 150)) = 405$ dollars. Finally, if we choose both buyers to serve, we may no longer be able to serve each buyer with their cheapest feasible option. In the first scenario, the best options for b_1 and b_2 would be h_1 and h_3, respectively, and the remaining value is 150 dollars. Similarly, the remaining values would be 225 and 150 dollars when serve both buyers in the second and third scenarios, respectively. Therefore, the expected total profit from serving both customers would be $125 + 100 + (0.4 \times 150 + 0.3 \times 225 + 0.3 \times 150) = 397.5$ dollars. Thus, our best option is to only serve b_2 for a total profit of 405 dollars, even though her offered price is less than the price b_1 is willing to pay us.

In some applications such as in the hotel-reservation industry, the value c_h^I can be interpreted as the cost of providing option h in scenario I. In these situations, we study the loss minimization problem rather than the profit maximization version. Therefore, we also consider a modified objective that we call *loss*, which has the form

$$L(S) = \sum_{b \in B \setminus S} v_b + \mathrm{E}[\sum_{h \in \mathcal{M}^I(S)} c_h^I].$$

[2]We may use "price" interchangeably with "value" herein.

Note that $L(S)$ is an affine transformation of $P(S)$. Intuitively, the loss objective tries to capture the idea of lost revenue, where we can lose revenue either by choosing not to serve a buyer, or by having to spend to pay for an option.

1.1 Our results

Since buyers may specify any pack of options they like, the marginal value of serving a particular customer becomes hard to quantify – they may conflict with other buyers in complex and arbitrary ways. Nevertheless, we prove that the profit objective function is submodular, and thus a polynomial-time algorithm approximates the optimum value within a factor of 0.5 due to the result of Buchbinder et al. [3].

Theorem (Theorem 2.3) The profit function is submodular.

To prove this theorem, we rewrite $P(S)$ as $\sum_{b\in S} v_b + \mathrm{E}[\sum_{h\in S} c_h^I] - C(S)$ where $C(S)$ is the expected value of the cheapest matching over scenarios or equivalently $C(S) = \sum_{h\in \mathcal{M}^I(S)} c_h^I$. The challenge is to prove that $C(S)$ is supermodular. It is enough to show that it is supermodular for each scenario individually. We first prove a lemma to demonstrate how for sets $S \subseteq T \subseteq B$ we can change a matching of S to a matching of T. Then we apply this lemma to the sets $T \cup \{b\}$ and S to show that the distance between the value of these two matchings $C(T \cup \{b\}) - C(S)$ can be broken into two disjoint matching distances. The first one between $S \cup \{b\}$ and S and the second one between the sets T and S. This gives us an inequality which immediately yields the supermodularity of $C(S)$.

We also study the loss objective function that has been used in the associated literature [16, 1, 11, 2]. The loss objective has the form of "missed" value; note that exactly minimizing loss is equivalent to exactly maximizing profit. Unfortunately, the loss object function is supermodular and does not have the nice structural property of the profit objective function. In Theorem 3.2 we show that it is not possible to optimally minimize the loss function in polynomial time unless $P = NP$. In order to approximate the solution, in Section 4, we show that we can use sampling to construct an integer program that, with high probability, provides a $(1 + O(\epsilon))$-approximation to the loss objective. We call this integer program the second-stage allocation IP (see Figure 2). Unfortunately, this does not directly lead to an approximation via the standard approach of linear-programming relaxations, as we show that the integrality gap of the corresponding linear program is quite high.

Theorem (Theorem 3.3) The integrality gap of the second-stage allocation IP is at least $\Omega(n)$ where the total number of buyers is $O(n)$.

We prove this theorem by constructing an example with $2n$ customers and $O(4^n)$ options in which the fractional solution is 2 and the integral solution cannot be better than $n + 1$. We consider all the values of customers to be equal to 1. The idea is to come up with the right edges and set of scenarios such that no n customers can be satisfied simultaneously. In other words, if we choose a set of n customers, we cannot match them at the same time in at least one scenario. For each set of n customers, we consider a scenario in which all of these customers have only edges to $n - 1$ affordable options, and therefore, we have to miss at least one of them in the contracts. However, we show there exists a solution to the LP which fractionally matches all customers in each instance, and does not have to miss any of them.

The high integrality gap of the aforementioned linear program leads us to consider bicriteria-style approximations; our main result is the following, which provides an approximation to the loss objective by relaxing the matching constraints between buyers and options.

Theorem (Theorem 3.5) Any fractional solution to the second-stage allocation integer program can be rounded to an integral solution while increasing the loss objective value by at most a factor of $1/f$, while ensuring that no option is matched to more than 2 buyers and at most a $\min\{\frac{f}{1-2f}, \frac{1}{2}\}$ fraction of buyers cannot be uniquely matched to an option, for any $0 < f < \frac{1}{2}$.

We propose an integer programming formulation for solving this problem. In order to obtain Theorem 3.5, we first relax the integer program to a linear program (LP), and leverage the sampling technique to propose a polynomial-time algorithm for solving the corresponding linear program. Then, we show how to round the LP-solution using an appropriate dependent rounding. One of the tools we use in rounding the LP-solution is a certain type of bipartite dependent-rounding procedure developed in [9]. In particular, (a) this helps show that with probability one, no option has more than two buyers assigned, and (b) gives us a handle both on the (expected) number of overbooked customers and on the probability of assigning a customer to an option. The "dependence" in the rounding helps with issue (a), while inheriting the property (b) from *independent* rounding schemes.

1.2 Related work

Our problem falls into the framework of two-stage stochastic optimization. This framework formalizes hedging against uncertainty into two stages: in the first, decisions have low cost but the exact input is uncertain; in the second, the input is known but decisions have high cost. Many problems have been cast in this framework, e.g., set cover, minimum spanning tree, Steiner tree, maximum weighted matching, facility location, and knapsack [5, 8, 15, 14]. Prior work has considered linear programming approaches in this framework [23, 25], for example the Sample Average Approximation (SAA) method to reduce the size of a linear program [20, 4]. Ensuring the reduced linear program is representative of the original problem is generally hard and requires problem-specific techniques for most combinatorial optimization settings, however, and so no unified framework has been developed so far.

Our problem is most closely related to bipartite matching problems in this literature. Katriel et al. [18] consider such a problem, where an optimizers wants to buy an edge set containing a maximum matching at the least cost, and must balance fixed first-stage edge costs against the potential risks and rewards of random second-stage edge costs. They propose a polynomial-time deterministic algorithm which approximates the expected cost of minimum matching within a factor of $O(n^2)$, where n is the size of the input graph. They also design a polynomial-time bicriteria randomized algorithm which returns, with probability $1 - e^{-n}$, a matching of size at most $(1 - \beta)n$ which approximates the optimum cost within a factor of $1/\beta$. In our setting, however, we *must* book a room for every buyer served in the first stage, and this bicriteria algorithm gives no guarantees on the set of served but unmatched buyers – they might even all have demanded the exact same option. We seek an algorithm assigning few customers to each option, even in the worst case, an objective that requires significant new insight compared to the setting of [18]. We design an algorithm which assigns at most two customers to each option. Kong and Schaefer [21] give results for the maximum-weighted matching problem, but this objective fails to capture either of our problems.

Maximizing a non-negative submodular function has been extensively studied in the literature (see, e.g., [6, 10, 7, 26]). This problem generalizes the NP-hard max-cut problem [12]. The first constant-factor approximation algorithm for maximizing a non-negative *non-monotone* submodular function was proposed by Feige, Mirrokni, and Vondrak [6]. They present a randomized local-search algorithm with an approximation factor of 0.4. They also show that it is impossible to get a better than 0.5 approximation for the submodular maximization problem with polynomially many oracle queries. Gharan and Vondrak [10] improve this approximation factor to 0.41 by a simulated annealing algorithm. This approximation ratio was further improved to 0.42 by Feldman, Naor, and Schwartz [7] based on a structural continuous greedy algorithm. Later, Buchbinder et al. [3] improved this approximation ratio to the optimal 0.5. It is worth mentioning that submodular maximization plays an important role in many optimization problems, e.g., influence maximization [19, 22], graph cut problems [24], and load balancing [24].

2. PROFIT MAXIMIZATION

Our first step is to consider the second-stage of the coordinator's optimization problem more closely. Note that we let customers form any pack of options they like. Since packs can now intersect in arbitrary ways, the problem of choosing how to assign buyers to options once prices are revealed becomes more complicated. We shall show, however, that it still has nice structure. In this section, we show that the coordinator's objective function has good structural properties. In particular, we show that the profit objective function is submodular. In order to show the submodularity of the profit function, we first prove the expected cost for satisfying a set of buyers $S \subseteq B$ in the second stage is supermodular in S, where the cost of satisfying a set of buyers $S \subseteq B$ is defines as follows:

$$\mathrm{C}(S) = \mathrm{E}[\textstyle\sum_{h \in \mathcal{M}^I(S)} c_h^I],$$

where $\mathcal{M}^I(S)$ is the minimum matching that covers buyers in S in scenario I, and the expectation is over which I occurs. We then leverage the supermodularity of the cost function and prove the profit function is submodular.

We now show that the expected cost for reserving a set of buyers $S \subseteq B$ in the second stage is supermodular in S. We begin by showing that for any fixed future scenario $I \in \mathcal{I}$, the cost $\mathrm{C}_I(S) = \sum_{h \in \mathcal{M}^I(S)} c_h^I$ of reserving options for a set $S \subseteq B$ is supermodular in S. Since our expected cost overall is just a weighted sum of the costs in each possible scenario, it immediately follows that the expected cost of serving a set of buys is supermodular as well. Thus, for the rest of this section, our discussion and arguments fall within the context of a single fixed future scenario $I \in \mathcal{I}$, and so omit it from our notation. Before we begin our proof, however, we first define some notation that will prove useful. First, given a set of buyers S, let $\mathcal{M}(S)$ denote the minimum-cost matching of buyers S to options. Note that after fixing a scenario, multiple matchings may give the same cost; careful tie-breaking is critical to our proofs, and so we defer further discussion of this matter until later. Lastly, we use $\mathrm{C}(S) = \sum_{h \in \mathcal{M}(S)} c_h$ to denote the minimum cost to serve a set of buyers S in our fixed scenario.

We now proceed to show that the function $\mathrm{C}(S)$ is supermodular in S, that is

$$\mathrm{C}(T \cup \{b\}) - \mathrm{C}(T) \geq \mathrm{C}(S \cup \{b\}) - \mathrm{C}(S)$$

for any $S \subseteq T \subseteq B$ and $b \in B \setminus T$. We start by finding a clean characterization of how adding buyers to our served set changes the optimal matching to options. In the following lemma, for any two sets A and B, $A \Delta B$ refers to the symmetric difference of A and B, i.e. an element exists in $A \Delta B$ if and only if, it exists in exactly one of A or B.

LEMMA 2.1. *For any $S \subseteq T \subseteq B$ and any choice of $\mathcal{M}(S)$, there exists a choice of $\mathcal{M}(T)$ such that $\mathcal{M}(S) \triangle \mathcal{M}(T)$ consists of $|T \setminus S|$ disjoint paths of odd length. Furthermore, each of these paths has one endpoint in $T \setminus S$.*

PROOF. Choose $\mathcal{M}(T)$ to be the minimum-cost matching covering T such that the size of $\mathcal{M}(S) \triangle \mathcal{M}(T)$ is minimized. First, note that in $\mathcal{M}(S) \triangle \mathcal{M}(T)$, every element of $T \setminus S$ has degree exactly one; every element of S has degree either zero or two; every other element of B has degree zero; and every element of H has degree zero, one, or two. As such, we can immediately see that $\mathcal{M}(S) \triangle \mathcal{M}(T)$ can be decomposed into a disjoint union of paths and cycles, and the latter must all be of even length since our underlying graph is bipartite. We shortly show that if an even length path or cycle exists, we can use it to modify $\mathcal{M}(T)$ and get a minimum-cost matching that covers T but has strictly smaller symmetric difference with $\mathcal{M}(S)$. The claim immediately follows, since this means $\mathcal{M}(S) \triangle \mathcal{M}(T)$ is a disjoint union of paths of odd length, and as we already observed the set of vertices in B with degree one is precisely $T \setminus S$.

Let $\mathcal{C}$ be any cycle of even length in $\mathcal{M}(S) \triangle \mathcal{M}(T)$. Consider what it represents in the context of our original problem. It means that both of our matchings assigned the customers incident to $\mathcal{C}$ to the options incident to $\mathcal{C}$, just in a different order. Thus, $\mathcal{M}(T) \triangle \mathcal{C}$ would still be a minimum-cost matching, but have strictly smaller symmetric difference with $\mathcal{M}(S)$. Similarly, let $\mathcal{P}$ be an even length path in $\mathcal{M}(S) \triangle \mathcal{M}(T)$. Note that the endpoints of the path must lie in H – otherwise, the set of buyers served by $\mathcal{M}(S)$ and $\mathcal{M}(T)$ would be incomparable, rather than the former being a subset of the latter. Thus, we can see that in the context of our problem, the path $\mathcal{P}$ represents that the two matchings used served the incident buyers using slightly different sets of options. If an option has degree one in $\mathcal{M}(S) \triangle \mathcal{M}(T)$, however, we may conclude that it is used in precisely one of the matchings. Thus, it follows that both $\mathcal{M}(S) \triangle \mathcal{P}$ and $\mathcal{M}(T) \triangle \mathcal{P}$ are valid matchings covering S and T, respectively. Since both $\mathcal{M}(S)$ and $\mathcal{M}(T)$ are minimum-cost matchings, however, we may conclude either of these assignments of the buyers incident to $\mathcal{P}$ to options have the same cost. As such, $\mathcal{M}(T) \triangle \mathcal{P}$ is a minimum-cost matching that has strictly smaller symmetric difference with $\mathcal{M}(S)$, contradicting our choice of $\mathcal{M}(T)$. Thus, we may conclude that no paths of cycle of even length exist in $\mathcal{M}(S) \triangle M(T)$. □

We may use the above lemma to show that the cost function is, in fact, supermodular.

LEMMA 2.2. *For any $S \subseteq T \subseteq B$, and any $b \in B \setminus T$, we have that $\mathrm{C}(T \cup \{b\}) - \mathrm{C}(T) \geq \mathrm{C}(S \cup \{b\}) - \mathrm{C}(S)$.*

PROOF. Consider applying Lemma 2.1 to the sets $T \cup \{b\}$ and S, and some minimum-cost matching $\mathcal{M}(S)$. Let $\mathcal{P}_b$ be the resulting path with endpoint b, and let $\mathcal{P}_{T \setminus S}$ be the union of the paths with endpoints in $T \setminus S$. Observe that each of these paths is an alternating path with respect to $\mathcal{M}(S)$, and that since they are disjoint they can be applied one-by-one to $\mathcal{M}(S)$ in any order to produce a sequence of matchings. Since every path has odd length, we can see that it will increase the size of the matching by one and the cost of the matching by precisely the cost of the option that is one of the path's endpoints. But then, $\mathcal{M}(S) \triangle \mathcal{P}_b$ is a matching covering $S \cup \{b\}$, and so has cost at least $\mathrm{C}(S \cup \{b\})$. Similarly, $\mathcal{M}(S) \triangle \mathcal{P}_{T \setminus S}$ is a matching covering T, and so has cost at least $\mathrm{C}(T)$. But then we can see that

$$\mathrm{C}(T \cup \{b\}) - \mathrm{C}(S) \geq (\mathrm{C}(S \cup \{b\}) - \mathrm{C}(S)) + (\mathrm{C}(T) - \mathrm{C}(S)).$$

Rearranging terms gives precisely the desired inequality. □

THEOREM 2.3. *The profit function is submodular.*

PROOF. We first write the profit objective function as follows:

$$P(S) = \sum_{b \in S} v_b + \mathrm{E}[\sum_{h \in H} c_h^I] - \mathrm{C}(S).$$

Knowing facts that $\mathrm{C}(S)$ is supermodular (based on Lemma 2.2), $\mathrm{E}[\sum_{h \in H} c_h^I]$ is a constant independent of S, and $\sum_{b \in S} v_b$ is just an additive function, we can conclude that the profit function is submodular. □

3. LOSS MINIMIZATION

Unfortunately, the loss objective remains hard to approximate as well. First, in Theorem 3.2 we show that it is not possible to optimally minimize the loss function in polynomial time unless $P = NP$. Moreover, while we can phrase our problem as an integer program, we can show that the integrality gap of this program is quite large. This motivates us to try relaxing some of the constraints in our problem, and find a bicriteria-style approximation. In fact, an optimum solution to the loss minimization problem is an optimum solution to the profit maximization problem as well. Thus, from Theorem 3.2, one may immediately conclude that, there is no polynomial time algorithm for the profit maximization problem unless $P = NP$.

In Theorem 3.2 we used the hardness of 3-*dimensional matching* problem to show that there is no polynomial algorithm for the loss minimization problem unless P=NP.

DEFINITION 3.1. *The 3-dimensional matching is defined as follow. Let R_1, R_2 and R_3 be disjoint and finite sets s.t. $|R_1| = |R_2| = |R_3| = n$ and let R be a subset of $R_1 \times R_2 \times R_3$. The problem is to check whether there exists $M \subseteq R$ s.t. $|M| = n$ and for any two distinct triples (r_1, r_2, r_3) and (r_1', r_2', r_3') in M we have $r_1 \neq r_1'$, $r_2 \neq r_2'$ and $r_2 \neq r_2'$.*

The 3-dimensional matching problem is known to be NP-complete [17].

THEOREM 3.2. *There is no polynomial algorithm for the loss minimization problem unless P=NP.*

PROOF. Consider the decision version of our loss minimization problem (DLMin), that we want to know weather the optimum solution is less than k or not. Here, we give a reduction from 3-dimensional matching problem to DLMin. This, in fact, means that DLMin is NP-hard and there is no polynomial algorithm for the loss minimization problem unless $P = NP$.

Let $R \subseteq R_1 \times R_2 \times R_3$ be an instance of 3-dimensional matching problem with $|R_1| = |R_2| = |R_3| = n$ and $R = m$. We create an instance of DLMin with three future scenarios as follow:

- For every item $r = (r_1, r_2, r_3) \in R$ we have one customer with value 1.
- For each element in $R_1 \cup R_2 \cup R_3$ we have an option.
- Each customer corresponds to an item $r = (r_1, r_2, r_3)$ accepts options correspond to elements r_1, r_2 and r_3.
- We have 3 scenarios s.t. in scenario i, the price of options in R_i are 0 (low cost) and price of all other options are 4 (high cost). Each of the scenarios happen with probability $\frac{1}{3}$.

Consider that, since $1 \leq \frac{1}{3} \times 4$, we prefer not to choose a customer rather than matching her to a high cost option even with probability $\frac{1}{3}$. Moreover, in the instance constructed above, each customer in each scenario has exactly one low cost option. This means that, items corresponds to the customers that we select in an optimal solution do not share any element r_i. Therefore, any optimum solution with loss k to the above instance gives a 3-dimensional matching of size $m - k$ in R.

On the other hand, if we choose the customers correspond to the items in a 3-dimensional matching of size $m-k$, we have a solution with loss k to the above instance. This completes the reduction and says that here is no polynomial algorithm for the loss minimization problem unless P=NP. □

$$\begin{aligned}
\text{min:} \quad & \Big(\sum_{b \in B} (1 - Y_b) v_b + \frac{1}{N} \sum_{1 \leq k \leq N} \sum_{(b,h) \in E} x_{hbk} c_{hk}\Big) \\
\text{s.t.} \quad & \sum_{h \in H} x_{hbk} \geq Y_b \qquad \forall b \in B, \forall 1 \leq k \leq N \qquad (1) \\
& \sum_{b \in B} x_{hbk} \leq 1 \qquad \forall h \in H, \forall 1 \leq k \leq N \qquad (2) \\
& Y_b, x_{hbk} \in \{0, 1\} \;\; \forall h \in H, \forall b \in B, \forall 1 \leq k \leq N
\end{aligned}$$

Figure 2: The second-stage allocation integer program

We first investigate how the coordinator can minimize the loss objective $L(S)$ via an integer program. One immediate challenge that we encounter is that there may be many possible future scenarios. This is problematic because calculating L requires computing the expected value of the maximum matching in every possible future scenario. We show that we can find an approximate solution $\hat{L}$ to function L using polynomially-many samples of scenarios (See Theorem 4.1) and solving the problem simultaneously for these samples based on a result of [4]. Therefore, our goal is to minimize function $\hat{L}$. The integer program for the problem of minimizing function $\hat{L}$ can be written as in Figure 2. We call it the second-stage allocation IP.

In the second-stage allocation IP: (i) N is the number of samples; (ii) c_{hk} is the known price of option h in the kth sample; (iii) variable Y_b is 1 if and only if $b \in S$, and $Y_b = 0$ otherwise; and (iv) variable x_{hbk} is 1 if and only if option h is assigned to buyer b in the kth sample and is 0 otherwise. Constraint (1) requires that if $Y_b = 1$, then at least one option should be assigned to this buyer in every sample $1 \leq k \leq N$. We call this family of constraints the *capacity* constraints. Constraint (2) for each option $h \in H$ and each scenario k requires that option h in sample k can be assigned to no more than one buyer; we call this family of constraints the *assignment* constraints. The objective function of this IP is exactly equal to $\hat{L}(S)$. Let $\sum_{b \in B} (1 - Y_b) v_b$ be the *lost* term, and $\sum_k \sum_{(b,h) \in E} x_{hbk} c_{hk}$ be the *cost* term of the objective function. In the following, we relax the last two constraints of this IP to their linear counterparts $x_{hbk} \in [0, 1]$ and $Y_b \in [0, 1]$ to obtain a linear program. Edge between buyer b and option h in sample k is a *fractional* edge in a LP solution $\langle \mathbf{x}, \mathbf{Y} \rangle$ if and only if $0 < x_{hbk} < 1$.

The first question that comes to mind when trying to find a minimizer of function $\hat{L}$ is whether we can use a solution to the LP to find an exact or an approximate solution to the IP. However, we show that the integrality gap between the IP and LP solutions can be quite high by the following theorem. Indeed, this theorem shows a linear gap base on the number of buyers, which is a logarithmic gap base on the number of scenarios.

THEOREM 3.3. *The integrality gap of the second-stage allocation IP is at least $\Omega(n)$ where the total number of buyers is $O(n)$.*

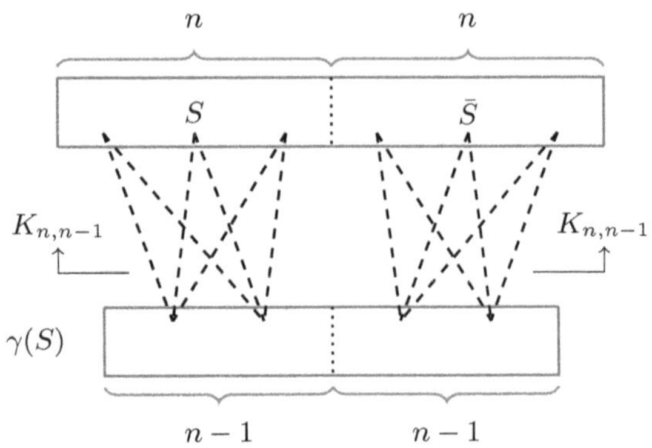

Figure 3: In this graph the upper vertices show the buyers with a subset of size n labeled as S and the rest of buyers labeled as $\bar{S}$. The lower vertices show the group of options $\gamma(S)$. Note that in exactly one scenario all the options in $\gamma(S)$ have a zero price and they have very high prices in all other scenarios. Therefore, we can only match the buyers to options in $\gamma(S)$ in one scenario, and no matching can use this set of options in any other scenario. The best LP solution requires us to assign an amount $\frac{1}{n}$ to each edge in this figure in the aforementioned scenario, and to assign a value equal to zero to all these edges in all other scenarios.

PROOF. Assume there are $2n$ buyers and $(2n-2)\binom{2n}{n}$ options. Suppose there are only two possible prices for each option: the *low* price for all options is 0 and the *high* price for all options is $(2n+1)\binom{2n}{n}$. For each buyer b, $v_b = 1$. Partition the options into $\binom{2n}{n}$ groups of size $2n-2$ each. Consider all the subsets of buyers of size n. There are $\binom{2n}{n}$ such subsets. Let γ denote any one to one mapping from these subsets to option groups. For each subset S and the group of options $\gamma(S)$ mapped to it add edges from each $b \in S$ to all the first $n-1$ options in $\gamma(S)$ and add edges from each $b \notin S$ to all the last $n-1$ options in $\gamma(S)$. Figure 3 illustrates the edges between the buyers and the group of options $\gamma(S)$ for an arbitrary subset of buyers S of size n. Consider $\binom{2n}{n}$ samples and in sample i suppose all the options in the i-th group have the low price (which is 0) and all other options have the high price.

Since the high price for options is very large, we can never assign a person to an option that has a high price. This is true because a trivial solution to the IP is when all the variables are equal to 0 in which case the objective value would be equal to $2n$. However, if we assign a buyer to an option with high price for even one sample, the objective would become at least $2n+1$, which is worse than the trivial solution. Therefore, in any optimal solution to the IP we can assume x_{hbk} is 1 only if option h in sample k has price 0. Thus, the second term in the objective function is always equal to 0, and the objective function for this example simplifies to $\sum_{b\in B}(1-Y_b)$, the number of buyers that we fail to serve.

Note that the objective of the IP in this example is to maximize the number of buyers served. Recall, however, our earlier observation that an optimal integral solution can never use an option with high cost. By construction, this means that an optimal IP solution can only serve at most $n-1$ buyers. Note this property is much less restrictive for LP solutions. Simply serving every buyer at a rate of $(1-1/n)$ will satisfy this requirement while serving a (fractional) total of $2n-2$ customers. We now proceed to formalize the above discussion and demonstrate that it yields the desired gap.

We present a feasible LP solution for which the objective value is equal to 2. Then we show no IP solution can achieve an objective value of less than $n+1$ and we conclude the integrality gap between the LP and IP solutions can be very large.

Here we present a feasible LP solution.

$$Y_b = \frac{n-1}{n} \qquad \forall b \in B \tag{3}$$

$$x_{hbk} = \begin{cases} \frac{1}{n} & \text{if } c_{hk} = 0 \\ 0 & \text{otherwise} \end{cases} \qquad \forall h \in H, \forall b \in B, \forall 1 \le k \le N$$

Consider the first set of constraints in the LP. For each buyer $b \in B$ and each sample, b has edges to $n-1$ options with low prices. Therefore, for $n-1$ options $x_{hbk} = \frac{1}{n}$. This means $\sum_{h\in H} x_{hbk}$ in each sample for each buyer b is $\frac{n-1}{n}$, which is equal to Y_b and the constraint holds. Now consider the second set of constraints. For each option $h \in H$ and each sample, at most n buyers have an edge to this option. The maximum possible value of the variables x is $\frac{1}{n}$. Therefore, $\sum_{b\in B} x_{hbk}$ cannot exceed 1. Thus the set of variables form a feasible LP solution. The objective value with this set of variables would be equal to $\sum_{b\in B}(1-\frac{n-1}{n}) = 2$.

On the other hand, assume an IP solution can achieve an objective value less than $n+1$. Since the objective function is equal to $\sum_{b\in B}(1-Y_b)$, this means for at least n buyers $Y_b = 1$. Consider S to be the set of these n buyers. Consider the sample which has the group of options $\gamma(S)$ as its low price options. In this sample, these n buyers have edges to only $n-1$ options with low prices. It means at least one of them is matched to an option with the high price. Therefore, Y_b can be equal to 1 for at most $n-1$ of them contradicting the fact that $Y_b = 1$ for all the buyers $b \in S$. Therefore, no IP solution can achieve an objective value less than $n+1$.

Therefore, while the optimum LP solution is less than or equal to 2, the optimum IP solution cannot be less than $n+1$. Since, the number of vertices is $2n + (2n-2)\binom{2n}{n} = O(4^n)$, we conclude the integrality between our LP and IP is linear in the total number of buyers and logarithmic in the total number of options. □

The result of Theorem 3.3 leads us to consider relaxations of our problem. In particular, we consider relaxing the constraint that requires matching at most one customer to each option. We will allow ourselves to match **up to two** buyers to an option, but try to minimize the fraction of buyers who are not matched uniquely. We say a buyer is **multi-covered** in a scenario if she is matched to the same option as a previous buyer in that scenario: if we match 2 buyers to an option then one of them is multi-covered. We formally define the bicriteria-style approximation below.

DEFINITION 3.4. *An (α,β)-approximate solution to the second-stage allocation packs IP is a solution which has an objective value at most α times the objective value of the optimal solution to this IP while the number of buyer vertices that it multi-covers in all graphs overall is no more than β times the number of buyer vertices that it covers in all graphs overall.*

THEOREM 3.5. *For any given f such that $0 < f < 1/2$, we can find in deterministic polynomial time, an $(1/f, \min\{\frac{f}{1-2f}, \frac{1}{2}\})$-approximate solution to the second-stage allocation IP in which in every scenario, any option is matched to at most two buyers.*

PROOF. The four-step algorithm supporting Theorem 3.5 is parametrized by $0 < f < 1/2$ and is described next. The primary work done is for Step 4, as seen below.

Step 1: Solving the LP. Solve the LP relaxation; let $x^{(1)}$ and $y^{(1)}$ denote the vectors x and Y of the LP, that occur as the optimal solution-vectors.

Step 2: Filtering. Update $y^{(1)}$ to $y^{(2)}$ as follows: for all b such that $y_b^{(1)} \leq 1-f$, set $y_b^{(2)} := 0$, with $y_b^{(2)} = y_b^{(1)}$ for all other b. Let $x^{(2)} := x^{(1)}$.

Step 3: Scaling up. Update $y^{(2)}$ to $y^{(3)}$ as follows: for all b such that $y_b^{(2)} > 0$, set $y_b^{(3)} := 1$ (we have $y_b^{(3)} = 0$ for all other b). Next update $x^{(2)}$ to $x^{(3)}$ in two sub-steps as follows:

- for all b such that $y_b^{(3)} = 1$, and for all (h, k), set $x_{hbk}^{(3)} := x_{hbk}^{(2)} / y_b^{(1)}$, so that the constraints (1) are satisfied; for all other (h, b, k), initialize $x_{hbk}^{(3)} := x_{hbk}^{(2)}$;
- arbitrarily decrease the $x_{hbk}^{(3)}$ values (subject to non-negativity) such that equality now holds in the constraints (1).

Step 4: Derandomized Dependent Rounding. Separately for each scenario k, we apply a certain derandomized version of the bipartite dependent-rounding procedure of [9] to the vector $x^{(3)}$ (restricted to the index k): the details are as follows. Let $\ell_k(h) = \sum_b x_{hbk}^{(3)}$ denote the fractional load on option h. This procedure rounds x_{hbk} for each (h, b) – recall that we are considering any fixed k now – to some $X_{hbk} \in \{0, 1\}$, such that the following properties hold, among others:

(P1) For all (h, b), $E[X_{hbk}] = x_{hbk}^{(3)}$;

(P2) For all b such that $y_b^{(3)} = 1$, $\sum_h X_{hbk} = 1$ with probability one, and

(P3) For all h, $\sum_b X_{hbk} \in \{\lfloor \ell_k(h) \rfloor, \lceil \ell_k(h) \rceil\}$ with probability one.

We will run a derandomized version of this procedure as follows. For $i = 1, 2, 3$, let L_i and C_i denote the "lost" and "cost" values of the objective function for scenario k, at the end of step i above. That is, for $i = 1, 2, 3$, at the **end** of Step i above, let

$$L_i = \sum_{b \in B} (1 - y_b^{(i)}) v_b \text{ and } C_i = \sum_{(b,h)} x_{hbk}^{(i)} c_{hk}.$$

Let $t = \sum_b y^{(3)} b$ be the final number of buyers chosen, and define $H_k = \{h : \ell_k(h) > 1\}$; let $s = |H_k|$. Consider the potential function

$$\Phi = \frac{f}{1-f} \cdot \frac{\sum_{(b,h)} X_{hbk} c_{hk}}{C_3} + \frac{1-2f}{1-f} \cdot \frac{\sum_{h \in H_k} [(\sum_b X_{hbk}) - 1]}{\min\{tf, sf/(1-f)\}}.$$

At every step of the dependent-rounding procedure of [9] – which randomizes among two choices and continually updates the vector X which initially starts at $x^{(3)}$ – deterministically make the choice that never increases Φ. As pointed out in [9], this is indeed possible ((P1) and the linearity of expectation, along with the nature of the choices made in [9], justify this).

Analysis of the algorithm. Let us start with L_i. It is easy to see that $L_2 \leq L_1/f$, and that L_i does not decrease any further. Thus, the "lost" value gets blown up by a factor of at most $1/f$, as compared to the initial LP value.

Note next that $x_{hbk}^{(3)} \leq x_{hbk}^{(1)}/(1-f)$. Combined with (2), this shows that $\ell_k(h) \leq 1/(1-f) \leq 2$ for all (h, k). Thus, property (P3) assures us that the final load $\sum_b X_{hbk}$ on option h in scenario k will be at most two.

To analyze the cost and overbooking, we first claim that for all $h \in H_k$,

$$\sum_h (\ell_k(h) - 1) \leq \min\{tf, sf/(1-f)\}. \quad (4)$$

To see this, start by recalling that $\ell_k(h) \leq 1/(1-f)$ and note that: (i) the LHS of (4) is

$$\sum_h \ell_k(h) \cdot (1 - 1/\ell_k(h)) \leq \sum_b \ell_k(h) \cdot (1 - (1-f)) \leq tf,$$

and (ii) since $\ell_k(h) \leq 1/(1-f)$, the LHS of (4) is at most $s \cdot (1/(1-f) - 1) = sf/(1-f)$. Thus we have (4).

Therefore we see that Φ is initially at most $\frac{f}{1-f} \cdot 1 + \frac{1-2f}{1-f} \cdot = 1$, and thus never exceeds 1. Thus, the final cost value is at most $\sum_k C_3 \cdot (1-f)/f$. However, since $x_{hbk}^{(3)} \leq x_{hbk}^{(1)}/(1-f)$, this implies that the final total cost is at most the LP's cost times $((1-f)/f) \cdot 1/(1-f)$; thus, just like the "lost" function, the "cost" function again gets blown up by a factor of at most f.

Finally for the multi-covering. It is easy to see that the fraction of people multi-covered at the end is at most $U = (1/t) \cdot \sum_{h \in H_k} [(\sum_b X_{hbk}) - 1]$. Since $\Phi \leq 1$ at the end, this implies that

$$U \leq \frac{1-f}{1-2f} \cdot (1/t) \cdot \min\{tf, sf/(1-f)\}. \quad (5)$$

However, property (P3) shows an additional upper-bound on U:

$$U \leq \frac{\min\{t, 2s\} - s}{t} \quad (6)$$

A case analysis of the minimum of these two upper-bounds (e.g., based on whether s/t is at least or at most $1/2$), we get the bound

$$U \leq \min\{\frac{f}{1-2f}, \frac{1}{2}\}$$

as desired. □

4. APPROXIMATE-OPTIMALITY VIA SAMPLING

Charikar et al. consider general 2-stage stochastic models. In these models, an optimizer must make a decision in the first stage which leads to a known cost in the first stage and an unknown cost in the second stage. For our problem, this first stage decision is choosing which customers to serve. In terms of the loss objective, our first stage cost is the values of customers we do not choose to serve, and our second stage cost is buying options for the customers we choose to serve. To that end, we use

$$g(S) = \sum_{b \notin S} v_b \qquad \text{and} \qquad w(S, I) = \sum_{h \in \mathcal{M}^I(S)} c_h^I$$

to denote the first and second stage costs, respectively, of choosing to serve a set of customers $S \subseteq B$ when second stage scenario $I \in \widehat{\mathcal{I}}$ happens. Recall that $\mathcal{M}_I(S)$ is the the minimum-cost matching between customers in S and the options in second stage scenario I. Thus the loss objective for a future scenario I is $L_I(S) = g(S) + w(S, I)$. The goal is to find a first stage decision $S \subseteq B$ so that $E_I(L_I(S)) = g(S) + E_I(w(S, I)) = L(S)$ is minimized. We call such an S a minimizer for the loss objective. Since the space $\mathcal{I}$ might be very large it is hard to solve the problem of minimizing the function L over the full space $\mathcal{I}$. Instead, we define an approximation $\hat{L}$ of L as follows. Given N independent samples of scenarios $I_1, I_2, ..., I_N$ from the space $\mathcal{I}$, we estimate the function L by $\hat{L}(S) = g(S) + \frac{1}{N} \sum_{1 \leq i \leq N} w(S, I_i)$.

In order to apply Charikar et al.'s theorem, we need to prove some properties on the first and second stage costs. These properties are as follows.

1. Both first and second stage costs must always be nonnegative for all first stage decisions and all future scenarios.
2. There must exist a first stage decision for which the first stage cost is zero and the second stage cost is more than that of any other first stage decision for any future scenarios. That is there must exist a first stage decision $S_0 \subseteq B$ for which $g(S_0) = 0$ and $w(S_0, I) \leq w(S, I)$ for all $S \subseteq B$ and all $I \in \widehat{\mathcal{I}}$. We call this S_0 the *null* decision.
3. There must be a bounded inflation factor. That is if S_0 is the null decision from the previous property, then $w(S_0, I) - w(S, I) \leq \eta g(S)$ should hold for all $S \subseteq B$ and a fixed finite real number η. This means the penalty that we have to pay in the second stage because of making a null first stage decision compared to any other first stage decision is no more than a constant factor of the cost of the other first decision.

In our problem, $g(S) = \sum_{b \notin S} v_b$. Since v_b is nonnegative for all customers $b \in B$, $g(S)$ should also be nonnegative for all S. Moreover, $w(S, I)$ is equal to the cost of the matching $\mathcal{M}_I(S)$; since the weights in this matching represent nonnegative option costs, this must be nonnegative as well. Thus, the first property holds. For the second property, we claim B gives the desired null decision for the first stage. Now, $g(B) = \sum_{b \notin B} v_b = 0$, and for a fixed future scenario I, the optimization problem on the future would be matching all the customers, which must be more costly than matching any other subset of customers. The third property holds for our problem with $\eta = \frac{Max^H}{Min^B}$, where Max^H is the maximum possible option price and Min^B is the minimum value of customers. We can see this because

$$\sum_{h \in \mathcal{M}_I(B)} c_h^I - \sum_{h \in \mathcal{M}_I(S)} c_h^I \leq \sum_{b \notin S} Max^H$$
$$\leq \eta \sum_{b \notin S} Min^B$$
$$\leq \eta \sum_{b \notin S} v_b = \eta g(S).$$

Thus, we may apply the following theorem, which is a restatement of a theorem from [4], specialized to our setting. Indeed, the number of samples is polynomial in η, $\frac{1}{\epsilon}$, $\log(|\mathcal{I}|)$ andlog$(\frac{1}{\delta})$, and may not be polynomial in the length of the input.

THEOREM 4.1. *Any exact minimizer $\hat{S}$ of function $\hat{L}$ using $\Theta(\eta^2 \frac{1}{\epsilon^4} \log(|\mathcal{I}|) \log(\frac{1}{\delta}))$ samples of scenarios is a $(1 + O(\epsilon))$-approximate minimizer of L with probability $1 - 2\delta$. That is with probability $1 - 2\delta$, the inequality $L(\hat{S}) \leq (1 + O(\epsilon))L(S)$ holds for all $S \subseteq B$.*

Acknowledgments

Supported in part by NSF CAREER award 1053605, NSF grant CCF-1161626, NSF award CNS-1010789, NSF award CCF-1422569, Google Faculty Research award, DARPA/AFOSR grant FA9550-12-1-0423.

REFERENCES

[1] Ajit Agrawal, Philip Klein, and R. Ravi. When trees collide: an approximation algorithm for the generalized Steiner problem on networks. *SIAM J. Comput.*, 24(3):440–456, 1995.

[2] Aaron Archer, MohammadHossein Bateni, MohammadTaghi Hajiaghayi, and Howard Karloff. Improved approximation algorithms for prize-collecting steiner tree and tsp. *SIAM J. Comput.*, 40(2):309–332, 2011.

[3] Niv Buchbinder, Moran Feldman, Joseph Naor, and Roy Schwartz. A tight linear time (1/2)-approximation for unconstrained submodular maximization. In *Foundations of Computer Science (FOCS), 2012 IEEE 53rd Annual Symposium on*, pages 649–658. IEEE, 2012.

[4] Moses Charikar, Chandra Chekuri, and Martin Pál. Sampling bounds for stochastic optimization. In *APPROX/RANDOM*, pages 610–610, 2005.

[5] Kedar Dhamdhere, Vineet Goyal, R. Ravi, and Mohit Singh. How to pay, come what may: Approximation algorithms for demand-robust covering problems. In *FOCS*, pages 367–378, 2005.

[6] Uriel Feige, Vahab S. Mirrokni, and Jan Vondrak. Maximizing non-monotone submodular functions. In *FOCS*, pages 461–471, 2007.

[7] Moran Feldman, Joseph Seffi Naor, and Roy Schwartz. Nonmonotone submodular maximization via a structural continuous greedy algorithm. In *ICALP*, pages 342–353, 2011.

[8] Abraham D. Flaxman, Alan Frieze, and Michael Krivelevich. On the random 2-stage minimum spanning tree. In *SODA*, pages 919–926, 2005.

[9] R. Gandhi, S. Khuller, S. Parthasarathy, and A. Srinivasan. Dependent rounding and its applications to approximation algorithms. *Journal of the ACM*, 53:324–360, 2006.

[10] Shayan Oveis Gharan and Jan Vondrák. Submodular maximization by simulated annealing. In *SODA*, pages 1098–1116, 2011.

[11] Michel X. Goemans and David P. Williamson. A general approximation technique for constrained forest problems. *SIAM J. Comput.*, 24(2):296–317, 1995.

[12] Michel X. Goemans and David P. Williamson. Improved approximation algorithms for maximum cut and satisfiability problems using semidefinite programming. *J. ACM*, 42(6):1115–1145, 1995.

[13] Guestmob. `http://guestmob.tumblr.com/ourstory`.

[14] Anupam Gupta, Martin Pál, R. Ravi, and Amitabh Sinha. Sampling and cost-sharing: Approximation algorithms for stochastic optimization problems. *SIAM J. Comput.*, 40(5):1361–1401, 2011.

[15] Nicole Immorlica, David Karger, Maria Minkoff, and Vahab S. Mirrokni. On the costs and benefits of procrastination: approximation algorithms for stochastic combinatorial optimization problems. In *SODA*, pages 691–700, 2004.

[16] David S. Johnson, Maria Minkoff, and Steven Phillips. The prize collecting steiner tree problem: theory and practice. In *SODA*, pages 760–769, 2000.

[17] RichardM. Karp. Reducibility among combinatorial problems. In RaymondE. Miller, JamesW. Thatcher, and JeanD. Bohlinger, editors, *Complexity of Computer Computations*, The IBM Research Symposia Series, pages 85–103. Springer US, 1972.

[18] Irit Katriel, Claire Kenyon-Mathieu, and Eli Upfal.

Commitment under uncertainty: Two-stage stochastic matching problems. *Theor. Comput. Sci.*, 408(2):213–223, 2008.

[19] David Kempe, Jon Kleinberg, and Éva Tardos. Maximizing the spread of influence through a social network. In *KDD*, pages 137–146, 2003.

[20] Anton J. Kleywegt, Alexander Shapiro, and Tito Homem-de Mello. The sample average approximation method for stochastic discrete optimization. *SIAM J. on Optim.*, 12(2):479–502, 2002.

[21] Nan Kong and Andrew J. Schaefer. A factor $\frac{1}{2}$approximation algorithm for two-stage stochastic matching problems. *Eur. J. Oper. Res.*, 172:740–746, 2004.

[22] Elchanan Mossel and Sebastien Roch. On the submodularity of influence in social networks. In *STOC*, pages 128–134, 2007.

[23] David B. Shmoys and Chaitanya Swamy. Stochastic optimization is (almost) as easy as deterministic optimization. In *FOCS*, pages 228–237, 2004.

[24] Zoya Svitkina and Lisa Fleischer. Submodular approximation: Sampling-based algorithms and lower bounds. *SIAM Journal on Computing*, 40(6):1715–1737, 2011.

[25] Chaitanya Swamy and David B Shmoys. Sampling-based approximation algorithms for multi-stage stochastic optimization. In *FOCS*, pages 357–366, 2005.

[26] Jan Vondrák. Symmetry and approximability of submodular maximization problems. *SIAM Journal on Computing*, 42(1):265–304, 2013.

Social Decision with Minimal Efficiency Loss: An Automated Mechanism Design Approach

Mingyu Guo, Hong Shen
School of Computer Science
University of Adelaide, Australia
{mingyu.guo, hong.shen}
@adelaide.edu.au

Taiki Todo, Yuko Sakurai, Makoto Yokoo
Graduate School of ISEE
Kyushu University, Japan
{todo,ysakurai,yokoo}
@inf.kyushu-u.ac.jp

ABSTRACT

We study the problem where a group of agents need to choose from a finite set of social outcomes. We assume every agent's valuation for every outcome is bounded and the bounds are public information. For our model, no mechanism simultaneously satisfies strategy-proofness, individual rationality, non-deficit, and efficiency. In light of this, we aim to design mechanisms that are strategy-proof, individually rational, non-deficit, and minimize the worst-case efficiency loss.

We propose a family of mechanisms called the shifted Groves mechanisms, which are generalizations of the Groves mechanisms. We first show that if there exist mechanisms that are strategy-proof, individually rational, and non-deficit, then there exist shifted Groves mechanisms with these properties. Our main result is an Automated Mechanism Design (AMD) approach for identifying the (unique) optimal shifted Groves mechanism, which minimizes the worst-case efficiency loss among all shifted Groves mechanisms. Finally, we prove that the optimal shifted Groves mechanism is globally optimal among all deterministic mechanisms that are strategy-proof, individually rational, and non-deficit.

Categories and Subject Descriptors

I.2.11 [**Distributed Artificial Intelligence**]: Multiagent Systems

General Terms

Algorithms, Economics, Theory

Keywords

Groves Mechanisms, Automated Mechanism Design, Social Decision

1. INTRODUCTION

Social decision-making is a fundamental problem in multiagent systems. This paper studies how to design economic mechanisms for implementing good social outcomes. We study the problem where a group of agents need to choose from a finite set of social outcomes. The agents' valuations for the outcomes are private information. We assume every agent's valuation for every outcome is bounded and the bounds are public information (*e.g.*, the bounds are prescribed by the nature of the outcomes). One example setting is the public project problem:

Example 1. Public Project Problem

n agents need to decide whether or not to build a public project (*e.g.*, a bridge accessible by everyone). The cost of the project is 1. There are two outcomes:

- Outcome 1: not build

  Every agent's valuation for this outcome equals 0.

- Outcome 2: build, and every agent is responsible for an equal share of the cost, which equals $\frac{1}{n}$

  Different agents value the project differently. We assume an agent's valuation for the project is between 0 (not appreciating at all) and 1 (as high as the cost of the whole project). That is, taking the cost share into consideration, every agent's valuation for this outcome is between $-\frac{1}{n}$ and $\frac{n-1}{n}$.

For social decision problems like the above, ideally, we prefer mechanisms that satisfy the following properties:

- *Strategy-proofness*: Every agent's dominant strategy is to report truthfully, regardless of the other agents' reports. It is without loss of generality to require strategy-proofness due to the revelation principle.

- *(Ex post) individual rationality*: Every agent's utility (valuation of the chosen outcome minus payment) is non-negative. Individual rationality is necessary when participation is voluntary.

- *Non-deficit property*: The agents' total payment is non-negative.[1] That is, no external subsidy is ever needed. Another related but stronger property is *budget balance*, which requires that the agents' total payment is exactly 0. We require non-deficit, otherwise the mechanism is not sustainable.

- *Efficiency*: The mechanism always chooses the outcome that maximizes the agents' total valuation. (For the public project problem, it means the project is built if and only if the agents' total valuation for outcome 2 is higher.

[1] An individual agent may still pay negative payment.

Appears in: *Proceedings of the 14th International Conference on Autonomous Agents and Multiagent Systems (AAMAS 2015), Bordini, Elkind, Weiss, Yolum (eds.), May 4–8, 2015, Istanbul, Turkey.*

For resource allocation settings, the above properties can be simultaneously achieved, *e.g.*, by the VCG redistribution mechanisms [1, 5, 13]. However, when it comes to social decision settings, sometimes an agent has to face an undesirable outcome that is forced onto him by the others (*e.g.*, an agent who does not appreciate the public project may be forced to chip in to build the project). The VCG redistribution mechanisms, when applied to the public project problem, are not individually rational (unless we change the definition of individual rationality) [7, 8, 14]. Actually, as we will discuss in more details later on, *for social decision settings, no mechanisms can be simultaneously strategy-proof, individual rational, non-deficit, and efficient.*

In light of the above, we choose to sacrifice efficiency.[2] Our aim is to design mechanisms that are strategy-proof, individually rational, non-deficit, and as close to efficiency as possible. Specifically, we try to minimize the *worst-case efficiency loss* (the loss of efficiency in the worst case, as the result of using an inefficient mechanism).

We adopt a (Computationally Feasible) Automated Mechanism Design approach [6, 2]. We propose a family of mechanisms called the shifted Groves mechanisms, which are generalizations of the Groves mechanisms. We first show that if there exist mechanisms that are strategy-proof, individually rational, and non-deficit, then there exist shifted Groves mechanisms with these properties. We use AMD to identify the (unique) optimal shifted Groves mechanism, which minimizes the worst-case efficiency loss among all shifted Groves mechanisms. Finally, we prove that the optimal shifted Groves mechanism is globally optimal among all deterministic mechanisms that are strategy-proof, individually rational, and non-deficit. Besides proposing optimal mechanisms for a fundamental mechanism design setting, our approach also demonstrates the effectiveness of using AMD to deliver new economic results.

2. FORMAL MODEL DESCRIPTION

There are n agents who need to choose from k outcomes. We use $\theta_i = (v_{i1}, v_{i2}, \ldots, v_{ik})$ to denote agent i's type, where v_{ij} represents agent i's valuation for outcome j.

We make the following assumptions:

- v_{ij} is bounded below and above by *known constants* L_{ij} and U_{ij}. It should be noted that both L_{ij} and U_{ij} may be negative.
- For every i, agent i's type space Θ_i is the whole of $[L_{i1}, U_{i1}] \times [L_{i2}, U_{i2}] \times \ldots \times [L_{ik}, U_{ik}]$.
- The set of type profiles is the whole of $\Theta_1 \times \Theta_2 \times \ldots \times \Theta_n$.
- There do not exist two outcomes, so that the agents always prefer one outcome than the other for all type profiles. That is, for every pair of j and j', we have $\sum_i U_{ij} \geq \sum_i L_{ij'}$.

Our analysis throughout the paper relies on the above assumptions (*e.g.*, we need the above to prove that our AMD approach produces optimal mechanisms). However, it should be noted that only the first assumption is needed to *apply* the AMD approach, which takes the bounds as input. For example, it could be that certain type values do not exist (*e.g.*, v_{ij}'s possible values do not form an interval or form a much narrower interval than $[L_{ij}, U_{ij}]$) and/or certain types/type profiles do not exist (*e.g.*, due to interdependence). For these cases, the AMD approach still lead to a feasible mechanism. Of course, the mechanism is generally not optimal, because we fail to recognize that certain profiles are impossible.

As mentioned earlier, it is impossible to simultaneously have strategy-proofness, individually rationality, non-deficit, and efficiency. Below we present the details. According to Holmström [9], for convex type space (our setting), the *Groves mechanisms* [4] are the only mechanisms that are efficient and strategy-proof. The Groves mechanisms are defined as follows:

- The mechanism chooses an outcome from $\arg\max_j \sum_i v_{ij}$. That is, the mechanism chooses an outcome that maximizes the agents' total valuation.
- Let j^* be the chosen outcome. For every i, agent i receives $\sum_{i' \neq i} v_{i'j^*}$. That is, the amount an agent receives is equal to the other agents' total valuation for j^*.
- For every i, agent i then pays an amount that is independent of i's own type, which is denoted by $h_i(\theta_{-i})$.[3] Different sets of h_i functions correspond to different Groves mechanisms.

Every Groves mechanism is efficient and strategy-proof, but no Groves mechanism is both individually rational and non-deficit. We need the $h_i(\theta_{-i})$ term to be small enough, so that agent i's utility is non-negative. We also need the $h_i(\theta_{-i})$ term to be large enough, so that the agents' total payment is non-negative. However, we cannot satisfy both. We use $E(\theta_i, \theta_{-i})$ to denote the agents' total valuation for the efficient outcome. Under the Groves mechanisms, agent i's utility is simply $E(\theta_i, \theta_{-i}) - h_i(\theta_{-i})$, which needs to be non-negative for ensuring individual rationality. Hence, we have $h_i(\theta_{-i}) \leq E(\theta_i, \theta_{-i})$ for all θ_i and all θ_{-i}. The left-hand side does not depend on θ_i, and the right-hand side is minimized when $\theta_i = (L_{i1}, L_{i2}, \ldots, L_{ik})$ (we use $\underline{\theta_i}$ to denote this type). Hence, individual rationality is equivalent to for all i and all type profiles,

$$h_i(\theta_{-i}) \leq E(\underline{\theta_i}, \theta_{-i}) = \max_j (L_{ij} + \sum_{i' \neq i} v_{i'j})$$

It does not hurt to set $h_i(\theta_{-i})$ to exactly $\max_j(L_{ij} + \sum_{i' \neq i} v_{i'j})$. As mentioned earlier, we want this term to be large enough for ensuring non-deficit. If we set it any larger, individual rationality is violated. Once we fix the $h_i(\theta_{-i})$ term, there is one Groves mechanism left. If this mechanism is not non-deficit, then no Groves mechanisms are both individually rational and non-deficit. We use the following example to show this.

Example 2. Let us consider a public project problem (described in Example 1) with 2 agents. We have $L_{i1} = U_{i1} = 0$,

[2]The Faltings' mechanism [3] also sacrifices efficiency. The mechanism works for both resource allocation settings and social decision settings, but again, it is not individually rational for our problem.

[3]When we run the mechanism, we simply combine the payment terms in step 2 and 3. Throughout this paper, they are presented separately as we analyze them separately.

$L_{i2} = -\frac{1}{2}$, and $U_{i2} = \frac{1}{2}$. Let $\theta_1 = \theta_2 = (0, \frac{1}{2})$. That is, $v_{i1} = 0$ and $v_{i2} = \frac{1}{2}$. For this type profile, the decision is to build, both agents receive $\frac{1}{2}$ (here, $h_i(\theta_{-i}) = 0$). The non-deficit property is violated here.

In conclusion, in light of the above impossibility result, our aim is to design social decision mechanisms that are strategy-proof, individually rational, non-deficit, and minimize the *worst-case efficiency loss.*[4]

Definition 1. Let M be a mechanism. Let $M(\theta_i, \theta_{-i})$ be the agents' total valuation under M for type profile (θ_i, θ_{-i}). We recall that $E(\theta_i, \theta_{-i})$ represents the agents' total valuation for the efficient outcome. Mechanism M's **worst-case efficiency loss** is defined as:

$$\max_{\theta_i, \theta_{-i}} \left(E(\theta_i, \theta_{-i}) - M(\theta_i, \theta_{-i})\right)$$

3. SHIFTED GROVES MECHANISMS

We revisit the public project example. As we have seen, if outcome 2 (build) is chosen, deficit may occur. On the other hand, if outcome 1 is chosen, deficit never occurs.[5] One idea is then to "discourage" outcome 2 by asking the agents to pay additional payments when outcome 2 is chosen (essentially changing the agents' valuations for outcome 2). For example, we may *shift* the outcome "build" to "build, and every agent pays x in addition to mechanism payments and building cost". This helps reducing deficit for two reasons. First, after introducing these additional payments, less type profiles are mapped to outcome 2, so the maximal deficit when outcome 2 is chosen may potentially decrease. Second, the additional payments also help offset the deficit. If outcome 2 is chosen, we know that we have nx additional payment to offset the deficit.

The above idea leads to the *shifted Groves mechanisms*:

- For every agent i, every outcome j, we introduce an additional payment t_{ij}. That is, if outcome j is chosen, agent i needs to pay t_{ij} in addition to her mechanism payment. The t_{ij} are constants set by the mechanism designer. The total additional payment for outcome j is $P_j = \sum_i t_{ij}$.
- Apply the Groves mechanisms on the modified outcomes.
  - The mechanism chooses an outcome from
    $$\arg\max_j \sum_i (v_{ij} - t_{ij}) = \arg\max_j \{-P_j + \sum_i v_{ij}\}$$
    That is, the mechanism chooses an outcome that maximizes the agents' total valuation, considering the additional payments.
  - Let j^* be the chosen outcome. For every i, agent i receives $\sum_{i' \neq i}(v_{i'j^*} - t_{i'j^*})$. That is, the amount an agent receives is equal to the other agents' total valuation for the chosen outcome j^*, considering the additional payments. We also keep in mind that agent i needs to pay the additional payment t_{ij^*}. Therefore, agent i's net income at this point should be
    $$\sum_{i' \neq i}(v_{i'j^*} - t_{i'j^*}) - t_{ij^*} = -P_{j^*} + \sum_{i' \neq i} v_{i'j^*}$$
  - For every i, agent i then pays an amount that is independent of i's own type, which is denoted by $h_i(\theta_{-i})$.

Similar to the case without additional payments, we can find an upper bound on $h_i(\theta_{-i})$. Agent i's utility equals $\max_j\{-P_j + \sum_i v_{ij}\} - h_i(\theta_{-i})$, which must be non-negative for ensuring individual rationality. Therefore, we have $h_i(\theta_{-i}) \leq \max_j\{-P_j + \sum_i v_{ij}\}$ for all θ_i. By setting $\theta_i = \underline{\theta_i} = (L_{i1}, L_{i2}, \ldots, L_{ik})$, we have

$$h_i(\theta_{-i}) \leq \max_j\{-P_j + L_{ij} + \sum_{i' \neq i} v_{i'j}\}$$

Again, it does not hurt to set $h_i(\theta_{-i})$ to be exactly the right-hand side. (This value does not affect strategy-proofness and allocative efficiency. We need it large for achieving the non-deficit property, but any larger value violates individual rationality.)

Once we fix the $h_i(\theta_{-i})$ terms, we observe that the shifted Groves mechanisms are completely characterized by the total additional payments for the outcomes (the P_j). Both the outcome and the payments do not depend on the individual additional payments (the t_{ij}). This leads to a conciser definition of shifted Groves mechanisms.

Definition 2. A **shifted Groves mechanism** is characterized by k constants $P_1, P_2, \ldots, P_k$.

- The mechanism chooses an outcome from
  $$\arg\max_j \{-P_j + \sum_i v_{ij}\}$$
- Let j^* be the chosen outcome. For every i, agent i pays
  $$\max_j\{-P_j + L_{ij} + \sum_{i' \neq i} v_{i'j}\} + P_{j^*} - \sum_{i' \neq i} v_{i'j^*}$$

We use $M(P_1, P_2, \ldots, P_k)$ to denote the shifted Groves mechanism characterized by the P_j.

It should be noted that the shifted Groves mechanisms are special cases of *Affine Maximizer Auctions (AMA)* [10, 11]. There are many works on characterizing strategy-proof mechanisms in social choice settings. Roberts [15] shows that when the type space of agents is unrestricted (and there exist three or more choices), the only strategy-proof mechanisms are affine maximizers (of which the shifted Groves mechanisms are special cases). In our setting, the type space of agents is bounded so the results in [15] do not apply. There also exist works on characterizing strategy-proof mechanisms in a restricted domain. For example, [12] showed that all strategy-proof mechanisms are affine maximizers if the agents' valuations are drawn from intervals. However, [12] requires that the intervals be open (we use close intervals in this paper), and more importantly, it also requires that an agent's interval for all outcomes are identical

[4]For mechanisms that need to deal with tie-breaking, we assume tie-breaking is done randomly, and the worst-case efficiency loss considers all possible tie-breaking scenarios.

[5]If the chosen outcome is 1 (not build), then both agents receive 0 and $h_i(\theta_{-i}) = 0$ (*e.g.*, $h_1(\theta_{-1}) = \max\{0, -\frac{1}{2} + v_{22}\} = 0$).

(we do not require this, *e.g.*, for the public project problem, the agents obviously have different intervals for not build and build). Therefore, [12] also does not apply. For our setting, it remains to see whether all strategy-proof mechanisms are affine maximizers. Nevertheless, in this paper, we show that the optimal shifted Groves mechanism is optimal among all strategy-proof mechanisms, without relying on such characterization results.[6]

Based on how they are defined, all shifted Groves mechanisms are strategy-proof and individual rational. Unlike the Groves mechanisms, some shifted Groves mechanisms can be non-deficit (while being individually rational).

THEOREM 1. *Given a setting, if there exist mechanisms that are strategy-proof, individually rational, and non-deficit, then there must exist shifted Groves mechanisms with these properties.*

To prove the above theorem, we introduce the following lemma. We recall that $\sum_i L_{ij^*}$ is the agents' lowest possible total valuation for outcome j^*.

LEMMA 1. *If $\sum_i L_{ij^*} \geq 0$, then under all shifted Groves mechanisms (for all values of the P_j), when outcome j^* is chosen, deficit never occurs.*

PROOF. When outcome j^* is chosen, agent i's payment equals

$$\max_j\{-P_j + L_{ij} + \sum_{i' \neq i} v_{i'j}\} + P_{j^*} - \sum_{i' \neq i} v_{i'j^*}$$

$$\geq -P_{j^*} + L_{ij^*} + \sum_{i' \neq i} v_{i'j^*} + P_{j^*} - \sum_{i' \neq i} v_{i'j^*} = L_{ij^*}$$

Therefore, the agents' total payment is at least $\sum_i L_{ij^*}$, which is non-negative. □

Without loss of generality, we assume $\sum_i L_{i1} \geq \sum_i L_{i2} \geq \ldots \geq \sum_i L_{ik}$. Now we are ready to prove the theorem.

PROOF. If $\sum_i L_{i1} < 0$, then for some type profiles, the agents' total valuation for every outcome is negative. For these type profiles, individual rationality and non-deficit cannot coexist.

If $\sum_i L_{i1} \geq 0$, then under any shifted Groves mechanism, outcome 1 never incurs deficit. We may simply "shift down" every outcome except for 1 (for all $j > 1$, set P_j to be really large), so that only outcome 1 can be possibly chosen (*e.g.*, ensure that for all $j > 1$, $-P_j + \sum_i U_{ij} < \sum_i L_{i1}$). The resulting mechanism simply always picks outcome 1, which guarantees the non-deficit property according to Lemma 1. We already know that all shifted Groves mechanisms are strategy-proof (they are part of the AMA family) and individually rational (the way we set the $h_i(\theta_{-i})$ term guarantees individual rationality).

In conclusion, if $\sum_i L_{i1} < 0$, no mechanisms can be both individually rational and non-deficit. If $\sum_i L_{i1} \geq 0$, there exist shifted Groves mechanisms that are strategy-proof, individually rational, and non-deficit. □

[6]It should be noted that even if all strategy-proof mechanisms are affine maximizers for our setting, we still need to prove that only "shifts" are needed to reach the optimal mechanism, since affine maximizers also rely on "weights" (multiplication).

Based on the proof of Theorem 1, from this point on, we assume $\sum_i L_{i1} \geq 0$. Otherwise, no feasible mechanisms exist. For many settings, there exists an outcome which corresponds to the *status quo* (*e.g.*, not build in the public project problem). The agents' valuations for the status quo are all equal to 0. If the status quo belongs to the set of outcomes, then according to Theorem 1, there exist mechanisms that are strategy-proof, individually rational, and non-deficit.

Given $\sum_i L_{i1} \geq 0$, we also have that for all j, $\sum_i U_{ij} \geq 0$, because our assumption is that there do not exist two outcomes, so that the agents always prefer one to the other for all type profiles.

We do not have to study all shifted Groves mechanisms. First of all, we only consider those that are non-deficit (we call these shifted Groves mechanisms *feasible*). We also ignore those that are not *onto*.

Definition 3. A shifted Groves mechanism $M(P_1, P_2, \ldots, P_k)$ is **onto** *iff* under it, for every outcome j, there exists at least one type profile for which j is chosen by the mechanism (or may be chosen by the mechanism assuming random tie-breaking).

Formally, this means that for every pair of outcomes a and b, we have

$$-P_a + \sum_i U_{ia} \geq -P_b + \sum_i L_{ib}$$

LEMMA 2. *Let $M(P_1, P_2, \ldots, P_k)$ be a shifted Groves mechanism that is feasible but not onto. There must exist another feasible shifted Groves mechanism that is onto, and has the same or higher allocative efficiency for all type profiles.*

PROOF. If $M(P_1, P_2, \ldots, P_k)$ is feasible but not onto, then there exist two outcomes a and b, so that

$$-P_a + \sum_i U_{ia} < -P_b + \sum_i L_{ib}$$

We can simply decrease P_a so that

$$-P_a + \sum_i U_{ia} = -P_b + \sum_i L_{ib}$$

This modification does not change the allocative efficiency of any type profile, except for maybe when $v_{ia} = U_{ia}$ and $v_{ib} = L_{ib}$ for all i. For this case, a may be chosen instead of b. We have that $\sum_i U_{ij} > \sum_i L_{ij'}$ for every pair of j and j'. That is, the above modification never decreases the allocative efficiency. The modification also does not change the payments of any agents when outcome a is not chosen. So for outcomes other than a, the modified mechanism is still non-deficit. Finally, when a is indeed chosen, agent i's payment equals

$$\max_j\{-P_j + L_{ij} + \sum_{i' \neq i} v_{i'j}\} + P_a - \sum_{i' \neq i} v_{i'a}$$

$$\geq -P_b + L_{ib} + \sum_{i' \neq i} v_{i'b} + P_a - \sum_{i' \neq i} v_{i'a}$$

$$\geq -P_a + \sum_i U_{ia} + P_a - \sum_{i' \neq i} v_{i'a} \geq U_{ia}$$

The total payment is then at least $\sum_i U_{ia}$, which is at least 0 (at least $\sum_i L_{i1}$). In summary, the modified mechanism remains feasible and has the same or higher allocative efficiency. We can repeat the above process until the mechanism becomes onto. □

THEOREM 2. *Let $M(P_1, P_2, \ldots, P_k)$ be a shifted Groves mechanism that is both feasible and onto. $M(P_1, P_2, \ldots, P_k)$'s worst-case efficiency loss is $\max_j P_j - \min_j P_j$.*

Theorem 2 directly follows from the following two lemmas:

LEMMA 3. *Let $M(P_1, P_2, \ldots, P_k)$ be a shifted Groves mechanism. $M(P_1, P_2, \ldots, P_k)$ and $M(P_1-\Delta, P_2-\Delta, \ldots, P_k-\Delta)$ are equivalent (Δ is an arbitrary constant).*

The above lemma directly follows from Definition 2. It implies that $M(P_1, P_2, \ldots, P_k)$ and $M(P_1 - \min_j P_j, P_2 - \min_j P_j, \ldots, P_k - \min_j P_j)$ are equivalent. That is, it is without loss of generality to focus on cases where the P_j are non-negative, and at least one of the P_j is 0.

LEMMA 4. *Let $M(P_1, P_2, \ldots, P_k)$ be a shifted Groves mechanism that is feasible and onto. The P_j are non-negative and $\min_j P_j = 0$. $M(P_1, P_2, \ldots, P_k)$'s worst-case efficiency loss is $\max_j P_j$.*

PROOF. If $\max_j P_j = 0$, then the mechanism is simply a Groves mechanism, which is efficient (worst-case efficiency loss is 0). We then analyze cases with $\max_j P_j > 0$.

First of all, it is easy to see that the worst-case efficiency loss is at most $\max_j P_j$. We only need to prove that it is also at least this much.

Let $P_a = 0$ and $P_b = \max_j P_j$. a and b are different. We construct the following type profile: $v_{ij} = L_{ij}$ for all i and all $j \neq a, b$. Due to the onto property, we have $\sum_i U_{ia} = -P_a + \sum_i U_{ia} \geq \max_j(-P_j + \sum_i L_{ij})$. We certainly have $\sum_i L_{ia} = -P_a + \sum_i L_{ia} \leq \max_j(-P_j + \sum_i L_{ij})$. Therefore, we can set the v_{ia} so that $\sum_i v_{ia} = \max_j(-P_j + \sum_i L_{ij})$. This ensures that a is at least tied with all $j \neq b$. Again, due to the onto property, we have $-P_b + \sum_i U_{ib} \geq \max_j(-P_j + \sum_i L_{ij}) \geq -P_b + \sum_i L_{ib}$. We set the v_{ib} so that outcome b is tied with a. For this type profile, since we assume random tie-breaking, a may be chosen ahead of b, which corresponds to an efficiency loss of $\max_j P_j$. □

Next we try to find the optimal shifted Groves mechanism. As mentioned earlier, we only need to consider shifted Groves mechanisms that are feasible and onto. Also, we only need to consider cases where the P_j are non-negative and at least one of the P_j is 0.

Definition 4. A shifted Groves mechanism $M(P_1, P_2, \ldots, P_k)$ is **optimal**, if there does not exist another shifted Groves mechanism $M(P_1', P_2', \ldots, P_k')$, so that $P_i' \leq P_i$ for all i.

Our aim is to minimize the worst-case efficiency loss. Based on Lemma 4. the optimal shifted Groves mechanism should minimize $\max_j P_j$. We will prove later on that this is indeed the case, and the optimal mechanism is unique. Before that, we first propose a linear program based AMD approach for identifying the optimal mechanism.

Given a shifted Groves mechanism $M(P_1, P_2, \ldots, P_k)$, we can calculate the maximal deficit for outcome j^* using the following linear program:

Constants: L_{ij}, U_{ij}, P_j, j^*
Variables: v_{ij}
Dummy Variables: d_i (d_i represents agent i's payment)
Maximize: $-\sum_i d_i$ (maximize deficit)
Subject to:
For all $j \neq j^*$,

$$-P_{j^*} + \sum_i v_{ij^*} \geq -P_j + \sum_i v_{ij} \quad (1)$$

For all j,

$$d_i \geq (-P_j + L_{ij} + \sum_{i' \neq i} v_{i'j}) + P_{j^*} - \sum_{i' \neq i} v_{i'j^*} \quad (2)$$

For all i and j,

$$L_{ij} \leq v_{ij} \leq U_{ij}$$

Constraint 1 ensures that we are dealing with type profiles where outcome j^* is chosen. Constraint 2 ensures that d_i represents agent i's payment. That is,

$$d_i = \max_j\{-P_j + L_{ij} + \sum_{i' \neq i} v_{i'j}\} + P_{j^*} - \sum_{i' \neq i} v_{i'j^*}$$

This is true because the linear program will minimize the d_i in order to maximize the objective.

The above linear program can be significantly simplified. We may divide Constraint 2 into the following two:

For all $j \neq j^*$,

$$d_i \geq (-P_j + L_{ij} + \sum_{i' \neq i} v_{i'j}) + P_{j^*} - \sum_{i' \neq i} v_{i'j^*} \quad (3)$$

For $j = j^*$,

$$d_i \geq (-P_j + L_{ij} + \sum_{i' \neq i} v_{i'j}) + P_{j^*} - \sum_{i' \neq i} v_{i'j^*} = L_{ij^*} \quad (4)$$

Constraint 4 has nothing to do with the v_{ij}. For Constraint 1 and 3, they are the most relaxed if we set $v_{ij} = L_{ij}$ for all i and all $j \neq j^*$, and we set $v_{ij^*} = U_{ij^*}$ for all i. After simplification, we have

Constants: L_{ij}, U_{ij}, P_j, j^*
Dummy Variables: d_i (d_i represents agent i's payment)
Maximize: $-\sum_i d_i$ (maximize deficit)
Subject to:
For all $j \neq j^*$,

$$-P_{j^*} + \sum_i U_{ij^*} \geq -P_j + \sum_i L_{ij} \quad (5)$$

For all $j \neq j^*$ and all i,

$$d_i \geq (-P_j + \sum_{i'} L_{i'j}) + P_{j^*} - \sum_{i' \neq i} U_{i'j^*} \quad (6)$$

$$d_i \geq L_{ij^*} \quad (7)$$

Constraint 5 is already guaranteed by the onto property. The objective value of the above linear program is simply

$$-\sum_i \max\{\max_{j \neq j^*}\{-P_j + \sum_{i'} L_{i'j}\} + P_{j^*} - \sum_{i' \neq i} U_{i'j^*}, L_{ij^*}\}$$

We use $D_{j^*}(P_1, P_2, \ldots, P_k)$ to denote the above objective value. That is, $D_{j^*}(P_1, P_2, \ldots, P_k)$ represents the maximal deficit under the shifted Groves mechanism $M(P_1, P_2, \ldots, P_k)$, when outcome j^* is chosen,

We notice that $D_{j^*}(P_1, P_2, \ldots, P_k)$ is non-increasing in P_{j^*} and non-decreasing in P_j for $j \neq j^*$. This leads to the following AMD approach.

- Start from $P_1 = P_2 = \ldots = P_k = 0$. That is, we start from the original Groves mechanism, which is onto but not necessarily feasible.
- For every outcome j^*, if $D_{j^*}(P_1, P_2, \ldots, P_k)$ is positive, then increase P_{j^*} until $D_{j^*}(P_1, P_2, \ldots, P_k)$ reaches 0. This move maintains the onto property. If after the modification, it is no longer onto, then we have $-P_j^* + \sum_i U_{ij^*} < \max_{j \neq j^*}\{-P_j + \sum_i L_{ij}\}$. For $D_{j^*}(P_1, P_2, \ldots, P_k)$, we then have

$$-\sum_i \max\{\max_{j \neq j^*}\{-P_j + \sum_{i'} L_{i'j}\} + P_{j^*} - \sum_{i' \neq i} U_{i'j^*}, L_{ij^*}\}$$

$$\leq -\sum_i (\max_{j \neq j^*}\{-P_j + \sum_{i'} L_{i'j}\} + P_{j^*} - \sum_{i' \neq i} U_{i'j^*})$$

$$< -\sum_i (\sum_i U_{ij^*} - \sum_{i' \neq i} U_{i'j^*}) = -\sum_i U_{ij^*} \leq 0$$

That is, $D_{j^*}(P_1, P_2, \ldots, P_k)$ is negative, which contradicts with the algorithm description.

THEOREM 3. *The AMD process produces a unique optimal shifted Groves mechanism that is feasible, onto, and has minimal worst-case efficiency loss among all shifted Groves mechanisms.*

PROOF. If we follow the AMD steps, then P_1 must remain 0, because according to Lemma 1, $D_1(P_1, P_2, \ldots, P_k)$ is never positive. This implies that in all calculations, for $j > 1$,

$$-P_1 + \sum_i L_{i1} = \sum_i L_{i1} \geq \sum_i L_{ij} \geq -P_j + \sum_i L_{ij}$$

This fact further simplifies $D_{j^*}(P_1, P_2, \ldots, P_k)$ for $j^* > 1$:

$$-\sum_i \max\{\max_{j \neq j^*}\{-P_j + \sum_{i'} L_{i'j}\} + P_{j^*} - \sum_{i' \neq i} U_{i'j^*}, L_{ij^*}\}$$

$$= -\sum_i \max\{\sum_{i'} L_{i'1} + P_{j^*} - \sum_{i' \neq i} U_{i'j^*}, L_{ij^*}\}$$

That is, the maximal deficit for outcome j^* depends only on P_{j^*} (the other P_j values are irrelevant). Therefore, the AMD algorithm does produce a feasible mechanism that is onto.

Next, we prove the optimal mechanism is unique. Let $M(P_1^*, P_2^*, \ldots, P_k^*)$ be an optimal mechanism. When we start the AMD process, we have $P_1 = P_2 = \ldots = P_k = 0$. That is, we have $P_j \leq P_j^*$ for all j. During the AMD, if $D_j(P_1, P_2, \ldots, P_k) > 0$. The AMD process increases P_j to $P_j + \Delta$ so that $D_j(P_1, P_2, \ldots, P_k) = 0$. We recall that $D_j(P_1, P_2, \ldots, P_k)$ is non-increasing in P_j and non-decreasing in $P_{j'}$ for $j' \neq j$. Therefore,

$$0 = D_j(P_1, \ldots, P_{j-1}, P_j + \Delta, P_{j+1}, \ldots, P_k) \leq$$

$$D_j(P_1^*, \ldots, P_{j-1}^*, P_j + \Delta, P_{j+1}^*, \ldots, P_k^*)$$

We also have

$$D_j(P_1^*, \ldots, P_{j-1}^*, P_j^*, P_{j+1}^*, \ldots, P_k^*) \leq 0$$

Therefore, we have $P_j^* \geq P_j + \Delta$. That is, after the AMD, we have $P_j \leq P_j^*$ for all j. Since we assumed $M(P_1^*, P_2^*, \ldots, P_k^*)$ to be optimal, we should have $P_j = P_j^*$ for all j after the AMD. Since $M(P_1^*, P_2^*, \ldots, P_k^*)$ is arbitrarily chosen, the optimal mechanism must be unique.

If there exists a non-optimal mechanism $M(P_1', P_2', \ldots, P_k')$ that minimize the worst-case efficiency loss. Then there must exist an optimal mechanism $M(P_1^*, P_2^*, \ldots, P_k^*)$ satisfying $P_j^* \leq P_j'$ for all j. Then by Lemma 4, $M(P_1^*, P_2^*, \ldots, P_k^*)$ should have the same or less worst-case efficiency loss. □

Finally, based on Lemma 1, for all j with $\sum_i L_{ij} \geq 0$, we have $D_j(P_1, P_2, \ldots, P_k) \leq 0$ for all the P_j. This implies that when conducting the AMD, if $\sum_i L_{ij} \geq 0$, we simply leave P_j to be 0.

4. GLOBAL OPTIMALITY

Theorem 3 only shows that the optimal shifted Groves mechanism is optimal *within* the family of shifted Groves mechanisms. Here, we show that it is also optimal among all deterministic mechanisms that are strategy-proof, individually rational, and non-deficit.

LEMMA 5. *When there are only two outcomes, the optimal shifted Groves mechanism has the lowest worst-case efficiency loss among all deterministic mechanisms that are strategy-proof, individually rational, and non-deficit.*

PROOF. We denote outcome 1 by a and outcome 2 by b. We have the usual assumptions that $\sum_i L_{ia} \geq \sum_i L_{ib}$ and $\sum_i L_{ia} \geq 0$. Let H be a deterministic mechanism that is strategy-proof, individually rational, and non-deficit. Let Δ be H's worst-case efficiency loss. We show that there exists a shifted Groves mechanism with the same or lower worst-case efficiency loss.

If $\Delta \geq \sum_i U_{ib} - \sum_i L_{ia}$, then we can simply construct a trivial shifted Groves mechanism that always chooses a (choosing a never results in deficit), and this mechanism's worst-case efficiency loss is at most Δ. Therefore, we only need to consider $\Delta < \sum_i U_{ib} - \sum_i L_{ia}$.

We consider the shifted Groves mechanism $M(0, \Delta + \epsilon)$, where ϵ is a small positive value ($\Delta + \epsilon < \sum_i U_{ib} - \sum_i L_{ia}$). For simplicity, we simply call this mechanism M. M's worst-case efficiency loss is at most $\Delta + \epsilon$. If we can show that M is non-deficit, then that means one feasible shifted Groves mechanism has a worst-case efficiency loss of at most $\Delta + \epsilon$. ϵ can be made arbitrary small, which means that there must exist a feasible shifted Groves mechanism with a worst-case efficiency loss of at most Δ. This proves that the optimal shifted Groves mechanism is globally optimal.

Now we prove that M is non-deficit. When outcome a is chosen, by Lemma 1, deficit will not occur. We only need to prove that when M chooses b, there will not be deficit.

Whenever M chooses b, we know that the agents prefer b to a by at least $\Delta + \epsilon$, which means that H must also choose b.

Let (θ_i, θ_{-i}) be a type profile for which M chooses b. For this type profile, H must also choose b. We analyze agent i's payment under H and M.

Case 1: Under M, given θ_{-i}, no matter what agent i reports, the outcome is always b. If this is the case, then under H, given θ_{-i}, no matter what agent i reports, the outcome is always b. (Whenever b is chosen under M, H must also choose b.) H is deterministic. Agent i's payment under H must be fixed (does not change with the report). Otherwise, H is not strategy-proof. Let x be agent i's payment. x must be at most L_{ib}. Otherwise, H is not individually rational. Agent i's payment under M is exactly L_{ib} according to the definition. That is, for Case 1, agent i pays the same or more under M.

Case 2: Under M, given θ_{-i}, both a and b may be chosen (depending on θ_i). When b is chosen, agent i pays

$$\max\{L_{ia} + \sum_{i' \neq i}(v_{i'a} - v_{i'b}) + \Delta + \epsilon, L_{ib}\}$$

We divide Case 2 into the following sub-cases.

Case 2i: If under H, given θ_{-i}, no matter what agent i reports, the outcome is always b, then as analyzed earlier, agent i pays at most L_{ib}. That is, for Case 2i, agent i pays the same or more under M.

Case 2ii: Under H, given θ_{-i}, for some θ_i, outcome a is chosen, and for some other θ_i, outcome b is chosen. We recall that H is deterministic. When a is chosen, agent i's payment must be a fixed amount that is independent of θ_i. Otherwise, H is not strategy-proof. We use p_a^H to denote this amount. Similarly, we use p_b^H to denote the fixed payment paid by i whenever b is chosen. Let $C^H = p_b^H - p_a^H$. This C^H value is a critical value: whenever agent i favors outcome b by more than C^H, outcome b will be chosen (otherwise, a is chosen). This critical value C^H must be less than $\sum_{i' \neq i}(v_{i'a} - v_{i'b}) + \Delta + \epsilon$. Otherwise, H may choose a when the agents favor b by more than Δ, which contradicts with the fact that H's worst-case efficiency loss is Δ. H is individually rational, which means that we either have $p_a^H \leq L_{ia}$ or $p_b^H \leq L_{ib}$. Otherwise, agent i may end up not able to afford either outcome. So we have $p_b^H - C^H \leq L_{ia}$ or $p_b^H \leq L_{ib}$. That is,

$$p_b^H \leq \max\{L_{ia} + C^H, L_{ib}\}$$

$$\leq \max\{L_{ia} + \sum_{i' \neq i}(v_{i'a} - v_{i'b}) + \Delta + \epsilon, L_{ib}\}$$

Therefore, for Case 2ii, agent i pays the same or more under M when b is chosen. □

THEOREM 4. *The optimal shifted Groves mechanism has the lowest worst-case efficiency loss among all deterministic mechanisms that are strategy-proof, individually rational, and non-deficit.*

PROOF. If there is only one outcome, then the optimal shifted Groves mechanism is the original Groves mechanism, which obviously minimizes the worst-case efficiency loss (as it is efficient). Lemma 5 already proved the case with two outcomes. We then consider cases with more than two outcomes.

We first analyze the worst-case efficiency loss of the optimal shifted Groves mechanism $M(P_1^*, P_2^*, \ldots, P_k^*)$. Reusing the analysis in the proof of Theorem 3, we must have $P_1^* = 0$. For $j > 1$, $P_j^* = 0$ if

$$-\sum_i \max\{\sum_{i'} L_{i'1} - \sum_{i' \neq i} U_{i'j}, L_{ij}\} \leq 0$$

Otherwise, P_j^* is the minimal value that makes

$$-\sum_i \max\{\sum_{i'} L_{i'1} + P_j^* - \sum_{i' \neq i} U_{i'j}, L_{ij}\} = 0$$

According to Lemma 4, the worst-case efficiency loss is simply $\max_j P_j^*$. Let $P_b^* = \max_j P_j^*$. If $P_b^* = 0$, then the shifted Groves mechanism is efficient, which obviously minimizes the worst-case efficiency loss. We only consider $P_b^* > 0$. When $P_b^* > 0$, P_b^* is the minimal value that makes

$$-\sum_i \max\{\sum_{i'} L_{i'1} + P_b^* - \sum_{i' \neq i} U_{i'b}, L_{ib}\} = 0$$

Let us then consider the following settings:

- Setting 1 is the original setting. That is, for all i and j, v_{ij} is in $[L_{ij}, U_{ij}]$.
- Setting 2 is a restricted version of setting 1.
  - Outcome 1: For all i, let $v_{i1} = L_{i1}$.
  - Outcome b: For all i, let v_{ib}'s range be the same as before, that is, in $[L_{ib}, U_{ib}]$.
  - Outcome j other than 1 and b: For all i, let $v_{ij} = C_{ij}$. C_{ij} is a constant chosen from $[L_{ij}, U_{ij}]$. We need $\sum_i C_{ij} = \sum_i L_{i1}$. The C_{ij} exist because $\sum_i L_{ij} \leq \sum_i L_{i1} \leq \sum_i U_{ij}$.
- Setting 3 is obtained by dropping all outcomes other than 1 and b.
  - Outcome 1: For all i, let $v_{i1} = L_{i1}$.
  - Outcome b: For all i, let v_{ib}'s range be $[L_{ib}, U_{ib}]$.

Let H_i be the strategy-proof, individually rational, and non-deficit mechanism that minimizes the worst-case efficiency loss in setting i. Let α_i be H_i's worst-case efficiency loss.

$\alpha_1 \geq \alpha_2$: Setting 2 is a restricted version of setting 1, so H_1 applies in setting 2, which means that the optimal worst-case efficiency loss in setting 2 is at most α_1.

$\alpha_2 \geq \alpha_3$: We first consider setting 2 and H_2. It is without loss of generality to assume that H_2 only chooses outcome 1 and b, because given a type profile, if H_2 chooses outcome $j \neq 1, b$, then we may simply change H_2 so that it chooses 1 instead. Then for all i, ask agent i to pay an additional payment equal to $L_{i1} - C_{ij}$. This makes the agents "as if" they are choosing outcome j. This change does not affect the agents' utilities (strategy-proofness and individual rationality are not affected). This change does not affect the total payment, as $\sum_i(L_{i1} - C_{ij}) = 0$ (non-deficit is not affected). This change does not affect the allocative efficiency, as the agents' total valuations for outcome 1 and j are the same. In conclusion, we can apply H_2 to setting 3, which implies that the optimal worst-case efficiency loss in setting 3 is at most α_2.

Above, we have proved that $\alpha_1 \geq \alpha_3$. According to Lemma 5, in setting 3, α_3 is achieved by the optimal shifted Groves mechanism. We run the AMD process on setting 3. We get that α_3 is the minimal value that makes

$$-\sum_i \max\{\sum_{i'} L_{i'1} + \alpha_3 - \sum_{i' \neq i} U_{i'b}, L_{ib}\} = 0$$

Now earlier we have shown that the optimal shifted Groves mechanism in setting 1 (the original setting) has the same worst-case efficiency loss as α_3. Given that $\alpha_1 \geq \alpha_3$, we must have that the optimal shifted Groves mechanism is optimal in the original setting, which concludes the proof. □

COROLLARY 1. *There exists a mechanism that is strategy-proof, individually rational, non-deficit, and efficient,* iff *for all $j > 1$, we have*

$$-\sum_i \max\{\sum_{i'} L_{i'1} - \sum_{i' \neq i} U_{i'j}, L_{ij}\} \leq 0$$

PROOF. According to Theorem 4, there exists a mechanism that is strategy-proof, individually rational, non-deficit, and efficient, iff the optimal shifted Groves mechanism is efficient.

Now the optimal shifted Groves mechanism is efficient iff it is $M(0, 0, \ldots, 0)$. That is, the optimal shifted Groves mechanism is efficient iff the AMD process carries out no updates at all, which is exactly when for all $j > 1$, we have

$$-\sum_i \max\{\sum_{i'} L_{i'1} - \sum_{i' \neq i} U_{i'j}, L_{ij}\} \leq 0$$

□

If for all $j > 1$, $\sum_i L_{ij} \geq 0$, then the above corollary applies. In this case, the original Groves mechanism $M(0, 0, \ldots, 0)$ (efficient) is the optimal shifted Groves mechanism.

5. NUMERICAL EXPERIMENTS

Given a setting, let the optimal shifted Groves mechanism be $M(P_1^*, P_2^*, \ldots, P_k^*)$. We recall that we must have $P_1^* = 0$. For $j > 1$, $P_j^* = 0$ if

$$-\sum_i \max\{\sum_{i'} L_{i'1} - \sum_{i' \neq i} U_{i'j}, L_{ij}\} \leq 0$$

Otherwise, P_j^* is the minimal value that makes

$$-\sum_i \max\{\sum_{i'} L_{i'1} + P_j^* - \sum_{i' \neq i} U_{i'j}, L_{ij}\} = 0$$

At the end, the maximal P_j^* defines the optimal worst-case efficiency loss.

We revisit Example 1 (the public project problem). There are only two outcomes. The optimal shifted Groves mechanism is $M(0, P_2^*)$. For $j = 2$, we have

$$-\sum_i \max\{\sum_{i'} L_{i'1} - \sum_{i' \neq i} U_{i'2}, L_{i2}\}$$

$$= -\sum_i \max\{-\sum_{i' \neq i} \frac{n-1}{n}, -\frac{1}{n}\} > 0$$

We then need to find the minimal P_2^* that makes

$$-\sum_i \max\{P_2^* - \sum_{i' \neq i} \frac{n-1}{n}, -\frac{1}{n}\} = 0$$

We get that $P_2^* = \frac{(n-1)^2}{n}$, which is then the optimal worst-case efficiency loss of the public project problem.

Resource allocations with externalities can also be modelled as social decision problems, for which our AMD approach can be applied. Below we present a variant of the k-winner selection problem described in [16].

Example 3. There are n agents. We need to choose at most 2 winners (*e.g.* there are 2 Ad slots for n advertisers). There are $1 + n + \frac{n(n-1)}{2}$ outcomes. There is 1 outcome that selects 0 winners. There are n outcomes that select 1 winner. Finally, there are $\frac{n(n-1)}{2}$ outcomes that select 2 winners.

Agent i's valuation for an outcome consists of two parts. One part is her valuation for winning, which is a value from 0 to 1. The other part is her "externality" toward the other agent selected by the outcome, if she is not the only winner. The externality value is from -1 to 1.

For outcome $\{\}$ (no winners), the agents' valuations are all 0. For outcome $\{a\}$ (the only winner is a), agent a's valuation is from 0 to 1, and the other agents' valuations are all 0. For outcome $\{a, b\}$ (the winners are a and b), agent a's valuation is from -1 to 2 (same for b), and the other agents' valuations are all 0.

As usual, we sort the outcomes according to the agents' minimal total valuations. So outcome 1 should be $\{\}$. We have $L_{i1} = U_{i1} = 0$. The next n outcomes should be $\{a\}$ for $a = 1, 2, \ldots, n$. For outcome j among these outcomes, we have $\sum_i L_{ij} = 0$, so these outcomes never cause deficit and can be ignored. Finally, the next $\frac{n(n-1)}{2}$ outcomes should be $\{a, b\}$ for every pair of a and b from $1, 2, \ldots, n$.

The worst-case efficiency loss is caused by one of the outcomes that selects 2 winners. Due to symmetry, we only consider the outcome $\{1, 2\}$. We denote this outcome by j. We have that the worst-case efficiency loss for this outcome is P_j, where P_j is the minimal value that makes

$$-\sum_i \max\{\sum_{i'} L_{i'1} + P_j - \sum_{i' \neq i} U_{i'j}, L_{ij}\} = 0$$

Plugging in the numbers, we have

$$-\sum_i \max\{P_j - \sum_{i' \neq i} U_{i'j}, L_{ij}\} = 0$$

Simplify it, we get

$$-2\max\{P_j - 2, -1\} - (n-2)\max\{P_j - 4, 0\} = 0$$

Solving the above equation, we get that P_j should be 2. That is, the optimal worst-case efficiency loss is 2.

6. CONCLUSION

For the problem where a group of agents need to choose from a finite set of outcomes, we proposed the optimal shifted Groves mechanism, which is strategy-proof, individually rational, non-deficit, and minimizes the worst-case efficiency loss. One immediate future research direction is to study other objectives, such as minimizing the expected efficiency loss given a prior distribution. We may also consider settings where we drop certain assumptions (*e.g.*, an agent's valuation space is not a closed interval, or the agents' valuations are interdependent).

7. ACKNOWLEDGMENTS

This work was partially supported by JSPS KAKENHI Grant Number 24220003 and 26730005, and JST PRESTO program.

REFERENCES

[1] R. Cavallo. Optimal decision-making with minimal waste: Strategyproof redistribution of VCG payments. In *Proceedings of the International Conference on Autonomous Agents and Multi-Agent Systems (AAMAS)*, pages 882–889, Hakodate, Japan, 2006.

[2] V. Conitzer and T. Sandholm. Complexity of mechanism design. In *Proceedings of the 18th Annual Conference on Uncertainty in Artificial Intelligence (UAI)*, pages 103–110, Edmonton, Canada, 2002.

[3] B. Faltings. A budget-balanced, incentive-compatible scheme for social choice. In *Agent-Mediated Electronic Commerce (AMEC), LNAI, 3435*, pages 30–43, 2005.

[4] T. Groves. Incentives in teams. *Econometrica*, 41:617–631, 1973.

[5] M. Guo and V. Conitzer. Worst-case optimal redistribution of VCG payments in multi-unit auctions. *Games and Economic Behavior*, 67(1):69–98, 2009.

[6] M. Guo and V. Conitzer. Computationally feasible automated mechanism design: General approach and case studies. In *Proceedings of the National Conference on Artificial Intelligence (AAAI)*, pages 1676–1679, Atlanta, GA, USA, 2010. NECTAR track.

[7] M. Guo, E. Markakis, K. R. Apt, and V. Conitzer. Undominated groves mechanisms. *Journal of Artificial Intelligence Research*, 46:129–163, 2013.

[8] M. Guo, V. Naroditskiy, V. Conitzer, A. Greenwald, and N. R. Jennings. Budget-balanced and nearly efficient randomized mechanisms: Public goods and beyond. In *Proceedings of the Seventh Workshop on Internet and Network Economics (WINE)*, Singapore, 2011.

[9] B. Holmström. Groves' scheme on restricted domains. *Econometrica*, 47(5):1137–1144, 1979.

[10] A. Likhodedov and T. Sandholm. Methods for boosting revenue in combinatorial auctions. In *Proceedings of the National Conference on Artificial Intelligence (AAAI)*, pages 232–237, San Jose, CA, USA, 2004.

[11] A. Likhodedov and T. Sandholm. Approximating revenue-maximizing combinatorial auctions. In *Proceedings of the National Conference on Artificial Intelligence (AAAI)*, Pittsburgh, PA, USA, 2005.

[12] D. Mishra and A. Sen. Roberts' theorem with neutrality: A social welfare ordering approach. *Games and Economic Behavior*, 75(1):283–298, 2012.

[13] H. Moulin. Almost budget-balanced VCG mechanisms to assign multiple objects. *Journal of Economic Theory*, 144(1):96–119, 2009.

[14] V. Naroditskiy, M. Guo, L. Dufton, M. Polukarov, and N. R. Jennings. Redistribution of VCG payments in public project problems. In *Proceedings of the Eighth Workshop on Internet and Network Economics (WINE)*, Liverpool, 2012.

[15] K. Roberts. The characterization of implementable social choice rules. In J.-J. Laffont, editor, *Aggregation and Revelation of Preferences*. North-Holland Publishing Company, 1979.

[16] Y. Sakurai, T. Okimoto, M. Oka, and M. Yokoo. Strategy-proof mechanisms for the k-winner selection problem. In *Principles and Practice of Multi-Agent Systems (PRIMA)*, Dunedin, New Zealand, 2013.

Complexity of Mechanism Design with Signaling Costs

Andrew Kephart
Dept. of Computer Science
Duke University
kephart@cs.duke.edu

Vincent Conitzer
Dept. of Computer Science
Duke University
conitzer@cs.duke.edu

ABSTRACT

In mechanism design, it is generally assumed that an agent can submit any report at zero cost (with the occasional further restriction that certain types can not submit certain reports). More generally, however, an agent of type θ may be able to report θ', but only at a cost $c(\theta, \theta')$. This cost may reflect the effort the agent would have to expend to be indistinguishable from an agent that truthfully reports θ'. Even more generally, the possible reports (or *signals*) may not directly correspond to types. In this paper, we consider the complexity of determining whether particular social choice functions can be implemented in this context.

Categories and Subject Descriptors

I.2.11 [**Distributed Artificial Intelligence**]: Multiagent Systems; J.4 [**Computer Applications**]: Social and Behavioral Sciences - Economics

General Terms

Algorithms, Economics, Theory

Keywords

game theory; mechanism design; automated mechanism design; signaling costs; partial verification; revelation principle; implementation; complexity

1. INTRODUCTION

In settings with multiple self-interested agents, making a desirable collective decision is complicated by the fact that agents will misrepresent their preferences if they perceive this to be in their interest. In such settings, we must design mechanisms for making decisions that result in good outcomes even when agents act strategically. One topic of particular interest to the AI community has been *automated mechanism design* [5, 6], where instead of analytically characterizing optimal mechanisms, we have a computer intelligently search through the space of possible mechanisms to find an optimal one.

In mechanism design, an agent's private information is represented by his type. Generally the focus is on mechanisms in which each agent's action consists simply of reporting his type, justified by the *revelation principle* which states that, under certain conditions, this does not come at a loss. Usually, an agent can report any type at zero cost. However, in some of the literature, which types an agent can report depends on his type. For example, in the design of online mechanisms [14], it is generally assumed that an agent cannot report an earlier arrival time than his true arrival time. Settings such as these are referred to as *mechanism design with partial verification* [11].

In these settings, it can be computationally hard even to check whether a given social choice function—the function mapping types to outcomes—can be implemented [1, 4]. This is in contrast to regular (automated) mechanism design where this is easy to check thanks to the revelation principle, which no longer holds with partial verification.

In this paper, we consider a more general model, where for every two types θ, θ', an agent with true type θ can misreport θ', but only at a cost $c(\theta, \theta')$. Reporting truthfully is free: $c(\theta, \theta) = 0$. Mechanism design with partial verification is the special case where all costs are 0 or ∞. We also consider the even more general case where the space of *signals* that the agent can send does not correspond naturally to the type space, so that there is a cost $c(\theta, s)$ for an agent of type θ to send signal s, without restrictions on c. We focus on determining, under various conditions, the complexity of deciding whether a particular social choice function can be implemented. Our positive results hold even in this most general case, and our negative results even in the less general case where signals are type reports and reporting truthfully is free (in which case we will also refer to the signals as *reports*).

The motivation for our model is quite different from that of mechanism design with partial verification (even though it is a straightforward mathematical extension). In mechanism design with partial verification, as the name suggests, the designer has access to information (e.g., login time) that allows her to directly detect certain types of misreporting. This motivation has pushed existing extensions of the model in a somewhat different direction from ours, such as mechanism design with probabilistic verification [4], where an agent can misreport but is caught with a probability that depends on the true and reported type, and if caught the agent can be punished.

The inspiration for our model primarily comes from settings where a principal assesses an agent, perhaps based on information provided by that agent, and makes a decision. Examples include university admission, dating, insurance rate-setting, taxation etc. In each case, the agent, who knows he is being evaluated, may be able to present himself more favorably (i.e., send a better signal) at some amount of effort that depends on his true type.

In economics, such *signaling games* are often studied, with perhaps the most famous example being Spence's education model [15].

Appears in: *Proceedings of the 14th International Conference on Autonomous Agents and Multiagent Systems (AAMAS 2015), Bordini, Elkind, Weiss, Yolum (eds.), May, 4–8, 2015, Istanbul, Turkey.*

In this model, education serves as a useful signal of an agent's abilities to a potential employer, but is otherwise useless. In equilibrium, high types end up more educated than lower types, thereby signaling their type to the employer – and it is not worth it to lower types to "pool" with the higher types by obtaining education, because doing so comes at a much greater cost to the lower types. A mechanism design model with signaling costs, similar to ours, has also been proposed [9]. They show conditions for implementability when the agent can send multiple signals and the cost of misrepresentation increases with the magnitude of it.

We believe that these types of consideration will also be increasingly important in machine learning. For example, consider an e-commerce setting where an algorithm classifies visitors to a website in order to determine whether to make them a special offer on a product. When users get wind of this, they may, at some cost to themselves, attempt to change their classification, for example by erasing their cookies, using a different URL to reach the website, etc. Indeed the problem of *adversarial classification* has already received some attention in machine learning, motivated by detecting spam, intrusions, fraud, etc. [7, 3]. Our contribution here is to make the link to mechanism design and create the right machinery for this on the mechanism design side. Another key difference is our work is motivated by classifying *agents* while adversarial classification emphasizes classifying *actions* taken by agents. This makes it much easier to for us to create this link. We can abstract away the classifier to the cost function, whereas, when classifying actions the specific form of the classifier matters more.

2. MODEL

Throughout, we focus on the case of a single agent. The agent draws a type θ from a set Θ. Subsequently, the agent chooses a single signal s to emit from a set S (possibly but not necessarily, $S = \Theta$). The agent experiences a cost $c(\theta, s)$ (possibly infinite) from doing so. The mechanism maps s to an outcome (e.g., allocation) $o \in O$, as well as, if we allow for transfers, a transfer t to the agent. The agent's resulting utility is $u(\theta, s, o, p) = v(\theta, o) + t - c(\theta, s)$, where $v(\theta, o)$ is the agent's valuation for the outcome.

Let $A : S \to O$ denote the mapping of signals to outcomes, let $T : S \to \mathbb{R}$ denote the mapping of signals to transfers to the agent, and let $M = (A, T)$ be the entire mechanism. We will simply drop t and T in cases where transfers are not possible. As always, the designer commits to M first, after which the agent responds with some $s^* \in \arg\max_{s \in S} u(\theta, s, A(s), T(s))$.

Let $F : \Theta \to O$ be a *social choice function (SCF)* that we seek to implement. We say that M *implements* F if for every $\theta \in \Theta$, there exists some $s^* \in S$ with $c(\theta^*, s) < \infty$ such that (1) $s^* \in \arg\max_{s \in S} u(\theta, s, A(s), T(s))$ and (2) $A(s) = F(\theta)$. In standard mechanism design, where $S = \Theta$ and $c(\cdot, \cdot) = 0$ everywhere, the revelation principle holds, so that one can assume without loss of generality that $A(\theta) = F(\theta)$. However, as is well known, this is already no longer true in the partial verification setting (where $c : \Theta \times \Theta \to \{0, \infty\}$ with $c(\theta, \theta) = 0$), and therefore also not in our more general setting.

2.1 Example: Car Insurance

We include an example to illustrate the model. Brad would like to buy car insurance from Sally. Brad is either a *safe* driver or a *risky* driver. Sally would like to sell to Brad if he is *safe* and not sell to him if he is *risky*. In the language of our model this gives:

$\Theta = \{safe, risky\}$
$O = \{sale, no\ sale\}$
$F = \{safe \to sale, risky \to no\ sale\}$

Sally requires that Brad take a driving test, the result of which can be *perfect*, *good*, or *bad*. How much effort he needs to put into the test depends on both his true type, and which result he wants to achieve. This effort could take many forms (getting a good night's sleep before the test, bribing the test proctor, etc). Specifically:

$c =$

	perfect	*good*	*bad*
safe	10	0	0
risky	30	15	0

Brad's value for insurance also depends on his type: the worse of a driver he really is, the more valuable insurance is to him. We have:

$v =$

	sale	*no sale*
safe	12	0
risky	20	0

Now, Sally must choose a mechanism that maps the result of the test to an outcome. In the case without transfers, the naïve mechanism, $A = \{perfect \to sale, good \to sale, bad \to no\ sale\}$ wouldn't implement F. This is because if Brad has the *risky* type, it would then be optimal for him to put in the 15 units of effort cost to a achieve a score of *good* and get the 20 units of value for being insured.

A mechanism (still without transfers) that would succeed at implementing F is $A = \{perfect \to sale, good \to no\ sale, bad \to no\ sale\}$. Under this mechanism, if Brad has type *safe* it would be worth it to him to put in the effort to achieve a score of *perfect* on the test and obtain insurance; but if he has type *risky*, it is not worth the 30 units of effort cost to do so.[1]

With transfers, we could of course use the above mechanism with transfers set to zero, but other possibilities emerge as well. For example, the mechanism $M(A, T)$ with $A = \{perfect \to sale, good \to sale, bad \to no\ sale\}$ and transfers $T = \{perfect \to 0, good \to -6, bad \to 0\}$ would implement F, for the following reasons. If Brad has the *risky* type then it is no longer worth it for him to test as *good* (the effort cost of 15 plus the required transfer of 6 would outweigh the 20 benefit from insurance), but if he has the *safe* type he is happy to pay 6 for being insured (with no effort cost).[2]

In the example above, there is a clear distinction between the type space and the signal space; in fact, they do not even have the same size. However, the example can be modified to make the type space and the signal space the same, by introducing a new type *supersafe* that can obtain a score of *perfect* (or any other score) at no cost, which naturally Sally would like to insure. Then, we can relabel *perfect* as a report of *supersafe*, *good* as *safe*, and *bad* as *risky*. Hence, Brad would always be able to report his true type at zero cost.

Because these modifications do not change the behavior of the *safe* and *risky* types at all, the analysis above remains unchanged. It follows that the revelation principle does not hold in this context (as is the case in the partial verification model): without transfers, F is not truthfully implementable but it is (nontruthfully) implementable. It also shows that we cannot solve the problem by reduc-

[1]Note that if the effort that Brad had to expend as a *safe* driver to achieve the *perfect* result were increased to anything greater than 12, then F would be no longer implementable (without transfers) at all.

[2]Note that if we set $c(safe, perfect) > 22$ and $c(safe, good) > 7$, then even with transfers, no mechanism could implement F. This is because under these conditions, whenever it is worth it for a *safe* type to obtain insurance, then it is also worth it for a *risky* type, no matter the transfers.

		Transfers (T)		No Transfers (NT)	
		Two Outcomes (TO)	*Injective SCF (FI)*	*Two Outcomes (TO)*	*Injective SCF (FI)*
Free Utilities (FU)	*Unrestricted Costs (U)*	NP-c	**NP-c**	NP-c	**NP-c**
	$\{0, \infty\}$ *Costs (ZI)*	NP-c	**NP-c**	NP-c	**P**
Targeted Utilities (TU)	*Unrestricted Costs (U)*	**NP-c**	**P**	NP-c	**P**
	$\{0, \infty\}$ *Costs (ZI)*	**NP-c**	**P**	NP-c	**P**

Figure 1: Complexity of implementation results with non-constant $|\Theta|$ and non-constant $|S|$. Bold font represents new results proven in this paper; others were proven in, or follow immediately from, work by Auletta et al.

ing it to mechanism design without costly signaling by somehow embedding the reporting costs into the valuations or transfers.

In the traditional setting without costs, it is straightforward to check whether a particular social choice function can be implemented, precisely due to the revelation principle; but as we will see, with general costs it is (in some cases) NP-hard.

3. COMPLEXITY OF IMPLEMENTATION

In this paper, we are interested in the complexity of the following problem.

DEFINITION 1 (IMPLEMENTATION). *We are given an instance I consisting of a type set Θ, a signal set S, an outcome set O, a cost function $c : \Theta \times S \to \mathbb{R}$, a valuation function $v : \Theta \times O \to \mathbb{R}$, an SCF $F : \Theta \to O$, and potentially some additional restrictions on the mechanism. We are asked whether F can be implemented.*

The restrictions correspond to (1) the case where transfers are not allowed and (2) the case where for every type, we have a "target" utility $g(\theta) \in \mathbb{R}$ that it should obtain.

The IMPLEMENTATION problem is in NP: given the outcome function $A : S \to O$ and a mapping $E : \Theta \to S$ with $A(E(\theta)) = F(\theta)$, we can check in polynomial time whether there is a transfer function (possibly required to be 0) such that (1) the agent is best off following E and (2, if necessary) each type gets its target utility. (One can write a linear program with the transfers as variables for this problem.[3]) As we will see, in general, it is NP-complete. We will be interested in special cases where the problem is tractable.

If $|\Theta|$ is constant, IMPLEMENTATION is in P, by the following argument. We can do a brute-force search over all E as $|E| = |S|^{|\Theta|}$. This will restrict A on the signals that are in the image of E. For the remaining signals, if transfers are allowed, we can impose a sufficiently negative transfer on such signals that the agent will never choose them. If transfers are not allowed, we can check for each such signal s separately whether we can set $A(s)$ so that no type will choose s. At this point, we have both A and E and can check whether they can be made to work as above.

If $|S|$ constant and we are in the setting without transfers, IMPLEMENTATION is in P, by the following argument. We can do a brute-force search over all $M = A$ as $|A| = |O|^{|S|}$ (a mechanism consists in assigning an outcome to each signal). It is easy to then check whether each type can maximize utility by choosing a signal that results in its assigned outcome.

We currently do not know the complexity of the case where transfers are allowed, and $|S|$ is constant but $|\Theta|$ is not. Of course, this cannot happen in mechanisms where $S = \Theta$.

[3]Note that this generalizes the observation that this problem is in P when $S = \Theta$ and $c(\cdot, \cdot) = 0$ everywhere, because by the revelation principle in that case it is sufficient to consider the case where E is the identity function and $A = F$.

In the remainder of the paper, we consider the following four different dimensions of the problem. For each dimension, we only consider its two extremes, leading to $2^4 = 16$ cases. Figure 1 shows our results.

Utilities We consider implementation with free utilities (FU) and with targeted utilities (TU). In the latter case we are given a function $g : \Theta \to \mathbb{R}$, and restrict attention to implementations where type θ gets utility $g(\theta)$.

Transfers We consider implementation with transfers (T) and without (NT).

Signaling Costs We consider instances where the signaling costs are unrestricted (U) and instances where signaling costs lie in $\{0, \infty\}$ (ZI).

Outcomes We consider SCFs with only two outcomes (TO) and SCFs that are injective (FI) – i.e., for every outcome there is at most one type that gets it.[4]

We refer to each of the 16 combinations with an acronym. For instance, FU/NT/U/FI is the combination of free utilities, no transfers, unrestricted signaling costs, and an SCF that is injective. Clearly, ZI is a special case of U, but for the other dimensions, it is not immediately clear which extreme point is easier. For example, one might think that TO cases are easier than FI cases because the former have only two outcomes—but, perhaps surprisingly, this is not the case: for example, we show that FU/NT/ZI/FI can be solved in polynomial time, even though FU/NT/ZI/TO is NP-complete as shown in [1].

3.1 Cases Implied by Earlier Work

For six of the two-outcome cases, NP-completeness results have either been proven in or follow immediately from [1]. (As in our paper, their hardness results hold in the setting where $S = \Theta$ and $c(\theta, \theta) = 0$ for all $\theta \in \Theta$.)

THEOREM 1 ([1]). *FU/T/ZI/TO is NP-complete.*

The hardness of FU/T/U/TO immediately follows.

THEOREM 2 ([1]). *FU/NT/ZI/TO is NP-complete.*

The hardness of FU/NT/U/TO immediately follows.

THEOREM 3. *TU/NT/ZI/TO is NP-complete.*

The hardness of TU/NT/U/TO immediately follows.

[4]These two cases are the extremes, in the sense that two is the smallest nontrivial number of outcomes and $|\Theta|$, which corresponds to the injective case, is the largest. Moreover, they both correspond to natural settings, as our examples illustrate.

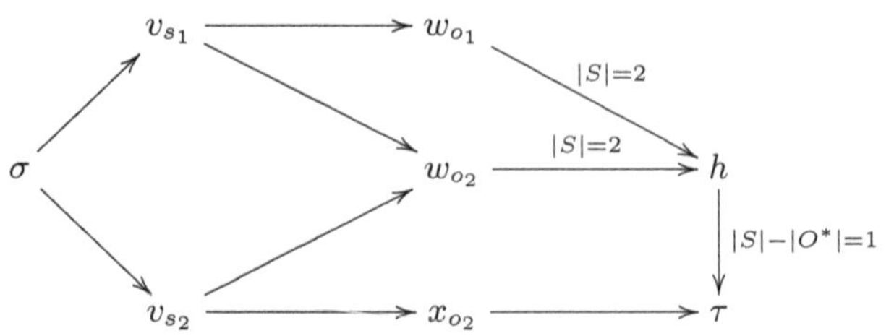

Figure 2: MAX-FLOW corresponding to instance where $O_{s_1}^{+} = \{o_1, o_2\}$, $O_{s_1}^{=} = \varnothing$, $O_{s_2}^{+} = \{o_2\}$, $O_{s_2}^{=} = \{o_2\}$, and $O^* = \{o_2\}$. Edges without a label have capacity 1.

PROOF. If a FU/NT/ZI/TO instance has a solution, then in any successful implementation, the agent's final utility when it draws type θ is $v(\theta, F(\theta))$. This is because in FU/NT/ZI/TO, there are no transfers or signaling costs. As a result, the FU/NT/ZI/TO instance is equivalent to the TU/NT/ZI/TO instance that has $g(\theta) = v(\theta, F(\theta))$ and is otherwise identical. Hence, TU/NT/ZI/TO is NP-complete. □

In the remainder of the paper, we prove our new results.

3.2 Easy Cases

We now turn to our cases where it is easy to find whether an implementation exists. As it turns out, if we set things up correctly, we can show all of them to be easy using the same algorithm. Say that a version of our problem *predetermines utilities* if given the instance, one can compute in polynomial time a utility for each type such that, *if* the instance has a solution, then that is the utility that that type has in all solutions. Any version of the problem with targeted utilities predetermines utilities. Also, any version of the problem with zero/infinity costs and no transfers predetermines utilities, because in this case, $u(\theta, s, f(\theta), p) = v(\theta, f(\theta)) + p - c(\theta, s) = v(\theta, f(\theta))$ in any solution. The main theorem we prove in this section is the following.

THEOREM 4. *If a variant of IMPLEMENTATION (1) predetermines utilities and (2) has injective SCFs (FI) then we can solve it in polynomial time by reduction to MAX-FLOW.*[5]

Theorem 4 allows us to solve TU/T/U/FI (and thus TU/T/ZI/FI), TU/NT/U/FI (and thus TU/NT/ZI/FI), and FU/NT/ZI/FI in polynomial time. To prove it, we first need the following lemma.

LEMMA 1. *Let $u^*(\theta)$ be the predetermined utility of θ. Then, we can compute in polynomial time a function $T^* : S \times O \to \mathbb{R}$ such that if I has a solution $M = (A, T)$, and $A(s) = o$, then $T(s) = T^*(s, o)$.*

PROOF. In variants of the problem without transfers, the lemma is trivially true by setting $T^* = 0$. In the remainder, we focus on variants where transfers are allowed. Set

$$T^*(s, o) = \max\{p : (\forall\theta) v(\theta, o) - c(\theta, s) + p \leq u^*(\theta)\}$$

This is easy to compute by computing for every θ separately $u^*(\theta) - v(\theta, o) + c(\theta, s)$, and taking the minimum of these.

[5]If, in addition, $|S| = |\Theta|$, then we can reduce to the problem of perfect bipartite matching. We omit the proof due to space constraint.

We must prove this function has the desired property. To do so, let $M = (A, T)$ be a mechanism that solves I. If for some s, $T(s) > T^*(s, A(s))$, then by the definition of T^* there exists some type θ with $T^*(s, A(s)) = u^*(\theta) - v(\theta, A(s)) + c(\theta, s)$, or equivalently, $v(\theta, A(s)) - c(\theta, s) + T^*(s, A(s)) = u^*(\theta)$. The utility that θ would get from sending s under M is therefore $v(\theta, A(s)) - c(\theta, s) + T(s) > v(\theta, A(s)) - c(\theta, s) + T^*(s, A(s)) = u^*(\theta)$, so it is able to (and therefore will) obtain a larger utility than it is supposed to.

Now, define $M^* = (A, T^*)$ (weakly increasing M's transfer function to T^*). If under M, it was optimal for θ to report s, then this is also the case for M^*, for the following reason. Reporting s will still give θ a utility of exactly $u^*(\theta)$ (it is at least this much because transfers have only increased, and at most this much by the definition of T^*). On the other hand, reporting another s' will give θ a utility of at most $u^*(\theta)$ by the definition of T^*. Because A is unchanged, it follows that M^* is also a solution to I. □

We are now ready to prove Theorem 4.

PROOF OF THEOREM 4. We will use u^* (which is available due to utilities being predetermined) and T^* (which is available by Lemma 1) to define, for every s and o, whether letting $A(s) = o$ is *safe* and whether it is *satisfying*. "Safe" means that no type will obtain a strictly higher utility from sending s than it is supposed to, and "satisfying" means that it is safe and allows the type that is supposed to get o to send s to get o at the right utility. Let $O^* = \{o | (\exists\theta) F(\theta) = o\}$. Then, a mechanism is a solution if and only if (1) all outcome assignments are safe and (2) for each $o \in O^*$ there is at least one satisfying assignment of it to a signal. This is so because every type is able to get the correct outcome at the correct utility, and is not able to do better by deviating.

Safe $O_s^+ \triangleq \{o | (\forall\theta)\, u^*(\theta) \geq v(\theta, o) - c(\theta, s) + T^*(s, o)\}$.

Satisfying $O_s^= \triangleq \{o \in O_s^+ \cap O^* \mid U^*(F^{-1}(o)) = v(F^{-1}(o), o) - c(F^{-1}(o), s) + T^*(s, o)\}$.

We use these definitions to create a MAX-FLOW instance $G = (V, E)$ as follows (an illustration is given in Figure 2). V consists of: A start node σ; a signal node v_s for each $s \in S$, an outcome node w_o; for each $o \in O$, another outcome node x_o for each o in O^*; a single helper node h; and a final node τ. E consists of: an edge between σ and each v_s; for each s, edges between v_s and each w_o with $o \in O_s^+$ and each x_o with $o \in O_s^=$; edges between each w_o and h (with capacity $|S|$); an edge between h and τ (with capacity $|S| - |O^*|$); and edges between each x_o and τ. Unless otherwise specified, edges have capacity 1. Our goal is to get a flow of $|S|$.

At a high level, solving MAX-FLOW on G tests whether a bipartite matching can be found between some subset of the signals and O^*, while simultaneously assigning to each unmatched signal an outcome that will not incentivise any type to deviate to it. We now prove the equivalence formally.

***I* has a solution $\implies$ *G* has a flow of $|S|$.** Let M be a mechanism which solves I with transfers T^*; we will create a flow of size $|S|$. Send one unit of flow from σ to each signal node v_s. Then, for each θ, there is a distinct s such that $F(\theta) \in O_s^=$; send one unit of flow from the corresponding v_s to $x_{F(\theta)}$ and then on to τ. For each remaining s, $A(s)$ must be a safe assignment; send one unit of flow from v_s to $w_{A(s)}$, and then via h on to τ. (Note there is at most $|S| - |O^*|$ such flow so that it does not exceed the capacity on the edge (h, τ).) It is straightforward to check that this is a valid flow of size $|S|$.

***G* has a flow of $|S|$ $\implies$ *I* has a solution.** Given a flow of size $|S|$, we will create a mechanism $M = (A, T^*)$ that is a solution to I. Due to the capacity on (h, τ), each edge (x_o, τ) must have one unit of flow on it. Thus, for each x_o, there exists some v_s such that (v_s, x_o) has a unit of flow on it (by flow integrality); moreover, these v_s are all distinct, because exactly one unit of flow passes through each v_s. If (v_s, x_o) has a unit of flow on it, set $A(s) = o$. Thereby, for each $o \in O^*$, there is a satisfying assignment of o to a signal s (Condition (2) above). For any remaining s, there must be some w_o such that there is a unit of flow on (v_s, w_o) (by flow integrality); in this case, set $A(s) = o$. This is a safe assignment (Condition (1) above). Thus, the mechanism meets the two conditions for it to solve I. $\square$

3.2.1 Example: Identification

This easiness result shows that we can solve (at scale) several special cases of mechanism design with signaling costs. In our opinion, the most interesting of these is free utilities, no transfers, $\{0, \infty\}$ signaling costs, and an injective SCF (FU/NT/ZI/FI).[6] Conceptually, the goal here is *identification*: the mechanism needs to learn the type of the agent exactly. The following example illustrates this.

It is early Christmas Morning and Santa Claus has almost finished delivering gifts to the small children of the world. There are only three left who have not received anything: Johnny, Molly, and Timmy. In his sack, Santa Claus has a specific gift for each, as well as a lump of coal. Each child should get its own gift and not anyone else's.[7] Thus:

$\Theta = \{Molly,\ Johnny,\ Timmy\}$
$O = \{G_{Johnny},\ G_{Molly},\ G_{Timmy},\ coal\}$
$F = \{* \rightarrow G_*\}$

Upon arriving inside a house Santa Claus must decide which gift to leave behind. Unfortunately, he does not know in which house each child lives. All he can observe is what food has been left out for him by whoever lives there. Luckily, Santa Claus knows which foods each child is capable of preparing and setting out. We refer to the set of foods that *child* can put out as S_{child}. We have:

$S = \{coffee,\ cookies,\ eggnog,\ gingerbread\}$

$S_{Johnny} = \{cookies,\ gingerbread\}$
$S_{Molly} = \{coffee,\ cookies\}$
$S_{Timmy} = \{coffee,\ eggnog,\ gingerbread\}$

Each child has preferences over the gifts. These only need to be specified up to order, as we do not have transfers or complex costs.

$v_{Johnny} = G_{Timmy} > G_{Molly} > G_{Johnny} > coal$
$v_{Molly} = G_{Timmy} > G_{Molly} > G_{Johnny} > coal$
$v_{Timmy} = G_{Johnny} > G_{Timmy} > G_{Molly} > coal$

When Santa arrives inside a house and sees what food has been put out for him, what gift should he leave? We can translate this problem instance into the appropriate MAX-FLOW instance (or work it out in our head) and solve for a mechanism that Santa can use. As it turns out, the only way that works is:

$M = \{coffee \rightarrow G_{Molly},\ cookies \rightarrow G_{Johnny},\ eggnog \rightarrow G_{Timmy},\ gingerbread \rightarrow coal\}$

Note the usefulness to Santa Claus of being able to give *coal*. Without *coal*, there is no mechanism that implements F: no matter which gift he gave for a signal of *gingerbread*, either *Johnny* or *Timmy* would want to set out *gingerbread* and receive a different gift than he was supposed to.

3.3 Free Utilities / Transfers / Injective Social Choice Function

We now move on to our cases where it is hard to find whether an implementation exists.

THEOREM 5. *FU/T/ZI/FI is NP-complete.*

This immediately implies FU/T/U/FI is NP-complete.

PROOF. We reduce from the MINSAT problem, in which we are given a Boolean formula in conjunctive normal form with m clauses and a number n, and are asked whether there is an assignment that satisfies at most n clauses. MINSAT is NP-complete [12]. Given an instance I of MINSAT, we construct the following instance I^* of FU/T/ZI/FI.

The types are:

- n "rescue" types $r_1, \ldots, r_n$.
- m clause types $k_1, \ldots, k_m$. In a slight abuse of notation, we will also refer to the corresponding clauses by $k_1, \ldots, k_m$.
- One variable gadget for each variable v in I. The gadget consists of three types: two literal types l, one for each of v^+ and v^-, and one "switch" type w_v.

We let $-l$ be the opposite literal of l (i.e., $-l = v^-$ if $l = v^+$, and $-l = v^+$ if $l = v^-$). We assume without loss of generality that no clause contains a pair of opposite literals. We will use $w_l = w_{-l}$ to indicate the switch type in the same clause as l.

The reporting cost structure c is:

All costs are symmetrical, i.e. $c(\theta, \theta') = c(\theta', \theta)$.
$\forall \theta,\ c(\theta, \theta) = 0$.
$\forall r \forall k,\ c(r, k) = 0$.
$\forall k \forall l \in k,\ c(k, l) = 0$.
$\forall l,\ c(w_l, l) = 0$. (And $c(w_l = w_{-l}, -l) = 0$).
All costs not defined above are infinite.

Figure 3 illustrates the reporting cost structure. The SCF is injective, so for each type θ there is a unique outcome $o_\theta = F(\theta)$.

The valuation function v is:

$v(\theta, o_\theta) = 0$.
$\forall k \forall l \in k,\ v(k, o_l) = 1$ and $v(l, o_k) = 0$.
$\forall l \forall k,\ v(w_l, o_k) = 24|\Theta| + 12$.
All valuations not defined above are -10.

I has a solution $\Rightarrow I^*$ has a solution. Given a MINSAT solution, we construct a mechanism $M = (A, T)$ that is a solution to I^* as follows.

- No more than n clauses are satisfied. Thus, for each clause k that is satisfied we can pick a different rescue node r and set $A(r) = o_k$, $A(k) = o_r$, and $T(r) = 2$.
- For each $l, -l$ pair one literal will be true and the other will be false. Assume without loss of generality that l is the true literal. Let $A(w_l) = o_l$, $A(l) = o_{w_l}$, and set $T(w_l) = 2$.
- For all $A(\theta)$ and $T(\theta)$ not defined above, let $A(\theta) = o_\theta$ and $T(\theta) = 0$.

[6]This setting restricts that of mechanism design with partial verification by requiring an injective SCF, and generalizes it by allowing $S \neq \Theta$ and $c(\theta, \theta) \neq 0$.
[7]Note that the fact that coal is a possible outcome does not pose a problem for the injectivity of the SCF, which specifies that no child should ever receive coal.

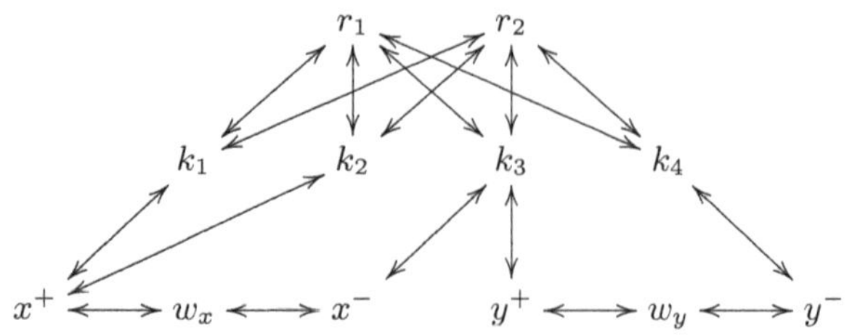

Figure 3: Reporting cost structure of the FU/T/ZI/FI instance corresponding to the MINSAT instance: $(x^+) \wedge (x^+) \wedge (x^- \vee y^+) \wedge (y^-)$ with n = 2. A (θ, θ') edge indicates that type θ can report type θ' at zero cost.

We now show $M = (A, T)$ solves I^*. Note that $c(\theta, A^{-1}(o_\theta)) = 0$ for all θ. Thus, each θ can report at zero cost the type that would lead to its intended outcome o_θ.

Because the largest transfer by the mechanism is 2, a switch or rescue type θ will obtain a utility of no higher than -8 from any outcome they could obtain other than o_θ , and thus will prefer to report $A^{-1}(o_\theta)$ for a utility of 0.

We now show that each literal type l will be best off reporting $A^{-1}(o_l)$. If l is false, then it will get a utility of 2 for reporting w_v, which leads to o_l. This is the maximum possible utility for a literal type, so this is an optimal course of action. On the other hand, if l is true, then each clause k that it is in must be satisfied. Thus, for each such k, $A(k) = o_r$ for some r. Thus l would get a utility of -10 for reporting k, -8 for reporting w_l (which would lead to o_{-l}), and 0 for reporting truthfully (which leads to o_l). So l will report truthfully and get the correct outcome.

Finally, we show that each clause type k is best off reporting $A^{-1}(o_k)$. If k is satisfied, k can get a utility of 2 by reporting the r such that $r = A^{-1}(o_k)$. Because 2 is the maximum transfer, k could only hope to achieve a larger utility by reporting in a way that results in some o_l with $l \in k$ and a transfer of 2; however, o_l only comes with a transfer when it results from reporting a switch type, which k cannot do. So k will report $A^{-1}(o_k)$. If k is not satisfied, all the literals in it must be false. Thus, if k were to report a literal, it would instead achieve some o_{w_v}, leading to a utility of -10. Reporting a rescue type would give a utility of at most -8. Hence, k is best off reporting truthfully and achieving a utility of 0.

I^* has a solution $\Rightarrow$ I has a solution. Let $M = (A, T)$ be the mechanism that constitutes a solution to I^*. We first prove a lemma, (a),: for any $\theta_1 \neq \theta_2$, if $A(\theta_2) = o_{\theta_1}$, then $T(\theta_2) - T(\theta_1) < 12|\Theta|$. This holds because of the following. First, because F is injective, A must decompose the type space into cycles of the form $o_{\theta_1} = A(\theta_2), o_{\theta_2} = A(\theta_3), \ldots, o_{\theta_j} = A(\theta_1)$, where $1 \leq j \leq |\Theta|$. Now suppose, for the sake of contradiction, that for some such cycle, $T(\theta_2) - T(\theta_1) \geq 12|\Theta|$.We know that $T(\theta_3) - T(\theta_2) > -12$, because for all o (including $o = o_{\theta_1}$), $v(\theta_2, o_{\theta_2}) - v(\theta_2, o) \leq 11 < 12$. Adding this inequality to the previous one, we obtain, $T(\theta_3) - T(\theta_1) > 12(|\Theta| - 1)$. Similarly, $T(\theta_4) - T(\theta_3) > -12$, and adding this, we obtain $T(\theta_4) - T(\theta_1) > 12(|\Theta| - 2)$. Continuing this, we eventually find $T(\theta_j) - T(\theta_1) > 12(|\Theta| - j + 2)$, and subsequently $T(\theta_1) - T(\theta_1) > 12(|\Theta| - j + 1)$—but this is a contradiction, because the left-hand side is 0 and the right-hand side is at least 12.

We use lemma (a) to prove another lemma, (b), which is that there can be no literal l and clause k such that $A(l) = o_k$. For the sake of contradiction, suppose this were the case. There are two possibilities. One is that $A(w_l) = o_l$. In this case, set $\theta_1 = l, \theta_2 = w_l, \theta_3 = A^{-1}(o_{w_l})$; these are part of a cycle. By two applications of lemma (a), we obtain $T(\theta_3) - T(\theta_1) < 24|\Theta|$. But $v(w_l, A(\theta_1)) - v(w_l, A(\theta_3)) = v(w_l, o_k) - v(w_l, o_{w_l}) = 24|\Theta| + 12$, so w_l would prefer reporting θ_1, and we have a contradiction. The other possibility is that $A(w_l) \neq o_l$. In this case, w_l and l belong to different cycles. For w_l not to misreport l (to obtain o_k), it must be the case that $T(A^{-1}(o_{w_l})) - T(l) \geq 24|\Theta| + 12$. By lemma (a), $T(A^{-1}(o_{w_l})) - T(w_l) < 12|\Theta|$, and also $T(A^{-1}(o_l) - T(l) < 12|\Theta|$. If we subtract the latter two inequalities from the one before it, we obtain $T(w_l) - T(A^{-1}(o_l) > 12$. But then l will prefer to report w_l instead of $A^{-1}(o_l)$, because $v(l, o_l) - v(l, A(w_l)) \leq 11$, and we again have a contradiction.

Next, we show that, for any literal l, either $A(l) = o_l$ or $A(-l) = o_{-l}$. This is because at least one of o_l and o_{-l} is not equal to $A(w_l)$; without loss of generality, suppose it is o_l. Two possibilities remain: $A(l) = o_l$ or $A(k) = o_l$ for some k. We must rule out the latter. If $A(k) = o_l$, then somewhere in the corresponding cycle of misreports there must be some l' and k' such that $A(l') = o_{k'}$—but this contradicts lemma (b).

Then, create a truth value assignment such that l = true implies that $A(l) = o_l$. This assignment must solve the MINSAT instance. For consider any clause k satisfied by this assignment. We show that $A^{-1}(o_k)$ must be a rescue node. Since k is satisfied, there must be some $l \in k$ such that k can obtain o_l by reporting l. Then, it cannot be the case that $A(k) = o_k$. For the sake of contradiction, suppose this were so; then on the one hand, $T(k) - T(l) \leq 0$ to keep l from misreporting k, and on the other hand, $T(k) - T(l) \geq 1$ to keep k from misreporting l—but this gives a contradiction. So $A^{-1}(o_k)$ cannot be k. It cannot be another clause node or a switch node, because these cannot be reported by k. It cannot be a literal by lemma (b). Hence, it must be a rescue node. Because there are only n rescue nodes, it follows that there are at most n satisfied clauses. $\square$

3.4 Free Utilities / No Transfers / Unrestricted Edge Costs / Injective Social Choice Function

THEOREM 6. *FU/NT/U/FI is NP-complete.*

PROOF. We reduce from satisfiability. Given an instance I of SAT, we construct the following instance I^* of FU/NT/U/FI.

The types are:

- For each clause k in I, a *clause gadget*, which consists of one clause type, k, and one "displacer" type, d_k.
- For each variable v in I, a *variable gadget* which contains a type (l, k) for every $l \in \{v^+, v^-\}$ and every $k \ni l$. (From here on, when we refer to (l, k), we implicitly assume $l \in k$.)

Let $-l$ be the opposite literal of l (i.e., $-l = v^-$ if $l = v^+$, and $-l = v^+$ if $l = v^-$). We assume without loss of generality that no clause contains a pair of opposite literals. The SCF is injective, so for each type θ there is a unique outcome $o_\theta = F(\theta)$.

The reporting cost structure c is:

$c(d_k, k) = 0.$

$\forall (l, k),\ c(k, (l, k)) = 0.$

$\forall (l, k) \forall (-l, k'),\ c((l, k), (-l, k')) = 2.$

$\forall (l, k),\ c((l, k), d_k) = 2.$

All other costs are infinite.

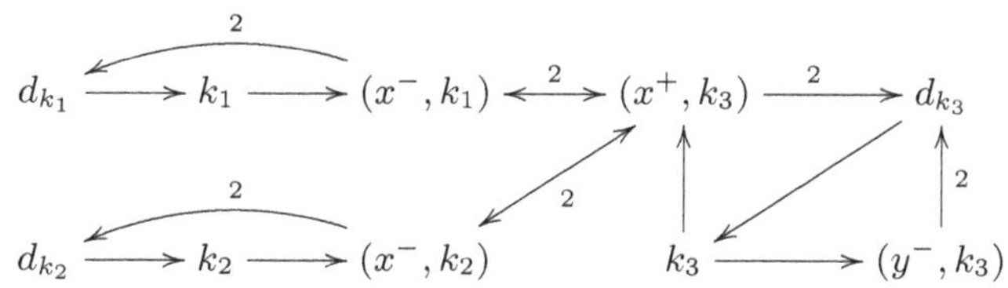

Figure 4: Reporting cost structure of the FU/NT/U/FI instance corresponding to the SAT instance: $(x^-) \wedge (x^-) \wedge (x^+ \vee y^-)$. Edges without a label have cost 0.

Figure 4 illustrates the reporting cost structure.

The valuation function v is:

$v(d_k, o_k) = 10.$

$v(d_k, o_{d_k}) = 5.$

$v(k, o_{d_k}) = -10.$

$\forall(l,k),\ v(k, o_{(l,k)}) = -1.$

$\forall(l,k)\forall k' \neq k,\ v((l,k), o_{k'}) = 1.$

$\forall(l,k), v((l,k), o_k) = -10.$

$\forall(l,k)\forall(l',k') \neq (l,k),\ v((l,k), o_{(l',k')}) = -10.$

All other valuations are 0.

I **has a solution** $\implies$ I^* **has a solution.** Given an assignment that solves I, we construct a mechanism $M = (A, T)$ (where necessarily $T = 0$) which solves I^*. For each clause k, choose some literal l that satisfies it, and let $A((l,k)) = o_k, A(k) = o_{d_k}$, and $A(d_k) = o_{(l,k)}$. For all remaining types θ that do not yet have $A(\theta)$ set by this (which are all of the form (l,k)) let $A(\theta) = o_\theta$. Note that if $A((l,k)) = o_k$, then $A((-l,k')) = o_{(-l,k')}$ for all $k' \ni -l$, because $-l$ must be set to *false*.

We now show that M solves I^*. If $A((l,k)) = o_{(l,k)}$, then the reporting options for (l,k) are (i) itself, for a utility of 0; (ii) d_k, for a utility of $-10-2=-12$; and (iii) some $(-l,k')$ for a utility of at most $1-2=-1$. Thus it will report itself, resulting in the appropriate outcome. If $A((l,k)) = o_k$, then the reporting options for (l,k) are (i) itself, for a utility of -10; (ii) d_k, for a utility of $0-2=-2$; and (iii) some $(-l,k')$, for a utility of $-10-8$ (because we know $A((-l,k')) = o_{(-l,k')}$). Thus it will report d_k, resulting in the appropriate outcome. For each clause k, it can report (i) itself, for a utility of -10; (ii) the (l,k) such that $A((l,k)) = o_k$, for a utility of $0-0=0$; or (iii) some (l,k) such that $A((l,k)) = o_{(l,k)}$, for a utility of $-1-0=-1$. Thus, it will report the (l,k) that results in the outcome o_k. Finally, a displacer type d_k can report (i) itself, for a utility of 0; or (ii) k, for a utility of $5-0=5$. Thus it will report k, resulting in the correct outcome. Hence, M solves I^*.

I^* **has a solution** $\implies$ I **has a solution.** Let $M = (A, T)$ (where necessarily $T = 0$) be a mechanism that solves I^*. For each clause k, its displacer type, d_k, values o_k more than o_{d_k}. Thus, we must have $M(k) \neq o_k$. It follows that to obtain o_k, k must report some (l,k) instead, so that $A((l,k)) = o_k$. For this l, we may then conclude for all $(-l,k')$ that $A((-l,k')) \neq o_{k'}$ This is because if it were the case that $A((-l,k')) = o_{k'}$, then (l,k) could report $(-l,k')$ to obtain a utility of $1-2=-1$, and this would be strictly higher than reporting the type $A^{-1}(o_{(l,k)}) \neq (l,k)$ (because $A((l,k)) = o_k$), which would give a utility of $0-2=-2$.

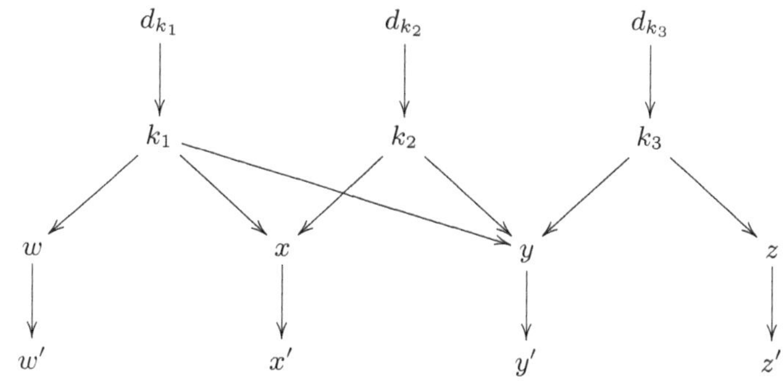

Figure 5: Reporting cost structure of the TU/T/ZI/TO instance corresponding to the Monotone SAT instance: $(w^+ \vee x^+ \vee y^+) \wedge (x^- \vee y^-) \wedge (y^+ \vee z^+)$. Edges indicate a zero cost report.

It follows that the following assignment is well defined: set l to *true* if and only if there exists some k such that $A((l,k)) = o_k$ (unless this results in a pair of opposite literals both being set to *false*, in which case arbitrarily choose one to set to *true*). Because for every k, there exists some $l \in k$ such that $A((l,k)) = o_k$, this is a satisfying assignment.[8] □

3.5 Target Utilities / Transfers / Two Outcomes

THEOREM 7. *TU/T/ZI/TO is NP-complete.*

This immediately implies that TU/T/U/TO is NP-complete as well.

PROOF. We reduce from the Monotone SAT problem (SAT where within each clause all the literals have the same sign, which is NP-complete [10]). Given an instance I of Monotone SAT we construct the following instance I^* of TU/T/ZI/TO.

The types are:

- For each clause k in I, a *clause gadget* which consists of one clause type, k, and one "displacer" type, d_k.
- For each variable w in I, a variable type w and slot type w'

The reporting cost structure c is:

$\forall\theta, c(\theta,\theta) = 0$

$\forall k,\ c(d_k, k) = 0.$

$\forall k \forall w \in k,\ c(k, w) = 0.$

$\forall w\ c(w, w') = 0$

All other costs are infinite.

Figure 5 illustrates the reporting cost structure.
The two outcomes are o^+ and o^-. Let $\neg o^+ = o^-$ and $\neg o^- = o^+$.

The social choice function F is:

$\forall k\ s.t.\ k$ only contains positive literals, $F(k) = o^+$.

$\forall k\ s.t.\ k$ only contains negative literals, $F(k) = o^-$.

$\forall d_k,\ (F(k) = o^+) \Rightarrow F(d_k) = o^-$ and $(F(k) = o^-) \Rightarrow F(d_k) = o^+$.

[8]Note that the mechanism could be quite different from the mechanism used in the first part of this proof; even so, our argument that it produces a satisfying assignment still holds.

$\forall w,\ F(w) = F(w') = o^+$.

The valuation function v is:

$\forall d_k,\ v(d_k, F(d_k)) = 0$ and $v(d_k, \neg F(d_k)) = 10$.
$\forall k,\ v(k, F(k)) = 0$ and $v(k, \neg F(k)) = -10$.
$\forall w\ v(w, o^+) = v(w', o^+) = 0$.
$\forall w\ v(w, o^-) = v(w', o^-) = -1$.

The target utility function g is simply: $\forall \theta,\ g(\theta) = 0$.

I has a solution $\Rightarrow$ I^* has a solution. We construct the mechanism $M = (A, T)$ as follows. Set all transfers to zero. For each d_k let $A(d_k) = F(d_k)$. For each k, let $A(k) = \neg F(k) = F(d_k)$. For each variable w that is positively instantiated in I, let $A(w) = o^+$, for each variable that is negatively instantiated, let $A(w) = o^-$. For each w' let $A(w') = o^+$.

We argue that M is a solution to I^*. Each w' recieves o^+. Each w will report w' to achieve an outcome of o^+. For each clause k which includes only negative literals there will be at least one variable w contained in k that is negatively instantiated in I. Thus, k can report w and receive a utility maximizing outcome of o^-. Similarly, each clause which contains only positive literals will be able to receive o^+. Finally, for each d_k, $A(d_k) = A(k) = F(d_k)$, so d_k has no choice but to give a report which leads to the appropriate outcome.

I^* has a solution $\Rightarrow$ I has a solution. Let $M = A$ be the mechanism that solves I^*. For each k, since d_k values $\neg F(d_k)$ more than $F(d_k)$, it must be the case that: $A(k) = F(d_k)$, or, there is large negative transfer for reporting k. Since $F(d_k) = \neg F(k)$ and $g(k) = 0$, either way each k cannot report itself. Thus each k must report a variable node to achieve the correct outcome—hence $\forall k \exists w\ s.t.\ A(w) = F(k)$.

Then, for each w in I, set w to *true* if $A(w) = o^+$ and to *false* if $A(w) = o^-$. This represents a solution to I, because $\forall k \exists w\ s.t.\ A(w) = F(k)$ implies that at least one of the variables in each clause will be set in a way that satisfies the clause. □

4. CONCLUSION

In this paper, we generalized the model of mechanism design with partial verification—where not every type can report every other type—to mechanism design with costly signaling, where there is a cost $c(\theta, \theta')$ for type θ to report another type θ' (or, more generally, a cost $c(\theta, s)$ for sending signal s). Building on earlier results for the partial-verification case, we characterized the complexity of determining whether a specific social choice function can be implemented under various conditions.

Future research could be devoted to expanding our complexity results, for example obtaining fixed-parameter tractability results. It could also be devoted to the case where the social choice function is not given, but rather has to be optimized as well with respect to some objective function, as is often done in automated mechanism design [5, 6]. Of course, insofar as any SCF may maximize the objective value, this problem can be no easier than the problem studied here, because the answer to the optimization version would tell us whether the SCF that maximizes the objective value is feasible or not. (In fact, in automated mechanism design with costless and unlimited misreporting, checking whether a given SCF can be implemented is easy, though the optimization problem is sometimes hard.) However, the optimization version may still allow efficient approximations. Other future research can be devoted to expanding the connection to machine learning, as discussed in the introduction. The techniques discussed in this paper may allow us to tailor classifiers to strategic agents based on our knowledge of the cost structure.[9] Also, in a companion (working) paper, we characterize when the revelation principle holds in the costly-signaling model (citation suppressed for anonymity). This generalizes earlier results for partial verification [1, 16].

Acknowledgments

We thank NSF and ARO for support under grants CCF-1101659, IIS-0953756, CCF-1337215, W911NF-12-1-0550, and W911NF-11-1-0332.

REFERENCES

[1] V. Auletta, P. Penna, G. Persiano, and C. Ventre. Alternatives to truthfulness are hard to recognize. *Autonomous Agents and Multi-Agent Systems*, 22(1):200–216, 2011.

[2] M. Balcan, A. Blum, J. D. Hartline, and Y. Mansour. Reducing mechanism design to algorithm design via machine learning. *Journal of Computer and System Sciences*, 74(8):1245–1270, 2008.

[3] M. Barreno, B. Nelson, A. D. Joseph, and J. D. Tygar. The security of machine learning. *Machine Learning*, 81(2):121–148, 2010.

[4] I. Caragiannis, E. Elkind, M. Szegedy, and L. Yu. Mechanism design: from partial to probabilistic verification. In *Proceedings of the ACM Conference on Electronic Commerce (EC)*, pages 266–283, Valencia, Spain, 2012.

[5] V. Conitzer and T. Sandholm. Complexity of mechanism design. In *Proceedings of the 18th Annual Conference on Uncertainty in Artificial Intelligence (UAI)*, pages 103–110, Edmonton, Canada, 2002.

[6] V. Conitzer and T. Sandholm. Self-interested automated mechanism design and implications for optimal combinatorial auctions. In *Proceedings of the ACM Conference on Electronic Commerce (EC)*, pages 132–141, New York, NY, USA, 2004.

[7] N. N. Dalvi, P. Domingos, Mausam, S. K. Sanghai, and D. Verma. Adversarial classification. In *Proceedings of the Tenth ACM SIGKDD International Conference on Knowledge Discovery and Data Mining*, pages 99–108, Seattle, WA, USA, 2004.

[8] O. Dekel, F. Fischer, and A. D. Procaccia. Incentive compatible regression learning. In *Proceedings of the Annual ACM-SIAM Symposium on Discrete Algorithms (SODA)*, pages 884–893, Philadelphia, PA, USA, 2008. Society for Industrial and Applied Mathematics.

[9] R. Deneckere and S. Severinov. Optimal screening with costly misrepresentation, 2007. Working paper available at http://www.severinov.com/working_papers/screening_costly_misrepresentation_jul07.pdf.

[10] M. Garey and D. Johnson. *Computers and Intractability*. W. H. Freeman and Company, 1979.

[11] J. Green and J.-J. Laffont. Partially verifiable information and mechanism design. *Review of Economic Studies*, 53:447–456, 1986.

[9]Note that the resulting setup is quite different from previous work on *incentive compatible machine learning* [8, 13] where an agent is not attempting to be misclassified himself, but rather is aiming to get a global classifier, constructed based on the data reported by multiple agents, to be as accurate as possible on his own data. Both this direction and ours are even more different from mechanism design *via* machine learning [2], where the approach is to use one set of bids to set prices for another set of bidders.

[12] R. Kohli, R. Krishnamurti, and P. Mirchandani. The minimum satisfiability problem. *SIAM Journal on Discrete Mathematics*, 7(2):275–283, 1994.

[13] R. Meir, A. D. Procaccia, and J. S. Rosenschein. Algorithms for strategyproof classification. *Artificial Intelligence*, 186:123–156, 2012.

[14] D. Parkes. Online mechanisms. In N. Nisan, T. Roughgarden, E. Tardos, and V. Vazirani, editors, *Algorithmic Game Theory*, chapter 16. Cambridge University Press, 2007.

[15] M. Spence. Job market signaling. *Quarterly Journal of Economics*, 87(3):355–374, 1973.

[16] L. Yu. Mechanism design with partial verification and revelation principle. *Autonomous Agents and Multi-Agent Systems*, 22(1):217–223, 2011.

To Ask, Sense, or Share: Ad Hoc Information Gathering

Adam Eck and Leen-Kiat Soh
Department of Computer Science and Engineering
University of Nebraska-Lincoln
Lincoln, Nebraska, USA
{aeck, lksoh}@cse.unl.edu

ABSTRACT

Agents operating in complex (e.g., dynamic, uncertain, partially observable) environments must gather information from various sources to inform their incomplete knowledge. Two popular types of sources include: (1) directly sensing the environment using the agent's sensors, and (2) sharing information between networked agents occupying the same environment. In this paper, we address agent reasoning for appropriately selecting between such types of sources to update agent knowledge over time. In particular, we consider ad hoc environments where agents cannot collaborate in advance to predetermine joint solutions for when to share vs. when to sense. Instead, we propose a solution where agents individually learn the benefits of relying on each type of source to maximize knowledge improvement. We empirically evaluate our learning-based solution in different environment configurations to demonstrate its advantages over other strategies.

Categories and Subject Descriptors

I.2.11 [**Artificial Intelligence**]: Distributed Artificial Intelligence – *intelligent agents, multiagent systems*

General Terms

Performance, Design, Experimentation

Keywords

Information Gathering; Information Sharing; Ad Hoc

1. INTRODUCTION

One of the most fundamental responsibilities of intelligent agents is *understanding their complex (e.g., dynamic, uncertain, partially observable) environments*, which guides agent reasoning, actuation, and goal accomplishment. Often, agents lack complete knowledge of their environment *a priori* and must update their understanding over time. These updates are informed by incorporating information gathered whilst operating in the environment. Two popular types of sources of information include (1) an agent independently *sensing* its environment, gathering direct observations as a result of the agent's actions and sensors, and (2) receiving *shared* information from other agents operating in the same environment (either cooperatively for the sake of the system or for individual profit by self-interested agents).

Depending on the application, these two types of sources might have different benefits (e.g., types of information provided, information quantity and quality) and costs (e.g., resource and time expenses). Sensing can be performed on demand, gathering information as soon as the agent needs, and the agent can do so in a timely fashion without taking away from other agents' activities. Information sharing, on the other hand, can propagate information through the entire system potentially faster and with less cost (not waiting for each agent to individually sense the same information). However, relying on sharing also means waiting for another agent to possess the desired information, and sharing takes time and resources away from other agent activities that could instead further the sharing agent's individual goals.

Because of these differences, agents in applications where both sources coexist face an interesting question: *when should I use sensing to update my understanding vs. when should I request information from other agents and rely on shared information?* Answering this question leads to a challenging tradeoff between using the two types of information sources that when properly balanced could lead to improved agent behavior and goal accomplishment (e.g., through lower cumulative cost and higher quality knowledge).

Traditionally, agents in a shared environment would pre-coordinate when they might be willing and able to share information so that each agent could plan appropriately to know when to sense vs. when to rely on shared information. However, in many applications, this pre-coordination might not be possible. Specifically, in **ad hoc environments** where pre-coordination is impossible and agents might not know the behaviors or capabilities of their peers in advance [24], agents cannot determine *a priori* the value of relying on shared information against the value of sensing alone. This is especially true in many types of ad hoc environments that are also *open environments*, where agents can join and leave the environment over time. Agent openness is especially problematic to information sharing because the availability of shared information changes over time and knowledge about the environment disappears with departing agents (who knew more than newly joining agents). Thus, determining when to sense vs. when to rely on shared information is especially difficult in ad hoc environments. In this paper, we study how agents should balance the sensing vs. sharing tradeoff in ad hoc environments, henceforth referred to as the ad hoc information gathering (AHIG) problem.

Appears in: *Proceedings of the 14th International Conference on Autonomous Agents and Multiagent Systems (AAMAS 2015), Bordini, Elkind, Weiss, Yolum (eds.), May 4–8, 2015, Istanbul, Turkey.*

In order to solve the AHIG, we propose a learning-based solution where agents individually learn over time how different types of information gathering actions (independently sensing vs. requesting shared information) improve their knowledge about the environment. Through learning, agents can find good information gathering strategies without relying on pre-coordination in ad hoc environments, instead treating other agents as part of the environment affecting the quality of their information gathering. Moreover, learning enables each agent to adapt its behavior as it interacts with different agents, which is valuable in open environments where agents join and leave over time. Thus, through learning, agents can individually adapt their behavior to maximize their own knowledge improvement by learning the benefits of using different types of information sources without requiring coordination between agents.

However, because agents are operating in complex environments with incomplete information, learning is generally a computationally complex problem: learning in partially observable environments is much harder than learning in fully observable environments. To simplify the agents' learning process, we show how the agents' general problem of *understanding the current state of the complex environment* can be transformed to a simpler problem of *improving agent knowledge over time*, in a transformation we term the **Knowledge State MDP** exploiting full observability of current measures of agent knowledge as intermediate states for guiding agent decision making. As a result, an agent can learn faster how to gather information in the environment to best refine knowledge. Moreover, this transformation is potentially useful in more general information gathering problems (beyond the AHIG).

To demonstrate the effectiveness of our transformation and learning-based solution, we empirically evaluate using different experimental environment configurations how well agents learn to select between different information sources over time to improve their knowledge. We discover that our solution outperforms baseline approaches maximizing either sensed or shared information, and does so by appropriately selecting between different information sources at different times to best refine agent knowledge. Furthermore, our results indicate that learning about how to gather information is most beneficial when information is most scarce (and careful information gathering is most necessary).

2. PROBLEM

The AHIG problem occurs whenever a set of agents observe the same environment and can share information but cannot coordinate in advance to determine when agents might share or what quality of information they might provide. This includes real world examples such as (1) intelligent ad hoc sensor networks, where agents are deployed on wireless sensors that are randomly dropped to monitor an open space, (2) robotic search and rescue operations, where different organizations might bring their own robots to explore the same disaster area, and (3) ad hoc traffic information networks, where intelligent agents on cars communicate with a road infrastructure system as they navigate through town to report and understand traffic conditions.

2.1 AHIG Formulation

We formalize the AHIG problem as follows. A set of agents $Ag = \{i\}$ exist in a shared environment and are connected by a bidirectional communication network. Because communication costs grow as the network becomes larger, each agent's local neighborhood $N(i)$ is relatively small compared to the size of the entire network. Occasionally, due to openness, some agents will leave the network and others will join. Thus, we represent the current set of agents at time t with Ag_t, and likewise for an agent i's neighborhood $N_t(i)$.

Also in the shared environment are a finite set of phenomena $P = \{j\}$ that represent objects, entities, or properties of the environment that the agents need to understand. Each phenomenon j can take states from a finite set $PS_j = \{ps\}$, and the current state of each phenomenon in the dynamic environment changes with probability cp each time step. In AHIG, the agents are tasked with always understanding the current state of each phenomenon, which requires forming correct knowledge about each phenomenon over time that is refined through gathering information.

To gather information about a particular phenomenon, agents can perform different actions that use different types of sources for information. In particular, each agent can (1) *sense* each phenomenon directly using its sensors, or the agent can (2) *request* that its neighbors $N_t(i)$ share their beliefs about a phenomenon. We assume that the agent's sensors are noisy and imperfect, returning correct observations about the sensed phenomenon's current state with accuracy acc (and an incorrect observation with probability $1 - acc$). Agents can also perform a third type of action: (3) agents can respond to requests from neighbors with a *share* action communicating the agent's uncertain current knowledge about the state of the phenomenon in question.

The goal of each agent is to form accurate knowledge about each phenomenon, representing good knowledge about the current state of the environment, while minimizing costs incurred in sensing. Agents are awarded a reward for each time point during which they have relatively certain knowledge about a phenomenon, whereas sensing actions and requests for information incur costs to the agent. To encourage self-interested agents to collaborate, the agents are also awarded a small reward for sharing information with their neighbors, but only when requested (to avoid unnecessarily consuming the communication resources) and when they are confident about the current state of the requested phenomenon (to avoid sharing unfruitful information). Otherwise, agents receive a penalty for sharing information.

To illustrate, consider a search and rescue (S&R) robotics example, where robot agents Ag_t explore a damaged building after a natural disaster. Here, the phenomena P represent different locations where victims might be trapped, and the phenomenon states PS_j indicate whether victims exist at location j. A robot i can either directly observe the environment with a noisy camera sensor (that consumes limited energy), or the agent can communicate with nearby robots $N_t(i)$ using line-of-sight communications. The goal of each robot is to determine with certainty whether victims exist in each location so that they can be rescued by human first responders, all-the-while minimizing energy and time costs.

Of final note: how agents represent their knowledge about the phenomena in the environment, as well as how they choose actions to refine their knowledge are not specified in the general AHIG formalization. Different domains, applications, and solutions might require different approaches to these features (knowledge and decision making) that are internal to the agent. Indeed, in real-world ad hoc environments, different agents produced by different developers might even use different approaches to these features in the same environment. However, agents must have some shared language that is consistent between agents for communicating shared information. In this paper, we choose the knowledge representation and decision making process as part of our solution, described in Section 4.

2.2 Related Work

The AHIG problem is closely related to several other problems in the multiagent systems literature. First, the Large Team Information Sharing (LTIS) problem (e.g., [11, 12, 19]) also considers a team of agents working together to observe at least one phenomenon in the environment, where agents both sense the current state of the phenomenon individually, as well as share information through the team's network. Prior research on LTIS has focused primarily on producing analytic models for the flow of information through the team of agents [11, 12], as well as developing distributed solutions for adapting information flow to achieve accurate, consistent, shared beliefs [11, 19]. However, LTIS differs from the AHIG in several key ways. First, in LTIS, the team of agents is constant over time (i.e., there is no agent openness), and agents follow a pre-coordinated strategy of when to share information. Second and most importantly, in LTIS agents do not choose between sensing, requesting, or sharing information. Instead, agents with sensors (which might not be all agents in the team) always receive observations from their sensors at every time point. Additionally, agents never request information; instead, they automatically share information with their neighbors whenever (and only when) they reach new highly certain knowledge about a phenomenon. Thus, LTIS does not consider the tradeoff between relying on different types of information as in the AHIG.

Another closely related problem studied in the multiagent systems literature is trust and reputation systems (e.g., [21, 22, 26]). In such systems, agents can also request and share information with one another to provide additional information to refine agent knowledge over time. The primary focus in trust and reputation systems is to determine how to incorporate such shared information: should the sharing agent be highly trusted and should their information heavily influence the receiving agent's knowledge, or should an agent be cautious when receiving information from another agent with which it has limited experience interacting? Like LTIS, this research does not focus on balancing information from other agents with the agent's own sensing, and thus does not solve the AHIG problem, but it is complementary in that reasoning about the trustworthiness and reputation of neighboring agents as information sources could be used to improve an AHIG agent's decision making process (which we intend to pursue as future work).

Finally, previous research in ad hoc environments has focused on problems such as how to lead teams of agents without communication [1, 10], as well as how to learn to interact with a single Markovian agent [6]. Since information sharing inherently requires communication, our research differs from the former (although in our work, agents still cannot pre-coordinate how they will interact, under the broad definition of ad hoc environments [24]). Similar to the latter, we also use reinforcement learning to determine how to interact with other agents, although our approach considers an agent working with multiple other agents in the environment.

3. POMDP FORMULATION

In order to solve the AHIG and gather the necessary information to understand the environment, each agent faces a sequential decision making problem of planning a sequence of actions to perform that refine its incomplete knowledge while minimizing costs incurred for gathering such information. In most partially observable environments (which includes AHIG since sensing phenomena returns noisy, imperfect observations), sequential decision making problems are generally solved by some variant of partially observable Markov decision processes (POMDPs) [15]. This is especially true of applications of single agent control of environment monitoring (e.g., [2, 4, 7, 8, 23], similar to our S&R robot example), which we extend in this paper to multiagent information gathering in ad hoc environments.

To setup our solution, in the following we first introduce background on the MDP and POMDP frameworks, then we provide a description of both how the AHIG problem could be cast as a POMDP and the problems with this formulation. Then, in Section 4, we will introduce our Knowledge State MDP transformation of the POMDP for sequential decision making for information gathering problems.

3.1 Background

Markov decision processes (both fully and partially observable) are mathematical descriptions of complex environment properties (e.g., dynamics, incomplete information, and uncertainty) that enable an agent to plan action sequences that maximize rewards (and/or minimize costs) in order to accomplish its goals [15].

Formally, a (discounted, finite state) MDP is represented by a tuple $\langle S, A, T, R, \gamma \rangle$ where $S = \{s\}$ is a set of states in which the agent needs to choose actions from the set $A = \{a\}$. Because the environment is dynamic, actions can change the current state according to a stochastic transition function $T : S \times A \times S \rightarrow [0,1]$ modeling the probability $T(s_t, a, s_{t+1}) = P(s_{t+1}|s_t, a)$ that the state changes from s_t to s_{t+1} after action a. To guide agent decision making, the agent receives rewards (or costs) according to a reward function $R : S \times A \rightarrow \mathbb{R}$ dependent on the current state and the action chosen. The agent's goal is to determine a plan of actions called a policy $\pi : S \rightarrow A$ that tells the agent what actions to perform (dependent on state) to maximize cumulative, discounted rewards, with $\gamma \in (0,1)$ a discount factor weighting uncertain future rewards:

$$\sum_{t=0}^{\infty} \gamma^t R(s_t, \pi(s_t)) \quad (1)$$

Because the current state is hidden in partially observable environments, a POMDP model is often used instead. Formally, a (discounted, finite state) POMDP is a tuple $\langle S, A, Z, T, O, R, \gamma, b_0 \rangle$ with S, A, T, R, γ as in a MDP. $Z = \{z\}$ represents a set of observations the agent receives (instead of perfect information about s), which are generated according to a stochastic observation function $O : S \times A \times Z \rightarrow [0,1]$ modeling the probability $O(s_{t+1}, a, z) = P(z|s_{t+1}, a)$ that the environment produces observation z after action a transitions the state to s_{t+1}. To handle uncertainty in the current state s_t, the agent maintains a belief state $b : S \rightarrow [0,1]$ representing its probabilistic knowledge in the current state. Using observations gathered from the environment, the agent updates its knowledge through belief updates:

$$b_{t+1}(s_{t+1}) = \frac{1}{\eta} O(s_{t+1}, a, z) \sum_{s_t \in S} T(s_t, a, s_{t+1}) b_t(s_t) \quad (2)$$

where η normalizes b_{t+1}. b_0 is the agent's initial belief state. Note, R can be chosen to provide rewards based on properties of the belief state b, instead of just individual environment states [2]. Likewise, policy π maps beliefs to actions.

3.2 AHIG as a POMDP

Since the AHIG is a sequential decision making problem in a partially observable environment (i.e., phenomenon states are partially observable), casting the AHIG as a POMDP is a natural starting point for a potential solution. In particular, we consider the POMDP formulation for the AHIG $\langle S, A, T, O, R, \gamma, b_0 \rangle$ summarized in Table 1.

In this POMDP, the state space S contains variables representing different information about situations faced by the agent: partially observable PS_j represent the different states each phenomenon can take (e.g., the presence of victims in different locations in our S&R example), and fully observable S_{Req} and S_{Rec} represent counts per phenomenon of how long it has been since the agent last requested that its neighbors share information or received a neighbor's request, respectively. These count variables are useful for tracking (1) whether the agent recently requested information, so that it doesn't request too frequently and disrupt other agents, and (2) whether a neighbor requested information so that the agent knows if it is appropriate to share its own knowledge. Given this S, the belief state b represents the agent's uncertain knowledge about each phenomenon's hidden state. This knowledge is refined using information Z collected from actions A using Eq. 2. Beliefs start with pure uncertainty (a uniform distribution over phenomenon states, e.g., a location is equally likely to contain a victim or not).

Since the environment is dynamic, the transition function T encodes the probability that phenomena change states at each time point (to a new state with probability cp, else phenomenon states stay the same with probability $1 - cp$, c.f., Section 2.1) (e.g., whether a previously safe location collapses and traps new victims, or trapped victims are rescued). The fully observable states transition deterministically each time step: the count for each phenomenon j in S_{Req} is incremented by one (up to k) unless the agent requests new information about j, and the count for each phenomenon j in S_{Rec} is incremented by one (up to k) unless the agent shares information (in which case it reverts to k to indicate no request from a neighbor is pending).

The observation function O, on the other hand, encodes the probability that the agent receives information about a particular phenomenon depending on the action taken. For $Sense_j$ actions, O encodes that the agent observes the correct state with probability acc (the agents' sensor's accuracy, c.f., Section 2.1) and a wrong state with probability $1 - acc$ (e.g., whether or not the robot's camera correctly identifies a victim in a room). Other actions return a null observation since they do not directly gather information about the state of any phenomenon in the environment.

The reward function R encodes (1) the rewards for having high certainty beliefs or sharing information when requested, and (2) the costs for information gathering actions or penalties for sharing unrequested or uncertain information as described in Section 2.1. Maximizing cumulative rewards leads the agent to highly certain knowledge (for which it receives a reward) while minimizing costs used to refine its knowledge.

However, a few problems exist in this solution formulation. First, the observation set Z only considers observations from the $Sense_j$ actions and does not handle shared information from neighbors, which would occur some delayed amount of time after a $Request_j$ action. Although Z could be modified to include additional variables for received information, this limits the types of shared information neighbors can provide to discrete quantifications of the neighbor's beliefs (e.g., the locations most likely to contain victims), which loses information about the neighbor's uncertainty (e.g., the probabilities of victims in each location). Otherwise, the observation space would be continuous (and thus very difficult to work with) if neighbors shared their full belief states.

Second, even if Z were extended to include shared information, there is no way for the observation function in a single agent POMDP to encode a probability that a neighbor shares a phenomenon state from its own beliefs (in response to a request) without some pre-coordination and agreement between agents. That is, agents must understand the likelihoods that a neighbor both (1) shares a particular piece of information (dependent on the neighbor's beliefs that change over time) and (2) any information at all (e.g., a robot might be busy and unwilling to share information at the current time). Without this information, an agent cannot calculate the overall probability that it receives any particular information from a neighbor at any point in time, necessary for updating its beliefs with Eq. 2 with shared information, nor plan what information it might receive over time. Therefore, a single agent POMDP formulation of the AHIG will not directly work in ad hoc environments.

Of note, traditional multiagent variants of POMDPs (e.g., DEC-POMDPs, Distributed POMDPs, and I-POMDPs [3, 13, 18]) provide some methods for handling both of the aforementioned problems; however, these types of POMDPs require pre-coordination so are inappropriate for ad hoc environments and do not scale well with the number of agents.

To resolve these problems inherent in a POMDP-based AHIG model, we need to add some method to incorporate shared information (which is inherently multiagent in nature) outside of the (single agent) POMDP framework's belief updates. Then, the agent should still make decisions based on its current knowledge, but it also needs a way to plan how its beliefs will change to form an action policy.

4. KNOWLEDGE STATE MDP

In this section, we first describe how we propose to incorporate shared information from other agents, building on the aforementioned POMDP formulation. Then, we describe a *transformation* of the POMDP into a MDP that looks at solving the AHIG from a metareasoning perspective, decoupled from how the agent refines its knowledge when it receives new information. Finally, we introduce a *learning process* for the MDP that enables an agent to learn how to choose actions to take to refine its knowledge in ad hoc environments without requiring pre-coordination about how and when other agents will share information.

4.1 Incorporating Shared Information

For agent knowledge about phenomenon states, we consider probability distributions over all possible phenomenon states very similar to belief states described in Section 3.2.

Table 1: POMDP Formulation of the AHIG Problem

POMDP	Values	AHIG Description
State Variables S	$S_{Req} \times S_{Rec} \times_{j \in P} PS_j$ $S_{Req} = \{0, \ldots, k\}^{\|P\|}$ $S_{Rec} = \{0, \ldots, k\}^{\|P\|}$	Counts of the number of time steps since the agent last requested (S_{Req}) or received a request for information (S_{Rec}), up to a maximum count k, and the phenomenon states (PS_j)
Actions A	$\bigcup_{j \in P} \{Sense_j, Request_j, Share_j\}$	Actions (1) sensing a particular phenomenon j, (2) requesting information from neighbors about phenomenon j, and (3) sharing information to neighbors about phenomenon j (for each $j \in P$)
Observations Z	$\{null\} \cup PS_j$	Observations about the phenomenon state of a particular phenomenon, or receiving no observation at all
Transition Function T	$[0, 1]$	Probability that request counts change (deterministically) and phenomenon states change (stochastically) after each action
Observation Function O	$[0, 1]$	Probability that the agent receives observations about partially observable phenomenon states from its actions
Reward Function R	$\mathbb{R}$	Rewards received for taking different actions based on the current state of the environment and the agent's knowledge.
Discount Factor γ	$(0, 1)$	A discount factor to use for weighting future, uncertain rewards
Initial Belief State b_0	$[0, 1]$	The probability ascribed to each phenomenon state being the correct initial state of each phenomenon (a uniform distribution)

We reuse notation with $b_t(j, ps)$ the probability that the agent believes phenomenon $j \in P$ is currently $ps \in PS_j$. For $Sense_j$ actions, beliefs update from b to b' after receiving observation z about phenomenon j using Bayes' rule:

$$b'(j, ps) = \frac{p}{\eta}\Big[(1-cp)b_t(j, ps) + \sum_{ps' \in PS_j / ps} \Big(\frac{cp}{|PS_j| - 1}\Big) b(j, ps')\Big] \quad (3)$$

where $p = acc$ when $z = ps$, else $p = 1 - acc$. This is equivalent to the belief updates performed with Eq. 2 using the POMDP formulation described in Section 3.2.

With respect to shared information, we assume[1] that agents share the full information about their beliefs: the probabilities ascribed to each phenomenon state for the particular phenomenon for which a neighbor sent a request. Then, the corresponding belief update for shared information b_{Sh} is:

$$b'(j, ps) = \frac{b(j, ps)\big[w \cdot b_{Sh}(j, ps) + (1 - w)(1 - b_{Sh}(j, ps))\big]}{\sum_{ps' \in PS_j} b(j, ps')\big[w \cdot b_{Sh}(j, ps') + (1 - w)(1 - b_{Sh}(j, ps'))\big]} \quad (4)$$

where constant weight[2] w dampens shared information so that uncertain shared beliefs do not cause agents to become certain too quickly from little gathered information.

Using these two rules, agents can incorporate information from both from (1) directly observing a phenomenon with its sensors, and (2) its neighbors sharing their knowledge.

4.2 Knowledge State MDP Transformation

At the core of AHIG, the agent's behavior does not necessarily depend on which *particular* phenomenon state is currently correct for each phenomenon, but instead the problem is really about how the agent should choose actions to improve its *knowledge* (noting that actions to improve knowledge could be equivalent for each actual phenomenon state). After all, the agents' goal is to form highly certain knowledge about each phenomenon using the information available in the environment. For instance, in our S&R example, a robot will base its information gathering on *how certain its knowledge is* about a location (looking to resolve its uncertainty so that it knows where all victims are as quickly as possible), which is *internal* to the agent and independent of whether or not an *external* unknown location actually contains victims. The robot isn't necessarily responsible for using the refined knowledge for a separate task (that is done by human first responders), but the goal of the agent in the AHIG is to develop high quality knowledge that could subsequently be used for other purposes, depending on the application.

Given this insight, we transform the above POMDP into what we call the **Knowledge State MDP**–an alternative formulation of the problem directly enabling an agent to make decisions of how to gather information based on considering the current state of its *knowledge*, as opposed to the state of the *environment* (including the states of phenomena under observation). This provides a ***metareasoning solution*** enabling the agent to choose how to gather information based on reflecting about the quality of its knowledge without worrying about the domain-specific contents of that knowledge. As a result, the agent's decision making (at a metareasoning level) is decoupled from its knowledge refinement (at a standard reasoning level), as desired.

The Knowledge State MDP can be mathematically described as a MDP $\langle S_{Req} \times S_{Rec} \times K, A, T, R \rangle$, summarized in Table 2. Here, the partially observable part of the state space is replaced with the different knowledge states K of the agent's knowledge (which are fully observable when reflecting on the agent's knowledge) as it gathers information to understand its environment. K is combined with the S_{Req} and S_{Rec} state variables representing counts of time since requests were sent or received, described in Section 3.2.

Recall that in the AHIG, the primary concern of the agent is to form highly certain beliefs, so the state of agent knowledge should reflect how much certainty exists in the agent's knowledge. Then, the agent can take actions that improve its certainty and result in better knowledge states (closer

[1]Other types of information might instead be shared, based on the domain, which we leave to consider as future work.

[2]Such weights are common in the information sharing literature (e.g., [11, 19]) and could be learned as in trust and reputation systems to further refine our solution, which we intend to explore in the future. Please see [11] for a more elaborate discussion of the impact of weight w.

Table 2: Knowledge State MDP Formulation

MDP	Values	AHIG Description
State Variables S	$S_{Req} \times S_{Rec} \times K$ $S_{Req} = \{0, \ldots, k\}^{\|P\|}$ $S_{Rec} = \{0, \ldots, k\}^{\|P\|}$ $K : H(b, j)$ in k bins	Counts of the number of time steps since the agent last requested information (S_{Req}) or received a request for information (S_{Rec}), up to a maximum count k, and the agents current certainty (K) in the current state of each phenomenon j
Actions A	$\bigcup_{j \in P} \{Sense_j, Request_j, Share_j\}$	Actions (1) sensing a particular phenomenon j, (2) requesting information from neighbors about phenomenon j, and (3) sharing information to neighbors about phenomenon j (for each $j \in P$)
Transition Function T	$T_{S_{Rec}, S_{Req}} \cdot T_K \in [0, 1]$	Probability of state changes, as the product of request state variable transitions and knowledge state transitions T_K
Reward Function R	$\mathbb{R}$	Rewards received for taking different actions based on the agent's knowledge.
Discount Factor γ	$(0, 1)$	A discount factor to use for weighting future, uncertain rewards

to full certainty). Given that the knowledge representation b described in Section 4.1 is a probability distribution over possible phenomenon states for each phenomenon, an appropriate measure of certainty in each phenomenon j's state (independent of application) is the entropy $H(b, j) \in [0, 1]$ of the probability distribution representing its knowledge [2]:

$$H(b, j) = 1 + \frac{1}{\log |PS_j|} \sum_{ps \in PS_j} b(j, ps) \log b(j, ps) \tag{5}$$

To create a set of finite knowledge states K using $H(b, j)$ so that the MDP is a discrete state MDP, and thus is much more tractable, we suggest discretizing the certainty values into equal sized bins so that there exist a desired number of states $|K|$. Note that a larger $|K|$ creates a finer grained separation between different knowledge states, potentially enabling better planning, whereas a smaller $|K|$ make the MDP faster to solve (and has implications on the learning process described in Section 4.3).

Given the rewards in the AHIG described in Section 2.1, it is important to note that the same reward encoding works for the Knowledge State MDP as well: knowledge states identifying high certainty earn a reward, and action-based costs, rewards, and penalties stay the same.

4.3 Learning Knowledge State Dynamics

Now, within the Knowledge State MDP, the key to guiding appropriate action selection is the dynamics of how knowledge states change based on each action $a \in A$. That is, how actions lead the agent to improve its certainty over time. This information is encoded in the knowledge state transition function T_K. Unfortunately, due to a lack of precoordination to determine how and when agents will share information, this function is undetermined initially. However, whereas this was a problem in our suggested POMDP-based solution in Section 3.2, the transformation into an MDP makes it feasible to perform model-based reinforcement learning[3] (MB-RL) [16] to learn this transition function through interactions with the environment and other agents (and adjust it over time as agent openness causes the environment to change), instead of having to rely on pre-coordination.

[3]Although MB-RL algorithms also exist for POMDPs (e.g., [20]), such algorithms have high complexity and are not generally applicable in practice for POMDPs of moderate to large state spaces (which grows quickly with phenomena P and their states PS_j for Section 3.2's POMDP).

In general, any MB-RL algorithm should be sufficient to learn the knowledge state transition function T_K. For our experimental setup in this paper, we use a learning approach for the transition function similar to recent variants [14, 25] of one of the most popular MB-RL algorithms: R-max [5]. In particular, this algorithm uses frequentist counting by maintaining a table counting the number of times $n(s_t, a, s_{t+1})$ that the agent observes a transition from state s_t to s_{t+1} after taking action a, then the algorithm updates the transition table to

$$T(s_t, a, s_{t+1}) = \frac{n(s_t, a, s_{t+1})}{n(s_t, a)} \tag{6}$$

whenever the total count of observed transitions for a state-action pair $n(s_t, a) = \sum_{s_{t+1} \in S} n(s_t, a, s_{t+1})$ equals a parameter m, after which the learning counts for the state-action pair are reset to 0. A smaller m enables *faster updates* to the transition table, whereas a larger m ensures *more precise updates* (by relying on more observed transitions before updating). Of note, smaller $|K|$ are also beneficial here, causing the same knowledge state to be encountered more frequently, and thus more frequent learning updates.

Considering the Knowledge State MDP, learning T_K amounts to learning exactly how the certainty in the agent's knowledge changes based on (1) each information gathering action, and (2) how long it has been since the agent requested information (since this alerts the agent both how timely neighbors respond, as well as whether or not they respond at all). Understanding such changes to agent knowledge is exactly the information the agent needs to determine which information gathering actions to perform in order to reach highly certain knowledge and achieve its primary goal–actions that are more likely to lead to high certainty knowledge states from the current knowledge state are actions that most improve the agent's knowledge, as desired.

This learning process only requires feedback from the agent's knowledge updates (using sensed or shared information) to observe exactly which knowledge state (i.e., certainty) transitions occur after taking each action. Thus, the agent can learn over time how its knowledge changes when it senses, as well as when it requests shared information (including how long such information takes to arrive), without having to know in advance when or how other agents will choose to share information. Therefore, this learning process bypasses the problems of other solutions in ad hoc environments without requiring pre-coordination to understand the behaviors of neighboring agents and their impact on knowledge refinement. Moreover, the agent also adapts its understanding of knowledge state transition changes over time, which is important for open environments where information sharing can become more or less prevalent over time, in which case a smaller m might be useful for more frequent learning and faster adaptation to the changing environment.

By planning with the reward function R, the agent plans to reach certainty as fast as possible (by maximizing rewards for certain knowledge) while also minimizing costs required for gathering information, making the agent both effective and efficient at its task. Thus, our Knowledge State MDP coupled with MB-RL is an appropriate solution for the AHIG.

It is important to note that this Knowledge State MDP transformation is closely related to a similar metareasoning framework in the literature: the Observer Effect POMDP [8], which combines fully observable knowledge states with partially observable environment states to guide agents to perform actions that refine knowledge over time. Our solution differs in that (1) it learns the transitions in knowledge over time, as opposed to the domain-specific value of information, and (2) extends this type of approach to a multiagent setting where learning enables the agent to reason about the affects of other agents on its own knowledge.

5. EXPERIMENTAL SETUP

To better understand our approach and investigate its performance in different AHIG settings, we conducted experiments empirically evaluating how well our Knowledge State MDP and MB-RL process guide agent information gathering using different information sources, including information sharing, without requiring pre-coordination. In particular, we considered a range of network configurations that might reflect different types of environments and applications.

That is, we varied the average neighborhood size $N_t(i)$, where larger neighborhoods made shared information more prevalent, whereas smaller neighborhoods represent more communication-constrained environments (e.g., our S&R robot example where only a few robots might be within line-of-sight of one another). The networks were randomly generated using an Erdos-Renyi model [9]. Since the environment was ad hoc, agents knew nothing about their neighbors in advance. Moreover, we made the environment open, where a predetermined percentage (10%) of the agents left periodically (every 100 time steps) and new agents joined. This agent openness also reduced the availability of information over time, making information sharing more or less valuable at different points in time. Within a neighborhood (and throughout the set of agents), agents differed in their capabilities: different agents had different sensing accuracies, making them better or worse at quickly gathering good information from the environment to share with their neighbors upon request. This follows in the tradition of other ad hoc environments (e.g., [6, 24]), where agents must work with agents with different capabilities than themselves.

The different opponents in our experiments included: (1) **KSMDP+MB-RL**: our Knowledge State MDP solution with MB-RL, using the UCT algorithm [17] to plan each time step using the learned MDP, (2) **KSMDP**: our Knowledge State MDP solution without MB-RL (also using UCT for planning, but only using the initial, uninformed K_T function where knowledge states only transition to the closest states), and two baselines: (3) **AlwaysSense**: where agents *maximized sensing* for information gathering and did not plan for information sharing since pre-coordination was not possible (which serves as a lower bound on acceptable agent performance), and (4) **RequestThenSense**: where agents requested information about each phenomenon every k steps to *maximize information sharing*, then either sensing the rest of the time to further inform agent knowledge or sharing if the agent had certain knowledge to help its neighbors.

We evaluated agent performance using three measures averaged per time step: (1) average belief certainty across all agents, (2) average proportion of agents with correct, highly certain knowledge, and (3) average total rewards earned by all agents. Each agent earned rewards: +10 whenever its b was sufficiently certain (i.e., $H(b) \geqslant 0.8$), -1 for every $Sense_i$ action, -1 for each $Request_j$ action (or -5 if $S^j_{Req} < k$), and +1 for each $Share_j$ action (whenever $S^j_{Rec} < k$, else -5). The other parameters were set: $|Ag| = 100$ (which is too large for multiagent POMDP solutions as a baseline), average $N_t(i) \in \{2, 4, 6, 8, 10\}$, $|P| = 1$, $|PS_j| = 3$, $cp = 1\%$, $acc \sim (0.5, 0.8)$, $\gamma = 0.99$, $k = 6$, $|K| = 100$. Each configuration repeated 50 times for 1000 time steps.

6. RESULTS

We begin our results analysis by considering the agent's average belief certainty, presented in Fig. 1. From these results, we first observe that our Knowledge State MDP solution with and without MB-RL (respectively KSMDP+MB-RL, KSMDP) achieved *higher amounts of belief certainty* than either of the baselines. This implies that, instead of trying to maximize either type of information gathering, our KSMDP formulation enabled agents to *appropriately select between information gathering actions using different sources to best refine their knowledge*, as opposed to either (1) requesting shared information as often as possible (RequestThenSense), or (2) independently relying only on sensed information (AlwaysSense).

Comparing across average neighborhood sizes, we observe that as neighborhood size increased and information became more available through sharing (due to each agent being connected to more potential information sources), the average certainty of the agents increased. Most notably, *certainty increased fastest for our KSMDP solutions*, implying that they became better at controlling information gathering as information became more readily available (although they also achieved the best performances when the neighborhoods were smallest and information was most limited).

Further comparing between the two variants of our solutions, we note that although adding MB-RL did not improve belief certainty very much, it did so at a 0.05 statistically significant level for the smaller average neighborhood sizes (2-6). This was when information was least available (due to fewer neighbors as sources) and thus more care was necessary for controlling information gathering. Therefore, *adding MB-RL to our Knowledge State MDP was most beneficial when information gathering most needed help.*

Next, we consider the average proportion of agents holding correct and highly certain beliefs, presented in Fig. 2. Maximizing this performance measure was the desired emergent behavior of solving the AHIG. From these results, we additionally observe that not only did our Knowledge State MDP-based solutions (KSMDP+MB-RL and KSMDP) lead

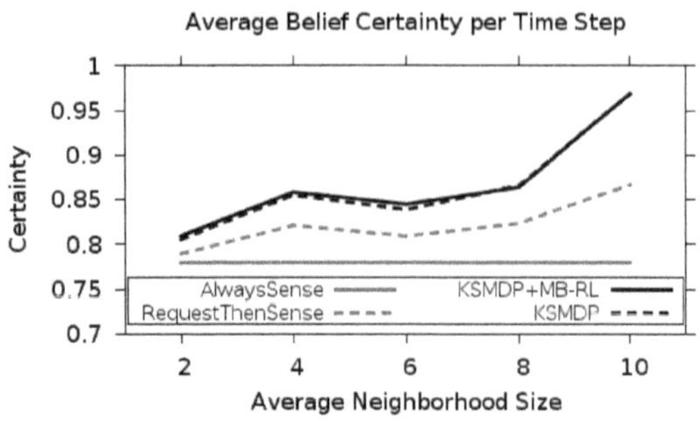

Figure 1: Average Belief Certainty

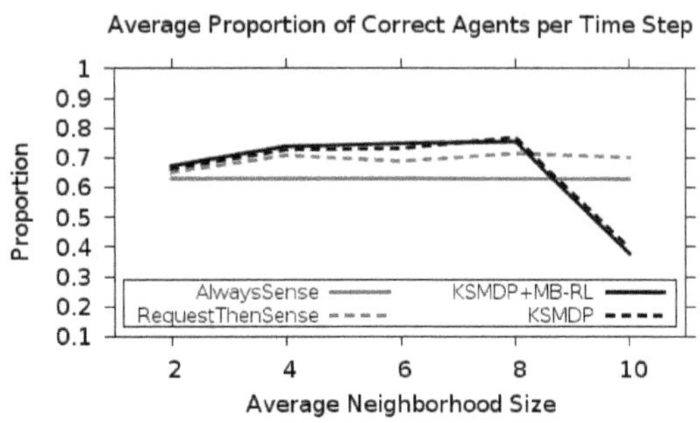

Figure 2: Average Proportion of Correct Agents Note: in all figs., 95% CI are too small to display

to more certainty in the agents' beliefs, but those beliefs were also correct. Thus, agents were *gathering the right information to understand their environments* over time. Additionally, we again find evidence of the benefits of using MB-RL to learn how agent knowledge changes based on different information gathering actions using different sources: the improvement over KSMDP (without MB-RL) for KSMDP+MB-RL *was more pronounced when information was most constrained* (i.e., at lowest neighborhood sizes).

Interestingly, we also observe that for the largest neighborhood size (10) considered in our experiments, our KSMDP solutions actually achieved very few correct agents compared to the baselines, which is in sharp contrast to the other neighborhood sizes. Upon further inspection, what happened is the agents fell victim to **institutional memory**: they converged to highly certain beliefs (as indicated in Fig. 1) because of the prevalence of shared information (favoring requesting information over continually sensing the environment). This caused the agents to become stuck with outdated beliefs that didn't adapt as the phenomenon changed over time since very few agents continued sensing the phenomenon directly. In the future, we intend to explore how we can adapt our solution to learn to avoid this problem.

Finally, we consider the average total rewards earned by all agents per time step, presented in Fig. 3. We observe that for all but the lowest neighborhood sizes, our KSMDP approaches–that directly maximized rewards to plan information gathering actions–earned the highest cumulative rewards due to achieving high certainty while trying to minimize costs. Of note, for the lowest neighborhood sizes (2-4) when information was most scarce, the KSMDP approaches were *willing to accept more information gathering cost in order to achieve higher certainty and correctness*, as displayed in Figs. 1-2, ultimately attaining the agents' primary goal.

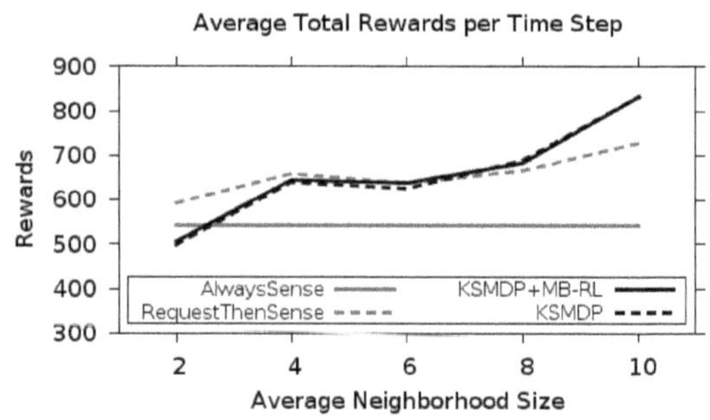

Figure 3: Average Total Reward

7. CONCLUSIONS

In summary, we introduced the ad hoc information gathering (AHIG) problem occurring when agents must balance relying on different types of information sources (knowing when to sense vs. when to rely on shared information from other agents) in order to understand their complex environment without pre-coordinating with one another. From the tradition of using POMDPs to guide agent decision making, we proposed a transformation called the Knowledge State MDP that enables agents to control information gathering by reflecting on (fully observable) changes to their knowledge. To address the inability of agents to pre-coordinate in ad hoc environments, we added a MB-RL process to the Knowledge State MDP that enables agents to learn how their knowledge changes when relying on different information sources. This includes learning how and when neighbors might be willing to share information to supplement an agent's own sensing of the environment. Using an experimental study, we investigated the performance of our Knowledge State MDP (with and without MB-RL) in a range of environment configurations (with varying number of information sources), and discovered: (1) our solution gathered better information and earned greater rewards than baseline strategies of trying to maximize the usefulness of either type of information source (sensing vs. shared information), and (2) adding MB-RL enabled agents to best guided their behavior when information availability was most limited (and high quality information gathering was most necessary).

In the future, we intend to: (1) combine our solution with trust and reputation systems to further learn not only *when to rely on different information sources*, but *how much weight to place in received information*, which could help overcome the institutional memory problem (where weight w could be adapted to avoid agents rapidly converging to certain beliefs when shared information is prevalent), and (2) study how to use the Knowledge State MDP to balance information gathering about different phenomena in the environment to avoid *imbalanced knowledge* potentially caused by favoring sources for one phenomenon over the others.

Acknowledgments

This material is based upon work partially supported by the NSF (grant SES-1132015) and was completed utilizing the Holland Computing Center of the University of Nebraska.

REFERENCES

[1] N. Agmon, S. Barrett, and P. Stone. Modeling uncertainty in leading ad hoc teams. In *Proceedings of the 13th International Conference on Autonomous Agents and Multiagent Systems (AAMAS'14)*, pages 397–404, Paris, France, May 5-9, 2014.

[2] M. Araya-Lopez, O. Buffet, V. Thomas, and F. Charpillet. A POMDP extension with belief-dependent rewards. In *Proceedings of the 24th Annual Conference on Neural Information Processing Systems (NIPS'10)*, pages 64–72, Vancouver, B.C., Canada, December 6-9, 2010.

[3] D. S. Bernstein, R. Givan, N. Immerman, and S. Zilberstein. The complexity of decentralized control of Markov decision processes. *Mathematics of Operations Research*, 27(4):819–840, 2002.

[4] C. Boutilier. A POMDP formulation of preference elicitation problems. In *Proceedings of the 18th National Conference on Artificial Intelligence (AAAI'02)*, pages 239–246, Edmonton, Alberta, Canada, July 28-August 1, 2002.

[5] R. I. Brafman and M. Tennenholtz. R-max – a general polynomial time algorithm for near-optimal reinforcement learning. *Journal of Machine Learning Research*, 3:213–231, 2002.

[6] D. Chakraborty and P. Stone. Cooperating with a Markovian ad hoc teammate. In *Proceedings of the 12th International Conference on Autonomous Agents and Multiagent Systems (AAMAS'13)*, pages 1085–1092, Saint Paul, MN, May 6-10, 2013.

[7] F. Doshi and N. Roy. The permutable POMDP: fast solutions to POMDPs for preference elicitation. In *Proceedings of the 7th International Conference on Autonomous Agents and Multiagent Systems (AAMAS'08)*, pages 493–500, Estoril, Portugal, May 12-16, 2008.

[8] A. Eck and L.-K. Soh. Observer effect from stateful resources in agent sensing. *Autonomous Agents and Multiagent Systems*, 26(2):202–244, 2013.

[9] P. Erdos and A. Renyi. On the evolution of random graphs. *Publication of the Mathematical Institute of the Hungarian Academy of Sciences*, pages 17–61, 1960.

[10] K. Genter, N. Agmon, and P. Stone. Ad hoc teamwork for leading a flock. In *Proceedings of the 12th International Conference on Autonomous Agents and Multiagent Systems (AAMAS'13)*, pages 531–538, Saint Paul, MN, May 6-10, 2013.

[11] R. Glinton, P. Scerri, and K. Sycara. Exploiting scale invariant dynamics for efficient information propagation in large teams. In *Proceedings of the 9th International Conference on Autonomous Agents and Multiagent Systems (AAMAS'10)*, pages 21–28, Toronto, Canada, May 10-14, 2010.

[12] R. Glinton, P. Scerri, and K. Sycara. An investigation of the vulnerabilities of scale invariant dynamics in large teams. In *Proceedings of the 10th International Conference on Autonomous Agents and Multiagent Systems (AAMAS'11)*, pages 21–28, Taipei, Taiwan, May 2-6, 2011.

[13] P. J. Gmytrasiewicz and P. Doshi. A framework for sequential planning in multi-agent settings. *Journal of Artificial Intelligence Research*, 24:49–79, 2005.

[14] P. Hernandez-Leal, E. M. de Cote, and L. E. Sucar. Exploration strategies to detect strategy switches. In *Proceedings of the 14th International Workshop on Adaptive and Learning Agents (ALA'2014)*, Paris, France, May 5-6, 2014.

[15] L. P. Kaelbling, M. L. Littman, and A. R. Cassandra. Planning and acting in partially observable stochastic domains. *Artificial Intelligence*, 101:99–134, 1998.

[16] L. P. Kaelbling, M. L. Littman, and W. Moore. Reinforcement learning: A survey. *Journal of Artificial Intelligence Research*, 4:237–285, 1996.

[17] L. Kocsis and C. Szepesvari. Bandit based Monte-Carlo planning. In *Proceedings of the 17th European Conference on Machine Learning (ECML'06)*, pages 282–293, Berlin, Germany, September 18-22, 2006.

[18] R. Nair, P. Varakantham, M. Tambe, and M. Yokoo. Networked distributed POMDPs: A synthesis of distributed constraint optimization and POMDPs. In *Proceedings of the 20th National Conference on Artificial Intelligence (AAAI'05)*, pages 133–139, Pittsburgh, PA, July 9-13, 2005.

[19] O. Pryymak, A. Rogers, and N. R. Jennings. Efficient opinion sharing in large decentralized teams. In *Proceedings of the 11th International Conference on Autonomous Agents and Multiagent Systems (AAMAS'12)*, Valencia, Spain, June 4-8, 2012.

[20] S. Ross, B. Chaib-draa, and J. Pineau. Bayes-adaptive POMDPs. In *Proceedings of the 21st Annual Conference on Neural Information Processing Systems (NIPS'07)*, Vancouver, B.C., Canada, December 3-6, 2007.

[21] J. Sabater and C. Sierra. Reputation and social network analysis in multi-agent systems. In *Proceedings of the 1st International Conference on Autonomous Agents and Multiagent Systems (AAMAS'02)*, pages 475–482, Bologna, Italy, July 15-19, 2002.

[22] M. Sensoy, A. Fokoue, J. Z. Pan, T. J. Norman, Y. Tang, N. Oren, and K. Sycara. Reasoning about uncertain information and conflict resolution through trust revision. In *Proceedings of the 12th International Conference on Autonomous Agents and Multiagent Systems (AAMAS'13)*, pages 837–844, Saint Paul, MN, May 6-10, 2013.

[23] M. T. J. Spaan, T. S. Veiga, and P. U. Lima. Active cooperative perception in networked robotic systems using POMDPs. In *Proceedings of the 2010 IEEE/RSJ International Conference on Intelligent Robots and Systems (IROS'10)*, pages 4800–4805, Taipei, Taiwan, October 18-22, 2010.

[24] P. Stone, G. A. Kaminka, S. Kraus, and J. S. Rosenschein. Ad hoc autonomous agent teams: Collaboration without pre-coordination. In *Proceedings of the 24th National Conference on Artificial Intelligence (AAAI'10)*, pages 1504–1509, Atlanta, GA, July 11-15, 2010.

[25] I. Szita and C. Szepesvari. Model-based reinforcement learning with nearly tight exploration complexity

bounds. In *Proceedings of the 27th International Conference on Machine Learning (ICML'2010)*, pages 1031–1038, Haifa, Israel, June 21-24, 2010.

[26] W. T. Teacy, J. Patel, N. R. Jennings, and M. Luck. TRAVOS: Trust and reputation in the context of inaccurate information sources. *Autonomous Agents and Multiagent Systems*, 12(2):183–198, 2006.

A Mechanism for Smoothly Handling Human Interrupts in Team Oriented Plans

Alessandro Farinelli, Nicolo' Marchi, Masoume M. Raeissi
Computer Science Department
University of Verona
Verona, Italy
alessandro.farinelli@univr.it
marchi.nicolo@gmail.com
masoume.raeissi@univr.it

Nathan Brooks, Paul Scerri
Robotics Institute
Carnegie Mellon University
Pittsburgh, PA USA
nbb@cs.cmu.edu
pscerri@cs.cmu.edu

ABSTRACT

Team oriented plans have become a popular tool for operators to control teams of autonomous agents (or robots) to pursue complex objectives in complex environments. Such plans allow an operator to specify high level directives and allow the team to autonomously determine how to implement such directives. However, the operators will often want to interrupt the activities of individual team members to deal with particular situations, such as a danger to a robot that the robot team cannot perceive. Previously, after such interrupt, the operator would usually need to restart the team plan to ensure its success. In this paper, we present an approach to encoding how unexpected interrupts can be smoothly handled within a team plan. Building on a team plan formalism that uses Colored Petri Net, we describe a mechanism that allows a range of interrupts to be handled smoothly, allowing the team to efficiently continue with its task, after the operator intervention. We validate the approach with an application of robotic watercraft and show improved overall efficiency. In particular, our interrupt mechanism decreases the time to complete the mission (up to 48% reduction) and decreases the operator load (up to 80% reduction in number of user actions).

Categories and Subject Descriptors

I.2.11 [**Distributed Artificial Intelligence**]: Multiagent Systems; I.2.9 [**Robotics**]: Operator Interfaces

General Terms

Experimentation

Keywords

Plan Monitoring; Petri Net; Cooperative Robotic Watercraft

1. INTRODUCTION

Robotics technology has matured sufficiently to make the idea of building robot teams for real environments a serious possibility. For applications ranging from disaster response to environmental monitoring to military operations, approaches are emerging to allow small numbers of humans to control teams of robots for achieving complex objectives. A common way of doing this is via team plans [1, 2, 3], which allow an operator to interact via high level objectives and plans and allow automation to work out the details. For example, a plan for environmental monitoring might tell robots to collect a certain type of information in a certain area, leaving the robots to work out who goes where to collect the information.

However, in most real domains, human operators will occasionally need to directly control a robot for some purpose, perhaps to protect a robot from a danger it cannot perceive or to achieve some specific objectives that the robot is not capable of understanding. Typically, when a robot plan is interrupted, any team plan that the robot was participating in will be terminally impacted. In some cases, the rest of the team can reorganize without the interrupted robot and then reorganize when the interruption is over, but this depends sensitively on the plan, the particular situation and nature of the interruption. In general, how to respond to an external interruption is very sensitive to the specific context of the plan and if the context is not taken into account when dealing with the interruption, overall performance will be poor.

In this paper, we are specifically looking at a domain of teams of robotic boats collecting information in bodies of water [4]. In such applications, one or a small number of experienced operators, perhaps water scientists, are managing between five and 25 boats on a body of water. Large manned boats and water phenomena are external dangers to the robots that the human operators might be able to help mitigate. In other cases, operators might have some external knowledge about what is going on in the water that allows them to direct resources in a very specific way to get very specific information. Hence, while it is necessary to utilize team plans to make use of multiple assets, interruptions are an inevitable and important part of operations.

We specifically adopt an approach for creating team plans with Petri Nets to allow specification of complex, parallel and multi-stage plans. To deal with external interruptions, two special events are created, indicating the start of two categories of interruptions, but not specifying the nature of the interruption. The approach allows transitions to be created from any place in the Petri Net to a place that waits for the interruption handling to be completed before sending the plan back to an appropriate place in the plan. Depending on the nature and timing of the interaction, relative to the specific context of the plan, the expressive approach allows a range of possibilities to be encoded, including restarting the plan, directly resuming or going through some intermediate steps to restart effectively. The key is that the plan designer can work out in advance

Appears in: *Proceedings of the 14th International Conference on Autonomous Agents and Multiagent Systems (AAMAS 2015), Bordini, Elkind, Weiss, Yolum (eds.), May 4–8, 2015, Istanbul, Turkey.*

how to handle interruptions at a particular place in the plan and encode efficient and effective resumptions.

In some interesting plans, there are specific roles for specific assets. Our team plan approach captures this by using a Colored Petri Net formalism and allowing the different colored tokens to represent specific roles. For such plans, we have a special event type which captures which role is being interrupted when the interruption occurs. The plan can then be designed to react differently to different roles being interrupted. For example, interruptions of non-critical roles might be ignored completely, while when one of a set of tightly coupled roles is interrupted, the other roles might be put into some sort of holding pattern. The key is that the design approach provides the representational power to handle the interruption effectively.

To evaluate the approach, we use a simulator of the robot boats and a novel technique for determining the value of the concept. The simulator is used for all development and testing of algorithms on the real robots, hence it is an accurate simulator of their capabilities. However, it is very difficult to design an experiment with real human operators where interrupts would be distributed over the whole length of the plan and vary in length in non-trivial ways. Moreover, this would require a proper evaluation of the operator interface which falls outside the scope of this contribution. Instead, our experimental approach simulates all possible interrupts multiple times. While in practice interrupts at some times might be more common than others, the concept of the approach is that any interrupt is handled smoothly hence the experimental setup provides a significant indication of the power offered by the interrupt mechanism without considering the skills of the human operators. In more detail, we compared the execution of team plans without specific interrupt handling to plans where interrupt handlers were explicitly encoded by using our framework and we found significant improvement in overall efficiency, i.e., up to a 48% reduction in time to complete a mission and up to a 80% reduction in operator load.

The rest of the paper is organized as follows, Section 2 provides necessary background on Colored Petri Net (CPN) and plan monitoring for multi-agent systems. Section 3 describes the robotic boat system we considered here and the plan specification language used in such system. Section 4 describes the interrupt mechanism we propose and Section 5 details our empirical methodology discussing obtained results. Finally, Section 6 concludes the paper.

2. BACKGROUND AND RELATED WORK

In this section we will first provide necessary mathematical background on Petri Net and Colored Petri Net and then discuss related work on plan monitoring in multi-agent systems.

2.1 Petri Net

Petri Net (PN) is a widely used mathematical and graphical modeling tool for describing concurrency and synchronization in distributed systems. Graphically, a PN is represented by a directed bipartite graph, in which nodes could be either places (states of the system) or transitions (system events), arcs connect places to transitions and vice versa. Places in a Petri net contain a discrete number of marks called *tokens*. A particular allocation of tokens to places is called a *marking* and it defines a specific state of the system that the Petri Net represents.

Formally, a PN is a tuple $PN = (P, T, F, W, M_0)$, where $P = \{p_1, p_2, \ldots, p_m\}$, is a finite set of places; $T = \{t_1, t_2, \ldots, t_n\}$, is a finite set of transitions; $F \subseteq (P \times T) \cup (T \times P)$, is a set of arcs; $W : F \to \mathbb{N}$, is a weight function; $M_0 : P \to \mathbb{N}_0$ is an initial marking.

The markings of a PN evolves based on the firing behavior of the transitions. A transition t can fire whenever it is enabled (i.e., when each input place p_i of the transition is marked with at least $W(p_i, t)$ tokens) and if the transition fires $W(p_i, t)$ tokens are removed from each input places p_i and $W(t, p_j)$ tokens are added to each output place p_j.

Colored Petri Net (CPN) [5] extends Petri Nets where tokens become more informative and each of them has attached a data value called the token *color*. The firing behaviors of transitions, and consequently the evolution of the markings, now depends on the colors of the tokens. In particular, tokens can now be identified and related to specific agents, thus providing a compact and convenient modeling language for team oriented plans.

Moreover, similar to PN, CPN can be analyzed and verified either by means of simulation or formal analysis methods[1] thus allowing validation of team oriented plans before their execution.

2.2 Plan monitoring in multi-agent systems

The problem of monitoring plan execution in agents and multi-agent systems has been addressed from different perspective throughout the years [7, 8, 9]. In particular here we focus on approaches that are most relevant to our work as they are explicitly designed for multi-agent systems. Hence, we discuss Belief Desire Intension (BDI) architectures [1, 2] and approaches based on Petri Net [10, 3].

Two successful BDI-based frameworks are STEAM and BITE which enable a coherent teamwork structure for multiple agents. The key aspect of STEAM [1] are team operators which are based on the Joint Intentions Theory, introduced by [11]. In STEAM, agents can monitor the team's performance and reorganize the team based on the current situation. BITE, which was introduced by Kaminka & Frenkel [2], specifies a library of social behaviors and offers different synchronization protocols that can be used interchangeably and mixed as needed. However, while both this works provide key contributions for building team oriented plans, they do not provide any specific mechanism for a human-operator to interrupt the execution of such plans.

One of the first approaches based on Petri Net for multi-agent plan monitoring was proposed by King et al. [10]. In particular they propose the use of automated planning methods to generate plans for multiple agents. Such plans are then compiled into Petri Nets for analysis, execution and monitoring. The approach handles possible failures during plan execution by re-planning at run-time. In particular, the agent which experienced a problem/failure informs the human-operator, who starts the re-planning process. Hence, the human operator intervention happens only after receiving a request from the agent; moreover, re-planning at run-time might be problematic for applications that must operate within real-time constraints.

Recently, Ziparo et al. proposed an approach for plan monitoring called Petri Net Plan (PNP) [3] . PNP takes inspiration from action languages and offers a rich collection of mechanisms for dealing with action failures, concurrent actions and cooperation in a multi-robot context. One important functionality offered by the formalism of PNP is the possibility to modify the execution of a plan at run-time using interrupts. Our work also focuses on interrupting multi-robot plans, however here we are mainly interested in human-operators interrupting the normal execution of a team-plan rather than action failures and plan synchronization. In more detail, here we take a different approach for plan representation as we encode team plans by using Colored Petri Nets in contrast to what is

[1] See for example CPN *Tools* [6]

proposed in [3] where a team-plan is a collection of several single-agent plans represented with standard Petri Nets. This is a significant difference as it allows us to represent plans involving several agents with a very compact structure as agents are represented by the colored tokens and not explicitly in the network. Moreover, by using CPN we can represent different types of interrupts, i.e., team-level and platform specific (see Section 4) thus providing a rich model to allow sophisticated interactions between the human operators and team plans.

3. THE COOPERATIVE ROBOTIC WATERCRAFT FRAMEWORK

This work focuses on a system of robotic boats developed as part of the Cooperative Robotic Watercraft project [4]. In this Section we describe the team plan specification language used in such system (SAMI) and provide a brief overview of the whole system.

3.1 SAMI Petri Net

The main components of the SAMI Petri Net specification language are illustrated in a sample plan in Figure 1. The language is based on Colored Petri Nets and Hierarchical Petri Nets and has several extensions to add the capability to send and receive commands and information from team members, to perform and reference task allocations, and to capture situational awareness and mixed initiative directives. In particular, the plan shown in Figure 1 reports places and transitions with associated output (OE) and input events (IE). When the plan starts the output event *Operator Select Robot List* is triggered asking the operator to select the list of boats that will participate in the plan. When the operator performs this action the input event *Operator Selects Boat List* is triggered, the corresponding transition will then fire moving the *relevant* tokens (i.e., the tokens that correspond to the selected boats) to the next place. The plan progresses in a similar way until the tokens reach the last place (i.e., all selected boats completed their path). When this happens the mission is over and the plan is no longer active.

Events fall under two categories: *output events* and *input events*. Output events are added to places in the Petri Net and contain commands or requests that are sent to human operators, robots, or agents. When a token(s) enter a place, all the output events on the place are triggered. The registered handler for that class of output event is sent the output event along with the tokens that just entered the place. For output event classes that contain data fields, there are 4 ways to specify the information, which are listed here with example usage in our outlined scenario: (1) Value defined offline by the petri net developer (the battery voltage threshold to send a low-energy alert to the operator). (2) Value defined by the operator at run-time when the plan is instantiated (the location boats should move to have their battery swapped). (3) Value defined by operator at run-time when the plan reaches place containing event (a safe temporary position for robots to move to in order to avoid an incoming manned boat). (4) Variable name defined by developer at plan design time, whose value is retrieved at run-time when plan reaches the place containing the event (a variable to retrieve the path planning results from a planning agent).

Input events are put on transitions and contain information received from human operators, robot proxies[2], or agent services, which perform assistive functions such as path planning, task allocation, and image processing. Input events on a transition are typically responses to an output event on a place preceding the transition. For input events that will contain information at run-time (such as a generated path or selection from an operator), a variable name is used so the information can be stored and accessed by output events. When an input event is received by the plan execution engine, it copies each piece of information held by the input event to the corresponding variable name that was specified by the plan developer. Input events also contain "relevant proxy" and "relevant task" fields, which contain the identities of the proxy(s) or task(s) that sent or triggered the input event.

Markup Each plan is "marked up" with context clues attached to individual events which provide information to the run-time GUI about which UI components and widgets are most appropriate for operator interaction, which set of priorities an agent service should consider when choosing from multiple algorithms, and which level of mixed-initiative autonomy to employ in making decisions. Each markup has a number of options and variables that the petri net developer must specify. UI components and agent services correspondingly indicate which markup options they support, allowing the most appropriate ones to be retrieved automatically at run-time. For example, the "relevant proxy" markup indicates to the UI that the locational data of certain proxies should be displayed to the operator in addition to any other information contained within the event. Settings include the proxy selection criteria (the event's relevant proxies or all proxies) and which data to visualize (including pose, current path, future paths, and past paths). The "mixed initiative trigger" markup is used to indicate when system autonomy should make a decision and if the operator should be informed. Options range from never using system autonomy, using autonomy after a timer expires, or using autonomy immediately without consulting the operator.

Tokens The Token class has 4 fields: a name (String), a token type (TokenType), a proxy (ProxyInt), and a task (Task). There are 3 TokenTypes: *Generic* tokens have no defined proxy or task and are used as counters. *Proxy* tokens contain a proxy but no task. These are created whenever a robot proxy is added to the system at run-time. *Task* tokens contain a task and might contain a proxy. Task tokens are created by the petri net execution engine when a plan is started, creating one for each task in the plan. When the task is allocated to a proxy, the proxy field of the task's corresponding token is set to the proxy assigned to the task. Representing proxies and tasks using tokens allows for multi-robot plans with arbitrary numbers of team members to be constructed and visualized compactly, compared to having individual Petri Net for each member of the team.

Edge Requirements In a standard Petri Net, incoming edges specify the tokens required for a transition to fire, which are then consumed, and outgoing edges specify the tokens that are added to the connected place. SAMI Petri Net edge labels have additional options designed to provide additional power. Labels on incoming edges specify tokens that must be present in the connected place in order for the connected transition to fire, but does not remove them upon firing as it could cause undesired interruption of behavior controlled by output events in the connected place. Labels on outgoing edges specify tokens that should be taken or consumed from the incoming places preceding the connected transition and/or tokens that should be added to the connected place. Taking a token removes it from its old place and adds it to the place connected to the outgoing edge. Consuming a token simply removes it from its old place, while adding a token will not modify the old place and just add a copy of the token to the connected place. In addition to generic tokens and specific task tokens, edge requirements can also refer to "relevant tokens" which are defined by the input events on the transition being evaluated. The list could contain proxy token(s), in the case of a "Path Completed" input event which spec-

[2]With the term *proxy* we refer to a software-service that connects a specific boat with the rest of the system

ifies the proxy token for the robot that finished, so that at run-time that proxy token can be moved forward in the Petri Net. It could also contain task token(s), in the case of a "Task Completed" input event signaling that a particular task has been completed and another task with a sequential completion constraint can begin.

Sub-missions The SAMI team plan language supports hierarchical team plans, allowing a "sub-mission" to be added on a place. When tokens enter the place an instance of the sub-mission is started, placing the tokens that entered the place into the start place of the sub-mission. Until the sub-mission finishes executing, transitions in the parent mission leaving the place holding the sub-mission are prevented from firing. Sub-missions can return values, return tokens, and write to variables shared with its parent mission, allowing sub-missions to reduce repeated creation of common Petri Net sequences and increase readability of the petri net.

3.2 System design

Figure 2 shows an airboat style robot, although differential drive propeller versions have also been developed. In addition to a battery based propulsion mechanism, each boat is equipped with an Android OS smartphone, custom electronics board, and sensor payload. The Android smartphone provides communication, either through a wireless local area network or 3G cellular network, GPS, compass, and multi-core processor. An optional prism can be mounted to the transparent lid of the waterproof electronics bay to use the phone's camera for obstacle avoidance and imaging. The Arduino Mega based electronics board receives commands from the Android phone over USB OTG and interfaces with the propulsion mechanism and sensor payload, as shown in Figure 3. The electronics board supports a wide variety of devices including acoustic doppler current profilers and sensors that measure electroconductivity, temperature, dissolved oxygen, and pH level. All sensor data is logged along with time and location.

The robot team is controlled from a nearby base station via a high power wireless antenna or remotely using 3G connectivity. The operator uses a SAMI compatible GUI to instantiate SAMI Petri Net plans, monitor their execution, and provide input as necessary. In this case, compatibility means the GUI contains a library of UI components listing which data classes and SAMI markups they support, allowing a custom "interaction panel" to be constructed for each event requiring operator input.

In order to assist the petri net developer, an intelligent plan editing tool named DREAAM was created. The editor was designed with three potential limitations of the plan language in mind: overwhelming visual clutter and developer errors resulting in invalid Petri Net or unexpected run-time behavior. DREAAM contains different visualization modes which selectively hide and compress sections of nets based on different tasks the developer may be performing. "Assistant agents" check for violations of Petri Net rules and flag errors, such as incomplete graphs and unlabeled start/end places, and warnings, such as suspicious edge labels.

Figure 2: Airboat robot platform

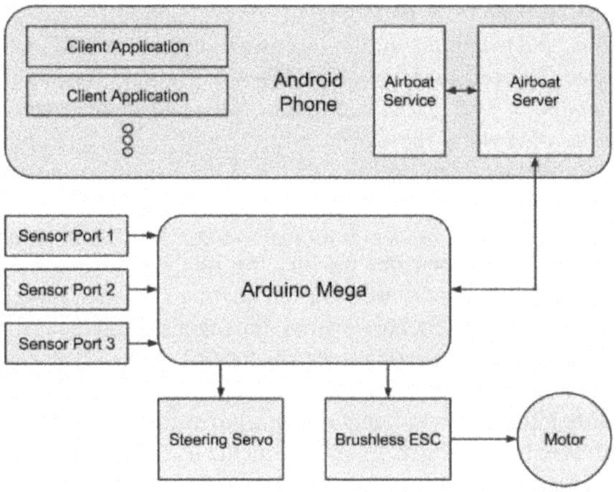

Figure 3: CRW system architecture

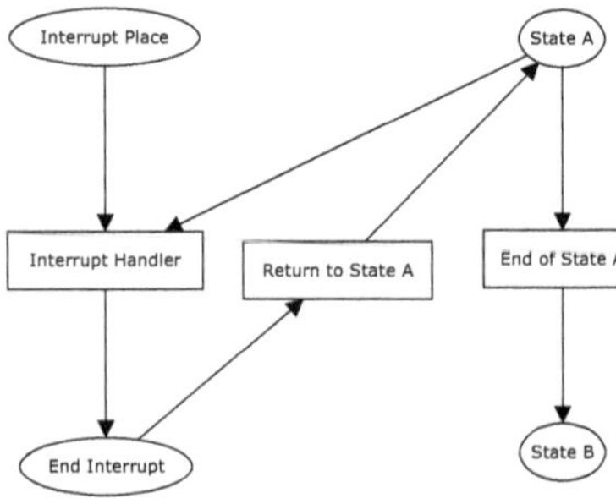

Figure 4: Interrupt implementation with Petri Net.

4. THE INTERRUPT MECHANISM

In this Section, we describe the basic ideas of the interrupt mechanism for Petri Net and how we realize such mechanism in SAMI. Then we discuss an exemplar multi-agent plan that makes use of such interrupt mechanism, i.e., the Cooperative Location Visit plan.

4.1 Modelling the interrupt Mechanism in Petri Net

The Petri Net paradigm does not offer a special construct to implement interrupts, but it is possible to replicate the behavior of an interrupt through a specific sequence of places and transitions [12].

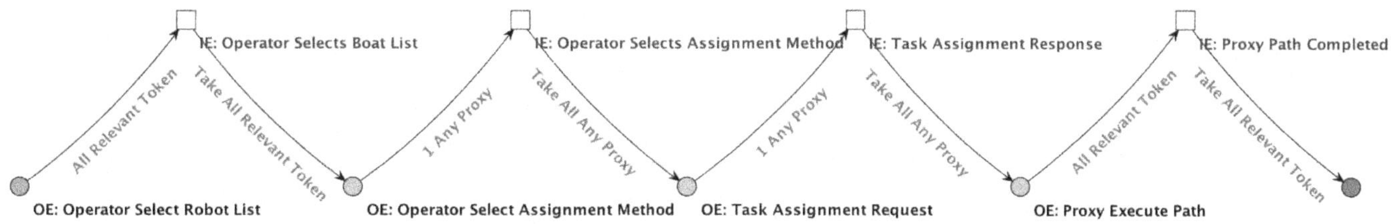

Figure 1: SAMI Petri Net "Cooperative Location Visit" plan (without the interrupts)

Figure 4 reports an example of an interrupt realized in the Petri Net framework. Essentially, the normal execution flow can be interrupted when the system is in *state A*. The interrupt can be triggered by the human operator simply placing a token in the *Interrupt Place*. This will enable the *Interrupt Handler* transition, hence changing the execution flow of the plan. If the *Interrupt Handler* transition fires, the system will place a token in the *End Interrupt* place, and, when the execution of such behavior is completed (i.e., when the *Return to State A* transition fires), the system resumes the normal execution by placing a token back to the *State A* place. Notice that, during the execution of the interrupt behavior, the transition *End of State A* is not enabled, therefore the flow of execution can not progress to *State B* until the interrupt handler behavior is completed.

4.2 Modeling the Interrupt mechanism in SAMI

Following the interrupt implementation idea described in Figure 4 we use three key elements to model the interrupt mechanism in the *SAMI* framework: i) a place (called *Interrupt Place*) ii) a transition that starts the interrupt handling procedure (*StartInterruptTransition*) and, iii) a transition that determines the end of the interrupt procedure (*EndInterruptTransition*). Now, consider a general plan that we represent with a *Source Place*, indicating the state of the system that could receive an interrupt, a general transition, indicating a general part of a plan, and a *Destination Place*, indicating the state of the system that should be reached when the interrupt handling procedures terminates (notice that the source and destination places could be the same). Figure 5 shows the structure we propose to add an interrupt to such general plan. As the figure shows, the *StartInterruptTransition* and the *EndInterruptTransition* are connected by a *Submission Interrupt Place* which represents a general sub-plan that models the appropriate interrupt handling behaviour. After the execution of the submission all the tokens that comes out from the submission move to the destination place of the interrupt, and restore the normal behaviour of the plan.

The structure described above can represent two types of interrupts: a *proxy* interrupt (see Figure 5(a)) and a *general* interrupt (see Figure 5(b)). As shown in Figures 5(a) and 5(b), the structure to realize these two types of interrupts is the same, however, the events attached to places/transitions and the labels to the edges of the net are different. In what follows we describe these two interrupt types in more detail.

The Proxy Interrupt The *proxy* interrupt relates to a specific subset of the platforms, and affects the execution flow of those platforms only (while the others continue the normal execution of the plan). This type of interrupt typically represents a procedure that should be activated in response to some proxy-level events, e.g., the battery of a boat reaches a critical level and the boat should stop the current plan to go to a recharge area.

In particular, the interrupt place generates a *ProxyInterruptEvent*, which is an output event[3]. The *ProxyInterruptEvent* encapsulates the information regarding which proxies should be involved in the event. Such information is used by the *Start Interrupt Transition* to consume only the relevant tokens from the *Source Place* and transfer them to the *Submission Interrupt Place*. Consequently, only the tokens specified by the *ProxyInterruptEvent* will stop their current mission to execute the interrupt submission. Such relevant tokens are selected with a mission specific procedure, and this often requires a user interaction (i.e., the user directly selects which platforms should execute the interrupt submission).

General Interrupt The *general* interrupt is a team-level interrupt that is not specific to a particular platform. The *general* interrupt represents a situation where all robotic-boats should perform a particular procedure, e.g., stop all current plans and go to a safe position as a manned boat is approaching.

In contrast to the *proxy* interrupt, the *general* interrupt will remove all tokens present in the *Source Place* and transfer them to the submission. Hence, the event generated by the *interrupt place* is a different output event, named *InterruptEvent*. Such event is generated to trigger the interrupt mechanism but does not contain any specific information regarding the relevant proxies (as all proxies are relevant in this case). Consequently, the *StartInterruptTransition* requires a *generic* token (and not a proxy token) and it will transfer all the *proxy* tokens from the *Source Place* to the *Submisison Interrupt Place*. A general interrupt is essentially a compact way of representing an interrupt for all proxies. Such compact representation is crucial for team level plans that must be designed and monitored by human operators.

4.3 Using interrupt in multi-agent plans

Here we provide an exemplar multi-agent plan, discussing the possible use of both interrupt types described above. In particular we consider a Cooperative Location Visit (CLV) plan where the operator selects a group of boats to visit a set of locations so to perform point measuring tasks. The boats should navigate to each location and acquire a specific measure (e.g., pH level, oxygen level, temperature). In this work, we assume that each boat is equipped with the same sensors, hence visiting the same location with different boats does not provide more information and should be avoided, in contrast, each boat can visit several locations (i.e., executing a path that goes through all such locations in sequence). The system offers various techniques to assign boats to locations and in this work we used a method which is based on Sequential Single Item auctions [13]. The method assign locations to boats sequentially, and for each location the system selects the boat that can provide the lowest path cost. Such path cost is computed as the minimum path cost that the boat can achieve when inserting the

[3]Recall from Section 3.1 that output events are associated to places and contain commands or requests for other modules. Input events are associated to transitions and encapsulate information that should be consumed by the module that receives such event

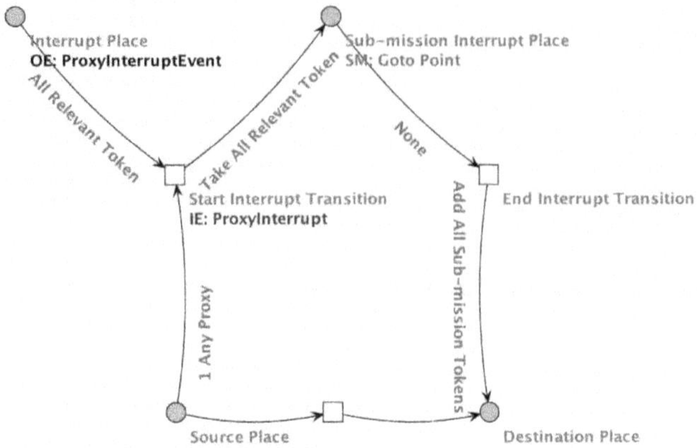

(a) Proxy Interrupt

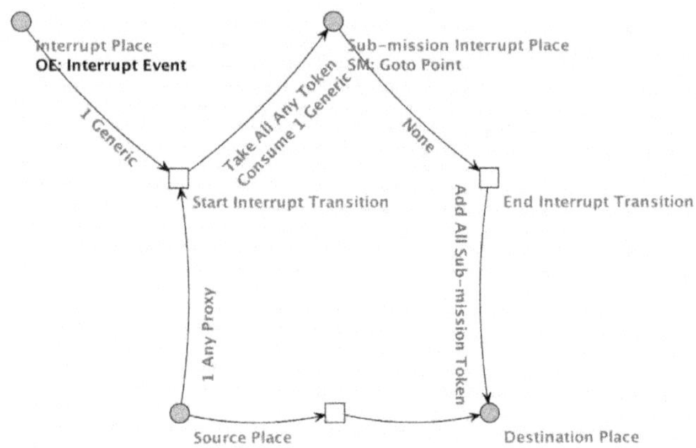

(b) General Interrupt

Figure 5: Types of interrupt implemented in the SAMI framework.

current location in the set of locations that are already assigned to such boat[4].

The CLV plan is reported in Figure 6. In such plan, the general interrupt handles a situation where the user decides to temporarily stop the current mission of all the boats to avoid a dangerous situation, i.e., a manned boat that enters the area where the boats are operating. The general interrupt starts from the *ProxyExecutePath* place and goes back to the same place. When the interrupt triggers, all the tokens present in the *ProxyExecutePath* place are transferred to the submission place. The submission associated to the interrupt (not shown in this picture) sends all the boats to a specific safe assemble position and then waits for an operator input to re-start the previous mission. When the operator decides that the dangerous situation is over, the boats are sent back to the *ProxyExecutePath* place where they resume executing their mission, maintaining their previous location assignment.

In contrast, the proxy interrupt allows the operator to stop the execution of a selected subset of the boats without interfering with the mission execution of the other boats. This is useful when the human operator should handle an event that influences the behavior of a specific group of boats, i.e., a boat that reaches a critical level of the battery. The proxy interrupt moves the set of selected proxies to the submission place while the others will continue their execution. In our exemplar plan, the submission associated to the interrupt is a recharge submission that stops the current plans of the selected proxies and sends the relevant proxies to a recharge station, where the batteries are replaced. Then the proxies re-start their previous mission.

By combining the team-level and proxy-level interrupts our approach provides a powerful and general model to allow sophisticated interactions between the human operators and the robotic system. As the empirical evaluation shows this results in a significant performance gain for the system.

5. EMPIRICAL RESULTS

In this section we present a quantitative evaluation of our approach to team plan monitoring for the CRW framework. We first describe our empirical methodology, then we present and discuss the results we obtained.

5.1 Empirical Methodology

The main goals of the empirical evaluation are: i) to validate the applicability of the interrupt mechanism to team-level plans that represent realistic use cases, ii) to evaluate the gain achieved by such mechanism, in terms of task specific performance as well as operator load, with respect to aborting the plan whenever an external event takes place.

As a first step, we consider the CLV plan discussed in Section 4.3 considering the "interrupt" version that encodes the interrupt within the plan (reported in Figure 6) and the "standard" version without the interrupts (reported in Figure 1). Next, we define two possible external events: i) *general alarm* and ii) *temporary boat pull-out* that should be handled at execution time by a human operator. We then simulate the execution of both versions of the CLV plan with both events, measuring indicators of task specific performance and operator work load. When we execute the standard plan and one of the external events takes place, the human operator must abort the entire mission execution, execute the plan that can handle the specific event, and then restart the original plan.

External Events As for the external events, the *general alarm* represents a danger that may significantly interfere with the plan execution of all the boats. An example of this could be a manned boat that enters the operative areas of the robotic boats. If this happens the human operator should signal to all the platforms that all plans should be suspended to avoid collisions. When the manned boat leaves the scene the human operator can then instruct the boats to recover the execution of their plans (e.g., executing the remaining tasks). This situation can be handled with a general interrupt as all the boats will have to execute the same specific sub-mission (i.e., reach a safe position) before recovering their plans. In our empirical evaluation we simulate the occurrences of several general alarm events while a CLV plan is running. In particular, we fix the number of events to happen and distribute them randomly during the mission execution,

In contrast, the *temporary boat pull out* represents an event that interferes with a specific subset of robotic platforms and that will not directly hinder the plan execution for the rest of the team. An example of this could be the need to recharge the battery for one robotic boat. Specifically, we simulate a discharge process for the boats, where the battery level is reduced based on distance traveled. The discharge process includes a random element that increases or decreases the units of battery consumed to simulate possible not-modeled situations (such as currents) that impact the amount of energy required to traverse a given distance. In more detail, if we

[4]Since computing the minimum path cost given a sequence of visit locations is in general NP-Hard here we use a simple nearest neighbor heuristic: the path is built incrementally by always selecting the next locations as the one that is closest to the current location. At the beginning the current location is the boat position.

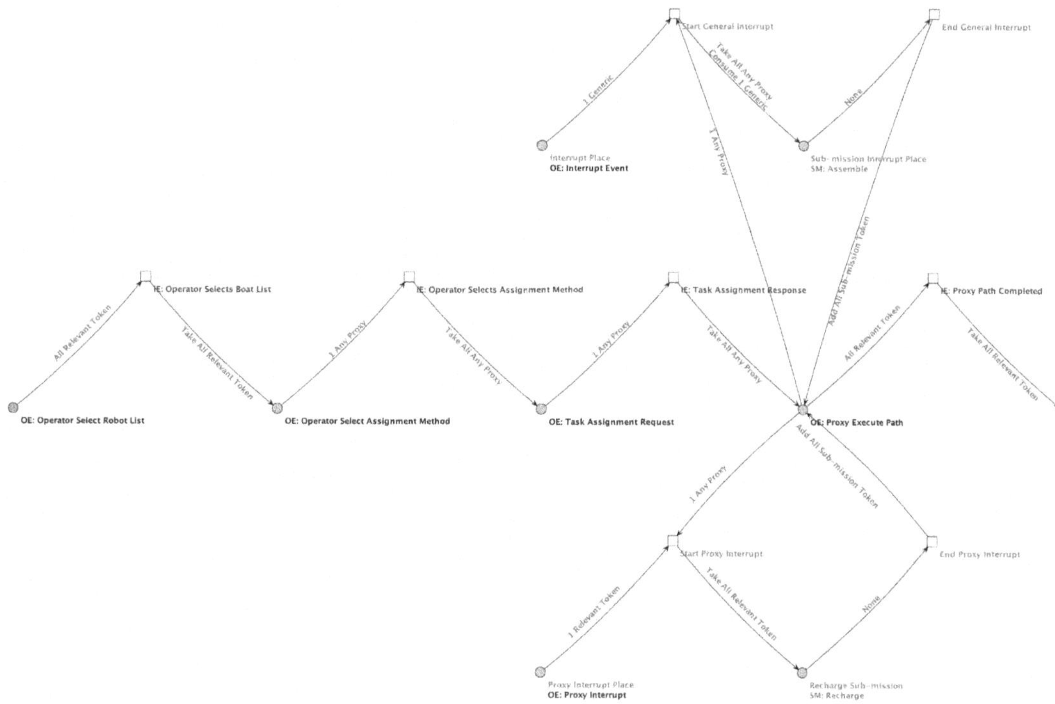

Figure 6: The Cooperative Location Visit plan specified in the SAMI framework, with both interrupts (general and proxy).

indicate with $b_i(t)$ the level of battery at time t for boat i, we have that $b_i(t+\tau) = b_i(t) - Kd_i(\tau)(1+R)$, where τ is a positive value that represents a time interval, $d_i(\tau)$ represents the distance (in meters) traveled by boat i in the time interval τ, K is a constant that expresses the units of battery required to travel one meter and $R \sim U(-0.1, 0.1)$ is a random variable drawn from a uniform probability distribution.

When we execute the plan with the interrupt mechanism in place, we assume that whenever an external event happens, the operator will trigger the corresponding interrupt. For example, when we execute the CLV plan and the battery level of a boat reaches a critical level, in our simulation the corresponding proxy interrupt will always be triggered and the correct boat will be selected. In other words, we assume the human operator will always do the correct actions that the framework offers to respond to the external events. This is because our intent here is to evaluate the interrupt mechanism and not the human interface. As mentioned in the intro, a proper evaluation of the human interface falls outside the scope of this contribution.

When we execute the plan without the interrupt, we assume that the human operator will abort the current plan, start the plan for the specific interrupts and, finally, start a new plan to complete the original mission once the interrupt has been handled. Note that, when we start a new plan the operator must re-insert all information required by the plan, such as the locations to be visited. In our experiments, we assume the operator can keep track of which locations have been visited and re-start the plan only with the locations yet to be visited (this reduces the number of interactions in favor of the standard approach). Moreover, we assume that the operator will start new plans only after the recharge mission has been completed. This means that the other boats will remain idle for the recharge mission duration. Another execution model could start new plans for the other boats while the recharging boat accomplishes its mission and then restart the plan with all the boats once the recharge process is over. While this would reduce the overall time of the mission it would significantly increase the number of interactions with the user.

Metrics The metrics we extract from the simulation combine task dependent metrics and metrics to evaluate the operator load. Specifically, the task dependent metric is the time to complete a mission while the load metric is the number of user actions required to start/abort the plan, trigger the interrupt, provide information to the boats (e.g., the locations to visit). In our experiments such interactions always take the form of a click (on a map or on a button), hence we measure the number of clicks that the operator performs. Since the main goal of the empirical evaluation is to compare the use of the interact mechanism with the standard execution model, we compute and report the percentage gain of the interrupt mechanism for both metrics. In particular, we compute $\frac{(v_{Std} - v_{Int})}{\max\{v_{Int}, v_{Std}\}} * 100$, where v_{Std} is the value of the metric obtained with the standard execution model and v_{Int} is the value of the metric obtained with the interrupt mechanism. Since for both metrics the lower the better, a positive value indicates superior performance of the interrupt mechanism over the standard execution model.

In the next section we report and discuss the results obtained with our empirical evaluation.

5.2 Results

Table 1 reports results obtained for the CLV plan and the boat pull out event. In particular, we consider a set of configurations, where each configuration is defined by three elements: i) the number of boats involved in the plan (3,5), ii) the number of locations to be visited (10,20) and iii) the time required to exchange a boat's battery expressed in seconds (10,20). For each configuration we executed 10 repetitions. We report the average values of the gain for both metrics and the standard error of the mean (shown in square brackets). In the tables, we report only the percentage gain for con-

Configurations	Std	Int.	% Gain (Interrupt vs Standard)	
#boat,#loc.,r.t.	#rec.	#rec.	Total Time	# interactions
3, 20, 10	6	6	6.3%	73%
5, 20, 10	5	5	23% [± 0.5]	68%
3, 20, 20	6	6	26% [± 2.5]	72% [± 0.8]
5, 20, 20	5	5	27% [± 6.6]	64% [± 3.7]
3, 30, 10	11	12	26% [± 1.2]	69% [± 9.5]
5, 30, 10	10	12	21%	75%
3, 30, 20	11	12	48% [± 0.8]	80% [± 0.1]
5, 30, 20	10	12	27% [± 2.9]	75% [± 0.5]

Table 1: Results for the CLV plan and boat pull out event. Each configuration specifies the number of boats, the number of locations, the time required to recharge the boat's battery (in seconds). The number of recharge (#rec) represents the number of times a boat required a recharge action for the standard execution (Std.) and for the plan with the interrupt (Int.)

Configurations	% Gain (Interrupt vs Standard)
#boat,#loc.,#alarms	# interactions
3, 20, 1	44% [± 0.6]
5, 20, 1	40% [± 1.4]
3, 20, 3	65% [± 0.6]
5, 20, 3	61% [± 1]
3, 30, 1	46% [± 0.3]
5, 30, 1	16% [± 1.9]
3, 30, 3	68% [± 0.23]
5, 30, 3	66% [± 0.4]

Table 2: Results for the CLV plan and the general alarm event. Each configuration specifies the number of boats, the number of locations and the number of alarms.

figurations that show a statistically significant difference between the values of the means[5].

As it is possible to see, for all configurations the plan with the interrupts achieves better performance both in terms of time to complete the mission as well as for the operator workload. In more detail, focusing on the time to complete the mission, we can see that the gain of the interrupt mechanism with respect to the standard mechanism increases when the recharge time increases, because in the standard execution model all plans must be aborted when a boat must recharge, while in the interrupt model the other boats can continue with their mission execution. As for the operator work load, the interrupt mechanism requires far fewer user actions than the standard plan. This is due to the fact that, in the standard execution model, the user must re-insert the locations that the boats must visit when the CLV plan is re-started. Notice that, the number of recharge actions is higher when using the interrupts model. This is because the battery discharge process depends on the travel distance, and since the interrupt model minimizes the idle time of the boats, each boat will on average travel more (this is confirmed by the positive gain in the total time).
Table 2 reports results achieved for the CLV plan and the general alarm event. We considered the same number of boats and number of tasks, and we vary the number of alarm events that will appear during the mission (1,3). As before, we report the average values of the gain and the standard error of the mean.

For what concerns the operator work load, these results confirm the superior performance of the approach that encodes interrupts in the plan. However, in this case, the difference in time to complete the mission does not show a statistical significance, consequently we do not report such values. This is because the procedure to handle the general alarm requires all boats to stop and wait until the original mission can be safely re-started. Hence, the actions that the boats perform when aborting a plan are very similar to the interrupt handling procedure. Notice that, in all the simulations we do not consider the time required by a human operator to perform the click actions but we simply count the number of clicks. This is because, a proper evaluation of such time would be highly dependent on the skills of the operator. However, in practice this time will not be negligible and would significantly increase the gain in favor of the interrupt mechanism.

Finally, a video showing an exemplar execution of the CLV plan presented in Figure 6 is reported here[6]. The video shows that, when the general interrupt is triggered all the boats move through the interrupt branch, and enters a recovery sub-mission that sends them all to a safe assemble location. When the alarm is over the boats restart their previous missions. In contrast, when the proxy interrupt is triggered, the selected boat proceeds to the recharge area while the execution of the other boats progresses unchanged. When such boat completes the recharge mission, it returns to finish executing its previous mission.

The video shows how our mechanism allows the human operator to smoothly handle different types of interrupts during the execution phase of complex team-level plans.

6. CONCLUSIONS

We consider the problem of handling human interrupts in team oriented plans. Team oriented plans are a key tool for allowing human operators to specify high level directives for teams of autonomous agents. However, in many scenarios an operator might need to interrupt the activities of individual team members to deal with particular situations (i.e., a danger that the team can not perceive). Previous to this work, after such interrupt the operator would usually need to restart the team plan manually to ensure its success.

Here, we proposed a mechanism that allows a range of interrupts to be handled smoothly, allowing the team to efficiently continue with its tasks after an operator intervention. In particular, we build on the SAMI framework, which proposes the use of Colored Petri Net for specifying team plans, and we define two types of interrupts: a *proxy* interrupt that affects the execution flow of a subset of the platforms, and a *general* interrupt that specifies a particular recovery procedure for all the platforms.

We validated our approach considering an application of robotic watercraft. In more detail, we provided a quantitative evaluation of our interrupt mechanism by simulating the plan execution with and without the interrupts in a set of selected use cases. The empirical results show that, by combining the team-level and proxy-level interrupts, our mechanism provides a powerful and general model to allow sophisticated interactions between the human operators and team plans, resulting in a significant performance gain for the system.

Acknowledgments

This work is funded by the Qatar National Research Fund NPRP grant 4-1330-1-213.

[5]To check whether results are statistically significant we run a t-test with $\alpha = 0.05$.

[6]`http://profs.sci.univr.it/~farinelli/videos/CLV.mp4`

REFERENCES

[1] M. Tambe, "Towards flexible teamwork," *Journal of Artificial Intelligence Research*, pp. 83–124, 1997.

[2] G. A. Kaminka and I. Frenkel, "Flexible teamwork in behavior-based robots," in *Proceedings, The Twentieth National Conference on Artificial Intelligence and the Seventeenth Innovative Applications of Artificial Intelligence Conference, July 9-13, 2005, Pittsburgh, Pennsylvania, USA*, 2005, pp. 108–113. [Online]. Available: http://www.aaai.org/Library/AAAI/2005/aaai05-018.php

[3] V. Ziparo, L. Iocchi, P. Lima, D. Nardi, and P. Palamara, "Petri net plans," *Autonomous Agents and Multi-Agent Systems*, vol. 23, no. 3, pp. 344–383, 2011. [Online]. Available: http://dx.doi.org/10.1007/s10458-010-9146-1

[4] P. Scerri, B. Kannan, P. Velagapudi, K. Macarthur, P. Stone, M. Taylor, J. Dolan, A. Farinelli, A. Chapman, B. Dias *et al.*, "Flood disaster mitigation: A real-world challenge problem for multi-agent unmanned surface vehicles," in *Advanced Agent Technology*. Springer, 2012, pp. 252–269.

[5] K. Jensen, *Coloured Petri nets: A high level language for system design and analysis*. Springer, 1991.

[6] A. V. Ratzer, L. Wells, H. M. Lassen, M. Laursen, J. F. Qvortrup, M. S. Stissing, M. Westergaard, S. Christensen, and K. Jensen, "Cpn tools for editing, simulating, and analysing coloured petri nets," in *Applications and Theory of Petri Nets 2003*. Springer, 2003, pp. 450–462.

[7] M. M. Veloso, M. E. Pollack, and M. T. Cox, "Rationale-based monitoring for continuous planning in dynamic environments," in *Proceedings of the Fourth International Conference on Artificial Intelligence Planning Systems*, Pittsburgh, PA, June 1998, pp. 171–179.

[8] R. Simmons and D. Apfelbaum, "A task description language for robot control," in *Proceedings of IEEE/RSJ International Conference on Intelligent Robots and Systems*, vol. 3, Oct 1998, pp. 1931–1937.

[9] F. Y. Wang, K. Kyriakopoulos, A. Tsolkas, and G. Saridis, "A petri-net coordination model for an intelligent mobile robot," *Systems, Man and Cybernetics, IEEE Transactions on*, vol. 21, no. 4, pp. 777–789, Jul 1991.

[10] J. King, R. K. Pretty, and R. G. Gosine, "Coordinated execution of tasks in a multiagent environment," *IEEE Transactions on Systems, Man, and Cybernetics, Part A*, vol. 33, no. 5, pp. 615–619, 2003. [Online]. Available: http://dx.doi.org/10.1109/TSMCA.2003.817387

[11] P. R. Cohen and H. J. Levesque, "Teamwork," *Special Issue in cognitive Science and Artificial Intelligence*, pp. 487–512, 1991.

[12] J. Desel, W. Reisig, and G. Rozenberg, *Lectures on concurrency and Petri nets: advances in Petri nets*. Springer, 2004, vol. 3098.

[13] C. Tovey, M. Lagoudakis, S. Jain, and S. Koenig, "The generation of bidding rules for auction-based robot coordination," in *Multi-Robot Systems: From Swarms to Intelligent Automata*, F. S. L. Parker and A. S. (editor), Eds., vol. 3, no. 14. Springer, 2005.

Bounty Hunters and Multiagent Task Allocation

Drew Wicke
Department of Computer Science
George Mason University
4400 University Drive MSN 4A5
Fairfax, VA 22030, USA
dwicke@gmu.edu

David Freelan
Department of Computer Science
George Mason University
4400 University Drive MSN 4A5
Fairfax, VA 22030, USA
dfreelan@gmu.edu

Sean Luke
Department of Computer Science
George Mason University
4400 University Drive MSN 4A5
Fairfax, VA 22030, USA
sean@cs.gmu.edu

ABSTRACT

We propose a system for multiagent task allocation inspired by the model used by bounty hunters and bail bondsmen. A bondsman posts tasks for agents to complete, along with bounties to be collected by an agent on completion. Multiple agents, taking the role of the bounty hunters, compete to finish tasks and collect their bounties. While a task remains uncompleted, its bounty gradually rises, making it more and more desirable to pursue. Unlike auctions, this model does not assume rationality in agents' bids (as there are none), and since tasks are not exclusive to given agents, the system is robust to highly noisy environments. We examine how agents may locally develop rational task valuations in such an environment, gradually adapting to dividing tasks according to the agents best suited to them. We compare different methods for building these valuations against approaches which are more "auction-like" in that they permit exclusivity, and we do so under both static environments and ones in which agents, and task details, change dynamically.

Categories and Subject Descriptors

I.2.11 [**Distributed Artificial Intelligence**]: Multiagent Systems

General Terms

Algorithms, Experimentation, Performance

Keywords

Bounty Hunting; Auctions; Task Allocation

INTRODUCTION

The *dynamic multiagent task allocation problem* is one in which one or more agents collectively perform tasks as they appear dynamically in the environment. The agents typically vary in their ability to perform various tasks, and as this is a *multiagent* problem, there is no one agent who decides how to allocate the tasks to them. Rather, the agents decide on their own what tasks they should vie for, with certain limitations on the degree to which they may consult one another to make these decisions. Ideally, out of a morass of individual greedy agent decisions, we would see a task allocation which approaches optimal global efficiency.

Scenarios such as these crop up throughout multiagent systems: they appear in robots divvying up room cleaning needs; or automated multiagent delivery services; or video games where a band of plucky outlaws must defend themselves against hordes of zombies. Considerable study over the years has focused on centralized approaches to globally optimal dynamic task allocation, involving areas such as register coloring and pebbling, multi-armed bandits, and bin packing. When the problem is restricted to the multiagent case, most work has focused on greedy methods, the most popular approach being *auctions*.

A simple auction method might work as follows. There is a single auctioneer who distributes tasks, and multiple agents who bid on the privilege to do them. As tasks come available, agents compete with bids in an auction, and after a clearing time has passed, the winning agent is given the task to complete. Typically the agents will bid their *valuation* of the task, that is, some estimate the agent has of how good the task would be for the agent to do.

This approach is intuitive and appealing at first glance, but it has some curiosities. First, in much of the literature, there is no incentive or reward for agents to complete a task. Second, agents generally have an infinite money supply, and so we must presume they are altruistic and non-strategic. Third, winning agents usually have exclusive ownership of tasks, so some other mechanism (perhaps real options) must be implemented to deal with agents with poor or noisy task performance. Fourth, agents typically must have some built-in ability to produce an accurate valuation of the tasks they are bidding on. Fifth, auction methods commonly assume that tasks are bid on sequentially as they arrive, perhaps necessitating a multi-task mechanism for each agent or a clearing time. For these reasons and others, auctions seem to us to be an odd approach to task allocation.

In this paper we study an alternative model which seems to us to be a closer fit to the dynamic multiagent task allocation problem: *bounty hunting*. Here, the auctioneer is replaced with a bail bondsman, and the agents are no longer bidders, but bounty hunters.

A quick explanation of these terms for those who may be unfamiliar with them. In the United States, an arrested man may be set free temporarily prior to his trial in return for some amount of money (*bail*) as collateral. Bail is often costly, so there is an industry of *bail bondsmen* who will, for a fee, post bail on behalf of the arrested man. If the man does not show for his trial, a bail bondsman can recover his posted bail only if he brings the fugitive back to be tried before the government has re-arrested him. To do this, the bail bondsman will offer some amount of reward (a *bounty*) to anyone who successfully captures the fugitive. The competing agents who try to capture the fugitive in return for this bounty are *bounty hunters*. While the fugitive is still at large, the bounty may be increased so as to make his capture more lucrative. This model appears elsewhere in different guises of course: for example, a reward for a lost cat, a Most Wanted Criminal list, a murder contract, or a software bug bounty.

Appears in: *Proceedings of the 14th International Conference on Autonomous Agents and Multiagent Systems (AAMAS 2015), Bordini, Elkind, Weiss, Yolum (eds.), May 4–8, 2015, Istanbul, Turkey.*

Bounties are an attractive approach to the dynamic multiagent task allocation problem for several reasons. First, because agents may compete for the same bounty, tasks are no longer exclusive. If an agent cannot successfully do a given task, eventually its bounty will rise and attract other agents to take it from him. Second, there is no bidding involved: agents can be self-interested, though still perhaps not hyperstrategic, and there is no need for a queue or clearing interval. Finally, since agents are not bidding their valuation, they don't need to have (at least initially) an accurate valuation mechanism in the first place.

But despite their seemingly natural fit, bounties have surprisingly been little studied in multiagent systems. In this paper we will try to remedy this. We first describe one possible formal model for a bounty system, and relax this model in two ways (notably adding exclusive ownership of tasks) which are more "auction like" (the scenarios we study do not lend themselves to classical auctions). In all these approaches agents have no initial valuation of tasks, so we then examine how they may adapt to develop a proper valuation, and thus improve global system performance. We will also examine how well this adaptation performs when the nature of tasks, or the agents, changes radically. The "auction like" models are slightly more efficient in common situations: but we then show that they are problematic in noisy situations. Finally, we study what might happen when agents are permitted to abandon tasks.

RELATED WORK

A taxonomy of solutions to the general multiagent task allocation problem has been offered [10] with three major dimensions: the type of task, the type of agent, and the information available to determine task assignment. This taxonomy has recently been improved to classify more task allocation problems, like those where tasks have dependencies [16]. Current solution methods include centralized approaches using k-armed bandits, integer programming, and combinatorial optimization; and decentralized approaches like auctions, markets, and task swapping [17, 18, 19, 22].

We are primarily interested in the decentralized case. The most common approach, auctions, were popularized by MURDOCH, an auction method which focused on minimizing resource usage, task completion time, and communication overhead [11]. This approach trusted agents to truthfully bid their task valuations, though sensor noise or an unknown environment could cause their bids to be inaccurate. TraderBots, another auction framework, was designed to be more flexible and extensible [8, 13]. Auctions have been augmented to be robust to robot malfunctions [23]. CoMutaR merged multiagent task allocation with coordination through the use of auctions under the assumption of truthful agents [29]. We are aware of only one paper that has considered approaches to extend auctions with non-exclusivity and non-commitment [20].

Markets have also been used in multi-robot task allocation [1, 27] and exploration [30, 32]. One paper describes a market based planning system in which the agents learn to bid their opportunity cost for doing a task, and tasks have rewards associated with them, allowing agents to re-auction them [28].

Another approach is *token-passing* [9]. This method, like auctions and markets, also assumes task exclusivity. But like some market methods, it allows the tasks to be reassigned by passing the token to other agents. Similarly, [7] used *vacancy chains* as a method for allocating tasks. A vacancy chain is a social construct where when one agent receives a task, he releases his previous task, which goes to another agent in the chain, who releases his task, and so on. Finally, L-ALLIANCE adapted threshold parameters determining how robots choose tasks [24, 25].

A few auction methods have agents that use adaptive mechanisms for bidding. For example, [14] use Support Vector Regression to formulate a bid for a task in domains where some tasks can't be completed due to a lack of resources. Another adaptive bidding procedure for task allocation was developed in [4] and was used to bid in a sequential auction with a clearing time. In a method developed by [26], the auctioneer, rather than the bidders, is adaptive and weights the bids for tasks based on each agent's success rate. This is very close to a centralized approach. One non-auction task allocation method [2] uses biologically inspired adaptive agents that have an upper and lower bound for going after tasks with particular difficulties (similar to L-ALLIANCE), where the lower threshold changes based on task difficulty distribution. Because of the strong assumptions these adaptive auctions make, they could be adapted to our target problem case only with radical modification. We have instead taken a different approach for comparison: adapting our proposed bounty mechanism into one which has certain the basic features (notably exclusivity) of an auction.

Bounties are a subset of *contests*, scenarios where agents are pit against one another to obtain a prize [6]. One type of contest, the *tournament*, is very common in sports and competitions [5], and contests are also found throughout economics, and in the managerial and political sciences [15]. Contests have not been applied much in multiagent task allocation to date. Contest theory has explored adjustable incentive mechanisms in terms of promotions within companies and cash prizes based on performance [3, 21, 31]. These incentive mechanisms are mainly used to manipulate the effort of the contestants. In contrast, the purpose of the bounty mechanism is not to increase the contestant effort, but to more effectively pair contestants to specific tasks.

To our knowledge, competitive bounty hunting has not been used as a mechanism for multiagent task allocation. Interestingly, while bounties have been studied in terms of public policy [12], not much work has been done examining them as an economic model either. Bounties share some relationships with *real options* where an agent may negotiate to have the option to exercise something in the future: for example, movie producers may purchase the rights to make a movie from a book; or mining companies may purchase the rights to use a parcel of public land. The option seller in some sense may be viewed as a bondsman and the buyer as a bounty hunter: however in a bounty system, the "option" is not exclusive, guaranteed, nor even negotiated. Options are more similar to market or token methods such as in [9, 28].

MODEL DESCRIPTION

The Bounties task allocation model involves two types of actors: a bondsman and one or more bounty hunter agents. The bondsman generates and maintains a list of available tasks. Tasks belong to *task classes*. Tasks in a given class are considered similar in some sense, and hence related in difficulty. Each task has an associated *bounty* which is posted with the task and which changes (we will assume it rises linearly) over time as long as the task is uncompleted.

A bounty hunter *commits* to at most one task at a time, which allows him to begin work on the task, and which announces to other agents that he has committed to it. Multiple agents may commit to a task, but they may not collaborate on it. For now we will presume that once an agent has committed to a task, he must complete the task, or be beaten out by some other agent, before he may commit to a new task. When a bounty hunter successfully completes a task, he receives a payment equal to the bounty of the task when he had committed to it.

Agents could refuse to commit to any task for some period of time. However in our experiments there is always at least one available task, and we have set the incentive structure to make refusal irrational. Thus the agents in our experiments by design never wait before committing to tasks.

More formally we have:

- A set of bounty hunter agents, denoted $A : \{a_1, a_2, ..., \}$.
- A set of task classes $S : \{S_1, S_2, ...\}$.
- For each task class S_i, there is an associated set of possible tasks $\{I_{i,1}, I_{i,2}, ...\}$.
- At each time step t there is some set $Q^{(t)}$ of uncompleted tasks available for bounty hunters to attempt to complete. We denote these tasks by the integers $1, 2, ..., i, ...$
- Each uncompleted task $i \in Q^{(t)}$ is associated with a *bounty* $b_i \in \mathbb{R}$. This bounty changes over time t according to some (typically monotonically nondecreasing) function $B_i(t)$. In our experiments we will assume that $B_i(t)$ is a simple linear function, and so denote the *rate* at which b_i increases per timestep as r_i.
- At any time t, a mapping $M_t(A) : A \times \{Q^{(t)} \cup \{\square\}\} \rightarrow \mathbb{R}$ from agents and the uncompleted tasks to which each is committed (or to none, denoted $\square$), to the bounty established when each agent committed to that task. The bounty on "none" ($\square$) is immaterial.

  In our model we will assume that an agent may commit to no more than a single task at any given time. Furthermore, in some methods, only a single agent may commit to a task (it is *exclusive*).

EXCLUSIVITY AND CLEARING TIME

Unlike a typical auction, a true bounty system is not exclusive: multiple agents may commit to a task. Exclusivity has an advantage in that agents are never wasting time simultaneously working on the same task. But bounties have a different advantage: they provide a straightforward way for agents to resolve situations where an agent cannot complete a task or complete it efficiently, as ultimately another agent will take it from him.

Similarly, a bounty system also does not require a *clearing time* for bids, since there are no bids at all. An auction-style clearing time is not easy to integrate into scenarios where tasks arrive at arbitrary times, levels of urgency, or rate; and where typically only a single agent is available to bid for them: and so agents would likely need to have multi-task queues. Our simple experimental scenario, defined later, is one such example. We failed to find an auction model from the distributed multiagent task allocation literature which could be straightforwardly adapted to it.

Lacking an easy way to compare against the auction literature, we can still tweak a bounty model into an "auction-like" environment, by adding task exclusivity and optionally a one-task queue of sorts. Such modified models are no longer true bounty systems, but retain much of their flexibility. We consider three possibilities:

- **Bounties** This is the model discussed earlier. Tasks are not exclusive.
- **Bounties with Exclusivity** This is the Bounties model, except that when an agent commits to a task, he owns it exclusively: no other agent may commit to it. If two or more agents simultaneously commit to a task, the winner is chosen at random, and the losers vie for the remaining tasks.
- **A Bounty "Auction"** This is the same as the Bounties with Exclusivity model, except that we change the procedure with which an agent decides to commit. When one or more agents are ready to commit to tasks at time t, all agents (committed or not) are queried for their valuations of the current uncommitted tasks in $Q^{(t)}$. We then iterate as follows: the highest-valued task is paired with the agent who valued it thus (breaking ties randomly). This task and agent are then discarded, and of the remaining tasks and agents, the highest-valued task is again paired with the agent who valued it, and so on. This continues until all tasks or all agents have been paired. An agent who wishes to commit then commits to the task to which he has been paired, if any. We assume that an agent will always commit to a new task immediately upon completion of his current task, if a new task exists.

Note that these three approaches run the gamut from a bounties model to one more closely resembling an exclusive multi-item auction of sorts, albeit one without a clearing time, nor one where agents necessarily receive tasks even if ones are available.

ADAPTIVE VALUATION

Because the bounty model does not presume that agents have an accurate valuation of the environment, nor of the nature of other agents, we have experimented with two methods which enable agents to learn this information in order to adapt to the tasks best suited to them. The *Simple* method only tries to learn the *estimated time to completion* of given task classes, and their corresponding *probability of completion*. The *Complex* method expands on the probability of completion to learn the probability of completion given the specific other agents that have also committed to the task.

These two methods provide us with several parameters to experiment with. ε is the probability that the agent will commit to a randomly-chosen task. α is the learning rate for the estimated time to completion. β is the learning rate for the estimated probability of completion. Finally, γ is a (small) *unlearning* rate for the estimated probability of completion: like ε, this promotes exploration.

Simple Method. Given a posted task i, let the estimated expected time to complete tasks of the class of i be T_i and the estimated probability of completion of tasks of the class of i be P_i. Initially, $\forall i : T_i = 1,\ P_i = 1$, to encourage the agent to explore all tasks. The agent then iterates as follows. First, the agent chooses a task to commit to and complete. With ε probability he will pick an entirely random available task. Otherwise he will choose task I^* as:

$$I^* \leftarrow \underset{i \,\in\, \text{Available Tasks}}{\operatorname{argmax}} \frac{b_i}{T_i} P_i$$

While the agent is working on a task, nothing is updated. Then at some point the agent either completes the task, or fails to do so because some other agent has completed it instead. In the first case, T_i and P_i are updated as:

$$T_i \leftarrow (1-\alpha)T_i + \alpha t$$
$$P_i \leftarrow (1-\beta)P_i + \beta$$

...where t is the amount of time it has taken to complete the task since the agent committed to it. In the second case, only P_i is updated as:

$$P_i \leftarrow (1-\beta)P_i$$

Finally upon completion or failure of a task, *all* tasks i are updated:

$$\forall i : P_i \leftarrow (1-\gamma)P_i + \gamma$$

The purpose of γ is to slowly drift probabilities towards 1 to make them more likely to try in the future. This, like ε, promotes exploration of the space.

We note that in the *Bounties with Exclusivity* and *Bounty "Auction"* approaches, since tasks are exclusively committed to, the probability table P serves no purpose. Thus for these approaches we fix $(\forall i) P_i = 1,\ \beta = 0,\ \gamma = 0$.

Complex Method. In the Complex Method we augment the task selection equation by including the probability that the agent will succeed given that certain other agents have committed to the task. We naively compute this as the product of the estimated probability, for each additional agent committed to the task, that our agent would defeat the additional agent. To do this, instead of P_i, let $P_{i,a}$ be the estimated probability that our agent will defeat another agent a at tasks of the class of i if both agents are committed to it. This (wrongly but conveniently) assumes that success rates against different agents are independent.

Initially we set $\forall i, a : T_i = 1,\ P_{i,a} = 1$. We select using ε as usual, but redefine I^* as:

$$I^* \leftarrow \underset{i \in \text{Available Tasks}}{\operatorname{argmax}} \frac{b_i}{T_i} \prod_{a \text{ presently committed to } i} P_{i,a}$$

We revised the update equations accordingly. When our agent succeeds at a task, T_i and $P_{i,a}$ are updated as:

$$T_i \leftarrow (1-\alpha)T_i + \alpha t$$
$$\forall a \text{ presently committed to } i : P_{i,a} \leftarrow (1-\beta)P_{i,a} + \beta$$

...where t is the amount of time it has taken to complete the task since the agent committed to it. When our agent fails at a task because a specific other agent a^* has beaten it to the task, we only update: P_{i,a^*}:

$$P_{i,a^*} \leftarrow (1-\beta)P_{i,a^*}$$

In either case, upon completion or failure of a task, all tasks i are then updated for all other agents a as:

$$\forall i, a : P_{i,a} \leftarrow (1-\gamma)P_{i,a} + \gamma$$

We note that the *Bounties with Exclusivity* and *Bounty "Auction"* approaches do not use this method, since it explicitly assumes that other agents may commit to the same task.

EXPERIMENTS

To test the effectiveness of the adaptive bounty methods and different exploration techniques, we performed tests in a simulated environment of agents and balls for them to retrieve. This scenario was derived from similar tasks we encountered in robot soccer experiments. Four agents (1, 2, 3, and 4) are placed at the corners $\langle 0,0\rangle$, $\langle 59,0\rangle$, $\langle 0,39\rangle$, and $\langle 59,39\rangle$ respectively on an infinite discrete grid. We define twenty task classes, each with a *mean location* uniformly randomly chosen somewhere within the 60×40 rectangle between the agents' corners. The simulation starts with twenty balls (the tasks, one task per class), which appear on the field randomly at locations using a gaussian distribution centered at their task class means and with a standard deviation in each direction using $\sigma = 5$.

When an agent commits to a task, he moves towards its ball. Agents can move one grid square (up, down, left, right) per timestep. When an agent reaches the ball, he completes the task, and everybody who was moving toward the ball is instantly teleported back to his corner. Teleportation was meant largely to speed up simulation. When the task is completed, another ball of the task class reappears in $p \sim \text{uniform}(0, 19)$ timesteps.

While a task remains uncompleted, its bounty gradually increases at a rate described later. Once an agent commits to a task, he is locked to the current bounty for that task and may not abandon that task until it is completed by some agent (not necessarily himself). It is legal for two agents to occupy the same square. If two agents complete the same task simultaneously, the winner is the agent with the lower agent ID (1, 2, 3, or 4).

We tested six scenarios. First, we used a *static environment* where agents played the game described above. Second, we tried a *dynamic agent environment* where periodically some agents would be removed from the game, then added back. Third, we tried a *dynamic task environment* where task complexities changed for each agent periodically. The fourth and fifth experiments focused on extreme situations. The fourth experiment had unreliable collaborators that were slower in going after tasks than the other agents. In the fifth experiment we randomly modified a task class to be unexpectedly harder to do for a particular agent by making that agent a tenth its normal speed. Finally, in the sixth experiment we examined the effect of allowing agents to abandon going after their chosen task.

Dynamic environments require that agents explore sufficiently in order to understand that the world has changed. We tested the two methods (Simple and Complex) using three different approaches to exploration. First, we simply relied on rising bounty values to trigger more exploration. We called these the *Simple* and *Complex* approaches. Second, we set $\varepsilon = 0.1$, which caused 10% of task selections to be completely random. We called these the *SimpleR* and *ComplexR* methods. Third, we set $\gamma = 0.001$, which gradually caused the agents to become more optimistic about their probabilities of success. We called these the *SimpleP* and *ComplexP* methods. We further fixed $\alpha = 0.1$ and $\beta = 0.2$. The settings of $\alpha, \beta, \varepsilon$, and γ were determined from calibration trials. We also included the *Bounties with Exclusivity* method, hereafter shortened to *Exclusive*, and the *Bounty "Auction"*, hereafter shortened to *Auction*.

We compared these eight methods and exploration techniques against two control methods, largely to serve as rough upper and lower bounds. In *Random*, agents commit to tasks entirely at random. This served as our worst case bound. In *Greedy*, each agent knows the expected time $E(T_i)$ to completion of tasks of the class of task i, and greedily commits to the task $I^* \leftarrow \operatorname{argmax}_{i \in \text{Uncommitted Tasks}} \frac{b_i}{E(T_i)}$. Only one agent will commit to a given task. This served as a moderate upper bound for comparison.

Simulations ran for 200,000 timesteps, yielding a minimum of 2000 tasks per agent. Each combination of method, exploration technique, and scenario was run for 100 independent trials. Statistical significance was verified using an ANOVA with a Tukey Post-hoc Test at $p = 0.05$. Bounty hunters were required to bring back all prisoners alive: no disintegrations!

Metric. The metric we used for global system efficiency was the sum total bounty $h(t)$ over outstanding tasks at a given time t, that is, $h(t) = \sum_{i \in Q^{(t)}} b_i$. This metric nicely reflects two objectives at once. First, as tasks pile up, $h(t)$ will grow. Second, if tasks are left stagnant in the queue, their bounty increases and again $h(t)$ grows. In many scenarios, the sum total bounty can also be considered an indication of urgency: essentially, it is a measure of the number of fires to put out, and their importance.

How Fast Should Bounties Increase? If the bail bondsman increases the bounty too rapidly, agents might reasonably choose to wait rather than commit to a task. With multiple competing agents, such task speculation is less common, but with a single agent, speculation is easy to demonstrate.

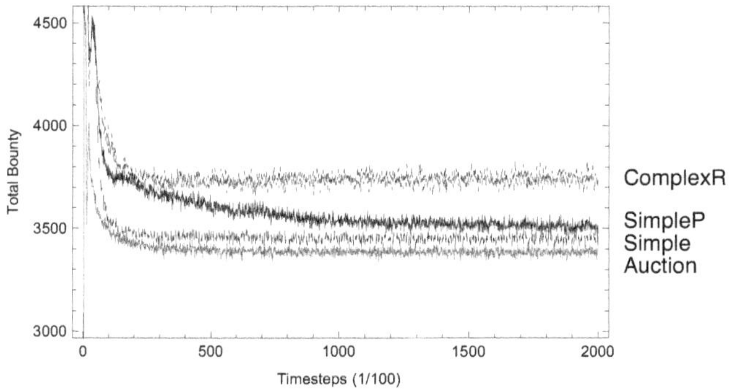

Figure 1: Experiment 1, Static Environment (Selected Results), 200,000 timesteps. Lower values are better.

Equivalence Classes	Method	γ	ε	Mean
+	Random	-	-	6139.72
+	ComplexR	0	0.1	3739.18
+	SimpleR	0	0.1	3641.62
+	ComplexP	0.001	0	3476.67
+	SimpleP	0.001	0	3475.81
+ +	Complex	0	0	3434.75
+ +	Simple	0	0	3408.04
+ +	Auction	-	-	3407.77
+ +	Exclusive	-	-	3403.4
+	Greedy	-	-	3372.64

Table 1: Experiment 1 results, Static Environment, at time=200,000. Lower mean values are better. Equivalence Classes show statistically insignificant differences between methods.

Imagine a scenario where a single agent is given the same task i over and over again. His only choice, then, is when to commit to the task. The longer he waits, the higher the bounty he receives on task completion. Let $b_{i,0}$ be the bounty for task i when it is first offered. Suppose the task takes $m_i > 0$ time to complete, and the bounty rises at a rate of $r_i \geq 0$ per timestep. If the agent waited for $n > 0$ time to begin the task, it would take $n + m_i$ time to finish it for a bounty of $b_{i,0} + nr_i$, yielding a bounty per timestep of $\frac{b_{i,0}+nr_i}{n+m_i}$. If he had started the task immediately, his bounty would be $b_{i,0}$, for a bounty per timestep of $\frac{b_{i,0}}{m_i}$. Thus we want $\frac{b_{i,0}+nr_i}{n+m_i} \leq \frac{b_{i,0}}{m_i}$ to discourage procrastination. Rearranging, we get $r_i \leq \frac{b_{i,0}}{m_i}$.

We have chosen to adopt this conservative rule. In our experiments, the maximum expected task length was approximately 100, and so the initial bounty on all task classes was set to 100 and increased at a rate of 1.

First Experiment: A Static Environment

The first experiment verified that the discussed methods could learn to adapt to the best task choices per-agent. Results are shown in Table 1, and selected results in Figure 1.

Results. The results made very clear that all techniques will converge to values near to our *Greedy* reference. We note an initial spike in bounty as the techniques spend time learning their best options.

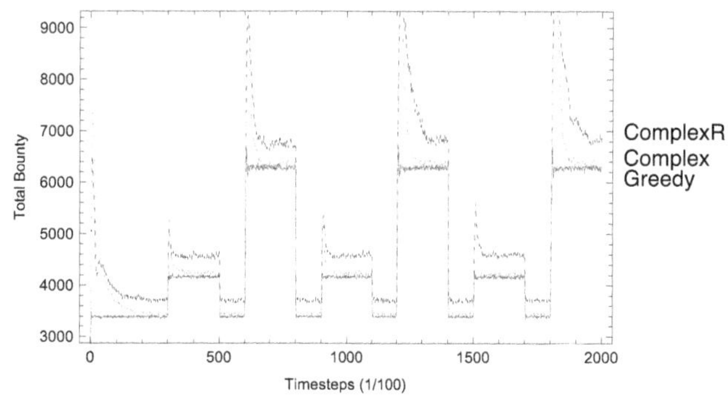

Figure 2: Experiment 2, Dynamic Agents (Selected Results), 200,000 timesteps. Lower values are better. Complex peaks exceed 9500, 10500, and 11500 respectively.

Equivalence Classes	Method	γ	ε	Mean
+	Random	-	-	11255.4
+	ComplexR	0	0.1	6904.13
+ +	SimpleR	0	0.1	6808.35
+ +	SimpleP	0.001	0	6572.01
+ +	ComplexP	0.001	0	6495.58
+ +	Simple	0	0	6437.8
+ +	Exclusive	-	-	6412.1
+ +	Complex	0	0	6383.45
+	Auction	-	-	6326.7
+	Greedy	-	-	6289.88

Table 2: Experiment 2 results, Dynamic Agents, at time=200,000. Lower values are better. Equivalence Classes show statistically insignificant differences between methods.

The best five methods were (in order but with statistically insignificant differences) *Greedy*, *Exclusive*, *Auction*, *Simple*, and *Complex*. While *Auction* and *Exclusive* outperformed our methods, the difference was statistically insignificant. We note that *Simple* (and to a lesser extent *Complex*) performed this well despite having no explicit exploration strategy. We also note here that *SimpleR* and *ComplexR* — which use a 10% random task exploration strategy — did poorly. This will be a continuing theme.

Second Experiment: Dynamic Agents

In the real world, agents are prone to failure. We tested each method's ability to adapt to a situation where agents were periodically removed from the game, then later reinstated. In this experiment, agent 1 was removed every 30,000 timesteps, and agent 2 was removed every 60,000 timesteps. Agents were reinserted 20,000 timesteps after removal. Ideally while agents were gone, teammates would adapt to cover for them.

Results. We discovered that all the methods would adapt quickly, as illustrated in Figure 2. The *Complex* method converged to the *Greedy* performance regardless of the number of agents in the game. This is verified in Table 2, which reflects the final timestep 200,000, when two agents were missing from the game.

We note in Figure 2 that *Complex* and *ComplexR* (shown Figure 2) had very high temporary peaks of poor performance compared to other methods whenever an agent would disappear: they had a larger

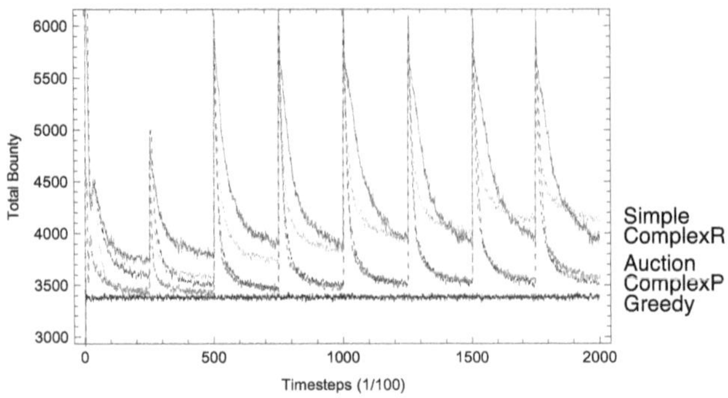

Figure 3: Experiment 3, Dynamic Tasks (Selected Results), 200,000 timesteps. Lower values are better.

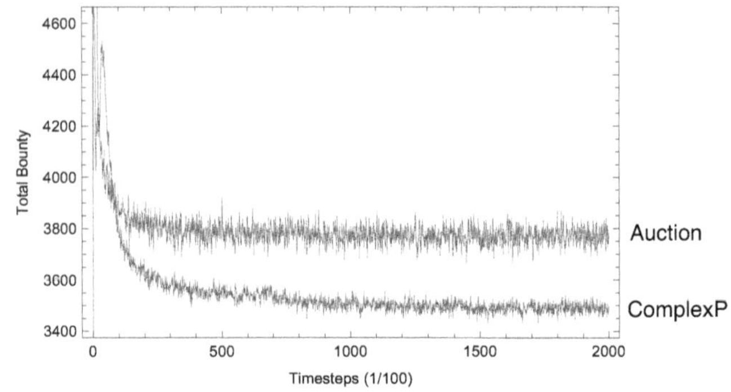

Figure 4: Experiment 4, Unreliable Collaborators (Selected Results), 200,000 timesteps. Lower values are better. *Exclusive* is omitted as its results are very similar to *Auction*.

Equivalence Classes					Method	γ	ε	Mean
				+	Random	-	-	6035.74
			+		Complex	0	0	4150.56
			+		Simple	0	0	4086.08
		+			ComplexR	0	0.1	3934.94
		+			SimpleR	0	0.1	3928.61
	+				Auction	-	-	3591.57
	+				SimpleP	0.001	0	3578.96
	+				Exclusive	-	-	3529.17
	+				ComplexP	0.001	0	3509.76
+					Greedy	-	-	3394.73

Table 3: Experiment 3 results, Dynamic Tasks, at time=200,000. Lower values are better. Equivalence Classes show statistically insignificant differences between methods.

Equivalence Classes		Method	γ	ε	Mean
	+	Exclusive	-	-	7652.40
	+	Auction	-	-	7334.31
+		ComplexP	0.001	0	5625.17

Table 4: Experiment 4 results, Unreliable Collaborators, at time=200,000. Lower values are better. Equivalence Classes show statistically insignificant differences between methods.

state table and would be expected to take longer to adapt. The 10% random task exploration strategy once again did poorly compared to other methods. Note that *Auction* outperformed *SimpleP* and *SimpleR*, but not *Complex*.

Third Experiment: Dynamic Tasks

If the distribution of tasks suddenly changes, we want the bounty system to recover. To test this, we occasionally rotated the corners among the four agents: that is, agent 1's corner would become agent 2's corner, whose old corner would now belong to agent 3, and so on. We did this every 25,000 timesteps, with a second rotation performed every 50,000 timesteps (a worst case scenario for task distribution, as the closest balls became the furthest and vice versa).

Results. This experiment, as shown in Figure 3 and Table 3, shows the weakness of relying solely on bounty for exploration: the *Simple* and *Complex* methods performed poorly. Following them were the remaining random exploration methods (*SimpleR*, and *ComplexR*). Finally, the best adaptive methods were *SimpleP*, *Auction*, *ComplexP*, and *Exclusive*. We note that, *SimpleP* and *ComplexP*, performed just as well as the *Exclusive* and *Auction* methods. Unfortunately, no adaptive method could consistently converge to *Greedy*'s performance.

We also note that after several iterations of rotations, the agents were unable to converge to the same (lower) value. This is because the rate of rotating was too fast for the adaptive methods to catch up and so the total bounty would gradually pile up. This was especially true for the *Auction* strategy. In the first few iterations *Auctions* started out better than *ComplexP*, but by the last iteration, they were equivalent.

Fourth Experiment: Unreliable Collaborators

The purpose of Experiments 4 and 5 is to show when exclusivity can fail. In the previous experiments exclusivity was favorable, since non-exclusive approaches potentially wasted time on tasks another agent was completing. However, in these next experiments we show there are situations where non-exclusivity is desirable.

Suppose a system has agents which do not perform nearly as well as other agents. In this experiment, there were 2 agents, placed in the top left corner of the grid world, who moved 10x slower than other agents, and 4 agents, placed in the corners (like normal), who moved at a normal speed. We chose to test *ComplexP* as our main bounty mechanism, and compared it to our two auction-like algorithms (*Auction* and *Exclusive*).

Results. The results are shown in Table 4 and illustrated in Figure 4. *ComplexP* was clearly the best in this test. The obvious underlying reason was that agents at normal speed would win a race to a ball (a task) against a slow, unreliable collaborator. The auction-like methods simply had no way to prevent the unreliable collaborator from holding things up. Also, *ComplexP* was naturally suited to this task due to the added information it learned about the other agents in the environment.

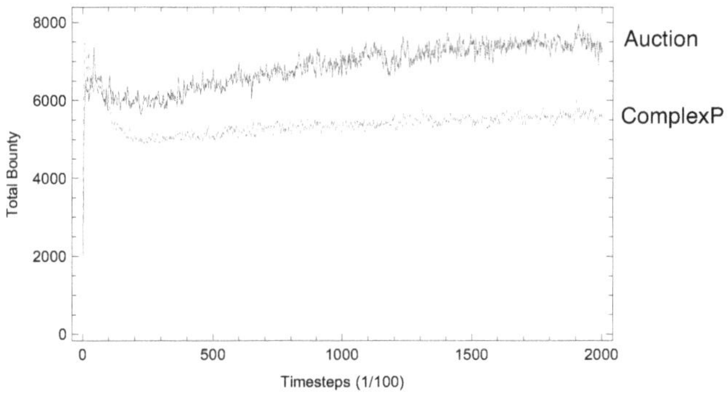

Figure 5: Experiment 5, Unexpectedly Bad Tasks (Selected Results), 200,000 timesteps. Lower values are better. *Exclusive* is omitted as its results are very similar to *Auction*.

Equivalence Classes		Method	γ	ε	Mean
	+	Exclusive	-	-	3779.05
	+	Auction	-	-	3762.39
+		ComplexP	0.001	0	3497.28

Table 5: Experiment 5 results, Unexpectedly Bad Tasks, at time=200,000. Lower values are better. Equivalence Classes show statistically insignificant differences between methods.

Fifth Experiment: Unexpectedly Bad Tasks

We now consider an experiment where some tasks suddenly change in difficulty for particular agents. We modified the scenario such that, every time a task class reappeared on the board, there was a 10% probability it would become "difficult" for a randomly-selected agent to complete. By "difficult" we mean that this agent, upon choosing this task, would move at one-tenth his normal speed.

We once again compared *ComplexP*, *Exclusive*, and *Auction*.

Results. The results are shown in Table 5 and illustrated in Figure 5. *ComplexP*, again, was the clear winner. Once again, the exclusivity of the auction-like methods prevented agents from taking over "difficult" tasks which have trapped helpless agents.

Sixth Experiment: Jumping Ship

We finally experimented with the effect of *jumping ship* on bounties, by which we mean that an agent may, at any time, abandon his current task and recommit to a different one, perhaps because its bounty is higher, or because a better agent has committed to the old one. If an agent abandons a task, he is teleported back to his corner, so as to counter speculation.

To discourage excess jumping, we modified each agent's estimate of remaining time left to complete his *current* task as $T_i' \leftarrow |T_i - t|$, where t is the amount of time the agent has spent on the task so far. Thus the closer the agent is to his expectation of completion, the more likely he would be to stay on the task. For the current task, T_i' substituted for T_i in the calculation of I^* (potential new tasks just used T_i).

We did not test jumping ship during learning, but rather after learning was completed. Thus we ran the *Complex* method in the Static Environment for 200,000 timesteps, and then turned off learning ($\alpha = 0$, $\beta = 0$) and turned *on* the ability to jump ship. We then ran the agents for 100,000 more timesteps.

Results. The results were not good. Jumping ship resulted in a total bounty of 4178.08 at timestep 300,000, compared to 3557.72 prior. This result was statistically significant.

CONCLUSIONS

We have demonstrated methods for agents to adapt to their best tasks in a bounty hunter system, thus improving the efficiency of the whole system. We have compared various approaches to adaptation, as well as both exclusive and non-exclusive task allocation strategies.

As we had imagined, the "complex" non-exclusive methods performed better in dynamic situations due to their additional per-agent information, since they retained knowledge of missing agents and could immediately re-use that information when the agents were re-introduced. While the exclusive and "auction-like" methods generally performed well in the static and basic dynamic scenarios, Experiments 4 and 5 showed that they would perform very poorly in situations where task exclusivity could saddle agents with leaden tasks. Without any additional information or communication, non-exclusive bounty agents naturally adapted to these situations. In the future, we will look at different scenarios which take advantage of this natural adaptation.

A bounty hunter system is a promising method for task allocation: it seems robust to loss of agents, changes in task difficulty, and other kinds of noise. The key properties of a bounty hunter system which distinguish it from other methods, and permits this robustness, is its non-exclusivity of task assignment, lack of a bidding structure, and the increasing attractiveness of outstanding tasks as the bounty on them rises. For this reason, it is surprising bounties have not been studied more: we hope this trend will change in the future.

ACKNOWLEDGMENTS

The work presented in this paper is supported by NSF NRI Grant 1317813.

REFERENCES

[1] S. C. Botelho and R. Alami. M+: a scheme for multi-robot cooperation through negotiated task allocation and achievement. In *IEEE International Conference on Robotics and Automation*, volume 2, pages 1234–1239, 1999.

[2] Adam Campbell, Annie S. Wu, and Randall Shumaker. Multi-agent task allocation: Learning when to say no. In *Proceedings of the 10th Annual Conference on Genetic and Evolutionary Computation*, pages 201–208, 2008.

[3] Pablo Casas-Arce and F. Asís Martínez-Jerez. Relative performance compensation, contests, and dynamic incentives. *Management Science*, 55(8):1306–1320, 2009.

[4] S.H. Choi and W.K. Zhu. A closed-loop bid adjustment method of dynamic task allocation of robots. In *Electrical Engineering and Intelligent Systems*, volume 130 of *Lecture Notes in Electrical Engineering*, pages 81–94. Springer, 2013.

[5] Brian L. Connelly, Laszlo Tihanyi, T. Russell Crook, and K. Ashley Gangloff. Tournament theory thirty years of contests and competitions. *Journal of Management*, 40(1):16–47, 2014.

[6] Luis C. Corchón. The theory of contests: a survey. *Review of Economic Design*, 11(2):69–100, 2007.

[7] T. S. Dahl, M. J. Matarić, and G. Sukhatme. Multi-robot task-allocation through vacancy chains. In *IEEE International Conference on Robotics and Automation*, volume 2, pages 2293–2298, 2003.

[8] M. Bernardine Dias. *Traderbots: A New Paradigm for Robust and Efficient Multirobot Coordination in Dynamic Environments*. PhD thesis, Carnegie Mellon University, Pittsburgh, PA, USA, 2004.

[9] Alessandro Farinelli, Luca Iocchi, Daniele Nardi, and Fabio Patrizi. Task assignment with dynamic token generation. In *Monitoring, Security, and Rescue Techniques in Multiagent Systems*, pages 467–477. Springer, 2005.

[10] B. P. Gerkey. A formal analysis and taxonomy of task allocation in multi-robot systems. *International Journal of Robotics Research*, 23(9):939–954, 2004.

[11] B. P. Gerkey and M. J. Matarić. Sold!: auction methods for multirobot coordination. *IEEE Transactions on Robotics and Automation*, 18(5):758–768, 2002.

[12] Eric Helland and Alexander Tabarrok. The fugitive: Evidence on public versus private law enforcement from bail jumping. *Journal of Law and Economics*, 47(1):93–122, 2004.

[13] E. Gil Jones, B. Browning, M. Bernardine Dias, B. Argall, M. Veloso, and A. Stentz. Dynamically formed heterogeneous robot teams performing tightly-coordinated tasks. In *IEEE International Conference on Robotics and Automation*, pages 570–575, 2006.

[14] E Gil Jones, M Bernardine Dias, and Anthony Stentz. Learning-enhanced market-based task allocation for oversubscribed domains. In *International Conference on Intelligent Robots and Systems*, pages 2308–2313, 2007.

[15] K.A. Konrad. *Strategy and dynamics in contests*. LSE perspectives in economic analysis. Oxford University Press, 2009.

[16] G. Ayorkor Korsah, A. Stentz, and M. Bernardine Dias. A comprehensive taxonomy for multi-robot task allocation. *International Journal of Robotics Research*, 32(12):1495–1512, 2013.

[17] M. G. Lagoudakis, M. Berhault, S. Koenigt, P. Keskinocak, and A. J. Kleywegt. Simple auctions with performance guarantees for multi-robot task allocation. In *IEEE/RSJ International Conference on Intelligent Robots and Systems*, volume 1, pages 698–705, 2004.

[18] Lantao Liu, Nathan Michael, and Dylan Shell. Fully decentralized task swaps with optimized local searching. In *Proceedings of Robotics: Science and Systems*, 2014.

[19] Lantao Liu and Dylan Shell. A distributable and computation-flexible assignment algorithm: From local task swapping to global optimality. In *Proceedings of Robotics: Science and Systems*, 2012.

[20] Maja J. Matarić, Gaurav S. Sukhatme, and Esben H. Østergaard. Multi-robot task allocation in uncertain environments. *Autonomous Robots*, 14(2-3):255–263, 2003.

[21] Barry J. Nalebuff and Joseph E. Stiglitz. Prizes and incentives: towards a general theory of compensation and competition. *The Bell Journal of Economics*, pages 21–43, 1983.

[22] M. Nanjanath and M. Gini. Dynamic task allocation for robots via auctions. In *Robotics and Automation, 2006. ICRA 2006. Proceedings 2006 IEEE International Conference on*, pages 2781–2786, 2006.

[23] Maitreyi Nanjanath and Maria Gini. Repeated auctions for robust task execution by a robot team. *Robotics and Autonomous Systems*, 58(7):900–909, 2010.

[24] L. E. Parker. L-ALLIANCE: a mechanism for adaptive action selection in heterogeneous multi-robot teams. Technical Report ORNL/TM–13000, Oak Ridge National Laboratory, 1995.

[25] L. E. Parker. ALLIANCE: an architecture for fault tolerant multi-robot cooperation. *IEEE Transactions on Robotics and Automation*, 14(2):220–240, 1998.

[26] Charles E. Pippin and Henrik Christensen. Learning task performance in market-based task allocation. In *Proceedings of the 12th International Conference on Intelligent Autonomous Systems*, volume 2, pages 613–621, 2012.

[27] A Pustowka and E.F. Caicedo. Market-based task allocation in a multi-robot surveillance system. In *Robotics Symposium and Latin American Robotics Symposium*, pages 185–189, 2012.

[28] Jeff Schneider, David Apfelbaum, J. Andrew (Drew) Bagnell, and Reid Simmons. Learning opportunity costs in multi-robot market based planners. In *IEEE International Conference on Robotics and Automation*, pages 1151–1156, 2005.

[29] P. M. Shiroma and M. F M Campos. Comutar: A framework for multi-robot coordination and task allocation. In *IEEE/RSJ International Conference on Intelligent Robots and Systems*, pages 4817–4824, 2009.

[30] R. Simmons, D. Apfelbaum, W. Burgard, D. Fox, M. Moors, S. Thrun, and H. Younes. Coordination for multi-robot exploration and mapping. In *Proceedings of the AAAI National Conference on Artificial Intelligence*, 2000.

[31] Christian Terwiesch and Yi Xu. Innovation contests, open innovation, and multiagent problem solving. *Management science*, 54(9):1529–1543, 2008.

[32] Robert Zlot, A. Stentz, M. Bernardine Dias, and Scott Thayer. Multi-robot exploration controlled by a market economy. In *IEEE International Conference on Robotics and Automation*, 2002.

How to Form a Task-Oriented Robust Team

Tenda Okimoto
Graduate School of Maritime Sciences, Kobe University
Kobe, Japan
tenda@maritime.kobe-u.ac.jp

Nicolas Schwind
Transdisciplinary Research Integration Center
Tokyo, Japan
schwind@nii.ac.jp

Maxime Clement
The Graduate University for Advanced Studies
Tokyo, Japan
Maxime-clement@nii.ac.jp

Tony Ribeiro
The Graduate University for Advanced Studies
Tokyo, Japan
tony_ribeiro@nii.ac.jp

Katsumi Inoue
National Institute of Informatics
Tokyo, Japan
inoue@nii.ac.jp

Pierre Marquis
CRIL - CNRS
Université d'Artois
Lens, France
marquis@cril.univ-artois.fr

ABSTRACT

How to form a team for achieving a given set of tasks is an important issue in multi-agent systems. Task-oriented team formation is the problem of selecting a group of agents, where each agent is characterized by a set of capabilities; the objective is to achieve a given set of tasks, where each task is made precise by a set of capabilities necessary for managing it. Robustness (i.e., the ability to reach the goal even if some agents break down) is an expected property of a team. In this paper, the focus is laid on the Task-Oriented Robust Team Formation (TORTF) problem. A formal framework is defined and some decision and optimization problems for TORTF are pointed out. The computational complexity of TORTF is then identified. Interestingly, TORTF does not prove more computationally demanding than the task-efficient team formation problem, i.e., robustness is in some sense "for free". In order to solve these TORTF problems, two algorithms, *ART* (Algorithm for Robust Team) for the decision problem and *AORT* (Algorithm for Optimal Robust Team) for bi-objective constraint optimization problems, are presented and evaluated on a number of benchmarks.

Categories and Subject Descriptors

I.2.11 [**Distributed Artificial Intelligence**]: Multi-agent Systems

General Terms

Theory

Keywords

Team Formation; Robustness; Complexity Analysis; Bi-Objective Constraint Optimization

Appears in: *Proceedings of the 14th International Conference on Autonomous Agents and Multiagent Systems (AAMAS 2015), Bordini, Elkind, Weiss, Yolum (eds.), May 4–8, 2015, Istanbul, Turkey.*

1. INTRODUCTION

Task-oriented team formation is the problem of forming the best possible team to accomplish some tasks of interest, given some limited resources. This problem is a key issue for many applications related to multi-agent cooperation, e.g., RoboCup rescue team [13], Unmanned Aerial Vehicles (UAVs) operations [9], team formation in social networks [15], and online soccer prediction games [21].

In the following, we are interested in the robustness issue for task-oriented team formation. Let us start with a motivating example. Assume that you are a project leader. There are a set of tasks to be achieved and a set of available agents, where each agent has different skills to achieve the tasks; the cost for hiring an agent typically varies with its capabilities, and you have a limited budget c. Your objective is to select a team (i.e., a subset of agents), which is able to achieve the tasks of interest. Considering a team with all agents is enough to determine efficiently whether the tasks will be achievable. But the great team does not meet the budget constraint in the general case: one looks for a *c-costly* team (i.e., a team which can accomplish the goal, but for an expense upper bounded by the limited budget c) or even for a team which minimizes the global expense.

Furthermore, what happens if some of the team members fall sick once the team has been formed? Clearly enough, some tasks might not be achieved and it becomes possible that the whole project ends in failure. This is obviously unexpected. In order to be able to manage the case when such failures occur, an approach consists in addressing the robustness issue for task-oriented team formation *at the team design step*. This is the main purpose of our work.

In this paper, a formal framework for the *Task-Oriented Robust Team Formation* (TORTF) problem is first defined and some decision and optimization problems for TORTF are pointed out. A team is viewed as *k-robust* (for a given non-negative integer k) if removing any k agents from it leads to a remaining team which can still accomplish the given tasks. For the decision problem, the aim is to compute (when it exists) one c-costly and k-robust team, for a given cost c and robustness k. For optimization problems, one can be interested in optimizing the robustness of the team, while keeping its cost below the given budget. Dually, one can also fix the robustness and try to find a cheapest team meeting the robustness requirement. We can also view the TORTF problem as a *bi-objective constraint optimization problem* (i.e., optimizing both the cost and the robustness of a team). Among these three optimization problems, this paper focuses on the last one.

First of all, the computational complexity of TORTF is identified. From a computational point of view, the task-oriented team formation problem is similar to some well-known **NP**-complete decision problems (e.g., SET COVER problem [12]). When TORTF is considered, the robustness property must be ensured on top of the task-oriented team formation problem. This explains why TORTF cannot be computationally easier than solving a task-oriented team formation problem, since it requires to solve the original task-oriented team formation problem and also to check the k-robustness of the obtained team by removing any k agents (i.e., any subset of size k) from it. However, we show that TORTF does not prove more computationally demanding than the task-oriented team formation problem since the decision problem TORTF is **NP**-complete; as a by-product, we get that the associated optimization problem TORTF is **NP**-hard.

In order to solve the decision and optimization problems for TORTF, two algorithms called *ART* (Algorithm for Robust Team) and *AORT* (Algorithm for Optimal Robust Team) are presented and evaluated on a number of benchmarks. *ART* is an algorithm which computes a *c-costly* and *k-robust* team when it exists. *AORT* is a bi-objective constraint optimization algorithm which aims at computing every trade-off team (Pareto optimal solution), i.e., a team T such that no other team is at the same time less expensive and more robust than T. We expect that the decision problem TORTF exhibits an easy-hard-easy phase transition pattern, which is well-known as phase transition behavior in Constraint Satisfaction Problem (CSP) [10]: for the given cost c and robustness k, there exist problems where the algorithm can easily find a team (or it can easily show that there exists no team), and there exist problems (called *critical points* in CSP) where finding a team is difficult. We also expect that for the bi-objective constraint optimization problem TORTF, the number of trade-off teams is small. For Multi-Objective Constraint Optimization Problem [20, 25], in general, the number of Pareto optimal solutions becomes larger when the number of objectives increases and it is often exponential in the number of agents, while the number of objectives is two, and the number of trade-off teams is bounded by the number of agents in TORTF problems.

As an application domain, we believe that forming rescue teams (i.e., the ability to continue rescue operations even if some rescue members are involved in an accident) is promising. Consider the problem of forming a rescue team in a disaster area. There are a set of tasks to be achieved and a set of available rescue robots, where each robot has different skills to achieve the tasks, e.g., providing medical treatment, acting as a firefighter, driving a vehicle, etc. Assume that their current positions are different (e.g., a robot is charging her battery in the robot station and some robots are outside and waiting for a command). Forming a rescue team which is both efficient (by considering the distance to the disaster area) and robust of the team (i.e., still able to accomplish the set of tasks even if some robots break down), amounts to a TORTF problem. Moreover, nurse scheduling problems [22] when the bounded working hours of each nurse is considered and the robustness of the whole team expected, also corresponds to TORTF problems. Finally, the design of fault tolerant system (i.e., the ability to continue operating tasks even if some components break down) is another application domain which is worth being investigated.

The rest of the paper is organized as follows. In the next section, our framework for the Task-Oriented Robust Team Formation TORTF problem is introduced and some decision and optimization problems for TORTF are provided. The computational complexity of TORTF is then identified. The next section presents the algorithm for TORTF. Afterwards, some empirical results are provided. Just before the concluding section, some related works are discussed.

2. FRAMEWORK FOR TASK-ORIENTED ROBUST TEAM FORMATION

In this section, the problem of task-oriented robust team formation is formally defined. Both the decision problem (finding out a team which is "sufficiently" robust and cheap) and the optimization problem (finding out every team which is optimally robust and/or cheap) are considered. Also, the computational complexity of TORTF is identified.

DEFINITION 1. (Team formation problem description) A *team formation problem description* is a tuple $TF = \langle A, P, f, \alpha\rangle$ where $A = \{a_1, a_2, ..., a_n\}$ is a set of agents, $P = \{p_1, p_2, ..., p_m\}$ is a set of tasks, $f : 2^A \to \mathbb{N}$ is a cost function, and α is a mapping from A to 2^P. Both f and α are supposed to be computable in polynomial time. A set of agents $T \subseteq A$ is called a *team*, and a set of tasks $G \subseteq P$ is said to be a *goal*.

We first recall two standard properties of expected teams, namely team cost and team efficiency, that both apply to any team $T \subseteq A$. These two properties are defined as follows.

DEFINITION 2. (Team affordability) Let $TF = \langle A, P, f, \alpha\rangle$ be a team formation problem description. Given a team $T \subseteq A$ and a non-negative integer c, T is said to be *c-costly* if the cost of T is less than c:

$$f(T) \leq c.$$

For simplicity, in this paper, we assume that the cost of a team is given by the sum of the costs of each agent a_i of the team T, i.e., $f(T) = \sum_{a_i \in T} f(a_i)$.

DEFINITION 3. (Team efficiency) Let $TF = \langle A, P, f, \alpha\rangle$ be a team formation problem description. Given a team $T \subseteq A$ and a goal $G \subseteq P$, T is said to be *efficient with respect to* G if T can accomplish G:

$$G \subseteq \bigcup_{a_i \in T} \alpha(a_i).$$

EXAMPLE 1. (Team affordability and efficiency) Consider the following TORTF instance: let $TF = \langle\{a_1, a_2, ..., a_6\}, \{p_1, p_2, ..., p_5\}, f, \alpha\rangle$ be a team formation description and $G = \{p_1, p_3\}$ be a goal. We set the cost c to $c = 8$. Table 1 shows a set of accomplishable tasks and the cost of each agent of A. We assume that a set of tasks is given by a mapping α (e.g., $\alpha(a_1) = \{p_1, p_2\}$, agent a_1 can accomplish the tasks p_1 and p_2), and the cost is provided by f (e.g.,

Table 1: Accomplishable tasks and cost of each agent.

agent	accomplishable tasks	cost
a_1	$\{p_1, p_2\}$	4
a_2	$\{p_1, p_3\}$	3
a_3	$\{p_1, p_2, p_3\}$	5
a_4	$\{p_3, p_4\}$	2
a_5	$\{p_1, p_2, p_4, p_5\}$	9
a_6	$\{p_5\}$	1

$f(a_1) = 4$). Consider a team $T' = \{a_2, a_3\}$. Since $f(T') = f(a_2) + f(a_3) = 8$, T' is 8-costly. Also, since $G = \{p_1, p_3\} \subseteq \alpha(T') = \{p_1, p_2, p_3\}$, T' is efficient w.r.t. G.

These two properties are standard ones. When considered together, they require the cost for a team to be kept under a certain threshold while covering the given set of tasks. The corresponding decision problem, namely *Task Efficient Team Formation* (TETF), is defined as follows:

DEFINITION 4. (TETF)

- **Input:** A team formation problem description $TF = \langle A, P, f, \alpha\rangle$, a non-negative integer c and a goal $G \subseteq P$,
- **Question:** Does there exist a team $T \subseteq A$ such that T is c-costly and efficient w.r.t G ?

We get the following complexity result:

PROPOSITION 1. TETF is **NP**-complete.

PROOF. Let $TF = \langle A, P, f, \alpha\rangle$, $G \subseteq P$ and $c, k \geq 0$. To check whether there exists a team $T \subseteq A$ that is c-costly and efficient w.r.t. G, it is enough to guess a team $T \subseteq A$ and check in polynomial time that T is c-costly and efficient w.r.t. G. Therefore, TETF $\in$ **NP**. Let us prove now that TETF is **NP**-hard. We consider the following polynomial reduction from the well-known **NP**-hard problem SET COVER [12]: given a collection C of subsets of a finite set S and a non-negative integer k, does C contain a cover for S of size c or less, i.e., a subset $C' \subseteq C$ with $|C'| \leq c$ such that every element of S belongs to at least one member of C'? Let $COV = \langle C, S, c\rangle$ where $C = \{C_1, C_2, \ldots, C_n\}$ is a collection of subsets from a finite set $S = \{p_1, p_2, \ldots, p_m\}$ and c be a non-negative integer. We associate with COV in polynomial time the tuple $\langle TF, G, c\rangle$ where TF is the team formation $TF = \langle A, S, F, \alpha\rangle$ defined as $A = \{a_1, a_2, \ldots, a_n\}$, $P = S$, for every $T \subseteq A$, $f(T) = |T|$ and for every $a_i \in A$, $\alpha(a_i) = C_i$, and $G = P$ (i.e., $G = S$). Additionally, we associate with every set $C' \subseteq C$ the team $T_{C'} \subseteq A$ defined as $T_{C'} = \{a_i \in A \mid C_i \in C'\}$. Now, let $C' \subseteq C$. On the one hand, C' has a size of c or less if and only if $|T_{C'}| \leq c$ if and only if $f(T_{C'}) \leq c$ if and only if $T_{C'}$ is c-costly. On the other hand, C' is a cover for S if and only if $S \subseteq \bigcup_{C_i \in C'} C_i$ if and only if for every $G \subseteq \bigcup_{a_i \in T_{C'}} \alpha(a_i)$, if and only if $T_{C'}$ is efficient w.r.t. G. Therefore, C contains a cover for S of size c or less if and only if there is a team $T \subseteq A$ that is c-costly and efficient w.r.t. G. This shows that TETF is **NP**-hard, thus TETF is **NP**-complete. □

The induced optimization problem can be expressed as follows: given a team formation problem description, find a subset of agents of minimal cost that is efficient w.r.t. a given goal. This problem is NP-hard, since the associated decision problem is NP-hard as well.

Robustness can now be defined in formal terms as follows:

DEFINITION 5. (Team robustness) Let $TF = \langle A, P, f, \alpha\rangle$ be a team formation problem description. Given a team $T \subseteq A$, a goal $G \subseteq P$ and a non-negative integer k, T is said to be *k-robust* w.r.t. G if for every set of agents $T' \subseteq T$, such that $|T'| \leq k$, the team $T \setminus T'$ is efficient w.r.t. G.

This property is a generalization of the property of team efficiency (Definition 3), considered at different strength degrees, depending on the choice of the value k. This will be more salient given the following observations:

OBSERVATION 1. Let $T \subseteq A$ and $G \subseteq P$. T is efficient w.r.t G if and only if it is 0-robust w.r.t. G.

To complete this observation, let us point out that team efficiency is the weakest version of team robustness, and that the property of k-robustness is monotonic when the values of k vary:

OBSERVATION 2. Let $T \subseteq A$, $G \subseteq P$ and $k > 0$. If T is k-robust w.r.t. G, then T is $(k-1)$-robust w.r.t. G.

Therefore, a team T is considered to be "more robust" than a team T' for a given goal G if and only if there is a non-negative integer k such that T is k-robust w.r.t. G while T' is not. Moreover, strengthening the notion of robustness for a given team w.r.t. a given goal comes to a limit, which is linearly bounded by the number of agents in the team:

OBSERVATION 3. Let $T \subseteq A$ and $G \subseteq P$. For every $k \geq |T|$, T is not k-robust w.r.t G.

Accordingly, the notion of k-robustness is non-trivial only when k takes its value within the set $\{0, \ldots, |T|-1\}$. [1] From Observations 2 and 3, for any given team $T \subseteq A$ and a non-empty goal G, we can conclude that when T is efficient w.r.t. G, there exists a unique, highest value $k \in \{0, \ldots, |T|-1\}$ such that T is k-robust. We call this value the "degree of robustness" of a team w.r.t. G:

DEFINITION 6. (Degree of robustness) Let $TF = \langle A, P, f, \alpha\rangle$ be a team formation problem description. Given a team $T \subseteq A$ and a goal $G \subseteq P$, the *degree of robustness* of T w.r.t. G, denoted $deg_G(T)$ is defined as $-\infty$ if T is not efficient w.r.t. G, and by $deg_G(T) = \max\{k \in \{0, |T| - 1 \mid T \text{ is } k\text{-robust w.r.t. } G\}$ otherwise.

When the robustness issue is added on top of this problem, the resulting problem cannot become computationally easier than the TETF problem since it requires to solve a TETF problem and also to check the k-robustness of the obtained solution (team)/ However, we show that the complexity of the resulting problem does not increase.

First, we show that for a given team $T \subseteq A$ and a goal $G \subseteq P$, whether T is k-robust w.r.t. G can be decided in

[1] Please note that Observation 3 holds for non-empty sets of tasks only; indeed k-robustness w.r.t. an empty set of tasks would be trivially satisfied for any team T. However, this specific case can be ignored since we initially assumed goals to be non-empty sets of tasks in Definition 7.

polynomial time. Before proving it, let us first introduce the following notation: for every task $p_i \in P$ and every team $T \subseteq A$, let $p_i(T)$ be the set of agents from T that can perform the task p_i, i.e., $p_i(T) = \{a_i \in T \mid p_i \in \alpha(a_i)\}$. The following proposition holds:

PROPOSITION 2. Given a team $T \subseteq A$, a non-negative integer k and a goal $G \subseteq P$, T is k-robust w.r.t. G if and only if for every task $p_i \in G$, we have : $|p_i(T)| > k$.

PROOF. Let $T \subseteq A$, k be a non-negative integer and $G \subseteq P$. (*If Part*) Assume T is not k-robust w.r.t. G. By Definition 5, there exists a subset $T' \subseteq T$ of agents such that $|T'| \leq k$ and such that the team $T \setminus T'$ is not G-efficient. Then from Definition 3, there exists a task $p_i \in G$ such that $p_i \notin \bigcup_{a_i \in T \setminus T'} \alpha(a_i)$, or equivalently, that $p_i \notin \alpha(a_i)$ for every $a_i \in T \setminus T'$, that is, $|p_i(T \setminus T')| = 0$. Yet $|T'| \leq k$, so $|p_i(T')| \leq k$, thus we get that $|p_i(T)| \leq k$.

(*Only If Part*) Assume that there exists a task $p_i \in G$ such that $|p_i(T)| \leq k$. Let $T' \subseteq T$ defined as $T' = p_i(T)$. Then by definition of $p_i(T \setminus T')$, we have $p_i \notin \bigcup_{a_i \in T \setminus T'} \alpha(a_i)$, thus from Definition 3, $T \setminus T'$ is not efficient w.r.t. G. Moreover, since $T' = p_i(T)$ and $|p_i(T)| \leq k$, we have $|T'| \leq k$. Hence, from Definition 5, $T \setminus T'$ is not k-robust w.r.t. G. □

As a direct consequence, the degree of robustness of a team w.r.t. a goal can be computed in polynomial time:

COROLLARY 1. Given a team $T \subseteq A$, and a goal $G \subseteq P$, we have $deg_G(T) = \min\{|p_i(T)| - 1 \mid p_i \in G\}$.

We can now generalize the decision problem TETF to the *Task-Oriented Robust Team Formation* (TORTF) problem. TORTF is formally defined as follows:

DEFINITION 7. (TORTF)

- **Input:** A team formation problem description $TF = \langle A, P, f, \alpha \rangle$, two non-negative integers c, k and a goal $G \subseteq P$,
- **Question:** Does there exist a team $T \subseteq A$ such that T is c-costly and k-robust w.r.t. G ?

From Observation 1 and Proposition 1, TORTF is a generalization of TETF, thus it is an **NP**-hard problem. However, from Proposition 2, since it turns out that TORTF is not harder than TETF, the following corollary holds.

COROLLARY 2. TORTF is **NP**-complete.

EXAMPLE 2. (Team robustness) We consider the same TORTF instance as in Example 1: let $TF = \langle \{a_1, a_2, ..., a_6\}, \{p_1, p_2, ..., p_5\}, f, \alpha \rangle$ be a team formation and $G = \{p_1, p_3\}$ be a goal. We set the cost c and the degree of robustness k to $c = 8$ and $k = 1$. Consider a team $T' = \{a_2, a_3\}$. Since $\alpha(T' \setminus \{a_2\}) = \alpha(a_3) = \{p_1, p_2, p_3\} \supset G$ and $\alpha(T' \setminus \{a_3\}) = \alpha(a_2) = \{p_1, p_3\} = G$, T' is 1-robust w.r.t. G. This means that T' can accomplish a goal G, even if any agent (i.e., $k = 1$), is removed from T'. Similarly, $T' = \{a_2, a_3\}$ is the team that is 8-costly (see example 1) and 1-robust. From Observation 3, the degree of robustness of this team is one.

Beyond the decision problem TORTF, several constraint optimization problems for TORTF are meaningful. Mainly, one can be interested in optimizing the degree of robustness of the team, while keeping its cost below the given budget. Dually, one can also fix the minimal degree of robustness which is expected, and try to point out a cheapest team meeting the robustness requirement.[2] We can also view the TORTF problem as a *bi-objective constraint optimization problem*, and be interested in computing Pareto optimal (i.e., non-dominated) robust teams. Clearly, all those optimization problems are NP-hard, since the associated decision problem is NP-hard as well. In the following, we focus on the bi-objective constraint optimization problem, only. To be more precise, we are interested in computing *all* the Pareto optimal solutions of a TORTF problem:

DEFINITION 8. (Dominance) Let $TF = \langle A, P, f, \alpha \rangle$ be a team formation problem description, $G \subseteq P$ be a goal and $T, T' \subseteq A$ be two teams. T *dominates* T' if and only if $deg_G(T) \geq deg_G(T')$ and $f(T) < f(T')$, or $deg_G(T) > deg_G(T')$ and $f(T) \leq f(T')$.

DEFINITION 9. (Pareto optimality) Let $TF = \langle A, P, f, \alpha \rangle$ be a team formation problem description, $G \subseteq P$ be a goal. A team $T \subseteq A$ which is efficient w.r.t. G is a *Pareto optimal robust team* (also called a "trade-off" team in the following) if no team $T' \subseteq A$ that is efficient w.r.t. G dominates T.

In order to solve it, our problem is modeled as a Multi-Objective Constraint Optimization Problem (MO-COP) [20, 25] (the extension of mono-objective Constraint Optimization Problem (COP) [7, 28] to multi-criteria decision making). A COP consists of a set of variables, and a value assignment of those variables is sought in such a way that the sum of the resulting costs is optimized. In our framework, each agent a_i is identified by a variable x_i. It takes its value from a finite, discrete domain $\{join, not\ join\}$, expressing whether the agent will participate or not to the team. A team is a set of agents who choose the value *join*. In case all agents choose *not join*, the (empty) team cannot achieve any tasks and its cost is 0. Deriving a trade-off team consists in finding a value assignment to all agents so that the cost of the team is minimized and the degree of robustness of the team is maximized. Compared to typical MO-COPs (i.e., problems with more than two objectives), the number of Pareto optimal solutions (trade-off teams) of TORTF problem is "small", since (i) our problem is a bi-objective COP[3], and (ii) the number of trade-off teams is bounded by the number of agents $|A|$, i.e., for each k, there exists at most one Pareto optimal robust team and k is bounded by $|A|$, while the number of Pareto optimal solutions in MO-COPs is exponential in the number of agents, i.e., every possible assignment can be Pareto optimal solution in the worst case.

EXAMPLE 3. (Bi-objective constraint optimization problem) We consider the same instance as in Example 1, but the goal is changed to $G = \{p_3\}$. The purpose is now to find the set of trade-off teams w.r.t. the cost c of the team and the number of removal agents k. Table 2 shows all Pareto optimal robust teams. There are three teams with one agent that can accomplish the goal, i.e., $T_1 = \{a_4\}$, $T_1' = \{a_3\}$, and

[2]These problems can be represented as Constraint Optimization Problems [28] and solved using existing COP solvers.

[3]In general, the number of Pareto optimal solutions becomes larger when the number of objectives increases.

Table 2: **All trade-off teams for bi-objective constraint optimization problem.**

team	agents	accomplishable tasks	cost	k
T_1	$\{a_4\}$	$\{p_3, p_4\}$	2	0
T_2	$\{a_2, a_4\}$	$\{p_1, p_3, p_4\}$	5	1
T_3	$\{a_2, a_3, a_4\}$	$\{p_1, p_2, p_3, p_4\}$	10	2

Algorithm 1 *AORT* (and *ART*)

```
1: INPUT : a team formation problem description TF and
   non-negative integers maxCost and k, (plus a Boolean
   value Decision when decision problems are to be handled).
2: OUTPUT : the set of all trade-off teams PF
3: PF ← ∅: // a set of teams
4: T ← ∅ // a set of agents
5: solve (1, T, PF, TF, maxCost, k, (Decision)) // start
   with the first agent of the ordering
6: Return PF
```

$T_1'' = \{a_2\}$ (see Table 1). Since the costs of T_1, T_1' and T_1'' are $f(T_1) = 2$, $f(T_1') = 5$ and $f(T_1'') = 3$, and all teams are 0-robust ones (from Observation 3), T_1 dominates T_1' and T_1'', i.e., the cost of T_1 ($f(T_1) = 2$) is smaller than 5 ($= f(T_1')$) and 3 ($= f(T_1'')$). Let v_i be the vector of values for T_i where $1 \leq i \leq 3$. The following three bi-objective vectors are obtained: $v_1 = (2, 0)$, $v_2 = (5, 1)$, and $v_3 = (10, 2)$ (the first coordinate represents the cost of each team and the second coordinate gives the degree of robustness). Clearly, no solution (team) is dominated by another one, hence $\{T_1, T_2, T_3\}$ is the set of Pareto optimal robust (trade-off) teams of this bi-objective constraint optimization problem.

3. ALGORITHMS FOR TASK-ORIENTED ROBUST TEAM FORMATION

In this section, in order to solve decision and optimization TORTF problems, we present a branch and bound search-based algorithm, which is a widely used technique for solving MO-COPs [20]. When the decision problem is considered, the algorithm is referred to as *ART*: this algorithm aims at computing one "satisfying" solution, i.e., a c-costly and k-robust team where c and k are given. When bi-objective constraint optimization problems are considered, the algorithm is referred to as *AORT*: this algorithm computes every Pareto optimal robust team (each of them corresponds to a trade-off between cost c and degree of robustness k). We mainly describe how *AORT* works, since *ART* can be viewed as a by-product of *AORT*.

Algorithms 1 and 2 give the pseudo-codes for *AORT* (and also *ART*). Initialization is made in Algorithm 1 where the input is a team formation problem description TF, two non-negative integers $maxCost$ and k, and the expected output is the set of all trade-off teams PF (lines 1 and 2). In this algorithm, we assume that a variable ordering (corresponding to an ordering over agents) is provided. The algorithm starts the search with the first agent w.r.t. this ordering (line 5). The search is based on a recursive call to *solve*, detailed in Algorithm 2. This algorithm successively considers each agent as part of the team (then out of the team), building partial teams until either one of the bounding functions is unsatisfied or a full assignment is reached.

Algorithm 2 solve(N,T,PF,TF,$maxCost$,k,($Decision$))

```
1: INPUT : a non-negative integer N, a team T, a set of
   teams PF, a team formation problem description TF,
   two non-negative integers maxCost and k (plus an additional
   Boolean value Decision when decision problems
   are to be handled).
2: // 1) Check whether all agents has been assigned
3: if N > |A| then
4:     if T is not efficient then
5:         Return
6:     end if
7:     if Decision then return {T} // for decision problem
8:     end if
9:     if T is not dominated by any element of PF then
10:        Remove all teams dominated by T from PF
11:        PF ← PF ∪ {T}
12:    end if
13:    Return
14: end if
15: // 2) Assign agent N
16: a: the N^th agent of A
17: T ← T ∪ {a}
18: // 3) Check the affordability
19: if cost(T) > maxCost then
20:     solve (N + 1, T \ {a}, PF, TF, maxCost, k)
21:     Return
22: end if
23: // 4) Check the efficiency
24: MinAgent := 0
25: if T is not efficient then
26:     MinAgent ← MinAgent + k + 1
27: end if
28: if T is k_T-robust and k_T < k then // k_T is the degree
    of robustness of the current team
29:     MinAgent ← MinAgent + (k − k_T)
30: end if
31: if (|A| − N) < MinAgent then
32:     T ← T \ {a}
33:     Return
34: end if
35: // 5) Check the dominance
36: Maxk := (|A| − N)
37: if T is k_T-robust then
38:     Maxk ← Maxk + k_T
39: end if
40: for all team T' of PF do
41:     if cost(T') < cost(T) and k_T' ≥ Maxk then
42:         solve(N + 1, T \ {a}, PF, TF, maxCost, k)
43:         Return
44:     end if
45: end for
46: // 6) Continue the search with the next agent
47: solve(N + 1, T, PF, TF, maxCost, k)
48: solve(N + 1, T \ {a}, PF, TF, maxCost, k)
49: Return
```

Let us first describe the optimization case where we consider parameters $k = 0$ and $maxCost = \infty$. Function *solve* takes an integer N as parameter and assigns the N-th agent of A to the team T (line 17 in Algorithm 2). It then checks the affordability, efficiency and dominance of the partial team. The team T is not affordable if its cost is superior to $maxCost$. In this case, the partial team T is ignored and the algorithm continues the search without considering the N-th agent as part of the team (line 20). For ensuring efficiency (line 23-34), the algorithm checks if the robustness k that is expected is reachable, based on the current robustness k_T of the team T and the remaining agents that can be added. In case k is not reachable, the current partial team T can be given up. Finally, the algorithm checks if T is not dominated by another team in PF (where the teams found previously are stored) (line 35-45). To do this, the maximum possible robustness (denoted $Maxk$) that T can reach is computed by adding the current robustness k_T to the number of remaining agents that can be added ($|A|-N$). The algorithm then checks if there exists a team T' in PF that has a cost lower than the one of T and for a degree of robustness higher or equal to $Maxk$. If such team T' exists, then T can be given up (line 42).

If the three conditions (i.e., affordability, efficiency and dominance) are satisfied, the search considers the N-th agent as part of team (line 47) and then not part of it (line 48). When the last agent (w.r.t. the ordering) has been assigned, an assignment to all agents is obtained (line 3). If T is efficient and not Pareto dominated by another team in PF, then T is added to PF (line 11) and the solutions of PF dominated by T are removed.

When the bi-objective constraint optimization problem with parameters $k = 0$ and $maxCost = \infty$ is considered, every team T will pass the affordability and efficiency checks (line 18 and 23). However, when the decision problem is considered instead, all checks must be performed and the algorithm must stop once the first efficient solution is found. We can easily obtain ART for the decision problem by removing the dominance check (line 35) and giving the fixed $maxCost$ and k. Clearly enough, the time complexities of ART and $AORT$ are exponential in the number of agents.

EXAMPLE 4. (AORT) We explain how $AORT$ works on Example 1. The input is a TORTF instance with $A = \{a_1, a_2, ..., a_6\}$ and $G = \{p_1, p_2, ..., p_5\}$. In order to find each Pareto optimal solution, every possible team in A must be considered; for each of them, its *cost* as well its *k-robustness* must be computed. During the search, a vector of solutions is maintained for each possible k and is updated whenever a new Pareto optimal solution is found. For example, assume that the assignment $A_1 = \{a_1, a_2, a_3, a_4, a_5, a_6\}$ has been found as a possible solution for $k = 1$ with $cost = 24$. When the assignment $A'_1 = \{a_3, a_4, a_5, a_6\}$ leading to $k = 1$ and $cost = 17$ is considered, the complete assignment A_1 can be replaced by A'_1 since, for the same value of k, A'_1 has an inferior cost. For $k = 0$, if $A_0 = \{a_1, a_4, a_5\}$ with $cost = 15$ has been previously found, and the assignment $A'_0 = \{a_1, a_4, a_6\}$ with $cost = 7$ is considered, A_0 can be replaced by A'_0 since, for the same value of k, A'_0 has an inferior cost. Finally, the algorithm returns two solutions A'_0 and A'_1 that are the cost minimal teams for $k = 0$ and $k = 1$ respectively.

EXAMPLE 5. (ART) We now explain how ART works, using again Example 1 where the set of agents $A = \{a_2, a_3, a_4\}$ is considered, only. We want to determine if there exists a team T that realizes $G = \{p_3\}$ so that T is 7-costly and 1-robust. ART starts with the empty set $\emptyset$ and tries adding agents until either it finds a 7-costly and 1-robust team or the team cost exceeds 7. Starting from the empty set $\emptyset$, the first agent a_2 is added and thus the algorithm checks the team $\{a_2\}$. This team accomplishes $\{p_3\}$ but it is not 1-robust. The search continues by adding the next agent a_3. The team $\{a_2, a_3\}$ which is 1-robust but not 7-costly ($cost = 8$), is obtained. The algorithm does not add any further agent to the team $\{a_2, a_3\}$. Indeed, this team is not 7-costly and since adding agents can only increase the cost, no supersets of $\{a_2, a_3\}$ are 7-costly. The algorithm then backtracks to the team $\{a_2\}$ and adds agent $\{a_4\}$. The team $\{a_2, a_4\}$ is obtained: this team accomplishes the tasks, is 1-robust and 7-costly ($cost = 5$). Thus ART stops the search and outputs $\{a_2, a_4\}$.

Table 3: Average number of trade-off teams obtained by $AORT$ (and also Naive) for $|G| = 3, 5, 7, 9, 11$.

# agents \\$|G|$	3	5	7	9	11
10	3.7	3.5	3.2	2.7	2.7
15	5.8	5.0	4.7	4.6	4.2
20	7.6	7.1	6.8	6.4	6.3
25	10.2	9.4	8.8	8.5	8.6
30	12.1	11.3	10.8	10.6	10.6

4. SOME EMPIRICAL RESULTS

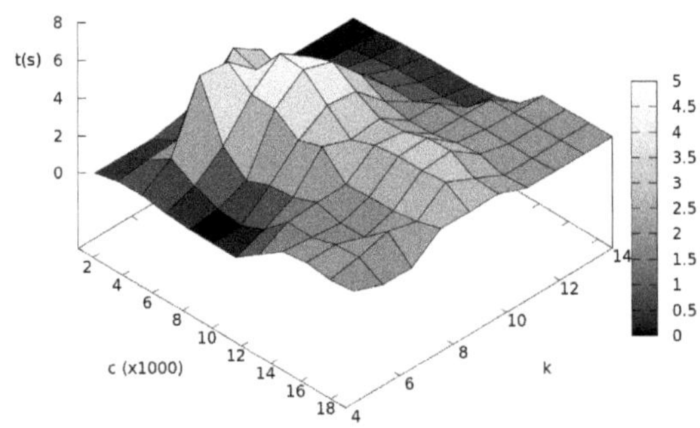

Figure 1: ART with heuristic $h1$.

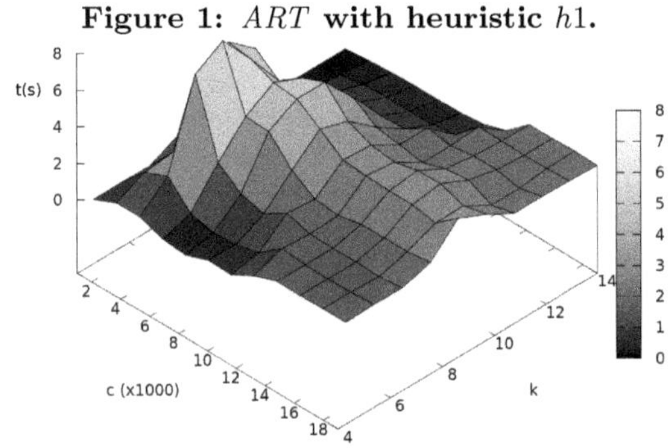

Figure 2: ART with heuristic $h2$.

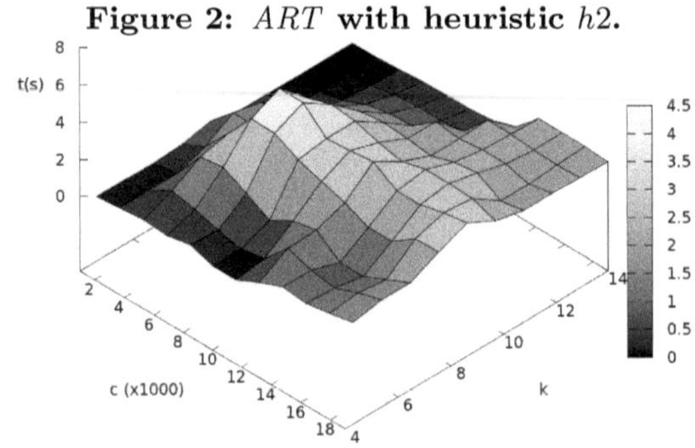

Figure 3: ART with heuristic $h3$.

Table 4: Average runtime of *AORT* and *Naive* for $|G| = 3, 5, 7, 9$ and 11.

	Naive					*AORT*				
# agents	$\|G\|=3$	$\|G\|=5$	$\|G\|=7$	$\|G\|=9$	$\|G\|=11$	$\|G\|=3$	$\|G\|=5$	$\|G\|=7$	$\|G\|=9$	$\|G\|=11$
10	0.01	0.01	0.01	0.01	0.01	0.001 (0.001)	0.002 (0.001)	0.003 (0.001)	0.01 (0.001)	0.01 (0.001)
15	0.1	0.11	0.12	0.13	0.14	0.05 (0.04)	0.05 (0.05)	0.06 (0.06)	0.07 (0.07)	0.06 (0.06)
20	3.2	3.5	3.7	4.0	4.3	0.8 (0.8)	1.3 (1.2)	1.2 (1.2)	1.4 (1.4)	1.5 (1.4)
25	94.6	103.5	111.7	121.2	129.6	17.4 (17.4)	22.0 (22.8)	23.2 (25.6)	25.2 (28.9)	29.1 (32.0)
30	3175	3412	3661	3965	4241	266 (340)	430 (486)	527 (555)	486 (650)	592 (734)

In this section, the performances of *ART* and *AORT* on a number of benchmarks are reported. The empirical protocol we considered is as follows. The number of accomplishable tasks per agent has been chosen uniformly at random within range [1...10]. The cost of each agent has also been chosen uniformly at random within range [1000:20000]. The cost $f(T)$ of a team T was defined additively: $f(T) = \sum_{a \in T} f(a)$. Tasks have been also chosen at random within range [1...10], considering a uniform distribution, for defining goals G. For bi-objective constraint optimization problems for TORTF, the domain of each variable is of size two, i.e., $\{join, not\ join\}$. We present some representative results.[4] Each data point in the graphs and tables is an average value over 100 instances. *ART* and *AORT* have been implemented in Python; experiments have been carried out on a One Core Computer running at 2.6GHz with 12GB RAM. For assessing the performances of *ART*, the following three agent ordering heuristics have been considered:

- h1 : random order.
- h2 : order the agents based on the number of skills.
- h3 : order the agents based on the costs.

Figures 1-3 present the results obtained by *ART* with $h1$, $h2$ and $h3$ with 25 agents and different values of the cost c and the degree of robustness k. As we expected, for all results, we can observe the shape of the curve (*easy-hard-easy transition*) in graphs, which is well-known as "phase transition behavior" in CSP [10]. For example, the peak (where the required runtime is maximum) occurs around 6000 for the costs and 9 for the degree of robustness in Fig.1. We call such a peak the *critical area*. In the critical area, we get the case where the search space is not greatly reduced (the cost is not low enough and the degree of robustness is not high enough) and also the case where finding a solution is the most difficult (the cost is not high enough to have a team with many agents and the degree of robustness is not low enough to be able to reach it with only a few agents). Also, we can see that before and after the critical area *ART* can find a solution quickly, i.e., it can easily find a team for the given cost c and the degree of robustness k (e.g., c is around 6000 and k is 4 in Fig.1), or it can easily find that there exists no team for the given c and k (e.g., c is around 6000 and k is 14 in Fig.1). Moreover, when we compare the effect of variable-ordering heuristics, $h3$ outperforms $h1$ and $h2$. The average runtime of *ART* with $h3$ at the critical area is 4.2s (Fig.3), while they are 5.3s and 7.5s for *ART* with $h1$ and $h2$ (Fig.1 and Fig.2).

We also compared the performances of *AORT* with those of a *naive* (brute-force) algorithm (without pruning) for several numbers of agents and goal tasks. Table 3 shows the number of trade-off teams (i.e., Pareto optimal solutions) obtained by these algorithms. As we expected, for all results, i.e., $|G| = 3, 5, 7, 9$ and 11, the number of trade-off teams increases slightly with the number of agents. Thus, for $|G| = 3$, there exist in average 3.7 trade-off teams for 10 agents, 7.6 trade-off teams for 20 agents, and 12.1 trade-off teams for 30 agents. Also, we can observe that the number of trade-off teams becomes smaller, when the number of goal tasks increases. Thus, when the number of agents is 30, the average number of trade-off teams for $|G| = 3$ is 12.1, while there exist 10.6 trade-off teams for $|G| = 11$. The results can be explained by the fact that the number of teams depends heavily on the maximal degree of robustness (denoted k_{max}) of the problem under consideration. For example, if the team containing all agents is 8-robust, we can expect to find a 9-robust team (one per possible k between 0 and k_{max}). Since a wide cost range per agent and a uniform distribution model have been considered in our experiments the cases when several teams exist for the same k and the same *cost* are avoided. Thus, increasing the number of agents increases the potential k_{max}, while increasing the number of tasks makes robustness more difficult to be achieved and decreases k_{max}.

Note that finding all trade-off teams of a TORTF problem is generally easier than solving a bi-objective COP. In TORTF problem, the number of solutions is bounded by the number of agents, i.e., there exist at most $|A| - 1$ trade-off teams where A is a set of agents. On the other hand, in a bi-objective COP, the number of Pareto optimal solutions is often exponential in the number of agents (i.e., all assignments are Pareto optimal solutions in the worst case).

Table 4 gives the average runtimes of *AORT* and of the naive algorithm. The results of *AORT* with h_3 and h_1 are reported. The results between brackets indicate the results of *AORT* with $h1$. The naive algorithm utilizes h_1 for agent ordering. In all cases (i.e. $|G| = 3, 5, 7, 9$ and 11), we can observe that the difference between the results of *AORT* and those of the naive algorithm becomes larger, when the number of agents increases. For example, in case $|G| = 3$, the average runtime of *AORT* is 0.001s for 10 agents, 0.8s for 20 agents and 266s for 30 agents, while the corresponding runtimes of the naive algorithm are respectively 0.01s, 3.2s and 3175s. For $|G| = 11$, the average runtime of *AORT* is 0.01s for 10 agents, 1.5s for 20 agents and 592s for 30 agents, while they are 0.01s, 4.3s and 4241s for the naive algorithm. Also, when the number of agents is at least 25, we can observe that the difference between the results of *AORT* and those of the naive algorithm increases with the number of goal tasks. Moreover, the effect of variable-ordering heuristics (i.e., $h1$ and $h3$) becomes significant, when the number of agents becomes larger. Thus, for $|G| = 11$, the average runtime of *AORT* with $h3$ is 592s for 30 agents, while it is 734s for *AORT* with $h1$.

[4]We observed similar results for other settings.

In summary, as we expected, these experimental results reveal that (i) there exists the easy-hard-easy transition for decision problems, and (ii) for bi-objective constraint optimization problems, the number of trade-off teams increases slightly with the number of agents. Additionally, we examined the effect of agent-ordering heuristics. For decision problems, we compared the performances of ART with three agent-ordering heuristics (i.e., random ordering $h1$, skill-based ordering $h2$ and cost-based ordering $h3$) and observed that $h3$ outperforms $h1$ and $h2$. For optimization problems, we also observed that $h3$ is more effective than $h1$, when the number of agents increases.

5. OTHER RELATED WORK

Many works have been devoted so far to the problem of forming teams. Classically, a set of tasks and a set of agents are given; each agent has some capabilities and some skills are required to achieve each task. The team performance is often viewed as the set of all capabilities of its members.

Thus, Nair et al. [23] worked on forming a team with the maximum expected value so that the team has all required skills to accomplish the tasks of interest. Vidal et al. [29] focused on task-oriented domain problems and showed how the benefits of teaming and selflessness arise in this domain. Bachrach et al. [4] introduced coalitional skill games, where the aim is to make a coalition among agents so that it can cover a set of required skills for a given task (team efficiency). Other works considered e.g., the optimal joint action with a new ad-hoc agent [1] where agents compute their actions based on the observations of their teammates, configuration of a network of agents [8], and minimal coordination cost for a single task [15]. Liemhetcharat et al. [16, 18] considered synergetic effects among agents, and introduced a (weighted) synergy graph model to capture interactions among agents in a team. Marcolino et al. [19] focused on the diversity of a team and showed that a diverse team can overcome a uniform team. In this work, the authors provided optimal voting rules for selecting a diverse team. This property is also important issue for team formation, when dynamic changes are considered, e.g., some agents break down because of the unexpected accident and injury. We plan to investigate the relationship between diverse and robust teams.

In the context of robot team formation, Kaminka et al. [11] introduced a behavior-based teamwork architecture that automates collaboration in physical robots. Liemhetcharat et al. [17] considered configurable robots that are composed of modules, e.g., motors and sensors; he focused on the probability of module failures of each robot and considered how to form a multi-robot team that is robust to failures.

Coalition Structure Generation (CSG) [3, 24, 27] involves partitioning a set of agents into groups (called coalitions) so that the sum of the values of all coalitions is maximized. A partition is called a coalition structure. In CSG, the value of a coalition is given by a black box function. It is well-known that finding an optimal coalition structure is NP-hard. Indeed, the decision problem associated with CSG is equivalent to the *complete set partition problem* [30]. The purpose is different from the one of team formation; indeed, the objective of teal formation is to select a team (a subset of agents), which can achieve the tasks of interest, while the aim of CSG is to find an optimal partition of all agents.

None of those works actually considers the robustness issue for team formation and multi-objective setting, making them quite different from the present work.

Related to our work are also task-allocation problems [14, 31], which involve deciding how to assign a set of tasks to a set of agents. The robustness issue has been considered for these problems, e.g., in [2, 5]. In [2], Ali et al. investigated how to determine a resource allocation so that the robustness of desired system features against perturbations is maximized. This research addressed the design of a robustness metric for resource allocations. In [5], Choi et al. worked on task allocation to coordinate a fleet of autonomous vehicles and presented decentralized task-allocation algorithms that provides conflict-free solutions independent of inconsistencies in Situational Awareness (i.e., robustness to inconsistent SA). Our notion of robustness is consistent with these works: some goal must still be accomplished even when some agents break down, i.e., the formed team is robust against some potential perturbations. However, our work differs from task-allocation problems in the sense that the agents forming a team are not effectively assigned to a specific task. In fact, they are associated with a set of tasks which they have the skill for. Therefore, our work can be used as an upstream step of a task-allocation problem. Making such a link between these two frameworks is worth being considered for further research, where the dependencies between both notions of robustness will be investigated.

6. CONCLUSION

How to form a team for achieving a given set of tasks is an important issue in multi-agent systems. Task-oriented team formation is the problem of forming the best possible team to achieve some tasks of interest, given some limited resources. This paper investigated the robustness issue for task-oriented team formation.

The contribution of this paper is mainly twofold:

- The concept of task-oriented robust team has been first defined and studied. Especially, the issue of computing a robust, yet affordable team has been investigated from a computational point of view. While robustness generalizes the usual notion of team efficiency, this generalization does not lead to a computational shift.
- Two algorithms for solving the TORTF problem have been provided and evaluated. ART for solving a decision problem which aims at computing one c-costly and k-robust team, for given cost c and robustness k. $AORT$ for solving a bi-objective constraint optimization problem which aims at computing every Pareto optimal robust solution. Experiments showed that (i) an easy-hard-easy phase transition pattern can be observed for decision problems, and (ii) for bi-objective constraint optimization problems, the number of trade-off teams increases slightly with the number of agents.

As a perspective for further research, we plan to develop some efficient heuristics and algorithms (based on Russian Doll Search [26]) for solving TORTF problems. Also, we intend to apply our approach to some real-world problems, especially rescue team formation, nurse scheduling problem and fault tolerant system design. Furthermore, we plan to extend our model to a dynamic setting in which goal tasks change with time. An objective will be to develop an algorithm that reconstructs the team after each change, and to apply it to a distributed robot team reconfiguration problem [6].

REFERENCES

[1] N. Agmon and P. Stone. Leading ad hoc agents in joint action settings with multiple teammates. In *AAMAS*, pages 341–348, 2012.

[2] S. Ali, A. Maciejewski, H. Siegel, and J. Kim. Measuring the robustness of a resource allocation. *Parallel and Distributed Systems*, 15(7):630–641, 2004.

[3] Y. Bachrach, P. Kohli, V. Kolmogorov, and M. Zadimoghaddam. Optimal coalition structure generation in cooperative graph games. In *AAAI*, pages 81–87, 2013.

[4] Y. Bachrach and J. Rosenschein. Coalitional skill games. In *AAMAS*, pages 1023–1030, 2008.

[5] H. Choi, L. Brunet, and J. How. Consensus-based decentralized auctions for robust task allocation. *IEEE Transactions on Robotics*, 25(4):912–926, 2009.

[6] P. Dasgupta and K. Cheng. Robust multi-robot team formations using weighted voting games. *Distributed Autonomous Robotic Systems*, 83:373–387, 2013.

[7] R. Dechter. *Constraint Processing*. Morgan Kaufmann Publishers, 2003.

[8] M. E. Gaston and M. desJardins. Agent-organized networks for dynamic team formation. In *AAMAS*, pages 230–237, 2005.

[9] J. George, J. Pinto, P. Sujit, and J. Sousa. Multiple UAV coalition formation strategies. In *AAMAS*, pages 1503–1504, 2010.

[10] T. Hogg, B. Huberman, and C. Williams. Phase transitions and the search problem. *Artificial Intelligence*, 81(1-2):1–15, 1996.

[11] G. Kaminka and I. Frenkel. Flexible teamwork in behavior-based robots. In *AAAI*, pages 108–113, 2005.

[12] R. M. Karp. Reducibility among combinatorial problems. In *Complexity of Computer Computations*, pages 85–103, 1972.

[13] H. Kitano and S. Tadokoro. Robocup rescue: A grand challenge for multiagent and intelligent systems. *AI Magazine*, 22(1):39–52, 2001.

[14] S. Koenig, C. Tovey, X. Zheng, and I. Sungur. Sequential bundle-bid single-sale auction algorithms for decentralized control. In *IJCAI*, pages 1359–1365, 2007.

[15] T. Lappas, K. Liu, and E. Terzi. Finding a team of experts in social networks. In *KDD*, pages 467–476, 2009.

[16] S. Liemhetcharat and M. Veloso. Modeling and learning synergy for team formation with heterogeneous agents. In *AAMAS*, pages 365–374, 2012.

[17] S. Liemhetcharat and M. Veloso. Forming an effective multi-robot team robust to failures. In *IROS*, pages 5240–5245, 2013.

[18] S. Liemhetcharat and M. Veloso. Weighted synergy graphs for effective team formation with heterogeneous ad hoc agents. *Artificial Intelligence*, 208:41–65, 2014.

[19] L. S. Marcolino, A. Jiang, and M. Tambe. Multi-agent team formation: Diversity beats strength? In *IJCAI*, pages 81–87, 2013.

[20] R. Marinescu. Best-first vs. depth-first and/or search for multi-objective constraint optimization. In *ICTAI*, pages 439–446, 2010.

[21] T. Matthews, S. Ramchurn, and G. Chalkiadakis. Competing with humans at fantasy football: Team formation in large partially-observable domains. In *AAAI*, pages 1394–1400, 2012.

[22] M. Moz and M. Pato. Solving the problem of rerostering nurse schedules with hard constraints: New multicommodity flow models. *Annals OR*, 128(1-4):179–197, 2004.

[23] R. Nair and M. Tambe. Hybrid bdi-pomdp framework for multiagent teaming. *Journal of Artificial Intelligent Research*, 23:367–420, 2005.

[24] T. Rahwan and N. Jennings. Coalition structure generation: Dynamic programming meets anytime optimization. In *AAAI*, pages 156–161, 2008.

[25] E. Rollon and J. Larrosa. Bucket elimination for multiobjective optimization problems. *Journal of Heuristics*, 12(4-5):307–328, 2006.

[26] E. Rollon and J. Larrosa. Multi-objective Russian doll search. In *AAAI*, pages 249–254, 2007.

[27] T. Sandholm, K. Larson, M. Andersson, O. Shehory, and F. Tohmé. Coalition structure generation with worst case guarantees. *Artificial Intelligence*, 111(1-2):209–238, 1999.

[28] T. Schiex, H. Fargier, and G. Verfaillie. Valued constraint satisfaction problems: Hard and easy problems. In *IJCAI*, pages 631–639, 1995.

[29] J. Vidal. The effects of co-operation on multiagent search in task-oriented domains. *Journal of Experimental and Theoretical Artificial Intelligence*, 16(1):5–18, 2004.

[30] D. Yeh. A dynamic programming approach to the complete set partitioning problem. *BIT Computer Science and Numerical Mathematics*, 26(4):467–474, 1986.

[31] R. Zlot and A. Stentz. Complex task allocation for multiple robots. In *ICRA*, pages 1515–1522, 2005.

Dynamic Theoretical Analysis of the Distributed Stochastic and Distributed Breakout Algorithms

Anton Ridgway
University of Tulsa
Tandy School of Computer Science
Tulsa, Oklahoma
anton-ridgway@utulsa.edu

Roger Mailler
University of Tulsa
Tandy School of Computer Science
Tulsa, Oklahoma
roger-mailler@utulsa.edu

ABSTRACT

The distributed constraint satisfaction problem is often used to model real-world situations and find agent-based solutions. A number of methods have been developed to solve these problems, including the well-known DSA and DBA algorithms. In many real scenarios, however, the problems are not static. This forces practitioners to adapt these protocols to solve dynamic distributed constraint satisfaction problems (DynDCSP). Surprisingly, despite long-running study of the problem, practically all analysis of DynDCSP algorithms has been experimental in nature. This work presents a new theoretical assessment of the DSA and DBA algorithms, leveraging a mapping of DynDCSP instances to a physical thermodynamics model to develop a deeper understanding of the algorithms' behavior.

Here, we assess the static versions of DSA and DBA, but focus on examining their rates of convergence, not just their final convergence points, as a means of understanding how they will perform in dynamic settings. We develop various theoretical approaches to show how the algorithms' convergence rates are affected by problem density and tightness, and examine the impact that problem size has on an algorithm's performance. Finally, we show the accuracy of our analytical predictions through comparison with experimental results.

Categories and Subject Descriptors

I.2.11 [**Artificial Intelligence**]: Distributed Artificial Intelligence-Multiagent systems, Coherence and coordination

General Terms

Algorithms, Performance, Experimentation, Theory

Keywords

Dynamics, Constraint Satisfaction, Thermodynamics

1. INTRODUCTION

In studying the applications of distributed constraint satisfaction problems (DCSP), it is often crucial to have algorithms available to us that are not only able to solve problems, but also able to adapt to a changing problem space. This has naturally led to the expansion of DCSP studies to the realm of dynamic distributed constraint satisfaction problems (DynDCSP). Under the DynDCSP model described by Mailler [6], these problems can be defined as DCSPs whose constraints change continuously over time during the problem solving process. This definition differs from the original definition presented by Dechter and Dechter [3], where changes to the problem occurred between subsequent executions of a problem solver. Several algorithms have been developed or modified to solve this problem, including the Distributed Breakout Algorithm (DBA) [11, 6], the Distributed Stochastic Algorithm [5] and the Asynchronous Partial Overlay (APO) protocol [6], but in every case the complex nature of the problem has limited the evaluation of these algorithms to empirical analysis.

In a recent work by Mailler and Zheng [7], they showed that DynDCSPs can be mapped to physical systems and therefore obey the laws of thermodynamic theory. This is an important finding because it allows researchers and practitioners to characterize an environment and protocol based on the rate at which they affect a problem and predict the equilibrium that the combination would establish. Their findings considerably reduce the amount of empirical evaluation needed to compare dynamic protocols, but still rely on measuring their behavior on static instances.

Moreover, this analysis drew attention to another important property of DynDCSP algorithms, which had not been considered important in the past. Not only should these algorithms be considered in terms of the quality of the solution they converge on (convergence point), but also in terms of how fast they reach these values (convergence rate). Consideration of both the rate and the point are crucial in determining which algorithms are best suited for any given application.

In this paper, we perform a theoretical analysis of DSA and DBA, two simple and well-known algorithms whose behavior is nevertheless challenging to analyze. Our analysis will focus on the impact that a problem's density, tightness, and size have on the convergence rate of these protocols. The results of this are bounds and approximations on these protocols' performance in dynamic environments. These bounds are then compared with empirical results to validate their accuracy.

The rest of this paper is organized as follows: In section 2, we will discuss background including introducing the DynDCSP problem, some useful terminology, and the mapping of DynDCSPs to thermodynamic systems. In section 3, we will reacquaint the reader with the DSA and DBA protocols and provide our analysis of their performance. This section also includes our empirical results including the test setup, findings, and comparison to our theoretical bounds. Finally, in section 4, we will present concluding remarks and provide some areas for future research.

Appears in: *Proceedings of the 14th International Conference on Autonomous Agents and Multiagent Systems (AAMAS 2015), Bordini, Elkind, Weiss, Yolum (eds.), May 4–8, 2015, Istanbul, Turkey.*

2. BACKGROUND AND TERMINOLOGY

In general, a static DCSP is described by $P =< V, A, D, C >$, where the following is true:

- V is a set of n variables: $V = \{v_1, \ldots, v_n\}$.
- A is a set of g agents: $A = \{a_1, \ldots, a_g\}$.
- D is a set of discrete, finite domains for each variable: $D = \{D_1, \ldots, D_n\}$.
- C is a set of constraints $C = \{c_1, \ldots, c_m\}$, where each $c_i(d_{i,1}, \ldots, d_{i,j})$ is a function $c_i : D_{i,1} \times \cdots \times D_{i,j} \rightarrow \{true, false\}$. That is, a constraint returns true if the values for its associated variables are such that the constraint is satisfied.

Given this, we seek to find a solution $\mathcal{S}^* = \{d_1, \ldots, d_n | d_i \in D_i\}$ such that no constraint is violated, or otherwise, to identify that this cannot be done. Each agent a_i is associated with at least one variable and its variables' constraints, and is primarily concerned with finding a violation-free solution for its own portion of the problem space. Agents coordinate together to solve their constraints, leading to a global problem solution.

Note that in this paper, unless otherwise stated, we consider binary constraints only. In general, it is straightforward to generalize n-ary constraints to binary [1], and while this does affect how an algorithm approaches a given n-ary constraint problem, it will still perform within the bounds we develop here.

We also make use of the following important variable assignments, commonly seen in the literature [8]:

- p_1 is the density of the problem. This indicates the percent of possible constraints that are actually present. Given n variables, we know that $\frac{n(n-1)}{2}$ constraints are possible, therefore $m = p_1 \frac{n(n-1)}{2}$.
- p_2 is the average tightness of the variables in the problem. This term represents the difficulty of an individual constraint being satisfiable, in terms of the percentage of constraint configurations that evaluate to $false$.
- The expected number of initially-violated constraints is $mp_2 = p_1 p_2 \frac{n(n-1)}{2}$.
- The degree of a problem is the average degree of its variables, in general $\frac{m}{n} = p_1 \frac{n-1}{2}$.
- p is the probability of change used in DSA. DBA does not use this variable.

We can build on the definition for DCSPs to define DynDCSPs as follows [6]:

- We introduce a dynamics function: $\Delta : P_t \mapsto P_{t+1}$
- This expression produces a *sequence* of individual DCSP problems: $\mathbf{P} = \{P_0, P_1, \cdots, P_\infty\}$
- Given this, we can characterize the *rate* of change of problems as
  $\frac{dP}{dt} = \lim_{\Delta t \rightarrow 0} \frac{P_{t+\Delta t} - P_t}{\Delta t} = \frac{1}{\Delta t} \sum_{i=t}^{t+\Delta t} (| f_i^a | + | f_i^r |)$

The reader should note that the Δ function is associated with time and that it works by adding a set of constraints, f_i^a, and removing another set of constraints, f_i^r at each step. This means that we cannot always solve any given problem before it changes, so our goal becomes to maximize the number of satisfied constraints, rather than necessarily to find a complete solution or determine its impossibility. Also, if these sets become imbalanced (i.e. $|f_i^a| \neq |f_i^r|$) or the tightness of the constraints within these sets change, then the the problem can change in difficulty as well. We refer to these types of changes as second-order dynamics and do not consider them in this work, although it is an important topic for future investigation.

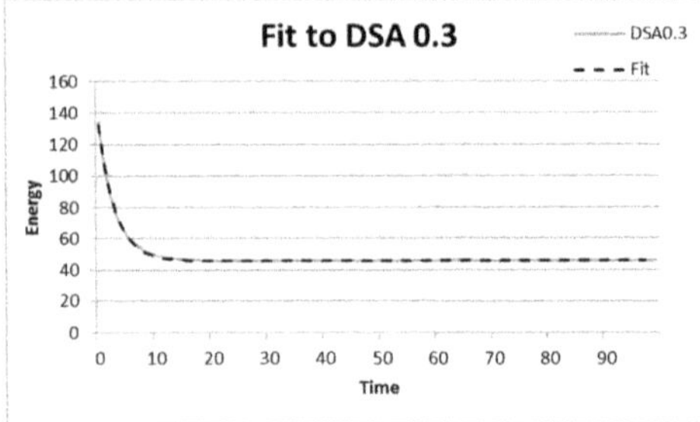

Figure 1: Function fit for DSA 0.3 (n=200, $|D_i|$=3, p_1=0.027, p_2=0.33)

Finally, we map DynDCSPs to thermodynamic theory.

- Variables are equivalent to particles.
- Constraints are equivalent to the interactions between particles.
- The quality of a solution—measured by the number of unsatisfied constraints—is equivalent to the energy of the system E.
- The entropy of a solution—measured by the number of assignments with a specific quality—is equivalent to the entropy of a physical system, generally measured by the number of states with a specific energy.

Mailler and Zheng found that this mapping allowed for a very close match between the empirical behavior of DynDCSP systems and that predicted by the thermodynamics-style equations implied by the mapping. First, they showed that the change in energy in a DynDCSP could be described effectively by Newton's cooling law [7].

$$E_Q = mp_2 - be^{-\frac{rate*t}{m}}$$

Here, b is a constant factor, t is time, and $rate$ is the rate of constraint-change at time t. By allowing A to represent the convergence rate, and B the convergence point, they then showed that the performance profile for distributed protocols could also be fit by the same function.

$$E_W = B + ke^{-\frac{t}{A}}, 0 < B < mp_2, 0 < k$$

This yields an expected change in energy per unit time of

$$\frac{dE_W}{dt} = \frac{B - E}{A}$$

Finally, using the First Law of Thermodynamics ($\Delta E = \delta Q - \delta W$) they showed that the expected equilibrium for a dynamically changing constraint system being simultaneously solved by a protocol is

$$E_0 = \frac{Amp_2 + \frac{mB}{rate}}{A + \frac{m}{rate}}$$

In practice, obtaining the values of A and B involves running numerous trials using static instances for various values of n, p_1, and p_2. The data produced by these runs is then processed. Processing involves computing the average energy for each time step over the test series, then calculating A and B using a program like Mathematica [10] to obtain a least squares fit. Figure 1 shows the result of this procedure for the DSA protocol with $p = 0.3, n = 200, |D_i| = 3$ for all $i, p_1 = 0.027, p_2 = 0.33$, which is fit quite well by $A = 2.95$ and $B = 45.7$.

3. ALGORITHM ANALYSIS

Being able to predict a system's dynamic performance using two parameters that are obtained by testing static instances is, in itself, a significant advance. However, we are still left with all of the parameters for static DCSPs— n, each $|D_i|$, p_1, and p_2— when evaluating a new protocol. Worse yet, some protocols like DSA have tunable parameters whose settings can be very problem specific. One way to address this problem is to perform exhaustive testing on the protocol in question using parameter settings that may be encountered in practice. The approach we follow here is to analyze the protocol to determine if estimates or bounds on its performance can be derived.

In this section, we present an analysis of two popular distributed protocols; DSA and DBA. For both of these protocols, we will derive functions that describe their convergence rate A as a function of problem density and tightness. Because the DSA and DBA algorithms remain fundamentally unchanged in the transition to their dynamic counterparts, our analysis, like the empirical studies described above, can provide valuable insights into their dynamic performance, even though they don't address the dynamic case specifically.

Note also that we necessarily address only the average-case behavior for these algorithms. For any DCSP algorithm, it is always possible to produce problem instances that converge arbitrarily fast, or not at all. As such, absolute bounds on algorithm performance are generally unhelpful for us, and we focus instead on characterizing how in the large scale each algorithm solves problems on average.

3.1 Distributed Stochastic Algorithm

The Distributed Stochastic Algorithm (DSA) is perhaps the simplest of all of DynDCSP algorithms (see figure 2). Because of its simplicity, it can remain fundamentally unchanged by the transition from a DCSP setting to that of DynDCSP, so it accommodates much simpler analysis approaches. The protocol works by having each agent determine if they could reduce the number of constraint violations by changing their variable's value. If they can, with some probability p, they change their value and inform their neighbors. There are several variants to DSA, with the most popular being DSA-B. In addition to operating like DSA, DSA-B also has a possibility of making lateral moves (i.e., changes when the potential for improvement is 0) if its constraints are not satisfied.

The optimal setting for p has been the subject of some experimentation [12, 5], and is generally believed to lie somewhere around 0.3. Prior studies, however, focused exclusively on the "final" quality produced by the protocol on static instances, where a slower approach to obtaining a solution might yield a superior answer, rather than on the convergence rate.

We expect the value of p to be strongly associated with the convergence rate of the algorithm, since if the value of p is small enough, agents will only change infrequently and converge on a final result after a longer time. However, if p is too large, DSA agents can cancel out each other's intended improvements—if both agents of a constraint change their values, it may or may not actually satisfy the constraint or cause an improvement. With DSA-B, we have to take into account the effect of a lateral move, which is more subtle. Lateral moves are not expected to directly affect the convergence rate, but can potentially affect the convergence point by allowing the algorithm to explore different regions of the search space.

Our basic methodology in analyzing DSA is constraint-centric, and takes a whole-system perspective, in which the number of unsatisfied constraints is always decreasing. Imagine a single constraint within the problem. At any given moment, this constraint is either satisfied or unsatisfied. If it is satisfied, then we do not consider it further. For other binary constraints, one of three things can occur (see figure 3); both agents do nothing, only one of the agents changes, or both agents change (often called a collision). Because variable changes are determined by the setting of p, it allows us to state simply that, taking the system as a whole, the probability for each of the cases for each unsatisfied constraint is $(1-p)^2$, $2p(1-p)$, and p^2, respectively. However, the resulting energy change of making these moves is dependent on the circumstances of each case.

Note that the convergence point B for a protocol represents the

```
procedure main
  while (not terminated) do
    update agent_view with incoming
      ok? (x_j, d_j) messages;
    new_value ← choose_value;
    if new_value ≠ d_i do
      d_i ← new_value;
      send ((ok?, (x_i, d_i)) to all x_j ∈ neighbors;
    end if;
  end do;
end main;

procedure choose_value
  if d_i has no conflicts do
    return d_i;
  v ← the value with the least conflict (v ≠ d_i);
  if v has fewer conflicts than d_i
      and random < p do
    return v;
  else
    return d_i;
end choose_value;
```

Figure 2: The procedures of the DSA algorithm.

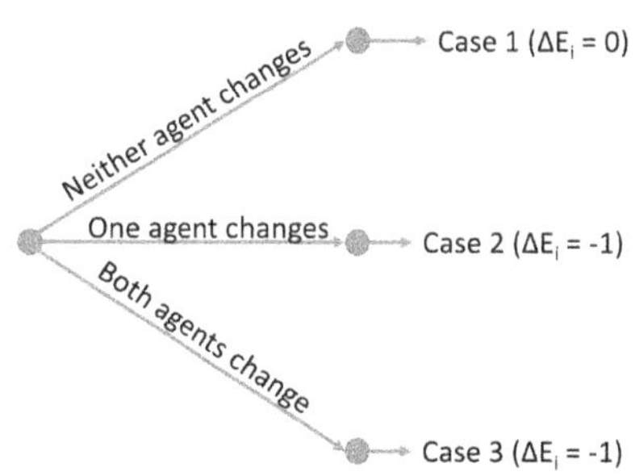

Figure 3: Probability tree for the upper bound analysis.

final energy that it can reach, given the current system parameters, on average. Therefore, we can assume that when the system has not yet reached the convergence point, there will on average always be an agent that can make an improvement, but not beyond that point. As such, we here make an overriding assumption that applies throughout our analysis— namely, at each time step, one or more of the agents *will* attempt to change values, as long as the system energy has not reached the convergence point. Without this assumption, the analysis would assume that every problem is eventually solvable, resulting in a sizable overestimate of the energy reduction per unit time.

Upper Bound Analysis.

We continue our analysis of DSA by attempting to derive an upper (optimistic) bound on how fast it can reduce the energy of a problem over time. To create our upper bound approximation, we have to employ another simplifying assumption— that when an agent changes value, it always leads to a reduction in energy. This first assumption is not unreasonable, since DSA only changes values if the energy can be reduced, but it ignores the fact that an agent may change its value to solve a different constraint then the one being considered. It also ignores the collision case, where two agents change their values at the same time and the constraint remains unsatisfied. Because these two caveats slow energy reduction, however, this is suitable for an upper bound. The resulting energy-change values for each case are represented in figure 3.

With these assumptions, we can compute an upper bound on the average convergence rate for DSA:

$$\frac{dE_w}{dt} \leq (E-B)*[(0)*(1-p)^2+(-1)*(2p(1-p))+(-1)*p^2]$$

$$\frac{dE_w}{dt} \leq (E-B)*[-2p+2p^2-p^2]$$

$$\frac{dE_w}{dt} \leq (E-B)*[p^2-2p]$$

Lower Bound Analysis.

The lower bound analysis is similar to that for the upper bound, except that it changes certain assumptions (see figure 4). First, when just one agent alters its value, we consider that the structure of the constraints will not always allow the removal of a violation. Instead, the expected likelihood of solving a constraint is $1-p_2$, in which case the energy decreases by one, producing an expected outcome of $\Delta E_i = (-1)*(1-p_2) = -1+p_2$. Second, we assume that when two agents change their values at the same time, the constraint between them is never satisfied. Both of these are quite pessimistic estimates of the actual behavior.

These assumptions lead to the lower bound on convergence rate for DSA:

$$\frac{dE_w}{dt} \geq (E-B)*[(0)*(1-p)^2+(-1+p_2)*(2p(1-p))+(0)*p^2]$$

$$\frac{dE_w}{dt} \geq (E-B)*[(p_2-1)(2p-2p^2)]$$

Approximate Analysis.

Although it is instructive to have upper and lower bounds, it is also much nicer to have an estimate of the algorithm's performance in practice. One way to achieve this is to assume that the actual convergence rate lies at the average of the predicated upper and lower bounds. For many circumstances, this is entirely reasonable. However, we can do better through a careful choice of terms. In considering the probability tree for our lower bound analysis, one might note that if one agent moves, it is actually more likely than just $1-p_2$ to solve the constraint in question, while if two agents move at the same time, they are at least somewhat likely to inadvertently solve the constraint. For our improved approximation, we assume that the constraint is solved (leading to a reduction in energy of 1) whenever only one agent changes value, and that if both agents change values, there is a $1-p_2$ probability that the constraint will be satisfied (see figure 5).

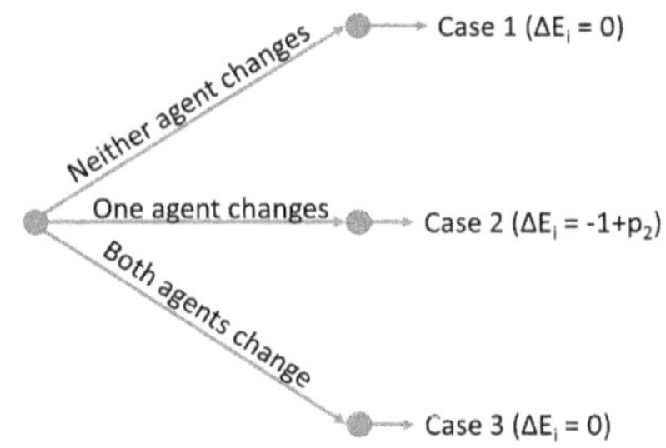

Figure 4: Probability tree for the lower bound analysis.

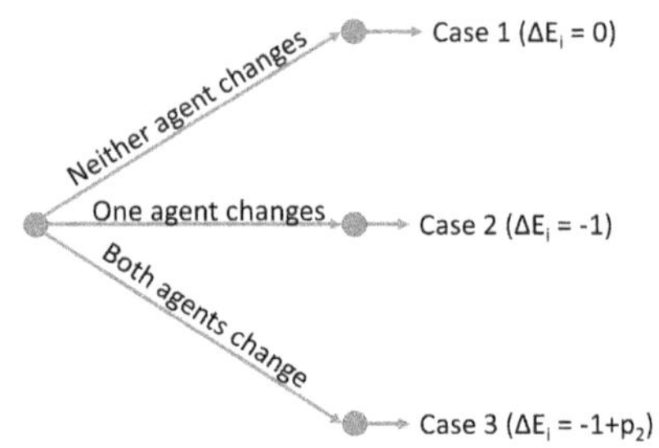

Figure 5: Probability tree for approximate analysis.

Having made these assumptions, we can create a simple approximation of energy change which follows directly from the probability tree:

$$\frac{dE_w}{dt} \approx (E-B)*[(0)*(1-p)^2+(-1)*(2p(1-p))+(-1+p_2)*p^2]$$

$$\frac{dE_w}{dt} \approx (E-B)*[-2p+2p^2-p^2+p_2p^2]$$

$$\frac{dE_w}{dt} \approx (E-B)*[(1+p_2)p^2-2p]$$

Experimental Results.

To evaluate our bounds and approximation, we conducted a series of experiments on static, DCSP instances using DSA. For our test setup, we chose to use $n = 200$ variables, with the domain of each variable v_i containing $|D_i| = 3$ values. We chose a fixed value of $p_2 = 0.33$ and varied the density of the problems $p_1 = \{0.02, 0.023, 0.027\}$. We tested DSA with probability settings in $p = \{0.3, 0.5, 0.7\}$, and for each combination of p_1 and p tested 100 random instances, measuring the number of constraint violations at each step. This resulted in 900 test runs overall.

```
when received (ok?, x_j, d_j) do
   add (x_j, d_j) to agent_view;
   when received ok? from all neighbors do
      send_improve;
      mode ← wait_improve;
   end do;
end do;

procedure send_improve
   compute best assignment and improve value;
   new_value ← best assignment;
   my_improve ← improve;
   send improve to neighbors;
end send_improve;
```

Figure 7: The procedures of the *wait_ok?* mode in Distributed Breakout.

Once we collected the data, we analyzed it using the method described at the end of section 2. The result of this analysis is a set of values for A and B, which can be seen in table 1. The values in this table show two general trends. First, as the problems become more dense, the problem solvers produce worse solutions, and do so at a slower pace. Both of these are to be expected, since denser problems decrease the likelihood of a variable being improvable at each step, and result in more constraints that cannot be satisfied. Interestingly, though, as the value of p increases, the convergence rate decreases (recall that smaller rate values mean faster convergence). Thus, despite the associated increase in the number of collisions that occur, the DSA with $p = 0.7$ operates faster than DSA with $p = 0.3$ and is therefore expected to perform better in highly dynamic setting.

	Density					
	0.201		0.023		0.027	
	A	**B**	**A**	**B**	**A**	**B**
DSA 0.3	2.47	24.89	2.70	32.96	2.94	45.81
DSA 0.5	1.51	24.92	1.58	32.17	1.72	44.37
DSA 0.7	1.14	23.00	1.20	30.90	1.28	42.17

Table 1: Measured values for convergence rate and point for DSA.

Using these values of A and B, we next plotted the convergence rate function along with our lower bound, upper bound, and approximation functions (see figure 6). Because of space limitations, we only show the graphs for density $p_1 = 0.027$, but the results for other configurations are similar.

These graphs show a plot of the expected energy change as a function of the current energy. In all of these graphs, the lower and upper bounds bracket the function fit as expected. The estimates that these bounds provide naturally diverge from the actual behavior considerably as the energy of the problem increases, since they are overly pessimistic and optimistic, respectively. The approximation function does fairly well at predicting the behavior of the protocol. For low values of p, the function tends to overestimate the energy reduction that is obtained, likely because it underestimates the impact of collisions, and overestimates the impact for single variable changes (again, it assumes that the change will fix the violation). As the value of p increases, the estimate becomes more accurate, and by the time the value of $p = 0.7$, we see that it is slightly underestimating the true value.

3.2 Distributed Breakout Algorithm

The Distributed Breakout Algorithm (DBA) [11] is a distributed

```
when received (improve, x_j, improve, eval) do
   record message;
   when received improve from all neighbors do
      send_ok;
      clear agent_view;
      mode ← wait_ok;
   end do;
end do;

procedure send_ok
   if my_improve is better than all of my neighbors
      current_value ← new_value;
   end if;
   when in a quasi-local-minimum do
      increase the weights on all violated constraints;
   end do;
   send (ok?, x_i, current_value) to neighbors;
end send_ok;
```

Figure 8: The procedures of the *wait_improve?* mode in Distributed Breakout.

adaptation of the centralized Breakout algorithm [9]. DBA works by alternating between two modes. The first mode (see figure 7) is called the *wait_ok?* mode. During this mode, agents collect *ok?* messages from each of their neighbors containing their current variable assignments. The agents then calculate the best new value for their own variables, along with the improvement to their local evaluation. The agents then send out *improve?* messages containing this improvement value to each of their neighbors and change to the *wait_improve?* mode.

In the *wait_improve* mode (see figure 8), the agents collect *improve?* messages from each of their neighbors. When all of these messages are received, the agents check to see if they have the best improvement amongst their neighbors. If an agent does, it is allowed to change its value. Finally, the agents send *ok?* messages to each of their neighbors and change back to the *wait_ok?* mode. The algorithm starts up with each agent sending *ok?* messages and going into the *wait_ok?* mode. By repeating this protocol again and again, the agents hill-climb to a better state.

However, like all hill-climbing algorithms, DBA is prone to getting trapped in local minima, so it employs a rather unusual escape mechanism. If an agent has at least one violated constraint, is not able to change its value to remove the violations, and has no neighbor that reports it can improve, then it is in a state called a quasi-local-minimum (QLM). A QLM is a weaker condition than what is typically thought of as a local minimum, since QLM *can* occur when the search is not in a true local minima. However, if the search is in a true local minima, it is guaranteed to be detected by the QLM mechanism.

When an agent believes it is in a quasi-local-minimum (QLM), it increases the weights on each of its violated constraints, placing higher priority on solving constraints with a higher weight. The DBA protocol without the QLM escape mechanism is sometimes referred to as the Maximum Gain Message (MGM) protocol [2].

Because of the strict locking mechanism employed in the algorithm, the overall behavior of the agents is to simultaneously switch back and forth between the two modes. If one or more of the agents reacts slowly or messages are delayed, the neighboring agents wait for the correct message to arrive. This also makes the protocol's communication usage very predictable, since in each mode, each agent sends exactly one message to each of its neighbors. Thus, if there are m constraints, exactly $2m$ messages are transmitted during each step.

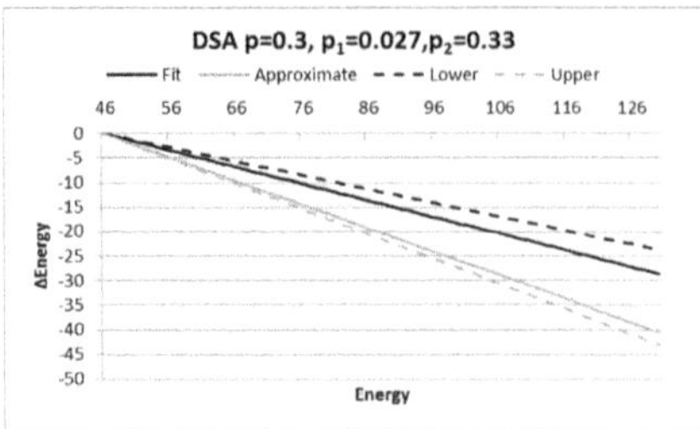

(a) DSA 0.3

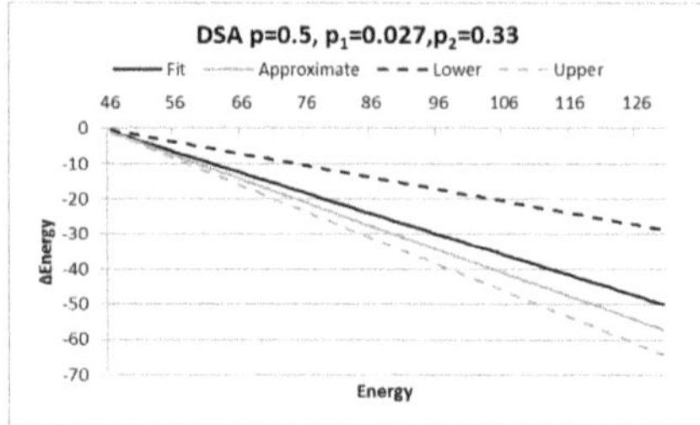

(b) DSA 0.5

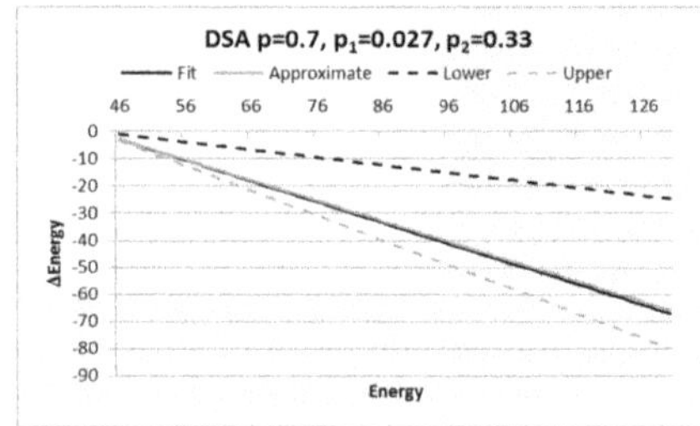

(c) DSA 0.7

Figure 6: Comparison of function fit versus lower, upper, and approximate functions for DSA

Protocol Analysis.

DBA is a more complex algorithm than DSA, but its analysis actually proves to be much simpler. We began our analysis by observing that because of the strict locking mechanism, the average degree of the problem is the limiting factor on the convergence rate. Taking a variable-centric view of the analysis, we started by estimating the maximum number of agents that can move during a single time step. Since only one out of a set of neighbors can move, we have:

$$moves \leq \frac{n}{degree} = \frac{n}{\frac{m}{n}} = \frac{n^2}{m}$$

Since we know how many variables are going to change, we need only estimate the impact of those changes. And since this is an upper bound approximation, we can assume that if a variable changes its value, all of the currently unsatisfied constraints that could be satisfied will be. This is not a particularly bad estimate, because we know that DBA will choose to change the variables that lead to the greatest overall reduction in energy.

To calculate the energy decrease for a single variable change, we only need to know how many constraints the variable has (which is simply the average degree), and the probability that each of those constraints is currently violated (i.e., the average energy of each constraint, which is the current energy divided by the number of constraints). However, since we know that we have to account for any unsatisfiable constraints in the problem, we subtract the convergence point from the current energy level.

What this leads to is that change in energy is the number of variable changes times the number of constraints per variable times the probability that those constraints can become satisfied. The formula is therefore:

$$\frac{dE_w}{dt} \leq \frac{n^2}{m} * \frac{m}{n} * \frac{E-B}{m} = \frac{n(E-B)}{m}$$

This formula is remarkably satisfying because it can easily be rewritten as $\frac{dE_w}{dt} \leq \frac{E-B}{degree}$, which says that the convergence rate is directly limited by the average degree of the problem, as we expect.

Experimental Results.

In a similar way to how we tested our bounds and approximation of DSA, we conducted a series of experiments on DBA. As before, we used $n = 200$ variables each with $|D_i| = 3$ values. We used a fixed value of $p_2 = 0.33$, and varied the density of the problems $p_1 = \{0.02, 0.023, 0.027\}$. For each of the values of p_1, we generated 100 random instances, and counted the number of constraint violations at each step. This test series consisted of 300 runs.

Following our standard procedure, we fit the results to Newton's cooling equation, and derived values for both A and B. These values are presented in table 2. Like DSA, DBA is affected by the density of the problem. However, density has a greater impact on the convergence rate of DBA than it does on DSA. This can be easily understood when we consider that density and degree are closely related, and that the higher the degree, the fewer the number of variables that can change during a time step.

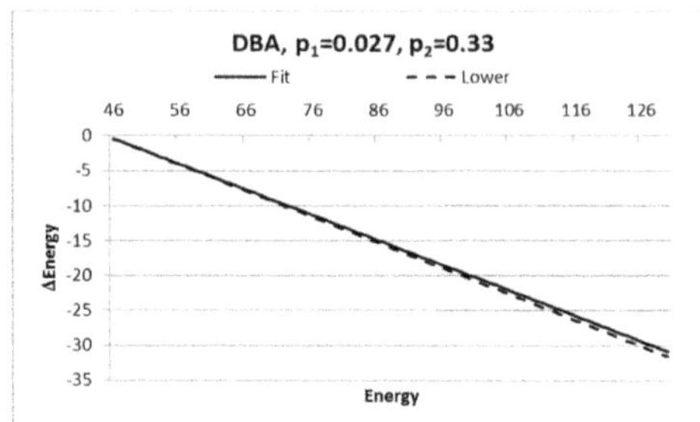

Figure 9: Comparison of function fit versus lower bound for DBA

	Density					
	0.201		0.023		0.027	
	A	**B**	**A**	**B**	**A**	**B**
DBA	1.97	24.92	2.37	33.54	2.77	44.72

Table 2: Measured values for convergence rate and point for DBA.

In figure 9, the results of the comparison between the fit and the upper bounds is shown. The graph clearly shows a very tight bounds on the actual performance of the protocol. Because our upper-bound analysis provides such a tight match, we decided not to pursue creating lower bounds or a tighter approximation.

3.3 Effects of Problem Size

As we mentioned in the introduction of this paper, our motivation for this work is to reduce the amount of empirical evaluation needed to estimate a protocol's performance. The work of Mailler and Zheng made it possible to eliminate one parameter by creating a procedure for estimating performance in dynamic environments. Our analysis thus far has shown that we can estimate the value for the parameter A given the value of p, for DSA, or the average degree for DBA. What's interesting about that statement is that our equations for convergence rate are all scale-independent. This is an important finding, because it says that if we determine the rate for a problem of one size, then as long as we don't change the degree or tightness of the problem as we scale it, the convergence rate A should remain unchanged.

To verify this interpretation, we ran another series of tests, varying the size of the problem from $n = 25 - 200$, for three set-

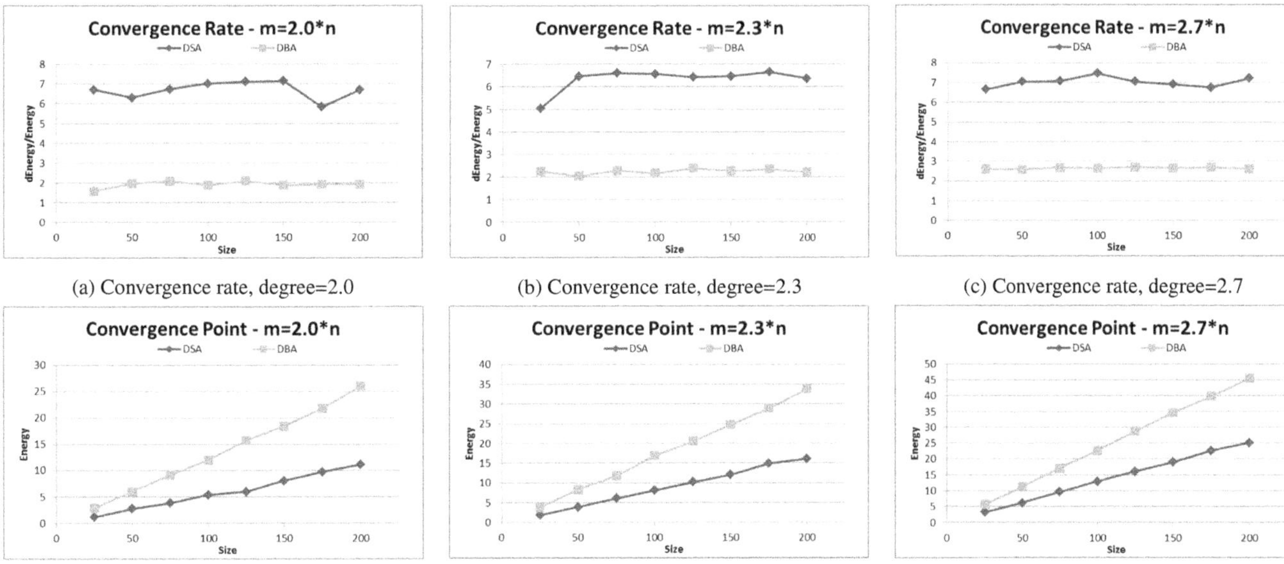

(a) Convergence rate, degree=2.0

(b) Convergence rate, degree=2.3

(c) Convergence rate, degree=2.7

(d) Convergence point, degree=2.0

(e) Convergence point, degree=2.3

(f) Convergence point, degree=2.7

Figure 10: Convergence rate and point versus problem size, for three problem degrees.

tings of average degree $\frac{m}{n} = \{2.0, 2.3, 2.7\}$ and a fixed tightness $p_2 = 0.33$. As in our previous experiments, we generated 100 random instances, produced performance profiles, and fit those profiles to Newton's cooling function. The results can be seen in figure 10.

As we suspected, the convergence rate of the protocols is unaffected by scale. Intuitively, this makes perfect sense, because both of these protocols work in a parallel manner. If we assume that on average the energy of the system is evenly spread, then it allows the agents to work nearly independently of one another.

When looking at the convergence point, another trend becomes apparent— the value of B scales linearly with the size of the problem. To understand why this occurs, consider two independent DCSPs, P_1 and P_2, that have the same values for n, each $|D_i|$, p_1, and p_2, but not necessarily the same structure. Now since P_1 and P_2 are statistically the same, if we ran DSA on them both, we would expect that the convergence points of the final solutions DSA produces, B_1 and B_2, would be, on average, the same.

Now, it is well understood that if you combine two independent thermodynamic systems together, the energy of the combined system is the sum of the energies of the individual systems, due to the law of conservation of energy [4]. In a similar manner, if we combine P_1 with P_2 without changing the ratio of constraints to variables, then the convergence point would become $B_1 + B_2 = 2 * B_1$.

For us, the implication is simple. If we take a static DCSP instance with a known degree, tightness, and domain size and compute the value for B, then we can extrapolate the value for B for any size problem. Combining this with our analysis, we can then recreate the performance profile, and predict the protocols' behavior in dynamic environments, without needing to perform additional empirical testing.

4. CONCLUSION AND DISCUSSIONS

In this paper, we made use of a thermodynamic analysis of DynDCSPs to develop analytical predictions—both approximations and bounds—for the behavior of DSA and DBA, two well-known algorithms for the problem. Through experimentation, we showed that these analyses are able to predict the algorithms' behavior with a high degree of accuracy. Having the ability to generate close predictions of convergence rate and convergence point is a huge asset to the development of DCSP systems, since it allows us to form a reasonable expectation of system behavior in advance of actual testing. Insight into the algorithms' convergence rate is also especially important, since it allows us to understand how they will behave in dynamic systems.

We also found that convergence point and convergence rate parameters, generated by testing with a single problem instance, can be reliably predicted for other problem sizes—convergence point increases linearly, while convergence rate generally remains constant. This is important, since it means that we are now able to derive parameters from testing with a single problem instance that allow us to accurately extrapolate algorithm behaviors for any size problem with the same density and parameter values.

In future work, we'd like to develop similar analyses for other well-known DCSP algorithms. This type of analysis is naturally deeply dependent on finding useful approaches based on each algorithm's structure, but we are confident that our current work provides a strong foothold to help approach this later research. We also plan to address the second-order dynamics of DCSPs—the effects of changes in density and tightness on algorithm behavior. This analysis will aid us in developing a fuller understanding of DCSP algorithms, and afford us power to extrapolate over a much wider variety of problem instances. Additionally, we'd like to look at a more formal development of hard bounds on these algorithms, as well as ways that we could tighten our overall approximations.

5. ACKNOWLEDGMENTS

We are deeply appreciative of the help of the National Science Foundation and the Air Force Research Laboratory for funding our work on this research.

This material is based on research sponsored by the Air Force Research Laboratory, under agreement number FA8750-13-1-0124 and the National Science Foundation under Grant No. IIS-1350671. The U.S. Government is authorized to reproduce and distribute reprints for Governmental purposes notwithstanding any copyright notation thereon. The views and conclusions contained herein are those of the authors and should not be interpreted as necessarily representing the official policies or endorsements, either expressed or implied, of the Air Force Research Laboratory or the U.S. Government.

REFERENCES

[1] F. Bacchus and P. van Beek. On the conversion between non-binary constraint satisfaction problems. *Proceedings of the 15th Nat'l/10th Conf. on Artificial Intelligence/Innovative Applications of Artificial Intelligence*, pages 311–318, 1998.

[2] E. Bowring, J. P. Pearce, C. Portway, M. Jain, and M. Tambe. On k-optimal distributed constraint optimization algorithms: New bounds and algorithms. In *Proceedings of the 7th International Joint Conference on Autonomous Agents and Multiagent Systems - Volume 2*, pages 607–614, 2008.

[3] R. Dechter and A. Dechter. Belief maintenance in dynamic constraint networks. In *Proceedings of the 6th National Conference on Artificial Intelligence (AAAI-88)*, pages 37–42, 1988.

[4] R. Fitzpatrick. *Thermodynamics and Statistical Mechanics: An intermediate level course*. Lulu Enterprises, Inc., 2006.

[5] S. Fitzpatrick and L. Meertens. *Distributed Sensor Networks: A Multiagent Perspective*, chapter Distributed Coordination Through Anarchic Optimization, pages 257–294. Kluwer Academic Publishers, 2003.

[6] R. Mailler. Comparing two approaches to dynamic, distributed constraint satisfaction. In *Proceedings of the Fourth International Joint Conference on Autonomous Agents and MultiAgent Systems (AAMAS)*, pages 1049–1056, 2005.

[7] R. Mailler and H. Zheng. A new analysis method for dynamic, distributed constraint satisfaction. In *Proceedings of the 2014 International Joint Conference on Autonomous Agents and MultiAgent Systems (AAMAS)*, pages 901–908, 2014.

[8] A. Meisels, I. Razgon, E. Kaplansky, and R. Zivan. Comparing performance of distributed constraints processing algorithms. In *Proc. AAMAS-2002 Workshop on Distributed Constraint Reasoning DCR*, pages 86–93, 2002.

[9] P. Morris. The breakout method for escaping local minima. In *Proceedings of the Eleventh National Conference on Artificial Intelligence*, pages 40–45, 1993.

[10] I. Wolfram Research. Mathematica version 8.0, 2010.

[11] M. Yokoo and K. Hirayama. Distributed breakout algorithm for solving distributed constraint satisfaction problems. In *Proceedings of the 2nd Int'l Conf. on Multiagent Systems*, pages 401–408, 1996.

[12] W. Zhang, G. Wang, Z. Xing, and L. Wittenburg. Chapter 13: A comparative study of distributed constraint algorithms. *Distributed Sensor Networks: A Multiagent Perspective*, 2003.

Efficient Inter-Team Task Allocation in RoboCup Rescue

Marc Pujol-Gonzalez
Jesus Cerquides
IIIA-CSIC
Campus de la UAB
Bellaterra, Spain
mpujol@iiia.cisc.es
cerquide@iiia.cisc.es

Alessandro Farinelli
Computer Science Department
University of Verona
Ca Vignal 2, Strada le Grazie 15
Verona, Italy
alessandro.farinelli@univr.it

Pedro Meseguer
Juan A. Rodriguez-Aguilar
IIIA-CSIC
Campus de la UAB
Bellaterra, Spain
pedro@iiia.cisc.es
jar@iiia.cisc.es

ABSTRACT

The coordination of cooperative agents involved in rescue missions is an important open research problem. We consider the RoboCup Rescue Simulation (RCS) challenge, where teams of agents perform urban rescue operations. Previous approaches typically cast such problem as separate single-team allocation problems. However, different teams have complementary capabilities, and therefore some kind of inter-team coordination is desirable for high-quality solutions. Our contribution considers inter-team coordination using Max-Sum. We present a methodology that allows teams in RCS to efficiently assess joint allocations. Furthermore, we show how to reduce the algorithm's computational complexity from exponential to polynomial time by using Tractable High Order Potentials. To the best of our knowledge this is the first time where it has been shown that MS can be run in polynomial time in the RCS challenge without relaxing the problem. Experiments with fire brigades and police agents show that teams employing inter-team coordination are significantly more effective than uncoordinated teams. Moreover, the evaluation shows that our BMS and THOPs method achieves up to 2.5 times better results than other state-of-the-art methods.

Categories and Subject Descriptors

I.2.11 [**Artificial Intelligence**]: Distributed Artificial Intelligence—*multiagent systems, coherence and coordination*

General Terms

Algorithms, Performance

Keywords

Multi-agent task allocation, Max-Sum, RoboCup Rescue

1. INTRODUCTION

In many practical applications, such as rescue, surveillance and environmental monitoring, agents with different capabilities must cooperate in dynamic and unpredictable environments [23]. Hence, the coordination problem faced by teams of rescue agents has been addressed in the literature from various perspectives and with a wide variety of solution techniques.

Appears in: *Proceedings of the 14th International Conference on Autonomous Agents and Multiagent Systems (AAMAS 2015), Bordini, Elkind, Weiss, Yolum (eds.), May 4–8, 2015, Istanbul, Turkey.*

However, most previous work either proposes approaches to enable teamwork between heterogeneous agents [25, 13, 10] or focuses on specific coordination techniques for a single team of agents (e.g., task assignment [22, 15] or resource allocation [12]).

In particular, a standard model for the task allocation problem in the context of rescue agent teams is the Extended Generalized Assignment Problem [22, 3]. However, such model cannot properly encode synergies and interferences among agents working on related tasks. For instance, EGAP cannot express that it is possible for two agents to perform the same task, but less desirable than letting them perform separate tasks (because otherwise they could interfere on each other). Since capturing such synergies is essential for effective cooperation in rescue missions, other works model such problem as a coalition formation problem [19, 20]. However, this approach suffers from the exponential growth of possible coalitions with the number of agents, hence its application to realistic, large-scale rescue scenarios is problematic.

Recently, a body of work focuses on ad-hoc teamwork [24, 9], where a team of agents must coordinate with very little or no prior information about their team mates (e.g., without having a shared communication protocol or knowing each other capabilities). Here, we take a different approach and focus on specific task assignment techniques for agents that might be part of different teams but have a relevant amount of prior information on each other capabilities, which is the typical case for urban rescue scenarios.

Task assignment problems in such settings can be conveniently formalized as a Distributed Constraint Optimization problem, as proposed in [8], where agents must compute a joint assignment that maximizes the team performance. For example, in the rescue domain, fire brigades must decide which fire to tackle so to mitigate damages to the buildings and civilians. While DCOPs offer a wealth of solution techniques, the dynamic nature of our reference scenario and the strict time constraints under which agents must operate favor the use of heuristic solutions [29, 11, 4]

An important advantage of using the DCOP model is that there exist several readily available heuristic approaches that typically provide good quality solutions. Moreover, the model is inherently distributed, providing the necessary robustness for such scenarios. In this perspective, we observe that the Max-Sum (MS) algorithm has been applied to a significant variety of application domains with successful results. Some examples include UAVs task assignment [2], Radar coordination [6], and task assignment in RoboCup Rescue [19, 8].

However, the use of MS for large scale applications and real-time constraints, such as the emergency response scenario we consider here, is significantly limited by the computational bottleneck associated with the message update operations. In particular, the MS algorithm has a computational complexity $O(d^n)$, where d is the number of tasks that each agent may perform (i.e., the size of associated variable domain) and n is the number of agents that can perform a given task (i.e., the arity of the associated constraint). Such issue has been addressed with various approaches that includes modifications to the algorithm, i.e., the Fast-Max-Sum approach [19], or simplifications of the DCOP model, i.e., the pruning approach proposed in [8] or the function meta reasoning method proposed in [28].

Specifically, the Fast Max-Sum (Fast MS) algorithm proposed in [19] is equivalent (in terms of solution quality) to the MS approach, but reduces the computational effort from $O(d^n)$ to $O(2^n)$ (and the message size from d to 2). However, the computation remains exponential and hence it can not be applied to scenarios where the number of agent that can execute the same task is high, as it is the case in our fire-fighter coordination problem, where each fire-fighting unit can potentially work on every possible fire. In contrast, the approaches that simplify the DCOP model [8, 28], essentially consider, in the message update phase, only a sub-set of the possible agents that can perform a task while completely ignoring the others. While this has the important benefit of reducing the arity of the constraint (and hence decouple the computational complexity of the message update phase from the number of agent in the system), such approaches can not guarantee that the quality of the returned solution is the same as the one that the MS approach working on the original model would provide.

Now, MS originates and is widely used in the graphical models community, where its exponentiality issue was also considered simultaneously. There, Tarlow et al. have shown [26] that the computation associated to MS can be reduced to polynomial time (between $O(n)$ and $O(n \log n)$) for some specific types of factors (or constraints), known as *Tractable Higher Order Potentials* (THOPs). Crucially, this approach do not simplify the model on which the MS approach is defined. In contrast, it exploits the specific structure of THOPs hence providing a faster approach to update messages that is guaranteed to return the same solution that the standard MS approach would return. While, not all DCOP functions can be represented using THOPs, previous work [16, 17] shows that THOPS are expressive enough for several application domains.

One important contribution of this paper is to propose a THOP only model for the task allocation problem related to the RCS challenge, hence obtaining a polynomial time approach that provides the same solution of the standard MS algorithm.

Now, a distinctive feature of THOPs is that they are defined over binary variables, and hence the approach is typically named Binary Max-Sum (BMS). While BMS is a promising approach for agent coordination, modeling large coordination problem using such approach is not straightforward nor intuitive. For example, usually a modeler finds much easier to work with a single d-valued variable that encodes which fire is a firefighter servicing than with d boolean variables encoding the same information. As the size of the problem grows, these issues become more evident, hampering the ability of the modeler to accurately do his work. Hence, it is crucial to devise effective design methodologies for BMS to become more widespread.

Against this background, in this paper we take an important step in that direction, by using BMS to enable effective multi-team coordination in the rescue scenario. Although the idea of coordinating different teams by means of coordination variables is not new (for instance in the loosely coupled planning literature [1], or the cooperative control community [21]), no methodology has been proposed up-to-date for building multi-team coordination models using BMS. To illustrate the methodology, we consider the realistic scenario represented by the RCS challenge, where a team of police officers and a team of firefighters must join forces to mitigate damages to a city after a natural disaster.

Furthermore our work shows that typical inter-team coordination interactions can be effectively modeled by means of THOPs allowing MS messages to be assessed in polynomial time in such complex scenarios.

The main contributions of this work are the following:

- We develop a THOP-only model for the firefighters task allocation problem associated to the RoboCup Simulation (RCS) domain. Despite previous work in this area [8, 19], to the best of our knowledge this is the first time where it has been shown that MS can be run in polynomial time for such task without simplifying the associated model (i.e., the DCOP representation).
- We present a methodology that eases the design of THOP-only models for large problems with several (interrelated) functional areas such as rescue teams. Following this methodology, we develop a THOP-only multi-team coordination model for the police and firefighters RCS problem.
- We empirically show that BMS obtains better results than other state-of-the-art DCOP algorithms (operating on a standard DCOP model), preventing more than twice as much damage to the city.

The rest of the paper is organized as follows. Section 2 provides background on MS and THOPs. Section 3 presents the RCS problem we tackle. Section 4 describes how the DCOP model to coordinate firefighters from [8] can be mapped to a THOP-only model. Section 5 presents our methodology to handle large problems, and develops a complete model for the police and firefighter forces. Section 6 reports our empirical findings. Finally, Section 7 concludes the paper.

2. BACKGROUND

MS is an approximate optimization algorithm that has been applied to different coordination problems with good empirical results. In this section we review MS and explain how, in some specific cases, its complexity can be reduced from exponential to polynomial time.

Let $T = \langle t_1, \dots, t_n \rangle$ be a sequence of variables, with each variable t_i taking values in a finite set $\mathcal{D}_i$, its *domain*. The joint domain $\mathcal{D}_T$ is the cartesian product of the domain of each variable. We use $\mathbf{t_i}$ to refer to a possible assignment of t_i, that is $\mathbf{t_i} \in \mathcal{D}_i$ and $\mathbf{T}$ to refer to a possible joint assignment for variables in T, that is $\mathbf{T} \in \mathcal{D}_T$. Given a sequence of variables $W \subseteq T$, a factor c is a function $c : \mathcal{D}_W \to [-\infty, \infty)$. We refer to the variables in the scope of c as T_c. The set of factors of the problem is denoted by C. A function $g : \mathcal{D}_X \to \mathbb{R}$ is said to *decompose additively* if it can be broken as a sum of local terms, that is, whenever there is a set of local terms F (referred to as the additive decomposition F) such that $g(\mathbf{X}) = \sum_{f \in F} f(\mathbf{X}_f)$,

As an example, say we have three variables, x_1 with domain $\mathcal{D}_1 = \{0, 1\}$, x_2 with domain $\mathcal{D}_2 = \{0, 1, 2\}$ and x_3 with domain $\mathcal{D}_3 = \{1, 2\}$. The possible states for x_1 are $\mathbf{x}_1 \in \mathcal{D}_1 = \{0, 1\}$. We can define the function $g(x_1, x_2, x_3) = x_1 \cdot x_1 + x_1 \cdot x_2 - x_2 \cdot x_3$. It is easy to see that g decomposes additively by taking $F = \{f_1, f_2, f_3\}$, where $f_1(x_1) = x_1 \cdot x_1$, $f_2(x_1, x_2) = x_1 \cdot x_2$, and $f_3(x_2, x_3) = -(x_2 \cdot x_3)$.

The MS algorithm provides an approximate solution to the problem of maximizing a function that decomposes additively as a sum of functions with smaller scope:

$$\begin{array}{lll} \text{maximize} & g(\mathbf{X}) = \sum_{c \in C} c(\mathbf{T}_c) & \\ \text{subject to} & \mathbf{t}_i \in \mathcal{D}_i & \forall i \in \{1, \ldots, n\}\,, \end{array}$$

where $\mathbf{T_c}$ contains the values assigned by $\mathbf{T}$ to the variables in the scope of factor c.

MS operates on the so-called *factor graph*, a bipartite graph between variables and factors. It provides an approximate solution in two stages. First, messages are sent from variables to factors and from factors to variables. This step is repeated until the messages no longer change or a specified number of iterations is reached. After that, MS determines the best state for each variable independently.

At the first stage, MS assesses the message from variable t to factor c as

$$\mu_{t \to c}(\mathbf{t}) = \sum_{c' \in \mathcal{N}(t) \setminus \{c\}} \mu_{c' \to t}(\mathbf{t})\,, \tag{1}$$

where $\mathcal{N}(t)$ stands for the factors that have variable x in its scope and $\mu_{c' \to t}$ stands for the last message received by variable t from factor c'. MS assesses the message from c to t as

$$\mu_{c \to t}(\mathbf{t}) = \max_{\mathbf{W}} \left(c(\mathbf{t}, \mathbf{W}) + \sum_{w \in W} \mu_{w \to c}(\mathbf{w}) \right)\,, \tag{2}$$

where W is the set of variables in the scope of factor c excluding t, and $\mathbf{W}$ is a joint assignment for the variables in W.

At the second stage, MS assesses the preferred assignment for each variable as

$$\mathbf{t}^* = \arg\max_{\mathbf{t}} \sum_{c \in \mathcal{N}(t)} \mu_{c \to t}(\mathbf{t}).$$

The standard MS algorithm can be binarized as follows. A standard variable with d possible values becomes d boolean variables, all connected by a new factor that assures that only one boolean variable will be active. A standard factor involving k standard variables has (in the worst case) d^k entries. With boolean variables the number of entries increases up to $2^{d \times k}$. It is clear that both, standard MS and BMS have the same expressive power and can solve the same kind of problems.

Now, the computational bottleneck for MS is in equation 2, that takes time exponential in the number of variables in the scope of the factor. Recently, several works [16, 17, 26] have shown that for some specific types of factors, called Tractable Higher Order Potentials (THOPs), this time can be reduced to polynomial provided that all the variables in the scope are binary. In the following we consider binary variables and say that a variable is active (resp. inactive) if it is assigned to value 1 (resp. 0). It is worth noting that not every factor can be expressed using THOPs. However, it turns out that the RCS coordination problem we consider here can be formulated using THOPs only.

In particular, here we will employ two types of THOPs, *cardinality potentials* and *composite potentials*. Cardinality Potentials (CP) are factors whose value for an assignment depends on how many variables are active in that assignment, but does not depend on which particular variables are active. In general a CP can be expressed as $c(\mathbf{T_c}) = c'(n_c(\mathbf{T_c}))$, where $n_c(\mathbf{T_c}) = \sum_{t_i \in T_c} \mathbf{t_i}$ stands for the number of active variables in assignment $\mathbf{T_c}$. Tarlow et al. have shown [26] that for CPs, messages from equation 2 can be assessed in time $O(N \log N)$ time, where N is the number of variables in the scope of the factor. Particular cases of CPs are strict cardinality constraints such as *OneAndOnlyOne*, *AtMostOne* and *AllZeros*. Tarlow et al. [26] note that for some of these strict cardinality constraints, even more efficient algorithms to assess the messages are available, and, in particular, Pujol-Gonzalez et al. [17] shows that for *OneAndOnlyOne factors* the messages can be assessed in time $O(N)$. Finally, Tarlow et al. [26] also propose a technique for the composition of THOPs that allows to efficiently assess messages for any factor that can be constructed by the context-specific composition of smaller THOPs. These THOPs are known as *composite potentials*.

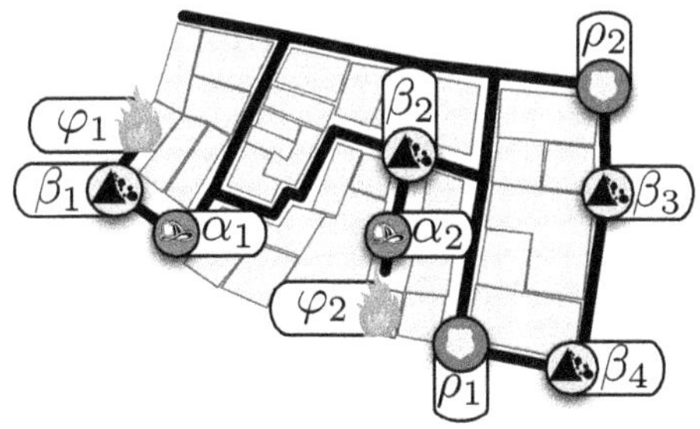

Figure 1: Example scenario.

3. PROBLEM DESCRIPTION

The RCS Platform is a benchmarking environment that simulates an urban search and rescue scenario where rescue forces (police patrols, ambulances and fire brigades) must coordinate their actions. Specifically, police patrols can unblock roads, fire brigades can extinguish fires, and ambulance agents can rescue trapped civilians. RCS creates a realistic simulation environment that presents significant aspects of dynamism (e.g., fires spread across a city), uncertainty (e.g., the behavior of fires is determined by a number of factors that may not be perfectly sensed or modeled), and issues of scale (e.g., tens of rescue agents and possibly hundreds of fires in a large urban area) [7].

In this paper we focus on the coordination problem of fire brigades, police patrols, and their interactions. Regarding fire brigades, a first element to consider is travel time: the closer a fire brigade is to a fire, the sooner they will be able to work on it. Moreover, the more fire brigades acting on one fire, the faster they will contain it. However, beyond a certain number of fire brigades, the contribution of each additional one is less significant. Now, a key issue for the fire fighting activity is that fires evolve and spread over time. A crucial insight on fire spreading is that new fires are more likely to extend than older ones, and older fires are fierier. Hence, fire brigades should try to prioritize new fires to prevent them from spreading as much as possible. Overall, fire brigades must cooperate to ensure that an adequate number of agents is allocated to each fire considering fire fieriness and travel time. Unlike fires, road blockades do not evolve over time unless some agent is acting on them. Moreover, in the version we used (2013), the simulation defines that having more police agents working on the same blockade is not beneficial. Hence, police patrols should spread out as much as possible to free roads as fast as they can.

Now, when we consider the whole picture, police patrols and fire brigades must coordinate their actions so that fire brigades can tackle important fires, which might be not reachable due to blockades, and police patrols should focus on blockades that might be far away but crucial for the fire fighting activity. For example, consider the scenario depicted in Figure 1, which will serve as a running example throughout our paper. In this scenario we have:

- two police patrols $P = \{\rho_1, \rho_2\}$ (blue circles);
- two fire brigades $A = \{\alpha_1, \alpha_2\}$ (red circles);

- four blockades $B = \{\beta_1, \beta_2, \beta_3, \beta_4\}$ (yellow circles) that prevent agents from transiting the road they are blocking; and
- two ignition points $F = \{\varphi_1, \varphi_2\}$, which are buildings that are on fire at the beginning of the simulation.

When considering the police patrol coordination problem without taking the fire fighting activity into account, a good allocation for this scenario would be $(\rho_1 \to \beta_4), (\rho_2 \to \beta_3)$ because both agents work on their closest blockade. However, if we consider the overall goal of the rescue agents (including fire fighters), a better allocation would be $(\rho_1 \to \beta_2), (\rho_2 \to \beta_1)$, enabling fire brigade agents to choose which fire to attend at their will.

4. THE FIRE BRIGADES TEAM MODEL

In this section we develop a THOP-only model for the coordination of the firefighters team, disregarding police forces entirely. With this aim, we first present an improved version of the general DCOP model in [8]. Thereafter we show how this model can be binarized, thus allowing us to run BMS instead of MS and reducing the complexity from exponential to linearithmic time.

4.1 DCOP model

Solving the firefighters problem amounts to deciding which fire should each fire brigade attend. These decisions can be encoded by a set of decision variables $Y = \{y_a | a \in A\}$, where each variable y_a takes values in F. Note that $y_{\alpha_1} = \varphi_2$ means that brigade α_1 is assigned to fire φ_2. Thus, our objective is to find an assignment $\mathbf{Y}$ that maximizes the team utility $u(\mathbf{Y})$, that is

$$\begin{array}{lll} \text{maximize} & u(\mathbf{Y}) & \\ \text{subject to} & \mathbf{y}_a \in F. & \forall a \in A \end{array}$$

In a DCOP model, the team's utility is expected to be decomposed as a sum of factors. In our case, a natural decomposition is to introduce two kinds of factors:

- *fire factors*, that specify the gain obtained when firefighters are allocated to some fire; and
- *cost factors*, that specify the cost for agents to reach different fires.

Thus, our team utility is

$$u(\mathbf{Y}) = \sum_{f \in F} e_f(\mathbf{Y}) - \sum_{f \in F} \sum_{a \in A} r_{af}(\mathbf{y_a}), \quad (3)$$

where $e_f(\mathbf{Y})$ are fire factors and $r_{af}(\mathbf{y_a})$ are cost factors.

4.1.1 Fire factors

As explained in Section 3, some fires are more relevant than others. Hence, to asses $e_f(\mathbf{Y})$, we first compute a value v_f for each fire f, corresponding to the utility obtained by assigning a brigade to put it out. Next, notice that more than one brigade can be assigned to the same fire. A simple model for e_f is to multiply v_f by the number of brigades that are assigned to fire f, namely $n_f(\mathbf{Y})$. Nonetheless, depending on the fieriness and size of a fire, there is a threshold t_f in the number of fire brigades that can successfully cooperate in extinguishing it. Thus, we consider that an assignment of fire brigades to a fire f is penalized when more than t_f fire brigades are assigned to fire f. Moreover, this penalty increases with the number of additional agents beyond the threshold. Combining all these assessments, $e_f(\mathbf{Y})$ is calculated as

$$e_f(\mathbf{Y}) = v_f \cdot n_f(\mathbf{Y}) - \kappa \cdot [\max(0, n_f(\mathbf{Y}) - t_f)]^\gamma, \quad (4)$$

where $\kappa > 0$ and $\gamma \geq 1$ are arbitrary coefficients.

4.1.2 Cost factors

All fire brigades are equally capable in RCS. Thus, the cost for agents to reach each fire depends only on their distance and whether that fire is reachable or not. As a result, we evaluate the cost of assigning a brigade to a fire as proportional to the square of the distance between them.[1] Additionally, a blockade may prevent fire brigade a from reaching fire f. We discourage choosing blocked fires by introducing an additional cost M when a cannot reach f. Thus, r_{af} is assessed as

$$r_{af}(\mathbf{y_a}) = \begin{cases} \nu d_{af}^2 + o_{af} M & \text{if } \mathbf{y_a} = f \\ 0 & \text{otherwise} \end{cases}, \quad (5)$$

where d_{af} is the normalized distance between brigade a and fire f, $\nu \geq 0$ is an arbitrary coefficient, and o_{af} is a constant with value 1 when agent a cannot reach fire f or 0 otherwise.

At this point we have a DCOP model. We can now compute allocations using MS by instantiating the e_f and r_{af} factors and exchanging messages between them and the variables in Y. However, recall that computing a factor's messages in MS takes exponential time on the number of variables involved in that factor. Because the e_f factors depend on all of the problem's variables, running MS on this model takes an exponential time on the number of fire brigades. From this follows that for most scenarios MS can not compute a solution within the one second time limit enforced by the RoboCup simulator.

4.2 THOP-only model

Next we show how to exactly encode the previous model in a binary form and only using THOPs. As a result, we will be able to run BMS in polynomial, instead of exponential, time. With this aim, we first split each decision variable y_a into $|F|$ binary variables z_{af}. Variable z_{af} is active (set to 1) in a solution whenever agent a is assigned to fire f, and it is inactive (set to 0) otherwise. Unlike our representation above, with this set of binary variables we can encode that a single brigade is assigned to two or more different fires simultaneously. Hence, we must add a set of constraints (one per brigade) to prevent this from happening:

$$\sum_{f \in F} \mathbf{z_{af}} = 1 \quad \forall a \in A\,. \quad (6)$$

With a slight abuse of notation, we now redefine the factors of the DCOP model to operate over the binary variables in Z instead of the n-ary variables in Y. Likewise equation (3), the utility function $u(\mathbf{Z})$ is split into fire factors e_f and cost factors r_{af}. The binarized versions of the utility functions in equations (4) and (5) are the following:

$$e_f(\mathbf{Z_{.f}}) = v_f \cdot n_f(\mathbf{Z_{.f}}) - \kappa \cdot [\max(0, n_f(\mathbf{Z_{.f}}) - t_f)]^\gamma \quad (7)$$

$$r_{af}(\mathbf{z_{af}}) = \mathbf{z_{af}}(\nu d_{af}^2 + o_{af} M) \quad (8)$$

where $Z_{.f} = \{z_{af} | a \in A\}$ is the set of variables that relate to fire f.

At this point, we can represent the entire firefighters coordination problem as the following optimization problem:

$$\begin{array}{lll} \text{maximize} & \sum_{f \in F} e_f(\mathbf{Z_{.f}}) - \sum_{f \in F} \sum_{a \in A} r_{af}(\mathbf{z_{af}}) & \\ \text{subject to} & \sum_{f \in F} \mathbf{z_{af}} = 1 & \forall a \in A \\ & \mathbf{z_{af}} \in \{0, 1\} & \forall a \in A \ \forall f \in F \end{array}$$

[1]We normalize distances so that the largest distance between any two points in a scenario is 1.

Notice that a fire factor e_f does not depend on the specific fire brigades attending it, but only on how many. Hence e_f factors fulfill the condition to be Cardinality Potentials, and their BMS messages can be computed in $O(N\log(N))$ time using the procedure described in [26]. Likewise, the consistency constraints in equation (6) are *OneAndOnlyOne* THOPs (as described in Section 2), and the agent factors r_{af} depend only on one variable.

As a result, it is now possible to assess an approximate solution to our problem by applying BMS to the THOP-only model. Furthermore, the complexity of each iteration of the algorithm is reduced from the $O(|F||F|^{|A|})$ time of MS over the DCOP model to $O(|F||A|\log|A|)$ time of BMS with the THOP-only model.

5. INTER-TEAM COORDINATION

In the rescue scenario we consider here, a single-team (i.e., the fire-fighters) can take better decisions by considering the operations of other rescue teams (i.e., the police forces). Consider our example in Figure 1. Fire brigades alone will try to avoid blocked fires. However, this completely disregards the fact that police agents will be removing blockades in the meantime so that fire brigades may be able to reach blocked fires in the near future. To capture the interdependencies between teams' decisions, we argue that it is necessary to perform inter-team coordination.

Here we present a methodology to enact inter-team coordination to make team decisions considering a shared goal. Our methodology is intended to help the designer build a representation of the complete inter-team coordination problem as a single utility function. This is not an easy endeavor because, as the number of "teams" grows, the global utility function becomes more and more complex, possibly becoming unmanageable. Our methodology proposes a modular construction of the global utility function following the next steps:

1. *Define independent coordination models* for each team involved in the inter-team coordination.

2. *Identify the coordination objects* that capture the interdependencies between teams. Such objects will serve to create coordination variables, which are meant to act as interfaces between single-team coordination models.

3. *Extend single-team coordination models* to connect them to the coordination variables.

At the end of this process, the global utility function is readily obtained by simply adding up the extended single-team coordination models into a single function. Since, as we show below, the resulting global utility function decomposes additively as a sum of functions, the teams involved will be able to apply MS to assess their decisions. A distinctive advantage of our methodology is that, once coordination variables are defined, the designer does not need to consider the whole inter-team coordination problem anymore. That is, each team independently connects its intra-team coordination model with the coordination variables. Therefore, our methodology avoids the design complexity explosion.

Next we exemplify the application of our methodology to the coordination of a team of fire brigades and a team of police forces. For space reasons, we only present the THOP model in this part.

5.1 Define Independent Coordination Models

The first step in our methodology consists in separately defining the coordination models for each individual team involved in inter-team coordination. In Section 4 we already introduced a coordination model for a team of fire brigades. Hence, we just need to develop a coordination model for a team of police forces.

The Police Team Model

Recall from section 3 that police patrols can remove blockades from roads, freeing the paths for other types of agents to move along. Hence, it is critical that policemen coordinate between them to remove blockades as quickly as possible. Thus, the coordination problem faced by the policemen team is to decide the assignment of patrols to blockade removal tasks. As in the case of fire brigades and fires, we encode an allocation of patrols to blockades using a set of binary variables $X = \{x_{pb} | p \in P, b \in B\}$ where x_{pb} is active if patrol p is assigned to blockade b and inactive otherwise. Obviously, a patrol can not remove more than one blockade at a time. Also, in RCS multiple patrols cannot work on the same blockade at the same time. Hence, the goal of the police team coordination problem is to compute the best allocation of patrols to blockades where each patrol is assigned to at most one blockade and each blockade is not assigned to more than one policemen. Thus, the following constraints must be enforced:

$$\sum_{b\in B} \mathbf{x_{pb}} \leq 1 \quad \forall p \in P \tag{9}$$

$$\sum_{p\in P} \mathbf{x_{pb}} \leq 1 \quad \forall b \in B \tag{10}$$

Similar to fire brigades, the utility of an allocation $u(\mathbf{X})$ can be decomposed in *blockade factors* e_b and *cost factors* r_{pb}, namely

$$u(\mathbf{X}) = \sum_{b\in B} e_b(\mathbf{X}_{.\mathbf{b}}) - \sum_{b\in B}\sum_{p\in P} r_{pb}(\mathbf{x_{pb}}). \tag{11}$$

Since all patrols are assumed equally capable in RCS and blockades do not have distinguishing characteristics, we assign a utility $v_B > 0$ to attending any blockade. This utility is obtained whenever some patrol is assigned to remove that blockade. Thus:

$$e_b(\mathbf{X}_{.\mathbf{b}}) = \begin{cases} v_B & \text{if } n_b(\mathbf{X}_{.\mathbf{b}}) \geq 1 \\ 0 & \text{otherwise.} \end{cases} \tag{12}$$

where $n_b(\mathbf{X}_{.b})$ is the number of patrols assigned to blockade b.

The cost of assigning a patrol p to service blockade b is analogous to what we did for the fire brigades. First, we introduce a constant o_{pb} that is 0 if the blockade is directly accessible to the patrol (no other blockade appears in the path between p and b), or 1 if the path from p to b is obstructed by some other blockade. Then the cost is proportional to the square of the distance d_{pb} between the patrol and the target blockade, with an additional penalty Q if the path is obstructed:

$$r_{pb}(\mathbf{x_{pb}}) = \mathbf{x_{pb}}(d_{pb}^2 + o_{pb}Q)\ . \tag{13}$$

With these definitions, we can represent the full police forces coordination model as the following optimization problem:

$$\begin{array}{lll} \text{maximize} & \sum_{b\in B} e_b(\mathbf{X}_{.\mathbf{b}}) - \sum_{b\in B}\sum_{p\in P} r_{pb}(\mathbf{x_{pb}}) & \\ \text{subject to} & \sum_{b\in B} \mathbf{x_{pb}} \leq 1 & \forall p \in P \\ & \sum_{p\in P} \mathbf{x_{pb}} \leq 1 & \forall b \in B \\ & \mathbf{x_{pb}} \in \{0,1\} & \forall p \in P\ \forall f \in F. \end{array}$$

This problem can also be entirely encoded with THOPs. The reasoning for the e_b and r_{pb} factors is analogous to the e_f and r_{af}

factors in the previous section. Then, the constraint in equation (9) can be mapped to a factor of the form

$$AtMostOne_p(\mathbf{X}_{.p}) = \begin{cases} 0 & \text{if } \sum_{b \in B} \mathbf{x}_{pb} \leq 1 \\ -\infty & \text{otherwise,} \end{cases} \quad (14)$$

and the same holds for the constraint in equation (10).

Although no reference to the *AtMostOne* factor as being a THOP appears in the literature, the expressions for the messages going out from it are simple and can be derived similarly to those of the *OneAndOnlyOne* factor in [17]. The assessment of the messages for an *AtMostOne* factor in a BMS iteration can then be done in time $O(|B|)$.

5.2 Identify the Coordination Objects

In our RoboCup example the coordination objects between fire brigades and policemen are blockades. On the one hand, police forces should prioritize blockades that are actually preventing fire brigades from performing their duties. On the other hand, fire brigades would like to know which blockades will be removed in the near future to make better decisions. Thus, we create a binary coordination variable c_b for each blockade b as a means of representing the coordination objects relating police patrols and fire brigades. The coordination variable for a blockade b must become active whenever the blockade is to be removed in the near future, or inactive otherwise.

In our particular example, these variables represent everything our police forces and fire brigades need to know to coordinate with each other. In other words, the coordination variables can be understood as representing the *common language* between our individual teams. Such language is intended to enable the fire brigades team and the policemen team to exchange information about their interdependencies regarding blockades.

5.3 Extending Single-Team Models

The third step in our methodology is to extend the independent team models by connecting them to the coordination variables. Hereafter we extend both the fire brigades team model and the police patrols team model to take coordination variables into account.

5.3.1 Extending the Fire Brigades Team Model

Fire brigades can modify their utility function provided that they know which blockades will be removed by police patrols. In particular, the penalty associated to a blocked fire should be removed whenever police patrols are planning to remove the blockade that prevents the fire brigade from accessing it. The interface between the fire brigades model and the coordination variables can be done by simply adding an additional factor s_{afb} whenever fire brigade a is being prevented from reaching fire f by blockade b.

$$s_{afb}(\mathbf{z_{af}}, \mathbf{c_b}) = \begin{cases} M & \text{if } \mathbf{c_b} \text{ is active and } \mathbf{z_{af}} \text{ is active} \\ 0 & \text{otherwise} \end{cases} . \quad (15)$$

The role of this factor is essentially to cancel out the penalty in equation 5 when the blockade b that is preventing fire fighter a to reach fire f is being attended by some police agent.

5.3.2 Extending the Police Team Model

The internal variables of the police team should be consistent with the semantics of the coordination variables c_b above. Specifically, c_b must only be active if some police agent is attending b. That is, variable c_b is an indicator of whether any of the variables in $X_{.b}$ are active. We can enforce this by adding a new *Indicator* factor $I_b(\mathbf{c_b}, \mathbf{X_{.b}})$ for each blockade, defined as

$$I_b(\mathbf{c_b}, \mathbf{X_{.b}}) = \begin{cases} 0 & \text{if } \mathbf{c_b} = 1 \text{ and } \sum_{p \in P} x_{pb} \geq 1 \\ 0 & \text{if } \mathbf{c_b} = 0 \text{ and } \sum_{p \in P} x_{pb} = 0 \\ -\infty & \text{otherwise} \end{cases} \quad (16)$$

I_b is not known to be a THOP, but we can derive expressions for its messages by noticing that it is a composite factor[2] where c_b defines two partitions depending on whether it is active or not. When c_b is active, the factor is a *Cardinality Potential* that yields a utility of 0 when exactly one of the $X_{.b}$ variables is active, or $-\infty$ otherwise. When c_b is inactive, the factor is an *AllInactive*[3] factor between the variables in $X_{.b}$. Since the *Indicator* potential is a composite factor, and in each of the partitions defined by c_b we have a THOP, we can efficiently assess the messages out of this factor in time $O(|B| \log |B|)$.

At this point, we can construct the global utility function for inter-team coordination. This results from adding the objective function that results from extending the fire brigades team coordination model with the objective function that results from extending the policemen team coordination model. Notice that such global utility function represents the whole problem. Since this function has been built as an additive composition of functions, we can readily apply BMS to solve the inter-team coordination problem. The execution of BMS yields an exchange of information from team to team regarding coordination variables. Messages from brigades to patrols will represent how much interested brigades are in police forces removing a blockade, whereas messages from patrols to brigades convey the police team's cost of removing a blockade.

6. EMPIRICAL EVALUATION

In this section we empirically evaluate the performance of our task allocation mechanism for the fire and police teams. With this aim, we compare BMS with the methods implemented in the RMAS-Bench [8] platform, namely DSA and Greedy. DSA is a local search algorithm executed in parallel by the participant agents. It employs a stochastic parameter, DSA_p, to control the amount of parallelism allowed while running. This simple algorithm provides surprisingly good results in many different problems, and its main advantage is that it requires very low computation and communication efforts. In contrast, Greedy represents a simple greedy allocation where each agent chooses the target that maximizes its individual utility, without coordinating at all. These algorithms operate over a standard (n-ary) DCOP model that suits them better and is equivalent to the binary one presented here. We omit the details for space reasons, but the entire source code used in this evaluation is available for the interested reader [18].

We do not compare against standard MS because as explained in [8] and in section 4.1.2, it incurs in exponential costs and fails to assess a solution within the one second time limit enforced by the simulator[4]. Although Fast MS [20] reduces this exponentiality from $O(d^n)$ to (2^n), unfortunately it is still unable to fulfill this time limit. Furthermore, note that BMS will assess the same solution as both MS and Fast MS only at a lower cost.

6.1 Experimental setup

We run experiments on the standard scenarios used in the 2013 RoboCup competition, namely Paris and Kobe. However, we dis-

[2] A composite potential in [26],

[3] The messages for the *AllInactive* factor are trivial to derive. The messages to all its variables are simply $-\infty$.

[4] As explained in section 1, they tame MS costs by relaxing version of the problem. In contrast, we work on the unrelaxed problem.

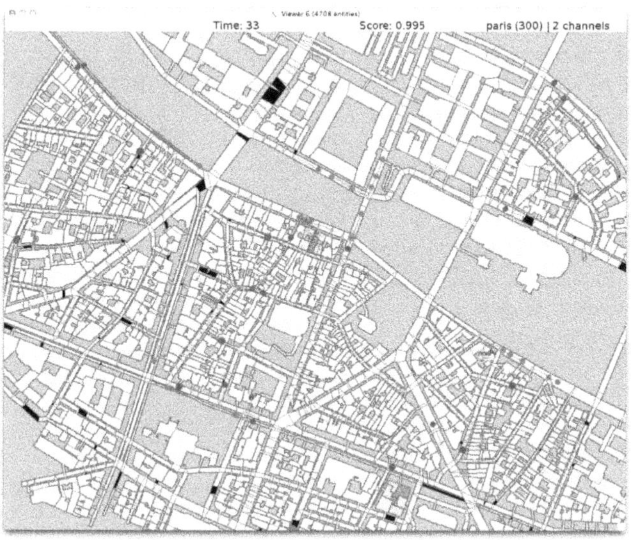

Figure 2: RCS viewer showing a running simulation. Red dots are fire brigades, blue dots are police patrols, blacked out areas are blocked roads and colored buildings are buildings on fire.

card the scenarios' elements that are irrelevant for our evaluation, i.e., everything but ignition points, police forces and fire brigades. The algorithms have one second to compute an allocation at each simulation step, and the simulation finishes either when all fires are extinguished or after 300 steps. Additionally, we randomly block 5% of the roads at the beginning of the simulation. Hence, the order in which police forces remove these blockades may have a noticeable impact on the results, depending on how well the coordination mechanism works.

After an extensive empirical evaluation, we fixed the utility function's parameters to κ=2, γ=1.4, and ν=10, because these provided the best results for all algorithms. Moreover, the utility of each fire is $v_f = 4 - I_f$, where $I_f \in \{1,2,3\}$ is the fieriness of fire f as reported by the simulator, and t_f is the area of fire f divided by 100. Intuitively, the fierier a fire is, the longer a building has been burning, and the less valuable it is to contain. Additionally, we scale all the utilities of the police forces model by 10^{-3} to give more relevance to the fire brigades team than to the police agents team. With the same objective, we set $M = 100$, and $Q = 50$, so that blockades preventing fire brigades from reaching fires are more important than blockades in the path of police agents.

Regarding algorithms' parameters we set the number of maximum iterations for DSA and BMS to 100. Lowering the number of iterations to 50 slightly decreased the quality of both algorithms, whereas increasing them to 1000 did not improve the results, wasting resources in both cases. We also employ the Anytime framework from [30] to keep track of the best global solution (assignment) each algorithm has found during all the iterations, and use that as the final result. After testing with DSA_p values ranging from 0.1 to 0.9 (in 0.1 increments), we chose 0.1 because it yielded the best results overall. In our DSA implementation agents always prefer to switch tasks whenever they are in conflict. In fact, agents tend to switch too much if a large p is used, explaining the rather low DSA_p value. It is well known that MS has problems to reach convergence on factor graphs containing many loops. To overcome these issues, we use a damping factor [5] of 0.9 in BMS. [5]

Figure 2 shows a snapshot of a running simulation in the Paris map. The white areas represent buildings and roads. A blacked out road is currently blocked, and cannot be transited until some police patrol (blue dot) clears it. In contrast, colored buildings represent fires that the firefighters (red dots) must extinguish.

Table 1: Statistics for Greedy, DSA and BMS averaged over 30 runs in the Paris scenario (agents start acting after 25 iterations).

Algorithm	Greedy	DSA	BMS
Score	5.29±0.79 %	2.94±0.43 %	1.13±0.18 %
NCCCs	0.00±0.00 k	7.51±0.11 k	79.62±0.81 k
Num. Msgs	0.00±0.00 k	91.08±0.92 k	536.31±8.84 k
Total bytes	0.00±0.00 Kb	711.60±7.16 Kb	4189.92±69.03 Kb
CPU time	16.14±0.45 ms	220.91±7.02 ms	726.37±15.09 ms

Against this background, we use the following metrics to evaluate the performance of the different algorithms:

- *Score*: is the main performance metric used by the RoboCup simulator. It evaluates the percentage of damage suffered by the city, with 100% meaning that it has been completely destroyed;
- *NCCCs [14]*: captures the per-iteration average amount of non-parallelizable computation performed by the agents;
- *Num msgs*: tracks the average number of messages sent between all agents in a single iteration;
- *Total bytes*: is the average number of bytes per iteration sent between all agents.

In the following section we summarize the main results of our experimental evaluation.

6.2 Results

Table 1 shows the results we obtained on the Paris map with a start time of 25 simulation steps[6] averaged over 30 simulations. BMS clearly achieves the best score, with only 1.13% of the city damaged. In contrast, more than twice as many buildings burn down when using DSA, and more than four times with the Greedy algorithm. This gain in quality comes at a cost though. Greedy agents obtain the worst results in quality but require no coordination resources. DSA requires few computational resources and relatively low communications, whereas BMS computes an order of magnitude more than DSA, and requires substantially more bandwidth. Nonetheless, taking into account that an iteration of the RCS represents one minute of real time, all these costs are within an acceptable range. We also experimented with a closest allocation method, where an agent is assigned to the closest task. Such method has been frequently used in the RCS as a benchmarking approach for task allocation (e.g., see [15]). With that method fire agents spend too much time watering down old fires (which are unlikely to spread), and an average of 49% of the city gets damaged. This result indicates that our utility function is properly capturing the characteristics of the problem.

Next we assess the behavior of the different algorithms when the amount of fire and police agents decreases. Overall, Figure 3(a)

[5] The use of a damping factor δ in max-sum is a well-known technique that helps stabilize the algorithm. When using damping, each sent message $\hat{\mu}^i_{c\to t}$ is a weighted average between the latest computed message and the message sent in the previous iteration, namely $\hat{\mu}^i_{c\to t} = \delta\mu^i_{c\to t} + (1-\delta)\hat{\mu}^{i-1}_{c\to t}$.

[6] This means prevent agents from executing any action before 25 time steps, so that fires have time to spread.

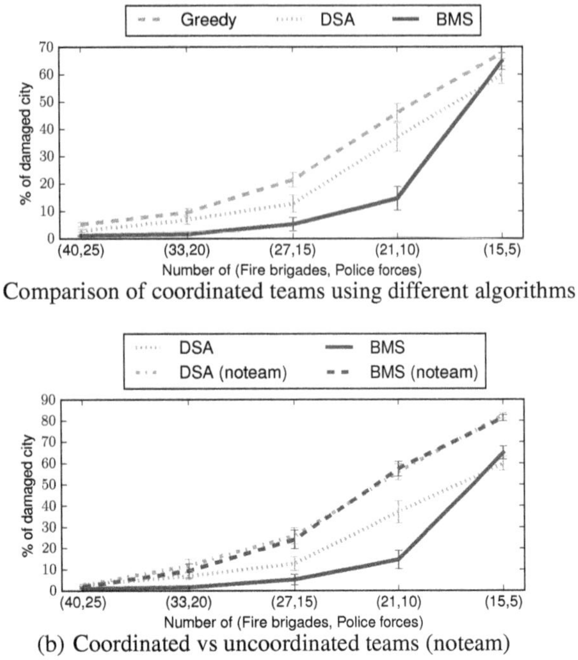

(a) Comparison of coordinated teams using different algorithms

(b) Coordinated vs uncoordinated teams (noteam)

Figure 3: Performance comparison when decreasing the agent resources. Results are averaged over 30 runs and error bars represent the standard error of the mean.

shows that BMS coordinated agents achieve significantly better results than DSA and Greedy in all but the worst conditions. Namely, BMS prevents around 2.5 times more damages than DSA, and around 4 times more damages than Greedy. This trend continues when the amount of available police and fire brigades decreases. For instance, BMS saves 85.4% of the city when there are only 21 fire brigades and 10 police patrols, whereas DSA saves only 62.9% of the buildings and Greedy an even lower 54%. However, there is a point where there are so few agents that the situation is helpless and most of the city gets damaged. In this scenario, we observe this effect when we reduce the resources to 15 fire brigades and 5 police agents. At this point all algorithms obtain fairly similar results, and DSA becomes the best strategy thanks to its greedy but still coordinated nature.

While Figure 3(a) shows that both DSA and BMS outperform the Greedy strategy given a sensible number of rescue agents, we cannot be sure whether this is purely because of the algorithm or thanks to the inter-team coordination. Therefore, we repeated the above experiments using BMS and DSA, but now without the inter-team coordination constraints. Figure 3(b) shows the results we obtained, where "DSA (noteam)" and "BMS (noteam)" represent the corresponding algorithms but without the inter-team constraints. The results are particularly revealing. On the one hand, the algorithms without inter-team coordination perform similarly. BMS provides slightly better results when there are more agents, but the differences become insignificant (according to a Wilcoxon signed-rank [27] test with $p = 0.01$) when the number of agents decreases past 27 fire brigades and 15 police patrols. On the other hand, both algorithms perform notably better when employing our inter-team coordination constraints, thus validating our inter-team methodology and the resulting model.

Furthermore, the gains from inter-team coordination are clearly larger for BMS than for DSA. This difference has a simple explanation. Notice that the inter-team constraints require an agent (especially police patrols) to temporarily worsen its own individual outcome (by attending a farther blockade) to realize the inter-team gains (to allow a firefighter to reach a more important fire). Now recall that DSA is essentially a greedy algorithm. In contrast, Max-Sum is the only known local-state DCOP algorithm that does not operate in a greedy manner. Therefore, the Max-Sum algorithm (and BMS by extension) is intrinsically better equipped to exploit these coordination situations where some temporary individual sacrifice must be made to achieve a greater outcome.

Finally, we conducted similar experiments in the 2013's Kobe scenario. The observed trends are the same, but the differences between algorithms are smaller because the problem is easier: in Kobe there is only one fire focus and the map is small and much easier to navigate.

7. CONCLUSIONS

We presented a methodology that allows multiple teams to make joint allocations by enabling them to coordinate during the task allocation process. Using this methodology, we developed a model for inter-team coordination of firefighters and police forces. We have shown that some typical inter-team coordination interactions can be effectively modeled by means of THOPs allowing MS messages to be assessed in polynomial time in such complex scenarios. To the best of our knowledge this is the first time where it has been shown that MS can be run in polynomial time without simplifying the associated model. Experiments with fire brigades and police agents show that teams employing inter-team coordination are significantly more effective than uncoordinated teams. Moreover, the evaluation shows that our BMS and THOPs method achieves up to 2.5 times better results than other state-of-the-art methods. Furthermore, the gains from inter-team coordination are clearly larger for BMS than for alternative algorithms with a greedy inspiration. Therefore, we have seen that the Max-Sum algorithm (and BMS by extension) is intrinsically better equipped to exploit these coordination situations.

Acknowledgments

Work funded by projects DAMAS (TIN2013-45732-C4-4-P), COR (TIN2012-38876-C02-01), MECER (201250E053), the Generalitat of Catalunya grant 2009-SGR-1434, and the Ministry of Economy and Competitivity grant BES-2010-030466.

REFERENCES

[1] Ri Brafman and Carmel Domshlak. From One to Many: Planning for Loosely Coupled Multi-Agent Systems. *International Conference on Automated Planning and Scheduling*, pages 28–35, 2008.

[2] F. M. Delle Fave, A. Rogers, Z. Xu, S. Sukkarieh, and N. R. Jennings. Deploying the max-sum algorithm for decentralised coordination and task allocation of unmanned aerial vehicles for live aerial imagery collection. In *2012 IEEE International Conference on Robotics and Automation*, pages 469–476, 2012.

[3] F. dos Santos and A.C. Bazzan. Towards efficient multiagent task allocation in the robocup rescue: a biologically-inspired approach. *Autonomous Agents and Multi-Agent Systems*, 22(3):465–486, 2011.

[4] A. Farinelli, A. Rogers, A. Petcu, and N. R. Jennings. Decentralised coordination of low-power embedded devices using the max-sum algorithm. In *Proceedings of the 7th international joint conference on Autonomous agents and*

multiagent systems-Volume 2, pages 639–646. International Foundation for Autonomous Agents and Multiagent Systems, 2008.

[5] B. Frey and D. Dueck. Clustering by passing messages between data points. *Science*, 315(5814):972–976, 2007.

[6] Y. Kim, M. Krainin, and V. Lesser. Application of max-sum algorithm to radar coordination and scheduling. In *Workshop on Distributed Constraint Reasoning*, 2010.

[7] H. Kitano, S. Tadokoro, I. Noda, H. Matsubara, T. Takahashi, A. Shinjou, and S. Shimada. Robocup rescue: Search and rescue in large-scale disasters as a domain for autonomous agents research. In *Systems, Man, and Cybernetics, 1999. IEEE SMC'99 Conference Proceedings.*, volume 6, pages 739–743. IEEE, 1999.

[8] A. Kleiner, A. Farinelli, S. Ramchurn, B. Shi, F. Maffioletti, and R. Reffato. Rmasbench: benchmarking dynamic multi-agent coordination in urban search and rescue. In *Proceedings of the 2013 international conference on Autonomous agents and multi-agent systems*, pages 1195–1196. International Foundation for Autonomous Agents and Multiagent Systems, 2013.

[9] Somchaya Liemhetcharat and Manuela Veloso. Modeling and learning synergy for team formation with heterogeneous agents. In *Proceedings of the 11th International Conference on Autonomous Agents and Multiagent Systems-Volume 1*, pages 365–374. International Foundation for Autonomous Agents and Multiagent Systems, 2012.

[10] Somchaya Liemhetcharat and Manuela Veloso. Weighted synergy graphs for effective team formation with heterogeneous ad hoc agents. *Artificial Intelligence*, 208:41–65, 2014.

[11] R. T. Maheswaran, J. P. Pearce, and M. Tambe. Distributed algorithms for DCOP: A graphical game-based approach. In *Proceedings of the Seventeenth International Conference on Parallel and Distributed Computing Systems*, pages 432–439, 2004.

[12] R. Mailler, V. Lesser, and B. Horling. Cooperative negotiation for soft real-time distributed resource allocation. In *Proceedings of AAMAS'03*, pages 576–583, 2003.

[13] Leandro Soriano Marcolino, Albert Xin Jiang, and Milind Tambe. Multi-agent team formation: diversity beats strength? In *Proceedings of the Twenty-Third international joint conference on Artificial Intelligence*, pages 279–285. AAAI Press, 2013.

[14] A. Meisels, E. Kaplansky, I. Razgon, and R. Zivan. Comparing performance of distributed constraints processing algorithms. In *Proc. AAMAS-2002 DCR Workshop*, pages 86–93, 2002.

[15] James Parker and Maria Gini. Tasks with cost growing over time and agent reallocation delays. In *Proceedings of the 2014 International Conference on Autonomous Agents and Multi-agent Systems*, AAMAS '14, pages 381–388, Richland, SC, 2014. International Foundation for Autonomous Agents and Multiagent Systems.

[16] T. Penya-Alba, J. Cerquides, J. A. Rodriguez-Aguilar, and M. Vinyals. A Scalable Message-Passing Algorithm for Supply Chain Formation. In *AAAI*, pages 1436–1442, 2012.

[17] M. Pujol-Gonzalez, J. Cerquides, P. Meseguer, J. A. Rodriguez-Aguilar, and M. Tambe. Engineering the decentralized coordination of UAVs with limited communication range. In *CAEPIA*, 2013.

[18] Marc Pujol-Gonzalez, Alexander Kleiner, Alessandro Farinelli, Sarvapali Ramchurn, Bing Shi, Fabio Maffioletti, and Riccardo Reffato. RMASBench: Multi-agent coordination benchmark. http://github.com/RMASBench/RMASBench, 2012–2014.

[19] S. D. Ramchurn, A. Farinelli, K. S. Macarthur, and N. R. Jennings. Decentralized coordination in robocup rescue. *The Computer Journal*, 53(9):1447–1461, 2010.

[20] S. D. Ramchurn, M. Polukarov, A. Farinelli, N. Jennings, and C. Trong. Coalition formation with spatial and temporal constraints. In *International Joint Conference on Autonomous Agents and Multi-Agent Systems (AAMAS 2010)*, pages 1181–1188, 2010.

[21] Wei Ren, Randal W. Beard, and Timothy W. McLain. Coordination Variables and Consensus Building in Multiple Vehicle Systems. *Lecture Notes in Control and Information Sciences*, 309/2005:439–442, 2005.

[22] P. Scerri, A. Farinelli, S. Okamoto, and M. Tambe. Allocating tasks in extreme teams. In *Proc. of AAMAS 05*, pages 727–734, Utrecht, Netherland, 2005.

[23] N. Schurr, J. Marecki, P. Scerri, J. P. Lewi, and M. Tambe. *Programming Multiagent Systems*, chapter The DEFACTO System: Coordinating Human-Agent Teams for the Future of Disaster Response, page 296. Springer, 2005.

[24] P. Stone, G. Kaminka, S. Kraus, and J. Rosenschein. Ad hoc autonomous agent teams: Collaboration without pre-coordination. In *Proceedings of the Twenty-Fourth Conference on Artificial Intelligence*, July 2010.

[25] M. Tambe. Towards flexible teamwork. *Journal of Artificial Intelligence Research (JAIR)*, 7:83–124, 1997.

[26] D. Tarlow, I. E. Givoni, and R. S. Zemel. HOP-MAP : Efficient Message Passing with High Order Potentials. In *13th AISTATS*, volume 9, pages 812–819, 2010.

[27] F Wilcoxon. Individual comparisons of grouped data by ranking methods. *Journal of economic entomology*, 39(6):269, 1946.

[28] Harel Yedidsion, Roie Zivan, and Alessandro Farinelli. Explorative max-sum for teams of mobile sensing agents. *Proceedings of the 2014 international conference on Autonomous agents and multi-agent systems*, pages 549–556, 2014.

[29] W. Zhang, G. Wang, Z. Xing, and L. Wittenburg. Distributed stochastic search and distributed breakout: properties, comparison and applications to constraint optimization problems in sensor networks. *Artificial Intelligence*, 161(1-2):55–87, January 2005.

[30] R. Zivan. Anytime local search for distributed constraint optimization. In *Proceedings of the 7th international joint conference on Autonomous agents and multiagent systems-Volume 3*, pages 1449–1452. International Foundation for Autonomous Agents and Multiagent Systems, 2008.

A Semantic Framework for Socially Adaptive Agents
Towards strong norm compliance

M. Birna van Riemsdijk[*]
Delft University of Technology,
The Netherlands
m.b.vanriemsdijk@tudelft.nl

Louise Dennis[†]
University of Liverpool, UK
l.a.dennis@liverpool.ac.uk

Michael Fisher
University of Liverpool, UK
mfisher@liverpool.ac.uk

Koen V. Hindriks
Delft University of Technology
k.v.hindriks@tudelft.nl

ABSTRACT

We address the question of how an agent can adapt its behavior to comply with newly adopted norms. This is particularly relevant in the case of open systems where agents may enter and leave norm-governed social contexts not known at design time. This requires norms to be explicitly and separately stated and presented to an agent as rules to which it then can try to adapt its behavior.

We propose a formal semantic framework that specifies an execution mechanism for such socially adaptive agents. This framework is based on expressing norms using Linear Temporal Logic. The formality of the framework allows us to rigorously study its norm compliance properties. A weak form of norm compliance allows agents to abort execution in order to prevent norm violation. In this paper we investigate a stronger notion of norm compliance that is evaluated over infinite traces. We show that it is not possible for all agents to be strongly compliant with any arbitrary set of norms. We then investigate situations when strong norm compliance can be guaranteed.

Categories and Subject Descriptors

I.2.11 [**Artificial Intelligence**]: Distributed Artificial Intelligence—*Intelligent agents, languages and structures, multiagent systems*; I.2.5 [**Artificial Intelligence**]: Programming Languages and Software; F.3.2 [**Logics and Meaning of Programs**]: Semantics of Programming Languages

General Terms

Theory, Languages

Keywords

Norm-aware agents; Agent programming languages; Norm compliance; Formal semantics; Executable temporal logic

[*]First author was supported by the NWO Vidi project CoreSAEP.

[†]Second and third authors supported by EPSRC Grant EP/L024845/1, "Verifiable Autonomy".

Appears in: *Proceedings of the 14th International Conference on Autonomous Agents and Multiagent Systems (AAMAS 2015), Bordini, Elkind, Weiss, Yolum (eds.), May, 4–8, 2015, Istanbul, Turkey.*

1. INTRODUCTION

Norms have been proposed as a way of regulating multi-agent systems in order to prevent undesirable or ineffective behavior [3]. Norms describe how agents should ideally behave. When agents enter a social context that is governed by a set of norms, they should be able to recognize the norms, decide whether they want to follow them, and if they decide to do so, adapt their behavior accordingly to generate norm-compliant behavior.

In this paper we address the latter issue, focusing on the following question: *how can agents adapt their behavior to comply with newly adopted norms?* We refer to such agents as *socially adaptive agents.* Creating socially adaptive agents is particularly relevant in the case of open systems [13] where agents may enter and leave norm-governed social contexts not known at design time. This means they have to be able to adapt to new norms at run-time. Examples are social robots and personal assistant agents that support people in their daily lives in various social contexts.

Our aim is to develop an *execution mechanism* for socially adaptive agents that can be integrated into existing agent programming languages [5]. As argued in [32], treating adopted norms "simply as additional beliefs, goals, or rules that the agent may adopt at run-time is insufficient, as it will be difficult (if not impossible) to do it in such a way that norm compliant behavior is generated". Since it is not known at design time which combinations of norms may arise, we need an execution mechanism that can adapt the agent's proactive and reactive behavior to arbitrary sets of norms (in some normative language) at run-time. Moreover, agent behavior should not be adapted if this is not required according to norms.

In this paper we propose a formal *semantic framework* that specifies such an execution mechanism for socially adaptive agents. Formally specifying the semantics allows us to rigorously study its norm compliance properties. In previous work [32] we proposed an execution semantics for agents that had the option of aborting in order to prevent norm violation (weak norm compliance). Compliance of an execution trace with norms was evaluated up to the point where a norm violation was about to occur. In this paper, we investigate a stronger notion that evaluates compliance over infinite traces. We argue that strong norm compliance corresponds to an intuitive idea of norm compliant behavior. Strong norm compliance requires that any (infinite) normative agent trace complies with norms. Not all agents can be strongly norm compliant with any set of norms, for example when norms are inconsistent. We investigate when strong norm compliance *can* be guaranteed.

We start by discussing related work on reasoning about norm

compliance and propose an architecture for socially adaptive agents that shows how the execution mechanism can be integrated with other types of norm compliance reasoning (Section 2). We use an *abstract decision mechanism* to define an agent's proactive and reactive behavior, and express norms using the next-fragment of *Linear Temporal Logic (LTL)* (Section 3). An agent satisfies a norm expressed as an LTL formula if it generates behavior that satisfies the formula. The main contributions of this paper are the following:

- A *normative agent semantics* that specifies how the agent's decision mechanism is adapted to comply with norms (Section 4). We introduce a number of desired properties of normative agent semantics and show that our semantics satisfies them.
- A definition and semantic exploration of *strong norm compliance* (Section 5). We show that satisfiability of norms corresponds to the existence of a strongly norm compliant agent, provide a semantic characterization of strong norm compliance by proving that it coincides with absence of conflict, and identify sets of "safe" norms that guarantee strong norm compliance.

2. NORM COMPLIANCE REASONING

We position our work in the broader area of reasoning about norm compliance by discussing related work (Section 2.1) and introducing an architecture to show how different types of reasoning about norm compliance can be integrated (Section 2.2).

2.1 Related Work

The term norm compliance has been used in different ways and in different contexts in the literature. There has been considerable research on how agents can *reason about whether they want to comply* with norms by determining whether the benefits from complying outweigh the expected costs of violation (e.g., induced by sanctions) or if complying is instrumental in achieving the agent's goals [9, 4, 17, 26, 27, 31, 1, 11]. Our aim is complementary: we focus on generating behavior that complies with norms, *once the agent has decided it wants to comply* with them.

In the context of business process modelling, techniques have been developed for *verifying whether a business process complies with a set of norms*, for example through model checking [22, 21, 23, 30, 12, 15]. These approaches are aimed at compliance checking at design time. In [21] the declarative representation of norms and goals for a business process is proposed in a modal defeasible theory. Compliance by design can be achieved if from this one creates a new process that satisfies goals and norms. There is also research on run-time verification of process models [28], in which business processes are monitored during execution in order to detect (potential) problems. Monitoring is also investigated in the area of normative multi-agent systems [7, 10, 8] in which mechanisms for detecting norm violations are developed. While verification and monitoring approaches *check* whether a given agent or business process complies with norms, our aim is to develop an execution mechanism that can *generate* norm compliant behavior (while preserving the original agent behavior if possible). In [21] it is suggested to generate a compliant business process from a declarative specification. This is different from defining an execution mechanism that generates norm compliant behavior by *adapting a given procedural specification.*

In [29] another technique is proposed that allows agents to adapt their behavior to newly adopted norms. The main difference with our work is that they do not specify norm compliance and the execution mechanism formally and consequently cannot formally investigate norm compliance properties. In [31] a norm-based planning approach is proposed for generating agent behavior that maximizes an agent's utility. Planning can be used to generate norm compliant behavior. However, it requires that agents are modelled as planners which is not always desirable. In particular, planning assumes a finite horizon which our semantic framework does not. We define an operational semantics of what it means that an agent adapts its behavior to norms, which facilitates integration of our execution mechanism into agent programming languages.

2.2 Architecture

In this section we illustrate how we envisage the execution mechanism for generating norm compliant behavior to be integrated into an overall architecture for socially adaptive agents. The architecture (Figure 1) shows how different types of reasoning about norm compliance, as discussed in Section 2.1, can be integrated.

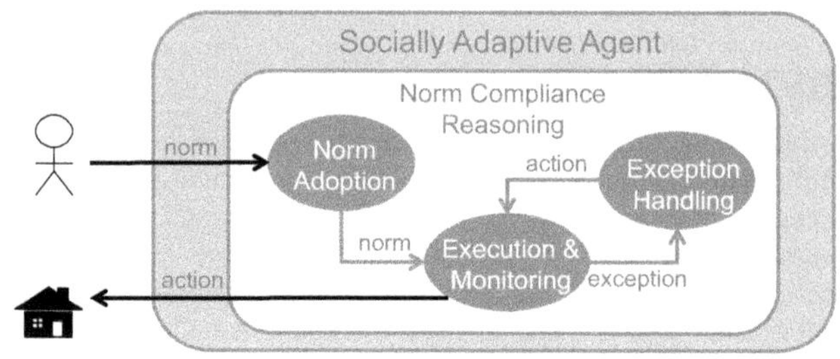

Figure 1: Socially Adaptive Agent Architecture

When an agent identifies new norms at run-time (called *normative beliefs* in [2]), it has to decide whether to adopt them by reasoning about whether it wants to comply. Once norms have been adopted (called *normative goals* in [2]), the agent's execution mechanism should ensure that norm compliant behavior is generated (if possible). This is the focus of this paper. Monitoring can be used to detect if norm violations (exceptions) unexpectedly occur. Exceptions may occur if the execution mechanism cannot fully guarantee norm compliant behavior. In this paper we analyze to what extent the execution mechanism can provide such guarantees. If a norm violation occurs, an exception handling process needs to be in place to determine the best way to respond. Exception handling is related to contrary-to-duty reasoning [24, 22], which concerns the derivation of new norms that should be fulfilled to repair or compensate for violation of the primary norm. Contrary-to-duty reasoning is outside the scope of this paper. Our architecture is in line with that proposed in [29].

3. PRELIMINARIES

We use the abstract agent semantics (Section 3.1) and normative language (Section 3.2) from [32], which we summarize here.

3.1 Abstract Agent Semantics

The semantic framework we propose comprises three "layers": 1) a transition function $\mathcal{T}$ specifying how the execution of an action changes a state, representing the actions that an agent can execute 2) an agent decision mechanism *Dec* specifying which actions enabled by $\mathcal{T}$ an agent would choose to execute if there were no norms in place, and 3) a normative agent semantics $[\![A]\!]_N$ specifying how *Dec* is adapted to comply with norms N. *Dec* can be generated, for example, through an agent program that specifies the agent's reactive and proactive behavior. We here abstract from how

Dec is generated to ensure that our normative agent semantics can be integrated with various agent programming frameworks.

We assume two mutually disjoint sets: a set of propositional atoms At with typical element p over which properties of states are defined, and a set of agent actions Act with typical element a. We assume a language of propositional logic $\mathcal{L}_{\mathsf{At}}$ with typical element ϕ defined over a finite set of atoms At, with $\top, \bot \in \mathcal{L}_{\mathsf{At}}$ denoting the true and false sentence, respectively. We also assume a finite set of abstract agent states S and an entailment relation $s \models_{\mathcal{L}_{\mathsf{At}}} \phi$, which defines when ϕ holds in s, such that for each $\phi \in \mathcal{L}_{\mathsf{At}}$ with $\phi \not\models_{\mathcal{L}_{\mathsf{At}}} \bot$ there is a state $s \in S$ such that $s \models_{\mathcal{L}_{\mathsf{At}}} \phi$. Moreover, states are complete, i.e., for each state $s \in S$ and $p \in \mathsf{At}$ either $s \models_{\mathcal{L}_{\mathsf{At}}} p$ or $s \models_{\mathcal{L}_{\mathsf{At}}} \neg p$. This is important to prove correspondence of the semantics with LTL. We also assume atoms are independent, i.e., for any two atoms, p and q both $p \wedge q$ and $p \wedge \neg q$ are consistent[1]. We provide no formal definition for $\models_{\mathcal{L}_{\mathsf{At}}}$ abstracting from this for the same reasons we abstracted from *Dec*.

The partial function $\mathcal{T}$ of type : $(\mathsf{Act} \times S) \rightarrow S$ specifies how the execution of an action changes a state. If an action a cannot be executed in state s, $\mathcal{T}(a, s)$ is undefined. We assume an abstract agent decision mechanism $Dec(\mathsf{Act}, S, \mathcal{T})$ as a set of transitions $s \xrightarrow{a} s'$ with $s, s' \in S$ and $a \in \mathsf{Act}$ for which $\mathcal{T}(a, s) = s'$. This set of transitions defines which actions may be executed in which state according to the agent's decision mechanism. This is a subset of the transitions that can occur according to $\mathcal{T}$.

3.2 Language of Norms

We use Linear Temporal Logic (LTL) [16] to specify norms and thus our syntax of norms is that of LTL. In order to comply with a norm expressed as an LTL formula, agents should exhibit behavior that satisfies the LTL formula. An important advantage of using LTL for specifying norms is that LTL is an expressive formal language for specifying properties of traces of computational systems. Norm compliance directly translates to satisfaction of the LTL formulas over the traces that the agent generates.

To facilitate executing a temporal logic specification, in [18] a normal form for temporal logic called Separated Normal Form (SNF) is introduced. SNF is a concise clausal form for temporal formulas which facilitates operationalization (see, e.g., METATEM [19, 20]). An SNF formula consists of an implication with a conjunction of propositional literals as the antecedent and a temporal formula as the consequent. The temporal formula consists of a temporal operator $\bigcirc$ (next) or $\Diamond$ (sometime/eventually) applied to a disjunction of propositional literals. Any LTL formula can be transformed into an equivalent set of Separated Normal Form (SNF) rules [18]. By way of example, the LTL formula

$$\Box(\phi \rightarrow (done(a_1) \text{ before } done(a_2)))$$

may represent a norm for a robot in a rescue scenario expressing that it should always ($\Box$) be the case if the robot enters a room (ϕ) it should send a message to the other agents ($done(a_1)$) before it leaves the room ($done(a_2)$). This is represented in SNF as follows:

$$\left.\begin{array}{l} \phi \Rightarrow \neg done(a_2) \\ \phi \Rightarrow (w \vee done(a_1)) \end{array}\right\} \quad \text{present time rules}$$

$$\left.\begin{array}{l} w \Rightarrow \bigcirc(\neg done(a_2)) \\ w \Rightarrow \bigcirc(w \vee done(a_1)) \end{array}\right\} \quad \text{step rules}$$

The present time rules informally specify that if the left-hand side (lhs) of the rule holds in a state, then the right-hand side (rhs) must also hold in that state. Step rules represent that if the lhs holds, the rhs should hold in the next ($\bigcirc$) state. For reasons of simplicity, in this paper we consider the "next-fragment" of LTL as represented by present time and step rules. This means that we do not include rules that express that something should hold sometime in the future. The advantage of present time and step rules is that they can be evaluated over individual transitions. This does mean that the formalism discussed here cannot represent all norms encoded in LTL, but we believe it includes a large useful subset.

In the translation process from LTL to SNF, an auxiliary atom w was introduced above which can be read as 'waiting'. A new atom is introduced whenever a complex temporal operator (e.g., before) is translated into SNF. These atoms do not refer to the environment state as atoms in At, but are introduced for technical reasons in order to facilitate model building for the temporal formula. Their role is to defer, from state to state, the satisfaction of some formula e.g., $done(a_1)$ above – so in every state either $done(a_1)$ is true or the system is still waiting for a_1 to be done (w). While w is true $done(a_2)$ is prohibited because it must take place after $done(a_1)$. Agent actions do not directly affect auxiliary atoms, and therefore we use a separate set At_{aux} to denote the set of auxiliary atoms, where $\mathsf{At} \cap \mathsf{At}_{aux} = \emptyset$.

We use $lit(\mathsf{At})$ and $lit(\mathsf{Act})$ to denote the set of positive and negative literals over At and Act, respectively. We use *propositional literals* to refer to literals containing atoms from At, *auxiliary atoms* to refer to atoms from At_{aux}, and *action literals* to refer to literals from Act. To clearly distinguish action literals from propositional literals, we denote the former as $done(a)$ or $\neg done(a)$. We define present time and step rules as follows.

DEFINITION 1. *(Present Time Rules) A present time rule has the form* $\bigwedge l \Rightarrow \bigvee l'$ *where* $l \in lit(\mathsf{At})$ *and* $l' \in lit(\mathsf{Act}) \cup \mathsf{At}_{aux}$.

DEFINITION 2. *(Step Rules) A step rule has the form* $\bigwedge l \Rightarrow \bigcirc(\bigvee l')$ *where* $l \in lit(\mathsf{At} \cup \mathsf{Act}) \cup \mathsf{At}_{aux}$ *and* $l' \in lit(\mathsf{Act}) \cup \mathsf{At}_{aux}$.

Step rules correspond to conditional norms that oblige or forbid the execution of actions. For example, the step rule $p \Rightarrow \bigcirc(done(a))$ ($\bigcirc \neg done(a)$) can be read as a norm that expresses that if p holds, the agent is obliged (forbidden) to execute a next. Our language of norms is, for example, comparable to the normative language of the norm-aware agent framework of [29]. Our language is more restrictive than [29] in that we only allow actions and no states in the consequent of norms. It is more expressive in that we allow disjunctions of actions (and auxiliary atoms) in the consequent, and we have present time rules. LTL has also been used to specify norms for the MOISE organizational modelling language [33]. Our normative language differs from temporal deontic logics (e.g., [14, 6]) in that norms are not expressed explicitly. Temporal deontic logics are aimed at reasoning *about* which norms are in force, while our normative language directly expresses the behavior that agents should exhibit.

4. NORMATIVE AGENT SEMANTICS

In this section we define the normative agent semantics that formally defines how we integrate norms and agent deliberation. The semantics is a declarative variant of the semantics of [32], with a number of changes needed for providing a definition and characterization of strong norm compliance. We summarize these at the end of the section. The semantics is defined with respect to a set of norms N. If the set N changes at run-time because new norms are adopted, the agent can immediately adapt its behavior according to the semantics. We do not define such an update mechanism because it is not required for studying strong norm compliance.

[1] This means we can exclude multiply defined norms from consideration – e.g., $\neg smoking$ and *refrain_from_smoking*.

We use N to denote a set of norms in SNF and use $N_{PTR} \subseteq N$ and $N_{SR} \subseteq N$ to denote the sets of present time and step rules of N $(= N_{PTR} \cup N_{SR})$, respectively. In order to represent which auxiliary atoms hold and to represent the action that has been executed[2], we extend the states $s \in S$ to *normative states* $n = \langle s, aux, a\rangle$ with $aux \subseteq \mathsf{At}_{aux}$ and $a \in \mathsf{Act}$. We use $\downharpoonright$ to denote the projection of a normative state transition to a transition in *Dec*, i.e., $(\langle s, aux, a\rangle \longrightarrow \langle s', aux', a'\rangle)\downharpoonright \; = s \xrightarrow{a'} s'$.

We define that a normative state $n = \langle s, aux, a\rangle$ satisfies a formula $\phi = \bigwedge l$, denoted as $n \models \phi$, iff *(i)* all propositional literals (both positive and negative) from ϕ follow from s (according to entailment relation $\models_{\mathcal{L}_{\mathsf{At}}}$ introduced above), *(ii)* all auxiliary atoms from ϕ are contained in *aux*, and *(iii)* all positive action literals from ϕ are equal to a and all negative action literals are unequal to a. Satisfaction for a formula $\phi = \bigvee l$ is defined similarly by replacing "for all" by "there exists".

One advantage of the transformation of temporal formulas into present time and step rules is that satisfaction of these rules can be evaluated on single normative transitions $n \longrightarrow n'$. A transition satisfies a present time rule if it is satisfied in n and n', and a step rule $\phi \Rightarrow \bigcirc(\psi)$ is satisfied if it is the case that when ϕ holds in n, ψ holds in n'. We formally define satisfaction of a present time rule ($\models_{PTR}$) in a normative state as follows:

$$n \models_{PTR} (\phi \Rightarrow \psi) \quad \text{iff} \quad n \models \phi \Rightarrow n \models \psi$$

. We define satisfaction of present time ($\models_{PTR}$) and step rules ($\models_{SR}$) over a normative transition as follows:

$$\begin{array}{lll} n \longrightarrow n' \models_{PTR} (\phi \Rightarrow \psi) & \text{iff} & n, n' \models (\phi \Rightarrow \psi) \\ n \longrightarrow n' \models_{SR} (\phi \Rightarrow \bigcirc\psi) & \text{iff} & n \models \phi \Rightarrow n' \models \psi \end{array}$$

We write $n \longrightarrow n' \models N$ to denote that a normative transition $n \longrightarrow n'$ satisfies all norms in N.

In defining a normative agent semantics one can make a range of choices that result in different semantics as well as computational properties. To guide and motivate the choices we make in this paper, we introduce a number of properties for such semantics. These are not the only desirable properties one may consider for such a semantics, and they do not uniquely characterize the semantics. However, by making these properties and the semantic choices explicit, we obtain a better understanding of the space of possibilities and its impact on norm compliance. The semantics in [32] was proven to satisfy the first two of the following properties.

- *Preservation of agent semantics:* If the set of norms $N = \emptyset$, then the generated normative traces correspond to those of the agent semantics.
- *Weak norm compliance:* Transitions derived by the transition rules should satisfy norms.
- *Preservation of norm compliance:* If a norm-compliant transition is possible according to $\mathcal{T}$, there should be a norm-compliant transition in the semantics[3]. Intuitively the semantics does not prevent the agent from executing a transition that is norm-compliant. This property is required for our characterization of strong norm compliance (Section 5.2).

In this paper we aim for a computational semantics that is "local", i.e., that takes into account only the current normative state in deriving a transition. The advantage of such a semantics over one that performs lookahead (and backtracking) to derive transitions is that it is computationally less intensive (see [25] for an example of a lookahead semantics to satisfy maintenance goals). A consequence is, however, that normative conflicts cannot always be prevented, which impacts norm compliance as we will see.

4.1 Semantics

Our normative agent semantics has two transition rules: one that allows us to derive transitions from *Dec* that are norm-compliant, and where no such transition exists one that allows the agent to take any norm-compliant action. The norm-constrained decision rule is introduced to satisfy preservation of the agent semantics. Its guard ensures that a transition can only be derived if it complies with the norms. In [32] the guard was used to construct the next state, while here we provide a simpler declarative constraint.

DEFINITION 3. *(Norm-Constrained Decision Rule)*

$$\frac{(n \longrightarrow n')\downharpoonright \in Dec \quad n \longrightarrow n' \models N}{n \longrightarrow n'}$$

This rule does not suffice to satisfy the preservation of norm compliance. Consider a step rule $\phi \Rightarrow \bigcirc done(b)$ and that in state $n = \langle s, aux, a\rangle$ we have $n \models \phi$, $\mathcal{T}(b, s) = s'$ and no other norms are applicable. In this case there is a norm-compliant transition to $n' = \langle s', \emptyset, b\rangle$, but unless $s \xrightarrow{b} s' \in Dec$, the transition cannot be derived. Thus we need a transition rule that allows *insertion* of actions into the agent semantics.

We also need to ensure that an agent always has an executable action that it can insert and that is not forbidden by norms. To this end we introduce an action `wait` $\notin$ Act and extend $\mathcal{T}$ to include this action such that for all $s \in S : \mathcal{T}(\texttt{wait}, s) = s$. Thus `wait` does not change the agent state but, importantly, it will allow auxiliary atoms to change. Consider, for example, step rules $w_0 \Rightarrow \bigcirc(\neg done(a)), \phi \Rightarrow \bigcirc(w_1)$ and $w_1 \Rightarrow \bigcirc(done(a))$, and an agent in state $n \models \phi \wedge w_0$ – so the norms state that in this state the agent should not do a next but should do it the time step after that. Also assume that a is the only action. In this case the agent would not be able to make a transition through actions from Act, but it can make a norm compliant transition to $n' \models w_1$ through `wait` (which will remove w_0 from the auxiliary atoms and add w_1 – thus waiting until it is allowed to perform a). In n' it may then execute a if the action is enabled, in order to satisfy the third step rule. Without `wait`, no transitions would be possible. As we will see below, this would mean that the agent is not strongly compliant. We require that the transition rule for action insertion is only executed when the norm-constrained decision rule cannot be applied. This is needed for preservation of the agent semantics. Without this constraint the agent may derive transitions that do not appear in *Dec* when $N = \emptyset$.

DEFINITION 4. *(Action Insertion Rule) Let* $n = \langle s, aux, a\rangle$, $\mathcal{T}(a', s) = s'$, *and* n' *be of the form* $\langle s', aux', a'\rangle$[4].

$$\frac{\begin{array}{c} n \longrightarrow n' \models N \\ \forall n''. ((n \longrightarrow n'')\downharpoonright \in Dec \Rightarrow n \longrightarrow n'' \not\models N) \end{array}}{n \longrightarrow n'}$$

[32] proposes a stronger variant of the action insertion rule which only allows the insertion of actions that appear positively in the rhs of step rules. The idea is that the agent will only insert actions that

[2] This is needed to evaluate applicability of present time and step rules, since they may contain conditions about which action has been executed.

[3] This includes vacuous norms, in fact such norms may be required, see our discussion of `wait`.

[4] Note that is is allowable for n to equal n' if such a transition otherwise complies with the norms.

it may, at some point, be required to take. Such a rule provides a semantics that satisfies preservation of the agent semantics without requiring that it can be applied only if the norm-constrained decision rule is inapplicable. However, the stronger rule makes it impossible to make norm-compliant transitions in situations where any transition in *Dec* is forbidden but no action is required according to step rules, as in the example above for $\phi \Rightarrow w_1$. This semantics would therefore violate preservation of norm compliance.

The transition relation $\longrightarrow$ on normative states n is the smallest relation induced by the two transition rules defined above.

We define an agent $A = \langle S_0, Dec(\mathsf{Act}, S, \mathcal{T})\rangle$ where $S_0 \subseteq S$ is a non-empty set of initial states and *Dec* is an abstract agent decision mechanism. We define the normative agent semantics for an agent as the set of all normative traces that can be derived from the initial states using the normative transition system. To this end we transform initial agent states into initial normative states.

DEFINITION 5. *(Initial Normative States) Let s be a state and N a set of norms. An initial normative state of s, denoted as init(s), is a tuple* $\langle s, aux, \epsilon\rangle$ *where aux is a set of auxiliary atoms for which* $\langle s, aux, \epsilon\rangle \models N_{PTR}$*, and* $\epsilon \notin \mathsf{Act}$ *is a special "empty" action.*

There are multiple initial states, for example representing different ways in which present time rules with more than one auxiliary atom in their rhs can be satisfied. An initial normative state does not always exist for any initial agent state – it may not be possible to create one that satisfies present time rules. The following proposition captures when an initial normative state exists.

PROPOSITION 1. *We use* lit^- *to denote the set of negative literals. Let N be a set of norms where for each* $r \in N_{PTR}$ *it holds that r has a disjunct* $l' \in lit^-(\mathsf{Act}) \cup \mathsf{At}_{aux}$ *in its right hand side. Then for any state* $s \in S$ *there is an initial normative state init(s).*

Proof: Consider a present time rule $\phi \Rightarrow \psi$. If $s \not\models \phi$, the result trivially holds. If $s \models \phi$, either there is a negative action literal in ψ which holds in all *init*(s) or there is an auxiliary atom w in ψ in which case there is an $init(s) = \langle s, aux, \epsilon\rangle$ where $w \in aux$. □

A trace in the normative agent semantics is a sequence of normative states where each consecutive state can be derived from the previous state through the transition rules defined above. If no transition can be derived then a special action `stop` is inserted that changes neither the agent state nor the auxiliary atoms. `stop` is thus different from `wait`, which allows changes to auxiliary atoms.

DEFINITION 6. *(Normative Agent Semantics)*
Let N be a set of norms and $A = \langle S_0, Dec(\mathsf{Act}, S, \mathcal{T})\rangle$ *be an agent. A trace from state s in the normative transition system, typically denoted by t and referred to as a* normative trace*, is an infinite sequence of normative states* $n_0, n_1, n_2, \ldots$ *such that* n_0 *is some init(s), and for each* $i \geq 0$ *the transition* $n_i \longrightarrow n_{i+1}$ *is in the transition relation on normative states (Definitions 3 and 4), or no transition from* $n_i = \langle s_i, aux_i, a_i\rangle$ *can be derived and* $n_{i+1} = \langle s_i, aux_i, \mathtt{stop}\rangle$ *where* $\mathtt{stop} \notin \mathsf{Act}$.
We define $S^N(s)$ *as the set of all normative traces under set of norms N starting in an initial state init(s). This set is empty if there is no initial normative state for s. The normative agent semantics* $[\![A]\!]_N$ *of an agent A under set of norms N is the set of associated normative traces starting in an initial state of A, i.e.,*

$$[\![A]\!]_N = \bigcup_{s \in S_0} S^N(s)$$

COROLLARY 1. *For each trace* $t \in [\![A]\!]_N$*, we have that the initial state of t satisfies* N_{PTR}*. Thus* $[\![A]\!]_N = \emptyset$ *iff all initial normative states violate present time rules* N_{PTR}*.*

Proof: Immediate from the definition of an initial normative state (Definition 5) and S^N (Definition 6). □

In contrast with [32], the normative agent semantics in this paper only yields infinite traces. The former yields finite traces if the agent cannot progress or would violate a norm. Besides yielding a more elegant semantics, it is required for investigating strong norm compliance which is defined over infinite traces.

4.2 Properties

We show that the normative agent semantics satisfies the three properties we introduced above. Preservation of the agent semantics is up to prefixes for finite traces of the agent. That is, if $N = \emptyset$ and for a state s there is no transition in *Dec*, then the normative semantics allows the agent to execute any action from Act[5].

PROPOSITION 2. *(Preservation of agent semantics) If A is an agent and* $N = \emptyset$ *then for each trace* $t \in [\![A]\!]_N$*, the maximal prefix of t for which each transition* $(n \longrightarrow n)\downharpoonright \in Dec$*, is a trace of A.*

Proof: Immediate from the fact that Definition 4 can only be applied if Definition 3 does not. If N is empty then norms do not impose constraints on the derivation of transitions from *Dec*. □

We define that a trace weakly complies with a set of norms if all non-stop transitions comply with norms.

DEFINITION 7. *(Weak norm compliance) A normative trace t* weakly complies *with a set of norms N iff all non-stop transitions* $n \longrightarrow n'$ *(i.e., where* n' *is of the form* $\langle s', aux', a'\rangle$ *and* $a' \neq \mathtt{stop}$*) in t satisfy N. An agent A weakly complies with set of norms N iff for all* $t \in [\![A]\!]_N$ *we have that t weakly complies with N.*

Defining weak norm compliance by referring only to non-stop transitions is justified because stop occurs iff the transition does not comply with norms. The inclusion of `wait` ensures that this proposition holds because it prevents the semantics deriving a `stop` transition just because no executable actions are available.

PROPOSITION 3. *(Stop signals norm violation) Let A be an agent and N a set of norms. Then a transition* $n \longrightarrow n'$ *on a trace* $t \in [\![A]\!]_N$ *is a stop transition (i.e., of the form* $\langle s, aux, a\rangle \longrightarrow \langle s, aux, \mathtt{stop}\rangle$*) iff* $n \longrightarrow n' \not\models N$*.*

Proof: Follows because a stop transition can only be derived iff no norm compliant transition exists by Definition 6. □

PROPOSITION 4. *The normative agent semantics is weakly norm compliant. That is, for any agent A and set of norms N, it holds that A weakly complies with N.*

Proof: The transition rules of Definitions 3 and 4 only allow the derivation of transitions that comply with norms. Weak compliance only concerns those transitions. □

PROPOSITION 5. *(Preservation of norm compliance) Let A be an agent, N a set of norms and* $n = \langle s, aux, a\rangle$ *a state on a trace* $t \in [\![A]\!]_N$*. If there is a normative state* $n' = \langle s', aux', a'\rangle$ *such that* $\mathcal{T}(a', s) = s'$ *and* $n \longrightarrow n' \models N$ *then there is a normative state* n'' *such that* $n \longrightarrow n''$ *is a norm compliant transition in t.*

[5]The semantics could be adapted so that, in this situation, only `wait` transitions were be selected if no transition from *Dec* were available, but we do not do that here for reasons of simplicity.

Proof: If $n \longrightarrow n'$ can be derived by Definition 3 we are done. Otherwise if $\mathcal{T}(a', s) = s'$ it can be derived by Definition 4 which encompasses all other norm compliant transitions in $\mathcal{T}$. □

In summary, we have obtained the following insights regarding the definition of a semantic framework for socially adaptive agents targeted at strong norm compliance:

- Preservation of norm compliance requires a weaker form of action insertion than proposed in [32] because satisfying norms may require progression without explicitly requiring the execution of an action.
- A consequence of using a weaker form of action insertion is that preservation of the agent semantics can only be proven up to maximal prefixes. That is, if $N = \emptyset$ and according to *Dec* the agent would terminate at some point, according to the normative agent semantics the agent would continue executing actions if possible. In [32] it was shown that the stronger action insertion rule yields exact preservation of the agent semantics, i.e., not only up to maximal prefixes.
- Defining weak norm compliance over infinite traces requires distinguishing norm compliant transitions that do not change the agent state (e.g., `wait`) from those that violate norms (`stop`). Intuitively, this highlights that there is a difference between refraining from doing an action in order to avoid norm violation (if certain actions are forbidden) and aborting the execution of the agent. The former is ok from the perspective of strong norm compliance, while the latter is problematic.

5. STRONG NORM COMPLIANCE

Weak norm compliance expresses that *if* the agent can derive a transition through the transition rules of Definitions 3 or 4, the transition is norm compliant. We argue that this notion is too weak to model what one would intuitively consider to be a norm compliant agent. Consider a robot in a care facility that is required by the family to leave the patient's room immediately when the family enters, and it is required by the physician to hold a device immediately when s/he asks it to do so. Now assume the family comes in and the physician asks it to hold a device. The robot can stop and be weakly norm compliant. However, from the perspective of the family and the physician, if the robot stops it violates both norms.

We introduce a strong notion of norm compliance to reflect this intuition. We define that an agent strongly complies with norms when all transitions on all traces of the agent satisfy the norms, and there is at least one such trace. The set of traces is empty iff all initial states of the agent violate present time rules (Corollary 1).

DEFINITION 8. *(Strong Norm Compliance)*
A normative trace t strongly complies *with a set of norms* N *iff all transitions* $n \longrightarrow n'$ *in* t *satisfy* N, *i.e.,* $n \longrightarrow n' \models N$. *An agent* A *strongly complies with a set of norms* N *iff there is a transition* $t \in [\![A]\!]_N$ *and for all* $t \in [\![A]\!]_N$, t *strongly complies with* N.

COROLLARY 2. *Strong compliance implies weak compliance, i.e., if an agent* A *strongly complies with a set of norms* N *then* A *weakly complies with* N.

In contrast with weak norm compliance, not all agents are strongly norm compliant with any set of norms. In our example above where N contained $\mathit{family} \Rightarrow \bigcirc(\mathit{done}(\mathit{leave}))$ and $\mathit{requestHold} \Rightarrow \bigcirc(\mathit{done}(\mathit{hold}))$, when both *family* and *requestHold* are satisfied, no norm compliant transition can be derived and the semantics introduces the `stop` transition. This transition does not comply with these step rules, and thus the robot is not strongly norm compliant.

Weak and strong norm compliance differ only with respect to the evaluation of stop transitions. Thus the traces of strongly norm compliant agents do not have stop transitions. This corresponds with the intuition that to be strongly norm compliant, agents should not be allowed to abort to prevent norm violation.

In this section we explore semantic characteristics of strong norm compliance from three perspectives. We provide a logical characterization of when a strongly norm compliant agent exists (Section 5.1), we provide a semantic characterization of strong norm compliance (Section 5.2), and based on this show that certain subclasses of norms ensure strong norm compliance (Section 5.3).

5.1 LTL Satisfiability

In this section we investigate how strong norm compliance relates to satisfiability of particular LTL expressions. Intuitively, strong norm compliance corresponds to satisfaction of norms expressed as LTL formulas. We investigate whether our semantics and notion of strong norm compliance indeed satisfy this property.

To this end, we define how normative states in our semantics can be translated to LTL states, and based on this how normative traces can be translated to LTL traces. LTL states consist of a valuation over the propositions in the language over which formulas are defined. In our case this means that for each atom, auxiliary atom, and action, either the atom or its negation is part of the state. Normative states can then be constructed from LTL states straightforwardly.

DEFINITION 9. *(Normative trace to LTL trace and vice versa) The function* $\mathit{ns2ltl}(n)$ *for some normative state* $n = \langle s, \mathit{aux}, a\rangle$ *yields an LTL state consisting of the set of literals* l *where* $l \in \mathit{lit}(\mathsf{At})$ *and* $s \models l$, *auxiliary atoms* w *for* $w \in \mathit{aux}$, *and negated auxiliary atoms* $\neg w$ *for* $w \in \mathsf{At}_{\mathit{aux}} \setminus \mathit{aux}$, *positive action literal* $\mathit{done}(a)$ *as well as* $\neg \mathit{done}(a')$ *for any* $a' \in \mathsf{Act}$ *with* $a' \neq a$. *The function* $\mathit{nt2ltl}(t)$ *transforms a normative trace* t *that does not include* `stop` *to a normative LTL trace by applying* $\mathit{ns2ltl}$ *to each state on the trace. The space of normative LTL traces consists of sequences of states defined over* At, $\mathsf{At}_{\mathit{aux}}$, *and actions* $\mathsf{Act} \cup \{\mathtt{wait}\}$. *Similarly, the functions* $\mathit{ltls2n}(n)$ *and* $\mathit{ltlt2n}(t)$ *transform an LTL state and trace to a normative state and trace.*

Because states are complete, for any $\mathit{ns2ltl}(n)$ and atom $p \in \mathsf{At}$ we have that either $p \in \mathit{ns2ltl}(n)$ or $\neg p \in \mathit{ns2ltl}(n)$. This is required for construction of an action transition function $\mathcal{T}$ from a trace.

One may expect that strong norm compliance corresponds to satisfiability of the set of norms N. However, it is not enough to consider only the set of norms. Our semantics adds a number of constraints on traces: no action has been executed in initial states (*init*); precisely one action at a time can be executed, which means that only one atom of the form $\mathit{done}(a)$ can hold in a state (*Single*); and at least one must hold (*Do*). Finally, the action `wait` does not change the state expressed over atoms (*Wait*). Below we describe these properties as LTL formulas.

1. $\mathit{init} \equiv (\bigwedge_{a \in \mathsf{Act}} \neg \mathit{done}(a)) \wedge \neg \mathit{done}(\mathtt{wait})$
2. $\mathit{Single} \equiv \Box(\bigwedge_{a_1, a_2 \in \mathsf{Act}} \neg(\mathit{done}(a_1) \wedge \mathit{done}(a_2)))$
3. $\mathit{Do} \equiv \Box(\neg \mathit{init} \rightarrow \bigvee_{a \in \mathsf{Act} \cup \{\mathtt{wait}\}} \mathit{done}(a))$
4. $\mathit{Wait} \equiv \Box(\bigwedge_{p \in \mathsf{At}}(p \wedge \bigcirc(\mathit{done}(\mathtt{wait})) \rightarrow \bigcirc(p))$
5. $N_{\mathit{spec}} \equiv \bigwedge_{r \in N} \Box(r)$

We prove that a formula representing the norms as well as the constraints on initial states and execution of actions is satisfiable iff there is an agent that strongly complies with these norms.

THEOREM 1. *(Satisfiable norms) Let N be a set of norms defined over a set of atoms* At*, set of auxiliary atoms* At_{aux}*, and actions* Act*. We then have that init $\wedge$ Single $\wedge$ Do $\wedge$ Wait $\wedge$ N_{spec} is satisfiable iff there is an action transition function $\mathcal{T}$ and set of initial states S_0 such that an agent $A = \langle S_0, Dec(\mathsf{Act}, S, \mathcal{T})\rangle$ strongly complies with N.*

Proof: (Sketch) ($\Rightarrow$) Assume *init* $\wedge$ *Single* $\wedge$ *Do* $\wedge$ *Wait* $\wedge$ N_{spec} is satisfiable. We can construct the appropriate agent from a trace that satisfies this formula using *ltls2n* to define the transitions in $\mathcal{T}$.

($\Leftarrow$) Because some agent, A, strongly complies with norms we know that there is a strongly norm compliant trace $t \in [\![A]\!]_N$ and thus a strongly compliant normative LTL trace $nt2ltl(t)$. This trace satisfies *Single* $\wedge$ *Do* $\wedge$ *Wait* $\wedge$ N_{spec}. □

5.2 Characterizing Strong Norm Compliance

In this section we provide a characterization of strong norm compliance by showing that an agent strongly complies with norms iff there are no states n on any trace of the agent that are in conflict with respect to the agent's norms and transition function. This yields a deeper understanding of the notion of strong norm compliance by identifying precisely when a problem occurs, and it provides the basis for identifying subsets of norms for which all agents are strongly norm compliant.

We say that a normative state is in conflict when all possible ways in which the agent could potentially progress to a next state are in conflict. To capture what it means to "potentially progress to a next state", we introduce the notion of a Potential Normative Future (PNF). The idea of a PNF is that it captures two states that *could* be paired by the transition system in a way that satisfies all those parts of the norms that do not explicitly restrict the actions that may be taken. A PNF is a tuple $\langle s', aux', A\rangle$ where s' and aux' represent the agent state and auxiliary atoms of the potential next state, and A is a set of action literals that represents the constraints that norms place on the actions that may be executed for this potential next state. The definition of a PNF is independent of $\mathcal{T}$. It implicitly assumes that any state can transition to any other.

DEFINITION 10. *(Potential Normative Future) Let N be a set of norms and $n = \langle s, aux, a\rangle$ a normative state. A potential normative future (PNF) of n is a tuple $\langle s', aux', A\rangle$ where $s' \in S$ is a state, $aux' \subseteq \mathsf{At}_{aux}$ is a set of auxiliary atoms and $A \subseteq lit(\mathsf{Act})$ is a set of action literals such that:*

1. *$\forall r = \phi \Rightarrow \psi \in N_{PTR}$: if $s' \models \phi$ then $\exists l \in \psi : l \in aux'$ or $\exists l \in \psi : l \in A$, and*
2. *$\forall r = \phi \Rightarrow \bigcirc\psi \in N_{SR}$: if $n \models \phi$ then $\exists l \in \psi : l \in aux'$ or $\exists l \in \psi : l \in A$*

Note that A may contain additional action literals not required by the norms. This is required for the proof of Lemma 1.

As an example consider the states s_1, s_2 such that $s_1 \models \phi$ and the norms we generated for $\Box(\phi \rightarrow (done(a_1)$ before $done(a_2)))$ in section 3.2. Then the potential normative futures for some normative state $\langle s_1, \{w\}, a\rangle$ include $\langle s_1, \{w\}, \{\neg done(a_2)\}\rangle$, $\langle s_1, \emptyset, \{done(a_1), \neg done(a_2)\}\rangle$ and $\langle s_2, \{w\}, \{\neg done(a_2)\}\rangle$. They also include "impossible" futures such as $\langle s_1, \{w\}, \{done(a_2), \neg done(a_2)\}\rangle$ – the only requirement is that all literals *required* by the norms be present.

We now define a notion of a conflicted normative state. We identify three possible causes of conflict: (i) the norms require the agent to perform an action that it cannot perform (*practical conflict*), (ii) the norms require the agent to do an action that is forbidden by another (*prohibition conflict*), or (iii) the norms require the agent to do multiple actions at the same time (*obligation conflict*). The latter two are together called a *normative conflict*. A PNF is in conflict if it is in practical or normative conflict.

DEFINITION 11. *(Normative State in Conflict) Let N be a set of norms, $\mathcal{T}$ be a transition function, and $n = \langle s, aux, a\rangle$ a normative state, and let pnf $= \langle s', aux', A\rangle$ be a PNF of n wrt. N.*

- *We say that pnf is in* practical conflict *with $\mathcal{T}$ iff there is an action a such that $done(a) \in A$ and there is no $done(a) \in A : \mathcal{T}(a, s) = s'$.*
- *We say that pnf is in* normative conflict *iff $\exists a, b : a \neq b$ and $done(a), done(b) \in A$ (obligation conflict), or $\exists a : done(a), \neg done(a) \in A$ (prohibition conflict).*

We say that a PNF is in conflict with $\mathcal{T}$ if it is in practical conflict with $\mathcal{T}$ or in normative conflict. We say that a normative state n is in conflict *wrt. set of norms N and action transition function $\mathcal{T}$ iff all PNFs of n with respect to N which contain positive action literals are in conflict with $\mathcal{T}$.*

Where $\mathcal{T}$ and N are obvious from the context we will say that, respectively, a PNF is in conflict or a normative state is in conflict.

COROLLARY 3. *Let pnf $= \langle s', aux', A\rangle$ be a PNF of n with respect to N. Then the following holds: if there is no action a such that $done(a) \in A$, then pnf is not in conflict with any $\mathcal{T}$.*

To prove the theorem that an agent strongly complies with norms iff none if its traces contain conflicting normative states, we first prove a lemma that shows that a transition $n \longrightarrow n'$ complies with norms iff there is a non-conflicting PNF of n.

LEMMA 1. *(Norm-compliance and non-conflicting PNFs) Let N be a set of norms, n a norm compliant state, and $n \longrightarrow n'$ with $n' = \langle s', aux', a'\rangle$ be a transition for an agent A with transition function $\mathcal{T}$. Then $n \longrightarrow n' \models N$ iff there is a PNF $\langle s', aux', A\rangle$ of n that contains a positive action literal and that is not in conflict.*

Proof: (Sketch) ($\Rightarrow$) We construct a non-conflicting PNF, $\langle s', aux', A \cup \{done(a')\}\rangle$, by examining the RHS of all applicable normative rules. If the RHS contains an auxiliary atom it is placed in aux' otherwise it is placed in A. It is simple to prove that this PNF is not in conflict.

($\Leftarrow$) We assume there is a potential normative future *pnf* $= \langle s', aux', A\rangle$ for $n = \langle s, aux, a\rangle$, which is not in conflict and which contains a positive action literal, $done(a')$. Since $done(a') \in A$ then $\mathcal{T}(a', s) = s'$ We show that $n \longrightarrow \langle s', aux', a'\rangle \models N$ which follows simply from the fact that *pnf* is not in conflict. □

We prove that an agent strongly complies with norms iff there are no conflicting states.

THEOREM 2. *An agent $A = \langle S_0, Dec(\mathsf{Act}, S, \mathcal{T})\rangle$ strongly complies with a set of norms N iff there is no normative state n on some trace $t \in [\![A]\!]_N$ that is in conflict.*

Proof: ($\Rightarrow$) Assume that an agent A strongly complies with a set of norms N. This means that all transitions $n \longrightarrow n'$ on all traces $t \in [\![A]\!]_N$ satisfy N. Then by Lemma 1 we know that n has a PNF that contains a positive action literal and is not in conflict, which means that n is not in conflict.

($\Leftarrow$) Assume that there is no normative state n on some trace $t \in [\![A]\!]_N$ that is in conflict. Then for all states n there is a PNF $\langle s', aux', A\rangle$ of n that contains a positive action literal and is not in conflict. Then by Lemma 1 we know that there is an $n' = \langle s', aux', a'\rangle$ such that $n \longrightarrow n' \models N$. By Proposition 5 we know that there is a transition, $n \longrightarrow n''$ on a trace $t \in [\![A]\!]_N$ and $n \longrightarrow n'' \models N$. Therefore there is a norm-compliant transition from all states n on all traces t, and if there is a norm-compliant transition from some state n then all transitions from n on all traces are norm compliant (since `stop` means no norm-compliant transition was possible). Hence A strongly complies with N. □

5.3 Safe Norms

In this section we analyze a number of subsets of norms for which any agent A is strongly norm compliant. This means by Theorem 2 that there can be no normative state of any A that is in conflict. We call these "safe" norms. The first proposition considers step rules with only negative action literals in the rhs.

PROPOSITION 6. *Let N be a set consisting only of step rules of the form $\phi \Rightarrow \bigcirc\neg done(a)$. Then any agent strongly complies with N.*

Proof: Immediate from Corollary 3. □

Proposition 7 concerns step rules that oblige the execution of an action in the next state. Such norms cannot give rise to a conflict when the lhs of the norm implies the precondition of the action (ought implies can), which means that whenever the norm is applicable, the action can be executed. To prevent two actions being obliged at the same time, the lhs of these rules are defined to be mutually exclusive. This is formalized in the following proposition.

PROPOSITION 7.
Let $\mathcal{T}$ be an action transition function and let N be a set consisting only of step rules of the form $\phi \Rightarrow \bigcirc done(a)$ such that:

- *for all $\phi \Rightarrow \bigcirc done(a) \in N$: if $s \models \phi$, then $\mathcal{T}(a, s)$ is defined (ought implies can), and*
- *for any two norms $\phi \Rightarrow \bigcirc done(a) \in N$ and $\phi' \Rightarrow \bigcirc done(a') \in N$ we have $\models \phi \Rightarrow \neg\phi'$ (mutually exclusive lhs).*

Then we have that any agent A with action transition function $\mathcal{T}$ strongly complies with N.

Proof: We have to show that none of the states on traces of A are in conflict. This is simple to show from the fact that at most one rule is applicable in any state. □

We note that the implication does not hold in the other direction. If an agent strongly complies with norms consisting of step rules of the form $\phi \Rightarrow \bigcirc done(a)$, this does not mean that these have to follow ought implies can nor that the lhs have to be mutually exclusive. For example, if the agent can avoid states where the lhs of these rules hold, then they are never applicable. If the lhs of these rules can be satisfied in initial states, which means they should not include positive action literals, and the initial states of the agent $A = \langle S_0, \langle \mathsf{Act}, S, \mathcal{T} \rangle \rangle$ are complete (i.e., $S_0 = S$), then the proposition holds in both directions.

The next proposition considers norms of the form introduced in Section 3.2 where an action has to be executed before another one.

PROPOSITION 8. *Let N be the SNF rules corresponding to a set of norms of the form $\phi \Rightarrow (done(a_1)$ before $done(a_2))$. Then any agent A strongly complies with N.*

Proof: The SNF rules for norms of this form were presented in Section 3.2. Consider a state n where both ϕ and w hold for all rules of this form, i.e., all norms are applicable. If there is no such state, similar reasoning applies for subsets of N. The question is now whether a conflict occurs in such a state. These norms can be satisfied (i.e., a PNF can be constructed accordingly) by not executing actions a_2 and satisfying w, because even if all actions from Act are included in these norms, the agent can execute `wait` to get to the next state in a norm compliant way. Thus a non-conflicting PNF $\langle s', aux', A \rangle$ of n is one where the action set A consists of negative action literals for all actions a_2, aux' is the set of auxiliary atoms w occurring in these rules, and s' is the result of executing some executable action from $\mathsf{Act} \cup \{\mathtt{wait}\}$ such that no norms are violated (and we know this exists due to `wait`). Therefore n is not in conflict, and we are done. □

We note that while any agent with these norms is strongly norm compliant, it may be so because it continues to execute `wait` and thus postpone the execution of $done(a_2)$. If we require that a_2 *is* executed eventually, then assumptions on $\mathcal{T}$ have to be introduced to ensure that a_2 can be executed. These "sometime" rules that require that an action is eventually executed take us out of the next fragment of LTL, and so are not considered in this paper.

6. CONCLUSION AND FUTURE WORK

If we want to ensure that an agent can follow norms in a range of different scenarios where norms may change at run-time, we cannot pre-program all such possible normative behaviours at design time. For this reason we propose a formal semantic framework that specifies an execution mechanism for socially adaptive agents that can adapt their behavior to comply with newly adopted norms at run-time.

Whether an agent can comply with norms is determined by the interplay between execution semantics, norms, and agent capabilities.[6] To arrive at a fundamental understanding of how the combination of these elements affects norm compliance we have provided a formal specification for them, and in doing so have made choices in defining the normative agent semantics, the language of norms and our notion of compliance. We have argued why these choices were made, and we have shown how these choices resulted in satisfaction of relevant properties of the resulting framework.

In summary, this paper provides the following main contributions: i) a set of properties that a normative agent semantics should satisfy, ii) a declarative *normative agent semantics* with proofs that the properties are satisfied, iii) a definition of *strong norm compliance* with an exploration of its semantic characteristics. In particular we provide a logical characterization, a semantic characterization, and an exploration of safe norm sets.

In future work we plan to explore other choices for defining a framework and how they affect norm compliance. In particular, extensions of the language of norms, such as larger fragments of SNF, and alternative notions of norm compliance, such as the *bounded* norm compliance corresponding to bounded rationality. We also aim to investigate the effect of complying with norms on goal achievement (see also [21]), and studying how an agent can comply with norms with minimal effort. Finally, we will explore how this framework can be integrated with techniques for reasoning about norm violation, working towards a comprehensive framework for normative agents.

REFERENCES

[1] N. Alechina, M. Dastani, and B. Logan. Programming norm-aware agents. In *Proceedings of the 11th International*

[6]Eventually we will also need to take into account environment characteristics and actions of other agents and study their effect on norm compliance. However, before we can embark upon studying such complex interactions we need a proper understanding of the fundamentals of norm compliance.

Conference on Autonomous Agents and Multiagent Systems (AAMAS'12), pages 1057–1064. IFAAMAS, 2012.

[2] G. Andrighetto, M. Campenni, F. Cecconi, and R. Conte. The complex loop of norm emergence: A simulation model. In *Simulating Interacting Agents and Social Phenomena: The second world congress*, volume 7 of *Agent-Based Social Systems*, pages 19–35. Springer, 2010.

[3] G. Andrighetto, G. Governatori, P. Noriega, and L. W. N. van der Torre, editors. *Normative Multi-Agent Systems*, volume 4 of *Dagstuhl Follow-Ups*. Schloss Dagstuhl–Leibniz-Zentrum fuer Informatik, 2013.

[4] G. Boella and R. Damiano. An architecture for normative reactive agents. In *Proceedings of the 5th Pacific Rim International Workshop on Intelligent Agents and Multi-Agent Systems (PRIMA'02)*, volume 2413 of *LNCS*, pages 1–17, 2002.

[5] R. H. Bordini, M. Dastani, J. Dix, and A. El Fallah Seghrouchni. *Multi-Agent Programming: Languages, Platforms and Applications*. Springer, Berlin, 2005.

[6] J. Broersen and J. Brunel. Preservation of obligations in a temporal and deontic framework. In *Proceedings of the 6th International Joint Conference on Autonomous Agents and Multiagent Systems (AAMAS'07)*, pages 1108–1110. ACM, 2007.

[7] J. Broersen, S. Cranefield, Y. Elrakaiby, D. Gabbay, D. Grossi, E. Lorini, X. Parent, L. W. N. van der Torre, L. Tummolini, P. Turrini, and F. Schwarzentruber. Normative reasoning and consequence. In G. Andrighetto, G. Governatori, P. Noriega, and L. W. N. van der Torre, editors, *Normative Multi-Agent Systems*, volume 4 of *Dagstuhl Follow-Ups*, pages 33–70. Schloss Dagstuhl–Leibniz-Zentrum fuer Informatik, 2013.

[8] N. Bulling, M. Dastani, and M. Knobbout. Monitoring norm violations in multi-agent systems. In *Proceedings of the twelfth international joint conference on autonomous agents and multiagent systems (AAMAS'13)*, pages 491–498. IFAAMAS, 2013.

[9] R. Conte, C. Castelfranchi, and F. Dignum. Autonomous norm acceptance. In *Proceedings of the 5th International Workshop on Agent Theories, Architectures, and Languages (ATAL'98)*, volume 1555 of *LNCS*, pages 99–112. Springer, 1999.

[10] S. Cranefield, M. Winikoff, and W. Vasconcelos. Modelling and monitoring interdependent expectations. In S. Cranefield, M. Riemsdijk, J. Vázquez-Salceda, and P. Noriega, editors, *Coordination, Organizations, Institutions, and Norms in Agent System VII*, volume 7254 of *LNCS*, pages 149–166. Springer, 2012.

[11] N. Criado, E. Argente, P. Noriega, and V. Botti. Human-inspired model for norm compliance decision making. *Information Sciences*, 245:218–239, 2013.

[12] D. D'Aprile, L. Giordano, V. Gliozzi, A. Martelli, G. Pozzato, and D. T. Dupré. Verifying business process compliance by reasoning about actions. In J. Dix, J. Leite, G. Governatori, and W. Jamroga, editors, *Computational Logic in Multi-Agent Systems*, volume 6245 of *Lecture Notes in Computer Science*, pages 99–116. Springer, 2010.

[13] F. Dignum, V. Dignum, J. Thangarajah, L. Padgham, and M. Winikoff. Open agent systems??? In *Proceedings of the 8th International Workshop on Agent-Oriented Software Engineering (AOSE'07)*, volume 4951 of *LNCS*, pages 73–87. Springer, 2008.

[14] F. Dignum and R. Kuiper. Combining dynamic deontic logic and temporal logic for the specification of deadlines. In *Proceedings of the Thirtieth Hawaii International Conference on System Sciences*, volume 5, pages 336–346. IEEE, 1997.

[15] A. Elgammal. *Towards a comprehensive framework for business process compliance*. PhD thesis, 2012.

[16] E. Emerson. Temporal and modal logic. In J. van Leeuwen, editor, *Handbook of Theoretical Computer Science*, volume B: Formal Models and Semantics, pages 996–1072. Elsevier, Amsterdam, 1990.

[17] M. S. Fagundes, H. Billhardt, and S. Ossowski. Normative reasoning with an adaptive self-interested agent model based on Markov Decision Processes. In *Proceedings of the 12th Ibero-American Conference on AI (IBERAMIA'10)*, volume 6433 of *LNCS*, pages 274–283. Springer, 2010.

[18] M. Fisher. A normal form for temporal logics and its applications in theorem-proving and execution. *Journal of Logic and Computation*, 7(4):429–456, 1997.

[19] M. Fisher. Agent deliberation in an executable temporal framework. *Journal of Applied Logic*, 9(4):223–238, 2011.

[20] M. Fisher and A. Hepple. Executing logical agent specifications. In R. H. Bordini, M. Dastani, J. Dix, and A. El Fallah Seghrouchni, editors, *Multi-Agent Programming: Languages, Tools and Applications*, pages 1–27. Springer, Berlin, 2009.

[21] G. Governatori, F. Olivieri, S. Scannapieco, and M. Cristani. Designing for compliance: Norms and goals. In F. Olken, M. Palmirani, and D. Sottara, editors, *5th International Symposium on Rule-Based Modeling and Computing on the Semantic Web (RuleML'11)*, pages 282–297. Springer, 2011.

[22] G. Governatori and S. Shazia. The journey to business process compliance. pages 426–454. IGI Global, 2009.

[23] H. Groefsema and D. Bucur. A survey of formal business process verification: From soundness to variability. In *International Symposium on Business Modeling and Software Design*, pages 198–203, 2013.

[24] J. Hansen, G. Pigozzi, and L. van der Torre. Ten philosophical problems in deontic logic. In G. Boella, L. van der Torre, and H. Verhagen, editors, *Normative Multi-agent Systems*, number 07122 in Dagstuhl Seminar Proceedings. Internationales Begegnungs- und Forschungszentrum für Informatik (IBFI), Schloss Dagstuhl, Germany, 2007.

[25] K. Hindriks and M. B. van Riemsdijk. Satisfying maintenance goals. In *Proceedings of the fifth International Workshop on Declarative Agent Languages and Technologies (DALT'07)*, volume 4897 of *LNAI*, pages 86–103. Springer, 2007.

[26] F. López y López, M. Luck, and M. d'Inverno. Constraining autonomy through norms. In *The First International Joint Conference on Autonomous Agents and Multiagent Systems (AAMAS'02)*, pages 674–681. ACM, 2002.

[27] F. López y López, M. Luck, and M. d'Inverno. Normative agent reasoning in dynamic societies. In *The Third International Joint Conference on Autonomous Agents and Multiagent Systems (AAMAS'04)*, pages 732–739. IEEE Computer Society, 2004.

[28] F. M. Maggi, M. Westergaard, M. Montali, and W. M. van der Aalst. Runtime verification of ltl-based declarative process models. In S. Khurshid and K. Sen, editors, *Runtime*

Verification, volume 7186 of *Lecture Notes in Computer Science*, pages 131–146. Springer, 2012.

[29] F. Meneguzzi and M. Luck. Norm-based behaviour modification in BDI agents. In *Proceedings of the eighth international joint conference on autonomous agents and multiagent systems (AAMAS'09)*, pages 177–184, Budapest, 2009.

[30] M. Montali, P. Torroni, F. Chesani, P. Mello, M. Alberti, and E. Lamma. Abductive logic programming as an effective technology for the static verification of declarative business processes. *Fundamenta Informaticae*, 102(3-4):325–361, 2010.

[31] S. Panagiotidi and J. Vázquez-Salceda. Norm-aware planning: Semantics and implementation. In *Proceedings of the 2011 IEEE/WIC/ACM International Conferences on Web Intelligence and Intelligent Agent Technology - Volume 03*, pages 33–36. IEEE, 2011.

[32] M. B. van Riemsdijk, L. Dennis, M. Fisher, and K. V. Hindriks. Agent reasoning for norm compliance: a semantic approach. In *Proceedings of the twelfth international joint conference on autonomous agents and multiagent systems (AAMAS'13)*, pages 499–506. IFAAMAS, 2013.

[33] M. B. van Riemsdijk, K. V. Hindriks, C. M. Jonker, and M. Sierhuis. Formalizing organizational constraints: A semantic approach. In *Proceedings of the nineth international joint conference on autonomous agents and multiagent systems (AAMAS'10)*, pages 823–830. IFAAMAS, 2010.

Synthesising Liberal Normative Systems

Javier Morales[1,2], Maite Lopez-Sanchez[1]
[1]Universitat de Barcelona
Barcelona, Spain
jmorales@iiia.csic.es
maite@maia.ub.es

Juan A. Rodriguez-Aguilar
[2]Artificial Intelligence Research Institute (IIIA-CSIC)
Campus UAB. Bellaterra, Spain
jar@iiia.csic.es

Michael Wooldridge
Dept. of Computer Science
University of Oxford
Oxford, UK
mjw@cs.ox.ac.uk

Wamberto Vasconcelos
Dept. of Computing Science
University of Aberdeen
Aberdeen, UK
wvasconcelos@acm.org

ABSTRACT

Norms have been extensively studied to coordinate multi-agent systems, and the literature has investigated two general approaches to norm synthesis: off-line (synthesising norms at design-time) and on-line (run-time synthesis). On-line synthesis is generally recognised to be appropriate for open systems, where aspects of the system remain unknown at design-time. In this paper we present LION, an algorithm aimed at synthesising *liberal* normative systems. LION's normative systems respect the agents' autonomy to the greatest possible extent, constraining their behaviour when only necessary to avoid undesirable system states. LION's norm synthesis is also driven by the need to construct *compact* normative systems. The key to the success of LION in this multi-objective synthesis process is that it learns about and exploits norm synergies. More precisely, LION can learn when norms are either substitutable or complementary. We show empirically that LION significantly outperforms the state of the art by synthesising normative systems that are more liberal while maintaining representation compactness.

Categories and Subject Descriptors

I.2.11 [**Artificial Intelligence**]: Distributed Artificial Intelligence —*Multiagent Systems*

General Terms

Algorithms

Keywords

Norms; Normative Systems; On-line Norm Synthesis

1. INTRODUCTION

Norms have been extensively studied as a technique for coordinating interactions within multi-agent systems (MAS) [6, 4]. However, computing a normative system (i.e., a set of norms) that will effectively coordinate a multi-agent system has been identified as a computationally complex (NP-hard) problem [21]. Two general approaches to the design of norms have been investigated in the literature: off-line [21, 7, 1] (design time synthesis) and on-line [17, 18, 8, 15, 3] (run-time synthesis). It is generally recognised that on-line synthesis is better suited than off-line synthesis for open systems, where aspects of the system (such as the system state space or the range of possible agent behaviours) are unknown at design-time.

Appears in: *Proceedings of the 14th International Conference on Autonomous Agents and Multiagent Systems (AAMAS 2015), Bordini, Elkind, Weiss, Yolum (eds.), May 4–8, 2015, Istanbul, Turkey.*

Recent research on on-line synthesis has focused on norm emergence [20, 19, 9, 23], which considers that agents collaborate to synthesise their own norms. However, this line of research makes several strong assumptions, namely that agents will participate in the norm synthesis process, and will have the appropriate computational capabilities to synthesise norms. These assumptions are not required in a family of alternative on-line norm synthesis approaches [11, 12, 13] that synthesise normative systems from the observation of agents' interactions. On the one hand, they synthesise norms that are *effective* to avoid undesirable states of a MAS (i.e., conflicts) as long as agents comply with them. On the other hand, they aim at avoiding over-regulation by preserving only those norms that are *necessary* to avoid such conflicts. Based on [11], the IRON [12] and SIMON [13] systems focus on synthesising *compact* normative systems. Compactness is concerned with minimising both the number of norms that are given to the agents as well as their norm reasoning computational effort. With this aim, they perform norm generalisations that represent several (specific) norms by means of general (abstract) norms. The normative systems that result have fewer and more general norms (and thus, easier to reason about) than [11]. In particular, SIMON proved to be the *best-in-class* approach, outperforming IRON in terms of compactness.

However, even though IRON and SIMON minimise the number of norms, they do not take into account agents' actual freedom, a key synthesis criterion that considers how norms constrain their behaviour. This is so because a general norm (such as, for example, "give way to any approaching car" in a traffic scenario), represents several specific norms ("give way to left", "give way to right", etc.) which together restrict agents' behaviour to a high extent. Therefore, the smaller the number of constraints in a normative system, the greater freedom for the agents. Along this line of preserving autonomy, the work in [7] proposes to minimise the number of constraints that agents are required to obey. Additionally, the work in [1] introduces *liberality* as a relationship between normative systems. It states that a normative system Ω is *more liberal* (less restrictive) than another one Ω' if it places fewer constraints on the agents. Thus, following the traffic example, we can state that a normative system with a "give way to left" norm is *more liberal* than one with a norm "give way to any approaching car".

Aiming at synthesising liberal normative systems without compromising compactness, we present LION (*LI*beral *O*n-line *N*orm synthesis). Based on [13], LION aims at synthesising normative systems that (i) avoid undesired states (i.e., conflicts) in a system; (ii) minimise the number of norms; and (iii) maximise agents' freedom (i.e., autonomy) by minimising the number of imposed constraints. The key to the success of LION in this multi-objective synthesis process is that it learns about and exploits norm synergies. More precisely, LION can learn when norms are either *substitutable* or *complementary*. Substitutability and complementarity [16, 10] are well-known concepts in economics that apply to a wide range of domains [2, 25, 22]. While two substitute goods may replace one another in use, complementary goods are better used together. By considering such relationships, LION outperforms SIMON in terms of liberality without compromising criteria (i) and (ii). In 96% of our simulations using a simple traffic domain LION synthesised normative systems that contained, on average, 90% fewer substitutability relationships than those synthesised by SIMON.

The remainder of this paper is organised as follows. Section 2 provides the necessary background about previous norm synthesis approaches. Next, Section 3 introduces concepts used in LION, which is presented in Section 4. Section 5 reports our empirical evaluation and Section 6 concludes the paper.

2. BACKGROUND

As previously introduced, the work reported in [11, 12, 13] constitutes a family of on-line norm synthesis approaches that synthesise normative systems from the observation of agents' interactions. In what follows, we present the key concepts of SIMON [13], which proved to be the best-in-class approach.

Briefly, SIMON synthesises norms by continuously monitoring a system at runtime, searching for undesirable states (which we refer to as *conflicts*). Whenever a conflict arises, it proposes a new norm (aimed at avoiding the conflict in the future) and provides the updated set of active norms to the agents. Agents can then decide whether to comply or not with those norms that apply to them at each time step. Norm fulfilment/infringement decisions may have effects in terms of future conflicts. SIMON gathers this information as norm performance is evidenced (i.e., if they where effective/necessary to avoid conflicts). Norm evaluation can then be used to refine the normative system by (i) generalising well-performing norms that can be represented in a more compact manner, and (ii) discarding (or specialising) under-performing norms.

SIMON considers a system populated by a set of agents Ag that can perform a set of actions $Ac \subseteq \mathcal{L}_{Ag}$. The *context* of an agent is a formula of a first-order logic language $\mathcal{L}_{Ag}$ that describes the local perception of that agent (i.e., the agent's own point of view). $\mathcal{L}_{Ag}$ is composed of first-order predicates $p(\tau_1, \dots, \tau_n)$, where p is a predicate symbol and $\tau_1, \dots, \tau_n$ are terms of $\mathcal{L}_{Ag}$. A *norm* is then defined so that it will apply to an agent whenever the context of that agent satisfies the precondition of the norm. Specifically, norms are of the form $\langle \varphi, \theta(ac) \rangle$, where φ is the norm's precondition and $\theta(ac)$ its post-condition (where φ is a formula of $\mathcal{L}_{Ag}$, θ is a deontic operator such as a *prohibition*, and $ac \in Ac$). We say $\theta(ac)$ holds for any agent whose context satisfies φ. Furthermore, we say a norm is *specific* iff all its terms are grounded.

SIMON keeps synthesised norms as nodes in a directed graph data structure called the *Normative Network* (NN), so that it represents current normative system Ω as its set of active norms. Moreover, edges in SIMON's NN stand for norm *generalisation* relationships. SIMON creates general norms that compactly represent specific norms. Generalisation may lead to over-generalisations that will be backtracked by specialization whenever one of the specific norms under-performs.

In order to illustrate these concepts, we introduce a traffic example scenario in which $ambulance$, $police$ represent different types of $emergency$ vehicles; car, $motorbike$ describe $private$ vehicles; and any represents both $emergency$ and $private$ terms. Figure 1a depicts a normative network composed of four specific active norms n_1 : *"Give way to ambulances"*, n_2 : *"Give way to police"*, n_3 : *"Give way to cars"*, and n_4 : *"Give way to motorbikes"*. Since *ambulances* and *police cars* are both *emergency* vehicles, SIMON

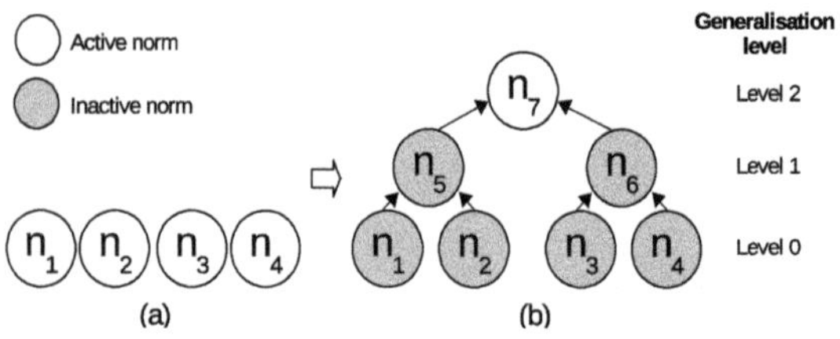

Figure 1: Generalisation of norms $n_1, n_2, n_3, n_4, n_5, n_6$.

will create a general norm n_5 : *"Give way to emergency vehicles"* to represent (and establish a generalisation relationship with) n_1 and n_2. Similarly, a new general norm n_6 : *"Give way to private vehicles"* will generalise norms n_3, n_4, which in turn will lead to the creation of a new norm n_7 : *"Give way to any vehicle"* with the highest generalisation level. Figure 1b shows the resulting normative network, where $\Omega = \{n_7\}$. Afterwards, in case n_1 underperforms, SIMON will deactivate n_1, n_5, n_7 and will activate n_2, n_6 so that the normative system becomes updated ($\Omega = \{n_2, n_6\}$).

Generalisation thus provides representation compactness but, as introduced in Section 1, general norms can represent an arbitrary number of constraints (i.e., specific norms) and, in particular, some of them may not be required to avoid conflicts. Thus, generalisations may over-constrain the system, restricting the freedom of agents. Indeed, in [13] SIMON was employed to synthesise norms and this was the case. There, a slightly different traffic scenario was used, where each car described its perceptions by means of predicates *left*, *front*, *right*, each predicate containing one term out of $\{car\text{-}to\text{-}left, car\text{-}to\text{-}right, car\text{-}same\text{-}heading, wall, nil, any\}$. The first three terms represent a car heading in different directions with respect to the reference car, term $wall$ represents the perception of a wall, nil means that a car does not perceive anything, and any stands for car, $wall$ or nil. Table 1 shows SIMON's most-frequently synthesised normative system, which was obtained by executing SIMON's publicly available code [14]. This normative system resulted in 90% of the tests and proved to avoid collisions when norms were fulfilled just by having five explicit general norms. Nevertheless, this compact normative system implicitly represents (i.e., includes) 18 different constraints[1] and not all of them are really required. In fact, n_a represents a general norm of giving way to the left (that is, a car should stop whenever it perceives a car to its left, and no matter what it perceives to its front and right positions) and n_b is a general norm to give way to the right[2]. It is worth noticing that n_a does not generalise n_b nor the other way around, and thus they are not related from SIMON's point of view. However, although they are neither syntactically related, if we could go a step further and consider semantics, then we could infer that the normative system could still prevent collisions by just having one of these two norms. Therefore, there is room for finding an alternative normative system that is more liberal (poses fewer constraints to agents) than that obtained by SIMON.

Nevertheless, removing constraints from a normative system is not straightforward, since norm synergies within the normative system need to be taken into account. In the previous example from Table 1, specific norms n_a and n_b can replace one another, and thus we say they are *substitutable*. However, the proper performance of some specific norms may depend on the existence of other specific norms. If this is the case, then we say that these specific norms complement each other: they are *complementary*. Furthermore,

[1] Notice that the addition of #Constr. column in Table 1 results in 28, but several general norms generalise to the same specific norm.

[2] The remaining norms n_c, n_d, n_e ensure a car stops whenever it perceives a car ahead with different headings.

Norm	Pre-condition (θ)	Norm target	#Constr.
n_a	*left(car-to-right), front(any), right(any)*	*prh(Go)*	6
n_b	*left(any), front(any), right(car-to-left)*	*prh(Go)*	6
n_c	*left(any), front(car-same-heading), right(any)*	*prh(Go)*	8
n_d	*left(any), front(car-to-left), right(any)*	*prh(Go)*	4
n_e	*left(any), front(car-to-right), right(any)*	*prh(Go)*	4

Table 1: A typical SIMON's normative system upon convergence, along with the number of constraints each norm represents.

there may be substitutable norms that are complementary to others, and this should be considered when discarding norms if we want to preserve the effectiveness of the normative system (i.e., its performance in avoiding undesired states).

We thus conclude that SIMON's normative systems are overconstrained, but that aiming at synthesising more liberal normative systems amounts to managing norm synergies in this multi-objective synthesis process. More precisely, substitutability and complementarity relationships between specific norms need to be successfully learned and exploited.

3. CHARACTERISING NORM SYNERGIES

This section formally characterises the notion of synergies between norms. In particular, we focus on two types of norm synergies: substitutability and complementarity. On the one hand, we consider that two norms are substitutable if they satisfy the same regulatory requirements and, therefore, can be used to replace one another. On the other hand, we consider that two norms are complementary if they are better when used together instead of separately. Next, in section 3.1 we provide some preliminary definitions, while in section 3.2 we provide the formal characterisation of both norm relationships. Finally, we also discuss the relationship between complementarity, substitutability, and generalisation.

3.1 Preliminary definitions

Our basic definitions follow those of [13] presented in Section 2. Thus, we consider a multi-agent system composed of a set of agents Ag; a set of actions $Ac = \{ac_1, \dots, ac_m\}$ available to the agents; a set S of states of the system, where a state s is a set of ground atomic formulae from $\mathcal{L}_{Ag}$; and a set $C \subset S$ of undesirable states. The set of active norms is made available to the agents as a normative system (e.g., Table 1).

Furthermore, we consider a *state transition function* $\mathbb{T} : S \times Ac^{|Ag|} \to S$ that leads the MAS to a state s' from a state s after the agents perform a collection of actions $A \subseteq Ac^{|Ag|}$. We will denote a transition from a state s to a state s' after the performance of A by $\langle s, A, s' \rangle$. For convenience, Ac includes a special action nil that stands for not performing any action. Then, given a transition $\langle s, A, s' \rangle$, function $action : Ag \times S \times S \to Ac$ returns the action that an agent performed during the transition. We assume each agent has its own perception of the MAS it is part of. Such perception is a partial representation of the MAS from the agent's local point of view. Thus, we consider that an agent ag perceives the MAS at a state s by means of its local function *context* $c : Ag \times S \to \mathcal{P}(\mathcal{L}_{Ag})$, which returns a set of predicates with terms of language $\mathcal{L}_{Ag}$. Besides, we will also consider that an agent can tell what other agents it can perceive. This is captured by the scope function $sc : Ag \times S \to \mathcal{P}(Ag)$, which returns the set of agents that an agent perceives at a given state. When an agent ag' is in the scope of agent ag, we say that ag' is detected by ag.

We now introduce the core concepts of norm fulfilment and norm infringement. We first establish when a norm applies: $\langle \varphi, \theta(ac) \rangle$ *applies* to agent ag at state s if the agent's local context $c(ag, s)$ satisfies the precondition of the norm, namely iff $c(ag, s) \models \varphi$. Let there be $\langle \varphi, \theta(ac) \rangle$ which applies to agent ag at state s, and a transition $\langle s, A, s' \rangle$; we then say that the agent *fulfilled* the norm during the state transition if either it did not perform an action prohibited by the norm or it performed an action obliged by the norm.

DEF. 1 (NORM FULFILMENT). *Let $s \in S$ be a state, $ag \in Ag$ an agent, and $n = \langle \varphi, \theta(ac) \rangle$ be a norm that applies to ag at s. We say that ag fulfilled norm n during a transition $\langle s, A, s' \rangle$ when either: (i) $\theta = prh$ and $action(ag, s, s') \neq ac$; or (ii) $\theta = obl$ and $action(ag, s, s') = ac$.*

As a dual concept to norm fulfilment, we consider that an agent *infringed* a norm during a state transition if it performed an action that the norm prohibited or it did not perform an action that the norm enforced.

DEF. 2 (NORM INFRINGEMENT). *Let $s \in S$ be a state, $ag \in Ag$ an agent, and $n = \langle \varphi, \theta(ac) \rangle$ a norm that applies to ag at s. We say that ag infringed norm n during a transition $\langle s, A, s' \rangle$ when either: (i) $\theta = prh$ and $action(ag, s, s') = ac$; or (ii) $\theta = obl$ and $action(ag, s, s') \neq ac$.*

Next, we provide our formal characterisation of norm synergies.

3.2 Substitutability and complementarity

As mentioned above, two norms are substitutable if they satisfy the same regulatory needs and, therefore, can be used to replace one another, whereas two norms are complementary if they perform better when used together. Therefore, in order to assess whether any of these two relationships holds between a pair of norms, we will have to assess the difference in outcome between the fulfilment of the two norms at the same time and their individual fulfilments. Thus, substitutability between two norms will hold when the concurrent fulfilment of the two norms avoids undesired states, but also does the individual fulfilment of any of the two norms (while the other one is infringed). By contrast, complementarity between two norms will hold when only the concurrent fulfilment of both norms avoids undesired states, whereas the individual fulfilment of any of the two norms does not.

However, before formalising substitutability and complementarity we need to establish when two norms concurrently apply. First, we consider the notion of joint context. We say that two agents share a joint context in a given state if they can detect (perceive) one another. Formally,

DEF. 3 (JOINT CONTEXT). *Let $s \in S$ be a state, and $ag, ag' \in Ag$ two agents with contexts $c(ag, s)$, $c(ag', s)$ and scopes $sc(ag, s)$, $sc(ag', s)$. We say that $\langle c(ag, s), c(ag', s) \rangle$ is a joint context shared by the agents iff $ag' \in sc(ag, s)$ and $ag \in sc(ag', s)$.*

Then, when two agents share a joint context and there are two norms such that there is one norm that applies to each agent, we say that the norms concurrently apply. Formally,

DEF. 4 (CONCURRENT APPLICABILITY). *Let $s \in S$ be a state, $ag, ag' \in Ag$ two agents that share a joint context $\langle c(ag, s), c(ag', s) \rangle$, and $n = \langle \varphi, \theta(ac) \rangle$, $n' = \langle \varphi', \theta'(ac') \rangle$ two different norms. We say that n, n' concurrently apply in the joint context iff $c(ag, s) \models \varphi$ and $c(ag', s) \models \varphi'$.*

We now formalise the notion of substitutability. We notice though that we will consider that substitutability only holds between *specific norms* as defined in Section 2. Thus, for example, $\langle \{left(car\text{-}to\text{-}right), front(nil), right(nil)\}, prh(Go) \rangle$ is a specific norm generalised (represented) by n_a in Table 1. Then, we say that two specific norms that concurrently apply are substitutable in a particular state when only one of them is required to avoid a transition to an undesired state. Formally,

DEF. 5 (SUBSTITUTABILITY). *Let $s \in S$ be a state, $C \subseteq S$ a set of undesired states, and $ag, ag' \in Ag$ two agents that share a joint context $\langle c(ag, s), c(ag', s)\rangle$. Let n, n' be two different, specific norms such that n applies to ag and n' applies to ag', and they concurrently apply in the agents' joint context. Let $\langle s, A, s'\rangle$ be the transition that results after ag and ag' perform actions $ac \in A$ and $ac' \in A$ respectively. Norms n, n' are substitutable in s iff the following conditions hold: (i) a conflict occurs ($s' \in C$) when both agents infringe their norms; and (ii) no conflict occurs ($s' \notin C$) when at least one of the agents fulfils its applicable norm.*

In Section 2 we illustrated substitutability with two norms n_a: "give way to left" and n_b: "give way to right". Notice that both norms concurrently apply together in a situation in which (i) two cars perceive each other; and (ii) each norm applies to only one of the cars. In this situation, collisions can be avoided by employing only one of the norms. Therefore, employing both norms would over-constrain the situation. We say then that both norms substitute one another, namely they are substitutable, since any of them could satisfactorily regulate the situation.

From the definition above, we say that two norms are substitutable in a set of states if they are substitutable at each state. Consider now all the states of a system where two norms concurrently apply, we say that the two norms are *fully substitutable* if they are substitutable in all those states. We notice that the substitutability relationship is irreflexive, and symmetric, but non-transitive.

Next we formalise the notion of complementarity. We say that two norms that concurrently apply are complementary in a particular state when the two of them are required to avoid a transition to an undesired state. Formally,

DEF. 6 (COMPLEMENTARITY). *Let $s \in S$ be a state, $C \subseteq S$ a set of undesired states, and $ag, ag' \in Ag$ two agents that share a joint context $\langle c(ag, s), c(ag', s)\rangle$. Let n, n' be two different, specific norms such that n applies to ag and n' applies to ag', and they concurrently apply in the agents' joint context. Say that $\langle s, A, s'\rangle$ is the transition that results after ag and ag' perform actions $ac \in A$ and $ac' \in A$ respectively. Norms n, n' are complementary in s iff the following conditions hold: (i) a conflict occurs ($s' \in C$) when at least one of the agents infringes its applicable norm; and (ii) no conflict occurs ($s' \notin C$) when both agents fulfil their norms.*

From the definition above, we say that two norms are complementary in a set of states if they are complementary at each state. We say that the two norms are *fully complementary* if they are complementary in all the states of the system where they concurrently apply. Like substitutability, the complementarity relationship is irreflexive, and symmetric, but non-transitive.

OBSERVATION 1. *Generalisation, substitutability, and complementarity are mutually exclusive relationships.*

To see this, first observe that substitutability and complementarity are mutually exclusive relationships: two norms that are substitutable cannot be complementary at the same time and the other way around. This directly follows from the conditions in definitions 5 and 6. Furthermore, generalisation and substitutability are mutually exclusive. This also comes from the definition of generalisation and substitutability. According to definition 5, substitutability only holds between specific norms, whereas generalisation always requires at least a non-specific norm. From this it follows that generalisation and substitutability cannot hold at the very same time between two norms. Following the same line of reasoning, since complementarity only holds between specific norms, generalisation and complementarity are mutually exclusive.

This observation tells us that the norm synthesis algorithm described in [13], which only learned generalisation relationships, never learned any substitutability relationship nor any complementarity relationship. In the next section we show how a norm synthesis process can take advantage of substitutability and complementarity relationships. The aim of our normative synthesis process will be: (i) to exploit generalisation relationships to yield a compact normative system; (ii) to exploit substitutability to disregard over-constraining norms; and (iii) to exploit complementarity to keep together norms that are better off together.

4. SYNTHESISING LIBERAL NORMATIVE SYSTEMS

We now describe LION (*LI*beral *O*n-line *N*orm synthesis), our novel multi-objective norm synthesis mechanism. LION aims to synthesise compact normative systems that avoid undesirable states (i.e., conflicts) while respecting the autonomy of agents to the greatest possible extent. The main feature of LION is that it is capable of learning and exploiting (benefitting from) norm synergies during the norm synthesis process. More precisely, LION identifies when norms are either substitutable or complementary, book-keeps these relationships between norms, and uses this knowledge (together with the generalisation relationships) to synthesise liberal normative systems that perform well and do not compromise compactness. This requires carefully handling the interplay between all norm relationships at synthesis time.

Specifically, LION continuously monitors agents' interactions at run-time, searching for conflicts and creating norms to avoid them. LION publishes the normative system that it currently handles (the current active norms) so that agents make their decision considering whether to fulfil or infringe its norms. The outcome of agents' decisions may (or may not) lead to conflicts. LION captures such outcomes to evaluate how norms perform individually and to detect pair-wise relationships between specific norms. From this, LION updates the current normative system as follows. On the one hand, LION employs the individual performance of norms to either perform generalisations (when norms perform well) or specialisations (when a norm performs poorly). On the other hand, LION exploits norm relationships to discard (deactivate) norms involved in substitutability relationships. The heuristic employed to make this decision is simple: given two substitutable norms, choose to discard the one that causes less *compactness loss* provided that it is not part of any complementarity relationships. Since deactivating a norm leads to specialisation, and hence to losing compactness, LION chooses to discard the norm that minimises such loss. Overall, generalisation pursues compactness, complementarity safeguards performance, and discarding substitutable norms provides liberality.

This section is thus organised as follows. Section 4.1 details how LION represents substitutability and complementarity relationships, Section 4.2 explains how it detects these relationships and Section 4.3 details how it exploits them. Finally, Section 4.4 presents LION's multi-objective norm synthesis strategy, and Section 4.5 defines metrics to evaluate normative systems.

4.1 Representing norm relationships

First, LION generalises the notion of *Normative Network* introduced in [12], and referred to in Section 2, to represent norm relationships as follows:

DEF. 7 (GENERALISED NORMATIVE NETWORK). *A generalised normative network (GNN) is a tuple* $\langle \mathcal{N}, \mathcal{E}_\mathcal{G}, \mathcal{E}_\mathcal{S}, \mathcal{E}_\mathcal{C}, \Delta, \delta \rangle$ *where:* (i) $(\mathcal{N}, \mathcal{E}_\mathcal{G} \cup \mathcal{E}_\mathcal{S} \cup \mathcal{E}_\mathcal{C})$ *is a graph such that:* $\mathcal{N}$ *is a set of norms that correspond to the nodes in the graph;* $\mathcal{E}_\mathcal{G} \subseteq \mathcal{N} \times \mathcal{N}$ *is a set of directed edges representing generalisation relationships* ($(n, n') \in \mathcal{E}_\mathcal{G}$ *means that* n' *generalises* n*);* $\mathcal{E}_\mathcal{S} \subseteq \mathcal{N} \times \mathcal{N}$ *is a set of undirected edges standing for substitutability relationships;* $\mathcal{E}_\mathcal{C} \subseteq \mathcal{N} \times \mathcal{N}$ *is a set of undirected edges standing for complementarity relationships; and* $\mathcal{E}_\mathcal{G}, \mathcal{E}_\mathcal{S}, \mathcal{E}_\mathcal{C}$ *are pair-wise disjoint.* (vi) $\Delta = \{Active, Inactive\}$ *is the set of possible states of a norm in* $\mathcal{N}$*;* (vii) $\delta : \mathcal{N} \to \Delta$ *yields the state of a norm in* $\mathcal{N}$.

Figure 2b shows a GNN built by LION after detecting substitutability and complementarity relationships between norms. We notice that specific norms n_9 and n_1 hold a substitutability relationship; specific norms n_9 and n_{11} hold a complementarity relationship; and the rest of relationships (directed edges) stand for generalisations (n_{10} generalises n_8, n_9 and n_7 generalises norms n_1–n_6 at different generalisation levels). Since norms n_{11}, n_{10}, n_7 are the only ones active (denoted by white circles), the GNN represents the normative system $\Omega = \{n_{11}, n_{10}, n_7\}$.

4.2 Detecting norm relationships

Next we describe how LION learns, at run-time, substitutability and complementarity relationships between specific norms in the GNN. We recall from Section 3.2 that a pair of concurrently applicable norms are *substitutable* if no conflicts arise whenever at least one of them is fulfilled. Similarly, they are considered *complementary* if any conflicts arise whenever at least one of them is infringed. LION is an on-line process that progressively gathers evidences, as they occur, to support whether a pair of norms are either substitutable or complementary. Thus, given a pair of norms, if the substitutability conditions in Def. 5 occur a sufficient number of times, namely for a sufficient number of states, LION considers that the relationship holds. The same applies to complementarity. When LION learns that either a substitutability or complementarity relationship holds, it does represent it in the GNN.

LION proceeds as follows. Whenever it detects a new pair of concurrently applicable norms (n, n'), it creates three utility series

$$\langle \mathcal{U}^{FF}_{n,n'}, \mathcal{U}^{FI}_{n,n'}, \mathcal{U}^{IF}_{n,n'} \rangle$$

that accumulate the frequency in avoiding conflicts along time whenever n, n' are fulfilled (F) or infringed (I). $\mathcal{U}^{FF}_{n,n'}$ is a binary series $\langle u^{FF}_1, \dots, u^{FF}_m \rangle$, where u^{FF}_i gathers the evidence related to the i-th time that n and n' were concurrently applicable and were both fulfilled (FF). Specifically, $u^{FF}_i = 1$ when both fulfilments did not lead to an undesired state, and 0 otherwise. Analogously, we define $\mathcal{U}^{FI}_{n,n'}$ and $\mathcal{U}^{IF}_{n,n'}$ for series where n is fulfilled and n' is infringed, and n is infringed and n' is fulfilled, respectively.

Gathering pair-wise evidences does not cover dependencies with other norms in the current normative system, although accounted undesired states may in fact be caused by third norms. This "noisy" evidences cause fluctuations in the binary series. Therefore, as it is usually the case for data streams, LION employs the *cumulative moving average* [5] to smooth out short-term fluctuations and highlight longer-term trends when detecting substitutability and complementarity. The cumulative average of a series $\mathcal{U}^{FF}_{n,n'}$ is another series $\hat{\mathcal{U}}^{FF}_{n,n'} = \langle \hat{u}_1, \dots \hat{u}_m \rangle$, where $\hat{u}^{FF}_i$ is computed as follows:

$$\hat{u}^{FF}_i = \frac{\sum\limits_{u_j \in \mathcal{U}^{FF}_{n,n'}, 0 \le j \le i} u_j}{i} \qquad (1)$$

the elements in $\hat{\mathcal{U}}^{FI}_{n,n'}$ and $\hat{\mathcal{U}}^{IF}_{n,n'}$ are computed analogously.

We consider that two concurrently applicable norms n, n' are substitutable whenever their cumulative averaged series *are similar*. Since the Euclidean distance is one of the most used and efficient time series (dis)similarity measures [24], we assess the similarity between our series by means of the *averaged Euclidean distance*, computed as follows:

$$Distance(\hat{\mathcal{U}}^{FF}_{n,n'}, \hat{\mathcal{U}}^{FI}_{n,n'}) = \frac{\sqrt{\sum\limits_{i=1}^{l_{min}} (\hat{u}^{FF}_i - \hat{u}^{FI}_i)^2}}{l_{min}} \qquad (2)$$

being l_{min} the minimum length of series $\hat{\mathcal{U}}^{FF}_{n,n'}$ and $\hat{\mathcal{U}}^{FI}_{n,n'}$, namely $l_{min} = min(|\hat{\mathcal{U}}^{FF}_{n,n'}|, |\hat{\mathcal{U}}^{FI}_{n,n'}|)$.

Thus, LION determines that two concurrently applicable norms n and n' are substitutable iff: (i) it accumulates *enough* evidence regarding the outcomes of the concurrent application of both norms; and (ii) the distance between series $\hat{\mathcal{U}}^{FF}_{n,n'}$ and $\hat{\mathcal{U}}^{FI}_{n,n'}$ as well as the distance between series $\hat{\mathcal{U}}^{FF}_{n,n'}$ and $\hat{\mathcal{U}}^{IF}_{n,n'}$ are both below a given threshold $\alpha_{sim} > 0$. This amounts to verifying whether the following conditions hold:

$$|\hat{\mathcal{U}}^{FF}_{n,n'}| \ge eval_{min}, |\hat{\mathcal{U}}^{FI}_{n,n'}| \ge eval_{min}, |\hat{\mathcal{U}}^{FI}_{n,n'}| \ge eval_{min} \qquad (3)$$

$$Distance(\hat{\mathcal{U}}^{FF}_{n,n'}, \hat{\mathcal{U}}^{FI}_{n,n'}) \le \alpha_{sim} \qquad (4)$$

$$Distance(\hat{\mathcal{U}}^{FF}_{n,n'}, \hat{\mathcal{U}}^{IF}_{n,n'}) \le \alpha_{sim} \qquad (5)$$

Along the same lines, LION considers that two concurrently applicable norms are complementary whenever their series $\hat{\mathcal{U}}^{FF}_{n,n'}$ is greater than series $\hat{\mathcal{U}}^{FI}_{n,n'}$ and $\hat{\mathcal{U}}^{IF}_{n,n'}$, and all them have a minimum number of evidences. Formally, it corresponds to satisfying equations 3, 6 and 7:

$$Distance(\hat{\mathcal{U}}^{FF}_{n,n'}, \hat{\mathcal{U}}^{FI}_{n,n'}) > \alpha_{sim} \qquad (6)$$

$$Distance(\hat{\mathcal{U}}^{FF}_{n,n'}, \hat{\mathcal{U}}^{IF}_{n,n'}) > \alpha_{sim} \qquad (7)$$

Whenever LION detects that two norms are substitutable or complementary, it establishes the corresponding relationship in the GNN.

4.3 Exploiting norm relationships

As previously discussed, generalisation pursues compactness, complementarity safeguards performance and discarding substitutable norms provides liberality. Hence, at run-time, when LION detects two substitutable norms, it should discard one of them, since it is over-constraining the agents in the MAS. Nevertheless, LION does not proceed directly, on the contrary, it exploits the relationships of both norms so that the less generalised substitutable norm is discarded provided that it is not complementary with another norm.

We recall from Section 2 that deactivating specific norms implies backtracking over (that is, undoing) norm generalisations, hence leading to less compact normative systems. Therefore, before discarding a substitutable norm, LION considers the ancestors of each norm to determine its corresponding *compactness loss* and to choose the norm having the lowest value. As detailed below, the compactness loss of a norm n is related to the decrement in compactness that the normative system will suffer in case norm n is deactivated, or, in other words, its associated specialisation cost.

As an example, consider the GNN in Figure 2a representing the normative system $\{n_7, n_{10}\}$. It contains two substitutable norms n_1, n_9 that are generalised by other norms. In particular, n_9 is represented by an active norm n_{10} whose generalisation level is 1, and n_1 is represented by an active norm n_7 whose generalisation level is 2. Because of being more general, n_7 compactly represents

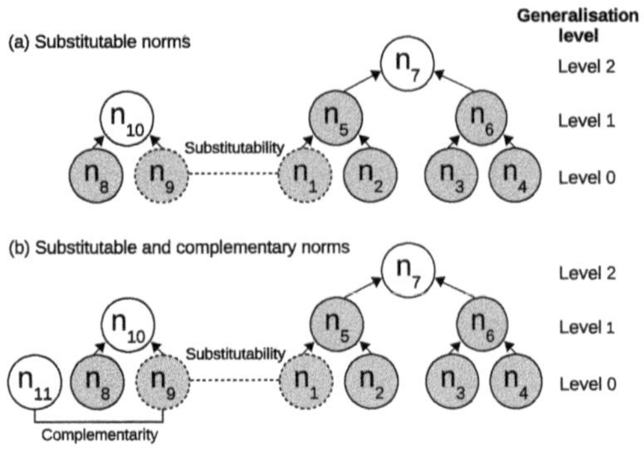

Figure 2: Norm relationships: solid arrows stand for (non-symmetric) generalisation; dashed lines for substitutability (symmetric) and solid lines for complementarity (symmetric).

a greater number of norms than n_{10}. At this point, LION must decide whether to discard n_9 or n_1 because they are substitutable. Since deactivating n_1 would imply in specialising n_7, we consider that n_1 has a higher specialisation cost than n_9, and thus, LION will deactivate norm n_9 instead.

Specifically, LION uses equation 8 to compute the compactness loss of a norm n as the sum of the generalisation degrees of its ancestors in the GNN graph.

$$\mathcal{C}_{loss}(n, GNN) = \sum_{n' \in \, ancestors(n)} g_{deg}(n', GNN) \tag{8}$$

where $g_{deg}(n', GNN)$ is the generalisation degree of a norm n' in the normative network, which is computed by means of equation 9:

$$g_{deg}(n, GNN) = |children(n)| \cdot k^{level(n)} \tag{9}$$

where: $children(n)$ is a function that assesses the norms that n directly generalises (those norms n has an incoming generalisation relationship with); $level(n)$ is the generalisation level of n; and $k > 1$ a constant factor.

Figure 2b helps to illustrate these computations. The compactness loss of norm n_1 is the sum of the generalisation degree of its ancestors n_5, n_7. In particular, since n_5 has a generalisation level of 1 and has two children (n_1, n_2), its generalisation degree is $g_{deg}(n_5, GNN) = 2k$. Analogously, norm n_7 has a generalisation degree $g_{deg}(n_5, GNN) = 2k^2$ because its generalisation level is 2 and it has 2 children (n_5 and n_6). As a result, $\mathcal{C}_{loss}(n_1, GNN) = 2k + 2k^2$, which is greater than $\mathcal{C}_{loss}(n_9, GNN) = 2k$. Therefore, LION chooses to deactivate n_9.

Regarding complementarity relationships, Figure 2b depicts an alternative situation during the synthesis process where the normative network contains, not only substitutable norms n_1, n_9, but also a complementarity relationship between norm n_9 and norm n_{11}. In this case, since LION prioritizes the preservation of complementary norms, it will keep n_9 active and will choose to deactivate n_1.

Algorithm 1 details how LION exploits norm relationships to choose which norm to discard (i.e., deactivate) from a pair of substitutable norms. Given two substitutable norms n_A, n_B, it first checks if any of them is complementary to other norms in the normative network (lines 3-4) in order to preserve complementary norms (lines 5-8). If none of them is complementary, then it marks to substitute the norm with the lowest compactness loss (lines 9-13). Otherwise, in case there are no complementarity relationships with other norms and their compactness losses are equal, then LION randomly marks to deactivate one of them (line 15). It then returns (line 16) the norm that has been chosen to be substituted.

Algorithm 1 Choosing a substitutable norm to discard

```
1: function CHOOSETODISCARD(nA, nB, GNN)
2:    toDiscard ← null
3:    nACompl ← hasComplementarity(nA, GNN)
4:    nBCompl ← hasComplementarity(nB, GNN)
5:    if nACompl and not nBCompl then
6:        toDiscard ← nB
7:    if nBCompl and not nACompl then
8:        toDiscard ← nA
9:    if not nACompl and not nBCompl then
10:       if Closs(nA, GNN) > Closs(nB, GNN) then
11:           toDiscard ← nB
12:       else if Closs(nA, GNN) < Closs(nB, GNN) then
13:           toDiscard ← nA
14:       else
15:           toDiscard ← random(nA, nB)
16:   return toDiscard
```

4.4 Norm synthesis strategy

We have so far described how to detect substitutability and complementarity relationships between norms. Furthermore, we have detailed how these relationships can be exploited to minimise the number of constraints imposed on the agents, while preserving the compactness of normative systems to the greatest possible extent. We now introduce a novel norm synthesis strategy that detects and exploits substitutability and complementarity relationships.

Algorithm 2 describes LION's norm synthesis strategy, which receives as input a transition $\langle s, A, s' \rangle$ with the system states before (s) and after (s') the performance of A; the set $C \in S$ of undesired states of the system; and the generalised normative network GNN. Initially, the strategy performs norm generation if the current state s' is undesired and LION has never generated norms aimed at avoiding it (line 2). If this is the case, it creates norms aimed at avoiding s' in the future (line 3). We borrow $normCreation$ and other basic operations such as $normApplicability$, $normEvaluation$, $generaliseUp$ or $specialiseDown$, from the SIMON algorithm [13]. Next, it retrieves those norms that have been applicable to the agents in state s (line 4), and computes concurrently applicable norms (line 5). Then, the strategy evaluates if applicable norms have succeeded in avoiding conflicts in s' (a norm is considered to perform well if it was applicable at the previous state s, and the current state s' is not undesired) (line 6). Afterwards, it classifies each applicable norm (line 9) to assess if (i) it is has performed well so far; (ii) it is *generalisable* with another norm in the normative system; (iii) it is *substitutable* with another norm in the normative network; and (iv) it is *complementary* with another norm in the normative network. Thereafter, the GNN is updated with the newly discovered substitutability and complementarity relationships (line 12). Next, the algorithm exploits norm classifications to refine the normative system. Different operations are carried out depending on the outcome of the classification:

- *Underperforming norm.* If a norm underperforms in terms of effectiveness or necessity, it must be specialised. Thus, the algorithm deactivates the norm and specialises down the norm's children in the GNN (lines 14-15). This undoes (backtracks over) all the generalisations involving the underperforming norm.
- *Generalisable norm.* If a norm is generalisable with another norm, it generalises them up in the GNN (lines 17-18).
- *Substitutable norm.* If a norm is substitutable with other norms, the algorithm retrieves all the norms it is substitutable with (lines 19-20). For each norm it is substitutable with, it invokes Algorithm 1 to choose which of them must be discarded (line 22). The chosen norm is subsequently deactivated and specialised down in the GNN (line 24).

Algorithm 2 LION's norm synthesis strategy

```
function LIONSTRATEGY(⟨s, A, s'⟩, C, GNN)
  if s' ∈ C and not regulated(s', GNN) then
    GNN ← normCreation(⟨s, A, s'⟩, GNN)
  applicableNorms ← normApplicability(s, GNN)
  concurrentNorms ← normConcurrency(s, GNN)
  performances ← normEvaluation(s', applicableNorms)
  classifiedNorms ← ∅
  for all n ∈ applicableNorms do
    n ← classify(n, performances, concurrentNorms)
    if isClassified(n) then
      classifiedNorms ← classifiedNorms ⋃{n}
      GNN ← update(GNN, n)
  for all n ∈ classifiedNorms do
    if underPerforms(n) then
      GNN ← specialiseDown(n, GNN)
    else
      if isGeneralisable(n) then
        GNN ← generaliseUp(n, GNN)
      if isSubstitutable(n) then
        substitutableNorms ← getSubstitutable(n, GNN)
        for all n' ∈ substitutableNorms do
          discard ← chooseToDiscard(n, n', GNN)
          if discard ≠ null then
            GNN ← specialiseDown(discard, GNN)
  return GNN
```

The algorithm ends by returning the possibly updated GNN, which contains the normative system that will be communicated to the agents.

4.5 Analysing normative systems

Next we establish how to measure and compare normative systems in terms of the synthesis objectives pursued by LION, namely in terms of *compactness*, *liberality*, and *regulative performance*.

The literature in norms research has considered different metrics to evaluate normative systems. In particular, [7] introduces *minimality* and *simplicity* as criteria for the off-line synthesis of norms. While minimality measures the number of *constraints* in a normative system, simplicity measures the cost of agent reasoning with its norms. Based on these concepts, in [13], normative systems are evaluated in terms of their minimality and simplicity. There, the minimality of a normative system is computed as the number of norms it contains, and simplicity is assessed as the total number of norm predicates. However, we recall that a norm may compactly represent several specific norms (e.g. in Figure 2a, norm n_7 represents four specific norms n_1, n_2, n_3, n_4). Therefore, the interpretation of minimality in [13] disregards the actual number of specific norms that a normative system represents. This requires a more fine-grained measure of minimality. Thus, we define the representation minimality of a normative system Ω as $\mathcal{R}(\Omega) = |\cup_{n \in \Omega} specific(n)|$, where $specific(n)$ stands for the specific norms represented by norm n. From this definition it follows that the less the representation minimality of a normative system, namely the fewer the number of constraining (specific) norms, the greater the freedom for the agents. We consider that the notion of representation minimality more accurately captures the concept of minimality originally introduced in [7].

We notice that minimality and simplicity provide *compactness measures*. In order to compare whether a normative system is more liberal than another, we rely on the *"more liberal than"* relationship between normative systems introduced by Ågotnes et al. in [1]. Hence, in this work we say that a normative system Ω is more liberal than another Ω' if the norms represented by Ω are included in those represented by Ω', namely if $\cup_{n \in \Omega} specific(n) \subset \cup_{n' \in \Omega'} specific(n')$. We will also assess the substitutability of a normative system as the number of substitutability relationships that it contains. This provides a measure of the lack of liberality of a normative system: the more substitutability of a normative system, the bigger the opportunity to synthesise a more liberal one.

Finally, regarding regulative performance, we resort to the measures of effectiveness and necessity defined in [13]. These allow us to quantify how good a normative system is at regulating a MAS and how necessary its norms are for regulating.

5. EMPIRICAL EVALUATION

We now compare LION with SIMON [13] along several dimensions. We first analyse the liberality of the normative systems synthesised by both approaches, and show that the normative systems synthesised by LION are more liberal than those synthesised by SIMON. We observe that the key to LION being more liberal than SIMON is that LION manages to detect and discard, on average, 90% of the substitutability relationships within SIMON's most-frequently synthesised normative system. Thereafter, we perform a further analysis to quantify the performance of SIMON's multi-objective synthesis. We observe that the representation compactness and performance obtained by LION is similar to SIMON's. This comes at some extra cost of LION's synthesis process.

Empirical settings. Our experiments use the same scenario and experimental settings described in [13]. We run a discrete-event simulation of a traffic junction, whose agents are autonomous cars, and undesired states are those where cars collided. Each simulation employs some norm synthesis mechanism (either LION or SIMON) that monitors the simulation and synthesises norms for the cars. Every time the norm synthesis mechanism at use changes the normative system, it sends the new normative system to the cars. At each tick, each car decides whether to fulfil or infringe norms according to some norm infringement probability, which is fixed to 0.3 and is the same for all cars. To detect substitutability and complementarity, we set the minimum number of samples for the utility series of a pair of norms ($\hat{\mathcal{U}}^{FF}_{n,n'}$, $\hat{\mathcal{U}}^{FI}_{n,n'}$ and $\hat{\mathcal{U}}^{IF}_{n,n'}$) to 20 ($eval_{min} = 20$). Moreover, we set α_{sim}, the threshold employed to detect substitutability and complementarity in equations 4, 5, 6, 7, to 0.05. Finally, we set to 10 the constant factor k employed to compute the generalisation degree of a norm in equation 9.

We performed 200 simulations with LION and 200 simulations with SIMON. Each simulation started with an empty normative system. The syntax of norms is the one described in Section 2: three predicates describe the perceptions of a reference car from its three front positions (relative heading of another car, a wall, nothing, or anything). We considered that a simulation converged to a normative system if during a 5000-tick period: (i) the normative system remained unchanged; and (ii) no new conflicts (those that had not been regulated by any norm yet) occurred. Thus, conflicts arising from norm violations are disregarded when assessing convergence.

Liberality analysis. Our first comparison focuses on the liberality of the normative systems that LION and SIMON managed to synthesise upon convergence. We notice that both LION and SIMON converged in all simulations. Figure 3 graphically represents the relationship *"more liberal than"* between LION's and SIMON's normative systems. Each circle represents a different normative system. The squared figure on top of each circle stands for the number of times (out of 200 simulations) it was synthesised. White circles represent LION's normative systems, while gray circles represent SIMON's normative systems. For instance, Ω_1 is a normative system that was synthesised by SIMON 179 times. The "more liberal than" relationship is represented by the subset relationship between circles. For instance, since Ω_7 is contained in Ω_1 then we say that Ω_7 is more liberal than Ω_1.

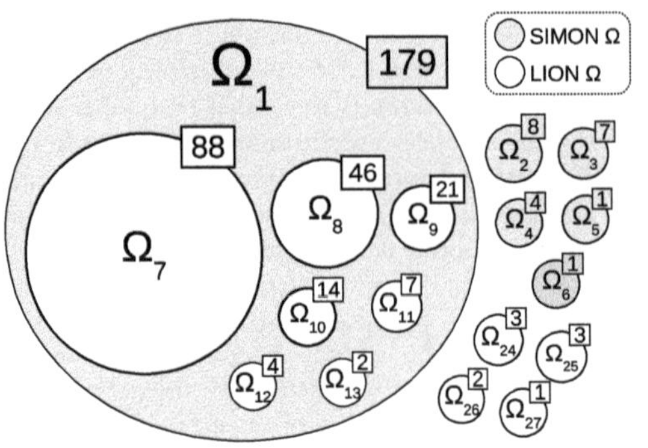

Figure 3: Normative systems synthesised by LION and SIMON.

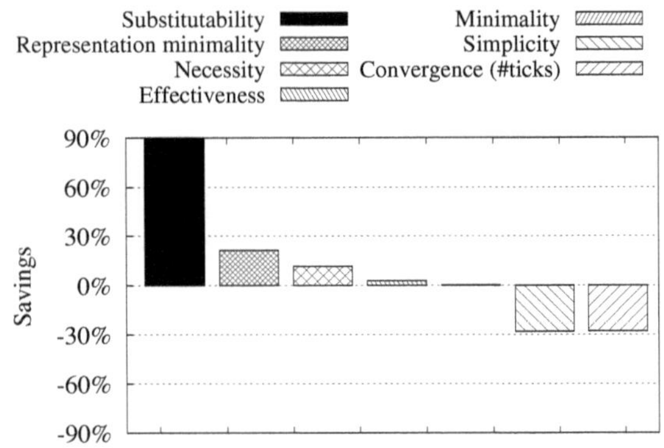

Figure 4: LION savings with respect to SIMON's most frequently synthesised normative system.

We observe that SIMON converged to 6 different normative systems ($\Omega_1, \ldots, \Omega_6$). Specifically, 90% of the times (179 out of 200 simulations), it converged to normative system Ω_1, which corresponds to the one previously depicted in Table 1. As to LION, it synthesised 21 different normative systems ($\Omega_7, \ldots, \Omega_{27}$). Nevertheless, those normative systems where not evenly distributed. Thus, 90% of the simulations (180 out of 200) synthesised just 6 normative systems ($\Omega_7, \ldots, \Omega_{12}$), whereas the remaining normative systems ($\Omega_{13}, \ldots, \Omega_{27}$) where only synthesised by 10% of the simulations. As shown in Figure 3, 81% of LION's normative systems (from Ω_7 to Ω_{23}) are more liberal than (are contained in) Ω_1, namely SIMON's most frequent normative system[3]. 81% of LION's normative systems were synthesised in 96% of simulations, and thus we can state that LION converged to normative systems more liberal than Ω_1 for 96% of simulations. The remaining normative systems have similar (slightly better) metrics than SIMON's Ω_1.

Now we analyse why 81% of LION's normative systems are more liberal than Ω_1. With this aim, we compute the number of substitutability relationships in LION's and SIMON's normative systems. We carry out this computation by means of simulation. For each normative system, we run a simulation that performs pairwise comparison between its norms to check if they are substitutable. For each pair of norms in the normative system, the simulation proceeds by having two cars fulfil/infringe the norms, checking whether conflicts arise or not after fulfilments/infringements, and hence detecting substitutability according to Definition 5. As depicted in Figure 4, on average, LION's normative systems manage to get rid of 90% of the substitutability relationships that SIMON's Ω_1 contains. Furthermore, it managed to detect and preserve the 100% of complementary norms in SIMON's Ω_1.

Multi-objective synthesis analysis. Figure 4 summarises the average savings obtained by LION's multi-objective synthesis process with respect to SIMON. First, following the observation above, the success in detecting and discarding substitutable norms translates into a reduction in representation minimality, which is our measure to quantify the gain in liberality. More precisely, the normative systems synthesised by LION contain 21% less specific norms than those synthesised by SIMON. Therefore, LION's normative systems are less restrictive than SIMON's normative systems. Second, regarding effectiveness and necessity, LION's normative systems are similarly effective in avoiding conflicts (in fact, slightly, 2.73%, more effective), while they are more necessary (11% higher). This comes at no surprise because SIMON's normative systems contain substitutable norms. We recall that two substitutable norms satisfy the same regulatory needs, and hence only one of them (but at least one of them) is actually necessary. Third, as to compactness, although LION's and SIMON's normative systems can be considered to be equally minimal (LION is 0.1% more minimal), the first ones are 28% less simple. In other words, LION's normative systems have as many norms as SIMON's, but the norms in LION's normative systems have more predicates. This is reasonable if we consider that discarding substitutable norms involves specialising general norms, and hence leads to normative systems whose norms are more specific (and thus have a larger number of predicates). Notice though that these benefits come at some extra cost: LION requires 27.81% extra time to converge, since it performs extra tasks to capture norm synergies, as well as to deactivate substitutable norms.

[3]For clarity, Figure 3 only shows 7 out of the 17 LION's normative systems that are more liberal than Ω_1. Normative systems $\Omega_{14}, \ldots, \Omega_{23}$ are all more liberal than Ω_1 but each one is only synthesised once by LION.

6. CONCLUSIONS AND FUTURE WORK

The aim of our work is to automatically synthesise compact, well-performing and liberal normative systems for open multi-agent systems that respect the autonomy of agents to the greatest extent possible. We argue that, on the one hand, the resulting normative system that is synthesised on-line should: i) be able to regulate agent interactions in a seamless way; ii) be as compact as possible to limit agents' norm reasoning effort; and iii) impose as few restrictions as possible, to respect the autonomy of agents to the greatest extent possible. On the other hand, we also highlight that norms within normative systems can present non-apparent synergies that have been hitherto unexplored in the literature. In this paper, in addition to considering generalisation relationships that have been proven to help to synthesise compact normative systems, we propose LION, a *LI*beral *O*n-line *N*orm mechanism that includes *substitutability* and *complementarity* norm relationships to pursue liberality without compromising efficiency.

We provided experimental evidence to assesses the quality and relevance of our proposal. In particular, we reported on experiments in which 96% of the time LION synthesised normative systems that are more liberal than those produced by the best-of-class approach, SIMON [13]. Specifically, they remove 90% of its substitutability relationships. This is accomplished without compromising minimality, effectiveness, or necessity. In future work we plan to study its application to other scenarios such as self-regulation of on-line communities as well as to employee-driven creation of best-practices for professional bodies.

Acknowledgements

Work funded by projects AT (CSD2007-0022), COR (TIN2012-38876-C02-01, TIN2012-38876-C02-02), and 2009-SGR-1434. Mike Wooldridge was supported by the ERC under Advanced Grant 291528 ("RACE").

REFERENCES

[1] T. Ågotnes, W. Van Der Hoek, C. Sierra, and M. Wooldridge. On the logic of normative systems. In *Proceedings of the 20th International Joint Conference on Artificial Intelligence*, IJCAI '07, pages 1175–1180, 2007.

[2] G. M. Ahlfeldt and W. Maennig. Substitutability and complementarity of urban amenities: External effects of built heritage in berlin. *Real Estate Economics*, 38(2):285–323, 2010.

[3] N. Alechina, M. Dastani, and B. Logan. Norm approximation for imperfect monitors. In *Proceedings of the 2014 International Conference on Autonomous Agents and Multi-agent Systems*, AAMAS '14, pages 117–124, Richland, SC, 2014. International Foundation for Autonomous Agents and Multiagent Systems.

[4] G. Boella, L. van der Torre, and H. Verhagen. Introduction to normative multiagent systems. *Computational & Mathematical Organization Theory*, 12(2-3):71–79, 2006.

[5] Y. Chou. *Statistical analysis: with business and economic applications*. Holt, Rinehart and Winston Quantitative Methods Series. Holt, Rinehart and Winston, 1969.

[6] F. Dignum. Autonomous agents with norms. *Artif. Intell. Law*, 7(1):69–79, 1999.

[7] D. Fitoussi and M. Tennenholtz. Minimal social laws. In *AAAI*, pages 26–31, 1998.

[8] H. Franks, N. Griffiths, and S. Anand. Learning agent influence in mas with complex social networks. *Autonomous Agents and Multi-Agent Systems*, 28(5):836–866, 2014.

[9] N. Griffiths and M. Luck. Norm Emergence in Tag-Based Cooperation. In *Proceedings of COIN*, 2010.

[10] G. McKenzie. Complementarity, substitutability, and independence. *Oxford Economic Papers*, 29(3):430–441, 1977.

[11] J. Morales, M. López-Sánchez, and M. Esteva. Using Experience to Generate New Regulations. In *IJCAI*, pages 307–312, 2011.

[12] J. Morales, M. Lopez-Sanchez, J. A. Rodriguez-Aguilar, M. Wooldridge, and W. Vasconcelos. Automated synthesis of normative systems. In *AAMAS 2013*, pages 483–490, 2013.

[13] J. Morales, M. Lopez-Sanchez, J. A. Rodriguez-Aguilar, M. Wooldridge, and W. Vasconcelos. Minimality and simplicity in the on-line automated synthesis of normative systems. In *AAMAS 2014*, pages 109–116, Richland, SC, 2014. IFAAMAS.

[14] J. Morales, M. Lopez-Sanchez, J. A. Rodriguez-Aguilar, M. Wooldridge, and W. Vasconcelos. Source code of minimality and simplicity in the on-line automated synthesis of normative systems. `https://github.com/NormSynthesis/NormSynthesisMachine`, 2014.

[15] A. Perotti, G. Boella, and A. d. Garcez. A framework for monitoring and learning in multiagent systems. 2014.

[16] P. A. Samuelson. Complementarity: An essay on the 40th anniversary of the hicks-allen revolution in demand theory. *Journal of Economic Literature*, pages 1255–1289, 1974.

[17] B. Savarimuthu, S. Cranefield, M. Purvis, and M. Purvis. Identifying prohibition norms in agent societies. *Artificial Intelligence and Law*, 21(1):1–46, 2013.

[18] T. Savarimuthu, S. Cranefield, M. A. Purvis, and M. K. Purvis. Obligation norm identification in agent societies. *Journal of Artificial Societies and Social Simulation*, 13(4):3, 2010.

[19] O. Sen and S. Sen. Effects of social network topology and options on norm emergence. In *Proceedings of COIN*, pages 211–222, 2010.

[20] S. Sen and S. Airiau. Emergence of norms through social learning. In *IJCAI*, pages 1507–1512, 2007.

[21] Y. Shoham and M. Tennenholtz. On social laws for artificial agent societies: off-line design. *Artificial Intelligence*, 73(1-2):231–252, February 1995.

[22] M. van Smoorenburg and R. van der Velden. The training of school-leavers: Complementarity or substitution? *Economics of Education Review*, 19(2):207 – 217, 2000.

[23] D. Villatoro, J. Sabater-Mir, and S. Sen. Social instruments for robust convention emergence. In *IJCAI*, pages 420–425, 2011.

[24] X. Wang, A. Mueen, H. Ding, G. Trajcevski, P. Scheuermann, and E. Keogh. Experimental comparison of representation methods and distance measures for time series data. *Data Mining and Knowledge Discovery*, 26(2):275–309, 2013.

[25] A. J. Ward, J. A. Brown, and D. Rodriguez. Governance bundles, firm performance, and the substitutability and complementarity of governance mechanisms. *Corporate Governance: An International Review*, 17(5):646–660, 2009.

Practical Run-Time Norm Enforcement with Bounded Lookahead

Natasha Alechina
University of Nottingham
Nottingham, UK
nza@cs.nott.ac.uk

Nils Bulling
Delft University of Technology
Delft, The Netherlands
n.bulling@tudelft.nl

Mehdi Dastani
Universiteit Utrecht
Utrecht, The Netherlands
M.M.Dastani@uu.nl

Brian Logan
University of Nottingham
Nottingham, UK
bsl@cs.nott.ac.uk

ABSTRACT

Norms have been widely proposed as a means of coordinating and controlling the behaviour of agents in a multi-agent system. A key challenge in normative MAS is norm enforcement: how and when to restrict the agents' behaviour in order to obtain a desirable outcome? Even if a norm can be enforced theoretically, it may not be enforceable in a grounded, practical setting. In this paper we study the problem of practical norm enforcement. The key notion is that of a *guard*. Guards are functions which restrict the possible actions after a history of events. We propose a formal, computational model of norms, guards and norm enforcement, based on linear-time temporal logic with past operators. We show that not all norms can be enforced by such guard functions, even in the presence of unlimited computational power to reason about future events. We analyse which norms can be enforced by guards if only a fixed lookahead is available. We investigate decision problems for this question with respect to specific classes of norms, related to safety and liveness properties.

Categories and Subject Descriptors

I.2.11 [**Artificial Intelligence**]: Distributed Artificial Intelligence—*Multi-agent systems*

Keywords

Norms; Run-time enforcement

1. INTRODUCTION

Multi-agent systems are often regulated using norms. Some norms can be violated (agents are able to perform an action which leads to a violation) and the violating behaviour is sanctioned. Some norms are regimented, that is, agents are prevented from performing an action that would lead to a violation. In this paper we focus on regimented norms, and in particular on the case when norms are temporal properties which potentially apply to infinite runs of the system (the simplest case of such a norm is an invariant property to be maintained). In a practical system, regimented norm enforcement involves having access to a finite run of the system, and having to decide which successor states should be disallowed since all the subsequent runs through those states would result in a norm violation.

We assume that the decision regarding which successor states should be enabled is provided by a *guard* function, which takes a finite run (history of the system's behaviour so far) and returns 'safe' successor states: the states from where it is possible to continue without violating the norm. The central problem in this setting is defining an appropriate guard function. The guard function should have several properties: (1) it must ensure that the resulting runs do not violate the norm; (2) it must not rule out behaviours that do not violate the norm; (3) it should be deadlock-free, that is every compliant history should have at least one successor state. Note that the problem of specifying the guard function is different from that of run-time verification [9], where the problem is to check whether a finite run violates a given property (rather than prevent a next step on the run if it leads to a violation).

Clearly, achieving the three properties above is not always possible. Not all norms can be perfectly enforced using a guard function (perfect enforcement means that the set of all infinite runs generated by the guard function is exactly the set of runs that conform to the norm). An obvious example of such norms are liveness properties (or, in normative terms, obligations without a deadline). Similarly, deadlock-free guard functions do not always exist: in the simplest case, a norm may not be enforceable on a given system.

We assume that the normative organisation has access to a finite transition system describing all possible multi-agent system behaviours, but only a bounded lookahead window that can be used to decide which successor states of the current state on a run should be disallowed. We study the minimal size of a lookahead window required for successful norm enforcement and show that it is surprisingly large for norms expressed in LTL.

The contributions of the paper are as follows.

- We define the notions of run-time norm enforcement, guard functions and the problem of establishing whether a given norm has a deadlock-free guard that (perfectly) enforces it on a given transition system.
- We study a special kind of guard function that correspond to LTL with past formulas, and characterise which norms can be perfectly enforced by LTL with past formulas and the computational complexity of checking whether an LTL with past formula is a deadlock-free guard.
- We show that liveness norms can always be enforced and

Appears in: *Proceedings of the 14th International Conference on Autonomous Agents and Multiagent Systems (AAMAS 2015), Bordini, Elkind, Weiss, Yolum (eds.), May 4–8, 2015, Istanbul, Turkey.*

safety norms can be perfectly enforced (in the sense of Definition 10 below) by the *canonical guard* with a sufficiently large lookahead.

- We show that state-based safety norms can be always enforced with a lookahead window of size 1 by explicitly listing 'prohibited' successor states; however some enforceable LTL norms cannot be enforced with a lookahead window that is smaller than the length of the longest cycle-free path is a model.

The structure of the paper is as follows. We first define the system model and LTL with past operators. Then, we introduce the three key concepts of this paper: norms, guards and norm enforcement, followed by a logic-based setting to define guards. In Section 5, we consider bounded lookahead, and discuss practical aspects in Section 6. Finally, we discuss related work in Section 7 and conclude.

2. PRELIMINARIES

System Model. Our system model is a transition system consisting of a set of states and a serial accessibility relation between states. Each state is labelled with a set of propositions, modelling the facts in the world.

DEFINITION 1 (TRANSITION SYSTEM). *Let Π be a finite set of atomic propositions. A (transition) system is defined as $M = \langle S, R, V\rangle$, where S is a set of states, $R \subseteq S \times S$ is a serial accessibility relation and $V : S \to 2^{\Pi}$ is a labelling function. In order to simplify the presentation, we sometimes implicitly assume that there is a non-empty set $S_0 \subseteq S$ of* initial states. *If not stated otherwise, it can be assumed that $S_0 = S$.*

A transition system M describes the computational behaviour of a (multi) agent system. The relation R corresponds to the actions agents may execute, sequentially or in parallel, in each state to bring the system to a new state. A *history* and a *run* in the transition system are finite and infinite sequences of states interconnected by the accessibility relation, respectively.

DEFINITION 2 (RUNS AND HISTORIES). *Given a transition system $M = \langle S, R, V\rangle$, a* run *of M is an infinite sequence of states $\rho = s_0s_1s_2\ldots$ such that for $i \geq 0$ we have $(s_i, s_{i+1}) \in R$. The set of* runs *of M starting in s is denoted by $\mathcal{R}_M(s)$. We simply write $\mathcal{R}_M := \bigcup_{s\in S}\mathcal{R}_M(s)$ for the set of all runs, and $\mathcal{R}_M(S_0)$ as the set of runs starting in S_0. A* history *h of M is a finite prefix of a run. We use $h \sqsubset \rho$ to indicate that h is a (prefix) history of the run ρ; $h \sqsubset h'$ to indicate that the history h is a prefix of the history h'; and $h \sqsubseteq h'$ if $h \sqsubset h'$ or $h = h'$. The set of histories of M starting in s is denoted by $\mathcal{H}_M(s)$ and, analogously to runs, we define $\mathcal{H}_M$ and $\mathcal{H}_M(S_0)$. Finally, the operator $\circ$ is used to concatenate a history h with another history h' ($h \circ h'$) and run ρ ($h \circ \rho$), respectively. We often omit $\circ$ and just write hs, hh', $h\rho$, etc.*

Given a run ρ we write $\rho[i]$, $\rho[i, j]$, $\rho[i, \infty]$, for $i \geq 0$, to refer to the ith state on ρ, the history starting at position i on ρ and ending at position j of ρ, and the suffix (run) of ρ starting at position i on ρ, respectively. We assume that i and j are non-negative integers with $i \leq j$. We use similar notation for histories; in particular, for a history h, $h[\infty]$ refers to the *last state of h*. We omit the formal details.

LTL with past operators. Below, we use LTL to specify norms and LTL with past operators [23] to specify guards: the temporal operator Y stands for "yesterday", P for "now or at some point in the past", S for "since", X for "tomorrow (next)", F for "now or sometime in the future", and U for "until". We denote LTL with past operators by LTL^{+p}.

DEFINITION 3 (LTL PLUS PAST, SIMPLE FORMULA). *Formulae of LTL^{+p} are defined by the grammar: $\phi ::= p \mid \neg\phi \mid \phi \wedge \phi \mid Y\phi \mid \phi S\phi \mid X\phi \mid \phi U\phi$ where $p \in \Pi$ is a proposition. We define $F\phi = \top U\phi$ and $P\phi = \top S\phi$ as macros. Given a transition system M, a run ρ, and a position $i \in \mathbb{N}_0$, the truth of LTL^{+p}-formulas is defied by the semantic relation $\models$ as follows:*

$M, \rho, i \models p$ *iff* $p \in V(\rho[i])$

$M, \rho, i \models \neg\phi$ *iff* $M, \rho, i \not\models \phi$

$M, \rho, i \models \phi \wedge \psi$ *iff* $M, \rho, i \models \phi$ *and* $M, \rho, i \models \phi$

$M, \rho, i \models Y\phi$ *iff* $i > 0$ *and* $M, \rho, i-1 \models \phi$,

$M, \rho, i \models \phi S\psi$ *iff* $\exists j \leq i$ *s.t.* $M, \rho, j \models \psi$ *and* $\forall k : j < k \leq i : M, \rho, k \models \phi$

$M, \rho, i \models X\phi$ *iff* $M, \rho, i+1 \models \phi$

$M, \rho, i \models \phi U\psi$ *iff* $\exists j, i \leq j$ *s.t.* $M, \rho, j \models \psi$ *and* $\forall k : i \leq k < j : M, \rho, k \models \phi$

LTL-formulae are LTL^{+p}-formulae that do not contain any past-time modalities, i.e. Y, P and S. We call an LTL^{+p}-formula simple *if it contains at most one temporal operator.*

We note that LTL^{+p} over infinite runs is no more expressive than pure LTL (without past operators). However, the past operators allow more intuitive and succinct specifications [20].

3. NORMS, GUARDS AND ENFORCEMENT

In this section, we introduce the three key concepts of this paper: norms, guards and norm enforcement. A *norm* can be seen as a linear-time property over a set of propositions, or as a set of 'good' runs of a transition system uniquely defining a linear time property. A *guard* is a means to control the system's run-time behaviour; it allows to disable transitions after a history. Finally, the notion of *enforcement* links norms and guards. We say that a guard enforces a norm if all possible behaviours resulting from the application of the guard are normative. Throughout this section we assume that $M = (S, R, V)$ is a finite transition system with initial states $S_0 \subseteq S$ over a finite set of propositions Π. We also assume that formulae are constructed over Π.

3.1 Specification of Regimentation Norms

We begin with our representation of norms. A *norm* describes the 'good', the *normative* behaviour of a system. In general, this behaviour can be defined independently of a transition system, just over a set of propositions Π. In this sense, a norm is a set of infinite words over 2^{Π}. For example, the norm "it is prohibited to take drugs" corresponds to the set of all infinite words $w_0w_1\ldots \in 2^{\Pi}$ such that *drugs* $\notin w_i$ for all $i \in \mathbb{N}_0$. If a norm is considered in the context of a transition system it is often convenient to identify a linear-time properties with a subset of the runs of the transition system, namely those runs which (given the labelling function V) correspond to one of the behaviours of the norm. In the remainder of this paper we use LTL-formulae φ to characterise a norm. This supports both views: if we talk about a norm independent of a model, the (LTL-)norm φ is identified with all linear-time behaviours satisfying φ (over a fixed set of proposition). In the context of a transition system M, we write φ_M to refer to a norm defined as the set of all runs $\rho \in \mathcal{R}_M(S_0)$ that satisfy the LTL-formula φ. The formal definition is given next.

DEFINITION 4 (REGIMENTATION NORM). *A (regimentation)* norm *is an LTL-formula φ. A* norm *φ* over a transition system M *is given by*

$$\varphi_M := \{\rho \in \mathcal{R}_M(S_0) \mid M, \rho, 0 \models \varphi\}.$$

As seen from this definition a norm has a descriptive flavour. It specifies, from a global point of view, which runs or linear time behaviours are good.

3.2 Guards

A transition system encodes all possible behaviours, both the 'good' ones as well as the 'bad'/undesirable ones according to a given norm. The system designer may wish to control the behaviour of the agents to ensure a desirable system outcome. Using the notation introduced above, the system designer needs a mechanism to ensure that all behaviours are normative, but which at the same time does not overly restrict the agents' autonomy. *Guards* are used to implement norms by disabling specific transitions following a history. It is important to note that guards operate and restrict behaviours at *run-time*. This is in general more flexible than approaches operating at *design-time*, in the sense that transitions in the (static) model are altered. Moreover, a run-time approach is in general less restrictive and offers agents more autonomy as the disabling of transitions dynamically depends on the history.

A *guard over a transition system* M is a function that maps histories to a set of states enabled after the history.

DEFINITION 5 (GUARD). *A guard over M is defined as $G_M : \mathcal{H}_M \to 2^S$.*

If the system restricts the actions according to the guard some histories are no longer possible. A history that is possible given the application of a guard is called *consistent (with the guard)*.

DEFINITION 6 (CONSISTENT HISTORY). *Let G_M be a guard and $h \in \mathcal{H}_M$. We call a history h* consistent with the guard G_M *if, and only if, $h = s \in S_0$ or $s \in G_M(h')$ for all $h' \in \mathcal{H}_M$, $s \in S$ with $h' \circ s \sqsubset h$.*

A guard is deadlock free if each consistent history can be extended to another consistent history.

DEFINITION 7 (DEADLOCK-FREE). *A guard G_M is called* deadlock-free, *or* df-guard *for short, if, and only if, $G_M(h) \neq \emptyset$ for all histories $h \in \mathcal{H}_M(S_0)$ that are consistent with G_M.*

The application of a guard restricts the set of runs of a transitions system as follows:

DEFINITION 8 (GUARD APPLICATION). *The* application of a df-guard G_M in s *restricts the runs starting in s to*

$$\mathcal{R}_M^G(s) = \{\rho \in \mathcal{R}_M(s) \mid \forall h \in \mathcal{H}_M, s' \in S, hs' \sqsubset \rho : s' \in G_M(h)\}.$$

It is easy to see that if G_M is a df-guard then $R_M(s) \neq \emptyset$ for all $s \in S_0$. We note that the transitions disabled by the guard are not disabled in the model but at run-time.

Clearly, a more general guard is preferable as it allows the agents greater autonomy. This is captured by the following definition.

DEFINITION 9 (GENERALITY ORDERING). *Given two guards G_M and G'_M we say that G'_M is at least as general as G_M, denoted by $G_M \leq G'_M$, if, for all $h \in \mathcal{H}_M$, $G_M(h) \subseteq G'_M(h)$. As usual, we use $<$ to refer to the strict variant.*

The following proposition captures the intuition that the application of a more general guard results in a larger set of system behaviours.

PROPOSITION 1. *If $G_M \leq G'_M$ for two df-guards, then $\mathcal{R}_M^G(s) \subseteq \mathcal{R}_M^{G'}(s)$ for all $s \in S_0$.*

3.3 Norm Enforcement

A key question is whether we can construct a guard such that, if the guard is applied, then all possible runs of the system are normative. This is formally captured by the following definition:

DEFINITION 10 ((PERFECT, OPTIMAL) NORM ENFORCEMENT). *We say that a df-guard G_M enforces a norm φ_M iff $\varphi_M = \emptyset$ or $\emptyset \neq \mathcal{R}_M^G(S_0) \subseteq \varphi_M$. The enforcement is* perfect *iff $\mathcal{R}_M^G(S_0) = \varphi_M$. The enforcement is* optimal *if there is no other df-guard G'_M such that $\mathcal{R}_M^G(S_0) \subsetneq \mathcal{R}_M^{G'}(S_0) \subseteq \varphi_M$.*

EXAMPLE 1 (A LIVENESS NORM). *Consider the transition system $M_0 = \langle S, R, V\rangle$ with $S = \{s_0, s_1\}$, $R = \{(s_0, s_0), (s_0, s_1), (s_1, s_1)\}$, and $V(s_0) = \emptyset$, $V(s_1) = \{p\}$, and $S_0 = S$. Possible runs in the transition system are: $s_0^\omega = s_0 s_0 \ldots$ (always stay in s_0), $s_0 s_1^\omega = s_0 s_1 s_1 \ldots$ (stay in s_0 once, then proceed to s_1 and stay there forever), $s_0^2 s_1^\omega = s_0 s_0 s_1^\omega$ (stay in s_0 twice, then proceed to s_1 and stay there forever), and s_1^ω (stay in s_1 forever). We consider the norm $\varphi_0 = Fp$, the set of all runs which eventually visit a state in which proposition p holds, formally: $(\varphi_0)_{M_0} = \{s_0^n s_1^\omega \mid n \in \mathbb{N}_0\}$. Intuitively, the norm states that it is prohibited to stay in s_0 forever. This is a* liveness property. *We would like to construct a guard which enforces the norm. We define the following guard function G_{1,M_0}: $G_{1,M_0}(h) = \{s_1\}$ for all histories h. It is easy to see that this norm enforces $(\varphi_0)_{M_0}$ as we have: $\mathcal{R}_{M_0}^{G_1} = \{s_0 s_1^\omega, s_1^\omega\} \subseteq (\varphi_0)_{M_0}$. Clearly, the guard does not perfectly nor optimally enforce $(\varphi_0)_{M_0}$ as for example $s_0 s_0 s_1^\omega \notin \mathcal{R}_{M_0}^{G_1}$ but the run is normative. Another alternative would be guard function G_{2,M_0} with $G_{2,M_0}(h) = \{s_0, s_1\}$ if h ends in s_0, and $G_{2,M_0}(h) = \{s_1\}$ ends in s_1. This norm, however, does not enforce $(\varphi_0)_{M_0}$. Actually, there is no guard function which can perfectly enforce $(\varphi_0)_{M_0}$. We will make this more formal in Section 4.2.*

EXAMPLE 2 (A SAFETY NORM). *Consider the transition system $M_1 = (S_1, R_1, V_1)$ with $S_1 = \{s_0, s_1, s_2, s_3, s_4, s_5\}$ with $R_1 = \{(s_0, s_1), (s_1, s_2), (s_2, s_3), (s_3, s_3), (s_0, s_4), (s_4, s_5), (s_5, s_5)\}$ and $V(s) = \{p\}$ for all $s \in S_1 \backslash \{s_3\}$ and $V(s_3) = \emptyset$. The norm $\varphi_1 = Gp$ with $(\varphi_1)_{M_1} = \{s_0 s_4 s_5^\omega\}$ is a safety property. The guard G_{3,M_1} with $G_{3,M_1}(s_0) = \{s_4\}$, $G_{3,M_1}(s_0 s_4) = \{s_5\}$, and $G_{3,M_1}(s_0 s_4 s_5^n) = \{s_5\}$ for all $n \in \mathbb{N}$ does perfectly enforce $(\varphi_1)_{M_1}$ for $S_0 = \{s_0\}$. In Section 6.2 we show that all safety properties can be perfectly enforced.*

4. LOGIC-BASED GUARDS

In this section we define guards in LTL^{+p} and introduce the important concept of a *canonical guard*. We investigate when guards are deadlock free and when norms can be perfectly enforced. As before, we assume that $M = (S, R, V)$ is a finite transition system with initial states S_0 over a finite set of propositions Π.

4.1 Guards in LTL+Past

We first show how LTL^{+p}-formulae can be used to define guards. The guard G_M^γ, defined by the *guard formula* γ, returns, for a history h, the set of states s such that, on some run ρ that extends the history hs, γ holds.

DEFINITION 11 (LTL^{+p}-DEFINED GUARD). *For a given LTL^{+p}-formula γ, we define the γ-*defined guard *over M G_M^γ by*

$$G_M^\gamma(h) = \{s \in S \mid \exists \rho \in \mathcal{R}_M : hs \sqsubset \rho \text{ and } M, \rho, |h| \models \gamma\}.$$

We sometimes refer to γ as the guard formula. *When G_M^γ is applied to M we simply write $\mathcal{R}_M^\gamma$ instead of $\mathcal{R}_M^{G^\gamma}$ to refer to the set of possible runs when the guard G_M^γ is applied.*

It is important to note that, in addition to the current history, such a guard can make use of additional information contained in the model. That is, the decision which transitions to disable can take into account the future and the past. In this sense the guard has *unbounded lookahead*. In Section 5 we consider guards with *bounded lookahead*.

REMARK 1. *We note that the guard γ is interpreted in/after the history hs. Equivalently, it would be possible to interpret it in history h.*

Deadlock-free guards are particularly important. According to the definition of a df-guard, the set of states returned must always be non-empty; that is, it must always be possible for the system to continue execution following a history. In general, this is not ensured for guards defined using guard formulas; consider, for example, a formula that is never true in the model. So, a key problem is to check whether a guard formula does actually define a df-guard. In Section 4.3 we show that this is a difficult problem.

EXAMPLE 3 (EXAMPLE 1 CONT.). *We consider the guard $G_M^{\gamma_1}$ with $\gamma_1 = p$. We have that $G^p_{M_0} = G_{1,M_0}$. We can also define G_{2,M_0} by $G^{\top}_{M_0}$. We consider the guard γ_{φ_0} (this guard will play an important role in the remainder of the paper and is formally introduce in Definition 12). The guard $G_{M_0}^{\gamma_{\varphi_0}}$ with $\gamma_{\varphi_0} = P(Y\bot \wedge \varphi_0)$ seems to be a good choice to enforce φ_{M_0}. Intuitively, it enables all paths that satisfy the norm. But the guard does not enforce $(\varphi_0)_{M_0}$, since it allows the run s_0^ω. In general, if a norm corresponds to a property that is not violated on any finite initial segment of a run, then it is not possible to perfectly enforce it using guards. This relates to run-time verification and the non-existence of finite bad prefixes for liveness properties [9].*

EXAMPLE 4 (EXAMPLE 2 CONT.). *The guard $G_{M_1}^{\gamma_3}$ with $\gamma_3 = Gp$ is equivalent to G_{3,M_1}. In this example, the* canonical guard *$\gamma_{\varphi_1} = P(Y\bot \wedge Gp)$ does enforce $(\varphi_1)_{M_1}$, perfectly and thus also optimally.*

4.2 Canonical Guards

Given a norm φ it is possible to define a specific guard from the norm itself: the *canonical guard*. We have already seen this guard in Examples 3 and 5. If the canonical guard enforces a norm then it is the most general guard which enforces the norm. The canonical guard has other interesting properties which we discuss below.

DEFINITION 12 (CANONICAL GUARD). *Let φ be a norm. The* canonical guard (formula) *of φ is defined as $\gamma_\varphi = P(Y\bot \wedge \varphi)$.*

Before studying properties of the canonical guard we make the following easy observation.

PROPOSITION 2. *If $\models \gamma \to \gamma'$ then for any transition system M, $G_M^\gamma \leq G_M^{\gamma'}$.*

The following result states that if the canonical guard of a norm is deadlock-free and enforces the norm, then it is the optimal df-guard in the sense that it leaves the agents with the greatest degree of autonomy.

PROPOSITION 3. *If the canonical guard $G_M^{\gamma_\varphi}$ of a norm φ is deadlock-free and enforces φ_M then it is optimal.*

PROOF. Consider a df-guard G_M^γ that enforces φ_M. That is, for all $\rho \in \mathcal{R}_M^\gamma$ we have that $\rho \in \varphi_M$ which means that $M, \rho, 0 \models \rho$. So, if $G_M^\gamma(h) \neq \emptyset$ there is a run ρ with $h \sqsubset \rho$ and $\rho \in \mathcal{R}_M^\gamma$. This show that $M, \rho, |h| \models \gamma_\varphi$ and thus $G_M^{\gamma_\varphi}(h) \neq \emptyset$. We conclude that $G_M^\gamma \leq G_M^{\gamma_\varphi}$. □

The canonical guard can also be used to show that there is no df-guard to enforce a norm from a given history. In other words, Proposition 3 tells us that, in order to enforce a norm from a history h with $G_M^{\gamma_\varphi}(h) = \emptyset$, we must define a df-guard which regiments the history h.

PROPOSITION 4. *Let φ be a norm. If there is a history $h \in \mathcal{H}_M$ with $G_M^{\gamma_\varphi}(h) = \emptyset$ then there is no df-guard which can enforce φ from history h on.*

PROOF. Suppose $G_M^{\gamma_\varphi}(h) = \emptyset$ and there were a df-guard G_M^γ with $G_M^\gamma(h) \neq \emptyset$ and for all runs $\rho \in \mathcal{R}_M^\gamma$ with $h \sqsubset \rho$ we have that $\rho \in \varphi_M$. Then, we must have that $M, \rho, |h| \models \gamma_\varphi$ and thus $\rho[|h|] \in G_M^{\gamma_\varphi}(h) = \emptyset$. Contradiction. □

Finally, the canonical guard suggests a decision method for determining whether a norm can be enforced perfectly: a norm cannot be perfectly enforced if the canonical guard does not enforce the norm.

PROPOSITION 5. *Given a norm φ. If $G_M^{\gamma_\varphi}$ does not enforce φ_M then φ_M cannot be perfectly enforced by any guard.*

PROOF. Suppose $\rho^* \in \mathcal{R}_M^{\gamma_\varphi} \backslash \varphi_M$ is a run witnessing that the canonical guard does not enforce the norm. Because $\rho^* \in \mathcal{R}_M^{\gamma_\varphi}$ we have that for any $h \sqsubset \rho^*$, $G_M^{\gamma_\varphi}(h) \neq \emptyset$. In particular, for any such h there must be a run ρ_h with $h \sqsubset \rho_h$ and $\rho_h \in \varphi_M$ because the guard is canonical. Now, suppose there were a guard G_M^γ that enforces φ_M. Then, it cannot be the case that $\rho^* \in \mathcal{R}_M^\gamma$. To avoid this, the guard has to regiment from some h the transition which results in ρ^*. Suppose h denotes this very history where the regimentation takes place and $hs \sqsubset \rho^*$. Then, however, the run $\rho_{hs} \in \varphi_M$ (using the notation above) would also not be in $\mathcal{R}_M^\gamma$. This shows that G_M^γ cannot perfectly enforce φ_M. □

4.3 Determining Deadlock Freeness

Many of these results rely on deadlock-free guards. Deadlock-free guards are also of practical importance, as it is often undesirable if a system deadlocks. Unfortunately, a LTL^{+p}-defined guard is not necessarily deadlock free. As a result, using a guard to regiment the behaviour of the system can result in deadlock. The following proposition suggests that, in general, verifying whether a guard is deadlock-free is a difficult problem. However, we can identify classes of guards with better computational properties.

PROPOSITION 6. *The problem of checking whether G_M^γ is deadlock-free is in **2EXPTIME**. If γ is simple (cf. Definition 3) and contains no future time operators, then it is in **PSPACE**, and if γ is a Boolean formula, then in **P**.*

PROOF. We have that G_M^γ is deadlock free, iff, for all $s \in S_0$ we have that $M, s, 0 \models EX\gamma \wedge AG(AX\neg\gamma \to P\neg\gamma)$. For an arbitrary LTL^{+p}-formula γ, this is a formula of $\mathsf{CTL}^* + \mathsf{past}$, and the model checking problem for $\mathsf{CTL}^* + \mathsf{past}$ is in **2EXPTIME** [10]. If γ is simple (cf. Definition 3) and contains no future time operators, then the formula above is equivalent to $EXE\gamma \wedge AG(AXA\neg\gamma \to EPE\neg\gamma)$ (where we assume linear past) which is a $\mathsf{CTL} + \mathsf{past}$ formula, and the model checking problem for $\mathsf{CTL} + \mathsf{past}$ is **PSPACE**-complete [19]. If γ is a Boolean formula, then the initial formula is equivalent to the future time CTL-formula $EX\gamma \wedge \neg E(\gamma U(\gamma \wedge AX\neg\gamma))$, and the CTL model checking problem is in **P** [12]. □

5. BOUNDED LOOKAHEAD

The application of guards assumes that in addition to a history, the guard has access to the state transition system. Using the information in the transition system, we attempt to construct guard functions that given a history, rule out certain successors of the last state on the history (intuitively, those leading to a norm violation). In this section, we consider a setting with *bounded lookahead*. Bounding the lookahead reduces the amount of computation required to enforce the norm, by restricting the ability of the normative organisation to reason about and to take into consideration the future evolution of the system. In Section 6 we consider the problem of the minimal size of the lookahead window required to perfectly enforce a given norm on a given model. In this section, we introduce the formal machinery to define guards which operate with a bounded lookahead, in contrast to guards which have unbounded lookahead. We introduce the notion of a *view*, as the part of a run considered by a guard. The length of a view is defined by a *window*. To simplify the presentation, we assume that windows only restrict the lookahead, and that all past events are remembered and can be perfectly observed. Note that a past-restricting window could be seen as a way to limit the amount of memory the normative organisation can use to store information about the past. While restricting the past window is important for resource-bounded systems, we leave it for future work. In the remainder of this section we again assume that $M = (S, R, V)$ is a finite transition system.

5.1 Windows and Views

We consider the case of a contiguous view consisting of the sequence of states before and some finite sequence of states after the current position on a run ρ. A *window* defines the size of the view and is just a natural number defining the future lookahead. A *view* maps a run together with the current position on the run to a history. Given a run ρ and a position i, the view $\mathsf{view}(\rho, i)$ with respect to window W returns the history consisting of all past events $\rho[0, i-1]$, the current state $\rho[i]$ and the future states $\rho[i, i+W]$ which fit into the window.

DEFINITION 13 (WINDOW AND VIEW). *A (future)* window *is given by $W \in \mathbb{N}$. Let ρ be a run, W a window and $i \in \mathbb{N}_0$ (the current position on ρ). The* view of ρ at i with respect to W, $\mathsf{view}^W(\rho, i)$, *is defined by the function:* $\mathsf{view}^W : \mathcal{R}_M \times \mathbb{N}_0 \to \mathcal{H}_M$ *with $(\rho, i) \mapsto \rho[0, i+W]$. We also lift the view with respect to a window to a set of runs X: $\mathsf{view}^{\mathsf{W}}(X, i) = \bigcup_{\rho \in X} \mathsf{view}^{\mathsf{W}}(\rho, i)$*

Consider for example the run $\rho = s_1 s_2 s_3 s_4 s_5 s_6^\omega$. Then, we have that: $\mathsf{view}^2(\rho, 1) = s_1 s_2 s_3 s_4$. The part $s_1 s_2$ is the current history where s_2 is the current state; and $s_3 s_4$ encodes the lookahead. The window has size 2.

5.2 Window-Filtered Guards

We now integrate windows with guards and their application. A guard applied in context of a window can only be evaluated on the current view and thus has to decide which actions to disable based on a history rather then on a run. The *W-filtered guard* of a guard formula γ takes as an input a history h and returns a set of enabled states. In order to give the formal definition we first need to introduce a *finite trace semantics* for LTL^{+p}-formulae.

DEFINITION 14 (FINITE TRACE SEMANTICS). *We define a finite trace semantics for LTL^{+p} with two truth values (t and f). Given a transition system M, a history h, and a position i $0 \leq i < h$, the truth of LTL^{+p} formulas is defined by the semantic relation $\models^f$:*

$M, h, i \models^f p$ *iff* $p \in V(\rho[i])$

$M, h, i \models^f \neg\phi$ *iff* $M, h, i \not\models^f \phi$

$M, h, i \models^f \phi \wedge \psi$ *iff* $M, h, i \models^f \phi$ *and* $M, \rho, i \models^f \phi$

$M, h, i \models^f Y\phi$ *iff* $i > 0$ *and* $M, \rho, i-1 \models^f \phi$,

$M, h, i \models^f \phi S \psi$ *iff* $\exists j, 0 \leq j \leq i$ *s.t.* $M, h, j \models^f \psi$ *and* $\forall k : j < k \leq i : M, h, k \models^f \phi$

$M, h, i \models^f X\phi$ *iff* $i < |h|$ *and* $M, \rho, i+1 \models^f \phi$

$M, h, i \models^f \phi U \psi$ *iff* $\exists j, i \leq j < |h|$ *s.t.* $M, \rho, j \models^f \psi$ *and* $\forall k : i \leq k < j : M, \rho, k \models^f \phi$

This semantics captures an essentially pessimistic view, meaning that *false positives* are not acceptable. This semantics is used to interpret guards on a finite trace because a transition should only be enabled if the guard is *definitely true* on the view. We note that if used for (future-time) LTL-formulae, this semantics coincides with the finite trace semantics given in [14].

We also note that the finite trace semantics would not always be appropriate when evaluating norms on a finite trace in order to detect norm violations. In this case, a violation should only be reported if the violation has or will definitely take place, that is *false negatives* are not appropriate. A formal definition of such a semantics can be easily obtained by slightly modifying the truth conditions given for $\models^f$. In the following we shall denote the 'optimistic variant' of $\models^f$ by $\models^f_o$.

We can now formally define the notion of window-filtered guard. Given a guard formula γ the *W-filtered guard* $G_M^{\gamma,W}$ returns, for an input history h, all states s such that there is a run ρ which extends hs in such a way that the history $\mathsf{view}^{\mathsf{W}}(\rho, |h|-1)$ satisfies the guard γ. For convenience, the evaluation of the guard takes place in the last state of the view. We note, however, that the guard formula γ could equivalently be evaluated at position $|h|$ on $\mathsf{view}^{\mathsf{W}}(\rho, |h|-1)$ as done in the unbounded setting.

DEFINITION 15 (WINDOW-FILTERED GUARDS). *Let γ be a guard formula and W a window. The W-filtered guard $G_M^{\gamma,W}$ is defined as follows:*

$$G_M^{\gamma,W}(h) = \{s \in S \mid \exists \rho \in \mathcal{R}_M : hs \sqsubset \rho \text{ and } M, \mathsf{view}^{\mathsf{W}}(\rho, |h|-1), |h|+W-1 \models^f \gamma\}$$

for all histories $h \in \mathcal{H}_M$. Analogously, $G_M^{\gamma,W}$ is called deadlock-free *if it is non-empty for all consistent histories h (now with respect to the W-filtered guard). The* application *of a W-filtered guard is defined as before, where we write $\mathcal{R}_M^{\gamma,W}$ instead of $\mathcal{R}_M^{G_M^{\gamma},W}$.*

EXAMPLE 5 (EXAMPLE 2 CONT.). *We consider the W-filtered guard $G' = G_{M_1}^{\gamma_3,W}$, with $\gamma_3 = Gp$. For $W = 3$ the guard G' (perfectly) enforces $(\varphi_1)_{M_1}$. Let us consider $G'(s_0)$. The views of the two possible runs from s_0 are $s_0 s_1 s_2 s_3$ and $s_0 s_4 s_5 s_5$. The first view is discarded as $M_1, s_0 s_1 s_2 s_3, 3 \not\models^f \gamma_3$. It is also easy to see that G' is deadlock-free for $W = 3$. For all $W < 3$ however, the guard G' is not deadlock free. Suppose e.g. $W = 2$. Then $s_1 \in G'(s_0)$ as $M_1, s_0 s_1 s_2, 2 \models^f \gamma_3$. In the next step, however, we have $G'(s_0 s_1) = \emptyset$ as $M_1, s_0 s_1 s_2 s_3, 3 \models^f \gamma_3$, and the system deadlocks after the history $s_0 s_1$.*

A key problem is to determine (a minimal) window W and a (as general as possible) guard γ such that $G_M^{\gamma,W}$ does (optimally) enforce a given norm φ_M. We consider this problem in the next section.

6. PRACTICAL ENFORCEMENT

In this section we study some practical aspects of norm enforcement. First, we show that, in general, norm enforcement is a difficult problem. Then we study canonical guards for bounded lookahead for liveness and safety properties. We show that the canonical guard can always enforce such norms if the window size is sufficiently large. We also look at other, more practical, guard functions with bounded lookahead.

6.1 The General Problem

The first problem we investigate is whether a guard function enforces a norm given unbounded lookahead. We show that this problem is intractable.

PROPOSITION 7 (ENFORCEMENT: UNBOUNDED CASE). *Let M be a transition system, G_M^γ be a LTL^{+p}-defined df-guard, and φ an LTL-defined norm. The problem whether G_M^γ enforces φ_M is **PSPACE**-hard and in **2EXPTIME**.*

PROOF IDEA. The guard γ is a pure LTL^{+p}-formula and φ is an LTL-formula; thus, $A(GXE\gamma \to \varphi)$ is a $\mathsf{CTL}^* + \mathsf{past}$-formula. The model checking problem for $\mathsf{CTL}^* + \mathsf{past}$ is shown to be in **2EXPTIME** [10]. Moreover, $M, s \models A(GXE\gamma \to \varphi)$ for all $s \in S_0$ iff G_M^γ enforces φ_M. To see this we analyse the formula: $M, s \models A(GXE\gamma \to \varphi)$ iff $\forall \rho \in \mathcal{R}_M(s)[(\forall i \forall \exists \rho' \in \mathcal{R}_M, \rho[0,i] \sqsubset \rho', M, \rho', i \models \gamma) \Rightarrow M, \rho, 0 \models \varphi]$ iff $\forall \rho \in \mathcal{R}_M(s)[(\forall hs' \in \mathcal{H}_M, hs' \sqsubset \rho, s' \in G_M^\gamma(h)) \Rightarrow M, \rho, 0 \models \varphi]$ iff $\forall \rho \in \mathcal{R}_M(s)[\rho \in \mathcal{R}_M^\gamma(s) \Rightarrow \rho \in \varphi_M]$.

Hardness. For $\varphi = \bot$ and $\gamma = P(Y\bot \wedge \gamma')$ for some LTL^{+p}-formula γ' we have: $M, s \models A(GXE\gamma \to \varphi)$ iff $M, s \models A(GXE\gamma \to \bot)$ iff forall runs $\rho \in \mathcal{R}_M(s)$, $M, \rho, 0 \not\models \gamma'$ iff there is no run $\rho \in \mathcal{R}_M$ with $M, \rho, 0, \models \gamma'$. The latter problem corresponds to (universal) model checking the LTL^{+p}-formula γ'. A **PSPACE**-complete problem [23]. □

In the case of bounded lookahead, a norm can be enforced given a window of size k, if it is possible to determine by looking only k steps ahead, whether the norm must be violated on all paths allowed by the guard from a given state s. Conversely, a norm cannot be enforced given a window of size k and a guard G if all paths consistent with the guard G from a state violate the norm but only after at least k steps. In that case, a transition is made which will inevitably violate the norm at some later moment.

Suppose the current history is h and we need to decide whether a transition to s should be allowed. For any LTL norm φ, this problem can be solved in a straightforward (but computationally expensive) way by checking: (1) for each finite trace t in the k-unraveling from the current state s, whether $M, ht, 0 \models_o^f \varphi$ (using the 'optimistic' finite trace semantics; that is, a violation is only reported if there is no way to satisfy the norm); (2) $M, ht, |h| + |t| - 1 \models^f \gamma$ and (3) $M, \rho, 0 \not\models \varphi$ for all ρ with $hs \sqsubset \rho$. That is, whether a transition to s inevitably results in the violation of the norm, but this cannot be detected in k steps. Such an approach has exponential complexity.

These results show that norm enforcement is in general a difficult problem. In the remainder of this section, we consider the special cases of *safety* and *liveness norms*. We use $LTL^+(T_1, T_2, \ldots)$ to refer to the fragment of LTL which only allows the temporal operators $T_1, T_2, \ldots$, and only outside the scope of negation. These fragments can be used to define safety and liveness properties:

DEFINITION 16 (SAFETY AND LIVENESS NORM). *We say that an LTL-formula φ is a* safety norm *if $\varphi \in LTL^+(G, X)$. The formula is a (finite)* liveness norm *if $\varphi \in LTL^+(F, U)$.*

For example, the formula $G(p \to Xq)$ is a safety property, and Fp and pUq are simple liveness properties.

We define prefixes which can be used to witness the truth/or non-truth of such a property with respect to a given model M. For a (finite) liveness property φ we say that $h \in \mathcal{H}_M$ is a *good prefix of φ in M* if for all $\rho \in \mathcal{R}_M$ with $h \sqsubset \rho$, $M, \rho, 0 \models \varphi$. Similarly, for a safety property φ we say that $h \in \mathcal{H}_M$ is a *bad prefix of φ in M* if for all $\rho \in \mathcal{R}_M$ with $h \sqsubset \rho$, $M, \rho, 0 \not\models \varphi$. We note that for a liveness property φ, each $\rho \in \varphi_M$ has a good prefix; and for a safety property φ, each $\rho \notin \varphi_M$ has a bad prefix (cf. [8] for a general discussion).

Unfortunately, even for safety and liveness properties the problem presented in Proposition 7 remains intractable. Even if the guards are given by Boolean formulae the problem is **PSPACE**-complete. This follows from [21], where it is shown that model checking formulae of $LTL^+(G, X)$ as well as of $LTL^+(U)$ is **PSPACE**-complete.

Given this observation, an interesting question is, whether we can construct a guard from which we *know* that it will enforce a safety property, without having to check whether it actually enforces the norm. More precisely, we consider two types of results:

- We show that we can compute an upper bound such that the canonical guard always enforces the norm. At *run-time* we simply have to check whether the canonical guard is satisfied. It is important to note, that this does not require *model-checking* the guard, which would again be intractable. Other techniques, like progression or automata theoretic approaches can be used to efficiently monitor the truth of safety and liveness norms [9]. Propositions 8, 9, and 12 are in line with this view.
- We show how to *precompute* a guard function which operates by simply disabling successor states which are in a list of prohibited states. Proposition 10 is a result in this direction.

6.2 Enforcement of Safety Norms

The next proposition gives a positive answer to the question above: if we choose a window of sufficient size, then the canonical guard for a safety norm guarantees that the norm will be enforced, moreover the enforcement is *perfect*.

Let φ be a safety norm of type $\varphi = Gp$. Then, a state s should be disabled from the current history h, if Gp cannot be ensured on any path from s. In order for a path satisfying Gp to exist, we need to find a cycle on which Gp holds. If such a cycle exists, it must be found within $|S|$ steps. This is an upper bound for the lookahead needed to decide whether safety norm $\varphi = Gp$ will be violated if state s is reached. For arbitrary safety norms, the reasoning for computing the lookahead is similar.

PROPOSITION 8 (SAFETY NORM: PERFECT ENFORCEMENT). *Let φ be an LTL-safety property and M a transition system. One can compute a window W such that the canonical guard of φ enforces perfectly φ_M under window size W.*

Earlier in Example 5 we have seen that, even with very simple norms such as Gp, enforcement may require arbitrary long lookahead windows, depending on the size of the model. However, depending on the class of models the lookahead can be significantly reduced as illustrated by the next example.

EXAMPLE 6 (CLASS OF MODELS WITH LOOKAHEAD ONE). *There is a special class of model where Gp can be perfectly enforced with a lookahead window of just one. This holds for models M that are reflexive and have at least one run from each state in*

S_0 satisfying Gp. For such an M, a df-guard for Gp can be defined as follows: $G_M(h) = \{s \mid (h[\infty], s) \in R \text{ and } p \in V(s)\}$ Clearly, this guarantees that the next state always exists (since $(h[\infty], h[\infty]) \in R$) and all states on runs consistent with G_M satisfy p.

We now show how to determine the minimal size of a lookahead for a simple kind of safety norms.

DEFINITION 17 (STATE-BASED SAFETY NORM). *A state-based safety norm is of the form $G\psi$ where $\psi \in LTL^+(X)$.*

State-based safety norms have a useful property: it is possible to define a set of states from which all paths inevitably violate the norm (do not satisfy ψ). Note that this is a CTL-definable property, using only AX operators. We call this set of states $Viol_M(\varphi)$.

EXAMPLE 7. *An example of a state-based safety norm is Gp. For this norm, the set $Viol_M(\varphi)$ is the set of states where p is false.*

Similarly, for a state-based safety norm $\varphi = G(p \to Xq)$ the set $Viol_M(\varphi)$ consist of all states s such that $p \in V(s)$ and for all states s' reachable from s in one step, $q \notin V(s')$. This is definable as $p \wedge AX\neg q$.

Clearly, a guard function for φ should not return successors in $Viol_M(\varphi)$. It should also disable states which are not themselves in $Viol_M(\varphi)$, but from which all paths lead inevitably to a $Viol_M(\varphi)$ state. We call the latter set of states $Viol^+_M(\varphi)$ states. This latter set is also CTL-definable as $AF\chi$ where χ describes $Viol_M(\varphi)$. To enforce a state-based safety norm, we need to avoid states in $Viol^+_M(\varphi)$.

In the following, we show how to compute the minimal window size k of Proposition 8, such that the canonical guard of a state-based safety norm enforces the norm. We show that the complexity of finding the minimal k is polynomial.

We give an algorithm to compute the minimum window size for enforcing φ on M (see Algorithm 1). The algorithm works by computing the set of states $\tau = Viol^+_M(\varphi)$ from which all paths lead to $Viol_M(\varphi)$. Starting from the states in $Viol_M(\varphi)$, υ, we repeatedly compute the set of transitions on a path leading to υ states, δ, the states τ from which all transitions lead to a υ state or a τ state, and the set of simple paths to states in τ, σ. Finally we compute the longest simple path between two states in τ, which gives us the required lookahead k.

Note that $Viol_M(\varphi)$ can be computed using CTL model-checking in time polynomial in the size of the φ and M. It is also possible to compute τ by computing the set of states satisfying $AF\chi$ where χ describes $Viol_M(\varphi)$. Instead we give an explicit algorithm, since it also computes the size of the longest simple path from a state to a state in τ. The complexity of Algorithm 1 is $O(|S| \times |R|)$.

From the algorithm the following proposition immediately follows:

PROPOSITION 9. *The problem of deciding whether window size k is sufficient for the canonical guard to enforce a state-based safety norm on a model M is in **P**.*

The most straightforward way to solve this problem is to find the minimal size of the window and compare it to k. We can also define a decision variant of Algorithm 1, which simply checks whether a given window size is sufficient to enforce the norm. Rather than looping until τ does not change, we repeat the loop $k + 1$ times (for a window size of k), and check if the length of the longest path returned is $> k$. However given the complexity of the algorithm, it is not clear that the reduction in computation is worthwhile.

Algorithm 1 Computing window size for state-based norm φ

> **function** WINDOW-SIZE($\varphi, M = \langle S, R, V\rangle$)
> $\upsilon \leftarrow Viol_M(\varphi)$
> $\delta \leftarrow \{(s,(s,s')) \mid (s,s') \in R \wedge s' \in \upsilon\}$
> $\tau \leftarrow \{s \mid \forall (s,s') \in R\ ((s,(s,s')) \in \delta)\}$
> $\sigma \leftarrow \{(s, s \circ [s']) \mid s \in \tau \wedge (s,(s,s')) \in \delta\}$
> $\epsilon \leftarrow \{(s,(s,s')) \mid (s,s') \in R \wedge s' \in \upsilon \cup \tau\}$
>   **while** $\delta \subset \epsilon$ **do**
> $\delta \leftarrow \epsilon$
> $\tau \leftarrow \tau \cup \{s \mid \forall (s,s') \in R\ ((s,(s,s')) \in \delta)\}$
> $\sigma \leftarrow \{(s, s \circ \rho) \mid s \in \tau \wedge \rho \in \operatorname{arg\,max}_{(s,(s,s')) \in \delta,\ (s',\rho) \in \sigma,\ s \notin \rho} |\rho|$
> $\epsilon \leftarrow \{(s,(s,s')) \mid (s,s') \in R \wedge s' \in \upsilon \cup \tau\}$
>   **end while**
>   **return** $\operatorname{arg\,max}_{(s,\rho) \in \sigma} |\rho|$
> **end function**

An alternative to computing the size of the window and using it at run-time in combination with the canonical guard, is to use the set of 'bad' states $Viol^+_M(\varphi)$ directly in implementing the enforcement of the norm. The guard is defined as follows:

$$G_M(h) = \{s' \mid (h[\infty], s') \in R \text{ and } s' \notin Viol^+_M(\varphi)\}$$

where $Viol^+_M(\varphi)$ is τ computed by Algorithm 1. We note that the guard can be implemented by looking only at the last state of the view, that is, whether the last state is prohibited (is in $Viol^+_M(\varphi)$). In this approach, enforcement effectively requires a window of size 1, since all that is required is to check if the state resulting from a transition is in $Viol^+_M(\varphi)$, so we have:

PROPOSITION 10. *State-based safety norms can be perfectly enforced by a guard which only requires one step lookahead.*

6.3 Enforcement of Liveness Norms

In Proposition 8 we have shown that safety norms can be perfectly enforced. This is not the case for liveness norm:

PROPOSITION 11. *Let M be a transition system. In general, an LTL-liveness property φ cannot be perfectly enforced.*

PROOF. In Example 3 we have shown that the norm $\varphi_0 = Fp$ which is a liveness property in M_0 is not enforced by the canonical guard $\gamma_{\varphi_0} = P(Y\bot \wedge \varphi_0)$. Thus, by Proposition 5 φ cannot be perfectly enforced by any guard. □

However, we can compute a lookahead that allows us to enforce (though not perfectly or optimally), a liveness norm. Let φ be a liveness property. Then, for each initial state $s \in S_0$, there is a minimal length good prefix of φ in M. We define function $d_M : S_0 \to \mathbb{N}_0^\infty$ which assigns to each initial state the length of a minimal length good prefix of φ. If such a history does not exist we set $d_M(s) = \infty$. That is, from each state s_0 the norm can be satisfied in $d_M(s_0)$-many transitions. Now, we define $L^\varphi_M = \max\{d_M(s) \mid s \in S_0, d_M(s) \neq \infty\}$ if for some $s \in S_0$ we have that $d(s) < \infty$; and $L^\varphi_M = \infty$ otherwise. Consequently, a lookahead of L^φ_M would be sufficient do decide whether a transition to the a next state should be enabled or not, if it is possible to satisfy the norm at all. So, the good news is that, in general, simple liveness norms can be enforced. Moreover, an upper bound for L^φ_M is $|\varphi| \cdot |S|$. This can be seen by decomposing φ into at most $|\varphi|$ independent checks of simpler liveness formulae. Each of these formula can be witnesses within $|S|$ steps in the model.

PROPOSITION 12 (LIVENESS CAN BE ENFORCED). *Let φ be an LTL liveness property and M a transition system. The canonical-guard of φ enforces φ_M under window size $W = L^{\varphi}_M$; in general, the enforcement is neither optimal nor perfect. An upper bound for L^{φ}_M is $|\varphi| \cdot |S|$.*

In order to use this result, we can either use the upper bound or compute the minimal lookahead L^{φ}_M. For liveness norms of type $\varphi = Fp$ and $\varphi = qUp$, for example, the value L^{φ}_M can be computed in polynomial time in the size of the model. For both types of formulae the upper bound for L^{φ}_M is $|S|$. Moreover, in both cases, we can use Dijkstra's algorithm [15] to compute the shortest path between an initial state s and a state s' with $p \in V(s')$. In the case of $\varphi = qUp$ the search simply ignores states s' with $\{q, p\} \cap V(s') = \emptyset$.

7. RELATED WORK

In the literature on multi-agent systems, many computational and programming frameworks for norms and norm enforcement have been proposed. Existing frameworks mainly focus on specific types of norms, and norm monitoring and enforcement mechanisms, e.g., [18, 16, 6, 13]. Of these, our approach is closest to that of [16]; however their approach does not support prediction of future violations, or attempt to ensure that violations do not occur. The focus of our paper is different, as we are interested in a formally defined computational model for a run-time enforcement mechanism that monitors LTL norms to prevent future norm violations at run-time. In particular, we are interested in formal models of run-time norm enforcement and their computational complexity. Our model can be applied to develop computational frameworks for run-time norm enforcement mechanisms.

Our work is closely related to [1] where multi-agent systems are modelled as transition systems and norm regimentation is modelled by removing bad transitions. However, in contrast to our approach, [1] considers norms semantically by means of a set of bad transitions that are removed at design time by updating the transition system with norms. In our work, norms are specified syntactically by means of LTL formulas, and bad transitions are disabled at run-time by means of a guard function.

Another related work on norm monitoring is [11, 5], where norms are considered in the context of imperfect monitors. Similar to our work, [11, 5] considers norms syntactically by means of LTL formulas, and monitors are assumed to be imperfect. However, [11, 5] consider imperfect monitors at an abstract level and by means of an indistinguishability relation between runs, while we consider imperfect monitors at a practical level and by means of a windowing mechanism. In particular, the window mechanism in our approach restricts the computational effort required to predict the future of the actual run. Moreover, [11] ignores the problem of run-time norm monitoring and focus on the notion of imperfect monitors, while [5] focuses on the problem of synthesising the closest approximation of a norm that can be monitored with a set of imperfect monitors. Finally, imperfect monitors in [11] can be improved by means of their combinations, while in our approach an imperfect monitor can be improved by increasing the size of its window.

It is obvious that our work is closely related to, and actually inspired by, the run-time verification literature, e.g., [9]. We build on this work to evaluate norms (LTL properties) on finite runs, but in contrast to run-time verification literature, we consider the construction of a guard function that enforces norms by avoiding norm violations. Our work also extends run-time verification approaches by proposing lookahead and windowing mechanisms to predict violations of LTL properties. Our work is also closely related to supervisory control theory for discrete event systems, e.g., [22, 7]. While supervisory control theory approaches the problem of synthesising control mechanisms at an abstract level by means of operations on formal languages (e.g., intersection, inclusion, product), our approach is more practical focusing on the construction of guard functions that disable violating transitions at run-time.

We would like to emphasise that our work differs from work on the verification of normative updates and and the compliance of protocols with norms as proposed in [17, 4, 13, 2]. One difference is that we focus on run-time norm enforcement while [17, 4, 13, 2] consider offline verification of normative updates and protocols. Second, [4] consider specific norms (conditional prohibitions/obligations with deadline) that can be expressed in a fragment of CTL* with Past, while we consider various types of norms that can be expressed by various fragments of LTL. Third, [4, 13] consider norm enforcement at design time by means of both regimentation and sanctioning, while our work focuses on run-time norm regimentation. Enforcing norms by sanctions allows norm to be violated, but imposes sanctions when norms are violated. We believe that our approach can be extended to model enforcement by sanctions. This can be done by, for example, imposing sanctions on the states that are reached by violating transitions, instead of disabling those transitions. We consider norm enforcement by means of sanctions as a future direction of our research.

In this work, we have focused on norm regimentation from an organisational perspective. Accordingly, the guard function is considered as a functionality of the agents' organisation, which enables/disables the options that are available to the agents at run-time. We did not focus on norm regimentation mechanism from an agent perspective and have ignored issues such as agents' norm awareness as studied in [24, 3]. Of course, our work can be applied to make individual agents norm aware in the sense that the agents themselves compute the options that cause norm violations. Using this ability the agents can decide whether to violate or to obey the norms at run-time. We consider the norm awareness issue as a future direction of our research.

8. CONCLUSIONS

This paper presents a formally defined computational model for run-time norm enforcement mechanism. The model is based on a guard function that enables/disables options that (could) violate norms after a system history. The guard function, which is characterised by LTL formulae with past operators, may use computational resources to reason about the future of the actual run in order to disable the options that cause norm violations. The computational resources that allow to reason about the future of the run is modelled by means of a window of a particular size. The model is formally analysed and the computational complexity for various types of run-time norm enforcement is provided.

Our approach can be extended in various directions. A possible extension would be to allow norm enforcement by means of sanctions. In this regard, the interaction between the predication of norm violations and sanctioning becomes an interesting but challenging issue. Another possible extension is to allow windows with limited size in the past. In this paper, a window covers the complete history from a starting state, but this is obviously not a practical assumption as this requires sufficient memory capacity to store the history; so we have already investigated cases where the full history is not used. Limiting the history size of a window may cause some norm violations to be undetected and not enforceable. Finally, our model can be used to allow agents to evaluate and to reason about the system behaviours in order to decide whether they obey or violate norms.

REFERENCES

[1] T. Ågotnes, W. van der Hoek, and M. Wooldridge. Robust normative systems and a logic of norm compliance. *Logic Journal of the IGPL*, 18(1):4–30, 2010.

[2] H. Aldewereld, J. Vázquez-Salceda, F. Dignum, and J. C. Meyer. Verifying norm compliancy of protocols. In O. Boissier, J. A. Padget, V. Dignum, G. Lindemann, E. T. Matson, S. Ossowski, J. S. Sichman, and J. Vázquez-Salceda, editors, *Coordination, Organizations, Institutions, and Norms in Multi-Agent Systems*, volume 3913 of *Lecture Notes in Computer Science*, pages 231–245. Springer, 2006.

[3] N. Alechina, M. Dastani, and B. Logan. Programming norm-aware agents. In *Proceedings of the 11th International Conference on Autonomous Agents and Multiagent Systems (AAMAS 2012)*, pages 1057–1064. IFAAMAS, 2012.

[4] N. Alechina, M. Dastani, and B. Logan. Reasoning about normative update. In *Proceedings of the Twenty Third International Joint Conference on Artificial Intelligence (IJCAI 2013)*, pages 20–26. AAAI Press, 2013.

[5] N. Alechina, M. Dastani, and B. Logan. Norm approximation for imperfect monitors. In *Proceedings of the 13th International Conference on Autonomous Agents and Multiagent Systems (AAMAS 2014)*, 2014.

[6] S. Alvarez-Napagao, H. Aldewereld, J. VÃązquez-Salceda, and F. Dignum. Normative monitoring: Semantics and implementation. In M. De Vos, N. Fornara, J. Pitt, and G. Vouros, editors, *Coordination, Organizations, Institutions, and Norms in Agent Systems VI*, volume 6541 of *Lecture Notes in Computer Science*, pages 321–336. Springer Berlin Heidelberg, 2011.

[7] G. Aucher. Supervisory control theory in epistemic temporal logic. In *Proceedings of the 13th International Conference on Autonomous Agents and Multiagent Systems (AAMAS 2014)*, 2014.

[8] C. Baier and J.-P. Katoen. *Principles of Model Checking*. The MIT Press, May 2008.

[9] A. Bauer, M. Leucker, and C. Schallhart. Runtime verification for LTL and TLTL. *ACM Transactions on Software Engineering and Methodology*, 20(4):14:1–14:68, 2011.

[10] L. Bozzelli. The complexity of CTL*+ linear past. In *Foundations of Software Science and Computational Structures*, pages 186–200. Springer, 2008.

[11] N. Bulling, M. Dastani, and M. Knobbout. Monitoring norm violations in multi-agent systems. In *Twelfth International conference on Autonomous Agents and Multi-Agent Systems (AAMAS'13)*, pages 491–498, 2013.

[12] E. Clarke, O. Grumberg, and D. Peled. *Model Checking*. MIT Press, 1999.

[13] M. Dastani, J.-J. C. Meyer, and D. Grossi. A logic for normative multi-agent programs. *Journal of Logic and Computation*, 23(2):335–354, 2013.

[14] G. De Giacomo and M. Y. Vardi. Linear temporal logic and linear dynamic logic on finite traces. In *Proceedings of the Twenty-Third international joint conference on Artificial Intelligence*, pages 854–860. AAAI Press, 2013.

[15] E. W. Dijkstra. A note on two problems in connexion with graphs. *Numerische mathematik*, 1(1):269–271, 1959.

[16] M. Esteva, J. Rodríguez-Aguilar, B. Rosell, and J. Arcos. AMELI: An agent-based middleware for electronic institutions. In *Proceedings of AAMAS 2004*, pages 236–243, New York, US, July 2004.

[17] M. Esteva, J. Rodriguez-Aguilar, C. Sierra, and W. Vasconcelos. Verifying norm consistency in electronic institions. In V. Dignum, D. Corkill, C. Jonker, and F. Dignum, editors, *Proceedings of the AAAI-04 Workshop on Agent Organizations: Theory And Practice*, volume Technical Report WS-04-02, San Jose, July 2004. AAAI, AAAI Press.

[18] J. Hübner, J. S. Sichman, and O. Boissier. $\mathcal{S}$-$\mathcal{M}$OISE$^+$: A middleware for developing organised multi-agent systems. In *Proceedings of the international workshop on Coordination, Organizations, Institutions, and Norms in Multi-Agent Systems*, volume 3913 of *LNCS*, pages 64–78. Springer, 2006.

[19] F. Laroussinie and P. Schnoebelen. Specification in CTL+ past for verification in CTL. *Information and Computation*, 156(1):236–263, 2000.

[20] N. Markey. Temporal logic with past is exponentially more succinct. *EATCS Bulletin*, 79:122–128, 2003.

[21] N. Markey. Past is for free: on the complexity of verifying linear temporal properties with past. *Acta Informatica*, 40(6-7):431–458, 2004.

[22] P. Ramadge and M. Wonham. The control of discrete event systems. In *Proceedings of the IEEE*, volume 77(1), 1989.

[23] A. P. Sistla and E. M. Clarke. The complexity of propositional linear temporal logics. *Journal of the ACM*, 32(3):733–749, 1985.

[24] M. B. van Riemsdijk, K. V. Hindriks, and C. M. Jonker. Programming organization-aware agents: A research agenda. In *Proceedings of the Tenth International Workshop on Engineering Societies in the Agents' World (ESAW'09)*, volume 5881 of *LNAI*, pages 98–112. Springer, 2009.

Generalized Commitment Alignment

Amit K. Chopra
Lancaster University
Lancaster LA1 4WA, United Kingdom
a.chopra1@lancaster.ac.uk

Munindar P. Singh
North Carolina State University
Raleigh, NC 27695-8206, USA
singh@ncsu.edu

ABSTRACT

The interoperability of interacting components means that their expectations of each other remain in agreement. A commitment captures what one agent (its creditor) may expect from another agent (its debtor). Chopra and Singh (C&S) motivate commitment alignment as a meaning-based form of interoperation and show how to ensure alignment among agents despite asynchrony.

Although C&S's approach demonstrates the key strengths of relying on commitment semantics, it suffers from key shortcomings, which limit its applicability in practice. One, C&S do not model commitments properly, causing unacceptable interference between commitments in different transactions. Two, they require that the communication infrastructure guarantee first-in first-out (FIFO) delivery of messages for every agent-agent channel. Three, C&S guarantee alignment only in quiescent states (where no messages are in transit); however, such states may never obtain in enactments of real systems.

Our approach retains and enhances C&S's key strengths and avoids their shortcomings by providing a declarative semantics-based generalized treatment of alignment. Specifically, we (1) motivate a declarative notion of alignment-relevant system states termed completeness; (2) prove that it coincides with alignment; and (3) provide the computations by which a system of agents provably progresses toward alignment assuming eventual delivery of messages.

Categories and Subject Descriptors

H.1.0 [**Information Systems**]: Models and Principles—*General*; I.2.11 [**Artificial Intelligence**]: Distributed Artificial Intelligence—*Multiagent systems*

General Terms

Theory

Keywords

Interoperability; Commitments; Protocols; Transactions

Appears in: *Proceedings of the 14th International Conference on Autonomous Agents and Multiagent Systems (AAMAS 2015), Bordini, Elkind, Weiss, Yolum (eds.), May, 4–8, 2015, Istanbul, Turkey.*

1. INTRODUCTION

This paper concerns decentralized multiagent systems in which autonomous agents interact with each other. Normally, each agent in such a system would represent an autonomous social principal, such as a human or an organization. Specification of interaction protocols and infrastructures for the distributed enactment of such protocols are major themes of research in multiagent systems.

An important class of approaches for specifying interaction protocols is that of commitment protocols [12, 25, 26]. The formula $\mathsf{C}(x, y, r, u)$ represents a commitment, meaning that x (the debtor) is committed to y (the creditor) that if r (the antecedent) holds, then u (the consequent) will hold [22]. A commitment protocol specifies the meanings of the messages in terms of their effects on commitments. For example, in a protocol for e-business, one could specify that the message *Offer* from a merchant to a customer means that the merchant is committed to the customer for delivering the goods offered if the customer pays the price quoted. A growing body of work has addressed various aspects of commitments and commitment protocols [2, 4, 8, 9, 13].

We address the challenges of enacting commitment protocols in decentralized settings where the agents communicate asynchronously and no central party maintains the definitive global state. Instead each agent maintains its own state based on the messages it has observed, both sent and received. Generally, in a distributed system, agents' observations may differ: agents may observe different sets of messages, and even when they observe the same messages, they may do so in different orders. Coupled with the fact that messages affect commitments, this means that the agents may infer different active commitments at any given moment. Since commitments reflect the expectations one agent has of another, such a difference in inferred commitments is an indication of a failure of interoperability at the semantic level. Preventing such interoperability failures would be important in business and security settings.

Chopra and Singh [6] (C&S, for short) define commitment misalignment as the following situation: an agent y infers it is the creditor of a commitment whose debtor is x, but x does not infer that it is the debtor of that commitment to y. For example, upon observing the *Offer* message Bob (a customer) may expect that if he pays the quoted price, then Alice (the merchant) will deliver the offered goods. If Alice does not also infer the same commitment, the two would be misaligned. And that would indicate a potential breakdown in interoperability. Commitment *alignment* is a novel and useful concept: it characterizes interoperability in terms of the meanings of interactions not merely in terms of message transmission as traditionally understood, e.g., [1].

C&S formalize alignment and provide a method for ensuring alignment among agents. Although we share C&S's intuitions about commitment alignment, we find that their formalization and method embody limiting assumptions that preclude practical application. Accordingly, we contribute a generalized approach that tackles the following situations.

Independent transactions. Informally, a transaction logically encapsulates a set of correlated commitments. Reasoning about commitments in one transaction ideally should not interfere with reasoning about commitments in another. Suppose a customer is involved in two transactions with a merchant, each involving a commitment to deliver some book for some payment. Then canceling one should not affect the other. C&S's approach does not support multiple transactions and generates erroneous interference between commitments of the same debtor-creditor pair.

We contribute a language that supports modeling commitments as belonging to different transactions. We formalize alignment for commitments in this language and present a method that guarantees alignment.

Message delivery order. C&S require ordered communication, i.e., each channel is first-in first-out (FIFO). FIFO delivery is not acceptable in every setting because it requires buffering messages to ensure in-order delivery. Specifically, it hinders applications that require extremely low latency (e.g., in finance) and that are storage-constrained (e.g., in the Internet of Things).

We contribute an approach that dispenses with FIFO channels, which additionally leads to looser coupling between agents with potential gains in performance.

System states under consideration. C&S define alignment to apply only in states that are *quiescent*, meaning those states where no message is in transit. Doing so eliminates false negatives. For instance, we should not expect alignment when a debtor of a commitment has sent a message to the creditor canceling the commitment, but which the creditor has not yet received. However, C&S's approach additionally eliminates true positives. Specifically, these are cases where we should determine that the agents are aligned even though some messages are in transit.

We contribute a notion of complete states that captures better where we expect alignment to hold. We show that under our method, completeness with respect to commitment implies alignment with respect to the commitment, and vice versa.

Complexity. C&S's approach mixes in procedural elements to describe the notifications required from agents and to model priority between debtors and creditors.

We contribute a significantly simplified, purely declarative approach that requires fewer notifications and avoids the notion of priority.

Organization. Section 2 motivates the challenge of alignment and provides a technical overview of C&S's approach. Section 3 describes the opportunities for improving over C&S. Section 4 describes the details of our approach. Section 5 discusses related work and directions for future work.

2. BACKGROUND ON ALIGNMENT

Fig. 1 reproduces C&S's scenarios to motivate commitment alignment. Each subfigure represents an enactment in the manner of a sequence diagram. Here, a vertical line represents an agent's history; an arrow represents a message exchange; time flows downward. Table 1 lists the messages that concern us in this paper.

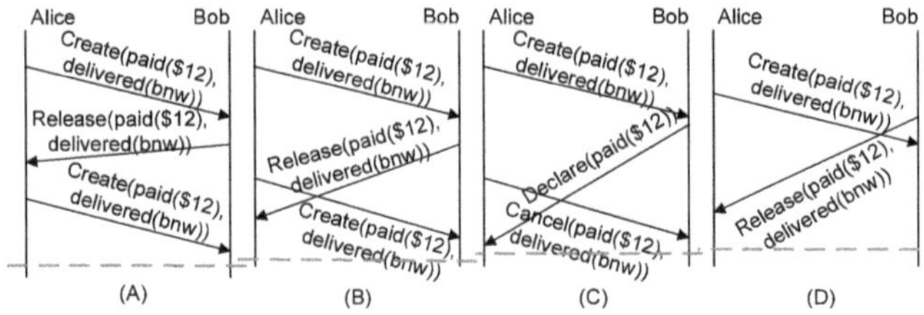

Figure 1: Alice and Bob are aligned in A, not in B, C, D.

Table 1: Messages and their effects; x and y are agents; r and u are propositions.

Message	Sender	Receiver	Naïve effect
$\mathsf{Create}(x, y, r, u)$	x	y	$\mathsf{C}(x, y, r, u)$
$\mathsf{Cancel}(x, y, r, u)$	x	y	$\neg\mathsf{C}(x, y, r, u)$
$\mathsf{Release}(x, y, r, u)$	y	x	$\neg\mathsf{C}(x, y, r, u)$
$\mathsf{Declare}(x, y, p)$	x	y	p

Table 1 lists the messages corresponding to commitment operations [21] and their naïve effects. We see below that this naïve formulation is inapplicable in distributed settings. Table 1 introduces Declare, by which a suitably empowered agent [14] brings about relevant conditions that feature in the antecedents or consequents of commitments. For example, declaring a payment or delivery would cause the detach or discharge of some commitments in Table 2. A received Declare may be forwarded by an agent to others. Since the identity of the declarer is not relevant for this paper, we use Declare for both purposes.

Table 2 lists the example commitments we use as running examples, especially to illustrate C&S's approach.

Table 2: Example commitments. When the antecedent is $\top$, the commitment is unconditional. Here, bnw, gow, and soc are names of books.

c_A	$\mathsf{C}(\mathsf{Alice}, \mathsf{Bob}, \mathsf{paid}(\$12), \mathsf{delivered}(\mathsf{bnw}))$
c_{UA}	$\mathsf{C}(\mathsf{Alice}, \mathsf{Bob}, \top, \mathsf{delivered}(\mathsf{bnw}))$
c_B	$\mathsf{C}(\mathsf{Alice}, \mathsf{Bob}, \mathsf{paid}(\$12), \mathsf{delivered}(\mathsf{gow}))$
c_{UB}	$\mathsf{C}(\mathsf{Alice}, \mathsf{Bob}, \top, \mathsf{delivered}(\mathsf{gow}))$
c_{AB}	$\mathsf{C}(\mathsf{Alice}, \mathsf{Bob}, \mathsf{paid}(\$12), \mathsf{delivered}(\mathsf{bnw}) \wedge \mathsf{delivered}(\mathsf{gow}))$
c_{UAB}	$\mathsf{C}(\mathsf{Alice}, \mathsf{Bob}, \top, \mathsf{delivered}(\mathsf{bnw}) \wedge \mathsf{delivered}(\mathsf{gow}))$
c_C	$\mathsf{C}(\mathsf{Alice}, \mathsf{Bob}, \mathsf{paid}(\$15), \mathsf{delivered}(\mathsf{soc}))$
c_{UC}	$\mathsf{C}(\mathsf{Alice}, \mathsf{Bob}, \top, \mathsf{delivered}(\mathsf{soc}))$
c_{UAC}	$\mathsf{C}(\mathsf{Alice}, \mathsf{Bob}, \top, \mathsf{delivered}(\mathsf{bnw}) \wedge \mathsf{delivered}(\mathsf{soc}))$

Following the naïve effects in Table 1, let us see how the enactments from Fig. 1 fare from the point of view of alignment at the moment denoted by the dashed line.

Example 1: In Fig. 1(A), there is no misalignment. Both Alice and Bob infer that c_A.

In Fig. 1(B), Alice and Bob are misaligned. Bob infers c_A but Alice does not. The reason is that Bob observes the second create after the release whereas Alice observes them in the opposite order.

In Fig. 1(C), Alice and Bob are misaligned. Bob infers c_{UA} (because of the detach when he sends the declare) but Alice does not because she had already canceled c_A by the time the declare arrives and so there is nothing to detach.

In Fig. 1(D), Alice and Bob are misaligned. Bob infers c_A but Alice does not.

2.1 Technical Preliminaries

We introduce some technical details. B_1–B_8 are postulates for commitment reasoning [22].

B_1. DISCHARGE. $u \rightarrow \neg \mathsf{C}(r, u)$

B_2. DETACH. $\mathsf{C}(r \wedge s, u) \wedge r \rightarrow \mathsf{C}(s, u)$

B_3. AUGMENT. From $\mathsf{C}(r, u)$, $s \vdash r$, $s \not\vdash u$ infer $\mathsf{C}(s, u)$

B_4. L-DISJOIN. $\mathsf{C}(r, u) \wedge \mathsf{C}(s, u) \rightarrow \mathsf{C}(r \vee s, u)$

B_5. R-CONJOIN. $\mathsf{C}(r, u) \wedge \mathsf{C}(r, v) \rightarrow \mathsf{C}(r, u \wedge v)$

B_6. CONSISTENCY. $\neg \mathsf{C}(r, \bot)$

B_7. NONVACUITY. From $r \vdash u$ infer $\neg \mathsf{C}(r, u)$

B_8. WEAKEN. $\mathsf{C}(r, u \wedge v) \wedge \neg u \rightarrow \mathsf{C}(r, u)$

Definition 1: A commitment $\mathsf{C}(r, u)$ is *stronger than* $\mathsf{C}(s, v)$ (with the same debtor and creditor), or $\mathsf{C}(r, u) \succeq \mathsf{C}(s, v)$, if and only if $u \vdash v$ and $s \vdash r$. If $\mathsf{C}(r, u) \succeq \mathsf{C}(s, v)$ but $\mathsf{C}(s, v) \not\succeq \mathsf{C}(r, u)$, $\mathsf{C}(r, u)$ is *strictly stronger than* $\mathsf{C}(s, v)$ or $\mathsf{C}(r, u) \succ \mathsf{C}(s, v)$.

For example, from Table 2, $c_{UAB} \succ c_{AB} \succ c_A$ and $c_{UAB} \succ c_{UA} \succ c_A$ but $c_B \not\succeq c_A$ and $c_A \not\succeq c_B$. Let's say an agent infers c_A and c_B. Then, by B_5, the agent infers c_{AB} as well, which is strictly stronger than both c_A and c_B.

2.2 C&S's Solution for Ensuring Alignment

In C&S's solution, agents can send any message at any time. The effects of the messages, however, are not computed according to Table 1 but by rules C&S provide. For instance, Bob's observation of the second create in Fig. 1(B) is a *noop* because it is not strictly stronger than commitments that held previously (*Principle of Novel Creation*). This solves the misalignment in Fig. 1(B). C&S address Fig. 1(D) by treating a released or canceled commitment as having held previously (*Principle of Accommodation*), thus making Bob's observation of the create a noop.

C&S characterize the problem in Fig. 1(C) as arising from a race between the debtor's (Alice's) cancelation and the creditor's (Bob's) detach. To address this misalignment, they assign priorities to actions as part of the protocol specification, and prescribe actions that agents must take depending on who has priority (*Principle of Priority*). In this example, if Alice has priority (for c_A's cancellation), then Bob must release Alice from c_{UA} upon observing the cancel. Alternatively, if Bob has priority, then Alice must explicitly create c_{UA}. In either case, the misalignment is avoided.

C&S introduce two additional principles, which we mention for completeness. The *Principle of Complete Erasure* states that canceling or releasing a commitment removes all weaker commitments if no strictly stronger commitment holds; otherwise, it is a noop. The *Principle of Notification* states that debtors must be notified by creditors of detaches and creditors must be notified by debtors of discharges.

C&S show that a multiagent system is aligned in states where all notifications have been sent ("integral"), and no messages are in transit ("quiescent"): if a creditor infers a commitment, then the debtor also infers it.

3. GENERALIZATION OPPORTUNITIES

We now motivate opportunities for improvements by discussing the limitations of C&S's approach.

3.1 Independent Transactions

Conceptually, the idea behind a transaction is that it encapsulates a set of related events or operations. Specifically, events in independent transactions will not affect each other. Thus, events concerning a commitment in one transaction should not affect a commitment in another transaction. For example, as illustrated in Section 1, canceling a commitment for a book in one transaction should not affect a commitment for a book in another transaction. A key limitation of C&S's approach is that it does not support multiple transactions. In effect, it treats all commitments as being in the same *implicit* transaction. Example 2 illustrates this.

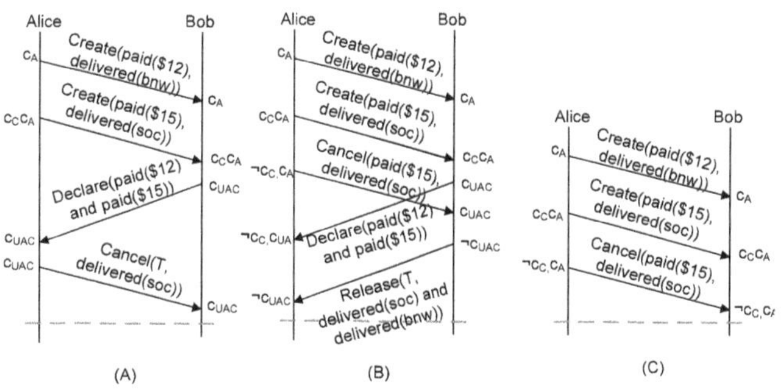

Figure 2: Aligned but unrealistic outcomes due to the lack of transactions in C&S.

Example 2: See Fig. 2(A). Alice creates c_A and c_C. Let's assume that the two commitments are in separate transactions. Accordingly, we expect no interference between them. Bob sends payment for both books (via a Declare message). Hence, Bob infers the unconditional versions of both commitments, c_{UA} and c_{UC}. Due to B_5, however, Bob infers c_{UAC}, which is strictly stronger than c_{UA} and c_{UC}. Therefore, Alice's cancelation of c_{UC} is ineffective (by C&S's *Principle of Complete Erasure*).

Interestingly, C&S advocate using domain identifiers in the content of the commitment to enable making the "same" commitment twice (Ex. 5 on p. 940). In the spirit of their example, Alice could have created $\mathsf{C}(\mathsf{Alice}, \mathsf{Bob}, \mathsf{paid}(\mathsf{id0}, \$12), \mathsf{delivered}(\mathsf{id0}, \mathsf{bnw}))$ and $\mathsf{C}(\mathsf{Alice}, \mathsf{Bob}, \mathsf{paid}(\mathsf{id1}, \$15), \mathsf{delivered}(\mathsf{id1}, \mathsf{soc}))$ instead of c_A and c_C, respectively; here, $\mathsf{id0}$ and $\mathsf{id1}$ serve to distinguish the transactions. However, notice that from their unconditional versions, one would still infer $\mathsf{C}(\mathsf{Alice}, \mathsf{Bob}, \top, \mathsf{delivered}(\mathsf{id0}, \mathsf{bnw}) \wedge \mathsf{delivered}(\mathsf{id1}, \mathsf{soc}))$ (again, by B_5). This means that, just as in Example 2, the unconditional commitment for soc cannot be canceled by Alice. This means that the two commitments, even with domain identifiers to help distinguish them, are not in separate transactions. In Section 4, we adopt C&S's intuition about using domain identifiers but treat it more fully in order to avoid such anomalies.

Example 3 shows an enactment where the outcome following C&S's approach is especially undesirable.

Example 3: See Fig. 2(B). Assume c_A and c_C are in different transactions. Alice's cancel is treated as a noop by Bob because Bob already infers the stronger c_{UAC}. Alice, in contrast, infers c_{UA} but not c_{UC} upon seeing Bob's declare because she had already canceled c_C. Therefore, Alice does not infer c_{UAC}. A potential misalignment ensues: Bob infers c_{UAC}, which Alice does not. C&S's *Principle of Priority* kicks in to handle this. Let's say Alice has priority. Accordingly, Bob releases Alice from c_{UAC}, thus fixing the misalignment. Notice that a release of just c_{UC} would not have worked—it would in fact be a noop because c_{UAC} holds (*Principle of Complete Erasure*). But releasing c_{UAC} gets rid of c_{UA} as well (by *Principle of Complete Erasure*). In effect, fixing a misalignment for one commitment c_C gets rid of an unrelated commitment in a different transaction, which is highly undesirable.

To bring out the magnitude of the problem highlighted in Example 3, imagine that instead of just c_{UA} there were a million unconditional commitments from Alice to Bob, each for the delivery of some item, that held for Bob at the point where Bob receives Alice's cancelation of c_C. Then, Bob would need to release Alice from all those—practically speaking, wipe the slate clean—to produce alignment.

Let us consider how we can avoid priority. Consider Example 4, which C&S support.

Example 4: See Fig. 2(C). Alice creates c_A and c_C. She then cancels c_C, which makes c_C go away. Only c_A remains.

At first glance, it appears reasonable to remove commitments piecemeal, as in Example 4. But what if Bob had detached the commitments concurrently with Alice's cancelation, as in Example 3?

In general, a conditional commitment may be detached at any time and thus its cancelation would inherently lead to an undefined state. C&S's notion of priority seeks to repair this undefined state. Instead we should prevent it. In this spirit, a simpler alternative is to treat cancelations and releases not at the level of commitments but at the level of the transaction. In other words, a cancelation wipes out all the commitments in a transaction. Notice that unlike the wipeout in Example 3, the scope of the wipeout is limited by the transaction. Applying this idea to Example 4, if c_A and c_C were part of the same transaction, canceling the transaction would remove them both; if they belonged to different transactions, then canceling the transaction of c_C would remove only c_C. Analogous reasoning applies to Example 3.

Once a transaction is removed by the observation of either a cancel or release, no commitment belonging to the transaction can hold again—the transaction is *used up*. This idea is especially important in non-FIFO settings, where messages can be delivered in any order (as we shall see below). In case a debtor changes it mind after sending the cancel and wants to "recreate" the commitments in a canceled transaction, it must do so in a new transaction.

3.2 Message Delivery Order

Fig. 3(A) shows a first-in first-out (FIFO) enactment, in which messages between any two agents are delivered in order. Fig. 3(B) shows a non-FIFO variant of the enactment. Bob sees the creates of c_A and c_B before the cancel of c_A. Therefore, Bob already infers c_A (by B_5) when the cancel arrives. Since the cancel is for a weaker commitment than

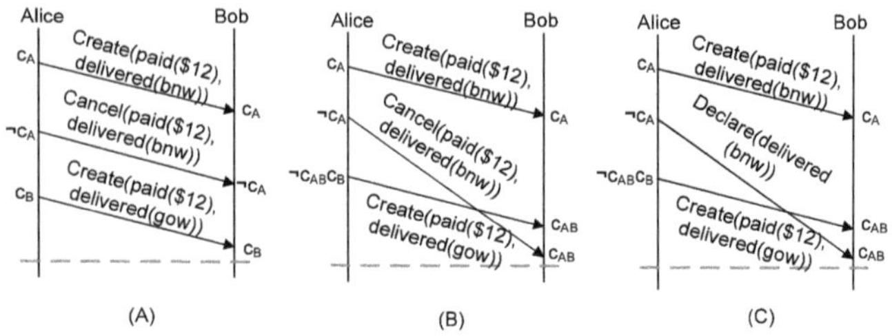

Figure 3: In (A), messages are delivered on FIFO basis; Alice and Bob are aligned. In (B) and (C) messages are not delivered on FIFO basis, which causes misalignment.

what already holds ($c_{AB} \succ c_A$), the cancel is a noop. Hence Alice and Bob are misaligned: Bob infers c_{AB} at the dashed line but Alice does not. An analogous situation obtains when Alice discharges c_A, as in Fig. 3(C).

When we deal with commitments in transactional scope, a general solution is to treat the observation of a cancel as removing all the commitments in that transaction (taking care of the problem in Fig. 3(B)), and to prohibit the sending of creates after some commitment in the transaction has been discharged (taking care of the problem in Fig. 3(C)).

C&S require FIFO message delivery. Although FIFO is supported in enterprise message queues, it limits applicability in settings where buffering is not appropriate, such as low-latency finance and sensing applications and settings where the infrastructure has reduced capabilities for storage. Our approach avoids assuming FIFO but without limiting the range of enactments that the agents can realize.

3.3 Systems States

C&S's notion of alignment exploits the inherent asymmetry of a commitment. Alignment requires only that a debtor meet a creditor's expectations, not that a creditor must have some expectation: introducing unnecessary expectations would only couple the parties unnecessarily.

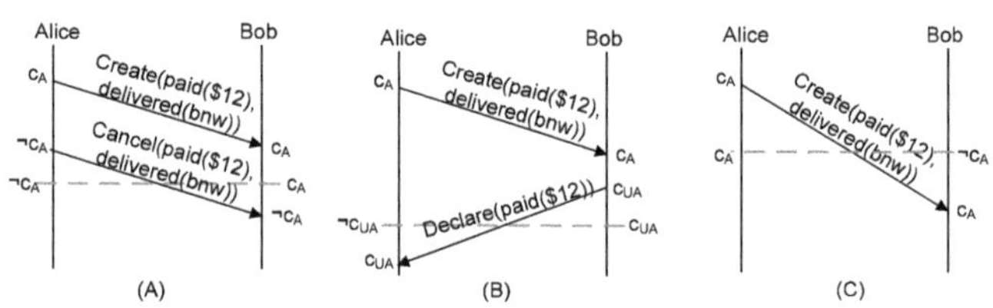

Figure 4: The dotted lines indicate nonquiescent system states. In (A) and (B), the agents are misaligned. However, in (C) the agents are aligned.

Asynchronous message transmission is causally asymmetric: the sender is aware of a message before the receiver is. Therefore, agents can be in disagreement in states where the relevant information has not propagated to the concerned agents. For example, when a debtor has sent a cancel message for a commitment but the creditor has not seen it yet, the creditor will infer the commitment but the debtor will not. Fig. 4(A) shows this state using a dashed line. In Fig. 4(B), the dashed line indicates a system state where the detach of a commitment has not propagated to the debtor. C&S formalize the idea that only *quiescent* states, where no message is in transit, are relevant for alignment. That is, the states denoted by the dashed lines in Fig. 4 are irrelevant.

However, the above formulation is too strong. In Fig. 4(C), even though the state indicated by the dashed line is not quiescent, the agents are aligned. Two commitments in different transactions would not affect each other. So even if a cancel for one is in transit, the agents may be aligned with respect to the other. In other words, we should able to claim alignment for each commitment independently.

Further, consider that in practice quiescent states may never obtain in a distributed system. Hence, to define alignment in quiescent states severely limits its practical value. Ideally, we would like to semantically characterize relevant states with respect to a commitment and show alignment in those states with respect to that commitment. Further, to show that our characterization is not too strong, we would like to show that if the agents are in agreement with respect to the commitment in some state, then the state is relevant in our characterization.

4. TECHNICAL FRAMEWORK

We now describe our framework in terms of a language and models of computation.

Let $\mathcal{P}$ be a finite set of predicates. Each predicate has a signature consisting of a list of domains. The first domain is the set of natural numbers ($\mathbb{N}$) and is treated as the ID of the predicate. Each domain is a set of values, written as constants in the syntax.

An *atom* is obtained from a predicate by applying the predicate on a list of constants, each constant representing a value drawn from the corresponding domain (the particular constants chosen would depend on an agent's internal reasoning, which is outside the scope of this paper). Let ι be the value of ID in an atom. Then we say that the atom belongs to the transaction whose identifier is ι. More simply, we will say the atom belongs to transaction ι. We require that any expression that involves two or more atoms, e.g., a DNF or a commitment expression, involves atoms with the same value for ID. Let ι be the value of ID in a commitment expression. Then we say that the commitment (expression) belongs to transaction ι. Any commitment belongs to only one transaction but one transaction may include multiple commitments. Below, we use ι as the generic transaction identifier in our formal definitions. For each transaction ι, we define a special atom $\top(\iota)$ that represents true in that transaction.

Table 3 introduces our syntax. Here $\mathcal{X}$ is a set of agents. As remarked above, we restrict our attention to expressions (Comm in Table 3) that involve atoms with the same ID. This is a reasonable restriction because otherwise there would be no way to correlate the events that discharge a commitment with those that detach it. Specifically, the commitment $\mathsf{C}(\mathsf{Alice}, \mathsf{Bob}, \mathsf{paid}(20, \$12), \mathsf{delivered}(15, \mathsf{bnw}))$ is malformed because it mixes transactions with IDs 20 and 15, respectively. But $\mathsf{C}(\mathsf{Alice}, \mathsf{Bob}, \mathsf{paid}(15, \$12), \mathsf{delivered}(15, \mathsf{bnw}))$ meets our restriction. $\mathsf{C}(\mathsf{Alice}, \mathsf{Bob}, \top(15), \mathsf{delivered}(15, \mathsf{bnw}))$ represents the unconditional variant of the commitment; it too meets our restriction. Unconditional commitments of the sort allowed in C&S, e.g., $\mathsf{C}(\mathsf{Alice}, \mathsf{Bob}, \top, \mathsf{delivered}(15, \mathsf{bnw}))$, are not included in our language.

The fact that the antecedent in an unconditional commitment is qualified with a transaction identifier is key to blocking reasoning across transactions. For example, from $\mathsf{C}(\mathsf{Alice}, \mathsf{Bob}, \top(15), \mathsf{delivered}(15, \mathsf{bnw}))$ and $\mathsf{C}(\mathsf{Alice}, \mathsf{Bob}, \top(16), \mathsf{delivered}(16, \mathsf{gow}))$, you cannot derive a stronger commitment by applying B_5, as you could with c_{UA} and c_{UB} to derive c_{UAB}. From $\mathsf{C}(\mathsf{Alice}, \mathsf{Bob}, \top(15), \mathsf{delivered}(15, \mathsf{bnw}))$ and $\mathsf{C}(\mathsf{Alice}, \mathsf{Bob}, \top(15), \mathsf{delivered}(15, \mathsf{gow}))$, however, you get $\mathsf{C}(\mathsf{Alice}, \mathsf{Bob}, \top(15), \mathsf{delivered}(15, \mathsf{bnw}) \wedge \mathsf{delivered}(15, \mathsf{gow}))$.

Table 3: Formal syntax.

Base	$\longrightarrow$	Comm | Atom | $\mathsf{removed}(\mathcal{X}, \mathcal{X}, \mathbb{N})$
Comm	$\longrightarrow$	$\mathsf{C}(\mathcal{X}, \mathcal{X}$, DNF, CNF)
DNF	$\longrightarrow$	And | And $\vee$ DNF
CNF	$\longrightarrow$	Or | Or $\wedge$ CNF
And	$\longrightarrow$	Atom | Atom $\wedge$ And
Or	$\longrightarrow$	Atom | Atom $\vee$ Or
Message	$\longrightarrow$	$\mathsf{Declare}(\mathcal{X}, \mathcal{X}$, And) | $\mathsf{Cancel}(\mathcal{X}, \mathcal{X}, \mathbb{N})$| $\mathsf{Create}(\mathcal{X}, \mathcal{X}$, DNF, CNF) | $\mathsf{Release}(\mathcal{X}, \mathcal{X}, \mathbb{N})$

Notice in Table 3, cancel and release take a transaction identifier as a parameter. And, removed is a stative that records that a cancel or release was observed.

Below, x, y, z are agents; $p \ldots w$ are DNF or CNF expressions; $\vee$, $\wedge$, and $\neg$ are the usual connectives; $\vdash$ is the usual propositional inference symbol. To reduce clutter, we omit the debtor and creditor from expressions when they are understood, e.g., writing $\mathsf{C}(r, u)$ instead of $\mathsf{C}(x, y, r, u)$.

Let ι be the ID of all atoms that appear in $\mathsf{C}(r, u)$; that is, let $\mathsf{C}(r, u)$ belong to transaction ι. Since all atoms have the same ID, if we need to refer to the ID, we need write it only once to make it explicit. Specifically, we will write $\mathsf{C}(\iota, r, u)$ when we wish to make the ID explicit.

4.1 Messages and Observations

Agents communicate by point-to-point messaging. Here $m(x, y)$ indicates a message m from x to y. An agent *observes* all and only those messages that it sends or receives. All facts relevant to an enactment arise from the observations an agent makes during its interactions with others. An agent's internal reasoning is irrelevant for our purposes.

An agent x's *observation sequence* $\langle m_0, \ldots, m_n \rangle_x$ describes the sequence of messages x observes in a particular execution. For an observation sequence $o = \langle \ldots, m \rangle$ and message m', we define the *concatenation* of o with m' as $\langle \ldots, m, m' \rangle$ and write it as $o; m'$.

Let $\mathcal{A}$ be a system of k agents. Then, $O = [O_0 \ldots O_i \ldots O_{k-1}]$ is an *observation vector* over $\mathcal{A}$, where the O_is are the observation sequences, one for each of the k agents. An observation vector is thus a snapshot of the system. Below, O is an observation vector and O_x is agent x's observation sequence within O. Now we define important concepts concerning observation sequences and vectors.

Definition 2: The length of an observation sequence is the number of observations it contains. The length of an observation vector is the sum of the lengths of its observation sequences. If $O = [O_0 \ldots O_i \ldots O_{k-1}]$ is of length n, then we write O^n to denote its length and O_i^n to denote the observation sequence of agent i.

Definition 3: Let o' be an observation sequence. Then o is a subsequence of o', denoted by $o \sqsubseteq o'$ iff

- $o' = o$, or
- for some message m, $o' = o; m$, or
- for some observation sequence o'', $o \sqsubseteq o'' \sqsubseteq o'$.

If $o \sqsubseteq o'$ but $o \neq o'$, then we say that o' strictly extends o and write it as $o \sqsubset o'$.

Definition 4: Let $O = [O_0 \ldots O_i \ldots O_{k-1}]$ and $O' = [O'_0 \ldots O'_i \ldots O'_{k-1}]$. We say that that O' extends O, denoted by $O \sqsubseteq O'$, iff each $O_i \sqsubseteq O'_i$. If $O \sqsubseteq O'$ but $O \neq O'$, then we say that O' strictly extends O and write it as $O \sqsubset O'$.

Finally, Definition 5 defines an operator that gives the remainder of an observation sequence after removing a prefix.

Definition 5: Let $o = \langle m_0, \ldots, m_l \rangle$ and $o' = \langle m_0, \ldots, m_l, m_{l+1}, \ldots, m_i \rangle$. Then $o' \setminus o = \langle m_{l+1}, \ldots, m_i \rangle$.

4.2 Agent Snapshots and Local Maintenance

We now formalize the treatment of an agent snapshot, its local state as arising from its observation sequence. In syntactic terms, a snapshot is a finite data structure. In semantic terms, a snapshot yields a set of propositions that an agent may logically infer from its observations. To enable how an agent's snapshot progresses based on its observations, we introduce two *update operators* called *addition* $\oplus$ and *subtraction* $\ominus$, which respectively "add" or "subtract" propositions from its snapshot. These operators ensure that the resulting representation is consistent according to the postulates of this paper, and that only the essential (i.e., minimal) changes are made due to each message. We now describe a way in which to implement the update operators.

Let S be a set of base propositions, i.e., atoms, commitments, or removeds. Specifically, S may represent the snapshot of an agent arising from a sequence of observations. In logical terms, the state of the agent is $[\![S]\!]$, the deductive closure of its snapshot. We extend $\vdash$ to apply to snapshots: $S \vdash p$ means $p \in [\![S]\!]$. We assume that $\vdash$ respects B_1 to B_8.

Then we define the operators to modify snapshots. Below, β is an atom or a $\mathsf{removed}(\iota)$. And, $\chi(S)$ is the set of commitments in S. That is, $\chi(S) = \{\mathsf{C}(r,u) : \mathsf{C}(r,u) \in S\}$. Definition 6 says that adding a β gets rid of all commitments that are discharged by the addition, and adding a commitment is only effective if the transaction has not been removed and if the commitment has not been discharged.

Definition 6: We define $\oplus$ as follows.

- Given snapshot S and β, $S \oplus \beta = (S \cup \{\beta\}) \setminus \{\mathsf{C}(r,u) : \mathsf{C}(r,u) \in \chi(S), S \cup \{\beta\} \not\vdash u\}$
- Given snapshot S and $\beta_1, \ldots, \beta_k$, $S \oplus (\beta_1 \wedge \ldots \wedge \beta_k) = (S \oplus \beta_1) \ldots \oplus \beta_k$
- Given snapshot S and $\mathsf{C}(\iota, r, u)$, $S \oplus \mathsf{C}(\iota, r, u) = S$ if $S \vdash \mathsf{removed}(\iota) \vee u$; else $S \cup \{\mathsf{C}(\iota, r, u)\}$.

Definition 7 says that removing a transaction amounts to removing all commitments with that transaction's identifier.

Definition 7: Given snapshot S and ι, we define $\ominus$ as follows: $S \ominus \iota = S \oplus \mathsf{removed}(\iota) \setminus \{\mathsf{C}(\iota, s, v) : \mathsf{C}(\iota, s, v) \in \chi(S)\}$.

Let $S(o)$ be the snapshot corresponding to the sequence of observations o. Then we compute $S(o; m)$ from $S(o)$ via one or more applications of the above update operators. The specific applications of the operators depend upon the semantics of the message m. In U_1–U_5, o is either x's or y's observation sequence. $S(\langle\,\rangle)$ is easily finitely stored.

U_1. $S(\langle\,\rangle) = \{\top[\iota]\}$, for every possible binding of ι

U_2. $S(o; \mathsf{Create}(r, u)) = S(o) \oplus \mathsf{C}(r, u)$

U_3. $S(o; \mathsf{Release}(\iota)) = S(o) \ominus \iota$

U_4. $S(o; \mathsf{Cancel}(\iota)) = S(o) \ominus \iota$

U_5. $S(o; \mathsf{Declare}(\beta_0 \wedge \ldots \wedge \beta_k) = S(o) \oplus \beta_0 \wedge \ldots \wedge \beta_k$

Our only constraint is that once an agent infers an atom with identifier ι, it no longer send any further creates for commitments with ι. This reflects the intuition that once an agent begins discharging commitments in a transaction, it should not introduce new commitments to the transaction. The constraint helps address the problem in Fig. 3(C).

Lemma 1 means that if observation sequence derives a commitment of identifier ι, then it cannot derive its consequent or $\mathsf{removed}(\iota)$.

Lemma 1: If $S(o) \vdash \mathsf{C}(\iota, r, u)$, then $S(o) \vdash \neg\mathsf{removed}(\iota) \wedge \neg u$.

4.3 Alignment in Relevant States

As discussed in Section 3, defining alignment as holding only in quiescent states is too strong. We need a notion that coincides with alignment. Definition 8 characterizes such a notion. It defines only those vectors to be complete with respect to a commitment where if the debtor does not infer the commitment, then the creditor does not infer it too or the creditor knows that it was either discharged or its transaction removed. Consider a vector where the creditor infers a commitment because of a detach but the debtor does not because it has not received information about the detach. Such a vector would be incomplete as well.

Definition 8: O is *complete* with respect to $\mathsf{C}(\iota, r, u)$ if and only if $S(O_x) \vdash \neg\mathsf{C}(r,u) \Rightarrow S(O_y) \vdash \neg\mathsf{C}(r,u) \vee u \vee \mathsf{removed}(\iota)$.

Notice that if O is complete with respect to $\mathsf{C}(s, v)$ and $\mathsf{C}(s, v) \succ \mathsf{C}(r, u)$, it does not imply that O is complete with respect to $\mathsf{C}(r, u)$. To see this, let O_x be $\langle \mathsf{Create}(x, y, r, u \wedge v), \mathsf{Declare}(z, x, u) \rangle$ and O_y be $\langle \mathsf{Create}(x, y, r, u \wedge v) \rangle$; this O is complete with respect to $\mathsf{C}(x, y, r, u \wedge v)$ but not complete with respect to $\mathsf{C}(x, y, r, u)$.

Definition 9 says that a vector is aligned for a commitment if and only if the following condition is met: if the creditor's observation sequence in the vector derives the commitment, then the debtor's observation sequence in the vector derives the commitment as well.

Definition 9: O is aligned with respect to $\mathsf{C}(r, u)$ if and only if $S(O_y) \vdash \mathsf{C}(r, u)$ implies $S(O_x) \vdash \mathsf{C}(r, u)$.

Notice that Definition 9 does not rely upon any internal reasoning or state of the agent. Whether a commitment holds or not for an agent is solely a property of the agent's observations.

Theorem 1 and Theorem 2 show that alignment and completeness coincide.

Theorem 1: [Alignment] If O is complete with respect to $\mathsf{C}(r, u)$, then O is aligned with respect to $\mathsf{C}(r, u)$.

Proof. Let ι be $\mathsf{C}(r, u)$'s identifier. If O is complete with respect to $\mathsf{C}(r, u)$, then by Definition 8, $S(O_x) \vdash \neg\mathsf{C}(r, u) \Rightarrow S(O_y) \vdash \neg\mathsf{C}(r, u) \vee u \vee \mathsf{removed}(\iota)$, that is either (i) $S(O_x) \vdash \mathsf{C}(r, u)$, or (ii) $S(O_y) \vdash \neg\mathsf{C}(r, u) \vee u \vee \mathsf{removed}(\iota)$. If (i), then O is aligned with respect to $\mathsf{C}(r, u)$. If (ii), then (a) if $S(O_y) \vdash \neg\mathsf{C}(r, u)$, then O is aligned with respect to $\mathsf{C}(r, u)$; (b) if $S(O_y) \vdash \vee u \vee \mathsf{removed}(\iota)$, then by the contraposition of Lemma 1, $S(O_y) \vdash \neg\mathsf{C}(r, u)$. Therefore, O is aligned with respect to $\mathsf{C}(r, u)$. □

Theorem 2: [Completeness] If O is aligned with respect to $\mathsf{C}(r, u)$, then O is complete with respect to $\mathsf{C}(r, u)$.

Proof. We identify two cases. Case 1: $S(O_y) \vdash \mathsf{C}(r,u)$. Then, because O is aligned with respect to $\mathsf{C}(r,u)$, $S(O_x) \vdash \mathsf{C}(r,u)$. Therefore, by Definition 8, O is complete with respect to $\mathsf{C}(r,u)$. Case 2: $S(O_y) \vdash \neg\mathsf{C}(r,u)$. By Definition 8, O is complete with respect to $\mathsf{C}(r,u)$. □

4.4 Progress

We proved that all vectors complete with respect to a commitment are aligned with the respect to a commitment. But what if a vector incomplete with respect to a commitment is realized by the agents' interactions? Can the agents take actions that will guarantee the realization of a vector that is complete with respect to the commitment? In other words, can we ensure that the system always progresses to completion (and, therefore, alignment) with respect to every commitment? To establish that a multiagent system will advance toward alignment, we formalize the elements of a decentralized enactment of a multiagent system.

An underlying assumption for messaging in decentralized settings is *causality*, namely, that each message is sent before being received [16]. Definition 10 captures causality in a recursive formulation of realizability, wherein an agent is always able to send a message (reflecting its autonomy in saying anything it chooses) and is able to receive a message only if the message has previously been sent.

Further, showing progress requires the assumption of *reliability*, namely, that each message that is sent arrives at its destination, i.e., every sent message is received.

Definition 10 (Realize)*:* A multiagent system $\mathcal{A}$ of n agents $\{1 \ldots i \ldots n\}$ *realizes* an observation vector $O = [O_1 \ldots O_n]$ if and only if one of these conditions holds:

- $O = [\langle\rangle \ldots \langle\rangle]$, a vector of n empty observation sequences;
- $O = [O_1 \ldots O_i; \text{send}(j,m) \ldots O_n]$ and $\mathcal{A}$ realizes $\langle O_1 \ldots O_i \ldots O_n \rangle$; or
- $O = [O_1 \ldots O_i; \text{receive}(j,m) \ldots O_n]$ and $\mathcal{A}$ realizes $[O_1 \ldots O_i \ldots O_n]$ and O_j contains send(i,m).

C&S give action rules that specify the messages an agent must send based upon its local observations to propagate the information necessary for alignment. Specifically, debtors must notify creditors of discharges and creditors must notify debtors of detaches. Their notifications are of four kinds. One, if a commitment holds and then is discharged (*Discharge Posterior*); two, if a commitment whose consequent already holds is created (*Discharge Prior*); three, if a commitment holds and then is detached (*Detach Posterior*); and four, if a commitment whose detach condition already holds is created (*Detach Prior*). We give declarative characterizations analogous to each notification kind, except *Discharge Prior*. *Discharge Prior* does not apply for us because we adopt the restriction to not send creates for commitments of identifier ι if some atom with identifier ι already holds.

Definition 11 characterizes the messages that a debtor should send to the creditors of commitments that are discharged upon the debtor making an observation, say $n+1$. We refer to this set of messages as the discharge notification set for observation $n+1$. The only caveat is that we must be careful to send notification only for every strongest commitment (because for any commitment that holds there are arbitrarily many weaker commitments that hold).

Below, to save space, we assume that the transaction identifier of the commitments involved is ι.

Definition 11*:* $DI(z,n)$, the discharge notification set of z at observation $n+1$ is $\{\mathsf{Declare}(z,y,u') : S(O^n_x) \vdash \mathsf{C}(z,y,r,u)$ and $S(O^n_z) \vdash \neg\mathsf{C}(z,y,s,v)$ such that $\mathsf{C}(z,y,s,v) \succ \mathsf{C}(z,y,r,u)$, and $S(O^{n+1}_z) \vdash u'$ such that $u' \vdash u\}$.

Definition 12 characterizes the messages a creditor should send to its debtors upon making an observation that detaches currently holding commitments (again, strongest).

Definition 12*:* $DEPO(z,n)$, the detach posterior notification set of z at $n+1$ is $\{\mathsf{Declare}(z,x,s) : S(O^n_z) \vdash \mathsf{C}(x,z,(r \wedge s) \vee t,u) \wedge \neg\mathsf{C}(x,z,w,v) \wedge \neg s$ such that $\mathsf{C}(x,z,w,v) \succ \mathsf{C}(x,z,(r \wedge s) \vee t,u)$ and $S(O^{n+1}_z) \vdash s \wedge \neg u \wedge \neg\mathsf{removed}(\iota)\}$.

Definition 13 characterizes the messages that a creditor should send to the debtor of a commitment upon receiving the create of a commitment that would be at least partially detached because parts of the antecedent already hold.

Definition 13*:* $DEPR(z,n)$, the detach prior notification set of z at $n+1$ is $\{\mathsf{Declare}(z,x,s) : S(O^n_z) \vdash s \wedge \neg\mathsf{C}(x,z,(r \wedge s) \vee t,u) \wedge \neg u \wedge \neg\mathsf{removed}(\iota)$ and $n+1$ is z's observation *receive*$(x, \mathsf{Create}(x,z,(r \wedge s) \vee t,u))$ such that $s \not\equiv \top(\iota)\}$.

Definition 14 characterizes the set of all messages that an agent must send upon making an observation.

Definition 14*:* $NS(z,n)$, the notification set of agent z at observation n is $DI(z,n) \cup DEPO(z,n) \cup DEPR(z,n)$.

Definition 15 captures the state of an agent that has sent messages in the notification set for an observation.

Definition 15*:* Agent z is notification-done for n at k iff $O^n_z \sqsubseteq O^k_z$ and for each message $m \in NS(z,n)$, $O^k_z \setminus O^n_z$ contains send(z,m).

Messages sent from the notification set may themselves generate notifications. Definition 16 characterizes the idea of a closure of notifications.

Definition 16*:* Agent z is notification-closed if and only if for any n there exists a k such that z is notification-done for each j $(n \leqslant j \leqslant k)$ at k.

Lemma 2 expresses an important property: If an agent merely sends the messages in the notification set for an observation n, without any other intervening observations, then the resulting sequence is guaranteed to be notification-closed. This enables us to treat the sending of notifications as atomic with the observation that made them necessary.

Lemma 2*:* Let k be the smallest number such that z is notification-done for n at k. Then, z is notification-closed.

Definition 17*:* A system $\mathcal{A}$ of n agents $\{1 \ldots i \ldots n\}$ acceptably realizes an observation vector $O = [O_1 \ldots O_n]$ iff

- $\mathcal{A}$ realizes $O = [O_1 \ldots O_i \ldots O_n]$, and
- each i is notification-closed.

Informally, Theorem 3 states that if the system acceptably realizes an observation vector that is incomplete with respect to a commitment, then the system will acceptably realize an observation vector that is complete with respect to the commitment. Theorem 3 guarantees completeness only with respect to strongest commitments. In other words, if the vector is complete with respect to, say, $\mathsf{C}(r, u \wedge v)$, then we do not care that it may be incomplete with respect to $\mathsf{C}(r,u)$ (which it may well be, as illustrated earlier).

Theorem 3*:* [Progress] If a system $\mathcal{A}$ acceptably realizes an observation vector O that is incomplete with respect to $\mathsf{C}(r,u)$ and $\mathsf{C}(r,u)$ is a strongest incomplete commitment, then either $\mathcal{A}$ acceptably realizes an observation vector O' such that $O \sqsubset O'$ and O' is complete with respect to $\mathsf{C}(r,u)$ or $(\exists i \in \mathcal{A}, \mathsf{C}(s,v) : \mathsf{C}(s,v) \succ \mathsf{C}(r,u)$ and $\mathcal{S}(o_i) \vdash \mathsf{C}(s,v))$.

Proof. We sketch out a proof here. The proof is by induction on the length of the commitment expression, which is defined as the number of atoms in the expression. Let $\mathsf{C}(p,q)$ be a minimum length commitment (that is, of length two). By Definition 8, O^0 is acceptably realizable and complete with respect to $\mathsf{C}(p,q)$. Consider any complete vector O^c. Let O^i be a smallest acceptable extension of O^c that is incomplete with respect to $\mathsf{C}(p,q)$. This means that the following condition holds by Definition 8: $S(O^i_x) \vdash \neg\mathsf{C}(p,q)$ and $S(O^i_y) \vdash \mathsf{C}(p,q) \wedge \neg q \wedge \neg\mathsf{removed}(\iota)$. There are two primary cases to consider. (1) $S(O^{i-1}_x) \vdash \mathsf{C}(p,q)$, meaning that what made O^i incomplete was that x stopped inferring $\mathsf{C}(p,q)$. In this case, either a Cancel or a discharge notification is on the way to y, which when y receives them will make the resulting vector complete. (2) $S(O^{i-1}_y) \vdash \neg\mathsf{C}(p,q)$, meaning that what made O^i incomplete was that y began inferring $\mathsf{C}(p,q)$. If it is because of a stronger create, we are done (by theorem statement). If it is by a detach, then acceptability means that a notification is on the way to x, which when it arrives will produce a complete vector.

Assume that the theorem holds for all commitments of length k. Then we must prove that it holds for commitments of length $k+1$. By inspection, we see that there two relevant cases. These correspond to B_4 and B_5, respectively.

Consider B_4 first. Let $\mathsf{C}(r,u)$ and $\mathsf{C}(s,u)$ be each of length k and $\mathsf{C}(r \vee s, u)$ of length $k+1$. We know that O^0 is complete with respect to $\mathsf{C}(r \vee s, u)$. Let O^c be any vector complete with respect to $\mathsf{C}(r \vee s, u)$. As before, let O^i be the smallest incomplete acceptably realized extension with respect to $\mathsf{C}(r, u \wedge v)$. Then, we want to prove that the system acceptably realizes a complete extension of O^i. From the inductive hypothesis, we know there there will be an extension O^j of O^i that will be complete with respect to both $\mathsf{C}(r,u)$ and $\mathsf{C}(s,v)$. This means that $S(O^j_x) \vdash \neg\mathsf{C}(r,u)$ and $S(O^j_y) \vdash \mathsf{C}(r,u) \wedge \neg u \wedge \neg\mathsf{removed}(\iota)$ and $S(O^j_x) \vdash \neg\mathsf{C}(s,u)$ and $S(O^j_y) \vdash \mathsf{C}(s,u) \wedge \neg u \wedge \neg\mathsf{removed}(\iota)$. From these we infer that, $S(O^j_x) \vdash \neg\mathsf{C}(r \vee s, u)$ and $S(O^j_y) \vdash \mathsf{C}(r \vee s, u) \wedge \neg u \wedge \neg\mathsf{removed}(\iota)$. In other words, O^j is complete with respect to $\mathsf{C}(r \vee s, u)$.

Reasoning about the other case with B_5 is analogous. □

4.5 Revisiting the Motivating Scenarios

It is worth revisiting the enactments in Fig. 1 to see what their outcomes would be under our approach, specifically, when the commitments and operations on commitments are expressed in our syntax and include identifiers. Assume they involve the same transaction identifier.

Consider Fig. 1(A). Then, the second create is ineffective because of the earlier release; Bob and Alice are aligned (with respect to all commitments). Consider Fig. 1(B). Bob's observation of the second create is a noop because of the earlier release; Bob and Alice are aligned.

Consider Fig. 1(C). Bob's observation of the cancel removes c_{UA}; therefore, no commitment holds for either Bob or Alice; so they are aligned. Reasoning for Fig. 1(D) is analogous to (B).

Instead, consider the case that follows Fig. 1(A), but where the first create and release involve the same identifier and the second create involves a distinct identifier. Then, the second create makes a commitment with its identifier hold. Hence, Bob and Alice are still aligned.

5. DISCUSSION

We develop a novel treatment of alignment that addresses important shortcomings in C&S via a more general and simpler treatment than C&S. Our approach supports multiple transactions and does not require FIFO delivery. Compared to C&S, we require fewer kinds of notifications, fewer kinds of statives, and fewer reasoning postulates. We avoid C&S's *Principle of Priority* and the associated action rules, which make C&S's approach unnecessarily complex. Although we adopt the broad intuitions of C&S, our formal development is almost entirely novel, including the formal language (Table 3) and the definition of alignment (Definition 9).

Several works express protocols and commitments in first-order languages, e.g., the event calculus [4, 26]. However, a systematic treatment of information in protocols and commitments has a more recent history [7, 18, 19, 23]. Important questions here concern the identification of instances—of events, commitment, and protocol enactments. This paper is in the same vein and contributes to the proper treatment of commitments despite decentralization.

Some works [9, 10, 11, 17, 20] propose a purely syntactic notion of commitment identifiers. These approaches place an identifier in an explicit slot in a commitment expression but do not associate the identifier with the content (antecedent and consequent) of the commitment. Further, because these are syntactic approaches, they give unique identifiers to commitments. As C&S explain, this is problematic for reasoning over commitments. For example, from a commitment for $p \wedge q$, one would not be able to infer a commitment for p (what would its identifier be?); nor would one be able to infer a commitment for $p \wedge q$ from commitments for p and q. C&S proposed the semantic solution that commitments be identified based upon identifiers in the content. We adopt their core intuition though with enhancements to be able to accommodate distinct transactions.

Winikoff [25] notes problems with interoperability among agents enacting commitment protocols but does not provide a general solution. Kafalı et al. [15] consider it an overhead to send notifications for detaches and discharges. In a distributed system, where parties have incomplete information about relevant events, we consider notifications as essential for correct reasoning and a pragmatic way to ensure alignment. However, there may be opportunities for reducing the cost of notifications, for example, via piggybacking.

We foresee four important directions. One, implement our approach in an agent-oriented programming platform, such as JaCaMo [3]. Two, develop a general theory of commitment-based transactions. A fuller treatment of transactions that covers nested and multiparty cases would require a richer modeling of information in commitments. Approaches such as Cupid [7] could potentially be applied for this purpose. Three, develop a methodology and tool support for specifying commitment-based transactions. Protos [5] is a methodology for deriving commitment-based specifications from stakeholder requirements; it could be extended to commitment-based transactions. Four, develop a approach for alignment that applies to all kinds of social expectations, including norms that capture security requirements [24].

Acknowledgments

Thanks to the anonymous reviewers for comments.

6. REFERENCES

[1] M. Baldoni, C. Baroglio, A. K. Chopra, N. Desai, V. Patti, and M. P. Singh. Choice, interoperability, and conformance in interaction protocols and service choreographies. In *Proceedings of the 9th International Conference on Autonomous Agents and Multiagent Systems*, pages 843–850, Budapest, 2009. IFAAMAS.

[2] M. Baldoni, C. Baroglio, E. Marengo, and V. Patti. Constitutive and regulative specifications of commitment protocols: A decoupled approach. *ACM Transactions on Intelligent Systems and Technologies*, 4(2):22:1–22:25, 2013.

[3] O. Boissier, R. H. Bordini, J. F. Hübner, A. Ricci, and A. Santi. Multi-agent oriented programming with JaCaMo. *Science of Computer Programming*, 78(6):747–761, June 2013.

[4] F. Chesani, P. Mello, M. Montali, and P. Torroni. Representing and monitoring social commitments using the event calculus. *Autonomous Agents and Multi-Agent Systems*, 27(1):85–130, 2013.

[5] A. K. Chopra, F. Dalpiaz, F. B. Aydemir, P. Giorgini, J. Mylopoulos, and M. P. Singh. Protos: Foundations for engineering innovative sociotechnical systems. In *Proceedings of the 18th IEEE International Requirements Engineering Conference (RE)*, pages 53–62, 2014. IEEE Computer Society.

[6] A. K. Chopra and M. P. Singh. Multiagent commitment alignment. In *Proceedings of the Eighth International Conference on Autonomous Agents and Multiagent Systems*, pages 937–944. IFAAMAS, 2009.

[7] A. K. Chopra and M. P. Singh. Cupid: Commitments in relational algebra. In *Proceedings of the 23rd Conference on Artificial Intelligence (AAAI)*, pages 1–8, Austin, Texas, Jan. 2015. AAAI Press.

[8] S. Cranefield and M. Winikoff. Verifying social expectations by model checking truncated paths. In *Coordination, Organizations, Institutions and Norms in Agent Systems IV*, volume 5428 of *LNCS*, pages 204–219. Springer, 2009.

[9] M. El-Menshawy, J. Bentahar, and R. Dssouli. A new semantics of social commitments using branching space-time logic. In *International Joint Conferences on Web Intelligence and Intelligent Agent Technologies*, pages 492–496, 2009.

[10] R. A. Flores, P. Pasquier, and B. Chaib-draa. Conversational semantics sustained by commitments. *Journal of Autonomous Agents and Multi-Agent Systems (JAAMAS)*, 14(2):165–186, Apr. 2007.

[11] N. Fornara and M. Colombetti. Operational specification of a commitment-based agent communication language. In *Proceedings of the 1st International Joint Conference on Autonomous Agents and Multiagent Systems (AAMAS)*, pages 535–542. ACM Press, July 2002.

[12] N. Fornara and M. Colombetti. A commitment-based approach to agent communication. *Applied Artificial Intelligence*, 18(9-10):853–866, 2004.

[13] A. Günay, M. Winikoff, and P. Yolum. Generating and ranking commitment protocols. In *Proceedings of the 12th International Conference on Autonomous Agents and Multiagent Systems*, pages 1323–1324. 2013.

[14] A. J. I. Jones and M. J. Sergot. A formal characterisation of institutionalised power. *Logic Journal of the IGPL*, 4(3):427–443, June 1996.

[15] Ö. Kafalı, F. Chesani, and P. Torroni. What happened to my commitment? Exception diagnosis among misalignment and misbehavior. In *Proceedings of the 11th International Workshop on Computational Logic in Multi-Agent Systems*, volume 6245 of *LNCS*, pages 82–98. Springer, 2010.

[16] L. Lamport. Time, clocks, and the ordering of events in a distributed system. *Communications of the ACM*, 21(7):558–565, July 1978.

[17] A. U. Mallya, P. Yolum, and M. P. Singh. Resolving commitments among autonomous agents. In F. Dignum, editor, *Advances in Agent Communication, International Workshop on Agent Communication Languages, ACL 2003*, volume 2922 of *LNCS*, pages 166–182. Springer, 2004.

[18] F. Meneguzzi, P. R. Telang, and M. P. Singh. A first-order formalization of commitments and goals for planning. In *Proceedings of the 23rd Conference on Artificial Intelligence (AAAI)*, pages 697–703, Bellevue, Washington, July 2013. AAAI Press.

[19] M. Montali, D. Calvanese, and G. D. Giacomo. Verification of data-aware commitment-based multiagent system. In *Proceedings of the 13th International Conference on Autonomous Agents and Multiagent Systems*, pages 157–164, Paris, May 2014.

[20] M. Rovatsos. Dynamic semantics for agent communication languages. In *Proceedings of the 6th International Conference on Autonomous Agents and MultiAgent Systems (AAMAS)*, pages 100–107, Honolulu, May 2007. IFAAMAS.

[21] M. P. Singh. An ontology for commitments in multiagent systems: Toward a unification of normative concepts. *Artificial Intelligence and Law*, 7(1):97–113, Mar. 1999.

[22] M. P. Singh. Semantical considerations on dialectical and practical commitments. In *Proceedings of the 23rd Conference on Artificial Intelligence*, pages 176–181, 2008.

[23] M. P. Singh. Information-driven interaction-oriented programming: BSPL, the blindingly simple protocol language. In *Proceedings of the 10th International Conference on Autonomous Agents and MultiAgent Systems*, pages 491–498, 2011.

[24] M. P. Singh. Cybersecurity as an application domain for multiagent systems. In *Proceedings of the 14th International Conference on Autonomous Agents and MultiAgent Systems (AAMAS)*, pages 1–4, Istanbul, May 2015. IFAAMAS. Blue Sky Ideas Track.

[25] M. Winikoff, W. Liu, and J. Harland. Enhancing commitment machines. In *Proceedings of the 2nd International Workshop on Declarative Agent Languages and Technologies (DALT)*, volume 3476 of *LNAI*, pages 198–220, Berlin, 2005. Springer-Verlag.

[26] P. Yolum and M. P. Singh. Flexible protocol specification and execution: Applying event calculus planning using commitments. In *Proceedings of the 1st International Joint Conference on Autonomous Agents and MultiAgent Systems*, pages 527–534. 2002.

Monitoring Hierarchical Agent-based Simulation Traces

Benjamin Herd, Simon Miles, Peter McBurney, Michael Luck
Department of Informatics
King's College London
London, United Kingdom
{benjamin.c.herd, simon.miles, peter.mcburney, michael.luck}@kcl.ac.uk

ABSTRACT

Due to their internal complexity, agent-based simulations are rarely amenable to conventional formal verification. With its focus on individual traces, *runtime verification* represents an interesting alternative for correctness assessment. Here, execution traces produced by the running system are observed by a monitor and checked for correctness *on-the-fly*. If the truth or falsity of a given property cannot be determined at time t, then the monitor creates an *obligation* that the current trace needs to satisfy at time $t+1$ in order for the whole property to become true.

With different observational levels, traces produced by agent-based simulations have an inherently *hierarchical* nature which complicates the structure and manipulation of obligations significantly. However, it turns out that this problem is general enough to be dealt with in an abstract, language-independent way.

In this paper, we provide a general framework for the monitoring of hierarchical traces. It introduces different types of obligations and appropriate manipulation procedures along with minimal requirements that a property specification language needs to satisfy in order to be monitorable. We provide a full formalisation of the framework and an example implementation of a subset in Haskell.

Categories and Subject Descriptors

D.2.5 [**Software Engineering**]: Testing and Debugging—*Monitors*; I.2.11 [**Artificial Intelligence**]: Distributed Artificial Intelligence—*Multiagent systems*

General Terms

Verification, Theory, Algorithms

Keywords

Runtime verification; agent-based simulation; monitoring; temporal logic

1. INTRODUCTION

Agent-based simulation (ABS) is rapidly emerging as a popular paradigm for the simulation of complex systems that exhibit non-linear and emergent behaviour [14]. Similar to other software systems, *correctness* also plays a central role in the development of ABSs and the demand for tailored verification techniques increases.

Appears in: *Proceedings of the 14th International Conference on Autonomous Agents and Multiagent Systems (AAMAS 2015), Bordini, Elkind, Weiss, Yolum (eds.), May 4–8, 2015, Istanbul, Turkey.*

In the more general area of multiagent systems (MAS), temporal logic model checking has been used successfully to verify a wide range of properties [13]. Despite impressive advances made in recent years, exponential growth of the underlying finite-state model (the so-called 'state space explosion') remains a central problem which renders the verification of large-scale real-world systems difficult or even impossible. Due to their high level of complexity, the exhaustive verification of ABSs is, in general, far beyond the capabilities of contemporary model checking techniques and tools.

Runtime verification represents a promising alternative for the evaluation of large-scale systems [8]. It refers to the idea of observing the execution of a program at runtime and perform correctness checks on-the-fly. A central component of any runtime verification approach is a *monitoring process* which observes an execution trace against the background of a given correctness criterion (e.g. a linear temporal logic formula) and reports for each state in the trace whether the given property has already been satisfied or violated or whether a clear verdict cannot be made yet. In the latter case, an *obligation* is produced; it describes those aspects of the original property that the system needs to satisfy in the next step in order to satisfy the overall property.

Runtime verification of software systems has been investigated extensively in the past twenty years, yet in the area of MAS in general and ABS in particular, approaches are still largely missing. One reason for that is complexity. Conventional runtime verification assumes traces to be *monolithic*, i.e. composed of atomic, individual states. In a multiagent setting, however, traces have a more fine-grained internal structure: Traces still represent sequences of states (*population states*) yet, at the same time, they also represent sets of sequences of *group states* as well as sets of sequences of *individual agent states*. This has significant implications on the nature of obligations and their manipulation at runtime. Whilst some existing approaches to runtime verification and monitoring in the area of general MAS have to deal with certain aspects of obligation manipulation, a general and specification language-independent treatment of the monitoring problem is still missing. It turns out that the nature of obligations in a multiagent context as well as their manipulation is *independent* of the underlying specification language and can (and should) thus be treated *entirely separately* from the latter's design and implementation.

This paper makes the following contributions:

- we present a *language-independent framework for the monitoring of hierarchical traces* with a particular focus on the *manipulation of obligations*. The framework serves as an *abstract description of a monitoring procedure* which, due to its general nature, can be used as a blueprint for developers to implement concrete monitors for different specification languages;

- we give a *full typechecked formalisation* of the framework using the Z notation; and
- we show the correspondence of the abstract framework and an implementation by translating a subset of the framework into executable Haskell code.

We start with an overview of related work in Section 2 and some background in Section 3. We then provide an informal description of the idea of hierarchical traces in Section 4 which is succeeded by a formal treatment of the obligation manipulation problem in Section 5. Instead of tying the monitoring problem to a particular specification language, we aim to be as *general* as possible and treat the problem in a *language-independent* way. The purpose of this endeavour is to isolate the problem of obligation manipulation in order to allow a language designer to focus solely on the core language. We do this by developing a *monitoring framework for ABS traces* for the purpose of runtime verification together with *requirements* that a specification language needs to satisfy in order to be usable within the framework. To this end, we introduce the concepts of *joinability*, *agent-monitorability*, and *multiagent-monitorability*. In order to show the closeness of the framework to an executable implementation, we translate a subset of the framework into Haskell code. The integration of a simple example specification language into the framework is illustrated in Section 6.

2. RELATED WORK

In the wider area of MAS, runtime verification has not yet been dealt with in a general way. Whereas a range of problem-specific and language-specific testing and debugging approaches have been proposed for general MAS [9], their simulation counterparts have been largely neglected to date. Simulation-specific monitoring and testing approaches that have been presented tackle the monitoring problem in an ad hoc fashion [16, 21, 4]; formal approaches to monitor construction are still missing.

The approach closest to ours is the one presented by Dastani and Meyer [5]. They propose MDL, a specification language for the formulation of properties about BDI-based multiagent programs together with a debugging, i.e. runtime verification procedure. MDL allows for the specification of temporal properties about BDI-based systems and, in addition to temporal operators, provides a means to limit the *scope* of a property to an individual agent, to a group of agents, or to the overall population[1]. As opposed to the approach described above, Dastani and Meyer give MDL a two-valued semantics, according to which properties are either true (if clearly satisfied) or false (if either violated or not yet satisfied). The algorithm is thus not optimal w.r.t. the early detection of violations. Furthermore, as opposed to producing obligations, they seem to re-verify the entire trace prefix produced so far once a new state has been processed. Giving t time steps, $(t + 1)/2$ states thus need to be verified. This offline nature of the verification procedure circumvents the obligation problem discussed in this paper, yet it also renders the approach non-optimal w.r.t. the number of checks necessary to answer a given property.

Sharpanskykh and Treur presented *TTL*, the *temporal trace language* [17]. It subsumes languages based on temporal logics and differential equations and thus allows for the expression of properties which go beyond purely temporal statements. The specification language takes into consideration the hierarchical nature of traces obtained from MAS executions and offers the possibility to observe behaviours on different levels of observation. The authors also describe a verification procedure on sets of traces. However, the procedure is *exhaustive* in nature, i.e. it expects full traces to be present prior to verification. Similar to Dastani and Meyer's work described above, this circumvents the need to deal with obligations.

[1]In that respect, it bears a strong similarity with *simLTL*, a property specification language for ABS traces [10, 11].

3. BACKGROUND

Linear temporal logic (LTL).

The treatment of time in temporal logic can be roughly subdivided into *branching time* (CTL, CTL*) and *linear temporal logic* (LTL) [2]. Branching time logics assume that there is a choice between different successor states at each time step and thus views time as an exponentially growing tree of possible worlds. Linear time logic views time as a linear sequence of states. The problem addressed in this paper is based upon the analysis of individual finite execution traces. Since each path comprises a sequence of states, it is natural to assume linear temporal flow. We thus focus on LTL, the syntax of which is given below:

$$\phi ::= \mathbf{true} \mid p \mid \phi \wedge \phi \mid \phi \vee \phi \mid \neg \phi \mid \mathbf{X}\phi \mid \phi\, \mathbf{U}\, \phi$$

The basic building blocks are atomic propositions p, the Boolean connectives $\wedge$ ('and'), $\vee$ ('or') and $\neg$ ('not') and the temporal connectives $\mathbf{X}$ ('next') and $\mathbf{U}$ ('until'). LTL formulae are evaluated over paths. For formula ϕ and state s, $\mathbf{true}$ always holds, p holds iff it is true in s, $\phi_1 \wedge \phi_2$ holds iff ϕ_1 holds and ϕ_2 holds, $\phi_1 \vee \phi_2$ holds iff either ϕ_1 or ϕ_2 holds, $\neg\phi$ holds iff ϕ does not hold and $\mathbf{X}\phi$ holds iff ϕ holds in the direct successor state of s. For formulae ϕ_1 and ϕ_2, $\phi_1\, \mathbf{U}\, \phi_2$ holds in state s iff ϕ_1 holds until ϕ_2 holds at some point in the future. Other logical connectives such as '$\Rightarrow$' or '$\Leftrightarrow$' can be derived in the usual manner: $\phi_1 \Rightarrow \phi_2 \equiv \neg\phi_1 \vee \phi_2$ and $\phi_1 \Leftrightarrow \phi_2 \equiv (\phi_1 \Rightarrow \phi_2) \wedge (\phi_2 \Rightarrow \phi_1)$. Additional temporal operators such as $\mathbf{F}$ ('eventually'), $\mathbf{G}$ ('always') and $\mathbf{W}$ ('weak until') can be derived as follows: $\mathbf{F}\phi \equiv \mathbf{true}\, \mathbf{U}\, \phi$ (*ϕ holds eventually*), $\mathbf{G}\phi \equiv \neg\mathbf{F}(\neg\phi)$ (*ϕ holds always*) and $\phi_1 \mathbf{W} \phi_2 \equiv (\phi_1\, \mathbf{U}\, \phi_2) \vee \mathbf{G}\phi_1$ (ϕ_1 may be succeeded by ϕ_2).

Runtime verification.

As indicated above, the application of conventional model checking is severely constrained by the size of the underlying system. Runtime verification attempts to circumvent this problem by focussing on the *current execution* of a system instead of its universal behaviour [12]. In that respect, runtime verification bears a strong similarity with testing. However, in contrast to conventional testing, runtime verification typically allows for the formulation of the system's desired behaviour in a less ad hoc and more rigorous, e.g. logic-based, way and can thus be considered more formal.

Runtime verification represents a large research area in its own right and we can only give a very superficial description here. A typical runtime verification approach has the following three characteristics: (i) the behaviour of the system under consideration is observed while the system is running; (ii) a property describing the system's desired behaviour is checked against the current execution trace; and (iii) a result is reported as soon as the property has been satisfied (or violated). Due to its focus on individual execution traces, runtime verification views time as a linear flow and properties are thus often formulated in a variant of LTL. Those properties are then translated into a *monitor* which is used to observe the execution of the system and report any satisfaction or violation that may occur. In order for a monitoring approach to be efficient, it necessarily needs to be *forward-oriented*; having to 'rewind' the execution of a system in order to determine the truth of a property is generally not an option. In terms of monitor construction, two

$$\mathbf{X}\phi \equiv \mathbf{true} \wedge \mathbf{X}\phi \quad (1)$$

$$\phi_1 \,\mathbf{U}\, \phi_2 \equiv \phi_2 \vee (\phi_1 \wedge \mathbf{X}(\phi_1 \,\mathbf{U}\, \phi_2)) \quad (2)$$

Table 1: Expansion laws for the elementary LTL operators

different approaches — *automaton-based* and *symbolic* — can be distinguished. They are briefly described below.

The automaton-based approach is related to automata-theoretic model checking of LTL properties and involves the construction of an automaton, for example a finite state automaton, a Büchi automaton or an alternating finite automaton [19]. The automaton represents the language $\mathcal{L}(\phi)$ defined by a given LTL property ϕ which describes all allowed traces of the system. One typical problem in runtime verification is that the truth of a property ϕ at time t may need additional information about the future behaviour of the trace which is not yet available. From the monitor's point of view at a particular point in time, the future is not foreseeable. Depending on the type of automaton being used, transitions may thus need to be taken nondeterministically which raises questions about the correct *traversal mode*. In the case of depth-first traversal, the automaton can only ever be in a single state, yet it may require backtracking if the wrong path has been taken. In the case of breadth-first traversal, the automaton can be in a number of states at the same time, yet the number of currently active states may grow exponentially over time.

The second, symbolic approach is based on the idea of *formula manipulation*. Instead of constructing a full automaton as mentioned above, the monitor is represented as a formula which describes (i) the requirements that the currently observed state needs to satisfy in order to either satisfy (or at least not violate) a given property ϕ, and (ii) those requirements which the rest of the trace needs to fulfil in order for ϕ to be eventually satisfied. To that end, the symbolic approach makes use of the recursive nature of temporal logic by exploiting *expansion laws* (the laws for the basic LTL operators are shown in Table 1). Informally, expansion laws allow for the decomposition of an LTL formulae into two parts: the fragment of the formula that needs to hold in the *current* state and the fragment that needs to hold in the *next* state in order for the whole formula to be true. It is useful to view both fragments as *obligations*, i.e. aspects of the formula that the trace under consideration needs to satisfy *immediately* and aspects that it promises to satisfy *in the next step*. Consider, for example, the expansion law for the 'until' operator shown in Table 1. The equivalence states that, in order for a formula $\phi_1 \,\mathbf{U}\, \phi_2$ to be satisfied at time t, either (i) ϕ_2 needs to be satisfied at time t, or (ii) ϕ_1 needs to be satisfied at time t and $\phi_1 \,\mathbf{U}\, \phi_2$ needs to be satisfied at time $t + 1$.

Expansion laws play an important role in the idea of runtime verification, since they form the basis of a decision procedure that a monitor can use to decide in a certain state whether a given property has already been satisfied or violated. By decomposing a formula into an immediate and a future obligation, optimality can be achieved: as soon as the immediate obligation is satisfied and no future obligation is created, the formula is satisfied and evaluation ends. Expansion laws work well if the trace under consideration is infinite. In the presence of finite traces, however, certain problems arise. A thorough discussion of the finite trace problem is beyond the scope of this paper, for further information, see e.g. [3].

4. HIERARCHICAL TRACES

Although the monitoring of hierarchical traces is a general problem in the area of MAS, we put a particular focus on simulations here. We can assume that simulation traces are, by definition, finite and therefore *maximal*, i.e. there is no 'unknown future' that a monitor needs to take into account. As a consequence, we can restrict our focus to a *three-valued* truth domain, i.e. $true$, $false$, and $undecided$ (the latter of which only occurs in the middle of a trace, not at its end) [3]; furthermore, in a simulation context, the focus is typically on the purely *state-based behaviour* of the system rather than on epistemic, deontic or doxastic issues, as it is often the case in the multiagent world [13].

As opposed to other types of software system, traces produced by an ABS are not monolithic but hierarchical in nature. In addition to describing the evolution of the overall *agent population*, each trace also describes at the same time the evolution of all possible *groups of agents* as well as the evolution of all *individual agents*. An example of a hierarchical trace is shown in Figure 1. It describes the temporal evolution of four agents in a simple epidemiological context. The agents are grouped into two categories (*male* and *female*) and can be in one of two states (*healthy* or *infected*). Each vertical sequence of boxes below an agent name can be seen as the evolution of the respective agent's state over time. For example, Agent 2 is initially healthy but becomes infected at time 3.

Due to the logical grouping of agents into a male and a female fragment, the simulation trace exhibits a hierarchical structure; it can be seen as comprising four agent traces, two group traces and one population trace. Each group can be understood as a *meta agent* which is characterised by its own state and its own behaviour. For example, the state of the group of male agents at time t is defined as the union of the states of male agents 1 and 2 at time t. The same holds for the entire population whose state at time t is defined as the union of the states of all agents at time t. It is important to note that groups are not just containers that host their children. They can also possess attributes which are functions of their children's states but nevertheless attributes of the group itself. For example, we might be interested in the *number of infected female agents*. This is clearly a group attribute that cannot be expressed as a combination of individual agent attributes. The same hierarchy that exists within a full trace also exists within a single time step. For example, the state of the entire population at time t can be subdivided into the state of all male agents and the state of all female agents, each of which in turn can be itself subdivided into the states of its constituents. The hierarchical structure thus permeates the trace on all levels — temporal and atemporal. The diagram on the right hand side of Figure 1 illustrates the tree structure of a hierarchical trace. The leaf nodes represent individual agents, the composite nodes represent groups of agents. Groups can be seen as meta agents which, besides serving as containers for other groups or individual agents, have their own state and behaviour.

In a verification context, the presence of hierarchical traces has important implications. It requires the ability to formulate hierarchical correctness properties, i.e. properties about *individual agents*, about *groups of agents*, as well as about the whole population. Consequently, when the correctness of a simulation model is to be assessed, this can (and, in fact, has to) be done on multiple levels. Each component of a hierarchical trace, i.e. each node in the tree structure, is a potential candidate for correctness assessment.

Formally, we view an agent's evolution over time as a simple sequence of states. We refer to such a sequence as an *agent trace*:

$$Tr_a == \mathrm{seq}\, AState$$

where $AState == Name \rightarrow Value$ is a mapping from the set of attribute names to the set of attribute values. Each group of agents is assumed to be finite and composed of n individual agents. Consequently, a *group state* is defined as a function from the set of

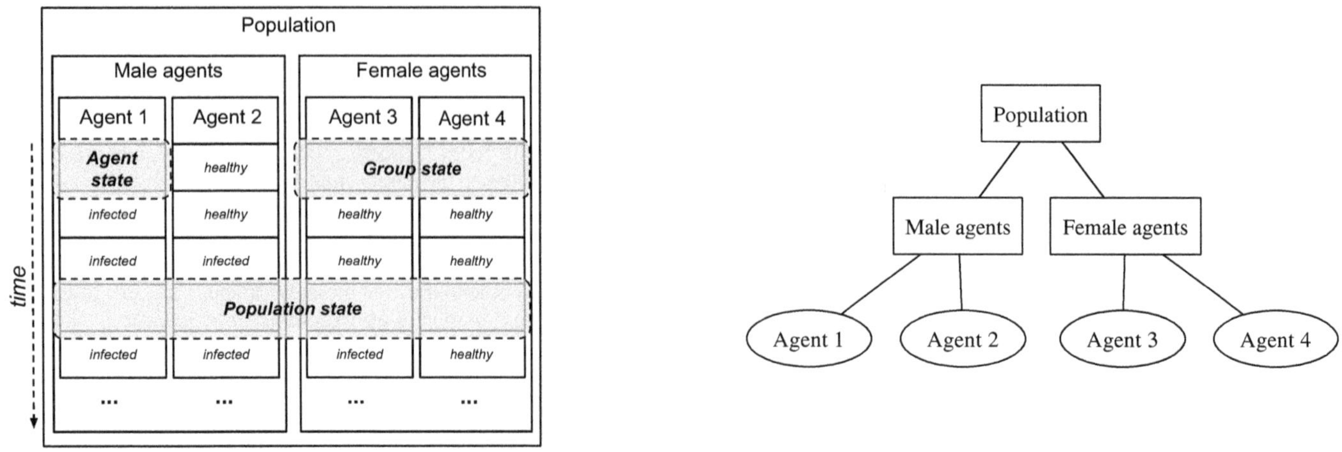

Figure 1: Example of a hierarchical trace (left) and its internal structure represented as a tree (right)

agent identifiers Ag to the set of agent states $AState$:

$$GState == Ag \rightarrow AState$$

Since agents evolve over time, groups also evolve. A *group trace* is thus defined as a sequence of group states:

$$Tr_g == \text{seq}\, GState$$

The next section discusses the verification of temporal multi-level properties on hierarchical traces.

5. MONITORING HIERARCHICAL TRACES

Due to the presence of individual agents as well as groups of agents which may themselves be arbitrarily nested, the analysis of hierarchical traces poses particular challenges. For example, in the presence of individual agents (each with its own distinct life history), obligations are no longer atomic but also hierarchical in nature. Furthermore, obligations referring to groups of agents may be understood in different ways — *collectively* or *individually*.

The crucial point is that those complications are essentially independent of the specification language being used. They are, in fact, common to all languages which allow for the formulation of statements about individuals as well as about groups. A developer of such a specification language is thus guaranteed to eventually face the problem of obligation manipulation which, given its generality, should be solved on a higher level of abstraction.

The purpose of this section is to address this problem and provide a formal treatment of the monitoring problem for hierarchical traces *independent of the concrete shape of the underlying specification language*. We tackle the problem in a layered manner, starting with the monitoring of individual agents in Section 5.1, followed by the monitoring of groups in Section 5.2. Our formalisation is based on the Z notation [18] which, together with its different extensions, has been shown to be useful as a specification language for MAS [6, 7, 15]. In order to keep the specifications as succinct as possible, we follow a functional style and make use of two commonly used functions, *map* and *zip*[2].

An essential ingredient of the subsequent formalisation is a distinction between *agent* and *group properties*. Before going into more detail we introduce the notion of a $Context == Agent \times Group$ which describes context information for the monitor about the current point in time. The context consists of the *agent in scope*, i.e. the currently focussed agent within a group (in the case of agent properties) as well as the *group* (i.e. a finite set of agents) that the monitor is currently operating on (in the case of group properties).

[2] *map* accepts a sequence and a function, applies the function to each element in the sequence and returns the resulting sequence; *zip* takes two sequences and combines them into a single sequence of tuples.

5.1 Monitoring agent properties

Agent properties — as the name suggests — are properties about individual agents. If one assumes atomic propositions to describe Boolean facts about agents, then LTL as described in Section 3 can, for example, be used as an agent property language. Our goal here is to abstract away from any concrete language and reduce it to a set of mere requirements that it needs to satisfy in order to be usable in a runtime verification context.

To that end, we first define what it means for a language to be *joinable*. Informally, for any language $\mathcal{L}$, we want to be able to both *conjoin* and *disjoin* instances of $\mathcal{L}$. This is important because — as illustrated further below — the manipulation of obligations for any language $\mathcal{L}$ may require the construction of logical conjunctions or disjunctions of any two formulae of type $\mathcal{L}$. In order for that to be possible, $\mathcal{L}$ needs to provide implementations of the logical 'and' and 'or' operators. This leads to the following definition.

Definition 1. A language $\mathcal{L}$ is **joinable** if it supports logical conjunction and disjunction, i.e. if implementations of both operators $\wedge$: $\mathcal{L} \times \mathcal{L} \rightarrow \mathcal{L}$ and $\vee$: $\mathcal{L} \times \mathcal{L} \rightarrow \mathcal{L}$ are given.

Essentially, the monitoring of individual agent properties is no different from the monitoring of conventional linear time properties as described in Section 3. In a three-valued setting and at any point in time, a linear time property $\phi : \mathcal{L}$ may be *satisfied*, *violated* or *undecided*. As a consequence, the result of a property check is either a definite truth value (**true**, **false**) or an obligation $\psi : \mathcal{L}$, the latter of which is again a property of language $\mathcal{L}$. In order to describe this formally, we define the following algebraic data type $AResult$ which describes the result of an individual agent property check of language $\mathcal{L}$:

$$AResult ::= ASuccess \mid AFailure \mid AO\langle\langle \mathcal{L} \rangle\rangle$$

The first two constructors, $ASuccess$ and $AFailure$ are obvious: they denote the immediate success or failure of the given agent property. The third constructor denotes an *agent obligation*, i.e. a property of type $\mathcal{L}$ that the respective agent promises to satisfy in the next step in order for the whole property to become true.

During verification, we may also need to conjoin and disjoin monitoring results; to that end, we need to define appropriate operators. We start with conjunction:

$$\_ \wedge \_ : AResult \times AResult \rightarrow AResult$$

$$\begin{array}{l} \forall a, b : AResult \bullet \\ \quad (ASuccess \wedge b = b \wedge \\ \quad a \wedge ASuccess = a \wedge \\ \quad a \wedge AFailure = AFailure \wedge \\ \quad AFailure \wedge b = AFailure) \vee \\ \quad a \wedge b = AO(\mathbf{a} \wedge \mathbf{b}) \end{array}$$

The definition states that a conjunction of $ASuccess$ with b always results in b, a conjunction of $AFailure$ with something else always results in $AFailure$, and all other cases result in a new obligation which represents the conjunction of the respected formulae. Disjunction can be defined accordingly:

$$\_ \vee \_ : AResult \times AResult \rightarrow AResult$$

$$\begin{array}{l} \forall a, b : AResult \bullet \\ \quad (ASuccess \vee b = ASuccess \wedge \\ \quad a \vee ASuccess = ASuccess \wedge \\ \quad a \vee AFailure = a \wedge \\ \quad AFailure \vee b = b) \vee \\ \quad a \vee b = AO(\mathbf{a} \vee \mathbf{b}) \end{array}$$

The definition states that the disjunction of $ASuccess$ with something else always results in $ASuccess$, a disjunction of $AFailure$ with b always results in b, and all other cases result in a new obligation which represents the disjunction of the respected formulae. We see here that the conjunction and disjunction of instances of $AResult$ requires $\mathcal{L}$ to be joinable, i.e. it has to provide appropriate conjunction and disjunction operators (in bold).

Formally, $AResult$ is now now closed under conjunction and disjunction. Theoretically, $AResult$ should also be closed under negation since it may be the case that an element of $AResult$ is to be negated as part of the obligation manipulation process. In the case of $AResult$, negation is trivial and can be defined easily; in the case of group properties described further below, however, negation becomes more intricate. In order to circumvent the problem of obligation negation altogether, we thus assume any specification language to be in *Positive Normal Form (PNF)* where negations are only allowed to appear in front of atomic predicates [2]. If the underlying language is in PNF, then the obligation manipulation does not need to take into account the negation of obligations.

According to the description above, once a property $\phi : \mathcal{L}$ is evaluated on a state of a trace at time t, a result of type $AResult$ is produced. In order to advance the monitoring process, this result now needs to be 'fed into' the evaluation of the next state at time $t + 1$. Again, this evaluation procedure is a general problem which is independent of the underlying specification language and can thus be treated in a general way. Intuitively, monitoring of a given formula $\phi : \mathcal{L}$ should stop once a definite result (success, failure) to ϕ has been found; if an obligation has been produced, it is to be fed into the evaluation of the next time step. We can thus devise the following evaluation function for instances of $AResult$:

$$evalAR : Context \times AResult \rightarrow AResult$$

$$\begin{array}{l} \forall c : Context;\ a : \mathcal{L} \bullet \\ \quad evalAR(c, ASuccess) = ASuccess \wedge \\ \quad evalAR(c, AFailure) = AFailure \wedge \\ \quad evalAR(c, AO(a)) = \mathbf{evalA}(c, a) \end{array}$$

As emphasised in bold in the last line, the definition of function $evalAR$ implies that a language $\mathcal{L}$ needs to provide an implementation of an evaluation function $evalA$ that accepts an instance of $\mathcal{L}$ as well as additional context information and returns either success, failure, or an individual obligation of type $\mathcal{L}$. This leads to the following general definition.

Definition 2. A language $\mathcal{L}$ is **agent-monitorable** if it provides the following components:

1. a representation in PNF;
2. logical conjunction and disjunction; and
3. an evaluation function that returns an instance of $AResult$, i.e. success, failure, or an obligation of type $\mathcal{L}$.

5.2 Monitoring group properties

The obligation manipulation problem is slightly more complex in the case of group properties. Similar to the agent layer, we first need to think about what a verification result looks like when a property is checked for a group of agents. Consider, for example, the following property: *"all agents will eventually satisfy ϕ"*. In this case, each agent within a given group is expected to satisfy *"eventually ϕ"* individually and separately. Obligations are thus also produced separately for each agent. As a consequence, we may end up with a set of n obligations (where n denotes the number of agents), each of which needs to be satisfied separately in order for the overall formula to be satisfied. We call this type of obligation a *group obligation*. Since group properties concern groups of individual agents, several possible results may arise:

1. the current group *as a whole* needs to satisfy an obligation in the next step;
2. several agents within the current group need to satisfy an obligation *as a group* in the next step;
3. several agents within the current group need to satisfy obligations *individually* in the next step;
4. a logical conjunction or disjunction of cases 1-3 needs to be satisfied in the next step; or
5. no future obligation exists (property is immediately satisfied or violated).

In order to formalise the idea of a group result, we define again an algebraic data type $GResult$ which captures these different cases:

$$\begin{array}{rl} GResult ::= & GSuccess \mid GFailure \\ & \mid CGO\langle\langle Group \times \mathcal{L}\rangle\rangle \\ & \mid IGO\langle\langle \mathbb{N} \times \mathrm{seq}(GResult \times Group)\rangle\rangle \\ & \mid GAnd\langle\langle GResult \times GResult\rangle\rangle \\ & \mid GOr\langle\langle GResult \times GResult\rangle\rangle \end{array}$$

The first two constructors are straightforward, they denote *group success* and *group failure*, respectively. The third constructor, CGO, describes a *collective group obligation*, i.e. an obligation which needs to be satisfied *collectively* by a certain group of agents; it accommodates the first two cases in the list above. As described above, an obligation of an individual agent in a language $\mathcal{L}$ is always another $\mathcal{L}$ formula. The first argument of constructor CGO is a group, i.e. a finite set of agents, for which the formula must be satisfied, the second argument is a formula $\phi \in \mathcal{L}$. This type of obligation may, for example, result from the evaluation of an *aggregate group property*, i.e. a property which makes a statement about the *group as a whole*. The fourth constructor, IGO represents an *individual group obligation* and accommodates the third case in the list above. Here, different obligations are to be satisfied by different groups of agents. The obligation accepts a sequence of tuples, each of which contains an obligation as well as an agent; it also contains a *satisfaction constraint* in the form of a natural number which describes the number of agents within the group that need to satisfy the given criterion. The evaluation of this type of obligation can be seen as an iteration over the given group of agents, for each of which the given sub-obligation is evaluated. This type of obligation may, for example, result from the evaluation of a universally quantified group formula. Similar to $AResult$ discussed above, it is necessary for instances $GResult$ to be closed under conjunction and disjunction. However, as opposed to $AResult$ where conjunction and disjunction always resulted in either $ASuccess$, $AFailure$, or AO, it is not always possible to simplify combinations of CGO and IGO such that the result can be described as a single $GSuccess$, $GFailure$, CGO, or IGO. In order to solve this problem, constructors 5 and 6, $GAnd$ and GOr, allow for the recursive description of conjunctions or disjunctions of obligations and thus accommodate the fourth case above.

We can now look at the conjunction and disjunction of instances of $GResult$. Similar to $AResult$, we define operators $\wedge$ and $\vee$ as shown below.

$$
\begin{array}{l}
\_ \wedge \_ : GResult \times GResult \rightarrow GResult \\
\hline
\forall a, b : GResult \bullet \\
\quad (GSuccess \wedge b = b \wedge \\
\quad a \wedge GFailure = GFailure \wedge \\
\quad GFailure \wedge b = GFailure \wedge \\
\quad a \wedge GSuccess = b \wedge \\
\quad (\forall g_1, g_2 : Group;\ a_1, a_2 : Lang \bullet \\
\qquad (CGO(g_1, a_1)) \wedge (CGO(g_2, a_2)) = \\
\qquad\quad \mathbf{if}\ g_1 = g_2\ \mathbf{then}\ CGO(g_1, a_1 \wedge g_2) \\
\qquad\quad \mathbf{else}\ (\mathbf{let}\ o_1 == CGO(g_1, a_1); \\
\qquad\qquad\qquad o_2 == CGO(g_2, a_2) \bullet \\
\qquad\qquad\qquad GAnd(o_1, o_2)))) \vee \\
\quad a \wedge b = GAnd(a, b)
\end{array}
$$

The definition states that a conjunction of $GSuccess$ and any other instance b always results in b, and a conjunction of $GFailure$ and any other instance always results in $GFailure$. Things are slightly more complex for the conjunction of collective group obligations. Here, we have to distinguish between different cases: if both obligations refer to the same group of agents, then we can create a single new obligation containing the conjunction of the respective formulae; otherwise, we cannot perform any further simplifications and thus construct an obligation of type $GAnd$ which represents a conjunction of obligations. This is also done for all other combinations of obligations, as described in the last line[3].

Disjunction can be given accordingly:

$$
\begin{array}{l}
\_ \vee \_ : GResult \times GResult \rightarrow GResult \\
\hline
\forall a, b : GResult \bullet \\
\quad (GSuccess \vee b = GSuccess \wedge \\
\quad a \vee GSuccess = GSuccess \wedge \\
\quad GFailure \vee b = b \wedge \\
\quad a \vee GFailure = a) \vee \\
\quad a \vee b = GOr(a, b)
\end{array}
$$

A disjunction of $GSuccess$ with any other instance always results in $GSuccess$, a disjunction of $GFailure$ with any other instance b always results in b, and a disjunction of all other combinations always results in GOr[3].

[3]Further simplifications are possible but, for clarity and space limitation, we keep the description simple.

We can now describe how instances of $GResult$ are to be manipulated over time. Similar to $AResult$, monitoring should stop once success or failure of a property has been determined. In all other cases, the obligations have to be fed into the evaluation of the next step. This is described by function $evalGR$ which accepts as an input the current context as well as an instance of $GResult$ and produces another instance of $GResult$:

$$
\begin{array}{l}
evalGR : Context \times GResult \rightarrow GResult \\
\hline
\forall c : Context \bullet \\
\quad evalGR(c, GSuccess) = GSuccess \wedge \\
\quad evalGR(c, GFailure) = GFailure \wedge \\
\quad (\forall a : Ag;\ g, g' : Group;\ o : Lang \bullet \\
\qquad evalGR((a, g), CGO(g', o)) = \mathbf{evalG}((a, g'), o)) \wedge \\
\quad (\forall a : Ag;\ g : Group;\ k : \mathbb{N};\ os : \mathrm{seq}(GResult \times Group) \bullet \\
\qquad evalGR((a, g), IGO(k, os)) = \\
\qquad\quad (\mathbf{let}\ fct == (\lambda t : (GResult \times Group) \bullet \\
\qquad\qquad evalGR((a, second\, t), first\, t)) \bullet \\
\qquad\qquad (\mathbf{let}\ chks == map(fct, os) \bullet \\
\qquad\qquad\quad kSat(k, zip(chks, snds(os)))))) \wedge \\
\quad (\forall x1, x2 : GResult \bullet \\
\qquad evalGR(c, GAnd(x1, x2)) = \\
\qquad\quad (\mathbf{let}\ r1 == evalGR(c, x1);\ r2 == evalGR(c, x2) \bullet \\
\qquad\qquad r1 \wedge r2)) \wedge \\
\quad (\forall x1, x2 : GResult \bullet \\
\qquad evalGR(c, GOr(x1, x2)) = \\
\qquad\quad (\mathbf{let}\ r1 == evalGR(c, x1);\ r2 == evalGR(c, x2) \bullet \\
\qquad\qquad r1 \vee r2))
\end{array}
$$

If the result to be checked is either $GSuccess$ or $GFailure$, then there is nothing else to be done. In the case of a collective group obligation (CGO), the two parameters of CGO (the group in scope together with the obligation to be fulfilled) are passed to a language-specific evaluation function $evalG$ (in bold) which itself returns an instance of $GResult$. In the case of an individual group obligation, the situation is slightly more complicated. As opposed to a collective group obligation which wraps a group *formula*, the individual group obligation wraps a *list of result-group tuples* together with a numeric value that describes a *satisfaction constraint*, i.e. the required number of successful checks. To this end, an individual, recursive call to $evalGR$ is performed for each entry in the list (using map). The resulting list of check results is then 'zipped' with the list of groups. This results in another list which is checked for satisfaction w.r.t. the numeric constraint using a function $kSat$ which checks whether at least k elements in the given list are equal to $GSuccess$. The manipulation of obligation conjunctions and disjunctions is straightforward and not described in further detail here. This leads to the following final conclusion.

Definition 3. A language $\mathcal{L}$ is **multiagent-monitorable** if it provides the following components:

1. a representation in positive normal form;
2. logical conjunction and disjunction;
3. a group evaluation function that returns an instance of $GResult$, i.e. *success*, *failure*, a *collective group obligation*, an *individual group obligation*, or a conjunction or disjunction of the previous two types of obligation; and
4. an agent evaluation function that returns an instance of $AResult$, i.e. *success*, *failure*, or an *individual agent obligation*.

This concludes the description and the formalisation of the monitoring framework. The next section illustrates the implementation of the agent layer of the framework in Haskell.

5.3 Implementation

The description of the monitoring framework has been purely formal in nature so far. As mentioned in the introduction, its purpose is to serve as a blueprint for developers to construct their own monitoring procedures. To illustrate this process and show that the formal description is sufficiently close to an executable implementation, we provide here a formulation of the framework in Haskell. The code shown below is part of MC^{2}MABS, a practical statistical runtime verification framework for large-scale agent-based simulation models [10, 1]. For space limitations, we restrict our description to the agent layer here; the group layer can be translated accordingly. A more comprehensive description of MC^{2}MABS including implementation details, complexity considerations, and case studies is given elsewhere [10]; the source code of MC^{2}MABS together with additional documentation is available online [1].

Haskell is a strongly typed, purely functional language, so we first need to think about the necessary types. In analogy to the Z description given above, $AResult$ can be defined as an algebraic data type with a generic parameter a that denotes the underlying language type:

```
AResult a ::= ASuccess | AFailure | AO a
```

Requirements that a type needs to satisfy can be described by means of *type classes* in Haskell; consequently, all types that belong to a given type class need to satisfy the given constraints. The notion of *joinability* can thus be described conveniently as follows.

```
class Joinable a where
  and  :: a → a → a
  or   :: a → a → a
```

The type class requires that any type a has to provide both an 'and' and an 'or' function, which is precisely the definition of joinability given above. Using this information, we can now describe the conjunction of elements of type AResult. As described in Section 5.1, in order for elements of type AResult to be conjoinable, formulae of the underlying language also need to provide an appropriate 'and' function. This can be formulated as a *type constraint* utilising the Joinable type class in the signature of the function:

```
andAR :: Joinable a ⇒ AResult a → AResult a → AResult a
andAR ASuccess b   = b
andAR _ AFailure   = AFailure
andAR AFailure _   = AFailure
andAR b ASuccess   = b
andAR b1 b2        = do r1 ← b1
                        r2 ← b2
                        return $ r1 `and` r2
```

Disjunction can be described accordingly:

```
orAR :: Joinable a ⇒ AResult a → AResult a → AResult a
orAR ASuccess _ = ASuccess
orAR _ ASuccess = ASuccess
orAR AFailure b = b
orAR b AFailure = b
orAR b1 b2      = do r1 ← b1
                     r2 ← b2
                     return $ r1 `or` r2
```

In order for elements of type $AResult$ to be evaluable by function $evalAR$, the underlying specification language also needs to provide an appropriate evaluation function $evalA$. This in combination with joinability (and the PNF which, for simplicity, is omitted here), provides the basis for the notion of *agent monitorability* which is described by the following type class[4]:

[4]Context information is dealth with using the *State Monad* [20].

```
class AgentMonitorable a
  evalA :: a → State Context (AResult a)
```

We now have everything that we need for evaluation of agent formulae which is described by function $evalAR$ (see Section 5.1). Similar to the functions above, it can be translated into a corresponding Haskell function in a straightforward way, utilising the constraint imposed upon the underlying language by type class AgentMonitorable.

```
evalAR :: AgentMonitorable a ⇒
          AResult a → State Context (AResult a)
evalAR ASuccess = return ASuccess
evalAR AFailure = return AFailure
evalAR (AO a)   = do res ← evalA a
                     return res
```

This concludes the implementation of the agent layer. Group-related types and functions can be translated accordingly. It is interesting to note that, despite exhibiting the same functionality and the same level of rigour, the Haskell notation is significantly more succinct than the Z description given above.

The next section illustrates the application of the ideas by describing how a simple example specification language can be made monitorable by satisfying the necessary requirements.

6. EXAMPLE: QUANTIFIED LTL

The nature of property specification languages depends critically on the type of system to be analysed. The concepts of joinability, agent-monitorability, and multiagent-monitorability introduced in the previous section serve as a basic interface that a specification language needs to implement in order to be monitorable in a three-valued runtime verification context.

In order to illustrate this idea, we introduce here *qLTL*, a variant of LTL which supports the formulation of properties about *individual agents* as well as about *groups of agents*. In order to achieve that, we make a syntactic distinction between *agent formulae* and *group formulae*, as described further below. It is important to note that the focus here is on illustration rather than on the development of a full specification language; the description is thus kept deliberately simple and superficial. A comprehensive description of $simLTL$, a conceptually similar, yet more complex and realistic specification language that is used within MC^{2}MABS is given elsewhere [10, 11]. The syntax of qLTL formulae is described by the following abstract data type.

$$\begin{aligned} QLTL ::= {} & Atom\langle\langle Prop\rangle\rangle \mid \\ & And\langle\langle QLTL \times QLTL\rangle\rangle \mid Or\langle\langle QLTL \times QLTL\rangle\rangle \mid \\ & Next\langle\langle QLTL\rangle\rangle \mid Until\langle\langle QLTL \times QLTL\rangle\rangle \mid \\ & ForAll\langle\langle QLTL\rangle\rangle \mid ForAgent\langle\langle QLTL\rangle\rangle \end{aligned}$$

The basic building blocks are atomic propositions $p \in Prop$, Boolean conjunction and disjunction, temporal operators 'next' and 'until', and quantifiers 'forAll' and 'forAgent'. In the case of 'forAll', the enclosed qLTL formula is checked for each agent in the current group; in the case of 'forAgent', the enclosed formula is checked on the agent that is currently in scope[5].

qLTL provides an implicit distinction between *agent* and *group formulae*. Agent formulae are those that are enclosed by a 'forAgent' statement; all other formulae are group formulae. The semantics of agent formulae are formulated over *agent traces* formally introduced in Section 4. Let $tr_a : Tr_a$ be an agent trace.

[5]Note that the syntax allows for the construction of semantically invalid formulae. For example, $ForAgent(ForAll(Prop(p)))$ is syntactically correct but, due to the enclosing of a 'forAll' statement in a 'forAgent' statement, semantically questionable. In a real-world scenario, the syntax would have to be crafted more carefully in order to avoid such problems.

Then, for all $p, p_1, p_2 : qLTL$, tr_a satisfies p (denoted $tr_a \models p$) iff p is true in state $tr_a[0]$, tr_a satisfies $Atom(p)$ (denoted $tr_a \models Atom(p)$) iff p is true in state $tr_a[0]$, tr_a satisfies $And(p_1, p_2)$ iff $tr_a \models p_1$ and $tr_a \models p_2$, tr_a satisfies $Or(p_1, p_2)$ iff $tr_a \models p_1$ or $tr_a \models p_2$, tr_a satisfies $Next(p)$ iff $tr_a[1..] \models p$ and, finally, $tr_a \models Until(p_1, p_2)$ iff $tr_a \models p_2$ or $tr_a \models p_1$ until eventually $tr_a \models p_2$. The semantics of group formulae are defined over *group traces*. The basic operators are similar to the agent case. Let $tr_g : Tr_g$ be a group trace. Then, tr_g satisfies $ForAll(p)$ iff p holds for all agents in the current group. and tr_g satisfies $ForAgent(p)$ iff p holds for the agent currently in scope.

As described in Section 5, any specification language needs to be *joinable*, *agent monitorable*, and *multiagent monitorable* in order to be usable in a runtime verification context for ABSs; furthermore, its formulae need to be in PNF. In the qLTL grammar given above, negation is not supported, so the PNF requirement is already satisfied. Furthermore, qLTL is closed under logical conjunction and disjunction, i.e. the requirement of joinability is also already satisfied. It remains just to discuss the requirements of agent and multiagent monitorability. In order to satisfy both requirements, we need to provide appropriate evaluation functions.

We start with the evaluation of qLTL agent formulae. Informally, in any state, an agent formula is either true, false, or not yet decidable. In the latter case, an obligation (which is again a qLTL agent formulae) is produced. This is described by the algebraic datatype $AResult$ that was introduced in Section 5.1 above. We can thus describe the evaluation of agent formulae by a function $evalA$ shown below; it accepts context information and an agent formula as input and returns an instance of $AResult$. Obligations are only produced in the case of formulae that contain temporal operators ('next' or 'until'); in all other cases, a verdict can be produced immediately.

$evalA : Context \times QLTL \rightarrow AResult$

$$
\begin{aligned}
&\forall c : Context \bullet \\
&\quad (\forall p : Prop \bullet evalA(c, Atom(p)) = holds(c, p)) \wedge \\
&\quad (\forall a, b : QLTL \bullet evalA(c, And(a, b)) = \\
&\qquad evalA(c, a) \wedge evalA(c, b)) \wedge \\
&\quad (\forall a, b : QLTL \bullet evalA(c, Or(a, b)) = \\
&\qquad evalA(c, a) \vee evalA(c, b)) \wedge \\
&\quad (\forall a : QLTL \bullet evalA(c, Next(a)) = AO(a)) \wedge \\
&\quad (\forall a, b : QLTL \bullet evalA(c, Until(a, b)) = \\
&\qquad \textbf{if } evalA(c, b) = ASuccess \textbf{ then } ASuccess \\
&\qquad \textbf{else if } evalA(c, a) = ASuccess \\
&\qquad \textbf{then } AO(Until(a, b)) \textbf{ else } AFailure)
\end{aligned}
$$

The evaluation of group formulae differs from that for agent formulae only w.r.t. the temporal operators and the quantifiers. The evaluation of a 'next' formula results in the creation of a collective group obligation CGO which can be explained as follows: if the group as a whole needs to satisfy formula p in the next step (as denoted by the 'next' operator), then this can only become true if it promises to satisfy p in the next step — hence the collective obligation. In the evaluation of an 'until' formula, if the second subformula b is satisfied, then the overall formula is satisfied. Otherwise, if the first subformula, a, is already satisfied, then the group as a whole promises to satisfy $Until(a, b)$ in the future. In this case, again, a collective group obligation is produced. If neither a nor b is satisfied, then there is no chance for the group to satisfy the overall property. The evaluation of a universally quantified formula is slightly different. Here, the nested agent formula p is evaluated *separately for each agent in the current group*. If we assume heterogeneity in the group then, clearly, there may also be different evaluation results for the agents. As a consequence, an individual group obligation IGO is returned. It represents a list of individual agent obligations that need to be satisfied in the next step. A formal description of function $evalG$ is given below.

$evalG : Context \times qLTL \rightarrow GResult$

$$
\begin{aligned}
&\ldots \\
&(\forall a : Agent;\ g : Group \bullet \\
&\quad (\forall p : QLTL \bullet evalG((a, g), Next(p)) = CGO(g, p)) \wedge \\
&\quad (\forall a, b : QLTL \bullet evalG((a, g), Until(a, b)) = \\
&\qquad \textbf{if } evalG((a, g), b) = GSuccess \textbf{ then } GSuccess \\
&\qquad\quad \textbf{else if } evalG((a, g), a) = GSuccess \\
&\qquad\qquad \textbf{then } CGO(g, Until(a, b)) \textbf{ else } GFailure) \wedge \\
&\quad (\forall p : QLTL \bullet evalG((a, g), ForAll(p)) = \\
&\qquad (\textbf{let } os == \{n : \mathbb{N};\ a' : Agent \mid n \in 1 \mathinner{..} \# g \wedge a' \in g \bullet \\
&\qquad\quad n \mapsto (evalG((a, g), p), g)\} \bullet IGO(\# g, os))) \wedge \\
&\quad (\forall p : QLTL \bullet evalG((a, g), ForAgent(a, p)) = \\
&\qquad (\textbf{let } res == evalA((a, g), p) \bullet \\
&\qquad\quad \textbf{if } res = ASuccess \textbf{ then } GSuccess \\
&\qquad\quad \textbf{else if } res = AFailure \textbf{ then } GFailure \\
&\qquad\quad \textbf{else } CGO(\{a\}, p))))
\end{aligned}
$$

This concludes the description of qLTL. With a PNF representation, joinability, agent monitorability and multiagent monitorability, qLTL now satisfies all requirements in order for it to be used in a three-valued runtime verification context.

7. CONCLUSIONS

Monitoring properties about hierarchical traces is a complex, yet essentially language-independent problem and can (and should) thus be tackled in a general way. This paper addresses the monitoring problem on a high level of abstraction and proposes a language-independent solution. We first introduced formally the notion of hierarchical which allows for the evaluation of properties on two different observational levels — *groups of agents* and *individual agents*. This serves as the semantic basis for a *general, language-independent monitoring framework* for hierarchical traces in a three-valued setting. The existence of observational levels has an important impact on the nature of *obligations* produced during monitoring. We introduced different *types of obligations* — both on the agent and the group level — together with *algorithms for their manipulation* at runtime. Language independence is achieved by the definition of *minimal requirements* or *contracts* which a specification language needs to satisfy in order to be used in a runtime verification setting. To this end, we introduced the concepts of *joinability*, *agent monitorability* and *multiagent monitorability*. Along with the conceptual description of the framework, we also provided a full typechecked formalisation in Z.

The overall purpose of the framework is to serve as an abstract description of a general monitoring procedure which can, for example, be implemented as a generic library in a particular programming language. In order to illustrate this and show the close correspondence between the formal description and the executable implementation, we gave an example implementation of the agent-related functions and data types in Haskell. The implementation is part of MC^2MABS, a practical statistical runtime verification framework for large-scale agent-based simulation models [10, 1].

The integration of an existing specification language into the framework by implementing appropriate evaluation functions as required by the notions of agent monitorability and multiagent monitorability was illustrated using a simple example language, conceptually similar to the one used by MC^2MABS.

REFERENCES

[1] MC^{2}MABS website. https://github.com/bherd/mc2mabs. Last access: 02/15.

[2] C. Baier and J.-P. Katoen. *Principles of Model Checking*. The MIT Press, 2008.

[3] A. Bauer, M. Leucker, and C. Schallhart. Comparing LTL semantics for runtime verification. *Journal of Logic and Computation*, 20(3):651–674, June 2010.

[4] I. Cakirlar, Ö. Gürcan, O. Dikenelli, and S. Bora. RatKit: A repeatable automated testing toolkit for agent-based modeling and simulation. In *Proc. 15th Int. Workshop on Multi-Agent-Based Simulation*, 2014.

[5] M. Dastani and J.-J. C. Meyer. Correctness of multi-agent programs: A hybrid approach. In M. Dastani, K. V. Hindriks, and J.-J. C. Meyer, editors, *Specification and Verification of Multi-agent Systems*, pages 161–194. Springer US, 2010.

[6] M. d'Inverno and M. Luck. *Understanding Agent Systems*. Springer, 2004.

[7] M. d'Inverno, M. Luck, M. Georgeff, D. Kinny, and M. Wooldridge. The dMARS architecture: A specification of the distributed multi-agent reasoning system. *Autonomous Agents and Multi-Agent Systems*, 9:5–53, July 2004.

[8] Y. Falcone, K. Havelund, and G. Reger. A tutorial on runtime verification. *Engineering Dependable Software Systems*, 34:141–175, 2012.

[9] M. A. C. Gatti and A. von Staa. Testing & debugging multi-agent systems: a state of the art report. Technical report, Departamento de Informatica, Pontifical Catholic University of Rio de Janeiro, 2006.

[10] B. Herd. *Statistical runtime verification of agent-based simulations*. PhD thesis, King's College London, 2015.

[11] B. Herd, S. Miles, P. McBurney, and M. Luck. An LTL-based property specification language for agent-based simulation traces. Technical Report 14-02, King's College London, Oct 2014.

[12] M. Leucker and C. Schallhart. A brief account of runtime verification. *The Journal of Logic and Algebraic Programming*, 78(5):293 – 303, 2009.

[13] A. Lomuscio and F. Raimondi. Model checking knowledge, strategies, and games in multi-agent systems. In *Proc. 5th Int. Joint Conf. on Autonomous Agents and Multiagent Systems*, pages 161–168, 2006.

[14] C. M. Macal and M. J. North. Tutorial on agent-based modelling and simulation. *Journal of Simulation*, 4(3):151–162, 2010.

[15] T. Miller and P. McBurney. Multi-agent system specification using TCOZ. In T. Eymann, F. KlÃijgl, W. Lamersdorf, M. Klusch, and M. Huhns, editors, *Multiagent System Technologies*, volume 3550 of *Lecture Notes in Computer Science*, pages 216–221. Springer, 2005.

[16] M. Niazi, A. Hussain, and M. Kolberg. Verification and validation of agent based simulations using the VOMAS approach. In *Proc. of the 3rd Workshop on Multi-Agent Systems and Simulation*, 2009.

[17] A. Sharpanskykh and J. Treur. A temporal trace language for formal modelling and analysis of agent systems. In M. Dastani, K. V. Hindriks, and J.-J. C. Meyer, editors, *Specification and Verification of Multi-agent Systems*, pages 317–352. Springer US, 2010.

[18] J. M. Spivey. *The Z notation: A Reference Manual*. Prentice Hall International (UK) Ltd., Hertfordshire, UK, 1992.

[19] M. Vardi. Automata-theoretic model checking revisited. In B. Cook and A. Podelski, editors, *Verification, Model Checking, and Abstract Interpretation*, volume 4349 of *LNCS*, pages 137–150. Springer, 2007.

[20] P. Wadler. Monads for functional programming. In J. Jeuring and E. Meijer, editors, *Advanced Functional Programming*, volume 925 of *Lecture Notes in Computer Science*, pages 24–52. Springer Berlin Heidelberg, 1995.

[21] C. J. Wright, P. McMinn, and J. Gallardo. Towards the automatic identification of faulty multi-agent based simulation runs using MASTER. In F. Giardini and F. Amblard, editors, *Multi-Agent-Based Simulation XIII*, volume 7838 of *LNCS*, pages 143–156. Springer, 2013.

A Framework for Institutions Governing Institutions

Thomas C. King[1], Tingting Li[2], Marina De Vos[3], Virginia Dignum[1], Catholijn M. Jonker[1], Julian Padget[3], M. Birna van Riemsdijk[1]

[1]*Delft University of Technology* {t.c.king-1, M.V.Dignum, C.M.Jonker, M.B.vanRiemsdijk}@tudelft.nl

[2]*Imperial College London* tingting.li@imperial.ac.uk

[3]*University of Bath* {mdv, jap}@cs.bath.ac.uk

ABSTRACT

Norms guide multi-agent systems away from being potentially anarchic towards a coordinated and collaborative society. Institutions provide an explicit, external representation of norms as well as the means to detect violations and other conditions. Each institution can be crafted individually to capture their designers' goals, but this creates a challenge at higher levels of authority in guiding the institutional design to be coordinated with other institutions and not imposing unacceptable limits on agents' rights. We propose to use institutions to govern and to revise institutions, following a principle widely encountered in the social world, where treaties, primary legislation, framework agreements and subsidiarity establish a regulatory space by defining norms on the form of a body of regulation. We set out a formal and computational framework, building on the InstAL model and implementation, to construct tiers of institutions, where the norms at each tier are governed by those at the tier above. Thus, agents' behaviour is governed and monitored by a tier-1 institution, whose norms are governed and monitored by a tier-2 institution, etc.. This allows us to check the compliance of an institution with the tier above. Compliance failure generates the necessary negative examples for automatic norm-revision.

Categories and Subject Descriptors

[**Knowledge representation and reasoning**]: Logic programming and answer set programming

General Terms

Legal Aspect; Verification

Keywords

Normative Systems; Institutions; Higher-order Norms

1. INTRODUCTION

An MAS (Multi-Agent System) is liable to exhibiting undesirable behaviour contrary to the system's goals, due to agents' intrinsic autonomy [27]. Institutions govern MAS, containing rules to impose norms (obligations and prohibitions) that guide agents' behaviour. However, institutions themselves can promote subjectively undesirable behaviour by imposing undesirable norms. This is due to the inherent autonomy of an institutions' designers who can specify an institution that, for example, imposes norms that violate agents' rights or lacks coordination with other institutions (e.g. national legislation not imposing an international policy).

To address this, we propose using institutions to govern, guide and revise institutions, with *tiers* of institutions, where the first-tier is an institution governed by the second-tier institution and so on. This is by each tier obliging and prohibiting the imposition of norms by the institution in the tier below, that is, imposing *higher-order* norms. Then, each tier *monitors* the tier below for whether its regulations impose norms that are compliant with these higher-order norms. To this end, we propose a vertical governance structure of institutions governing other institutions, which we call a *multi-tier* institution. This consists of a first-tier institution imposing *first-order* norms on an MAS' members, a second-tier institution imposing *second-order* norms on the first-tier and each tier-i imposing ith-order norms on the tier below.

Multi-tier governance is widely found in the social world, also known as vertical and multi-level governance, with benefits widely identified in Political Science literature [18]. The main benefit being, following the subsidiarity principle, what can be done at the local level is left up to the local level. So, an institution prescribing to a lower-tier institution the norms it should impose gives flexibility to the lower-tier designers in how and whether to comply without the redesign of the institution being regimented. For example, the designers can choose to remove a prohibited norm, replace it with a permitted norm that achieves the same goal, or forego redesign if the prohibited norm's benefits outweigh the costs of a non-compliant institution. Examples include service policies governing contracts offered for the provision of services, where service policy compliance is a prerequisite for contractual agreement; and in the political sphere EU Directives [24] governing member states' legislation, and the UK's Financial Conduct Authority governing financial institutions and the obligations they impose on clients [25].

The problem is that AI frameworks for modelling normative systems have focussed on institutions governing MAS (see [1] for a review), while work in Political Science has not operationalised institutions governing institutions. This raises the question, to what extent do institutional modelling techniques in AI model multi-tier institutions and higher-order norms? We address this with a framework for the representation, modelling and automated compliance-checking of multi-tier institutions that extends the InstAL framework [7] and provides input for existing norm revision techniques to make a multi-tier institution compliant.

In the rest of the paper, we first introduce a contracting case-study (2) and then an informal overview of the framework (3). Then, we propose a formal framework (4) that extends the InstAL framework for individual institutions [7] to institutions governing other institutions (4.1), to represent and model multi-tier institu-

Appears in: *Proceedings of the 14th International Conference on Autonomous Agents and Multiagent Systems (AAMAS 2015), Bordini, Elkind, Weiss, Yolum (eds.), May 4–8, 2015, Istanbul, Turkey.*

tions (4.2). The formal framework is implemented with a computational framework in ASP (Answer-Set Programming) for automated compliance checking (5). The computational framework then provides input for ILP (Inductive-Logic Programming) based norm revision to make institutions compliant (6). We compare our framework with others (7) and conclude discussing the framework's implications and wider applications (8).

2. CASE STUDY: SERVICE CONTRACTS

The case study we look at focuses on crowdsensing, the crowdsourcing of people's services and mobile sensors [10], for obtaining a large number of photographic weather damage reports over a wide geographic area on demand over a period of time. We specifically look at the interaction between two agents, the service *requestor* and the potential *service provider*.

Since it is uncertain whether the service provider will provide photographic weather reports, the idea is to make a binding agreement (contract), potentially with rewards and punishments. A contract is a type of legal institution [22] (modelled as such in e.g. [4]) and in this case if accepted governs the interaction between the requestor and service provider, an MAS, and is therefore a *first-tier* institution. However, contracts can contain terms imposing undesirable norms from the service provider's point of view. To address this, the service provider has in turn specified a *service policy*, a *second-tier* institution governing any contracts offered where compliance is a prerequisite for agreement. We begin with a description of a contract for the provision of photographic weather report services.

Contract. The proposed contract is for the service provider to provide photographic weather damage reports on-demand. The service requestor wants to determine the service provider's location and request photographs if they are in an area of interest. Thus, when requested the provider is obliged to provide their location before they leave the area. Additionally, when requested, the service provider is obliged to provide a photographic report before leaving their current location.

The service provider has in turn defined a *service policy* governing the contract by obliging and prohibiting it from imposing norms, where any non-compliant contract is rejected. Outside of the norms the service policy obliges and prohibits, the service requestor has freedom in the contract specification whilst remaining compliant.

Service Policy. The service policy prescribes which norms should be imposed by a contract and in what order. The service provider should only be obliged to provide a photograph after *accepting* a request. Thus, after a photograph is requested, the service policy imposes a second-order norm obliging the request is accepted *before* the the obligation to provide the photograph is imposed. The provider does not want to provide their location if it is sensitive, so when the service provider is in a sensitive location, it is prohibited to oblige them to reveal their location.

Composing the contract and service policy gives us a multi-tier institution with two tiers, that is, a *two-tier* institution. The case study is intentionally simple for illustrative purposes (for example we assume a trusted third-party can verify the service provider is in a sensitive location without revealing it). In principle, the framework can be applied to cases with further institutional tiers. For example, if the service provider is employed by an organisation to engage in contracts with clients and provide the service, then the employer could give them the task of crafting the service policy, whilst guiding them in including certain second-order norms with a third-tier institution imposing third-order norms (e.g. the service policy should demand payment for services).

3. OVERVIEW

This section overviews the framework for representing individual institutions, composing multi-tier institutions from individual institutions and modelling multi-tier institutions. Following Searle's definition [23], an individual institution is a set of regulative and constitutive rules that govern a system. The idea is then that, since individual institutions govern systems, be it an MAS or another institution, they can be placed in different tiers of a multi-tier institution. The different tiers are then linked such that each tier monitors the legality of the tier below (an MAS or another institution). Thus, some institutions govern other institutions and through monitoring we can determine the compliance of the norms one institution imposes, such as on an MAS, with the institution it is governed by.

Each institution specifies the events that can occur and the fluents that can hold (properties whose truth value changes over time) in the institution, and how it evolves over time. An institution's evolution is specified in terms of which institutional events and state changes occur when - in response to specific external events occurring in specific institutional contexts. The occurrence of an institutional event is according to the specification of what Searle calls *constitutive rules* [23, p. 35] stating when one event counts as another in a given institutional context (e.g. killing someone when not at a time of war counts as murder). The evolution of the institutional state is described by which fluents do and do not hold from one state to the next state following the occurrence of events. The specification of an institution's evolution is used to produce an institutional model: a sequence of events and a sequence of states, where events transition between states, in response to the events and state changes occurring in the tiers below.

An institution's norms are rules that impose obligations and prohibitions, thus we model permissive societies which permit anything not prohibited, represented as fluents. The following describes their meaning:

- **Obligation:** Expresses an event/fluent should occur/hold before a deadline event/fluent. If neither the aim nor deadline are normative fluents, it is a first-order norm. Otherwise it is a normative fluent about *other* normative fluents and thus a higher-order normative fluent. It is discharged when the event/fluent it obliges occurs/holds strictly before the deadline, and violated if the deadline occurs/holds before the aim.
- **Prohibition:** The same as obligation but is discharged if the deadline occurs/holds first, and violated if the aim it prohibits occurs/holds before or at the same time as the deadline.

The approach we take to *representing* multi-tier institutions is to compose them from individual institutions structured as follows. Tier-0 is the MAS and represented as a domain of propositions denoting observable events, and fluents. Each tier above is an institution governing the tier below by imposing norms about the events/fluents occurring in the tier below. Tier-1 imposes first-order norms about the MAS events and fluents. Each tier-i above imposes ith-order norms about the normative fluents in the tier below.

The approach we take to *modelling* multi-tier institutions is to extend the InstAL [7] framework from modelling normative fluents about events to normative fluents about events and fluents. This includes other normative fluents and thus allows us to model higher-order norms. Then, we model a multi-tier institution as a whole by linking each tier with a vertical governance structure such that the normative events that occur and fluents that hold in one tier are 'sent up' to the tier above for monitoring, and each tier is modelled

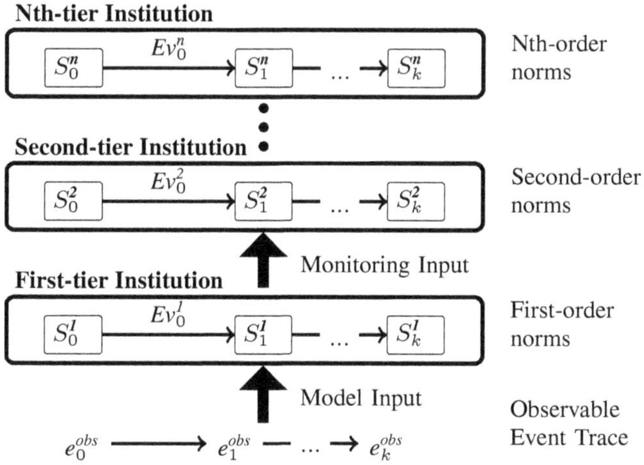

Figure 1: Modelling a multi-tier institution

as an individual institution with input from the tier below.

In more detail, a multi-tier institution model, depicted in Figure 1, is produced in response to a trace of observable events occurring in the MAS. The first-tier is modelled in response to the trace of observable events, such that the MAS' initial event (e_0^{obs}) causes events to occur in the first-tier institution (at Ev_0^1), such as norm dischargement/violation, according to the initial institutional state (S_0^1). This advances the first-tier institution to the next state (S_1^1). This continues for every event and state in the observable event trace until a corresponding sequence of sets of events and a sequence of events is produced, that is, the model of the first-tier is produced. Each tier above the first is also modelled in response to the observable event trace with additional input from the normative events and state changes in the tier below.

Each institutional model also acts as a legal monitor for the tier below, the first-tier monitors the legality of events in the observable event trace and the fluents they cause to hold, non-compliance causing a first-order norm violation event. Higher tiers, meanwhile, monitor the legality of the normative fluents in the tier below, non-compliance causing higher-order norm violation events. For example, if in the second-tier institution's state S_0^2 a second-order normative fluent prohibits a first-order normative fluent being imposed, but the first-tier's state S_0^1 imposes the prohibited norm, then a corresponding second-order norm violation event occurs next (in Ev_0^2). A multi-tier institutional model shows the compliance of each tier with the tier above for an event trace.

4. FORMAL FRAMEWORK

This section presents the formal framework for representing and operationalising individual (4.1) and multi-tier institutions (4.2).

4.1 Individual Institutions

The formal framework for *individual institutions*, consists of two main parts: the specification of individual institutions and their operational semantics. We start with the representation of normative fluents, which oblige/prohibit an event occurring or another fluent holding (the aim) before an event occurs or fluent holds (the deadline). The language of normative fluents is over a set of propositions denoting fluents and events describing the system being governed. If the set of propositions includes only non-normative events and fluents, then only first-order normative fluents can be expressed. If, however, the set of propositions contains first-order normative fluents, then second-order normative fluents can be expressed and so on. Such higher-order normative fluents are categorised as: obliging/prohibiting a normative fluent holds before an event or non-normative fluent holds, obliging/prohibiting an event or non-normative fluent before a normative fluent holds, and obliging/prohibiting a normative fluent to hold before another normative fluent holds.

Definition 1. **Normative Fluents** Let P be a set of propositions denoting fluents and events, a be the norm's aim, d the deadline and $a, d \in P$. The set of normative fluents $\mathcal{N}|_P$ is the set of all norms n expressed as:

$$n \ ::= \ obl(a,d) \ | \ pro(a,d)$$

The contract imposes a normative fluent obliging the service provider to share their location, when requested, before they leave the area. The corresponding normative fluent is below (upper-case terms denote variables acting as shorthand for their instantiations):

$$obl(provide\_photo(Location, Agent\_1, Agent\_2), \\ leave(Location, Agent\_1))$$

The normative fluents the second-tier institution specifies always include, in the aim or the deadline, a first-order normative fluent. Thus, they are second-order normative fluents. The following second-order normative fluent prohibits the aforementioned first-order norm, when the service provider enters a sensitive area, until the service provider leaves the area.

$$pro(obl(provide\_location(Location, Agent\_1, Agent\_2), \\ leave(Location, Agent\_1)), \\ leave(Location, Agent\_1))$$

Second-order normative fluents can also oblige an event or fluent before a normative fluent is imposed. The following second-order normative fluent is imposed when the service provider is requested to provide a photograph, obliging the request is *accepted* before the service provider is obliged to provide a photograph.

$$obl(accept\_photo\_request(Location, Agent\_1, Agent\_2), \\ obl(provide\_photo(Location, Agent\_1, Agent\_2), \\ leave(Location, Agent\_1)))$$

An institutional specification gives the *signature* of events ($\mathcal{E}$) that can occur and fluents ($\mathcal{F}$) that can hold in the institution. The signature is specified from a set of propositions P to which the institution $\mathcal{I}|_P$ is restricted to (just $\mathcal{I}$ is used if P is unimportant). The events $\mathcal{E}$ is the set of observable events ($\mathcal{E}_{obs}$), and the set of institutional events ($\mathcal{E}_{inst}$) which consists of events signifying something unrelated to a norm has happened ($\mathcal{E}_{instact}$), or a norm has been discharged/violated ($\mathcal{E}_{norm}$). The set of an institution's fluents ($\mathcal{F}$), describe the state of a domain ($\mathcal{F}_{dom}$) such as that being governed (e.g. an agent is at a location), and the normative fluents ($\mathcal{F}_{norm}$) that can hold in the institution.

An institutional specification also describes how the institution evolves over time starting with an initial state (Δ). This is in terms of the events and state changes that occur in response to the occurrence of events, where, an institutional state is a set of fluents that are true at that point in time, $\Sigma = 2^{\mathcal{F}}$ denoting the set of all possible institutional states. Describing the events and state changes that occur are an *event generation* function and *state consequence* function. Both functions' arguments are a condition on a state, describing the things that must and must not hold in a state to cause the events/state change, and a set of events. A condition on a state is described with state formulae, $\mathcal{X} = 2^{\mathcal{F} \cup \neg \mathcal{F}}$ denoting the set of all state formulae, where $\neg \mathcal{F} = \{\neg f \mid f \in \mathcal{F}\}$ is the weak negation of all fluents denoting they do not hold. The event generation function ($\mathcal{G} : \mathcal{X} \times \mathcal{E} \rightarrow 2^{\mathcal{E}_{inst}}$) states when, conditional on a state, one event counts-as another. The consequence function ($\mathcal{C} : \mathcal{X} \times \mathcal{E} \rightarrow 2^{\mathcal{F}} \times 2^{\mathcal{F}}$) provides the fluents that are initiated and terminated by events from one state to the next. We use $\mathcal{C}(X, e) = \langle \mathcal{C}^{\uparrow}(X, e), \mathcal{C}^{\downarrow}(X, e) \rangle$ to denote the consequence function's result, where $\mathcal{C}^{\uparrow}(X, e)$ is the set of fluents initiated and $\mathcal{C}^{\downarrow}(X, e)$ is the set of fluents terminated by the event e when the state entails the state condition X.

Definition 2. **Individual Institution** An institution is a tuple $\mathcal{I}|_P = \langle \mathcal{E}, \mathcal{F}, \mathcal{C}, \mathcal{G}, \Delta \rangle$, restricted to the set of propositions P, given $\mathcal{E}_{obs}, \mathcal{E}_{instact}, \mathcal{F}_{dom} \subseteq P$, $\mathcal{I}|_P$ is defined as:

- $\mathcal{F}_{norm} \subseteq \mathcal{N}|_P$ is a set of normative fluents.
- $\mathcal{F} = \mathcal{F}_{dom} \cup \mathcal{F}_{norm}$ is a set of fluents.
- $\mathcal{E}_{norm} = \{disch(n), viol(n) \mid n \in \mathcal{F}_{norm}\}$
- $\mathcal{E}_{inst} = \mathcal{E}_{instact} \cup \mathcal{E}_{norm}$ where $\mathcal{E}_{instact}$ and $\mathcal{E}_{norm}$ are disjoint.
- $\mathcal{E} = \mathcal{E}_{obs} \cup \mathcal{E}_{inst}$.
- $\mathcal{C} : \mathcal{X} \times \mathcal{E} \rightarrow 2^{\mathcal{F}} \times 2^{\mathcal{F}}$ is a state consequence function.
- $\mathcal{G} : \mathcal{X} \times \mathcal{E} \rightarrow 2^{\mathcal{E}_{instact}}$ is an event generation function.
- $\Delta \subseteq \mathcal{F}$ is the initial institutional state.

To ascertain an institution's evolution over time, we extend InstAL's [7] operational semantics from producing models for institutions governing MAS to models of institutions governing other institutions. The main changes are modelling normative fluents about events or other fluents and thereby modelling higher-order norms. We also introduce norm dischargement events and model permissive societies (anything not prohibited is permitted) with prohibitions rather than prohibitive societies containing just obligations and permissions (anything not permitted is prohibited). Given these minor changes we describe rather than reintroduce InstAL's operational semantics, and how we extend them.

The operational semantics for an institution $\mathcal{I}$ are defined with an *event generation operation* and a *state transition operation*. The event generation operation, $GR : \Sigma \times 2^{\mathcal{E}} \rightarrow 2^{\mathcal{E}}$, takes as input a state and a set of events and outputs: the events input, events generated by the institution's event generation function, and norm dischargement/violation events caused by an event occurring or a fluent holding. The event generation function's fixpoint is denoted with GR^{ω}, representing all the events that occur in response to a set of events in a state.

The state transition operation, $TR : \Sigma \times 2^{\mathcal{E} \cup \{e_{null}\}} \rightarrow \Sigma$ is a total function producing the next state, from the current state $S_i \in \Sigma$ and a set of events E. If only the null event e_{null} occurs then the next state S_{i+1} is the same as the previous. Otherwise, S_{i+1} contains all the fluents in S_i not terminated (inertia), all initiated fluents according to the institution's consequent function $\mathcal{C}$, ($f \in \mathcal{C}^{\uparrow}(X, e)$) due to the occurrence of an event $e \in E$ for some X entailed by the state S_i. The next state S_{i+1} does not contain any fluents terminated by the institution's consequence function ($f \in \mathcal{C}^{\downarrow}(X, e)$) or discharged/violated normative fluents ($disch(f) \in E$ or $viol(f) \in E$).

Together, these operations allow an individual institution model to be produced in response to a trace of events. Since we focus on multi-tier institutions, we use these operations to give the multi-tier operational semantics in the next section.

4.2 Multi-tier Institutions

In this section we present the specification of *multi-tier* institutions as a composition of individual institutions in a vertical governance structure, and their operational semantics.

The approach we take to representing a multi-tier institution is to restrict each ith-tier such that it can contain events and fluents from all the tiers below for monitoring, but can only govern the tier directly below by imposing ith-order norms. This restriction is defined by, starting with a set of propositions P which describe the MAS' events and fluents, the first-tier $\mathcal{I}^1|_{P^1}$ imposes normative fluents over the events and fluents of the MAS (i.e. first-order normative fluents) such that $P^1 = P$.

Then, each ith-tier above the first $\mathcal{I}^i|_{P^i}$ can contain the normative fluents and events (dischargement and violation) from the tiers below for monitoring ($P^i = P^{i-1} \cup \mathcal{N}|_{P^{i-1}} \cup \mathcal{E}^{i-1}_{norm}$), but each ith-tier is restricted in only initiating and terminating normative fluents over these (i.e. ith-order norms). This means, an institution can potentially also impose norms about the dischargement and violation of norms in the tier below. We leave this to the discretion of the designer, since in some cases it can make sense, for example obliging a norm is violated before an obligation to pay a fine is imposed. Finally, for monitoring, to ensure the ith-tier contains the events and fluents produced from the tier below, a function $\mathcal{GX}^i$ provides all the normative events recognised from the tier below, and $\mathcal{CX}^i$ provides normative fluents from the tier below.

Definition 3. **Multi-tier Institution** Let P be a set of propositions denoting the domain, a multi-tier institution is a tuple $\mathcal{M} = \langle \mathcal{T}, \mathcal{GX}^i, \mathcal{CX}^i \rangle$ where:

- $\mathcal{T} = \langle \mathcal{I}^1|_{P^1}, ..., \mathcal{I}^n|_{P^n} \rangle$ is an n-tuple of institutions s.t. $\forall i \in [n] : \mathcal{I}^i|_{P^i} = \langle \mathcal{E}^i, \mathcal{F}^i, \mathcal{C}^i, \mathcal{G}^i, \Delta^i \rangle, \mathcal{X}^i = 2^{\mathcal{F}^i \cup \neg \mathcal{F}^i}$, $\Sigma^i = 2^{\mathcal{F}^i}$
- $P^1 = P$ and $\forall i \in [2, n]$, $P^i = P^{i-1} \cup \mathcal{N}|_{P^{i-1}} \cup \mathcal{E}^{i-1}_{norm}$ - each ith-tier can contain the events and fluents that can be defined in the tier below and normative fluents over these.
- $\forall i \in [2, n], \forall S \in \mathcal{X}^i, \forall e \in \mathcal{E}^i : \mathcal{C}^{i\uparrow}(S, e) \cap \mathcal{N}|_{P^{i-1}} = \emptyset, \mathcal{C}^{i\downarrow}(S, e) \cap \mathcal{N}|_{P^{i-1}} = \emptyset$ - the ith-tier can only initiate and terminate ith-order norms.
- $\forall i \in [n-1] : \mathcal{GX}^i : 2^{\mathcal{E}^i} \rightarrow 2^{\mathcal{E}^{i+1}}$ is an event filtering function defined as $\forall i \in [n-1], \forall E \in 2^{\mathcal{E}^i} : \mathcal{GX}^i(E) = E \cap \mathcal{E}^i_{norm} \cap \mathcal{E}^{i+1}$
- $\forall i \in [n-1] : \mathcal{CX}^i : \Sigma^i \rightarrow \Sigma^{i+1}$ is a fluent filtering function defined as $\forall i \in [n-1], \forall F \in \Sigma^i : \mathcal{CX}^i(F) = F \cap \mathcal{F}^i_{norm} \cap \mathcal{F}^{i+1}$

To exemplify, the running example is formalised in Table 1. For brevity we leave out the observable events $\mathcal{E}^i_{obs}$ which correspond to institutional events in $\mathcal{E}^i_{inst}$ prepended with *ext_*. Similarly, the generation function does not include institutional events generated from observable events. Finally, the set of fluents is left out, which are inferred from the generation and consequence functions.

A multi-tier institution model is produced, consisting of a model of each individual institution, in response to a *composite trace* [16] of events, where each event is observable to at least one tier.

Definition 4. **Composite Event Trace** Let $\mathcal{M} = \langle \mathcal{T}, \mathcal{GX}, \mathcal{CX} \rangle$ be a multi-tier institution s.t. $\mathcal{T} = \langle \mathcal{I}^1, ..., \mathcal{I}^n \rangle$. $ctr = \langle e_0, ..., e_k \rangle$ is a composite trace for $\mathcal{M}$ iff $\forall j \in [0, k], \exists i \in [n] : e_j \in \mathcal{E}^i_{obs}$

Service Contract

$\mathcal{E}_{inst} = \{enter(Location\_1, Agent\_1)), leave(Location\_1, Agent\_1),$
$\quad provide\_location(Location\_1, Agent\_1, Agent\_2),$
$\quad provide\_photo(Location\_1, Agent\_1, Agent\_2)),$
$\quad request\_location(Agent\_1, Agent\_2)$
$\quad request\_photo(Location\_1, Agent\_1, Agent\_2)$
$\quad accept\_photo\_request(Location\_1, Agent\_1, Agent\_2)\}\}$
$\mathcal{G}(\mathcal{X}, \mathcal{E}):$
$\langle\{at(Location\_1, Agent\_1)\}, enter(Location\_2, Agent\_1)\rangle \rightarrow$
$\quad \{leave(Location\_1, Agent\_1)\}$
$\mathcal{C}^{\uparrow}(\mathcal{X}, \mathcal{E}):$
$\langle\emptyset, enter(Location\_1, Agent\_1)\rangle \rightarrow \{at(Location\_1, Agent\_1)\}$
$\langle\emptyset, request\_photo(Location\_1, Agent\_1, Agent\_2)\rangle$
$\rightarrow \{obl(provide\_photo(Location\_1, Agent\_1, Agent\_2),$
$\quad leave(Location\_1, Agent\_1))\}$
$\langle\{at(Location\_1, Agent\_2)\}, request\_location(Agent\_1, Agent\_2)\rangle$
$\rightarrow \{obl(provide\_location(Location\_1, Agent\_2, Agent\_1),$
$\quad leave(Location\_1, Agent\_2))\}$
$\mathcal{C}^{\downarrow}(\mathcal{X}, \mathcal{E}):$
$\langle\emptyset, leave(Location\_1, Agent\_1)\rangle \rightarrow \{at(Location\_1, Agent\_1)\}$

Service Policy

$\mathcal{E}_{inst} = \{enter(Location\_1, Agent\_1), leave(Location\_1, Agent\_1),$
$\quad request\_photo(Location\_1, Agent\_1, Agent\_2),$
$\quad request\_location(Agent\_1, Agent\_2),$
$\quad accept\_photo\_request(Location\_1, Agent\_1, Agent\_2)\}$
$\mathcal{G}(\mathcal{X}, \mathcal{E}):$
$\langle\{at(Location\_1, Agent\_1)\}, enter(Location\_2, Agent\_1)\rangle \rightarrow$
$\quad \{leave(Location\_1, Agent\_1)\}$
$\mathcal{C}^{\uparrow}(\mathcal{X}, \mathcal{E}):$
$\langle\emptyset, enter(Location\_1, Agent\_1)\rangle \rightarrow \{at(Location\_1, Agent\_1)\}$
$\langle\{sensitive(Location\_1)\}, enter(Location\_1, Agent\_1)\rangle \rightarrow$
$\quad \{pro(obl(provide\_location(Location\_1, Agent\_1, Agent\_2),$
$\quad\quad leave(Location\_1, Agent\_1)),$
$\quad\quad leave(Location\_1, Agent\_1))\}$
$\langle\{\emptyset, request\_photo(Location\_1, Agent\_1, Agent\_2)\rangle \rightarrow$
$\quad \{obl(accept\_photo\_request(Location\_1, Agent\_1, Agent\_2),$
$\quad\quad obl(provide\_photo(Location\_1, Agent\_1, Agent\_2),$
$\quad\quad leave(Location\_1, Agent\_1)))\}$
$\mathcal{C}^{\downarrow}(\mathcal{X}, \mathcal{E}):$
$\langle\emptyset, leave(Location\_1, Agent\_1)\rangle \rightarrow \{at(Location\_1, Agent\_1)\}$

Table 1: Formalisation of the service policy governing a service contract

Only events an institution recognises advance its state, potentially causing unsynchronised institutions. We address this with a *synchronised trace* for each institution [16] replacing unrecognised events in the composite trace with a null event e_{null} to advance the institution's state.

Definition 5. **Synchronised Trace** Let $\mathcal{I}$ be an institution, and $ctr = \langle e_0, ..., e_k\rangle$ be a composite trace. A trace $str = \langle se_0, ..., se_k\rangle$ is a *synchronised trace* of ctr for $\mathcal{I}$ iff $\forall i \in [0, k]$: if $e_k \in \mathcal{E}_{obs}$, $se_k = e_k$ and $se_k = e_{null}$ otherwise.

A multi-tier institutional model in response to a composite event trace consists of a model for each tier-i institution ($M^i = \langle S^i, E^i\rangle$) - a sequence of states (S^i) and a sequence of sets of events (E^i) in response to the synchronised event trace str^i. The model for each tier-i institution represents its evolution over time, where each set of events E^i_j causes a transition from one state S^i_j to the next S^i_{j+1}.
Each institutional model starts with an initial state. For the first-tier this is the same initial state in its specification (Δ^1), for all the other tier-i institutions it is the initial state in its specification Δ^i combined with the initial state of the tier below filtered to only contain normative fluents by $\mathcal{CX}^{i-1}$. Each set of events E^i_j in each tier-i institution's model is produced by the institution's event generation operation fixpoint ($GR^{i\omega}$). The arguments for the first tier's event generation operation are the current institutional state (S^1_j) and an event in the synchronised event trace (se^1_j), for all other tier-i institutions the events used also include those produced by the tier below (E^{i-1}_j) filtered to only normative events by $\mathcal{GX}^{i-1}$. Each succeeding state S^i_{j+1} for each tier-i institution is produced with tier-i's state transition operation TR^i. For the first-tier, the arguments for the state transition operation are its current state S^1_{j+1} and the set of events produced E^1_j, for all other tier-i institutions the successor state S^i_{j+1} also includes the fluents of the state in the tier below S^{i-1}_{j+1} filtered to only normative fluents by $\mathcal{CX}^{i-1}$, minus any normative fluents that no longer hold in the tier below.

Definition 6. **Multi-tier Institution Model** Let $\mathcal{M} = \langle \mathcal{T}, \mathcal{GX}^i, \mathcal{CX}^i\rangle$ be a multi-tier institution s.t. $\mathcal{T} = \langle \mathcal{I}^1, ..., \mathcal{I}^n\rangle$. Let ctr be a composite trace for $\mathcal{M}$ and $\forall i \in [n]$: $str^i = \langle se^i_0, ..., se^i_k\rangle$ be a synchronised trace of ctr for $\mathcal{I}^i$. A model of $\mathcal{M}$ in response to ctr is $M^{\mathcal{M}} = \langle M^1, ..., M^n\rangle$, of the form $\forall i \in [n] : M^i = \langle S^i, E^i\rangle, S^i = \langle S^i_0, ..., S^i_{k+1}\rangle, E^i = \langle E^i_0, ..., E^i_k\rangle$ where:

- $\forall i \in [n] : GR^i : \Sigma^i \times 2^{\mathcal{E}^i} \rightarrow 2^{\mathcal{E}^i}$ - is the event generation operation for $\mathcal{I}^i$.
- $\forall i \in [n] : TR^i : \Sigma^i \times 2^{\mathcal{E}^i \cup \{e_{null}\}} \rightarrow \Sigma^i$ - is the state transition operation for $\mathcal{I}^i$.
- $S^1_0 = \Delta^1$ - the first state of the tier-1.
- $\forall j \in [0, k] : E^1_j = GR^{1\omega}(S^1_j, se^1_j)$ - events produced by the tier-1 institution.
- $\forall j \in [0, k] : S^1_{j+1} = TR^1(S^1_j, E^1_j)$ - states produced by the tier-1 institution
- $\forall i \in [2, n] : S^i_0 = \Delta^i \cup \mathcal{CX}^{i-1}(S^{i-1}_0)$ - the first state of each tier-i institution above tier-1.
- $\forall i \in [2, n], \forall j \in [0, k] : E^i_j = GR^{i\omega}(S^i_j, \{se^i_j\} \cup \mathcal{GX}^{i-1}(E^i_j))$ - events produced by each tier-i institution above the first.
- $\forall i \in [2, n], \forall j \in [0, k] : S^i_{j+1} = (TR^i(S^i_j, E^i_j) \cup \mathcal{CX}^{i-1}(S^{i-1}_{j+1})) \backslash (S^{i-1}_j \backslash S^{i-1}_{j+1})$ - states produced by each tier-i institution above the first.

An objective of modelling a multi-tier institution is assessing each tier's compliance with the tier above. This supports revising legislation to be compliant, which conducted pre-runtime for a contract makes it acceptable to the party governing the contract. A partial-compliance check can be performed for a single composite trace deemed interesting, or a full-compliance check can be performed for all possible composite traces. A multi-tier institution is non-compliant for a composite trace if a higher-order norm is violated, otherwise it is compliant for that trace. A compliance check provides the set of violations between institutions.

Definition 7. **Multi-tier Institution Violation** Let $\mathcal{M} = \langle \mathcal{T}, \mathcal{GX}, \mathcal{CX}\rangle$ be a multi-tier institution, $\mathcal{T} = \langle \mathcal{I}^1, ..., \mathcal{I}^n\rangle$ and $\forall i \in [n] : \mathcal{I}^i = \langle \mathcal{E}^i, \mathcal{F}^i, \mathcal{C}^i, \mathcal{G}^i, \Delta^i\rangle$. Let ctr be a composite trace for $\mathcal{M}$ and $M^{\mathcal{M}} = \langle M^1, ..., M^n\rangle$ be a model for $\mathcal{M}$ w.r.t. ctr. The tuple of multi-tier violation sets $V(\mathcal{M}, ctr) = \langle V^1, ..., V^{n-1}\rangle$ is defined as:

- $\forall i \in [n-1] : V^i = (\mathcal{E}^{i+1}_{viol} \backslash \bigcup^i_{j=1} \mathcal{E}^j_{viol}) \cap \bigcup^n_{i=0} E_i$

ctr is identified as an ith-tier institution *non-compliance trace* for $i \in [n-1]$ if there is at least one violation between the ith-tier institution and the institution above, s.t. $V^{i+1} \neq \emptyset$.

5. COMPUTATIONAL FRAMEWORK

In this section we provide the computational framework for multi-tier institutions representation and operational semantics as a set of ASP rules (5.1), or in some places examples of rules due to space constraints. Then, we give the results of using the computational framework for a compliance check on the running example (5.2).

ASP [2, 12], is a non-monotonic logic programming language, that given a problem description as an ASP program, grounds the program and then goes about finding solutions (answer-sets) computed according to the stable-model semantics [12]. There are many answer set solvers available (e.g. [9, 11]), we adhere to CLINGO's syntax [11] described as follows. A CLINGO ASP program is built from atoms and predicates, where predicates containing variables are ground instance schemas. Atoms and predicates can be preceded with any sequence of weak negation (`not`) and classical negation ($-$). A horn clause `p_0 :- p_1, ..., p_n.` states that `p_0` is true when `p_1, ..., p_n` is true. Constraints, expressed with `:- p_1, ..., p_n.`, are shorthand for falsity in the head, meaning the body cannot be true in any answer set. Finally a choice construct of the form $l\{$`p_1, ..., p_n`$\}u$, where l and u are positive integers, states that at least l and at most u number of literals $p\_1, ..., p\_n$ need to be true in order for the choice construct to be true (when omitted l is 0 and u is infinity).

5.1 Representation and Operational Semantics in ASP

In this section, we first describe the operational semantics of individual institutions as ASP rules for producing institutional events, reflecting the formal framework's event generation operation, and states, reflecting the formal framework's state transition operation. Then, we provide a translation of multi-tier institutions from their formal to ASP rule representation, by translating each individual institution and linking them in a vertical governance structure with a set of ASP rules. Finally, we provide a set of rules for producing composite, synchronised, traces. The rules comprise an ASP program that produces an Answer-Set for a composite trace, reflecting a multi-tier institution model in the formal framework.

Beginning with event generation, institutional events are generated from ASP rules that produce, from an observable event, institutional events, and from the legality of the events that occur and fluents that hold norm dischargement and violation events. The following rule produces an institution event from an observable event if it occurs externally and is recognised by the institution.

```
occurred(E,In,I) :- evtype(E,In,ex), observed(E,In,I),
   instant(I), inst(In).
```

Rules producing norm dischargement/violation events check to see if a norm holds, and whether an event occurs or fluent holds that discharges/violates the norm, producing the norm dischargement/violation event if it does and terminating the norm at the same time. For brevity, we give an example rule for obligation discharge-ment and termination below, in total there are four rules for obligation and prohibition dischargement and violation.

```
2{occurred(disch(obl(A, D)),In,I),
  terminated(obl(A, D), In, I)} :-
   holdsat(obl(A, D),In,I), 1{holdsat(A,In,I),
   occurred(A, In, I)}, inst(In), not holdsat(D,In,I),
   not occurred(D, In, I), instant(I).
```

The rules to produce institutional states define the predicate `holdsat(P, In, I)`. As in [16], it states that the fluent `P` holds in an institution with the name `In` represented with a fact `inst(In)`, at time `I`. It is true if `P` was initiated in the previous state, or it held in the previous state and was not terminated (inertia).

```
holdsat(P,In,J) :- holdsat(P,In,I),
   not terminated(P,In,I),next(I,J),
   ifluent(P, In),instant(I), instant(J), inst(In).
holdsat(P,In,J) :- initiated(P,In,I), next(I,J),
   ifluent(P, In),instant(I), instant(J), inst(In).
```

$\mathcal{M} = \langle \mathcal{T}, \mathcal{GX}^i, \mathcal{CX}^i \rangle, \mathcal{T} = \langle \mathcal{I}^1, ..., \mathcal{I}^n \rangle, \forall i \in [n]$
$(\mathcal{I}^i = \langle \mathcal{E}^i, \mathcal{F}^i, \mathcal{C}^i, \mathcal{G}^i, \Delta^i \rangle)$:

$\mathcal{I}^i$	$\Leftrightarrow$	`tier`(*In*,*i*). `inst`(*In*).
$e \in \mathcal{E}^i_{obs}$	$\Leftrightarrow$	`evtype(e,`*In*`, ex)`.
$f \in \mathcal{F}^i$	$\Leftrightarrow$	`ifluent(f,`*In*`)`.
$\mathcal{C}^{i\uparrow}(X,e) = P$	$\Leftrightarrow$	$\forall p \in P$: `initiated`(p,*In*, `I`) : $-$ `occurred`(e,*In*, `I`), *EX(X, In, I)*.
$\mathcal{C}^{i\downarrow}(X,e) = P$	$\Leftrightarrow$	$\forall p \in P$: `terminated`(p,*In*, `I`) : $-$ `occurred`(e,In,I), *EX(X, In, I)*.
$\mathcal{G}^i(X,e) = E$	$\Leftrightarrow$	$\forall e' \in E$: `occurred`(e',*In*, `I`) : $-$ `occurred`(e,*In*, `I`), *EX(X, In, I)*.
$f \in \Delta^i$	$\Leftrightarrow$	`holdsat`(f,*In*, `I`) : $-$`start(I)`.

Figure 3: Multi-tier institution translation into ASP.

A multi-tier institution's translation from its formal representation into ASP rules is given in Figure 3. The ASP rules state when a fluent is initiated (`initiated/3`) and terminated (`terminated/3`), when one event causes an institutional event to occur (`occurred/3`), and the set of fluents (`ifluent/2`) and events (`evtype/3`) recognised by the institution. Keeping with InstAL's convention, for some $X \in \mathcal{X}^i$, *EX(X, In*, `I`) is shorthand for a comma delimited set of ASP literals of the form `holdsat(`*f*, `In, I)` for all positive fluents in X and `not holdsat(`*f*, `In, I)` for all negated fluents in X denoting negation as failure.

Further rules in ASP link tiers by passing up norm dischargement and violation events, this reflects the formal definition of a multi-tier institution where, according to $\mathcal{GX}^i$, normative events are 'sent upwards'. An example of the rule ensuring norm dischargement occurring in one tier occurs in all tiers above is given below, for brevity we leave out the rule for norm violation.

```
occurred(disch(N), In_2, I) :-
    occurred(disch(N), In_1, I),
    tier(In_1, I_1), tier(In_2, I_2), I_2 == I_1 + 1.
```

ASP rules also reflect the formal framework's passing up of normative fluents according to $\mathcal{CX}^i$ and the definition of a multi-tier model. The rules ensure that if a normative fluent is initiated by the tier below it is also initiated by the tier above, and likewise for termination. The rule for obligation initiation is given below, further rules we do not include 'pass up' obligation termination, and prohibition initiation and termination.

```
initiated(obl(A, D), In_2, I) :-
   initiated(obl(A, D), In_1, I),
   ifluent(obl(A,D), In_2),
   tier(In_2, I_1), tier(In_2, I_2), I_2 == I_1 + 1.
```

A multi-tier institution is modelled by providing a composite event trace and then producing the answer-set reflecting the formal multi-tier institution model. To define and generate a compos-

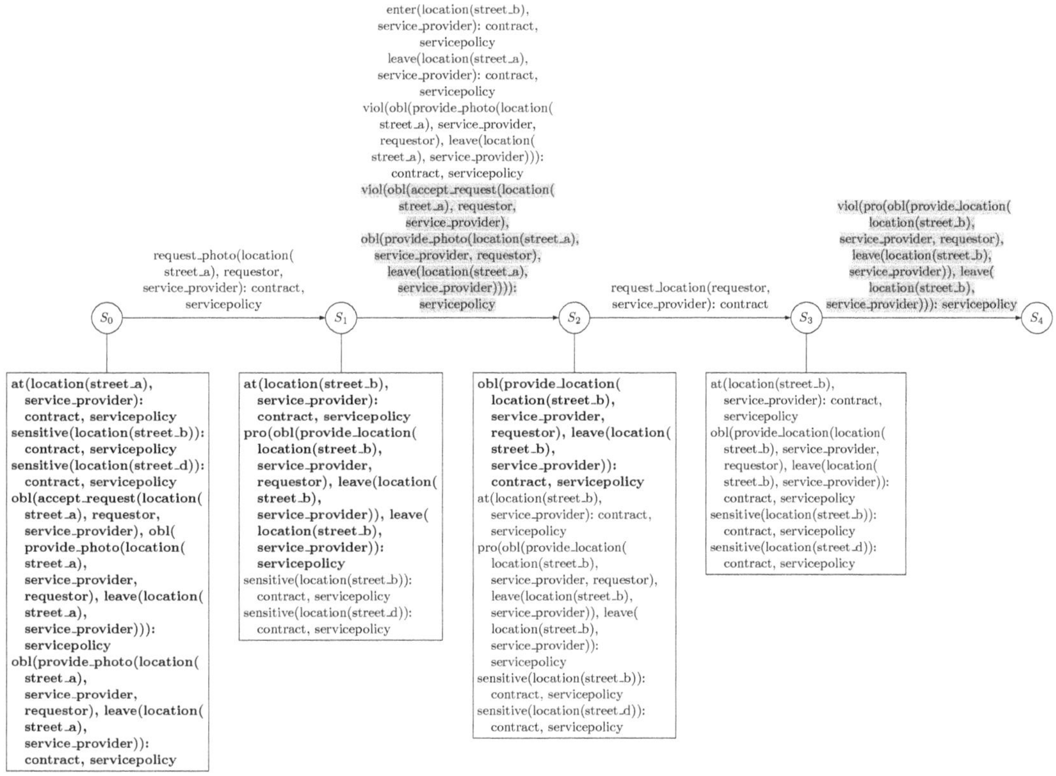

Figure 2: Results for a trace, highlighting violated second-order norms in the second-tier institution.

ite trace we provide a set of rules taken from modelling composite institutions in ASP [17]. These rules produce a composite trace where at each time point only one observable event occurs and it is recognised by at least one institution, and a synchronised trace for each institution such that each event not recognised is replaced with a null event. We assume a timeline is supplied to ground the variables for **instant/1**, **start/1**, **final/1** and **next/2**.

```
{compObserved(E, J)} :- evtype(E,In,ex),
  instant(J), not final(J), inst(In).
:- compObserved(E,J),compObserved(F,J),
  instant(J),evtype(E,InX,ex),
  evtype(F,InY,ex), E!=F,inst(InX;InY).
obs(I):- compObserved(E,I),evtype(E,In,ex),
  instant(I),inst(In).
:- not obs(I), not final(I), instant(I), inst(In).
observed(E,In,I) :- compObserved(E,I),
  inst(In), instant(I).
occurred(null,In,I) :- not evtype(E,In,ex),
  observed(E,In,I), instant(I), inst(In).
```

These rules produce answer-sets for all composite traces up to length T. If we are only interested in specific traces, we can supply a trace with **compObserved(E, I)** predicates. Alternatively, a constraint can limit traces to just those that produce at least one higher-order norm violation, such as given below, assuming **norm_order/2** defines each norm's order:

```
n_tier_violation :- occurred(viol(N), In, T),
  instant(T), tier(In, I), norm_order(N, I), I > 1.
:- not n_tier_violation.
```

5.2 Results: Monitoring the Contract and Service Policy

The results of translating the formalised example into a corresponding ASP program are given graphically in Figure 2, for a specific trace encoded in ASP below with **compObserved**.

```
compObserved(ex_request_photo(location(street_a),
            requestor, service_provider), 0).
compObserved(ex_enter(location(street_b),
            service_provider), 1).
compObserved(ex_request_location(requestor,
            service_provider), 2).
```

The results show the first-tier is non-compliant with the second with two highlighted second-order norm violations. The first service policy violation occurs in the trace because when the service provider is requested to provide a photograph, a first-order obligation to provide a photograph before leaving the area is initiated in S_0. Yet, simultaneously, a second-order norm is initiated obliging the request is accepted before such an obligation is imposed.

The second service policy violation occurs in the trace because when the agent enters a new location *street_b*, a second-order norm prohibiting an obligation for the service provider to provide their location is initiated in state S_1 , since *sensitive*(*street_b*) also holds. Yet, the service requestor then requests the service provider's location, initiating in state S_2 an obligation on the service provider to provide their location. This causes the second-order norm prohibiting such an obligation to be violated in state S_3.

If the contract is accepted as it is, then the service provider would be obliged to provide photographs regardless of if they had accepted the request, and they would be obliged to reveal their location when requested even if in a sensitive location. To resolve this the compliance check's results are used as input for a revision for compliance process, we give the output of in the next section.

6. ILP REVISION FOR COMPLIANCE

When any non-compliance is detected via the monitoring process outlined in Section 5.1, we then need a way to *revise* the non-compliant ith-tier institution to be consistent with the institution it is governed by. We use an *Inductive Logic Programming* (ILP) based approach for norm revision, which provides a suitable solution for our computational framework due to its implementation in ASP [8, 16]. This involves using the results of compliance failure produced by the computational framework as input for an ILP norm revision process, which due to space considerations we provide the results of rather than detail in full.

In the preceding section the running example was formalised in ASP (5.2). This gave us a non-compliance trace leading to two second-order norm violations in the second-tier, due to the contract obliging the service provider to provide a photo before they have accepted a request, and obliging the service provider to reveal their location even if they are in a sensitive location. The idea is that, ILP norm revision is provided a cost of a revision, such as the number of literals added and removed, and examples of undesirable properties for a trace, in our case the automatically detected second-tier violations. Then, ILP searches for all possible minimal revisions of the institution that resolve the undesirable properties (non-compliance) for a trace. In our case, two suitable suggestions are provided (of several) for the results from the previous section.

One suggestion is to revise the rule initiating the obligation to provide a photo by removing the body literal for the request photograph event occurrence. Then, replacing it with the body literal denoting the occurrence of the provider *accepting* the request:

```
initiated(obl(provide_photo(location(L),X,Y),
              leave(location(L),X)),contract,I):-
  occurred(request_photo(location(L),Y,X),contract,I),
  occurred(accept_request(location(L),Y,X),contract,I)),
  instant(I), agent(X;Y).
```

The second suggestion is initiating the obligation to provide locations only when the service provider's location is not sensitive.

```
initiated(obl(provide_location(location(L),X,Y),
              leave(location(L), X)), contract, I) :-
  occurred(request_location(Y,X),contract,I),
  not holdsat(sensitive(location(L)), contract, I),
  holdsat(at(location(L), X), contract, I),
  instant(I), agent(X;Y).
```

By using our computational framework we are able to automatically provide the required examples of undesirable properties, non-compliance of the first-tier with the second in this case. In turn, by using ILP-based norm revision, we are able to automatically revise the two-tier institution to be compliant, making the service contract acceptable to the service provider.

7. RELATED WORK

To the best of our knowledge, there are no frameworks for reasoning about institutions governing institutions or multi-tier institutions. Thus, the most closely related work is on authority hierarchies, legislating the legislators and interacting institutions, with less closely related work focussing on governing MAS.

Boella and van der Torre [3] formalise normative systems with authority hierarchies and the relationship between permissions and obligations. They use what they call 'meta-norms', which are not norms in the deontic sense but instead describe the hierarchical relationship between norms issued by different authorities. Then, permissions from a higher authority *derogate* obligations to the contrary issued by a lower authority. In comparison, we address the autonomy of institutional designers, using higher-tier institutions to govern lower-tiers in the norms they impose with *violatable*, rather than derogative, higher-order norms and a vertical governance structure for higher-tier institutions monitoring lower-tiers.

Lopez and Luck [19] provide a representation for different norm categories including *legislative norms* which describe what norm rule creation/abolishment actions are permitted. In contrast, our approach is not to govern rule change but rather the normative effects of rules. This is by imposing higher-order norms in some contexts which can be discharged and violated when lower-order norm rules are *invoked*. Whilst our approach focuses on the effects rather than existence of rules, it can then be used to determine if adding or removing an institutional rule causes the institution to be non-compliant in some circumstances and therefore whether a specific institutional change action is non-compliant.

Li [15] looks at the problem of agents governed by multiple interacting institutions which being designed by separate people are liable to collectively impose conflicting norms. Like us, Li also uses the InstAL framework, in her case to detect conflicts between institutions. The main difference is that Li looks at the interaction between institutions (for example, the event in one triggering a change in the other) but not the governance of institutions by institutions, and not the imposition of higher-order norms.

Further afield, our framework bears *some* similarities to modelling social commitments [6,28] and King et al. 'meta-norms' [14] in the Event Calculus, since we use EC-like constructs; agent compliance monitoring [5,20], rather than *institution* compliance; and detecting and resolving normative conflicts [13,21,26], rather than higher-order norm *violation* and revision for compliance.

8. CONCLUSIONS

This paper addressed the problem of guiding institutions towards imposing desirable norms, with a novel framework for the representation and operationalization of multi-tier institutions. Taking the InstAL framework for institutions governing MAS, we generalised it to also model institutions governing other institutions. Then, the representation and modelling of multi-tier institutions was provided, where institutions govern other institutions with higher-order norms and monitor them for whether the norms they impose are compliant. We then showed how this provides results for automatic norm-revision of an institution to be compliant, giving suggestions to institutional designers to resolve the *cause* of non-compliance. Consequently we automated *guiding* and supporting rather than regimenting compliant institution design.

The framework proposal has addressed one part of institutional design and governance, we note there are other institutional design considerations for institution designing agents. One factor is the cost of remaining non-compliant before a deadline, for a contract offer this is rejection, but in other cases it invites punishment. Another factor is if multiple-tier institutions are non-compliant, which to revise first. Whilst it makes sense to resolve highest non-compliant tier first, this depends on which institutions the designer has the power to effect change.

For future work it will be interesting to formalise more complex case studies (e.g. EU Directives) and multi-institution system coordination where multiple institutions occupy each tier. Another aspect is extending the representation and reasoning to handle punishment for non-compliance after a runtime deadline. The framework can perform pre-runtime checks that create higher-order norm violations due to the *invocation* of rules. However, violations of instruments such as EU Directives occur not when rules in an institution are invoked, but due to legislation as a whole being non-compliant.

Acknowledgments

This work is partially supported by the SHINE[1] project funded by TU Delft.

[1]http://shine.tudelft.nl

REFERENCES

[1] G. Andrighetto, G. Governatori, P. Noriega, and L. van der Torre. Normative Multi-Agent Systems. *Dagstuhl Follow-Ups*, 4, 2013.

[2] C. Baral. *Knowledge Representation, Reasoning and Declarative Problem Solving*. Cambridge University Press, Cambridge, 2003.

[3] G. Boella and L. van der Torre. Permissions and obligations in hierarchical normative systems. In *Proceedings of the 9th International Conference on Artificial Intelligence and Law*, pages 109–118, 2003.

[4] G. Boella and L. van der Torre. Contracts as Legal Institutions in Organizations of Autonomous Agents. In *AAMAS 2004*, pages 948 – 955, 2004.

[5] N. Bulling, M. Dastani, and M. Knobbout. Monitoring norm violations in multi-agent systems. In *AAMAS 2013*, pages 491–498, 2013.

[6] F. Chesani, P. Mello, M. Montali, and P. Torroni. Representing and monitoring social commitments using the event calculus. *Autonomous Agents and Multi-Agent Systems*, 27(1):85–130, June 2012.

[7] O. Cliffe, M. De Vos, and J. Padget. Answer set programming for representing and reasoning about virtual institutions. *Computational Logic in Multi-Agent Systems*, 4371:60–79, 2006.

[8] D. Corapi, A. Russo, M. De Vos, J. Padget, and K. Satoh. Normative design using inductive learning. *TPLP*, 4-5:783–799, 2011.

[9] T. Eiter, W. Faber, N. Leone, and G. Pfeifer. The diagnosis frontend of the dlv system. *AI Communications*, 12(1):99–111, 1999.

[10] R. Ganti, F. Ye, and H. Lei. Mobile crowdsensing: current state and future challenges. *IEEE Communications Magazine*, 49(11):32–39, Nov. 2011.

[11] M. Gebser, B. Kaufmann, and R. Kaminski. Potassco: The Potsdam answer set solving collection. *AI Communications*, 24(2):107 – 124, 2011.

[12] M. Gelfond and V. Lifschitz. The stable model semantics for logic programming. In *Logic Programming, Proceedings of the Fifth International Conference and Symposium*, pages 1070 – 1080, 1988.

[13] G. Governatori, M. Palmirani, R. Riveret, A. Rotolo, and G. Sartor. Norm modifications in defeasible logic. In *In Proceedings of JURIX'05*, pages 13–22, 2005.

[14] T. C. King, M. B. V. Riemsdijk, V. Dignum, and C. M. Jonker. Supporting Request Acceptance with Use Policies. In *COIN @ AAMAS 2014 Pre-proceedings*, 2014.

[15] T. Li. *Normative Conflict Detection and Resolution in Cooperating Institutions*. PhD thesis, University of Bath, 2014.

[16] T. Li, T. Balke, M. De Vos, J. Padget, and K. Satoh. A model-based approach to the automatic revision of secondary legislation. In *Proceedings of the Fourteenth International Conference on Artificial Intelligence and Law*, pages 202–206. ACM, 2013.

[17] T. Li, T. Balke, M. De Vos, K. Satoh, and J. Padget. Detecting conflicts in legal systems. *New Frontiers in Artificial Intelligence*, pages 174 – 189, 2013.

[18] H. Liesbet and M. Gary. Unraveling the central state, but how? Types of multi-level governance. *American political science review*, 97(2):233–243, 2003.

[19] F. L. y. López and M. Luck. Modelling Norms for Autonomous Agents. In *Proceedings of The Fourth Mexican Conference on Computer Science*, pages 238–245. IEEE Computer Society, 2003.

[20] S. Modgil, N. Faci, and F. Meneguzzi. A framework for monitoring agent-based normative systems. In *AAMAS 2009: Proceedings of the 8th International Conference on Autonomous Agents and Multiagent Systems*, pages 153–160. IFAAMAS, 2009.

[21] N. Oren, M. Luck, S. Miles, and T. Norman. An argumentation inspired heuristic for resolving normative conflict. In *Proc. of the 5th Workshop on Coordination, Organization, Institutions and Norms in Agent Systems (COIN@AAMAS)*, Estoril, Portugal, 2008.

[22] D. Ruiter. A basic classification of legal institutions. *Ratio Juris*, 10(4):357 – 372, 1997.

[23] J. R. Searle. *Speech acts: An essay in the philosophy of language*. Cambridge university press, 1969.

[24] The EU Member States. Treaty and Functioning of the European Union, 1958.

[25] UK Government. Financial Services Act, 2012.

[26] W. W. Vasconcelos, M. J. Kollingbaum, and T. J. Norman. Normative conflict resolution in multi-agent systems. *Autonomous Agents and Multi-Agent Systems*, 19(2):124–152, Nov. 2009.

[27] M. Wooldridge. *An Introduction to Multi-Agent Systems*. Wiley, 2002.

[28] P. Yolum and M. Singh. Reasoning about commitments in the event calculus: An approach for specifying and executing protocols. *Annals of Mathematics and Artificial Intelligence*, 42(1-3):227–253, 2004.

DIRECT: A Scalable Approach for Route Guidance in Selfish Orienteering Problems

Pradeep Varakantham, Hala Mostafa, Na Fu, Hoong Chuin Lau
School of Information Systems
Singapore Management University
{pradeepv,halamostafa,nafu,hclau}@smu.edu.sg

ABSTRACT

We address the problem of crowd congestion at venues like theme parks, museums and world expos by providing route guidance to multiple selfish users (with budget constraints) moving through the venue simultaneously. To represent these settings, we introduce the Selfish Orienteering Problem (SeOP) that combines two well studied problems from literature, namely Orienteering Problem (OP) and Selfish Routing (SR). OP is a single agent routing problem where the goal is to minimize latency (or maximize reward) in traversing a subset of nodes while respecting budget constraints. SR is a game between selfish agents looking for minimum latency routes from source to destination along edges of a network available to all agents. Thus, SeOP is a multi-agent planning problem where agents have selfish interests and individual budget constraints. As with Selfish Routing, we employ Nash Equilibrium as the solution concept in solving SeOP. A direct mathematical program formulation to find a Nash equilibrium in SeOP cannot scale because the number of constraints is quadratic in the number of paths, which itself is an exponential quantity. To address scalability issues, we make two key contributions. First, we provide a compact non-pairwise formulation with linear number of constraints in the number of paths to enforce the equilibrium condition. Second, we introduce DIRECT, an incremental and iterative master-slave decomposition approach to compute an approximate equilibrium solution. Similar to existing flow based approaches, DIRECT is scale invariant in the number of agents. We also provide a theoretical discussion of our approximation quality and present extensive empirical results on synthetic and real-world graphs demonstrating the scalability of combining DIRECT with our non-pairwise formulation.

Categories and Subject Descriptors

J.m [**Computing Application**]: Game Theory

General Terms

Leisure and Entertainment, Decision Support

Appears in: *Proceedings of the 14th International Conference on Autonomous Agents and Multiagent Systems (AAMAS 2015), Bordini, Elkind, Weiss, Yolum (eds.), May 4–8, 2015, Istanbul, Turkey.*

Keywords

Game Theory; Selfish Routing; Orienteering; Network Congestion Games, Constraint Generation

1. INTRODUCTION

A fundamental problem in the management of large-scale transportation and communication networks is that of routing traffic to optimize network performance, given that performance degrades when network users act greedily and myopically. Game-theoretic equilibrium strategies are shown to provide good performance [10], achieving more than 75% of optimal social welfare in environments where the latency on an edge is linear in the number of agents using it (also referred to as *flow*). We therefore focus on the computation of game-theoretic equilibrium strategies.

We consider the routing of selfish individuals each of whom is interested in a set of nodes and is operating under a resource or time budget (minimum number of attractions to visit or maximum time to spend). This problem arises in crowd coordination for theme parks, museums and world expos. For the operators of such facilities, one important concern is the real-time coordination of visitors to provide customized route guidance that reduces visitor wait times while respecting their budgets. With the prevalence of smart devices, this coordination is realizable by delivering guidance to visitors' mobile phones.

The computation of routes (sequence through all or a subset of nodes of interest) in such scenarios has traditionally been studied in the context of the Orienteering Problem (OP). OP is a generalization of the Traveling Salesman Problem where the goal is to find a route that maximizes utility (or minimizes latency) while respecting budget constraints on resources or time [13]. OP has been extensively studied by the Operations Research and AI communities (a survey of OP and its variants is given in [15]). While efficient algorithms for OP exist, the model and its solution approaches are inapplicable in our setting because they do not address or represent the effects of interactions among selfish agents traversing common edges whose latencies depend on the number of agents using them, thereby linking the decision problems of individual agents.

On the other hand, there are related multi agent models such as Network Congestion Games (NCG) and Selfish Routing (SR) [10, 9, 3] which consider the interactions among selfish agents on a network. The goal for each agent is to compute the minimum latency path from a designated start node to a designated end node, where the latency of an edge depends on the number of agents traversing it. However, neither NCG nor SR considers each agent's resource or time budget constraints that limit the number of nodes this agent can visit.

To fill this gap, we introduce the Selfish Orienteering Problem (SeOP) where we represent the problem of finding a path (sequence of nodes) for each selfish agent to satisfy their resource and budget constraints as a game. An assignment of paths to agents results in certain flows on the edges of the graph. As in NCG and SR, the goal is to compute the set of paths that give rise to flows describing an (approximate) Nash equilibrium where no agent can achieve lower latency/higher reward by deviating from the prescribed (possibly non-deterministic) path strategies.

To that end, we first present a formulation for finding a Nash equilibrium in SeOP as an optimization problem. However, the resulting Mixed Integer Linear Program has limited scalability because it enforces the equilibrium condition using a number of constraints quadratic in the number of available paths. To address this, we make the following contributions:

1. We provide a compact optimization formulation for SeOP that enforces the equilibrium condition using a number of constraints linear in the size of the path set.
2. We present DIRECT, an iterative master-slave decomposition approach that computes an approximate equilibrium in a scalable manner by incrementally growing the set of paths that constitute the support set of mixed strategies for each agent type. Since SeOP is a generalization of SR problems, our approach can also be used to solve SR problems efficiently.

We provide a theoretical discussion of our approximation quality and present extensive empirical results demonstrating the scalability of combining DIRECT with our compact formulation. We report results from both synthetic and real-world graphs.

2. SELFISH ORIENTEERING PROBLEM

In the Selfish Orienteering Problem (SeOP), as with Selfish Routing (SR), each agent optimizes their individual objective (maximizing utility or minimizing latency). Orienteering problems of different agents are interdependent since the reward or latency of an edge is a function of the number of agents using that edge.

Formally, SeOP is a tuple: $<\Gamma, \mathbf{N}, \mathcal{V}, \mathcal{E}, \mathbf{L}, \mathbf{D}, \mathbf{B}>$. Γ is the set of agent types and $\mathbf{N} = \{\mathcal{N}^\tau\}_{\tau\in\Gamma}$ is a vector representing the number of agents of each type τ. $\langle\mathcal{V}, \mathcal{E}\rangle$ represents the underlying network graph with vertices/nodes $\mathcal{V}$ and edges $\mathcal{E}$. $\mathbf{L} = \{\mathcal{L}^\tau_{ij}\}_{\tau\in\Gamma, ij\in\mathcal{E}}$ is a vector of latency functions, one per agent type and edge. The latency experienced by type τ on path p is the sum of latencies experienced on each edge in the path:

$$\mathcal{L}^\tau_p = \sum_{ij\in p} \mathcal{L}^\tau_{ij}(x_{ij})$$

where each edge latency is a function of the flow x_{ij} on it. In the context of guidance at theme parks, the latency function for an agent type τ on an edge captures the tolerance of τ for congestion on this edge; the higher the latency the lower the tolerance. $\mathbf{D} = \{\mathcal{D}^\tau\}_{\tau\in\Gamma}$ is a vector where each $\mathcal{D}^\tau$ is the set of nodes that agents of type τ want to visit and $\mathcal{B}^\tau \in \mathbf{B}$ is the budget for each agent type. For example, $\mathcal{B}^\tau$ can be the minimum number of nodes in $\mathcal{D}^\tau$ that type τ wants to visit.

The goal is for each agent of type τ to find one or more paths that have minimum total latency from a designated start node to a designated end node and cover at least $\mathcal{B}^\tau$ nodes in $\mathcal{D}^\tau$. SeOP differs from network congestion games in multiple respects, namely budget on nodes to be visited and the path should cover a subset or all nodes in the list of interested nodes.

A solution of SeOP is an assignment of flows of every agent type to edges and, consequently, paths. We focus on computing equilibrium solutions, i.e. the calculated agent flows are such that each agent is prescribed a path with minimum latency and thus has no incentive to deviate from this path given the paths of other agents.

EXAMPLE 1. *To give a concrete example, we present SeOP in the context of the problem of providing route guidance to visitors at a theme park:*

- *Visitors to the theme park are the agents and examples of agent types, Γ, are adults, families with kids, families with senior citizens, etc.*
- *The nodes, $\mathcal{V}$, are theme park attractions.*
- *Latencies, $\mathbf{L}$, represent the wait times on edges[1].*
- *$\mathbf{B}$ is the resource (maximum number of nodes in the final path) or time (total time available to visit attractions) budget for each visitor type.*
- *$\mathbf{D}$ is the set of interesting attractions for each visitor type. For example, a family with children prefers child rides and moderately thrill rides.*

The goal is to compute a sequence of nodes (selected from $\mathcal{D}^\tau$) for each agent type τ such that no agent of any type has incentive to deviate from the prescribed sequence, i.e. the prescribed sequence has minimum latency in the context of sequences prescribed to other types.

3. SEOP AS AN OPTIMIZATION PROBLEM

To formulate SeOP as an optimization problem, we use the following observation, due to Wardrop [16], on equilibrium flows in traffic routing.

OBSERVATION 1. *At equilibrium, if a path p has positive flow, then no other path can have a strictly lower latency than the latency on path p [16] .*

3.1 Pairwise Formulation of SeOP

Based on Observation 1, we propose the optimization formulation for calculating equilibrium flows for SeOPs[2] given in Table 1. x^τ_p and x^τ_{ij} are the flows of agents of type τ on path p and edge ij, respectively. x_{ij} is the total flow of all agent types on edge ij. Note that if we generate the path set $\mathcal{P}^\tau$ for each agent type τ to only contain paths that meet the budget $\mathcal{B}^\tau$, we do not have to include explicit budget constraints.

Since our goal is to compute any equilibrium solution, our optimization problem is essentially a feasibility problem, with an option to include an objective function that

[1]At a theme park wait times are at attractions. While we consider wait times or latencies as being associated with edges, our model and approach can easily be modified to account for wait times at nodes as shown in Section 7.2.

[2]This is an extension of the SR formulation [10] to account for budget constraints and agent types.

Table 1: Pairwise SeOP formulation

$$\min \ \mathbf{0} \quad \text{subject to}$$

$$x_{ij} = \sum_{\tau} x_{ij}^{\tau} \ \ \forall (i,j) \in \mathcal{E} \tag{1}$$

$$\forall \tau \in \Gamma;$$

$$x_{ij}^{\tau} = \sum_{p \in \mathcal{P}^{\tau} | ij \in p} x_p^{\tau} \ \ \forall (i,j) \in \mathcal{E} \tag{2}$$

$$\sum_j x_{0j}^{\tau} = \sum_j x_{j|\mathcal{V}|}^{\tau} = \mathcal{N}^{\tau} \tag{3}$$

$$\sum_i x_{ij}^{\tau} = \sum_k x_{jk}^{\tau} \ \ \forall j \in \mathcal{V} \tag{4}$$

$$\forall p \in \mathcal{P}^{\tau} \textbf{if } x_p^{\tau} > 0:$$

$$\sum_{ij \in p} \mathcal{L}_{ij}^{\tau}(x_{ij}) \leq \sum_{kl \in p'} \mathcal{L}_{kl}^{\tau}(x_{kl}) \ \ \forall p' \in \mathcal{P}^{\tau} \tag{5}$$

$$x_p^{\tau}, x_{ij}^{\tau}, x_{ij} \geq 0 \tag{6}$$

Table 2: Non-pairwise SeOP formulation

$$\min \ \mathbf{0} \quad \text{subject to}$$

$$\forall \tau \in \Gamma, p \in \mathcal{P}^{\tau}$$

flow conservation and identity constraints

$$y_p^{\tau} \cdot M \geq x_p^{\tau} \tag{7}$$

$$y_p^{\tau} \leq x_p^{\tau} \cdot M \tag{8}$$

$$\sum_{ij \in p} \mathcal{L}_{ij}^{\tau}(x_{ij}) \geq d^{\tau} \tag{9}$$

$$\sum_{ij \in p} \mathcal{L}_{ij}^{\tau}(x_{ij}) - d^{\tau} \leq u_p^{\tau} \cdot M \tag{10}$$

$$y_p^{\tau} \leq w_p^{\tau} \cdot M \tag{11}$$

$$u_p^{\tau} + w_p^{\tau} \leq 1 \tag{12}$$

$$x_{ij}^{\tau}, x_{ij}, x_p^{\tau}, d^{\tau} \geq 0$$

$$y_p^{\tau}, u_p^{\tau}, w_p^{\tau} \in \{0,1\}$$

measures the quality of an equilibrium solution (e.g. the social welfare of a solution). In Table 1, constraints 1 and 2 are identity constraints to ensure that agent flows on edges and paths are consistent. They specify that the flow on an edge is the sum of flows on path that include this edge and define edge flow as the sum of agents of all types that traverse this edge.

Constraints 3 and 4 enforce flow conservation for each type:

- Total flow out of the start node 0 equals total flow into the end node $|\mathcal{V}|$ equals the number of agents of this type.
- Total flow into a node equals total flow out of it.

Constraint 5 implements Observation 1 by enforcing a pairwise relation between the latencies of every pair of paths. It states that the latency of a path with positive flow should be no larger than the latency of any other path. Although constraint 5 is a logical constraint, it can easily be represented as a set of linear constraints (similar to the complementarity constraint in the next subsection).

3.2 Non-pairwise Formulation of SeOP

The formulation in Table 1 suffers from limited scalability due to $\mathcal{O}(|\mathcal{P}|^2)$ latency equilibrium constraints (5). We now propose a formulation that does not perform pairwise comparisons of path latencies and uses only $\mathcal{O}(|\mathcal{P}|)$ constraints. d^{τ} represents the minimum latency achieved by type τ.

First, we rephrase the equilibrium condition: at equilibrium, if the minimum attainable latency for type τ on any path is d^{τ}, then each path with positive flow of type τ agents must have latency d^{τ}. Table 2 shows our **non-pairwise (NPW)** SeOP formulation as a feasibility problem.

For each path p, let the binary variable y_p^{τ} indicate whether there is positive flow of agents of type τ on path p:

$$y_p^{\tau} = 1 \quad \text{iff } x_p^{\tau} > 0$$

The above relation can be enforced using the linear constraints (7) and (8), where M is a large positive number.

The constraint that each path with positive flow must have minimum latency can be seen as a complementarity constraint between the indicator y_p^{τ} on the one hand and the gap between a path's latency $\mathcal{L}_p^{\tau}$ and the minimal latency d^{τ} on the other hand. If there is a gap, the indicator must be 0 (path must have zero flow), and if the path has positive flow, the gap must be zero.

$$y_p^{\tau} \cdot (\mathcal{L}_p^{\tau} - d_p^{\tau}) = 0$$

A complementarity constraint $pq = 0$ can be expressed using the linear constraints

$$\begin{aligned} p &\leq wM \\ q &\leq uM \\ u + w &\leq 1 \end{aligned}$$

where M is again a large positive number and u and w are binary variables. Constraints (10), (11) and (12) apply the same linearization to enforce complementarity between y_p^{τ} and the gap $\mathcal{L}_p^{\tau} - d_p^{\tau}$. Constraint (9) ensures that d^{τ} is indeed the minimum latency.

4. ITERATIVE DECOMPOSITION

Even though NPW reduces the number of constraints from quadratic to linear in the number of paths, it is not enough to ensure scalability, since the number of paths is itself exponential in the number of nodes in $\mathcal{D}^{\tau}$ and the budget $\mathcal{B}^{\tau}$. To overcome this problem, we do not compute equilibria using the entire support set $\mathcal{P}^{\tau}$ of each type. Instead, we propose Deviation Incentive based Restricted dECompositiTion (DIRECT), an iterative master-slave decomposition approach where the master computes equilibria over a relatively small support set and the slave searches for better paths to be included in the support set in the next iteration. DIRECT computes ϵ-equilibrium solutions where ϵ is controlled using the input parameter $\delta \in [0,1]$.

As shown in Table 3, we start by initializing a seed path set for each type, for example by randomly choosing a predefined number of paths that meet the budget, or incorporating domain knowledge to generate an initial set of promising paths. In each iteration and for each type τ, DIRECT performs the following steps:

1. The master computes equilibrium flows for all agents except for a **fraction** δ **of an agent** of type τ. Note that δ is not a fraction of all agents of type τ. Instead, it is a fraction of only one agent of type τ.
2. The slave finds the minimum latency path for the remaining δ of an agent given the other flows computed by the master.
3. If the slave path has lower latency than the minimum latency for type τ calculated by the master, the agent has incentive to deviate and we need to add this path to the support.

The algorithm converges when no more paths can be added to the support. At convergence, we solve the master problem with the final support set of paths for all $\mathcal{N}$ agents. The resulting approximate equilibrium flows are such no agent has incentive to deviate for more than fraction δ of the time.

EXAMPLE 2. *Consider a problem with 10 agents all of one type and* $\delta = 0.2$. *Consider an iteration where* $\hat{\mathcal{P}}^\tau = \{p_1, p_2\}$ *and the equilibrium flows returned by the master in this iteration are 6.3 agents on* p_1 *and 3.5 agents on* p_2 *for a total of* 9.8 $(= 10 - \delta)$ *agents. Let the latency of each of these paths (which must be equal since they have positive flow) be 20. The slave then checks if* δ $(= 0.2)$ *fraction of one agent has incentive to use a path other than* p_1 *and* p_2. *The slave computes the shortest non-divisible flow path for* δ *given the flows computed for the other 9.8 agents. If this new shortest path has latency 18, it is added to the support set and the next iteration's master uses the larger support to compute an equilibrium with lower latency than the current iteration.*

The example illustrates the following two key approximations we make in DIRECT:

1. Every call to the master computes equilibria using a *restricted* set of paths $\hat{\mathcal{P}}$ rather than the full set $\mathcal{P}$. As we show empirically, $|\hat{\mathcal{P}}|$ is typically orders of magnitude smaller than $|\mathcal{P}|$, leading to significant reductions in run times.

2. The second approximation allows the slave to check if an agent has an incentive to deviate from the equilibrium computed by the master in a scalable manner. This is done by restricting the slave to only use binary flow variables x_{ij}, thereby finding the minimum latency path among the set of deterministic paths only.

The master problem MASTER($\hat{\mathcal{P}}, \delta, \tau$) has the same form as Table 2 with two key differences; the path sets are $\hat{\mathcal{P}}^\tau$ rather than $\mathcal{P}^\tau$; and the flow conservation constraints (3) are modified such that the total flow for type τ is only $\mathcal{N}^\tau - \delta$. Table 4 provides the slave as an integer linear program. The objective function is the latency over all edges given current flows $\mathbf{x}^{\hat{\mathcal{P}}}$ from the master in addition to the planned flow for δ fraction of an agent of type τ. Constraints (13) and (14) ensure indivisible flow conservation for the δ fraction of an agent. Constraints (15) and (16) ensure that the returned path only visits desirable nodes and satisfies the budget.

Ideally, we want to know if there is incentive for any one agent to switch to any *set* of paths; i.e., search the space of non-deterministic strategies. But this would require the slave to allow fractional flows and the branching of flow at some nodes. Expressing the overall latency experienced by the agent would then require an indicator variable for each possible path and the slave problem would have the same complexity as the original master over the full set of paths. Therefore, instead of computing fractional flows for one agent, we compute non-divisible flow for a fraction δ of an agent, thereby avoiding the exponential enumeration of paths at the expense of introducing the approximation error discussed in the next section.

While we consider latency (reward) functions to be linear, as long as they are convex, our decomposition approach can use off-the-shelf solvers to obtain a solution. For non-convex and non-linear latency (or reward) functions, we can employ piecewise constant or piecewise linear approximations. Extending DIRECT to these function classes is a topic for future research.

Table 3: DIRECT (δ)

//Initialize subset of paths for each type
$\hat{\mathcal{P}} = \{\hat{\mathcal{P}}^1, \hat{\mathcal{P}}^2, .., \hat{\mathcal{P}}^{|\Gamma|}\}$
converged $\leftarrow$ **false**
while !*converged* **do**
  converged $\leftarrow$ **true**
  for all $\tau \in \Gamma$ **do**
    $< \mathbf{x}^{\hat{\mathcal{P}}}, d^\tau > \leftarrow$ MASTER($\hat{\mathcal{P}}, \delta, \tau$)
    $p^\tau \leftarrow$ SLAVE($\mathbf{x}^{\hat{\mathcal{P}}}, \delta, \tau$)
    if $p^\tau \notin \hat{\mathcal{P}}^\tau$ **and** $\mathcal{L}^\tau_{p^\tau} < d^\tau$ **then**
      $\hat{\mathcal{P}}^\tau \leftarrow \hat{\mathcal{P}}^\tau \cup \{p^\tau\}$
      converged $\leftarrow$ **false**
return MASTER($\hat{\mathcal{P}}, 0, -1$)

Table 4: Slave($\mathbf{x}^{\hat{\mathcal{P}}}, \delta, \tau$)

$$\min_{x \in \{0,1\}} \sum_{(ij)} x_{ij} \cdot \mathcal{L}^\tau_{ij}(\mathbf{x}^{\hat{\mathcal{P}}}_{ij} + \delta)$$

$$\sum_j x_{0j} = \sum_i x_{i|\mathcal{V}|} = 1 \tag{13}$$

$$\sum_i x_{ij} = \sum_k x_{jk} \quad \forall j \tag{14}$$

$$\sum_i x^\tau_{ij} = 0 \quad \forall j \notin \mathcal{D}^\tau \tag{15}$$

$$\sum_{i,j \in \mathcal{D}^\tau} x^\tau_{ij} \geq \mathcal{B}^\tau \tag{16}$$

5. THEORETICAL RESULTS

In this section, we provide an *a posteriori* (after computing the solution) bound on the approximation error, ϵ for a given value of δ with our DIRECT algorithm.

PROPOSITION 1. *DIRECT(δ) converges to an* ϵ *equilibrium with*

$$\epsilon \leq \delta \cdot \max_\tau \left(\mathcal{L}^{\tau,\#}(\delta) - \mathcal{L}^{\tau,\#}(0)\right) \tag{17}$$

where $\mathcal{L}^{\tau,\#}(\delta)$ *and* $\mathcal{L}^{\tau,\#}(0)$ *are the latency values obtained by solving* SLAVE($\boldsymbol{x}^{\hat{\mathcal{P}}}, \delta, \tau$) *and* SLAVE($\boldsymbol{x}^{\hat{\mathcal{P}}}, 0, \tau$) *respectively at convergence.* $\boldsymbol{x}^{\hat{\mathcal{P}}}$ *is the flow obtained by solving the master at the last iteration for* $\mathcal{N} - \delta$ *agents, with* δ *representing a fraction of type* τ *agent.*

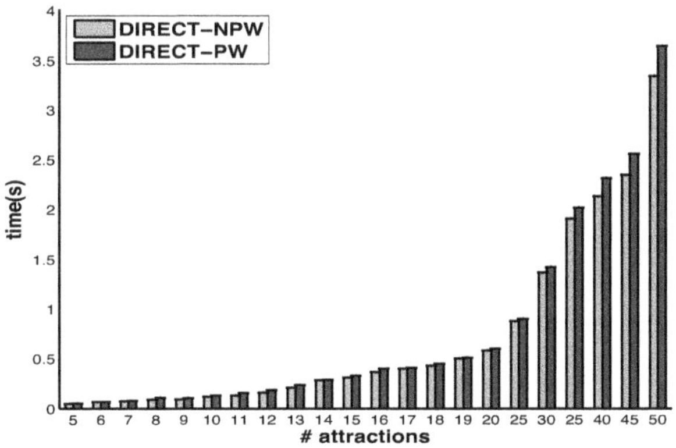

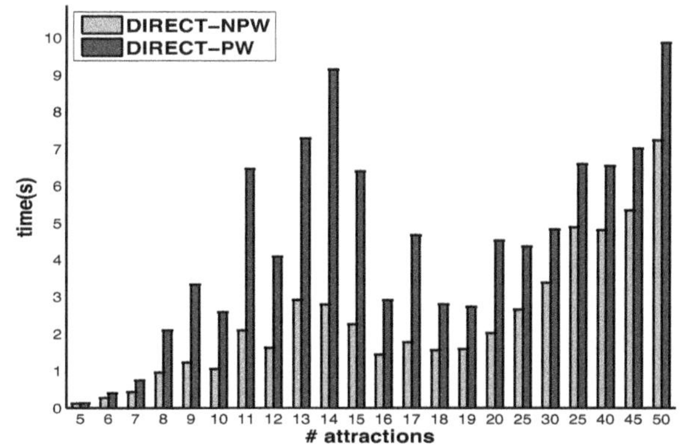

Figure 1: Effect of number of attractions $|\mathcal{V}|$ on runtime for 1 (L) and 2 (R) types. $\delta = 0.5$

Proof. There is an approximation error with DIRECT for an input parameter of δ, because potentially less than δ fraction of an agent can find a path that has lower latency value given the flows for the rest of the agents. A lower bound on the lowest latency value for a type τ agent is obtained by solving the shortest path problem given flow for $\mathcal{N} - \delta$ agents (equivalent to $\text{SLAVE}(\mathbf{x}^{\hat{\mathcal{P}}}, 0, \tau)$) and considering that δ agents do not contribute to the flow on paths. This is a lower bound because latency without adding δ fraction of the agent will only be smaller than the latency obtained by adding the δ fraction of the agent. Therefore for agent of type τ, the error would be given by:

$$\epsilon_\tau \leq \delta \cdot \left(\mathcal{L}^{\tau,\#}(\delta) - \mathcal{L}^{\tau,\#}(0)\right)$$

We multiply by the δ factor because $1 - \delta$ fraction of the agent remains the same in both components of the difference. Approximation error over all types is the maximum over the error for each individual type and hence the bound on error given in Equation 17. ■

6. EXPERIMENTAL RESULTS

We now compare 3 approaches for solving SeOP. **Full-NPW** formulates SeOP as the non-pairwise feasibility problem in Table 2 using the full path set and no decomposition[3]. **DIRECT-PW** uses master-slave decomposition with pairwise formulation in the master (Table 1). **DIRECT-NPW** combines decomposition with the compact non-pairwise formulation in Table 2[4].

We change 3 parameters: $\delta \in \{0.2, 0.5, 0.9\}$ changes the tightness of the approximate equilibrium while the number of attractions in the theme park $|\mathcal{V}|$ and the number of agent types $|\Gamma|$ change the size of the problem. For the different approaches, we compare 1) runtime; 2) latency of the (approximate) equilibria; and 3) number of paths in the support set.

6.1 Synthetic graphs

For each parameter combination, we generate 10 instances that vary in the latency functions of their edges, which have the form $ax + b$ where a, b are randomly drawn from the range 1 to 10. Unless stated otherwise, we set the budget $\mathcal{B}^\tau$ of each type to be $|\mathcal{V}|$, so the full set of possible paths is the set of permutations of all attractions. In DIRECT-PW and DIRECT-NPW, the set $\hat{\mathcal{P}}^\tau$ for each type is initialized with a single path traversing all nodes in order.

Impact of number of attractions $|\mathcal{V}|$

We first consider the effect of the number of attractions on runtime. Figure 1 shows run times for 1 and 2 agent types and $\delta = 0.5$. With 1 type, Full-NPW is faster only for very small problems (up to $|\mathcal{V}| = 8$) that do not need decomposition. For $|\mathcal{V}| = 9, 10$, Full-NPW takes 17 and 401 seconds, respectively and runs out of time (aborted after 1 hour) and/or memory while generating the full set of paths for larger problems. For 2 types, Full-NPW could only handle 5 and 6 attractions. For the rather large value of 0.5 for δ, both DIRECT approaches scale very well with $|\mathcal{V}|$, handling up to 50 attractions in a few seconds.

The figures clearly show the significant impact of the number of types on runtime. To understand the effects of $|\mathcal{V}|$ and $|\Gamma|$, note that DIRECT's gradual increase of the support size largely mitigates the main challenge posed by a large set of attractions, namely the exponential explosion of the set of paths. Increasing the number of types, however, increases the number of times the master and slave problems are solved in each iteration of DIRECT, in addition to each master problem being larger, since we have a set of variables per type per path. Moreover, a path introduced by 1 type's slave can give all other types incentives to deviate, upon which paths are added to their respective sets.

Impact of input parameter δ

Tables 5 and 6 show the effect of δ ($\delta = 0$ refers to Full-NPW) on the latency of the equilibrium paths $\mathcal{L}$ and the size of the support set $|\hat{\mathcal{P}}|$ (for DIRECT-*, this is also the number of iterations). As explained earlier, lower values of δ result in tighter approximations. Entries marked '-' indicate running out of time/memory. To have a meaningful comparison of these quantities, Table 5 is for $|\Gamma|$=1. DIRECT-PW and DIRECT-NPW have the same $\mathcal{L}$ and $|\hat{\mathcal{P}}|$, which confirms that the pairwise and non-pairwise constraints enforce the same semantics on flows. As expected, higher δ leads to fewer iterations (thus smaller path sets) because given

[3]We were only able to run **Full-PW** on very small problems and hence is not described in experimental results.
[4]Using a Mac with 3.4 GHz Intel Core i7, 32 GB 1600 MHz DDR3. All optimization problems were solved using IBM ILOG CPLEX Optimization Studio V12.4.

Table 5: Effect of δ on latency at equilibrium and support size. $|\Gamma| = 1$

	$|\mathcal{V}|$=8		$|\mathcal{V}|$=10		$|\mathcal{V}|$=20	
δ	$\mathcal{L}$	$|\hat{\mathcal{P}}|$	$\mathcal{L}$	$|\hat{\mathcal{P}}|$	$\mathcal{L}$	$|\hat{\mathcal{P}}|$
0	91.8	720	100.9	40,320	-	-
0.2	92	12.7	101.2	15.7	143.6	20.6
0.5	93.3	8.6	103.7	10	153.1	12
0.9	97.8	6.2	110.5	7.5	169.3	7.8

Table 6: Effect of δ on runtime (seconds). $|\Gamma| = 2$

	$|\mathcal{V}|$=10		$|\mathcal{V}|$=20	
δ	NPW	PW	NPW	PW
0	-	-	-	-
0.2	25	108	90	496
0.5	1.0	2.6	2.0	4.5
0.9	0.3	0.5	0.8	0.9

Table 7: Tightness of error bound

$|\mathcal{V}|$	Upper bound on ϵ (Proposition 1)	Observed ϵ	Final Latency
8	1.212	0.15	91.84
9	1.416	0.37	95.58
10	1.802	0.31	100.89

flows for other agents, an agent can have no incentive to deviate 0.9 of the time, but have incentive to deviate 0.2 of the time, so the slave can find a path to add to the support with $\delta = 0.2$, but not with $\delta = 0.9$. Table 5 also shows the increasing approximation gap between $\mathcal{L}$ of Full-NPW and the DIRECT approaches as δ and $|\mathcal{V}|$ increase[5]. Noting how little the support size changes as $|\mathcal{V}|$ increases explains the scalability of DIRECT demonstrated in Figure 1. The timing results in Table 6 show that DIRECT-PW takes much longer to achieve the same result as DIRECT-NPW, with the difference in runtime growing with $|\mathcal{V}|$.

To investigate how the quest for tighter approximation affects the scalability of DIRECT approaches, we set $\delta = 0.2$ to generate Figure 2(a) which strongly suggests that if the goal is better approximate equilibria, the pairwise formulation can get prohibitively expensive while the non-pairwise formulation continues to scale very well with $|\mathcal{V}|$.

Impact of number of types $|\Gamma|$

We next investigate the scalability of our approaches with the number of types $|\Gamma|$. Based on our observations from a real life theme park, patrons of different types (e.g., age, nationality) are interested in different subsets of attractions. We experiment with 16 attractions and for each type, generate a set of 8 random attraction that agents of this type want to visit, so $|\mathcal{D}|^\tau = \mathcal{B}^\tau = 8\ \forall \tau$. Figure 2(b) again exhibits the observation from Figure 1 that the number of types has a strong impact on runtime, and shows the limitation of DIRECT-PW as $|\Gamma|$ increases.

Tightness of error bound

We now demonstrate the tightness of the error bound on ϵ by providing the difference in observed value of ϵ and upper bound on ϵ computed using Propostion 1. Since, we can only run Full-NPW for small problems, we consider $|\Gamma| = 1$ and $|\mathcal{V}| = \{8, 9, 10\}$. As can be noted from Table 7, the predicted upper bound on ϵ using Proposition 1 is a tight bound and the difference in predicted and observed is less than 1.5% of the final latency (last column).

[5]We assume the all 3 approaches are converging to the same equilibrium.

Table 8: Real Network: Runtime and support size

δ	DIRECT-NPW Runtime	DIRECT-PW Runtime	$|\hat{\mathcal{P}}|$ /type
$|\Gamma| = 1$			
0.2	22.1354	22.6016	13.1
0.5	9.545	10.0806	8.4
0.9	4.1876	4.3091	5.9
$|\Gamma| = 2$			
0.2	53.4626	80.0936	9.4
0.5	21.329	26.081	6.85
0.9	10.7274	11.7274	5.1

Table 9: Real Network: Impact of initial path set. $|\Gamma| = 1$

Initial Path Set	Final Latency	Support Set Size
1	121.31	9
2	121.16	9
3	121.16	10
4	121.22	10
5	120.04	9
6	119.18	10
7	120.31	10
8	122.26	8
9	120.50	9
10	119.99	11

6.2 Graph of a real-world theme park

To demonstrate the applicability of our approach to real networks, we present results of running our formulations using graphs obtained from a major theme park in Singapore with 12 attractions/nodes. The graph is based on analysing movement dynamics of visitors among attractions over a one year period. Although this graph is not a complete graph, the comparison results between DIRECT-PW and DIRECT-NPW with respect to runtime are qualitatively the same as those obtained on complete synthetic graphs.

As can be noted from Table 8, the runtime results are similar to the ones obtained for synthetic graphs. We have also considered benchmarks for single and team orienteering problems [14] from literature. All these problems are fully connected graphs with 21 and 32 nodes. Since we show results on problems with up to 50 nodes that have randomly generated latency functions, we do not explicitly provide results on these benchmark instances.

Impact of initial path set

As explained earlier, DIRECT-* approaches rely on an initial path set that is incrementally expanded at each iteration. Here, we experiment with DIRECT-NPW using 10 different initial path sets for $\delta = 0.5$ on both the real theme park graph introduced earlier and a fully connected syn-

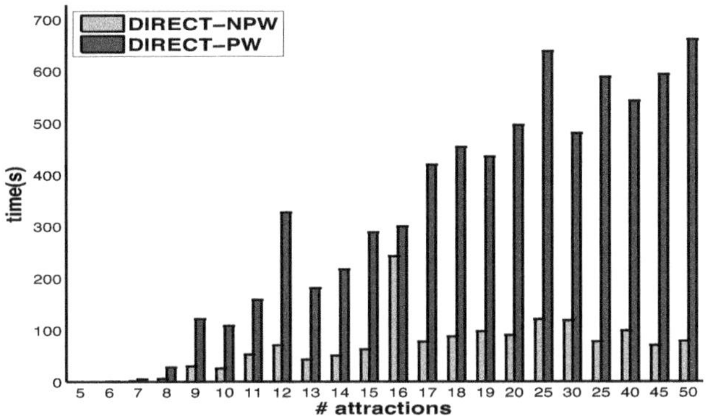

(a) Effect of number of attractions $|\mathcal{V}|$ on runtime for $|\Gamma|$=2 $\delta = 0.2$

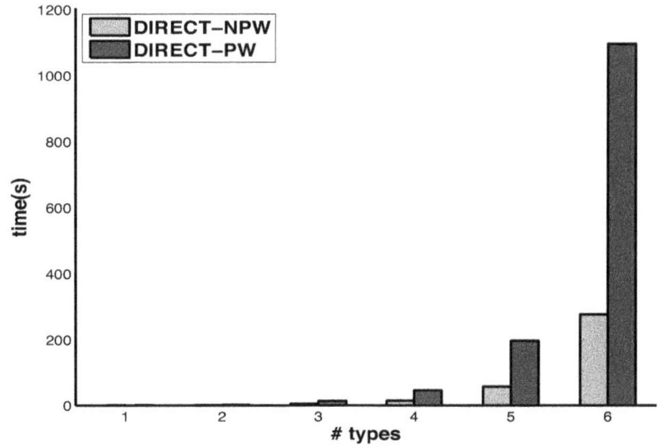

(b) Effect of number of types $|\Gamma|$ on runtime for $|\mathcal{V}|$=16 $\delta = 0.5$ and $\mathcal{B}^{\tau}$=8

Figure 2: DIRECT-NPW vs DIRECT-PW

Table 10: Real Network: Impact of Initial Path Set. $|\Gamma| = 2$

Initial Path Set	Final Latencies	Support Set Sizes
1	195.82 ; 155.82	6 ; 6
2	192.79 ; 158.47	7 ; 8
3	195.66 ; 155.61	7 ; 7
4	199.48 ; 152.52	5 ; 7
5	194.59 ; 152.85	6 ; 8
6	196.04 ; 157.08	7 ; 7
7	198.86 ; 151.65	8 ; 8
8	197.70 ; 151.37	7 ; 7
9	193.69 ; 156.99	6 ; 8
10	197.35 ; 155.29	7 ; 7

Table 11: Synthetic Network: Impact of initial path set. $|\Gamma| = 1$

Initial Path Set	Final Latency	Support Set Size
1	106.70	11
2	106.86	10
3	107.00	11
4	107.02	11
5	106.71	11
6	107.70	11
7	108.14	9
8	106.98	11
9	107.36	10
10	107.25	10

thetic graph, both of which have 12 nodes. Tables 9, 10, 11 and 12 show the results on one and two types of agents. As can be seen, differences in the final latencies for both real and synthetic examples are minimal. The run-time results are also very similar for different initial path sets, which is to be expected, since the final support set size are similar.

It is interesting to note that we converge to a very similar equilibrium even though we start from vastly different path sets. While we cannot make general claims from this result, it potentially suggests a low price of anarchy for SeOPs. We leave the study of price of anarchy in SeOPs for future work.

7. DISCUSSION

In this section, we discuss variants and extensions of our model and approach.

7.1 Maximizing Reward with Time Budget

It should be noted that while we have described SeOP in terms of minimizing latency constrained by a resource budget on nodes to be visited, our optimization approach and its enhancement are directly applicable to the following variants of SeOP:

- The budget for each agent type τ is on the maximum time available to visit the nodes in $\mathcal{D}^{\tau}$.
- Each agent maximizes the reward accumulated (instead of minimizing latency) in visiting a subset of attractions/nodes within the given time budget.

Table 1 can be modified as follows when each agent maximizes a reward function $\mathcal{R}$ instead of minimizing latency $\mathcal{L}$ and budget constraints are on the maximum time available instead of the minimum number of desirable nodes to visit:

- We replace the latency constraint 5 with the reward constraint

$$\textbf{if } x_p > 0 : \sum_{ij \in p} \mathcal{R}^{\tau}_{ij}(x_{ij}) \geq \sum_{(kl) \in p'} \mathcal{R}^{\tau}_{kl}(x_{kl}), \forall \tau \in \Gamma, p, p' \in \mathcal{P}^{\tau}$$

  Similar to the latency functions, $\mathcal{R}^{\tau}_{ij}(x_{ij})$ is the reward obtained by agents of type τ for travelling on edge ij when the flow on this edge is x_{ij}. The path sets $\mathcal{P}^{\tau}$ are no longer computed from the budget, and include all possible paths for agents of type τ.
- Unlike the budget constraint on resources which is implicit in the set of available paths, the budget constraint on time requires the following new constraint:

$$\textbf{if } x_p > 0 : \sum_{ij \in p} \mathcal{L}^{\tau}_{ij}(x_{ij}) \leq \mathcal{B}^{\tau}$$

Table 12: Synthetic Network: Impact of initial path set. $|\Gamma| = 2$

Initial Path Set	Final Latencies	Support Set Sizes
1	135.00 ; 118.02	10 ; 10
2	135.32 ; 117.32	9 ; 10
3	134.97 ; 119.11	10 ; 10
4	133.5 ; 118.78	9 ; 10
5	136.88 ; 118.89	9 ; 9
6	134.34 ; 117.54	10 ; 11
7	133.46 ; 121.88	9 ; 8
8	135.53 ; 118.46	10 ; 9
9	134.6 ; 118.8	10 ; 10
10	133.73 ; 118.72	10 ; 10

7.2 Wait Times at Nodes Instead of Edges

To accurately represent the theme park setting, we need to consider wait times at nodes instead of at edges. For this, the key change is in the computation of latency for any path, p. Instead of summing over all edges in the path, we sum over latencies at all nodes in the path, i.e., $\sum_{i\in p} \mathcal{L}_i^\tau(\sum_j x_{ij})$. It should be noted that the latency for a node, i will be calculated based on the incoming flow into that node i.e., $\sum_j x_{ij}$ and not on x_{ij}. All other constraints in the optimization problems (Table 1 and Table 2) remain the same. In fact, considering latency at nodes may be an easier problem than considering latency on edges.

8. RELATED WORK

The Team Orienteering Problem (TOP) [1, 6, 14, 11] represents OP for teams of agents and is different from the work in this paper due to selfishness of our agents.

The optimization formulation for Selfish Routing by Roughgarden *et al.* [10] is the closest work to this paper. However, we address budget constraints (additional knapsack constraints) and use decomposition to handle larger SeOP instances. While decomposition approaches such as column generation for optimizing social welfare in traffic routing [12] exist, it is non-trivial to adapt these approaches to account for equilibrium constraints since a column refers to a path and two paths with overlapping edges are not completely independent of each other as these approaches assume.

Although the master-slave decomposition in DIRECT has an iterative best response (IBR) flavor, we cannot use IBR as a baseline since 1) at each iteration IBR needs to compute best response and as we have shown (with the performance of centralised optimization formulations) optimising even for a single agent over the entire path set becomes practically infeasible very quickly; and 2) iterating to compute pure strategies for individual agents is expensive (as we consider domains with thousands and thousands of agents), while iterating at the level of types can be easily shown to not converge to strategies that are stable at the individual agent level. DIRECT addresses both issues: 1) the master incrementally builds the support set and 2) the slave finds candidate paths by trying to route a fraction of an agent, guaranteeing at convergence that no agent prefers to deviate more than δ of the time.

Fictitious play [2] and other adaptive learning approaches can potentially be used to solve SeOPs. However, they also run into the same issues as IBR and furthermore, with multiple agent types, they do not guarantee convergence because the game becomes atomic. Hence there is no guarantee on the existence of a potential function [7]. Since there exists an equilibrium for every finite game and our approach is based in optimization, we do not have issues with convergence. In contrast to variational inequality models [4] commonly used for traffic equilibrium problems in transportation networks, our approach is much more scalable computationally as demonstrated in the experimental results.

While SeOP is similar to network congestion games (NCGs), it has the following complicating requirements: 1) an agent needs to visit a given set of nodes and 2) different agent types have different latency functions (cost vectors) for a given edge. As such, the proof of existence of pure NE that holds for NCGs [9, 3] does not necessarily hold in SeOP. Unlike symmetric NCGs where agents have the same strategy spaces and for which a polynomial time algorithm exists [3], asymmetric NCGs are PLS-complete. So even if SeOPs have pure NE, because each agent in SeOP must visit certain nodes (and thus has a different set of valid strategies), SeOP is likely to be PLS-complete or harder. Another complexity argument is that OP is NP-hard [5], so our multi-agent version is at least in this complexity class. Milchtaich [8] considered congestion games with player-specific utilities, but each player selects exactly one resource and the game is not networked.

DIRECT is similar to column generation in that we gradually increase the size of the support set. In order to compute reduced cost of adding a column (a path in this case), column generation needs to have columns that are independent of each other. However, because multiple paths (columns) can share edges, the independence assumption does not hold.

9. CONCLUSION

This paper proposes a new model for the Selfish Orienteering Problem (SeOP) to combine the Orienteering Problem and Selfish Routing/network congestion games. We first give a direct formulation of finding a Nash equilibrium in SeOP as an optimization problem and address its limited scalability through two main contributions: a compact formulation with a linear number of constraints to enforce the equilibrium condition without pairwise comparisons of path latencies and DIRECT, an iterative master-slave decomposition approach that incrementally grows the set of paths to compute an approximate equilibrium. We provide a theoretical discussion of our approximation quality and present experimental results clearly showing that 1) our non-pairwise formulation achieves the same solution quality as the pairwise one using a fraction of the number of constraints; and 2) our master-slave decomposition achieves solutions with adjustable approximation gap using a fraction of the full path set. Together, these two contributions form an approach to solving SeOP that is highly scalable in the number of attractions and types of agents, while also being scale invariant in number of agents of each type.

Acknowledgements This research is supported by the Singapore National Research Foundation under its International Research Centre @ Singapore Funding Initiative and administered by the IDM Programme Office, Media Development Authority (MDA).

REFERENCES

[1] C. Archetti, A. Hertz, and M. G. Speranza. Metaheuristics for the team orienteering problem. *Journal of Heuristics*, 13(1):49–76, 2007.

[2] G. W. Brown. Iterative solution of games by fictitious play. *Activity Analysis of Production and Allocation*, 13(1):374–376, 1951.

[3] A. Fabrikant, C. Papadimitriou, and K. Talwar. The complexity of pure nash equilibria. In *Proc. of STOC*, 2004.

[4] T. L. Friesz, D. Bernstein, T. E. Smith, R. L. Tobin, and B. W. Wie. A variational inequality formulation of the dynamic network user equilibrium problem. *Operations Research*, 41(1):179–191, 1993.

[5] B. L. Golden, L. Levy, and R. Vohra. The orienteering problem. *Naval Research Logistics (NRL)*, 34(3):307–318, 1987.

[6] L. Ke, C. Archetti, and Z. Feng. Ants can solve the team orienteering problem. *Computers & Industrial Engineering*, 54(3):648–665, 2008.

[7] K. Kollias and T. Roughgarden. Restoring pure equilibria to weighted congestion games. In *Proceedings of the 38th international conference on Automata, languages and programming - Volume Part II*, ICALP'11, pages 539–551, Berlin, Heidelberg, 2011. Springer-Verlag.

[8] I. Milchtaich. Congestion games with player-specific payoff functions. *Games and Economic Behavior*, 13:111–124, 1996.

[9] R. W. Rosenthal. A class of games possessing pure-strategy nash equilibria. *International Journal of Game Theory*, 2:65–67, 1973.

[10] T. Roughgarden and E. Tardos. How bad is selfish routing? *Journal of the ACM*, 49(2):236–259, Mar. 2002.

[11] W. Souffriau, P. Vansteenwegen, G. Vanden Berghe, and D. Van Oudheusden. A path relinking approach for the team orienteering problem. *Computers & Operations Research*, 37(11):1853–1859, 2010.

[12] G. N. T. Leventhal and L. Trotter. A column generation algorithm for optimal traffic assignment. *Transportation Science*, 7(2):168–176, 1973.

[13] T. Tsiligirides. Heuristic methods applied to orienteering. *The Journal of the Operational Research Society*, 35(9):797–809, 1984.

[14] P. Vansteenwegen, W. Souffriau, G. V. Berghe, and D. V. Oudheusden. A guided local search metaheuristic for the team orienteering problem. *European Journal of Operational Research*, 196(1):118–127, 2009.

[15] P. Vansteenwegen, W. Souffriau, and D. V. Oudheusden. The orienteering problem: A survey. *European Journal of Operational Research*, 209(1):1 – 10, 2011.

[16] J. G. Wardrop and J. I. Whitehead. Correspondence. some theoretical aspects of road traffic research. *ICE Proceedings: Engineering Divisions*, 1, 1952.

Coordinating Measurements for Air Pollution Monitoring in Participatory Sensing Settings

Alexandros Zenonos, Sebastian Stein and Nicholas R. Jennings
Electronics and Computer Science
University of Southampton, UK
{az2g13,ss2,nrj}@ecs.soton.ac.uk

ABSTRACT

Environmental monitoring is important, as it allows authorities to understand the impact of potentially harmful environmental phenomena, such as air pollution, noise or temperature, on public health. To achieve this effectively, participatory sensing is a promising paradigm for large-scale data collection. In this approach, ordinary citizens (non-expert contributors) collect environmental data using low-cost mobile devices. However, these participants are generally self-interested agents having their own goals and making local decisions about where and when to take measurements, if any at all. This can lead to a highly inefficient outcome, where observations are either taken redundantly or do not provide sufficient information about key areas of interest. To address these challenges, a coordination system is necessary to guide and to coordinate participants. This paper proposes such a participatory sensing framework and presents a novel algorithm based on entropy and mutual information criteria, called Local Greedy Search (LGS), that takes into consideration knowledge about human mobility patterns and the inconvenience cost that is incurred by taking measurements. In particular, the algorithm uses a local search technique to map participants to measurements that need to be taken. We empirically evaluate our algorithm on real-world human mobility and air quality data and show that our coordination algorithm outperforms the state-of-the-art greedy and myopic algorithms. In particular, LGS gains 33.4% more information than the best benchmark in realistic city-scale scenarios with hundreds of agents.

Categories and Subject Descriptors

I.2.8 [**Problem Solving, Control Methods, and Search**]: Heuristic Methods; I.2.11 [**Distributed Artificial Intelligence**]: Coherence and Coordination; Intelligent Agents

General Terms

Algorithms, Experimentation, Measurement, Performance, Theory

Appears in: *Proceedings of the 14th International Conference on Autonomous Agents and Multiagent Systems (AAMAS 2015), Bordini, Elkind, Weiss, Yolum (eds.), May 4–8, 2015, Istanbul, Turkey.*

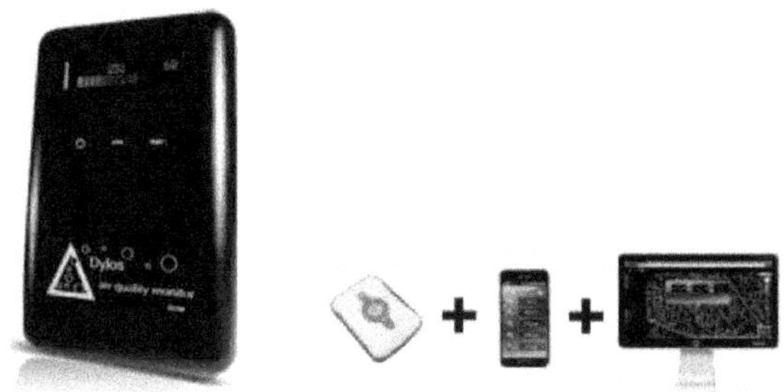

(a) (b)

Figure 1: Examples of portable devices that measure air quality in terms of atmospheric particulate matter (PM).

Keywords

Participatory Sensing; Collective Intelligence; Coordination; Gaussian Processes; Emissions; Air Quality; Teamwork; Human Mobility; Approximation Algorithms; Dynamic Environments

1. INTRODUCTION

Applications involving the placement of sensors for monitoring environmental phenomena, especially air pollution, are receiving considerable attention [5, 12], as it is a subject that concerns many, from environmental organisations to policy-makers and the general public. Air pollution is responsible for a range of heart-related diseases and leads to approximately 7 million annual deaths[1]. Given this, understanding the situation and predicting how it is going to change, in the long term as well as on a daily or even hourly basis, i.e., achieving *situational awareness*, is crucial in allowing decision makers to take action. For example, in terms of urban planning, city councils can make decisions about where to build parks and plant trees to minimize the effect of high pollution areas in cities. They can also make planning decisions about new roads so as to handle traffic efficiently based on air pollution measurements. Furthermore, it can help doctors link environmental factors with symptoms and thus affect potential patients' treatment [1].

At present, the problem of monitoring air pollution is mainly tackled with networks of static stations. These are funded and operated by government authorities collecting measurements on a continuous basis, and they are controlled by a number of experts. These stations are very costly to

[1] `http://www.who.int/mediacentre/news/releases/2014/air-pollution/en/`

acquire and maintain, resulting in the collection of limited information [5].

However, another way to monitor environmental phenomena is to exploit participatory sensing, which is a promising paradigm for data collection [1]. Instead of making use of expensive equipment and employing a number of experts to work for hours to collect data, the burden is divided between a higher number of individuals (not necessarily experts), carrying cheap sensor devices, such as mobile phones and 'Senspod'[2], 'Sensordrone'[3] or 'Dylos'[4] as shown in Figure 1. This paradigm enables the public to gather and share local knowledge. The benefits of this approach are firstly that it is cheaper than the traditional approach of using static stations. Secondly, static sensors are located away from streets and emission sources in order to reflect the average pollution over an area [5]. Consequently, it might underestimate the true exposure of people to air pollution. Participatory sensing alleviates this by enabling people to directly make measurements at the sources of air pollution.

While delivering impressive results [3, 15], existing participatory campaigns lack an important element. They do not provide a coordination system that can efficiently guide or suggest to participants where and when to take measurements in order to fill coverage gaps throughout time in the area of interest, exploiting in this way the 'collective intelligence' of the crowd. This is a major problem because some areas remain unexplored, which leads to a false or partial picture of the situation over the entire environment that the campaign initiator is interested in. Also, people may provide redundant information by taking measurements at the same time and place, which can waste participants' effort as well as communication and processing resources.

However, people participate in environmental campaigns either for their own personal/social interest, or for monetary incentives [4]. Crucially, it cannot be assumed that participants can provide an unlimited number of measurements for free as they cannot be seen as robotic entities that behave exactly as instructed. Instead, they act as self-interested agents having their own personal goals and limited information about the environment. Thus, in order to take measurements they typically incur inconvenience costs or even require financial compensation. In our work, we capture this by assuming a cost, different for each agent, for taking measurements. Moreover, humans are typically predictable in terms of their mobility habits [8]. So, even though knowledge about their daily routines could be available, no participatory sensing platform exploits it to suggest to individuals where to take measurements based on their future location.

Most current coordination mechanisms are computationally intensive and do not apply in participatory sensing as they focus on finding informative paths for autonomous agents and do not consider the mobility patterns of agents nor the cost of taking a measurement [13]. Some coordination approaches focus on decentralised approximations and deal with communication limitations [14], which is not a concern in this work because participants do not need to communicate with each other. Recent work [2], uses mobility patterns to coordinate agents in a different problem domain. The focus of that paper is assigning agents to tasks based on their mobility patterns, so as to maximize the payoff of the tasks within a given time limit. However, no cost is associated with each agent to correspond to the inconvenience or the incentive needed to execute the task and tasks are completely independent from each other. Furthermore, once executed, they are no longer available, which is not the case when monitoring environmental phenomena.

In this paper, we address these shortcomings by proposing a complete participatory sensing framework which includes a novel algorithm that decides who should take measurements where and when, in order to achieve better situational awareness for a specified time period, while at the same time taking into consideration the cost of doing so. The algorithm is also able to incorporate knowledge available about human mobility patterns. Our algorithm uses local search and a greedy approach, extending them to trade off utility for speed, in order to make our approach feasible in city-scale scenarios. In more detail, the contributions of this paper are:

- We define the problem of coordinating measurements for participatory sensing applications and propose a framework for building participatory sensing applications for environmental monitoring.
- We develop a novel local search greedy algorithm that is the first to incorporate human mobility patterns to make decisions about who should take a measurement, when they should take it and where, so that more information about the area of interest is learned while balancing this with the cost of taking the measurements.
- We empirically evaluate our algorithm on real human mobility pattern data and real air quality sensor data and show that it is 33.4% better in terms of total utility gained than the state-of-the-art greedy algorithm. We also demonstrate the generality of our approach by evaluating our algorithm on different environments by varying the dynamism of the observed phenomenon and showing that it is consistently better than the benchmarks in all scenarios.

The remainder of this paper is organised as follows: In Section 2 we introduce our framework. In Section 3 we formally define the problem. In Section 4 we introduce the technical details of the Gaussian process model we use. In Section 5 we detail our algorithm. In Section 6 we empirically evaluate it and present our experimental results, and finally we conclude in Section 7.

2. PARTICIPATORY SENSING FRAMEWORK

Our framework is designed to provide a platform for participatory sensing campaigns in order to efficiently monitor an environment while taking into consideration knowledge available about the participants. In particular our framework consists of four components: (a) the main component is the coordination algorithm, which is the main contribution of this work, (b) the human mobility patterns component, which is a system for making predictions about the mobility patterns of the participants, (c) the cost component, which captures the cost incurred by each participant for taking

[2]http://v2.sensaris.com/products/
[3]http://sensorcon.com/products/sensordrone-multisensor-tool
[4]http://www.dylosproducts.com/

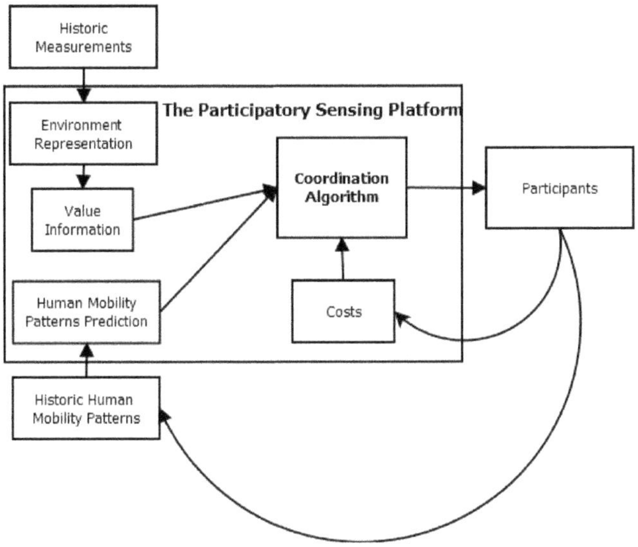

Figure 2: A conceptual architecture of the coordination system

measurements and (d) the environmental phenomenon component, which supplies the system with information about the environment being monitored, given past measurements. Figure 2 shows the overall architecture of the participatory sensing framework and illustrates how each component interacts with each other.

Anyone willing to take part in the campaign would own or be provided with a smartphone with Internet connectivity and specialised equipment, depending on the phenomenon and environment to be monitored. The participatory sensing platform is responsible for contacting the participants over the Internet in advance in order to inform them about the measurements they need to take.

The participants are in a feedback loop, where they provide the platform with their mobility patterns and cost value. Specifically, intelligent agents on participants' devices can monitor their behaviour and provide the platform with the mobility patterns. Also, each participant is associated with a cost of taking measurements per timestep, which can be given directly by participants or learned from their participation in previous campaigns with the assistance of the intelligent agents.

A mobility pattern prediction system infers their future mobility patterns for a specific time horizon producing a number of possible routines according to a probability distribution. Also, the cost of each participant at each time is associated with uncertainty since some participants might be more predictable than others in terms of their willingness to take specific measurements. The coordination algorithm suggests to participants where and when to take measurements, in order to efficiently monitor the environment for a time period. In this paper, we do not focus on a complete implementation of the aforementioned framework but rather focus on the algorithmic challenge of developing an efficient coordination algorithm that exploits knowledge about participants' mobility patterns as well as the cost for taking measurements. Specifically, due to the regularities that human mobility patterns exhibit [8], we assume that only a single routine is predicted for each agent for a specific period of time. Therefore, the full probabilistic treatment of mobility patterns is left for future work. Also, for simplicity but without violating the underpinning idea of the framework we assume deterministic cost to each agent, leaving the uncertainty about costs for future work.

3. THE COORDINATION PROBLEM

This section formally introduces the problem that the coordination algorithm needs to solve. Let a participatory sensing campaign be a collection of observations[5] $\mathbf{O}$ constrained on geography, duration, context and users such that $\mathbf{O}$ is collected participatively by a set of agents $\mathbf{A}$. An environment is denoted by a tuple $\mathcal{E} = (\mathbf{A}, L, T)$, which consists of: a set of agents $\mathbf{A}= \{\mathcal{A}_1, \dots, \mathcal{A}_M\}$, a set of spatial coordinates $L = \{l_1, \dots, l_N\}$ where measurements can be taken, and a discrete set of temporal coordinates $T = \{1, 2, 3, \dots E\}$ that specify when a measurement can be taken, where E is the end of the campaign.

In order to define the problem of coordinating agents to monitor an environment $\mathcal{E}$ we must firstly define the following:

Definition 1. A set of spatio-temporal observation coordinates $O = (L \cup \{\perp\}) \times T$.

An element $o \in O$ is called an observation. The observation made by $\mathcal{A}_i$ at time t is denoted by $o_{i,t}$. The set of observations made by all agents at, or before, time t is denoted as $\mathbf{O}_t \subseteq O$. The set of observations made by all agents at time t is denoted as $O_t \subseteq \mathbf{O}_t$. If no observations at a time step are made by an agent i, we record a null observation $o_{i,t} = (\perp, t)$.

Each location $l \in L$ and time $t \in T$ is associated with a random variable $X_{l,t}$ which describes the environmental phenomenon. We use $X_{l,t} = x_{l,t}$ to refer to the realisation of that variable for specific spatio-temporal coordinates. When an observation is made at some spatio-temporal coordinate, the realisation $x_{l,t}$ becomes known. All observations made are associated with a utility value as follows:

Definition 2. A utility function $u : 2^O \to \mathbb{R}^+$, assigns a utility value to a set of observations.

The real value assigned by the utility function is based on the entropy given by the Bayesian D-optimality criterion [6]. This is a criterion similar to mutual information described in the aforementioned work, but since we are interested in dynamic environments rather than static ones, we take into consideration all the locations at all timesteps instead of predicting the values only at unobserved locations. The D-optimality criterion, in the context of environmental monitoring, measures the reduction of entropy at all locations L within the environment by making a set of observations O_t. In other words, this criterion provides the mutual information between observation sets $\mathbf{O}_{t-1}$, which represents the observations made until the previous timestep, and O_t, which represents the observations made at the current timestep. Intuitively, it is proportional to the uncertainty without making any observations minus the uncertainty when making those observations. This will result in a number of values, one for each spatial location $l_1, \dots, l_N$, representing the information gained at those coordinates by making the aforementioned observations. In particular, we use $X_{L,t|\mathbf{O}_{t-1}}$ to describe the belief at time t about the random variable over

[5]Observations and measurements are used interchangeably.

the set of all locations, given that the agents made certain observations in the past $\mathbf{O}_{t-1}$. We also denote by $X_{L,t|O_t}$ the belief at time t at all the locations given that a set of observations has actually been made at time t. For simplicity in the notation, and unless stated otherwise we use $X_y = X_{L,t|\mathbf{O}_{t-1}}$ and $X_A = X_{L,t|O_t}$. Therefore, realised measurements over all locations given a set of observations can be expressed as $X_A = x_A$. The D-optimality criterion is given by:

$$I_l(X_y; X_A) = H_l(X_y) - H_l(X_y|X_A) \tag{1}$$

where $H_l(X_y)$ is a scalar representing the entropy at a specific location of the environment taking into consideration the set of observations made in the past, and $H_l(X_y|X_A)$ is a scalar representing the entropy at a specific location of the environment given that observations are made at time t. Finally, the utility for a set of observations made at time t, can be expressed as follows:

$$u(O_t) = \sum_{l=l_1}^{l_N} I_l(X_y; X_A) \tag{2}$$

where $u(O_t)$ is the summation of the mutual information from all the locations. This results in a single utility value for all the locations. However, by making an observation users incur a cost, which can be defined in terms of our model as follows:

Definition 3. A cost function $c_i : O \rightarrow \mathbb{R}^+$ assigns a cost to each agent for making an observation at a particular location.

So, asking an agent i to take an observation at location l and time t incurs a cost $c_i(l,t)$. This could represent the inconvenience incurred by users when making the observation, the financial compensation that is offered or the distance users have to travel to make that observation. We also define the cost function for an agent i that makes no observation at time t to be $c_i(\perp, t) = 0$. We denote by $\mathbb{U}$ the total utility earned by all the agents at time t which is given by:

$$\mathbb{U}(O_t) = \left(u(O_t) - \sum_{i=1}^{M} c_i(l,t)\right) \tag{3}$$

where M is the total number of agents in the campaign. Since users are never asked to deviate from their routes in our problem, we simplify the cost notation to $c_i(t)$. The utility earned so far up to time t from all the agents can be expressed as:

$$\mathbb{U}(\mathbf{O}_t) = \sum_{j=1}^{t} \mathbb{U}(O_j) = \sum_{j=1}^{t} \left[u(O_j) - \sum_{i=1}^{M} c_i(j)\right] \tag{4}$$

Given this nomenclature, the optimisation problem can be described as follows: at a set of spatio-temporal coordinates $W \subseteq L \times T$, we ask a set of agents $\mathbf{A}$ to take observations that maximize the difference between the utility and the cost functions $\mathbb{U}(\mathbf{O}_E)$ throughout the campaign. Concretely, we are looking for a mapping $s : \mathbf{A} \times T \rightarrow (L \cup \{\perp\})$ that is a total function and determines which agents should make which observations to reach an optimal solution to the problem. Formally,

$$S^* = arg\, max_s\, \mathbb{U}(\mathbf{O}_E) \tag{5}$$

Note that the mapping s gives us the set of observations $\mathbf{O}_E$, which is the union of all the observations taken from all the agents. Thus, a solution to this problem is a policy S^* that associates a number of agents participating in the campaign with a number of observations taken from each one of them. In order to apply this problem in practice a model of the environment is needed that our utility function will be based on. Concretely, a mathematical way of expressing the utility defined is needed. Gaussian processes provide a straightforward relationship between the D-optimality criterion and predictive variance, as described next.

4. MODELLING THE PHENOMENON

As shown in [6], we can assume that the measurements of an environmental phenomenon, i.e., air pollution measurements ($\mathbf{O}_E$), have a multivariate Gaussian joint distribution over all the locations and timesteps where a measurement is taken. It is an effective way of capturing the relationship of different spatio-temporal coordinates with respect to an environmental phenomenon. Since we are interested in the air pollution values over the entire environment (L) for a time period and not just on the locations where measurements are taken, we make use of a regression technique to do so. In particular, we use Gaussian processes (GPs), which are a class of nonparametric probabilistic models and can generalise the multivariate Gaussians to an infinite number of random variables and thus generalise over the entire set of locations (L) and timesteps (T)[10]. The main advantages of GPs are that they can capture structural correlations of a spatio-temporal phenomenon as well as provide a value of certainty on the predictions, i.e., predictive uncertainty. Crucially, it is sufficient to know the locations of the observations but not the actual value of the measurement, to get the variance over the environment. The GP can be fully specified by its mean function $m(\mathbf{x})$ and a covariance function (also referred to as kernel) $k(\mathbf{x},\mathbf{x}')$. It can be viewed as a distribution over functions, where every random variable represents a value of a function f at a specific point. Formally,

$$f(\mathbf{x}) \sim \mathcal{GP}(m(\mathbf{x}), k(\mathbf{x},\mathbf{x}')) \tag{6}$$

For simplicity in notation we denote the mean vector of some set of random variables X_A as μ_A. Suppose that a column vector x_A of realised measurements is available. The GP can then exploit these observations to make predictions for any location as well as provide their corresponding predictive uncertainty. The distribution of X_y, given these observations, is Gaussian with mean $\mu_{y|A}$ and variance $\Sigma_{y|A}$ which are given by:

$$\begin{aligned} \mu_{y|A} &= \mu_y + \Sigma_{yA}\Sigma_{AA}^{-1}(x_A - \mu_A) \\ \Sigma_{y|A} &= \Sigma_{yy} - \Sigma_{yA}\Sigma_{AA}^{-1}\Sigma_{Ay} \end{aligned} \tag{7}$$

There is a lot of discussion around which kernel to use for each problem. Admittedly, air pollution could be modelled using a composite non-stationary covariance function taking into consideration the atmospheric diffusion and the change of smoothness of the function depending on the location. However, in order to preserve time efficiency a common choice of covariance function is Matérn [5, 9]:

$$k(\mathbf{x},\mathbf{x}') = \sigma_f^2(1 + \sqrt{3}r)\exp(-\sqrt{3}r) + \sigma_n^2\delta_{\mathbf{x},\mathbf{x}'} \tag{8}$$

where $r = \sqrt{(\mathbf{x}-\mathbf{x}')^T\mathbf{P}^{-1}(\mathbf{x}-\mathbf{x}')}$, $\mathbf{P} = \begin{bmatrix} l_1 & 0 & 0 \\ 0 & l_2 & 0 \\ 0 & 0 & l_3 \end{bmatrix}$ and $\theta = \{l_1, l_2, l_3, \sigma_f^2, \sigma_n^2\}$ are the hyperparameters (parameters of the covariance function) that need to be learned. Specifically, l_1 is the length-scale that controls the smoothness of the regression function over the x-axis, l_2 over y-axis, l_3 over time[6]. Intuitively, (l_1, l_2, l_3) capture the dynamism of the phenomenon in both the spatial and the temporal dimension. Also, σ_f^2 is the signal variance that controls the uncertainty about predictions made further away from the observed points, σ_n^2 is the noise variance that controls the percentage of the data variation that can be attributed to noise, and $\delta_{\mathbf{x},\mathbf{x}'}$ is the Kronecker delta defined as follows:

$$\delta_{xx'} = \begin{cases} 1, & \text{if } \mathbf{x} = \mathbf{x}', \\ 0, & \text{if } \mathbf{x} \neq \mathbf{x}' \end{cases} \tag{9}$$

This approach enables the GP to be updated both with the spatial aspect, as well as the temporal aspect of the phenomenon. In our work, hyperparameters are assumed to be initially unknown, but we exploit historic data provided from a number of static air pollution stations [16] to train the model. In particular, in order to learn the hyperparameters we use maximum likelihood estimation (MLE). That is finding the parameters θ that maximize the log marginal likelihood (ML) $\log p(x_A|\theta) =$

$$-\frac{1}{2}(x_A-\mu_A)^T\Sigma_{AA}^{-1}(x_A-\mu_A) - \frac{1}{2}\log|\Sigma_{AA}| - \frac{n}{2}\log 2\pi \tag{10}$$

In terms of Gaussian processes, the conditional entropy of a random variable X_y given a set of variables X_A is expressed as follows:

$$\begin{aligned} H(X_y|X_A) &= \frac{1}{2}\log(2\pi e\sigma^2_{X_y|X_A}) \\ H(X_y|X_A) &= \frac{1}{2}\log(\sigma^2_{X_y|X_A}) + \frac{1}{2}(\log(2\pi)+1) \end{aligned} \tag{11}$$

Using a GP to model the environment, we develop an algorithm to exploit predictive uncertainty and the information metric designed.

5. GREEDY LOCAL SEARCH ALGORITHM

Finding an optimal solution to this particular problem is computationally infeasible, especially when large geographic areas are monitored for a number of days with hundreds of agents. This is because this category of optimisation problems is known to be NP-hard [6]. Thus, in this work, we concentrate on heuristic methods and in particular local search and greedy approach. In this section, we describe our algorithm in detail.

5.1 Algorithm Design

For each timestep all agents are assigned a binary value. This value indicates whether or not the specific individual should take a measurement at that specific time. In this paper, we assume knowledge of the mobility patterns of the participants in order to efficiently plan ahead in terms of where and when to take measurements. This is feasible as shown in [8, 7] by analysing the historic movements of participants. In our work, we can only ask someone to take a measurement if we know their exact location at that point in time. So, each agent has either a single GPS location at any point or no information is available at all[7]. Also, given that it is sufficient to know the locations of the observations, but not the actual value of the measurement, to get the variance over the environment, we are able to construct policies of people taking measurements at different locations and times in an offline manner. Thus, a policy can be represented by a binary matrix where each row represents a timestep (T) and each column an agent ($\mathcal{A}_i$). The null policy, which is the policy where nobody takes any measurements, is represented by the zero matrix.

The algorithm uses a local search technique to reach a local maximum [11]. The idea is to find the best state among a set of possible states according to the objective function defined. Generally, the way local search achieves finding the best state is by starting at a state, say the zero matrix, and move to another candidate solution by applying local changes, i.e., move to a neighbour of that state as defined in the context of each particular problem, say adding a bit in different positions of the matrix at a time, until an acceptance criterion is met. Given this brief introduction to the local search technique, we will, both formally (Algorithm 1) and intuitively, describe the algorithm developed.

The algorithm initially starts with no measurements at all. So, initially a zero matrix is created (line 2). At this point, the utility is known to be zero by definition. Next, the algorithm checks what the total utility would be by adding a single measurement to the matrix, i.e., setting that position in the matrix to 1 based on the utility function defined in Equation 4. In this way, a subset p of possible measurements, other than cases where agents are known to be unavailable, are checked one by one (lines 6). This enables the algorithm to look ahead in time and check what the utility will be if a measurement is taken in the future. The fact that only a subset is checked reduces the overall runtime of the algorithm. If the utility of any of the produced matrices (line 23) is greater than the utility of the zero matrix (line 25), then the matrix resulting in the highest utility is selected (line 28). If the utility of the zero matrix is higher, then the algorithm stops (line 26)[8]. In the same fashion, assuming that the zero matrix does not produce a higher utility than any of the newly produced matrices, the algorithm keeps the best configuration so far (line 28), and attempts to add another measurement to the matrix (line 10), and again all possible positions, but the one already selected, are evaluated (line 6). However, it is possible to evaluate another policy (line 8) by removing one measurement previously selected, and thus backtracking to a previous iteration. This will enable the algorithm to avoid local maxima. The algorithm works greedily, in the sense that it starts by considering the null policy, and when a measurement is chosen it cannot be altered unless a very bad choice is made. For example, if a measurement at the last position of the matrix produces the best result in the first iteration, it is set to one and it cannot be changed back to zero in later iterations unless removing a single observation from a previous matrix results in better utility. This approach limits the number of policies that are evaluated and thus leads to a faster runtime. The procedure continues until no further increase in the utility can be gained.

We have $2^{(M \cdot E)}$ possible combinations since we have an independent option for whether or not to take a measure-

[6]Note that l_1, l_2, l_3 may also be used in the context of problem description denoting locations 1, 2, 3 of L.

[7]When no information is available for an agent at a specific timestep, the value is automatically set to 0 which means no measurement should be taken.

[8]It might be the case that any single observation at any timestep is very costly compared to the utility gained.

Algorithm 1 Local Greedy Search Algorithm (LGS)

input: E (timesteps), A (agents)
Initialise $M = |A|$, $maxU' = 0$, $S^* \leftarrow null\ matrix(E, M)$, $obsList = null$
for $k = 1\ to\ (M \cdot E)$ **do**
  $z \leftarrow null\ positions\ of\ S^*$, $newobs = S^*$
  $p \subset z$, $sz \leftarrow |p|$
  for $l = 1\ to\ sz + 1$ **do**
    if $l = sz + 1$ **then**
      Change $obsList(k - 2)$ to 0 in $newobs$ matrix
    else
      Change l^{th} zero bit to 1 in $newobs$ matrix
    end if
    Set $C = 0$
    for $i = 1\ to\ E$ **do**
      for $j = 1\ to\ M$ **do**
        if $newobs(i, j) = 1$ **then**
          $C \leftarrow c_j(i) + C$ {calculate the cost for each agent and add it to the total cost}
        end if
      end for
      $\mathbb{U}(O_i) \leftarrow [u(O_i) - C]$ {calculate the total utility given what observations are made}
    end for
    $s_l \leftarrow \mathbb{U}(\mathbf{O}_E)$
  end for
  Keep the maximum $\mathbb{U}(\mathbf{O}_E)$ of s_l in $maxU$ variable
  Add/Remove observation from $obsList$
  if $maxU < maxU'$ **then**
    return: S^*
  else
    Set S^* to be the best configuration
  end if
  $maxU' \leftarrow maxU$
end for
return: S^*

ment by an agent at any timestep. However, since our algorithm is greedy, its runtime is polynomial in the number of agents and timesteps. Specifically, it will run for a maximum of $(M \cdot E)$ iterations and at each one of them compute $(M \cdot E) - l'$ policies, assuming that $(|p| = |z|)$, where M is the number of agents, E the duration of the campaign and l' is the number of observations already chosen. Initially, $l' = 0$. The total number of iterations can be expressed as follows:

$$\frac{M \cdot E(M \cdot E + 1)}{2} \tag{12}$$

6. EMPIRICAL EVALUATION

In this section, we will evaluate the algorithm developed in the previous section in different participatory sensing scenarios. In the first part of the empirical evaluation we present the benchmarks our algorithm is contrasted with. Next, we state our hypotheses and describe the experiments performed. Finally, we present and analyze our findings.

6.1 Benchmarks

The algorithm developed is benchmarked against six algorithms which are described below:

- **Greedy**: This algorithm checks which measurements should be taken in order to maximize the utility at each timestep, i.e., maximize $\mathbb{U}(O_1), \mathbb{U}(O_2), \cdots, \mathbb{U}(O_E)$ sequentially. It does so in a greedy way, i.e., select the single observation among the number of agents that maximizes the utility but only at a specific timestep, instead of looking ahead as in LGS, and then the next best observation until no further improvement can be achieved for that timestep. The final policy produced, S^*, is the concatenation of the outcome of each timestep. The Greedy algorithm is the simplest approximation algorithm and it is used in determining where to place sensors in static environments [6].
- **Patrol**: This algorithm assumes that measurements are taken at each timestep by all agents no matter the cost. It is an algorithm that replicates the behavior of mobile sensors, i.e., patrolling an area in order to monitor environmental phenomena as in the work of [14].
- **Myopic Optimal (MyopicOpt)**: This algorithm makes decisions myopically, i.e., considers only the current timestep, but it computes all the possible combinations of agents making an observation for a particular timestep thus, finding the optimal assignment of agents to observations that maximize utility $\mathbb{U}(O_t)$ for that timestep. Like Greedy, it produces a policy S^* that is the concatenation of the outcome of each timestep.
- **Random**: This algorithm assumes that measurements are made randomly by agents throughout time. It is an algorithm that creates a policy that could have potentially been created by participants making local decisions, i.e., without coordination, in environmental monitoring campaigns.
- **Random100**: This algorithm runs 100 random policies S^* and selects the best one of those.
- **Optimal (Brute Force)**: This algorithm produces the optimal policy S^* for coordinating measurements by evaluating all the possible combinations of those. This is only feasible to do in small-scale scenarios.

6.2 Experimental Hypotheses

Given the benchmarks above, we formulate the following experimental hypotheses:

- *Hypothesis 1:* The total utility earned by the LGS algorithm will consistently be higher than that of the Greedy, Patrol, Random100 and Random algorithms, irrespective of the number of agents participating.

  Outperforming Greedy is a result of the fact that LGS looks ahead in time and thus is able to select measurements that should increase the total utility earned by the end of the campaign. Outperforming the rest is caused by the fact that the Patrol and Random algorithms ignore the costs of taking measurements and thus taking a measurement at every time-step or randomly results in a suboptimal behaviour.
- *Hypothesis 2:* LGS will be faster than the optimal.

This is due to the fact that the optimal policy is found by evaluating all possible coordination policies, which is exponential in terms of the number of the participants and the timesteps of the campaign.

- *Hypothesis 3:* The total utility earned by the LGS algorithm will be higher than Greedy, MyopicOpt, Patrol, Random100 and Random in all scenarios of varying dynamism.

  This is because LGS aims at increasing the total utility by computing policies irrespective of the phenomenon. Even though Greedy and MyopicOpt are expected to perform better as the phenomenon becomes more dynamic, i.e., the phenomenon is almost independent at each timestep, LGS will still outperform them, because it is able to greedily add measurements in a similar way but at the same time look ahead and thus make decisions that lead to a higher utility over time.

6.3 Experimental Setup

In order to empirically evaluate our algorithm, we compare its performance against the six algorithms described above. In particular, we focus on air quality in terms of fine particulate matter (PM2.5) in Beijing, where the levels of air pollution are known to be high. Table 1 shows the air quality index for air quality in Beijing. We use an air quality dataset [16] which contains one year's (2013-2014) fine grained air quality data from static air quality monitoring stations in Beijing. We use this data to train our GP model, and in particular learn the hyperparameters. These include the dynamism of the phenomenon (l_3) and smoothness over latitude and longitude (l_1, l_2). The sensors are scattered in Beijing and take measurements every hour. Figure 3 shows the stations and the state of the environment represented by a GP for a particular timestep. Air quality exhibits spatial variations, i.e., PM2.5 is different depending on where you are in Beijing, as well as temporal variations, i.e., it is different depending on the time of the day.

Ideally, at the same time the human mobility patterns are learned using a human mobility prediction system. In this work, however, we use data from Geolife trajectories dataset [17] which contains sequences of time-stamped locations of 182 humans in Beijing over a period of 5 years (2007-2012). For our experiments, we extracted the patterns of 108 humans over a period so as to get as much overlap between collected patterns as possible. In order to test our system for more than 108 agents, we take patterns of different months from the same pool of agents' trajectories. Humans are assumed to be equipped with the necessary equipment and they are able to take measurements when necessary if their spatial coordinates are available. Our system simulates human mobility patterns by getting the location of people every hour. However, as described in the problem description, taking a measurement involves a cost which is different for each agent. The cost is randomly assigned to each agent. In addition, we assume there are peak and off-peak hours where measurements are more expensive or cheaper for all agents respectively. This way we capture the cost which would be associated with participants in a real deployment.

The next section presents our findings from two different experiments. In the first experiment we simulate a varying number of agents in a 5-day campaign and compare the utility gained from LGS, Greedy, MyopicOpt, Random and Random100. The optimal algorithm is infeasible to run in city-scale scenarios.

To make our system generally applicable, we experiment with a number of artificial environments by altering the hyperparameters, and in particular l_3, which controls the dynamism of the environment. This change shows how our algorithm will perform potentially in other cities or for phenomena with other levels of dynamism. In the second experiment we simulate a varying number of dynamism for a single day with 5 agents and compare LGS against all of the six benchmarks both in terms of utility gained as well as runtime. Experimenting with small-scale scenarios will enable us to compare our algorithm with the optimal one.

6.4 Evaluation

6.4.1 Effect of the number of agents

Figure 4 shows results of the performance of varying the number M of agents participating in the system. The dy-

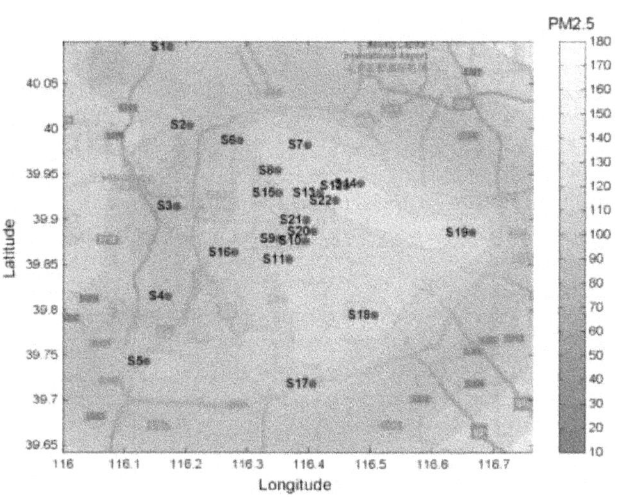

Figure 3: Air quality measurement stations in Beijing overlaid by air quality measurements predicted by GP.

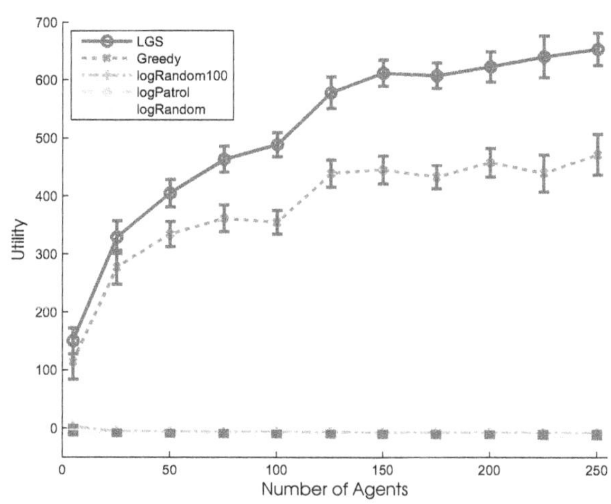

Figure 4: Total utility gained for a 5-day participatory sensing campaign. The error bars indicate the 95% confidence interval.

AQI Category	PM2.5 Level	Associated Health Impacts
0-50	Excellent	Little or no risk.
51-100	Moderate	Few hypersensitive individuals should reduce outdoor exercise.
101-150	Unhealthy for Sensitive Groups	Slight irritations may occur.
151-200	Unhealthy	Everyone may begin to experience health effects.
201-300	Very unhealthy	Healthy people will be noticeably affected.
300+	Hazardous	Healthy people will experience reduced endurance in activities.

Table 1: Air Quality Index (AQI) for air pollution (`http://airnow.gov/index.cfm?action=aqibasics.aqi`)

namism in this experiment is fixed at $l_3 = 10.6$, which was found using the MLE technique. The results confirm our first hypothesis that LGS will outperform the rest of the algorithms. We can observe that LGS is 33.4% better on average than the Greedy algorithm. This is because LGS can look ahead in time, and thus make choices that will increase the total utility by the end of the participatory sensing campaign.

6.4.2 *Effect of the dynamism of the phenomenon*

Figure 5 shows results of the performance of the algorithms when varying the time-scale (l_3) which controls the dynamism of the phenomenon. Originally, time-scale was found to be ($l_3 = 10.6$) using the MLE technique. The smaller the time-scale, the more dynamic the phenomenon is. Consequently, as time-scale approaches zero, each timestep is more independent from the other. Thus, MyopicOpt is similar to the optimal algorithm and Greedy performs near-optimally. Intuitively, the more dynamic the phenomenon is the more information is gained by taking observations consecutively (in every timestep). However, the dynamism of air pollution was at the scale of tens of hours, which make Greedy and far from optimal. The results confirm our third hypothesis as LGS is better than the rest of the algorithms in all scenarios. However, as time-scale approaches zero, LGS's performance tends to be similar to MyopicOpt and Greedy. Also, the utility gained from LGS is near the optimal one. Figure 6 shows results of the time efficiency of the algorithms when varying time-scale (l_3). LGS needs more time in dynamic environments as more measurements need to be taken and is generally slower than Greedy, MyopicOpt, Patrol and Random algorithms. However, the optimal algorithm requires a lot more time, confirming our second hypothesis. Specifically, Figure 6 includes the natural logarithms of LGS, Greedy and the optimal algorithm's runtime.

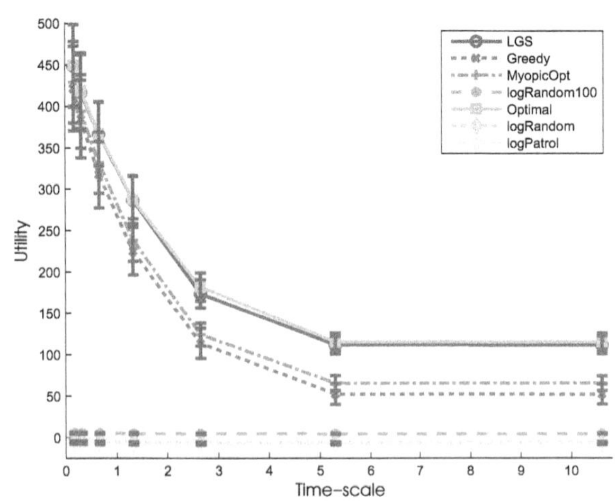

Figure 5: Total utility gained for a 1-day participatory sensing campaign. The error bars indicate the 95% confidence interval.

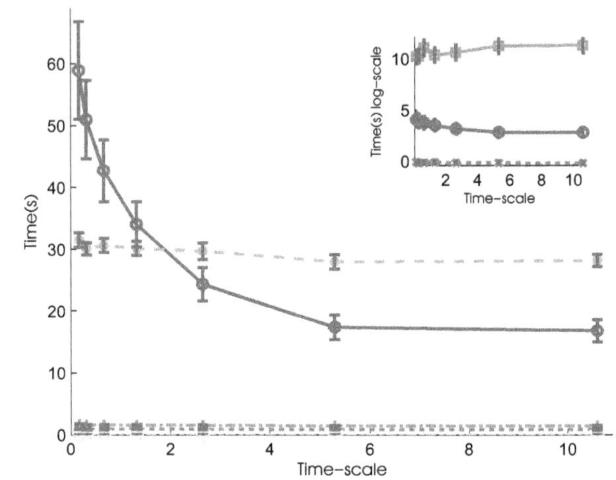

Figure 6: Average runtime for a 1-day participatory sensing campaign. The error bars indicate the 95% confidence interval.

7. CONCLUSIONS

In this paper, we introduced the problem of coordinating measurements in participatory sensing settings and developed a novel algorithm that maximizes the total utility gained over a period of time while at the same time minimizing the cost incurred by taking measurements. In particular, we demonstrate how efficient the algorithm is compared to the state-of-the-art Greedy algorithm and Brute force approach. An empirical evaluation on real data showed that (a) LGS is 33.4% better than the Greedy algorithm (b) LGS is faster than the Brute Force approach (c) dynamic environment affects the performance of LGS algorithm and the total utility gained, but still outperforms the benchmarks in all scenarios. Our future work in this area is to extend the algorithm to deal with more agents in campaigns running for a longer period of time. Also, we need to deal with the problem of having uncertainty over the human mobility patterns and inconvenience cost. Furthermore, we would like to investigate the performance of other algorithms including variations of our algorithm. Finally, conducting a real-world trial would be an interesting avenue to follow.

8. ACKNOWLEDGMENTS

This research was undertaken as part of the ORCHID project funded by EPSRC (EP/I011587/1).

REFERENCES

[1] J. Burke, D. Estrin, M. Hansen, A. Parker, N. Ramanathan, S. Reddy, and M. B. Srivastava. Participatory sensing. In *Workshop on World-Sensor-Web: Mobile Device Centric Sensor Networks and Applications*, pages 117–134, 2006.

[2] C. Chen, S.-F. Cheng, A. Gunawan, A. Misra, K. Dasgupta, and D. Chander. Traccs: Trajectory-aware coordinated urban crowd-sourcing. In *Second AAAI Conference on Human Computation & Crowdsourcing (HCOMP)*, pages 30–40, 2014.

[3] E. D'Hondt, M. Stevens, and A. Jacobs. Participatory noise mapping works! an evaluation of participatory sensing as an alternative to standard techniques for environmental monitoring. *Pervasive and Mobile Computing*, 9(5):681–694, 2013.

[4] L. Jaimes, I. Vergara-Laurens, and M. Labrador. A location-based incentive mechanism for participatory sensing systems with budget constraints. In *Pervasive Computing and Communications (PerCom), 2012 IEEE International Conference on*, pages 103–108, March 2012.

[5] A. Jutzeler, J. J. Li, and B. Faltings. A region-based model for estimating urban air pollution. In *Proceedings of the Twenty-Eighth AAAI Conference on Artificial Intelligence, July 27 -31, 2014, Québec City, Québec, Canada.*, pages 424–430, 2014.

[6] A. Krause, A. Singh, and C. Guestrin. Near-optimal sensor placements in gaussian processes: Theory, efficient algorithms and empirical studies. *J. Mach. Learn. Res.*, 9:235–284, June 2008.

[7] J. McInerney, A. Rogers, and N. R. Jennings. Learning periodic human behaviour models from sparse data for crowdsourcing aid delivery in developing countries. In *Conference on Uncertainty in Artificial Intelligence (UAI)*, pages 401–410, July 2013.

[8] J. McInerney, S. Stein, A. Rogers, and N. R. Jennings. Breaking the habit: Measuring and predicting departures from routine in individual human mobility. *Pervasive Mob. Comput.*, 9(6):808–822, Dec. 2013.

[9] R. Ouyang, K. H. Low, J. Chen, and P. Jaillet. Multi-robot active sensing of non-stationary gaussian process-based environmental phenomena. In *Proceedings of the 2014 International Conference on Autonomous Agents and Multi-agent Systems*, AAMAS '14, pages 573–580, Richland, SC, 2014. International Foundation for Autonomous Agents and Multiagent Systems.

[10] C. E. Rasmussen and C. K. I. Williams. *Gaussian Processes for Machine Learning.* The MIT Press, 2006.

[11] S. J. Russell and P. Norvig. *Artificial Intelligence: A Modern Approach.* Pearson Education, 2003.

[12] J. H. Seinfeld and S. N. Pandis. *Atmospheric chemistry and physics: from air pollution to climate change.* John Wiley & Sons, 2012.

[13] A. Singh, A. Krause, and W. J. Kaiser. Nonmyopic adaptive informative path planning for multiple robots. In *IJCAI*, pages 1843–1850, 2009.

[14] R. Stranders, E. Munoz De Cote, A. Rogers, and N. R. Jennings. Near-optimal continuous patrolling with teams of mobile information gathering agents. *Artif. Intell.*, 195:63–105, Feb. 2013.

[15] M. Whitney and H. Richter Lipford. Participatory sensing for community building. In *CHI '11 Extended Abstracts on Human Factors in Computing Systems*, CHI EA '11, pages 1321–1326, New York, NY, USA, 2011. ACM.

[16] Y. Zheng, F. Liu, and H.-P. Hsieh. U-air: When urban air quality inference meets big data. In *Proceedings of the 19th ACM SIGKDD International Conference on Knowledge Discovery and Data Mining*, KDD '13, pages 1436–1444, New York, NY, USA, 2013. ACM.

[17] Y. Zheng, L. Zhang, X. Xie, and W.-Y. Ma. Mining interesting locations and travel sequences from gps trajectories. In *Proceedings of the 18th International Conference on World Wide Web*, WWW '09, pages 791–800, New York, NY, USA, 2009. ACM.

Factored MDPs for Optimal Prosumer Decision-Making

Angelos Angelidakis
Electronic and Computer Engineering
Technical University of Crete
Greece, GR73100
aggelos@intelligence.tuc.gr

Georgios Chalkiadakis
Electronic and Computer Engineering
Technical University of Crete
Greece, GR73100
gehalk@intelligence.tuc.gr

ABSTRACT

Tackling the decision-making problem faced by a prosumer (i.e., a producer that is simultaneously a consumer) when selling and buying energy in the emerging smart electricity grid, is of utmost importance for the economic profitability of such a business entity. In this paper, we model, for the first time, this problem as a factored Markov Decision Process. By so doing, we are able to represent the problem compactly, and provide an exact optimal solution via dynamic programming—notwithstanding its large size. Our model successfully captures the main aspects of the business decisions of a prosumer corresponding to a community microgrid of *any* size. Moreover, it includes appropriate sub-models for prosumer production and consumption prediction. Experimental simulations verify the effectiveness of our approach; and show that our exact value iteration solution matches that of a state-of-the-art method for stochastic planning in very large environments, while outperforming it in terms of computation time.

Categories and Subject Descriptors

I.2.11 [**Distributed Artificial Intelligence**]: Multiagent Systems

General Terms

Algorithms, Experimentation

Keywords

energy; smart grid; factored MDPs; decision-making

1. INTRODUCTION

In recent years, the term *prosumer* has been coined in order to describe an entity that both produces and consumes energy, implying that prosumers possess the ability to play a key role to the stabilization of the electricity network [4, 20]. As such, and assuming prosumers are able to adjust their behaviour according to dynamic indicators, their smooth integration into the shaping *Smart Grid* is of critical importance [22]. Viewed as a business entity, a prosumer could correspond to a single residence, a specific industry, or to whole neighborhoods of houses that are served by a dedicated microgrid—which may or may not be connected to the rest of the electricity Grid. Our focus of attention in this paper will be optimizing the business decisions of a micro grid-corresponding prosumer, producing electricity from (mainly) renewable energy resources, and which has the option of buying and selling energy from utility companies residing in the larger electricity Grid. Paradigms of such community-oriented and renewable energy-relying microgrids are expected to be commonplace in the near future [4]. Naturally, the viability (economic and otherwise) of such an entity is tightly connected to the quality of its business decisions: i.e., whether to buy, sell, or store energy, within some decisions horizon, in order to possibly make a profit while ensuring the smooth operation of its energy-consuming units; and ensuring this viability is key to the smooth integration of prosumers into the Smart Grid.

Notwithstanding its importance, essentially no work to date has, to the best of our knowledge, attacked this specific problem heads on. By contrast, in this paper, we model, for the first time, the decision problem faced by a microgrid-prosumer planning its energy production, storage and usage strategy for the day ahead as a *factored Markov Decision Process* [7]. Our formulation enables us to provide *an exact optimal solution* (bar certain discretization-related modeling decisions) for the problem faced by a prosumer corresponding to a microgrid of essentially *any* size. In addition, we equip our consumer with specific consumption and production-predicting submodels, which provide it with the necessary input signals on which to base its decisions. As part of our work, we show that *Gaussian processes* and *Bayesian linear regression* techniques can be successfully used for consumption prediction.

Given our model, the solution to the prosumer decision problem can then be computed using standard dynamic programming techniques. In this work, we employed value iteration to this purpose. The effectiveness and efficiency of our approach is verified by comparisons to the performance of *SPUDD*, a state-of-the-art method for stochastic planning in large environments. Our value iteration method, operating over a problem horizon corresponding to 24 hours, is shown to produce policies that coincide with those produced by SPUDD [12]. However, as we explain in Section 6 of the paper, SPUDD has to operate over a state space that is artificially larger, while, at the same time, it does not possess enough structure. This creates a need to build huge input files for SPUDD to operate on, resulting to a huge pre-processing time for the algorithm. As a result, while our method can scale to larger state spaces for our problem, SPUDD cannot produce a solution in such cases within the required 24-hour timeframe.

The rest of this paper is organized as follows. Section 2 provides a brief background on factored MDPs and reviews related work; Section 3 then describes our model, while the value iteration algorithm is described in Section 4; Section 5 presents our methods for predicting the future production and consumption of the prosumer; Section 6 presents our simulation experiments; and, finally, Section 7 concludes this paper and outlines future work.

Appears in: *Proceedings of the 14th International Conference on Autonomous Agents and Multiagent Systems (AAMAS 2015), Bordini, Elkind, Weiss, Yolum (eds.), May 4–8, 2015, Istanbul, Turkey.*

2. BACKGROUND AND RELATED WORK

Factored Markov Decision Processes (FMDPs) [7] provide a *compact* alternative to standard MDP representation. Specifically, they decompose states into sets of *state variables* in order to represent the transition and model compactly—since transitions and rewards may rely on specific model aspects, corresponding to subsets of variables only. Thus, the set of states in a factored MDP representation correspond to multivariate random variables, $\boldsymbol{s} = \langle s_i \rangle$, with the s_i variables taking on values in their corresponding $DOM(s_i)$ domains. Intuitively, state variables correspond to a selection of *features* which are sufficient to describe the system state. In FMDPs, actions are also quite often described as random variables, while reward functions used are assumed to be factored into specific (usually additive) components. Furthermore, FMDP models allow for *external signals*, described by *signal variables*, affecting state variables; while *temporal Bayesian networks (TBNs)* and *influence diagrams* can be employed to represent the effects of actions on state transitions and rewards. A multitude of techniques that exploit the resulting representational structure can then be used to solve large problems, at least approximately (e.g., linear value functions, approximate linear programming, stochastic algebraic decision diagrams, and so on) [11, 7].

Stochastic Planning Using Decision Diagrams (SPUDD) [12], in particular, is a well-known algorithm for finding (near-)optimal policies in very large problems represented as factored MDPs. It is essentially a value iteration algorithm that uses algebraic decision diagrams (ADDs) [5] to represent value functions and policies, assuming an ADD input representation of the FMDP. Specifically, SPUDD operates over an input script describing the factored states and actions, and the FMDP transition model and reward function.

Now there have been a few recent papers dealing with optimal decision-making when buying and selling energy in the Smart Grid. However, most of them do not focus on prosumers. For instance, TacTex [24] was the champion agent for the 2013 Power Trading Agent Competition (PowerTAC). In PowerTAC, several self-interested, autonomous agents corresponding to *brokers* compete with each other with the goal of maximizing profits through energy trading. TacTex does not model the decision making problem of a microgrid prosumer, as we do, but that of a broker simultaneously participating in tariff and wholesale markets. As such, its utility measure is the cash amount existing in a bank, while the energy amount to buy is not considered part of the decision making problem: it is simply set to the difference between predicted demand and the energy that is already procured for the targeted time period. Moreover, there are only 26 states in the MDP solved by TacTex, and a state transition leads to one of only two potential states (by contrast, we tackle MDPs with state-action spaces encompassing hundreds of thousands of elements).

Similarly to TacTex, the work of Peters *et al.* [19] also deals with optimising the long-term behaviour of broker agents during retail electricity trading. They employ the classic SARSA reinforcement learning algorithm [23] for selecting actions in a tariff market. However, it is less flexible than TacTex's tariff market strategy, which is not constrained to a finite set of actions.

We are only aware of two papers that focus on prosumer decision-making. First, Nikovski and Zhang [17] propose a method for finding the optimal conditional operational schedule for a set of power generators, assuming stochastic electricity demand and stochastic generator output. However, in contrast to our work here, they do not tackle the problem of selling or storing the generated power. Second, Kanchev *et al.* [13] propose an energy management system which could be employed by a prosumer managing photovoltaic generators, storage units, and a gas microturbine. However, they assume a deterministic system, not accounting for uncertainty and errors that may occur during the prosumer's operation time.

3. OUR MODEL

The prosumer we consider in this work corresponds to a *microgrid* distributing power to a community. As such, it produces energy by means of *renewable energy sources*, and is responsible for the well-being of *residential consumers*. Moreover, the prosumer has access to *storage devices (batteries)*, which it can use to store energy for future use. Our prosumer is connected to the wider Grid, and it has to take decisions regarding the amounts of energy to purchase or sell to the Grid at pre-specified intervals during the next day. We assume that the Grid is represented by some utility company that can specify *tariffs* determining the sell and buy prices of electricity, to which the prosumer can subscribe (at any one of the aforementioned time intervals). The tariffs available to prosumers for the day-ahead are announced by the utility company at the beginning of each day. Then, the problem facing the prosumer is taking the right decisions as to which tariff to subscribe to and what amounts of energy to buy, sell, or store at any given interval of the day-ahead—so as to meet demand at a minimum cost and make a profit by selling the electricity to the utilities.

We acknowledge that this model formulation, presented in detail below, seemingly disregards the complexity of modern and anticipated electricity markets. Indeed, prosumers could be faced with complex decisions during their simultaneous participation in markets of various types (e.g., *spot*, *forward*, *balancing*, or even *futures*). Despite this fact, we believe that solving the simpler problem of viewing the prosumer as an entity interacting with the wider electricity Grid via pre-specified tariffs determining energy prices (which, however, can be "variable" or to an extent "real-time" themselves), is key to determining behaviour in more complex business environments. In addition, ours is a model that corresponds to conceivable situations in the immediate near future, where (largely) energy self-sufficient communities will be operating their private microgrids, and only occasionally use energy from the wider Grid—essentially as a fallback strategy.

In the rest of this section, we first describe our factored states and actions, and present certain physical constraints they have to adhere to; and we then present the transition model, and our choices for representing the reward function so that it realistically captures the gains and costs from selling and purchasing energy. Importantly, our reward function takes into account periodic operation costs of the prosumer related with subscription to a tariff, as well as its costs because of accumulating battery life losses due to discharging. Moreover, there is nothing in the formulation below that precludes the applicability of our model and proposed solution to microgrid prosumers of a particular size or type.

3.1 Factored Representation

We now describe our problem's factored representation in detail. To begin, the factored states can be described as a multivariate random variable $\boldsymbol{s} = \langle s_i \rangle$, where each variable s_i can take a value in its domain DOM(s_i). There are three factored state variables, listed in Table 1. The first one, *tms*, takes as values the specific time steps at which the prosumer is able to act. Its domain is originally set to [1 ... 24] (one time step per hour in the day). However, as we later explain, we can drop this state variable altogether from the representation, and incorporate it in the problem horizon over which our value iteration method operates; moreover, we also conduct experiments that require the prosumer to act on a half-hourly basis. The second one, *bat*, corresponds to the amount of energy available in the batteries, and its domain is [0 ... $Battery_{max}$], with

$Battery_{max}$ corresponding to the maximum capacity of the storage device(s). Note that *bat* is a naturally continuous state variable, but it was discretized in order to enable its processing by existing FMDP solvers (such as SPUDD). Finally, *tf* corresponds to the tariff the prosumer has assigned to at the moment, and its domain is the enumerated tariffs that the utility offers during the day. That is, DOM(*tf*)=$\{tf_1, \cdots, tf_i, \cdots, tf_K\}$, with K being the number of tariffs available on a specific day. Each tf_i tariff is characterized by a buying and a selling price, denoted $buying_i$ and $selling_i$ respectively, and communicated to the prosumer via external signals.[1]

Then, actions can be described as a multivariate random variable $\boldsymbol{a} = \langle a_i \rangle$ where each variable a_i affects the transition from some factored state to another, and takes a value in its domain DOM(a_i). The discretization for each DOM(a_i) is performed dynamically: it is based on the discretization of the DOM(s_i) domains, in a way that from any given state, actions can lead to any other.

There are three factored actions. First, action *buy*, which describes the amount of energy bought from the electric utility. Positive values for *buy* denote the actual buying of energy from the utility, while negative values mean the prosumer sells energy to the utility. With $Load_{max}$ being the maximum total expected residential consumption load, and the nominal power generating capacity of the renewable energy sources denoted by RES_{nom}, the domain for *buy* is set to [-RES_{nom} ... $Load_{max}$]. Second, factored action *chg*, which signifies the attempt to store an amount of energy to the batteries. Its value range is [-$Battery_{max} \dots Battery_{max}$]. Positive values represent charging the battery, and negative values represent discharging the battery. Finally, the third action, sel_{tf}, corresponds to a selection of tariff by the prosumer. Its domain is [0 ... K]. The value 0 signifies a choice to remain attached to its current tariff, while values 1 to K signify a choice to move to some other of the K tariffs available.[2]

Now, there are three types of external signals the prosumer receives. These are listed in Table 3, and can be described as multivariate random variable $\boldsymbol{sg} = \langle signal_i \rangle$ where each variable $signal_i$ can take a value in its domain DOM($signal_i$). The prosumer employs these signals to help her determine her actions. The first two, *prod* and *cons*, specify the current estimates about the production and consumption levels of the prosumer (at a specific time step). Their domains are defined given the RES_{nom} and $Load_{max}$ values introduced above. Thus, DOM(*prod*)= [0 ... RES_{nom}] , and DOM(*cons*)=[0 ... $Load_{max}$]. The third signal type, $price_{tf}$, specifies, once a day, the buy and sell prices ($buying_i$ and $selling_i$) for each one of the K tariffs, and for each t time step of the day ahead.

Notice that all factored variables in our formulation are independent of the size of the prosumer microgrid—i.e., they are not affected by the number of generators or homes populating it. Moreover, despite the complexity of the problem, the temporal dependencies among the state variables in our model are in fact quite simple, as seen in the 2-stages temporal Bayesian network (2-TBN) of Fig. 1. It can be seen there that a variable value at $t+1$ depends only on the variable's value at t (with value changes triggered, for *bat* and *tf*, by actions *chg* and sel_{tf} respectively).

[1]Notice that tariffs can be key to group together a range of consumer preferences, that would have had to be represented by distinct state or action variables otherwise. For instance, one would have wished to represent preferences to consume when buying prices are low, e.g. at night, and sell when selling prices are high—and distinct sell and buy variables would have been required to allow this. Tariffs could potentially incorporate more information, such as special discounts, and so on. Thus, the use of tariffs can be key at reducing the state-action space in such problems.

[2]The additional 'stay-with-current-tariff' action is required as subscribing and resubcribing would entail a subscription cost (thus the action protects the prosumer from that cost).

Features	Denoted	Description
time-step	*tms*	current time step within the operational day
battery	*bat*	amount of stored energy (at a specific time step)
tariff	*tf*	tariff currently in effect (at a specific time step)

Table 1: Factored states

Actions	Denoted	Description
buy	*buy*	buy from the utility
charge	*chg*	charge battery
select tariff	sel_{tf}	select a tariff to subscribe to

Table 2: Factored actions

Signals	Denoted	Description
production	*prod*	predicted levels of energy production
consumption	*cons*	predicted levels of energy consumption
$\{buying_i, selling_i\}$	$price_{tf}$	buying and selling price for tariff i

Table 3: Signal types

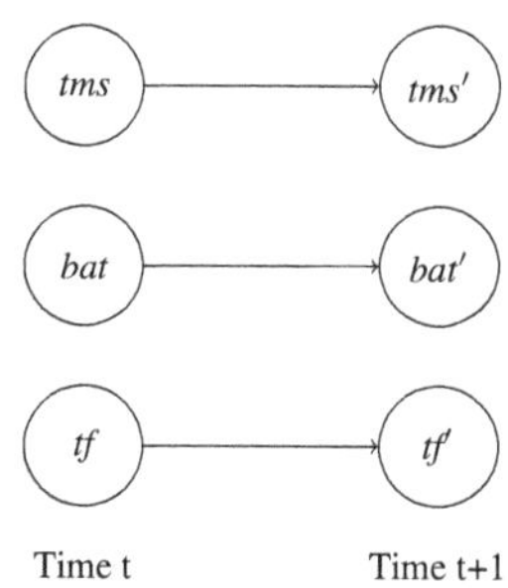

Figure 1: Temporal dependencies among state variables

In what follows, we use the notation x_t to denote the value of a state, action, or signal variable at time t.

3.2 Physical Constraints

There are certain constraints that our state and action variables must adhere to. First, in a setting involving energy exchanges, the *balance energy constraint* [14, 2] must be respected at all times. This means that, at any time step t, power produced (including that bought) should match power consumed (including that stored):

$$prod_t - cons_t - chg_t + buy_t = 0 \tag{1}$$

The second constraint refers to the storage unit(s) of the prosumer. A storage unit cannot be charged over its capacity:

$$chg_t \leq Battery_{max} - bat_t \tag{2}$$

Similarly, the energy quantity discharged from a unit cannot exceed that currently stored in the unit:

$$-chg_t \leq bat_t \tag{3}$$

Finally, for safety reasons, the battery storage level must be always kept between 20% and 100% [10]:

$$0.2 \leq bat_t / Battery_{max} \leq 1 \tag{4}$$

3.3 Transition Function

State transitions in our model will be in general stochastic, since faults may occur while taking actions like charging or discharging the storage devices and buying or selling energy to the utility. The variable *tms* is an exception to this rule—since one specific time step is always followed by the next one. That is, $Pr(tms_{t+1} = t+1|tms_t = t) = 1$. For the rest of the variables, we define certain *bounded regions* (with distinct boundaries for each variable), which include a subset of discrete factored states lying close to the factored state intended to transition to by performing a factored action taken at time t. The boundaries can be set to any values required.

Thus, (factored) actions are assumed to have the intended result with some probability p (arbitrarily set to 0.9 in our experiments); while, with probability $1-p$, they transition to some (factored) state within the bounded region (chosen uniformly at random). For instance, assuming that N *bat* states lie within a prespecified bound_{bat} bounded region, the action of charging the battery with an energy amount c at time t (action $chg_t = c$) is successful with probability p:

$$Pr(bat_{t+1} = bat_t + c \mid chg_t = c, bat_t) = p$$

whereas with probability $1-p$ it fails, leading to any potential factored battery state within the bound_{bat} region:

$$Pr(bat_{t+1} = bat \in \text{bound}_{bat} \mid chg_t = c, bat_t) = (1-p)/N$$

Since distinct factored actions can be simultaneously utilized—i.e., the prosumer can select a new tariff, buy energy, and charge the battery at the same time step t— the overall transition probability is given by Eq. 5 as follows.

$$Pr(tms_{t+1}, bat_{t+1}, tf_{t+1} | tms_t, bat_t, tf_t, chg_t, sel_{tf,t}) = Pr(bat_{t+1}|bat_t, chg_t) \cdot Pr(tf_{t+1}|tf_t, sel_{tf,t}) \quad (5)$$

given that the battery level at any time step depends on the previous battery level state and on whether a *chg* action was used, while the tariff in place is affected by a tariff selection action. Notice also that, in our model, buying or selling energy does not have a direct effect on a state variable, thus no state transitions need to be defined for action *buy*. It is thus implicitly assumed that *buy* (a positive or negative energy amount) always succeeds. This assumption is quite realistic, and it is motivated from the need to respect the constraint in Eq. 1 above: choosing how much energy to buy/sell depends on the production and consumption estimates, and on the results of charging the battery. In practice, the latter is an action whose outcome is indeed more uncertain than that of buying/selling energy.

3.4 Factored Reward Representation

The next step is to determine the reward function for our factored MDP. The reward function is associated with *(a)* either the gain from selling power to the utility or the cost of buying power in a certain price; *(b)* the running costs for being subscribed to a tariff; and *(c)* the operation costs of using the storage devices. As such, we choose to represent the reward function as a cost function with three main components. Specifically, the function describing the immediate cost for a transition from state $\boldsymbol{s}_t$ to $\boldsymbol{s}'_{t+1}$ by executing some $\boldsymbol{a}_t$ at time-step t, is defined as follows:

$$Cost(\boldsymbol{s}_t, \boldsymbol{a}_t, \boldsymbol{s}'_{t+1}) = C_{energy} + C_{period} + C_{bl} \quad (6)$$

We now explain its components in turn. The first component, C_{energy}, captures the cost per Wh for buying electricity (or the profits from selling it to the utility), given the buy/sell rates prescribed by the tariff in effect:

$$C_{energy}(tf_{t+1}, buy_t) = \begin{cases} buy_t \cdot \text{buying}_{tf_{t+1}} & \text{if } buy_t \geq 0 \\ buy_t \cdot \text{selling}_{tf_{t+1}} & \text{if } buy_t < 0 \end{cases} \quad (7)$$

The second component captures the periodic costs $C_{periodic}$ inflicted on the prosumer for being subscribed into a tariff. Naturally, one would expect that "better" tariffs for a prosumer—that is, tariffs specifying high selling prices and low buy prices—will actually incur higher periodic costs (flat rates). Due to this, in our model we make the assumption that periodic costs drop exponentially with decreasing tariff quality (i.e., as the difference between buying price and selling price increases):

$$C_{period}(tf_{t+1}, price_{tf}^{t+1}) = C_1 \exp\{-C_2 \cdot (\text{buying}_{tf}^{t+1} - \text{selling}_{tf}^{t+1})\} \quad (8)$$

with $C_1 = 0.013$, $C_2 = -2.7$. The function is plotted in Fig. 2.

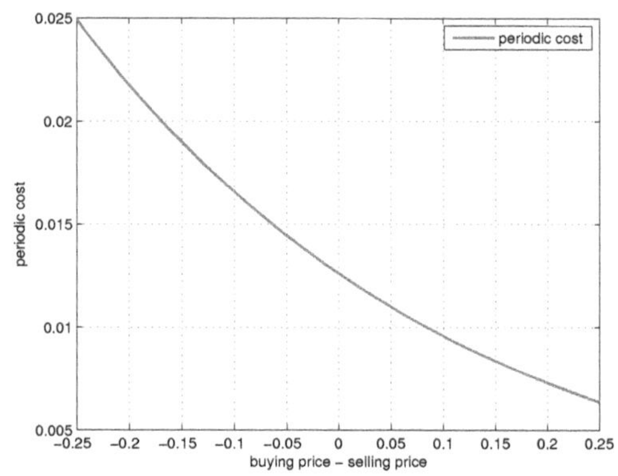

Figure 2: Periodic costs as a function of tariff quality.

The third component of the cost function, C_{bl}, captures the costs associated with *battery life losses*. That is, the costs inflicted from charging (or discharging) the storage devices (batteries) with a charge amount of chg_t, at a given time-step t when the stored energy amount is at bat_t. To estimate this component, we assume the use of deep-cycle batteries, which are lead-acid batteries designed to be regularly deeply discharged (using most of their capacity) [25].

The C_{bl} cost of an attempted *chg* action can then be viewed as a fraction of the $C_{init-bat}$ *initial investment cost* for the batteries:

$$C_{bl} = L_{loss} \cdot C_{init-bat} \quad (9)$$

The "life loss" L_{loss} factor in the above equation is affected by the *effective throughput* A_c of the battery over a certain charge period (measured in Ah) [25]:

$$L_{loss} = \frac{A_c}{A_{total}}$$

Here, A_{total} is the total cumulative throughput (in Ah) during the battery's lifetime. A battery size of Q Ah will deliver an effective $A_{total} = 390 \cdot QAh$ over its lifetime [25].

Now, A_c above related to the operating *state of charge* (SOC) and the *actual throughput* A'_c. The latter can be calculated, given the voltage of the battery, as:

$$A'_c = \frac{chg_t}{V_{battery}}$$

To calculate A_c, we first have to define the *state of charge* (SOC) of the battery, as the fraction of its total $Battery_{max}$ capacity covered by its currently stored energy amount, bat_t:

$$SOC = \frac{bat_t}{Battery_{max}}$$

and its value has to be kept always between 0.2 and 1, for safety reasons [25]. A_c is then expressed as

$$A_c = \lambda_{soc} A'_c$$

where λ_{soc} is an *effective weighting factor* given the battery's state of charge. When SOC is between 0.2 and 1, λ_{soc} is approximately linear with SOC [25], which can be expressed as

$$\lambda_{soc} = k \cdot SOC + d$$

In our work, the values of k and d in the previous equation were set to -0.7594 and 1.43 respectively, as a result of applying linear fitting over certain empirically set (SOC, λ_{SOC}) data points reported in [25]. The resulting fitted line is depicted at Fig. 3.

With λ_{soc} at hand, we can then fully determine the C_{bl} component, and use it to determine the life loss cost incurred on batteries during their charge (or discharge) by the application of a chg_t action at time-step t.

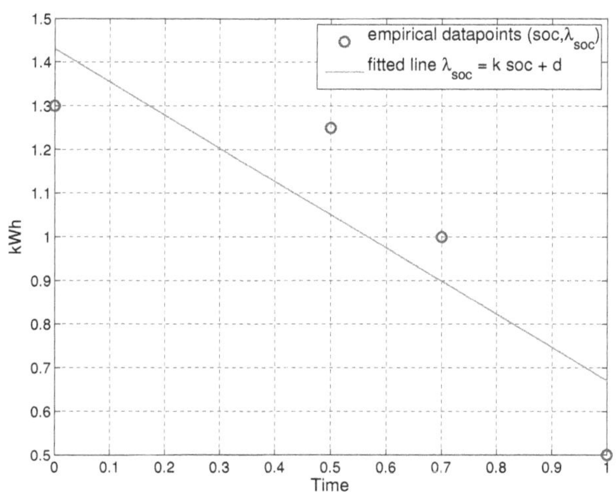

Figure 3: Estimating the λ_{soc} weighting factor.

4. SOLVING THE FMDP

With the above FMDP at hand, the optimal policy can be derived by solving the corresponding Bellman equations. Dynamic programming (DP) methods can be used to obtain the optimal solution [23]. In our work here we used *value iteration (VI)* as the DP method of choice. Interestingly, our experiments confirm that our formulation permits VI to provide us with the solution within a reasonable time, when run on everyday desktops or laptops. This is despite the large state-action space (in the order of hundreds of thousands)–while, at the same time, SPUDD sometimes fails to compute a solution within a reasonable time, when taking its pre-processing requirements into account. We will discuss our experimental results in length in Section 6. For now, we simply outline the instantiation of the VI algorithm in this domain.

Our problem is naturally a finite-horizon problem, thus we employed a finite-horizon VI method. By setting the horizon T to be

for *all instantiations of* $\boldsymbol{s}$ **do**
  set $V_{T+1}(\boldsymbol{s}) = 0$
end
for *all time-steps t in descending order (i.e., with* $1, \cdots, T$ *stages-to-go)* **do**
  for *all instantiations of* $\boldsymbol{s}_t$ **do**

$$V_t(\boldsymbol{s}_t) \leftarrow \max_{\boldsymbol{a}_t} \sum_{\boldsymbol{s}'_{t+1}} Pr(\boldsymbol{s}'_{t+1} | \boldsymbol{a}_t, \boldsymbol{s}_t) \cdot \left(R(\boldsymbol{s}_t, \boldsymbol{a}_t, \boldsymbol{s}'_{t+1}) + V_{t+1}(\boldsymbol{s}'_{t+1})\right)$$

  end
end
for *all instantiations of* $\boldsymbol{s}$ *and all time-steps t* **do**

$$\pi(\boldsymbol{s}, t) = \arg\max_{\boldsymbol{a}} \sum_{\boldsymbol{s}'} Pr(\boldsymbol{s}' | \boldsymbol{a}, \boldsymbol{s}) \left(R(\boldsymbol{s}, \boldsymbol{a}, \boldsymbol{s}') + V_{t+1}(\boldsymbol{s}')\right)$$

end

Algorithm 1: Value iteration for solving the FMDP

equal to the number of time steps at which the prosumer is required to act, we can incorporate the *tms* factored state into the problem's horizon, thus effectively reducing the size of the state space.

Then, with $\boldsymbol{s}'_t$ denoting the potential successor states of $\boldsymbol{s}_t$; with $Pr(\boldsymbol{s}'_{t+1} | \boldsymbol{a}_t, \boldsymbol{s}_t)$ denoting the probability of state transitions from $\boldsymbol{s}_t$ to possible successor states $\boldsymbol{s}'_{t+1}$, given that action $\boldsymbol{a}_t$ was taken; and $R(\boldsymbol{s}_t, \boldsymbol{a}_t, \boldsymbol{s}'_{t+1}) = -Cost(\boldsymbol{s}_t, \boldsymbol{a}_t, \boldsymbol{s}'_{t+1})$ denoting the corresponding immediate reward (the negative immediate cost), the VI algorithm iteratively estimates the value function for the factored states, and outputs an optimal policy π, as shown in Alg. 1.

5. PROSUMER PRODUCTION AND CONSUMPTION MODELS

Naturally, the estimated production from the renewable energy sources distributed on the microgrid, and the predicted load consumption of the connected consumers, affect the policy of the prosumer. The prosumer is notified about the expected production and consumption values via the *prod* and *cons* signals. Thus, it is necessary to predict values for those signals that are as accurate as possible, to assist the decision-making process of the prosumer.

5.1 Production Prediction

To obtain the production estimates of the photovoltaic systems (PVS) and wind turbine generators (WTG) of our microgrid, we employ *RENES* [18], a web-based PVS and WTG production prediction tool. RENES generates PVS and WTG production estimates given time, geographical coordinates and online weather forecasts, and it comes with specific performance guarantees. For PVS production predictions, RENES utilizes non-linear approximation components for turning cloud-coverage into radiation forecasts, which are then used for production prediction. It has an interactive web-based interface, along with an API providing XML responses to prediction requests. New production estimates are provided every half an hour. RENES predictions are provided free-of-charge. The tool and API can be accessed at www.intelligence.tuc.gr/renes/ .

5.2 Consumption Prediction

Here we show how to employ two regression methods to predict the load consumption of the prosumer: Gaussian Process (GP) and Bayesian Linear Regression. To begin, the input data of our model, and the output data whose values we are trying to predict, correspond to the factored state *tms* and the signal variable *cons* :

$$\boldsymbol{x} = (tms_1, \ldots, tms_n) \quad (10)$$

$$\boldsymbol{y} = (cons_1, \ldots, cons_n) \quad (11)$$

that is, they are sequences of consumption data, containing information about time-steps and the respective load consumption.

Our goal in regression, is to make predictions of the target variables for new inputs. Given a set of output data

$$\boldsymbol{y} = (y_1, \ldots, y_n)^T$$

corresponding to input values $(x_1, \ldots, x_n)$, where n is the length of the time sequence we use, we predict the target variable y_{n+1} for a new input vector with an additional x_{n+1} value.

Bayesian Linear Regression.

The first method we use for prediction is *Bayesian linear regression.* To begin, we define a model parameter $\boldsymbol{w}$

$$\boldsymbol{w} = [\boldsymbol{x}\ \boldsymbol{y}]$$

with x, y as in Eqs. 10 and 11 above. For a set of training samples, $\mathcal{D} = \{(x_j, y_j), j = 1, ..., n\}$ (x_j inputs and y_j outputs) we need to predict the posterior distribution of w given the target values y.

Now, the conjugate prior of $\boldsymbol{w}$ is a *Gaussian distribution*:

$$p(\boldsymbol{w}) = \mathcal{N}(\boldsymbol{w}|\mu_0, \sigma_0^2)$$

where μ_0 is the mean and σ_0^2 the variance noise; while the *likelihood function* $p(y|w)$ is given also by a *Gaussian distribution* of the form

$$p(\boldsymbol{y}|\boldsymbol{w}) = \mathcal{N}(\boldsymbol{y}|\ \Phi\boldsymbol{w}, \beta^{-1}I)$$

where β is noise single precision parameter, and Φ is a polynomial basis function.

With conjugate prior and likelihood function at hand, the *posterior distribution* is computed using Bayes theorem for Gaussians [6]. In order to find the posterior distribution, we just require the mean and the variance:

$$p(\boldsymbol{w}|\boldsymbol{y}) = \mathcal{N}(\boldsymbol{w}|\mu_n, S_n),\ where$$

$$\mu_n = S_n(S_0^{-1}\mu_0 + \beta\Phi^T\boldsymbol{y})$$

$$S_n^{-1} = S_0^{-1} + \beta\Phi^T\Phi$$

In this work, we adopt a zero-mean isotropic Gaussian, governed by a single precision parameter α, so that:

$$p(\boldsymbol{w}|\alpha) = \mathcal{N}(w|0, \alpha^{-1}I)$$

Then, the corresponding posterior distribution $p(\boldsymbol{w}|\boldsymbol{y})$ has:

$$\mu_n = \beta S_n\Phi^T\boldsymbol{y}$$

$$S_n^{-1} = \alpha I + \beta\Phi^T\Phi$$

Evidence approximation [6] is utilised to calculate the optimal values of the hyper-parameters α and β.

Gaussian Process Regression.

The second regression method that we use is Gaussian Process (GP) with two form of kernels, a gaussian and a polynomial one. The use of a GP with a Gaussian kernel appears to be the better choice for our setting, as we demonstrate in Sec. 5.3 below. We note that Gaussian Processes have also been recently applied for consumption reduction prediction in electricity demand management settings [3, 16, 21].

Gaussian processes can be used for regression and classification without a parametric model assumption. For a set $\mathcal{D} = \{(x_j, y_j), j = 1, ..., n\}$ of training samples, with x_j inputs and y_j noisy outputs, we need to predict the distribution of the noisy output at some test locations. We assume the model:

$$y_j = f(x_j) + \epsilon_j,\ \text{where}\ \epsilon_j \sim \mathcal{N}(0, \sigma_{noise}^2)$$

with σ_{noise}^2 the variance noise.

GP regression is a Bayesian approach that assumes a priori that function values follow: $p(\mathbf{f}|x_1, x_2, ..., x_n) = \mathcal{N}(\mathbf{0}, K)$ where $\mathbf{f} = [f_1, f_2, ..., f_n]^T$ is the vector of latent function values, $f_j = f(x_j)$ and K is the covariance matrix that is computed by a "kernel" covariance function $k(\cdot,\cdot)$: $K_{jk} = k(x_j, x_k)$.

The kernel functions used in this work are given by a polynomial and Gaussian form [6] respectively:

$$k(x_j, x_k) = \theta_0 + \theta_1(x_j^T x_k) + \theta_2(x_j^T x_k)^2$$

$$k(x_j, x_k) = \theta_0\ \exp\big(-\frac{(x_j - x_k)^T(x_j - x_k)}{2(\theta_1)^2}\big)$$

where the θ_* are the model's hyper parameters. Their optimal values can be found by maximizing the log likelihood [6], for instance using *backtracking line search* [8], as we do in this work.

Finally, in order to proceed to the inference, we must combine the joint GP prior obtained by the test values with the likelihood $p(\mathbf{y}|\mathbf{f})$, via Bayes rule. The joint GP prior and the independent likelihood are both Gaussian with mean and variance at a test point x_* as follows:

$$GP_\mu(x_*, \mathcal{D}) = K_{*,f}(K_{f,f} + \sigma_{noise}^2 I)^{-1}\mathbf{y} \quad (12a)$$

$$GP_\sigma(x_*, \mathcal{D}) = K_{*,*} - K_{*,f}(K_{f,f} + \sigma_{noise}^2 I)^{-1}K_{f,*} \quad (12b)$$

5.3 Comparing Regression Methods

To choose a Φ polynomial basis function to use for Bayesian linear regression (BLR), we performed cross-validation with random subsampling repeated 10 times for different polynomial functions [15]. For this, we split our consumption dataset (described in Section 6 below) to an 80% part for training, and a 20% one for testing. The results, in terms of *mean square error (MSE)*, are shown of Table 4. The degree of the polynomial with the minimum average MSE is D=5: thus, this was the polynomial of choice for *BLR*. We then compared the performance of *BLR* against that of a Gaussian process (GP) that employed either the polynomial (GP-poly) or the Gaussian (GP-G) kernel mentioned above. The prediction performance of the methods is depicted in Fig. 4; and Table 5 contains the methods' MSE. Results show that *GP-G* does much better than *GP-poly* and *BLR* in terms of MSE, achieving a quite low MSE value. Moreover, the prediction mean of the *GP-G* method apparently follows more closely the actual consumption pattern, as emerging from the actual (x, y) data points.

6. EXPERIMENTS AND RESULTS

We evaluate our model by examining a residential prosumer at New Hampshire, New England, northeastern United States. The data used in our prediction of residential load consumption for the area, comes from the Public Service Company of New Hampshire, and is freely available in their website (http://www.psnh.com/). Our simulated prosumer serves 30 households and includes 20 photovoltaic modules with nominal power 60kW, 2 windturbines with nominal power 1000kW and 24 deep cycle 12Volts batteries 212AH C20 /

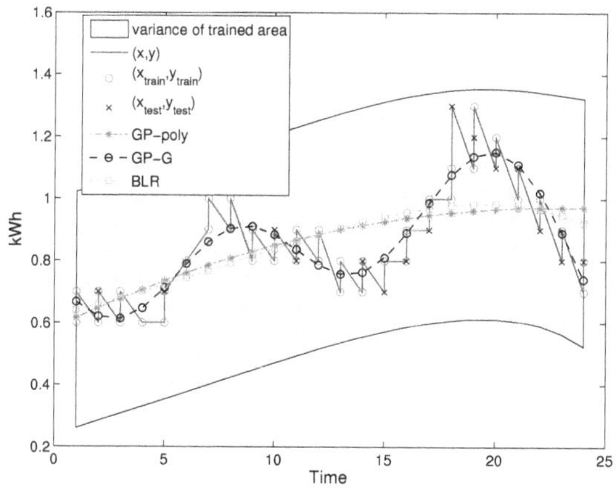

Figure 4: Prediction performance of *GP-poly*, *GP-G*, and *BLR*. The (x, y) input-target pairs are actual consumption data points. The *GP-G* mean matches the (typical) daily electricity demand curve of our dataset, with two consumption peaks.

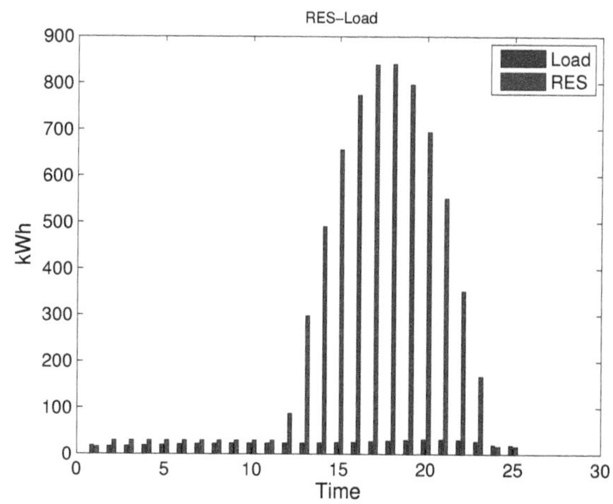

Figure 5: Predicted production of renewable energy sources (RES) and predicted load consumption of prosumer (Load)

Degree of Polynomial	MSE
1	0.022372
2	0.021312
3	0.020175
4	0.017679
5	0.016861
6	0.017329
7	0.017355
8	0.017167
9	0.017399
10	0.017611

Table 4: MSE of Bayesian linear regression Φ functions

FMD200 – VRLA/AGM, with cost of each battery 269,00 €. Estimated battery lifetime is 10-12 years. As mentioned earlier, we employ RENES (www.intelligence.tuc.gr/renes/) to obtain predictions regarding the power production of the prosumer's renewable energy generators; the services provided by RENES are also free of charge. Our simulations were conducted with data regarding a specific day-ahead (24 / 10 / 2014), at which date the predicted electricity consumption and electricity production profile of the particular residential prosumer was as presented in Fig. 5. All experiments were conducted on a 2.10 GHz x 4 Intel Core i3-2310M processor, with 8GB of memory.

We now discuss our choices for the factored MDP representation for our simulated prosumer, and proceed to compare the performance of our value iteration solution method with that of SPUDD.

We initially adopted the following discretisation for our state and action variables (signals are not discretised, but simply communicate the production and consumption predictions, and tariff characteristics to the prosumer). The discretisation step size is shown inside the range of the factored state *bat* (corresponding to the prosumer's batteries' array), and the action *chg* below:

$$bat = [0kWh \ : \ 1kWh \ : \ 60kWh]$$

$$chg = [-60kWh \ : \ 1kWh \ : \ 60kWh]$$

GP with polynomial kernel (GP-poly)	0.0173
GP with Gaussian kernel (GP-G)	0.006943
Bayesian linear Regression (BLR)	0.0169

Table 5: MSE of GP & Bayesian Linear Regression

We also defined nine tariffs, which are as follows:

$$tf_1 = \{0.1€, 0.1€\} \ tf_4 = \{0.2€, 0.1€\} \ tf_7 = \{0.3€, 0.1€\}$$

$$tf_2 = \{0.1€, 0.2€\} \ tf_5 = \{0.2€, 0.2€\} \ tf_8 = \{0.3€, 0.2€\}$$

$$tf_3 = \{0.1€, 0.3€\} \ tf_6 = \{0.2€, 0.3€\} \ tf_9 = \{0.3€, 0.3€\}$$

which thus give rise to 10 possible sel_{tf} tariff selection actions (9 corresponding to choosing one of the tariffs+1 for choosing to stay with their current one).

The transition boundaries for our state variables were initially set to boundary$_{bat}$=1kWh and boundary$_{tf}$=0.1€. Given those boundaries, the maximum number of transitions leading from one state to another are ~ 15.

Now, the discretisation above resulted to a state-action space size of $|S \times A| = 664290$. Notice, however, that in order for SPUDD to be able to model our problem, there was a need to add an additional state variable, *tms* , due to the fact that SPUDD does not allow us to incorporate the time-step into the problem horizon, but requires a complete representation for all states. Simply put, formulating the problem requires the states to be "stamped" by the time-step, so as to keep them distinct from each other, for the SPUDD solver to be able to operate upon the representation. Thus, in the case of SPUDD, state-action spaces shown in Table 6 are expanded by a factor of $|DOM(tms)|$ (i.e., 24 or 48, for our experiments). We also note that a policy extracted by SPUDD can be presented through policy diagrams and the *pquery* SPUDD GUI tool. Figure 6 provides an insight on how such diagrams look like, for a toy example (a smaller instance of our problem).

Horizon	$\|S \times A\|$	bounded region size	value iteration (hours)	SPUDD (hours)	
				Script	Runtime
24	664290	15	1.76	13.4992	0.184
		90	15.84	46.9188	1.19
	2624490	15	8.7603	36.98	0.73975
48	664290	15	3.5	16.8221	0.4271

Table 6: Running time of value iteration and SPUDD for four different scenarios. "Script" refers to the pre-processing time required for the SPUDD input files to be generated, while "Runtime" denotes the subsequent SPUDD execution time.

We compared SPUDD to value iteration for this initial discretisation, and observed that the optimal policy computed through value iteration and SPUDD for the day-ahead coincide with each other. Nevertheless, value iteration produced the optimal policy in approximately 15% of the required time for SPUDD to extract the same policy. The exact running times are presented in Table 6.

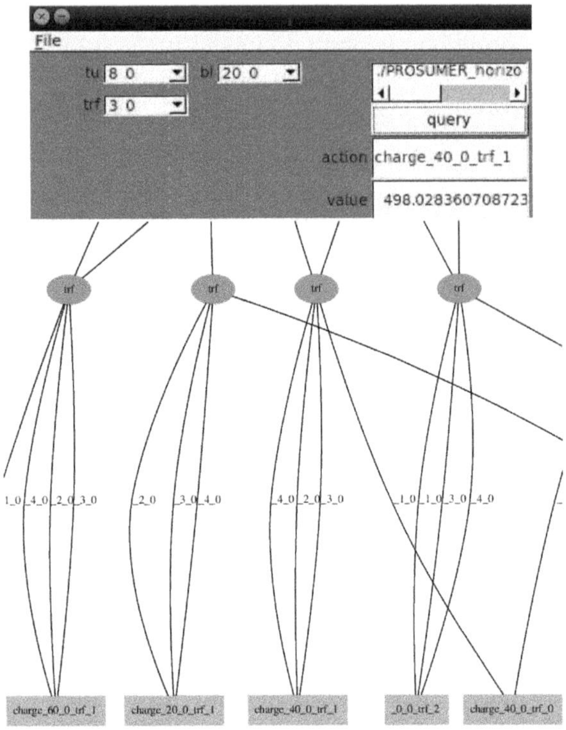

Figure 6: Part of the SPUDD's optimal policy (below), for a toy example with $|S| \cdot |A| = 63000$, and 15 factored states at most within any bounded region. Running time to create the script was: 29.7 sec and to execute it: 1.46 sec. Variables tu, bl and trf presented in pquery correspond to the factored states *tms*, *bat* and *tf* respectively. Variables are presented in blue bubbles, with factored actions in yellow squares, e.g. $charge\_40\_0\_trf\_1$ represents the actions *chg*= 40kWh and sel_{tf} = 1. The pquery GUI tool is shown above.

Following that, we increased the size of the transition boundaries so as to contain 90 state variables instead of 15. The boundaries used for the transitions from one state to another in this case are: $boundary_{bat}$=10kWh and $boundary_{tf}$=0.2€. SPUDD could not produce a solution within the time that our "planning-for-the-day-ahead" problem must be solved (maximum 24 hours). By contrast, the running time for the simple value iteration method was approximately 15.8 hours, as shown in Table 6.

We then increased the size of state and action spaces to $|S \times A| = 2624490$ (by reducing the discretisation step sizes for our factored variables), but kept the bounded regions for state transitions quite small ($boundary_{bat}$=1kWh and $boundary_{tf}$=0.1€). SPUDD, once more, was not able to produce a solution within 24 hours, and could not generate a final policy with the available memory, in contrast to our value iteration method (Table 6).

Finally, we also experimented with a scenario involving 48 (half-hour) time steps at which the prosumer is required to act (as is usually the case in electricity markets). In this case, we had $|S \times A| = 664290$, $boundary_{bat}$=1kWh , and $boundary_{tf}$=0.1€. Once again, value iteration provided us with the same (optimal) policy as SPUDD, but in approximately 25% of the time (Table 6).

The experiments above demonstrate the limitations of SPUDD when used for problems that do not possess enough structure to allow for a compact enough representation of the required transitions in its input files. Both SPUDD and value iteration provide us with the same optimal policies in all experiments–that is, policies which intuitively maximize profits from selling/buying decisions while ensuring that consumer needs are satisfied. Nevertheless, value iteration required a fraction of SPUDD's total required time to produce the solution. We note that this is despite the fact that we took special care to make our factored representation as compact as possible for SPUDD to operate upon.

7. CONCLUSIONS

This paper employs, for the first time, factored MDPs to model the decision problem faced by a prosumer planning its energy flow management for the day-ahead. Our model incorporates the key factors responsible for the effective operation of a microgrid prosumer, regardless of its size; and allows us to obtain the exact optimal solution to the problem. We used a simple value iteration algorithm to compute the solution to this sequential decision making problem, and demonstrated our method's effectiveness and efficiency by comparing it to the performance of *SPUDD*. By so doing, we exposed the limitations of this particular FMDP solver. While our model enables the simple VI method to compute the optimal solution within a reasonable time, the problem does not have enough structure to allow the creation of a compact input file for SPUDD to operate on, resulting to poor performance. In addition, this work provides specific predictive tools for obtaining prosumer consumption and production estimates, and exhibits how *Gaussian processes* and *Bayesian linear regression* techniques can be used for consumption prediction in this setting (with Gaussian processes emerging as the most successful).

Our model and solution technique allow the determination of optimal policies regarding the main prosumer activities. However, additional state and action variables can be added to the model, to allow for additional operations to take place (e.g., choosing to alter the projected production and consumption levels for increased economic benefits). In future work, we intend to enrich our model in that direction, and also study the performance of more-powerful-than-VI factored MDP solution techniques, such as approximate linear programming and approximate policy iteration [11]. Applying these techniques in this domain is not a straightforward task, since it requires the careful determination of appropriate basis value functions. Finally, we intend to use these ideas in order to smoothly incorporate prosumers within *cooperatives* that are fast emerging in the Smart Grid [9, 1].

8. ACKNOWLEDGEMENTS

We are grateful to Dr. Jesse Hoey for help with using SPUDD and fruitful discussions.

REFERENCES

[1] Federation of groups and cooperatives of citizens for renewable energy in Europe. http://www.rescoop.eu.

[2] T. Ackermann (ed.). *Wind power in power systems*. J. Wiley & Sons, 2005.

[3] C. Akasiadis and G. Chalkiadakis. Stochastic filtering methods for predicting agent performance in the Smart Grid. In *Proc. of ECAI/PAIS-2014*, pages 1205–1206, 2014.

[4] P. Asmus. Microgrids, virtual power plants and our distributed energy future. *The Electricity Journal*, pages 72–82, 2010.

[5] R. Bahar, E. Frohm, C. Gaona, G. Hachtel, E. Macii, A. Pardo, and F. Somenzi. Algebric decision diagrams and their applications. *Formal methods in system design*, pages 171–206, 1997.

[6] C. M. Bishop. *Pattern Recognition and Machine Learning*. Springer, 2006.

[7] C. Boutilier, T. Dean, and S. Hanks. Decision-theoretic planning: Structural assumptions and computational leverage. *Journal of Artificial Intelligence Research (JAIR)*, pages 1–94, 1999.

[8] S. Boyd and L. Vandenberghe. *Convex Optimization*. 2004.

[9] G. Chalkiadakis, V. Robu, R. Kota, A. Rogers, and N. Jennings. Cooperatives of distributed energy resources for efficient virtual power plants. In *Proc. of AAMAS-2011 - Volume 2*, pages 787–794, 2011.

[10] J. Chiasson and B. Vairamohan. Estimating the state of charge of a battery. *IEEE Transactions on Control Systems Technology*, pages 465–470, 2005.

[11] C. Guestrin, D. Koller, R. Parr, and S. Venkataraman. Efficient solution algorithms for factored MDPs. *Journal of Artificial Intelligence Research (JAIR)*, pages 399–468, 2003.

[12] J. Hoey, R. St-Aubin, A. J. Hu, and C. Boutilier. SPUDD: Stochastic planning using decision diagrams. Proc. of UAI-1999, pages 279–288, 1999.

[13] H. Kanchev, D. Lu, F. Colas, V. Lazarov, and B. Francois. Energy management and operational planning of a microgrid with a PV-based active generator for Smart Grid applications. *Industrial Electronics, IEEE Transactions on*, pages 4583–4592, 2011.

[14] D. Kirschen and G. Strbac. *Fundamentals of Power System Economics*. J. Wiley & Sons, 2005.

[15] R. Kohavi. A study of cross-validation and bootstrap for accuracy estimation and model selection. In *Proc. of IJCAI-95*, pages 1137–1143, 1995.

[16] J. Kolter and J. Ferreira. A large-scale study on predicting and contextualizing building energy usage. In *AAAI*, pages 1349–1356, 2011.

[17] D. Nikovski and W. Zhang. Factored markov decision process models for stochastic unit commitment. In *IEEE Conference on Innovative Technologies for an Efficient and Reliable Electricity Supply (CITRES)*, pages 28–35, 2010.

[18] A. Panagopoulos, G. Chalkiadakis, and E. Koutroulis. Predicting the power output of distributed renewable energy resources within a broad geographical region. In *Proc. of ECAI/PAIS 2012*, pages 981–986, 2012.

[19] M. Peters, W. Ketter, M. Saar-Tsechansky, and J. Collins. A reinforcement learning approach to autonomous decision-making in smart electricity markets. *Machine learning*, 92(1), pages 5–39, 2013.

[20] S. D. Ramchurn, P. Vytelingum, A. Rogers, and N. Jennings. Putting the 'smarts' into the Smart Grid: A grand challenge for Artificial Intelligence. *Commun. ACM*, 55(4), pages 86-97, 2012.

[21] A. Rogers, S. Maleki, S. Ghosh, and N. Jennings. Adaptive home heating control through gaussian process prediction and mathematical programming. In *Proc. of ATES 2011*, pages 71–78, 2011.

[22] A. Rogers, S. Ramchurn, and N. Jennings. Delivering the Smart Grid: Challenges for autonomous agents and multi-agent systems research. In *Proc. of AAAI-2012*, pages 2166–2172, 2012.

[23] R. S. Sutton and A. G. Barto. Reinforcement learning: An introduction, 1998.

[24] D. Urieli and P. Stone. Tactex'13: a champion adaptive power trading agent. In *Proc. of AAMAS-2014*, pages 1447–1448, 2014.

[25] B. Zhao, X. Zhang, J. Chen, C. Wang, and L. Guo. Operation optimization of standalone microgrids considering lifetime characteristics of battery energy storage system. *Sustainable Energy, IEEE Transactions on*, pages 934–943, 2013.

Data-Driven Agent-Based Modeling, with Application to Rooftop Solar Adoption

Haifeng Zhang and Yevgeniy Vorobeychik
Electrical Engineering and Computer Science
Vanderbilt University
Nashville, TN
{haifeng.zhang,yevgeniy.vorobeychik}@vanderbilt.edu

Joshua Letchford and Kiran Lakkaraju
Sandia National Laboratories
Albuquerque, NM
{jletchf,klakkar}@sandia.gov

ABSTRACT

Agent-based modeling is commonly used for studying complex system properties emergent from interactions among many agents. We present a novel data-driven agent-based modeling framework applied to forecasting individual and aggregate residential rooftop solar adoption in San Diego county. Our first step is to learn a model of individual agent behavior from combined data of individual adoption characteristics and property assessment. We then construct an agent-based simulation with the learned model embedded in artificial agents, and proceed to validate it using a holdout sequence of collective adoption decisions. We demonstrate that the resulting agent-based model successfully forecasts solar adoption trends and provides a meaningful quantification of uncertainty about its predictions. We utilize our model to optimize two classes of policies aimed at spurring solar adoption: one that subsidizes the cost of adoption, and another that gives away free systems to low-income households. We find that the optimal policies derived for the latter class are significantly more efficacious, whereas the policies similar to the current California Solar Initiative incentive scheme appear to have a limited impact on overall adoption trends.

Categories and Subject Descriptors

I.2.11 [**Artificial Intelligence**]: Distributed Artificial Intelligence—*Multiagent systems, Agent-based Modeling*; I.6.5 [**Simulation and Modeling**]: Model Development—*Modeling methodologies*

Keywords

Machine Learning; Agent-based Modeling; Innovation Diffusion; Rooftop Solar; Policy Optimization

Appears in: *Proceedings of the 14th International Conference on Autonomous Agents and Multiagent Systems (AAMAS 2015), Bordini, Elkind, Weiss, Yolum (eds.), May 4–8, 2015, Istanbul, Turkey.*

1. INTRODUCTION

The rooftop solar market in the US, and especially in California, has experienced explosive growth in last decade. At least in part this growth can be attributed to the government incentive programs which effectively reduce the system costs. One of the most aggressive incentive programs is the California Solar Initiative (CSI), a rooftop solar subsidy program initiated in 2007 with the goal of creating 1940 megawatts of solar capacity by 2016 [7]. The CSI program has been touted as a great success, and it certainly seems so: over 2000 megawatts have been installed to date. However, in a rigorous sense, success would have to be measured in comparison to some baseline; for example, in comparison to the same world, but without incentives. Such an experiment is, of course, impossible, but it is also critical to understand how one would evaluate success of any policy vis-a-vis its stated goals, so that we can both learn from past experience and identify high-quality policy alternatives in future settings with similar goals.

Agent-based modeling (ABM) has long been a common framework of choice for studying aggregate, or emergent, properties of complex systems as they arise from microbehaviors of a multitude of agents in social and economic contexts [4, 20, 25]. ABM appears well-suited to policy experimentation of just the kind needed for the rooftop solar market. Indeed, there have been several attempts to develop agent-based models of solar adoption trends [9, 22, 28]. Both traditional agent-based modeling, as well as the specific models developed for solar adoption, use data to calibrate aspects of the models (for example, features of the social network, such as density, are made to match real networks), but not the entire model. Moreover, validation is often qualitative, or, if quantitative, using the same data as used for calibration.

The emergence of "Big Data" offers new opportunities to develop agent-based models in a way that is entirely data-driven, both in terms of model calibration and validation. In the particular case of rooftop solar adoption, the CSI program, in addition to subsidies, also provides for a collection of a significant amount of data by the program administrators, such as Center for Sustainable Energy (CSE) in San Diego county, about specific (individual-level) characteristics of adopters. While by itself insufficient, we combine this data with property assessment characteristics for all San Diego county residents to yield a high-fidelity data set which we use to calibrate artificial agent models using machine learning techniques. A data-driven ABM is then constructed using exclusively such learned agent models, with no additional hand-tuned variables. Moreover, following standard practice in machine learning, we separate the calibration data from the data used for validation.

This paper makes the following contributions:

1. A framework for data-driven agent-based modeling,
2. methods for learning individual-agent models of solar adoption, addressing challenges posed by the market structure and the nature of the data,
3. a data-driven agent-based model of solar adoption in (a portion of) San Diego county, with forecasting efficacy evaluated on data not used for model learning,
4. a quantitative evaluation of the California Solar Initiative subsidy program, a broad class of incentive policies, and a broad class of solar system "seeding" policies.

2. RELATED WORK

Agent-based modeling methodology has a substantial, active, literature [4, 20, 25], ranging from methodological to applied. Somewhat simplistically, the approach is characterized by the development of models of agent behavior, which are integrated within a simulation environment. The common approach is to make use of relatively simple agent models (for example, based on qualitative knowledge of the domain, qualitative understanding of human behavior, etc.), so that complexity arises primarily from agent interactions among themselves and with the environment. For example, Thiele et al. [30] document that only 14% of articles published in the Journal of Artificial Societies and Social Simulation include parameter fitting. Our key methodological contribution is a departure from developing simple agent models based on relevant *qualitative* insights to *learning* such models entirely on data. Due to its reliance on data about *individual agent behavior*, our approach is not universally applicable. However, we contend that such data is becoming increasingly prevalent, as individual behavior is now continuously captured in the plethora of virtual environments, as well as through the use of mobile devices. As such, we are not concerned about simplicity of agent models *per se*; rather, it is "bounded" by the amount of data available (the more data we have, the more complex models we can reliably calibrate on it). Thiele et al. [30], as well as Dancik et al. [8] propose methods for calibrating model parameters to data. However, unlike our work, neither offers methodology for *validation*, and both operate at model-level, requiring either extremely costly simulations (making calibration of many parameters intractable), or, in the case of Dancik et al., a multi-variate Normal distribution as a proxy, losing any guarantees about the quality of the original model in the process. Our proposal of calibration at the *agent level*, in contrast, enables us to leverage state-of-the-art machine learning techniques, as well as obtain more reliable, and interpretable, models at the individual agent level.

A number of agent-based modeling efforts are specifically targeted at the rooftop solar adoption domain [5, 9, 22, 28, 27, 23, 34]. Denholm et al. [9] and Boghesi et al. [5] follow a relatively traditional methodological approach (i.e., simple rule-based behavior model), and their focus is largely on financial considerations in rooftop solar adoption. Palmer et al. [22] and Zhao et al. [34], likewise use a traditional approach, but consider several potentially influential behavioral factors, such as social influence and household income. Palmer et al. calibrate their model using total adoption data in Italy (unlike our approach, they do not separate calibration from validation). Zhao et al. set model parameters based on a combination of census and survey data, but without performing higher-level model calibration with actual adoption trends. None of these past approaches makes use of machine learning to develop agent models (indeed, none except Palmer et al. calibrate the model using actual adoption data, and even they do not seem to do so in a systematic way, using instead "trial and error"). Much of this previous work on agent-based models of rooftop solar adoption attempts to use the models to investigate alternative policies. Unlike us, however, none (to our knowledge) consider the *dynamic* optimization problem faced by policy makers (i.e., how much of the budget to spend at each time period), nor compare alternative incentive schemes with "seeding" policies (i.e., giving systems away, subject to a budget constraint).

There have also been a number of models of innovation diffusion in general, as well as rooftop solar adoption in particular, that are not agent-based in nature, but instead aspire only to anticipate aggregate-level trends. Bass [2] introduce the classic "S-curve" quantitative model, building on the qualitative insights offered by Rogers [29] and others. In the context of rooftop solar, noteworthy efforts include Lobel and Perakis [18], Bollinger and Gillingham [3], and van Benthem et al. [32]. Lobel and Perakis calibrate a simple model of aggregate solar adoption in Germany on total adoption data; their model, like ours, includes both economics (based on the feed-in tariff as well as learning-by-doing effects on solar system costs) and peer effects. We therefore use their model, adapted to *individual* agent behavior, as our "baseline". Bollinger and Gillingham demonstrate causal influence of peer effects on adoption decisions, and van Benthem et al. focus on identifying and quantifying learning-by-doing effects.

Three related efforts are somewhat closer in spirit to our work. Kearns and Wortman [16] developed a theoretical model of learning from collective behavior, making the connection between learning individual agent models and models of aggregate behavior. However, this effort does not address the general problem of learning from a single observed sequence of collective behavior which is of key interest to us. Judd et al. [15] use machine learning to predict behavior of participants in social network coordination experiments, but are only able to match the behavior qualitatively. Another effort in a similar vein uses machine learning to calibrate walking models from real and synthetic data, which are then aggregated in an agent-based simulation [31]. Aside from the fundamental differences in application domains from our setting, Torrens et al. [31] largely eschew model validation, and do not consider the subsequent problem of policy evaluation and optimization, both among our key contributions.

Finally, there has been substantial literature that considers the problem of marketing on social networks [17, 6]. Almost universally, however, the associated approaches rely on the structure of specific, very simple, influence models, without specific context or attempting to learn the individual behavior from data (indeed, we find that simple baseline models are not sufficiently reliable to be a basis for policy optimization in our setting). Moreover, most such approaches are static (do not consider the dynamic marketing problem, as we do), although an important exception is the work by Golovin and Krause [13].

3. DATA-DRIVEN AGENT-BASED MODELING

The overwhelming majority of agent-based modeling efforts in general, as well as in the context of innovation/solar adoption modeling in particular,, involve a) *manual* development of an agent model, which is usually rule-based (follows simple behavior rules), b) ad hoc tuning of a large number of parameters, pertaining to both the agent behaviors, as well as the overall model (environment characteristics, agent interactions, etc), and c) validation usually takes the form of qualitative expert assessment, or is in terms of overall fit of aggregate behavior (e.g., total number of rooftop solar adoptions) to ground truth, *using the data on which the model was calibrated* [4, 20, 25, 5, 9, 22, 28, 34]. We break with this tradition, offering instead a framework for *data-driven agent-based modeling (DDABM)*, where agent models are learned from data about individual (typically, human) behavior, and the agent-based model is thereby fully data-driven, with *no additional parameters to govern its behavior*. We now present our general framework for *data-driven agent-based modeling (DDABM)*, which we subsequently apply to the problem of modeling residential rooftop solar diffusion in San Diego county, California. The key features of this framework are: a) explicit division of data into "calibration" and "validation" to ensure sound and reliable model validation and b) automated agent model training and cross-validation. In this framework, we make three assumptions. The first is that time is discrete. While this assumption is not of fundamental importance, it will help in presenting the concepts, and is the assumption made in our application. The second assumption is that agents are homogeneous. This may seem a strong assumption, but in fact it is quite weak. To see this, suppose that $h(x)$ is our model of agent behavior, where x is *state*, or all information that conditions the agent's decision. Heterogeneity can be embedded in h by considering individual characteristics in state x, such as personality traits and socio-economic status, or, as in our application domain, housing characteristics. Our third assumption is that each individual makes independent decisions at each time t, conditional on state x. Again, if x includes all features relevant to an agent's decision, this assumption is relatively innocuous.

Given these assumptions, DDABM proceeds as follows. We start with a data set of individual agent behavior over time, $D = \{(x_{it}, y_{it})\}_{i,t=0,\ldots,T}$, where i indexes agents, t time through some horizon T and y_{it} indicates agent i's decision, i.e., 1 for "adopted" and 0 for "did not adopt" at time t.

1. Split the data D into *calibration* D_c and *validation* D_v parts along the time dimension: $D_c = \{(x_{it}, y_{it})\}_{i,t\leq T_c}$ and $D_v = \{(x_{it}, y_{it})\}_{i,t>T_c}$ where T_c is a time threshold.
2. Learn a model of agent behavior h on D_c. Use cross-validation on D_c for model (e.g., feature) selection.
3. Instantiate agents in the ABM using h learned in step 2.
4. Initialize the ABM to state x_{jT_c} for all artificial agents j.
5. Validate the ABM by running it from x_{T_c} using D_v.

One may wonder how to choose the initial state x_{jT_c} for the artificial agents. This is direct if the artificial agents in the ABM correspond to actual agents in the data. For example, in rooftop solar adoption we know which agents have adopted solar at time T_c, can use actual housing characteristics, etc. Alternatively, one can run the ABM from the initial state, and start evaluation upon reaching time $T_c + 1$.

Armed with the underlying framework for DDABM, we now proceed to apply it in the context of spatial-temporal solar adoption dynamics in San Diego county.

4. DDABM FOR SOLAR ADOPTION

4.1 Data

In order to construct the DDABM for rooftop solar adoption, we made use of three data sets provided by the Center for Sustainable Energy: individual-level adoption characteristics of residential solar projects installed in San Diego county as a part of the California Solar Initiative (CSI), property assessment data for the entire San Diego county, and electricity utilization data for most of the San Diego county CSI participants spanning twelve months prior to solar system installation. Our CSI data, covering projects completed between May 2007 and April 2013 (about 6 years and 8,500 adopters), contains detailed information about the rooftop solar projects, including system size, reported cost, incentive (subsidy) amount, whether the system was purchased or leased, the date of incentive reservation, and the date of actual system installation, among others. The assessment data includes comprehensive housing characteristics of San Diego county residents (about 440,000 households), including square footage, acreage, number of bedrooms and bathrooms, and whether or not the property has a pool. The CSI and assessment data were merged so that we could associate all property characteristics with adoption decisions.

4.2 Modeling Individual Agent Behavior

Our DDABM framework presupposes a discrete-time data set of individual adoption decisions. At face value, this is not what we have: rather, our data only appears to identify static characteristics of individuals, and their adoption timing. This is, of course, not the full story. Much previous literature on innovation diffusion in general [2, 12, 26, 29], and solar adoption in particular [3, 18, 24, 33], identifies two important factors that influence an individual's decision to adopt: economic benefits and peer effects. We quantify economic benefits using *net present value (NPV)*, or discounted net of benefits less costs of adoption: $NPV = \sum_t \delta^t(b_t - c_t)$, where b_t correspond to benefits (net savings) in month t, and c_t are costs incurred in month t; we used a $\delta = 0.95$ discount factor. Peer, or social, effects in adoption decisions arise from social influence, which can take many forms. Most pertinent in the solar market is *geographic* influence, or the number/density of adopters that are geographically close to an individual making a decision. Both economic benefits and peer effects are dynamic: the former changes as system costs change over time, while the latter changes directly in response to adoption decision by others. In addition, peer effects create interdependencies among agent decisions, so that aggregate adoption trends are not simply averages of individual decisions, but evolve through a highly non-linear process. Consequently, even if we succeed in learning individual agent models, this by no means guarantees success when they are jointly instantiated in simulation, especially in the context of a forecasting task. Next, we describe in detail how we quantify economic and peer effect variables in our model.

4.2.1 Quantifying Peer Effects

We start with the simpler issue of quantifying peer effects. The main challenge is that there are many ways to measure these: for example, total number of adopters in a zip code (a measure used previously [3]), fraction of adopters in the entire area of interest (used by [18]), which is San Diego county in our case, as well as the number/density of adopters within a given radius of the individual making a decision. Because we ultimately utilize feature selection methods such as regularization, our models consider a rather large collection of these features, including both the number and density of adoptions in San Diego county, the decision maker's zip code, as well as within a given radius of the decision maker for several radii. Because we are ultimately interested in policy evaluation, we need to make sure that policy-relevant features can be viewed as causal. While we can never fully guarantee this, our approach for computing peer effect variables follows the methodology of Bollinger and Gillingam [3], who tease out causality from the fact that there is significant spatial separation between the adoption decision, which is indicated by the incentive reservation action, and installation, which is used in measuring peer effects.

4.2.2 Quantifying Net Present Value

To compute NPV in our DDABM framework we need to know costs and benefits *that would have been perceived* by an individual i adopting a system at time t. Of course, our data does not actually offer such counterfactuals, but only provides information for adopters *at the time of adoption.* The structure of solar adoption markets introduces another complication: there are two principal means of adoption, buying and leasing. In the former, the customer pays the costs up-front (we ignore any financing issues), while in the latter, the household pays an up-front cost *and a monthly cost* to the installer. Moreover, CSI program incentives are only offered to system buyers, who, in the case of leased systems, are the installers. Consequently, incentives directly offset the cost to those buying the system outright, but at best do so indirectly for leased systems. In the case of leased systems, there is also an additional data challenge: the system costs reported in the CSI data do not reflect actual leasing expenses, but the estimated market value, and are therefore largely useless for our purposes. Finally, both costs and benefits depend on the capacity (in watts) of the installed system, and this information is only available for individuals who have previously adopted.

Our first step is to estimate system capacity using property assessment features. We do so using step-wise linear regression [10], arriving at a relatively compact model, shown in Table 1. The adjusted R^2 of this model is about 0.27, which is acceptable for our purposes.

Table 1: Linear model of solar system capacity (size). All coefficients are significant at $p = 0.05$ level.

Predictor	Estimate
(Intercept)	1.59
Owner Occupied (binary)	-0.25
Has a Pool (binary)	0.63
Livable Square Footage	7.58e-04
Acreage	1.32
Average Electricity Utilization in Zipcode	8.25e-04

Next, we use the system size variable to estimate system costs separately for the purchased and leased systems. For the purchased systems, the cost at the time of purchase is available and reasonably reliable in the CSI data, but only during the actual purchase time. However, costs of solar systems decrease significantly over time. A principal theory for this phenomenon is *learning-by-doing* [1, 14, 19, 18, 32], in which costs are a decreasing function of aggregate technology adoption (representing, essentially, economies of scale). In line with the learning-by-doing theory, we model the cost of a purchased system as a function of property assessment characteristics, predicted system size, and peer effect features, including total adoption in San Diego county. We considered a number of models for ownership cost and ultimately found that the linear model is most effective. In all cases, we used l_1 regularization for feature selection [11]. The resulting model is shown in Table 2.

Table 2: Ownership cost linear model.

Predictor	Coefficient
(Intercept)	1.14e+04
Property Value	7.38e-04
Livable Square Footage	0.15
System Capacity	6.21e+03
Total Adoption in SD County	-1.06

In order to estimate total discounted lease costs, we extracted cost details from 227 lease contracts, and used this data to estimate the total discounted leasing costs $C^l = \sum_t \delta^t c_t$ through the duration of the lease contract in a manner similar to our estimation of ownership costs. One interesting finding in our estimation of lease costs is that they appear to be largely insensitive to the economic subsidies; more specifically, system capacity turned out to be the only feature with a non-zero coefficient (the coefficient value was 1658, with the intercept value of 10447). In particular, this implies that solar installers do not pass down their savings to customers of leased systems.

Having tackled estimation of costs, we now turn to the other side of NPV calculation: benefits. In the context of solar panel installation, economic benefits are monthly savings, which are the total electricity costs offset by solar system production. These depend on two factors: the size of the system, which we estimate as described above, and the electricity rate. The latter seems simple in principle, but the rate structure used by SDG&E (San Diego Gas and Electric company) makes this a challenge. The SDG&E rates have over the relevant time period a four-tier structure, with each tier depending on monthly electricity utilization relative to a baseline. Tiers 1 and 2 have similar low rates, while tiers 3 and 4 have significantly higher rates. Tier rates are marginal: for example, tier-3 rates are only paid for electricity use above the tier-3 threshold. The upshot is that we need to know electricity utilization of an individual in order to estimate marginal electricity costs offset by the installed solar system. For this purpose, we use the electricity utilization data for the adopters. Here, we run into a technical problem: after running a regression model, we found that average predicted electricity rates for San Diego zip codes significantly exceed observed zip code averages—in other words, our data is biased. To reduce this bias, we modified the linear model as follows. Let (X, y) represent the feature matrix and corresponding vector of energy utilizations for a given month for adopters, and let $(\bar{X}, \bar{y})$ be the matrix of average feature values and average energy use for all San Diego county zip codes. A typical linear model chooses a weight vector w to minimize $(Xw - y)^T(Xw - y)$. In our model, we extend this to solve

$$\min_{w} \quad (Xw - y)^T(Xw - y) + \lambda(\bar{X}w - \bar{y})^T(\bar{X}w - \bar{y}),$$

which is equivalent to a linear regression with the augmented data set (Z, z), where

$$Z = \begin{pmatrix} X \\ \sqrt{\lambda}\bar{X} \end{pmatrix} \quad \text{and} \quad z = \begin{pmatrix} y \\ \sqrt{\lambda}\bar{y} \end{pmatrix}.$$

When λ is small, our model is better able to capture fidelity of individual-level data, but exhibits greater bias. We used deviance ratio to choose a value of λ in the context of the overall individual-agent model.

Now that we can predict both system size and electricity utilization, we can correspondingly predict, for an arbitrary individual, their monthly savings from having installed rooftop solar. Along with the predicted costs, this gives us a complete evaluation of NPV for each potential adopter.

4.2.3 *Learning the Individual-Agent Model*

In putting everything together to learn an individual-agent model, we recognize that there is an important difference between the decision to buy and the decision to lease, as described above. In particular, we have to compute net present value differently in the two models. Consequently, we actually learn two models: one to predict the decision to lease, and another for the decision to buy, each using its respective NPV feature, along with all of the other features, including peer effects and property assessment, which are shared between the models. For each decision model, we used l_1-regularized logistic regression. Taking x_l and x_o to be the feature vectors and $p_l(x_l)$ and $p_o(x_o)$ the corresponding logistic regression models of the lease and own decision respectively, we then compute the probability of adoption

$$p(x) = p_l(x_l) + p_o(x_o) - p_l(x_l)p_o(x_o),$$

where x includes the NPV values for lease and own decisions.

To train the two logistic regression models, we can construct the data set (x_{it}, y_{it}), where i correspond to the households in San Diego county and t to months, with x_{it} the feature vector of the relevant model and y_{it} the lease (own) decision, encoded as a 1 if the system is leased (owned) and 0 otherwise. To separate calibration and validation we used only the data through 04/2011 for calibration, and the rest (through 04/2013) for ABM validation below. The training set was comprised of nearly 7,000,000 data points, of which we randomly chose 30% for calibration (due to scalability issues of standard logistic regression implementation in R).[1] All model selection was performed using 10-fold cross-validation. Since leases only became available in 2008, we introduced a dummy variable that was 1 if the lease option was available at the time and 0 otherwise. We also introduced seasonal dummy variables (Winter, Spring, Summer) to account for seasonal variations in the adoption patterns. The final model for the propensity to purchase a solar system is shown in Table 3, and a model for leasing is shown in Table 4.

Table 3: Ownership Logistic Regression Model

Predictor	Coefficient
(Intercept)	-10.19
Owner Occupied (binary)	0.94
# Installations Within 2 Mile Radius	-3.05e-04
# Installations Within 1 Mile Radius	2.60e-03
# Installations Within $\frac{1}{4}$ Mile Radius	6.78e-03
Lease Option Available (binary)	0.69
Winter (binary)	-0.59
Spring (binary)	-0.19
Summer (binary)	-0.28
Installation Density in Zipcode	100.11
NPV (Purchase)	7.58e-06

Table 4: Lease Logistic Regression Model

Predictor	Coefficient
(Intercept)	-13.22
Owner Occupied (binary)	0.73
# Installations Within 2 Mile Radius	2.21e-03
# Installations Within $\frac{1}{4}$ Mile Radius	7.87e-03
Lease Option Available (binary)	1.65
Winter (binary)	-0.39
Spring (binary)	0.29
Summer (binary)	-0.20
Installation Density in Zipcode	85.69
NPV (Lease)	7.07e-06

4.3 Agent-Based Model

The models developed above were implemented in the Repast ABM simulation toolkit [21].

4.3.1 *Agents*

The primary agent type in the model represents residential households (implemented as a Java class in Repast). In the ABM we do not make the distinction between leasing and buying solar systems, so that each agent acts according the the stochastic model $p(x_{it})$ derived as described in the previous section, where x_{it} is the system state relevant to agent i's at time (iteration) t. In addition, in order to flexibly control the execution of simulation, we defined a special *updater* agent type which is responsible for updating state attributes of household agents x_{it} at each time step t.

[1]In fact, we have sampled the process multiple times, and can confirm that there is little variance in the model or final results.

4.3.2 *Time Step*

Time steps of the simulation correspond to months. At each tick of the simulation, updater agent first updates features x_{it} for all agents, such as purchase and lease costs, incentive (which may depend on time), NPVs, and peer effects, for all agents based on the state of world (e.g., the set of agents having adopted thus far in the simulation). Lease and ownership cost are computed using the lease and ownership cost models as described above, while the incentives may follow an arbitrary subsidy scheme, and in particular can mirror the CSI rate schedule. Next, each non-adopter household is asked to make a decision. When a household agent i is called upon to make the adoption decision at time t, this agent adopts with probability $p(x_{it})$. If an agent chooses to adopt, this agent switches from being a non-adopter to becoming an adopter in the simulation environment. Moreover, when we thereby create a new adopter, we also assign an installation period of the solar system. Specifically, just as in reality, adoption decision only involves the reservation of the incentive, while actual installation of the system takes place several months later. Since peer effect variables are only affected by completed installations, it is important to capture this lag time. We capture the delay between adoption and installation using a random variable distributed uniformly in the interval $[1, 6]$, which is the typical lag time range in the training data.

4.3.3 *Computing Peer Effect Variables*

In order to compute geography-based peer effects, we need information about geographic location of the households. To this end we use a Repast GIS package. A naive way to compute peer effect variables would update these for each non-adopter agent in each iteration. However, this approach is very inefficient and scales poorly, as there are vastly more non-adopters than adopters in typical simulations. Therefore, we instead let adopter agents update peer effect variables for their neighbors at the time of system installation, dramatically reducing the corresponding overhead.

5. ABM VALIDATION

We have now reached Step 5 of the DDABM framework: validation. Our starting point is quantitative validation, *using data that is the "future" relative to the data used for model learning (calibration)*. Given that our agent model and, consequently, the ABM are stochastic, we validate the model by comparing its performance to a baseline in terms of *log-likelihood of observed adoption sequence* in validation data. Specifically, suppose that $D_v = \{(x_{it}, y_{it})\}$ is the sequence of adoption decisions by individuals in the validation data, where x_{it} evolves in part as a function of past adoption decisions, $\{y_{i,t-k}, \ldots, y_{i,t-1}\}$ (where k is the installation lag time). Letting all aspects relevant to the current decision be a part of the current state x_{it}, we can compute the likelihood of the adoption sequence given a model p as:

$$L(D_v; p) = \prod_{i,t \in D_v} p(x_{it})^{y_{it}}(1 - p(x_{it}))^{(1-y_{it})}.$$

Quality of a model p relative to a baseline b can then be measured using likelihood ratio, $R = \frac{L(D_v;p)}{L(D_v;b)}$. If $R > 1$, the model p outperforms the baseline. As this discussion implies, we need a baseline. We consider two baseline models: a NULL model, which estimates the probability of adoption as the overall fraction of adopters, and a model using only the NPV and zip code adoption density features for the purchase and lease decisions (referred to as *baseline* below). The latter baseline is somewhat analogous to the model used by Lobel and Perakis [18], although it is adapted to our setting, with all its associated complications discussed above. As we found the NULL model to be substantially worse, we only present the comparison with the more sophisticated *baseline*.

To enable us to execute many runs within a reasonable time frame, we restricted the ABM to a representative zip code in San Diego county (approximately 13000 households). We initialized the simulation with the assessors features, GIS locations, and adoption states (that is, identifies of adopters) in this zip code. To account for stochasticity of our model, we executed 1000 sample runs for all models.

Figure 1 shows the likelihood ratio of our model (namely *lasso*) to the *baseline*. From this figure, it is clear that our model significantly outperforms the baseline in its ability to forecast rooftop solar adoption: the models are relatively similar in their quality for a number of months as the adoption trend is relatively predictable, but diverge significantly after 9/12, with our model ultimately outperforming the baseline by an order of magnitude.[2] In other words, both models predict near-future (from the model perspective) relatively well, but our model significantly outperforms the baseline in forecasting the more distance future.

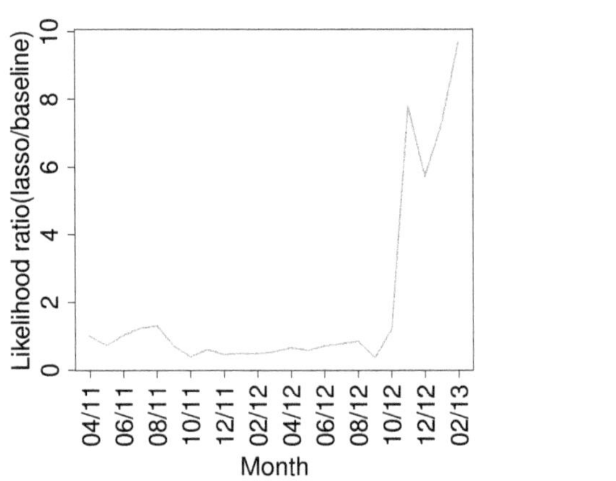

Figure 1: Likelihood ratio R of our model relative to the baseline.

Thus, quantitative validation already strongly suggests that the DDABM model we developed performs quite well in terms of forecasting the probability distribution of *individual decisions*.

In addition, we assess model performance in terms of aggregate behavior in more qualitative terms. Specifically we can consider Figure 2 , which shows *stochastic realizations* of our model (recall that agent behavior is stochastic), where heavier regions correspond to greater density, in comparison with the actual average adoption path. First, we can observe that the actual adoption path is in the "high-likelihood" region of our model realizations. This is a crucial observation: when behavior is stochastic, it would be unreasonable to

[2] 9/12 is where the aggregate adoption becomes highly non-linear, so that the added value of the extra features used by our model sharply increases.

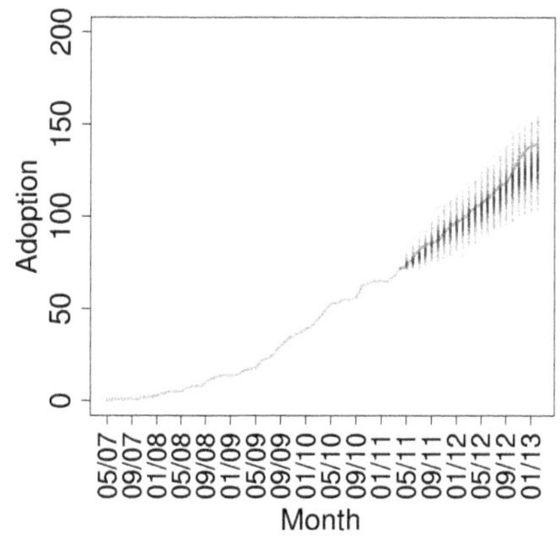

Figure 2: Spread of sample runs of our model, with heavier colored regions corresponding to higher density, and the observed average adoption trend.

expect a prediction to be "spot-on": in fact, every particular realization of behavior path has a minuscule probability. Instead, model correctness is well assessed in terms of how likely observed adoption path is *according to the model*; we observe that our model is *very likely to produce an outcome similar to what was actually observed.* Second, our model offers a meaningful quantification of uncertainty, which is low shortly after the observed initial state, but fans out further into the future. Given that adoption is, for practical purposes, a stochastic process, it is extremely useful to be able to quantify uncertainty, and we therefore view this as a significant feature of our model. Note also that we expect variation in the actual adoption path as well, so one would not therefore anticipate this to be identical to the model average path, just as individual sample paths typically deviate from the average.

6. POLICY ANALYSIS

The model of residential rooftop solar we developed and validated can now be used both as a means to evaluate the effectiveness of a policy that had been used (in our case, California Solar Initiative solar subsidy program), and consider the effectiveness of alternative policies. Our evaluation here is restricted to a single representative zip code in San Diego county, as discussed above. We begin by considering the problem of designing the incentive (subsidy) program.

6.1 Incentive Design

Financial subsidies have been among the principal tools in solar policy aimed at promoting solar adoption. One important variable in this policy landscape is budget: in particular, how much budget should be allocated to the program to achieve a desired adoption target? Our first experiment, therefore, compares the impact of incentive programs based on the California Solar Initiative, but with varying budget in multiples of the actual CSI program budget.[3] Specifically, we consider multiples of 0 (that is, no incentives), 1 (which corresponds to the CSI program budget), as well as 2, 4, and 8, which amplify the original budget. To significantly speed up the evaluation (and reduce variance), rather than taking many sample adoption paths for each policy, we compare policies in terms of expected adoption path. This is done as follows: still generate 1000 sample paths at each time step, but only use the state with average number of adopters as initial state for the next time step.

Figure 3 shows the effectiveness of a CSI-based subsidy program on expected adoption trends over the full length of the program. As one would expect, increasing the budget uniformly shifts average adoption up. Remarkably, however, the shift is relatively limited, even with 8x the original budget level. Even more surprisingly, the difference in adoption between no subsidies and incentives at the CSI program levels is quite small: only several more individuals adopt in this zip code, on average.

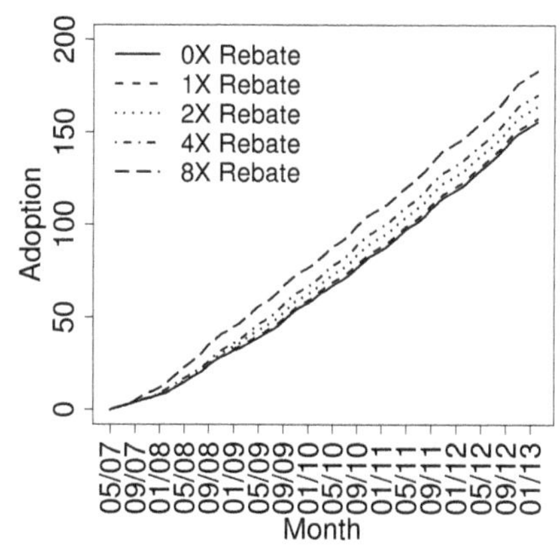

Figure 3: Adoption trends for the CSI-based subsidy structure.

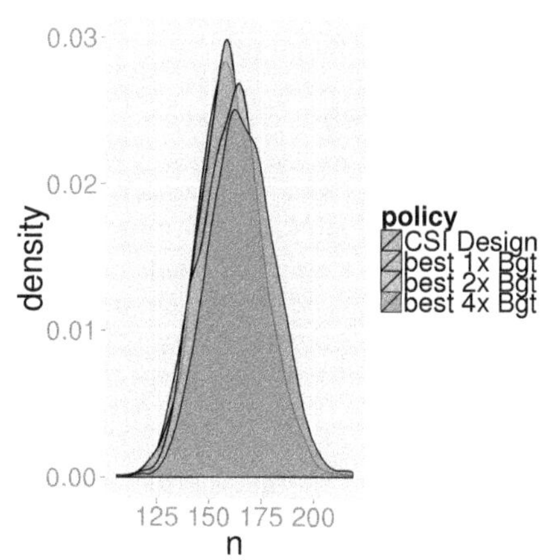

Figure 4: Comparison of distributions of the number of adopters (n) up to 4/13 for "optimal" incentive policies.

[3]It is important to note that the CSI program has many facets, and promoting solar adoption directly is only one of its many goals. For example, much of the program is focused on improving marketplace conditions for solar installers. Our analysis is therefore limited by the closed world assumption of our simulation model, and focused on only a single aspect of the program.

Since we found that the CSI-like solar system subsidies have rather limited effect, a natural question is whether we can design a better subsidy scheme. We proceed by creating a parametric space of subsidy schemes that are similar in nature to the CSI incentive program. Specifically, suppose we have a budget B and a megawatt target M, and we wish to achieve this mega watt goal in T steps. We assign each step a subgoal m^i with the constraint that $\sum_{i=0}^{T-1} m^i = M$. Additionally, we associate with each step i an incentive rate r^i (that is, the subsidy per megawatt), implying a budget constraint $\sum_{i=0}^{N-1} r^i m^i \leq B$. Our goal is to design an incentive schedule (r^i, m^i) which abides by the two constraints above. We restrict the design space by assuming that $r^{i+1} = \gamma r^i$ for all time steps i. In addition, we let each megawatt step m^i to be a multiple of the CSI program megawatt levels in the corresponding step, where the multiplicative factor corresponds to the budget multiple of the CSI program budget. With these restrictions, our only decision is about the choice of r^0, which then uniquely determines the value of γ based on the budget constraint. To choose the (approximately) optimal value of r^0, we simply considered a finely discretized space ranging from 1 to 8 \$/watt for 1x, 2x, and 4x CSI budget. The results, shown in Figure 4 show that the impact of subsidies is quite limited even in this one-dimensional optimization context. Of course, we cannot rule out that more complex optimization schemes would result in significantly greater benefits. However, there are two reasons we do not expect that to be the case, and which explain the relatively small impact that incentives have on adoption. First, the economic factor in our model appears to be relatively weak. This could be due to a host of reasons, including limited availability of data about electricity utilization of non-adopters (we only have this data aggregated by zip code). Indeed, we found that incentive effect increases as we partially de-bias our prediction of electricity rate (as described above), but it does so only slightly. Second, incentives have no effect on leased systems (obviously, no direct effect, but also, we found, they have no appreciable effect on lease prices), which is becoming an increasingly dominant force in the solar market. Next, we examine an alternative space of policies to subsidies, which appears to have a greater impact on adoption.

6.2 Seeding the Solar Market

Suppose that we can give away free solar systems. Indeed, there are policies of this kind already deployed, such as the SASH program in California [7], fully or partially subsidizing systems to low-income households. To mirror such programs, we consider a fixed budget B, a time horizon T, and consider seeding the market with a collection of initial systems in increasing order of cost in specific time periods (a reasonable proxy for low-income households). There is a twofold tension in such a policy: earlier seeding implies greater peer effect impact, as well as greater impact on costs through learning-by-doing. Later seeding, however, can have greater direct effect as prices come down (i.e., more systems can be seeded later with the same budget). We consider, therefore, a space of policies where a fraction of the budget α is used at time 0, and the rest at time $T-1$, and compute a near-optimal value of α using discretization.[4] Our findings, for different budget levels (as before, as multiples of the original CSI budget), are shown in Figure 5. We can make two

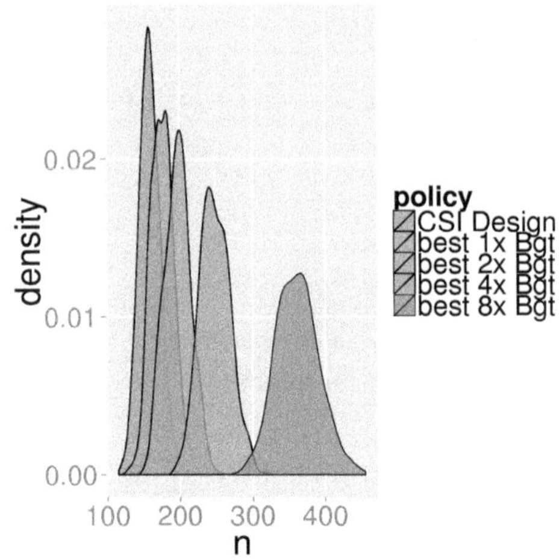

Figure 5: Distribution of final adoptions (n) for optimal split of the seeding budgets.

key observations: first, we can achieve significantly greater adoption using a seeding policy as compared to the CSI program baseline, and second, this class of policies is far more responsive to budget increase than the incentive program.

7. CONCLUSION

We introduced a data-driven agent-based modeling framework, and used it to develop a model of residential rooftop solar adoption in San Diego county. Our model was validated quantitatively in comparison to a baseline, and qualitatively by considering its predictions and quantified uncertainty in comparison with the observed adoption trend *temporally beyond the data used to calibrate the model.* We used this model to analyze the existing solar incentive program in California, as well as a class of alternative incentive programs, showing that subsidies appear to have little impact on adoption trends. We considered another class of policies commonly known as "seeding", showing that adoption is far more sensitive to such policies than to subsidies.

Looking ahead, there are many ways to improve and extend our model. Better data, for example, electricity use data by non-adopters, would undoubtedly help. More sophisticated models of individual behavior are likely to help, though how much is unclear. Additionally, other sources of data can be included, for example, survey data about adoption characteristics, as well as results from behavior experiments in this or similar settings. The importance of promoting renewable energy, such as solar, is now widely recognized. Studies, such as ours, enable rigorous evaluation of a wide array of policies, improving the associated decision process and the increasing the chances of successful diffusion of sustainable technologies.

8. ACKNOWLEDGMENTS

This work was partially supported by the U.S. Department of Energy (DOE) office of Energy Efficiency and Renewable Energy, under the Solar Energy Evolution and Diffusion Studies (SEEDS) program.

[4]In fact, we optimize over discrete choices of alpha (at 0.1 intervals), and the optimal alpha varies with budget.

REFERENCES

[1] Kenneth J. Arrow. The economic implications of learning by doing. *Review of Economic Studies*, 29(3):155–173, 1962.

[2] Frank M. Bass. A new product growth for model consumer durables. *Management Science*, 15(5):215–227, 1969.

[3] Brian Bollinger and Kenneth Gillingham. Peer effects in the diffusion of solar photovoltaic panels. *Marketing Science*, 31(6):900–912, 2012.

[4] E. Bonabeau. Agent-based modeling: Methods and techniques for simulating human systems. *Proceedings of the National Academy of Sciences*, 99(Supp 3):7280–7287, 2002.

[5] Andrea Borghesi, Michela Milano, Marco Gavanelli, and Tony Woods. Simulation of incentive mechanisms for renewable energy policies. In *European Conference on Modeling and Simulation*, 2013.

[6] Wei Chen, Yajun Wang, and Siyu Yang. Efficient influence maximization in social networks. In *Proceedings of the 15th ACM SIGKDD International Conference on Knowledge Discovery and Data Mining*, pages 199–208, 2009.

[7] CPUC. California solar initiative program handbook, 2013.

[8] Garrett M. Dancik, Douglas E. Jones, and Karin S. Dorman. Parameter estimation and sensitivity analysis in an agent-based model of leishmania major infection. *Journal of Theoretical Biology*, 262(3):398–412, 2011.

[9] Paul Denholm, Easan Drury, and Robert Margolis. The solar deployment system (SolarDS) model: Documentation and sample results. Technical report, National Renewable Energy Laboratory, 2009.

[10] N. Draper and H. Smith. *Applied Regression Analysis*. John Wiley & Sons, 2nd edition, 1981.

[11] J. Friedman, T. Hastie, , and R. Tibshirani. *The Elements of Statistical Learning*. Springer Series in Statistics, 2001.

[12] P. A. Geroski. Models of technology diffusion. *Research Policy*, 29(4):603–625, 2000.

[13] Daniel Golovin and Andreas Krause. Adaptive submodularity: Theory and applications in active learning and stochastic optimization. *Journal of Artificial Intelligence Research*, 42:427–486, 2011.

[14] C. Harmon. Experience curves of photovoltaic technology. Technical report, International Institute for Applied Systems Analysis, 2000.

[15] Stephen Judd, Michael Kearns, and Yevgeniy Vorobeychik. Behavioral dynamics and influence in networked coloring and consensus. *Proceedings of the National Academy of Sciences*, 107(34):14978–14982, 2010.

[16] Michael Kearns and Jennifer Wortman. Learning from collective behavior. In *Conference on Learning Theory*, 2008.

[17] David Kempe, Jon Kleinberg, and Éva Tardos. Maximizing the spread of influence through a social network. In *Proceedings of the Ninth ACM SIGKDD International Conference on Knowledge Discovery and Data Mining*, pages 137–146, 2003.

[18] Ruben Lobel and Georgia Perakis. Consumer choice model for forecasting demand and designing incentives for solar technology. Working paper, 2011.

[19] A. McDonald and L. Schrattenholzer. Learning rates for energy technologies. *Energy Policy*, 29(4):255–261, 2001.

[20] John H. Miller and Scott E. Page. *Complex Adaptive Systems: An Introduction to Computational Models of Social Life*. Princeton University Press, 2007.

[21] M.J. North, N.T. Collier, J. Ozik, E. Tatara, M. Altaweel, C.M. Macal, M. Bragen, and P. Sydelko. Complex adaptive systems modeling with repast simphony. In *Complex Adaptive Systems Modeling*. Springer, 2013.

[22] J. Palmer, G. Sorda, and R. Madlener. Modeling the diffusion of residential photovoltaic systems in italy: An agent-based simulation. Working paper, 2013.

[23] V Rai and S.A. Robinson. Determinants of spatio-temporal patterns of energytechnology adoption: An agent-based modelingapproach. Working paper, 2014.

[24] Varun Rai and Ben Sigrin. Diffusion of environmentally-friendly energy technologies: buy versus lease differences in residential pv markets. *Environmental Research Letters*, 8(1):014022, 2013.

[25] W. Rand and R.T. Rust. Agent-based modeling in marketing: Guidelines for rigor. *International Journal of Research in Marketing*, 28(3):181–193, 2011.

[26] K.U. Rao and V. Kishore. A review of technology diffusion models with special reference to renewable energy technologies. *Renewable and Sustainable Energy Reviews*, 14(3):1070–1078, 2010.

[27] S.A. Robinson and V Rai. Agent-based modeling of energy technology adoption:empirical integration of social, behavioral, economic,and environmental factors. Working paper, 2014.

[28] S.A. Robinson, M. Stringer, V. Rai, and A. Tondon. GIS-integrated agent-based model of residential solar pv diffusion. Working paper, 2013.

[29] Everett M. Rogers. *Diffusion of Innovations*. Free Press, 5th edition, 2003.

[30] Jan C. Thiele, Winfried Kurth, and Volker Grimm. Facilitating parameter estimation and sensitivity analysis of agent-based models: A cookbook using NetLogo and R. *Journal of Artificial Societies and Social Simulation*, 17(3), 2014.

[31] Paul Torrens, Xun Li, and William A. Griffin. Building agent-based walking models by machine-learning on diverse databases of space-time trajectory samples. *Transactions in GIS*, 15(s1):67–94, 2011.

[32] Arthur van Benthem, Kenneth Gillingham, and James Sweeney. Learning-by-doing and the optimal solar policy in california. *Energy Journal*, 29(3):131–151, 2008.

[33] P. Zhai and E.D. Williams. Analyzing consumer acceptance of photovoltaics (pv) using fuzzy logic model. *Renewable Energy*, 41:350–357, 2012.

[34] Jiayun Zhao, Esfandyr Mazhari, Nurcin Celik, and Young-Jun Son. Hybrid agent-based simulation for policy evaluation of solar power generation systems. *Simulation Modelling Practice and Theory*, 19:2189–2205, 2011.

Optimizing Efficiency of Taxi Systems: Scaling-up and Handling Arbitrary Constraints

Jiarui Gan
University of Chinese Academy of Sciences
The Key Laboratory of Intelligent Information Processing, ICT, CAS, Beijing 100190, China
ganjr@ics.ict.cn

Bo An, Chunyan Miao
School of Computer Engineering
Nanyang Technological University
Singapore 639798
{boan,ascymiao}@ntu.edu.sg

ABSTRACT

Taxi service is an indispensable part of public transport in modern cities. However, due to its decentralized operation mode, taxi services in many cities are inefficient. Besides, the decentralized nature also poses significant challenges to analyzing and regulating taxi services. State of the art computational methods for optimizing taxi market efficiency suffer from two important limitations: 1) they cannot be scaled up efficiently; and 2) they cannot address complex real-world market situations where additional scheduling constraints need to be handled. In this paper, we propose two novel algorithms—FLORA and FLORA-A—to address the inadequacies. Using convex polytope representation techniques, FLORA provides a fully compact representation for taxi drivers' strategy space and scales up more efficiently than existing algorithms. FLORA-A avoids enumerating the entire exponentially large pure strategy space by gradually expanding the strategy space. It is the first known method capable of handling arbitrary scheduling constraints for optimizing taxi system efficiency. Experimental results show orders of magnitude improvement in speed FLORA provides, and the necessity of using FLORA-A as suggested by changes in the taxi drivers' operation strategy under different market conditions.

Categories and Subject Descriptors

I.2.11 [**Artificial Intelligence**]: Intelligent agents, Multiagent systems

Keywords

Taxi System; Game Theory; Optimization

1. INTRODUCTION

Taxi service has long been an indispensable part of public transport in modern cities. However, taxi systems are quite inefficient and are very difficult to analyze and regulate since they are highly decentralized and are operated by profit-driven drivers (unlike other types of public transport, such as bus and metro systems, operation schedules and movements of taxis can hardly be controlled by regulators). Besides, taxi service can be affected by many factors such as road condition, customer demand, fare price, etc. These factors not only depend on each other in complex ways, but also vary with time. Analyzing, regulating, and optimizing taxi systems are thus important but challenging problems, which have attracted many research interests over the past decades [9, 3, 4, 7]. In this paper, we study the taxi system efficiency optimization problem (through adjusting taxi fare price) with a focus on the computational challenges.

Figure 1: People waiting for taxis during rush hours in Beijing (left) and Chongqing (right) in China.

There has been some existing work concerning taxi system efficiency optimization and taxi pricing. For instance, Schaller studied the effects of fare price increase on taxi market in New York [17]. Kim and Hwang studied an incremental discount policy on the taxi fare with the objective of maximizing average profit of taxis [15]. Yang et al. examined a nonlinear fare structure and showed its advantages over the existing linear fare structure in Hong Kong [21]. These work focused on modeling the interdependencies among market factors, but ignored taxi drivers' profit-driven behaviors and their competitive relations, which are the key to the decentralized nature and the low efficiency of taxi markets. Recent successful applications of AI techniques in the transportation domain (i.e., AI-based traffic control and intersection management [10, 2, 16, 20], and decision support for taxi drivers [19]) have indicated a promising way to analyze the intelligent human behaviors and to address the limitation of above work. Indeed, Gan et al. have proposed a game theoretic approach to address a taxi fare price optimization problem [13, 12]. A time-varying taxi market model was proposed, and taxi drivers' profit-driven and competing behaviors were considered in the model. This work has opened a new door to AI-based taxi market studies.

Unfortunately, the current state of the art algorithms proposed by Gan et al. (e.g., the *atom schedule method* [13]) for computing optimal taxi fare structure are inadequate for dealing with real-world taxi system efficiency optimization problems. Firstly, the algorithm scales up poorly with the

Appears in: *Proceedings of the 14th International Conference on Autonomous Agents and Multiagent Systems (AAMAS 2015), Bordini, Elkind, Weiss, Yolum (eds.), May 4–8, 2015, Istanbul, Turkey.*

number of periods (in order to model a time-varying taxi market, the optimization horizon is discretized into a set of periods, and fine-grained discretization indicates more periods). Secondly, their work only considered taxi drivers' scheduling constraints on maximum total/continuous working time, which is insufficient for some specific cases. For example, in some cities, taxi drivers are not allowed to switch from working to resting during peak hours, and the regulation is effectively implemented with heavy fines and intensive supervision. The effects of the market regulations on taxi drivers' decision-making cannot be ignored, and new algorithms are needed to compute solution under these effects.

In this paper, we propose two novel algorithms to address the limitations of existing work. The first algorithm, FLORA, provides a *fully* compact representation for the complex optimization problem associated with taxi drivers' decision-making process. It utilizes convex polytope representation conversion techniques and reduces the number of variables and constraints to $O(n)$ in the number n of periods. Our second algorithm, FLORA-A, is the first known method for solving taxi system optimization problems with *arbitrary* scheduling constraints. FLORA-A takes advantage of the small support size of the taxi drivers' mixed strategies and the concavity and differentiability of the taxi drivers' utility function. It avoids enumerating the entire exponentially large pure strategy space by gradually expending the strategy space with useful pure strategies. Using FLORA-A, we are able to consider additional constraints existing algorithms fail to handle, such as disabling state switching during rush hours, and setting the minimum continuous working/resting time to eliminate unrealistic schedules where the drivers switch states in a very frequent manner. Experimental results show that 1) FLORA provides orders of magnitude improvement in speed over existing algorithms; and 2) significant changes in the market caused by additional scheduling constraints, which suggests the necessity of using FLORA-A to handle additional constraints when they indeed exist.

2. TAXI SYSTEM EFFICIENCY OPTIMIZATION PROBLEM

The goal of the Taxi system Efficiency optiMization Problem (**TEMP**) is to maximize the *efficiency* of a taxi system through adjusting the *taxi fare*. To this end, the first step is to know how system efficiency is affected by fare price in a taxi market. Results from transportation researches [22, 23] suggest that a taxi market is determined by two key factors—the *fare price* and the *number of working taxis* (i.e., taxis in service, either vacant or occupied). Furthermore, when the taxi drivers' profit-driven behavior is taken into consideration, it turns out that the number of taxis in service also relies on the fare price, because the taxi drivers always adjust their strategies to fit the given fare price, and keep their profits maximized. In this section, we first present a taxi market model based on transportation science researches. Then we model the taxi drivers' profit-driven behavior, and formulate TEMP.

2.1 A Multi-period Taxi Market Model

A taxi market is a dynamic time-varying system. Consider the peak time and the non-peak time of a day, there are huge variances in factors such as the number of potential

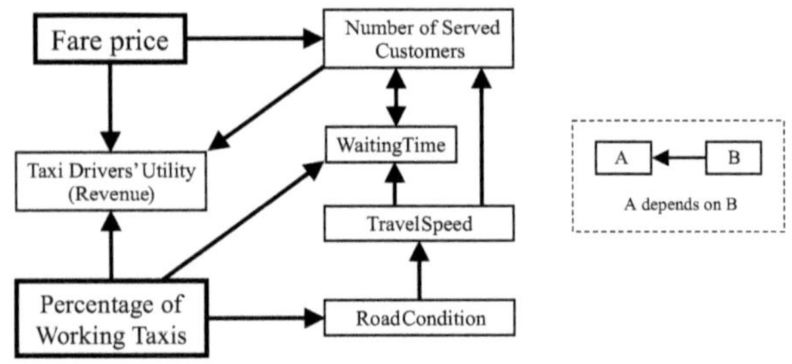

Figure 2: Complex interdependencies among factors in the taxi market.

customers and the travel speed on road. To deal with such variances, we discretize the optimization horizon T (e.g., a whole day) into a set of n equal-length periods, such that when the duration of each period is sufficiently short, the market can be treated as static in each period. We adopt a static taxi market model to each period i. The model involves many factors, and the factors depend on each other in very complex ways (see Figure 2). We start with the number of served customers. The number of customers served by the whole taxi system is determined by average monetary and time cost of a trip [22], i.e.,

$$D^i(F^i, L^i, W^i) = \bar{D}^i \exp\{-\beta(\frac{F^i}{\gamma} + \phi_1 L^i + \phi_2 W^i)\}, \quad (1)$$

where F^i is the average fare price, L^i is the average travel time, and W^i is the average customer waiting time; $\beta > 0$ is a sensitivity parameter; ϕ_1 and ϕ_2 are parameters used for converting time costs into monetary costs; γ is the average number of passengers per ride; $\bar{D}^i$ is the number of potential customers, which is obtained when the total cost is zero. The waiting time W^i is negatively related to the number of vacant taxis available, and in turn depends on D^i as

$$W^i(D^i, L^i, p^i) = \frac{\omega}{p^i \cdot N_T - \frac{D^i L^i}{\gamma \cdot \tau}}, \quad (2)$$

where $\omega > 0$ is a parameter depending on the density of taxi stands; p^i is the Percentage of Working taxis (**PoW**), and given a fixed number N_T of total licensed taxis, $p^i \cdot N_T - D^i L^i/(\gamma \cdot \tau)$ represents vacant taxis available in period i. It can be proven that when F^i, L^i and p^i are fixed, D^i and W^i are uniquely determined by Eqs. (1) and (2) [23]. Therefore, D^i and W^i are in fact implicit functions of F^i, L^i and p^i. We can thus denote them as $D^i = D^i(F^i, L^i, p^i)$ and $W^i = W^i(F^i, L^i, p^i)$.

Given the average trip distance d^i, the travel time is then determined by travel speed V^i as $L^i = d^i/V^i$. Travel speed in a road network can be approximated by a linear function of number of on-road vehicles [18], which is furthermore linear to PoW p^i as we assume that the number N_v^i of non-taxi vehicles on the road is a period-specified constant. Thus, V^i is a linear function of p^i, i.e.,

$$V^i(p^i) = \mu(p^i \cdot N_T + N_v^i) + \lambda,$$

where μ and λ are parameters depending on the road condition. Similarly, we denote L^i, D^i, and W^i as $L^i = L^i(p^i)$, $D^i = D^i(F^i, p^i)$, and $W^i = W^i(F^i, p^i)$, respectively.

We adopt a *distance-based* fare structure (the model can also be extended to other fare structures):

$$F^i = f_0 + f^i \cdot (d^i - d_0),$$

where f_0 is the initial charge and d_0 is the distance covered by f_0; f^i is the charge rate for period i, i.e., the per unit distance charge. We optimize the fare structure through adjusting the charge rate f^i, and thus treat F^i as a function $F^i(f^i)$. Accordingly, all the market factors, particularly the number D^i of served customers, now depend on f^i and p^i, i.e., $D^i = D^i(f^i, p^i)$. For ease of description, we denote a market factor over T as a column vector with each component corresponding to a period. For example, we denote charge rate over all periods as $\mathbf{f} = \langle f^i \rangle$.

2.2 Modeling the Taxi drivers' Strategy

From a game theoretic perspective, the taxi drivers have a set $\mathcal{S}$ of *pure strategies*, and they adopt a *mixed strategy* (*strategy* for simplicity), which is a probability distribution $\mathbf{x}$ over their pure strategies in $\mathcal{S}$. Each pure strategy is a schedule that specifies working and resting periods. Formally, a pure strategy can be denoted as a 0/1 vector $\mathbf{s}\in\{0,1\}^n$, where s^i=1 (resp. s^i=0) represents working (resp. not working) in period i. Each pure strategy has to satisfy some constraints to ensure its feasibility in practice. For example:

- **Constraint 1 (C1):** A taxi driver cannot work for more than $\hat{n}_w$ periods in any schedule in $\mathcal{S}$.
- **Constraint 2 (C2):** A taxi driver cannot work *continuously* for more than $\hat{n}_c$ periods in any schedule in $\mathcal{S}$.

As we will show later, more realistic constraints might be needed in specific scenarios, and different algorithms are developed to cope with different constraint settings. We assume that the taxi drivers adopt the same mixed strategy. Thus when they choose strategy $\mathbf{x}$, PoW is determined as:

$$\mathbf{p}(\mathbf{x}) = \sum\nolimits_{\mathbf{s}\in\mathcal{S}} x_{\mathbf{s}} \cdot \mathbf{s}. \tag{3}$$

Furthermore, since taxi drivers are profit-driven, they always choose the best strategy which maximizes their utility, i.e.,

$$\mathbf{x}^* \in \arg \max_{\mathbf{x}:\, \mathbf{x}\geq \mathbf{0},\, \mathbf{1}^\mathsf{T}\mathbf{x}=1} U\big(\mathbf{f}, \mathbf{p}(\mathbf{x})\big). \tag{4}$$

The utility function $U(\mathbf{f}, \mathbf{p})$ is defined as the sum of utilities in all periods, i.e., $U = \sum_i U^i$, and U^i is defined as

$$U^i(f^i, p^i) = \frac{D^i}{\gamma \cdot N_T} \cdot F^i - p^i \cdot c_f \cdot \tau,$$

where $D^i \cdot F^i/(\gamma \cdot N_T)$ represents the income as $D^i/(\gamma \cdot N_T)$ is the average number of trips each taxi serves, and c_f is the cost of gasoline per unit time. In such a way, the fare price determines the taxi drivers' strategy via the optimization in Eq. (4), and taxi drivers' strategy in turn determines PoW via Eq. (3). Particularly, as shown in Figure 3(a), for a realistic range of charge rates, the second-order partial derivative $\frac{\partial^2 U^i}{\partial {p^i}^2} < 0$ only except for a very small part where PoW is very close to 0. We exclude this part of the function since it occurs when U^i is very close to 0 and has negligible affect on the overall shape of the curve of U^i (Figure 3(b)). Therefore, for a given charge rate f^i, U^i can be treated as a *concave* function with respect to p^i; and U is concave with respect to $\mathbf{p}$ since the Hessian matrix $\nabla^2 U = \text{diag}(\frac{\partial^2 U^1}{\partial (p^1)^2}, \ldots, \frac{\partial^2 U^n}{\partial (p^n)^2})$ is positive definite. Given a convex feasible set of $\mathbf{p}$ there is only one $\mathbf{p}$ that maximizes U [6]. This means even if there are different solutions to Eq. (4), the solutions must all yield the same PoW, such that a one-to-one correspondence from $\mathbf{f}$ to $\mathbf{p}$ is guaranteed.

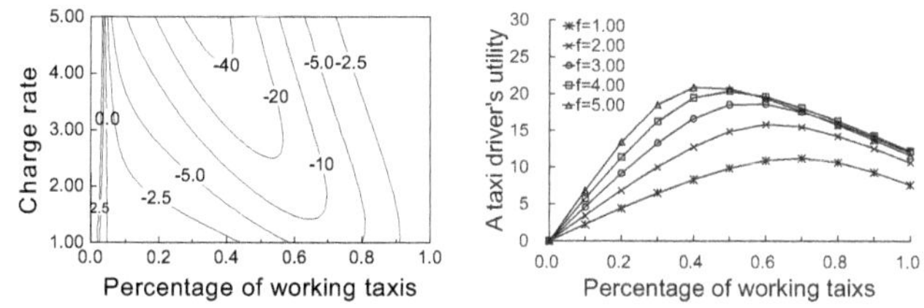

(a) Contours of $\frac{\partial^2 U^i}{\partial {p^i}^2}$ (b) Strict concaveness of U^i

Figure 3: Properties of taxi drivers' utility function

2.3 A Bilevel Optimization Problem

We measure the system efficiency with the total number of served customers, i.e., $D(\mathbf{f}, \mathbf{p}) = \sum_i D^i(f^i, p^i)$, and formulate a TEMP as the following bilevel optimization program.

$$\max_{\mathbf{f}, \mathbf{x}} \quad D\big(\mathbf{f}, \mathbf{p}(\mathbf{x}^*)\big) \tag{5}$$

$$\text{s.t.} \quad \mathbf{x}^* = \arg \max_{\mathbf{x}:\, \mathbf{x}\geq \mathbf{0},\, \mathbf{1}^\mathsf{T}\mathbf{x}=1} U\big(\mathbf{f}, \mathbf{p}(\mathbf{x})\big) \tag{6}$$

The model can also handle other measures of the system efficiency with the same form of optimization program as long as the optimization objective is a function of $\mathbf{f}$ and $\mathbf{p}$. To solve this bilevel optimization problem, a practical way is to discretize the continuous fare price space into a small set of candidate prices, e.g. $\{¥1.00, ¥1.20, \ldots, ¥5.00\}^n$, and solve the lower level program (Eq. (6)) under each of the candidate prices to find the optimal fare price. Thus the key is to compute the lower level program. Unfortunately, the lower level program suffers from a scalability issue caused by the exponential explosion of the taxi drivers' pure strategy space. Next, we present our algorithms to deal with the scalability issue under different circumstances.

3. ALGORITHM WITH FULLY COMPACT REPRESENTATION

In this section, we present our first algorithm FLORA (FuLly cOmpact RepresentAtion). FLORA deals with the scalability issue under constraints **C1** and **C2**. It reduces the scale of the lower level program to $O(n)$ and avoids enumerating any schedule by utilizing a *fully* compact representation of the taxi drivers' strategy space, which is in contrast with the partially compact representation offered by the state-of-the-art algorithm [13].

3.1 FLORA

According to the bilevel program in Eqs. (5)–(6), PoW acts a bridge linking the taxi drivers' strategy and the rest of the system. FLORA uses PoW to compactly represent the taxi drivers' strategy and reformulate the bilevel program as:

$$\max_{\mathbf{f}, \mathbf{p}} \quad D(\mathbf{f}, \mathbf{p}^*) \tag{7}$$

$$\text{s.t.} \quad \mathbf{p}^* = \arg\max_{\mathbf{p}\in\mathcal{P}} U(\mathbf{f}, \mathbf{p}) \tag{8}$$

Thus the number of variables of the lower level program is reduced to n. The major challenge of this approach is to guarantee that the PoW obtained can always be implemented by a feasible mixed strategy of the taxi drivers, namely, to define the feasible set $\mathcal{P}$ of PoW. In an implicit way, $\mathcal{P}$ can be defined as:

$$\mathcal{P} = \left\{ \mathbf{p} \in \mathbb{R}^n \;\middle|\; \begin{array}{l} \mathbf{p} = \sum_{\mathbf{s} \in \mathcal{S}} x_{\mathbf{s}}, \\ \mathbf{0} \le \mathbf{x} \le \mathbf{1} \text{ and } \mathbf{1}^{\mathsf{T}}\mathbf{x} = 1 \end{array} \right\}, \tag{9}$$

which is a convex polytope of $\mathcal{S}$ as a set of n-dimensional points. A convex polytope can be defined in two ways: 1) **V**ertex Representation (V-rep), as the convex hull of a set of points (the set of points contains at least all the vertices of the convex hull); 2) **H**alf-space Representation (H-rep), as the intersection of the set of its facet-inducing half-spaces [14]. Eq. (9) is the V-rep of $\mathcal{P}$. When $\mathcal{S}$ satisfies **C1** and **C2**, the H-rep of $\mathcal{P}$ is the following inequality set, where each inequality defines a half-space.

$$\left(\begin{array}{ccccc} & & I_n & & \\ \hdashline & & -I_n & & \\ \hdashline 1 & & \cdots & & 1 \\ \hdashline 1\ \cdots\ 1 & & & & \\ & \ddots & \ddots & \ddots & \\ & & & & \underbrace{1\ \cdots\ 1}_{\hat{n}_c+1} \end{array}\right) \mathbf{p} \le \left(\begin{array}{c} 1 \\ \vdots \\ 1 \\ \hdashline 0 \\ \vdots \\ 0 \\ \hdashline \hat{n}_w \\ \hdashline \hat{n}_c \\ \vdots \\ \hat{n}_c \end{array}\right). \tag{10}$$

Let the convex polytope defined by the above H-rep be $\mathcal{P}_{\mathrm{H}}$. $\mathcal{P}_{\mathrm{H}}$ is equivalent to $\mathcal{P}$ because:

1. $\mathcal{P} \subseteq \mathcal{P}_{\mathrm{H}}$, since all the vertices of $\mathcal{P}$, i.e., points in $\mathcal{S}$, satisfy Eq. (10). Specifically, the inequality set is divided into four parts by the dashed lines. The first two parts, i.e., $\mathbf{0} \le \mathbf{p} \le \mathbf{1}$, are obviously satisfied by all 0/1 vectors. The third and the fourth parts are equivalent to **C1** and **C2** respectively, and are thus satisfied for all points in $\mathcal{S}$.

2. $\mathcal{P}_{\mathrm{H}} \subseteq \mathcal{P}$, since it can be proven that all the vertices of $\mathcal{P}_{\mathrm{H}}$ are 0/1 vectors (Proposition 1), and they are all in $\mathcal{S}$ since $\mathcal{S}$ contains all 0/1 vectors satisfying **C1** and **C2**.

Thus using the H-rep (written as $\mathbf{Ap} \le \mathbf{b}$ for simplicity), the lower level program is compactly represented as

$$\max_{\mathbf{p}} \quad U(\mathbf{f}, \mathbf{p}) \tag{11}$$

$$\text{s.t.} \quad \mathbf{Ap} \le \mathbf{b} \tag{12}$$

which only has n variables and less than $3n$ constraints.

PROPOSITION 1. *Let $\mathcal{P}_{\mathrm{H}}$ be the convex polytope defined by Eq. (10). All the vertices of $\mathcal{P}_{\mathrm{H}}$ are 0/1 vectors.*

PROOF. Let $\mathbf{v} = (v_1, \ldots, v_n)^{\mathsf{T}}$ be a vertex of $\mathbf{P}_{\mathrm{H}}$. We show that $\mathbf{v} \in \{0,1\}^n$. A vertex of a polytope in an n-dimensional space is in n of the polytope's facets, and is the only solution to an equality system with n equalities each corresponding to a facet. For $\mathbf{v}$, each of the equalities is derived from a row of Eq. (10) by setting inequality to equality. We write the equality system as

$$H'\mathbf{v} = \mathbf{b}, \tag{13}$$

and the augmented form as

$$\widetilde{H}' = \left(\, H' \; \middle| \; \mathbf{b} \, \right). \tag{14}$$

Since H' is part of the matrix in the left of Eq. (10), it has the following properties:

a) it contains only 0 and 1 as its elements;

b) all the 1s in each row are consecutive.

According to these properties, for the ith row $\widetilde{\mathbf{h}}'_i = [\mathbf{h}'_i \,|\, b_i]$ of $\widetilde{H}'$, we define $L(\mathbf{h}'_i) = \min\{j \,|\, h'_{ij} = 1,\, j \in \{1, \ldots, n\}\}$, where h'_{ij} is the jth element of $\mathbf{h}'_i$; and $R(\mathbf{h}'_i) = \max\{j \,|\, h'_{ij} = 1,\, j \in \{1, \ldots, n\}\}$. Namely, $L(\mathbf{h}'_i)$ and $R(\mathbf{h}'_i)$ are the indices of the leftmost and rightmost 1 in $\mathbf{h}'_i$, respectively.

Algorithm 1: Row reduction

1 **for** $k = 1$ *to* n **do**
2 $\quad \mathcal{L}_k \leftarrow \{i \,|\, L(\mathbf{h}'_i) = k,\, i \in \{1, \ldots, n\}\}$;
3 **while** *some* $\mathcal{L}_k$ *contains more than one element* **do**
4 $\quad i_0 \leftarrow \arg\min_i \{R_i \,|\, i \in \{1, \ldots, n\}\}$;
5 $\quad$ **for** *each* $i \in \mathcal{L}_k \setminus \{i_0\}$ **do**
6 $\quad\quad \widetilde{\mathbf{h}}'_i \leftarrow \widetilde{\mathbf{h}}'_i - \widetilde{\mathbf{h}}'_{i_0}$;
7 $\quad\quad \mathcal{L}_k \leftarrow \mathcal{L}_k \setminus \{i\}$;
8 $\quad\quad l \leftarrow L(\mathbf{h}'_i)$;
9 $\quad\quad \mathcal{L}_l \leftarrow \mathcal{L}_l \cup \{i\}$;
10 Rearrange the rows of $\widetilde{H}'$ by the index of the leftmost 1 in ascending order;
11 **for** $i = n - 1$ *to* 1 **do**
12 $\quad$ **for** $j = n$ *to* 1 **do**
13 $\quad\quad \widetilde{\mathbf{h}}'_i \leftarrow \widetilde{\mathbf{h}}'_i - \widetilde{h}'_{ij} \widetilde{\mathbf{h}}'_j$;

We perform row reduction on $\widetilde{H}'$ in the way described by Algorithm 1. Throughout the process, $\widetilde{H}'$ is transformed into the patterns shown in Eq. (15), where entries marked as $*$ are integers. The first step (Lines 1 to 10) is explained as follows:

1. Throughout Lines 1 to 10, $\widetilde{H}'$ always maintains its two properties. This is because the only operation that might break the properties is the subtraction in Line 6, but they always hold since $L(\mathbf{h}'_i) = L(\mathbf{h}'_{i_0})$ and $R(\mathbf{h}'_i) \ge R(\mathbf{h}'_{i_0})$.

2. Line 3 indicates that each $\mathcal{L}_k$ contains less than one element. Moreover, if some $\mathcal{L}_k$ contains no element, then the rank of $\widetilde{H}'$ will be smaller than n, which contradicts the fact that Eq. (13) has only one solution. Therefore, each $\mathcal{L}_k$ contains exactly one row at the end of the while-loop, i.e., there is one and exactly one row in H' where the leftmost 1 has index k, for all $k = 1, \ldots, n$.

$$\widetilde{H}' \xrightarrow{\text{Lines 1 to 10,}} \left(\begin{array}{cccc|c} 1 & * & \cdots & * & * \\ & \ddots & \ddots & \vdots & \vdots \\ & & 1 & * & * \\ & & & 1 & * \end{array}\right)$$

$$\xrightarrow{\text{Lines 11 to 13,}} \left(\begin{array}{cccc|c} 1 & & & & * \\ & 1 & & & * \\ & & \ddots & & \vdots \\ & & & 1 & * \end{array}\right) \quad (15)$$

Lines 11 to 13 further transform $\widetilde{H}'$ into the final pattern. All the entries in the rightmost column remain to be integers, because all the operands in Line 13 are integers. Therefore, the solution to Eq. (13) are integers. We have $\mathbf{v} \in \mathbb{Z}^n$. Since the first two parts of Eq. (10) require that $\mathbf{0} \leq \mathbf{v} \leq \mathbf{1}$, we conclude that $\mathbf{v} \in \{0,1\}^n$. □

4. ARBITRARY CONSTRAINTS

To enhance the practical effectiveness of the optimized fare, we need to build a realistic model of the taxi system and one important modeling component is the scheduling constraints of taxi drivers. FLORA and existing algorithms are all designed for TEMPs with scheduling constraints **C1** and **C2**. In some other cases, it is also necessary to consider other types of scheduling constraints. For example, when the model is more fine-grained, a period has a shorter duration (e.g., half an hour), and it is thus unrealistic that a taxi driver rests or works for only one period each time as it takes time and efforts to find parking when they switch. Therefore, the following constraints need to be considered.

- **C3:** In all schedules in $\mathcal{S}$, if a taxi driver switch to work, she should work continuously for at least $\check{n}_c$ periods.
- **C4:** A taxi driver should rest for at least $\check{n}_r$ periods before she works again in all schedules in $\mathcal{S}$.

Besides, in a well regulated market, it is essential to take into account the impact of market regulations. For example, in some cities in China, such as Chongqing, Fuzhou, Hefei, and Harbin, taxi drivers are not allowed to switch from working to resting during peak hours. The regulation was introduced because it was frequently reported that large numbers of taxi drivers refuse to take passengers in the name of a daily working switch.[1] Such regulations can be effectively implemented (if not in megacities such as Beijing and Shanghai) with the help of intensive supervision and heavy fines, so that their effects are not negligible. Knowing how taxi drivers react to the regulations is thus essential for optimization. Specially, we consider the following constraint.

- **C5:** A taxi driver cannot switch off during peak time in any schedule in $\mathcal{S}$.

However, the existing atom schedule method cannot handle the above constraints. It is not known whether FLORA can be extended to handle them due to the complexity of polytope representation conversion. Generally, the problem of converting a convex polytope from its V-rep to its H-rep is known as the *facet enumeration problem*. The problem is unpredictable in time complexity and the size of output H-rep. No algorithm that runs in time polynomial in the sizes of input V-rep and output H-rep is known [1]; and an n-dimensional 0/1-polytope may contain as many as $O\big((n-2)!\big)$ hyperplanes [11]. These facts make the approach of FLORA unsuitable for dealing with additional scheduling constraints. Next, we present FLORA-A (FLORA with Arbitrary scheduling constraints) to handle *arbitrary* scheduling constraints, given that the utility function is *differentiable* and *concave*. Here by saying arbitrary scheduling constraints, we mean any constraint that can be seen as a function $g : \{0,1\}^n \mapsto \{0,1\}$ that tells whether every schedule (as an n-dimensional 0/1 vector) is feasible or not.

[1]In these cities, a taxi is usually operated by two drivers working on alternative days. When one's shift ends, the driver needs to hand the taxi to the other driver.

Algorithm 2: FLORA-A

1 $\mathcal{S}' \leftarrow n+1$ randomly chosen pure strategies in $\mathcal{S}$;
2 **repeat**
3 $\quad \mathbf{x}^* \leftarrow \arg\max_{\mathbf{x}:\text{ a distribution over }\mathcal{S}'} U\big(\mathbf{f}, \mathbf{p}(\mathbf{x})\big)$;
4 $\quad \mathbf{p}^* \leftarrow \mathbf{p}(\mathbf{x}^*)$;
5 $\quad \mathbf{s} \leftarrow \arg\max_{\mathbf{s}\in\mathcal{S}} (\mathbf{s}-\mathbf{p}^*)^\mathsf{T} \nabla U(\mathbf{p}^*)$;
6 $\quad \mathcal{S}' \leftarrow \mathcal{S}' \cup \{\mathbf{s}\}$;
7 **until** $(\mathbf{s}-\mathbf{p}^*)^\mathsf{T} \nabla U(\mathbf{p}^*) \leq 0$;

4.1 FLORA-A

FLORA-A is outlined in Algorithm 2. Recall that calculating the taxi drivers' optimal strategy suffers from the scalability issue due to the exponential explosion of taxi drivers' pure strategy space. In contrast, to support an optimal mixed strategy, the taxi drivers only need a small fraction of pure strategies out of the exponentially large pure strategy set. This can be explained by the Carathéodory's theorem (Theorem 2), as any point in the convex polytope of PoW (Eq. (9)) falls in a convex hull of $n+1$ or fewer points in $\mathcal{S}$, and can thus be 'implemented' by these points as their convex combination. Therefore, the general idea of FLORA-A is to restrict the pure strategy set to a *small* subset $\mathcal{S}' \subset \mathcal{S}$, e.g., a subset of $n+1$ randomly chosen pure strategies, and calculate taxi drivers' optimal mixed strategy under the restriction. When $\mathcal{S}'$ is very small, the optimal strategy can be simply calculated with the program defined by Eq. (6) (with $\mathbf{x}$ being a probabilistic distribution over pure strategies $\mathcal{S}'$). Since the solution is only optimal against a restricted pure strategy set $\mathcal{S}'$, not being necessarily optimal when the entire pure space $\mathcal{S}$ is considered, FLORA-A furthermore searches for a point $\mathbf{s} \in \mathcal{S}$, such that when $\mathbf{s}$ is added to $\mathcal{S}'$, the solution of the restricted problem can be improved; and FLORA-A repeats the processes of solving the restricted problem and searching for a new pure strategy, until no pure strategy can be added to improve the solution, when the solution obtained must be optimal against the entire strategy space.

The problem thus reduces to how to find a new pure strategy to improve the solution of the restricted problem. To accomplish this, FLORA-A takes advantage of the concavity and differentiability of the objective function. Let $\mathbf{x}^*$ be the optimal mixed strategy of the restricted problem defined over $\mathcal{S}'$. FLORA-A evaluates the gradient of the objective function U at $\mathbf{p}^* = \mathbf{p}(\mathbf{x}^*)$ in the PoW space, and searches for a point $\mathbf{s} \in \mathcal{S}$ such that $(\mathbf{s}-\mathbf{p}^*)^\mathsf{T} \nabla U(\mathbf{p}^*) > 0$ (For ease of description, we write $U(\mathbf{f}, \mathbf{p})$ as $U(\mathbf{p})$, since $\mathbf{f}$ is actually fixed in the lower level program). In such a way:

- If a satisfying point $\mathbf{s}$ is found, $\mathcal{S}'$ is expanded to $\mathcal{S}'' = \mathcal{S}' \cup \{\mathbf{s}\}$, and correspondingly, the PoW space is expanded from the convex polytope of $\mathcal{S}'$, say $\mathcal{P}'$, to that of $\mathcal{S}''$, say $\mathcal{P}''$. The optimal value of U over $\mathcal{P}''$ must be strictly larger than that over $\mathcal{P}'$, because the optimality criterion (Theorem 3) does not hold for $\mathbf{p}^*$ at $\mathbf{s} \in \mathcal{P}''$. Therefore, the solution of the restricted problem is improved when the pure strategy set expands from $\mathcal{S}'$ to $\mathcal{S}''$.
- If no satisfying point exists, then $(\mathbf{s} - \mathbf{p}^*)^{\mathsf{T}} \nabla U(\mathbf{p}') \leq 0$ holds for all $\mathbf{s} \in \mathcal{S}$, and in turn for all points in the convex polytope of $\mathcal{S}$, say polytope $\mathcal{P}$. According to the optimality criterion, $\mathbf{p}^*$ must be optimal over $\mathcal{P}$, which means that the solution of the current restricted problem is already optimal against the entire strategy space.

THEOREM 2 (CARATHÉODORY'S THEOREM [8]). *If point $\mathbf{p} \in \mathbb{R}^n$ lies in the convex hull of a set $\mathcal{S}$, there is a subset $\mathcal{S}'$ of $\mathcal{S}$ consisting of $n+1$ or fewer points such that $\mathbf{p}$ lies in the convex hull of $\mathcal{S}'$.*

THEOREM 3 (OPTIMALITY CRITERION [6]). *Suppose in a concave maximization problem (i.e., a program of maximizing a concave objective function over a convex feasible set) the objective function $f(\mathbf{x})$ is differentiable. Let X be the convex feasible set. Then $\mathbf{x}^*$ is optimal in X if and only if $(\mathbf{x} - \mathbf{x}^*)^{\mathsf{T}} \nabla f(\mathbf{x}^*) \leq 0$ for all $\mathbf{x} \in X$.*

4.2 FLORA-A with Linear Constraints

Notably, when all the scheduling constraints can be expressed as linear constraints, a *mixed-integer programming* (MILP) structured as follows can be employed to facilitate the process of searching for new pure strategies.

$$\max_{\mathbf{s} \in \{0,1\}^n} \quad (\mathbf{s} - \mathbf{p}^*)^{\mathsf{T}} \nabla U(\mathbf{p}^*)$$
$$\text{s.t.} \quad \textit{scheduling constraints as linear constraints}$$

If the optimal solution of the above MILP has a positive objective value, then it can be taken as the new pure strategy; otherwise, we can conclude that no satisfying pure strategy exists. Indeed, constraints **C1**–**C5** can all be expressed as linear constraints:

- **C1 and C2:** As we have shown in Section 3, schedules violating **C1** and **C2** can be eliminated by linear constraints defined in the third and the fourth parts of Eq. (10), respectively.
- **C3:** A schedule where continuous working of $m < \check{n}_c$ periods occurs has the following structure:

$$(\ \dots,\ \ 0,\ \underbrace{1,\ 1, \dots, 1,}_{m}\ \ 0,\ \dots)^{\mathsf{T}}$$

Thus we can define the following linear constraints for all $m = 1, \dots, \check{n}_c - 1$ to eliminate schedules violating **C3**:

$$\begin{pmatrix} 1 & \cdots & 1 & -1 & & & \\ -1 & 1 & \cdots & 1 & -1 & & \\ & \ddots & \ddots & \ddots & \ddots & \ddots & \\ & & -1 & 1 & \cdots & 1 & -1 \\ & & & -1 & \underbrace{1 \ \cdots \ 1}_{m} & & \end{pmatrix} \mathbf{s} < \begin{pmatrix} m \\ m \\ \vdots \\ m \\ m \end{pmatrix}$$

It can be easily verified that a schedule satisfying **C3** satisfies all of the above linear constraints, while one violating **C3** should violates at least one of them. There are $O(n^2)$ such constraints in total.

- **C4:** Similarly, a schedule where a taxi driver rests for $m < \check{n}_r$ periods has the following structure:

$$(\ \dots,\ 1,\ \ \underbrace{0,\ \ 0, \dots,\ \ 0,}_{m}\ 1,\ \dots)^{\mathsf{T}}$$

We can define the following constraints for $m = 1, \dots, \check{n}_r - 1$ to eliminate schedules violating **C4**:

$$\begin{pmatrix} 1 & -1 & \cdots & -1 & 1 & & \\ & \ddots & \ddots & \ddots & \ddots & \ddots & \\ & & 1 & \underbrace{-1 \ \cdots \ -1}_{m} & & 1 & \end{pmatrix} \mathbf{s} < \begin{pmatrix} 2 \\ \vdots \\ 2 \end{pmatrix}$$

There are $O(n^2)$ such constraints in total.

- **C5:** A schedule where taxi drivers switch off during peak time has the following structure:

$$(\ \underbrace{\dots,\ \dots,\ 1,\ 0, \dots,}_{\text{peak periods}}\ \dots)^{\mathsf{T}}$$

We can eliminate schedules violating **C5** with the following linear constraints:

$$\Bigg(\quad \underbrace{\begin{array}{:cccc:} 1 & -1 & & \\ & \ddots & \ddots & \\ & & 1 & -1 \end{array}}_{\text{Peak periods}} \quad \Bigg) \mathbf{s} < \begin{pmatrix} 2 \\ \vdots \\ 2 \end{pmatrix}$$

The number of such constraints is less than the number of peak periods.

5. EXPERIMENTAL EVALUATION

Government data on Beijing's transportation [5] are used for the experiments, and are listed in Tables 1 and 2. The data have also been used by existing work [13]. It provides statistics for 18 one-hour-long periods ranging from 5:00 a.m. to 11:00 p.m. We use the non-linear programming solver KNITRO (8.0.0) to solve all the standard form optimization programs; and we use the solver CPLEX (12.0.4) to solve all the MILPs. All results are obtained on a machine with a 3.10GHz quad core CPU and a 4.00GB memory.

5.1 Scalability of FLORA

The first set of experiments compare the scalability of FLORA with the existing atom schedule method. Models with up to 100 periods are generated with the 18-period data. For an n-period setting, we fix the horizon T to 18 hours, and fix the maximum total and continuous working time to 9 hours and 5 hours, respectively. We use $\tau = 18/n$ (hour) as the duration for each period, and use $\hat{n}_w = \lceil 9 \times \tau \rceil$ and $\hat{n}_c = \lceil 5 \times \tau \rceil$ for **C1** and **C2**. We use linear interpolation to generate period-dependent parameters from the 18-period raw data. Other period-independent parameters remain the same as the 18-period setting.

Table 1: Period-independent parameters

	Value	Description
N_t	6.66×10^4	Total number of licensed taxis
$\bar{N}$	1.00×10^6	Road network capacity
$\bar{d}$	$7.2\ km$	Average trip distance
τ	$1\ hour$	Duration of a period (in hour)
n	18	Total number of periods
n_w	9	Maximum number of working periods
n_c	5	Maximum number of continuous working periods
V_0	$50\ km/hour$	Free-flow speed
β	0.06	Demand sensitive parameter
ϕ_1	¥$20/hour$	Parameter for converting travel time to monetary cost
ϕ_2	¥$40/hour$	Parameter for converting waiting time to monetary cost
ω	400	Parameter for calculating waiting time
γ	1.5	Average number of passengers per trip
c_f	¥$20/hour$	Fuel cost per hour

Table 2: Period-dependent parameters

i	$\bar{D}^i$ ($\times 10^4$)	N_v^i ($\times 10^4$)	i	$\bar{D}^i$ ($\times 10^4$)	N_v^i ($\times 10^4$)	i	$\bar{D}^i$ ($\times 10^4$)	N_v^i ($\times 10^4$)
1	8.99	8.53	7	64.70	59.53	13	159.44	81.53
2	49.43	54.64	8	49.27	47.14	14	112.40	75.95
3	151.93	81.75	9	41.45	43.13	15	34.97	44.31
4	106.87	78.14	10	50.46	46.38	16	45.96	47.95
5	55.42	53.34	11	63.72	54.96	17	28.88	37.42
6	68.76	58.99	12	52.90	59.48	18	21.13	21.99

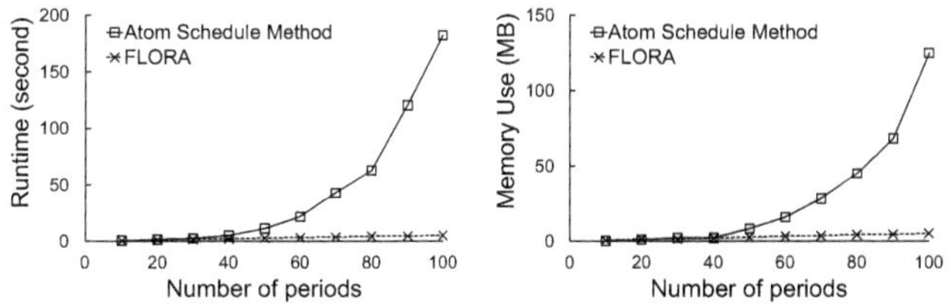

(a) Runtime (b) Memory use

Figure 4: Runtime and memory scalability

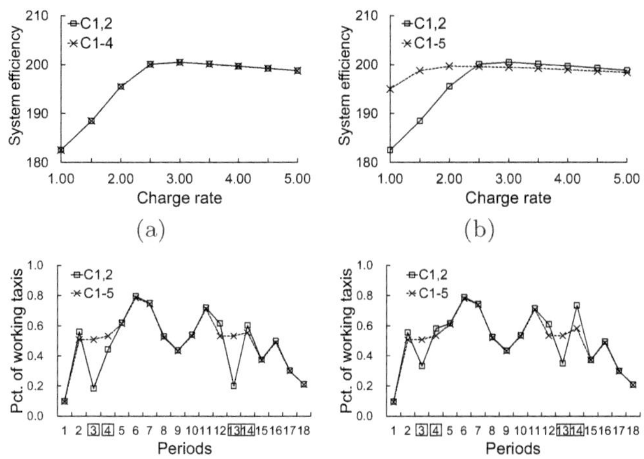

(a) (b) (c) (d)

Figure 5: Market conditions under different constraints: (a) and (b), variations in system efficiency under different constraint settings; (c) and (d), PoW under current and optimal fare, respectively (peak periods are labelled with boxes).

Experimental results show that FLORA returns exactly the same solution as the existing algorithm, verifying the theoretical correctness of FLORA. In Figure 4, FLORA shows orders of magnitude improvement in speed and memory efficiency over the existing atom schedule method. Each result of the experiments is averaged over 50 runs.

5.2 Effects of Additional Constraints

The second set of experiments uses FLORA-A to examine the necessity of considering other constraints.

5.2.1 *Effects of* C3 *and* C4

We first consider the effects of **C3** and **C4**. Experiments conducted by the previous work have only considered **C1** and **C2** (**C1,2** for short) in a 18-period problem where each period lasts for one hour [13]. Under this setting, it is reasonable to not consider **C3** and **C4**, since a working or resting section would naturally last for at least one hour (i.e., one period), which is quite realistic. To examine the effects of **C3** and **C4**, we use a more fine-grained 36-period data generated in the first set of experiments, where each period lasts for only 0.5 hour, and set the minimum durations in **C3** and **C4** as $\check{n}_c$=2 and $\check{n}_r$=2, which amounts to one hour and is in line with the 18-period setting. We fix the charge rate of non-peak periods, and optimize the peak periods (i.e., periods 5–8 and period 25–28) charge rate within {¥1.00, ¥1.20, ..., ¥5.00}. The results show that market conditions under **C1,2** and **C1–4** are the same. As depicted in Figure 5(a), the system efficiency (i.e., total number of served customers ($\times 10^3$)) are exactly the same such that the two curves overlap completely. This suggests that even if **C3** and **C4** are considered, the taxi drivers still have the flexibility to implement the best strategy under **C1,2** as the limitation of **C3** and **C4** are not likely to be reached. We can thus relax **C3** and **C4** and use FLORA, which is more efficient, to compute the approximately optimal solution.

5.2.2 *Effects of* C5

Next, we consider constraint **C5** to check the impact of market regulations. We use the 18-period data and consider all **C1** to **C5** to optimize the peak-time fare price as existing work did [13]. 07:00–09:00 a.m. and 05:00–07:00 p.m. are identified as peak time. Figure 5(b) depicts the variations in system efficiency under different constraint settings, where differences as a result of additional constraints can be easily observed. The **C1–5** curve tends to be flatter because the taxi drivers have less flexibility in arranging their schedule in the presence of market regulation defined by **C5**, and are thus less sensitive to the price change. Different optimal charge rates are also obtained (¥2.80 as for **C1,2**, and ¥2.20 as for **C1–5**). In addition, Figure 5(c) depicts PoW in each period with different constraint settings under the current charge rate (f=¥2.00). The valleys in peak periods in the **C1,2** curve are leveled up in the **C1–5** curve when taxi drivers are not allowed to switch off during peak time. Similar patterns can be observed under optimal charge rates in Figure 5(d). These differences suggest inaccuracy as a result of not considering **C5** in scenarios where market regulation takes effect.

5.2.3 *Performance of FLORA-A*

In addition, we show the performance of FLORA-A in the above experiments. Figure 6(a) shows the convergence of 20 runs, where each run solves an 18-period problem with **C1–5** being considered. All the runs end in less than 50 iterations, and converge very quickly to the optimal value. Figure 6(b) depicts the scalability of FLORA-A in comparison with that of FLORA. FLORA-A is less efficient than FLORA as a tradeoff for being more general.

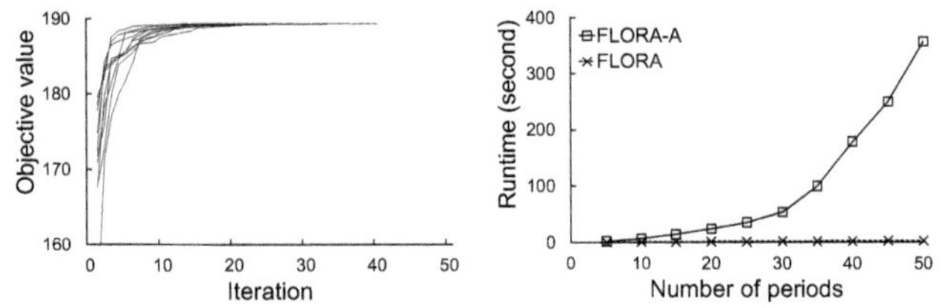

(a) Convergence (b) Runtime

Figure 6: Performance of FLORA-A

5.3 Discussions

As we can see from the above experiments, while FLORA-A is more general and can be used to solve TEMPs with arbitrary scheduling constraints, FLORA is more efficient in dealing with problems with constraints **C1** and **C2**. Even if in the presence of some other constraints, such as **C3** and **C4**, FLORA provides good approximate solutions as shown in Figure 5(a). Therefore, FLORA can be used for solving TEMPs in cities with normal constraints (e.g., **C1** and **C2**) and constraints that FLORA could provide good approximate solutions (e.g., **C3** and **C4**). For TEMPs in cities where other constraints exists (e.g., regulation constraint **C5**), the more general algorithm FLORA-A has to be used.

6. CONCLUSIONS

Our key contributions in this paper are two novel algorithms: 1) FLORA provides a fully compact representation of the taxi drivers' strategy space, which scales up the model far more efficiently than existing algorithms as is shown both theoretically and experimentally; 2) FLORA-A is the first known method for solving taxi system efficiency optimization problems with arbitrary scheduling constraints. It allows us to examine more extensive market conditions, and we believe that it can also be applied to similar large scale optimization problems in other domains.

Acknowledgments

This work is supported by NSFC grant No. 61202212 and Singapore MOE AcRF Tier 1 grant MOE RG33/13. This research is supported by the National Research Foundation, Prime Ministerạ́s Office, Singapore under its IDM Futures Funding Initiative and administered by the Interactive and Digital Media Programme Office.

REFERENCES

[1] D. Avis, D. Bremner, and R. Seidel. How good are convex hull algorithms? *Computational Geometry*, 7(5):265–301, 1997.

[2] A. L. Bazzan. Opportunities for multiagent systems and multiagent reinforcement learning in traffic control. *Proceedings of the International Conference on Autonomous Agents and Multiagent Systems (AAMAS)*, 18:342–375, 2009.

[3] M. E. Beesley. Regulation of taxis. *The Economic Journal*, 83(329):150–172, 1973.

[4] M. E. Beesley and S. Glaister. Information for regulating: the case of taxis. *The Economic Journal*, 93(371):594–615, 1983.

[5] Beijing Transportation Research Center (BTRC). Annual transportation report of Beijing (2011), 2011.

[6] S. P. Boyd and L. Vandenberghe. *Convex optimization*. Cambridge university press, 2004.

[7] R. D. Cairns and C. Liston-Heyes. Competition and regulation in the taxi industry. *Journal of Public Economics*, 59(1):1–15, 1996.

[8] G. Danninger-Uchida. Carathéodory theorem. In C. Floudas and P. Pardalos, editors, *Encyclopedia of Optimization*, pages 236–237. Springer US, 2001.

[9] G. W. Douglas. Price regulation and optimal service standards: The taxicab industry. *Journal of Transport Economics and Policy*, pages 116–127, 1972.

[10] K. Dresner and P. Stone. A multiagent approach to autonomousintersection management. *Journal of Artificial Intelligence Research*, 31:591–656, 2008.

[11] T. Fleiner, V. Kaibel, and G. Rote. Upper bounds on the maximal number of facets of 0/1-polytopes. *European Journal of Combinatorics*, 21(1):121–130, 2000.

[12] J. Gan and B. An. Game theoretic considerations for optimizing efficiency of taxi systems. In *AAAI-15 Workshop on Computational Sustainability*, 2015.

[13] J. Gan, B. An, H. Wang, X. Sun, and Z. Shi. Optimal pricing for improving efficiency of taxi systems. In *Proceedings of the Twenty-Third International Joint Conference on Artificial Intelligence*, pages 2811–2818, 2013.

[14] B. Grunbaum, V. Klee, M. A. Perles, and G. C. Shephard. *Convex polytopes*, volume 2. Springer, 1967.

[15] Y.-J. Kim and H. Hwang. Incremental discount policy for taxi fare with price-sensitive demand. *International Journal of Production Economics*, 112(2):895–902, 2008.

[16] N. Pulter, H. Schepperle, and K. Böhm. How agents can help curbing fuel combustion: a performance study of intersection control for fuel-operated vehicles. In *Proceedings of the 10th International Conference on Autonomous Agents and Multiagent Systems (AAMAS'11)*, pages 795–802, 2011.

[17] B. Schaller. Issues in fare policy: Case of the new york taxi industry. *Transportation Research Record:*

Journal of the Transportation Research Board, 1618(1):139–142, 1998.

[18] J. M. Smith and F. Cruz. State dependent travel time models, properties, & kernerąŕs three-phase traffic theory. 2012.

[19] P. Varakantham, S.-F. Cheng, G. J. Gordon, and A. Ahmed. Decision support for agent populations in uncertain and congested environments. In *Proceedings of the 26th AAAI Conference on Artificial Intelligence (AAAI'12)*, pages 1471–1477, 2012.

[20] X.-F. Xie, S. Smith, and G. Barlow. Schedule-driven coordination for real-time traffic network control. In *Proceedings of the International Conference on Automated Planning and Scheduling (ICAPS)*, pages 323–331, 2012.

[21] H. Yang, C. Fung, K. Wong, and S. Wong. Nonlinear pricing of taxi services. *Transportation Research Part A: Policy and Practice*, 44(5):337–348, 2010.

[22] H. Yang, S. C. Wong, and K. Wong. Demand–supply equilibrium of taxi services in a network under competition and regulation. *Transportation Research Part B: Methodological*, 36(9):799–819, 2002.

[23] H. Yang, M. Ye, W. H.-C. Tang, and S. C. Wong. A multiperiod dynamic model of taxi services with endogenous service intensity. *Operations research*, 53(3):501–515, 2005.

HAC-ER: A Disaster Response System based on Human-Agent Collectives*

Sarvapali D. Ramchurn, Trung Dong Huynh, Yuki Ikuno, Jack Flann, Feng Wu, Luc Moreau, Nicholas R. Jennings
Electronics and Computer Science
University of Southampton
Southampton, UK

Joel E. Fischer, Wenchao Jiang, Tom Rodden
Mixed Reality Lab
University of Nottingham
Nottingham, UK

Edwin Simpson, Steven Reece, Stephen Roberts
Pattern Recognition Group
University of Oxford
Oxford, UK

ABSTRACT

This paper proposes a novel disaster management system called HAC-ER that addresses some of the challenges faced by emergency responders by enabling humans and agents, using state-of-the-art algorithms, to collaboratively plan and carry out tasks in teams referred to as human-agent collectives. In particular, HAC-ER utilises crowdsourcing combined with machine learning to extract situational awareness information from large streams of reports posted by members of the public and trusted organisations. We then show how this information can inform human-agent teams in coordinating multi-UAV deployments as well as task planning for responders on the ground. Finally, HAC-ER incorporates a tool for tracking and analysing the provenance of information shared across the entire system. In summary, this paper describes a prototype system, validated by real-world emergency responders, that combines several state-of-the-art techniques for integrating humans and agents, and illustrates, for the first time, how such an approach can enable more effective disaster response operations.

Categories and Subject Descriptors

I.2.11 [**Distributed Artificial Intelligence**]: Intelligent agents; H.5.2 [**User Interfaces**]: User-centered design

General Terms

Applications

Keywords

Innovative Applications; Human and Agents; Disaster Response.

1. INTRODUCTION

In the aftermath of major disasters (man-made or natural), such as the Haiti earthquake of 2010 or typhoon Haiyan in 2013, emergency response agencies face a number of key challenges [19]. First, it is vital to gain *situational awareness* of the unfolding event to determine where aid is required and how it can be delivered, given that infrastructure may be damaged. Useful information can come from a variety of sources, including people on the ground, relief agencies, or satellite imagery. However, making sense of this information is a painstaking process, particularly as the information sources are liable to noise, bias, and delays. Second, emergency response agencies typically need to gather additional information by deploying unmanned aerial vehicles (UAVs). Using multiple UAVs avoids risking human life but involves additional complexity in controlling the vehicles and visualising the information they feed back [2]. Tasks should be allocated to maximise the amount of information collected, whilst considering limited battery capacity and ensuring human coordinators are not overwhelmed by the need to manually operate individual UAVs. The third challenge is to use situational awareness to allocate relief tasks to emergency responders, for example, digging people out of rubble, moving water treatment units to populated areas, or extinguishing fires. It is crucial to consider the travelling time required for each task, as this blocks responders from performing other tasks [9]. However, the capabilities of individual responders must be considered to ensure that all tasks can be performed effectively and that no one is put in harm's way. For example, it may not be suitable to allocate medics to densely built-up areas where a fire is spreading, or to attend casualties during riots. Finally, given that the disaster environment is highly uncertain and liable to change significantly, it is crucial that emergency response agencies can track and verify the information and decisions that they use, allowing them to modify or reinforce the current course of action whenever new information is detected or previously trusted information is invalidated, e.g. through direct verification by other organisations.

Against this background, we propose a prototype disaster management system called Human-Agent Collectives for Emergency Response, or HAC-ER (pronounced 'hacker'), that demonstrates how humans and agents can be coalesced into teams called *Human-Agent Collectives* (HACs) [8] to address the above challenges. We designed our system collaboratively with emergency responders from Rescue Global[1] and other defence organisations in the UK, and trialled our system with over 100 users, to determine how HACs can support emergency response in different activities. In more detail, this paper first demonstrates a HAC that integrates crowdsourcing to gather, interpret and fuse information from both trusted agencies and members of the public on the ground, and thereby determine priority areas for responders. We then develop a system for multi-UAV coordination using a HAC, which involves both a distributed coordination algorithm and a number of human operators to prioritise search areas. Rescue targets identified by UAVs are then passed to a HAC composed of a planning agent and responders on the ground, who work together to determine a schedule for

*Watch a video on HAC-ER here: http://bit.ly/17aDRqt.

Appears in: *Proceedings of the 14th International Conference on Autonomous Agents and Multiagent Systems (AAMAS 2015), Bordini, Elkind, Weiss, Yolum (eds.), May 4–8, 2015, Istanbul, Turkey.*

[1] http://www.rescueglobal.org.

the completion of tasks. Finally, we employ a provenance tracking and analysis tool to allow the HACs to react to events and provide accountability for both human and agent-based decision making.

The rest of this paper is structured as follows. Section 2 discusses the decision making challenges addressed by HAC-ER. Section 3 presents our crowdsourcing support tool, while Section 4 describes our mixed-initiative UAV command interfaces. Section 5 then shows how to allocate emergency responders to rescue targets and Section 6 describes how information and decisions are tracked by a provenance manager to guarantee system reliability in dynamic environments. Finally, Section 7 concludes the paper.

2. DECISION MAKING IN DISASTER RESPONSE

Emergency response agencies are typically hierarchical, military-style organisations that employ the OODA framework[2] [5, 6]. A command and control structure is established whereby decision making is divided into strategic, tactical, and operational levels. The teams responsible for each are sometimes referred to as Gold, Silver, and Bronze respectively.[3] At the strategic (Gold) level, decision makers from all major response agencies involved decide on the main objectives of the response effort. At the tactical level, based on the specified objectives, the Silver command team decides on the allocation of resources and tasks to be carried out, while at the operational level, Bronze first responders (FRs), on the ground, determine the logistics required to carry out those tasks. Information gathered from the ground is also passed back up from Bronze, through Silver, to Gold.

In this paper, we focus on the challenges faced by the Silver and Bronze levels of these organisations respectively. The Silver commanders need to gain *situational awareness*, that is, gather information from the disaster scene, ensure this information is reliable, and then attempt to efficiently schedule resources and tasks on the ground to meet their objectives. Thus, situational awareness may be gathered using a combination of: (i) crowdsourced reports from members of the public, (ii) deployments of UAVs in collaboration with Bronze FRs to collect aerial imagery and locate key targets (iii) deployments of FRs to gather first-hand information, while carrying out response efforts in collaboration with other agencies and citizens.

These different information sources come with different levels of reliability and at different costs. For example, gathering data from online crowdsourcing platforms such as Twitter[4] or Ushahidi[5] only requires relatively cheap web technology, but the reports from such platforms can be posted by unverified sources. Instead, deploying UAVs or FRs on the ground helps gather more reliable data and information but this may turn out to be an expensive exercise if the UAVs get damaged, or even tragic if FRs are put in danger. Hence, it is important to avoid deploying FRs to the ground, and instead focus on gathering as much high quality data from crowds and UAVs as quickly as possible. To this end, we design HAC-ER with the aim to support the work of human emergency responders with a number of agent-based tools. In more detail, we first develop machine learning agents to annotate crowdsourced reports and generate heatmaps for Silver commanders to visualise key priority areas

[2]OODA stands for Observe-Orientate-Decide-Act. It is a well established information gathering and decision making process for deployments in dynamic environments.

[3]Variants of this organisational structure do exist but we find that the Gold, Silver, Bronze model is the most prevalent from our interactions with emergency responders such as Rescue Global and Hampshire County Council.

[4]`www.twitter.com`.

[5]`www.ushahidi.com`.

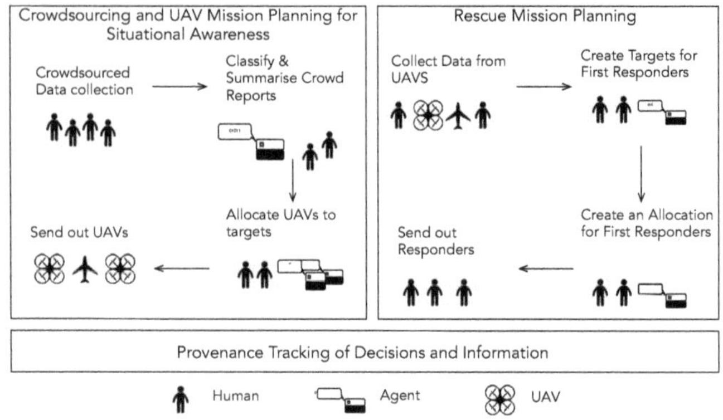

Figure 1: Information gathering and decision making process in the HAC-ER disaster management system.

(see Section 3). We then show how information from heatmaps can be used in determining UAV deployment plans that are generated using a decentralised coordination algorithm (see Section 4). Fig. 1 describes these two steps (top-left box) as part of an OODA loop, where the information gathered from the crowd (Observe) is used to decide on a plan for the UAV deployment (Orientate/Decide), which is then is carried out (Act).

During UAV missions, Silver operators at headquarters will typically monitor the video feeds coming back from the UAVs, while Bronze operators will supervise individual UAVs, and, at times, tele-operate them to gather more detailed information. As targets on the ground (e.g., casualties, collapsed buildings, fuel sources) are identified through this process, these targets are used by Silver commanders to allocate tasks to FRs. To help make these decisions, we developed interfaces for mixed-initiative task allocation, whereby human commanders interact with planning agents running coordination algorithms that exploit sensor data. Through this interaction, planning agents can compute plans that are efficient and *acceptable*, i.e. satisfy human preferences. The different steps of the mission planning process are graphically expressed in Fig. 1 (top-right box).

In general, a large amount of information is generated by various actors (humans, software agents, and UAVs) in a disaster response operation. Hence, a major contribution of this paper is the method by which provenance is tracked and used to improve the decision making process, providing accountability and ensuring dependencies between information and decisions are continuously recorded. This tracking system underlies all the decision making processes in our disaster management system (the bottom box in Fig. 1).

In this section, we have described how different components of HAC-ER fit into the organisation of emergency response agencies during major disasters. The following sections elaborate on each element of the HAC-ER system, namely the CrowdScanner, the Mixed-Initiative UAV Controller, the Mixed-Initiative Task Allocation System, and the Provenance Tracking System.

3. CROWDSCANNER

With the widespread popularity of mobile networks and the Internet, people affected by a disaster nowadays routinely post text messages or photographs to platforms such as Twitter or Ushahidi, reporting the situations on the ground in real time covering a wide area before FRs even arrive [12]. Thus, first-hand reports by members of the public has become a key source of information during a disaster, in addition to reports from FRs and aerial imagery of the effected areas. Vast quantities of data can be produced very rapidly as the disaster unfolds, which can overwhelm the silver commanders who require situational awareness to plan operations.

Only some of the information may be relevant and reports may be erroneous, out of date or duplicated (e.g. retweets). To overcome information overload, we design a software agent for situational awareness, the CrowdScanner, which uses machine learning to fuses heterogeneous reports into a common picture of the disaster, or a *heatmap of incidents*. Our approach is able to automatically combine information from both unreliable and trusted sources, filter out erroneous data, and help Silver commanders visualise the relevant information via a series of map overlays on a computer screen (see Fig. 2).

Our approach takes a large set of *unstructured data* from across a disaster zone, including geo-tagged text reports or images, and converts this to structured data with the help of a crowd of non-experts. The crowd answers key questions about each image or report and either (a) classifies it as one of several types of emergency, such as a collapsed building or medical emergency, or (b) indicates no emergency at that location, or (c) marks it as irrelevant. The crowd may also correct locations associated with reports if places are mentioned in the text do not correspond with their geotags. Machine learning algorithms then interpret this crowdsourced structured data to build a statistical model of the disaster area.

Our approach combines two key machine learning techniques, independent Bayesian classifier combination (IBCC) [17] and the Gaussian Process (GP) [14] into an algorithm that uses the principled Bayesian information framework to:

- efficiently combine classifications from different members of the crowd to remove erroneous information and rectify misclassifications,
- predict the location of emergencies across an entire disaster area by interpolating between sparse reports, and
- select subsets of reports to pass to the crowd for labelling and thus minimise the work undertaken by the crowd.

The IBCC algorithm combines crowd-classified reports from heterogeneous sources at each location to estimate the probability of an emergency at those locations. To do this, IBCC learns a *confusion matrix* [17] that encodes the reliability of each information source, such as an individual reporter or an NGO. By accounting for variations in accuracy of reports from different sources, we can fuse both highly trusted reports and weaker, error-prone data. Our prototype application demonstrates this by combining real Ushahidi reports written by people in Haiti after the 2010 earthquake, with simulated FR reports. Each FR is given a separate confusion matrix, but we do not have identifiers for the authors of Ushahidi reports. Instead, we have several classes of reports corresponding to different emergency categories,[6] which we treat as distinct information sources with separate confusion matrices. We can thereby account for the relevance of each type of report when predicting emergencies at a specific location.

IBCC does not require training with ground truth labels, but is instead an unsupervised approach that fits a model given only crowdsourced data and prior distributions over the confusion matrices and *emergency occurrence probability*, κ. We set the confusion matrix priors for Ushahidi reports to have a weak bias towards correctly indicating emergencies, encoding our initial uncertainty about their reliability. For the FRs, the priors are set to reflect our greater prior confidence in the accuracy of their reports. As more data is assimilated, IBCC is updated, and uncertainty in both κ and the confusion matrices decreases.

Now, we note that disasters can impact neighbouring areas in very similar ways. For instance, an earthquake will affect similar infrastructure in neighbouring locations, and a flood can impact adjacent areas in similar ways. Hence, we extend the standard IBCC model to accommodate this insight into a novel algorithm that can make predictions at locations where we are missing reports. Our extended model assumes that the emergency occurrence probability varies reasonably smoothly from location to location. To model this, we assume that $\kappa(x, y) \in [0, 1]$ at coordinates (x, y) is drawn from a Gaussian process (GP), which is a distribution over smooth functions defined over the entire spatial disaster zone. The GP is mapped through a sigmoid function so that the distribution over $\kappa(x, y)$ is in the range $[0, 1]$ as detailed in [15]. We choose a low order isotropic, stationary Matérn covariance function to model the emergency occurrence probability over the two dimensional disaster zone as this does not impose a too stringent smoothness on $\kappa()$. The GP is fully integrated within the IBCC framework and consequently, inference of the combined IBCC/GP model is performed efficiently by variational Bayes. The length scales of the GPs are the most likely values found using the Nelder-Mead algorithm to optimise the variational lower bound. Our algorithm uses the GP to aggregate neighbouring reports and interpolate between them to determine the posterior distribution of $\kappa(x, y)$ across the entire space.

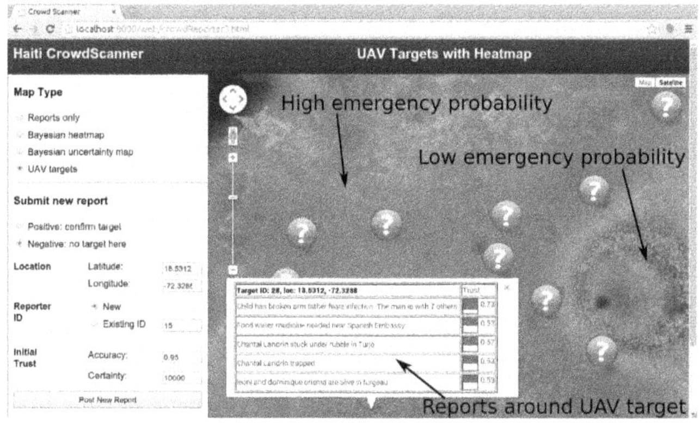

Figure 2: Heatmap user interface for Port-au-Prince after the 2010 Earthquake, showing high probability of emergency (red) and low probability (blue). The area marked as low emergency probability was identified using reports from FRs. Targets for UAVs are marked identified by red '?' icons.

We plot the posterior distribution of emergencies over the entire disaster zone as a heatmap, as shown in Fig. 2, to highlight areas that require emergency aid. We can also show a heatmap of the variance in $\kappa()$, where high variance indicates regions for which little information about the emergency status is available. By fully exploiting information between neighbourhoods, our new method reduces uncertainty in the emergency situation at each location and consequently decreases the number of reports that must be labelled by the crowd. Furthermore, we use our algorithm to prioritise crowd labelling of reports at highly uncertain locations, and, when such reports are not available, to identify locations for further reconnaissance. From the heatmaps, we can automatically extract targets for UAVs to gather aerial imagery from likely emergency locations, to either confirm the precise nature of the emergency or invalidate reports and refocus response efforts. Targets are extracted by marking the peaks of the heatmap within the flight range of a UAV. These are depicted by red '?' icons in Fig. 2. The next section details our HAC approach for deploying UAVs to these targets.

[6]The Ushahidi dataset does not contain labels indicating 'no emergency here'; such reports were collected but not marked in the original Ushahidi project, although this would be useful in future.

4. MIXED-INITIATIVE UAV CONTROLLER

The targets suggested by the CrowdScanner come with varying degrees of certainty. Hence, the emergency response team will aim to verify these targets with first-hand knowledge. UAVs are typically used for this purpose to avoid putting personnel in harm's way. However, in most cases, the number of UAV operators available will be limited and the team will aim to send as many UAVs out as possible to gather information as quickly and effectively as possible. Hence, in what follows, we describe HAC-ER's UAV mission planning and command system that provides Silver commanders with supervisory control to allocate multiple UAVs to fly over points of interest in a disaster area so as to verify the potential targets. Moreover, we develop interfaces for low-level UAV tele-operation by individual Bronze operators on the ground to identify specific items of interest from the UAVs' camera feeds.

In more detail, the interaction between Silver and Bronze operators is mediated through voice-based communication as well as interface elements (see Section 4.2). This is an important part of the system as Bronze and Silver operators may have diverging views on how to operate the UAVs. For example, in the dynamic conditions of a disaster scenario, a Bronze operator may ground a UAV if she thinks the weather conditions are inappropriate, or she may take control to focus the UAV on a particular area to gather imagery. This may disrupt the plan decided by the Silver operators. We address this in Section 4.2.3 by designing the interaction to support dynamic handover of control between Silver and Bronze.

Furthermore, the human team is supported by coordinating agents that are individually in charge of the UAVs. More specifically, agents employ a decentralised coordination algorithm to allocate tasks among themselves. Thus, Silver operators are able to specify goals for the UAVs to achieve (fly to a point, scan a region) and the algorithm (distributively run by individual agents) allows the UAVs to decide which of them is best suited for each task. Crucially, our approach coordination implements the notion of flexible autonomy [8], whereby the agents' plan can be influenced by the human operators. We elaborate on this in the following section.

4.1 Flexible Decentralised Coordination

The flexible coordination module continuously monitors the state of the UAVs and tasks defined in the system and dynamically determines a task allocation plan to minimise the time that the UAVs take to complete their allocated task(s). We employ *max-sum* as the de facto coordination algorithm given that UAVs are naturally distributed in the scenario. As shown in [16], max-sum provides good approximate solutions to challenging dynamic decentralised optimisation.[7] However, max-sum does not explicitly handle constraints imposed by human operators. For example, if after running max-sum, agent A is tasked to go to point X, agent B to point Y, and agent C to point Z, there is no explicit method for human operators to partially modify the plan such that agent A goes to point Y, and B and C *automatically* re-allocate points Y and Z among themselves in the best way possible. Hence, to cater for such situations, we extend the max-sum algorithm to include constraints specified by human operators. In what follows, we provide a brief overview of the max-sum algorithm.[8]

4.1.1 The Max-Sum Algorithm

The max-sum algorithm works by first constructing a factor graph representation of a set of tasks (each representing a point or waypoints UAVs are meant to fly to) and the set of agents (each representing a UAV) and then sets a protocol for an exchange of messages between different nodes in the factor-graph. The factor graph is a bipartite graph where vertices represent agents and tasks, and edges the dependencies between them. Given a set of tasks, D, max-sum determines a subset of these tasks $D_i \subseteq D$ that are most appropriate for each UAV, i, using branch-and-bound techniques [16]. Effectively, this means pruning the factor graph to generate an acyclic graph over which max-sum is guaranteed to converge to a solution. Given this graph, agent and task nodes exchange messages that capture the utility of different allocations. Eventually, each agent node determines its best allocation by maximising over the sum of all messages it receives.

4.1.2 Integrating Human Input

Using a utility function defined from the time required for a UAV to fly to tasks, the priority of each task, and its urgency, max-sum allocates each UAV to a task to maximise the overall utility as per [3]. However, this assignment may not be accepted by the human operators as it may not consider the qualitative and quatitative priorities that humans attribute to tasks [18] as well as flight paths. For example, a UAV may be allocated by max-sum to fly from its position in the East to a task in the West but the human operators may, instead, prefer a UAV to fly from the South to the same task to provide imagery over the area covered by that path, which may be more important than the lateral traversal from East to West.

Against this background, given a plan computed by max-sum, through our planner interfaces (see Section 4.2), users can specify *manual* allocations of UAVs to tasks. These manual allocations specify a task-agent pair. Given this, for each agent i, we then define a set of tasks $D_i = \{j\}$. This effectively results in the deletion of all edges in the factor graph that connect the agent node i with other task nodes apart from that of j. This, in turn, forces max-sum to only allocate agent i to task j, and if two or more agents are required by task j, another agent will be chosen based on this restriction.

4.2 Interaction Design

We designed a number of fully functional, web-based user interfaces to allow a human-agent team to coordinate the UAVs. Through these interfaces, Silver operators visualise the plans suggested by max-sum and modify these plans as required. We also provide an interface for the Bronze operator to tele-operate a selected UAV. We next detail the interactions within each view.

4.2.1 Camera View

The camera view provides multiple live video streams from the UAVs (an MPEG stream is available from typical UAV camera modules). In a simulation of the system, we employed Google Maps[9] *aerial* view (see left of Fig. 3 for feeds from six UAVs). The images displayed are taken at real GPS locations of the UAVs in the disaster area. Targets, as identified by the CrowdScanner, are positioned at specific points in the area considered and displayed on the aerial view whenever the UAV flies over it. The user can then click on the map and create an annotation with the matching description as perceived by the Silver or Bronze operator. Once a target has been identified, an icon describing the target is then displayed across all views to ensure immediate situational awareness across the team.

An important feature of the interface is the flagging system, which Silver operators can use to alert Bronze operators when specific items of interest appear in the camera view. A special (clickable) button on each camera view highlights to the Bronze operator that

[7]Other decentralised coordination algorithms could be used here (e.g., DPOP, ADOPT, BnB-ADOPT) as we only adapt the tree over which they run to compute a solution.

[8]A detailed description of max-sum is beyond the scope of this paper. The reader is referred to [3, 10, 16] for more details on the implementation of max-sum for UAVs and task allocation domains.

[9]http://maps.google.com.

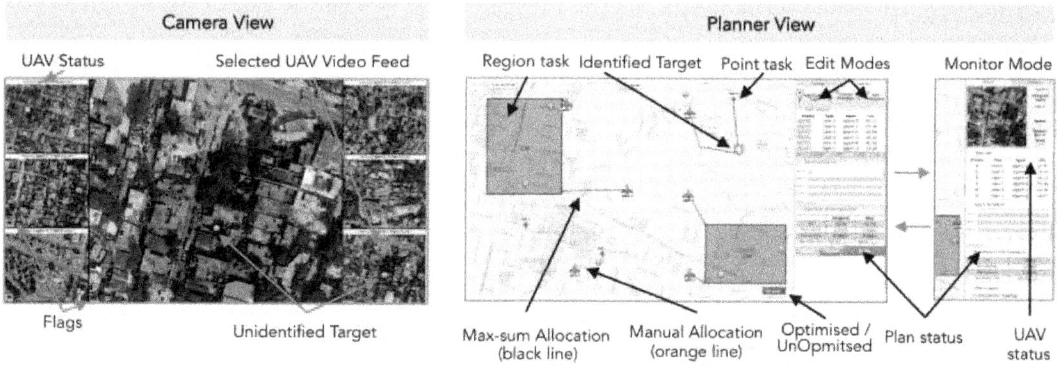

Figure 3: Silver operators' views including the camera view and the two modes of the planner view.

a specific UAV needs attention (see Section 4.2.3). Moreover, if a Bronze operator takes over control of a particular UAV, this UAV's camera view updates its status to 'tele-operated'. By so doing, we allow Silver and Bronze operators to coordinate their actions.

4.2.2 *Planner View*

This is the main planning tool that provides both monitoring and planning capabilities (see right of Fig. 3). Operators can choose to create two types of tasks for the UAVs; *point* tasks with way points for UAVs to fly to specific points in the space and scan the area along the way, and *region* tasks that define areas that teams of UAVs can self-organise to sweep-scan (i.e., they automatically divide the area between themselves and scan their individual sections). The operator can decide, either using max-sum or manually, which UAV should go to each of these tasks. These capabilities are accessible in two modes accessible through the tabs on the top right, namely 'Monitor' and 'Task Edit'. We describe each of these modes in turn.

Monitor Mode

This mode shows the current status of the allocation (see the right part of Fig. 3). The allocation of UAVs to tasks is represented as lines with arrowheads. Region tasks are marked as grey boxes and point tasks using icons. Paths chosen by the max-sum algorithm are shown in black, while paths chosen manually by the users are shown in orange. Once a region task has been completed, the grey box turns green. A region task is deemed completed when UAVs have covered its area, and a point task is considered completed when the allocated UAV has reached that task and hovered for 5 seconds. Once a point task is completed, the task disappears from the map. The right side of the monitor displays the current allocation of agents to tasks, the expected completion times and the schedule (as a Gantt chart) of the UAVs going to the tasks.

Task Edit Mode

This mode provides the user with a number of planning options (see right part of Fig. 3) through a number of sub-modes. The user can:

1. add/delete tasks (region or point): Users can create two types of tasks: (i) region tasks — this task requires two UAVs to carry out a sweep scan of the area selected by the user, and (ii) point tasks — a point selected in the map.

2. change/adapt the allocation of tasks to agents: the allocation automatically computed by max-sum can be changed by the user by clicking on a UAV and allocating it to another task. Max-sum then adapts its allocation to fit to the constraint set by the user (as per Section 4.1.1). For each allocation, a straight line is drawn from the selected UAV to the selected task (unless way points are specified).

3. add way points to the paths taken by the UAVs: this applies to paths chosen to point tasks, whereby users can adjust the path taken by a UAV to cover areas in more complex ways than in region tasks.

Once an allocation of UAVs to tasks has been chosen, the user can verify the completion time of the tasks using the side bar widgets and then decide to execute the plan.

4.2.3 *Bronze Operator View*

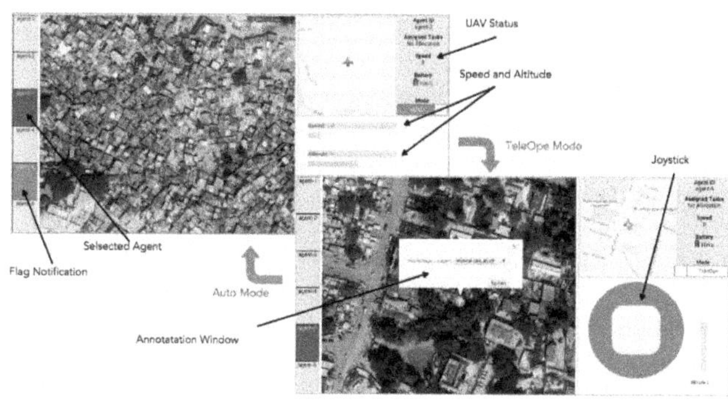

Figure 4: Tablet-based Bronze Operator Views.

The Bronze operator view is displayed on a tablet interface. In this view (see Fig. 4), the Bronze operator can select the specific UAV she may want to tele-operate or supervise more closely. Each UAV's camera view is accessible under different tabs (left of the screen). Additionally, in this view, we provide a notification mechanism for the Silver commanders to alert the Bronze operators, whereby the tab related to a specific UAV can be made to flash when the Silver commander 'flags' the UAV in their screen.

The view also incorporates a simulated joystick that controls the direction and speed of the UAV (pushing further in a given direction speeds up the UAV) and a slider that regulates the altitude of the UAV. The Bronze view is designed to receive live video feed from any drone that transmits an MPEG video stream.

5. MIXED-INITIATIVE TASK ALLOCATION

Having confirmed the locations of key targets in the disaster area through the UAVs, we next consider the deployment of FRs on the ground. More specifically, in this section we describe the system for Silver commanders to compute task allocations for Bronze FRs using the help of a planning agent. In this section, we first provide an overview of the model used by the planner agent, then describe the interaction mechanisms for the planner agent to allocate tasks to the FRs.

5.1 The Planner Agent

We developed an algorithm for a planner agent, that computationally models the behaviour of FRs in terms of the actions they take and the teams they form to complete their tasks. In contrast to the UAV task allocation problem where operators (Bronze or Silver) control UAVs at will, allocating human FRs requires judging whether they are fit to perform their tasks and whether there are any constraints that prevent them, individually, from doing so.

Given such uncertainties due to human behaviour, we model the task allocation problem using decision theoretic techniques. In more detail, the algorithm receives GPS locations of targets from the Mixed-Initiative UAV Controller and the location of FRs through their mobile responder tool (see Section 5.2.2). We model the problem of allocating FRs to targets using a *Multi-Agent Markov Decision Process* (MMDP). In what follows we only describe the MMDP model we use to solve the planning problem as the implementation details are beyond the scope of this paper.

Formally, an MMDP is defined as tuple $\langle I, S, \{A_i\}, T, R, s^0, \gamma \rangle$, where: $I = \{1, 2, \cdots, n\}$ is the set of n FRs as described above; S is a set of system states (e.g., where the FRs are positioned, their current task); A_i is the action set of FR $i \in I$; $T : S \times \vec{A} \times S \to [0, 1]$ is the transition function where $\vec{A} = \times_{i \in I} A_i$ is the set of joint actions; $R : S \times \vec{A} \to \Re$ is the reward function (e.g., the level of completion of a rescue mission or the time it takes to distribute vital resources); $s^0 \in S$ is the initial state; and $\gamma \in (0, 1]$ is the discount factor. Here, an action $a_i \in A_i$ is what an FR can do in one step in a fixed amount of time so all FRs complete their actions at the same time as commonly assumed in other MMDP applications. If some task takes much longer than others, FRs only need to repeat their actions several times until the task is finished. The outcome of solving an MMDP is a policy $\pi : S \to \vec{A}$ that maps from states to joint actions. Starting in state s^0, a joint action $\vec{a}$ is selected based on policy π. Each agent executes its component a_i of the joint action and the system transitions to next state s' based on the transition function. This process repeats with the new state s'. The objective of solving an MMDP is to find a policy that maximises the discounted expected values.

This MMDP can be fed to standard solvers (e.g., UCT [1]). However, this will be very inefficient due to the large search space of the model. Hence, we decompose the decision-making process into a hierarchical planning process: at the top level, a task planning algorithm is run for the whole team to assign the best task to each FR given the current state of the world; at the lower level, given a task, a path planning algorithm is run by each FR to find the best path to the task from her current location. Furthermore, since not all states of MMDPs are relevant to the problem, we only need to consider the reachable states given the current state. Hence, we compute the policy online, starting from the current state. This reduces computation significantly because the number of the reachable states is usually much smaller than the overall state space.

In more detail, we define the team values that reflect the level of performance of FR teams in performing tasks. This is computed from the estimated rewards that the teams obtain for performing the tasks. The expected values after completing the tasks are estimated by Monte-Carlo simulations. Given the team values, we assign a task to each team by solving a *mixed integer linear program* that maximises the overall team performance given the current state, subject to the requirements of each task to FRs. In the path planning phase, we compute the best path for a FR to her assigned task. Since there are uncertainties in the environment and the responders' actions, we model this problem as a single-agent MDP that can be solved by *real-time dynamic programming*. By so doing, we assign tasks to FRs such that their long term effects are rewarding while reduce the search space to a tractable size.

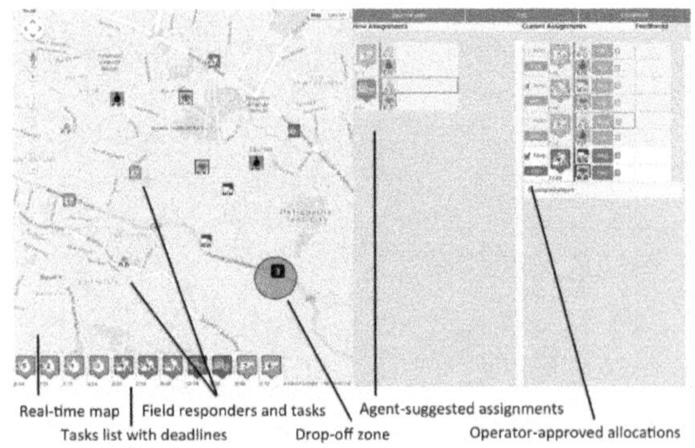

Figure 5: The Silver commanders' task allocation interface.

The output of our algorithm is a set of actions that describes which task each FR should undertake and their best paths given the tasks in the current state. This plan can then be provided on demand to Silver commanders. The challenge, however, is that such plans do not factor (i) whether the FRs are tired — if FRs are tired they may not be able to do the task allocated and may prefer to do easier (closer) tasks, and (ii) existing relationships between FRs — this can result in some FRs preferring to work together and leave others out. Crucially, it is not possible for the planner agent to model all the aspects of human collaboration and perception which could mean that plans may not make sense in the real world. Hence, in the next section we develop methods for interactions with the planner agent as well as between Silver commanders and Bronze FRs to help them converge on an effective plan.

5.2 Interaction Design

Following the Haiti scenario, once the UAVs have identified the targets on the ground (see Section 4), FRs with specific roles have to be allocated to these targets to further investigate, evacuate, rescue, repair, etc., depending on the nature of the target. To exemplify how this system would work, we assume four different types of FR roles (medics, fire fighters, soldiers, and transporters), and four different types of targets (injured personnel, social unrest, infrastructural damage, and water shortage). Mimicking real-world complexity, different targets have different role requirements, e.g., to rescue an 'injured personnel' target, a medic and a transporter are required. For Silver commanders, this creates the aforementioned task allocation problem under time pressure (due to task deadlines). In order to support Silver commanders with their coordination work to allocate tasks to FRs, we designed a set of interactive tools that both integrate the agent-based task allocation and path planning algorithm in the previous section, as well as situation awareness and communication capabilities for Silver commanders and FRs.

Fundamentally, these capabilities are enabled by two applications: (a) a web-based task allocation interface to support Silver coordination of FRs; and (b) a Mobile Responder Tool for FRs to respond to task assignments and messages from Silver commanders, to find each other, and to navigate the environment to evacuate targets. The following sections illustrate the ways in which we implemented a *human-in-the-loop* rationale for intelligent task allocation. Findings from earlier user studies showed that an effective interaction strategy leaves routine task assignment to the agent, but human input is required to confirm allocations or change these on demand, and, in particular, to deal with contingencies that may arise in the disaster setting.

5.2.1 Task allocation UI

The web-based task allocation interface for Silver commanders is depicted in Fig. 5. The operator uses the real-time map to locate responders and targets 'on the ground', to keep track of tasks and

Figure 6: The Mobile Responder Tool.

their deadlines, to request assignments from the agent, and to inspect and confirm which of them get sent to the FRs. The task assignments may be edited 'manually', for example to prioritise a specific target due to type or deadline.

Due to relative complexity of the 'work flow' and the resulting target states, we implemented interactive elements to make the UI effective and guide the attention of the operator as follows:

- **FR feedback**. FRs accept or reject tasks (e.g., due to local knowledge unavailable to the operator). Rejection leads to a red, flashing signal, signalling to the operator that immediate attention is required. The operator may then decide to call upon the planner agent for a new allocation based on certain constraints or manually create an assignment of tasks to FR.
- **Hover-over alignment**. Hovering the cursor over task or FR icons in the task list or in the allocation list highlights the corresponding icon on the map, so as to facilitate aligning the views.
- **Drag-and-drop editing**. Silver commanders allocate FRs to tasks by drag-and-drop. Once a task is dropped into the assignment column, the responders' required roles are visualised to further guide the operator.
- **Task-based comms channels**. Operators have a channel for each team allocated to a task, to provide task-specific messaging (see Fig. 6).

5.2.2 Mobile Responder Tool

The mobile responder tool is depicted in Fig. 6. It provides the Bronze FRs with the same real-time map as the Silver commanders, with some convenience methods to facilitate focusing important elements on the limited mobile screen size, such as 'find me' and 'show task'. In addition, it provides task allocation information in a separate tab (shown), which users have to accept. In case they reject the allocation, they are first alerted to the task deadline in a modal ('are you sure?' dialogue) so as to discourage rejection.

Our pilot studies of different versions of our Mixed-Initiative Task Allocation system have demonstrated that FRs are more likely to accept plans computed by the planner agent if the plans are first analysed, modified, and validated by the Silver commanders [13]. Moreover, in our workshops with emergency responders from Rescue Global, it was particularly highlighted that such a disaster response system is an opportunity to provide, in real-time, an up-to-date picture of the disaster zone. Crucially, they highlighted the fact that the information generated by FRs on the ground, UAVs, and the CrowdScanner, needed to be tracked and analysed continually to identify potential discrepancies in decision making. Given this, we discuss next our approach to managing such information and decisions within the HAC-ER system.

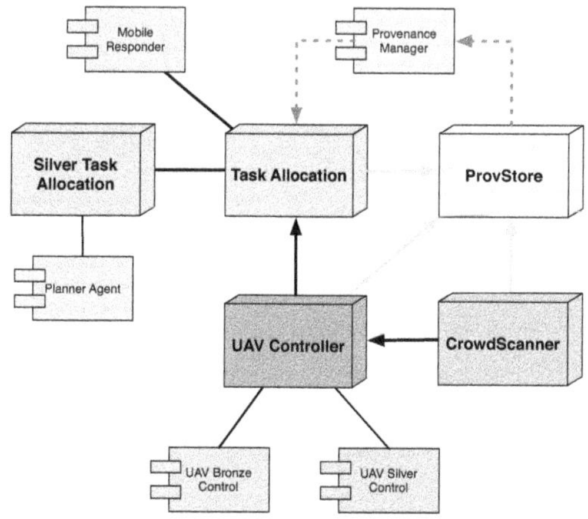

Figure 7: Information flows between HAC-ER's components.

6. TRACKING INFORMATION AND DECISIONS IN HAC-ER

As discussed earlier, HAC-ER consists of loosely-coupled components that involve collectives of humans and agents. For an overview, Fig. 7 presents the components and information flows between them. Given the significant costs of making mistakes in our domain, tracking provenance of the information fed into decision making is a critical requirement. In this section, we describe how provenance in HAC-ER is tracked (Section 6.1) and used to improve awareness of changes across its components (Section 6.2).

6.1 Tracking Provenance

The World Wide Web Consortium (W3C) defines provenance as "a record that describes the people, institutions, entities, and activities involved in producing, influencing, or delivering a piece of data or a thing" [11]. In this system, when a piece of information is produced by one of the components, it records which inputs were used in the production of that piece of information and the agent(s) and/or human(s) that were involved. Fig. 8a shows an example of such provenance. In the example, the entity `uav/target/33.1` was generated by a "UAV Verification" activity; it was attributed to the UAV Bronze commander, was derived from another entity called `cs/target/33.0` (which was previously created by the CrowdScanner, but this is not shown in the figure), and has a property to represent its type as an "Infrastructure Damage." Examining this provenance, either when the entity `uav/target/33.1` is used or in a much later audit when the operation has finished, allows us and to track back to the origin of the information and to answer questions such as "who was responsible for the information", "on which other information it depended."

In our system, the provenance of information is stored in a purpose built repository for provenance, called ProvStore [7]. Individual components (i.e., the CrowdScanner, UAV Controller, and Task Allocation) record the provenance of information and data generated in each of their activities and report the provenance to ProvStore once the activity completes. The provenance of any entity can then be retrieved from ProvStore when required. Fig. 8b, for instance, shows the result of a query for all the dependencies of the entity `comfimed_plan/178`, which is a task allocation plan that has been confirmed by a commander. As can be seen, the result goes back all the way to the crowd reports aggregated by the CrowdScanner (some entities omitted due to space constraints).

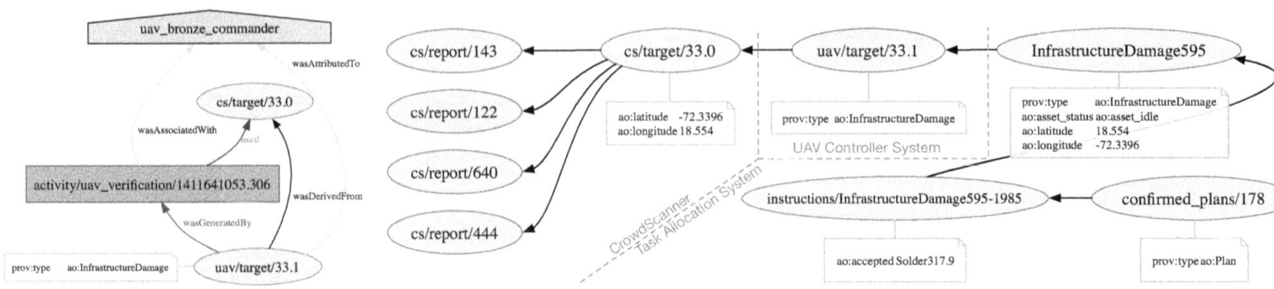

(a) The provenance of a target (`uav/target/33.1`).

(b) A chain of derived information tracked across HAC-ER's three components.

Figure 8: Provenance graphs in HAC-ER. In (a) ellipses are entities, boxes are activities, and houses are agents.

Should any information in a derivation chain as the one shown in Fig. 8b later be discovered unreliable or incorrect, it would be possible to assess its potential impact by querying from ProvStore all of its dependents. This is indeed what our Provenance Manager monitors in order to ensure that the responders on the ground and their commanders are aware of potentially adverse information in dynamic situations typically in the area of disaster response. In the next section, we describe how this is achieved.

6.2 Monitoring Decisions

In an ongoing operation, the available information is typically uncertain and/or incomplete [19]. In HAC-ER, for instance, targets identified from aggregating crowd reports are inherently uncertain (see Section 3); new (and more trustworthy) reports from FRs, for example, can invalidate targets that are already assigned to UAVs. UAV operators can also make mistakes when annotating targets and later correct them. However, the incorrect information may have already propagated to the Planner agent, resulting in assignments for FRs. Those assignments may have subsequently confirmed by a Silver commander before the incorrect information is discovered. In order to be in control of such dynamic situations and to effectively manage such changes, we develop a *Provenance Manager* that tracks significant information changes at ProvStore that may have impacts on decisions already made. It works as follows:

- **Listening to information invalidation**: ProvStore provides an API for external services to register to be notified when an event of interest occurs. Whenever prior information is invalidated, decisions and actions must be revised immediately. Therefore, the Provenance Agent asks ProvStore to notify it with any invalidation of existing information asserted by one of HAC-ER's components.
- **Identifying potential impacts**: Once an entity is invalidated, ProvStore sends a notification to the Provenance Manager which identifies all the dependents of the invalidated entity by querying ProvStore for the transitive closure of the wasDerivedFrom relations of the entity. If any of the dependents are confirmed decisions, the entity `confirmed_plan/178` in Fig. 8b for example, their owners will be notified next.
- **Notifying affected actors**: As each entity (e.g. a decision) is attributed to a human or agent actor, when its validity may be affected by now-invalid input(s), the actors may need to re-evaluate their decision. Hence, the Provenance Agent will send a notification to the affected actor, informing them of the fact that an entity has just become invalid, the other entities potentially affected by this, and the provenance information that has all the details for further investigation. For example, the entity `uav/target/33.1` (in Fig. 8a), may have been mistakenly identified as an "Infrastructure Damage". The error was later corrected, resulting in a new version of the target (`uav/target/33.2`) and the original version invalidated. The same chain of derivations as shown in Fig. 8b was identified by the Provenance Manager, and a notification was generated and sent to the commander who had confirmed the task allocation specified in `confirmed_plan/178`.

With the information and decision tracking provided by the Provenance Manager in tandem with ProvStore, our pilot tests have demonstrated that the system maintains situation awareness of the participants in a timely manner whenever the information used for task planning is invalidated. Silver commanders were notified of the changes in less than a minute after they occurred. More importantly, the generic provenance tracking and monitoring mechanisms implemented here are flexible and do not depend on this particular domain. Future changes in HAC-ER's individual components, or even the addition of new components, will not affect the existing operation of the Provenance Manager as long as the components report provenance information from their operation to ProvStore as previously described in Section 6.1.

7. CONCLUSIONS

In this paper, we presented HAC-ER, a prototype disaster management system based on Human-Agent Collectives. The individual components of HAC-ER demonstrate how humans and agents can be coalesced in flexible and social relationships to manage information and decisions, in order to address specific challenges faced in gathering a high level of situational awareness from crowds and UAVs, and in allocating tasks to first responders on the ground. Our prototype has been field tested with more than 100 users so far and validated by real-world emergency responders. Our field trials of the HAC-ER system have so far shown that the performance of the system is improved when greater control over autonomy is given to users (e.g., in the multi-UAV and the planner system in particular). Furthermore, emergency responders found that tracking the provenance of information from the Crowdscanner would significantly improve their confidence in information coming from crowds. The reader is referred to [13] and [4] for further details. Future work will look at deploying HAC-ER in disaster response training exercises and evaluating our interaction mechanisms and agents *in situ*.

Acknowledgements

This work was done as part of the EPSRC-funded ORCHID project (EP/I011587/1). We also thank RescueGlobal and BAE Systems for their feedback on initial versions of the system.

REFERENCES

[1] A. G. Barto, S. J. Bradtke, and S. P. Singh. Learning to act using real-time dynamic programming. *Artificial Intelligence*, 72(1):81–138, 1995.

[2] M. Cummings, A. Brzezinski, and J. D. Lee. The impact of intelligent aiding for multiple unmanned aerial vehicle schedule management. *IEEE Intelligent Systems: Special Issue on Interacting with Autonomy*, 22(2):52–59, 2007.

[3] F. M. Delle Fave, A. Rogers, Z. Xu, S. Sukkarieh, and N. R. Jennings. Deploying the max-sum algorithm for decentralised coordination and task allocation of unmanned aerial vehicles for live aerial imagery collection. In *Robotics and Automation (ICRA), 2012 IEEE International Conference on*, pages 469–476. IEEE, 2012.

[4] J. E. Fischer, S. Reeves, T. Rodden, S. Reece, S. D. Ramchurn, and D. Jones. Building a bird's eye view: Collaborative work. In *Proceedings of SIGCHI (To appear)*, 2015.

[5] T. Grant. Unifying planning and control using an ooda-based architecture. In *Proceedings of the 2005 annual research conference of the South African institute of computer scientists and information technologists on IT research in developing countries*, pages 159–170. South African Institute for Computer Scientists and Information Technologists, 2005.

[6] T. Grant and B. Kooter. Comparing ooda & other models as operational view c2 architecture topic: C4isr/c2 architecture. *ICCRTS2005, Jun*, 2005.

[7] T. D. Huynh and L. Moreau. ProvStore: A public provenance repository. In *5th International Provenance and Annotation Workshop (IPAW'14)*, Cologne, Germany, 2014.

[8] N. R. Jennings, L. Moreau, D. Nicholson, S. D. Ramchurn, S. Roberts, T. Rodden, and A. Rogers. On human-agent collectives. *Communications of the ACM*, 57(12):33–42, 2014.

[9] H. Kitano and S. Tadokoro. Robocup rescue: A grand challenge for multiagent and intelligent systems. *AI Magazine*, 22(1):39–52, 2001.

[10] K. S. Macarthur, R. Stranders, S. D. Ramchurn, and N. R. Jennings. A distributed anytime algorithm for dynamic task allocation in multi-agent systems. In W. Burgard and D. Roth, editors, *AAAI*. AAAI Press, 2011.

[11] L. Moreau and P. Missier. PROV-DM: The PROV data model. Technical report, World Wide Web Consortium, 2013. W3C Recommendation.

[12] N. Morrow, N. Mock, A. Papendieck, and N. Kocmich. Independent Evaluation of the Ushahidi Haiti Project. *Development Information Systems International*, 8:2011, 2011.

[13] S. D. Ramchurn, F. Wu, W. Jiang, J. E. Fischer, S. Reece, S. Roberts, C. Greenhalgh, T. Rodden, and N. R. Jennings. Human-agent collaboration for disaster response. *Autonomous Agents and Multi-Agent Systems: Special Issue on Human-Agent Interaction (to appear)*, 2015.

[14] C. E. Rasmussen and C. K. I. Williams. *Gaussian Processes for Machine Learning*. The MIT Press, 2006.

[15] S. Reece, S. Roberts, D. Nicholson, and C. Lloyd. Determining intent using hard/soft data and gaussian process classifiers. In *Information Fusion (FUSION), 2011 Proceedings of the 14th International Conference on*, pages 1–8. IEEE, 2011.

[16] A. Rogers, A. Farinelli, R. Stranders, and N. R. Jennings. Bounded approximate decentralised coordination via the max-sum algorithm. *Artificial Intelligence*, 175(2):730–759, 2011.

[17] E. Simpson, S. J. Roberts, A. Smith, and C. Lintott. Bayesian combination of multiple, imperfect classifiers. In *NIPS 2011*, Oxford, December 2011.

[18] P. Smith, C. McCoy, and C. Layton. Brittleness in the design of cooperative problem-solving systems: the effects on user performance. *Systems, Man and Cybernetics, Part A: Systems and Humans, IEEE Transactions on*, 27(3):360–371, May 1997.

[19] J. Villaveces. Disaster response 2.0. *Forced Migration Review*, 38:7–9, 2011.

Adaptive Advice in Automobile Climate Control Systems*

Ariel Rosenfeld
Department of Computer Science, Bar-Ilan University
Ramat Gan, Israel
rosenfa5@cs.biu.ac.il

Amos Azaria
Machine Learning Department
Carnegie Mellon University
Pittsburgh, PA, USA
amos.azaria@gmail.com

Sarit Kraus
Department of Computer Science, Bar-Ilan University
Ramat Gan, Israel
sarit@cs.biu.ac.il

Claudia V. Goldman
General Motors Advanced Technical Center
Herzliya, Israel
claudia.goldman@gm.com

Omer Tsimhoni
General Motors Advanced Technical Center
Herzliya, Israel
omer.tsimhoni@gm.com

ABSTRACT

Reducing an automobile's energy consumption will lower its dependency on fossil fuel and extend the travel range of electric vehicles. Automobile Climate Control Systems (CCS) are known to be heavy energy consumers. To help reduce CCS energy consumption, this paper presents an adaptive automated agent, MDP Agent for Climate control Systems (MACS), which provides drivers with advice as to how to set their CCS. First, we present a model which has 78% accuracy in predicting drivers' reactions to different advice in different situations. Using the prediction model, we designed a Markov Decision Process which solution provided the advising policy for MACS. Through empirical evaluation using an electric car, with 83 human subjects, we show that MACS successfully reduced the energy consumption of the subjects by 33% compared to subjects who were not equipped with MACS. MACS also outperformed the state-of-the-art Social agent for Advice Provision (SAP).

Categories and Subject Descriptors

I.2.m [**Computing Methodologies**]: ARTIFICIAL INTELLIGENCE—*Miscellaneous*

General Terms

Human Factors, Experimentation

Keywords

Energy Aware Systems; Advice Provision; Human-Agent Interaction

1. INTRODUCTION

According to Lee and Lovellette [18], by 2030 a rising middle class in China and India will cause a high demand for passenger cars which will result in approximately 1.1 billion cars on the road worldwide, compared to 750 million in 2010. Such a fleet would probably not be able to rely on fossil fuels alone for long. The growing interest in electrical cars seems to offer a great solution to the escalating number of cars on the road [18]. Between 2012 and mid-2014, there was an increase of 170% in electrical cars worldwide [26, 21]. Yet, one of the most reported reasons for refraining from switching to electric cars is the relatively limited travel range it has (w.r.t petrol cars). Auto experts have reported that the car's climate control system (CCS) reduces the cars power efficiency by up to 10 percent [23, 12]. Thus, reducing energy consumption of the CCS is important in order to reduce the human ecological footprint and extend the travel distance of electric vehicles.

There is a broad consensus that modifying a driver's behavior may allow a reduction in vehicle fuel consumption [9]. Inspired by these results, in this paper, we propose an automated agent that advises a driver how to set the car's CCS, in a way that would reduce energy consumption while keeping the driver comfortable. The agent operates in a repeated interaction environment, in which it offers *adaptive* advice to the driver. While the agent is mainly concerned with the car's energy consumption, the driver is usually more interested in her own comfort level—an interest which changes from one driver to another. This partial conflict, which may occur, is a challenge in the advice provision process—the agent must consider the driver's comfort in order to provide reasonable advice. Furthermore, the agent should consider the trust the driver has in it and take into account the long term effect of each piece of advice.

We present a methodology which combines a *driver model*, a *CCS model* and an *environment model* in a Markov Decision Process (MDP) setting [27] in order to generate adaptive advice for the driver on how to set her CCS. In this work we mainly focus on the *driver model*, which considers the driver's preferences, the dynamically changing environment and the repeated interaction process between the driver and the agent. Modeling the driver in a personalized manner is very challenging. First, different drivers may have different preferences when it comes to CCS settings. Their preferences vary according to the environment changes and can even change during the ride itself. Second, the interaction between the driver and the agent also affects the driver's preferences and her future reactions to new advice suggested by the agent.

*This work was supported in part by ERC grant #267523.

Appears in: *Proceedings of the 14th International Conference on Autonomous Agents and Multiagent Systems (AAMAS 2015), Bordini, Elkind, Weiss, Yolum (eds.), May 4–8, 2015, Istanbul, Turkey.*

In order to learn drivers' preferences and behavior while they interact with an agent in repeated interactions, we used 2 simple repeatedly interacting agents that were tested with 38 human subjects using a GM Chevrolet Volt electrical car. These agents use different advising procedures and examine different advice as well as different interaction sequences from which we can learn about the aforementioned factors. Generalizing findings from only 38 subjects is extremely difficult in repeated interaction settings, especially because we cannot simulate all of the different advice and interactions with our subjects.

Using machine learning techniques and careful selection of predicative features we were able to overcome the above challenges and construct a personalized driver model for predicting drivers' reactions to advice depending on its content, the context in which it was given and the previous agent-driver interactions. Predicting drivers' reactions necessitates the identification of predicative features which describe the driver's preferences, the environmental factors that influence her decision-making and a representation of the trust between the driver and the agent which affect her decision-making as well. We were able to identify a set of features with which we can provide a probability assessment for each specific driver of whether she will accept the given advice, based on the details of the advice, the current setting inside and outside the car and interactions before the advice was given. In a similar fashion, an environment model was constructed. A CCS model was obtained from previous work on a single interaction advice provision in CCS settings [5].

We used an MDP modeling, which utilizes the aforementioned models to account for the dynamic and changing environment in which the agent operates, and solved it to calculate an advising policy. The resulting policy, which is used by our proposed agent, MDP Agent for Climate control Systems — MACS, was tested and compared to the state-of-the-art Social agent for Advice Provision (SAP) modeling [4] and a non-advising agent (Silent). Our experiments, with 83 human drivers, show that subjects equipped with our agent significantly saved energy compared to both competing agents. Subjects equipped with MACS reduced their CCS energy consumption by 33% (on average) compared to subjects using a non-advising agent (Silent). These results were unexpected compared to the limited savings reported in [5] for a single interaction advising agent.

MACS can be deployed in petrol and electric cars alike and hold both long-term and short-term benefits for the driver and the environment.

Our proposed strategic advice provision approach can also be implemented in other human interacting systems where there is tension between the users' and system's goals.

2. RELATED WORK

Persuasive technologies have been used in different domains that target behaviors; from a healthy/safe lifestyle and the ecological behavior of an individual (see [13] for an excellent review) to changing a group's decision in voting [11]. These technologies use different techniques to persuade humans to change how they think or what they do [6] and differ in their theoretical background [20]. Among these persuasive technologies, one can find many agents for the improvement of energy efficiency. In many of these works, the agent is not required to provide *advice* as to how to achieve the goal, but persuade the user into doing so by providing socio-feedback or eco-feedback [10, 8]. For example, in [7] a mobile application is presented that senses and reveals information about transportation behavior, in an attempt to persuade people to increase their use of green transportation. In [2] the authors investigate the design and evaluation of an intelligent agent that helps to persuade family members to conserve energy in their home. Other agents negotiate with humans in order to conserve energy, for example in the work-place [17, 1]. In the context of automobiles, some agents use drivers' observed behavior to automatically elicit the drivers' intention and goals [29, 25, 19, 16]. Yet, to the best of our knowledge, the only work that deals directly with advice provision concerning CCSs is [5].The authors propose CARE—a method to persuade a driver to reduce the energy consumption of the climate control system of her electric car. CARE is designed for a *single round interaction* with a driver, and is not *adaptive* to the driver's actions. That is, the driver receives advice which does not change throughout the ride. Furthermore, CARE requires the driver to report her "initial comfort level" (how comfortable the driver feels at the beginning of the ride) in order to personalize the advice such that different drivers receive different advice depending on their initial comfort level. Without obtaining this initial comfort level, CARE is *not personalized*, and all drivers would receive advice depending solely on the external and internal temperatures. In real world implementation we would like the agent to be able to personalize and adapt the advice to the drivers' actions and refrain from explicitly requesting data from the driver, as requesting such information may be annoying and even dangerously distracting [28]. In this work, the agent elicits the drivers' preferences implicitly from their observed actions and interactions with the system and does not require any additional information from the driver, prior to or during the ride.

Agents who consider their own utility while offering advice are common in the literature. While most of these works assume one-shot interactions, some do consider the long term effect of the advice in repeated interactions [24, 4]. The two state-of-the-art approaches for the latter used MDP modeling and maximized a weighted social utility function in a Social agent for Advice Provision model (SAP). The MDP and SAP models were compared in [3] in a *simulated* CCS environment, yet their results are inapplicable in our setting as the authors assumed explicitly given utility functions for both the agent and the user. In our work, we confront a much greater challenge: first, we assume no prior knowledge of the driver's preferences and utility. Second, the utility which the driver gains from the different climate control settings is not homogeneous among the drivers. Thus, an extensive context and preference-related analysis of observed actions was conducted in this work to provide a probabilistic estimation of the driver's reactions to possible advice. This estimation was in turn combined into an advice provision model in which the human driver could be persuaded to save the energy consumed by her electric car's climate control system.

3. THE CHEVROLET VOLT CLIMATE CONTROL SYSTEM

Our study is based on the GM Chevrolet Volt climate control system. In this system the drivers have control over the setting S which is a tuple (T, F, D, M) consisting of the following variables:

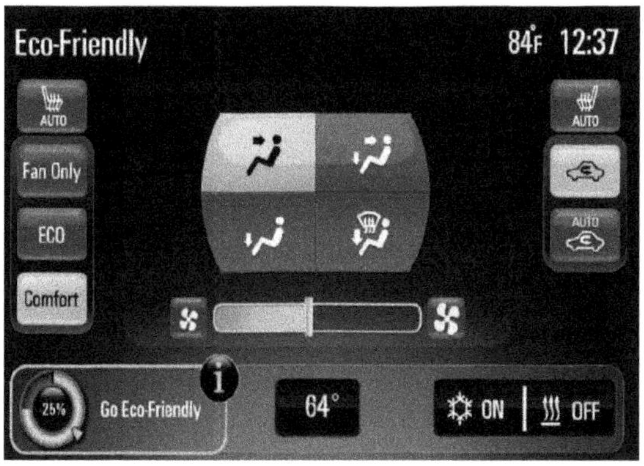

Figure 1: Main screen.

- Temperature (T): this variable can receive values between 16 and 35, and is associated with a temperature in Celsius.
- Fan strength (F): this variable can receive values between 1 and 6 and is associated with the fan blower power.
- Air delivery (D): in the Volt climate control system, the air delivery may be set to face (panel), face and feet, only feet and windshield and feet. In our study we limited the air delivery to either the face (in which D is set to 0) or the face and feet (in which D is set to 1).
- Mode (M): This variable may either be set to 'eco' (when M is set to 0) or to 'comfort' (when M is set to 1).

The Volt climate control system also allows the following additional variables to be set, which we did not include in this study. These variables are heating of the driver and passenger seats, recirculation to either manual or automatic, and a 'fan only' mode which does not use the climate control's compressor. We set the air source to recirculation in all of the experiments. Figure 1 presents the climate control system panel.

Additional important parameters are E, which is the external temperature as displayed in the central stack, and I, which is the internal temperature as we measured with a manual thermometer located between the 2 front seats. We denote these two parameters together as *world state* $v \in V$, where V is the set of all possible world states.

Given a setting s, we use subscript s_T to refer to the temperature in that setting, s_F to refer to the fan strength, s_D for the air delivery and s_M for the mode of the setting.

3.1 Energy Consumption Model

We followed the model of the CCS energy consumption as described in [5]. This model was compared by the authors to others and yielded the greatest fit for the data they collected.

$$e(T,F,D,M,E,I) = (w_1 \cdot (-T) + w_2 \cdot F + w_3 \cdot D + w_4 \cdot E + w_5 \cdot I) \cdot (1 + w_6 \cdot M) \quad (1)$$

We use the same $w_1, w_2, ..., w_6$ calculated by the authors.

4. THE REPEATED ADVICE PROVISION PROBLEM

In our setting, there is a repeated interaction between a receiver (the driver) and a sender (the agent). The interaction is composed of *rounds* (intuitively, different rides in the car). In round t, after i interactions in that round, the sender observes the state of the world $v = (E, I) \in V$, the current climate control settings $s = (T, F, D, M) \in S$ and the history of interactions with the agent, $h^{t,i}$, and suggests that the receiver change its climate control setting to some $d \in S$. The agent is also allowed to "keep silent" and not offer any suggestion. After observing advice d from the sender (if given) the receiver chooses one of the following reactions $\{accept, reject\}$. Regardless of d and the timing, the receiver can choose any $s' \in S$ at her discretion.

The prediction model, which we will soon describe, is intended to assess $P(accept \mid d, t, v, s, h^{t,i})$, the probability that the receiver will choose to *accept* the sender's suggestion d at the time and context in which d was provided.

For a given world state v, settings s and history $h^{t,i-1}$, we define the sender's expected cost for advice d as follows:

$$EC_S^{t,i}(v,s,h^{t,i-1},d) = \sum_{a \in \{accept,reject\}} P(a \mid d,t,v,s,h^{t,i-1}) \left(R(a,v,s,d) + \gamma(t,i) \sum_{v' \in V, s' \in S} p(v',s' \mid a,v,s,d)(\min_{d'} EC_s^{\alpha(t,i),\beta(t,i)}(v',s',h^{t,i},d'))\right) \quad (2)$$

$R(a, v, s, d)$ is the immediate reward/cost function, which in our domain is the expected energy consumption given the current world state v, setting s, advice d and the driver's reaction a. $\gamma(t, i)$ is the discount factor, which represents the difference in the significance between future rewards and present rewards. $p(v', s' \mid a, v, s, d)$ is the probability of reaching world state v' and setting s' from state v and setting s, when the receiver takes action a and the advice was d, which in our case corresponds to the probability that the world state will change from v to v' and the setting will change from s to s' between consecutive interactions. Note that not only may the settings s change according to the receiver's action, but also the world state v. For example, acceptance ($a = accept$) of suggestion d while in state v may change the internal temperature.

Intuitively, $EC_s^{\alpha(t,i),\beta(t,i)}$ sums up the expected utility in the current time period and in the future. $\alpha(t,i) = t + \left\lfloor \frac{t_l - mod(i/t_l)}{t_l} \right\rfloor$ and $\beta(t,i) = \begin{cases} i+1, & \text{if } i < t_l \\ 1, & \text{otherwise} \end{cases}$ where t_l is the limit on the number of interactions per round. $EC_s^{\alpha(t,i),\beta(t,i)}$ considers the possible responses and multiplies the probability that the receiver will choose this action ($P(a \mid d, t, v, s, h^{t,i})$) with the sum of two elements: The first specifies the immediate reward ($R(a, v, s, d)$) and the second specifies the expected future reward. The future expected reward first depends on whether the interactions will continue at all, which will happen with a probability depending on the number of rounds and interactions $\gamma(t, i)$. Then, it depends heavily on the future world state v' and setting s'. For any possible future world state v' and settings s' that will occur with a probability of $p(v', s' \mid a, v, s, d)$ the agent will choose the best advice d' and will obtain, recursively, the expected utility from giving this advice in the next interaction $i + 1$ with the updated history $h^{t,i}$.

The advice that minimizes the sender's cost is

$$\pi^*(v,s,h^{t,i-1}) = \text{argmin}_d EC_S^{\alpha(t,i),\beta(t,i)}(v,s,h^{t,i-1},d) \quad (3)$$

where π^* is the advice function.

Hitherto, we have dealt with all variables in the optimization problem except $P(a \mid d,t,v,s,h^{t,i})$ and $p(v',s' \mid a,v,s,d)$ which require estimations. The next subsection is dedicated to the data collection and analysis which in turn resulted in prediction models for the above.

4.1 Data Collection

In order to estimate $P(a \mid d,t,v,s,h^{t,i})$ we recruited 38 subjects, of whom 20 were males and 18 were females[1] ranging in age between 23 and 67, with a mean of 35.

Each subject was given 10 minutes to be in the car and he or she was free to tell the experimenter what settings to set in the climate control system once the experiment began. The experiment screen (see Figure 1) was displayed on a laptop while the central stack screen was covered. The system presented advice (if available) as a small "Go Eco-Friendly" button on the bottom left side of the experiment screen. The subject could choose to click on that button at any given moment, and thereby change the climate control setting to the advice suggested by the agent (see Figure 2). Notice that the advice itself is not presented to the driver *before* "Go Eco-Friendly" is applied. At that point, the system merely presents the energy saving that the advice would yield if applied. During the next 10 seconds the drivers could choose whether to accept the advice (keep the new settings) or reject it (return to her previous setting). If for the next 10 seconds the driver does not react, the new setting is automatically accepted[2]. Regardless of the advice, the subject could change the climate control settings in whichever way she saw fit – the experimenter updated the climate control of the car as many times as requested by the driver. While in the car the subject was given a cell phone with a driving simulator "Bus Simulator 3D"[3] to be played while the experiment was conducted. The motivation was to set the conditions similar to regular driving conditions and give the subjects something to do. After 10 minutes, the subject had to exit the car and wait until the inside of the car was warm again to simulate initial conditions. This phase took about 10 minutes while the car was switched off and the car doors and trunk were left open. Then, the subject reentered the car to simulate a new trip. This process was then repeated again. That is, each subject spent 30 minutes in the car in three 10-minute sessions and an additional 20 minutes waiting between the different rounds. Including the collection of demographic data and payment (the subjects were paid 100 NIS each, the price of a fancy lunch in Israel), each subject spent about 60 minutes in our garage.

In order to have a variety of advice and drivers' responses, we had to develop algorithms for repeated advice provision. The goal of these algorithms was to simulate varying interactions between the agent and different subjects. Simulating different interactions is challenging. The time with each driver is limited, thus testing all possible advice in every possible order is impossible. Consequently, we needed to collect data on "reasonable" interactions, that is, interactions which we believed people might consider accepting as the agent's advice.

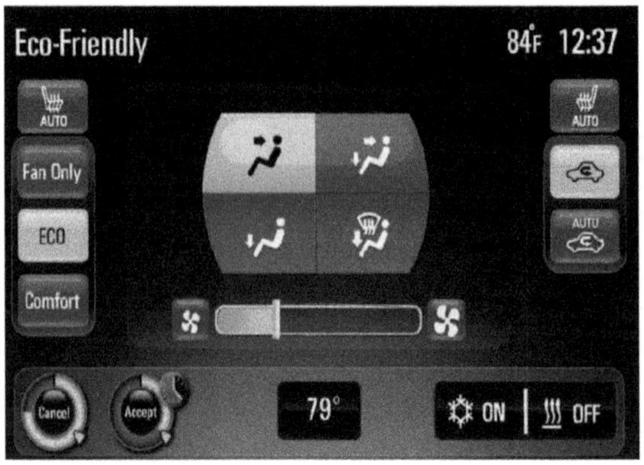

Figure 2: Advised screen.

We used the advice that would have been generated by CARE [5] as a starting point. We removed the initial comfort level parameter from CARE's comfort model and retrained the model using the data that the authors originally collected. We emphasize that the goal of the experiment was not to evaluate these algorithms but rather to collect data on drivers' behavior as the basis for the development of a methodology for advice provision in repeated interactions. During the experiment we logged all of the actions performed by the agent, all of the actions performed by the subjects and the energy consumption of the car.

We implemented two algorithms; The *Pusher* algorithm, which advises the settings that maximize the comfort level but consume no more than the average between the current consumption and the "ideal consumption" – that is, CARE's advice. The intuition behind this algorithm is that the system will always try to persuade the subject to choose the "ideal" settings. The *Lenient* algorithm, which advises the settings that maximize the comfort level but consume no more than the "ideal consumption" (CARE's advice) plus the delta between the user's maximal consumption and the current consumption. The intuition behind this algorithm is that if the driver is willing to compromise and consume less energy (than her maximal consumption) the system is also willing to compromise and offer more "generous" advice (in terms of energy consumption).

Nineteen subjects participated in the experiments with the Pusher algorithm. The average number of times in which new advice was suggested to a subject per session was 3.44. In 74% of the cases the subject chose to consider the advice and clicked the "Go Eco-Friendly" button. Furthermore, in 59% of these cases she chose to accept the advice. Similarly, 19 subjects participated in the experiments with Lenient. The average number of times that new advice was given to a subject per session was only 1.18. Moreover, in only 59% of the cases in which new advice was proposed, the subject chose to consider the advice and chose the "Go Eco-Friendly" button. Furthermore, in 59% of these cases she chose to accept the advice. There was no significant change between the sessions.

We compared the energy consumption per condition. While in the first condition the consumption was slightly higher (0.1605KWH vs 0.1525KWH), the difference was not statistically significant. It is also interesting to observe that the

[1] All experiments with human subjects were approved by the corresponding IRB.

[2] We designed several GUI's to provide advice and carried out an experiment to identify the most preferred GUI.

[3] Available free at Google Play store.

Table 1: List of Features

notation	meaning
$save$	d's energy saving percentage of the advice.
Δ_T	d's temperature difference from current s_T.
Δ_F	d's fan difference from current s_F.
Δ_I	d's temperature difference from current I.
$d\%$	the advice acceptance rate thus far.
$d\%^t$	the advice acceptance rate in round t.
$acc\Delta_T$	the average Δ_T of accepted advice so far.
$acc\Delta_F$	the average Δ_F of accepted advice so far.
$rej\Delta_T$	the average Δ_T of rejected advice so far.
$rej\Delta_F$	the average Δ_F of rejected advice so far.
$acc\Delta_T^t$	the average Δ_T of accepted advice in round t.
$acc\Delta_F^t$	the average Δ_F of accepted advice in round t.
$rej\Delta_T^t$	the average Δ_T of rejected advice in round t.
$rej\Delta_F^t$	the average Δ_F of rejected advice in round t.

energy saving average "Go Eco-Friendly" suggested to the subject was -16.86% with Pusher and -36.91% with Lenient.

As for the rounds: in the first round 0.76 of the times that new advice appeared, the subjects clicked on it, however, only 0.69 of the times that the subjects clicked on new advice in rounds 2 and 3. In the first round the subjects rejected 0.37 of the advice received, in the second round 0.46 and in the third 0.42. The number of pieces of advice received per subject dropped from 2.8 in round 1 to 2.6 in round 2 and 2.2 in round 3. The average saving of the advice offered dropped from -22.5% in round 1 to -20.8% in round 2 and -18.1% in round 3. The average consumption was reduced from 0.162 in round 1 to 0.155 in rounds 2 and 3. Combining all of this data, it seems that although the subjects received less advice in the latter rounds, they apparently consumed less energy. This is because the subjects were probably influenced by the first round and consumed less energy to begin with and therefore required less advice. However, the advice still seemed to have a large impact on the subjects also in the later rounds.

We also separated all rounds according to the algorithms used (Pusher, Lenient). With the Pusher algorithm the acceptance rate of new advice (percent of advice in which the subjects also clicked on "Go Eco-Friendly" and also accepted the advice) did not vary much in the rounds (0.45 in the first round, 0.41 in the second and 0.49 in the third). Lenient demonstrated a major drop from the first round's acceptance rate, from 0.57 to 0.1 in the last round's acceptance rate.

4.2 Prediction Model

Recall that in order to calculate Equation 2 we need to estimate $P(a \mid d, t, v, s, h^{t,i-1})$. Given the data obtained in the Data Collection phase, denoted Λ, we extracted features, as described in Table 1, which help predict the driver's response given the advice d, the round t, the world state v, and the interaction history $h^{t,i-1}$. For each d,t,v,s,$h^{t,i-1}$ we encountered in the data we extracted the features and labeled the instances *accepted* or *rejected* according to their status. This process merely translated the interaction (which was in a textual format) to a set of vectors, whereby each is a set of features and a label – the subject's response. This vector represents a single interaction in the experiment and was used in the prediction model.

The resulting labeled set ψ was divided in a one-left-out fashion, where for every subject j we created ψ_j as a test set and ψ_{-j} as a training set. Then, a prediction model using K-Nearest-Neighbors algorithm (KNN) was created. The Algorithm was trained on ψ_{-j} and tested over ψ_j for every j. KNN is a classical non-parametric lazy classifying algorithm in which an object is classified according to its k nearest neighbors (k is a positive integer, typically small). If k = 1, then the object is simply assigned to the class of that single nearest neighbor. The classes in our settings were *accepted* and *rejected*, and k was set to 21 as it provided the highest prediction accuracy on ψ.

Unfortunately, ψ turned out to be very unbalanced; out of the 436 instances in ψ, 324 where *accepted* and 112 were *rejected* instances. This was caused due to the use of the Pusher and Lenient agents that only advised settings which we a priori believed the driver would accept (predicted comfort of at least 7). We used 2 methods to overcome this problem: 1) We oversampled the minority group (*rejected*). 2) We synthetically injected instances in the following manner – for every *rejected* labeled instance in ψ we added rejected instances for any warmer[4] advice than the one rejected. For example, if a subject rejected a setting of $T = 23, F = 1$ she would most likely reject $T = 24, F = 1$ and $T = 25, F = 1$ as well. We were very careful with this injection and ensured that the suggestion was rejected because it was too hot and not because it was too cold. We only synthetically created instances for actual rejected instances with temperatures higher than 22 and fan lower than 3.

Of the 436 suggestions, we correctly classified 337 instances (78%), where we had greater success with *accepted* instances (85%) than with the *rejected* group (59%). Moreover, we identified which features were good predicative features and which were not. Namely, $save$,Δ_T,Δ_F,Δ_I,Δ_F,$d\%$ features were found to be influential whereas the rest had little (if any) effect on the accuracy rate (features appear in Table 1).

We note that the use of different machine learning algorithms such as SVM and Decision Trees provided very similar yet lower prediction rates (72%, 63%, respectively).

The use of the KNN algorithm also provided a probability measurement of $P(a \mid d, t, v, s, h^{t,i-1})$, which was needed to design the agent. We estimated $P(a \mid d, t, v, s, h^{t,i-1})$ as the number of *accepted* labeled instances among the 21 nearest neighbors divided by 21. That is, if 7 of the 21 nearest neighbors are labeled *accept* we would assume that the probability of the current advice d to be accepted, in the context in which it is given, would be 1/3. This method achieved a Mean Absolute Error of 0.37 and a Root Mean Squared Error of 0.42.

4.3 Agents

Based on both the prediction model and the energy consumption model we constructed two agents, *SAP agent* and *MACS*. MACS tries to solve the optimization problem given in Equation 3 whereas the SAP agent does not.

4.3.1 MACS

An MDP [27] is a tuple $(\mathcal{O}, \mathcal{A}, \mathcal{T}, \mathcal{R})$ where

1. $\mathcal{O}$ is the set of possible states of the system (S);
2. $\mathcal{A}$ is the set of possible advice the agent can suggest; in our case it is $S \cup \{\text{"silent"}\}$;

[4]Data collection and experiments were conducted during the summer period.

3. $\mathcal{T}$ represents the interaction dynamics – the driver's reactions to advice and the environmental changes;

4. $\mathcal{R}$ is the energy consumption function for each $s \in S$.

Acting in an MDP results in a sequence of states and actions $o_0, a_0, o_1, a_1, o_2, \ldots$

A policy π is a sequence of mappings $(\mu_0, \mu_1, \mu_2, \ldots, \mu_{t_l})$, where, at time t, the mapping $\mu_t(\cdot)$ determines the action $a_t = \mu_t(o_t)$ to take when in state o_t. t_l denotes the limit on the amount of advice the agent can suggest.

The objective is to find an optimal policy that minimizes the expected cost accumulated over time. In particular, a policy π is good if its *Expected Cost* is low. Expected Cost is defined as:

$$ExpectedCost(\pi) = \mathbb{E}[\sum_{t=1}^{t_l} \gamma^t \mathcal{R}(o_t)|\pi] \quad (4)$$

γ is the probability of continuing to the next round. In our environment the decision maker is the *advisor* (the agent), which has to decide which, if any, advice to provide. The driver controls the actual dynamics of the system as she controls the actual climate control settings.

We model this environment using an MDP. Each state $o \in \mathcal{O}$ consists of a world state v, the current climate control setting s, interaction number i, round number t and the advice acceptance rate thus far, d%. These states cover all possible scenarios in which the agent is required to provide advice or to keep silent. There is an infinite number of states, which require discretization. We discretized the environment by rounding degrees to the closest integer and the acceptance rate was restricted to 2 digits after the floating point. This process resulted in about 100,000 states. The current state is completely observable by the agent from the car's data and the previous interaction with the driver. As such, no uncertainty is induced as to the state in which the agent works.

The agent can only suggest climate control settings to the driver or it can keep silent, i.e. $\mathcal{A} = T \times F \times D \times M \cup \{silent\}$, where $T \times F \times D \times M$ is the space of all possible climate control settings. Notice that all of these actions are possible at each state.

$\mathcal{T}(o, d, o')$ provides the probability of reaching MDP state o' given advice d in MDP state o. In our environment this transition is controlled mainly by the driver. The driver is free to change the climate control settings whenever she chooses to, and as shown in [5], drivers are also influenced by the agent's advice, even when it is rejected. Because the drivers are free to change the climate control settings regardless of advice, it is hard to model these changes. Furthermore, the external and internal temperatures may vary during the experiment. This makes it extremely hard to accurately assess $\mathcal{T}$. For example, after advice is rejected the climate control settings are automatically switched back to the previous ones. Before the next advice appears, a time we configured to 60 seconds (as proposed by our engineers) to avoid distracting the driver, the driver can change the CCS setting in whichever way she wants and the internal temperatures tend to decline. We could not detect any clear behavior of the driver's setting changes except for when a driver was considering whether to accept or reject advice. Thus, we assumed that the climate control settings change only by explicitly accepting them and/or at the beginning of each round. This assumption is restricted only for modeling — in actual implementation the driver receives advice according to her actual state, regardless of how she reached that state — namely by advice or by manual changes. Due to the short time intervals in which the experiment is conducted (10-minute episodes), the external temperature is unlikely to change and therefore was assumed to remain constant. The internal temperature on the other hand tended to change, mostly decreasing during the experiment. We estimated these changes using $p_c(v' \mid a, v, s, d)$ which was estimated using another KNN model (with k again set to 21). Each instance in ψ was translated into a feature vector containing a, v, s, d and was labeled with the change of the I during the 60 second intervals between the different suggestions. For example, given $I = 35, E = 36$, $T = 19, F = 2, D = 0, M = 0$, the advice of $T = 22, F = 1, D = 0, M = 0$ which was *accepted*, we estimated a 9.5% chance of I decreasing by 1 degree Celsius and a 90.5% chance of I not changing. This was due to the fact that 2 of the 21 nearest neighbors experienced a decline of 1 degree Celsius and 19 did not. In addition, the driver can choose to ignore the advice by avoiding clicking on the "Go Eco-Friendly" button. This factor was also learned statistically by a Maximum Likelihood Estimator, denoted $p_s(stop \mid t, i)$. That is, given t, i, we estimated the probability of an interaction to stop at t, i (not to continue to $i+1$) by dividing the number of instances in round t and interaction i which did not continue to $i+1$ by the number of instances of round t and interaction i in ψ.

$\mathcal{T}$ is derived from the prediction model described above, $p_c(\cdot)$ and $p_s(\cdot)$. The prediction model provides us with the probability of suggestion d being accepted in state o, which leads us to a new state – o'. Yet, regardless of the estimation, $p_c(\cdot)$ and $p_s(\cdot)$ are applied and therefore there are multiple possible outcomes: "accept" with I declining by 1 degree Celsius, "accept" with no change to I, "ignore" etc... If we predict that the driver will stop the interaction we again assume she will keep the current setting of the climate control system.

The $\mathcal{R}$ function is naturally derived from the previously described Energy Consumption Model. At each phase the agent faces a cost, which is the energy consumed by the CCS. The accumulation of all costs encountered during the interaction is the payoff to the agent, which it tries to minimize.

Recall that t_l is the horizon of the interaction, which in our experimental setting is set to 9 (3 rounds, 3 pieces of advice per round). t_l was chosen according to GM's experience in designing driver-interaction systems. γ is 1 if $t \leq 9$, and otherwise 0. This is due to the fact that we do not distinguish between the different rounds in terms of energy consumption. t in Equation 4 indicates the current number of the interaction ($t \leq 9$).

We solved the MDP problem using Dynamic Programming [22] and received a policy π^*, which determines which advice d (if any) to provide in every state o. We note again that π^*, an optimal policy for the given MDP, does not take into account the manual changes the driver can perform. Nevertheless, if the driver reconfigures the climate control setting manually (by changing her climate control setting) the suggestion will be according to her new state. We anticipate that π^* will still provide solid recommendations.

To deploy π^* in the GM Chevrolet Volt car, we enumerated all states and advice as $< o, \Pi^*(o) >$ pairs and saved them in a table. The agent loads the table at the beginning of the interaction and simply identifies each state (when needed) and provides the specified advice.

4.3.2 SAP agent

According to social preference theory, people consider the outcomes of others as well as their own when making strategic decisions. SAP modeling explicitly reasons about the trade-offs between the costs to both participants in the selection process based on a social weight [3]. SAP modeling provides advice that maximizes a social utility function which is a weighted sum of the agent and human's utilities. SAP uses simulation runs of repeated human-agent interaction to identify the weights that maximize the agent's utility over time.

In climate control settings the agent's utility is based on the energy consumption and the driver's utility is based mainly on her comfort level. Unfortunately, the driver's comfort level (even if the driver is able to quantify it) is not available to the agent in a real car deployment. In [3], the authors asked the participants explicitly to quantify their comfort level on a scale of 1 to 10 where 7 means —"I'm comfortable; I would like to drive under these conditions". However, preferences over final outcomes vary according to the reference point from which those outcomes are judged [15]. That is, the comfort level setting s provided depends heavily on the last setting the driver experienced. Therefore, the proposed comfort level function is *not adaptive* to the reference point and the projected comfort level from setting s relies solely on s's components – s_T, s_F, s_D and s_M. Nevertheless, we wanted to test the predicative ability of the comfort level function (as calculated in [3]). An analysis of Λ (see Section Data Collection) reveals that although suggesting only settings in which the comfort level suggested will result in a comfort level of 7 (at least), we encountered 41% misclassifications – that is, 41% of the suggestions were rejected despite their expected comfort level being 7 or more.

In order to work around this problem we propose to estimate the driver's comfort using the prediction model described above. We assume that there is a strong correlation between the acceptance probability of a suggestion and the utility that the suggestion provides to the driver – the higher the probability of acceptance, the higher the utility of the driver and vice versa.

The SAP agent provides advice d which maximizes the following social utility function u, given a defined weight w.

$$u(d) = -w \cdot e(d) + (1-w) \cdot P(accept \mid d, t, v, s, h^{t,i-1}) \quad (5)$$

That is, given w (which is defined offline) and $t, v, s, h^{t,i-1}$ the SAP agent searches for advice d which maximizes u. This advice will be presented to the driver.

In order to compute the optimal weight w^* of the social utility function we performed an (offline) exhaustive search over all possible weights in the interval $[0, 1]$ in steps of 0.01, each simulated with 100,000 games of 9 interactions. At each interaction in the simulation, similar to MACS, the SAP agent provides advice while maximizing Esquation 5. If the advice is considered by the simulated driver (using $p_s(\cdot)$), $P(accept \mid d, t, v, s, h^{t,i-1})$ was applied to simulate the driver's response. Immediately thereafter, the change in I using $p_c(\cdot)$ is simulated.

In order to avoid online calculations we generated all states offline and created a table of $< s, d >$.

4.4 Empirical Evaluation

The aforementioned agents, MACS and SAP agent, alongside a *Silent* agent (that does not provide any advice), were tested in the exact same fashion as described in the Data Collection section above.

We recruited 45 subjects in order to evaluate the 3 agents. Of the 45 subjects, 23 were males and 22 were females ranging in age from 23 to 72 with a mean of 41.

Each subject spent about 60 minutes in our garage. Due to that fact, we could not implement a within-subject experimental setting (it would take too long). In our between-subjects experimental setting the testing of policies in extremely similar world-states is important for the integrity of the results. All subjects who took part in this stage of the research participated in the experiments between mid-August 2014 and mid-September 2014. In these 4 weeks, between $11:00-15:00$ (the time of the experiment), temperatures in our garage were almost constant. All participants experienced temperatures between 35-37 degrees Celsius, *without any exceptions.*

4.4.1 Results

The MACS and SAP agent were limited to 3 pieces of advice per round (9 overall), yet neither of them reached the 9 suggestion limitation. MACS offered 6.07 pieces of advice to each subject whereas the SAP agent offered 6.13 suggestions (on average). Of the 91 suggestions MACS offered its 15 subjects, 84% of the time (76) "Go Eco-Friendly" was clicked, and 58% of such clicks resulted in the suggestion being accepted (44). On the other hand, SAP offered 92 pieces of advice to its 15 subjects, yet only 64% of the time "Go Eco-Friendly" was clicked (59), and 54% of such clicks resulted in the suggestion being accepted (32).

When we break down the data according to rounds, we can see that the low click rate of the SAP agent starts from the first round and keeps declining. In the first round 67% of the time new advice was presented, the subjects clicked on "Go Eco-Friendly". However, in the second and third rounds a decline was recorded – 65% and 59%, respectively. The amount of advice given per round also declined from 2.2 in the first round to 2.1 in the second and 1.8 in the third. However, the average savings from the advice offered increased from 32.5% in the first round to 33.3% and 35.8% in the second and third rounds, respectively. The average energy consumption varied across the rounds, where in round 1 an average consumption of 0.249KWH was recorded and only 0.216KWH was recorded in the second round. In the third round the consumption increased to 0.247KWH.

MACS, on the other hand, kept a relatively constant click rate (the percentage of times new advice was considered via the "Go Eco-Friendly" button) across the different rounds — 85%,82%,83%, respectively. Similarly to the SAP agent, in the first round 2.2 pieces of advice were presented to the subject (on average). Yet in the second round it offered only 1.8 pieces of advice and 2 in the third round. As for the energy consumption, in the first round 0.191KWH on average was recorded whereas in the second and third rounds 0.158KWH and 0.173KWH were recorded, respectively.

4.4.2 Analysis

A total of 45 participants took part in the experiment. We used a between-subject design, with three levels of conditions (MACS, SAP agent, and Silent). Each participant

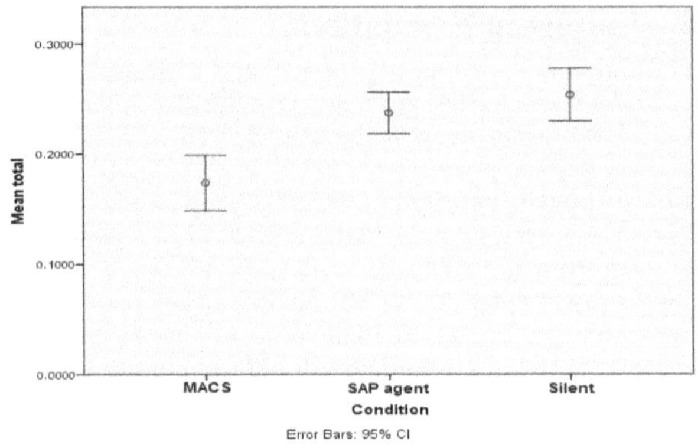

Figure 3: Agents' energy consumption per round (on average, in KWH).

performed the task under one of the three conditions and performed three consecutive runs. The data was analyzed with a univariate ANOVA, with condition and repetition as the independent factors and the energy consumption as the dependent variable. Post-hoc comparisons among the three conditions were also run.

The energy consumption was significantly affected by the condition, $F(2,126)=14.0$, $p < 0.001$, $\eta^2 = 0.18$. Figure 3 shows the mean energy consumption (per round) and 95% confidence intervals under the three experimental conditions. Post-hoc comparisons among the conditions (using Bonferroni correction for multiple comparisons) showed that MACS was significantly different from both SAP and Silent agents, $p < 0.001$. On average, a subject using MACS consumed 33% less energy than the benchmark group of Silent. Subjects who used the SAP agent consumed 5% less energy than subjects equipped with Silent, though this difference was not found to be statistically significant using the post-hoc comparison.

4.5 Discussion

A decline in the clicking rate (the percentage of times new advice was considered by clicking on "Go Eco-Friendly") is natural as the subjects learn different settings and perhaps find a setting in which they are unwilling to compromise. Therefore, there is a small decline in the pieces of advice provided by the agents as the experiment proceeds. Both MACS and the SAP agent offered 33 pieces of advice in the first round opposed to 30 and 27 in the last round (respectively).

Our results show that MACS outperforms the SAP agent in our repeated interaction CCS settings. This result contradicts previous results presented in [4], which have shown that the authors SAP based agent outperformed their MDP based agent. However, recall that in our implementation of SAP we used the probability estimation of the driver to accept a suggestion rather than the driver's actual utility function which we could not articulate. Learning the driver's precise utility function, if one even exists, may be possible, but would certainly require a lot more data on each driver.

Our findings show that the SAP agent was much more *aggressive* in its suggestions than MACS. On average, the SAP agent offered to reduce 33.7% of the energy consumption in its advice, whereas MACS offered to reduce the energy by 23.1%. It seems that this aggressiveness was the reason why some subjects stopped trying the advice. Those who did choose to continue to click on the "Go Eco-Friendly" button demonstrated a relatively good acceptance rate (54%).

In the implementation of both MACS and SAP agents, we used a KNN prediction model to assess $P(a \mid d, t, v, s, h^{t,i-1})$. We reevaluated the model to examine whether its predictions of drivers' reactions to advice were accurate w.r.t the observed interaction with MACS and SAP agents. When we tested the model on the data collected by the Pusher and Lenient algorithms (using the 1-left-out methodology) we revealed a prediction accuracy of 78%, a Mean Absolute Error of 0.37 and a Root Mean Squared Error of 0.42. We retested the prediction model using the interactions with MACS and SAP agents as a *test-set*. The model's prediction accuracy was found to be 76% while its Mean Absolute Error and Root Mean Squared Error were 0.39 and 0.41, respectively. These findings suggest that our prediction model is able to generalize across different drivers and agents.

It has been shown in literature that women are more likely to "express thermal dissatisfaction" and are more sensitive to cooler conditions in *indoor* experimentation than men [14]. Our data also shows a significant difference between men and women in automotive CCS settings. On average, a woman equipped with one of the three agents (MACS, SAP agent and Silent) set her CCS to 22 degrees and a fan speed of 2, whereas a man, set his CCS to 20 degrees temperature and a fan speed of between 3 and 4 on average. Consequently, men consumed 0.72KWH and women consumed 0.59KWH (on average, per subject) in 3 rounds total. This difference was statistically significant using post-hoc testing ($p = 0.02$). Although women accepted more advice than men on average (59% vs. 51%) the difference was not statistically significant and does not provide an explanation for the difference in energy consumption.

5. CONCLUSIONS

In this work we present a methodology for the development of a repeated interacting agent for automobile climate control systems, MACS. MACS offers adaptive advice which considers the drivers' reactions and the long term effect of each piece of advice. The use of machine learning techniques enabled us to satisfactorily predict different drivers' reactions to different advice, which in turn was used for the modeling of MACS. This prediction and modeling resulted in an adaptive policy which was found to be beneficiary – drivers equipped with MACS consumed 33% less energy (on average) than those who were not.

We can conclude that an MDP modeling for the long-term effect of advice is good practice for advising agents operating in environments with repeated settings. The use of machine learning techniques helped us bridge over the lack of prior knowledge of the human's preferences and desires which is required to correctly model interactions. Despite the very few examples, which required simulating different repeated interactions in a reasonable fashion, and having limited prediction accuracy over the minority group we were able to generalize our findings to provide solid prediction accuracy and beneficiary adaptive advising policies.

The methodology presented herein can be used in different domains and settings which require strategic advice provision by self-interested agents and is not restricted to automotive climate control systems.

Our agent and methodology are being considered for implementation in future GM cars.

REFERENCES

[1] S. Abras, S. Ploix, S. Pesty, and M. Jacomino. A multi-agent home automation system for power management. In *Informatics in Control Automation and Robotics*, pages 59–68. Springer, 2008.

[2] A. Al Mahmud, P. Dadlani, O. Mubin, S. Shahid, C. Midden, and O. Moran. iparrot: towards designing a persuasive agent for energy conservation. In *Persuasive Technology*, pages 64–67. Springer, 2007.

[3] A. Azaria, Z. Rabinovich, S. Kraus, and C. V. Goldman. Strategic information disclosure to people with multiple alternatives. In *AAAI*, 2011.

[4] A. Azaria, Z. Rabinovich, S. Kraus, C. V. Goldman, and Y. Gal. Strategic advice provision in repeated human-agent interactions. In *AAAI*, 2012.

[5] A. Azaria, A. Rosenfeld, S. Kraus, C. V. Goldman, and O. Tsimhoni. Advice provision for energy saving in automobile climate control systems. In *AI-magazine*, 2015.

[6] B. Fogg. *Persuasive Technology: Using Computers to Change What We Think and Do (Interactive Technologies)*. Morgan Kaufmann, 2002.

[7] J. Froehlich, T. Dillahunt, P. Klasnja, J. Mankoff, S. Consolvo, B. Harrison, and J. A. Landay. Ubigreen: investigating a mobile tool for tracking and supporting green transportation habits. In *Pro. of the SIGCHI Conference on Human Factors in Computing Systems*, pages 1043–1052. ACM, 2009.

[8] J. Froehlich, L. Findlater, and J. Landay. The design of eco-feedback technology. In *Proc. of the SIGCHI Conference on Human Factors in Computing Systems*, pages 1999–2008. ACM, 2010.

[9] J. Gonder, M. Earleywine, and W. Sparks. Analyzing vehicle fuel saving opportunities through intelligent driver feedback. Technical report, SAE Technical Paper, 2012.

[10] J. Ham and C. Midden. A robot that says bad!: using negative and positive social feedback from a robotic agent to save energy. In *Proc. of the 4th ACM/IEEE international conference on HRI*, pages 265–266. ACM, 2009.

[11] N. Hazon, R. Lin, and S. Kraus. How to change a group's collective decision? In *Proc. of the Twenty-Third international joint conference on Artificial Intelligence*, pages 198–205, 2013.

[12] W. Hill, D. Lebut, G. Major, and F. Schenkel. Affect of windows down on vehicle fuel economy as compared to AC load. Technical report, IEA, 2004.

[13] F. Jazizadeha, G. Kavulyaa, J.-Y. Kwakb, B. Becerik-Gerberc, M. Tambe, and W. Woode. Human-building interaction for energy conservation in office buildings. In *Proc. of the Construction Research Congress*, pages 1830–1839, 2012.

[14] S. Karjalainen. Thermal comfort and gender: a literature review. *Indoor air*, 22(2):96–109, 2012.

[15] B. Kőszegi and M. Rabin. A model of reference-dependent preferences. *The Quarterly Journal of Economics*, 121(4):1133–1165, 2006.

[16] J. Krumm and E. Horvitz. Predestination: Inferring destinations from partial trajectories. In *UbiComp*, pages 243–260. Springer, 2006.

[17] J.-y. Kwak, P. Varakantham, R. Maheswaran, M. Tambe, F. Jazizadeh, G. Kavulya, L. Klein, B. Becerik-Gerber, T. Hayes, and W. Wood. Saves: A sustainable multiagent application to conserve building energy considering occupants. In *AAMAS*, pages 21–28. International Foundation for Autonomous Agents and Multiagent Systems, 2012.

[18] H. Lee and G. Lovellette. *Will electric cars transform the US vehicle market?: An analysis of the key determinants.* Harvard Kennedy School, Belfer Center for Science and International Affairs, 2011.

[19] J. Letchner, J. Krumm, and E. Horvitz. Trip router with individualized preferences (TRIP): Incorporating personalization into route planning. In *Proc. of the IAAI*, volume 21, pages 1795–1800, 2006.

[20] H. Oinas-Kukkonen. A foundation for the study of behavior change support systems. *Personal and ubiquitous computing*, 17(6):1223–1235, 2013.

[21] J. Pontes. World Top 10, May 2014. Technical report, EVSales.com, 2014.

[22] M. L. Puterman. *Markov decision processes: discrete stochastic dynamic programming*, volume 414. John Wiley & Sons, 2009.

[23] P. Reed and B. Romans. We test the tips part ii, save gas with smart driving and slick aerodynamics. Technical report, edmunds.com, 2009.

[24] G. Shani, R. I. Brafman, and D. Heckerman. An MDP-based recommender system. In *Proc. of the Eighteenth conference on Uncertainty in artificial intelligence*, pages 453–460. Morgan Kaufmann Publishers Inc., 2002.

[25] K. Torkkola, K. Zhang, H. Li, H. Zhang, C. Schreiner, and M. Gardner. Traffic advisories based on route prediction. In *Proc. of Workshop on Mobile Interaction with the Real World*, pages 33–36, 2007.

[26] T. Trigg and P. Telleen. Global ev outlook 2013 - understanding the electric vehicle landscape to 2020. Technical report, International Energy Agency, 2013.

[27] C. C. White III and D. J. White. Markov decision processes. *European Journal of Operational Research*, 39(1):1–16, 1989.

[28] K. Young, M. Regan, and M. Hammer. Driver distraction: A review of the literature. *Distracted driving. Sydney, NSW: Australasian College of Road Safety*, pages 379–405, 2007.

[29] B. D. Ziebart, A. L. Maas, A. K. Dey, and J. A. Bagnell. Navigate like a cabbie: Probabilistic reasoning from observed context-aware behavior. In *Proc. of the 10th international conference on Ubiquitous computing*, pages 322–331. ACM, 2008.

Are Aggressive Agents as Scary as Aggressive Humans?

Romy Blankendaal[1], Tibor Bosse[1], Charlotte Gerritsen[2], Tessa de Jong[1] and Jeroen de Man[1]
[1] VU University Amsterdam, Agent Systems Research Group
De Boelelaan 1081a, 1081 HV Amsterdam, The Netherlands
[2] Netherlands Institute for the Study of Crime and Law Enforcement
De Boelelaan 1077a, 1081 HV Amsterdam, The Netherlands
romy.blankendaal@gmail.com, t.bosse@vu.nl,
cgerritsen@nscr.nl, tessadejong71@msn.com, j.de.man@vu.nl

ABSTRACT
Most research into intelligent virtual agents focuses on agents with a positive stance towards the user. Nevertheless, the development of virtual agents that show aggressive behavior may also be interesting for a range of application domains, varying from aggression de-escalation training to anti-bullying education. However, ensuring that such aggressive agents achieve the desired effect is not easy, as they need to be believable in a number of aspects. In particular, they need to bring their human conversation partners into a serious state of anxiety. To investigate to what extent this can be achieved using state-of-the-art virtual agent technology, an experiment was performed in which the impact of an aggressive virtual agent was compared with that of an aggressive human. By randomly distributing a group of 28 participants over two conditions (virtual and human) and measuring their physiological and subjective emotional state before and after an aggressive outburst of their conversation partner, the difference between virtual and human aggression was studied. The results point out that both types of aggression induced a substantial stress response, but that the impact of the human aggression was higher than that of the virtual aggression.

Categories and Subject Descriptors
[**Human-centered computing**]: Empirical studies in HCI.

General Terms
Experimentation, Human Factors.

Keywords
Human-agent interaction; Aggression; Anxiety

1. INTRODUCTION
"You are about to finish your daily surveillance route, when you notice a middle-aged man with a baseball cap, who seems to be harassing a young lady. You politely ask the couple whether everything is OK. Suddenly, the man starts behaving aggressively towards you: he approaches you with clenched fists, shouting at you to mind your own business. The angry look on his face gives you the shivers. As he moves closer, you literally feel your blood running cold. Just when you are considering drawing your weapon, you realize he is just a character in a Virtual Reality environment. With a sigh of relief, you switch off your head-mounted display."

Appears in: *Proceedings of the 14th International Conference on Autonomous Agents and Multiagent Systems (AAMAS 2015), Bordini, Elkind, Weiss, Yolum (eds.), May, 4–8, 2015, Istanbul, Turkey.*

Although this example sounds futuristic, it illustrates the impact that intelligent virtual agents (IVAs) may have on the mental and physical state of the human beings that interact with them. IVAs can be defined as 'interactive characters that exhibit human-like qualities and communicate with humans or with each other using natural human modalities such as facial expressions, speech and gesture' [2]. Recently, IVAs have become widely used for numerous applications, in particular within serious games [27]. They have been successfully applied in a variety of games, in domains ranging from military missions [33] to negotiation [20]. In such applications, IVAs play various roles in which they interact with users (mostly via conversations), for instance as a coach, instructor, mentor, therapist, or teammate [26].

Despite these developments, we are only scratching the surface of potential applications. Interestingly, the majority of the research into IVAs addresses agents with a 'positive' attitude towards the user; i.e., they aim to support or collaborate with her in one way or the other. Instead, the area of IVAs with a 'negative' attitude has received less attention. This is a missed opportunity, because in our everyday reality, encounters with negative individuals are strikingly common, especially within the public domain [13, 32]. Indeed, in the past few years we can observe an increasing interest in the use of IVAs that also display negative, or even *aggressive* behavior. For instance, recent applications include virtual training of aggression de-escalation skills (e.g., for security personnel or clinical care providers) [6], Virtual Reality exposure therapy [29], and anti-bullying education [36]. In line with these developments, the current paper is part of a project that aims to develop a serious game for aggression de-escalation training in the public domain. The main idea is that trainees will learn to apply appropriate communication techniques by placing them in situations where they have to interact with aggressive virtual characters.

Nevertheless, ensuring that such training applications (and more specifically, the virtual agents involved) achieve the desire effect is a nontrivial issue. In general, it is now commonly accepted that, for an IVA to be effective, it needs to be *believable* [4]. This is particularly true when it comes to aggressive virtual agents, who are expected to induce some 'state of anxiety' in the humans they interact with. After all, in case users (e.g., of an aggression de-escalation training environment) do not experience their virtual conversation partners as scary, such an application will be of little use to prepare the person for aggressive confrontations in the real world.

Hence, an important challenge within this area of research is to develop aggressive virtual agents that induce a state of anxiety in their human conversation partners that approximates the state of anxiety they experience during real world confrontations with aggressive individuals. To reach this (long-term) goal, as a starting point it is useful to know how far we are currently away from it. In other words, to what extent is it already possible to induce the desired state of anxiety by using state-of-the-art virtual agent technology? This is the main purpose of the current paper. An experiment has been set up in which 28 participants were asked to listen to a story told by a conversation partner that would suddenly show an outburst of aggression. For half of the participants, the storyteller was a real human (an actress), whereas for the other half it was a virtual agent. Other than that, the difference between both conditions was kept to a minimum. By measuring physiological responses as well as subjective opinions of the participants, the difference in impact between the real and the virtual aggressive agent could be determined.

The remainder of this article is structured as follows. In Section 2, some background information about our project on aggression de-escalation training is provided. After that, Section 3 summarizes the recent literature on believable agents in the context of aggression de-escalation. Section 4 discusses the concept of anxiety as well as possibilities to induce and measure this emotional state. Next, Section 5 introduces the experiment that is central to our study, and Section 6 presents the results. Section 7 and 8 conclude the paper with a discussion and conclusion.

2. AGGRESSION DE-ESCALATION TRAINING

Aggressive behavior against public service workers (e.g. police officers, ambulance personnel, public transport employees) is an ongoing concern in many countries [13, 32]. Most incidents of aggression are of a verbal nature (e.g., insulting, swearing, intimidating), but in about 10% of the cases the conflicts escalate into physical aggression (e.g., threatening, abusing, robbing). To prepare employees to deal with such aggressive confrontations in an effective manner, dedicated training is required.

An important goal of such training is to help trainees develop their *emotional intelligence*: they should be able to recognize the emotional state of the conversation partner, and act upon this. In this respect, an important factor is the distinction between *reactive* and *pro-active* aggression: reactive aggression is characterized as an emotional reaction to a negative event that frustrates a person's desires, whereas pro-active aggression is the instrumental use of aggression to achieve a certain goal [14]. Based on the observed type of aggression, the employee should either apply a more empathic communication style or a more dominant style [1, 6].

To learn to effectively apply such techniques, employees in different domains within the public sector receive dedicated training in communication, both directly on-the-job and in artificial environments. Since on-the-job training is not considered sufficient because of limited possibilities to create the desired learning scenarios, 'offline' training receives much attention. Such training often uses role-play, where the roles are played either by co-students or by professional actors. Although reasonably successful, these types of training have important drawbacks. First, they are very costly, both in terms of money and time. As a result, the frequency by which they are offered is low. And second, there are large differences in the successfulness of role-play-based training: for some students the learning effect is large, whereas for others it is minimal. In conclusion, existing training is expensive, and hard to tailor to individual needs.

As a complementary approach to real world training, the current paper is part of a project that aims to develop a simulation-based serious game for public service workers, by which they can train their aggression de-escalation skills[1]. Users of the system will be placed in front of a 3D Virtual Reality (VR) environment (see Figure 1) that is either projected on a computer screen or on a head-mounted display[2]. During the training, users will be placed in a virtual scenario in a particular domain (e.g., issuing parking tickets, or selling tram tickets), which involves one or more virtual agents that at some point in time start behaving aggressively (e.g., insulting the tram driver because he is late). The user's task is to de-escalate the aggressive behavior of the virtual agents by applying the appropriate communication techniques. Users will be able to communicate with the agents via multiple modalities (e.g., text, speech, facial expression). Meanwhile, they will be monitored by intelligent software that observes and analyzes the behavior and physiological state (e.g., heart rate, skin conductance, brain activity) of the trainee and provides tailored feedback (e.g., as in [18]). Feedback will consist of two categories, namely hints and prompts on the one hand, and run-time modifications in the scenarios on the other hand. An example of the former would be to inform the trainee that (s)he should use a more empathic communication style, whereas an example of the latter would be to decrease the difficulty level in case the trainee makes many mistakes.

Figure 1. Screenshot of the VR environment used for training.

As explained in the introduction, aggression de-escalation is a prototypical example of a domain in which virtual training can only be successful if the virtual environment used is sufficiently realistic. For the most part, this has to do with the fact that the type of training addressed can be categorized as 'training with anxiety'. For such tasks, previous research (e.g., in the domain of shooting behavior) has pointed out that a certain level of

[1] More information on this project 'Simulation-based Training of Resilience in Emergencies and Stressful Situations' can be found at http://stress.few.vu.nl.

[2] The VR Environment has been developed by IC3D Media (http://www.ic3dmedia.com).

'simulated threat' is a necessary criterion to realize an adequate *transfer of training* from the simulated to the real world [22]. For our training environment, this simulated threat can be achieved by enhancing the believability of the aggressive virtual agents that interact with the user[3]. This topic is discussed in more detail in the following section.

3. BELIEVABLE AGGRESSIVE AGENTS

In 1996, Reeves and Nass put forward their Media Equation theory, stating that people have a tendency to treat computers (and other media) as if they were real humans [25]. This is a promising message for the IVA community, as it confirms that it is - in principle - not unnatural for people to interact with virtual agents, which is a good point of departure for applications that make use of such agents, such as simulation-based training. Nevertheless, the extent to which humans perceive virtual agents as realistic may vary, depending on a number of characteristics. Important concepts in this regard are *believability*, *immersion* and *presence*.

Believability is a property of virtual agents that refers to the extent to which they provide the illusion of being alive, hence permit the audience's suspension of disbelief [4]. In [12], believability is defined by three dimensions, namely *aesthetic*, *functional*, and *social* qualities of agents, which can be related, respectively, to the agent's *body* (its physical appearance), *mind* (the mechanisms that drive its behavior), and *personality* (the traits that determine its interaction style). Believability has some similarities to, but is not the same as immersion. Immersion can be considered a property of virtual environments as a whole (not necessarily of virtual agents), and describes the extent to which the environment is 'capable of delivering an inclusive, extensive, surrounding and vivid illusion of reality to the senses of a human participant' [30]. One way to create an immersive environment is, for instance, to make use of a head-mounted display (HMD). Presence, finally, is defined by Slater and Wilbur as a 'psychological sense of being in the virtual environment' [30], although this is just one out of many existing definitions. As such, presence can be considered a property of a human, rather than of a technology, which is indeed the perspective taken in this paper.

To relate these concepts to the current paper, we aim to study how virtual agents that show believable aggressive behavior in a (possibly immersive) virtual environment affect the state of presence of the human user (with an emphasis on her state of anxiety). Believability of the agents is realized in a number of ways: to create believable aesthetics, we make use of highly realistic 3D virtual characters that are provided by a commercial company. To create believable functional and social abilities, the agents' behavior is generated based on state-of-the-art commercial motion capture technology, which can be used to animate the entire facial motion of the virtual characters and synchronize it with recorded human speech (see Section 5). With the help of a professional actress, pre-recorded speech fragments were created in which the agent shows a sudden outburst of aggression during an otherwise neutral story. Immersion is realized (to some extent) by displaying the virtual character on a 19" computer monitor[4], and providing the auditory modality via a circumaural headphone. Our main interest is to investigate whether this setup results in a strong sense of presence (or more precisely: a sense of anxiety, which can be viewed as a more specific psychological state with a negative valence), and whether this experienced anxiety is similar to the anxiety experienced in the same circumstance in the real world.

Previous work in this area suggests that, under certain conditions, virtual environments and IVAs may indeed trigger physiological, experiential and behavioral responses in humans. For instance, Houtkamp and colleagues [19] found visual dynamics and sounds to be important factors influencing a user's affective appraisal of 3D virtual environments, although their studies did not focus on virtual agents. In contrast, Prendinger et al. [23] did focus on the interaction between humans and virtual agents. They demonstrated, among others, that electrodermal activity (EDA) is a useful indicator for arousal during such interactions. Following up on these developments Choi et al. [10] recently found that affective virtual agents strongly influence people's decision making through a combination of affective and cognitive processes. Additionally, they found physiological evidence that electrodermal lability, an individual trait, predicts which of these processes will dominate. Nevertheless, none of these studies explicitly compared the impact of virtual agents with that of real humans. A welcome exception is the work by Villani et al. [34]. This study indicated that, for the case of a simulated job interview, it is possible to induce physiological and experiential responses in humans that approximate (and on some aspects are even stronger than) the responses triggered by a comparable situation in the real world. However, this study differs from ours in the sense that these authors deliberately added some elements to the virtual condition (such as technological mediation and social and cultural cues) that were not present in the real world condition. In contrast, we aim to set up our experiment in such a way that the virtual and the real condition are as similar as possible.

In sum, despite a body of interesting literature in the area of human-agent interaction and physiological measurements, not many studies compare the impact of virtual agents on (physiological, experiential and behavioral) responses in humans in a systematic manner with the impact of real people; let alone that they focus on the specific impact of aggressive behavior on the spectator's state of anxiety. This is exactly the purpose of the current paper. Before we describe the setup of our experiment, we will provide a more precise definition of anxiety, and discuss possibilities to induce and measure it.

4. ANXIETY

The literature on anxiety mentions a number of closely related concepts, which are used in similar contexts. To avoid confusion on what the targeted mental state is in our experiment, in this section a more detailed explanation of the concept is provided.

Firstly, to reach a high state of presence a trainee needs to experience arousal [3]. In the broadest sense, arousal is considered a physiological and psychological state of alertness and readiness for action, often in response to a particular stimulus.

[3] There are numerous ways in which this 'simulated threat' can be enhanced, e.g. using air blast devices or electric surges. Discussing this in detail however goes beyond the scope of this paper.

[4] No HMD was used in the current study, as this will not be used in the initial version of the aggression de-escalation training system either.

In this paper however, the focus lies on a specific type of arousal underlying the fight-or-flight reaction or acute stress response, where the arousal is specifically caused by a threatening stimulus [8]. This negatively valenced arousal is what we will refer to as (state) anxiety.

A large body of research exists on the physiological effects of anxiety [31], as well as on related work using stress [7] or fear [11] as a denomination for a similar state. Since arousal is an activation of the sympathetic nervous system, electrodermal activity and cardiovascular responses are often used as measurements thereof, as covered in the previous section. For electrodermal activity, tonic changes - changes over longer time-intervals, often referred to as skin conductance levels - are assumed to be indicative of a general level of arousal [15]. Even though cardiovascular activity is influenced by both the sympathetic and parasympathetic nervous system and thus provides a less clear picture of arousal [16], measurements such as heart rate (variability) or blood pressure are reliably used for estimations of arousal [9]. Other modalities that are regularly used as a measurement of arousal include the eye (i.e. pupil size [5]), muscles (i.e. activity [35]) and recently also EEG (i.e. alpha asymmetry [7]).

To induce anxiety using virtual stimuli, a wide variety of methods can be used. For instance, the International Affective Picture Set (IAPS) is composed of a large number of pictures that have been rated on their arousal, valance and dominance [21]. By offering the most negatively valenced and highly arousing pictures to human viewers, a state of negative arousal can be induced which arguably is similar to a state of anxiety. However, the passive nature of viewing still images is at a disadvantage in inducing emotional states compared to viewing video clips [17]. Taking it another step further, videogames are used more and more for emotion elicitation [24]. By using virtual reality in combination with a HMD, presence can be increased further, thus providing a great opportunity for emotion elicitation [28].

As the quality of virtual reality keeps improving, the question raised in the introduction (i.e., 'how far we are currently away from inducing a state of anxiety that approximates the experience of real world confrontations?'), becomes increasingly relevant. In the following sections, as a first step towards answering this question, an experiment and its results are described to compare virtually elicited anxiety with that induced by a real human.

5. EXPERIMENT

The main question to be addressed by the experiment is roughly as follows: does a virtual agent elicit as much anxiety as a human being does during an aggressive outburst towards a human conversation partner? This will be tested in a between-subjects experiment, involving one independent variable (agent type: human or virtual) and several dependent variables that are indicative for anxiety, including physiological (heart rate and EDA) and subjective measurements.

5.1 Preparation

As preparation for the experiment, two video fragments of a virtual agent have been created. To this end, the Faceshift motion capture technology (http://www.faceshift.com/) has been used, in combination with a Microsoft Xbox 360 Kinect camera. The Faceshift software can be used to animate the entire facial motion of virtual characters, including facial expression, head orientation and eye gaze, and synchronize it with recorded human speech. To create the required content for the experiment, a professional actress was hired; she was asked to read a story about the history of the personal computer, while her voice and motion was being recorded. The first fragment lasted about 5 minutes; during this fragment, the actress simply read the text in a calm manner, while making eye contact with the camera from time to time, as if she was reading the text to an audience. After that, a second fragment was recorded. During this fragment, the actress read another part of the story (which followed the first fragment), but after 1 minute she would suddenly get extremely angry towards the camera, while shouting and accusing the listener of not paying attention. The exact text used for this was as follows (translated from her original language): '*What the hell! Just look at me when I'm talking to you, that's the least you can do! It's not difficult, just listen to me, or at least pretend you're listening!*'. After recoding both fragments, they were projected on a 3D virtual character (taken from http://www.rocketbox-libraries.com/) that was selected to resemble the real actress (see Figure 2).

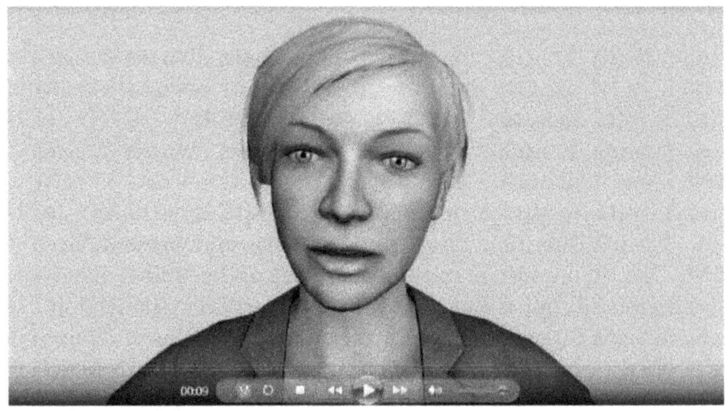

Figure 2. Screenshot of the virtual agent.

5.2 Participants

As participants for the experiment, 28 Computer Science students, all aged between 18 and 25, were recruited. The participants were randomly distributed over two groups of 14 participants, to which we will refer as the 'real' and the 'virtual' condition. The real group consisted of 8 male and 6 female students; the virtual group consisted of 7 male and 7 female students.

5.3 Design

The experiment took place in two ordinary office rooms, of which the physical setup is depicted in Figure 3 (left: real condition; right: virtual condition).

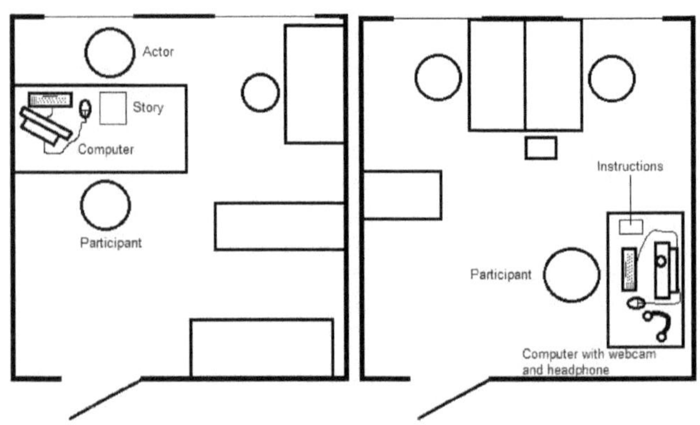

Figure 3. Experimental setup: real (left) and virtual (right).

The rectangles denote tables and the circles denote chairs. In both conditions, the chair that was intended for the participants was placed in front of a table. In the real condition, a real person (the same actress that played the behavior of the virtual agent) was sitting at the other end of the table. In the virtual condition, a computer monitor was placed on the table, on which the virtual agent would be displayed. In this condition, also a (non-working) webcam was attached to the computer, to make it appear as if the participants were monitored by the system (they were told beforehand that the agent was 'intelligent' in the sense that it would use these observations to adapt its own behavior towards the participant).

A summary of the different steps of the experiment is as follows. Before the start of the experiment, the participants had to read a text with instructions and sign an informed consent form. They were told that the experiment focused on measuring their attention and working memory. They were instructed to pay close attention to the story that they were about to hear, since they would have to answer some questions about it afterwards[5]. After that, they entered the experiment room, and took a seat on the chair. The experimenter then attached some physiological sensors (www.plux.info) to their body, which were used to measure their heart rate and electrodermal activity. After testing the sensors, the experimenter left the room.

At this moment, the storyteller (i.e., the human or virtual agent, depending on the condition) started reading the text about the history of the personal computer. As mentioned earlier, the first fragment of this story would take about five minutes. The main goal of this first part was to allow the participant to recover from the initial stress induced by the start of the experiment. After this first part, a short break followed. Then, the second part was read and at this moment physiological measurements were recorded; after one minute, suddenly the aggressive outburst would take place. In the virtual condition, this happened in the way described above. In the real condition, the actress would use the exact same wordings as used for the fragments of the virtual agent. She was also instructed to keep her performance as constant as possible across trials, by always using the exact same intonation, facial and bodily expressions. Then, after the aggressive outburst, the actress would leave the room. In the virtual condition, a 'connection lost' message would appear. This happened approximately 50 seconds after the start of the outburst. A few seconds later (at 1 minute after the outburst), recordings of physiological measurements were stopped and the actress and/or experimenter would re-enter the room, to explain to the participant that the aggressive outburst was just an act and provide comfort when necessary.

After the experiment was terminated, the participants had to fill out a questionnaire. This was done to obtain some information about their subjective experience, in addition to the physiological measurements only. The questionnaire consisted of the following questions:

- Q1: Did you listen carefully when the story was told?
- Q2: Did the aggressive outburst scare you?
- Q3: Although the actual goal of the experiment was to investigate your reaction to aggression, we told you in advance that the experiment focused on attention and memory. Did you believe this?
- Q4: Did you find the aggressive outburst believable?
- Q5: Did you feel personally addressed by the storyteller?

The participants had to rate these questions and score them on a 10-point Likert scale (with 1 = 'absolutely not' and 10 = 'absolutely'). They could also fill out an empty text box for every question, in case they had additional remarks.

6. RESULTS

The results of the physiological measurements are depicted in Figure 4. These graphs depict the dynamics of the heart rate in beats per minute (upper figure) and electrodermal activity in microSiemens (lower figure) over time during the relevant part of the experiment, averaged over all participants in each group. The horizontal axis denotes a period of 2 minutes, i.e., 1 minute before the start of the aggressive outburst and 1 minute after it. The vertical line indicates the moment the outburst started.

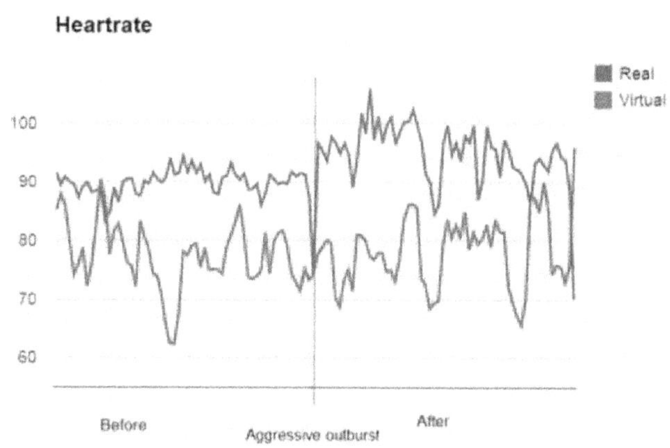

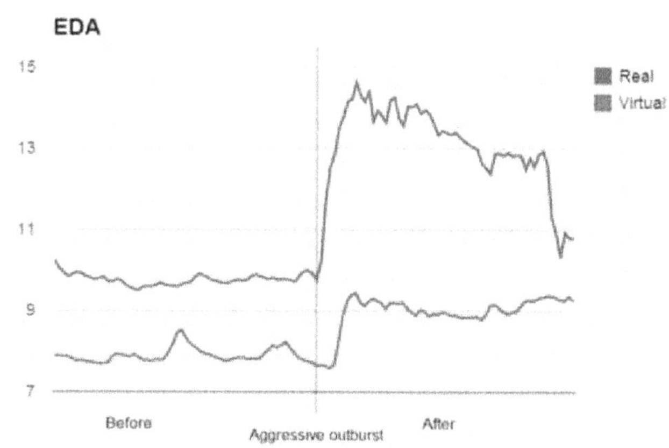

Figure 4. Development of heart rate (above) and EDA (below) during the experiment, averaged over all participants/group.

As can be seen from the figures, it seems that the participants in the real condition already start with a higher level of arousal (on

[5] The participants were asked not to talk back to the (virtual or human) storyteller, as this would result in a too much variation in conversations, which would make the trials incomparable. For the same reason, the actress was instructed to ignore the behavior of the participants.

average) than those in the virtual condition[6]. Indeed, this difference turns out to be significant, both for heart rate and for EDA. During the minute before the outburst, the average heart rate of the real group was 89.7 BPM (σ=10.5), whereas it was 77.3 BPM (σ=11.9) for the virtual group. An independent t-test confirms that this is a significant difference ($p<0.01$). For EDA, the average value of the real group was 10.2 μS (σ=6.0) during that minute, whereas it was 7.9 μS (σ=3.8) for the virtual group. Again, this difference is significant, although the effect is less pronounced than for heart rate ($p<0.05$).

Next, within-group comparisons are made between the average response before and after the aggressive outburst, both for heart rate and the EDA. This is done to find out for each group whether the aggressive outburst caused a significant stress reaction. For the real condition, the average heart rate increased from 89.7 (during the minute before the outburst, as reported above) to 94.8 (during the minute after the outburst). A paired t-test confirmed that this increase is fairly significant ($p<0.05$). The average EDA for this group increased from 10.2 to 13.4, which is strongly significant ($p<0.001$). For the virtual condition, the average heart rate increased only mildly, namely from 77.3 to 78.2; this increase is not significant ($p=0.37$). However, the average EDA for this group did increase significantly ($p<0.001$), namely from 7.9 to 9.0.

The obvious next step is to test whether the increase in responses in the real condition is significantly larger than the increase in the virtual condition. To this end, for both groups and both types of physiological measurements, the differences in response between the minute before and the minute after have been calculated, and these have been compared between the groups using independent t-tests. For heart rate, the average change over time was +5.11 for the real condition, and +0.95 for the virtual condition. Although this difference may seem large, it turned out to be not significant ($p=0.14$), probably due to the large individual differences. For EDA, the average change over time was +3.14 for the real condition, and +1.05 for the virtual condition. In contrast to the situation for the heart rate, this difference is strongly significant ($p<0.001$).

Regarding the subjective measurements, the answers given to all questions in the questionnaire were averaged and visualized in Figure 5. For each question, the difference in ratings between the real and the virtual condition was compared using an independent t-test. There appeared to be a significant difference for question Q1 ($p<0.05$), indicating that the participants in the real condition reported paying significantly more attention to the storyteller than those in the virtual condition. For question Q2, addressing the extent to which the participants experienced being scared, the difference turned out the be just above the significance level ($p=0.13$). For the other three questions, the differences were clearly not significant (all p-values higher than 0.4).

Finally, we tested whether there were any correlations between the answers given in the questionnaire. This was done by calculating Pearson's correlation coefficient for all combinations of questions. For both conditions, there turned out to be moderate to strong relationships between several combinations of questions, most notably between Q2, Q4 and Q5. As an illustration, a scatterplot of the strongest relation, which is between Q2 and Q5 in the real condition ($r=0.61$), is shown in Figure 6. This figure indicates that (for the exception of one outlier) the participants that claimed to feel more personally addressed by the storyteller generally reported to be more scared by the outburst.

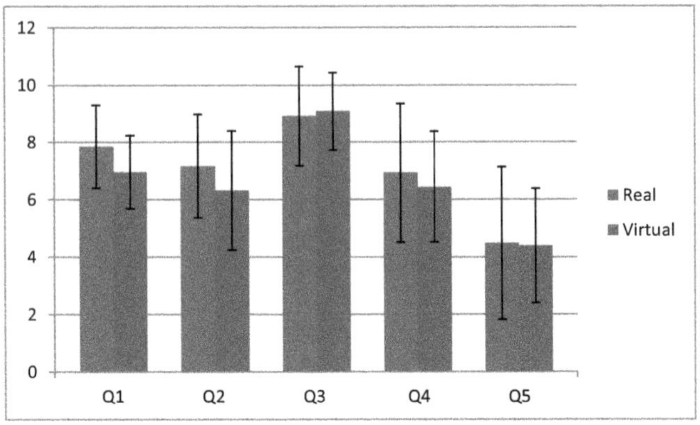

Figure 5. Results of the questionnaire.

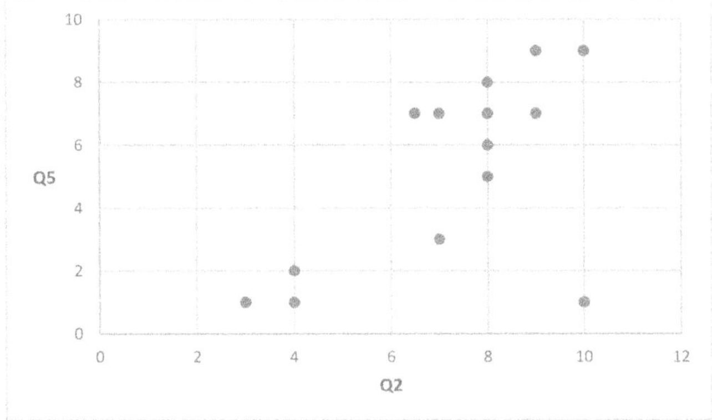

Figure 6. Correlation between Q2 and Q5 (real condition).

7. DISCUSSION

Before discussing the physiological measurements, a discussion on the subjective results is given first. Here, only one result appeared statistically significant, indicating that participants in the real condition reported paying more attention compared to the virtual condition (question Q1). It is not a stretch to consider that there is more pressure on the participant to pay attention when confronted with a real human agent due to social convention. This is consistent with the additional remarks given by some of the participants in the virtual condition, who reported having some difficulties in maintaining a high level of concentration during the experiment. Interestingly however, the other questions did not show any significant results. Thus, no significant differences were found in the scariness (Q2) and the believability of the aggressive outburst (Q4), and in the extent to which the participants felt personally addressed (Q5). One factor that should be taken into account here is a potential bias of the participants in the virtual condition; for instance, these participants may have (unconsciously) interpreted question Q2 as "Did the aggressive outburst scare you, *considering that it was a virtual agent*?".

[6] Hence, in a way the two groups have different 'baseline' measurements. To give an impression about the difference with a 'true' baseline measurement: in a pilot study, where subjects were brought in a state at rest by watching a 'relaxing' movie, we found this baseline to have a mean value of 70 BPM for heart rate and of about 7.5 μS for EDA.

Not finding a significant difference in the scariness is interesting, as it might indicate that there is already very little difference between the virtual and the real condition. Also with regard to believability, it is promising that no significant differences were found. However, it is important to note that the sample size in the experiment (28 participants) was limited, which makes it difficult to draw crisp conclusions about this. Additionally, with an average score between 6 and 7 it could be argued that a participant does not experience the same threat in such an experimental condition as it would in a real situation. Nonetheless, this same difference holds for actor-based training versus on-the-job training.

Regarding correlations between the questions, the most pronounced result is the strong correlation between Q2 and Q5, indicating that people who felt more personally addressed by the storyteller generally reported to be more scared by the outburst. This is an interesting finding with our training application in mind. Although correlation does not necessarily mean causation, it may be worthwhile to design the virtual agent in such a way that users have the impression that it addresses them in person.

Next up are the physiological results. A striking first find is that for both the heart rate and electrodermal activity, average values in the real condition are overall higher compared to the virtual group. This might indicate that when confronted with a real human, participants were already more aroused than those who were put in front of a virtual agent. This finding is consistent with the fact that participants in this condition paid more attention to the storyteller (see results for question Q1 in the questionnaire), as attentional effort is typically paired with physiological reactions.

Looking at the impact of the aggressive outburst (by comparing the response levels before and after this moment), a clear effect can be seen in the graph of the electrodermal activity[7]. Even though the aggressive outburst only covers part of the post-measurements, the effect lasts for the entire time in the virtual condition and only at the very end a drop occurs in the real condition. For heart rate the outburst seems to have less impact, although it still resulted in a significant increase in average heart rate in the real condition. This could be caused because cardiovascular measurements not only reflect the sympathetic nervous system, but are of a more complex nature, as explained earlier. A noteworthy result is the short, sudden and extreme drop in heart rate in the real condition at the exact time of the aggressive outburst. This effect is not seen in the virtual group, and could reflect a literal skip of a heartbeat.

To check how sensitive the results are to the time frame used for the physiological measurements, (e.g., due to peculiarities of the specific measures, like EDA having a much slower time decay than heart rate), we investigated whether using measurements over shorter time frames (e.g. 30 seconds before and after the outburst) changed the results, but in general it did not. For instance, using 30 instead of 60 seconds changes the average heart rate before the outburst from 89.7 to 89.8 (see also Fig.4). In summary, physiological measurements seem to indicate that in both conditions, the outburst is sufficient to trigger an emotional response. Both the average level of arousal as well as the reaction to the aggressive outburst are larger in the real condition than in the virtual condition. However, these conclusions should be handled with care, as there was already a difference in the 'baseline' measurement between the two groups. Furthermore, a subjective evaluation of the difference between the two groups with regard to anxiety was inconclusive.

With this in mind, some of the potential weaknesses in this experimental setup seem minor. Even though the virtual agent was designed to be as realistic as possible, some important drawbacks of the fragments need some consideration. First, only the face of the actress was recorded and no gestures were animated in the clips. Second, subtle non-verbal cues displayed in the real world setting, might have gone lost in recording. Third, a regular monitor was used instead of an HMD, which has possibly limited immersion. Nonetheless, the virtual group experienced a physical and emotional reaction to the aggressive outburst. By improving the virtual condition, it can only be expected to decrease differences further, or even surpass the real condition with respect to evoking anxiety.

Although the actress was instructed to keep her performance as constant as possible across participants, it is possible that some small differences appeared, e.g. in the precise tone or volume of her voice or her non-verbal behavior. In any case, similar to the virtual condition, participants in the real condition did not interact with the actress (as instructed) and as a result she was able to consistently give a steady performance, with hardly any interference from the participant. To prevent this discussion entirely, for follow-up studies it may be interesting to add another condition in which participants are confronted with a pre-recorded video fragment of the actress (comparable to a 'teleconference' setting). On the other hand, this would be of less relevance for our project, as in the end the aim is to train people that are confronted with real world, face-to-face aggression.

Another difficult aspect of this type of research is pinpointing or describing the exact emotional state that is being targeted. Here, anxiety was used for the state of negative arousal as described before. In the current setup, there could be a difference between the initial (unconscious) 'shock' experienced when the actress or agent suddenly bursts out in anger compared to the 'higher-order emotion' (of shame perhaps) that is felt afterwards, because of the reprimand. In reality, there is probably a gradual transition from the former state to the latter, which makes it difficult to assess which of the (subjective and physiological) measurements relate to which state. In some sense, this is not a problem for our research, as our main focus is on minimizing the difference between the real and the virtual condition, for all possible responses. At some point however, it might become useful to gain a deeper understanding about the relation between the different measurements and the emotional states that are induced.

Related to this, an interesting point of discussion addresses the question which aspects of the (real and virtual) storyteller's aggressive behaviour contribute to the state of anxiety. Potential components include facial expression, sound, and the content of the utterances. For instance, it is possible that the main part of the participants' reaction (both in the real and the virtual condition) was caused by an acute stress response triggered by the loud sound of the shouting storyteller, independent from what she said and the look on her face. In follow-up experiments, we aim to study these aspects in more detail.

[7] The slight delay of the response in the virtual condition appeared to be caused by a timing issue in the fragments of the virtual agent.

8. CONCLUSION

In this paper, an experiment was described to compare the impact of an aggressive virtual agent with that of a real human actor with respect to the listener's anxiety. A group of 28 participants took part in the experiment, which were randomly assigned to the 'real' or the 'virtual' condition. Results show a physiological response to the aggressive outburst in both conditions, although it is larger in the real group. In contrast, a post-activity questionnaire did not show any differences in subjectively experienced anxiety between both groups. In all, these findings show that virtual agents are able to elicit similar responses as a real human actress, when showing aggressive behavior. Although there are still some differences in the physiological response induced, this provides strong support for using virtual agents for aggression de-escalation training.

With multiple possibilities to enhance the realism of the virtual agent, in the future the emotion experienced by the user could be intensified even further, which provides more possibilities into exploring the differences (or lack thereof) between the real and the virtual world. Currently, a virtual environment for training aggression de-escalation techniques is being implemented, which will be used to investigate the potential of using virtual agents for training compared to role-play further. Here, in addition to the currently used facial animations, agents will be able to make gestures. Moreover, in addition to evaluating the impact on users' emotional and physiological state, transfer of learning from the virtual training environment to the real world will be evaluated.

Parallel to this, it is important to also consider the possible risks of using virtual reality. As it is not yet known what the limits are that can be reached using this technology, care should be taken not to reach a situation in which the virtual experience becomes equally (or more) frightening than real-life, hence introducing similar (psychological) risks such as posttraumatic stress disorder. As this research has shown, there lies great power in using virtual reality and virtual agents for training purposes, but it is important we also learn to understand and harness this power well.

ACKNOWLEDGEMENTS

This research was supported by funding from the National Initiative Brain and Cognition, coordinated by the Netherlands Organization for Scientific Research (NWO), under grant agreement No. 056-25-013. The authors are very grateful to Maaike Schuilenburg for her contribution to the experiment. Additionally, they wish to thank Marco Otte for his technical support, as well as all students who participated in the experiment.

9. REFERENCES

[1] Anderson, L.N. and Clarke, J.T. (1996). De-escalating verbal aggression in primary care settings. Nurse Pract. 21(10):95, 98, 101-2.

[2] Aylett, R., Krenn, B., Pelachaud, C., and Shimodaira, H. (eds.) (2013). Intelligent Virtual Agents. Proceedings of the 13th International Conference on Intelligent Virtual Agents, IVA'13. Lecture Notes on Computer Science, Springer Verlag, vol. 8108.

[3] Baños, R.M., Botella, C., Alcañiz, M., Liaño, V., Guerrero, B., Rey, B. (2004). Immersion and Emotion: Their Impact on the Sense of Presence. CyberPsychology & Behavior 7(6), 734–741.

[4] Bates, J. (1994). The role of emotions in believable agents. Communications of the ACM, vol. 37, issue 7, pp. 122-125.

[5] Bradley, M., Miccoli, L., Escrig, M., and Lang, P. (2008). The pupil as a measure of emotional arousal and autonomic activation. Psychophysiology , 45, 602-607.

[6] Bosse, T. and Provoost, S. (2014). Towards Aggression De-escalation Training with Virtual Agents: A Computational Model. In: Proceedings of the 16th Int. Conference on Human-Computer Interaction, HCI'14. Lecture Notes in Computer Science, Springer Verlag, pp. 375-387.

[7] Brouwer, A.M., Neerincx, M.A., Kallen, V.L., van der Leer, L., ten Brinke, M. (2011). EEG alpha asymmetry, heart rate variability and cortisol in response to virtual reality induced stress. Journal of Cybertherapy & Rehabilitation 4(1), 21–34.

[8] Cannon, W. (1932). Wisdom of the Body. United States: W.W. Norton & Company.

[9] Chida, Y. and Hamer, M. (2008). Chronic psychosocial factors and acute physiological responses to laboratory-induced stress in healthy populations: a quantitative review of 30 years of investigations. Psychological Bulletin, 134 (6), 829-885.

[10] Choi, A., Melo, C.M. de, Khooshabeh, P., Woo, W., and Gratch, J. (2015). Physiological evidence for a dual process model of the social effects of emotion in computers. International Journal of Human-Computer Studies 74, pp. 41-53.

[11] Courtney, C. G., Dawson, M. E., Schell, A. M., Iyer, A., and Parsons, T. D. (2010). Better than the real thing: Eliciting fear with moving and static computer-generated stimuli. International Journal of Psychophysiology, 78(2), 107-114.

[12] De Angeli, A., Lynch, P., and Johnson, G. (2001). Personifying the e-market: A framework for social agents. In: M. Hirose (Ed.), Proceedings of Interact 2001. IOS Press, pp. 198-205.

[13] DelBel, J. (2003). De-escalating workplace aggression. Nurning Management (USA) 34, 31-34.

[14] Dodge, K.A. (1990). The structure and function of reactive and proactive aggression. In D. Pepler and H. Rubin, (eds.), The development and treatment of childhood aggression (pp. 201-218). Hillsdale, NJ: Erlbaum.

[15] Figner, B. and Murphy, R. (2011). Using skin conductance in judgment and decision making research. In M. Schulte-Mecklenbeck, A. Kuehberger, & R. Ranyard (Eds.), A handbook of process tracing methods for decision research (pp. 163-184). New York: Psychology Press.

[16] Geus, E. de and Doornen, L. van (1996). Ambulatory assessment of parasympathetic/sympathetic balance by impedance cardiography. In J. Fahrenberg, & M. Myrtek, Ambulatory Assessment. Computer assisted psychological and psychophysiological methods in monitoring and field studies (pp. 141-164). Berlin: Hogrefe & Huber.

[17] Gross, J.J. and Levenson, R.W. (1995). Emotion elicitation using films. Cognition & Emotion, 9(1), 87-108.

[18] Heuvelink, A. and Mioch, T. (2008). FeGA: A cognitive Feedback Generating Agent. In Proceedings of the Seventh

IEEE/WIC/ACM International Conference on Intelligent Agent Technology (IAT 2008) (pp. 567-572). IEEE Computer Society Press.

[19] Houtkamp, J.M., Schuurink, E.L., and Toet, A. (2008). Thunderstorms in my computer: the effect of visual dynamics and sound in a 3D environment. In: Bannatyne, M. & Counsell, J. (Eds.), Proc. of the Int. Conference on Visualisation in Built and Rural Environments BuiltViz'08, IEEE Computer Society, Los Alamitos, USA.

[20] Kim, J., Hill, R.W., Durlach, P., Lane, H.C., Forbell, E., Core, C., Marsella, S. Pynadeth, D. and Hart, J. (2009) BiLAT: A game-based environment for practicing negotiation in a cultural context. International Journal of AI in Education, vol. 19, issue 3, pp. 289-308.

[21] Lang, P.J, Bradley, M.M., and Cuthberth, B.N. (1999). International Affective Picture System (IAPS): Technical Manual and Affective ratings. Gainesville, Fl. The Cennter for Research in Psychophysiology, University of Florida

[22] Nieuwenhuys, A. and Oudejans, R.R.D. (2011). Training with anxiety: Short- and long-term effects on police officers' shooting behaviour under pressure. Cognitive Processing, 23 March 2011, 1-12.

[23] Prendinger, H., Becker-Asano, C., and Ishizuka, M. (2006). A study in users' physiological response to an empathic interface agent. International Journal of Humanoid Robotics, 3(3):371–391.

[24] Reekum, C. van, Johnstone, T., Banse, R., Etter, A., Wehrle, T., and Scherer, K. (2004). Psychophysiological responses to appraisal dimensions in a computer game. Cognition and Emotion, 18(5), 663-688.

[25] Reeves, B. and Nass, C. (1996). The media equation: How people treat computers, television, and new media like real people and places. Stanford, CA : CSLI Publications.

[26] Rickel, J. (2001). Intelligent virtual agents for education and training: Opportunities and challenges. In A. de Antonio, R. Aylett, and D. Ballin (eds.), Intelligent Virtual Agents, Lecture Notes in Computer Science, Springer Verlag, vol. 2190, pp. 15–22.

[27] Ritterfeld, U., Cody, M., and Vorderer, P. (eds.) (2009). Serious Games: Mechanisms and Effects. New York/London: Routledge.

[28] Riva, G., Mantovani, F., Capideville, C. S., Preziosa, A., Morganti, F., Villani, Gaggioli, A., D., Botella, C. and Alcañiz, M. (2007). Affective interactions using virtual reality: The link between presence and emotions. CyberPsychology & Behavior, 10(1), 45-56.

[29] Rizzo, A.A., Reger, G., Gahm, G., Difede, J., and Rothbaum, B.O. (2008). Virtual Reality Exposure Therapy for Combat Related PTSD. In: Shiromani, P., Keane, T., and LeDoux, J. (eds.), Post-Traumatic Stress Disorder: Basic Science and Clinical Practice, Springer Verlag.

[30] Slater, M. and Wilbur, S. (1997). A framework for immersive virtual environments (FIVE): Speculations on the role of presence in virtual environments. Presence: Teleoperators and Virtual Environments, 6(6).

[31] Smith, J.C., Bradley, M.M., and Lang, P.J. (2005). State anxiety and affective physiology: effects of sustained exposure to affective pictures. Biological Psychology, 69(3), 247-260.

[32] Smith, M.J. and Clarke, R.V. (2000). Crime and public transport. In R. Clarke (Ed.), Crime and Justice: A Review of Research (pp. 169-234). Chicago, IL: The University of Chicago Press.

[33] Traum, D. and Rickel, J. (2002). Embodied agents for multi-party dialogue in immersive virtual worlds. Proceedings of the International Joint Conference on Autonomous Agents and Multi-agent Systems (AAMAS 2002), pp. 766–773.

[34] Villani, D., Repetto, C., Cipresso, P., and Riva, G. (2012). May I experience more presence in doing the same thing in virtual reality than in reality? An answer from a simulated job interview. Interacting with Computers, 24 (4), 265-272.

[35] Visser, B., Looze, M. de, Graaff, M. de, and Dieën, J. van (2004). Effects of precision demands and mental pressure on muscle activation and hand forces in computer mouse tasks. Ergonomics , 47 (2), 202-217.

[36] Zoll, C., Enz, S., Schaub, H., Aylett, R., and Paiva, A. (2006). Fighting Bullying with the Help of Autonomous Agents in a Virtual School Environment. In: Proceedings of the 7th International Conference on Cognitive Modelling (ICCM).

The Fallacy of Endogenous Discounting of Trust Recommendations

Tim Muller, Yang Liu, Jie Zhang
School of Computer Engineering, Nanyang Technological University
50, Nanyang Avenue, Singapore
{tmuller,yangliu,zhangj}@ntu.edu.sg

ABSTRACT

Recommendations are widely used in recommender systems, reputation systems, and trust-based security systems. Some existing reputation systems and trust-based security systems use the flawed notion of endogenous discounting. Endogenous discounting is the idea that claims deviating from prior expectations should be ignored or discounted, which introduces confirmation bias. To show the fallacy of endogenous discounting, we construct a semantic meta-model that captures the key notions surrounding recommendations. We prove that any model covered by the meta-model can be formulated in a divide-and-conquer fashion. We show how divide-and-conquer clashes with endogenous discounting. Lastly, we discuss the implications on existing work that applies endogenous discounting, and provide suggestions for future work.

Categories and Subject Descriptors

I.2.11 [**Distributed Artificial Intelligence**]: Multiagent Systems

Keywords

Endogenous Discounting; Recommendation; Trust System; Rating

1. INTRODUCTION

Recommendations are an increasingly common source of information for decision making over the Internet. There are different models for reasoning with different forms of recommendations. Some models are designed for a particular goal, e.g., for recommending movies [13], books (amazon.com), music (last.fm) or security. Some models apply in a particular setting, e.g., for peer to peer networks [1] or mobile ad-hoc networks [15]. Other models are generic trust models, e.g., Subjective Logic [10], TRAVOS [27], or HMM-based models [5, 7]. Whether recommendations are deceitful is an important question in all. Recommendations that are deceitful must be filtered out (qualitatively or quantitatively), and the remainder must be combined into an informed decision.

There are two ways to filter recommendations: *exogenous discounting* and *endogenous discounting*, as named in [30]. In exogenous discounting, recommendations from unreliable sources are filtered out[1]. In endogenous discounting, recommendations are filtered out when they deviate from other recommendations and/or first-hand experience. Examples of endogenous discounting are: "This seller did not scam me, therefore I can ignore the warnings from others" or "9 people loved the movie, and 1 person hated it; that single person's opinion can be ignored". These two are clear examples of fallacious reasoning, due to confirmation bias. In this work, we prove the fallacy of endogenous discounting, in generality.

We did not find examples of endogenous discounting in recommender systems in the literature – presumably, there, examples are too obviously fallacious. We did, however, find a significant number of examples in reputation systems and trust-based security systems (discussed in Section 5.4). Since the fallacy occurs in reputation systems and trust-based security systems, our formalism more closely matches their paradigm. Nevertheless, the formalism is sufficiently general to cover all collusion-free systems with recommendations. The impact of collusion is discussed in Section 5.2.

Our main contributions are three-fold:

1. We introduce a generic semantics for dealing with opinions and recommendations. The semantics is generalised over the possible behaviours of the agents.
2. We prove viability of modular/incremental/algebraic approaches in systems with recommendations – approaches where users maintain opinions about agents, which are updated when new information arrives.
3. We show that endogenous discounting should not be applied to evaluate recommendations. We discuss the impact of this fallacy.

Results 1 and 2 corroborate results found in parts of the literature: Result 1 supports the approaches based on Bayesian methods [7, 26], based on HMM models [5, 28], and based on model-based collaborative filtering [25]. Result 2 indicates that decentralised and dynamic approaches to forming opinions, e.g., [10, 26], are viable. Result 3 has a direct impact to a significant fraction of research on trust models that apply endogenous discounting. Endogenous discounting is applied in (recent) work on: reputation systems [3, 30, 32], security protocols – like secure routing [14], mobile ad-hoc networks [9], access control [8], specific domains – like cloud computing [6], peer to peer networks [31] – and general analysis of recommendations [23].

Organization. In Section 2, we introduce a simple trust model with endogenous filtering, to exemplify the notions used in this paper, as well as exemplify how endogenous filtering can introduce error. To generalise that, we need to introduce a general notion that covers the relevant models. The meta-model is introduced in Section 3 for this purpose. Using the meta-model, we prove decompositionality in Section 4. In Section 5, we complete the argument against

[1]E.g. in collaborative filtering [2], unreliable sources are people with different tastes; e.g. with referral trust [11], unreliable sources are typically people with hidden agendas.

Appears in: *Proceedings of the 14th International Conference on Autonomous Agents and Multiagent Systems (AAMAS 2015), Bordini, Elkind, Weiss, Yolum (eds.), May, 4–8, 2015, Istanbul, Turkey.*

endogenous discounting. We discuss the impact of decompositionality on endogenous discounting in Section 5.1, the relation with collusion in Section 5.2, why endogenous discounting is used despite being fallacious in Section 5.3, the impact of our results to existing work in Section 5.4 and the implications for future research in Section 5.5.

2. CONFIRMATION BIAS

The confirmation bias is the fallacy where an agent accepts or rejects evidence, not on the basis of the quality of the evidence, but on whether or not it fits in the agent's view. Weighting evidence against counter-evidence and deciding the former outweighs the latter does not suffer from confirmation bias. However, discarding the counter-evidence is an instance of confirmation bias. When the counter-evidence is not considered, the resulting opinion will be overconfident. Moreover, in the case that the opinion is wrong, correcting it is difficult. In this section, we show these characteristics of the confirmation bias using a simplified model. The general idea that endogenous filtering is fallacious is discussed in the remainder of the paper.

In this work, we assume that trust models contain *interactions* between *users* and *targets*. The users cannot determine the *outcome* of the interaction, therefore, they first form an *opinion* about the target. In order to form an opinion, users use past interactions, and users may consult with *recommenders*, who provide *recommendations*. Agents in the system may be users, recommenders, targets, or possibly fulfill multiple roles. The interactions are, typically, only visible to the user and the target involved. In this section, we set up a simple trust model that incorporates and links these notions. The notions are generalised in Section 3.

Ad-hoc Trust Model with Endogenous Discounting.

The *ad-hoc trust model* exemplifies a trust model, where we can exhibit our general results in a concrete manner. The details of the model are not important, but for concrete data, strong assumptions must be made. The assumptions are chosen for being both representative for reputation systems, yet easy to compute with.

The outcome of an interaction Q is denoted with a quality parameter $q \in (0,1)$. A high *quality* interaction (e.g., stay at a nice hotel, or receive the timely delivery of intact goods) has a value q near 1. Targets with high *integrity* (e.g., good hotels or honest salesmen), denoted with R, tend to provide higher a quality interaction Q. We assume that given integrity R, the quality Q of an outcome is determined as $p_Q(q|R=r) = \max(2-4\cdot|r-q|, 0) + \max(2-4\cdot(r+q), 0) + \max(-6+4\cdot(r+q), 0)$. We depict the distribution for $R = 0.1$, $R = 0.3$ and $R = 0.5$, in Figure 1(a). This particular distribution is chosen for its convenient computational properties, but the general argument holds for all distributions of Q given R, and even for subjective notions of quality. The crucial notion is that a target has a (random) integrity, which determines the distribution of the quality, where higher integrity targets tend to provide higher quality interactions.

In the ad-hoc trust model, we assert that a trustworthy recommender y provides a recommendation $C_y \in (0,1)$ close to the quality parameter R of the target. We partition $(0,1)$ into ten intervals of size 0.1, called bins. "Close to" simply means that C_y and R are in the same bin. We introduce the parameter P_y to capture the trustworthiness of recommender y; y is trustworthy with probability P_y. Both trustworthy and untrustworthy recommendations are uniformly distributed. The distribution of C_y is, therefore:

$$P_{C_y}(c_y|P_y{=}p_y, R{=}r) = \begin{cases} 10\cdot p_y & \text{if } r \text{ and } c_y \text{ share a bin.} \\ \frac{1-p_y}{0.9} & \text{otherwise.} \end{cases}$$

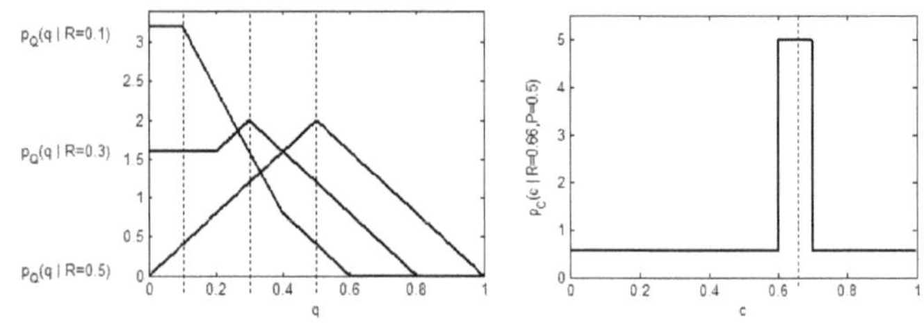

(a) Distrib. $p_Q(q|R{=}0.1)$, $p_Q(q|R{=}0.3)$, $p_Q(q|R{=}0.5)$ (b) Dist. $p_{C_y}(c_y|R=0.66)$

Figure 1: Distribution of the quality and the recommendations, given the integrity of the target.

The distribution of recommendations is depicted in Figure 1(b), with $P_y = 0.5$ and $R = 0.66$.

Remark 1. For simplicity, we let all integrity values be equiprobable a priori, i.e., $p_R(r)$ is uniformly distributed. Using Bayes' theorem, with $p_R(r) = 1$, we obtain $p_R(r|Q{=}q) = p_Q(q|R{=}r)$. Similarly, $p_R(r|C_y{=}c_y, P_y{=}p_y) = p_{C_y}(c_y|R{=}r, P_y{=}p_y)$ These equations do not hold in full generality, but are a direct consequence of the convenient choices of our distributions.

A user may form an opinion about a target x, based on an interaction with quality Q, and some recommendations C_{y_0}, C_{y_1}. We denote this as the opinion $\tau_x(Q{=}q, C_{y_0}{=}c_{y_0}, C_{y_1}{=}c_{y_1})$. This opinion may not correspond to single values, it simply succinctly denotes the perspective of a user in a system. For such an opinion about a target to be relevant, it must have implications on the integrity R of the target.

We implement endogenous discounting in the ad-hoc trust model using statistical hypothesis testing. The null hypothesis is that recommenders are trustworthy – the recommendation and the target's integrity share a bin. The alternative hypothesis is its negation. We let $\alpha = 0.05$, meaning that we reject recommendations c_y, if the probability of getting c_y from a trustworthy recommender y is smaller than 5%, given a distribution over R. Thus, given distribution f over R, we reject when the bin of c_y has probability mass under 0.05, or formally: $\int_{\frac{\lceil 10c \rceil}{10}}^{\frac{\lfloor 10c \rfloor}{10}} f(r)\mathbf{d}r \le \alpha$. This function resembles the form of endogenous filtering used in TRAVOS [27]. Recommendations are provided to the system in chronological order, and hypothesis testing is performed in that order.

Experimental Analysis of the Ad-hoc Trust Model.

The purpose of the experimental analysis, is to provide a concrete interpretation of the general results that we prove in the paper. Therefore, we simplify the experimental analysis, to expose the core issues: decompositionality and the confirmation bias. In particular, this means that we discretise the random variables, and that we set all $P_{y_i} = 0.5$ as public knowledge. Setting P_{y_i} as a fixed value precludes exogenous discounting, since all recommenders are equally helpful, thus exposing endogenous discounting.

A target has integrity R with probability $p_R(r)$. In the ad-hoc trust model, only the integrity determines the quality of the interactions, so the integrity of the target is of great interest to the user. By obtaining evidence (recommendations or interactions), the probabilities change, since generally $p_R(r) \neq p_R(r|E)$, where E is some evidence. Decompositionality is the notion that we can derive $p_R(r|E_1, E_2)$ from $p_R(r|E_1)$ and $p_R(r|E_2)$. The computation that allows us to derive the former is called aggregation (Definition 3). In the ad-hoc trust model, aggregation is simply normalised multiplication. That means that $p_R(r|E_1, E_2)$ is proportional to $p_R(r|E_1)\cdot p_R(r|E_2)$.

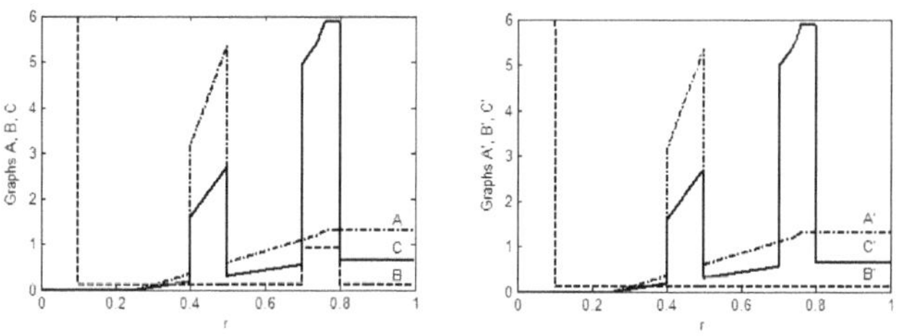

(a) Graphs A, B, C (b) Graphs A', B' C'

Figure 2: Probability distributions of the integrity of the target, given different evidence.

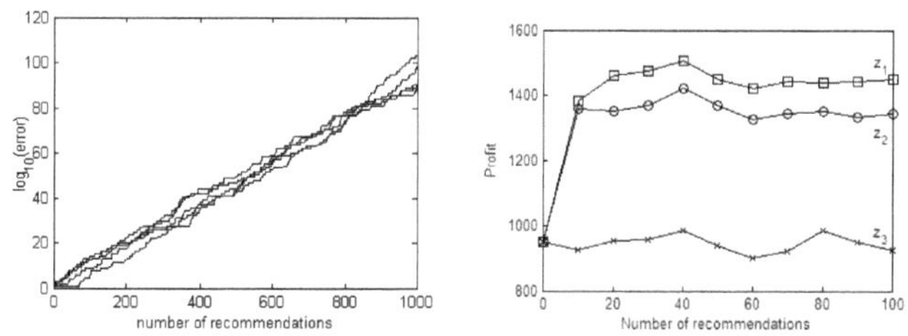

(a) Error after n rec. (b) Profit of z_1, z_2 and z_3

Figure 3: Simulations demonstrating that endogenous discounting introduces an error, and decreases profit.

To show concretely what decompositionality means, consider the following simulation: We have two bodies of evidence, one body consists of an interaction with quality $q = 0.76$ and $C_{y_1} = 0.43$, thus $\tau_x(Q{=}0.76, C_{y_0}{=}0.43)$, and one body is recommendations $C_{y_1} = 0.04$, $C_{y_2} = 0.07$ and $C_{y_3} = 0.72$, thus $\tau_x(C_{y_1}{=}0.04, C_{y_2}{=}0.07, C_{y_3}{=}0.72)$. We run a Monte Carlo simulation, generating R, Q and $C_{y_0}, \ldots C_{y_3}$. In variation A, we drop all samples except those where $\tau_x(q{=}0.76, C_{y_0}{=}0.43)$ – thus where there is one interaction with quality 0.76 and only recommender y_0 provides a recommendation, namely 0.43. In variation B, we drop all samples except those where $\tau_x(C_{y_1}{=}0.04, C_{y_2}{=}0.07, C_{y_3}{=}0.72)$. In variation C both must hold, thus samples are kept only if $\tau_x(Q{=}0.76, C_{y_0}{=}0.43, C_{y_1}{=}0.04, C_{y_2}{=}0.07, C_{y_3}{=}0.72)$. Figure 2(a) shows the probability of the integrity, in A, B and C. Note that graph B exceeds the dimensions of the figure. Figure 2(a) furthermore reveals that C is proportional to the pointwise product of A and B, decompositionality holds. Thus, in reality, there exists a link between A&B and C. There is no reason why a trust model should not break this link.

Endogenous discounting, as proposed in the ad-hoc trust model, does break the link between A&B and C. We run the same Monte Carlo simulation as before, with one difference: If we are not confident in the trustworthiness of the recommender, then we reject the recommendation (thus ignore the effect of the recommendation on the samples). Figure 2(b) shows A', B', C', which correspond to A, B, C with endogenous discounting. Here B' is cut off too. In particular, observe that in graph B', the dashed block spanning from 0.7 to 0.8 disappeared, compared to B. This is because after receiving recommendations $C_{y_1} = 0.04$ and $C_{y_2} = 0.07$, the recommendation $C_{y_3} = 0.72$ is rejected (confidence 0.99). However, in C', $C_{y_1} = 0.04$ and $C_{y_2} = 0.07$ are rejected, and as a consequence $C_{y_3} = 0.72$ is accepted. It is immediate that A'&B' are no longer linked with C'. The ad-hoc trust model with endogenous discounting failed to uphold decompositionality.

The two preceding simulations make the main argument of this paper concrete: decompositionality is a natural property, but endogenous discounting breaks decompositionality. The next two simulations demonstrate that endogenous discounting can be harmful. Notice that the difference between B and B', is that B' puts more probability density on what it believes to be the likely integrity value, $c < 0.1$. This is caused by the confirmation bias, as B' rejects evidence ($C_{y_3}{=}0.72$) due to the fact that the evidence does not match expectations. First, we show that arbitrarily large errors can be introduced by the confirmation bias with a bounded probability. Second, we show that endogenous discounting actually leads to impaired decision making.

We take a simplistic view on error, namely the inverse of the probability density assigned to the integrity of the target, $\frac{1}{p_R(r|\ldots)}$. A distribution with high density on r gives error close to 0, and a distribution with low density on r gives increasingly high error. We initialise every simulation by selecting random r, and two recommendations C_{y_0}, C_{y_1}, such that C_{y_0} and C_{y_1} are in the same bin, but in a different bin from R. This happens with probability $\frac{(1-P_{y_0})\cdot(1-P_{y_1})}{9} = \frac{1}{36}$. The remainder of the simulation uses n randomly generated recommendations (using $p_{C_{y_i}}(c_{y_i}|R = r, P_{y_i} = p_{y_i})$). Figure 3(a) show the error as n increases. The reason the error increases rapidly, is because of an unfortunate false start, whereafter the truth is rejected for being unlikely, and further misleading evidence may be accepted. The error grows exponentially in with respect to n, and the probability of the false start remains a constant $\frac{1}{36}$.

To show that endogenous discounting negatively impacts decision making, consider a game between three users, z_1, z_2 and z_3. Users z_1, z_2 and z_3 are offered the same interactions, with a certain payoff in case of success, and cost in case of failure. If they believe the interaction is profitable, they interact, otherwise they do not. User z_1 does not apply endogenous discounting, z_2 does, and z_3 is the baseline, as he ignores all recommendations. We perform a Monte Carlo simulation of $10,000$ runs, in which we generate an integrity, and k recommendations according to the assumptions (e.g. a random $\tau_t(Q{=}q, C_{y_1}{=}c_{y_1}, \ldots, C_{y_k}{=}c_{y_k})$) and payoff and cost of interaction uniformly in $[0, 1]$ and $[-1, 0]$. The users z_1 and z_2 typically make the same decision, for $k = 10$, users z_1 and z_2 make different decisions in less than 5% - 10% of the potential interactions. This is despite the fact that user z_2 falls for the confirmation bias in 15% - 20% of the cases. Specifically, in 15% - 20% of the cases, the user z_2 rejects recommendations that were in the correct bin.

We see, in Figure 3(b), that if $k = 0$, the profit is identical for all users, as no user actually uses any recommendations. User z_3 ignores all further recommendations, meaning that any variation in the graph is pure chance. We see that z_1 and z_2 increase and rapidly stabilise, with z_1 stabilising consistently higher than z_2. The stabilisation is because the additional impact of extra recommendations quickly decreases. The absolute difference between z_1 and z_2 is fairly small. However, relative to the baseline, z_3, we see a difference that roughly corresponds with the 15% of the cases in which z_1 falls for the confirmation bias. This implies that falling for the confirmation bias has a real and detrimental effect on trust-based decision making. It is important to note that fallaciously using recommendations (z_2) is significantly better than not using recommendations at all (z_3).

Observe that the unbounded error from Figure 3(a) has a bounded effect on the profit, in Figure 3(b). The reason is that the maximal size of a mistake is bounded, and even an exponentially large error cannot increase the size of the mistake.

When we introduce the formalism in full generality, we refer to this concrete example. Whenever we refer to the running example, we refer to the ad-hoc trust model, and specifically to the experiments from Figure 2(a).

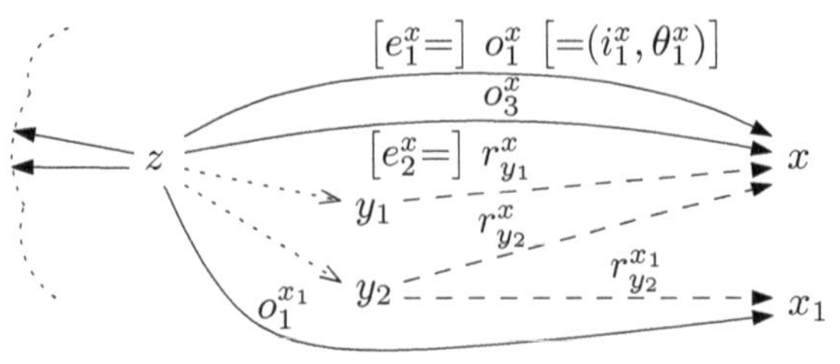

Figure 4: Example of a network from user z's perspective

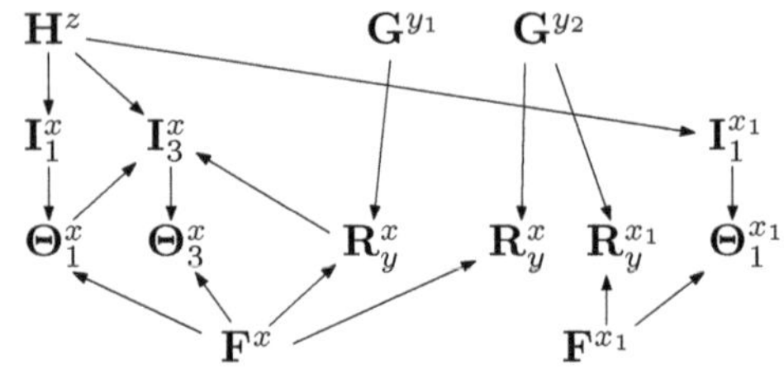

Figure 5: A Bayesian network depicting the relationships.

3. META-MODEL

In this section, we introduce the meta model, which aims to capture the key semantics of the recommendation related components and concepts. As it is a meta-model, we leave some details unspecified and use them to reason about abstract entities and relationships. Consequently, our meta-model requires only the bare assumptions, found often in reputation systems and trust-based security systems. Concretely, we reason about strategies and probabilities, without assigning strategies to agents, nor selecting prior distributions.

3.1 Setting

The main assumption of our meta-model, is that models deal with *opinions* based on evidence. Specifically, $\tau_x(e_1, \ldots, e_n)$ is the opinion about x based on evidence $e_1, \ldots, e_n$. These opinions have a semantics, which:

R1 makes predictions about the agent (or product) that the opinion applies to.

R2 can be updated when additional evidence arises.

A significant number of reputation systems, recommender systems and trust management systems aim to satisfy R1 and R2. Not all models, however, satisfy R1 and R2, e.g., models of human cognition may purposely implement the confirmation bias or other fallacies. In this section, we provide a meta-model that provides semantics that satisfy both R1 and R2.

Before introducing the meta model, we first formally define the notations for the concepts introduced in the previous section. Let Z be a set of users, Y be the set of recommenders and X be the set of targets. Interactions are a pair consisting of an initiation $i_j^x \in I$ and an outcome $\theta_j^x \in \Theta$ of one interaction (e.g., purchasing a laptop is an interaction, consisting of an initiation in the form of a prepayment of the price of a laptop, and an outcome in the form of a timely delivery of the offered laptop). Throughout the paper, we adopt the viewpoint of a user – therefore, it suffices to identify an interaction (or initiation or outcome) by the target x and an index j. We may also omit the target or the index, if they are not relevant.

We use O to denote the set of observations of the interactions between the users and targets $o_j^x \in O$ is short for the interaction between user j and target x. (One observation is about exactly one interaction.) We use R to denote the set of recommendations of recommenders provide. $r_y^x \in R$ represents the recommendation from recommender y about target x. Observations and recommendations collectedly form the evidence E, i.e., $E = O \cup R$. Users have opinions $\tau_x(e_1, e_2, \ldots)$ about x based on *evidence*, $e_j \in E$.

Figure 4 depicts an example of a network with user z, two recommenders y_1 and y_2, and two targets x and x_1. In the network the user has two pieces of direct evidence about x: $e_1^x{=}o_1^x{=}(i_1^x, \theta_1^x)$ and $e_3^x{=}o_3^x{=}(i_3^x, \theta_3^x)$ – we omit the equivalent notations of o_3^x in the figure, to avoid cluttering. The user, further, has two recommendations about x, from agents y_1 and y_2, namely $e_2^x{=}r_{y_1}^x$ and $e_4^x{=}r_{y_2}^x$. In order to establish the reliability of the recommenders, the user may look at other recommendations by the recommenders. In the example, recommender y_2 also makes a recommendation about x_1, $e_2^{x_1}{=}r_{y_2}^{x_1}$, and the user has direct evidence about x_1, namely $e_1^{x_1}{=}o_1^{x_1}$.

In our meta-model, we are not necessarily interested in the behaviour of the agents. We are interested in which factors may influence the decisions of the agents. Events unobserved by an agent, for example, cannot influence the behaviour of that agent. Here, we could use Bayesian network to visualise the influence. A Bayesian network is a graphical notation to show the conditional independence between random variables. Intuitively, an arrow can be interpreted as meaning that the source influences the sink.

Figure 5 represents the relations of the random variables corresponding to the entities in Figure 4. We use random variables $\mathbf{E}_i^x$, $\mathbf{O}_i^x$, $\mathbf{R}_y^x$, $\mathbf{I}_i^x$ and $\mathbf{\Theta}_i^x$ for evidence, observations, recommendations, initiations and outcomes, respectively. There are 5 additional random variables, $\mathbf{H}^z$, $\mathbf{G}^{y_1}$, $\mathbf{G}^{y_2}$, $\mathbf{F}^x$ and $\mathbf{F}^{x_1}$, representing the behaviour of z, y_1, y_2, x and x_1, that will be discussed later. This Bayesian network represents the essentials of a typical trust system, with two caveats: there is no collusion and no recommendations about recommendations. The relevance of these caveats is discussed after the formalism and results.

The meta-model presented in this work encodes the relations between the entities, and which events are visible to whom. If an agent performs an action under some circumstances, then the behaviour of that agent is more likely to be the sort of behaviour in which he performs that action under those circumstances with high probability – this is Bayes' theorem. However, the circumstances are typically only partially known, and subtle hidden connections may exist. Notions like cost, benefit, taste and discrimination must be gracefully handled by the meta-model, without explicitly modeling these. As a consequence, the precise formulation of the meta-model contains a fair amount of technicalities.

3.2 Formal Meta-model

In the meta-model, users, recommenders and targets have reactive strategies. A user strategy takes into account a collection of evidence, in order to decide whether to interact with a target. A recommender strategy takes into account the target of the recommendation, when recommending. A target strategy takes into account the interaction at hand, in order to decide the outcome of the interaction. Thus, a reactive strategy allows (the probability of) the outcome to depend, e.g., on the value of the interaction (as in the value imbalance attack [12]).

Remark 2. The reactive strategy is stateless, it cannot (naively) model, e.g., performing ten successes and only then a failure (as in the playbook attack [12]). Decompositionality also holds for a meta-model allowing the more technically involved stateful reactive strategies (similar to [16]). See our technical report [17].

We use some shorthand notations. A list $\langle a_1, \ldots, a_n \rangle$ may be shorthanded to $\overline{a}$. We define $\triangleleft(\Phi)$ to be the set of distributions over the arbitrary set Φ. If Φ is discrete, $\triangleleft(\Phi) = (\Phi \to [0,1])$, where for all $f : \triangleleft(\Phi)$, $\sum_{\varphi\in\Phi} f(\varphi) = 1$, and if Φ is continuous, $\triangleleft(\Phi) = (\Phi \to \mathbb{R}^{\geq 0})$, where $\int_\Phi f(\varphi)\mathbf{d}\varphi = 1$. We use P and p for probability mass and probability density functions. For random variable $\mathbf{A}$ and outcome a, rather than writing $P(\mathbf{A}{=}a)$ or $p_{\mathbf{A}}(a)$, we write $P(a)$ or $p(a)$, whenever this introduces no ambiguity.

Rather than explicitly assigning strategies to agents, we merely define the shape of the strategies. A target finalises an interaction, based on the initiation of that interaction. A recommender provides recommendations based on the target that the recommendation is about (be it truthful or not). A user initiates interactions with targets, based on the evidence he has about the target. From game theory, we learn that agents may want to perform actions with probabilities between 0 and 1; so-called mixed moves. In our definition, we assert that a strategy is simply a function from the input, to a distribution over the output:

Definition 1. The *strategy of a target* is a function $f : I \to \triangleleft(\Theta)$. The *strategy of a recommender* is a function $g : F \to \triangleleft(R)$. The *strategy of a user* is a function $h : E \times \cdots \times E \to \triangleleft(I)$.

In the technical report [17], the strategy is extended to a form probabilistic automata, similar to hidden Markov models.

Running Example 1. In the ad-hoc trust model, it is assumed that every target x has an internal parameter r_x that determines the quality of its interactions. The outcomes are denoted with a quality, between 0 and 1, thus $\Theta = (0,1)$. The probability of the outcome being θ, is equal to $\min(\frac{2\theta}{r}, \frac{2(1-\theta)}{1-r})$. Thus, we can identify each r_x with exactly one strategy f_r^x, such that $f_r^x(i)(\theta) = \min(\frac{2\theta}{r}, \frac{2(1-\theta)}{1-r})$. Similarly, we can identify every p_y with exactly one strategy g_p^y, such that

$$g_p^y(r)(c) = \begin{cases} 10 \cdot p & \text{if } r \text{ and } c \text{ share a bin.} \\ \frac{1-p}{0.9} & \text{otherwise.} \end{cases}$$

In some systems, particularly reputation systems, recommenders cannot observe the target's strategy, but only perform interactions and observe these. Thus, we may propose a function from interactions to recommendations, rather than from a strategy to recommendations: $(\hat{g}^y \in \hat{G}) : \overline{O} \to \triangleleft(R)$. Each target strategy f^x (in conjunction with the recommender strategy) yields a distribution over the interactions $(P(\overline{o^x}|\hat{g}^y, f^x))$. Therefore, given the target's strategy f^x, for every $\hat{g}^y$, there exists an identical g^y, namely: $g^y(f^x)(r_y^x) = \sum_{\overline{o^x}\in\overline{O}} P(\overline{o^x}|\hat{g}^y, f^x) \cdot \hat{g}^y(\overline{o^x})(r_y^x)$. Hence, as long as the user has no direct information about the interactions between the recommender and the target, every $\hat{g} \in \hat{G}$ can be substituted by some $g \in G$. Thus, without loss of generality we can assert the shape of the input of the recommender strategy to be the as in Definition 1.

Running Example 2. We can alter the ad-hoc trust system, such that the recommender interacts with the target, and receives an interaction with quality q' based on r. The recommender then bases his recommendation on q' (rather than r), as many reputation systems assert. Specifically, the trustworthy recommenders provide a recommendation c in the same bin as q' (rather than r). Thus, as before $\hat{g}_p^y(q')(r) = \begin{cases} 10 \cdot p & \text{if } q' \text{ and } c \text{ share a bin.} \\ \frac{1-p}{0.9} & \text{otherwise.} \end{cases}$ Now, since the link between r and q' is known to be $P(q'|r)$ and q' is not visible to any of the users: $g_p^y(r)(r) = \int_0^1 P(q'|r) \cdot \hat{g}_p^y(q')(r)\mathbf{d}q'$.

We use the random variables $\mathbf{F}^x$, $\mathbf{G}^y$ and $\mathbf{H}^z$, for the strategies of the targets x, recommenders y and users z. As we assume agents do not collude, we assume mutual independence between $\overline{\mathbf{F}}, \overline{\mathbf{G}}, \overline{\mathbf{H}}$; any collection of strategies is independent of any collection of different strategies.

By the definition of the strategy, $\mathbf{I}^x = h(\overline{e^x})$, $\mathbf{\Theta}^x = f^x(i^x)$, and $\mathbf{R}_y^x = g^y(f^x)$. The strategy completely determines the actions of the agents. That means, in particular, that the probability that an agent performs an action a, under the condition that his strategy is φ and the input is b, equals $\varphi(b)(a)$ – as long as a does not appear in the condition. Formally, $P(a|\varphi, b, \overline{c}) = \varphi(b)(a)$, if $\overline{c}$ does not contain a. (Note that variables may be nested, e.g. $c_i = \psi(a)$.)

Based on these random variables, we can introduce the semantics of an opinion, called a valuation:

Definition 2. The *valuation* $[\![\tau_x(e_1, \ldots, e_n)]\!]$ is the semantics of the opinion $\tau_x(e_1, \ldots, e_n)$. The valuation $[\![\tau_x(e_1, \ldots, e_n)]\!]$ is the distribution $p(f^x|e_1, \ldots, e_n)$.

In the technical report [17], valuations are extended to stateful valuations, which are distributions over states that the target may be in.

Running Example 3. Opinion $\tau_x(Q{=}0.76, C_{y_0}{=}0.43)$ was introduced in Section 2. The opinion $\tau_x(Q{=}0.76, C_{y_0}{=}0.43)$ occurs when the user observes $Q = 0.76$ and recommendations $C_{y_0} = 0.43$ about the target x. Graph A, in Figure 2(a) depicts the true distribution of the integrity parameter, given $Q = 0.76$ and $C_{y_0} = 0.43$, namely $p_R(r|Q{=}0.76, C_{y_0}{=}0.43)$. Definition 2 states that graph A – $p_R(r|Q{=}0.76, C_{y_0}{=}0.43)$ – is the semantics of $\tau_x(Q{=}0.76, C_{y_0}{=}0.43)$.

We introduce aggregation to denote the required operation for updating opinions:

Definition 3. The *aggregation* of two opinions $\tau_x(\overline{e}), \tau_x(\overline{e'})$ is denoted $\tau_x(\overline{e})\bowtie\tau_x(\overline{e'})$ and equals $\tau_x(\overline{e}, \overline{e'})$.

Definitions 1 and 2 are sufficient to prove that for direct observations, valuations are updateable:

PROPOSITION 1. *For arbitrary two observations $\overline{o^x}$ and $\overline{o'^x}$, $[\![\tau_x(\overline{o^x})\bowtie\tau_x(\overline{o'^x})]\!] \propto \frac{[\![\tau_x(\overline{o^x})]\!]\cdot[\![\tau_x(\overline{o'^x})]\!]}{[\![\tau_x(\emptyset)]\!]}$.*

PROOF. We first apply induction over n to prove

$$p(f^x|o_1^x, \ldots, o_n^x) = p(f^x) \cdot \prod_{j=1}^{n} f^x(i_j^x)(\theta_j^x). \tag{1}$$

The base case trivially holds. The induction step is as follows:

$$\begin{aligned} & p(f^x|o_1^x, \ldots, o_n^x) \\ & \propto P(\theta_n^x, i_n^x|f^x, o_1^x, \ldots, o_{n-1}^x) \cdot p(f^x|o_1^x, \ldots, o_{n-1}^x) \\ & = P(\theta_n^x|i_n^x, f^x, o_1^x, \ldots, o_{n-1}^x) \cdot P(i_n^x|f^x, o_1^x, \ldots, o_{n-1}^x) \\ & \qquad \cdot p(f^x|o_1^x, \ldots, o_{n-1}^x) \\ & = f^x(i_n^x)(\theta_n^x) \cdot h^z(o_1^x, \ldots, o_{n-1}^x)(i_n^x) \cdot p(f^x|o_1^x, \ldots, o_{n-1}^x) \\ & \propto f^x(i_n^x)(\theta_n^x) \cdot p(f^x|o_1^x, \ldots, o_{n-1}^x) \end{aligned}$$

From equation (1), the proposition follows as:

$$\begin{aligned} & [\![\tau_x(o_1^x, \ldots, o_k^x)\bowtie\tau_x(o_{k+1}^x, \ldots, o_n^x)]\!] \\ & = [\![\tau_x(o_1^x, \ldots, o_n^x)]\!] \\ & \propto p(f^x) \cdot \prod_{j=1}^{n} f^x(i_j^x)(\theta_j^x) \\ & = \frac{p(f^x)\cdot\prod_{j=1}^{k} f^x(i_j^x)(\theta_j^x)\cdot p(f^x)\cdot\prod_{j=k+1}^{n} f^x(i_j^x)(\theta_j^x)}{p(f^x)} \\ & = \frac{[\![\tau_x(o_1^x, \ldots, o_k^x)]\!]\cdot[\![\tau_x(o_{k+1}^x, \ldots, o_n^x)]\!]}{[\![\tau_x(\emptyset)]\!]} \quad \square \end{aligned}$$

This proposition is proven for stateful valuations in the technical report [17].

Proposition 1 proves that aggregation's semantics are the pointwise multiplication of the valuations, corrected for prior distributions. Bayesian updates are pointwise multiplications. Hence, the pointwise multiplication of two valuations contains both their Bayesian updates. However, the prior distribution is contained twice – it is pointwise squared. Hence, we need to divide by the prior, $p(f^x)$.

Running Example 4. Aggregation is the link between A&B and C (see Figure 2(a)). It states that $\tau_x(Q{=}0.76, C_{y_0}{=}0.43)$ aggregated with $\tau_x(C_{y_1}{=}0.04, C_{y_2}{=}0.07, C_{y_3}{=}0.72)$ is $\tau_x(Q{=}0.76, C_{y_0}{=}0.43, C_{y_1}{=}0.04, C_{y_2}{=}0.07, C_{y_3}{=}0.72)$. Proposition 1 is the formalisation of the notion that the link between A&B and C can be computed using only the values of $p_R(r|Q{=}0.76, C_{y_0}{=}0.43)$, $p_R(r|C_{y_1}{=}0.04, C_{y_2}{=}0.07, C_{y_3}{=}0.72)$ and $p_R(r|Q{=}0.76, C_{y_0}{=}0.43, C_{y_1}{=}0.04, C_{y_2}{=}0.07, C_{y_3}{=}0.72)$. The computation is a normalised pointwise multiplication, which is independent from the evidence. The same does not hold for A'&B' and C'.

The meta-model ensures that the semantics of every model it covers satisfies R1 and R2. Users can predict (R1) the probability that a target performs action θ upon our initiation i, when our opinion is $\tau_x(e_1, \ldots, e_n)$. First take the semantics: $[\![\tau_x(e_1, \ldots, e_n)]\!] = p(f^x|e_1, \ldots, e_n)$, then take the expected value of the probability that θ happens: $\int_0^1 p(f^x|e_1, \ldots, e_n) \cdot f^x(i)(\theta)\mathbf{d}f^x$. The latter formula provides the exact probability that θ happens, whenever the assumptions about the prior distribution are correct. For observations, the opinions can be updated in a straightforward manner, as Proposition 1 proves. In Section 4, we generalise Proposition 1 to Lemma 1, and ultimately Theorem 1, and show that R2 holds in full generality. Not only can the trust opinions be updated without reevaluating the evidence, the procedure for updating is aggregation as defined in Definition 3.

4. DECOMPOSITIONALITY

A scenario where an opinion is computed based on recommendations (and possibly direct observations) is called a *chain*. In a *basic chain*, all evidence the user has about the target, is one single recommendation. Since a basic chain is a chain, any system that computes chains can compute the basic chain. Endogenous discounting cannot be applied to the basic chain, since there is nothing to compare the recommendation to. We prove that any chain can be decomposed into basic chains with aggregation. Neither basic chains nor aggregation need endogenous discounting. Therefore, any chain can be computed (via decomposition) without endogenous discounting.

Decompositionality has been proven in a special case – the Beta model – in [18]. Our Lemma 1 and Theorem 1 are proper generalisations of the Modularity Proposition and Modularity Theorem.

Proposition 1 can be generalised to prove that the user's direct observations can be isolated from the recommendations. We refer to the ability to separate direct observations and recommendations as *weak decompositionality*.

LEMMA 1. *Let $\overline{e^{\overline{x}}}$ be evidence about targets $x_1, \ldots, x_\ell \neq x$, $\overline{o^x}$ be observations about the target x, and $r^x_{\overline{y}}$ be recommendations about x from recommenders $\overline{y} = y_1, \ldots, y_k$. Then:*
$[\![\tau_x(\overline{o^x}, r^x_{\overline{y}}, \overline{e^{\overline{x}}})]\!] = [\![\tau_x(\overline{o^x}, \overline{e^{\overline{x}}}) \bowtie \tau_x(r^x_{\overline{y}}, \overline{e^{\overline{x}}})]\!]$

PROOF. The induction in the proof of Proposition 1 can be straightforwardly adapted to prove:

$$p(f^x|o^x_1, \ldots, o^x_n, r^x_{\overline{y}}, \overline{e^{\overline{x}}}) = p(f^x|r^x_{\overline{y}}, \overline{e^{\overline{x}}}) \cdot \prod_{j=1}^{n} f^x(i^x_j)(\theta^x_j)$$

Note that $p(f^x|r^x_{\overline{y}}, \overline{e^{\overline{x}}}) = p(f^x|r^x_{\overline{y}})$, as follows:

$$\begin{aligned}
p(f^x|r^x_{\overline{y}}, \overline{e^{\overline{x}}}) &\propto P(\overline{e^{\overline{x}}}, r^x_{\overline{y}}|f^x) \cdot p(f^x)\\
&= \int_{\overline{F}}\int_{\overline{G}} P(\overline{e^{\overline{x}}}, r^x_{\overline{y}}|f^x, \overline{f^{x'}}, \overline{g^y}) \cdot p(\overline{f^{x'}}, \overline{g^y}|f^x)\mathbf{d}\overline{f^{x'}}\mathbf{d}\overline{g^y} \cdot p(f^x)\\
&= \int_{\overline{F}}\int_{\overline{G}} \left(\prod_i \left(\prod_j f^{x'_i}(i^{x'_i}_j)(\theta^{x'_i}_j)\right) \cdot \left(\prod_j g^{y_j}(f^{x'_i})(r^{x'_i}_j)\right)\right)\\
&\qquad \cdot \left(\prod_j f^x(i^x_j)(\theta^x_j)\right) \cdot p(\overline{f^{x'}}, \overline{g^y})\mathbf{d}\overline{f^{x'}}\mathbf{d}\overline{g^y} \cdot p(f^x)\\
&\propto \left(\prod_j f^x(i^x_j)(\theta^x_j)\right) \cdot p(f^x) \quad \propto \quad p(f^x|r^x_{\overline{y}})
\end{aligned}$$

Using equation (1), $\prod_{j=1}^n f^x(i^x_j)(\theta^x_j) = \frac{p(f^x|r^x_{\overline{y}})}{p(f^x)}$, and thus $\prod_{j=1}^n f^x(i^x_j)(\theta^x_j) = \frac{p(f^x|r^x_{\overline{y}}, \overline{e^{\overline{x}}})}{p(f^x)}$, proving the lemma. □

Weak decompositionality, Lemma 1, states that user's own observations can be ignored without loss of generality, with respect to analysing recommendations. Decompositionality requires that recommendations can furthermore be treated in isolation from each other.

THEOREM 1. *Let $\overline{e^{\overline{x}}}$ be evidence about targets $x_1, \ldots, x_\ell \neq x$, and $e^x_1, \ldots, e^x_n$ be evidence about target x. Then:*
$[\![\tau_x(e^x_1, \ldots, e^x_n, \overline{e^{\overline{x}}})]\!] = [\![\tau_x(e^x_1, \overline{e^{\overline{x}}}) \bowtie \ldots \bowtie \tau_x(e^x_n, \overline{e^{\overline{x}}})]\!]$

PROOF. Via Lemma 1, we assume w.l.o.g. $e^x_j = r^x_{y_j}$. Thus, it suffices to prove that $p(f^x|r^x_{y_1}, \ldots, r^x_{y_k}, \overline{e^{\overline{x}}}) = p(f^x|r^x_{y_1}, \overline{e^{\overline{x}}}) \bowtie \ldots \bowtie p(f^x|r^x_{y_k}, \overline{e^{\overline{x}}})$.

Suppose $\frac{p(f^x|\overline{e^{\overline{x}}})}{p(f^x)} \propto 1$ and $p(\overline{g^y}|f^x, \overline{e^{\overline{x}}}) = p(\overline{g^y}|\overline{e^{\overline{x}}})$, then:

$$\begin{aligned}
&p(f^x|r^x_{y_1}, \ldots r^x_{y_n}, \overline{e^{\overline{x}}})\\
&\propto P(r^x_{y_1}, \ldots r^x_{y_n}|f^x, \overline{e^{\overline{x}}}) \cdot p(f^x|\overline{e^{\overline{x}}})\\
&= \int_{\overline{G}} P(r^x_{y_1}, \ldots, r^x_{y_n}|f^x, \overline{g^y}, \overline{e^{\overline{x}}}) \cdot p(\overline{g^y}|f^x, \overline{e^{\overline{x}}})\mathbf{d}\overline{g^y} \cdot p(f^x|\overline{e^{\overline{x}}})\\
&\propto \int_{\overline{G}} \left(\prod_j g^{y_j}(f^x)(r^x_{y_j})\right) \cdot p(g^{y_1}, \ldots, g^{y_k}|\overline{e^{\overline{x}}}) \cdot p(f^x|\overline{e^{\overline{x}}})\mathbf{d}\overline{g^y}\\
&\propto \frac{\prod_j p(f^x|r^x_{y_j}, \overline{e^{\overline{x}}})}{p(f^x)^{n-1}}
\end{aligned}$$

In Lemma 1, we find $p(f^x|r^x_{\overline{y}}, \overline{e^{\overline{x}}}) = p(f^x|r^x_{\overline{y}})$. Letting $e^{\overline{x}}$ be empty, this is our first assertion. The second assertion holds too:

$$\begin{aligned}
&p(\overline{g^y}|f^x, \overline{e^{\overline{x}}})\\
&\propto p(\overline{e^{\overline{x}}}|f^x, \overline{g^y}) \cdot p(\overline{g^y})\\
&= \int_{\overline{F}} p(\overline{e^{\overline{x}}}|f^x, \overline{g^y}, \overline{f^{x'}}) \cdot p(\overline{f^{x'}}|f^x, \overline{g^y})\mathbf{d}\overline{f^{x'}} \cdot p(\overline{g^y})\\
&= \int_{\overline{F}} p(\overline{e^{\overline{x}}}|\overline{g^y}, \overline{f^{x'}}) \cdot p(\overline{f^{x'}}|\overline{g^y})\mathbf{d}\overline{f^{x'}} \cdot p(\overline{g^y})\\
&\propto p(\overline{g^y}|\overline{e^{\overline{x}}}) \quad \square
\end{aligned}$$

5. FALLACY OF ENDOGENOUS DISCOUNTING

We have introduced a meta-model, and proven a divide-and-conquer approach to evaluating recommendations. In this section, we show that endogenous discounting is indeed fallacious, then relate these theoretical results to existing work and extract useful data for future work.

5.1 Endogenous Discounting is Fallacious

To show that endogenous discounting is fallacious, we need to show that:

H1 Our meta-models cover the relevant models.

H2 Decompositionality is not an artifact from our choice of formalism.

H3 Decompositionality precludes endogenous discounting.

Our meta-models are a semantic model. Thus, for claim H1, it suffices to argue that the meaning of an opinion in a trust model[2] coincides with our semantics. Some trust models explicitly reason about strategies and/or probability, and are trivially covered by our meta-models. Examples under the meta model are Subjective Logic [10], TRAVOS [27], HABIT [26], BLADE [21], PRep [7], and recommender systems using model-based collaborative filtering [25] or memory-based collaborative filtering [33], whereas HMM models [5, 28] fall under the stateful extension of the meta-model.

Typically, probabilistic trust and reputation systems ascribe a fixed quality or integrity to agents, and construct a distribution over that parameter. Take the set of strategies f_p, for $p \in [0,1]$, such that $f_p(i)(\theta{=}1) = p$, for arbitrary initiations and $\Theta = \{0,1\}$. The strategy f_p corresponds to the behaviour of an agent with integrity p; in both interpretations, the agent succeeds with probability p. BLADE and HABIT require more parameters, but are still captured by the meta-model. The HMM models are instances of the stateful meta-model, where the distribution over the initial parameterisations can be transformed to the distribution over the root nodes in the valuation.

In the probabilistic recommender systems, users, recommenders and targets have hidden profiles, features or classifications. The outcomes of interactions are assumed to be determined by these profiles, in a relatively straightforward process. The strategy merely emulates this process. (Thus, our strategies may simply be a modelling tool, as, e.g., movies cannot be ascribed to a strategy.)

For the remaining (non-probabilistic) models, as long as they aim to be predictive (R1) and updatable (R2), our results are useful. The model aims to be able to combine opinions based on different recommendations (R2). Since the result should be accurate (R1), its semantics must resemble the semantics of the aggregated opinions. As the latter can be computed without endogenous discounting, the model need not apply endogenous discounting.

Concerning claim H2, note that any (meta) model, introduces some relations and assumptions. The implications of our meta-model are only as good as its assumptions. The notion that agents have strategies is straightforward, as is the notion that these strategies can only use facts that are observed by the agent. An apparent weakness is our assumption that agents operate independently (non-collusion); perhaps decompositionality is a trivial consequence of this. However, all that we assume is that an agent cannot access another agent's private information, except through the system. Thus, two agents can cooperate (benevolently or maliciously) in our meta-model, as long as they only coordinate using the system. In reality, collusion – users coordinating outside of the system – does occur. It is important to notice that although decompositionality breaks, weak decompositionality (Lemma 1) remains true. We discuss collusion in more detail in Section 5.2. Thus, we see no reason to believe that decompositionality is an artificial result of our formalism, affirming claim H2.

[2]Meaning the model used in reputation systems, in recommender systems or in trust management systems.

Per decompositionality, pointwise multiplication forms the provably correct semantics of aggregation (Theorem 1). Pointwise multiplication does not actually evaluate the evidence. Thus, if two opinions are aggregated, and the individual opinions are free of endogenous discounting, then the result is also free of endogenous discounting. The opinion based on an individual piece of evidence, particularly a single recommendation, can trivially not apply endogenous discounting. Therefore, decompositionality precludes endogenous discounting, affirming claim H3.

5.2 Collusion

Agents may collude for all kinds of reasons. Usually agents attempt to increase their gains. A recommender does not need to be part of a coaction to provide informative recommendations. Thus, when recommenders collude, they typically mislead other agents[3]. Moreover, it is reasonable to assume that colluding agents are sufficiently smart to avoid lying in a way that is detrimental to their goals.

The proof of Theorem 1 obviously fails in the presence of colluding agents, since $p(\overline{f},\overline{g}|f^x) \neq p(\overline{f},\overline{g})$, invalidating decompositionality. However, since Lemma 1 still holds, weak decompositionality holds even under collusion. Since weak decompositionality holds even in systems where collusion occurs, endogenous discounting based on the user's direct observations remains fallacious regardless of collusion. Without loss of generality, we consider only endogenous discounting where recommendations are compared to each other.

A naive endogenous discounting approach weights recommendations with how common they are. A rational coalition lets all its members provide similar recommendations, to increase their weight. Naive endogenous discounting, therefore, becomes less effective as the size of the coalition increases – and we have proven it fallacious for coalitions of size one.

More sophisticated notions of endogenous discounting have to take into account possible strategies of the target and of the coalition (members). If the target strategy is not taken into account, the target may discriminate a group of agents to make it appear they are colluding. If the coalition strategy is not taken into account, the coalition may exploit the inner workings of the endogenous discounting mechanism. Therefore, we need to model the probabilities of strategies of agents and coalitions, given the user's observations. Thus, simply comparing the contents of the recommendations is insufficient.

The argument does not constitute a proof that endogenous discounting is fallacious, in systems with collusion. However, the argument is sufficiently powerful to indicate that endogenous discounting should be avoided, even in systems with collusion. Collaborative filtering algorithms and clustering algorithms have proven to be effective tools to find coalitions – see, e.g., [20]. We, therefore, advise using these algorithms, and to avoid endogenous discounting.

5.3 Intuition behind Endogenous Discounting

The reason why endogenous discounting is occasionally applied, is the intuition that deviant recommendations are probably lies. Our results do not disprove this intuition. The effect that deviant recommendations are likely lies exists. Our results, however, do imply that we do not need to filter this effect.

Intuitively, there is little information conveyed by a fake recommendation r. According to information theory, the valuation of

[3]In atypical situations, coalitions lie to assist the user [4]. In our domain, however, it is assumed that helpful agents simply provide truthful recommendations.

a known fake recommendation is intuitively close to the uniform distribution, call it p_u. The valuation of a known true recommendation intuitively matches the valuation based on the evidence from the claim, call it p_r. Let q be the probability that the recommendation is true. Then the probability that the strategy of the target equals f is $q \cdot p_r(f) + (1-q) \cdot p_u(f)$.

Now, let p_o be a valuation, such that r is a conflicting recommendation. In other words, p_o and p_r do not agree on which strategies are probable; for arbitrary f, $p_r(f) \approx 0$ or $p_o(f) \approx 0$. (Since, if neither $p_r(f)$ nor $p_o(f)$ is close to 0, then they agree that f is probable.) Aggregating p_o and p_r, we get $p_t(f) \propto p_o(f) \cdot (q \cdot p_r(f) + (1-q) \cdot p_u(f))$. By distributivity, we obtain two summands, $q \cdot p_r(f) \cdot p_o(f)$ and $(1-q) \cdot p_u(f) \cdot p_o(f)$. Since, for all f, $p_r(f) \approx 0$ or $p_o(f) \approx 0$, the first summand is close to zero. Thus $p_t(f) \approx c \cdot (1-q) \cdot p_u(f) \cdot p_o(f)$, and as p_u is close to uniform, $p_t(f) \approx p_o(f)$. In conclusion, when the conflict is sufficiently high, the aggregated opinion p_t tends towards the original opinion p_o, meaning that the impact of the conflicting recommendation diminishes.

Nowhere did we need to apply endogenous discounting, to obtain the result that conflicting recommendations should have a reduced impact. That is how it is possible that on one hand, the intuition behind endogenous discounting is valid, while on the other hand, endogenous discounting is fallacious.

5.4 Implications on Existing Work

Endogenous discounting is applied in classical trust models [27, 30, 32], recent trust models [22, 23] and in domain specific work [6, 8, 9, 14, 31], but – fortunately – not typically applied in recommender systems. The fallacy can enter a model in subtle ways, particularly if the primary objective of the model is to find the reliability of the recommender (rather than the target), as in [22, 29]. In fact, the fallacy may lay outside of the work in question, but arise when the work is naively applied, as possible with [19, 24].

Endogenous discounting is first defined in the Beta Reputation System [30]. The BRS shares many of the assumptions of the stateless meta-model. However, being one of the first Beta models, the authors do not yet attempt to capture recommendations using Bayesian methods. Rather, their chained opinions are based on intuition, and, fallaciously implement the intuition described in the previous section. The notion of endogenous discounting, as a heuristic, was still an improvement over no filtering. Thus, endogenous discounting gained some traction.

Prob-Cog is an example of a system with a wider scope than just evaluating and combining recommendations. Its primary goal is to encode human dispositions into a probabilistic setting [19]. The authors introduce a notion of credibility for recommenders to deal with unfair ratings. Credibility is computed using a variation of collaborative filtering [2], with modifications to allow tendencies such as optimism. Naively, the most precise value for credibility would use all recommendations. Our results help avoid this pitfall, and, thus, assist in applying systems like Prob-Cog correctly.

HABIT [26] is a probabilistic model that uses Bayesian inference. HABIT, like many Bayesian and beta models, does not support endogenous discounting. The reason is that such models are a direct sub-model of our meta-models. For HABIT, all assumptions of the stateless meta-model, are assumptions of HABIT. Therefore, Theorem 1 can be directly translated into HABIT's formalism.

In conclusion, our results prove that work based on endogenous discounting is flawed. Using our results, one can avoid incorrectly interpreting work that focusses on specialised issues. We corroborate existing work that does not apply endogenous discounting, by showing that it can be correct without endogenous discounting.

5.5 Recommendations for Future Work

The obvious implication of our work, is that future work should avoid endogenous discounting solutions. As we saw in the previous section, some heuristics can be improved with endogenous discounting (i.e., BRS with endogenous discounting). Therefore, we do not oppose future work that uses endogenous discounting per se. However, we advise authors to establish that endogenous discounting is the better alternative in their heuristic. It is insufficient to show that endogenous discounting provides better results than no filtering.

A major implication of our work, is the proof that for non-colluding recommenders, their recommendations can be evaluated in isolation. This means that divide-and-conquer approaches, such as Subjective Logic [10], are viable approaches. Divide-and-conquer methods are efficient, adaptive and easy to parallelise or decentralise. We advise researchers, therefore, to use decompositionality in their favour.

Bayesian and other probabilistic models are powerful, well-studied and general. In particular, recent work allows agents with increasingly rich behaviour; dynamic [5, 7], adaptive [21] or interactive [26]. Strategies straightforwardly model dynamic, adaptive and interactive behaviour. Therefore, we believe that strong theoretical and practical results can be obtained using our semantics.

6. CONCLUSION

When there is no collusion, it is fallacious to discount deviating recommendations, despite the fact that they more probably are lies (e.g. despite the majority opinion being more likely true). The reason is that, given a correct aggregation procedure, all recommendations can be treated in isolation and then aggregated, without post-hoc correction for lies. Filtering out deviating recommendations may, therefore, lead to confirmation bias.

When there is collusion, recommendations cannot be treated in isolation. We argue that this is a limitation in our approach to disproving endogenous discounting, rather than a scenario where endogenous discounting may work. Naive endogenous discounting is fallacious even under collusion.

An important necessity in proving our result is a sufficiently general meta-model. The meta-model is kept abstract, and assumes the bare minimum. What it does assume is in-line with modern probabilistic models. It assumes that agents have a local view that determines their actions, and that a user tries to determine the probability of agents' strategies. We considered both stateless and perfect-recall strategies.

We have formal proofs that recommendations can be treated in isolation and aggregated naively. We refer to this result as decompositionality. Decompositionality indicates that models that apply divide-and-conquer techniques are feasible. Therefore, our work impacts current work that applies endogenous discounting; current work that uses divide-and-conquer methods; and Bayesian or probabilistic models.

Acknowledgements

This research is supported (in part) by the National Research Foundation, Prime Minister's Office, Singapore under its National Cybersecurity R&D Program (Award No. NRF2014NCR-NCR001-30) and administered by the National Cybersecurity R&D Directorate. This research is also partially supported by "Formal Verification on Cloud" project under Grant No: M4081155.020, and the ASTAR/I2R - SERC, Public Sector Research Funding (PSF) Singapore (M4070212.020) awarded to Dr. Jie Zhang.

7. REFERENCES

[1] Karl Aberer and Zoran Despotovic. Managing trust in a peer-2-peer information system. In *International conference on Information and knowledge management*, pages 310–317. ACM, 2001.

[2] John S Breese, David Heckerman, and Carl Kadie. Empirical analysis of predictive algorithms for collaborative filtering. In *Proceedings of the Fourteenth conference on Uncertainty in artificial intelligence*, pages 43–52. Morgan Kaufmann Publishers Inc., 1998.

[3] Chrysanthos Dellarocas. Immunizing online reputation reporting systems against unfair ratings and discriminatory behavior. In *ACM conference on Electronic commerce*, pages 150–157. ACM, 2000.

[4] Naipeng Dong, Hugo Jonker, and Jun Pang. Enforcing privacy in the presence of others: Notions, formalisations and relations. In *European Symposium on Research in Computer Security (ESORICS)*, pages 499–516, 2013.

[5] Ehab ElSalamouny, Vladimiro Sassone, and Mogens Nielsen. Hmm-based trust model. In *International Workshop on Formal Aspects in Security and Trust (FAST2009)*, volume 5983, pages 21–35. LNCS, Springer, July 2009.

[6] Wenjuan Fan and Harry Perros. A reliability-based trust management mechanism for cloud services. In *Trust, Security and Privacy in Computing and Communications (TrustCom)*, pages 1581–1586. IEEE, 2013.

[7] Yasaman Haghpanah and Marie Desjardins. Prep: a probabilistic reputation model for biased societies. In *International Conference on Autonomous Agents and Multiagent Systems*, volume 1, pages 315–322. International Foundation for Autonomous Agents and Multiagent Systems, 2012.

[8] Naima Iltaf, Abdul Ghafoor, and Uzman Zia. A mechanism for detecting dishonest recommendation in indirect trust computation. *EURASIP Journal on Wireless Communications and Networking*, 2013(1), 2013.

[9] Mr Rahul A Jichkar and MB Chandak. An implementation on detection of trusted service provider in mobile ad-hoc networks. *International Journal of Engineering Trends and Technology (IJETT)*, 11(2):64–74, 2014.

[10] Audun Jøsang. A logic for uncertain probabilities. *International Journal of Uncertainty, Fuzziness and Knowledge-Based Systems*, 9(03):279–311, 2001.

[11] Audun Jøsang and Simon Pope. Semantic constraints for trust transitivity. In *Proceedings of the 2nd Asia-Pacific conference on Conceptual modelling-Volume 43*, pages 59–68. Australian Computer Society, Inc., 2005.

[12] Reid Kerr and Robin Cohen. Smart cheaters do prosper: defeating trust and reputation systems. In *Autonomous Agents and Multiagent Systems*, volume 2, pages 993–1000. International Foundation for Autonomous Agents and Multiagent Systems, 2009.

[13] Joseph A Konstan, Bradley N Miller, David Maltz, Jonathan L Herlocker, Lee R Gordon, and John Riedl. Grouplens: applying collaborative filtering to usenet news. *Communications of the ACM*, 40(3):77–87, 1997.

[14] Mohamed MEA Mahmoud and Xuemin Sherman Shen. Secure routing protocols. In *Security for Multi-hop Wireless Networks*, chapter 4, pages 63–93. Springer, 2014.

[15] Sergio Marti, Thomas J Giuli, Kevin Lai, and Mary Baker. Mitigating routing misbehavior in mobile ad hoc networks. In *International conference on Mobile computing and networking*, pages 255–265. ACM, 2000.

[16] Tim Muller, Yang Liu, Sjouke Mauw, and Jie Zhang. On robustness of trust systems. In *Trust Management VIII*, pages 44–60. Springer, 2014.

[17] Tim Muller, Yang Liu, and Jie Zhang. The fallacy of endogenous discounting of trust recommendations with dynamic agents. Technical report, Nanyang Technological University: http://pat.sce.ntu.edu.sg/tim/papers/fallacytechreport.pdf, 2015.

[18] Tim Muller and Patrick Schweitzer. On beta models with trust chains. In *Trust Management VII*, pages 49–65. Springer, 2013.

[19] Zeinab Noorian, Stephen Marsh, and Michael Fleming. Prob-cog: An adaptive filtering model for trust evaluation. In *Trust Management V*, pages 206–222. Springer, 2011.

[20] Grzegorz Orynczak and Zbigniew Kotulski. On a mechanism of detection of coalitions for reputation systems in p2p networks. In *Performance Evaluation of Computer and Telecommunication Systems (SPECTS 2014), International Symposium on*, pages 578–584. IEEE, 2014.

[21] Kevin Regan, Pascal Poupart, and Robin Cohen. Bayesian reputation modeling in e-marketplaces sensitive to subjectivity, deception and change. In *National Conference on Artificial Intelligence*, volume 21, page 1206. Menlo Park, CA; Cambridge, MA; London; AAAI Press; MIT Press; 1999, 2006.

[22] Raha Sadeghi and Mohammad Abdollahi Azgomi. A method for fair propagation of user perceptions for trust management in composite services. *Service Oriented Computing and Applications*, pages 1–20, 2014.

[23] Murat Şensoy, Geeth de Mel, Lance Kaplan, Tien Pham, and Timothy J Norman. Tribe: Trust revision for information based on evidence. In *Information Fusion (FUSION)*, pages 914–921. IEEE, 2013.

[24] Murat Şensoy, Jie Zhang, Pinar Yolum, and Robin Cohen. Poyraz: Context-aware service selection under deception. *Computational Intelligence*, 25(4):335–366, 2009.

[25] Xiaoyuan Su and Taghi M Khoshgoftaar. Collaborative filtering for multi-class data using belief nets algorithms. In *Tools with Artificial Intelligence (ICTAI)*, pages 497–504. IEEE, 2006.

[26] WT Teacy, Michael Luck, Alex Rogers, and Nicholas R Jennings. An efficient and versatile approach to trust and reputation using hierarchical bayesian modelling. *Artificial Intelligence*, 193:149–185, 2012.

[27] WT Luke Teacy, Jigar Patel, Nicholas R Jennings, and Michael Luck. Travos: Trust and reputation in the context of inaccurate information sources. *Autonomous Agents and Multi-Agent Systems*, 12(2):183–198, 2006.

[28] George Vogiatzis, Ian MacGillivray, and Maria Chli. A probabilistic model for trust and reputation. In *International Conference on Autonomous Agents and Multiagent Systems*, volume 1, pages 225–232. International Foundation for Autonomous Agents and Multiagent Systems, 2010.

[29] Yonghong Wang, Chung-Wei Hang, and Munindar P Singh. A probabilistic approach for maintaining trust based on evidence. *Journal of Artificial Intelligence Research*, 40(1):221–267, 2011.

[30] Andrew Whitby, Audun Jøsang, and Jadwiga Indulska. Filtering out unfair ratings in bayesian reputation systems. In *Proc. 7th Int. Workshop on Trust in Agent Societies*, volume 6, 2004.

[31] Qingui Xu and Guixiong Liu. Weakening unreliable ratings in p2p reputation systems based on an honest majority. *Advances in information Sciences and Service Sciences*, 4:418–425, 2012.

[32] Bin Yu and Munindar P Singh. Detecting deception in reputation management. In *International joint conference on Autonomous agents and multiagent systems*, pages 73–80. ACM, 2003.

[33] Kai Yu, Anton Schwaighofer, Volker Tresp, Xiaowei Xu, and H-P Kriegel. Probabilistic memory-based collaborative filtering. *Knowledge and Data Engineering, IEEE Transactions on*, 16(1):56–69, 2004.

Composing Social Interactions via Social Games

Daniel Shapiro[1], Larry LeBron[1], Michael Mateas[1], Kerry Moffitt[3]
Karen Tanenbaum[1], Craig Reynolds[1], Bill Ferguson[3], Will Coon[3]
Josh McCoy[2], Andrew Stern[1], David Diller[3], Bruce Roberts[3]

[1]Computational Media Dept.
UCSC, Santa Cruz, CA 95064
+1-831-459-3181
dgs at ucsc.edu

[2]Computer Science and Game Lab
American University,Washington D.C.
+1-202-885-6438
jam at american.edu

[3]Raytheon-BBN Technologies
10 Moulton St., Cambridge MA 02138
+1-617-873-2208
wferguson at bbn.com

ABSTRACT

This paper addresses the problem of enabling non-scripted social interaction with virtual characters, and of authoring the underlying behavior in reusable form. We hypothesize that social behavior can be decomposed into *social games*, which are collections of affordances surrounding social state, and claim that non-scripted player interactions can be generated by the execution of social games in various combinations. We describe three social games (for alliance, authority, and threat management), the implementation architecture that executes these games, and the resulting behavior, which is set in a military house-search scenario. The architecture consists of a decision process that selects motivations appropriate to the games, selects social moves appropriate to the motivations, and finally performs behaviors that implement social moves, all in a situation-responsive, dynamic fashion. We show that social games form a loosely coupled system that generates a space of possible interactions.

Categories and Subject Descriptors

I.2.11 [**Artificial Intelligence**]: Distributed Artificial Intelligence – *Intelligent Agents.*

General Terms

Algorithms, Design

Keywords

Virtual Agents and Humans; Socio-Cultural Behavior; Human-Agent Interaction; Agent-Based Simulation; Social Simulation

1. INTRODUCTION

Social interaction is a core element of human experience, but it is difficult to achieve with virtual characters. The underlying issues are both technical and theoretical. In particular, social phenomena are inherently complex and require sophisticated mechanisms to express in automated form. While the social sciences provide inspiration in the form of explanatory analyses of social behavior, we have yet to transform those models into generative forms that can drive synthetic characters. Finally, although there is a growing interest in the games, training, and autonomous agent communities, there is little prior work on social characters.

Despite these difficulties, a number of projects have taken important steps. Work in games and training systems has made progress on enhancing the social presence of virtual characters, and on improving the dynamic (vs predetermined) quality of interactive social experiences. For example, AAA games like Bioware's Mass Effect create social presence through highly scripted interactions and nuanced visual performances [2]. Microsoft's Kinectimals [17] pursue the opposite strategy; they enhance the believability of virtual pets by supporting simple unscripted interactions. Several ICT projects employ a combination of agent technology and structured narrative to enhance social presence. The museum guides, Ada and Grace, respond socially to visitors, while occasionally taking initiative, using technology that maps utterances into available next actions [24]. Gunslinger lets players converse freely with characters in an augmented reality setting en route to an impending gunfight, although the narrative is strongly controlled [7]. BiLat provides negotiation training across culture boundaries, with automated choice of tactics, but the experience relies on a strong narrative flow [8]. A few games, like PromWeek [15] and Versu [9] employ explicit models of social practices to enhance believability, while Façade [14] emphasizes real-time, dynamic flow to create social presence. Several research efforts have developed other forms of social agent models to create believable characters. For example, Prada and Paiva [20] model individual and group dynamics to create believable autonomous agents, Callejas et al. [3] employ social attitudes to drive training interactions within a virtual recruiter, and Osborne pursues a model based on "social masks". Overall, the vector of development is towards the use of sophisticated social models to support increasingly dynamic and believable interactions with virtual characters.

This paper describes work towards the goal of supporting emergent social behavior for use in games, training, and simulation contexts. We pursue a generative approach based on an explicit model of social practices that enables non-scripted interactions with characters who possess a social agenda. We are simultaneously interested in the problem of authoring such interactions, that is, of constructing social competencies from component parts. Towards that end, we take inspiration from Berne [1] and Goffman [6] by pursuing the metaphor of *social games*.

In more detail, we define a social game as a family of practices surrounding particular elements of social state, and associate social motivations, moves, and preference logic with each game, as well as a body of executable behaviors that implement social moves. We define an architecture for utilizing social games that selects motivations appropriate to characters and their situations, and then resolves them through moves into executable behaviors.

Appears in: *Proceedings of the 14th International Conference on Autonomous Agents and Multiagent Systems (AAMAS 2015), Bordini, Elkind, Weiss, Yolum (eds.), May, 4–8, 2015, Istanbul, Turkey.*

These behaviors flow into a social simulation that supports real-time, whole-body interaction with virtual characters that exhibit nuanced performances.

In addition, we show that social games can be executed individually, or in combination to generate increasingly complex social behavior. We demonstrate this with behavioral examples, and by graphically depicting the space of possible interactions. In particular, because social games are weakly coupled through social state, the set of active games defines a space of possible trajectories. As a result, the interaction follows a dynamic sequence determined by the social consequences of the player's and characters' joint action.

The following sections describe an interactive experience produced by social games, the architecture for representing and executing social games, and our approach to authoring behavior by composing social games (including illustrations of the interaction space). Following this, we examine related work in more detail, and conclude with a discussion of this work's implications and limitations, plus directions for future research.

2. BREAKING BREAD EXPERIENCE

Breaking Bread is an interactive experience conducted via a whole body gestural interface, where the player takes on the role of a US soldier deployed in a foreign country to which the US military is providing aid and training (See Figure 1). The player is accompanying a local national soldier (LNS) through a village to do house inspections, looking for contraband weapons and drugs. While the player has some authority over the local national, her role is to watch and advise as the LNS takes the lead in conducting the search. The local national soldier speaks some English but not much; the civilians in the village do not speak any English. At the start of the Breaking Bread scenario, the player and the LNS have entered the home of a villager while the rest of the squad waits outside.

Breaking Bread presents the player with a social puzzle. She wants to complete her house search mission, achieve cooperation from the civilians in the house (rather than resistance), and assist the LNS, who is supposed to lead the search but is unfortunately badge-heavy. If the player takes no action, due either to inattention or failure to understand the social conventions, the scenario plays out as follows: The head of the household (HoH), a middle-aged man who speaks no English, warily allows the player and LNS into his home and gives a greeting of a small bow. He offers a bowl of fruit to the player and is offended when the gift is not accepted. The LNS begins wandering around the house and touching objects, agitating the head of household. The LNS, who seems to enjoy demonstrating his power and role in the local military, continues to provoke the villager by touching his things and arguing with him about his right to do so. He arrogantly commands the HoH to open a set of cabinets, and the HoH grudgingly complies, revealing an empty interior. The situation crosses a line when the LNS picks up a piece of bread and eats it, enraging the HoH. He grabs a bowl of fruit from the table and smashes it to the ground, yelling. Shortly thereafter, the HoH's son enters the tense room and begins yelling at the player and LNS to get out. Both the man and his son become increasingly agitated, shooing the intruders out the door.

Figure 1. A snapshot from Breaking Bread

Throughout all of these interactions, the player has an opportunity to observe passively, or to intervene. Several de-escalation moves are possible to either calm down the HoH in the face of the LNS's transgressions, or to dissuade the LNS from provoking the homeowner. Successful de-escalation can lead to a less volatile situation. If the LNS is sufficiently controlled and the HoH is placated, the scenario ends much more positively.

A more active player might generate a runthrough that plays out as follows: Upon entering the kitchen, the HoH greets the LNS and player with a small bow, which the player returns, garnering a favorable response. The HoH then offers a piece of fruit to the player, which the player accepts, further pleasing the HoH. As the LNS begins wandering around and touching things, the player asks him to stop and put the objects down. The player apologizes to the HoH for these infractions. The player then asks the HoH to open the cabinets, successfully communicating through mimed gestures. The HoH complies and reveals an empty cabinet. The LNS persists in touching objects and attempting to eat the bread, so the player calls him over to stand near her by the door, which prevents further transgressions. The player asks the HoH to open a second set of cabinets, which reveals medicine of questionable legality. At this point, the son enters the room, alarmed by the presence of strangers in the house. Because the situation is not nearly as tense as the previous example run-through, the HoH calms the son down and introduces him to the visitors. The player thanks him and leaves courteously, deciding to preserve the cordial relationship with the HoH and the successful restraint of the LNS rather than push the issue of the dubious drugs. The drugs have at least been found in this scenario, whereas in the previous iteration they were not even uncovered before the player and LNS were forced to leave the kitchen.

An active, but less socially adept player can produce a noticeably worse outcome by ignoring the LNS's excesses and actively suppressing the HoH's pleas. As before, the plate smashes and the son enters the room at the maximally tense moment, but now with an interaction history where the player has allied heavily with the LNS. The LNS or the player can raise their weapon in this circumstance, resulting in a dangerous standoff. Overall, the goal of Breaking Bread is to give the player experience and training with interpreting social interactions across language and cultural barriers. If the player picks up on social conventions, like returning the bow and accepting the offered fruit, the interaction is generally positive. If the player can also recognize and respond to non-verbal cues like forceful gestures, raised voices, and physical pleas for assistance, the situation can be controlled. In order to support the variety of interactions within Breaking Bread, characters must be able to take social initiative and respond to the player in a dynamic and essentially unscripted way. The following sections describe the technology underlying Breaking Bread, which is produced by a set of *social games* that model a character's social knowledge, motivations and actions.

3. SOCIAL GAME ARCHITECTURE

A social game is a family of practices surrounding social state. We have defined three social games for use in Breaking Bread: *Alliance, Authority,* and *Threat.* The *Alliance* game deals with forging and damaging relationships, while *Authority* concerns power dynamics and ownership over objects and space. *Threat* deals with the management of physical force and danger. Each game monitors certain elements of state, and contains representations of relevant social motivations and abstract social actions called moves, together with rules for prioritizing them.

Figure 2 illustrates the architecture for executing social games. It consists of a memory (for holding background knowledge, observations, and inferred beliefs), an intention formation process for selecting motivations and moves for characters across games, and a performance mechanism for executing and interleaving the associated behaviors. We discuss social game content (state, motivations, moves, and ranking rules) and the process of utilizing games to select social moves, below. Shapiro et al. [21] examines the performance system, viewed as an interactive, real-time, immersive simulation, so we only comment on its structure with respect to social games here.

We represent the social game state via binary predicates or continuously valued relations. For example, the *Alliance* game monitors a *degree of alliance* (a scalar-valued directed relation between two NPCs, or the NPC and the player), and a binary predicate encoding whether those agents are *allies.* Each social game also contains a characteristic set of motivations to create (increase) or remove (decrease) that state, as well as to express its value through agent actions in the virtual world. The Alliance game supports *AllianceUp*, *AllianceDown*, and *AllianceExpress* relative to the degree of alliance, and *AlliesMake*, *AlliesBreak*, and *AlliesExpress* relative to the allies distinction. The moves within a social game represent abstract actions for pursuing motivations. In general, there are multiple moves for each motivation. For example, *Greet* and *GiveAGift* address *AllianceUp*, while *BackupAlly* and *FriendlyGoodbye* address *AllianceExpress*.

As a second example, the *Authority* game governs interactions related to power dynamics and ownership over objects and spaces. The underlying state consists of *AuthorityOver(X,Y, val)* relations, and permission levels for access to objects ranging from "no access" (0) to "can consume/destroy" (5). The motivations are *AuthorityUp, AuthorityDown, AuthorityExpress.* The Authority game contains a wide variety of moves for the house search scenario. These include *MessWithOthersStuff, OpenYourCabinets, EatOthersStuff, HoardMyStuff, Outburst, PutMyStuffDown, GiveMyStuffBack, DirtyLook,* and *DerisiveChuckle.*

3.1 Ranking Motivations and Moves

Each social game contains a set of preference rules for ranking motivations. For example, the following rules simultaneously nominate and rank motivations:

```
Alliance(X, Y, <50)
→ AllianceUp(X,Y) + 2

Alliance(X, Y, >50) ^
Alliance(Y, Z, >50) ^
Alliance(X, Z, <50)
→ AllianceUp(X,Z) + 3
```

The first rule acts to elevate the importance (called volition) of increasing the degree of alliance between two characters whose

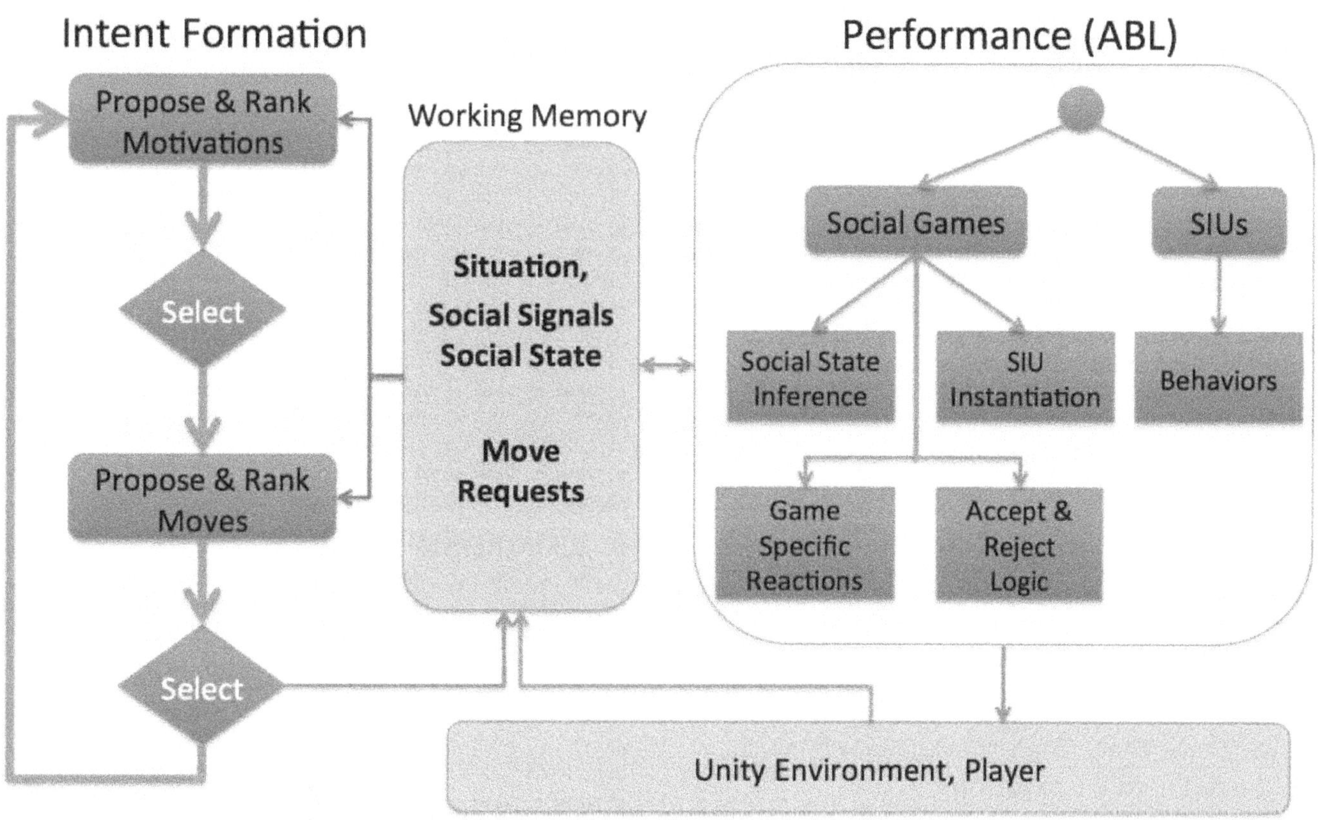

Figure 2. The architecture for executing social games

bond is suffering. The second motivates a character to build networks of alliances. X observes that he is friendly with Y but not Z and Y *is* friendly to Z, so he reaches out to Z. Similarly, the Authority game contains these two rules:

```
Arrogant(X) ^
Authority(Y,X,<50) ^
Authority(X,Y,<80)
→ AuthorityUp(X,Y) + 6

Permission(X, Obj, Owns) ^
Permission(Y, Obj,  LookAt) ^
Touch(Y, Obj)
→ AuthorityUp(X,Y) + 8
```

The first expresses an inclination for one character to dominate another, while the second expresses a desire to reassert authority when a character exceeds its allowed permission to manipulate an object. An analogous set of preference rules govern moves. For example:

```
AllianceUp(X,Y) ^
GiftingAppropriate(X,Y) ^
Object(tag=="gift", Obj)
→ GiveAGift(X, Y, Obj) + 5

AuthorityUp(X, Y) ^
Permission(Y, Obj,  Owns) ^
Permission(X, Obj, <Touch)
→ ViolateObjNorm(X, Obj) + 7
```

These rules simultaneously nominate and rank moves. The first suggests X give an appropriate object to Y as means of increasing the degree of alliance between those two characters. The second rule incites X to deliberately exceed permission levels with respect to Y's belongings in a bid to increase authority.

In general, social games contain a large number of rules for ranking motivations and moves, and these rules can depend upon accumulated knowledge, character status, and current environmental state. For example, *GiftingAppropriate(X, Y)* only becomes true after characters have greeted one another, and the environment must contain objects tagged as giftable for the GiveAGift rule to apply. Similarly, only characters flagged as *Arrogant* seek to dominate others within the Authority game.

Volition values add across rules. For example, the player and LNS begin with an *Alliance* in Breaking Bread, so if the player and HoH become allies, the motivation rules for *AllianceUp* (above) combine to influence the HoH to increase his alliance with the LNS, and vice versa. However, the *AuthorityUp* motivations have higher volition; the LNS will care more about dominating the HoH, and the HoH more about increasing his authority over the LNS in response to his prior bad behavior.

Taken together, the rules that assign volition to motivations and moves represent an agent-held utility function. Their additive semantics mediate situation specific influences, while the specific volition values (large or small) follow authoring conventions.

3.2 Social Game Execution

The mechanism for executing social games begins with an iterated intention formation process that reasons top-down from games, through motivations, to moves. This process gathers and applies all motivation rules across games, and outputs a ranking for all situation relevant motivations for all characters. The algorithm down-selects this set to the top two motivations for each character whose volition scores exceed a preset threshold. The next step nominates and ranks all motivation and situation relevant moves via an analogous computation. The final stage of the decision process filters this set to the single best move for each character above the same threshold. The architecture repeats this decision process on a regular basis. Since each move invokes relatively fine-grained behaviors, we set the decision interval to 1 second.

The performance side of the architecture in Figure 2 enacts social moves selected by the intention formation process. It provides a real-time, interactive, multi-agent simulation that accepts whole-body gestural input from the player as well as limited speech, and it realizes character behavior in a 3D virtual world based on the Unity engine [21]. From the perspective of the performance system, moves correspond to plans to pursue in response to player input. They are implemented as hierarchical, reactive, parallel programs in the ABL language [13]. Each social move involves 5 - 30 seconds of interactive performance, and is analogous to a dramatic beat. We call the ball of behaviors that implement a move a Social Interaction Unit (SIU). As an example, *GiveAGift* causes a character to navigate to an object, pick it up, approach the player, and interact with the player to transact the object. The SIU also encodes the nuances that lend emotive quality to that performance. These include glances at the object and the player, facial expressions, choice of motion styles (bold, hesitant), and more. A single SIU can control the behavior of multiple non-player characters. The intention formation process outputs a stream of SIUs that arrive in a dynamic, non-scripted order. As a result, their performances must interleave with ongoing activities. The performance system contains a priority based resource allocation mechanism that achieves this interleaving while resolving conflicts. The individual SIUs are written such that they can be smoothly interrupted and resumed.

In addition to executing SIUs, the performance architecture manages more durative aspects of social games. These include background behaviors (demons) that observe and infer the elements of state monitored by social games or that are referenced by rules in the intention formation process. They also include character reactions consistent with games, viewed as states of mind. For example, the *Authority* game contains a demon that observes when owned objects are touched, and deduces an object norm violation when permission was absent. The *Threat* game contains an alarm reaction to any sudden move, which is not present outside of the threat context. Finally, the performance system employs volition rules to determine character responses to an enforced choice, e.g., if the player asks an NPC to provide an object, the NPC must either accept or reject. This mechanism is separate from the top-down, intention formation process.

4. COMPOSING SOCIAL GAMES

Taken in isolation, each social game captures a family of practices surrounding a common theme. However, taken together, the games form a weakly interacting set. Social games couple through social state; the execution of an SIU motivated by one game may impact the state utilized in another to nominate and rank motivations or moves. Moreover, social games can be activated in in arbitrary combinations, so as the games are composed, more interactions are exposed, resulting in a form of emergent social behavior. This section describes that interaction space, first graphically and then in terms of the resulting behavior.

Taken in isolation, each social game captures a family of practices surrounding a common theme. However, taken together, the games form a weakly interacting set. Social games couple through social state; the execution of an SIU motivated by one game may impact the state utilized in another to nominate and rank motivations or moves. Moreover, social games can be activated in in arbitrary combinations, so as the games are composed, more interactions are exposed, resulting in a form of emergent social behavior. This section describes that interaction space, first graphically, and then in terms of the resulting behavior.

As mentioned earlier, we utilized three social games in Breaking Bread, and provided detail on Alliance and Authority. The third game, *Threat,* concerns the management of physical force and danger. Threat tracks two key elements of state: *Might*, and *PerceivedDanger*. *Might* represents a character's level of power (e.g., is it armed or unarmed), while *PerceivedDanger* captures both the likelihood and the magnitude of the force that others characters could apply if a conflict arises. The Threat game contains the standard three motivations, *Threat_Up*, *Threat_Down*, and *Threat_Express*, plus moves for *ProtectSelf*, *GetHelpWithOutburster*, *HelpMeOut*, *AdvanceOn*, *WardThreat* and *AcknowledgeThreat*. It also contains multiple rules for ranking *Threat* motivations and moves.

Figure 3 provides a graphical illustration of the interaction space enabled by the Alliance, Authority, and Threat games. This diagram elides some of elements of state, motivations and moves, and only shows relational terms (suppressing arguments) in order to highlight the coupling between games. The top row of the figure lists elements of social state input to the intention formation process. The second row (boxed, with graduated shading) identifies motivations the characters can choose. The next four rows name moves that address motivations, while the bottom row shows state altered by the execution of moves. The figure also sorts the elements from left to right by social game, in the order of Alliance (in purple), Authority (green), and Threat (pink). The arrows show data flow imposed by nomination and ranking rules, or by execution of the SIUs associated with moves. More exactly, the arrows show the aggregate of the data flow across all rules (meaning a fan-in may represent multiple rules).

The main thing to note about the figure is that the data flow stays mostly in columns; *Threat* state flows through *Threat* motivations, into *Threat* moves and back to state. For example, *PerceivedDanger* effects the importance of *ThreatDown*, which impacts the volition to *ProtectSelf.* Execution of *ProtectSelf* may alter the character's *Might* and *PerceivedDanger*, depending upon how it unfolds in the world. (There is no guarantee; the SIU for *ProtectSelf* contains alternate methods, the situation enables some paths, and the player can impact the outcomes.)

The diagram also contains multiple instances of cross-talk. At the motivational layer, *PerceivedDanger* decreases the volition of motivations in all other games (as a means of highlighting the relevance of a threat, no matter its severity). If a character has Alliances, their presence tends to decrease the importance of *ThreatDown* (to counter perceived danger). A character with an *Alliance* to an authority figure looks to that figure for support via *ThreatExpress* (as the LNS does to the player in response to the HoH's outburst in Breaking Bread). While moves are almost wholly owned by games, some rules employ state from the *Authority* game called *AuthorityOver* to nominate and assign volition to *GiveAGift.*

Similarly, Alliance levels are relevant to *HelpMeOut*. The cross-talk from moves to state is more profound. Within the *Alliance* game, completing social rituals (via *GiveAGift* or *Greet*) impacts

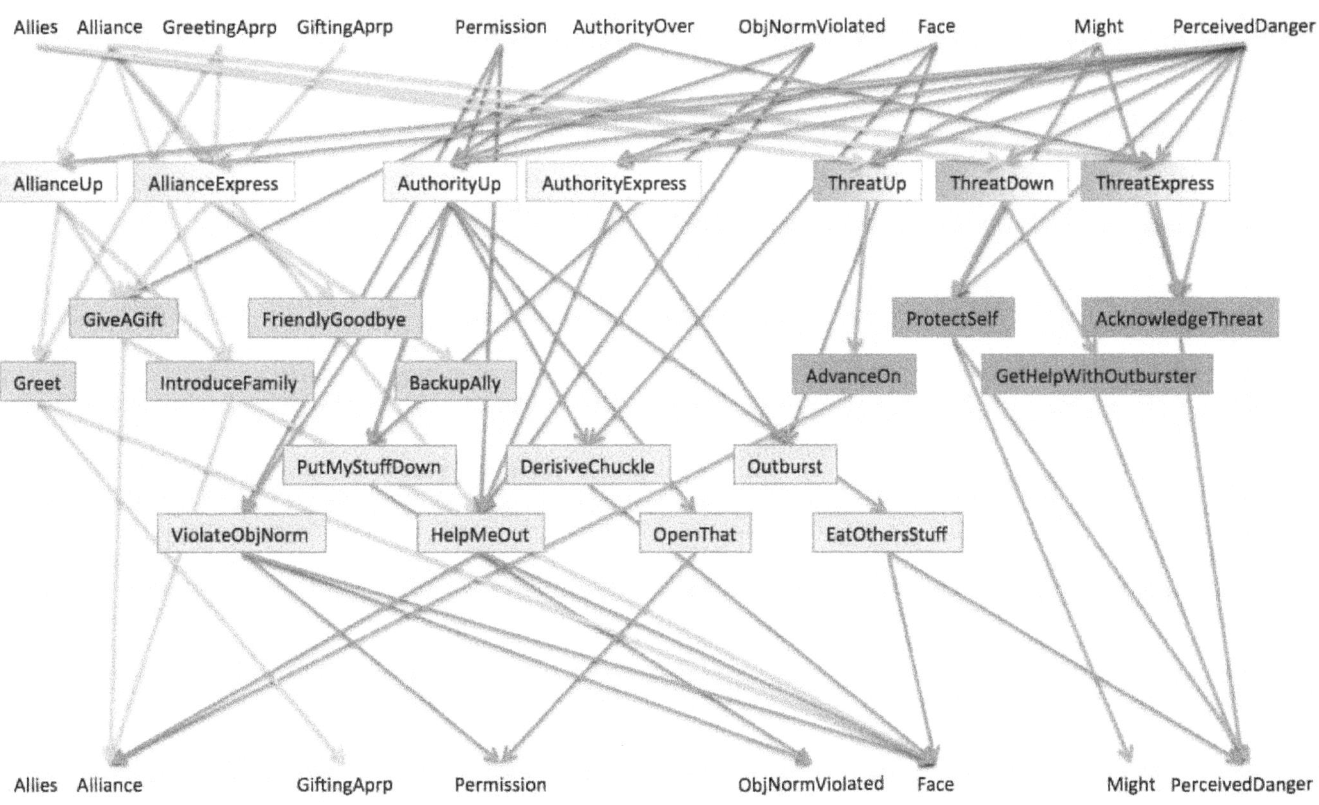

Figure 3. Social game composition

Face in the *Authority* game. Within *Authority*, requesting others to *HelpMeOut* builds *Alliance* with the helper, while *EatOthersStuff* impacts others' *PerceivedDanger* through the impression that the character is willing to take aggressive action (as seen between the LNS and the HoH in Breaking Bread). Similarly, the move to *AdvanceOn* a character within *Threat* clearly impacts any prior *Alliance*.

4.1 Layered Demonstrations of Social Games

Because social games only interact through shared state and soft constraints, no game is required to execute another. Moreover, social games can be activated in arbitrary combinations; a given combination defines a space of possible actions, and an agent can initiate any move in that space that is both motivated and feasible at any time. In order to demonstrate this point, we changed the context for executing social games to a "Sandbox" scenario where the interactions are more visible than in Breaking Bread. The Sandbox contains fewer elements; it supports interaction between a player, two non-player characters (NPC01 and NPC02), and a handful of objects on a pedestal. We illustrate social game composition through three, layered demonstrations, viewable online [23]. The first generates behavior by *Alliance*, alone, while the next two add *Authority* and *Threat* in turn.

The interaction based solely on the *Alliance* game unfolds as follows. We give NPC02 a positive *Alliance* value towards the player and mark the objects on the table as "giftable". After the player greets NPC02 in a friendly manner, *GiftingAppropriate* is created between NPC02 and the player. This *Alliance* state motivates a simple *Alliance* building move, *GiveAGift*, for NPC02 to offer the player one of the objects from the pedestal.

The interaction generated by Alliance plus Authority follows a different path. We initialize the starting state required by the *Authority* game as follows NPC01 is given ownership over the objects on the pedestal by setting *Permission* values for all the objects to the highest tier, 5, and "granted", the player and NPC02 are assigned Permission values of 1 with the status "granted", (which enables them to freely "look at" objects in the environment), and the player is marked as having *AuthorityOver* NPC02 and NPC02 is given the character trait, *Arrogant*. When the scenario starts, the player greets NPC01, and again triggers a friendly gift offer through the *Alliance* mechanics outline above. Meanwhile, *AuthorityUp* motivations coming from NPC02's Arrogant trait make him touch items owned by NPC01 without permission. NPC02's actions trigger a permission update for that object to "ungranted, pick up". The first time this violation occurs, NPC01 gives NPC02 a *DirtyLook*, a move motivated by an *AuthorityUp* response to the object violation. When NPC02 picks up the bread, this second ownership violation motivates a stronger *AuthorityUp* response. NPC01 angrily asks NPC02 to put down the bread (via *RequestPutThatDown*). NPC02 refuses to comply (a local accept/reject decision), due to his *Arrogant* trait. Finally, because of previous alliance building through gifting and greeting, NPC01 turns to the player and asks for help, an *Authority* move that is also sensitive to *Alliance* state. The player asks NPC02 to stop his annoying behavior, and this time, NPC02 complies (accepts) because the player has *AuthorityOver* relation with him. This move by the player raises his *Alliance* with NPC01 but reduces NPC02's *Face*.

Finally, adding the *Threat* game makes the fact that the player is holding a rifle salient. In this run-through, the player greets as before, but then rejects the offered gift, offending NPC01 and failing to build *Alliance*. When the wrangling over objects starts, NPC01 does not look to the player for assistance because of the lack of built up *Alliance*. Instead, he simply gets more and more upset, and continues to apply *AuthorityUp* moves in response to NPC02's provocations. NPC02's *PerceivedDanger* elevates due to NPC01's yelling and he reacts with fear. He forms the motivation to *Threat_Down*, which triggers the move to *ProtectSelf*, causing NPC02 to raise his hands in an attempt to surrender. When the player raises her weapon to take control of the situation, her *Might* and the resulting perceptions of danger motivate both NPCs to *ProtectSelf* in response to *Threat_Down*, now orienting on the player.

5. RELATED WORK

This section examines theory from psychology and sociology that underlies social games and related work on social agents. We provide a survey of similar systems that attempt to create social interaction with dynamic, autonomous agents.

5.1 Theory of Social Games

Support for approaching agent interaction as "social games" comes from literature on psychology and sociology. Goffman's dramaturgical analysis is a sociological theory that posits people's everyday behavior can be understood as inherently performative through the metaphor of a dramatic production [6]. This perspective provides the conceptual framework for our take on social games. The concept of social games originated as character performance patterns featured in the interactive drama, Façade [14]. In Façade, social games are interactions where the player is put in the position of changing the relationships between the characters. Because every possible outcome and nuance had to be individually authored, this version of social games came with a high burden on the author of the experience. Work by McCoy et al. [16] on Comme il Faut (CiF) develops a variant where each social game is authored once and is procedurally tailored to fit the participating characters and social context. Other works in psychology and sociology have looked at the role of game-like interactions and social dynamics, such as Berne's work on the "games people play" and transactional analysis [1]. Berne's categorization of social interaction includes the concept of a game, meaning a series of complementary transactions that are ongoing and organized towards a predictable outcome. Additionally, transactional analysis decouples the performance of a game from its intent (via ego and psychological states), which inspired the covert and parallel aspects of social games. French and Raven's psychological study claims that people respond to five categories of social power: reward, coercive, legitimate, referent and expert power [5]. Pereira et al. [19] embed these distinctions in a framework through which agents become aware and capable of manipulating social power. Our work on social games builds on these models, and on the viewpoint that agents should recognize practices for exploiting social power.

5.2 Related Work on Social Agents

A few games, like Prom Week [15] and Versu [9] have built social game models, but not in the context of real-time interaction where it could be employed to add a new dimension of realism to game characters. The Sims is one of the most commercially successful agent based games, where individual characters are driven to pursue autonomous goals related to their personality, needs, skills and relationships [4]. However, their memory is short, and the rules for determining goals and how to achieve them are simple. Gunslinger features movement and exploration of a virtual world via rich multi-modal input but lacks social simulation and remains bound to a pre-set narrative [7]. The Synthetic Group Dynamics Model uses theories of group dynamics to make interactions between groups of agents more believable [20].

Other works approach social interaction by modeling the social and emotional states of characters and using that state to drive behavior. For example, emotional responses of agents are simulated via appraisal dynamics by EMA [12][11] Thespian [21] and the system it is built on, PsychSim [10], are multi-agent capable systems that realize social interactions from models of social influence. Osborne takes an approach to social modeling that is also partially based on Goffman, proposing "the mask model", which controls NPC behavior through three overlapping layers of social masks: the self-perception layer, the social layer and the interpersonal layer [18]. These efforts employ psychological and affective models to produce believable characters. As our work relies on a social agent model, they represent complementary avenues for future work.

6. DISCUSSION

Our goal for this work has been to prototype a capability that supports social interaction with synthetic characters in a non-scripted, generative form. While this is a very large problem, we have demonstrated progress along two fronts. First, we have shown that we can drive character behavior from a model of social practices called social games, via a mechanism that inputs social state, chooses situation relevant motivations, and resolves those motivations into actionable moves. Second, we have shown that social games can be combined to generate more complex social behavior. We demonstrated this effect by layering the Alliance, Authority, and Threat games, and by graphically depicting the space of social behaviors enabled by their (weak) interaction. In addition, we have utilized social games to produce a complex playable interaction set in a house search scenario.

While our work demonstrates feasibility, it raises several key questions. First, it is natural to ask if social games are general, in the sense of supporting reuse across scenarios. To date, we have a small amount of positive, anecdotal evidence from our experience porting the games to the Sandbox from Breaking Bread. This shift preserved virtually all elements of the games, with minor tweaks. However, the Sandbox environment is noticeably simpler than Breaking Bread, so a port to a more complex scenario would likely expose limitations. In general, we would like the process of porting a social game to require minimal massaging of inputs and outputs, i.e., to map available character observations and knowledge into the state required by social games, and to instantiate the moves output by social games into executable behaviors. From this perspective, the current vocabulary of social moves is a bit suspect. Looking at Figure 3, the terms *Greet*, *ViolateObjNorm*, and *ProtectSelf* suggest domain independent, abstract actions, while *IntroduceFamily*, *EatOthersStuff* and *GetHelpWithOutburster* appear too scenario-specific.

A second key question concerns the coverage of social games. Are there 3, 30, or 300 of them, and if so, what is their content? We have begun to investigate this question by considering 10-20 vignettes of social interaction in the Sandbox setting, e.g., "a woman is agitated and wants to talk to you, her companion (a man) does not approve - what happens, and what social games are involved?" Anecdotally, variants on Alliance, Authority, and Threat have a great deal of coverage. One explanation is to view games as practices for exerting categories of social power. As described above, French and Raven [5] claim there are five kinds of social power: reward, coercive, legitimate, referent and expert power. *Alliance* expresses Referent power (acting to please others), *Authority* exploits Legitimate power (the influence of social norms), and *Threat* exerts Coercive power (the ability to influence behavior through force/punishment), implying that our games implement instances of most basic types. This line of reasoning also suggests a way forward; we should encode one game for exerting each type of social power containing a family of abstract practices, and author mechanisms for applying those games in specific contexts. An alternate approach is to build a great many social games in the style of Berne [1], e.g., a victimization game, an envy game, a co-dependency game, etc. This repertoire would form a library of social strategies with associated state and internal sequence, that might be easier to define but less portable across scenarios.

More broadly, this paper makes claims about authoring social interactions as opposed to the behavior produced. That said, examining the quality of the interactions produced by social games is an important goal. Two reasonable approaches would be to (a) collect subjective assessments of player experience, and (b) measure achievement of targeted simulation states. Within (a), we could employ metrics on social and system engagement, and player questionnaires. Within (b), since Breaking Bread was created for pedagogic goals, we could measure student achievements - e.g., if the player finds the contraband, or achieves a given HoH-player alliance value. Overall, player ability to solve social puzzles reflects on the quality of the social interaction enabled by social games, and on the sufficiency of social games as an authoring construct. It would also provide insight on the feasibility of using virtual characters to teach human social interaction skills.

7. FUTURE WORK

Going forward, we intend to continue investigation of reusable social games. We plan to pursue that investigation by porting social games to new contexts, e.g., some of the vignettes we alluded to above that are easy to instantiate in the Sandbox environment. In the process, we expect to re-examine the vocabulary for social moves to make them more general, and to expand/clarify the suite of social games. We plan to examine the problem of instantiating abstract social games in more specific contexts. At a more detailed level, we hope to refine our treatment of coupling across games, e.g., by employing the concept of "counts as" to relate elements of social state.

8. SUMMARY

This work explores the question of authoring non-scripted social interaction with virtual characters. We envision application to games, social and cross-cultural training, and social simulation in general. Our work on social games connects to this vision by modularizing the capacity for social interaction. Our ultimate goal is to export an authoring tool, plus content for instantiating social games that will let authors easily create virtual social characters in contexts where that capability had not existed before.

9. ACKNOWLEDGMENTS

We gratefully acknowledge the contribution to this work of our collaborators at SRI International at Princeton, and SoarTech. This work was sponsored by the DARPA Strategic Social Interaction Modules program, under U.S. Army Research Office contract W911NF-12-C-0002. The contents of this paper are the responsibility of the authors, and do not necessarily reflect the position or the policy of the US Government. No official endorsement should be inferred.

10. REFERENCES

[1] Berne, Eric (1966) Games People Play – The Basic Hand Book of Transactional Analysis. New York: Ballantine Books.

[2] Bioware (2007) Mass Effect.

[3] Callejas, Z. et al. (2014). A computational model of social attitudes for a virtual recruiter. AAMAS '14 Proceedings of the 2014 international conference on Autonomous agents and multi-agent systems (May 2014), 93–100.

[4] Electronic Arts (2000) The Sims.

[5] French Jr., J., Raven, B.: The bases of social power. Studies in Social Power, 150–167 (1959)

[6] Goffman, E. (1974). Frame Analysis. (K. Brown, Ed.) Harvard University Press.

[7] Hartholt, A; Gratch, J. and Weiss, L. (2009) At the virtual frontier: Introducing Gunslinger, a multi-character, mixed-reality, story-driven experience. In Proceedings of Conference on Intelligent Virtual Agents.

[8] Kim, J. M., Hill, R. W., Jr., Durlach, P. J., Lane, H. C., Forbell, E., Core, M., Hart, J. (2009). BiLAT: A Game-Based Environment for Practicing Negotiation in a Cultural Context. Int. J. Artif. Intell. Ed., 19(3), 289–308.

[9] Linden Lab, (2013) Versu.

[10] Marsella, S., Pynadath, D., & Read, S. (2004). PsychSim: Agent-based modeling of social interactions and influence. Proceedings the International Conference on Cognitive Modeling. Pittsburg.

[11] Marsella, S. and Gratch, J. 2003. Modeling coping behavior in virtual humans. Proceedings of the second international joint conference on Autonomous agents and multiagent systems - AAMAS '03. (2003), 313.

[12] Marsella, S. & Gratch, J. (2006). EMA: A computational model of appraisal dynamics. In Proceedings of Agent Construction and Emotions. Vienna, Austria.

[13] Mateas, M., & Stern, A. (2002). A behavior language for story-based believable agents. IEEE Intelligent Systems, 17(4), 39–47.

[14] Mateas, M., & Stern, A. (2005). Structuring Content in the Façade Interactive Drama Architecture. Artificial Intelligence and Interactive Digital Entertainment (AIIDE 2005) (Vol. 3). Marina del Rey, CA.

[15] McCoy, J; Treanor, M.; Samuel, B; Reed, A; Wardrip-Fruin, N; Mateas, M (2012) PromWeek, Center for Games and Playable Media.

[16] McCoy, J., Treanor, M., Samuel, B., Wardrip-Fruin, N., & Mateas, M. (2011). Comme il Faut: A System for Authoring Playable Social Models. In *AIIDE*.

[17] Microsoft Game Studios (2010) Kinectimals.

[18] Osborne, F. (2011). A New Approach to Social Behavior Simulation: The Mask Model. In M. Si, D. Thue, E. Andre, J. Lester, J. Tanenbaum, & V. Zammitto (Eds.), *Interactive Storytelling 4th International Conference on International Digital Storytelling* (pp. 97–108).

[19] Pereira, G; Prada, R & Santos, P. (2013) Conceptualizing Social Power For Agents, in Intelligent Virtual Agents 2013 - IVA 2013, pg. 313-324, Springer / Heidelberg, Edinburgh, UK, August, 2013

[20] Prada, R. and Paiva, A. (2005). Believable groups of synthetic characters. AAMAS 05 Proceedings of the fourth international joint conference on Autonomous agents and multiagent systems. (2005), 37–43.

[21] Shapiro, D., McCoy, J., Grow, A., Samuel, B., Stern, A., Swanson, R., Treanor, M., and Mateas, M., *Creating Playable Social Experiences through Whole-body Interaction with Virtual Characters* (2013). Proceedings of the Ninth AAAI Conference on Artificial Intelligence and Interactive Digital Entertainment (AIIDE-13), Boston, MA.

[22] Si, M., Marsella, S. C., & Pynadath, D. V. (2005). Thespian: Using Multi-agent Fitting to Craft Interactive Drama. In *Proceedings of the Fourth International Joint Conference on Autonomous Agents and Multiagent Systems* (pp. 21–28). New York, NY, USA: ACM.

[23] Social Game Videos (2014)
Alliance: https://vimeo.com/112014884
Alliance & Authority: https://vimeo.com/112080014
Alliance, Authority & Threat: https://vimeo.com/112080518

[24] Swartout, W., Traum, D., Artstein, R., Noren, D., Debevec, P., Bronnenkant, K., Williams, J., Leuski, A., Narayanan, S., Piepol, D., Lane, C., Morie, J., Aggarwal, P., Liewer, M., Chiang, J., Gerten, J., Chu, S., and White, K. *Ada and Grace: Toward Realistic and Engaging Virtual Museum Guides*, in J. Allbeck et al. (Eds.): IVA 2010, LNAI 6356, pp. 286–300, 2010. Springer-Verlag Berlin Heidelberg 2010

Human Behavior Models for Virtual Agents in Repeated Decision Making under Uncertainty

Ming Yin*
Harvard University
mingyin@fas.harvard.edu

Yu-An Sun
PARC
YuAn.Sun@xerox.com

ABSTRACT

To design virtual agents that simulate humans in repeated decision making under uncertainty, we seek to quantitatively characterize the actual human behavior in these settings. We collect our data from 800 real human subjects through a large-scale randomized online experiment. We evaluate the performance of a wide range of computational models in fitting the data by both conducting a scalable search through the space of two-component models (i.e. inference + selection model) and investigating a few rules of thumb.

Our results suggest that across different decision-making environment, an average human decision maker can be best described by a two-component model, which is composed of an inference model that relies heavily on more recent information (i.e. displays recency bias) and a selection model which assumes cost-proportional errors and reluctance to change in subsequent trials (i.e. displays status-quo bias). Additionally, while a large portion of individuals behave like the average decision maker, how they differ from each other is greatly influenced by the environment. These results imply the possibility of constructing agents with a single type of model that is robust against the context, and provide insights into adjusting heterogeneity among multiple agents based on the context.

Categories and Subject Descriptors

I.2.0 [**Artificial Intelligence**]: General – *Cognitive simulation*

Keywords

Repeated Decision Making; Human-like Virtual Agents; Behavior Model; Cognitive Biases; Online Experiment

1. INTRODUCTION

Autonomous virtual agents that exhibit human-like behaviors have been widely applied in various domains, including multi-agent based simulations, serious games, arts and digital entertainment, education and virtual training [15, 4, 14]. One challenging problem with virtual agent design is how these agents should be modeled to resemble human behavior when they face uncertainty in decision-making, and in particular, when they have to make such decisions repeatedly. While most existing paradigms assume agents are rational decision makers hence display optimal behavior [28, 9], there is a large literature in behavioral economics and psychology showing that real humans are irrational as they are subject to cognitive biases and limitations [25, 23].

Thus, searching for a more realistic design of virtual agents in the setting of repeated decision making under uncertainty, a key question that needs to be addressed first is how real human beings *actually* behave in these conditions. For instance, how does a horse-racing gambler place bets on horses while observing their fluctuating performance over time; and how does a house owner choose her preferred electricity tariff scheme among multiple alternatives, such as the flat rate scheme (unit price is the same for usage in different time intervals) and different Time of Use (ToU) schemes (unit price is different for usage in different time intervals), while she periodically reviews her electricity bills?

To answer this question, in this paper, we aim at finding a computational model which best characterizes human behavior in repeated decision making under uncertainty. In particular, we focus on the following scenario which we refer to as the *environment learning problem*: There are N random variables in an environment (e.g. the amount of time for each of the N horses to finish a race, the electricity usage in each of the N time intervals of a day), and each random variable follows a *fixed* distribution that is *unknown* to the decision maker (DM). In each trial, the DM is first asked to choose among M options. Then, the DM observes an *independent* sample of *each* random variable for the trial. The DM's utility in a trial depends both on her choice and on the realized samples of all random variables in that trial. While the DM learns about the environment (i.e. random variable distributions) through the noisy samples, her objective is to maximize her cumulative utility in the whole decision period of T trials[1]. To the best of our knowledge, there is no previous work on modeling human behavior in this problem, though it generalizes real-life decision making in various domains like financial investment and security resource allocation.

*This work was done during a PARC internship.

[1]Note the difference with the multi-armed bandit problem (MAB): In MAB, the DM can only observe the realized sample of *one* random variable (corresponds to the chosen option) per trial and thus faces the tradeoff between exploration and exploitation.

Appears in: *Proceedings of the 14th International Conference on Autonomous Agents and Multiagent Systems (AAMAS 2015), Bordini, Elkind, Weiss, Yolum (eds.), May 4–8, 2015, Istanbul, Turkey.*

To examine a wide range of candidate human behavior models for the environment learning problem, we define a "model space" by decomposing a human DM's cognitive reasoning process in each trial into two components, i.e the *inference* component and the *selection* component. The inference component describes how DMs aggregate historic information and make forecast for the current trial, while the selection component models how DMs compare different options based on the forecasts and make decisions. Such decomposition provides us with the possibility to conduct a scalable search through the vast space of decision-making models. Moreover, inference and selection models that we evaluate in this paper vary in their assumptions on rationality and thus enable us to pinpoint a few key irrationalities that lead to suboptimal human behavior. As a complementary, we also investigate another family of models, which instead assumes that human DMs simply follow different rules of thumb *without* actively predicting future outcomes in preparation for evaluating alternatives.

From an agent designer's perspective, however, understanding a particular human DM's behavior in a specific decision-making environment is not the whole story. In fact, human DMs' behavior in real life can be influenced by characteristics of the decision-making environment like the degree of uncertainty in the environment [3, 1], as well as DMs' own characteristics. Both of these variations pose new challenges for virtual agent design, as they may imply the needs for creating a huge number of different agents that are tailored to all kinds of contexts and individuals. To better leverage our understanding on human behavior for agent design, we further ask two questions: First, if the goal is to design an agent which resembles an average human DM, does a single type of model exist which is robust against different environment? Second, when creating multiple agents to reproduce the behavior of a population of heterogeneous human beings, how many agents can still be described by an average DM's behavior model and how should we adjust the degree of heterogeneity in the agent population according to the environment?

To this end, we design and conduct a large-scale randomized online experiment, through which we collect data on 24 sequential decisions in an environment learning problem from each of 800 unique human subjects on Amazon Mechanical Turk (MTurk). Each subject of our experiment is randomly assigned to one of the eight treatments with different predefined decision-making environment characteristics. Performance of various computational models is then examined for the "average subject" in each treatment (by assuming an one-size-fit-all model for all subjects in one treatment) and for each individual subject.

Our results suggest that across different decision-making environment, a specific type of two-component model generally outperforms other models, including different rules of thumb, in explaining an average human DM's behavior in the environment learning problem. According to this model, the average DM relies on the most recent information heavily to update their understanding of the uncertain environment, tends to stick with their previous choices, and is inclined to select suboptimal options with higher forecasted utilities. On the other hand, in characterizing each human DM's behavior, we find that while the behavior of a significant portion of individual DMs can be described by the model for the average DM, the degree to which individuals differ from each other is largely affected by the environment. For example, in a less uncertain environment where the sequence of noisy observations implies consistent information, individual DMs are more heterogeneous and display varying levels of rationality; while in a more uncertain environment, they tend to be more homogeneous and behave uniformly naive.

These findings provide valuable implications for designing human-like virtual agents in repeated decision making under uncertainty. On the one hand, the existence of a single type of robust model (against the environment contexts) for resembling average human beings and the fact that this model can also explain the behavior of a large number of individuals indicates a possible decrease of computational burdens for virtual agent design, as we may not need to use a different model to construct an agent every time given a new problem instance. On the other hand, our observations on the relationship between the decision-making environment characteristics and the degree of heterogeneity among human DMs suggest possible principles on tuning behavior in the agent population for context adaptation.

2. RELATED WORK

Various frameworks have been adopted to create virtual agents in uncertain environment, including Fuzzy Logic [9], rule-based or experience-based inference [9, 14], decision network [28], BDI (i.e. belief-desire-intention) and E-BDI (i.e. Emotional BDI) models [15, 13]. In particular, to generate more human-like behavior under uncertainty, [15] integrated the prospect theory [10] with a BDI model and drew a distinction between risk and ambiguity. Our work is different from these studies in two perspectives: First, we focus on a setting where agents have to *repeatedly* make decisions under uncertainty, hence the agent's decision in one trial can be explicitly influenced by not only the current imperfect observation of the environment, but also historic observations and decisions. Second, instead of providing a generic decision-making framework with certain human behavior models embedded a priori, we take a different approach by focusing on a specific decision-making scenario (i.e. the environment learning problem) and examining a variety of different behavior model alternatives in searching for the one which *actually* characterizes real human behavior the best.

Decision-making under uncertainty is a field that is extensively studied in economics. The first, and for a long time the only model in this field, is the expected utility model, which is based on the hypothesis that in an uncertain environment individuals always choose the options that maximize their expected utilities [26]. However, as empirical evidence that violates this hypothesis being consistently observed (e.g. the Allais paradox [2]), new theories have been proposed. One of the alternatives is the random utility model [16], which states that the utility of an option is composed by an observable part (e.g. expected utility) and an unobservable stochastic error term. With different underlying structure in the error terms, various discrete choice models are proposed to account for the choices over multiple options [24]. In our study, while we investigate two selection models that are directly derived from the expected utility and random utility models (i.e. the ϵ-Greedy and the Logit model), given the nature of repeated decision-making in our scenario, we also propose two new selection models (i.e. the Single Hurdle and the Double Hurdle model), with the assumption that subsequent decisions are not independent with each other.

There is an important distinction between these classical decision making under uncertainty settings in economics and the environment learning problem, however. That is, in the environment learning problem, the utility of each option is *unknown* at the decision time[2]. Thus, a decision maker has to *predict* how "good" each option is by inferring from her previous experiences, or equivalently, by forecasting the random variable values based on historic observations. A large number of approaches can be found in statistical inference literatures along this direction, including time-series analysis techniques [7], reinforcement learning methods [22] and the Bayesian inference framework [8]. While most existing virtual agent systems apply the Bayesian inference framework to reason about uncertainty [15, 28], we also consider the other two possibilities and investigate three inference models in this paper (i.e. the Last-K, the TDRL and the Bayesian updating model).

Finally, it has been suggested by behavioral economists and psychologists that people often make decisions based on approximate rules of thumb rather than rational thoughts [25, 23]. In the context of repeated decision-making under uncertainty, a number of rules of thumb have also been specified for other scenarios (e.g. the multi-arm bandit problem) in previous studies [21, 29]. By adapting them into our scenario, we are able to compare the performance of two families of models: two-component models and rules of thumb.

3. EXPERIMENTAL DESIGN

We first introduce our experimental design. Our study is based on the human subjects' choice data that we collect in this experiment on an environment learning problem.

To begin with, we now formally define the environment learning problem: Each of the N random variables in the environment is denoted as X_i, which follows a stationary distribution. The initial observation on X_i is x_i^0. In each trial t ($t \geq 1$), the DM chooses among M options. When the chosen option is $Y_t = j$, the DM's utility in trial t is $U_t = f_j(x_{1:N}^t)$[3], where $f_j(\cdot)$ is the payoff function of option j, and x_i^t is the value of X_i in trial t which will be realized *after* the DM's choice. Both the initial observation and the realized values of X_i in each trial are generated by drawing random samples from its distribution independently. The DM's objective is to maximize her cumulative utility $\sum_{t=1}^{T} U_t$ in all T trials.

3.1 Task

Since our goal is to understand the actual human behavior, in our experiment, we are interested in creating a realistic setting of repeated decision making under uncertainty for the subjects. Thus, we frame the environment learning problem as a game on periodically reviewing the electricity bills and choosing the preferred tariff scheme, which is a common practice in daily life. Specifically, each subject is told that the energy company of her community begins to provide three (i.e. $M = 3$) different electricity tariff schemes:

- *Flat-rate scheme*: Unit price is \$0.25/kWh for electricity usage at any time in a day.
- *Cheaper in the day scheme*: Unit price is \$0.20/kWh during the daytime (7am–7pm) and \$0.30/kWh during the nighttime (7pm–7am).
- *Cheaper in the night scheme*: Unit price is \$0.30/kWh during the daytime and \$0.20/kWh during the nighttime.

One trial in the game corresponds to one "month". In each trial, the subject can review the "electricity bill" of the last month, which includes information on the daytime (nighttime) usage and costs, and choose her preferred tariff scheme for the current month. The game lasts for $T = 24$ trials (i.e. 2 "years"). Figure 1 shows the interface of one trial.

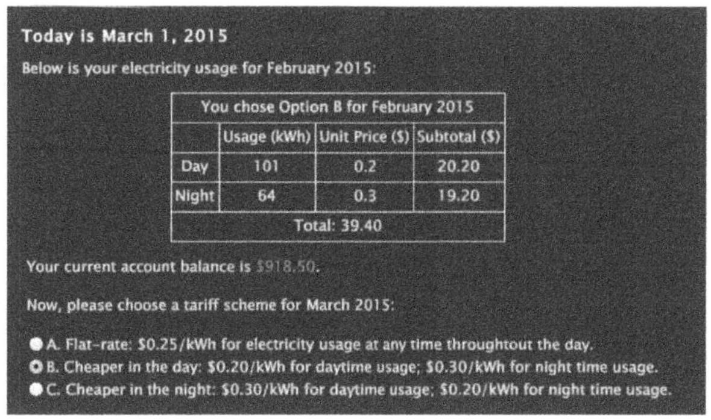

Figure 1: Interface of one trial in the game.

3.2 Treatments

Two random variables (i.e. $N = 2$) are used to represent the daytime (X_1) and nighttime (X_2) electricity usage in each month. We further assume that the electricity usage follows a normal distribution, that is, $X_i \sim N(\mu_i, \sigma_i^2), i \in \{1, 2\}$. To simulate a rich variety of decision-making environment, we control 3 "environment characteristics" to create eight treatments. These characteristics include:

- *Mean usage difference*: the difference between the expected daytime and nighttime electricity usage in a month (i.e. $\Delta\mu = |\mu_2 - \mu_1|$) can be either small or large.
- *Usage variance*: the variance of daytime and nighttime electricity usage (i.e. σ_i^2) can be either small or large.
- *Default option*: when making decisions in each trial, there may or may not exist a default option.

The first two characteristics give us the flexibility to vary the easiness for people to distinguish the underlying distributions of the daytime and nighttime electricity usage, which further influence people's perception on the degree of uncertainty in the environment. The concept of *discriminability*, defined as $d = \frac{|\mu_2 - \mu_1|}{\sqrt{\sigma_1^2 + \sigma_2^2}}$, formally captures this idea [1]: With a larger value of $\Delta\mu$ or a smaller value of σ_i^2 (hence larger d), the sequence of noisy samples are more likely to be consistent (e.g. $x_1^t > x_2^t$ in most trials or vice versa) and it's easier for the subjects to figure out their electricity usage is generally higher in one time interval than that in another interval, thus the subjects may perceive the environment to be less uncertain. Different values of these

---

[2]In classical settings, an option is often presented as a "prospect" (o_1, p_1; ...; o_n, p_n), for which the outcome o_i is yielded with probability p_i and $\sum_{i=1}^{n} p_i = 1$. While the value for p_i may be either known (risk) or unknown (uncertainty), a decision maker is usually aware of the utility of each possible outcome, $u(o_i)$.

[3]The colon notation is used to refer to a range of elements, e.g. $x_{1:N}^t = x_1^t, ..., x_i^t, ..., x_N^t$. In addition, the assumption of a DM's utility being linearly correlated with option payoffs implies that DMs are risk-neutral. Concave/convex utility functions are also tested to account for other risk preferences and results are similar.

two characteristics lead to 4 *electricity usage conditions* and parameter values in each condition are specified in Table 1. Note that within one condition, whether a subject's daytime usage is generally higher (i.e. whether $\mu_1 > \mu_2$) is randomly decided.

Moreover, we include the third characteristic to examine whether human subjects' decisions are affected by the explicit existence of the default (or status-quo) option. A prevalent observation in previous studies is that individuals disproportionately stick with the status-quo option when it exists, which is referred to as the *status-quo bias* [20]. In our experiment, we test 2 *default option conditions*: In the "no default" condition, pre-selected option doesn't exist and an active choice is required for each trial; in the "default" condition, starting from the second trial, the chosen option in the last trial will be pre-selected as the default, yet the subject can choose to switch to other options.

Finally, the combination of an electricity usage condition and a default option condition creates one treatment. Thus, there are 8 treatments in our experiment.

Table 1: Parameter values for the 4 electricity usage conditions.

Conditions	Distributions of X_i	d
Small difference, small variance	$N(70, 10^2)$; $N(90, 10^2)$	1.41
Small difference, large variance	$N(70, 20^2)$; $N(90, 20^2)$	0.71
Large difference, small variance	$N(60, 10^2)$; $N(100, 10^2)$	2.83
Large difference, large variance	$N(60, 30^2)$; $N(100, 30^2)$	0.94

3.3 Experimental Control

Upon arrival, a subject is randomly assigned to one treatment. While the subject understands there may exist some regularities for her electricity usage, she is unaware of the exact forms of the electricity usage distributions in the assigned treatment. In the game, the subject decides only her monthly tariff scheme but *not* the amount of daytime (nighttime) electricity usage shown on the bills, which is actually generated by drawing random samples from the distributions of X_1 (X_2) independently, and the subject has been trained to read the bills. To simulate the real world in which people can benefit from smartly-chosen tariff schemes due to the electricity cost savings, we introduce performance-contingent bonuses in our game. Specifically, Each subject is initially endowed with 1000 dollars of game money and she can observe her account balance in each trial. At the end of the game, besides a fixed payment of $0.15, the subject may earn a bonus up to $0.70 by converting the final balance (if positive) with a 100:1 rate. We recommend subjects to keep close track of their monthly bills so as to find out possible regularities hence minimize the costs.

3.4 Data

In total, 800 unique U.S. subjects are recruited from MTurk and 100 subjects are assigned to each treatment, with half of the subjects generally using more electricity in the day (i.e. $\mu_1 > \mu_2$) and the other half consuming more at night (i.e. $\mu_1 < \mu_2$). For each subject, we record the history of daytime (nighttime) electricity usage that she observes (i.e. $x_i^{0:T}$) and her decisions in each trial (i.e. $Y_{1:T}$).

4. MODELS

We now list the formal definitions of all computational models that we examine. In all models, the payoff function of an option j is $f_j(x_{1:N}^t) = -\sum_{i=1}^{N} w_i^j x_i^t$, where w_i^j is the unit price of daytime or nighttime usage stated in option j[4].

4.1 Two-Component Models: Inference + Selection

When a DM makes decision in trial t, she has observed the realized values of *each* X_i for *all* previous trials (i.e. $x_i^{0:t-1}$), yet her utility in the current trial depends on the unknown value of x_i^t which will be revealed in the future. We hence define our first family of models in a "model space" such that each model consists of two separate components to enable a scalable search over all kinds of decision-making models: the *inference* component is represented by a function that maps the DM's previous observations to forecasts on the random variable values in the current trial, i.e. $\hat{x}_i^t = h(x_i^{0:t-1})$, where $\hat{x}_i^t$ is the predicted value of X_i in trial t; the *selection* component refers to the DM calculating the forecasted utility of each option $\hat{u}_j^t = f_j(\hat{x}_{1:N}^t)$ and stochastically making a choice, i.e. $r_j^t = g(\hat{u}_{1:M}^t)$, r_j^t is the probability of choosing option j in trial t and $\sum_{j=1}^{M} r_j^t = 1$.

4.1.1 Inference Models

For the inference component, we consider 3 models:

DEFINITION 1 (LAST-K). *The predicted value of random variable X_i in trial t is the average of its realized values in a sliding window of (at most) last K trials: $\hat{x}_i^t = \frac{1}{t-s}\sum_{k=s}^{t-1} x_i^k$, where $s = max(0, t-K)$.* ■

The Last-K model is commonly used in time series analysis (typically referred to as moving average). In addition, an important cognitive foundation of the Last-K model is that humans have limited memory. The widely-known finding of "the magical number 7" suggests that the working memory capacity of an average human is 7±2 [17]. In the limits, when $K = 1$, we have a "*recency model*" in which a DM can only remember the most recent observation; and when $K = t$, we get an "*average model*" that a DM recalls everything from the very beginning.

DEFINITION 2 (TDRL). *The temporal difference reinforcement learning (TDRL) model suggests that a DM predicts the value of a random variable X_i in trial t according to $\hat{x}_i^t = \hat{x}_i^{t-1} + \alpha(x_i^{t-1} - \hat{x}_i^{t-1})$, where α is a learning rate parameter.* ■

TDRL is a prediction method mostly used for solving reinforcement learning problems [22, 6]. The core idea is that in each trial, the prediction is adjusted to better match the most recent observation, with a larger α indicating a higher discount on the old information.

Both the Last-K and the TDRL model imply that DMs may have bounded rationality so they apply heuristics like trimming and weighting when aggregating information and making inference. On the contrary, Bayesian inference, which is the framework frequently used in existing virtual agent systems, presents a idealistic inference mechanism by assuming that DMs have sufficient prior knowledge (e.g. the

[4]The negative sign converts a cost minimizing problem into a utility maximizing problem.

models that generate the observations) and rationally make inferences by applying the Bayesian updating scheme given the sequential observations.

DEFINITION 3 (BAYESIAN UPDATING). *In each trial, a DM updates her posterior belief on parameter values for the distribution of X_i by integrating the realized value of X_i with the prior belief using the Bayes rule, and her prediction $\hat{x}_i^t$ for trial t is the expected value of X_i conditioned on its posterior parameter distribution in trial $t-1$.* ■

For our case, a DM's initial belief on the two parameters for the distribution of X_i (i.e. μ_i and the precision parameter $\lambda_i = 1/\sigma_i^2$) is assumed to be a Normal-Gamma distribution as the conjugate prior[5].

4.1.2 Selection Models

For the selection component, we study 4 different models:

DEFINITION 4 (ϵ-GREEDY). *A DM chooses the (set of) optimal option(s) with probability ϵ:*

$$r_j^t = \begin{cases} \frac{\epsilon}{|J^*|} & j \in J^* \\ \frac{1-\epsilon}{M-|J^*|} & j \notin J^* \end{cases}$$

where J^* is the set of options with the maximal forecasted utility $\hat{u}_j^t$ in trial t. ■

The ϵ-Greedy model corresponds to a stochastic version of the expected utility model by stating that DMs will choose the option with maximal utility, yet there is a constant chance of making errors (i.e. $1-\epsilon$).

DEFINITION 5 (LOGIT). *The probability for a DM to choose option j is given by $r_j^t = \frac{exp(\beta \hat{u}_j^t)}{\sum_{j'=1}^M exp(\beta \hat{u}_{j'}^t)}$, where β is a precision parameter.* ■

The Logit model is a prominent type of discrete choice model in economics [24], which is based on a random utility model assuming that the stochastic error term in utility follows a Gumbel distribution (i.e. type I generalized extreme value distribution). It uses a softmax function to convert option utility into choice probability. The parameter β indicates a DM's sensitivity to utilities: when $\beta \to 0$, the DM chooses randomly; when $\beta \to \infty$, the DM almost always chooses the forecasted optimal option. On the cognitive level, the Logit model implies a property called *cost-proportional errors*, that is, human DMs can be more likely to err when the error costs are lower (i.e. choose suboptimal options more often when they have larger utilities), and this property has also been modeled as the *quantal best response* in behavior theory [27].

Both the ϵ-Greedy and the Logit model assume that human DMs evaluate options in each trial independently. However, when a DM makes decisions repeatedly, her choice in a specific trial may be affected by her previous decisions, for example, she may be inclined to keep her previous choice. Inspired by the hurdle and zero-inflated model in statistics, which are developed to characterize count data with extra zero-valued observations [18, 11], we propose the following two models to take such limitation into account:

[5]That is, $NG(\mu, \lambda|\mu_0, \kappa_0, \alpha_0, \beta_0) = N(\mu|\mu_0, (\kappa_0\lambda)^{-1}) \cdot Ga(\lambda|\alpha_0, \beta_0)$, where $N(\cdot)$ and $Ga(\cdot)$ are the probability density functions of Normal and Gamma distributions, respectively.

DEFINITION 6 (SINGLE HURDLE). *When $t = 1$, the Single Hurdle model is the same as the Logit model. Otherwise, the probability for a DM to choose option j is given by:*

$$r_j^t = \begin{cases} \pi & j = Y_{t-1} \\ \frac{(1-\pi)exp(\beta \hat{u}_j^t)}{\sum_{j' \neq Y_{t-1}} exp(\beta \hat{u}_{j'}^t)} & j \neq Y_{t-1} \end{cases}$$

where β is a precision parameter and Y_{t-1} is the DM's choice in trial $t-1$. ■

DEFINITION 7 (DOUBLE HURDLE). *When $t = 1$, the Double Hurdle model is the same as the Logit model. Otherwise, the probability for a DM to choose option j is given by:*

$$r_j^t = \begin{cases} \pi + \frac{(1-\pi)exp(\beta \hat{u}_j^t)}{\sum_{j'=1}^M exp(\beta \hat{u}_{j'}^t)} & j = Y_{t-1} \\ \frac{(1-\pi)exp(\beta \hat{u}_j^t)}{\sum_{j'=1}^M exp(\beta \hat{u}_{j'}^t)} & j \neq Y_{t-1} \end{cases}$$

where β is a precision parameter and Y_{t-1} is the DM's choice in trial $t-1$. ■

These two models implicitly assume 2 steps in selecting options. In Step 1, the DM decides whether to stick with her choice in the last trial regardless of its forecasted utility, and this is governed by a binomial distribution with parameter π. In Step 2, the DM makes further evaluations if the previous choice is not preserved in Step 1: For the Double Hurdle model, *all* options are evaluated; yet for the Single Hurdle model, the previous choice is *excluded* from the evaluation. The conditional probability of selecting an option in Step 2 follows the Logit model.

4.2 Rules of Thumb

The second family of models is a few rules of thumb, assuming that human DMs don't explicitly predict future outcomes and make decisions based on the forecasted utility of each option. Four rules are examined in this study:

RULE 1 (RANDOM). *A DM chooses an option uniformly randomly in each trial. That is, option j is selected in trial t with probability $\frac{1}{M}$.* ■

The random rule suggests a naive way of making decisions in regardless of utilities. Thus, it is a baseline rule of thumb.

RULE 2 (PROBABILITY MATCHING). *A DM initially assigns a "success count" n_j^0 to each option j. Upon the observation of $x_{1:N}^{t-1}$ before trial t, if $f_j(x_{1:N}^{t-1}) \geq f_{j'}(x_{1:N}^{t-1})$ for any j', the DM updates the success count of option j as $n_j^t = n_j^{t-1}+1$; otherwise $n_j^t = n_j^{t-1}$. Option j is then selected in trial t with probability $\frac{n_j^t}{\sum_{j'=1}^M n_{j'}^t}$.* ■

Probability matching suggests a suboptimal decision strategy that has been widely observed among humans: Instead of consistently choosing the maximizing option, the DM assigns a probability to each option by matching its likelihood of being optimal [21].

RULE 3 (GOOD-STAY-BAD-SHIFT). *Upon the observation of $x_{1:N}^{t-1}$ before trial t, if the DM's previous choice Y_{t-1} turns out to be "good", the DM will keep that choice with probability p; otherwise, the DM will shift to the (set of) optimal option(s) (according to $x_{1:N}^{t-1}$) with probability p. Other options are selected uniformly randomly in both cases.* ■

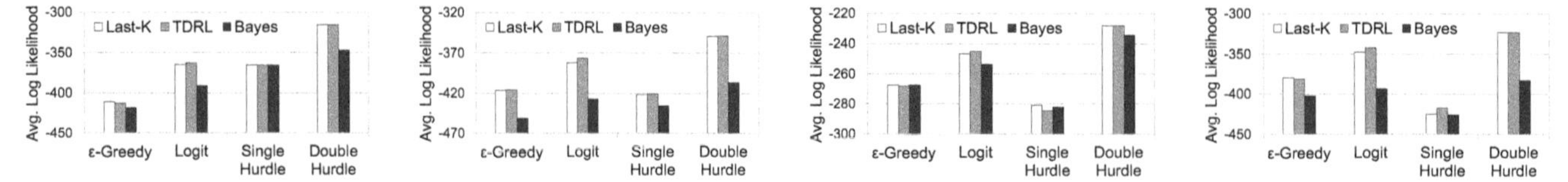

(a) T1: Small difference, small variance, no default (b) T2: Small difference, large variance, no default (c) T3: Large difference, small variance, no default (d) T4: Large difference, large variance, no default

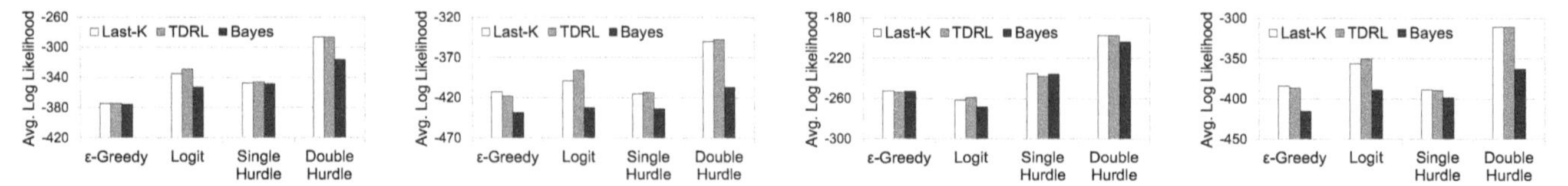

(e) T5: Small difference, small variance, default (f) T6: Small difference, large variance, default (g) T7: Large difference, small variance, default (h) T8: Large difference, large variance, default

Figure 2: Mean log likelihood in 5-fold cross validation when modeling an average DM using two-component models.

We test two ways to define a "good" option: an aggressive DM requires Y_{t-1} to have the highest utility among all options given $x^{t-1}_{1:N}$, yet a conservative DM considers Y_{t-1} to be good as long as its utility is not the lowest. This rule is adapted from the "win-stay-lose-shift" heuristics in previous studies for the two-armed bandit problem [29].

Finally, we consider a fourth rule which describes the DM as constantly choosing a "safe choice" unless another option can be significantly better.

RULE 4 (SAFE CHOICE). *A DM has a safe choice j_s in mind. Upon the observation of $x^{t-1}_{1:N}$, the DM will only switch to the optimal option j^* (according to $x^{t-1}_{1:N}$) in trial t with probability q if $\frac{f_{j^*}(x^{t-1}_{1:N})-f_{j_s}(x^{t-1}_{1:N})}{|max(f_{j^*}(x^{t-1}_{1:N}),f_{j_s}(x^{t-1}_{1:N}))|} > 0$; otherwise, the DM will stay with her safe choice with probability q. Other options are selected uniformly randomly in both cases.* ■

A natural safe choice in our setting is the "flat-rate scheme" as it can't be the worst option at any time. Such preference for the flat-rate scheme is also observed empirically, which may because humans tend to avoid variations [12].

5. RESULTS

In this section, we present the performance of each computational model in explaining human DMs' behavior, both for an average DM and for each individual DM.

5.1 Modeling for an Average DM

Our first research question is how to design an agent to resemble an *average* human DM in repeated decision making under uncertainty. Therefore, we start with the evaluation on the performance of different models (including both two-component models and rules of thumb) in terms of explaining the average human DM's behavior in various decision-making environment.

To evaluate the performance of a specific type of model in a particular decision-making environment (i.e. treatment), we conduct a 5-fold cross validation, and an *one-size-fit-all* model of the given type is used to account for the average human DM's behavior. That is, given the dataset for one treatment (i.e. all choice data for all subjects in that treatment), we first create 5 folds by randomly partitioning the subjects into 5 groups and collecting all data for a subject to her group. Next, we retain one fold of the dataset as the validation dataset while the other 4 folds are used as training data, and the cross-validation process is repeated 5 times by using each fold as the validation dataset once. Within one round of cross validation, given a model type (e.g. Last-K + ϵ-Greedy), we first train an average DM's model of this type using maximum likelihood estimation, with the assumption that all subjects in the training dataset share the same model parameters and thus search for the optimal parameter values which give us the largest probability of observing the training data. Then, we calculate the log likelihood value of the validation data given the obtained model. The mean log likelihood value of all 5 folds is used to represent how well this type of model fits an average DM's behavior in this treatment, with a larger value indicating a better model. Hence, by comparing the mean log likelihood values of different models within each treatment, we can understand what is the best model to characterize the average DM's behavior in each decision-making environment.

5.1.1 *The Best Two-Component Model*

We first examine the performance of different two-component models in various environment, and the results are shown in Figure 2(a)-2(h). When the Last-K model is used for the inference component, we test on a number of different K values (i.e. $K = 1, 2, 3, 6, 12, t$) and the largest log likelihood value for the corresponding two-component model is reported. As the figures suggest, in *all* eight decision-making environment, the combination of the TDRL (or the best Last-K) inference model and the Double Hurdle selection model consistently has a better performance than other two-component models in capturing an average DM's behavior.

Particularly, for the inference component, it is interesting to see that the widely-used model for virtual agents, that is, the Bayesian updating model, actually describes an average real human DM's behavior relatively poor. This can be possibly attributed to human DMs' limited prior information and rationality. Indeed, a closer look at the other two inference models suggest that the average DM is irrational in the reasoning process: While the TDRL model consistently reports very high learning rates (e.g. estimated α values are in the range of 0.86-0.99), we also find that the recency model (i.e. $K = 1$) almost always provides the highest log likelihood among all Last-K models when combined with a selection model (except in $T3$). These observations indicate that the average human DM is subject to the *recency bias* severely when she predicts the future based on the history, that is, she reacts strongly to the new information and discounts old information heavily [5, 6].

On the other hand, when we focus on the selection component, one of the models that we propose, i.e. the Double Hurdle model, clearly outperforms other models. The implications are two-folds: First, instead of being a strict utility maximizer, the average DM makes cost-proportional errors (e.g. estimated β values are in the range of 0.72-1.52); Second, when the average DM makes decisions repeatedly, she doesn't take each of them independently. In fact, the average DM is affected by the status-quo bias and is reluctant to change decisions in subsequent trials, even if the previous choice is *not* explicitly set as the default (e.g. estimated π values suggests a 25%-50% chance of sticking with the previous choice). The average DM's bias towards the status-quo option also serves as an add-on to her analysis on the forecasted utility of each option, which leads to the advantage of the Double Hurdle model over the Single Hurdle model.

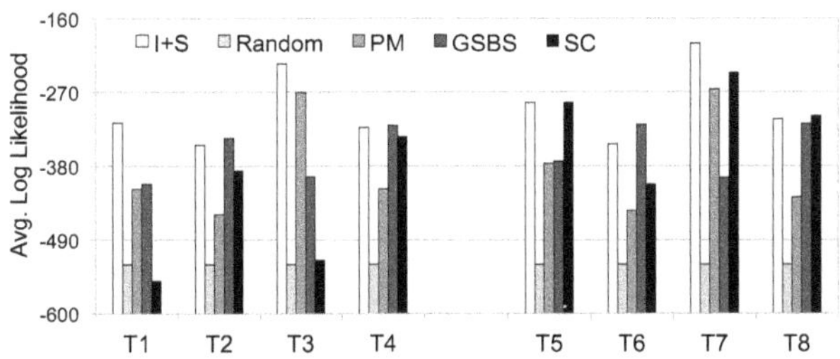

Figure 3: Comparison between the best two-component model and different rules of thumb.

5.1.2 *Inference+Selection vs. Rules of Thumb*

Figure 3 presents the comparison between the two families of models in fitting an average DM's behavior, where $T1$-$T4$ are treatments without the default option and $T5$-$T8$ are treatments with the default option. When variations exist for a model (e.g. different combinations of inference and selection component for the two-component model, the aggressive and conservative way to define a "good" option in a Good-Stay-Bad-Shift rule, etc.), the one with the highest log likelihood value is reported.

Clearly, the best two-component model fits the data reasonably well for *all* 8 treatments, which essentially suggests the combination of a TDRL inference model and a Double Hurdle selection model can be generally recommended for designing a virtual agent to simulate an average DM in the environment learning problem, no matter what the specific decision-making environment is. In contrast, different rules of thumb may capture the average human DM's behavior accurately in *some* specific environment, for example, the Safe Choice rule performs well in treatments with the default option. However, none of these rules provides robustly good fitting performance across all treatments, indicating that for the average DM, the activation of rules of thumb, if any, is highly context-dependent, which is also consistent with the literatures [19].

5.2 Modeling for Individual DMs

Our second research question is when designing an agent population to reproduce the behavior of a group of heterogeneous human DMs, how many agents in the population can still adopt the best-performing model for the average DM and how should we adjust the degree of heterogeneity within the population based on the decision-making environment. We hence proceed on to characterize *individual* DM's behavior using various two-component models. That is, we treat each individual DM as a unique entity and explore a "personalized" behavior model for every one of them. As subjects don't exhibit significantly different behavior in the 2 default option conditions, in this subsection, we combine subjects together for each of the 4 electricity usage conditions.

5.2.1 *Validity of the Average DM's Model on the Individual Level*

To answer the question of to what degree the best-performing average DM's behavior model can be used if we aim at creating a population of heterogeneous agents, we seek to find out the fittest inference model and the fittest selection model among individual DMs, respectively.

For the fittest inference model, we first set each DM's selection model to be the Double Hurdle model and compare the fitness of different inference models (i.e. the log likelihood value) in explaining the individual DM's decisions. Figure 4(a) reports the percentage of subjects in each electricity usage condition that the best inference model is Last-K, TDRL and Bayesian updating, respectively. As shown in the figure, across all four different environment, the fittest inference model is the TDRL model for the majority of individual DMs, which is consistent with the inference component choice in the best-performing model for the average DM.

Moreover, for the fittest selection model among individuals, we fix a DM's inference model to be the TDRL model and compare the performance of different selection models for each individual. Results are presented in Figure 4(b). While we observe more diversity in DM's choice on the selection model, we still find the Double Hurdle model to be the fittest selection model for the largest percentage of individual DMs. That is, the selection model in the best-performing model for the average DM can also be used for a large portion of individual DMs.

In sum, through the examination on the fittest inference and selection model for each individual DM, we validate the feasibility of the best-performing average DM's behavior model on the individual level by showing that it can actually be used to characterize the behavior of a large number of individual DMs.

5.2.2 *Heterogeneity and the Environment*

The existence of individual differences in a heterogeneous population indicates that there are always some individuals who "deviate" from the average. For example, as Figure 4(a) shows, depending on the decision-making environment, 11%-35% of individual DMs actually display consistency with the Bayesian inference framework, suggesting a subgroup of individuals with possibly higher levels of rationality. We hence ask how is the degree of heterogeneity among individual DMs affected by the decision-making environment.

Take the heterogeneity among individuals on making inferences about the uncertain environment as an example. Figure 4(a) seem to indicate that DMs are more heterogeneous in the "Large difference, small variance" condition, as more individuals are able to avoid the recency bias hence behave more rationally. More formally, the degree of het-

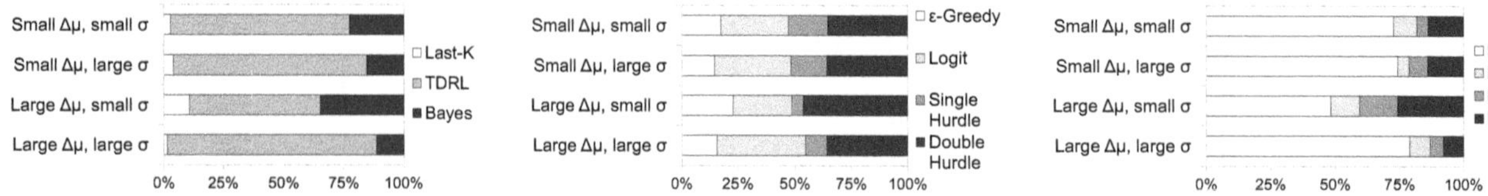

(a) The inference component (b) The selection component (c) The Last-K model

Figure 4: Individual DM's behavior in the environment learning problem.

erogeneity within a population can be measured by Shannon's entropy. In particular, given a population of L types of individuals, if the probability of an individual belonging to type l is p_l, the heterogenous degree of this population can be defined as $H = -\sum_{l=1}^{L} p_l log(p_l)$, with a larger value representing a higher degree of heterogeneity. The heterogenous degree for each population in the four decision-making environment in Figure 4(a) is reported in the H_{inf} column of Table 2. As we expect, the values differ a lot across various environment, while individuals in the "Large difference, small variance" environment have the highest degree of heterogeneity.

Recall from Table 1 that the "Large difference, small variance" environment has the highest discriminability in all 4 conditions, implying that the sequence of observations are likely to provide consistent information and DMs may perceive this environment to be less uncertain. Thus, we make a conjecture on the relationship between the decision-making environment and the degree of heterogeneity among human DMs: In an environment of high discriminability (i.e. less perceived uncertainty), individuals are capable of leveraging their varying levels of rationality hence are more heterogeneous; however, in an environment of low discriminability (i.e. more perceived uncertainty), individuals uniformly display their irrationality hence are more homogeneous.

As another supporting evidence, we set each DM's inference and selection model to be the Last-K and Double Hurdle model, respectively. We then test different K values (i.e. $K = 1, 3, 6, t$) and rank the fitness of each model for each DM. Figure 4(c) shows the percentage of subjects for whom the best K value is $1, 3, 6, t$, respectively, when the Last-K model is used as the inference component, and the heterogenous degree of each population in this figure is also reported in the H_{Last-K} column of Table 2. Again, we find that in a less uncertain environment, DMs are more heterogeneous and more individuals consider a longer sequence of previous observations, or even the entire observation history, to predict the future. Yet, in a more uncertain environment, most of DMs display recency bias and as a result, the population is more homogeneous.

Table 2: The degree of heterogeneity among individual DMs on making inferences for the 4 electricity usage conditions.

Conditions	H_{inf}	H_{Last-K}
Small difference, small variance	0.6558	0.8586
Small difference, large variance	0.5925	0.8246
Large difference, small variance	0.9378	1.2282
Large difference, large variance	0.4269	0.7453

6. DISCUSSIONS AND CONCLUSIONS

In this paper, we evaluate and compare the performance of a variety of computational models in fitting the data of real human behavior in an environment learning problem. Based on our evaluation results, we list two guidelines for designing human-like virtual agents in repeated decision making under uncertainty:

1. To resemble an average person, the agent should be designed with a few human irrationalities, like the recency and status-quo bias and tendency to make cost-proportional errors.
2. While the same behavior model can be used across different decision-making environment for agents that resemble average human beings, when designing an agent population to simulate a group of heterogenous people, we should adjust the degree of heterogeneity within the population (i.e. the use of different models for each individual agent) according to the decision-making environment.

The first guideline advocates for deeper considerations of the cognitive limitations and biases of human beings for the design of human-like virtual agents. Essentially, the question is whether a fully rational agent is really "human-like", and we think the answer is "No".

The second guideline is based on our findings that the combination of the TDRL inference model and the Double Hurdle selection model provides accurate description of an average DM's behavior across all decision-making environment, yet the specific environment characteristics largely influence how much individual DMs differ from each other. Particularly, we observe that people seem to be more heterogeneous in a less uncertain environment while more homogeneous in a more uncertain environment.

There are many interesting work that can be done in the future. For example, in this paper, we provide a methodology to conduct scalable search through the vast space of human behavior models in repeated decision making under uncertainty by decomposing the decision-making process into two components. While we strive to cover a wide range of both inference and selection models in the study, our search may not be comprehensive. More sophisticated models, such as various complicated time-series and discrete choice models, can be integrated into the space and be evaluated in the future. Furthermore, designing virtual agents which have these human behavior models in mind and target to interactively train or "nudge" real people towards better decisions would be another very exciting future direction.

Acknowledgements

The authors are grateful to Yiling Chen and Barbara Grosz for helpful discussions and feedback. Any opinions, findings, conclusions, or recommendations expressed here are those of the authors alone.

REFERENCES

[1] H.-i. Ahn and R. W. Picard. Modeling subjective experience-based learning under uncertainty and frames. In *Twenty-Eighth AAAI Conference on Artificial Intelligence*, 2014.

[2] M. Allais. Le comportement de l'homme rationnel devant le risque: critique des postulats et axiomes de l'école américaine. *Econometrica: Journal of the Econometric Society*, pages 503–546, 1953.

[3] A. Bechara, H. Damasio, D. Tranel, and A. R. Damasio. Deciding advantageously before knowing the advantageous strategy. *Science*, 275(5304):1293–1295, 1997.

[4] T. Bosse, C. Gerritsen, and J. Treur. Combining rational and biological factors in virtual agent decision making. *Applied intelligence*, 34(1):87–101, 2011.

[5] C. Camerer. *Behavioral Game Theory: Experiments in Strategic Interaction*. Princeton University Press, 2003.

[6] D. Fudenberg and A. Peysakhovich. Recency, records and recaps: learning and non-equilibrium behavior in a simple decision problem. In *Proceedings of the fifteenth ACM conference on Economics and Computation*, pages 971–986. ACM, 2014.

[7] J. D. Hamilton. *Time series analysis*, volume 2. Princeton university press Princeton, 1994.

[8] C. Howson and P. Urbach. *Scientific reasoning: the Bayesian approach*. Open Court Publishing, 2006.

[9] I. Hupont, R. Del-Hoyo, S. Baldassarri, E. Cerezo, F. J. Serón, and D. Romero. Towards an intelligent affective multimodal virtual agent for uncertain environments. In *Proceedings of the International Workshop on Affective-Aware Virtual Agents and Social Robots*, page 4. ACM, 2009.

[10] D. Kahneman and A. Tversky. Prospect theory: An analysis of decision under risk. *Econometrica: Journal of the Econometric Society*, pages 263–291, 1979.

[11] D. Lambert. Zero-inflated poisson regression, with an application to defects in manufacturing. *Technometrics*, 34(1):1–14, 1992.

[12] A. Lambrecht and B. Skiera. Paying too much and being happy about it: Existence, causes, and consequences of tariff-choice biases. *Journal of Marketing Research*, 43(2):212–223, 2006.

[13] H. Lejmi-Riahi, F. Kebair, and L. B. Said. Agent decision-making under uncertainty: Towards a new e-bdi agent architecture based on immediate and expected emotions.

[14] L. Luo, S. Zhou, W. Cai, M. Lees, and M. Y.-H. Low. Modeling human-like decision making for virtual agents in time-critical situations. In *Cyberworlds (CW), 2010 International Conference on*, pages 360–367. IEEE, 2010.

[15] N. Marques, F. Melo, S. Mascarenhas, J. Dias, R. Prada, and A. Paiva. Towards agents with human-like decisions under uncertainty. In *The Annual Meeting of the Cognitive Science Society*, 2013.

[16] D. McFadden. Economic choices. *American Economic Review*, pages 351–378, 2001.

[17] G. A. Miller. The magical number seven, plus or minus two: some limits on our capacity for processing information. *Psychological Review*, 63(2):81, 1956.

[18] J. Mullahy. Specification and testing of some modified count data models. *Journal of Econometrics*, 33(3):341–365, 1986.

[19] J. W. Payne, J. R. Bettman, and E. J. Johnson. *The adaptive decision maker*. Cambridge University Press, 1993.

[20] W. Samuelson and R. Zeckhauser. Status quo bias in decision making. *Journal of Risk and Uncertainty*, 1(1):7–59, 1988.

[21] L. P. Sugrue, G. S. Corrado, and W. T. Newsome. Matching behavior and the representation of value in the parietal cortex. *Science*, 304(5678):1782–1787, 2004.

[22] R. S. Sutton and A. G. Barto. *Introduction to Reinforcement Learning*. MIT Press, 1998.

[23] R. H. Thaler and C. R. Sunstein. *Nudge: Improving decisions about health, wealth, and happiness*. Yale University Press, 2008.

[24] K. E. Train. *Discrete Choice Methods with Simulation*. Cambridge university press, 2009.

[25] A. Tversky and D. Kahneman. Judgment under uncertainty: Heuristics and biases. *science*, 185(4157):1124–1131, 1974.

[26] J. Von Neumann and O. Morgenstern. Theory of games and economic behavior (2nd rev). 1947.

[27] J. R. Wright and K. Leyton-Brown. Beyond equilibrium: Predicting human behavior in normal-form games. In *AAAI*, 2010.

[28] Q. Yu and D. Terzopoulos. A decision network framework for the behavioral animation of virtual humans. In *Proceedings of the 2007 ACM SIGGRAPH/Eurographics symposium on Computer animation*, pages 119–128. Eurographics Association, 2007.

[29] S. Zhang and J. Y. Angela. Forgetful bayes and myopic planning: Human learning and decision-making in a bandit setting. In *Advances in Neural Information Processing Systems*, pages 2607–2615, 2013.

DJ-MC: A Reinforcement-Learning Agent for Music Playlist Recommendation

Elad Liebman
Computer Science Department
The University of Texas at Austin
eladlieb@cs.utexas.edu

Maytal Saar-Tsechansky
McCombs School of Business
The University of Texas at Austin
maytal@mail.utexas.edu

Peter Stone
Computer Science Department
The University of Texas at Austin
pstone@cs.utexas.edu

ABSTRACT

In recent years, there has been growing focus on the study of automated recommender systems. Music recommendation systems serve as a prominent domain for such works, both from an academic and a commercial perspective. A fundamental aspect of music perception is that music is experienced in temporal context and in sequence. In this work we present DJ-MC, a novel reinforcement-learning framework for music recommendation that does not recommend songs individually but rather song sequences, or playlists, based on a model of preferences for both songs and song transitions. The model is learned online and is uniquely adapted for each listener. To reduce exploration time, DJ-MC exploits user feedback to initialize a model, which it subsequently updates by reinforcement. We evaluate our framework with human participants using both real song and playlist data. Our results indicate that DJ-MC's ability to recommend sequences of songs provides a significant improvement over more straightforward approaches, which do not take transitions into account.

1. INTRODUCTION

Music is one of the most widespread and prevalent expressions of human culture. It has accompanied the human experience throughout history, and the enjoyment of music is one of the most common human activities. As an activity, music listening sessions commonly span over a sequence of songs, rather than a single song in isolation. Importantly, it is well established that music is experienced in temporal context and in sequence [11,12]. This phenomenon not only underlies the notion of structure in music (as in the canonical sonata form [9]), but also implies that the pleasure one derives from a complete song is directly affected by its relative position in a sequence. This notion also underlies the manner in which DJs construct playlists [8], and indeed, research on automated playlist construction has aimed to produce generally appealing playlists [10, 19]. However, such works have not considered the construction of personalized playlists tailored to *individual* users' preferences.

In the field of recommender systems, [1] music has been of particular interest, both academically [1,18] and commercially [3]. Pandora, Jango, and Last.fm are some examples of popular contemporary commercial applications. To the best of our knowledge, however, research on *personalized* music recommendations has focused mostly on predicting users' preferences over *individual* songs, rather than song *sequences*.

Overall, there has been little effort to relate learning individual listener preferences with holistic playlist generation. In this paper, we aim to bridge this gap and present DJ-MC, a novel framework for *adaptive, personalized* music playlist recommendation. In this framework, we formulate the playlist recommendation problem as a sequential decision making task, and borrow tools from the reinforcement learning literature to learn preferences over both songs and song transitions on the fly. Our contributions are as follows. First, we formulate the problem of selecting which sequence of songs to play as a Markov Decision Process, and demonstrate the potential effectiveness of a reinforcement-learning based approach in a new practical domain. Second, we test the hypothesis that sequence does have a significant effect on listener experience through a user study. Third, we show empirically that DJ-MC's account for song order allows it to outperform recommendations based strictly on individual song preferences, implying such preferences can be learned efficiently with limited user information. In particular, we demonstrate that starting with no knowledge of a new user's preferences, DJ-MC is able to generate personalized song sequences within a single listening session of just 25–50 songs.

The remainder of this paper is organized as follows. In Section 2 we discuss our reformulation of playlist generation as a reinforcement learning task. In Section 3 we describe how the DJ-MC agent models different aspects of the MDP for the purpose of learning. In Section 4 we present the real-world data sources we used in this paper. In Section 5 we present the full DJ-MC agent architecture. In Section 6 we discuss the performance of DJ-MC in simulation, and in Section 7 we present the results of applying DJ-MC in a user study with human participants. In Section 8 we discuss related work and put our contributions in a broader context, and finally in Section 9 we summarize and discuss our results.

Appears in: *Proceedings of the 14th International Conference on Autonomous Agents and Multiagent Systems (AAMAS 2015), Bordini, Elkind, Weiss, Yolum (eds.), May 4–8, 2015, Istanbul, Turkey.*

2. REINFORCEMENT LEARNING FRAMEWORK

We consider the adaptive playlist generation problem formally as an episodic Markov Decision Process (MDP). An episodic MDP is a tuple (S, A, P, R, T) where S is the set of states; A the set of actions, $P : S\times A\times S \rightarrow [0,1]$ is the state transition probability function where $P(s,a,s') = r$ denotes the probability of transitioning from state s to state s' when taking action a. $R : S \times A \rightarrow \mathbb{R}$ is the state-action reward function, where $R(s,a) = r$ means that taking action a from state s will yield reward r. T is the set of terminal states, which end the episode.

For the purposes of our specific application, consider a finite set of n musical tracks (songs) $\mathcal{M} = \{a_1, a_2, \ldots, a_n\}$ and assume that playlists are of length k. Our MDP formulation of the music playlist recommendation task is then as follows.

- To capture the complex dependency of listener experience on the entire sequence of songs heard, a Markov state must include an ordered list of all prior songs in the playlist. Thus, the state space S is the entire ordered sequence of songs played, $S = \{(a_1, a_2, \ldots, a_i)|1 \leq i \leq k; \forall j \leq i, a_j \in \mathcal{M}\}$.

  That is, a state $s \in S$ is an ordered tuple of songs ranging in length from 0 when choosing the first song of the playlist to k when the playlist is complete.

- The set of actions A is the selection of the next song to play, $a_k \in A$. This means that the action space is exactly the set of songs: $A = \mathcal{M}$.

- These definitions of S and A induce a deterministic transition function P. As such, we can use the shorthand notation $P(s,a) = s'$ to indicate that when taking action a in state s, the probability of transitioning to s' is 1, and to $s'' \neq s'$ is 0. Specifically, $P((a_1, a_2, \ldots, a_i), a^*) = (a_1, a_2, \ldots, a_i, a^*)$.

- $R(s,a)$ is the utility (or pleasure) the current listener derives from hearing song a when in state s. Note that this formulation implies that each listener induces a unique reward function. A key challenge addressed in this paper is enabling efficient learning of R for a new listener.

- $T = \{(a_1, a_2, \ldots m_k)\}$: the set of playlists of length k.

Solving an MDP typically refers to finding a policy $\pi : S \rightarrow A$ such that from any given state s, executing action $\pi(s)$ and then acting optimally (following the optimal policy π^*) thereafter, yields the highest (expected) sum of rewards over the length of the episode. In our case, since P is deterministic, $\pi*$ corresponds to the single sequence of songs that would be most pleasing to the listener.[1] However, we assume that the listener's reward function R is initially unknown. We consider the fundamental challenge of playlist generation as being efficiently modeling R.

In particular, in the reinforcement learning literature, there are two high-level approaches to approximating (learning) π^*: model-free and model-based. *Model-free* approaches learn the value of taking an action a from state s directly. Typical approaches, such as Q-learning and SARSA [21] are computationally efficient and elegant, but require a lot of experiential data to learn. *Model-based* approaches alternatively learn the transition and reward functions (P and R) so as to be able to *simulate* arbitrary amounts of experiential data in order to find an approximate solution to the MDP in an approach that can be thought of as *planning* through forward lookahead search. Compared to model-free methods, most model-based algorithms are significantly more computationally expensive, especially if they re-solve the MDP whenever the model changes. However, in many applications, including playlist recommendation, where data is considerably more scarce than computation, this tradeoff of computational expense for data efficiency is a good one. We therefore adopt a model-based learning approach in this paper (see Sections 3 and 5 for details).

In the MDP defined above, the transition function P is trivially known. Therefore the only unknown element of the model necessary for model-based learning is R, the current listener's utility (enjoyment) function. Indeed modeling R in such a way that generalizes aggressively and accurately across both songs and song transitions is the biggest technical challenge in this work. Consider that even for a moderately sized music corpus of 10^3 songs, and for playlist horizons of 10 songs, the size of the state space alone would be 10^{30}. It is impractical for a learning agent to even explore any appreciable size of this state space, let alone learn the listener's utility for each possible state (indeed our objective is to learn a new user's preferences and generate a personalized song sequence within a single listening session of 25–50 songs). Therefore to learn efficiently, the agent must internally represent states and actions in such a way that enables generalization of the listener's preferences.

Section 3 presents how DJ-MC compactly represents R by 1) generalizing across songs via a factored representation; and 2) separating R into two distinct components, one dependent only on the current song (a), and one dependent on the transition from the past history of songs to the current song (s to a). Recognizing that DJ-MC's specific representation of R is just one of many possible options, we also evaluate the extent to which the representational choices made are effective for generalization and learning.

3. MODELING

As motivated in the previous section, learning a listener's preference function over a large set of songs and sequences requires a compact representation of songs that is still rich enough to capture meaningful differences in how they are perceived by listeners. To this end, we represent each song as a vector of song *descriptors*.

Specifically DJ-MC uses spectral auditory descriptors that include details about the spectral fingerprint of the song, its rhythmic characteristics, its overall loudness, and their change over time. We find that these descriptors enable a great deal of flexibility (for instance, in capturing similarities between songs from vastly different backgrounds, or the ability to model songs in unknown languages). Nonetheless, our framework is in principle robust to using any sufficiently expressive vector of song descriptors. Section 3.1 specifies in detail the descriptors used by DJ-MC.

In order to further speed up learning, we make a second key representational choice, namely that the reward function R corresponding to a listener can be factored as the sum of two distinct components: 1) the listener's preference over *songs* in isolation, $R_s : A \rightarrow \mathbb{R}$ and 2) his preference over

[1]We consider the problem as finding a single playlist in isolation, ignoring the fact that the same listener may not want to hear similar sequences repeatedly. In practice, the stochasticity of our approach makes it exceedingly unlikely that the same sequence would be presented to a given listener multiple times, as will become clear below.

Descriptors	Descriptor Indices
10th and 90th percentiles of tempo	1,2
average and variance of tempo	3,4
10th and 90th percentiles of loudness	5,6
average and variance of loudness	7,8
pitch dominance	9–20
variance of pitch dominance	21
average timbre weights	22–33
variance in timbre	34

Table 1: Descriptors used for song representation. Tempo data was based on beat durations. Thus the first descriptor is the 10th percentile of beat durations in the song. Loudness was straightforwardly obtained from amplitude. Pitch dominance weights each of the 12 possible pitch classes based on their presence in the song averaged over time. Timbre weights are the average weights of the 12 basis functions used by the Echo Nest analysis tool to capture the spectro-temporal landscape of the song.

transitions from past songs to a new song, $R_t : S \times A \to \mathbb{R}$. That is, $R(s,a) = R_s(a) + R_t(s,a)$.

Section 3.2 describes DJ-MC's reward model in detail. Section 3.3 then evaluates the extent to which the chosen descriptors are able to differentiate meaningfully between song sequences that are clearly good and clearly bad.

3.1 Modeling Songs

As motivated above, we assume each song can be factored as a vector of scalar descriptors that reflect details about the spectral fingerprint of the song, its rhythmic characteristics, its overall loudness, and their change over time. For the purpose of our experiments, we used the acoustic features in the Million Song Dataset representation [5] to extract 12 meta-descriptors, out of which 2 are 12-dimensional, resulting in a 34-dimensional song descriptor vector. The complete set of descriptors is summarized in Table 1.

3.2 Modeling The Listener Reward Function

Despite an abundance of literature on the psychology of human musical perception [22], there is no canonical model of the human listening experience. In this work we model listening as being dependent not only on preferences over the descriptors laid out above, but also over feature *transitions*. This model is fairly consistent with many observed properties of human perception, such as the stochastic dependence on remembering earlier events, and evidence of working memory having greater emphasis on the present [6,11,22].

We now proceed to specify the two components of R: R_s and R_t.

3.2.1 Listener Reward Function over Songs R_s

To model R_s, we use a sparse encoding of the song descriptors to generate a binary feature vector. R_s is then a linear function of this feature vector: that is, we assume that each feature contributes independently to the listener's utility for the song.

Specifically, for each song descriptor, we collect statistics over the entire music database, and quantize the descriptor into 10-percentile bins. Following standard reinforcement learning notation, we denote the feature vector for song a as $\theta_s(a)$. It is a vector of size $\#bins \times \#descriptors = 10 \times 34 = 340$ consisting of $\#descriptors$ containing 1's at coordinates that correspond to the bins song a populates, and 0 otherwise, meaning $\theta_s(a)$ behaves as an indicator function (the weight of $\theta_s(a)$ will be 34 overall).

For each feature, we assume the listener has a value representing the pleasure they obtains from songs with that feature active. These values are represented as a weight vector $\phi_s(u)$. Thus $R_s(a) = \phi_s(u) \cdot \theta_s(a)$. The parameters of $\phi_s(u)$ must be learned afresh for each new user.

3.2.2 Listener Reward Function over Transitions R_t

A main premise of this work is that in addition to the actual songs played, a listener's enjoyment depends on the *sequence* in which they are played. To capture this dependence, we assume that

$$E[R_t((a_1,\ldots,a_{t-1}),a_t)] = \sum_{i=1}^{t-1} \frac{1}{i^2} r_t(a_{t-i}, a_t)$$

where $r_t(a_i,a_j)$ represents the listener's utility for hearing song a_j sometime after having heard a_i. The term $\frac{1}{i^2}$ represents the notion that a song that was played i songs in the past has a probability of $\frac{1}{i}$ of affecting the transition reward (i.e. being "remembered"), and when it does, its impact decays by a second factor of $\frac{1}{i}$ (its impact decays over time).

It remains only to specify the song to song transition reward function $R_t(a_i,a_j)$. Like R_s, we can describe R_t as a linear function of a sparse binary feature vector: $R_t(a_i,a_j) = \phi_t(u) \cdot \theta_t(a_i,a_j)$ where $\phi_t(u)$ is a user-dependent weight vector and θ_t is a binary feature vector.

Were we to consider the transitions between all 340 features of both a_i and a_j, θ_t would need to be of length $340^2 > 100{,}000$. For the sake of learnability, we limit θ_t and ϕ_t to only represent transitions between 10-percentile bins of the same song descriptors. That is, there is for each of the 34 song descriptors, there are 100 features, one of which is 1 and 99 of which are 0, indicating which pair of 10-percentile bins were present in songs a_i and a_j. Therefore, overall, θ_t consists of 3,400 binary features, 34 of which are 1's.

Clearly, this representation is limiting in that it cannot capture the joint dependence of listener utility on transitions between multiple song descriptors. Especially for the pitch class features, these are likely to be relevant. We make this tradeoff in the interest of enabling learning from relatively few examples. Empirical results indicate that this representation captures enough of real peoples' transition reward to make a difference in song recommendation quality.

Like $\phi_s(u)$, the parameters of $\phi_t(u)$ must be learned afresh for each new user. Thus all in all, there are 3740 weight parameters to learn for each listener.

With even that many parameters, it is infeasible to experience songs and transitions with all of them active in just 25 songs. However DJ-MC is able to leverage knowledge of even a few transition examples to plan a future sequence of songs that is biased in favor of the positive ones and against the negative ones.

3.3 Expressiveness of the Listener Model

This representation of the listener's utility function as a 3740-dimensional sparse binary feature vector is just one of many possible representations. A necessary property of a useful representation is that its features are able to differentiate between commonly perceived "good" vs. "bad" sequences, and the DJ-MC agent internally relies on this property when modeling the listener reward function. To evaluate whether our features are expressive enough to allow this differentiation, we examine the transition profile for two types of transitions, "poor" vs. "fair", both derived from the same population of songs. We generate "fair" transitions by sampling pairs of songs that appeared in an actual sequence. We generate "poor" transitions by interleaving songs so that each one is distinctly different in character (for instance, a fast, loud track followed by a soft piece). The difference between the two profiles can be seen in Figure *1*. More definitive evidence in favor of the adequacy of our representation is provided by the successful empirical application of our framework, discussed in Section 7.

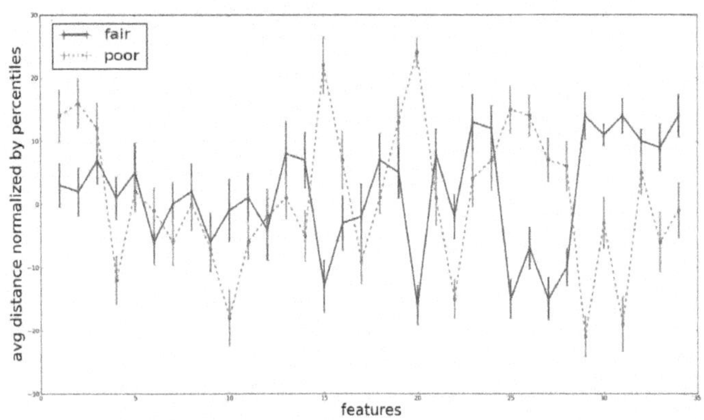

Figure 1: **Example of fair vs. poor transition profiles, based on the same set of 20 songs. The plot shows the average transition delta for each feature. Both the fair transitions and the poor ones are constructed from the same core set of 20 songs taken from 5 different albums. In the case of fair transitions, we maintain the original order. In the case of poor transitions, the albums are randomly interleaved. The results indicate that qualitatively different sequences are indeed distinguishable in our feature model. In this specific example, 19 of the 34 features are discriminative (confidence intervals do not overlap). We expect different features to be discriminative for different transition profiles.**

4. DATA

A significant component of this work involves extracting real-world data for both songs and playlists to rigorously test our approach. In this section we discuss the different data sources we used to model both songs and playlists. For songs, we relied on the Million Song Dataset [5], a freely-available collection of audio features and metadata for a million contemporary popular music tracks. The dataset covers 44,745 different artists and 10^6 different tracks. All the features described in Table *1* are derived from this representation. An example of the audio input for a single track is provided in Figure *2*. It should be noted that our agent architecture (described in detail in Section 5) is agnostic to the choice of a specific song corpus, and we could have easily used a different song archive.

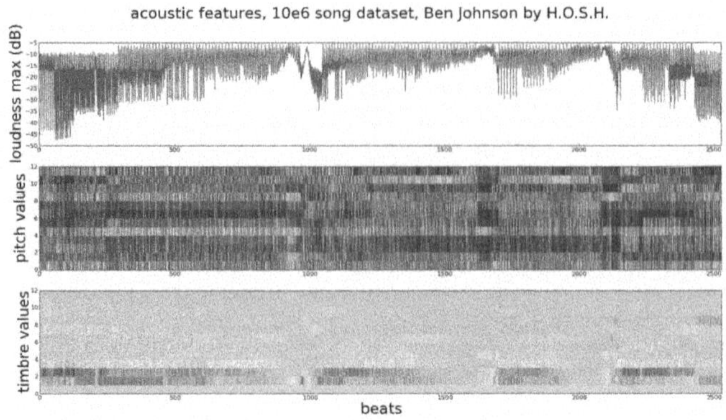

Figure 2: **Example of loudness, pitch and timbre data for an example track over time (time units are in beats). Loudness is in dB, pitch measurements are represented as a vector of 12 values between 0 and 1 representing dominance per pitch class. Timbre is approximated as the decomposition of the spectro-temporal surface of the song according to 12 pre-computed basis functions.**

To initially test our approach in simulation (a process described in detail in Section 6), we also needed real playlists to extract song transition data from. A good source of playlists needs to be sufficiently rich and diverse, but also reflect real playlists "in the wild". In this paper, we used two separate sources. The first, the Yes.com archive, is corpus collected by Chen et al. [7]. These playlists and related tag data were respectively crawled from Yes.com and Last.fm. Chen et al. harvested data between December 2010 and May 2011, yielding 75,262 songs and 2,840,553 transitions. The second source is the Art of the Mix Archive, collected by Berenzweig et al [4]. Berenzweig et al. gathered 29,000 playlists from The Art of the Mix (`www.artofthemix.org`), a repository and community center for playlist hobbyists. These playlists were (ostensibly) generated by real individual users, rather than a commercial radio DJ or a recommendation system, making this corpus particularly appealing for listener modeling.

5. DJ-MC

In this section we introduce DJ-MC, a novel reinforcement learning approach to a playlist-oriented, personalized music recommendation system. The DJ-MC agent architecture contains two major components: learning of the listener parameters (ϕ_s and ϕ_t) and planning a sequence of songs. The learning part is in itself divided into two parts - initialization and learning on the fly. Initialization is critical if we wish to engage listeners quickly without losing their interest before the agent has converged on a good enough model. Learning on the fly enables the system to continually improve until it converges on a reliable model for that listening session. In simulation, we assume the user is able to specify an initial list of songs that they like (this is similar to most initialization practices used by commercial music recommendation systems). However, in Section 7 we show this step can be replaced with random exploration, while still reaching compelling results at the exploitation stage.

The planning step enables the selection of the next appropriate song to play. As pointed out in Section 2, given

Algorithm 1 Initialize Song Preferences R_s

```
1: Input: Song corpus, M
   Number of preferred songs to be provided by listener, k_s
2: initialize all coordinates of φ_s to 1/(k_s + #bins)
3: preferredSet = {a_1, ..., a_{k_s}} (chosen by the listener)
4: for i = 1 to k_s do
5:     φ_s = φ_s + 1/(k_s+1) · θ_s(a_i)
6: end for
```

Algorithm 2 Initialize Transition Preferences R_t

```
1: Input: Song corpus M
   Number of transitions to poll the listener, k_t
2: initialize all coordinates of φ_t to 1/(k_t + #bins)
3: Select upper median of M, M*, based on R_s
4: δ = 10th percentile of all pairwise distances between
   songs in M
5: representative set C = δ -medoids (M*)
6: song_0 = choose a song randomly from C
7: for i = 1 to k_t do
8:     song_i ← chosen by the listener from C
9:     φ_t = φ_t + 1/(k_t+1) · θ_t(song_{i-1}, song_i)
10: end for
```

the sheer scope of the learning problem, even after various abstraction steps, solving the MDP exactly is intractable. For this reason we must approximate the solution. From a practical perspective, from any given state, the objective is to find a song that is "good enough" to play next. For this purpose we utilize Monte Carlo Tree Search.

In Sections 5.1 and 5.2 we describe the initialization steps taken by DJ-MC. In Section 5.3 we describe the core of the learning algorithm, which learns on the fly. in Section 5.4 we describe the planning step. The full agent pseudocode is provided in Algorithm 5.

5.1 Learning Initial Song Preferences

To initialize the listener's song model, DJ-MC polls the listener for his k_s favorite songs in the database and passes them as input to Algorithm 1. As a form of smoothing (or of maintaining a uniform prior), each element of $\phi_s(u)$ is initialized to $1/(k_s + \#bins)$, where $\#bins$ is the granularity of discretization of each song descriptor – in our case 10 (line 2). Then for each favorite song a, $\phi_s(u)$ is incremented by $1/(k + \#bins) \cdot \theta_s(a)$ (line 5). At the end of this process, the weights in $\phi_s(u)$ corresponding to each song descriptor sum to 1.

5.2 Learning Initial Transition Preferences

In the second stage, the listener is queried for preferences regarding transitions, following the procedure in Algorithm 2. As in the case of initializing song preferences, the predicted value of a transition from bin i to bin j for each feature is initialized to $1/(k_t + \#bins)$ where k_t is the number of transitions queried and $\#bins$ is the number of feature transition bins – in our case 100 (line 2).

We wouldn't want to query transitions for too small a subset of preferred songs, because that won't necessarily reveal enough about the preferred transitions. For this reason we explore the preferences of the listener in a targeted fashion, by presenting them with different possible transitions that encapsulate the variety in the dataset, and directly asking which of a possible set of options the listener would prefer. On the other hand, we would also like to exclude regions in the search space where expected song rewards are low.

To accomplish both ends, DJ-MC first chooses a 50-% subset of the songs $\mathcal{M}^*$ of the song corpus $\mathcal{M}$ which, based on its song rewards model, obtains the highest song reward R_s (line 3). Then, DJ-MC queries transition preferences over this upper median of songs by eliciting user feedback. It does so by applying the δ-medoids algorithm, a novel method for representative selection (line 5) [13]. This algorithm returns a compact but close-fitting subset of representatives such that no sample in the dataset is more than a parameter δ away from a representative, thus providing a diverse sample of the upper median of songs. δ is initialized to be the 10-th percentile of the distance histogram between all pairs of songs in the database (line 4). We denote the representative subset $\mathcal{C}$. To model transitions, DJ-MC chooses songs from $\mathcal{C}$, and queries the listener which song $a_i \in \mathcal{C}$ they would like to listen to next (line 8).[2] For modeling purposes, we assume the listener chooses the next song he would prefer by simulating the listening experience, including the non-deterministic history-dependent transition reward, and choosing the one with the maximal total reward. DJ-MC then proceeds to update the characteristics of this transition, by increasing the weight of transition features by $1/(k + \#bins)$ (line 9) , similarly to how it updated the model for song preferences (so again, the weights of each individual descriptor sum up to 1). The full details of the algorithm are described in Algorithm 2.

5.3 Learning on the fly

After initialization, DJ-MC begins playing songs for the listener, requesting feedback, and updating ϕ_s and ϕ_t accordingly. For ease of use DJ-MC does not require separate ratings for songs and transitions. Rather, it can assign credit to each component individually from a single unified reward signal. It does so by computing the relative contributions of the song and transition rewards to the total reward as predicted by its model. This update procedure is presented in Algorithm 3.

Specifically, let r be the reward the user assigns after hearing song a in state s, and $\bar{r}$ be the average rewards assigned by this listener so far (line 4). We define $r_{incr} = log(\frac{r}{\bar{r}})$ (line 5). This factor determines both direction and magnitude for the update (negative if $r < \bar{r}$, positive otherwise, and greater the farther r is from average). Let $R_s(a_i)$ and $R_t(a_{i-1}, a_i)$ be the expected song and transition rewards yielded by our model, respectively. DJ-MC uses the proportions of these values to set weights for credit assignment (this is essentially a maximum likelihood estimate). Concretely, we define the update weights for the song and transition to be

$w_s = \frac{R_s(a_i)}{R_s(a_i)+R_t(a_{i-1},a_i)}$ and

$w_t = \frac{R_t(a_{i-1},a_i)}{R_s(a_i)+R_t(a_{i-1},a_i)}$ respectively (lines 6-7).

Finally, the agent uses the credit assignment values determined at the previous step to partition the given reward between song and transition weights, and update their values (lines 8-9). Following this step, DJ-MC normalizes both the song and transition reward models so that the weights for each feature sum up to 1 (line 10). This update proce-

[2] If $\mathcal{C}$ is too large, it can be replaced at this step with a smaller subset, depending on the parameters of the system and the size of $\mathcal{C}$.

Algorithm 3 Model Update

1: **Input:** Song corpus, $\mathcal{M}$
Planned playlist duration, K
2: **for** $i \in \{1, \dots, K\}$ **do**
3: Use Algorithm 4 to select song a_i, obtaining reward r_i
4: let $\bar{r} = average(\{r_1, \dots, r_{i-1}\})$
5: $r_{incr} = log(r_i/\bar{r})$
weight update:
6: $w_s = \frac{R_s(a_i)}{R_s(a_i)+R_t(a_{i-1},a_i)}$
7: $w_t = \frac{R_t(a_{i-1},a_i)}{R_s(a_i)+R_t(a_{i-1},a_i)}$
8: $\phi_s = \frac{i}{i+1} \cdot \phi_s + \frac{1}{i+1} \cdot \theta_s \cdot w_s \cdot r_{incr}$
9: $\phi_t = \frac{i}{i+1} \cdot \phi_t + \frac{1}{i+1} \cdot \theta_t \cdot w_t \cdot r_{incr}$
10: Per $d \in$ descriptors, normalize ϕ_s^d, ϕ_t^d
(where ϕ_x^d denotes coordinates in ϕ_x corresponding to 10-percentile bins of descriptor d)
11: **end for**

dure as a whole can be perceived as a temporal-difference update with an attenuating learning rate, which balances how much the model "trusts" the previous history of observations compared to the newly obtained signal. It also guarantees convergence over time.

5.4 Planning

Equipped with the listener's learned song and transition utility functions R_s and R_t, which determine the MDP reward function $R(s,a) = R_s(a) + R_t(s,a)$, DJ-MC employs a tree-search heuristic for planning, similar to that used in [23]. As in the case of initializing the transition weights (Algorithm 2), DJ-MC chooses a subset of 50-percent of the songs in the database, which, based on R_s, obtain the highest song reward (line 2). At each point, it simulates a trajectory of future songs selected at random from this "high-yield" subset (lines 7-11). The DJ-MC architecture then uses R_s and R_t to calculate the expected payoff of the song trajectory (line 12). It repeats this process as many times as possible, finding the randomly generated trajectory which yields the highest expected payoff (lines 13-16). DJ-MC then selects the first song of this trajectory to be the next song played (line 19). It uses just the first song and not the whole sequence because as modeling noise accumulates, its estimates become farther off. Furthermore, as we discussed in Subsection 5.3, DJ-MC actively adjusts ϕ_s and ϕ_t online based on user feedback using Algorithm 3. As a result, replanning at every step is advisable.

If the song space is too large or the search time is limited, it may be infeasible to sample trajectories starting with all possible songs. To mitigate this problem, DJ-MC exploits the structure of the song space by clustering songs according to song types (line 9).[3] It then plans over abstract song types rather than concrete songs, thus drastically reducing search complexity. Once finding a promising trajectory, DJ-MC selects a concrete representative from the first song type in the trajectory to play (line 18).

Combining initialization, learning on the fly, and planning, the full DJ-MC agent architecture is presented in Algorithm 5.

[3] In principle, any clustering algorithm could work. For our experiments, we use the canonical k-means algorithm [14].

Algorithm 4 Plan via Tree Search

1: **Input:** Song corpus $\mathcal{M}$, planning horizon q
2: Select upper median of $\mathcal{M}$, $\mathcal{M}^*$, based on R_s
3: *BestTrajectory* = *null*
4: *HighestExpectedPayoff* = $-\infty$
5: **while** computational power not exhausted **do**
6: *trajectory* = []
7: **for** 1.... q **do**
8: *song* $\leftarrow$ selected randomly from $\mathcal{M}^*$
(avoiding repetitions)
9: optional:
song_type $\leftarrow$ selected randomly from *song_types*($\mathcal{M}^*$)
(avoiding repetitions, song_types(·) reduces the set to clusters)
10: add *song* to *trajectory*
11: **end for**
12: expectedPayoffForTrajectory = $R_s(song_1) + \sum_{i=2}^{q}(R_t((song_1, \dots, song_{i-1}), song_i) + R_s(song_i))$
13: **if** expectedPayoffForTrajectory > HighestExpectedPayoff **then**
14: HighestExpectedPayoff = expectedPayoffForTrajectory
15: *BestTrajectory* = *trajectory*
16: **end if**
17: **end while**
18: optional: if planning over song types, replace *BestTrajectory*[0] with concrete song.
19: return *BestTrajectory*[0]

Algorithm 5 Full DJ-MC Architecture

1: **Input:** $\mathcal{M}$ - song corpus, K - planned playlist duration, k_s - number of steps for song preference initialization, k_t - the number of steps for transition preference initialization

Initialization:
2: Call Algorithm 1 with corpus $\mathcal{M}$ and parameter k_s to initialize song weights ϕ_s.
3: Call Algorithm 2 with corpus $\mathcal{M}$ and parameter k_t to initialize transition weights ϕ_t.

Planning and Model Update:
4: Run Algorithm 3 with corpus $\mathcal{M}$ and parameter K
(Algorithm 3 iteratively selects the next song to play by calling algorithm 4, and then updates R_s and R_t. This is repeated for K steps.)

6. EVALUATION IN SIMULATION

Due to the time and difficulty of human testing, especially in listening sessions lasting hours, it is important to first validate DJ-MC in simulation. To this end, we tested DJ-MC on a large set of listener models built using real playlists made by individuals and included in The Art of the Mix archive. For each experiment, we sample a 1000-song corpus from the Million Song Dataset.

One of the issues in analyzing the performance of DJ-MC was the nonexistence of suitable competing approaches to compare against. Possible alternatives are either commercial and proprietary, meaning their mechanics are unknown, or they do not fit the paradigm of online interaction with an unknown individual user. Still, we would like our evaluation to give convincing evidence that DJ-MC is capable of learning not only song preferences but also transition preferences to a reasonable degree, and that by taking transition into account DJ-MC is able to provide listeners with a significantly more enjoyable experience (see Section 8 for related work).

In order to measure the improvement offered by our agent, we compare DJ-MC against two alternative baselines: an agent that chooses songs randomly, and a greedy agent that always plays the song with the highest song reward, as determined by Algorithm 1. As discussed in the introduction, we expect that the greedy agent will do quite well since song reward is the primary factor for listeners. However we find that by learning preferences over transitions, DJ-MC yields a significant improvement over the greedy approach.

To represent different listener types, we generate 10 different playlist clusters by using k-means clustering on the playlists (represented as artist frequency vectors). We generate 1000 different listeners by first sampling a random cluster, second sampling 70% of the song transition pairs in that cluster, and third inputting this data to Algorithms 1 and 2 to train the listener's song and transition weights. For the experiments reported here we used a playlist length of 30 songs, a planning horizon of 10 songs ahead, a computational budget of 100 random trajectories for planning, a query size of 10 songs for song reward modeling and 10 songs for transition rewards. As shown in Figure *3*, DJ-MC performs significantly better than the baselines, most noticeably in the beginning of the session.

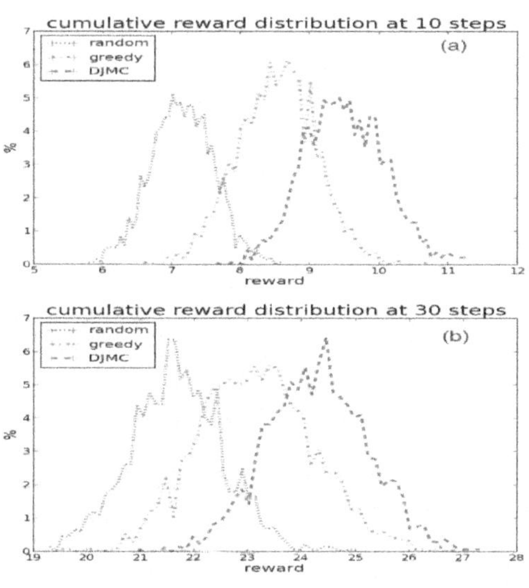

Figure 3: Cumulative reward histograms for playlists of length 10 (*a*) **and** 30 (*b*)**, with listeners based on real playlist data. The DJ-MC agent outperforms both random and greedy agents, particularly for the first** 10 **songs. Results are highly significant (*p*-value** $<< 0.01$**).**

7. EVALUATION ON HUMAN LISTENERS

While using simulated listeners allows for extensive analysis, ultimately the true measure of DJ-MC is whether it succeeds when applied on real listeners. To test whether this is the case, we ran two rounds of lab experiments with *47* human participants. The participants pool was comprised of graduate students at the McCombs School of Business at the University of Texas at Austin.

7.1 Experimental Setup

Each participant interacted with a playlist generator. As a song corpus we used songs with corresponding Million Song Dataset entries that also appeared in Rolling Stone Magazine's list of 500 greatest albums of all time.[4] To keep the duration of the experiment reasonable, each song played for *60* seconds before transitioning (with a cross-fade) to the next song. After each song the participants were asked, via a graphic user interface, to specify whether they liked or disliked the played song, as well as the transition to it. This provided us with separate (albeit not independent) signals for song quality and song transition quality to test how well DJ-MC actually did. Since asking users for their selection of 10 songs was impractical in this setting, in order to seed the learning the agent explored randomly for *25* songs, and then began exploiting the learned model (while continuing to learn) for *25* songs. The participants were divided into *2* groups - *24* interacted with the greedy baseline, whereas *23* interacted with DJ-MC. Though we expect the greedy agent to perform well based on song preferences only, we test whether DJ-MC's attention to transition preferences improves performance.

7.2 Results

Since our sample of human participants is not large, and given the extremely noisy nature of the input signals, and the complexity of the learning problem, it should come as no surprise that a straightforward analysis of the results can be difficult and inconclusive. To overcome this issue, we take advantage of bootstrap resampling, which is a highly common tool in the statistics literature to estimate underlying distributions using small samples and perform significance tests.

At each stage we treat a "like" signal for either the transition or the song as $+1$ reward value vs. 0 for a "dislike". We continue to reconstruct an approximate distribution of the aggregate reward for each condition by sampling subsets of *8* participants with repetition for $N = 250000$ times and estimating the average reward value for the subset. Figures *4a* and *4c* compare the reward distributions for the greedy and DJ-MC agents from song reward and transition reward respectively, during the first 25 episodes. Since both act identically (randomly) during those episodes, the distributions are very close (and indeed testing the hypothesis that the two distributions have means more than 0.25 apart by offsetting the distributions and running an appropriate t-test does not show significance).

During the exploitation stage (episodes 26-50), the agents behave differently. With regards to song reward, we see that both algorithms are again comparable (and better in expectation than in the exploration stage, implying some knowledge of preference has been learned), as seen in Figure *4b*. In Figure *4d*, however, we see that DJ-MC significantly outperforms the greedy algorithm in terms of transition reward, as expected, since the greedy algorithm does not learn transition preferences. The results are statistically significant

[4]`http://www.rollingstone.com/music/lists/500-greatest-albums-of-all-time-20120531`

using an unpaired t-test ($p << 0.01$), and are also significant when testing to see if the difference is greater than 0.25.

Interestingly, the average transition reward is higher for the greedy algorithm at the exploitation stage (apparent by higher average reward comparing Figures *4a* and *4b*). From this result we can deduce that either people are more likely to enjoy a transition if they enjoy the song, or that focusing on given tastes immediately reduces the "risk" of poor transitions by limiting the song space. All in all, these findings, made with the interaction of human listeners, corroborate our findings based on simulation, that reasoning about transition preferences gives DJ-MC a small but significant boost in performance compared to only reasoning about song preferences.

8. RELATED WORK

Though not much work has attempted to model playlists directly, there has been substantial research on modeling similarity between artists and between songs. Platt et al. [20] use semantic tags to learn a Gaussian process kernel function between pairs of songs. Weston et al. [25] learn an embedding in a shared space of social tags, acoustic features and artist entities by optimizing an evaluation metric for various music retrieval tasks. Aizenberg et al. [2] model radio stations as probability distributions of items to be played, embedded in an inner-product space, using real playlist histories for training.

In the academic literature, several recent papers have tried to tackle the issue of playlist prediction. Maillet et al. [15] approach the playlist prediction problem from a supervised binary classification perspective, with pairs of songs in sequence as positive examples and random pairs as negative ones. Mcfee and Lanckriet [16] consider playlists as a natural language induced over songs, training a bigram model for transitions and observing playlists as Markov chains. Chen et al. [7] take on a similar Markov approach, treating playlists as Markov chains in some latent space, and learn a metric representation (or multiple representations) for each song in that space, without relying on audio data. In somewhat related work, Zheleva et al. [26] adapt a Latent Dirichlet Allocation model to capture music taste from listening activities across users, and identify both the groups of songs associated with the specific taste and the groups of listeners who share the same taste. In a more recent related work, Natarajan et al. [17] generalize this approach to the problem of collaborative filtering for interactional context. Users are clustered based on a one-step transition probability between items, and then transition information is generalized across clusters. Another recent work by Wang et al. [24] also borrows from the reinforcement learning literature, and considers the problem of song recommendations as a bandit problem. Applying this approach, the authors attempt to balance the tradeoff between exploration and exploitation in personalized song recommendation.

The key difference between these approaches and our methodology is that to the best of our knowledge, no one has attempted to model entire playlists *adaptively*, while interacting with a human listener individually and learning his preferences over both individual songs and song transitions online. By explicitly modeling transitions and exploiting user reinforcement, our framework is able to learn preference models for playlists on the fly without any prior knowledge.

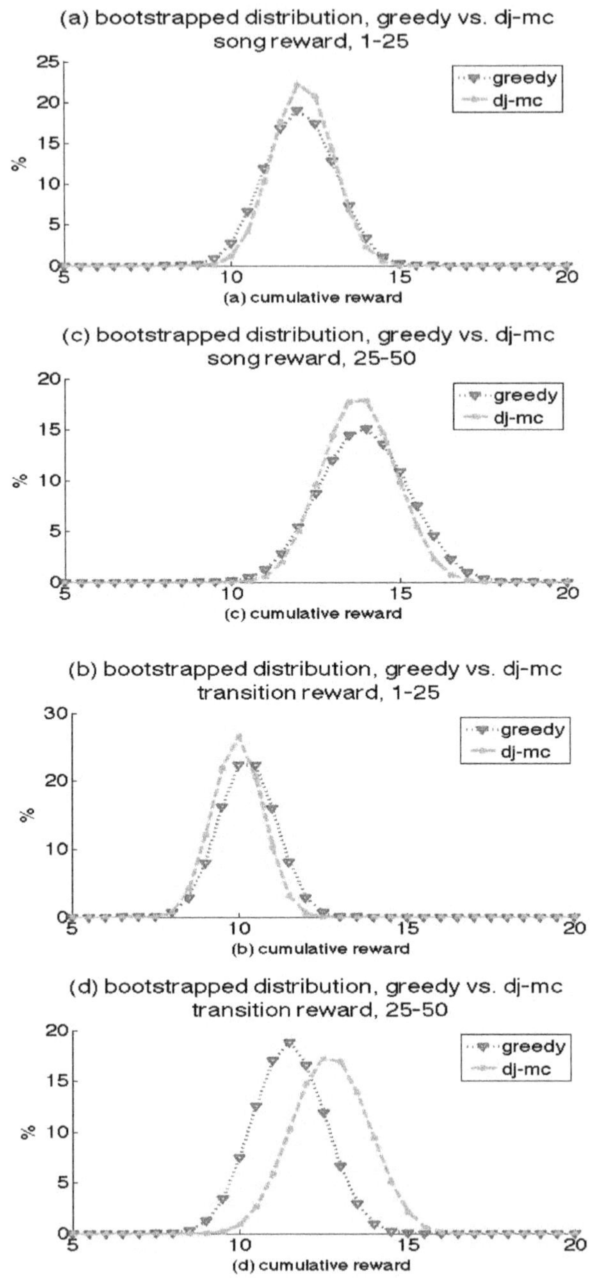

Figure 4: (a) Histogram of cumulative song rewards for the first 25 songs (b) Histogram of cumulative song rewards for the songs 25-50. (c) Histogram of cumulative transition rewards for the first 25 songs. (d) Histogram of cumulative transition rewards for the songs 25-50. Histograms computed via bootstrap resampling the original data 250,000 times.

9. SUMMARY AND DISCUSSION

In this work we present DJ-MC, a full DJ framework, meant to learn the preferences of an individual listener online, and generate suitable playlists adaptively. In the experimental sections we show that our approach offers significant improvement over a more standard approach, which only considers song rewards. DJ-MC, which focuses on the audio properties of songs, has the advantage of being able to generate pleasing playlists that are unexpected with respect to traditional classifications based on genre, period, etc. In future work, it would be of interest to combine intrinsic sonic features with varied sources of metadata (e.g. genre, period, tags, social data, artist co-occurrence rates, etc). It would also be of interest to test our framework on specific types of listeners and music corpora. This work shows promise for both creating better music recommendation systems, and demonstrating the effectiveness of a reinforcement-learning based approach in a new practical domain.

Acknowledgements

This work has taken place in the Learning Agents Research Group (LARG) at the Artificial Intelligence Laboratory, The University of Texas at Austin. LARG research is supported in part by grants from the National Science Foundation (CNS-1330072, CNS-1305287), ONR (21C184-01), AFOSR (FA8750-14-1-0070, FA9550-14-1-0087), and Yujin Robot.

REFERENCES

[1] G. Adomavicius and A. Tuzhilin. Toward the next generation of recommender systems: A survey of the state-of-the-art and possible extensions. *Knowledge and Data Engineering, IEEE Transactions on*, 17(6):734–749, 2005.

[2] N. Aizenberg, Y. Koren, and O. Somekh. Build your own music recommender by modeling internet radio streams. In *Proceedings of the 21st international conference on World Wide Web*, pages 1–10. ACM, 2012.

[3] L. Barrington, R. Oda, and G. Lanckriet. Smarter than genius? human evaluation of music recommender systems. In *International Symposium on Music Information Retrieval*, 2009.

[4] A. Berenzweig, B. Logan, D. P. Ellis, and B. Whitman. A large-scale evaluation of acoustic and subjective music-similarity measures. *Computer Music Journal*, 28(2):63–76, 2004.

[5] T. Bertin-Mahieux, D. P. Ellis, B. Whitman, and P. Lamere. The million song dataset. In *ISMIR 2011: Proceedings of the 12th International Society for Music Information Retrieval Conference, October 24-28, 2011, Miami, Florida*, pages 591–596. University of Miami, 2011.

[6] W. L. Berz. Working memory in music: A theoretical model. *Music Perception*, pages 353–364, 1995.

[7] S. Chen, J. L. Moore, D. Turnbull, and T. Joachims. Playlist prediction via metric embedding. In *Proceedings of the 18th ACM SIGKDD international conference on Knowledge discovery and data mining*, pages 714–722. ACM, 2012.

[8] D. Cliff. Hang the dj: Automatic sequencing and seamless mixing of dance-music tracks. *HP LABORATORIES TECHNICAL REPORT HPL*, (104), 2000.

[9] N. Cook. *A guide to musical analysis.* Oxford University Press, 1994.

[10] M. Crampes, J. Villerd, A. Emery, and S. Ranwez. Automatic playlist composition in a dynamic music landscape. In *Proceedings of the 2007 international workshop on Semantically aware document processing and indexing*, pages 15–20. ACM, 2007.

[11] J. B. Davies and J. B. Davies. *The psychology of music.* Hutchinson London, 1978.

[12] B. Kahnx, R. Ratner, and D. Kahneman. Patterns of hedonic consumption over time. *Marketing Letters*, 8(1):85–96, 1997.

[13] E. Liebman, B. Chor, and P. Stone. Representative selection in non metric datasets. *eprint arXiv:1502.07428*, 2015.

[14] J. MacQueen et al. Some methods for classification and analysis of multivariate observations. In *Proceedings of the fifth Berkeley symposium on mathematical statistics and probability*, volume 1, pages 281–297. California, USA, 1967.

[15] F. Maillet, D. Eck, G. Desjardins, P. Lamere, et al. Steerable playlist generation by learning song similarity from radio station playlists. In *ISMIR*, pages 345–350, 2009.

[16] B. McFee and G. R. Lanckriet. The natural language of playlists. In *ISMIR*, pages 537–542, 2011.

[17] N. Natarajan, D. Shin, and I. S. Dhillon. Which app will you use next?: collaborative filtering with interactional context. In *Proceedings of the 7th ACM conference on Recommender systems*, pages 201–208. ACM, 2013.

[18] J. O'Donovan and B. Smyth. Trust in recommender systems. In *Proceedings of the 10th international conference on Intelligent user interfaces*, pages 167–174. ACM, 2005.

[19] N. Oliver and L. Kreger-Stickles. Papa: Physiology and purpose-aware automatic playlist generation. In *Proc. 7th Int. Conf. Music Inf. Retrieval*, pages 250–253, 2006.

[20] J. C. Platt. Fast embedding of sparse similarity graphs. In *Advances in Neural Information Processing Systems*, page None, 2003.

[21] R. S. Sutton and A. G. Barto. *Introduction to Reinforcement Learning.* MIT Press, Cambridge, MA, USA, 1st edition, 1998.

[22] S.-L. Tan, P. Pfordresher, and R. Harré. *Psychology of music: From sound to significance.* Psychology Press, 2010.

[23] D. Urieli and P. Stone. A learning agent for heat-pump thermostat control. In *Proceedings of the 12th International Conference on Autonomous Agents and Multiagent Systems (AAMAS)*, May 2013.

[24] X. Wang, Y. Wang, D. Hsu, and Y. Wang. Exploration in interactive personalized music recommendation: A reinforcement learning approach. *arXiv preprint arXiv:1311.6355*, 2013.

[25] J. Weston, S. Bengio, and P. Hamel. Multi-tasking with joint semantic spaces for large-scale music annotation and retrieval. *Journal of New Music Research*, 40(4):337–348, 2011.

[26] E. Zheleva, J. Guiver, E. Mendes Rodrigues, and N. Milić-Frayling. Statistical models of music-listening sessions in social media. In *Proceedings of the 19th international conference on World wide web*, pages 1019–1028. ACM, 2010.

Author Index

Abolhassani, Melika 337
Abushark, Yoosef 1071
Agmon, Noa 861, 889
Agrawal, Pritee 1275
Ahrndt, Sebastian 1691
Ahuja, Garima 1883
Aknine, Samir 1791
Alam, Muddasser 1295
Albayrak, Sahin ... 1691, 1905, 1937
Alden, Matthew 155
Alechina, Natasha 443, 1809
Alkoby, Shani 635
Allen, John A. 781, 1907
Alqithami, Saad 1981
Al-Zinati, Mohammad 1031
Amanatidis, Georgios 715
Ambukovski, Nik 1929
Amgoud, Leila 1511
Amigoni, Francesco 821, 1815
An, Bo 523, 753, 1803
Anagnostopoulos, Aris 1767
Anai, Hirokazu 1885
Anand, Ankit 1901
Ancona, Davide 1019
Andrea, Kevin 287
Angelidakis, Angelos 503
Antunes, Luis 1747
Antzoulatos, Nikolas 1957
Arco, Leticia 1917
Auffenberg, Frederik 1799
Aumann, Yonatan 901
Avellana, Narcís 1917
Aylett, Ruth 1711, 1923
Azaria, Amos 543, 1655
Aziz, Haris 107, 939, 1451, 1639
Bachrach, Yoram 919
Balbo, Flavien 1801
Balcan, Maria Florina 3
Baldoni, Matteo 1705, 1739
Bálint-Benczédi, Ferenc ... 871, 1941
Bard, Nolan 17
Baroglio, Cristina 1705, 1739
Barrett, Samuel 1625
Barrot, Nathanaël 715
Bartels, Georg 1925
Bastianelli, Emanuele 851
Battaglino, Cristina 1669
Baumeister, Dorothea 1707
Bazzan, Ana L. C. 1723
Beetz, Michael 871, 1891, 1925, 1941
Beheshti, Rahmatollah 1731
Belardinelli, Francesco 237
Bell, Nathan 257
Ben-Naim, Jonathan 1511
Beßler, Daniel 1925, 1941
Beynier, Aurélie 625
Bezunartea, Maite 1917
Bhat, Satyanath 1789
Bhatnagar, Shalabh 1371
Bhattacharyya, Arnab 1421
Bhouri, Neïla 1791
Biancardi, Beatrice 1817
Bilgin, Ayse 1701
Bilò, Vittorio 1239
Biswas, Arpita 1101
Blankendaal, Romy 553
Bloembergen, Daan 1699
Bogert, Kenneth 1837, 1919
Boissier, Olivier 1801
Bonnet, Grégory 1797
Borrego, Carlos 1697, 1943
Bošanský, Branislav 1773, 1813
Bosse, Tibor 553
Boutilier, Craig 605
Bowling, Michael 17, 27
Brandl, Florian 1219, 1411
Brandt, Felix 1219, 1411, 1915
Bredereck, Robert 67
Brill, Markus 1213, 1401
Brink, Laura 811
Briola, Daniela 1019
Broecker, Bastian 1775
Brooks, Nathan 377
Brown, Noam 7
Brys, Tim 181, 1641, 1913
Bulling, Nils 443, 1781
Burke, Damian 1905
Burnett, Christopher 1845
Cahill, Vinny 1897
Cai, Wentong 801
Cai, Yi 1647
Caliskanelli, Ipek 1775
Campano, Sabrina 1649
Campeotto, Federico 1835
Campillo-Sanchez, Pablo 1949
Camurri, Antonio 1817
Cañadas, Adrian 1917
Capuzzimati, Federico 1705
Caragiannis, Ioannis 675
Cardoza, Colleen 1041
Caridroit, Thomas 1677
Casanova, Guillaume 1171
Castellano, Ginevra 1923
Castelletti, Andrea 821
Castro, Elkin 1957
Cavazza, Marc 1547
Ceballos, Hector G. 1651
Centeno, Roberto 1805
Čermák, Jiří 1813
Cerquides, Jesus 413, 1285, 1855
Cerutti, Federico 781, 1845
Chabin, Guillaume 1915
Chakraborty, Nilanjan 1751
Chalkiadakis, Georgios 503
Charrier, Tristan 1471
Chen, Bin 1861
Chen, Binyi 327
Chen, Cen 1715
Chen, Guihai 1111
Chen, Liang 1821
Chen, Lijie 1673
Chen, Po-An 1721
Chen, Xi 1861
Chen, Xiaoping 1667
Chen, Xujin 1765
Chen, Yingke 1161
Cheng, Shih-Fen 1715
Chevaleyre, Yann 625
Chira, Camelia 1723
Chitre, Mandar 267
Chli, Maria 1735
Cholvy, Laurence 1643
Chopra, Amit K. 453, 1739
Chow, Yinlam 1829
Christensen, Anders Lyhne 297, 735, 2017
Ciná, Giovanni 1009
Cittern, David 1727
Claes, Daniel 881
Claessens, Rik 1933

Clarke, Siobhán 1897
Clavel, Chloé 1649
Clement, Maxime 395
Coheur, Luísa 1521
Colby, Mitchell K. . 171, 1659, 1661
Collins, John 1131
Conitzer, Vincent ... 357, 1213, 1401
Coon, Will 573
Cornelio, Cristina 969
Correia, Luís 735, 2017
Corrigan, Lee J. 1923
Cossentino, Massimo 1061
Cranefield, Stephen 1743
Cruz-Mencia, Francisco 1855
Curran, William 1659
da Costa Pereira, Célia 1849
da Silva, Viviane Torres 2013
Damamme, Anastasia 625
Damiano, Rossana 1669
Darty, Kévin 1683
Das, Sanmay 635
Dastani, Mehdi 443, 1781
Davami, Erfan 145
Davies, Toby O. 1141
Dayama, Pankaj 1091
De Giacomo, Giuseppe 1675
de Haan, Ronald 117, 127
de Jong, Tessa 553
de Lima, Tiago 1677
de Man, Jeroen 553
De Nardi, Renzo 1607
de Nijs, Frits 1979
de Silva, Lavindra 1957
de Villiers, Pieter 1933
De Vos, Marina 473
de Waal, Alta 1933
De Weerdt, Mathijs 1769
Delahaye, Jean-Paul 1665
Delaney, Brendan 1819
Delias, Pavlos 1693
Delle Fave, Francesco Maria ... 1381
Dennis, Louise 423
Dennisen, Sophie 1707
Deshmukh, Amol 1711, 1923
Deshmukh, Jayati 1717
Dey, Palash 87, 1421, 1441, 1973
Dhamal, Swapnil 1787
Di Napoli, Claudia 1779
Di Nocera, Dario 1779
Di Tullio, Eugenio 1923
Dignum, Virginia 473
Diller, David 573
Ding, Yu 1817
Dobson, Richard J.B. 831
Dorigo, Marco 1305
Doshi, Prashant 1161, 1837, 1839, 1919
Doucette, John A. 1841
Dovier, Agostino 1835
Draief, Moez 1481
Dropps, Timothy 781, 1907
Durfee, Edmund H. 1267
Durkota, Karel 1773
Dusparic, Ivana 1897
Dutta, Partha Sarathi 1759
Eck, Adam 367
Edalat, Abbas 1727
Efthymiadis, Kyriakos 763
Ellen Foster, Mary 1923
Elogeel, Abdelrahman 155
Endriss, Ulle 117, 127, 1009
Esfandiari, Hossein 337
Espinosa, Antonio 1855
Etuk, Anthony 781, 1807
Everaere, Patricia 999
Evertsz, Rick 1051, 1929
Fähndrich, Johannes 1691
Faliszewski, Piotr 67
Faltings, Boi 1081
Fanelli, Angelo 1239
Fang, Fei 1381, 1663
Farinelli, Alessandro 377, 413
Feigh, Karen M. 1873
Felli, Paolo 1461
Feng, Yuan 209
Ferguson, Bill 573
Fernández de la Cruz, Lorena 831
Ferraioli, Diodato 1767
Ferrando, Angelo 1019
Fioretto, Ferdinando 1823, 1835, 2007
Fischer, Joel E. 533, 1921
Fisher, Michael 423
Flacher, Fabien 1939
Flammini, Michele 1239
Flann, Jack 533, 1921
Flores-Solorio, Victor 1651
Foster, Mary Ellen 1711
Fotakis, Dimitris 307
Freelan, David 387
Freeman, Rupert 1213, 1401
Fu, Na 483
Fu, Qiming 1685
Fujita, Etsushi 1885
Gaciarz, Matthis 1791
Gal, Ya'akov (Kobi) 665
Galand, Lucie 1895
Galland, Stéphane 1801
Gan, Jiarui 523
Ganzfried, Sam 7, 37
Gao, Yang 753
Garcia-Vandellós, Gerard 1943
Garcia-Vazquez, Juan P. 1651
Garg, Dinesh 1091
Gasparini, Luca 1821
Gaspers, Serge 107, 1451
Gatti, Nicola 1813, 1831
Gattinger, Malvin 1795
Gaud, Nicolas 1801
Geist, Christian 1915
Gemignani, Guglielmo 851, 1879
Genter, Katie 247, 1745
Gerritsen, Charlotte 553
Gertler, Ethan 685
Ghosh, Sujata 1491
Gierasimczuk, Nina 1853
Gini, Maria 1577
Giouroukis, Dimitris 1945
Giuliani, Matteo 821
Gmytrasiewicz, Piotr J. 1875
Godoy, Julio 1577, 1995
Goebel, Rainer 1953
Goh, Chi Keong 1759
Goldman, Claudia V. 543, 1655
Goldsmith, Judy 969, 1851
Gomes, Jorge 297
Gomez-Sanz, Jorge J. 1949
Goodman, Robert 831
Goodrich, Michael A. 1041, 1615
Goto, Masahiro 1887
Goyal, Ripple 1911
Grandi, Umberto 969, 989
Gratch, Jonathan 1567
Grau, Isel 1917
Griffiths, Nathan 1653, 1785
Groß, Roderich 279
Grossi, Davide 237
Grover, Aditya 1901
Grzes, Marek 1249
Gudmundsson, Joachim 107
Gujar, Sujit 1789

Guo, Jiong 1431, 1725, 1729
Guo, Mingyu 347, 1885
Gupta, Anshul 1361
Guy, Stephen J. 1577
Habibi, Golnaz 1315
Hajiaghayi, MohammadTaghi ... 337
Hamada, Naoto 1887
Hamann, Heiko 1305
Han, The Anh 1657, 1719
Hanna, Nader 1701, 1777
Hao, Jianye 1647
Harel, David 1
Harland, James 1071, 1645
Harrenstein, Paul 655
Harutyunyan, Anna 181, 1641, 1913
Haskell, William 1341
Hassidim, Avinatan 705, 901
Hastie, Helen 1711, 1923, 1959
Hawes, Nick 745
Hazon, Noam 705
Hemberg, Erik 1825
Hennes, Daniel 881, 1699, 1775
Herd, Benjamin 463
Hermoso, Ramón 1805
Hernandez-Leal, Pablo ... 1709, 1989
Heßler, Axel 1905
Hindriks, Koen V. 423
Hofbauer, Johannes 1411
Holbrook, Jon 1041
HolmesParker, Chris 171
Hoogland, Jasper 1769
Hopkins, Jack 1927
Horvitz, Eric 1191
Hosseini, Hadi 1841, 2005
How, Jonathan P. 1793
Hrabia, Christopher-Eyk 1937
Hu, Xiaodong 1765
Hu, Yujing 753
Huang, Dongping 1647
Hung, Hayley 1771
Hunt III, Harry B. 1501
Huynh, Trung Dong 533, 1921
Ibrahim, Zina M. 831
Ikuno, Yuki 533, 1921
Inam, Wardah 1833
Inoue, Katsumi 395
Irissappane, Athirai A. 791
Isbell Jr., Charles L. 1873
Iwane, Hidenao 1885
Iwasaki, Atsushi 1885, 1887
Jabbour, Said 1749
Jain, Manish 645, 1911
Jain, Shweta 1101, 1789
Jamroga, Wojciech 227
Janarthanam, Srinivasan .1711, 1923
Jarrah, Moath 1811
Jennings, Nicholas R. 493, 533, 1295, 1607, 1719, 1921
Ji, Jianmin 1667
Jiang, Albert Xin 645
Jiang, Guifei 979, 1975
Jiang, Nan 1181
Jiang, Wenchao 533, 1921
Jones, Aidan 1923
Jonker, Catholijn M. 473, 1201
Julier, Simon J. 1607
Jurado, Sergio 1917
K. J., Prabuchandran 1787
Kafalı, Özgür 1927
Kalociński, Dariusz 1853
Kamar, Ece 1191
Kambhampati, Subbarao 1151
Kaminka, Gal A. 861, 1867
Kang, Yilin 1871
Kar, Debarun 1381
Karamouzas, Ioannis 1577
Karapinar, Sertac 1843
Karlapalem, Kamalakar ..1761, 1883
Kephart, Andrew 357
Ketter, Wolfgang 1131
Khandelwal, Piyush 1625
Kharaghani, Sepideh 171
Kiekintveld, Christofer 1773
Kiekintveld, Christopher 1877
King, Thomas C. 473, 2011
Kingston, Zachary 1315
Klee, Steven D. 1879
Kobti, Ziad 1869
Kochanowicz, Jaroslaw 1529
Koenig, Sven 1757
Kökciyan, Nadin 2019
Kollingbaum, Martin J. 1821
Kolobov, Andrey 155
Konieczny, Sébastien 999, 1677
Korkinof, Dimitrios 1481
Kraus, Sarit 543, 705, 1655
Krimpas, George A. 675
Krishnan, Ramayya 1121
Kroer, Christian 47, 317
Krysta, Piotr 307
Kuate, Rodrigue T. 1735
Kudenko, Daniel 763
Kuiper, Dane 1955
Kulesza, Alex 1181
Kumar, Akshat 1275
Kurata, Ryoji 1887
Küster, Tobias 1783, 1937
L.A., Prashanth 1371
La Poutré, Han 1769
Labreuche, C. 959
Lakkaraju, Kiran 513, 1863
Lanctot, Marc 27
Lang, Jérôme 715, 1229
Lau, Hoong Chuin .. 483, 1121, 1715
Laue, Tim 1745
Le, Truc Viet 1121
LeBron, Larry 573
Leeke, Matthew 1785
Lenaerts, Tom 1657
Leonardi, Stefano 1767
Leonetti, Matteo 725
Lesire, Charles 1171
Lespérance, Yves 1675
Lesser, Victor 1201
Letchford, Joshua 513
Leung, Cyril 1689, 1991
Lev, Omer 1733
Lewenberg, Yoad 919
Lewis, Richard 1181
Li, Guangliang 1771
Li, Hengfei 1907
Li, Minming 615
Li, Tingting 473
Liebman, Elad 591, 1983
Liemhetcharat, Somchaya 1325, 1695
Lim, Mei Yii 1711
Lim, Su Fang 1687
Lima, Pedro U. 1827
Lin, Han 1687
Lin, Jun 1687, 1947
Lin, Lanny 1615
Lindsay, Alan 1547
Lisý, Viliam 27, 1773
Liu, Jiangchuan 1667
Liu, Qipeng 1741
Liu, Quan 1685
Liu, Siyuan 1121
Liu, Tie-Yan 327, 1755, 1765

Liu, Yang 563, 791
Liu, Yicheng 1741
Liu, Yunlong 1259
Lodato, Carmelo 1061
Logan, Brian 443, 1809
Lomuscio, Alessio 189, 1713
Lopes, Salvatore 1061
López-Sánchez, Maite 433, 1931
Loreggia, Andrea 1737
Lorini, Emiliano 989
Loscalzo, Steven 163
Lu, Chi-Jen 1721
Lu, Dongcai 1667
Lucas, Gale 1567
Luck, Michael 463, 831, 1819
Luke, Sean 287, 387
Luo, Linbo 801
Luo, Yicheng 1695
Lust, Thibaut 1895
Lützenberger, Marco 1691, 1783
Ly, Thanh Chi 1051
Ma, Weidong 1765
Ma, Yue 1749
Mackenzie, Simon . 107, 1451, 1639
Mackin, Erika 685
Magdon-Ismail, Malik 685
Magessi, Nuno 1747
Mahini, Hamid 337
Mahmoud, Samhar 1819
Mailler, Roger 405
Malec, David 337
Mancini, Maurizio 1817
Mandal, Debmalya 1101, 1753
Marathe, Madhav V. 1501
Marchant, James 1785
Marchi, Nicolo' 377
Mariano, Pedro 297
Marinescu, Andrei 1897
Markakis, Evangelos 715, 1733
Marquis, Pierre 395, 999, 1677
Mascardi, Viviana 1019
Mascarenhas, Samuel 1899
Mateas, Michael 573
Mathieu, Philippe 1665
Mattei, Nicholas 107, 969, 1451
Maudet, N. 959
Maudet, Nicolas 625
Mausam 1901
McBurney, Peter 463
McCoy, Josh 573
McLurkin, James 1315
Meir, Reshef 665, 929
Mell, Johnathan 1567, 2015
Melo, Francisco S. 1521, 1899
Menashe, Jacob 771, 1985
Mendizabal, Iosu 1931
Mendoza, Juan Pablo 1587, 1999
Meneguzzi, Felipe 1681, 1743
Mercer, Eric 1041
Meseguer, Pedro 413
Meyer, Christophe 1939
Meyer, Joachim 1655
Meyer, John-Jules Ch. 1821
Miao, Chunyan 523, 1687, 1689, 1947
Micalizio, Roberto 1705
Michalak, Tomasz 1893
Michaliszyn, Jakub 189
Mihaylov, Mihail 1917
Miles, Simon 463, 1653, 1819
Miller, Tim 1071, 1461
Misra, Archan 1715
Misra, Neeldhara 87, 97, 1441
Mitakides, Nektarios 1693
Möckel, Rico 1953
Moffitt, Kerry 573
Mokom, Felicitas 1869
Monaco, Gianpiero 1239
Montagna, Sara 1763
Morales, Javier 433, 1931
Moreau, Luc 533, 1921
Moscardelli, Luca 1239
Mostafa, Hala 483
Mostarda, Leonardo 1809
Mostowski, Marcin 1853
Mota, Pedro 1521
Moure, Juan Carlos 1855
Muise, Christian 1461
Muller, Tim 563, 791
Munoz de Cote, Enrique 1709, 1989
Murano, Aniello 227
Myagmarjav, Batbold 1865, 1993
Nabeel, Arshed 97
Nagarajan, Vaishnavh 695, 1909
Narahari, Y 87, 1091, 1101, 1441
Narahari, Yadati ...1753, 1787, 1789
Narayanam, Ramasuri 1679
Narayanaswamy, Balakrishnan 1091
Nardi, Daniele 851, 1879
Narodytska, Nina 1451, 1737
Narvekar, Sanmit 725
Naumov, Pavel 219
Navarro, Laurent 1939
Nguyen, Hoang Nga 1809
Nguyen, Thanh H. 1963
Nicholas, Deon 17
Niedermeier, Rolf 67
Nieścieruk, Agata 1893
Norman, Timothy J. 781, 1807, 1821, 1907
Nowé, Ann ... 181, 1641, 1913, 1917
Obraztsova, Svetlana 1733
Oka, Masaaki 909
Okimoto, Tenda 395
Oliehoek, Frans A. 881, 1703
Omicini, Andrea 1763
Ondráček, Jakub 1597
Oommen, B. John 257
O'Reilly, Una-May 1825
Oren, Nir 781, 1743, 1807, 1845, 1907
Ouerdane, W. 959
Ouyang, Robin Wentao 781, 1907
Padget, Julian 473
Padgham, Lin 1903, 1935
Paiva, Ana 1847, 1899, 1923
Panagopoulos, Athanasios Aris 1295
Panda, Swetasudha 1391, 2003
Panella, Alessandro 1875
Papadopoulos, Fotios 1923
Paquet, Hugo 1713
Parkes, David 929
Parons, S. 959
Parsons, Simon 1699
Pasumarthi, Ramakumar 1679
Pathania, Deepika 1761
Pavlin, Gregor 1933
Pearce, Adrian R. . 1141, 1461, 1675
Pěchouček, Michal 1597
Pecune, Florian 1817
Pelachaud, Catherine .. 5, 1649, 1817
Penders, Ate 1933
Pereira, Gonçalo 1857, 1951
Pereira, Gonçalo Duarte Garcia 1861
Perez-Diaz, Fernando 279
Perrussel, Laurent 979, 989, 1643
Pianini, Danilo 1763
Picard, Gauthier 1285, 1801

Pitt, Jeremy 1481
Platis, Nikos 1945
Pontelli, Enrico 1823, 1835
Porteous, Julie 1539, 1547
Poupart, Pascal 1249
Pozo Pardo, Francisco Denis ... 1937
Prada, Rui 1857, 1861, 1951
Pralet, Cédric 1171
Prasad, H. L. 1371
Procaccia, Ariel D. 949
Pujol-Gonzalez, Marc 413
Qian, Yundi 1341, 1961
Qiao, Xingye 163
Qin, Tao 327, 1755, 1765, 1803
Qiu, Guoping 1755
Qu, Hongyang 1889
Qu, Xia 1839
Quattrini Li, Alberto 1815
Rabinovich, Zinovi 645, 1733
Radanovic, Goran 1081
Raddaoui, Badran 1749
Raeissi, Masoume M. 377
Rahwan, Talal 1893
Raimondi, Franco 1041, 1809
Ramchurn, Sarvapali D. 533, 841, 1921
Ratchev, Svetan 1957
Ravi, S. S. 1501
Ravindran, Balaraman 1679
Ray, Arupratan 1753
Raynaut, William 1643
Razo-Zapata, Iván 1917
Read, Jonathon 1547
Reece, Steven 533, 1921
Rey, Anja 1229
Reynolds, Craig 573
Ribeiro, Tiago 1923
Ribeiro, Tony 395
Ribino, Patrizia 1061
Richards, Deborah 1701, 1777
Ridgway, Anton 137, 405
Ries, Bernard 715
Ripley, Michael 137
Riva, Alessandro 1815
Riveret, Regis 1481
Robbel, Philipp 881
Roberts, Bruce 573
Roberts, Stephen J. 533, 1921
Robles, Sergi 1697, 1943
Rocco, Marco 1831
Rodden, Tom 533, 1921
Rodriguez, Sebastian 1801
Rodríguez-Aguilar, Juan A. 413, 433, 1285, 1931
Rodriguez-Aguilar, Juan Antonio 1855
Rogers, Alex 1295, 1607, 1799
Rong, Jiang 1803
Rosalia, Jesse 1873
Rosen, Jacob B. 1825
Rosenfeld, Ariel 543
Rosenkrantz, Daniel J. 1501
Rosenschein, Jeffrey S. 919, 1733
Rossi, Francesca 969, 1737
Rossi, Silvia 1779
Rothe, Jörg 1229
Roxas, Jon Cedric 1701
Rubin, Sasha 199
Rungta, Neha 1041
Russell, Katherine 287
Saarinen, Sam 1851
Saar-Tsechansky, Maytal 591
Sabouret, Nicolas 1683
Sais, Lakhdar 1749
Sakurai, Yuko 347, 909
Salhi, Yakoub 1749
Salisbury, Elliot 841
Salmon, Charles Thomas 1991
Sánchez-Carmona, Adrián 1697, 1943
Sánchez-Pinsach, David 1931
Sandholm, Tuomas 7, 37, 47, 317
Santos, Fernando P. 1847
Santos, Francisco C. 1847
Santos, Pedro A. ... 1857, 1861, 1951
Sariel, Sanem 1843
Sarne, David 635
Saunier, Julien 1683
Savarimuthu, Tony 1743
Scerri, Paul 377
Schader, Michael 287
Schadrack, Hilmar 1229
Schend, Lena 1229
Schewe, Sven 1361
Schwager, Mac 1315
Schwarzentruber, François 1471
Schwind, Nicolas 395
Seedig, Hans Georg 939
Segal, Avi 2001
Segal-Halevi, Erel 901
Seidita, Valeria 1061
Sen, Sandip 137
Şensoy, Murat 1807
Sequeira, Pedro 1899, 1923
Serafino, Paolo 1831, 1977
Sha, Meng 1759
Shapiro, Daniel G. 573
Shaukat, Mansoor 267
Shen, Hong 347
Shen, Zhiqi 1687, 1689, 1947
Shorten, Robert 811
Shrestha, Yash Raj 1431, 1725
Shvartzon, Avraham 1655
Silva, Fernando 735, 2017
Silvestre, Eduardo Augusto 2013
Simmons, Reid 1587
Simpson, Edwin 533, 1921
Sina, Sigal 705
Sinapov, Jivko 725
Singh, Dhirendra 1903
Singh, Harman 97
Singh, Munindar P. 453, 1207, 1739
Singh, Satinder 1181
Singla, Parag 1901
Sinha, Arunesh 1351, 1911
Sintov, Nicole 1381
Sklar, Elizabeth 1775
Sleight, Jason 1267
Smyrnakis, Michalis 1889
Soh, Leen-Kiat 367, 1861
Solaimanpour, Sina 1919
Sompolinsky, Yonatan 919
Søndergaard, Harald 1141
Sonenberg, Liz 1461
Song, Lei 209
Sorger, Bettina 1953
Soriano Marcolino, Leandro 695, 1909, 1967
Spaan, Matthijs T. J. 1703, 1827
Spanoudakis, Nikolaos 1693
Sreedharan, Sarath 1151
Sridharan, Mohan 1865, 1993
Srinivasa, Srinath 1719
Srinivasan, Aravind 337
Srivastava, Mani 781, 1907
Srour, F. Jordan 1637
Stathis, Kostas 1927
Stearns, Richard E. 1501
Steel, Travis 1955
Stein, Sebastian 493, 841, 1799
Stern, Andrew 573

Stocker, Richard 1041
Stone, Peter 247, 591, 725, 771, 1625, 1663, 1745, 1985
Strawser, Daniel 1833
Stringaris, Argyris 831
Strobel, Martin 1219
Stuckey, Peter J. 1141
Sucar, L. Enrique 1709, 1989
Suffern, Zachary 1757
Sui, Xin 605
Sukthankar, Gita 145, 1731
Sullivan, Paul 781, 1907
Sun, Jun 1647
Sun, Yu-An 581
Sycara, Katia 1751
Szeider, Stefan 127
Szepesvári, Csaba 17
Tal, Maor 665
Talmon, Nimrod 67
Tambe, Milind 695, 1341, 1351, 1381, 1663, 1909, 1911, 1963, 1967
Tan, Ah-Hwee 1529, 1871
Tanenbaum, Karen 573
Tang, Pingzhong 1673, 1741
Tang, Yun 1259
Tao, Bingyang 1111
Tao, Jia 219
Taweel, Adel 1819
Taylor, Adam 1897
Taylor, Matthew E. 181, 1709
Teacy, W. T. Luke 1607
Tee, Keng Peng 1325
Telang, Pankaj R. 1681
Tenorth, Moritz 1925, 1941
Teredesai, Ankur 155
Testerink, Bas 1781
Tettamanzi, Andrea G. B. 1849
Teutenberg, Jonathan 1539
Thalmann, Daniel 1529
Thangarajah, John 1051, 1071, 1645, 1929
Thévenin, Jean-Marc 1643
Thomaz, Andrea 1873
Timsina, Anish 1861
Todo, Taiki 347, 909, 1885
Tokadli, Guliz 1873
Toniolo, Alice 781, 1907
Tovey, Craig 1757, 1851
Tran-Thanh, Long 1719
Truran, Mark 1547
Tryfonopoulos, Christos 1945
Tsang, Alan 1841
Tsimhoni, Omer 543, 1655
Tsuruta, Shunsuke 909
Tumanov, Kirill 1953
Tumer, Kagan 171, 1635, 1659, 1661
Turrini, Paolo 655
Tuyls, Karl 881, 1699, 1775, 1933
Ure, N. Kemal 1793
Valentini, Gabriele 1305
Vallée, Thibaut 1797
Valogianni, Konstantina .1131, 1965
van der Hoek, Wiebe 881
van Eijck, Jan 1795
Van Moffaert, Kristof 1917
van Riemsdijk, M. Birna ...423, 473, 1201
Vaněk, Ondřej 1597
Varakantham, Pradeep 483, 1275
Varni, Giovanna 1817
Vasconcelos, Wamberto ...433, 1931
Veiga, Tiago S. 1827
Velázquez-Quesada, Fernando R. 1491
Veliz, Oscar 1877
Veloso, Manuela 1587, 1879
Venable, K. Brent 969, 1737
Ventre, Carmine 307, 1831
Vered, Mor 1867
Veres, Sandor M. 1889
Vian, John 1793
Villata, Serena 1849
Volpe, Gualtiero 1817
von Wedel, Jana Karina 939
Vorobeychik, Yevgeniy 513, 949, 1391, 2003
Voudouris, Alexandros A. 675
Vrancx, Peter 1641, 1913
Wah, Elaine 57, 1987
Walsh, Toby 107, 1451, 1737
Wang, Changjun 1765
Wang, Dongxia 791, 1997
Wang, Hai H. 1735
Wang, Zhuoran 1959
Wang, Zijian 1315
Waniek, Marcin 1893
Warner, Geoff 1825
Weiss, Gerhard 1953
Wellman, Michael P. 57, 1881
Wenkstern, Rym 1031, 1955
Whiteson, Shimon 1771
Wicke, Drew 387
Wiedemeyer, Thiemo 871, 1941
Wiedenbeck, Bryce 1881
Wijesinghe, Sanith 1825
Williams, Brian C. 1833
Wilson, Drew 1635
Winikoff, Michael 1071, 1935
Winkler, Jan 1925
Winkler, Jan Oliver 1891
Witwicki, Stefan J. 1703
Wooldridge, Michael 433, 655, 1931
Woźna-Szcześniak, Bożena 1671
Wright, Robert 163
Wu, Fan 1111
Wu, Feng 533, 1921
Xi, Hui 1759
Xia, Lirong 685, 1639
Xu, Bolei 1755
Xu, Haifeng 645
Xu, Ying 1751
Yadav, Nitin 1051, 1935
Yan, Rui 1325
Yang, Feidiao 1765
Yang, Yongjie 77, 1431, 1725, 1729
Ye, Chun 1639
Yehoshua, Roi 861, 891, 1969
Yeoh, William 1823, 1835
Yi, Yuan 685
Yin, Haiyan 801
Yin, Ming 581
Yliniemi, Logan 1635
Yokoo, Makoto 347, 909, 1885, 1887
Yorke-Smith, Neil 1637, 1645, 1681
Young, Jay 745
Yu, Chao 1647
Yu, Han 1687, 1689, 1947
Yu, Jia Yuan 1829
Yu, Lei 163
Yu, Xinjia 1991
Yuan Yu, Jia 811
Zbrzezny, Agnieszka M. 1671, 2021
Zeng, Yifeng 1161, 1259
Zenonos, Alexandros 493
Zhang, Chao 1351, 1911, 1971
Zhang, Dongmo 979
Zhang, Haifeng 513, 949, 2009

Zhang, Heng 979
Zhang, Jie 563, 791, 1759, 1811
Zhang, Li 1557
Zhang, Lijun 209
Zhang, Shun 247
Zhang, Yang 1557
Zhang, Yu 1151
Zhang, Zongzhang 1685
Zheng, Ronghuo 1751
Zhong, Jinghui 801
Zhou, Yicheng 1685
Zillmer, Ruediger 279
Zohar, Aviv 919
Zou, Shaokun 615

AAMAS 2016

9-13 May 2016, Singapore

AAMAS is the leading scientific conference for research in autonomous agents and multiagent systems. The AAMAS conference series was initiated in 2002 by merging three highly respected meetings: the International Conference on Multi-Agent Systems (ICMAS); the International Workshop on Agent Theories, Architectures, and Languages (ATAL); and the International Conference on Autonomous Agents (AA). The aim of the joint conference is to provide a single, high-profile, internationally respected archival forum for scientific research in the theory and practice of autonomous agents and multiagent systems.

AAMAS 2016, the fifteenth conference in the AAMAS series, seeks the submission of high-quality papers limited to 8 pages in length. Reviews will be double blind; authors must avoid including anything that can be used to identify them. Please note that submitting an abstract is required to submit a full paper. However, the abstracts will not be reviewed and full (8-page) papers must be submitted for the review process to begin. All work must be original, i.e., it must not have appeared in a conference proceedings, book, or journal and may not be under review for another archival conference. In addition to submissions in the main track, AAMAS 2016 will be soliciting papers in special tracks. The review process for the special tracks will be similar to the main track, but with programme committee members specially selected for each track. All accepted papers for the special tracks will be included in the proceedings.

General Chairs: Catholijn Jonker (Delft University of Technology, Netherlands)
Stacy Marsella (Northeastern University, USA)

Program Chairs: Karl Tuyls (University of Liverpool, UK)
John Thangarajah (RMIT University, Australia)

The full call for papers, along with descriptions of the special tracks and all topics of interest, and the important dates will be made available at: **http://sis.smu.edu.sg/aamas2016**

www.ingramcontent.com/pod-product-compliance
Ingram Content Group UK Ltd.
Pitfield, Milton Keynes, MK11 3LW, UK
UKHW051418290926
15471UKWH00009B/1661

9 781450 337694